1964

SELECT BRITISH ELOQUENCE

Essay and Monograph Series
of The Liberal Arts Press
OSKAR PIEST, FOUNDER

SELECT
BRITISH ELOQUENCE:

EMBRACING

THE BEST SPEECHES ENTIRE

OF THE

MOST EMINENT ORATORS OF GREAT BRITAIN

FOR THE LAST TWO CENTURIES;

WITH SKETCHES OF THEIR LIVES, AN ESTIMATE OF THEIR GENIUS, AND NOTES, CRITICAL AND EXPLANATORY.

BY CHAUNCEY A. GOODRICH, D.D.

PROFESSOR IN YALE COLLEGE

With an Introduction by

BOWER ALY

PROFESSOR OF SPEECH, UNIVERSITY OF OREGON

THE BOBBS-MERRILL COMPANY, INC.
A SUBSIDIARY OF HOWARD W. SAMS & CO., INC.
Publishers • INDIANAPOLIS • NEW YORK

Printed in the United States of America
Library of Congress Catalog Card Number: 63-7978

PREFACE

Mr. Hume has somewhere remarked, that "he who would teach eloquence must do it chiefly by *examples*." The author of this volume was forcibly struck with this remark in early life; and in entering on the office of Professor of Rhetoric in Yale College, more than thirty years ago, besides the ordinary instructions in that department, he took Demosthenes' Oration for the Crown as a *text-book* in the Senior Class, making it the basis of a course of informal lectures on the principles of oratory. Modern eloquence came next, and he endeavored, in a distinct course, to show the leading characteristics of the great orators of our own language, and the best mode of studying them to advantage. His object in both courses was, not only to awaken in the minds of the class that love of genuine eloquence which is the surest pledge of success, but to aid them in catching the spirit of the authors read, and, by analyzing passages selected for the purpose, to initiate the pupil in those higher principles which (whether they were conscious of it or not) have always guided the great masters of the art, till he should learn the *unwritten* rules of oratory, which operate by a kind of instinct upon the mind, and are far more important than any that are found in the books.

Such is the origin of this volume, which contains the matter of the second course of lectures mentioned above, cast into another form, in connection with the speeches of the great British orators of the first and second class. A distinct volume would be necessary for American eloquence, if the lectures on that subject should ever be published.

The speeches selected are those which, by the general suffrage of the English public, are regarded as the master-pieces of their respective authors. They are in almost every instance given *entire*, because the object is to have each of them studied as a complete system of thought. Detached passages of extraordinary force and beauty may be useful as exercises in elocution; but, if dwelt upon exclusively as models of style, they are sure to vitiate the taste. It is like taking all one's nutriment from highly-seasoned food and stimulating drinks.

As to the orators chosen, Chatham, Burke, Fox, and Pitt stand, by universal consent, at the head of our eloquence, and to these Erskine may be added as the greatest of our forensic orators. Every thing, however imperfect, from a man like Chatham is of interest to the student in oratory, and therefore *all* his speeches are here inserted, including eight never before published in this country. All of Burke's speeches which he prepared for the press have also found a place, except that on Economical Reform, which, relating to mere matters of English finance, has less interest for an American. In room of this, the reader will find the most striking passages in his works on the French Revolution, so that this volume contains nearly every thing which most persons can have any desire to study in the pages of Mr. Burke. Six of Fox's great speeches are next given, and three of Pitt's, with copious extracts from the early efforts of the latter; together with nine of Erskine's ablest arguments, being those on which his reputation mainly rests. Among the orators of the second class, the reader will find in this volume four speeches of Lord Mansfield; two of Mr. Grattan's, with his invectives against Flood and Corry; Mr. Sheridan's celebrated speech against Hastings; three of Mr. CURRAN'S; Sir JAMES MACKINTOSH s famous speech for Peltier; four of Mr. CANNING'S; and five of Lord BROUGHAM'S, including his instructive discourse on the study of eloquence in the Greek orators. Some of the most finished letters of JUNIUS are given in their proper place, with remarks on his style as an admirable model of condensation, elegance, and force. In the first fifty pages will be found nearly all the celebrated speeches before the days of Lord Chatham, from Sir ROBERT WALPOLE, Lord CHESTERFIELD, Mr. PULTENEY, Lord BELHAVEN, Sir JOHN DIGBY, the Earl of STRAFFORD, and Sir JOHN ELIOT. The selections in this volume extend through a period of two hundred years, and embrace a very large proportion of the most powerful eloquence of Great Britain.

The following are the aids afforded for the study of these speeches:

(1.) A memoir of each orator, designed to show his early training in eloquence, the leading events of his public life, the peculiar cast of his genius, and the distinctive characteristics of his oratory. It ought to be said, in justice to the author, that these sketches were completed in every essential particular, long before the publication of Lord Brougham's work upon British Statesmen.

(2.) A historical introduction to each of the speeches, explaining minutely the circumstances of the case, the state of parties, and the exact point at issue, being intended to place the reader in the midst of the scene as an actual spectator of the contest. These introductions, with the memoirs just mentioned, form a slight but continuous thread of political history, embracing the most important topics discussed in the British Parliament for more than a century.

(3.) An analysis of the longer speeches in side-notes, giving the divisions and subdivisions of thought, and thus enabling the reader to perceive at once the connection and bearing of the several parts.

(4.) A large body of explanatory notes, bringing out minuter facts or relations of the parties, without a knowledge of which many passages lose all their force and application.

(5.) Critical notes, as specimens of the kind of analysis which the author has been accustomed to apply to the several parts of an oration, and which every student in oratory should be continually making out for himself.

(6.) Translations of the passages quoted from the ancient and foreign languages, with the poetry rendered into English verse. The passages are usually traced to their sources, and the train of thought given as it appears in the original, without a knowledge of which most quotations have but little force or beauty. For the same reason, the classical and other allusions are traced out and explained.

(7.) A concluding statement of the way in which the question was decided, with occasional remarks upon its merits, or the results produced by the decision.

Great compression has been used in preparing this volume, that all who are interested in the study of eloquence may be able to possess it. Each page contains the matter of three ordinary octavo pages in Pica type; and the whole work has in it one sixth more than Chapman's Select Speeches, or Willison's American Eloquence, in five octavo volumes each.

In conclusion, the author may be permitted to say, that while he has aimed to produce a volume worthy of lying at all times on the table of every one engaged in speaking or writing for the public, he has hoped it might prove peculiarly useful to men of his own profession; since nothing is more desirable, at the present day, than a larger infusion into our sacred eloquence of the freedom, boldness, and strength which distinguish our secular oratory.

***Sept. 1st*, 1852.**

INTRODUCTION

I

An understanding of Chauncey Allen Goodrich as a rhetorician is to be gained chiefly from three sources: his lectures on rhetoric delivered at Yale College;[1] the critical apparatus to be found in his *Select British Eloquence;* and his concept of oratory as revealed in the speeches that he chose for *Select British Eloquence.* For the modern student, the effort to understand Goodrich should prove rewarding, for although the texts of the speeches are not well established by current standards, and although his critical system antedates Marx, Freud, social Darwinism, and nuclear fission, he presents in *Select British Eloquence* a compendium of ideas and demonstrations developed from theories of rhetoric—and hence of the human being—that have proved viable in many centuries and many lands. It is fortunate that the book is now presented in a new and complete edition, since the contents are of abiding interest to historians of American and British culture and to all concerned with rhetoric and oratory.

Select British Eloquence deserves to be considered, however, primarily in the form in which its author devised it, that is, as a textbook. In a sense, it is an extension of the life and thought of a teacher who regarded the study of speechmaking as a matter of consequence in the education of young men. What can Chauncey Goodrich teach today? He can teach many lessons; the most important of these are the oldest and the most obvious, yet perhaps also the most needed.

II

Foremost among the lessons taught by Goodrich is the Aristotelian principle that the hearer is the speech's end and object. In his selection of speeches as well as in his commentaries, Goodrich assumes that a speech is designed to effect a purpose—first with an immediate audience and perhaps eventually with a remote one.

It is almost impossible to read the texts of the speeches provided by Goodrich without being constantly reminded that here is discourse intended to be heard. Sir James Mackintosh, pleading before the King's Bench in behalf of Jean Peltier, speaks not in general nor in the abstract. He speaks not to the past nor to the future but to the present purpose of defending his client against the pending charge of a libel against Napoleon Bonaparte. Thomas Erskine, in the case of the Dean of Asaph, addresses a listening judge specifically and directly on the rights of juries. Every part of his speech is imbued with the spirit of direct and forceful communication to a court sit-

[1] For the opportunity to study Goodrich's lectures on rhetoric, scholars are indebted to Professor John P. Hoshor, of the University of Hawaii, who in 1940 located the manuscript notes of the lectures in an attic in Pasadena, California, arranged to have them transferred to the library of Yale University, transcribed them, and provided an introduction and annotations. See John P. Hoshor, "The Rhetorical Theory of Chauncey Allen Goodrich" (Unpublished Dissertation; State University of Iowa, 1947), pp. 234-398; see also *Speech Monographs,* XIV (1947), 1-37.

ting in present judgment. John Philpot Curran, engaged in the defense of Archibald Hamilton Rowan, talks to the jurors with the clear intention of influencing their immediate decision. George Canning, speaking to his constituents in Liverpool, leaves no doubt that he is addressing them energetically and with an immediate realization of the content of his words. The inimitable Charles James Fox, in passionate protest against the ministry's rejection of Bonaparte's overtures for peace, employs his masterful talent for refutation in language urgently directed to the members of the House of Commons. Even the letters of Junius, wisely included by Goodrich in this volume, seem to talk, for, although never spoken, they are speeches delivered in print, and they argue their case most shrewdly indeed.

In his commentaries, Goodrich likewise assumes the indispensable audience and almost equally indispensable adversary. In a characteristic instance, he thus describes the elder Pitt before the House of Commons:

> By degrees he completely subdued the House, until a murmur of applause broke forth from every quarter. Seizing the favorable moment, he drew back with the utmost dignity, and placing himself in an attitude of defiance, exclaimed, in his loudest tone, "Is there an *Austrian* among you? Let him come forward and reveal himself!" The effect was irresistible. "Universal silence," says Walpole, "left him arbiter of his own terms." [2]

In *Select British Eloquence,* Goodrich merely put into practice what he professed. In his lectures at Yale College, he set forth his theory:

> The end of public speaking is *not* to be eloquent. I say this because an error on this subject has had great influence in corrupting eloquence. . . . It has produced a tendency to speak for the sake of delivery, of attracting the attention of constituents, of establishing a reputation for eloquence. But this attitude always defeats its object. . . .The true end is to address just and pertinent remarks on the subject under contemplation. To this, genius is not indispensable—sound sense and thorough knowledge, with good style and clear arrangement, are sufficient. But one more quality is necessary—a certain degree of *vivacity* without which men will not listen.[3]

The style throughout *Select British Eloquence* is unmistakably that of a speaker addressing a hearer. Because the language is of a former time, it may sometimes seem quaint to the modern ear, but the style would be oral in any language. It is the discourse of men talking. It says, "Listen, listen to me: we have business together."

III

Consistently in his commentaries, and almost invariably in his selection of speeches, Goodrich discloses his assumption that a sound rhetoric is deeply involved with dialectic. Indeed, the commentaries, read in sequence, suggest that in the United Kingdom rhetoric and oratory have developed in one long adversary proceeding. For the most part, the speeches included in *Select British Eloquence* are taken from debates in the House of Commons or from pleas to judges or juries. Goodrich obviously assumes that true dialectic is necessary to sound rhetoric. If it follows that a sound

[2] *Select British Eloquence,* p. 61.

[3] John P. Hoshor (ed.), "Lectures on Rhetoric and Public Speaking by Chauncey Allen Goodrich" (Unpublished Dissertation; State University of Iowa, 1947), pp. 3-4.

rhetoric is prerequisite to useful oratory, Goodrich would seem here to have adopted a highly significant criterion, for no speaker can argue against himself quite so well as an adversary can argue against him. If a speaker really wishes to get to the bottom of any matter, he must prepare himself to deal with the strongest possible opposition to his proposal. In a tyranny, the official truth can be manufactured overnight by a Bureau of Public Enlightenment and published next morning in an official newspaper. In a free country, truth is the survivor of conflict. It is not singular but plural, and it cannot be official.

If useful oratory presupposes sound rhetoric, and if sound rhetoric requires dialectic, then vigorous opposition would seem to be helpful, if not indispensable. Great speeches may thus be sought in their natural habitat—controversy in which the requisite dialectic is provided by more speakers than one. Great speeches are likely to be found, therefore, as parts of a whole, of a dialogue involving thrust and counterthrust, argument and refutation, question and answer, proposal and denial, affirmation and negation. That Goodrich's choices were not inadvertent is manifest in his lectures to his students at Yale. "Every work of art," he said, "is a *system,* a combination of various subordinate parts, which combine to produce one harmonious *whole.* Each distinct part therefore is nothing in itself—its value is *relative.*"[4] Goodrich thus clearly states for rhetoric and oratory a holistic theory, and the principle of the whole embracing the union of rhetoric and dialectic is implicit in *Select British Eloquence.* Perhaps in conscious deference to this principle, Goodrich provided a memoir of each orator, a historical introduction to each speech, an analysis of the longer speeches, critical and explanatory notes, and a concluding statement. The application of this principle is to be found also in the selection of the speeches for the book and in the providing of the texts in their entirety.

Among the speeches delivered in the House of Commons, where opposition was not wanting, the student will find the following: Sir John Eliot's address on the Petition of Right; Sir William Wyndham's attack on Sir Robert Walpole and Walpole's reply; the elder Pitt's speeches on the marriage of the Prince of Wales, on the Spanish Convention, on the impressment of seamen, on taking the Hanoverian troops into the pay of Great Britain, on the removal of the British troops from Boston, as well as other speeches on the question of the American commonwealths. The student will also find Burke's speeches on American taxation, on the East India Bill, and on the Nabob of Arcot's debts. He will find Grattan's speech moving a declaration of Irish right, Sheridan's speech against Warren Hastings, and the younger Pitt's speeches on dealing with France. He will also find speeches by Canning and by Brougham, and, notably, speeches by Charles James Fox on the East India Bill, on the Westminster Scrutiny, and on Parliamentary reform.

Each of these speeches was delivered, presumably, under the rule that sound rhetoric is involved in dialectic. Each was delivered in the heat of genuine debate under the pressures of immediate circumstance. Nor were the speeches in the House of Commons the only ones delivered in legislative assembly. Goodrich has included in his volume Lord Belhaven's eloquent but unavailing speech to the Parliament of Scotland and an address by Lord Chesterfield to the House of Lords.

The most rigorous reasoning and the strictest evidence in speeches are

[4] "Lectures," *op. cit.*, pp. 10-11.

sometimes to be found in those delivered in the courtroom, especially, according to tradition, in the speeches delivered before learned judges. Goodrich has included in his book examples of the great legal oratory of Lord Erskine, represented by his speech in behalf of Lord George Gordon and by others in behalf of Stockdale, Frost, Bingham, Hardy, Hadfield, and Markham. John Philpot Curran is represented by his speeches in behalf of Rowan and Finnerty and by his speech against the Marquess of Headfort. Sir James Mackintosh appears in behalf of Peltier.

The speeches of Erskine, Curran, and Mackintosh were delivered against opposition, present and vocal, in the courtroom. They must surely have been preceded, as they were accompanied, by thorough dialectic. Indeed, in *Select British Eloquence* the single discourse is the exception. Doubtless Lord Brougham did not anticipate opposition when he gave his inaugural address as Lord Rector of the University of Glasgow. Perhaps Lord Mansfield did not anticipate the opposition he met from the mob that surrounded him during the trial of John Wilkes. Yet, while his address to the mob is obviously extempore, it clearly exemplifies the experience of dialectic that comes from a lifetime spent with the law.

The Goodrich volume thus offers few speeches that were not delivered in debate, either in a legislative chamber or in a courtroom. Among the exceptions is the magnificent speech delivered by Edmund Burke before the electors of Bristol on September 6, 1780. This speech might well be required reading for every member of the United States Senate, and at least the following section should be posted in every Congressional office:

> It is certainly not pleasing to be put out of the public service. But I wish to be a member of Parliament, to have my share of doing good, and resisting evil. It would therefore be absurd to renounce my objects in order to obtain my seat. I deceive myself, indeed, most grossly, if I had not much rather pass the remainder of my life hidden in the recesses of the deepest obscurity, feeding my mind even with the visions and imaginations of such things, than to be placed on the most splendid throne of the universe, tantalized with the denial of the practice of all which can make the greatest situation any other than the greatest curse.[5]

IV

Goodrich regarded oratory as one of the liberal arts, indeed as an art more noble than poetry, painting, sculpture, music, or architecture, since its object is not merely to please but also to direct the soul, to enforce the truth. Oratory is the great and genuine drama of mankind, presented on a stage as wide as the world and as old as time. In the view of Goodrich, oratory, as a great liberal art, is also ". . . the adaptation of means to an end, on the immutable principles of human nature."[6]

Goodrich's concept of oratory as an especially human art undoubtedly explains the care he takes throughout his commentaries to describe the incidents and provide the anecdotes that make speeches real and bring orators to life. Certainly students reading Goodrich will see much of Lord Chatham as the imperious human being who could put even the King out of countenance. They will also see Chatham taunted before the House of Commons for having received a pension from the Crown and for having recommended

[5] *Select British Eloquence,* p. 310.
[6] "Lectures," *op. cit.*, p. 9.

pensions for others. They will discover him earning, through his actions, year by year, the title of the "Great Commoner." They will observe Chatham in a facetious moment devastating George Grenville's earnest plea, "Tell me, tell me where you can lay another tax!" by breaking into a popular song, "Gentle Shepherd Tell Me Where." They will see Chatham undergo the intense pain of gout and will observe the House of Commons unanimously urging that he speak while seated—an unprecedented privilege. They will see Chatham insist on kneeling before the King despite the King's willingness to relieve him of his obligation. They will hear the crippled Chatham say to those members of the House of Commons who foolishly imagine that they can disperse the continental armies of America, "I might as well talk of driving them before me with this crutch."[7] They will see Chatham dismiss an error with contempt and cow an adversary with a glance. And as with Chatham, so with Burke, Fox, Grattan, the younger Pitt, Erskine, Curran, and Brougham.

To young people studying orators and oratory, the forensic triumphs of the great must surely become tedious if unrelieved by evidence of the humanity of the speakers. As a playwright provides comic relief, so Goodrich in his drama of oratory lets the students see the passion, the pain, and the humanity of the great British orators who have carried on the tradition of free men in the parliament, in the courtroom, and on the public platform.

V

As all speeches are human events, Goodrich views great speeches on great occasions as great events deserving the notice of historians, for he sees speechmaking as a force, like wealth or generalship. No lesson taught by Goodrich is more significant to the student, more useful to the teacher, than his quiet assumption, throughout *Select British Eloquence,* that speeches are truly significant transactions in the commonwealth of humanity. Much too sophisticated to attribute the winning or losing of a parliamentary contest to a single speech or even to a series of speeches, Goodrich rightly divines the power of public speaking in the formation of the opinion that ultimately governed eighteenth-century England, as well as the United States of his own day. "All agree," he said, "that in no country is the power of impressing thought on others through the medium of language so controlling in its influence as here [in the United States]. All our institutions and our government are suspended on the contest of mind going on around us."[8]

In his commentaries, Goodrich demonstrates the way in which speeches are woven into the fabric of human affairs. In spite of adversity, Goodrich says, Erskine was able to keep Horne Tooke from being hanged; Lord Chatham's speech in the case of Wilkes, though failing in its immediate purpose, gained the support of the Lord Chancellor; the younger Pitt's speech so electrified the House of Commons that "Sir John Sinclair . . . withdrew his motion for an amendment, and the address was passed . . . without one dissenting voice."[9]

In the texts chosen for this book, Goodrich also demonstrates that speeches may be highly influential transactions. The speeches show the

[7] *Select British Eloquence,* p. 71, note 16. For the memoir of Chatham, see pp. 52-75.
[8] "Lectures," *op. cit.,* p. 2.
[9] *Select British Eloquence,* pp. 761, 113, 603.

Commons, in session after the illegal seizure of Sir John Eliot, meeting only to determine "not to do any more business until they were righted in their privileges." They show Sir John Eliot himself courageously speaking from and for the wisdom of his ancestors, as well as for the Petition of Right, in defiance of the threat of the Tower that ominously awaited him on the dissolution of the Parliament. They show the unfortunate Earl of Strafford, deserted by his King, pleading his defense against the charge of treason before the House of Lords. They show Lord Digby abandoning his role as one of the managers of Strafford's impeachment to argue on principle that the Commons had no right to try Strafford legislatively in avoidance of judicial proceedings. The student may hear Lord Digby saying:

> Of all these corruptives of judgment, Mr. Speaker, I do, before God, discharge myself to the utmost of my power; and do now, with a clear conscience, wash my hands of this man's blood by this solemn protestation, *that my vote goes not to the taking of the Earl of Strafford's life.*[10]

War as well as oratory is a human transaction, and sometimes war and oratory conjoin. In *Select British Eloquence,* the reader may hear Lord Chatham address the throne, in a last great effort to stop the American war. In words as vigorous as the English language can supply, Lord Chatham brings all his English patriotism to the succor of the American commonwealths. The reader may also hear the reasoned and reasonable eloquence of Edmund Burke pleading for conciliation with the American colonies. Speaking to an obdurate audience in the House of Commons, Burke bases his argument for conciliation with America squarely on the rights of Englishmen and on the grounds of expediency. With faultless cogency, but without success, he argues his proposal for a peace that would place the Americans on an equal footing with other Englishmen. And the student may observe the younger Pitt bringing the full power of his administration to bear in support of William Wilberforce's proposal for the abolition of the slave trade. As they deal with treason, with war, and with slavery—serious events in the human commonwealth—speeches are likewise events, and, as human affairs go, profoundly grave events.

VI

Implicit in Goodrich's thought is the assumption that great speeches are concerned chiefly and characteristically with matters of probability, with the taking of action in those questions on which policies must be formed and decisions made without benefit of all the facts, without opportunity to obtain truly valid evidence, even, perhaps, without the comfort of knowing afterward whether the right decision was taken. Yet Goodrich seems to share with John Donne the faith that ". . . rhetorique will make absent and remote things present to your understanding." [11]

In such a view, speeches are events that influence and are influenced by other events. They thus bear a discernible relationship to history, which is also concerned with things absent or remote. Indeed, it may be observed that rhetoric, considered as the theory of speechmaking, is to the future as history is to the past. Both arts—history and rhetoric—deal with distant countries. History maps a land once visited and now remembered—per-

[10] *Ibid.*, p. 18.

[11] John Donne, "Sermon XXVI," *Complete Poetry and Selected Prose,* ed. John Hayward (London: The Nonesuch Press, 1929), p. 615.

haps but dimly—and rhetoric, a land not yet seen, save in the mind's eye. As history endeavors to sustain the memory of a country lost, so rhetoric endeavors to describe the shape of an undiscovered country and, often as occasion affords, to alter or determine that shape. In the great issues of probability that are the special province of rhetoric and oratory, the speechmaker has characteristically relied on history, as well as upon rhetoric, to make absent things present to his understanding. Patrick Henry thus declared, in the great speech attributed to him, "I have but one lamp by which my feet are guided, and that is the lamp of experience. I know of no way of judging the future but by the past." [12]

The poet and the scientist also endeavor to make absent things present to the understanding—but with a difference. The scientist in his laboratory may design his procedures with relatively little interference from the public. The poet, if he likes, may express his inmost thoughts in solitude. But, as Goodrich constantly demonstrates, the orator is engaged before the public in the public business. He is not free to be silent. He must declare himself, for a speech is an act; and failure to act may have consequences that, far from being negative, are as affirmative as the consequences of any act that could possibly be envisioned. The orator, like the physician or the commander of an army, thus has problems that must be embraced and contained, even though they may never be solved beyond question. The scientist may demonstrate empirically the validity of his hypothesis, but the orator and his audience must be content with apparent solutions for which validity may never be truly demonstrated. The orator deals in symbols, albeit very potent symbols, to influence policies that, once established, cannot be undone.

The involvement of oratory with things absent and remote, with questions of probability, is a teaching and a learning implicit in *Select British Eloquence.* Rhetoric brings to the understanding of Charles James Fox—and he attempts to bring to the understanding of the Commons—a vision of peace, of nations relieved from the horrors of war. Serious even to sadness, Edmund Burke constructs a future that would admit "Americans to an equal interest in the British constitution, and place them at once on the footing of other Englishmen." The younger Pitt foresees and warns against a time of great peril when every subject of the King must exert himself to protect Britain against the forces of Napoleon Bonaparte. Perhaps no British orator has excelled Lord Chatham in the statesman's prescience described by Demosthenes: "And what is the duty of a statesman? to watch the inception of events, to descry their tendency, and to forewarn his countrymen." [13] On April 7, 1778, Lord Chatham came before the Commons, in his own words, old and infirm, with one foot—more than one foot—in the grave.[14] He came to perform his duty, as he saw it, and to reject a future that would give America complete independence from Britain. He was unable, unwilling, to bring to his understanding an absent world in which Britain and America were to be dissevered. Lord Chatham's dying speech illustrates well the way in which visions of the future can conflict and assumptions concerning the future may influence the present moment. A person (or a nation) confident of the approval of destiny is an entirely

[12] Patrick Henry, "Address to the Virginia Delegation to the Continental Congress."

[13] Demosthenes, "On the Crown," *The Oration of Demosthenes on the Crown,* translated by the Right Hon. Sir Robert Collier (London: Longmans, Green, and Co., 1875), p. 94.

[14] *Select British Eloquence,* p. 142.

different creature from one whose vision of the future is limited, timorous, or confused. Absent and remote things brought to understanding will affect the present as well as future times. As Goodrich perceived, the rhetoricians and the orators have in their keeping, for better or for worse, their several visions of the future and the task of resolving the conflicts among them.

VII

To summarize, the qualified student who utilizes *Select British Eloquence* as a textbook may expect to learn much that is taught directly: names, dates, places. He may expect to learn something of metaphor and enthymeme. He may gain some knowledge of history, of parliamentary institutions, and of human nature. But perhaps the most valuable lessons are those taught by indirection. Like all great teachers, Goodrich is most useful when he seems not to be teaching at all. The most significant lessons in his book are to be found in what he implies, in what he discloses in passing, in what he assumes to be true. The perceptive student of Goodrich's *Select British Eloquence* may thus see demonstrated that the hearer *is* the speech's end and object; that sound rhetoric is deeply involved with dialectic; that speechmaking is a humanistic study, a great liberal art; that great speeches are great events deserving the notice of historians; and that great speeches are concerned with questions of probability. As Chauncey Goodrich's present-day pupils learn the lessons he has to teach, they may find fulfilled John Morley's hope "that your professors of rhetoric will teach you to cultivate that golden art—the steadfast use of a language in which truth can be told; a speech that is strong by natural force, and not merely effective by declamation; an utterance without trick, without affectation, without mannerism. . . ."[15]

Bower Aly

University of Oregon

February, 1963

[15] John Morley, "On the Study of Literature," *Literary Essays* (London: Arthur L. Humphreys, 1906), p. 382.

CONTENTS

SELECT BRITISH ELOQUENCE.

SIR JOHN ELIOT.

John Eliot was descended from a family of great respectability in Cornwall, and was born on the 20th of April, 1590. After enjoying the best advantages for education which England could afford, and spending some years in foreign travel, he was elected to Parliament at the age of thirty-three, and became one of the most prominent members in the House of Commons under Charles I.

The House embraced at this time, some of the ablest and most learned men of the age, such as Sir Edward Coke, John Hampden, Selden, St. John, Pym, &c. Among these, Sir John Eliot stood pre-eminent for the force and fervor of his eloquence. The general style of speaking at that day was weighty, grave, and sententious, but tinctured with the pedantry of the preceding reign, and destitute of that warmth of feeling which is essential to the character of a great orator. Eliot, Wentworth, and a few others were exceptions; and Eliot especially spoke at times with all the enthusiasm and vehemence of the early days of Greece and Rome.

Hence he was appointed one of the managers of the House when the Duke of Buckingham was impeached in 1626, and had the part assigned him of making the closing argument against the Duke before the House of Lords. This he did with such energy and effect as to awaken the keenest resentment of the Court; so that two days after he was called out of the House, as if to receive a message from the King, and was instantly seized and hurried off by water to the Tower. The Commons, on hearing of this breach of privilege, were thrown into violent commotion. The cry "Rise!" "Rise!" was heard from every part of the hall. They did immediately adjourn, and met again only to record their resolution, "Not to do any more business until they were righted in their privileges." This decisive measure brought the government to a stand, and reduced them to the humiliating necessity of releasing Sir John Eliot, and also Sir Dudley Diggs, another of the managers who had been arrested on the same occasion. Eliot and his companion returned in triumph to the House, which voted that "they had not exceeded the commission intrusted to them."

In consequence of this defeat, and the backwardness of the Commons to grant the supplies demanded, Charles soon after dissolved Parliament, and determined to raise money by "forced loans." Great numbers resisted this imposition, and among them Eliot and Hampden, who, with seventy-six others of the gentry, were thrown into prison for refusing to surrender their property to the Crown; while hundreds of inferior rank were impressed into the army or navy by way of punishment. The King found, however, that with all this violence he could not raise the necessary supplies, and was compelled to call another Parliament within eight months. Eliot, Hampden, and many others who had been lying under arrest, were elected members of the new House of Commons while thus confined in prison, and were released only a few days before the meeting of Parliament.

These violent invasions of the rights of property and person, naturally came up for consideration at an early period of the session. The Commons, as the result of their discussions, framed, on the 27th of May, 1628, that second Great Charter of the liberties of England the PETITION OF RIGHT; so called because drawn up, in the humble spirit of the day, in the form of a petition to the King, but having, when ratified by his concurrence, all the authority of a fundamental law of the kingdom. This document was prepared by Sir Edward Coke at the age of eighty-three, and was one of the last public acts of that distinguished lawyer. It provided, that no loan or tax might be levied but by consent of Parliament; that no man might be imprisoned but by legal process; that soldiers might not be quartered on people contrary to their wills; and that no commissions be granted for executing martial law. On the 2d of June, Charles returned an evasive answer, in which he endeavored to satisfy the Commons without giving a legal and binding assent to the petition. The next day, Sir John Eliot made the following speech. It breathes throughout, that spirit of affection and reverence for the King's person which was still felt by both houses of Parliament. It does not dwell, therefore, on those recent acts of arbitrary power in which the King might be supposed to have reluctantly concurred; and the fact is a striking one, that Eliot does not even allude to his late cruel imprisonment, a decisive proof that he was not actuated by a spirit of personal resentment. The entire speech was directed against the royal Favorite, the Duke of Buckingham. Its object was, to expose his flagrant misconduct during the preceding ten years, under the reign of James as well as Charles; and to show that through his duplicity, incompetency, and rash counsels, the honor of the kingdom had been betrayed, its allies sacrificed, its treasures wasted, and those necessities of the King created which gave rise to the arbitrary acts referred to in the Petition of Right. The facts which Eliot adduces in proof, are very briefly mentioned, or barely alluded to, because they were fresh in the minds of all, and had created a burning sense of wrong and dishonor throughout the whole kingdom. They will be explained in brief notes appended to the speech; but, to feel their full force, the reader must go back to the history of the times, and place himself in the midst of the scene.

There is in this speech, a union of dignity and fervor which is highly characteristic of the man. "His mind," says Lord Nugent, "was deeply imbued with a love of philosophy and a confidence in religion which gave a lofty tone to his eloquence." His fervor, acting on a clear and powerful understanding, gives him a simplicity, directness, and continuity of thought, a rapidity of progress, and a vehemence of appeal, which will remind the reader of the style of Demosthenes. His whole soul is occupied with the subject. He seizes upon the strong points of his case with such absorbing interest, that all those secondary and collateral trains of thought with which a speaker like Burke, amplifies and adorns the discussion, are rejected as unworthy of the stern severity of the occasion. The eloquence lies wholly in the thought; and the entire *bareness* of the expression, the absence of all ornament, adds to the effect, because there is nothing interposed to break the force of the blow. The antique air of the style heightens the interest of the speech; and will recommend it particularly to those who have learned to relish the varied construction and racy English of our early writers.

SPEECH

OF SIR JOHN ELIOT ON THE PETITION OF RIGHT, DELIVERED IN THE HOUSE OF COMMONS, JUNE 3, 1628.

Mr. Speaker,—We sit here as the great Council of the King, and in that capacity, it is our duty to take into consideration the state and affairs of the kingdom, and when there is occasion, to give a true representation of them by way of counsel and advice, with what we conceive necessary or expedient to be done.

In this consideration, I confess many a sad thought hath affrighted me, and that not only in respect of our dangers from abroad (which yet I know are great, as they have been often prest and dilated to us), but in respect of our disorders here at home, which do enforce those dangers, and by which they are occasioned. For I believe I shall make it clear to you, that both at first, the cause of these dangers were our disorders, and our disorders now are yet our greatest dangers—that not so much the potency of our enemies as the weakness of ourselves, doth threaten us: so that the saying of one of the Fathers may be assumed by us, "*non tam potentiâ suâ quam negligentiâ nostrâ*," "not so much by their power as by our neglect." Our want of true devotion to heaven—our insincerity and doubling in religion—our want of councils—our precipitate actions—the insufficiency or unfaithfulness of our generals abroad—the ignorance or corruption of our ministers at home—the impoverishing of the sovereign—the oppression and depression of the subject—the exhausting of our treasures—the waste of our provisions—consumption of our ships—destruction of our men—*these* make the advantage to our enemies, not the reputation of their arms; and if in these there be not reformation, we need no foes abroad: *Time itself will ruin us.*

To show this more fully, I believe you will all hold it necessary that what I say, should not seem an aspersion on the state or imputation on the government, as I have known such motions misinterpreted. But far is this from me to propose, who have none but clear thoughts of the excellency of the King; nor can I have other ends but the advancement of his Majesty's glory. I shall desire a little of your patience extraordinary, as I lay open the particulars, which I shall do with what brevity I may, answerable to the importance of the cause and the necessity now upon us; yet with such respect and observation to the time, as I hope it shall not be thought troublesome.

I. For the first, then, our insincerity and doubling in religion, is the greatest and most dangerous disorder of all others. This hath never been unpunished; and of this we have many strong examples of all states and in all times to awe us. What testimony doth it want? Will you have authority of books? Look on the collections of the Committee for Religion; *there* is too clear an evidence. See there the commission procured for composition with the papists of the North! Mark the proceedings thereupon, and you will find them to little less amounting than a toleration in effect: the slight payments, and the easiness of them, will likewise show the favor that is intended. Will you have proofs of *men?* Witness the hopes, witness the presumptions, witness the reports of all the papists generally. Observe the dispositions of commanders, the trust of officers, the confidence in secretaries to employments in this kingdom, in Ireland, and elsewhere. These will all show that it hath too great a certainty. And to this add but the incontrovertible evidence of that All-powerful Hand, which we have felt so sorely, that gave it full assurance; for as the heavens oppose themselves to our impiety, so it is we that first opposed the heavens.[1]

II. For the second, our want of councils, that great disorder in a state under which there can not be stability. If effects may show their causes (as they are often a perfect demonstration of them), our misfortunes, our disasters, serve to prove our deficiencies in council, and the consequences they draw with them. If reason be allowed in this dark age, the judgment of dependencies and foresight of contingencies in affairs, do confirm my position. For, if we view ourselves at home, are we in strength, are we in reputation, equal to our ancestors? If we view ourselves abroad, are our friends as many? are our enemies no more? Do our friends retain their safety and possessions? Do not our enemies enlarge themselves, and gain from them and us? To what council owe we the loss of the Palatinate, where we sacrificed both our honor and our men sent thither, stopping those greater powers appointed for the service, by which it might have been defended?[2] What council gave

[1] The gun-powder plot for blowing up both houses of Parliament, and extirpating the Protestant religion at a single stroke, was still fresh in the minds of all. It is not, therefore, surprising, at a period when correct views of religious liberty were as yet unknown in England, that any remissness in executing the laws against Catholics, was regarded with great jealousy by Eliot and his friends, especially as the mother of Buckingham was of that communion.

[2] Frederick V., the Elector Palatine, who married "the beautiful Elizabeth," sister of Charles I., had been attacked on religious grounds by a union of Catholic states in Germany, with Austria at their head, stripped of the Palatinate, and driven as an exile into Holland, with his wife and child Al'

direction to the late action, whose wounds are yet bleeding, I mean the expedition to Rhé, of which there is yet so sad a memory in all men? What design for us, or advantage to our state, could that impart?

You know the wisdom of your ancestors, and the practice of their times, how they preserved their safeties. We all know, and have as much cause to doubt [i. e., distrust or guard against] as they had, the greatness and ambition of that kingdom, *which the Old World could not satisfy*.[3] Against this greatness and ambition, we likewise know the proceedings of that princess, that never-to-be-forgotten, excellent Queen Elizabeth, whose name, without admiration, falls not into mention even with her enemies. You know how she advanced herself, and how she advanced the nation in glory and in state; how she depressed her enemies, and how she upheld her friends; how she enjoyed a full security, and made those our scorn who now are made our terror.

Some of the principles she built on were these; and if I mistake, let reason and our statesmen contradict me.

First, to maintain, in what she might, a unity in France, that the kingdom, being at peace within itself, might be a bulwark to keep back the power of Spain by land.

Next, to preserve an amity and league between that state and us, that so we might come in aid of the Low Countries [Holland], and by that means receive their ships, and help them by sea.

This triple cord, so working between France, the States [Holland], and England, might enable us, as occasion should require, to give assistance unto others. And by this means, as the experience of that time doth tell us, we were not only free from those fears that now possess and trouble us, but then our names were fearful to our enemies. See now what correspondency our action had with this. Try our conduct by these rules. It did induce, as a necessary consequence, a division in France between the Protestants and their king, of which there is too woful and lamentable experience.[4] It hath made an absolute breach between that state and us, and so entertains us against France, and France in preparation against us, that we have nothing to promise to our neighbors, nay, hardly to ourselves. Next, observe the *time* in which it was attempted, and you shall find it not only varying from those principles, but directly contrary and opposite to those ends; and such, as from the issue and success, rather might be thought a conception of Spain than begotten here with us.

[Here there was an interruption made by Sir Humphrey May, Chancellor of the Duchy and of the Privy Council, expressing a dislike; but the House ordered Sir John Eliot to go on, whereupon he proceeded thus:]

Mr. Speaker, I am sorry for this interruption, but much more sorry if there hath been occasion on my part. And, as I shall submit myself wholly to your judgment, to receive what censure you may give me, if I have offended, so, in the integrity of my intentions and the clearness of my thoughts, I must still retain this confidence, *that no greatness shall deter me from the duties I owe to the service of my king and country; but that, with a true English heart, I shall discharge myself as faithfully and as really, to the extent of my poor power, as any man whose honors or whose offices most strictly oblige him.*

You know the dangers of Denmark,[5] and how much they concern us; what in respect of our alliance and the country; what in the importance of the Sound; what an advantage to our enemies the gain thereof would be! What loss, what prejudice to us by this disunion; we breaking in upon France, France enraged by us, and the Netherlands at amazement between both![6] Neither could we intend to aid that luckless king [Christian IV., of Denmark], whose loss is our disaster.

Can those [the King's ministers] that express their trouble at the hearing of these things, and have so often told us in this place of their knowledge in the conjunctures and disjunctures of affairs—can they say they advised in this? Was this an act of council, Mr. Speaker? I have more

Protestant Christendom was indignant at these wrongs; and the King of England was expected to sustain the injured Elector on the double ground of family alliance and a community of religion. These expectations had all been disappointed by the weak, indecisive, and fluctuating counsels of Buckingham. Twelve thousand English troops were indeed sent to assist Frederick, under Count Mansfeldt, but nearly all of them perished on the way, from mere want of foresight and preparation on the part of the English government. This wanton sacrifice of life is alluded to at the close of the speech in a single word —"*Mansfeldt!*"—a name which at that time smote on the heart of the whole English nation. The expedition to the Isle of Rhé, mentioned in the next sentence, will be explained hereafter.

[3] To understand the force and beauty of this allusion to Spain, we must go back to the time when all Europe was filled with dismay at the power of the Spanish arms on both continents. Few things in English eloquence, as Forster remarks, are finer in expression or purpose, than this allusion and the subsequent train of thought, as addressed to Englishmen of that day.

[4] This refers to the expedition against the Isle of Rhé, respecting which see note 8.

[5] Christian IV., King of Denmark, as a leading Protestant prince, and uncle to Elizabeth, wife of Frederick, the Elector Palatine, had entered warmly into their cause, and marched with a large army to reinstate them in the Palatinate. After some partial successes, however, he was repulsed by the Austrians, driven back into his own dominions, and reduced to imminent danger of being stripped of all his possessions. The English trade through the Sound into the Baltic, which was of great value, was thus on the point of being entirely cut off by the establishment of a hostile power on the ruins of Denmark. Yet England had done nothing to sustain her ally, or to protect her rights and interests in that quarter; and the English people were justly incensed against Buckingham for this neglect.

[6] Here, as above, allusion is made to the disgraceful expedition against the Isle of Rhé, by which France was enraged, and no diversion in favor of Denmark either made or intended.

charity than to think it; and unless they make confession of it themselves, I can not believe it.

III. For the next, the insufficiency and unfaithfulness of our generals (that great disorder abroad), what shall I say? I wish there were not cause to mention it; and, but for the apprehension of the danger that is to come, if the like choice hereafter be not prevented, I could willingly be silent. But my duty to my sovereign, my service to this House, and the safety and honor of my country, are above all respects; and what so nearly trenches to the prejudice of these, must not, shall not be forborne.

At Cadiz,[7] then, in that first expedition we made, when we arrived and found a conquest ready—the Spanish ships, I mean, fit for the satisfaction of a voyage, and of which some of the chiefest then there, themselves have since assured me, that the satisfaction would have been sufficient, either in point of honor or in point of profit—*why was it neglected?* Why was it not achieved, it being granted on all hands how feasible it was?

Afterward, when, with the destruction of some of our men and the exposure of others, who (though their fortune since has not been such), by chance, came off safe—when, I say, with the loss of our serviceable men, that unserviceable fort was gained, and the whole army landed, *why was there nothing done?* Why was there nothing *attempted?* If nothing was intended, wherefore did they land? If there *was* a service, wherefore were they shipped again? Mr. Speaker, it satisfies me too much [*i. e.*, I am over-satisfied] in this case—when I think of their dry and hungry march into that drunken quarter (for so the soldiers termed it), which was the period [termination] of their journey—that divers of our men being left as a sacrifice to the enemy, *that labor was at an end.*

For the next undertaking, at Rhé,[8] I will not trouble you much; only this, in short. Was not that whole action carried against the judgment and opinion of those officers that were of the council? Was not the first, was not the last, was not all in the landing—in the intrenching—in the continuance there—in the assault—in the retreat—without their assent? Did any advice take place of such as were of the council? If there should be made a particular inquisition thereof, these things will be manifest and more. I will not instance the manifesto that was made, giving the reason of these arms; nor by whom, nor in what manner, nor on what grounds it was published, nor what effects it hath wrought, drawing, as it were, almost the whole world into league against us. Nor will I mention the leaving of the wines, the leaving of the salt, which were in our possession, and of a value, as it is said, to answer much of our expense. Nor will I dwell on that great wonder (which no Alexander or Cæsar[9] ever did), the enriching of the enemy by courtesies when our soldiers wanted help; nor the private intercourse and parleys with the fort, which were continually held. What they intended may be read in the success; and upon due examination thereof, they would not want their proofs.

For the last voyage to Rochelle, there need no observations, it is so fresh in memory; nor will I make an inference or corollary on all. Your own knowledge shall judge what truth or what sufficiency they express.

IV. For the next, the ignorance and corruption of our ministers, where can you miss of instances? If you survey the court, if you survey the country; if the church, if the city be exam-

[7] Buckingham, at the close of 1625, had fitted out a fleet of eighty sail, to intercept the Spanish treasure ships from America, to scour the coasts of Spain, and destroy the shipping in her ports. Owing to the utter incompetency of the commander, there was no concert or subordination in the fleet. The treasure-ships were not intercepted; but seven other large and rich Spanish ships, which would have repaid all the expenses of the expedition, were suffered to escape, when they might easily have been taken. At length a landing was effected in the neighborhood of Cadiz, and the paltry fort of Puntal was taken. The English soldiers broke open the wine-cellars of the country around, and became drunk and unmanageable; so that the Spanish troops, if they had known their condition, might easily have cut the whole army to pieces. Their commander, as the only course left him, retreated to the ships, leaving some hundreds of his men to perish under the knives of the enraged peasantry.

[8] Buckingham, from motives of personal resentment against the French king, undertook, in June, 1627, to aid the Huguenots at Rochelle, who were in a state of open rebellion. He therefore sailed with a fleet of one hundred ships and seven thousand land forces, taking the command of the expedition himself, and expecting to be received with open arms. But the Rochellers, having no previous arrangement with him on the subject, and probably distrusting his intentions, refused to admit him into the town, and advised him to take possession of the Isle of Rhé, in the neighborhood. This he did, and immediately issued a manifesto, inciting the Protestants throughout France to rebel against their government. Great indignation was awakened in Europe by this attempt to rekindle the flames of civil war in that country. His appeal was, unfortunately, successful. The Protestants in the south of France rose almost to a man. A bloody conflict ensued, in which they were completely crushed, and their condition rendered far more wretched than before. Buckingham, in the mean time, conducted every thing wildly and at random. In October, a reenforcement of fifteen hundred men was sent out, mentioned in the speech as "the last voyage to Rochelle;" but the Duke was still repulsed, with loss at every point, till he was compelled to return in disgrace, with the loss of one third of his troops, in the month of November, 1627. This speech was delivered in June of the next year, while the nation was still smarting under the sense of the disasters and disgraces of this mad expedition.

[9] This sneer at the generalship of Buckingham was keenly felt, and derived its peculiar force from the lofty pretensions and high-sounding titles he assumed. He had also made himself ridiculous, and even suspected of treachery, by his affectation of courtesy in the interchange of civilities with the French commanders. To this Eliot alludes with stinging effect in the remaining part of the sentence.

ined; if you observe the bar, if the bench, if the ports, if the shipping, if the land, if the seas—all these will render you variety of proofs; and that in such measure and proportion as shows the greatness of our disease to be such that, if there be not some speedy application for remedy, our case is almost desperate.

V. Mr. Speaker, I fear I have been too long in these particulars that are past, and am unwilling to offend you: therefore in the rest I shall be shorter; and as to that which concerns the impoverishing of the King, no other arguments will I use than such as all men grant.

The exchequer, you know, is empty, and the reputation thereof gone; the ancient lands are sold; the jewels pawned; the plate engaged;[10] the debts still great; almost all charges, both ordinary and extraordinary, borne up by *projects!* What poverty can be greater? What necessity so great? *What perfect English heart is not almost dissolved into sorrow for this truth?*

VI. For the oppression of the subject, which, as I remember, is the next particular I proposed, it needs no demonstration. The whole kingdom is a proof; and for the exhausting of our treasures, that very oppression speaks it. What waste of our provisions, what consumption of our ships, what destruction of our men there hath been; witness that expedition to Algiers[11]—witness that with Mansfeldt—witness that to Cadiz—witness the next—witness that to Rhé—witness the last (I pray God we may never have more such witnesses)—witness, likewise, the Palatinate—witness Denmark—witness the Turks—witness the Dunkirkers—WITNESS ALL! What losses we have sustained! How we are impaired in munitions, in ships, in men!

It is beyond contradiction that we were never so much weakened, nor ever had less hope how to be restored.

These, Mr. Speaker, are our dangers, these are they who do threaten us; and these are, like the Trojan horse, brought in cunningly to surprise us. In these do lurk the strongest of our enemies, ready to issue on us; and if we do not speedily expel them, these are the signs, these the invitations to others! These will so prepare their entrance, that we shall have no means left of refuge or defense; for if we have these enemies at home, how can we strive with those that are abroad? If we be free from these, no other can impeach us. Our ancient English virtue (like the old Spartan valor), cleared from these disorders—our being in sincerity of religion and once made friends with heaven; having maturity of councils, sufficiency of generals, incorruption of officers, opulency in the King, liberty in the people, repletion in treasure, plenty of provisions, reparation of ships, preservation of men—our ancient English virtue, I say, thus rectified, will secure us; and unless there be a speedy reformation in these, I know not what hopes or expectations we can have.

These are the things, sir, I shall desire to have taken into consideration; that as we are the great council of the kingdom, and have the apprehension of these dangers, we may truly represent them unto the King; which I conceive we are bound to do by a triple obligation—of duty to God, of duty to his Majesty, and of duty to our country.

And therefore I wish it may so stand with the wisdom and judgment of the House, that these things may be drawn into the body of a REMONSTRANCE, and in all humility expressed, with a prayer to his Majesty that, for the safety of himself, for the safety of the kingdom, and for the safety of religion, he will be pleased to give us time to make perfect inquisition thereof, or to take them into his own wisdom, and there give them such timely reformation as the necessity and justice of the case doth import.

And thus, sir, with a large affection and loyalty to his Majesty, and with a firm duty and service to my country, I have suddenly (and it may be with some disorder) expressed the weak apprehensions I have; wherein if I have erred, I humbly crave your pardon, and so submit myself to the censure of the House.

The King, finding, after the delivery of this speech, that he could no longer resist the demands of the Commons, gave his public assent to the Petition of Right, on the 7th of June, 1628. But he never forgave Sir John Eliot for his freedom of speech. At the expiration of nine months he dissolved Parliament, determining to rule from that time without their aid or interference; and, two days after, committed Sir John Eliot and other members to the Tower for words spoken during the sitting of Parliament. In this flagrant breach of privilege, and violation of the Petition of Right, he was sustained by servile courts; and Eliot, as "the greatest offender and ringleader," was sentenced to pay a fine of £2000, and be imprisoned in the Tower of London.

After two years his health gave way under the rigor of his confinement. He then petitioned the King for a temporary release, that he might recover strength; but this was denied him, unless he made the most humbling concessions. He refused, and sunk, at last, under the weight of his sufferings, at the end of three years, in November, 1632, "the most illustrious confessor in the cause of liberty," says Hallam, "whom the times produced." One of his sons petitioned for liberty to remove his body to Cornwall for burial in his native soil, and received for answer these insulting words, written at the bottom of his petition: "Let him be buried in the parish where he died;" that is, in the *Tower*, the place of his imprisonment. No wonder that such a spirit brought Charles to the block!

---

[10] Buckingham had taken the crown jewels and plate to Holland, and pawned them for £300,000.

[11] Buckingham, some years before, had sent out an expedition for the capture of Algiers. It resulted in a total failure, and so incensed the Algerines, that the commerce of England suffered ten-fold loss in consequence; thirty-five ships, engaged in the Mediterranean trade, having been captured within a few months, and their crews sold for slaves.

THE EARL OF STRAFFORD.

Thomas Wentworth, first Earl of Strafford, was descended from an ancient family in Yorkshire, and was born at the house of his maternal grandfather, in London, on the 13th of April, 1593. At St. John's College, Cambridge, where he received his education, he was distinguished not only for the strength and versatility of his genius, but for his unwearied efforts to improve his mind by the severest discipline, and especially to prepare himself for the duties of public life, as an orator and a statesman. The leading features of his character were strongly marked. He had an ardor of temperament, a fixedness of will, a native impetuosity of feeling, and a correspondent energy of action, which united to make him one of the most daring and determined men of the age. To those who rendered him the deference he expected, who were ready to co-operate in his plans or become subservient to his purposes, he was kind and liberal. But he was quick and resentful when his will was crossed; and even Clarendon admits that "he manifested a nature excessively imperious."

He was trained from childhood, to a belief in those extravagant doctrines respecting the royal prerogative, which were so generally prevalent at that day. It was therefore natural that Wentworth, in entering on public life, should seek employment at Court. The King seems, from the first, to have regarded him with favor; but Buckingham, who was then in power, was secretly jealous and hostile. Hence he was treated at times with great confidence, and raised to important offices, and again stripped suddenly of his employments, and subjected to the most mortifying rebuffs. Under these circumstances, he came out for a time as a "patriot," and joined the popular party. That he did so, however, only in opposition to Buckingham, as the most effectual means of putting down a rival—that there was no change in his principles, no real sympathy between him and the illustrious men who were resisting the tyranny of Charles, is obvious from his subsequent conduct, and from the whole tenor of his private correspondence, as afterward given to the world.[1] But such was the strength of his passions, and the force of imagination (so characteristic of the highest class of orators) with which he could lay hold of, and for the time being, appropriate to himself, all the principles and feelings which became his new character, that he appeared to the world, and perhaps even to himself, to have become a genuine convert to the cause of popular liberty. In the Parliament of 1627–8, during the great discussion on the public grievances, he came forth in all his strength, "amid the delighted cheers of the House, and with a startling effect on the Court." After entering upon the subject with a calm and solemn tone befitting the greatness of the occasion, he rose in power as he advanced, until, when he came to speak of forced loans, and the billeting of soldiers upon families, he broke forth suddenly, with that kind of dramatic effect which he always studied, in a rapid and keen invective, which may be quoted as a specimen of his early eloquence. "They have rent from us the light of our eyes! enforced companies of guests, worse than the ordinances of France! vitiated our wives and children before our eyes! brought the Crown to greater want than ever it was in, by anticipa-

[1] This is shown at large by Mr. Forster in his Life of Strafford, which forms part of Lardner's Cabinet Cyclopedia.

ting the revenue! and can the shepherd be thus smitten, and the sheep not scattered? They have introduced a Privy Council, ravishing at once the spheres of all ancient government! imprisoning without bail or bond! They have taken from us —what shall I say? Indeed, *what have they left us?* They have taken from us all means of supplying the King, and ingratiating ourselves with him, by tearing up the roots of all property; which if they be not seasonably set again into the ground by his Majesty's hand, we shall have, instead of beauty, baldness!"

He next, in the boldest language, proposes his remedy. "By one and the same thing hath the King and the people been hurt, and by the same must they be cured: to vindicate—What? New things? No! Our ancient, lawful, and vital liberties, by re-enforcing the ancient laws, made by our ancestors; by setting such a stamp upon them, that no licentious spirit shall dare hereafter to enter upon them. And shall we think this a way to *break* a Parliament?[2] No! our desires are modest and just. I speak truly for the interests of the King and the people. If we enjoy not these, it will be impossible to relieve him." "Let no man," said he, in conclusion, "judge this way 'a break-neck' of Parliaments; but a way of honor to the King, nay, of profit; for, besides the supply we shall readily give him, suitable to his occasions, we give him our hearts—*our hearts*, Mr. Speaker; *a gift that* God *calls for, and fit for a King.*"

In the same spirit, he united with Eliot in urging forward the Petition of Right; and when the Lords proposed an additional clause, that it was designed "to leave entire that *sovereign power* with which his Majesty is intrusted," he resisted its insertion, declaring, "If we admit of the addition, we leave the subject worse than we found him. These laws are not acquainted with 'Sovereign Power!'"

The Court were now thoroughly alarmed. But they knew the man. There is evidence from his own papers, that within *ten days* from this time, he was in negotiation with the speaker, Finch; and "almost before the burning words which have just been transcribed, had cooled from off the lips of the speaker, a transfer of his services to the Court was decided on." In a few days Parliament was prorogued; and shortly after, Sir Thomas Wentworth was created Baron Wentworth, and appointed a member of that same Privy Council which he had just before denounced, as "ravishing at once the spheres of all ancient government!" The death of Buckingham about a month after, placed him, in effect, at the head of affairs. He was made a Viscount, and Lord President of the North; and at a subsequent period, Lord Deputy, and Lord Lieutenant of Ireland, and Earl of Strafford.

The twelve years that followed, during which Charles undertook to reign without the aid of Parliaments, were filled up with arbitrary exactions, destructive monopolies, illegal imprisonments, and inhuman corporal punishments, which Strafford was known to have recommended or approved; while his presidency in the North was marked by numerous acts of high-handed injustice, and his government of Ireland carried on with such violence and oppression as "gave men warning," in the words of Clarendon, "how they trusted themselves in the territories where he commanded."

In 1640 Charles was compelled by his necessities to convene another Parliament. The day of retribution had at length arrived. The voice of three kingdoms called for vengeance on the author of their calamities; and not a man was found, except Charles and Laud, to justify or excuse his conduct. Even Digby, who sought only to save his life, speaks of Strafford, as "a name of hatred in the present age by his practices, and fit to be made a name of terror to future ages by his punishment." At the moment when, governed by his accustomed policy, he was preparing to

[2] Alluding to the threats of the Parliament being dissolved for their freedom of speech.

strike the first blow, and to impeach the leaders of the popular party, as the surest means to avert the coming storm, he was himself impeached by the House of Commons, stripped of all his dignities, and thrown into the Tower. The 22d of March, 1641, was fixed upon for his trial. The great object of his accusers was to establish against him the charge of "attempting to subvert the fundamental laws of the realm." In doing so, they brought forward many offenses of inferior magnitude, as an index of his intentions; and they never pretended that more than two or three of the articles contained charges which amounted strictly to high treason.

In conducting the impeachment, they had great difficulties to encounter. They could find precedents in abundance to justify the doctrine of *constructive* treason. Still, it was a doctrine which came with an ill grace from the friends of civil liberty; and it gave wide scope to the eloquence of Strafford, in some of the most powerful and touching appeals of his masterly defense. In addition to this, the time had not yet arrived when treason against the state, as distinguished from an assault upon the life or personal authority of the king, was distinctly recognized in England. Strafford had undoubtedly, as a sworn counselor of Charles, given him unconstitutional advice; had told him that he was absolved from the established rules of government; that he might use his simple prerogative for the purpose of raising money, above or against the decisions of Parliament. Such an attempt to subvert the fundamental laws of the kingdom, if connected with any overt act, would now be treason. But the doctrine was a new one. The idea of considering the sovereign as only the *representative* of the state; of treating an encroachment on the established rights of the people as a crime of equal magnitude with a violation of the King's person and authority, had not yet become familiar to the English mind. We owe it to the men who commenced this impeachment; and it is not wonderful that Strafford, with his views, and those of most men at that day, could declare with perfect sincerity that he was utterly unconscious of the crime of treason.

The trial lasted from the 22d of March to the 13th of April, 1641, during which time the Earl appeared daily before the court, clothed in black, and wearing no badge or ornament but his George. "The stern and simple character of his features accorded with the occasion; his countenance 'manly black,' as Whitlocke describes it, and his thick hair cut short from his ample forehead." He was tall in person, but through early disease had contracted a stoop of the shoulders, which would have detracted from his appearance on any other occasion; but being now ascribed to intense suffering from the stone and the gout, which he was known to have endured during the progress of the trial, it operated in his favor, and excited much sympathy in his behalf. During eighteen days he thus stood alone against his numerous accusers, answering in succession the twenty-eight articles of the impeachment, which of themselves filled two hundred sheets of paper, examining the witnesses, commenting on their evidence, explaining, defending, palliating his conduct on every point with an adroitness and force, a dignity and self-possession, which awakened the admiration even of his enemies. On the last day of the trial, he summed up his various defenses in a speech of which the report given below is only an imperfect outline. It enables us, however, to form some conception of the eloquence and pathos of this extraordinary man. There is in it a union of dignity, simplicity, and force—a felicity in the selection of topics—a dexterity of appeal to the interests and feelings of his judges—a justness and elevation in every sentiment he utters—a vividness of illustration, a freshness of imagery, an elasticity and airiness of diction—an appearance of perfect sincerity, and a pervading depth of passion breaking forth at times in passages of startling power or tenderness, which belongs only to the highest class of oratory. The pathos of the conclusion has been much admired; and if we go back in imagination to the scene as presented in Westminster Hall—the once proud Earl standing amid the wreck of his fortunes, with that splendid court around him which so lately bowed submissive to his will; with his humbled monarch looking on from behind the screen that concealed his person, unable to interpose or arrest the proceedings; with that burst of tenderness at the thought of earlier days and of his wife, the Lady Arabella Hollis, "that saint in heaven," to whose memory he had always clung amid the power and splendor of later life; with his body bowed down under the pressure of intense physical suffering, and his strong spirit utterly subdued and poured out like water in that startling cry, "My Lords, my *Lords*, my LORDS, something more I had intended to say, but my voice and my spirit fail me"—we can not but feel that there are few passages of equal tenderness and power in the whole range of English eloquence. We are strongly reminded of Shakspeare's delineation of Wolsey under similar circumstances, in some of the most pathetic scenes which poetry has ever depicted. We feel that Strafford, too, with his "heart new opened," might have added *his* testimony to the folly of ambition, and the bitter fruits of seeking the favor of a king, at the expense of the people's rights, and the claims of justice and truth.

Cromwell, I charge thee, fling away ambition!
By that sin fell the angels; how can man, then,
The image of his Maker hope to win by't?
Love thyself last! Cherish those hearts that hate thee!
Corruption wins not more than honesty!
Still in thy right hand carry gentle peace,
To silence envious tongues! Be just and fear not!
Let all the ends thou aim'st at be thy country's,
Thy God's, and Truth's! Then if thou fallest, O Cromwell,
Thou fallest a blessed martyr."

SPEECH

OF THE EARL OF STRAFFORD WHEN IMPEACHED FOR HIGH TREASON BEFORE THE HOUSE OF LORDS, APRIL 13, 1641.[1]

MY LORDS, — This day I stand before you charged with high treason. The burden of the charge is heavy, yet far the more so because it hath borrowed the authority of the House of Commons. If *they* were not interested, I might expect a no less easy, than I do a safe, issue. But let neither my weakness plead my innocence, nor their power my guilt. If your Lordships will conceive of my defenses, as they are in themselves, without reference to either party —and I shall endeavor so to present them—I hope to go hence as clearly justified by you, as I now am in the testimony of a good conscience by myself.

My Lords, I have all along, during this charge, watched to see that poisoned arrow of Treason, which some men would fain have feathered in my heart; but, in truth, it hath not been my quickness to discover any such evil yet within my breast, though now, perhaps, by sinister information, sticking to my clothes.

They tell me of a two-fold treason, one against the statute, another by the common law; this direct, that consecutive; this individual, that accumulative; this in itself, that by way of construction.

As to this charge of treason, I must and do acknowledge, that if I had the least suspicion of my own guilt, I would save your Lordships the pains. I would cast the first stone. I would pass the first sentence of condemnation against myself. And whether it be so or not, I now refer to your Lordships' judgment and deliberation. You, and you *only*, under the care and protection of my gracious master, are my judges. Under favor, none of the Commons are my peers, nor can they be my judges. I shall ever celebrate the providence and wisdom of your noble ancestors, who have put the keys of life and death, so far as concerns you and your posterity, into your own hands. *None but your own selves, my Lords, know the rate of your noble blood: none but yourselves must hold the balance in disposing of the same.*[2]

I shall now proceed in repeating my defenses as they are reducible to the two main points of treason. And,

I. For treason against the statute, which is the only treason in effect, there is nothing alleged for that but the fifteenth, twenty-second, and twenty-seventh articles.

[Here the Earl brought forward the replies which he had previously made to these articles, which contained all the charges of individual acts of treason. The fifteenth article affirmed that he had "inverted the ordinary course of justice in Ireland, and given immediate sentence upon the lands and goods of the King's subjects, under pretense of disobedience; had used a military way for redressing the contempt, and laid soldiers upon the lands and goods of the King's subjects, to their utter ruin." There was a deficiency of proofs as to the facts alleged. The Earl declared that "the customs of England differed exceedingly from those of Ireland; and therefore, though *cessing* of men might seem strange here, it was not so there;" and that "nothing was more common there than for the governors to appoint soldiers to put all manner of sentences into execution," as he proved by the testimony of Lord Dillon, Sir Adam Loftus, and Sir Arthur Teringham.

The twenty-seventh article charged him with having, as lieutenant general, charged on the county of York eight pence a day for supporting the train-bands of said county during one month, when called out; and having issued his warrants without legal authority for the collection of the same. The Earl replied that "this money was freely and voluntarily offered by them of Yorkshire, in a petition; and that he had done nothing but on the petition of the county, the King's special command, and the connivance, at least, of the Great Council, and upon a present necessity for the defense and safety of the county, when about to be invaded from Scotland."

The twenty-second and twenty-third articles were the most pressing. Under these he was charged with saying in the Privy Council that "the Parliament had forsaken the King; that the King ought not to suffer himself to be overmastered by the stubbornness of the people; and that, if his Majesty pleased to employ forces, he had some in Ireland that might serve to reduce

---

[1] There are in the Parliamentary History two reports of this speech, one by Whitlocke, and the other by some unknown friend of Strafford. As each has important passages which are not contained in the other, they are here combined by a slight modification of language, in order to give more completeness to this masterly defense.

[2] Strafford had no chance of acquittal except by inducing the Lords, from a regard to their dignity and safety, to rise above the influence of the Commons as his prosecutors, and of the populace who surrounded Westminster Hall by thousands, demanding his condemnation. In this view, his exordium has admirable dexterity and force. He reverts to the same topic in his peroration, assuring them, with the deepest earnestness and solemnity (and, as the event showed, with perfect truth), that if they gave him up, they must expect to perish with him in the general ruin of the peerage.

this kingdom," thus counseling to his Majesty to put down Parliament, and subvert the fundamental laws of the kingdom by force and arms. To this the Earl replied, (1.) That there was only one witness adduced to prove these words, viz., Sir Henry Vane, secretary of the Council, but that two or more witnesses are necessary by statute to prove a charge of treason. (2.) That the others who were present, viz., the Duke of Northumberland, the Marquess of Hamilton, Lord Cottington, and Sir Thomas Lucas, did not, as they deposed under oath, remember these words. (3.) That Sir Henry Vane had given his testimony as if he was in doubt on the subject, saying "as I do remember," and "such or such like words," which admitted the words might be "*that* kingdom," meaning Scotland.]

II. As to the other kind, viz., constructive treason, or treason by way of *accumulation;* to make this out, many articles have been brought against me, as if in a heap of mere felonies or misdemeanors (for they reach no higher) there could lurk some prolific seed to produce what is treasonable! But, my Lords, when a thousand misdemeanors will not make one felony, shall twenty-eight misdemeanors be heightened into treason?

I pass, however, to consider these charges, which affirm that I have designed the overthrow both of religion and of the state.

1. The first charge seemeth to be used rather to make me odious than guilty; for there is not the least proof alleged—nor *could* there be any—concerning my confederacy with the popish faction. Never was a servant in authority under my lord and master more hated and maligned by these men than myself, and that for an impartial and strict execution of the laws against them; for observe, my Lords, that the greater number of the witnesses against me, whether from Ireland or from Yorkshire, were of that religion. But for my own resolution, I thank God I am ready every hour of the day to seal my dissatisfaction to the Church of Rome with my dearest blood.

Give me leave, my Lords, here to pour forth the grief of my soul before you. These proceedings against me seem to be exceeding rigorous, and to have more of prejudice than equity—that upon a supposed charge of hypocrisy or errors in religion, I should be made so odious to three kingdoms. A great many thousand eyes have seen my accusations, whose ears will never hear that when it came to the upshot, *those very things were not alleged against me!* Is this fair dealing among Christians? But I have lost nothing by that. Popular applause was ever nothing in my conceit. The uprightness and integrity of a good conscience ever was, and ever shall be, my continual feast; and if I can be justified in your Lordships' judgments from this great imputation—as I hope I am, seeing these gentlemen have thrown down the bucklers—I shall account myself justified by the whole kingdom, because absolved by you, who are the better part, the very soul and life of the kingdom.

2. As for my designs against the state, I dare plead as much innocency as in the matter of religion. I have ever admired the wisdom of our ancestors, who have so fixed the pillars of this monarchy that each of them keeps a due proportion and measure with the others—have so admirably bound together the nerves and sinews of the state, that the straining of any one may bring danger and sorrow to the whole economy. The Prerogative of the Crown and the Propriety of the Subject have such natural relations, that *this* takes nourishment from *that*, and *that* foundation and nourishment from *this*. And so, as in the lute, if any one string be wound up too high or too low, you have lost the whole harmony; so here the excess of prerogative is oppression, of pretended liberty in the subject is disorder and anarchy. The prerogative must be used as God doth his omnipotence, upon extraordinary occasions; the laws must have place at all other times. As there must be prerogative because there must be extraordinary occasions, so the propriety of the subject is ever to be maintained, if it go in equal pace with the other. They are fellows and companions that are, and ever must be, inseparable in a well-ordered kingdom; and no way is so fitting, so natural to nourish and entertain both, as the frequent use of Parliaments, by which a commerce and acquaintance is kept up between the King and his subjects.[3]

These thoughts have gone along with me these fourteen years of my public employments, and shall, God willing, go with me to the grave! God, his Majesty, and my own conscience, yea, and all of those who have been most accessary to my inward thoughts, can bear me witness that I ever did inculcate this, that the happiness of a kingdom doth consist in a just poise of the King's prerogative and the subject's liberty, and that things could never go well till these went hand in hand together. I thank God for it, by my master's favor, and the providence of my ancestors, I have an estate which so interests me in the commonwealth, that I have no great mind to be a *slave*, but a *subject*. Nor could I wish the cards to be shuffled over again, in hopes to fall upon a better set; nor did I ever nourish such base and mercenary thoughts as to become a pander to the tyranny and ambition of the greatest man living. No! I have, and ever shall, aim at a fair but *bounded* liberty; remembering always that I am a freeman, yet a subject—that I have rights, but under a monarch. It hath been my misfortune, now when I am gray-headed, to be charged by the *mistakers* of the times, who are so highly bent that all appears to them to be in the extreme for monarchy which is not for themselves. Hence it is that designs, words, yea, *intentions*, are brought out as demonstrations of my misdemeanors. Such a multiplying-glass is a prejudicate opinion!

[3] Strafford was generally regarded as the secret author of the King's aversion to Parliaments, which had led him to dispense with their use for many years. Hence the above declaration, designed to relieve him from the effects of this prejudice.

The articles against me refer to *expressions* and *actions*—my expressions either in Ireland or in England, my actions either before or after these late stirs.

(1.) Some of the expressions referred to were uttered in private, and I do protest against their being drawn to my injury in this place. If, my Lords, words spoken to friends in familiar discourse, spoken at one's table, spoken in one's chamber, spoken in one's sick-bed, spoken, perhaps, to gain better reason, to gain one's self more clear light and judgment by reasoning—if these things shall be brought against a man as treason, this (under favor) takes away the comfort of all human society. By this means we shall be debarred from speaking—the principal joy and comfort of life—with wise and good men, to become wiser and better ourselves. If these things be strained to take away life, and honor, and all that is desirable, *this will be a silent world!* A city will become a hermitage, and sheep will be found among a crowd and press of people! No man will dare to impart his solitary thoughts or opinions to his friend and neighbor!

Other expressions have been urged against me, which were used in giving counsel to the King. My Lords, these words were not wantonly or unnecessarily spoken, or whispered in a corner; they were spoken in full council, when, by the duty of my oath, I was obliged to speak according to my heart and conscience in all things concerning the King's service. If I had forborne to speak what I conceived to be for the benefit of the King and the people, I had been perjured toward Almighty God. And for delivering my mind openly and freely, shall I be in danger of my life as a traitor? If *that* necessity be put upon me, I thank God, by his blessing, I have learned not to stand in fear of him who can only kill the body. If the question be whether I must be traitor to man or perjured to God, I will be faithful to my Creator. And whatsoever shall befall me from popular rage or my own weakness, I must leave it to that almighty Being, and to the justice and honor of my judges.

My Lords, I conjure you not to make yourselves so unhappy as to disable your Lordships and your children, from undertaking the great charge and trust of this Commonwealth. You inherit that trust from your fathers. You are born to great thoughts. You are nursed for the weighty employments of the kingdom. But if it be once admitted that a counselor, for delivering his opinion with others at the council board, *candide et caste*, with candor and purity of motive, under an oath of secrecy and faithfulness, shall be brought into question, upon some misapprehension or ignorance of law—if every word that he shall speak from sincere and noble intentions shall be drawn against him for the attainting of him, his children and posterity—I know not (under favor I speak it) any wise or noble person of fortune who will, upon such perilous and unsafe terms, adventure to be counselor to the King. Therefore I beseech your Lordships so to look on me, that my misfortune may not bring an inconvenience to yourselves. And though my words were not so advised and discreet, or so well weighed as they ought to have been, yet I trust your Lordships are too honorable and just to lay them to my charge as High Treason. *Opinions may make a heretic, but that they make a traitor I have never heard till now.*

(2.) I am come next to speak of the actions which have been charged upon me.

[Here the Earl went through with the various overt acts alleged, and repeated the sum and heads of what had been spoken by him before. In respect to the twenty-eighth article, which charged him with "a malicious design to engage the kingdoms of England and Scotland in a national and bloody war," but which the managers had not urged in the trial, he added more at large, as follows:]

If that one article had been proved against me, it contained more weighty matter than all the charges besides. It would not only have been treason, but villainy, to have betrayed the trust of his Majesty's army. But as the managers have been sparing, by reason of the times, as to insisting on that article, I have resolved to keep the same method, and not utter the least expression which might disturb the happy agreement intended between the two kingdoms. I only admire how I, being an incendiary against the Scots in the twenty-third article, am become a confederate with them in the twenty-eighth article! how I could be charged for betraying Newcastle, and also for fighting with the Scots at Newburne, since fighting against them was no possible means of betraying the town into their hands, but rather to hinder their passage thither! I never advised war any further than, in my poor judgment, it concerned the very life of the King's authority, and the safety and honor of his kingdom. Nor did I ever see that any advantage could be made by a war in Scotland, where nothing could be gained but hard blows. For my part, I honor that nation, but I wish they may ever be *under their own climate*. I have no desire that they should be *too well acquainted with the better soil of England.*

My Lords, you see what has been alleged for this constructive, or, rather, *de*structive treason. For my part, I have not the judgment to conceive, that such treason is agreeable to the fundamental grounds either of reason or of law. Not of reason, for how can that be treason in the lump or mass, which is not so in any of its parts? or how can that make a thing treasonable which is not so in *itself?* Not of law, since neither statute, common law, nor practice hath from the beginning of the government ever mentioned such a thing.

It is hard, my Lords, to be questioned upon a law which can not be shown! Where hath this fire lain hid for so many hundred years, without smoke to discover it, till it thus bursts forth to consume me and my children? My Lords, do we not live under laws? and must we be punished by laws before they are made? Far better were it to live by no laws at all; but to be governed by those characters of virtue and discretion, which Nature hath stamped upon us, than to put this necessity of *divination* upon a man, and to accuse him of a breach of law *before it is a law at all!* If a waterman upon the Thames split his boat by grating upon an anchor, and the same have no buoy appended to it, the owner of the anchor is to pay the loss; but if a buoy be set there, every man passeth upon his own peril. Now where is the mark, where is the token set upon the crime, to declare it to be high treason?

My Lords, be pleased to give that regard to the peerage of England as never to expose yourselves to such moot points, such constructive interpretations of law. If there must be a trial of wits, let the subject matter be something else than the lives and honor of peers! It will be wisdom for yourselves and your posterity to cast into the fire these bloody and mysterious volumes of constructive and arbitrary treason, as the primitive Christians did their books of curious arts; and betake yourselves to the plain letter of the law and statute, which telleth what is and what is not treason, without being ambitious to be more learned in the art of killing than our forefathers. These gentlemen tell us that they speak in defense of the Commonwealth against my arbitrary laws. Give me leave to say it, I speak in defense of the Commonwealth against their arbitrary treason!

It is now full two hundred and forty years since any man was touched for this alleged crime to this height before myself. Let us not awaken those sleeping lions to our destruction, by taking up a few musty records that have lain by the walls for so many ages, forgotten or neglected.

My Lords, what is my present misfortune may be forever yours! It is not the smallest part of my grief that not the crime of treason, but my other sins, which are exceeding many, have brought me to this bar; and, except your Lordships' wisdom provide against it, the shedding of my blood may make way for the tracing out of yours. YOU, YOUR ESTATES, YOUR POSTERITY, LIE AT THE STAKE!

For my poor self, if it were not for your Lordships' interest, and the interest of a saint in heaven, who hath left me here two pledges on earth—[at this his breath stopped, and he shed tears abundantly in mentioning his wife]—I should never take the pains to keep up this ruinous cottage of mine. It is loaded with such infirmities, that in truth I have no great pleasure to carry it about with me any longer. Nor could I ever leave it at a fitter time than this, when I hope that the better part of the world would perhaps think that by my misfortunes I had given a testimony of my integrity to my God, my King, and my country. I thank God, I count not the afflictions of the present life to be compared to that glory which is to be revealed in the time to come!

My Lords! my Lords! my Lords! something more I had intended to say, but my voice and my spirit fail me. Only I do in all humility and submission cast myself down at your Lordships' feet, and desire that I may be a beacon to keep you from shipwreck. Do not put such rocks in your own way, which no prudence, no circumspection can eschew or satisfy, but by your utter ruin!

And so, my Lords, even so, with all tranquillity of mind, I submit myself to your decision. And whether your judgment in my case—I wish it were not the case of you all—be for life or for death, it shall be righteous in my eyes, and shall be received with a *Te Deum laudamus*, we give God the praise.

The House of Lords, after due deliberation, voted that the main facts alleged in the impeachment had been proved in evidence; and referred the question whether they involved the crime of treason, to the decision of the judges of the Court of the King's Bench. Previous to this, however, and even before the Earl had made his closing argument, a new course of proceedings was adopted in the House of Commons. When the managers had finished their evidence and arguments as to the *facts* alleged, a bill of attainder against the Earl was brought into the House by Sir Arthur Haselrig. The reason for this procedure can not now be ascertained with any degree of certainty. The friends of Strafford have always maintained, that such an impression had been made on the minds of the judges and audience during the progress of the trial, as to turn the tide in his favor; and that his accusers, fearing he might be acquitted, resorted to this measure for the purpose of securing his condemnation. Such may have been the fact; but the Commons, in their conference with the Lords, April 15, declared that this was the course they had originally intended to pursue, "that the evidences of the fact being given, it was proposed *from the beginning* to go by way of bill, and that they had accordingly brought in a bill for his attainder." St. John, their legal manager, positively denied that they were seeking to avoid the judicial mode of proceeding; and, "what is stronger," as Hallam remarks, "the Lords voted on the articles *judicially*, and not as if they were enacting a legislative measure." Still the bill of attainder was strenuously opposed by a few individuals in the House, and especially by Lord Digby, in his celebrated speech on the subject, which will next be given.

LORD DIGBY.

George Digby, oldest son of the Earl of Bristol, was born at Madrid in 1612, during the residence of his father in that city as English embassador to the Court of Spain. He was educated at Magdalen College, Oxford; and entered into public life at the age of twenty-eight, being returned member of Parliament for the county of Dorset, in April, 1640. In common with his father, who had incurred the displeasure of the King by his impeachment of Buckingham in 1626, Lord Digby came forward at an early period of the session, as an open and determined enemy of the Court. Among the "Speeches relative to Grievances," his, as representative of Dorsetshire, was one of the most bold and impassioned. His argument shortly after in favor of triennial Parliaments, was characterized by a still higher order of eloquence; and in the course of it he made a bitter attack upon Strafford, in showing the necessity of frequent Parliaments as a control upon ministers, declaring "he must not expect to be pardoned in this world till he is dispatched to the other."

From the ardor with which he expressed these sentiments, and the leading part he took in every measure for the defense of the people's rights, Lord Digby was appointed one of the managers for the impeachment of Strafford. Into this he entered, for a time, with the utmost zeal. He is described by Clarendon as a man of uncommon activity of mind and fertility of invention; bold and impetuous in whatever designs he undertook; but deficient in judgment, inordinately vain and ambitious, of a volatile and unquiet spirit, disposed to separate councils, and governed more by impulse than by fixed principles. Whether the course he took in respect to the attainder of Strafford ought to be referred in any degree to the last-mentioned traits of character, or solely to a sense of justice, a conviction forced upon him in the progress of the trial that the testimony had failed to sustain the charge of treason, can not, perhaps, be decided at the present day. The internal evidence afforded by the speech, is strongly in favor of his honesty and rectitude of intention. He appears throughout like one who was conscious of having gone too far; and who was determined to retrieve his error, at whatever expense of popular odium it might cost him. Had he stopped here, there would have been no ground for imputations on his character. But he almost instantly changed the whole tenor of his political life. He abandoned his former principles; he joined the Court party; and did more, as we learn from Clarendon, to ruin Charles by his rashness and pertinacity, than any other man. But, whatever may be thought of Digby, the speech is one of great manliness and force. It is plausible in its statements, just in its distinctions, and weighty in its reasonings. Without exhibiting any great superiority of genius, and especially any richness of imagination, it presents us with a rapid succession of striking and appropriate thoughts, clearly arranged and vividly expressed In one respect, the diction is worthy of being studied. It abounds in those direct and pointed forms of speech, which sink at once into the heart; and by their very plainness give an air of perfect sincerity to the speaker, which of all things is the most important to one who is contending (as he was) against the force of popular prejudice. Much of the celebrity attached to this speech is owing, no doubt, to the circumstances under which it was delivered. The House of Commons must have presented a scene of the most exciting nature when, at the moment of taking the final vote on the bill, one of the managers of the impeachment came forward to abandon his ground; to disclose the proceedings of the committee in secret session; and to denounce the condemnation of Strafford by a bill of attainder, as an act of murder.

SPEECH

OF LORD DIGBY ON THE BILL OF ATTAINDER AGAINST THE EARL OF STRAFFORD, DELIVERED IN THE HOUSE OF COMMONS, APRIL 21, 1641.

WE are now upon the point of giving, as much as in us lies, the final sentence unto death or life, on a great minister of state and peer of this kingdom, Thomas, Earl of Strafford, a name of hatred in the present age for his practices, and fit to be made a terror to future ages by his punishment.

I have had the honor to be employed by the House in this great business, from the first hour that it was taken into consideration. It was a matter of great trust; and I will say with confidence that I have served the House in it, not only with industry, according to my ability, but with most exact faithfulness and justice.

And as I have hitherto discharged my duty to this House and to my country in the progress of this great cause, so I trust I shall do now, in the last period of it, to God and to a good conscience. I do wish the peace of *that* to myself, and the blessing of Almighty God to me and my posterity, according as my judgment on the life of this man shall be consonant with my heart, and the best of my understanding in all integrity.

I know well that by some things I have said of late, while this bill was in agitation, I have raised some prejudices against me in the cause. Yea, some (I thank them for their plain dealing) have been so free as to tell me, that I have suffered much by the backwardness I have shown in the bill of attainder of the Earl of Strafford, against whom I have formerly been so keen, so active.

I beg of you, Mr. Speaker, and the rest, but a suspension of judgment concerning me, till I have opened my heart to you, clearly and freely, in this business. Truly, sir, I am still the same in my opinion and affections as to the Earl of Strafford. I confidently believe him to be the most dangerous minister, the most insupportable to free subjects, that can be charactered. I believe his practices in themselves to have been as high and tyrannical as any subject ever ventured on; and the malignity of them greatly aggravated by those rare abilities of his, whereof God hath given him the use, but the devil the application. In a word, I believe him to be still that grand apostate to the Commonwealth, who must not expect to be pardoned in this world till he be dispatched to the other.

And yet let me tell you, Mr. Speaker, *my hand must not be to that dispatch*. I protest, as my conscience stands informed, I had rather it were off.

Let me unfold to you the mystery, Mr. Speaker: I will not dwell much upon justifying to you my seeming variance at this time from what I was formerly, by putting you in mind of the difference between prosecutors and judges—how misbecoming that fervor would be in a judge which, perhaps, was commendable in a prosecutor. Judges we are now, and must, therefore, put on another personage. It is honest and noble to be earnest in order to the discovery of truth; but when that hath been brought so far as it can be to light, our judgment thereupon ought to be calm and cautious. In prosecution upon probable grounds, we are accountable only for our industry or remissness; but in *judgment* we are deeply responsible to Almighty God for its rectitude or obliquity. In cases of life, the judge is God's steward of the party's blood, and must give a strict account for every drop.

But, as I told you, Mr. Speaker, I will not insist long upon this ground of difference in me now from what I was formerly. The truth of it is, sir, the same ground whereupon I with the rest of the few to whom you first committed the consideration of my Lord Strafford, brought down our opinion that it was fit he should be accused of treason—upon the same ground, I was engaged with earnestness in his prosecution; and had the same ground remained in that force of belief in me, which till very lately it did, I should not have been tender in his condemnation. But truly, sir, to deal plainly with you, that ground of our accusation—that which should be the basis of our judgment of the Earl of Strafford as to *treason*—is, to my understanding, quite vanished away.

This it was, Mr. Speaker—his advising the King to employ the army in Ireland to reduce England. This I was assured would be proved, before I gave my consent to his accusation. I was confirmed in the same belief during the prosecution, and fortified most of all in it, after Sir Henry Vane's preparatory examination, by assurances which that worthy member Mr. Pym gave me, that his testimony would be made convincing by some notes of what passed at the Junto [Privy Council] concurrent with it. This I ever understood would be of some other counselor; but you see now, it proves only to be a copy of the same secretary's notes, discovered and produced in the manner you have heard; and those such disjointed fragments of the venomous part of discourses—no results, no conclusions of councils, which are the only things that secretaries should register, there being no use of the other but to accuse and bring men into danger.[1]

[1] See Strafford's reply on this subject, p. 12.

But, sir, this is not that which overthrows the evidence with me concerning the army in Ireland, nor yet that all the rest of the Junto remember nothing of it; but this, sir, which I shall tell you, is that which works with me, under favor, to an utter overthrow of his evidence as touching the army of Ireland. Before, while I was prosecutor, and under tie of secrecy, I might not discover [disclose] any weakness of the cause, which now, as judge, I must.

Mr. Secretary Vane was examined thrice upon oath at the preparatory committee. The first time he was questioned as to all the interrogatories; and to that part of the seventh which concerns the army in Ireland, he said positively these words: "I can not charge him with that;" but for the rest, he desired time to recollect himself, which was granted him. Some days after, he was examined a second time, and then deposed these words concerning the King's being absolved from rules of government, and so forth, very clearly. But being pressed as to that part concerning the Irish army, again he said he could say "nothing to that." Here we thought we had done with him, till divers weeks after, my Lord of Northumberland, and all others of the Junto, denying to have heard any thing concerning those words of reducing England by the Irish army, it was thought fit to examine the secretary once more; and then he deposed these words to have been spoken by the Earl of Strafford to his Majesty: "You have an army in Ireland, which you may employ here to reduce (or some word to that sense) this kingdom." Mr. Speaker, these are the circumstances which I confess with my conscience, thrust quite out of doors that grand article of our charge concerning his desperate advice to the King of employing the Irish army here.

Let not this, I beseech you, be driven to an aspersion upon Mr. Secretary, as if he should have sworn otherwise than he knew or believed. He is too worthy to do that. Only let this much be inferred from it, that he, who twice upon oath, with time of recollection, could not remember any thing of such a business, might well, a third time, misremember somewhat; and in this business the difference of one word "here" for "there," or "that" for "this," quite alters the case; the latter also being the more probable, since it is confessed on all hands that the debate then was concerning a war with Scotland. And you may remember, that at the bar he once said "employ *there*." And thus, Mr. Speaker, have I faithfully given you an account what it is that hath blunted the edge of the hatchet, or bill, with me, toward my Lord Strafford.

This was that whereupon I accused him with a free heart; prosecuted him with earnestness; and had it to my understanding been proved, should have condemned him with innocence; whereas now I can not satisfy my conscience to do it. I profess I can have no notion of any body's intent to subvert the laws treasonably, but by force; and this design of force not appearing, all his other wicked practices can not amount so high with me. I can find a more easy and natural spring from whence to derive all his other crimes. than from an intent to bring in tyranny, and make his own posterity, as well as us, slaves; viz., from revenge, from pride, from passion, and from insolence of nature. But had this of the Irish army been proved, it would have diffused a complexion of treason over all. It would have been a withe indeed, to bind all those other scattered and lesser branches, as it were, into a fagot of treason.

I do not say but the rest of the things charged may represent him a man as worthy to die, and perhaps worthier than many a traitor. I do not say but they may justly direct us to enact that they *shall* be treason for the future. But God keep me from giving judgment of death on any man, and of ruin to his innocent posterity, upon a law made *à posteriori*. Let the mark be set on the door where the plague is, and then let him that will enter, die.[2]

I know, Mr. Speaker, there is in Parliament a double power of life and death by bill; a judicial power, and a legislative. The measure of the one is, what is legally just; of the other, what is prudentially and politically fit for the good and preservation of the whole. But these two, under favor, are not to be confounded in judgment. We must not piece out want of legality with matter of convenience, nor the defailance of prudential fitness with a pretense of legal justice.

To condemn my Lord of Strafford *judicially*, as for treason, my conscience is not assured that the matter will bear it; and to do it by the *legislative* power, my reason consultively can not agree to that, since I am persuaded that neither the Lords nor the King will pass this bill; and, consequently, that our passing it will be a cause of great divisions, and contentions in the state.

Therefore my humble advice is, that, laying aside this bill of attainder, we may think of another, saving only life; such as may secure the state from my Lord of Strafford, without endangering it as much by division concerning his punishment, as he hath endangered it by his practices.

If this may not be hearkened unto, let me conclude in saying that to you all, which I have thoroughly inculcated upon mine own conscience, on this occasion. Let every man lay his hand upon his own heart, and seriously consider what we are going to do with a breath: *either justice or murder*—justice on the one side, or murder, heightened and aggravated to its supremest extent, on the other! For, as the casuists say, He who lies with his sister commits incest; but he that marries his sister, sins higher, by applying God's ordinance to his crime; so, doubtless, he that commits murder with the sword of justice, heightens that crime to the utmost.

[2] This image was peculiarly appropriate and forcible at that time, when the plague had recently prevailed in London, and a mark was placed by the magistrates on infected dwellings as a warning not to enter.

The danger being so great, and the case so doubtful, that I see the best lawyers in diametrical opposition concerning it; let every man wipe his heart as he does his eyes, when he would judge of a nice and subtle object. The eye, if it be pre-tinctured with any color, is vitiated in its discerning. Let us take heed of a blood-shotten eye in judgment. Let every man purge his heart clear of all passions. I know this great and wise body politic can have none; but I speak to individuals from the weakness which I find in myself. Away with personal animosities! Away with all flatteries to the people, in being the sharper against him because he is odious to them! Away with all fears, lest by sparing his blood they may be incensed! Away with all such considerations, as that it is not fit for a Parliament that one accused by it of treason, should escape with life! Let not former vehemence of any against him, nor fear from thence that he can not be safe while that man lives, be an ingredient in the sentence of any one of us.

Of all these corruptives of judgment, Mr. Speaker, I do, before God, discharge myself to the utmost of my power; and do now, with a clear conscience, wash my hands of this man's blood by this solemn protestation, *that my vote goes not to the taking of the Earl of Strafford's life.*

Notwithstanding this eloquent appeal, the bill of attainder was carried the same day in the House, by a vote of two hundred and four to fifty-nine.

The Lords had already decided in their judicial capacity that the main *facts* alleged in the indictment were proved, and referred the points of law to the decision of the judges of the Court of the King's Bench. On the seventh of May, "the Lord Chief Justice of the King's Bench delivered in to the Lords the *unanimous* decision of all the judges present, 'That they are of opinion upon all which their Lordships had voted to be proved, that the Earl of Strafford doth deserve to undergo the pains and forfeitures of high treason by law.' "—Parl. Hist., vol. ii., p. 757. The Lords now yielded the point of form to the Commons; and as the penal consequences were the same, instead of giving sentence under the impeachment, they passed the bill of attainder the next day, May 8th, by a vote of twenty-six to nineteen.

It was still in the power of Charles to save Strafford by refusing his assent to the bill; and he had made a solemn and written promise to deliver him from his enemies in the last extremity, by the exercise of the royal prerogative. But, with his constitutional fickleness, he yielded; and then, to pacify his conscience, he sent a letter to the Lords asking the consent of Parliament, that he might "moderate the severity of the law in so important a case." Still, with that weakness, amounting to fatuity, which so often marked his conduct, he nullified his own request by that celebrated postscript, "If he must die, it were charity to reprieve him till Saturday!" As might have been expected, the Earl was executed the next day, May 12th, 1641. The House of Commons, however, with a generosity never manifested before or since in such a case, immediately passed a bill to relieve his descendants from the penalties of forfeiture and corruption of blood.

It is now generally admitted that, in a moral point of view, Strafford richly merited the punishment he received. On the question of legal right, it may be proper to say, that while the doctrine of constructive treason under an impeachment can not be too strongly condemned, the proceedings under a bill of attainder were of a different nature. "Acts of Parliament," says Blackstone, "to attaint particular persons of treason, are to all intents and purposes *new* laws made *pro re nata*, and by no means an execution of such as are already in being." They are, from their very nature, *ex post facto* laws. They proceed on the principle that while judicial courts are to be governed by the strict letter of the law, as previously known and established, Parliament, in exercising the high sovereignty of the state, may, "on great and crying occasions," arrest some enormous offender in the midst of his crimes, and inflict upon him the punishment he so richly deserves, even in cases where, owing to a defect in the law, or to the arts of successful evasion, it is impossible to reach him by means of impeachment, or through the ordinary tribunals of justice. Such a power is obviously liable to great abuses; and it is, therefore, expressly interdicted to Congress in the Constitution of the United States. But it has always belonged, and still belongs, to the Parliament of Great Britain, though for many years it has ceased to be exercised in this form. The principle of retrospective punishment (the only thing really objectionable in this case) has, indeed, come down in a milder form to a very late period of English history. We find it in those bills of "pains and penalties," which, as Hallam observes, "have, in times of comparative moderation and tranquillity, been sometimes thought necessary to visit some unforeseen and anomalous transgression, beyond the reach of our penal code." Mr. Macaulay maintains that the Earl's death, under existing circumstances, was absolutely necessary; "that, during the civil wars, the Parliament had reason to rejoice that an irreversible law and an impassable barrier protected them from the valor and rapacity of Strafford." Those who think differently on this point must at least agree with Hallam, that "he died justly before God and man; though we may deem the precedent dangerous, and the better course of a magnanimous lenity rejected; and in condemning the bill of attainder, *we can not look upon it as a crime.*"

LORD BELHAVEN.

The author of this speech belonged to the Hamilton family. He was one of the old Presbyterian lords, of high education, especially in classical literature; lofty in his demeanor; dauntless in spirit; and wholly devoted to the peculiar interests of his country. The speech owes much of its celebrity to the circumstances under which it was delivered. It embodies the feelings of a proud and jealous people, when called upon to surrender their national independence, and submit to the authority of the British Parliament.

A century had now elapsed since the union of the English and Scottish crowns in the person of James I., and Scotland still remained a distinct kingdom, with its own Parliament, its own judicial system, its own immemorial usages which had all the force of law. This state of things, though gratifying to the pride of the Scottish people, was the source of endless jealousies and contentions between the two countries; and, as commonly happens in such cases, the weaker party suffered most. Scotland was governed by alternate corruption and force. Her nobility and gentry were drawn to England in great numbers by the attractions of the Court, as the seat of fashion, honor, and power. The nation was thus drained of her wealth; and the drain became greater, as her merchants and tradesmen were led to transfer their capital to the sister kingdom, in consequence of the superior facilities for trade which were there enjoyed.

It was now apparent that Scotland could never flourish until she was permitted to share in those commercial advantages, from which she was debarred as a distinct country, by the Navigation Act of England. The Scotch were, therefore, clamorous in their demands for some arrangement to this effect. But the English had always looked with jealousy upon any intermeddling with trade, on the part of Scotland. They had crushed her African and India Company by their selfish opposition, and had left her Darien settlement of twelve hundred souls to perish for want of support and protection; so that few families in the Lowlands had escaped the loss of a relative or friend. Exasperated by these injuries, and by the evident determination of the English to cut them off from all participation in the benefits of trade, the Scotch were hurried into a measure of alarming aspect for the safety of the empire. Noble and burgher, Jacobite and Presbyterian, were for once united. There was one point where England was vulnerable. It was the succession to the crown. This had been settled by the English Parliament on the Protestant line in the house of Hanover, and the fullest expectations were entertained that the Parliament of Scotland would readily unite in the same measure. Instead of this, the Scotch, in 1704, passed their famous Act of Security, in which they threw down the gauntlet to England, and enacted, that "the same person should be *incapable* of succeeding in both kingdoms, unless a free communication of trade, the benefits of the Navigation Act, and liberty of the Plantations [*i. e.*, of trading with the British West Indies and North America] was first obtained." They also provided conditionally for a separate successor, and passed laws for arming the whole kingdom in his defense.

It was now obvious that concessions must be made on both sides, or the contest be decided by the sword. The ministry of Queen Anne, therefore, proposed that commissioners from the two kingdoms should meet at London, to devise a plan of

Union, which should be mutually advantageous to the two countries. This was accordingly done, in the month of April, 1706; and, after long negotiations, it was agreed, that the two kingdoms should be united into one under the British Parliament, with the addition of sixteen Scottish peers to the House of Lords, and of forty-five Scottish members to the House of Commons; that the Scotch should be entitled to all the privileges of the English in respect to trade, and be subject to the same excise and duties; that Scotland should receive £398,000 as a compensation or "equivalent" for the share of liability she assumed in the English debt of £20,000,000; and that the churches of England and Scotland respectively should be confirmed in all their rights and privileges, as a fundamental condition of the Union.

These arrangements were kept secret until October, 1706, when the Scottish Parliament met to consider and decide on the plan proposed. The moment the Articles were read in that body, and given to the public in print, they were met with a burst of indignant reprobation from every quarter. A federal union which should confer equal advantages for trade, was all that the Scotch in general had ever contemplated: an *incorporating* union, which should abolish their Parliament and extinguish their national existence, was what most Scotchmen had never dreamed of. Nor is it surprising, aside from all considerations of national honor, that such a union should have been regarded with jealousy and dread. "No past experience of history," says Hallam, "was favorable to the absorption of a lesser state (at least where the government partook so much of a republican form) in one of superior power and ancient rivalry. The representation of Scotland in the united Legislature, was too feeble to give any thing like security against the English prejudices and animosities, if they should continue or revive. The Church of Scotland was exposed to the most apparent perils, brought thus within the power of a Legislature so frequently influenced by one which held her, not as a sister, but rather as a bastard usurper of a sister's inheritance; and though her permanence was guaranteed by the treaty, yet it was hard to say how far the legal competence of Parliament might hereafter be deemed to extend, or, at least, how far she might be abridged of her privileges and impaired in her dignity."

It was with sentiments like these that, when the first article of the treaty was read, Lord Belhaven arose, and addressed the Parliament of Scotland in the following speech. It is obviously reported in a very imperfect manner, and was designed merely to open the discussion which was expected to follow, and not to enter at large into the argument. It was a simple burst of feeling, in which the great leader of the country party, who was equally distinguished for "the mighty sway of his talents and the resoluteness of his temper," poured out his emotions in view of that act of *parricide*, as he considered it, to which the Parliament was now called. He felt that no regard to consequences, no loss or advancement of trade, manufactures, or national wealth, ought to have the weight of a feather, when the honor and existence of his country were at stake. He felt that Scotland, if only united, was abundantly able to work out her own salvation. These two thoughts, therefore—NATIONAL HONOR and NATIONAL UNION—constitute the burden of his speech.

SPEECH

OF LORD BELHAVEN AGAINST THE LEGISLATIVE UNION OF ENGLAND AND SCOTLAND, DELIVERED IN THE PARLIAMENT OF SCOTLAND, NOV. 2, 1706.

My Lord Chancellor,—When I consider the affair of a union betwixt the two nations, as expressed in the several articles thereof, and now the subject of our deliberation at this time, I find my mind crowded with a variety of melancholy thoughts; and I think it my duty to disburden myself of some of them by laying them before, and exposing them to the serious consideration of this honorable House.

I think I see a free and independent kingdom delivering up that which all the world hath been fighting for since the days of Nimrod; yea, that for which most of all the empires, kingdoms, states, principalities, and dukedoms of Europe, are at this time engaged in the most bloody and cruel wars; to wit, a *power to manage their own affairs by themselves, without the assistance and counsel of any other.*

I think I see a national church, founded upon a rock, secured by a claim of right, hedged and fenced about by the strictest and most pointed legal sanctions that sovereignty could contrive, voluntarily descending into a plain, upon an equal level with Jews, Papists, Socinians, Arminians, Anabaptists, and other sectaries.

I think I see the noble and honorable peerage of Scotland, whose valiant predecessors led armies against their enemies upon their own proper charges and expense, now devested of their followers and vassalages; and put upon such an equal foot with their vassals, that I think I see a petty English exciseman receive more homage and respect than what was paid formerly to their *quondam* Mackalamores.

I think I see the present peers of Scotland, whose noble ancestors conquered provinces, overran countries, reduced and subjected towns and fortified places, exacted tribute through the greatest part of England, now walking in the Court of Requests, like so many English attorneys; laying aside their walking swords when in company with the English peers, lest their self-defense should be found murder.

I think I see the honorable estate of barons, the bold assertors of the nation's rights and liberties in the worst of times, now setting a watch upon their lips, and a guard upon their tongues, lest they may be found guilty of *scandalum magnatum*, a speaking evil of dignities.

I think I see the royal state of burghers walking their desolate streets, hanging down their heads under disappointments, wormed out of all the branches of their old trade, uncertain what hand to turn to, necessitated to become prentices to their unkind neighbors; and yet, after all, finding their trade so fortified by companies, and secured by prescriptions, that they despair of any success therein.

I think I see our learned judges laying aside their pratiques and decisions, studying the common law of England, graveled with certioraris, nisi priuses, writs of error, verdicts, injunctions, demurs, &c., and frightened with appeals and avocations, because of the new regulations and rectifications they may meet with.

I think I see the valiant and gallant soldiery either sent to learn the plantation trade abroad, or at home petitioning for a small subsistence, as a reward of their honorable exploits; while their old corps are broken, the common soldiers left to beg, and the youngest English corps kept standing.

I think I see the honest industrious tradesman loaded with new taxes and impositions, disappointed of the equivalents,[1] drinking water in place of ale, eating his saltless pottage, petitioning for encouragement to his manufactures, and answered by counter petitions.

In short, I think I see the laborious plowman, with his corn spoiling upon his hands for want of sale, cursing the day of his birth, dreading the expense of his burial, and uncertain whether to marry or do worse.

I think I see the incurable difficulties of the landed men, fettered under the golden chain of "equivalents," their pretty daughters petitioning for want of husbands, and their sons for want of employment.

I think I see our mariners delivering up their ships to their Dutch partners; and what through presses and necessity, earning their bread as underlings in the royal English navy!

But above all, my Lord, I think I see our ancient mother, Caledonia, like Cesar, sitting in the midst of our Senate, ruefully looking round about her, covering herself with her royal garment, attending the fatal blow, and breathing out her last with an *et tu quoque mi fili!*[2]

---

[1] The "equivalent," or compensation, of £398,000, spoken of above, was to be distributed, a great portion of it, to the shareholders of the African and India Company, who had suffered so severely by the breaking up of the Darien settlement. As the shares must, in many instances, have changed hands, great inequality and disappointment was to be expected in the distribution of this money; which was likely, in most cases, to go into the hands of the friends of government, as a bribe or recompense for services on this occasion.

[2] The actual exclamation of Cesar, as stated by Suetonius, was in Greek, Και συ τεκνον; and *thou also, my child?* The Latin version was undoubtedly made at the time, by those who reported the

Are not these, my Lord, very afflicting thoughts? And yet they are but the least part suggested to me by these dishonorable articles. Should not the consideration of these things vivify these dry bones of ours? Should not the memory of our noble predecessors' valor and constancy rouse up our drooping spirits? Are our noble predecessors' souls got so far into the English cabbage stalk and cauliflowers, that we should show the least inclination that way? Are our eyes so blinded, are our ears so deafened, are our hearts so hardened, are our tongues so faltered, are our hands so fettered, that in this our day—I say, my Lord, in this *our* day—we should not mind the things that concern the very being, and well-being of our ancient kingdom, before the day be hid from our eyes?

No, my Lord, God forbid! Man's extremity is God's opportunity: he is a present help in time of need—a deliverer, and that right early! Some unforeseen providence will fall out, that may cast the balance; some Joseph or other will say, "Why do ye strive together, since ye are brethren?" None can destroy Scotland save Scotland's self. Hold your hands from the *pen*, and you are secure! There will be a Jehovah-Jireh; and some ram will be caught in the thicket, when the bloody knife is at our mother's throat. Let us, then, my Lord, and let our noble patriots behave themselves like men, and we know not how soon a blessing may come.

I design not at this time to enter into the merits of any one particular article. I intend this discourse as an introduction to what I may afterward say upon the whole debate, as it falls in before this honorable House; and therefore, in the further prosecution of what I have to say, I shall insist upon a few particulars, very necessary to be understood before we enter into the detail of so important a matter.

I shall therefore, in the first place, endeavor to encourage a free and full deliberation, without animosities and heats. In the next place, I shall endeavor to make an inquiry into the nature and source of the unnatural and dangerous divisions that are now on foot within this isle, with some motives showing that it is our interest to lay them aside at this time. And all this with all deference, and under the correction of this honorable House.

My Lord Chancellor, the greatest honor that was done unto a Roman, was to allow him the glory of a triumph; the greatest and most dishonorable punishment was that of parricide. He that was guilty of parricide was beaten with rods upon his naked body, till the blood gushed out of all the veins of his body; then he was sewed up in a leathern sack called a *culeus*, with a cock, a viper, and an ape, and thrown headlong into the sea.

My Lord, *patricide is a greater crime than parricide, all the world over.*

In a triumph, my Lord, when the conqueror was riding in his triumphal chariot, crowned with laurels, adorned with trophies, and applauded with huzzas, there was a monitor appointed to stand behind him, to warn him not to be high-minded, nor puffed up with overweening thoughts of himself; and to his chariot were tied a whip and a bell, to remind him that, notwithstanding all his glory and grandeur, he was accountable to the *people* for his administration, and would be punished as other men, if found guilty.

The greatest honor among *us*, my Lord, is to represent the sovereign's sacred person [as High Commissioner] in Parliament; and in one particular it appears to be greater than that of a triumph, because the whole legislative power seems to be intrusted with him. If he give the royal assent to an act of the estates, it becomes a law obligatory upon the subject, though contrary to or without any instructions from the sovereign. If he refuse the royal assent to a vote in Parliament, it can not be a law, though he has the sovereign's particular and positive instructions for it.

His Grace the Duke of Queensbury, who now represents her Majesty in this session of Parliament, hath had the honor of that great trust as often, if not more, than any Scotchman ever had. He hath been the favorite of two successive sovereigns; and I can not but commend his constancy and perseverance, that, notwithstanding his former difficulties and unsuccessful attempts, and maugre some other specialities not yet determined, his Grace has yet had the resolution to undertake the most unpopular measure last. If his Grace succeed in this affair of a union, and that it prove for the happiness and welfare of the nation, then he justly merits to have a statue of gold erected for himself; but if it shall tend to the entire destruction and abolition of our nation, and that we, the nation's trustees, shall go into it, then I must say, that a whip and a bell, a cock, a viper, and an ape, are but too small punishments for any such bold, unnatural undertaking and complaisance.[3]

I. That I may pave the way, my Lord, to a full, calm, and free reasoning upon this affair, which is of the last consequence unto this nation, I shall mind this honorable House, that we are the successors of those noble ancestors who founded our monarchy, framed our laws, amended, altered, and corrected them from time to

words. By many at the present day, "*Et tu Brute*," has been given as the expression; but for this, it is believed, there is no classical authority.

[3] The High-Commissioner Queensbury, though by birth a Scotchman, had by long employment in the service of the Court, lost all regard for the distinctive interests and honor of his native country. He was conciliating in his manners, cool, enterprising, and resolute, expert in all the arts and intrigues of politics, and lavish of the public money for the accomplishment of his purposes. He had been the agent of the Court for attempting many unpopular measures in the Scottish Parliament; and he had now "the resolution to undertake the most unpopular measure last." He was generally hated and suspected as a renegade; and hence the bitterness with which he is here assailed, as seeking "the entire destruction and abolition of the nation."

time, as the affairs and circumstances of the nation did require, without the assistance or advice of any foreign power or potentate; and who, during the time of two thousand years, have handed them down to us, a free, independent nation, with the hazard of their lives and fortunes. Shall not we, then, argue for that which our progenitors have purchased for us at so dear a rate, and with so much immortal honor and glory? God forbid. Shall the hazard of a father unbind the ligaments of a dumb son's tongue and shall we hold our peace when our *patria*, our country, is in danger?[4] I say this, my Lord, that I may encourage every individual member of this House to speak his mind freely. There are many wise and prudent men among us, who think it not worth their while to open their mouths; there are others, who can speak very well, and to good purpose, who shelter themselves under the shameful cloak of silence from a fear of the frowns of great men and parties. I have observed, my Lord, by my experience, the greatest number of speakers in the most trivial affairs; and it will always prove so, while we come not to the right understanding of the oath *de fideli*, whereby we are bound not only to give our vote, but our *faithful advice* in Parliament, as we should answer to God. And in our ancient laws, the representatives of the honorable barons and the royal boroughs are termed "*spokesmen.*" It lies upon your Lordships, therefore, particularly to take notice of such, whose modesty makes them bashful to speak. Therefore I shall leave it upon you, and conclude this point with a very memorable saying of an honest private gentleman to a great Queen, upon occasion of a state project, contrived by an able statesman, and the favorite to a great King, against a peaceful, obedient people, because of the diversity of their laws and constitutions: "If at this time thou hold thy peace, salvation shall come to the people from another place; but thou and thy house shall perish." I leave the application to each particular member of this House.[5]

II. My Lord, I come now to consider our divisions. We are under the happy reign, blessed be God, of the best of queens, who has no evil design against the meanest of her subjects; who loves all her people, and is equally beloved by them again; and yet, that under the happy influence of our most excellent Queen, there should be such divisions and factions, more dangerous and threatening to her dominions than if we were under an arbitrary government, is most strange and unaccountable. Under an arbitrary prince all are willing to serve, because all are under a necessity to obey, whether they will or not. He chooses, therefore, whom he will, without respect to either parties or factions; and if he think fit to take the advice of his councils or Parliaments, every man speaks his mind freely, and the prince receives the faithful advice of his people, without the mixture of self-designs. If he prove a good prince, the government is easy; if bad, either death or a revolution brings a deliverance: whereas here, my Lord, there appears no end of our misery, if not prevented in time. Factions are now become independent, and have got footing in councils, in Parliaments, in treaties, in armies, in incorporations, in families, among kindred; yea, man and wife are not free from their political jars.

It remains, therefore, my Lord, that I inquire into the nature of these things; and since the names give us not the right idea of the thing, I am afraid I shall have difficulty to make myself well understood.

The names generally used to denote the factions are Whig and Tory; as obscure as that of Guelfs and Ghibellines; yea, my Lord, they have different significations, as they are applied to factions in each kingdom. A Whig in England is a heterogeneous creature: in Scotland he is all of a piece. A Tory in England is all of a piece, and a statesman: in Scotland he is quite otherwise; an anti-courtier and anti-statesman.

A Whig in England appears to be somewhat like Nebuchadnezzar's image, of different metals, different classes, different principles, and different designs; yet, take them altogether, they are like a piece of some mixed drugget of different threads; some finer, some coarser, which, after all, make a comely appearance and an agreeable suit. Tory is like a piece of loyal home-made English cloth, the true staple of the nation, all of a thread; yet if we look narrowly into it, we shall perceive a diversity of colors, which, according to the various situations and positions, make various appearances. Sometimes Tory is like the moon in its full; as appeared in the affair of the Bill of Occasional Conformity. Upon other occasions, it appears to be under a cloud, and as if it were eclipsed by a greater body; as it did in the design of calling over the illustrious Princess Sophia. However, by this we may see their designs are to outshoot Whig in his own bow.

[4] Allusion is here made to the story of Crœsus and his dumb child, as related by Herodotus. At the storming of Sardis, a Persian soldier, through ignorance of the King's person, was about to kill Crœsus; when his dumb son, under the impulse of astonishment and terror, broke silence, and exclaimed, "Oh man, do not kill my father Crœsus!" There was evidently in the mind of the speaker, and perhaps in the language actually employed, a play on the words *pater*, father, and *patria*, country, which gave still greater force to the allusion.

[5] An appeal is here made, not merely to those members of Parliament who were at first awed into silence by the authority of the Court, but to the Squadroné Volanté, or Flying Squadron, a party headed by the Marquess of Tweddale, who held the balance of power, and were accustomed to throw themselves, during the progress of a debate, on that side where they could gain most. This party had thus far maintained a cautious silence; and the object of Lord Belhaven was to urge them, under the pressure of a general and indignant public sentiment, to declare themselves at once on the popular side, before the influence of the Court had time to operate through patronage or bribery.

Whig, in Scotland, is a true blue Presbyterian, who, without considering time or power, will venture his all for the Kirk, but something less for the State. The greatest difficulty is how to describe a Scots Tory. Of old, when I knew them first, Tory was an honest-hearted, comradish fellow, who, provided he was maintained and protected in his benefices, titles, and dignities by the State, was the less anxious who had the government of the Church. But now, what he is since *jure divino* came in fashion, and that Christianity, and by consequence salvation, comes to depend upon episcopal ordination, I profess I know not what to make of him; only this I must say for him, that he endeavors to do by opposition that which his brother in England endeavors by a more prudent and less scrupulous method.[6]

Now, my Lord, from these divisions there has got up a kind of aristocracy, something like the famous triumvirate at Rome. They are a kind of undertakers and pragmatic statesmen, who, finding their power and strength great, and answerable to their designs, will make bargains with our gracious sovereign; they will serve her faithfully, but upon their own terms; they must have their own instruments, their own measures. This man must be turned out, and that man put in, and then they will make her the most glorious queen in Europe.

Where will this end, my Lord? Is not her Majesty in danger by such a method? Is not the monarchy in danger? Is not the nation's peace and tranquillity in danger? Will a change of parties make the nation more happy? No, my Lord. The seed is sown that is like to afford us a perpetual increase. It is not an annual herb, it takes deep root; it seeds and breeds; and if not timely prevented by her Majesty's royal endeavors, will split the whole island in two.

III. My Lord, I think, considering our present circumstances at this time, the Almighty God has reserved this great work for us. We may bruise this hydra of division, and crush this cockatrice's egg. Our neighbors in England are not yet fitted for any such thing; they are not under the afflicting hand of Providence, as we are. Their circumstances are great and glorious; their treaties are prudently managed, both at home and abroad; their generals brave and valorous, their armies successful and victorious; their trophies and laurels memorable and surprising; their enemies subdued and routed, their strongholds besieged and taken. Sieges relieved, marshals killed and taken prisoners, provinces and kingdoms are the results of their victories. Their royal navy is the terror of Europe; their trade and commerce extended through the universe, encircling the whole habitable world, and rendering their own capital city the emporium for the whole inhabitants of the earth.[7] And which is yet more than all these things, the subjects freely bestowing their treasure upon their sovereign; and above all, these vast riches, the sinews of war, and without which all the glorious success had proved abortive, these treasures are managed with such faithfulness and nicety, that they answer seasonably all their demands, though at never so great a distance. Upon these considerations, my Lord, how hard and difficult a thing will it prove to persuade our neighbors to a self-denying bill.

'Tis quite otherwise with us, my Lord, as we are an obscure poor people, though formerly of better account, removed to a distant corner of the world, without name, and without alliances; our posts mean and precarious; so that I profess I don't think any one post in the kingdom worth the briguing [seeking] after, save that of being commissioner to a long session of a factious Scots Parliament, with an antedated commission, and that yet renders the rest of the ministers more miserable.[8] What hinders us then,

[6] A few words of explanation will make this description clearer. The English Whigs effected the Revolution of 1688 by combining various interests against James II., and in favor of King William. Hence the party was composed of discordant materials; and Belhaven therefore describes it as a "mixed drugget of different threads," although, as a Scotch Presbyterian, he would naturally consider it as adapted to make "a comely appearance and an agreeable suit," from its Low-Church character, and its support of the Protestant succession. The English Tories were "the true staple of the nation," being chiefly the old and wealthy families of the Establishment, holding to High-Church principles and the divine right of kings. They gained the ascendency on the accession of Queen Anne to the throne, and were thus "like the moon in its full." They showed their sense of this ascendency, and their determination to maintain it, by the Bill of Occasional Conformity, which excluded from office all persons who had attended a dissenting place of worship. Afterward they changed their policy, and sought favor with the Hanover family, by a proposal for "calling over the Princess Sophia," who was the next successor to the crown. This gave great offense to Queen Anne, so that now they were under a cloud, and as it were eclipsed. This courting of the Hanover family (which had hitherto been supported by the Whigs alone) showed the English Tory to be "a statesman," or statemonger, bent on having power from supporting the state. A Scotch Tory, on the contrary, was a Jacobite, an "anti-courtier and anti-statesman," opposed to the very existence of the new government; while a Scotch Whig was a true blue Presbyterian, resolving his entire politics into the advancement of his Kirk and his country. The object of this satire on parties was to create a national spirit among the Scotch, which should put an end to their factions, and unite them all in maintaining their country's independence.

[7] The battle of Blenheim and other victories of Marlborough had recently taken place, and had raised England to the height of her military renown, while her naval superiority had been recently established by equally decisive victories at sea.

[8] By an act passed near the close of King William's reign, the duration of the existing Scottish Parliament was to be prolonged for the period of *six* months after his death. But it did not actually meet, on the accession of Queen Anne, until the end

my Lord, to lay aside our divisions, to unite cordially and heartily together in our present circumstances, when our all is at stake. Hannibal, my Lord, is at our gates—Hannibal is come within our gates—Hannibal is come the length of this table—he is at the foot of the throne. He will demolish the throne, if we take not notice. He will seize upon these regalia. He will take them as our *spolia opima*,[9] and whip us out of this house, never to return again.

For the love of God, then, my Lord, for the safety and welfare of our ancient kingdom, whose sad circumstances I hope we shall yet convert into prosperity and happiness! We want no means if we unite. God blessed the peacemakers. We want neither men, nor sufficiency of all manner of things necessary to make a nation happy. All depends upon management. *Concordia res parvæ crescunt*—small means increase by concord. I fear not these Articles, though they were ten times worse than they are, if we once cordially forgive one another, and that according to our proverb, *Bygones be bygones*, and fair play for time to come. For my part, in the sight of God, and in the presence of this honorable House, I heartily forgive every man, and beg that they may do the same to me. And I do most humbly propose that his Grace my Lord Commissioner may appoint an *Agape*, may order a Love-feast for this honorable House, that we may lay aside all self-designs, and after our fasts and humiliations, may have a day of rejoicing and thankfulness; may eat our meat with gladness, and our bread with a merry heart. Then shall we sit each man under his own fig-tree, and the voice of the turtle shall be heard in our land, a bird famous for constancy and fidelity.

My Lord, I shall pause here, and proceed no further in my discourse, till I see if his Grace my Lord Commissioner [Queensbury] will receive any humble proposals for removing misunderstandings among us, and putting an end to our fatal divisions. Upon my honor, I have no other design; and I am content to beg the favor upon my bended knees.[10]

No answer.

My Lord Chancellor, I am sorry that I must pursue the thread of my sad and melancholy story. What remains is more afflictive than what I have already said. Allow me, then, to make this meditation—that if our posterity, after we are all dead and gone, shall find themselves under an ill-made bargain, and shall have recourse to our records for the names of the managers who made that treaty by which they have suffered so much, they will certainly exclaim, "Our nation must have been reduced to the last extremity at the time of this treaty! All our great chieftains, all our noble peers, who once defended the rights and liberties of the nation, must have been killed, and lying dead on the bed of honor, before the nation could ever condescend to such mean and contemptible terms! Where were the great men of the noble families—the Stewarts, Hamiltons, Grahams, Campbells, Johnstons, Murrays, Homes, Kers? Where were the two great officers of the Crown, the Constable and the Marischal of Scotland? Certainly all were extinguished, *and now we are slaves forever!*"

But the English records—how will they make their posterity reverence the names of those illustrious men who made that treaty, and forever brought under those fierce, warlike, and troublesome neighbors who had struggled so long for independency, shed the best blood of their nation, and reduced a considerable part of their country to become waste and desolate!

I see the English Constitution remaining firm—the same two houses of Parliament; the same taxes, customs, and excise; the same trade in companies; the same municipal laws; while all ours are either subjected to new regulations, or annihilated forever! And for what? Only that we may have the honor to pay their old debts; and may have some few persons present [in Parliament] as witnesses to the validity of the deed, when they are pleased to contract more!

Good God! What? *Is* this an entire surrender?

My Lord, I find my heart so full of grief and indignation, that I must beg pardon not to finish the last part of my discourse; but pause that I may drop a tear as the prelude to so sad a story!

This fervent appeal had no effect. The Treaty of Union was ratified by a majority of thirty-three out of two hundred and one members. That it was carried by bribery is now matter of history. Documents have been brought to light, showing that the sum of £20,000 was sent to Queensbury for this purpose by the English ministers; and the names of those to whom the money was paid, belonging chiefly to the Squadroné, are given in full.

---

of *nine* months. Hence the legality of its assembling was denied by the Duke of Hamilton the moment it convened; and he, with eighty other members, withdrew before it was constituted. Queensbury, however, proceeded, as High Commissioner, to open Parliament. This, undoubtedly, is the transaction here alluded to. The commission under which he acted was dated back, probably, within the six months prescribed; and hence the sneer about "an antedated commission." Violent animosities were created by this procedure.

[9] The *spolia opima*, or "richest spoils" of war among the Romans, consisted, according to Livy, of the armor and trappings which a supreme commander had stripped, on the field of battle, from the leader of the foe. Plutarch says that, down to his time, only three examples of this kind had occurred in Roman history. The image is, therefore, a very striking one, representing Scotland as prostrate, and stripped of her regalia (objects of almost superstitious veneration to the people), which would be borne off by England as her *spolia opima*, to grace her triumph.

[10] Lord Brougham, it seems from this passage, was not without precedent, when he sunk on his knees before the House of Lords, in urging the adoption of the Reform Bill.

The fate of Belhaven was a melancholy one. He submitted quietly to what he considered the ruin and dishonor of his country. Two years after, a French fleet, with the Pretender on board, appeared off the coast of Scotland, and menaced an invasion of the country. The government was thrown into the utmost disorder; and though the fleet withdrew without venturing on the proposed descent, numerous arrests were made of suspected persons. Among these were Belhaven and others who had opposed the Union. Without a particle of proof against him, he was dragged to London. At the end of some weeks, however, he was released; but expired almost immediately after, of grief and indignation at this unworthy treatment.[11]

The evils anticipated by Lord Belhaven, and depicted in such glowing colors, never actually occurred. Nor were the benefits of the Union so immediate or great as were anticipated by its friends. The nation remained for a long time in an angry and mutinous state. Two rebellions took place in behalf of the Stuart family, one in 1715, and the other in 1745. It became at length apparent that the worst evils of Scotland arose from her system of *clanship;* which divided most of the country, especially the Highlands, into numerous small sovereignties, with the right of "pit and gallows," or imprisonment and death, under the name of "heritable jurisdictions." The course of justice was thus effectually impeded; and a large part of Scotland was kept in a state of perpetual disorder by the jealousies and contentions of rival clans. Immediately after the rebellion of 1745, the right of "heritable jurisdiction" was abolished by an act of Parliament, and the whole kingdom brought under the control of the same courts. "From the time that this act came into full operation," says Lord Campbell, "and not from the Union, commences the prosperity of Scotland; which having been the idlest, poorest, and most turbulent country in Europe, has become one of the most industrious, the most improving, and most orderly."

[11] Laing, iv., 375.

SIR ROBERT WALPOLE.

The administration of Walpole was the longest which has occurred since the days of Queen Elizabeth. He was probably the most dexterous party leader which England ever had; "equally skilled to win popular favor, to govern the House of Commons, and to influence and be influenced by public opinion."

Descended from an ancient and respectable family, he was born at Houghton, in Norfolkshire, on the 26th day of August, 1676. Part of his boyhood was spent at Eton, and he was for two years a member of the University of Cambridge; but in neither of these places did he give any indications of superior talents. In early life he was remarkable for nothing but his high spirits and dislike of study. The only benefit he seems to have obtained from his early education, was a facility which he acquired at Eton of conversing in Latin. This became to him afterward an important instrument of power. George I. could speak no English, and Walpole no German: so they compromised the matter when he was made Prime Minister; and all the communications between him and his master, involving the highest interests of the kingdom, were carried on in "very bad Latin."

The first impulse given to the mind of Walpole arose from his being elected a member of Parliament at the age of twenty-four. A vein was now struck which laid open the master principle of his character. It was a spirit of intense ambition. From this moment he laid aside all his sluggishness and love of ease; he threw himself at once into the arena of political strife; and the whole cast of his mind and feelings, as well as the character of the times, went to secure his early ascendency. He had naturally great force and penetration of intellect; a clear judgment; a dauntless spirit; a thorough knowledge of human nature, especially on its weak side; infinite dexterity in carrying on or counteracting political intrigues; a self-possession which never forsook him in the most trying circumstances; and a perfectly unscrupulous freedom in the adoption of every means that seemed necessary to the accomplishment of his designs. The only acquired knowledge which he brought with him into public life, was a thorough acquaintance with finance. It was precisely the knowledge that was needed at that juncture; and it laid the foundation, at no distant period, of the long and almost despotic sway which he exercised over English affairs.

On taking his seat in Parliament, in 1710, he joined himself to the Whig party, and was almost immediately brought into office as Secretary at War. Thrown out soon after by a change of ministry, which arose from the silly prosecution of Sacheverell, he was restored to office in 1714, when the Whigs came into power under George I. From this time, for nearly thirty years, he was an active member of the government, during twenty of which he was Prime Minister. To this office he was called, by general consent, in 1721, on the explosion of the South Sea project, which filled the whole island with consternation and ruin. He had opposed the scheme and predicted its failure from the outset, though he had the sagacity to profit largely by speculating in the stock; and now that his predictions were fulfilled, every eye was turned to Walpole, as the only one fitted, by his financial skill, to repair the shattered credit of the country. He was made First Lord of the Treasury, and Chancellor of the Exchequer, on the second of April, 1721.

Walpole had now reached the summit of his ambition; and if he had only been just and liberal to his political associates, he might, pernaps. even in that faithless and intriguing age, have gone on to enjoy an undisputed supremacy. But his ambition was domineering and exclusive. He was jealous of every man in his own party, whose growing influence or force of character seemed likely to raise him above the station of a humble dependant. In about two years he quarreled with Carteret, one of the most gifted men of the age, who came in with him as Secretary of State, simply because he would allow of no colleague, but was resolved to rule at the council board as sole master. Within two years more, he endeavored to put Pulteney out of the way by a specious offer of the peerage ; and thus made the most eloquent speaker in the House, before the time of Chatham, his enemy for life. Chesterfield was turned out from his station as Lord Steward of the Household, with circumstances of personal insult, because he voted against the Excise Bill, which Walpole himself soon after abandoned. Others of the nobility, with a number of military officers, among whom was Lord Chatham, were treated with the same indignity. Thus he alienated from him, by degrees, nearly all the talent of the Whig party.

The Opposition which he had to encounter was, therefore, composed of singularly discordant materials. To his natural opponents, the Jacobites and Tories, was added a large body of disaffected Whigs, who took the name of "Patriots." Bolingbroke, after the pardon of his treasons by George I., and his return to England in 1724, though not restored to his seat in the House of Lords, and therefore unable to share in public debate, was the acknowledged leader of the Tories and Jacobites ; and, by a coalition which he soon after made with Pulteney, became for nearly ten years the real head of the Opposition. He was qualified for this station by extraordinary abilities and matured experience. He was a veteran in the arts of popular delusion. Such was the ascendency of his genius over the strongest minds, that he could unite Wyndham and Pulteney in the same measures ; and from his station behind the scenes, could move the machinery of Opposition with the greater coolness because he had no share in public measures. Men were thus brought into one body, under the strictest party discipline, who could never have acted together for a moment on any other subject. They comprised a large part of the talent of the kingdom ; and were engaged for years in the struggle to put Walpole down, animated, in most instances, not only by an intense desire for office, but by personal resentment and a spirit of revenge.

It was certainly a proof of consummate ability in Walpole, that he was able to stand for a single year against such an Opposition. That he sustained himself, to a considerable extent, by the systematic bribery of the leading members of Parliament, there can be no doubt. Nor is he to be tried by the standard of the present day on that subject. Charles II. commeneed the system ; it was continued under his successor ; and when William III. was placed on the throne by the Revolution of 1688, he found it impossible to carry on the government without resorting to the same means. "It was not, therefore," as remarked by Cooke in his History of Party, "the minister who corrupted the age ; his crime was that he pandered to the prevailing depravity." But bribery alone could never have given Walpole so complete an ascendency. A ministerial majority, even when part of its members are bribed, demand of their leader at least plausible reasons for the vote they give. Against such an Opposition as he had to encounter, nothing but extraordinary talents, and a thorough knowledge of affairs, could have maintained him for a single month at the head of the government. And it is a remarkable fact, as to the leading measures for which he was so vehemently assailed, his Excise Bill, Wood's Patent, a Standing Army, Septennial Parliaments, the Hanover Treaty, and the Spanish Convention, that the verdict of posterity has been decidedly in his favor.. Even

Lord Chatham, who in early life was drawn under the influence of the Opposition leaders by their extraordinary talents and specious pretensions to patriotism, publicly declared, at a later period, that he had changed his views of the principal measures of Walpole.

But while posterity have thus decided for Walpole, on the main questions in debate between him and the Opposition, they have been far from awarding to him the honors of a great statesman. He undoubtedly rendered a most important service to his country, by the skill and firmness with which he defeated the machinations of the Jacobites, and held the house of Brunswick on the throne. It was not without reason that Queen Caroline, on her dying bed, commended, not Walpole to the favor of the King, but the King to the protection and support of Walpole. Still, it is apparent, from the whole tenor of his conduct, that in this, as in every other case, he was governed by the absorbing passion of his life, the love of office. "He understood," says Lord Campbell, "the *material* interests of the country, and, so far as was consistent with the retention of power, he was desirous of pursuing them." We have here the key to every measure of his administration—"*the retention of power!*" It was this that dictated his favorite maxim, *ne quieta moveas*, because he felt that change, however useful, might weaken his hold on office. Hence his scandalous treatment of the Dissenters, whom he deluded for years with solemn promises of deliverance from the galling yoke of the Test Act, and thus held them as firm supporters of his ministry in the most trying seasons; but when driven at last to say, "*When* will the time come?" he answered, as he always meant, "Never!" He was afraid of the High Church party; and he chose rather to break his word, than to venture on what he acknowledged to be a simple act of justice. It was so in every thing. He would run no personal risk to secure the most certain and valuable improvements. He would do nothing to provide against remote dangers, if it cost any great and immediate sacrifice. He therefore did nothing for the advancement of English institutions. He was the minister of the Present, not of the Future. His conduct in respect to the Spanish war furnishes a complete exhibition of his character, and has covered his memory with indelible disgrace. He knew it to be unnecessary and unjust—"the most unprovoked and unjustifiable war," as a great writer has observed, "in the English annals." Any other minister, rather than be forced into it by the popular clamor, would have instantly resigned. But in the words of Lord Mahon, who was disposed, in general, to judge favorably of Walpole, "He still clung unworthily to his darling office; thus proving that a love of power, and not a love of peace (as has been pretended), was his ruling principle. It was a sin against light. No man had a clearer view of the impending mischief and misery of the Spanish war. On the very day of the Declaration, when joyful peals were heard from every steeple of the city, the minister muttered, 'They may ring the bells now; before long they will be *wringing* their hands.' Yet of this mischief and misery he could stoop to be the instrument!"

The selfish and temporizing policy of Walpole, on this occasion, proved his ruin. The war, which he never intended should take place, and for which he had, therefore, made no preparation, proved disastrous to the English; and the Opposition had the art to turn the popular odium with double violence upon the minister, for the failure of a measure which they had themselves forced upon him. The circumstances attending his fall from power will be detailed hereafter, in connection with his speech on a motion for his removal from office. He resigned all his employments on the 11th of February, 1742, and died about three years after, just as he was entering his sixty-ninth year.

The age of Walpole was an age rather of keen debate than impassioned eloquence. If we except Lord Chatham, whose greatest efforts belong to a later period, we shall find but little in the leading orators of the day that was lofty or imposing. They were emphatically business speakers, eagerly intent upon their object, but destitute of any principles or feelings, which could raise them above the level of the most selfish minds, engaged in a desperate struggle for office and power. We find, therefore, in their speeches, no large views, no generous and elevated sentiments, none of those appeals to the higher instincts of our nature, which are the crowning excellence of our English oratory. Any thing of this kind would have been laughed down by Walpole, as sheer affectation. Even patriotism, which is too often a limited and selfish virtue, he regarded as mere pretense. "Patriots," says he, "spring up like mushrooms! I could raise fifty of them within the twenty-four hours. I have raised many of them in a single night. It is but refusing to gratify an unreasonable or an insolent demand, and up starts a *patriot!*" The reasonings of that day were brief and pointed; with no attempts at philosophy; with but little breadth of illustration; with scarcely any disposition to discuss a subject in its principles. Parliamentary speaking was literally "a keen encounter of the wits," in which the ball of debate was tossed to and fro between men of high talent, who perfectly understood each other's motives, and showed infinite dexterity in twisting facts and arguments to serve a purpose. It was the maxim of the day, that every thing was fair in politics.—The best speeches abounded in wit and sarcasm, in sly insinuations or cutting invective, all thrown off with a light, bold, confident air, in racy English, and without any apparent effort. The language of debate approached as near to that of actual conversation, as the nature of the topics, and the flow of continuous discourse, would permit. It was direct and idiomatic; the language of men who had lived in the society of Addison and Swift; and who endeavored to unite the ease and simplicity of the one with the pungency and force of the other. It is a style of speaking which has always been a favorite one in the British Senate; and notwithstanding the examples of a loftier strain of eloquence in that body since the days of Chatham, it is still (though connected with more thorough discussion) the style which is cultivated by a majority of speakers down to the present day in both houses of Parliament.

WYNDHAM AND WALPOLE ON THE SEPTENNIAL ACT.

INTRODUCTION.

THE Septennial Act was passed in 1716, extending the duration of Parliaments from three to seven years. By an extraordinary stretch of power, the Act was made applicable to the Parliament that *passed it*, whose members, by their own vote, thus added four years to their tenure of office. This they did on the ground that the nation had just emerged from a dangerous rebellion, and that the public mind was still in so agitated a state, as to render the exciting scenes of a general election hazardous to the public safety. Whatever may be thought of this plea (and perhaps most men at the present day would unite with Mr. Hallam in justifying the measure), no one can doubt that the provisions of the Septennial Act, in respect to subsequent Parliaments, were strictly legal.

This Act has now been in operation eighteen years; and Bolingbroke, who planned the leading measures of the Opposition, saw that a motion to repeal it would embarrass the ministry, and gratify at once the landholders and the mob. The landholders, who were almost to a man Jacobites or Tories, would be zealous for the repeal, since they were not only indignant at the Act, as originally directed against themselves, but had found by experience, that it was greatly for their interest to have frequent elections. The influence they possessed over their tenantry, could be exerted at any moment, and cost them little or nothing. This influence the Whigs in power could overcome only at an enormous expense. Every general election was, therefore, a scene of general licentiousness and bribery, to which the common people looked forward as their harvest season; and so vast was the pecuniary sacrifice to which the Whigs were thus subjected, that they could never endure it if the elections were of frequent occurrence. Thus, according to Bolingbroke's calculations, if the Act was repealed, the Whigs would be driven from power; if it was not repealed, they would be loaded with the resentment of all classes, from the highest to the lowest.

There was a part of the Opposition, however, who were delicately situated in respect to this Act. It was a measure of their own. They had argued and voted for it as essential to the public security. Such was the case with Pulteney and most of the disaffected Whigs; and it was a long time before Bolingbroke succeeded in wheedling or driving them into his plan. At last, however, party discipline and the desire of office prevailed. The motion was made on the 13th of March, 1734, and gave rise to one of the most celebrated debates in English history.

It was on this occasion that Sir William Wyndham, the leader of the Tories in the House, delivered what was undoubtedly his master-piece of eloquence. This speech, however, is remembered with interest at the present day, only on account of the altercation to which it gave rise between him and Walpole. He closed with a bitter *personal* attack on the minister, and thus drew forth a reply of equal bitterness, which concluded the debate. In this reply, however, Walpole, instead of retaliating upon Wyndham, turned adroitly upon Bolingbroke as the real author of all the maneuvers against him; and while he thus threw contempt on Wyndham, by treating him as the mere mouth-piece of another, he inflicted a castigation upon Bolingbroke which, for stinging effect and perfect adherence to truth, has rarely been surpassed in the British Parliament. This, in connection with the attack of Wyndham, will now be given; and the reader will observe how dexterously Walpole, in going on, as he does, briefly to defend the Septennial Act, argues with the Tories on their own ground; showing that frequent Parliaments serve to extend and perpetuate the democratic principle in the English Constitution—a thing against which every true Tory must feel himself bound to contend.

SIR WILLIAM WYNDHAM'S[1] ATTACK

ON SIR ROBERT WALPOLE, DELIVERED IN THE HOUSE OF COMMONS ON A MOTION FOR THE REPEAL OF THE SEPTENNIAL ACT, MARCH 13, 1734.

[Mr. Wyndham, after dwelling on a variety of arguments (chiefly in reply to others), which, from a change of circumstances, are of but little interest at the present day, concluded in the following manner:]

We have been told, sir, in this House, that no faith is to be given to prophecies, therefore I shall not pretend to prophesy; but I may *suppose* a case, which, though it has not yet happened, may possibly happen. Let us then suppose, sir, a man abandoned to all notions of virtue or honor, of no great family, and of but a

[1] Wyndham was born in 1687, of an ancient family, and was heir to one of the richest baronetcies in England. He entered Parliament at the age of twenty-one, and immediately attached himself to Bolingbroke, under whose instruction he soon became expert in all the arts of oratory and intrigue.

mean fortune, raised to be chief minister of state by the concurrence of many whimsical events; afraid or unwilling to trust any but creatures of his own making, and most of them equally abandoned to all notions of virtue or honor; ignorant of the true interest of his country, and consulting nothing but that of enriching and aggrandizing himself and his favorites; in foreign affairs, trusting none but those whose education makes it impossible for them to have such knowledge or such qualifications, as can either be of service to their country, or give any weight or credit to their negotiations. Let us suppose the true interest of the nation, by such means, neglected or misunderstood; her honor and credit lost; her trade insulted; her merchants plundered; and her sailors murdered; and all these things overlooked, only for fear his administration should be endangered. Suppose him, next, possessed of great wealth, the plunder of the nation, with a Parliament of his own choosing, most of their seats purchased, and their votes bought at the expense of the public treasure. In such a Parliament, let us suppose attempts made to inquire into his conduct, or to relieve the nation from the distress he has brought upon it; and when lights proper for attaining those ends are called for, not perhaps for the information of the particular gentlemen who call for them, but because nothing can be done in a parliamentary way, till these things be in a proper way laid before Parliament; suppose these lights refused, these reasonable requests rejected by a corrupt majority of his creatures, whom he retains in daily pay, or engages in his particular interest, by granting them those posts and places which ought never to be given to any but for the good of the public. Upon this scandalous victory, let us suppose this chief minister pluming himself in defiances, because he finds he has got a Parliament, like a packed jury, ready to acquit him at all adventures. Let us further suppose him arrived to that degree of insolence and arrogance, as to domineer over all the men of ancient families, all the men of sense, figure, or fortune in the nation, and as he has no virtue of his own, ridiculing it in others, and endeavoring to destroy or corrupt it in all.

I am still not prophesying, sir; I am only supposing; and the case I am going to suppose I hope never will happen. But with such a minister and such a Parliament, let us suppose a prince upon the throne, either for want of true information, or for some other reason, ignorant and unacquainted with the inclinations and the interest of his people; weak, and hurried away by unbounded ambition and insatiable avarice. This case, sir, has never yet happened in this nation. I hope, I say, it will never exist. But as it is possible it may, could there any greater curse happen to a nation, than such a prince on the throne, advised, and solely advised, by such a minister, and that minister supported by such a Parliament? The nature of mankind can not be altered by human laws; the existence of such a prince or such a minister we can not prevent by act of Parliament; but the existence of such a Parliament I think we may. And as such a Parliament is much more likely to exist, and may do more mischief while the septennial law remains in force, than if it were repealed, therefore I am most heartily for the repeal of it.

SPEECH

OF SIR ROBERT WALPOLE ON A MOTION TO REPEAL THE SEPTENNIAL BILL, DELIVERED IN THE HOUSE OF COMMONS, 1734, IN REPLY TO SIR WILLIAM WYNDHAM.

Sir,—I do assure you, I did not intend to have troubled you on this occasion. But such incidents now generally happen toward the end of our debates, nothing at all relating to the subject; and gentlemen make such suppositions (meaning some person, or perhaps, as they say, no person now in being), and talk so much of wicked ministers, domineering ministers, ministers pluming themselves in defiances—which terms, and such like, have been of late so much made use of in this House—that if they really mean nobody either in the House or out of it, yet it must be supposed they at least mean to call upon some gentleman in this House to make them a reply. I hope, therefore, I may be allowed to draw a picture in my turn; and I may likewise say, that I do not mean to give a description of any particular person now in being. When gentlemen talk of ministers abandoned to all sense of virtue or honor, other gentlemen may, I am sure, with equal justice, and, I think, more justly, speak of anti-ministers and mock-patriots, who never had either virtue or honor; but in the whole course of their opposition are actuated only by motives of envy, and of resentment against those who have disappointed them in their views, or may not perhaps have complied with all their desires.

But now, sir, let me too suppose, and the House being cleared, I am sure no one that hears me can come within the description of the person I am to suppose. Let us suppose in this, or in some other unfortunate country, an anti-minister, who thinks himself a person of so great and extensive parts, and of so many eminent qualifications, that he looks upon himself as the only person in the kingdom capable to conduct the public affairs of the nation; and therefore christening every other gentleman who has the honor to be employed in the administration by the name of Blunderer. Suppose this fine gentleman lucky enough to have gained over to his party some persons really of fine parts, of ancient families, and of great fortunes, and others of desperate views, arising from disappointed and malicious hearts; all these gentlemen, with respect to their political behavior, moved by him, and by him solely; all they say, either in private or public, being only a repetition of the words he has put into their mouths, and a spitting out of that venom which he has infused into them; and yet we may suppose this leader not really liked by any, even of those who so blindly follow him, and hated by all the rest of mankind. We will suppose this anti-minister to be in a country where he really ought not to be, and where he could not have been but by an effect of too much goodness and mercy; yet endeavoring, with all his might and with all his art, to destroy the fountain from whence that mercy flowed. In that country suppose him continually contracting friendships and familiarities with the embassadors of those princes who at the time happen to be most at enmity with his own; and if at any time it should happen to be for the interest of any of those foreign ministers to have a secret divulged to them, which might be highly prejudicial to his native country, as well as to all its friends; suppose this foreign minister applying to him, and he answering, "I will get it you; tell me but what you want, I will endeavor to procure it for you." Upon this he puts a speech or two in the mouths of some of his creatures, or some of his new converts. What he wants is moved for in Parliament, and when so very *reasonable* a request as this is refused, suppose him and his creatures and tools, by his advice, spreading the alarm over the whole nation, and crying out, "Gentlemen, our country is at present involved in many dangerous difficulties, all which we would have extricated you from, but a wicked minister and a corrupt majority refused us the proper materials!" And upon "this scandalous victory," this minister became so insolent as "to plume himself in defiances!" Let us further suppose this anti-minister to have traveled, and at every court where he was, thinking himself the greatest minister, and making it his trade to betray the secrets of every court where he had before been; void of all faith or honor, and betraying every master he ever served. I could carry my suppositions a great deal further, and I may say I mean no person now in being; but if we can suppose such a one, can there be imagined a greater disgrace to human nature than such a wretch as this?[1]

Now, to be serious, and to talk really to the subject in hand. Though the question has been already so fully and so handsomely opposed by my worthy friend under the gallery, by the learned gentleman near me, and by several others, that there is no great occasion to say any thing further against it; yet, as some new matter has been stated by some of the gentlemen who have since that time spoke upon the other side of the question, I hope the House will indulge me the liberty of giving some of those reasons which induce me to be against the motion.

In general, I must take notice, that the nature of our constitution seems to be very much mistaken by the gentlemen who have spoken in favor of this motion. It is certain that ours is a mixed government; and the perfection of our constitution consists in this, that the monarchical, aristocratical, and democratical forms of government are mixed and interwoven in ours, so as to give us all the advantages of each, without subjecting us to the dangers and inconveniences of either. The democratical form of government, which is the only one I have now occasion to take notice of, is liable to these inconveniences, that they are generally too tedious in their coming to any resolution, and seldom brisk and expeditious enough in carrying their resolutions into execution. That they are always wavering in their resolutions, and never steady in any of the measures they resolve to pursue; and that they are often involved in factions, seditions, and insurrections, which expose them to be made the tools, if not the prey of their neighbors. Therefore, in all the regulations we make with respect to our constitution, we are to guard against running too much into that form of government which is properly called democratical. This was, in my opinion, the effect of the triennial law, and will again be the effect, if it should ever be restored.

That triennial elections would make our government too tedious in all their resolves is evident; because, in such case, no prudent administration would ever resolve upon any measure of consequence till they had felt, not only the pulse of the Parliament, but the pulse of the people. The ministers of state would always labor under this disadvantage, that as secrets of state must not be immediately divulged, their enemies (and enemies they will always have) would have a handle for exposing their measures, and rendering them disagreeable to the people, and thereby carrying perhaps a new election against them, before they could have an opportunity of justifying their measures, by divulging those facts and circumstances from whence the justice and the wisdom of their measures would clearly appear.

Then it is by experience well known, that what is called the populace of every country are apt to

1 "How must Wyndham and Pulteney," says Lord Mahon, "have quailed before this terrible invective! How must it have wrung the haughty soul of Bolingbroke!" Every word of it was true. While Secretary of State under Queen Anne, he maintained a treasonable correspondence with the Pretender, though he contrived, at the time, to conceal the evidence, which has since been made public. On the accession of George I. he fled to France, and was made the Pretender's Secretary of State. Having quarreled with his new master, after some years, such were his powers of insinuation, that he obtained a pardon from George I., and was thus restored to a country "where he could not have been, but by the effect of too much goodness and mercy." Here he did the very things described by Walpole; his friends did not deny it, or attempt his defense. As he soon after gave up the contest, and announced his intention to quit England forever, it has been understood that this speech of Walpole drove him from the country. Lord Mahon has indeed shown that he had other reasons for going; but this does not prove that Walpole's invective was not one important cause, by destroying all his hopes of future success.

be too much elated with success, and too much dejected with every misfortune. This makes them wavering in their opinions about affairs of state, and never long of the same mind. And as this House is chosen by the free and unbiased voice of the people in general, if this choice were so often renewed, we might expect that this House would be as wavering and as unsteady as the people usually are. And it being impossible to carry on the public affairs of the nation without the concurrence of this House, the ministers would always be obliged to comply, and consequently would be obliged to change their measures as often as the people changed their minds.

With septennial Parliaments we are not exposed to either of these misfortunes, because, if the ministers, after having felt the pulse of the Parliament (which they can always soon do), resolve upon any measures, they have generally time enough, before the new election comes on, to give the people proper information, in order to show them the justice and the wisdom of the measures they have pursued. And if the people should at any time be too much elated or too much dejected, or should, without a cause, change their minds, those at the helm of affairs have time to set them right before a new election comes on.

As to faction and sedition, I will grant, that in monarchical and aristocratical governments, it generally arises from violence and oppression; but in popular or mixed governments, it always arises from the people's having too great a share in the government. For in all countries, and in all governments, there always will be many factious and unquiet spirits, who can never be at rest, either in power or out of power. When in power they are never easy, unless every man submits entirely to their directions; and when out of power, they are always working and intriguing against those that are in, without any regard to justice, or to the interest of their country. In popular governments such men have too much game. They have too many opportunities for working upon and corrupting the minds of the people, in order to give them a bad impression of, and to raise discontents against those that have the management of the public affairs for the time; and these discontents often break out into seditions and insurrections. This would, in my opinion, be our misfortune, if our Parliaments were either annual or triennial. By such frequent elections, there would be so much power thrown into the hands of the people, as would destroy that equal mixture, which is the beauty of our constitution. In short, our government would really become a democratical government, and might from thence very probably diverge into a tyrannical. Therefore, in order to preserve our constitution, in order to prevent our falling under tyranny and arbitrary power, we ought to preserve this law, which I really think has brought our constitution to a more equal mixture, and consequently to a greater perfection, than it was ever in before that law took place

As to bribery and corruption, if it were possible to influence, by such base means, the majority of the electors of Great Britain, to choose such men as would probably give up their liberties—if it were possible to influence, by such means, a majority of the members of this House to consent to the establishment of arbitrary power—I should readily allow, that the calculations made by the gentlemen of the other side were just, and their inference true. But I am persuaded that neither of these is possible. As the members of this House generally are, and must always be, gentlemen of fortune and figure in their country, is it possible to suppose that any of them could, by a pension or a post, be influenced to consent to the overthrow of our constitution, by which the enjoyment, not only of what he got, but of what he before had, would be rendered altogether precarious? I will allow, that with respect to bribery, the price must be higher or lower, generally in proportion to the virtue of the man who is to be bribed; but it must likewise be granted that the humor he happens to be in at the time, and the spirit he happens to be endowed with, adds a great deal to his virtue. When no encroachments are made upon the rights of the people, when the people do not think themselves in any danger, there may be many of the electors who, by a bribe of ten guineas, might be induced to vote for one candidate rather than another. But if the court were making any encroachments upon the rights of the people, a proper spirit would, without doubt, arise in the nation; and in such a case I am persuaded that none, or very few, even of such electors, could be induced to vote for a court candidate—no, not for ten times the sum.

There may be some bribery and corruption in the nation; I am afraid there will always be some. But it is no proof of it that strangers [*i. e.*, non-residents] are sometimes chosen; for a man may have so much natural influence over a borough in his neighborhood, as to be able to prevail with them to choose any person he pleases to recommend. And if upon such recommendation they choose one or two of his friends, who are perhaps strangers to them, it is not from thence to be inferred that the two strangers were chosen their representatives by the means of bribery and corruption.

To insinuate that money may be issued from the public treasury for bribing elections, is really something very extraordinary, especially in those gentlemen who know how many checks are upon every shilling that can be issued from thence; and how regularly the money granted in one year for the service of the nation must always be accounted for the very next session in this House, and likewise in the other, if they have a mind to call for any such account.[2] And as to gentlemen in office, if they have any advantage over country gentlemen, in having something else to depend on besides their own private for-

[2] Walpole's notorious system of bribery was certainly not conducted in so bungling a manner.

tunes, they have likewise many disadvantages. They are obliged to live here at London with their families, by which they are put to a much greater expense, than gentlemen of equal fortune who live in the country. This lays them under a very great disadvantage in supporting their interest in the country. The country gentleman, by living among the electors, and purchasing the necessaries for his family from them, keeps up an acquaintance and correspondence with them, without putting himself to any extraordinary charge. Whereas a gentleman who lives in London has no other way of keeping up an acquaintance and correspondence among his friends in the country, but by going down once or twice a year, at a very extraordinary expense, and often without any other business; so that we may conclude, a gentleman in office can not, even in seven years, save much for distributing in ready money at the time of an election. And I really believe, if the fact were narrowly inquired into, it would appear, that the gentlemen in office are as little guilty of bribing their electors with ready money, as any other set of gentlemen in the kingdom.

That there are ferments often raised among the people without any just cause, is what I am surprised to hear controverted, since very late experience may convince us of the contrary. Do not we know what a ferment was raised in the nation toward the latter end of the late Queen's reign? And it is well known what a fatal change in the affairs of this nation was introduced, or at least confirmed, by an election coming on while the nation was in that ferment.[3] Do not we know what a ferment was raised in the nation soon after his late Majesty's accession? And if an election had then been allowed to come on while the nation was in that ferment, it might perhaps have had as fatal effects as the former. But, thank God, this was wisely provided against by the very law which is now sought to be repealed.

It has, indeed, been said, that the chief motive for enacting that law now no longer exists. I can not admit that the motive they mean, was the chief motive; but even that motive is very far from having entirely ceased. Can gentlemen imagine, that in the spirit raised in the nation [against the Excise Bill] not above a twelvemonth since, Jacobitism and disaffection to the present government had no share? Perhaps some who might wish well to the present establishment, did co-operate; nay, I do not know but they were the first movers of that spirit; but it can not be supposed that the spirit then raised should have grown up to such a ferment, merely from a proposition which was honestly and fairly laid before the Parliament, and left entirely to their determination! No; the spirit was perhaps begun by those who are truly friends to the illustrious family we have now upon the throne. But it was raised to a much greater height than, I believe, even they designed, by Jacobites, and such as are enemies to our present establishment; who thought they never had a fairer opportunity of bringing about what they had so long and so unsuccessfully wished for, than that which had been furnished them by those who first raised that spirit. I hope the people have now in a great measure come to themselves; and therefore I doubt not but the next elections will show, that when they are left to judge coolly, they can distinguish between the real and the pretended friends to the government. But I must say, if the ferment then raised in the nation had not already greatly subsided, I should have thought a new election a very dangerous experiment. And as such ferments may hereafter often happen, I must think that frequent elections will always be dangerous; for which reason, in so far as I can see at present, I shall, I believe, at all times think it a very dangerous experiment to repeal the Septennial Bill.

The motion for repeal was rejected by a large majority, and the bill has remained untouched down to the present time. Most reflecting men will agree with Mr. Macaulay, that "the repeal of the Septennial Act, unaccompanied by a complete reform of the constitution of the elective body, would have been an unmixed curse to the country."

SPEECH

OF SIR ROBERT WALPOLE ON A MOTION FOR ADDRESSING THE KING FOR HIS REMOVAL, DELIVERED IN THE HOUSE OF COMMONS, FEBRUARY, 1741.

INTRODUCTION.

The unpopularity of Walpole was greatly increased by the disasters of the Spanish war, all of which were ascribed to his bad management or want of preparation. The Opposition, therefore, decided, early in 1741, on the extreme measure of proposing an address to the King for his removal. Accordingly, Mr. Sandys, who was designated to take the lead, gave notice of a motion to that effect on the 11th of February, 1741. Walpole rose immediately and thanked him for the information. He went on with great calmness and dignity, to assure the House that he was ready to meet every charge that could be brought

---

[3] Allusion is here made to the ferment created by the trial of Sacheverell, and the fall of the Whig administration of Godolphin, Somers, &c., consequent thereon. This change of ministry led to the Peace of Utrecht, by which the English gained far less, and their opponents more, than had been generally expected under the Whig administration.

against him; that he desired no favor, but simply a fair hearing; and concluded by laying his hand on his breast, and declaring, in the words of his favorite Horace, that he was "conscious of no crime, and dreaded no accusation."[1] At the end of two days the motion was made; and such was the eagerness of public expectation, that the galleries were filled before daybreak, and many of the members took their places in the House at six o'clock in the morning to secure themselves a seat. At one o'clock, when the debate opened, nearly five hundred members of Parliament were present.

On bringing forward his motion, Sandys, in a speech of great length and considerable ability, went over all the charges which from time to time had been urged against the minister. As to none of them did he attempt any new proofs; and nearly all were of that general nature which would certainly justify inquiry, but hardly authorize any decisive action. His main argument, after all, was, that Walpole had been at the head of affairs for twenty years, and that the people were tired of him as a minister, and hated him as a man. He ended by saying, "I have not, at present, any occasion for showing that the Favorite I am now complaining of has been guilty of heinous crimes, yet I will say that there is a very general suspicion against him; that this suspicion is justified by the present situation of our affairs both at home and abroad; and that it is ridiculous to expect that any proper discovery should be made as long as he is in possession of all the proofs, and has the distribution of all the penalties the crown can inflict, as well as of all the favors the crown can bestow. Remove him from the King's councils and presence; remove him from those high offices and power he is now possessed of. If he has been guilty of any crimes, the proofs may then be come at, and the witnesses against him will not be afraid to appear. Till you do this, it is impossible to determine whether he is guilty or innocent; and, considering the universal clamor against him, it is high time to reduce him to such a condition that he may be brought to a fair, an impartial, and a strict account. If he were conscious of his being entirely innocent, and had a due regard to the security and glory of his master and sovereign, he would have chosen to have put himself into this condition long before this time. Since he has not thought fit to do so, it is our duty to endeavor to do it for him; and, therefore, I shall conclude with moving, 'That an humble address be presented to his Majesty, that he would be graciously pleased to remove the right honorable Sir Robert Walpole, knight of the most noble order of the garter, first commissioner for executing the office of treasurer of the exchequer, chancellor and under-treasurer of the exchequer, and one of his Majesty's most honorable privy council, from his Majesty's presence and councils forever.'"

A few days after, Walpole made a speech of four hours, in reply to Sandys and others, by whom he had been attacked. We have only an imperfect outline of his argument in the speech given below, but there is reason to believe that the introductory part and the conclusion are very nearly in his own words.

SPEECH, &c.

It has been observed by several gentlemen, in vindication of this motion, that if it should be carried, neither my life, liberty, nor estate will be affected. But do the honorable gentlemen consider my character and reputation as of no moment? Is it no imputation to be arraigned before this House, in which I have sat forty years, and to have my name transmitted to posterity with disgrace and infamy? I will not conceal my sentiments, that to be *named* in Parliament as a subject of inquiry, is to me a matter of great concern. But I have the satisfaction, at the same time, to reflect, that the impression to be made depends upon the consistency of the charge and the motives of the prosecutors.

Had the charge been reduced to specific allegations, I should have felt myself called upon for a specific defense. Had I served a weak or wicked master, and implicitly obeyed his dictates, obedience to his commands must have been my only justification. But as it has been my good fortune to serve a master who wants no bad ministers, and would have hearkened to none, my defense must rest on my own conduct. The consciousness of innocence is also a sufficient support against my present prosecutors. A further justification is derived from a consideration of the views and abilities of the prosecutors. Had I been guilty of great enormities, they want neither zeal and inclination to bring them forward, nor ability to place them in the most prominent point of view. But as I am conscious of no crime, my own experience convinces me that none can be justly imputed.

I must therefore ask the gentlemen, From whence does this attack proceed? From the passions and prejudices of the parties combined

[1] In quoting the words of Horace (Epistle I., 61), Walpole gave them thus:

Nil conscire sibi, null*i* pallescere culp*æ*.

Pulteney, who sat by, cried out, "Your Latin is as bad as your logic!" "Null*á* pallescere culp*á*!" Walpole defended his quotation, and offered to bet a guinea on its correctness. The question was accordingly referred to Sir Nicholas Hardinge, clerk of the House, whose extraordinary erudition was acknowledged by all, and he at once decided in favor of Pulteney. Walpole tossed him the guinea, and Pulteney, as he caught it, held it up before the House, exclaiming, "It is the only money I have received from the treasury for many years, and it shall be the last." He kept the guinea to the end of his life, as a memento of this occurrence, and left it to his children, with a paper stating how it was won, and adding, "This guinea I desire may be kept as an heir-loom. It will prove to my posterity the use of knowing Latin, and will encourage them in their learning." It is now deposited in the medal-room of the British Museum.

against me, who may be divided into three classes, the Boys, the riper Patriots, and the Tories.[1] The Tories I can easily forgive. They have unwillingly come into the measure; and they do me honor in thinking it necessary to remove me, as their only obstacle. What, then, is the inference to be drawn from these premises? That demerit with my opponents ought to be considered as merit with others. But my great and principal crime is my long continuance in office; or, in other words, the long exclusion of those who now complain against me. This is the heinous offense which exceeds all others. I keep from them the possession of that power, those honors, and those emoluments, to which they so ardently and pertinaciously aspire. I will not attempt to deny the reasonableness and necessity of a party war; but in carrying on that war, all principles and rules of justice should not be departed from. The Tories must confess that the most obnoxious persons have felt few instances of extra-judicial power. Wherever they have been arraigned, a plain charge has been exhibited against them. They have had an impartial trial, and have been permitted to make their defense. And will they, who have experienced this fair and equitable mode of proceeding, act in direct opposition to every principle of justice, and establish this fatal precedent of parliamentary inquisition? Whom would they conciliate by a conduct so contrary to principle and precedent?

Can it be fitting in them [the Tories], who have divided the public opinion of the nation, to share it with those who now appear as their competitors? With the men of yesterday, the boys in politics, who would be absolutely contemptible did not their audacity render them detestable? With the mock patriots, whose practice and professions prove their selfishness and malignity; who threatened to pursue me to destruction, and who have never for a moment lost sight of their object? These men, under the name of Separatists, presume to call themselves exclusively the *nation* and the *people*, and under that character assume all power. In their estimation, the King, Lords, and Commons are a faction, and *they* are the government. Upon these principles they threaten the destruction of all authority, and think they have a right to judge, direct, and resist all legal magistrates. They withdraw from Parliament because they succeed in nothing; and then attribute their want of success, not to its true cause, their own want of integrity and importance, but to the effect of places, pensions, and corruption.[2] May it not be asked on this point, Are the people on the court side more united than on the other? Are not the Tories, Jacobites, and Patriots equally determined? What makes this strict union? What cements this heterogeneous mass? Party engagements and personal attachments. However different their views and principles, they all agree in opposition. The Jacobites distress the government they would subvert; the Tories contend for party prevalence and power. The Patriots, from discontent and disappointment, would change the ministry, that themselves may exclusively succeed. They have labored this point twenty years unsuccessfully. They are impatient of longer delay. They clamor for change of measures, but mean only change of ministers.

In party contests, why should not both sides be equally steady? Does not a Whig administration as well deserve the support of the Whigs as the contrary? Why is not *principle* the cement in one as well as the other; especially when my opponents confess that all is leveled against one man? Why this one man? Because they think, vainly, nobody else could withstand them. All others are treated as tools and vassals. The one is the corrupter; the numbers corrupted. But whence this cry of corruption, and exclusive claim of honorable distinction? Compare the estates, characters, and fortunes of the Commons on one side with those on the other. Let the matter be fairly investigated. Survey and examine the individuals who usually support the measures of government, and those who are in opposition. Let us see to whose side the balance preponderates. Look round both Houses, and see to which side the balance of virtue and talents preponderates! Are all these on one side, and not on the other? Or are all these to be counterbalanced by an affected claim to the exclusive title of patriotism? Gentlemen have talked a great deal of patriotism. A venerable word, when duly practiced. But I am sorry to say that of late it has been so much hackneyed about, that it is in danger of falling into disgrace. The very idea of true patriotism is lost, and the term has been prostituted to the very worst of purposes. A patriot, sir! Why, patriots spring up like mushrooms! I could raise fifty of them within the four-and-twenty hours. I have raised many of them in one night. It is but refusing to gratify an unreasonable or an insolent demand, and up starts a patriot. I have never been afraid of making patriots; but I disdain and despise all their efforts. This pretended virtue proceeds from personal malice and disappointed ambition. There is not a man among them whose particular aim I am not able to ascertain, and from what motive they have entered into the lists of opposition.

I shall now consider the articles of accusation which they have brought against me, and which they have not thought fit to reduce to specific charges; and I shall consider these in the same

[1] By the Boys he means Pitt, Lyttleton, &c., who were recently from college, with an ardent love of liberty, and much under the influence of Pulteney and others of more mature age, who were the "riper Patriots."

[2] This refers to a secession from the House headed by Wyndham, after the debate on the Spanish convention in 1739. It placed those who withdrew in a very awkward and even ridiculous position, from which they were glad to escape with consistency some months after, when war was declared against Spain.

order as that in which they were placed by the honorable member who made the motion. First, in regard to foreign affairs; secondly, to domestic affairs; and, thirdly, to the conduct of the war.

I. As to foreign affairs, I must take notice of the uncandid manner in which the gentlemen on the other side have managed the question, by blending numerous treaties and complicated negotiations into one general mass.

To form a fair and candid judgment of the subject, it becomes necessary not to consider the treaties merely *insulated*; but to advert to the time in which they were made, to the circumstances and situation of Europe when they were made, to the peculiar situation in which I stand, and to the power which I possessed. I am called repeatedly and insidiously prime and sole minister. Admitting, however, for the sake of argument, that I am prime and sole minister in this country, am I, therefore, prime and sole minister of all Europe? Am I answerable for the conduct of other countries as well as for that of my own? Many words are not wanting to show, that the particular view of each court occasioned the dangers which affected the public tranquillity; yet the whole is charged to my account. Nor is this sufficient. Whatever was the conduct of England, I am equally arraigned. If we maintained ourselves in peace, and took no share in foreign transactions, we are reproached for tameness and pusillanimity. If, on the contrary, we interfered in these disputes, we are called Don Quixotes, and dupes to all the world. If we contracted guarantees, it was asked why is the nation wantonly burdened? If guarantees were declined, we were reproached with having no allies.

I have, however, sir, this advantage, that all the objections now alleged against the conduct of the administration to which I have the honor to belong, have already been answered to the satisfaction of a majority of both houses of Parliament, and I believe to the satisfaction of a majority of the better sort of people in the nation. I need, therefore, only repeat a few of these answers that have been made already, which I shall do in the order of time in which the several transactions happened; and consequently must begin with our refusing to accept of the sole mediation offered us by Spain, on the breach between that court and the court of France, occasioned by the dismission of the Infanta of Spain.[3]

I hope it will not be said we had any reason to quarrel with France upon that account; and therefore, if our accepting of that mediation might have produced a rupture with France, it was not our duty to interfere unless we had something very beneficial to expect from the acceptance. A reconciliation between the courts of Vienna and Madrid, it is true, was desirable to all Europe as well as to us, provided it had been brought about without any design to disturb our tranquillity or the tranquillity of Europe. But both parties were then so high in their demands that we could hope for no success; and if the negotiation had ended without effect, we might have expected the common fate of arbitrators, the disobliging of both. Therefore, as it was our interest to keep well with both, I must still think it was the most prudent part we could act to refuse the offered mediation.

The next step of our foreign conduct, exposed to reprehension, is the treaty of Hanover.[4] Sir if I were to give the true history of that treaty, which no gentleman can desire I should, I am sure I could fully justify my own conduct. But as I do not desire to justify my own without justifying his late Majesty's conduct, I must observe that his late Majesty had such information as convinced not only him, but those of his council, both at home and abroad, that some dangerous designs had been formed between the Emperor and Spain at the time of their concluding the treaty at Vienna, in May, 1725; designs, sir, which were dangerous not only to the liberties of this nation, but to the liberties of Europe. They were not only to wrest Gibraltar and Port Mahon from this nation, and force the Pretender upon us; but they were to have Don Carlos married to the Emperor's eldest daughter, who would thereby have had a probability of uniting in his person, or in the person of some of his successors, the crowns of France and Spain, with the imperial dignity and the Austrian dominions. It was therefore highly reasonable, both in France and us, to take the alarm at such designs, and to think betimes of preventing their being carried into execution. But with regard to us, it was more particularly our business to take the alarm, because we were to have been immediately attacked. I shall grant, sir, it would have been very difficult, if not impossible, for Spain

[3] The Infanta of Spain was betrothed to Louis XV., king of France, when four years old, and was sent to Paris to be educated there. At the end of two years, Louis broke off the engagement and sent her back to Madrid. This indignity awakened the keenest resentment at the Spanish court, which sought to involve England in the quarrel by offering to make her sole mediator in respect to existing differences between Spain and the Emperor of Germany, thus throwing Spain entirely into the hands of England. The English government, for the reasons here assigned by Walpole, wisely rejected the mediation, and this was now imputed to him as a crime.

[4] Spain now turned her resentment against England, and settled her differences with the Emperor of Germany on terms so favorable to the latter, as to awaken suspicions (which were confirmed by secret intelligence) that some hidden compact had been made, for conjointly attacking the dominions of England. To counteract this, England, in 1725, united with France, Prussia, Denmark, and Holland, in an opposing league, by a compact called the treaty of Hanover, from the place where it was made. The evidence of these facts could not then be brought forward to defend the ministry; and hence the treaty of Hanover, and the consequent expenditures on the Continent, were extremely unpopular in England. But subsequent disclosures have made it nearly or quite certain, that every thing here alleged by Walpole was strictly true.

and the Emperor joined together, to have invaded or made themselves masters of any of the British dominions. But will it be said they might not have invaded the King's dominions in Germany, in order to force him to a compliance with what they desired of him as King of Great Britain? And if those dominions had been invaded on account of a quarrel with this nation, should we not have been obliged, both in honor and interest, to defend them? When we were thus threatened, it was therefore absolutely necessary for us to make an alliance with France; and that we might not trust too much to their assistance, it was likewise necessary to form alliances with the northern powers, and with some of the princes in Germany, which we never did, nor ever could do, without granting them immediate subsidies. These measures were, therefore, I still think, not only prudent, but necessary; and by these measures we made it much more dangerous for the Emperor and Spain to attack us, than it would otherwise have been.

But still, sir, though by these alliances we put ourselves upon an equal footing with our enemies in case of an attack, yet, in order to preserve the tranquillity of Europe as well as our own, there was something else to be done. We knew that war could not be begun and carried on without money; we knew that the Emperor had no money for that purpose without receiving large remittances from Spain; and we knew that Spain could make no such remittances without receiving large returns of treasure from the West Indies. The only way, therefore, to render these two powers incapable of disturbing the tranquillity of Europe, was by sending a squadron to the West Indies to stop the return of the Spanish galleons; and this made it necessary, at the same time, to send a squadron to the Mediterranean for the security of our valuable possessions in that part of the world. By these measures the Emperor saw the impossibility of attacking us in any part of the world, because Spain could give him no assistance either in money or troops; and the attack made by the Spaniards upon Gibraltar was so feeble, that we had no occasion to call upon our allies for assistance. A small squadron of our own prevented their attacking it by sea, and from their attack by land we had nothing to fear. They might have knocked their brains out against inaccessible rocks to this very day, without bringing that fortress into any danger.

I do not pretend, sir, to be a great master of foreign affairs. In that post in which I have the honor to serve his Majesty, it is not my business to interfere; and as one of his Majesty's council, I have but one voice. But if I had been the sole adviser of the treaty of Hanover, and of all the measures which were taken in pursuance of it, from what I have said I hope it will appear that I do not deserve to be censured either as a weak or a wicked minister on that account.

The next measures which incurred censure were the guarantee of the Pragmatic Sanction by the second treaty of Vienna, and the refusal of the cabinet to assist the house of Austria, in conformity with the articles of that guarantee.[5]

As to the guarantee of the Pragmatic Sanction, I am really surprised to find that measure objected to. It was so universally approved of, both within doors and without, that till this very day I think no fault was ever found with it, unless it was that of being too long delayed. If it was so necessary for supporting the balance of power in Europe, as has been insisted on in this debate, to preserve entire the dominions of the house of Austria, surely it was not our business to insist upon a partition of them in favor of any of the princes of the empire. But if we had, could we have expected that the house of Austria would have agreed to any such partition, even for the acquisition of our guarantee? The King of Prussia had, it is true, a claim upon some lordships in Silesia; but that claim was absolutely denied by the court of Vienna, and was not at that time so much insisted on by the late King of Prussia. Nay, if he had lived till this time, I believe it would not now have been insisted on; for he acceded to that guarantee without any reservation of that claim; therefore I must look upon this as an objection which has since arisen from an accident that could not then be foreseen or provided against.

I must therefore think, sir, that our guarantee of the Pragmatic Sanction, or our manner of doing it, can not now be objected to, nor any person censured by Parliament for advising that measure. In regard to the refusal of the cabinet to assist the house of Austria, though it was prudent and right in us to enter into that guarantee, we were not therefore obliged to enter into every broil the house of Austria might afterward lead themselves into. And therefore, we were not in honor obliged to take any share in the war which the Emperor brought upon himself in the year 1733; nor were we in interest obliged to take a share in that war as long as neither side attempted to push their conquests farther than was consistent with the balance of power in Europe, which was a case that did not happen. For the power of the house of Austria was not diminished by the event of that war, because they got Tuscany, Parma, and Placentia in lieu of Naples and Sicily; nor was the power of France much increased, because Lor-

[5] Charles VI., emperor of Germany, having no male issue, made an instrument called a Pragmatic Sanction, by which all his hereditary estates were to devolve on his female descendants. To give this instrument greater force, he induced nearly all the powers of Europe (and England among the rest, for reasons assigned by Walpole) to unite in a *guarantee* for carrying it into effect. But this, although designed to secure Austria against a partition between various claimants, in case of his death, was certainly not intended to pledge England or any other power to interfere in all the quarrels in which the Emperor might engage. When he became involved in war with France, therefore, in 1733, by supporting Augustus for the vacant throne of Poland, against the remonstrances of Walpole, the latter was under no obligation to afford him aid.

raine was a province she had taken and kept possession of during every war in which she had been engaged.

As to the disputes with Spain, they had not then reached such a height as to make it necessary for us to come to an open rupture. We had then reason to hope, that all differences would be accommodated in an amicable manner; and while we have any such hopes, it can never be prudent for us to engage ourselves in war, especially with Spain, where we have always had a very beneficial commerce. These hopes, it is true, sir, at last proved abortive; but I never heard it was a crime to hope for the best. This sort of hope was the cause of the late Convention. If Spain had performed her part of that preliminary treaty, I am sure it would not have been wrong in us to have hoped for a friendly accommodation; and for that end to have waited nine or ten months longer, in which time the plenipotentiaries were, by the treaty, to have adjusted all the differences subsisting between the two nations. But the failure of Spain in performing what had been agreed to by this preliminary, put an end to all our hopes, and then, and not till then, it became prudent to enter into hostilities, which were commenced as soon as possible after the expiration of the term limited for the payment of the £95,000.[6]

Strong and virulent censures have been cast on me for having commenced the war without a single ally; and this deficiency has been ascribed to the multifarious treaties in which I have bewildered myself. But although the authors of this imputation are well apprised, that all these treaties have been submitted to and approved by Parliament, yet they are now brought forward as crimes, without appealing to the judgment of Parliament, and without proving or declaring that all or any of hem were advised by me. A supposed sole minister is to be condemned and punished as the author of all; and what adds to the enormity is, that an attempt was made to convict him uncharged and unheard, without taking into consideration the most arduous crisis which ever occurred in the annals of Europe. Sweden corrupted by France; Denmark tempted and wavering; the Landgrave of Hesse Cassel almost gained; the King of Prussia, the Emperor, and the Czarina, with whom alliances had been negotiating, dead; the Austrian dominions claimed by Spain and Bavaria; the Elector of Saxony hesitating whether he should accede to the general confederacy planned by France; the court of Vienna irresolute and indecisive. In this critical juncture, if France enters into engagements with Prussia, and if the Queen of Hungary hesitates and listens to France, are all or any of those events to be imputed to English counsels?[7] And if to English counsels, why are they to be attributed to one man?

II. I now come, sir, to the second head, the conduct of domestic affairs. And here a most heinous charge is made, that the nation has been burdened with unnecessary expenses, for the sole purpose of preventing the discharge of our debts and the abolition of taxes. But this attack is more to the dishonor of the whole cabinet council than to me. If there is any ground for this imputation, it is a charge upon King, Lords, and Commons, as corrupted, or imposed upon. And they have no *proof* of these allegations, but affect to substantiate them by common fame and public notoriety!

No expense has been incurred but what has been approved of, and provided for, by Parliament. The public treasure has been duly applied to the uses to which it was appropriated by Parliament, and regular accounts have been annually laid before Parliament, of every article of expense. If by foreign accidents, by the disputes of foreign states among themselves, or by their designs against us, the nation has often been put to an extraordinary expense, that expense can not be said to have been unnecessary; because, if by saving it we had exposed the balance of power to danger, or ourselves to an attack, it would have cost, perhaps, a hundred times that sum before we could recover from that danger, or repel that attack.

In all such cases there will be a variety of opinions. I happened to be one of those who thought all these expenses necessary, and I had the good fortune to have the majority of both houses of Parliament on my side. But this, it seems, proceeded from bribery and corruption. Sir, if any one instance had been mentioned, if it had been shown that I ever offered a reward to any member of either House, or ever threatened to deprive any member of his office or employment, in order to influence his vote in Parliament, there might have been some ground for this charge. But when it is so generally laid, I do not know what I can say to it, unless it be to deny it as generally and as positively as it has

[6] This is the only point on which Walpole is tame and weak. It is exactly the point where, if he had acted a manly part eighteen months before, his defense would have been most triumphant. He knew there was no ground for a war with Spain; and he ought to have held to the truth on that point, even at the sacrifice of his office.

[7] This "critical juncture" was occasioned by the recent death of the Emperor Charles VI. Under the Pragmatic Sanction, his Austrian possessions fell to his daughter Maria Theresa, queen of Hungary; but were claimed in part by Spain, though chiefly by the Elector of Bavaria, supported by France. Frederick of Prussia, afterward called the Great, who had just succeeded his father, was fluctuating between France and the Queen; but offered to support the latter if she would cede to him Silesia. Walpole, who wished to defeat the plans of France, advised her to yield to this demand, though unjust, and thus prevent a general war. Her ministers were weak and irresolute, and the affairs of Europe were in utter confusion. The proud spirit of the Queen soon decided the question. She refused the surrender of Silesia, was attacked by Frederick and the French, and was on the brink of ruin; when she made, seven months after this speech was delivered, her celebrated appeal for support to the Diet of Hungary, by which, in the words of Johnson, "The Queen, the Beauty, set the *world in arms*."

been asserted. And, thank God! till some proof be offered, I have the laws of the land, as well as the laws of charity, in my favor.

Some members of both Houses have, it is true, been removed from their employments under the Crown; but were they ever told, either by me, or by any other of his Majesty's servants, that it was for opposing the measures of the administration in Parliament? They were removed because his Majesty did not think fit to continue them longer in his service. His Majesty had a right so to do; and I know no one that has a right to ask him, "What doest thou?" If his Majesty had a mind that the favors of the Crown should circulate, would not this of itself be a good reason for removing any of his servants? Would not this reason be approved of by the whole nation, except those who happen to be the present possessors? I can not, therefore, see how this can be imputed as a crime, or how any of the King's ministers can be blamed for his doing what the public has no concern in; for if the public be well and faithfully served, it has no business to ask by whom.

As to the particular charge urged against me, I mean that of the army debentures, I am surprised, sir, to hear any thing relating to this affair charged upon me. Whatever blame may attach to this affair, it must be placed to the account of those that were in power when I was, as they call it, the country gentleman.[8] It was by them this affair was introduced and conducted, and I came in only to pay off those public securities, which their management had reduced to a great discount; and consequently to redeem our public credit from that reproach which they had brought upon it. The discount at which these army debentures were negotiated, was a strong and prevalent reason with Parliament to apply the sinking fund first to the payment of those debentures; but the sinking fund could not be applied to that purpose till it began to produce something considerable, which was not till the year 1727. That the sinking fund was then to receive a great addition, was a fact publicly known in 1726; and if some people were sufficiently quick-sighted to foresee that the Parliament would probably make this use of it, and cunning enough to make the most of their own foresight, could I help it, or could they be blamed for doing so? But I defy my most inveterate enemy to prove that I had any hand in *bringing* these debentures to a discount, or that I had any share in the profits by *buying* them up.

In reply to those who confidently assert that the national debt is not decreased since 1727, and that the sinking fund has not been applied to the discharge of the public burdens, I can with truth declare, that a part of the debt *has* been paid off; and the landed interest has been very much eased with respect to that most unequal and grievous burden, the land tax. I say so, sir, because upon examination it will appear, that within these sixteen or seventeen years, no less than £8,000,000 of our debt has been actually discharged, by the due application of the sinking fund; and at least £7,000,000 has been taken from that fund, and applied to the ease of the land tax. For if it had not been applied to the current service, we must have supplied that service by increasing the land tax; and as the sinking fund was originally designed for paying off our debts, and easing us of our taxes, the application of it in ease of the land tax, was certainly as proper and necessary a use as could be made. And I little thought that giving relief to landed gentlemen, would have been brought against me as a crime.[9]

III. I shall now advert to the third topic of accusation: the conduct of the war. I have already stated in what manner, and under what circumstances, hostilities commenced; and as I am neither general nor admiral—as I have nothing to do either with our navy or army—I am sure I am not answerable for the prosecution of it. But were I to answer for every thing, no fault could, I think, be found with my conduct in the prosecution of the war. It has from the beginning been carried on with as much vigor, and as great care of our trade, as was consistent with our safety at home, and with the circumstances we were in at the beginning of the war. If our attacks upon the enemy were too long delayed, or if they have not been so vigorous or so frequent as they ought to have been, those only are to blame who have for many years been haranguing against standing armies; for, without a sufficient number of regular troops in proportion to the numbers kept up by our neighbors, I am sure we can neither defend ourselves nor offend our enemies. On the supposed miscarriages of the war, so unfairly stated, and so unjustly imputed to me, I could, with great ease, frame an incontrovertible defense. But as I have trespassed so long on the time of the House, I shall not weaken the effect of that forcible exculpation, so generously and disinterestedly advanced by the right honorable gentleman who so meritoriously presides at the Admiralty.

If my whole administration is to be scrutinized and arraigned, why are the most favorable parts to be omitted? If facts are to be accumulated on one side, why not on the other? And why

8 One who held himself bound to neither party.

9 Here Walpole dexterously avoids the main point of the difficulty. In 1717, it was provided by law that all the surplus income of the government should be converted into what was called the *Sinking Fund*, which was to be used for paying off the public debt. This principle was strictly adhered to down to 1729, when more than a million of this fund was used for current expenses, instead of laying taxes to meet them. The same thing was done in six other instances, under Walpole's administration. Now it is true, as Walpole says, that by thus applying the fund, he lessened the land tax. Still, it was a perversion of the fund from its original design; and if the taxes had been uniformly laid for all current expenses, and the fund been faithfully applied to its original purpose, the debt (small as it then was) might perhaps have wholly been extinguished.

may not I be permitted to speak in my own favor? Was I not called by the voice of the King and the nation to remedy the fatal effects of the South Sea project, and to support declining credit? Was I not placed at the head of the treasury when the revenues were in the greatest confusion? Is credit revived, and does it now flourish? Is it not at an incredible height, and if so, to whom must that circumstance be attributed? Has not tranquillity been preserved both at home and abroad, notwithstanding a most unreasonable and violent opposition? Has the true interest of the nation been pursued, or has trade flourished? Have gentlemen produced one instance of this exorbitant power; of the influence which I extend to all parts of the nation; of the tyranny with which I oppress those who oppose, and the liberality with which I reward those who support me? But having first invested me with a kind of mock dignity, and styled me a prime minister, they impute to me an unpardonable abuse of that chimerical authority which they only have created and conferred. If they are really persuaded that the army is annually established by me, that I have the sole disposal of posts and honors, that I employ this power in the destruction of liberty and the diminution of commerce, let me awaken them from their delusion. Let me expose to their view the real condition of the public weal. Let me show them that the Crown has made no encroachments, that all supplies have been granted by Parliament, that all questions have been debated with the same freedom as before the fatal period in which my counsels are said to have gained the ascendency; an ascendency from which they deduce the loss of trade, the approach of slavery, the preponderance of prerogative, and the extension of influence. But I am far from believing that they feel those apprehensions which they so earnestly labor to communicate to others; and I have too high an opinion of their sagacity not to conclude that, even in their own judgment, they are complaining of grievances that they do not suffer, and promoting rather their private interest than that of the public.

What is this unbounded sole power which is imputed to me? How has it discovered itself, or how has it been proved?

What have been the effects of the corruption, ambition, and avarice with which I am so abundantly charged?

Have I ever been suspected of being corrupted? A strange phenomenon, a corrupter himself not corrupt! Is ambition imputed to me? Why then do I still continue a commoner? I, who refused a white staff and a peerage. I had, indeed, like to have forgotten the little ornament about my shoulders [the garter], which gentlemen have so repeatedly mentioned in terms of sarcastic obloquy. But surely, though this may be regarded with envy or indignation in another place, it can not be supposed to raise any resentment in *this* House, where many may be pleased to see those honors which their ancestors have worn, restored again to the Commons.

Have I given any symptoms of an avaricious disposition? Have I obtained any grants from the Crown, since I have been placed at the head of the treasury? Has my conduct been different from that which others in the same station would have followed? Have I acted wrong in giving the place of auditor to my son, and in providing for my own family? I trust that their advancement will not be imputed to me as a crime, unless it shall be proved that I placed them in offices of trust and responsibility for which they were unfit.

But while I unequivocally deny that I am sole and prime minister, and that to my influence and direction all the measures of the government must be attributed, yet I will not shrink from the responsibility which attaches to the post I have the honor to hold; and should, during the long period in which I have sat upon this bench, any one step taken by government be proved to be either disgraceful or disadvantageous to the nation, I am ready to hold myself accountable.

To conclude, sir, though I shall always be proud of the honor of any trust or confidence from his Majesty, yet I shall always be ready to remove from his councils and presence when he thinks fit; and therefore I should think myself very little concerned in the event of the present question, if it were not for the encroachment that will thereby be made upon the prerogatives of the Crown. But I must think that an address to his Majesty to remove one of his servants, without so much as alleging any particular crime against him, is one of the greatest encroachments that was ever made upon the prerogatives of the Crown. And therefore, for the sake of my master, without any regard for my own, I hope all those that have a due regard for our constitution, and for the rights and prerogatives of the Crown, without which our constitution can not be preserved, will be against this motion.

This speech had a great effect. The motion for an address was negatived by a large majority.

But the advantage thus gained was only temporary. A spirit of disaffection had spread throughout the kingdom; and the next elections, which took place a few months after, showed that the power and influence of Walpole were on the decline. Still he clung to office with a more desperate grasp than ever. He used some of the most extraordinary expedients ever adopted by a minister, to divide the Opposition and retain his power. He even opened a negotiation with the Pretender at Rome, to obtain the support of the Jacobites. But his efforts were in vain. He lost his majority in the House; he was compelled to inform the King that he could no longer administer the government; he was created Earl of Orford with a pension of £4000 a year, and resigned all his offices on the 11th of February, 1742.

MR. PULTENEY.

William Pulteney, first Earl of Bath, was born in 1682. He was elected a member of Parliament in early life, and applied himself to the diligent study of the temper of the House, and the best mode of speaking in so mixed and discordant an assembly. He made no attempts to dazzle by any elaborate display of eloquence; for it was his maxim, that "there are few real orators who commence with set speeches." His powers were slowly developed. He took part in almost every important debate, more (at first) for his own improvement than with any expectation of materially changing the vote. He thus gradually rose into one of the most dexterous and effective speakers of the British Senate.

His speeches, unfortunately, have been worse reported, in respect to the peculiar characteristics of his eloquence, than those of any of his contemporaries. The following one, however, though shorter than might be wished, is undoubtedly a fair specimen of the bold, direct, and confident, though not overbearing manner, in which he ordinarily addressed himself to the judgment and feelings of the House. The language is uncommonly easy, pointed, and vigorous. The sentences flow lightly off in a clear and varied sequence, without the slightest appearance of stateliness or mannerism. It is the exact style for that conversational mode of discussion which is best adapted to the purposes of debate.

Walpole, when displaced by the exertions of Pulteney in 1742, had the satisfaction of dragging down his adversary along with him. He saw that the Opposition must go to pieces the moment they were left to themselves; that a new administration could never be framed out of such discordant materials; and that whoever should undertake it would be ruined in the attempt. He therefore induced the King to lay that duty upon Pulteney. The result was just what he expected. The King insisted on retaining a large proportion of Walpole's friends. Comparatively few offices remained for others, and both Whigs and Tories were disappointed and enraged. Pulteney shrunk from taking office himself, under these circumstances. He professed great disinterestedness; he had no desire for power; he would merely accept a peerage, which all parties regarded as the reward of his perfidy. He was created Earl of Bath; and the name of *Patriot*, as Horace Walpole tells us, became a term of derision and contempt throughout all the kingdom. When the newly-created earls met for the first time in the House of Lords, Walpole walked up to Pulteney, and said to him, with a mixture of pleasantry and bitterness, for which he was always distinguished, "Here we are, my Lord, the two most insignificant fellows in England." Pulteney died on the 8th of June, 1764.

SPEECH

OF MR. PULTENEY ON A MOTION FOR REDUCING THE ARMY, DELIVERED IN THE HOUSE OF COMMONS.

Sir,—We have heard a great deal about Parliamentary armies, and about an army continued from year to year. I have always been, sir, and always shall be, against a standing army of any kind. To me it is a terrible thing, whether under that of Parliamentary or any other designation. A standing army is still a standing army, whatever name it be called by. They are a body of men distinct from the body of the people; they are governed by different laws; and blind obedience, and an entire submission to the orders of their commanding officer, is their only principle.

The nations around us, sir, are already enslaved, and have been enslaved by these very means: by means of their standing armies they have every one lost their liberties. It is indeed impossible that the liberties of the people can be preserved in any country where a numerous standing army is kept up. Shall we, then, take any of our measures from the examples of our neighbors? No, sir, on the contrary, from their misfortunes we ought to learn to avoid those rocks upon which they have split.

It signifies nothing to tell me, that our army is commanded by such gentlemen as can not be supposed to join in any measures for enslaving their country. It may be so. I hope it is so! I have a very good opinion of many gentlemen now in the army. I believe they would not join in any such measures. But their lives are uncertain, nor can we be sure how long they may be continued in command; they may be all dismissed in a moment, and proper tools of power put in their room. Besides, sir, we know the passions of men; we know how dangerous it is to trust the best of men with too much power. Where was there a braver army than that under Julius Cesar? Where was there ever an army that had served their country more faithfully? That army was commanded generally by the best citizens of Rome—by men of great fortune and figure in their country; yet *that* army enslaved their country. The affections of the soldiers toward their country, the honor and integrity of the under officers, are not to be depended on. By the military law, the administration of justice is so quick, and the punishments so severe, that neither officer nor soldier dares offer to dispute the orders of his supreme commander; he must not consult his own inclinations. If an officer were commanded to pull his own father out of this House, he must do it; he dares not disobey; immediate death would be the sure consequence of the least grumbling. And if an officer were sent into the Court of Requests, accompanied by a body of musketeers with screwed bayonets, and with orders to tell us what we ought to do, and how we were to vote, I know what would be the duty of this House; I know it would be our duty to order the officer to be taken and hanged up at the door of the lobby. But, sir, I doubt much if such a spirit could be found in the House, or in any House of Commons that will ever be in England.

Sir, I talk not of imaginary things. I talk of what *has* happened to an English House of Commons, and from an English army; and not only from an English army, but an army that was raised by that very House of Commons, an army that was paid by them, and an army that was commanded by generals appointed by them. Therefore do not let us vainly imagine that an army raised and maintained by authority of Parliament will always be submissive to them. If an army be so numerous as to have it in their power to overawe the Parliament, they will be submissive as long as the Parliament does nothing to disoblige their favorite general; but when that case happens, I am afraid that, in place of Parliament's dismissing the army, the army will dismiss the Parliament, as they have done heretofore. Nor does the legality or illegality of that Parliament, or of that army, alter the case. For with respect to that army, and according to their way of thinking, the Parliament dismissed by them was a legal Parliament; they were an army raised and maintained according to law; and at first they were raised, as they imagined, for the preservation of those liberties which they afterward destroyed.

It has been urged, sir, that whoever is for the Protestant succession must be for continuing the army: for that very reason, sir, I am against continuing the army. I know that neither the Protestant succession in his Majesty's most illustrious house, nor any succession, can ever be safe so long as there is a standing army in the country. Armies, sir, have no regard to hereditary successions. The first two Cesars at Rome did pretty well, and found means to keep their armies in tolerable subjection, because the generals and officers were all their own creatures. But how did it fare with their successors? Was not every one of them named by the army, without any regard to hereditary right, or to any right? A cobbler, a gardener, or any man who happened to raise himself in the army, and could gain their affections, was made Emperor of the world. Was not every succeeding Emperor raised to the throne, or tumbled headlong into the dust, according to the mere whim or mad phrensy of the soldiers?

We are told this army is desired to be continued but for one year longer, or for a limited term of years. How absurd is this distinction! Is there any army in the world continued for any term of years? Does the most absolute monarch tell his army, that he is to continue them any number of years, or any number of months? How long have we already continued our army from year to year? And if it thus continues, wherein will it differ from the standing armies of those countries which have already submitted their necks to the yoke? We are now come to the Rubicon. Our army is now to be reduced, or never will. From his Majesty's own mouth we are assured of a profound tranquillity abroad, and we know there is one at home. If this is not a proper time, if these circumstances do not afford us a safe opportunity for reducing at least a part of our regular forces, we never can expect to see any reduction. This nation, already overburdened with debts and taxes, must be loaded with the heavy charge of perpetually supporting a numerous standing army; and remain forever exposed to the danger of having its liberties and privileges trampled upon by any future king or ministry, who shall take in their head to do so, and shall take a proper care to model the army for that purpose.

The bill for continuing the army on the same footing was passed by a large majority.

LORD CHESTERFIELD.

Philip Dormer Stanhope, fourth Earl of Chesterfield, was born in 1694. He was equally distinguished for his love of polite literature, the grace of his manners, the pungency of his wit, and the elegance of his literary productions. In later times he has been most known by his Letters to his Son. These, though admirable models of the epistolary style, are disfigured by a profligacy of sentiment which has cast a just odium on his character; while the stress they lay upon mere accomplishments has created a very natural suspicion, among those who have seen him only in that correspondence, as to the strength and soundness of his judgment. He was unquestionably, however, a man of great acuteness and force of intellect. As an orator, Horace Walpole gave him the preference over all the speakers of his day. This may have arisen, in part, from the peculiar dexterity with which he could play with a subject that he did not choose to discuss—a kind of talent which Walpole would be very apt to appreciate. It often happens that weak and foolish measures can be exposed more effectually by wit than by reasoning. In this kind of attack Lord Chesterfield had uncommon power. His fancy supplied him with a wide range of materials, which he brought forward with great ingenuity, presenting a succession of unexpected combinations, that flashed upon the mind with all the liveliness and force of the keenest wit or the most poignant satire. The speech which follows is a specimen of his talent for this kind of speaking. "It will be read with avidity by those who relish the sprightly sallies of genius, or who are emulous of a style of eloquence which, though it may not always convince, will never fail to delight."

The speech relates to a bill for granting licenses to gin-shops, by which the ministry hoped to realize a very large annual income. This income they proposed to employ in carrying on the German war of George II., which arose out of his exclusive care for his Electorate of Hanover, and was generally odious throughout Great Britain. Lord Chesterfield made two speeches on this subjcct, which are here given together, with the omission of a few unimportant paragraphs. It has been hastily inferred, from a conversation reported by Boswell, that these speeches, as here given, were written by Johnson. Subsequent inquiry, however, seems to prove that this was not the fact; but, on the contrary, that Lord Chesterfield prepared them for publication himself.

Lord Chesterfield filled many offices of the highest importance under the reign of George II. In 1728 he was appointed embassador to Holland; and, by his adroitness and diplomatic skill, succeeded in delivering Hanover from the calamities of war which hung over it. As a reward for his services, he was made Knight of the Garter and Lord Steward of the Royal Household. At a later period he was appointed Lord Lieutenant of Ireland. This difficult office he discharged with great dexterity and self-command, holding in check the various factions of that country with consummate skill. On his return to England in 1746, he was called to the office of Secretary of State; but, having become wearied of public employments, he soon resigned, and devoted the remainder of his life to the pursuits of literature and the society of his friends. He now carried on the publication of a series of papers in imitation of the Spectator, entitled the World, in which some of the best specimens may be found of his light, animated, and easy style of writing. Toward the close of his life he became deaf, and suffered from numerous bodily infirmities, which filled his latter days with gloom and despondency. He bore the most emphatic testimony to the folly and disappointment of the course he had led, and died in 1773, at the age of seventy-nine.

SPEECH

OF LORD CHESTERFIELD ON THE GIN ACT, DELIVERED IN THE HOUSE OF LORDS, FEBRUARY 21, 1743.

THE bill now under our consideration appears to me to deserve a much closer regard than seems to have been paid to it in the other House, through which it was hurried with the utmost precipitation, and where it passed almost without the formality of a debate. Nor can I think that earnestness with which some lords seem inclined to press it forward here, consistent with the importance of the consequences which may with great reason be expected from it.

To desire, my Lords, that this bill may be considered in a committee, is only to desire that it may gain one step without opposition; that it may proceed through the forms of the House by stealth, and that the consideration of it may be delayed, till the exigences of the government shall be so great as not to allow time for raising the supplies by any other method.

By this artifice, gross as it is, the patrons of this wonderful bill hope to obstruct a plain and open detection of its tendency. They hope, my Lords, that the bill shall operate in the same manner with the liquor which it is intended to bring into more general use; and that, as those who drink spirits are drunk before they are well aware that they are drinking, the effects of this law shall be perceived before we know that we have made it. Their intent is, to give us a dram of policy, which is to be swallowed before it is tasted, and which, when once it is swallowed, will turn our heads.

But, my Lords, I hope we shall be so cautious as to examine the draught which these state empirics have thought proper to offer us; and I am confident that a very little examination will convince us of the pernicious qualities of their new preparation, and show that it can have no other effect than that of poisoning the public.

The law before us, my Lords, seems to be the effect of that practice of which it is intended likewise to be the cause, and to be dictated by the liquor of which it so effectually promotes the use; for surely it never before was conceived, by any man intrusted with the administration of public affairs, to raise taxes by the destruction of the people.

Nothing, my Lords, but the destruction of all the most laborious and useful part of the nation can be expected from the license which is now proposed to be given, not only to drunkenness, but to drunkenness of the most detestable and dangerous kind; to the abuse not only of intoxicating, but of poisonous liquors.

Nothing, my Lords, is more absurd than to assert that the use of spirits will be hindered by the bill now before us, or indeed that it will not be in a very great degree promoted by it. For what produces all kind of wickedness but the prospect of impunity on one part, or the solicitation of opportunity on the other? Either of these have too frequently been sufficient to overpower the sense of morality, and even of religion; and what is not to be feared from them, when they shall unite their force, and operate together, when temptations shall be increased, and terror taken away?

It is allowed, by those who have hitherto disputed on either side of this question, that the people appear obstinately enamored of this new liquor. It is allowed on both parts that this liquor corrupts the mind and enervates the body, and destroys vigor and virtue, at the same time that it makes those who drink it too idle and feeble for work; and, while it impoverishes them by the present expense, disables them from retrieving its ill consequences by subsequent industry.

It might be imagined, my Lords, that those who had thus far agreed would not easily find any occasions of dispute. Nor would any man, unacquainted with the motives by which parliamentary debates are too often influenced, suspect that after the pernicious qualities of this liquor, and the general inclination among the people to the immoderate use of it, had been thus fully admitted, it could be afterward inquired whether it ought to be made more common; whether this universal thirst for poison ought to be encouraged by the Legislature, and whether a new statute ought to be made, to secure drunkards in the gratification of their appetites.

To pretend, my Lords, that the design of this bill is to prevent or diminish the use of spirits, is to trample upon common sense, and to violate the rules of decency as well as of reason. For when did any man hear that a commodity was prohibited by licensing its sale, or that to offer and refuse is the same action?

It is indeed pleaded that it will be made dearer by the tax which is proposed, and that the increase of the price will diminish the number of the purchasers; but it is at the same time expected that this tax shall supply the expense of a war on the Continent. It is asserted, therefore, that the consumption of spirits will be hindered; and yet that it will be such as may be expected to furnish, from a very small tax, a revenue sufficient for the support of armies, for the re-establishment of the Austrian family, and the repressing of the attempts of France.

Surely, my Lords, these expectations are not

very consistent; nor can it be imagined that they are both formed in the same head, though they may be expressed by the same mouth. It is, however, some recommendation of a statesman, when, of his assertions, *one* can be found reasonable or true; and in this, praise can not be denied to our present ministers. For though it is undoubtedly false that this tax will lessen the consumption of spirits, it is certainly true that it will produce a very large revenue—a revenue that will not fail but with the people from whose debaucheries it arises.

Our ministers will therefore have the same honor with their predecessors, of having given rise to a new fund; not indeed for the payment of our debts, but for much more valuable purposes; for the cheering of our hearts under oppression, and for the ready support of those debts which we have lost all hopes of paying. They are resolved, my Lords, that the nation which no endeavors can make wise, shall, while they are at its head, at least be very merry; and, since public happiness is the end of government, they seem to imagine that they shall deserve applause by an expedient which will enable every man to lay his cares asleep, to drown sorrow, and lose in the delights of drunkenness both the public miseries and his own.

Luxury, my Lords, is to be taxed, but vice prohibited, let the difficulties in executing the law be what they will. Would you lay a tax on the breach of the ten commandments? Would not such a tax be wicked and scandalous; because it would imply an indulgence to all those who could pay the tax? Is not this a reproach most justly thrown by Protestants upon the Church of Rome? Was it not the chief cause of the Reformation? And will you follow a precedent which brought reproach and ruin upon those that introduced it? This is the very case now before us. You are going to lay a tax, and consequently to indulge a sort of drunkenness, which almost necessarily produces a breach of every one of the ten commandments? Can you expect the reverend bench will approve of this? I am convinced they will not; and therefore I wish I had seen it full upon this occasion. I am sure I have seen it much fuller upon other occasions, in which religion had no such deep concern.

We have already, my Lords, several sorts of funds in this nation, so many that a man must have a good deal of learning to be master of them. Thanks to his Majesty, we have now among us the most learned man of the nation in this way. I wish he would rise up and tell us what name we are to give this new fund. We have already the Civil List Fund, the Sinking Fund, the Aggregate Fund, the South Sea Fund, and God knows how many others. What name we are to give this new fund I know not, unless we are to call it the Drinking Fund. It may perhaps enable the people of a certain foreign territory [Hanover] to drink claret, but it will disable the people of this kingdom from drinking any thing else but gin; for when a man has, by gin drinking, rendered himself unfit for labor or business, he can purchase nothing else; and then the best thing he can do is to drink on till he dies.

Surely, my Lords, men of such unbounded benevolence as our present ministers deserve such honors as were never paid before: they deserve to bestride a butt upon every sign-post in the city, or to have their figures exhibited as tokens where this liquor is to be sold by the license which they have procured. They must be at least remembered to future ages as the "happy politicians" who, after all expedients for raising taxes had been employed, discovered a new method of draining the last relics of the public wealth, and added a new revenue to the government. Nor will those who shall hereafter enumerate the several funds now established among us, forget, among the benefactors to their country, the illustrious authors of the Drinking Fund.

May I be allowed, my Lords, to congratulate my countrymen and fellow-subjects upon the happy times which are now approaching, in which no man will be disqualified from the privilege of being drunk; when all discontent and disloyalty shall be forgotten, and the people, though now considered by the ministry as enemies, shall acknowledge the leniency of that government under which all restraints are taken away?

But, to a bill for such desirable purposes, it would be proper, my Lords, to prefix a preamble, in which the kindness of our intentions should be more fully explained, that the nation may not mistake our indulgence for cruelty, nor consider their benefactors as their persecutors. If, therefore, this bill be considered and amended (for why else should it be considered?) in a committee, I shall humbly propose that it shall be introduced in this manner: "Whereas, the designs of the present ministry, whatever they are, can not be executed without a great number of mercenaries, which mercenaries can not be hired without money; and whereas the present disposition of this nation to drunkenness inclines us to believe that they will pay more cheerfully for the undisturbed enjoyment of distilled liquors than for any other concession that can be made by the government; be it enacted, by the King's most excellent Majesty, that no man shall hereafter be denied the right of being drunk on the following conditions."

This, my Lords, to trifle no longer, is the proper preamble to this bill, which contains only the conditions on which the people of this kingdom are to be allowed henceforward to riot in debauchery, in debauchery licensed by law and countenanced by the magistrates. For there is no doubt but those on whom the inventors of this tax shall confer authority, will be directed to assist their masters in their design to encourage the consumption of that liquor from which such large revenues are expected, and to multiply without end those licenses which are to pay a yearly tribute to the Crown.

By this unbounded license, my Lords, that price will be lessened, from the increase of which the expectations of the efficacy of this law are pretended; for the number of retailers will lessen the value, as in all other cases, and lessen it more than this tax will increase it. Besides, it is to be considered, that at present the retailer expects to be paid for the danger which he incurs by an unlawful trade, and will not trust his reputation or his purse to the mercy of his customer without a profit proportioned to the hazard; but, when once the restraint shall be taken away, he will sell for common gain, and it can hardly be imagined that, at present, he subjects himself to informations and penalties for less than sixpence a gallon.

The specious pretense on which this bill is founded, and, indeed, the only pretense that deserves to be termed specious, is the propriety of taxing vice; but this maxim of government has, on this occasion, been either mistaken or perverted. Vice, my Lords, is not properly to be taxed, but suppressed; and heavy taxes are sometimes the only means by which that suppression can be attained. Luxury, my Lords, or the excess of that which is pernicious only by its excess, may very properly be taxed, that such excess, though not strictly unlawful, may be made more difficult. But the use of those things which are simply hurtful, hurtful in their own nature, and in every degree, is to be prohibited. None, my Lords, ever heard, in any nation, of a tax upon theft or adultery, because a tax implies a license granted for the use of that which is taxed to all who shall be willing to pay it.

* * * * *

During the course of this long debate, I have endeavored to recapitulate and digest the arguments which have been advanced, and have considered them both separately and conjointly; but find myself at the same distance from conviction as when I first entered the House.

In vindication of this bill, my Lords, we have been told that the present law is ineffectual; that our manufacture is not to be destroyed, or not this year; that the security offered by the present bill has induced great numbers to subscribe to the new fund; that it has been approved by the Commons; and that, if it be found ineffectual, it may be amended another session.

All these arguments, my Lords, I shall endeavor to examine, because I am always desirous of gratifying those great men to whom the administration of affairs is intrusted, and have always very cautiously avoided the odium of disaffection, which they will undoubtedly throw, in imitation of their predecessors, upon all those whose wayward consciences shall oblige them to hinder the execution of their schemes.

With a very strong desire, therefore, though with no great hopes, of finding them in the right, I venture to begin my inquiry, and engage in the examination of their first assertion, that the present law against the abuse of strong liquors is without effect.

I hope, my Lords, it portends well to my inquiry that the first position which I have to examine is true; nor can I forbear to congratulate your Lordships upon having heard from the new ministry *one* assertion not to be contradicted.

It is evident, my Lords, from daily observation, and demonstrable from the papers upon the table, that every year, since the enacting of the last law, that vice has increased which it was intended to repress, and that no time has been so favorable to the retailers of spirits as that which has passed since they were prohibited.

It may therefore be expected, my Lords, that having agreed with the ministers in their fundamental proposition, I shall concur with them in the consequence which they draw from it; and having allowed that the present law is ineffectual, should admit that another is necessary.

But, my Lords, in order to discover whether this consequence be necessary, it must first be inquired why the present law is of no force. For, my Lords, it will be found, upon reflection, that there are certain degrees of corruption that may hinder the effect of the best laws. The magistrates may be vicious, and forbear to enforce that law by which themselves are condemned; they may be indolent, and inclined rather to connive at wickedness, by which they are not injured themselves, than to repress it by a laborious exertion of their authority; or they may be timorous, and, instead of awing the vicious, may be awed by them.

In any of these cases, my Lords, the law is not to be condemned for its inefficacy, since it only fails by the defect of those who are to direct its operations. The best and most important laws will contribute very little to the security or happiness of a people, if no judges of integrity and spirit can be found among them. Even the most beneficial and useful bill that ministers can possibly imagine, a bill for laying on our estates a tax of the fifth part of their yearly value, would be wholly without effect if collectors could not be obtained.

I am therefore, my Lords, yet doubtful whether the inefficacy of the law now subsisting necessarily obliges us to provide another; for those that declared it to be useless, owned, at the same time, that no man endeavored to enforce it, so that perhaps its only defect may be that it will not execute itself.

Nor, though I should allow that the law is at present impeded by difficulties which can not be broken through, but by men of more spirit and dignity than the ministers may be inclined to trust with commissions of the peace, yet it can only be collected that another law is necessary, not that the law now proposed will be of any advantage.

Great use has been made of the inefficacy of the present law to decry the proposal made by the noble Lord [a member of the Opposition] for laying a high duty upon these pernicious liquors. High duties have already, as we are informed, been tried without advantage. High duties are at this hour imposed upon those spirits which are retailed, yet we see them every day sold in the streets without the payment of the tax required, and therefore it will be folly to make a second essay of means, which have been found, by the essay of many years, unsuccessful.

It has been granted on all sides in this debate, nor was it ever denied on any other occasion, that the consumption of any commodity is most easily hindered by raising its price, and its price is to be raised by the imposition of a duty. This, my Lords, which is, I suppose, the opinion of every man, of whatever degree of experience or understanding, appears likewise to have been thought of by the authors of the present law; and therefore they imagined that they had effectually provided against the increase of drunkenness, by laying upon that liquor which should be retailed in small quantities, a duty which none of the inferior classes of drunkards would be able to pay.

Thus, my Lords, they conceived that they had reformed the common people without infringing the pleasures of others; and applauded the happy contrivance by which spirits were to be made dear only to the poor, while every man who could afford to purchase two gallons was at liberty to riot at his ease, and, over a full flowing bumper, look down with contempt upon his former companions, now ruthlessly condemned to disconsolate sobriety.

But, my Lords, this intention was frustrated, and the project, ingenious as it was, fell to the ground; for, though they had laid a tax, they unhappily forgot this tax would make no addition to the price unless it was paid, and that it would not be paid unless some were empowered to collect it.

Here, my Lords, was the difficulty: those who made the law were inclined to lay a tax from which themselves should be exempt, and therefore would not charge the liquor as it issued from the still; and when once it was dispersed in the hands of petty dealers, it was no longer to be found without the assistance of informers, and informers could not carry on the business of prosecution without the consent of the people.

It is not necessary to dwell any longer upon the law, the repeal of which is proposed, since it appears already that it failed only from a partiality not easily defended, and from the omission of what we now propose—the collecting the duty from the still-head.

If this method be followed, there will be no longer any need of informations or of any rigorous or new measures; the same officers that collect a smaller duty may levy a greater; nor can they be easily deceived with regard to the quantities that are made; the deceits, at least, that can be used, are in use already; they are frequently detected and suppressed; nor will a larger duty enable the distillers to elude the vigilance of the officers with more success.

Against this proposal, therefore, the inefficacy of the present law can be no objection. But it is urged that such duties would destroy the trade of distilling; and a noble Lord has been pleased to express great tenderness for a manufacture so beneficial and extensive.

That a large duty, levied at the still, would destroy, or very much impair, the trade of distilling, is certainly supposed by those who defend it, for they proposed it only for that end: and what better method can they propose, when they are called to deliberate upon a bill for the prevention of the excessive use of distilled liquors?

The noble Lord has been pleased kindly to inform us that the trade of distilling is very extensive; that it employs great numbers; and that they have arrived at an exquisite skill, and therefore—note well the consequence—the trade of distilling is not to be discouraged.

Once more, my Lords, allow me to wonder at the different conceptions of different understandings. It appears to me that since the spirits which the distillers produce are allowed to enfeeble the limbs and vitiate the blood, to pervert the heart and obscure the intellects, that the number of distillers should be no argument in their favor; for I never heard that a law against theft was repealed or delayed because thieves were numerous. It appears to me, my Lords, that if so formidable a body are confederated against the virtue or the lives of their fellow-citizens, it is time to put an end to the havoc, and to interpose, while it is yet in our power to stop the destruction.

So little, my lords, am I affected with the merit of the wonderful skill which the distillers are said to have attained, that it is, in my opinion, no faculty of great use to mankind to prepare palatable poison; nor shall I ever contribute my interest for the reprieve of a murderer, because he has, by long practice, obtained great dexterity in his trade.

If their liquors are so delicious that the people are tempted to their own destruction, let us at length, my Lords, secure them from these fatal draughts, by bursting the vials that contain them. Let us crush at once these artists in slaughter, who have reconciled their countrymen to sickness and to ruin, and spread over the pitfalls of debauchery such baits as can not be resisted.

The noble Lord has, indeed, admitted that this bill may not be found sufficiently coercive, but gives us hopes that it may be improved and enforced another year, and persuades us to endeavor a reformation of drunkenness by degrees, and, above all, to beware at present of hurting the *manufacture*.

I am very far, my Lords, from thinking that there are, this year, any peculiar reasons for tolerating murder; nor can I conceive why the manufacture should be held sacred now, if it be to be destroyed hereafter. We are, indeed, desired to try how far this law will operate, that we may be more able to proceed with due regard to this valuable manufacture.

With regard to the operation of the law, it appears to me that it will only enrich the government without reforming the people; and I believe there are not many of a different opinion. If any diminution of the sale of spirits be expected from it, it is to be considered that this diminution will, or will not, be such as is desired for the reformation of the people. If it be sufficient, the manufacture is at an end, and all the reasons against a higher duty are of equal force against this; but if it is not sufficient, we have, at least, omitted part of our duty, and have neglected the health and virtue of the people.

I can not, my Lords, yet discover why a reprieve is desired for this manufacture—why the present year is not equally propitious to the reformation of mankind as any will be that may succeed it. It is true we are at war with two nations, and perhaps with more; but war may be better prosecuted without money than without men. And we but little consult the military glory of our country if we raise supplies for paying our armies by the destruction of those armies that we are contriving to pay.

We have heard the necessity of reforming the nation by degrees urged as an argument for imposing first a lighter duty, and afterward a heavier. This complaisance for wickedness, my Lords, is not so defensible as that it should be battered by arguments in form, and therefore I shall only relate a reply made by Webb, the noted walker, upon a parallel occasion.

This man, who must be remembered by many of your Lordships, was remarkable for vigor, both of mind and body, and lived wholly upon water for his drink, and chiefly upon vegetables for his other sustenance. He was one day recommending his regimen to one of his friends who loved wine, and who perhaps might somewhat contribute to the prosperity of this spirituous manufacture, and urged him, with great earnestness, to quit a course of luxury by which his health and his intellects would equally be destroyed. The gentleman appeared convinced, and told him "that he would conform to his counsel, and thought he could not change his course of life at once, but would leave off strong liquors by degrees." "By degrees!" says the other, with indignation. "If you should unhappily fall into the fire, would you caution your servants not to pull you out but by degrees?"

This answer, my Lords, is applicable to the present case. The nation is sunk into the lowest state of corruption; the people are not only vicious, but insolent beyond example. They not only break the laws, but defy them; and yet some of your Lordships are for reforming them *by degrees!*

I am not so easily persuaded, my Lords, that our ministers really intend to supply the defects that may hereafter be discovered in this bill. It will doubtless produce money, perhaps much more than they appear to expect from it. I doubt not but the licensed retailers will be more than fifty thousand, and the quantity retailed must increase with the number of retailers. As the bill will, therefore, answer all the ends intended by it, I do not expect to see it altered; for I have never observed ministers desirous of amending their own errors, unless they are such as have caused a deficiency in the revenue.

Besides my Lords, it is not certain that, when this fund is mortgaged to the public creditors, they can prevail upon the Commons to change the security. They may continue the bill in force for the reasons, whatever they are, for which they have passed it; and the good intentions of our ministers, however sincere, may be defeated, and drunkenness, legal drunkenness, established in the nation.

This, my Lords, is very reasonable, and therefore we ought to exert ourselves for the safety of the nation while the power is yet in our own hands, and, without regard to the opinion or proceedings of the other House, show that we are yet the chief guardians of the people.

The ready compliance of the Commons with the measures proposed in this bill has been mentioned here, with a view, I suppose, of influencing us, but surely by those who had forgotten our independence, or resigned their own. It is not only the right, but the duty of either House, to deliberate, without regard to the determinations of the other; for how should the nation receive any benefit from the distinct powers that compose the Legislature, unless the determinations are without influence upon each other? If either the example or authority of the Commons can divert us from following our own convictions, we are no longer part of the Legislature; we have given up our honors and our privileges, and what then is our concurrence but slavery, or our suffrage but an echo?

The only argument, therefore, that now remains, is the expediency of gratifying those, by whose ready subscription the exigencies our new statesmen have brought upon us have been supported, and of continuing the security by which they have been encouraged to such liberal contributions.

Public credit, my Lords, is indeed of very great importance; but public credit can never be long supported without public virtue; nor indeed, if the government could mortgage the morals and health of the people, would it be just and rational to confirm the bargain. If the ministry can raise money only by the destruction of their fellow-subjects, they ought to abandon those schemes for which the money is necessary; for what calamity can be equal to unbounded wickedness?

But, my Lords, there is no necessity for a choice which may cost our ministers so much regret; for the same subscriptions may be procured by an offer of the same advantages to a fund of any other kind, and the sinking fund will easily supply any deficiency that might be suspected in another scheme.

To confess the truth, I should feel very little pain from an account that the nation was for some time determined to be less liberal of their contributions; and that money was withheld till it was known in what expeditions it was to be employed, to what princes subsidies were to be paid, and what advantages were to be purchased by it for our country. I should rejoice, my Lords, to hear that the lottery by which the deficiencies of this duty are to be supplied was not filled, and that the people were grown at last wise enough to discern the fraud and to prefer honest commerce, by which all may be gainers, to a game by which the greatest number must certainly be losers.

The lotteries, my Lords, which former ministers have proposed, have always been censured by those who saw their nature and their tendency. They have been considered as legal cheats, by which the ignorant and the rash are defrauded, and the subtle and avaricious often enriched; they have been allowed to divert the people from trade, and to alienate them from useful industry. A man who is uneasy in his circumstanoes and idle in his disposition, collects the remains of his fortune and buys tickets in a lottery, retires from business, indulges himself in laziness, and waits, in some obscure place, the event of his adventure. Another, instead of employing his stock in trade, rents a garret, and makes it his business, by false intelligence and chimerical alarms, to raise and sink the price of tickets alternately, and takes advantage of the lies which he has himself invented.

Such, my Lords, is the traffic that is produced by this scheme of getting money; nor were these inconveniences unknown to the present ministers in the time of their predecessors, whom they never ceased to pursue with the loudest clamors whenever the exigencies of the government reduced them to a lottery.

If I, my Lords, might presume to recommend to our ministers the most probable method of raising a large sum for the payment of the troops of the Electorate, I should, instead of the tax and lottery now proposed, advise them to establish a certain number of licensed wheel-barrows, on which the laudable trade of thimble and button might be carried on for the support of the war, and shoe-boys might contribute to the defense of the house of *Austria* by raffling for apples.

Having now, my Lords, examined, with the utmost candor, all the reasons which have been offered in defense of the bill, I can not conceal the result of my inquiry. The arguments have had so little effect upon my understanding, that, as every man judges of others by himself, I can not believe that they have any influence even upon those that offer them, and therefore I am convinced that this bill must be the result of considerations which have been hitherto concealed, and is intended to promote designs which are never to be discovered by the authors before their execution.

With regard to these motives and designs, however artfully concealed, every Lord in this House is at liberty to offer his conjectures.

When I consider, my lords, the tendency of this bill, I find it calculated only for the propagation of diseases, the suppression of industry, and the destruction of mankind. I find it the most fatal engine that ever was pointed at a people; an engine by which those who are not killed will be disabled, and those who preserve their limbs will be deprived of their senses.

This bill therefore, appears to be designed only to thin the ranks of mankind, and to disburden the world of the multitudes that inhabit it; and is perhaps the strongest proof of political sagacity that our new ministers have yet exhibited. They well know, my lords, that they are universally detested, and that, whenever a Briton is destroyed, they are freed from an enemy; they have therefore opened the flood-gates of gin upon the nation, that, when it is less numerous, it may be more easily governed.

Other ministers, my Lords, who had not attained to so great a knowledge in the art of making war upon their country, when they found their enemies clamorous and bold, used to awe them with prosecutions and penalties, or destroy them like burglars, with prisons and with gibbets. But every age, my Lords, produces some improvement; and every nation, however degenerate, gives birth, at some happy period of time, to men of great and enterprising genius. It is our fortune to be witnesses of a new discovery in politics. We may congratulate ourselves upon being contemporaries with those men, who have shown that hangmen and halters are unnecessary in a state; and that ministers may escape the reproach of destroying their enemies by inciting them to destroy themselves.

This new method may, indeed, have upon different constitutions a different operation; it may destroy the lives of some and the senses of others; but either of these effects will answer the purposes of the ministry, to whom it is indifferent, provided the nation becomes insensible, whether pestilence or lunacy prevails among them. Either mad or dead the greatest part of the people must quickly be, or there is no hope of the continuance of the present ministry.

For this purpose, my Lords, what could have been invented more efficacious than an establishment of a certain number of shops at which poison may be vended—poison so prepared as to please the palate, while it wastes the strength, and only kills by intoxication? From the first instant that any of the enemies of the ministry shall grow clamorous and turbulent, a crafty hireling may lead him to the ministerial slaughter-house, and ply him with their wonder-working liquor till he is no longer able to speak or think; and, my Lords, no man can be more agreeable to our ministers than he that can neither speak nor think, except those who *speak without thinking*.

But, my Lords, the ministers ought to reflect, that though all the people of the present age are their enemies, yet they have made no trial of the temper and inclinations of posterity. Our successors may be of opinions very different from ours. They may *perhaps* approve of wars on the Continent, while our plantations are insulted and our trade obstructed; they may think the support of the house of Austria of more importance to us than our own defense; and may perhaps so far differ from their fathers, as to imagine the treasures of Britain very properly employed in supporting the troops, and increasing the splendor, of a foreign Electorate.

LORD CHATHAM.

THE name of CHATHAM is the representative, in our language, of whatever is bold and commanding in eloquence. Yet his speeches are so imperfectly reported, that it is not so much from them as from the testimony of his contemporaries, that we have gained our conceptions of his transcendent powers as an orator. We measure his greatness, as we do the height of some inaccessible cliff, by the shadow it casts behind. Hence it will be proper to dwell more at large on the events of his political life; and especially to collect the evidence which has come down to us by tradition, of his astonishing sway over the British Senate.

WILLIAM PITT, first Earl of Chatham, was descended from a family of high respectability in Cornwall, and was born at London, on the 15th of November, 1708. At Eton, where he was placed from boyhood, he was distinguished for the quickness of his parts and for his habits of unwearied application, though liable, much of his time, to severe suffering from a hereditary gout. Here he acquired that love of the classics which he carried with him throughout life, and which operated so powerfully in forming his character as an orator. He also formed at Eton those habits of easy and animated conversation for which he was celebrated in after life. Cut off by disease from the active sports of the school, he and Lord Lyttleton, who was a greater invalid than himself, found their chief enjoyment during the intervals of study, in the lively interchange of thought. By the keenness of their wit and the brilliancy of their imaginations, they drew off their companions, Fox, Hanbury Williams, Fielding, and others, from the exercises of the play-ground, to gather around them as eager listeners; and gained that quickness of thought, that dexterity of reply, that ready self-possession under a sudden turn of argument or the sharpness of retort, which are indispensable to success in public debate. Almost every great orator has been distinguished for his conversational powers.

At the age of eighteen, Mr. Pitt was removed to the University of Oxford. Here, in connection with his other studies, he entered on that severe course of rhetorical training which he often referred to in after life, as forming so large a part of his early discipline. He took up the practice of writing out translations from the ancient orators and historians, on the broadest scale. Demosthenes was his model; and we are told that he rendered a large part of his orations again and again into English, as the best means of acquiring a forcible and expressive style. The practice was highly recommended by Cicero, from his own experience. It aids the young orator far more effectually in catching the spirit of his model, than any course of mere reading, however fervent or repeated. It is, likewise, the severest test of his command of language. To clothe the thoughts of another in a dress which is at once "close and easy" (an excellent, though quaint description of a good translation) is a task of extreme difficulty. As a means of acquiring copiousness of diction and an exact choice of words, Mr. Pitt also read and re-read the sermons of Dr. Barrow, till he knew many of them by heart. With the same view, he performed a task to which, perhaps, no other student in oratory has ever submitted. He went *twice* through the folio Dictionary of Bailey (the best before that of Johnson), examining each word attentively, dwelling on its peculiar import and modes of construction, and thus endeavoring to bring the whole range of our language completely under his control.

At this time, also, he began those exercises in elocution by which he is known to have obtained his extraordinary powers of delivery. Though gifted by nature with a commanding voice and person, he spared no effort to add every thing that art could confer for his improvement as an orator. His success was commensurate with his zeal. Garrick himself was not a greater actor, in that higher sense of the term in which Demosthenes declared *action* to be the first, and second, and third thing in oratory. The labor which he bestowed on these exercises was surprisingly great. Probably no man of genius since the days of Cicero, has ever submitted to an equal amount of drudgery.

Leaving the University a little before the regular time of graduation, Mr. Pitt traveled on the Continent, particularly in France and Italy. During this tour, he enriched his mind with a great variety of historical and literary information, making every thing subservient, however, to the one great object of preparing for public life. "He thus acquired," says Lord Chesterfield, "a vast amount of premature and useful knowledge." On his return to England, he applied a large part of his slender patrimony to the purchase of a commission in the army, and became a Cornet of the Blues. This made him dependent on Sir Robert Walpole, who was then Prime Minister; but, with his characteristic boldness and disregard of consequences, he took his stand, about this time, in the ranks of Opposition. Walpole, by his jealousy, had made almost every man of talents in the Whig party his personal enemy. His long continuance in office, against the wishes of the people, was considered a kind of tyranny; and young men like Pitt, Lyttleton, &c., who came fresh from college, with an ardent love of liberty inspired by the study of the classics, were naturally drawn to the standard of Pulteney, Carteret, and the other leading "Patriots," who declaimed so vehemently against a corrupt and oppressive government. The Prince of Wales, in consequence of a quarrel with his father, had now come out as head of the Opposition. A rival court was established at Leicester House, within the very precincts of St. James's Palace, which drew together such an assemblage of wits, scholars, and orators, as had never before met in the British empire. Jacobites, Tories, and Patriots were here united. The insidious, intriguing, but highly-gifted Carteret; the courtly Chesterfield; the impetuous Argyle; Pulteney, with a keenness of wit, and a familiarity with the classics which made him as brilliant in conversation as he was powerful in debate; Sir John Barnard, with his strong sense and penetrating judgment; Sir William Wyndham, with his dignified sentiments and lofty bearing; and "the all-accomplished Bolingbroke, who conversed in language as elegant as that he wrote, and whose lightest table-talk, if transferred to paper, would, in its style and matter, have borne the test of the severest criticism"—these, together with the most distinguished literary men of the age, formed the court of Frederick, and became the intimate associates of Mr. Pitt. On a mind so ardent and aspiring, so well prepared to profit by mingling in such society, so gifted with the talent of transferring to itself the kindred excellence of other minds, the company of such men must have acted with extraordinary power; and it is probable that all his rhetorical studies had less effect in making him the orator that he was, than his intimacy with the great leaders of the Opposition at the court of the Prince of Wales.

Mr. Pitt became a member of Parliament in 1735, at the age of twenty-six. For nearly a year he remained silent, studying the temper of the House, and waiting for a favorable opportunity to come forward. Such an opportunity was presented by the marriage of the Prince of Wales, in April, 1736. It was an event of the highest interest and joy to the nation; but such was the King's animosity against his son, that he would not suffer the address of congratulation to be moved, as usual, by the ministers of the Crown. The motion was brought forward by Mr. Pulteney; and it shows the high estimate put upon Mr. Pitt, that, when he had not as yet opened his lips in Parliament, he should be selected to second the motion, in preference to some of the most able and experienced members of the House. His speech was received with the highest applause, and shows that Mr. Pitt's imposing manner and fine command of language gave him from the first that sort of fascination for his audience, which he seemed always to exert over a popular assembly. The speech, which will be found below, if understood literally, is only a series of elegant and high-sounding compliments. If, however, as seems plainly the case, there runs throughout it a deeper meaning; if the glowing panegyric on "the *filial virtue*" of the Prince, and "the *tender* paternal delight" of the King, was intended to reflect on George II. for his harsh treatment of his son—and it can hardly be otherwise—we can not enough admire the dexterity of Mr. Pitt in so managing his subject, as to give his compliments all the effect of the keenest irony, while yet he left no pretense for taking notice of their application as improper or disrespectful. Certain it is that the whole speech was wormwood and gall to the King. It awakened in his mind a personal hatred of Mr. Pitt, which, aggravated as it was by subsequent attacks of a more direct nature, excluded him for years from the service of the Crown, until he was forced upon a reluctant monarch by the demands of the people.

Sir Robert Walpole, as might be supposed, listened to the eloquence of his youthful opponent with anxiety and alarm; and is said to have exclaimed, after hearing the speech, "We must, at all events, muzzle that terrible Cornet of Horse." Whether he attempted to bribe him by offers of promotion in the army (as was reported at the time), it is impossible now to say; but finding him unalterably attached to the Prince and the Opposition, he struck the blow without giving him time to make another speech, and deprived him of his commission within less than eighteen days. Such a mode of punishing a political opponent has rarely been resorted to, under free governments, in the case of military and naval officers. It only rendered the Court more odious, while it created a general sympathy in favor of Mr. Pitt, and turned the attention of the public with new zest and interest to his speeches in Parliament. Lord Lyttleton, at the same time, addressed him in the following lines, which were eagerly circulated throughout the country, and set him forth as already leader of the Opposition.

Long had thy virtues marked thee out for fame,
Far, far superior to a Cornet's name;
This generous Walpole saw, and grieved to find
So mean a post disgrace the human mind,
The servile standard from the free-born hand
He took, and bade thee *lead the Patriot Band*.

As a compensation to Mr. Pitt for the loss of his commission, the Prince appointed him Groom of the Bed-chamber at Leicester House.

Thus, at the age of twenty-seven, Mr. Pitt was made, by the force of his genius and the influence of concurrent circumstances, one of the most prominent members of Parliament, and an object of the liveliest interest to the great body, especially the middling classes, of the English nation. These classes were now rising into an importance never before known. They regarded Sir Robert Walpole, sustained as he was in power by the will of the sovereign and the bribery of Parliament, as their natural enemy. Mr. Pitt shared in all their feelings. He was the exponent of their principles. He was, in *truth*, "the Great Commoner." As to many of the measures for which Walpole was hated by the people and opposed by Mr. Pitt, time has shown that he was in the right and they in the wrong. It has also shown, that nearly all the great leaders of the Opposition, the Pulteneys and the Carterets, were unprincipled men, who played on the generous sympathies of Pitt and Lyttleton, and lashed the prejudices of the nation into rage against the minister, simply to obtain his place. Still the struggle of the people, though in many respects a blind one, was prompted by a genuine instinct of their nature, and was prophetic of an onward movement in English society. It was the Commons of England demanding their place in the Constitution; and happy it was that they had a leader like Mr. Pitt, to represent their principles and animate their exertions. To face at once the Crown and the Peerage demanded not only undaunted resolution, but something of that imperious spirit, that haughty self-assertion, which was so often complained of in the greatest of English orators. In him, however, it was not merely a sense of personal superiority, but a consciousness of the cause in which he was engaged. *He was set for the defense of the popular part of the Constitution.*

In proceeding to trace briefly the course of Mr. Pitt as a statesman, we shall divide his public life into distinct periods, and consider them separately with reference to his measures in Parliament.

The *first* period consists of nearly ten years, down to the close of 1744. During the whole of this time, he was an active member of the Opposition, being engaged for nearly seven years in unwearied efforts to put down Sir Robert Walpole, and when this was accomplished, in equally strenuous exertions for three years longer, to resist the headlong measures of his successor, Lord Carteret. This minister had rendered himself odious to the nation by encouraging the narrow views and sordid policy of the King, in respect to his Continental possessions. George II. was born in Hanover, and he always consulted its interests at the expense of Great Britain; seeking to throw upon the national treasury the support of the Hanoverian troops during his wars on the Continent, and giving the Electorate, in various other ways, a marked preference over the rest of the empire. To these measures, and the minister who abetted them, Mr. Pitt opposed himself with all the energy of his fervid argumentation, and the force of his terrible invective. It was on this subject that he first came into collision, December 10th, 1742, with his great antagonist Murray, afterward Lord Mansfield. Mr. Oswald, a distinguished literary man who was present, thus describes the two combatants: "Murray spoke like a pleader, who could not divest himself of the appearance of having been employed by others. Pitt spoke like a gentleman—like a statesman who felt what he said, and possessed the strongest desire of conveying that feeling to others, for their own interest and that of their country. Murray gains your attention by the perspicuity of his statement and the elegance of his diction; Pitt commands your attention and respect by the nobleness and greatness of his sentiments, the strength and energy of his expressions, and the certainty of his always rising to a greater elevation both of thought and sentiment. For, this talent he possesses, beyond any speaker I ever heard, of never *falling* from the beginning to the end of his speech, either in thought or expression. And as in this session he has begun to speak like a man of business as well as an orator, he will in all probability be, or rather *is*, allowed to make as great an appearance as ever man did in that House."

Mr. Pitt incessantly carried on the attack upon Carteret, who, strong in the King's favor, was acting against the wishes of his associates in office. He exclaimed against him as "a *sole* minister, who had renounced the British nation, and seemed to have drunk of that potion described in poetic fictions, which made men forget their country." He described the King as "hemmed in by German officers, and *one* English minister without an English heart." It was probably about this time that he made his celebrated retort on Sir William Yonge, a man of great abilities but flagitious life, who had interrupted him while speaking by crying out "Question! Question!" Turning to the insolent intruder with a look of inexpressible disgust he exclaimed, "Pardon me, Mr. Speaker, my agitation! When that gentleman calls for the *question*, I think I hear the knell of my country's ruin." Mr. Pitt soon gained a complete ascendency over the House. No man could cope with him; few ventured even to oppose him; and Carteret was given up by all as an object of merited reprobation. Under these circumstances, Mr. Pelham and the other colleagues of the minister, opened a negotiation for a union with Mr. Pitt and the dismissal of Carteret. The terms were easily arranged, and a memorial was at once presented to the King by Lord Hardwicke, supported by the rest of the ministry, demanding the removal of the obnoxious favorite. The King refused, wavered, temporized, and at last yielded. Mr. Pelham became Prime Minister in November, 1744, with the understanding that Mr. Pitt should be brought into office at the earliest moment that the King's prejudices would permit. During the same year, the Duchess of Marlborough died, leaving Mr. Pitt a legacy of £10,000, "on account of his merit in the noble defense of the laws of England, and to prevent the ruin of the country." This was a seasonable relief to one who never made any account of money, and whose circumstances, down to this time, were extremely limited. It may as well here be mentioned, that about twenty years after, he received a still more ample testimony of the same kind from Sir William Pynsent, who bequeathed him an estate of £2500 a year, together with £30,000 in ready money.

We now come to the *second* period of Mr. Pitt's political life, embracing the ten years of Mr. Pelham's ministry down to the year 1754. So strong was the hostility of the King to his old opponent, that no persuasions could induce him to receive Mr. Pitt into his service. On the contrary, when pressed upon the subject, he took decided measures for getting rid of his new ministers. This led Mr. Pelham and his associates, who knew their strength, instantly to resign. The King was now powerless. The Earl of Bath (Pulteney), to whom he had committed the formation of a ministry, could get nobody to serve under him; the retired ministers looked with derision on his fruitless efforts; and some one remarked sarcastically, "that it was unsafe to walk the streets at night, for fear of being pressed for a cabinet counselor." The *Long* Administration came to an end in just forty-eight hours! The King was compelled to go back to Mr. Pelham, and to take Mr. Pitt along with him; he stipulated, however, that the man who was thus forced upon him should not, at least for a time, be brought into immediate contact with his person. He could not endure the mortification of meeting with him in private. Mr. Pitt, therefore, received provisionally the situation of Joint Treasurer of Ireland. He now resigned the office of Groom of the Chamber to the Prince of Wales, and entered heartily into the interests of the Pelham ministry. A contemporary represents him as "swaying the House of Commons, and uniting in himself the dignity of Wyndham, the wit of Pulteney, and the knowledge and judgment of Walpole." He was "right [conciliatory] toward the King, kind and respectful to the old corps, and resolute and contemptuous to the Tory Opposition." About a year after (May, 1746), on the death of Mr. Winnington, he was made Paymaster of the Forces, as originally agreed on.

In entering upon his new office, Mr. Pitt gave a striking exhibition of disinterestedness, which raised him in the public estimation to a still higher level as a man, than he had ever attained by his loftiest efforts as an orator. It was then the custom, that £100,000 should constantly lie as an advance in the hands of the Paymaster, who invested the money in public securities, and thus realized about £4000 a year for his private benefit. This was obviously a very dangerous practice; for if the funds were suddenly depressed, through a general panic or any great public calamity, the Paymaster might be unable to realize his investments, and would thus become a public defaulter. This actually happened during the rebellion of 1745, when the army, on whose fidelity depended the very existence of the government, was for a time left without pay. Mr. Pitt, therefore, on assuming the duties of Paymaster, placed all the funds at his control in the Bank of England, satisfied with the moderate compensation attached to his office.

He also gave another proof of his elevation above pecuniary motives, by refusing a certain per centage, which had always been attached to his office, on the enormous subsidies then paid to the Queen of Austria and the King of Sardinia. The latter, when he heard of this refusal, requested Mr. Pitt to accept, as a token of royal favor, what he had rejected as a perquisite of office. Mr. Pitt still refused. It was this total disregard of the ordinary means of becoming rich, that made Mr. Grattan say, "his character astonished a corrupt age." Politicians were indeed puzzled to understand his motives; for bribery in Parliament and corruption in office had become so universal, and the spirit of public men so sordid, that the cry of the horse-leech was heard in every quarter, Give! give! Ambition itself had degenerated into a thirst for gold. Power and preferment were sought chiefly as the means of amassing wealth. Well might George II. say, when he heard of Mr. Pitt's noble disinterestedness, "His conduct does honor to human nature!"

In joining the Pelham ministry, Mr. Pitt yielded more than might have been expected, to the King's wishes in regard to German subsidies and Continental alliances. For this he has been charged with inconsistency. He thought, however, that the case was materially changed. The war had advanced so far, that nothing remained but to fight it through, and this could be done only by German troops. In addition to this, the Electorate was now in danger; and though he had resisted Carteret's measures for aggrandizing Hanover at the expense of Great Britain, he could, without any change of principles, unite with Pelham to prevent her being wrested from the empire by the ambition of France. He saw, too, that the King grew more obstinate as he grew older; and that if the government was to be administered at all, it must be by those who were willing to make some concessions to the prejudices, and even to the weakness, of an aged monarch. That he was influenced in all this by no ambitious motives, that his desire to stand well with the King had no connection with a desire to stand highest in the state, it would certainly be unsafe to affirm. But his love of power had nothing in it that was mercenary or selfish. He did not seek it, like Newcastle, for patronage, or, like Pulteney and Fox, for money. He had lofty conceptions of the dignity to which England might be raised as the head of European politics; he felt himself equal to the achievement; and he panted for an opportunity to enter on a career of service which should realize his brightest visions of his country's glory. With these views, he supported Pelham and endeavored to conciliate the King, waiting with a prophetic spirit for the occasion which was soon to arrive.

Mr. Pelham died suddenly in March, 1754; and this leads us to the *third* period of Mr. Pitt's public life, embracing about three years, down to 1757. The death of Pelham threw every thing into confusion. "Now I shall have no more peace," said the old King, when he heard the news. The event verified his predictions. The Duke of Newcastle, brother of Mr. Pelham, demanded the office of Prime Minister, and was enabled, by his borough interest and family connections, to enforce his claim. The "lead" of the House of Commons was now to be disposed of; and there were only three men who had the slightest pretensions to the prize, viz., Pitt, Fox, and Murray, afterward Lord Mansfield. And yet Newcastle, out of a mean jealousy of their superior abilities, gave it to Sir Thomas Robinson, who was so poor a speaker, that "when he played the orator," says Lord Waldegrave, "which he frequently attempted, it was so exceedingly ridiculous, that even those who loved him could not always preserve a friendly composure of countenance." "Sir Thomas Robinson lead us?" said Pitt to Fox; "the Duke might as well send his jack-boot to lead us!" He was accordingly baited on every side, falling perpetually into blunders which provoked the stern animadversions of Pitt, or the more painful irony of Fox. Robinson was soon silenced, and Murray was next brought forward. Mr. Pitt did not resign; but after this second rejection he felt absolved from all obligations to Newcastle, and determined to make both him and Murray feel his power. An opportunity was soon presented, and he carried out his design with a dexterity and effect which awakened universal admiration. At the trial of a contested election [that of the Dalavals], when the debate had degenerated into mere buffoonery, which kept the members in a continual roar, Mr. Pitt came down from the gallery where he was sitting, says Fox, who was present, and took the House to task for their conduct "in his highest tone." He inquired whether the dignity of the House stood on such sure foundations, that they might venture to shake it thus. He intimated, that the tendency of things was to degrade the House into a mere French Parliament; and exhorted the Whigs of all conditions to defend their attacked and expiring liberties, "unless," said he, "you are to degenerate into a little assembly, serving no other purpose than to register the arbitrary edicts of *one* too powerful *subject*" (laying, says Fox, a most remarkable emphasis on the words *one* and *subject*). The application to Newcastle was seen and felt by all. "It was the finest speech," adds Fox, "that was ever made; and it was observed that by his first two sentences, he brought the House to a silence and attention that you might have heard a pin drop. I just now learn that the Duke of Newcastle was in the utmost fidget, and that it spoiled his stomach yesterday."[1] According to another who was present, "this thunderbolt, thrown in a sky so long clear, confounded the audience. Murray crouched silent and terrified." Nor without reason, for *his* turn came next. On the following day, November 27, 1754, Mr. Pitt made two other speeches, ostensibly against Jacobitism, but intended for Murray, who had just been raised from the office of Solicitor to that of Attorney General. "In both speeches," says Fox, "every word was MURRAY, yet so managed that neither he nor any body else could take public notice of it, or in any way reprehend him. I sat near Murray, who *suffered* for an hour." It was, perhaps, on this occasion, says Charles Butler, in his Reminiscences, that Pitt used an expression which was once in every mouth. After Murray had "suffered" for a time, Pitt stopped, threw his eyes around, then fixing their whole power on Murray, exclaimed, "I must now address a few words to Mr. Attorney; they shall be few, but shall be daggers." Murray was agitated; the look was continued; the agitation increased. "Felix trembles!" exclaimed Pitt, in a tone of thunder; "*he shall hear me some other day!*" He sat down. Murray made no reply; and a languid debate showed the paralysis of the House.[2]

[1] It is surprising that Charles Butler should insist, in his Reminiscences, that "it was the *manner*, and not the *words*, that did the wonder" in this allusion to Newcastle's overbearing influence with the King. Had he forgotten the jealousy of the English people as to their monarch's being ruled by a favorite? What changed the attachment of the nation for George III., a few years after, into anger and distrust, but the apprehension that he was governed by Lord Bute? And what was better calculated to startle the House of Commons than the idea of sinking, like the once free Parliaments of France, "into a little assembly, serving no other purpose than to register the arbitrary edicts of *one* too powerful *subject?*

[2] It is not difficult to conjecture what were the "daggers" referred to by Mr. Pitt. The Stormont family, to which Murray belonged, was devotedly attached to the cause of James II. His brother was confidential secretary to the Pretender during the rebellion of 1745; and when the rebel lords were brought to London for trial in 1746, Lord Lovat, who was one of them, addressed Murray, to his great dismay, in the midst of the trial, "*Your mother was very kind to my clan as we marched through Perth to join the Pretender!*" Murray had been intimate, while a student in the Temple, with Mr. Vernon, a rich Jacobite citizen; and it was affirmed that when Vernon and his friends drank the Pretender's health *on their knees* (as they often did), Murray was present and joined in the act. When he entered life, however, he saw that the cause of James was hopeless, and espoused the interests of the reigning family. There was no reason to doubt his sincerity; but

Newcastle found it impossible to go on without adding to his strength in debate. He therefore bought off Fox in April, 1755, by bringing him into the Cabinet, while Pitt was again rejected with insult. To this incongruous union Mr. Pitt alluded, a short time after, in terms which were much admired for the felicity of the image under which the allusion was conveyed. Newcastle, it is well known, was feeble and tame, while Fox was headlong and impetuous. An address, prepared by the ministry, was complained of as obscure and incongruous. Mr. Pitt took it up, saying, "There are parts of this address which do not seem to come from the same quarter with the rest. I can not unravel the mystery." Then, as if suddenly recollecting the two men thus brought together at the head of affairs, he exclaimed, clapping his hand to his forehead, "Now it strikes me! I remember at Lyons to have been carried to see the conflux of the Rhone and the Saone—the one a feeble, languid stream, and, though languid, of no great depth; the other a boisterous and impetuous torrent. But, different as they are, they *meet at last;* and long," he added, with the bitterest irony, "*long* may they continue united, to the *comfort* of each other, and to the *glory, honor*, and *security* of this nation!" In less than a week Mr. Pitt was dismissed from his office as Paymaster.

This was the signal for open war—Pitt against the entire ministry. Ample occasion for attack was furnished by the disasters which were continually occurring in the public service, and the dangers resulting therefrom—the loss of Minorca, the defeat of General Braddock, the capture of Calcutta by Sujah Dowlah, and the threatened invasion by the French. These topics afforded just ground for the terrible onset of Mr. Pitt. "During the whole session of 1755–6," says an eye-witness, "Mr. Pitt found occasion, in every debate, to confound the ministerial orators. His vehement invectives were awful to Murray, terrible to Hugh Campbell; and no malefactor under the stripes of the executioner, was ever more helpless and forlorn than Fox, shrewd and able in Parliament as he confessedly is. Doddington sheltered himself in silence." With all this vehemence, however, he was never betrayed into any thing coarse or unbecoming the dignity of his character. Horace Walpole, writing to Gerard Hamilton, says of his appearance on one of these occasions, "There was more humor, wit, vivacity, fine language, more boldness, in short more astonishing perfection than even you, who are used to him, can conceive." And again, "He surpassed himself, as I need not tell you he surpassed Cicero and Demosthenes. What a figure would they make, with their formal, labored, cabinet orations, by the side of his manly vivacity and dashing eloquence at *one o'clock in the morning*, after a sitting of eleven hours!" The effect on the ministerial ranks was soon apparent. Murray was the first to shrink. The ablest by far among the supporters of the ministry—much abler, indeed, as a reasoner, than his great opponent, and incomparably more learned in every thing pertaining to the science of government, he could stand up no longer before the devouring eloquence of Pitt. On the death of Chief-justice Ryder, which took place in November, 1756, he instantly demanded the place. Newcastle resisted, entreated, offered, in addition to the profits of the Attorney Generalship, a pension of £2000, and, at last, of £6000 a year. It was all in vain. Nothing could induce Murray to remain longer in the House. He was accordingly made Chief Justice,

these early events of his life gave Mr. Pitt immense advantage over him in such attacks. Junius cast them into his teeth sixteen years after. "Your zeal in the cause of an unhappy prince was expressed with *the sincerity of wine and some of the solemnities of religion.*"

In quoting from Butler, I have modified his statement in two or three instances. By a slip of the pen he wrote *Festus* for Felix, and Solicitor for Attorney. He also makes Pitt say "*Judge* Festus," when Murray was not made judge until a year later. It is easy to see how the title judge might have slipped into the story after Murray was raised to the bench; but Mr. Pitt could never have addressed the same person as judge, and yet as prosecuting officer of the Crown.

and a Peer with the title of Lord Mansfield; and on the day he took his seat upon the bench, Newcastle *resigned as minister*.

Nothing now remained for the King but to transfer the government to Mr. Pitt. It was a humiliating necessity, but the condition of public affairs was dark and threatening, and no one else could be found of sufficient courage or capacity to undertake the task. Pitt had said to the Duke of Devonshire, "My Lord, I am sure that I can save this country, and that nobody else can." The people believed him. "The eyes of an afflicted and despairing nation," says Glover, who was far from partaking in their enthusiasm, "were now lifted up to a private gentleman of slender fortune, wanting the parade of birth or title, with no influence except marriage with Lord Temple's sister, and even confined to a narrow circle of friends and acquaintances. Yet, under these circumstances, Mr. Pitt was considered the savior of England." His triumph was the triumph of the popular part of the Constitution. It was the first instance in which the middling classes, the true Commons of Great Britain, were able to break down in Parliament that power which the great families of the aristocracy had so long possessed, of setting aside or sustaining the decisions of the Throne.

Mr. Pitt's entrance on the duties of Prime Minister in December, 1756, brings us to the *fourth* period of his political life, which embraces nearly five years, down to October, 1761. For about four months, however, during his first ministry, his hands were in a great measure tied. Though supported by the unanimous voice of the people, the King regarded him with personal dislike; Newcastle and his other opponents were able to defeat him in Parliament; and in April, 1757, he received the royal mandate to retire. This raised a storm throughout the whole of England. The stocks fell. The Common Council of London met and passed resolutions of the strongest kind. The principal towns of the kingdom, Bath, Chester, Norwich, Salisbury, Worcester, Yarmouth, Newcastle, and many others, sent Mr. Pitt the freedom of their respective cities, as a token of their confidence and as a warning to the King. "For some weeks," says Horace Walpole, "it rained gold boxes!" The King, in the mean time, spent nearly three months in the vain attempt to form another administration. It was now perfectly apparent, that nothing could be done without concessions on both sides. Mr. Pitt therefore consented, June 30th, 1757, to resume his office as Principal Secretary of State and Prime Minister, in conjunction with Newcastle as head of the Treasury, satisfied that he could more easily overrule and direct the Duke as a member of the Cabinet than as leader of the Opposition. The result verified his expectations. His second ministry now commenced, that splendid era which raised England at once, as if by magic, from the brink of ruin and degradation. The genius of one man completely penetrated and informed the mind of a whole people. "From the instant he took the reins, the panic, which had paralyzed every effort, disappeared. Instead of mourning over former disgrace and dreading future defeats, the nation assumed in a moment the air of confidence, and awaited with impatience the tidings of victory." In every thing he undertook,

"He put so much of his soul into his act
That his example had a magnet's force,
And all were prompt to follow whom all loved."

To this wonderful power of throwing his spirit into other minds, Colonel Barré referred at a later period, in one of his speeches in Parliament: "He was possessed of the happy talent of transfusing his own zeal into the souls of all those who were to have a share in carrying his projects into execution; and it is a matter well known to many officers now in the House, that no man ever entered his closet who did not feel himself, if possible, *braver at his return* than when he went in." He knew, also, how to use fear, as well as affection, for the accomplishment of his designs. "It will be impossible to have so many ships prepared so soon," said Lord

Anson, when a certain expedition was ordered. "If the ships are not ready," said Mr. Pitt, "I will impeach your Lordship in presence of the House." They were ready as directed. Newcastle, in the mean time, yielded with quiet submission to the supremacy of his genius. All the Duke wanted was the patronage, and this Mr. Pitt cheerfully gave up for the salvation of the country. Horace Walpole says, in his lively manner, "Mr. Pitt *does* every thing, and the Duke of Newcastle *gives* every thing. As long as they can agree in this partition, they may do what they will."[3]

One of the first steps taken by Mr. Pitt was to grant a large subsidy to Frederick the Great, of Prussia, for carrying on the war against the Empress of Austria. This was connected with a total change which had already taken place in the Continental policy of George II., and was intended to rescue Hanover from the hands of the French. Still, there were many who had a traditional regard for the Empress of Austria, in whose defense England had expended more than ten millions of pounds sterling. The grant was, therefore, strenuously opposed in the House, and Mr. Pitt was taunted with a desertion of his principles. In reply, he defended himself, and maintained the necessity of the grant with infinite dexterity. "It was," says Horace Walpole, "the most artful speech he ever made. He provoked, called for, defied objections—promised enormous expense—demanded never to be tried by events." By degrees he completely subdued the House, until a murmur of applause broke forth from every quarter. Seizing the favorable moment, he drew back with the utmost dignity, and placing himself in an attitude of defiance, exclaimed, in his loudest tone, "Is there an *Austrian* among you? Let him come forward and reveal himself!" The effect was irresistible. "Universal silence," says Walpole, "left him arbiter of his own terms." Another striking instance of Mr. Pitt's mastery over the House is said also to have occurred about this time. Having finished a speech, he walked out with a slow step, being severely afflicted with the gout. A silence ensued until the door was opened to let him pass into the lobby, when a member started up, saying, "Mr. Speaker, I rise to reply to the right honorable gentleman." Pitt, who had caught the words, turned back and fixed his eye on the orator, who instantly sat down. He then returned toward his seat, repeating, as he hobbled along, the lines of Virgil, in which the poet, conducting Æneas through the shades below, describes the terror which his presence inspired among the ghosts of the Greeks who had fought at Troy:

> Ast Danaum proceres, Agamemnoniæque phalanges,
> Ut vidêre VIRUM, fulgentiaque arma per umbras,
> Ingenti trepidare metu; pars vertere terga,
> Ceu quondam petière rates; pars tollere vocem
> Exiguam: *inceptus clamor frustratur hiantes.*[4]
>
> VIRGIL, *Æn.*, vi., 489.

[3] A curious anecdote illustrates the ascendency of Pitt over Newcastle. The latter was a great valetudinarian, and was so fearful of taking cold, especially, that he often ordered the windows of the House of Lords to be shut in the hottest weather, while the rest of the Peers were suffering for want of breath. On one occasion he called upon Pitt, who was confined to his bed by the gout. Newcastle, on being led into the bed-chamber, found the room, to his dismay, *without fire* in a cold, wintery afternoon. He begged to have one kindled, but Pitt refused: it might be injurious to his gout. Newcastle drew his cloak around him, and submitted with the worst possible grace. The conference was a long one. Pitt was determined on a naval expedition, under Admiral Hawke, for the annihilation of the French fleet. Newcastle opposed it on account of the lateness of the season. The debate continued until the Duke was absolutely shivering with cold; when, at last, seeing another bed in the opposite corner, he slipped in, and covered himself with the bed-clothes! A secretary, coming in soon after, found the two ministers in this curious predicament, with their faces only visible, bandying the argument with great eagerness from one bed-side to the other.

[4] The Grecian chiefs, and Agamemnon's host,
When they beheld the MAN with shining arms

Reaching his seat, he exclaimed, "Now let me hear what the honorable gentleman has to say to me!" One who was present, being asked whether the House was not convulsed with laughter at the ludicrous situation of the poor orator and the aptness of the lines, replied, "No, sir; we were all too much awed to laugh."

There was, however, very little debate after his administration had fairly commenced. All parties united in supporting his measures. It is, indeed, a remarkable fact, that the Parliamentary History, which professes to give a detailed report of all the debates in Parliament, contains not a single speech of Mr. Pitt, and only two or three by any other person, during the whole period of his ministry. The supplies which he demanded were, for that day, enormous—twelve millions and a half in one year, and nearly twenty millions the next—"a most incredible sum," says Walpole, respecting the former, "and yet already all subscribed for, and even more offered! Our unanimity is prodigious. You would as soon hear 'No' from an old maid as from the House of Commons." "Though Parliament has met," says Walpole again, in 1759, "no politics are come to town. One may describe the House of Commons like the stocks: Debates, nothing done; Votes, under par; Patriots, no price; Oratory, books shut!"

England now entered into the war with all the energy of a new existence. Spread out in her colonies to the remotest parts of the globe, she resembled a strong man who had long been lying with palsied limbs, and the blood collected at the heart; when the stream of life, suddenly set free, rushes to the extremities, and he springs to his feet with an elastic bound to repel injury or punish aggression. In the year 1758, the contest was carried on at once in Europe, Asia, Africa, and America—wherever France had possessions to be attacked, or England to be defended. Notwithstanding some disasters at first, victory followed upon victory in rapid succession. Within little more than two years, all was changed. In Africa, France was stripped of every settlement she had on that continent. In India, defeated in two engagements at sea, and driven from every post on land, she gave up her long contest for the mastery of the East, and left the British to establish their government over a hundred and fifty millions of people. In America, all her rich possessions in the West Indies passed into the hands of Great Britain. Louisburg, Quebec, Ticonderoga, Crown Point, Oswego, Niagara, Fort Duquesne [now PITTSBURGH], were taken; and the entire chain of posts with which France had hemmed in and threatened our early settlements, fell before the united arms of the colonists and the English, and not an inch of territory was left her in the Western World. In Europe, Hanover was rescued; the French were defeated at Creveldt, and again at Minden with still greater injury and disgrace; the coasts of France were four times invaded with severe loss to the English, but still with a desperate determination to strike terror into the hearts of the enemy; Hâvre was bombarded; the port and fortifications of Cherbourg were demolished; Brest and the other principal sea-ports were blockaded; the Toulon fleet was captured or destroyed; and the brilliant victory of Admiral Hawke off Quiberon, annihilated the French navy for the remainder of the war.[5] At home, the only part of the empire which continued hostile to the

---

Amid those shades, trembled with sudden fear.
Part turned their backs in flight, as when they sought
Their ships. * * * * Part raised
A feeble outcry; but the sound commenced,
Died on their gasping lips.

[5] One of those brilliant sallies for which Mr. Pitt was distinguished, occurred at this time, and related to Sir Edward Hawke. In proposing a monument for General Wolfe, Mr. Pitt paid a high compliment to Admiral Saunders: "a man," said he, "equaling those who have beaten Armadas—may I anticipate? those who *will* beat Armadas!" The words were prophetic. It was the very day of Hawke's victory, November 20th, 1759.

government, the Highlanders of Scotland, who had been disarmed for their rebellions, and insulted by a law forbidding them to wear their national costume, were forever detached from the Stuarts, and drawn in grateful affection around the Throne, by Mr. Pitt's happy act of confidence in putting arms into their hands, and sending them to fight the battles of their country in every quarter of the globe. Finally, the commercial interests of the kingdom, always the most important to a great manufacturing people, prospered as never before; and "COMMERCE," in the words inscribed by the city of London on the statue which they erected to Mr. Pitt, "COMMERCE, for the *first* time, was united with, and made to flourish by, WAR!"

France was now effectually humbled. In 1761 she sought for peace; and Mr. Pitt declared to his friends, when entering on the negotiation, that "no Peace of Utrecht should again stain the annals of England." He therefore resisted every attempt of France to obtain a restoration of conquests, and was on the point of concluding a treaty upon terms commensurate with the triumphs of the English arms, when the French succeeded in drawing Spain into the contest. After a season of long alienation, an understanding once more took place between the two branches of the house of Bourbon. The French minister instantly changed his tone. He came forward with a proposal that Spain should be invited to take part in the treaty, specifying certain claims of that country upon England which required adjustment. Mr. Pitt was indignant at this attempt of a prostrate enemy to draw a third party into the negotiation. He spurned the proposal. He declared, that "he would not relax one syllable from his terms, until the Tower of London was taken by storm." He demanded of Spain a disavowal of the French minister's claims. This offended the Spanish court, and France accomplished her object. The celebrated Family Compact was entered into, which once more identified the two nations in all their interests; and Spain, by a subsequent stipulation, engaged to unite in the war with France, unless England should make peace on satisfactory terms before May, 1762. Mr. Pitt, whose means of secret intelligence were hardly inferior to those of Oliver Cromwell, was apprised of these arrangements (though studiously concealed) almost as soon as they were made. He saw that a war was inevitable, that he had just ground of war; and he resolved to strike the first blow—to seize the Spanish treasure-ships which were then on their way from America; to surprise Havana, which was wholly unprepared for defense; to wrest the Isthmus of Panama from Spain, and thus put the keys of her commerce between the two oceans forever into the hands of the English. But when he proposed these measures to the Cabinet, he was met, to his surprise, with an open and determined resistance. George II. was dead. Lord Bute, the favorite of George III., was jealous of Mr. Pitt's ascendency. The King probably shared in the same feelings; and in the language of Grattan, "conspired to remove him, in order to be relieved from his superiority." An obsequious cabinet voted down Mr. Pitt's proposal. He instantly resigned; and Spain, as if to prove his sagacity, and justify the measure he had urged, declared war herself within three months!

The King, however, in thus ending the most glorious ministry which England had ever seen, manifested a strong desire to conciliate Mr. Pitt. The very next day he sent a message to him through Lord Bute, declaring that he was "impatient" to bestow upon him some mark of the royal favor. Mr. Pitt was melted by these unexpected tokens of kindness. He replied in terms which have often been censured as unbecoming a man of spirit under a sense of injury—terms which would certainly be thought obsequious at the present day, but which were probably dictated by the sudden revulsion of his feelings, and the courtly style which he always maintained in his intercourse with the sovereign.[6] On the day after his resignation, he accepted

[6] In his long and frequent interviews with George II., Mr. Pitt, though often commanded to sit

a pension of £3000 (being much less than was offered him), together with a peerage for his wife. Some, indeed, complained that, acting as he did for the people, he should have allowed the King to place him under any pecuniary obligations. "If he had gone into the city," said Walpole, "and told them he had a poor wife and children unprovided for, and opened a subscription, he would have got £500,000 instead of £3000 a year." He could never have done so, until he had ceased to be William Pitt. Mr. Burke has truly said, "With regard to the pension and the title, it is a shame that any defense should be necessary. What eye can not distinguish, at the first glance, between this and the exceptionable case of titles and pensions? What Briton, with the smallest sense of honor or gratitude, but must blush for his country, if such a man had retired unrewarded from the public service, let the motives of that retirement be what they would? It was not *possible* that his sovereign should let his eminent services pass unrequited; and the quantum was rather regulated by the moderation of the great mind that received, than by the liberality of that which bestowed it."[7] It is hardly necessary to add, that the tide of public favor, which had ebbed for a moment, soon returned to its ordinary channels. The city of London sent him an address in the warmest terms of commendation. On Lord Mayor's day, when he joined the young King and Queen in their procession to dine at Guildhall, the eyes of the multitude were turned from the royal equipage to the modest vehicle which contained Mr. Pitt and his brother-in-law, Lord Temple. The loudest acclamations were reserved for the Great Commoner. The crowd, says an eye-witness, clustered around his carriage at every step, "hung upon the wheels, hugged his footmen, and even kissed his horses." Such were the circumstances under which he retired from office, having resigned on the 5th of October, 1761.

We now come to the *fifth* and last period of Mr. Pitt's life, embracing about sixteen years, down to his decease in 1778. During the whole of this period, except for a brief season when he was called to form a new ministry, he acted with the Opposition. When a treaty of peace was concluded by Lord Bute, in 1762, he was confined to his bed by the gout; but his feelings were so excited by the concessions made to France, that he caused himself to be conveyed to the House in the midst of his acutest sufferings, and poured out his indignation for three hours and a half, exposing in the keenest terms the loss and dishonor brought upon the country by the conditions of peace. This was called his "Sitting Speech;" because, after having stood for a time supported by two friends, "he was so excessively ill," says the Parliamentary History, "and his pain became so exceedingly acute, that the House unanimously desired he might be permitted to deliver his sentiments *sitting*—a circumstance that was unprecedented."[8] But whether the peace was disgraceful or not, the ministry had no alternative. Lord Bute could not raise money to carry on the war. The merchants, who had urged upon Mr. Pitt double the amount he needed whenever he asked a loan, refused their assistance to a minister whom they could not trust.

Under these circumstances, Lord Bute was soon driven to extremities; and as a means of increasing the revenues, introduced a bill subjecting cider to an excise. An Excise Bill has always been odious to the English. It brings with it the right of search. It lays open the private dwelling, which every Englishman has been taught to regard as his "castle." "You give to the dipping-rod," said one, arguing against such a law, "what you deny to the scepter!" Mr. Pitt laid hold of this feeling, and opposed the bill with his utmost strength. There is no report of his

while suffering severe pain from the gout, never obeyed. When unable any longer to stand, he always kneeled on a cushion before the King.

[7] Annual Register for 1761.

[8] Parliamentary History, xv., 1262. The report of this speech is too meager and unsatisfactory to merit insertion in this work.

speech, but a single passage has come down to us. containing one of the finest bursts of his eloquence. "The poorest man in his cottage may bid defiance to all the forces of the Crown. It may be frail; its roof may shake; the wind may blow through it; the storm may enter it; but *the King of England can not enter it!* All his power dares not cross the threshold of that ruined tenement!" It was on this occasion, as stated in the Parliamentary History, that Mr. Pitt uttered a *bon mot* which was long remembered for the mirth it occasioned. Mr. George Grenville replied to Mr. Pitt, and, though he admitted that an excise was odious, contended that the tax was unavoidable. "The right honorable gentleman," said he, "complains of the hardship of the tax—why does he not tell us *where* we can lay another in its stead?" "Tell me," said he, repeating it with strong emphasis, "tell me where you can lay another tax! Tell me where!" Mr. Pitt, from his seat, broke out in a musical tone, quoting from a popular song of the day, "*Gentle shepherd, tell me where!*" The House burst into a fit of laughter, which continued for some minutes, and Mr. Grenville barely escaped the *sobriquet* of Gentle Shepherd for the rest of his life. After six divisions, the bill was passed, but it drove Lord Bute from power. He resigned a few weeks after, and in May, 1763, was succeeded by Mr. Grenville, whose mistakes as minister, in connection with the peculiar temperament of the King, opened a new era in the history of Great Britain.

It was the misfortune of George III., in the early part of his life, to be governed first by favorites and then by his own passions. He was naturally of a quick and obstinate temper. During the first twenty years of his reign (for he afterward corrected this error), he allowed his feelings as a man to mingle far too much with his duties as a sovereign. This led him into two steps, one of which agitated, and the other dismembered his empire—the persecution of John Wilkes, and the attempt to force taxation on the American colonies. It is now known, that he sent a personal order to have Wilkes arrested under a general warrant, against the advice of Lord Mansfield, and insisted on all the subsequent violations of law which gave such notoriety and influence to that restless demagogue. And although he did not originate the plan of taxing America, the moment the *right* was questioned, he resolved to maintain the principle to the utmost extremity. This it was that forced the "Declaratory Act" on Lord Rockingham, and held Lord North so long to the war, as it now appears, against his own judgment and feelings. In respect to both these subjects, Mr. Pitt took, from the first, an open and decided stand against the wishes of the King. He did it on the principle which governed his whole political life; which led him, nearly thirty years before, to oppose so violently the issue of search-warrants for seamen[9]—the principle of resisting arbitrary power in every form; of defending, at all hazards, the rights and liberties of the subject, "however mean, however remote." During the remainder of his life, all his speeches of any importance, with a single exception, related to one or the other of these topics. It was his constant aim, in his own emphatic language, "*to restore, to save, to confirm* the CONSTITUTION."

This attachment of Mr. Pitt to the popular part of the government gave rise to an attack (it is not known on what occasion), which called forth one of those keen and contemptuous retorts with which he so often put down his opponents. Mr. Moreton, Chief Justice of Chester, having occasion to mention "the King, Lords, and Commons," paused, and, turning toward Mr. Pitt, added, "or, as the right honorable member would call them, Commons, Lords, and King." Mr. Pitt, says Charles Butler, in relating the story, rose (as he always did) with great deliberation, and called to *order*. "I have," he said, "heard frequently in this House doctrines which surprised me; but now my blood runs cold! I desire the words

[9] See page 80.

of the honorable member may be taken down." The clerk wrote down the words. "Bring them to me!" said Mr. Pitt, in his loudest voice. By this time Mr. Moreton was frightened out of his senses. "Sir," said he, addressing the Speaker, "I meant nothing! King, Lords, and Commons; Lords, King, and Commons; Commons, Lords, and King—*tria juncta in uno*. I meant nothing! Indeed, I meant nothing!" "I don't wish to push the matter further," said Mr. Pitt, in a tone but little above a whisper. Then, in a higher note, "The moment a man acknowledges his error, he ceases to be guilty. I have a great regard for the honorable gentleman, and, as an instance of that regard, I give him this advice— a pause of some moments; then, assuming a look of unspeakable derision, he added, in a colloquial tone, "Whenever that gentleman *means* nothing, I recommend to him to *say* nothing!"

It has already been intimated that, during the period now under review, Mr. Pitt was called, for a brief season, into the service of the Crown. George Grenville, who succeeded Lord Bute, after acting as minister about two years, and inflicting on his country the evils of the American Stamp Act, became personally obnoxious to the King, and was dismissed from office about the middle of 1765. The eyes of the whole country were now turned toward Mr. Pitt, and the King asked the terms upon which he would accept office. Mr. Pitt replied that he was ready to go to St. James's, if he could "carry the Constitution along with him." But upon entering into details, it was found impossible to reconcile his views with that court influence which still overruled the King. Lord Rockingham was then called upon to form a ministry; and Mr. Pitt has been censured by many, and especially by his biographer, Mr. Thackeray, for not joining heartily in the design, and lending the whole weight of his influence to establish, under his Lordship, another great Whig administration. This might, perhaps, have been an act of magnanimity. But, considering his recent splendid services, the known wishes of the people, and his acknowledged superiority over every other man in the empire, it could hardly be expected of Mr. Pitt that he should make himself a stepping-stone for the ambition of another. Lord Rockingham, though a man of high integrity and generous sentiments, had not that force of character, that eloquence in debate, that controlling influence over the minds of others which could alone reanimate the Whig party, and restore their principles and their policy under a Tory King. Mr. Pitt did not oppose the new ministers; but he declared, at the opening of Parliament, that he could not give them his confidence. "Pardon me, gentlemen," said he, bowing to the ministry, "*confidence is a plant of slow growth in an aged bosom!*"[10] The event justified his delay and hesitation. "The Cabinet," says Cooke, in his History of Party, "was formed from the rear-guard of the Whigs—men who were timorous and suspicious of their own principles; who were bound in the chains of aristocratic expediency and personal interest, and who dared not to loose them, because they knew not the power of their principles or their ultimate tendency." The Rockingham administration performed one important service—they repealed the Stamp Act. But they held together only a year, and were dissolved on the 5th of August, 1766.

Mr. Pitt was now called upon to frame a ministry. It was plainly impossible for him to succeed; and no one but a man of his sanguine temperament would have thought of making the attempt. The Rockingham Whigs, forming the wealthy and aristocratic section of the party, might of course be expected to oppose. Lord Temple, who had hitherto adhered to Mr. Pitt in every emergency, now deserted him, and joined his brother, George Grenville, in justifying American taxation.

[10] See page 103 for the speech containing this passage, and a description of Mr. Pitt's impressive manner in thus declaring off from Lord Rockingham. This single sentence decided the fate of that ministry.

Lord Camden and a few others, the pioneers of Whiggism as it now exists, supported Mr. Pitt, and carried with them the suffrages of the people. But the Tories were favorites at Court. They filled all the important stations of the household; they had the readiest access to the royal presence; and, though Mr. Pitt might, at first, undoubtedly rely on the King for support, he could hardly expect to enjoy it long without gratifying his wishes in the selection of the great officers of state. Under these circumstances, the moment Mr. Pitt discovered his real situation, he ought to have relinquished the attempt to form a ministry. But he was led on step by step. His proud spirit had never been accustomed to draw back. He at last formed one on coalition principles. He drew around him as many of his own friends as possible, and filled up the remaining places with Tories, hoping to keep the peace at the council-board by his personal influence and authority. He had put down Newcastle by uniting with him, and he was confident of doing the same with his new competitors. But he made one mistake at the outset, which, in connection with his subsequent illness, proved the ruin of his ministry. It related to the "lead" of the House of Commons. *His* voice was the only one that could rule the stormy discussions of that body, and compose the elements of strife which were thickening around him. And yet he withdrew from the House, and gave the lead to Charles Townsend. Never was a choice more unfortunate. Townsend was, indeed, brilliant, but he was rash and unstable; eaten up with the desire to please every body; utterly devoid of firmness and self-command; and, therefore, the last man in the world for giving a lead and direction to the measures of the House. But Mr. Pitt's health was gone. He felt wholly inadequate, under his frequent attacks of the gout, to take the burden of debate; he therefore named himself Lord Privy Seal, and passed into the Upper House with the title of Lord Chatham. As might be expected, his motives in thus accepting the peerage were, for a time, misunderstood. He was supposed to have renounced his principles, and become a creature of the Court. The city of London, where he had ruled with absolute sway as the Great Commoner, refused him their support or congratulations as Lord Chatham. The press teemed with invectives; and the people, who considered him as having betrayed their cause, loaded him with maledictions. Such treatment, in connection with his sufferings from disease, naturally tended to agitate his feelings and sour his temper. He was sometimes betrayed into rash conduct and passionate language. His biographer has, indeed, truly said, that, "highly as Lord Chatham was loved and respected by his own family, and great as were his talents and virtues, he possessed not the art of cementing political friendships. A consciousness of his superior abilities, strengthened by the brilliant successes of his former administration, and the unbounded popularity he enjoyed, imparted an austerity to his manners which distressed and offended his colleagues."

Such were the circumstances under which Lord Chatham formed his third ministry. It would long since have passed into oblivion, had not Mr. Burke handed it down to posterity in one of the most striking pictures (though abounding in grotesque imagery) which we have in our literature. "He made an administration," says Mr. Burke, in his speech on American Taxation, "so checkered and speckled; he put together a piece of joinery so crossly indented and whimsically dovetailed; a cabinet so variously inlaid; such a piece of diversified mosaic; such a tesselated pavement without cement, here a bit of black stone, and there a bit of white; patriots and courtiers, King's friends and Republicans, that it was indeed a very curious show, but utterly unsafe to touch and unsure to stand on. The colleagues whom he assorted at the same boards stared at each other, and were obliged to ask, 'Sir, your name?' 'Sir, you have the advantage of me.' 'Mr. Such-a-one, I beg a thousand pardons.' I venture to say it did so happen, that persons had a single office divided between them who had never spoke to each other in their lives until they found themselves (they knew not how) pigging together, heads and points, in the same truckle-bed."[11] * * * "If ever he fell into a fit of the gout, or if any other cause withdrew him from public cares, principles directly the contrary were sure to predominate. When he had executed his plan, he had not an inch of ground to stand on. When he had accomplished his scheme of administration, *he was no longer a minister*."

Such was literally the fact. Only a few weeks after his final arrangements were made, he was seized with a paroxysm of the gout at Bath, which threatened his immediate dissolution. Having partially recovered, he set out on his return for London, in February, 1767. But he was violently attacked on the road, and was compelled to retire to his country seat at Hayes, where he lay in extreme suffering, with a mind so agitated and diseased that all access to him was denied for many months. It was during this period that Charles Townsend, in one of his rash and boastful moods, committed himself to Mr. Grenville in favor of taxing the colonies; and was induced to lay those duties on tea, glass, &c., which revived the contest, and led to the American Revolution. It is, indeed, a singular circumstance, that such a bill should have passed under an administration bearing the name of Chatham. But he had ceased to be minister except in name. Some months before, he had sent a verbal message to the King (for he was unable to write), that "such was the ill state of his health, that his majesty must not expect from him any further advice or assistance in any arrangement whatever." When Grafton became minister, he sent in his formal resignation by the hands of Lord Camden. It is striking to observe how soon great men are forgotten when they fall from power, and withdraw, in the decay of their faculties, from the notice of the public. Lord Chatham's former resignation was an era in Europe. The news of it awakened the liveliest emotions throughout the civilized world. The time of his second resignation was hardly known in London. His sun appeared to have sunk at mid-day amid clouds and gloom Little did any one imagine, that it was again to break forth with a purer splendor, and to fill the whole horizon around with the radiance of its setting beams.[12]

[11] Supposed to refer to Lord North and Mr. George Cooke, who were made joint paymasters.

[12] There was a mystery connected with Lord Chatham's long confinement which has created many surmises. A writer in the London Quarterly Review for 1840 has endeavored to show that it was, to a great extent, a thing of pretense and affectation; that he was shocked at the sudden loss of his popularity after accepting the peerage; disconcerted by the opposition which sprung up; mortified at the failure of his attempts to strengthen his government; and that, under these circumstances, "he felt some reluctance to come forward in his new character, and perhaps clung to office only that he might find some *striking and popular occasion for resignation*." To an enemy of Lord Chatham's fame and principles this may seem probable; but it is a mere hypothesis, without the least evidence to support it. It is probably true that Lord Chatham's withdrawal from public business was not owing to *direct* sufferings from the gout during the whole space of two years. Lord Chesterfield, who was no friend of Chatham, and not the least inclined to shelter him, attributed "his inactivity to the effects of the injudicious treatment of his physician, who had prevented a threatened attack of the gout by dispersing the humor throughout the whole system. The experiment caused a severe fit of illness, which chiefly affected his nerves." Whether this was the cause or not, it is certain that his nervous system was in a very alarming state, and that his mind became greatly diseased. He was gloomy in the extreme, and perhaps yielded to unreasonable jealousies and suspicions. Such seems to have been at one time the opinion of Lord Camden, who says, in a confidential letter, "Lord Chatham is at Hayes, brooding over his own suspicions and discontents—his return to business almost desperate—inaccessible to every body; but under a persuasion that he is given up and abandoned." But Lord Camden soon after received information which probably changed his views. "On his return to London," says his biographer, "he heard such an account of Lord Chatham as to convince him that the country was forever deprived of the services of that illustrious man." This refers, undoubtedly, to a report of his being *deranged*, which was then prevalent. It now appears that this was not literally the fact, though his mind was certainly in such a state that Lady Chatham did not allow him to be master

After an entire seclusion from the world for nearly three years, Lord Chatham, to the surprise of all, made his appearance in Parliament with his health greatly improved, and in full possession of his gigantic powers. He was still so infirm, however, that he went on crutches, and was swathed in flannels, when he entered the House of Lords at the opening of the session, January 9, 1770. In commenting on the address, he came out at once in a loftier strain of eloquence than ever in reply to Lord Mansfield on the case of John Wilkes.[13] This speech gave a decisive turn to political affairs. A leader had now appeared to array the Whigs against the Duke of Grafton. Lord Camden, who as Chancellor had continued in the Cabinet, though hostile to the measures which prevailed, came down from the wool-sack at the close of Lord Chatham's speech, and declared against the minister. "I have," said he, "hung down my head in council, and disapproved by my looks those steps which I knew my avowed opposition could not prevent. I will do so no longer. I now proclaim to the world that I entirely coincide in the opinion expressed by my noble friend—whose presence again reanimates us—respecting this unconstitutional vote of the House of Commons." He was of course dismissed; and united with Lord Chatham, Lord Rockingham, and the rest of the Whigs, to oppose the Grafton ministry. They succeeded in nineteen days: the Duke resigned on the twenty-eighth of the same month. But the Whigs did not profit by their victory. The hostility of the King excluded them from power, and Lord North was placed at the head of affairs. An attempt was now made to put down Lord Chatham by personal insult. He was taunted before the House, March 14, 1770, with having received a pension from the Crown, and having unjustifiably recommended pensions for others. He rose upon his antagonist, as he always did on such occasions, and turned his defense into an attack. He at once took up the case of Lord Camden, whom he had brought in as Chancellor three years before, with a pension of fifteen hundred pounds. "I could not," said he, "expect such a man to quit the Chief-justiceship of the Common Pleas, which he held for life, and put himself in the power of those who were not to be trusted, to be dismissed from the Chancery at any moment, without making some slight provision for such an event. The public has not been deceived by his conduct. My suspicions have been justified. His integrity has made him once more a poor and a private man; *he was dismissed for the vote he gave in favor of the right of election in the people.*" Here an attempt was made to overwhelm him with clamor. Some Lords called out, "To the bar! to the bar!" and Lord Marchmont moved that his words be taken down. Lord Chatham seconded the motion; and went on to say, "I neither deny, retract, nor explain these words. I do *re-affirm* the fact, and I desire to meet the sense of the House. I appeal to the honor of every Lord in this House whether he has not the same conviction." Lord Rockingham, Lord Temple, and many others, rose, and, upon their honor, affirmed the same. The ministry were now desirous to drop the subject; but Lord Marchmont, encouraged by Lord Mansfield, persisted, and moved that nothing had appeared to justify the assertion. Lord Chatham again declared, "My words remain unretract-

of his own actions. It is, therefore, uncandid in the extreme to represent Lord Chatham as feigning illness in order to escape from the responsibilities of his station.

[13] Though Lord Chatham had a high sense of Mansfield's learning and abilities, he continued to regard him with aversion and distrust on account of his extreme Tory sentiments. In reply to Mansfield, when the case of Wilkes again came up at a late evening session, he quoted Lord Somers and Chief-justice Holt on the points of law, and drew their characters in his own masterly style. He pronounced them "*honest* men who knew and loved the Constitution." Then turning to Mansfield, he said, "I vow to God, I think the noble Lord equals them both—*in abilities!*" He complained bitterly, in conclusion, of the motion being pressed by Lord Marchmont and Lord Mansfield at so unreasonable an hour, and called for an adjournment. "If the Constitution must be wounded," said he, "let it not receive its mortal stab at this dark and midnight hour, when honest men are asleep in their beds, and when only felons and assassins are seeking for prey!"

ed, unexplained, and reaffirmed. I desire to know whether I am condemned or acquitted; and whether I may still presume to hold my head as high as the noble Lord who moved to have my words taken down." To this no answer was given. It was easy for the ministry to pass what vote they pleased; but they found that every attempt to disgrace such a man only recoiled on themselves. His glowing defense of the people's rights regained him the popularity he had lost by his accession to the peerage. The city of London addressed him in terms of grateful acknowledgment, thanking him for "the zeal he had shown in support of those most valuable privileges, the right of election and the right of petition." The people looked up to him again as their best and truest friend; and though promoted to an earldom, they felt, in the language of his grandson, Lord Mahon, "that his elevation over them was like that of Rochester Castle over his own shores of Chatham—that he was raised above them only for their protection and defense."

After this session, Lord Chatham was unable to attend upon Parliament except occasionally and at distant intervals. He spent his time chiefly on his estate at Burton Pynsent, superintending the education of his children, and mingling in their amusements with the liveliest pleasure, notwithstanding his many infirmities. He sought to interest them not only in their books, but in rural employments and rural scenery. He delighted in landscape gardening; and, in speaking of its fine arrangements for future effect, called it, with his usual felicity of expression, "the prophetic eye of Taste." "When his health would permit," says the tutor of his son, "he never suffered a day to pass without giving instruction of some sort to his children, and seldom without reading the Bible with them." He seems, indeed, to have studied the Scriptures with great care and attention from early life. He read them not only for the guidance of his faith, but for improvement in oratory. "Not content," says Lord Lyttleton, "to correct and instruct his imagination by the works of men, he borrowed his noblest images from the language of inspiration." His practice, in this respect, was imitated by Burke, Junius, and other distinguished writers of the day. At no period in later times, has secular eloquence gathered so many of her images and allusions from the pages of the Bible.

Thus withdrawn from the cares and labors of public life, there was only one subject that could ever induce him to appear in Parliament. It was the contest with America. He knew more of this country than any man in England except Burke. During the war in which he wrested Canada from the French, he was brought into the most intimate communication with the leading men of the colonies. He knew their spirit and the resources of the country. Two of the smallest states (Massachusetts and Connecticut) had, in answer to his call, raised *twelve thousand* men for that war in a single year. Feelings of personal attachment united, therefore, with a sense of justice, to make him the champion of America. Feeble and decrepit as he was, he forgot his age and sufferings. He stood forth, in presence of the whole empire, to arraign, as a breach of the Constitution, every attempt to tax a people who had no representatives in Parliament. It was the era of his sublimest efforts in oratory. With no private ends or party purposes to accomplish, with a consciousness of the exalted services he had rendered to his country, he spoke "as one having authority," and denounced the war with a prophetic sense of the shame and disaster attending such a conflict. His voice of warning was lost, indeed, upon the ministry and on the great body of the nation, who welcomed a relief from their burdens at the expense of America. But it rang throughout every town and hamlet of the colonies; and when he proclaimed in the ears of Parliament, "I rejoice that America has resisted," millions of hearts on the other side of the Atlantic swelled with a prouder determination to resist even to the end.[14]

[14] Lord Chatham received numerous tokens of respect and gratitude from the colonies. At

But while he thus acted as the champion of America, he never for a moment yielded to the thought of her separation from the mother country. When the Duke of Richmond, therefore, brought forward his motion, in April, 1778, advising the King to withdraw his fleets and armies, and to effect a conciliation with America involving her independence, Lord Chatham heard of his design "with unspeakable concern," and resolved to go once more to the House of Lords for the purpose of resisting the motion. The effort cost him his life. A detailed account of the scene presented on that occasion will be given hereafter, in connection with his speech. At the close, he sunk into the arms of his attendants, apparently in a dying state. He revived a little when conveyed to his dwelling; and, after lingering for a few days, died on the 11th of May, 1778, in the seventieth year of his age.

Lord Chatham has been generally regarded as the most powerful orator of modern times. He certainly ruled the British Senate as no other man has ever ruled over a great deliberative assembly. There have been stronger minds in that body, abler reasoners, profounder statesmen, but no man has ever controlled it with such absolute sway by the force of his eloquence. He did things which no human being but himself would ever have attempted. He carried through triumphantly, what would have covered any other man with ridicule and disgrace.

His success, no doubt, was owing, in part, to his extraordinary personal advantages. Few men have ever received from the hand of Nature so many of the outward qualifications of an orator. In his best days, before he was crippled by the gout, his figure was tall and erect; his attitude imposing; his gestures energetic even to vehemence, yet tempered with dignity and grace.[15] Such was the power of his eye, that he very often cowed down an antagonist in the midst of his speech, and threw him into utter confusion, by a single glance of scorn or contempt. Whenever he rose to speak, his countenance glowed with animation, and was lighted up with all the varied emotions of his soul, so that Cowper describes him, in one of his bursts of patriotic feeling,

"With all his country beaming in his face."

"His voice," says a contemporary, "was both full and clear. His lowest whisper was distinctly heard; his middle notes were sweet and beautifully varied; and, when he elevated his voice to its highest pitch, the House was completely filled with the volume of sound. The effect was awful, except when he wished to cheer or animate; then he had spirit-stirring notes which were perfectly irresistible." The prevailing character of his delivery was majesty and force. "The crutch in his hand became a weapon of oratory."[16]

Much, however, as he owed to these personal advantages, it was his character as

Charleston, S. C., a colossal statue of him, in white marble, was erected by order of the Commons, who say, in their inscription upon the pedestal,

TIME
SHALL SOONER DESTROY
THIS MARK OF THEIR ESTEEM,
THAN
ERASE FROM THEIR MINDS
THE JUST SENSE
OF HIS PATRIOTIC VIRTUE.

15 Lord Brougham speaks of him as having "a peculiarly defective and even awkward action." This is directly opposed to the testimony of all his contemporaries. Hugh Boyd speaks of "the persuasive gracefulness of his action;" and Lord Orford says, that his action, on many occasions, was worthy of Garrick. The *younger* Pitt had an awkwardness of the kind referred to; and Lord Brougham, who was often hasty and incorrect, probably confounded the father and the son.

16 Telum Oratoris.—Cicero. "You talk, my Lords, of conquering America; of your numerous friends there to annihilate the Congress; of your powerful forces to disperse her armies; *I might as well talk of driving them before me with this crutch.*"

a man which gave him his surprising ascendency over the minds of his countrymen. There was a fascination for all hearts in his lofty bearing; his generous sentiments; his comprehensive policy; his grand conceptions of the height to which England might be raised as arbiter of Europe; his preference of her honor over all inferior *material* interests. There was a fascination, too, for the hearts of all who loved freedom, in that intense spirit of liberty which was the animating principle of his life. From the day when he opposed Sir Charles Wager's bill for breaking open private houses to press seamen, declaring that he would *shoot* any man, even an officer of justice, who should thus enter his dwelling, he stood forth, to the end of his days, the Defender of the People's Rights. It was no vain ostentation of liberal principles, no idle pretense to gain influence or office. The nation saw it; and while Pulteney's defection brought disgrace on the name of "Patriot," the character of Pitt stood higher than ever in the public estimation. His political integrity, no less than his eloquence, formed "an era in the Senate;" and that comparative elevation of principle which we now find among English politicians, dates back for its commencement to his noble example. It was his glory as a statesman, not that he was always in the right, or even consistent with himself upon minor points; but that, in an age of shameless profligacy, when political principle was universally laughed at, and every one, in the words of Walpole, "had his price," he stood forth to "stem the torrent of a downward age." He could truly say to an opponent, as the great Athenian orator did to Æschines, 'Εγὼ *δή σοι λέγω, ὅτι τῶν πολιτευομένων παρὰ τοῖς* "Ελλησι *διαφθαρέντων ἁπάντων, ἀρξαμένων ἀπὸ σοῦ, πρότερον μὲν ὑπὸ Φιλίππου, νῦν δ' ὑπ'* 'Αλεξάνδρου, *ἐμὲ οὔτε καιρὸς, οὔτε φιλανθρωπία λόγων, οὔτε ἐπαγγελιῶν μέγεθος, οὔτ' ἐλπὶς, οὔτε φόβος, οὔτε χάρις, οὔτ' ἄλλο οὐδὲν ἐπῆρεν, οὐδὲ προηγάγετο, ὧν ἔκρινα δικαίων καὶ συμφερόντων τῇ πατρίδι, οὐδὲν προδοῦναι*: "When all our statesmen, beginning with yourself, were corrupted by bribes or office, no convenience of opportunity, or insinuation of address, or magnificence of promises—or hope, or fear, or favor—could induce me to give up for a moment what I considered the rights and interests of the people." Even his enemies were forced to pay homage to his noble assertion of his principles—his courage, his frankness, his perfect sincerity. Eloquent as he was, he impressed every hearer with the conviction, that there was in him something higher than all eloquence. "Every one felt," says a contemporary, "that the man was infinitely greater than the orator." Even Franklin lost his coolness when speaking of Lord Chatham. "I have sometimes," said he, "seen eloquence without wisdom, and often wisdom without eloquence; but in him I have seen them united in the highest possible degree."

The range of his powers as a speaker was uncommonly wide. He was equally qualified to conciliate and subdue. When he saw fit, no man could be more plausible and ingratiating; no one had ever a more winning address, or was more adroit in obviating objections and allaying prejudice. When he changed his tone, and chose rather to subdue, he had the sharpest and most massy weapons at command—wit, humor, irony, overwhelming ridicule and contempt. His *forte* was the terrible; and he employed with equal ease the indirect mode of attack with which he so often tortured Lord Mansfield, and the open, withering invective with which he trampled down Lord Suffolk. His burst of astonishment and horror at the proposal of the latter to let loose the Indians on the settlers of America, is without a parallel in our language for severity and force. In all such conflicts, the energy of his will and his boundless self-confidence secured him the victory. Never did that "erect countenance" sink before the eye of an antagonist. Never was he known to hesitate or falter. He had a feeling of superiority over every one around him, which acted on his mind with the force of an inspiration. He *knew* he was right! He *knew* he could save England, and that no one else could do it! Such a spirit, in great crises, is the unfailing instrument of command both to the general and the orator. We may call it arrogance; but even arrogance here operates upon most minds with the potency of a charm; and when united to a vigor of genius and a firmness of purpose like his, men of the strongest intellect fall down before it, and admire—perhaps hate—what they can not resist.

The leading characteristic of eloquence is *force;* and force in the orator depends mainly on the action of strongly-excited feeling on a powerful intellect. The intellect of Chatham was of the highest order, and was peculiarly fitted for the broad and rapid combinations of oratory. It was at once comprehensive, acute, and vigorous; enabling him to embrace the largest range of thought; to see at a glance what most men labor out by slow degrees; and to grasp his subject with a vigor, and hold on to it with a firmness, which have rarely, if ever, been equaled. But his intellect never acted alone. It was impossible for him to speak on any subject in a dry or abstract manner; all the operations of his mind were pervaded and governed by intense feeling. This gave rise to certain characteristics of his eloquence which may here be mentioned.

First, he did not, like many in modern times, divide a speech into distinct copartments, one designed to convince the understanding, and another to move the passions and the will. They were too closely united in his own mind to allow of such a separation. All went together, conviction and persuasion, intellect and feeling, like chain-shot.

Secondly, the rapidity and abruptness with which he often flashed his thoughts upon the mind arose from the same source. Deep emotion strikes directly at its object. It struggles to get free from all secondary ideas—all mere accessories. Hence the simplicity, and even bareness of thought, which we usually find in the great passages of Chatham and Demosthenes. The whole turns often on a single phrase, a word, an allusion. They put forward a few great objects, sharply defined, and standing boldly out in the glowing atmosphere of emotion. They pour their burning thoughts instantaneously upon the mind, as a person might catch the rays of the sun in a concave mirror, and turn them on their object with a sudden and consuming power.

Thirdly, his mode of reasoning, or, rather, of dispensing with the forms of argument, resulted from the same cause. It is not the fact, though sometimes said, that Lord Chatham never reasoned. In most of his early speeches, and in some of his later ones, especially those on the right of taxing America, we find many examples of argument; brief, indeed, but remarkably clear and stringent. It is true, however, that he endeavored, as far as possible, to escape from the trammels of formal reasoning. When the mind is all a-glow with a subject, and sees its conclusions with the vividness and certainty of intuitive truths, it is impatient of the slow process of logical deduction. It seeks rather to reach the point by a bold and rapid progress, throwing away the intermediate steps, and putting the subject *at once* under such aspects and relations as to carry its own evidence along with it. Demosthenes was remarkable for thus crushing together proof and statement in a single mass. When, for example, he calls on his judges, *μὴ τὸν ἀντίδικον σύμβουλον ποιήσασθαι περὶ τοῦ πῶς ἀκούειν ὑμᾶς ἐμοῦ δεῖ*, 'not to make his enemy their counselor as to the manner in which they should hear his reply,' there is an argument involved in the very ideas brought together—in the juxtaposition of the words *ἀντίδικον* and *σύμβουλον*—an argument the more forcible because not drawn out in a regular form. It was so with Lord Chatham. The strength of his feelings bore him directly forward to the *results* of argument. He affirmed them earnestly, positively; not as mere assertions, but on the ground of their intrinsic evidence and certainty. John Foster has finely remarked, that "Lord Chatham struck on the results of reasoning as a cannon-shot strikes the mark, without your seeing its course through the air." Perhaps a *bomb-shell* would have furnished even a better illustration. It explodes when it strikes, and thus becomes the most powerful of *arguments*.

Fourthly, this ardor of feeling, in connection with his keen penetration of mind, made him often indulge in political prophecy. His predictions were, in many instances, surprisingly verified. We have already seen it in the case of Admiral Hawke's victory, and in his quick foresight of a war with Spain in 1762. Eight years after, in the midst of a profound peace, he declared to the House of Lords that the inveterate enemies of England were, at the moment he spoke, striking "a blow of hostility" at her possessions in some quarter of the globe. News arrived at the end of four months that the Spanish governor of Buenos Ayres was, at that very time, in the act of seizing the Falkland Islands, and expelling the English. When this prediction was afterward referred to in Parliament, he remarked, "I will tell these young ministers the true secret of intelligence. It is sagacity—sagacity to compare causes and effects; to judge of the present state of things, and discern the future by a careful review of the past. Oliver Cromwell, who astonished mankind by his intelligence, did not derive it from spies in the cabinet of every prince in Europe; he drew it from the cabinet of his own sagacious mind." As he advanced in years, his tone of admonition, especially on American affairs, became more and more lofty and oracular. He spoke as no other man ever spoke in a great deliberative assembly—as one who felt that the time of his departure was at hand; who, withdrawn from the ordinary concerns of life, in the words of his great eulogist, "came *occasionally* into our system to *counsel and decide*."

Fifthly, his great preponderance of feeling made him, in the strictest sense of the term, an extemporaneous speaker. His mind was, indeed, richly furnished with thought upon every subject which came up for debate, and the matter he brought forward was always thoroughly matured and strikingly appropriate; but he seems never to have studied its arrangement, much less to have bestowed any care on the language, imagery, or illustrations. Every thing fell into its place at the moment. He poured out his thoughts and feelings just as they arose in his mind; and hence, on one occasion, when dispatches had been received which could not safely be made public, he said to one of his colleagues, "I must not speak to day; I shall let out the secret." It is also worthy of remark, that nearly all these great passages, which came with such startling power upon the House, arose out of some unexpected turn of the debate, some incident or expression which called forth, at the moment, these sudden bursts of eloquence. In his attack on Lord Suffolk, he caught a single glance at "the tapestry which adorned the walls" around him, and one flash of his genius gave us the most magnificent passage in our eloquence. His highest power lay in these sudden bursts of passion. To call them *hits*, with Lord Brougham, is beneath their dignity and force. "They form," as his Lordship justly observes, "the grand charm of Lord Chatham's oratory; they were the distinguishing excellence of his great predecessor, and gave him at will to wield the fierce democratie of Athens and to fulmine over Greece."

To this intense emotion, thus actuating all his powers, Lord Chatham united a vigorous and lofty imagination, which formed his crowning excellence as an orator. It is this faculty which exalts *force* into the truest and most sublime eloquence. In this respect he approached more nearly than any speaker of modern times, to the great master of Athenian art. It was here, chiefly, that he surpassed Mr. Fox, who was not at all his inferior in ardor of feeling or robust vigor of intellect. Mr. Burke had even more imagination, but it was wild and irregular. It was too often on the wing, circling around the subject, as if to display the grace of its movements or the beauty of its plumage. The imagination of Lord Chatham struck directly at its object. It "flew an eagle flight, forth and right on." It never became his master. Nor do we ever find it degenerating into *fancy*, in the limited sense of that term: it was never *fanciful*. It was, in fact, so perfectly blended with the other powers of his mind—so simple, so true to nature even in its loftiest flights—that we rarely think of it as imagination at all.

The style and language of Lord Chatham are not to be judged of by the early speeches in this volume, down to 1743. Reporters at that day made little or no attempt to give the exact words of a speaker. They sought only to convey his sentiments, though they might occasionally be led, in writing out his speeches, to catch some of his marked peculiarities of thought or expression. In 1766, his speech against the American Stamp Act was reported, with a considerable degree of verbal accuracy, by Sir Robert Dean, aided by Lord Charlemont. Much, however, was obviously omitted; and passages having an admirable felicity of expression were strangely intermingled with tame and broken sentences, showing how imperfectly they had succeeded in giving the precise language of the speaker. Five speeches (to be mentioned hereafter) were written out, from notes taken on the spot by Sir Philip Francis and Mr. Hugh Boyd. One of them is said to have been revised by Lord Chatham himself. These are the best specimens we possess of his style and diction; and it would be difficult, in the whole range of our literature, to find more perfect models for the study and imitation of the young orator. The words are admirably chosen. The sentences are not rounded or balanced periods, but are made up of short clauses, which flash themselves upon the mind with all the vividness of distinct ideas, and yet are closely connected together as tending to the same point, and uniting to form larger masses of thought. Nothing can be more easy, varied, and natural than the style of these speeches. There is no mannerism about them. They contain some of the most vehement passages in English oratory; and yet there is no appearance of effort, no straining after effect. They have this infallible mark of genius—they make every one feel, that if placed in like circumstances, he would have said exactly the same things in the same manner. "Upon the whole," in the words of Mr. Grattan, "there was in this man something that could create, subvert, or reform; an understanding, a spirit, and an eloquence to summon mankind to society, or to break the bonds of slavery asunder, and rule the wildness of free minds with unbounded authority; something that could establish or overwhelm empire, and strike a blow in the world that should resound through its history."

SPEECH

OF LORD CHATHAM ON A MOTION FOR AN ADDRESS ON THE MARRIAGE OF THE PRINCE OF WALES, DELIVERED IN THE HOUSE OF COMMONS, APRIL, 29, 1736.

INTRODUCTION.

THIS was Mr. Pitt's maiden speech; and, literally understood, it is a mere string of courtly compliments, expressed in elegant diction. But it seems plainly to have had a deeper meaning. The King, who was extremely irritable, had quarreled with the Prince of Wales, and treated him with great severity. There was an open breach between them. They could not even speak to each other; and although the King desired the marriage, he would not allow the usual Address of Congratulation to be brought in by his ministers. In view of this extraordinary departure from established usage, and the feelings which it indicated on the King's part, Mr. Pitt's emphatic commendations of the young prince have a peculiar significance; while the manner in which he speaks of "the tender, paternal delight" which the King *must* feel in yielding to "the most dutiful application" of his son, has an air of the keenest irony. Viewed in this light, the speech shows great tact and talent in asserting the cause of the Prince, and goading the feelings of the King, in language of the highest respect—the very language which could alone be appropriate to such an occasion.

SPEECH, &c.

I am unable, sir, to offer any thing suitable to the dignity and importance of the subject, which has not already been said by my honorable friend who made the motion. But I am so affected with the prospect of the blessings to be derived by my country from this most desirable, this long-desired measure—the marriage of his Royal Highness the Prince of Wales—that I can not forbear troubling the House with a few words expressive of my joy. I can not help mingling my offering, inconsiderable as it is, with this oblation of thanks and congratulation to His Majesty.

However great, sir, the joy of the public may be—and great undoubtedly it is—in receiving this benefit from his Majesty, it must yet be inferior to that high satisfaction which he himself enjoys in bestowing it. If I may be allowed to suppose that any thing in a royal mind can transcend the pleasure of gratifying the earnest wishes of a loyal people, it can only be the tender, paternal delight of indulging the most dutiful application, the most humble request, of a submissive and obedient son. I mention, sir, his Royal Highness's having asked a marriage, because something is in justice due to him for having asked what we are so strongly bound, by all the ties of duty and gratitude, to return his Majesty our humble acknowledgments for having granted.

The marriage of a Prince of Wales, sir, has at all times been a matter of the highest importance to the public welfare, to present and to future generations. But at no time (if a character at once amiable and respectable can embellish, and even dignify, the elevated rank of a Prince of Wales) has it been a more important, dearer consideration than at this day. Were it not a sort of presumption to follow so great a personage through his hours of retirement, to view him in the milder light of domestic life, we should find him engaged in the noblest exercise of humanity, benevolence, and every social virtue. But, sir, however pleasing, however captivating such a scene may be, yet, as it is a private one, I fear I should offend the delicacy of that virtue to which I so ardently desire to do justice, were I to offer it to the consideration of this House. But, sir, filial duty to his royal parents, a generous love of liberty, and a just reverence for the British Constitution—these are public virtues, and can not escape the applause and benedictions of the public. These are virtues, sir, which render his Royal Highness not only a noble ornament, but a firm support, if any could possibly be wanting, of that throne so greatly filled by his royal father.

I have been led to say thus much of his Royal Highness's character, because it is the consideration of that character which, above all things, enforces the justice and goodness of his Majesty in the measure now before us—a measure which the nation thought could never be taken too soon, because it brings with it the promise of an additional strength to the Protestant succession in his Majesty's illustrious and royal house. The spirit of liberty dictated that succession; the same spirit now rejoices in the prospect of its being perpetuated to the latest posterity. It rejoices in the wise and happy choice which his Majesty has been pleased to make of a princess so amiably distinguished in herself, so illustrious in the merit of her family, the glory of whose great ancestor it is to have sacrificed himself in the noblest cause for which a prince can draw a sword—the cause of liberty and the Protestant religion.

Such, sir, is the marriage for which our most

humble acknowledgments are due to his Majesty. May it afford the comfort of seeing the royal family, numerous as, I thank God, it is, still growing and rising up into a third generation! A family, sir, which I most earnestly hope may be as immortal as those liberties and that constitution which they came to maintain. Sir, I am heartily for the motion.

The motion was unanimously agreed to.

SPEECH

OF LORD CHATHAM ON THE SPANISH CONVENTION, DELIVERED IN THE HOUSE OF COMMONS MARCH 8, 1739.

INTRODUCTION.

Difficulties had arisen between England and Spain, from the measures adopted by the latter to suppress an illicit trade carried on by English adventurers with the coast of South America. The Spanish cruisers searched British merchantmen found in that quarter, and in so doing, either through mistake or design, committed outrages to a considerable extent upon lawful traders. Exaggerated accounts of these outrages were circulated throughout England. The public mind became greatly inflamed on the subject, and many went so far as to contend that the British flag covered her merchant ships and protected them from search under all circumstances.

Walpole opened a negotiation with the Court of Madrid for the redress and removal of these grievances. After due examination, the just claims of the English merchants upon Spain were set down at £200,000. On the other hand, the sum of £60,000 was now adjudged, under the stipulations of a former treaty, to be due from England to Spain, for captures made in 1718 by Admiral Byng. The balance due to England was thus settled at £140,000; and Walpole, to avoid the usual delay of the Spaniards in money matters, offered to make an abatement of £45,000 for prompt payment, thus reducing the entire amount to £95,000. To this the Spanish government gave their assent, but on the express condition that this arrangement should be considered as in no way affecting certain claims of Spain on the English South Sea Company.

As the result of this negotiation, a *Convention* was drawn up on the 14th of January, 1739, stipulating for the payment of £95,000 within four months from the exchange of ratifications. It also provided for the removal of all remaining difficulties, by agreeing that commissioners from England and Spain should meet within six weeks, to adjust all questions respecting trade between Europe and the colonies in America; and also to establish the boundary lines between Florida and the English settlements in Carolina, then embracing Georgia. It further stipulated that, during the sitting of this commission, the erection of fortifications should be suspended, both in Carolina and Florida. At the moment when this Convention was to be signed, the Spanish government gave notice, that as the South Sea Company was not embraced in this arrangement, the King of Spain held them to be his debtors to the amount of £68,000, for his share of the profits they had realized under previous engagements; and that, unless payment was made within a specified time, he would deprive them of the *Assiento*, or contract, which he had granted them for supplying South America with slaves. Such were the provisions of the famous Spanish Convention, and the circumstances under which it was signed.

The House of Commons appointed March 6th, 1739, for considering this Convention. The public mind was greatly agitated on the subject. There was a general outcry against it, as betraying at once the interests of the merchants and the honor of the country. Such was the excitement and expectation when the day arrived, that four hundred members took their seats in the House at 8 o'clock A.M., five hours before the time appointed for entering upon business. Two days were spent in examining witnesses and hearing numerous written documents relating to the subject. On the 8th of March, Mr. Horace Walpole, brother to the minister, after a long and able speech, moved in substance that "the House return thanks to his Majesty for communicating the Convention; for having taken measures to obtain speedy payment for the losses sustained by the merchants; and also for removing similar abuses in future, and preserving a lasting peace." After a number of members had expressed their views, Mr. Pitt rose and delivered the following speech, which gave him at once, and at the age of thirty, that ascendency as a speaker in the House of Commons which he afterward maintained.

SPEECH, &c.

Sir,—There certainly has never been in Parliament a matter of more high national concern than the Convention referred to the consideration of this committee; and, give me leave to say, there can not be a more indirect manner of taking the sense of the committee upon it than by the complicated question that is now before you.

We have here the soft name of an humble address to the Throne proposed, and for no other end than to lead gentlemen into an approbation of the Convention. Is this that full, deliberate examination, which we were with defiance called upon to give to this Convention? Is this cursory, blended disquisition of matters of such variety and extent, all that we owe to ourselves and to our country? When trade is at stake, it is your last intrenchment; you must defend it or perish; and whatever is to decide *that*, deserves the most distinct consideration, and the most direct, undisguised sense of Parliament. But how are we now proceeding? Upon an artificial, ministerial question. Here is all the confidence, here is the conscious sense of the greatest service that ever was done to this country![1] to be complicating questions, to be lumping sanction and approbation, like a commissary's account! to be covering and taking sanctuary in the royal name, instead of meeting openly, and standing fairly, the direct judgment and sentence of Parliament upon the several articles of this Convention.

You have been moved to vote an humble address of thanks to his Majesty for a measure which (I will appeal to gentlemen's conversation in the world) is odious throughout the kingdom. Such thanks are only due to the fatal influence that framed it, as are due for that low, unallied condition abroad which is now made a plea for this Convention.

To what are gentlemen reduced in support of it? They first try a little to defend it upon its own merits; if that is not tenable, they throw out general terrors—the House of Bourbon is united, who knows the consequence of a war? Sir, Spain knows the consequence of a war in America. Whoever gains, it must prove fatal to her. She knows it, and must therefore avoid it; but she knows that England does not dare to make it. And what is a delay, which is all this magnified Convention is sometimes called, to produce? Can it produce such conjunctures as those which you lost while you were giving kingdoms to Spain, and all to bring her back again to that great branch of the house of Bourbon which is now held out to you as an object of so much terror? If this union be formidable, are we to delay only till it becomes more formidable, by being carried farther into execution, and by being more strongly cemented? But be it what it will, *is this any longer a nation?* Is this any longer an English Parliament, if, with more ships in your harbors than in all the navies of Europe; with above two millions of people in your American colonies, you will bear to hear of the expediency of receiving from Spain an insecure, unsatisfactory, dishonorable Convention? Sir, I call it no more than it has been proved in this debate; it carries fallacy or downright subjection in almost every line. It has been laid open and exposed in so many strong and glaring lights, that I can not pretend to add any thing to the conviction and indignation which it has raised.

Sir, as to the great national objection, the searching of your ships, that favorite word, as it was called, is not, indeed, omitted in the preamble to the Convention, but it stands there as the reproach of the whole, as the strongest evidence of the fatal submission that follows. On the part of Spain, a usurpation, an inhuman tyranny, claimed and exercised over the American seas; on the part of England, an undoubted right by treaties, and from God and nature declared and asserted in the resolutions of Parliament, are referred to the discussion of plenipotentiaries upon one and the same equal footing! Sir, I say this undoubted right is to be *discussed* and to be *regulated!* And if to regulate be to prescribe rules (as in all construction it is), this right is, by the express words of this Convention, to be given up and sacrificed; for it must cease to be any thing from the moment it is submitted to limits.

The court of Spain has plainly told you (as appears by papers upon the table), that you shall steer a due course, that you shall navigate by a line to and from your plantations in America—if you draw near to her coast (though, from the circumstances of the navigation, you are under an unavoidable necessity of doing so), you shall be seized and confiscated. If, then, upon these terms only she has consented to refer, what becomes at once of all the security we are flattered with in consequence of this reference? Plenipotentiaries are to regulate finally the respective pretensions of the two crowns with regard to trade and navigation in America; but does a man in Spain reason that these pretensions must be regulated to the satisfaction and honor of England? No, sir, they conclude, and with reason, from the high spirit of their administration, from the superiority with which they have so long treated you, that this reference must end, as it has begun, to their honor and advantage.

But, gentlemen say, the treaties subsisting are to be the measure of this regulation. Sir, as to treaties, I will take part of the words of Sir William Temple, quoted by the honorable gentleman near me; *it is vain to negotiate and to make treaties, if there is not dignity and vigor sufficient to enforce their observance.* Under the misconstruction and misrepresentation of these very treaties subsisting, this intolerable grievance has arisen. It has been growing upon you, treaty after treaty, through twenty years of negotiation, and even under the discussion of commissaries, to whom it was referred. You have heard from Captain Vaughan, at your bar, at what time these injuries and indignities were continued. As a kind of explanatory comment upon this Convention which Spain has thought fit to grant you, as another insolent protest, under the validity and force of which she has suffered this Convention to be proceeded upon, she seems to say, "We will treat with you, but we will search and take your ships; we will sign a Convention, but we will keep your subjects prisoners in Old Spain; the West Indies are remote; Europe shall witness in what manner we use you."

Sir, as to the inference of an admission of our right not to be searched, drawn from a reparation made for ships unduly seized and confis-

[1] Alluding to the extravagant terms of praise in which Mr. H. Walpole had spoken of the Convention, and of those who framed it.

cated, I think that argument very inconclusive. The right claimed by Spain to search our ships is one thing, and the excesses admitted to have been committed in consequence of this pretended right is another. But surely, sir, to reason from inference and implication only, is below the dignity of your proceedings upon a right of this vast importance. What this reparation is, what sort of composition for your losses forced upon you by Spain, in an instance that has come to light, where your own commissaries could not in conscience decide against your claim, has fully appeared upon examination; and as for the payment of the sum stipulated (all but seven-and-twenty thousand pounds, and that, too, subject to a drawback), it is evidently a fallacious nominal payment only. I will not attempt to enter into the detail of a dark, confused, and scarcely intelligible account; I will only beg leave to conclude with one word upon it, in the light of a submission as well as of an adequate reparation. Spain stipulates to pay to the Crown of England ninety-five thousand pounds; by a preliminary protest of the King of Spain, the South Sea Company is at once to pay sixty-eight thousand of it: if they refuse, Spain, I admit, is still to pay the ninety-five thousand pounds; but how does it stand then? The Assiento Contract is to be suspended. You are to purchase this sum at the price of an exclusive trade, pursuant to a national treaty, and of an immense debt of God knows how many hundred thousand pounds, due from Spain to the South Sea Company. Here, sir, is the submission of Spain by the payment of a stipulated sum; a tax laid upon subjects of England, under the severest penalties, with the reciprocal accord of an English minister as a preliminary that the Convention may be signed; a condition imposed by Spain in the most absolute, imperious manner, and most tamely and abjectly received by the ministers of England. Can any verbal distinctions, any evasions whatever, possibly explain away this public infamy? To whom would we disguise it? To ourselves and to the nation! I wish we could hide it from the eyes of every court in Europe. They see that Spain has talked to you like your master. They see this arbitrary fundamental condition standing forth with a pre-eminence of shame, as a part of this very Convention.

This Convention, sir, I think from my soul, is nothing but a stipulation for national ignominy; an illusory expedient to baffle the resentment of the nation; a truce, without a suspension of hostilities, on the part of Spain; on the part of England, a suspension, as to Georgia, of the first law of nature, self-preservation and self-defense; a surrender of the rights and trade of England to the mercy of plenipotentiaries, and, in this infinitely highest and most sacred point—future security—not only inadequate, but directly repugnant to the resolutions of Parliament and the gracious promise from the Throne. The complaints of your despairing merchants, and the voice of England, have condemned it. Be the guilt of it upon the head of the adviser: God forbid that this committee should share the guilt by approving it!

The motion was carried by a very small majority, the vote being 260 to 232. Mr. Burke's statement respecting the merits of this question, as it afterward appeared, even to those who took the most active part against the Convention, may be found in his Regicide Peace. Whether Lord Chatham was one of the persons referred to by Mr. Burke as having changed their views, does not appear, but it is rather presumed not.

SPEECH

OF LORD CHATHAM AGAINST SEARCH-WARRANTS FOR SEAMEN, DELIVERED IN THE HOUSE OF COMMONS, MARCH 6, 1741.

INTRODUCTION.

War was declared against Spain in October, 1739, and it soon became extremely difficult to man the British fleets. Hence a bill was brought forward by Sir Charles Wager, in January, 1741, conferring authority on Justices of the Peace to issue search-warrants, under which constables might enter private dwellings either by day or by night—and, if need be, might force the doors—for the purpose of discovering seamen, and impressing them into the public service. So gross an act of injustice awakened the indignation of Mr. Pitt, who poured out the following invective against the measure, and those who were endeavoring to force it on the House.

SPEECH, &c.

Sir,—The two honorable and learned gentlemen[1] who spoke in favor of this clause, were pleased to show that our seamen are half slaves already, and now they modestly desire you should make them *wholly so.* Will this increase your number of seamen? or will it make those you have more willing to serve you? Can you expect that any man will make himself a slave if he can avoid it? Can you expect that any man will breed his child up to be a slave? Can you expect that seamen will venture their lives or their limbs for a country that has made them slaves?

[1] The Attorney and Solicitor General, Sir Dudley Ryder and Sir John Strange. The former was subsequently Lord Chief Justice of the King's Bench, and the latter Master of the Rolls.

or can you expect that any seaman will stay in the country, if he can by any means make his escape? Sir, if you pass this law, you must, in my opinion, do with your seamen as they do with their galley-slaves in France—you must chain them to their ships, or chain them in couples when they are ashore. But suppose this should both increase the number of your seamen, and render them more willing to serve you, it will render them incapable. It is a common observation, that when a man becomes a slave, he loses half his virtue. What will it signify to have your ships all manned to their full complement? Your men will have neither the courage nor the temptation to fight; they will strike to the first enemy that attacks them, because their condition can not be made worse by a surrender. Our seamen have always been famous for a matchless alacrity and intrepidity in time of danger; this has saved many a British ship, when other seamen would have run below deck, and left the ship to the mercy of the waves, or, perhaps, of a more cruel enemy, a pirate. For God's sake, sir, let us not, by our new projects, put our seamen into such a condition as must soon make them worse than the cowardly slaves of France or Spain.

The learned gentlemen were next pleased to show us that the government were already possessed of such a power as is now desired. And how did they show it? Why, sir, by showing that this was the practice in the case of felony, and in the case of those who are as bad as felons, I mean those who rob the public, or dissipate the public money. Shall we, sir, put our brave sailors upon the same footing with felons and public robbers? Shall a brave, honest sailor be treated as a felon, for no other reason but because, after a long voyage, he has a mind to solace himself among his friends in the country, and for that purpose absconds for a few weeks, in order to prevent his being pressed upon a Spithead, or some such pacific expedition? For I dare answer for it, there is not a sailor in Britain but would immediately offer his services, if he thought his country in any real danger, or expected to be sent upon an expedition where he might have a chance of gaining riches to himself and glory to his country. I am really ashamed, sir, to hear such arguments made use of in any case where our seamen are concerned. Can we expect that brave men will not resent such treatment? Could we expect they would stay with us, if we should make a law for treating them in such a contemptible manner?

But suppose, sir, we had no regard for our seamen, I hope we shall have some regard for the rest of the people, and for ourselves in particular; for I think I do not in the least exaggerate when I say, we are laying a trap for the lives of all the men of spirit in the nation. Whether the law, when made, is to be carried into execution, I do not know; but if it is, we are laying a snare for our own lives. Every gentleman of this House must be supposed, I hope justly, to be a man of spirit. Would any of you, gentlemen, allow this law to be executed in its full extent? If, at midnight, a petty constable, with a press-gang, should come thundering at the gates of your house in the country, and should tell you he had a search-warrant, and must search your house for seamen, would you at that time of night allow your gates to be opened? I protest I would not. What, then, would be the consequence? He has by this law a power to break them open. Would any of you patiently submit to such an indignity? Would not you fire upon him, if he attempted to break open your gates? I declare I would, let the consequence be never so fatal; and if you happened to be in the bad graces of a minister, the consequence would be your being either killed in the fray, or hanged for killing the constable or some of his gang. This, sir, may be the case of even some of us here; and, upon my honor, I do not think it an exaggeration to suppose it may.

The honorable gentlemen say no other remedy has been proposed. Sir, there have been several other remedies proposed. Let us go into a committee to consider of what has been, or may be proposed. Suppose no other remedy should be offered: to tell us we must take this, because no other remedy can be thought of, is the same with a physician's telling his patient, "Sir, there is no known remedy for your distemper, therefore you shall take poison—I'll cram it down your throat." I do not know how the nation may treat its physicians; but, I am sure, if my physician told me so, I should order my servants to turn him out of doors.

Such desperate remedies, sir, are never to be applied but in cases of the utmost extremity, and how we come at present to be in such extremity I can not comprehend. In the time of Queen Elizabeth we were not thought to be in any such extremity, though we were then threatened with the most formidable invasion that was ever prepared against this nation. In our wars with the Dutch, a more formidable maritime power than France and Spain now would be, if they were united against us, we were not supposed to be in any such extremity, either in the time of the Commonwealth or of King Charles the Second. In King William's war against France, when her naval power was vastly superior to what it is at present, and when we had more reason to be afraid of an invasion than we can have at present, we were thought to be in no such extremity. In Queen Anne's time, when we were engaged in a war both against France and Spain, and were obliged to make great levies yearly for the land service, no such remedy was ever thought of, except for one year only, and then it was found to be far from being effectual.

This, sir, I am convinced, would be the case now, as well as it was then. It was at that time computed that, by means of such a law as this, there were not above fourteen hundred seamen brought into the service of the government; and, considering the methods that have been already taken, and the reward proposed by this bill to be offered to volunteers, I am convinced that the most strict and general search would not bring in half the number. Shall we, then, for the sake of adding six or seven hundred, or even fourteen hundred seamen to his Majesty's navy, expose our Constitution to so much danger, and every housekeeper in the kingdom to the danger of being disturbed at all hours in the night?

But suppose this law were to have a great effect, it can be called nothing but a temporary expedient, because it can in no way contribute toward increasing the number of our seamen, or toward rendering them more willing to enter into his Majesty's service. It is an observation made by Bacon upon the laws passed in Henry the Seventh's reign, that all of them were calculated for futurity as well as the present time.[2] This showed the wisdom of his councils; I wish I could say so of our present. We have for some years thought of nothing but expedients for getting rid of some present inconvenience by running ourselves into a greater. The ease or convenience of posterity was never less thought of, I believe, than it has been of late years. I wish I could see an end of these temporary expedients; for we have been pursuing them so long, that we have almost undone our country and overturned our Constitution. Therefore, sir, I shall be for leaving this clause out of the bill, and every other clause relating to it. The bill will be of some service without them; and when we have passed it, we may then go into a committee to consider of some lasting methods for increasing our stock of seamen, and for encouraging them upon all occasions to enter into his Majesty's service.

In consequence of these remarks, all the clauses relating to search-warrants were ultimately struck out of the bill.

It was during this debate that the famous altercation took place between Mr. Pitt and Horatio Walpole, in which the latter endeavored to put down the young orator by representing him as having too little experience to justify his discussing such subjects, and charging him with "petulancy of invective," "pompous diction," and "theatrical emotion." The substance of Mr. Pitt's reply was reported to Johnson, who wrote it out in his own language, forming one of the most bitter retorts in English oratory. It has been so long connected with the name of Mr. Pitt, that the reader would regret its omission in this work. It is therefore given below, not as a specimen of his style, which was exactly the reverse of the sententious manner and balanced periods of Johnson, but as a general exhibition of the sentiments which he expressed.

REPLY

OF LORD CHATHAM WHEN ATTACKED BY HORATIO WALPOLE, DELIVERED MARCH 6, 1741.

SIR,—The atrocious crime of being a young man, which the honorable gentleman has, with such spirit and decency, charged upon me, I shall neither attempt to palliate nor deny, but content myself with wishing that I may be one of those whose follies may cease with their youth, and not of that number who are ignorant in spite of experience. Whether youth can be imputed to any man as a reproach, I will not, sir, assume the province of determining; but surely age may become justly contemptible, if the opportunities which it brings have passed away without improvement, and vice appears to prevail when the passions have subsided. The wretch who, after having seen the consequences of a thousand errors, continues still to blunder, and whose age has only added obstinacy to stupidity, is surely the object of either abhorrence or contempt, and deserves not that his gray hairs should secure him from insult. Much more, sir, is he to be abhorred, who, as he has advanced in age, has receded from virtue, and becomes more wicked with less temptation; who prostitutes himself for money which he can not enjoy, and spends the remains of his life in the ruin of his country. But youth, sir, is not my only crime; I have been accused of acting a theatrical part. A theatrical part may either imply some peculiarities of gesture, or a dissimulation of my real sentiments, and an adoption of the opinions and language of another man.

In the first sense, sir, the charge is too trifling to be confuted, and deserves only to be mentioned to be despised. I am at liberty, like every other man, to use my own language; and though, perhaps, I may have some ambition to please this gentleman, I shall not lay myself under any restraint, nor very solicitously copy *his* diction or *his* mien, however matured by age, or modeled by experience. If any man shall, by charging me with theatrical behavior, imply that I utter any sentiments but my own, I shall treat him as a calumniator and a villain; nor shall any protection shelter him from the treatment he deserves. I shall, on such an occasion, without scruple, trample upon all those forms with which wealth and dignity intrench themselves.

[2] "Certainly his (Henry the Seventh's) times for good commonwealth's laws did excel, so as he may justly be celebrated for the best lawgiver to this nation after King Edward the First; for his laws, whoso marks them well, are deep, and not vulgar; not made upon the spur of a particular occasion for the present, but out of providence for the future, to make the estate of his people still more and more happy, after the manner of the legislators in ancient and heroical times."—Bacon's Works, vol. iii., p. 233, edition 1834.

nor shall any thing but age restrain my resentment—age, which always brings one privilege, that of being insolent and supercilious without punishment. But with regard, sir, to those whom I have offended, I am of opinion, that if I had acted a borrowed part, I should have avoided their censure. The heat that offended them is the ardor of conviction, and that zeal for the service of my country which neither hope nor fear shall influence me to suppress. I will not sit unconcerned while my liberty is invaded, nor look in silence upon public robbery. I will exert my endeavors, at whatever hazard, to repel the aggressor, and drag the thief to justice, whoever may protect them in their villainy, and whoever may partake of their plunder. And if the honorable gentleman—

[At this point Mr. Pitt was called to order by Mr. Wynnington, who went on to say, "No diversity of opinion can justify the violation of decency, and the use of rude and virulent expressions, dictated only by resentment, and uttered without regard to—"

Here Mr. Pitt called to order, and proceeded thus:] Sir, if this be to preserve order, there is no danger of indecency from the most licentious tongues. For what calumny can be more atrocious, what reproach more severe, than that of speaking with regard to any thing but truth. Order may sometimes be broken by passion or inadvertency, but will hardly be re-established by a monitor like this, who can not govern his own passions while he is restraining the impetuosity of others.

Happy would it be for mankind if every one knew his own province. We should not then see the same man at once a criminal and a judge; nor would this gentleman assume the right of dictating to others what he has not learned himself.

That I may return in some degree the favor he intends me, I will advise him *never hereafter to exert himself on the subject of order;* but whenever he feels inclined to speak on such occasions, to remember how he has now succeeded, and condemn in silence what his censures will never amend.

SPEECH

OF LORD CHATHAM ON A MOTION FOR INQUIRING INTO THE CONDUCT OF SIR ROBERT WALPOLE, DELIVERED IN THE HOUSE OF COMMONS, MARCH 9, 1742.

INTRODUCTION.

Sir Robert Walpole was driven from power on the 11th of February, 1742. So greatly were the public excited against him, that the cry of "blood" was heard from every quarter; and a motion was made by Lord Limerick, on the 9th of March, 1742, for a committee "to inquire into the conduct of affairs at home and abroad during the last twenty years." This, of course, gave the widest scope for arraigning the conduct of the ex-minister; while, at the same time, no specific charges were requisite, because the question was simply on an *inquiry*, which was expected to develop the evidence of his guilt.

This motion was strongly opposed by Walpole's friends, and especially by Mr. Henry Pelham, who remarked, in allusion to one of the preceding speakers, that "it would very much shorten the debate if gentlemen would keep close to the argument, and not run into long harangues or flowers of rhetoric, which might be introduced upon any other subject as well as the present." Mr. Pitt followed, and took his exordium from this sarcasm of Mr. Pelham. He then went fully, and with great severity of remark, into a review of the most important measures of Walpole's administration. This led him over the same ground which had been previously traversed by Walpole, in his defense against the attack of Mr. Sandys and others about a year before. The reader will therefore find it interesting to compare this speech on the several points, as they come up, with that of Walpole, which is given on a preceding page. He will there see some points explained in the notes, by means of evidence which was not accessible to the public at the time of this discussion.

SPEECH, &c.

What the gentlemen on the other side mean by long harangues or flowers of rhetoric, I shall not pretend to determine. But if they make use of nothing of the kind, it is no very good argument of their sincerity, because a man who speaks from his heart, and is sincerely affected with the subject upon which he speaks (as every honest man must be when he speaks in the cause of his country), such a man, I say, falls naturally into expressions which may be called flowers of rhetoric; and, therefore, deserves as little to be charged with affectation, as the most stupid sergeant-at-law that ever spoke for a half-guinea fee. For my part, I have heard nothing in favor of the question but what I think very proper, and very much to the purpose. What has been said, indeed, on the other side of the question, especially the long justification that has been made of our late measures, I can not think so proper; because this motion is founded upon the present melancholy situation of affairs, and upon the general clamor without doors, against the conduct of our late public servants. Either of these, with me, shall always be a sufficient reason for agreeing to a parliamentary inquiry; because, without such inquiry, I can not, even in my own mind, enter into the disquisition whether our public measures have been right or not; without such inquiry, I can not be furnished with the necessary information.

But the honorable gentlemen who oppose this motion seem to mistake, I do not say willfully, the difference between a motion for an impeachment and a motion for an inquiry. If any member of this House were to stand up in his place, and move to impeach a minister, he would be obliged to charge him with some particular crimes or misdemeanors, and produce some proof, or declare that he was ready to prove the facts. But any gentleman may move for an *inquiry*, without any particular allegation, and without offering any proof, or declaring what he is ready to prove; because the very design of an inquiry is to find out particular facts and particular proofs. The general circumstances of things, or general rumors without doors, are a sufficient foundation for such a motion, and for the House agreeing to it when it is made. This, sir, has always been the practice, and has been the foundation of almost all the inquiries that have ever been set on foot in this House, especially those that have been carried on by secret and select committees. What other foundation was there for the secret committee appointed in the year 1694 (to go no further back), to inquire into, and inspect the books and accounts of the East India Company, and of the Chamberlain of London?[1] Nothing but a general rumor that some corrupt practices had been made use of. What was the foundation of the inquiry in the year 1715?[2] Did the honorable gentleman who moved the appointment of the secret committee upon the latter occasion, charge the previous administration with any particular crimes? Did he offer any proofs, or declare that he was ready to prove any thing? It is said, the measures pursued by that administration were condemned by a great majority of the House of Commons. What, sir! were those ministers condemned before they were heard? Could any gentleman be so unjust as to pass sentence, even in his own mind, upon a measure before he had inquired into it? He might, perhaps, dislike the Treaty of Utrecht, but, upon inquiry, it might appear to be the best that could be obtained; and it has since been so far justified, that it appears at least as good, if not better, than any treaty we have subsequently made.

Sir, it was not the Treaty of Utrecht, nor any measure openly pursued by the administration which negotiated it, that was the foundation or the cause of an inquiry into their conduct. It was the loud complaints of a great party against them; and the general suspicion of their having carried on treasonable negotiations in favor of the Pretender, and for defeating the Protestant succession. The inquiry was set on foot in order to detect those practices, if any such existed, and to find proper evidence for convicting the offenders. The same argument holds with regard to the inquiry into the management of the South Sea Company in the year 1721.[3] When that affair was first moved in the House by Mr. Neville, he did not, he could not, charge the directors of that company, or any of them, with any particular delinquencies; nor did he attempt to offer, or say that he was ready to offer, any particular proofs. His motion was, "That the directors of the South Sea Company should forthwith lay before the House an account of their proceedings," and it was founded upon the general circumstances of things, the distress brought upon the public credit of the nation, and the general and loud complaints without doors. This motion, indeed, reasonable as it was, we know was opposed by the Court party at the time, and, in particular, by two doughty brothers,[4] who have been attached to the Court ever since; but their opposition raised such a warmth in the House, that they were glad to give it up, and never after durst directly oppose that inquiry. I wish I could now see the same zeal for public justice. The circumstances of affairs I am sure deserve it. Our public credit was then, indeed, brought into distress; but now the nation itself, nay, not only this nation, but all our friends upon the Continent, are brought into the most imminent danger.

This, sir, is admitted even by those who oppose this motion; and if they have ever lately conversed with those that dare speak their minds, they must admit, that the murmurs of the people against the conduct of the administration are now as general and as loud as ever they were upon any occasion. But the misfortune is, that gentlemen who are in office seldom converse with any but such as either are, or want to be, in office; and such men, let them think as they will, will always applaud their superiors; consequently, gentlemen who are in the administration, or in any office under it, can rarely know the voice of the people. The voice of this House was formerly, I grant, and always ought to be, the voice of the people. If new Parliaments were more frequent, and few placemen, and no pensioners, admitted, it would be so still; but if long Parliaments be continued, and a corrupt influence should prevail, not only at elections, but in this House, the voice of this House will generally be very different from, nay, often directly contrary to, the voice of the people. However, as this is not, I believe, the case at present, I hope there is a majority of us who know what is the voice of the people. And if it be admitted by all that the nation is at present in the utmost distress and danger, if it be admitted by a majority that the voice of the people is loud against the conduct of our late administration, this motion must be agreed to, because I have shown that these two circumstances, without any par-

[1] See Parl. Hist., vol. v., p. 896 and 900.

[2] Ibid., vol. vii., p. 53.

[3] Ibid., p. 685.

[4] Sir Robert and Mr. Horatio Walpole.

ticular charge, have been the foundation of almost every parliamentary inquiry.

I readily admit, sir, that we have very little to do with the character or reputation of a minister, but as it always does, and must affect our sovereign. But the people may become disaffected as well as discontented, when they find the King continues obstinately to employ a minister who, they think, oppresses them at home and betrays them abroad. We are, therefore, in duty to our sovereign, obliged to inquire into the conduct of a minister when it becomes generally suspected by the people, in order that we may vindicate his character if he be innocent of the charges brought against him, or, if he be guilty, that we may obtain his removal from the councils of our sovereign, and also condign punishment on his crimes.

After having said thus much, sir, I need scarcely answer what has been asserted, that no parliamentary inquiry ought ever to be instituted, unless we are convinced that something has been done amiss. Sir, the very name given to this House of Parliament proves the contrary. We are called The Grand Inquest of the Nation; and, as such, it is our duty to inquire into every step of public management, both abroad and at home, in order to see that nothing has been done amiss. It is not necessary, upon every occasion, to establish a secret committee. This is never necessary but when the affairs to be brought before it, or some of those affairs, are supposed to be of such a nature as to require secrecy. But, as experience has shown that nothing but a superficial inquiry is ever made by a general committee, or a committee of the whole House, I wish that all estimates and accounts, and many other affairs, were respectively referred to select committees. Their inquiries would be more exact, and the receiving of their reports would not occupy so much of our time as is represented. But, if it did, our duty being to make strict inquiries into every thing relative to the public, our assembling here being for that purpose, we must perform our duty before we break up; and his present Majesty, I am sure, will never put an end to any session till that duty has been fully performed.

It is said by some gentlemen, that by this inquiry we shall be in danger of discovering the secrets of our government to our enemies. This argument, sir, by proving too much, proves nothing. If it were admitted, it would always have been, and its admission forever will be, an argument against our inquiring into any affair in which our government can be supposed to be concerned. Our inquiries would then be confined to the conduct of our little companies, or of inferior custom-house officers and excisemen; for, if we should presume to inquire into the conduct of commissioners or of great companies, it would be said the government had a concern in their conduct, and the secrets of government must not be divulged. Every gentleman must see that this would be the consequence of admitting such an argument. But, besides, it is false in fact, and contrary to experience. We have had many parliamentary inquiries into the conduct of ministers of state; and yet I defy any one to show that any state affair which ought to have been concealed was thereby discovered, or that our affairs, either abroad or at home, ever suffered by any such discovery. There are methods, sir, of preventing papers of a very secret nature from coming into the hands of the servants attending, or even of all the members of a secret committee. If his Majesty should, by message, inform us, that some of the papers sealed up and laid before us required the utmost secrecy, we might refer them to our committee, instructing them to order only two or three of their number to inspect such papers, and to report from them nothing but what they thought might safely be communicated to the whole. By this method, I presume, the danger of discovery would be effectually removed; this danger, therefore, is no good argument against a parliamentary inquiry.

The other objection, sir, is really surprising, because it is founded upon a circumstance which, in all former times, has been admitted as a strong argument in favor of an immediate inquiry. The honorable gentlemen are so ingenuous as to confess that our affairs, both abroad and at home, are at present in the utmost embarrassment; but, say they, you ought to free yourselves from this embarrassment before you inquire into the cause of it. Sir, according to this way of arguing, a minister who has plundered and betrayed his country, and fears being called to an account in Parliament, has nothing to do but to involve his country in a dangerous war, or some other great distress, in order to prevent an inquiry into his conduct; because he may be dead before that war is at an end, or that distress is surmounted. Thus, like the most detestable of all thieves, after plundering the house, he has only to set it on fire, that he may escape in the confusion. It is really astonishing to hear such an argument seriously urged in this House. But, say these gentlemen, if you found yourself upon a precipice, would you stand to inquire how you were led there, before you considered how to get off? No, sir; but if a guide had led me there, I should very probably be provoked to throw him over, before I thought of any thing else. At least I am sure I should not trust to the same guide for bringing me off; and this, sir, is the strongest argument that can be used for an inquiry.

We have been, for these twenty years, under the guidance, I may truly say, of one man—of one single minister. We now, at last, find ourselves upon a dangerous precipice. Ought we not, then, immediately to inquire, whether we have been led upon this precipice by his ignorance or wickedness; and if by either, to take care not to trust to his guidance for our safety? This is an additional and a stronger argument for this inquiry than ever was urged for any former one, for, if we do not inquire, we shall probably remain under his guidance; because, though he be removed from the Treasury Board, he is not removed from the King's Court, nor will he be, probably, unless it be by our advice, or unless we lodge him in a place at the other end of the town [*i. e.*, the Tower], where he can not so well injure his country. Sir, our distress *at home* evidently proceeds from want of economy, and from our having incurred many unnecessary expenses. Our distress and danger *abroad* are evidently owing to the misconduct of the war with Spain, and to the little confidence which our natural and ancient allies have reposed in our councils. This is so evident, that I should not think it necessary to enter into any particular explanation, if an honorable gentleman on the other side had not attempted to justify most of our late measures both abroad and at home. But as he has done so, though not, in my opinion, quite to the purpose of the present debate, I hope I shall be allowed to make some remarks upon what he has said on the subject; beginning, as he did, with the measures taken for punishing the South Sea directors, and restoring public credit after the terrible shock it received in the year 1720.

As those measures, sir, were among the first exploits of our late (I fear I must call him our present) prime minister, and as the committee proposed, if agreed to, will probably consist of one-and-twenty members, I wish the motion had extended one year further back, that the number of years might have corresponded with the number of inquirers, and that it might have comprehended the first of those measures to which I have before alluded. As it now stands, it will not comprehend the methods taken for punishing the directors [of the South Sea Company], nor the first regulation made for restoring public credit; and with regard to both, some practices might be discovered that would deserve a much severer punishment than any of those directors experienced. Considering the many frauds made use of by the directors and their agents for luring people to their ruin, I am not a little surprised to hear it now said that their punishment was considered too severe. Justice by the lump was an epithet given to it, not because it was thought too severe, but because it was an artifice to screen the most heinous offenders, who, if they did not deserve death, deserved, at least, to partake of that total ruin which they had brought upon many unthinking men. They very ill deserved, sir, those allowances which were made them by Parliament.

Then, sir, as to public credit, its speedy restoration was founded upon the conduct of the nation, and not upon the wisdom or justice of the measures adopted. Was it a wise method to remit to the South Sea Company the whole seven millions, or thereabouts, which they had solemnly engaged to pay to the public? It might as well be said, that a private man's giving away a great part of his estate to those who no way deserved it, would be a wise method of reviving or establishing his credit. If those seven millions had been distributed among the poor sort of annuitants, it would have been both generous and charitable; but to give it among the proprietors in general was neither generous nor just, because most of them deserved no favor from the public. As the proceedings of the directors were authorized by general courts, those who were then the proprietors were in some measure accessary to the frauds of the directors, and therefore deserved to be punished rather than rewarded, as they really were; because every one of them who continued to hold stock in that company received nearly fifty per cent., added to his capital, most part of which arose from the high price annuitants were, by act of Parliament, obliged to take stock at, and was therefore a most flagrant piece of injustice done to the annuitants. But we need not be at a loss for the true cause of this act of injustice, when we consider that a certain gentleman had a great many friends among the old stockholders, and few or none among the annuitants.

Another act of injustice, which I believe we may ascribe to the same cause, relates to those who were engaged in heavy contracts for stock or subscription, many of whom groan under the load to this very day. For after we had, by act of Parliament, quite altered the nature, though not the name, of the stock they had bought, and made it much less valuable than it was when they engaged to pay a high price for it, it was an act of public injustice to leave them liable to be prosecuted at law for the whole money which they had engaged to pay. I am sure this was not the method to restore that private credit upon which our trade and navigation so much depend. Had the same regulation been here adopted which was observed toward those who had borrowed money of the company, or had a sort of *uti possidetis* been enacted, by declaring all such contracts void so far as related to any future payments, this would not have been unjust; on the contrary, such a regulation, sir, was extremely necessary for quieting the minds of the people, for preventing their ruining one another at law, and for restoring credit between man and man. But there is reason to suppose that a certain gentleman [Walpole] had many friends among the *sellers* in those contracts, and very few among the *buyers*, which was the reason that the latter could obtain little or no relief or mercy by any public law or regulation.

Then, sir, with regard to the extraordinary grants made to the civil list, the very reason given by the honorable gentleman for justifying those grants is a strong reason for an immediate inquiry. If considerable charges have arisen upon that revenue, let us see what they are; let us examine whether they were necessary. We have the more reason to do this, because the revenue settled upon his late Majesty's civil list was at least as great as that which was settled upon King William or Queen Anne. Besides, there is a general rumor without doors, that the civil list is now greatly in arrear, which, if true, renders an inquiry absolutely necessary. For it is inconsistent with the honor and dignity of the Crown of these kingdoms to be in arrear to its tradesmen and servants; and it is the duty of this House to take care that the revenue which we have settled for supporting the honor and dignity of the Crown, shall not be squandered or misapplied. If former Parliaments have failed in this respect, they must be censured, though they can not be punished; but we ought now to atone for their neglect.

I come now, in course, to the Excise Scheme, which the honorable gentleman says ought to be forgiven, because it was easily given up.[5] Sir, it was not easily given up. The promoter of that scheme did not easily give it up; he gave it up with sorrow, with tears in his eyes, when he saw, and not until he saw, it was impossible to carry it through the House. Did not his majority decrease upon every division? It was almost certain that if he had pushed it farther, his majority would have turned against him. His sorrow showed his disappointment; and his disappointment showed that his design was deeper than simply to prevent frauds in the customs. He was, at that time, sensible of the influence of the excise laws and excise men with regard to elections, and of the great occasion he should have for that sort of influence at the approaching general election. His attempt, sir, was most flagrant against the Constitution; and he deserved the treatment he met with from the people. It has been said that there were none but what gentlemen are pleased to call the *mob* concerned in burning him in effigy;[6] but, as the mob consists chiefly of children, journeymen, and servants, who speak the sentiments of their parents and masters, we may thence judge of the sentiments of the higher classes of the people.

The honorable gentleman has said, these were all the measures of a domestic nature that could be found fault with, because none other have been mentioned in this debate. Sir, he has already heard one reason assigned why no other measures have been particularly mentioned and condemned in this debate. If it were necessary, many others might be mentioned and condemned. Is not the maintaining so numerous an army in time of peace to be condemned? Is not the fitting out so many expensive and useless squadrons to be condemned? Are not the encroachments made upon the Sinking Fund;[7] the reviving the salt duty; the rejecting many useful bills and motions in Parliament, and many other domestic measures, to be condemned? The weakness or the wickedness of these measures has often been demonstrated. Their ill consequences were at the respective times foretold, and those consequences are now become visible by our distress.

Now, sir, with regard to the foreign measures which the honorable gentleman has attempted to justify. The Treaty of Hanover deserves to be first mentioned, because from thence springs the danger to which Europe is now exposed; and it is impossible to assign a reason for our entering into that treaty, without supposing that we then resolved to be revenged on the Emperor for refusing to grant us some favor in Germany. It is in vain now to insist upon the secret engagements entered into by the courts of Vienna and Madrid as the cause of that treaty. Time has fully shown that there never were any such engagements,[8] and his late

[5] The Excise Scheme of Sir Robert Walpole was simply a warehousing system, under which the duties on tobacco and wine were payable, not when the articles were imported, but when they were taken out to be consumed. It was computed, that, in consequence of the check which this change in the mode of collecting the duties on these articles would give to smuggling, the revenue would derive an increase which, with the continuance of the salt tax (revived the preceding year), would be amply sufficient to compensate for the total abolition of the land tax. The political opponents of Sir Robert Walpole, by representing his proposition as a scheme for a *general* excise, succeeded in raising so violent a clamor against it, and in rendering it so unpopular, that, much against his own inclination, he was obliged to abandon it. It was subsequently approved of by Adam Smith; and Lord Chatham, at a later period of his life, candidly acknowledged, that his opposition to it was founded in misconception. For an interesting account of the proceedings relative to the Excise Scheme, see Lord Hervey's Memoirs of the Court of George II., chaps. viii. and ix.

[6] See Lord Hervey's Memoirs of the Court of George II., vol. i., p. 203.

[7] In the year 1717, the surplus of the public income over the public expenditure, was converted into what was called *The Sinking Fund*, for the purpose of liquidating the national debt. During the whole reign of George I., this fund was invariably appropriated to the object for which it had been created; and, rather than encroach upon it, money was borrowed upon new taxes, when the supplies in general might have been raised by dedicating the surplus of the old taxes to the current services of the year. The first direct encroachment upon the Sinking Fund took place in the year 1729, when the interest of a sum of £1,250,000, required for the current service of the year, was charged on that fund, instead of any new taxes being imposed upon the people to meet it. The second encroachment took place in the year 1731, when the income arising from certain duties which had been imposed in the reign of William III., for paying the interest due to the East India Company, and which were now no longer required for that purpose, in consequence of their interest being reduced, was made use of in order to raise a sum of £1,200,000, instead of throwing such income into the Sinking Fund, as ought properly to have been done. A third perversion of this fund took place in the year 1733, before the introduction of the Excise Scheme. In the previous year the land tax had been reduced to one shilling in the pound; and, in order to maintain it at the same rate, the sum of £500,000 was taken from the Sinking Fund and applied to the services of the year. In 1734 the sum of £1,200,000, the whole produce of the Sinking Fund, was taken from it; and in 1735 and 1736, it was anticipated and alienated.—Sinclair's Hist. of the Revenue, vol. i., p. 484, *et seq.* Coxe's Walpole, chap. xl.

[8] Here Lord Chatham was mistaken. It is now certainly known that secret engagements did exist,

Majesty's speech from the throne can not here be admitted as any evidence of the fact. Every one knows that in Parliament the King's speech is considered as the speech of the minister; and surely a minister is not to be allowed to bring his own speech as an evidence of a fact in his own justification. If it be pretended that his late Majesty had some sort of information, that such engagements had been entered into, that very pretense furnishes an unanswerable argument for an inquiry. For, as the information now appears to have been groundless, we ought to inquire into it; because, if it appears to be such information as ought not to have been believed, that minister ought to be punished who advised his late Majesty to give credit to it, and who, in consequence, has precipitated the nation into the most pernicious measures.

At the time this treaty was entered into, we wanted nothing from the Emperor upon our own account. The abolition of the Ostend Company was a demand we had no right to make, nor was it essentially our interest to insist upon it, because that Company would have been more hostile to the interests both of the French and Dutch East India trades than to our own; and if it had been a point that concerned us much, we might probably have gained it by acceding to the Vienna treaty between the Emperor and Spain, or by guaranteeing the Pragmatic Sanction,[9] which we afterward did in the most absolute manner, and without any conditions.[10] We wanted nothing from Spain but a relinquishment of the pretense she had just begun, or, I believe, hardly begun, to set up, in an express manner, with regard to searching and seizing our ships in the American seas; and this we did not obtain, perhaps did not desire to obtain, by the Treaty of Seville.[11] By that treaty we obtained nothing; but we advanced another step toward that danger in which Europe is now involved, by uniting the courts of France and Spain, and by laying a foundation for a new breach between the courts of Spain and Vienna.

I grant, sir, that our ministers appear to have been forward and diligent enough in negotiating, and writing letters and memorials to the court of Spain; but, from all my inquiries, it appears that they never rightly understood (perhaps they would not understand) the point respecting which they were negotiating. They suffered themselves to be amused with fair promises for ten long years; and our merchants plundered, our trade interrupted, now call aloud for inquiry. If it should appear that ministers allowed themselves to be amused with answers which no man of honor, no man of common sense, in such circumstances, would take, surely, sir, they must have had some secret motive for being thus grossly imposed on. This secret motive we may perhaps discover by an inquiry; and as it must be a wicked one, if it can be discovered, the parties ought to be severely punished.

But, in excuse for their conduct, it is said that our ministers had a laudable repugnance to involving their country in a war. Sir, this repugnance could not proceed from any regard to their country. It *was* involved in a war. Spain *was* carrying on a war against our trade, and that in the most insulting manner, during the whole time of their negotiations. It was this very repugnance, at least it was the knowledge of it which Spain possessed, that at length made

---

and there is no reason to doubt that the most important of them were correctly stated by Walpole. They were said to have been to the effect, that the Emperor should give in marriage his daughters, the two arch-duchesses, to Don Carlos and Don Philip, the two Infants of Spain; that he should assist the King of Spain in obtaining by force the restitution of Gibraltar, if good offices would not avail; and that the two courts should adopt measures to place the Pretender on the throne of Great Britain. The fact of there having been a secret treaty, was placed beyond doubt by the Austrian embassador at the court of London having shown the article relating to Gibraltar in that treaty, in order to clear the Emperor of having promised any more than his good offices and mediation upon that head. (Coxe's History of the House of Austria, chap. xxxvii.) With reference to the stipulation for placing the Pretender on the throne of Great Britain, Mr. J. W. Croker, in a note to Lord Hervey's Memoirs of the Court of George II., vol. i., p. 78, says that its existence "is very probable;" but that it is observable that Lord Hervey, who revised his Memoirs some years after the 29th of March, 1734, when Sir Robert Walpole asserted in the House of Commons that there was such a document, and who was so long in the full confidence of Walpole, speaks very doubtfully of it.

[9] On the 2d of August, 1718, the Emperor Charles VI. promulgated a new law of succession for the inheritance of the house of Austria, under the name of the Pragmatic Sanction. In this he ordained that, in the event of his having no male issue, his own daughters should succeed to the Austrian throne, in preference to the daughters of his elder brother, as previously provided; and that such succession should be regulated according to the order of primogeniture, so that the elder should be preferred to the younger, and that she should inherit his entire dominions.

[10] By the second Treaty of Vienna, concluded on the 16th of March, 1731, England guaranteed the Pragmatic Sanction on the condition of the suppression of the Ostend Company, and that the archduchess who succeeded to the Austrian dominions should not be married to a prince of the house of Bourbon, or to a prince so powerful as to endanger the balance of Europe.—Coxe's House of Austria, chap. lxxxviii.

[11] By the Treaty of Seville, concluded between Great Britain, France, and Spain, on the 9th of September, 1729, and shortly after acceded to by Holland, all former treaties were confirmed, and the several contracting parties agreed to assist each other in case of attack. The King of Spain revoked the privileges of trade which he had granted to the subjects of Austria by the Treaty of Vienna, and commissioners were to be appointed for the final adjustment of all commercial difficulties between Spain and Great Britain. In order to secure the succession of Parma and Tuscany to the Infant Don Carlos, it was agreed that 6000 Spanish troops should be allowed to garrison Leghorn, Porto Ferrajo, Parma, and Placentia. This treaty passed over in total silence the claim of Spain to Gibraltar.

it absolutely necessary for us to commence the war. If ministers had at first insisted properly and peremptorily upon an explicit answer, Spain would have expressly abandoned her new and insolent claims and pretensions. But by the long experience we allowed her, she found the fruits of those pretensions so plentiful and so gratifying, that she thought them worth the hazard of a war. Sir, the damage we had sustained became so considerable, that it really was worth that hazard. Besides, the court of Spain was convinced, while we were under such an administration, that either nothing could provoke us to commence the war, or, that if we did, it would be conducted in a weak and miserable manner. Have we not, sir, since found that their opinion was correct? Nothing, sir, ever more demanded a parliamentary inquiry than our conduct in the war. The only branch into which we have inquired we have already censured and condemned. Is not this a good reason for inquiring into every other branch? Disappointment and ill success have always, till now, occasioned a parliamentary inquiry. Inactivity, of itself, is a sufficient cause for inquiry. We have now all these reasons combined. Our admirals abroad desire nothing more; because they are conscious that our inactivity and ill success will appear to proceed, not from their own misconduct, but from the misconduct of those by whom they were employed.

I can not conclude, sir, without taking notice of the two other foreign measures mentioned by the honorable gentleman. Our conduct in the year 1734, with regard to the war between the Emperor and France, may be easily accounted for, though not easily excused. Ever since the last accession of our late minister to power, we seem to have had an enmity to the house of Austria. Our guarantee of the Pragmatic Sanction was an effect of that enmity, because we entered into it when, as hath since appeared, we had no intention to perform our engagement; and by that false guarantee we induced the Emperor to admit the introduction of the Spanish troops into Italy, which he would not otherwise have done.[12] The preparations we made in that year, the armies we raised, and the fleet we fitted out, were not to guard against the event of the war abroad, but against the event of the ensuing elections at home. The new commissions, the promotions, and the money laid out in these preparations, were of admirable use at the time of a general election, and in some measure atoned for the loss of the excise scheme. But France and her allies were well convinced, that we would in no event declare against them, otherwise they would not then have dared to attack the Emperor; for Muscovy, Poland, Germany, and Britain would have been by much an over-match for them. It was not our preparations that set bounds to the ambition of France, but her getting all she wanted at that time for herself, and all she desired for her allies. Her own prudence suggested that it was not then a proper time to push her views further; because she did not know but that the spirit of this nation might overcome (as it since has with regard to Spain) the spirit of our administration; and should this have happened, the house of Austria was then in such a condition, that our assistance, even though late, would have been of effectual service.

I am surprised, sir, to hear the honorable gentleman now say, that we gave up nothing, or that we acquired any thing, by the infamous Convention with Spain. Did we not give up the freedom of our trade and navigation, by submitting it to be regulated by plenipotentiaries? Can freedom be regulated without being confined, and consequently in some part destroyed? Did we not give up Georgia, or some part of it, by submitting to have new limits settled by plenipotentiaries? Did we not give up all the reparation of the damage we had suffered, amounting to five or six hundred thousand pounds, for the paltry sum of twenty-seven thousand pounds? This was all that Spain promised to pay, after deducting the sixty-eight thousand pounds which we, by the declaration annexed to that treaty, allowed her to insist on having from our South Sea Company, under the penalty of stripping them of the Assiento Contract, and all the privileges to which they were thereby entitled. Even this sum of twenty-seven thousand pounds, or more, they had before acknowledged to be due on account of ships they allowed to have been unjustly taken, and for the restitution of which they had actually sent orders: so that by this infamous treaty we acquired nothing, while we gave up every thing. Therefore, in my opinion, the honor of this nation can never be retrieved, unless the advisers and authors of it be censured and punished. This, sir, can not regularly be done without a parliamentary inquiry.

By these, and similar weak, pusillanimous, and wicked measures, we are become the ridicule of every court in Europe, and have lost the confidence of all our ancient allies. By these measures we have encouraged France to extend her ambitious views, and now at last to attempt carrying them into execution. By bad economy, by extravagance in our domestic measures, we have involved ourselves in such distress at home, that we are almost wholly incapable of entering into a war; while by weakness or wickedness in our foreign measures, we have brought the affairs of Europe into such distress that it is almost impossible for us to avoid it. Sir, we have been brought upon a dangerous precipice. Here we now find ourselves; and shall we trust to be led safely off by the same guide who has led us on? Sir, it is impossible for him to lead

[12] See Walpole's explanation of his reason for remaining neutral, in his speech, page 39. Although England remained neutral during the progress of these hostilities, she augmented her naval and military forces, "in order," said Mr. Pelham, in the course of the debate, "to be ready to put a stop to the arms of the victorious side, in case their ambition should lead them to push their conquests further than was consonant with the balance of power in Europe."—Parl. Hist., vol. xii., p. 479.

us off. Sir, it is impossible for us to get off, without first recovering that confidence with our ancient allies which formerly we possessed. This we can not do, so long as they suppose that our councils are influenced by our late minister; and this they will suppose so long as he has access to the King's closet—so long as his conduct remains uninquired into and uncensured. It is not, therefore, in revenge for our past disasters, but from a desire to prevent them in future, that I am now so zealous for this inquiry. The punishment of the minister, be it ever so severe, will be but a small atonement for the past. But his impunity will be the source of many future miseries to Europe, as well as to his country. Let us be as merciful as we will, as merciful as any man can reasonably desire, when we come to pronounce sentence; but sentence we must pronounce. For this purpose, unless we are resolved to sacrifice our own liberties, and the liberties of Europe, to the preservation of one guilty man, we must make the inquiry.

The motion was rejected by a majority of two. A second motion was made a fortnight after, for an inquiry into the last *ten* years of Walpole's administration, which gave rise to another speech of Mr. Pitt. This will next be given.

SECOND SPEECH

OF LORD CHATHAM ON A MOTION TO INQUIRE INTO THE CONDUCT OF SIR ROBERT WALPOLE, DELIVERED IN THE HOUSE OF COMMONS, MARCH 23, 1742.

INTRODUCTION.

LORD LIMERICK's first motion for an inquiry into the conduct of Walpole was lost chiefly through the absence of Mr. Pulteney from the House during the illness of a favorite daughter. On the return of Pulteney at the end of a fortnight, the motion was renewed, with a variation in one respect, viz., that the inquiry be extended only to the last *ten* years of Walpole's continuance in office.

On that occasion, Mr. Pitt made the following speech in answer to Mr. Cook Harefield, who had recently taken his seat in the House. In it he shows his remarkable power of reply; and argues with great force the propriety of inquiry, as leading to a decision whether an impeachment should be commenced.

SPEECH, &c.

As the honorable gentleman who spoke last against the motion has not been long in the House, it is but charitable to believe him sincere in professing that he is ready to agree to a parliamentary inquiry when he thinks the occasion requires it. But if he knew how often such professions are made by those who upon all occasions oppose inquiry, he would now avoid them, because they are generally believed to be insincere. He may, it is true, have nothing to dread, on his own account, from inquiry. But when a gentleman has contracted, or any of his near relations have contracted, a friendship with one who may be brought into danger, it is very natural to suppose that such a gentleman's opposition to an inquiry does not entirely proceed from public motives; and if that gentleman follows the advice of some of his friends, I very much question whether he will ever think the occasion requires an inquiry into the conduct of our public affairs.

As a parliamentary inquiry must always be founded upon suspicions, as well as upon facts or manifest crimes, reasons may always be found for alleging those suspicions to be without foundation; and upon the principle that a parliamentary inquiry must necessarily lay open the secrets of government, no time can ever be proper or convenient for such inquiry, because it is impossible to suppose a time when the government has no secrets to disclose.

This, sir, would be a most convenient doctrine for ministers, because it would put an end to all parliamentary inquiries into the conduct of our public affairs; and, therefore, when I hear it urged, and so much insisted on, by a certain set of gentlemen in this House, I must suppose their hopes to be very extensive. I must suppose them to expect that they and their posterity will forever continue in office. Sir, this doctrine has been so often contradicted by experience, that I am surprised to hear it advanced by gentlemen now. This very session has afforded us a convincing proof that very little foundation exists for asserting, that a parliamentary inquiry must necessarily reveal the secrets of the government. Surely, in a war with Spain, which must be carried on principally by sea, if the government have secrets, the Lords of the Admiralty must be intrusted with the most important of them. Yet, sir, in this very session, we have, without any secret committees, made inquiry into the conduct of the Lords Commissioners of the Admiralty. We have not only inquired into their conduct, but we have censured it in such a manner as to put an end to the trust which was before reposed in them. Has that inquiry discovered any of the secrets of our government? On the contrary, the committee found that there was no occasion to probe into such secrets. They found cause enough for censure without it; and none of the Commissioners pretended to justify their conduct by the assertion that the papers contained secrets which ought not to be disclosed.

This, sir, is so recent, so strong a proof that there is no necessary connection between a parliamentary inquiry and a discovery of secrets which it behooves the nation to conceal, that I trust gentlemen will no longer insist upon this danger as an argument against the inquiry. Sir, the First Commissioner of the Treasury has nothing to do with the application of secret service money. He is only to take care that it be regularly issued from his office, and that no more be issued than the conjuncture of affairs appears to demand. As to the particular application, it properly belongs to the Secretary of State, or to such other persons as his Majesty employs. Hence we can not suppose the proposed inquiry will discover any secrets relative to the application of that money, unless the noble lord has acted as Secretary of State, as well as First Commissioner of the Treasury; or unless a great part of the money drawn out for secret service has been delivered to himself or persons employed by him, and applied toward gaining a corrupt influence in Parliament or at elections. Of both these practices he is most grievously suspected, and both are secrets which it very much behooves him to conceal. But, sir, it equally behooves the nation to discover them. His country and he are, in this cause, equally, although oppositely concerned. The safety or ruin of one or the other depends upon the fate of the question; and the violent opposition which this question has experienced adds great strength to the suspicion.

I admit, sir, that the noble lord [Walpole], whose conduct is now proposed to be inquired into, was one of his Majesty's most honorable Privy Council, and consequently that he must have had a share at least in advising all the measures which have been pursued both abroad and at home. But I can not from this admit, that an inquiry into his conduct must necessarily occasion a discovery of any secrets of vital importance to the nation, because we are not to inquire into the measures themselves.

But, sir, suspicions have gone abroad relative to his conduct as a Privy Counselor, which, if true, are of the utmost consequence to be inquired into. It has been strongly asserted that he was not only a Privy Counselor, but that he usurped the whole and sole direction of his Majesty's Privy Council. It has been asserted that he gave the Spanish court the first hint of the unjust claim they afterward advanced against our South Sea Company, which was one chief cause of the war between the two nations. And it has been asserted that this very minister has advised the French in what manner to proceed in order to bring our Court into their measures; particularly, that he advised them as to the numerous army they have this last summer sent into Westphalia. What truth there is in these assertions, I pretend not to decide. The facts are of such a nature, and they must have been perpetrated with so much caution and secrecy, that it will be difficult to bring them to light even by a parliamentary inquiry; but the very suspicion is ground enough for establishing such inquiry, and for carrying it on with the utmost strictness and vigor.

Whatever my opinion of past measures may be, I shall never be so vain, or bigoted to that opinion, as to determine, without any inquiry, against the majority of my countrymen. If I found the public measures generally condemned, let my private opinions of them be ever so favorable, I should be for inquiry in order to convince the people of their error, or at least to furnish myself with the most authentic arguments in favor of the opinion I had embraced. The desire of bringing others into the same sentiments with ourselves is so natural, that I shall always suspect the candor of those who, in politics or religion, are opposed to free inquiry. Besides, sir, when the complaints of the people are general against an administration, or against any particular minister, an inquiry is a duty which we owe both to our sovereign and the people. We meet here to communicate to our sovereign the sentiments of his people. We meet here to redress the grievances of the people. By performing our duty in both respects, we shall always be enabled to establish the throne of our sovereign in the hearts of his people, and to hinder the people from being led into insurrection and rebellion by misrepresentations or false surmises. When the people complain, they must either be right or in error. If they be right, we are in duty bound to inquire into the conduct of the ministers, and to punish those who appear to have been most guilty. If they be in error, we ought still to inquire into the conduct of our ministers, in order to convince the people that they have been misled. We ought not, therefore, in any question relating to inquiry, to be governed by our own sentiments. We must be governed by the sentiments of our constituents, if we are resolved to perform our duty, both as true representatives of the people, and as faithful subjects of our King.

I perfectly agree with the honorable gentleman, that if we are convinced that the public measures are wrong, or that if we suspect them to be so, we ought to make inquiry, although there is not much complaint among the people. But I wholly differ from him in thinking that notwithstanding the administration and the minister are the subjects of complaint among the people, we ought not to make inquiry into his conduct unless we are ourselves convinced that his measures have been wrong. Sir, we can no more determine this question without inquiry, than a judge without a trial can declare any man innocent of a crime laid to his charge. Common fame is a sufficient ground for an inquisition at common law; and for the same reason, the general voice of the people of England ought always to be regarded as a sufficient ground for a parliamentary inquiry.

But, say gentlemen, of what is this minister

accused? What crime is laid to his charge? For, unless some misfortune is said to have happened, or some crime to have been committed, no inquiry ought to be set on foot. Sir, the ill posture of our affairs both abroad and at home; the melancholy situation we are in; the distresses to which we are now reduced, are sufficient causes for an inquiry, even supposing the minister accused of no particular crime or misconduct. The nation lies bleeding, perhaps expiring. The balance of power has been fatally disturbed. Shall we acknowledge this to be the case, and shall we not inquire whether it has happened by mischance, or by the misconduct, perhaps by the malice prepense, of the minister? Before the Treaty of Utrecht, it was the general opinion that in a few years of peace we should be able to pay off most of our debts. We have now been very nearly thirty years in profound peace, at least we have never been engaged in any war but what we unnecessarily brought upon ourselves, and yet our debts are almost as great as they were when that treaty was concluded.[1] Is not this a misfortune, and shall we not make inquiry into its cause?

I am surprised to hear it said that no inquiry ought to be set on foot unless it is known that some public crime has been committed. Sir, the *suspicion* that a crime has been committed has always been deemed a sufficient reason for instituting an inquiry. And is there not now a suspicion that the public money has been applied toward gaining a corrupt influence at elections? Is it not become a common expression, "The flood-gates of the Treasury are opened against a general election?" I desire no more than that every gentleman who is conscious that such practices have been resorted to, either for or against him, should give his vote in favor of the motion. Will any gentleman say that this is no crime, when even private corruption has such high penalties inflicted by express statute against it? Sir, a minister who commits this crime—who thus abuses the public money, adds breach of trust to the crime of corruption; and as the crime, when committed by him, is of much more dangerous consequence than when committed by a private man, it becomes more properly the object of a parliamentary inquiry, and merits the severest punishment. The honorable gentleman may with much more reason tell us that *Porteous* was never murdered by the mob at Edinburgh, because, notwithstanding the high reward as well as pardon proffered, his murderers were never discovered,[2] than tell us that we can not suppose our minister, either personally or by others, has ever corrupted an election, because no information has been brought against him. Sir, nothing but a pardon, upon the conviction of the offender, has ever yet been offered in this case; and how could any informer expect a pardon, and much less a reward, when he knew that the very man against whom he was to inform had not only the distribution of all public rewards, but the packing of a jury or a Parliament against him? While such a minister preserves the favor of the Crown, and thereby the exercise of its power, this information can never be expected.

This shows, sir, the impotence of the act, mentioned by the honorable gentleman, respecting that sort of corruption which is called bribery. With regard to the other sort of corruption, which consists in giving or taking away those posts, pensions, or preferments which depend upon the arbitrary will of the Crown, the act is still more inefficient. Although it would be considered most indecent in a minister to tell any man that he gave or withheld a post, pension, or preferment, on account of his voting for or against any ministerial measure in Parliament, or any ministerial candidate at an election; yet, if he makes it his constant rule never to give a post, pension, or preferment, but to those who vote for his measures and his candidates; if he makes a few examples of dismissing those who vote otherwise, it will have the same effect as when he openly declares it.[3] Will any gentleman say that this has not been the practice of the minister? Has he not declared, in the face of this House, that he will continue the practice? And will not this have the same effect as if he went separately to every particular man, and told him in express terms, "Sir, if you vote for such a measure or such a candidate, you shall have the first preferment in the gift of the Crown; if you vote otherwise, you must not expect to keep what you have?" Gentlemen may deny that the sun shines at noon-day; but if they have eyes, and do not willfully shut them, or turn their backs, no man will believe them to be ingenuous in what they say. I think, therefore, that the honorable gentleman was in the right who endeavored to justify the practice. It was more candid than to deny it. But as his arguments have already been fully answered, I shall not farther discuss them.

Gentlemen exclaim, "What! will you take from the Crown the power of preferring or cashiering the officers of the army?" No, sir, this is neither the design, nor will it be the effect of our agreeing to the motion. The King at pres-

[1]

Debt on the accession of George the First, in 1714	£54,145,363
Debt at the commencement of the Spanish war, in 1739	£46,954,623
Decrease during the peace	£7,190,740

[2] The case of Porteous, here referred to, was the one on which Sir Walter Scott founded his "Heart of Midlothian." Porteous had been condemned to death for firing on the people of Edinburgh, but was reprieved at the moment when the execution was to have taken place. Exasperated at this, the mob, a few nights after, broke open his prison, and hanged him on the spot where he had fired. A reward of £200 was offered, but the perpetrators could not be discovered.

[3] It will be recollected that, in consequence of his parliamentary opposition to Sir Robert Walpole, Mr. Pitt had been himself dismissed from the army. The Duke of Bolton and Lord Cobham had also, for a similar reason, been deprived of the command of their regiments.

ent possesses the absolute power to prefer or cashier the officers of our army. It is a prerogative which he may employ for the benefit or safety of the public; but, like other prerogatives, it may be abused, and when it is so abused, the minister is responsible to Parliament. When an officer is preferred or cashiered for voting in favor of or against any court measure or candidate, it is an abuse of this prerogative, for which the minister is answerable. We may judge from circumstances or outward appearances—from these we may condemn, and I hope we have still a power to punish a minister who dares to advise the King to prefer or cashier from such motives! Sir, whether this prerogative ought to remain as it is, without any limitation, is a question foreign to this debate. But I must observe, that the argument employed for it might, with equal justice, be employed for giving our King an absolute power over every man's property; because a large property will always give the possessor a command over a great body of men, whom he may arm and discipline if he pleases. I know of no law to restrain him—I hope none will ever exist—I wish our gentlemen of estates would make more use of this power than they do, because it would tend to keep our domestic as well as our foreign enemies in awe. For my part, I think that a gentleman who has earned his commission by his services (in his military capacity, I mean), or bought it with his money, has as much a property in it as any man has in his estate, and ought to have it as well secured by the laws of his country. While it remains at the absolute will of the Crown, he must, unless he has some other estate to depend on, be a slave to the minister; and if the officers of our army long continue in that state of slavery in which they are at present, I am afraid it will make slaves of us all.

The only method to prevent this fatal consequence, as the law now stands, is to make the best and most constant use of the power we possess as members of this House, to prevent any minister from daring to advise the King to make a bad use of his prerogative. As there is such a strong suspicion that this minister has done so, we ought certainly to inquire into it, not only for the sake of punishing him if guilty, but as a terror to all future ministers.

This, sir, may therefore be justly reckoned among the many other sufficient causes for the inquiry proposed. The suspicion that the civil list is greatly in debt is another; for if it is, it must either have been misapplied, or profusely thrown away, which abuse it is our duty both to prevent and to punish. It is inconsistent with the honor of this nation that the King should stand indebted to his servants or tradesmen, who may be ruined by delay of payment. The Parliament has provided sufficiently to prevent this dishonor from being brought upon the nation, and, if the provision we have made should be lavished or misapplied, we must supply the deficiency. We ought to do it, whether the King makes any application for that purpose or not; and the reason is plain, because we ought first to inquire into the management of that revenue, and punish those who have occasioned the deficiency. They will certainly choose to leave the creditors of the Crown and the honor of the nation in a state of suffering, rather than advise the King to make an application which may bring censure upon their conduct, and condign punishment upon themselves. Besides this, sir, another and a stronger reason exists for promoting an inquiry. There is a strong suspicion that the public money has been applied toward corrupting voters at elections, and members when elected; and if the civil list be in debt, it affords reason to presume that some part of this revenue has, under the pretense of secret service money, been applied to this infamous purpose.

I shall conclude, sir, by making a few remarks upon the last argument advanced against the proposed inquiry. It has been said that the minister delivered in his accounts annually; that these accounts were annually passed and approved by Parliament; and that therefore it would be unjust to call him now to a general account, because the vouchers may be lost, or many expensive transactions have escaped his memory. It is true, sir, estimates and accounts were annually delivered in. The forms of proceeding made that necessary. But were any of these estimates and accounts properly inquired into? Were not all questions of that description rejected by the minister's friends in Parliament? Did not Parliament always take them upon trust, and pass them without examination? Can such a superficial passing, to call it no worse, be deemed a reason for not calling him to a new and general account? If the steward to an infant's estate should annually, for twenty years together, deliver in his accounts to the guardians; and the guardians, through negligence, or for a share of the plunder, should annually pass his accounts without examination, or at least without objection; would that be a reason for saying that it would be unjust in the infant, when he came of age, to call his steward to account? Especially if that steward had built and furnished sumptuous palaces, living, during the whole time, at a much greater expense than his visible income warranted, and yet amassing great riches? The public, sir, is always in a state of infancy; therefore no prescription can be pleaded against it—not even a general release, if there is the least cause for supposing that it was surreptitiously obtained. Public vouchers ought always to remain on record; nor ought any public expense to be incurred without a voucher—therefore the case of the public is still stronger than that of an infant. Thus, sir, the honorable gentleman who made use of this objection, must see how little it avails in the case before us; and therefore I trust we shall have his concurrence in the question.

The motion prevailed by a majority of seven. A committee of twenty-one was appointed, composed of Walpole's political and personal opponents. They entered on the inquiry with great zeal and expectation. But no documentary proofs of importance could be found. Witnesses were called up for examination as to their transactions with the treasury; but they refused to testify, unless previously indemnified against the consequences of the evidence they might be required to give. The House passed a bill of indemnity, but the Lords rejected it, as dangerous in its tendency, and calculated to invite accusation from peculators and others, who might wish to cover their crimes by making the minister a partaker in their guilt. "The result of all their inquiries," says Cooke, "was charges so few and so ridiculous, when compared with those put forward at the commencement of the investigation, that the promoters of the prosecution were themselves ashamed of their work. Success was found impracticable, and Lord Orford enjoyed his honors unmolested."—Hist. of Party, ii., 316.

SPEECH

OF LORD CHATHAM ON TAKING THE HANOVERIAN TROOPS INTO THE PAY OF GREAT BRITAIN, DELIVERED IN THE HOUSE OF COMMONS, DEC. 10, 1742.

INTRODUCTION.

George II., when freed from the trammels of Walpole's pacific policy, had a silly ambition of appearing on the Continent, like William III., at the head of a confederate army against France, while he sought, at the same time, to defend and aggrandize his Electorate of Hanover at the expense of Great Britain. In this he was encouraged by Lord Carteret, who succeeded Walpole as prime minister. The King therefore took sixteen thousand Hanoverian troops into British pay, and sent them with a large English force into Flanders. His object was to create a diversion in favor of Maria Theresa, queen of Hungary, to whom the English were now affording aid, in accordance with their guarantee of the Pragmatic Sanction.[1] Two subsidies, one of £300,000 and another of £500,000, had already been transmitted for her relief; and so popular was her cause in England, that almost any sum would have been freely given. But there was a general and strong opposition to the King's plan of shifting the burdens of Hanover on to the British treasury. Mr. Pitt, who concurred in these views, availed himself of this opportunity to come out as the opponent of Carteret. He had been neglected and set aside in the arrangements which were made after the fall of Walpole; and he was not of a spirit tamely to bear the arrogance of the new minister. Accordingly, when a motion was made to provide for the payment of the Hanoverian troops, he delivered the following speech, in reply to Henry Fox, who had said that he should "continue to vote for these measures till better could be proposed."

SPEECH, &c.

Sir, if the honorable gentleman determines to abandon his present sentiments as soon as any better measures are proposed, the ministry will quickly be deprived of one of their ablest defenders; for I consider the measures hitherto pursued so weak and so pernicious, that scarcely any alteration can be proposed that will not be for the advantage of the nation.

The honorable gentleman has already been informed that no necessity existed for hiring auxiliary troops. It does not appear that either justice or policy required us to engage in the quarrels of the Continent; that there was any need of forming an army in the Low Countries; or that, in order to form an army, auxiliaries were necessary.

But, not to dwell upon disputable points, I think it may justly be concluded that the measures of our ministry have been ill concerted, because it is undoubtedly wrong to squander the public money without effect, and to pay armies, only to be a show to our friends and a scorn to our enemies.

The troops of Hanover, whom we are now expected to pay, marched into the Low Countries, sir, where they still remain. They marched to the place most distant from the enemy, least in danger of an attack, and most strongly fortified, had an attack been designed. They have, therefore, no other claim to be paid, than that they left their own country for a place of greater security. It is always reasonable to judge of the future by the past; and therefore it is probable that next year the services of these troops will not be of equal importance with those for which they are now to be paid. I shall not, therefore, be surprised, if, after such another glorious campaign, the opponents of the ministry be challenged to propose better measures, and be told that the money of this nation can not be more properly employed than in hiring Hanoverians to eat and sleep.

But to prove yet more particularly that better measures may be taken—that more useful troops may be retained—and that, therefore, the honorable gentleman may be expected to quit those to whom he now adheres, I shall show that, in hiring the forces of Hanover, we have obstructed our own designs; that, instead of assisting the Queen of Hungary, we have withdrawn from her a part of the allies, and have burdened the nation with troops from which no service can reasonably be expected.

[1] See note to Walpole's speech, p. 40.

The advocates of the ministry have, on this occasion, affected to speak of the balance of power, the Pragmatic Sanction, and the preservation of the Queen of Hungary, not only as if they were to be the chief care of Great Britain, which (although easily controvertible) might, in compliance with long prejudices, be possibly admitted; but as if they were to be the care of Great Britain alone. These advocates, sir, have spoken as if the power of France were formidable to no other people than ourselves; as if no other part of the world would be injured by becoming a prey to a universal monarchy, and subject to the arbitrary government of a French deputy; by being drained of its inhabitants only to extend the conquests of its masters, and to make other nations equally wretched; and by being oppressed with exorbitant taxes, levied by military executions, and employed only in supporting the state of its oppressors. They dwell upon the importance of public faith and the necessity of an exact observation of treaties, as if the Pragmatic Sanction had been signed by no other potentate than the King of Great Britain; as if the public faith were to be obligatory upon ourselves alone.

That we should inviolably observe our treaties—observe them although every other nation should disregard them; that we should show an example of fidelity to mankind, and stand firm in the practice of virtue, though we should stand alone, I readily allow. I am, therefore, far from advising that we should recede from our stipulations, whatever we may suffer in their fulfillment; or that we should neglect the support of the Pragmatic Sanction, however we may be at present embarrassed, or however disadvantageous may be its assertion.

But surely, sir, for the same reason that we observe our stipulations, we ought to excite other powers also to observe their own; at the least, sir, we ought not to assist in preventing them from doing so. But how is our present conduct agreeable to these principles? The Pragmatic Sanction was guaranteed, not only by the King of Great Britain, but by the Elector of Hanover also, who (if treaties constitute obligation) is thereby equally obliged to defend the house of Austria against the attacks of any foreign power, and to send his proportion of troops for the Queen of Hungary's support.

Whether these troops *have* been sent, those whose province obliges them to possess some knowledge of foreign affairs, are better able to inform the House than myself. But, since we have not heard them mentioned in this debate, and since we know by experience that none of the merits of that Electorate are passed over in silence, it may, I think, be concluded that the distresses of the Queen of Hungary have yet received no alleviation from her alliance with Hanover; that her complaints have excited no compassion at that court, and that the justice of her cause has obtained no attention.

To what can be attributed this negligence of treaties, this disregard of justice, this defect of compassion, but to the pernicious counsels of those who have advised his Majesty to hire and to send elsewhere those troops which should have been employed for the Queen of Hungary's assistance. It is not to be imagined, sir, that his Majesty has more or less regard to justice as King of Great Britain, than as Elector of Hanover; or that he would not have sent his proportion of troops to the Austrian army, had not the temptation of greater profit been laid industriously before him. But this is not all that may be urged against such conduct. For, can we imagine that the power, that the designs of France, are less formidable to Hanover than Great Britain? Is it less necessary for the security of Hanover than of ourselves, that the house of Austria should be re-established it its former splendor and influence, and enabled to support the liberties of Europe against the enormous attempts at universal monarchy by France?

If, therefore, our assistance to the Queen of Hungary be an act of honesty, and granted in consequence of treaties, why may it not be equally required of Hanover? If it be an act of generosity, why should this country alone be obliged to sacrifice her interests for those of others? or why should the Elector of Hanover exert his liberality at the expense of Great Britain?

It is now too apparent, sir, that this great, this powerful, this mighty nation, is considered only as a province to a despicable Electorate; and that in consequence of a scheme formed long ago, and invariably pursued, these troops are hired only to drain this unhappy country of its money. That they have hitherto been of no use to Great Britain or to Austria, is evident beyond a doubt; and therefore it is plain that they are retained only for the purposes of Hanover.

How much reason the transactions of almost every year have given for suspecting this absurd, ungrateful, and perfidious partiality, it is not necessary to declare. I doubt not that most of those who sit in this House can recollect a great number of instances in point, from the purchase of part of the Swedish dominions, to the contract which we are now called upon to ratify. Few, I think, can have forgotten the memorable stipulation for the Hessian troops: for the forces of the Duke of Wolfenbuttle, which we were scarcely to march beyond the verge of their own country: or the ever memorable treaty, the tendency of which is discovered in the name. A treaty by which we disunited ourselves from Austria; destroyed that building which we now endeavor, perhaps in vain, to raise again; and weakened the only power to which it was our interest to give strength.

To dwell on all the instances of partiality which have been shown, and the yearly visits which have been paid to that *delightful* country; to reckon up all the sums that have been spent to aggrandize and enrich it, would be an irksome and invidious task—invidious to those who are afraid to be told the truth, and irksome to those who are unwilling to hear of the dishonor and injuries of their country. I shall not dwell farther on this unpleasing subject than to express my hope, that we shall no longer suffer ourselves to be deceived and oppressed: that we shall at length perform our duty as representatives of the people: and, by refusing to ratify this contract, show, that however the interests of Hanover have been preferred by the ministers, the Parliament pays no regard but to the interests of Great Britain.

The motion was carried by a considerable majority; but Mr. Pitt's popularity was greatly increased throughout the country by his resistance of this obnoxious measure.

SPEECH

OF LORD CHATHAM ON A MOTION FOR AN ADDRESS OF THANKS AFTER THE BATTLE OF DETTINGEN, DELIVERED IN THE HOUSE OF COMMONS, DECEMBER 1, 1743.

INTRODUCTION.

THE battle of Dettingen was the last in which any English monarch has appeared personally in the field. It was fought near a village of this name in Germany, on the banks of the Mayn, between Mayence and Frankfort, on the 19th of June, 1743. The allied army, consisting of about thirty-seven thousand English and Hanoverian troops, was commanded, at the time of this engagement, by George II. Previous to his taking the command, it had been brought by mismanagement into a perilous condition, being hemmed in between the River Mayn on the one side and a range of precipitous hills on the other, and there reduced to great extremities for want of provisions. The French, who occupied the opposite side of the Mayn in superior force, seized the opportunity, and threw a force of twenty-three thousand men across the river to cut off the advance of the allies through the defile of Dettingen, and shortly after sent twelve thousand more into their rear, to preclude the possibility of retreat. The position of the French in front was impregnable, and, if they had only retained it, the capture of the entire allied army would have been inevitable. But the eagerness of Grammont, who commanded the French in that quarter, drew him off from his vantage ground, and induced him to give battle to the allies on more equal terms. When the engagement commenced, George II., dismounting from his horse, put himself at the head of his infantry, and led his troops on foot to the charge. "The conduct of the King in this conflict," says Lord Mahon, "deserves the highest praise; and it was undoubtedly through him and through his son [the Duke of Cumberland], far more than through any of his generals, that the day was won." The British and Hanoverian infantry vied with each other under such guidance, and swept the French forces before them with an impetuosity which soon decided the battle, and produced a complete rout of the French army. The exhausted condition of the allies, however, and especially their want of provisions, rendered it impossible for them to pursue the French, who left the field with the loss of six thousand men.

The King, on his return to England, opened the session of Parliament in person; and in reply to his speech, an Address of Thanks was moved, "acknowledging the goodness of Divine Providence to this nation in protecting your Majesty's sacred person amid imminent dangers, in defense of the common cause and liberties of Europe." In opposition to this address, Mr. Pitt made the following speech. In the former part of it, either from erroneous information or prejudice, he seems unwilling to do justice to the King's intrepidity on that occasion. But the main part of the speech is occupied with an examination,

I. Of Sir Robert Walpole's policy (which was that of the King) in respect to the Queen of Hungary and the balance of power.

II. Of the conduct of the existing ministry (that of Lord Carteret) in relation to these subjects.

III. Of the manner in which the war in Germany had been carried on; and,

IV. Of the consequences to be anticipated from the character and conduct of the ministry.

The speech will be interesting to those who have sufficient acquaintance with the history of the times to enter fully into the questions discussed. It is characterized by comprehensive views and profound reflection on the leading question of that day, the balance of power, and by a high sense of national honor. It has a continuous line of argument running throughout it; and shows the error of those who imagine that "Lord Chatham never reasoned.'

SPEECH, &c.

From the proposition before the House, sir, we may perceive, that whatever alteration has been, or may be produced with respect to foreign measures, by the late change in administration, we can expect none with regard to our domestic affairs. In foreign measures, indeed, a most extraordinary change has taken place. From one extreme, our administration have run to the very verge of another. Our former minister [Walpole] betrayed the interests of his country by his pusillanimity; our present minister [Carteret] would sacrifice them by his Quixotism. Our former minister was for negotiating with all the world; our present minister is for fighting against all the world. Our former minister was for agreeing to every treaty, though never so dishonorable; our present minister will give ear to none, though never so rea sonable. Thus, while both appear to be extravagant, this difference results from their opposite conduct: that the wild system of the one must subject the nation to a much heavier expenditure than was ever incurred by the pusillanimity of the other.

The honorable gentleman who spoke last [Mr. Yorke] was correct in saying, that in the beginning of the session we could know nothing, in a parliamentary way, of the measures that had been pursued. I believe, sir, we shall know as little, in that way, at the end of the session; for our new minister, in this, as in every other step of his domestic conduct, will follow the example of his predecessor, and put a negative upon every motion which may tend toward our acquiring any parliamentary knowledge of our late proceedings. But if we possess no knowledge of these proceedings, it is, surely, as strong an argument for our not approving, as it can be for our not condemning them. Sir, were nothing relating to our late measures proposed to be inserted in our address upon this occasion, those measures would not have been noticed by me. But when an approbation is proposed, I am compelled to employ the knowledge I possess, whether parliamentary or otherwise, in order that I may join or not in the vote of approbation. What though my knowledge of our late measures were derived from foreign and domestic newspapers alone, even of that knowledge I must avail myself, when obliged to express my opinion; and when from that knowledge I apprehend them to be wrong, it is my duty, surely, to withhold my approbation. I am bound to persist in thus withholding it, till the minister be pleased to furnish me with such parliamentary knowledge as may convince me that I have been misinformed. This would be my proper line of conduct when, from the knowledge I possess, instead of approving any late measures, I think it more reasonable to condemn them. But supposing, sir, from the knowledge within my reach, that I consider those measures to be sound, even then I ought not to approve, unless such knowledge can warrant approval. Now, as no sort of knowledge but a parliamentary knowledge can authorize a parliamentary approbation, for this reason alone I ought to refuse it. If, therefore, that which is now proposed contain any sort of approbation, my refusing to agree to it contains no censure, but is a simple declaration that we possess not such knowledge of past measures as affords sufficient grounds for a parliamentary approbation. A parliamentary approbation, sir, extends not only to all that our ministers have advised, but to the acknowledgment of the truth of several facts which inquiry may show to be false; of facts which, at least, have been asserted without authority and proof. Suppose, sir, it should appear that his Majesty was exposed to few or no dangers abroad, but those to which he is daily liable at home, such as the overturning of his coach, or the stumbling of his horse, would not the address proposed, instead of being a compliment, be an affront and an insult to the sovereign? Suppose it should appear that our ministers have shown no regard to the advice of Parliament; that they have exerted their endeavors, not for the preservation of the house of Austria, but to involve that house in dangers which otherwise it might have avoided, and which it is scarcely possible for us now to avert. Suppose it should appear that a body of Dutch troops, although they marched to the Rhine, have never joined our army. Suppose it should appear that the treaty with Sardinia is not yet ratified by all the parties concerned, or that it is one with whose terms it is impossible they should comply. If these things should appear on inquiry, would not the address proposed be most ridiculously absurd? Now, what assurance have we that all these facts will not turn out as I have imagined?

I. Upon the death of the late Emperor of Germany, it was the interest of this nation, I grant, that the Queen of Hungary should be established in her father's dominions, and that her husband, the Duke of Lorraine, should be chosen Emperor. This was our interest, because it would have been the best security for the preservation of the balance of power; but we had no other interest, and it was one which we had in common with all the powers of Europe, excepting France. We were not, therefore, to take upon us the sole support of this interest. And, therefore, when the King of Prussia attacked Silesia—when the King of Spain, the King of Poland, and the Duke of Bavaria laid claim to the late Emperor's succession, we might have seen that the establishment of the Queen of Hungary in all her father's dominions was impracticable, especially as the Dutch refused to interfere, excepting by good offices. What, then, ought we to have done? Since we could not preserve the whole, is it not evident that, in order to bring over some of the claimants to our side, we ought to have advised her to yield up part? Upon this we ought to have insisted, and the claimant whom first we should have considered was the King of Prussia, both because he was one of the most neutral, and one of the most powerful allies with whom we could treat. For this reason it was certainly incumbent upon us to advise the Queen of Hungary to accept the terms offered by the King of Prussia when he first invaded Silesia.[1] Nay, not only should we have advised, we should have insisted upon this as the condition upon which we would assist her against the claims of others. To this the court of Vienna must have assented; and, in this case, whatever protestations the other claimants might have made, I am persuaded that the Queen of Hungary would to this day have re-

Walpole's policy.

[1] This, it is now known. was the course urged by Walpole on the Queen of Hungary. He strongly advised her to give up Silesia rather than involve Europe in a general war. She replied that she "would sooner give up her under petticoat;" and, as this put an end to the argument, he could do nothing but give the aid which England had promised —See Coxe's Walpole iii., 148.

mained the undisturbed possessor of the rest of her father's dominions, and that her husband, the Duke of Lorraine, would have been now seated on the imperial throne.

This salutary measure was not pursued. This appears, sir, not only from the Gazettes, but from our parliamentary knowledge. For, from the papers which have been either accidentally or necessarily laid before Parliament, it appears, that instead of insisting that the court of Vienna should agree to the terms offered by Prussia, we rather encouraged the obstinacy of that court in rejecting them. We did this, sir, not by our memorials alone, but by his Majesty's speech to his Parliament, by the consequent addresses of both houses, and by speeches directed by our courtiers against the King of Prussia. I allude, sir, to his Majesty's speech on the 8th of April, 1741, to the celebrated addresses on that occasion for guaranteeing the dominions of Hanover, and for granting £300,000 to enable his Majesty to support the Queen of Hungary. The speeches made on that occasion by several of our favorites at court, and their reflections on the King of Prussia, must be fresh in the memory of all. All must remember, too, that the Queen of Hungary was not then, nor for some months after, attacked by any one prince in Europe excepting the King of Prussia. She must, therefore, have supposed that both the court and nation of Great Britain were resolved to support her, not only against the King of Prussia, but against all the world. We can not, therefore, be surprised that the court of Vienna evinced an unwillingness to part with so plenteous a country as that claimed by the King of Prussia—the lordship of Silesia.

But, sir, this was not all. Not only had we promised our assistance to the Queen of Hungary, but we had actually commenced a negotiation for a powerful alliance against the King of Prussia, and for dividing his dominions among the allies. We had solicited, not only the Queen of Hungary, but also the Muscovites and the Dutch, to form parts of this alliance. We had taken both Danes and Hessians into our pay, in support of this alliance. Nay, even Hanover had subjected herself to heavy expenses on this occasion, by adding a force of nearly one third to the army she had already on foot. This, sir, was, I believe, the first extraordinary expense which Hanover had incurred since her fortunate conjunction with England; the first, I say, notwithstanding the great acquisitions she has made, and the many heavy expenses in which England has been involved upon her sole account.

If, therefore, the Queen of Hungary was obstinate in regard to the claims of Prussia, her obstinacy must be ascribed to ourselves. To us must be imputed those misfortunes which she subsequently experienced. It was easy to promise her our assistance while the French seemed determined not to interfere with Germany. It was safe to engage in schemes for her support, and for the enlargement of the Hanoverian dominions, because Prussia could certainly not oppose an equal resistance to the Queen of Hungary alone, much less so to that Queen when supported by Hanover and the whole power of Great Britain. During this posture of affairs, it was safe for us, I say, it was safe for Hanover, to promise assistance and to concert schemes in support of the Queen of Hungary. But no sooner did France come forward than our schemes were at an end, our promises forgotten. The safety of Hanover was then involved; and England, it seems, is not to be bound by promises, nor engaged in schemes, which, by possibility, may endanger or distress the Electorate! From this time, sir, we thought no more of assisting the Queen of Hungary, excepting by grants which were made by Parliament. These, indeed, our ministers did not oppose, because they contrive to make a job of every parliamentary grant. But from the miserable inactivity in which we allowed the Danish and Hessian troops to remain, notwithstanding that they received our pay; and from the insult tamely submitted to by our squadron in the Mediterranean, we must conclude that our ministers, from the time the French interfered, resolved not to assist the Queen of Hungary by land or sea. Thus, having drawn that princess forward on the ice by our promises, we left her to retreat as she could. Thus it was, sir, that the Duke of Bavaria became Emperor.[2] Thus it was that the house of Austria was stripped of great part of its dominions, and was in the utmost danger of being stripped of all, had France been bent on its destruction. Sir, the house of Austria was saved by the policy of France, who wished to reduce, but not absolutely to destroy it. Had Austria been ruined, the power of the Duke of Bavaria, who had been elected Emperor, would have risen higher than was consistent with the interests of France. It was the object of France to foment divisions among the princes of Germany, to reduce them by mutual strife, and then to render the houses of Bavaria, Austria, and Saxony nearly equal by partitions.

It was this policy which restrained the French from sending so powerful an army into Germany as they might otherwise have sent. And then, through the bad conduct of their generals, and through the skill and bravery of the officers and troops of the Queen of Hungary, a great improvement in her affairs was effected. This occurred about the time of the late changes in our administration; and this leads me to consider the origin of those measures which are now proceeding, and the situation of Europe at that particular time, February, 1742. But, before I enter upon that consideration, I must lay this down as a maxim to be ever observed by this nation, that, although it be our own interest to preserve a balance of power in Europe, yet, as we are the most remote from danger, we have the least reason to be jealous as to the adjustment of that balance, and should be the last to take alarm on its

[2] The Duke of Bavaria was elected Emperor on the 12th of February, 1742.

account. Now the balance of power may be supported, either by the existence of one single potentate capable of opposing and defeating the ambitious designs of France, or by a well-connected confederacy adequate to the same intent. Of these two methods, the first, when practicable, is the most eligible, because on that method we may most safely rely; but when it can not be resorted to, the whole address of our ministers and plenipotentiaries should tend to establish the second.

The wisdom of the maxim, sir, to which I have adverted, must be acknowledged by all who consider, that when the powers upon the Continent apply to us to join them in a war against France, we may take what share in the war we think fit. When we, on the contrary, apply to them, they will prescribe to us. However some gentlemen may affect to alarm themselves or others by alleging the dependency of all the European powers upon France, of this we may rest assured, that when those powers are really threatened with such dependency, they will unite among themselves, and call upon us also to prevent it. Nay, sir, should even that dependence imperceptibly ensue; so soon as they perceived it, they would unite among themselves, and call us to join the confederacy by which it might be shaken off. Thus we can never be reduced to stand single in support of the balance of power; nor can we be compelled to call upon our continental neighbors for such purpose, unless when our ministers have an interest in pretending and asserting imaginary dangers.

The posture of Europe since the time of the Romans is wonderfully changed. In those times each country was divided into many sovereignties. It was then impossible for the people of any one country to unite among themselves, and much more impossible for two or three large countries to combine in a general confederacy against the enormous power of Rome. But such confederacy is very practicable now, and may always be effected whenever France, or any one of the powers of Europe, shall endeavor to enslave the rest. I have said, sir, that the balance of power in Europe may be maintained as securely by a confederacy as it can be by opposing any one rival power to the power of France. Now, let us examine to which of these two methods we ought to have resorted in February, 1742. The imperial diadem was then fallen from the house of Austria; and although the troops of the Queen of Hungary had met with some success during the winter, that sovereign was still stripped of great part of the Austrian dominions. The power of that house was therefore greatly inferior to what it was at the time of the late emperor's death; and still more inferior to what it had been in 1716, when we considered it necessary to add Naples and Sardinia to its former acquisitions, in order to render it a match for France. Besides this, there existed in 1742 a very powerful confederacy against the house of Austria, while no jealousy was harbored by the powers of Europe against the ambition of France. For France, although she had assisted in depressing the house of Austria, had shown no design of increasing her own dominions. On the other hand, the haughty demeanor of the court of Vienna, and the height to which that house had been raised, excited a spirit of disgust and jealousy in the princes of Germany. That spirit first manifested itself in the house of Hanover, and at this very time prevailed not only there, but in most of the German sovereignties. Under such circumstances, however weak and erroneous our ministers might be, they could not possibly think of restoring the house of Austria to its former splendor and power. They could not possibly oppose that single house as a rival to France. No power in Europe would have cordially assisted them in that scheme They would have had to cope, not only with France and Spain, but with all the princes of Germany and Italy, to whom Austria had become obnoxious.

In these circumstances, what was this nation to do? It was impossible to establish the balance of power in Europe upon the single power of the house of Austria. Surely, then, sir, it was our business to think of restoring the peace of Germany as soon as possible by our good offices, in order to establish a confederacy sufficient to oppose France, should she afterward discover any ambitious intentions. It was now not so much our business to prevent the lessening the power of the house of Austria, as it was to bring about a speedy reconciliation between the princes of Germany; to take care that France should get as little by the treaty of peace as she said she expected by the war. This, I say, should have been our chief concern; because the preservation of the balance of power was now no longer to depend upon the house of Austria, but upon the joint power of a confederacy then to be formed; and till the princes of Germany were reconciled among themselves, there was scarcely a possibility of forming such a confederacy. If we had made this our scheme, the Dutch would have joined heartily in it. The Germanic body would have joined in it; and the peace of Germany might have been restored without putting this nation to any expense, or diverting us from the prosecution of our just and necessary war against Spain, in case our differences with that nation could not have been adjusted by the treaty for restoring the peace of Germany.

Carteret's policy.

II. But our new minister, as I have said, ran into an extreme quite opposite to that of the old. Our former minister thought of nothing but negotiating when he ought to have thought of nothing but war; the present minister has thought of nothing but war, or at least its resemblance, when he ought to have thought of nothing but negotiation.

A resolution was taken, and preparations were made, for sending a body of troops to Flanders, even before we had any hopes of the King of Prussia's deserting his alliance with France, and without our being called on to do so by any one power in Europe. I say, sir, by any one power in Europe; for I defy our ministers to show that even the Queen of Hungary desired any such thing before it was resolved on. I believe some of her ministers were free enough to declare that the money those troops cost would have done her much more service; and I am sure we were so far from being called on by the Dutch to do so, that it was resolved on without their participation, and the measures carried into execution, I believe, expressly contrary to their advice.

This resolution, sir, was so far from having any influence on the King of Prussia, that he continued firm to his alliance with France, and fought the battle of Czaslau after he knew such a resolution was taken. If he had continued firm in the same sentiments, I am very sure our troops neither would nor could have been of the least service to the Queen of Hungary. But the battle of Czaslau fully convinced him that the French designed chiefly to play one German prince against another, in order to weaken both; and perhaps he had before this discovered, that, according to the French scheme, his share of Silesia was not to be so considerable as he expected. These considerations, and not the eloquence or address of any of our ministers, inclined him to come to an agreement with the Queen of Hungary. As she was now convinced that she could not depend upon our promises, she readily agreed to his terms, though his demands were now much more extravagant than they were at first; and, what is worse, they were now unaccompanied with any one promise or consideration, except that of a neutrality; whereas his first demands were made palatable by the tender of a large sum of money, and by the promise of his utmost assistance, not only in supporting the Pragmatic Sanction, but in raising her husband, the Duke of Lorraine, to the imperial throne. Nay, originally, he even insinuated that he would embrace the first opportunity to assist in procuring her house an equivalent for whatever part of Silesia she should resign to him.

This accommodation between the Queen of Hungary and the King of Prussia, and that which soon after followed between her and the Duke of Saxony, produced a very great alteration in the affairs of Europe. But, as these last powers promised nothing but a neutrality, and as the Dutch absolutely refused to join, either with the Queen of Hungary or with ourselves, in any offensive measures against France, it was still impossible for us to think of restoring the house of Austria to such power as to render it a match for the power of France. We ought, therefore, still to have thought only of negotiation, in order to restore the peace of Germany by an accommodation between her and the Emperor. The distresses to which the Bavarian and French armies in Germany were driven furnished us with such an opportunity: this we ought by all means to have embraced, and to have insisted on the Queen of Hungary's doing the same, under the pain of being entirely deserted by us. A peace was offered both by the Emperor and the French, upon the terms of *uti possidetis*, with respect to Germany; but, for what reason I can not comprehend, we were so far from advising the Queen of Hungary to accept, that I believe we advised her to reject it.

This, sir, was a conduct in our ministers so very extraordinary, so directly opposite to the interest of this nation, and the security of the balance of power, that I can suggest to myself no one reason for it, but that they were resolved to put this nation to the expense of maintaining sixteen thousand Hanoverians. This I am afraid was the true motive with our new ministers for all the warlike measures they resolved on. Nothing would now satisfy us but a conquest of Alsace and Lorraine in order to give them to the Queen of Hungary, as an equivalent for what she had lost. And this we resolved on, or at least pretended to resolve on, at a time when France and Prussia were in close conjunction; at a time when no one of the powers of Europe could assist us; at a time when none of them entertained a jealousy of the ambitious designs of France; and at a time when most of the princes of Germany were so jealous of the power of the house of Austria, that we had great reason to apprehend that the most considerable of these would join against us, in case we should meet with any success.

Sir, if our ministers were really serious in this scheme, it was one of the most romantic that ever entered the head of an English Quixote. But if they made it only a pretext for putting this nation to the expense of maintaining sixteen thousand Hanoverians, or of acquiring some new territory for the Electorate of Hanover, I am sure no British House of Commons can approve their conduct. It is absurd, sir, to say that we could not advise the Queen of Hungary to accept of the terms offered by the Emperor and France, at a time when their troops were cooped up in the city of Prague, and when the terms were offered with a view only to get their troops at liberty, and to take the first opportunity to attack her with more vigor. This, I say, is absurd, because, had she accepted the terms proposed, she might have had them guaranteed by the Dutch, by the German body, and by all the powerful princes of Germany; which would have brought all these powers into a confederacy with us against the Emperor and France, if they had afterward attacked her in Germany; and all of them, but especially the Dutch, and the King of Prussia, would have been ready to join us, had the French attacked her in Flanders. It is equally absurd to say that she could not accept of these terms, because they contained nothing for the security of her dominions in Italy. For suppose the war had continued in Italy, if the Queen of Hungary had been safe upon the side of Germany, she could have poured such a number of troops into Italy as would have been sufficient to oppose and defeat all the armies that both the French and Spaniards could send to and maintain in that country; since we could, by our superior fleets, have made it impossible for the French and Spaniards to maintain great armies in that country.

No other reason can therefore be assigned for the Queen of Hungary's refusal of the terms proposed to her for restoring the tranquillity of Germany than this alone, that we had promised to assist her so effectually as to enable her to conquer a part of France, by way of equivalent for what she had lost in Germany and Italy. Such assistance it was neither our interest nor in our power to give, considering the circumstances of Europe. I am really surprised that the Queen of Hungary came to trust a second time to our promises; for I may venture to prophesy that she will find herself again deceived. We shall put ourselves to a vast unnecessary expense, as we did when she was first attacked by Prussia; and without being able to raise a jealousy in the other powers of Europe, we shall give France a pretense for conquering Flanders, which, otherwise, she would not have done. We may bring the Queen of Hungary a second time to the verge of destruction, and leave her there; for that we certainly shall do, as soon as Hanover comes to be a second time in danger. From all which I must conclude, that our present scheme of politics is fundamentally wrong, and that the longer we continue to build upon such a foundation, the more dangerous it will be for us. The whole fabric will involve this unfortunate nation in its ruins.

III. But now, sir, let us see how we have prosecuted this scheme, bad as it is, during the last campaign. As this nation must bear the chief part of the expense, it was certainly our business to prosecute the war with all possible vigor; to come to action as soon as possible, and to push every advantage to the utmost. Since we soon found that we could not attack the French upon the side of Flanders, why were our troops so long marching into Germany? Or, indeed, I should ask, why our armies were not first assembled in that country? Why did they continue so long inactive upon the Mayn? If our army was not numerous enough to attack the French, why were the Hessians left behind for some time in Flanders? Why did we not send over twenty thousand of those regular troops that were lying idle here at home? How to answer all those questions I can not tell; but it is certain we never thought of attacking the French army in our neighborhood, and, I believe, expected very little to be attacked ourselves. Nay, I doubt much if any action would have happened during the whole campaign, if the French had not, by the misconduct of some one or other of our generals, caught our army in a hose-net, from which it could not have escaped, had all the French generals observed the direction of their commander-in-chief; had they thought only of guarding and fortifying themselves in the defile [Dettingen], and not of marching up to attack our troops. Thank God, sir, the courage of some of the French generals got the better of their discretion, as well as of their military discipline. This made them attack, instead of waiting to be attacked; and then, by the bravery of the English foot, and the cowardice of their own, they met with a severe repulse, which put their whole army into confusion, and obliged them to retire with precipitation across the Mayn. Our army thus escaped the snare into which they had been led, and was enabled to pursue its retreat to Hanau.

Conduct of the war.

This, sir, was a signal advantage; but was it followed up? Did we press upon the enemy in their precipitate retreat across a great river, where many of them must have been lost had they been closely pursued? Did we endeavor to take the least advantage of the confusion into which their unexpected repulse had thrown them? No, sir; the ardor of the British troops was restrained by the cowardice of the Hanoverians; and, instead of pursuing the enemy, we ourselves ran away in the night with such haste that we left all our wounded to the mercy and care of the enemy, who had the honor of burying our dead as well as their own. This action may, therefore, on our side, be called a fortunate *escape;* I shall never give my consent to honor it with the name of *victory*.

After this escape, sir, our army was joined by a very large re-enforcement. Did this revive our courage, or urge us on to give battle? Not in the least, sir; though the French continued for some time upon the German side of the Rhine, we never offered to attack them, or to give them the least disturbance. At last, upon Prince Charles's approach with the Austrian army, the French not only repassed the Rhine, but retired quite out of Germany. And as the Austrian army and the allied army might then have joined, and might both have passed the Rhine without opposition at Mentz, or almost any where in the Palatinate, it was expected that both armies would have marched together into Lorraine, or in search of the French army. in order to force them to a battle. Instead of this, sir, Prince Charles marched up the German side of the Rhine—to do what? To pass that great river, in the sight of a French army equal in number to his own, which, without some extraordinary neglect in the French, was impracticable; and so it was found by experience. Thus the whole campaign upon that side was consumed in often attempting what so often appeared to be impracticable.

On the other side—I mean that of the allied army—was there any thing of consequence performed? I know of nothing, sir, but that of sending a party of hussars into Lorraine with a manifesto. The army, indeed, passed the Rhine at Mentz, and marched up to the French lines upon the frontier of Alsace, but never offered to pass those lines until the French had abandoned them, I believe with a design to draw our army into some snare; for, upon the return of the French toward those lines, we retired with much greater haste than we had advanced, though the Dutch auxiliaries were then come up and pretended, at least, to be ready to join our army. I have heard, however, that they found a pretext for never coming into the line; and I doubt much if they would have marched with us to attack the French army in their own territories, or to invest any of the fortified places; for I must observe that the French lines upon the Queich were not all of them within the territories of France. But suppose this Dutch detachment had been ready to march with us to attack the French in their own territories, or to invest some of their fortified places, I can not join in any congratulation upon that event; for a small detachment of Dutch troops can never enable us to execute the vast scheme we have undertaken. The whole force of that republic would not be sufficient for the purpose, because we should have the majority of the empire against us; and, therefore, if the Dutch had joined *totis viribus*[3] in our scheme, instead of congratulating, I should have bemoaned their running mad by our example and at our instigation.

Prospects for the future.

IV. Having now briefly examined our past conduct, from the few remarks I have made, I believe, sir, it will appear that, supposing our scheme to be in itself possible and practicable, we have no reason to hope for success if it be not prosecuted with more vigor and with better conduct than it was during the last campaign. While we continue in the prosecution of this scheme, whoever may lose, the Hanoverians will be considerable gainers. They will draw four or five hundred thousand pounds yearly from this nation over and above what they have annually drawn, ever since they had the good fortune to be united under the same sovereign with ourselves. But we ought to consider—even the Hanoverians ought to consider—that this nation is not now in a condition to carry on an expensive war for ten or twelve years, as it did in the reign of Queen Anne. We may fund it out for one, two, or three years; but the public debt is now so large that, if we go on adding millions to it every year, our credit will at last (sooner, I fear, than some among us may imagine) certainly be undone; and if this misfortune should occur, neither Hanover nor any other foreign state would be able to draw another shilling from the country. A stop to our public credit would put an end to our paper currency. A universal bankruptcy would ensue, and all the little ready money left among us would be locked up in iron chests, or hid in by-corners by the happy possessors. It would then be impossible to raise our taxes, and consequently impossible to maintain either fleets or armies. Our troops abroad would be obliged to enter into the service of any prince that could maintain them, and our troops at home would be obliged to live upon free quarter. But this they could not do long; for the farmer would neither sow nor reap if he found his produce taken from him by the starving soldier. In these circumstances, I must desire the real friends of our present happy establishment to consider what might be the consequence of the Pretender's landing among us at the head of a French army. Would he not be looked upon by most men as a savior? Would not the majority of the people join with him, in order to rescue the nation from those that had brought it into such confusion? This danger, sir, is, I hope, imaginary, but I am sure it is far from being so imaginary as that which has been held out in this debate, the danger of all the powers of the continent of Europe being brought under such a slavish dependence upon France as to join with her in conquering this island, or in bringing it under the same slavish dependence with themselves.

I had almost forgotten, sir (I wish future nations may forget), to mention the Treaty of Worms.[4] I wish that treaty could be erased from our annals and our records, so as never to be mentioned hereafter: for that treaty, with its appendix, the convention that followed, is one of the most destructive, unjust, and absurd that was ever concluded. By that treaty we have taken upon ourselves a burden which I think it impossible for us to support; we have engaged in such an act of injustice toward Genoa as must alarm all Europe, and give to the French a most signal advantage. From this, sir, all the princes of Europe will see what regard we have to justice when we think that the power is on our side; most of them, therefore, will probably join with France in curtailing our power, or, at least, in preventing its increase.

[3] With all their forces.

[4] The Treaty of Worms was an offensive and defensive alliance, concluded on the 2d of September, 1743, between England, Austria, and Sardinia. By it the Queen of Hungary agreed to transfer to the King of Sardinia the city and part of the duchy of Placentia, the Vigevanesco, part of the duchy of Pavia, and the county of Anghiera, as well as her claims to the marquisate of Finale, which had been ceded to the Genoese by the late Emperor Charles VI. for the sum of 400,000 golden crowns, for which it had been previously mortgaged. The Queen of Hungary also engaged to maintain 30,000 men in Italy, to be commanded by the King of Sardinia. Great Britain agreed to pay the sum of £300,000 for the cession of Finale, and to furnish an annual subsidy of £200,000, on the condition that the King of Sardinia should employ 45,000 men. In addition to supplying these sums, Great Britain agreed to send a strong squadron into the Mediterranean, to act in concert with the allied forces. By a separate and secret convention, agreed to at the same time and place as the treaty, but which was never ratified nor publicly avowed, it was stipulated that Great Britain should pay to the Queen of Hungary an annual subsidy of £300,000, not merely during the war, but so long "as the necessity of her affairs should require." The terms of the Treaty of Worms relative to the cession of the marquisate of Finale to Sardinia were particularly unjust to the Genoese, since that territory had been guaranteed to them by the fourth article of the Quadruple Alliance, concluded on the 2d of August, 1718, between Great Britain, France, Austria, and Holland.—Coxe's Austria, chap. civ. Lord Mahon's Hist. of England, vol. iii., p. 231. Belsham's Hist. of England, vol. iv., p. 82, *et seq.*

The alliance of Sardinia and its assistance may, I admit, be of great use to us in defeating the designs of the Spaniards in Italy. But gold itself may be bought too dear; and I fear we shall find the purchase we have made to be but precarious, especially if Sardinia should be attacked by France as well as by Spain, the almost certain consequence of our present scheme of politics. For these reasons, sir, I hope there is not any gentleman, nor even any minister, who expects that I should declare my satisfaction that this treaty has been concluded.

It is very surprising, sir, to hear gentlemen talk of the great advantages of unanimity in our proceedings, when, at the time, they are doing all they can to prevent unanimity. If the honorable gentleman had intended that what he proposed should be unanimously agreed to, he would have returned to the ancient custom of Parliament which some of his new friends have, on former occasions, so often recommended. It is a new doctrine to pretend that we ought in our address to return some sort of answer to every thing mentioned in his Majesty's speech. It is a doctrine that has prevailed only since our Parliaments began to look more like French than English Parliaments; and now we pretend to be such enemies of France, I supposed we should have laid aside a doctrine which the very method of proceeding in Parliament must show to be false. His Majesty's speech is not now so much as under our consideration, but upon a previous order for that purpose; therefore we can not now properly take notice of its contents, any farther than to determine whether we ought to return thanks for it or not. Even this we may refuse, without being guilty of any breach of duty to our sovereign; but of this, I believe, no gentleman would have thought, had the honorable gentleman who made this motion not attached to it a long and fulsome panegyric upon the conduct of our ministers. I am convinced no gentleman would have objected to our expressing our duty to our sovereign, and our zeal for his service, in the strongest and most affectionate terms: nor would any gentleman have refused to congratulate his Majesty upon any fortunate event happening to the royal family. The honorable gentleman would have desired no more than this, had he intended that his motion should be unanimously agreed to. But ministers are generally the authors and drawers up of the motion, and they always have a greater regard for themselves than for the service of their sovereign; that is the true reason why such motions seldom meet with unanimous approbation.

As to the danger, sir, of our returning or not returning to our national custom upon this occasion, I think it lies wholly upon the side of our not returning. I have shown that the measures we are now pursuing are fundamentally wrong, and that the longer we pursue them, the heavier our misfortunes will prove. Unless some signal providence interpose, experience, I am convinced, will confirm what I say. By the immediate intervention of Providence, we may, it is true, succeed in the most improbable schemes; but Providence seems to be against us. The sooner, therefore, we repent and amend, the better it will be for us; and unless repentance begins in this House, I shall no where expect it until dire experience has convinced us of our errors.

For these reasons, sir, I wish, I hope, that we may now begin to put a stop to the farther prosecution of these disastrous measures, by refusing them our approbation. If we put a negative upon this question, it may awaken our ministers from their deceitful dreams. If we agree to it, they will dream on till they have dreamed Europe their country, and themselves into utter perdition. If they stop now, the nation may recover; but if by such a flattering address we encourage them to go on, it may soon become impossible for them to retreat. For the sake of Europe, therefore, for the sake of my country, I most heartily join in putting a negative upon the question.

After a protracted debate, the address was carried by a vote of 279 to 149.

SPEECH

OF LORD CHATHAM ON AN ADDRESS TO THE THRONE, IN WHICH THE RIGHT OF TAXING AMERICA IS DISCUSSED, DELIVERED IN THE HOUSE OF COMMONS, JANUARY 14, 1766.

INTRODUCTION.

Mr. George Grenville, during his brief administration from 1763 to 1765, adopted a plan for replenishing the exhausted treasury of Great Britain, which had been often proposed before, but rejected by every preceding minister. It was that of levying direct taxes on the American colonies. His famous Stamp Act was brought forward February 7th, 1765. It was strongly opposed by Colonel Barré, who thus indignantly replied to the charge of ingratitude, brought by Charles Townsend against the Americans, as "children planted by our care, nourished by our indulgence, and protected by our arms," &c. "*They planted by your care?*" said Colonel Barré: "No! Your oppressions planted them in America. They fled from your tyranny to a then uncultivated and inhospitable country, where they exposed themselves to almost all the hardships to which human nature is liable; and, among others, to the cruelties of a savage foe, the most subtle, and, I will take it upon me to say, the most formidable of any people on earth; and yet, actuated by principles of true English liberty, they met all hardships with pleasure, compared with those they suffered in their native land from the hands of those who should have been their friends. *They nourished by your indulgence?* They grew by your neglect of them! As soon as you began to care about them, that care was exercised in sending persons to rule them, who were, perhaps, the deputies of deputies to some members of this House—sent to spy out their liberties, to misrepresent their actions, and to prey upon them—men promoted to the highest seats of justice; some of whom, to my knowledge, were glad, by going to a foreign country, to escape being brought to the bar of a court of justice in their own. *They protected by your arms?* They have nobly taken up arms in your defense; have exerted a valor, amid their constant and laborious industry, for the defense of a country whose frontier was drenched in blood, while its interior yielded all its little savings to your emolument. And—believe me—remember I this day told you so—that same spirit of freedom which actuated that people at first, will accompany them still. But prudence forbids me to say more. God knows I do not, at this time, speak from motives of party heat. What I deliver are the genuine sentiments of my heart. However superior to me in general knowledge and experience the respectable body of this House may be, I claim to know more of America than most of you, having seen and been conversant with that country. The people are, I believe, as truly loyal as any subjects the King has; but a people jealous of their liberties, and who will vindicate them, if they should ever be violated."

This prophetic warning was in vain. The bill was passed on the 22d of March, 1765.

A few months after, the ministry of Mr. Grenville came abruptly to an end, and was followed by the administration of Lord Rockingham. That able statesman was fully convinced that nothing but the repeal of the Stamp Act could restore tranquillity to the colonies, which, according to Colonel Barré's predictions, were in a state of almost open resistance. The news of this resistance reached England at the close of 1765, and Parliament was summoned on the 17th of December. The plan of the ministry was to repeal the Stamp Act; but, in accordance with the King's wishes, to re-assert (in doing so) the *right* of Parliament to tax the colonies. Against this course Mr. Pitt determined to take his stand; and when the ordinary address was made in answer to the King's speech, he entered at once on the subject of American taxation, in a strain of the boldest eloquence. His speech was reported by Sir Robert Dean, assisted by Lord Charlemont, and, though obviously broken and imperfect, gives us far more of the language actually used by Mr. Pitt than any of the preceding speeches.

SPEECH, &c.

Mr. Speaker,—I came to town but to-day. I was a stranger to the tenor of his Majesty's speech, and the proposed address, till I heard them read in this House. Unconnected and unconsulted, I have not the means of information. I am fearful of offending through mistake, and therefore beg to be indulged with a second reading of the proposed address. [The address being read, Mr. Pitt went on:] I commend the King's speech, and approve of the address in answer, as it decides nothing, every gentleman being left at perfect liberty to take such a part concerning America as he may afterward see fit. One word only I can not approve of: an "early," is a word that does not belong to the notice the ministry have given to Parliament of the troubles in America. In a matter of such importance, the communication ought to have been *immediate!*

I speak not now with respect to parties. I stand up in this place single and independent. As to the late ministry [turning himself to Mr. Grenville, who sat within one of him], every capital measure they have taken has been entirely wrong! As to the present gentlemen, to those at least whom I have in my eye [looking at the bench where General Conway sat with the lords of the treasury], I have no objection. I have never been made a sacrifice by any of them. Their characters are fair; and I am always glad when men of fair character engage in his Majesty's service. Some of them did me the honor to ask my opinion before they would engage. These will now do me the justice to own, I advised them to do it—but, notwithstanding (for I love to be explicit), *I can not give them my confidence.* Pardon me, gentlemen [bowing to the ministry], confidence is a plant of slow growth in an aged bosom. Youth is the season of credulity. By comparing events with each other, reasoning from effects to causes, methinks I plainly discover the traces of an *overruling* influence.[1]

There is a clause in the Act of Settlement obliging every minister to sign his name to the advice which he gives to his sovereign. Would it were observed! I have had the honor to serve the Crown, and if I could have submitted to *influence*, I might have still continued to serve: but I would not be responsible for others. I have no local attachments. It is indifferent to me whether a man was rocked in his cradle on this side or that side of the Tweed. I sought for merit wherever it was to be found. It is my boast, that I was the first minister who looked for it, and found it, in the mountains of the North. I called it forth, and drew into your service a hardy and intrepid race of men—men, who, when left by your jealousy, became a prey to the artifices of your enemies, and had gone nigh

[1] Chas. Butler says in his Reminiscences, "Those who remember the air of condescending protection with which the bow was made and the look given, will recollect how much they themselves, at the moment, were both delighted and awed; and what they themselves conceived of the immeasurable superiority of the speaker over every other human being that surrounded him."

to have overturned the state in the war before the last. These men, in the last war, were brought to combat on your side. They served with fidelity, as they fought with valor, and conquered for you in every part of the world. Detested be the national reflections against them! They are unjust, groundless, illiberal, unmanly! When I ceased to serve his Majesty as a minister, it was not the *country* of the man by which I was moved — but the *man* of that country wanted wisdom, and held principles incompatible with freedom.[2]

It is a long time, Mr. Speaker, since I have attended in Parliament. When the resolution was taken in this House to tax America, I was ill in bed. If I could have endured to be carried in my bed—so great was the agitation of my mind for the consequences—I would have solicited some kind hand to have laid me down on this floor, to have borne my testimony against it! It is now an act that has passed. I would speak with decency of every act of this House; but I must beg the indulgence of the House to speak of it with freedom.

I hope a day may soon be appointed to consider the state of the nation with respect to America. I hope gentlemen will come to this debate with all the temper and impartiality that his Majesty recommends, and the importance of the subject requires; a subject of greater importance than ever engaged the attention of this House, that subject only excepted, when, near a century ago,[3] it was the question, whether you yourselves were to be bond or free. In the mean time, as I can not depend upon my health for any future day (such is the nature of my infirmities), I will beg to say a few words at present, leaving the justice, the equity, the policy, the expediency of the act to another time.

I will only speak to one point, a point which seems not to have been generally understood. I mean to the *right*. Some gentlemen [alluding to Mr. Nugent] seem to have considered it as a point of honor. If gentlemen consider it in that light, they leave all measures of right and wrong, to follow a delusion that may lead to destruction. It is my opinion, that this kingdom has no right to lay a tax upon the colonies. At the same time, I assert the authority of this kingdom over the colonies to be sovereign and supreme, in every circumstance of government and legislation whatsoever. They are the subjects of this kingdom; equally entitled with yourselves to all the natural rights of mankind and the peculiar privileges of Englishmen; equally bound by its laws, and equally participating in the constitution of this free country. The Americans are the sons, not the bastards of England! Taxation is no part of the governing or legislative power. The taxes are a voluntary *gift* and *grant* of the Commons alone. In legislation the three estates of the realm are alike concerned; but the concurrence of the peers and the Crown to a tax is only necessary to clothe it with the form of a law. The gift and grant is of the Commons alone. In ancient days, the Crown, the barons, and the clergy possessed the lands. In those days, the barons and the clergy gave and granted to the Crown. They gave and granted what was their own! At present, since the discovery of America, and other circumstances permitting, the Commons are become the proprietors of the land. The Church (God bless it!) has but a pittance. The property of the lords, compared with that of the commons, is as a drop of water in the ocean; and this House represents those commons, the proprietors of the lands; and those proprietors virtually represent the rest of the inhabitants. When, therefore, in this House, we give and grant, we give and grant what is our own. But in an American tax, what do we do? "We, your Majesty's Commons for Great Britain, give and grant to your Majesty"—what? Our own property? No! "We give and grant to your Majesty" the property of your Majesty's commons of America! It is an absurdity in terms.

The distinction between legislation and taxation is essentially necessary to liberty. The Crown and the peers are equally legislative powers with the Commons. If taxation be a part of simple legislation, the Crown and the peers have rights in taxation as well as yourselves; rights which they will claim, which they will exercise, whenever the principle can be supported by power.

There is an idea in some that the colonies are *virtually* represented in the House. I would fain know by whom an American is represented here. Is he represented by any knight of the shire, in any county in this kingdom? *Would to God that respectable representation was aug-*

[2] It need hardly be said that Lord Bute is aimed at throughout the whole of these two paragraphs. The passage illustrates a mode of attack which Lord Chatham often used, that of *pointing at* an individual in a manner at once so significant as to arrest attention, and yet so remote as to involve no breach of decorum—saying the severest things by *implication*, and leaving the hearer to apply them; thus avoiding the coarseness of personal invective, and giving a wide scope for ingenuity in the most stinging allusions. In the present case, the allusion to Bute as having "made a sacrifice" of Chatham, by driving him from power through a secret ascendency over the King; to "the traces of an overruling influence" from the same quarter as a reason for withholding confidence from the new ministry; and to Bute's shrinking from that responsibility which the Act of Settlement imposed upon all advisers of the King—these and other allusions to the favorite of George III. would be instantly understood and keenly felt among a people who have always regarded the character of a *favorite* with dread and abhorrence. Lord Chatham, to avoid the imputation of being influenced in what he said by the prevailing prejudices against Bute as a Scotchman, refers to himself, in glowing language, as the first minister who employed Highlanders in the army; calling "from the mountains of the North" "a hardy and intrepid race of men," who had been alienated by previous severity, but who, by that one act of confidence, were indissolubly attached to the house of Hanover.

[3] At the Revolution of 1688.

mented to a greater number! Or will you tell him that he is represented by any representative of a borough? a borough which, perhaps, its own representatives never saw! This is what is called *the rotten part of the Constitution.* It can not continue a century. If it does not drop, it must be amputated.[4] The idea of a virtual representation of America in this House is the most contemptible idea that ever entered into the head of a man. It does not deserve a serious refutation.

The Commons of America, represented in their several assemblies, have ever been in possession of the exercise of this, their constitutional right, of giving and granting their own money. They would have been slaves if they had not enjoyed it! At the same time, this kingdom, as the supreme governing and legislative power, has always bound the colonies by her laws, by her regulations, and restrictions in trade, in navigation, in manufactures, in every thing, except that of taking their money out of their pockets without their consent.

Here I would draw the line,

Quam ultra citraque neque consistere rectum.[5]

[As soon as Lord Chatham concluded, General Conway arose, and succinctly avowed his entire approbation of that part of his Lordship's speech which related to American affairs, but disclaimed altogether that "secret overruling influence which had been hinted at." Mr. George Grenville, who followed in the debate, expatiated at large on the tumults and riots which had taken place in the colonies, and declared that they bordered on rebellion. He condemned the language and sentiments which he had heard as encouraging a *revolution.* A portion of his speech is here inserted, as explanatory of the replication of Lord Chatham.[6]]

I can not, said Mr. Grenville, understand the difference between external and internal taxes. They are the same in effect, and differ only in name. That this kingdom has the sovereign, the supreme legislative power over America, is granted; it can not be denied; and taxation is a part of that sovereign power. It is one branch of the legislation. It is, it has been, exercised over those who are not, who were never represented. It is exercised over the India Company, the merchants of London, the proprietors of the stocks, and over many great manufacturing towns. It was exercised over the county palatine of Chester, and the bishopric of Durham, before they sent any representatives to Parliament. I appeal for proof to the preambles of the acts which gave them representatives; one in the reign of Henry VIII., the other in that of Charles II. [Mr. Grenville then quoted the acts, and desired that they might be read; which being done, he said,] When I proposed to tax America, I asked the House if any gentleman would object to the right; I repeatedly asked it, and no man would attempt to deny it. Protection and obedience are reciprocal. Great Britain protects America; America is bound to yield obedience. If not, tell me when the Americans were emancipated? When they want the protection of this kingdom, they are always very ready to ask it. That protection has always been afforded them in the most full and ample manner. The nation has run herself into an immense debt to give them their protection; and now, when they are called upon to contribute a small share toward the public expense—an expense arising from themselves—they renounce your authority, insult your officers, and break out, I might almost say, into open rebellion. The seditious spirit of the colonies owes its birth to the factions in this House. Gentlemen are careless of the consequences of what they say, provided it answers the purposes of opposition. We were told we trod on tender ground. We were bid to expect disobedience. What is this but telling the Americans to stand out against the law, to encourage their obstinacy with the expectation of support from hence? "Let us only hold out a little," they would say, "our friends will soon be in power." Ungrateful people of America! Bounties have been extended to them. When I had the honor of serving the Crown, while you yourselves were loaded with an enormous debt, you gave bounties on their lumber, on their iron, their hemp, and many other articles. You have relaxed in their favor the Act of Navigation, that palladium of the British commerce; and yet I have been abused in all the public papers as an enemy to the trade of America. I have been particularly charged with giving orders and instructions to prevent the Spanish trade, and thereby stopping the channel by which alone North America used to be supplied with cash for remittances to this country. I defy any man to produce any such orders or instructions. I discouraged no trade but what was illicit, what was prohibited by an act of Parliament. I desire a West India merchant (Mr. Long), well known in the city, a gentleman of character, may be examined. He will tell you that I offered to do every thing in my power to advance the trade of America. I was above giving an answer to anonymous calumnies; but in this place it becomes one to wipe off the aspersion.

[Here Mr. Grenville ceased. Several members got up to speak, but Mr. Pitt seeming to rise, the House was so clamorous for Mr. *Pitt!* Mr. *Pitt!* that the speaker was obliged to call to order.]

Mr. Pitt said, I do not apprehend I am speaking twice. I did expressly reserve a part of my subject, in order to save the time of this House; but I am compelled to proceed in it. I do not

[4] We have here the first mention made by any English statesman of a *reform* in the borough system. A great truth once uttered never dies. The Reform Bill of Earl Grey had its origin in the mind of Chatham.

[5] On neither side of which we can rightly stand.

[6] Mr. Grenville, it will be remembered, had now no connection with the ministry, but was attempting to defend his Stamp Act against the attack of Mr. Pitt.

speak twice; I only finish what I designedly left imperfect. But if the House is of a different opinion, far be it from me to indulge a wish of transgression against order. I am content, if it be your pleasure, to be silent. [Here he paused. The House resounding with *Go on! go on!* he proceeded:]

Gentlemen, sir, have been charged with giving birth to *sedition* in America. They have spoken their sentiments with freedom against this unhappy act, and that freedom has become their crime. Sorry I am to hear the liberty of speech in this House imputed as a crime. But the imputation shall not discourage me. It is a liberty I mean to exercise. No gentleman ought to be afraid to exercise it. It is a liberty by which the gentleman who calumniates it might have profited. He ought to have desisted from his project. The gentleman tells us, America is obstinate; America is almost in open rebellion. I rejoice that America has resisted. Three millions of people, so dead to all the feelings of liberty as voluntarily to submit to be slaves, would have been fit instruments to make slaves of the rest. I come not here armed at all points, with law cases and acts of Parliament, with the statute book doubled down in dog's ears, to defend the cause of liberty. If I had, I myself would have cited the two cases of Chester and Durham. I would have cited them to show that, even under former arbitrary reigns, Parliaments were ashamed of taxing a people without their consent, and allowed them representatives. Why did the gentleman confine himself to Chester and Durham? He might have taken a higher example in Wales—Wales, that never was taxed by Parliament till it was incorporated. I would not debate a particular point of law with the gentleman. I know his abilities. I have been obliged to his diligent researches. But, for the defense of liberty, upon a general principle, upon a constitutional principle, it is a ground on which I stand firm—on which I dare meet any man. The gentleman tells us of many who are taxed, and are not represented—the India Company, merchants, stockholders, manufacturers. Surely many of these are represented in other capacities, as owners of land, or as freemen of boroughs. It is a misfortune that more are not equally represented. But they are all inhabitants, and, as such, are they not virtually represented? Many have it in their option to be actually represented. They have connections with those that elect, and they have influence over them. The gentleman mentioned the stockholders. I hope he does not reckon the debts of the nation as a part of the national estate.

Since the accession of King William, many ministers, some of great, others of more moderate abilities, have taken the lead of government. [Here Mr. Pitt went through the list of them, bringing it down till he came to himself, giving a short sketch of the characters of each, and then proceeded:] None of these thought, or even dreamed, of robbing the colonies of their constitutional rights. That was reserved to mark the era of the late administration. Not that there were wanting some, when I had the honor to serve his Majesty, to propose to me to burn my fingers with an American stamp act. With the enemy at their back, with our bayonets at their breasts, in the day of their distress, perhaps the Americans would have submitted to the imposition; but it would have been taking an ungenerous, an unjust advantage. The gentleman boasts of his bounties to America! Are not these bounties intended finally for the benefit of this kingdom? If they are not, he has misapplied the national treasures!

I am no courtier of America. I stand up for this kingdom. I maintain that the Parliament has a right to bind, to restrain America. Our legislative power over the colonies is sovereign and supreme. When it ceases to be sovereign and supreme, I would advise every gentleman to sell his lands, if he can, and embark for that country. When two countries are connected together like England and her colonies, without being incorporated, the one must necessarily govern. The greater must rule the less. But she must so rule it as *not to contradict the fundamental principles that are common to both.*

If the gentleman does not understand the difference between external and internal taxes, I can not help it. There is a plain distinction between taxes levied for the purposes of raising a revenue, and duties imposed for the regulation of trade, for the accommodation of the subject; although, in the consequences, some revenue may incidentally arise from the latter.

The gentleman asks, When were the colonies emancipated? I desire to know, when were they made slaves? But I dwell not upon words. When I had the honor of serving his Majesty, I availed myself of the means of information which I derived from my office. I speak, therefore, from knowledge. My materials were good. I was at pains to collect, to digest, to consider them; and I will be bold to affirm, that the profits to Great Britain from the trade of the colonies, through all its branches, is two millions a year. This is the fund that carried you triumphantly through the last war. The estates that were rented at two thousand pounds a year, threescore years ago, are at three thousand at present. Those estates sold then from fifteen to eighteen years purchase; the same may now be sold for thirty. You owe this to America. This is the price America pays you for her protection. And shall a miserable financier come with a boast, that he can bring "a pepper-corn" into the exchequer by the loss of millions to the nation?[7] I dare not say how much higher these profits may be augmented. Omitting [*i. e.*, not taking into account] the immense increase of people, by natural population, in the northern colonies, and the emigration from every part of

[7] Alluding to Mr. Nugent, who had said that "a pepper-corn in acknowledgment of the *right* to tax America, was of more value than millions without it."

Europe, I am convinced [on other grounds] that the commercial system of America may be altered to advantage. You have prohibited where you ought to have encouraged. You have encouraged where you ought to have prohibited. Improper restraints have been laid on the continent in favor of the islands. You have but two nations to trade with in America. Would you had twenty! Let acts of Parliament in consequence of treaties remain; but let not an English minister become a custom-house officer for Spain, or for any foreign power. Much is wrong! Much may be amended for the general good of the whole!

Does the gentleman complain he has been misrepresented in the public prints? It is a common misfortune. In the Spanish affair of the last war, I was abused in all the newspapers for having advised his Majesty to violate the laws of nations with regard to Spain. The abuse was industriously circulated even in handbills. If administration did not propagate the abuse, administration never contradicted it. I will not say what advice I did give the King. My advice is in writing, signed by myself, in the possession of the Crown. But I will say what advice I did not give to the King. I did *not* advise him to violate any of the laws of nations.

As to the report of the gentleman's preventing in some way the trade for bullion with the Spaniards, it was spoken of so confidently that I own I am one of those who did believe it to be true.

The gentleman must not wonder he was not contradicted when, as minister, he asserted the right of Parliament to tax America. I know not how it is, but there is a modesty in this House which does not choose to contradict a minister. Even your chair, sir, looks too often toward St. James's. I wish gentlemen would get the better of this modesty. If they do not, perhaps the collective body may begin to abate of its respect for the representative. Lord Bacon has told me, that a great question would not fail of being agitated at one time or another. I was willing to agitate such a question at the proper season, viz., that of the German war—*my* German war, they called it! Every session I called out, Has any body any objection to the German war?[8] Nobody would object to it, one gentleman only excepted, since removed to the Upper House by succession to an ancient barony [Lord Le Despencer, formerly Sir Francis Dashwood]. He told me he did not like a German war. I honored the man for it, and was sorry when he was turned out of his post.

A great deal has been said without doors of the power, of the strength of America. It is a topic that ought to be cautiously meddled with. In a good cause, on a sound bottom, the force of this country can crush America to atoms. I know the valor of your troops. I know the skill of your officers. There is not a company of foot that has served in America, out of which you may not pick a man of sufficient knowledge and experience to make a governor of a colony there. But on this ground, on the Stamp Act, which so many here will think a crying injustice, I am one who will lift up my hands against it.

In such a cause, your success would be hazardous. America, if she fell, would fall like the strong man; she would embrace the pillars of the state, and pull down the Constitution along with her. Is this your boasted peace—not to sheathe the sword in its scabbard, but to sheathe it in the bowels of your countrymen? Will you quarrel with yourselves, now the whole house of Bourbon is united against you; while France disturbs your fisheries in Newfoundland, embarrasses your slave trade to Africa, and withholds from your subjects in Canada their property stipulated by treaty; while the ransom for the Manillas is denied by Spain, and its gallant conqueror basely traduced into a mean plunderer! a gentleman (Colonel Draper) whose noble and generous spirit would do honor to the proudest grandee of the country? The Americans have not acted in all things with prudence and temper: they have been wronged; they have been driven to madness by injustice. Will you punish them for the madness you have occasioned? Rather let prudence and temper come first from this side. I will undertake for America that she will follow the example. There are two lines in a ballad of Prior's, of a man's behavior to his wife, so applicable to you and your colonies, that I can not help repeating them:

> "Be to her faults a little blind;
> Be to her virtues very kind."

Upon the whole, I will beg leave to tell the House what is my opinion. It is, that the Stamp Act be repealed absolutely, totally, and immedi-

[8] This speech is so much condensed by the reporter as sometimes to make the connection obscure, Mr. Pitt is answering Mr. Grenville's complaints by a reference to his own experience when minister. Had Mr. Grenville been misrepresented in the public prints? So was Mr. Pitt in respect to "the Spanish affair of the last war." Had the Stamp Act been drawn into discussion, though originally passed without contradiction? Mr. Grenville might easily understand that there was a reluctance to contradict the minister; and he might learn from Lord Bacon that a great question like this *could not* be avoided; it *would* be "agitated at one time or another." Mr. Pitt, when minister, had a great question of this kind, viz., the "German war," and he did not shrink from meeting it, or complain of the misrepresentation to which he was subjected. He had originally resisted the disposition of George II. to engage in wars on the Continent. But when things had wholly changed, when England had united with Prussia to repress the ambition of Austria sustained by France and Russia, he *did* carry on "a German war," though not one of his own commencing. And he was always ready to meet the question. He challenged discussion. He called out, "Has any body objections to the German war?" Probably Mr. Pitt here alludes to an incident already referred to, page 62, when, putting himself in an attitude of defiance, he exclaimed, "Is there an *Austrian* among you? Let him come forward and reveal himself!"

ately. That the reason for the repeal be assigned, viz., because it was founded on an erroneous principle. At the same time, let the sovereign authority of this country over the colonies be asserted in as strong terms as can be devised, and be made to extend to every point of legislation whatsoever; that we may bind their trade, confine their manufactures, and exercise every power whatsoever, except that of taking their money out of their pockets without their consent.

The motion for the address received the approbation of all. About a month after, February 26th, 1766, a bill was introduced repealing the Stamp Act; but, instead of following Mr. Pitt's advice, and abandoning all claim to the right of taxing the colonies, a Declaratory Act was introduced, asserting the authority of the King and Parliament to make laws which should "bind the colonies and people of America *in all cases whatsoever!*" Lord Camden, when the Declaratory Act came into the House of Lords, took the same ground with Mr. Pitt in the House of Commons. "My position," said he, "is this—I repeat it—I will maintain it to the last hour: *Taxation and representation are inseparable.* This position is founded on the laws of nature. It is more; it is in itself an eternal law of nature. For whatever is a man's own is absolutely his own. No man has a right to take it from him without his consent, either expressed by himself or his representative. Whoever attempts to do this, attempts an injury. Whoever does it, commits a robbery. He throws down and destroys the distinction between liberty and slavery." Other counsels, however, prevailed. The Stamp Act was repealed, but the Declaratory Act was passed; its principles were carried out by Charles Townsend the very next year, by imposing new taxes; and the consequences are before the world.

SPEECH

OF LORD CHATHAM IN REPLY TO LORD MANSFIELD, IN RELATION TO THE CASE OF JOHN WILKES, DELIVERED IN THE HOUSE OF LORDS, JANUARY 9, 1770.

INTRODUCTION.

THIS was the first appearance of Lord Chatham in the House of Lords after his illness in 1767. The Duke of Grafton, his former friend and ally, was now minister, and had come out a virtual Tory. The case of John Wilkes agitated the whole kingdom. He had been expelled from the House of Commons for a "seditious libel," in February, 1769, and a new writ was issued for the election of a member from Middlesex. Wilkes was almost unanimously re-elected, and the House of Commons resolved, on the day after his election, that he was *incapable* of being chosen to that Parliament. Another election was therefore held; he was again chosen, and his election again declared void. A third was ordered, and the ministry now determined to contest it to the utmost. They prevailed upon Colonel Luttrell, son of Lord Irnham, to vacate his seat in the House, and become their candidate; but, with all their influence and bribery, they could obtain only 296 votes, while Wilkes numbered 1143. The latter, of course, was again returned as a member; but the House passed a resolution directing the clerk of the Crown to amend the return, by erasing the name of Mr. Wilkes and inserting that of Colonel Luttrell, who accordingly took his seat, in April, 1769.

There is, at the present day, no difference of opinion as to these proceedings. "All mankind are agreed," says Lord Campbell, in his Lives of the Chancellors, "that the House of Commons acted illegally and unconstitutionally in expelling Mr. Wilkes for a supposed offense, committed before his re-election, and in seating Mr. Luttrell as representative for Middlesex." With Mr. Wilkes as an individual, Lord Chatham had no connection, either personal or political. He had, on the contrary, expressed his detestation of his character and principles, some years before, in the presence of Parliament. But he felt that one of the greatest questions had now arisen which was ever agitated in England, and that the House of Lords ought to enter their protest against this flagrant breach of the Constitution. He, perhaps, considered himself the more bound to come forward, because in his late ministry he had given the Duke of Grafton the place which he now held of First Lord of the Treasury, and had thus opened the way for the advancement of his grace to the station of Prime Minister. At all events, he determined, on the first day of his appearance in Parliament after his late ministry, to express his disapprobation of two measures which had been adopted by his former colleagues, viz., the taxation of America, and the expulsion of Mr. Wilkes. When, therefore, an address to the Throne was moved, January 9th, 1770, he came forward on both these subjects in one of his most celebrated speeches, but which, unfortunately, is very imperfectly preserved.

He commenced with great impressiveness of manner: "At my advanced period of life, my Lords, bowing under the weight of my infirmities, I might, perhaps, have stood excused if I had continued in my retirement, and never taken part again in public affairs. But the alarming state of the country calls upon me to execute the duty which I owe to my God, my sovereign, and my country." He then took a rapid view of the external and internal state of the country. He lamented the measures which had alienated the colonies, and driven them to such excesses. But he still insisted that they should be treated with tenderness. "These excesses," he said, "are the mere eruptions of liberty, which break out upon the skin, and are a sign, if not of perfect health, at least of a vigorous constitution, and must not be repelled too suddenly, lest they should strike to the heart."

He then passed to the case of Mr. Wilkes, and the prevailing discontent throughout the kingdom, in consequence of his expulsion from the House of Commons. The privileges of the House of Peers, he said, however transcendent, stood on the same broad bottom as the rights of the people. It was, therefore, their highest interest, as well as their duty, to watch over and protect the people; for when the people had lost their rights, the peerage would soon become insignificant. He referred, as an illustration, to the case of Spain, where the grandees, from neglecting and slighting the rights of the people, had been enslaved themselves. He concluded with the following remarkable passage: "My Lords, let this example be a lesson to us all. Let us be cautious how we admit an idea, that our rights stand on a footing different from those of the people. Let us be cautious how we invade the liberties of our fellow-subjects, however mean, however remote. For be assured, my Lords, in whatever part of the empire you suffer slavery to be established, whether it be in America, or in Ireland, or here at home, you will find it a disease which spreads by contact, and soon reaches from the extremities to the heart. The man who has lost his own freedom, becomes, from that moment, an instrument in the hands of an ambitious prince to destroy the freedom of others. These reflections, my Lords, are but too applicable to our present situation. The liberty of the subject is invaded, not only in the provinces, but here at home! The English people are loud in their complaints; they demand redress; and, depend upon it, my Lords, that, one way or another, *they will have redress*. They will never return to a state of tranquillity till they are redressed. Nor ought they. For in my judgment, my Lords, and I speak it boldly, it were better for them to perish in a glorious contention for their rights, than to purchase a slavish tranquillity at the expense of a single iota of the Constitution. Let me entreat your Lordships, then, by all the duties which you owe to your sovereign, to the country, and to yourselves, to perform the office to which you are called by the Constitution, by informing his Majesty truly of the condition of his subjects, and the real cause of their dissatisfaction."

With this view, Lord Chatham concluded his speech by moving an amendment to the address, "That we will, with all convenient speed, take into our most serious consideration the causes of the discontents which prevail in so many parts of your Majesty's dominions, and particularly the late proceedings of the House of Commons touching the incapacity of John Wilkes, Esq., expelled by that House, to be re-elected a member to serve in the present Parliament, thereby refusing, by a resolution of one branch of the Legislature only, to the subject his common right, and depriving the electors of Middlesex of their free choice of a representative."

This amendment was powerfully resisted by Lord Mansfield. Nothing remains, however, of his speech, except a meager account of the general course of his argument. He contended "that the amendment violated every form and usage of Parliament, and was a gross attack on the privileges of the House of Commons. That there never was an instance of the Lords *inquiring* into the proceedings of that House with respect to their own members, much less of their taking upon themselves to *censure* such proceedings, or of their advising the Crown to take notice of them. 'If, indeed, it be the purpose of the amendment to provoke a quarrel with the House of Commons, I confess,' said his Lordship, 'it will have that effect certainly and immediately. The Lower House will undoubtedly assert their privileges, and give you vote for vote. I leave it, therefore, to your Lordships, to consider the fatal effects which, in such a conjuncture as the present, may arise from an open breach between the two houses of Parliament."

Lord Chatham immediately arose and delivered the following speech in reply.

SPEECH, &c.[1]

My Lords,—There is one plain maxim, to which I have invariably adhered through life: that in every question in which my liberty or my property were concerned, I should consult and be determined by the dictates of common sense. I confess, my Lords, that I am apt to distrust the refinements of learning, because I have seen the ablest and the most learned men equally liable to deceive themselves and to mislead others. The condition of human nature would be lamentable indeed, if nothing less than the greatest learning and talents, which fall to the share of so small a number of men, were sufficient to direct our judgment and our conduct. But Providence has taken better care of our happiness, and given us, in the simplicity of common sense, a rule for our direction, by which we can never be misled. I confess, my Lords, I had no other guide in drawing up the amendment which I submitted to your consideration; and, before I heard the opinion of the noble Lord who spoke last, I did not conceive that it was even within the limits of possibility for the greatest human genius, the most subtle understanding, or the acutest wit, so strangely to misrepresent my meaning, and to give it an interpretation so entirely foreign from what I intended to express, and from that sense which the very terms of the amendment plainly and distinctly carry with them. If there be the smallest foundation for the censure thrown upon me by that noble Lord;

[1] This is the best reported and most eloquent speech of Lord Chatham, except that of November 18th, 1777. It was published at the time from manuscript notes taken by an unknown individual, who is now ascertained with almost absolute certainty to have been the celebrated Sir Philip Francis, considered by so many as the author of Junius's Letters.

if, either expressly, or by the most distant implication, I have said or insinuated any part of what the noble Lord has charged me with, discard my opinions forever, discard the motion with contempt.

My Lords, I must beg the indulgence of the House. Neither will my health permit me, nor do I pretend to be qualified to follow that learned Lord minutely through the whole of his argument. No man is better acquainted with his abilities and learning, nor has a greater respect for them than I have. I have had the pleasure of sitting with him in the other House, and always listened to him with attention. I have not now lost a word of what he said, nor did I ever. Upon the present question I meet him without fear. The evidence which truth carries with it is superior to all argument; it neither wants the support, nor dreads the opposition of the greatest abilities. If there be a single word in the amendment to justify the interpretation which the noble Lord has been pleased to give it, I am ready to renounce the whole. Let it be read, my Lords; let it speak for itself. [It was read.] In what instance does it interfere with the privileges of the House of Commons? In what respect does it question their jurisdiction, or suppose an authority in this House to arraign the justice of their sentence? I am sure that every Lord who hears me will bear me witness, that I said not one word touching the *merits* of the Middlesex election. So far from conveying any opinion upon that matter in the amendment, I did not even in discourse deliver my own sentiments upon it. I did not say that the House of Commons had done either right or wrong; but, when his Majesty was pleased to recommend it to us to cultivate unanimity among ourselves, I thought it the duty of this House, as the great hereditary council of the Crown, to state to his Majesty the distracted condition of his dominions, together with the events which had destroyed unanimity among his subjects. But, my Lords, I stated events merely as facts, without the smallest addition either of censure or of opinion. They *are* facts, my Lords, which I am not only convinced are true, but which I know are indisputably true. For example, my Lords: will any man deny that discontents prevail in many parts of his Majesty's dominions? or that those discontents arise from the proceedings of the House of Commons touching the declared incapacity of Mr. Wilkes? It is impossible. No man can deny a truth so notorious. Or will any man deny that those proceedings refused, by a resolution of one branch of the Legislature only, to the subject his common right? Is it not indisputably true, my Lords, that Mr. Wilkes had a common right, and that he lost it no other way but by a resolution of the House of Commons? My Lords, I have been tender of misrepresenting the House of Commons. I have consulted their journals, and have taken the very words of their own resolution. Do they not tell us in so many words, that Mr. Wilkes having been expelled, was thereby rendered incapable of serving in that Parliament? And is it not their resolution alone which refuses to the subject his common right? The amendment says farther, that the electors of Middlesex are deprived of their free choice of a representative. Is this a false fact, my Lords? Or have I given an unfair representation of it? Will any man presume to affirm that Colonel Luttrell is the free choice of the electors of Middlesex? We all know the contrary. We all know that Mr. Wilkes (whom I mention without either praise or censure) was the favorite of the county, and chosen by a very great and acknowledged majority to represent them in Parliament. If the noble Lord dislikes the manner in which these facts are stated, I shall think myself happy in being advised by him how to alter it. I am very little anxious about terms, provided the substance be preserved; and these are facts, my Lords, which I am sure will always retain their weight and importance, in whatever form of language they are described.

Now, my Lords, since I have been forced to enter into the explanation of an amendment, in which nothing less than the genius of penetration could have discovered an obscurity, and having, as I hope, redeemed myself in the opinion of the House, having redeemed my motion from the severe representation given of it by the noble Lord, I must a little longer entreat your Lordships' indulgence. The Constitution of this country has been openly invaded in fact; and I have heard, with horror and astonishment, that very invasion defended upon principle. What is this mysterious power, undefined by law, unknown to the subject, which we must not approach without awe, nor speak of without reverence—which no man may question, and to which all men must submit? My Lords, I thought the slavish doctrine of passive obedience had long since been exploded; and, when our Kings were obliged to confess that their title to the Crown, and the rule of their government, had no other foundation than the known laws of the land, I never expected to hear a divine right, or a divine infallibility, attributed to any other branch of the Legislature. My Lords, I beg to be understood. No man respects the House of Commons more than I do, or would contend more strenuously than I would to preserve to them their just and legal authority. Within the bounds prescribed by the Constitution, that authority is necessary to the well-being of the people. Beyond that line, every exertion of power is arbitrary, is illegal; it threatens tyranny to the people, and destruction to the state. Power without right is the most odious and detestable object that can be offered to the human imagination. It is not only pernicious to those who are subject to it, but tends to its own destruction. It is what my noble friend [Lord Lyttleton] has truly described it, "Res detestabilis et caduca."[2] My Lords, I acknowledge the just power, and reverence the constitution of the House of Com-

[2] A thing hateful, and destined to destruction.

mons. It is for their own sakes that I would prevent their assuming a power which the Constitution has denied them, lest, by grasping at an authority they have no right to, they should forfeit that which they legally possess. My Lords, I affirm that they have betrayed their constituents, and violated the Constitution. Under pretense of declaring the law, they have *made* a law, and united in the same persons the office of legislator and of judge!

I shall endeavor to adhere strictly to the noble Lord's doctrine, which is, indeed, impossible to mistake, so far as my memory will permit me to preserve his expressions. He seems fond of the word jurisdiction; and I confess, with the force and effect which he has given it, it is a word of copious meaning and wonderful extent. If his Lordship's doctrine be well founded, we must renounce all those political maxims by which our understandings have hitherto been directed, and even the first elements of learning taught in our schools when we were schoolboys. My Lords, we knew that jurisdiction was nothing more than "jus dicere." We knew that "*legem facere*" and "*legem dicere*" [to make law and to declare it] were powers clearly distinguished from each other in the nature of things, and wisely separated by the wisdom of the English Constitution. But now, it seems, we must adopt a new system of thinking! The House of Commons, we are told, have a supreme jurisdiction, and there is no appeal from their sentence; and that wherever they are competent judges, their decision must be received and submitted to, as *ipso facto*, the law of the land. My Lords, I am a plain man, and have been brought up in a religious reverence for the original simplicity of the laws of England. By what sophistry they have been perverted, by what artifices they have been involved in obscurity, is not for me to explain. The principles, however, of the English laws are still sufficiently clear; they are founded in reason, and are the masterpiece of the human understanding; but it is in the text that I would look for a direction to my judgment, not in the commentaries of modern professors. The noble Lord assures us that he knows not in what code the law of Parliament is to be found; that the House of Commons, when they act as judges, have no law to direct them but their own wisdom; that their decision is law; and if they determine wrong, the subject has no appeal but to Heaven. What then, my Lords? Are all the generous efforts of our ancestors, are all those glorious contentions, by which they meant to secure to themselves, and to transmit to their posterity, a *known* law, a certain rule of living, reduced to this conclusion, that instead of the arbitrary power of a King, we must submit to the arbitrary power of a House of Commons? If this be true, what benefit do we derive from the exchange? Tyranny, my Lords, is detestable in every shape, but in none so formidable as when it is assumed and exercised by a number of tyrants. But, my Lords, this is not the fact; this is not the Constitution. We *have* a law of Parliament. We have a code in which every honest man may find it. We have Magna Charta. We have the Statute Book, and the Bill of Rights.

If a case should arise unknown to these great authorities, we have still that plain English reason left, which is the foundation of all our English jurisprudence. That reason tells us, that every judicial court, and every political society, must be vested with those powers and privileges which are necessary for performing the office to which they are appointed. It tells us, also, that no court of justice can have a power inconsistent with, or paramount to the known laws of the land; that the people, when they choose their representatives, never mean to convey to them a power of invading the rights, or trampling on the liberties of those whom they represent. What security would they have for their rights, if once they admitted that a court of judicature might determine every question that came before it, not by any known positive law, but by the vague, indeterminate, arbitrary rule of what the noble Lord is pleased to call *the wisdom of the court?* With respect to the decision of the courts of justice, I am far from denying them their due weight and authority; yet, placing them in the most respectable view, I still consider them, not as law, but as an *evidence* of the law. And before they can arrive even at that degree of authority, it must appear that they are founded in and confirmed by reason; that they are supported by precedents taken from good and moderate times; that they do not contradict any positive law; that they are submitted to without reluctance by the people; that they are unquestioned by the Legislature (which is equivalent to a tacit confirmation); and what, in my judgment, is by far the most important, that they do not violate the spirit of the Constitution. My Lords, this is not a vague or loose expression. We all know what the Constitution is. We all know that the first principle of it is, that the subject shall not be governed by the *arbitrium* of any one man or body of men (less than the whole Legislature), but by certain laws, to which he has virtually given his consent, which are open to him to examine, and not beyond his ability to understand. Now, my Lords, I affirm, and am ready to maintain, that the late decision of the House of Commons upon the Middlesex election is destitute of every one of those properties and conditions which I hold to be essential to the legality of such a decision. (1.) It is not founded in reason; for it carries with it a contradiction, that the representative should perform the office of the constituent body. (2.) It is not supported by a single precedent; for the case of Sir Robert Walpole is but a half precedent, and even that half is imperfect. Incapacity was indeed declared, but his crimes are stated as the ground of the resolution, and his opponent was declared to be not duly elected, even after his incapacity was established. (3.) It contradicts Magna Charta and the Bill of Rights, by which it is provided, that no subject shall be deprived of his freehold, unless by the judgment of his peers, or the law of the land; and that elections of members to serve in Parliament shall be free. (4.) So far is this decision from being submitted to by the people, that they have taken the strongest measures, and adopted the most positive language, to express their discontent. Whether it will be questioned by the Legislature, will depend upon your Lordships' resolution; but that it violates the spirit of the Constitution, will, I think, be disputed by no man who has heard this day's debate, and who wishes well to the freedom of his country. Yet, if we are to believe the noble Lord, this great grievance, this manifest violation of the first principles of the Constitution, will not admit of a remedy. It is not even capable of redress, unless we appeal at once to Heaven! My Lords, I have better hopes of the Constitution, and a firmer confidence in the wisdom and constitutional authority of this House. It is to *your* ancestors, my Lords, it is to the English barons, that we are indebted for the laws and Constitution we possess. Their virtues were rude and uncultivated, but they were great and sincere. Their understandings were as little polished as their manners, but they had hearts to distinguish right from wrong; they had heads to distinguish truth from falsehood; they understood the rights of humanity, and they had spirit to maintain them.

My Lords, I think that history has not done justice to their conduct, when they obtained from their sovereign that great acknowledgment of national rights contained in Magna Charta: they did not confine it to themselves alone, but delivered it as a common blessing to the whole people. They did not say, these are the rights of the great barons, or these are the rights of the great prelates. No, my Lords, they said, in the simple Latin of the times, "nullus liber homo" [no free man], and provided as carefully for the meanest subject as for the greatest. These are uncouth words, and sound but poorly in the ears of scholars; neither are they addressed to the criticism of scholars, but to the hearts of free men. These three words, "nullus liber homo," have a meaning which interests us all. They deserve to be remembered—they deserve to be inculcated in our minds—*they are worth all the classics.* Let us not, then, degenerate from the glorious example of our ancestors. Those iron barons (for so I may call them when compared with the silken barons of modern days) were the guardians of the people; yet *their* virtues, my Lords, were never engaged in a question of such importance as the present. A breach has been made in the Constitution—the battlements are dismantled—the citadel is open to the first invader—the walls totter—the Constitution is not tenable. What remains, then, but for us to stand foremost in the breach, and repair it, or perish in it?

Great pains have been taken to alarm us with the consequences of a difference between the two houses of Parliament; that the House of Commons will resent our presuming to take notice of their proceedings; that they will resent our daring to advise the Crown, and never forgive us for attempting to save the state. My Lords, I am sensible of the importance and difficulty of this great crisis: at a moment such as this, we are called upon to do our duty, without dreading the resentment of any man. But if apprehensions of this kind are to affect us, let us consider which we ought to respect most, the representative or the collective body of the people. My Lords, five hundred gentlemen are not ten millions; and if we *must* have a contention, let us take care to have the English nation on our side. If this question be given up, the freeholders of England are reduced to a condition baser than the peasantry of Poland. If they desert their own cause, they deserve to be slaves! My Lords, this is not merely the cold opinion of my understanding, but the glowing expression of what I feel. It is my heart that speaks. I know I speak warmly, my Lords; but this warmth shall neither betray my argument nor my temper. The kingdom is in a flame. As mediators between the King and people, it is our duty to represent to him the true condition and temper of his subjects. It is a duty which no particular respects should hinder us from performing; and whenever his Majesty shall demand our advice, it will then be our duty to inquire more minutely into the causes of the present discontents. Whenever that inquiry shall come on, I pledge myself to the House to prove that, since the first institution of the House of Commons, not a single precedent can be produced to justify their late proceedings. My noble and learned friend (the Lord Chancellor Camden) has pledged himself to the House that he will support that assertion.

My Lords, the character and circumstances of Mr. Wilkes have been very improperly introduced into this question, not only here, but in that court of judicature where his cause was tried—I mean the House of Commons. With one party he was a patriot of the first magnitude; with the other, the vilest incendiary. For my own part, I consider him merely and indifferently as an English subject, possessed of certain rights which the laws have given him, and which the laws alone can take from him. I am neither moved by his private vices nor by his public merits. In *his* person, though he were the *worst* of men, I contend for the safety and security of the best. God forbid, my Lords, that there should be a power in this country of measuring the civil rights of the subject by his moral character, or by any other rule but the fixed laws of the land! I believe, my Lords, *I* shall not be suspected of any personal partiality to this unhappy man. I am not very conversant in pamphlets or newspapers; but, from what I have heard, and from the little I have read, I may venture to affirm, that I have had my share in the compliments which have come from that quarter.[3] As for motives of ambition (for I must

[3] Lord Chatham here refers, among others, to Junius, who had attacked him about a year before in his first letter. At a later period Junius changed

take to myself a part of the noble Duke's insinuation), I believe, my Lords, there have been times in which I have had the honor of standing in such favor in the closet, that there must have been something extravagantly unreasonable in my wishes if they might not *all* have been gratified. After neglecting those opportunities, I am now suspected of coming forward, in the decline of life, in the anxious pursuit of wealth and power which it is impossible for me to enjoy. Be it so! There is one ambition, at least, which I ever will acknowledge, which I will not renounce but with my life. It is the ambition of delivering to my posterity those rights of freedom which I have received from my ancestors. I am not now pleading the cause of an individual, but of every freeholder in England. In what manner this House may constitutionally interpose in their defense, and what kind of redress this case will require and admit of, is not at present the subject of our consideration. The amendment, if agreed to, will naturally lead us to such an inquiry. That inquiry may, perhaps, point out the necessity of an act of the Legislature, or it may lead us, perhaps, to desire a conference with the other House; which one noble Lord affirms is the only parliamentary way of proceeding, and which another noble Lord assures us the House of Commons would either not come to, or would break off with indignation. Leaving their Lordships to reconcile that matter between themselves, I shall only say, that before we have inquired, we can not be provided with materials; consequently, we are not at present prepared for a conference.

It is not impossible, my Lords, that the inquiry I speak of may lead us to advise his Majesty to dissolve the present Parliament; nor have I any doubt of our right to give that advice, if we should think it necessary. His Majesty will then determine whether he will yield to the united petitions of the people of England, or maintain the House of Commons in the exercise of a legislative power, which heretofore abolished the House of Lords, and overturned the monarchy. I willingly acquit the present House of Commons of having actually formed so detestable a design; but they can not themselves foresee to what excesses they may be carried hereafter; and, for my own part, I should be sorry to trust to their future moderation. Unlimited power is apt to corrupt the minds of those who possess it; and this I know, my Lords, that *where law ends, tyranny begins!*

Lord Chatham's motion was rejected; but he was sustained in his views by Lord Camden, who was still Lord Chancellor, and of course a leading member of the Grafton ministry. He came down from the woolsack, and broke forth in the following indignant terms: "I accepted the great seal without conditions; I meant not, therefore, to be trammeled by his Majesty[4]—I beg pardon, by his ministers—but I have suffered myself to be so too long. For some time I have beheld with silent indignation the arbitrary measures of the minister. I have often drooped and hung down my head in council, and disapproved by my looks those steps which I knew my avowed opposition could not prevent. I will do so no longer, but openly and boldly speak my sentiments. I now proclaim to the world that I entirely coincide in the opinion expressed by my noble friend—whose presence again reanimates us—respecting this unconstitutional vote of the House of Commons. If, in giving my opinion as a judge, I were to pay any respect to that vote, I should look upon myself as a traitor to my trust, and an enemy to my country. By their violent and tyrannical conduct, ministers have alienated the minds of the people from his Majesty's government—I had almost said from his Majesty's person—insomuch, that if some measures are not devised to appease the clamors so universally prevalent, I know not, my Lords, whether the people, in despair, may not become their own avengers, and take the redress of grievances into their own hands." After such a speech, Lord Camden could not, of course, expect to hold office. He was instantly dismissed. It was a moment of extreme excitement. Lord Shelburne went so far as to say in the House, "After the dismission of the present worthy Lord Chancellor, the seals will go begging; but I hope there will not be found in this kingdom a wretch so base and mean-spirited as to accept them on the conditions on which they must be offered." This speech of Lord Chatham decided the fate of the Duke of Grafton. The moment a leader was found to unite the different sections of the Opposition, the attack was too severe for him to resist. The next speech will show the manner in which he was driven from power.

Lord Mansfield had a difficult part to act on this occasion. He could not but have known that the expulsion of Wilkes was illegal; and this is obvious from the fact that he did not attempt to defend it. He declared that, on this point, "he had never given his opinion, he would not now give it, and he did not know but he might carry it to the grave with him." All he contended was, that "if the Commons had passed an unjustifiable vote, it was a matter between God and their own consciences, and that nobody else had any thing to do with it." Lord Chatham rose a second time, and replied, "It plainly appears, from what the noble Lord has said, that he concurs in sentiment with the Opposition; for, if he had concurred with the ministry, he would no doubt have avowed his opinion—that it now equally behooves him to avow it in behalf of the people. He ought to do so as an honest man, an independent man, as a man of

his ground, and published his celebrated eulogium on Lord Chatham.

[4] This hasty expression shows, what has since been more fully known, that the King dictated the measures against Wilkes. He entered with all the feelings of a personal enemy into the plan of expelling him from the House, and was at last beaten by the determination of his own subjects.

courage and resolution. To say, that if the House of Commons has passed an unjustifiable vote, it is a matter between God and their own consciences, and that nobody else has any thing to do with it, is such a strange assertion as I have never before heard, and involves a doctrine subversive of the Constitution. What! If the House of Commons should pass a vote abolishing this House, and surrendering to the Crown all the rights and interests of the people, would it be only a matter between them and their conscience, and would nobody have any thing to do with it? *You* would have to do with it! *I* should have to do with it! Every man in the kingdom would have to do with it! Every man would have a right to insist on the repeal of such a treasonable vote, and to bring the authors of it to condign punishment. I would, therefore, call on the noble Lord to declare his opinion, *unless he would lie under the imputation of being conscious of the illegality of the vote*, and yet of being restrained by some unworthy motive from avowing it to the world." Lord Mansfield *replied not*."—Gentleman's Magazine for January, 1770.

SPEECH

OF LORD CHATHAM ON A MOTION OF LORD ROCKINGHAM TO INQUIRE INTO THE STATE OF THE NATION, DELIVERED IN THE HOUSE OF LORDS, JANUARY 22, 1770.

INTRODUCTION.

THE preceding speech of Lord Chatham, in connection with the decisive step taken by Lord Camden, threw the Duke of Grafton and his ministry into the utmost confusion; and an adjournment of a week was resorted to, for the purpose of making new arrangements. During this time, the Marquess of Granby deserted the administration, apologizing for the vote he had given for seating Colonel Luttrell in the House, and deploring it as the greatest misfortune of his life. He resigned all his places, except his commission as Colonel. Mr. Grenville, Mr. Dunning, the Dukes of Beaufort and Manchester, the Earls of Coventry and Huntington, and a number of others, followed his example. A reconciliation took place between Lord Chatham and Lord Rockingham, and the Opposition was completely organized under their guidance. It was decided to follow up the blow at once, by a motion from Lord Rockingham for an "inquiry into the state of the nation," which allows the utmost latitude for examining into the conduct of a minister. Accordingly, Lord Rockingham moved such an inquiry, almost immediately after the Lords again met. In supporting this motion, he maintained, that the existing discontents did not spring from any immediate temporary cause, but from a maxim which had grown up by degrees from the accession of George III., viz., "that the royal prerogative was sufficient to support the government, whatever might be the hands to which the administration was committed."[1] He exposed this Tory principle as fatal to the liberties of the people. The Duke of Grafton followed in a few explanatory remarks; and Lord Chatham then delivered the following speech, which contains some passages of remarkable boldness and even vehemence.

SPEECH, &c.[2]

MY LORDS,—I meant to have arisen immediately to second the motion made by the noble Lord [Rockingham]. The charge which the noble Duke [Grafton] seemed to think affected himself particularly, did undoubtedly demand an early answer. It was proper he should speak before me, and I am as ready as any man to applaud the decency and propriety with which he has expressed himself.

I entirely agree with the noble Lord, both in the necessity of your Lordships' concurring with the motion, and in the principles and arguments by which he has very judiciously supported it. I see clearly that the complexion of our government has been materially altered; and I can trace the origin of the alteration up to a period which ought to have been an era of happiness and prosperity to this country.[3]

My Lords, I shall give you my reasons for concurring with the motion, not methodically, but as they occur to my mind. I may wander, perhaps, from the exact parliamentary debate, but I hope I shall say nothing but what may deserve your attention, and what, if not strictly proper at present, would be fit to be said when the state of the nation shall come to be considered. My uncertain state of health must plead my excuse. I am now in some pain, and very probably may not be able to attend to my duty when I desire it most, in this House. I thank

[1] This is the topic so powerfully discussed in Mr. Burke's pamphlet, entitled, "Thoughts on the Cause of the Present Discontents," one of the most ingenious and able productions of that great writer.

[2] This speech, like the last, was reported at the time by a gentleman, who is now ascertained to have been Sir Philip Francis.

[3] When George III. came to the throne, England was in the midst of that splendid career of victories by which Lord Chatham humbled the enemies of his country, and established her power in every quarter of the globe. The peace which was made two years after, under the influence of Lord Bute, was generally considered a disgrace to the nation, and from that time dissatisfaction began to prevail in all classes of society.

God, my Lords, for having thus long preserved so inconsiderable a being as I am, to take a part upon this great occasion, and to contribute my endeavors, such as they are, to restore, to save, to confirm the Constitution.

My Lords, I need not look abroad for grievances. The grand capital mischief is fixed at home. It corrupts the very foundation of our political existence, and preys upon the vitals of the state. The Constitution has been grossly violated. *The Constitution at this moment stands violated.* Until that wound be healed, until the grievance be redressed, it is in vain to recommend union to Parliament, in vain to promote concord among the people. If we mean seriously to unite the nation within itself, we must convince them that their complaints are regarded, that their injuries shall be redressed. On that foundation I would take the lead in recommending peace and harmony to the people. On any other, I would never wish to see them united again. If the breach in the Constitution be effectually repaired, the people will of themselves return to a state of tranquillity; if not, *may discord prevail forever.* I know to what point this doctrine and this language will appear directed. But I feel the principles of an Englishman, and I utter them without apprehension or reserve. The crisis is indeed alarming. So much the more does it require a prudent relaxation on the part of government. If the King's servants will not permit a constitutional question to be decided on according to the forms and on the principles of the Constitution, it must then be decided in some other manner; and, rather than it should be given up, rather than the nation should surrender their birthright to a despotic minister, I hope, my Lords, old as I am, I shall see the question brought to issue, and fairly tried between the people and the government. My Lord, this is not the language of faction. Let it be tried by that criterion by which alone we can distinguish what is factious from what is not—by the principles of the English Constitution. I have been bred up in these principles, and know, that when the liberty of the subject is invaded, and all redress denied him, resistance is justified. If I had a doubt upon the matter, I should follow the example set us by the most reverend bench, with whom I believe it is a maxim, when any doubt in point of faith arises, or any question of controversy is started, to appeal at once to the greatest source and evidence of our religion—I mean the Holy Bible. The Constitution has its Political Bible, by which, if it be fairly consulted, every political question may, and ought to be determined. Magna Charta, the Petition of Rights, and the Bill of Rights, form that code which I call the *Bible of the English Constitution.* Had some of his Majesty's unhappy predecessors trusted less to the comments of their ministers; had they been better read in the text itself, the glorious revolution would have remained only possible in theory, and would not now have existed upon record a formidable example to their successors.

My Lords, I can not agree with the noble Duke, that nothing less than an immediate attack upon the honor or interest of this nation can authorize us to interpose in defense of weaker states, and in stopping the enterprises of an ambitious neighbor.[4] Whenever that narrow, selfish policy has prevailed in our councils, we have constantly experienced the fatal effects of it. By suffering our natural enemies to oppress the powers less able than we are to make resistance, we have permitted them to increase their strength, we have lost the most favorable opportunities of opposing them with success, and found ourselves at last obliged to run every hazard in making that cause our own, in which we were not wise enough to take part while the expense and danger might have been supported by others. With respect to Corsica, I shall only say, that France has obtained a more useful and important acquisition in one *pacific* campaign than in any of her *belligerent* campaigns—at least while I had the honor of administering war against her. The word may, perhaps, be thought singular. I mean only while I was the minister chiefly intrusted with the conduct of the war. I remember, my Lords, the time when Lorraine was united to the crown of France. That, too, was in some measure a pacific conquest; and there were people who talked of it as the noble Duke now speaks of Corsica. France was permitted to take and keep possession of a noble province; and, according to his grace's ideas, we did right in not opposing it. The effect of these acquisitions is, I confess, not immediate; but they unite with the main body by degrees, and, in time, make a part of the national strength. I fear, my Lords, it is too much the temper of this country to be insensible of the approach of danger, until it comes with accumulated terror upon us.

My Lords, the condition of his Majesty's affairs in Ireland, and the state of that kingdom within itself, will undoubtedly make a very material part of your Lordship's inquiry. I am not sufficiently informed to enter into the subject so fully as I could wish; but by what appears to the public, and from my own observation, I confess I can not give the ministry much credit for the spirit or prudence of their conduct. I see that even where their measures are well chosen, they are incapable of carrying them through without some unhappy mixture of weakness or imprudence. They are incapable of doing entirely right. My Lords, I do, from my conscience, and from the best weighed principles of my understanding, applaud the augmentation of the army. As a military plan, I believe it has been judiciously arranged. In a political

[4] In the year 1768, France, under pretense of a transfer from the Genoese (who claimed the island), had seized upon Corsica. General Paoli made a brave resistance, but was overpowered, and fled to England, where his presence excited a lively interest in the oppressed Corsicans. Lord Chatham maintained that France ought to have been resisted in this shameful act of aggression.

view, I am convinced it was for the welfare, for the safety of the whole empire. But, my Lords, with all these advantages, with all these recommendations, if I had the honor of advising his Majesty, I never would have consented to his accepting the augmentation, with that absurd, dishonorable condition which the ministry have submitted to annex to it.[5] My Lords, I revere the just prerogative of the Crown, and would contend for it as warmly as for the rights of the people. They are linked together, and naturally support each other. I would not touch a feather of the prerogative. The expression, perhaps, is too light; but, since I have made use of it, let me add, that the entire command and power of directing the local disposition of the army is to the royal prerogative, as the *master feather in the eagle's wing;* and, if I were permitted to carry the allusion a little farther, I would say, they have disarmed the imperial bird, the "Ministrum Fulminis Alitem."[6] The army is the thunder of the Crown. The ministry have tied up the hand which should direct the bolt.

My Lords, I remember that Minorca was lost for want of four battalions.[7] They could not be spared from hence, and there was a delicacy about taking them from Ireland. I was one of those who promoted an inquiry into that matter in the other House; and I was convinced we had not regular troops sufficient for the necessary service of the nation. Since the moment the plan of augmentation was first talked of, I have constantly and warmly supported it among my friends. I have recommended it to several members of the Irish House of Commons, and exhorted them to support it with their utmost interest in Parliament. I did not foresee, nor could I conceive it possible, the ministry would accept of it, with a condition that makes the plan itself ineffectual, and, as far as it operates, defeats every useful purpose of maintaining a standing military force. His Majesty is now so confined by his promise, that he must leave twelve thousand men locked up in Ireland, let the situation of his affairs abroad, or the approach of danger to this country, be ever so alarming, unless there be an actual rebellion or invasion in Great Britain. Even in the two cases excepted by the King's promise, the mischief must have already begun to operate, must have already taken effect, before his Majesty can be authorized to send for the assistance of his Irish army. He has not left himself the power of taking any preventive measures, let his intelligence be ever so certain, his apprehensions of invasion or rebellion be ever so well founded. Unless the traitor be actually in arms, unless the enemy be in the heart of your country, he can not move a single man from Ireland.

I feel myself compelled, my Lords, to return to that subject which occupies and interests me most. I mean the internal disorder of the Constitution, and the remedy it demands. But first I would observe, there is one point upon which I think the noble Duke has not explained himself. I do not mean to catch at words, but, if possible, to possess the sense of what I hear. I would treat every man with candor, and should expect the same candor in return. For the noble Duke, in particular, I have every personal respect and regard. I never desire to understand him but as he wishes to be understood. His Grace, I think, has laid much stress upon the diligence of the several public offices, and the assistance given them by the administration in preparing a state of the expenses of his Majesty's civil government, for the information of Parliament and for the satisfaction of the public. He has given us a number of plausible reasons for their not having yet been able to finish the account; but, as far as I am able to recollect, he has not yet given us the smallest reason to hope that it ever will be finished, or that it ever will be laid before Parliament.

My Lords, I am not unpracticed in business; and if, with all that apparent diligence, and all that assistance which the noble Duke speaks of, the accounts in question have not yet been made up, I am convinced there must be a defect in some of the public offices, which ought to be strictly inquired into, and severely punished. But, my Lords, the waste of the public money is not, of itself, so important as the pernicious purpose to which we have reason to suspect that money has been applied. For some years past, there has been an influx of wealth into this country, which has been attended with many fatal consequences, because it has not been the regular, natural produce of labor and industry.[8] The riches of Asia have been poured in upon us, and have brought with them not only Asiatic luxury, but, I fear, Asiatic principles of government. Without connections, without any natural interest in the soil, the importers of foreign gold have forced their way into Parliament by such a tor-

[5] This refers to an engagement on the part of the King, that a number of effective troops, not less than 12,000 men, should at all times, except in cases of invasion or rebellion in Great Britain, be kept in Ireland for its better defense.

[6] "The winged minister of thunder." This is one of the most beautiful instances in our literature of rising at once from a casual and familiar expression, which seemed below the dignity of the occasion, into a magnificent image, sustained and enforced by a quotation from Horace, which has always been admired for its sublimity and strength.

The image of a *feather* here applied to the King may have suggested to Junius (who was obviously an attentive hearer of Lord Chatham) a similar application of it to the same personage a few months after, in what has generally been considered the finest of his images. "The King's honor is that of his people. Their real honor and interest are the same. * * * * *The feather that adorns the royal bird supports its flight. Strip him of his plumage, and you fix him to the earth.*"

[7] In January, 1756.

[8] Much of the wealth which was brought from India about this time, was used for the purchase of seats in Parliament by men who went out mere adventurers.

rent of private corruption, as no private hereditary fortune could resist. My Lords, not saying but what is within the knowledge of us all, the corruption of the people is the great original cause of the discontents of the people themselves, of the enterprise of the Crown, and the notorious decay of the internal vigor of the Constitution. For this great evil some immediate remedy must be provided; and I confess, my Lords, I did hope that his Majesty's servants would not have suffered so many years of peace to relapse without paying some attention to an object which ought to engage and interest us all. I flattered myself I should see some barriers thrown up in defense of the Constitution; some impediment formed to stop the rapid progress of corruption. I doubt not we all agree that something must be done. I shall offer my thoughts, such as they are, to the consideration of the House; and I wish that every noble Lord that hears me would be as ready as I am to contribute his opinion to this important service. I will not call my own sentiments crude and undigested. It would be unfit for me to offer any thing to your Lordships which I had not well considered; and this subject, I own, has not long occupied my thoughts. I will now give them to your Lordships without reserve.

Whoever understands the theory of the English Constitution, and will compare it with the fact, must see at once how widely they differ. We must reconcile them to each other, if we wish to save the liberties of this country; we must reduce our political practice, as nearly as possible, to our principles. The Constitution intended that there should be a permanent relation between the constituent and representative body of the people. Will any man affirm that, as the House of Commons is now formed, that relation is in any degree preserved? My Lords, it is not preserved; it is destroyed. Let us be cautious, however, how we have recourse to violent expedients.

The boroughs of this country have properly enough been called "the rotten parts" of the Constitution. I have lived in Cornwall, and, without entering into any invidious particularity, have seen enough to justify the appellation. But in my judgment, my Lords, these boroughs, corrupt as they are, must be considered as the natural infirmity of the Constitution. Like the infirmities of the body, we must bear them with patience, and submit to carry them about with us. The limb is mortified, but the amputation might be death.

Let us try, my Lords, whether some gentler remedies may not be discovered. Since we can not cure the disorder, let us endeavor to infuse such a portion of new health into the Constitution as may enable it to support its most inveterate diseases.

The representation of the counties is, I think, still preserved pure and uncorrupted. That of the greatest cities is upon a footing equally respectable; and there are many of the larger trading towns which still preserve their independence. The infusion of health which I now allude to would be to permit every county to elect one member more, in addition to their present representation. The knights of the shires approach nearest to the constitutional representation of the county, because they represent the soil. It is not in the little dependent boroughs, it is in the great cities and counties that the strength and vigor of the Constitution resides; and by them alone, if an unhappy question should ever arise, will the Constitution be honestly and firmly defended. It would increase that strength, because I think it is the only security we have against the profligacy of the times, the corruption of the people, and the ambition of the Crown.[9]

I think I have weighed every possible objection that can be raised against a plan of this nature; and I confess I see but one which, to me, carries any appearance of solidity. It may be said, perhaps, that when the act passed for uniting the two kingdoms, the number of persons who were to represent the whole nation in Parliament was proportioned and fixed on forever. That this limitation is a fundamental article, and can not be altered without hazarding a dissolution of the Union.

My Lords, no man who hears me can have a greater reverence for that wise and important act than I have. I revere the memory of that great prince [King William III.] who first formed the plan, and of those illustrious patriots who carried it into execution. As a contract, every article of it should be inviolable; as the common basis of the strength and happiness of two nations, every article of it should be sacred. I hope I can not be suspected of conceiving a thought so detestable as to propose an advantage to one of the contracting parties at the expense of the other. No, my Lords, I mean that the benefit should be universal, and the consent to receive it unanimous. Nothing less than a most urgent and important occasion should persuade me to vary even from the letter of the act; but there is no occasion, however urgent, however important, that should ever induce me to depart from the spirit of it. Let that spirit be religiously preserved. Let us follow the principle upon which the representation of the two countries was proportioned at the Union; and when we increase the number of representatives for the English counties, let the shires of Scotland be allowed an equal privilege. On these terms, and while the proportion limited by the Union is preserved by the two nations, I apprehend that no man who is a friend to either will

[9] This is the first distinct proposal that was ever made for a reform of Parliament. It left the borough system as it was, in all its rottenness, and aimed to "infuse a portion of new health into the Constitution," sufficient to counteract the evil, by increasing the representation from the counties. The plan was never taken up by later reformers The rotten part was amputated in 1832, as Lord Chatham himself predicted it would be before the expiration of a century.

object to an alteration so necessary for the security of both. I do not speak of the authority of the Legislature to carry such a measure into effect, because I imagine no man will dispute it. But I would not wish the Legislature to interpose by an exertion of its power alone, without the cheerful concurrence of all parties. My object is the happiness and security of the two nations, and I would not wish to obtain it without their mutual consent.

My Lords, besides my warm approbation of the motion made by the noble Lord, I have a natural and personal pleasure in rising up to second it. I consider my seconding his Lordship's motion (and I would wish it to be considered by others) as a public demonstration of that cordial union which I am happy to affirm subsists between us, of my attachment to those principles which he has so well defended, and of my respect for his person. There has been a time, my Lords, when those who wished well to neither of us, who wished to see us separated forever, found a sufficient gratification for their malignity against us both. But that time is happily at an end. The friends of this country will, I doubt not, hear with pleasure that the noble Lord and his friends are now united with me and mine upon a principle which, I trust, will make our union indissoluble. It is not to possess, or divide the emoluments of government, but, if possible, to save the state. Upon this ground we met; upon this ground we stand, firm and inseparable. No ministerial artifices, no private offers, no secret seduction, can divide us. United as we are, we can set the profoundest policy of the present ministry, their grand, their only arcanum of government, their "divide et impera,"[10] at defiance.

I hope an early day will be agreed to for considering the state of the nation. My infirmities must fall heavily upon me, indeed, if I do not attend to my duty that day. When I consider my age and unhappy state of health, I feel how little I am personally interested in the event of any political question. But I look forward to others, and am determined, as far as my poor ability extends, to convey to them who come after me the blessings which I can not hope to enjoy myself.

It was impossible to resist the motion, and therefore the Duke of Grafton yielded to it with the best grace possible, naming two days from that time, January 24th, as the day for the enquiry. He afterward deferred it until February 2d; but, finding it impossible to resist the pressure, he resigned on the 28th of January, 1770. Lord North took his place. The administration now became more decidedly Tory than before. Lord North continued at the head of the government for about twelve years.

SPEECH

OF LORD CHATHAM ON A MOTION CALLING FOR PAPERS IN RELATION TO THE SEIZURE OF THE FALKLAND ISLANDS BY SPAIN, DELIVERED IN THE HOUSE OF LORDS, NOVEMBER 2, 1770.

INTRODUCTION.

The Falkland Islands, lying about three hundred miles east of the Straits of Magellan, were discovered by the English in the days of Queen Elizabeth, but so dreary and deterring was their appearance, that no steps were taken for their settlement during the next two hundred years. At length, in 1765, they were occupied in form by the British government, who soon after erected a small block-house, named Fort Egmont, on one of the islands, and there stationed a few troops. This gave much offense to the court of Spain, which claimed all the Magellanic regions; and, after sundry protests, Buccarelli, the governor of Buenos Ayres, sent an expedition which drove the English from the islands in the early part of 1770. It is a remarkable fact, as already mentioned, that Lord Chatham predicted this event at the close of the preceding Parliament, during the very month in which the Spanish fleet arrived at the Falkland Islands. "I do now pledge myself," said he, "to this honorable House for the truth of what I am going to assert, that, at this very hour that we are sitting together, a blow of hostility has been struck against us by our old inveterate enemies in some quarter of the world."

When the intelligence of this seizure reached England, the whole nation was fired at the indignity offered to the British flag, and in every quarter the utmost eagerness was manifested to vindicate the national honor. Lord Chatham, who had always cherished a strong antipathy and contempt for the Spaniards, shared largely in these feelings. Accordingly, when the Duke of Richmond moved for papers on this subject, he made the following speech, in which he first considers the outrage committed by Spain, and then expatiates on the want of spirit exhibited by the ministry, their neglect of naval and military preparations, the depressed condition of the country, and some of the causes which had led to this result.

SPEECH, &c.[1]

My Lords,—I rise to give my hearty assent to the motion made by the noble Duke. By his Grace's favor I have been permitted to see it, before it was offered to the House. I have fully considered the necessity of obtaining from the

[10] Divide and rule.

[1] This speech is understood to have been reported by Sir Philip Francis.

King's servants a communication of the papers described in the motion, and I am persuaded that the alarming state of facts, as well as the strength of reasoning with which the noble Duke has urged and enforced that necessity, must have been powerfully felt by your Lordships. What I mean to say upon this occasion may seem, perhaps, to extend beyond the limits of the motion before us. But I flatter myself, my Lords, that if I am honored with your attention, it will appear that the meaning and object of this question are naturally connected with considerations of the most extensive national importance. For entering into such considerations, no season is improper, no occasion should be neglected. Something must be done, my Lords, and immediately, to save an injured, insulted, undone country; if not to save the state, my Lords, at least to mark out and drag to public justice those servants of the Crown, by whose ignorance, neglect, or treachery this once great, flourishing people are reduced to a condition as deplorable at home as it is despicable abroad. Examples are wanted, my Lords, and should be given to the world, for the instruction of future times, even though they be useless to ourselves. I do not mean, my Lords, nor is it intended by the motion, to impede or embarrass a negotiation which we have been told is now in a prosperous train, and promises a happy conclusion.

[*Lord Weymouth.*—I beg pardon for interrupting the noble Lord; but I think it necessary to remark to your Lordships that I have not said a single word tending to convey to your Lordships any information or opinion with regard to the state or progress of the negotiation. I did, with the utmost caution, avoid giving to your Lordships the least intimation upon that matter.]

I perfectly agree with the noble Lord. I did not mean to refer to any thing said by his Lordship. He expressed himself, as he always does, with moderation and reserve, and with the greatest propriety. It was another noble Lord, very high in office, who told us he understood that the negotiation was in a favorable train.

[*Earl of Hillsborough.*—I did not make use of the word *train*. I know the meaning of the word too well. In the language from which it was derived, it signifies protraction and delay, which I could never mean to apply to the present negotiation.]

This is the second time that I have been interrupted. I submit to your Lordships whether this be fair and candid treatment. I am sure it is contrary to the orders of the House, and a gross violation of decency and politeness. I listen to every noble Lord in this House with attention and respect. The noble Lord's design in interrupting me is as mean and unworthy as the manner in which he has done it is irregular and disorderly. He flatters himself that by breaking the thread of my discourse, he shall confuse me in my argument. But, my Lords, I will not submit to this treatment. I will not be interrupted. When I have concluded, let him answer me, if he can. As to the word which he has denied, I still affirm that it was the word he made use of; but if he had used any other, I am sure every noble Lord will agree with me, that his meaning was exactly what I have expressed it. Whether he said course or train is indifferent. He told your Lordships that the negotiation was in a way that promised a happy and honorable conclusion. His distinctions are mean, frivolous, and puerile. My Lords, I do not understand the exalted tone assumed by that noble Lord. In the distress and weakness of this country, my Lords, and conscious as the ministry ought to be how much they have contributed to that distress and weakness, I think a tone of modesty, of submission, of humility, would become them better; "quædam causæ modestiam desiderant."[2] Before this country they stand as the greatest criminals. Such I shall prove them to be; for I do not doubt of proving, to your Lordships' satisfaction, that since they have been intrusted with the King's affairs, they have done every thing that they ought not to have done, and hardly any thing that they ought to have done.

The noble Lord talks of Spanish punctilios in the lofty style and idiom of a Spaniard. We are to be wonderfully tender of the Spanish point of honor, as if they had been the complainants, as if they had received the injury. I think he would have done better to have told us what care had been taken of the English honor. My Lords, I am well acquainted with the character of that nation—at least as far as it is represented by their court and ministry, and should think this country dishonored by a comparison of the English good faith with the punctilios of a Spaniard. My Lords, the English are a candid, an ingenuous people. The Spaniards are as mean and crafty as they are proud and insolent. The integrity of the English merchant, the generous spirit of our naval and military officers, would be degraded by a comparison with their merchants or officers. With their ministers I have often been obliged to negotiate, and never met with an instance of candor or dignity in their proceedings; nothing but low cunning, trick, and artifice. After a long experience of their want of candor and good faith, I found myself compelled to talk to them in a peremptory, decisive language. On this principle I submitted my advice to a trembling council for an immediate declaration of a war with Spain.[3] Your Lordships well know what were the consequences of not following that advice. Since, however, for reasons unknown to me, it has been thought advisable to negotiate with the court of Spain, I should have conceived that the great and single object of such a negotiation would have been, to obtain complete satisfaction for the injury done to the crown and people of England. But, if I understand the noble Lord, the only object of the present negotiation is to find a salvo for the punctilious honor of the Spaniards. The absurdity of such an idea is of it-

[2] Some causes call for modesty.

[3] In 1761. See p. 63.

self insupportable. But, my Lords, I object to our negotiating at all, in our present circumstances. We are not in that situation in which a great and powerful nation is permitted to negotiate. A foreign power has forcibly robbed his Majesty of a part of his dominions. Is the island restored? Are you replaced in *statu quo?* If that had been done, it might then, perhaps, have been justifiable to treat with the aggressor upon the satisfaction he ought to make for the insult offered to the Crown of England. But will you descend so low? Will you so shamefully betray the King's honor, as to make it matter of negotiation whether his Majesty's possessions shall be restored to him or not?

I doubt not, my Lords, that there are some important mysteries in the conduct of this affair, which, whenever they are explained, will account for the profound silence now observed by the King's servants. The time will come, my Lords, when they shall be dragged from their concealments. There are some questions which, sooner or later, must be answered. The ministry, I find, without declaring themselves explicitly, have taken pains to possess the public with an opinion, that the Spanish court have constantly disavowed the proceedings of their governor; and some persons, I see, have been shameless and daring enough to advise his Majesty to support and countenance this opinion in his speech from the throne. Certainly, my Lords, there never was a more odious, a more infamous falsehood imposed on a great nation. It degrades the King's honor. It is an insult to Parliament. His Majesty has been advised to confirm and give currency to an absolute falsehood. I beg your Lordship's attention, and I hope I shall be understood, when I repeat, that the court of Spain's having disavowed the act of their governor is an absolute, a palpable falsehood.[4] Let me ask, my Lords, when the first communication was made by the court of Madrid of their being apprised of the taking of Falkland's Island, was it accompanied with an offer of instant restitution, of immediate satisfaction, and the punishment of the Spanish governor? If it was not, they have adopted the act as their own, and the very mention of a disavowal is an impudent insult offered to the King's dignity. The King of Spain disowns the thief, while he leaves him unpunished, and profits by the theft. In vulgar English, he is the receiver of stolen goods, and ought to be treated accordingly.

If your Lordships will look back to a period of the English history in which the circumstances are reversed, in which the Spaniards were the complainants, you will see how differently they succeeded. You will see one of the ablest men, one of the bravest officers this or any other country ever produced (it is hardly necessary to mention the name of Sir Walter Raleigh), sacrificed by the meanest prince that ever sat upon the throne, to the vindictive jealousy of that haughty court. James the First was base enough, at the instance of Gondomar, to suffer a sentence against Sir Walter Raleigh, for another supposed offense, to be carried into execution almost twelve years after it had been passed. This was the pretense. His real crime was, that he had mortally offended the Spaniards, while he acted by the King's express orders, and under his commission.

My Lords, the pretended disavowal by the court of Spain is as ridiculous as it is false. If your Lordships want any other proof, call for your own officers who were stationed at Falkland Island. Ask the officer who commanded the garrison, whether, when he was summoned to surrender, the demand was made in the name of the Governor of Buenos Ayres or of his Catholic Majesty? Was the island said to belong to Don Francisco Buccarelli or to the King of Spain? If I am not mistaken, we have been in possession of these islands since the year 1764 or 1765. Will the ministry assert, that, in all that time, the Spanish court have never once claimed them? That their right to them has never been urged, or mentioned to our ministry? If it has, the act of the Governor of Buenos Ayres is plainly the consequence of our refusal to acknowledge and submit to the Spanish claims. For five years they negotiate; when that fails, they take the island by force. If that measure had arisen out of the general instructions constantly given to the Governor of Buenos Ayres, why should the execution of it have been deferred so long?

My Lords, if the falsehood of this pretended disavowal had been confined to the court of Spain, I should have admitted it without concern. I should have been content that they themselves had left a door open for excuse and accommodation. The King of England's honor is not touched till he adopts the falsehood, delivers it to his Parliament, and adopts it as his own.

I can not quit this subject without comparing the conduct of the present ministry with that of a gentleman [Mr. George Grenville] who is now no more. The occasions were similar. The French had taken a little island from us [in 1764] called Turk's Island. The minister then at the head of the treasury [Mr. Grenville] took the business upon himself. But he did not negotiate. He sent for the French embassador and made a peremptory demand. A courier was dispatched to Paris, and returned in a few days, with orders for instant restitution, not only of the island, but of every thing that the English subjects had lost.[5]

Such, then, my Lords, are the circumstances

[4] History confirms this statement. Adolphus says that when Lord Weymouth inquired "whether Grimaldi had instructions to disavow the conduct of Buccarelli, he received an answer in the *negative*." —Vol. i., p. 431. It was not until January 22d, 1771, nearly three months after, that the disavowal was made. See Adolphus, i.. 435.

[5] A similar measure of spirit was adopted by the same minister with the Spaniards, who had driven our settlers from Honduras, to whom fourteen days had been allowed; upon which, all was instantly and amicably adjusted.

of our difference with Spain; and in this situation, we are told that a negotiation has been entered into; that this negotiation, which must have commenced near three months ago, is still depending, and that any insight into the actual state of it will impede the conclusion. My Lords, I am not, for my own part, very anxious to draw from the ministry the information which they take so much care to conceal from us. I very well know where this honorable negotiation *will* end—where it *must* end. We may, perhaps, be able to patch up an accommodation for the present, but we shall have a Spanish war in six months. Some of your Lordships may, perhaps, remember the Convention. For several successive years our merchants had been plundered; no protection given them; no redress obtained for them. During all that time we were contented to complain and to negotiate. The court of Madrid were then as ready to disown their officers, and as unwilling to punish them, as they are at present. Whatever violence happened was always laid to the charge of one or other of their West India governors. To-day it was the Governor of Cuba, to-morrow of Porto Rico, Carthagena, or Porto Bello. If in a particular instance redress was promised, how was that promise kept? The merchant who had been robbed of his property was sent to the West Indies, to get it, if he could, out of an empty chest. At last, the Convention was made; but, though approved by a majority of both houses, it was received by the nation with universal discontent. I myself heard that wise man [Sir Robert Walpole] say in the House of Commons, "'Tis true we have got a Convention and a vote of Parliament; but what signifies it? We shall have a Spanish war upon the back of our Convention." Here, my Lords, I can not help mentioning a very striking observation made to me by a noble Lord [Granville], since dead. His abilities did honor to this House and to this nation. In the upper departments of government he had not his equal; and I feel a pride in declaring, that to his patronage, his friendship, and instruction, I owe whatever I am. This great man has often observed to me, that, in all the negotiations which preceded the Convention, our ministers never found out that there was no ground or subject for any negotiation That the Spaniards had not a right to search our ships, and when they attempted to regulate that right by treaty, they were regulating a thing which did not exist. This I take to be something like the case of the ministry. The Spaniards have seized an island they have no right to; and his Majesty's servants make it a matter of negotiation, whether his dominions shall be restored to him or not.

From what I have said, my Lords, I do not doubt but it will be understood by many Lords, and given out to the public, that I am for hurrying the nation, at all events, into a war with Spain. My Lords, I disclaim such counsels, and I beg that this declaration may be remembered. Let us have peace, my Lords, but let it be honorable, let it be secure. A patched-up peace will not do. It will not satisfy the nation, though it may be approved of by Parliament. I distinguish widely between a solid peace, and the disgraceful expedients by which a war may be deferred, but can not be avoided. I am as tender of the effusion of human blood as the noble Lord who dwelt so long upon the miseries of war. If the bloody politics of some noble Lords had been followed, England, and every quarter of his Majesty's dominions would have been glutted with blood—the blood of our own countrymen.

My Lords, I have better reasons, perhaps, than many of your Lordships for desiring peace upon the terms I have described. I know the strength and preparation of the house of Bourbon; I know the defenseless, unprepared condition of this country. I know not by what mismanagement we are reduced to this situation; but when I consider who are the men by whom a war, in the outset at least, must be conducted, can I but wish for peace? Let them not screen themselves behind the want of intelligence. They *had* intelligence: I know they had. If they had not, they are criminal, and their excuse is their crime. But I will tell these young ministers the true source of intelligence. It is sagacity. Sagacity to compare causes and effects; to judge of the present state of things, and discern the future by a careful review of the past. Oliver Cromwell, who astonished mankind by his intelligence, did not derive it from spies in the cabinet of every prince in Europe: he drew it from the cabinet of his own sagacious mind. He observed facts, and traced them forward to their consequences. From what was, he concluded what must be, and he never was deceived. In the present situation of affairs, I think it would be treachery to the nation to conceal from them their real circumstances, and, with respect to a foreign enemy, I know that all concealments are vain and useless. They are as well acquainted with the actual force and weakness of this country as any of the King's servants. This is no time for silence or reserve. I charge the ministers with the highest crimes that men in their stations can be guilty of. I charge them with having destroyed all content and unanimity at home by a series of oppressive, unconstitutional measures; and with having betrayed and delivered up the nation defenseless to a foreign enemy.

Their utmost vigor has reached no farther than to a fruitless, protracted negotiation. When they should have acted, they have contented themselves with talking "*about it, goddess, and about it.*" If we do not stand forth, and do our duty in the present crisis, the nation is irretrievably undone. I despise the little policy of concealments. You ought to know the whole of your situation. If the information be new to the ministry, let them take care to profit by it. I

[6] The Convention here referred to was the one made by Sir Robert Walpole in 1739, which Lord Chatham at the time so strenuously resisted.

mean to rouse, to alarm the whole nation; to rouse the ministry, if possible, who seem to awake to nothing but the preservation of their places—to awaken the King.

Early in the last spring, a motion was made in Parliament for inquiring into the state of the navy, and an augmentation of six thousand seamen was offered to the ministry. They refused to give us any insight into the condition of the navy, and rejected the augmentation. Early in June they received advice of a commencement of hostilities by a Spanish armament, which had warned the King's garrison to quit an island belonging to his Majesty. From that to the 12th of September, as if nothing had happened, they lay dormant. Not a man was raised, not a single ship was put into commission. From the 12th of September, when they heard of the first blow being actually struck, we are to date the beginning of their preparations for defense. Let us now inquire, my Lords, what expedition they have used, what vigor they have exerted. We have heard wonders of the diligence employed in impressing, of the large bounties offered, and the number of ships put into commission. These have been, for some time past, the constant topics of ministerial boast and triumph. Without regarding the description, let us look to the substance. I tell your Lordships that, with all this vigor and expedition, they have not, in a period of considerably more than two months, raised ten thousand seamen. I mention that number, meaning to speak largely, though in my own breast I am convinced that the number does not exceed eight thousand. But it is said they have ordered forty ships of the line into commission. My Lords, upon this subject I can speak with knowledge. I have been conversant in these matters, and draw my information from the greatest and most respectable naval authority that ever existed in this country—I mean the late Lord Anson. The merits of that great man are not so universally known, nor his memory so warmly respected as he deserved. To his wisdom, to his experience and care (and I speak it with pleasure), the nation owes the glorious naval successes of the last war. The state of facts laid before Parliament in the year 1756, so entirely convinced me of the injustice done to his character, that in spite of the popular clamors raised against him, in direct opposition to the complaints of the merchants, and of the whole city (whose favor I am supposed to court upon all occasions), I replaced him at the head of the Admiralty, and I thank God that I had resolution enough to do so. Instructed by this great seaman, I do affirm, that forty ships of the line, with their necessary attendant frigates, to be properly manned, require forty thousand seamen. If your Lordships are surprised at this assertion, you will be more so when I assure you, that in the last war, this country maintained eighty-five thousand seamen, and employed them all.

Now, my Lords, the peace establishment of your navy, supposing it complete and effective (which, by-the-by, ought to be known), is sixteen thousand men. Add to these the number newly raised, and you have about twenty-five thousand men to man your fleet. I shall come presently to the application of this force, such as it is, and compare it with the services which I know are indispensable. But first, my Lords, let us have done with the boasted vigor of the ministry. Let us hear no more of their activity. If your Lordships will recall to your minds the state of this country when Mahon was taken, and compare what was done by government at that time with the efforts now made in very similar circumstances, you will be able to determine what praise is due to the vigorous operations of the present ministry. Upon the first intelligence of the invasion of Minorca, a great fleet was equipped and sent out, and near double the number of seamen collected in half the time taken to fit out the present force, which, pitiful as it is, is not yet, if the occasion was ever so pressing, in a condition to go to sea. Consult the returns which were laid before Parliament in the year 1756. I was one of those who urged a parliamentary inquiry into the conduct of the ministry. That ministry, my Lords, in the midst of universal censure and reproach, had honor and virtue enough to promote the inquiry themselves. They scorned to evade it by the mean expedient of putting a previous question. Upon the strictest inquiry, it appeared that the diligence they had used in sending a squadron to the Mediterranean, and in their other naval preparations, was beyond all example.

My Lords, the subject on which I am speaking seems to call upon me, and I willingly take this occasion, to declare my opinion upon a question on which much wicked pains have been employed to disturb the minds of the people and to distress government. My opinion may not be very popular; neither am I running the race of popularity. I am myself clearly convinced, and I believe every man who knows any thing of the English navy will acknowledge, that without impressing, it is impossible to equip a respectable fleet within the time in which such armaments are usually wanted. If this fact be admitted, and if the necessity of arming upon a sudden emergency should appear incontrovertible, what shall we think of those men who, in the moment of danger, would stop the great defense of their country? Upon whatever principle they may act, the act itself is more than faction—it is laboring to cut off the right hand of the community. I wholly condemn their conduct, and am ready to support any motion that may be made for bringing those aldermen, who have endeavored to stop the execution of the Admiralty warrants, to the bar of this House. My Lords, I do not rest my opinion merely upon necessity. I am satisfied that the power of impressing is founded upon uninterrupted usage. It is the "consuetudo regni" [the custom of the realm], and part of the common law prerogative of the Crown. When I condemn the proceedings of some persons upon this occasion, let me do justice to a man whose character and conduct have been most infamously traduced; I mean the late Lord Mayor, Mr. Treacothick. In the midst of reproach and clamor, he had firmness enough to persevere in doing his duty. I do not know in office a more upright magistrate, nor, in private life, a worthier man.

Permit me now, my Lords, to state to your Lordships the extent and variety of the service which must be provided for, and to compare them with our apparent resources. A due attention to, and provision for these services, is prudence in time of peace; in war it is necessity. Preventive policy, my Lords, which obviates or avoids the injury, is far preferable to that vindictive policy which aims at reparation, or has no object but revenge. The precaution that meets the disorder is cheap and easy; the remedy which follows it, bloody and expensive. The first great and acknowledged object of national defense in this country is to maintain such a superior naval force at home, that even the united fleets of France and Spain may never be masters of the Channel. If that should ever happen, what is there to hinder their landing in Ireland, or even upon our own coast? They have often made the attempt. In King William's time it succeeded. King James embarked on board a French fleet, and landed with a French army in Ireland. In the mean time the French were masters of the Channel, and continued so until their fleet was destroyed by Admiral Russel. As to the probable consequences of a foreign army landing in Great Britain or Ireland, I shall offer your Lordships my opinion when I speak of the actual condition of our standing army.

The second naval object with an English minister should be to maintain at all times a powerful Western squadron. In the profoundest peace it should be respectable; in war it should be formidable. Without it, the colonies, the commerce, the navigation of Great Britain, lie at the mercy of the house of Bourbon. While I had the honor of acting with Lord Anson, that able officer never ceased to inculcate upon the minds of his Majesty's servants, the necessity of constantly maintaining a strong Western squadron; and I must vouch for him, that while he was at the head of the marine, it was never neglected.

The third object indispensable, as I conceive, in the distribution of our navy, is to maintain such a force in the Bay of Gibraltar as may be sufficient to cover that garrison, to watch the motions of the Spaniards, and to keep open the communication with Minorca. The ministry will not betray such a want of information as to dispute the truth of any of these propositions. But how will your Lordships be astonished when I inform you in what manner they have provided for these great, these essential objects? As to the first—I mean the defense of the Channel—I take upon myself to affirm to your Lordships, that, at this hour (and I beg that the date may be taken down and observed), we can not send out eleven ships of the line so manned and equipped, that any officer of rank and credit in the service shall accept of the command and stake his reputation upon it. We have one ship of the line at Jamaica, one at the Leeward Islands, and one at Gibraltar! Yet at this very moment, for aught that the ministry know, both Jamaica and Gibraltar may be attacked; and if they are attacked (which God forbid), they must fall. Nothing can prevent it but the appearance of a superior squadron. It is true that, some two months ago, four ships of the line were ordered from Portsmouth and one from Plymouth, to carry a relief from Ireland to Gibraltar. These ships, my Lords, a week ago were still in port. If, upon their arrival at Gibraltar, they should find the bay possessed by a superior squadron, the relief can not be landed; and if it could be landed, of what force do your Lordships think it consists? Two regiments, of four hundred men each, at a time like this, are sent to secure a place of such importance as Gibraltar! a place which it is universally agreed can not hold out against a vigorous attack from the sea, if once the enemy should be so far masters of the bay as to make a good landing even with a moderate force. The indispensable service of the lines requires at least four thousand men. The present garrison consists of about two thousand three hundred; so that if the relief should be fortunate enough to get on shore, they will want eight hundred men of their necessary complement.

Let us now, my Lords, turn our eyes homeward. When the defense of Great Britain or Ireland is in question, it is no longer a point of honor; it is not the security of foreign commerce or foreign possessions; we are to contend for the being of the state. I have good authority to assure your Lordships that the Spaniards have now a fleet at Ferrol, completely manned and ready to sail, which we are in no condition to meet. We could not this day send out eleven ships of the line properly equipped, and to-morrow the enemy may be masters of the Channel. It is unnecessary to press the consequences of these facts upon your Lordships' minds. If the enemy were to land in full force, either upon this coast or in Ireland, where is your army? Where is your defense? My Lords, if the house of Bourbon make a wise and vigorous use of the actual advantages they have over us, it is more than probable that on this day month we may not be a nation. What military force can the ministry show to answer any sudden demand? I do not speak of foreign expeditions or offensive operations; I speak of the interior defense of Ireland and of this country. You have a nominal army of seventy battalions, besides guards and cavalry. But what is the establishment of these battalions? Supposing they were complete in the numbers allowed, which I know they are not, each regiment would consist of something less than four hundred men, rank and file. Are these battalions complete? Have any orders been given for an augmentation, or do the ministry mean to continue them upon their present low establishment? When America, the West Indies, Gibraltar, and

Minorca, are taken care of, consider, my Lords, what part of this army will remain to defend Ireland and Great Britain? This subject, my Lords, leads me to considerations of foreign policy and foreign alliance. It is more connected with them than your Lordships may at first imagine. When I compare the numbers of our people, estimated highly at seven millions, with the population of France and Spain, usually computed at twenty-five millions, I see a clear, self-evident impossibility for this country to contend with the united power of the house of Bourbon merely upon the strength of its own resources. They who talk of confining a great war to naval operations only, speak without knowledge or experience. We can no more command the disposition than the events of a war. Wherever we are attacked, there we must defend.

I have been much abused, my Lords, for supporting a war which it has been the fashion to call *my* German war. But I can affirm with a clear conscience, that that abuse has been thrown on me by men who were either unacquainted with facts, or had an interest in misrepresenting them. I shall speak plainly and frankly to your Lordships upon this, as I do upon every occasion. That I did in Parliament oppose, to the utmost of my power, our engaging in a German war, is most true; and if the same circumstance were to recur, I would act the same part, and oppose it again. But when I was called upon to take a share in the administration, that measure was already decided. Before I was appointed Secretary of State, the first treaty with the King of Prussia was signed, and not only ratified by the Crown, but approved of and confirmed by a resolution of both houses of Parliament. It was a weight fastened upon my neck. By that treaty the honor of the Crown and the honor of the nation were equally engaged. How I could recede from such an engagement—how I could advise the Crown to desert a great prince in the midst of those difficulties in which a reliance upon the good faith of this country had contributed to involve him, are questions I willingly submit to your Lordships' candor. That wonderful man might, perhaps, have extricated himself from his difficulties without our assistance. He has talents which, in every thing that touches the human capacity, do honor to the human mind. But how would England have supported that reputation of credit and good faith by which we have been distinguished in Europe? What other foreign power would have sought our friendship? What other foreign power would have accepted of an alliance with us?

But, my Lords, though I wholly condemn our entering into any engagements which tend to involve us in a continental war, I do not admit that alliances with some of the German princes are either detrimental or useless. They may be, my Lords, not only useful, but necessary. I hope, indeed, I never shall see an army of foreign auxiliaries in Great Britain; we do not want it. If our people are united—if they are attached to the King, and place confidence in his government, we have an internal strength sufficient to repel any foreign invasion. With respect to Ireland, my Lords, I am not of the same opinion. If a powerful foreign army were landed in that kingdom, with arms ready to be put into the hands of the Roman Catholics, I declare freely to your Lordships that I should heartily wish it were possible to collect twenty thousand German Protestants, whether from Hesse, or Brunswick, or Wolfenbuttle, or even the unpopular Hanoverians, and land them in Ireland. I wish it, my Lords, because I am convinced that, whenever the case happens, we shall have no English army to spare.

I have taken a wide circuit, my Lords, and trespassed, I fear, too long upon your Lordships' patience. Yet I can not conclude without endeavoring to bring home your thoughts to an object more immediately interesting to us than any I have yet considered; I mean the internal condition of this country. We may look abroad for wealth, or triumphs, or luxury; but England, my Lords, is the main stay, the last resort of the whole empire To this point every scheme of policy, whether foreign or domestic, should ultimately refer. Have any measures been taken to satisfy or to unite the people? Are the grievances they have so long complained of removed? or do they stand not only unredressed, but aggravated? Is the right of free election restored to the elective body? My Lords, I myself am one of the people. I esteem that security and independence, which is the original birthright of an Englishman, far beyond the privileges, however splendid, which are annexed to the peerage. I myself am by birth an English elector, and join with the freeholders of England as in a common cause. Believe me, my Lords, we mistake our real interest as much as our duty when we separate ourselves from the mass of the people. Can it be expected that Englishmen will unite heartily in the defense of a government by which they feel themselves insulted and oppressed? Restore them to their rights; that is the true way to make them unanimous. It is not a ceremonious recommendation from the Throne that can bring back peace and harmony to a discontented people. That insipid annual opiate has been administered so long that it has lost its effect. Something substantial, something effectual must be done.

The public credit of the nation stands next in degree to the rights of the Constitution; it calls loudly for the interposition of Parliament. There is a set of men, my Lords, in the city of London, who are known to live in riot and luxury upon the plunder of the ignorant, the innocent, the helpless—upon that part of the community which stands most in need of, and best deserves the care and protection of the Legislature. To me, my Lords, whether they be miserable jobbers of 'Change Alley, or the lofty Asiatic plunderers of Leadenhall Street, they are all equally detestable. I care but little whether a man walks on foot, or is drawn by eight horses or six horses; if his luxury is supported by the plunder of his country, I despise and detest him. My Lords, while I had the honor of serving his Majesty, I never ventured to look at the treasury but at a distance; it is a business I am unfit for, and to which I never could have submitted. The little I know of it has not served to raise my opinion of what is vulgarly called the *moneyed interest;* I mean that blood-sucker, that muck-worm, which calls itself the friend of government—that pretends to serve this or that administration, and may be purchased, on the same terms, by any administration—that advances money to government, and takes special care of its own emoluments. Under this description I include the whole race of commissaries, jobbers, contractors, clothiers, and remitters. Yet I do not deny that, even with these creatures, some management may be necessary. I hope, my Lords, that nothing that I have said will be understood to extend to the honest and industrious tradesman, who holds the middle rank, and has given repeated proofs that he prefers law and liberty to gold. I love that class of men. Much less would I be thought to reflect upon the fair merchant, whose liberal commerce is the prime source of national wealth. I esteem his occupation and respect his character.

My Lords, if the general representation, which I have had the honor to lay before you, of the situation of public affairs, has in any measure engaged your attention, your Lordships, I am sure, will agree with me, that the season calls for more than common prudence and vigor in the direction of our councils. The difficulty of the crisis demands a wise, a firm, and a popular administration. The dishonorable traffic of places has engaged us too long. Upon this subject, my Lords, I speak without interest or enmity. I have no personal objection to any of the King's servants. I shall never be minister; certainly not without full power to cut away all the rotten branches of government. Yet, unconcerned as I truly am for myself, I can not avoid seeing some capital errors in the distribution of the royal favor. There are men, my Lords, who, if their own services were forgotten, ought to have an hereditary merit with the house of Hanover; whose ancestors stood forth in the day of trouble, opposed their persons and fortunes to treachery and rebellion, and secured to his Majesty's family this splendid power of rewarding. There are other men, my Lords [looking sternly at Lord Mansfield], who, to speak tenderly of them, were not quite so forward in the demonstrations of their zeal to the reigning family. There was another cause, my Lords, and a partiality to it, which some persons had not at all times discretion enough to conceal. I know I shall be accused of attempting to revive distinctions. My Lords, if it were possible, I would abolish all distinctions. I would not wish the favors of the Crown to flow invariably in one channel. But there are some distinctions which are inherent in the nature of things. There is a distinction between right and wrong—between WHIG and TORY.

When I speak of an administration, such as the necessity of the season calls for, my views are large and comprehensive. It must be popular, that it may begin with reputation. It must be strong within itself, that it may proceed with vigor and decision. An administration, formed upon an exclusive system of family connections or private friendships, can not, I am convinced, be long supported in this country. Yet, my Lords, no man respects or values more than I do that honorable connection, which arises from a disinterested concurrence in opinion upon public measures, or from the sacred bond of private friendship and esteem. What I mean is, that no single man's private friendships or connections, however extensive, are sufficient of themselves either to form or overturn an administration. With respect to the ministry, I believe they have fewer rivals than they imagine. No prudent man will covet a situation so beset with difficulty and danger.

I shall trouble your Lordships with but a few words more. His Majesty tells us in his speech that he will call upon us for our advice, if it should be necessary in the farther progress of this affair. It is not easy to say whether or no the ministry are serious in this declaration, nor what is meant by the *progress* of an affair which rests upon one fixed point. Hitherto we have not been called upon. But, though we are not consulted, it is our right and duty, as the King's great hereditary council, to offer him our advice. The papers mentioned in the noble Duke's motion will enable us to form a just and accurate opinion of the conduct of his Majesty's servants, though not of the actual state of their honorable negotiations. The ministry, too, seem to want advice upon some points in which their own safety is immediately concerned. They are now balancing between a war which they ought to have foreseen, but for which they have made no provision, and an ignominious compromise. Let me warn them of their danger. If they are forced into a war, they stand it at the hazard of their heads. If by an ignominious compromise they should stain the honor of the Crown, or sacrifice the rights of the people, let them look to the consequences, and consider whether they will be able to walk the streets in safety.

The Duke of Richmond's motion was negatived by a vote of 65 to 21. The ministry, however, took from this time more decided ground, and demanded a restoration of the islands, and a disavowal of their seizure, as the only course on the part of Spain which could prevent immediate war. It is now known that the Spanish court, in adopting these measures, had acted in concert with the court of France, and had reason to expect her support, whatever might be the consequences. Had this support been afforded, the war predicted by Lord Chatham would inevitably have taken place. But the King of France found himself involved in great pecuniary difficulties, and could not be induced to enter into the war. The Spaniards were therefore compelled to yield. They disavowed the seizure and restored the islands, on condition that this restoration should not affect any claim of right on the part of Spain. Three years after, they were abandoned by the English; and it is now understood that Lord North secretly *agreed* to do this, when the arrangement was made for the restoration of the islands by the Spanish.

SPEECH

OF LORD CHATHAM ON THE BILL AUTHORIZING THE QUARTERING OF BRITISH SOLDIERS ON THE INHABITANTS OF BOSTON, DELIVERED IN THE HOUSE OF LORDS, MAY 27, 1774.

INTRODUCTION.

THE health of Lord Chatham had for some time prevented him from taking any active part in public affairs. During two years he had rarely made his appearance in the House of Lords, and nothing but the rash and headlong measures of Lord North in regard to America, could have drawn him again from his retirement.

In speaking of those measures, it may be proper briefly to remind the reader of some of the preceding events. When Charles Townsend was left at the head of affairs, by Lord Chatham's unfortunate illness during the winter of 1766–7, he was continually goaded by Mr. Grenville on the subject of American taxation.[1] "You are cowards! You are afraid of the Americans. You dare not tax America!" The rash spirit of Townsend was roused by these attacks. "Fear?" said he. "Cowards? *Dare* not tax America? *I dare tax America!*" Grenville stood silent for a moment, and then said, "Dare you tax America? I wish to God you would do it." Townsend replied, "I will, I will." This hasty declaration could not be evaded or withdrawn, and in June, 1767, Townsend brought in a bill imposing duties on glass, paper, pasteboard, white and red lead, painters' colors, and tea, imported into the colonies. The preamble declared that it was "expedient to raise a revenue in America." A spirit of decided resistance to these taxes was at once manifested throughout all the colonies, and Lord North, on coming into power about two years after, introduced a bill repealing all the duties imposed by the act of 1767, except that on tea. But this was unsatisfactory, for it put the repeal on "commercial grounds" alone, and expressly reserved the *right* of taxation. At the close of 1773, the East India Company, encouraged by the ministry, sent large quantities of tea to Boston and some other American ports. The people resolved that the tea should not be landed, but should be sent back to England in the ships that brought it. As this was forbidden by the Custom-house, all the tea on board the ships lying in Boston harbor was thrown into the water by men disguised as Indians. on the evening of December 18th, 1773. This daring act awakened the keenest resentment of the British ministry. In March, 1774, laws were passed depriving Massachusetts of her charter, closing the port of Boston, and allowing persons charged with capital offenses to be carried to England for trial. As a means of farther enforcement, a bill was introduced in the month of May, 1774, for quartering troops on the inhabitants of the town of Boston, and other parts of the American colonies. This state of things gave rise to a number of Lord Chatham's most celebrated speeches, of which the following was the first in order.

SPEECH, &c.

MY LORDS,—The unfavorable state of health under which I have long labored, could not prevent me from laying before your Lordships my thoughts on the bill now upon the table, and on the American affairs in general.

If we take a transient view of those motives which induced the ancestors of our fellow-subjects in America to leave their native country, to encounter the innumerable difficulties of the unexplored regions of the Western World, our astonishment at the present conduct of their descendants will naturally subside. There was no corner of the world into which men of their free and enterprising spirit would not fly with alacrity, rather than submit to the slavish and tyrannical principles which prevailed at that period in their native country. And shall we wonder, my Lords, if the descendants of such illustrious characters spurn with contempt the hand of unconstitutional power, that would snatch from them such dear-bought privileges as they now contend for? Had the British colonies been planted by any other kingdom than our own, the inhabitants would have carried with them the chains of slavery and spirit of despotism; but as they are, they ought to be remembered as great instances to instruct the world what great exertions mankind will naturally make, when they are left to the free exercise of their own powers. And, my Lords, notwithstanding my intention to give my hearty negative to the question now before you, I can not help condemning in the severest manner the late turbulent and unwarrantable conduct of the Americans in some instances, particularly in the late riots of Boston. But, my Lords, the mode which has been pursued to bring them back to a sense of their duty to their parent state, has been so diametrically

[1] See Burke's admirable sketches of Grenville, Townsend, and Lord Chatham's third ministry, in his Speech on American Taxation.

opposite to the fundamental principles of sound policy, that individuals possessed of common understanding must be astonished at such proceedings. By blocking up the harbor of Boston, you have involved the innocent trader in the same punishment with the guilty profligates who destroyed your merchandise; and instead of making a well-concerted effort to secure the real offenders, you clap a naval and military extinguisher over their harbor, and visit the crime of a few lawless depredators and their abettors upon the whole body of the inhabitants.

My Lords, this country is little obliged to the framers and promoters of this tea tax. The Americans had almost forgot, in their excess of gratitude for the repeal of the Stamp Act, any interest but that of the mother country; there seemed an emulation among the different provinces who should be most dutiful and forward in their expressions of loyalty to their real benefactor, as you will readily perceive by the following letter from Governor Bernard to a noble Lord then in office.

"The House of Representatives," says he, "from the time of opening the session to this day, has shown a disposition to avoid all dispute with me, every thing having passed with as much good humor as I could desire. They have acted in all things with temper and moderation; they have avoided some subjects of dispute, and have laid a foundation for removing some causes of former altercation."

This, my Lords, was the temper of the Americans, and would have continued so, had it not been interrupted by your fruitless endeavors to tax them without their consent. But the moment they perceived your intention was renewed to tax them, under a pretense of serving the East India Company, their resentment got the ascendant of their moderation, and hurried them into actions contrary to law, which, in their cooler hours, they would have thought on with horror; for I sincerely believe the destroying of the tea was the effect of despair.

But, my Lords, from the complexion of the whole of the proceedings, I think that administration has purposely irritated them into those late violent acts, for which they now so severely smart, purposely to be revenged on them for the victory they gained by the repeal of the Stamp Act; a measure in which they seemingly acquiesced, but at the bottom they were its real enemies. For what other motive could induce them to dress taxation, that father of American sedition, in the robes of an East India director, but to break in upon that mutual peace and harmony which then so happily subsisted between them and the mother country?

My Lords, I am an old man, and would advise the noble Lords in office to adopt a more gentle mode of governing America; for the day is not far distant when America may vie with these kingdoms, not only in arms, but in arts also. It is an established fact that the principal towns in America are learned and polite, and understand the Constitution of the empire as well as the noble Lords who are now in office; and, consequently, they will have a watchful eye over their liberties, to prevent the least encroachment on their hereditary rights.

This observation is so recently exemplified in an excellent pamphlet, which comes from the pen of an American gentleman, that I shall take the liberty of reading to your Lordships his thoughts on the competency of the British Parliament to tax America, which, in my opinion, puts this interesting matter in the clearest view.

"The high court of Parliament," says he, "is the supreme legislative power over the whole empire; in all free states the Constitution is fixed; and as the supreme Legislature derives its power and authority from the Constitution, it can not overleap the bounds of it without destroying its own foundation. The Constitution ascertains and limits both sovereignty and allegiance; and therefore his Majesty's American subjects, who acknowledged themselves bound by the ties of allegiance, have an equitable claim to the full enjoyment of the fundamental rules of the English Constitution; and that it is an essential, unalterable right in nature, ingrafted into the British Constitution as a fundamental law, and ever held sacred and irrevocable by the subjects within this realm, that what a man has honestly acquired is absolutely his own; which he may freely give, but which can not be taken from him without his consent."

This, my Lords, though no new doctrine, has always been my received and unalterable opinion, and I will carry it to my grave, *that this country had no right under heaven to tax America*. It is contrary to all the principles of justice and civil polity, which neither the exigencies of the state, nor even an acquiescence in the taxes, could justify upon any occasion whatever. Such proceedings will never meet their wished-for success. Instead of adding to their miseries, as the bill now before you most undoubtedly does, adopt some lenient measures, which may lure them to their duty. Proceed like a kind and affectionate parent over a child whom he tenderly loves, and, instead of those harsh and severe proceedings, pass an amnesty on all their youthful errors, clasp them once more in your fond and affectionate arms, and I will venture to affirm you will find them children worthy of their sire. But, should their turbulence exist after your proffered terms of forgiveness, which I hope and expect this House will immediately adopt, I will be among the foremost of your Lordships to move for such measures as will effectually prevent a future relapse, and make them feel what it is to provoke a fond and forgiving parent! a parent, my Lords, whose welfare has ever been my greatest and most pleasing consolation. This declaration may seem unnecessary; but I will venture to declare, the period is not far distant when she will want the assistance of her most distant friends; but should the all-disposing hand of Providence prevent me from affording her my poor assistance, my prayers shall be ever for her welfare—*Length of days be in her right hand, and in her left riches and honor; may her ways be the ways of pleasantness, and all her paths be peace!*

Notwithstanding these warnings and remonstrances, the bill was passed by a majority of 57 to 16.

SPEECH

OF LORD CHATHAM ON A MOTION FOR AN ADDRESS TO HIS MAJESTY, TO GIVE IMMEDIATE ORDERS FOR REMOVING HIS TROOPS FROM BOSTON, DELIVERED IN THE HOUSE OF LORDS, JANUARY 20, 1775.

INTRODUCTION.

On the 20th of January, 1775, Lord Dartmouth, Secretary of State, laid before the House of Lords various papers relating to American affairs. Upon this occasion Lord Chatham moved an "address to his Majesty for the immediate removal of his troops from Boston," and supported it by the following speech.

When he arose to speak, says one who witnessed the scene, "all was silence and profound attention. Animated, and almost inspired by his subject, he seemed to feel his own unrivaled superiority. His venerable figure, dignified and graceful in decay, his language, his voice, his gesture, were such as might, at this momentous crisis, big with the fate of Britain seem to characterize him as the guardian genius of his country."

SPEECH, &c.[1]

My Lords,—After more than six weeks' possession of the papers now before you, on a subject so momentous, at a time when the fate of this nation hangs on every hour, the ministry have at length condescended to submit to the consideration of this House, intelligence from America with which your Lordships and the public have been long and fully acquainted.

The measures of last year, my Lords, which have produced the present alarming state of America, were founded upon misrepresentation. They were violent, precipitate, and vindictive. The nation was told that it was only a faction in Boston which opposed all lawful government; that an unwarrantable injury had been done to private property, for which the justice of Parliament was called upon to order reparation; that the least appearance of firmness would awe the Americans into submission, and upon only passing the Rubicon we should be "sine clade victor."[2]

That the people might choose their representatives under the influence of those misrepresentations, the Parliament was precipitately dissolved. Thus the nation was to be rendered instrumental in executing the vengeance of administration on that injured, unhappy, traduced people.

But now, my Lords, we find that, instead of suppressing the opposition of the faction at Boston, these measures have spread it over the whole continent. They have united that whole people by the most indissoluble of all bands—intolerable wrongs. The just retribution is an indiscriminate, unmerciful proscription of the innocent with the guilty, unheard and untried. The bloodless victory is an impotent general with his dishonored army, trusting solely to the pickax and the spade for security against the just indignation of an injured and insulted people.

My Lords, I am happy that a relaxation of my infirmities permits me to seize this earliest opportunity of offering my poor advice to save this unhappy country, at this moment tottering to its ruin. But, as I have not the honor of access to his Majesty, I will endeavor to transmit to him, through the constitutional channel of this House, my ideas on American business, to rescue him from the misadvice of his present ministers. I congratulate your Lordships that the business is at last entered upon by the noble Lord's [Lord Dartmouth] laying the papers before you. As I suppose your Lordships are too well apprised of their contents, I hope I am not premature in submitting to you my present motion. [The motion was read.]

I wish, my Lords, not to lose a day in this urgent, pressing crisis. An hour now lost in allaying ferments in America may produce years of calamity. For my own part, I will not desert, for a moment, the conduct of this weighty business, from the first to the last. Unless nailed to my bed by the extremity of sickness, I will give it unremitted attention. I will knock at the door of this sleeping and confounded ministry, and will rouse them to a sense of their danger.

When I state the importance of the colonies to this country, and the magnitude of danger hanging over this country from the present plan of misadministration practiced against them, I desire not to be understood to argue for a reciprocity of indulgence between England and America. I contend not for indulgence, but justice to America; and I shall ever contend that the Americans justly owe obedience to us in a limited degree—they owe obedience to our ordinances of trade and navigation; but let the line be skillfully drawn between the objects of those ordinances

---

[1] This speech was reported by Mr. Hugh Boyd, a man of high literary attainments, and bears very strong marks of accuracy.

[2] Victorious without slaughter.

and their private internal property. Let the sacredness of their property remain inviolate. Let it be taxable only by their own consent, given in their provincial assemblies, else it will cease to be property. As to the metaphysical refinements, attempting to show that the Americans are equally free from obedience and commercial restraints, as from taxation for revenue, as being unrepresented here, I pronounce them futile, frivolous, and groundless.

When I urge this measure of recalling the troops from Boston, I urge it on this pressing principle, that it is necessarily preparatory to the restoration of your peace and the establishment of your prosperity. It will then appear that you are disposed to treat amicably and equitably; and to consider, revise, and repeal, if it should be found necessary (as I affirm it will), those violent acts and declarations which have disseminated confusion throughout your empire.

Resistance to your acts was necessary as it was just; and your vain declarations of the omnipotence of Parliament, and your imperious doctrines of the necessity of submission, will be found equally impotent to convince or to enslave your fellow-subjects in America, who feel that tyranny, whether *ambitioned* by an individual part of the Legislature, or the bodies who compose it, is equally intolerable to British subjects.

The means of enforcing this thraldom are found to be as ridiculous and weak in practice as they are unjust in principle. Indeed, I can not but feel the most anxious sensibility for the situation of General Gage, and the troops under his command; thinking him, as I do, a man of humanity and understanding; and entertaining, as I ever will, the highest respect, the warmest love for the British troops. Their situation is truly unworthy; penned up—pining in inglorious inactivity. They are an army of impotence. You may call them an army of safety and of guard; but they are, in truth, an army of impotence and contempt; and, to make the folly equal to the disgrace, they are an army of irritation and vexation.

But I find a report creeping abroad that ministers censure General Gage's inactivity. Let them censure him — it becomes them — it becomes their justice and their honor. I mean not to censure his inactivity. It is a prudent and necessary inaction; but it is a miserable condition, where disgrace is prudence, and where it is necessary to be contemptible. This tameness, however contemptible, can not be censured; for the first drop of blood shed in civil and unnatural war might be "immedicabile vulnus."[3]

I therefore urge and conjure your Lordships immediately to adopt this conciliating measure. I will pledge myself for its immediately producing conciliatory effects, by its being thus well timed; but if you delay till your vain hope shall be accomplished of triumphantly dictating reconciliation, you delay forever. But, admitting that this hope (which in truth is desperate) should be accomplished, what do you gain by the imposition of your victorious amity? You will be untrusted and unthanked. Adopt, then, the grace, while you have the opportunity, of reconcilement—or at least prepare the way. Allay the ferment prevailing in America, by removing the obnoxious hostile cause—obnoxious and unserviceable; for their merit can be only inaction: "Non dimicare est vincere,"[4] their victory can never be by exertions. Their force would be most disproportionately exerted against a brave, generous, and united people, with arms in their hands, and courage in their hearts: three millions of people, the genuine descendants of a valiant and pious ancestry, driven to those deserts by the narrow maxims of a superstitious tyranny. And is the spirit of persecution never to be appeased? Are the brave sons of those brave forefathers to inherit their sufferings, as they have inherited their virtues? Are they to sustain the infliction of the most oppressive and unexampled severity, beyond the accounts of history or description of poetry: "Rhadamanthus habet durissima regna, castigatque *auditque*."[5] So says the wisest poet, and perhaps the wisest statesman and politician. But our ministers say *the Americans must not be heard.* They have been condemned *unheard.* The indiscriminate hand of vengeance has lumped together innocent and guilty; with all the formalities of hostility, has blocked up the town [Boston], and reduced to beggary and famine thirty thousand inhabitants.

But his Majesty is advised that the union in America can not last. Ministers have more eyes than I, and should have more ears; but, with all the information I have been able to procure, I can pronounce it a union solid, permanent, and effectual. Ministers may satisfy themselves, and delude the public, with the report of what they call commercial bodies in America. They are *not* commercial. They are your packers and factors. They live upon nothing, for I call commission nothing. I speak of the ministerial authority for this American intelligence—the runners for government, who are paid for their intelligence. But these are not the men, nor this the influence, to be considered in America, when we estimate the firmness of their union. Even to extend the question, and to take in the

[3] Nil prosunt artes; erat *immedicabile vulnus.*

All arts are vain: *incurable the wound.*

Ovid's Metamorphoses, book x., 189.

[4] Not to fight is to conquer.

[5] The passage is from the Æneid of Virgil, book vi., 366–7.

Gnosius hæc Rhadamanthus habet durissima regna,
Castigâtque auditque dolos.

O'er these dire realms
The Cretan Rhadamanthus holds his sway,
And lashes guilty souls, whose wiles and crimes
He hears.

Lord Chatham, from the order of the words, gives them an ingenious turn, as if the punishment came *before* the hearing; which was certainly true of justice as then administered in America, though not in the infernal regions of Virgil.

really mercantile circle, will be totally inadequate to the consideration. Trade, indeed, increases the wealth and glory of a country; but its real strength and stamina are to be looked for among the cultivators of the land. In their simplicity of life is found the simpleness of virtue—the integrity and courage of freedom. These true, genuine sons of the earth are invincible; and they surround and hem in the mercantile bodies, even if these bodies (which supposition I totally disclaim) could be supposed disaffected to the cause of liberty. Of this general spirit existing in the British nation (for so I wish to distinguish the real and genuine Americans from the pseudo-traders I have described)—of this spirit of independence, animating the *nation* of America, I have the most authentic information. It is not new among them. It is, and has ever been, their established principle, their confirmed persuasion. It is their nature and their doctrine.

I remember, some years ago, when the repeal of the Stamp Act was in agitation, conversing in a friendly confidence with a person of undoubted respect and authenticity, on that subject, and he assured me with a certainty which his judgment and opportunity gave him, that these were the prevalent and steady principles of America—that you might destroy their towns, and cut them off from the superfluities, perhaps the conveniences of life, but that they were prepared to despise your power, and would not lament their loss, while they have—what, my Lords?—their *woods* and their *liberty*. The name of my authority, if I am called upon, will authenticate the opinion irrefragably.[6]

If illegal violences have been, as it is said, committed in America, prepare the way, open the door of possibility for acknowledgment and satisfaction; but proceed not to such coercion, such proscription; cease your indiscriminate inflictions; amerce not thirty thousand—oppress not three millions for the fault of forty or fifty individuals. Such severity of injustice must forever render incurable the wounds you have already given your colonies; you irritate them to unappeasable rancor. What though you march from town to town, and from province to province; though you should be able to enforce a temporary and local submission (which I only suppose, not admit), how shall you be able to secure the obedience of the country you leave behind you in your progress, to grasp the dominion of eighteen hundred miles of continent, populous in numbers, possessing valor, liberty, and resistance?

This resistance to your arbitrary system of taxation might have been foreseen. It was obvious from the nature of things, and of mankind; and, above all, from the Whiggish spirit flourishing in that country. The spirit which now resists your taxation in America is the same which formerly opposed loans, benevolences, and ship-money in England; the same spirit which called all England "on its legs," and by the Bill of Rights vindicated the English Constitution; the same spirit which established the great fundamental, essential maxim of your liberties, *that no subject of England shall be taxed but by his own consent*.

This glorious spirit of Whiggism animates three millions in America, who prefer poverty with liberty, to gilded chains and sordid affluence; and who will die in defense of their rights as men, as freemen. What shall oppose this spirit, aided by the congenial flame glowing in the breast of every Whig in England, to the amount, I hope, of double the American numbers? Ireland they have to a man. In that country, joined as it is with the cause of the colonies, and placed at their head, the distinction I contend for is and must be observed. This country superintends and controls their trade and navigation; but they *tax themselves*. And this distinction between external and internal control is sacred and insurmountable; it is involved in the abstract nature of things. Property is private, individual, absolute. Trade is an extended and complicated consideration: it reaches as far as ships can sail or winds can blow: it is a great and various machine. To regulate the numberless movements of its several parts, and combine them into effect for the good of the whole, requires the superintending wisdom and energy of the supreme power in the empire. But this supreme power has no effect toward internal taxation; for it does not exist in that relation; there is no such thing, no such idea in this Constitution, as a supreme power operating upon property. Let this distinction then remain forever ascertained; taxation is theirs, commercial regulation is ours. As an American, I would recognize to England her supreme right of regulating commerce and navigation; as an Englishman by birth and principle, I recognize to the Americans their supreme, unalienable right in their property: a right which they are justified in the defense of to the last extremity. To maintain this principle is the common cause of the Whigs on the other side of the Atlantic and on this. "'Tis liberty to liberty engaged," that they will defend themselves, their families, and their country. In this great cause they are immovably allied: it is the alliance of God and nature—immutable, eternal—fixed as the firmament of heaven.

To such united force, what force shall be opposed? What, my Lords? A few regiments in America, and seventeen or eighteen thousand men at home! The idea is too ridiculous to take up a moment of your Lordships' time. Nor can such a national and principled union be resisted by the tricks of office, or ministerial maneuver. Laying of papers on your table, or counting numbers on a division, will not avert or postpone the hour of danger. It must arrive, my Lords, unless these fatal acts are done away; it must arrive in all its horrors, and then these boastful ministers, spite of all their confidence and all their maneuvers, shall be forced to hide their heads. They shall be forced to a disgrace-

[6] It was Dr. Franklin.

ful abandonment of their present measures and principles, which they avow, but can not defend; measures which they presume to attempt, but can not hope to effectuate. They can not, my Lords, they can not stir a step; they have not a move left; they are *check-mated!*

But it is not repealing this act of Parliament, it is not repealing a piece of parchment, that can restore America to our bosom. You must repeal her fears and her resentments, and you may then hope for her love and gratitude. But now, insulted with an armed force posted at Boston, irritated with a hostile array before her eyes, her concessions, if you *could* force them, would be suspicious and insecure; they will be "irato animo" [with an angry spirit]; they will not be the sound, honorable passions of freemen; they will be the dictates of fear and extortions of force. But it is more than evident that you can not force them, united as they are, to your unworthy terms of submission. It is impossible. And when I hear General Gage censured for inactivity, I must retort with indignation on those whose intemperate measures and improvident counsels have betrayed him into his present situation. His situation reminds me, my Lords, of the answer of a French general in the civil wars of France—Monsieur Condé opposed to Monsieur Turenne. He was asked how it happened that he did not take his adversary prisoner, as he was often very near him. "J'ai peur," replied Condé, very honestly, "j'ai peur qu'il ne me prenne;" *I'm afraid he'll take me.*

When your Lordships look at the papers transmitted us from America—when you consider their decency, firmness, and wisdom, you can not but respect their cause, and wish to make it your own. For myself, I must declare and avow, that in all my reading and observation—and it has been my favorite study—I have read Thucydides, and have studied and admired the master-states of the world—that for solidity of reasoning, force of sagacity, and wisdom of conclusion, under such a complication of difficult circumstances, no nation or body of men can stand in preference to the general Congress at Philadelphia. I trust it is obvious to your Lordships that all attempts to impose servitude upon such men, to establish despotism over such a mighty continental nation, must be vain, must be fatal. We shall be forced ultimately to retract; let us retract while we can, not when we must. I say we must necessarily undo these violent, oppressive acts.[7] They must be repealed. You *will* repeal them. I pledge myself for it, that you will, in the end, repeal them. I stake my reputation on it. I will consent to be taken for an idiot if they are not finally repealed.[8] Avoid, then, this humiliating, disgraceful necessity. With a dignity becoming your exalted situation, make the first advances to concord, to peace, and happiness; for that is your true dignity, to act with prudence and justice. That *you* should first concede is obvious, from sound and rational policy. Concession comes with better grace and more salutary effect from superior power. It reconciles superiority of power with the feelings of men, and establishes solid confidence on the foundations of affection and gratitude.

So thought a wise poet and a wise man in political sagacity—the friend of Mecænas, and the eulogist of Augustus. To him, the adopted son and successor of the first Cesar—to him, the master of the world, he wisely urged this conduct of prudence and dignity: "Tuque prior, tu parce; projice tela manu."[9]

Every motive, therefore, of justice and of policy, of dignity and of prudence, urges you to allay the ferment in America by a removal of your troops from Boston, by a repeal of your acts of Parliament, and by demonstration of amicable dispositions toward your colonies. On the other hand, every danger and every hazard impend to deter you from perseverance in your

[7] The Boston Port Bill, and the act taking away the charter of Massachusetts.

[8] This prediction was verified. After a war of three years, a repeal of these acts was sent out to propitiate the Americans, but it was too late.

[9] If Lord Chatham's memory had not failed him in respect to these words, his taste and genius would have suggested a still finer turn. They were addressed, not by Virgil to Augustus Cesar, but to a parent advancing in arms against a child; and would, therefore, have been applied with double force and beauty to the contest of England against America. The words are taken from that splendid passage at the close of the sixth book of Virgil's Æneid, where Anchises is showing to Æneas, in the world of spirits, the souls of those who were destined to pass within "the gates of life," and to swell, as his descendants, the long line of Roman greatness. After pointing out the Decii and Drusii, Torquatus with his bloody ax, and Camillus with his standards of glory, he comes at last to Julius Cesar, and Pompey, his son-in-law, preparing for the battle of Pharsalia. As if the conflict might yet be averted, he addresses his future children, and entreats them not to turn their arms against their country's vitals. He appeals especially to Cesar as "descended from Olympian Jove," and exhorts him "Tuque prior, tu parce; projice tela manu."

Illæ autem, paribus quas fulgere cernis in armis,
Concordes animæ nunc et dum nocte premuntur,
Heu! quantum inter se bellum, si limina vitæ
Attingerint, quantas acies stragemque ciebunt,
Aggeribus socer Alpinis atque arce Monœci
Descendens, gener adversis instructus Eois!
Ne, pueri, ne tanta animis assuecite bella;
Neu patriæ validas in viscera vertite vires!
Tuque prior, tu parce, genus qui ducis Olympo;
Projice tela manu, sanguis meus!—826–835.

Those forms which now thou seest in equal arms
Shining afar—united souls while here
Beneath the realm of night—what fields of blood
And mutual slaughter shall mark out their course,
If once they pass within the Gates of Life!
See, from the Alpine heights the father comes
Down by Monaco's tower, to meet the son
Equipped with hostile legions from the East.
Nay! nay, my children! Train not thus your minds
To scenes of blood! Turn not those arms of strength
Against your country's vitals!
Thou! thou, descended from Olympian Jove!
Be first to spare! Son of my blood! *cast down
Those weapons from thy hand!*

present ruinous measures. Foreign war hanging over your heads by a slight and brittle thread; France and Spain watching your conduct, and waiting for the maturity of your errors, with a vigilant eye to America and the temper of your colonies, more than to their own concerns, be they what they may.

To conclude, my Lords, if the ministers thus persevere in misadvising and misleading the King, I will not say that they can alienate the affections of his subjects from his crown, but I will affirm *that they will make the crown not worth his wearing*. I will not say that the King is betrayed, but I will pronounce *that the kingdom is undone*.

The motion, after a long debate, was lost by a vote of 68 to 18.

SPEECH

OF LORD CHATHAM ON A MOTION FOR AN ADDRESS TO THE CROWN, TO PUT A STOP TO HOSTILITIES IN AMERICA, DELIVERED IN THE HOUSE OF LORDS, MAY 30, 1777.

INTRODUCTION.

Lord Chatham had now been prevented by his infirmities from taking his place in the House of Lords for more than two years. Anxious to make one effort more for ending the contest with America, he made his appearance in the House on the 30th of May, 1777, wrapped in flannels, and supported on crutches, and moved an address to the King, recommending that speedy and effectual measures be taken to put an end to the war between the colonies and the mother country. He spoke as follows:

SPEECH, &c.

My Lords, this is a flying moment; perhaps but six weeks left to arrest the dangers that surround us. The gathering storm may break; it has already opened, and in part burst. It is difficult for government, after all that has passed, to shake hands with defiers of the King, defiers of the Parliament, defiers of the people. I am a defier of nobody; but if an end is not put to this war, there is an end to this country. I do not trust my judgment in my present state of health; this is the judgment of my better days—the result of forty years' attention to America. They are rebels; but for what? Surely not for defending their unquestionable rights! What have these rebels done heretofore? I remember when they raised four regiments on their own bottom, and took Louisbourg from the veteran troops of France. But their excesses have been great: I do not mean their panegyric; but must observe, in extenuation, the erroneous and infatuated counsels which have prevailed; the door to mercy and justice has been shut against them; but they may still be taken up upon the grounds of their former submission. [Referring to their petition.]

I state to you the importance of America: it is a double market—the market of consumption, and the market of supply. This double market for millions, with naval stores, you are giving to your hereditary rival. America has carried you through four wars, and will now carry you to your death, if you don't take things in time. In the sportsman's phrase, when you have found yourselves at fault, you must try back. You have ransacked every corner of Lower Saxony; but forty thousand German boors never can conquer ten times the number of British freemen. You may ravage—you can not conquer; it is impossible; you can not conquer the Americans. You talk, my Lords, of your numerous friends among them to annihilate the Congress, and of your powerful forces to disperse their army. I *might as well talk of driving them before me with this crutch!* But what would you conquer—the map of America? I am ready to meet any general officer on the subject [looking at Lord Amherst.] What will you do out of the protection of your fleet? In the winter, if together, they are starved; and if dispersed, they are taken off in detail. I am experienced in spring hopes and vernal promises; I know what ministers throw out; but at last will come your equinoctial disappointment. You have got nothing in America but stations. You have been three years teaching them the art of war; they are apt scholars; and I will venture to tell your Lordships that the American gentry will make officers enough, fit to command the troops of all the European powers. What you have sent there are too many to make peace—too few to make war. If you conquer them, what then? You can not make them respect you; you can not make them wear your cloth; you will plant an invincible hatred in their breasts against you. Coming from the stock they do, they can never respect you. If ministers are founded in saying there is no sort of treaty with France, there is still a moment left; the point of honor is still safe. France must be as self-destroying as England, to make a treaty while you are giving her America, at the expense of twelve millions a year. The intercourse has produced every thing to France; and England, Old England, must pay for all. I have, at different times, made different propositions, adapted to the circumstances in which they were offered. The plan contained in the former bill is now impracticable; the present motion will tell you where you are, and what you have now to depend upon. It may produce a respectable division in America, and unanimity at home; it will give America an option; she has yet had no option. You have said, Lay down your arms; and she has given you the Spartan answer, "Come, take." [Here he read his motion.] "That an humble address be presented to his Majesty, most dutifully representing to his royal wisdom that this House is deeply penetrated with the view of impending ruin to the kingdom, from the continuation of an unnatural war against the British colonies in America; and most humbly to advise his Majesty to take the most speedy and effectual measures for putting a stop to such fatal hostilities, upon the only just and solid foundation, namely, the removal of accumulated grievances; and to assure his Majesty that this House will enter upon this great and necessary work with cheerfulness and dispatch, in order to open to his Majesty the only means of regaining the affections of the British colonies, and of securing to Great Britain the commercial advantages of these valuable possessions; fully persuaded that to heal and to redress will be more congenial to the goodness and magnanimity of his Majesty, and more prevalent over the hearts of generous and free-born subjects, than the rigors of chastisement and the horrors of a civil war, which hitherto have served only to sharpen resentments and consolidate union, and, if continued, must end in finally dissolving all ties between Great Britain and the colonies."

[His Lordship rose again.] The proposal, he said, is specific. I thought this so clear, that I did not enlarge upon it. I mean the redress of all their grievances, and the right of disposing of their own money. This is to be done instantaneously. I will get out of my bed to move it on Monday. This will be the herald of peace; this will open the way for treaty; this will show Parliament sincerely disposed. Yet still much must be left to treaty. Should you conquer this people, you conquer under the cannon of France—under a masked battery then ready to open. The moment a treaty with France appears, you must declare war, though you had only five ships of the line in England; but France will defer a treaty as long as possible. You are now at the mercy of every little German chancery; and the pretensions of France will increase daily, so as to become an avowed party in either peace or war. We have tried for unconditional submission; try what can be gained by unconditional redress. Less dignity will be lost in the repeal, than in submitting to the demands of German chanceries. We are the aggressors. We have invaded them. We have invaded them as much as the Spanish Armada invaded England. Mercy can not do harm; it will seat the King where he ought to be, throned on the hearts of his people; and millions at home and abroad, now employed in obloquy or revolt, would pray for him.

[In making his motion for addressing the King, Lord Chatham insisted frequently and strongly on the absolute necessity of immediately making peace with America. Now, he said, was the crisis, before France was a party to the treaty. This was the only moment left before the fate of this country was decided. The French court, he observed, was too wise to lose the opportunity of effectually separating America from the dominions of this kingdom. War between France and Great Britain, he said, was not less probable because it had not yet been declared. It would be folly in France to declare it now, while America gave full employment to our arms, and was pouring into her lap her wealth and produce, the benefit of which she was enjoying in peace. He enlarged much on the importance of America to this country, which, in peace and in war, he observed, he ever considered as the great source of all our wealth and power. He then added (raising his voice), Your trade languishes, your taxes increase, your revenues diminish. France at this moment is securing and drawing to herself that commerce which created your seamen, fed your islands, &c. He reprobated the measures which produced, and which had been pursued in the conduct of the civil war, in the severest language; infatuated measures giving rise to, and still continuing a cruel, unnatural, self-destroying war. Success, it is said, is hoped for in this campaign. Why? Because our army will be as strong this year as it was last, when it was not strong enough. The notion of conquering America he treated with the greatest contempt.

After an animated debate, in which the motion was opposed by Lords Gower, Lyttelton, Mansfield, and Weymouth, and the Archbishop of York, and supported by the Dukes of Grafton and Manchester, Lord Camden and Shelburne, and the Bishop of Peterborough,

The Earl of Chatham again rose, and in reply to what had fallen from Lord Weymouth, said:] My Lords, I perceive the noble Lord neither apprehends my meaning, nor the explanation given by me to the noble Earl [Earl Gower] in the blue ribbon, who spoke early in the debate. I will, therefore, with your Lordships' permission, state shortly what I meant. My Lords, my motion was stated generally, that I might leave the question at large to be amended by your Lordships. I did not dare to point out the specific means. I drew the motion up to the best of my poor abilities; but I intended it only as the herald of conciliation, as the harbinger of peace to our afflicted colonies. But as the noble Lord seems to wish for something more specific on the subject, and through that medium seeks my particular sentiments, I will tell your Lordships very fairly what I wish for. I wish for a repeal of every oppressive act which your Lordships have passed since 1763. I would put our brethren in America precisely on the same footing they stood at that period. I would expect, that, being left at liberty to tax themselves, and dispose of their own property, they would, in return, contribute to the common burdens according to their means and abilities. I will move your Lordships for a bill of repeal, as the only means left to arrest that approaching destruction which threatens to overwhelm us. My Lords, I shall no doubt hear it objected, "Why should we submit or concede? Has America done any thing on her part to induce us to agree to so large a ground of concession?" I will tell you, my Lords, why I think you should. You have been the aggressors from the beginning. I shall not trouble your Lordships with the particulars; they have been stated and enforced by the noble and learned Lord who spoke last but one (Lord Camden), in a much more able and distinct manner than I could pretend to state them. If, then, we are the aggressors, it is your Lordships' business to make the first overture. I say again, this country has been the aggressor. You have made descents upon their coasts; you have burned their towns, plundered their country, made war upon the inhabitants, confiscated their property, proscribed and imprisoned their persons. I do therefore affirm, my Lords, that instead of exacting unconditional submission from the colonies, we should grant them unconditional redress. We have injured them; we have endeavored to enslave and oppress them. Upon this ground, my Lords, instead of chastisement, they are entitled to redress. A repeal of those laws, of which they complain, will be the first step to that redress. The people of America look upon Parliament as the authors of their miseries; their affections are estranged from their sovereign. Let, then, reparation come from the hands that inflicted the injuries; let conciliation succeed chastisement; and I do maintain, that Parliament will again recover its authority; that his Majesty will be once more enthroned in the hearts of his American subjects; and that your Lordships, as contributing to so great, glorious, salutary, and benignant a work, will receive the prayers and benedictions of every part of the British empire.

The motion was lost by a vote of 99 to 28.

SPEECH

OF LORD CHATHAM ON A MOTION FOR AN ADDRESS TO THE THRONE, AT THE OPENING OF PARLIAMENT, DELIVERED IN THE HOUSE OF LORDS, NOVEMBER 18, 1777.

INTRODUCTION.

THIS was Lord Chatham's greatest effort. Though sinking under the weight of years and disease, he seems animated by all the fire of youth. It would, indeed, be difficult to find in the whole range of parliamentary history a more splendid blaze of genius, at once rapid, vigorous, and sublime.

SPEECH, &c.[1]

I RISE, my Lords, to declare my sentiments on this most solemn and serious subject. It has imposed a load upon my mind, which, I fear, nothing can remove, but which impels me to endeavor its alleviation, by a free and unreserved communication of my sentiments.

In the first part of the address, I have the honor of heartily concurring with the noble Earl who moved it. No man feels sincerer joy than I do; none can offer more genuine congratulations on every accession of strength to the Protestant succession. I therefore join in every congratulation on the birth of another princess, and the happy recovery of her Majesty.

But I must stop here. My courtly complaisance will carry me no farther. I will not join in congratulation on misfortune and disgrace. I can not concur in a blind and servile address, which approves, and endeavors to sanctify the monstrous measures which have heaped disgrace and misfortune upon us. This, my Lords, is a perilous and tremendous moment! It is not a time for adulation. The smoothness of flattery can not now avail—can not save us in this rugged and awful crisis. It is now necessary to instruct the Throne in the language of truth. We must dispel the illusion and the darkness which envelop it, and display, in its full danger and true colors, the ruin that is brought to our doors.

This, my Lords, is our duty. It is the proper function of this noble assembly, sitting, as we do, upon our honors in this House, the hereditary council of the Crown. *Who* is the minister—*where* is the minister, that has dared to suggest to the Throne the contrary, unconstitutional language this day delivered from it? The accustomed language from the Throne has been application to Parliament for advice, and a reliance on its constitutional advice and assistance. As it is the right of Parliament to give, so it is the duty of the Crown to ask it. But on this day, and in this extreme momentous exigency, no reliance is reposed on our constitutional counsels! no advice is asked from the sober and enlightened care of Parliament! but the Crown, from itself and by itself, declares an unalterable determination to pursue measures — and what measures, my Lords? The measures that have produced the imminent perils that threaten us; the measures that have brought ruin to our doors.

Can the minister of the day now presume to expect a continuance of support in this ruinous infatuation? Can Parliament be so dead to its dignity and its duty as to be thus deluded into the loss of the one and the violation of the other? To give an unlimited credit and support for the steady perseverance in measures not proposed

[1] This was reported by Hugh Boyd, and is said to have been corrected by Lord Chatham himself.

for our parliamentary advice, but dictated and forced upon us—in measures, I say, my Lords, which have reduced this late flourishing empire to ruin and contempt! "But yesterday, and England might have stood against the world: now none so poor to do her reverence."[2] I use the words of a poet; but, though it be poetry, it is no fiction. It is a shameful truth, that not only the power and strength of this country are wasting away and expiring, but her well-earned glories, her true honor, and substantial dignity are sacrificed.

France, my Lords, has insulted you; she has encouraged and sustained America; and, whether America be wrong or right, the dignity of this country ought to spurn at the officious insult of French interference. The ministers and embassadors of those who are called rebels and enemies are in Paris; in Paris they transact the reciprocal interests of America and France. Can there be a more mortifying insult? Can even our ministers sustain a more humiliating disgrace? Do they dare to resent it? Do they presume even to hint a vindication of their honor, and the dignity of the state, by requiring the dismission of the plenipotentiaries of America? Such is the degradation to which they have reduced the glories of England! The people whom they affect to call contemptible rebels, but whose growing power has at last obtained the name of enemies; the people with whom they have engaged this country in war, and against whom they now command our implicit support in every measure of desperate hostility—this people, despised as rebels, or acknowledged as enemies, are abetted against you, supplied with every military store, their interests consulted, and their embassadors entertained, by your inveterate enemy! and our ministers dare not interpose with dignity or effect. Is this the honor of a great kingdom? Is this the indignant spirit of England, who "but yesterday" gave law to the house of Bourbon? My Lords, the dignity of nations demands a decisive conduct in a situation like this. Even when the greatest prince that perhaps this country ever saw, filled our throne, the requisition of a Spanish general, on a similar subject, was attended to, and complied with; for, on the spirited remonstrance of the Duke of Alva, Elizabeth found herself obliged to deny the Flemish exiles all countenance, support, or even entrance into her dominions; and the Count Le Marque, with his few desperate followers, were expelled the kingdom. Happening to arrive at the Brille, and finding it weak in defense, they made themselves masters of the place; and this was the foundation of the United Provinces.

My Lords, this ruinous and ignominious situation, where we can not act with success, nor suffer with honor, calls upon us to remonstrate in the strongest and loudest language of truth, to rescue the ear of majesty from the delusions which surround it. The desperate state of our arms abroad is in part known. No man thinks more highly of them than I do. I love and honor the English troops. I know their virtues and their valor. I know they can achieve any thing except impossibilities; and I know that the conquest of English America *is an impossibility*. You can not, I venture to say it, *you can not* conquer America. Your armies last war effected every thing that could be effected; and what was it? It cost a numerous army, under the command of a most able general [Lord Amherst], now a noble Lord in this House, a long and laborious campaign, to expel five thousand Frenchmen from French America. My Lords, *you can not conquer America*. What is your present situation there? We do not know the worst; but we know that in three campaigns we have done nothing and suffered much. Besides the sufferings, perhaps *total loss* of the Northern force,[3] the best appointed army that ever took the field, commanded by Sir William Howe, has retired from the American lines. *He was obliged* to relinquish his attempt, and with great delay and danger to adopt a new and distant plan of operations. We shall soon know, and in any event have reason to lament, what may have happened since. As to conquest, therefore, my Lords, I repeat, it is impossible. You may swell every expense and every effort still more extravagantly; pile and accumulate every assistance you can buy or borrow; traffic and barter with every little pitiful German prince that sells and sends his subjects to the shambles of a foreign prince; your efforts are forever vain and impotent—doubly so from this mercenary aid on which you rely; for it irritates, to an incurable resentment, the minds of your enemies, to overrun them with the mercenary sons of rapine and plunder, devoting them and their possessions to the rapacity of hireling cruelty! If I were an American, as I am an Englishman, while a foreign troop was landed in my country, I never would lay down my arms—never—never—never.

Your own army is infected with the contagion of these illiberal allies. The spirit of plunder and of rapine is gone forth among them. I know it; and, notwithstanding what the noble Earl [Lord Percy] who moved the address has given as his opinion of the American army, I know from authentic information, and the *most experienced officers*, that our discipline is deeply wounded. While this is notoriously our sinking situation, America grows and flourishes; while our strength and discipline are lowered, hers are rising and improving.

But, my Lords, who is the man that, in addition to these disgraces and mischiefs of our army, has dared to authorize and associate to our arms the tomahawk and scalping-knife of the savage? to call into civilized alliance the wild and inhuman savage of the woods; to delegate to the merciless Indian the defense of disputed rights, and to wage the horrors of his barbarous war

[2] "But yesterday the word of Cesar might
Have stood against the world; now lies he there,
And none so poor to do him reverence."
Julius Cesar, Act III., Sc. 6.

[3] General Burgoyne's army.

against our brethren? My Lords, these enormities cry aloud for redress and punishment. Unless thoroughly done away, it will be a stain on the national character. It is a violation of the Constitution. I believe it is against law. It is not the least of our national misfortunes that the strength and character of our army are thus impaired. Infected with the mercenary spirit of robbery and rapine; familiarized to the horrid scenes of savage cruelty, it can no longer boast of the noble and generous principles which dignify a soldier; no longer sympathize with the dignity of the royal banner, nor feel the pride, pomp, and circumstance of glorious war, "that make ambition virtue!" What makes ambition virtue?—the sense of honor. But is the sense of honor consistent with a spirit of plunder, or the practice of murder? Can it flow from mercenary motives, or can it prompt to cruel deeds? Besides these murderers and plunderers, let me ask our ministers, What other allies have they acquired? What *other powers* have they associated to their cause? Have they entered into alliance with the *king of the gipsies?* Nothing, my Lords, is too low or too ludicrous to be consistent with their counsels.

The independent views of America have been stated and asserted as the foundation of this address. My Lords, no man wishes for the due dependence of America on this country more than I do. To preserve it, and not confirm that state of independence into which *your measures* hitherto have *driven them*, is the object which we ought to unite in attaining. The Americans, contending for their rights against arbitrary exactions, I love and admire. It is the struggle of free and virtuous patriots. But, contending for independency and total disconnection from England, as an Englishman, I can not wish them success; for in a due constitutional dependency, including the ancient supremacy of this country in regulating their commerce and navigation, consists the mutual happiness and prosperity both of England and America. She derived assistance and protection from us; and we reaped from her the most important advantages. She was, indeed, the fountain of our wealth, the nerve of our strength, the nursery and basis of our naval power. It is our duty, therefore, my Lords, if we wish to save our country, most seriously to endeavor the recovery of these most beneficial subjects; and in this perilous crisis, perhaps the present moment may be the only one in which we can hope for success. For in their negotiations with France, they have, or think they have, reason to complain; though it be notorious that they have received from that power important supplies and assistance of various kinds, yet it is certain they expected it in a more decisive and immediate degree. America is in ill humor with France; on some points they have not entirely answered her expectations. Let us wisely take advantage of every possible moment of reconciliation. Besides, the natural disposition of America herself still leans toward England; to the old habits of connection and mutual interest that united both countries. This *was* the established sentiment of all the Continent; and still, my Lords, in the great and principal part, the sound part of America, this wise and affectionate disposition prevails. And there is a very considerable part of America yet sound—the middle aud the southern provinces. Some parts may be factious and blind to their true interests; but if we express a wise and benevolent disposition to commuuicate with them those immutable rights of nature and those constitutional liberties to which they are equally entitled with ourselves, by a conduct so just and humane we shall confirm the favorable and conciliate the adverse. I say, my Lords, the rights and liberties to which they are equally entitled with ourselves, *but no more.* I would participate to them every enjoyment and freedom which the colonizing subjects of a free state can possess, or wish to possess; and I do not see why they should not enjoy every fundamental right in their property, and every original substantial liberty, which Devonshire, or Surrey, or the county I live in, or any other county in England, can claim; reserving always, as the sacred right of the mother country, the due constitutional dependency of the colonies. The inherent supremacy of the state in regulating and protecting the navigation and commerce of all her subjects, is necessary for the mutual benefit and preservation of every part, to constitute and preserve the prosperous arrangement of the whole empire.

The sound parts of America, of which I have spoken, must be sensible of these great truths and of their real interests. America is not in that state of desperate and contemptible rebellion which this country has been deluded to believe. It is not a wild and lawless banditti, who, having nothing to lose, might hope to snatch something from public convulsions. Many of their leaders and great men have a great stake in this great contest. The gentleman who conducts their armies, I am told, has an estate of four or five thousand pounds a year; and when I consider these things, I can not but lament the inconsiderate violence of our penal acts, our declarations of treason and rebellion, with all the fatal effects of attainder and confiscation.

As to the disposition of foreign powers which is asserted [in the King's speech] to be pacific and friendly, let us judge, my Lords, rather by their actions and the nature of things than by interested assertions. The uniform assistance supplied to America by France, suggests a different conclusion. The most important interests of France in aggrandizing and enriching herself with what she most wants, supplies of every naval store from America, must inspire her with different sentiments. The extraordinary preparations of the house of Bourbon, by land and by sea, from Dunkirk to the Straits, equally ready and willing to overwhelm these defenseless islands, should rouse us to a sense of their real disposition and our own danger. Not five thousand troops in England! hardly three thousand in Ireland! What can we oppose to the combined force of our enemies? Scarcely twenty ships of the line so fully or sufficiently manned, that any admiral's reputation would permit him to take the command of. The river of Lisbon in the possession of our enemies! The seas swept by American privateers! Our Channel trade torn to pieces by them! In this complicated crisis of danger, weakness at home, and calamity abroad, terrified and insulted by the neighboring powers, unable to act in America, or acting only to be destroyed, where is the man with the forehead to promise or hope for success in such a situation, or from perseverance in the measures that have driven us to it? Who has the forehead to do so? Where is that man? I should be glad to see his face.

You can not *conciliate* America by your present measures. You can not *subdue* her by your present or by any measures. What, then, can you do? You can not conquer; you can not gain; but you can *address;* you can lull the fears and anxieties of the moment into an ignorance of the danger that should produce them. But, my Lords, the time demands the language of truth. We must not now apply the flattering unction of servile compliance or blind complaisance. In a just and necessary war, to maintain the rights or honor of my country, I would strip the shirt from my back to support it. But in such a war as this, unjust in its principle, impracticable in its means, and ruinous in its consequences, I would not contribute a single effort nor a single shilling. I do not call for vengeance on the heads of those who have been guilty; I only recommend to them to make their retreat. Let them walk off; and let them make haste, or they may be assured that speedy and condign punishment will overtake them.

My Lords, I have submitted to you, with the freedom and truth which I think my duty, my sentiments on your present awful situation. I have laid before you the ruin of your power, the disgrace of your reputation, the pollution of your discipline, the contamination of your morals, the complication of calamities, foreign and domestic, that overwhelm your sinking country. Your dearest interests, your own liberties, the Constitution itself, totters to the foundation. All this disgraceful danger, this multitude of misery, is the monstrous offspring of this unnatural war. We have been deceived and deluded too long. Let us now stop short. This is the crisis—the only crisis[4] of time and situation, to give us a possibility of escape from the fatal effects of our delusions. But if, in an obstinate and infatuated perseverance in folly, we slavishly echo the peremptory words this day presented to us, nothing can save this devoted country from complete and final ruin. We madly rush into multiplied miseries, and "confusion worse confounded."

Is it possible, can it be believed, that ministers are yet blind to this impending destruction? I did hope, that instead of this false and empty vanity, this overweening pride, engendering high conceits and presumptuous imaginations, ministers would have humbled themselves in their errors, would have confessed and retracted them, and by an active, though a late repentance, have endeavored to redeem them. But, my Lords, since they had neither sagacity to foresee, nor justice nor humanity to shun these oppressive calamities—since not even severe experience can make them feel, nor the imminent ruin of their country awaken them from their stupefaction, the guardian care of Parliament must interpose. I shall therefore, my Lords, propose to you an amendment of the address to his Majesty, to be inserted immediately after the two first paragraphs of congratulation on the birth of a princess, to recommend an immediate cessation of hostilities, and the commencement of a treaty to restore peace and liberty to America, strength and happiness to England, security and permanent prosperity to both countries. This, my Lords, is yet in our power; and let not the wisdom and justice of your Lordships neglect the happy, and, perhaps the only opportunity. By the establishment of irrevocable law, founded on mutual rights, and ascertained by treaty, these glorious enjoyments may be firmly perpetuated. And let me repeat to your Lordships, that the strong bias of America, at least of the wise and sounder parts of it, naturally inclines to this happy and constitutional reconnection with you. Notwithstanding the temporary intrigues with France, we may still be assured of their ancient and confirmed partiality to us. America and France can not be congenial. There is something decisive and confirmed in the honest American, that will not assimilate to the futility and levity of Frenchmen.

My Lords, to encourage and confirm that innate inclination to this country, founded on every principle of affection, as well as consideration of interest; to restore that favorable disposition into a permanent and powerful reunion with this country; to revive the mutual strength of the empire; again to awe the house of Bourbon, instead of meanly truckling, as our present calamities compel us, to every insult of French caprice and Spanish punctilio; to re-establish our commerce; to reassert our rights and our honor; to confirm our interests, and renew our glories forever—a consummation most devoutly to be endeavored! and which, I trust, may yet arise from reconciliation with America—I have the honor of submitting to you the following amendment, which I move to be inserted after the two first paragraphs of the address:

"And that this House does most humbly advise and supplicate his Majesty to be pleased to cause the most speedy and effectual measures to be taken for restoring peace in America; and that no time may be lost in proposing an imme-

[4] It can not have escaped observation, says Chapman, with what urgent anxiety the noble speaker has pressed this point throughout his speech; the critical necessity of instantly treating with America. But the warning voice was heard in vain; the address triumphed; Parliament adjourned; ministers enjoyed the festive recess of a long Christmas; and America ratified her alliance with France.

diate cessation of hostilities there, in order to the opening of a treaty for the final settlement of the tranquillity of these invaluable provinces, by a removal of the unhappy causes of this ruinous civil war, and by a just and adequate security against the return of the like calamities in times to come. And this House desire to offer the most dutiful assurances to his Majesty, that they will, in due time, cheerfully co-operate with the magnanimity and tender goodness of his Majesty for the preservation of his people, by such explicit and most solemn declarations, and provisions of fundamental and irrevocable laws, as may be judged necessary for the ascertaining and fixing forever the respective rights of Great Britain and her colonies."

[In the course of this debate, Lord Suffolk, secretary for the northern department, undertook to defend the employment of the Indians in the war. His Lordship contended that, besides its *policy* and *necessity*, the measure was also allowable on *principle;* for that "it was perfectly justifiable to use all the means that *God and nature put into our hands!*"]

I am astonished! (exclaimed Lord Chatham, as he rose), shocked! to hear such principles confessed—to hear them avowed in this House, or in this country; principles equally unconstitutional, inhuman, and unchristian!

My Lords, I did not intend to have encroached again upon your attention, but I can not repress my indignation. I feel myself impelled by every duty. My Lords, we are called upon as members of this House, as men, as Christian men, to protest against such notions standing near the Throne, polluting the ear of Majesty. "That God and nature put into our hands!" I know not what ideas that Lord may entertain of God and nature, but I know that such abominable principles are equally abhorrent to religion and humanity. What! to attribute the sacred sanction of God and nature to the massacres of the Indian scalping-knife—to the cannibal savage torturing, murdering, roasting, and eating—literally, my Lords, *eating* the mangled victims of his barbarous battles! Such horrible notions shock every precept of religion, divine or natural, and every generous feeling of humanity. And, my Lords, they shock every sentiment of honor; they shock me as a lover of honorable war, and a detester of murderous barbarity.

These abominable principles, and this more abominable avowal of them, demand the most decisive indignation. I call upon that right reverend bench, those holy ministers of the Gospel, and pious pastors of our Church—I conjure them to join in the holy work, and vindicate the religion of their God. I appeal to the wisdom and the law of this learned bench, to defend and support the justice of their country.. I call upon the Bishops, to interpose the unsullied sanctity of their lawn; upon the learned Judges, to interpose the purity of their ermine, to save us from this pollution. I call upon the honor of your Lordships, to reverence the dignity of your ancestors, and to maintain your own. I call upon the spirit and humanity of my country, to vindicate the national character. I invoke the genius of the Constitution. From the tapestry that adorns these walls, the immortal ancestor of this noble Lord frowns with indignation at the disgrace of his country.[5] In vain he led your victorious fleets against the boasted Armada of Spain; in vain he defended and established the honor, the liberties, the religion—the *Protestant religion*—of this country, against the arbitrary cruelties of popery and the Inquisition, if these more than popish cruelties and inquisitorial practices are let loose among us—to turn forth into our settlements, among our ancient connections, friends, and relations, the merciless cannibal, thirsting for the blood of man, woman, and child! to send forth the infidel savage—against whom? against your Protestant brethren; to lay waste their country, to desolate their dwellings, and extirpate their race and name with these horrible hell-hounds of savage war—*hell-hounds, I say, of savage war!* Spain armed herself with blood-hounds to extirpate the wretched natives of America, and we improve on the inhuman example even of Spanish cruelty; we turn loose these savage hell-hounds against our brethren and countrymen in America, of the same language, laws, liberties, and religion, endeared to us by every tie that should sanctify humanity.

My Lords, this awful subject, so important to our honor, our Constitution, and our religion, demands the most solemn and effectual inquiry. And I again call upon your Lordships, and the united powers of the state, to examine it thoroughly and decisively, and to stamp upon it an indelible stigma of the public abhorrence. And I again implore those holy prelates of our religion to do away these iniquities from among us. Let them perform a lustration; let them purify this House, and this country, from this sin.

My Lords, I am old and weak, and at present unable to say more; but my feelings and indignation were too strong to have said less. I could not have slept this night in my bed, nor reposed my head on my pillow, without giving this vent to my eternal abhorrence of such preposterous and enormous principles.

This speech had no effect. The amendment was rejected by a vote of 97 to 24.

5 The tapestry of the House of Lords represented the English fleet led by the ship of the lord admiral, Effingham Howard (ancestor of Suffolk), to engage the Spanish Armada.

SPEECH

OF LORD CHATHAM AGAINST A MOTION FOR ADJOURNING PARLIAMENT, DELIVERED IN THE HOUSE OF LORDS, DECEMBER 11, 1777.

INTRODUCTION.

One of the ministry having moved that the Parliament do adjourn for the space of six weeks, Lord Chatham opposed the motion in the following speech, in which he dwelt on the dangerous condition of the country, as demanding the immediate attention of Parliament.

SPEECH, &c.

It is not with less grief than astonishment I hear the motion now made by the noble Earl, at a time when the affairs of this country present on every side prospects full of awe, terror, and impending danger; when, I will be bold to say, events of a most alarming tendency, little expected or foreseen, will shortly happen; when a cloud that may crush this nation, and bury it in destruction forever, is ready to burst and overwhelm us in ruin. At so tremendous a season, it does not become your Lordships, the great hereditary council of the nation, to neglect your duty, to retire to your country seats for six weeks, in quest of joy and merriment, while the real state of public affairs calls for grief, mourning, and lamentation—at least, for the fullest exertions of your wisdom. It is your duty, my Lords, as the grand hereditary council of the nation, to advise your sovereign, to be the protectors of your country, to feel your own weight and authority. As hereditary counselors, as members of this House, you stand between the Crown and the people. You are nearer the Throne than the other branch of the Legislature; it is your duty to surround and protect, to counsel and supplicate it. You hold the balance. Your duty is to see that the weights are properly poised, that the balance remains even, that neither may encroach on the other, and that the executive power may be prevented, by an unconstitutional exertion of even constitutional authority, from bringing the nation to destruction.

My Lords, I fear we are arrived at the very brink of that state, and I am persuaded that nothing short of a spirited interposition on your part, in giving speedy and wholesome advice to your sovereign, can prevent the people from feeling beyond remedy the full effects of that ruin which ministers have brought upon us. These calamitous circumstances ministers have been the cause of; and shall we, in such a state of things, when every moment teems with events productive of the most fatal narratives, shall we trust, during an adjournment of six weeks, to those men who have brought those calamities upon us, when, perhaps, our utter overthrow is plotting, nay, ripe for execution, without almost a possibility of prevention? Ten thousand brave men have fallen victims to ignorance and rashness.[1] The only army you have in America may, by this time, be no more. This very nation remains no longer safe than its enemies think proper to permit. I do not augur ill. Events of a most critical nature may take place before our next meeting. Will your Lordships, then, in such a state of things, trust to the guidance of men who in every step of this cruel, wicked war, from the very beginning, have proved themselves weak, ignorant, and mistaken? I will not say, my Lords, nor do I mean any thing personal, or that they have brought premeditated ruin on this country. I will not suppose that they foresaw what has since happened, but I do contend, my Lords, that their want of wisdom, their incapacity, their temerity in depending on their own judgment, or their base compliances with the orders and dictates of others, perhaps caused by the influence of one or two individuals, have rendered them totally unworthy of your Lordships' confidence, of the confidence of Parliament, and those whose rights they are the constitutional guardians of, the people at large. A remonstrance, my Lords, should be carried to the Throne. The King has been deluded by his ministers. They have been imposed on by false information, or have, from motives best known to themselves, given apparent credit to what they have been convinced in their hearts was untrue. The nation has been betrayed into the ruinous measure of an American war by the arts of imposition, by their own credulity, through the means of false hopes, false pride, and promised advantages, of the most romantic and improbable nature.

My Lords, I do not wish to call your attention entirely to that point. I would fairly appeal to your own sentiments whether I can be justly charged with arrogance or presumption if I say, great and able as ministers think themselves, that all the wisdom of the nation is not confined to the narrow circle of their petty cabinet. I might, I think, without presumption, say, that your Lordships, as one of the branches of the Legislature, may be supposed as capable of advising your sovereign, in the moment of difficulty and danger, as any lesser council, composed of a fewer number, and who, being already so fatally trusted, have betrayed a want of honesty or a want of talents. Is it, my Lords, within the utmost stretch of the most sanguine expectation, that the same men who have plunged you into your present perilous and calamitous situation are the prop-

[1] This refers to the surrender of Burgoyne's army, which took place October 17th, 1777.

er persons to rescue you from it? No, my Lords, such an expectation would be preposterous and absurd. I say, my Lords, you are now specially called upon to interpose. It is your duty to forego every call of business and pleasure, to give up your whole time to inquire into past misconduct; to provide remedies for the present; to prevent future evils; to rest on your arms, if I may use the expression, to watch for the public safety; to defend and support the Throne, and, if Fate should so ordain it, to fall with becoming fortitude, with the rest of your fellow-subjects, in the general ruin. I fear this last must be the event of this mad, unjust, and cruel war. It is your Lordships' duty to do every thing in your power that it shall not; but, if it must be so, I trust your Lordships and the nation will fall gloriously.

My Lords, as the first and most immediate object of your inquiry, I would recommend to you to consider the true state of our home defense. We have heard much from a noble Lord in this House of the state of our navy. I can not give an implicit belief to all I have heard on that important subject. I still retain my former opinion relative to the number of line of battle ships; but as an inquiry into the real state of the navy is destined to be the subject of future consideration, I do not wish to hear any more about it till that period arrives. I allow, in argument, that we have thirty-five ships of the line fit for actual service. I doubt much whether such a force would give us full command of the Channel. I am certain, if it did, every other part of our possessions must lie naked and defenseless, in every quarter of the globe.

I fear our utter destruction is at hand.[2] What, my Lords, is the state of our military defense? I would not wish to expose our present weakness; but, weak as we are, if this war should be continued, as the public declaration of persons in high confidence with their sovereign would induce us to suppose, is this nation to be entirely stripped? And if it should, would every soldier now in Britain be sufficient to give us an equality to the force of America? I will maintain they would not. Where, then, will men be procured? Recruits are not to be had in this country. Germany will give no more. I have read in the newspapers of this day, and I have reason to believe it true, that the head of the Germanic body has remonstrated against it, and has taken measures accordingly to prevent it. Ministers have, I hear, applied to the Swiss Cantons. The idea is preposterous. The Swiss never permit their troops to go beyond sea. But, my Lords, even if men were to be procured in Germany, how will you march them to the water side? Have not our ministers applied for the port of Embden, and has it not been refused? I say, you will not be able to procure men even for your home defense, if some immediate steps be not taken. I remember, during the last war, it was thought advisable to levy independent companies. They were, when completed, formed into two battalions, and proved of great service. I love the army. I know its use. But I must nevertheless own that I was a great friend to the measure of establishing a national militia. I remember, the last war, that there were three camps formed of that corps at once in this kingdom. I saw them myself—one at Winchester, another in the west, at Plymouth, and a third, if I recollect right, at Chatham. Whether the militia is at present in such a state as to answer the valuable purposes it did then, or is capable of being rendered so, I will not pretend to say; but I see no reason why, in such a critical state of affairs, the experiment should not be made, and why it may not be put again on the former respectable footing.[3] I remember, all circumstances considered, when appearances were not near so melancholy and alarming as they are, that there were more troops in the county of Kent alone, for the defense of the kingdom, than there are now in the whole island.

My Lords, I contend that we have not, nor can procure any force sufficient to subdue America. It is monstrous to think of it. There are several noble Lords present, well acquainted with military affairs. I call upon any one of them to rise and pledge himself that the military force now within the kingdom is adequate to its defense, or that any possible force to be procured from Germany, Switzerland, or elsewhere, will be equal to the conquest of America. I am too perfectly persuaded of their abilities and integrity to expect any such assistance from them. Oh! but if America is not to be conquered, she may be treated with. Conciliation is at length thought of. Terms are to be offered. Who are the persons that are to treat on the part of this afflicted and deluded country? The very men who have been the authors of our misfortunes. The very men who have endeavored, by the most pernicious policy, the highest injustice and oppression, the most cruel and devastating war, to enslave those people they would conciliate, to gain the confidence and affection of those who have survived the Indian tomahawk and German bayonet. Can your Lordships entertain the most distant prospect of success from such a treaty and such negotiations? No, my Lords, the Americans have virtue, and they must detest the principles of such men. They have understanding, and too much wisdom to trust to the cunning and narrow politics which must cause such overtures on the part of their merciless persecutors. My Lords, I maintain that they would shun, with a mixture of prudence and detestation, any proposition coming from that quarter. They would receive terms from such men as snares to allure and betray. They would dread them as ropes meant to be put about their legs, in order to entangle and overthrow them in certain ruin. My Lords, supposing that our domestic danger, if at all, is far distant; that our enemies will leave us at liberty to prosecute this

[2] Here, and in many other parts of his speech, his Lordship broadly hinted that the house of Bourbon was meditating some important and decisive blow near home.

[3] This was afterward done.

war to the utmost of our ability; suppose your Lordships should grant a fleet one day, an army another; all these, I do affirm, will avail nothing, unless you accompany it with advice. Ministers have been in error; experience has proved it; and, what is worse, they continue it. They told you, in the beginning, that 15,000 men would traverse all America, without scarcely an appearance of interruption. Two campaigns have passed since they gave us this assurance. Treble that number have been employed; and one of your armies, which composed two thirds of the force by which America was to be subdued, has been totally destroyed, and is now led captive through those provinces you call rebellious. Those men whom you called cowards, poltroons, runaways, and knaves, are become victorious over your veteran troops; and, in the midst of victory, and the flush of conquest, have set ministers an example of moderation and magnanimity well worthy of imitation.

My Lords, no time should be lost which may promise to improve this disposition in America, unless, by an obstinacy founded in madness, we wish to stifle those embers of affection which, after all our savage treatment, do not seem, as yet, to have been entirely extinguished. While on one side we must lament the unhappy fate of that spirited officer, Mr. Burgoyne, and the gallant troops under his command, who were sacrificed to the wanton temerity and ignorance of ministers, we are as strongly compelled, on the other, to admire and applaud the generous, magnanimous conduct, the noble friendship, brotherly affection, and humanity of the victors, who, condescending to impute the horrid orders of massacre and devastation to their true authors, supposed that, as soldiers and Englishmen, those cruel excesses could not have originated with the general, nor were consonant to the brave and humane spirit of a British soldier, if not compelled to it as an act of duty. They traced the first cause of those diabolic orders to their true source; and, by that wise and generous interpretation, granted their professed destroyers terms of capitulation which they could be only entitled to as the makers of fair and honorable war.

My Lords, I should not have presumed to trouble you, if the tremendous state of this nation did not, in my opinion, make it necessary. Such as I have this day described it to be, I do maintain it is. The same measures are still persisted in; and ministers, because your Lordships have been deluded, deceived, and misled, presume that, whenever the worst comes, they will be enabled to shelter themselves behind Parliament. This, my Lords, can not be the case. They have committed themselves and their measures to the fate of war, and they must abide the issue. I tremble for this country. I am almost led to despair that we shall ever be able to extricate ourselves. At any rate, the day of retribution is at hand, when the vengeance of a much-injured and afflicted people will, I trust, fall heavily on the authors of their ruin; and I am strongly inclined to believe, that before the day to which the proposed adjournment shall arrive, the noble earl who moved it will have just cause to repent of his motion.

This appeal was unavailing. The motion to adjourn was carried by a vote of 47 to 18.

LAST SPEECH

OF LORD CHATHAM, DELIVERED IN THE HOUSE OF LORDS, APRIL 7, 1778.

INTRODUCTION.

After the delivery of the preceding speech, Lord Chatham continued to decline in health, and would probably never have appeared again in the House of Lords, had not a measure been proposed, against which he felt bound to enter a public remonstrance, even at the hazard of his life. Ignorant of the real state of feeling in America, he thought the colonies might be still brought back to their former allegiance and affection, if their wrongs were redressed. He learned, therefore, "with unspeakable concern," that his friend the Duke of Richmond was about to move an address to the King, advising his Majesty to make a peace involving American independence, which Lord Chatham thought would be the ruin of his country. On the 7th of April, 1778, therefore, the day appointed for the Duke of Richmond's motion, he came to Westminster, and refreshed himself for a time in the room of the Lord Chancellor, until he learned that business was about to commence. "He was then led into the House of Peers," says his biographer, "by his son, the Honorable William Pitt, and his son-in-law, Lord Mahon. He was dressed in a rich suit of black velvet, and covered up to the knees in flannel. Within his large wig, little more of his countenance was seen than his aquiline nose, and his penetrating eye, which retained all its native fire. He looked like a dying man, yet never was seen a figure of more dignity. He appeared like a being of a superior species. The Lords stood up and made a lane for him to pass to his seat, while, with a gracefulness of deportment for which he was so eminently distinguished, he bowed to them as he proceeded. Having taken his seat, he listened with profound attention to the Duke of Richmond's speech."

After Lord Weymouth had replied in behalf of the ministry, Lord Chatham rose with slowness and difficulty from his seat, and delivered the following speech. It is very imperfectly reported, and is interesting chiefly as showing "the master spirit strong in death;" for he sunk under the effort, and survived only a few days. Supported by his two relations, he lifted his hand from the crutch on which he leaned, raised it up, and, casting his eyes toward heaven, commenced as follows:

SPEECH, &c.

I THANK God that I have been enabled to come here to-day—to perform my duty, and speak on a subject which is so deeply impressed on my mind. I am old and infirm. I have one foot—*more* than one foot—in the grave. I have risen from my bed to stand up in the cause of my country—perhaps never again to speak in this House.

["The reverence, the attention, the stillness of the House," said an eye-witness, "were here most affecting: had any one dropped a handkerchief, the noise would have been heard."

As he proceeded, Lord Chatham spoke at first in a low tone, with all the weakness of one who is laboring under severe indisposition. Gradually, however, as he warmed with the subject, his voice became louder and more distinct, his intonations grew more commanding, and his whole manner was solemn and impressive in the highest degree. He went over the events of the American war with that luminous and comprehensive survey for which he was so much distinguished in his best days. He pointed out the measures he had condemned, and the results he had predicted, adding at each stage, as he advanced, "And so it proved! And *so it proved!*" Adverting, in one part of his speech, to the fears entertained of a foreign invasion, he recurred to the history of the past: "A Spanish invasion, a French invasion, a Dutch invasion, many noble Lords must have read of in history; and some Lords" (looking keenly at one who sat near him, with a last reviving flash of his sarcastic spirit), "some Lords may remember a *Scotch* invasion!" He could not forget Lord Mansfield's defense of American taxation, and the measures of Lord Bute, which had brought down the country to its present degraded state, from the exalted position to which he had raised it during his brief but splendid administration. He then proceeded in the following terms:] My Lords, I rejoice that the grave has not closed upon me; that I am still alive, to lift up my voice against the dismemberment of this ancient and most noble monarchy! Pressed down as I am by the hand of infirmity, I am little able to assist my country in this most perilous conjuncture; but, my Lords, while I have sense and memory, I will never consent to deprive the offspring of the royal house of Brunswick, the heirs of the Princess Sophia, of their fairest inheritance. I will first see the Prince of Wales, the Bishop of Osnaburgh, and the other rising hopes of the royal family, brought down to this committee, and assent to such an alienation. Where is the man who will dare to advise it? My Lords, his Majesty succeeded to an empire as great in extent as its reputation was unsullied. Shall we tarnish the luster of this nation by an ignominious surrender of its rights and fairest possessions? Shall this great nation, that has survived, whole and entire, the Danish depredations, the Scottish inroads, the Norman conquest—that has stood the threatened invasion of the Spanish Armada, now fall prostrate before the house of Bourbon? Surely, my Lords, this nation is no longer what it was! Shall a people that seventeen years ago was the terror of the world, now stoop so low as to tell its ancient inveterate enemy, *Take all we have, only give us peace?* It is impossible!

I wage war with no man or set of men. I wish for none of their employments; nor would I co-operate with men who still persist in unretracted error, or who, instead of acting on a firm, decisive line of conduct, halt between two opinions, where there is no middle path. In God's name, if it is absolutely necessary to declare either for peace or war, and the former can not be preserved with honor, why is not the latter commenced without delay? I am not, I confess, well informed as to the resources of this kingdom, but I trust it has still sufficient to maintain its just rights, though I know them not. But, my Lords, any state is better than despair. Let us at least make one effort, and, if we must fall, let us fall like men!

When Lord Chatham had taken his seat, Lord Temple remarked to him, "You have forgotten to mention what we have been talking about. Shall I get up?" "No," replied Lord Chatham, "*I* will do it by-and-by."

Lord Richmond replied to Lord Chatham, telling him that the country was in no condition to continue the war; and that, even if he himself were now (as formerly) at the head of affairs, his name, great as it was, could not repair the shattered fortunes of the country. Lord Chatham listened with attention, but gave indications, at times, both by his countenance and his gestures, that he felt agitated or displeased.

When the Duke of Richmond had ended his speech, Lord Chatham made a sudden and strenuous attempt to rise, as if laboring under the pressure of painful emotions. He seemed eager to speak; but, after repeated efforts, he suddenly pressed his hand on his heart, and sunk down in convulsions. Those who sat near him caught him in their arms. His son William Pitt, then a youth of seventeen, who was standing without the bar, sprang forward to support him. It is this moment which Copley has chosen for his picture of the death of Lord Chatham. "History," says an able writer, "has no nobler scene to show than that which now occupied the House of Lords. The unswerving patriot, whose long life had been devoted to his country, had striven to the last. The aristocracy of the land stood around, and even the brother of the sovereign thought himself honored in being one of his supporters; party enmities were remembered no more; every other feeling was lost in admiration of the great spirit which seemed to be passing away from among them." He was removed in a state of insensibility from the House, and carried to Hayes, where he lingered a few days, and died on the 11th of May, 1778, aged seventy.

LORD MANSFIELD.

William Murray, first Earl of Mansfield, was born at Scone Castle, near Perth, in Scotland, on the 2d of March, 1705. He was the fourth son of Lord Stormont, head of an ancient but decayed family, which had been reduced to comparative poverty by a long course of extravagance. The title having been conferred by James I., Lord Stormont, like his predecessors, remained true to the cause of the Stuarts. His second son, Lord Dunbar, was private secretary to the Pretender.

William was sent to London for his education at a very early age; and hence Johnson used sportively to maintain, that his success in after life ought not to be put to the credit of his country, since it was well known that "much might be made of a Scotchman if he was *caught young*." Not a little, however, had been done for William before he left the grammar-school of Perth. Though but fourteen years old, he could read quite freely in the Latin classics; he knew a large part of Sallust and Horace by heart; and was able not only to write Latin correctly, but to speak it with accuracy and ease. It is not surprising, therefore, considering his native quickness of mind, that within a year after he joined Westminster school, he gained its highest distinction, that of being chosen one of the King's scholars. He soon stood as "dux," or leader of the school; and, at the end of four years, after a rigorous examination, was put first on the list of those who were to be sent to Oxford, on the foundation at Christ Church. His choice had for some time been firmly fixed upon the law as a profession; and nothing could so gratify his feelings or advance his interests as to enter the University. But the straitened circumstances of his father seemed to forbid the thought; and he was on the point of giving up his most ardent wishes in despair, when a casual conversation with a young friend opened the way for his being sent to Oxford, with an honorable provision for his support. Lord Foley, father of the friend referred to, having heard of his superior abilities, and his strong attachment to the law, generously offered to assist him with the requisite means, to be repaid only in the event of his succeeding in after life.

During his residence at Oxford, he gave himself to study with that fervor and diligence for which he was always distinguished, quickened by a sense of the responsibilities he had incurred, and by a fixed resolve to place himself at the head of his profession. He made every thing subservient to a preparation for the bar; and while, in the spirit of that university, he studied Aristotle with delight as the great master of reasoning and thought, he devoted his most earnest efforts to improvement in oratory. He read every thing that had been written on the principles of the art; he made himself familiar with all the great masters of eloquence in Greece and Rome, and spent much of his time in translating their finest productions as the best means of improving his style. Cicero was his favorite author; and he declared, in after life, that there was not one of his orations which he had not, while at Oxford, translated into English, and, after an interval, according to the best of his ability, re-translated into Latin.

Having taken his degree at the age of twenty-two, he entered on the study of the law at Lincoln's Inn in 1737. His labors were now conducted on the broadest scale. While law had the precedence, he carried on the practice of oratory with the utmost zeal. To aid him in extemporaneous speaking, he joined a debating society, where the most abstruse legal points were fully discussed. For these exercises, he prepared himself beforehand with such copiousness and accuracy, that the notes he used proved highly valuable in after life, both at the bar and on the bench. He found time, also, to pursue his historical studies to such an extent, that Lord Campbell speaks of his familiarity with modern history as "astounding and even *appalling*, for it produces a painful consciousness of inferiority, and creates remorse for time misspent." When called to the bar in 1730, "he had made himself acquainted not only with international law, but with the codes of all the most civilized nations, ancient and modern; he was an elegant classical scholar; he was thoroughly imbued with the literature of his own country; he had profoundly studied our mixed constitution; he had a sincere desire to be of service to his country; and he was animated by a noble aspiration after honorable fame."

When he first came to London as a boy in Westminster school, he was introduced by his countryman, Lord Marchmont, to Mr. Pope, then at the height of his unrivaled popularity. The poet took a lively interest in the young Scotchman, attracted not only by the quickness of his parts and the fineness of his manners and person, but by "the silvery tones of his voice," for which he continued to be distinguished to the end of life. Mr. Pope entered with the warmest concern into all his employments, and assisted especially in his rhetorical studies during his preparation for the bar. One day says his biographer, he was surprised by a friend, who suddenly entered the room, in "the act of practicing before a glass, while Pope sat by to aid him in the character of an instructor!" Their friendship continued throughout life; and in a new edition of the Dunciad Mr. Pope introduced his name, with that of other distinguished men, complaining that law and politics should have drawn them off from the more congenial pursuits of literature.

"Whate'er the talents and howe'er designed,
We hang one jingling padlock on the mind.
A poet the first day he dips his quill;
And what the last? a very poet still.
Pity the charm works only in our wall,
Lost—too soon lost—in yonder *House* or *Hall*:
There truant Wyndham ev'ry muse gave o'er;
There Talbot sank, and was a wit no more;
How sweet an Ovid, MURRAY, *was our boast!*
How many Martials were in Pulteney lost!"

Some years elapsed after Mr. Murray's call to the bar before he had any business of importance; and then, after a few successful cases, it poured in upon him to absolute repletion. "From a few hundred pounds a year," said he, "I found myself in the receipt of thousands." Retainers came in from every quarter; and one of a thousand guineas was sent by Sarah, Duchess of Marlborough, with that ostentatious munificence which she sometimes affected. Nine hundred and ninety-five guineas were returned by Mr. Murray, with the significant remark that "a retaining fee was never more nor less than five guineas." He found her a very troublesome client. Not unfrequently she made her appearance at his chambers after midnight, crowding the street with her splendid equipage and her attendants with torches; and on one occasion when he was absent, his clerk, giving an account of her visit the next morning, said, "I could not make out, sir, who she was, for she would not tell me her name; but she *swore* so dreadfully that she must have been a lady of quality!"

Soon after the fall of Sir Robert Walpole in 1742, Mr. Murray was appointed Solicitor General, and elected a member of Parliament through the influence of the Duke of Newcastle. His powerful talents were needed for the support of the new administration, which was suffering under the vehement attacks of Mr. Pitt. Here commenced that long series of conflicts which divided for life the two most accomplished orators of the age. It could not be otherwise, for never were two men more completely the antipodes of each other. Pitt was a Whig; Murray was a High Tory. Pitt was ardent, open, and impetuous; Murray was cool, reserved, and circumspect. The intellect of Pitt was bold and commanding; that of Murray was subtle, penetrating, and refined. Pitt sought power; Murray, office and emolument. Two such men could not but differ; and differing as they did for life, it was natural that the one should distrust or despise, and the other fear, perhaps hate. In native talent, it would be difficult to say which had the advantage; but the mind of Murray was more perfectly trained, and his memory enriched with larger stores of knowledge. "In closeness of argument," says an able writer, "in happiness of illustration, in copiousness and grace of diction, the oratory of Murray was unsurpassed: and, indeed, in all the qualities which conspire to form an able *debater*, he is allowed to have been Pitt's superior. When measures were attacked, no one was better capable of defending them; when reasoning was the weapon employed, none handled it with such effect; but against declamatory invective, his very temperament incapacitated him for contending with so much advantage. He was like an accomplished fencer, invulnerable to the thrusts of a small sword, but not equally able to ward off the downright stroke of a bludgeon."

In 1754 Mr. Murray was appointed Attorney General, and soon after made leader of the House of Commons under the Duke of Newcastle. "At the beginning of the session," says Horace Walpole, "Murray was awed by Pitt; but, finding himself supported by Fox, he surmounted his fears, and convinced the House, and Pitt too, of his superior abilities. Pitt could only attack, Murray only defend. Fox, the boldest and ablest champion, was still more forward to worry; but the keenness of his saber was blunted by the difficulty with which he drew it from the scabbard—I mean, the hesitation and ungracefulness of his delivery took off from the force of his arguments. Murray, the brightest genius of the three, had too much and too little of the lawyer; he refined too much and could wrangle too little for a popular assembly." We have seen already, in the life of Lord Chatham, what difficulties Murray had to encounter that session in sustaining the ministry of Newcastle, and the crushing force with which he was overwhelmed by his opponent. In 1756 he resolved to endure it no longer, and on the death of Sir Dudley Ryder he demanded the office of Chief Justice of the King's Bench. Newcastle refused, remonstrated, supplicated. "The writ for creating Murray," he declared, "would be the death-warrant of his own administration." He resisted for several months, offering the most tempting bribes, including a pension of £6000 a year, if he would only remain in the House until the new session was opened, and the address voted in reply to the King's speech. Murray declared, in the most peremptory terms, that he would not remain "a month or a day even to support the address;" that "he never again would enter that assembly." Turning with indignation to Newcastle, he exclaimed, "What merit have I, that you should lay on this country, for which so little is done with spirit, the additional burden of £6000 a year;" and concluded with declaring his unalterable determination, if he was not made Chief Justice, to serve no longer as Attorney General. This brought Newcastle to a decision. On the 8th of November, 1756, Murray was sworn in as Chief Justice, and created a peer with the title of Baron Mansfield. At a later period he was raised to the earldom.

In entering on his new career, he was called upon to take public leave of his associates of Lincoln's Inn. On that occasion he was addressed in an elegant speech by the Honorable Charles Yorke. The reader will be interested in Mr. Murray's reply, as showing with what admirable dignity and grace he could receive the compliments bestowed upon him, and turn them aside in favor of another.

"I am too sensible, sir, of my being undeserving of the praises which you have so elegantly bestowed upon me, to suffer commendations so delicate as yours to insinuate themselves into my mind; but I have pleasure in that kind of partiality which is the occasion of them. To deserve such praises is a worthy object of ambition, and from such a tongue flattery itself is pleasing.

"If I have had, in any measure, success in my profession, it is owing to the great man who has presided in our highest courts of judicature the whole time I attended the bar.[1] It was im-

[1] Lord Hardwicke, father of Mr. Yorke.

possible to attend to him, to sit under him every day, without catching some beams from his light. The disciples of Socrates, whom I will take the liberty to call the great lawyer of antiquity, since the first principles of all law are derived from his philosophy, owe their reputation to their having been the reporters of the sayings of their master. If we can arrogate nothing to ourselves, we can boast the school we were brought up in; the scholar may glory in his master, and we may challenge past ages to show us his equal. My Lord Bacon had the same extent of thought, and the same strength of language and expression, but his life had a stain. My Lord Clarendon had the same ability, and the same zeal for the Constitution of his country, but the civil war prevented his laying *deep* the foundations of law, and the avocations of politics interrupted the business of the chancellor. My Lord Somers came the nearest to his character, but his time was short, and envy and faction sullied the luster of his glory. It is the peculiar felicity of the great man I am speaking of to have presided very near twenty years, and to have shone with a splendor that has risen superior to faction and that has subdued envy.

"I did not intend to have said, I should not have said so much on this occasion, but that in this situation, with all that hear me, what I say must carry the weight of testimony rather than appear the voice of panegyric.

"For you, sir, you have given great pledges to your country; and large as the expectations of the public are concerning you, I dare say you will answer them.

"For the society, I shall always think myself honored by every mark of their esteem, affection, and friendship; and shall desire the continuance of it no longer than while I remain zealous for the Constitution of this country and a friend to the interests of virtue."

Lord Mansfield now entered on that high career of usefulness which has made his name known and honored throughout the civilized world. Few men have ever been so well qualified for that exalted station. He had pre-eminently a legal intellect, great clearness of thought, accuracy of discrimination, soundness of judgment, and strength of reasoning, united to a scientific knowledge of jurisprudence, a large experience in all the intricacies of practice, unusual courtesy and ease in the dispatch of business, and extraordinary powers of application. He came to the bench, not like most lawyers, trusting to his previous knowledge and the aid afforded by counsel in forming his decisions, but as one who had just entered on the real employment of his life. "On the day of his inauguration as Chief Justice, instead of thinking that he had won the prize, he considered himself as only starting in the race."

How he discharged the duties of his high station, it belongs especially to men of his own profession to determine. One fact, however, may stand in the place of many authorities. Out of the thousands of cases which he decided in the Court of King's Bench, there were only *two* in which his associates of that court did not unanimously agree with him in opinion. Yet they were, as all the world knows, men of the highest ability and the most perfect independence of mind. Junius, indeed, assailed him with malignant bitterness, but it is the universal decision of the bar that his charges were false as they were malignant. Against this attack we may set off the opinion of Chief Justice Story. "England and America, and the civilized world, lie under the deepest obligations to him. Wherever commerce shall extend its social influences; wherever justice shall be administered by enlightened and liberal rules; wherever contracts shall be expounded upon the eternal principles of right and wrong; wherever moral delicacy and judicial refinement shall be infused into the municipal code, at once to persuade men to be honest and to keep them so; wherever the intercourse of mankind shall aim at something more elevated than that groveling spirit of barter, in which meanness, and avarice, and fraud strive for the mastery over ignorance, credulity, and folly, the name of Lord Mansfield will be held in reverence by the good and the wise, by the honest merchant, the enlightened lawyer, the just statesman, and the conscientious judge. The proudest monument of his fame is in the volumes of Burrow, and Cowper, and Douglas, which we may fondly hope will endure as long as the language in which they are written shall continue to instruct mankind. His judgments should not be merely referred to and read on the spur of particular occasions, but should be studied as models of juridical reasoning and eloquence."

As a speaker in the House of Lords, the success of Lord Mansfield was greater than in the House of Commons. The calmness and dignity of the assembly were better suited to his habits of thought. Here, after a few years, he had again to encounter his great antagonist, who was raised to the same dignity in 1766. As Chatham was the advocate of the people's rights, Mansfield was the champion of the King's prerogative. He defended the Stamp Act, and maintained the right of Parliament to tax the Americans as being virtually represented in the House of Commons. A speech on that subject, corrected by himself, is given below. Lord Campbell, notwithstanding his strong predilections as a Whig, does not hesitate to pronounce it unanswerable. His speech in favor of taking away the protection extended to the servants of peers is the most finished of his productions, and will also be found in this volume. To these will be added his argument in the case of the Chamberlain of London *vs.* Allan Evans, which has often been spoken of as the most perfect specimen of juridical reasoning in our language. His address from the bench, when surrounded by a mob, during the trial of the outlawry of Wilkes, will also form part of the extracts.

After discharging his duties as Chief Justice nearly thirty-two years, he resigned his office on the 4th of June, 1788. His faculties were still unimpaired, though his strength was gone; and he continued in their unclouded exercise nearly five years longer, when he died, after an illness of ten days, on the 20th of March, 1793, in the eighty-ninth year of his age.

"The countenance of Lord Mansfield," says a friend and contemporary, "was uncommonly beautiful, and none could ever behold it, even in advanced years, without reverence. Nature had given him an eye of fire; and his voice, till it was affected by the years which passed over him, was perhaps unrivaled in the sweetness and variety of its tones. There was a similitude between his action and that of Mr. Garrick. In speaking from the bench, there was sometimes a confusion in his periods, and a tendency to involve his sentences in parentheses; yet, such was the charm of his voice and action, and such the general beauty, propriety, and force of his expressions, that, while he spoke, all these defects passed unnoticed."

The eloquence of Lord Mansfield, especially in his best speeches in the House of Lords, was that of a judge rather than an advocate or a party leader. He had the air of addressing the House of Lords, according to the theory of that body, as one who spoke *upon honor*. He sought not to drive, but to lead; not to overwhelm the mind by appeals to the passions, but to aid and direct its inquiries; so that his hearers had the satisfaction of seeming, at least, to form their own conclusions. He was peculiarly happy in his statement of a case. "It was worth more," said Mr. Burke, "than any other man's argument." Omitting all that was unnecessary, he seized, with surprising tact, on the strong points of a subject; he held them steadily before the mind; and, as new views opened, he led forward his hearers, step by step, toward the desired result, with almost the certainty of intuitive evidence. "It was extremely difficult," said Lord Ashburton, "to answer him when he was wrong, and impossible when he was in the right." His manner was persuasive, with enough of force and animation to secure the closest attention. His illustrations were always apposite, and sometimes striking and beautiful. His language, in his best speeches, was select and graceful; and his whole style of speaking approached as near as possible to that dignified conversation which has always been considered appropriate to the House of Lords.

SPEECH

OF LORD MANSFIELD ON THE RIGHT OF TAXING AMERICA, DELIVERED IN THE HOUSE OF LORDS, FEBRUARY 3, 1766.

INTRODUCTION.

In January, 1776, a bill was brought into the House of Commons, under Lord Rockingham's ministry, for the repeal of the American Stamp Act; and in order to mollify the King, who was opposed to that measure, it was accompanied by a Declaratory Act, affirming that "Parliament had full power and right to make laws of sufficient force to bind the colonies." Lord Chatham, then Mr. Pitt, remarked with severity on this Declaratory Act when before the Commons. Lord Camden did the same when it came before the House of Lords, February 3d, 1766. He said, "In my opinion, my Lords, the Legislature have no right to make this law. The sovereign authority, the omnipotence of the Legislature, is a favorite doctrine; but there are some things which you can not do. You can not take away a man's property without making him a compensation. You have no right to condemn any man by bill of attainder without hearing him. But, though Parliament can not take any man's private property, yet every subject must make contribution; and this he consents to do by his representative. Notwithstanding the King, Lords, and Commons could in ancient times tax other persons, they could not tax the clergy." He then went on to consider the case of the counties palatine of Wales and of Berwick, showing that they were never taxed till they sent representatives to the House of Commons, observing that the Irish tax themselves, and that the English Parliament could not tax them. "But," said he, "even supposing the Americans have no exclusive right to tax themselves, it would be good policy to give it to them, instead of offensively exerting a power which you ought never to have exercised. America feels that she can do better without us than we can do without her."

Lord Northington, the Chancellor, made some coarse and bitter remarks in reply; and Lord Mansfield then rose to defend his favorite doctrine of the right of Great Britain to tax the colonies. His speech is by far the most plausible and argumentative one ever delivered on that side of the question; and Lord Campbell, in referring to the subject, says, "Lord Mansfield goes on with great calmness, and with arguments to which I have never been able to find an answer, to deny, as far as the *power* is concerned, the distinction between a law to tax and a law for any other purpose."[1] The speech was corrected for the press by Lord Mansfield, and may therefore be relied on as authentic.

SPEECH, &c.

The question one of right, not expediency.

My Lords,—I shall speak to the question strictly as a matter of right; for it is a proposition in its nature so perfectly distinct from the expediency of the tax, that it must necessarily be taken separate, if there is any true logic in the world; but of the expediency or inexpediency I will say nothing. It will be time enough to speak upon that subject when it comes to be a question.

I shall also speak to the distinctions which have been taken, without any real difference, as to the nature of the tax; and I shall point out, lastly, the necessity there will be of exerting the force of the superior authority of government, if opposed by the subordinate part of it.

I am extremely sorry that the question has ever become necessary to be agitated, and that there should be a decision upon it. No one in this House will live long enough to see an end put to the mischief which will be the result of the doctrine which has been inculcated; but the arrow is shot, and the wound already given. I shall certainly avoid personal reflections. No one has had more cast upon him than myself; but I never was biased by any consideration of applause from without, in the discharge of my public duty; and, in giving my sentiments according to what I thought law, I have relied upon my own consciousness. It is with great pleasure I have heard the noble Lord who moved the resolution express himself in so manly and sensible a way, when he recommended a dispassionate debate, while, at the same time, he urged the necessity of the House coming to such a resolution, with great dignity and propriety of argument.

Refutation of arguments from ancient records and practices.

I shall endeavor to clear away from the question, all that mass of dissertation and learning displayed in arguments which have been fetched from speculative men who have written upon the subject of government, or from ancient records, as being little to the purpose. I shall insist that these records are no proofs of our present Constitution. A noble Lord has taken up his argument from the settlement of the Constitution at the Revolution; I shall take up my argument from the Constitution as it now is. The Constitution of this country has been always in a moving state, either gaining or losing something,

[1] Lives of the Chancellors. v., 206.

and with respect to the modes of taxation, when we get beyond the reign of Edward the First, or of King John, we are all in doubt and obscurity. The history of those times is full of uncertainties. In regard to the writs upon record, they were issued some of them according to law, and some not according to law; and such [*i. e.*, of the latter kind] were those concerning ship-money, to call assemblies to tax themselves, or to compel benevolences. Other taxes were raised from escuage, fees for knights' service, and by other means arising out of the feudal system. Benevolences are contrary to law; and it is well known how people resisted the demands of the Crown in the case of ship-money, and were persecuted by the Court; and if any set of men were to meet now to lend the King money, it would be contrary to law, and a breach of the rights of Parliament.

I shall now answer the noble Lord particularly upon the cases he has quoted. With respect to the Marches of Wales, who were the borderers, privileged for assisting the King in his war against the Welsh in the mountains, their enjoying this privilege of taxing themselves was but of a short duration, and during the life of Edward the First, till the Prince of Wales came to be the King; and then they were annexed to the Crown, and became subject to taxes like the rest of the dominions of England; and from thence came the custom, though unnecessary, of naming Wales and the town of Monmouth in all proclamations and in acts of Parliament. Henry the Eighth was the first who issued writs for it to return two members to Parliament. The Crown exercised this right *ad libitum*, from whence arises the inequality of representation in our Constitution at this day. Henry VIII. issued a writ to Calais to send one burgess to Parliament. One of the counties palatine (I think he said Durham) was taxed fifty years to subsidies, before it sent members to Parliament. The clergy were at no time unrepresented in Parliament. When they taxed themselves, it was done with the concurrence and consent of Parliament, who permitted them to tax themselves upon their petition, the Convocation sitting at the same time with the Parliament. They had, too, their representatives always sitting in this House, bishops and abbots; and, in the other House, they were at no time without a right of voting singly for the election of members; so that the argument fetched from the case of the clergy is not an argument of any force, because they were at no time unrepresented here.

The colonies of antiquity not a case in point.

The reasoning about the colonies of Great Britain, drawn from the colonies of antiquity, is a mere useless display of learning; for the colonies of the Tyrians in Africa, and of the Greeks in Asia, were totally different from our system. No nation before ourselves formed any regular system of colonization, but the Romans; and their system was a military one, and of garrisons placed in the principal towns of the conquered provinces. The states of Holland were not colonies of Spain; they were states dependent upon the house of Austria in a feudal dependence. Nothing could be more different from our colonies than that flock of men, as they have been called, who came from the North, and poured into Europe. Those emigrants renounced all laws, all protection, all connection with their mother countries. They chose their leaders, and marched under their banners to seek their fortunes and establish new kingdoms upon the ruins of the Roman empire.

Direct Arguments. 1. The colonies created by charter, and therefore dependent on Great Britain.

But our colonies, on the contrary, emigrated under the sanction of the Crown and Parliament. They were modeled gradually into their present forms, respectively, by charters, grants, and statutes; but they were never separated from the mother country, or so emancipated as to become *sui juris*. There are several sorts of colonies in British America. The charter colonies, the proprietary governments, and the King's colonies. The first colonies were the charter colonies, such as the Virginia Company; and these companies had among their directors members of the privy council and of both houses of Parliament; they were under the authority of the privy council, and had agents resident here, responsible for their proceedings. So much were they considered as belonging to the Crown, and not to the King personally (for there is a great difference, though few people attend to it), that when the two Houses, in the time of Charles the First, were going to pass a bill concerning the colonies, a message was sent to them by the King that they were the King's colonies, and that the bill was unnecessary, for that the privy council would take order about them; and the bill never had the royal assent. The Commonwealth Parliament, as soon as it was settled, were very early jealous of the colonies separating themselves from them; and passed a resolution or act (and it is a question whether it is not in force now) to declare and establish the authority of England over its colonies.

2. They have submitted to English law, and thus acknowledged their dependence.

But if there was no express law, or reason founded upon any necessary inference from an express law, yet the usage alone would be sufficient to support that authority; for, have not the colonies submitted ever since their first establishment to the jurisdiction of the mother country? In all questions of property, the appeals from the colonies have been to the privy council here; and such causes have been determined, not by the law of the colonies, but by the law of England. A very little while ago, there was an appeal on a question of limitation in a devise of land with remainders; and, notwithstanding the intention of the testator appeared very clear, yet the case was determined contrary to it, and that the land should pass according to the law of England. The colonies have been obliged to recur very frequently to the jurisdiction here, to settle the disputes among their own governments. I well remember several references on this head, when the late Lord

Hardwicke was attorney general, and Sir Clement Wearg solicitor general. New Hampshire and Connecticut were in blood about their differences; Virginia and Maryland were in arms against each other. This shows the necessity of one superior decisive jurisdiction, to which all subordinate jurisdictions may recur. Nothing, my Lords, could be more fatal to the peace of the colonies at any time, than the Parliament giving up its authority over them; for in such a case, there must be an entire dissolution of government. Considering how the colonies are composed, it is easy to foresee there would be no end of feuds and factions among the several separate governments, when once there shall be no one government here or there of sufficient force or authority to decide their mutual differences; and, government being dissolved, nothing remains but that the colonies must either change their Constitution, and take some new form of government, or fall under some foreign power. At present the several forms of their Constitution are very various, having been produced, as all governments have been originally, by accident and circumstances. The forms of government in every colony were adopted, from time to time, according to the size of the colony; and so have been extended again, from time to time, as the numbers of their inhabitants and their commercial connections outgrew the first model. In some colonies, at first there was only a governor assisted by two or three counsel; then more were added; afterward courts of justice were erected; then assemblies were created. Some things were done by instructions from the secretaries of state; other things were done by order of the King and council; and other things by commissions under the great seal. It is observable, that in consequence of these establishments from time to time, and of the dependency of these governments upon the supreme Legislature at home, the lenity of each government in the colonies has been extreme toward the subject; and a great inducement has been created for people to come and settle in them. But, if all those governments which are now independent of each other, should become independent of the mother country, I am afraid that the inhabitants of the colonies are very little aware of the consequences. They would feel in that case very soon the hand of power more heavy upon them in their own governments, than they have yet done, or have ever imagined.

3. The laws to which they submitted affected their pecuniary interests vitally.

The Constitutions of the different colonies are thus made up of different principles. They must remain dependent, from the necessity of things, and their relations to the jurisdiction of the mother country; or they must be totally dismembered from it, and form a league of union among themselves against it, which could not be effected without great violences. No one ever thought the contrary till the trumpet of sedition was blown. Acts of Parliament have been made, not only without a doubt of their legality, but with universal applause, the great object of which has been ultimately to fix the trade of the colonies, so as to center in the bosom of that country from whence they took their original. The Navigation Act shut up their intercourse with foreign countries. Their ports have been made subject to customs and regulations which have cramped and diminished their trade. And duties have been laid, affecting the very inmost parts of their commerce, and, among others, that of the post; yet all these have been submitted to peaceably, and no one ever thought till now of this doctrine, that the colonies are not to be taxed, regulated, or bound by Parliament. A few particular merchants were then, as now, displeased at restrictions which did not permit them to make the greatest possible advantages of their commerce in their own private and peculiar branches. But, though these few merchants might think themselves losers in articles which they had no right to gain, as being prejudicial to the general and national system, yet I must observe, that the colonies, upon the whole, were benefited by these laws. For these restrictive laws, founded upon principles of the most solid policy, flung a great weight of naval force into the hands of the mother country, which was to protect its colonies. Without a union with her, the colonies must have been entirely weak and defenseless, but they thus became relatively great, subordinately, and in proportion as the mother country advanced in superiority over the rest of the maritime powers in Europe; to which both mutually contributed, and of which both have reaped a benefit, equal to the natural and just relation in which they both stand reciprocally, of dependency on one side, and protection on the other.

4. The colonies are *virtually* represented in Parliament.

There can be no doubt, my Lords, but that the inhabitants of the colonies are as much represented in Parliament, as the greatest part of the people of England are represented; among nine millions of whom there are eight which have no votes in electing members of Parliament. Every objection, therefore, to the dependency of the colonies upon Parliament, which arises to it upon the ground of representation, goes to the whole present Constitution of Great Britain; and I suppose it is not meant to new model *that* too. People may form speculative ideas of perfection, and indulge their own fancies or those of other men. Every man in this country has his particular notion of liberty; but perfection never did, and never can exist in any human institution. To what purpose, then, are arguments drawn from a distinction, in which there is no real difference—of a virtual and actual representation? A member of Parliament, chosen for any borough, represents not only the constituents and inhabitants of that particular place, but he represents the inhabitants of every other borough in Great Britain. He represents the city of London, and all other the commons of this land, and the inhabitants of all the colonies and dominions of Great Britain; and is, in duty and conscience, bound to take care of their interests.

I have mentioned the customs and the post tax. This leads me to answer another distinction, as false as the above; the distinction of internal and external taxes. The noble Lord who quoted so much law, and denied upon those grounds the right of the Parliament of Great Britain to lay internal taxes upon the colonies, allowed at the same time that restrictions upon trade, and duties upon the ports, were legal. But I can not see a real difference in this distinction; for I hold it to be true, that a tax laid in any place is like a pebble falling into and making a circle in a lake, till one circle produces and gives motion to another, and the whole circumference is agitated from the center. For nothing can be more clear than that a tax of ten or twenty per cent. laid upon tobacco, either in the ports of Virginia or London, is a duty laid upon the inland plantations of Virginia, a hundred miles from the sea, wheresoever the tobacco grows.

5. The distinction of external and internal taxation is a false one.

I do not deny but that a tax may be laid injudiciously and injuriously, and that people in such a case may have a right to complain. But the nature of the tax is not now the question; whenever it comes to be one, I am for lenity. I would have no blood drawn. There is, I am satisfied, no occasion for any to be drawn. A little time and experience of the inconveniences and miseries of anarchy, may bring people to their senses.

Mr. Otis's book.

With respect to what has been said or written upon this subject, I differ from the noble Lord, who spoke of Mr. Otis and his book with contempt, though he maintained the same doctrine in some points, while in others he carried it farther than Otis himself, who allows every where the supremacy of the Crown over the colonies.[2] No man, on such a subject, is contemptible. Otis is a man of consequence among the people there. They have chosen him for one of their deputies at the Congress and general meeting from the respective governments. It was said, the man is mad. What then? One madman often makes many. Masaniello was mad. Nobody doubts it; yet, for all that, he overturned the government of Naples. Madness is catching in all popular assemblies and upon all popular matters. The book is full of wildness. I never read it till a few days ago, for I seldom look into such things. I never was actually acquainted with the contents of the Stamp Act, till I sent for it on purpose to read it before the debate was expected. With respect to authorities in *another House*, I know nothing of them. I believe that I have not been in that House more than once since I had the honor to be called up to this; and, if I did know any thing that passed in the other House, I could not, and would not, mention it as an authority here. I ought not to mention any such authority. I should think it beneath my own and your Lordships' dignity to speak of it.

I am far from bearing any ill will to the Americans; they are a very good people, and I have long known them. I began life with them, and owe much to them, having been much concerned in the plantation causes before the privy council; and so I became a good deal acquainted with American affairs and people. I dare say, their heat will soon be over, when they come to feel a little the consequences of their opposition to the Legislature. Anarchy always cures itself; but the ferment will continue so much the longer, while hot-headed men there find that there are persons of weight and character to support and justify them here.

Force must be used if the disturbances continue.

Indeed, if the disturbances should continue for a great length of time, force must be the consequence, an application adequate to the mischief, and arising out of the necessity of the case; for force is only the difference between a superior and subordinate jurisdiction. In the former, the whole force of the Legislature resides collectively, and when it ceases to reside, the whole connection is dissolved. It will, indeed, be to very little purpose that we sit here enacting laws, and making resolutions, if the inferior will not obey them, or if we neither can nor dare enforce them; for then, and then, I say, of necessity, the matter comes to the sword. If the offspring are grown too big and too resolute to obey the parent, you must try which is the strongest, and exert all the powers of the mother country to decide the contest.

Examples of popular dislikes on other subjects.

I am satisfied, notwithstanding, that time and a wise and steady conduct may prevent those extremities which would be fatal to both. I remember well when it was the violent humor of the times to decry standing armies and garrisons as dangerous, and incompatible with the liberty of the subject. Nothing would do but a regular militia. The militia are embodied; they march; and no sooner was the militia law thus put into execution, but it was then said to be an intolerable burden upon the subject, and that it would fall, sooner or later, into the hands of the Crown. That was the language, and many counties petitioned against it. This may be the case with the colonies. In many places they begin already

[2] The celebrated James Otis is here referred to, who in 1764 published a pamphlet, which was reprinted in England, entitled The Rights of the British Colonies. In this pamphlet, while he admitted the supremacy of the Crown over the colonies, he strenuously maintained, with Lord Chatham, that as long as America remained unrepresented in the House of Commons, Parliament had no right to tax the colonies.

Mr. Otis, who was a man of fervid eloquence, expressed himself so strongly respecting the rights of America, that some persons (as Lord Mansfield mentions) treated him as a madman. There is a speech (to be found in most of our collections of eloquence) which bears his name, and begins, "England may as well dam up the waters of the Nile with bulrushes, as fetter the step of freedom," &c. It first appeared in a work entitled The Rebels, written by Mrs. Child, and was designed as a fancy sketch, like the speeches put by Mr. Webster into the mouth of Adams and Hancock, in his oration on the death of John Adams and Thomas Jefferson.

to feel the effects of their resistance to government. Interest very soon divides mercantile people; and, although there may be some mad, enthusiastic, or ill-designing people in the colonies, yet I am convinced that the greatest bulk, who have understanding and property, are still well affected to the mother country. You have, my Lords, many friends still in the colonies; and take care that you do not, by abdicating your own authority, desert them and yourselves, and lose them forever.

In all popular tumults, the worst men bear the sway at first. Moderate and good men are often silent for fear or modesty, who, in good time, may declare themselves. Those who have any property to lose are sufficiently alarmed already at the progress of these public violences and violations, to which every man's dwelling, person, and property are hourly exposed. Numbers of such valuable men and good subjects are ready and willing to declare themselves for the support of government in due time, if government does not fling away its own authority.

My Lords, the Parliament of Great Britain has its rights over the colonies; but it may abdicate its rights.

There was a thing which I forgot to mention. I mean, the manuscript quoted by the noble Lord. He tells you that it is there said, that, if the act concerning Ireland had passed, the Parliament might have abidicated its rights as to Ireland. In the first place, I heartily wish, my Lords, that Ireland had not been named, at a time when that country is of a temper and in a situation so difficult to be governed; and when we have already here so much weight upon our hands, encumbered with the extensiveness, variety, and importance of so many objects in a vast and too busy empire, and the national system shattered and exhausted by a long, bloody, and expensive war, but more so by our divisions at home, and a fluctuation of counsels. I wish Ireland, therefore, had never been named.

Notice of a manuscript of Lord Hale's, which had been quoted by Lord Camden.

I pay as much respect as any man to the memory of Lord Chief Justice Hale; but I did not know that he had ever written upon the subject; and I differ very much from thinking with the noble Lord, that this manuscript ought to be published. So far am I from it, that I wish the manuscript had never been named; for Ireland is too tender a subject to be touched. The case of Ireland is as different as possible from that of our colonies. Ireland was a conquered country; it had its *pacta conventa* and its *regalia*. But to what purpose is it to mention the manuscript? It is but the opinion of one man. When it was written, or for what particular object it was written, does not appear. It might possibly be only a work of youth, or an exercise of the understanding, in sounding and trying a question problematically. All people, when they first enter professions, make their collections pretty early in life; and the manuscript may be of that sort. However, be it what it may, the opinion is but problematical; for the act to which the writer refers never passed, and Lord Hale only said, that, if it had passed, the Parliament might have abdicated their right.

But, my Lords, I shall make this application of it. You may abdicate your right over the colonies. Take care, my Lords, how you do so; for such an act will be irrevocable. Proceed, then, my Lords, with spirit and firmness; and, when you shall have established your authority, it will then be a time to show your lenity. The Americans, as I said before, are a very good people, and I wish them exceedingly well; but they are heated and inflamed. The noble Lord who spoke before ended with a prayer. I can not end better than by saying to it, Amen; and in the words of Maurice, prince of Orange, concerning the Hollanders, "*God bless this industrious, frugal, and well-meaning, but easily-deluded people.*"

The Stamp Act was repealed, and the Declaratory Act, thus advocated by Lord Mansfield, was also passed by a large majority.

As Lord Campbell has pronounced the above argument *unanswerable*, it may interest the young reader to know how it was actually answered by the Americans, and why they denied the right of Parliament to lay internal taxes upon them.

1. They owed their existence not to Parliament, but to the Crown. The King, in the exercise of the high sovereignty then conceded to him, had made them by charter *complete civil communities*, with Legislatures of their own having power to lay taxes and do all other acts which were necessary to their subsistence as distinct governments. Hence,

2. They stood substantially on the same footing as Scotland previous to the Union. Like her they were subject to the Navigation Act, and similar regulations touching the *external* relations of the empire; and like her the ordinary legislation of England did not reach them, nor did the common law any farther than they chose to adopt it. Hence,

3. They held themselves amenable in their internal concerns, not to Parliament, but to the Crown alone. It was to the *King* in council or to *his* courts, that they made those occasional references and appeals, which Lord Mansfield endeavors to draw into precedents. So "the post tax" spoken of above, did not originate in Parliament, but in a charter to an individual which afterward reverted to the Crown, and it was in this way alone that the post-office in America became connected with that of England. It was thus that the Americans answered the first three of Lord Mansfield's direct arguments (p. 149–50). Their charters made them dependent not on Parliament, but on the Crown; and their submission to English authority, much as it involved their pecuniary interests, was rendered only to the *latter*. Weak as they were, the colonists had sometimes to temporize, and endure an occasional over-reaching by Parliament. It was not always easy

to draw the line between the laws of trade, to which they held themselves subject, and the general legislation of Parliament. But they considered it clear that their charters exempted them from the latter, giving it to their own Legislatures. — See *Massachusetts State Papers*, p. 351. On this ground, then, they denied the right of Parliament to tax them. It is a striking fact in confirmation of these views, as mentioned by Mr. Daniel Webster, that the American Declaration of Independence does not once refer to the British Parliament. They owed it no allegiance, their only obligations were to the King; and hence the causes which they assigned for breaking off from the British empire consisted in *his* conduct alone, and in his confederating with others in "*pretended* acts of legislation."

They had, however, a second argument, that from *long-continued usage*. Commencing their existence as stated above, the British Parliament had never subjected them to internal taxation. When this was attempted, at the end of one hundred and fifty years, they used the argument of Mr. Burke, "*You were not* WONT *to do these things from the beginning;*" and while his inference was, "Your taxes are inexpedient and unwise," theirs was, "You have no *right* to lay them." Long-continued usage forms part of the English Constitution. Many of the rights and privileges of the people rest on no other foundation; and a usage of this kind, commencing with the very existence of the colonies, had given them the *exclusive* right of internal taxation through their own Legislatures, since they maintained their institutions at their own expense without aid from the mother country. To give still greater force to this argument, the Americans appealed to the monstrous consequences of the contrary supposition. If, as colonies, after supporting their own governments, they were liable to give England what part she chose of their earnings to support her government—one twentieth, one tenth, one half each year, at her bidding—they were no longer Englishmen, they were vassals and slaves. When George the Third, therefore, undertook to lay taxes in America and collect them at the point of the bayonet, he invaded their privileges, he dissolved the connection of the colonies with the mother country, and they were of right free.

A third argument was that of Lord Chatham. "Taxation," said his Lordship, "is no part of the governing or legislative power." A tax bill, from the very words in which it is framed, is "a gift and grant of the Commons alone," and the concurrence of the Peers and Crown is only necessary to give it the *form* of law. "When, therefore, in this House," said his Lordship, "we give and grant, we give and grant what is our own. But in an American tax what do we do? We, your Majesty's Commons for Great Britain, give and grant to your Majesty—What? Our own property? No. We give and grant to your Majesty the property of your Majesty's subjects in *America!* It is an absurdity in terms!" To this Lord Mansfield could only reply, as he does in his fourth direct argument (p. 150). "America is *virtually* represented in the House of Commons." But this, as Lord Campbell admits, is idle and false. A virtual representation there may be of particular classes (as of minors and females), who live intermingled in the same community with those who vote; but a virtual representation of a whole people three thousand miles off, with no intermingling of society or interests, is beyond all doubt "an absurdity in terms." The idea is contrary to all English usage in such cases. When the Scotch were incorporated with the English in 1705, they were not considered as "virtually represented" in the English Parliament, but were allowed to send representatives of their own. It was so, also, with Wales, Chester, and Durham, at an earlier period. Nothing, in fact, could be more adverse to the principles of the English Constitution than the idea of the "virtual representation" of three millions of people living at the distance of three thousand miles from the body of English electors. But if not virtually represented, the Americans were not represented at all. A bill giving away their property was, therefore, null and void—as much so as a bill would be if passed by the House of Lords, levying taxes on the Commons of England. Under the English Constitution, *representation* of some kind is essential to taxation.

Lord Mansfield's last argument (p. 151) is, that "the distinction between external and internal taxation is a false one." According to him, as Parliament, in carrying out the Navigation Act, laid external taxes affecting the colonies, Parliament was likewise authorized to lay internal taxes upon them. The answer is given by Mr. Burke. The duties referred to were simply *incidental* to the Navigation Act. They were used solely as instruments of carrying it out, of checking trade and directing its channels. They had never from the first been regarded as a means of *revenue*. They stood, therefore, on a footing entirely different from that of internal taxes, which were "the *gift* and *grant* of the Commons alone." The distinction between them was absolute and entire; and any attempt to confound them, and to take money on this ground from those who are not represented in Parliament, was subversive of the English Constitution.[1]

Such were the arguments of the Americans; and the world has generally considered them as forming a complete answer to the reasonings of Lord Mansfield.

---

[1] The reader will find this distinction fully drawn out in Mr. Burke's Speech on American Taxation, page 249, 250. He there shows, that during the whole operation of the Navigation Laws, down to 1764, "a parliamentary revenue thence was never once in contemplation; that "the words which distinguish revenue laws, specifically as such, were premeditatedly avoided;" and that all duties of this kind previous to that period, stood on the ground of mere "*commercial regulation and restraint.*"

SPEECH

OF LORD MANSFIELD WHEN SURROUNDED BY A MOB IN THE COURT OF THE KING'S BENCH, ON A TRIAL RESPECTING THE OUTLAWRY OF JOHN WILKES, ESQ., DELIVERED JANUARY 8, 1768.

INTRODUCTION.

In 1764, Mr. Wilkes was prosecuted for a seditious libel upon the King, and for an obscene and impious publication entitled an Essay on Women. Verdicts were obtained against him under both these prosecutions, and, as he had fled the country, and did not appear to receive sentence, he was *outlawed* in the sheriff's court for the county of Middlesex on the 12th of July, 1764. In 1768 he returned to England, and applied to the Court of the King's Bench for a reversal of the outlawry; alleging, among other things, that the sheriff's writ of exegent was not technically correct in its wording, since he merely described the court as "my county court," whereas he ought to have added a description of the place, viz., "*of Middlesex.*" Mr. Wilkes was now the favorite of the populace. Tumultuous meetings were held in his behalf in various parts of the metropolis; riots prevailed to an alarming extent; the Mansion House of the Lord Mayor was frequently assailed by mobs; members of Parliament were attacked or threatened in the streets; and great fears were entertained for the safety of Lord Mansfield and the other judges of the Court of the King's Bench during the trial. On the 8th of June, 1768, the decision was given, the court being surrounded by an immense mob, waiting the result in a highly excited state. Under these circumstances, Lord Mansfield, after reading his decision for a time, broke off suddenly, and, turning from the case before him, addressed to all within the reach of his voice a few words of admonition, in which we can not admire too much the dignity and firmness with which he opposed himself to the popular rage, and the perfect willingness he showed to become a victim, if necessary, for the support of law.

SPEECH, &c.[1]

But here let me pause.

It is fit to take some notice of various terrors being out—the numerous crowds which have attended and now attend in and about the hall, out of all reach of hearing what passes in court, and the tumults which, in other places, have shamefully insulted all order and government. Audacious addresses in print dictate to us, from those they call the *people*, the judgment to be given now, and afterward upon the conviction. Reasons of policy are urged, from danger in the kingdom by commotions and general confusion.

Give me leave to take the opportunity of this great and respectable audience to let the whole world know *all such attempts are vain*. Unless we have been able to find an error which bears us out to reverse the outlawry, it must be affirmed. The Constitution does not allow reasons of state to influence our judgments: God forbid it should! We must not regard political consequences how formidable soever they might be. If rebellion was the certain consequence, we are bound to say, "Fiat justitia, ruat cœlum."[2] The Constitution trusts the King with reasons of state and policy. He may stop prosecutions; he may pardon offenses; it is his to judge whether the law or the criminal shall yield. *We* have no election. None of us encouraged or approved the commission of either of the crimes of which the defendant is convicted. None of us had any hand in his being prosecuted. As to myself, I took no part (in another place) in the addresses for that prosecution. *We* did not advise or assist the defendant to fly from justice; it was his own act, and he must take the consequences. None of us have been consulted or had any thing to do with the present prosecution. It is not in our power to stop it; it was not in our power to bring it on. We can not pardon. We are to say what we take the law to be. If we do not speak our real opinions, we prevaricate with God and our own consciences.

I pass over many anonymous letters I have received. Those in print are public, and some of them have been brought judicially before the court. Whoever the writers are, *they take the wrong way!* I will do my duty unawed. What am I to fear? That "mendax infamia" [lying scandal] from the press, which daily coins false facts and false motives? The lies of calumny carry no terror to me. I trust that the temper of my mind, and the color and conduct of my life, have given me a suit of armor against these arrows. If during this King's reign I have ever supported his government, and assisted his measures, I have done it without any other reward than the consciousness of doing what I thought right. If I have ever opposed, I have done it upon the points themselves, without mixing in party or faction, and without any collateral views. I honor the King and respect the people; but many things acquired by the favor of either are, in my account, objects not worthy of ambition. I wish popularity, but it is that popularity which follows, not that which is run after. It is that popularity which, sooner or later, never fails to do justice to the pursuit of noble

[1] From Burrow's Reports, iv., 2561.

[2] Be justice done, though heaven in ruins fall.

ends by noble means. I will not do that which my conscience tells me is wrong upon this occasion, to gain the huzzas of thousands, or the daily praise of all the papers which come from the press. I will not avoid doing what I think is right, though it should draw on me the whole artillery of libels—all that falsehood and malice can invent, or the credulity of a deluded populace can swallow. I can say with a great magistrate, upon an occasion and under circumstances not unlike, "Ego hoc animo semper fui, ut invidiam virtute partam, gloriam non invidiam, putarem."[3]

The threats go farther than abuse—personal violence is denounced. I do not believe it. It is not the genius of the worst of men of this country, in the worst of times. But I have set my mind at rest. The last end that can happen to any man never comes too soon, if he falls in support of the law and liberty of his country (for liberty is synonymous with law and government). Such a shock, too, might be productive of public good. It might awake the better part of the kingdom out of that lethargy which seems to have benumbed them, and bring the mad part back to their senses, as men intoxicated are sometimes stunned into sobriety.

Once for all, let it be understood, that no endeavors of this kind will influence any man who at present sits here. If they had any effect, it would be contrary to their intent; leaning against their impression might give a bias the other way. But I hope and I know that I have fortitude enough to resist even that weakness. No libels, no threats, nothing that has happened, nothing that can happen, will weigh a feather against allowing the defendant, upon this and every other question, not only the whole advantage he is entitled to from substantial law and justice, but every benefit from the most critical nicety of form which any other defendant could claim under the like objection. The only effect I feel is an anxiety to be able to explain the grounds on which we proceed, so as to satisfy all mankind "that a flaw of form given way to in this case, could not have been got over in any other."

Lord Mansfield now resumed the discussion of the case, and stated in respect to the insertion of the qualifying phrase "of Middlesex," mentioned above, that "a series of authorities, unimpeached and uncontradicted, have said such words are *formally necessary;* and such authority, though begun without law, reason, or common sense, ought to avail the defendant." He therefore (with the concurrence of the other judges) declared a *reversal;* adding, "I beg to be understood, that I ground my opinion *singly* on the authority of the cases adjudged; which, as they are on the favorable side, in a criminal case highly penal, I think ought not to be departed from."

This reversal, however, did not relieve Mr. Wilkes from the operations of the verdicts already mentioned. Ten days after, Mr. Justice Yates pronounced the judgment of the court, sentencing him to be imprisoned for twenty-two months, and to pay a fine of one thousand pounds.

SPEECH

OF LORD MANSFIELD IN THE CASE OF THE CHAMBERLAIN OF LONDON AGAINST ALLAN EVANS, ESQ., DELIVERED IN THE HOUSE OF LORDS, FEBRUARY 4, 1769.

INTRODUCTION.

THIS case affords a striking example of the abuses which spring up under a religious establishment.

The city of London was in want of a new mansion house for the Lord Mayor, and resolved to build one on a scale of becoming magnificence. But, as the expense would be great, some ingenious churchmen devised a plan for extorting a large part of the money out of the Dissenters, who had for a number of years been growing in business and property, under the protection of the Toleration Act. The mode was this. A by-law of the city was passed, imposing a fine of £600 on any person who should be elected as sheriff and decline to serve. Some wealthy individual was then taken from the dissenting body, and, by a concert among the initiated, was chosen to the office of sheriff. Of course he was not expected to serve, for the Test and Corporation Acts rendered him incapable. He was, therefore, compelled to decline; and was then fined £600, under a by-law framed for the very purpose of extorting this money![1] Numerous appointments were thus made, and £15,000 were actually paid in; until it came to be a matter of mere sport to "roast a Dissenter," and bring another £600 into the treasury toward the expenses of the mansion house.

At length Allan Evans, Esq., a man of spirit, who had been selected as a victim, resolved to try the question. He refused to pay the fine, and was sued in the Sheriff's Court. Here he pleaded his rights

---

[3] This is one of those sentences of Cicero, in his first oration against Catiline, which it is impossible to translate. Striking as the sentiment is, it owes much of its force and beauty to the fine antithesis with which it flashes upon the mind, and even to the paronomasia on the word *invidiam,* while its noble rhythmus adds greatly to the effect. To those who are not familiar with the original, the following may give a conception of the meaning: Such have always been my feelings, that I look upon odium incurred by the practice of virtue, not as odium, but as the highest glory.

[1] See Parliamentary History.

under the Toleration Act, but lost his cause. He appealed to the Court of Hustings, where the decision was affirmed. He then appealed to the Court of Common Pleas, where judgment went in his favor; the decisions of the courts below being unanimously reversed. The city now brought a writ of error through their Chamberlain, and carried the case before the House of Lords. Here the subject was taken up by Lord Mansfield, who, in common with all the judges but one, of the Court of the King's Bench, was of opinion that Evans was protected by the Toleration Act, and exempted from the obligation to act as sheriff. These views he maintained in the following speech, which had great celebrity at the time, and is spoken of by Lord Campbell as "one of the finest specimens of forensic eloquence to be found in our books."[2] It was published from notes taken by Dr. Philip Furneaux, "with his Lordship's consent and approbation." Though it has not, in every part, that perfection of style for which Lord Mansfield was distinguished, it is certainly an admirable model of juridical eloquence, being equally remarkable for the clearness of its statements, the force of its reasonings, and the liberal and enlightened sentiments with which it abounds. It rises toward the close into a strain of indignant reprobation, and administers a terrible rebuke to the city of London for suffering its name to be connected with so despicable a system of extortion.

SPEECH, &c.

My Lords,—As I made the motion for taking the opinion of the learned judges, and proposed the question your Lordships have been pleased to put to them, it may be expected that I should make some farther motion, in consequence of the opinions they have delivered.

In moving for the opinion of the judges, I had two views. The first was, that the House might have the benefit of their assistance in forming a right judgment in this cause now before us, upon this writ of error. The next was, that, the question being fully discussed, the grounds of our judgment, together with their exceptions, limitations, and restrictions, might be clearly and certainly known, as a rule to be followed hereafter in all future cases of the like nature; and this determined me as to the manner of wording the question, "How far the defendant might, in the present case, be allowed to plead his disability in bar of the action brought against him?"

The question, thus worded, shows the point upon which your Lordships thought this case turned; and the answer necessarily fixes a criterion, under what circumstances, and by what persons, such a disability may be pleaded as an exemption from the penalty inflicted by this by-law, upon those who decline taking upon them the office of sheriff.

In every view in which I have been able to consider this matter, I think this action can not be supported.

Preliminary view of the grounds of argument.

I. If they rely on the Corporation Act; by the literal and express provision of that act, no person can be elected who hath not within a year taken the sacrament in the Church of England. The defendant hath not taken the sacrament within a year; he is not, therefore, elected. Here they fail.

If they ground it on the general design of the Legislature in passing the Corporation Act; the design was to exclude Dissenters from office, and disable them from serving. For, in those times, when a spirit of intolerance prevailed, and severe measures were pursued, the Dissenters were reputed and treated as persons ill affected and dangerous to the government. The defendant, therefore, a Dissenter, and in the eye of this law a person dangerous and ill affected, is excluded from office, and disabled from serving. Here they fail.

If they ground the action on their own by-law; that by-law was professedly made to procure fit and able persons to serve the office, and the defendant is not fit and able, being expressly disabled by statute law. Here, too, they fail.

If they ground it on his disability's being owing to a neglect of taking the sacrament at church, when he ought to have done it, the Toleration Act having freed the Dissenters from all obligation to take the sacrament at church, the defendant is guilty of no neglect—no *criminal* neglect. Here, therefore, they fail.

These points, my Lords, will appear clear and plain.

Intent and effect of the Corporation Act.

II. The Corporation Act, pleaded by the defendant as rendering him ineligible to this office, and incapable of taking it upon him, was most certainly intended by the Legislature to *prohibit* the persons therein described being elected to any corporation offices, and to disable them from taking such offices upon them. The act had two parts: first, it appointed a commission for turning out all that were at that time in office, who would not comply with what was required as the condition of their continuance therein, and even gave a power to turn them out though they should comply; and then it farther enacted, that, from the termination of that commission, no person hereafter, who had not taken the sacrament according to the rites of the Church of England within one year preceding the time of such election, should be placed, chosen, or elected into any office of, or belonging to, the government of any corporation; and this was done, as it was expressly declared in the preamble to the act, in order to perpetuate the succession in corporations in the hands of persons well affected to government in church and state.

It was not their design (as hath been said) "to *bring* such persons into corporations by inducing them to take the sacrament in the Church of England;" the Legislature did not mean to tempt persons who were ill affected to the gov-

[2] Lives of the Chancellors, v., 287.

ernment occasionally to conform. It was not, I say, their design to bring them in. They could not trust them, lest they should use the power of their offices to distress and annoy the state. And the reason is alleged in the act itself. It was because there were "evil spirits" among them; and they were afraid of evil spirits, and determined to keep them out. They therefore put it out of the power of electors to choose such persons, and out of their power to serve; and accordingly prescribed a mark or character, laid down a description whereby they should be known and distinguished by their conduct previous to such an election. Instead of appointing a condition of their serving the office, resulting from their future conduct, or some consequent action to be performed by them, they declared such persons incapable of being chosen as had not taken the sacrament in the Church within a year before such election; and without this mark of their affection to the Church, they could not be in office, and there could be no election. But as the law *then* stood, no man could have pleaded this disability, resulting from the Corporation Act, in bar of such an action as is now brought against the defendant, because this disability was owing to what was then, in the eye of the law, a crime; every man being required by the canon law (received and confirmed by the statute law) to take the sacrament in the Church at least once a year. The law would not then permit a man to say that he had not taken the sacrament in the Church of England; and he could not be allowed to plead it in bar of any action brought against him.

Effect of the Toleration Act.

III. But the case is quite altered since the Act of Toleration. It is now no crime for a man, who is within the description of that act, to say he is a Dissenter; nor is it any crime for him not to take the sacrament according to the rites of the Church of England; nay, the crime is, if he does it contrary to the dictates of his conscience.

If it is a crime not to take the sacrament at church, it must be a crime by some *law;* which must be either common or statute law, the canon law enforcing it being dependent wholly upon the statute law. Now the statute law is repealed as to persons capable of pleading [under the Toleration Act] that they are so and so qualified; and therefore the canon law is repealed with regard to those persons.

If it is a crime by common law, it must be so either by usage or principle. But there is no usage or custom, independent of positive law, which makes nonconformity a crime. The eternal principles of natural religion are part of the common law. The essential principles of revealed religion are part of the common law; so that any person reviling, subverting, or ridiculing them, may be prosecuted at common law. But it can not be shown, from the principles of natural or revealed religion, that, independent of positive law, temporal punishments ought to be inflicted for mere opinions with respect to particular modes of worship.

Persecution for a sincere though erroneous conscience is not to be deduced from reason or the fitness of things. It can only stand upon positive law.

Refutation of plaintiff's arguments.

IV. It has been said (1.) That "the Toleration Act only amounts to an exemption of the Protestant Dissenters from the *penalties* of certain laws therein particularly mentioned, and to nothing more; that, if it had been intended to bear, and to have any operation upon the Corporation Act, the Corporation Act ought to have been mentioned therein; and there ought to have been some enacting clause, exempting Dissenters from prosecution in consequence of this act, and enabling them to plead their not having received the sacrament according to the rites of the Church of England in bar of such action." But this is much too limited and narrow a conception of the Toleration Act, which amounts consequentially to a great deal more than this; and it hath consequentially an inference and operation upon the Corporation Act in particular. The Toleration Act renders *that which was illegal before, now legal.* The Dissenters' way of worship is permitted and allowed by this act. It is not only exempted from punishment, but rendered innocent and lawful. It is established; it is put under the protection, and is not merely under the connivance of the law. In case those who are appointed by law to register dissenting places of worship refuse on any pretense to do it, we must, upon application, send a mandamus to compel them.

Now there can not be a plainer position than that the law protects nothing in that very respect in which it is (in the eye of the law) at the same time a crime. Dissenters, within the description of the Toleration Act, are restored to a legal consideration and capacity; and a hundred consequences will from thence follow, which are not mentioned in the act. For instance, previous to the Toleration Act, it was unlawful to devise any legacy for the support of dissenting congregations, or for the benefit of dissenting ministers; for the law knew no such assemblies, and no such persons; and such a devise was absolutely void, being left to what the law called superstitious purposes. But will it be said in any court in England that such a devise is not a good and valid one now? And yet there is nothing said of this in the Toleration Act. By this act the Dissenters are freed, not only from the pains and penalties of the laws therein particularly specified, but from all ecclesiastical censures, and from all penalty and punishment whatsoever, on account of their nonconformity, which is allowed and protected by this act, and is therefore, in the eye of the law, no longer a crime. Now, if the defendant may say he is a Dissenter; if the law doth not stop his mouth; if he may declare that he hath not taken the sacrament according to the rites of the Church of England, without being considered as criminal; if, I say, his mouth is not stopped by the law, he may then plead his not having taken the sacrament according to the rites of the Church of England, in bar of this action. It is such a disability as doth not leave him liable to any action, or to any penalty whatsoever.

(2.) It is indeed said to be "a maxim in law, that a man shall not be allowed to disable himself." But, when this maxim is applied to the present case, it is laid down in too large a sense. When it is extended to comprehend a legal disability, it is taken in too great a latitude. What! Shall not a man be allowed to plead that he is not fit and able? These words are inserted in the by-law, as the ground of making it; and in the plaintiff's declaration, as the ground of his action against the defendant. It is alleged that the defendant was fit and able, and that he refused to serve, not having a reasonable excuse. It is certain, and it is hereby in effect admitted, that if he is not fit and able, and that if he hath a reasonable excuse, he may plead it in bar of this action. Surely he might plead that he was not worth £15,000, provided that was really the case, as a circumstance that would render him not fit and able. And if the law allows him to say that he hath not taken the sacrament according to the rites of the Church of England, being within the description of the Toleration Act, he may plead *that* likewise to show that he is not fit and able. It is a reasonable, it is a lawful excuse.

My Lords, the meaning of this maxim, "that a man shall not disable himself," is solely this: that a man shall not disable himself by his own willful crime; and such a disability the law will not allow him to plead. If a man contracts to sell an estate to any person upon certain terms at such a time, and in the mean time he sells it to another, he shall not be allowed to say, "Sir, I can not fulfill my contract; it is out of my power; I have sold my estate to another." Such a plea would be no bar to an action, because the act of his selling it to another is the very breach of contract. So, likewise, a man who hath promised marriage to one lady, and afterward marries another, can not plead in bar of a prosecution from the first lady that he is already married, because his marrying the second lady is the very breach of promise to the first. A man shall not be allowed to plead that he was drunk in bar of a criminal prosecution, though perhaps he was at the time as incapable of the exercise of reason as if he had been insane, because his drunkenness was itself a crime. He shall not be allowed to excuse one crime by another. The Roman soldier, who cut off his thumbs, was not suffered to plead his disability for the service to procure his dismission with impunity, because his incapacity was designedly brought on him by his own willful fault. And I am glad to observe so good an agreement among the judges upon this point, who have stated it with great precision and clearness.

When it was said, therefore, that "a man can not plead his crime in excuse for not doing what he is by law required to do," it only amounts to this, that he can not plead in excuse what, when pleaded, *is* no excuse; but there is not in this the shadow of an objection to his pleading what is an excuse—pleading a legal disqualification. If he is nominated to be a justice of the peace, he may say, I can not be a justice of the peace, for I have not a hundred pounds a year. In like manner, a Dissenter may plead, "I have not qualified, and I can not qualify, and am not obliged to qualify; and you have no right to fine me for not serving."

(3.) It hath been said that "the King hath a right to the service of all his subjects." And this assertion is very true, provided it be properly qualified. But surely, against the operation of this general right in particular cases, a man may plead a natural or civil disability. May not a man plead that he was upon the high seas? May not idiocy or lunacy be pleaded, which are natural disabilities; or a judgment of a court of law, and much more a judgment of Parliament, which are civil disabilities?

(4.) It hath been said to be a maxim "that no man can plead his being a lunatic to avoid a deed executed, or excuse an act done, at that time, because," it is said, "if he was a lunatic, he could not remember any action he did during the period of his insanity;" and this was doctrine formerly laid down by some judges. But I am glad to find that of late it hath been generally exploded. For the reason assigned for it is, in my opinion, wholly insufficient to support it; because, though he could not remember what passed during his insanity, yet he might justly say, if he ever executed such a deed, or did such an action, it *must* have been during his confinement or lunacy, for he did not do it either before or since that time.

As to the case in which a man's plea of insanity was actually set aside, it was nothing more than this: it was when they pleaded *ore tenus* [or verbally]; the man pleaded that he was at the time out of his senses. It was replied, How do you know that you were out of your senses? No man that is so, knows himself to be so. And accordingly his plea was, upon this quibble, set aside; not because it was not a valid one, if he *was* out of his senses, but because they concluded he was not out of his senses. If he had alleged that he was at that time confined, being apprehended to be out of his senses, no advantage could have been taken of his manner of expressing himself, and his plea must have been allowed to be good.

(5.) As to Larwood's case, he was not allowed the benefit of the Toleration Act, because he did not plead it. If he had insisted on his right to the benefit of it in his plea, the judgment must have been different. His inserting it in his *replication* was not allowed, not because it was not an allegation that would have excused him if it had been originally taken notice of in his plea, but because its being not mentioned till afterward was a departure from his plea.

In the case of the Mayor of Guilford, the Toleration Act was pleaded. The plea was allowed good, the disability being esteemed a lawful one; and the judgment was right.

And here the defendant hath likewise insisted on his right to the benefit of the Toleration Act. In his plea he saith he is *bona fide* a Dissenter, within the description of the Toleration Act; that he hath taken the oaths, and subscribed the declaration required by that act, to show that he is not a popish recusant; that he hath never received the sacrament according to the rites of the Church of England, and that he can not in conscience do it; and that for more than fifty years past he hath not been present at church at the celebration of the established worship, but hath constantly received the sacrament and attended divine service among the Protestant Dissenters. These facts are not denied by the plaintiff, though they might easily have been traversed; and it was incumbent upon them to have done it, if they had not known they should certainly fail in it. There can be no doubt, therefore, that the defendant is a Dissenter—an honest, conscientious Dissenter; and no conscientious Dissenter can take the sacrament at church. The defendant saith he can not do it, and he is not obliged to do it. And as this is the case, as the law allows him to say this, as it hath not stopped his mouth, the plea which he makes is a lawful plea, his disability being through no crime or fault of his own. I say, he is disabled by act of Parliament, without the concurrence or intervention of any fault or crime of his own; and therefore he may plead this disability in bar of the present action.

(6.) The case of "atheists and infidels" is out of the present question; they come not within the description of the Toleration Act. And this is the sole point to be inquired into in all cases of the like nature with that of the defendant, who here pleads the Toleration Act. Is the man *bona fide* a Dissenter within the description of that act? If not, he can not plead his disability in consequence of his not having taken the sacrament in the Church of England. If he is, he may lawfully and with effect plead it in bar of such an action; and the question on which this distinction is grounded must be tried by a jury.

(7.) It hath been said that "this being a matter between God and a man's own conscience, it can not come under the cognizance of a jury." But certainly it may; and, though God alone is the absolute judge of a man's religious profession and of his conscience, yet there are some marks even of sincerity, among which there is none more certain than *consistency*. Surely a man's sincerity may be judged of by overt acts. It is a just and excellent maxim, which will hold good in this, as in all other cases, "by their fruits ye shall know them." Do they, I do not say go to meeting now and then, but do they frequent the meeting-house? Do they join generally and statedly in divine worship with dissenting congregations? Whether they do or not, may be ascertained by their neighbors, and by those who frequent the same places of worship. In case a man hath occasionally conformed for the sake of places of trust and profit; in that case, I imagine, a jury would not hesitate in their verdict. If a man then alleges he is a Dissenter, and claims the protection and the advantages of the Toleration Act, a jury may justly find that he is not a Dissenter within the description of the Toleration Act, so far as to render his disability a lawful one. If he takes the sacrament for his interest, the jury may fairly conclude that this scruple of conscience is a false pretense when set up to avoid a burden.

The defendant in the present case pleads that he is a Dissenter within the description of the Toleration Act; that he hath not taken the sacrament in the Church of England within one year preceding the time of his supposed election, nor ever in his whole life; and that he can not in conscience do it.

Conscience is not controllable by human laws, nor amenable to human tribunals. Persecution, or attempts to force conscience, will never produce conviction, and are only calculated to make hypocrites or martyrs.

Concluding observations.

V. My Lords, there never was a single instance, from the Saxon times down to our own, in which a man was ever punished for erroneous opinions concerning rites or modes of worship, but upon some positive law. The common law of England, which is only common reason or usage, knows of no prosecution for mere opinions. For atheism, blasphemy, and reviling the Christian religion, there have been instances of persons prosecuted and punished upon the common law. But bare nonconformity is no sin by the common law; and all positive laws inflicting any pains or penalties for nonconformity to the established rites and modes, are repealed by the Act of Toleration, and Dissenters are thereby exempted from all ecclesiastical censures.

What bloodshed and confusion have been occasioned, from the reign of Henry the Fourth, when the first penal statutes were enacted, down to the revolution in this kingdom, by laws made to force conscience! There is nothing, certainly, more unreasonable, more inconsistent with the rights of human nature, more contrary to the spirit and precepts of the Christian religion, more iniquitous and unjust, more impolitic, than persecution. It is against natural religion, revealed religion, and sound policy.

Sad experience and a large mind taught that great man, the President De Thou, this doctrine. Let any man read the many admirable things which, though a Papist, he hath dared to advance upon the subject, in the dedication of his History to Harry the Fourth of France, which I never read without rapture, and he will be fully convinced, not only how cruel, but how impolitic it is to prosecute for religious opinions. I am sorry that of late his countrymen have begun to open their eyes, see their error, and adopt his sentiments. I should not have broken my heart (I hope I may say it without breach of Christian charity) if France had continued to cherish the Jesuits and to persecute the Huguenots.[3]

[3] This is a most dexterous preparation for the cut-

There was no occasion to revoke the Edict of Nantes. The Jesuits needed only to have advised a plan similar to what is contended for in the present case, *Make a law to render them incapable of office, make another to punish them for not serving.* If they accept, punish them (for it is admitted on all hands that the defendant, in the cause before your Lordships, is prosecutable for taking the office upon him)—if they accept, punish them; if they refuse, punish them. If they say yes, punish them; if they say no, punish them. My Lords, this is a most exquisite dilemma, from which there is no escaping. It is a trap a man can not get out of; it is as bad persecution as that of Procrustes. If they are too short, stretch them; if they are too long, lop them. Small would have been their consolation to have been gravely told, "The Edict of Nantes is kept inviolable. You have the full benefit of that act of toleration; you may take the sacrament in your own way with impunity; you are not compelled to go to mass." Were this case but told in the city of London, as of a proceeding in France, how would they exclaim against the Jesuitical distinction? And yet, in truth, it comes from themselves. The Jesuits never thought of it. When they meant to persecute by their act of toleration, the Edict of Nantes was repealed.

This by-law, by which the Dissenters are to be reduced to this wretched dilemma, is a by-law of the city, a local corporation, contrary to an act of Parliament, which is the law of the land; a modern by-law of a very modern date, made long since the Corporation Act, long since the Toleration Act, in the face of them, for they knew these laws were in being. It was made in some year in the reign of the late King—I forget which; but it was made about the time of *building the mansion house!!* Now, if it could be supposed the city have a power of making such a by-law, it would entirely subvert the Toleration Act, the design of which was to exempt the Dissenters from all penalties; for by such a by-law they have it in their power to make every Dissenter pay a fine of six hundred pounds, or any sum they please, for it amounts to that.

The professed design of making this by-law was to get fit and able persons to serve the office; and the plaintiff sets forth in his declaration, that, if the Dissenters are excluded, they shall want fit and able persons to serve the office. But, were I to deliver my own suspicion, it would be, that they did not so much wish for their services as their fines. Dissenters have been appointed to this office, one who was blind, another who was bed-ridden; not, I suppose, on account of their being fit and able to serve the office. No: they were disabled both by nature and by law.

We had a case lately in the courts below, of a person chosen mayor of a corporation while he was beyond seas with his Majesty's troops in America, and they knew him to be so. Did they want him to serve the office? No; it was impossible. But they had a mind to continue the former mayor a year longer, and to have a pretense for setting aside him who was now chosen, on all future occasions, as having been elected before.

In the case before your Lordships, the defendant was by law incapable at the time of his pretended election; and it is my firm persuasion that he was chosen because he was incapable. If he had been capable, he had not been chosen, for they did not want him to serve the office. They chose him because, without a breach of the law, and a usurpation on the Crown, he could not serve the office. They chose him, that he might fall under the penalty of their by-law, made to serve a particular purpose; in opposition to which, and to avoid the fine thereby imposed, he hath pleaded a legal disability, grounded on two acts of Parliament. As I am of opinion that his plea is good, I conclude with moving your Lordships,

"That the judgment be affirmed."

The judgment was accordingly affirmed, and an end put to a system of extortion so mean and scandalous, that it seems difficult to understand, at the present day, how an English community could have endured, or English courts have upheld, it for a single hour.

SPEECH

OF LORD MANSFIELD ON A BILL TO DEPRIVE PEERS OF THE REALM OF CERTAIN PRIVILEGES, DELIVERED IN THE HOUSE OF LORDS, MAY 8, 1770.

INTRODUCTION.

THIS speech is the best specimen extant of Lord Mansfield's parliamentary eloquence. It has that felicity of statement and clearness of reasoning for which he was so much distinguished, connected with an ardor and elevation of sentiment, that give double force to every argument he uses. The style is uncommonly chaste and polished. It has a conversational ease, and yet entire dignity throughout, which have made it the favorite of all who love pure and simple English.

---

ting rebuke which follows. Nothing could be more mortifying to the citizens of London, among whom the fires of Smithfield had left a traditional horror of Popish cruelty, than to be thus held out to the world as more cruel and Jesuitical than the detested persecutors of the French Huguenots.

SPEECH, &c.

My Lords,—When I consider the importance of this bill to your Lordships, I am not surprised it has taken so much of your consideration. It is a bill, indeed, of no common magnitude. It is no less than to take away from two thirds of the Legislative body of this great kingdom, certain privileges and immunities of which they have been long possessed. Perhaps there is no situation the human mind can be placed in, that is so difficult, and so trying, as where it is made a judge in its own cause. There is something implanted in the breast of man so attached to itself, so tenacious of privileges once obtained, that, in such a situation, either to discuss with impartiality, or decide with justice, has ever been held as the summit of all human virtue. The bill now in question puts your Lordships in this very predicament; and I doubt not but the wisdom of your decision will convince the world, that, where self-interest and justice are in opposite scales, the latter will ever preponderate with your Lordships.

Privileges have been granted to legislators in all ages and in all countries. The practice is founded in wisdom; and, indeed, it is peculiarly essential to the Constitution of this country, that the members of both Houses should be free in their persons in cases of civil suits; for there may come a time when the safety and welfare of this whole empire may depend upon their attendance in Parliament. God forbid that I should advise any measure that would in future endanger the state. But the bill before your Lordships has, I am confident, no such tendency, for it expressly secures the *persons* of members of either House in all civil suits. This being the case, I confess, when I see many noble Lords, for whose judgment I have the greatest respect, standing up to oppose a bill which is calculated merely to facilitate the recovery of just and legal debts, I am astonished and amazed. They, I doubt not, oppose the bill upon public principles. I would not wish to insinuate that private interest has the least weight in their determination.

This bill has been frequently proposed, and as frequently miscarried; but it was always lost in the Lower House. Little did I think, when it had passed the Commons, that it possibly could have met with such opposition here. Shall it be said that you, my Lords, the grand council of the nation, the highest judicial and legislative body of the realm, endeavor to evade by *privilege* those very laws which you enforce on your fellow-subjects? Forbid it, justice. I am sure, were the noble Lords as well acquainted as I am with but half the difficulties and delays that are every day occasioned in the courts of justice, under pretense of privilege, they would not, nay, they could not, oppose this bill.

I have waited with patience to hear what arguments might be urged against the bill; but I have waited in vain. The truth is, there is no argument that can weigh against it. The justice and expediency of this bill are such as render it self-evident. It is a proposition of that nature that can neither be weakened by argument, nor entangled with sophistry. Much, indeed, has been said by some noble Lords on the wisdom of our ancestors, and how differently they thought from us. They not only decreed that privilege should prevent all civil suits from proceeding during the sitting of Parliament, but likewise granted protection to the very servants of members. I shall say nothing on the wisdom of our ancestors. It might perhaps appear invidious, and is not necessary in the present case. I shall only say, that the noble Lords that flatter themselves with the weight of that reflection, should remember, that, as circumstances alter, things themselves should alter. Formerly it was not so fashionable either for masters or servants to run in debt as it is at present; nor formerly were merchants or manufacturers members of Parliament, as at present. The case now is very different. Both merchants and manufacturers are, with great propriety, elected members of the Lower House. Commerce having thus got into the legislative body of the kingdom, privilege must be done away. We all know that the very soul and essence of trade are regular payments; and sad experience teaches us that there are men who will not make their regular payments without the compulsive power of the laws. The law, then, ought to be equally open to all. Any exemption to particular men, or particular ranks of men, is, in a free commercial country, a solecism of the grossest nature.

But I will not trouble your Lordships with arguments for that which is sufficiently evident without any. I shall only say a few words to some noble Lords, who foresee much inconvenience from the persons of their servants being liable to be arrested. One noble Lord observes, that the coachman of a peer may be arrested while he is driving his master to the House, and consequently he will not be able to attend his duty in Parliament. If this was actually to happen, there are so many methods by which the member might still get to the House, I can hardly think the noble Lord to be serious in his objection. Another noble Lord said, that by this bill one might lose his most valuable and honest servants. This I hold to be a contradiction in terms; for he neither can be a valuable servant, nor an honest man, who gets into debt, which he neither is able nor willing to pay till compelled by law. If my servant, by unforeseen accidents, has got in debt, and I still wish to retain him, I certainly would pay the debt. But upon no principle of liberal legislation whatever can my servant have a title to set his creditors at defiance, while, for forty shillings only, the honest tradesman may be torn from his family and locked up in jail. It is monstrous injustice! I flatter myself, however, the determination of this day will entirely put an end to all such partial proceedings for the future, by passing into a law the bill now under your Lordships' consideration.

I now come to speak upon what, indeed, I would have gladly avoided, had I not been particularly *pointed* at for the part I have taken in this bill. It has been said by a noble Lord on my left hand that I likewise am running the race of popularity. If the noble Lord means by popularity that applause bestowed by after ages on good and virtuous actions, I have long been struggling in that race, to what purpose all-trying time can alone determine. But if the noble Lord means that mushroom popularity which is raised without merit, and lost without a crime, he is much mistaken in his opinion. I defy the noble Lord to point out a single action in my life where the popularity of the times ever had the smallest influence on my determinations. I thank God I have a more permanent and steady rule for my conduct — the dictates of my own breast. Those that have foregone that pleasing adviser, and given up their mind to be the slave of every popular impulse, I sincerely pity. I pity them still more if their vanity leads them to mistake the shouts of a mob for the trumpet of their fame. Experience might inform them that many who have been saluted with the huzzas of a crowd one day, have received their execrations the next; and many who, by the popularity of their times, have been held up as spotless patriots, have nevertheless appeared upon the historian's page, when truth has triumphed over delusion, the assassins of liberty.

Why, then, the noble Lord can think I am ambitious of present popularity, that echo of folly and shadow of renown, I am at a loss to determine. Besides, I do not know that the bill now before your Lordships will be popular. It depends much upon the caprice of the day. It may not be popular to compel people to pay their debts; and in that case the present must be an unpopular bill. It may not be popular, neither, to take away any of the privileges of Parliament; for I very well remember, and many of your Lordships may remember, that not long ago the popular cry was for the extension of privilege. And so far did they carry it at that time, that it was said that privilege protected members from criminal actions; nay, such was the power of popular prejudices over weak minds, that the very decisions of some of the courts were tinctured with that doctrine.[1] It was undoubtedly an abominable doctrine. I thought so then, and think so still. But, nevertheless, it was a popular doctrine, and came immediately from those who were called the friends of liberty, how deservedly time will show. True liberty, in my opinion, can only exist when justice is equally administered to all—to the King and to the beggar. Where is the justice, then, or where is the law, that protects a member of Parliament more than any other man from the punishment due to his crimes? The laws of this country allow no place nor employment to be a sanctuary for crimes; and, where I have the honor to sit as judge, neither royal favor nor popular applause shall ever protect the guilty.

I have now only to beg pardon for having employed so much of your Lordships' time; and I am very sorry a bill, fraught with so good consequences, has not met with an abler advocate; but I doubt not your Lordships' determination will convince the world that a bill, calculated to contribute so much to the equal distribution of justice as the present, requires, with your Lordships, but very little support.

The act was finally passed.

[1] This refers to the case of Mr. Wilkes, who was arrested under a general warrant for a seditious libel on the King. He was taken before the Court of Common Pleas by a writ of Habeas Corpus, and there pleaded his privilege against arrest as a member of Parliament. The court, with Lord Camden at their head, unanimously decided, that members were free from arrest in all cases except treason, felony, and actual breach of the peace. Whatever may have been the merits of this case, it was unworthy of Lord Mansfield to sneer at Lord Camden and his associates as "weak minds." "As authorities then stood," says Lord Campbell, "I think a court of law was *bound* to decide in favor of privilege in such a case." This, it is believed, has been the general sentiment of the English bar; while all agree that this extension of privilege to criminal cases was wrong in principle, and was very properly set aside a short time after, by a joint resolution of the two houses of Parliament.

JUNIUS.

STAT NOMINIS UMBRA.[1]

The Letters of Junius have taken a permanent place in the eloquence of our language. Though often false in statement and malignant in spirit, they will never cease to be read as specimens of powerful composition: For the union of brilliancy and force, there is nothing superior to them in our literature. Nor is it for his style alone that Junius deserves to be studied. He shows great rhetorical skill in his mode of developing a subject. There is an arrangement of a given mass of thought, which serves to throw it upon the mind with the greatest possible effect. There is another arrangement which defeats its object, and renders the impression feeble or indistinct. Demosthenes was, of all men, most perfectly master of the one; the majority of extemporaneous speakers are equally good examples of the other.

Junius had evidently studied this subject with great care; and it is for the sake of urging it upon the young orator that some of the ablest of his productions will now be given. Happily, the selection is easy. There are ten or twelve of his letters which stand far above the rest for strength of thought and elegance of diction. These will be found below, with the exception of his Letters to Lord Mansfield, which, though highly finished in respect to style, are now universally condemned for their errors, both in law and fact, and their unmerited abuse of the greatest of English jurists. In regard to his treatment of others, it is hardly necessary to say that the statements of Junius are to be taken with great allowance. He was an unscrupulous political partisan; and though much that he said of the Duke of Grafton and the other objects of his vengeance was strictly true, they were by no means so weak or profligate as he here represents them. We might as well take Pope's Satires for a faithful exhibition of men and manners in the days of George II.

It is, therefore, only as an orator—for such he undoubtedly was in public life, and such he truly is in these letters—that we are now to consider him. In this character his writings are worthy of the closest study, especially in respect to the quality alluded to above. Each of these letters was the result of severe and protracted labor. We should have known it, if he had not himself avowed the fact, for we see every where the marks of elaborate forecast and revision; and we learn, from his private correspondence with Woodfall, that he expended on their composition an amount of anxiety and effort which hardly any other writer, especially one so proud, would have been willing to acknowledge. Yet it is certain that by far the greater part of all this toil was bestowed, not upon the language, but on the selection and arrangement of his ideas. His mind, in early life, had clearly been subjected to the severest logical training. Composition, with him, was the creation of a *system* of thought, in which every thing is made subordinate to a just order and sequence of ideas. One thought grows out of another in regular succession. His reasonings

1 This celebrated motto was taken from the first book of Lucan's Pharsalia, line 135. The poet there speaks of Pompey, when he entered into the war with Cesar, as having his name, or reputation, chiefly in the *past;* and adds, in reference to this idea, "Stat magni nominis umbra" — He stands the shadow of a mighty name. When the author of these letters collected them into a volume, he beautifully appropriated these words to himself, with the omission of the word *magni*, and a change of application. He placed them on the title-page, in connection with the word Junius, which "stands the shadow of a name," whose secret was intrusted to no one, and was never to be revealed.

often take the form of a syllogism, though usually with the omission of one of the terms; and we never find him betrayed into that careless diffusion of style so common with those who are ignorant of the principles of logic. In this respect, the writings of Junius will amply repay the closest study and analysis. Let the young orator enter completely into the scope and design of the author. Let him watch the under-current of his thoughts and feelings. Let him observe how perfectly every thing coincides to produce the desired impression—the statement of principles and the reference to facts, the shadings of thought and the colorings of imagery. Let him take one of the more striking passages, and remark the dexterous *preparation* by which each of its several parts is so shaped that the leading thoughts come forward to the best advantage; clear in all their relations, standing boldly out, unencumbered by secondary ideas, and thus fitted to strike the mind with full and undivided force. Such a study of Junius will prepare the young reader to enter into the Logic of Thought. It will lead to the formation of a severe intellectual taste, which is the best guard against the dangers of hasty composition, and the still greater dangers of extemporaneous speaking. Such speaking can not be dispensed with. On the contrary, it is becoming more and more essential to the success of public men in every department of life. It is, therefore, of the highest importance for the student in oratory to be familiar with models which shall preserve the purity of his style, and aid him in the formation of those intellectual habits without which there can be neither clearness, nor force, nor continuity of thought in extemporaneous speaking. One of our most eloquent advocates, the late William Wirt, whose early training was of a different kind, remarked, in an address delivered not long before his death, that here lay the chief deficiency of our public speakers—that the want of severe intellectual discipline was the great want of American orators.

There is also another lesson to be learned from Junius, viz., *the art of throwing away unnecessary ideas*. A large proportion of the thoughts which rise to the mind in first considering a subject, are not really essential to its clear and full development. No one ever felt this more strongly than Junius. He had studied in the school of the classics; he had caught the spirit of the Grecian oratory; and he knew that the first element of its power was a rigid scrutiny of the ideas to be brought forward, and a stern rejection of every form of thought, however plausible or attractive, which was not clearly indispensable to the attainment of his object. He learned, too, in the same school, another lesson of equal importance, in relation to the ideas selected for use. He saw how much could be done to abridge their statement, and set aside the necessity of qualifying terms and clauses, by such an arrangement of the leading thoughts that each should throw light upon the other, and all unite in one full, determinate impression. Our language is, indeed, poorly fitted for such purposes. It is a weak and imperfect instrument compared with others, whose varied inflections and numerous illative particles afford the readiest means of graceful transition, and of binding ideas together in close-compacted masses. Such as it is, however, Junius has used it to the utmost advantage. In his best passages, there is a fine compression of thought, arising from the skillful disposition of his materials, which it is far more easy to admire than to imitate. Not an idea is excluded which could promote his object. It is all there, but in the narrowest compass. The stroke is a single one, because nothing more is needed; and it takes its full effect, because there is nothing in the way to weaken the force of the blow. He has thus given us some of the best specimens in our language of that "rich economy of expression," which was so much studied by the great writers of antiquity.

There is only one more characteristic of Junius which will here be noticed. It is the wonderful power he possessed of *insinuating* ideas into the mind without giving them a formal or direct expression. Voltaire is the only writer who ever enjoyed this power in an equal degree, and he used it chiefly in his hours of gayety and sport. Junius used it for the most serious purposes of his life. He made it the instrument of torturing his victims. It is a curious inquiry why this species of indirect attack is so peculiarly painful to persons of education and refinement. The question is not why they suffer more than others from contempt and ridicule, but why sarcasm, irony, and the other forms of attack by *insinuation*, have such extraordinary power to distress their feelings. Perhaps the reason is, that such persons are peculiarly qualified to understand and appreciate these forms of ingenious derision. The ignorant and vulgar have no power to comprehend them, and are therefore beyond their reach. But it is otherwise with men of cultivated minds. It is impossible for such men not to admire the efforts of genius; and when they find these efforts turned against themselves, and see all the force of a subtle intellect employed in thus dexterously insinuating suspicion or covering them with ridicule, whatever may be their consciousness of innocence, they can not but feel deeply. Coarse invective and reproachful language would be a relief to the mind. Any one can cry "fool," "liar," or "scoundrel." But to sketch a picture in which real traits of character are so ingeniously distorted that every one will recognize the likeness and apply the name, requires no ordinary force of genius; and it is not wonderful that men of the firmest spirit shrink from such an assailant. We have seen how Lord Mansfield "suffered" under inflictions of this kind from Lord Chatham, till he could endure them no longer, and abruptly fled the contest. In addition to this, he who is thus assailed knows that the talent which he feels so keenly will be perfectly understood by others, and that attacks of this kind diffuse their influence, like a subtle poison, throughout the whole republic of letters. They will be read, he is aware, not only by that large class who dwell with malicious delight on the pages of detraction, but by multitudes whose good opinion he prizes most highly—in whose minds all that is dear to him in reputation will be mingled with images of ridicule and contempt, which can not fail to be remembered for their ingenuity, how much soever they may be condemned for their spirit. For these and perhaps other reasons, this covert mode of attack has always been the most potent engine of wounding the feelings and destroying character. Junius had not only the requisite talent and bitterness to wield this engine with terrible effect, but he stood on a vantage ground in using it, such as no other writer ever enjoyed. He had means of secret information, which men have labored in vain to trace out or conceive of. His searching eye penetrated equally into the retired circles of domestic life, the cabinets of ministers, and the closet of the King.[2] Persons of the highest rank and most callous feelings were filled with alarm when they found their darkest intrigues laid open, their most hidden motives detected, their duplicity and tergiversation exposed to view, and even their private vices blazoned before the eyes of the public. Nor did Junius, on these points, very scrupulously confine himself to the truth. He gave currency to some of the basest slanders of the day, which he could not but know were unfounded, in order to blacken the char-

[2] The following is a curious instance. About two years after these Letters were commenced, Garrick learned confidentially from Woodfall that it was doubtful whether Junius would continue to write much longer. He flew instantly with the news to Mr. Ramus, one of the royal pages, who hastened with it to the King, then residing at Richmond. Within two days, Garrick received, through Woodfall, the following note from Junius:

"I am very exactly informed of your impertinent inquiries, and of the information you so busily sent to Richmond, and with what triumph and exultation it was received. I knew every particular of it the next day. Now, mark me, vagabond! keep to your pantomimes, or be assured you shall hear of it. Meddle no more, thou busy informer! It is in my power to make you curse the hour in which you dared to interfere with JUNIUS."

Miss Seward states, in her Letters, that on the evening after the receipt of this note, Garrick, for once in his life, played badly.

acter of his opponents. He stood, in the mean time, unassailable himself, wrapped, like Æneas at the court of Dido, in the cloud around him, affording no opportunity for others to retort his accusations, to examine his past conduct, or to scan his present motives. With all these advantages, he toiled as few men ever toiled, to gain that exquisite finish of style, that perfect union of elegance and strength, which could alone express the refined bitterness of his feelings. He seemed to exult in gathering up the blunted weapons of attack thrown aside by others, and giving them a keener edge and a finer polish. "Ample justice," says he to one whom he assailed, "has been done by abler pens than mine to the separate merits of your life and character. Let it be my humble office to collect the scattered sweets, *till their united virtue tortures the sense.*" In the success of these labors he felt the proud consciousness that he was speaking to other generations besides his own, and declared concerning one of his victims, "I would pursue him through life, and try the last exertion of my abilities to *preserve the perishable infamy of his name, and make it immortal.*"[3]

This reliance of Junius on his extraordinary powers of composition, naturally leads us to consider his style. We might pronounce it perfect, if it were only free from a slight appearance of labor, and were as easy and idiomatic as it is strong, pointed, and brilliant. But it seems hardly possible to unite all these qualities in the highest degree. Where strength and compactness are carried to their utmost limit, there will almost of necessity be something rigid and unbending. A man in plate armor can not move with the freedom and lightness of an athlete. But Junius, on the whole, has been wonderfully successful in overcoming these difficulties. His sentences have generally an easy flow, with a dignified and varied rhythmus, and a harmonious cadence. Clear in their construction, they grow in strength as they advance, and come off at the close always with liveliness, and often with a sudden, stinging force. He is peculiarly happy in the *choice of words.* It has been said of Shakspeare, that one might as well attempt to push a brick out of its place in a well-constructed wall, as to alter a single expression. In his finest passages, the same is true of Junius. He gives you the exact word, he brings out the most delicate shadings of thought, he throws it upon the mind with elastic force, and you say, "What is written is written!" There are, indeed, instances of bad grammar and inaccurate expression, but these may be ascribed, in most cases, to the difficulty and danger of his correcting the press. Still, there is reason to believe that he was not an author by profession. Certain words and forms of construction seem plainly to show, that he had never been trained to the minuter points of authorship. And, perhaps, for this very reason, he was a better writer. He could think of nothing but how to express his ideas with the utmost vividness and force. Hence he gave them a frank and fearless utterance, which, modified by a taste like his, has imparted to his best passages a perfection of style which is never reached by mere mechanical labor. Among other things, Junius understood better than most writers where the true strength of language lies, viz., in the nouns and verbs. He is, therefore, sparing in the use of qualifying expressions.[4] He relies mainly for effect on the frame-work of thought. In the filling out of his ideas, where qualifying terms must of course be employed, he

[3] How much Junius relied for success on the perfection of his statement, may be learned from the following fact. When he had hastily thrown off a letter containing a number of coarse and unguarded expressions, of which he was afterward ashamed, he coolly requested Woodfall to say in a subsequent number, "We have some reason to suspect, that the last letter signed Junius in this paper *was not written by the real Junius,* though the observation escaped us at the time!" There is nothing equal to this in all the annals of literature, unless it be Cicero's famous letter to Lucceius, in which he asks the historian to *lie* a little in his favor in recording the events of his consulship, for the sake of making him a greater man!

[4] Voltaire somewhere remarks, that the adjective is the greatest enemy of the substantive, though they agree together in gender, number, and case.

rarely uses intensives. His adverbs and adjectives are nearly all descriptive, and are designed to shade or to color the leading thoughts with increased exactness, and thus set them before the mind in bolder relief or with more graphic effect. He employs contrast also, with much success, to heighten the impression. No one has shown greater skill in crushing discordant thoughts together in a single mass, and giving them, by their juxtaposition, a new and startling force. Hardly any one but Demosthenes has made so happy a use of antithesis. His only fault is, that he now and then allows it to run away with his judgment, and to sink into epigram. The *imagery* of Junius is uncommonly brilliant. It was the source of much of his power. He showed admirable dexterity in working his bold and burning metaphors into the very texture of his style. He was also equally happy in the use of plainer images, drawn from the ordinary concerns of life, and intended not so much to adorn, as to illustrate and enforce. A few instances of each will show his wide and easy command of figurative language. In warning his countrymen against a readiness to be satisfied with some temporary gain, at the expense of great and permanent interests, he says, "In the shipwreck of the state, trifles float and are preserved, while every thing solid and valuable sinks to the bottom and is lost forever." Speaking of the numerous writers in favor of the ministry, he says, "They pile up reluctant quarto upon solid folio, as if their labors, because they are gigantic, could contend with truth and heaven."[5] Again, "The very sunshine you live in is a prelude to your dissolution: when you are ripe, you shall be plucked." Exhorting the King no longer to give importance to Wilkes by making him the object of royal persecution, he says, "The gentle breath of peace would leave him on the surface neglected and unremoved. It is only the tempest that lifts him from his place." And again, in a higher strain, "The rays of royal indignation collected upon him, served only to illuminate and could not consume." The last instance of this kind which will now be cited, has been already referred to on a preceding page, as perhaps suggested by a classical allusion of Lord Chatham. If so, it is a beautiful example of the way in which one man of genius often improves upon another. Many have pronounced it the finest metaphor in our language. Speaking of the King's sacrifice of honor in not instantly resenting the seizure of the Falkland Islands, he says, "A clear, unblemished character comprehends not only the integrity that will not offer, but the spirit that will not submit to an injury; and whether it belongs to an individual or to a community, it is the foundation of peace, of independence, and of safety. Private credit is wealth; public honor is security. *The feather that adorns the royal bird supports his flight. Strip him of his plumage, and you fix him to the earth.*" Such are some of the characteristics of the style of Junius, which made Mr. Mathias, author of the Pursuits of Literature, rank him among the English classics, in the place assigned to Livy and Tacitus among the ancients.

Reference has already been made to the violent passions of Junius, and his want of candor toward most of his opponents. Still it will be seen, from the following sentiments contained in a private letter, that in his cooler moments he had just and elevated views concerning the design of political discussions. He is speaking of an argument he had just stated in favor of rotten boroughs, and goes on to say, "The man who fairly and completely answers this argument, shall have my thanks and my applause. My heart is already with him. I am ready to be converted. I admire his morality, and would gladly subscribe to the articles of his faith. Grateful as I am to the GOOD BEING, whose bounty has imparted to me this reasoning intellect, whatever it is, I hold myself proportionably indebted to him, whose enlightened understanding communicates another ray of knowledge to mine. But neither should

[5] Referring to the story of the giants' tearing up mountains, and piling Pelion upon Ossa, in their contest with the gods.

I think the most exalted faculties of the human mind a gift worthy of the divinity, nor any assistance in the improvement of them a subject of gratitude to my fellow-creatures, if I were not satisfied that *really to inform the understanding, corrects and enlarges the heart.*" "Si sic omnia!" Would that all were thus! Happy were it for the character of Junius as a man, if he had always been guided as a writer by such views and feelings!

Who was Junius? Volumes have been written to answer this question, and it remains still undecided. At the end of eighty years of inquiry and discussion, after the claims of nearly twenty persons have been examined and set aside, only two names remain before the public as candidates for this distinction.[6] They are Sir Philip Francis, and Lord George Sackville, afterward Lord George Germain. In favor and against each of these, there is circumstantial evidence of considerable weight. Neither of them has left any specimens of style which are equal in elegance and force to the more finished productions of Junius. Lord George Sackville, however, is far inferior in this respect. He was never a practical writer; and it seems impossible to believe, that the mind which expressed itself in the compositions he has left us, could ever have been raised by any excitement of emotion or fervor of effort, into a capacity to produce the Letters of Junius. Sir Philip Francis was confessedly a far more able writer. He had studied composition from early life. He was diligent in his attendance on Parliament; and he reported some of Lord Chatham's speeches with uncommon elegance and force. If we must choose between the two—if there is no other name to be brought forward, and this seems hardly possible—the weight of evidence is certainly in his favor. Mr. Macaulay has summed it up with his usual ability in the following terms:

"Was he the author of the Letters of Junius? Our own firm belief is, that he was. The external evidence is, we think, such as would support a verdict in a civil, nay, in a criminal proceeding. The handwriting of Junius is the very peculiar handwriting of Francis, slightly disguised. As to the position, pursuits, and connections of Junius, the following are the most important facts which can be considered as clearly proved: First, that he was acquainted with the technical forms of the Secretary of State's office; secondly, that he was intimately acquainted with the business of the War office; thirdly, that he, during the year 1770, attended debates in the House of Lords, and took notes of speeches, particularly of the speeches of Lord Chatham; fourthly, that he bitterly resented the appointment of Mr. Chamier to the place of deputy Secretary at War; fifthly, that he was bound by some strong tie to the first Lord Holland. Now Francis passed some years in the Secretary of State's office. He was subsequently chief clerk of the War office. He repeatedly mentioned that he had himself, in 1770, heard speeches of Lord Chatham; and some of those speeches were actually printed from his notes. He resigned his clerkship at the War office from resentment at the appointment of Mr. Chamier. It was by Lord Holland that he was first introduced into the public service. Now, here are five marks, all of which ought to be found in Junius. They are all five found in Francis. We do not believe that more than two of them can be found in any other person whatever. If this argument does not settle the question, there is an end of all reasoning on circumstantial evidence.

"The internal evidence seems to us to point the same way. The style of Francis bears a strong resemblance to that of Junius; nor are we disposed to admit, what is generally taken for granted, that the acknowledged compositions of Francis are very decidedly inferior to the anonymous letters. The argument from inferiority, at all events, is one which may be urged with at least equal force against every claim-

[6] It has been shown in the London Athenæum, that the recent attempts to make the younger Lyttleton Junius, and also a Scottish surgeon named Maclain, are entire failures.

ant that has ever been mentioned, with the single exception of Burke, who certainly was not Junius. And what conclusion, after all, can be drawn from mere inferiority? Every writer must produce his best work; and the interval between his best work and his second best work may be very wide indeed. Nobody will say that the best letters of Junius are more decidedly superior to the acknowledged works of Francis, than three or four of Corneille's tragedies to the rest; than three or four of Ben Jonson's comedies to the rest; than the Pilgrim's Progress to the other works of Bunyan; than Don Quixote to the other works of Cervantes. Nay, it is certain that the Man in the Mask, whoever he may have been, was a most unequal writer. To go no farther than the Letters which bear the signature of Junius—the Letter to the King, and the Letters to Horne Tooke, have little in common except the asperity; and asperity was an ingredient seldom wanting either in the writings or in the speeches of Francis.

"Indeed, one of the strongest reasons for believing that Francis was Junius, is the moral resemblance between the two men. It is not difficult, from the letters which, under various signatures, are known to have been written by Junius, and from his dealings with Woodfall and others, to form a tolerably correct notion of his character. He was clearly a man not destitute of real patriotism and magnanimity—a man whose vices were not of a sordid kind. But he must also have been a man in the highest degree arrogant and insolent—a man prone to malevolence, and prone to the error of mistaking his malevolence for public virtue. 'Doest thou well to be angry?' was the question asked in old time of the Hebrew prophet. And he answered, 'I do well.' This was evidently the temper of Junius; and to this cause we attribute the savage cruelty which disgraces several of his Letters. No man is so merciless as he who, under a strong self-delusion, confounds his antipathies with his duties. It may be added, that Junius, though allied with the democratic party by common enmities, was the very opposite of a democratic politician. While attacking individuals with a ferocity which perpetually violated all the laws of literary warfare, he regarded the most defective parts of old constitutions with a respect amounting to pedantry—pleaded the cause of Old Sarum with fervor, and contemptuously told the capitalists of Manchester and Leeds that, if they wanted votes, they might buy land and become freeholders of Lancashire and Yorkshire. All this, we believe, might stand, with scarcely any change, for a character of Philip Francis."[7]

[7] Charles Butler, in his Reminiscences, suggests a mixed hypothesis on this subject. He thinks that Sir Philip Francis was too young to have produced these Letters, which indicate very thorough and extensive reading, and especially a profound knowledge of human character. He mentions, likewise, that Junius shows himself in the most unaffected manner, throughout his private correspondence with Woodfall, to have been not only a man of high rank, but of ample fortune—promising to indemnify him against any loss he might suffer from being prosecuted, a thing which Francis, with a mere clerkship in the War office, was unable to do. He therefore thinks that Sir Philip may have been the organ of some older man of the highest rank and wealth, who has chosen to remain in proud obscurity. It is certain that some one acted in conjunction with Junius, for he says in his fifty-first note to Woodfall, "The gentleman who transacts the conveyancing part of this correspondence, tells me there was much difficulty last night." This person was once seen by a clerk of Woodfall, as he withdrew from the door, after having thrown in a Letter of Junius. He was a person who "wore a bag and a sword," showing that he was not a mere servant, but, as Junius described him, a "gentleman." It seems probable, also, that the hand of another was used in transcribing these Letters, for Junius says concerning one of them, "You shall have the Letter some time to-morrow; it can not be corrected and *copied* before;" and again, of another, "The inclosed, though begun within these few days, has been greatly labored. It is very *correctly copied*." This, though not decisive, has the air of one who is speaking of what another person had been doing, not himself. If this be admitted, Mr. Butler suggests that these Letters may actually have been sent to Woodfall in the handwriting of Francis, without his being the original author. Still, he by no means considers him a mere copyist. Francis may have collected valuable information; may have given very important hints; may even have shared, to some extent, in the composition,

But, whatever may be thought of the origin of these Letters, it is not difficult to understand the political relations of the writer, and the feelings by which he was actuated. A few remarks on this subject will close the present sketch.

The author of these Letters, as we learn from Woodfall, had been for some years an active political partisan. He had written largely for the public prints under various signatures, and with great ability. A crisis now arrived which induced him to come forward under a new name, and urged him by still higher motives to the utmost exertion of his powers. Lord Chatham's " checkered and dovetailed" cabinet had fallen to pieces, and the Duke of Grafton, as Junius expressed it, became " minister by accident," at the close of 1767. He immediately endeavored to strengthen himself on every side. He yielded to the wishes of the King by making Lord North Chancellor of the Exchequer, and by raising Mr. Jenkinson, the organ of Lord Bute, to higher office and influence. Thus he gave a decided ascendency to the Tories. On the other hand, he endeavored to conciliate Lord Rockingham and the Duke of Bedford by very liberal proposals. But these gentlemen differing as to the lead of the House, the Bedford interest prevailed ; Lord Weymouth, a member of that family, was made Secretary of the Home Department ; while Lord Rockingham was sent back to the ranks of Opposition under a sense of wrong and insult. Six months, down almost to the middle of 1768, were spent in these negotiations and arrangements.

These things wrought powerfully on the mind of Junius, who was a Grenville or Rockingham Whig. But in addition to this, he had strong private animosities. He not only saw with alarm and abhorrence the triumph of Tory principles, but he cherished the keenest personal resentment toward the King and most of his ministers. Those, especially, who had deserted their former Whig associates, he regarded as traitors to the cause of liberty. He therefore now determined to give full scope to his feelings, and to take up a system of attack far more galling to his opponents than had ever yet been adopted. One thing was favorable to such a design. Parliament was to expire within a few months ; and every blow now struck would give double alarm and distress to the government, while it served also to inflame the minds of the people, and rouse them to a more determined resistance in the approaching elections. Accordingly, at the close of the Christmas holidays, when the business of the session really commences, he addressed his first Letter to the printer of the Public Advertiser, under date of January 21, 1769. It was elaborated with great care ; but its most striking peculiarity was the daring spirit of personal attack by which it was characterized. Junius, for the first time, broke through the barriers thrown around the monarch by the maxim, " the King can do no wrong." He assailed him like any other man, though in more courtly and guarded language. Assuming an air of great respect for his motives, he threw out the most subtle insinuations, mingled with the keenest irony, as to his " love of low intrigue," and " the treacherous amusement of double and triple negotiations." It was plainly his intention not only to distress, but to terrify. He represented the people as driven to the verge of desperation. He hinted at the possible consequences. He spoke of the crisis as one " from which a reasonable man can expect no remedy but *poison*, no relief but *death*." He attacked the ministry in more direct terms, commenting with great severity on the

or, at least, the revision of the Letters ; for the writer was plainly not an author by profession. In short, Francis may have been to him, in respect to these Letters, what Burke was more fully to Lord Rockingham, and what Alexander Hamilton was at times to Washington. On this theory the government would have the same motives to buy off Sir Philip Francis, a thing they seem plainly to have done when these Letters stopped so suddenly in 1772. It may have been a condition made by Junius in favor of his friend. To have made it for himself seems inconsistent with his whole character and bearing, both in his Letters to the public and his confidential communications to Woodfall. The theory is, at least, an ingenious one, and has therefore been here stated. It has, however, very serious difficulties, as the reader will easily perceive.

character of those who filled the principal departments of state, and declaring, "We need look no farther for the cause of every mischief which befalls us." "It is not a casual concurrence of calamitous circumstances—it is the pernicious hand of government alone, that can make a whole people desperate." All this was done with a dignity, force, and elegance entirely without parallel in the columns of a newspaper. The attention of the public was strongly arrested. The poet Gray, in his correspondence, speaks of the absorbing power of this Letter over his mind, when he took it up casually for the first time at a country inn, where he had stopped for refreshment on a journey. He was unable to lay it down, or even to think of the food before him, until he had read it over and over again with the most painful interest. The same profound sensation was awakened in the higher political circles throughout the kingdom.

Still it may be doubted whether the writer, at this time, had formed any definite plan of continuing these Letters. Very possibly, except for a circumstance now to be mentioned, he might have stopped here; and the name of Junius have been known only in our literature by this single specimen of eloquent vituperation. But he was instantly attacked. As if for the very purpose of compelling him to go on, and of giving notoriety to his efforts, Sir William Draper, Knight of the Bath, came out under his *own signature*, charging him with "maliciously traducing the best characters of the kingdom," and going on particularly to defend the Commander in Chief, the Marquess of Granby, against the severe imputations of this Letter. Junius himself could not have asked, or conceived of, any thing more perfectly suited to make him conspicuous in the eyes of the public. Sir William had the character of being an elegant scholar, and had gained high distinction as an officer in the army by the capture of Manilla, the capital of the Philippine Islands, in 1762. It was no light thing for such a man to throw himself into the lists without any personal provocation, and challenge a combat with this unknown champion. It was the highest possible testimony to his powers. Junius saw his advantage. He perfectly understood his antagonist—an open-hearted and incautious man, vain of his literary attainments, and uncommonly sensitive to ridicule and contempt. He seized at once on the weak points of Sir William's letter. He turned the argument against him. He overwhelmed him with derision. He showed infinite dexterity in wresting every weapon from his hands, and in turning all his praises of the Marquess, and apologies for his failings, into new instruments of attack. "It is *you*, Sir William, who make your friend appear awkward and ridiculous, by giving him a *laced suit of tawdry qualifications* which Nature never intended him to wear!" "It is you who have taken pains to represent your friend *in the character of a drunken landlord*, who deals out his promises as liberally as his liquor, and will suffer no man to leave his table either sorrowful or sober!" He then turned upon Sir William himself. He glanced at some of the leading transactions of his life. He goaded him with the most humiliating insinuations and interrogatories. He hinted at the motives which the public would impute to him, in thus coming out from his retirement at Clifton; and concluded by asking in a tone of lofty contempt, "And do you now, after a retreat not very like that of Scipio, presume to intrude yourself, unthought of, uncalled for, upon the patience of the public?" Never was an assailant so instantaneously put on the defensive. Instead of silencing the "traducer," and making him the object of public indignation, he was himself dragged to the confessional, or rather placed as a culprit at the bar of the public. His feelings at this sudden change seem much to have resembled those of a traveler in the forests of Africa, when he finds himself, without a moment's warning, wrapped in the folds of a boa constrictor, darting from above, and crushed beneath its weight. He exclaimed piteously against this "uncandid Junius," his "abominable scandals," his delight in putting men to "the rack," and "mangling their carcasses with a hatchet." He quoted Virgil, and made a feeling allusion to Æsop's Fables : " You bite against a file ; cease, viper !" Junius replied in three Letters, two of which will be found below. He tells Sir William that an " academical education had given him an unlimited command over the most beautiful figures of speech." " Masks, hatchets, racks, and vipers dance through your letters in all the mazes of metaphorical confusion. These are the gloomy companions of a disturbed imagination ; the melancholy madness of poetry, without the inspiration." As the correspondence went on, Sir William did, indeed, clear himself of the imputations thrown out by Junius affecting his personal honesty, but he was so shocked and confounded by the overmastering power of his antagonist, that he soon gave up the contest. Some months after, when he saw these Letters collected and republished in a volume, he again came forward to complain of their injustice. "*Hæret lateri lethalis arundo,*"[8] was the savage exclamation of Junius, when he saw the writhings of his prostrate foe. Such was the first encounter of Junius before the public. The whole nation looked on with astonishment ; and from this hour his name was known as familiarly in every part of the kingdom as that of Chatham or Johnson. It was a name of terror to the King and his ministers ; and of pride and exultation to thousands throughout the empire, not only of those who sympathized in his malignant feelings, but those who, like Burke, condemned his spirit, and yet considered him engaged in a just cause, and hailed him as a defender of the invaded rights of the people.

Junius now resumed his attack on the ministry with still greater boldness and virulence. After assailing the Duke of Grafton repeatedly on individual points, he came out in two Letters, under date of May 30th and July 8th, 1769, with a general review of his Grace's life and conduct. These are among his most finished productions, and will be given below. On the 19th of September, he attacked the Duke of Bedford, whose interests had been preferred to those of Lord Rockingham in the ministerial arrangements mentioned above. This Letter has even more force than the two preceding ones, and will also be found in this collection. Three months after, December 19th, 1769, appeared his celebrated Letter to the King, the longest and most elaborate of all his performances. The reader will agree with Mr. Burke in saying, " it contains many *bold truths* by which a wise prince might profit." Lord Chatham now made his appearance on the stage, after an illness of three years ; and at the opening of Parliament, January 9th, 1770, took up the cause with more than his accustomed boldness and eloquence. Without partaking of the bitter spirit of Junius, he maintained his principles on all the great questions of the day, in their fullest extent. He at once declared in the face of the country, " A breach has been made in the Constitution—the battlements are dismantled—the citadel is open to the first invader—the walls totter—the Constitution is not tenable. What remains, then, but for us to stand foremost in the breach, to repair it, or perish in it ?" The result has already been stated in connection with that and his other speech on this subject, p. 114–18. At the end of *nineteen* days, January 28th, 1770, the Duke of Grafton was driven from power ! About a fortnight after, Junius addressed his fallen adversary in a Letter of great force, which closes the extracts from his writings in this volume. Lord North's ministry now commenced. Junius continued his labors with various ability, but with little success, nearly two years longer, until, in the month of January, 1772, the King remarked to a friend in confidence, " Junius is known, and will write no more." Such proved to be the fact. His last performance was dated January 21st, 1772, three years to a day from his first great Letter to the printer of the Public Advertiser. Within a few months Sir PHILIP FRANCIS was appointed to one of the highest stations of profit and trust in India, at a distance of fifteen thousand miles from the seat of English politics !

[8] Still rankles in his side the fatal dart.

LETTERS OF JUNIUS.

LETTER

TO THE PRINTER OF THE PUBLIC ADVERTISER.[1]

SIR,—The submission of a free people to the executive authority of government is no more than a compliance with laws which they themselves have enacted. While the national honor is firmly maintained abroad, and while justice is impartially administered at home, the obedience of the subject will be voluntary, cheerful, and, I might say, almost unlimited. A generous nation is grateful even for the preservation of its rights, and willingly extends the respect due to the office of a good prince into an affection for his person. Loyalty, in the heart and understanding of an Englishman, is a rational attachment to the guardian of the laws. Prejudices and passion have sometimes carried it to a criminal length; and, whatever foreigners may imagine, we know that Englishmen have erred as much in a mistaken zeal for particular persons and families, as they ever did in defense of what they thought most dear and interesting to themselves.

It naturally fills us with resentment to see such a temper insulted and abused.[2] In reading the history of a free people, whose rights have been invaded, we are interested in their cause. Our own feelings tell us how long they ought to have submitted, and at what moment it would have been treachery to themselves not to have resisted. How much warmer will be our resentment, if experience should bring the fatal example home to ourselves!

The situation of this country is alarming enough to rouse the attention of every man who pretends to a concern for the public welfare. Appearances justify suspicion; and, when the safety of a nation is at stake, suspicion is a just ground of inquiry. Let us enter into it with candor and decency. Respect is due to the station of ministers; and if a resolution must at last be taken, there is none so likely to be supported with firmness as that which has been adopted with moderation.

The ruin or prosperity of a state depends so

---

[1] Dated January 21, 1769. There is great regularity in the structure of this letter. The first two paragraphs contain the *exordium.* The *transition* follows in the third paragraph, leading to the main *proposition*, which is contained in the fourth, viz., "that the existing discontent and disasters of the nation were justly chargeable on the King and ministry." The next eight paragraphs are intended to give the *proof* of this proposition, by reviewing the chief departments of government, and endeavoring to show the incompetency or maladministration of the men to whom they were intrusted. A *recapitulation* follows in the last paragraph but one, leading to a restatement of the proposition in still broader terms. This is strengthened in the *conclusion* by the remark, that if the nation should escape from its desperate condition through some signal interposition of Divine Providence, posterity would not believe the history of the times, or consider it possible that England should have survived a crisis "so full of terror and despair."

[2] We have here the starting point of the exordium, as it lay originally in the mind of Junius, viz., that the English nation was "insulted and abused" by the King and ministers. But this was too strong a statement to be brought out abruptly. Junius therefore went back, and prepared the way by showing in successive sentences, (1.) Why a free people obey the laws—"because they have themselves enacted them." (2.) That this obedience is ordinarily cheerful, and almost unlimited. (3.) That such obedience to the guardian of the laws naturally leads to a strong affection for his person. (4.) That this affection (as shown in their history) had often been excessive among the English, who were, in fact, peculiarly liable to a "mistaken zeal for particular persons and families." Hence they were equally liable (this is not said, but implied) to have their loyalty imposed upon; and therefore the feeling then so prevalent was well founded, that the King, in his rash counsels and reckless choice of ministers, *must* have been taking advantage of the generous confidence of his people, and playing on the easiness of their temper. If so, they were *indeed* insulted and abused. The exordium, then, is a complete chain of logical deduction, and the case is fully made out, provided the popular feeling referred to was correct. And here we see where the fallacy of Junius lies, whenever he is in the wrong. It is in *taking for granted* one of the steps of his reasoning. He does not, in this case, even mention the feeling alluded to in direct terms. He knew it was beating in the hearts of the people; his whole preceding train of thought was calculated to justify and inflame it; and he therefore leaps at once to the conclusion it involves, and addresses them as actually filled with *resentment* "to see such a temper insulted and abused." The feeling, in this instance, was to a great extent well founded, and so far his logic is complete. In other cases his assumption is a false one. He lays hold of some slander of the day, some distorted statement of facts, some maxim which is only half true, some prevailing passion or prejudice, and, dexterously intermingling them with a train of thought which in every other respect is logical and just, he hurries the mind to a conclusion which seems necessarily involved in the premises. Hardly any writer has so much art and plausibility in thus misleading the mind.

much upon the administration of its government, that, to be acquainted with the merit of a ministry, we need only observe the condition of the people. If we see them obedient to the laws, prosperous in their industry, united at home, and respected abroad, we may reasonably presume that their affairs are conducted by men of experience, abilities, and virtue. If, on the contrary, we see a universal spirit of distrust and dissatisfaction, a rapid decay of trade, dissensions in all parts of the empire, and a total loss of respect in the eyes of foreign powers, we may pronounce, without hesitation, that the government of that country is weak, distracted, and corrupt. The multitude, in all countries, are patient to a certain point. Ill usage may rouse their indignation, and hurry them into excesses, *but the original fault is in government.*[3] Perhaps there never was an instance of a change in the circumstances and temper of a whole nation, so sudden and extraordinary as that which the misconduct of ministers has, within these very few years, produced in Great Britain. When our gracious sovereign ascended the throne, we were a flourishing and a contented people. If the personal virtues of a king could have insured the happiness of his subjects, the scene could not have altered so entirely as it has done. The idea of uniting all parties, of trying all characters, and distributing the offices of state by rotation, was gracious and benevolent to an extreme, though it has not yet produced the many salutary effects which were intended by it. To say nothing of the wisdom of such plan, it undoubtedly arose from an unbounded goodness of heart, in which folly had no share. It was not a capricious partiality to new faces; it was not a natural turn for low intrigue, nor was it the treacherous amusement of double and triple negotiations. No, sir, it arose from a continued anxiety in the purest of all possible hearts for the general welfare.[4] Unfortunately for us, the event has not been answerable to the design. After a rapid succession of changes, we are reduced to that change which hardly any change can mend. Yet there is no extremity of distress which of itself ought to reduce a great nation to despair. It is not the disorder, but the physician; it is not a casual concurrence of calamitous circumstances, it is the pernicious hand of government, which alone can make a whole people desperate.

Without much political sagacity, or any extraordinary depth of observation, we need only mark how the principal departments of the state are bestowed [distributed], and look no farther for the true cause of every mischief that befalls us.

The finances of a nation, sinking under its debts and expenses, are committed to a young nobleman already ruined by play.[5] Introduced

---

[3] Here is the central idea of the letter—the *proposition* to be proved in respect to the King and his ministers. The former part of this paragraph contains the major premise, the remainder the minor down to the last sentence, which brings out the conclusion in emphatic terms. In order to strengthen the minor, which was the most important premise, he rapidly contrasts the condition of England before and after the King ascended the throne. In doing this, he dilates on those errors of the King which led to, and which account for, so remarkable a change. Thus the conclusion is made doubly strong. This union of severe logic with the finest rhetorical skill in filling out the premises and giving them their utmost effect, furnishes an excellent model for the student in oratory.

[4] In this attack on the King, there is a refined artifice, rarely if ever equaled, in leading the mind gradually forward from the slightest possible insinuation to the bitterest irony. First we have the "uniting of all parties," which is proper and desirable; next, "trying all characters," which suggests decidedly a want of judgment; then "distributing the offices of state by *rotation*," a charge rendered plausible, at least, by the frequent changes of ministers, and involving (if true) a weakness little short of absolute fatuity. The way being thus prepared, what was first insinuated is now openly expressed in the next sentence. The word "*folly*" is applied to the conduct of the King of England in the face of his subjects, and the application rendered doubly severe by the gravest irony. Still, there is one relief. Allusion is made to his "unbounded goodness of heart," from which, in the preceding chain of insinuations, these errors of judgment had been deduced. The next sentence takes this away. It directly ascribes to the King, with an increased severity of ironical denial, some of the meanest passions of royalty, "a capricious partiality for new faces," a "natural love of low intrigue," "the treacherous amusement of double and triple negotiations!" It is unnecessary to remark on the admirable precision and force of the language in these expressions, and, indeed, throughout the whole passage. There had been just enough in the King's conduct for the last seven years to make the people suspect all this, and to weaken or destroy their affection for the Crown. It was all connected with that system of favoritism introduced by Lord Bute, which the nation so much abhorred. Nothing but this would have made them endure for a moment such an attack on their monarch, and especially the absolute mockery with which Junius concludes the whole, by speaking of "the anxiety of the purest of all *possible* hearts for the general welfare!" His entire Letter to the King, with all the rancor ascribed to it by Burke, does not contain so much bitterness and insult as are concentrated in this single passage. While we can not but condemn its spirit, we are forced to acknowledge that there is in this and many other passages of Junius, a rhetorical skill in the evolution of thought which was never surpassed by Demosthenes.

[5] The Duke of Grafton, first Lord of the Treasury. It is unnecessary to remark on the dexterity of connecting with this mention of a treasury, "sinking under its debts and expenses," the idea of its head being a gambler loaded with his own debts, and liable continually to new distresses and temptations from his love of play. The thought is wisely left here. The argument which it implies would be weakened by any attempt to expand it. Junius often reminds us of the great Athenian orator, in thus striking a single blow, and then passing on to some other subject, as he does here to the apostasy of the Duke of Grafton, his inconsistency, caprice, and irresolution.

to act under the auspices of Lord Chatham, and left at the head of affairs by that nobleman's retreat, he became a minister by accident; but, deserting the principles and professions which gave him a moment's popularity, we see him, from every honorable engagement to the public, an apostate by design. As for business, the world yet knows nothing of his talents or resolution, unless a wavering, wayward inconsistency be a mark of genius, and caprice a demonstration of spirit. It may be said, perhaps, that it is his Grace's province, as surely it is his passion, rather to distribute than to save the public money, and that while Lord North is Chancellor of the Exchequer, the first Lord of the Treasury may be as thoughtless and extravagant as he pleases. I hope, however, he will not rely too much on the fertility of Lord North's genius for finance. His Lordship is yet to give us the first proof of his abilities. It may be candid to suppose that he has hitherto voluntarily concealed his talents; intending, perhaps, to astonish the world, when we least expect it, with a knowledge of trade, a choice of expedients, and a depth of resources equal to the necessities, and far beyond the hopes of his country. He must now exert the whole power of his capacity, if he would wish us to forget that, since he has been in office, no plan has been formed, no system adhered to, nor any one important measure adopted for the relief of public credit. If his plan for the service of the current year be not irrevocably fixed on, let me warn him to think seriously of consequences before he ventures to increase the public debt. Outraged and oppressed as we are, this nation will not bear, after a six years' peace, to see new millions borrowed, without any eventual diminution of debt or reduction of interest. The attempt might rouse a spirit of resentment, which might reach beyond the sacrifice of a minister. As to the debt upon the civil list, the people of England expect that it will not be paid without a strict inquiry how it was incurred.[6] If it must be paid by Parliament, let me advise the Chancellor of the Exchequer to think of some better expedient than a lottery. To support an expensive war, or in circumstances of absolute necessity, a lottery may perhaps be allowable; but, besides that it is at all times the very worst way of raising money upon the people, I think it ill becomes the royal dignity to have the debts of a prince provided for, like the repairs of a country bridge or a decayed hospital. The management of the King's affairs in the House of Commons can not be more disgraced than it has been. A leading minister repeatedly called down for absolute ignorance—ridiculous motions ridiculously withdrawn—deliberate plans disconcerted, and a week's preparation of graceful oratory lost in a moment, give us some, though not an adequate idea of Lord North's parliamentary abilities and influence.[7] Yet, before he had the misfortune of being Chancellor of the Exchequer, he was neither an object of derision to his enemies, nor of melancholy pity to his friends.

A series of inconsistent measures had alienated the colonies from their duty as subjects and from their natural affection to their common country. When Mr. Grenville was placed at the head of the treasury, he felt the impossibility of Great Britain's supporting such an establishment as her former successes had made indispensable, and, at the same time, of giving any sensible relief to foreign trade and to the weight of the public debt. He thought it equitable that those parts of the empire which had benefited most by the expenses of the war, should contribute something to the expenses of the peace, and he had no doubt of the constitutional right vested in Parliament to raise the contribution. But, unfortunately for this country, Mr. Grenville was at any rate to be distressed because he was minister, and Mr. Pitt and Lord Camden were to be patrons of America, because they were in opposition. Their declaration gave spirit and argument to the colonies; and while, perhaps, they meant no more than the ruin of a minister, they in effect divided one half of the empire from the other.[8]

[6] Within about seven years, the King had run up a debt of £513,000 beyond the ample allowance made for his expenses on the civil list, and had just applied, at the opening of Parliament, for a grant to pay it off. The nation were indignant at such overreaching. The debt, however, was paid this session, and in a few years there was another contracted. Thus it went on, from time to time, until 1782, when £300,000 more were paid, in addition to a large sum during the interval. At this time a partial provision was made, in connection with Mr. Burke's plan of economical reform, for preventing all future encroachments of this kind on the public revenues.

[7] Notwithstanding these early difficulties, Lord North became at last a very dexterous and effective debater.

[8] This attack on Lord Chatham and his friend shows the political affinities of Junius. He believed with Mr. Grenville and Lord Rockingham in the *right* of Great Britain to tax America; and in referring to Mr. Grenville's attempt to enforce that right by the Stamp Act, he adopts his usual course of interweaving an argument in its favor into the language used. He thus prepares the way for his censures on Lord Chatham and Lord Camden, affirming that they acted on the principle that "Mr. Grenville was at *any rate* to be distressed because he was minister and they were in opposition," thus implying that they were actuated by factious and selfish views in their defense of America. About a year after this letter was written, Lord Rockingham was reconciled to Lord Chatham and Lord Camden, and all united to break down the Grafton ministry. Junius now turned round and wrote his celebrated eulogium on Lord Chatham, contained in his fifty-fourth letter, in which he says, "Recorded honors shall gather round his monument, and thicken over him. It is a solid fabric, and will support the laurels that adorn it. I am not conversant in the language of panegyric. These praises are extorted from me; but they will wear well, for they have been dearly earned." The last of his letters was addressed to Lord Camden, in which he says, "I turn with pleasure from that barren waste, in which no solitary plant takes root, no verdure quickens, to a charac-

Under one administration the Stamp Act is made, under the second it is repealed, under the third, in spite of all experience, a new mode of taxing the colonies is invented, and a question revived, which ought to have been buried in oblivion. In these circumstances, a new office is established for the business of the Plantations, and the Earl of Hillsborough called forth, at a most critical season, to govern America. The choice at least announced to us a man of superior capacity and knowledge. Whether he be so or not, let his dispatches as far as they have appeared, let his measures as far as they have operated, determine for him. In the former we have seen strong assertions without proof, declamation without argument, and violent censures without dignity or moderation, but neither correctness in the composition, nor judgment in the design. As for his measures, let it be remembered that he was called upon to conciliate and unite, and that, when he entered into office, the most refractory of the colonies were still disposed to proceed by the constitutional methods of petition and remonstrance. Since that period they have been driven into excesses little short of rebellion. Petitions have been hindered from reaching the Throne, and the continuance of one of the principal assemblies put upon an arbitrary condition, which, considering the temper they were in, it was impossible they should comply with, and which would have availed nothing as to the general question if it had been complied with.[9] So violent, and I believe I may call it so unconstitutional an exertion of the prerogative, to say nothing of the weak, injudicious terms in which it was conveyed, gives us as humble an opinion of his Lordship's capacity as it does of his temper and moderation. While we are at peace with other nations, our military force may perhaps be spared to support the Earl of Hillsborough's measures in America. Whenever that force shall be necessarily withdrawn or diminished, the dismission of such a minister will neither console us for his imprudence, nor remove the settled resentment of a people, who, complaining of an act of the Legislature, are outraged by an unwarrantable stretch of prerogative, and, supporting their claims by argument, are insulted with declamation.

Drawing lots would be a prudent and reasonable method of appointing the officers of state, compared to a late disposition of the secretary's office. Lord Rochford was acquainted with the affairs and temper of the Southern courts; Lord Weymouth was equally qualified for either department. By what unaccountable caprice has it happened, that the latter, who pretends to no experience whatsoever, is removed to the most important of the two departments, and the former, by preference, placed in an office where his experience can be of no use to him?[10] Lord Weymouth had distinguished himself in his first employment by a spirited, if not judicious conduct. He had animated the civil magistrate beyond the tone of civil authority, and had directed the operations of the army to more than military execution. Recovered from the errors of his youth, from the distraction of play, and the bewitching smiles of Burgundy, behold him exerting the whole strength of his clear, unclouded faculties in the service of the Crown. It was not the heat of midnight excesses, nor ignorance of the laws, nor the furious spirit of the house of Bedford; no, sir; when this respectable minister interposed his authority between the magistrate and the people, and signed the mandate on which, for aught he knew, the lives of thousands depended, he did it from the deliberate motion of his heart, supported by the best of his judgment.[11]

ter fertile, as I willingly believe, in every great and good qualification." Political men have certainly a peculiar faculty of viewing the characters of others under very different lights, as they happen to affect their own interests and feelings.

[9] The "arbitrary condition" was that the General Court of Massachusetts should rescind one of their own resolutions and expunge it from their records. The whole of this passage in relation to Hillsborough is as correct in point of fact, as it is well reasoned and finely expressed.

[10] The changes here censured had taken place about three months before. The office of Foreign Secretary for the Southern Department was made vacant by the resignation of Lord Shelburne. Lord Rochford, who had been minister to France, and thus made "acquainted with the temper of the Southern courts," ought naturally to have been appointed (if at all) to this department. Instead of this, he was made Secretary of the Northern Department, for which he had been prepared by no previous knowledge; while Lord Weymouth was taken from the Home Department, and placed in the Southern, being "*equally* qualified" [that is, wholly unqualified by any "experience whatsoever"] for either department in the Foreign office, whether Southern or Northern.

[11] As Secretary of the Home Department, Lord Weymouth had addressed a letter to the magistrates of London, early in 1768, advising them to call in the military, provided certain disturbances in the streets should continue. The idea of setting the soldiery to fire on masses of unarmed men has always been abhorrent to the English nation. It was, therefore, a case admirably suited to the purposes of this Letter. In using it to inflame the people against Lord Weymouth, Junius charitably supposes that he was not repeating the errors of his youth—that he was neither drunk, nor ignorant of what he did, nor impelled by "the furious spirit" of one of the proudest families of the realm—all of which Lord Weymouth would certainly say—and therefore (which his Lordship must also admit) that he did, from "the deliberate motion of his heart, supported by the best of his judgment," sign a paper which the great body of the people considered as authorizing promiscuous murder, and which actually resulted in the death of fourteen persons three weeks after. The whole is so wrought up as to create the feeling, that Lord Weymouth was in *both* of these states of mind—that he acted with *deliberation* in carrying out the dictates of headlong or drunken passion.

All this, of course, is greatly exaggerated. Severe measures did seem indispensable to suppress the mobs of that day, and, whoever stood forth to direct them, must of necessity incur the popular in-

It has lately been a fashion to pay a compliment to the bravery and generosity of the Commander-in-chief [the Marquess of Granby] at the expense of his understanding. They who love him least make no question of his courage, while his friends dwell chiefly on the facility of his disposition. Admitting him to be as brave as a total absence of all feeling and reflection can make him, let us see what sort of merit he derives from the remainder of his character. If it be generosity to accumulate in his own person and family a number of lucrative employments; to provide, at the public expense, for every creature that bears the name of Manners; and, neglecting the merit and services of the rest of the army, to heap promotions upon his favorites and dependents, the present Commander-in-chief is the most generous man alive. Nature has been sparing of her gifts to this noble Lord; but where birth and fortune are united, we expect the noble pride and independence of a man of spirit, not the servile, humiliating complaisance of a courtier. As to the goodness of his heart, if a proof of it be taken from the facility of never refusing, what conclusion shall we draw from the indecency of never performing? And if the discipline of the army be in any degree preserved, what thanks are due to a man, whose cares, notoriously confined to filling up vacancies, have degraded the office of Commander-in-chief into [that of] a broker of commissions.[12]

With respect to the navy, I shall only say, that this country is so highly indebted to Sir Edward Hawke, that no expense should be spared to secure him an honorable and affluent retreat.

The pure and impartial administration of justice is perhaps the firmest bond to secure a cheerful submission of the people, and to engage their affections to government. It is not sufficient that questions of private right or wrong are justly decided, nor that judges are superior to the vileness of pecuniary corruption. Jefferies himself, when the court had no interest, was an upright judge. A court of justice may be subject to another sort of bias, more important and pernicious, as it reaches beyond the interest of individuals, and affects the whole community. A judge, under the influence of government, may be honest enough in the decision of private causes, yet a traitor to the public. When a victim is marked out by the ministry, this judge will offer himself to perform the sacrifice. He will not scruple to prostitute his dignity, and betray the sanctity of his office, whenever an arbitrary point is to be carried for government, or the resentment of a Court to be gratified.

These principles and proceedings, odious and contemptible as they are, in effect are no less injudicious. A wise and generous people are roused by every appearance of oppressive, unconstitutional measures, whether those measures are supported openly by the power of government, or masked under the forms of a court of justice. Prudence and self-preservation will oblige the most moderate dispositions to make common cause, even with a man whose conduct they censure, if they see him persecuted in a way which the real spirit of the laws will not justify. The facts on which these remarks are founded, are too notorious to require an application.[13]

This, sir, is the detail. In one view, behold a nation overwhelmed with debt; her revenues wasted; her trade declining; the affections of her colonies alienated; the duty of the magistrate transferred to the soldiery; a gallant army, which never fought unwillingly but against their fellow-subjects, moldering away for want of the direction of a man of common abilities and spirit; and, in the last instance, the administration of justice become odious and suspected to the whole body of the people. This deplorable scene admits but of one addition—that we are governed by councils, from which a reasonable man can expect no remedy but poison, no relief but death.

If, by the immediate interposition of Providence, it were [be] possible for us to escape a

dignation. Still, it was a question among the most candid men, whether milder means might not have been effectual.

[12] The Marquess of Granby, personally considered, was perhaps the most popular member of the cabinet, with the exception of Sir Edward Hawke. He was a warm-hearted man, of highly social qualities and generous feelings. As it was the object of Junius to break down the ministry, it was peculiarly necessary for him to blast and destroy his popularity. This he attempts to do by discrediting the character of the Marquess, as a man of firmness, strength of mind, and disinterestedness in managing the concerns of the army. This attack is distinguished for its plausibility and bitterness. It is clear that Junius was in some way connected with the army or with the War Department, and that in this situation he had not only the means of very exact information, but some private grudge against the Commander-in-chief. His charges and insinuations are greatly overstrained; but it is certain that the army was moldering away at this time in a manner which left the country in a very defenseless condition. Lord Chatham showed this by incontestible evidence, in his speech on the Falkland Islands, delivered about a year after this Letter was written.

[13] It is unnecessary to say that Lord Mansfield is here pointed at. No one now believes that this great jurist ever did the things here ascribed to him by Junius. All that is true is, that he was a very high Tory, and was, therefore, naturally led to exalt the prerogatives of the Crown; and that he was a very politic man (and this was the great failing in his character), and therefore unwilling to oppose the King or his ministers, when he knew in heart they were wrong. This was undoubtedly the case in respect to the issuing of a general warrant for apprehending Wilkes, which he ought publicly to have condemned; but, as he remained silent, men naturally considered him, in his character of Chief Justice, as having approved of the course directed by the King. Hence Mansfield was held responsible for the treatment of Wilkes, of whom Junius here speaks in very nearly the terms used by Lord Chatham, as a man whose "conduct" he censured, but with whom every moderate man must "make common cause," when he was "persecuted in a way which the real spirit of the laws will not justify."

crisis so full of terror and despair, posterity will not believe the history of the present times. They will either conclude that our distresses were imaginary, or that we had the good fortune to be governed by men of acknowledged integrity and wisdom. They will not believe it possible that their ancestors could have survived, or recovered from so desperate a condition, while a Duke of Grafton was Prime Minister, a Lord North Chancellor of the Exchequer, a Weymouth and a Hillsborough Secretaries of State, a Granby Commander-in-chief, and a Mansfield chief criminal judge of the kingdom.

JUNIUS.

LETTER

TO SIR WILLIAM DRAPER, KNIGHT OF THE BATH.[1]

SIR,—The defense of Lord Granby does honor to the goodness of your heart. You feel, as you ought to do, for the reputation of your friend, and you express yourself in the warmest language of the passions. In any other cause, I doubt not, you would have cautiously weighed the consequences of committing your name to the licentious discourses and malignant opinions of the world. But here, I presume, you thought it would be a breach of friendship to lose one moment in consulting your understanding; as if an appeal to the public were no more than a military *coup de main*, where a brave man has no rules to follow but the dictates of his courage. Touched with your generosity, I freely forgive the excesses into which it has led you; and, far from resenting those terms of reproach, which, considering that you are an advocate for decorum, you have heaped upon me rather too liberally, I place them to the account of an honest, unreflecting indignation, in which your cooler judgment and natural politeness had no concern. I approve of the spirit with which you have given your name to the public, and, if it were a proof of any thing but spirit, I should have thought myself bound to follow your example. I should have hoped that even *my* name might carry some authority with it, if I had not seen how very little weight or consideration a printed paper receives even from the respectable signature of Sir William Draper.[2]

You begin with a general assertion, that writers, such as I am, are the real cause of all the public evils we complain of. And do you really think, Sir William, that the licentious pen of a political writer is able to produce such important effects? A little calm reflection might have shown you that national calamities do not arise from the description, but from the real character and conduct of ministers. To have supported your assertion, you should have proved that the present ministry are unquestionably the *best and brightest* characters of the kingdom; and that, if the affections of the colonies have been alienated, if Corsica has been shamefully abandoned, if commerce languishes, if public credit is threatened with a new debt, and your own Manilla ransom most dishonorably given up, it has all been owing to the malice of political writers, who will not suffer the best and brightest of characters (meaning still the present ministry) to take a single right step for the honor or interest of the nation.[3] But it seems you were a

---

[1] Dated February 7, 1769. It is unnecessary to give the letters of Sir William Draper, since their contents will be sufficiently understood from the replies, and our present concern is not with the merits of the controversy, but the peculiarities of Junius as a writer.

[2] The reader will be interested in the following brief sketch of Sir William Draper's life by a contemporary:

"Sir William, as a scholar, had been bred at Eton and King's College, Cambridge, but he chose the sword for his profession. In India he ranked with those famous warriors, Clive and Lawrence. In 1761 he acted at Belleisle as a brigadier. In 1762 he commanded the troops who conquered Manilla, which place was saved from plunder by the promise of a ransom of £1,000,000, that was never paid. His first appearance as an able writer was in his clear refutation of the objections of the Spanish court to the payment of that ransom. His services were rewarded with the command of the sixteenth regiment of foot, which he resigned to Colonel Gisborne for his half-pay of £200 Irish. This common transaction furnished Junius with many a sarcasm. Sir William had scarcely closed his contest with that formidable opponent, when he had the misfortune to lose his wife, who died on the 1st of September, 1769. As he was foiled, he was no doubt mortified; and he set out, in October of that year, to make the tour of the American colonies, which had now become objects of notice and scenes of travel. He arrived at Charleston, South Carolina, in January, 1770; and, traveling northward, he arrived, during the summer of that year, in Maryland, where he was received with that hospitality which she always paid to strangers, and with the attentions that were due to the merit of such a visitor. From Maryland Sir William passed on to New York, where he married Miss De Lancey, a lady of great connections there, and agreeable endowments, who died in 1778, leaving him a daughter. In 1779 he was appointed Lieutenant Governor of Minorca—a trust which, however discharged, ended unhappily. He died at Bath, on the 8th of January, 1787."

[3] A few words of explanation may be necessary on two of the points here mentioned.

The Corsicans had risen against their former masters and oppressors, the Genoese, and, through the bravery and conduct of their leader, General Paoli, had nearly recovered their liberties. Genoa now called in the aid of France, and finally sold her the island. Public sentiment in England was strongly in favor of the Corsicans; and the general feeling was that of Lord Chatham, that England ought to interfere, and prevent France from being aggrandized at the expense of the Corsicans. Instead of

little tender of coming to particulars. Your conscience insinuated to you that it would be prudent to leave the characters of Grafton, North, Hillsborough, Weymouth, and Mansfield to shift for themselves; and truly, Sir William, the part you *have* undertaken is at least as much as you are equal to.

Without disputing Lord Granby's courage, we are yet to learn in what articles of military knowledge Nature has been so very liberal to his mind. If you have served with him, you ought to have pointed out some instances of able disposition and well-concerted enterprise, which might fairly be attributed to his capacity as a general. It is you, Sir William, who make your friend appear awkward and ridiculous, by giving him a laced suit of tawdry qualifications which Nature never intended him to wear.

You say, he has acquired nothing but honor in the field. Is the ordnance nothing? Are the Blues nothing? Is the command of the army, with all the patronage annexed to it, nothing? Where he got these *nothings* I know not; but you, at least, ought to have told us where he deserved them.

As to his bounty, compassion, &c., it would have been but little to the purpose, though you had proved all that you have asserted. I meddle with nothing but his character as Commander-in-chief; and though I acquit him of the baseness of selling commissions, I still assert that his military cares have never extended beyond the disposal of vacancies; and I am justified by the complaints of the whole army, when I say that, in this distribution, he consults nothing but parliamentary interests, or the gratification of his immediate dependents. As to his servile submission to the reigning ministry, let me ask, whether he did not desert the cause of the whole army when he suffered Sir Jeffery Amherst to be sacrificed? and what share he had in recalling that officer to the service?[4] Did he not betray the just interest of the army in permitting Lord Percy to have a regiment? and does he not at this moment give up all character and dignity as a gentleman, in receding from his own repeated declarations in favor of Mr. Wilkes?

In the two next articles I think we are agreed. You candidly admit that he often makes such promises as it is a virtue in him to violate, and that no man is more assiduous to provide for his relations at the public expense. I did not urge the last as an absolute vice in his disposition, but to prove that a *careless, disinterested spirit* is no part of his character; and as to the other, I desire it may be remembered that I never descended to the indecency of inquiring into his *convivial hours*. It is you, Sir William Draper, who have taken pains to represent your friend in the character of a drunken landlord, who deals out his promises as liberally as his liquor, and will suffer no man to leave his table either sorrowful or sober. None but an intimate friend, who must frequently have seen him in these unhappy, disgraceful moments, could have described him so well.

The last charge, of the neglect of the army, is indeed the most material of all. I am sorry to tell you, Sir William, that in this article your first fact is false;[5] and as there is nothing more painful to me than to give a direct contradiction to a gentleman of your appearance, I could wish that, in your future publications, you would pay a greater attention to the truth of your premises, before you suffer your genius to hurry you to a conclusion. Lord Ligonier *did not* deliver the army (which you, in classical language, are pleased to call a Palladium) into Lord Granby's hands. It was taken from him, much against his inclination, some two or three years before Lord Granby was Commander-in-chief. As to the state of the army, I should be glad to know where you have received your intelligence. Was it in the rooms at Bath, or at your retreat at Clifton? The reports of reviewing generals comprehend only a few regiments in England, which, as they are immediately under the royal inspection, are perhaps in some tolerable order. But do you know any thing of the troops in the West Indies, the Mediterranean, and North America, to say nothing of a whole army absolutely ruined in Ireland? Inquire a little into facts, Sir William, before you publish your next panegyric upon Lord Granby, and believe me you will find there is a fault at head-quarters, which even the acknowledged care and abilities of the Adjutant General [General Harvey] can not correct.

this, the Grafton ministry had decided three months before to give her up, and the great body of the nation were indignant at this decision.

In respect to the Manilla ransom, it has already been stated, that the Spanish court, in their usual spirit, had endeavored to evade the debt. Year after year had been spent in fruitless negotiations, when the decided tone recommended by Lord Chatham would have at once secured payment. The nation felt disgraced by this tame endurance. Sir William Draper was indeed rewarded with the order of the Bath, whose "blushing ribbon" is so stingingly alluded to at the close of this letter. He also received the pecuniary emoluments here mentioned. But all this was considered by many as mere favoritism, and the reward of his silence; for Admiral Cornish, who commanded the fleet in that expedition, together with the inferior officers and troops, was left to languish and die without redress.

[4] Sir Jeffery Amherst was a favorite general of Lord Chatham, and conducted most of his great enterprises in America. He was rewarded with the office of Governor of Virginia, but was abruptly displaced in 1768, through the interposition of Hillsborough, chiefly on account of his friendship for Chatham. He was, however, speedily raised to a higher station in the army, through the determined interposition of his friends, but not (as Junius intimates) through that of Lord Granby.

In respect to Lord Percy, it was bitterly complained of in the army that he should receive a regiment "plainly by way of pension to the noble, disinterested house of Percy," for their support of the ministry, while the most meritorious officers were passed over in neglect, and suffered, after years of arduous service, to languish in want.

[5] It is hardly correct to say that a *fact* is false, but rather the statement which affirms it.

Permit me now, Sir William, to address myself personally to you, by way of thanks for the honor of your correspondence. You are by no means undeserving of notice; and it may be of consequence even to Lord Granby to have it determined, whether or no the man, who has praised him so lavishly, be himself deserving of praise. When you returned to Europe, you zealously undertook the cause of that gallant army, by whose bravery at Manilla your own fortune had been established. You complained, you threatened, you even appealed to the public in print. By what accident did it happen that, in the midst of all this bustle, and all these clamors for justice to your injured troops, the name of the Manilla ransom was suddenly buried in a profound, and, since that time, an uninterrupted silence? Did the ministry suggest any motives to you strong enough to tempt a man of honor to desert and betray the cause of his fellow-soldiers? Was it that blushing ribbon, which is now the perpetual ornament of your person? Or was it that regiment, which you afterward (a thing unprecedented among soldiers) sold to Colonel Gisborne? Or was it that government [of Yarmouth], the full pay of which you are contented to hold, with the half-pay of an Irish colonel? And do you now, after a retreat not very like that of Scipio, presume to intrude yourself, unthought of, uncalled for, upon the patience of the public? Are your flatteries of the Commander-in-chief directed to another regiment, which you may again dispose of on the same honorable terms? We know your prudence, Sir William, and I should be sorry to stop your preferment. JUNIUS.

Sir William Draper, in reply to this Letter, said, concerning Lord Granby, "My friend's political engagements I know not, so can not pretend to explain them, or assert their consistency." He does, however, reassert "his military skill and capacity." As to the Manilla ransom, he says that he had complained, and even appealed to the public, but his efforts with the ministry were in vain. "Some were ingenuous enough to own that they could not think of involving this distressed nation into another war for our private concerns. In short, our rights, for the present, are sacrificed to national convenience; and I must confess that, although I may lose five-and-twenty thousand pounds by their acquiescence to this breach of faith in the Spaniards, I think they are in the right to temporize, considering the critical situation of this country, convulsed in every part by poison infused by anonymous, wicked, and incendiary writers."

His pecuniary transactions he explained in a manner which ought to have satisfied any candid mind, that there was nothing in them either dishonest or dishonorable. As to his being rewarded with office and preferment, while his companions in arms were neglected, this was certainly not to be imputed to him as a crime, since his services merited all he received. Still, he may, on this account, have been more willing (as Junius insinuated) to remain quiet. He closed his second letter thus: "Junius makes much and frequent use of interrogations: they are arms that may be easily turned against himself. I could, by malicious interrogation, disturb the peace of the most virtuous man in the kingdom. I could take the Decalogue, and say to one man, 'Did you never steal?' to the next, 'Did you never commit murder?' and to Junius himself, who is putting my life and conduct to the rack, 'Did you never bear false witness against thy neighbor?' Junius must easily see, that unless he affirms to the contrary in his real name, some people, who may be as ignorant of him as I am, will be apt to suspect him of having deviated a little from the truth; therefore let Junius ask no more questions. You bite against a file; cease, viper!"

LETTER

TO SIR WILLIAM DRAPER, KNIGHT OF THE BATH.[1]

SIR,—An academical education has given you an unlimited command over the most beautiful figures of speech. Masks, hatchets, racks, and vipers dance through your letters in all the mazes of metaphorical confusion. These are the gloomy companions of a disturbed imagination—the melancholy madness of poetry without the inspiration. I will not contend with you in point of composition. You are a scholar, Sir William, and, if I am truly informed, you write Latin with almost as much purity as English. Suffer me, then, for I am a plain unlettered man, to continue that style of interrogation which suits my capacity, and to which, considering the readiness of your answers, you ought to have no objection. Even Mr. Bingley promises to answer, if put to the torture.[2]

Do you then really think that, if I were to ask a *most virtuous man* whether he ever committed theft, or murder, it would disturb his peace of mind? Such a question might perhaps discompose the gravity of his muscles, but I believe it

---

[1] Dated March 3, 1769. This was the *Io Triumphe* of Junius in closing the correspondence.

[2] This man was a bookseller, who had been subpœnaed by the government in the case of Wilkes. For some reason, he refused to answer the questions put by either party, and made himself the laughing-stock of both, by declaring under oath that he would never answer until *put to the torture.* He was imprisoned a number of months for contempt of court, and at last released.

would little affect the tranquillity of his conscience. Examine your own breast, Sir William, and you will discover that reproaches and inquiries have no power to afflict either the man of unblemished integrity, or the abandoned profligate. It is the middle, compound character which alone is vulnerable: the man who, without firmness enough to avoid a dishonorable action, has feeling enough to be ashamed of it.

I thank you for the hint of the Decalogue, and shall take an opportunity of applying it to some of your *most virtuous* friends in both houses of Parliament.

You seem to have dropped the affair of your regiment; so let it rest. When you are appointed to another, I dare say you will not sell it, either for a gross sum, or for any annuity upon lives.

I am truly glad (for really, Sir William, I am not your enemy, nor did I begin this contest with you) that you have been able to clear yourself of a crime, though at the expense of the highest indiscretion. You say that your half pay was given you by way of pension. I will not dwell upon the singularity of uniting in your own person two sorts of provision, which, in their own nature, and in all military and parliamentary views, are incompatible; but I call upon you to justify that declaration, wherein you charge your prince with having done an act in your favor notoriously against law. The half pay, both in Ireland and in England, is appropriated by Parliament; and if it be given to persons who, like you, are legally incapable of holding it, it is a breach of law. It would have been more decent in you to have called this dishonorable transaction by its true name; a job to accommodate two persons, by particular interest and management at the Castle. What sense must government have had of your services, when the rewards they have given you are only a disgrace to you!

And now, Sir William, I shall take my leave of you forever. Motives, very different from any apprehension of your resentment, make it impossible you should ever know me. In truth, you have some reason to hold yourself indebted to me. From the lessons I have given, you may collect a profitable instruction for your future life. They will either teach you so to regulate your conduct as to be able to set the most malicious inquiries at defiance, or, if that be a lost hope, they will teach you prudence enough not to attract the public attention to a character which will only pass without censure when it passes without observation. JUNIUS.

Junius added the following note when the letters were collected into a volume, after the death of the Marquess of Granby:

"It has been said, and I believe truly, that it was signified to Sir William Draper, at the request of Lord Granby, that he should desist from writing in his Lordship's defense. Sir William Draper certainly drew Junius forward to say more of Lord Granby's character than he originally intended. He was reduced to the dilemma of either being totally silenced, or of supporting his first letter. Whether Sir William had a right to reduce him to this dilemma, or to call upon him for his name, after a voluntary attack on his side, are questions submitted to the candor of the public. The death of Lord Granby was lamented by Junius. He undoubtedly owed some compensations to the public, and seemed determined to acquit himself of them. In private life, he was unquestionably that good man, who, for the interest of his country, ought to have been a great one, 'Bonum virum facile dixeris; magnum libenter.'[3] I never spoke of him with resentment. His mistakes in public conduct did not arise either from want of sentiment or want of judgment, but in general from the difficulty of saying No! to the bad people who surrounded him. As for the rest, the friends of Lord Granby should remember, that he himself thought proper to condemn, retract, and disavow, by a most solemn declaration in the House of Commons, that very system of political conduct which Junius had held forth to the disapprobation of the public."[4]

LETTER

TO HIS GRACE THE DUKE OF GRAFTON.[1]

MY LORD,—If the measures in which you have been most successful had been supported

---

[3] "You would readily call him a good man, and be glad to call him a great one."

[4] This refers to the change of Lord Granby's views and feelings after Lord Chatham's speech of January 9th, 1770: see page 114. As already stated, page 114, he withdrew from the Duke of Grafton's administration, apologizing for the vote he had given for seating Colonel Luttrell in the House, deploring it as the greatest misfortune of his life.

[1] Dated May 30th, 1769. This, like the first letter, has great regularity of structure. It begins with an artful apology for its bitterness, representing the Duke as utterly incorrigible; as having such a reliance on his purchased majority in Parliament, and such audacity in vice, as made him treat with contempt all endeavors for his good, and left room only for the writer "to consider his character and conduct as a subject of *curious speculation.*" Junius then goes on to speak of, (1.) The stain which rested on the Duke's descent, and his resemblance to his reputed ancestors. (2.) His education under Lord Chatham, and his early desertion of his patron and of all others who had ever confided in him. (3.) His management under the third ministry of Chatham, to engross power and influence by a union with the Duke of Bedford and a marriage into his family. (4.) His supposed design, by this union, to obtain the mastery of the closet, and take the place of the Favorite. (5.)

by any tolerable appearance of argument, I should have thought my time not ill employed in continuing to examine your conduct as a minister, and stating it fairly to the public. But when I see questions of the first national importance carried as they have been, and the first principles of the Constitution openly violated without argument or decency, I confess I give up the cause in despair. The meanest of your predecessors had abilities sufficient to give a color to their measures. If they invaded the rights of the people, they did not dare to offer a direct insult to their understanding; and, in former times, the most venal Parliaments made it a condition, in their bargain with the minister, that he should furnish them with some plausible pretenses for selling their country and themselves. You have had the merit of introducing a more compendious system of government and logic. You neither address yourself to the passions nor to the understanding, but simply to the *touch*. You apply yourself immediately to the feelings of your friends, who, contrary to the forms of Parliament, never enter heartily into a debate until they have divided.[2]

Relinquishing, therefore, all idle views of amendment to your Grace, or of benefit to the public, let me be permitted to consider your character and conduct merely as a subject of curious speculation. There is something in both which distinguishes you not only from all other ministers, but all other men. It is not that you do wrong by design, but that you should never do right by mistake. It is not that your indolence and your activity have been equally misapplied, but that the first uniform principle, or, if I may so call it, the genius of your life, should have carried you through every possible change and contradiction of conduct, without the momentary imputation or color of a virtue; and that the wildest spirit of inconsistency should never once have betrayed you into a wise or honorable action. This, I own, gives an air of singularity to your fortune, as well as to your disposition. Let us look back together to a scene, in which a mind like yours will find nothing to repent of. Let us try, my Lord, how well you have supported the various relations in which you stood, to your sovereign, your country, your friends, and yourself. Give us, if it be possible, some excuse to posterity, and to ourselves, for submitting to your administration. If not the abilities of a great minister, if not the integrity of a patriot, or the fidelity of a friend, show us, at least, the firmness of a man. For the sake of your mistress, the lover shall be spared. I will not lead her into public, as you have done, nor will I insult the memory of departed beauty. Her sex, which alone made her amiable in your eyes, makes her respectable in mine.[3]

The character of the reputed ancestors of some men has made it possible for their descendants to be vicious in the extreme, without being degenerate. Those of your Grace, for instance, left no distressing examples of virtue, even to their *legitimate* posterity; and you may look back with pleasure to an illustrious pedigree, in which heraldry has not left a single good quality upon record to insult or upbraid you. You have better proofs of your descent, my Lord, than the register of a marriage, or any troublesome inheritance of reputation. There are some hereditary strokes of character, by which a family may be as clearly distinguished as by the blackest features in the human face. Charles the First lived and died a hypocrite. Charles the Second was a hypocrite of another sort, and should have died upon the same scaffold. At the distance of a century, we see their different characters happily revived and blended in your Grace. Sullen and severe without religion, profligate without gayety, you live like Charles the Second, without being an amiable companion, and, for aught I know, may die as his father did, without the reputation of a martyr.[4]

You had already taken your degrees with credit in those schools in which the English nobility are formed to virtue, when you were introduced to Lord Chatham's protection. From Newmarket, White's, and the Opposition, he gave you to the world with an air of popularity,

His fluctuating policy in respect to America. (6.) His betrayal of the Corsicans into the hands of France, and his permitting the French to gain the ascendency in the Turkish Divan. (7.) His alienating the affections of the people from the King by his home administration, "sometimes allowing the laws to be scandalously relaxed, and sometimes violently stretched beyond their tone." He concludes by telling the Duke, as the only hope of his being rendered useful to mankind, "I mean to make you a *negative* instructor to your successors forever."

[2] About this time, as appears from the Court Calendar, *one hundred and ninety-two* members of the House of Commons had places under government, and were thus held in absolute subserviency to the minister; to say nothing of the more direct use of money alluded to above.

[3] The Duke of Grafton had outraged public decency a few months before, by appearing openly with his mistress, Miss Parsons, in places of general resort and amusement. Junius attacked him on the subject at that time (though not under his present signature), remarking ironically, "You have exceeded my warmest expectations. I did not think you capable of exhibiting the 'lovely Thais' at the Opera House, of sitting a whole night by her side, of calling for her carriage yourself, and of leading her to it through a crowd of the first men and women in this kingdom. To a mind like yours, such an outrage to your wife, such a triumph over decency, such an insult to the company, must have afforded the highest gratification. It was, I presume, your *novissima voluptas.*" Junius very dexterously throws in this mention of the Duke of Grafton's dissolute habits to introduce the next paragraph, which traces his origin from the most debauched of English monarchs.

[4] The first Duke of Grafton was a natural son of Charles II., and the present Duke a great-grandchild of that debauched monarch. This reference to the fact was of itself sufficiently mortifying; but it derives double severity from the ingenious turn by which the discordant qualities of his two royal ancestors are made to meet and mingle in the person of his Grace.

which young men usually set out with, and seldom preserve; grave and plausible enough to be thought fit for business; too young for treachery; and, in short, a patriot of no unpromising expectations. Lord Chatham was the earliest object of your political wonder and attachment; yet you deserted him, upon the first hopes that offered of an equal share of power with Lord Rockingham. When the Duke of Cumberland's first negotiation failed, and when the Favorite was pushed to the last extremity, you saved him, by joining with an administration in which Lord Chatham had refused to engage.[5] Still, however, he was your friend, and you are yet to explain to the world why you consented to act without him, or why, after uniting with Lord Rockingham, you deserted and betrayed him. You complained that no measures were taken to satisfy your patron, and that your friend, Mr. Wilkes, who had suffered so much for the party, had been abandoned to his fate. They have since contributed, not a little, to your present plenitude of power; yet, I think, Lord Chatham has less reason than ever to be satisfied; and as for Mr. Wilkes, it is, perhaps, the greatest misfortune of his life that you should have so many compensations to make in the closet for your former friendship with him. Your gracious master understands your character, and makes you a persecutor, because you have been a friend.[6]

Lord Chatham formed his last administration upon principles which you certainly concurred in, or you could never have been placed at the head of the treasury. By deserting those principles, and by acting in direct contradiction to them, in which he found you were secretly supported in the closet, you soon forced him to leave you to yourself, and to withdraw his name from an administration which had been formed on the credit of it.[7] You had then a prospect of friendships better suited to your genius, and more likely to fix your disposition. Marriage is the point on which every rake is stationary at last; and truly, my Lord, you may well be weary of the circuit you have taken, for you have now fairly traveled through every sign in the political zodiac, from the Scorpion in which you stung Lord Chatham, to the hopes of a Virgin in the house of Bloomsbury. One would think that you had had sufficient experience of the frailty of nuptial engagements, or, at least, that such a friendship as the Duke of Bedford's might have been secured to you by the auspicious marriage of your late Duchess with his nephew. But ties of this tender nature can not be drawn too close; and it may possibly be a part of the Duke of Bedford's ambition, after making *her* an honest woman, to work a miracle of the same sort upon your Grace. This worthy nobleman has long dealt in virtue. There has been a large consumption of it in his own family; and in the way of traffic, I dare say, he has bought and sold more than half the representative integrity of the nation.[8]

In a political view this union is not imprudent. The favor of princes is a perishable commodity. You have now a strength sufficient to command the closet; and if it be necessary to betray one friendship more, you may set even Lord Bute at defiance. Mr. Stuart Mackenzie may possibly remember what use the Duke of Bedford usually makes of his power;[9] and our gracious sover-

[5] See on this subject the sketch of Lord Chatham's life, p. 66. The Duke of Grafton had been the protégé and adherent of his Lordship; but he joined the administration of Lord Rockingham in 1765, as Secretary of State, while Chatham declared to the House that he could not give his confidence or support to the new ministers. Still, he stated in the same speech that "some of them asked his opinion before they accepted, and that he advised them to do it." The Duke of Grafton may have been one of the number, and in that case, the present is one of the many instances in which Junius perverts facts for the sake of wounding an adversary.

[6] Cooke, speaking of this period in his History of Party, vol. iii., 105, says, "The Duke of Grafton, the present premier, although still a young man, had passed through several shades of politics. During the struggle upon the subject of general warrants, he had strenuously supported Wilkes; and he had, since that time, repeated his assurances of protection and friendship. When placed by Lord Chatham at the head of the treasury, he had, through his own brother, conveyed a similar message to the impatient democrat, who, inflated with hope, returned to England to receive his pardon. He found, however, upon his arrival, that nothing was intended in his favor. He revenged himself by writing and publishing a severe letter to the Duke of Grafton, taxing him with faithlessness and prevarication; and he returned in bitter disappointment to his exile and his poverty."

[7] Lord Chatham did ultimately withdraw his name for this reason, October, 1768; though his previous illness had prevented him from taking the lead of the government, and had thus given the Duke of Grafton an opportunity to gain the King's favor, which could be permanently secured only by abandoning the principles and friendship of Lord Chatham.

[8] The facts here referred to betray a shameless profligacy in all the parties concerned. While the Duke of Grafton was parading his mistress before the public at the Opera House, his wife had an adulterous connection with Lord Upper Ossory, nephew of the Duke of Bedford. For this she was divorced, and was soon after married by her paramour, who thus brought her into the Bedford circle. Incredible as it may seem, the Duke of Grafton became in a short time affianced to a member of the same circle, Miss Wrottesley, a niece of the Duchess of Bedford ("a virgin of the house of Bloomsbury"); so that Junius represents it as the ambition of the Duke of Bedford, after making the adultress "an honest woman, to work a miracle of the same sort" on her former husband, the Duke of Grafton! This exposure of their shame would have satisfied most persons; but Junius, in the next paragraph, dexterously turns the whole to a new purpose, viz., that of inflaming the public mind against the minister, as designing, by this connection, to "gain strength sufficient to command the closet;" imputing to him the unpopular friendship of Lord Bute, and a design to betray it!

[9] When the Duke of Bedford became minister in 1763, he forced the King, against his wishes (as it

eign, I doubt not, rejoices at this first appearance of union among his servants. His late Majesty, under the happy influence of a family connection between his ministers, was relieved from the cares of government. A more active prince may, perhaps, observe with suspicion, by what degrees an artful servant grows upon his master, from the first unlimited professions of duty and attachment to the painful representation of the necessity of the royal service, and soon, in regular progression, to the humble insolence of dictating in all the obsequious forms of peremptory submission. The interval is carefully employed in forming connections, creating interests, collecting a party, and laying the foundation of double marriages, until the deluded prince, who thought he had found a creature prostituted to his service, and insignificant enough to be always dependent upon his pleasure, finds him at last too strong to be commanded, and too formidable to be removed.

Your Grace's public conduct, as a minister, is but the counterpart of your private history—the same inconsistency, the same contradictions. In America we trace you, from the first opposition to the Stamp Act, on principles of convenience, to Mr. Pitt's surrender of the right; then forward to Lord Rockingham's surrender of the fact; then back again to Lord Rockingham's declaration of the right; then forward to taxation with Mr. Townsend; and, in the last instance, from the gentle Conway's undetermined discretion, to blood and compulsion with the Duke of Bedford.[10] Yet, if we may believe the simplicity of Lord North's eloquence, at the opening of next sessions you are once more to be patron of America. Is this the wisdom of a great minister, or is it the vibration of a pendulum? *Had* you no opinion of your own, my Lord? Or was it the gratification of betraying every party with which you had been united, and of deserting every political principle in which you had concurred?

Your enemies may turn their eyes without regret from this admirable system of provincial government: they will find gratification enough in the survey of your domestic and foreign policy.

If, instead of disowning Lord Shelburne, the British court had interposed with dignity and firmness, you know, my Lord, that Corsica would never have been invaded.[11] The French saw the weakness of a distracted ministry, and were justified in treating you with contempt. They would probably have yielded in the first instance rather than hazard a rupture with this country; but, being once engaged, they can not retreat without dishonor. Common sense foresees consequences which have escaped your Grace's penetration. Either we suffer the French to make an acquisition, the importance of which you have probably no conception of, or we oppose them by an underhand management, which only disgraces us in the eyes of Europe, without answering any purpose of policy or prudence. From secret, indiscreet assistance, a transition to some more open, decisive measures becomes unavoidable, till at last we find ourselves principals in the war, and are obliged to hazard every thing for an object which might have originally been obtained without expense or danger. I am not versed in the politics of the North; but this I believe is certain, that half the money you have distributed to carry the expulsion of Mr. Wilkes, or even your secretary's share in the last subscription, would have kept the Turks at your devotion.[12] Was it economy, my Lord? or did the coy resistance you have constantly met with in the British Senate make you despair of corrupting the Divan? Your friends, indeed, have the first claim upon your bounty; but if five hundred pounds a year can be spared in pension to Sir John Moore, it would not have disgraced you to have allowed something to the secret service of the public.[13]

You will say, perhaps, that the situation of affairs at home demanded and engrossed the whole of your attention. Here, I confess you have been active. An amiable, accomplished prince ascends the throne under the happiest of all auspices, the acclamations and united affections of his subjects. The first measures of his reign, and even the odium of a Favorite, were not able to shake their attachments. *Your* services, my Lord, have been more successful. Since you were permitted to take the lead, we have seen the natural effects of a system of government at once both odious and contemptible. We have seen the laws sometimes scandalously relaxed, sometimes violently stretched beyond their tone. We have

---

was understood), to dismiss Mr. Stuart Mackenzie, brother of Lord Bute. Mr. Mackenzie was restored as soon as the Duke retired; and Junius here describes, in the most graphic manner, the way in which the same man and his associates might be expected to go on again, till he reached "the humble insolence of *dictating* in all the obsequious forms of peremptory submission," as was done to George II.

[10] This is substantially true. "The Duke of Grafton," says a well-informed writer, "occasionally favored Mr. Pitt's opinion, occasionally the Marquess of Rockingham's, and at last sided with Charles Townsend in a determined resolution to carry the system of taxation into effect at all hazards."

[11] Lord Shelburne, then Secretary of Foreign Affairs, had instructed the English embassador at the court of France to remonstrate in spirited terms against the occupation of Corsica by the French. But Grafton and the rest of the ministry disavowed the instructions of their own secretary, and Lord Shelburne resigned on the 21st of October, 1768, under a sense of injury.

[12] It was the policy of Great Britain, touching "the politics of the North," to prevent Russia from being weakened by Turkey in the war then existing between them. French officers were aiding the Turks and disciplining their troops. Junius intimates that a small sum comparatively might have prevented this, and served not only to curtail the growing power of the French in the Divan, but to have transferred the ascendency to the English.

[13] Sir John Moore was an old Newmarket acquaintance of the Duke, who had squandered his private fortune, and had recently obtained from his Grace a pension of £500 a year.

seen the sacred person of the sovereign insulted; and, in profound peace, and with an undisputed title, the fidelity of his subjects brought by his own servants into public question.[14] Without abilities, resolution, or interest, you have done more than Lord Bute could accomplish with all Scotland at his heels.

Your Grace, little anxious, perhaps, either for present or future reputation, will not desire to be handed down in these colors to posterity. You have reason to flatter yourself that the memory of your administration will survive even the forms of a constitution which our ancestors vainly hoped would be immortal; and as for your personal character, I will not, for the honor of human nature, suppose that you can wish to have it remembered. The condition of the present times is desperate indeed; but there is a debt due to those who come after us, and it is the historian's office to punish, though he can not correct. I do not give you to posterity as a pattern to imitate, but as an example to deter; and as your conduct comprehends every thing that a wise or honest minister should avoid, I mean to make you a negative instruction to your successors forever.

JUNIUS.

LETTER

TO HIS GRACE THE DUKE OF GRAFTON.[1]

MY LORD,—If nature had given you an understanding qualified to keep pace with the wishes and principles of your heart, she would have made you, perhaps, the most formidable minister that ever was employed, under a limited monarch, to accomplish the ruin of a free people. When neither the feelings of shame, the reproaches of conscience, nor the dread of punishment, form any bar to the designs of a minister, the people would have too much reason to lament their condition, if they did not find some resource in the weakness of his understanding. We owe it to the bounty of Providence, that the completest depravity of the heart is sometimes strangely united with a confusion of the mind, which counteracts the most favorite principles, and makes the same man treacherous without art, and a hypocrite without deceiving. The measures, for instance, in which your Grace's activity has been chiefly exerted, as they were adopted without skill, should have been conducted with more than common dexterity. But truly, my Lord, the execution has been as gross as the design. By one decisive step you have defeated all the arts of writing. You have fairly confounded the intrigues of Opposition, and silenced the clamors of faction. A dark, ambiguous system might require and furnish the materials of ingenious illustration, and, in doubtful measures, the virulent exaggeration of party must be employed to rouse and engage the passions of the people. You have now brought the merits of your administration to an issue, on which every Englishman, of the narrowest capacity, may determine for himself. It is not an alarm to the passions, but a calm appeal to the judgment of the people upon their own most essential interests. A more experienced minister would not have hazarded a direct invasion of the first principles of the Constitution, before he had made some progress in subduing the spirit of the people. With such a cause as yours, my Lord, it is not sufficient that you have the court at your devotion, unless you can find means to corrupt or intimidate the jury. The collective body of the people form that jury, and from their decision there is but one appeal.

Whether you have talents to support you at a crisis of such difficulty and danger, should long since have been considered. Judging truly of your disposition, you have perhaps mistaken the extent of your capacity. Good faith and folly have so long been received as synonymous terms, that the reverse of the proposition has grown into credit, and every villain fancies himself a man of abilities. It is the apprehension of your friends, my Lord, that you have drawn some hasty conclusion of this sort, and that a partial reliance upon your moral character has betrayed you beyond the depth of your understanding. You have now carried things too far to retreat. You have plainly declared to the people what they are to expect from the continuance of your administration. It is time for your Grace to consider what you also may expect in return from *their* spirit and *their* resentment.

Since the accession of our most gracious sovereign to the throne, we have seen a system of government which may well be called a reign of experiments. Parties of all denominations have been employed and dismissed. The advice of the ablest men in this country has been repeatedly called for and rejected; and when the royal displeasure has been signified to a minister, the marks of it have usually been proportioned to his abilities and integrity. The spirit of the FA-

---

[14] As the King became unpopular through his persecution of Wilkes and for other causes, the Duke of Grafton had made exertions to procure addresses from various parts of the kingdom, expressive of the people's attachment to the Crown. In this he signally failed, except in Scotland, and thus brought the fidelity of his Majesty's subjects into "public question."

[1] Dated July 8th, 1769. This Letter is directed chiefly to one point—the daring step just taken by the ministry, of seating Mr. Luttrell in the House of Commons to the exclusion of Mr. Wilkes, when the former had received only 296 votes, and the latter 1143 votes, and had been returned by the sheriff of Middlesex as the elected member. Junius does not enter into the argument, for the case was too clear to admit of extended reasoning. His object was to convince the King and the ministry, that the people would not *endure* so flagrant an act of violence.

VORITE had some apparent influence upon every administration; and every set of ministers preserved an appearance of duration as long as they submitted to that influence.[2] But there were certain services to be performed for the Favorite's security, or to gratify his resentments, which your predecessors in office had the wisdom or the virtue not to undertake. The moment this refractory spirit was discovered, their disgrace was determined. Lord Chatham, Mr. Grenville, and Lord Rockingham have successively had the honor to be dismissed, for preferring their duty, as servants of the public, to those compliances which were expected from their station. A submissive administration was at last gradually collected from the deserters of all parties, interests, and connections; and nothing remained but to find a leader for these gallant, well-disciplined troops. *Stand forth, my Lord, for thou art the man!* Lord Bute found no resource of dependence or security in the proud, imposing superiority of Lord Chatham's abilities, the shrewd, inflexible judgment of Mr. Grenville, nor in the mild but determined integrity of Lord Rockingham. His views and situation required a creature void of all these properties; and he was forced to go through every division, resolution, composition, and refinement of political chemistry, before he happily arrived at the *caput mortuum* of vitriol in your Grace. Flat and insipid in your retired state, but, brought into action, you become vitriol again. Such are the extremes of alternate indolence or fury which have governed your whole administration. Your circumstances with regard to the people soon becoming desperate, like other honest servants, you determined to involve the best of masters in the same difficulties with yourself. We owe it to your Grace's well-directed labors, that your sovereign has been persuaded to doubt of the affections of his subjects, and the people to suspect the virtues of their sovereign, at a time when both were unquestionable. You have degraded the royal dignity into a base, dishonorable competition with Mr. Wilkes, nor had you abilities to carry even this last contemptible triumph over a private man, without the grossest violation of the fundamental laws of the Constitution and

[2] If the reader wishes to understand the true state of parties at this time, and the real merits of the so much agitated question of *favoritism*, he will be aided by a consideration of the following facts:

William III. was placed on the throne in the revolution of 1688, by a union of the great Whig families; and his successors were held there against the efforts of the Jacobites by the same power. Hence the government of the country "on Revolution principles," so often spoken of, was really, to a great extent, the government of the King himself as well as the country, by a union of these families powerful enough to control Parliament. Junius has very graphically described, in the preceding Letter, the process by which George II., "under the happy influence of a connection between his ministers, was *relieved of the cares of government*." When George III. came to the throne, he determined to break away from these shackles, and to rule according to his own views and feelings, selecting such men from all parties as he considered best fitted to administer the government. If he had thrown himself into the hands of Lord Chatham for the accomplishment of this design, he would probably have succeeded. That great statesman, by the splendor of his abilities, and his unbounded influence with the body of the people, might have raised up a counterpoise against the weight of those great family combinations in the peerage. But George III. disliked the Great Commoner, and had no resource but his early friend, Lord Bute. But this nobleman had neither the abilities nor the political influence which were necessary for the accomplishment of such a scheme. As a Scotchman, particularly, he had to encounter the bitterest jealousy of the English. After a brief effort to administer the government, he gave up the attempt in despair. Still, there was a wide-spread suspicion that he maintained an undue influence over the King by secret advice and intercourse. It seems now to be settled, however, that such was not the fact. The complaint of his continuing to rule as *Favorite*, is now admitted to have been chiefly or wholly unfounded. But the King, if he persevered in his plan, must have some agents and advisers. Hence, it was maintained by Mr. Burke, in his celebrated pamphlet entitled Thoughts on the Present Discontents, that there was a regular organization, a "cabinet behind the throne," which overruled the measures of the ostensible ministry. Such, substantially, were the views of Junius, though he chose to give prominence to Lord Bute as most hated by the people. He represents one ministry after another to have been sacrificed through the influence of his Lordship. He treats the Duke of Grafton as the willing tool of this system of favoritism. All this was greatly exaggerated. Private influence did probably exist to a limited extent; but the King's frequent changes of ministers resulted partly from personal disgust, and partly from his inability to carry on the government without calling in new strength. The great Whig families, in the mean time, felt indignant at these attempts of the King to free himself from their control. Junius represented the feelings of these men; and there was much less of real patriotism in his attack on the King than he pretends. It was a struggle for power. "There were many," says an able writer, "among the Whig party, who rejoiced at the King's resolute determination to free himself from the thraldom in which 'the great Revolution families' were prepared to bind him. They felt that the reign of a haughty oligarchy was not merely degrading to the sovereign, but ruinous to the claims of 'new men' endowed with genius and capacity for affairs." The King, however, had not the requisite largeness or strength of understanding to carry out the design, and he had rejected the only man who could have enabled him to do it. He therefore threw himself into the hands of the Tories. But his quarrel with Wilkes was the great misfortune of his life. He seems at first to have been ignorant of the law on the points in question, and his ministers had not the honesty and firmness to set him right. On the contrary, they went forward, at his bidding, into the most flagrant violations of the Constitution. The great body of the nation became alienated in their affections. On these points the attacks of Junius were just, and his services important in defending the rights of the people. The King was defeated; he was compelled to give up the contest; and subsequent votes of Parliament established the principles for which Junius contended.

rights of the people. But these are rights, my Lord, which you can no more annihilate than you can the soil to which they are annexed. The question no longer turns upon points of national honor and security abroad, or on the degrees of expediency and propriety of measures at home. It was not inconsistent that you should abandon the cause of liberty in another country [Corsica], which you had persecuted in your own; and in the common arts of domestic corruption, we miss no part of Sir Robert Walpole's system except his abilities. In this humble, imitative line you might long have proceeded, safe and contemptible. You might probably never have risen to the dignity of being hated, and you might even have been despised with moderation. But, it seems, you meant to be distinguished; and to a mind like yours there was no other road to fame but by the destruction of a noble fabric, which you thought had been too long the admiration of mankind. The use you have made of the military force, introduced an alarming change in the mode of executing the laws. The arbitrary appointment of Mr. Luttrell invades the foundation of the laws themselves, as it manifestly transfers the right of legislation from those whom the people have chosen to those whom they have rejected. With a succession of such appointments, we may soon see a House of Commons collected, in the choice of which the other towns and counties of England will have as little share as the devoted county of Middlesex.

Yet I trust your Grace will find that the people of this country are neither to be intimidated by violent measures, nor deceived by refinement. When they see Mr. Luttrell seated in the House of Commons by mere dint of power, and in direct opposition to the choice of a whole county, they will not listen to those subtleties by which every arbitrary exertion of authority is explained into the law and privilege of Parliament. It requires no persuasion of argument, but simply the evidence of the senses, to convince them, that to transfer the right of election from the collective to the representative body of the people, contradicts all those ideas of a House of Commons which they have received from their forefathers, and which they had already, though vainly, perhaps, delivered to their children. The principles on which this violent measure has been defended have added scorn to injury, and forced us to feel that we are not only oppressed, but insulted.

With what force, my Lord, with what protection, are you prepared to meet the united detestation of the people of England? The city of London has given a generous example to the kingdom, in what manner a King of this country ought to be addressed; and I fancy, my Lord, it is not yet in your courage to stand between your sovereign and the addresses of his subjects. The injuries you have done this country are such as demand not only redress, but vengeance. In vain shall you look for protection to that venal vote which you have already paid for: another must be purchased; and, to save a minister, the House of Commons must declare themselves not only independent of their constituents, but the determined enemies of the Constitution. Consider, my Lord, whether this be an extremity to which their fears will permit them to advance; or, if their protection should fail you, how far you are authorized to rely upon the sincerity of those smiles, which a pious court lavishes without reluctance upon a libertine by profession. It is not, indeed, the least of the thousand contradictions which attend you, that a man, marked to the world by the grossest violation of all ceremony and decorum, should be the first servant of a court, in which prayers are morality, and kneeling is religion.[3] Trust not too far to appearances, by which your predecessors have been deceived, though they have not been injured. Even the best of princes may at last discover that this is a contention in which every thing may be lost, but nothing can be gained; and, as you became minister by accident, were adopted without choice, and continued without favor, be assured that, whenever an occasion presses, you will be discarded without even the forms of regret. You will then have reason to be thankful if you are permitted to retire to that seat of learning, which, in contemplation of the system of your life, the comparative purity of your manners with those of their high steward [Lord Sandwich], and a thousand other recommending circumstances, has chosen you to encourage the growing virtue of their youth, and to preside over their education.[4] Whenever the spirit of distributing prebends and bishoprics shall have departed from you, you will find that learned seminary perfectly recovered from the delirium of an installation, and, what in truth it ought to be, once more a peaceful scene of slumber and meditation. The venerable tutors of the university will no longer distress your modesty by proposing you for a pattern to their pupils. The learned dullness of declamation will be silent; and even the venal muse, though happiest in fiction, will forget your virtues. Yet, for the benefit of the succeeding age, I could wish that your retreat might be deferred until your morals shall happily be ripened to that maturity of corruption at which, philosophers tell us, the worst examples cease to be contagious.

JUNIUS.

---

[3] This attack on the moral and religious character of the King was wholly unmerited. A sovereign can not always find ministers able to carry on the government, whose private character he approves. George III. had no grimace in his religion; he was sincere and conscientious; and he at last wrought a surprising change in the outward morals of the higher classes, by the purity of his own household. All England has borne testimony to the wide-spread and powerful influence of his reign in this respect.

[4] The Duke of Grafton had recently been installed Chancellor of the University of Cambridge with great pomp. The poet Gray, who owed his professorship to the unsolicited patronage of the Duke, had composed his Ode for Music, to be performed on that occasion, commencing,

Hence! avaunt! 'tis holy ground!
Comus and his nightly crew, &c.

LETTER

TO HIS GRACE THE DUKE OF BEDFORD.[1]

MY LORD,—You are so little accustomed to receive any marks of respect or esteem from the public, that if, in the following lines, a compliment or expression of applause should escape me, I fear you would consider it as a mockery of your established character, and perhaps an insult to your understanding. You have nice feelings, my Lord, if we may judge from your resentments. Cautious, therefore, of giving offense, where you have so little deserved it, I shall leave the illustration of your virtues to other hands. Your friends have a privilege to play upon the easiness of your temper, or possibly they are better acquainted with your good qualities than I am. You have done good by stealth. The rest is upon record. You have still left ample room for speculation, when panegyric is exhausted.

You are indeed a very considerable man. The highest rank, a splendid fortune, and a name, glorious till it was yours, were sufficient to have supported you with meaner abilities than I think you possess. From the first, you derived a constitutional claim to respect; from the second, a natural extensive authority; the last created a partial expectation of hereditary virtues. The use you have made of these uncommon advantages might have been more honorable to yourself, but could not be more instructive to mankind. We may trace it in the veneration of your country, in the choice of your friends, and in the accomplishment of every sanguine hope which the public might have conceived from the illustrious name of Russell.

The eminence of your station gave you a commanding prospect of your duty.[2] The road, which led to honor, was open to your view. You could not lose it by mistake, and you had no temptation to depart from it by design. Compare the natural dignity and importance of the richest peer of England; the noble independence which he might have maintained in Parliament; and the real interest and respect which he might have acquired, not only in Parliament, but through the whole kingdom; compare these glorious distinctions with the ambition of holding a share in government, the emoluments of a place, the sale of a borough, or the purchase of a corporation; and, though you may not regret the virtues which create respect, you may see, with anguish, how much real importance and authority you have lost. Consider the character of an independent, virtuous Duke of Bedford; imagine

[1] Dated September 19th, 1769. The Bedford family was at this time the richest in England, and, through its borough interest and wide-spread alliances, stood foremost in political influence. The present Duke was now sixty years old, and had spent half his life in the conflicts of party. He first held office under Lord Carteret, then under Mr. Pelham, and was made Viceroy of Ireland by Lord Chatham in his first administration. Thus far he had acted as a Whig. But when Lord Bute drove out Lord Chatham in 1761, he took the office of Privy Seal, made vacant by the resignation of Chatham's brother-in-law. Lord Temple, and was now considered as uniting his interests to those of the Favorite. When Lord Bute resigned in 1763, the influence of the Duke became ascendant in the cabinet, and the administration, though ostensibly that of Mr. Grenville, has often been spoken of as the Duke of Bedford's. It was extremely unpopular, from the general belief that Lord Bute still ruled as Favorite; and in 1765 it gave way to the administration of Lord Rockingham, which threw the Duke of Bedford wholly into the back-ground. The Duke of Grafton, when he became minister in 1767, through the illness of Lord Chatham and the death of Charles Townsend, found it necessary to call in new strength, and opened negotiations, as already mentioned, with Lord Rockingham on the one hand and the Duke of Bedford on the other. The Rockingham Whigs had the strongest hopes of prevailing in these new arrangements, and of being made virtual masters of the government. But the influence of the Duke of Bedford prevailed. Three of his dependents, Lords Weymouth, Gower, and Sandwich, were received into the ministry; and the Duke of Bedford drew upon himself the bitterest resentment of the Rockingham Whigs for thus depriving them of power, and becoming, as they conceived, the savior of Lord Bute and the Tories, and thus re-establishing the system of secret influence in the closet. These events, as stated above, were the immediate cause which led the writer of these Letters to come out under a new signature, and in a bolder style of attack. After assailing the Duke of Grafton, as we have seen in the preceding letters, he now turns upon the Duke of Bedford in a spirit of still fiercer resentment. He reviews the whole public and private conduct of his Grace, and endeavors to call up all the odium of past transactions to enkindle new jealousies against him, as about to give increased effect to a system of favoritism in the closet; and seeks at the same time to overwhelm the Duke himself with a sense of dishonor, baseness, and folly, which might make him shrink from the public eye. There is nothing in all the writings of Junius that is more vehemently eloquent than the close of this letter. It is proper to add, that this eloquence is, in far too many cases, unsupported by facts.

[2] This and the next three paragraphs are among the finest specimens of composition to be found in Junius. Nowhere has he made so happy a use of *contrast*. Commencing with a natural and expressive image, he first sketches with admirable discrimination the character and conduct to be expected in the first peer of England, and then sets off against it an artful and exaggerated representation of the political errors and private weaknesses of the Duke of Bedford during the preceding thirty years.

what he might be in this country, then reflect one moment upon what you are. If it be possible for me to withdraw my attention from the fact, I will tell you in theory what such a man might be.

Conscious of his own weight and importance, his conduct in Parliament would be directed by nothing but the constitutional duty of a peer. He would consider himself as a guardian of the laws. Willing to support the just measures of government, but determined to observe the conduct of the minister with suspicion, he would oppose the violence of faction with as much firmness as the encroachments of prerogative. He would be as little capable of bargaining with the minister for places for himself or his dependents, as of descending to mix himself in the intrigues of Opposition. Whenever an important question called for his opinion in Parliament, he would be heard, by the most profligate minister, with deference and respect. His authority would either sanctify or disgrace the measures of government. The people would look up to him as to their protector, and a virtuous prince would have one honest man in his dominions, in whose integrity and judgment he might safely confide. If it should be the will of Providence to afflict him with a domestic misfortune, he would submit to the stroke with feeling, but not without dignity.[3] He would consider the people as his children, and receive a generous, heart-felt consolation in the sympathizing tears and blessings of his country.

Your Grace may probably discover something more intelligible in the negative part of this illustrious character. The man I have described would never prostitute his dignity in Parliament by an indecent violence either in opposing or defending a minister. He would not at one moment rancorously persecute, at another basely cringe to the Favorite of his sovereign. After outraging the royal dignity with peremptory conditions, little short of menace and hostility, he would never descend to the humility of soliciting an interview with the Favorite, and of offering to recover, at any price, the honor of his friendship.[4] Though deceived, perhaps, in his youth, he would not, through the course of a long life, have invariably chosen his friends from among the most profligate of mankind. His own honor would have forbidden him from mixing his private pleasures or conversation with jockeys, gamesters, blasphemers, gladiators, or buffoons. He would then have never felt, much less would he have submitted to the dishonest necessity of engaging in the interests and intrigues of his dependents—of supplying their vices, or relieving their beggary at the expense of his country. He would not have betrayed such ignorance or such contempt of the Constitution as openly to avow, in a court of justice, the purchase and sale of a borough.[5] He would not have thought it consistent with his rank in the state, or even with his personal importance, to be the little tyrant of a little corporation.[6] He would never have been insulted with virtues which he had labored to extinguish, nor suffered the disgrace of a mortifying defeat, which has made him ridiculous and contemptible, even to the few by whom he was not detested. I reverence the afflictions of a good man—his sorrows are sacred. But how can we take part in the distresses of a man whom we can neither love nor esteem, or feel for a calamity of which he himself is insensible? Where was the father's heart when he could look for, or find an immediate consolation for the loss of an only son in consultations and bargains for a place at court, and even in the misery of balloting at the India House?[7]

Admitting, then, that you have mistaken or deserted those honorable principles which ought to have directed your conduct; admitting that you have as little claim to private affection as to public esteem, let us see with what abilities, with what degree of judgment you have carried your own system into execution. A great man, in the success, and even in the magnitude of his crimes, finds a rescue from contempt. Your Grace is every way unfortunate. Yet I will not look back to those ridiculous scenes, by which, in your earlier days, you thought it an honor to be distinguished; the recorded stripes, the public infamy, your own sufferings, or Mr. Rigby's fortitude.[8] These events undoubtedly left an im-

---

[3] The Duke had lately lost his only son, Lord Tavistock, by a fall from his horse. There is great beauty in the turn of the next sentence, "he would consider the *people* as his children," which might well be done by a descendant of Lord William Russell, whose memory was venerated by the people as a martyr in the cause of liberty. This thought gives double severity to the contrast that follows, in which the character and conduct of the Duke are presented in such a light, that, instead of being able to repose his sorrows on the bosom of the people, he had made himself an object of their aversion or contempt. As to the justice of these insinuations respecting a want of "feeling" and "dignity" under this calamity, see the remarks at the end of this Letter.

[4] It is stated in a note by Junius, "At this interview, which passed at the house of the late Lord Eglintoun, Lord Bute told the Duke that he was determined never to have any connection with a man who had so basely betrayed him." Horace Walpole confirms this statement.

[5] This he did in an answer in Chancery, when sued for a large sum paid him by a gentleman, whom he had undertaken (but failed) to return as a member of Parliament. He was obliged to refund the money.

[6] The town of Bedford had been greatly exasperated by the overbearing disposition of the Duke. To deliver themselves from the thraldom in which he had held them, they admitted a great number of strangers to the freedom of the corporation, and the Duke was defeated.

[7] As to the justice of this cruel attack, see the remarks at the end of the present Letter.

[8] Note by Junius. "Mr. Heston Humphrey, a country attorney, horsewhipped the Duke, with equal justice, severity, and perseverance, on the course at Litchfield. Rigby and Lord Trentham were also cudgeled in a most exemplary manner. This gave

pression, though not upon your mind. To such a mind, it may perhaps be a pleasure to reflect, that there is hardly a corner of any of his Majesty's kingdoms, except France, in which, at one time or other, your valuable life has not been in danger. Amiable man! we see and acknowledge the protection of Providence, by which you have so often escaped the personal detestation of your fellow-subjects, and are still reserved for the public justice of your country.

Your history begins to be important at that auspicious period at which you were deputed to represent the Earl of Bute at the court of Versailles.[9] It was an honorable office, and executed with the same spirit with which it was accepted. Your patrons wanted an embassador who would submit to make concessions without daring to insist upon any honorable condition for his sovereign. Their business required a man who had as little feeling for his own dignity as for the welfare of his country; and they found him in the first rank of the nobility. Belleisle, Goree, Guadaloupe, St. Lucia, Martinique, the Fishery, and the Havana, are glorious monuments of your Grace's talents for negotiation. My Lord, we are too well acquainted with your pecuniary character to think it possible that so many public sacrifices should have been made without some private compensation. Your conduct carries with it an interior evidence, beyond all the legal proof of a court of justice. Even the callous pride of Lord Egremont was alarmed. He saw and felt his own dishonor in corresponding with you; and there certainly was a moment at which he meant to have resisted, had not a fatal lethargy prevailed over his faculties, and carried all sense and memory away with it.

I will not pretend to specify the secret terms on which you were invited to support an administration which Lord Bute pretended to leave in full possession of their ministerial authority, and perfectly masters of themselves.[10] He was not of a temper to relinquish power, though he retired from employment. Stipulations were certainly made between your Grace and him, and certainly violated. After two years' submission, you thought you had collected a strength sufficient to control his influence, and that it was your turn to be a tyrant, because you had been a slave.[11] When you found yourself mistaken in your opinion of your gracious master's firmness, disappointment got the better of all your humble discretion, and carried you to an excess of outrage to his person, as distant from true spirit, as from all decency and respect. After robbing him of the rights of a King, you would not permit him to preserve the honor of a gentleman. It was then Lord Weymouth was nominated to Ireland, and dispatched (we well remember with what indecent hurry) to plunder the treasury of the first fruits of an employment which you well knew he was never to execute.[12]

This sudden declaration of war against the Favorite might have given you a momentary merit with the public, if it had been either adopted upon principle, or maintained with resolution. Without looking back to all your former servil-

rise to the following story: When the late King heard that Sir Edward Hawke had given the French a *drubbing*, his Majesty, who had never received that kind of chastisement, was pleased to ask Lord Chesterfield the meaning of the word. 'Sir,' said Lord Chesterfield, 'the meaning of the word—But here comes the Duke of Bedford, who is better able to explain it to your Majesty than I am.'"

9 Soon after Lord Chatham was driven from office in the midst of his glorious ministry, Lord Bute sent the Duke of Bedford to negotiate a treaty of peace with France, which was signed November 3d, 1762. The concessions then made, which are here enumerated by Junius, were generally considered as highly dishonorable to the country. They were not, however, chargeable to the Duke of Bedford personally, though he may have been liable to censure for consenting to negotiate such a treaty.

The insinuation which follows, respecting the Duke's having received "some private compensation," refers to a report in circulation soon after the treaty was signed, that the Duke had been bribed by the French, in common with the Princess Dowager of Wales, Lord Bute, and Mr. Henry Fox. The story was too ridiculous to be seriously noticed, but the matter was investigated by a committee of the House of Commons, and found to rest solely on the statement of a man named Musgrave, who had "no credible authority for the imputations of treachery and corruption which he was willing to propagate."—See Heron's Junius, i., 269. Still, Junius revived the story at the end of six years, and, when called upon for proof, had nothing to allege, except that the Duke was understood to love money. "I combined the known temper of the man with the extravagant concessions of the embassador." There was another and perfectly well-known reason for these "concessions." Lord Bute could not raise funds to carry on the war. The moneyed men would not trust him. He was, therefore, compelled to make peace on such terms as he could obtain. The downright dishonesty of Junius in this case naturally leads us to receive *all* his statements with distrust, unless supported by other evidence.

10 Junius here refers to the time when Lord Bute resigned, April 8th, 1763, and the Duke of Bedford and his friends came into power in connection with Mr. George Grenville. It was at this period that the Duke compelled the King, as mentioned in a former letter, to displace Mr. Stuart Mackenzie, brother of Lord Bute, who had received the royal promise of never being removed. This arose out of the Duke's jealousy of Lord Bute at that time, and a determination to show that he was not governed by him.

11 Note by Junius. "The ministry having endeavored to exclude the Dowager out of the Regency Bill, the Earl of Bute determined to dismiss them. Upon this the Duke of Bedford demanded an audience of the King—reproached him in plain terms with his duplicity, baseness, falsehood, treachery, hypocrisy—repeatedly gave him the lie, and left him in convulsions." How far there is any truth in this statement, it is not easy now to say. It is probable there was a rumor of this kind at the time; but no one will believe that the King would ever have invited the Duke of Bedford again into his service (as he afterward did), if a tenth part of these indignities had been offered him.

12 He received three thousand pounds for plate and equipage money.

ity, we need only observe your subsequent conduct, to see upon what motives you acted. Apparently united with Mr. Grenville, you waited until Lord Rockingham's feeble administration should dissolve in its own weakness. The moment their dismission was suspected, the moment you perceived that another system was adopted in the closet, you thought it no disgrace to return to your former dependence, and solicit once more the friendship of Lord Bute. You begged an interview, at which he had spirit enough to treat you with contempt.[13]

It would now be of little use to point out by what a train of weak, injudicious measures it became necessary, or was thought so, to call you back to a share in the administration.[14] The friends, whom you did not in the last instance desert, were not of a character to add strength or credit to government; and at that time your alliance with the Duke of Grafton was, I presume, hardly foreseen. We must look for other stipulations, to account for that sudden resolution of the closet, by which three of your dependents (whose characters, I think, can not be less respected than they are) were advanced to offices, through which you might again control the minister, and probably engross the whole direction of affairs.

The possession of absolute power is now once more within your reach. The measures you have taken to obtain and confirm it are too gross to escape the eyes of a discerning, judicious prince. His palace is besieged; the lines of circumvallation are drawing round him; and unless he finds a resource in his activity, or in the attachment of the real friends of his family, the best of princes must submit to the confinement of a state prisoner, until your Grace's death, or some less fortunate event, shall raise the siege. For the present, you may safely resume that style of insult and menace, which even a private gentleman can not submit to hear without being contemptible. Mr. Mackenzie's history is not yet forgotten, and you may find precedents enough of the mode in which an imperious subject may signify his pleasure to his sovereign. Where will this gracious monarch look for assistance, when the wretched Grafton could forget his obligations to his master, and desert him for a hollow alliance with *such* a man as the Duke of Bedford?

Let us consider you, then, as arrived at the summit of worldly greatness.[15] Let us suppose that all your plans of avarice and ambition are accomplished, and your most sanguine wishes gratified, in the fear as well as the hatred of the people. Can age itself forget that you are now in the last act of life? Can gray hairs make folly venerable? and is there no period to be reserved for meditation and retirement? For shame, my Lord! Let it not be recorded of you, that the latest moments of your life were dedicated to the same unworthy pursuits, the same busy agitations, in which your youth and manhood were exhausted. Consider, that, although you can not disgrace your former life, you are violating the character of age, and exposing the impotent imbecility, after you have lost the vigor of the passions.

Your friends will ask, perhaps, Whither shall this unhappy old man retire? Can he remain in the metropolis, where his life has been so often threatened, and his palace so often attacked? If he returns to Woburn [his country seat], scorn and mockery await him. He must create a solitude round his estate, if he would avoid the face of reproach and derision. At Plymouth, his destruction would be more than probable; at Exeter, inevitable. No honest Englishman will ever forget his attachment, nor any honest Scotchman forgive his treachery, to Lord Bute. At every town he enters, he must change his liveries and his name. Whichever way he flies, the *Hue and Cry* of the country pursues him.

In another kingdom, indeed, the blessings of his administration have been more sensibly felt; his virtues better understood; or, at worst, they will not, for him alone, forget their hospitality.[16] As well might Verres have returned to Sicily. You have twice escaped, my Lord; beware of a third experiment. The indignation of a whole people, plundered, insulted, and oppressed as they have been, will not always be disappointed.

---

[13] A negotiation was opened between Lord Temple and Mr. Grenville on the one hand, and Lord Bute on the other. Mr. Grenville, however, refused to go forward without the Duke of Bedford, and Lord Bute, as stated above, refused to have any connection with his Grace. Horace Walpole makes a similar statement in his Memoirs of George III.

[14] This refers to the call of the Duke of Bedford into the administration about a year before, which created so much disappointment to the Rockingham Whigs, and was probably the occasion, as already stated, of the first letter of Junius. The King is understood to have recommended that measure; and Junius intimates that the close existing alliance with the Duke of Grafton had not then been contemplated. Three of the Duke of Bedford's dependents, viz., Lords Weymouth, Gower, and Sandwich, were now placed in very important stations. The Duke of Bedford was also suspected of being again united in full confidence with Lord Bute. Thus Junius insinuates, a plan was formed for giving him the absolute control over the government in conjunction with the Duke of Grafton, but with authority over him. The whole paragraph was intended to alarm the people on the one hand, and those who were considered "the King's friends" on the other. It need not be repeated that these suspicions of Lord Bute's continued secret influence were, to a great extent, unfounded.

[15] This and the remaining paragraphs are the most eloquent parts of the Letter. It is hardly necessary to remark how much there is in them of art, of passion, and of keen discernment into human character. There is a rapidity and glow of expression that is truly admirable. The several places are enumerated where the Duke had formerly met with tokens of public aversion, and where he might expect again to be received with reproach and derision.

[16] The Duke had been once in Ireland as Viceroy, and again when he was appointed to the principal honorary office in the University of Dublin.

It is in vain, therefore, to shift the scene. You can no more fly from your enemies than from yourself. Persecuted abroad, you look into your own heart for consolation, and find nothing but reproaches and despair. But, my Lord, you may quit the field of business, though not the field of danger; and though you can not be safe, you may cease to be ridiculous. I fear you have listened too long to the advice of those pernicious friends with whose interests you have sordidly united your own, and for whom you have sacrificed every thing that ought to be dear to a man of honor. They are still base enough to encourage the follies of your age, as they once did the vices of your youth. As little acquainted with the rules of decorum as with the laws of morality, they will not suffer you to profit by experience, nor even to consult the propriety of a bad character. Even now they tell you that life is no more than a dramatic scene, in which the hero should preserve his consistency to the last, and that, as you lived without virtue, you should die without repentance. JUNIUS.

The Duke of Bedford died four months after the publication of this letter, and Junius has succeeded in handing down his character to posterity, as a monstrous compound of baseness and folly. It has been shown, however, in the preceding notes, that some of his statements were gross falsehoods, while others were equally gross exaggerations.

The Duke was certainly a very unpopular man. He did experience the public indignities mentioned in this Letter. He was mobbed by the Spitalfield weavers; his life was more than once put in danger; and his palace in Bloomsbury Square was assaulted by congregated thousands. This was done because the price of silk goods fell greatly after the peace which he negotiated with France in 1762, and men like Junius taught those ignorant mechanics to believe that the Duke of Bedford was the cause, when the fault, if there was any, lay with Lord Bute. In like manner, his administration in Ireland was unfortunate. His manners were shy and cold; his temper was quick and imperious; he had bad friends and advisers. The Primate of Ireland united the factions of the country against him; and mobs were stirred up to break into the public buildings and set his authority at defiance. And yet Horace Walpole, who, from being his friend, had become his political enemy, states, without hesitation, that the Duke went to Ireland with the best intentions, and was really desirous to improve the condition of that miserable and distracted country. He was charged with meanness in his pecuniary concerns, and Junius sneers at his doing good "by stealth." Walpole adverts to this, and says, "his great economy was called avarice; if so, it was blended with more generosity and goodness than that passion will commonly unite with." A writer in his favor stated, without contradiction, that "he had paid his brother's debts to the amount of £100,000; had made a splendid provision for the son whom he lost, and afterward for his widow; and that he was distinguished for his bounty to his dependents and domestics." The most cruel charge in this Letter was that of insensibility to the loss of his son: a charge which Junius repeated with great vehemence on a subsequent occasion. Upon this subject, it will be sufficient to give a note of Sir Dennis Le Marchant, editor of Walpole's Memoirs of George III., vol. ii., p. 443. "The Duke's memory has been repeatedly vindicated from this cruel aspersion, and never with more generous and indignant eloquence than by Lord Brougham, in his Political Sketches, vol. iii. It has always been understood in the quarters likely to be best informed, that he felt his son's loss deeply to the last hour of his life.[17] Instead, however, of yielding to his grief, he endeavored to employ his thoughts upon public business, and the natural fervor of his disposition insensibly engaged him in the scenes before him, perhaps more deeply than he was aware. The meeting he attended at the India House must, as appears from the Company's books, have been that of April 8th, which determined the course to be taken by the Company on the government propositions: a great question, in which he took a lively interest. The force of mind he thus displayed is noticed with commendation in a letter written at the time by David Hume, who, from his connection with Conway, is assuredly an impartial witness. The absurd charge brought by Junius [Letter xxix.] against the Duchess, of making money by her son Lord Tavistock's wardrobe, originated in its having been sold for the benefit of his valet and Lady Tavistock's maid, according to the general practice of that day."

Horace Walpole, speaking of this subject, while he censures the Duke for going to the balloting at the India House, says he "was *carried* there by his creatures, Lord Sandwich, Earl Gower, and Mr. Rigby, to vote." He speaks also of these men and their associates, usually called "the Bloomsbury gang," as having been shunned by Lord Tavistock, and says, "the indecent indifference with which such a catastrophe [his sudden death] was felt by the faction of the family, spoke too plainly that Lord Tavistock had lived a reproach and terror to them." We have here the secret of a considerable portion of the Duke's misfortunes for life—those "pernicious friends" spoken of by Junius, who had "a privilege to play on the easiness of his temper." He was a very ardent politician; and was reduced to "the necessity of engaging in the interest and intrigues of his dependents; of supplying their vices and relieving their beggary at the expense of his country." His ardor in politics led him into the borough-mongering alluded to in this Letter. It also made him "at one time rancorously persecute, and at another basely cringe to, the Favorite of the Sovereign." In connection

[17] Walpole says that, "on hearing of his death, the Duke for a few days almost lost his senses."

with the impetuosity of his feelings and his sudden bursts of passion, it betrayed him into "indecent violence in opposing or defending ministers." These were his real faults, and they were great ones; but they by no means imply that depravity of heart imputed to him by Junius; and it will be observed, that this writer, in all the bitterness of his satire, does not charge the Duke with being personally an immoral man. Walpole says "he was a man of inflexible honesty and good will to his country." "His parts were certainly far from shining, and yet he spoke readily, and upon trade, well. His foible was speaking upon every subject, and imagining he understood it, as he must have done, by inspiration. He was always governed—generally by the Duchess; though immeasurably obstinate when once he had formed or had an opinion instilled into him. His manner was impetuous, of which he was so little sensible, that, being told Lord Halifax was to succeed him, he said, 'He is too warm and overbearing: the King will never endure him.' If the Duke of Bedford would have thought less of himself, the world would probably have thought better of him."—Memoirs of George II., vol. i., p. 186.

LETTER

TO THE KING.[1]

When the complaints of a brave and powerful people are observed to increase in proportion to the wrongs they have suffered—when, instead of sinking into submission, they are roused to resistance—the time will soon arrive at which every inferior consideration must yield to the security of the sovereign and to the general safety of the state. There is a moment of difficulty and danger, at which flattery and falsehood can no longer deceive, and simplicity itself can no longer be misled. Let us suppose it arrived. Let us suppose a gracious, well-intentioned prince, made sensible at last of the great duty he owes to his people, and of his own disgraceful situation; that he looks round him for assistance, and asks for no advice but how to gratify the wishes, and secure the happiness of his subjects. In these circumstances it may be matter of curious SPECULATION to consider, if an honest man were permitted to approach a King, in what terms he would address himself to his sovereign. Let it be imagined, no matter how improbable, that the first prejudice against his character is removed, that the ceremonious difficulties of an audience are surmounted, that he feels himself animated by the purest and most honorable affections to his King and country, and that the great person whom he addresses has spirit enough to bid him speak freely, and understanding enough to listen to him with attention. Unacquainted with the vain impertinence of forms, he would deliver his sentiments with dignity and firmness, but not without respect.[2]

[1] Dated December 19th, 1769. The Whigs had now effected a union among themselves. Lord Chatham had so far recovered from his three years' illness as to make it certain that he would soon be able to appear in the House of Lords. A reconciliation had taken place between him and the Grenville and Rockingham Whigs; a new session of Parliament was about to commence; and that voice was again to be heard in its councils which had so often summoned the nation to the defense of its rights. Junius, though acting by himself, would of course be acquainted with these arrangements; and to prepare the way for the approaching struggle, he now turns from the ministry to the Throne, and endeavors at once to intimidate the King, and to rouse the people to a determined resistance of the government.

The leading object of this Letter is to show the King, (1.) How great an error he had committed in making the Tories (the hereditary supporters of the Stuarts) the depositories of his power, and in choosing a Favorite from among them, while he rejected the Whigs, who had brought in the Hanover family, and thus far held them on the throne. (2.) How dishonorable was the contest he was then carrying on against a man of corrupt principles and abandoned life, whose cause good men were nevertheless compelled to take up against their sovereign, in defense of the dearest rights of the subject. (3.) That the breach of the Constitution in seating Mr. Luttrell, to the exclusion of Mr. Wilkes, in the House of Commons, was one which the nation could not long endure; that a contest was coming on between the King and the English people, in which all his reliances throughout the empire would certainly fail him; and that he ought in time to remember that "as his title to the throne was acquired by one revolution, it may be lost by another." Junius therefore exhorts him to turn from his ministers to the nation; to *dissolve Parliament* (a measure which the Whigs had now determined to press as their main point), and thus leave the people to decide the question by the choice of a new House of Commons. There is but little to condemn in this Letter, except the ridiculous charge that "England had been sold to France" in making the peace of 1762, and the attempt to create a national animosity against the Scotch. The King had fallen into great errors, although there were palliating circumstances in his early education, and his strong aversion to Wilkes as a licentious and profligate man. Still, they were errors which involved the safety of the empire; it was right to expose them; and while Junius does it with the utmost plainness, he shows comparatively little of that insulting and malignant spirit which characterized his attack upon the King in his first Letter.

[2] It will repay the student in oratory to review this introduction, and see how skillfully the reasons which justified so remarkable an address to the sovereign, are summed up and presented. He will observe, too, how adroitly Junius assumes the air of one engaged in "a curious speculation" on a supposed case, giving what follows as a mere *fancy-*

Sir,—It is the misfortune of your life, and originally the cause of every reproach and distress which has attended your government, that you should never have been acquainted with the language of truth until you heard it in the complaints of your people. It is not, however, too late to correct the error of your education. We are still inclined to make an indulgent allowance for the pernicious lessons you received in your youth, and to form the most sanguine hopes from the natural benevolence of your disposition.[3] We are far from thinking you capable of a direct, deliberate purpose to invade those original rights of your subjects, on which all their civil and political liberties depend. Had it been possible for us to entertain a suspicion so dishonorable to your character, we should long since have adopted a style of remonstrance very distant from the humility of complaint. The doctrine inculcated by our laws, *that the King can do no wrong*, is admitted without reluctance. We separate the amiable, good-natured prince from the folly and treachery of his servants, and the private virtues of the man from the vices of his government. Were it not for this just distinction, I know not whether your Majesty's condition, or that of the English nation, would deserve most to be lamented. I would prepare your mind for a favorable reception of truth. by removing every painful, offensive idea of personal reproach. Your subjects, sir, wish for nothing but that, as *they* are reasonable and affectionate enough to separate your person from your government, so *you*, in your turn, should distinguish between the conduct which becomes the permanent dignity of a King, and that which serves only to promote the temporary interest and miserable ambition of a minister.

You ascended the throne with a declared, and, I doubt not, a sincere resolution of giving universal satisfaction to your subjects. You found them pleased with the novelty of a young prince, whose countenance promised even more than his words, and loyal to you not only from principle, but passion. It was not a cold profession of allegiance to the first magistrate, but a partial, animated attachment to a favorite prince, the native of their country. They did not wait to examine your conduct, nor to be determined by experience, but gave you a generous credit for the future blessings of your reign, and paid you in advance the dearest tribute of their affections. Such, sir, was once the disposition of a people, who now surround your throne with reproaches and complaints. Do justice to yourself. Banish from your mind those unworthy opinions with which some interested persons have labored to possess you. Distrust the men who tell you that the English are naturally light and inconstant; that they complain without a cause. Withdraw your confidence equally from all parties—from ministers, favorites, and relations; and let there be one moment in your life in which you have consulted your own understanding.

When you affectedly renounced the name of Englishman,[4] believe me, sir, you were persuaded to pay a very ill-judged compliment to one part of your subjects, at the expense of another. While the natives of Scotland are not in actual rebellion, they are undoubtedly entitled to protection; nor do I mean to condemn the policy

---

sketch, in order to take off the appearance of intending any thing personally offensive to the King. He will be struck, also, with the dexterity shown in assuming just the requisite appearance of playing with the subject, when he says, "if an honest man were permitted to approach a King;" and the delicacy and apparent respect with which he enters on the task of administering to his sovereign unsought-for counsel and humiliating reproof.

[3] Note by Junius. The plan of tutelage and future dominion over the heir-apparent, laid many years ago at Carlton House between the Princess Dowager and her favorite the Earl of Bute, was as gross and palpable as that which was concerted between Anne of Austria and Cardinal Mazarin to govern Louis the Fourteenth, and in effect to prolong his minority until the end of their lives. That prince had strong natural parts, and used frequently to blush for his own ignorance and want of education, which had been willfully neglected by his mother and her minion. A little experience, however, soon showed him how shamefully he had been treated, and for what infamous purposes he had been kept in ignorance. Our great Edward, too, at an early period, had sense enough to understand the nature of the connection between his abandoned mother and the detested Mortimer. But, since that time, human nature, we may observe, is greatly altered for the better. Dowagers may be chaste, and minions may be honest. When it was proposed to settle the present King's household as Prince of Wales, it is well known that the Earl of Bute was forced into it, in direct contradiction to the late King's inclination. *That* was the salient point from which all the mischiefs and disgraces of the present reign took life and motion. From that moment, Lord Bute never suffered the Prince of Wales to be an instant out of his sight. We need not look farther.

On this statement Mr. Heron makes the following remarks in his edition of Junius, vol. ii., 43: "There was, therefore, no dishonest plan for keeping the King in perpetual pupilage formed between his mother and the Earl of Bute. Neither had George the Second nor the Princess Dowager of Wales committed the education of the young Prince to the Jacobites and Tories. His education was not neglected, but managed with admirable success and care. Not the young King, but their incapacity and unpopularity, drove the Newcastle party from power. Not the King, but his own arrogance, and the opposition and dislike of the Newcastle party and others, dismissed Mr. Pitt from the administration. The union of parties, and the breaking down of the great Whig party, was originally the measure of Pitt, and arose from the natural progress of things. So unjust are the imputations with which this Letter commences." The truth lies between the two.

[4] Junius here lays hold of and perverts the language used by the King in his first speech after coming to the throne: "Born and educated in this country, I glory in the name of *Briton*," &c. The prevailing hostility to the Scotch led many to comment on this avoidance of the word Englishman, as probably dictated by Lord Bute, and as indicating too much anxiety to conciliate the people of Scotland.

of giving some encouragement to the novelty of their affections for the house of Hanover. I am ready to hope for every thing from their new-born zeal, and from the future steadiness of their allegiance. But hitherto they have no claim to your favor. To honor them with a determined predilection and confidence, in exclusion of your English subjects, who placed your family, and, in spite of treachery and rebellion, have supported it upon the throne, is a mistake too gross even for the unsuspecting generosity of youth. In this error we see a capital violation of the most obvious rules of policy and prudence. We trace it, however, to an original bias in your education, and are ready to allow for your inexperience.

To the same early influence we attribute it, that you have descended to take a share not only in the narrow views and interests of particular persons, but in the fatal malignity of their passions. At your accession to the throne, the whole system of government was altered, not from wisdom or deliberation, but because it had been adopted by your predecessor. A little personal motive of pique and resentment was sufficient to remove the ablest servants of the Crown; but it is not in this country, sir, that such men can be dishonored by the frowns of a King.[5] They were dismissed, but could not be disgraced. Without entering into a minuter discussion of the merits of the peace, we may observe, in the imprudent hurry with which the first overtures from France were accepted, in the conduct of the negotiation, and terms of the treaty, the strongest marks of that precipitate spirit of concession with which a certain part of your subjects have been at all times ready to purchase a peace with the natural enemies of this country. On *your* part we are satisfied that every thing was honorable and sincere, and if England was sold to France, we doubt not that your Majesty was equally betrayed. The conditions of the peace were matter of grief and surprise to your subjects, but not the immediate cause of their present discontent.

Hitherto, sir, you had been sacrificed to the prejudices and passions of others. With what firmness will you bear the mention of your own?

A man, not very honorably distinguished in the world, commences a formal attack upon your Favorite, considering nothing but how he might best expose his person and principles to detestation, and the national character of his countrymen to contempt. The natives of that country, sir, are as much distinguished by a peculiar character as by your Majesty's favor. Like another chosen people, they have been conducted into the Land of Plenty, where they find themselves effectually marked, and divided from mankind. There is hardly a period at which the most irregular character may not be redeemed. The mistakes of one sex find a retreat in patriotism; those of the other in devotion. Mr. Wilkes brought with him into politics the same liberal sentiments by which his private conduct had been directed, and seemed to think, that, as there are few excesses in which an English gentleman may not be permitted to indulge, the same latitude was allowed him in the choice of his political principles, and in the spirit of maintaining them. I mean to state, not entirely to defend his conduct. In the earnestness of his zeal, he suffered some unwarrantable insinuations to escape him. He said more than moderate men would justify, but not enough to entitle him to the honor of your Majesty's personal resentment. The rays of royal indignation, collected upon him, served only to illuminate, and could not consume. Animated by the favor of the people on one side, and heated by persecution on the other, his views and sentiments changed with his situation. Hardly serious at first, he is now an enthusiast. The coldest bodies warm with opposition, the hardest sparkle in collision. There is a wholly mistaken zeal in politics as well as religion. By persuading others, we convince ourselves. The passions are engaged, and create a maternal affection in the mind, which forces us to love the cause for which we suffer. Is this a contention worthy of a King? Are you not sensible how much the meanness of the cause gives an air of ridicule to the serious difficulties into which you have been betrayed? The destruction of one man has been now, for many years, the sole object of your government; and, if there can be any thing still more disgraceful, we have seen, for such an object, the utmost influence of the executive power, and every ministerial artifice, exerted without success. Nor can you ever succeed, unless *he* should be imprudent enough to forfeit the protection of those laws to which you owe your crown, or unless your ministers should persuade you to make it a question of force alone, and try the whole strength of government in opposition to the people. The lessons *he* has received from experience will probably guard him from such excess of folly; and in your Majesty's virtues we find an unquestionable assurance that no illegal violence will be attempted.

Far from suspecting you of so horrible a design, we would attribute the continued violation of the laws, and even this last enormous attack upon the vital principles of the Constitution, to an ill-advised, unworthy personal resentment. From one false step you have been betrayed into another, and, as the cause was unworthy of you, your ministers were determined that the prudence of the execution should correspond with the wisdom and dignity of the design. They have reduced you to the necessity of choosing out of a variety of difficulties—to a situation so unhappy, that you can neither do wrong without ruin, nor right without affliction. These worthy servants have undoubtedly given you many singular proofs of their abilities. Not contented with making Mr. Wilkes a man of importance,

[5] Note by Junius. One of the first acts of the present reign was to dismiss Mr. Legge, because he had some years before refused to yield his interest in Hampshire to a Scotchman recommended by Lord Bute. This was the reason publicly assigned by his Lordship.

they have judiciously transferred the question from the rights and interests of one man to the most important rights and interests of the people, and forced your subjects, from wishing well to the cause of an individual, to unite with him in their own. Let them proceed as they have begun, and your Majesty need not doubt that the catastrophe will do no dishonor to the conduct of the piece.

The circumstances to which you are reduced will not admit of a compromise with the English nation. Undecisive, qualifying measures will disgrace your government still more than open violence, and, without satisfying the people, will excite their contempt. They have too much understanding and spirit to accept of an indirect satisfaction for a direct injury. Nothing less than a repeal, as formal as the resolution itself, can heal the wound which has been given to the Constitution, nor will any thing less be accepted. I can readily believe that there is an influence sufficient to recall that pernicious vote. The House of Commons undoubtedly consider their duty to the Crown as paramount to all other obligations. To *us* they are only indebted for an accidental existence, and have justly transferred their gratitude from their parents to their benefactors—from those who gave them birth, to the minister from whose benevolence they derive the comforts and pleasures of their political life; who has taken the tenderest care of their infancy, relieves their necessities without offending their delicacy, and has given them, what they value most, a virtuous education. But, if it were possible for their integrity to be degraded to a condition so vile and abject, that, compared with it, the present estimation they stand in is a state of honor and respect, consider, sir, in what manner you will afterward proceed? Can you conceive that the people of this country will long submit to be governed by so flexible a House of Commons? It is not in the nature of human society that any form of government, in such circumstances, can long be preserved. In ours, the general contempt of the people is as fatal as their detestation. Such, I am persuaded, would be the necessary effect of any base concession made by the present House of Commons; and, as a qualifying measure would not be accepted, it remains for you to decide whether you will, at any hazard, support a set of men, who have reduced you to this unhappy dilemma, or whether you will gratify the united wishes of the whole people of England by dissolving the Parliament.

Taking it for granted, as I do very sincerely, that you have personally no design against the Constitution, nor any views inconsistent with the good of your subjects, I think you can not hesitate long upon the choice which it equally concerns your interest and your honor to adopt. On one side, you hazard the affections of all your English subjects; you relinquish every hope of repose to yourself, and you endanger the establishment of your family forever. All this you venture for no object whatsoever, or for such an object as it would be an affront to you to name. Men of sense will examine your conduct with suspicion; while those who are incapable of comprehending to what extent they are injured, afflict you with clamors equally insolent and unmeaning. Supposing it possible that no fatal struggle should ensue, you determine at once to be unhappy, without the hope of a compensation either from interest or ambition. If an English king be hated or despised, he *must* be unhappy; and this, perhaps, is the only political truth which he ought to be convinced of without experiment. But if the English people should no longer confine their resentment to a submissive representation of their wrongs; if, following the glorious example of their ancestors, they should no longer appeal to the creature of the Constitution, but to that high Being who gave them the rights of humanity, whose gifts it were sacrilege to surrender, let me ask you, sir, upon what part of your subjects would you rely for assistance?

The people of Ireland have been uniformly plundered and oppressed. In return, they give you every day fresh marks of their resentment. They despise the miserable governor [Viscount Townsend] you have sent them, because he is the creature of Lord Bute; nor is it from any natural confusion in their ideas that they are so ready to confound the original of a king with the disgraceful representation of him.

The distance of the colonies would make it impossible for them to take an active concern in your affairs, if they were as well affected to your government as they once pretended to be to your person. They were ready enough to distinguish between *you* and your ministers. They complained of an act of the Legislature, but traced the origin of it no higher than to the servants of the Crown. They pleased themselves with the hope that their Sovereign, if not favorable to their cause, at least was impartial. The decisive, personal part you took against them, has effectually banished that first distinction from their minds.[6] They consider you as united with your servants against America, and know how to distinguish the sovereign and a venal Parliament on one side, from the real sentiments of the English people on the other. Looking forward to independence, they might possibly receive you for their king; but, if ever you retire to America, be assured they will give you such a Covenant to digest, as the presbytery of Scotland would have been ashamed to offer to Charles the Second. They left their native land in search of freedom, and found it in a desert. Divided as they are into a thousand forms

[6] In the King's speech of 8th November, 1768, it was declared "that the spirit of faction had broken out afresh in some of the colonies, and, in one of them, proceeded to acts of violence and resistance to the execution of the laws; that Boston was in a state of disobedience to all law and government, and had proceeded to measures subversive of the Constitution, and attended with circumstances that manifested a disposition to throw off their dependence on Great Britain."

of policy and religion, there is one point in which they all agree: they equally detest the pageantry of a King, and the supercilious hypocrisy of a bishop.

It is not, then, from the alienated affections of Ireland or America, that you can reasonably look for assistance; still less from the people of England, who are actually contending for their rights, and, in this great question, are parties against you. You are not, however, destitute of every appearance of support. You have all the Jacobites, Nonjurors, Roman Catholics, and Tories of this country, and all Scotland without exception. Considering from what family you are descended, the choice of your friends has been singularly directed; and truly, sir, if you had not lost the Whig interest of England, I should admire your dexterity in turning the hearts of your enemies. Is it possible for you to place any confidence in men, who, before they are faithful to you, must renounce every opinion, and betray every principle, both in church and state, which they inherit from their ancestors, and are confirmed in by their education? whose numbers are so inconsiderable, that they have long since been obliged to give up the principles and language which distinguished them as a party, and to fight under the banners of their enemies? Their zeal begins with hypocrisy, and must conclude in treachery. At first they deceive, at last they betray.

As to the Scotch, I must suppose your heart and understanding so biased, from your earliest infancy, in their favor, that nothing less than *your own* misfortunes can undeceive you. You will not accept of the uniform experience of your ancestors; and when once a man is determined to believe, the very absurdity of the doctrine confirms him in his faith. A bigoted understanding can draw a proof of attachment to the house of Hanover from a notorious zeal for the house of Stuart, and find an earnest of future loyalty in former rebellions. Appearances are, however, in their favor; so strongly, indeed, that one would think they had forgotten that you are their lawful King, and had mistaken you for a Pretender to the crown. Let it be admitted, then, that the Scotch are as sincere in their present professions as if you were in reality not an Englishman, but a Briton of the North—you would not be the first prince of their native country against whom they have rebelled, nor the first whom they have basely betrayed. Have you forgotten, sir, or has your Favorite concealed from you that part of our history, when the unhappy Charles (and he, too, had private virtues) fled from the open, avowed indignation of his English subjects, and surrendered himself at discretion to the good faith of his own countrymen? Without looking for support in their affections as subjects, he applied only to their honor as gentlemen, for protection. They received him as they would your Majesty, with bows, and smiles, and falsehood, and kept him until they had settled their bargain with the English Parliament; then basely sold their native king to the vengeance of his enemies. This, sir, was not the act of a few traitors, but the deliberate treachery of a Scotch Parliament representing the nation. A wise prince might draw from it two lessons of equal utility to himself. On one side he might learn to dread the undisguised resentment of a generous people, who dare openly assert their rights, and who, in a just cause, are ready to meet their sovereign in the field. On the other side, he would be taught to apprehend something far more formidable—a fawning treachery, against which no prudence can guard, no courage can defend. The insidious smiles upon the cheek would warn him of the canker in the heart.

From the uses to which one part of the army has been too frequently applied, you have some reason to expect that there are no services they would refuse. Here, too, we trace the partiality of your understanding. You take the sense of the army from the conduct of the Guards, with the same justice with which you collect the sense of the people from the representations of the ministry. Your marching regiments, sir, will not make the Guards their example, either as soldiers or subjects. They feel and resent, as they ought to do, that invariable, undistinguishing favor with which the Guards are treated; while those gallant troops, by whom every hazardous, every laborious service is performed, are left to perish in garrisons abroad, or pine in quarters at home, neglected and forgotten.[7] If they had no sense of the great original duty they owe their country, their resentment would operate like patriotism, and leave your cause to be defended by those to whom you have lavished the rewards and honors of their profession. The Pretorian bands, enervated and debauched as they were, had still strength enough to awe the Roman populace; but when the distant legions took the alarm, they marched to Rome, and gave away the Empire.[8]

On this side, then, whichever way you turn your eyes, you see nothing but perplexity and distress. You may determine to support the very ministry who have reduced your affairs to this deplorable situation; you may shelter yourself under the forms of Parliament, and set your

---

[7] Note by Junius. The number of commissioned officers in the Guards are to the marching regiments as *one* to eleven; the number of regiments given to the Guards, compared with those given to the line, is about three to one, at a moderate computation; consequently, the partiality in favor of the Guards is as thirty-three to one. So much for the officers. The private men have fourpence a day to subsist on, and five hundred lashes if they desert. Under this punishment they frequently expire. With these encouragements, it is supposed they may be depended upon, whenever a certain person thinks it necessary to butcher his *fellow-subjects*.

[8] This is one of the passages which show the familiarity of Junius with Tacitus, when composing these Letters. The event referred to was the march of the German legions to Rome, under Vitellius, and their defeat of the Pretorian Bands, who had previously given the imperial dignity to Otho, from whom it passed to Vitellius.

people at defiance. But, be assured, sir, that such a resolution would be as imprudent as it would be odious. If it did not immediately shake your establishment, it would rob you of your peace of mind forever.

On the other, how different is the prospect! How easy, how safe and honorable is the path before you! The English nation declare they are grossly injured by their representatives, and solicit your Majesty to exert your lawful prerogative, and give them an opportunity of recalling a trust, which, they find, has been so scandalously abused. You are not to be told that the power of the House of Commons is not original, but delegated to them for the welfare of the people, from whom they received it. A question of right arises between the constituent and the representative body. By what authority shall it be decided? Will your Majesty interfere in a question in which you have properly no immediate concern? It would be a step equally odious and unnecessary. Shall the Lords be called upon to determine the rights and privileges of the Commons? They can not do it without a flagrant breach of the Constitution. Or will you refer it to the judges? They have often told your ancestors that the law of Parliament is above them. What party then remains, but to leave it to the people to determine for themselves? They alone are injured; and since there is no superior power to which the cause can be referred, they alone ought to determine.

I do not mean to perplex you with a tedious argument upon a subject already so discussed, that inspiration could hardly throw a new light upon it. There are, however, two points of view in which it particularly imports your Majesty to consider the late proceedings of the House of Commons. By depriving a subject of his birthright, they have attributed to their own vote an authority equal to an act of the whole Legislature; and, though perhaps not with the same motives, have strictly followed the example of the Long Parliament, which first declared the regal office useless, and soon after, with as little ceremony, dissolved the House of Lords. The same pretended power which robs an English subject of his birthright, may rob an English King of his crown. In another view, the resolution of the House of Commons, apparently not so dangerous to your Majesty, is still more alarming to your people. Not contented with divesting one man of his right, they have arbitrarily conveyed that right to another. They have set aside a return as illegal, without daring to censure those officers who were particularly apprised of Mr. Wilkes's incapacity, not only by the declaration of the House, but expressly by the writ directed to them, and who nevertheless returned him as duly elected.[9] They have rejected the majority of votes, the only criterion by which our laws judge of the sense of the people; they have transferred the right of election from the collective to the representative body; and by these acts, taken separately or together, they have essentially altered the original constitution of the House of Commons. Versed, as your Majesty undoubtedly is, in the English history, it can not easily escape you, how much it is to your interest, as well as your duty, to prevent one of the three estates from encroaching upon the province of the other two, or assuming the authority of them all. When once they have departed from the great constitutional line by which all their proceedings should be directed, who will answer for their future moderation? Or what assurance will they give you, that, when they have trampled upon their equals, they will submit to a superior? Your Majesty may learn hereafter how nearly the slave and tyrant are allied.

Some of your council, more candid than the rest, admit the abandoned profligacy of the present House of Commons, but oppose their dissolution upon an opinion, I confess not very unwarrantable, that their successors would be equally at the disposal of the treasury. I can not persuade myself that the nation will have profited so little by experience. But if that opinion were well founded, you might then gratify our wishes at an easy rate, and appease the present clamor against your government without offering any material injury to the favorite cause of corruption.

You have still an honorable part to act. The affections of your subjects may still be recovered. But, before you subdue *their* hearts, you must gain a noble victory over your own. Discard those little personal resentments which have too long directed your public conduct. Pardon this man the remainder of his punishment, and, if resentment still prevails, make it, what it should have been long since, an act, not of mercy, but contempt.[10] He will soon fall back into his natural station—a silent senator, and hardly supporting the weekly eloquence of a newspaper. The gentle breath of peace would leave him on

9 There is force in this remark. If there was any blame in the Middlesex election, it certainly rested with the returning officers. They ought to have known, better than the common people of Middlesex could be presumed to know, whether Mr. Wilkes was disqualified by his expulsion from the House. But they received the votes, and returned him as member, and then the House of Commons punished the electors by setting aside their votes, without a word of censure on the returning officers.

10 He *was* pardoned and released from prison within less than four months. This Letter probably convinced the King that he could no longer maintain the contest. A general illumination took place throughout London on the night following his release. His debts had been previously paid or compromised by the Society of the People's Rights. Wilkes was soon after chosen an alderman of London, and subsequently Lord Mayor. At the next general election in 1774, he was returned again as member for Middlesex, and took his seat without opposition. On the dismissal of Lord North's administration in 1782, the obnoxious resolutions which gave Colonel Luttrell his seat were expunged, on his own motion, from the journals of the House of Commons.

the surface, neglected and unremoved. It is only the tempest that lifts him from his place.

Without consulting your minister, call together your whole council. Let it appear to the public that you can determine and act for yourself. Come forward to your people. Lay aside the wretched formalities of a King, and speak to your subjects with the spirit of a man, and in the language of a gentleman. Tell them you have been fatally deceived. The acknowledgment will be no disgrace, but rather an honor to your understanding. Tell them you are determined to remove every cause of complaint against your government; that you will give your confidence to no man who does not possess the confidence of your subjects; and leave it to themselves to determine, by their conduct at a future election, whether or no it be in reality the general sense of the nation, that their rights have been arbitrarily invaded by the present House of Commons, and the Constitution betrayed. They will then do justice to their representatives and to themselves.

These sentiments, sir, and the style they are conveyed in, may be offensive, perhaps, because they are new to you. Accustomed to the language of courtiers, you measure their affections by the vehemence of their expressions; and when they only praise you indirectly, you admire their sincerity. But this is not a time to trifle with your fortune. They deceive you, sir, who tell you that you have many friends, whose affections are founded upon a principle of personal attachment. The first foundation of friendship is not the power of conferring benefits, but the equality with which they are received, and *may* be returned. The fortune which made you a King forbade you to have a friend. It is a law of nature which can not be violated with impunity. The mistaken prince, who looks for friendship, will find a Favorite, and in that Favorite the ruin of his affairs.

The people of England are loyal to the house of Hanover, not from a vain preference of one family to another, but from a conviction that the establishment of that family was necessary to the support of their civil and religious liberties. This, sir, is a principle of allegiance equally solid and rational, fit for Englishmen to adopt, and well worthy of your Majesty's encouragement. We can not long be deluded by national distinctions. The name of Stuart, of itself, is only contemptible; armed with the sovereign authority, their principles were formidable. The Prince, who imitates their conduct, should be warned by their example; and while he plumes himself upon the security of his title to the crown, should remember that, as it was acquired by one revolution, it may be lost by another.

Junius.

This letter was published just before the Christmas holidays, and immediately after their close, Parliament commenced its session. Lord Chatham came out at once as leader of the Whigs, now united into one body, and within nineteen days the Duke of Grafton was compelled to resign. But Junius and his friends were bitterly disappointed. The King had, indeed, the wisdom to remove the great source of contention by pardoning Wilkes; but he clung to his Tory advisers; he placed Lord North at the head of affairs, and for twelve years persisted in his favorite measures, and especially his resolution to force taxation on America, until he drove her out of the empire.

Before leaving this letter, it will be proper to give a brief account of the celebrated trial to which it gave rise. Woodfall, the publisher, was prosecuted for a seditious libel, and brought before the Court of King's Bench on the 13th of June, 1770. Lord Mansfield, in charging the jury, told them "that there were only two points for their consideration: the first, the printing and publishing of the paper in question; the second, the sense and meaning of it. That as to the charges of its being malicious, seditious, &c., these were *inferences of law*. That, therefore, the printing and sense of the paper were alone what the jury had to consider of; and that, if the paper should really contain no breach of law, that was a matter which might afterward be moved in arrest of judgment." This put the prisoner completely in the power of the judges. The jury had no right to inquire into his motives or the real merits of the case. As the fact of publication was admitted, and the meaning of the words was clear, they must pronounce him *guilty*, although perfectly satisfied that he had spoken the truth, and had been governed by upright intentions. This, certainly, made the trial by jury in cases of libel a mere farce. In the present instance, the jury got round the difficulty by bringing in a verdict, "Guilty of the printing and publishing *only*." The question now arose, "What is the legal effect of this finding?" The Attorney General claimed that it was to be taken as a *conviction;* the counsel of Woodfall, that it amounted to an *acquittal*. The case was argued at length, and the court decided for neither party. They set the verdict aside, and ordered a new trial. This, however, was the same to Woodfall as an acquittal; for it was perfectly well known that no jury could ever be found in the city of London to return a verdict against the publisher. The matter was therefore dropped, and Junius came off victorious.

Much blame was thrown upon Lord Mansfield for this decision. The subject was brought before the House of Lords by Lord Chatham, and Lord Mansfield said in reply, "His Lordship tells the House that doctrines no less new than dangerous have been inculcated in this court, and that, particularly in a charge which I delivered to the jury on Mr. Woodfall's trial, my directions were contrary to law, repugnant to practice, and injurious to the dearest liberties of the people. This is an alarming picture, my Lords; it is drawn with great parade, and colored to affect the passions amazingly. Unhappily, however, for the painter, it wants the essential circumstance of *truth* in the design, and must, like many other political pictures, be thrown, notwithstanding the reputation of the artist, among the miserable daubings of faction. So far, my Lords, is the accusation without truth, that the directions now given to juries are the same that they have ever been. There is no novelty introduced—no chicanery attempted; nor has there, till very lately, been any complaint of the integrity of the King's Bench."

The opinion of enlightened jurists at the present day, as to the merits of the case, is expressed by Lord Campbell in his Lives of the Chief Justices, vol. ii., p. 480.

"Lord Mansfield, in the course of these trials, had done nothing to incur moral blame. I think his doctrine—that the jury were only to find the fact of publication and the *innuendos*—contrary to law as well as liberty. His grand argument for making the question of 'libel or not' exclusively one of law, that the defendant may demur or move in arrest of judgment, and so refer it to the court, admits of the easy answer, that, although there may be a writing set out in the information as libelous which it could under no circumstances be criminal to publish, yet that an information may set out a paper the publication of which may or may not be criminal, according to the intention of the defendant and the circumstances under which it is published. Therefore, supposing judges to be ever so pure, upright, and intelligent, justice could not be done by leaving to them the criminality or innocence of the paper alleged to be libelous, as a mere abstract question of law, to be decided by reading the record. Nevertheless, there were various authorities for the rule which Lord Mansfield had laid down; and, in laying it down, he not only followed the example of his immediate predecessors, but he was supported by the unanimous opinion of his brethren who sat by him. There was no pretense for representing him as a daring innovator, who, slavishly wishing to please the government, tried to subvert trial by jury, and to extinguish the liberty of the press."

Junius, as might be expected, attacked Lord Mansfield soon after in the most vehement terms. If he had confined himself to the legal question and the rights of juries, no one could have condemned him for using strong language; but he followed his ordinary method of assailing character and motives. He revived the exploded story of Mansfield's having drunk the Pretender's health on his knees. He tortured him by the most cruel insinuations. But he overshot his mark, and fell into the grossest errors, especially in his grand controversy about the right of Lord Mansfield to bail a man named Eyre, in which, as Lord Campbell remarks, "Junius was egregiously in the wrong, clearly showing that he was not a lawyer, his mistakes not being designedly made for disguise, but palpably proceeding from an ignorant man affecting knowledge." —Ibid., p. 402.

The trial of Woodfall was ultimately productive of good. It roused the public mind to the rights of juries. A similar case came up in 1784, when the Dean of St. Asaph was tried for a libel; and at this time Mr. Erskine made his celebrated argument on the subject, which prepared the way for an act of Parliament, declaring the right of juries to decide on the law as well as the facts in cases of libel.

LETTER

TO HIS GRACE THE DUKE OF GRAFTON.[1]

My Lord,—If I were personally your enemy, I might pity and forgive you. You have every claim to compassion that can arise from misery and distress. The condition you are reduced to would disarm a private enemy of his resentment, and leave no consolation to the most vindictive spirit, but that such an object as you are would disgrace the dignity of revenge. But, in the relation you have borne to this country, you have no title to indulgence; and, if I had followed the dictates of my own opinion, I never should have allowed you the respite of a moment. In your public character, you have injured every subject of the empire; and, though an individual is not authorized to forgive the injuries done to society, he *is* called upon to assert his separate share in the public resentment. I submitted, however, to the judgment of men, more moderate, perhaps more candid than myself. For my own part, I do not pretend to understand those prudent forms of decorum, those gentle rules of discretion, which some men endeavor to unite with the conduct of the greatest and most hazardous affairs. Engaged in the defense of an honorable cause, I would take a decisive part. I should scorn to provide for a future retreat, or to keep terms with a man who preserves no measures with the public. Neither the abject submission of deserting his post in the hour of danger, nor even the sacred shield of cowardice,[2]

[1] Dated February 14th, 1770. This Letter must have been commenced within a week after the resignation of the Duke of Grafton. It is Junius' first shout of triumph over the fall of his adversary. He evidently regarded Lord North's ministry as a mere modification of the Bedford party; and, as he always underrated his talents, he now treats him, at the close of this Letter, with great contempt, expressing (what he undoubtedly felt) a firm conviction that the whole concern must soon fall to pieces, and the Whigs be called into office.

This is one of the most finished productions of Junius. It has more eloquence than the Letter to the King, and would deserve our unqualified admiration, if it were as just as it is eloquent.

[2] *Sacro tremuere timore.* Every coward pretends to be planet-struck.

should protect him. I would pursue him through life, and try the last exertion of my abilities to preserve the perishable infamy of his name, and make it immortal.

What then, my Lord, is this the event of all the sacrifices you have made to Lord Bute's patronage, and to your own unfortunate ambition? Was it for this you abandoned your earliest friendships—the warmest connections of your youth, and all those honorable engagements, by which you once solicited, and might have acquired, the esteem of your country? Have you secured no recompense for such a waste of honor? Unhappy man! What party will receive the common deserter of all parties? Without a client to flatter, without a friend to console you, and with only one companion from the honest house of Bloomsbury, you must now retire into a dreadful solitude, [which you have created for yourself].[3] At the most active period of life, you must quit the busy scene, and conceal yourself from the world, if you would hope to save the wretched remains of a ruined reputation. The vices never fail of their effect. They operate like age—bring on dishonor before its time, and, in the prime of youth, leave the character broken and exhausted.

Yet your conduct has been mysterious as well as contemptible. Where is now that firmness, or obstinacy, so long boasted of by your friends, and acknowledged by your enemies? We were taught to expect that you would not leave the ruin of this country to be completed by other hands, but were determined either to gain a decisive victory over the Constitution, or to perish, bravely at least, in the last dike of the prerogative. You knew the danger, and might have been provided for it. You took sufficient time to prepare for a meeting with your Parliament, to confirm the mercenary fidelity of your dependents, and to suggest to your Sovereign a language suited to his dignity, at least, if not to his benevolence and wisdom. Yet, while the whole kingdom was agitated with anxious expectation upon one great point, you meanly evaded the question, and, instead of the explicit firmness and decision of a King, you gave us nothing but the misery of a ruined grazier,[4] and the whining piety of a Methodist. We had reason to expect that notice would have been taken of the petitions which the King has received from the English nation; and, although I can conceive some personal motives for not yielding to them, I can find none, in common prudence or decency, for treating them with contempt. Be assured, my Lord, the English people will not tamely submit to this unworthy treatment. They had a right to be heard; and their petitions, if not granted, deserved to be considered. Whatever be the real views and doctrine of a court, the Sovereign should be taught to preserve some forms of attention to his subjects, and, if he will not redress their grievances, not to make them a topic of jest and mockery among the lords and ladies of the bedchamber. Injuries may be atoned for and forgiven; but insults admit of no compensation. They degrade the mind in its own esteem, and force it to recover its level by revenge. This neglect of the petitions was, however, a part of your original plan of government; nor will any consequences it has produced account for your deserting your Sovereign in the midst of that distress in which you and your new friends [the Bedfords] had involved him. One would think, my Lord, you might have taken this spirited resolution before you had dissolved the last of those early connections which once, even in your own opinion, did honor to your youth—before you had obliged Lord Granby to quit a service he was attached to—before you had discarded one Chancellor and killed another.[5]

[3] The words in brackets were contained in the Letter as it originally appeared in the Public Advertiser, but were struck out by Junius in his revised edition. As they add an important idea, and give the period an easier cadence, it may be doubted whether the author did wisely to omit them. It is unnecessary to remark on the animated flow and condensed energy of this paragraph. An able critic has said, in rather strong terms, "No language, ancient or modern, can afford a specimen of impressive eloquence superior to this."

[4] The King's speech, which was drawn up by the Duke of Grafton for the opening of this session, went by the name of the "horned-cattle speech," because it commenced with referring to a prevalent distemper among the *horned cattle* of the kingdom, as a matter of great importance, requiring the attention of Parliament. This created universal merriment; and Junius could not deny himself the pleasure of throwing it in the teeth of the Duke, especially as the petitions and remonstrances of London, Westminster, Surrey, York, and other parts of the kingdom, respecting the most urgent political concerns, were passed over in silence, and thus treated with contempt.

[5] Lord Granby had resigned his office as Commander-in-chief about a month before, affirming that he had been wholly misled under the administration of the Duke of Grafton as to the affair of Wilkes, and declaring that he considered his vote on that subject as the greatest misfortune of his life.

When Lord Camden was discarded and compelled to resign, for saying in Parliament that he had long disapproved the measures of the cabinet, but had been unable to resist them, the King found it difficult to induce any one to accept the office of Lord Chancellor. He applied to Mr. Charles Yorke, son of the celebrated Lord Hardwicke, but could not prevail with him, because an acceptance would have been a virtual abandonment of his principles. After trying in other quarters, the King again requested a private interview with Mr. Yorke, and made such appeals to him (it is believed) as no monarch ought ever to address to a subject, declaring that, if he would only accept the seals, "an administration might soon be formed which the nation would entirely approve." Mr. Yorke was at length overpowered; he sunk on his knees in token of submission; and the King gave him his hand to kiss, saluting him as Lord Chancellor of England. Mr. Yorke instantly repaired to the house of his brother, Lord Hardwicke, to explain the step he had taken, and, to his great surprise, found Lord Rockingham, and the other leaders of Opposition, there, concerting with his brother the best means

To what an abject condition have you labored to reduce the best of princes, when the unhappy man, who yields at last to such personal instance and solicitation as never can be fairly employed against a subject, feels himself degraded by his compliance, and is unable to survive the disgraceful honors which his gracious Sovereign had compelled him to accept. He was a man of spirit, for he had a quick sense of shame, and death has redeemed his character. I know your Grace too well to appeal to your feelings upon this event; but there is another heart, not yet, I hope, quite callous to the touch of humanity, to which it ought to be a dreadful lesson forever.

Now, my Lord, let us consider the situation to which you have conducted, and in which you have thought it advisable to abandon your royal master. Whenever the people have complained, and nothing better could be said in defense of the measures of government, it has been the fashion to answer us, though not very fairly, with an appeal to the private virtues of your sovereign. "Has he not, to relieve the people, surrendered a considerable part of his revenue? Has he not made the judges independent by fixing them in their places for life?" My Lord, we acknowledge the gracious principle which gave birth to these concessions, and have nothing to regret but that it has never been adhered to. At the end of seven years, we are loaded with a debt of above five hundred thousand pounds upon the civil list, and we now see the Chancellor of Great Britain tyrannically forced out of his office, not for want of abilities, not for want of integrity, or of attention to his duty, but for delivering his honest opinion in Parliament upon the greatest constitutional question that has arisen since the Revolution. We care not to whose private virtues you appeal; the theory of such a government is falsehood and mockery; the practice is oppression. You have labored, then (though I confess to no purpose), to rob your master of the only plausible answer that ever was given in defense of his government—of the opinion which the people have conceived of his personal honor and integrity. The Duke of Bedford was more moderate than your Grace. He only forced his master to violate a solemn promise made to an individual [Mr. Stuart Mackenzie]. But you, my Lord, have successfully extended your advice to every political, every moral engagement that could bind either the magistrate or the man. The condition of a King is often miserable; but it required your Grace's abilities to make it contemptible. You will say, perhaps, that the faithful servants in whose hands you have left him are able to retrieve his honor and to support his government. You have publicly declared, even since your resignation, that you approved of their measures and admired their conduct, particularly that of the Earl of Sandwich.[6] What a pity it is that, with all this appearance, you should think it necessary to separate yourself from such amiable companions! You forget, my Lord, that while you are lavish in the praise of men whom you desert, you are publicly opposing your conduct to your opinions, and depriving yourself of the only plausible pretense you had for leaving your sovereign overwhelmed with distress—I call it plausible, for, in truth, there is no reason whatsoever, less than the frowns of your master, that could justify a man of spirit for abandoning his post at a moment so critical and important! It is in vain to evade the question. If you will not speak out, the public have a right to judge from appearances. We are authorized to conclude that you either differed from your colleagues, whose measures you still affect to defend, or that you thought the administration of the King's affairs no longer tenable. You are at liberty to choose between the hypocrite and the coward. Your best friends are in doubt which way they shall incline. Your country unites the characters, and gives you credit for them both. For my own part, I see nothing inconsistent in your conduct. You began with betraying the people—you conclude with betraying the King.

In your treatment of particular persons, you have preserved the uniformity of your character. Even Mr. Bradshaw declares that no man was ever so ill used as himself. As to the provision you have made for his family, he was entitled to it by the house he lives in.[7] The successor of one chancellor might well pretend to be the rival of another. It is the breach of private friendship which touches Mr. Bradshaw; and, to say the truth, when a man of his rank and abilities had taken so active a part in your affairs, he ought not to have been let down at last with a miserable pension of fifteen hundred pounds a

---

of carrying on their attack upon the government. When he told his story, they all turned upon him with a burst of indignation, and reproached him as guilty of a flagrant breach of honor. He returned to his house overwhelmed with grief, and within two days his death was announced. There was a general suspicion of suicide, and it has never yet been made certain that he died a natural death. Well might Junius say, in reference to the King, "There is another heart not yet, I hope, quite callous to the touch of humanity, to which it ought to be a dreadful lesson forever."

[6] This nobleman was notoriously profligate in his life. Such was the case also, to a great extent, with Gower, Rigby, and all the Bedford men in the Duke of Grafton's ministry.

[7] Mr. Bradshaw, a dependent of the Duke of Grafton, received a pension of £1500 a year for his own life and the lives of all his sons, while Sir Edward Hawke, who had saved the state, received what was actually worth a less sum. Junius, alluding to Bradshaw's complaints, sneeringly says that he was certainly entitled to a large pension on account of "the house he lives in," referring to a fact which occasioned considerable speculation, viz., that Bradshaw had just taken a very costly residence, previously occupied by Lord Chancellor Northington. The whole passage is obviously a sneering one, though Heron takes it seriously, and then represents Junius as inconsistent with himself, because he alludes, in a note, to the largeness of Bradshaw's pension as compared with Admiral Hawke's.

year. Colonel Luttrell, Mr. Onslow, and Mr. Burgoyne were equally engaged with you, and have rather more reason to complain than Mr. Bradshaw. These are men, my Lord, whose friendship you should have adhered to on the same principle on which you deserted Lord Rockingham, Lord Chatham, Lord Camden, and the Duke of Portland. We can easily account for your violating your engagements with men of honor, but why should you betray your natural connections? Why separate yourself from Lord Sandwich, Lord Gower, and Mr. Rigby, or leave the three worthy gentlemen above mentioned to shift for themselves? With all the fashionable indulgence of the times, this country does not abound in characters like theirs; and you may find it a difficult matter to recruit the black catalogue of your friends.

The recollection of the royal patent you sold to Mr. Hine obliges me to say a word in defense of a man [Mr. Vaughan] whom you have taken the most dishonorable means to injure.[8] I do not refer to the sham prosecution which you affected to carry on against him. On that ground, I doubt not he is prepared to meet you with tenfold recrimination, and to set you at defiance. The injury you have done him affects his moral character. You knew that the offer to purchase the reversion of a place which has hitherto been sold under a decree of the Court of Chancery, however imprudent in his situation, would no way tend to cover him with that sort of guilt which you wished to fix upon him in the eyes of the world. You labored then, by every species of false suggestion, and even by publishing counterfeit letters, to have it understood that he had proposed terms of accommodation to you, and had offered to abandon his principles, his party, and his friends. You consulted your own breast for a character of consummate treachery, and gave it to the public for that of Mr. Vaughan. I think myself obliged to do this justice to an injured man, because I was deceived by the appearances thrown out by your Grace, and have frequently spoken of his conduct with indignation. If he really be, what I think him, honest, though mistaken, he will be happy in recovering his reputation, though at the expense of his understanding. Here, I see, the matter is likely to rest. Your Grace is afraid to carry on the prosecution. Mr. Hine keeps quiet possession of his purchase; and Governor Burgoyne, relieved from the apprehension of refunding the money, sits down, for the remainder of his life, INFAMOUS and CONTENTED.

I believe, my Lord, I may now take my leave of you forever. You are no longer that resolute minister who had spirit to support the most violent measures; who compensated for the want of good and great qualities by a brave determination (which some people admired and relied on) to maintain himself without them. The reputation of obstinacy and perseverance might have supplied the place of all the absent virtues. You have now added the last negative to your character, and meanly confessed that you are destitute of the common spirit of a man. Retire then, my Lord, and hide your blushes from the world; for, with such a load of shame, even BLACK may change its color. A mind such as yours, in the solitary hours of domestic enjoyment, may still find topics of consolation. You may find it in the memory of violated friendship, in the afflictions of an accomplished prince, whom you have disgraced and deserted, and in the agitations of a great country, driven by your councils to the brink of destruction.

The palm of ministerial firmness is now transferred to Lord North. He tells us so himself, with the plenitude of the *ore rotundo*;[9] and I am ready enough to believe that, while he can keep his place, he will not easily be persuaded to resign it. Your Grace was the firm minister of yesterday: Lord North is the firm minister of to-day. To-morrow, perhaps, his Majesty, in his wisdom, may give us a rival for you both.

---

[8] This alludes to the patent of an office granted for the benefit of Mr. Burgoyne, who, with the Duke of Grafton's permission, sold out the annual income for a gross sum to a person named Hine. The prosecution mentioned in the next sentence is thus spoken of by Woodfall, in his Junius, vol. i., 322: "Mr. Samuel Vaughan was a merchant in the city, of hitherto unblemished character, and strongly attached to the popular cause. The office he attempted to procure had at times been previously disposed of for a pecuniary consideration, and had, on one particular occasion, been sold by an order of a Court of Chancery, and consisted in the reversion of the clerkship to the Supreme Court in the island of Jamaica. A Mr. Howell was, in fact, at this very time in treaty with the patentee for the purchase of his resignation, which clearly disproved any criminal intention in Mr. Vaughan. He was, however, prosecuted, obviously from political motives, but the prosecution was dropped after the affair of Hine's patent was brought before the public." Mr. Heron states, however, that "the office itself had never been directly or avowedly sold by the Crown, though the *life-interest* had been, under a decree of Chancery." It is not surprising (if this were so) that Mr. Vaughan, not being a professional man, should have failed to discern the difference. His application, therefore, may have been made without any criminal intention. To prosecute in such a case does seem a very severe measure; and, as the prosecution was dropped from this time, it would seem that the Duke himself considered it a bad business.

It may be added, that Sir Dennis Le Marchant, in his edition of Walpole's Memoirs of George III., says, "Junius's account of the prosecution [of Vaughan] is fair—making the usual deductions." Walpole censures the prosecution as foolish. As to Hine's patent, he says, "It was proved that he [the Duke] had bestowed on Colonel Burgoyne a place, which the latter *was to sell* to reimburse himself for the expenses of his election at Preston."—Vol. iii., 400. This was the statement made by Junius; and it is not, therefore, wonderful that, after the exposure of such a transaction, the Duke thought best to say as little as possible about Mr. Vaughan.

[9] Note by Junius. "This eloquent person has got as far as the *discipline* of Demosthenes. He constantly speaks with pebbles in his mouth, to improve his articulation."—This refers to a peculiarity of Lord North, whose "tongue was too large for his mouth."

You are too well acquainted with the temper of your late allies to think it possible that Lord North should be permitted to govern this country. If we may believe common fame, they have shown him their superiority already. His Majesty is indeed too gracious to insult his subjects by choosing his first minister from among the domestics of the Duke of Bedford. That would have been too gross an outrage to the three kingdoms. Their purpose, however, is equally answered by pushing forward this unhappy figure, and forcing it to bear the odium of measures which they in reality direct. Without immediately appearing to govern, they possess the power, and distribute the emoluments of government as they think proper. They still adhere to the spirit of that calculation which made Mr. Luttrell representative of Middlesex. Far from regretting your retreat, they assure us very gravely that it increases the real strength of the ministry. According to this way of reasoning, they will probably grow stronger, and more flourishing, every hour they exist; for I think there is hardly a day passes in which some one or other of his Majesty's servants does not leave them to improve by the loss of his assistance. But, alas! their countenances speak a different language. When the members drop off, the main body can not be insensible of its approaching dissolution. Even the violence of their proceedings is a signal of despair. Like broken tenants, who have had warning to quit the premises, they curse their landlord, destroy the fixtures, throw every thing into confusion, and care not what mischief they do to the estate.

JUNIUS.

The character of the Duke of Grafton, as given by Horace Walpole in his Memoirs of George III., accords in most respects with the representations of Junius. "His fall from power was universally ascribed to his pusillanimity; but whether betrayed by his fears or his friends, he had certainly been the chief author of his own disgrace. His haughtiness, indolence, reserve, and improvidence, had conjured up the storm; but his obstinacy and fickleness always *relaying* each other, and always *mal a propos*, were the radical causes of the numerous absurdities that discolored his conduct and exposed him to deserved reproaches—nor had he a depth of understanding to counterbalance the defects of his temper."—Vol. iv., 69. His love of the turf brought him into habits of intimacy with low and unprincipled men, whose wants he was compelled to supply, and whose characters often reflected dishonor upon his own. His immoralities, though public, appeared less disgraceful at that day, when the standard of sentiment on this subject was extremely low; and in this respect he was so far outdone by Lord Sandwich and others of "the Bloomsbury gang," with whom he was connected, that his vices were thrown comparatively into the shade. It ought to be stated, in justice to the Duke of Grafton, that he entered very early into public life, when his judgment was immature, and his strength of purpose unequal to the control of his passions. He was only thirty-four years old when he was driven from power. During a long life which followed, he retrieved his character. He showed himself, as Sir Dennis Le Marchant states, to be "by no means the insignificant or worthless personage that he appears in the pages of Walpole and Junius. A genuine love of peace, and hatred of oppression, either civil or religious, marked his whole political life; and great as were the errors which Walpole and Junius have justly denounced in his private conduct, it is only just to say, that from the date of these Memoirs [1771] to his death, which comprises a period of near forty years, there were few individuals more highly and more generally esteemed."—Note to Walpole's Memoirs of George III., vol. iv., p. 73.

In leaving Junius, the reader will be gratified to see the following estimates of his character and writings from the two most distinguished literary men of that day, Mr. Burke, a Whig, and Dr. Johnson, a Tory.

ESTIMATE OF JUNIUS, BY MR. BURKE.[1]

How comes this JUNIUS to have broke through the cobwebs of the law, and to range uncontrolled, unpunished through the land? The myrmidons of the Court have been long, and are still, pursuing him in vain. They will not spend their time upon me, or you, or you. No; they disdain such vermin, when the mighty boar of the forest, that has broken through all their toils, is before them. But what will all their efforts avail? No sooner has he wounded one than he lays another dead at his feet. For my part, when I saw his attack upon the King, I own my blood ran cold. I thought that he had ventured too far, and there was an end of his triumphs. Not that he had not asserted many truths. Yes, sir, there are in that composition many bold truths, by which a wise prince might profit. It was the rancor and venom with which I was struck. In these respects the North Briton is as much inferior to him, as in strength, wit, and judgment. But while I expected in this daring flight his final ruin and fall, behold him rising still higher, and coming down souse upon both houses of Parliament. Yes, he did make *you* his quarry, and you still bleed from the wounds of his talons. You crouched, and still crouch, beneath his rage. Nor has he dreaded the terrors of your brow, sir;[2] he has attacked even you—he has—and I believe you have no reason to triumph in the encounter. In short, after carrying away our Royal Eagle in his pounces, and dashing him against a rock, he has laid you prostrate. Kings, Lords, and Commons are but the sport of his fury. Were he a member of this House, what might not be expected from his

[1] From a speech delivered in the House of Commons.

[2] Sir Fletcher Norton, Speaker of the House, was distinguished for the largeness of his overhanging eyebrows.

knowledge, his firmness, and integrity? He would be easily known by his contempt of all danger, by his penetration, by his vigor. Nothing would escape his vigilance and activity. Bad ministers could conceal nothing from his sagacity; nor could promises nor threats induce him to conceal any thing from the public.

Estimate of Junius, by Dr. Johnson.[3]

This thirst of blood, however the visible promoters of sedition may think it convenient to shrink from the accusation, is loudly avowed by Junius, the writer to whom his party owes much of its pride, and some of its popularity. Of Junius it can not be said, as of Ulysses, that he scatters ambiguous expressions among the vulgar;[4] for he cries *havoc* without reserve, and endeavors to let slip the dogs of foreign and of civil war, ignorant whither they are going, and careless what may be their prey.[5] Junius has sometimes made his satire felt; but let not injudicious admiration mistake the venom of the shaft for the vigor of the blow. He has sometimes sported with lucky malice; but to him that knows his company, it is not hard to be sarcastic in a mask. While he walks like Jack the Giant Killer in a coat of darkness, he may do much mischief with little strength. Novelty captivates the superficial and thoughtless; vehemence delights the discontented and turbulent. He that contradicts acknowledged truth will always have an audience; he that vilifies established authority will always find abettors.

Junius burst into notice with a blaze of impudence which has rarely glared upon the world before, and drew the rabble after him as a monster makes a show. When he had once provided for his safety by impenetrable secrecy, he had nothing to combat but truth and justice, enemies whom he knows to be feeble in the dark. Being then at liberty to indulge himself in all the immunities of invisibility—out of the reach of danger, he has been bold; out of the reach of shame, he has been confident. As a rhetorician, he has the art of persuading when he seconded desire; as a reasoner, he has convinced those who had no doubt before; as a moralist, he has taught that virtue may disgrace; and as a patriot, he has gratified the mean by insults on the high. Finding sedition ascendant, he has been able to advance it; finding the nation combustible, he has been able to inflame it. Let us abstract from his wit the vivacity of insolence, and withdraw from his efficacy the sympathetic favor of plebeian malignity; I do not say that we shall leave him nothing; the cause that I defend scorns the help of falsehood; but if we leave him only his merit, what will be his praise?

It is not by his liveliness of imagery, his pungency of periods, or his fertility of allusion, that he detains the cits of London and the boors of Middlesex. Of style and sentiment they take no cognizance. They admire him for virtues like their own, for contempt of order and violence of outrage, for rage of defamation and audacity of falsehood. The supporters of the Bill of Rights feel no niceties of composition nor dexterities of sophistry; their faculties are better proportioned to the bawl of Bellas or barbarity of Beckford; but they are told that Junius is on their side, and they are therefore sure that Junius is infallible. Those who know not whither he would lead them, resolve to follow him; and those who can not find his meaning, hope he means rebellion.

Junius is an unusual phenomena, on which some have gazed with wonder, and some with terror; but wonder and terror are transitory passions. He will soon be more closely viewed or more attentively examined, and what folly has taken for a comet, that from its flaming hair shook pestilence and war, inquiry will find to be only a meteor formed by the vapors of putrefying democracy, and kindled into flame by the effervescence of interest struggling with conviction, which, after having plunged its followers in a bog, will leave us inquiring why we regarded it.

Yet, though I can not think the style of Junius secure from criticism—though his expressions are often trite, and his periods feeble—I should never have stationed him where he has placed himself, had I not rated him by his morals rather than his faculties. "What," says Pope, "must be the priest, where the monkey is a god?" What must be the drudge of a party, of which the heads are Wilkes and Crosby, Sawbridge and Townsend?

---

[3] From a pamphlet on the seizure of the Falkland Islands, published in 1771.

[4] Hinc semper Ulysses
Criminibus terrere novis; hinc spargere voces
In vulgum ambiguas.—*Virgil, Æneid,* ii., 97.

[5] And Cesar's spirit, ranging for revenge,
With Até by his side, come hot from hell,
Shall in these confines, with a monarch's voice,
Cry Havoc, and let slip the dogs of war.
Shakspeare's Julius Cesar, Act iii., Sc. ii.

EDMUND BURKE.

EDMUND BURKE was the son of a respectable barrister in Dublin, and was born in that city on the first day of January, 1730. Being of a delicate and consumptive habit, he was unable to share in the ordinary sports of childhood ; and was thus led to find his earliest enjoyment in reading and thought.

When eleven years old, he was sent to a school at Ballitore, about twenty miles from Dublin, under the care of a Quaker named Shackleton, who was distinguished, not only for the accuracy of his scholarship, but for his extraordinary power of drawing forth the talents of his pupils, and giving a right direction to their moral principles. Mr. Burke uniformly spoke of his instructor in after life with the warmest affection, and rarely failed, during forty years, whenever he went to Ireland, to pay him a visit. He once alluded to him in the House of Commons, in the following terms : "I was educated," said he, "as a Protestant of the Church of England, by a Dissenter who was an honor to his sect, though that sect has ever been considered as one of the purest. Under his eye, I read the Bible, morning, noon, and night ; and have ever since been a happier and better man for such reading." Under these influences, the development of his intellect and of his better feelings was steady and rapid. He formed those habits of industry and perseverance, which were the most striking traits in his character, and which led him to say in after life, "*Nitor in adversum*, is the motto for a man like me." He learned that simplicity and frankness, that bold assertion of moral principle, that reverence for the Word of God, and the habit of going freely to its pages for imagery and illustration, by which he was equally distinguished as a man and an orator. At this period, too, he began to exhibit his extraordinary powers of memory. In every task or exercise dependent on this faculty, he easily outstripped all his competitors ; and it is not improbable that he gained, under his early Quaker discipline, those habits of systematic thought, and that admirable arrangement of all his acquired knowledge, which made his memory one vast storehouse of facts, principles, and illustrations, ready for use at a moment's call. At this early period, too, the imaginative cast of his mind was strongly developed. He delighted above all things in works of fancy. The old romances, such as Palmerin of England and Don Belianis of Greece, were his favorite study ; and we can hardly doubt, considering the peculiar susceptibility of his mind, that such reading had a powerful influence in producing that gorgeousness of style which characterized so many of his productions in after life.

Quitting school at the end of three years, he became a member of Trinity College, Dublin, in 1744. Here he remained six years, engaged chiefly in a course of study of his own, though not to the neglect of his regular college duties. It was said by Goldsmith, perhaps to excuse his own indolence, that Burke's scholarship at college was low. This could not have been the case ; for in his third year he was elected Scholar of the House, which, his biographer assures us, "confers distinction in the classics throughout life." Still, he gave no peculiar promise of his future eminence. Leland, the translator of Demosthenes, who was then a fellow, used to say, that "he was known as a young man of superior but unpretending talents, and more anxious to acquire knowledge than to display it." That his college life was one of severe study, is evident from the extent and accuracy of his knowledge when he left the University.

A few things have come down to us, as to his course of reading. He had mastered most of the great writers of antiquity. Demosthenes was his favorite orator, though he was led in after life, by the bent of his genius, to form himself on the model of Cicero, whom he more resembled in magnificence and copiousness of thought. He delighted in Plutarch. He read most of the great poets of antiquity; and was peculiarly fond of Virgil, Horace, and Lucretius, a large part of whose writings he committed to memory.[1] In English he read the essays of Lord Bacon again and again with increasing admiration, and pronounced them "the greatest works of that great man." Shakspeare was his daily study. But his highest reverence was reserved for Milton, "whose richness of language, boundless learning, and scriptural grandeur of conception," were the first and last themes of his applause. The philosophical tendency of his mind began now to display itself with great distinctness, and became, from this period, the master principle of his genius. "Rerum cognoscere *causas*," seems ever to have been his delight, and soon became the object of all his studies and reflections. He had an exquisite sensibility to the beauties of nature, of art, and of elegant composition, but he could never rest here. "Whence this enjoyment?" "On what principle does it depend?" "How might it be carried to a still higher point?"—these are questions which seem almost from boyhood to have occurred instinctively to his mind. His attempts at philosophical criticism commenced in college, and led to his producing one of the most beautiful works of this kind to be found in any language. In like manner, history to him, even at this early period, was not a mere chronicle of events, a picture of battles and sieges, or of life and manners: to make it *history*, it must bind events together by the causes which produced them. The science of politics and government was in his mind the science of man; not a system of arbitrary regulations, or a thing of policy and intrigue, but founded on a knowledge of those principles, feelings, and even prejudices, which unite a people together in one community—"ties," as he beautifully expresses it, "which, though light as air, are strong as links of iron." Such were the habits of thought to which his mind was tending even from his college days, and they made him pre-eminently the great PHILOSOPHICAL ORATOR of our language.[2]

Being intended by his father for the bar, Mr. Burke was sent to London at the age of twenty, to pursue his studies at the Middle Temple. But he was never interested in the law. He saw enough of it to convince him that it is "one of the first and noblest of human sciences—a science which does more to quicken and invigorate the understanding, than all other kinds of learning put together." Still, it was too dry and technical for a mind like his; and he felt, that, "except in persons very happily born, it was not apt to open and liberalize the mind in the same proportion." He therefore soon gave himself up, with all the warmth of his early attachment, to the pursuits of literature and philosophy. His diligence in study was now carried to its

[1] Notwithstanding the extent of his reading in the classics, Mr. Burke (like many Irish scholars) paid but little attention to the subject of quantity, and a blunder in this respect, which was charged upon him in the House of Commons, gave rise to one of his happiest retorts. In attacking Lord North for being in want of still larger supplies, in the midst of the most lavish expenditure, he quoted the words of Cicero, "Magnum vectigal est parsimonia," accenting the word *vectigal* on the first syllable. Lord North cried out in a contemptuous tone from the Treasury Bench, *vectīgal, vectīgal*. Mr. Burke instantly replied, "I thank the right honorable gentleman for his correction; and, that he may enjoy the benefit of it, I repeat the words, Magnum *vectīgal* est parsimonia."

[2] These early tendencies of Mr. Burke's genius explain a fact which has been spoken of with surprise by all his biographers; namely, that he preferred the Æneid of Virgil to the Iliad of Homer, though he admitted, at the same time, the superiority of the latter in invention, force, and sublimity. To a mind like his, so full of sentiment and philosophy, there is something more delightful in the description of the world of spirits, in the sixth book of the Æneid, and the almost Christian anticipations of the Pollio, than in all the battle scenes of Homer. His extravagant attachment to Young's Night Thoughts, in early life, may be accounted for in the same way.

highest point. He devoted every moment to severe labor; spending his evenings, however, in conversation with the ablest men engaged in the same employments, and thus varying, perhaps increasing, the demand for mental exertion. Few men ever studied to greater effect. He early acquired a power which belongs peculiarly to superior minds—that of *thinking* at all times and in every place, and not merely at stated seasons in the retirement of the closet. His mind seems never to have floated on the current of passing events. He was always *working out trains of thought.* His reading, though wide and multifarious, appears from the first to have been perfectly digested. His views on every subject were formed into a complete system; and his habits of daily discussing with others whatever he was revolving in his own mind, not only quickened his powers, but made him guarded in statement, and led him to contemplate every subject under a great variety of aspects. His exuberant fancy, which in most men would have been a fatal impediment to any attempt at speculation, was in him the ready servant of the intellect, supplying boundless stores of thought and illustration for every inquiry. Such were his habits of study from this period, during nearly fifty years, down to the time of his death. Once only, as he stated to a friend, did his mind ever appear to flag. At the age of forty-five, he felt weary of this incessant struggle of thought. He resolved to pause and rest satisfied with the knowledge he had gained. But a week's experience taught him the misery of being idle; and he resumed his labors with the noble determination of the Greek philosopher, *γηράσκειν διδασκόμενος*, to grow old in learning. Gifted as he was with pre-eminent genius, it is not surprising that diligence like this, which would have raised even moderate abilities into talents of a high order, should have made him from early life an object of admiration to his friends, and have laid the foundation of that richness and amplitude of thought in which he far surpassed every modern orator.

Being on a journey to Scotland in 1753, Mr. Burke learned that the office of Professor of Logic had become vacant in the University of Glasgow, and would be awarded to the successful competitor at a public disputation. He at once offered himself as a candidate. Farther inquiries, however, showed that private arrangements in the city and University precluded all possibility of his being elected. He therefore withdrew from the contest; and the name of Mr. James Clow has come down to posterity as the man who succeeded when Edmund Burke failed.

Soon after his return from Scotland, the literary world was much excited by the publication of Lord Bolingbroke's philosophical works. Unwilling to incur the odium of so atrocious an attack on morals and religion, his Lordship had left his manuscripts, with a small legacy, in the hands of Mallet, to be published immediately after his death. This gave rise to Johnson's remark, that "Bolingbroke was a scoundrel and a coward—a scoundrel, for charging a blunderbuss against religion and morality; and a coward, because he had not resolution to fire it himself, but left half a crown to a beggarly Scotchman to draw the trigger." Mr. Burke took this occasion to make his first appearance before the public. He wrote a pamphlet of one hundred and six pages, under the title of a Vindication of Natural Society, which came out in the spring of 1756, and had all the appearance of being a posthumous work of Bolingbroke. His object was to expose his Lordship's mode of reasoning, by running it out into its legitimate consequences. He therefore applied it to civil society. He undertook in the person of Bolingbroke, and with the closest imitation of his impetuous and overbearing eloquence, to expose the crimes and wretchedness which have prevailed under every form of government, and thus to show that society is itself an evil, and the savage state the only one favorable to virtue and happiness. In this pamphlet he gave the most perfect specimen which the world has ever seen, of the art of imitating the style and manner of another. He went beyond the mere choice of words, the structure of sentences, and the cast of imagery, into the deepest recesses of thought; and so completely had he imbued himself with the spirit of Bolingbroke, that he brought out precisely what every one sees his Lordship *ought* to have said on his own principles, and might be expected to say, if he dared to express his sentiments. The work, therefore, can hardly be called ironical, for irony takes care to make its object known, by pressing things, at times, into open extravagance. But such was the closeness of the imitation, that Chesterfield and Warburton were for a while deceived, and even Mallet felt called upon to deny its authenticity. If he had made it professedly ironical, it would undoubtedly have taken better with the public. Every one would have enjoyed its keenness, had it come in the form of satire. But, as it was, some were vexed to find they had mistaken the author's meaning, and others regarded it only as "a clever imitation." Thus it happened to Mr. Burke in his first appearance before the public, as in some cases of greater importance in after life, that the very ability with which he executed his task, was for a time the reason of its being less highly appreciated. If his Vindication of Natural Society was at first a failure, his speech on the Nabob of Arcot's debts was so little understood at the time of delivery, and heard with so much impatience by the House of Commons, that Mr. Pitt and Lord Grenville considered it as needing no reply!

At the close of the same year, 1756, Mr. Burke published his celebrated treatise on the Sublime and Beautiful. This was the first attempt in our language to discuss the subject with philosophical accuracy and precision. Addison had, indeed, written a series of papers on the Pleasures of the Imagination; but his object was rather to exemplify and illustrate, than to trace those pleasures to any specific source. Mr. Burke boldly propounded a theory designed to account, upon a few simple principles, for all the diversified enjoyments of taste. His treatise shows great ingenuity, surprising accuracy of observation, and an exquisite sense of the sublime and beautiful, both in the works of nature and art. Like all his writings, it abounds in rich trains of thought, and observations of great value in themselves, whatever we may think of his theory. It contains, also, many things which are purely fanciful, as when he traces the pleasures of taste to states of the bodily system; and maintains that the sublime is connected with "an unnatural *tension* and certain violent motions of the nerves," while beauty acts "by *relaxing* the solids of the whole body!" These are some of the things which he learned to laugh at himself, in after life. His theory, as a whole, is rather defective than erroneous. It is one of those hasty generalizations which we are always to expect in the first stages of a new science. The work, however, was an extraordinary production for a youth of twenty-six; and in style and manner, was regarded by Johnson as "a model of philosophical criticism." With some few blemishes, such as we always look for in the writings of Burke, it has a clearness of statement, a purity of language, an ease and variety in the structure of sentences, and an admirable richness of imagery, which place it in the foremost rank of our elegant literature.

Such a work, from one who had been hitherto unknown to the public, excited a general and lively interest. Its author was every where greeted with applause. His acquaintance was sought by the most distinguished literary men and friends of learning, such as Pulteney, Earl of Bath; Markham, soon after Archbishop of York; Lord Lyttleton, Soame Jenyns, Johnson, and many others. In such society, his remarkable talents for conversation secured his success. Every one was struck with the activity of his mind, the singular extent and variety of his knowledge, his glowing power of thought, and the force and beauty of his language. Even Johnson, whose acknowledged supremacy made him in most cases

> "Bear, like the Turk, no brother near the throne,"

was soon conciliated or subdued by the conversational powers of Burke. It was a striking spectacle to see one so proud and stubborn, who had for years been accustomed to give forth his *dicta* with the authority of an oracle, submit to contradiction from a youth of twenty-seven. But, though Johnson differed from Burke on politics, and occasionally on other subjects, he always did him justice. He spoke of him from the first in terms of the highest respect. "Burke," said he, "is an extraordinary man. His stream of talk is perpetual; and he does not talk from any desire of distinction, but because his mind is full." "He is the *only* man," said he, at a later period, when Burke was at the zenith of his reputation, "whose common conversation corresponds with the general fame which he has in the world. Take him up where you please, he is ready to meet you." "No man of sense," he said, "could meet Burke by accident under a gateway to avoid a shower, without being convinced that he was the first man in England." A striking confirmation of this remark occurred some years after, when Mr. Burke was passing through Litchfield, the birth-place of Johnson. Wishing to see the Cathedral during the change of horses, he stepped into the building, and was met by one of the clergy of the place, who kindly offered to point out the principal objects of curiosity. "A conversation ensued; but, in a few moments, the clergyman's pride of local information was completely subdued by the copious and minute knowledge displayed by the stranger. Whatever topic the objects before them suggested, whether the theme was architecture or antiquities, some obscure passage in ecclesiastical history, or some question respecting the life of a saint, he touched it as with a sun-beam. His information appeared universal; his mind, clear intellect, without one particle of ignorance. A few minutes after their separation, the clergyman was met hurrying through the street. 'I have had,' said he, 'quite an adventure. I have been conversing for this half hour past with a man of the most extraordinary powers of mind and extent of information which it has ever been my fortune to meet with; and I am now going to the inn, to ascertain, if possible, who this stranger is.'"

In 1757, Mr. Burke married a daughter of Dr. Nugent, of Bath, and took up literature as a profession. The colonies upon the American coast being now an object of public interest, he prepared, during this year (perhaps in conjunction with his two brothers), a work in two octavo volumes, entitled an Account of the European Settlements of America. These labors, thus casually undertaken, had great influence in shaping his subsequent course as a statesman. He became deeply interested in the early history of the British colonies; and was led naturally, by his habits of thought, to trace the character of their institutions to the spirit of their ancestors, and to follow out that spirit in the enterprise, perseverance, and indomitable love of liberty, which animated the whole body of the people. He saw, too, the boundless resources of the country, and the irrepressible strength to which it must soon attain. Thus was he prepared, when the troubles came on, ten years after, and when there was hardly a man in England, except Lord Chatham, who had the least conception of the force and resolution of the colonies, to come forward with those rich stores of knowledge, and those fine trains of reasoning, conceived in the truest spirit of philosophy, which astonished and delighted, though they failed to convince, the Parliament of Great Britain.

In the next year, 1758, Mr. Burke projected the Annual Register, a work of great utility, which has been continued for nearly a century, down to the present time. The plan was admirable, presenting for each year a succinct statement of the debates in Parliament; a historical sketch of the principal occurrences in every part of the world connected with European politics; and a view of the progress of literature and science, with brief notices of the most important works published during the year. Such an undertaking required all the resources and self-reliance of a man like Burke, and would never have been commenced except by one of his extraordinary vigor and enterprise. It was entirely successful. So great was the demand, that some of the early volumes were reprinted five or six times. At first, Mr. Burke prepared the entire volume for the vear, containing five or six hundred pages, with hardly any assistance. He finally confined himself to the debates and the historical sketches, which for quite a number of years were written by himself, and afterward by others under his direction and superintendence. No employment could have been suited more perfectly to train him for his subsequent duties as a statesman. His attendance on the debates in Parliament made him familiar with the rules of business. Questions were continually arising in respect to trade, finance, the relations of other countries, or the past history of his own, which, to one of his ardent and inquisitive mind, would furnish unnumbered topics for study and reflection. His views were enlarged by the nature of his task, so as to embrace the entire range of European politics. His disposition to philosophize was hemmed in and directed by the great facts in politics and history, with which he had constantly to deal. The result was, that he became, in the strictest sense of the term, a *practical* statesman, whose philosophy was that of man in the concrete, and as he exists in society; so that no one had ever a greater contempt of abstract principles, or was more completely governed in his reasonings by the lessons of time and experience. Rarely has any work been of so much benefit, at once to its author and the public, as the Annual Register in its earlier volumes.

Mr. Burke's first entrance on political life was in 1761. Lord Halifax, being appointed Lord Lieutenant of Ireland, took with him William Gerard Hamilton (commonly called *single-speech* Hamilton) as Principal Secretary of State.[3] Hamilton, from the nature of his office, was the acting minister for Ireland, and needed the assistance of some able adviser who was well acquainted with the country. He therefore induced Mr. Burke to accompany him in this character, under the title of private secretary. Halifax was highly successful in his administration, showing great dexterity in disarming or neutralizing the various factions into which Ireland was divided. How far he was indebted for this success to the counsels of Mr. Burke, it is impossible to say, since the principal secretary would, of course, have the credit of every suggestion which came from that quarter. One thing, however, is certain; Hamilton perfectly understood the value of Mr. Burke's services. He obtained for him a pension of £300 on the Irish establishment; and after the secretaryship expired, and both had returned to England, in 1763, he actually endeavored to make this pension the means of attaching Mr. Burke to him for life, as a coadjutor and humble dependent. "It was," said Mr. Burke, in a letter on the subject, "an insolent and intolerable demand, amounting to no less than a claim of *servitude* during the whole course of my life, without leaving me at any time a power either of getting forward with honor, or of retiring with tranquillity." Such a demand was of course met with an indignant re-

[3] Hamilton gained this title in the following manner. When Newcastle's administration was suffering from Lord Chatham's tremendous attacks in 1755, Hamilton (who voted with the ministry), finding their cause in extreme danger one evening, suddenly arose, though he had never spoken in the House before, and poured forth a speech of surprising cogency of argument and fervor of emotion, with all the ease and self-command of a practiced orator. Every one expected that he would take his place at once among the leading debaters of the day. But, excepting a few words on the same subject soon after, he never made a speech of any length in the British Parliament, though he was a member for thirty years; nor did he speak elsewhere, except twice or three times, when compelled to do so, in the Irish Parliament. He was undoubtedly a man of talents; but, having gained so high a reputation by his maiden speech, he was afraid to make another—ever preparing, but never ready, for a second effort which should outdo the first. He left nothing as the result of sitting thirty years in the British Parliament, except a meager treatise on parliamentary logic. His example furnishes one lesson to young orators, worth more than all the precepts of his book, viz., *that he who would succeed as a speaker must be content sometimes to fail.*

fusal. Mr. Burke's nice sense of honor made him propose, without the least reason or propriety, to surrender the pension which his services had richly merited. Hamilton had the meanness to accept it; and whether he pocketed the money himself, or gave it to some miserable dependent, he deserves a title more stinging and contemptuous even than the one he bears.

About two years after, in the month of July, 1765, Mr. Burke entered permanently on the duties of public life. The administration of Lord Rockingham was now formed; and the new minister, being desirous to avail himself of Mr. Burke's splendid abilities, invited him to become his confidential adviser, with a seat in Parliament, and the office of private secretary. The arrangement was gratifying, in a high degree, to the friends of Rockingham. "The British dominions," says one who knew perfectly the character of the political men of the time, "did not furnish a more able and fit person for that important and confidential situation; the only man since the days of Cicero, who united the graces of speaking and writing with irresistible force and elegance." Mr. Burke, on his part, though pleased with this unlooked-for token of confidence, had no very sanguine expectations of the success or permanency of the new ministry. Highly as he estimated Lord Rockingham himself, he knew the discordant materials of which the cabinet was composed. But there was a question at issue with which he was better acquainted than any man in the kingdom—AMERICAN TAXATION; and no opportunity of influencing the decision of such a question was to be lost or neglected. Accordingly, having taken his seat as member for Wendover, Mr. Burke came forward, at the opening of the session, January, 1766, in a maiden speech of great compass and power, on the absorbing topic of the day, the Stamp Act. He was followed by Mr. Pitt (Lord Chatham), who commenced by saying, that "the young member had proved a very able advocate. He had himself intended to enter at length into the details, but he had been anticipated with such ingenuity and eloquence, that there was but little left for him to say. He congratulated him on his success, and his friends on the value of the acquisition they had made." Such an encomium, from the greatest of English orators, gave him at once a high reputation in the House and in the country. To a mind like Mr Burke's, it afforded an ample recompense for all his labors. "Laudari a laudato viro,"[4] is perhaps the highest gratification of genius.

The ministry had determined to repeal the Stamp Act, but in doing so, to pass a declaration affirming the *right* of Parliament to lay taxes on America. This put them between two fires. The courtiers and landed interest resisted the repeal; Lord Chatham and Lord Camden condemned the declaration. "Every thing on every side," to use the highly figurative language of Mr. Burke, "was full of traps and mines. Earth below shook; heaven above menaced; all the elements of ministerial safety were dissolved." The motion for repeal was made by General Conway; and Mr. Burke, who took a leading part in the debate, thus described the scene in one of his speeches at a later period. "I knew well enough the true state of things; but in my life, I never came with such spirits into this House. It was a time for a *man* to act in. We had a great battle to fight, but we had the means of fighting it. We did fight, that day, and conquer. * * * In that crisis, the whole trading interest of this empire, crammed in your lobbies, with a trembling and anxious expectation, waited almost to a winter's return of light their fate from your resolution. When, at length, you had determined in their favor, and your doors, thrown open, showed them the figure of their deliverer [General Conway] in the well-earned triumph of his important victory, from the whole of that grave multitude there arose an involuntary burst of gratitude and transport. They jumped upon him like children on a long-absent father. All England, all America, joined in his applause. Nor did he seem insensible

[4] Praise from the praised.

to the best of all earthly rewards. '*Hope elevated and joy brightened his crest.*'[5] I stood near him; and his face, to use the expression of the Scripture of the first martyr, 'his face was as if it had been the face of an angel.' I do not know how others feel; but if I had stood in that situation, I would never have exchanged it for all that kings in their profusion could bestow." Notwithstanding the generosity of Mr. Burke in thus transferring to another the honor of that victory, every one knows that he was himself the chief agent in providing "the means" of fighting the battle; and if Charles Townsend had not soon after thrown every thing into confusion by his rashness, posterity might have looked back to Edmund Burke, in his connection with Rockingham, as the great instrument of putting an end to the contest with America.

The King, much against his will, though pacified in some degree by the Declaration, signed the act for repeal, March 18th, 1766. But the fate of the ministry was sealed. Four months after, Lord Rockingham was dismissed.

Lord Chatham now followed with his third administration. Under this, Mr. Burke was offered a very important and lucrative office, that of one of the Lords of Trade. But, though "free to choose another connection as any man in the country," and even advised by Lord Rockingham to accept the offer, he had that delicate sense of honor which forbade him to share in the titles and emoluments of those who had united to remove his patron. The death of Charles Townsend thirteen months after, September 2d, 1767, put an end to this ministry, and that of the Duke of Grafton succeeded. Here commenced the ascendency of the Tories, which lasted about two years under the Duke of Grafton, and more than twelve years under Lord North, down to the close of the American war in 1782. During this whole period, Mr. Burke was the acknowledged leader of the Rockingham Whigs in the House, comprising the great body of the Opposition. He took part in every important debate, and, next to Chatham, who had now passed into the House of Lords, was universally regarded as the most eloquent speaker in Parliament.

The political career of Mr. Burke may be divided into three periods, corresponding to the three great subjects, AMERICA, INDIA, and FRANCE, which successively occupied the anxieties and labors of his life. A brief notice of each of these periods is all that can be attempted in a sketch like this.

The *first* period, which is equal in length to both the others, consists of about sixteen years, extending from 1766, when he took his seat in Parliament, to the end of the American war in 1782. It was, on the whole, the happiest and most successful part of his life. Though he had many difficulties to encounter, from his want of wealth, rank, and family connections, in addition to the strong prejudice under which he labored as an Irishman, he rose from year to year in the estimation of the House. Every one admired his talents; every one was delighted with his eloquence. The country cheered him on, as the great advocate of popular rights. His connection with Lord Rockingham secured him the support of a large proportion of the Whigs—a support which could not indeed, have made him minister under a change of administration, but which enabled him to carry many important measures in their name and through their influence. It rendered him formidable, also, as leader of the Opposition; for those who are eager to gain office will rally under almost any one who has great powers of attack. In this respect, Mr. Burke stood for many years without a rival in the House of Commons. And, though inferior to Lord Chatham in that fire and condensed energy which are the highest characteristics of oratory, he far surpassed him in the patient examination of every subject in debate, the accuracy of his knowledge, the variety and force of his reasonings, and his views of policy, at once comprehensive and practical in the highest degree. Nor was his influence as a leader confined to the discussions of the House. No man, probably, in the whole history

[5] Milton.

of English politics, ever did so much to instruct his friends in private on the questions in debate. His exuberant stores of information were open to every one. Mr. Fox declared toward the close of his life, that he had learned more in conversation with Mr. Burke, than from all the books he had ever read, and all the other men with whom he had ever associated.

In 1771, Mr. Burke received the appointment of agent for the colony of New York, with a salary of about £1000 a year. This office he held nearly four years, till the commencement of the American war. It gave him great advantages for obtaining a minute knowledge of the spirit and resources of the colonies, while, at the same time, it lessened the influence of his speeches on American affairs, by awakening the prejudice which is always felt against the arguments of a paid advocate.

Mr. Burke's first published speech was that on American Taxation, delivered April 19th, 1774. Often as he had dwelt on this topic in preceding years, no attempt had been made to give any regular report of his speeches. In the present instance, the evening was far advanced before he rose to address the House. The opening of the debate was dull, and many of the members had withdrawn into the adjoining apartments or places of refreshment. But the first few sentences of his stinging exordium awakened universal attention. The report of what was going on spread in every quarter; and the members came crowding back, till the hall was filled to the utmost, and resounded throughout the speech with the loudest expressions of applause. Highly as they had estimated Mr. Burke's talents, the House were completely taken by surprise. Lord John Townsend exclaimed aloud, at the close of one of those powerful passages in which the speech abounds, "Heavens! what a man this is! Where could he acquire such transcendent powers!" The opening of his peroration, especially, came with great weight on the minds of all. "Let us embrace," said he, "some system or other before we end this session. Do you mean to tax America, and draw a productive revenue from thence? If you do, speak out; name, fix, ascertain this revenue; settle its quantity; define its objects; provide for its collection; and then fight, when you have something to fight for. If you murder, rob; if you kill, take possession; and do not appear in the character of madmen as well as assassins, violent, vindictive, bloody, and tyrannical, *without an object*."

The moment Mr. Burke closed, his friends crowded around his seat, and urged him to commit his speech to writing, and give it immediately to the world, as a protest against the headlong measures which threatened the dismemberment of the empire. He did so, and on five other occasions he repeated the task; thus leaving us *six* speeches as representatives of several hundreds, many of which are said to have been equal, if not superior, in eloquence to those which were thus preserved. One especially, delivered about four years after, on the employment of the Indians in the war, was spoken of by his friends as the most powerful appeal which he ever made. Colonel Barré, in the fervor of his excitement, declared that, if it could be written out, he would nail it on every church door in the kingdom. Sir George Savile said, "He who did not hear that speech, has failed to witness the greatest triumph of eloquence within my memory." Governor Johnstone said on the floor of the House, "It was fortunate for the noble Lords [North and Germaine] that spectators had been excluded during that debate, for if any had been present, they would have excited the people to tear the noble Lords in pieces in their way home."

Parliament being dissolved in the autumn of 1774, Mr. Burke was invited to offer himself as a candidate for Bristol, in connection with Mr. Henry Cruger, a merchant largely engaged in the American trade. The contest was a sharp one, requiring Mr. Burke and Mr. Cruger to appear daily on the hustings for nearly a month, ready to answer questions of every sort, and to address the electors at a moment's call. Mr. Burke, of course, took the lead; and a laughable incident occurred on one of these occasions, showing the power with which he so often absorbed and bore away the minds of others in his glowing trains of thought. Mr. Cruger, being called upon to follow him after one of these harangues, was so lost in admiration that he could only cry out, with the genuine enthusiasm of the counting-house, "I say *ditto* to Mr. Burke, I say *ditto* to Mr. Burke!" It was undoubtedly the best speech that any man could have made under such circumstances.

The contest terminated in their favor, and Mr. Burke had the gratification of being declared a member from the second commercial city of the kingdom, November 3d, 1774. But at the moment of returning thanks, he offended a large part of his supporters by a manly assertion of his rights. It was a doctrine much insisted upon at Bristol, that a representative was bound to act and vote according to the instructions of his constituents. To this doctrine Mr. Cruger gave a public assent at the close of the poll. Mr. Burke, in adverting to the subject, remarked, "My worthy colleague says his will ought to be subject to yours. If that be all, the thing is innocent. If government were a matter of *will* upon any side, yours, without question, ought to be superior. But government and legislation are matters of reason and judgment, and not of inclination; and what sort of reason is that in which determination precedes discussion, in which one set of men deliberate and another decide, and where those who form the conclusion are perhaps three hundred miles distant from those who hear the arguments?" These sentiments, as we shall see hereafter, lost him the vote of Bristol at the next general election.

America was the all-absorbing topic during the first session of the new Parliament. On the 20th of February, 1775, Lord North brought forward an artful scheme, professedly for the purpose of "conciliating the differences with America," but really intended to divide the colonies among themselves, by exempting from taxation those who, through their General Assemblies, should "contribute their proportion to the common defense." Mr. Burke seized the opportunity thus presented, and endeavored to turn the scheme into its true and proper shape—that of leaving all taxes levied within the colonies, to be laid by their General Assemblies; and thus establishing the great principle of English liberty, that *taxation and representation are inseparably conjoined.* This gave rise to his celebrated speech on Conciliation with America, delivered March 22d, 1775. It would seem hardly possible that, in speaking so soon again on the same subject, he could avoid making this speech, to some extent, an echo of his former one. But never were two productions more entirely different. His "stand-point" in the first was *England.* His topics were the inconsistency and folly of the ministry in their "miserable circle of occasional arguments and temporary expedients" for raising a revenue in America. His object was to recall the House to the original principles of the English colonial system—that of *regulating* the trade of the colonies, and making it subservient to the interests of the mother country, while in other respects she left them "every characteristic mark of a free people in all their internal concerns." His "stand-point" in the second speech was *America.* His topics were her growing population, agriculture, commerce, and fisheries; the causes of her fierce spirit of liberty; the impossibility of repressing it by force; and the consequent necessity of some concession on the part of England. His object was (waiving all abstract questions about the right of taxation) to show that Parliament ought "to admit the people of the colonies into an interest in the Constitution," by giving them (like Ireland, Wales, Chester, and Durham) a share in the representation; and to do this, by leaving internal taxation to the colonial Assemblies, since no one could think of an actual representation of America in Parliament at the distance of three thousand miles. The two speeches were equally diverse in their spirit. The first was in a strain of incessant attack, full of the keenest sarcasm, and shaped from beginning to end for the purpose of putting down the ministry. The second, like the plan it proposed, was conciliatory; temperate and respectful toward Lord North; designed to inform those who were ignorant of the real strength and feelings of America; instinct with the finest philosophy of man and of social institutions; and intended, if possible, to lead the House, *through* Lord North's scheme, into a final adjustment of the dispute on the true principles of English liberty. It is the most finished of Mr. Burke's speeches; and though it contains no passage of such vividness and force as the description of Hyder Ali in his speech on the Nabob of Arcot's debts, it will be read probably more than any of his other speeches, for the richness of its style and the lasting character of the instruction it conveys. Twenty years after, Mr. Fox said, in applying its principles to the subject of parliamentary reform, "Let gentlemen read this speech by day and meditate on it by night; let them peruse it again and again, study it, imprint it on their minds, impress it on their hearts—they will there learn that *representation* is the sovereign remedy for every evil." Both of Mr. Burke's speeches on America, indeed, are full of materials for the orator and the statesman. After all that has been written on the origin of our Revolution, there is nowhere else to be found so admirable a summation of the causes which produced it. They both deserve to be studied with the utmost diligence by every American scholar.

The next speech which Mr. Burke wrote out for publication was that on Economical Reform, delivered February 20th, 1780. The subject is one which has no interest for the American reader, and the speech is therefore omitted in this collection. Like all his great efforts, it is distinguished by comprehensiveness of design and a minute knowledge of details. It has an exuberance of fancy, and too much of that coarse humor in which Mr. Burke sometimes indulged. His proposal was to reduce the expenses of the government by abolishing a large number of those sinecure offices which gave such enormous patronage to the Crown. But he had the most formidable difficulties to encounter. Lord Talbot had previously attempted to reform a single class of expenses—those of the royal kitchen; but was foiled at the outset, as Mr. Burke tells us in his speech, "because the King's *turnspit* was a *member of Parliament!*" Against the present scheme were arrayed, not only every turnspit in the palace, but the keepers of the stag, buck, and fox hounds, in the shape of honorable members, or lords in waiting, together with scores of others among the nobility and gentry, who were living on offices now fallen into total disuse, which once ministered to the pleasure or safety of the monarch. As might be expected, the plan, though highly approved of by the public, was voted down in the House; and Mr. Burke was left to console himself under his defeat with the popularity of his proposals, and the praises bestowed on his eloquence.

Six years had now elapsed since Mr. Burke's election as member for Bristol; and he was suddenly called upon, by the dissolution of Parliament, September 1st, 1780, to appear again before his constituents, and solicit their favor. It was a difficult task. He had differed from them widely on several important subjects. Many had taken offense at the course he pursued, not only in respect to America, but to the opening of the Irish trade, and other measures affecting the interests of Bristol. On some of these points he had explained and justified his conduct, in three able pamphlets, to be found in his works, addressed to the Sheriffs of Bristol, or to citizens of that place. Still, there was a violent hostility to his re-election. He had disobeyed the instructions of his constituents; he had, as they imagined, sacrificed some of their most important interests; he had wounded their pride by neglecting to visit them since the previous election. Hence, when he arrived in town to commence his canvass, he found himself met by the most formidable opposition. It was on this occasion that he came forward, September 6th, 1780, with his celebrated speech previous to the election at Bristol; "the best ever uttered on such an occasion, and perhaps never excelled by any thing he ever delivered elsewhere." Sir Samuel Romilly speaks of it as "perhaps the best piece of oratory in our language."—Works, i., 213. Being addressed to plain men, it has less fancy, less of studied ornament and classical allusion, than his speeches in Parliament. It is more business-like, simple, and direct. At the same time, it has all the higher qualities of Mr. Burke's mind; his thorough knowledge of human nature; his deep insight into political and social institutions; his enlarged views; his generous sentiments; his keen sensibility to the sufferings and wrongs of others; and his inflexible determination to do right, at all hazards and under all circumstances. Its *manliness* is, after all, its most striking characteristic. He had the strongest motives to shuffle, to evade, to conciliate. But he met every thing full in the face. "I did not obey your instructions. No! I conformed to the instructions of truth and nature, and maintained your interests against your opinions, with a constancy that became me. A representative worthy of you, ought to be a person of stability. I am to look, indeed, to your opinions, but to such opinions as you and I *must* have five years hence. I was not to look to the flash of the day. I knew that you chose me, in my place, along with others, to be a pillar of the state, and not a weathercock on the top of the edifice, exalted for my levity and versatility, and of no use but to indicate the shiftings of every fashionable gale."

It was apparent, at the close of his speech, that although the main body of the Corporation and of the Dissenters were with him, together with much of the wealth and respectability of the city, there was no chance of his being re-elected. He therefore determined at once to decline the contest, and did so, the next day, in a short speech, containing one of those touching reflections, embalmed in the most beautiful imagery, which occur so often in the writings of Mr. Burke. One of his competitors, Mr. Coombe, overcome by the excitement and agitation of the canvass, had died the preceding night. Such an event was indeed "an awful lesson against being too much troubled about any of the objects of ordinary ambition." Well might Mr. Burke say, in taking leave, "The worthy gentleman who has been snatched from us at the moment of the election, and in the middle of the contest, while his desires were as warm, and his hopes as eager as ours, has feelingly told us *what shadows we are, and what shadows we pursue!*"

Through the influence of Lord Rockingham, Mr. Burke was returned at once as member for Malton, and sat for this place during the remainder of his public life. "That humble borough," as Mr. Adolphus has remarked in his History of England, "gained by such a member an honor which the greatest commercial city might reasonably envy."

On the 27th of November, 1781, Mr. Burke, in animadverting on the King's speech, delivered one of his most eloquent philippics against the continuance of the American war. It was not, however, reported with any degree of fullness or accuracy, and is remembered only for the striking figure which it contained of "shearing the wolf." "The noble Lord tells us that we went to war for the maintenance of *rights:* the King's speech says, we will *go on* for the maintenance of our rights. Oh, invaluable rights, that have cost Great Britain thirteen provinces, four islands, a hundred thousand men, and seventy millions of money! Oh, inestimable rights, that have taken from us our rank among nations, our importance abroad, and our happiness at home; that have taken from us our trade, our manufactures, our commerce; that have reduced us from the most flourishing empire in the world, to be one of the most miserable and abject powers on the face of the globe! All this we did because we had a *right* to tax America! Miserable and infatuated ministers! Wretched and undone country! not to know that right signifies nothing without might—that the claim, without the power of enforcing it, is nugatory and idle! We had a right to tax America! Such is the reasoning by which the noble Lord justifies his conduct. Similar was the reasoning of him who was resolved to *shear the wolf!* What! shear a wolf? Have you considered the difficulty, the resistance, the danger? No! says the madman, I have considered nothing but the *right!* Man has a right of dominion over the inferior animals. A wolf has wool; animals that have wool are to be shorn; therefore I will shear the wolf!"

Well might Mr. Burke employ such language; for the news had reached London only two days before, that Lord Cornwallis had capitulated at Yorktown, with the loss of his entire army. When the intelligence was carried to Lord North, he received it, says an eye-witness, "as he would have taken a ball into his breast!" He threw open his arms, exclaiming wildly, as he paced the room, "It is all over! it is all over!" And yet the war was to go on! Such was the inflexible determination of the King, who came forward the next day in his speech at the opening of Parliament, with increased demands for "concurrence and assistance" to carry on the contest. Such obstinacy justified the remarks of Mr. Burke, and the still greater severity with which Mr. Fox, in the same debate, pointed directly at the King himself. "We have heard a speech," said he, "breathing vengeance, blood, misery, and rancor. It speaks exactly this language: 'Much has been lost; much blood, much treasure has been squandered; the burdens of my people are almost intolerable; but my passions are yet ungratified; my object of subjugation and revenge is yet unfulfilled; and therefore I am determined to persevere.'" And he did persevere. He compelled his ministers to persevere three months longer, during which the attack in the House of Commons was carried on with increased vehemence by Mr. Burke, Mr. Fox, and their associates, until, on the 27th of February, 1782, Lord North was voted down by a majority of 234 to 215. When the result was declared, there arose, says an eye-witness, a shout of triumph throughout the House, which seemed to pierce the roof, and then rolled away into the remotest parts of Westminster Hall. The King was conquered! At the close of March, a new ministry was formed, with Lord Rockingham at its head, having a cabinet composed of five Rockingham and five Shelburne Whigs. As the two parties could not agree on the disposal of the great seal, Lord Thurlow, with all his violent Tory feelings, was retained as Lord Chancellor, much to the satisfaction of the King.

We now come to the *second* period of Mr. Burke's political life. It would naturally be supposed that he who had borne nearly all the labor of this protracted contest, and had for years been the acknowledged head of the Opposition, would now be rewarded with a seat in the cabinet and the leadership of the House. Had Lord North resigned three years before, such might perhaps have been the case; but the pupil had risen above the master. Mr. Fox was now actuated by the keenest desire for popularity and power; and at this juncture he enjoyed peculiar advantages for placing himself at the head of the Whig party. His manners were highly conciliating; he was universally popular among the middle classes; while, as the favorite son of Lord Holland, he had unbounded influence with many of the most powerful families of the kingdom among the nobility and gentry. Though far inferior to Mr. Burke in richness of thought and copiousness of eloquence, he was a much more effective *debater*. He had made himself, by long practice, a perfect master of the science of attack and defense. When we add to this that he had a peculiar tact, beyond any of his contemporaries, for training and directing a political party, it is not surprising that he obtained the leadership of the House, and was made Secretary of State, while Mr. Burke was appointed Paymaster-general of the Forces. Whatever pain it may have cost him, Burke submitted to this arrangement with that noble generosity of feeling which was one of the brightest traits in his character. His biographer has truly said, "A vain man would have resented this treatment; a weak man would have complained of it; an ambitious or selfish man would have taken advantage of the first opportunity to quit the connection, and throw the weight of his name and talents into the opposite scale;" but Mr. Burke quietly yielded the precedence. He gave all the force of his transcendent abilities for the support and advancement of one who had crowded into his place. The whole history of politics affords hardly another instance of such a sacrifice, made in a spirit so truly noble and magnanimous. Nor did he ever separate himself, in action or feeling, from Mr. Fox, until the French Revolution put an end at once to their political connection and their private friendship.

Under the new ministry, measures of the highest importance were immediately brought forward, and carried successfully through Parliament. In most of these measures Mr. Burke took the lead and responsibility far more than Mr. Fox. His plan of Economical Reform, which had previously been defeated, was now revived. Though narrowed in some of its provisions, it was strenuously resisted by the adherents of the Court, but ultimately passed by a large majority. Many useless offices were abolished in the royal household, with a saving of nearly a hundred thousand pounds a year. Provision was thus made for paying off the King's debts, which already amounted to £300,000; and a check was put to the recurrence of such exorbitant demands in future. His bill for regulating the duties of the Paymaster's department, was considered an extraordinary specimen of tact and ingenuity in arrranging the details of a most complicated business. Any material reform here had been regarded as hopeless. And so it would have proved, if he had not commenced with himself; if he had not swept away at once enormous perquisites attached to his own office, arising out of profits on contracts, &c., together with the use of nearly a million of the public money, which made the situation of Paymaster the most lucrative one under the government. Considering his straitened circumstances, this was an extraordinary sacrifice. Lord Chatham alone had declined to use the public money, and placed it on deposit in the bank. Mr. Burke did more. He stripped himself of all his perquisites. He abolished them forever, and thus made a saving to the public which a pension of ten thousand pounds a year would have poorly recompensed.

Lord Rockingham died suddenly on the first of July, 1782, at the end of thirteen weeks from the commencement of his administration. Lord Shelburne, without a word of consultation with his colleagues, instantly seized the reins. Mr. Fox and Mr. Burke, together with the Rockingham Whigs, considered themselves ill treated, and at once resigned. The Shelburne administration, which will be spoken of more fully hereafter, lasted hardly eight months. It was overthrown February the 21st, 1783, by the famous coalition between Mr. Fox and Lord North, which, giving the nominal headship to the Duke of Portland, made Mr. Fox the real and responsible minister. To this ill-advised union with their former enemy, Mr. Burke acceded with reluctance, overcome, as his biographer declares, by "the persuasions of Mr. Fox, who was both eloquent and urgent with him on that occasion." Under the coalition ministry, he again became Paymaster of the Forces.

The great measure of this administration, on which its fate at last turned, was the celebrated East India Bill of Mr. Fox. As this measure originated with Mr. Burke, who was the animating spirit of every party to which he belonged, it will be proper to speak briefly on the subject in this place. More than ten years before, his attention was strongly drawn to the affairs of India. He studied the subject with his accustomed assiduity, and showed so intimate an acquaintance with its minutest details, when the affairs of the East India Company came before the House in 1772, that Lord North, with a view, no doubt, to get rid of a troublesome opponent, sound-

[6] See page 56.

ed him on the question "whether he was willing to go out at the head of a commission for revising the whole interior administration of India." About four years after, his brother William went to that country, where he became agent for the Rajah of Tanjore, and afterward Deputy Paymaster-general of India. Through him Mr. Burke obtained much minute information respecting the Company's concerns, which could only have been collected by a person living on the spot. These studies were pursued with still greater diligence after he was appointed a member of the Select Committee to inquire into the concerns of the East India Company, and the result has been thus graphically described by Mr. Macaulay, who was qualified, by a residence of some years on the banks of the Ganges, to speak decisively on the subject: "Mr. Burke's knowledge of India was such as few, even of those Europeans who have passed many years in that country, have attained, and such as certainly was never attained by any public man who had not quitted Europe. He had studied the history, the laws, and the usages of the East with an industry such as is seldom found united to so much genius and so much sensibility. In every part of those huge bales of Indian information, which repelled almost all other readers, his mind, at once philosophical and poetical, found something to instruct or to delight. His reason analyzed and digested those vast and shapeless masses; his imagination animated and colored them. He had in the highest degree that noble faculty whereby man is able to live in the past and the future, in the distant and the unreal. India and its inhabitants were not to him, as to most Englishmen, mere names and abstractions, but a real country and a real people. The burning sun; the strange vegetation of the palm and cocoa-nut tree; the rice-fields and the tank; the huge trees, older than the Mogul empire, under which the village crowds assemble; the thatched roof of the peasant's hut, and the rich tracery of the mosque, where the imaum prayed with his face toward Mecca; the drums, and banners, and gaudy idols; the devotee swinging in the air; the graceful maiden, with the pitcher on her head, descending the steps to the river side; the black faces, the long beards, the yellow streaks of sect; the turbans and the flowing robes; the spears and the silver maces; the elephants, with their canopies of state; the gorgeous palanquin of the prince, and the close litter of the lady, all these things were to him as the objects amid which his own life had been passed, as the objects which lay on the road between Beaconsfield and St. James's Street. All India was present to the eye of his mind, from the halls where suitors laid gold and perfumes at the feet of sovereigns, to the wild moor where the gipsy-camp was pitched; from the bazars, humming like bee-hives with the crowd of buyers and sellers, to the jungle, where the lonely courier shakes his bunch of iron rings to scare away the hyenas. He had just as lively an idea of the insurrection at Benares as of Lord George Gordon's riots, and of the execution of Nuncomar as of the execution of Dr. Dodd. Oppression in Bengal was to him the same thing as oppression in the streets of London."[7]

And why should it not be? Under the government of India, as now administered, the crimes of Englishmen abroad are punished on the same principles as the crimes of Englishmen at home. If a hundredth part of the cruelty and extortion of which Burke complained, were now found to exist among the Company's servants in India, all England would be moved with indignation, and nothing but the severest punishment could satisfy the demands of public justice. This change has been wrought mainly by the eloquence of Mr. Burke. The perpetrators of those crimes were indeed suffered to escape, for the nation had shared too largely in the profit to be fit executioners of the guilty. But every one felt that such enormities must cease; and the high ground taken by Mr. Burke was, perhaps, the only one which could have produced so entire a change of public sentiment. He was satisfied that the East India Com-

[7] Miscellanies, Warren Hastings.

pany, from its very constitution, was unable to redress these evils; and he therefore proposed at once to set aside their charter, and commit all their concerns, with the entire government of India, to Commissioners to be appointed by the House of Commons. Such, in substance, was the intent of Mr. Fox's East India Bill; and whatever ambitious designs that gentleman may have been charged with in bringing forward this measure, no one suspects Mr. Burke of having been actuated by any other motives but those of justice and humanity. On the question of going into a committee on the bill, December 1st, 1783, he delivered a speech of more than three hours in length, which completely exhausted the subject. As a piece of lucid and powerful reasoning, entering into the minutest details, and yet bringing every position to the test of general principles, it is incomparably superior to both of Mr. Fox's speeches in explanation and defense of his bill. This speech was committed to writing, and published by Mr. Burke soon after its delivery. It will be found below, with the omission of some of the numerous details which were necessary to make out the argument, but which have no longer any interest for the general reader. The bill, it is well known, passed the House of Commons by a large majority, but was defeated in the House of Lords by the direct interposition of the King. The details of this subject will be given hereafter in the sketch of Mr. Fox's life. Suffice it to say, that the coalition ministry was dismissed on the 18th of December, 1783, and Mr. William Pitt placed at the head of affairs. Mr. Burke went into opposition with Mr. Fox, under a deep sense of wrong as to the means employed for driving them from office; and from this time, for nearly ten years, he was one of the most strenuous opponents of Mr. Pitt's administration.

On the 28th of February, 1785, Mr. Burke delivered the last of the six great speeches which he wrote out for publication. It was that on the Nabob of Arcot's debts. The theme was unpromising, and he rose to speak under every possible disadvantage. It was late at night, or rather early in the morning, and the House was so exhausted by the previous debate, and so weary of the whole subject, that they seemed almost to a man determined not to hear him. He proceeded, however, amid much noise and interruption, and poured out his feelings, for nearly five hours, with an ardor and impetuosity which he had never before equaled. In this speech we have the most surprising exhibition to be found in any of Mr. Burke's productions, of the compass and variety of thought which he was able to crowd into a single effort. In rhetorical address, vivid painting, lofty declamation, bitter sarcasm, and withering invective, it surpasses all his former speeches. It has also more of the peculiar faults which belonged to his extemporaneous speaking. In some passages there is a violence of attack which seems almost savage, and a coarseness of imagery, where he seeks to degrade, which he never allowed himself to use in any other of his printed productions.

Warren Hastings, whom he regarded as the responsible author of nearly all the calamities of India, landed in England about three months after, on the 16th of June, 1785. Within four days, Mr. Burke gave notice that, *if no one else came forward* as his accuser, he should himself move for an inquiry into his conduct as Governor General of India, with a view to his impeachment before the House of Lords. In thus challenging the ministry to take up the prosecution, he acted wisely; for it is hardly possible for any one, except those in power, to command the necessary evidence in such a case, or to use it with effect. Until within a brief period, the leading members of the administration had been nearly or quite as hostile to Mr. Hastings as Mr. Burke himself. Mr. Dundas, when chairman of a committee on Indian affairs, had moved a series of the severest resolutions against him, recommending, among other things, his immediate recall. But times were now changed. Mr. Pitt's East India Bill had virtually placed the government of India in the hands of Mr. Dundas, as head of the Board of Control. It was now the interest of the ministry to keep things quiet. They could not decently refuse an inquiry, but they had no wish to promote it. Mr. Pitt's policy was to gain credit by assuming the character of an umpire, and to defeat the impeachment, if he saw fit, during the course of the introductory proceedings in the House.

To go forward under such circumstances required a degree of courage in Mr. Burke bordering upon rashness. It seemed almost certain that he must fail. Hastings was a personal favorite of the King. He had gained the confidence of the Board of Control, who were willing to overlook his past delinquencies in view of the stability he had given to the British empire in India. He had the warm support of the East India Company, which was saved from ruin and enriched with the spoils of kingdoms by his unscrupulous devotion to its interests. He was popular with the British residents in India, many of whom had gained immense fortunes under his administration at the expense of the natives, and were therefore ready to testify in his favor. He had friends of the highest rank in England, and among them Lord Thurlow, the favorite Chancellor of George III., who had pledged all their influence for his elevation to the peerage, and even higher honors which it was supposed the King was ready to bestow. Intrenched as Mr. Hastings thus was on every side, what could seem more hopeless than Mr. Burke's attempt to obtain the evidence of his crimes? Accordingly, when he and Mr. Fox called for the requisite papers in February, 1786, they were met by the ministry with impediments at every step, showing the strong reluctance of Mr. Pitt and Mr. Dundas to go on with the inquiry. A stormy debate ensued, which only increased the difficulty. Mr. Burke next brought forward (June, 1786) the Rohilla war as his first charge. Mr. Hastings' conduct in relation to this war had been pointedly condemned by Mr. Dundas himself in the resolutions mentioned above. It was a simple contract for blood, under which Mr. Hastings, in consideration of £400,000 received from Sujah Dowlah, *gave him a British army with which to subjugate, or rather destroy, the neighboring nation of the Rohillas*, who had never done the slightest injury to the British. Such were the facts, as admitted by all parties. The only defense was "state necessity!" The £400,000 were wanted to maintain the British conquests in India! It was, indeed, the price of blood. Nearly all the nation was exterminated. "More than a hundred thousand people fled from their homes to pestilential jungles, preferring famine, and fever, and the haunts of tigers, to the tyranny of him to whom an English and a Christian government had for shameful lucre sold their substance and their blood, and the honor of their wives and children!" And yet Mr. Dundas, admitting that "the Rohilla war was an unjustifiable measure," talked of "*state policy*" as the grand rule by which the sovereigns of powerful nations generally governed their public conduct, dwelt on "the essential services Mr. Hastings had rendered his country in the latter part of the war," and spoke of him as "THE SAVIOR OF INDIA!" Mr. Pitt *said nothing!* His friend, Mr. Wilberforce, did indeed support Mr. Burke's motion, declaring Mr. Hastings' contract with Sujah Dowlah "indefensible, and for an end inhuman and scandalous;" but the adherents of the minister understood how they were to vote, and absolved Mr. Hastings by a majority of 119 to 67.[8]

It is surprising that Mr. Burke and his friends did not instantly drop the prosecution. Hastings felt sure of the victory; and when Mr. Fox, supported by Sir Philip Francis, came forward, ten days after, with the charge of extortion in the case of Cheyte Sing, Rajah of Benares, the public universally expected a second acquittal, especially as the supporters of government in the House had received a note requesting them to be present, and to vote *against* Mr. Fox's motion. But, to the astonishment of all, the charge had hardly been made, when Mr. Pitt rose and declared that he should vote *in favor* of the motion for inquiring into Mr. Hastings' conduct. A few independent men on the ministerial benches were so completely scandalized by this

[8] Parliamentary History, vol. xxvi., 91.

sudden change, that they refused him their vote; but the great body remained true to the principles of party discipline, and the minister carried with him precisely the same number (119) for condemning Mr. Hastings, which he had used ten days before to acquit him, when charged with an offense incomparably more atrocious! Such a change must, of course, have been owing to some new light which had suddenly broke in upon the minds of Mr. Pitt and Mr. Dundas, in the doubtful game of politics in which they were then engaged. It is thus alluded to by Mr. Macaulay in his elaborate sketch of the life and character of Hastings, first published in the Edinburgh Review: "It was asserted," he says, "by Mr. Hastings, that, early on the morning of that very day on which the debate took place, Dundas called on Pitt, woke him, and was closeted with him many hours. The result of this conference was a determination to give up the late Governor-general to the vengeance of the Opposition. * * The friends of Mr. Hastings, most of whom, it is to be observed, generally supported the administration, affirmed that the motive of Pitt and Dundas was jealousy. Hastings was personally a favorite with the King. He was the idol of the East India Company. If he were absolved by the Commons, seated among the Lords, admitted to the Board of Control, closely allied with the strong-minded and imperious Thurlow, was it not almost certain that he would soon draw to himself the entire management of Indian affairs? Was it not possible that he might become a formidable rival in the cabinet? If the Commons impeached Hastings, all danger was at an end. The proceeding, however it might terminate, would probably last some years. In the mean time, the accused person would be excluded from honors and public employments, and could scarcely venture even to pay his service at court. Such were the motives attributed by a great part of the public to the young minister, whose ruling passion was generally believed to be avarice of power." From this time forth there was no more difficulty in the reception of charges. On the 7th of February, 1787, Mr. Sheridan delivered his brilliant speech on the cruelties practiced upon the Begums, or Princesses of Oude, and a Committee of Impeachment was soon after formed. This committee consisted of Burke, Fox, Sheridan, Windham, and Charles Grey, afterward Earl Grey, who acted as managers; together with fifteen others, who took no active part in the prosecution. The articles of impeachment were drawn up by Mr. Burke, and delivered to the House on the 25th of April. After a brief discussion, they were adopted; and on the 10th of May, 1787, Mr. Burke, attended by the members of the House of Commons, went to the bar of the House of Lords, and there in form impeached Warren Hastings of high crimes and misdemeanor.

The trial commenced in Westminster Hall on the 13th of February, 1788. After two days spent in the preliminary ceremonies, Mr. Burke opened the case in a speech which lasted four days, and was designed to give the members of the court a view of the character and condition of the people of India; the origin of the power exercised by the East India Company; the situation of the natives under the government of the English; the miseries they had endured through the agency of Mr. Hastings; and the motives by which he was influenced in his multiplied acts of cruelty and oppression. This speech has, perhaps, been truly characterized as the greatest intellectual effort ever made before the Parliament of Great Britain. A writer adverse to the impeachment has remarked, that "Mr. Burke astonished even those who were most intimately acquainted with him by the vast extent of his reading, the variety of his resources, the minuteness of his information, and the lucid order in which he arranged the whole for the support of his subject, and to make a deep impression on the minds of his auditory." On the third day, when he described the cruelties inflicted upon the natives by Debi Sing, one of Mr. Hastings' agents, a convulsive shudder ran throughout the whole assembly. "In this part of his speech," says the reporter, "his descriptions were more vivid, more harrowing, more horrific, than human utterance, on either fact or fancy, perhaps ever formed before." Mr. Burke himself was so much overpowered at one time that he dropped his head upon his hands, and was unable for some minutes to proceed; while "the bosoms of his auditors became convulsed with passion, and those of more delicate organs or a weaker frame swooned away." Even Mr. Hastings himself, who, not having ordered these inflictions, had always claimed that he was not involved in their guilt, was utterly overwhelmed. In describing the scene afterward, he said, "For half an hour I looked up at the orator in a revery of wonder, and actually felt myself to be the most culpable man on earth." "But at length," he added (in reference to the grounds just mentioned), "I recurred to my own bosom, and there found a consciousness that consoled me under all I heard and all I suffered."

Such a speech it was impossible for any reporter adequately to record, and Mr. Burke never wrote it out for publication. He left numerous papers, however, from which, after his death, a continuous report was framed of this and his other speeches against Hastings, chiefly in his own language, though we can not suppose that, in the vehement passages mentioned above, we have the exact expressions, the vivid painting, or impassioned energy with which he electrified Westminster Hall, and filled that vast assembly with mingled emotions of indignation and horror. The peroration of this speech, as delivered by Mr. Burke, will be given below.

The trial lasted one hundred and forty-seven days. If conducted in an ordinary court of justice, it would have been finished in less than three months; but in the House of Lords, being taken up only three or four hours at a time, in the intervals of other business, it extended through seven years. Mr. Burke made his closing speech in behalf of the managers on the 16th of July, 1794. It was in the darkest season of the French Revolution, a few days before the fall of Robespierre, when the British empire was agitated with conflicting passions, and fears were entertained by many of secret conspiracies to overthrow the government. To these things he referred at the close of his peroration, which has a grandeur and solemnity becoming the conclusion of such a trial.

"My Lords, I have done! The part of the Commons is concluded! With a trembling hand, we consign the product of these long, *long* labors to your charge. *Take it!* TAKE IT! It is a sacred trust! Never before was a cause of such magnitude submitted to any human tribunal!

"My Lords, at this awful close, in the name of the Commons, and surrounded by them, I attest the retiring, I attest the advancing generations, between which, as a link in the chain of eternal order, we stand. We call this nation, we call the world, to witness, that the Commons have shrunk from no labor; that we have been guilty of no prevarications; that we have made no compromise with crime; that we have not feared any odium whatsoever, in the long warfare which we have carried on with the crimes, the vices, the exorbitant wealth, the enormous and overpowering influence, of Eastern corruption.

"A business which has so long occupied the councils and tribunals of Great Britain, can not possibly be hurried over in the course of vulgar, trite, and transitory events. Nothing but some of those great revolutions that break the traditionary chain of human memory, and alter the very face of nature itself, can possibly obscure it. My Lords, we are all elevated to a degree of importance by it. The meanest of us will, by means of it, become more or less *the concern of posterity*.

"My Lords, your House yet stands; it stands, a great edifice; but, let me say, it stands in the midst of ruins—in the midst of ruins that have been made by the greatest moral earthquake that ever convulsed and shattered this globe of ours. My Lords, it has pleased Providence to place us in such a state, that we appear every moment to be on the verge of some great mutation. There is one thing, and one thing only, that defies mutation—that which existed before the world itself. I mean JUSTICE; that justice which, emanating from the Divinity, has a place in the breast of every one of us, given us for our guide with regard to ourselves, and with regard to others; and which will stand after this globe is burned to ashes, our advocate or our accuser before the great Judge, when he comes to call upon us for the tenor of a well-spent life.

"My Lords, the Commons will share in every fate with your Lordships. There is nothing sinister which can happen to you, in which we are not involved. And if it should so happen that your Lordships, stripped of all the decorous distinctions of human society, should, by hands at once base and cruel, be led to those scaffolds and machines of murder upon which great kings and glorious queens have shed their blood, amid the prelates, the nobles, the magistrates who supported their thrones, may you in those moments feel that consolation which I am persuaded they felt in the critical moments of their dreadful agony! * * *

"My Lords, if you must fall, may you so fall! But if you stand—and stand I trust you will, together with the fortunes of this ancient monarchy; together with the ancient laws and liberties of this great and illustrious kingdom—may you stand as unimpeached in honor as in power! May you stand, not as a substitute for virtue; may you stand, and long stand, the terror of tyrants; may you stand, the refuge of afflicted nations; may you stand, a sacred temple for the perpetual residence of inviolable JUSTICE!"

Mr. Hastings, it is well known, was acquitted by the House of Lords. This, however, does not imply that the atrocities so eloquently described by Mr. Burke were found to be overstated. Far from it. They are now matters of undisputed history.[9] One difficulty lay in the mode of proof. In previous cases of impeachment, the High Court of Parliament had never been bound by those strict rules of evidence which prevail in the lower courts. Proof of every kind was admitted which goes to satisfy men in the ordinary concerns of life, as to the truth or falsity of a charge. But it was now decided to adhere to the strict rules of legal evidence. The decision marks an advance in English justice. If these rules are wrong, they should be altered; but they should be one and the same in the highest and the lowest courts. The managers, however, were prepared for no such decision; and the moment it was made, the acquittal of Mr. Hastings became morally certain. Hundreds whom we know to be guilty, are acquitted every year in our courts of justice for want of legal proof. Much of the proof relied upon by the managers was ruled out on the principles now adopted, and what every body believed to be true, and history has recorded as fact, the court could not receive in evidence. In addition to this, the cruelty and injustice in such cases must be chiefly exercised through intermediate agents; and it is often impossible to connect those agents by legal proof with the real author of the crimes. There was still another difficulty. These crimes, in most instances, as the court were made to believe, were the only possible means of upholding the British government in India. They were committed for the sake of raising money in crises of extreme danger, and often of sudden rebellion, when, without money to support his troops, Mr. Hastings and his government would have been swept out of India in a single month. These considerations were powerfully urged by Mr. Erskine in his defense of Stockdale for publishing a pamphlet in favor of Hastings. "It may and must be true that Mr. Hastings has repeatedly offended against the rights and privileges of Asiatic government, if he was the faithful deputy of a power which could not maintain itself for an hour without trampling upon both. He may and must have offended against the laws of God and nature, if he was the faithful viceroy of an empire wrested in blood from the people to whom God and nature had given it. He may and must have preserved that unjust dominion over timorous and abject nations by a terrifying, overbearing, insulting superiority, if he was the faithful administrator of your government, which, having no root in consent or affection, no foundation in similarity of interests, no support from any one principle which cements men together in society, can be upheld only by alternate stratagem and force." Such were the considerations which turned the tide of popular sentiment in favor of Mr. Hastings, and made it impossible to convict him, though morally guilty, if not of all the crimes laid to his charge, at least of numerous and most flagrant acts of cruelty and oppression. But if Mr. Burke failed in the impeachment, he succeeded in the main object which he had in view, that of laying open to the indignant gaze of the public the enormities practiced under the British government in India. Nothing more was necessary to secure their correction; and his "long, long labors" in this cause became the means, though not so

9 See Mill's British India, vol. v., passim.

P

directly as he intended, of great and lasting benefits to a hundred and fifty millions of people.

In addition to these labors, and during their greatest urgency, Mr. Burke was drawn into a new conflict with Mr. Pitt, of the most exciting nature. The King became deranged in October, 1788, and the "Regency Question" instantly arose to agitate and divide the empire. The Opposition took the ground that the Prince of Wales had the inherent right, as heir of the crown, to act as regent during his father's loss of reason. Mr. Pitt denied this right, affirming that it lay with Parliament alone to provide for such an exigency—that they might commit the custody of the King's person and the administration of the government to other hands, if they saw fit; and might impose whatever restrictions they thought proper on the authority of the Prince of Wales, if they declared him regent. The subject more naturally belongs to the measures of Mr. Fox, and will be dwelt upon hereafter in the sketch of his life. It is necessary in this place only to say, that Mr. Burke took up the question, which was debated nearly two months, with more than his ordinary zeal and strength of feeling. He thought the Prince of Wales was treated with harshness and injustice. He maintained his cause with consummate ability; and it is now known that he drew up the celebrated letter on the subject, addressed by the Prince to Mr. Pitt, which has been so much admired, not only as a fine specimen of English composition, but as showing "the true, transmigrating power of genius, which enabled him thus to pass his spirit into the station of royalty, and to assume the calm dignity, both of style and feeling, that became it."

It has been already remarked that the first period of Mr. Burke's political life was the happiest. He was on the ascendent scale of influence and usefulness. His faculties were fresh; his hopes were high; and whenever he rose to speak, he was cheered by the consciousness of being listened to with interest and respect. But after the defeat of Mr. Fox's East India Bill, all was changed. In common with Mr. Fox, he was loaded with unpopularity; and, being retired in his habits, he never attempted, like his great leader, to cast off the odium thus incurred by a familiar intercourse with his political opponents. On the contrary, he was often drawn into personal altercations with Mr. Pitt, in which he lost his temper, and thus became doubly exposed to that cutting sarcasm or withering contempt with which the young minister knew how, better than any man of his age, to overwhelm an antagonist. A course of systematic insult was likewise adopted by certain members of the House, for the purpose of putting him down. "Muzzling the lion" was the term applied to such treatment of the greatest genius of the age. When he arose to speak, he was usually assailed with coughing, ironical cheers, affected laughter, and other tokens of dislike. Such things, of course, he could not ordinarily notice; though he did, in one instance, stop to remark, that "he could teach a pack of hounds to yelp with more melody and equal comprehension." George Selwyn used to tell a story with much effect, of a country member who exclaimed, as Mr. Burke rose to speak with a paper in his hand, "I hope the gentleman does not mean to read that large bundle of papers, and bore us with a speech into the bargain!" Mr. Burke was so much overcome, or rather suffocated with rage, that he was incapable of utterance, and rushed at once out of the House. "Never before," said Selwyn, "did I see the fable realized, of a lion put to flight by the braying of an ass." Such treatment soured his mind; and as he advanced in years, he was sometimes betrayed into violent fits of passion before the House, which were a source of grief to his friends, and of increased insult from his enemies. Under all these discouragements, however, "Nitor in adversum" was still his motto. His public labors were such as no other man of the age could have performed. Besides his attendance on the House, he had nearly all the burden of carrying forward Mr. Hastings' impeachment; involving charges more complicated in their nature, and embracing a wider range of proof, than had ever been submitted to an English tribunal. Seven years were spent in this drudgery; and it shows the unconquerable spirit of Mr. Burke, that he never once faltered, but brought his impeachment to a close with a dignity becoming his own character and the greatness of the interests involved.

In thus reaching forward to the end of Mr. Hastings' trial, we have already entered on the *third* period of Mr. Burke's political life. As America was the leading object of interest in the first, and India in the second of these great divisions of his public labors, FRANCE and its portentous revolution occupied the third stage of his eventful career, and called forth, at the close of life, the most brilliant efforts of his genius. It is a striking fact, that Mr. Burke was the only man in England who regarded the French Revolution of 1789, from its *very commencement*, with jealousy and alarm. Most of the nation hailed it with delight, and Mr. Pitt, no less than Mr. Fox, was carried away for a time in the general current of sympathy and admiration. But Mr. Burke, in writing to a friend only two months after the assembling of the States-General, expressed his fears of the result in the following terms: "Though I thought I saw something like this in progress for several years, it has something in it paradoxical and mysterious. The spirit it is impossible not to admire; but the Parisian ferocity has broken out in a shocking manner. It is true this *may* be no more than a sudden explosion; if so, no indication can be taken from it. But if it should be *character* rather than accident, the *people are not fit for liberty*." A few months confirmed his worst apprehensions. The levity, rashness, and presumption which had so long characterized the French nation, gained a complete ascendency. The better class of men who shared in the early movement were at first set aside, and soon after driven away or murdered. The States-General, breaking up the original balance of the Constitution, resolved the three chambers into one, under the name of the National Assembly; and the Third Estate, or Commons, became not only the sole legislative, but the sole *governing* power of the country. The galleries of that assembly were filled with a Parisian mob, which dictated to the representatives of the people the measures to be adopted. The sway of a ferocious populace became unrestrained. The King and Queen were dragged in triumph from Versailles to Paris, where they were virtually held as prisoners from the first, in fearful expectation of the fate which ultimately befell them. All this took place within little more than three months![10]

It may be said, however, that the Revolution was at last productive of important benefits to France; and some persons seem for this reason to have a vague impres-

10 The States-General resolved themselves into the National Assembly on the 17th of June, and the King and Queen were taken from Versailles to Paris on the 6th of October, 1789.

The following extracts from the diary and correspondence of Mr. Gouverneur Morris, the American minister at Paris during the early stages of the Revolution, show that his views of the French people at this time coincided with those of Mr. Burke. "There is one fatal principle which pervades all ranks. *It is, a perfect indifference to the violation of engagements.* Inconstancy is so mingled in the blood, marrow, and very essence of this people, that, when a man of high rank and importance laughs to-day at what he seriously asserted yesterday, it is considered the natural order of things."—Sparks' Life of Morris, vol. ii., p. 68. It is not, therefore, wonderful, that Mr. Morris had no faith in the Revolution. He told Lafayette, in reference to the leaders of it, "Their views respecting this nation are totally inconsistent with the materials of which it is composed, and the worst thing which could possibly happen would be to grant their wishes." Lafayette acknowledged the fact. "He tells me he is sensible that his party are mad, and tells them so."—Vol. i., 314. At a later period, speaking of Lafayette as commander of the National Guards, he says, "Lafayette has marched [to Versailles] by compulsion, guarded by his own troops, who suspect and threaten him. Dreadful situation! Obliged to do what he abhors, or suffer an ignominious death, with the certainty that the sacrifice of his life will not prevent the mischief."—Vol. i., 327. Mr. Morris seems to have anticipated from the first, what happened at no very distant period, that Lafayette would be obliged to flee from France, to escape the dagger of the assassin.

sion that Mr. Burke did wrong in opposing it. There is no doubt that this utter disruption of society was the means of removing great and manifold abuses, just as the fire of London burned out the corruptions of centuries in the heart of that city. But no one hesitates, on this account, to condemn the spirit of the incendiary. It should also be remembered, that these benefits were not the natural or direct results of the rash spirit of innovation opposed by Mr. Burke. On the contrary, they were never experienced until the nation had fled for protection against that spirit, to one of the sternest forms of despotism. Nor can any one prove that the benefits in question could be purchased only at this terrible expense. Lafayette, at least, always maintained the contrary; and the writer has reason to know that, in recommending Mignet's History of the Revolution to a friend as worthy of confidence, he made a distinct exception on this point, censuring in the strongest terms a kind of fatalism which runs through the pages of that historian, who seems to have regarded the whole series of crimes and miseries which marked that frightful convulsion, as the only possible means of doing away the evils of the old *régime*. But, even if this were so, who, at that early period, was to discover such a fact? And who is authorized, at the present day, to speak slightingly of Mr. Burke as rash and wanting in sagacity, because, while his predictions were so many of them fulfilled to the very letter, an overruling Providence brought good out of evil, in a way which no human forecast could anticipate? It should be remembered, too, that Mr. Burke never looked on the Revolution as an isolated fact, a mere struggle for power or for a new form of government, involving the interests of the French people alone. Considered in this light, he would have left it to take its course; he would never probably have written a syllable on the subject. But an event of this kind could not fail to affect the whole system of European politics, as a fire, breaking out in the heart of a forest, endangers the habitations of all who dwell on its borders. Whatever he said and wrote respecting France was, therefore, primarily intended for England. "Urit proximus Ucalegon," was his own account of his reasons for coming forward. "Whenever our neighbor's house is on fire, it can not be amiss for the engines to play a little on our own. Better be despised for too anxious apprehensions, than ruined by too confident a security." There were many in Great Britain who not only justified the early excesses of the Revolution, and exulted when they saw the King and Queen of France led to prison by a mob, but significantly pointed to a repetition of similar scenes upon English ground. Dr. Price, in a sermon before the Constitutional Society, said, in respect to the King of France, "led in triumph, and surrendering himself to his subjects," "I am thankful that I have lived to see this period. I could almost say, 'Lord, now lettest thou thy servant depart in peace, for mine eyes have seen thy salvation.'" When clergymen went so far, men of the world very naturally went farther. Societies were soon formed in London and the other large towns of the kingdom, "with the avowed purpose of obtaining political reformation by other means than those which the Constitution pointed out as legitimate."[11] Some of them maintained a correspondence with the Jacobin clubs of Paris; and, at a somewhat later period, five thousand persons belonging to the united societies of London, Manchester, and other places, held the following language, in a public address to the French National Assembly: "We are of opinion that it is the duty of every true Briton to *assist*, to the utmost of our power, the defenders of the rights of man, and to swear inviolable friendship to a nation which proceeds on the plan you have adopted. Frenchmen, you are already free, and Britons are *preparing to become so*."[12] It was under these circumstances, and

[11] Wade's British History, p. 551.

[12] It is stated in the London Christian Observer for 1807, which was edited at that time by Zachary Macaulay, Esq., father of the celebrated historian, "there seems to be but little doubt of the formation of a plan to raise an insurrection in London about the close of 1792 or the beginning of 1793."

while such a spirit was beginning to prevail in the country, that Mr. Burke came forward to guard the people of England against the infection of principles which tended to such results. Whatever may have been his errors at a later period, who will question whether he was right in warning his countrymen against every thing that could engender a spirit of insurrection? Without deciding whether the liberties of the people can ever be established on the Continent of Europe except by open rebellion, all will agree that nothing could be more disastrous to the cause of free principles than any attempts at reform in England by violence and bloodshed. The Revolution of 1688 has opened a new era on this subject. The progress of the English in throwing off the abuses which still belong to their political system, will take place hereafter in a series of *peaceful* revolutions, like that of Parliamentary Reform in 1832. The right of petition among such a people has more force than the bayonet. When they are once united in a good cause, neither the crown nor the peerage can stand before them.

The first reference to the French Revolution on the floor of the House of Commons was made by Mr. Fox in a debate on the army estimates, February 5th, 1790. He spoke of it in terms of eulogy and of high expectation, applauding especially the *defection of the French soldiery* from their officers and government. "It is now known throughout all Europe," he said, "that a man, by becoming a soldier, does not cease to be a citizen." These last remarks were certainly unfortunate. Unqualified as they were, they might naturally be understood to recommend a similar course to British soldiers in the event of civil commotions. It was still more unfortunate that, when Colonel Phipps, who followed, reminded him of this, stating the entire difference between the situation of things in England and France, and pointing, as a better example, to the conduct of the English troops during the London riots of 1780, "who patiently submitted to insult, and, in defiance of provocation, maintained the laws of the realm, acting under the authority of the civil power," Mr. Fox did not instantly avail himself of the opportunity to explain his remarks, and guard them against such an application. On the contrary, *he remained silent!* In justice to Mr. Burke, this fact ought to be kept in view as we approach the period of his separation from Mr. Fox. The leader of the Whig party, if he expected the continued support of his adherents, was bound to free them from all imputations on a subject like this. Four days after, when the question came up again, Mr. Burke felt bound to express his feelings at large, in view of Mr. Fox's remarks. In the course of his speech, he said,

"Since the House was prorogued in the summer, much work has been done in France. The French have shown themselves the greatest architects of ruin that have hitherto existed in the world. In that very short space of time they have completely pulled down to the ground their monarchy, their Church, their nobility, their law, their revenue, their army, their navy, their commerce, their arts, and their manufactures. They have done their business for us as rivals in a way which twenty Ramillies and Blenheims could never have done.

"In the last age we were in danger of being entangled by the example of France in a net of relentless despotism. That no longer exists. Our present danger arises from the example of a people whose character knows no medium. It is, with regard to government, a danger from anarchy—a danger of being led, through admiration of successful fraud and violence, to imitation of the excesses of an irrational, unprincipled, proscribing, confiscating, plundering, ferocious, bloody, and tyrannical democracy. On the side of religion, the danger of their example is no longer in intolerance, but atheism—a foul, unnatural vice, foe to all the dignity and consolation of mankind, which seems in France, for a long time, to have been embodied into a faction, accredited and almost avowed. These are our present dangers from France.

"But the very worst part of the example set is, in the late assumption of citizenship by the army, and the whole of the arrangement of their military. I am sorry that my right honorable friend has dropped even a word expressive of exultation on that circumstance. I attribute this opinion of Mr. Fox entirely to his own zeal for the best of all causes—liberty. It is with pain inexpressible I am obliged to have even a shadow of a difference with my friend, whose authority would be always great with me and with all thinking people. My confidence in Mr. Fox is such and so ample as to be almost implicit. I am not ashamed to avow that degree of docility, for, when the choice is well made, it strengthens instead of oppressing our intellect. He who calls in the aid of an equal understanding doubles his own. He who profits of a superior understanding, raises his power to a level with the height of the superior understanding he unites with. I have found the benefit of such a junction, and would not lightly depart from it. I wish almost on all occasions my sentiments were understood to be conveyed in Mr. Fox's words, and wish, among the greatest benefits I can wish the country, an eminent share of power to that right honorable gentleman, because I know that to his great and masterly understanding he has joined the greatest possible degree of that natural moderation which is the best corrective of power. He is of the most artless, candid, open, and benevolent disposition; disinterested in the extreme; of a temper mild and placable even to a fault, without one drop of gall in his whole constitution. The House must perceive, from my coming forward to mark an expression or two of my best friend, how anxious I am to keep the distemper of France from the least countenance in England, where some wicked persons have shown a strong disposition to recommend an imitation of the French spirit of reform.

"I am so strongly opposed to any the least tendency toward the means of introducing a democracy like theirs, as well as to the end itself, that, much as it would afflict me if such a thing could be attempted, and that any friend of mine should concur in such measures, *I would abandon my best friends and join with my worst enemies to oppose either the means or the end.*"[13]

Mr. Fox replied in kind and respectful language, but he did not explain or modify his expressions respecting the soldiery (referred to by Mr. Burke) in those full and explicit terms which the occasion seemed to require. He certainly looked for no reforms in England, except through the regular channels provided by the Constitution. He ought, therefore, to have accepted the distinction suggested by Colonel Phipps, and declared at once, that whatever might be proper in France, the English soldiery ought not to turn upon their officers, or resist the civil magistrate. Such a declaration would have been useful in the excited state of the public mind at that period, and it seems to have been absolutely demanded by the shape which the question had assumed. Instead of this, he simply said, "He never would lend himself to support any cabal or scheme formed in order to introduce any *dangerous* innovation into our excellent Constitution"—language which was at least rather indefinite; and declared as to the soldiery, that "when he described himself as exulting over the success of some of the late attempts in France, he certainly meant to pay a just tribute of applause to those who, feelingly alive to a sense of the oppressions under which their countrymen had groaned, disobeyed the despotic commands of their leaders, and gallantly espoused the cause of their fellow-citizens, in a struggle for the acquisition of that liberty, the sweets of which we all enjoyed." He said, also, that while he lamented the scenes of bloodshed and cruelty among the French, he thought these excesses should be "spoken of with some degree of compassion;" and that he believed "their present state, unsettled as it was, to be preferable to their former condition." Such views were so entirely different from those of Mr. Burke, that it was already apparent they could not act much longer in concert.

Mr. Sheridan now came forward to widen the breach. His remarks are given very differently by different reporters. One of them represents him as charging Mr. Burke with "deserting from the camp; with assaulting the principles of freedom itself; with defending despotism; with loving to obtrude himself as the libeler of liberty, and the enemy of men laboring for the noblest objects of mankind." His language, as afterward given in the Parliamentary History, is less harsh; but, whatever may have been his exact expressions, they were such as induced Mr. Burke to rise at once, and declare, in calm but indignant terms, that "such language ought to have been spared, were it only as a sacrifice to the ghost of *departed friendship.* The language itself was not new to him; it was but a repetition of what was to be perpetually heard at the reforming clubs and societies with which the honorable gentleman had lately become entangled, and for whose plaudits he had chosen to sacrifice his friends, though he might in time find that the value of such praise was not worth the price at which it was purchased. Henceforward *they were separated in politics forever.*"[14]

[13] Parliamentary History, vol. xxviii., p. 356.

[14] Moore ascribes this to *jealousy*, a fault never before charged on Burke. Sheridan's *habits* were bad, and this made it easy for Burke to give him up.

This debate has been given at greater length, because it was the immediate occasion of Mr. Burke's writing his work on the French Revolution, and more remotely of his separation from Mr. Fox and the Whig party. His breach with Mr. Sheridan put him on the defensive, and he at once determined to carry the question before the public. Accordingly, in the month of November, 1790, he published his "Reflections on the Revolution in France," in an octavo volume of four hundred pages. No political treatise in the English tongue has ever awakened so lively an interest, or met with so wide-spread and rapid a circulation. Thirty thousand copies were sold in Great Britain alone, at a time when the reading public embraced hardly a third of its present number. Some of the principles of this work, whether true or false, in regard to European society, can, of course, have no application to America, such as the necessity of an established Church, and the benefits of a titled aristocracy, which last is beautifully described as "the Corinthian capital" of the state. It must also be admitted that, in exposing the crimes of the revolutionists, Mr. Burke was betrayed into an error which his warmest admirers should be the first to acknowledge, since it arose from those generous sensibilities which are peculiarly liable to be misled. *All his sympathies were on one side.* The horror he felt at the atrocities of the Revolution made him forget the wrongs by which it was occasioned. It led him to think too favorably of the immediate sufferers, to overlook, and even palliate their vices or crimes. He felt only for princes and nobles, and forgot the body of the people, who had for ages been held down by Feudalism in ignorance, wretchedness, and degradation. The same feeling led him to defend institutions which, under other circumstances, he would have regarded only with abhorrence. This accounts for his arguing so strenuously in favor of monastic establishments, which the whole history of Europe has shown to be cancers on the body politic. It accounts, also, for his maintaining that the old *régime* was "a despotism rather in appearance than in reality," an assertion which will awaken the reader's astonishment just in proportion as he is acquainted with the history of France, and remembers the *lettres de cachet*, the *corvée*, the *gabelle*, and the thousand other instruments of tyranny, which had held the nation for centuries under the most grinding oppression. These one-sided views were the result of a peculiarity of mind in Mr. Burke which we have seen strikingly exemplified at a later period in Sir Walter Scott, that of looking with an excess of veneration upon every thing old. His prolific fancy covered all the early forms of society with romantic and venerable associations, so that abuses which would elsewhere have called forth his keenest reprobation seemed to him in old governments, if not positive benefits, at least evils to be touched with a trembling hand, like the weaknesses of an aged parent.

While we can not, for these reasons, give our sympathy or assent to every part of this volume, facts have shown that Mr. Burke was in the right far more than Mr. Fox as to the main point at issue, the character and prospects of the Revolution in France. Mr. Fox lived to see this, and when Lord Lauderdale once remarked in his presence, that Burke was a splendid madman, Mr. Fox replied, "It is difficult to say whether he is mad or inspired, but whether the one or the other, every one must agree that he is a *prophet*." Lord Brougham observed at a much later period, "All his predictions, except one momentary expression [relative to the martial spirit of the French], have been more than fulfilled." And down to the present day (for the Revolution is still in progress), what has been the result of the experiments which the French have been making in government for the last sixty years? They took refuge from their republic in a military despotism; they received back one branch of the Bourbons and exchanged it for another; they again tried a republic for a little more than three years; and they have now submitted to the usurpation of another Bonaparte, as weak in intellect and despicable in character as the former one was powerful and illustrious. In all this they have shown—and it was this, in reality, that Mr. Burke set out to inculcate—that a people who cast off the fear of God and are governed by impulse, not by fixed principle, who have extravagant hopes of regenerating society by a mere change of its outward forms, and have learned from a scoffing philosophy to despise those great original instincts of our nature and those finer sensibilities of the heart, which are the ultimate security of social order, can not, in the nature of things, be "fit for freedom." This was the real scope of Mr. Burke's "Reflections on the Revolution in France." He erred, indeed, in connecting these truths with church establishments and monarchical institutions, but the truths themselves were of imperishable value, not only for the age in which he wrote, but for all coming ages in that long struggle on which the world has entered for the establishment of free institutions.

In a literary view, there can be but one opinion of this work. Though desultory in its character, and sometimes careless or prolix in style, it contains more richness of thought, splendor of imagination, and beauty of diction than any volume of the same size in our language. Robert Hall has truly said, "Mr. Burke's imperial fancy has laid all nature under tribute, and has collected riches from every scene of the creation and every walk of art. His eulogium on the Queen of France is a masterpiece of pathetic composition, so select in its images, so fraught with tenderness, and so rich with colors 'dipt in heaven,' that he who can read it without rapture may have merit as a reasoner, but must resign all pretensions to taste and sensibility." At the present day, however, when the topics discussed are no longer of any practical importance, it is a book, like Milton's Paradise Lost, to be *once* resolutely gone through with by every literary man, and then read and re-read *for life* in select passages, which will awaken an ever-growing admiration of Mr. Burke for his compass of thought, his keen sagacity, his profound wisdom, his generous sentiments, his truth to nature and the best feelings of the heart. It is, indeed, the great peculiarity of his writings, that every reflecting man learns to estimate them more highly as he advances in knowledge and in years.

We now come to the most painful event of Mr. Burke's life, except the loss of his son—his separation from Mr. Fox. After the emphatic declaration he had made before the House, that "he would abandon his best friends and join with his worst enemies" to oppose French principles, we should naturally expect that the Whigs would treat him with great tenderness and forbearance if they did not mean to drive him from their ranks, and especially would not goad him on the subject, and provoke a quarrel, by bringing it up unnecessarily in debate. But such was the warmth and frankness of Mr. Fox, that whatever was upon his mind was on his tongue; and as he was conscious of having only the kindest feelings toward Mr. Burke, and was slow to take offense himself, he seems never once to have dreamed that any liberties he might use could lead, by any possibility, to a breach between him and his old friend. He therefore expressed his dissent from the principles of Mr. Burke's work in the strongest terms; and during a debate on the formation of a government for Canada he made a pointed allusion to certain well-known passages of the volume, speaking in a sarcastic manner of "those titles of honor the extinction of which some gentlemen so much deplored," and of "that *spirit of chivalry* which had fallen into disgrace in a neighboring country." In a debate a few evenings after, he went out of his way to praise the new Constitution of France, declaring, with a direct reference to Mr. Burke's strictures on that instrument, "I for one admire the new Constitution, considered altogether, *as the most glorious fabric ever raised by human integrity since the creation of man!*" Mr. Burke instantly rose with visible emotion to give vent to his feelings, but his Whig friends interposed to prevent him; the cry of "Question, question" became general throughout the House; and as it was then three o'clock in the morning, Mr. Burke at last gave way, and reserved himself for another occasion.

Great efforts were now made by the Whigs to prevent Mr. Burke from coming out in reply; but he felt himself pledged to the House and country; it would look like cowardice, he said, to shrink from a contest which was thus provoked. Still he spoke kindly and with honor of Mr. Fox, and, at a private interview between them, "talked over the plan of all he intended to say, opened the different branches of his argument, and explained the limitations which he meant to impose upon himself."[15] They then walked together to the House, and Mr. Fox took occasion almost immediately to say, that "he was extremely sorry to differ from any of his friends, but that he should never be backward in declaring his opinion, and that he did not wish to recede from any thing he had formerly said." This was generally considered as a direct challenge, if not a defiance of Mr. Burke, who was desirous instantly to reply; but, finding that the House preferred to adjourn the question over the holidays, which were then commencing, he again postponed his remarks.

When the recess was over and the Canada Bill came up (May 6th, 1791), Mr. Burke opened the debate. But the moment he touched on the French Revolution, in reply to Mr. Fox, he was called to order by a friend of the latter, and Mr. Fox himself immediately interposed in a strain of the bitterest irony, remarking, "that his right honorable friend could hardly be said to be out of order. It seemed this was a day of privilege, when any gentleman might stand up, select his mark, and abuse any government he pleased. Although nobody had said a word on the subject of the French Revolution (*sic!*), his friend had risen up and abused that event. Every gentleman had a right that day to abuse the government of every country, whether ancient or modern, as much as he pleased, and in as gross terms as he thought proper, with his right honorable friend." A very extraordinary scene ensued. Mr. Burke attempted to explain and to discuss the question of order, but was continually interrupted from his own side of the House. Seven times were his remarks broken in upon by renewed calls of "order." Mr. Fox repeated his irony about "the gentleman's right to discuss the Constitution of France;" and when Mr. Pitt defended his old opponent, affirming that Mr. Burke, in examining the government proposed for Canada, had a right to draw his illustrations from that of France, Mr. Fox took the floor, and, after a series of very severe remarks, said that Mr. Burke had once told the House, in a speech on American affairs, that he did not know how to draw up a bill of indictment against a whole people, but "he had now learned to do it, and to crowd it with all the technicalities which disgraced our statute-book, such as 'false,' 'wicked,' 'by instigation of the devil,' &c.; that no book his friend could cite, no words he could deliver in debate, however ingenious or eloquent, could induce him to change or abandon his opinions; he differed on that subject with his right honorable friend, *toto cœlo*."[16] Mr. Burke now rose and made an extended reply, commencing in "a grave and governed tone of voice." Among other things, he remarked, that "his friend had treated him in every sentence with uncommon harshness," and "had endeavored to crush him at once by declaring a censure upon his whole life and opinions." "It was certainly an indiscretion," he said, "at any period, and especially at his time of life, to provoke enemies, or to give his friends occasion to desert him; yet if his firm and steady adherence to the British Constitution placed him in this dilemma, he would risk all; and as public duty and public prudence taught him, with his last words he would exclaim, 'Fly from the French Constitution.'" [Mr. Fox here whispered that "there was no loss of friends."] Mr. Burke replied, emphatically, "Yes, there *is* a loss of friends! I know the price of my conduct. I have done my duty at the price of my friend. *Our friendship is at an end!*" Mr.

15 Annual Register, vol. xxxiii., p. 116. 16 Parliamentary History, vol. xxix., p. 389.

Fox rose in the utmost agitation, showing that he had never once suspected the extremities to which he was driving Mr. Burke. "For some minutes he could not proceed. Tears trickled down his cheeks, and he strove in vain to give utterance to his feelings." When at last he was able to speak, he adverted, in the most tender and generous terms, to their early friendship and his obligations to Mr. Burke, and expressed his hope "that, notwithstanding what had happened, his friend would think on past times, and, however any imprudent words or intemperance of his might have offended him, it would show that it had not been, at least, intentionally his fault." Unfortunately, however, when he came to reassert and defend his own views, he did it with some very pointed allusions to the former opinions of his friend, as inconsistent with his present ones. This grated so harshly on Mr. Burke's feelings, that he remarked, in entering on his reply, that "the tenderness which had been displayed in the beginning and conclusion of Mr. Fox's speech had been quite obliterated by what had occurred in the middle." The breach was irreparable. They never met again except in public; and even on his death-bed, Mr. Burke declined an interview which Mr. Fox solicited in the kindest terms, declaring, that "it had cost him the most heartfelt pain to obey the stern voice of duty in rending asunder a long friendship; that his principles continued the same, and *could be enforced only by the general persuasion of his sincerity.*" This last consideration appears to have governed him chiefly in breaking away from his old friend. It was not the irritability of his temper, as represented by Mr. Fox's adherents, nor was it mere wounded feeling, which time would easily have assuaged; it was a sense of duty (though carried, certainly, to an extreme), which impelled him, with all the force of a religious sentiment, to bear public testimony against one whose opinions he thought dangerous to the state; like the aged apostle, who is said to have hurried from one of the public baths when he saw Cerinthus enter it, declaring that he would not remain for a moment under the same roof with a man who inculcated such fatal errors.

From this time Mr. Burke began to act with Mr. Pitt, and, though he never took office under his old opponent, his son, whom he had long been training for public life, had an important station assigned him in the government of Ireland.

There is no page in the history of our English statesmen more full of tenderness and melancholy than that which records the disappointment of Mr. Burke in regard to this son. He was an only child, on whom all his parents' hopes were centered. In the prospect of a speedy retirement from public life, it was the last fond wish of the father that his son should take his place, especially as he was one who "had within him" (and would carry into the service of his country) "a salient, living spring of generous and manly action." "*He*," as the father thought, "would have supplied every deficiency, and symmetrized every disproportion" in his own political life. No doubt he overrated his son's abilities, for he considered them greater than his own; but there is the best evidence that Richard Burke had not only a heart full of tenderness and generosity, but a finely-balanced mind, much knowledge, great firmness and decision, united to strict integrity and high moral principle. Without his father's suspecting it, his constitution had given way before his appointment to Ireland. He was sinking into consumption, and his physicians detained him from his post; not daring, however, to apprise Mr. Burke of the danger, for they knew that, like the patriarch of old, "his life was bound up in the lad's life," and were convinced that a knowledge of the truth would prove fatal to him sooner than to his son. He was, therefore, kept in ignorance until a week before the closing scene, and from that time until all was over, "he slept not, he scarcely tasted food, or ceased from the most affecting lamentations." The last moments of young Burke present one of those striking cases in which nature seems to rally all her powers at the approach of dissolution, as the taper often burns brightest in the act of going out. His parents were waiting his departure in an adjoining room (for they were unable to bear the sight), when he rose from his bed, dressed himself completely, and leaning on his nurse, entered the apartment where they were sitting. "Speak to me, my dear father," said he, as he saw them bowed to the earth under the poignancy of their grief. "I am in no terror; I feel myself better and in spirits; yet my heart flutters, I know not why! Pray talk to me—of religion—of morality—of indifferent subjects." Then turning, he exclaimed, "What noise is that? Does it rain? Oh no, it is the rustling of the wind in the trees;" and broke out at once, with a clear, sweet voice, in that beautiful passage (the favorite lines of his father) from the Morning Hymn in Milton:

> His praise, ye winds, that from four quarters blow,
> Breathe soft or loud; and wave your tops, ye pines,
> With every plant in sign of worship wave!

He began again, and again repeated them with the same tenderness and fervor, bowing his head as in the act of worship, and then "sunk into the arms of his parents as in a profound and sweet sleep." It would be too painful to dwell on the scenes that followed, until the father laid all that remained to him of his child beneath the Beaconsfield church, adjoining his estate. From that hour he never looked, if he could avoid it, toward that church! Eighteen months after, when he had somewhat recovered his composure, he thus adverted to his loss in his celebrated "Letter to a Noble Lord:" "The storm has gone over me, and I lie like one of those old oaks which the late hurricane has scattered around me. I am stripped of all my honors; I am torn up by the roots, and lie prostrate on the earth! There, and prostrate there, I most unfeignedly recognize the divine justice, and in some degree submit to it." "*I am alone! I have none to meet my enemies in the gate!*"

The "Letter" referred to was called forth by an ungenerous attack from the Duke of Bedford, a young man who had just entered upon life. At the age of sixty-five, after devoting more than thirty years to the service of his country, Mr. Burke found himself oppressed with debts, arising chiefly from his kindness and liberality to indigent men of genius who sought his aid. This fact being known, a pension of £3600 a year was granted him in October, 1795, by the express order of the King, without the slightest solicitation of Mr. Burke or his friends. The Duke of Bedford, who had become infected with French principles in politics and religion, made a very offensive allusion to this grant in a debate soon after, and has immortalized his name (the only way he could ever have done it) by the castigation which he thus provoked. Of this "Letter" Mr. Mathias says, in his "Pursuits of Literature," "I perceive in it genius, ability, dignity, imagination; sights more than youthful poets when they dreamed; and sometimes the philosophy of Plato and the wit of Lucan."

Within less than a year, Mr. Burke commenced his last work, being "Thoughts on the Prospect of a Regicide Peace," which came out in three successive letters in 1796–7. His object was to animate his countrymen to a zealous prosecution of the contest with France, and he now brought out with astonishing ingenuity and eloquence those extreme principles respecting a war with the French Republic which constituted the chief error of his life. In his "Reflections" he dwelt mainly on the rashness of the French in their experiments upon government, as a warning to his own countrymen against repeating the error. He now took the ground of shutting France out from the society of nations! "This pretended republic is founded in crimes, and exists by wrong and robbery; and wrong and robbery, far from giving a title to any thing, is a war with mankind." *War*, therefore, to the utmost and to the end, was the only measure to be pursued with the French Republic! "To be at peace with robbery," said he, "is to be an accomplice with it!" It seems wonderful how a man like Burke could have fallen into this confusion of ideas between the crimes of individuals against the community in which they live, and the acts of an organized government, however wrongly constituted, and however cruel or oppressive in the treatment of those within its borders. If the Republic robbed England or her subjects, there was just ground of war. But if the *internal* policy of a government—its crimes (however great) against those who live under it—can justify an attack from surrounding nations, what government in Europe could escape ? or what would Europe itself be but a field of blood ? The principle of Mr. Burke was that on which Austria and Prussia sent the Duke of Brunswick, in 1792, to invade France. And what was the consequence ? Prostrate as she was—broken down so completely in her military spirit and resources, that Mr. Burke seemed justified in his famous sarcasm, "Gallos quoque in bellis floruisse audivimus," we have *heard* that the French were *once* distinguished in war—France, in a little more than a month, chased every foreign soldier from her borders ; the Republican leaders learned the art of composing every dissension by turning the passions of the people into a rage for foreign conquest, until seven hundred and fifty thousand men stood ready to carry their principles throughout Europe by fire and sword ; and, what was worse than all, the sympathy of the friends of freedom in every country on the Continent was turned against their own governments, and given for a time with the warmest zeal and confidence to this republic of blood. Still, Mr. Burke adhered to his principle. His only inference from the disasters of the allies was, that they had used means which were shamefully inadequate to the occasion ; that all they had done or attempted was only like "pelting a volcano with pebble stones ;" and that the whole of Europe ought to combine in one grand confederacy to "let loose the ministers of vengeance in famine, fever, plagues, and death upon a guilty race, to whose frame, and to all whose habit, order, peace, religion, and virtue were alien and abhorrent."

It is remarkable that this was the only subject on which Mr. Burke was ever betrayed into extreme opinions. Though many have thought otherwise from looking exclusively at this period of his life, his whole history shows that he was pre-eminently a man of cautious and moderate views. Lord Brougham has truly said, "It would be difficult to find any statesman of any age whose opinions were more habitually marked by moderation ; by a constant regard to the dictates of an enlarged reason ; by a fixed determination to be practical at the time he was giving scope to the most extensive general views ; by a cautious and prudent abstinence from all extremes. He brought this spirit of moderation into public affairs with him ; and if we except the very end of his life, when he had ceased to live much in public, it stuck by him to the last." And why did it now desert him ? Because, apparently, the dangers of the French Revolution, magnified by his powerful imagination, turned his caution into terror ; and all experience shows that nothing is so rash, so headlong, so cruel even, as extreme terror when it takes full possession of a vigorous and determined intellect. Even our virtues in such cases go to swell our excesses ; and we thus see how a man of Mr. Burke's justice, humanity, and love of genuine freedom, could become the advocate of war upon principles which would make it eternal, and be led to justify that doctrine of *intervention*, which absolute governments have ever since been using to arrest the progress of liberal institutions in the world.

Before he had finished his "Regicide Peace," Mr. Burke found his health rapidly declining, and in February, 1797, he removed to Bath to try the effect of its waters. But his constitution was gone ; and after remaining there three months, confined almost entirely to his bed, he made a last effort to return to Beaconsfield, that his bones might there rest with those of his son. "It will be so far, at least," said he, "on my way to the tomb, and I may as well travel it alive as dead !" During the short period that remained to him of life, he gave directions with the utmost calmness about the disposal of his papers ; he bore his sufferings with placid resignation, hoping for divine mercy through the intercession of the Redeemer, which, in his own words, he "had long sought with unfeigned humiliation, and to which he looked with trembling hope." He died on the 9th of July, 1797, in the sixty-eighth year of his age, and was interred, according to his own directions, in the same grave with his son. It was the wish of his friends, and even proposed by Mr. Fox in the House of Commons, that he should be buried in Westminster Abbey, but the plan was abandoned when the provisions of his will were made known.

Pains have been taken in this memoir to bring out the most striking qualities of Mr. Burke's mind in connection with the principal events of his life, and thus to avoid the necessity of an extended summation at the close. He was what the Germans would call a "many-sided man," so that any general analysis of his character must of necessity be imperfect. We can form a correct estimate of most orators from three or four of their best speeches, but fully to know Mr. Burke one must take into view all that he ever spoke, all that he ever wrote.

As an orator he derived little or no advantage from his personal qualifications. He was tall, but not robust; his gait and gesture were awkward; his countenance, though intellectual, was destitute of softness, and rarely relaxed into a smile; and as he always wore spectacles, his eye gave him no command over an audience. "His enunciation," says Wraxall, "was vehement and rapid; and his Irish accent, which was as strong as if he had never quitted the banks of the Shannon, diminished to the ear the effect of his eloquence on the mind."

The variety and extent of his powers in debate was greater than that of any other orator in ancient or modern times. No one ever poured forth such a flood of thought—so many original combinations of inventive genius; so much knowledge of man and the working of political systems; so many just remarks on the relation of government to the manners, the spirit, and even the prejudices of a people; so many wise maxims as to a change in constitutions and laws; so many beautiful effusions of lofty and generous sentiment; such exuberant stores of illustration, ornament, and apt allusion; all intermingled with the liveliest sallies of wit or the boldest flights of a sublime imagination. In actual debate, as a contemporary informs us, he passed more rapidly from one exercise of his powers to another, than in his printed productions. During the same evening, sometimes in the space of a few moments, he would be pathetic and humorous, acrimonious and conciliating, now giving vent to his indignant feelings in lofty declamation, and again, almost in the same breath, convulsing his audience by the most laughable exhibitions of ridicule or burlesque. In respect to the versatility of Mr. Burke as an orator, Dr. Parr says, "Who among men of eloquence and learning was ever more profoundly versed in every branch of science? Who is there that can transfer so happily the results of laborious research to the most familiar and popular topics? Who is there that possesses so extensive yet so accurate an acquaintance with every transaction recent or remote? Who is there that can deviate from his subject for the purposes of delight with such engaging ease, and insensibly conduct his hearers or readers from the severity of reasoning to the festivity of wit? Who is there that can melt them, if the occasion requires, with such resistless power to grief or pity? Who is there that combines the charm of inimitable grace and urbanity with such magnificent and boundless expansion?"

A prominent feature in the character of Mr. Burke, which prepared him for this wide exercise of his powers, was *intellectual independence*. He leaned on no other man's understanding, however great. In the true sense of the term, he never borrowed an idea or an image. Like food in a healthy system, every thing from without was perfectly assimilated; it entered by a new combination into the very structure of his thoughts, as when the blood, freshly formed, goes out to the extremities under the strong pulsations of the heart. On most subjects, at the present day, this is all we can expect of *originality;* the thoughts and feelings which a man expresses must be *truly his own.*

In the structure of his mind he had a strong resemblance to Bacon, nor was he greatly his inferior in the leading attributes of his intellect. In imagination he went far beyond him. He united more perfectly than any other man the discordant qualities of the philosopher and the poet, and this union was equally the source of some of his greatest excellencies and faults as an orator.

The first thing that strikes us in a survey of his understanding is its remarkable *comprehensiveness.* He had an amplitude of mind, a power and compass of intellectual vision, beyond that of most men that ever lived. He looked on a subject like a man standing upon an eminence, taking a large and rounded view of it on every side, contemplating each of its parts under a vast variety of relations, and those relations often extremely complex or remote. To this wide grasp of original thought he added every variety of information gathered from abroad. There was no subject on which he had not read, no system relating to the interests of man as a social being which he had not thoroughly explored. All these treasures of acquired knowledge he brought home to amplify and adorn the products of his own genius, as the ancient Romans collected every thing that was beautiful in the spoils of conquered nations, to give new splendor to the seat of empire.

To this largeness of view he added a surprising *subtlety of intellect.* So quick and delicate were his perceptions that he saw his way clearly through the most complicated relations, following out the finest thread of thought without once letting go his hold, or becoming lost or perplexed in the intricacies of the subject. This subtlety, however, did not usually take the form of mere logical acuteness in the detection of fallacies. He was not remarkable for his dexterity as a disputant. He loved rather to build up than to pull down; he dwelt not so much on the differences of things, as on some hidden agreement between them when apparently most dissimilar. The association of *resemblance* was one of the most active principles of his nature. While it filled his mind with all the imagery of the poet, it gave an impulse and direction to his researches as a philosopher. It led him, as his favorite employment, to trace out analogies, correspondencies, or contrasts (which last, as Brown remarks, are the necessary result of a quick sense of resemblance); thus filling up his originally comprehensive mind with a beautiful series of associated thoughts, showing often the identity of things which appeared the most unlike, and binding together in one system what might seem the most unconnected or contradictory phenomena. To this he added another principle of association, still more characteristic of the philosopher, that of *cause and effect.* "Why?" "Whence?" "By what means?" "For what end?" "With what results?" these questions from childhood were continually pressing upon his mind. To answer them in respect to *man* in all his multiplied relations as the creature of society, to trace out the working of political institutions, to establish the principles of wise legislation, to lay open the sources of national security and advancement, was the great object of his life; and he here found the widest scope for that extraordinary subtlety of intellect of which we are now speaking. In the two principles just mentioned, we see the origin of Mr. Burke's inexhaustible richness of invention. We see, also, how it was that in his mode of viewing a subject there was never any thing ordinary or commonplace. If the topic was a trite one, the manner of presenting it was peculiarly his own. As in the kaleidoscope, the same object takes a thousand new shapes and colors under a change of light, so in his mind the most hackneyed theme was transformed and illuminated by the radiance of his genius, or placed in new relations which gave it all the freshness of original thought.

This amplitude and subtlety of intellect, in connection with his peculiar habits of association, prepared the way for another characteristic of Mr. Burke, his remarkable *power of generalization*. Without this he might have been one of the greatest of poets, but not a philosopher or a scientific statesman. "To generalize," says Sir James Mackintosh, "is to philosophize; and comprehension of mind, joined to the habit of careful and patient observation, forms the true genius of philosophy." But it was not in his case a mere "habit," it was a kind of instinct of his nature, which led him to gather all the results of his thinking, as by an elective affinity, around their appropriate centers; and, knowing that truths are valuable just in proportion as they have a wider reach, to rise from particulars to generals, and so to shape his statements as to give them the weight and authority of universal propositions. His philosophy, however, was not that of abstract truth; it was confined to things in the *concrete*, and chiefly to man, society, and government. He was no metaphysician; he had, in fact, a dislike, amounting to weakness, of all abstract reasonings in politics, affirming, on one occasion, as to certain statements touching the rights of man, that just "in proportion as they were metaphysically true, they were morally and politically false!" He was, as he himself said, "a philosopher in *action*;" his generalizations embraced the great facts of human society and political institutions as affected by all the interests and passions, the prejudices and frailties of a being like man. The impression he made was owing, in a great degree, to the remoteness of the ideas which he brought together, the startling novelty and yet justness of his combinations, the heightening power of contrast, and the striking manner in which he connected truths of imperishable value with the individual case before him. It is here that we find the true character and office of Mr. Burke. He was the *man of principles*; one of the greatest teachers of "civil prudence" that the world has ever seen. A collection of maxims might be made from his writings infinitely superior to those of Rochefoucauld; equally true to nature, and adapted, at the same time, not to produce selfishness and distrust, but to call into action all that is generous, and noble, and elevated in the heart of man. His high moral sentiment and strong sense of religion added greatly to the force of these maxims; and, as a result of these fine generalizations, Mr. Burke has this peculiarity, which distinguishes him from every other writer, that he is almost equally instructive whether he is right or wrong as to the particular point in debate. He may fail to make out his case; opposing considerations may induce us to decide against him; and yet every argument he uses is full of instruction: it contains great truths, which, if they do not turn the scale here, may do it elsewhere; so that he whose mind is filled with the maxims of Burke has within him not only one of the finest incentives of genius, but a fountain of the richest thought, which may flow forth through a thousand channels in all the efforts of his own intellect, to whatever subject those efforts may be directed.

With these qualities and habits of mind, the oratory of Mr. Burke was of necessity *didactic*. His speeches were *lectures*, and, though often impassioned, enlivened at one time with wit, and rising at another into sublimity or pathos, they usually became wearisome to the House from their minuteness and subtlety, as

> "He went on refining,
> And thought of convincing while they thought of dining."

We see, then, in the philosophical habits of his mind (admirable as the results were in most respects), why he spoke so often to empty benches, while Fox, by seizing on the strong points of the case, by throwing away intermediate thoughts, and striking at the heart of the subject, never failed to carry the House with him in breathless attention.

His *method* was admirable, in respect at least to his published speeches. No man ever bestowed more care on the arrangement of his thoughts. The exceptions to this remark are apparent, not real. There is now and then a slight irregularity in his mode of transition, which seems purposely thrown in to avoid an air of sameness; and the subordinate heads sometimes spread out so widely, that their connection with the main topic is not always obvious. But there is reigning throughout the whole a massive unity of design like that of a great cathedral, whatever may be the intricacy of its details.

In his *reasonings* (for he was one of the greatest masters of reason in our language, though some have strangely thought him deficient in this respect) Mr. Burke did not usually adopt the outward forms of logic. He has left us, indeed, some beautiful specimens of dialectical ability, but his arguments, in most instances, consisted of the amplest enumeration and the clearest display of all the facts and principles, the analogies, relations, or tendencies which were applicable to the case, and were adapted to settle it on the immutable basis of the nature and constitution of things. Here again he appeared, of necessity, more as a teacher than a logician, and hence many were led to underrate his argumentative powers. The exuberance of his fancy was likewise prejudicial to him in this respect. Men are apt to doubt the solidity of a structure which is covered all over with flowers. As to this peculiarity of his eloquence, Mr. Fox truly said, "It injures his reputation; it casts a vail over his wisdom. Reduce his language, withdraw his images, and you will find that he is more wise than eloquent; you will have your full weight of metal though you melt down the chasing."

In respect to Mr. Burke's *imagery*, however, it may be proper to remark, that a large part of it is not liable to any censure of this kind; many of his figures are so finely wrought into the texture of his style, that we hardly think of them as figures at all. His great fault in other cases is that of giving them too bold a relief, or dwelling on them too long, so that the primary idea is lost sight of in the image. Sometimes the prurience of his fancy makes him low and even filthy. He is like a man depicting the scenes of nature, who is not content to give us those features of the landscape that delight the eye, but fills out his canvas with objects which are coarse, disgusting, or noisome. Hence no writer in any language has such extremes of imagery as Mr. Burke, from his picture of the Queen of France, "glittering like the morning star, full of life, and splendor, and joy," or of friendship, as "the soft green of the soul, on which the eye loves to repose," to Lord Chatham's administration "pigging together in the same truckle-bed," and Mr. Dundas, with his East India bills, "exposed like the imperial sow of augury, lying in the mud with the prodigies of her fertility about her, as evidences of her delicate amours."

His *language*, though copious, was not verbose. Every word had its peculiar force and application. His chief fault was that of overloading his sentences with secondary thoughts, which weakened the blow by dividing it. His style is, at times, more careless and inaccurate than might be expected in so great a writer. But his mind was on higher things. His idea of a truly fine sentence, as once stated to a friend, is worthy of being remembered. It consists, said he, in a union of thought, feeling, and imagery — of a striking truth and a corresponding sentiment, rendered doubly striking by the force and beauty of figurative language. There are more sentences of this kind in the pages of Mr. Burke than of any other writer.

In conclusion, we may say, without paradox, since oratory is only one branch of the quality we are now considering, that while Mr. Burke was inferior as an orator to Lord Chatham and Mr. Fox, he has been surpassed by no one in the richness and splendor of his eloquence; and that he has left us something greater and better than all eloquence in his countless lessons of moral and civil wisdom.

SPEECH

OF MR. BURKE ON AMERICAN TAXATION, DELIVERED IN THE HOUSE OF COMMONS, APRIL 9, 1774.

INTRODUCTION.

THE measures of the different British ministers respecting American taxation, from the passing of the Stamp Act in 1765 to the repeal of all taxes except that on tea in 1770, have been detailed already, in connection with the speeches of Lord Chatham. Lord North's policy in respect to America was arbitrary and fluctuating. It was well described by a contemporary writer as "a heterogeneous mixture of concession and coercion; of concession not tending to conciliate, and of coercion that could not be carried into execution—at once exciting hatred for the intention and contempt for the weakness." After the destruction of the tea in the harbor of Boston, violent measures prevailed. In March, 1774, laws were passed depriving Massachusetts of her charter, and closing the port of Boston against all commerce. Some, however, who had supported Lord North in these measures, thought they should be accompanied by an act indicative of a desire to conciliate. Accordingly, Mr. Rose Fuller, of Rye, who usually voted with the ministry, moved on the 19th of April, 1774, "that the House resolve itself into a committee of the whole House, to take into consideration the duty of threepence per pound on tea, payable in all his Majesty's dominions in America," with a view to repealing the same. Mr. Burke seconded the proposal, and sustained it in the following speech. The unfavorable circumstances under which he commenced, and the complete mastery which he soon gained over his audience, have been already described. The applause so lavishly bestowed upon this speech was richly merited. No one had ever been delivered in the Parliament of Great Britain so full at once of deep research, cogent reasoning, cutting sarcasm, graphic description, profound political wisdom, and fervid declamation. Lord Chatham alone had surpassed it in glowing and impassioned eloquence.

In discussing the subject, Mr. Burke confined himself to the single question, "Ought the tax on tea to be abandoned, and with it the entire scheme of raising a parliamentary revenue out of the colonies?" The measure had been popular throughout all England, except in a few commercial cities; and, whether wisely adopted or not, there were strong objections to an abandonment of the system while America remained in the attitude of open resistance. Instead of reserving these objections to be answered in form at the close of the main argument, Mr. Burke disposes of them at once in a preliminary head, under what he calls "the narrow" view of the subject; *i.e*, the mere question of *repeal*. Here he obviates the difficulties referred to; not speaking to the several points, however, under the *name* of objections, but rather turning the tables on Lord North with admirable dexterity, and showing that by his previous concessions he had himself opened the way for an immediate and entire repeal. Mr. Burke next enters on his main argument by giving a historical sketch of the colonial system of England from the passing of the Navigation Act in 1651. He shows that this system did not originally contemplate any direct taxation of the colonies. He traces the steps by which the scheme of obtaining a revenue from America was introduced and modified; sketches the character of the men concerned; and urges a return to the original principles of the Navigation Act, as the only means of restoring peace to the empire.

It would be difficult to find any oration, ancient or modern, in which the matter is more admirably arranged. The several parts support each other, and the whole forms a complete system of thought. The sketches of Mr. Grenville, Mr. Townsend, Lord Chatham, and his administration, are not strictly excrescences, though it would be unsafe for any man less gifted than Mr. Burke to arrest the progress of the discussion, and conduct the audience through such a picture-gallery of statesmen. They do, in one sense, form a part of the argument; for it was the character of the men that decided the character of the measures, and showed how England had been led to adopt a system which ought forever to be abandoned. Even the glowing picture of General Conway's reception by "the trading interest," as they "jumped upon him like children on a long-absent father," and "clung upon him as captives about their redeemer," when he carried through the repeal of the Stamp Act, adds force to the argument, for it shows how American taxation was regarded by those who were best informed on the subject.

The language of this speech is racy and pungent. It is nowhere so polished or rounded off as to lose its sharpness. The folly of American taxation is exposed in the keenest terms, from the opening paragraph, where the House is spoken of as having, "for nine long years," been "lashed round and round this miserable circle of occasional arguments and temporary expedients," to the closing sentence, in which Mr. Burke tells the ministry, "Until you come back to that system [the system of the Navigation Act], there will be no peace for England."

SPEECH, &c.

Sir,—I agree with the honorable gentleman[1] who spoke last, that this subject is not new in this House. Very disagreeably to this House, very unfortunately to this nation, and to the peace and prosperity of this whole empire, no topic has been more familiar to us. For nine long years, session after session, we have been lashed round and round this miserable circle of occasional arguments and temporary expedients. I am sure our heads must turn, and our stomachs nauseate with them. We have had them in every shape; we have looked at them in every point of view. Invention is exhausted; reason is fatigued; experience has given judgment; but obstinacy is not yet conquered.

The honorable gentleman has made one endeavor more to diversify the form of this disgusting argument. He has thrown out a speech composed almost entirely of challenges. Challenges are serious things; and, as he is a man of prudence as well as resolution, I dare say he has very well weighed those challenges before he delivered them. I had long the happiness to sit at the same side of the House, and to agree with the honorable gentleman on all the American questions. My sentiments, I am sure, are well known to him; and I thought I had been perfectly acquainted with his. Though I find myself mistaken, he will still permit me to use the privilege of an old friendship; he will permit me to apply myself to the House under the sanction of his authority; and on the various grounds he has measured out, to submit to you the poor opinions which I have formed upon a matter of importance enough to demand the fullest consideration I could bestow upon it.

Two modes of discussion.

He has stated to the House two grounds of deliberation, one narrow and simple, and merely confined to the question on your paper; the other more large and complicated; comprehending the whole series of the parliamentary proceedings with regard to America, their causes, and their consequences. With regard to the latter ground, he states it as useless, and thinks it may be even dangerous to enter into so extensive a field of inquiry. Yet, to my surprise, he has hardly laid down this restrictive proposition, to which his authority would have given so much weight, when directly, and with the same authority, he condemns it, and declares it absolutely necessary to enter into the most ample historical detail. His zeal has thrown him a little out of his usual accuracy. In this perplexity, what shall we do, sir, who are willing to submit to the law he gives us? He has reprobated in one part of his speech the rule he had laid down for debate in the other; and, after narrowing the ground for all those who are to speak after him, he takes an excursion himself, as unbounded as the subject and the extent of his great abilities.

The broad view the proper one.

Sir, when I can not obey all his laws, I will do the best I can. I will endeavor to obey such of them as have the sanction of his example; and to stick to that rule, which, though not consistent with the other, is the most rational. He was certainly in the right when he took the matter largely. I can not prevail on myself to agree with him in his censure of his own conduct. It is not, he will give me leave to say, either useless or dangerous. He asserts that retrospect is not wise; and the proper, the only proper subject of inquiry is, "not how we got into this difficulty, but how we are to get out of it." In other words, we are, according to him, to consult our invention and to reject our experience. The mode of deliberation he recommends is diametrically opposite to every rule of reason, and every principle of good sense established among mankind; for that sense and that reason I have always understood absolutely to prescribe, whenever we are involved in difficulties from the measures we have pursued, that we should take a strict review of those measures, in order to correct our errors, if they should be corrigible; or at least to avoid a dull uniformity in mischief, and the unpitied calamity of being repeatedly caught in the same snare.

Sir, I will freely follow the honorable gentleman in his historical discussion, without the least management for men or measures, farther than as they shall seem to me to deserve it. But before I go into that large consideration, because I would omit nothing that can give the House satisfaction, I wish to tread,

Objections to the repeal.

I. The NARROW GROUND, to which alone the honorable gentleman, in one part of his speech, has so strictly confined us.

Will not the Americans demand more?

(1.) He desires to know whether, if we were to repeal this tax agreeably to the proposition of the honorable gentleman who made the motion, the Americans would not *take post on this concession*, in order to make a new attack on the next body of taxes; and whether they would not call for a re peal of the duty on wine as loudly as they do now for the repeal of the duty on tea? Sir, I can give no security on this subject. But I will do all that I can, and all that can be fairly demanded. To the experience which the honorable gentleman reprobates in one instant and re verts to in the next; to that experience, without the least wavering or hesitation on my part, I steadily appeal; and would to God there was no other arbiter to decide on the vote with which the House is to conclude this day!

When Parliament repealed the Stamp Act in the year 1766, I affirm, first, that the Americans did *not*, in consequence of this measure, call upon you to give up the former parliamentary revenue which subsisted in that country, or even any one

[1] Chas. Wolfran Cornwall, Esq., one of the Lords of the Treasury, and afterward Speaker of the House of Commons.

of the articles which compose it.[2] I affirm, also, that when, departing from the maxims of that repeal, you revived the scheme of taxation, and thereby filled the minds of the colonists with new jealousy, and all sorts of apprehension, then it was that they quarreled with the old taxes as well as the new; then it was, and not till then, that they questioned all the parts of your legislative power; and by the battery of such questions have shaken the solid structure of this empire to its deepest foundations.

Of those two propositions I shall, before I have done, give such convincing, such damning proof, that, however the contrary may be whispered in circles, or bawled in newspapers, they never more will dare to raise their voices in this House. I speak with great confidence. I have reason for it. The ministers are with me. *They*, at least, are convinced that the repeal of the Stamp Act had not, and that no repeal can have, the consequences which the honorable gentleman who defends their measures is so much alarmed at. To their conduct I refer him for a conclusive answer to his objection. I carry my proof irresistibly into the very body of both ministry and Parliament; not on any general reasoning growing out of collateral matter, but on the conduct of the honorable gentleman's ministerial friends on the new revenue itself.

The act of 1767, which grants this tea duty, sets forth in its preamble that it was expedient to raise a revenue in America for the support of the civil government there, as well as for purposes still more extensive. To this support the act assigns six branches of duties. About two years after this act passed, the ministry—I mean the present ministry—thought it expedient to repeal five of the duties, and to leave, for reasons best known to themselves, only the sixth standing. Suppose any person, at the time of that repeal, had thus addressed the minister:[3] "Condemning, as you do, the repeal of the Stamp Act, why do you venture to repeal the duties upon glass, paper, and painters' colors? Let your pretense for the repeal be what it will, are you not thoroughly convinced that your concessions will produce, not satisfaction, but insolence, in the Americans; and that the giving up these taxes will necessitate the giving up of all the rest?" This objection was as palpable then as it is now; and it was as good for preserving the five duties as for retaining the sixth. Besides, the minister will recollect, that the repeal of the Stamp Act had but just preceded his repeal; and the ill policy of that measure (had it been so impolitic as it has been represented), and the mischiefs it produced, were quite recent. Upon the principles, therefore, of the honorable gentleman, upon the principles of the minister himself, the minister has nothing at all to answer. He stands condemned by himself, and by all his associates, old and new, as a destroyer, in the first trust of finance, in the revenues; and in the first rank of honor, as a betrayer of the dignity of his country.

Most men, especially great men, do not always know their well-wishers. I come to rescue that noble Lord out of the hands of those he calls his friends, and even out of his own. I will do him the justice he is denied at home. He has not been this wicked or imprudent man. He knew that a repeal had no tendency to produce the mischiefs which give so much alarm to his honorable friend. His work was not bad in its principle, but imperfect in its execution; and the motion on your paper presses him only to complete a proper plan, which, by some unfortunate and unaccountable error, he had left unfinished.

I hope, sir, the honorable gentleman who spoke last is thoroughly satisfied, and satisfied out of the proceedings of the ministry on their own favorite act, that his fears from a repeal are groundless. If he is not, I leave him, and the noble Lord who sits by him, to settle the matter, as well as they can, together; for if the repeal of American taxes destroys all our government in America—he is the man!—and he is the worst of all the repealers, because he is the last.[4]

Will consistency permit a repeal?

(2.) But I hear it continually rung in my ears, now and formerly, "the *preamble!* what will become of the preamble, if you repeal this tax?" I am sorry to be compelled so often to expose the calamities and disgraces of Parliament. The preamble of this law, standing as it now stands, has the lie direct given to it by the provisionary part of the act; if that can be called provisionary which makes no provision. I should be afraid to express myself in this manner, especially in the face of such a formidable array of ability as is now drawn up before me, composed of the ancient household troops of that side of the House, and the new recruits from this, if the matter were not clear and indisputable. Nothing but truth could give me this firmness; but plain truth and clear evidence can be beat down by no ability. The clerk will be so good as to turn to the act, and to read this favorite preamble.

[It was read in the following words:

"Whereas it is expedient that a revenue should be raised in your Majesty's dominions in America, for making a more certain and adequate provision for defraying the charge of the administration of justice and support of civil government in such provinces where it shall be found necessary, and toward farther defraying the expenses of defending, protecting, and securing the said dominions."]

You have heard this pompous performance. Now where is the revenue which is to do all these mighty things? Five sixths repealed—abandoned—sunk—gone—lost forever. Does

[2] There is reason to believe that the colonies would not have made any opposition to duties imposed for the mere regulation of trade.

[3] Lord North, then Chancellor of the Exchequer, was minister at the time of this repeal, March 5th, 1770.

[4] The pungency of this *argumentum ad hominem* is increased by the ingenious turn given to it by Mr. Burke, that he is defending Lord North against his own friends and adherents.

the poor solitary tea duty support the purposes of this preamble? Is not the supply there stated as effectually abandoned as if the tea duty had perished in the general wreck? Here, Mr. Speaker, is a precious mockery—a preamble without an act—taxes granted in order to be repealed—and the reasons of the grant still carefully kept up! This is raising a revenue in America! This is preserving dignity in England! If you repeal this tax in compliance with the motion, I readily admit that you lose this fair preamble. Estimate your loss in it. The object of the act is gone already; and all you suffer is the purging the statute-book of the opprobrium of an empty, absurd, and false recital.

Pretense that those taxes were repealed on *commercial* principles.

It has been said again and again, that the five taxes were repealed on commercial principles. It is so said in the paper in my hand[5]—a paper which I constantly carry about, which I have often used, and shall often use again. What is got by this paltry pretense of commercial principles I know not; for, if your government in America is destroyed by the repeal of taxes, it is of no consequence upon what ideas the repeal is grounded. Repeal this tax, too, upon commercial principles, if you please. These principles will serve as well now as they did formerly. But you know that, either your objection to a repeal from these supposed consequences has no validity, or that this pretense never could remove it. This commercial motive never was believed by any man, either in America, which this letter is meant to soothe, or in England, which it is meant to deceive. It was impossible it should; because every man, in the least acquainted with the detail of commerce, must know, that several of the articles on which the tax was repealed were fitter objects of duties than almost any other articles that could possibly be chosen; without comparison more so than the tea that was left taxed, as infinitely less liable to be eluded by contraband. The tax upon red and white lead was of this nature. You have, in this kingdom, an advantage in lead that amounts to a monopoly. When you find yourself in this situation of advantage, you sometimes venture to tax even your own export. You did so, soon after the last war, when, upon this principle, you ventured to impose a duty on coals. In all the articles of American contraband trade, who ever heard of the smuggling of red lead and white lead? You might, therefore, well enough, without danger of contraband, and without injury to commerce (if this were the whole consideration), have taxed these commodities. The same may be said of glass. Besides, some of the things taxed were so trivial, that the loss of the objects themselves, and their utter annihilation out of American commerce, would have been comparatively as nothing. But is the article of tea such an object in the trade of England as not to be felt, or felt but slightly, like white lead, and red lead, and painters' colors? Tea is an object of far other importance. Tea is perhaps the most important object, taking it with its necessary connections, of any in the mighty circle of our commerce. If commercial principles had been the true motives to the repeal, or had they been at all attended to, *tea would have been the last article we should have left taxed for a subject of controversy.*

Sir, it is not a pleasant consideration; but nothing in the world can read so awful and so instructive a lesson, as the conduct of ministry in this business, upon the mischief of not having large and liberal ideas in the management of great affairs.[6] Never have the servants of the state looked at the whole of your complicated interests in one connected view. They have taken things by bits and scraps, some at one time and one pretense, and some at another, just as they pressed, without any sort of regard to their relations or dependencies. They never had any kind of system, right or wrong, but only invented occasionally some miserable tale for the day, in order meanly to sneak out of difficulties into which they had proudly strutted. And they were put to all these shifts and devices, full of meanness and full of mischief, in order to pilfer piecemeal a repeal of an act which they had not the generous courage, when they found and felt their error, honorably and fairly to disclaim. By such management, by the irresistible operation of feeble counsels, so paltry a sum as threepence in the eyes of a financier, so insignificant an article as tea in the eyes of a philosopher, have shaken the pillars of a commercial empire that circled the whole globe.

The wants of the East India Company forbid the tax.

Do you forget that, in the very last year, you stood on the precipice of a general bankruptcy? Your danger was indeed great. You were distressed in the affairs of the East India Company; and you well know what sort of things are involved in the comprehensive energy of that significant appellation. I am not called upon to enlarge to you on that danger, which you thought proper yourselves to aggravate, and to display to the world with all the parade of indiscreet declamation. The monopoly of the most lucrative trades and the possession of imperial revenues had brought you to the verge of beggary and ruin. Such was your representation — such, in some measure, was your case. The vent of ten millions of pounds of this commodity, now locked up by the

[5] Lord Hillsborough's circular letter to the governors of the colonies concerning the repeal of some of the duties laid in the act of 176~

[6] Mr. Burke here pauses for a moment in the progress of his argument, to give us one of those fine generalizations with which he so often strengthens and dignifies his discussion of a particular point, by rising to some broader truth with which it is connected. The stinging force of his imagery in some parts, and the beauty of it in others, are worthy of attention. In the next paragraph he puts the argument on a new ground, viz., that the wants of the East India Company ought to have prevented a quarrel about tea with the colonies, which would have furnished an immense market, if they had not been led to combine against the use of it by abhorrence of the tax: he then returns to the subject of the preamble.

operation of an injudicious tax, and rotting in the warehouses of the Company, would have prevented all this distress, and all that series of desperate measures which you thought yourselves obliged to take in consequence of it. America would have furnished that vent, which no other part of the world can furnish but America; where tea is next to a necessary of life, and where the demand grows upon the supply. I hope our dear-bought East India committees have done us at least so much good as to let us know, that without a more extensive sale of that article, our East India revenues and acquisitions can have no certain connection with this country. It is through the American trade of tea that your East India conquests are to be prevented from crushing you with their burden. They are ponderous indeed; and they must have that great country to lean upon, or they tumble upon your head. It is the same folly that has lost you at once the benefit of the West and of the East. This folly has thrown open folding doors to contraband, and will be the means of giving the profits of the trade of your colonies to every nation but yourselves. Never did a people suffer so much for the empty words of a preamble. It must be given up. For on what principle does it stand? This famous revenue stands, at this hour, on all the debate, as a description of revenue not as yet known in all the comprehensive, but too comprehensive! vocabulary of finance—*a preambulary tax*. It is, indeed, a tax of sophistry, a tax of pedantry, a tax of disputation, a tax of war and rebellion, a tax for any thing but benefit to the imposers, or satisfaction to the subject.

Ought so small a tax to be complained of?

(3.) Well! but, whatever it is, gentlemen will force the colonists to take the teas. You will force them? Has seven years' struggle been yet able to force them? O, but it seems we are yet in the *right*. The tax is "*trifling*—in effect, it is rather an exoneration than an imposition; three fourths of the duty formerly payable on teas exported to America is taken off; the place of collection is only shifted; instead of the retention of a shilling from the drawback here, it is threepence custom paid in America." All this, sir, is very true. But this is the very folly and mischief of the act. Incredible as it may seem, you know that you have deliberately thrown away a large duty which you held secure and quiet in your hands, for the vain hope of getting one three fourths less, through every hazard, through certain litigation, and possibly through war.

Shown to be foolish by this very fact that it is small.

The manner of proceeding in the duties on paper and glass imposed by the same act, was exactly in the same spirit. There are heavy excises on those articles when used in England. On export, these excises are drawn back. But instead of withholding the drawback, which might have been done, with ease, without charge, without possibility of smuggling; and instead of applying the money (money already in your hands) according to your pleasure, you began your operations in finance by flinging away your revenue; you allowed the whole drawback on export, and then you charged the duty (which you had before discharged) payable in the colonies, where it was certain the collection would devour it to the bone, if any revenue were ever suffered to be collected at all. One spirit pervades and animates the whole mass.

Could any thing be a subject of more just alarm to America than to see you go out of the plain high road of finance, and give up your most certain revenues and your clearest interest merely for the sake of insulting your colonies? No man ever doubted that the commodity of tea could bear an imposition of threepence. But no commodity will bear threepence, or will bear a penny, when the general feelings of men are irritated, and two millions of people are resolved not to pay. The feelings of the colonies were formerly the feelings of Great Britain. Theirs were formerly the feelings of Mr. Hampden when called upon for the payment of twenty shillings.[7] Would twenty shillings have ruined Mr. Hampden's fortune? No! but the payment of half twenty shillings, on the principle it was demanded, would have made him a slave. It is the weight of that preamble, of which you are so fond, and not the weight of the duty, that the Americans are unable and unwilling to bear.

It is then, sir, upon the principle of this measure, and nothing else, that we are at issue. It is a principle of political expediency. Your act of 1767 asserts that it is expedient to raise a revenue in America; your act of 1769 [March, 1770], which takes away that revenue, contradicts the act of 1767; and, by something much stronger than words, asserts that it is not expedient. It is a reflection upon your wisdom to persist in a solemn parliamentary declaration of the expediency of any object, for which, at the same time, you make no sort of provision. And pray, sir, let not this circumstance escape you—it is very material—that the preamble of this act, which we wish to repeal, is not declaratory of a right, as some gentlemen seem to argue it; it is only a recital of the expediency of a certain exercise of a right supposed already to have been asserted; an exercise you are now contending for by ways and means, which you confess, though they were obeyed, to be utterly insufficient for their purpose. You are, therefore, at this moment in the awkward situation of fighting for a phantom—a quiddity—a thing that wants not only a substance, but even a name; for a thing which is neither abstract right, nor profitable enjoyment.

Will dignity permit a repeal?

(4.) They tell you, sir, that your *dignity* is tied to it. I know not how it happens, but this dignity of yours is a terrible encumbrance to you, for it has of late been at war with your interest, your equity, and every idea of your policy. Show the thing you

[7] The refusal of this celebrated man to pay "ship-money," when illegally demanded by Charles I., is known to all.

contend for to be reason; show it to be common sense; show it to be the means of attaining some useful end; and then I am content to allow it what dignity you please. But what dignity is derived from the perseverance in absurdity, is more than ever I could discern. The honorable gentleman has said well—indeed, in most of his general observations I agree with him—he says, that this subject does not stand as it did formerly. Oh, certainly not! every hour you continue on this ill-chosen ground, your difficulties thicken on you; and, therefore, my conclusion is, remove from a bad position as quickly as you can. The disgrace, and the necessity of yielding, both of them, grow upon you every hour of your delay.

Dignity did not prevent the promise of a repeal in the very same circumstances.

But will you repeal the act, says the honorable gentleman, at this instant, when America is in open resistance to your authority, and that you have just revived your system of taxation? He thinks he has driven us into a corner. But thus pent up, I am content to meet him, because I enter the lists supported by my old authority, his new friends, the ministers themselves. The honorable gentleman remembers that about five years ago as great disturbances as the present prevailed in America on account of the new taxes. The ministers represented these disturbances as treasonable; and this House thought proper, on that representation, to make a famous address for a revival and for a new application of a statute of Henry VIII. We besought the King, in that *well-considered* address, to inquire into treasons, and to bring the supposed traitors from America to Great Britain for trial.[8] His Majesty was pleased graciously to promise a compliance with our request. All the attempts from this side of the House to resist these violences, and to bring about a repeal, were treated with the utmost scorn. An apprehension of the very consequences now stated by the honorable gentleman was then given as a reason for shutting the door against all hope of such an alteration. And so strong was the spirit for supporting the new taxes, that the session concluded with the following remarkable declaration. After stating the vigorous measures which had been pursued, the speech from the throne proceeds:

"You have assured me of your firm support in the prosecution of them. Nothing, in my opinion, could be more likely to enable the well-disposed among my subjects in that part of the world effectually to discourage and defeat the designs of the factious and seditious, than the hearty concurrence of every branch of the Legislature in maintaining the execution of the laws in every part of my dominions."

After this, no man dreamed that a repeal under this ministry could possibly take place. The honorable gentleman knows as well as I that the idea was utterly exploded by those who sway the House. This speech was made on the 9th day of May, 1769. Five days after this speech, that is, on the 13th of the same month, the public circular letter, a part of which I am going to read to you, was written by Lord Hillsborough, secretary of state for the colonies. After reciting the substance of the King's speech, he goes on thus:

"I can take upon me to assure you, notwithstanding insinuations to the contrary, from men with factious and seditious views, that his Majesty's present administration have at no time entertained a design to propose to Parliament to lay any farther taxes upon America for the purpose of raising a revenue; and that it is at present their intention to propose, the next session of Parliament, to take off the duties upon glass, paper, and colors, upon consideration of such duties having been laid contrary to the true principles of commerce.

"These have always been, and still are, the sentiments of his Majesty's present servants, and by which their conduct in respect to America has been governed. And his Majesty relies upon your prudence and fidelity for such an explanation of his measures as may tend to remove the prejudices which have been excited by the misrepresentations of those who are enemies to the peace and prosperity of Great Britain and her colonies, and to re-establish that mutual confidence and affection upon which the glory and safety of the British empire depend."

Here, sir, is a canonical book of ministerial scripture; the General Epistle to the Americans. What does the gentleman say to it? Here a repeal is promised; promised without condition, and while your authority was actually resisted. I pass by the public promise of a peer relative to the repeal of taxes by this House. I pass by the use of the King's name in a matter of supply—that sacred and reserved right of the Commons. I conceal the ridiculous figure of Parliament, hurling its thunders at the gigantic rebellion of America, and then, five days after, prostrate at the feet of those assemblies we affected to despise, begging them, by the intervention of our ministerial sureties, to receive our submission, and heartily promising amendment. These might have been serious matters formerly; but we are grown wiser than our fathers. Passing, therefore, from the constitutional consideration to the mere policy, does not this letter imply that the idea of taxing America for the purpose of revenue is an abominable project, when the ministry suppose none but factious men, and with seditious views, could charge them with it? Does not this letter adopt and sanctify the American distinction of taxing for a revenue? Does it not state the ministerial rejection of such principle of taxation, not as the occasional, but the constant opinion of the King's servants? Does it not say—I care not how consistently—but does it not say that their conduct with regard to America has been always governed by this policy? It goes a great deal farther. These excellent and trusty servants of the King, justly fearful lest they

[8] In February, 1769, Parliament addressed the King, at the suggestion of ministers, requesting him to exercise the powers here mentioned, under an obsolete act of the 35th of Henry VIII.

themselves should have lost all credit with the world, bring out the image of their gracious Sovereign from the inmost and most sacred shrine, and they pawn him as a security for their promises. "His Majesty relies on your prudence and fidelity for such an explanation of his measures." These sentiments of the minister, and these measures of his Majesty, can only relate to the principle and practice of taxing for a revenue; and, accordingly, Lord Botetourt, stating it as such, did, with great propriety, and in the exact spirit of his instructions, endeavor to remove the fears of the Virginian assembly, lest the sentiments which it seems (unknown to the world) had always been those of the ministers, and by which their conduct in respect to America had been governed, should, by some possible revolution, favorable to wicked American taxers, be hereafter counteracted. He addresses them in this manner:

"It may possibly be objected that, as his Majesty's present administration are not immortal, their successors may be inclined to attempt to undo what the present ministers shall have attempted to perform; and to that objection I can give but this answer: that it is my firm opinion that the plan I have stated to you will certainly take place, and that it will never be departed from; and so determined am I forever to abide by it, that I will be content to be declared infamous if I do not, to the last hour of my life, at all times, in all places, and upon all occasions, exert every power with which I either am, or ever shall be legally invested, in order to obtain and maintain for the continent of America that satisfaction which I have been authorized to promise this day, by the confidential servants of our gracious Sovereign; who, to my certain knowledge, rates his honor so high, that he would rather part with his crown than preserve it by deceit."[9]

A glorious and true character! which (since we suffer his ministers with impunity to answer for his ideas of taxation) we ought to make it our business to enable his Majesty to preserve in all its luster. Let him have character, since ours is no more! Let some part of government be kept in respect!

This epistle is not the letter of Lord Hillsborough solely, though he held the official pen. It was the letter of the noble Lord upon the floor, [Lord North], and of all the King's then ministers, who (with, I think, the exception of two only) are his ministers at this hour. The very first news that a British Parliament heard of what it was to do with the duties which it had given and granted to the King, was by the publication of the votes of American assemblies. It was in America that your resolutions were predeclared. It was from thence that we knew to a certainty how much exactly, and not a scruple more or less, we were to repeal. We were unworthy to be let into the secret of our own conduct. The assemblies had *confidential* communications from his Majesty's *confidential* servants. We were nothing but instruments. Do you, after this, wonder that you have no weight and no respect in the colonies? After this, are you surprised that Parliament is every day and every where losing (I feel it with sorrow, I utter it with reluctance) that reverential affection which so endearing a name of authority ought ever to carry with it; that you are obeyed solely from respect to the bayonet; and that this House, the ground and pillar of freedom, is itself held up only by the treacherous under-pinning and clumsy buttresses of arbitrary power?

If this dignity, which is to stand in the place of just policy and common sense, had been consulted, there was a time for preserving it, and for reconciling it with any concession. If, in the session of 1768, that session of idle terror and empty menaces, you had, as you were often pressed to do, repealed those taxes, then your strong operations would have come justified and enforced, in case your concessions had been returned by outrages. But, preposterously, you began with violence; and before terrors could have any effect, either good or bad, your ministers immediately begged pardon, and promised that repeal to the obstinate Americans which they had refused in an easy, good-natured, complying British Parliament. The assemblies, which had been publicly and avowedly dissolved for their contumacy, are called together to receive your submission. Your ministerial directors blustered like tragic tyrants here; and then went mumping with a sore leg in America, canting, and whining, and complaining of faction, which represented them as friends to a revenue from the colonies. I hope nobody in this House will hereafter have the impudence to defend American taxes in the name of ministry. The moment they do, with this letter of attorney in my hand, I will tell them, in the authorized terms, they are wretches, "with factious and seditious views; enemies to the peace and prosperity of the mother country and the colonies," and subverters "of the mutual affection and confidence on which the glory and safety of the British empire depend."

After this letter, the question is no more on propriety or dignity. They are gone already. The faith of your sovereign is pledged for the political principle. The general declaration in the letter goes to the whole of it. You must

[9] A material point is omitted by Mr. Burke in this speech, viz., the manner in which the Americans received this royal assurance. The Assembly of Virginia, in their address in answer to Lord Botetourt's speech, express themselves thus: "We will not suffer our present hopes, arising from the pleasing prospect your Lordship hath so kindly opened and displayed to us, to be dashed by the bitter reflection that any future administration will entertain a wish to depart from that plan which affords the surest and most permanent foundation of public tranquillity and happiness. No, my Lord, we are sure our most gracious Sovereign, under whatever changes may happen in his confidential servants, will remain immutable in the ways of truth and justice, and that he is incapable of deceiving his faithful subjects; and we esteem your Lordship's information not only as warranted, but even sanctified by the royal word."

therefore either abandon the scheme of taxing, or you must send the ministers tarred and feathered to America, who dared to hold out the royal faith for a renunciation of all taxes for revenue. Them you must punish, or this faith you must preserve. The preservation of this faith is of more consequence than the duties on red lead, or white lead, or on broken glass, or atlas-ordinary, or demy-fine, or blue royal, or bastard, or fool's-cap, which you have given up, or the three-pence on tea which you have retained. The letter went stamped with the public authority of this kingdom. The instructions for the colony government go under no other sanction; and America can not believe, and will not obey you, if you do not preserve this channel of communication sacred. You are now punishing the colonies for acting on distinctions held out by that very ministry which is here shining in riches, in favor, and in power, and urging the punishment of the very offense to which they had themselves been the tempters.

Sir, if reasons respecting simply your own commerce, which is your own convenience, were the sole grounds of the repeal of the five duties, why does Lord Hillsborough, in disclaiming in the name of the King and ministry their ever having had an intent to tax for revenue, mention it as the means of "re-establishing the confidence and affection of the colonies?" Is it a way of soothing others to assure them that you will take good care of yourself? The medium, the only medium, for regaining their affection and confidence is, that you will take off something oppressive to their minds. Sir, the letter strongly enforces that idea; for, though the repeal of the taxes is promised on commercial principles, yet the means of counteracting "the insinuations of men with factious and seditious views," is by a disclaimer of *the intention of taxing for* REVENUE, as a constant invariable sentiment and rule of conduct in the government of America.

Proof from the taxes on the Isle of Man, that those on America were not repealed on commercial principles.

I remember that the noble Lord [Lord North] on the floor—not in a former debate, to be sure (it would be disorderly to refer to it—I suppose I read it somewhere)—but the noble Lord was pleased to say that he did not conceive how it could enter into the head of man to impose such taxes as those of 1767 (I mean those taxes which *he* voted for imposing and voted for repealing), as being taxes, contrary to all the principles of commerce, laid on British manufactures.

I dare say the noble Lord is perfectly well read, because the duty of his particular office requires he should be so, in all our revenue laws, and in the policy which is to be collected out of them. Now, sir, when he had read this act of American revenue, and a little recovered from his astonishment, I suppose he made one step retrograde (it is but one), and looked at the act which stands just before in the statute-book. The American revenue is the forty-fifth chapter; the other to which I refer is the forty-fourth of the same session. These two acts are both to the same purpose; both revenue acts; both taxing out of the kingdom; and both taxing British manufactures exported. As the forty-fifth is an act for raising a revenue in America, the forty-fourth is an act for raising a revenue in the Isle of Man. The two acts perfectly agree in all respects except one. In the act for taxing the Isle of Man, the noble Lord will find (not, as in the American act, four or five articles, but) almost the whole body of British manufactures taxed from two and a half to fifteen per cent., and some articles, such as that of spirits, a great deal higher. You did not think it uncommercial to tax the whole mass of your manufactures, and, let me add, your agriculture too; for, I now recollect, British corn is there also taxed up to ten per cent., and this, too, in the very head-quarters, the very citadel of smuggling, the Isle of Man. Now, will the noble Lord condescend to tell me why he repealed the taxes on your manufactures sent out to America, and not the taxes on the manufactures exported to the Isle of Man? The principle was exactly the same, the objects charged infinitely more extensive, the duties without comparison higher. Why? why, notwithstanding all his childish pretexts, *because the taxes were quietly submitted to in the Isle of Man; and because they raised a flame in America.* Your reasons were political, not commercial. The repeal was made, as Lord Hillsborough's letter well expresses it, to regain "the confidence and affection of the colonies, on which the glory and safety of the British empire depend." A wise and just motive surely, if ever there was such. But the mischief and dishonor is, that you have not done what you had given the colonies just cause to expect, when your ministers disclaimed the idea of taxes for a revenue. There is nothing simple, nothing manly, nothing ingenuous, open, decisive, or steady in the proceeding, with regard either to the continuance or the repeal of the taxes. The whole has an air of littleness and fraud. The article of tea is slurred over in the circular letter, as it were by accident. Nothing is said of a resolution either to keep that tax or to give it up. There is no fair dealing in any part of the transaction.

If you mean to follow your true motive and your public faith, give up your tax on tea for raising a revenue, the principle of which has, in effect, been disclaimed in your name, and which produces you no advantage—no, not a penny. Or, if you choose to go on with a poor pretense instead of a solid reason, and will still adhere to your cant of commerce, you have ten thousand times more strong commercial reasons for giving up this duty on tea than for abandoning the five others that you have already renounced.

The American consumption of teas is annually, I believe, worth £300,000, at the least farthing. If you urge the American violence as a justification of your perseverance in enforcing this tax, you know that you can never answer this plain question, "Why did you repeal the others given in the same act, while the very same violence subsisted?" But you did not find the violence cease upon that concession? No! because the concession was far short of satisfying the principle which Lord Hillsborough had abjured, or even the pretense on which the repeal of the other taxes was announced; and because, by enabling the East India Company to open a shop for defeating the American resolution not to pay that specific tax, you manifestly showed a hankering after the principle of the act which you formerly had renounced. Whatever road you take leads to a compliance with this motion. It opens to you at the end of every vista. Your commerce, your policy, your promises, your reasons, your pretenses, your consistency, your inconsistency—all jointly oblige you to this repeal.[10]

But still it sticks in our throats. If we go so far, the Americans will go farther. We do not know that. We ought, from experience, rather to presume the contrary. Do we not know for certain that the Americans are going on as fast as possible, while we refuse to gratify them? Can they do more, or can they do worse, if we yield this point? I think this concession will rather fix a turnpike to prevent their farther progress. It is impossible to answer for bodies of men. But I am sure the natural effect of fidelity, clemency, kindness, in governors, is peace, good will, order, and esteem, on the part of the governed. I would certainly, at least, give these fair principles a fair trial, which, since the making of this act to this hour, they never have had.

Broad and historical view of the subject.

II. Sir, the honorable gentleman having spoken what he thought necessary upon the narrow part of the subject, I have given him, I hope, a satisfactory answer. He next presses me, by a variety of direct challenges and oblique reflections, to say something on the HISTORICAL PART. I shall therefore, sir, open myself fully on that important and delicate subject; not for the sake of telling you a long story (which I know, Mr. Speaker, you are not particularly fond of), but for the sake of the weighty instruction that, I flatter myself, will necessarily result from it. It shall not be longer, if I can help it, than so serious a matter requires.

First Period: policy of the Navigation Act.

(1.) Permit me then, sir, to lead your attention very far back—back to the Act of Navigation—the corner-stone of the policy of this country with regard to its colonies.[11] Sir, that policy was, from the beginning, purely commercial; and the commercial system was wholly restrictive. It was the system of a monopoly. No trade was let loose from that constraint, but merely to enable the colonists to dispose of what, in the course of your trade, you could not take; or to enable them to dispose of such articles as we forced upon them, and for which, without some degree of liberty, they could not pay. Hence all your specific and detailed enumerations; hence the innumerable checks and counter checks; hence that infinite variety of paper chains by which you bind together this complicated system of the colonies. This principle of commercial monopoly runs through no less than twenty-nine acts of Parliament, from the year 1660 to the unfortunate period of 1764.

The laws under that system not *revenue* bills.

In all those acts the system of commerce is established, as that from whence alone you proposed to make the colonies contribute (I mean directly and by the operation of your superintending legislative power) to the strength of the empire. I venture to say, that during that whole period, a parliamentary revenue from thence was never once in contemplation. Accordingly, in all the number of laws passed with regard to the plantations, the words which distinguish revenue laws, specifically as such, were, I think, premeditatedly avoided. I do not say, sir, that a form of words alters the nature of the law, or abridges the power of the law-giver. It certainly does not. However, titles and formal preambles are not always idle words; and the lawyers frequently argue from them. I state these facts to show, not what was your right, but what has been your settled policy. Our revenue laws have usually a *title*, purporting their being *grants;* and the words *give and grant* usually precede the enacting parts. Although duties were imposed on America in acts of King Charles the Second, and in acts of King William, no one title of giving "an aid to his Majesty," or any of the usual titles to revenue acts, was to be found in any of them till 1764; nor were the words "give and grant" in any preamble until the 6th of George the Second. However, the title of this act of George the Second, notwithstanding the words of donation, considers it merely as a regulation—"an act for the better securing of the trade of his Majesty's sugar colonies in America." This act was made on a compromise of all, at the express desire of a part of the colonies themselves. It was therefore in some measure with their consent; and having a title directly purporting only a *commercial regulation*, and being in truth nothing more, the words were passed by, at a time

---

10 If any man has been accustomed to regard Mr. Burke as more of a rhetorician than a reasoner, let him turn back and study over the series of arguments contained in this first head. There is nothing in any of the speeches of Mr. Fox or Mr. Pitt which surpasses it for close reasoning on the facts of the case, or the binding force with which, at every step, the conclusion is linked to the premises. It is unnecessary to speak of the pungency of its application, or the power with which he brings to bear upon Lord North the whole course of his measures respecting the colonies, as an argument for repealing this "solitary duty on tea."

11 This celebrated act was passed during the sway of Cromwell in 1651, at the suggestion of St. John, the English embassador to Holland, who had been treated with gross indignity by the Dutch. It was designed to deprive the Dutch of the immense carrying trade which they enjoyed, and therefore prohibited the importation into England or any of her dependencies, in *foreign* vessels, of any commodities which were not the growth of the respective countries in whose vessels they were imported. At a subsequent period, other acts were passed for the increased advantage of British shipping.

when no jealousy was entertained and things were little scrutinized. Even Governor Bernard, in his second printed letter, dated in 1763, gives it as his opinion, that "it was an act of *prohibition*, not of revenue." This is certainly true, that no act avowedly for the purpose of revenue, and with the ordinary title and recital taken together, is found in the statute-book until the year I have mentioned, that is, the year 1764. All before this period stood on commercial regulation and restraint. The scheme of a colony revenue by British authority appeared therefore to the Americans in the light of a great innovation; the words of Governor Bernard's ninth letter, written in November, 1765, state this idea very strongly; "it must," says he, "have been supposed, such *an innovation* as a parliamentary taxation would cause a great alarm, and meet with much opposition in most parts of America. It was quite *new* to the people, and had no *visible bounds* set to it." After stating the weakness of government there, he says, "Was this a time to introduce so great a novelty as a parliamentary inland taxation in America?" Whatever the right might have been, this mode of using it was absolutely new in policy and practice.

No answer to say that the navigation laws were oppressive.

Sir, they who are friends to the schemes of American revenue say that the commercial restraint is full as hard a law for America to live under. I think so too. I think it, if uncompensated, to be a condition of as rigorous servitude as men can be subject to. But America bore it from the fundamental Act of Navigation until 1764. Why? Because men do bear the inevitable constitution of their original nature with all its infirmities. The Act of Navigation attended the colonies from their infancy, grew with their growth, and strengthened with their strength. They were confirmed in obedience to it, even more by usage than by law. They scarcely had remembered a time when they were not subject to such restraint.

There were compensations.

Besides, they were indemnified for it by a pecuniary compensation. Their monopolist happened to be one of the richest men in the world. By his immense capital (primarily employed, not for their benefit, but his own), they were enabled to proceed with their fisheries, their agriculture, their ship-building, and their trade too, within the limits, in such a manner as got far the start of the slow, languid operations of unassisted nature. This capital was a hot-bed to them. Nothing in the history of mankind is like their progress. For my part, I never cast an eye on their flourishing commerce, and their cultivated and commodious life, but they seem to me rather ancient nations grown to perfection through a long series of fortunate events, and a train of successful industry, accumulating wealth in many centuries, than the colonies of yesterday—than a set of miserable outcasts, a few years ago, not so much sent as thrown out, on the bleak and barren shore of a desolate wilderness three thousand miles from all civilized intercourse.

All this was done by England, while England pursued trade and forgot revenue. You not only acquired commerce, but you actually created the very objects of trade in America; and by that creation you raised the trade of this kingdom at least four-fold. America had the compensation of your capital, which made her bear her servitude. She had another compensation, which you are now going to take away from her. She had, except the commercial restraint, every characteristic mark of a free people in all her internal concerns. She had the image of the British Constitution. She had the substance. She was taxed by her own representatives. She chose most of her own magistrates. She paid them all. She had, in effect, the sole disposal of her own internal government. This whole state of commercial servitude and civil liberty, taken together, is certainly not perfect freedom; but, comparing it with the ordinary circumstances of human nature, it was a happy and a liberal condition.

America submitted to these laws.

I know, sir, that great and not unsuccessful pains have been taken to inflame our minds by an outcry, in this House and out of it, that in America the Act of Navigation neither is, nor ever was obeyed. But if you take the colonies through, I affirm that its authority never was disputed; that it was nowhere disputed for any length of time; and, on the whole, that it was well observed. Wherever the act pressed hard, many individuals indeed evaded it. This is nothing. These scattered individuals never denied the law, and never obeyed it. Just as it happens whenever the laws of trade, whenever the laws of revenue, press hard upon the people in England; in that case all your shores are full of contraband. Your right to give a monopoly to the East India Company, your right to lay immense duties on French brandy, are not disputed in England. You do not make this charge on any man. But you know that there is not a creek from Pentland Firth to the Isle of Wight, in which they do not smuggle immense quantities of teas, East India goods, and brandies. I take it for granted that the authority of Governor Bernard on this point is indisputable. Speaking of these laws, as they regarded that part of America now in so unhappy a condition, he says, "I believe they are nowhere better supported than in this province. I do not pretend that it is entirely free from a breach of these laws; but that such a breach, if discovered, is justly punished." What more can you say of the obedience to any laws in any country? An obedience to these laws formed the acknowledgment, instituted by yourselves, for your superiority, and was the payment you originally imposed for your protection.

Whether you were right or wrong in establishing the colonies on the principles of commercial monopoly, rather than on that of revenue, is at this day a problem of mere speculation. You can not have both by the same authority. To join together the restraints of a universal internal and external monopoly, with a universal internal and external taxation, is an unnatural union—perfect uncompensated slavery. You have long since decided for yourself and them; and you and they have prospered exceedingly under that decision.

Second Period. Attempts to raise a revenue from America.

(2.) This nation, sir, never thought of departing from that choice until the period immediately on the close of the last war. Then a scheme of government new in many things seemed to have been adopted. I saw, or thought I saw, several symptoms of a great change, while I sat in your gallery, a good while before I had the honor of a seat in this House. At that period the necessity was established of keeping up no less than twenty new regiments, with twenty colonels capable of seats in this House. This scheme was adopted with very general applause from all sides, at the very time that, by your conquests in America, your danger from foreign attempts in that part of the world was much lessened, or, indeed, rather quite over. When this huge increase of military establishment was resolved on, a revenue was to be found to support so great a burden. Country gentlemen, the great patrons of economy, and the great resisters of a standing armed force, would not have entered with much alacrity into the vote for so large and expensive an army, if they had been very sure that they were to continue to pay for it. But hopes of another kind were held out to them; and in particular, I well remember that Mr. Townsend, in a brilliant harangue on this subject, did dazzle them, by playing before their eyes the image of a revenue to be raised in America.

Here began to dawn the first glimmerings of this new colony system. It appeared more distinctly afterward, when it was devolved upon a person [Mr. Grenville] to whom, on other accounts, this country owes very great obligations. I do believe that he had a very serious desire to benefit the public. But with no small study of the detail, he did not seem to have his view, at least equally, carried to the total circuit of our affairs. He generally considered his objects in lights that were rather too detached. Whether the business of an American revenue was imposed upon him altogether; whether it was entirely the result of his own speculation; or, what is more probable, that his own ideas rather coincided with the instructions he had received, certain it is, that, with the best intentions in the world, he first brought this fatal scheme into form, and established it by act of Parliament.

No man can believe that at this time of day I mean to lean on the venerable memory of a great man, whose loss we deplore in common. Our little party differences have been long ago composed; and I have acted more with him, and certainly with more pleasure with him, than ever I acted against him. Undoubtedly Mr. Grenville was a first-rate figure in this country. With a masculine understanding, and a stout and resolute heart, he had an application undissipated and unwearied. He took public business, not as a duty which he was to fulfill, but as a pleasure he was to enjoy; and he seemed to have no delight out of this House, except in such things as in some way related to the business that was to be done within it. If he was ambitious, I will say this for him, his ambition was of a noble and generous strain. It was to raise himself, not by the low, pimping politics of a court, but to win his way to power through the laborious gradations of public service, and to secure himself a well-earned rank in Parliament by a thorough knowledge of its constitution, and a perfect practice in all its business.

Sir, if such a man fell into errors, it must be from defects not intrinsical; they must be rather sought in the particular habits of his life, which, though they do not alter the groundwork of character, yet tinge it with their own hue. He was bred in a profession. He was bred to the law, which is, in my opinion, one of the first and noblest of human sciences—a science which does more to quicken and invigorate the understanding than all the other kinds of learning put together; but it is not apt, except in persons very happily born, to open and to liberalize the mind exactly in the same proportion. Passing from that study, he did not go very largely into the world, but plunged into business; I mean, into the business of office, and the limited and fixed methods and forms established there. Much knowledge is to be had undoubtedly in that line; and there is no knowledge which is not valuable. But it may be truly said that men too much conversant in office are rarely minds of remarkable enlargement. Their habits of office are apt to give them a turn to think the substance of business not to be much more important than the forms in which it is conducted. These forms are adapted to ordinary occasions; and, therefore, persons who are nurtured in office do admirably well, as long as things go on in their common order; but when the high-roads are broken up, and the waters out, when a new and troubled scene is opened, and the file affords no precedent, then it is that a greater knowledge of mankind, and a far more extensive comprehension of things is requisite than ever office gave, or than office can ever give.[12] Mr. Grenville thought better of the wisdom and power of human legislation than in truth it deserves. He conceived, and many conceived along with him, that the flourishing trade of this country was greatly owing to law and institution, and not quite so much to liberty; for but too many are apt to believe regulation to be commerce, and taxes to be rev-

[12] This admirable sketch has one peculiarity which is highly characteristic of Mr. Burke. It does not so much describe the objective qualities of the man, as the formative principles of his character. The traits mentioned were *causes* of his being what he was, and doing what he did. They account (and for this reason they are brought forward) for the course he took in respect to America. The same, also, is true respecting the sketch of Charles Townsend which follows, and, to some extent, respecting the sketch of Lord Chatham. This is one of the thousand exhibitions of the philosophical tendencies of Mr. Burke's mind, his absorption in the idea of cause and effect, of the action and reaction of principles and feelings.

enue. Among regulations, that which stood first in reputation was his idol. I mean the Act of Navigation. He has often professed it to be so. The policy of that act is, I readily admit, in many respects well understood. But I do say, that if the act be suffered to run the full length of its principle, and is not changed and modified according to the change of times and the fluctuation of circumstances, it must do great mischief, and frequently even defeat its own purpose.

After the [French] war, and in the last years of it, the trade of America had increased far beyond the speculations of the most sanguine imaginations. It swelled out on every side. It filled all its proper channels to the brim. It overflowed with a rich redundance, and, breaking its banks on the right and on the left, it spread out upon some places where it was indeed improper, upon others where it was only irregular. It is the nature of all greatness not to be exact; and great trade will always be attended with considerable abuses. The contraband will always keep pace in some measure with the fair trade. It should stand as a fundamental maxim, that no vulgar precaution ought to be employed in the cure of evils which are closely connected with the cause of our prosperity. Perhaps this great person turned his eye somewhat less than was just toward the incredible increase of the fair trade, and looked with something of too exquisite a jealousy toward the contraband. He certainly felt a singular degree of anxiety on the subject, and even began to act from that passion earlier than is commonly imagined. For, while he was first Lord of the Admiralty, though not strictly called upon in his official line, he presented a very strong memorial to the Lords of the Treasury (my Lord Bute was then at the head of the board), heavily complaining of the growth of the illicit commerce in America. Some mischief happened even at that time from this over-earnest zeal. Much greater happened afterward, when it operated with greater power in the highest department of the finances. The bonds of the Act of Navigation were straitened so much, that America was on the point of having no trade, either contraband or legitimate.[13] They found, under the construction and execution then used, the act no longer tying, but actually strangling them. All this coming with new enumerations of commodities; with regulations which in a manner put a stop to the mutual coasting intercourse of the colonies; with the appointment of Courts of Admiralty under various improper circumstances; with a sudden extinction of the paper currencies;[14] with a compulsory provision for the quartering of soldiers, the people of America thought themselves proceeded against as delinquents, or at best as people under suspicion of delinquency, and in such a manner as they imagined their recent services in the war did not at all merit.[15] Any of these innumerable regulations, perhaps, would not have alarmed alone; some might be thought reasonable; the multitude struck them with terror.

But the grand maneuver in that business of new regulating the colonies was the 15th act of the fourth of George III., which, besides containing several of the matters to which I have just alluded, opened a new principle; and here properly began the second period of the policy of this country with regard to the colonies, by which the scheme of a regular plantation parliamentary revenue was adopted in theory and settled in practice. A revenue, not substituted in the place of, but superadded to a monopoly; which monopoly was enforced at the same time with additional strictness, and the execution put into military hands.

This act, sir, had for the first time the title of "granting duties in the colonies and plantations of America;" and for the first time it was asserted in the preamble, "that it was *just* and *necessary* that a revenue should be raised there." Then came the technical words of "giving and granting;" and thus a complete American revenue act was made in all the forms, and with a full avowal of the right, equity, policy, and even necessity of taxing the colonies, without any formal consent of theirs. There are contained also in the preamble to that act these very remarkable words: the Commons, &c.—"being desirous to make *some* provision in the *present* session of Parliament *toward* raising the said revenue." By these words it appeared to the colonies that this act was but a beginning of sorrows; that every session was to produce something of the same kind; that we were to go on from day to day, in charging them with such taxes as we pleased, for such a military force as we should think proper. Had this plan been pursued, it was evident that the provincial assemblies, in which the Americans felt all their portion of importance, and beheld their sole image of freedom, were *ipso facto* annihilated. This ill prospect before them seemed to be boundless in extent, and endless in duration. Sir, they were not mistaken. The ministry valued themselves when this act passed, and when they gave notice of the Stamp Act, that both of the duties came very short of their ideas of American taxation. Great was the applause of this measure here. In England we cried out for new taxes

[13] For some years previous to the peace of 1763, the American colonies carried on an extensive trade in British manufactured articles with the colonies of Spain and France. This, though not against the spirit of the Navigation Act, was a violation of its letter, and was stopped for a time, though afterward allowed under duties amounting to a prohibition. In carrying out these regulations, the accused were to be prosecuted in the Admiralty Courts, and thus deprived of a trial by jury.

[14] Paper money was issued by most of the colonies to supply a currency, when the coin was withdrawn in the course of trade to England. Regulations putting a sudden stop to this currency produced great trouble in America.

[15] The colonies had entered warmly into the war against France; and such was their zeal, that of their own accord they advanced for carrying it on, much larger sums than were allotted as their quota by the British government.

on America, while they cried out that they were nearly crushed with those which the war and their own grants had brought upon them.

Pretense that the Americans did not at first object to being taxed.

Sir, it has been said in the debate, that when the first American revenue act (the act in 1764, imposing the port duties) passed, the Americans did not object to the principle.[16] It is true they touched it but very tenderly. It was not a direct attack. They were, it is true, as yet novices; as yet unaccustomed to direct attacks upon any of the rights of Parliament. The duties were port duties, like those they had been accustomed to bear, with this difference, that the title was not the same, the preamble not the same, and the spirit altogether unlike. But of what service is this observation to the cause of those that make it? It is a full refutation of the pretense for their present cruelty to America; for it shows, out of their own mouths, that our colonies were backward to enter into the present vexatious and ruinous controversy.

Pretense that then the option was given them of taxing themselves.

There is also another circulation abroad (spread with a malignant intention, which I can not attribute to those who say the same thing in this House), that Mr. Grenville gave the colony agents an option for their assemblies to tax themselves, which they had refused. I find that much stress is laid on this as a fact. However, it happens neither to be true nor possible. I will observe, first, that Mr. Grenville never thought fit to make this apology for himself in the innumerable debates that were had upon the subject. He might have proposed to the colony agents that they should agree in some mode of taxation as the ground of an act of Parliament, but he never could have proposed that they should tax themselves on requisition, which is the assertion of the day. Indeed, Mr. Grenville well knew that the colony agents could have no general powers to consent to it; and they had no time to consult their assemblies for particular powers before he passed his first revenue act. If you compare dates, you will find it impossible. Burdened as the agents knew the colonies were at that time, they could not give the least hope of such grants. His own favorite governor was of opinion that the Americans were not then taxable objects.

"Nor was the time less favorable to the equity of such a taxation. I don't mean to dispute the reasonableness of America contributing to the charges of Great Britain when she is able; nor, I believe, would the Americans themselves have disputed it, at a proper time and season. But it should be considered that the American governments themselves have, in the prosecution of the late war, contracted very large debts, which it will take some years to pay off, and in the mean time, occasion very burdensome taxes for that purpose only. For instance, this government, which is as much beforehand as any, raises every year £37,500 sterling for sinking their debt, and must continue it for four years longer at least before it will clear."

These are the words of Governor Bernard's letter to a member of the old ministry, and which he has since printed. Mr. Grenville could not have made this proposition to the agents for another reason. He was of opinion, which he has declared in this House a hundred times, that the colonies could not legally grant any revenue to the crown; and that infinite mischiefs would be the consequence of such a power. When Mr. Grenville had passed the first revenue act, and in the same session had made this House come to a resolution for laying a stamp duty on America, between that time and the passing the Stamp Act into a law, he told a considerable and most respectable merchant, a member of this House, whom I am truly sorry I do not now see in his place, when he represented against this proceeding, that if the stamp duty was disliked, he was willing to exchange it for any other equally productive; but that, if he objected to the Americans being taxed by Parliament, he might save himself the trouble of the discussion, as he was determined on the measure. This is the fact, and, if you please, I will mention a very unquestionable authority for it.

Pretense that the opposition of the Americans could not be forseeen.

Thus, sir, I have disposed of this falsehood. But falsehood has a perennial spring. It is said that no conjecture could be made of the dislike of the colonies to the principle. This is as untrue as

[16] It is far from being true that "the Americans did not object to the principle" of the act of 1764; nor is Mr. Burke correct in saying they "touched it very tenderly." The first act of the British Parliament for the avowed purpose of raising a revenue in America was passed April 5th, 1764. Within a month after the news reached Boston, the General Court of Massachusetts met, and on the 13th of June, 1764, addressed a letter to Mr Mauduit, their agent in England, giving him spirited and decisive instructions on the subject. It seems he had misconstrued their silence respecting another law, and had not, therefore, come forward in their behalf against the act. They say, "No agent of the province has power to make concessions in any case without express orders; and that the silence of the province should have been imputed to any cause, even to despair, rather than to have been construed into a tacit cession of their rights, or an acknowledgment of a right in Parliament to *impose duties and taxes upon a people who are not represented in the House of Commons*." A committee was also chosen with power to sit in the recess of the General Court, and directed to correspond with the other provinces on the subject, acquainting them with the instructions sent to Mr. Mauduit, and requesting the concurrence of the other provincial assemblies in resisting "any impositions and taxes upon this and the other American provinces." Accordingly, in November of the same year, the House of Burgesses in Virginia sent an address to the House of Lords and a remonstrance to the House of Commons on the same subject. Remonstrances were likewise sent from Massachusetts and New York to the Privy Council. James Otis also published during this year his pamphlet against the right of Parliament to tax the colonies while unrepresented in the House of Commons. This was printed in London in 1765, about the time when the Stamp Act was passed.—See Holmes's American Annals, 2d ed., vol. ii., p. 225–6.

the other. After the resolution of the House, and before the passing of the Stamp Act, the colonies of Massachusetts Bay and New York did send remonstrances, objecting to this mode of parliamentary taxation. What was the consequence? They were suppressed; they were put under the table—notwithstanding an order of council to the contrary—by the ministry which composed the very council that had made the order: and thus the House proceeded to its business of taxing without the least regular knowledge of the objections which were made to it. But, to give that House its due, it was not over-desirous to receive information or to hear remonstrance. On the 15th of February, 1765, while the Stamp Act was under deliberation, they refused with scorn even so much as to receive four petitions presented from so respectable colonies as Connecticut, Rhode Island, Virginia, and Carolina, besides one from the traders of Jamaica. As to the colonies, they had no alternative left to them but to disobey, or to pay the taxes imposed by that Parliament which was not suffered, or did not suffer itself, even to hear them remonstrate upon the subject.

Third Period. Lord Rockingham's administration. Repeal of the Stamp Act.

(3.) This was the state of the colonies before his Majesty thought fit to change his ministers. It stands upon no authority of mine. It is proved by incontrovertible records. The honorable gentleman has desired some of us to lay our hands upon our hearts, and answer to his queries upon the historical part of this consideration; and by his manner (as well as my eyes could discern it) he seemed to address himself to me.

Sir, I will answer him as clearly as I am able, and with great openness. I have nothing to conceal. In the year sixty-five, being in a very private station, far enough from any line of business, and not having the honor of a seat in this House, it was my fortune, unknowing and unknown to the then ministry, by the intervention of a common friend, to become connected with a very noble person [Lord Rockingham], and at the head of the treasury department.[17] It was indeed in a situation of little rank and no consequence, suitable to the mediocrity of my talents and pretensions; but a situation near enough to enable me to see, as well as others, what was going on; and I did see in that noble person such sound principles, such an enlargement of mind, such clear and sagacious sense, and such unshaken fortitude, as have bound me, as well as others much better than me, by an inviolable attachment to him from time forward. Sir, Lord Rockingham very early in that summer received a strong representation from many weighty English merchants and manufacturers, from governors of provinces and commanders of men of war, against almost the whole of the American commercial regulations; and particularly with regard to the total ruin which was threatened to the Spanish trade. I believe, sir, the noble Lord soon saw his way in this business. But he did not rashly determine against acts which it might be supposed were the result of much deliberation. However, sir, he scarcely began to open the ground, when the whole veteran body of office took the alarm. A violent outcry of all (except those who knew and felt the mischief) was raised against any alteration. On one hand, his attempt was a direct violation of treaties and public law. On the other, the Act of Navigation and all the corps of trade laws were drawn up in array against it.

The first step the noble Lord took was to have the opinion of his excellent, learned, and ever-lamented friend, the late Mr. Yorke, then attorney general, on the point of law.[18] When he knew that formally and officially, which in substance he had known before, he immediately dispatched orders to redress the grievance. But I will say it for the then minister, he is of that constitution of mind, that I know he would have issued, on the same critical occasion, the very same orders, if the acts of trade had been, as they were not, directly against him; and would have cheerfully submitted to the equity of Parliament for his indemnity.

On the conclusion of this business of the Spanish trade, the news of the troubles, on account of the Stamp Act, arrived in England. It was not until the end of October that these accounts were received. No sooner had the sound of that mighty tempest reached us in England, than the whole of the then Opposition, instead of feeling humbled by the unhappy issue of their measures, seemed to be infinitely elated, and cried out that the ministry, from envy to the glory of their predecessors, were prepared to repeal the Stamp Act. Near nine years after, the honorable gentleman takes quite opposite ground, and now challenges me to put my hand to my heart, and say whether the ministry had resolved on the repeal till a considerable time after the meeting of Parliament. Though I do not very well know what the honorable gentleman wishes to infer from the admission or from the denial of this fact, on which he so earnestly adjures me, I do put my hand on my heart, and assure him that they did *not* come to a resolution directly to repeal. They weighed this matter as its difficulty and importance required. They considered maturely among themselves. They consulted with all who could give advice or information. It was not determined until a little before the meeting of Parliament; but it was determined, and the main lines of their own plan marked out, before that meeting. Two questions arose. I hope I am not going into a narrative troublesome to the House.

[A cry of go on, go on.]

The first of the two considerations was whether the repeal should be total, or whether only par-

[17] Mr. Burke became private secretary to Lord Rockingham in July, 1765, and was thus united with him in his political measures.

[18] Mr. Charles Yorke, whose sudden death in 1770, after having had the office of Lord Chancellor forced upon him by the King, is mentioned in a Letter of Junius to the Duke of Grafton. See page 201.

tial; taking out every thing burdensome and productive, and reserving only an empty acknowledgment, such as a stamp on cards or dice. The other question was, on what principle the act should be repealed. On this head, also, two principles were started: one, that the legislative rights of this country, with regard to America, were not entire, but had certain restrictions and limitations. The other principle was, that taxes of this kind were contrary to the fundamental principles of commerce on which the colonies were founded, and contrary to every idea of political equity; by which equity we are bound as much as possible to extend the spirit and benefit of the British Constitution to every part of the British dominions. The option, both of the measure and of the principle of repeal, was made before the session; and I wonder how any one can read the King's speech at the opening of that session without seeing in that speech both the repeal and the Declaratory Act very sufficiently crayoned out. Those who can not see this can see nothing.

Surely the honorable gentleman will not think that a great deal less time than was then employed ought to have been spent in deliberation, when he considers that the news of the troubles did not arrive till toward the end of October. The Parliament sat to fill the vacancies on the 14th day of December, and on business the 14th of the following January.

Sir, a partial repeal, or, as the *bon ton* of the Court then was, a *modification*, would have satisfied a timid, unsystematic, procrastinating ministry, as such a measure has since done such a ministry [Lord North's]. A modification is the constant resource of weak, undeciding minds. To repeal by a denial of our right to tax in the preamble (and this, too, did not want advisers), would have cut, in the heroic style, the Gordian knot with a sword. Either measure would have cost no more than a day's debate. But when the total repeal was adopted, and adopted on principles of policy, of equity, and of commerce, this plan made it necessary to enter into many and difficult measures. It became necessary to open a very large field of evidence commensurate to these extensive views. But then this labor did knight's service. It opened the eyes of several to the true state of American affairs; it enlarged their ideas, it removed their prejudices, and it conciliated the opinions and affections of men. The noble Lord who then took the lead in the administration, my honorable friend [Mr. Dowdeswell] under me, and a right honorable gentleman [General Conway] (if he will not reject his share, and it was a large one, of this business), exerted the most laudable industry in bringing before you the fullest, most impartial, and least garbled body of evidence that was ever produced to this House. I think the inquiry lasted in the committee for six weeks; and, at its conclusion, this House, by an independent, noble, spirited, and unexpected majority—by a majority that will redeem all the acts ever done by majorities in Parliament, in the teeth of all the old mercenary Swiss of state, in despite of all the old speculators and augurs of political events, in defiance of the whole embattled legion of veteran pensioners and practiced instruments of a court, gave a total repeal to the Stamp Act, and (if it had been so permitted) a lasting peace to this whole empire.

I state, sir, these particulars, because this act of spirit and fortitude has lately been, in the circulation of the season, and in some hazarded declamations in this House, attributed to timidity. If, sir, the conduct of ministry, in proposing the repeal, had arisen from timidity with regard to themselves, it would have been greatly to be condemned. Interested timidity disgraces as much in the cabinet as personal timidity does in the field. But timidity, with regard to the well-being of our country, is heroic virtue. The noble Lord who then conducted affairs, and his worthy colleagues, while they trembled at the prospect of such distresses as you have since brought upon yourselves, were not afraid steadily to look in the face that glaring and dazzling influence at which the eyes of eagles have blenched. He looked in the face of one of the ablest, and, let me say, not the most scrupulous Oppositions that, perhaps, ever was in this House, and withstood it, unaided by even one of the usual supporters of administration. He did this when he repealed the Stamp Act. He looked in the face of a person he had long respected and regarded, and whose aid was then particularly wanting. I mean Lord Chatham. He did this when he passed the Declaratory Act.[19]

It is now given out, for the usual purposes, by the usual emissaries, that Lord Rockingham did not consent to the repeal of this act until he was bullied into it by Lord Chatham; and the reporters have gone so far as publicly to assert, in a hundred companies, that the honorable gentleman under the gallery [General Conway], who proposed the repeal in the American committee, had another set of resolutions in his pocket directly the reverse of those he moved. These artifices of a desperate cause are, at this time, spread abroad with incredible care, in every part of the town, from the highest to the lowest companies; as if the industry of the circulation were to make amends for the absurdity of the report.

Sir, whether the noble Lord is of a complexion to be bullied by Lord Chatham, or by any man, I must submit to those who know him. I confess, when I look back at that time, I consider him as placed in one of the most trying situations in which, perhaps, any man ever stood. In the House of Peers there were very few of the ministry, out of the noble Lord's particular connection (except Lord Egmont, who acted, as far as I could discern, an honorable and manly part), that did not look to some other future arrangement, which warped his politics. There were in both Houses new and menacing appearances, that might very naturally drive any other than a most

[19] See Lord Chatham's speech on the Stamp Act, page 103, in which he explicitly declared to Lord Rockingham and his associates that he could not give them his support.

resolute minister from his measure or from his station. The household troops openly revolted. The allies of ministry (those, I mean, who supported some of their measures, but refused responsibility for any) endeavored to undermine their credit, and to take ground that must be fatal to the success of the very cause which they would be thought to countenance. The question of the repeal was brought on by ministry in the committee of this House, in the very instant when it was known that more than one court negotiation was carrying on with the heads of the Opposition. Every thing, upon every side, was full of traps and mines. Earth below shook; heaven above menaced; all the elements of ministerial safety were dissolved. It was in the midst of this chaos of plots and counter-plots—it was in the midst of this complicated warfare against public opposition and private treachery, that the firmness of that noble person was put to the proof. He never stirred from his ground—no, not an inch. He remained fixed and determined, in principle, in measure, and in conduct. He practiced no managements. He secured no retreat. He sought no apology.[20]

I will likewise do justice—I ought to do it—to the honorable gentleman who led us in this House [General Conway]. Far from the duplicity wickedly charged on him, he acted his part with alacrity and resolution. We all felt inspired by the example he gave us, down even to myself, the weakest in that phalanx. I declare for one, I knew well enough (it could not be concealed from any body) the true state of things; but, in my life, I never came with so much spirits into this House. It was a time for a *man* to act in. We had powerful enemies, but we had faithful and determined friends, and a glorious cause. We had a great battle to fight, but we had the means of fighting; not as now, when our arms are tied behind us. We did fight that day, and conquer.

I remember, sir, with a melancholy pleasure, the situation of the honorable gentleman [General Conway], who made the motion for the repeal, in that crisis, when the whole trading interest of this empire, crammed into your lobbies, with a trembling and anxious expectation, waited, almost to a winter's return of light, their fate from your resolutions. When, at length, you had determined in their favor, and your doors, thrown open, showed them the figure of their deliverer in the well-earned triumph of his important victory, from the whole of that grave multitude there arose an involuntary burst of gratitude and transport. They jumped upon him like children on a long-absent father. They clung upon him as captives about their redeemer. All England, all America, joined to his applause. Nor did he seem insensible to the best of all earthly rewards, the love and admiration of his fellow-citizens.

> "Hope elevated and joy
> Brightened his crest."
>
> *Milton's Par. Lost*, ix., 634.

I stood near him; and his face, to use the expression of the scripture of the first martyr, "his face was as if it had been the face of an angel." I do not know how others feel, but if I had stood in that situation, I never would have exchanged it for all that Kings in their profusion could bestow.[21] I did hope that that day's danger and honor would have been a bond to hold us all together forever. But, alas! that, with other pleasing visions, is long since vanished.

Sir, this act of supreme magnanimity has been represented as if it had been a measure of an administration that, having no scheme of their own, took a middle line, pilfered a bit from one side and a bit from the other. Sir, they took *no* middle lines. They differed fundamentally from the schemes of both parties, but they preserved the objects of both. They preserved the authority of Great Britain. They preserved the equity of Great Britain. They made the Declaratory Act. They repealed the Stamp Act. They did both *fully;* because the Declaratory Act was without qualification, and the repeal of the Stamp Act total. This they did in the situation I have ascribed.

Now, sir, what will the adversary say to both these acts? If the principle of the Declaratory Act was not good, the principle we are contending for this day is monstrous. If the principle of the repeal was not good, why are we not at war for a real, substantial, effective revenue? If both were bad, why has this ministry incurred all the inconveniences of both and of all schemes? Why have they enacted, repealed, enforced, yielded, and now attempt to enforce again?

Refutation of the pretense that the repeal produced the disturbances in America.

Sir, I think I may as well now, as at any other time, speak to a certain matter of fact, not wholly unrelated to the question under your consideration. We, who would persuade you to revert to the ancient policy of this kingdom, labor

[20] The Rockingham administration was distracted by internal dissensions, and obnoxious to the King because they had determined to repeal the Stamp Act, and also on personal grounds, because they neglected to apply to Parliament for an allowance to the younger brothers of his Majesty. The Declaratory Act was passed for the purpose of propitiating the King when the Stamp Act was repealed. But it failed of its object; and the administration of Lord Rockingham was dissolved a few months after.

[21] General Conway must have felt this passage keenly, and he deserved it. He was now connected with Lord North, and had gratified the King by going the whole length of the most violent measures against Wilkes. About three weeks before, he had said respecting the Boston Port Bill, that he "was particularly happy in the mode of punishment adopted in it." He was then enjoying his reward in the emoluments pertaining to the office of Governor of Jersey, to which he had been promoted after holding for some years that of Lieutenant General of the Ordnance. In justice to Conway, it ought, however, to be said, that notwithstanding his hasty remark in favor of the Boston Port Bill, he was always opposed to American taxation. He differed from Lord North at every step as to carrying on the war, and made the motion for ending it, February 22d, 1782, which drove Lord North from power.

under the effect of this short current phrase, which the court leaders have given out to all their corps, in order to take away the credit of those who would prevent you from that frantic war you are going to wage upon your colonies. Their cant is this: "All the disturbances in America have been created by the repeal of the Stamp Act." I suppress for a moment my indignation at the falsehood, baseness, and absurdity of this most audacious assertion. Instead of remarking on the motives and character of those who have issued it for circulation, I will clearly lay before you the state of America, antecedently to that repeal, after the repeal, and since the renewal of the schemes of American taxation.

The disturbances were great before the repeal.

It is said that the disturbances, if there were any before the repeal, were slight, and without difficulty or inconvenience might have been suppressed. For an answer to this assertion, I will send you to the great author and patron of the Stamp Act, who, certainly meaning well to the authority of this country, and fully apprised of the state of that, made, before a repeal was so much as agitated in this House, the motion which is on your journals; and which, to save the clerk the trouble of turning to it, I will now read to you. It was for an amendment to the address of the 17th of December, 1765.

"To express our just resentment and indignation at the outrageous tumults and insurrections which have been excited and carried on in North America; and at the resistance given by open and rebellious force to the execution of the laws in that part of his Majesty's dominions; and to assure his Majesty that his faithful commons, animated with the warmest duty and attachment to his royal person and government, will firmly and effectually support his Majesty in all such measures as shall be necessary for preserving and supporting the legal dependence of the colonies on the mother country," &c., &c.

Here was certainly a disturbance preceding the repeal; such a disturbance as Mr. Grenville thought necessary to qualify by the name of an insurrection, and the epithet of a rebellious force: terms much stronger than any by which those who then supported his motion have ever since thought proper to distinguish the subsequent disturbances in America. They were disturbances which seemed to him and his friends to justify as strong a promise of support as hath been usual to give in the beginning of a war with the most powerful and declared enemies. When the accounts of the American governors came before the House, they appeared stronger even than the warmth of public imagination had painted them; so much stronger, that the papers on your table bear me out in saying, that all the late disturbances, which have been at one time the minister's motives for the repeal of five out of six of the new court taxes, and are now his pretenses for refusing to repeal that sixth, did not amount—why do I compare them? no, not to a tenth part of the tumults and violence which prevailed long before the repeal of that act.

Ministry can not refuse the authority of the commander-in-chief, General Gage, who, in his letter of the 4th of November, from New York, thus represents the state of things:

"It is difficult to say, from the highest to the lowest, who has not been accessory to this insurrection, either by writing or mutual agreements to oppose the act, by what they are pleased to term all legal opposition to it. Nothing effectually has been proposed, either to prevent or quell the tumult. The rest of the provinces are in the same situation as to a positive refusal to take the stamps; and threatening those who shall take them, to plunder and murder them; and this affair stands in all the provinces, that unless the act, from its own nature, enforce itself, nothing but a very considerable military force can do it."

It is remarkable, sir, that the persons who formerly trumpeted forth the most loudly the violent resolutions of assemblies; the universal insurrections; the seizing and burning the stamped papers; the forcing stamp officers to resign their commissions under the gallows; the rifling and pulling down of the houses of magistrates; and the expulsion from their country of all who dared to write or speak a single word in defense of the powers of Parliament—these very trumpeters are now the men that represent the whole as a mere trifle, and choose to date all the disturbances from the repeal of the Stamp Act, which put an end to them. Hear your officers abroad, and let them refute this shameless falsehood, who, in all their correspondence, state the disturbances as owing to their true causes, the discontent of the people, from the taxes. You have this evidence in your own archives; and it will give you complete satisfaction, if you are not so far lost to all parliamentary ideas of information as rather to credit the lie of the day than the records of your own House.

Did not spring from opposition in the House to the Stamp Act when passed.

Sir, this vermin of court reporters, when they are forced into day upon one point, are sure to burrow in another; but they shall have no refuge; I will make them bolt out of all their holes Conscious that they must be baffled, when they attribute a precedent disturbance to a subsequent measure, they take other ground, almost as absurd, but very common in modern practice, and very wicked; which is, to attribute the ill effect of ill-judged conduct to the arguments which had been used to dissuade us from it. They say that the opposition made in Parliament to the Stamp Act, at the time of its passing, encouraged the Americans to their resistance. This has even formally appeared in print in a regular volume, from an advocate of that faction, a Doctor Tucker. This Doctor Tucker is already a dean, and his earnest labors in this vineyard will, I suppose, raise him to a bishopric. But this assertion, too, just like the rest, is false. In all the papers which have loaded your table; in all the vast crowd of verbal witnesses that appeared at your bar—witnesses which were indiscriminately produced from both sides of the House—not the least hint of such a cause of disturbance has ever appeared. As to the fact of a strenuous opposition to the Stamp Act, I sat as a stranger in your gallery when the act was under consideration. Far from any thing inflammatory, I never heard a more languid debate in this House. No more than two or three gentlemen, as I remember, spoke against the act, and that with great reserve and remarkable temper. There was but one division in the whole progress of the bill; and the minority did not reach to more than thirty-nine or forty. In the House of Lords I do not recollect that there was any debate or division at all. I am sure there was no protest. In fact, the affair passed with so very, very little noise, that in town they scarcely knew the nature of what you were doing. The opposition to the bill in England never could have done this mischief, because there scarcely ever was less of opposition to a bill of consequence.

Nor from the dismissal of Mr. Grenville's ministry.

Sir, the agents and distributors of falsehoods have, with their usual industry, circulated another lie of the same nature of the former. It is this, that the disturbances arose from the account which had been received in America of the change in the ministry. No longer awed, it seems, with the spirit of the former rulers, they thought themselves a match for what our calumniators choose to qualify by the name of so feeble a ministry as succeeded. Feeble in one sense these men certainly may be called; for, with all their efforts, and they have made many, they have not been able to resist the distempered vigor and insane alacrity with which you are rushing to your ruin. But it does so happen, that the falsity of this circulation is, like the rest, demonstrated by indisputable dates and records.

So little was the change known in America, that the letters of your governors, giving an account of these disturbances long after they had arrived at their highest pitch, were all directed to the *old* ministry, and particularly to the Earl of Halifax, the secretary of state corresponding with the colonies, without once in the smallest degree intimating the slightest suspicion of any ministerial revolution whatsoever. The ministry was not changed in England until the 10th day of July, 1765. On the 14th of the preceding June, Governor Fauquier, from Virginia, writes thus, and writes thus to the Earl of Halifax: "Government is set at defiance, not having strength enough in her hands to enforce obedience to the laws of the country. The private distress which every man feels, increases the general dissatisfaction at the duties laid by the Stamp Act, which breaks out and shows itself upon every trifling occasion." The general dissatisfaction had produced some time before, that is, on the 29th of May, several strong public resolves against the Stamp Act; and those resolves are assigned by Governor Bernard as the cause of the insurrections in Massachusetts Bay, in his letter of the 15th of August, still addressed to the Earl of Halifax; and he continued to address such accounts to that minister quite to the 7th of September of the same year. Similar accounts, and of as late a date, were sent from other governors, and all directed to Lord Halifax. Not one of these letters indicates the slightest idea of a change, either known, or even apprehended.

Thus are blown away the insect race of courtly falsehoods! thus perish the miserable inventions of the wretched runners for a wretched cause, which they have flyblown into every weak and rotten part of the country, in vain hopes that when their maggots had taken wing, their importunate buzzing might sound something like the public voice!

The disturbances ceased immediately after the repeal.

Sir, I have troubled you sufficiently with the state of America before the repeal. Now I turn to the honorable gentleman who so stoutly challenges us to tell whether, after the repeal, the provinces were quiet? This is coming home to the point. Here I meet him directly, and answer most readily: *They were quiet*. And I, in my turn, challenge him to prove when, where, and by whom, and in what numbers, and with what violence, the other laws of trade, as gentlemen assert, were violated in consequence of your concession? or that even your other revenue laws were attacked? But I quit the vantage ground on which I stand, and where I might leave the burden of proof upon him. I walk down upon the open plain, and undertake to show that they were not only quiet, but showed many unequivocal marks of acknowledgment and gratitude. And, to give him every advantage, I select the obnoxious colony of Massachusetts Bay, which at this time (but without hearing her) is so heavily a culprit before Parliament. I will select their proceedings even under circumstances of no small irritation; for, a little imprudently, I must say, Governor Bernard mixed in the administration of the lenitive of the repeal no small acrimony arising from matters of a separate nature. Yet see, sir, the effect of that lenitive, though mixed with these bitter ingredients; and how this rugged people can express themselves on a measure of concession:

"If it is not in our power," say they, in their address to Governor Bernard, "in so full a manner as will be expected, to show our respectful gratitude to the mother country, or to make a dutiful and affectionate return to the indulgence of the King and Parliament, it shall be no fault of ours; for this we intend, and hope we shall be able fully to effect."

Would to God that this temper had been cultivated, managed, and set in action! Other effects than those which we have since felt would have resulted from it. On the requisition for compensation to those who had suffered from the violence of the populace, in the same address they say: "The recommendation enjoined by Mr. Secretary Conway's letter, and in consequence thereof made to us, we will embrace the first convenient opportunity to consider and act upon." They did consider; they did act upon it. They obeyed the requisition. I know the mode has been chicaned upon; but it was substantially obeyed, and much better obeyed than I fear the parliamentary requisition of this session will be, though enforced by all your rigor, and backed with all your power. In a word, the damages of popular fury were compensated by legislative gravity. Almost every other part of America in various ways demonstrated their gratitude. I am bold to say, that so sudden a calm recovered after so violent a storm is without parallel in history. To say that no other disturbance should happen from any other cause, is folly. But, as far as appearances went, by the judicious sacrifice of one law, you procured an acquiescence in all that remained. After this experience, nobody shall persuade me, when a whole people are concerned, that acts of lenity are not means of conciliation.

I hope the honorable gentleman has received a fair and full answer to his question.

Fourth Period. New taxes laid by Charles Townsend, under Lord Chatham's third ministry.

(4.) I have done with the third period of your policy—that of your repeal; and the return of your ancient system, and your ancient tranquillity and concord. Sir, this period was not as long as it was happy. Another scene was opened, and other actors appeared on the stage. The state, in the condition I have described it, was delivered into the hands of Lord Chatham—a great and celebrated name—a name that keeps the name of this country respectable in every other on the globe. It may be truly called

Clarum et venerabile nomen,
Gentibus, et multum nostræ quod proderat urbi.[22]

Sir, the venerable age of this great man, his merited rank, his superior eloquence, his splendid qualities, his eminent services, the vast space he fills in the eye of mankind, and, more than all the rest, his fall from power, which, like death, canonizes and sanctifies a great character, will not suffer me to censure any part of his conduct. I am afraid to flatter him; I am sure I am not disposed to blame him. Let those who have betrayed him by their adulation, insult him with their malevolence. But what I do not presume to censure, I may have leave to lament. For a wise man, he seemed to me at that time to be governed too much by general maxims. I speak with the freedom of history, and, I hope, without offense. One or two of these maxims, flowing from an opinion not the most indulgent to our unhappy species, and surely a little too general, led him into measures that were greatly mischievous to himself; and, for that reason, among others, perhaps, fatal to his country; measures, the effects of which, I am afraid, are forever incurable. He made an administration so checkered and speckled; he put together a piece of joinery so crossly indented and whimsically dovetailed; a cabinet so variously inlaid; such a piece of diversified mosaic; such a tesselated pavement without cement; here a bit of black stone, and there a bit of white; patriots and courtiers, king's friends and Republicans, Whigs and Tories, treacherous friends and open enemies; that it was indeed a very curious show, but utterly unsafe to touch, and unsure to stand on. The colleagues whom he had assorted at the same boards, stared at each other, and were obliged to ask, "Sir, your name? Sir, you have the advantage of me—Mr. Such-a-one—I beg a thousand pardons." I venture to say, it did so happen, that persons had a single office divided between them, who had never spoke to each other in their lives, until they found themselves, they knew not how, pigging together, heads and points, in the same truckle-bed.[23]

Sir, in consequence of this arrangement, having put so much the larger portion of his enemies and opposers in power, the confusion was such, that his own principles could not possibly have any effect or influence in the conduct of affairs. If ever he fell into a fit of the gout, or if any other cause withdrew him from public cares, principles directly the contrary were sure to predominate. When he had executed his plan, he had not an inch of ground to stand upon. When he had accomplished his scheme of administration, he was no longer a minister.

When his face was hid but for a moment, his whole system was on a wide sea, without chart or compass. The gentlemen, his particular friends, who, with the names of various departments of ministry, were admitted to seem as if they acted under him, with a modesty that becomes all men, and with a confidence in him which was justified, even in its extravagance, by his superior abilities, had never, in any instance, presumed upon any opinion of their own. Deprived of his guiding influence, they were whirled about, the sport of every gust, and easily driven into any port; and as those who joined with them in manning the vessel were the most directly opposite to his opinions, measures, and character, and far the most artful and most powerful of the set, they easily prevailed, so as to seize upon the vacant, unoccupied, and derelict minds of his friends; and instantly they turned the vessel wholly out of the course of his policy. As if it were to insult as well as to betray him, even long before the close of the first session of his administration, when every thing was publicly transacted, and with great parade, in his name, they made an act declaring it highly just and expedient to raise a revenue in America. For even then, sir, even before this splendid orb was entirely set, and while the western horizon was in a blaze with his descending glory, on the opposite quarter of the heavens arose another luminary, and, for his hour, became lord of the ascendant.

This light, too, is passed and set forever. You understand, to be sure, that I speak of Charles

---

[22] A name illustrious and revered by nations,
And rich in blessings for our country's good.

The passage may be found in Lucan's Pharsalia, book ix., v. 202, and forms part of the character of Pompey, as put by the poet in the mouth of Cato.

[23] Supposed to allude to the Right Honorable Lord North, and George Cooke, Esq., who were made joint paymasters in the summer of 1766, on the removal of the Rockingham administration.

Townsend, officially the reproducer of this fatal scheme, whom I can not even now remember without some degree of sensibility. In truth, sir, he was the delight and ornament of this House, and the charm of every society which he honored with his presence. Perhaps there never arose in this country, nor in any country, a man of a more pointed and finished wit, and (where his passions were not concerned) of a more refined, exquisite, and penetrating judgment. If he had not so great a stock as some have had who flourished formerly, of knowledge long treasured up, he knew better by far, than any man I ever was acquainted with, how to bring together within a short time all that was necessary to establish, to illustrate, and to decorate that side of the question he supported. He stated his matter skillfully and powerfully. He particularly excelled in a most luminous explanation and display of his subject. His style of argument was neither trite and vulgar, nor subtle and abstruse. He hit the House just between wind and water; and, not being troubled with too anxious a zeal for any matter in question, he was never more tedious or more earnest than the preconceived opinions and present temper of his hearers required, to whom he was always in perfect unison. He conformed exactly to the temper of the House; and he seemed to guide, because he was always sure to follow it.

I beg pardon, sir, if, when I speak of this and other great men, I appear to digress in saying something of their characters. In this eventful history of the revolutions of America, the characters of such men are of much importance. *Great men are the guide-posts and land-marks in the state.* The credit of such men at court, or in the nation, is the sole cause of all the public measures. It would be an invidious thing (most foreign, I trust, to what you think my disposition) to remark the errors into which the authority of great names has brought the nation, without doing justice at the same time to the great qualities whence that authority arose. The subject is instructive to those who wish to form themselves on whatever of excellence has gone before them. There are many young members in the House (such of late has been the rapid succession of public men) who never saw that prodigy, Charles Townsend, nor, of course, know what a ferment he was able to excite in every thing, by the violent ebullition of his mixed virtues and failings. For failings he had, undoubtedly. Many of us remember them. We are this day considering the effect of them. But he had no failings which were not owing to a noble cause—to an ardent, generous, perhaps an immoderate passion for fame—a passion which is the instinct of all great souls. He worshiped that goddess wheresoever she appeared; but he paid his particular devotions to her in her favorite habitation, in her chosen temple, the House of Commons. Besides the characters of the individuals that compose our body, it is impossible, Mr. Speaker, not to observe, that this House has a collective character of its own. That character, too, however imperfect, is not unamiable. Like all great public collections of men, you possess a marked love of virtue, and an abhorrence of vice. But among vices, there is none which the House abhors in the same degree with *obstinacy*. Obstinacy, sir, is certainly a great vice; and, in the changeful state of political affairs, it is frequently the cause of great mischief. It happens, however, very unfortunately, that almost the whole line of the great and masculine virtues, constancy, gravity, magnanimity, fortitude, fidelity, and firmness, are closely allied to this disagreeable quality, of which you have so just an abhorrence; and, in their excess, all these virtues very easily fall into it. He who paid such a punctilious attention to all your feelings, certainly took care not to shock them by *that* vice which is the most disgustful to you.

That fear of displeasing those who ought most to be pleased, betrayed him sometimes into the other extreme. He had voted, and, in the year 1765, had been an advocate for the Stamp Act. Things and the disposition of men's minds were changed. In short, the Stamp Act began to be no favorite in this House. He therefore attended at the private meeting in which the resolutions moved by a right honorable gentleman were settled—resolutions leading to the repeal. The next day he voted for that repeal—and he would have spoken for it, too, if an illness (not, as was then given out, a political, but, to my knowledge, a very real illness) had not prevented it.

The very next session, as the fashion of this world passeth away, the repeal began to be in as bad an odor in this House as the Stamp Act had been in the session before. To conform to the temper which began to prevail, and to prevail mostly among those most in power, he declared, very early in the winter, that a revenue must be had out of America. Instantly he was tied down to his engagements by some who had no objections to such experiments, when made at the cost of persons for whom they had no particular regard.[24] The whole body of courtiers drove him onward. They always talked as if the King stood in a sort of humiliated state until something of the kind should be done.

Here this extraordinary man, then Chancellor of the Exchequer, found himself in great straits. To please universally was the object of his life; but to tax and to please, no more than to love and to be wise, is not given to men. However, he attempted it. To render the tax palatable to the partisans of American revenue, he made a preamble stating the necessity of such a revenue. To close with the American distinction, this revenue was *external*, or port duty; but again, to soften it to the other party, it was a duty of *supply*. To gratify the *colonists*, it was laid on British manufactures; to satisfy the *merchants of Britain*, the duty was trivial, and, except that on tea, which touched only the devoted East India Company, on none of the grand objects of

[24] See the introduction to Lord Chatham's speech on taxing America, p. 102, where the circumstances of this engagement are stated.

commerce. To counterwork the American contraband, the duty on tea was reduced from a shilling to threepence. But, to secure the favor of those who would tax America, the scene of collection was changed, and, with the rest, it was levied in the colonies. What need I say more? This fine-spun scheme had the usual fate of all exquisite policy. But the original plan of the duties, and the mode of executing that plan, both arose singly and solely from a love of our applause. He was truly the child of the House. He never thought, did, or said any thing but with a view to you. He every day adapted himself to your disposition, and adjusted himself before it as at a looking-glass.[25]

He had observed (indeed, it could not escape him) that several persons, infinitely his inferiors in all respects, had formerly rendered themselves considerable in this House by one method alone. They were a race of men (I hope in God the species is extinct) who, when they rose in their place, no man living could divine, from any known adherence to parties, to opinions, or to principles, from any order or system in their politics, or from any seqnel or connection in their ideas, what part they were going to take in any debate. It is astonishing how much this uncertainty, especially at critical times, called the attention of all parties on such men. All eyes were fixed on them, all ears open to hear them. Each party gaped, and looked alternately for their vote, almost to the end of their speeches. While the House hung in this uncertainty, now the *hear-him's* rose from this side—now they rebellowed from the other; and that party to whom they fell at length from their tremulous and dancing balance, always received them in a tempest of applause. The fortune of such men was a temptation too great to be resisted by one to whom a single whiff of incense withheld gave much greater pain than he received delight in the clouds of it which daily rose about him, from the prodigal superstition of innumerable admirers. He was a candidate for contradictory honors, and his great aim was to make those agree in admiration of him who never agreed in any thing else.

Hence arose this unfortunate act, the subject of this day's debate; from a disposition which, after making an American revenue to please one, repealed it to please others, and again revived it in hopes of pleasing a third, and of catching some thing in the ideas of all.

(4.) The revenue act of 1767 formed the fourth period of American policy. How we have fared since then; what woeful variety of schemes have been adopted; what enforcing and what repealing; what bullying and what submitting; what doing and undoing; what straining and what relaxing; what assemblies dissolved for not obeying, and called again without obedience; what troops sent out to quell resistance, and, on meeting that resistance, recalled; what shiftings, and changes, and jumblings of all kinds of men at home, which left no possibility of order, consistency, vigor, or even so much as a decent unity of color in any one public measure—It is a tedious, irksome task. My duty may call me to open it out some other time; on a former occasion I tried your temper on a part of it;[26] for the present I shall forbear.

After all these changes and agitations, your immediate situation upon the question on your paper is at length brought to this. You have an act of Parliament, stating that "it is *expedient* to raise a revenue in America." By a partial repeal you annihilated the greatest part of that revenue, which this preamble declares to be so expedient. You have substituted no other in the place of it. A secretary of state has disclaimed, in the King's name, all thoughts of such a substitution in future. The principle of this disclaimer goes to what has been left as well as what has been repealed. The tax which lingers after its companions (under a preamble declaring an American revenue expedient, and for the sole purpose of supporting the theory of that preamble) militates with the assurance authentically conveyed to the colonies, and is an exhaustless source of jealousy and animosity. On this state, which I take to be a fair one, not being able to discern any grounds of honor, advantage, peace, or power, for adhering either to the act or to the preamble, I shall vote for the question which leads to the repeal of both.

A final and total repeal now demanded.

If you do not fall in with this motion, then secure something to fight for, consistent in theory and valuable in practice. If you must employ your strength, employ it to uphold you in some honorable right or some profitable wrong. If you are apprehensive that the concession recommended to you, though proper, should be a means of drawing on you farther but unreasonable claims, why then employ your force in supporting that reasonable concession against those unreasonable demands. You will employ it with more grace, with better effect, and with great probable concurrence of all the quiet and rational people in the provinces, who are now united

[25] Mr. Burke has here touched with great tenderness and forbearance on the peculiar faults of Townsend. Horace Walpole has given them with perhaps too much prominence in the following sketch: "He had almost every great talent and every little quality. His vanity exceeded even his abilities, and his suspicions seemed to make him doubt whether he had any. With such a capacity, he must have been the greatest man of his age, and perhaps inferior to no man in any age, had his faults been only in a moderate proportion—in short, if he had had but common truth, common sincerity, common honesty, common modesty, common steadiness, common courage, and common sense." Sir Dennis Le Marchant remarks in a note: "This portrait has the broad lines of truth, and is more to be depended upon than Mr. Burke's splendid and affectionate panegyric (Speech on American Taxation); and yet, who can blame the warmth with which this great man claims admiration for a genius which in some points resembled his own?"

[26] By moving certain resolutions relative to the disturbances in America, in May, 1770.

with and hurried away by the violent; having, indeed, different dispositions, but a common interest. If you apprehend that on a concession you shall be punished by metaphysical process to the extreme lines, and argued out of your whole authority, my adviee is this: When you have recovered your old, your strong, your tenable position, then face about—stop short—do nothing more—reason not at all—oppose the ancient policy and practice of the empire as a rampart against the speculations of innovators on both sides of the question, and you will stand on great, manly, and sure ground. On this solid basis fix your machines, and they will draw worlds toward you.

Your ministers, in their own and his Majesty's name, have already adopted the American distinction of internal and external duties. It is a distinction, whatever merit it may have, that was originally moved by the Americans themselves; and I think they will acquiesce in it, if they are not pushed with too much logic and too little sense in all the consequences; that is, if external taxation be understood as they and you understand it when you please, to be, not a distinction of geography, but of policy; that it is a power for regulating trade, and not for supporting establishments. The distinction, which is as nothing with regard to right, is of most weighty consideration in practice. Recover your old ground and your old tranquillity. Try it. I am persuaded the Americans will compromise with you. When confidence is once restored, the odious and suspicious *summum jus*[27] will perish of course. The spirit of practicability, of moderation, and mutual convenience, will never call in geometrical exactness as the arbitrator of an amicable settlement. Consult and follow your experience. Let not the long story with which I have exercised your patience prove fruitless to your interests.

For my part, I should choose (if I could have my wish) that the proposition of the honorable gentleman [Mr. Fuller] for the repeal could go to America without the attendance of the penal bills. Alone, I could almost answer for its success. I can not be certain of its reception in the bad company it may keep. In such heterogeneous assortments, the most innocent person will lose the effect of his innocency. Though you should send out this angel of peace, yet you are sending out a destroying angel too; and what would be the effect of the conflict of these two adverse spirits, or which would predominate in the end, is what I dare not say: whether the lenient measures would cause American passion to subside, or the severe would increase its fury. All this is in the hand of Providence. Yet now, even now, I should confide in the prevailing virtue and efficacious operation of lenity, though working in darkness, and in chaos, in the midst of all this unnatural and turbid combination. I should hope it might produce order and beauty in the end.

[27] Referring to the adage, "Summum jus et summa injuria"—Right, when pressed to an extreme, becomes the height of injustice.

Let us, sir, embrace some system or other before we end this session. Do you mean to tax America, and to draw a productive revenue from thence? If you do, speak out: name, fix, ascertain this revenue; settle its quantity; define its objects; provide for its collection; and then fight, when you have something to fight for. If you murder, rob! If you kill, take possession; and do not appear in the character of madmen, as well as assassins, violent, vindictive, bloody, and tyrannical, without an object. But may better counsels guide you!

Peroration.

Again and again revert to your old principles. Seek peace and ensue it. Leave America, if she has taxable matter in her, to tax herself. I am not here going into the distinctions of rights, nor attempting to mark their boundaries. I do not enter into these metaphysical distinctions. I hate the very sound of them. Leave the Americans as they anciently stood, and these distinctions, born of our unhappy contest, will die along with it. They and we, and their and our ancestors, have been happy under that system. Let the memory of all actions, in contradiction to that good old mode, on both sides, be extinguished forever. Be content to bind America by laws of trade; you have always done it. Let this be your reason for binding their trade. Do not burden them with taxes; you were not used to do so from the beginning. Let this be your reason for not taxing. These are the arguments of states and kingdoms. Leave the rest to the schools, for there only they may be discussed with safety. But if, intemperately, unwisely, fatally, you sophisticate and poison the very source of government, by urging subtle deductions, and consequences odious to those you govern, from the unlimited and illimitable nature of supreme sovereignty, you will teach them by these means to call that sovereignty itself in question. When you drive him hard, the boar will surely turn upon the hunters. If that sovereignty and their freedom can not be reconciled, which will they take? They will cast your sovereignty in your face. Nobody will be argued into slavery. Sir, let the gentlemen on the other side call forth all their ability; let the best of them get up and tell me what one character of liberty the Americans have, and what one brand of slavery they are free from, if they are bound in their property and industry by all the restraints you can imagine on commerce, and at the same time are made pack-horses of every tax you choose to impose, without the least share in granting them? When they bear the burdens of unlimited monopoly, will you bring them to bear the burdens of unlimited revenue too? The Englishman in America will feel that this is slavery—that it is *legal* slavery will be no compensation either to his feelings or his understanding.

A noble Lord [Lord Carmarthen], who spoke some time ago, is full of the fire of ingenuous youth; and when he has modeled the ideas of a lively imagination by farther experience, he will be an ornament to his country in either House. He has said that the Americans are our children, and how can they revolt against their parent? He says that if they are not free in their present state, England is not free, because Manchester, and other considerable places, are not represented. So, then, because some towns in England are not represented, America is to have no representative at all. They are "our children;" but when children ask for bread, we are not to give a stone. Is it because the natural resistance of things, and the various mutations of time, hinders our government, or any scheme of government, from being any more than a sort of approximation to the right, is it therefore that the colonies are to recede from it infinitely? When this child of ours wishes to assimilate to its parent, and to reflect with a true filial resemblance the beauteous countenance of British liberty, are we to turn to them the shameful parts of our Constitution? Are we to give them our weakness for their strength—our opprobrium for their glory; and the slough of slavery, which we are not able to work off, to serve them for their freedom?

If this be the case, ask yourselves this question: Will they be content in such a state of slavery? If not, look to the consequences. Reflect how you ought to govern a people who think they ought to be free, and think they are not. Your scheme yields no revenue; it yields nothing but discontent, disorder, disobedience; and, such is the state of America, that, after wading up to your eyes in blood, you could only end just where you began; that is, to tax where no revenue is to be found; to—my voice fails me; my inclination, indeed, carries me no farther—all is confusion beyond it. [Here Mr. Burke was compelled by illness to stop for a short time, after which he proceeded:]

Well, sir, I have recovered a little, and, before I sit down, I must say something to another point with which gentlemen urge us: What is to become of the Declaratory Act, asserting the entireness of British legislative authority, if we abandon the practice of taxation?

Declaratory Act not set aside by a repeal of the Tea Act.

For my part, I look upon the rights stated in that act exactly in the manner in which I viewed them on its very first proposition, and which I have often taken the liberty, with great humility, to lay before you. I look, I say, on the imperial rights of Great Britain, and the privileges which the colonists ought to enjoy under these rights, to be just the most reconcilable things in the world. The Parliament of Great Britain sits at the head of her extensive empire in two capacities: one as the local Legislature of this island, providing for all things at home, immediately, and by no other instrument than the executive power. The other, and, I think, her nobler capacity, is what I call her imperial character, in which, as from the throne of heaven, she superintends all the several inferior Legislatures, and guides and controls them all without annihilating any. As all these provincial Legislatures are only co-ordinate to each other, they ought all to be subordinate to her; else they can neither preserve mutual peace, nor hope for mutual justice, nor effectually afford mutual assistance. It is necessary to coerce the negligent, to restrain the violent, and to aid the weak and deficient by the overruling plenitude of her power. She is never to intrude into the place of others while they are equal to the common ends of their institution. But, in order to enable Parliament to answer all these ends of provident and beneficent superintendence, her powers must be boundless. The gentlemen who think the powers of Parliament limited, may please themselves to talk of requisitions. But suppose the requisitions are not obeyed. What! shall there be no reserved power in the empire to supply a deficiency which may weaken, divide, and dissipate the whole? We are engaged in war; the Secretary of State calls upon the colonies to contribute; some would do it—I think most would cheerfully furnish whatever is demanded; one or two, suppose, hang back, and, easing themselves, let the stress of the draught lie on the others: surely it is proper that some authority might legally say, "Tax yourselves for the common supply, or Parliament will do it for you." This backwardness was, as I am told, actually the case of Pennsylvania for some short time toward the beginning of the last war, owing to some internal dissensions in the colony. But, whether the fact were so or otherwise, the case is equally to be provided for by a competent sovereign power. But then this ought to be no ordinary power, nor ever used in the first instance. This is what I meant when I have said at various times that I consider the power of taxing in Parliament as an instrument of empire, and not as a means of supply.

Such, sir, is my idea of the constitution of the British empire, as distinguished from the constitution of Britain; and on these grounds I think subordination and liberty may be sufficiently reconciled through the whole; whether to serve a refining speculatist or a factious demagogue, I know not; but enough, surely, for the ease and happiness of man.

Sir, while we held this happy course, we drew more from the colonies than all the impotent violence of despotism ever could extort from them. We did this abundantly in the last war. It has never been once denied; and what reason have we to imagine that the colonies would not have proceeded in supplying government as liberally, if you had not stepped in and hindered them from contributing, by interrupting the channel in which their liberality flowed with so strong a course; by attempting to take, instead of being satisfied to receive? Sir William Temple says, that Holland has loaded itself with ten times the impositions which it revolted from Spain rather than submit to. He says true. Tyranny is a poor provider. It knows neither how to accumulate nor how to extract.

I charge, therefore, to this new and unfortunate system, the loss not only of peace, of union, and of commerce, but even of revenue, which its friends are contending for. It is morally certain that we have lost at least a million of free grants since the peace. I think we have lost a great deal more; and that those who look for a revenue from the provinces, never could have pursued, even in that light, a course more directly repugnant to their purposes.

Now, sir, I trust I have shown, first, on that narrow ground which the honorable gentleman measured, that you are like to lose nothing by complying with the motion except what you have lost already. I have shown afterward, that in time of peace you flourished in commerce, and when war required it, had sufficient aid from the colonies, while you pursued your ancient policy; that you threw every thing into confusion when you made the Stamp Act; and that you restored every thing to peace and order when you repealed it. I have shown that the revival of the system of taxation has produced the very worst effects; and that the partial repeal has produced, not partial good, but universal evil. Let these considerations, founded on facts, not one of which can be denied, bring us back to our reason by the road of our experience.

I can not, as I have said, answer for mixed measures; but surely this mixture of lenity would give the whole a better chance of success. When you once regain confidence, the way will be clear before you. Then you may enforce the Act of Navigation when it ought to be enforced. You will yourselves open it where it ought still farther to be opened. Proceed in what you do, whatever you do, from policy, and not from rancor. Let us act like men, let us act like statesmen. Let us hold some sort of consistent conduct. It is agreed that a revenue is not to be had in America. If we lose the profit, let us get rid of the odium.

On this business of America, I confess I am serious even to sadness. I have had but one opinion concerning it since I sat, and before I sat, in Parliament. The noble Lord [Lord North] will, as usual, probably attribute the part taken by me and my friends in this business to a desire of getting his places. Let him enjoy this happy and original idea. If I deprived him of it, I should take away most of his wit, and all his argument. But I had rather bear the brunt of all his wit, and, indeed, blows much heavier, than stand answerable to God for embracing a system that tends to the destruction of some of the very best and fairest of his works. But I know the map of England as well as the noble Lord, or as any other person; and I know that the way I take is not the road to preferment. My excellent and honorable friend under me on the floor [Mr. Dowdeswell] has trod that road with great toil for upward of twenty years together. He is not yet arrived at the noble Lord's destination. However, the tracks of my worthy friend are those I have ever wished to follow, because I know they lead to honor. Long may we tread the same road together, whoever may accompany us, or whoever may laugh at us on our journey. I honestly and solemnly declare, I have in all seasons adhered to the system of 1766, for no other reason than that I think it laid deep in your truest interests; and that, by limiting the exercise, it fixes on the firmest foundations a real, consistent, well-grounded authority in Parliament. Until you come back to that system, there will be no peace for England.

Mr. Burke's motion was negatived by a vote of 182 to 49. The ministry were bent on violent measures, and the act for quartering troops in Boston was passed about a month after.

The name of Lord North occurs so often in this speech and in other parts of this volume, that the reader will be interested in a brief notice of his life and character. He was the eldest son of the Earl of Guilford, and was born in 1732. Having completed his education at Oxford, and traveled extensively on the Continent, he became a member of Parliament in 1754, and in 1759 was brought into office by Lord Chatham as a Commissioner of the Treasury. This office he continued to hold during Lord Bute's administration, and at the close of it was made head of the board by Mr. Grenville, who could always rely on him as a determined advocate of American taxation. He was thrown out of office in 1766, when Lord Rockingham came into power; but the next year was made Paymaster of the Forces by Lord Chatham, in his third administration, so graphically described in this speech. In 1767 he became Chancellor of the Exchequer under the Duke of Grafton, and when the latter resigned in 1770, took his place as First Lord of the Treasury and prime minister. The King felt greatly indebted to Lord North for thus saving him the necessity of going back to the Whigs under Lord Chatham and Lord Rockingham; and Lord North, on his part, yielded implicitly to the King's wishes, and carried on the war long after he was convinced that the contest was hopeless. At the end of twelve years he was defeated on this subject in the House of Commons, and, although urged by the King to persevere, he resigned his office on the 19th of March, 1782. Within a year from this time he formed his coalition with Mr. Fox, and came again into power as joint Secretary of State with his old opponent. They were dismissed, however, within less than nine months, and from this time Lord North held no responsible office under government.

As leader of the House of Commons, he showed much more talent than his early opponents, especially Junius, supposed him to possess. He never rose into high eloquence, but he succeeded admirably in managing the House. He had extraordinary tact, perfect self-command, and inflexible courage. To these was added a great fund of wit, which he used with much effect in allaying the violence of debate, when rendered almost savage, as it was at times, by the impetuous attacks of Mr. Fox and his other opponents. Often, when assailed with the bitterest invectives, threatened with impeachment, or held out as a fit object of popular violence, he would rise at the close of a debate and turn the laugh on his opponents by his good-humored pleasantry, while he furnished the ministerial benches with plausible reasons, at least, for carrying him through by their votes. He sometimes refreshed himself with a nap during these attacks; and on one occasion, when the orator, who had been threatening him with the block for his crimes, poured out an invective against him for being able to slumber over the ruin of his country, Lord North rose and complained of it as cruel that he should be denied a privilege always granted to criminals, that of a good night's rest before going to execution. After his union with Mr. Fox, when Mr. Martin, who harped continually on the subject, said "he wished he could see a starling perched on the right elbow of the speaker's chair, to repeat incessantly to the Treasury Bench '*disgraceful, shameless* COALITION,'" Lord North suggested it would be a saving of expense to have the honorable gentleman *himself* perform the service, as deputy to the starling. In one instance, when the worst possible spirit prevailed in the House, arising out of an attack made by Colonel Fullerton on Lord Shelburne, and Mr. Adam on Mr. Fox (leading to a duel in the latter case), Lord North attempted to allay the feeling, and check the prevailing disposition to take offense at what was said in debate. He referred to the attacks on himself, and the manner in which he was accustomed to treat them. "A gentleman," he remarked, "spoke of me some time ago as that *thing* called a minister. Now," said he, looking down at his large, round form, and patting his side, "I certainly *am* a thing: the member, when he called me so, said what was true. I can not, therefore, be angry with him. And when he spoke of me as the thing called a *minister*, he called me that which of all things he wished to be himself, and therefore *I took it as a compliment*." In private life, Lord North was beloved by all; and, notwithstanding the incessant attacks to which he was subjected in the House of Commons, it is probably true, as Charles Butler remarks, that "among all his political adversaries he had not a single enemy." On the death of his father in 1790, he succeeded to the earldom of Guilford, and died about two years after, at the age of sixty.

SPEECH

OF MR. BURKE ON MOVING HIS RESOLUTIONS FOR CONCILIATION WITH AMERICA, DELIVERED IN THE HOUSE OF COMMONS, MARCH 22, 1775.

INTRODUCTION.

THIS speech was occasioned by one of those sudden changes of policy which occurred so often in Lord North's treatment of the colonies.

In the midst of violent measures, and at the moment when bills were before Parliament for extinguishing the entire trade of America, he came forward, to the astonishment of his nearest friends, with a plan for *conciliation!* It was in substance this, that, whenever a colony, in addition to providing for its own government, should raise a fair proportion for the common defense, and place this sum at the disposal of Parliament, that colony should be exempted from all farther taxation, except such duties as might be necessary for the regulation of commerce. This was obviously an insidious scheme for sowing dissension among the Americans. Lord North's design was to open the way for treating *separately* with the different provinces. He could thus favor the loyal and burden the disaffected. He could array them against each other by creating hostile interests; and thus taking them in detail, he could reduce them all to complete subjection. There was cunning in the scheme, but it proceeded on a false estimate of American character. It sprung from a total ignorance of the spirit which actuated the colonies in resisting the mother country; and exemplified in a striking manner the truth of the remarks made by Mr. Burke in the preceding speech, on "the mischief of not having large and liberal ideas in the management of great affairs."

While Mr. Burke saw through this scheme, he thought it presented a favorable opportunity for bringing forward a plan of conciliation suited to the exigencies of the case; a plan which, if not adopted, might at least put the ministry wholly in the wrong. The idea of conciliating, and even of conceding, before America had submitted, was certainly admissible, for the minister himself had founded his scheme upon it. Mr. Burke, therefore, proposed "*to admit the Americans to an equal interest in the British Constitution, and place them at once on the footing of other Englishmen.*" In urging this measure, he discusses two questions:

1st. "Ought we to concede?" and if so,

2dly. "What should the concession be?"

In considering the first question, he enters minutely, and with surprising accuracy of detail, into the condition of the colonies, (1.) their population, (2.) commerce, (3.) agriculture, and (4.) fisheries. He shows that force is an improper and inadequate instrument for holding such a people in subjection to the mother country; especially considering their spirit of liberty, which he traces to (1.) their descent, (2.) their forms of government, (3.) the religious principles of the North, (4.) the social institutions of the South, (5.) the peculiarities of their education, and (6.) their remoteness from Great Britain. He concludes this head by showing that it is vain to think either (1.) of extinguishing this spirit by removing the causes mentioned above (since this is plainly impossible), or (2.) of putting it down by proceeding against it as criminal. He comes, therefore, to the conclusion that it must be *propitiated;* or, in other words, that England *must concede.* He now considers,

2dly. "What should the concession be?"

He remarks that it must obviously relate to taxation, since this was the origin of the contest; and then appeals to the case of Ireland, which was early allowed a Parliament of its own, and of Wales, Chester, and Durham, which were admitted to a representation in the Parliament of England. After obviating objections, and exposing the evils of Lord North's scheme, he comes to the conclusion that the Americans ought (as in the cases adduced) to be admitted to the peculiar privilege of Englishmen, that of "giving and granting," through their *own* Legislatures, whatever they contributed in aid of the Crown; and not be subjected to the imposition of taxes by a Parliament in which they were not represented. He therefore offers six main resolutions asserting these principles, and three subordinate ones for rescinding the penal statutes against America, thus carrying the plan of conciliation into full effect.

After the sketch here given, it is hardly necessary to say that this speech is distinguished for the felicitous selection of its topics; the lucid order in which they are arranged; their close connection; the ease with which one thought grows out of another in a regular and progressive series; and the tendency of the whole to a single point, with all the force and completeness of a moral demonstration. The argument throughout is founded on facts; and yet never was there a speech which had less the character of a mere "matter of fact" production than the one before us. The outline just given is filled up with thoughts fresh from a mind teeming with original and profound reflections on the science of government and the nature of man. There are more passages in this than in any other of Mr. Burke's speeches, which have been admired and quoted for the richness of their imagery, or the force and beauty of their descriptions. The language was evidently elaborated with great care; and Sir James Mackintosh has pronounced it "the most faultless of Mr. Burke's productions."

SPEECH, &c.

I HOPE, sir, that, notwithstanding the austerity of the chair, your good nature will incline you to some degree of indulgence toward human frailty.[1] You will not think it unnatural that those who have an object depending, which strongly engages their hopes and fears, should be somewhat inclined to superstition. As I came into the House full of anxiety about the event of my motion, I found, to my infinite surprise, that the grand penal bill, by which we had passed sentence on the trade and sustenance of America, is to be returned to us from the other House.[2] I do confess, I could not help looking on this event as a fortunate omen. I look upon it as a sort of providential favor, by which we are put once more in possession of our deliberative capacity, upon a business so very questionable in its nature, so very uncertain in its issue. By the return of this bill, which seemed to have taken its flight forever, we are, at this very instant, nearly as free to choose a plan for our American government, as we were on the first day of the session. If, sir, we incline to the side of conciliation, we are not at all embarrassed (unless we please to make ourselves so) by any incongruous mixture of coercion and restraint. We are therefore called upon, as it were by a superior warning voice, again to attend to America; to attend to the whole of it together; and to review the subject with an unusual degree of care and calmness.

The subject one that requires systematic views.

Surely it is an awful subject, or there is none so on this side of the grave. When I first had the honor of a seat in this House, the affairs of that continent pressed themselves upon us as the most important and most delicate object of parliamentary attention. My little share in this great deliberation oppressed me. I found myself a partaker in a very high trust; and having no sort of reason to rely on the strength of my natural abilities for the proper execution of that trust, I was obliged to take more than common pains to instruct myself in every thing which relates to our colonies. I was not less under the necessity of forming some fixed ideas concerning the general policy of the British empire. Something of this sort seemed to be indispensable, in order, amid so vast a fluctuation of passions and opinions, to concenter my thoughts; to ballast my conduct; to preserve me from being blown about by every wind of fashionable doctrine. I really did not think it safe, or manly, to have fresh principles to seek upon every fresh mail which should arrive from America.

At that period I had the fortune to find myself in perfect concurrence with a large majority in this House.[3] Bowing under that high author-

[1] There is too much that is *fanciful* in some parts of this exordium. A man who was wholly absorbed in his subject would not talk thus about himself, or about "the austerity of the chair," "indulgence toward human frailty," being "inclined to superstition," "a fortunate omen," "a superior warning voice," &c. It was this that made Mr. Hazlitt say, "Most of his speeches have a sort of parliamentary preamble to them: there is an air of affected modesty, and ostentatious trifling in them: he seems fond of coqueting with the House of Commons, and is perpetually calling the speaker out to dance a minuet with him before he begins." This is strongly stated, but it shows a fault in Mr. Burke, which was often spoken of by his contemporaries. Hazlitt attributes it to his having been "*raised* into public life: he was prouder of his new dignity than became so great a man." Perhaps a truer solution is, that Mr. Burke's fancy too often outran his judgment, which was certainly the occasion of most of his errors in composition.

[2] An act interdicting the trade and fisheries of all the New England colonies.

[3] This was in 1766, when the Stamp Act was repealed by the Rockingham administration.

ity, and penetrated with the sharpness and strength of that early impression, I have continued ever since in my original sentiments without the least deviation. Whether this be owing to an obstinate perseverance in error, or to a religious adherence to what appears to me truth and reason, it is in your equity to judge.

Sir, Parliament having an enlarged view of objects, made, during, this interval, more frequent changes in their sentiment and their conduct than could be justified in a particular person upon the contracted scale of private information. But though I do not hazard any thing approaching to a censure on the motives of former Parliaments to all those alterations, one fact is undoubted—that under them the state of America has been kept in continual agitation. Every thing administered as remedy to the public complaint, if it did not produce, was at least followed by, a heightening of the distemper; until, by a variety of experiments, that important country has been brought into her present situation—a situation which I will not miscall, which I dare not name, which I scarcely know how to comprehend in the terms of any description.

In this posture, sir, things stood at the beginning of the session. About that time, a worthy member [Mr. Rose Fuller] of great parliamentary experience, who, in the year 1766, filled the chair of the American committee with much ability, took me aside, and, lamenting the present aspect of our politics, told me, things were come to such a pass, that our former methods of proceeding in the House would be no longer tolerated. That the public tribunal (never too indulgent to a long and unsuccessful Opposition) would now scrutinize our conduct with unusual severity. That the very vicissitudes and shiftings of ministerial measures, instead of convicting their authors of inconstancy and want of system, would be taken as an occasion of charging us with a predetermined discontent, which nothing could satisfy; while we accused every measure of vigor as cruel, and every proposal of lenity as weak and irresolute. The public, he said, would not have patience to see us play the game out with our adversaries: we must produce our hand. It would be expected, that those who for many years had been active in such affairs, should show that they had formed some clear and decided idea of the principles of colony government, and were capable of drawing out something like a platform of the ground which might be laid for future and permanent tranquillity.

Mr. Burke invited to come forward.

I felt the truth of what my honorable friend represented, but I felt my situation too. His application might have been made with far greater propriety to many other gentlemen. No man was, indeed, ever better disposed or worse qualified for such an undertaking than myself. Though I gave so far into his opinion that I immediately threw my thoughts into a sort of parliamentary form, I was by no means equally ready to produce them. It generally argues some degree of natural impotence of mind, or some want of knowledge of the world, to hazard plans of government, except from a seat of authority. Propositions are made, not only ineffectually, but somewhat disreputably, when the minds of men are not properly disposed for their reception; and, for my part, I am not ambitious of ridicule—not absolutely a candidate for disgrace.

Reluctance to do so.

Besides, sir, to speak the plain truth, I have in general no very exalted opinion of the virtue of paper government, nor of any politics in which the plan is to be wholly separated from the execution. But when I saw that anger and violence prevailed every day more and more, and that things were hastening toward an incurable alienation of our colonies, I confess my caution gave way. I felt this, as one of those few moments in which decorum yields to a higher duty. Public calamity is a mighty leveler, and there are occasions when any, even the slightest, chance of doing good, must be laid hold on, even by the most inconsiderable person.

To restore order and repose to an empire so great and so distracted as ours, is, merely in the attempt, an undertaking that would ennoble the flights of the highest genius, and obtain pardon for the efforts of the meanest understanding. Struggling a good while with these thoughts, by degrees I felt myself more firm. I derived, at length, some confidence from what in other circumstances usually produces timidity. I grew less anxious, even from the idea of my own insignificance. For, judging of what you are by what you ought to be, I persuaded myself that you would not reject a reasonable proposition because it had nothing but its reason to recommend it. On the other hand, being totally destitute of all shadow of influence, natural or adventitious, I was very sure that if my proposition were futile or dangerous—if it were weakly conceived or improperly timed, there was nothing exterior to it of power to awe, dazzle, or delude you. You will see it just as it is, and you will treat it just as it deserves.

The PROPOSITION is peace. Not peace through the medium of war; not peace to be hunted through the labyrinth of intricate and endless negotiations; not peace to arise out of universal discord, fomented from principle, in all parts of the empire; not peace to depend on the juridical determination of perplexing questions, or the precise marking the shadowy boundaries of a complex government. It is simple peace, sought in its natural course and its ordinary haunts. It is peace sought in the spirit of peace, and laid in principles purely pacific. I propose, by removing the ground of the difference, and by restoring the former unsuspecting confidence of the colonies in the mother country, to give permanent satisfaction to your people; and, far from a scheme of ruling by discord, to reconcile them to each other in the same act, and by the bond of the very same interest, which reconciles them to British government.

The thing proposed.

My idea is nothing more. Refined policy ever has been the parent of confusion, and ever will be so as long as the world endures. Plain good intention, which is as easily discovered at the first view as fraud is surely detected at last, is (let me say) of no mean force in the government of mankind. Genuine simplicity of heart is a healing and cementing principle. My plan, therefore, being formed upon the most simple grounds imaginable, may disappoint some people when they hear it. It has nothing to recommend it to the pruriency of curious ears. There is nothing at all new and captivating in it. It has nothing of the splendor of the project which has been lately laid upon your table by the noble Lord in the blue ribbon[4] [Lord North]. It does not propose to fill your lobby with squabbling colony agents, who will require the interposition of your mace at every instant to keep the peace among them. It does not institute a magnificent auction of finance, where captivated provinces come to general ransom by bidding against each other, until you knock down the hammer, and determine a proportion of payments beyond all the powers of algebra to equalize and settle.

The plan justified by Lord North's project.

The plan which I shall presume to suggest derives, however, one great advantage from the proposition and registry of that noble Lord's project. The idea of conciliation is admissible. First, the House, in accepting the resolution moved by the noble Lord, has admitted, notwithstanding the menacing front of our address,[5] notwithstanding our heavy bill of pains and penalties, that we do not think ourselves precluded from all ideas of free grace and bounty.

The House has gone farther; it has declared conciliation admissible, *previous* to any submission on the part of America. It has even shot a good deal beyond that mark, and has admitted that the complaints of our former mode of exerting the right of taxation were not wholly unfounded. That right, thus exerted, is allowed to have had something reprehensible in it, something unwise, or something grievous; since, in the midst of our heat and resentment, we, of ourselves, have proposed a capital alteration, and, in order to get rid of what seemed so very exceptionable, have instituted a mode that is altogether new; one that is, indeed, wholly alien from all the ancient methods and forms of Parliament.

The *principle* of this proceeding is large enough for my purpose. The means proposed by the noble Lord for carrying his ideas into execution, I think, indeed, are very indifferently suited to the end; and this I shall endeavor to show you before I sit down. But, for the present, I take my ground on the admitted principle. I mean to give peace. Peace implies reconciliation; and, where there has been a material dispute, reconciliation does in a manner always imply concession on the one part or on the other. In this state of things I make no difficulty in affirming that the proposal ought to originate from us. Great and acknowledged force is not impaired, either in effect or in opinion, by an unwillingness to exert itself. The superior power may offer peace with honor and with safety. Such an offer from such a power will be attributed to magnanimity. But the concessions of the weak are the concessions of fear. When such a one is disarmed, he is wholly at the mercy of his superior, and he loses forever that time and those chances which, as they happen to all men, are the strength and resources of all inferior power.

The capital leading questions on which you must this day decide, are these two: *First, whether you ought to concede; and, secondly, what your concession ought to be.*

I. On the first of these questions we have gained, as I have just taken the liberty of observing to you, some ground. But I am sensible that a good deal more is still to be done. Indeed, sir, to enable us to determine both on the one and the other of these great questions with a firm and precise judgment, I think it may be necessary to consider distinctly,

First general consideration: State and circumstances of America.

The true *nature* and the peculiar *circumstances* of the object which we have before us; because, after all our struggle, whether we will or not, we must govern America according to that nature and to those circumstances, and not according to our imaginations; not according to abstract ideas of right; by no means according to mere general theories of government, the resort to which appears to me, in our present situation, no better than arrant trifling. I shall therefore endeavor, with your leave, to lay before you some of the most material of these circumstances in as full and as clear a manner as I am able to state them.

(1.) The first thing that we have to consider with regard to the nature of the object, is the

4 That when the governor, council, or Assembly, or General Court of any of his Majesty's provinces or colonies in America, shall propose to make provision, according to the condition, circumstances, and situation of such province or colony, for contributing their proportion to the common defense (such proportion to be raised under the authority of the General Court or General Assembly of such province or colony, and disposable by Parliament), and shall engage to make provision also for the support of the civil government and the administration of justice in such province or colony, it will be proper, if such proposal shall be approved by his Majesty and the two houses of Parliament, and for so long as such provision shall be made accordingly, to forbear, in respect of such province or colony, to levy any duty, tax, or assessment, or to impose any farther duty, tax, or assessment, except such duties as it may be expedient to continue to levy or impose for the regulation of commerce: the net produce of the duties last mentioned to be carried to the account of such province or colony respectively.—Resolution moved by Lord North in the committee, and agreed to by the House, 27th February, 1775.

5 The ministry had previously procured the passing of an address to the King, declaring that a rebellion existed in Massachusetts; requesting his Majesty to take effectual means for its suppression; and pledging the zealous co-operation of Parliament in whatever measures he might adopt for that purpose.

Population. number of people in the colonies. I have taken for some years a good deal of pains on that point. I can by no calculation justify myself in placing the number below two millions of inhabitants of our own European blood and color, besides at least five hundred thousand others, who form no inconsiderable part of the strength and opulence of the whole. This, sir, is, I believe, about the true number. There is no occasion to exaggerate, where plain truth is of so much weight and importance. But whether I put the present numbers too high or too low, is a matter of little moment. Such is the strength with which population shoots in that part of the world, that, state the numbers as high as we will, while the dispute continues, the exaggeration ends. While we are discussing any given magnitude, they are grown to it. While we spend our time in deliberating on the mode of governing two millions, we shall find we have two millions more to manage. Your children do not grow faster from infancy to manhood, than they spread from families to communities, and from villages to nations.[6]

I put this consideration of the present and the growing numbers in the front of our deliberation; because, sir, this consideration will make it evident to a blunter discernment than yours, that no partial, narrow, contracted, pinched, occasional system will be at all suitable to such an object. It will show you that it is not to be considered as one of those *minima* which are out of the eye and consideration of the law; not a paltry excrescence of the state; not a mean dependent, who may be neglected with little damage, and provoked with little danger. It will prove that some degree of care and caution is required in the handling such an object; it will show that you ought not, in reason, to trifle with so large a mass of the interests and feelings of the human race. You could at no time do so without guilt; and, be assured, you will not be able to do it long with impunity.

(2.) But the population of this country, the great and growing population, though a very important consideration, will lose much of its weight, if not combined with other circumstances. The commerce of your colonies is out of all proportion beyond the numbers of the people. This ground of their commerce, indeed, has been trod some days ago, and

Commerce.

with great ability, by a distinguished person [Mr. Gower] at your bar. This gentleman, after thirty-five years—it is so long since he appeared at the same place to plead for the commerce of Great Britain—has come again before you to plead the same cause, without any other effect of time, than that, to the fire of imagination and extent of erudition which even then marked him as one of the first literary characters of his age, he has added a consummate knowledge in the commercial interest of his country, formed by a long course of enlightened and discriminating experience.

Sir, I should be inexcusable in coming after such a person with any detail, if a great part of the members who now fill the House had not the misfortune to be absent when he appeared at your bar. Besides, sir, I propose to take the matter at periods of time somewhat different from his. There is, if I mistake not, a point of view, from whence, if you will look at this subject, it is impossible that it should not make an impression upon you.

I have in my hand two accounts: one a comparative state of the export trade of England to its colonies as it stood in the year 1704, and as it stood in the year 1772; the other a state of the export trade of this country to its colonies alone, as it stood in 1772, compared with the whole trade of England to all parts of the world, the colonies included, in the year 1704. They are from good vouchers; the latter period from the accounts on your table, the earlier from an original manuscript of Davenant, who first established the inspector general's office, which has been ever since his time so abundant a source of parliamentary information.

The export trade to the colonies consists of three great branches: the African, which, terminating almost wholly in the colonies, must be put to the account of their commerce; the West Indian, and the North American. All these are so interwoven, that the attempt to separate them would tear to pieces the contexture of the whole, and, if not entirely destroy, would very much depreciate the value of all the parts. I therefore consider these three denominations to be, what in effect they are, one trade.

The trade to the colonies, taken on the export side, at the beginning of this century, that is, in the year 1704, stood thus:

Exports to North America and the West Indies................	£483,265
To Africa......................	86,665
	£569,930

In the year 1772, which I take as a middle year between the highest and lowest of those lately laid on your table, the account was as follows:

To North America and the West Indies..........................	£4,791,734
To Africa..........................	866,398
To which, if you add the export trade from Scotland, which had in 1704 no existence....	364,000
	£6,022,398

[6] This is in Mr. Burke's best style. The comparison beautifully illustrates the idea, and justifies his assertion, that while "the dispute continues, the exaggeration ends." It is curious to observe, as one of the artifices of language, how Johnson treats the same idea in his Taxation no Tyranny, where he contrives to cover it with contempt in the minds of the Tories, for whom he wrote, by a dexterous use of sneers and appropriate imagery. "We are told that the continent of North America contains three millions, not merely of men, but of *Whigs*—of Whigs fierce for liberty and disdainful of dominion; that *they multiply with the fecundity of their rattlesnakes*, so that every quarter of a century they double their numbers!" His conclusion is, that they must be crushed in the egg.

From five hundred and odd thousand, it has grown to six millions. It has increased no less than twelve-fold. This is the state of the colony trade, as compared with itself at these two periods, within this century; and this is matter for meditation. But this is not all. Examine my second account. See how the export trade to the colonies alone in 1772 stood in the other point of view, that is, as compared to the whole trade of England in 1704.

The whole export trade of England, including that to the colonies, in 1704	£6,509,000
Exported to the colonies alone, in 1772	6,024,000
Difference..	£485,000

The trade with America alone is now within less than £500,000 of being equal to what this great commercial nation, England, carried on at the beginning of this century with the whole world! If I had taken the largest year of those on your table, it would rather have exceeded. But, it will be said, is not this American trade an unnatural protuberance, that has drawn the juices from the rest of the body? The reverse. It is the very food that has nourished every other part into its present magnitude. Our general trade has been greatly augmented, and augmented more or less in almost every part to which it ever extended, but with this material difference, that of the six millions which in the beginning of the century constituted the whole mass of our export commerce, the colony trade was but one twelfth part; it is now (as a part of sixteen millions) considerably more than a third of the whole. This is the relative proportion of the importance of the colonies at these two periods; and all reasoning concerning our mode of treating them must have this proportion as its basis, or it is a reasoning weak, rotten, and sophistical.

Mr. Speaker, I cannot prevail on myself to hurry over this great consideration. It is good for us to be here. We stand where we have an immense view of what is, and what is past. Clouds, indeed, and darkness, rest upon the future. Let us, however, before we descend from this noble eminence, reflect that this growth of our national prosperity has happened within the short period of the life of man. It has happened within sixty-eight years. There are those alive whose memory might touch the two extremities. For instance, my Lord Bathurst might remember all the stages of the progress. He was in 1704 of an age at least to be made to comprehend such things. He was then old enough "acta parentum jam legere, et quæ sit poterit cognoscere virtus."[7] Suppose, sir, that the angel of this auspicious youth, foreseeing the many virtues, which made him one of the most amiable, as he is one of the most fortunate men of his age, had opened to him in vision, that when, in the fourth generation, the third prince of the house of Brunswick had sat twelve years on the throne of that nation, which, by the happy issue of moderate and healing councils, was to be made Great Britain, he should see his son, Lord Chancellor of England, turn back the current of hereditary dignity to its fountain, and raise him to a higher rank of peerage, while he enriched the family with a new one. If, amid these bright and happy scenes of domestic honor and prosperity, that angel should have drawn up the curtain, and unfolded the rising glories of his country, and while he was gazing with admiration on the then commercial grandeur of England, the genius should point out to him a little speck, scarce visible in the mass of the national interest, a small seminal principle rather than a formed body, and should tell him, "Young man, there is America—which at this day serves for little more than to amuse you with stories of savage men and uncouth manners; yet shall, before you taste death, show itself equal to the whole of that commerce which now attracts the envy of the world. Whatever England has been growing to by a progressive increase of improvement, brought in by varieties of people, by succession of civilizing conquests and civilizing settlements in a series of seventeen hundred years, you shall see as much added to her by America in the course of a single life!" If this state of his country had been foretold to him, would it not require all the sanguine credulity of youth, and all the fervid glow of enthusiasm, to make him believe it? Fortunate man, he has lived to see it! Fortunate indeed, if he live to see

[7] Mr. Burke in adapting this passage to the context, has changed some of the words and omitted others, so as to render the construction obscure. When he made the first infinitive, *legere*, dependent on the preceding English phrase, he should have done the same with *cognoscere*, omitting *poterit*. Thus it would read, "He was then old enough *to read the exploits of his ancestors, and learn what virtue is.*"

The quotation is taken from Virgil's fourth Eclogue, where the poet predicts the birth of a child who should restore the peace and plenty of the Golden Age. The passage has been commonly referred to a child whose birth was expected from the sister of Augustus, and which the Emperor designed to adopt as his own. Hence the "acta parentis" in the words below.

At simul heroum laudes *et acta Parentis*
Jam legere, et quæ sit poteris cognoscere virtus,
Molli paulatim flavescet campus aristâ,
Incultisque rubens pendebit sentibus riva,
Et duræ quercus sudabunt roscida mella.

When thou can'st read
Our heroes' praises and thy Father's deeds,
And know what virtue is, o'er all our plains
Shall golden harvests wave with ripened corn;
The ruddy grape hang from uncultured thorns,
And dewy honey flow from rugged oaks.

In thus alluding to Lord Bathurst, Mr. Burke undoubtedly thought of him only as advanced in years, without reflecting on his exact age. He was born in 1684, and was therefore, in 1704, not only "of an age to be *made* to comprehend such things," but on the verge of manhood, and actually took his seat in Parliament the next year, 1705. The son of Lord Bathurst, referred to above, was Henry, created Lord Apsley, and raised to the dignity of Lord Chancellor in 1771.

nothing to vary the prospect and cloud the setting of his day![8]

Excuse me, sir, if, turning from such thoughts, I resume this comparative view once more. You have seen it on a large scale; look at it on a small one. I will point out to your attention a particular instance of it in the single province of Pennsylvania. In the year 1704 that province called for £11,459 in value of your commodities, native and foreign. This was the whole. What did it demand in 1772? Why nearly fifty times as much; for in that year the export to Pennsylvania was £507,909, nearly equal to the export to all the colonies together in the first period.

I choose, sir, to enter into these minute and particular details, because generalities, which, in all other cases are apt to heighten and raise the subject, have here a tendency to sink it. When we speak of the commerce with our colonies, fiction lags after truth; invention is unfruitful, and imagination cold and barren.

So far, sir, as to the importance of the object in the view of its commerce, as concerned in the exports from England. If I were to detail the imports, I could show how many enjoyments they procure, which deceive the burden of life; how many materials which invigorate the springs of national industry, and extend and animate every part of our foreign and domestic commerce. This would be a curious subject indeed; but I must prescribe bounds to myself in a matter so vast and various.

Agriculture.

(3.) I pass, therefore, to the colonies in another point of view—their agriculture. This they have prosecuted with such a spirit, that, besides feeding plentifully their own growing multitude, their annual export of grain, comprehending rice, has, some years ago, exceeded a million in value. Of their last harvest I am persuaded they will export much more. At the beginning of the century, some of these colonies imported corn from the mother country. For some time past the old world has been fed from the new. The scarcity which you have felt would have been a desolating famine, if this child of your old age, with a true filial piety, with a Roman charity, had not put the full breast of its youthful exuberance to the mouth of its exhausted parent.[9]

Fisheries.

(4.) As to the wealth which the colonies have drawn from the sea by their fisheries, you had all that matter fully opened at your bar. You surely thought those acquisitions of value, for they seemed even to excite your envy; and yet, the spirit by which that enterprising employment has been exercised, ought rather, in my opinion, to have raised your esteem and admiration. And pray, sir, what in the world is equal to it? Pass by the other parts, and look at the manner in which the people of New England have of late carried on the whale fishery. While we follow them among the tumbling mountains of ice, and behold them penetrating into the deepest frozen recesses of Hudson's Bay and Davis's Straits—while we are looking for them beneath the arctic circle, we hear that they have pierced into the opposite region of polar cold—that they are at the antipodes, and engaged under the frozen Serpent of the south.[10] Falkland Island, which seemed too remote and romantic an object for the grasp of national ambition, is but a stage and resting-place in the progress of their victorious industry. Nor is the equinoctial heat more discouraging to them than the accumulated winter of both the poles. We know that while some of them draw the line and strike the harpoon on the coast of Africa, others run the longitude, and pursue their gigantic game along the coast of Brazil. No sea but what is vexed by their fisheries. No climate that is not witness to their toils. Neither the perseverance of Holland, nor the activity of France, nor the dexterous and firm sagacity of English enterprise, ever carried this most perilous mode of hardy industry to the extent to which it has been pushed by this recent people—a people who are still, as it were, but in the gristle, and not yet hardened into the bone of manhood. When I contemplate these things—when I know that the colonies in general owe little or nothing to any care of ours, and that they are not squeezed into this happy form by the constraints of watchful and suspicious government, but that, through a wise and salutary neglect, a generous nature has been suffered to

[8] It may be doubted whether this amplification, and the more graphic one which follows in respect to the fisheries of New England, are not out of place in an argument of this kind before the House of Commons. They would have been perfectly appropriate in an address like that of Daniel Webster on the landing of the Pilgrims at Plymouth, since the audience had met for the very purpose of being delighted with rich trains of thought, beautifully expressed. We who read the speech at the present day, dwell on such passages with unmingled gratification, because we peruse them much in the same spirit. But they would certainly be unsafe models for a business speaker.

[9] The deed of "Roman charity" referred to in this beautiful image was celebrated in the annals of the republic, and is related by Pliny in his Natural History, lib. vii., 36, and also, more at large, by Valerius Maximus, lib. v., 4. A woman was condemned for some atrocious crime to be strangled in prison; but the jailer, disliking to execute the sentence, left her without food to perish of hunger. Her daughter, with great importunity, obtained permission to visit her from time to time, but only after being carefully searched to prevent the introduction of food. As the woman lived beyond all expectation, the jailer resolved to discover the secret; and, coming suddenly upon them, found the daughter (who had a little before given birth to a child) sustaining the mother from her own breast. The magistrates, struck with admiration at this instance of filial piety, pardoned the mother for the daughter's sake, and provided for the support of both at the public expense. Festus and Solinus, writers of a later age, represent it to have been a father, not a mother, who was thus sustained; and in this form the story has been more generally received in modern times.

[10] The Hydrus, or Water Serpent, is a small constellation lying very far to the south, within the antarctic circle.

take her own way to perfection—when I reflect upon these effects—when I see how profitable they have been to us, I feel all the pride of power sink, and all presumption in the wisdom of human contrivances melt, and die away within me. My rigor relents. I pardon something to the spirit of liberty.

I am sensible, sir, that all which I have asserted in my detail is admitted in the gross; but that quite a different conclusion is drawn from it. America, gentlemen say, is a noble object. It is an object well worth fighting for. Certainly it is, if fighting a people be the best way of gaining them. Gentlemen in this respect will be led to their choice of means by their complexions and their habits. Those who understand the military art will, of course, have some predilection for it. Those who wield the thunder of the state may have more confidence in the efficacy of arms. But I confess, possibly for want of this knowledge, my opinion is much more in favor of prudent management than of force; considering force not as an odious, but a feeble instrument, for preserving a people so numerous, so active, so growing, so spirited as this, in a profitable and subordinate connection with us.

Second general consideration: Force ought not to be used in such a case.

(1.) First, sir, permit me to observe, that the use of force alone is but *temporary*. It may subdue for a moment, but it does not remove the necessity of subduing again; and a nation is not governed which is perpetually to be conquered.

(2.) My next objection is its *uncertainty*. Terror is not always the effect of force; and an armament is not a victory. If you do not succeed, you are without resource; for, conciliation failing, force remains; but, force failing, no farther hope of reconciliation is left. Power and authority are sometimes bought by kindness, but they can never be begged as alms by an impoverished and defeated violence.

(3.) A farther objection to force is, that you *impair the object* by your very endeavors to preserve it. The thing you fought for is not the thing which you recover; but depreciated, sunk, wasted, and consumed in the contest. Nothing less will content me than *whole* America. I do not choose to consume its strength along with our own, because in all parts it is the British strength that I consume. I do not choose to be caught by a foreign enemy at the end of this exhausting conflict, and still less in the midst of it. I may escape; but I can make no insurance against such an event. Let me add, that I do not choose wholly to break the American spirit, because it is the spirit that has made the country.

(4.) Lastly, we have no sort of *experience* in favor of force as an instrument in the rule of our colonies. Their growth and their utility has been owing to methods altogether different. Our ancient indulgence has been said to be pursued to a fault. It may be so; but we know, if feeling is evidence, that our fault was more tolerable than our attempt to mend it; and our sin far more salutary than our penitence.

These, sir, are my reasons for not entertaining that high opinion of untried force, by which many gentlemen, for whose sentiments in other particulars I have great respect, seem to be so greatly captivated.[11]

But there is still behind a third consideration concerning this object, which serves to determine my opinion on the sort of policy which ought to be pursued in the management of America, even more than its population and its commerce—I mean its temper and character. In this character of the Americans *a love of freedom* is the predominating feature, which marks and distinguishes the whole; and, as an ardent is always a jealous affection, your colonies become suspicious, restive, and untractable, whenever they see the least attempt to wrest from them by force, or shuffle from them by chicane, what they think the only advantage worth living for. This fierce spirit of liberty is stronger in the English colonies, probably, than in any other people of the earth, and this from a variety of powerful causes, which, to understand the true temper of their minds, and the direction which this spirit takes, it will not be amiss to lay open somewhat more largely.[12]

Third general consideration: The spirit of America and its causes.

(1.) First, the people of the colonies are descendants of Englishmen. England, sir, is a nation which still, I hope, respects, and formerly adored her freedom. The colonists emigrated from you when this part of your character was most predominant; and they took this bias and direction the moment they parted from your hands. They are, therefore, not only devoted to liberty, but to liberty according to English ideas and on English principles. Abstract liberty, like other mere abstractions, is not to be found. Liberty inheres in some sensible object; and every nation has formed to itself some favorite point which, by way of eminence, becomes the criterion of their happiness. It happened, you know, sir, that the great contests for freedom in this country were, from the earliest times, chiefly upon the question of taxing. Most of the contests in the ancient commonwealths turned pri-

Origin

---

[11] These four arguments show how admirably Mr. Burke could *condense* when he saw fit.

[12] We here see the secret of Mr. Burke's richness of thought. It consisted, to a great extent, in his habit of viewing things in their *causes*, or tracing them out in their *results*. Let the reader study these pages with reference to this fact. Let him observe how Mr. Burke brings out the leading characteristics of the colonists, not as isolated facts, but as dependent upon certain *forming influences* in the mind of the English people: their early contests, civil and religious; the necessary results of certain relations of society and forms of mental development. Such habits of thought, if well directed, furnish an endless variety of valuable remarks in filling out a subject. If not abstract in their statement, but rendered intelligible and striking by a proper reference to individual cases, they always interest at the same time that they instruct. It is with reference to this subject, especially, that Mr. Burke should be studied by the young orator.

marily on the right of election of magistrates, or on the balance among the several orders of the state. The question of money was not with them so immediate. But in England it was otherwise. On this point of taxes the ablest pens and most eloquent tongues have been exercised; the greatest spirits have acted and suffered. In order to give the fullest satisfaction concerning the importance of this point, it was not only necessary for those who in argument defended the excellence of the English Constitution, to insist on this privilege of granting money as a dry point of fact, and to prove that the right had been acknowledged in ancient parchments and blind usages to reside in a certain body called the House of Commons. They went much farther: they attempted to prove (and they succeeded) that in theory it ought to be so, from the particular nature of a House of Commons, as an immediate representative of the people, whether the old records had delivered this oracle or not. They took infinite pains to inculcate, as a fundamental principle, that, in all monarchies, the people must, in effect, themselves, mediately or immediately, possess the power of granting their own money, or no shadow of liberty could subsist. The colonies draw from you, as with their life-blood, those ideas and principles. Their love of liberty, as with you, fixed and attached on this specific point of taxing. Liberty might be safe or might be endangered in twenty other particulars, without their being much pleased or alarmed. Here they felt its pulse; and, as they found that beat, they thought themselves sick or sound. I do not say whether they were right or wrong in applying your general arguments to their own case. It is not easy, indeed, to make a monopoly of theorems and corollaries. The fact is, that they did thus apply those general arguments; and your mode of governing them, whether through lenity or indolence, through wisdom or mistake, confirmed them in the imagination that they, as well as you, had an interest in these common principles.

Form of government.

(2.) They were further confirmed in this pleasing error by the form of their provincial legislative assemblies. Their governments are popular in a high degree; some are merely popular; in all, the popular representative is the most weighty;[13] and this share of the people in their ordinary government never fails to inspire them with lofty sentiments, and with a strong aversion from whatever tends to deprive them of their chief importance.

Religion.

(3.) If any thing were wanting to this necessary operation of the form of government, religion would have given it a complete effect. Religion, always a principle of energy, in this new people is no way worn out or impaired; and their mode of professing it is also one main cause of this free spirit. The people are Protestants; and of that kind which is the most adverse to all implicit submission of mind and opinion. This is a persuasion not only favorable to liberty, but built upon it. I do not think, sir, that the reason of this averseness in the dissenting churches from all that looks like absolute government, is so much to be sought in their religious tenets as in their history. Every one knows that the Roman Catholic religion is at least coeval with most of the governments where it prevails; that it has generally gone hand in hand with them; and received great favor and every kind of support from authority. The Church of England, too, was formed from her cradle under the nursing care of regular government. But the dissenting interests have sprung up in direct opposition to all the ordinary powers of the world, and could justify that opposition only on a strong claim to natural liberty. Their very existence depended on the powerful and unremitted assertion of that claim. All Protestantism, even the most cold and passive, is a kind of dissent. But the religion most prevalent in our northern colonies is a refinement on the principle of resistance; it is the dissidence[14] of dissent; and the Protestantism of the Protestant religion. This religion, under a variety of denominations, agreeing in nothing but in the communion of the spirit of liberty, is predominant in most of the northern provinces; where the Church of England, notwithstanding its legal rights, is in reality no more than a sort of private sect, not composing most probably the tenth of the people. The colonists left England when this spirit was high, and in the emigrants was the highest of all; and even that stream of foreigners, which has been constantly flowing into these colonies, has, for the greatest part, been composed of dissenters from the establishments of their several countries, and have brought with them a temper and character far from alien to that of the people with whom they mixed.

Domestic institutions.

(4.) Sir, I can perceive by their manner that some gentlemen object to the latitude of this description, because in the southern colonies the Church of England forms a large body, and has a regular establishment. It is certainly true. There is, however, a circumstance attending these colonies, which, in my opinion, fully counterbalances this difference, and makes the spirit of liberty still more high and haughty than in those to the northward. It is that in Virginia and the Carolinas they have a vast multitude of *slaves*. Where this is the case in any part of the world, those who are free are by far the most proud and jealous of their freedom. Freedom is to them not only an enjoyment, but a kind of rank and privilege. Not seeing there that freedom, as in countries where it is a common blessing, and as broad

[13] In some of the colonies all the officers of government were chosen directly by the people. In others, the governor and some of the magistrates were appointed by the Crown, but were unable to act without the co-operation of Assemblies elected by the colonists.

[14] In Chapman's Select Speeches, and in some editions of Burke, both in this country and in England, this word has been strangely altered into *diffidence.*

and general as the air, may be united with much abject toil, with great misery, with all the exterior of servitude, liberty looks, among them, like something that is more noble and liberal. I do not mean, sir, to commend the superior morality of this sentiment, which has at least as much pride as virtue in it; but I can not alter the nature of man. The fact is so; and these people of the southern colonies are much more strongly, and with a higher and more stubborn spirit, attached to liberty than those to the northward. Such were all the ancient commonwealths; such were our Gothic ancestors; such, in our days, were the Poles;[15] and such will be all masters of slaves, who are not slaves themselves. In such a people the haughtiness of domination combines with the spirit of freedom, fortifies it, and renders it invincible.

Education.

(5.) Permit me, sir, to add another circumstance in our colonies, which contributes no mean part toward the growth and effect of this untractable spirit—I mean their *education*. In no country perhaps in the world is the law so general a study. The profession itself is numerous and powerful; and in most provinces it takes the lead. The greater number of the deputies sent to Congress were lawyers. But all who read, and most do read, endeavor to obtain some smattering in that science. I have been told by an eminent bookseller, that in no branch of his business, after tracts of popular devotion, were so many books as those on the law exported to the Plantations. The colonists have now fallen into the way of printing them for their own use. I hear that they have sold nearly as many of Blackstone's Commentaries in America as in England. General Gage marks out this disposition very particularly in a letter on your table. He states, that all the people in his government are lawyers, or smatterers in law; and that in Boston they have been enabled, by successful chicane, wholly to evade many parts of one of your capital penal constitutions.[16] The smartness of debate will say, that this knowledge ought to teach them more clearly the rights of legislature, their obligations to obedience, and the penalties of rebellion. All this is mighty well. But my honorable and learned friend [Mr., afterward Lord Thurlow] on the floor, who condescends to mark what I say for animadversion, will disdain that ground. He has heard, as well as I, that when great honors and great emoluments do not win over this knowledge to the service of the state, it is a formidable adversary to government. If the spirit be not tamed and broken by these happy methods, it is stubborn and litigious. *Abeunt studia in mores.*[17] This study renders men acute, inquisitive, dexterous, prompt in attack, ready in defense, full of resources. In other countries, the people, more simple and of a less mercurial cast, judge of an ill principle in government only by an actual grievance. Here they anticipate the evil, and judge of the pressure of the grievance by the badness of the principle. They augur misgovernment at a distance; and snuff the approach of tyranny in every tainted breeze.

Remoteness.

(6.) The last cause of this disobedient spirit in the colonies is hardly less powerful than the rest, as it is not merely moral, but laid deep in the natural constitution of things. Three thousand miles of ocean lie between you and them. No contrivance can prevent the effect of this distance in weakening government. Seas roll, and months pass, between the order and the execution; and the want of a speedy explanation of a single point is enough to defeat the whole system. You have, indeed, "winged ministers" of vengeance, who carry your bolts in their pounces to the remotest verge of the sea.[18] But there a power steps in, that limits the arrogance of raging passions and furious elements, and says, "So far shalt thou go, and no farther." Who are you, that should fret and rage, and bite the chains of nature? Nothing worse happens to you than does to all nations who have extensive empire; and it happens in all the forms into which empire can be thrown. In large bodies, the circulation of power must be less vigorous at the extremities. Nature has said it. The Turk can not govern Egypt, and Arabia, and Koordistan, as he governs Thrace; nor has he the same dominion in Crimea and Algiers which he has at Broosa and Smyrna. Despotism itself is obliged to truck and huckster. The Sultan gets such obedience as he can. He governs with a loose rein, that he may govern at all; and the whole of the force and vigor of his authority in his center, is derived from a prudent relaxation in all his borders. Spain, in her provinces, is, perhaps, not so well obeyed as you are in yours. She complies too; she submits; she watches times. This is the immutable condition, the eternal law, of extensive and detached empire.

Then, sir, from these six capital sources of descent, of form of government, of religion in the northern provinces, of manners in the southern, of education, of the remoteness of situation from the first mover of government—from all

[15] When this speech was delivered, Poland had recently been struck from the list of nations, the first partition of her territory having been made by Austria, Prussia, and Russia in 1772.

[16] An amusing case of this kind may be mentioned. General Gage, in carrying out the coercive statutes, forbade by proclamation the calling of any town meetings after August 1st, 1774. One was held by the Bostonians, however, in defiance of the proclamation; and when measures were taken by the government to disperse it, the legality of the meeting was strenuously asserted, on the ground that it had not been "*called*" since the first of August, but had been only *adjourned* over from time to time!

[17] Studies pass into habits.

[18] Ministrum fulminis alitem.—Horace, Odes, book iv., ode i. We have seen (p. 116) Lord Chatham's application of this image to the army of England. Mr. Burke here applies it, in an expanded form, to her ships of war.

these causes a fierce spirit of liberty has grown up. It has grown with the growth of the people in your colonies, and increased with the increase of their wealth; a spirit that, unhappily meeting with an exercise of power in England, which, however lawful, is not reconcilable to any ideas of liberty, much less with theirs, has kindled this flame, that is ready to consume us.

The spirit of the Americans firm and intractable.

I do not mean to commend either the spirit in this excess, or the moral causes which produce it. Perhaps a more smooth and accommodating spirit of freedom in them would be more acceptable to us. Perhaps ideas of liberty might be desired, more reconcilable with an arbitrary and boundless authority. Perhaps we might wish the colonists to be persuaded that their liberty is more secure when held in trust for them by us, as guardians during a perpetual minority, than with any part of it in their own hands. But the question is not whether their spirit deserves praise or blame. What, in the name of God, shall we do with it? You have before you the object, such as it is, with all its glories, with all its imperfections on its head. You see the magnitude, the importance, the temper, the habits, the disorders. By all these considerations we are strongly urged to determine something concerning it. We are called upon to fix some rule and line for our future conduct, which may give a little stability to our politics, and prevent the return of such unhappy deliberations as the present. Every such return will bring the matter before us in a still more untractable form. For, what astonishing and incredible things have we not seen already? What monsters have not been generated from this unnatural contention? While every principle of authority and resistance has been pushed, upon both sides, as far as it would go, there is nothing so solid and certain, either in reasoning or in practice, that has not been shaken. Until very lately, all authority in America seemed to be nothing but an emanation from yours. Even the popular part of the colony constitution derived all its activity, and its first vital movement, from the pleasure of the Crown. We thought, sir, that the utmost which the discontented colonists could do, was to disturb authority. We never dreamed they could of themselves supply it, knowing in general what an operose business it is to establish a government absolutely new. But having, for our purposes in this contention, resolved that none but an obedient assembly should sit, the humors of the people there, finding all passage through the legal channel stopped, with great violence broke out another way. Some provinces have tried their experiment, as we have tried ours; and theirs has succeeded. They have formed a government sufficient for its purposes, without the bustle of a revolution, or the troublesome formality of an election. Evident necessity and tacit consent have done the business in an instant. So well they have done it, that Lord Dunmore (the account is among the fragments on your table) tells you, that the new institution is infinitely better obeyed than the ancient government ever was in its most fortunate periods. Obedience is what makes government, and not the names by which it is called; not the name of governor, as formerly, or committee, as at present. This new government has originated directly from the people, and was not transmitted through any of the ordinary artificial media of a positive constitution. It was not a manufacture ready formed, and transmitted to them in that condition from England. The evil arising from hence is this: that the colonists having once found the possibility of enjoying the advantages of order in the midst of a struggle for liberty, such struggles will not henceforward seem so terrible to the settled and sober part of mankind as they had appeared before the trial.

Pursuing the same plan of punishing by the denial of the exercise of government to still greater lengths, we wholly abrogated the ancient government of Massachusetts. We were confident that the first feeling, if not the very prospect of anarchy, would instantly enforce a complete submission. The experiment was tried. A new, strange, unexpected face of things appeared. Anarchy is found tolerable. A vast province has now subsisted, and subsisted in a considerable degree of health and vigor, for near a twelvemonth, without governor, without public council, without judges, without executive magistrates. How long it will continue in this state, or what may arise out of this unheard-of situation, how can the wisest of us conjecture? Our late experience has taught us, that many of those fundamental principles, formerly believed infallible, are either not of the importance they were imagined to be, or that we have not at all adverted to some other far more important and far more powerful principles, which entirely overrule those we had considered as omnipotent. I am much against any farther experiments, which tend to put to the proof any more of these allowed opinions, which contribute so much to the public tranquillity. In effect, we suffer as much at home by this loosening of all ties, and this concussion of all established opinions, as we do abroad. For, in order to prove that the Americans have no right to their liberties, we are every day endeavoring to subvert the maxims which preserve the whole spirit of our own. To prove that the Americans ought not to be free, we are obliged to depreciate the value of freedom itself; and we never seem to gain a paltry advantage over them in debate, without attacking some of those principles, or deriding some of those feelings, for which our ancestors have shed their blood.

Only three possible modes of dealing with the American spirit.

But, sir, in wishing to put an end to pernicious experiments, I do not mean to preclude the fullest inquiry. Far from it. Far from deciding on a sudden or partial view, I would patiently go round and round the subject, and survey it minutely in every possible aspect. Sir, if I were capable of engaging you to an equal attention, I would state that, as far as I am capable of discerning, there are but three ways of proceeding relative to this stubborn spirit which prevails in your colonies and disturbs your government. These are, to change that spirit, as inconvenient, by removing the causes; to prosecute it as criminal; or to comply with it as necessary. I would not be guilty of an imperfect enumeration. I can think of but these three. Another has, indeed, been started—that of giving up the colonies; but it met so slight a reception, that I do not think myself obliged to dwell a great while upon it. It is nothing but a little sally of anger, like the frowardness of peevish children, who, when they can not get all they would have, are resolved to take nothing.

To change it by removing the *causes* enumerated.

(1.) The *first* of these plans, to change the spirit, as inconvenient, by removing the causes, I think is the most like a systematic proceeding. It is radical in its principle, but it is attended with great difficulties, some of them little short, as I conceive, of impossibilities. This will appear by examining into the plans which have been proposed.

As the growing population of the colonies is evidently one cause of their resistance, it was last session mentioned in both houses by men of weight, and received, not without applause, that, in order to check this evil, it would be proper for the Crown to make no farther grants of land. But to this scheme there are two objections. The first, that there is already so much unsettled land in private hands as to afford room for an immense future population, although the Crown not only withheld its grants, but annihilated its soil. If this be the case, then the only effect of this avarice of desolation, this hoarding of a royal wilderness, would be to raise the value of the possessions in the hands of the great private monopolists without any adequate check to the growing and alarming mischief of population.

But if you stopped your grants, what would be the consequence? The people would occupy without grants. They have already so occupied in many places. You can not station garrisons in every part of these deserts. If you drive the people from one place, they will carry on their annual tillage, and remove with their flocks and herds to another. Many of the people in the back settlements are already little attached to particular situations. Already they have topped the Apalachian Mountains. From thence they behold before them an immense plain, one vast, rich, level meadow—a square of five hundred miles. Over this they would wander without a possibility of restraint. They would change their manners with the habits of their life; would soon forget a government by which they were disowned; would become hordes of English Tartars; and, pouring down upon your unfortified frontiers a fierce and irresistible cavalry, become masters of your governors and your counselors, your collectors and controllers, and of all the slaves that adhered to them.[19] Such would, and, in no long time, must be the effect of attempting to forbid as a crime, and to suppress as an evil, the command and blessing of Providence, "Increase and multiply." Such would be the happy result of an endeavor to keep as a lair of wild beasts that earth which God by an express charter has given to the children of men. Far different, and surely much wiser, has been our policy hitherto. Hitherto we have invited our people, by every kind of bounty, to fixed establishments. We have invited the husbandman to look to authority for his title. We have taught him piously to believe in the mysterious virtue of wax and parchment. We have thrown each tract of land, as it was peopled, into districts, that the ruling power should never be wholly out of sight. We have settled all we could, and we have carefully attended every settlement with government.

Adhering, sir, as I do, to this policy, as well as for the reasons I have just given, I think this new project of hedging in population to be neither prudent nor practicable.

To impoverish the colonies in general, and in particular to arrest the noble course of their marine enterprises, would be a more easy task. I freely confess it. We have shown a disposition to a system of this kind; a disposition even to continue the restraint after the offense, looking on ourselves as rivals to our colonies, and persuaded that of course we must gain all that they shall lose. Much mischief we may certainly do. The power inadequate to all other things is often more than sufficient for this. I do not look on the direct and immediate power of the colonies to resist our violence as very formidable. In this, however, I may be mistaken. But when I consider that we have colonies for no purpose but to be serviceable to us, it seems to my poor understanding a little preposterous to make them unserviceable in order to keep them obedient. It is, in truth, nothing more than the old, and, as I thought, exploded problem of tyranny, which proposes to beggar its subjects into submission. But, remember, when you have completed your system of impoverishment, that nature still proceeds in her ordinary course; that discontent will increase with misery; and that there are critical moments in the fortune of all states, when they who are too weak to contribute to your prosperity may be strong enough to complete your ruin "Spoliatis arma supersunt."[20]

The temper and character which prevail in our colonies are, I am afraid, unalterable by any human art. We can not, I fear, falsify the pedigree of this fierce people, and persuade them that they are not sprung from a nation in whose veins the blood of freedom circulates. The language in which they would hear you tell them this tale would detect the imposition. Your speech would betray you. An Englishman is the unfittest person on earth to argue another Englishman into slavery.

I think it is nearly as little in our power to

[19] It is in descriptions of this kind that Mr. Burke is more truly admirable than in those of a brilliant and imaginative character which precede.

[20] Arms remain to the plundered.

change their republican religion as their free descent; or to substitute the Roman Catholic as a penalty, or the Church of England as an improvement. The mode of inquisition and dragooning is going out of fashion in the old world, and I should not confide much to their efficacy in the new. The education of the Americans is also on the same unalterable bottom with their religion. You can not persuade them to burn their books of curious science; to banish their lawyers from their courts of law; or to quench the lights of their assemblies, by refusing to choose those persons who are best read in their privileges. It would be no less impracticable to think of wholly annihilating the popular assemblies in which these lawyers sit. The army, by which we must govern in their place, would be far more chargeable to us; not quite so effectual; and perhaps, in the end, full as difficult to be kept in obedience.

With regard to the high aristocratic spirit of Virginia and the southern colonies, it has been proposed, I know, to reduce it, by declaring a general enfranchisement of their slaves. This project has had its advocates and panegyrists, yet I never could argue myself into an opinion of it. Slaves are often much attached to their masters. A general wild offer of liberty would not always be accepted. History furnishes few instances of it. It is sometimes as hard to persuade slaves to be free as it is to compel freemen to be slaves; and in this auspicious scheme we should have both these pleasing tasks on our hands at once. But when we talk of enfranchisement, do we not perceive that the American master may enfranchise too, and arm servile hands in defense of freedom? A measure to which other people have had recourse more than once, and not without success, in a desperate situation of their affairs.

Slaves as these unfortunate black people are, and dull as all men are from slavery, must they not a little suspect the offer of freedom from that very nation which has sold them to their present masters? From that nation, one of whose causes of quarrel with those masters is their refusal to deal any more in that inhuman traffic? An offer of freedom from England would come rather oddly, shipped to them in an African vessel, which is refused an entry into the ports of Virginia or Carolina, with a cargo of three hundred Angola negroes. It would be curious to see the Guinea captain attempt at the same instant to publish his proclamation of liberty and to advertise his sale of slaves.

But let us suppose all these moral difficulties got over. The ocean remains. You can not pump this dry; and as long as it continues in its present bed, so long all the causes which weaken authority by distance will continue.

"Ye gods! annihilate but space and time,
And make two lovers happy!"

was a pious and passionate prayer, but just as reasonable as many of these serious wishes of very grave and solemn politicians.

(2.) If then, sir, it seems almost desperate to think of any alterative course for changing the moral causes (and not quite easy to remove the natural) which produce the prejudices irreconcilable to the late exercise of our authority, but that the spirit infallibly will continue, and, continuing, will produce such effects as now embarrass us, the *second* mode under consideration is to prosecute that spirit in its overt acts as *criminal*.

To prosecute it as criminal.

At this proposition I must pause a moment. The thing seems a great deal too big for my ideas of jurisprudence. It should seem, to my way of conceiving such matters, that there is a very wide difference in reason and policy between the mode of proceeding on the irregular conduct of scattered individuals, or even of bands of men, who disturb order within the state, and the civil dissensions which may, from time to time, on great questions, agitate the several communities which compose a great empire. It looks to me to be narrow and pedantic to apply the ordinary ideas of criminal justice to this great public contest. I do not know the method of drawing up an indictment against a whole people. I can not insult and ridicule the feelings of millions of my fellow-creatures, as Sir Edward Coke insulted one excellent individual [Sir Walter Raleigh] at the bar.[21] I am not ripe to pass sentence on the gravest public bodies, intrusted with magistracies of great authority and dignity, and charged with the safety of their fellow-citizens, upon the very same title that I am. I really think that, for wise men, this is not judicious; for sober men, not decent; for minds tinctured with humanity, not mild and merciful.

Perhaps, sir, I am mistaken in my idea of an empire, as distinguished from a single state or kingdom. But my idea of it is this: that an empire is the aggregate of many states, under one common head, whether this head be a monarch or a presiding republic. It does, in such constitutions, frequently happen (and nothing but the dismal, cold, dead uniformity of servitude can prevent its happening) that the subordinate parts have many local privileges and immunities. Between these privileges and the supreme common authority, the line may be extremely nice. Of course, disputes—often, too, very bitter disputes, and much ill blood, will arise. But though every privilege is an exemption, in the case, from the ordinary exercise

Distinction between an empire and a kingdom.

[21] See Howell's State Trials, vol. ii., p. 7, *et seq.*, for an exhibition of coarse and brutal treatment, which Jeffries never surpassed. The following may serve as a specimen: *Coke.* I will prove you the notoriest traitor that ever came to the bar. *Raleigh.* Your words can not condemn me; my innocency is my defense. *Coke.* Thou art a monster. Thou hast an English face, but a Spanish heart. *Raleigh.* Let me answer for myself. *Coke.* Thou shalt not. *Raleigh.* It concerneth my life. *Coke.* Oh! Do I touch you? Now see the most horrible practices that ever came out of the bottomless pit of the lowest hell. *Raleigh.* Here is no treason of mine. If Lord Cobham be a traitor, what is that to me? *Coke.* All that he did was by thy instigation, thou viper. Such was the language by which officers of justice recommended themselves to the favor of James I.

of the supreme authority, it is no denial of it. The claim of a privilege seems rather, *ex vi termini*,[22] to imply a superior power; for to talk of the privileges of a state or of a person who has no superior, is hardly any better than speaking nonsense. Now, in such unfortunate quarrels among the component parts of a great political union of communities, I can scarcely conceive any thing more completely imprudent than for the head of the empire to insist that, if any privilege is pleaded against his will or his acts, that his *whole* authority is denied; instantly to proclaim rebellion, to beat to arms, and to put the offending provinces under the ban. Will not this, sir, very soon teach the provinces to make no distinctions on their part? Will it not teach them that the government against which a claim of liberty is tantamount to high treason, is a government to which submission is equivalent to slavery? It may not always be quite convenient to impress dependent communities with such an idea.

We are, indeed, in all disputes with the colonies, by the necessity of things, the judge. It is true, sir; but I confess that the character of judge in my own cause is a thing that frightens me. Instead of filling me with pride, I am exceedingly humbled by it. I can not proceed with a stern, assured, judicial confidence, until I find myself in something more like a judicial character. I must have these hesitations as long as I am compelled to recollect that, in my little reading upon such contests as these, the sense of mankind has at least as often decided against the superior as the subordinate power. Sir, let me add, too, that the opinion of my having some abstract right in my favor would not put me much at my ease in passing sentence, unless I could be sure that there were no rights which, in their exercise under certain circumstances, were not the most odious of all wrongs, and the most vexatious of all injustice. Sir, these considerations have great weight with me, when I find things so circumstanced that I see the same party at once a civil litigant against me in point of right and a culprit before me; while I sit as criminal judge on acts of his whose moral quality is to be decided on upon the merits of that very litigation. Men are every now and then put, by the complexity of human affairs, into strange situations; but justice is the same, let the judge be in what situation he will.

There is, sir, also a circumstance which convinces me that this mode of criminal proceeding is not, at least in the present stage of our contest, altogether expedient, which is nothing less than the conduct of those very persons who have seemed to adopt that mode, by lately declaring a rebellion in Massachusetts Bay, as they had formerly addressed to have traitors brought hither, under an act of Henry the Eighth, for trial. For, though rebellion is declared, it is not proceeded against as such; nor have any steps been taken toward the apprehension or conviction of any individual offender, either on our late or our former address; but modes of *public* coercion have been adopted, and such as have much more resemblance to a sort of qualified hostility toward an independent power than the punishment of rebellious subjects. All this seems rather inconsistent; but it shows how difficult it is to apply these juridical ideas to our present case.

In this situation, let us seriously and coolly ponder. What is it we have got by all our menaces, which have been many and ferocious? What advantage have we derived from the penal laws we have passed, and which, for the time, have been severe and numerous? What advances have we made toward our object by the sending of a force which, by land and sea, is no contemptible strength? Has the disorder abated? Nothing less. When I see things in this situation, after such confident hopes, bold promises, and active exertions, I can not, for my life, avoid a suspicion that the plan itself is not correctly right.

If, then, the removal of the causes of this spirit of American liberty be, for the greater part, or rather entirely, impracticable; if the ideas of criminal process be inapplicable, or, if applicable, are in the highest degree inexpedient, what way yet remains? No way is open but the third and last—to comply with the American spirit as necessary, or, if you please, to submit to it as a necessary evil.

If we adopt this mode, if we mean to conciliate and concede, let us see,

II. Of what nature the concession ought to be. To ascertain the nature of our concession, we must look at their complaint. The colonies complain that they have not the characteristic mark and seal of British freedom. They complain that they are taxed in Parliament in which they are not represented. If you mean to satisfy them at all, you must satisfy them with regard to this complaint. If you mean to please any people, you must give them the boon which they ask; not what you may think better for them, but of a kind totally different. Such an act may be a wise regulation, but it is no concession, whereas our present theme is the mode of giving satisfaction.

The concession to be made.

Sir, I think you must perceive that I am resolved this day to have nothing at all to do with the question of the right of taxation.[23] Some gentlemen startle, but it is true. I put it totally out of the question. It is less than nothing in my consideration. I do not, indeed, wonder, nor will you, sir, that gentlemen of profound learning are fond of displaying it on this profound subject. But my consideration is narrow, confined, and whol-

Right of taxation not to be discussed.

22 From the very import of the term.

23 Mr. Burke here shows one of his most striking peculiarities as a reasoner on political subjects, viz., his fixed determination never to discuss them on the ground of mere abstract right. His mind fastened upon *prescription* as the principal guide in all such cases. We see it as fully in his early speeches as in his Reflections on the French Revolution.

ly limited to the policy of the question. I do not examine whether the giving away a man's money be a power excepted and reserved out of the general trust of government, and how far all mankind, in all forms of polity, are entitled to an exercise of that right by the charter of nature; or whether, on the contrary, a right of taxation is necessarily involved in the general principle of legislation, and inseperable from the ordinary supreme power. These are deep questions, where great names militate against each other; where reason is perplexed; and an appeal to authorities only thickens the confusion; for high and reverend authorities lift up their heads on both sides, and there is no sure footing in the middle. This point is

That Serbonian bog
Betwixt Damieta and Mount Cassius old,
Where armies whole have sunk.
Milton's Par. Lost, ii., 594.

I do not intend to be overwhelmed in this bog, though in such respectable company. The question with me is, not whether you have a right to render your people miserable, but whether it is not your interest to make them happy. It is not what a lawyer tells me I *may* do, but what humanity, reason, and justice tell me I *ought* to do. Is a politic act the worse for being a generous one? Is no concession proper but that which is made from your want of right to keep what you grant? Or does it lessen the grace or dignity of relaxing in the exercise of an odious claim, because you have your evidence-room full of titles, and your magazines stuffed with arms to enforce them? What signify all those titles and all those arms? Of what avail are they, when the reason of the thing tells me that the assertion of my title is the loss of my suit, and that I could do nothing but wound myself by the use of my own weapons?

Such is steadfastly my opinion of the absolute necessity of keeping up the concord of this empire by a unity of spirit, though in a diversity of operations, that, if I were sure the colonists had, at their leaving this country, sealed a regular compact of servitude; that they had solemnly abjured all the rights of citizens; that they had made a vow to renounce all ideas of liberty for them and their posterity to all generations, yet I should hold myself obliged to conform to the temper I found universally prevalent in my own day, and to govern two millions of men, impatient of servitude, on the principles of freedom. I am not determining a point of law. I am restoring tranquillity, and the general character and situation of a people must determine what sort of government is fitted for them. That point nothing else can or ought to determine.

The Americans to be allowed the rights of Englishmen.

My idea, therefore, without considering whether we yield as matter of right, or grant as matter of favor, is *to admit the people of our colonies into an interest in the constitution*, and, by recording that admission in the journals of Parliament, to give them as strong an assurance as the nature of the thing will admit, that we mean forever to adhere to that solemn declaration of systematic indulgence.

Taxation for revenue must be publicly renounced.

Some years ago, the repeal of a revenue act, upon its understood principle, might have served to show that we intended an unconditional abatement of the exercise of a taxing power. Such a measure was then sufficient to remove all suspicion, and to give perfect content. But unfortunate events, since that time, may make something farther necessary, and not more necessary for the satisfaction of the colonies, than for the dignity and consistency of our own future proceedings.

I have taken a very incorrect measure of the disposition of the House, if this proposal in itself would be received with dislike. I think, sir, we have few American financiers. But our misfortune is, we are too acute; we are too exquisite in our conjectures of the future, for men oppressed with such great and present evils. The more moderate among the opposers of parliamentary concession freely confess that they hope no good from taxation, but they apprehend the colonists have farther views, and, if this point were conceded, they would instantly attack the Trade Laws. These gentlemen are convinced that this was the intention from the beginning, and the quarrel of the Americans with taxation was no more than a cloak and cover to this design. Such has been the language even of a gentleman [Mr. Rice] of real moderation, and of a natural temper well adjusted to fair and equal government. I am, however, sir, not a little surprised at this kind of discourse, whenever I hear it; and I am the more surprised, on account of the arguments which I constantly find in company with it, and which are often urged from the same mouths and on the same day.

Inconsistency of those who insist on taxation.

For instance, when we allege that it is against reason to tax a people under so many restraints in trade as the Americans, the noble Lord [Lord North] in the blue ribbon shall tell you that the restraints on trade are futile and useless; of no advantage to us, and of no burden to those on whom they are imposed; that the trade of America is not secured by the acts of navigation, but by the natural and irresistible advantage of a commercial preference.

Such is the merit of the trade laws in this posture of the debate. But when strong internal circumstances are urged against the taxes; when the scheme is dissected; when experience and the nature of things are brought to prove, and do prove, the utter impossibility of obtaining an effective revenue from the colonies; when these things are pressed, or rather press themselves, so as to drive the advocates of colony taxes to a clear admission of the futility of the scheme; then, sir, the sleeping trade laws revive from their trance, and this useless taxation is to be kept sacred, not for its own sake, but as a counterguard and security of the laws of trade.

Then, sir, you keep up revenue laws which are mischievous, in order to preserve trade laws that are useless. Such is the wisdom of our plan in both its members. They are separately given up as of no value, and yet one is always to be defended for the sake of the other. But I can not agree with the noble Lord, nor with the pamphlet from whence he seems to have borrowed these ideas, concerning the inutility of the trade laws; for, without idolizing them, I am sure they are still, in many ways, of great use to us; and in former times, they have been of the greatest. They do confine, and they do greatly narrow the market for the Americans; but my perfect conviction of this does not help me in the least to discern how the revenue laws form any security whatsoever to the commercial regulations, or that these commercial regulations are the true ground of the quarrel, or that the giving way in any one instance of authority is to lose all that may remain unconceded.

The contest sprung from taxation.

One fact is clear and indisputable. The public and avowed origin of this quarrel was on taxation. This quarrel has indeed brought on new disputes on new questions, but certainly the least bitter, and the fewest of all, on the trade laws. To judge which of the two be the real radical cause of quarrel, we have to see whether the commercial dispute did, in order of time, precede the dispute on taxation. There is not a shadow of evidence for it. Next, to enable us to judge whether at this moment a dislike to the trade laws be the real cause of quarrel, it is absolutely necessary to put the taxes out of the question by a repeal. See how the Americans act in this position, and then you will be able to discern correctly what is the true object of the controversy, or whether any controversy at all will remain. Unless you consent to remove this cause of difference, it is impossible, with decency, to assert that the dispute is not upon what it is avowed to be. And I would, sir, recommend to your serious consideration, whether it be prudent to form a rule for punishing people, not on their own acts, but on your conjectures. Surely it is preposterous at the very best. It is not justifying your anger by their misconduct, but it is converting your ill will into their delinquency.

Objection that the colonies will resist the Navigation Act.

But the colonies will go farther. Alas! alas! when will this speculating against fact and reason end? What will quiet these panic fears which we entertain of the hostile effect of a conciliatory conduct? Is it true that no case can exist in which it is proper for the sovereign to accede to the desires of his discontented subjects? Is there any thing peculiar in this case to make a rule for itself? Is all authority of course lost, when it is not pushed to the extreme? Is it a certain maxim, that the fewer causes of dissatisfaction are left by government the more the subject will be inclined to resist and rebel?

All these objections being, in fact, no more than suspicions, conjectures, divinations, formed in defiance of fact and experience, they did not, sir, discourage me from entertaining the idea of a conciliatory concession, founded on the principles which I have just stated.

Principles and practice of the Constitution a safe guide.

In forming a plan for this purpose, I endeavored to put myself in that frame of mind which was the most natural and the most reasonable, and which was certainly the most probable means of securing me from all error. I set out with a perfect distrust of my own abilities; a total renunciation of every speculation of my own; and with a profound reverence for the wisdom of our ancestors, who have left us the inheritance of so happy a constitution and so flourishing an empire, and, what is a thousand times more valuable, the treasury of the maxims and principles which formed the one and obtained the other.

During the reigns of the Kings of Spain of the Austrian family, whenever they were at a loss in the Spanish councils, it was common for their statesmen to say, that they ought to consult the genius of Philip the Second. The genius of Philip the Second might mislead them; and the issue of their affairs showed that they had not chosen the most perfect standard. But, sir, I am sure that I shall not be misled, when, in a case of constitutional difficulty, I consult the genius of the English constitution. Consulting at that oracle (it was with all due humility and piety), I found four capital examples in a similar case before me: those of Ireland, Wales, Chester, and Durham.

First example.

(1.) Ireland, before the English conquest, though never governed by a despotic power, had no Parliament. How far the English Parliament itself was at that time modeled according to the present form, is disputed among antiquarians.[24] But we have all the reason in the world to be assured, that a form of Parliament, such as England then enjoyed, she instantly communicated to Ireland; and we are equally sure that almost every successive improvement in constitutional liberty, as fast as it was made here, was transmitted thither. The feudal baronage and the feudal knighthood, the roots of our primitive constitution, were early transplanted into that soil, and grew and flourished there. Magna Charta, if it did not give us originally the House of Commons, gave us, at least, a House of Commons of weight and consequence. But your ancestors did not churlishly sit down alone to the feast of Magna Charta. Ireland was made immediately a partaker. This

---

[24] The Witenagemote, or national council, whose consent was requisite for the enactment of laws, may be considered as the Parliament of the Anglo-Saxon times. It was composed of the bishops and abbots, the aldermen or governors of counties (afterward called earls), and those landed proprietors who were possessed of about four or five thousand acres. The boroughs do not appear, at this early period, to have sent any representatives. Magna Charta expressly provided, that "no scutage or aid" (with three exceptions) "shall be raised in our kingdom but by the *general council* of the nations," and this was described as composed of "the prelates and greater barons." The first representation of the Commons in Parliament is now generally agreed to have taken place toward the close of the reign of Henry III., or about A.D. 1264.

benefit of English laws and liberties, I confess, was not at first extended to *all* Ireland. Mark he consequence. English authority and English liberty had exactly the same boundaries. Your standard could never be advanced an inch before your privileges.[25] Sir John Davis shows beyond a doubt, that the refusal of a general communication of these rights was the true cause why Ireland was five hundred years in subduing; and after the vain projects of a military government, attempted in the reign of Queen Elizabeth, it was soon discovered that nothing could make that country English, in civility and allegiance, but your laws and your forms of legislature. It was not English arms, but the English constitution, that conquered Ireland. From that time, Ireland has ever had a general Parliament, as she had before a partial Parliament. You changed the people; you altered the religion; but you never touched the form or the vital substance of free government in that kingdom. You deposed kings; you restored them; you altered the succession to theirs, as well as to your own crown; but you never altered their constitution; the principle of which was respected by usurpation; restored with the restoration of monarchy, and established, I trust, forever, by the glorious revolution. This has made Ireland the great and flourishing kingdom that it is; and from a disgrace and a burden intolerable to this nation, has rendered her a principal part of our strength and ornament. This country can not be said to have ever formally taxed her. The irregular things done in the confusion of mighty troubles, and on the hinge of great revolutions, even if all were done that is said to have been done, form no example. If they have any effect in argument, they make an exception to prove the rule. None of your own liberties could stand a moment if the casual deviations from them, at such times, were suffered to be used as proofs of their nullity. By the lucrative amount of such casual breaches in the constitution, judge what the stated and fixed rule of supply has been in that kingdom. Your Irish pensioners would starve, if they had no other fund to live on than taxes granted by English authority. Turn your eyes to those popular grants from whence all your great supplies are come, and learn to respect that only source of public wealth in the British empire.

Second example.

(2.) My next example is Wales. This country was said to be reduced by Henry the Third.[26] It was said more truly to be so by Edward the First. But though then conquered, it was not looked upon as any part of the realm of England. Its old constitution, whatever that might have been, was destroyed, and no good one was substituted in its place. The care of that tract was put into the hands of lords marchers—a form of government of a very singular kind; a strange heterogeneous monster, something between hostility and government; perhaps it has a sort of resemblance, according to the modes of those times, to that of commander-in-chief at present, to whom all civil power is granted as secondary. The manners of the Welsh nation followed the genius of the government. The people were ferocious, restive, savage, and uncultivated; sometimes composed, never pacified. Wales, within itself, was in perpetual disorder; and it kept the frontier of England in perpetual alarm. Benefits from it to the state there were none. Wales was only known to England by incursion and invasion.

Sir, during that state of things, Parliament was not idle. They attempted to subdue the fierce spirit of the Welsh by all sorts of rigorous laws. They prohibited by statute the sending all sorts of arms into Wales, as you prohibit by proclamation (with something more of doubt on the legality) the sending arms to America. They disarmed the Welsh by statute, as you attempted (but still with more question on the legality) to disarm New England by an instruction. They made an act to drag offenders from Wales into England for trial, as you have done (but with more hardship) with regard to America. By another act, where one of the parties was an Englishman, they ordained that his trial should be always by English. They made acts to restrain trade, as you do; and they prevented the Welsh from the use of fairs and markets, as you do the Americans from fisheries and foreign ports. In short, when the statute-book was not quite so much swelled as it is now, you find no less than fifteen acts of penal regulation on the subject of Wales.

Here we rub our hands. A fine body of precedents for the authority of Parliament and the use of it! I admit it fully; and pray add likewise to these precedents, that all the while Wales rid this kingdom like an *incubus;* that it was an unprofitable and oppressive burden; and that an Englishman traveling in that country could not go six yards from the highroad without being murdered.

The march of the human mind is slow. Sir, it was not until after two hundred years discovered that, by an eternal law, Providence had decreed vexation to violence, and poverty to rapine. Your ancestors did, however, at length open their eyes to the ill husbandry of injustice. They found that the tyranny of a free people could of all tyrannies the least be endured, and that laws made against a whole nation were not the most effectual methods for securing its obedience. Accordingly, in the twenty-seventh year of Henry VIII., the course was entirely altered. With a preamble stating the entire and perfect rights of the Crown of England, it gave to the Welsh all the

[25] The English settlers in Ireland, after the invasion of Strongbow, kept themselves within certain limits distinct from the natives, called "the Pale." They enjoyed English law, while the natives were for a long time denied it; and this gave rise to incessant contentions. By an act of James I., the privileges of the Pale were extended to all Ireland.

[26] Wales was held in *vassalage* by Henry III. through its Prince Llewellen, who in this way purchased the aid of Henry against a rebellious son; but was not reduced under English sway as part of the kingdom till the time of Edward I.

rights and privileges of English subjects. A political order was established; the military power gave way to the civil; the marches were turned into counties. But that a nation should have a right to English liberties, and yet no share at all in the fundamental security of these liberties, the grant of their own property, seemed a thing so incongruous, that, eight years after, that is, in the thirty-fifth of that reign, a complete and not ill-proportioned representation by counties and boroughs was bestowed upon Wales by act of Parliament. From that moment, as by a charm, the tumults subsided; obedience was restored; peace, order, and civilization followed in the train of liberty. When the day-star of the English Constitution had arisen in their hearts, all was harmony within and without.

> Simul alba nautis
> Stella refulsit,
> Defluit saxis agitatus humor:
> Concidunt venti, fugiuntque nubes;
> Et minax (quod sic voluere) ponto
> Unda recumbit.[27]

(3.) Third example. The very same year the county palatine of Chester received the same relief from its oppressions and the same remedy to its disorders. Before this time Chester was little less distempered than Wales. The inhabitants, without rights themselves, were the fittest to destroy the rights of others; and from thence Richard II. drew the standing army of archers with which for a time he oppressed England. The people of Chester applied to Parliament in a petition penned as I shall read to you:

"To the King our sovereign lord, in most humble wise shown unto your excellent Majesty, the inhabitants of your grace's county palatine of Chester; that where the said county palatine of Chester is and hath been always hitherto exempt, excluded and separated out and from your high court of Parliament, to have any knights and burgesses within the said court; by reason whereof the said inhabitants have hitherto sustained manifold disherisons, losses, and damages, as well in their lands, goods, and bodies, as in the good, civil, and politic governance and maintenance of the commonwealth of their said country: (2.) And, forasmuch as the said inhabitants have always hitherto been bound by the acts and statutes made and ordained by your said highness and your most noble progenitors, by authority of the said court, as far forth as other counties, cities, and boroughs have been, that have had their knights and burgesses within your said court of Parliament, and yet have had neither knight ne burgess there for the said county palatine; the said inhabitants, for lack thereof, have been oftentimes touched and grieved with acts and statutes made within the said court, as well derogatory unto the most ancient jurisdictions, liberties, and privileges of your said county palatine, as prejudicial unto the common wealth, quietness, rest, and peace of your grace's most bounden subjects inhabiting within the same."

What did Parliament with this audacious address? Reject it as a libel? Treat it as an affront to government? Spurn it as a derogation from the rights of legislature? Did they toss it over the table? Did they burn it by the hands of the common hangman? They took the petition of grievance, all rugged as it was, without softening or temperament, unpurged of the original bitterness and indignation of complaint; they made it the very preamble to their act of redress, and consecrated its principle to all ages in the sanctuary of legislation.

Here is my third example. It was attended with the success of the two former. Chester, civilized as well as Wales, has demonstrated that freedom, and not servitude, is the cure of anarchy, as religion, and not atheism, is the true remedy for superstition. Sir, this pattern of Chester was followed in the reign of Charles II. with regard to the county palatine of Durham, which is my fourth example. Fourth example. This county had long lain out of the pale of free legislation. So scrupulously was the example of Chester followed, that the style of the preamble is nearly the same with that of the Chester act; and without affecting the abstract extent of the authority of Parliament, it recognizes the equity of not suffering any considerable district in which the British subjects may act as a body to be taxed without their own voice in the grant.

Now, if the doctrines of policy contained in these preambles, and the force of these examples in the acts of Parliament, avail any thing, what can be said against applying them with regard to America? Are not the people of America as much Englishmen as the Welsh? The preamble of the act of Henry VIII. says the Welsh speak a language no way resembling that of his Majesty's English subjects. Are the Americans not as numerous? If we may trust the learned and accurate Judge Barrington's account of North Wales, and take that as a standard to measure the rest, there is no comparison. The people can not amount to above two hundred thousand; not a tenth part of the number in the colonies. Is America in rebellion? Wales was hardly ever free from it. Have you attempted to govern America by penal statutes? You made fifteen for Wales. But your legislative authority is perfect with regard to America. Was it less perfect in Wales, Chester, and Durham? But America is virtually represented. What! does the electric force of virtual representation more easily pass over the Atlantic than pervade Wales, which lies in your neighborhood; or than Chester

[27] The passage is taken from an Ode of Horace to Augustus Cesar, lib. i., 12, in which the poet celebrates the praises of his imperial master by placing him on a level with gods and deified heroes. With a delicate allusion to the peaceful influence of Augustus, he refers to Castor and Pollux, the patron deities of mariners, and the effect of their constellation (the Twins) in composing tempests.

> When *their* auspicious star
> To the sailor shines afar,
> The troubled waters leave the rocks at rest:
> The clouds are gone, the winds are still,
> The angry wave obeys their will,
> And calmly sleeps upon the ocean's breast.

and Durham, surrounded by abundance of representation that is actual and palpable? But, sir, your ancestors thought this sort of virtual representation, however ample, to be totally insufficient for the freedom of the inhabitants of territories that are so near, and comparatively so inconsiderable. How, then, can I think it sufficient for those which are infinitely greater and infinitely more remote?

America not to be represented in Parliament.

You will now, sir, perhaps imagine that I am on the point of proposing to you a scheme for representation of the colonies in Parliament. Perhaps I might be inclined to entertain some such thought, but a great flood stops me in my course. Opposuit natura.[28] I can not remove the eternal barriers of the creation. The thing in that mode I do not know to be possible. As I meddle with no theory, I do not absolutely assert the impracticability of such a representation; but I do not see my way to it; and those who have been more, confident have not been more successful. However, the arm of public benevolence is not shortened, and there are often several means to the same end. What nature has disjoined in one way wisdom may unite in another. When we can not give the benefit as we would wish, let us not refuse it altogether. If we can not give the principal, let us find a substitute. But how? Where? What substitute?

Fortunately I am not obliged for the ways and means of this substitute to tax my own unproductive invention. I am not even obliged to go to the rich treasury of the fertile framers of imaginary commonwealths; not to the Republic of Plato, not to the Utopia of More, not to the Oceana of Harrington. It is before me. It is at my feet,

And the dull swain
Treads daily on it with his clouted shoon.[29]
Milton's Comus.

I only wish you to recognize, for the theory, the ancient constitutional policy of this kingdom with regard to representation, as that policy has been declared in acts of Parliament; and, as to the practice, to return to that mode which a uniform experience has marked out to you as best, and in which you walked with security, advantage, and honor, until the year 1763.

But to aid the Crown by grants of their Provincial Assemblies.

My resolutions, therefore, mean to establish the equity and justice of a taxation of America by *grant*, and not by *imposition*. To mark the *legal competency* of the colony assemblies for the support of their government in peace, and for public aids in time of war. To acknowledge that this legal competency has had *a dutiful and beneficial exercise*; and that experience has shown the *benefit of their grants*, and the *futility of parliamentary taxation as a method of supply.*

These solid truths compose six fundamental propositions. There are three more resolutions corollary to these. If you admit the first set, you can hardly reject the others. But if you admit the first, I shall be far from solicitous whether you accept or refuse the last. I think these six massive pillars will be of strength sufficient to support the temple of British concord. I have no more doubt than I entertain of my existence, that, if you admitted these, you would command an immediate peace; and, with but tolerable future management, a lasting obedience in America. I am not arrogant in this confident assurance. The propositions are all mere matters of fact; and if they are such facts as draw irresistible conclusions even in the stating, this is the power of truth, and not any management of mine.

Purport of Mr. Burke's resolutions.

Sir, I shall open the whole plan to you together, with such observations on the motions as may tend to illustrate them where they may want explanation. The first is a resolution "That the colonies and plantations of Great Britain in North America, consisting of fourteen separate governments, and containing two millions and upward of free inhabitants, have not had the liberty and privilege of electing and sending any knights and burgesses or others to represent them in the high court of Parliament." This is a plain matter of fact, necessary to be laid down, and (excepting the description) it is laid down in the language of the Constitution: it is taken nearly *verbatim* from acts of Parliament.

The second is like unto the first, "That the said colonies and plantations have been liable to and bounden by several subsidies, payments, rates, and taxes, given and granted by Parliament, though the said colonies and plantations have not their knights and burgesses in the said high court of Parliament, of their own election, to represent the condition of their country; by lack whereof they have been oftentimes touched and grieved by subsidies given granted, and assented to, in said court, in a manner prejudicial to the commonwealth, quietness, rest, and peace of the subjects inhabiting within the same."

Is this description too hot or too cold, too strong or too weak? Does it arrogate too much to the supreme Legislature? Does it lean too much to the claims of the people? If it runs into any of these errors, the fault is not mine. It is the language of your own ancient acts of Parliament.

Non meus hic sermo est sed quæ præcipit Ofellus,
Rusticus, abnormis sapiens.[30]

It is the genuine produce of the ancient, rustic, manly, home-bred sense of this country. I did not dare to rub off a particle of the venerable rust that rather adorns and preserves, than destroys the metal. It would be a profanation to touch with a tool the stones which construct the sacred altar of peace.[31] I would not violate with modern polish the ingenuous and noble roughness of

---

[28] Nature forbids.

[29] Obsolete plural of *shoe.*

[30] The precept is not mine.
Ofellus gave it in his rustic strain,
Irregular, but wise.—*Horace, Sat.*, i., 2.
Ofellus is a Sabine peasant, in whose mouth the poet puts this satire.

[31] "If thou lift thy tool upon it [the altar], thou hast polluted it."—*Exodus*, xx., 25

these truly constitutional materials. Above all things, I was resolved not to be guilty of tampering, the odious vice of restless and unstable minds. I put my foot in the tracks of our forefathers, where I can neither wander nor stumble. Determining to fix articles of peace, I was resolved not to be wise beyond what was written; I was resolved to use nothing else than the form of sound words, to let others abound in their own sense, and carefully to abstain from all expressions of my own. What the law has said, I say. In all things else I am silent. I have no organ but for her words. This, if it be not ingenious, I am sure, is safe.

There are, indeed, words expressive of grievance in this second resolution, which those who are resolved always to be in the right will deny to contain matter of fact, as applied to the present case, although Parliament thought them true with regard to the counties of Chester and Durham. They will deny that the Americans were ever "touched and grieved" with the taxes. If they consider nothing in taxes but their weight as pecuniary impositions, there might be some pretense for this denial. But men may be sorely touched and deeply grieved in their privileges as well as in their purses. Men may lose little in property by the act which takes away all their freedom. When a man is robbed of a trifle on the highway, it is not the twopence lost that constitutes the capital outrage. This is not confined to privileges. Even ancient indulgences withdrawn, without offense on the part of those who enjoyed such favors, operate as grievances. But were the Americans, then, not touched and grieved by the taxes, in some measure, merely as taxes? If so, why were they almost all either wholly repealed or exceedingly reduced? Were they not touched and grieved, even by the regulating duties of the sixth of George II.? Else why were the duties first reduced to one third in 1764, and afterward to a third of that third in the year 1766? Were they not touched and grieved by the Stamp Act? I shall say they were, until that tax is revived. Were they not touched and grieved by the duties of 1767, which were likewise repealed, and which Lord Hillsborough tells you, for the ministry, were laid contrary to the true principle of commerce? Is not the assurance given by that noble person to the colonies of a resolution to lay no more taxes on them an admission that taxes would touch and grieve them? Is not the resolution of the noble Lord in the blue ribbon, now standing on your journals, the strongest of all proofs that parliamentary subsidies really touched and grieved them? Else why all these changes, modifications, repeals, assurances, and resolutions?

The next proposition is, "That, from the distance of the said colonies, and from other circumstances, no method hath hitherto been devised for procuring a representation in Parliament for the said colonies." This is an assertion of a fact. I go no farther on the paper; though, in my private judgment, a useful representation is impossible; I am sure it is not desired by them, nor ought it, perhaps, by us; but I abstain from opinions.

The fourth resolution is, "That each of the said colonies hath within itself a body, chosen in part, or in the whole, by the freemen, freeholders, or other free inhabitants thereof, commonly called the General Assembly, or General Court, with powers legally to raise, levy, and assess, according to the several usages of such colonies, duties and taxes toward the defraying all sorts of public services."

This competence in the colony assemblies is certain. It is proved by the whole tenor of their acts of supply in all the assemblies, in which the constant style of granting is, "an aid to his Majesty;" and acts granting to the Crown have regularly for near a century passed the public offices without dispute. Those who have been pleased parodoxically to deny this right, holding that none but the British Parliament can grant to the Crown, are wished to look to what is done, not only in the colonies, but in Ireland, in one uniform, unbroken tenor every session. Sir, I am surprised that this doctrine should come from some of the law servants of the Crown. I say that if the Crown could be responsible, his Majesty—but certainly the ministers, and even these law officers themselves, through whose hands the acts pass biennially in Ireland, or annually in the colonies, are in a habitual course of committing impeachable offenses. What habitual offenders have been all presidents of the council, all secretaries of state, all first lords of trade, all attorneys, and all solicitors general! However, they are safe, as no one impeaches them; and there is no ground of charge against them except in their own unfounded theories.

The fifth resolution is also a resolution of fact: "That the said General Assemblies, General Courts, or other bodies legally qualified as aforesaid, have at sundry times freely granted several large subsidies and public aids for his Majesty's service, according to their abilities, when required thereto by letter from one of his Majesty's principal secretaries of state. And that their right to grant the same, and their cheerfulness and sufficiency in the said grants, have been at sundry times acknowledged by Parliament." To say nothing of their great expenses in the Indian wars; and not to take their exertion in foreign ones, so high as the supplies in the year 1695, not to go back to their public contributions in the year 1710, I shall begin to travel only where the journals give me light; resolving to deal in nothing but fact authenticated by parliamentary record, and to build myself wholly on that solid basis.

Proof that such grants are sanctioned by usage.

On the 4th of April, 1748,[32] a committee of this House came to the following resolution:

"*Resolved*, That it is the opinion of this committee, *that it is just and reasonable* that the several provinces and colonies of Massachusetts Bay, New Hampshire, Connecticut, and Rhode

[32] Journals of the House, vol. xxv.

Island, be reimbursed the expenses they have been at in taking and securing to the Crown of Great Britain the island of Cape Breton and its dependencies."

These expenses were immense for such colonies. They were above £200,000 sterling; money first raised and advanced on their public credit.

On the 28th of January, 1756,[33] a message from the King came to us, to this effect: "His Majesty, being sensible of the zeal and vigor with which his faithful subjects of certain colonies in North America have exerted themselves in defense of his Majesty's just rights and possessions, recommends it to this House to take the same into their consideration, and to enable his Majesty to give them such assistance as may be a *proper reward and encouragement.*"

On the third of February, 1756,[34] the House came to a suitable resolution, expressed in words nearly the same as those of the message; but with the farther addition, that the money then voted was an *encouragement* to the colonies to exert themselves with vigor. It will not be necessary to go through all the testimonies which your own records have given to the truth of my resolutions. I will only refer you to the places in the journals:

Vol. xxvii. 16th and 19th May, 1757.

Vol. xxviii. June 1st, 1758—April 26th and 30th, 1759—Mar. 26th and 31st, and April 28th, 1760—Jan. 9th and 20th, 1761.

Vol. xxix. Jan. 22d and 26th, 1762—March 14th and 17th, 1763.

Sir, here is the repeated acknowledgment of Parliament, that the colonies not only gave, but gave to satiety. This nation has formally acknowledged two things; first, that the colonies had gone beyond their abilities, Parliament having thought it necessary to reimburse them; secondly, that they had acted legally and laudably in their grants of money, and their maintenance of troops, since the compensation is expressly given as reward and encouragement.[35] Reward is not bestowed for acts that are unlawful; and encouragement is not held out to things that deserve reprehension. My resolution, therefore, does nothing more than collect into one proposition what is scattered through your journals. I give you nothing but your own, and you can not refuse in the gross what you have so often acknowledged in detail. The admission of this, which will be so honorable to them and to you, will, indeed, be mortal to all the miserable stories by which the passions of the misguided people have been engaged in an unhappy system. The people heard, indeed, from the beginning of these disputes, one thing continually dinned in their ears, that reason and justice demanded that the Americans, who paid no taxes, should be compelled to contribute. How did that fact of their paying nothing stand, when the taxing system began? When Mr. Grenville began to form his system of American revenue, he stated in this House that the colonies were then in debt two million six hundred thousand pounds sterling money, and was of opinion they would discharge that debt in four years. On this state, those untaxed people were actually subject to the payment of taxes to the amount of six hundred and fifty thousand a year. In fact, however, Mr. Grenville was mistaken. The funds given for sinking the debt did not prove quite so ample as both the colonies and he expected. The calculation was too sanguine: the reduction was not completed till some years after, and at different times in different colonies. However, the taxes after the war continued too great to bear any addition, with prudence or propriety; and when the burdens imposed in consequence of former requisitions were discharged, our tone became too high to resort again to requisition. No colony, since that time, ever has had any requisition whatsoever made to it.

We see the sense of the Crown, and the sense of Parliament, on the productive nature of a *revenue by grant.* Now search the same journals for the produce of the *revenue by imposition.* Where is it? Let us know the volume and the page. What is the gross, what is the net produce? To what service is it applied? How have you appropriated its surplus? What, can none of the many skillful index-makers that we are now employing, find any trace of it? Well, let them and that rest together. But are the journals, which say nothing of the revenue, as silent on the discontent? Oh no! a child may find it. It is the melancholy burden and blot of every page.

I think, then, I am, from those journals, justified in the sixth and last resolution, which is: "That it hath been found by experience, that the manner of granting the said supplies and aids, by the said general assemblies, hath been more agreeable to the said colonies, and more beneficial and conducive to the public service, than the mode of giving and granting aids in Parliament, to be raised and paid in the said colonies." This makes the whole of the fundamental part of the plan. The conclusion is irresistible. You can not say, that you were driven by any necessity to an exercise of the utmost rights of legislature. You can not assert, that you took on yourselves the task of imposing colony taxes, from the want of another legal body, that is competent to the purpose of supplying the exigencies of the state without wounding the prejudices of the people. Neither is it true that the body so qualified, and having that competence, had neglected the duty.

33 Journals of the House, vol. xxvii. 34 Ibid.

35 It had been asserted, against Mr. Burke's plan, that the colonies *could* not legally make grants to the Crown; that it tended to render the King independent of Parliament, and stood on the same footing as the ancient benevolences; and that Parliament *must,* therefore, impose the tax on the colonies if it was in any way to benefit the empire as a whole. Mr. Grenville and others were of this opinion. Hence Mr. Burke insists so strongly on these precedents.

The question now, on all this accumulated matter, is—whether you will choose to abide by a profitable experience, or a mischievous theory; whether you choose to build on imagination or fact; whether you prefer enjoyment or hope; satisfaction in your subjects or discontent?

If these propositions are accepted, every thing which has been made to enforce a contrary system must, I take it for granted, fall along with it. On that ground I have drawn the following resolution, which, when it comes to be moved, will naturally be divided in a proper manner: "That it may be proper to repeal an act, made in the seventh year of the reign of his present Majesty, entitled, An act for granting certain duties in the British colonies and plantations in America; for allowing a drawback of the duties of customs upon the exportation from this kingdom, of coffee and cocoa-nuts of the produce of the said colonies or plantations; for discontinuing the drawbacks payable on China earthenware exported to America, and for more effectually preventing the clandestine running of goods in the said colonies and plantations; and that it may be proper to repeal an act, made in the fourteenth year of the reign of his present Majesty, entitled, An act to discontinue, in such manner, and for such time as are therein mentioned, the landing and discharging, lading or shipping, of goods, wares, and merchandise, at the town and within the harbor of Boston, in the province of Massachusetts Bay, in North America; and that it may be proper to repeal an act, made in the fourteenth year of the reign of his present Majesty, entitled, An act for the impartial administration of justice in the cases of persons questioned for any acts done by them in the execution of the law, or for the suppression of riots and tumults in the province of Massachusetts Bay, in New England; and that it may be proper to repeal an act, made in the fourteenth year of the reign of his present Majesty, entitled, An act for the better regulating the government of the province of Massachusetts Bay, in New England; and also, that it may be proper to explain and amend an act, made in the thirty-fifth year of the reign of King Henry the Eighth, entitled, An act for the trial of treasons committed out of the King's dominions."

I wish, sir, to repeal the Boston Port Bill, because (independently of the dangerous precedent of suspending the rights of the subject during the King's pleasure) it was passed, as I apprehend, with less regularity, and on more partial principles, than it ought. The corporation of Boston was not heard before it was condemned. Other towns, full as guilty as she was, have not had their ports blocked up. Even the restraining bill of the present session does not go to the length of the Boston Port Act. The same ideas of prudence which induced you not to extend equal punishment to equal guilt, even when you were punishing, induce me, who mean not to chastise, but to reconcile, to be satisfied with the punishment already partially inflicted.

Ideas of prudence, and accommodation to circumstances, prevent you from taking away the charters of Connecticut and Rhode Island, as you have taken away that of Massachusetts Colony, though the Crown has far less power in the two former provinces than it enjoyed in the latter; and though the abuses have been full as great and as flagrant in the exempted as in the punished. The same reasons of prudence and accommodation have weight with me in restoring the charter of Massachusetts Bay. Besides, sir, the act which changes the charter of Massachusetts is in many particulars so exceptionable, that if I did not wish absolutely to repeal, I would by all means desire to alter it, as several of its provisions tend to the subversion of all public and private justice. Such, among others, is the power in the Governor to change the Sheriff at his pleasure, and to make a new returning officer for every special cause. It is shameful to behold such a regulation standing among English laws.

The act for bringing persons accused of committing murder under the orders of government to England for trial, is but temporary. That act has calculated the probable duration of our quarrel with the colonies, and is accommodated to that supposed duration. I would hasten the happy moment of reconciliation, and therefore must, on my principle, get rid of that most justly obnoxious act.

The act of Henry the Eighth, for the trial of treasons, I do not mean to take away, but to confine it to its proper bounds and original intention; to make it expressly for trial of treasons (and the greatest treasons may be committed) in places where the jurisdiction of the Crown does not extend.

Having guarded the privileges of local legislature, I would next secure to the colonies a fair and unbiased judicature; for which purpose, sir, I propose the following resolution: "That, from the time when the General Assembly or General Court of any colony or plantation in North America, shall have appointed by act of assembly, duly confirmed, a settled salary to the offices of the Chief Justice and other judges of the Superior Court, it may proper that the said Chief Justice and other judges of the Superior Courts of such colony, shall hold his and their office and offices during their good behavior; and shall not be removed therefrom, but when the said removal shall be adjudged by his Majesty in council, upon a hearing on complaint from the General Assembly, or on a complaint from the Governor, or Council, or the House of Representatives severally, of the colony in which the said Chief Justice and other judges have exercised the said offices."

The next resolution relates to the Courts of Admiralty.

It is this: "That it may be proper to regulate the Courts of Admiralty, or Vice Admiralty, authorized by the 15th chapter of the 4th of George the Third, in such a manner as to make the same more commodious to those who sue, or are sued, in the said courts, and to provide for the more decent maintenance of the judges in the same."

These courts I do not wish to take away. They are in themselves proper establishments. This court is one of the capital securities of the Act of Navigation. The extent of its jurisdiction, indeed, has been increased; but this is altogether as proper, and is, indeed, on many accounts, more eligible, where new powers were wanted, than a court absolutely new. But courts incommodiously situated, in effect, deny justice; and a court, partaking in the fruits of its own condemnation, is a robber. The Congress complain, and complain justly, of this grievance.[36]

These are the three consequential propositions. I have thought of two or three more, but they come rather too near detail, and to the province of executive government, which I wish Parliament always to superintend, never to assume. If the first six are granted, congruity will carry the latter three. If not, the things that remain unrepealed will be, I hope, rather unseemly encumbrances on the building, than very materially detrimental to its strength and stability.

Objections refuted.

Here, sir, I should close, but that I plainly perceive some objections remain, which I ought, if possible, to remove. The first will be, that, in resorting to the doctrine of our ancestors, as contained in the preamble to the Chester act, I prove too much; that the grievance from a want of representation stated in that preamble, goes to the whole of legislation as well as to taxation. And that the colonies, grounding themselves upon that doctrine, will apply it to all parts of legislative authority.

To this objection, with all possible deference and humility, and wishing as little as any man living to impair the smallest particle of our supreme authority, I answer, that *the words are the words of Parliament, and not mine;* and that all false and inconclusive inferences drawn from them are not mine, for I heartily disclaim any such inference. I have chosen the words of an act of Parliament, which Mr. Grenville, surely a tolerably zealous and very judicious advocate for the sovereignty of Parliament, formerly moved to have read at your table, in confirmation of his tenets. It is true that Lord Chatham considered these preambles as declaring strongly in favor of his opinions. He was a no less powerful advocate for the privileges of the Americans. Ought I not from hence to presume that these preambles are as favorable as possible to both, when properly understood; favorable both to the rights of Parliament, and to the privilege of the dependencies of this crown? But, sir, the object of grievance in my resolution I have not taken from the Chester, but from the Durham act, which confines the hardship of want of representation to the case of subsidies, and which, therefore, falls in exactly with the case of the colonies. But whether the unrepresented counties were *de jure* or *de facto* bound, the preambles do not accurately distinguish; nor indeed was it necessary; for, whether *de jure* or *de facto*, the Legislature thought the exercise of the power of taxing, as of right, or as of fact without right, equally a grievance, and equally oppressive.

I do not know that the colonies have, in any general way or in any cool hour, gone much beyond the demand of immunity in relation to taxes. It is not fair to judge of the temper or dispositions of any man, or any set of men, when they are composed and at rest, from their conduct or their expressions in a state of disturbance and irritation. It is, besides, a very great mistake to imagine that mankind follow up practically any speculative principle, either of government or freedom, as far as it will go in argument and logical illation. We Englishmen stop very short of the principles upon which we support any given part of our Constitution, or even the whole of it together. I could easily, if I had not already tired you, give you very striking and convincing instances of it. This is nothing but what is natural and proper. All government, indeed every human benefit and enjoyment, every virtue and every prudent act, is founded on compromise and barter. We balance inconveniences; we give and take; we remit some rights that we may enjoy others; and we choose rather to be happy citizens than subtle disputants. As we must give away some natural liberty to enjoy civil advantages, so we must sacrifice some civil liberties for the advantages to be derived from the communion and fellowship of a great empire. But, in all fair dealings, the thing bought must bear some proportion to the purchase paid. None will barter away "the immediate jewel of his soul."[36] Though a great house is apt to make slaves haughty, yet it is purchasing a part of the artificial importance of a great empire too dear to pay for it all essential rights and all the intrinsic dignity of human nature. None of us who would not risk his life rather than fall under a government purely arbitrary. But, although there are some among us who think our Constitution wants many improvements to make it a complete system of liberty, perhaps none who are of that opinion would think it right to aim at such improvement by disturbing his country, and risking every thing that is dear to him. In every arduous enterprise we consider what we are to lose as well as what we are to gain; and the more and better stake of liberty every people possess, the less they will hazard in a vain attempt to make it more. These are *the cords of man.* Man acts from adequate motives relative to his interest, and not on metaphysical speculations. Aristotle, the great master of reasoning,

[36] The Solicitor General informed Mr. B., when the resolutions were separately moved, that the grievance of the judges partaking of the profits of the seizure had been redressed by office; accordingly, the resolution was amended.

[36] Good name in man and woman, dear my Lord,
Is the immediate jewel of their souls.
Shakspeare's Othello, Act iii., Sc. 5.

cautions us, and with great weight and propriety, against this species of delusive geometrical accuracy in moral arguments as the most fallacious of all sophistry.

The Americans will have no interest contrary to the grandeur and glory of England, when they are not oppressed by the weight of it; and they will rather be inclined to respect the acts of a superintending Legislature, when they see them the acts of that power which is itself the security, not the rival, of their secondary importance. In this assurance my mind most perfectly acquiesces, and I confess I feel not the least alarm from the discontents which are to arise from putting people at their ease; nor do I apprehend the destruction of this empire from giving, by an act of free grace and indulgence, to two millions of my fellow-citizens, some share of those rights upon which I have always been taught to value myself.

It is said, indeed, that this power of granting, vested in American assemblies, would dissolve the unity of the empire, which was preserved entire, although Wales, and Chester, and Durham were added to it. Truly, Mr. Speaker, I do not know what this unity means, nor has it ever been heard of, that I know, in the constitutional policy of this country. The very idea of subordination of parts excludes this notion of simple and undivided unity. England is the head, but she is not the head and the members too. Ireland has ever had from the beginning a separate, but not an independent Legislature, which, far from distracting, promoted the union of the whole. Every thing was sweetly and harmoniously disposed through both islands for the conservation of English dominion and the communication of English liberties. I do not see that the same principles might not be carried into twenty islands, and with the same good effect. This is my model with regard to America, as far as the internal circumstances of the two countries are the same. I know no other unity of this empire than I can draw from its example during these periods, when it seemed to my poor understanding more united than it is now, or than it is likely to be by the present methods.

Lord North's scheme examined.

But since I speak of these methods, I recollect, Mr. Speaker, almost too late, that I promised, before I finished, to say something of the proposition of the noble Lord [Lord North] on the floor, which has been so lately received, and stands on your journals. I must be deeply concerned whenever it is my misfortune to continue a difference with a majority of this House. But as the reasons for that difference are my apology for thus troubling you, suffer me to state them in a very few words. I shall compress them into as small a body as I possibly can, having already debated that matter at large when the question was before the committee.

First, then, I can not admit that proposition of a ransom by auction, because it is a mere project. It is a thing new; unheard of; supported by no experience; justified by no analogy; without example of our ancestors, or root in the Constitution. It is neither regular parliamentary taxation nor colony grant. "Experimentum in corpore vili"[37] is a good rule, which will ever make me adverse to any trial of experiments on what is certainly the most valuable of all subjects, the peace of this empire.

Secondly, it is an experiment which must be fatal, in the end, to our Constitution. For what is it but a scheme for taxing the colonies in the ante-chamber of the noble Lord and his successors? To settle the quotas and proportions in this House is clearly impossible. You, sir, may flatter yourself you shall sit a state auctioneer, with your hammer in your hand, and knock down to each colony as its bids. But to settle (on the plan laid down by the noble Lord) the true proportional payment for four or five-and-twenty governments, according to the absolute and the relative wealth of each, and according to the British proportion of wealth and burden, is a wild and chimerical notion. This new taxation must therefore come in by the back door of the Constitution. Each quota must be brought to this House ready formed; you can neither add nor alter. You must register it. You can do nothing farther. For on what grounds can you deliberate, either before or after the proposition? You can not hear the counsel for all these provinces, quarreling each on its own quantity of payment, and its proportion to others. If you should attempt it, the committee of provincial ways and means, or by whatever other name it will delight to be called, must swallow up all the time of Parliament.

Thirdly, it does not give satisfaction to the complaint of the colonies. They complain that they are taxed without their consent; you answer, that you will fix the sum at which they shall be taxed. That is, you give them the very grievance for the remedy. You tell them, indeed, that you will leave the mode to themselves. I really beg pardon. It gives me pain to mention it; but you must be sensible that you will *not perform* this part of the contract. For, suppose the colonies were to lay the duties which furnished their contingent upon the importation of your manufactures; you know you would never suffer such a tax to be laid. You know, too, that you would not suffer many other modes of taxation; so that, when you come to explain yourself, it will be found that you will neither leave to themselves the quantum nor the mode, nor, indeed, any thing. The whole is delusion from one end to the other.

Fourthly, this method of ransom by auction, unless it be *universally* accepted, will plunge you into great and inextricable difficulties. In what year of our Lord are the proportions of payments to be settled, to say nothing of the impossibility, that colony agents should have general powers of taxing the colonies at their discretion? Consider, I implore you, that the com-

[37] This was an old maxim among physical inquirers, "An experiment should be made upon some worthless object."

munication by special messages, and orders between these agents and their constituents on each variation of the case, when the parties come to contend together, and to dispute on their relative proportions, will be a matter of delay, perplexity, and confusion that never can have an end.

If all the colonies do not appear at the outcry, what is the condition of those assemblies, who offer, by themselves or their agents, to tax themselves up to your ideas of their proportion? The refractory colonies who refuse all composition will remain taxed only to your old impositions, which, however grievous in principle, are trifling as to production. The obedient colonies in this scheme are heavily taxed; the refractory remain unburdened. What will you do? Will you lay new and heavier taxes by Parliament on the disobedient? Pray consider in what way you can do it. You are perfectly convinced that in the way of taxing you can do nothing but at the ports. Now suppose it is Virginia that refuses to appear at your auction, while Maryland and North Carolina bid handsomely for their ransom, and are taxed to your quota. How will you put these colonies on a par? Will you tax the tobacco of Virginia? If you do, you give its death wound to your English revenue at home, and to one of the very greatest articles of your own foreign trade. If you tax the import of that rebellious colony, what do you tax but your own manufactures, or the goods of some other obedient and already well-taxed colony? Who has said one word on this labyrinth of detail, which bewilders you more and more as you enter into it? Who has presented, who can present you with a clew to lead you out of it? I think, sir, it is impossible that you should not recollect that the colony bounds are so implicated in one another (you know it by your own experiments in the bill for prohibiting the New England fishery), that you can lay no possible restraints on almost any of them which may not be presently eluded, if you do not confound the innocent with the guilty, and burden those whom, upon every principle, you ought to exonerate. He must be grossly ignorant of America who thinks that, without falling into this confusion of all rules of equity and policy, you can restrain any single colony, especially Virginia and Maryland, the central and most important of them all.

Let it also be considered, that either in the present confusion you settle a permanent contingent which will and must be trifling, and then you have no effectual revenue; or, you change the quota at every exigency, and then on every new repartition you will have a new quarrel.

Reflect, besides, that when you have fixed a quota for every colony, you have not provided for prompt and punctual payment. Suppose one, two, five, ten years arrears. You can not issue a treasury extent against the failing colony. You must make new Boston Port bills, new restraining laws, new acts for dragging men to England for trial. You must send out new fleets, new armies. All is to begin again. From this day forward the empire is never to know an hour's tranquillity. An intestine fire will be kept alive in the bowels of the colonies, which one time or other must consume this whole empire. I allow, indeed, that the empire of Germany raises her revenue and her troops by quotas and contingents; but the revenue of the Empire, and the army of the Empire, is the worst revenue and the worst army in the world.

Instead of a standing revenue, you will therefore have a perpetual quarrel. Indeed, the noble Lord, who proposed this project of a ransom by auction, seemed himself to be of that opinion. His project was rather designed for breaking the union of the colonies than for establishing a revenue. He confessed that he apprehended that his proposal would not be to *their taste*. I say this scheme of disunion seems to be at the bottom of the project; for I will not suspect that the noble Lord meant nothing but merely to delude the nation by an airy phantom which he never intended to realize. But, whatever his views may be, as I propose the peace and union of the colonies as the very foundation of my plan, it can not accord with one whose foundation is perpetual discord.

The two schemes compared.

Compare the two. This I offer to give you, is plain and simple. The other full of perplexed and intricate mazes. This is mild; that harsh. This is found by experience effectual for its purposes; the other is a new project. This is universal; the other calculated for certain colonies only. This is immediate in its conciliatory operation; the other remote, contingent, full of hazard. Mine is what becomes the dignity of a ruling people; gratuitous, unconditional, and not held out as matter of bargain and sale. I have done my duty in proposing it to you. I have indeed tired you by a long discourse; but this is the misfortune of those to whose influence nothing will be conceded, and who must win every inch of their ground by argument. You have heard me with goodness. May you decide with wisdom! For my part, I feel my mind greatly disburdened by what I have done to day. I have been the less fearful of trying your patience, because on this subject I mean to spare it altogether in future. I have this comfort, that in every stage of the American affairs, I have steadily opposed the measures that have produced the confusion, and may bring on the destruction of this empire. I now go so far as to risk a proposal of my own. If I can not give peace to my country, I give it to my conscience.

Mr. Burke's scheme most productive to the country.

But what, says the financier, is peace to us without money? Your plan gives us no revenue. No! But it does. For it secures to the subject the power of *refusal*—the first of all revenues. Experience is a cheat, and fact a liar, if this power in the subject of proportioning his grant, or of not granting at all, has not been found the richest mine of revenue ever discovered by the skill or by the fortune of man. It does not indeed vote you £152,750 11*s*. $2\frac{3}{4}$*d*., nor any other paltry limited sum, but it gives the strong box itself, the fund, the bank, from whence only revenues can arise among a people sensible of freedom: *Posita luditur arca.*[39] Can not you in England; can not you at this time of day; can not you—a House of Commons—trust to the principle which has raised so mighty a revenue, and accumulated a debt of near one hundred and forty millions in this country? Is this principle to be true in England and false every where else? Is it not true in Ireland? Has it not hitherto been true in the colonies? Why should you presume, that in any country, a body duly constituted for any functions will neglect to perform its duty, and abdicate its trust? Such a presumption would go against all government in all modes. But, in truth, this dread of penury of supply, from a free assembly, has no foundation in nature. For first observe, that, besides the desire, which all men have naturally, of supporting the honor of their own government, that sense of dignity, and that security of property, which ever attends freedom, has a tendency to increase the stock of the free community. Most may be taken where most is accumulated. And what is the soil or climate where experience has not uniformly proved that the voluntary flow of heaped-up plenty, bursting from the weight of its own rich luxuriance, has ever run with a more copious stream of revenue, than could be squeezed from the dry husks of oppressed indigence, by the straining of all the politic machinery in the world.

Next, we know that parties must ever exist in a free country. We know, too, that the emulations of such parties, their contradictions, their reciprocal necessities, their hopes, and their fears, must send them all in their turns to him that holds the balance of the state. The parties are the gamesters, but government keeps the table, and is sure to be the winner in the end. When this game is played, I really think it is more to be feared that the people will be exhausted, than that government will not be supplied; whereas, whatever is got by acts of absolute power, ill obeyed, because odious, or by contracts ill kept, because constrained, will be narrow, feeble, uncertain, and precarious.

Ease would retract
Vows made in pain, as violent and void.—*Milt.*

I, for one, protest against compounding our demands. I declare against compounding, for a poor limited sum, the immense, ever-growing, eternal debt[40] which is due to generous government from protected freedom. And so may I speed in the great object I propose to you, as I think it would not only be an act of injustice, but would be the worst economy in the world, to compel the colonies to a sum certain, either in the way of ransom or in the way of compulsory compact.

But to clear up my ideas on this subject: a revenue from America transmitted hither—do not delude yourselves—you never can receive it—no, not a shilling. We have experience that from remote countries it is not to be expected. If, when you attempted to extract revenue from Bengal, you were obliged to return in loan what you had taken in imposition, what can you expect from North America? for certainly, if ever there was a country qualified to produce wealth, it is India; or an institution fit for the transmission, it is the East India Company. America has none of these aptitudes. If America gives you taxable objects on which you lay your duties *here*, and gives you, at the same time, a surplus by a foreign sale of her commodities to pay the duties on these objects which you tax at home, she has performed her part to the British revenue. But with regard to her own internal establishments, she may, I doubt not she will, contribute in moderation; I say in moderation; for she ought not to be permitted to exhaust herself. She ought to be reserved to a war, the weight of which, with the enemies that we are most likely to have, must be considerable in her quarter of the globe. There she may serve you, and serve you essentially.

No *direct* revenue ever to be expected from America.

For that service, for all service, whether of revenue, trade, or empire, my trust is in her interest in the British Constitution. My hold of the colonies is in the close affection which grows from common names, from kindred blood, from similar privileges, and equal protection. These are ties which, though light as air, are as strong as links of iron. Let the colonies always keep the idea of their civil rights associated with your government; they will cling and grapple to you, and no force under heaven will be of power to tear them from their allegiance. But let it be once understood that your government may be one thing, and their privileges another; that these two things may exist without any mutual relation; the cement is gone; the cohesion is loosened; and every thing hastens to decay and dissolution. As long as you have the wisdom to keep the sovereign authority of this country as the sanctuary of liberty, the sacred temple consecrated to our common faith, wherever the chosen race and sons of England worship Freedom, they will turn their faces toward you.[41] The more they multiply, the more

Peroration.

[39] The quotation is taken from the first Satire of Juvenal, the ninetieth line, where the poet describes the excess to which gambling was then carried on at Rome.

Neque enim loculis comitantibus itur
Ad casum tabulæ, *positâ sed luditur arcâ.*

For now no more the pocket's stores supply
The boundless charges of the desperate die;
The chest is staked!—Gifford.

[40] "The debt immense of endless gratitude."
Milton's Par. Lost, iv., 53.

[41] This is one of those beautiful allusions to the Scriptures with which Mr. Burke so often adorns his pages. The practice among the Jews of worshiping toward the temple in all their dispersions, was founded on the prayer of Solomon at its dedication: "If thy people go out to battle, or whithersoever thou shalt send them, and *shall pray unto the Lord toward the city which thou hast chosen, and toward*

friends you will have. The more ardently they love liberty, the more perfect will be their obedience. Slavery they can have any where. It is a weed that grows in every soil. They may have it from Spain; they may have it from Prussia; but, until you become lost to all feeling of your true interest and your natural dignity, freedom they can have from none but you. This is the commodity of price, of which you have the monopoly. This is the true Act of Navigation, which binds to you the commerce of the colonies, and through them secures to you the wealth of the world. Deny them this participation of freedom, and you break that sole bond which originally made, and must still preserve, the unity of the empire. Do not entertain so weak an imagination as that your registers and your bonds, your affidavits and your sufferances, your cockets and your clearances, are what form the great securities of your commerce. Do not dream that your letters of office, and your instructions, and your suspending clauses, are the things that hold together the great contexture of this mysterious whole. These things do not make your government. Dead instruments, passive tools as they are, it is the spirit of the English communion that gives all their life and efficacy to them. It is the spirit of the English Constitution, which, infused through the mighty mass, pervades, feeds, unites, invigorates, vivifies every part of the empire, even down to the minutest member.[42]

Is it not the same virtue which does every thing for us here in England? Do you imagine, then, that it is the land tax which raises your revenue? that it is the annual vote in the Committee of Supply, which gives you your army? or that it is the Mutiny Bill which inspires it with bravery and discipline? No! surely no! It is the love of the people; it is their attachment to their government, from the sense of the deep stake they have in such a glorious institution, which gives you your army and your navy, and infuses into both that liberal obedience, without which your army would be a base rabble, and your navy nothing but rotten timber.

All this, I know well enough, will sound wild and chimerical to the profane herd of those vulgar and mechanical politicians, who have no place among us; a sort of people who think that nothing exists but what is gross and material, and who therefore, far from being qualified to be directors of the great movement of empire, are not fit to turn a wheel in the machine. But to men truly initiated and rightly taught, these ruling and master principles, which, in the opinion of such men as I have mentioned, have no substantial existence, are in truth every thing and all in all. Magnanimity in politics is not seldom the truest wisdom; and a great empire and little minds go ill together. If we are conscious of our situation, and glow with zeal to fill our place as becomes our station and ourselves, we ought to auspicate all our public proceedings on America with the old warning of the Church, *Sursum corda!*[43] We ought to elevate our minds to the greatness of that trust to which the order of Providence has called us. By adverting to the dignity of this high calling, our ancestors have turned a savage wilderness into a glorious empire, and have made the most extensive and the only honorable conquests, not by destroying, but by promoting, the wealth, the number, the happiness of the human race. Let us get an American revenue as we have got an American empire. English privileges have made it all that it is; English privileges alone will make it all it can be.

In full confidence of this unalterable truth, I now (*quod felix faustumque sit*)[44] lay the first stone in the temple of peace; and I move you,

"That the colonies and plantations of Great Britain in North America, consisting of fourteen separate governments, and containing two millions and upward of free inhabitants, have not had the liberty and privilege of electing and sending any knights and burgesses, or others, to represent them in the high court of Parliament."

On this resolution the previous question was demanded, and was carried against Mr. Burke by a majority of 270 to 78. The other resolutions, of course, fell to the ground.

---

the House that I have built for thy name, then hear thou in heaven their prayer and their supplication, and maintain their cause."—1st Kings, ix., 44–5. Accordingly, "When Daniel knew that the writing was signed, he went into his house; *and his windows being open toward Jerusalem*, he kneeled upon his knees three times a day, and prayed and gave thanks before his God, as he did aforetime."—Dan., vi., 10.

[42] The reader of Virgil will trace the origin of this beautiful sentence to the poet's description of the Animus Mundi, or soul of the universe, in the sixth book of the Æneid, lines 926–7.

Spiritus intus alit; totamque infusa per artus
Mens agitat molem et magno se corpore miscit.

Within a Spirit lives: a Mind infused
Through every member of that mighty mass,
Pervades, sustains, and actuates the whole.

Mr. Burke's application of this image to the Spirit of Freedom in the English Constitution is one of the finest conceptions of his genius. The thought rises into new dignity and strength when we view it (as it lay in the mind of Burke) in connection with the sublime passage by which it was suggested.

[43] "Let your hearts rise upward," a call to silent prayer, at certain intervals of the Roman Catholic service.

[44] This was a form of prayer among the Romans at the commencement of any important undertaking, "that it may be happy and prosperous."

SPEECH

OF MR. BURKE AT BRISTOL, PREVIOUS TO THE ELECTION, DELIVERED SEPTEMBER 6, 1780.

INTRODUCTION.

Mr. Burke did not originally seek the honor of representing the city of Bristol in the House of Commons. On the dissolution of Parliament in 1774, he was chosen member for Malton in Yorkshire, through the influence of Lord Rockingham; and was in the act of returning thanks to his constituents, when a deputation arrived from Bristol, informing him that he had been put in nomination by his friends there. He repaired immediately to the spot, and after a severe contest was elected by a considerable majority.

During the six years which followed, Mr. Burke was laboriously engaged in his duties as a member of Parliament. His time was so fully occupied, that while he never neglected the interests of his constituents, he found but little leisure or opportunity to see them in person. He was, indeed, ill fitted, in some respects, for conciliating popular favor by visits and entertainments. His studious habits and refined tastes led him to shrink from the noise and bustle of a progress among the people of Bristol, which, in so large a city, would almost of necessity assume the character of a regular canvass. In addition to this, he had offended a majority of his constituents by his political conduct, especially by opposing the American war—by voting (against their positive instructions) for the grant of increased privileges to the Irish trade—by supporting Lord Beauchamp's bill for the relief of insolvent debtors—and by the share he took in the repeal of some very cruel enactments against the Roman Catholics.

In this state of things, Parliament was unexpectedly dissolved about a year before its regular term of expiration, and Mr. Burke found himself suddenly thrown, under every possible disadvantage, into the midst of a contested election. He immediately repaired to Bristol; and, as a preliminary step, in order to try his ground, he requested a meeting of the corporation, at which he delivered the following speech in explanation and defense of his conduct. Never was there a more manly or triumphant vindication. Conscious of the rectitude of his intentions, he makes no attempt to shuffle or evade. "No," he exclaims, "*I did not obey your instructions*. I conformed to the instructions of truth and nature, and maintained your interest against your opinions, with the constancy that became me. A representative that was worthy of you ought to be a person of stability. I am to look, indeed, to your opinions; but to such opinions as you and I must have five years hence. I was not to look at the flash of the day. I knew that you chose me in my place, along with others, *to be a pillar of the state, and not a weather-cock on the top of the edifice, exalted for my levity and versatility, and of no use but to indicate the shiftings of every fashionable gale*." The voice of posterity has decided in Mr. Burke's favor upon all the topics here discussed; and the wonder is, that these masterly reasonings should ever have been necessary, in defense of measures which were equally demanded by justice and humanity, and perhaps by the very existence of the empire.

This is, in many respects, the best speech of Mr. Burke for the study and imitation of a young orator. It is more simple and direct than any of his other speeches. It was addressed to merchants and business-men; and while it abounds quite as much as any of his productions in the rich fruits of political wisdom, and has occasionally very bold and striking images, it is less ambitious in style, and less profluent in illustration, than his more elaborate efforts in the House of Commons.

SPEECH, &c.

Mr. Mayor and Gentlemen,—I am extremely pleased at the appearance of this large and respectable meeting. The steps I may be obliged to take will want the sanction of a considerable authority; and in explaining any thing which may appear doubtful in my public conduct, I must naturally desire a very full audience.

I have been backward to begin my canvass. The dissolution of the Parliament was uncertain; and it did not become me, by an unseasonable importunity, to appear diffident of the fact of my six years' endeavors to please you. I had served the city of Bristol honorably; and the city of Bristol had no reason to think that the means of honorable service to the public were become indifferent to me.

Reasons for requesting the meeting.

I found, on my arrival here, that three gentlemen had been long in eager pursuit of an object which but two of us can obtain. I found that they had all met with encouragement. A contested election in such a city as this is no light thing. I paused on the brink of the precipice. These three gentlemen, by various merits, and on various titles, I made no doubt were worthy of your favor. I shall never attempt to raise myself by depreciating the merits of my competitors. In the complexity and confusion of these cross pursuits, I wished to take the authentic public sense of my friends upon a business of so much delicacy. I wished to take your opinion along with me; that if I should give up the contest at the very beginning, my surrender of my post may not seem the effect of inconstancy, or timidity, or anger, or disgust, or indolence, or any other temper unbecoming a man who has engaged in the public service. If, on the contrary, I should undertake the election, and fail of success, I was full as anxious that it should be manifest to the whole world that the peace of the city had not been broken by my rashness, presumption, or fond conceit of my own merit.

I am not come, by a false and counterfeit show of deference to your judgment, to seduce it in my favor. I ask it seriously and unaffectedly. If you wish that I should retire, I shall not consider that advice as a censure upon my conduct, or an alteration in your sentiments, but as a rational submission to the circumstances of affairs. If, on the contrary, you should think it proper for me to proceed on my canvass, if you will risk the trouble on your part, I will risk it on mine. My pretensions are such as you can not be ashamed of, whether they succeed or fail.

If you call upon me, I shall solicit the favor of the city upon manly ground. I come before you with the plain confidence of an honest servant in the equity of a candid and discerning master. I come to claim your approbation, not to amuse you with vain apologies, or with professions still more vain and senseless. I have lived too long to be served by apologies, or to stand in need of them. The part I have acted has been in open day; and to hold out to a conduct, which stands in that clear and steady light for all its good and all its evil, to hold out to that conduct the paltry winking tapers of excuses and promises, I never will do it. They may obscure it with their smoke, but they never can illumine sunshine by such a flame as theirs.

I am sensible that no endeavors have been left untried to injure me in your opinion. But the

Transition: Public men should not be treated captiously.

use of character is to be a shield against calumny. I could wish, undoubtedly (if idle wishes were not the most idle of all things), to make every part of my conduct agreeable to every one of my constituents. But in so great a city, and so greatly divided as this, it is weak to expect it. In such a discordancy of sentiments, it is better to look to the nature of things than to the humors of men. The very attempt toward pleasing every body, discovers a temper always flashy, and often false and insincere. Therefore, as I have proceeded straight onward in my conduct, so I will proceed in my account of those parts of it which have been most excepted to. But I must first beg leave just to hint to you, that we may suffer very great detriment by being open to every talker. It is not to be imagined how much of service is lost from spirits full of activity and full of energy, who are pressing, who are rushing forward to great and capital objects, when you oblige them to be continually looking back. While they are defending one service, they defraud you of a hundred. Applaud us when we run; console us when we fall; cheer us when we recover; but let us pass on—for God's sake, let us pass on.

Do you think, gentlemen, that every public act in the six years since I stood in this place before you—that all the arduous things which have been done in this eventful period, which has crowded into a few years' space the revolutions of an age, can be opened to you on their fair grounds in half an hour's conversation?

But it is no reason, because there is a bad mode of inquiry, that there should be no examination at all. Most certainly it is our duty to examine; it is our interest too. But it must be with discretion; with an attention to all the circumstances, and to all the motives; like sound judges, and not like caviling pettifoggers and quibbling pleaders, prying into flaws and hunting for exceptions. Look, gentlemen, to the *whole tenor* of your member's conduct. Try whether his ambition or his avarice have justled him out of the straight line of duty, or whether that grand foe of the offices of active life—that master-vice in men of business, a degenerate and inglorious sloth—has made him flag, and languish in his course. This is the object of our inquiry. If our member's conduct can bear this touch, mark it for sterling. He may have fallen into errors; he must have faults; but our error is greater, and our fault is radically ruinous to ourselves, if we do not bear, if we do not even applaud the whole compound and mixed mass of such a character. Not to act thus is folly; I had almost said, it is impiety. *He censures God who quarrels with the imperfections of man.*

Gentlemen, we must not be peevish with those who serve the people; for none will serve us while there is a Court to serve, but those who are of a nice and jealous honor. They who think every thing, in comparison of that honor, to be dust and ashes, will not bear to have it soiled and impaired by those for whose sake they make a thousand sacrifices to preserve it immaculate and whole. We shall either drive such men from the public stage, or we shall send them to the Court for protection, where, if they must sacrifice their reputation, they will at least secure their interest. Depend upon it, that the lovers of freedom will be free. None will violate their conscience to please us in order afterward to discharge that conscience which they have violated by doing us faithful and affectionate service. If we degrade and deprave their minds by servility, it will be absurd to expect that they who are creeping and abject toward us will ever be bold and incorruptible asserters of our freedom against the most seducing and the most formidable of all powers. No! Human nature is not so formed; nor shall we improve the faculties or better the morals of public men by our possession of the most infallible receipt in the world for making cheats and hypocrites.

It will drive them from the service of the people.

Let me say with plainness, I, who am no longer in a public character, that if by a fair, by an indulgent, by a gentlemanly behavior to our representatives, we do not give confidence to their minds and a liberal scope to their understandings; if we do not permit our members to act upon a *very* enlarged view of things, we shall at length infallibly degrade our national representation into a confused and shuffling bustle of local agency. When the popular member is narrowed in his ideas, and rendered timid in his proceedings, the service of the Crown will be the sole nursery of statesmen. Among the frolics of the Court, it may at length take that of attending to its business. Then the monopoly of mental power will be added to the power of all other kinds it possesses. On the side of the people there will be nothing but impotence; for ignorance is impotence; narrowness of mind is impotence; timidity is itself impotence, and makes all other qualities that go along with it impotent and useless.

At present it is the plan of the Court to make its servants insignificant. If the people should fall into the same humor, and should choose their servants on the same principles of mere obsequiousness, and flexibility, and total vacancy or indifference of opinion in all public matters, then no part of the state will be sound, and it will be in vain to think of saving it.[1]

I thought it very expedient at this time to give you this candid counsel; and with this counsel I would willingly close, if the matters which at various times have been objected to me in this city concerned only myself and my own election. These charges, I think, are four in number: my

Subject: Charges against Mr. Burke as representative of Bristol.

neglect of a due attention to my constituents; the not paying more frequent visits here; my conduct on the affairs of the first Irish trade acts; my opinion and mode of proceeding on Lord Beauchamp's debtor's bills; and my votes on the late affairs of the Roman Catholics. All of these (except, perhaps, the first) relate to matters of very considerable public concern; and it is not lest you should censure me improperly, but lest you should form improper opinions on matters of some moment to you, that I trouble you at all upon the subject. My conduct is of small importance.

I. With regard to the first charge, my friends

First Charge: Neglect of constituents.

have spoken to me of it in the style of amicable expostulation; not so much blaming the thing, as lamenting the effects. Others, less partial to me, were less kind in assigning the motives. I admit, there is a decorum and propriety in a member of Parliament's paying a respectful court to his constituents. If I were conscious to myself that pleasure or dissipation, or low, unworthy occupations had detained me from personal attendance on you, I would readily admit my fault, and quietly submit to the penalty. But, gentlemen, I live a hundred miles distance from Bristol; and at the end of a session I come to my own house, fatigued in body and in mind, to a little repose, and to a very little attention to my family and my private concerns. A visit to Bristol is always a sort of canvass, else it will do more harm than good. To pass from the toils of a session to the toils of a canvass is the farthest thing in the world from repose. I could hardly serve you as I have done and court you too. Most of you have heard that I do not very remarkably spare myself in public business; and in the *private* business of my constituents I have done very near as much as those who have nothing else to do. My canvass of you was not on the 'change, nor in the county meetings, nor in the clubs of this city. It was in the House of Commons; it was at the Custom-house; it was at the Council; it was at the Treasury; it was at the Admiralty. I canvassed you through your affairs, and not your persons. I was not only your representative as a body; I was the agent, the solicitor of individuals. I ran about wherever your affairs could call me; and in acting for you, I often appeared rather as a ship-broker than as a member of Parliament. There was nothing too laborious or too low for me to undertake. The meanness of the business was raised by the dignity of the object. If some lesser matters have slipped through my fingers, it was because I filled my hands too full, and, in my eagerness to serve you, took in more than my hands could grasp. Several gentlemen stand round me who are my willing witnesses, and there are others who, if they were here, would be still better, because they would be unwilling witnesses to the same truth. It was in the middle of a summer residence in London, and in the middle of a negotiation at the Admiralty for your trade, that I was called to Bristol; and this late visit, at this late day, has been possibly in prejudice to your affairs.

His services in London.

Since I have touched upon this matter, let me say, gentlemen, that if I had a disposition or a right to complain, I have some cause of complaint on my side. With a petition of this city in my hand, passed through the corporation without a dissenting voice, a petition in unison with almost the whole voice of the kingdom (with whose formal thanks I was covered over), while I labored on no less than five bills for a public reform,[2] and fought against the opposition of great abilities, and of the greatest power, every clause, and every word of the largest of those bills, almost to the very last day of a very long session—all this time a canvass in Bristol was as calmly carried on as if I were dead. I was considered as a man wholly out of the question. While I watched, and fasted, and sweated in the House of Commons, by the most easy and ordinary arts of election, by dinners and visits, by "How-do-you-dos" and "My worthy friends," I was to be quietly moved out of my seat; and promises were made, and engagements entered into, without

Mr. Burke, on his part, had reason to complain.

[1] It is hardly necessary to remark how much striking and just thought is crowded into this exordium and transition. It would be difficult to find any where in the same space an equal amount of weighty considerations so perfectly suited to introduce such a discussion.

[2] Mr. Burke here refers to his bills for economical reform, which were advocated in his speech on this subject, delivered February 11th, 1780.

any exception or reserve, as if my laborious zeal in my duty had been a regular abdication of my trust.

Grounds of reluctance to visit Bristol.

To open my whole heart to you on this subject, I do confess, however, that there were other times besides the two years in which I did visit you, when I was not wholly without leisure for repeating that mark of my respect; but I could not bring my mind to see you. You remember that in the beginning of this American war (that era of calamity, disgrace, and downfall—an era which no feeling mind will ever mention without a tear for England) you were greatly divided; and a very strong body, if not the strongest, opposed itself to the madness which every art and every power were employed to render popular, in order that the errors of the rulers might be lost in the general blindness of the nation. This opposition continued until after our great, but most unfortunate victory at Long Island.[3] Then all the mounds and banks of our constancy were borne down at once, and the phrensy of the American war broke in upon us like a deluge. This victory, which seemed to put an immediate end to all difficulties, perfected in us that spirit of domination which our unparalleled prosperity had but too long nurtured. We had been so very powerful, and so very prosperous, that even the humblest of us were degraded into the vices and follies of kings. We lost all measure between means and ends; and our headlong desires became our politics and our morals. All men who wished for peace, or retained any sentiments of moderation, were overborne or silenced; and this city was led by every artifice (and probably with more management, because I was one of your members) to distinguish itself by its zeal for that fatal cause. In this temper of yours and of my mind, I should have sooner fled to the extremities of the earth than have shown myself here. I, who saw in every American victory (for you have had a long series of these misfortunes) the germ and seed of the naval power of France and Spain, which all our heat and warmth against America was only hatching into life—I should not have been a welcome visitant with the brow and the language of such feelings. When afterward the other face of your calamity was turned upon you, and showed itself in defeat and distress, I shunned you full as much. I felt sorely this variety in our wretchedness, and I did not wish to have the least appearance of insulting you with that show of superiority which, though it may not be assumed, is generally suspected in a time of calamity from those whose previous warnings have been despised. I could not bear to show you a representative whose face did not reflect that of his constituents; a face that could not joy in your joys and sorrow in your sorrows. But time at length has made us all of one opinion; and we have all opened our eyes on the true nature of the American war, to the true nature of all its successes and all its failures.

In that public storm, too, I had my private feelings. I had seen blown down and prostrate on the ground several of those houses to whom I was chiefly indebted for the honor this city has done me. I confess, that while the wounds of those I loved were yet green, I could not bear to show myself in pride and triumph in that place into which their partiality had brought me, and to appear at feasts and rejoicings, in the midst of the grief and calamity of my warm friends, my zealous supporters, my generous benefactors. This is a true, unvarnished, undisguised state of the affair. You will judge of it.

This is the only one of the charges in which I am personally concerned. As to the other matters objected against me, which in their turn I shall mention to you, remember once more I do not mean to extenuate or excuse. Why should I, when the things charged are among those upon which I found all my reputation? What would be left to me, if I myself was the man who softened, and blended, and diluted, and weakened, all the distinguishing colors of my life, so as to leave nothing distinct and determinate in my whole conduct?[4]

Second charge: Giving free trade to Ireland.

II. It has been said, and it is the second charge, that in the questions of the Irish trade I did not consult the interest of my constituents, or, to speak out strongly, that I rather acted as a native of Ireland, than as an English member of Parliament.

I certainly have very warm, good wishes for the place of my birth. But the sphere of my duties is my true country. It was as a man attached to your interests, and zealous for the conservation of your power and dignity, that I acted on that occasion, and on all occasions. You were involved in the American war. A new world of policy was opened, to which it was necessary we should conform, whether we would or not; and my only thought was how to conform to our situation in such a manner as to unite to this kingdom, in prosperity and in affection, whatever remained of the empire. I was true to my old, standing, invariable principle, that all things which came from Great Britain should issue as a gift of her bounty and benefi-

[3] This occurred in August, 1776, when the army under Washington was defeated, and New York taken by the British. This success made the war popular throughout England, and created an expectation of the immediate reduction of the colonies.

[4] It is an old adage, that the audience makes the orator; and it is certainly the fact that Mr. Burke, in speaking thus largely of himself before a body of plain men like the people of Bristol, was entirely free from that appearance of display, and that intrusion of what is purely fanciful, which sometimes marked his performances in the House of Commons. Never was a defense more ingenious, and yet more simple and manly. There is no affected modesty about it, nor is there the slightest appearance of vanity or arrogance. If any one should consider beforehand what kind of answer was to be given to so frivolous an objection, it would hardly seem possible to frame one containing so much solid and ingenious thought, and yet so perfectly suited to the nature of the case.

cence, rather than as claims recovered against a struggling litigant; or at least, that if your beneficence obtained no credit in your concessions, yet that they should appear the salutary provisions of your wisdom and foresight; not as things wrung from you with your blood, by the cruel gripe of a rigid necessity. The first concessions, by being (much against my will) mangled and stripped of the parts which were necessary to make out their just correspondence and connection in trade, were of no use. The next year a feeble attempt was made to bring the thing into better shape. This attempt (countenanced by the Minister), on the very first appearance of some popular uneasiness, was, after a considerable progress through the House, thrown out by *him.*[5]

Demanded by the Irish in arms.

What was the consequence? The whole kingdom of Ireland was instantly in a flame. Threatened by foreigners, and, as they thought, insulted by England, they resolved at once to resist the power of France, and to cast off yours. As for us, we were able neither to protect nor to restrain them. Forty thousand men were raised and disciplined without commission from the Crown. Two illegal armies were seen with banners displayed at the same time, and in the same country. No executive magistrate, no judicature in Ireland, would acknowledge the legality of the army which bore the King's commission; and no law, or appearance of law, authorized the army commissioned by itself. In this unexampled state of things, which the least error, the least trespass on the right or left, would have hurried down the precipice into an abyss of blood and confusion, the people of Ireland demand a freedom of trade with arms in their hands. They interdict all commerce between the two nations. They deny all new supply in the House of Commons, although in time of war. They stint the trust of the old revenue, given for two years to all the King's predecessors, to six months. The British Parliament, in a former session frightened into a limited concession by the menaces of Ireland, frightened out of it by the menaces of England, was now frightened back again, and made a universal surrender of all that had been thought the peculiar, reserved, uncommunicable rights of England—the exclusive commerce of America, of Africa, of the West Indies—all the enumerations of the Acts of Navigation—all the manufactures, iron, glass, even the last pledge of jealousy and pride, the interest hid in the secret of our hearts, the inveterate prejudice molded into the constitution of our frame, even the sacred fleece itself,[6] all went together. No reserve; no exception; no debate; no discussion. A sudden light broke in upon us all. It broke in, not through well-contrived and well-disposed windows, but through flaws and breaches; through the yawning chasms of our ruin. We were taught wisdom by humiliation. No town in England presumed to have a prejudice, or dared to mutter a petition. What was worse, the whole Parliament of England, which retained authority for nothing but surrenders, was despoiled of every shadow of superintendence. It was, without any qualification, denied in theory, as it had been trampled upon in practice. This scene of shame and disgrace has, in a manner while I am speaking ended by the perpetual establishment of military power, in the dominions of this Crown, without consent of the British Legislature, contrary to the policy of the constitution, contrary to the declaration of right;[7] and by this your liberties

[5] Ireland was reduced to so much distress by the stoppage of trade during the American war, that Lord Nugent offered a number of resolutions in 1778 for removing the restrictions of the Navigation Act, and allowing her a large participation in the commerce of the world. This was vehemently opposed by Bristol, in common with the other great commercial towns; but Mr. Burke felt himself bound to support the measure against the wishes and instructions of his constituents. The ministry, however, became alarmed by the clamor, and nothing effectual was done. In 1779, another attempt of the same nature was made by Lord Nugent, with Lord North's approbation; but the minister became alarmed again, and defeated the plan. The Irish, indignant at this treatment, now formed associations (after the example of the Americans) to abstain from the use of all English manufactured articles. Associations of a still more alarming character had already commenced. The French and Spanish fleets effected a junction in August, 1779, and, driving back the English fleet (which was much inferior), swept the channel without resistance or molestation, and threatened a descent on Ireland. The people, left without protection by the English government, flew to arms; a part of them under an implied authority from the magistrates, and part with no authority but the necessity of national defense. The celebrated corps of IRISH VOLUNTEERS, consisting of between forty and fifty thousand men, was embodied, armed, and officered, within a few weeks. The Irish Parliament met shortly after, and approved their conduct by a unanimous vote of thanks. With these troops at their command, they sent a significant address to the King, declaring that "it was not by temporary expedients, but by a *free trade* that the nation was to be saved from impending ruin." To enforce this address, they limited their supplies to the period of six months, instead of the ordinary term of two years. It was now obvious that a rebellion in Ireland would be added to that in the colonies, unless the ministry yielded at once. The whole nation "had their face toward America, and their back toward England." Hence the instantaneous concessions so graphically described by Mr. Burke. Even the woolen trade—"the sacred fleece"—which the English had guarded with such jealous care, was thrown open to the Irish.

[6] The allusion here is to the story of the Argonauts, and the golden fleece of Colchis, which was guarded by a dragon that never slept. Many have supposed this to be a historical myth, relating to the first introduction of sheep into Greece from the Euxine for the sake of their wool, and Mr. Burke perhaps so regarded it. The image that follows is one of the strongest to be found in the speeches of Mr. Burke or any other orator.

[7] The Irish Parliament, flushed by their success in respect to trade, passed a bill enacting that the

are swept away along with your supreme authority—and both, linked together from the beginning, have, I am afraid, both together perished forever.

Course of Mr. Burke.

What! gentlemen, was I not to foresee, or, foreseeing, was I not to endeavor to save you from all these multiplied mischiefs and disgraces? Would the little, silly, canvass prattle of obeying instructions, and having no opinions but yours, and such idle, senseless tales, which amuse the vacant ears of unthinking men, have saved you from "that pelting of the pitiless storm," to which the loose improvidence, the cowardly rashness of those who dare not look danger in the face, so as to provide against it in time, and therefore throw themselves headlong into the midst of it, have exposed this degraded nation, beat down and prostrate on the earth, unsheltered, unarmed, unresisting? Was I an Irishman on that day, that I boldly withstood our pride? or on the day that I hung down my head, and wept in shame and silence over the humiliation of Great Britain? I became unpopular in England for the one, and in Ireland for the other.[8] What then? What obligation lay on me to be popular? I was bound to serve both kingdoms. To be pleased with my service was their affair, not mine.

He acted in respect to Ireland as he had previously done in regard to America.

I was an Irishman in the Irish business, just as much as I was an American, when, on the same principles, I wished you to concede to America, at a time when she prayed concession at our feet. Just as much was I an American, when I wished Parliament to offer terms in victory, and not to wait the well-chosen hour of defeat, for making good, by weakness and by supplication, a claim of prerogative, pre-eminence, and authority.

Instead of requiring it from me as a point of duty to kindle with your passions, had you all been as cool as I was, you would have been saved disgraces and distresses that are unutterable. Do you remember our commission? We sent out a solemn embassy across the Atlantic Ocean, to lay the crown, the peerage, the Commons of Great Britain, at the feet of the American Congress.[9] That our disgrace might want no sort of brightening and burnishing, observe who they were that composed this famous embassy. My Lord Carlisle is among the first ranks of our nobility. He is the identical man who, but two years before, had been put forward at the opening of a session in the House of Lords, as the mover of a haughty and rigorous address against America. He was put in the front of the embassy of submission. Mr. Eden was taken from the office of Lord Suffolk, to whom he was then under Secretary of State; from the office of that Lord Suffolk, who, but a few weeks before, in his place in Parliament, did not deign to inquire where a congress of vagrants was to be found. This Lord Suffolk sent Mr. Eden to find these vagrants, without knowing where his King's generals were to be found, who were joined in the same commission of supplicating those whom they were sent to subdue. They enter the capital of America only to abandon it; and these assertors and representatives of the dignity of England, at the tail of a flying army, let fly their Parthian shafts of memorials and remonstrances at random behind them. Their promises and their offers, their flatteries and their menaces, were all despised; and we were saved the disgrace of their formal reception, only because the Congress scorned to receive them; while the State House of independent Philadelphia opened her doors to the public entry of the embasador of France. From war and blood we went to submission; and from submission plunged back again to war and blood; to desolate and be desolated, without measure, hope, or end. I am a Royalist: I blushed for this degradation of the Crown. I am a Whig: I blushed for the dishonor of Parliament. I am a true Englishman: I felt to the quick for the disgrace of England. I am a man: I felt for the melancholy reverse of human affairs, in the fall of the first power in the world.

To read what was approaching in Ireland, in the black and bloody characters of the American war, was a painful, but it was a necessary part of my public duty; for, gentlemen, it is not your fond desires or mine that can alter the nature of things; by contending against which what have we got, or shall ever get, but defeat and shame? I did not obey your instructions! No, I conformed to the instructions of truth and nature, and maintained your interest against your opinions with a constancy that became me. A representative worthy of you ought to be a person of stability. I am to look, indeed, to your opinions; but to such opinions as you and I *must* have five years hence. I was not to look to the flash of the day: I knew that you chose me, in my place along with others, to be a pillar of the state, and not a weather-cock on the top of the edifice, exalted for my levity and versatility, and of no use but to indicate the shiftings of every fashionable gale. Would to God, the value of my sentiments on Ireland and on America had been at this day a subject of doubt and discussion!

---

military force of Ireland should be governed by laws of their own country, and not of the English Parliament. Lord North yielded, and introduced an alteration by which the law was made perpetual. It was hence called the Irish Perpetual Mutiny Act, and was strongly condemned by Mr. Burke and many of the best friends of Ireland, for the reasons here given.

[8] Mr. Burke "withstood the pride" of England, when he insisted on the grant of free trade to the Irish, who had always been treated as a conquered people; and "wept in shame and silence over the humiliation of Great Britain," when the Irish Perpetual Mutiny Act was passed. The former made him unpopular in England, the latter in Ireland.

[9] This was soon after the defeat of Burgoyne; and Mr. Burke argues, that as the people of Bristol now saw he was right in wishing to conciliate America, and prevent these disgraces, so he was also right in voting for an extension of trade to Ireland, as a measure of conciliation for that country.

No matter what my sufferings had been, so that this kingdom had kept the authority I wished it to maintain, by a grave foresight, and by an equitable temperance in the use of its power.

Third Charge: Relief of insolvent debtors.

III. The next article of charge on my public conduct, and that which I find rather the most prevalent of all, is Lord Beauchamp's bill.[10] I mean his bill of last session, for reforming the law-process concerning imprisonment. It is said (to aggravate the offense) that I treated the petition of this city with contempt, even in presenting it to the House, and expressed myself in terms of marked disrespect. Had this latter part of the charge been true, no merits on the side of the question which I took could possibly excuse me. But I am incapable of treating this city with disrespect. Very fortunately, at this minute (if my bad eyesight does not deceive me), the worthy gentleman [Mr. Williams], deputed on this business, stands directly before me. To him I appeal, whether I did not, though it militated with my oldest and my most recent public opinions, deliver the petition with a strong and more than usual recommendation to the consideration of the House, on account of the character and consequence of those who signed it. I believe the worthy gentleman will tell you, that the very day I received it I applied to the solicitor, now the attorney general, to give it an immediate consideration, and he most obligingly and instantly consented to employ a great deal of his very valuable time to write an explanation of the bill. I attended the committee with all possible care and diligence, in order that every objection of yours might meet with a solution, or produce an alteration. I entreated your learned recorder (always ready in business in which you take a concern) to attend. But what will you say to those who blame me for supporting Lord Beauchamp's bill, as a disrespectful treatment of your petition, when you hear that, out of respect to you, I myself was the cause of the loss of that very bill? For the noble Lord who brought it in, and who, I must say, has much merit for this and some other measures, at my request consented to put it off for a week, which the speaker's illness lengthened to a fortnight; and then the frantic tumult about popery drove that and every rational business from the House.[11] So that if I chose to make a defense of myself, on the little principles of a culprit, pleading in his exculpation, I might not only secure my acquittal, but make merit with the opposers of the bill. But I shall do no such thing. The truth is, that I did occasion the loss of the bill, and by a delay caused by my respect to you. But such an event was never in my contemplation; and I am so far from taking credit for the defeat of that measure, that I can not sufficiently lament my misfortune, if but one man who ought to be at large has passed a year in prison by my means. I am a debtor to the debtors: I confess judgment: I owe what, if ever it be in my power, I shall most certainly pay—ample atonement, and usurious amends to liberty and humanity for my unhappy lapse. For, gentlemen, Lord Beauchamp's bill was a law of justice and policy, as far as it went; I say as far as it went, for its fault was its being, in the remedial part, miserably defective.

Errors of the law for the recovery of debts.

There are two capital faults in our law with relation to civil debts. One is, that every man is presumed solvent: a presumption, in innumerable cases, directly against truth. Therefore the debtor is ordered, on a supposition of ability and fraud, to be coerced his liberty until he makes payment. By this means, in all cases of civil insolvency without a pardon from his creditor, he is to be imprisoned for life; and thus a miserable, mistaken invention of artificial science, operates to change a civil into a criminal judgment, and to scourge misfortune or indiscretion with a punishment which the law does not inflict on the greatest crimes.

The next fault is, that the inflicting of that punishment is not on the opinion of an equal and public judge, but is referred to the arbitrary discretion of a private, nay, interested and irritated individual. He who formally is, and substantially ought to be the judge, is in reality no more than ministerial, a mere executive instrument of a private man, who is at once judge and party. Every idea of judicial order is subverted by this procedure. If the insolvency be no crime, why is it punished with arbitrary imprisonment? If it be a crime, why is it delivered into private hands to pardon without discretion, or to punish without mercy and without measure?

Remedy proposed by Lord Beauchamp.

To these faults, gross and cruel faults in our law, the excellent principle of Lord Beauchamp's bill applied some sort of remedy. I know that credit must be preserved, but equity must be preserved too; and it is impossible that any thing should be necessary to commerce which is inconsistent with justice. The principle of credit was not weakened by that bill. God forbid! The enforcement of that credit was only put into the same public *judicial* hands on which we depend for our lives, and all that makes life dear to us. But, indeed, this business was taken up too warmly, both here and elsewhere. The bill was extremely mistaken. It was supposed to enact what it never enacted; and complaints were made of clauses in

[10] This bill (introduced Feb. 10, 1780) allowed an imprisoned debtor, who gave up all his property, and made oath that he was not worth five pounds in the world, except the bedding of his wife and the clothes of his children, to appear before a court. This court was strictly to investigate the facts, and release him if they saw fit, from *imprisonment*, though not from his debt, for which his future earnings were still liable. This bill Mr. Burke supported. It was lost, however, in the way mentioned above. And yet at Bristol he was overwhelmed with obloquy, for giving his countenance to this imperfect measure of justice and humanity, and actually lost his election chiefly on this ground.

[11] The "No Popery" riots which for some days involved Parliament in danger, and brought London to the verge of a general conflagration.

it as novelties, which existed before the noble Lord that brought in the bill was born. There was a fallacy that ran through the whole of the objections. The gentlemen who opposed the bill always argued as if the option lay between that bill and the ancient law; but this is a grand mistake; for practically the option is between, not that bill and the old law, but between that bill and those occasional laws called "acts of grace." For the operation of the old law is so savage, and so inconvenient to society, that, for a long time past, once in every Parliament, and lately twice, the Legislature has been obliged to make a general arbitrary jail-delivery, and at once to set open, by its sovereign authority, all the prisons in England.

Acts of grace the worst possible remedy.

Gentlemen, I never relished acts of grace, nor ever submitted to them, but from despair of better. They are a dishonorable invention, by which, not from humanity, not from policy, but merely because we have not room enough to hold these victims of the absurdity of our laws, we turn loose upon the public three or four thousand naked wretches, corrupted by the habits, debased by the ignominy of a prison. If the creditor had a right to those carcasses as a natural security for his property, I am sure we have no right to deprive him of that security; but if the few pounds of flesh were not necessary to his security, we had not a right to detain the unfortunate debtor, without any benefit at all to the person who confined him. Take it as you will, we commit injustice. Now Lord Beauchamp's bill intended to do deliberately, and with great caution and circumspection, upon each several case, and with all attention to the just claimant, what acts of grace do in a much greater measure, and with very little care, caution, or deliberation.

The existing system too bad to be long endured.

I suspect that here, too, if we contrive to oppose this bill, we shall be found in a struggle against the nature of things; for, as we grow enlightened, the public will not bear, for any length of time, to pay for the maintenance of whole armies of prisoners; nor, at their own expense, submit to keep jails as a sort of garrisons, merely to fortify the absurd principle of making men judges in their own cause. For credit has little or no concern in this cruelty. I speak in a commercial assembly. You know that credit is given because capital *must* be employed; that men calculate the chances of insolvency; and they either withhold the credit or make the debtor pay the risk in the price. The counting-house has no alliance with the jail. Holland understands trade as well as we, and she has done much more than this obnoxious bill intended to do. There was not, when Mr. Howard visited Holland, more than one prisoner for debt in the great city of Rotterdam. Although Lord Beauchamp's [other] act (which was previous to this bill, and intended to feel the way for it) has already preserved liberty to thousands, and though it is not three years since the last act of grace passed, yet, by Mr. Howard's last account, there were near three thousand again in jail. I can not name this gentleman without remarking that his labors and writings have done much to open the eyes and hearts of mankind. He has visited all Europe, not to survey the sumptuousness of palaces or the stateliness of temples; not to make accurate measurements of the remains of ancient grandeur, nor to form a scale of the curiosity of modern art; not to collect medals, or collate manuscripts, but to dive into the depths of dungeons; to plunge into the infection of hospitals; to survey the mansions of sorrow and pain, to take the gage and dimensions of misery, depression, and contempt; to remember the forgotten, to attend to the neglected, to visit the forsaken, and to compare and collate the distresses of all men in all countries. His plan is original, and it is as full of genius as it is of humanity. It was a voyage of discovery; a circumnavigation of charity. Already the benefit of his labor is felt more or less in every country: I hope he will anticipate his final reward, by seeing all its effects fully realized in his own. He will receive, not by retail, but in gross, the reward of those who visit the prisoner; and he has so forestalled and monopolized this branch of charity, that there will be, I trust, little room to merit by such acts of benevolence hereafter.[12]

Fourth Charge: Relief of Roman Catholics.

IV. Nothing now remains to trouble you with but the fourth charge against me—the business of the Roman Catholics.[13] It is a business closely connected with the rest. They are all on one and the same principle. My little scheme of conduct, such as it is, is all arranged. I could do nothing but what I have done on this subject, without confounding the whole train of my ideas and disturbing the whole order of my life. Gentlemen, I ought to apologize to you for seeming to think any thing at all necessary to be said upon this matter. The calumny is fitter to be scrawled with the midnight chalk of incendiaries, with "No popery," on walls and doors of devoted houses, than to be mentioned in any civilized company. I had heard that the spirit of discontent on that subject was very prevalent here. With pleasure I find that I have been grossly misinformed. If it exists at all in this city, the laws have crushed its exertions, and our morals have shamed its appearance in daylight. I have pursued this spirit wherever I could trace it, but it still fled from me.

---

[12] This admirable sketch forms not only a just tribute to the labors of Mr. Howard, and a beautiful rounding off of the present head, but it has all the force of an *argument from admitted facts;* for Lord Beauchamp's bill was designed to prevent tens of thousands from being immured in those very prisons whose filth and wretchedness Mr. Howard had laid open before the public. Mr. Burke's image of "a voyage of discovery, a circumnavigation of charity," was suggested by the exploring expedition of Captain Cooke, whose recent death at Owyhee had just been heard of in England. This made the allusion one of double interest to the public, who were at that time lamenting his death.

[13] This charge relates to Mr. Burke's vote in 1778 for repealing a cruel law against the Roman Catholics. This repeal gave rise to the No Popery riots.

It was a ghost which all had heard of, but none had seen. None would acknowledge that he thought the public proceeding with regard to our Catholic Dissenters to be blamable, but several were sorry it had made an ill impression upon others, and that my interest was hurt by my share in the business. I find with satisfaction and pride, that not above four or five in this city (and I dare say these misled by some gross misrepresentation) have signed that symbol of delusion and bond of sedition, that libel on the national religion and English character, the Protestant Association.[14] It is, therefore, gentlemen, not by way of cure, but of prevention, and lest the arts of wicked men may prevail over the integrity of any one among us, that I think it necessary to open to you the merits of this transaction pretty much at large; and I beg your patience upon it; for, although the reasonings that have been used to depreciate the act are of little force, and though the authority of the men concerned in this ill design is not very imposing, yet the audaciousness of these conspirators against the national honor, and the extensive wickedness of their attempts, have raised persons of little importance to a degree of evil eminence, and imparted a sort of sinister dignity to proceedings that had their origin in only the meanest and blindest malice.

In explaining to you the proceedings of Parliament which have been complained of, I will state to you, first, the thing that was done; next, the persons who did it; and, lastly, the grounds and reasons upon which the Legislature proceeded in this deliberate act of public justice and public prudence.

Causes which led to severe measures against Roman Catholics.

1. Gentlemen, the condition of our nature is such, that we buy our blessings at a price. The Reformation, one of the greatest periods of human improvement, was a time of trouble and confusion. The vast structure of superstition and tyranny which had been for ages in rearing, and which was combined with the interest of the great and of the many; which was molded into the laws, the manners, and civil institutions of nations, and blended with the frame and policy of states, could not be brought to the ground without a fearful struggle; nor could it fall without a violent concussion of itself and all about it. When this great revolution was attempted in a more regular mode by government, it was opposed by plots and seditions of the people; when by popular efforts, it was repressed as rebellion by the hand of power; and bloody executions (often bloodily returned) marked the whole of its progress through all its stages. The affairs of religion, which are no longer heard of in the tumult of our present contentions, made a principal ingredient in the wars and politics of that time; the enthusiasm of religion threw a gloom over the politics, and political interests poisoned and perverted the spirit of religion upon all sides. The Protestant religion, in that violent struggle, infected, as the Popish had been before, by worldly interests and worldly passions, became a persecutor in its turn, sometimes of the new sects, which carried their own principles farther than it was convenient to the original reformers, and always of the body from whom they parted; and this persecuting spirit arose not only from the bitterness of retaliation, but from the merciless policy of fear.

It was long before the spirit of true piety and true wisdom, involved in the principles of reformation, could be depurated from the dregs and feculence of the contention with which it was carried through. However, until this be done, the reformation is not complete; and those that think themselves good Protestants, from their animosity to others, are in that respect no Protestants at all. It was at first thought necessary, perhaps, to oppose to popery another popery, to get the better of it. Whatever was the cause, laws were made in many countries, and in this kingdom in particular, against Papists, which are as bloody as any of those which had been enacted by the popish princes and states; and where those laws were not bloody, in my opinion they were worse, as they were slow, cruel outrages on our nature, and kept men alive only to insult in their persons every one of the rights and feelings of humanity. I pass those statutes, because I would spare your pious ears the repetition of such shocking things; and I come to that particular law the repeal of which has produced so many unnatural and unexpected consequences.

Character of the law in question.

A statute was fabricated in the year 1699 by which the saying mass (a church service in the Latin tongue, not exactly the same as our Liturgy, but very near it, and containing no offense whatsoever against the laws or against good morals) was forged into a crime punishable with perpetual imprisonment. The teaching school, a useful and virtuous occupation, even the teaching in a private family, was in every Catholic subjected to the same unproportioned punishment. Your industry and the bread of your children was taxed for a pecuniary reward to stimulate avarice to do what nature refused; to inform and prosecute on this law. Every Roman Catholic was, under the same act, to forfeit his estate to his nearest Protestant relation, until, through a profession of what he did not believe, he redeemed by his hypocrisy what the law had transferred to the kinsman as the recompense of his profligacy. When thus turned out of doors from his paternal estate, he was disabled from acquiring any other by any industry, donation, or charity, but was rendered a foreigner in his native land, only because he retained the religion along with the property handed down to him from those who had been the old inhabitants of that land before him.

Does any one who hears me approve this scheme of things, or think there is common justice, common sense, or common honesty in any part of it? If any does, let him say it, and I am ready to discuss the point with temper and can-

[14] Those who signed the articles of this association became pledged to use all the efforts in their power to obtain the re-enactment of the law in question.

dor. But instead of approving, I perceive a virtuous indignation beginning to rise in your minds on the mere cold stating of the statute.

Reasons for passing that law, and mode of doing it.

But what will you feel when you know from history how this statute passed, and what were the motives, and what the mode of making it? A party in this nation, enemies to the system of the Revolution, were in opposition to the government of King William. They knew that our glorious deliverer was an enemy to all persecution. They knew that he came to free us from slavery and popery, out of a country where a third of the people are contented Catholics under a Protestant government. He came, with a part of his army composed of those very Catholics, to overset the power of a Popish prince. Such is the effect of a tolerating spirit; and so much is liberty served in every way, and by all persons, by a manly adherence to its own principles. While freedom is true to itself, every thing becomes subject to it, and its very adversaries are an instrument in its hands.

The party I speak of (like some among us who would disparage the best friends of their country) resolved to make the king either violate his principles of toleration, or incur the odium of protecting Papists. They therefore brought in this bill, and made it purposely wicked and absurd, that it might be rejected. The then Court party, discovering their game, turned the tables on them, and returned their bill to them stuffed with still greater absurdities, that its loss might lie upon its original authors. They, finding their own ball thrown back to them, kicked it back again to their adversaries; and thus this act, loaded with the double injustice of two parties, *neither of whom intended to pass* what they hoped the other would be persuaded to reject, went through the Legislature, contrary to the real wish of all parts of it, and of all the parties that composed it. In this manner these insolent and profligate factions, as if they were playing with balls and counters, made a sport of the fortunes and the liberties of their fellow-creatures. Other acts of persecution have been acts of malice. This was a subversion of justice from wantonness and petulance. Look into the history of Bishop Burnet. He is a witness without exception.

Operation of the law.

The effects of the act have been as mischievous as its origin was ludicrous and shameful. From that time every person of that communion, lay and ecclesiastic, has been obliged to fly from the face of day. The clergy, concealed in garrets of private houses, or obliged to take shelter (hardly safe to themselves, but infinitely dangerous to their country) under the privileges of foreign ministers, officiated as their servants, and under their protection. The whole body of the Catholics, condemned to beggary and to ignorance in their native land, have been obliged to learn the principles of letters, at the hazard of all their other principles, from the charity of your enemies.[15] They have been taxed to their ruin at the pleasure of necessitous and profligate relations, and according to the measure of their necessity and profligacy. Examples of this are many and affecting. Some of them are known to a friend who stands near me in this hall. It is but six or seven years since a clergyman of the name of Malony, a man of morals, neither guilty nor accused of any thing noxious to the state, was condemned to perpetual imprisonment for exercising the functions of his religion, and, after lying in jail two or three years, was relieved by the mercy of government from perpetual imprisonment, on condition of perpetual banishment. A brother of the Earl of Shrewsbury, a Talbot, a name respectable in this country while its glory is any part of its concern, was hauled to the bar of the Old Bailey among common felons, and only escaped the same doom, either by some error in the process, or that the wretch who brought him there could not correctly describe his person; I now forget which. In short, the persecution would never have relented for a moment, if the judges, superseding (though with an ambiguous example) the strict rule of their artificial duty by the higher obligation of their conscience, did not constantly throw every difficulty in the way of such informers. But so ineffectual is the power of legal evasion against legal iniquity, that it was but the other day that a lady of condition, beyond the middle of life, was on the point of being stripped of her whole fortune by a near relation, to whom she had been a friend and benefactor; and she must have been totally ruined, without a power of redress or mitigation from the courts of law, had not the Legislature itself rushed in, and, by a special act of Parliament, rescued her from the injustice of its own statutes. One of the acts authorizing such things was that which we in part repealed, knowing what our duty was, and doing that duty as men of honor and virtue, as good Protestants, and as good citizens! Let him stand forth that disapproves what we have done!

Peculiar malignity of a bad law in England.

Gentlemen, bad laws are the worst sort of tyranny. In such a country as this, they are of all bad things the worst: worse by far than any where else; and they derive a particular malignity even from the wisdom and soundness of the rest of our institutions. For very obvious reasons, you can not trust the Crown with a dispensing power over any of your laws. However, a government, be it as bad as it may, will, in the exercise of a discretionary power, discriminate times and persons; and will not ordinarily pursue any man, when its own safety is not concerned. A mercenary informer knows no distinction. Under such a system, the obnoxious people are slaves, not only to the government, but they live at the mercy of every individual. They are at once the slaves of the whole community, and of every

[15] Hundreds were sent to the college at St. Omer and other institutions in France, where a sense of wrong conspiring with the instructions of men attached to absolute monarchy, made them enemies of the English government.

part of it; and the worst and most unmerciful men are those on whose goodness they most depend.

In this situation men not only shrink from the frowns of a stern magistrate, but they are obliged to fly from their very species. The seeds of destruction are sown in civil intercourse, in social habitudes. The blood of wholesome kindred is infected. Their tables and beds are surrounded with snares. All the means given by Providence to make life safe and comfortable are perverted into instruments of terror and torment. This species of universal subserviency, that makes the very servant who waits behind your chair the arbiter of your life and fortune, has such a tendency to degrade and abase mankind, and to deprive them of that assured and liberal state of mind, which alone can make us what we ought to be, that I vow to God I would sooner bring myself to put a man to immediate death for opinions I disliked, and so to get rid of the man and his opinions at once, than to fret him with a feverish being, tainted with the jail distemper of a contagious servitude, to keep him above ground, an animated mass of putrefaction; corrupted himself, and corrupting all about him.[16]

Author of the repeal.

2. The act repealed was of this direct tendency, and it was made in the manner which I have related to you. I will now tell you by whom the bill of repeal was brought into Parliament. I find it has been industriously given out in this city (from kindness to me, unquestionably) that I was the mover or the seconder. The fact is, I did not once open my lips on the subject during the whole progress of the bill. I do not say this as disclaiming my share in that measure. Very far from it. I inform you of this fact, lest I should seem to arrogate to myself the merits which belong to others. To have been the man chosen out to redeem our fellow-citizens from slavery; to purify our laws from absurdity and injustice; and to cleanse our religion from the blot and stain of persecution, would be an honor and happiness to which my wishes would undoubtedly aspire, but to which nothing but my wishes could possibly have entitled me. That great work was in hands in every respect far better qualified than mine. The mover of the bill was Sir George Savile.

When an act of great and signal humanity was to be done, and done with all the weight and authority that belonged to it, the world could cast its eyes upon none but him. I hope that few things which have a tendency to bless or adorn life have wholly escaped my observation in my passage through it. I have sought the acquaintance of that gentleman, and have seen him in all situations. He is a true genius; with an understanding vigorous, and acute, and refined, and distinguishing even to excess; and illuminated with a most unbounded. peculiar, and original cast of imagination. With these he possesses many external and instrumental advantages, and he makes use of them all. His fortune is among the largest—a fortune which, wholly unincumbered, as it is, with one single charge from luxury, vanity, or excess, sinks under the benevolence of its dispenser. This private benevolence, expanding itself into patriotism, renders his whole being the estate of the public, in which he has not reserved a *peculium* for himself of profit, diversion, or relaxation.[17] During the session, the first in, and the last out of the House of Commons; he passes from the senate to the camp; and, seldom seeing the seat of his ancestors, he is always in Parliament to serve his country, or in the field to defend it. But in all well-wrought compositions, some particulars stand out more eminently than the rest; and the things which will carry his name to posterity are his two bills—I mean that for a limitation of the claims of the Crown upon landed estates,[18] and this for the relief of the Roman Catholics. By the former, he has emancipated property; by the latter, he has quieted conscience; and by both, he has taught that grand lesson to government and subject—no longer to regard each other as adverse parties.

[16] Mr. Burke's mode of treating a subject will be seen more clearly, if we compare him with such a speaker as Mr. Fox. In the present case, for instance: (1.) He prepares the way by a beautiful narration, full of thought, in which he shows how it was *possible* for Protestants, in defiance of all their principles, to become persecutors. (2.) He states at large the cruel enactments of the law in question. (3.) He describes the manner in which it was passed amid the conflicts of "insolent and profligate factions," who on both sides had "made it purposely wicked and absurd, that it might be rejected" by the opposing party. (4.) He shows that this law, instead of being suffered to sink at once into abeyance as too bad to be executed, had been carried into effect with terrible fidelity. (5.) He adds force and dignity to these individual statements by rising to a general truth, that "bad laws are the worst sort of tyranny," converting "all that makes life safe and comfortable into instruments of terror and torment." Now Mr. Fox, from his habit of striking directly at the heart of a subject, would probably have thrown away the first of these heads, and commenced at once with the third; showing the atrociously wicked manner in which the law was passed, and interweaving with his statement just enough of the provisions of the act and the cruelties of its execution, to make it stand forth in all its enormity as deserving public execration. Experience showed that Mr. Fox's method was best suited to the purposes of actual debate; while Mr. Burke's speeches have come down to posterity as objects of far greater interest to reflecting men for the depth, and compass, and richness of their thoughts.

[17] The *peculium* among the Romans was that small amount of property which a slave was allowed to possess and call his own, as distinct from his master's estate.

[18] This bill, passed in 1769, was called the Nullum Tempus Act, because it set aside the old maxim, "Nullum Tempus Regi occurrit," no length of possession bars the King. It provided that the Crown should have no claim upon any estate which had been enjoyed by any one during sixty years of undisputed possession.

Such was the mover of the act that is complained of by men who are not quite so good as he is; an act, most assuredly, not brought in by him from any partiality to that sect which is the object of it; for, among his faults, I really can not help reckoning a greater degree of prejudice against that people than becomes so wise a man. I know that he inclines to a sort of disgust, mixed with a considerable degree of asperity, to the system; and he has few, or rather no habits [in common] with any of its professors. What he has done was on quite other motives. The motives were these, which he declared in his excellent speech on his motion for the bill; namely, his extreme zeal to the Protestant religion, which he thought utterly disgraced by the act of 1699; and his rooted hatred to all kind of oppression, under any color or upon any pretense whatsoever.

The seconder was worthy of the mover and the motion. I was not the seconder. It was Mr. Dunning, recorder of this city. I shall say the less of him, because his near relation to you makes you more particularly acquainted with his merits. But I should appear little acquainted with them, or little sensible of them, if I could utter his name on this occasion without expressing my esteem for his character. I am not afraid of offending a most learned body, and most jealous of its reputation for that learning, when I say he is the first of his profession. It is a point settled by those who settle every thing else; and I must add (what I am enabled to say from my own long and close observation) that there is not a man, of any profession, or in any situation, of a more erect and independent spirit; of a more proud honor; a more manly mind; a more firm and determined integrity. Assure yourselves that the names of two such men will bear a great load of prejudice in the other scale, before they can be entirely outweighed.

With this mover and this seconder agreed the *whole* House of Commons; the *whole* House of Lords; the *whole* bench of Bishops; the King; the Ministry; the Opposition; all the distinguished clergy of the establishment; all the eminent lights (for they were consulted) of the dissenting churches. This according voice of national wisdom ought to be listened to with reverence. To say that all these descriptions of Englishmen unanimously concurred in a scheme for introducing the Catholic religion, or that none of them understood the nature and effects of what they were doing, so well as a few obscure clubs of people whose names you never heard of, is shamelessly absurd. Surely it is paying a miserable compliment to the religion we profess, to suggest that every thing eminent in the kingdom is indifferent, or even adverse to that religion, and that its security is wholly abandoned to the zeal of those who have nothing but their zeal to distinguish them. In weighing this unanimous concurrence of whatever the nation has to boast of, I hope you will recollect that all these concurring parties do by no means love one another enough to agree in any point which was not both evidently and importantly right.

3. To prove this—to prove that the measure was both clearly and materially proper, I will next lay before you (as I promised) the *political* grounds and reasons for the repeal of that penal statute, and the motives to its repeal at that particular time.

Reasons for the repeal.

(1.) Gentlemen, America—when the English nation seemed to be dangerously, if not irrecoverably divided; when one, and that the most growing branch, was torn from the parent stock, and ingrafted on the power of France, a great terror fell upon this kingdom. On a sudden we awakened from our dreams of conquest, and saw ourselves threatened with an immediate invasion; which we were, at that time, very ill prepared to resist. You remember the cloud that gloomed over us all. In that hour of our dismay, from the bottom of the hiding-places into which the indiscriminate rigor of our statutes had driven them, came out the Roman Catholics. They appeared before the steps of a tottering throne with one of the most sober, measured, steady, and dutiful addresses that was ever presented to the Crown.[19] It was no holiday ceremony; no anniversary compliment of parade and show. It was signed by almost every gentleman of that persuasion of note or property in England. At such a crisis, nothing but a decided resolution to stand or fall with their country could have dictated such an address; the direct tendency of which was to cut off all retreat, and to render them peculiarly obnoxious to an invader of their own communion. The address showed, what I long languished to see, that all the subjects of England had cast off all foreign views and connections, and that every man looked for his relief from every grievance at the hands only of his own natural government.

(1.) It was due to the generous loyalty of the Roman Catholics.

It was necessary, on our part, that the natural government should show itself worthy of that name. It was necessary, at the crisis I speak of, that the supreme power of the state should meet the conciliatory dispositions of the subject. To delay protection would be to reject allegiance. And why should it be rejected, or even coldly and suspiciously received? If any independent Catholic state should choose to take part with this kingdom in a war with France and Spain, that bigot (if such a bigot could be found) would be heard with little respect who could dream of objecting his religion to an ally, whom the nation would not only receive with its freest thanks, but purchase with the last remains of its exhausted treasure. To such an ally we should not dare

[19] This address may be found in Belsham's George III., vol. ii., p. 496. It is all that Mr. Burke represents it. Among other things it says, "In a time of public danger, when your Majesty's subjects can have but one interest, and ought to have but one wish and sentiment, we humbly hope it will not be deemed improper to assure your Majesty of our unreserved affection to your government, of our unalterable attachment to the cause and welfare of our common country, and our utter detestation of the designs and views of any foreign power against the dignity of your Majesty's Crown, the safety and tranquillity of your Majesty's subjects."

to whisper a single syllable of those base and invidious topics, upon which some unhappy men would persuade the state to reject the duty and allegiance of its own members. Is it, then, because foreigners are in a condition to set our malice at defiance, that with *them* we are willing to contract engagements of friendship, and to keep them with fidelity and honor; but that, because we conceive some descriptions of our countrymen are not powerful enough to punish our malignity, we will not permit them to support our common interest? Is it on that ground that our anger is to be kindled by their offered kindness? Is it on that ground that they are to be subjected to penalties, because they are willing by actual merit to purge themselves from imputed crimes? Lest by an adherence to the cause of their country they should acquire a title to fair and equitable treatment, are we resolved to furnish them with causes of eternal enmity, and rather supply them with just and founded motives to disaffection, than not to have that disaffection in existence to justify an oppression, which, not from policy but disposition, we have predetermined to exercise?

What shadow of reason could be assigned, why, at a time when the most Protestant part of this Protestant empire [America] found it for its advantage to unite with the two principal Popish states, to unite itself in the closest bonds with France and Spain for our destruction, that we should refuse to unite with our own Catholic countrymen for our own preservation? Ought we, like madmen, to tear off the plasters that the lenient hand of prudence had spread over the wounds and gashes, which, in our delirium of ambition, we had given to our own body? No person ever reprobated the American war more than I did, and do, and ever shall. But I never will consent that we should lay additional voluntary penalties on ourselves for a fault which carries but too much of its own punishment in its own nature. For one, I was delighted with the proposal of internal peace. I accepted the blessing with thankfulness and transport; I was truly happy to find *one* good effect of our civil distractions, that they had put an end to all religious strife and heart-burning in our own bowels. What must be the sentiments of a man, who would wish to perpetuate domestic hostility, when the causes of dispute are at an end; and who, crying out for peace with one part of the nation on the most humiliating terms, should deny it to those who offer friendship without any terms at all?

(2.) Due to the claims of humanity.

(2.) But if I was unable to reconcile such a denial to the contracted principles of local duty, what answer could I give to the broad claims of general humanity? I confess to you freely, that the sufferings and distresses of the people of America in this cruel war have at times affected me more deeply than I can express. I felt every gazette of triumph as a blow upon my heart, which has a hundred times sunk and fainted within me at all the mischiefs brought upon those who bear the whole brunt of war in the heart of their country. Yet the Americans are utter strangers to me; a nation among whom I am not sure that I have a single acquaintance. Was I to suffer my mind to be so unaccountably warped; was I to keep such iniquitous weights and measures of temper and of reason, as to sympathize with those who are in open rebellion against an authority which I respect, at war with a country which by every title ought to be, and is most dear to me; and yet to have no feeling at all for the hardships and indignities suffered by men, who, by their very vicinity, are bound up in a nearer relation to us; who contribute their share, and more than their share, to the common prosperity; who perform the common offices of social life, and who obey the laws to the full as well as I do? Gentlemen, the danger to the state being out of the question (of which, let me tell you, statesmen themselves are apt to have but too exquisite a sense), I could assign no one reason of justice, policy, or feeling, for not concurring most cordially, as most cordially I did concur, in softening some part of that shameful servitude, under which several of my worthy fellow-citizens were groaning.

(3.) Justified by its beneficial effects on the British Empire.

(3.) Important effects followed this act of wisdom. They appeared at home and abroad to the great benefit of this kingdom; and, let me hope, to the advantage of mankind at large. It betokened union among ourselves. It showed soundness even on the part of the persecuted, which generally is the weak side of every community. But its most essential operation was not in England. The act was immediately, though very imperfectly, copied in Ireland; and this imperfect transcript of an imperfect act, this first faint sketch of toleration, which did little more than disclose a principle, and mark out a disposition, completed in a most wonderful manner the re-union to the state of all the Catholics of that country. It made us, what we ought always to have been, one family, one body, one heart and soul, against the family combination, and all other combinations of our enemies. We have indeed obligations to that people, who received such small benefits with so much gratitude; and for which gratitude and attachment to us, I am afraid, they have suffered not a little in other places.[20]

(a.) Conciliating the people of Ireland.

I dare say you have all heard of the privileges indulged to the Irish Catholics residing in Spain. You have likewise heard with what circumstances of severity they have been lately expelled from the sea-ports of that kingdom, driven into the inland cities, and there detained as a sort of prisoners of state. I have good reason to believe that it was the zeal to our government and our cause (some-

[20] This remark Mr. Burke goes on to illustrate in the next paragraph, by referring to a recent persecution of Irish Catholics in Spain, and then argues that if they are persecuted abroad for their attachment to the English government, it is doubly cruel to persecute them at home as if enemies of the state. Unless this connection is noticed, the remarks which follow may seem a useless digression.

what indiscreetly expressed in one of the addresses of the Catholics of Ireland) which has thus drawn down on their heads the indignation of the Court of Madrid, to the inexpressible loss of several individuals, and, in future, perhaps, to the great detriment of the whole of their body. Now, that our people should be persecuted in Spain for their attachment to this country, and persecuted in this country for their supposed enmity to us, is such a jarring reconciliation of contradictory distresses, is a thing at once so dreadful and ridiculous, that no malice short of diabolical would wish to continue any human creatures in such a situation. But honest men will not forget either their merit or their sufferings. There are men (and many, I trust, there are) who, out of love to their country and their kind, would torture their invention to find excuses for the mistakes of their brethren, and who, to stifle dissension, would construe even doubtful appearances with the utmost favor. Such men will never persuade themselves to be ingenious and refined in discovering disaffection and treason in the manifest, palpable signs of suffering loyalty. Persecution is so unnatural to them, that they gladly snatch the very first opportunity of laying aside all the tricks and devices of penal politics, and of returning home, after all their irksome and vexatious wanderings, to our natural family mansion, to the grand social principle that unites all men, in all descriptions, under the shadow of an equal and impartial justice.

Men of another sort—I mean, the bigoted enemies to liberty—may perhaps, in their politics, make no account of the good or ill affection of the Catholics of England, who are but a handful of people (enough to torment, but not enough to fear), perhaps not so many, of both sexes and of all ages, as fifty thousand. But, gentlemen, it is possible you may not know that the people of that persuasion in Ireland amount at least to sixteen or seventeen hundred thousand souls. I do not at all exaggerate the number A *nation* to be persecuted! While we were masters of the sea, embodied with America, and in alliance with half the powers of the Continent, we might perhaps, in that remote corner of Europe, afford to tyrannize with impunity. But there is a revolution in our affairs which makes it prudent to be just. In our late awkward contest with Ireland about trade, had religion been thrown in, to ferment and imbitter the mass of discontents, the consequences might have been truly dreadful; but, very happily, that cause of quarrel was previously quieted by the wisdom of the acts I am commending.

(b.) Keeping valuable men in England.

Even in England, where I admit the danger from the discontent of that persuasion to be less than in Ireland; yet, even here, had we listened to the counsels of fanaticism and folly, we might have wounded ourselves very deeply, and wounded ourselves in a very tender part. You are apprised that the Catholics of England consist mostly of your best manufacturers. Had the Legislature chosen, instead of returning their declarations of duty with correspondent good will, to drive them to despair, there is a country at their very door to which they would be invited; a country in all respects as good as ours, and with the finest cities in the world ready built to receive them; and thus the bigotry of a free country, and in an enlightened age, would have repeopled the cities of Flanders, which, in the darkness of two hundred years ago, had been desolated by the superstition of a cruel tyrant. Our manufactures were the growth of the persecutions in the Low Countries. What a spectacle would it be to Europe to see us, at this time of day, balancing the account of tyranny with those very countries, and, by our persecutions, driving back trade and manufacture, as a sort of vagabonds, to their original settlement! But I trust we shall be saved this last of disgraces.

(4.) Justified by its beneficial example in foreign countries.

(4.) So far as to the effect of the act on the interests of this nation. With regard to the interests of mankind at large, I am sure the benefit was very considerable. Long before this act, indeed, the spirit of toleration began to gain ground in Europe. In Holland the third part of the people are Catholics; they live at ease, and are a sound part of the state. In many parts of Germany, Protestants and Papists partake the same cities, the same councils, and even the same churches. The unbounded liberality of the King of Prussia's conduct on this occasion is known to all the world, and it is of a piece with the other grand maxims of his reign. The magnanimity of the imperial court, breaking through the narrow principles of its predecessors, has indulged its Protestant subjects not only with property, with worship, with liberal education, but with honors and trusts, both civil and military. A worthy Protestant gentleman of this country now fills, and fills with credit, a high office in the Austrian Netherlands. Even the Lutheran obstinacy of Sweden has thawed at length, and opened a toleration to all religions. I know, myself, that in France the Protestants begin to be at rest. The army, which in that country is every thing, is open to them; and some of the military rewards and decorations which the laws deny, are supplied by others, to make the service acceptable and honorable. The first minister of finance in that country [Necker] is a Protestant. Two years' war without a tax is among the first fruits of their liberality. Tarnished as the glory of this nation is, and as far as it has waded into the shades of an eclipse, some beams of its former illumination still play upon its surface, and what is done in England is still looked to as argument, and as example. It is certainly true, that no law of this country ever met with such universal applause abroad, or was so likely to produce the perfection of that tolerating spirit, which, as I observed, has been long gaining ground in Europe; for abroad it was universally thought that we had done what, I am sorry to say, we had not; they thought we had granted a full toleration. That opinion was, however, so far from hurting the Protestant cause, that I declare, with the most serious solemnity, my firm belief, that no one thing done for these fifty years past was so likely to prove deeply beneficial to our religion at large as Sir George Savile's act. In its effects it was "an act for tolerating and protecting Protestantism throughout Europe;" and I hope that those who were taking steps for the quiet and settlement of our Protestant brethren in other countries will, even yet, rather consider the steady equity of the greater and better part of the people of Great Britain, than the vanity and violence of a few.

The question answered, Why was not the toleration made more complete?

I perceive, gentlemen, by the manner of all about me, that you look with horror on the wicked clamor which has been raised on this subject, and that, instead of an apology for what was done, you rather demand from me an account why the execution of the scheme of toleration was not made more answerable to the large and liberal grounds on which it was taken up. The question is natural and proper; and I remember that a great and learned magistrate [Lord Thurlow], distinguished for his strong and systematic understanding, and who at that time was a member of the House of Commons, made the same objection to the proceeding. The statutes, as they now stand, are, without doubt, perfectly absurd; but I beg leave to explain the cause of this gross imperfection in the tolerating plan as well and as shortly as I am able. It was universally thought that the session ought not to pass over without doing *something* in this business. To revise the whole body of the penal statutes was conceived to be an object too big for the time. The penal statute, therefore, which was chosen for repeal (chosen to show our disposition to conciliate, not to perfect a toleration) was this act of ludicrous cruelty, of which I have just given you the history. It is an act which, though not by a great deal so fierce and bloody as some of the rest, was infinitely more ready in the execution. It was the act which gave the greatest encouragement to those pests of society, mercenary informers, and interested disturbers of household peace; and it was observed, with truth, that the prosecutions, either carried to conviction or compounded, for many years, had been all commenced upon that act. It was said, that while we were deliberating on a more perfect scheme, the spirit of the age would never come up to the execution of the statutes which remained, especially as more steps, and a co-operation of more minds and powers, were required toward a mischievous use of them, than for the execution of the act to be repealed; that it was better to unravel this texture from below than from above, beginning with the latest, which, in general practice, is the severest evil. It was alleged that this slow proceeding would be attended with the advantage of a progressive experience, and that the people would grow reconciled to toleration, when they should find, by the effects, that justice was not so irreconcilable an enemy to convenience as they had imagined.

These, gentlemen, were the reasons why we left this good work in the rude, unfinished state in which good works are commonly left, through the tame circumspection with which a timid prudence so frequently enervates beneficence. In doing good, we are generally cold, and languid, and sluggish, and, of all things, afraid of being too much in the right. But the works of malice and injustice are quite in another style. They are finished with a bold, masterly hand; touched, as they are, with the spirit of those vehement passions that call forth all our energies whenever we oppress and persecute.

Thus this matter was left for the time, with the full determination in Parliament not to suffer other and worse statutes to remain, for the purpose of counteracting the benefits proposed by the repeal of one penal law; for nobody then dreamed of defending what was done as a benefit, on the ground of its being no benefit at all. We were not then ripe for so mean a subterfuge.

Farther action prevented by the No Popery riots.

I do not wish to go over the horrid scene that was afterward acted.[21] Would to God it could be expunged forever from the annals of this country! but, since it must subsist for our shame, let it subsist for our instruction. In the year 1780 there were found in this nation men deluded enough (for I give the whole to their delusion), on pretenses of zeal and piety, without any sort of provocation whatsoever, real or pretended, to make a desperate attempt, which would have consumed all the glory and power of this country in the flames of London, and buried all law, order, and religion, under the ruins of the metropolis of the Protestant world. Whether all this mischief done, or in the direct train of doing, was in their original scheme, I can not say. I hope it was not; but this would have been the unavoidable consequence of their proceedings, had not the flames they lighted up in their fury been extinguished in their blood.

All the time that this horrid scene was acting or avenging, as well as for some time before, and ever since, the wicked instigators of this unhappy multitude, guilty, with every aggravation, of all their crimes, and screened in a cowardly darkness from their punishment, continued, without interruption, pity, or remorse, to blow up the blind rage of the populace with a continued blast of pestilential libels, which infected and poisoned the very air we breathed in.

Reasons for not re-enacting these persecuting laws, as demanded by the rioters.

The main drift of all the libels and all the riots was, to force Parliament (to persuade us was hopeless) into an act of national perfidy which has no example; for, gentlemen, it is

[21] The powerful descriptions of Dickens in his Barnaby Rudge have made the public familiar with the terrible scenes enacted in London during the "No Popery" riots of 1780. Those who first framed the Protestant Association were actuated, no doubt, by a mistaken zeal for religion, but those who took up the cause afterward had far other designs. Dr. Johnson truly said: "Those who in age of infidelity exclaim, "Popery! Popery! would have cried *fire* in the midst of the general deluge."

proper you should all know what infamy we escaped by refusing that repeal, for a refusal of which, it seems, I, among others, stand somewhere or other accused. When we took away, on the motives which I had the honor of stating to you, a few of the innumerable penalties upon an oppressed and injured people, the relief was not absolute, but given on a stipulation and compact between them and us; for we bound down the Roman Catholics with the most solemn oaths to bear true allegiance to this government; to abjure all sort of temporal power in any other; and to renounce, under the same solemn obligations, the doctrines of systematic perfidy with which they stood (I conceive very unjustly) charged. Now our modest petitioners came up to us, most humbly praying nothing more than that we should break our faith, without any one cause whatsoever of forfeiture assigned; and when the subjects of this kingdom had on their part fully performed their engagement, we should refuse on our part the benefit we had stipulated on the performance of those very conditions that were prescribed by our own authority, and taken on the sanction of our public faith, that is to say, when we had inveigled them with fair promises within our door, we were to shut it on them, and, adding mockery to outrage, to tell them "Now we have got you fast; your consciences are bound to a power resolved on your destruction. We have made you swear that your religion obliges you to keep your faith. Fools, as you are! we will now let you see that our religion enjoins us to keep no faith with you." They who would advisedly call upon us to do such things must certainly have thought us not only a convention of treacherous tyrants, but a gang of the lowest and dirtiest wretches that ever disgraced humanity. Had we done this, we should have indeed proved that there were *some* in the world whom no faith could bind; and we should have *convicted* ourselves of that odious principle of which Papists stood *accused* by those very savages, who wished us, on that accusation, to deliver them over to their fury.

In this audacious tumult, when our very name and character, as gentlemen, was to be canceled forever, along with the faith and honor of the nation, I, who had exerted myself very little on the quiet passing of the bill, thought it necessary then to come forward. I was not alone; but though some distinguished members on all sides, and particularly on ours, added much to their high reputation by the part they took on that day (a part which will be remembered as long as honor, spirit, and eloquence have estimation in the world), I may and will value myself so far, that, yielding in abilities to many, I yielded in zeal to none. With warmth and with vigor, and animated with a just and natural indignation, I called forth every faculty that I possessed, and I directed it in every way which I could possibly employ it. I labored night and day. I labored in Parliament. I labored out of Parliament. If, therefore, the resolution of the House of Commons, refusing to commit this act of unmatched turpitude, be a crime, I am guilty among the foremost; but indeed, whatever the faults of that House may have been, no one member was found hardy enough to propose so infamous a thing; and, on full debate, we passed the resolution against the petitions with as much unanimity as we had formerly passed the law of which these petitions demanded the repeal.

Exemplary deportment of the Roman Catholics during the riots.

There was a circumstance (justice will not suffer me to pass it over) which, if any thing could enforce the reasons I have given, would fully justify the act of relief, and render a repeal, or any thing like a repeal, unnatural, impossible. It was the behavior of the persecuted Roman Catholics under the acts of violence and brutal insolence which they suffered. I suppose there are not in London less than four or five thousand of that persuasion from my country, who do a great deal of the most laborious works in the metropolis, and they chiefly inhabit those quarters which were the principal theater of the fury of the bigoted multitude. They are known to be men of strong arms and quick feelings, and more remarkable for a determined resolution than clear ideas or much foresight; but though provoked by every thing that can stir the blood of men, their houses and chapels in flames, and with the most atrocious profanations of every thing which they hold sacred before their eyes, not a hand was moved to retaliate, or even to defend. Had a conflict once begun, the rage of their persecutors would have redoubled. Thus, fury increasing by the reverberation of outrages, house being fired for house, and church for chapel, I am convinced that no power under heaven could have prevented a general conflagration, and at this day London would have been a tale; but I am well informed, and the thing speaks it, that their clergy exerted their whole influence to keep their people in such a state of forbearance and quiet, as, when I look back, fills me with astonishment; but not with astonishment only. Their merits on that occasion ought not to be forgotten; nor will they, when Englishmen come to recollect themselves. I am sure it were far more proper to have called them forth and given them the thanks of both houses of Parliament, than to have suffered those worthy clergymen and excellent citizens to be hunted into holes and corners, while we are making low-minded inquisitions into the number of their people; as if a tolerating principle was never to prevail, unless we were very sure that only a few could possibly take advantage of it. But indeed we are not yet well recovered of our fright. Our reason, I trust, will return with our security, and this unfortunate temper will pass over like a cloud.[22]

Objections to the repeal examined.

Gentlemen, I have now laid before you a few of the reasons for taking away the penalties of the act of 1699, and for refusing to establish them on the riotous requisition of 1780. Because I would not suf-

[22] Παρελθεῖν ὥσπερ νεφός.—Demosthenes, de Coronâ.

fer any thing which may be for your satisfaction to escape, permit me just to touch on the objections urged against our act and our resolves, and intended as a justification of the violence offered to both houses. "Parliament," they assert, "was too hasty, and they ought, in so essential and alarming a change, to have proceeded with a far greater degree of deliberation." The direct contrary. Parliament was too slow. They took fourscore years to deliberate on the repeal of an act which ought not to have survived a second session. When at length, after a procrastination of near a century, the business was taken up, it proceeded in the most public manner, by the ordinary stages, and as slowly as a law, so evidently right as to be resisted by none, would naturally advance. Had it been read three times in one day, we should have shown only a becoming readiness to recognize by protection the undoubted dutiful behavior of those whom we had but too long punished for offenses of presumption or conjecture. But for what end was that bill to linger beyond the usual period of an unopposed measure? Was it to be delayed until a rabble in Edinburgh should dictate to the Church of England what measure of persecution was fitting for her safety?[23] Was it to be adjourned until a fanatical force could be collected in London, sufficient to frighten us out of all our ideas of policy and justice? Were we to wait for the profound lectures on the reason of state, ecclesiastical and political, which the Protestant Association have since condescended to read to us? Or were we, seven hundred peers and commoners, the only persons ignorant of the ribald invectives which occupy the place of argument in those remonstrances, which every man of common observation had heard a thousand times over, and a thousand times over had despised? All men had before heard what they have to say; and all men at this day know what they dare to do; and I trust, all honest men are equally influenced by the one and by the other.

(a) That Parliament acted in haste.

But they tell us, that those our fellow-citizens, whose chains we have a little relaxed, are enemies to liberty and our free constitution—not enemies, I presume, to their *own* liberty; and as to the constitution, until we give them some share in it, I do not know on what pretense we can examine into their opinions about a business in which they have no interest or concern. But after all, are we equally sure that they are adverse to our constitution, as that our statutes are hostile and destructive to them? For my part, I have reason to believe their opinions and inclinations in that respect are various, exactly like those of other men; and if they lean more to the Crown than I, and than many of you think *we* ought, we must remember that he who aims at another's life is not to be surprised if he flies into any sanctuary that will receive him. The tenderness of the executive power is the natural asylum of those upon whom the laws have declared war; and to complain that men are inclined to favor the means of their own safety, is so absurd that one forgets the injustice in the ridicule.

(b) That the Roman Catholics were hostile to the government, and *ought* to be held down.

I must fairly tell you, that, so far as my principles are concerned (principles that I hope will only depart with my last breath), I have no idea of a liberty unconnected with honesty and justice. Nor do I believe that any good constitutions of government or of freedom, can find it necessary for their security to doom any part of the people to a permanent slavery. Such a constitution of freedom, if such can be, is in effect no more than another name for the tyranny of the strongest faction; and factions in republics have been, and are, full as capable as monarchs, of the most cruel oppression and injustice. It is but too true that the love, and even the very idea, of genuine liberty is extremely rare. It is but too true that there are many whose whole scheme of freedom is made up of pride, perverseness, and insolence. They feel themselves in a state of thraldom; they imagine that their souls are cooped and cabined in, unless they have some man, or some body of men, dependent on their mercy. This desire of having some one below them descends to those who are the very lowest of all—and a Protestant cobbler, debased by his poverty, but exalted by his share of the ruling Church, feels a pride in knowing it is by his generosity alone that the peer, whose footman's instep he measures, is able to keep his chaplain from a jail. This disposition is the true source of the passion which many men in very humble life have taken to the American war. *Our* subjects in America! *our* colonies! *our* dependants! This lust of party power is the liberty they hunger and thirst for, and this siren song of ambition has charmed ears that one would have thought were never organized to that sort of music.[24]

Pernicious disposition of men to lord it over others.

This way of *proscribing the citizens by denominations and general descriptions*, dignified by the name of reason of state, and security for constitutions and commonwealths, is nothing better at bottom than the miserable invention of an ungenerous ambition, which would fain hold the sacred trust of power without any of the virtues, or any of the energies, that give a title to it; a receipt of policy made up of a detestable compound of malice, cowardice, and sloth. They would govern men against their will; but in that government they would be discharged from the exercise of vigilance, providence, and fortitude; and therefore, that they may sleep on their watch, they consent to take some one division of the society

Proscription of men by *classes* cruelly unjust.

[23] The Protestant Association originated at Edinburgh.

[24] No man ever touched with such force that proud and cruel spirit which actuates a people who hold others in subjection. It was just the spirit of the Athenian mob toward their colonies, and of every Roman toward the provinces of the empire; and it was no doubt one principal cause of the American war.

into partnership of the tyranny over the rest. But let government, in what form it may be, comprehend the whole in its justice, and restrain the suspicious by its vigilance; let it keep watch and ward; let it discover by its sagacity, and punish by its firmness, all delinquency against its power, whenever delinquency exists in the overt acts; and then it will be as safe as ever God and nature intended it should be. Crimes are the acts of individuals, and not of denominations; and, therefore, arbitrarily to class men under general descriptions, in order to proscribe and punish them in the lump for a presumed delinquency, of which perhaps but a part, perhaps none at all, are guilty, is indeed a compendious method, and saves a world of trouble about proof; but such a method, instead of being law, is an act of unnatural rebellion against the legal dominion of reason and justice; and this vice, in any constitution that entertains it, at one time or other will certainly bring on its ruin.

We are told that this is not a religious persecution, and its abettors are loud in disclaiming all severities on account of conscience. Very fine, indeed! Then let it be so. They are not persecutors; they are only tyrants. With all my heart. I am perfectly indifferent concerning the pretexts upon which we torment one another; or whether it be for the constitution of the Church of England, or for the constitution of the state of England, that people choose to make their fellow-creatures wretched. When we were sent into a place of authority, you that sent us had yourselves but one commission to give. You could give us none to wrong or oppress, or even to suffer any kind of oppression or wrong, on any grounds whatsoever: not on political, as in the affairs of America: not on commercial, as in those of Ireland; not in civil, as in the laws for debt; not in religious, as in the statutes against Protestant or Catholic dissenters. The diversified but connected fabric of universal justice is well cramped and bolted together in all its parts; and, depend upon it, I never have employed, and I never shall employ, any engine of power which may come into my hands to wrench it asunder. All shall stand if I can help it, and all shall stand connected. After all, to complete this work, much remains to be done; much in the east, much in the west. But great as the work is, if our will be ready, our powers are not deficient.

(c.) That the consequence of the repeal had been unfortunate.

Since you have suffered me to trouble you so much on this subject, permit me, gentlemen, to detain you a little longer. I am, indeed, most solicitous to give you perfect satisfaction. I find there are some of a better and softer nature than the persons with whom I have supposed myself in debate, who neither think ill of the act of relief, nor by any means desire the repeal; not accusing but lamenting what was done, on account of the consequences, have frequently expressed their wish that the late Act had never been made. Some of this description, and persons of worth, I have met with in this city. They conceive that the prejudices, whatever they might be, of a large part of the people, ought not to have been shocked; that their opinions ought to have been previously taken, and much attended to; and that thereby the late horrid scenes might have been prevented.

I confess my notions are widely different; and I never was less sorry for any action of my life. I like the bill the better on account of the events of all kinds that followed it. It relieved the real sufferers; it strengthened the state; and by the disorders that ensued, we had clear evidence that there lurked a temper somewhere, which ought not to be fostered by the laws. No ill consequences whatever could be attributed to the Act itself. We knew beforehand, or we were poorly instructed, that toleration is odious to the intolerant; freedom to oppressors; property to robbers; and all kinds and degrees of prosperity to the envious. We knew that all these kinds of men would gladly gratify their evil dispositions under the sanction of law and religion, if they could; if they could not, yet, to make way to their objects, they would do their utmost to subvert all religion and all law. This we certainly knew; but knowing this, is there any reason because thieves break in and steal, and thus bring detriment to you and draw ruin on themselves, that I am to be sorry that you are in possession of shops, and of warehouses, and of wholesome laws to protect them? Are you to build no houses because desperate men may pull them down upon their own heads? Or, if a malignant wretch will cut his own throat because he sees you give alms to the necessitous and deserving, shall his destruction be attributed to your charity, and not to his own deplorable madness? If we repent of our good actions, what, I pray you, is left for our faults and follies? It is not the beneficence of the laws, it is the unnatural temper which beneficence can fret and sour, that is to be lamented. It is this temper which, by all rational means, ought to be sweetened and corrected. If froward men should refuse this cure, can they vitiate any thing but themselves? Does evil so react upon good, as not only to retard its motion, but to change its nature? If it can so operate, then good men will always be in the power of the bad; and virtue, by a dreadful reverse of order, must lie under perpetual subjection and bondage to vice.

As to the opinion of the people, which some think, in such cases, is to be implicitly obeyed; near two years' tranquillity, which followed the Act, and its instant imitation in Ireland, proved abundantly that the late horrible spirit was, in a great measure, the effect of insidious art, and perverse industry, and gross misrepresentation. But suppose that the dislike had been much more deliberate, and much more general than I am persuaded it was. When we know that the opinions of even the greatest multitudes are the standard of rectitude, I shall think myself obliged to make those opinions the masters of my conscience. But if it may be doubted whether omnipotence itself is competent to alter the essential constitution of right and wrong, sure I am that such *things* as they and I are possessed of no such power. No man carries farther than I do the policy of making government pleasing to the people; but the widest range of this politic complaisance is confined within the limits of justice. I would not only consult the interests of the people, but I would cheerfully gratify their humors. We are all a sort of children that must be soothed and managed. I think I am not austere or formal in my nature. I would bear—I would even myself play my part in any innocent buffooneries to divert them; but I never will act the tyrant for their amusement. If they will mix malice in their sports, I shall never consent to throw them any living, sentient creature whatsoever: no, not so much as a kitling, to torment.

If such views must exclude the speaker from Parliament, he is willing to remain out.

"But if I profess all this impolitic stubbornness, I may chance never to be elected into Parliament." It is certainly not pleasing to be put out of the public service. But I wish to be a member of Parliament, to have my share of doing good, and resisting evil. It would therefore be absurd to renounce my objects in order to obtain my seat. I deceive myself, indeed, most grossly, if I had not much rather pass the remainder of my life hidden in the recesses of the deepest obscurity, feeding my mind even with the visions and imaginations of such things, than to be placed on the most splendid throne of the universe, tantalized with the denial of the practice of all which can make the greatest situation any other than the greatest curse. Gentlemen, I have had my day. I can never sufficiently express my gratitude to you for having set me in a place wherein I could lend the slightest help to great and laudable designs. If I have had my share in any measure giving quiet to private property, and private conscience; if, by my vote, I have aided in securing to families the best possession, peace; if I have joined in reconciling kings to their subjects, and subjects to their prince; if I have assisted to loosen the foreign holdings of the citizen, and taught him to look for his protection to the laws of his country, and for his comfort to the good-will of his countrymen; if I have thus taken my part with the best of men in the best of their actions, I can shut the book. I might wish to read a page or two more; but this is enough for my measure. I have not lived in vain.

And now, gentlemen, on this serious day, when I come, as it were, to make up my account with you, let me take to myself some degree of honest pride on the nature of the charges that are against me. I do not here stand before you accused of venality, or of neglect of duty. It is not said that, in the long period of my service, I have, in a single instance, sacrificed the slightest of your interests to my ambition, or to my fortune. It is not alleged that, to gratify any anger, or revenge of my own, or of my party, I have had a share in wronging or oppressing any description of men, or any one man in any description. No! The charges against me are all of one kind, that I have pushed the principles of general justice and benevolence too far; farther than a cautious policy would warrant, and farther than the opinions of many would go along with me. In every accident which may happen through life—in pain, in sorrow, in depression, and distress—I will call to mind this accusation, and be comforted.

Gentlemen, I submit the whole to your judgment. Mr. Mayor, I thank you for the trouble you have taken on this occasion. In your state of health, it is particularly obliging. If this company should think it advisable for me to withdraw, I shall respectfully retire. If you think otherwise, I shall go directly to the council-house and to the 'change, and, without a moment's delay, begin my canvass.

At the close of this speech Mr. Burke was encouraged by his friends to proceed with the canvass; but it was soon apparent that the opposition he had to encounter could not be conciliated or resisted. He therefore, on the second day of the election, declined the poll in the speech which follows:

SPEECH

OF MR. BURKE ON DECLINING THE ELECTION AT BRISTOL, DELIVERED SEPTEMBER 9, 1780.

Gentlemen,—I decline the election. It has ever been my rule through life to observe a proportion between my efforts and my objects. I have never been remarkable for a bold, active, and sanguine pursuit of advantages that are personal to myself.

I have not canvassed the whole of this city in form; but I have taken such a view of it as satisfies my own mind that your choice will not ultimately fall upon me. Your city, gentlemen, is in a state of miserable distraction; and I am resolved to withdraw whatever share my pretensions may have had in its unhappy divisions. I have not been in haste. I have tried all prudent means. I have waited for the effect of all contingencies. If I were fond of a contest, by the partiality of my numerous friends (whom you know to be among the most weighty and respectable people of the city) I have the means of a sharp one in my hands; but I thought it far better, with my strength unspent, and my reputation unimpaired, to do early and from foresight that which I might be obliged to do from necessity at last.

I am not in the least surprised, nor in the least angry at this view of things. I have read the book of life for a long time, and I have read other books a little. Nothing has happened to me but what has happened to men much better than me, and in times and in nations full as good as the age and country that we live in. To say that I am no way concerned would be neither decent nor true. The representation of *Bristol* was an object on many accounts dear to me, and

I certainly should very far prefer it to any other in the kingdom. My habits are made to it; and it is in general more unpleasant to be rejected after a long trial than not to be chosen at all.

But, gentlemen, I will see nothing except your former kindness, and I will give way to no other sentiments than those of gratitude. From the bottom of my heart I thank you for what you have done for me. You have given me a long term, which is now expired. I have performed the conditions, and enjoyed all the profits to the full; and I now surrender your estate into your hands without being in a single tile or a single stone impaired or wasted by my use. I have served the public for fifteen years. I have served you, in particular, for six. What is past is well stored. It is safe, and out of the power of fortune. What is to come is in wiser hands than ours, and He in whose hands it is, best knows whether it is best for you and me that I should be in Parliament, or even in the world.

Gentlemen, the melancholy event of yesterday reads to us an awful lesson against being too much troubled about any of the objects of ordinary ambition. The worthy gentleman who has been snatched from us at the moment of the election, and in the middle of the contest, while his desires were as warm and his hopes as eager as ours, has feelingly told us what shadows we are, and what shadows we pursue.[1]

It has been usual for a candidate who declines, to take his leave by a letter to the sheriffs; but I received your trust in the face of day, and in the face of day I accept your dismission. I am not—I am not at all ashamed to look upon you, nor can my presence discompose the order of business here. I humbly and respectfully take my leave of the sheriffs, the candidates, and the electors, wishing heartily that the choice may be for the best at a time which calls, if ever time did call, for service that is not nominal. It is no plaything you are about. I tremble when I consider the trust I have presumed to ask. I confided perhaps too much in my intentions. They were really fair and upright; and I am bold to say that I ask no ill thing for you when, on parting from this place, I pray that whomever you choose to succeed me, he may resemble me exactly in all things except in my abilities to serve and my fortune to please you.

SPEECH

OF MR. BURKE ON THE EAST INDIA BILL OF MR. FOX, DELIVERED IN THE HOUSE OF COMMONS, DECEMBER 1, 1783.

INTRODUCTION.

So enormous were the abuses of the British power in India, that men of all parties demanded strong measures to secure an effectual remedy. Those embraced in the East India bill of Mr. Fox, as matured between him and Mr. Burke, were certainly of this character. All the concerns of the Company were taken into the hands of the English government. Seven commissioners, to be appointed for four years by Parliament, were intrusted with the civil and military government of the country; while the commercial concerns of the Company were committed to the hands of nine assistant directors, to be chosen out of the proprietors of East India stock. A second bill provided for the correction of numerous abuses in the administration of Indian affairs.

The first bill was brought into the House of Commons by Mr. Fox, on the 18th of November, 1783, and was strenuously opposed at every stage of its progress. The principal objections were, that it set aside the charter of the East India Company, threw too much patronage into the hands of the ministry, and might operate injuriously to the national credit. Mr. Fox's coalition with Lord North, which had brought the ministry into power, was also a subject of the severest animadversion. When the question came up, on the 1st of December, for going into a committee on the bill, Mr. Powys, a former friend and adherent of Mr. Fox, opposed it with all his strength. He had great authority in the House, as a country gentleman representing an extensive county, and sustained by a reputation for strong sense and unimpeachable integrity. He denounced the measure in the strongest terms, as a violation of chartered rights, and as designed to make Mr. Fox minister for life, by giving him an amount of patronage which would render it impossible for the King to remove him.

Mr. Wraxall, who was then a member of the House, and who was equally opposed with Mr. Powys to the passing of the bill, observes, in his Historical Memoirs, vol. iv., p. 566, "Burke, unable longer to observe silence after such reflections, then rose; and, in a dissertation rather than a speech, which lasted more than three hours, exhausted all the powers of his mighty mind in the justification of his friend's measure. The most ignorant member of the House, who had attended to the mass of information, historical, political, and financial, which fell from the lips of Burke on that occasion, must have departed rich in knowledge of Hindostan. It seemed impossible to crowd a greater variety of matter applicable to the subject into a smaller compass; and those who differed most widely from him in opinion did not render the less justice to his gigantic range of ideas, his lucid exposition of events, and the harmonic flow of his

---

[1] Mr. Burke here refers to Mr. Coombe, one of his competitors, who, overcome by the excitement and exhaustion of the contest, had died suddenly the evening before.

periods. There were portions of his harangue in which he appeared to be animated by feelings and considerations the most benign, as well as elevated; and the classic language in which he made Fox's panegyric, for having dared to venture on a measure so beset with dangers, but so pregnant, as he asserted, with benefits to mankind, could not be exceeded in beauty."

In giving this speech, those parts are omitted which contain minute details of the abuses of power on the part of the Company's servants in India. Though essential to the argument as originally stated, they would only be tedious at the present day, and, indeed, can hardly be understood without an intimate acquaintance with the concerns of the East India Company.

SPEECH, &c.

Mr. Speaker,—I thank you for pointing to me; I really wished much to engage your attention in an early stage of the debate. I have been long very deeply, though perhaps ineffectually, engaged in the preliminary inquiries which have continued without intermission for some years. Though I have felt, with some degree of sensibility, the natural and inevitable impressions of the several matters of fact, as they have been successively disclosed, I have not at any time attempted to trouble you on the merits of the subject, and very little on any of the points which incidentally arose in the course of our proceedings. But I should be sorry to be found totally silent upon this day. Our inquiries are now come to their final issue. It is now to be determined whether the three years of laborious parliamentary research,[1] whether the twenty years of patient Indian suffering, are to produce a substantial reform in our Eastern administration; or, whether our knowledge of the grievances has abated our zeal for the correction of them, and our very inquiry into the evil was only a pretext to elude the remedy which is demanded from us by humanity, by justice, and by every principle of true policy. Depend upon it, this business can not be indifferent to our fame. It will turn out a matter of great disgrace or great glory to the whole British nation. We are on a conspicuous stage, and the world marks our demeanor.

Mode in which the bill was opposed.

I am therefore a little concerned to perceive the spirit and temper in which the debate has been all along pursued upon one side of the House. The declamation of the gentlemen who oppose the bill has been abundant and vehement; but they have been reserved, and even silent about the fitness or unfitness of the plan to attain the direct object it has in view. By some gentlemen it is taken up (by way of exercise, I presume) as a point of law on a question of private property and corporate franchise; by others it is regarded as the petty intrigue of a faction at court, and argued merely as it tends to set this man a little higher, or that a little lower in situation and power. All the void has been filled up with invectives against coalition; with allusions to the loss of America; with the activity and inactivity of ministers. The total silence of these gentlemen concerning the interest and well-being of the people of India, and concerning the interest which this nation has in the commerce and revenues of that country, is a strong indication of the value which they set upon these objects.

It has been a little painful to me to observe the intrusion into this important debate of such company as *quo warranto*, and *mandamus*, and *certiorari;* as if we were on a trial about mayors and aldermen, and capital burgesses; or engaged in a suit concerning the borough of Penryn, or Saltash, or St. Ives, or St. Mawes. Gentlemen have argued with as much heat and passion, as if the first things in the world were at stake; and their topics are such as belong only to matter of the lowest and meanest litigation. It is not right, it is not worthy of us, in this manner to depreciate the value, to degrade the majesty of this grave deliberation of policy and empire.

For my part, I have thought myself bound, when a matter of this extraordinary weight came before me, not to consider (as some gentlemen are so fond of doing) whether the bill originated from a Secretary of State for the Home Department, or from a secretary for the foreign; from a minister of influence or a minister of the people; from Jacob or from Esau.[2] I asked myself, and I asked myself nothing else, what part it was fit for a member of Parliament, who has supplied a mediocrity of talents by the extreme of diligence, and who has thought himself obliged, by the research of years, to wind himself into the inmost recesses and labyrinths of the Indian detail, what part, I say, it became such a member of Parliament to take, when a minister of state, in conformity to a recommendation from the Throne, has brought before us a system for the better government of the territory and commerce of the East. In this light, and in this only, I will trouble you with my sentiments.

Measure called for.

It is not only agreed but demanded, by the right honorable gentleman [Mr. Pitt], and by those who act with him, that a whole system ought to be produced; that it ought not to be a *half measure;* that it ought to be no *palliative;* but a legislative provision, vigorous, substantial, and effective. I believe that no man who understands the subject can doubt for a moment that those must be the conditions of any thing deserving the name of a reform in the Indian government; that any thing short of them would not only be delusive, but, in this matter, which admits no medium, noxious in the extreme.

[1] Mr. Burke had taken a very active part in these researches as a member of a committee of the House.

[2] Mr. Powys, who retained a lingering affection for Mr. Fox, had ascribed the bill to the influence of Lord North, saying, "the voice is Jacob's, but the hands are the hands of Esau."

To all the conditions proposed by his adversaries the mover of the bill perfectly agrees; and on his performance of them he rests his cause. On the other hand, not the least objection has been taken with regard to the efficiency, the vigor, or the completeness of the scheme. I am, therefore, warranted to assume, as a thing admitted, that the bills accomplish what both sides of the House demand as essential. The end is completely answered, so far as the direct and immediate object is concerned.

But though there are no direct, yet there are various collateral objections made; objections from the effects which this plan of reform for Indian administration may have on the privileges of great public bodies in England; from its probable influence on the constitutional rights, or on the freedom and integrity of the several branches of the Legislature.

Answer to objections.

Before I answer these objections, I must beg leave to observe, that if we are not able to contrive some method of governing India *well*, which will not of necessity become the means of governing Great Britain *ill*, a ground is laid for their eternal separation; but none for sacrificing the people of that country to our constitution. I am, however, far from being persuaded that any such incompatibility of interest does at all exist. On the contrary, I am certain that every means effectual to preserve India from oppression is a guard to preserve the British Constitution from its worst corruption. To show this, I will consider the objections, which I think are four:

1st. That the bill is an attack on the chartered rights of men.

2dly. That it increases the influence of the Crown.

3dly. That it does *not* increase, but diminishes the influence of the Crown, in order to promote the interests of certain ministers and their party.

4thly. That it deeply affects the national credit.

Violation of the Company's Charter.

I. As to the first of these objections, I must observe that the phrase of "the chartered rights *of men*" is full of affectation, and very unusual in the discussion of privileges conferred by charters of the present description. But it is not difficult to discover what end that ambiguous mode of expression, so often reiterated, is meant to answer.

The rights of *men*, that is to say, the natural rights of mankind, are indeed sacred things; and if any public measure is proved mischievously to affect them, the objection ought to be fatal to that measure, even if no charter at all could be set up against it. If these natural rights are farther affirmed and declared by express covenants, if they are clearly defined and secured against chicane, against power, and authority, by written instruments and positive engagements, they are in a still better condition; they partake not only of the sanctity of the object so secured, but of that solemn public faith itself, which secures an object of such importance. Indeed, this formal recognition, by the sovereign power, of an original right in the subject, can never be subverted but by rooting up the holding radical principles of government, and even of society itself. The charters which we call, by distinction, "great," are public instruments of this nature; I mean the charters of King John and King Henry the Third. The things secured by these instruments may, without any deceitful ambiguity, be very fitly called the *chartered rights of men*.[3]

These charters have made the very name of a charter dear to the heart of every Englishman. But, sir, there may be, and there are charters, not only different in nature, but formed on principles the very reverse of those of the great charter. Of this kind is the charter of the East India Company. Magna Charta is a charter to restrain power, and to destroy monopoly. The East India charter is a charter to establish monopoly, and to create power. Political power and commercial monopoly are *not* the rights of men; and the rights to them derived from charters, it is fallacious and sophistical to call "the chartered rights of men." These chartered rights (to speak of such charters and of their effects in terms of the greatest possible moderation) do at least *suspend* the natural rights of mankind at large, and in their very frame and constitution are liable to fall into a direct violation of them.

It is a charter of this latter description (that is to say, a charter of power and monopoly) which is affected by the bill before you. The bill, sir, does, without question, affect it; it does affect it essentially and substantially; but, having stated to you of what description the chartered rights are which this bill touches, I feel no difficulty at all in acknowledging the existence of those chartered rights in their fullest extent. They belong to the Company in the surest manner, and they are secured to that body by every sort of public sanction. They are stamped by the faith of the King; they are stamped by the faith of Parliament; they have been bought for money, for money honestly and fairly paid; they have been bought for valuable consideration, over and over again.

I therefore freely admit to the East India Company their claim to exclude their fellow-subjects from the commerce of half the globe. I admit their claim to administer an annual territorial revenue of seven millions sterling, to command an army of sixty thousand men, and to dispose (under the control of a sovereign imperial discretion, and with the due observance of the natural and local law) of the lives and fortunes of thirty millions of their fellow-creatures. All this they possess by charter and by acts of Parliament (in my opinion) without a shadow of controversy.

Those who carry the rights and claims of the Company the farthest do not contend for more than this, and all this I freely grant; but, grant-

[3] This opening of the subject with a distinction thus clearly drawn and illustrated, is highly characteristic of Mr. Burke, and lays the foundation of his entire argument.

ing all this, they must grant to me in my turn that all political power which is set over men, and that all privilege claimed or exercised in exclusion of them, being wholly artificial, and for so much a derogation from the natural equality of mankind at large, ought to be some way or other exercised ultimately for their benefit. If this is true with regard to every species of political dominion and every description of commercial privilege, none of which can be original, self-derived rights, or grants for the mere private benefit of the holders, then such rights, or privileges, or whatever else you choose to call them, are all in the strictest sense a *trust;* and it is of the very essence of every trust to be rendered accountable, and even totally to cease, when it substantially varies from the purposes for which alone it could have a lawful existence.

That charter is a *trust* for the benefit of the public.

This I conceive, sir, to be true of trusts of power vested in the highest hands, and of such as seem to hold of no human creature;[4] but about the application of this principle to subordinate *derivative* trusts, I do not see how a controversy can be maintained. To whom, then, would I make the East India Company accountable? why, to Parliament, to be sure; to Parliament, from whom their trust was derived; to Parliament, which alone is capable of comprehending the magnitude of its object and its abuse, and alone capable of an effectual legislative remedy. The very charter which is held out to exclude Parliament from correcting malversation with regard to the high trust vested in the Company is the very thing which at once *gives a title* and *imposes a duty* on us to interfere with effect wherever power and authority originating from ourselves are perverted from their purposes, and become instruments of wrong and violence.

If Parliament, sir, had nothing to do with this charter, we might have some sort of Epicurean excuse to stand aloof, indifferent spectators of what passes in the Company's name in India and in London; but if we are the very cause of the evil, we are in a special manner engaged to the redress; and for us passively to bear with oppressions committed under the sanction of our own authority is, in truth and reason, for this House to be an active accomplice in the abuse.

That the power notoriously, grossly abused has been bought from us, is very certain; but this circumstance, which is urged against the bill, becomes an additional motive for our interference, lest we should be thought to have sold the blood of millions of men for the base consideration of money. We sold, I admit, all that we had to sell, that is our authority, not our control. *We had not a right to make a market of our duties.*

I ground myself, therefore, on this principle, that if the abuse is proved, the contract is broken, and we re-enter into all our rights, that is, into the exercise of all our duties. Our own authority is indeed as much a trust originally as the Company's authority is a trust derivatively; and it is the use we make of the resumed power that must justify or condemn us in the resumption of it. When we have perfected the plan laid before us by the right honorable mover, the world will then see what it is we destroy, and what it is we create. By that test we stand or fall, and by that test I trust that it will be found in the issue, that we are going to supersede a charter abused to the full extent of all the powers which it could abuse, and exercised in the plenitude of despotism, tyranny, and corruption; and that, in one and the same plan, we provide a real chartered security for the *rights of men* cruelly violated under that charter.

Is liable to be revoked if the trust be abused.

This bill, and those connected with it, are intended to form the *Magna Charta* of Hindostan.[5] Whatever the treaty of Westphalia is to the liberty of the princes and free cities of the empire, and to the three religions there professed; whatever the great charter, the statute of tallage, the petition of right, and the declaration of right, are to Great Britain, these bills are to the people of India. Of this benefit, I am certain, their condition is capable, and when I know that they are capable of more, my vote shall most assuredly be for our giving to the full extent of their capacity of receiving, and no charter of dominion shall stand as a bar in my way to their charter of safety and protection.

The strong admission I have made of the Company's rights (I am conscious of it) binds me to do a great deal. I do not presume to condemn those who argue *à priori* against the propriety of leaving such extensive political powers in the hands of a company of merchants. I know much is, and much more may be said against such a system; but with my particular ideas and sentiments, I can not go that way to work.[6] I feel an insuperable reluctance in giving my hand to destroy any established institution of government upon a theory, however plausible it may be. My experience in life teaches me nothing clear upon the subject. I have known merchants with the sentiments and the abilities of great statesmen, and I have seen persons in the rank of statesmen, with the conception and character of peddlers. Indeed, my observation has furnished me with nothing that is to be found in any habits of life or education,

4 Mr. Burke here alludes to regal authority, and hints at the argument drawn from the exclusion of James II. at the Revolution of 1688, on which Mr. Fox insisted so powerfully in his speech the same evening.

5 This is an instance of Mr. Burke's habit of rising from the particular case before him, and connecting it with a higher range of collateral thought. It is in this way that he adds great dignity to his subject, and often enriches it with venerable associations.

6 We have here an instance of Mr. Burke's utter repugnance to argue any question on the ground of mere abstract right. Some might deny the binding force of a charter which gave such ample powers; but his habits of mind led him to abide by all established institutions until driven from them by the most obvious necessity.

which tends wholly to disqualify men for the functions of government, but that by which the power of exercising those functions is very frequently obtained, I mean a spirit and habits of low cabal and intrigue, which I have never, in one instance, seen united with a capacity for sound and manly policy.

What abuse justifies a revocation.

To justify us in taking the administration of their affairs out of the hands of the East India Company, on my principles, I must see several conditions. 1st. The object affected by the abuse should be great and important. 2d. The abuse affecting this great object ought to be a great abuse. 3d. It ought to be habitual, and not accidental. 4th. It ought to be utterly incurable in the body as it now stands constituted. All this ought to be made as visible to me as the light of the sun, before I should strike off an atom of their charter. A right honorable gentleman [Mr. Pitt] has said, and said, I think, but once, and that very slightly (whatever his original demand for a plan might seem to require), that "there are abuses in the Company's government." If that were all, the scheme of the mover of this bill, the scheme of his learned friend, and his own scheme of reformation (if he has any), are all equally needless. There are, and must be, abuses in all governments. It amounts to no more than a nugatory proposition. But before I consider of what nature these abuses are of which the gentleman speaks so very lightly, permit me to recall to your recollection the map of the country which this abused chartered right affects. This I shall do, that you may judge whether in that map I can discover any thing like the first of my conditions, that is, whether the object affected by the abuse of the East India Company's power be of importance sufficiently to justify the measure and means of reform applied to it in this bill.

Magnitude of the object effected

(1.) With very few, and those inconsiderable intervals, the British dominion, either in the Company's name, or in the names of princes absolutely dependent upon the Company, extends from the mountains that separate India from Tartary to Cape Comorin, that is, one-and-twenty degrees of latitude!

Extent.

In the northern parts it is a solid mass of land, about eight hundred miles in length, and four or five hundred broad. As you go southward, it becomes narrower for a space. It afterward dilates; but, narrower or broader, you possess the whole eastern and northeastern coast of that vast country, quite from the borders of Pegu. Bengal, Bahar, and Orissa, with Benares (now unfortunately in our immediate possession), measure 161,978 square English miles; a territory considerably larger than the whole kingdom of France.[7] Oude, with its dependent provinces, is 53,286 square miles, not a great deal less than England. The Carnatic, with Tanjore and the Circars, is 65,948 square miles, very considerably larger than England; and the whole of the Company's dominions, comprehending Bombay and Salsette, amounts to 281,412 square miles, which forms a territory larger than any European dominion, Russia and Turkey excepted. Through all that vast extent of country there is not a man who eats a mouthful of rice but by permission of the East India Company.

Population.

So far with regard to the extent. The population of this great empire is not easy to be calculated. When the countries of which it is composed came into our possession, they were all eminently peopled and eminently productive, though at that time considerably declined from their ancient prosperity. But since they are come into our hands—! However, if we take the period of our estimate immediately before the utter desolation of the Carnatic, and if we allow for the havoc which our government had even then made in these regions, we can not, in my opinion, rate the population at much less than thirty millions of souls;[8] more than four times the number of persons in the island of Great Britain.

Character of the people.

My next inquiry to that of the number is the quality and description of the inhabitants. This multitude of men does not consist of an abject and barbarous populace, much less of gangs of savages, like the Guaranies and Chiquitos, who wander on the waste borders of the River of Amazon or the Plate, but a people for ages civilized and cultivated; cultivated by all the arts of polished life, while we were yet in the woods. There have been (and still the skeletons remain) princes once of great dignity, authority, and opulence. There are to be found the chiefs of tribes and nations. There is to be found an ancient and venerable priesthood, the depository of their laws, learning, and history, the guides of the people while living, and their consolation in death; a nobility of great antiquity and renown; a multitude of cities not exceeded in population and trade by those of the first class in Europe; merchants and bankers, individual houses of whom have once vied in capital with the Bank of England, whose credit had often supported a tottering state, and preserved their governments in the midst of war and desolation; millions of ingenious manufacturers and mechanics; millions of the most diligent, and not the least intelligent, tillers of the earth. Here are to be found almost all the religions professed by men; the Braminical, the Mussulmen, the Eastern and the Western Christians.

If I were to take the whole aggregate of our possessions there, I should compare it, as the nearest parallel I can find, with the empire of Germany. Our immediate possessions I should compare with the Austrian dominions, and they would not suffer in the comparison. The Nabob of Oude might stand for the King of Prussia; the Nabob of Arcot I would compare, as superior in territory and equal in revenue, to the Elector

[7] France has since been materially enlarged, its extent being at present two hundred and four thousand square miles.

[8] Now one hundred and fifty millions, great additions having been made to the territory.

of Saxony. Cheyte Sing, the Rajah of Benares, might well rank with the Prince of Hesse, at least; and the Rajah of Tanjore (though hardly equal in extent of dominion, superior in revenue) to the Elector of Bavaria. The Polygars, and the northern Zemindars, and other great chiefs, might well class with the rest of the princes, dukes, counts, marquesses, and bishops in the empire, all of whom I mention to honor, and surely without disparagement to any or all of those most respectable princes and grandees.[9]

All this vast mass, composed of so many orders and classes of men, is again infinitely diversified by manners, by religion, by hereditary employment, through all their possible combinations. This renders the handling of India a matter in a high degree critical and delicate. But oh! it has been handled rudely indeed. Even some of the reformers seem to have forgot that they had any thing to do but to regulate the tenants of a manor, or the shop-keepers of the next county town.

It is an empire of this extent, of this complicated nature, of this dignity and importance, that I have compared to Germany and the German government; not for an exact resemblance, but as a sort of a middle term, by which India might be approximated to our understandings, and, if possible, to our feelings, in order to awaken something of sympathy for the unfortunate natives, of which I am afraid we are not perfectly susceptible while we look at this very remote object through a false and cloudy medium.

(2.) My second condition, necessary to justify me in touching the charter, is, whether the Company's abuse of their trust, with regard to this great object, be an abuse of great atrocity. I shall beg your permission to consider their conduct in two lights: first, the political, and then the commercial. Their political conduct (for distinctness) I divide again into two heads: the external, in which I mean to comprehend their conduct in their federal capacity, as it relates to powers and states independent, or that not long since were such; the other internal, namely, their conduct to the countries either immediately subject to the Company, or to those who, under the apparent government of native sovereigns, are in a state much lower, and much more miserable, than common subjection.

Greatness of the abuse.

The attention, sir, which I wish to preserve to method will not be considered as unnecessary or affected.[10] Nothing else can help me to selection, out of the infinite mass of materials which have passed under my eye, or can keep my mind steady to the great leading points I have in view.

With regard, therefore, to the abuse of the external federal trust, I engage myself to you to make good these three positions. First, I say, that from Mount Imaus (or whatever else you call that large range of mountains that walls the northern frontier of India), where it touches us in the latitude of twenty-nine, to Cape Comorin, in the latitude of eight, there is not a single prince, state, or potentate, great or small, in India, with whom they have come into contact, whom they have not sold. I say *sold*, though sometimes they have not been able to deliver according to their bargain. Secondly, I say, that there is not a single treaty they have ever made which they have not broken. Thirdly, I say, that there is not a single prince or state, who ever put any trust in the Company, who is not utterly ruined; and that none are in any degree secure or flourishing, but in the exact proportion to their settled distrust and irreconcilable enmity to this nation.

Political abuses.

These assertions are universal. I say, in the full sense, *universal*. They regard the external and political trust only; but I shall produce others fully equivalent in the internal. For the present, I shall content myself with explaining my meaning; and if I am called on for proof while these bills are depending (which I believe I shall not), I will put my finger on the appendices to the reports, or on papers of record in the House, or the committees, which I have distinctly present to my memory, and which I think I can lay before you at half an hour's warning.

The first potentate sold by the Company for money was the Great Mogul, the descendant of Tamerlane. This high personage, as high as human veneration can look at, is, by every account, amiable in his manners, respectable for his piety according to his mode, and accomplished in all the Oriental literature.

Sale of princes and states.

All this, and the title derived under his *charter* to all that we hold in India, could not save him from the general sale. Money is coined in his name; in his name justice is administered; he is prayed for in every temple through the countries we possess—but he was sold!

It is impossible, Mr. Speaker, not to pause here for a moment, to reflect on the inconstancy of human greatness, and the stupendous revolutions that have happened in our age of wonders. Could it be believed, when I entered into existence, or when you, a younger man, were born, that on this day, in this House, we should be employed in discussing the conduct of those British subjects who had disposed of the power and person of the Grand Mogul? This is no idle speculation. Awful lessons are taught by it, and by other events, of which it is not yet too late to profit. [Mr. Burke here goes on to state the terms on which the Great Mogul was betrayed

[9] This attempt to illustrate the relation of the states of India, by comparing them with those of Germany, is highly characteristic of Mr. Burke, whose mind was ever full of correspondences; but there is something rather fanciful in it, especially when carried out to so great a length. Indeed, Mr. Burke himself seems to have felt that the comparison might appear a little ludicrous, for he adds, with a slight sneer at the counts, marquesses, and bishops, "all of whom I mention *to honor*."

[10] This apology for the exactness of his method reminds us of the extraordinary care bestowed by Mr. Burke on the orderly arrangement of his ideas. He sometimes takes pains to conceal it, lest his speeches should seem too formal; but every where we see traces of elaborate forecast in the disposition of his materials.

into the hands of his chief minister Sujah Dowlah, and adds:] The descendant of Tamerlane now stands in need almost of the common necessaries of life, and in this situation we do not allow him, as bounty, the smallest portion of what we owe him in justice.

The next sale was that of the whole nation of the Rohillas, which the grand salesman, without a pretense of quarrel, and contrary to his own declared sense of duty and rectitude, sold to the same Sujah ul Dowlah. He sold the people to utter *extirpation* for the sum of four hundred thousand pounds. Faithfully was the bargain performed on our side. Hafiz Rhamet, the most eminent of their chiefs, one of the bravest men of his time, and as famous throughout the East for the elegance of his literature, and the spirit of his poetical compositions (by which he supported the name of Hafiz), as for his courage, was invaded with an army of a hundred thousand men and an English brigade. This man, at the head of inferior forces, was slain, valiantly fighting for his country. His head was cut off, and delivered, for money, to a barbarian. His wife and children, persons of that rank, were seen begging a handful of rice through the English camp. The whole nation, with inconsiderable exceptions, was slaughtered or banished. The country was laid waste with fire and sword; and that land, distinguished above most others by the cheerful face of paternal government and protected labor, the chosen seat of cultivation and plenty, is now almost throughout a dreary desert, covered with rushes and briers, and jungles full of wild beasts. * * * *

[Mr. Burke next speaks of numerous other instances in which chiefs and countries had been sold by the Company's agents, and adds:]

All these bargains and sales were regularly attended with the waste and havoc of the country, always by the buyer, and sometimes by the object of the sale. This was explained to you by the honorable mover when he stated the mode of paying debts due from the country powers to the Company. An honorable gentleman, who is not now in his place, objected to his jumping near two thousand miles for an example; but the southern example is perfectly applicable to the northern claim, as the northern is to the southern; for, throughout the whole space of these two thousand miles, take your stand where you will, the proceeding is perfectly uniform, and what is done in one part will apply exactly to the other.

My second assertion is, that the Company never has made a treaty which they have not broken. This position is so connected with that of the sales of provinces and kingdoms, with the negotiation of universal distraction in every part of India, that a very minute detail may well be spared on this point. [The details given by Mr. Burke under this head abundantly support his position, but are here omitted, as of no present interest to the reader.]

Violation of treaties.

My third assertion, relative to the abuse made of the right of war and peace, is, that there are none who have ever confided in us who have not been utterly ruined. There is proof more than enough in the condition of the Mogul; in the slavery and indigence of the Nabob of Oude; the exile of the Rajah of Benares; the beggary of the Nabob of Bengal; the undone and captive condition of the Rajah and kingdom of Tanjore; the destruction of the Polygars; and, lastly, in the destruction of the Nabob of Arcot himself, who, when his dominions were invaded, was found entirely destitute of troops, provisions, stores, and (as he asserts) money, being a million in debt to the Company, and four millions to others; the many millions which he had extorted from so many extirpated princes and their desolated countries having, as he has frequently hinted, been expended for the ground-rent of his mansion-house in an alley in the suburbs of Madras. Compare the condition of all these princes with the power and authority of all the Mahratta states; with the independence and dignity of the Soubah [Prince] of the Deccan; and the mighty strength, the resources, and the manly struggle of Hyder Ali; and then the House will discover the effects, on every power in India, of an easy confidence, or of a rooted distrust in the faith of the Company.

All who confided in the Company have been ruined.

These are some of my reasons, grounded on the abuse of the external political trust of that body, for thinking myself not only justified, but bound to declare against those chartered rights which produce so many wrongs. I should deem myself the wickedest of men if any vote of mine could contribute to the continuance of so great an evil.

Now, sir, according to the plan I proposed, I shall take notice of the Company's internal government, as it is exercised first on the dependent provinces, and then as it affects those under the direct and immediate authority of that body. And here, sir, before I enter into the spirit of their interior government, permit me to observe to you upon a few of the many lines of difference which are to be found between the vices of the Company's government, and those of the conquerors who preceded us in India, that we may be enabled a little the better to see our way in an attempt to the necessary reformation.

Abuses in the internal government

The several irruptions of Arabs, Tartars, and Persians into India were, for the greater part, ferocious, bloody, and wasteful in the extreme.[11] Our entrance into the dominion of that country was, as generally, with small comparative effusion of blood, being introduced by various frauds and delusions, and by taking advantage of the incurable, blind, and senseless animosity which the several country powers bear toward each other, rather than by open force. But the difference in favor of the first conquerors is this: the

Early invaders of India compared with the English.

[11] This comparison is in Mr. Burke's finest style, exhibiting not only admirable powers of description, but of philosophical observation as to the sources of national prosperity.

Asiatic conquerors very soon abated of their ferocity, because they made the conquered country their own. They rose or fell with the rise or fall of the territory they lived in. Fathers there deposited the hopes of their posterity; and children there beheld the monuments of their fathers. Here their lot was finally cast; and it is the natural wish of all that their lot should not be cast in a bad land. Poverty, sterility, and desolation are not a recreating prospect to the eye of man; and there are very few who can bear to grow old among the curses of a whole people. If their passion or their avarice drove the Tartar hordes to acts of rapacity or tyranny, there was time enough, even in the short life of man, to bring round the ill effects of an abuse of power upon the power itself. If hoards were made by violence and tyranny, they were still domestic hoards; and domestic profusion, or the rapine of a more powerful and prodigal hand, restored them to the people. With many disorders, and with few political checks upon power, nature had still fair play; the sources of acquisition were not dried up; and therefore the trade, the manufactures, and the commerce of the country flourished. Even avarice and usury itself operated, both for the preservation and the employment of national weath. The husbandman and manufacturer paid heavy interest, but then they augmented the fund from whence they were again to borrow. Their resources were dearly bought, but they were sure; and the general stock of the community grew by the general effort.

But, under the English government, all this order is reversed. The Tartar invasion was mischievous, but it is our protection that destroys India. It was their enmity, but it is our friendship. Our conquest there, after twenty years, is as crude as it was the first day. The natives scarcely know what it is to see the gray head of an Englishman. Young men (boys almost) govern there, without society, and without sympathy with the natives. They have no more social habits with the people than if they still resided in England, nor, indeed, any species of intercourse but that which is necessary to making a sudden fortune, with a view to a remote settlement. Animated with all the avarice of age, and all the impetuosity of youth, they roll in one after another, wave after wave; and there is nothing before the eyes of the natives but an endless, hopeless prospect of new flights of birds of prey and passage, with appetites continually renewing for a food that is continually wasting.[12] Every rupee of profit made by an Englishman is lost forever to India. With us are no retributory superstitions, by which a foundation of charity compensates, through ages, to the poor, for the rapine and injustice of a day. With us, no pride erects stately monuments which repair the mischiefs which pride had produced, and which adorn a country out of its own spoils. England has erected no churches, no hospitals,[13] no palaces, no schools; England has built no bridges, made no high-roads, cut no navigations, dug out no reservoirs. Every other conqueror of every other description has left some monument, either of state or beneficence, behind him. Were we to be driven out of India this day, nothing would remain to tell that it had been possessed, during the inglorious period of our dominion, by any thing better than the orang-outang or the tiger.

There is nothing in the boys we send to India worse than the boys whom we are whipping at school, or that we see trailing a pike or bending over a desk at home. But as English youth in India drink the intoxicating draught of authority and dominion before their heads are able to bear it, and as they are full grown in fortune long before they are ripe in principle, neither nature nor reason have any opportunity to exert themselves for remedy of the excesses of their premature power. The consequences of their conduct, which in good minds (and many of theirs are probably such) might produce penitence or amendment, are unable to pursue the rapidity of their flight. Their prey is lodged in England; and the cries of India are given to seas and winds, to be blown about, in every breaking up of the monsoon, over a remote and unhearing ocean. In India, all the vices operate by which sudden fortune is acquired; in England are often displayed, by the same persons, the virtues which dispense hereditary wealth. Arrived in England, the destroyers of the nobility and gentry of a whole kingdom will find the best company of this nation at a board of elegance and hospitality. Here the manufacturer and husbandman will bless the just and punctual hand that in India has torn the cloth from the loom, or wrested the scanty portion of rice and salt from the peasant of Bengal, or wrung from him the very opium in which he forgot his oppressions and his oppressor. They marry into your families; they enter into your senate; they ease your estates by loans; they raise their value

Influence on England.

---

[12] There is here a mixture of incongruous images, which is not common with Mr. Burke. The English adventurers are in the same sentence *waves* of the sea, and yet *birds of prey!* But, passing by this, we have at the close of the sentence a fault into which Mr. Burke does very often fall, that of running out his images into too many particulars. "New flights of birds of prey" was a striking metaphor to represent the successive arrivals of English adventurers. The extension of the idea to birds of "passage" was perhaps unfortunate, because it draws off the mind from the main object, to mark the difference between the two classes of birds. But Mr. Burke goes much farther. He introduces the image by speaking of "an *endless, hopeless* prospect" of these flights; and then represents them as having "*appetites*"—these are "continually *renewing*"—the "food" of these "appetites" is next referred to, and this food is then described as "continually *wasting*." By these details, the mind is drawn off from the principal object to a mere picture. Such images may dazzle, but they do not illustrate or enforce the leading thought, which is the appropriate object of figurative language.

[13] The paltry foundation at Calcutta is scarcely worth naming as an exception.

by demand; they cherish and protect your relations which lie heavy on your patronage; and there is scarcely a house in the kingdom that does not feel some concern and interest that makes all reform of our Eastern government appear officious and disgusting, and, on the whole, a most discouraging attempt. In such an attempt, you hurt those who are able to return kindness or to resent injury. If you succeed, you save those who can not so much as give you thanks. All these things show the difficulty of the work we have on hand, but they show its necessity too. Our Indian government is, in its best state, a grievance. It is necessary that the correctives should be uncommonly vigorous, and the work of men sanguine, warm, and even impassioned in the cause. But it is an arduous thing to plead against abuses of a power which originates from your own country, and affects those whom we are used to consider as strangers.

I shall certainly endeavor to modulate myself to this temper, though I am sensible that a cold style of describing actions which appear to me in a very affecting light, is equally contrary to the justice due to the people, and to all genuine human feelings about them. I ask pardon of truth and nature for this compliance; but I shall be very sparing of epithets either to persons or things. It has been said (and, with regard to one of them, with truth) that Tacitus and Machiavel, by their cold way of relating enormous crimes, have in some sort appeared not to disapprove them; that they seem a sort of professors of the art of tyranny, and that they corrupt the minds of their readers by not expressing the detestation and horror that naturally belong to horrible and detestable proceedings. But we are in general, sir, so little acquainted with Indian details; the instruments of oppression under which the people suffer are so hard to be understood; and even the very names of the sufferers are so uncouth and strange to our ears, that it is very difficult for our sympathy to fix upon these objects. I am sure that some of us have come down stairs from the committee-room with impressions on our minds which to us were the inevitable results of our discoveries; yet, if we should venture to express ourselves in the proper language of our sentiments to other gentlemen not at all prepared to enter into the cause of them, nothing could appear more harsh and dissonant, more violent and unaccountable, than our language and behavior. All these circumstances are not, I confess, very favorable to the idea of our attempting to govern India at all; but there we are; there we are placed by the Sovereign Disposer; and we must do the best we can in our situation. The situation of man is the preceptor of his duty.

Upon the plan which I laid down, and to which I beg leave to return, I was considering the conduct of the Company to those nations which are indirectly subject to their authority. [Mr. Burke here goes into very ample details of the injuries inflicted on states and monarchs connected with the East India Company. Some of these will come up again in his speech on the Nabob of Arcot's debts, and in Mr. Sheridan's speech on the treatment of the Begums or Princesses of Oude. Having made out his case by the enumeration of these atrocities, he proceeds to his conclusion as follows:]

As the Company has made this use of their trust, I should ill discharge mine if I refused to give my most cheerful vote for the redress of these abuses, by putting the affairs of so large and valuable a part of the interests of this nation, and of mankind, into some steady hands, possessing the confidence and assured of the support of this House, until they can be restored to regularity, order, and consistency.

I have touched the heads of some of the grievances of the people and the abuses of government, but I hope and trust you will give me credit when I faithfully assure you that I have not mentioned one fourth part of what has come to my knowledge in your committee; and, farther, I have full reason to believe that not one fourth part of the abuses are come to my knowledge, by that or by any other means. Pray consider what I have said only as an index to direct you in your inquiries.

Commercial management of the Company.

If this, then, sir, has been the use made of the trust of political powers, internal and external, given by you in the charter, the next thing to be seen is the conduct of the Company with regard to the commercial trust. And here I will make a fair offer: If it can be proved that they have acted wisely, prudently, and frugally, as merchants, I shall pass by the whole mass of their enormities as statesmen. That they have not done this, their present condition is proof sufficient. Their distresses are said to be owing to their wars. This is not wholly true; but if it were, is not that readiness to engage in war which distinguishes them, and for which the Committee of Secrecy has so branded their politics, founded on the falsest principles of mercantile speculation?

Tests of good mercantile management.

The principle of buying cheap and selling dear is the first, the great foundation of mercantile dealing.[14] Have they ever attended to this principle? Nay, for years have they not actually authorized in their servants a total indifference as to the prices they were to pay?

A great deal of strictness in driving bargains for whatever we contract is another of the principles of mercantile policy. Try the Company by that test! Look at the contracts that are

[14] There is great ingenuity in throwing the argument to show the commercial incompetency and mismanagement of the Company into this form. The idea of *tests* was calculated to arrest attention. Those selected commend themselves to the good sense of all, as indispensable requisites in a good merchant. Curiosity is excited as Mr. Burke, in stating each test, goes on to apply it to the conduct of the Company. The inference is irresistible, *they are not fit to be intrusted with such vast commercial interests.*

made for them. Is the Company so much as a good commissary for their own armies? I engage to select for you, out of the innumerable mass of their dealings, all conducted very nearly alike, one contract only, the excessive profits on which, during a short term, would pay the whole of their year's dividend. I shall undertake to show that, upon two others, the inordinate profits given, with the losses incurred in order to secure those profits, would pay a year's dividend more.

It is a third property of trading men to see that the clerks do not divert the dealings of the master to their own benefit. It was the other day, only, when their governor and council taxed the Company's investment with a sum of fifty thousand pounds, as an inducement to persuade only seven members of their Board of Trade to give their *honor* that they would abstain from such profits upon that investment as must have violated their *oaths* if they had made at all!

It is a fourth quality of a merchant to be exact in his accounts. What will be thought when you have fully before you the mode of accounting made use of in the treasury of Bengal? I hope you will have it soon. With regard to one of their agencies, when it came to the material part, the prime cost of the goods on which a commission of fifteen per cent. was allowed, to the astonishment of the factory to whom the commodities were sent, the accountant general reports that he did not think himself authorized to call for vouchers relative to this and other particulars, because the agent was upon his *honor* with regard to them! A new principle of account upon honor seems to be regularly established in their dealings and their treasury, which in reality amounts to an entire annihilation of the principle of all accounts.

It is a fifth property of a merchant who does not meditate a fraudulent bankruptcy to calculate his probable profits upon the money he takes up to vest in business. Did the Company, when they bought goods on bonds bearing eight per cent. interest, at ten and even twenty per cent. discount, even ask themselves a question concerning the possibility of advantage from dealing on these terms?

The last quality of a merchant I shall advert to is the taking care to be properly prepared, in cash or goods, in the ordinary course of sale, for the bills which are drawn on them. Now I ask whether they have ever calculated the clear produce of any given sales, to make them tally with the four millions of bills which are come and coming upon them, so as at the proper periods to enable the one to liquidate the other? No, they have not. They are now obliged to borrow money of their own servants to purchase their investment. The servants stipulate five per cent. on the capital they advance if their bills should not be paid at the time when they become due; and the value of the rupee on which they charge this interest is taken at two shillings and a penny. Has the Company ever troubled themselves to inquire whether their sales can bear the payment of that interest, and at that rate of exchange? Have they once considered the dilemma in which they are placed—the ruin of their credit in the East Indies if they refuse the bills—the ruin of their credit and existence in England if they accept them? Indeed, no trace of equitable government is found in their politics; not one trace of commercial principle in their mercantile dealing; and hence is the deepest and maturest wisdom of Parliament demanded, and the best resources of this kingdom must be strained to restore them; that is, to restore the countries destroyed by the misconduct of the Company, and to restore the Company itself, ruined by the consequences of their plans for destroying what they were bound to preserve.

(3.) I required, if you remember, at my outset, a proof that these abuses were habitual; but surely this is not necessary for me to consider as a separate head, because I trust I have made it evident beyond a doubt, in considering the abuses themselves, that they are regular, permanent, and systematical.

The abuses habitual,

(4.) I now come to my last condition, without which, for one, I will never readily lend my hand to the destruction of any established government, which is, that in its present state the government of the East India Company is absolutely incorrigible.

And incurable.

Of this great truth I think there can be little doubt, after all that has appeared in this House. It is so very clear, that I must consider the leaving any power in their hands, and the determined resolution to continue and countenance every mode and every degree of peculation, oppression, and tyranny, to be one and the same thing. I look upon that body incorrigible, from the fullest consideration both of their uniform conduct, and their present real and virtual constitution.

If they had not constantly been apprised of all the enormities committed in India under their authority; if this state of things had been as much a discovery to them as it was to many of us, we might flatter ourselves that the detection of the abuses would lead to their reformation. I will go farther: if the court of directors had not uniformly condemned every act which this House or any of its committees had condemned; if the language in which they expressed their disapprobation against enormities and their authors had not been much more vehement and indignant than any ever used in this House, I should entertain some hopes. If they had not on the other hand, as uniformly commended all their servants who had done their duty and obeyed their orders, as they had heavily censured those who rebelled, I might say these people have been in error, and when they are sensible of it they will mend. But when I reflect on the uniformity of their support to the objects of their uniform censure, and the state of insignificance and disgrace to which all of those have been reduced whom they approved, and that even utter ruin and premature death have been among the fruits of their favor, I must be convinced that,

The abuses fully known but not redressed.

in this case as in all others, hypocrisy is the only vice that never can be cured.

Attend, I pray you, to the situation and prosperity of Benfield,[15] Hastings, and others of that sort. The last of these had been treated by the Company with an asperity of reprehension that has no parallel. They lament "that the power of disposing of their property for perpetuity should fall into such hands." Yet for fourteen years, with little interruption, he has governed all their affairs, of every description, with an absolute sway. He has had himself the means of heaping up immense wealth; and during that whole period, the fortunes of hundreds have depended on his smiles and frowns. He himself tells you he is encumbered with two hundred and fifty young gentlemen, some of them of the best families in England, all of whom aim at returning with vast fortunes to Europe in the prime of life. He has, then, two hundred and fifty of your children as his hostages for your good behavior;[16] and loaded for years, as he has been, with the execrations of the natives, with the censures of the court of Directors, and struck and blasted with the resolutions of this House, he still maintains the most despotic power ever known in India. He domineers with an overbearing sway in the assemblies of his pretended masters; and it is thought in a degree rash to venture to name his offenses in this House, even as grounds of a legislative remedy.

On the other hand, consider the fate of those who have met with the applauses of the Directors. Colonel Monson, one of the best of men, had his days shortened by the applauses, destitute of the support of the Company. General Clavering, whose panegyric was made in every dispatch from England, whose hearse was bedewed with the tears and hung round with the eulogies of the court of Directors, burst an honest and indignant heart at the treachery of those who ruined him by their praises. Uncommon patience and temper supported Mr. Francis a while longer under the baneful influence of the commendation of the court of Directors. His health, however, gave way at length, and in utter despair he returned to Europe. At his return the doors of the India House were shut to this man, who had been the object of their constant admiration. He has indeed escaped with life, but he has forfeited all expectation of credit, consequence, party, and following. He may well say, "Me nemo ministro fur erit, atque ideo nulli comes exeo."[17] This man, whose deep reach of thought, whose large legislative conceptions, and whose grand plans of policy make the most shining part of our reports, from whence we have all learned our lessons, if we have learned any good ones; this man, from whose materials those gentlemen who have least acknowledged it have yet spoken as from a brief; this man, driven from his employment, discountenanced by the Directors, has had no other reward and no other distinction but that inward "sunshine of the soul" which a good conscience can always bestow upon itself. He has not yet had so much as a good word, but from a person too insignificant to make any other return for the means with which he has been furnished for performing his share of a duty which is equally urgent on us all.[18]

Add to this, that from the highest in place to the lowest, every British subject who, in obedience to the Company's orders, has been active in the discovery of peculations, has been ruined. They have been driven from India. When they made their appearance at home, they were not heard; when they attempted to return, they were stopped. No artifice of fraud, no violence of power, has been omitted to destroy them in character as well as in fortune.

Worse, far worse, has been the fate of the poor creatures, the natives of India, whom the hypocrisy of the Company has betrayed into complaint of oppression and discovery of peculation. The first women in Bengal, the Ranny [Princess] of Rajeshahi, the Ranny of Burdwan, the Ranny of Amboa, by their weak and thoughtless trust in the Company's honor and protection, are utterly ruined. The first of these women, a person of princely rank and once of correspondent fortune, who paid above two hundred thousand a year quit-rent to the state, is, according to very credible information, so completely beggared as to stand in need of the relief of alms. Mahomed Reza Khan, the second Mussulman in Bengal, for having been distinguished by the ill-omened honor of the countenance and protection of the court of Directors, was, without the pretense of any inquiry whatsoever into his conduct, stripped of all his employments, and reduced to the lowest condition. His ancient rival for power, the Rajah Nuncomar, was, by an insult on every thing which India holds respectable and sacred, hanged in the face of all his nation by the judges you sent to protect that people; hanged for a pretended crime, upon an *ex post facto* British act of Parliament, in the midst of his evidence against Mr. Hastings. The accuser they saw hanged. The culprit, without acquittal or inquiry, triumphs on the ground of that murder—a murder not of Nuncomar only,

15 The reader will enter fully into the character of Paul Benfield when he comes to the speech on the Nabob of Arcot's debts. He was originally a servant of the Company in a low situation, with an income of only a few hundred pounds a year. He afterward became a banker at Madras, and so ingratiated himself with the Nabob of Arcot as to obtain at last the complete control of his actions, and to run up pretended debts against him to the amount of millions.

16 Mr. Burke here refers to the writers in the East India Company, who belonged generally to some of the best families in England, and who were wholly dependent on the governor general.

17 No one shall plunder through my instrumentality, and therefore I go out as the companion of no one.

18 Did Mr. Burke, when he delivered this glowing eulogy on Sir Philip Francis, suspect that he was the man on whom he had previously bestowed his praises under the name of *Junius?*

but of all living testimony, and even of evidence yet unborn. From that time not a complaint has been heard from the natives against their governors. All the grievances of India have found a complete remedy.[19]

Men will not look to acts of Parliament, to regulations, to declarations, to votes, and resolutions. No, they are not such fools. They will ask, What is the road to power, credit, wealth, and honors? They will ask, What conduct ends in neglect, disgrace, poverty, exile, prison, and the gibbet? These will teach them the course which they are to follow. It is your distribution of these that will give the character and tone to your government. All the rest is miserable grimace.

A part of the Directors not concerned in these abuses.

When I accuse the court of Directors of this habitual treachery in the use of reward and punishment, I do not mean to include all the individuals in that court. There have been, sir, very frequently, men of the greatest integrity and virtue among them, and the contrariety in the declarations and conduct of that court has arisen, I take it, from this: that the honest Directors have, by the force of matter of fact on the records, carried the reprobation of the evil measures of the servants in India. This could not be prevented while these records stared them in the face; nor were the delinquents, either here or there, very solicitous about their reputation, as long as they were able to secure their power. The agreement of their partisans to censure them, blunted for a while the edge of a severe proceeding. It obtained for them a character of impartiality, which enabled them to recommend, with some sort of grace, what will always carry a plausible appearance, those treacherous expedients called moderate measures. While these were under discussion, new matter of complaint came over, which seemed to antiquate the first. The same circle was here trod round once more; and thus, through years, they proceeded in a compromise of censure for punishment, until, by shame and despair, one after another, almost every man who preferred his duty to the Company to the interest of their servants, has been driven from that court.

Change in the constitution of the Company

This, sir, has been their conduct; and it has been the result of the alteration which was insensibly made in their constitution. The change was made insensibly, but it is now strong and adult, and as public and declared as it is fixed beyond all power of reformation; so that there is none who hears me that is not as certain as I am that the Company, in the sense in which it was formerly understood, has no existence. The question is not, what injury you may do to the proprietors of India stock, for there are no such men to be injured. If the active, ruling part of the Company, who form the general court, who fill the offices, and direct the measures (the rest tell for nothing), were persons who held their stock as a means of their subsistence; who, in the part they took, were only concerned in the government of India for the rise or fall of their dividend, it would be indeed a defective plan of policy. The interest of the people who are governed by them would not be their primary object—perhaps a very small part of their consideration at all; but then they might well be depended on, and perhaps more than persons in other respects preferable, for preventing the peculations of their servants to their own prejudice. Such a body would not easily have left their trade as a spoil to the avarice of those who received their wages. But now things are totally reversed. The stock is of no value, whether it be the qualification of a Director or Proprietor; and it is impossible that it should. A Director's qualification may be worth about two thousand five hundred pounds, and the interest, at eight per cent., is about one hundred and sixty pounds a year. Of what value is that, whether it rise to ten, or fall to six, or to nothing, to him whose son, before he is in Bengal two months, and before he descends the steps of the council chamber, sells the grant of a single contract for forty thousand pounds? Accordingly, the stock is bought up in qualifications. The vote is not to protect the stock, but the stock is bought to acquire the vote; and the end of the vote is to cover and support, against justice, some man of power who has made an obnoxious fortune in India, or to maintain in power those who are actually employing it in the acquisition of such a fortune, and to avail themselves in return of his patronage, that he may shower the spoils of the East, "barbaric pearl and gold,"[20] on them, their families, and dependents; so that all the relations of the Company are not only changed, but inverted. The servants in India are not appointed by the Directors, but the Directors are chosen by them. The trade is carried on with their capitals. To them the revenues of the country are mortgaged. The seat of the supreme power is in Calcutta. The house in Leadenhall Street is nothing more than a 'change for their agents, factors, and deputies to meet in,

[19] The case was this. Nuncomar was a Hindoo of the highest rank, who accused Mr. Hastings to the council at Calcutta (falsely, it is now believed) of putting up offices for sale, and receiving bribes. While the matter was in progress, Nuncomar was himself arrested on a charge of having forged a bond five years before; and though his accuser was a native, no one doubts that Mr. Hastings caused the accusation to be made. Forgery is a very common offense among the Hindoos, and was punished but slightly by their laws. But Mr. Hastings had Nuncomar prosecuted in an *English* court at Calcutta, and thus made him amenable to English laws, under which the crime is punished with death. Nuncomar was condemned and actually executed in the face of the whole native population of Calcutta, who looked on with astonishment and horror. Never was there a more flagrant act of injustice. The English law respecting forgery was not made with reference to the natives of India; they knew nothing of it; and the whole proceeding was little, if at all, short of deliberate murder under the forms of law.

[20] "Or where the gorgeous East with richest hand
Showers on her kings barbaric pearl and gold."
Milton's Par. Lost, ii., 4.

to take care of their affairs and support their interests; and this so avowedly, that we see the known agents of the delinquent servants marshaling and disciplining their forces, and the prime spokesmen in all their assemblies.

Facts confirming these statements.

Every thing has followed in this order, and according to the natural train of events. I will close what I have to say on the incorrigible condition of the Company by stating to you a few facts that will leave no doubt of the obstinacy of that corporation, and of their strength too, in resisting the reformation of their servants. By these facts you will be enabled to discover the sole grounds upon which they are tenacious of their charter. It is now more than two years that, upon account of the gross abuses and ruinous situation of the Company's affairs (which occasioned the cry of the whole world long before it was taken up here), that we instituted two committees to inquire into the mismanagements by which the Company's affairs had been brought to the brink of ruin. These inquiries had been pursued with unremitting diligence; and a great body of facts was collected and printed for general information. In the result of those inquiries, although the committees consisted of very different descriptions, they were unanimous. They joined in censuring the conduct of the Indian administration, and enforcing the responsibility upon two men,[21] whom this House, in consequence of these reports, declared it to be the duty of the Directors to remove from their stations, and recall to Great Britain, "*because they had acted in a manner repugnant to the honor and policy of this nation, and thereby brought great calamities on India, and enormous expenses on the East India Company.*"

The Company forbade the Directors to carry out the resolution.

Here was no attempt on the charter. Here was no question of their privileges. To vindicate their own honor, to support their own interests, to enforce obedience to their own orders—these were the sole object of the monitory-resolution of this House. But as soon as the General Court could assemble, they assembled to demonstrate who they really were. Regardless of the proceedings of this House, they ordered the Directors not to carry into effect any resolution they might come to for the removal of Mr. Hastings and Mr. Hornby. The Directors, still retaining some shadow of respect to this House, instituted an inquiry themselves, which lasted from June to October; and, after an attentive perusal and full consideration of papers, resolved to take steps for removing the persons who had been the objects of our resolution, but not without a violent struggle against evidence. Seven Directors went so far as to enter a protest against the vote of their court. Upon this the General Court takes the alarm; it reassembles; it orders the Directors to rescind their resolution, that is, not to recall Mr. Hastings and Mr. Hornby, and to despise the resolution of the House of Commons. Without so much as the pretense of looking into a single paper, without the formality of inquiry, they superseded all the labors of their own Directors and of this House.

It will naturally occur to ask how it was possible that they should not attempt some sort of examination into facts as a color for their resistance to a public authority, proceeding so very deliberately, and exerted, apparently at least, in favor of their own. The answer, and the only answer which can be given, is, that they were afraid that their true relations should be mistaken. They were afraid that their patrons and masters in India should attribute their support of them to an opinion of their cause, and not to an attachment to their power. They were afraid it should be suspected that they did not mean blindly to support them in the use they made of that power. They determined to show that they, at least, were set against reformation; that they were firmly resolved to bring the territories, the trade, and the stock of the Company to ruin, rather than be wanting in fidelity to their nominal servants and real masters in the ways they took to their private fortunes.

Even since the beginning of this session, the same act of audacity was repeated, with the same circumstances of contempt of all the decorum of inquiry on their part, and of all the proceedings of this House. They again made it a request to their favorite [Mr. Hastings] and your culprit to keep his post, and thanked and applauded him, without calling for a paper which could afford light into the merit or demerit of the transaction, and without giving themselves a moment's time to consider, or even to understand, the articles of the Mahratta peace. The fact is, that for a long time there was a struggle, a faint one indeed, between the Company and their servants; but it is a struggle no longer. For some time the superiority has been decided. The interests abroad are become the settled preponderating weight both in the court of Proprietors and the court of Directors. Even the attempt you have made to inquire into their practices and to reform abuses has raised and piqued them to a far more regular and steady support. The Company has made a common cause and identified themselves with the destroyers of India. They have taken on themselves all that mass of enormity; they are supporting what you have reprobated; those you condemn they applaud; those you order home to answer for their conduct, they request to stay, and thereby encourage to proceed in their practices. Thus the servants of the East India Company triumph, and the representatives of the people of Great Britain are defeated.

I therefore conclude, what you all conclude, that this body, being totally perverted from the purposes of its institution, is utterly incorrigible; and because they are incorrigible, both in conduct and constitution, power ought to be taken out of their hands, just on the same principles on which have been made all the just changes

[21] Mr. Hastings, the Governor General, and Mr. Hornby, President of Bombay.

and revolutions of government that have taken place since the beginning of the world.

I will now say a few words to the general principle of the plan which is set up against that of my right honorable friend. It is to re-commit the government of India to the court of Directors. Those who would commit the reformation of India to the destroyers of it, are the enemies to that reformation. They would make a distinction between Directors and Proprietors, which, in the present state of things, does not, can not exist. But a right honorable gentleman says he would keep the present government of India in the court of Directors, and would, to curb them, provide salutary regulations. Wonderful! That is, he would appoint the old offenders to correct the old offenses, and he would render the vicious and the foolish wise and virtuous by salutary regulations! He would appoint the wolf as guardian of the sheep; but he has invented a curious muzzle, by which this protecting wolf shall not be able to open his jaws above an inch or two at the utmost. Thus his work is finished. But I tell the right honorable gentleman that controlled depravity is not innocence, and that it is not the labor of delinquency in chains that will correct abuses. Will these gentlemen of the direction animadvert on the partners of their own guilt? Never did a serious plan of amending of any old tyrannical establishment propose the authors and abettors of the abuses as the reformers of them. If the undone people of India see their old oppressors in confirmed power, even by the reformation, they will expect nothing but what they will certainly feel—a continuance, or rather an aggravation, of all their former sufferings. They look to the seat of power, and to the persons who fill it; and they despise those gentlemen's regulations as much as the gentlemen do who talk of them.

Scheme opposed to Mr. Fox's bill.

But there is a cure for every thing. Take away, say they, the court of Proprietors, and the court of Directors will do their duty. Yes, as they have done it hitherto! That the evils in India have solely arisen from the court of Proprietors, is grossly false. In many of them, the Directors were heartily concurring; in most of them, they were encouraging, and sometimes commanding; in all, they were conniving.

But who are to choose this well-regulated and reforming court of Directors? Why, the very proprietors who are excluded from all management for the abuse of their power. They will choose, undoubtedly, out of themselves, men like themselves; and those who are most forward in resisting your authority, those who are most engaged in faction or interest with the delinquents abroad, will be the objects of their selection. But gentlemen say that when this choice is made the Proprietors are not to interfere in the measures of the Directors, while those Directors are busy in the control of their common patrons and masters in India. No, indeed, I believe they will not desire to interfere. They will choose those whom they know may be trusted, safely trusted, to act in strict conformity to their common principles, manners, measures, interests, and connections. They will want neither monitor nor control. It is not easy to choose men to act in conformity to a public interest against their private, but a sure dependence may be had on those who are chosen to forward their private interest at the expense of the public. But if the Directors should slip, and deviate into rectitude, the punishment is in the hands of the General Court, and it will surely be remembered to them at their next election.

If the government of India wants no reformation, but gentlemen are amusing themselves with a theory, conceiving a more democratic or aristocratic mode of government for these dependencies, or if they are in a dispute only about patronage, the dispute is with me of so little concern, that I should not take the pains to utter an affirmative or negative to any proposition in it. If it be only for a theoretical amusement that they are to propose a bill, the thing is at best frivolous and unnecessary. But if the Company's government is not only full of abuse, but is one of the most corrupt and destructive tyrannies that probably ever existed in the world (as I am sure it is), what a cruel mockery would it be in me, and in those who think like me, to propose this kind of remedy for this kind of evil!

II. I now come to the second objection: That this bill will increase the influence of the Crown. An honorable gentleman has demanded of me whether I was in earnest when I proposed to this House a plan for the reduction of that influence.[22] Indeed, sir, I was much, very much in earnest. My heart was deeply concerned in it, and I hope the public has not lost the effect of it. How far my judgment was right for what concerned personal favor and consequence to myself, I shall not presume to determine, nor is its effect upon *me* of any moment. But as to this bill, whether it increases the influence of the Crown or not, is a question I should be ashamed to ask. If I am not able to correct a system of oppression and tyranny, that goes to the utter ruin of thirty millions of my fellow-creatures and fellow-subjects, but by some increase to the influence of the Crown, I am ready here to declare that I, who have been active to reduce it, shall be at least as active and strenuous to restore it again. I am no lover of names; I contend for the substance of good and protecting government, let it come from what quarter it will.

Second objection.

But I am not obliged to have recourse to this expedient. Much, very much the contrary. I am sure that the influence of the Crown will by no means aid a reformation of this kind, which can neither be originated nor supported but by the uncorrupt public virtue of the representatives of the people of England. Let it once get into the ordinary course of administration, and to me all

No evidence that the bill will increase the influence of the Crown.

[22] Referring to Mr. Burke's plan of economical reform.

hopes of reformation are gone. I am far from knowing or believing that this bill will increase the influence of the Crown. We all know that the Crown has ever had some influence in the court of Directors, and that it has been extremely increased by the acts of 1773 and 1780. The gentlemen (Mr. Dundas, &c.) who, as part of their reformation, propose "a more active control on the part of the Crown," which is to put the Directors under a Secretary of State specially named for that purpose, must know that their project will increase it farther. But that old influence has had, and the new will have, incurable inconveniences, which can not happen under the parliamentary establishment proposed in this bill. An honorable gentleman (Governor Johnstone) not now in his place, but who is well acquainted with the India Company, and by no means a friend to this bill, has told you that a ministerial influence has always been predominant in that body; and that to make the Directors pliant to their purposes, ministers generally caused persons meanly qualified to be chosen Directors. According to his idea, to secure subserviency they submitted the Company's affairs to the direction of incapacity. This was to ruin the Company in order to govern it. This was certainly influence in the very worst form in which it could appear. At best it was clandestine and irresponsible. Whether this was done so much upon system as that gentleman supposes, I greatly doubt. But such, in effect, the operation of government on that court unquestionably was, and such, under a similar constitution, it will be forever. Ministers must be wholly removed from the management of the affairs of India, or they will have an influence in its patronage. The thing is inevitable. Their scheme of a new Secretary of State, "with a more vigorous control," is not much better than a repetition of the measure which we know by experience will not do. Since the year 1773 and the year 1780, the Company has been under the control of the Secretary of State's office, and we had then three Secretaries of State. If more than this is done, then they annihilate the direction which they pretend to support, and they augment the influence of the Crown, of whose growth they affect so great a horror. But, in truth, this scheme of reconciling a direction really and truly deliberative, with an office really and substantially controlling, is a sort of machinery that can be kept in order but a very short time. Either the Directors will dwindle into clerks, or the Secretary of State, as hitherto has been the course, will leave every thing to them, often through design, often through neglect. If both should affect activity, collision, procrastination, delay, and, in the end, utter confusion, must ensue.

A worse kind of influence.

But, sir, there is one kind of influence far greater than that of the nomination to office. This, gentlemen in opposition have totally overlooked, although it now exists in its full vigor; and it will do so, upon their scheme, in at least as much force as it does now. That influence this bill cuts up by the roots; I mean the *influence of protection*. I shall explain myself: The office given to a young man going to India is of trifling consequence; but he that goes out an insignificant boy, in a few years returns a great nabob. Mr. Hastings says he has two hundred and fifty of that kind of raw materials, who expect to be speedily manufactured into the merchantable quality I mention. One of these gentlemen, suppose, returns hither, loaded with odium and with riches. When he comes to England, he comes as to a prison or as to a sanctuary, and either is ready for him, according to his demeanor. What is the influence in the grant of any place in India, to that which is acquired by the protection or compromise with such guilt, and with the command of such riches, under the dominion of the hopes and fears which power is able to hold out to every man in that condition? That man's whole fortune—half a million, perhaps—becomes an instrument of influence, without a shilling of charge to the civil list; and the influx of fortunes which stand in need of this protection is continual. It works both ways; it influences the delinquent, and it may corrupt the minister. Compare the influence acquired by appointing, for instance, even a Governor General, and that obtained by protecting him. I shall push this no farther; but I wish gentlemen to roll it a little in their own minds.

The bill before you cuts off this source of influence. Its design and main scope is to regulate the administration of India upon the principles of a court of judicature, and to exclude, as far as human prudence can exclude, all possibility of a corrupt partiality, in appointing to office, or supporting in office, or covering from inquiry and punishment, any person who has abused or shall abuse his authority. At the board, as appointed and regulated by this bill, reward and punishment can not be shifted and reversed by a whisper. That commission becomes fatal to cabal, to intrigue, and to secret representation, those instruments of the ruin of India. He that cuts off the means of premature fortune, and the power of protecting it when acquired, strikes a deadly blow at the great fund, the bank, the capital stock of Indian influence, which can not be vested any where, or in any hands, without the most dangerous consequences to the public.

Third objection.

III. The third contradictory objection is, that this bill does not increase the influence of the Crown; on the contrary, that the just power of the Crown will be lessened and transferred to the use of a party, by giving the patronage of India to a commission nominated by Parliament and independent of the Crown. The contradiction is glaring, and it has been too well exposed to make it necessary for me to insist upon it; but, passing the contradiction, and taking it without any relation, of all objections, that is the most extraordinary. Do not gentlemen know that the Crown has not at present the grant of a single office under the Company, civil or military, at home or abroad? So far as the Crown is concerned, it is certainly rather a gainer, for the vacant offices are to be filled up by the King.

The tenure for four years defended.

It is argued, as a part of the bill derogatory to the prerogatives of the Crown, that the Commissioners named in the bill are to continue for a short term of years (too short, in my opinion), and because, during that time, they are not at the mercy of every predominant faction of the Court. Does not this objection lie against the present Directors, none of whom are named by the Crown, and a proportion of whom hold for this very term of four years? Did it not lie against the Governor General and council named in the act of 1773, who were invested by name, as the present Commissioners are to be appointed in the body of the act of Parliament, who were to hold their places for a term of years, and were not removable at the discretion of the Crown? Did it not lie against the reappointment, in the year 1780, upon the very same terms? Yet at none of these times, whatever other objections the scheme might be liable to, was it supposed to be a derogation to the just prerogative of the Crown, that a commission created by act of Parliament should have its members named by the authority which called it into existence? This is not the disposal by Parliament of any office derived from the authority of the Crown, or now disposable by that authority. It is so far from being any thing new, violent, or alarming, that I do not recollect, in any parliamentary commission, down to the commissioners of the land tax, that it has ever been otherwise.

The objection of the tenure for four years is an objection to all places that are not held during pleasure; but in that objection I pronounce the gentlemen, from my knowledge of their complexion and of their principles, to be perfectly in earnest. The party (say these gentlemen) of the minister who proposes this scheme will be rendered powerful by it, for he will name his party friends to the commission. This objection against party is a party objection; and in this, too, these gentlemen are perfectly serious. They see that if, by any intrigue, they should succeed to office, they will lose the *clandestine* patronage, the true instrument of clandestine influence, enjoyed in the name of subservient Directors, and of wealthy, trembling Indian delinquents. But as often as they are beaten off this ground, they return to it again. The minister will name his friends, and persons of his own party. Who should he name? Should he name those whom he can not trust? Should he name those to execute his plans who are the declared enemies to the principles of his reform? His character is here at stake. If he proposes for his own ends (but he never will propose) such names as, from their want of rank, fortune, character, ability, or knowledge, are likely to betray or to fall short of their trust, he is in an independent House of Commons; in a House of Commons which has, by its own virtue, destroyed the instruments of parliamentary subservience.

Answer to the objection that the minister will appoint his friends as Commissioners.

This House of Commons would not endure the sound of such names. He would perish by the means which he is supposed to pursue for the security of his power. The first pledge he must give of his sincerity in this great reform will be in the confidence which ought to be reposed in those names.

For my part, sir, in this business I put all indirect questions wholly out of my mind. My sole question, on each clause of the bill, amounts to this: Is the measure proposed required by the necessities of India? I can not consent totally to lose sight of the real wants of the people who are the objects of it, and to hunt after every matter of party squabble that may be started on the several provisions. On the question of the duration of the commission I am clear and decided. Can I, can any one who has taken the smallest trouble to be informed concerning the affairs of India, amuse himself with so strange an imagination as that the habitual despotism and oppression, that the monopolies, the peculations, the universal destruction of all the legal authority of this kingdom, which have been for twenty years maturing to their present enormity, combined with the distance of the scene, the boldness and artifice of delinquents, their combination, their excessive wealth, and the faction they have made in England, can be fully corrected in a shorter term than four years? None has hazarded such an assertion; none who has a regard for his reputation will hazard it.

The Commissioners have a great work to perform.

Sir, the gentlemen, whoever they are, who shall be appointed to this commission, have an undertaking of magnitude on their hands, and their stability must not only be, but it must be thought, real; and who is it will believe that any thing short of an establishment made, supported, and fixed in its duration with all the authority of Parliament, can be thought secure of a reasonable stability? The plan of my honorable friend is the reverse of that of reforming by the authors of the abuse. The best we could expect from them is, that they should not continue their ancient pernicious activity. To those we could think of nothing but applying *control*, as we are sure that even a regard to their reputation (if any such thing exists in them) would oblige them to cover, to conceal, to suppress, and consequently to prevent, all cure of the grievances of India. For what can be discovered which is not to their disgrace? Every attempt to correct an abuse would be a satire on their former administration. Every man they should pretend to call to an account would be found their instrument or their accomplice. They can never see a beneficial regulation but with a view to defeat it. The shorter the tenure of such persons, the better would be the chance of some amendment.

But the system of the bill is different. It calls in persons nowise concerned with any act censured by Parliament; persons generated with, and for the reform of which they are themselves the most essential part. To these the chief regulations in the bill are helps, not fetters; they are authorities to support, not regulations to restrain them. From these we look for much more than innocence. From these we expect zeal, firmness, and unremitted activity. Their duty, their character, binds them to proceedings of vigor; and they ought to have a tenure in their office which precludes all fear, while they are acting up to the purposes of their trust; a tenure without which none will undertake plans that require a series and system of acts. When they know that they can not be whispered out of their duty, that their public conduct can not be censured without a public discussion, that the schemes which they have begun will not be committed to those who will have an interest and credit in defeating and disgracing them, then we may entertain hopes. The tenure is for four years, or during their good behavior. That good behavior is as long as they are true to the principles of the bill; and the judgment is in either house of Parliament. This is the tenure of your judges; and the valuable principle of the bill is, to make a judicial administration for India. It is to give confidence in the execution of a duty which requires as much perseverance and fortitude as can fall to the lot of any that is born of woman.

Answer to objection as to party gain.

As to the gain by party from the right honorable gentleman's bill, let it be shown that this supposed party advantage is pernicious to its object, and the objection is of weight; but until this is done, and this has not been attempted, I shall consider the sole objection, from its tendency to promote the interest of a party, as altogether contemptible. The kingdom is divided into parties, and it ever has been so divided, and it ever will be so divided; and if no system for relieving the subjects of this kingdom from oppression, and snatching its affairs from ruin, can be adopted until it is demonstrated that no party can derive an advantage from it, no good can ever be done in this country. If party is to derive an advantage from the reform of India (which is more than I know or believe), it ought to be that party which alone in this kingdom has its reputation, nay, its very being, pledged to the protection and preservation of that part of the empire. Great fear is expressed that the Commissioners named in this bill will show some regard to a minister out of place [Lord North]. To men like the objectors, this must appear criminal. Let it, however, be remembered by others, that if the Commissioners should be his friends, they can not be his slaves. But dependents are not in a condition to adhere to friends, nor to principles, nor to any uniform line of conduct. They may begin censors, and be obliged to end accomplices. They may be even put under the direction of those whom they were appointed to punish.

Fourth objection.

IV. The fourth and last objection is, that the bill will hurt public credit. I do not know whether this requires an answer; but if it does, look to your foundations. The sinking fund is the pillar of credit in this country; and let it not be forgot, that the distresses, owing to the mismanagement of the East India Company, have already taken a million from that fund by the non-payment of duties. The bills drawn upon the Company, which are about four millions, can not be accepted without the consent of the treasury. The treasury, acting under a parliamentary trust and authority, pledges the public for these millions. If they pledge the public, the public must have a security in its hands for the management of this interest, or the national credit is gone; for otherwise it is not only the East India Company, which is a great interest, that is undone, but, clinging to the security of all your funds, it drags down the rest, and the whole fabric perishes in one ruin. If this bill does not provide a direction of integrity and of ability competent to that trust, the objection is fatal. If it does, public credit must depend on the support of the bill.

It has been said, if you violate this charter, what security has the charter of the Bank, in which public credit is so deeply concerned, and even the charter of London, in which the rights of so many subjects are involved? I answer, in the like case they have no security at all—no—no security at all. If the Bank should, by every species of mismanagement, fall into a state similar to that of the East India Company; if it should be oppressed with demands it could not answer, engagements which it could not perform, and with bills for which it could not procure payment, no charter should protect the mismanagement from correction, and such public grievances from redress. If the city of London had the means and will of destroying an empire, and of cruelly oppressing and tyrannizing over millions of men as good as themselves, the charter of the city of London should prove no sanction to such tyranny and such oppression. Charters are kept when their purposes are maintained; they are violated when the privilege is supported against its aim and object.

Peroration.

Now, sir, I have finished all I proposed to say, as my reasons for giving my vote to this bill. If I am wrong, it is not for want of pains to know what is right. This pledge, at least, of my rectitude, I have given to my country.

Eulogium on Mr. Fox.

And now, having done my duty to the bill, let me say a word to the author. I should leave him to his own noble sentiments, if the unworthy and illiberal language with which he has been treated, beyond all example of parliamentary liberty, did not make a few words necessary, not so much in justice to him as to my own feelings. I must say, then, that it will be a distinction honorable to the age, that the rescue of the greatest number of the human race that ever were so grievously oppressed, from the greatest tyranny that was ever exercised, has fallen to the lot of abilities and dispositions equal to the task; that it has fallen to one who has the enlargement to comprehend, the spirit to undertake, and the eloquence to support so great a measure of hazardous benevolence. His spirit is not owing to his ignorance of the state of men and things; he well knows what snares are spread about his path, from personal animosity, from court intrigues, and possibly from popular delusion. But he has put to hazard his ease, his security, his interest, his power, even his darling popularity, for the benefit of a people whom he has never seen. This is the road that all heroes have trod before him. He is traduced and abused for his supposed motives. He will remember that obloquy is a necessary ingredient in the composition of all true glory; he will remember that it was not only in the Roman customs, but it is in the nature and constitution of things, that calumny and abuse are essential parts of a triumph.[21] These thoughts will support a mind, which only exists for honor, under the burden of temporary reproach. He is doing, indeed, a great good, such as rarely falls to the lot, and almost as rarely coincides with the desires of any man. Let him use his time. Let him give the whole length of the reins to his benevolence.[22] He is now on a great eminence, where the eyes of mankind are turned to him. He may live long; he may do much. But here is the summit. He never can exceed what he does this day.

He has faults, but they are faults that, though they may in a small degree tarnish the luster and sometimes impede the march of his abilities, have nothing in them to extinguish the fire of great virtues. In those faults there is no mixture of deceit, of hypocrisy, of pride, of ferocity, of complexional despotism, or want of feeling for the distresses of mankind. His are faults which might exist in a descendant of Henry the Fourth of France, as they did exist in that father of his country. Henry the Fourth wished that he might live to see a fowl in the pot of every peasant of his kingdom. That sentiment of homely benevolence was worth all the splendid sayings that are recorded of kings; but he wished, perhaps, for more than could be obtained, and the goodness of the man exceeded the power of the king. But this gentleman, a subject, may this day say this, at least, with truth, that he secures the rice in his pot to every man in India. A poet of antiquity thought it one of the first distinctions to a prince whom he meant to celebrate, that, through a long succession of generations, he had been the progenitor of an able and virtuous citizen [Cicero], who, by force of the arts of peace, had corrected governments of oppression and suppressed wars of rapine.

Indole proh quantâ juvenis, quantumque daturus
Ausoniæ populis, ventura in sæcula civem.
Ille super Gangem, super exauditus et Indos,
Implebit terras voce; et furialia bella
Fulmine compescet linguæ.[23]

This was what was said of the predecessor of the only person to whose eloquence it does not wrong that of the mover of this bill to be compared. But the Ganges and the Indus are the patrimony of the fame of my honorable friend, and not of Cicero. I confess I anticipate with joy the reward of those whose whole consequence, power, and authority exist only for the benefit of mankind; and I carry my mind to all the people, and all the names and descriptions that, relieved by this bill, will bless the labors of this Parliament and the confidence which the best House of Commons has given to him who the best deserves it. The little cavils of party will not be heard where freedom and happiness will be felt. There is not a tongue, a nation, or religion in India which will not bless the presiding care and manly beneficence of this House, and of him who proposes to you this great work. Your names will never be separated before the throne of the Divine Goodness, in whatever language, or with whatever rites pardon is asked for sin, and reward for those who imitate the Godhead in his universal bounty to his creatures. These honors you deserve, and they will surely be paid, when all the jargon of influence, and party, and patronage are swept into oblivion.

I have spoken what I think and what I feel of the mover of this bill. An honorable friend of mine, speaking of his merits, was charged with having made a studied panegyric. I don't know what his was. Mine, I am sure, is a studied panegyric; the fruit of much meditation; the result of the observation of near twenty years. For my own part, I am happy that I have lived to see this day. I feel myself overpaid for the labors of eighteen years, when, at this late period, I am able to take my share, by one humble vote, in destroying a tyranny that exists to the disgrace of this nation and the destruction of so large a part of the human species.

The bill passed the House of Commons by a very large majority, but was defeated in the House of Lords by a resort to means which are fully explained in the sketch of Mr. Fox's life.

In connection with this defeat, Mr. Fox was dismissed, and Mr. William Pitt placed at the head of affairs. Mr. Burke went out of office with his friend, and was engaged for some years in a most active opposition to Mr. Pitt, whom he attacked with great force in the speech which immediately follows.

---

[21] During the procession in a Roman triumph, the soldiers and spectators proclaimed the praises of the conqueror, or indulged in keen sarcasms and coarse ribaldry at his expense, the most perfect freedom of speech being exercised on this occasion.—Smith's Dictionary of Antiquities, p. 1018.

[22] Mr. Burke seems to have been partial to this image. Elsewhere he speaks of "pouring out all the length of the reins," &c., using the image in various forms a number of times. It is derived from the "laxas habenas," "effundere habenas" of Virgil, in speaking of the management of steeds in chariot races, &c.

[23] The poet here addresses Tullus Attius, one of the early kings of the Volsci, who, according to some accounts, was the progenitor of Cicero, and congratulates him, in this character, on the greatness of his future descendant.

Rich in the gifts of nature, favored youth!
Thou to the Italian race shalt give the MAN
In ages far remote their city's pride; [streams,
Whose voice sublime shall ring o'er Ganges'
Through both the Indies, to Earth's utmost bound,
And still, with lightning-force, the rage of war.

SPEECH

OF MR. BURKE ON THE NABOB OF ARCOT'S DEBTS, DELIVERED IN THE HOUSE OF COMMONS, FEBRUARY 28, 1785.

INTRODUCTION.

THE design of this speech was to convict Mr. Pitt of a scandalous abuse of power. It charges him with allowing the claims of a set of unprincipled speculators in India to the amount of *four millions* of pounds, in direct defiance of an act of Parliament drawn up by Mr. Pitt himself.

Men of all parties had agreed that these claims were of a highly suspicious character, and ought never to be paid until they were severely scrutinized. Mr. Pitt, in his East India Bill, had therefore provided, that "whereas large sums of money are claimed to be due to British subjects by the Nabob of Arcot, the Court of Directors, as soon as may be, shall take into consideration the origin and justice of these demands." And yet, one of the first acts of the Board of Control created by that bill, was to take the whole matter out of the hands of the Directors just as they had commenced the investigation! This was done by Mr. Henry Dundas, President of the Board of Control, and it is, therefore, against him more immediately that the force of this speech is directed, though Mr. Pitt, as prime minister, was justly held responsible. A mandate was issued for paying all these claims without farther inquiry, and the Directors of the East India Company, notwithstanding their most earnest remonstrances, were compelled to sign an order for disbursing what proved to be nearly five millions of pounds sterling (interest included) on account of these debts.—Mill's British India, v., 26.

A few words only will be necessary to explain their origin. Mohammed Ali, Nabob of the Carnatic, or, as he was more commonly called, Nabob of Arcot, from the town where he held his court, was a man of weak judgment but strong passions, who was established in his dominions, to the prejudice of an elder brother, by the policy and arms of the Presidency of Madras. At an early period, he fell under the influence of Paul Benfield and a few other English residents, who played upon his passions, encouraged his schemes of conquest, and ruled him with absolute authority. They no doubt lent him money to some extent; but, as their means were limited, the amount could not have been very great. Every thing which they did lend, however, was put upon extravagant interest; and when he failed to pay, the amount was sometimes doubled or tripled in taking new securities. There is also reason to believe, that, in order to obtain their favor, he gave them acknowledgments of debts to an immense amount, which were understood by both parties to be purely fictitious. Thus, from time to time, enormous sums were put upon interest, at the rate of twenty or thirty per cent. a year, until the annual proceeds of the debts thus accumulated were equal, as Mr. Burke remarks, to "the revenue of a respectable kingdom." The Directors of the Company, in the mean time, had no knowledge of these proceedings, which were studiously concealed from all but the immediate agents in this system of usury and peculation. The Nabob at last became wholly unable to protect the dominions over which he had been placed, and the Company were compelled, in self-defense, and for the accomplishment of their designs, to take the military operations of the country into their own hands. In doing this, they received from the Nabob an assignment of his revenues, for the purpose of defraying the expense. But it now came out that these very revenues, to a great extent, had been previously assigned to Benfield and his friends, to secure the interest on their claims. Hence it was important for the Company to inquire how far these claims had any real foundation. Under Mr. Pitt's East India Bill, this inquiry became equally important to the whole British nation, because the civil and military concerns of India had now passed into the hands of the government at home. Whatever allowance was made to Benfield and his associates on the score of these debts, was so much money deducted from the resources provided for the government of India. Any deficit that occurred was of course to be supplied out of the general treasury of the empire; and the question was, therefore, truly stated by Mr. Burke to be this, "Whether the Board of Control could transfer the *public revenue* to the private emolument of certain servants of the East India Company, without the inquiry into the origin and justice of their claims, prescribed by an act of Parliament."

Mr. Fox brought the subject before the House in a call for papers, supported by a powerful speech, on the evening of the 28th of February, 1785. Mr. Dundas replied at great length, and was followed by Sir Thomas Rumbold, formerly President of Madras, who condemned the decision of the Board in brief but energetic terms. It was now late, and the cry of "Question!" "Question!" was heard from every quarter. At this moment Mr. Burke rose and commenced the speech before us, which lasted *five hours!* Never did a man speak under such adverse circumstances. The House was completely wearied out by the preceding discussion; and the majority, besides being prejudiced against Mr. Burke on other grounds, were so vexed at the unfortunate timing and length of his speech, that the more he dilated on the subject, the more firmly they were resolved to vote him down. In fact, no one that night seems to have had any conception of the real character of the speech which was delivered in their hearing. Lord Grenville was asked by Mr. Pitt, toward the close, whether it was best to reply, and instantly said, "No! not the slightest impression has been made. The speech may with perfect safety be passed over in silence." And yet, if Lord Grenville had been called upon, at a subsequent period of his life, to name the most remarkable speech in our language for its triumph over the difficulties of the subject, for the union of brilliancy and force, of comprehensive survey and minute detail, of vivid description and impassioned eloquence, he would at once, probably, have mentioned the speech on the Nabob of Arcot's debts. It does not, however, contain as much fine philosophy, or profound remark, as some of Mr. Burke's earlier speeches. Nor is it faultless in style, though it is generally distinguished by an elastic energy of expression admirably suited to the subject. Still, there are passages which mark a transition into greater profluence of imagery on the one hand, and greater coarseness of language on the other, arising from the excited state of Mr. Burke's mind. Never had his feelings been so completely roused. In none of his speeches do we find so much of cutting sarcasm. In none, except that against Warren Hastings, has he poured out his whole soul in such fervid declamation. His description of Hyder Ali, sweeping over the Carnatic with fire and sword, is the most eloquent passage which he ever produced. Lord Brougham has pronounced this speech "by far the first of all Mr. Burke's orations."

SPEECH, &c.

The times we live in, Mr. Speaker, have been distinguished by extraordinary events. Habituated, however, as we are, to uncommon combinations of men and of affairs, I believe nobody recollects any thing more surprising than the spectacle of this day. The right honorable gentleman [Mr. Dundas], whose conduct is now in question, formerly stood forth in this House the prosecutor of the worthy baronet [Sir Thomas Rumbold] who spoke after him. He charged him with several grievous acts of malversation in office; with abuses of a public trust of a great and heinous nature. In less than two years we see the situation of parties reversed, and a singular revolution puts the worthy baronet in a fair way of returning the prosecution in a recriminatory bill of pains and penalties, grounded on a breach of public trust, relative to the government of the very same part of India. If he should undertake a bill of that kind, he will find no difficulty in conducting it with a degree of skill and vigor fully equal to all that have been exerted against him.[1]

But the change of relation between these two gentlemen is not so striking as the total difference of their deportment under the same unhappy circumstances. Whatever the merits of the worthy baronet's defense might have been, he did not shrink from the charge. He met it with manliness of spirit and decency of behavior. What would have been thought of him if he had held the present language of his old accuser? When articles were exhibited against him by that right honorable gentleman, he did not think proper to tell the House that we ought to institute no inquiry, to inspect no paper, to examine no witness. He did not tell us (what at that time he might have told us with some show of reason) that our concerns in India were matters of delicacy; that to divulge any thing relative to them would be mischievous to the state. He did not tell us that those who would inquire into his proceedings were disposed to dismember the empire. He had not the presumption to say that, for his part, having obtained, in his Indian presidency, the ultimate object of his ambition, his honor was concerned in executing with integrity the trust which had been legally committed to his charge; that others, not having been so fortunate, could not be so disinterested, and therefore their accusations could spring from no other source than faction, and envy to his fortune.

Had he been frontless enough to hold such vain, vaporing language, in the face of a grave, a detailed, a specified matter of accusation, while he violently resisted every thing which could bring the merits of his cause to the test; had he been wild enough to anticipate the absurdities of this day; that is, had he inferred, as his late accuser has thought proper to do, that he could not have been guilty of malversation in office, for this sole and curious reason, that he had been in office; had he argued the impossibility of his abusing his power on this sole principle, that he had power to abuse, he would have left but one impression on the mind of every man who heard him, and who believed him in his senses—that, in the utmost extent, he was guilty of the charge.[2]

[1] It requires a minute knowledge of the times to understand this reference. Mr. Dundas, in 1782, had brought in a bill of pains and penalties against Sir Thomas Rumbold for high crimes and misdemeanors as Governor of Madras; but he managed it so badly, that he was at last compelled to give it up in disgrace. Hence Mr. Burke's reference to his "skill and energy" was a cutting sarcasm which Mr. Dundas could not but feel most keenly.

[2] This is the best of Mr. Burke's exordiums; it would be difficult, indeed, to find a better in any oration, ancient or modern, except that of Demosthenes for the Crown. It springs directly out of a turn in the debate, and has therefore all the freshness and interest belonging to a real transaction which has just taken place before the audience. It turns upon a striking circumstance, the sudden and remarkable change in the relative position of the two parties; and puts Mr. Dundas in the wrong from the very outset. Before a syllable is said touching the merits of the case, it presents him in the worst possible attitude—that of shuffling and evading, instead of "meeting the charge," like his old antagonist, "with manliness of spirit and decency of behavior." There is great ingenuity in selecting the various points of contrast between the deportment of Mr. Dundas and of Sir Thomas Rumbold in the two cases. The attack is

But, sir, leaving these two gentlemen to alternate, as criminal and accuser, upon what principles they think expedient, it is for us to consider whether the Chancellor of the Exchequer [Mr. Pitt] and the Treasurer of the Navy [Mr. Dundas], acting as a Board of Control, are justified, by law or policy, in suspending the legal arrangements made by the court of Directors, in order to transfer the public revenues to the private emolument of certain servants of the East India Company, without the inquiry into the origin and justice of their claims prescribed by an act of Parliament.

Preliminary discussion of the law.

I. It is not contended that the act of Parliament did not expressly ordain an inquiry. It is not asserted that this inquiry was not, with equal precision of terms, specially committed, under particular regulations, to the court of Directors. I conceive, therefore, the Board of Control had no right whatsoever to intermeddle in that business. (1.) There is nothing certain in the principles of jurisprudence, if this be not undeniably true, that when a special authority is given to any persons by name, to do some particular act, no others, by virtue of *general* powers, can obtain a legal title to intrude themselves into that trust, and to exercise those special functions in their place. I therefore consider the intermeddling of ministers in this affair as a downright usurpation. But if the strained construction by which they have forced themselves into a suspicious office (which every man, delicate with regard to character, would rather have sought constructions to avoid) were perfectly sound and perfectly legal, of this I am certain, (2.) That they can not be justified in declining the *inquiry* which had been prescribed to the court of Directors. If the Board of Control did lawfully possess the right of executing the special trust given to that court, they must take it as they found it, subject to the very same regulations which bound the court of Directors. It will be allowed that the court of Directors had no authority to dispense with either the substance or the mode of inquiry prescribed by the act of Parliament. If they had not, where, in the act, did the Board of Control acquire that capacity? Indeed, it was impossible they should acquire it. What must we think of the fabric and texture of an act of Parliament which should find it necessary to prescribe a strict inquisition; that should descend into minute regulations for the conduct of that inquisition; that should commit this trust to a particular description of men, and in the very same breath should enable another body, at their own pleasure, to supersede all the provisions the Legislature had made, and to defeat the whole purpose, end, and object of the law? This can not be supposed even of an act of Parliament conceived by the ministers themselves, and brought forth during the delirium of the last session.[3]

Subject—Debts of the Nabob of Arcot: Not involved in any peculiar mystery.

II. My honorable friend [Mr. Fox] has told you in the speech which introduced his motion, that, fortunately, this question is not a great deal involved in the labyrinths of Indian detail. Certainly not; but if it were, I beg leave to assure you that there is nothing in the Indian detail which is more difficult than the detail of any other business. I admit, because I have some experience of the fact, that, for the interior regulation of India, a minute knowledge of India is requisite; but, on any specific matter of delinquency in its government, you are as capable of judging as if the same thing were done at your door. Fraud, injustice, oppression, peculation, engendered in India, are crimes of the same blood, family, and cast with those that are born and bred in England. To go no farther than the case before us: you are just as competent to judge whether the sum of four millions sterling ought, or ought not, to be passed from the public treasury into a private pocket, without any title except the claim of the parties, when the issue of fact is laid in Madras, as when it is laid in Westminster. Terms of art, indeed, are different in different places, but they are generally understood in none. The technical style of an Indian treasury is not one jot more remote than the jargon of our own exchequer, from the train of our ordinary ideas, or the idiom of our common language. The difference, therefore, in the two cases is not in the comparative difficulty or facility of the two subjects, but in our attention to the one and our total neglect of the other. Had this attention and neglect been regulated by the value of the several objects, there would be nothing to complain of. But the reverse of that supposition is true. The scene of the Indian abuse is distant, indeed; but we must not infer that the value of our interest in it is decreased in proportion as it recedes from our view. In our politics, as in our common conduct, we shall be worse than infants, if we do not put our senses under the tuition of our judgment, and effectually cure ourselves of that optical illusion which

infinitely more severe from the *indirect* form which it assumes—showing what Sir Thomas Rumbold did *not* do, and turning each of these negatives into a cutting reflection upon Mr. Dundas, as having "left but one impression on the mind of every man who heard him, and who believed him in his senses—that, *in the utmost extent, he was guilty of the charge.*'

[3] That session was one of which we could not expect Mr. Burke to speak in any other terms than those of bitter disappointment and the keenest asperity. It was the first meeting of Parliament after the elections of 1784, which had annihilated the power of Mr. Fox, and put his young rival in complete possession of the House, as prime minister. One of its most important acts was the passing of Mr. Pitt's East India Bill, which dexterously adopted the most valuable features of Mr. Fox's bill. We may easily conceive of Mr. Burke's mortification at seeing the results of his labors thus turned to the advantage of one by whom he was driven from power. Early in this session the well-known case of the Westminster election came up, in respect to which Mr. Fox was certainly treated with arrogance and injustice by Mr. Pitt. To this, undoubtedly, Mr. Burke here alludes in part.

makes a brier at our nose, of greater magnitude than an oak at five hundred yards' distance.

Narrowness of view in public men the great source of calamity to the empire.

I think I can trace all the calamities of this country to the single source of our not having had steadily before our eyes a general, comprehensive, well-connected, and well-proportioned view of the whole of our dominions, and a just sense of their true bearings and relations. After all its reductions, the British empire is still vast and various. After all the reductions of the House of Commons (stripped as we are of our brightest ornaments and of our most important privileges),[4] enough are yet left to furnish us, if we please, with means of showing to the world that we deserve the superintendence of as large an empire as this kingdom ever held, and the continuance of as ample privileges as the House of Commons, in the plenitude of its power, had been habituated to assert. But if we make ourselves too little for the sphere of our duty; if, on the contrary, we do not stretch and expand our minds to the compass of their object, be well assured that every thing about us will dwindle by degrees, until at length our concerns are shrunk to the dimensions of our minds. It is not a predilection to mean, sordid, home-bred cares, that will avert the consequences of a false estimation of our interest, or prevent the shameful dilapidation into which a great empire must fall, by mean reparations upon mighty ruins.[5]

Illustration from two bills before the House.

I confess I feel a degree of disgust, almost leading to despair, at the manner in which we are acting in the great exigencies of our country. There is now a bill in this House appointing a rigid inquisition into the minutest detail of our offices at home. The collection of sixteen millions annually, a collection on which the public greatness, safety, and credit have their reliance; the whole order of criminal jurisprudence, which holds together society itself, have at no time obliged us to call forth such powers; no, nor any thing like them. There is not a principle of the law and constitution of this country that is not subverted to favor the execution of that project. And for what is all this apparatus of bustle and terror? Is it because any thing substantial is expected from it? No: the stir and bustle itself is the *end proposed!* The eye-servants of a short-sighted master will employ themselves, not on what is most essential to his affairs, but on what is nearest to his ken. Great difficulties have given a just value to economy; and our minister of the day must be an economist, whatever it may cost us. But where is he to exert his talents? At home, to be sure; for where else can he obtain a profitable credit for their exertion? It is nothing to him whether the object on which he works under our eye be promising or not. If he does not obtain any public benefit, he may make regulations without end. Those are sure to pay in present expectation, while the effect is at a distance, and may be the concern of other times and other men. On these principles he chooses to suppose (for he does not pretend more than to suppose) a naked possibility, that he shall draw some resource out of crumbs dropped from the trenchers of penury; that something shall be laid in store from the short allowance of revenue officers overloaded with duty and famished for want of bread; by a reduction from officers who are at this very hour ready to batter the treasury with what breaks through stone walls for an *increase* of their appointments. From the marrowless bones of these skeleton establishments, by the use of every sort of cutting, and of every sort of fretting tool, he flatters himself that he may chip and rasp an empirical alimentary powder, to diet into some similitude of health and substance the languishing chimeras of fraudulent reformation.

(1.) That on the management of the public accounts.

While he is thus employed according to his policy and to his taste, he has not leisure to inquire into those abuses in India that are drawing off money by millions from the treasures of this country, which are exhausting the vital juices from members of the state, where the public inanition is far more sorely felt than in the local exchequer of England. Not content with winking at these abuses, while he attempts to squeeze the laborious, ill-paid drudges of English revenue, he lavishes in one act of corrupt prodigality, upon those who never served the

[4] Mr. Burke, in speaking of the loss of some of "our brightest ornaments," refers no doubt to a number of very able men of the Whig party, about one hundred and sixty of whom lost their election, in 1784, through their adherence to Mr. Fox and his East India Bill. The "privileges" here referred to were those denied to Mr. Fox in respect to the Westminster election.

[5] In this paragraph we have one of those fine generalizations which give so much richness and force to the eloquence of Mr. Burke. In the preceding paragraph he exposes one of the most common errors among men, that of allowing their interest in an object *to decrease as it recedes from view;* and this error he places in the strongest light, by his image of the brier and the oak when seen at different distances. Here most orators would have stopped; not so Mr. Burke; his observation had taught him that this was peculiarly the error of English politicians. In his first great speech, that on American taxation, he had, eleven years before, pointed out a similar error, as the leading characteristic of Lord North. He dwelt on the "mischief of not having large and liberal ideas in the management of great affairs." "Never," says he, "have the servants of the state looked at the whole of your complicated interests in one view. They have taken things by bits and scraps, some at one time and one pretense, and some at another, *just as they are pressed,* without any sort of regard to their relations and dependencies." It was thus that America was lost to England through the folly of Lord North; and it was by the same narrowness of view, "the same predilection to mean, sordid, home-bred cares," that Parliament, under the guidance of Mr. Pitt, were sacrificing the highest interests of the empire by their neglect of Indian affairs, and seeking to sustain the fabric of government "by mean reparations upon mighty ruins."

public in any honest occupation at all, an annual income equal to two thirds of the whole collection of the revenues of this kingdom.

(2.) That on commercial intercourse between Great Britain and Ireland.

Actuated by the same principle of choice, he has now on the anvil another scheme, full of difficulty and desperate hazard, which totally alters the commercial relation of two kingdoms; and what end soever it shall have, may bequeath a legacy of heart-burning and discontent to one of the countries, perhaps to both, to be perpetuated to the latest posterity. This project is also undertaken on the hope of profit. It is provided, that out of some (I know not what) remains of the Irish hereditary revenue, a fund at some time, and of some sort, should be applied to the protection of the Irish trade. Here we are commanded again to tax our faith, and to persuade ourselves, that out of the surplus of deficiency, out of the savings of habitual and systematic prodigality, the minister of wonders will provide support for this nation, sinking under the mountainous load of two hundred and thirty millions of debt. But while we look with pain at his desperate and laborious trifling—while we are apprehensive that he will break his back in stooping to pick up chaff and straws, he recovers himself at an elastic bound, and with a broad-cast swing of his arms, he squanders over his Indian field a sum far greater than the clear produce of the whole hereditary revenue of the kingdom of Ireland.[6]

[6] The reader can not but notice the rhetorical skill with which these two instances, taken from measures then before the House, and therefore the more striking, are brought forward by Mr. Burke to illustrate his general principle, as stated above. They are both put, especially the former one, with great power of language and thought. They add all the liveliness and pungency of individual application to the weight and authority of a general truth. But they do more—and here is part of the skill—they reach forward as well as backward. They not only illustrate the past, but prepare for the future. They lay the foundation of another attack. They furnish the ground of the fine contrast here drawn between Mr. Pitt's penuriousness at home and prodigality abroad. They open the way for the keen philosophy of the next paragraph, which shows how "the economy of injustice" is made to "furnish resources for the fund of corruption." Thus they lead on to the next great portion of the speech, which insists on "an economy of quite another order," and demands the strictest inquiry into grants thus lavishly made to a band of Indian peculators.

This fine adjustment of the several parts of an oration, mutually to support or prepare the way for each other, is one of the most striking characteristics of the great orators of antiquity, and especially of Demosthenes. Most readers overlook it, and are wholly unconscious that there is any art in the case. The orator seems so completely to "speak right on," that they are not in the least aware of the skill with which he has selected and arranged his materials with a view to bring every thing forward in its proper place, and to give every thing the appearance of an unpremeditated and spontaneous effusion of thought.

Strange as this scheme of conduct in ministry is, and inconsistent with all just policy, it is still true to itself, and faithful to its own perverted order. Those who are bountiful to crimes will be rigid to merit and penurious to service. Their penury is even held out as a blind and cover to their prodigality. The economy of injustice is to furnish resources for the fund of corruption. Then they pay off their protection to great crimes and great criminals, by being inexorable to the paltry frailties of little men; and these modern Flagellants are sure, with a rigid fidelity, to whip their own enormities on the vicarious back of every small offender.[7]

The moneyed concerns of India more worthy of attention.

It is to draw your attention to economy of quite another order—it is to animadvert on offenses of a far different description, that my honorable friend [Mr. Fox] has brought before you the motion of this day. It is to perpetuate the abuses which are subverting the fabric of your empire, that the motion is opposed. It is therefore with reason (and, if he has power to carry himself through, I commend his prudence) that the right honorable gentleman [Mr. Dundas] makes his stand at the very outset, and boldly refuses all parliamentary information. Let him admit but one step toward inquiry, and he is undone. You must be ignorant, or he can not be safe. But, before his curtain is let down, and the shades of eternal night shall vail our Eastern dominions from our view, permit me, sir, to avail myself of the means which were furnished in anxious and inquisitive times, to demonstrate out of this single act of the present minister what advantages you are to derive from permitting the greatest concern of this nation to be separated from the cognizance, and exempted even out of the competence, of Parliament. The greatest body of your revenue, your most numerous armies, your most important commerce, the richest sources of your public credit (contrary to every idea of the known settled policy of England), are on the point of being converted into a mystery of state. You are going to have one half of the globe hid even from the common liberal curiosity of an English gentleman. Here a grand revolution commences.[8] Mark the period, and mark the

[7] The Flagellants were a sect of the thirteenth century, who sought to expiate their crimes by the discipline of the scourge. They traversed Europe, whipping themselves through the principal cities and at the doors of churches, and creating great commotion wherever they appeared.

[8] This prediction proved true. The establishment of the Board of Control, under Mr. Pitt's bill, merged the civil and political concerns of India in those of the British government. "The President of the Board of Control," says Mill, in his British India, "is essentially a new Secretary of State, a Secretary for the Indian Department. * * * The other five members of the Board are seldom called to deliberate, or, even for form's sake, to assemble. * * * Of this pretended Board, and real Secretary, the sphere of action extends to the whole of the civil and military government exercised by the Company, but not to their commercial transactions."—iv., 487.

circumstances. In most of the capital changes that are recorded in the principles and system of any government, a public benefit of some kind or other has been pretended. The revolution commenced in something plausible, in something which carried the appearance at least of punishment of delinquency, or correction of abuse. But here, in the very moment of the conversion of a department of British government into an Indian mystery, and in the very act in which the change commences, a corrupt private interest is set up in direct opposition to the necessities of the nation. A diversion is made of millions of the public money from the public treasury to a private purse. It is not into secret negotiations for war, peace, or alliance, that the House of Commons is forbidden to inquire. It is a matter of account; it is a pecuniary transaction; it is the demand of a suspected steward upon ruined tenants and an embarrassed master, that the Commons of Great Britain are commanded not to inspect. The whole tenor of the right honorable gentleman's argument is consonant to the nature of his policy. The system of concealment is fostered by a system of falsehood. False facts, false colors, false names of persons and things, are its whole support.

Sir, I mean to follow the right honorable gentleman over that field of deception, clearing what he has purposely obscured, and fairly stating what it was necessary for him to misrepresent. For this purpose, it is necessary you should know, with some degree of distinctness, a little of the locality, the nature, the circumstances, the magnitude of the pretended debts on which this marvelous donation is founded, as well as of the persons from whom and by whom it is claimed.

History of the debts.

III. Madras, with its dependencies, is the second (but with a long interval, the second) member of the British empire in the East. The trade of that city and of the adjacent territory was, not very long ago, among the most flourishing in Asia. But since the establishment of the British power, it has wasted away under a uniform, gradual decline, insomuch that in the year 1779 not one merchant of eminence was to be found in the whole country. During this period of decay, about six hundred thousand sterling pounds a year have been drawn off by English gentlemen, on their private account, by the way of China alone. If we add four hundred thousand as probably remitted through other channels and in other mediums, that is, in jewels, gold, and silver, directly brought to Europe, and in bills upon the British and foreign companies, you will scarcely think the matter overrated. If we fix the commencement of this extraction of money from the Carnatic at a period no earlier than the year 1760, and close it in the year 1780, it probably will not amount to a great deal less than twenty millions of money.

During the deep, silent flow of this steady stream of wealth, which set from India into Europe, it generally passed on with no adequate observation; but happening at some periods to meet rifts of rocks that checked its course, it grew more noisy, and attracted more notice.[9] The pecuniary discussions caused by an accumulation of part of the fortunes of their servants in a debt from the Nabob of Arcot, was the first thing which very particularly called for, and long engaged, the attention of the court of Directors This debt amounted to eight hundred and eighty thousand pounds sterling, and was claimed, for the greater part, by English gentlemen residing at Madras. This grand capital, settled at length by order at ten *per cent.*, afforded an annuity of eighty-eight thousand pounds.

While the Directors were digesting their astonishment at this information, a memorial was presented to them from three gentlemen, informing them that their friends had lent likewise to merchants of Canton, in China, a sum of not more than one million sterling. In this memorial they called upon the Company for their assistance and interposition with the Chinese government for the recovery of the debt. This sum, lent to Chinese merchants, was at twenty-four per cent., which would yield, if paid, an annuity of two hundred and forty thousand pounds.[10]

Perplexed as the Directors were with these demands, you may conceive, sir, that they did not find themselves very much disembarrassed by being made acquainted that they must again exert their influence for a new reserve of the happy parsimony of their servants, collected into a second debt from the Nabob of Arcot, amounting to two millions four hundred thousand pounds, settled at an interest of twelve per cent. This is known by the name of the Consolidation of 1777, as the former of the Nabob's debts was by the title of the Consolidation of 1767. To this was added, in a separate parcel, a little reserve called the Cavalry debt, of one hundred and sixty thousand pounds, at the same interest. The whole of these four capitals, amounting to four millions four hundred and forty thousand pounds, produced, at their several rates, annuities amounting to six hundred and twenty three thousand pounds a year; a good deal more than one third of the clear land tax of England at four shillings in the pound; a good deal more than double the whole annual dividend of the East India Company, the nominal masters to the proprietors in these funds. Of this interest, three hundred and eighty three thousand two hundred

[9] It may be doubted whether this image is not run out too far, so as to turn off the attention from the idea to be enforced to the *picture* here presented.

[10] These claims on China merchants are not mentioned as having any direct connection with the debts of the Nabob of Arcot; they are enumerated merely as part of the twenty millions abstracted from the Carnatic by English residents, and as having been urged upon the East India Company for aid in their collection. In this view alone are they brought into the sum total of £4,440,000 mentioned below. The China debts are then deducted, leaving, as will be seen at the close of the statement, the debts of the Nabob of Arcot with "an interest of £383,200 a year, chargeable on the public revenues of the Carnatic."

pounds a year stood chargeable on the public revenues of the Carnatic.

These debts suspicious from their magnitude alone.

Sir, at this moment, it will not be necessary to consider the various operations which the capital and interest of this debt have successively undergone. I shall speak to these operations when I come particularly to answer the right honorable gentleman on each of the heads, as he has thought proper to divide them. But this was the exact view in which these debts first appeared to the court of Directors and to the world. It varied afterward; but it never appeared in any other than a most questionable shape. When this gigantic phantom of debt first appeared before a young minister, it naturally would have justified some degree of doubt and apprehension. Such a prodigy would have filled any common man with superstitious fears. He would exorcise that shapeless, nameless form, and by every thing sacred would have adjured it to tell by what means a small number of slight individuals, of no consequence or situation, possessed of no lucrative offices, without the command of armies, or the known administration of revenues, without profession of any kind, without any sort of trade sufficient to employ a peddler, could have, in a few years (as to some even in a few months), amassed treasures equal to the revenues of a respectable kingdom. Was it not enough to put these gentlemen, in the novitiate of their administration, on their guard, and to call upon them for a strict inquiry (if not to justify them in a reprobation of those demands without any inquiry at all), that when all England, Scotland, and Ireland had for years been witness to the immense sums laid out by the servants of the Company in stocks of all denominations, in the purchase of lands, in the buying and building of houses, in the securing quiet seats in Parliament, or in the tumultuous riot of contested elections, in wandering throughout the whole range of those variegated modes of inventive prodigality, which sometimes have excited our wonder, sometimes roused our indignation, that after all India was four millions still in debt to *them?* India in debt to *them!* For what? Every debt for which an equivalent of some kind or other is not given, is, on the face of it, a fraud. What is the equivalent they have given? What equivalent had they to give? What are the articles of commerce or the branches of manufacture which those gentlemen have carried hence to enrich India? What are the sciences they beamed out to enlighten it? What are the arts they introduced to cheer and to adorn it? What are the religious, what the moral institutions they have taught among that people as a guide to life, or as a consolation when life is to be no more, that there is an eternal debt—a debt "still paying, still to owe," which must be bound on the present generation in India, and entailed on their mortgaged posterity forever?[11] A debt of millions, in favor of a set of men whose names, with few exceptions, are either buried in the obscurity of their origin and talents, or dragged into light by the enormity of their crimes.[12]

These suspicions justified by the Nabob of Arcot's declarations.

In my opinion, the courage of the minister was the most wonderful part of the transaction, especially as he must have read, or rather the right honorable gentleman says he has read for him, whole volumes upon the subject. The volumes, by-the-way, are not one tenth part so numerous as the right honorable gentleman has thought proper to pretend, in order to frighten you from inquiry; but in these volumes, such as they are, the minister must have found a full authority for a suspicion (at the very least) of every thing relative to the great fortunes made at Madras. What is that authority? Why, no other than the standing authority for all the claims which the ministry has thought fit to provide for—the grand debtor—the Nabob of Arcot himself Hear that prince, in the letter written to the court of Directors, at the precise period while the main body of these debts were contracting. In his letter he states himself to be, what undoubtedly he is, a most competent witness to this point. After speaking of the war with Hyder Ali in 1768 and 1769, and of other measures which he censures (whether right or wrong, it signifies nothing), and into which he says he had been led by the Company's servants, he proceeds in this manner: "If all these things were against the real interests of the Company, they are ten thousand times more against mine, and against the prosperity of my country, and the happiness of my people, for your interests and mine are the same. What were they owing to, then? To the private views of a few individuals, who have enriched themselves at the expense of your influence and of my country; for your servants *have no trade in this country;* neither do you pay them high wages, yet in a few years they return to England with many lacs of pagodas. How can you or I account for such immense fortunes, acquired in so short a time, without any visible means of getting them?"

When he asked this question, which involves its answer, it is extraordinary that curiosity did not prompt the Chancellor of the Exchequer to that inquiry, which might come in vain recommended to him by his own act of Parliament. Does not the Nabob of Arcot tell us, in so many words, that there was no fair way of making the enormous sums sent by the Company's servants to England? And do you imagine that there was or could be more honesty and good faith in

[11] The debt immense of endless gratitude;
————still paying, still to owe.—*Milton.*

[12] It is unnecessary to remark on the beauty of this amplification, which has all the force of the severest logic, since it enumerates the only proper and legitimate means by which such a debt could have been entailed upon a people. The passage is peculiarly characteristic of Mr. Burke's genius. It was dictated by that penetrating philosophy of his which was always searching into the *causes* of things, and thus furnishing the materials of profound remark and exuberant illustration.

the demands for what remained behind in India? Of what nature were the transactions with himself? If you follow the train of his information, you must see that, if these great sums were at all lent, it was not property, but *spoil* that was lent; if not lent, the transaction was not a contract, but a fraud. Either way, if light enough could not be furnished to authorize a full condemnation of these demands, they ought to have been left to the parties who best knew and understood each other's proceedings. It is not necessary that the authority of government should interpose in favor of claims whose very foundation was a defiance of that authority, and whose object and end was its entire subversion.

It may be said that this letter was written by the Nabob of Arcot in a moody humor, under the influence of some chagrin. Certainly it was; but it is in such humors that truth comes out; and when he tells you, from his own knowledge, what every one must presume, from the extreme probability of the thing, whether he told it or not, one such testimony is worth a thousand that contradict that probability, when the parties have a better understanding with each other, and when they have a point to carry that may unite them in a common deceit.

These debts not to be paid by the Nabob.

If this body of private claims of debt, real or devised, were a question, as it is falsely pretended, between the Nabob of Arcot as debtor, and Paul Benfield and his associates as creditors, I am sure I should give myself but little trouble about it. If the hoards of oppression were the fund for satisfying the claims of bribery and peculation, who would wish to interfere between such litigants? If the demands were confined to what might be drawn from the treasures which the Company's records uniformly assert that the Nabob is in possession of, or if he had mines of gold, or silver, or diamonds (as we know that he has none), these gentlemen might break open his hoards, or dig in his mines, without any disturbance from me. But the gentlemen on the other side of the House know as well as I do, and they dare not contradict me, that the Nabob of Arcot and his creditors are not adversaries, but collusive parties, and that the whole transaction is under a false color and false names. The litigation is not, nor ever has been, between their rapacity and his hoarded riches. No! It is between him and them combining and confederating on one side, and the public revenues and the miserable inhabitants of a ruined country on the other. These are the real plaintiffs and the real defendants in the suit. Refusing a shilling from his hoards for the satisfaction of any demand, the Nabob of Arcot is always ready—nay, he earnestly, and with eagerness and passion, contends for delivering up to these pretended creditors his territory and his subjects. It is, therefore, not from treasuries and mines, but from the food of your unpaid armies, from the blood withheld from the veins and whipped out of the backs of the most miserable of men, that we are to pamper extortion, usury, and peculation, under the false names of debtors and creditors of state.[13]

Examination of the debts.

IV. The great patron of these creditors (to whose honor they ought to erect statues), the right honorable gentleman [Mr. Dundas], in stating the merits which recommended them to his favor, has ranked them under three grand divisions—the first, the creditors of 1767; then the creditors of the cavalry loan; and, lastly, the creditors of the loan in 1777. Let us examine them, one by one, as they pass in review before us.

Consolidation of 1767.

(1.) The first of these loans, that of 1767, he insists, had an indisputable claim upon the public justice. The creditors, he affirms, lent their money publicly; they advanced it with the express knowledge and approbation of the Company; and it was contracted at the moderate interest of ten per cent. In this loan the demand is, according to him, not only just, but meritorious in a very high degree; and one would be inclined to believe he thought so, because he has put it *last* in the provision he has made for these claims!

I readily admit this debt to stand the fairest of the whole; for, whatever may be my suspicions concerning a part of it, I can convict it of nothing worse than the most enormous usury. But I can convict, upon the spot, the right honorable gentleman of the most daring misrepresentation in every one fact, without any exception, that he has alleged in defense of this loan, and of his own conduct with regard to it. I will show you that this debt was never contracted with the knowledge of the Company; that it had not their approbation; that they received the first intelligence of it with the utmost possible surprise, indignation, and alarm.

Concealed from the Company.

So far from being previously apprised of the transaction from its origin, it was two years before the court of Directors obtained any official intelligence of it. "The dealings of the servants with the Nabob were concealed, from the first, until they were found out" (says Mr. Sayer, the Company's counsel) "by the report of the country." The presidency, however, at last thought proper to send an official account. On this the Directors tell them, "To your great reproach, it has been *concealed from us*. We can not but suspect this debt to have had its weight in *your proposed aggrandizement of Mohammed Ali* [the Nabob of Arcot]; but whether it has or has not, certain it is, you are guilty of a high breach of duty in *concealing* it from us."

[13] The ascendency gained by Mr. Benfield over the Nabob of Arcot was represented, by a select committee at Madras in 1783, to have been of the most absolute kind. They say that, to secure the permanency of his power and profit, he kept the Nabob an entire stranger to the state of his own affairs; that he kept the accounts and correspondence in the English language, which neither the Nabob nor his son could read; that he had surrounded the Nabob on every side, "*making him believe what was not true, and subscribe to what he did not understand.*"

These expressions concerning the ground of the transaction, its effect, and its clandestine nature, are in the letters bearing date March 17, 1769. After receiving a more full account on the 23d of March, 1770, they state that "Messrs. John Pybus, John Call, and James Bourchier, as trustees for themselves and others of the Nabob's private creditors, had proved a deed of assignment upon the Nabob and his son of *fifteen* districts of the Nabob's country, the revenues of which yielded, in time of peace, eight lacs of pagodas (£320,000 sterling) annually; and likewise an assignment of the yearly tribute paid the Nabob from the Rajah of Tanjore, amounting to four lacs of rupees (£40,000)." The territorial revenue at that time possessed by these gentlemen, without the knowledge or consent of their masters, amounted to three hundred and sixty thousand pounds sterling annually. They were making rapid strides to the entire possession of the country, when the Directors, whom the right honorable gentleman states as having authorized these proceedings, were kept in such profound ignorance of this royal acquisition of territorial revenue by their servants, that in the same letter they say, "This assignment was obtained by three of the members of your board in January, 1767, yet we do not find the *least trace* of it upon your consultations until August, 1768, nor do any of your letters to us afford any information relative to such transactions till the 1st of November, 1768. By your last letters of the 8th of May, 1769, you bring the whole proceedings to light in one view."

Never ratified by the Directors.

As to the previous knowledge of the Company, and its sanction to the debts, you see that this assertion of that knowledge is utterly unfounded. But did the Directors approve of it, and ratify the transaction when it was known? The very reverse. On the same third of March the Directors declare, "Upon an impartial examination of the whole conduct of our late governor and council of Fort George [Madras], and on the fullest consideration, that the said governor and council have, *in notorious violation of the trust* reposed in them, manifestly *preferred the interest of private individuals to that of the Company*, in permitting the assignment of the revenues of certain valuable districts, to a very large amount, from the Nabob to individuals"—and then highly aggravating their crimes, they add: "We order and direct that you do examine, in the most impartial manner, all the above-mentioned transactions, and that you *punish*, by suspension, degradation, dismission, or otherwise, as to you shall seem meet, all and every such servant or servants of the Company who may by you be found guilty of any of the above offenses." "We had (say the Directors) the mortification to find that the servants of the Company, who had been *raised*, *supported, and owed their present opulence to the advantages* gained in such service, have in this instance most *unfaithfully betrayed* their trust, *abandoned* the Company's interest, and *prostituted* its influence to accomplish the *purposes of individuals, while the interest of the Company is almost wholly neglected*, and payment to us rendered extremely precarious." Here, then, is the rock of approbation of the court of Directors, on which the right honorable gentleman says this debt was founded. Any member, Mr. Speaker, who should come into the House, on my reading this sentence of condemnation of the court of Directors against their unfaithful servants, might well imagine that he had heard a harsh, severe, unqualified invective against the present ministerial Board of Control. So exactly do the proceedings of the patrons of this abuse tally with those of the actors in it, that the expressions used in the condemnation of the one may serve for the reprobation of the other, without the change of a word.

To read you all the expressions of wrath and indignation fulminated in this dispatch against the meritorious creditors of the right honorable gentleman, who, according to him, have been so fully approved by the Company, would be to read the whole.

Action of the presidency of Madras a different thing.

The right honorable gentleman, with an address peculiar to himself, every now and then slides in the "Presidency of Madras," as synonymous to the Company. That the presidency did approve the debt is certain. But the right honorable gentleman, as prudent in suppressing as skillful in bringing forward his matter, has not chosen to tell you that the presidency were the very persons guilty of contracting this loan; creditors themselves, and agents and trustees for all the other creditors. For this, the court of Directors accuse them of breach of trust; and for this, the right honorable gentleman considers them as perfectly good authority for those claims. It is pleasant to hear a gentleman of the law quote the approbation of creditors as an authority for their own debt!

How they came to contract the debt to themselves; how they came to act as agents for those whom they ought to have controlled, is for your inquiry. The policy of this debt was announced to the court of Directors by the very persons concerned in creating it. "Till very lately" (say the presidency), "the Nabob placed his dependence on the Company. Now he has been taught by ill advisers that an interest out of doors may stand him in good stead. He has been made to believe that *his private creditors have power and interest to overrule the court of Directors*." The Nabob was not misinformed. The private creditors [Benfield, &c.] instantly qualified a vast number of votes; and having made themselves masters of the court of Proprietors, as well as extending a powerful cabal in other places as important, they so completely overturned the authority of the court of Directors at home and abroad, that this poor, baffled government was soon obliged to lower its tone. It was glad to be admitted into partnership with its own servants. The court of Directors, establishing the debt which they had reprobated as a breach of

The Directors overruled, and the debts thus sanctioned.

trust, and which was planned for the subversion of their authority, settled its payments on a par with those of the public; and even so, were not able to obtain peace, or even equality in their demands. All the consequences lay in a regular and irresistible train. By employing their influence for the recovery of this debt, their orders, issued in the same breath, against creating new debts, only animated the strong desires of their servants to this prohibited prolific sport, and it soon produced a swarm of sons and daughters not in the least degenerated from the virtue of their parents.

From that moment the authority of the court of Directors expired in the Carnatic, and every where else. "Every man," says the presidency, "who opposes the government and its measures, finds an immediate countenance from the Nabob; even our discarded officers, however unworthy, are received into the Nabob's service. It was, indeed, a matter of no wonderful sagacity to determine whether the court of Directors, with their miserable salaries to their servants of four or five hundred pounds a year, or the distributor of millions, was most likely to be obeyed. It was an invention beyond the imagination of all the speculatists of our speculating age, to see a government quietly settled in one and the same town, composed of two distinct members; one to pay scantily for obedience, and the other to bribe high for rebellion and revolt.[14]

The debt run up by enormous interest.

The next thing which recommends this particular debt to the right honorable gentleman is, it seems, the moderate interest of ten per cent. It would be lost labor to observe on this assertion. The Nabob, in a long apologetic letter for the transaction between him and the body of the creditors, states the fact as I shall state it to you. In the accumulation of this debt, the first interest paid was from thirty to thirty-six per cent.; it was then brought down to twenty-five per cent.; at length it was reduced to twenty; and there it found its rest. During the whole process, as often as any of these monstrous interests fell into an arrear (into which they were continually falling), the arrear, formed into a new capital, was added to the old, and the same interest of twenty per cent. accrued upon both. The Company, having got some scent of the enormous usury which prevailed at Madras, thought it necessary to interfere, and to order all interests to be lowered to ten per cent. This order, which contained no exception, though it by no means pointed particularly to this class of debts, came like a thunder-clap on the Nabob. He considered his political credit as ruined; but, to find a remedy to this unexpected evil, he again added to the old principal twenty per cent. interest accruing for the last year. Thus a new fund was formed; and it was on that accumulation of various principals, and interests heaped upon interests, not on the sum originally lent, as the right honorable gentleman would make you believe, that ten per cent. was settled on the whole.

When you consider the enormity of the interest at which these debts were contracted, and the several interests added to the principal I believe you will not think me so skeptical if I should doubt whether for this debt of £880,000 the Nabob ever saw £100,000 in real money. The right honorable gentleman, suspecting, with all his absolute dominion over fact, that he never will be able to defend even this venerable patriarchal job, though sanctified by its numerous issue, and hoary with prescriptive years, has recourse to recrimination, the last resource of guilt. He says that this loan of 1767 was provided for in Mr. Fox's India Bill; and, judging of others by his own nature and principles, he more than insinuates that this provision was made, not from any sense of merit in the claim, but from partiality to General Smith, a proprietor, and an agent for that debt. If partiality could have had any weight against justice and policy with the then ministers and their friends, General Smith had titles to it. But the right honorable gentleman knows as well as I do that General Smith was very far from looking on himself as partially treated in the arrangements of that time; indeed, what man dared to hope for private partiality in that sacred plan for relief to nations?

It is not necessary that the right honorable gentleman should sarcastically call that time [Mr. Fox's East India Bill] to our recollection. Well do I remember every circumstance of that memorable period. God forbid I should forget it. O, illustrious disgrace! O, victorious defeat! May your memorial be fresh and new to the latest generations! May the day of that generous conflict be stamped in characters never to be canceled or worn out from the records of time! Let no man hear of us who shall not hear that, in a struggle against the intrigues of courts, and the perfidious levity of the multitude, we fell in the cause of honor, in the cause of our country, in the cause of human nature itself! But if fortune should be as powerful over

[14] Soon after the concessions thus forcibly extorted from the Directors, Lord Pigot was sent out as Governor to Madras, with instructions to restore the authority of the Company. He was immediately met with new demands from Mr. Benfield to an enormous amount. He hesitated to admit them; and immediately a majority of the council, who were in Mr. Benfield's interest, turned against Lord Pigot. He endeavored to maintain his power by impeaching two of the majority, and thus excluding them from the council. This produced a breach in the council, as stated by Mr. Burke, one part adhering to Lord Pigot, and the other (being the majority) denying and resisting his power. The latter determined at last to proceed to extremities. Having met and declared themselves vested with the government, they actually arrested their own governor in 1776, held him in close confinement, and assumed supreme authority. This outrage awakened great indignation in Great Britain. Orders were immediately sent out for his release and return to England, that the facts might be investigated; but before these orders could reach India *he was dead.* He sunk under the effect of anxiety and prolonged imprisonment.

fame, as she has been prevalent over virtue, at least our conscience is beyond her jurisdiction. My poor share in the support of that great measure no man shall ravish from me. It shall be safely lodged in the sanctuary of my heart, never, never to be torn from thence but with those holds that grapple it to life!

I say, I well remember that bill, and every one of its honest and its wise provisions. It is not true that this debt was ever protected or enforced, or any revenue whatsoever set apart for it. It was left in that bill just where it stood, to be paid or not to be paid out of the Nabob's private treasures, according to his own discretion. The Company had actually given it their sanction, though always relying for its validity on the sole security of the faith of him who, without their knowledge or consent, entered into the original obligation. It had no other sanction; it ought to have had no other. So far was Mr. Fox's bill from providing *funds* for it, as this ministry have wickedly done for this, and for ten times worse transactions, out of the public estate, that an express clause immediately preceded positively forbidding any British subject from receiving assignments upon any part of the territorial revenue, on any pretense whatsoever.[15]

This debt not protected by Mr. Fox's bill.

You recollect, Mr. Speaker, that the Chancellor of the Exchequer [Mr. Pitt] strongly professed to retain every part of Mr. Fox's bill which was intended to prevent abuse; but in *his* India bill, which (let me do justice) is as able and skillful a performance for its own purposes as ever issued from the wit of man, premeditating this iniquity—"hoc ipsum ut strueret Trojamque aperiret Achivis"[16] expunged this essential clause, broke down the fence which was raised to cover the public property against the rapacity of his partisans, and thus leveling every obstruction, he made a firm, broad highway for "Sin and Death," for usury and oppression, to renew their ravages throughout the devoted revenues of the Carnatic.[17]

(2.) The tenor, the policy, and the consequences of this debt of 1767, are, in the eyes of the ministry, so excellent, that its merits are irresistible; and it takes the lead to give credit and countenance to all the rest. Along with this chosen body of heavy-armed infantry, and to support it in the line, the right honorable gentleman has stationed his corps of black cavalry. If there be any advantage between this debt and that of 1769, according to him the Cavalry Debt has it. It is not a subject of defense; it is a theme of panegyric. Listen to the right honorable gentleman, and you will find it was contracted to save the country; to prevent mutiny in armies; to introduce economy in revenues; and for all these honorable purposes, it originated at the express desire, and by the representative authority of the Company itself.

Cavalry Debt.

First, let me say a word to the authority. This debt was contracted, not by the authority of the Company, not by its representatives (as the right honorable gentleman has the unparalleled confidence to assert), but in the ever memorable period of 1777, by the usurped power of those who rebelliously, in conjunction with the Nabob of Arcot, had overturned the lawful government of Madras.[18] For that rebellion, this House unanimously directed a public prosecution. The delinquents, after they had subverted the government in order to make themselves a party to support them in their power, are universally known to have dealt jobs about to the right and to the left, and to any who were willing to receive them. This usurpation, which the right honorable gentleman well knows was brought about by and for the great mass of these pretended debts, is the authority which is set up by him to represent the Company; to represent that Company which, from the first moment of their hearing of this corrupt and fraudulent transaction to this hour, have uniformly disowned and disavowed it!

Not authorized by the Company, but by a faction which had usurped the government at Madras.

So much for the authority. As to the facts, partly true and partly colorable, as they stand recorded, they are in substance these. The Nabob of Arcot, as soon as he had thrown off the superiority of this country by means of these creditors, kept up a great army, which he never paid. Of course, his soldiers were generally in a state of mutiny. The usurping council say that they labored hard with their master, the Nabob, to persuade him to reduce these mutinous and useless troops. He consent-

Real origin of the debt.

15 The following were the words of Mr. Fox's bill. "And be it further enacted by the authority aforesaid, that the Nabob of Arcot, the Rajah of Tanjore, or any other protected prince of India, shall not assign, mortgage, or pledge any territory or land whatsoever. or the revenue or produce thereof to any British subject whatsoever; nor shall it be lawful for any British subject whatsoever to take or receive any such assignment, mortgage, or pledge; and the same are hereby declared null and void. And all payments, or deliveries of produce or revenue under any such assignment, shall and may be recovered back by such native prince paying or delivering the same from the person or persons receiving the same, or from his or their representatives."

16 The passage is taken from Virgil's Æneid, book ii., line 60, and relates to Sinon, the Greek spy, when brought in by the shepherds.

—qui se ignotum venientibus ultro,
Hoc ipsum ut strueret Trojamque aperiret Achivis,
Obtulerat.

He offered himself unknown to them approaching,
This very end to gain, and open Troy
To the Greeks.

17 The allusion here is to Satan's first passage to this earth, as described by Milton in his Paradise Lost, near the close of the second Book.

Sin and Death amain
Following his track (such was the will of Heaven),
Paved after him a broad and beaten way
Over the dark abyss.

18 The circumstances of this usurpation have been already detailed in note 14, page 338.

ed; but, as usual, pleaded inability to pay them their arrears. Here was a difficulty: the Nabob had no money; the Company had no money; every public supply was empty. But there was one resource which no season has ever yet dried up in that climate. The *soucars* [money lenders] were at hand; that is, private English money-jobbers offered their assistance. Messrs. Taylor, Majendie, and Call proposed to advance the small sum of £160,000, to pay off the Nabob's black cavalry, provided the Company's authority was given for their loan. This was the great point of policy always aimed at and pursued through a hundred devices by the servants at Madras. The presidency, who themselves had no authority for the functions they presumed to exercise,[19] very readily gave the sanction of the Company to those servants who knew that the Company (whose sanction was demanded) had positively prohibited all such transactions.

However, so far as the reality of the dealing goes, all is hitherto fair and plausible; and here the right honorable gentleman concludes, with commendable prudence, his account of the business. But here it is I shall beg leave to commence my supplement, for the gentleman's discreet modesty has led him to cut the thread of the story somewhat abruptly. One of the most essential parties is quite forgotten. Why should the episode of the poor Nabob be omitted? When that prince chooses it, nobody can tell his story better. Excuse me if I apply again to my book, and give it you from the first hand—from the Nabob himself.

Documentary proofs.

"Mr. Stratton [one of the members of the council at Madras] became acquainted with this, and got Mr. Taylor and others to lend me four lacs of pagodas toward discharging the arrears of pay of my troops. Upon this, I wrote a letter of thanks to Mr. Stratton; and, upon the faith of this money being paid immediately, I ordered many of my troops to be discharged by a certain day, and lessened the number of my servants. Mr. Taylor, &c., some time after acquainted me that they had no ready money, but they would grant *teeps* [notes of hand], payable in four months. This astonished me; for I did not know what might happen when the sepoys were dismissed from my service. I begged of Mr. Taylor and the others to pay this sum to the officers of my regiments at the time they mentioned; and desired the officers, at the same time, to pacify and persuade the men belonging to them that their pay would be given to them *at the end of four months;* and that till those arrears were discharged their pay should be continued to them. *Two years* are nearly expired since that time, but Mr. Taylor has not yet entirely discharged the arrears of those troops, and I am obliged to continue their pay from that time till this. I hoped to have been able, by this expedient, to have lessened the number of my troops, and discharged the arrears due to them, considering the trifle of interest to Mr. Taylor and the others as of no great matter; but instead of this, *I am oppressed with the burden of pay due to those troops, and the interest which is going on to Mr. Taylor from the day the teeps were granted to him.*" What I have read to you is an extract of a letter from the Nabob of the Carnatic to Governor Rumbold, dated the 22d, and received the 24th of March, 1779.

Suppose his Highness not to be well broken in to things of this kind, it must, indeed, surprise so known and established a bond vender as the Nabob of Arcot, one who keeps himself the largest bond warehouse in the world, to find that he was now to receive in kind; not to take money for his obligations, but to give his bond in exchange for the bond of Messrs. Taylor, Majendie, and Call, and to pay, beside, a good smart interest, legally 12 per cent. [in reality perhaps twenty or twenty-four per cent.], for this exchange of paper. But his troops were not to be so paid or so disbanded; they wanted bread, and could not live by cutting and shuffling of bonds. The Nabob still kept the troops in service, and was obliged to continue, as you have seen, the whole expense; to exonerate himself from which, he became indebted to the *soucars.*

Had it stood here, the transaction would have been of the most audacious strain of fraud and usury perhaps ever before discovered, whatever might have been practiced and concealed. But the same authority (I mean the Nabob's) brings before you something, if possible, more striking. He states that, for this their paper, he immediately handed over to these gentlemen something very different from paper; that is, the receipt of a territorial revenue, of which it seems they continued as long in possession as the Nabob himself continued in possession of any thing. Their payments, therefore, not being to commence before the end of four months, and not being completed in two years, it must be presumed (unless they proved the contrary) that their payments to the Nabob were made out of the revenues they had received from his assignment. Thus they condescended to accumulate a debt of £160,000, with an interest of 12 per cent., in compensation for a lingering payment to the Nabob of £160,000 of his own money!

Still we have not the whole. About two years after the assignment of those territorial revenues to these gentlemen, the Nabob receives a remonstrance from his chief manager, in a principal province, of which this is the tenor: "The entire revenue of those districts is by your Highness's order set apart to discharge the *tunkaws* [assignments] granted to the Europeans. The *gomastahs* [agents] of Mr. Taylor, to Mr. De Fries, are there in order to collect those *tunkaws;* and as they receive all the revenue that is collected, your Highness's troops have seven or eight months' pay due which they can not receive, and are thereby reduced to the greatest distress. *In such times,* it is highly necessary to provide for the sustenance of the troops, that they

[19] The acting presidency were the usurping ones who had imprisoned Lord Pigot.

may be ready to exert themselves in the service of your Highness."

Here, sir, you see how these causes and effects act upon one another. One body of troops mutinies for want of pay; a debt is contracted to pay them, and they still remain unpaid. A territory destined to pay other troops is assigned for this debt, and these other troops fall into the same state of indigence and mutiny with the first. Bond is paid by bond; arrear is turned into new arrear; usury engenders new usury; mutiny suspended in one quarter, starts up in another; until all the revenues and all the establishments are entangled into one inextricable knot of confusion, from which they are only disengaged by being entirely destroyed. In that state of confusion, in a very few months after the date of the memorial I have just read to you, things were found, when the Nabob's troops, famished to feed English *soucars*, instead of defending the country, joined the invaders, and deserted in entire bodies to Hyder Ali.[20]

The manner in which this transaction was carried on shows that good examples are not easily forgot, especially by those who are bred in a great school. One of those splendid examples give me leave to mention at a somewhat more early period, because one fraud furnishes light to the discovery of another, and so on, until the whole secret of mysterious iniquity bursts upon you in a blaze of detection. The paper I shall read you is not on record. If you please, you may take it on my word. It is a letter written from one of undoubted information in Madras, to Sir John Clavering, describing the practice that prevailed there, while the Company's allies were under sale, during the time of Governor Winch's administration.

"One mode," says Clavering's correspondent, "of amassing money at the Nabob's cost is curious. He is generally in arrears to the Company. Here the Governor, being cash-keeper, is generally on good terms with the banker, who manages matters thus: The Governor presses the Nabob for the balance due from him; the Nabob flies to his banker for relief; the banker engages to pay the money, and grants his notes accordingly, which he puts in the cash-book as ready money; the Nabob pays him an interest for it at two and three per cent. a month, till the *tunkaws* [assignments] he grants on the particular districts for it are paid. Matters in the mean time are so managed, that there is no call for this money for the Company's service, till the *tunkaws* become due. By this means not a cash is advanced by the banker, though he receives a heavy interest from the Nabob, which is divided as lawful spoil."

Here, Mr. Speaker, you have the whole art and mystery, the true Free-mason secret of the profession of *soucaring;* by which a few innocent, inexperienced young Englishmen, such as Mr. Paul Benfield, for instance, without property upon which any one would lend to themselves a single shilling, are enabled at once to take provinces in mortgage, to make princes their debtors, and to become creditors for millions!

But it seems the right honorable gentleman's favorite *soucar* cavalry have proved the payment before the Mayor's Court at Madras! Have they so? Why, then, defraud our anxiety and their characters of that proof? Is it not enough that the charges which I have laid before you have stood on record against these poor injured gentlemen for eight years? Is it not enough that they are in print by the orders of the East India Company for five years? After these gentlemen have borne all the odium of this publication, and all the indignation of the Directors, with such unexampled equanimity, now that they are at length stimulated into feeling, are you to deny them their just relief? But will the right honorable gentleman be pleased to tell us how they came not to give this satisfaction to the court of Directors, their lawful masters, during all the eight years of this litigated claim? Were they not bound, by every tie that can bind man, to give them this satisfaction? This day, for the first time, we hear of the proofs. But when were these proofs offered? In what cause? Who were the parties? Who inspected? Who contested this belated account? Let us see something to oppose to the body of record which appears against them. The Mayor's Court! The Mayor's Court? Pleasant! Does not the honorable gentleman know that the first corps of creditors [the creditors of 1767] stated it as a sort of hardship to them, that they could not have justice at Madras, from the impossibility of their supporting their claims in the Mayor's Court? Why? Because, say they, the members of that court were themselves creditors, and therefore could not sit as judges! Are we ripe to say that no creditor under similar circumstances was a member of the court when the payment which is the ground of this cavalry debt was put in proof? Nay, are we not in a manner compelled to conclude that the court was so constituted, when we know there is scarcely a man in Madras who has not some participation in these transactions? It is a shame to hear such proofs mentioned, instead of the honest, vigorous scrutiny which the circumstances of such an affair so indispensably call for.[21]

Exposure of the pretense that the debt had been proved in court.

But his Majesty's ministers, indulgent enough to other scrutinies, have not been satisfied with

[20] This took place in 1780, during that terrible devastation of the Carnatic by Hyder Ali, which Mr. Burke so vividly describes toward the close of this speech.

[21] As to this pretended proof before the Mayor's Court at Madras, the fact turned out to be just as Mr. Burke supposed. It was wholly collusive. It consisted merely of an affidavit of the money-lenders themselves, who swore (what no one ever doubted) that they had *engaged,* and *agreed* to pay (not that they had actually paid), the sum of £160,000 to the Nabob of Arcot. This affidavit was made two years after the transaction, before George Proctor, mayor, who was also agent for some of the creditors.

authorizing the payment of this demand without such inquiry as the act has prescribed; but they have added the arrear of twelve per cent. interest, from the year 1777 to the year 1784, to make a new capital, raising thereby £160,000 to £294,000. Then they charge a new twelve per cent. on the whole from that period, for a transaction in which it will be a miracle if a single penny will be ever found really advanced from the private stock of the pretended creditors.

(3.) In this manner, and at such an interest, the ministers have thought proper to dispose of £294,000 of the public revenues, for what is called the *Cavalry Loan.* After dispatching this, the right honorable gentleman leads to battle his last grand division, the consolidated debt of 1777. But having exhausted all his panegyric on the two first, he has nothing at all to say in favor of the last. On the contrary, he admits that it was contracted in defiance of the Company's orders, without even the pretended sanction of any pretended representatives. Nobody, indeed, has yet been found hardy enough to stand forth avowedly in its defense. But it is little to the credit of the age, that what has not plausibility enough to find an advocate, has influence enough to obtain a protector. Could any man expect to find that protector any where? But what must every man think, when he finds that protector in the chairman of the Committee of Secrecy [Mr. Dundas], who had published to the House, and to the world, the facts that condemn these debts—the orders that forbid the incurring of them—the dreadful consequences which attended them. Even in his official letter, when he tramples on his parliamentary report, yet his general language is the same. Read the preface to this part of the ministerial arrangement, and you would imagine that this debt was to be crushed, with all the weight of indignation which could fall from a vigilant guardian of the public treasury, upon those who attempted to rob it. What must be felt by every man who has feeling, when, after such a thundering preamble of condemnation, this debt is ordered to be paid without any sort of inquiry into its authenticity? without a single step taken to settle even the amount of the demand? without an attempt so much as to ascertain the real persons claiming a sum, which rises in the accounts from one million three hundred thousand pounds sterling to two millions four hundred thousand pounds principal money? without an attempt made to ascertain the proprietors, of whom no list has ever yet been laid before the court of Directors; of proprietors who are known to be in a collusive shuffle, by which they never appear to be the same in any two lists, handed about for their own particular purposes?

Consolidation of 1777.

Authorized by no one.

My honorable friend [Mr. Fox] who made you the motion has sufficiently exposed the nature of this debt. He has stated to you that *its own agents,* in the year 1781, in the arrangement *they proposed* to make at Calcutta, were satisfied to have twenty-five per cent at once struck off from the capital of a great part of this debt, and prayed to have a provision made for this reduced principal, without any interest at all! This was an arrangement of their *own*—an arrangement made by those who best knew the true constitution of their own debt; who knew how little favor it merited, and how little hopes they had to find any persons in authority abandoned enough to support it as it stood.

Abandoned, to a great extent, by the claimants themselves.

But what corrupt men, in the fond imaginations of a sanguine avarice, had not the confidence to propose, they have found a Chancellor of the Exchequer in England hardy enough to undertake for them. He has cheered their drooping spirits. He has thanked the peculators for not despairing of their commonwealth.[22] He has told them they were too modest. He has replaced the twenty-five per cent. which, in order to lighten themselves, they had abandoned in their conscious terror. Instead of cutting off the interest, as they had themselves consented to do, with one fourth of the capital, he has added the whole growth of four years' usury of twelve per cent. to the first overgrown principal, and has again grafted on this meliorated stock a perpetual annuity of six per cent., to take place from the year 1781. Let no man hereafter talk of the decaying energies of nature. All the acts and monuments in the records of peculation; the consolidated corruption of ages, the patterns of exemplary plunder in the heroic times of Roman iniquity, never equaled the gigantic corruption of this single act. Never did Nero, in all the insolent prodigality of despotism, deal out to his Pretorian guards a donation fit to be named with the largess showered down by the bounty of our Chancellor of the Exchequer on the faithful band of his Indian Sepoys.

Yet allowed in full.

The right honorable gentleman [Mr. Dundas] lets you freely and voluntarily into the whole transaction. So perfectly has his conduct confounded his understanding, that he fairly tells you that through the course of the whole business he has never conferred with any but the agents of the pretended creditors! After this, do you want more to establish a secret understanding with the parties? to fix, beyond a doubt, their collusion and participation in a common fraud?

If this were not enough, he has furnished you with other presumptions that are not to be shaken. It is one of the known indications of guilt to stagger and prevaricate in a story, and to vary in the motives that are assigned to conduct. Try these ministers by this rule. In their official dispatch, they tell the presidency of Madras that they have established the debt for two reasons; first, because the Nabob (the party indebted) does not dispute it; secondly, because it is mischievous to keep it longer afloat, and that the payment of the European creditors will promote circulation in the country. These two motives (for the plainest reasons in the world) the right honora-

Contradictory reasons assigned for allowing them.

[22] —ne de republica desperandum sit.

ble gentleman has this day thought fit totally to abandon. In the first place, he rejects the authority of the Nabob of Arcot. It would indeed be pleasant to see him adhere to this exploded testimony. He next, upon grounds equally solid, abandons the benefits of that circulation, which was to be produced by drawing out all the juices of the body. Laying aside, or forgetting these pretenses of his dispatch, he has just now assumed a principle totally different, but to the full as extraordinary. He proceeds upon a supposition that many of the claims may be fictitious. He then finds that, in a case where many valid and many fraudulent claims are blended together, the best course for their discrimination is indiscriminately to establish them all! He trusts (I suppose), as there may not be a fund sufficient for every description of creditors, that the best warranted claimants will exert themselves in bringing to light those debts which will not bear an inquiry. What he will not do himself, he is persuaded will be done by others; and for this purpose he leaves to any person a general power of excepting to the debt. This total change of language and prevarication in principle is enough, if it stood alone, to fix the presumption of unfair dealing. His dispatch assigns motives of policy, concord, trade, and circulation. His speech proclaims discord and litigations, and proposes, as the ultimate end, detection.

But he may shift his reasons, and wind and turn as he will, confusion waits him at all his doubles. Who will undertake this detection? Will the Nabob? But the right honorable gentleman has himself this moment told us that no prince of the country can by any motive be prevailed upon to discover any fraud that is practiced upon him by the Company's servants. He says what (with the exception of the complaint against the cavalry loan) all the world knows to be true; and without that prince's concurrence, what evidence can be had of the fraud of any, the smallest of these demands? The ministers never authorized any person to enter into his exchequer and to search his records. Why, then, this shameful and insulting mockery of a pretended contest? Already contests for a preference have arisen among these rival bond creditors. Has not the Company itself struggled for a preference for years, without any attempt at detection of the nature of those debts with which they contended? Well is the Nabob of Arcot attended to in the only specific complaint he has ever made. He complained of unfair dealing in the cavalry loan. It is fixed upon him with interest on interest, and this loan is excepted from all power of litigation.

This day, and not before, the right honorable gentleman thinks that the general establishment of all claims is the surest way of laying open the fraud of some of them. In India this is a reach of deep policy; but what would be thought of this mode of acting on a demand upon the treasury in England? Instead of all this cunning, is there not one plain way open, that is, to put the burden of the proof on those who make the demand? Ought not ministry to have said to the creditors, "The person who admits your debt stands excepted as to evidence; he stands charged as a collusive party, to hand over the public revenues to you for sinister purposes? You say you have a demand of some millions on the Indian treasury. Prove that you have acted by lawful authority; prove, at least, that your money has been *bona fide* advanced; entitle yourself to my protection by the fairness and fullness of the communications you make." Did an honest creditor ever refuse that reasonable and honest test?

Undoubtedly some honest creditors.

There is little doubt that several individuals have been seduced by the purveyors to the Nabob of Arcot to put their money (perhaps the whole of honest and laborious earnings) into their hands, and that such high interest, as, being condemned at law, leaves them at the mercy of the great managers whom they trusted. These seduced creditors are probably persons of no power or interest, either in England or India, and may be just objects of compassion. By taking, in this arrangement, no measures for discrimination and discovery, the fraudulent and the fair are, in the first instance, confounded in one mass. The subsequent selection and distribution is left to the Nabob! With him the agents and instruments of his corruption, whom he sees to be omnipotent in England, and who may serve him in future, as they have done in times past, will have precedence, if not an exclusive preference. These leading interests domineer, and have always domineered, over the whole. By this arrangement the persons seduced are made dependent on their seducers; honesty (comparative honesty, at least) must become of the party of fraud, and must quit its proper character and its just claims, to entitle itself to the alms of bribery and peculation.

But chiefly natives of India.

But be these English creditors what they may, the creditors most certainly not fraudulent are the natives, who are numerous and wretched indeed: by exhausting the whole revenues of the Carnatic, nothing is left for them. They lent *bona fide;* in all probability, they were even forced to lend, or to give goods and service for the Nabob's obligations. They had no trust to carry to his market. They had no faith of alliances to sell. They had no nations to betray to robbery and ruin. They had no lawful government seditiously to overturn; nor had they a governor, to whom it is owing that you exist in India, to deliver over to captivity and to death in a shameful prison.[23]

These were the merits of the principal part of the debt of 1777, and the universally conceived cause of its growth; and thus the unhappy natives are deprived of every hope of payment for their real debts, to make provision for the arrears of unsatisfied bribery and treason. You see in

[23] For the circumstances attending the imprisonment and death of Lord Pigot, Governor of Madras, see note 14, page 338.

this instance that the presumption of guilt is not only no exception to the demands on the public treasury, but, with these ministers, it is a necessary condition to their support. But that you may not think this preference solely owing to their known contempt of the natives, who ought, with every generous mind, to claim their first charities, you will find the same rule religiously observed with Europeans too. Attend, sir, to this decisive case. Since the beginning of the war, besides arrears of every kind, a bond debt has been contracted at Madras, uncertain in its amount, but represented from four hundred thousand pounds to a million sterling. It stands only at the low interest of eight per cent. Of the legal authority on which this debt was contracted, of its purposes for the very being of the state, of its publicity and fairness, no doubt has been entertained for a moment. For this debt, no sort of provision whatever has been made! It is rejected as an outcast, while the whole undissipated attention of the minister has been employed for the discharge of claims entitled to his favor by the merits we have seen!

Impossible to determine the amount of these debts.

I have endeavored to find out, if possible, the amount of the whole of those demands, in order to see how much, supposing the country in a condition to furnish the fund, may remain to satisfy the public debt and the necessary establishments; but I have been foiled in my attempt. About one fourth, that is, about £220,000 of the loan of 1767, remains unpaid. How much interest is in arrear I could never discover; seven or eight years, at least, which would make the whole of that debt about £396,000. This stock, which the ministers, in their instructions to the Governor of Madras, state as the least exceptionable, they have thought proper to distinguish by a marked severity, leaving it the only one on which the interest is not added to the principal, to beget a new interest.

The cavalry loan, by the operation of the same authority, is made up to £294,000, and this £294,000, made up of principal and interest, is crowned with a new interest of twelve per cent.

What the grand loan, the bribery loan of 1777, may be, is among the deepest mysteries of state. It is probably the first debt ever assuming the title of consolidation that did not express what the amount of the sum consolidated was. It is little less than a contradiction in terms. In the debt of the year 1767 the sum was stated in the act of consolidation, and made to amount to £880,000 capital. When this consolidation of 1777 was first announced at the Durbar [Court], it was represented authentically at £2,400,000. In that, or rather in a higher state, Sir Thomas Rumbold found and condemned it. It afterward fell into such a terror as to sweat away a million of its weight at once; and it sunk to £1,400,000. However, it never was without a resource for recruiting it to its old plumpness. There was a sort of floating debt of about four or five hundred thousand pounds more, ready to be added as occasion should require.

In short, when you pressed this sensitive plant, it always contracted its dimensions. When the rude hand of inquiry was withdrawn, it expanded in all the luxuriant vigor of its original vegetation. In the treaty of 1781, the whole of the Nabob's debt to private Europeans is, by Mr. Sullivan, agent to the Nabob and the creditors, stated at £2,800,000, which (if the cavalry loan and the remains of the debt of 1767 be subtracted) leaves it nearly at the amount originally declared at the Durbar in 1777; but then there is a private instruction to Mr. Sullivan, which, it seems, will reduce it again to the lower standard of £1,400,000. Failing in all my attempts, by a direct account, to ascertain the extent of the capital claimed (where, in all probability, no capital was ever advanced), I endeavored, if possible, to discover it by the interest which was to be paid. For that purpose, I looked to the several agreements for assigning the territories of the Carnatic to secure the principal and interest of this debt. In one of them I found a sort of postscript, by way of an additional remark (not in the body of the obligation), the debt represented at £1,400,000; but when I computed the sums to be paid for interest by installments in another paper, I found they produced the interest of two millions, at twelve per cent., and the assignment supposed that if these installments might exceed, they might also fall short of the real provision for that interest.

Another installment bond was afterward granted. In that bond the interest exactly tallies with a capital of £1,400,000. But, pursuing this capital through the correspondence, I lost sight of it again, and it was asserted that this installment bond was considerably short of the interest that ought to be computed to the time mentioned. Here are, therefore, two statements of equal authority, differing at least a million from each other; and as neither persons claiming, nor any special sum as belonging to each particular claimant is ascertained in the instruments of consolidation or in the installment bonds, a large scope was left to throw in any sums for any persons, as their merits in advancing the interest of that loan might require; a power was also left for reduction, in case a harder hand or more scanty funds might be found to require it. Stronger grounds for a presumption of fraud never appeared in any transaction. But the ministers, faithful to the plan of the interested persons, whom alone they thought fit to confer with on this occasion, have ordered the payment of the whole mass of these unknown, unliquidated sums, without an attempt to ascertain them. On this conduct, sir, I leave you to make your own reflections.

It is impossible (at least I have found it impossible) to fix on the real amount of the pretended debts with which your ministers have thought proper to load the Carnatic. They are obscure; they shun inquiry; they are enormous. That is all you know of them.

That you may judge what chance any honorable and useful end of government has for a provision that comes in for the leavings of these gluttonous demands, I must take it on myself to bring before you the real condition of that abused, insulted, racked, and ruined country; though in truth my mind revolts from it; though you will hear it with horror; and I confess I tremble when I think on these awful and confounding dispensations of Providence. I shall first trouble you with a few words as to the cause.

State and resources of the Carnatic.

The great fortunes made in India in the beginnings of conquest naturally excited an emulation in all the parts, and through the whole succession of the Company's service; but in the Company it gave rise to other sentiments. They did not find the new channels of acquisition flow with equal riches to them. On the contrary, the high flood-tide of private emolument was generally in the lowest ebb of their affairs. They began also to fear that the fortune of war might take away what the fortune of war had given. Wars were accordingly discouraged by repeated injunctions and menaces; and, that the servants might not be bribed into them by the native princes, they were strictly forbidden to take any money whatsoever from their hands. But vehement passion is ingenious in resources. The Company's servants were not only stimulated, but better instructed by the prohibition. They soon fell upon a contrivance which answered their purposes far better than the methods which were forbidden, though in this also they violated an ancient, but, they thought, an abrogated order. They reversed their proceedings. Instead of receiving presents, they made loans. Instead of carrying on wars in their own name, they contrived an authority, at once irresistible and irresponsible, in whose name they might ravage at pleasure; and, being thus freed from all restraint, they indulged themselves in the most extravagant speculations of plunder. The cabal of creditors who have been the object of the late bountiful grant from his Majesty's ministers, in order to possess themselves, under the name of creditors and assignees, of every country in India, as fast as it should be conquered, inspired into the mind of the Nabob of Arcot (then a dependent on the Company of the humblest order) a scheme of the most wild and desperate ambition that, I believe, ever was admitted into the thoughts of a man so situated. First they persuaded him to consider himself as a principal member in the political system of Europe. In the next place they held out to him, and he readily imbibed the idea, of the general empire of Hindostan. As a preliminary to this undertaking, they prevailed on him to propose a tripartite division of that vast country—one part to the Company, another to the Mahrattas, and the third to himself. To himself he reserved all the southern part of the great peninsula, comprehended under the general name of the Deccan.

Introductory remarks on the mode of plundering the country.

On this scheme of their servants, the Company was to appear in the Carnatic in no other light than as contractor for the provision of armies, and the hire of mercenaries for his use and under his direction. This disposition was to be secured by the Nabob's putting himself under the guarantee of France, and, by the means of that rival nation, preventing the English forever from assuming an equality, much less a superiority, in the Carnatic. In pursuance of this treasonable project (treasonable on the part of the English), they extinguished the Company as a sovereign power in that part of India; they withdrew the Company's garrisons out of all the forts and strong-holds of the Carnatic; they declined to receive the embassadors from foreign courts, and remitted them to the Nabob of Arcot; they fell upon and totally destroyed the oldest ally of the Company, the King of Tanjore, and plundered the country to the amount of near five millions sterling; one after another, in the Nabob's name, but with English force, they brought into a miserable servitude all the princes and great independent nobility of a vast country. In proportion to these treasons and violences, which ruined the people, the fund of the Nabob's debt grew and flourished.

Among the victims to this magnificent plan of universal plunder, worthy of the heroic avarice of the projectors, you have all heard (and he has made himself to be well remembered) of an Indian chief called Hyder Ali Khan. This man possessed the western [Mysore], as the Company, under the name of the Nabob of Arcot, does the eastern division of the Carnatic. It was among the leading measures in the design of this cabal (according to their own emphatic language) to *extirpate* this Hyder Ali. They declared the Nabob of Arcot to be his sovereign, and himself to be a rebel, and publicly invested their instrument with the sovereignty of the kingdom of Mysore. But their victim was not of the passive kind. They were soon obliged to conclude a treaty of peace and close alliance with this rebel at the gates of Madras.[24] Both before and since that treaty, every principle of policy pointed out this power as a natural alliance, and on his part it was courted by every sort of amicable office. But the cabinet council of English creditors would not suffer their Nabob of Arcot to sign the treaty, nor even to give to a prince, at least his equal, the ordinary titles of respect and courtesy. From that time forward a continued plot was carried on within the divan, black and white, of the Nabob of Arcot, for the destruction of Hyder Ali. As to the outward members of the double, or rather treble government of Madras, which had signed the treaty,[25]

Hyder Ali.

[24] This took place in 1769, when Hyder Ali artfully drew off the British army to a great distance from Madras, and then suddenly, by a forced march of one hundred and twenty miles in three days, surprised the city in a defenseless state. No resistance could be offered, and the Council of Madras was compelled to conclude a treaty, which provided for a restitution of its conquests, and a co-operation with Hyder Ali for their mutual benefit.

[25] This triple government seems to have been the Nabob of Arcot, the nominal sovereign, and the two factions into which the Council was divided.

they were always prevented by some overruling influence (which they do not describe, but which can not be misunderstood) from performing what justice and interest combined so evidently to enforce.

His invasion of the Carnatic in 1780.

When at length Hyder Ali found that he had to do with men who either would sign no convention, or whom no treaty and no signature could bind, and who were the determined enemies of human intercourse itself, he decreed to make the country possessed by these incorrigible and predestinated criminals a memorable example to mankind. He resolved, in the gloomy recesses of a mind capacious of such things, to leave the whole Carnatic an everlasting monument of vengeance, and to put perpetual desolation as a barrier between him and those against whom the faith which holds the moral elements of the world together was no protection. He became at length so confident of his force, so collected in his might, that he made no secret whatsoever of his dreadful resolution. Having terminated his disputes with every enemy and every rival, who buried their mutual animosities in their common detestation against the creditors of the Nabob of Arcot, he drew from every quarter whatever a savage ferocity could add to his new rudiments in the arts of destruction; and compounding all the materials of fury, havoc, and desolation into one black cloud, he hung for a while on the declivities of the mountains. While the authors of all these evils were idly and stupidly gazing on this menacing meteor, which blackened all their horizon, it suddenly burst, and poured down the whole of its contents upon the plains of the Carnatic. Then ensued a scene of woe, the like of which no eye had seen, no heart conceived, and which no tongue can adequately tell. All the horrors of war before known or heard of were mercy to that new havoc. A storm of universal fire blasted every field, consumed every house, destroyed every temple. The miserable inhabitants, flying from their flaming villages, in part were slaughtered; others, without regard to sex, to age, to the respect of rank, or sacredness of function; fathers torn from children, husbands from wives, enveloped in a whirlwind of cavalry, and, amid the goading spears of drivers and the trampling of pursuing horses, were swept into captivity, in an unknown and hostile land. Those who were able to evade this tempest fled to the walled cities, but, escaping from fire, sword, and exile, they fell into the jaws of famine.[26]

The alms of the settlement [Madras], in this dreadful exigency, were certainly liberal, and all

---

[26] The reader will find it interesting to compare this passage with the most eloquent one in Mr. Fox's speeches, beginning "And all this without an intelligible motive," page 549; and also with Demosthenes' description (about the middle of his Oration for the Crown) of the terror and confusion at Athens, when the news arrived that Elateia had been seized by Philip.

Mr. Fox does not attempt to describe; he simply shows us a man on a field of battle, asking *why it is fought;* and, as the inquiry goes on, we catch glimpses of the scene around, while Mr. Fox (after his usual manner) turns the whole into *argument,* mingled with the severest irony and sarcasm.

Demosthenes gives us a picture of the scene by a few distinct characteristic touches—the Presidents starting from their seats in the midst of supper—rushing into the market-place—tearing down the booths around it—burning up the hurdles even, though the space would not be wanted till the next day—sending for the generals—crying out for the trumpeter: The Council meeting on the morrow at break of day—the people (usually so reluctant to attend) pouring along to the assembly before the Council had found a moment's opportunity to inquire or agree on measures—the entering of the Council into the assembly—their announcing the news—their bringing forward the messenger to tell his story: And then the proclamation of the herald, "*Who will speak?*"—the silence of all—the voice of their common country crying out again through the herald, "Who will speak for our deliverance?"—all remaining silent—when Demosthenes arose, and suggested measures which caused all these dangers to pass away ωσπερ νέφος, like a cloud!

Mr. Burke had no individual scene of this kind to depict; his description was of necessity a general one, embracing those elements of terror and destruction which attend the progress of an invading army. There are three central points around which the description gathers as it advances. First, the forces of Hyder Ali (like those of Fabius at the approach of Hannibal), hanging in "one *black cloud* on the declivities of the mountains." Secondly, "the *storm of universal fire,*" which did in fact lay waste the Carnatic from one extremity to the other. Thirdly, the "*whirlwind of cavalry*"—how apt an image of Hyder Ali's terrible band of Abyssinian horsemen, which swept the whole country around, and hurried tens of thousands "into captivity in an unknown and hostile land!" Lord Brougham, in a criticism on this passage, pointedly remarks, that some of the secondary touches which fill up the picture, such as "blackening of all the horizon," "the menacing meteor," the "goading spears of drivers," and "the trampling of pursuing horses," rather diminish than increase the effect. He mentions, also, "the storm of *unusual* fire"—an expression flat enough certainly, if Mr. Burke had used it, to merit all his censures. But if his Lordship had recalled the circumstances of Hyder Ali's march, he would have seen that *fire* was one of his chief instruments of destruction; and therefore that the "storm of universal fire," no less than the black cloud and the whirlwind of cavalry, should occupy a prominent place in the picture.

Without wishing, however, to criticise so admirable a passage too closely, or agreeing with Lord Brougham in all his remarks, the Editor would suggest that the first two sentences of this paragraph are too much clogged with qualifying thoughts. In a passage leading to so animated a description, the ideas should be few and simple; there should be nothing to occupy or detain the mind; every thing should bear it forward to one point. But instead of this, Mr. Burke, when he had spoken of men who would sign no convention, goes on to describe them as those "whom no treaty and no signature could bind, and who were the determined enemies of human intercourse itself;" he then represents them as "incorrigible and predestinated criminals," and in the next sentence speaks of them as those "against

was done by charity that private charity could do; but it was a people in beggary; it was a nation which stretched out its hands for food. For months together these creatures of sufferance, whose very excess and luxury in their most plenteous days had fallen short of the allowance of our austerest fasts, silent, patient, resigned, without sedition or disturbance, almost without complaint, perished by a hundred a day in the streets of Madras; every day seventy at least laid their bodies in the streets, or on the glacis of Tanjore, and expired of famine in the granary of India. I was going to awake your justice toward this unhappy part of our fellow-citizens, by bringing before you some of the circumstances of this plague of hunger. Of all the calamities which beset and waylay the life of man, this comes the nearest to our heart, and is that wherein the proudest of us all feels himself to be nothing more than he is. But I find myself unable to manage it with decorum. These details are of a species of horror so nauseous and disgusting; they are so degrading to the sufferers and to the hearers; they are so humiliating to human nature itself, that, on better thoughts, I find it more advisable to throw a pall over this hideous object, and to leave it to your general conceptions.

For eighteen months, without intermission, this destruction raged from the gates of Madras to the gates of Tanjore; and so completely did these masters in their art, Hyder Ali, and his more ferocious son [Tippoo Saib], absolve themselves of their impious vow, that when the British armies traversed, as they did, the Carnatic, for hundreds of miles in all directions, through the whole line of their march they did not see one man—not one woman—not one child—not one four-footed beast of any description whatever! One dead, uniform silence reigned over the whole region. With the inconsiderable exceptions of the narrow vicinage of some few forts, I wish to be understood as speaking literally. I mean to produce to you more than three witnesses, above all exception, who will support this assertion in its full extent. That hurricane of war passed through every part of the central provinces of the Carnatic. Six or seven districts to the north and to the south (and these not wholly untouched) escaped the general ravage.

Extent of the Carnatic.

The Carnatic is a country not much inferior in extent to England. Figure to yourself, Mr. Speaker, the land in whose representative chair you sit; figure to yourself the form and fashion of your sweet and cheerful country from Thames to Trent, north and south, and from the Irish to the German Sea, east and west, emptied and emboweled (may God avert the omen of our crimes!) by so accomplished a desolation. Extend your imagination a little farther, and then suppose your ministers taking a survey of this scene of waste and desolation! What would be your thoughts if you should be informed that they were computing how much had been the amount of the excises, how much the customs, how much the land and malt tax, in order that they should charge (take it in the most favorable light) for public service upon the relics of the satiated vengeance of relentless enemies the *whole* of what England had yielded in the most exuberant seasons of peace and abundance? What would you call it? To call it tyranny, sublimed into madness, would be too faint an image. Yet this very madness is the principle upon which the ministers at your right hand have proceeded in their estimate of the revenues of the Carnatic, when they were providing, not supply for the establishments of its protection, but rewards for the authors of its ruin.

Not easily resuscitated.

Every day you are fatigued and disgusted with this cant, "The Carnatic is a country that will soon recover, and become instantly as prosperous as ever." They think they are talking to innocents, who will believe that, by sowing of dragons' teeth, men may come up ready grown and ready armed.[27] They who will give themselves the trouble of considering (for it requires no great reach of thought, no very profound knowledge) the manner in which mankind are increased and countries cultivated, will regard all this raving as it ought to be regarded. In order that the people, after a long period of vexation and plunder, may be in a condition to maintain government, government must begin by maintaining them. Here the road to economy lies, not through receipt, but through expense; and in that country nature has given no short cut to your object. Men must propagate, like other animals, by the mouth. Never did oppression light the nuptial torch—never did extortion and usury spread out the genial bed. Does any of you think that England, so wasted, would, under such a nursing attendance, so rapidly and cheaply recover? But he is meanly acquainted with either England or India, who does not know that England would a thousand times sooner resume population, fertility, and what ought to be the ultimate secretion from both, revenue, than such a country as the Carnatic.

Requires constant irrigation at great expense.

The Carnatic is not by the bounty of nature a fertile soil. The general size of its cattle is proof enough that it is much otherwise. It is some days since I moved that a curious and interesting map, kept in the India House, should be laid before you.[28]

whom the faith which holds the moral elements of the world together was no protection." All this, or nearly all, were better omitted in such a place, and perhaps, also, his description of Hyder Ali's confederates as those "who buried their mutual animosities in their common detestation of the creditors of the Nabob of Arcot." Every one must feel, especially in reading these sentences aloud, that there is a heaviness about them which is any thing but fitted to introduce a description like that which follows.

[27] Cadmus, having slain a dragon which guarded the fountain of Mars, sowed its teeth by command of Minerva, and instantly full-grown men sprang up, armed, from the ground.

[28] Mr. Barnard's map of the Jaghire. By *Jaghire* is here meant a tract of country whose reve-

The India House is not yet in readiness to send it; I have therefore brought down my own copy, and there it lies for the use of any gentleman who may think such a matter worthy of his attention. It is, indeed, a noble map, and of noble things; but it is decisive against the golden dreams and sanguine speculations of avarice run mad. In addition to what you know must be the case in every part of the world (the necessity of a previous provision of habitation, seed, stock, capital), that map will show you that the use of the influences of Heaven itself are in that country a work of art. The Carnatic is refreshed by few or no living brooks or running streams, and it has rain only at a season; but its product of rice exacts the use of water subject to perpetual command. This is the national bank of the Carnatic, on which it must have a perpetual credit, or it perishes irretrievably. For that reason, in the happier times of India, a number almost incredible of reservoirs have been made in chosen places throughout the whole country. They are formed for the greater part of mounds of earth and stones, with sluices of solid masonry; the whole constructed with admirable skill and labor, and maintained at a mighty charge. In the territory contained in that map alone, I have been at the trouble of reckoning the reservoirs, and they amount to upward of eleven hundred, from the extent of two or three acres to five miles in circuit. From these reservoirs currents are occasionally drawn over the fields, and these water-courses again call for a considerable expense to keep them properly scoured and duly leveled. Taking the district in that map as a measure, there can not be in the Carnatic and Tanjore fewer than ten thousand of these reservoirs of the larger and middling dimensions, to say nothing of those for domestic services and the use of religious purifications. These are not the enterprises of your power, nor in a style of magnificence suited to the taste of your minister. These are the monuments of real kings, who were the fathers of their people; testators to a posterity which they embraced as their own. These are the grand sepulchers built by ambition; but by the ambition of an insatiable benevolence, which, not contented with reigning in the dispensation of happiness during the contracted term of human life, had strained, with all the reachings and graspings of a vivacious mind, to extend the dominion of their bounty beyond the limits of nature, and to perpetuate themselves through generations of generations, the guardians, the protectors, the nourishers of mankind!

The reservoirs every where needed reparation.

Long before the late invasion, the persons who are objects of the grant of public money now before you had so diverted the supply of the pious funds of culture and population, that every where the reservoirs were fallen into a miserable decay. But after those domestic enemies had provoked the entry of a cruel and foreign foe into the country, he did not leave it until his revenge had completed the destruction begun by their avarice. Few, very few indeed, of these magazines of water that are not either totally destroyed, or cut through with such gaps as to require a serious attention, and much cost to re-establish them as the means of present subsistence to the people, and of future revenue to the state.

No aid afforded by the ministry for this purpose.

What, sir, would a virtuous and enlightened ministry do on the view of the ruins of such works before them? on the view of such a chasm of desolation as that which yawned in the midst of those countries, to the north and south, which still bore some vestiges of cultivation? They would have reduced all their most necessary establishments; they would have suspended the justest payments; they would have employed every shilling derived from the producing to reanimate the powers of the unproductive parts. While they were performing this fundamental duty—while they were celebrating these mysteries of justice and humanity, they would have told the corps of fictitious creditors, whose crimes were their claims, that they must keep an awful distance; that they must silence their inauspicious tongues; that they must hold off their profane and unhallowed paws from this holy work. They would have proclaimed, with a voice that should make itself heard, that in every country the first creditor is the plow; that this original, indefeasible claim supersedes every other demand.

This is what a wise and virtuous ministry would have done and said. This, therefore, is what our minister could never think of saying or doing. A ministry of another kind would have first improved the country, and have thus laid a solid foundation for future opulence and future force. But on this grand point of the restoration of the country there is not one syllable to be found in the correspondence of our ministers, from the first to the last. They felt nothing for a land desolated by fire, sword, and famine; their sympathies took another direction. They were touched with pity for bribery, so long tormented with a fruitless itching of its palms;[29] their bowels yearned for usury, that had long missed the harvest of its returning months;[30] they felt for peculation, which had been for so many years raking in the dust of an empty treasury; they were melted into compassion for rapine and oppression, licking their dry, parched, unbloody jaws. These were the objects of their solicitude! These were the necessities for which they were studious to provide!

To state the country and its revenues in their real condition, and to provide for those fictitious claims, consistently with the support of an army

nues are permanently assigned to some individual or company for a specific purpose. The Jaghire referred to in this case was an extensive district in the neighborhood of Madras, which had been granted by the Nabob to the East India Company for military service.

[29] "Yet let me tell you, Cassius, you yourself
Are much condemned to have an *itching palm*." *Julius Cesar.*

[30] Interest is rated by the month in India.

and a civil establishment, would have been impossible; therefore the ministers are silent on that head, and rest themselves on the authority of Lord Macartney, who, in a letter to the court of Directors, written in the year 1781, speculating on what might be the result of a wise management of the countries assigned by the Nabob of Arcot, rates the revenue as in time of peace at twelve hundred thousand pounds a year, as he does those of the King of Tanjore (which had not been assigned) at four hundred and fifty.[31] On this Lord Macartney grounds his calculations, and on this they choose to ground theirs. It was on this calculation that the ministry, in direct opposition to the remonstrances of the court of Directors, have compelled that miserable, enslaved body to put their hands to an order for appropriating the enormous sum of £480,000 annually as a fund for paying to their rebellious servants a debt contracted in defiance of their clearest and most positive injunctions.

Revenues of the Carnatic: erroneously estimated by the ministry.

The authority and information of Lord Macartney is held high on this occasion, though it is totally rejected in every other particular of this business. I believe I have the honor of being almost as old an acquaintance as any Lord Macartney has. A constant and unbroken friendship has subsisted between us from a very early period; and I trust he thinks that, as I respect his character, and in general admire his conduct, I am one of those who feel no common interest in his reputation; yet I do not hesitate wholly to disallow the calculation of 1781, without any apprehension that I shall appear to distrust his veracity or his judgment. This peace estimate of revenue was not grounded on the state of the Carnatic as it then, or as it had recently stood. It was a statement of former and better times. There is no doubt that a period did exist, when the large portion of the Carnatic held by the Nabob of Arcot might be fairly held to produce a revenue to that, or to a greater amount; but the whole had so melted away by the slow and silent hostility of oppression and mismanagement, that the revenues, sinking with the prosperity of the country, had fallen to about £800,000 a year, even before an enemy's horse had imprinted his hoof on the soil of the Carnatic.[32] From that view, and independently of the decisive effects of the war which ensued, Sir Eyre Coote conceived that years must pass before the country could be restored to its former prosperity and production. It was that state of revenue (namely, the actual state before the war) which the Directors have opposed to Lord Macartney's speculation. They refused to take the revenues for more than £800,000. In this they are justified by Lord Macartney himself, who, in a subsequent letter, informs the court that his sketch is a matter of speculation; it supposes the country restored to its ancient prosperity, and the revenue to be in a course of effective and honest collection. If, therefore, the ministers have gone wrong, they were not deceived by Lord Macartney; they were deceived by no man. The estimate of the Directors is nearly the very estimate furnished by the right honorable gentleman himself [Mr. Dundas], and published to the world in one of the printed reports of his own committee; but as soon as he obtained his power, he chose to abandon his account. No part of his official conduct can be defended on the ground of his parliamentary information.

Lord Macartney's estimate made in a different state of the country.

The estimate of the Directors.

In this clashing of accounts and estimates, ought not the ministry, if they wished to preserve even appearances, to have waited for information of the actual result of these speculations, before they laid a charge, and such a charge, not conditionally and eventually, but positively and authoritatively, upon a country which they all knew, and which one of them had registered on the records of this House, to be wasted beyond all example, by every oppression of an abusive government, and every ravage of a desolating war. But that you may discern in what manner they use the correspondence of office, and that thereby you may enter into the true spirit of the ministerial Board of Control, I desire you, Mr. Speaker, to remark, that through their whole controversy with the court of Directors, they do not so much as hint at their ever having seen any other paper from Lord Macartney, or any other estimate of revenue, than this of 1781. To this they hold. Here they take post; here they intrench themselves.

The ministry ought, in these circumstances, to have delayed a decision.

When I first read this curious controversy between the ministerial board and the court of Directors,[33] common candor obliged me to attribute their tenacious adherence to the estimate of 1781 to a total ignorance of what had appeared upon the records. But the right honorable gentleman has chosen to come forward with an uncalled-for declaration; he boastingly tells you that he has seen, read, digested, compared every thing, and that, if he has sinned, he has sinned with his eyes broad open. Since, then, the ministers will obstinately "shut the gates of mercy" on themselves, let them add to their crimes what aggravations they please. They have, then (since it must be so), willfully and corruptly suppressed the information which they ought to have produced, and, for the support of peculation, have made themselves guilty of spoliation and suppression of evidence. The paper I hold in my hand, which totally overturns (for the present, at least) the estimate of 1781, they have no more taken notice of in their controversy with the court of Directors than if it had

But they suppressed the most reliable estimate, that of the Madras committee.

[31] Lord Macartney was at that time Governor of Madras.

[32] The manner in which Mr. Burke here individualizes, by mentioning the horse's *hoof*, is peculiarly appropriate and beautiful, after the description given above of the "whirlwind of *cavalry*" which had swept over the Carnatic.

[33] This controversy arose out of the resistance made by the Directors to the order of the Board of Control for the payment of these debts.

no existence. It is the report made by a committee appointed at Madras to manage the whole of the six countries assigned to the Company by the Nabob of Arcot. This committee was wisely instituted by Lord Macartney, to remove from himself the suspicion of all improper management in so invidious a trust, and it seems to have been well chosen. This committee has made a comparative estimate of the only six districts which were in a condition to be let to farm. In one set of columns they state the gross and net produce of the districts as let by the Nabob. To that statement they oppose the terms on which the same districts were rented for five years under their authority. Under the Nabob, the gross farm was so high as £570,000 sterling. What was the clear produce? Why, no more than about £250,000; and this was the whole profit to the Nabob's treasury, under his own management, of all the districts which were in a condition to be let to farm on the 27th of May, 1782. Lord Macartney's leases stipulated a gross produce of no more than about £530,000, but then the estimated net amount was nearly double the Nabob's. It, however, did not then exceed £480,000; and Lord Macartney's commissioners take credit for an annual revenue amounting to this clear sum. Here is no speculation; here is no inaccurate account clandestinely obtained from those who might wish, and were enabled to deceive. It is the authorized, recorded state of a real recent transaction. Here is not twelve hundred thousand pounds—not eight hundred. The whole revenue of the Carnatic yielded no more in May, 1782, than four hundred and eighty thousand pounds; nearly the very precise sum which your minister, who is so careful of the public security, has carried from all descriptions of establishment, to form a fund for the private emolument of his creatures.[34]

In this estimate we see, as I have just observed, the Nabob's farms rated so high as £570,000. Hitherto all is well; but follow on to the effective net revenue—there the illusion vanishes; and you will not find nearly so much as half the produce. It is with reason, therefore, Lord Macartney invariably, throughout the whole correspondence, qualifies all his views and expectations of revenue, and all his plans for its application, with this indispensable condition, that the management is not in the hands of the Nabob of Arcot. Should that fatal measure take place, he has over and over again told you that he has no prospect of realizing any thing whatsoever for any public purpose. With these weighty declarations, confirmed by such a state of indisputable fact before them, what has been done by the Chancellor of the Exchequer and his accomplices? Shall I be believed? They have delivered over those very territories, on the keeping of which in the hands of the committee the defense of our dominions, and, what was more dear to them, possibly, their own job, depended; they have delivered back again, without condition, without arrangement, without stipulation of any sort for the natives of any rank, the whole of those vast countries, to many of which he had no just claim, into the ruinous mismanagement of the Nabob of Arcot! To crown all, according to their miserable practice whenever they do any thing transcendently absurd, they preface this their abdication of their trust by a solemn declaration, that they were not obliged to it by any principle of policy, or any demand of justice whatsoever.

I have stated to you the estimated produce of the territories of the Carnatic, in a condition to be farmed in 1782, according to the different managements into which they fall, and this estimate the ministers have thought proper to suppress. Since that, two other accounts have been received. The first informs us that there has been a recovery of what is called arrear, as well as of an improvement of the revenue of one of the six provinces [Tinnevelly] which were let in 1782. It was brought about by making a new war. After some sharp actions, by the resolution and skill of Colonel Fullarton, several of the petty princes of the most southerly of the unwasted provinces were compelled to pay very heavy rents and tributes, who for a long time before had not paid any acknowledgment. After this reduction, by the care of Mr. Irwin, one of the committee, that province was divided into twelve farms. This operation raised the income of that particular province; the others remain as they were first farmed. So that, instead of producing only their original rent of £480,000, they netted, in about two years and a quarter, £1.320,000 sterling, which would be about £660,000 a year if the recovered arrear was not included. What deduction is to be made on account of that arrear I can not determine, but certainly what would reduce the annual income considerably below the rate I have allowed.

Subsequent estimates.

The second account received is the letting of the wasted provinces of the Carnatic. This, I understand, is at a growing rent, which may or may not realize what it promises; but if it should answer, it will raise the whole, at some future time, to £1,200,000.

You must here remark, Mr. Speaker, that this revenue is the produce of *all* the Nabob's dominions. During the assignment the Nabob paid nothing, because the Company had all. Supposing the whole of the lately-assigned territory to yield up to the most sanguine expectations of the right honorable gentleman; and suppose £1,200,000 to be annually realized (of which we actually know of no more than the realizing of six hundred thousand), out of this you must

[34] The Company were, of course, unable to pay the Nabob's debts at once, and the Board of Control therefore exacted from the Directors a paper setting apart for this purpose twelve lacs of pagodas, or about £480,000 a year. It appears, from the above computation, that the *entire* revenue of the Carnatic would be absorbed by this assignment. Nothing remained for its government and defense. This was left to come out of the other means of the Company, and if these failed, from the public treasury at home.

deduct the subsidy and rent which the Nabob paid before the assignment, namely, £340,000 a year. This reduces back the revenue, applicable to the new distribution made by his Majesty's ministers, to about £800,000. Of that sum, five eighths are by them surrendered to the debts. The remaining three are the only fund left for all the purposes so magnificently displayed in the letter of the Board of Control; that is, for the new-cast peace establishment; a new fund for ordnance and fortifications; and a large allowance for what they call "the splendor of the Durbar" [Court of the Nabob].

You have heard the account of these territories as they stood in 1782. You have seen the *actual* receipt since the assignment in 1781, of which I reckon about two years and a quarter productive. I have stated to you the expectation from the wasted part. For realizing all this, you may value yourselves on the vigor and diligence of a governor and committee that have done so much. If these hopes from the committee are rational, remember that the committee is no more. Your ministers, who have formed their fund for these debts on the presumed effect of the committee's management, have put a complete end to that committee. Their acts are rescinded; their leases are broken; their renters are dispersed. Your ministers knew, when they signed the death-warrant of the Carnatic, that the Nabob would not only turn all these unfortunate farmers of revenue out of employment, but that he has denounced his severest vengeance against them for acting under British authority. With a knowledge of this disposition, a British Chancellor of the Exchequer and Treasurer of the Navy, incited by no public advantage, impelled by no public necessity, in a strain of the most wanton perfidy which has ever stained the annals of mankind, have delivered over to plunder, imprisonment, exile, and death itself, according to the mercy of such execrable tyrants as Amir ul Omra and Paul Benfield, the unhappy and deluded souls who, untaught by uniform example, were still weak enough to put their trust in English faith.[35] They have gone farther; they have thought proper to mock and outrage their misery by ordering them protection and compensation. From what power is this protection to be derived? And from what fund is this compensation to arise? The revenues are delivered over to their oppressor; the territorial jurisdiction, from whence that revenue is to arise, and under which they live, is surrendered to the same iron hands; and that they shall be deprived of all refuge and all hope, the minister has made a solemn, voluntary declaration that he never will interfere with the Nabob's internal government.

The Company's Debt.

VI. The last thing considered by the Board of Control, among the debts of the Carnatic, was that arising to the East India Company, which, after the provision for the cavalry and the consolidation of 1777, was to divide the residue of the fund of £480,000 a year with the lenders of 1767. This debt the worthy chairman, who sits opposite to me, contends to be three millions sterling. Lord Macartney's account of 1781 states it to be, at that period, £1,200,000. The first account of the court of Directors makes it £900,000. This, like the private debt, being without any solid existence, is incapable of any distinct limits. Whatever its amount or its validity may be, one thing is clear; it is of the nature and quality of a public debt. In that light, nothing is provided for it but an eventual surplus to be divided with one class of the private demands, after satisfying the two first classes. Never was a more shameful postponing a public demand, which, by the reason of the thing, and the uniform practice of all nations, supersedes every private claim.[36]

Those who gave this preference to private claims consider the Company's as a lawful demand; else, why did they pretend to provide for it? On their own principles they are condemned.

This debt ought not to be charged on the revenues of the Carnatic.

But I, sir, who profess to speak to your understanding and to your conscience, and to brush away from this business all false colors, all false appellations, as well as false facts, do positively deny that the Carnatic owes a shilling to the Company, whatever the Company may be indebted to that undone country. It owes nothing to the Company, for this plain and simple reason: *The territory charged with the debt is their own!* To say that their revenues fall short, and owe them money, is to say they are in debt to themselves, which is only talking nonsense. The fact is, that by the invasion of an enemy, and the ruin of the country, the Company, either in its own name or in the names of the Nabob of Arcot and Rajah of Tanjore, has lost for several years what it might have looked to receive from its own estate. If men were allowed to credit themselves, upon such principles any one might soon grow rich by this mode of accounting. A flood comes down upon a man's estate in the Bedford level of a thousand pounds a year, and drowns his rents for ten years. The chancellor would put that man into the hands of a trustee, who would gravely make up his books, and for this loss credit

[35] The favorite son of the Nabob, Amir ul Omra, was so vicious and cruel, that, although destined to succeed his father, the Company set him aside on the death of the Nabob in 1795, and gave the government to his brother.

[36] The civil and military government of India, and the charge of its revenues, had been taken from the Company by Mr. Pitt's bill, and placed in the hands of the British government. All debts due to the Company had, therefore, become *public* debts; and if brought into the account at all, ought, on established principles, to have taken the precedence of every other. Instead of this, they had been put after most of the others! Mr. Burke, however, contends that they ought not to be brought into the account at all. The Company were now masters of the country; and whatever sums they had expended in thus adding to their dominions ought to be carried to the account of "profit and loss." They ought not to be brought in as *debts*, to squeeze more revenue out of the natives, or to be saddled on the public, if that revenue should fail.

himself in his account for a debt due to him of £10,000. It is, however, on this principle the Company makes up its demands on the Carnatic. In peace they go the full length, and indeed more than the full length, of what the people can bear for current establishments; then they are absurd enough to consolidate all the calamities of war into debts; to metamorphose the devastations of the country into demands upon its future production. What is this but to avow a resolution utterly to destroy their own country, and to force the people to pay for their sufferings, to a government which has proved unable to protect either the share of the husbandman or their own? In every lease of a farm, the invasion of an enemy, instead of forming a demand for arrear, is a release of rent; nor for that release is it at all necessary to show that the invasion has left nothing to the occupier of the soil, though in the present case it would be too easy to prove that melancholy fact. I therefore applaud my right honorable friend, who, when he canvassed the Company's accounts, as a preliminary to a bill that ought not to stand on falsehood of any kind, fixed his discerning eye and his deciding hand on these debts of the Company, from the Nabob of Arcot and Rajah of Tanjore, and at one stroke expunged them all, as utterly irrecoverable; he might have added, as utterly unfounded.

On these grounds I do not blame the arrangement this day in question, as a preference given to the debt of individuals over the Company's debt. In my eye, it is no more than the preference of a fiction over a chimera; but I blame the preference given to those fictitious private debts over the standing defense and the standing government. It is there the public is robbed. It is robbed in its army; it is robbed in its civil administration; it is robbed in its credit; it is robbed in its investment, which forms the commercial connection between that country and Europe. There is the robbery.

This debt made the pretext for others of the most unjustifiable nature.

But my principal objection lies a good deal deeper. That debt to the Company is the pretext under which all the other debts lurk and cover themselves. That debt forms the foul, putrid mucus, in which are engendered the whole brood of creeping ascarides, all the endless involutions, the eternal knot, added to a knot of those inexpugnable tape-worms which devour the nutriment, and eat up the bowels of India. It is necessary, sir, you should recollect two things: first, that the Nabob's debt to the Company carries no interest. In the next place you will observe, that whenever the Company has occasion to borrow, she has always commanded whatever she thought fit at eight per cent. Carrying in your mind these two facts, attend to the process with regard to the public and private debt, and with what little appearance of decency they play into each other's hands a game of utter perdition to the unhappy natives of India. The Nabob falls into an arrear to the Company. The presidency presses for payment. The Nabob's answer is, I have no money. Good! But there are *soucars* who will supply you on the mortgage of your territories. Then steps forward some Paul Benfield, and from his grateful compassion to the Nabob, and his filial regard to the Company, he unlocks the treasures of his virtuous industry, and for a consideration of twenty-four or thirty-six per cent. on a mortgage of the territorial revenue, becomes security to the Company for the Nabob's arrear.

All this intermediate usury thus becomes sanctified by the ultimate view to the Company's payment. In this case, would not a plain man ask this plain question of the Company: If you know that the Nabob must annually mortgage his territories to your servants to pay his annual arrear to you, why is not the assignment or mortgage made directly to the Company itself? By this simple, obvious operation, the Company would be relieved and the debt paid, without the charge of a shilling interest to that prince. But if that course should be thought too indulgent, why do they not take that assignment with such interest to themselves as they pay to others; that is, eight per cent.? Or, if it were thought more advisable (why it should I know not) that he must borrow, why do not the Company lend their own credit to the Nabob for their own payment? That credit would not be weakened by the collateral security of his territorial mortgage. The money might still be had at eight per cent. Instead of any of these honest and obvious methods, the Company has for years kept up a show of disinterestedness and moderation, by suffering a debt to accumulate to them from the country powers, without any interest at all; and at the same time have seen before their eyes, on a pretext of borrowing to pay that debt, the revenues of the country charged with a usury of twenty, twenty-four, thirty-six, and even eight-and-forty per cent., with compound interest, for the benefit of their servants! All this time they know that by having a debt subsisting without any interest, which is to be paid by contracting a debt on the highest interest, they manifestly render it necessary to the Nabob of Arcot to give the private demand a preference to the public; and, by binding him and their servants together in a common cause, they enable him to form a party to the utter ruin of their own authority and their own affairs. Thus their false moderation and their affected purity, by the natural operation of every thing false and every thing affected, becomes pander and bawd to the unbridled debauchery and licentious lewdness of usury and extortion.

Extreme oppression of the natives the necessary result.

In consequence of this double game, all the territorial revenues have, at one time or other, been covered by those locusts, the English *soucars*. Not one single foot of the Carnatic has escaped them; a territory as large England! During these operations, what a scene has that country presented! The usurious European assignee supersedes the Nabob's native farmer of the revenue; the farmer flies to the Nabob's presence to claim his bargain; while his servants murmur for wages, and his soldiers mutiny for pay.[37] The mortgage to the European assignee is then resumed, and the native farmer replaced; replaced, again to be removed on the new clamor of the European assignee. Every man of rank and landed fortune being long since extinguished, the remaining miserable last cultivator, who grows to the soil, after having his back scored by the farmer, has it again flayed by the whip of the assignee, and is thus, by a ravenous, because a short-lived succession of claimants, lashed from oppressor to oppressor, while a single drop of blood is left as the means of extorting a single grain of corn. Do not think I paint. Far, very far from it; I do not reach the fact, nor approach to it. Men of respectable condition, men equal to your substantial English yeomen, are daily tied up and scourged to answer the multiplied demands of various contending and contradictory titles, all issuing from one and the same source. Tyrannous exaction brings on servile concealment, and that, again, calls forth tyrannous coercion. They move in a circle, mutually producing and produced; till at length nothing of humanity is left in the government, no trace of integrity, spirit, or manliness in the people, who drag out a precarious and degraded existence under this system of outrage upon human nature. Such is the effect of the establishment of a debt to the Company, as it has hitherto been managed, and as it ever will remain, until ideas are adopted totally different from those which prevail at this time.

Your worthy ministers, supporting what they are obliged to condemn, have thought fit to renew the Company's old order against contracting private debts in future. They begin by rewarding the violation of the ancient law; and then they gravely re-enact provisions, of which they have given bounties for the breach. This inconsistency has been well exposed by Mr. Fox. But what will you say to their having gone the length of giving positive directions for contracting the debt which they positively forbid?

I will explain myself. They order the Nabob, out of the revenues of the Carnatic, to allot four hundred and eighty thousand pounds a year as a fund for the debts before us. For the punctual payment of this annuity, they order him to give *soucar* security. When a *soucar*, that is, a money-dealer, becomes security for any native prince, the course is, for the native prince to counter-secure the money-dealer by making over to him in mortgage a portion of his territory equal to the sum annually to be paid, with an interest of at least twenty-four per cent. The point fit for the House to know is, who are these *soucars* to whom this security on the revenues in favor of the Nabob's creditors is to be given? The majority of the House, unaccustomed to these transactions, will hear with astonishment that these *soucars* are no other than the creditors themselves. The minister, not content with authorizing these transactions in a manner and to an extent unhoped for by the rapacious expectations of usury itself, loads the broken back of the Indian revenues, in favor of his worthy friends the *soucars*, with an additional twenty-four per cent. for being security to themselves for their own claims; for condescending to take the country in mortgage to pay to themselves the fruits of their extortions!

The orders of the ministry render new debts necessary, at an enormous rate of interest.

The interest to be paid for this security, according to the most moderate strain of *soucar* demand, comes to one hundred and eighteen thousand pounds a year, which, added to the £480,000 on which it is to accrue, will make the whole charge on account of these debts on the Carnatic revenues amount to £598,000 a year, as much as even a long peace will enable those revenues to produce. Can any one reflect for a moment on all those claims of debt, which the minister exhausts himself in contrivances to augment with new usuries, without lifting up his hands and eyes in astonishment of the impudence both of the claim and of the adjudication? Services of some kind or other these servants of the Company must have done, so great and eminent, that the Chancellor of the Exchequer can not think that all they have brought home is half enough. He halloos after them, "Gentlemen, you have forgot a large packet behind you, in your hurry; you have not sufficiently recovered yourselves; you ought to have, and you shall have, interest upon interest, upon a prohibited debt that is made up of interest upon interest. Even this is too little; I have thought of another character for you, by which you may add something to your gains; you shall be security to yourselves; and hence will arise a new usury, which shall efface the memory of all the usuries suggested to you by your own dull inventions."

VII. I have done with the arrangement relative to the Carnatic. After this, it is to little purpose to observe on what the ministers have done to Tanjore. Your ministers have not observed even form and ceremony in their outrageous and insulting robbery of that country, whose only crime has been its early and constant adherence to the power of this, and the suffering of a uniform pillage in consequence of it. The debt of the Company from the Rajah of Tanjore is just of the same stuff with that of the Nabob of Arcot.[38]

Treatment of Tanjore.

[37] The books of the Company, in 1781, show that the Nabob's farmers of revenue rarely continued in office three months. What must have been the state of the country under such a system of exaction!

[38] Tanjore was a small kingdom on the southeastern coast of India, bordering on the Carnatic. Hyder Ali was eager to bring it into subjection to himself; and the presidency at Madras (then under the control of Benfield and his associates) united in the design, and sent an army for this purpose. At a later period they changed their policy, and sent another army to seize and hold it for the Company. "Never," says Mill, "was the resolution taken to make war upon a lawful sovereign with a view of stripping him of his dominions, and either putting him and his family to death, or making them prisoners for life, on a more accommodating principle. We

The Tanjore debt of £400,000 utterly without foundation.

The subsidy from Tanjore, on the arrear of which this pretended debt (if any there be) has accrued to the Company, is not, like that paid by the Nabob of Arcot, a compensation for vast countries obtained, augmented, and preserved for him; not the price of pillaged treasuries, ransacked houses, and plundered territories. It is a large grant from a small kingdom not obtained by our arms; robbed, not protected by our power; a grant for which no equivalent was ever given, or pretended to be given. The right honorable gentleman [Mr. Dundas], however, bears witness in his reports to the punctuality of the payments of this grant of bounty, or, if you please, of fear. It amounts to one hundred and sixty thousand pounds sterling net annual subsidy. He bears witness to a farther grant of a town and port, with an annexed district of thirty thousand pounds a year, surrendered to the Company since the first donation. He has not borne witness, but the fact is (he will not deny it), that, in the midst of war, and during the ruin and desolation of a considerable part of his territories, this prince made many very large payments. Notwithstanding these merits and services, the first regulation of ministry is to force from him a territory of an extent which they have not yet thought proper to ascertain for a military peace establishment, the particulars of which they have not yet been pleased to settle.

Penalty against the Rajah if engaged in war.

The next part of their arrangement is with regard to war. As confessedly this prince had no share in stirring up any of the former wars, so all future wars are completely out of his power; for he has no troops whatever, and is under a stipulation not so much as to correspond with any foreign state, except through the Company. Yet, in case the Company's servants should be again involved in war, or should think proper again to provoke any enemy, as in times past they have wantonly provoked all India, he is to be subjected to a new penalty. To what penalty? Why, to no less than the confiscation of all his revenues. But this is to end with the war, and they are to be faithfully returned? Oh, no; nothing like it. The country is to remain under confiscation until all the debt which the Company shall think fit to incur in such war shall be discharged; that is to say, forever. His sole comfort is to find his old enemy, the Nabob of Arcot, placed in the very same condition.

Revenues of Tanjore.

The revenues of that miserable country were, before the invasion of Hyder, reduced to a *gross* annual receipt of three hundred and sixty thousand pounds. From this receipt the subsidy I have just stated is taken. This again, by payments in advance, by extorting deposits of additional sums to a vast amount for the benefit of their *soucars*, and by an endless variety of other extortions, public and private, is loaded with a debt, the amount of which I never could ascertain, but which is large undoubtedly, generating a usury the most completely ruinous that probably was ever heard of; *that is, forty-eight per cent., payable monthly, with compound interest!*

Tanjore compelled to pay an annual tribute of £40,000 to the Nabob of Arcot.

Such is the state to which the Company's servants have reduced that country. Now come the reformers, restorers, and comforters of India. What have they done? In addition to all these tyrannous exactions, with all these ruinous debts in their train, looking to one side of an agreement while they willfully shut their eyes to the other, they withdraw from Tanjore all the benefits of the treaty of 1762, and they subject that nation to a perpetual tribute of forty thousand a year to the Nabob of Arcot—a tribute never due, or pretended to be due to *him*, even when he appeared to be something—a tribute, as things now stand, not to a real potentate, but to a shadow, a dream, an incubus of oppression. After the Company has accepted in subsidy, in grant of territory, in remission of rent, as a compensation for their own protection, at least two hundred thousand pounds a year, without discounting a shilling for that receipt, the ministers condemn this harassed nation to be tributary to a person [the Nabob of Arcot] who is himself, by their own arrangement, deprived of the right of war or peace; deprived of the power of the sword; forbid to keep up a single regiment of soldiers; and is, therefore, wholly disabled from all protection of the country which is the object of the pretended tribute. Tribute hangs on the sword. It is an incident inseparable from real sovereign power. In the present case, to suppose its existence is as absurd as it is cruel and oppressive. And here, Mr. Speaker, you have a clear exemplification of the use of those false names and false colors which the gentlemen who have lately taken possession of India choose to lay on for the purpose of disguising their plan of oppression. The Nabob of Arcot and Rajah of Tanjore have, in truth and substance, no more than a merely civil authority, held in the most entire dependence on the Com-

have done the Rajah great injury; we have no intention of doing him right. This constitutes a full and sufficient reason for going on to his destruction." Such was the doctrine! As Tanjore was thus seized without any authority from the Directors at London, the presidency at Madras was ordered to restore it; and Lord Pigot was sent out to carry the restoration into effect. A statement has already been given of the violence which ensued, and the imprisonment of Lord Pigot by the majority of the Council, who were in the interest of Benfield and his partisans. When the restoration was at last effected, it was only partial; some of the territory was withheld; and no part of the goods, money, or revenues, so unjustly taken from the Rajah, were restored. The Directors of the East India Company were ordered, in Mr. Pitt's East India Bill, to examine into the subject, and came to the conclusion that certain portions of territory should be restored to the Rajah. The Board of Control overruled this decision, and, though Tanjore had been repeatedly plundered, and reduced to a state of extreme destitution, levied upon the country about £400,000 as a pretended debt for arrearage of tribute. Other wrongs inflicted on Tanjore are enumerated by Mr. Burke.

pany. The Nabob, without military, without federal capacity, is extinguished as a potentate; but then he is carefully kept alive as an independent and sovereign power, for the purpose of rapine and extortion; for the purpose of perpetuating the old intrigues, animosities, usuries, and corruptions.

It was not enough that this mockery of tribute was to be continued without the correspondent protection, or any of the stipulated equivalents, but ten years of arrear, to the amount of £400,000 sterling, is added to all the debts to the Company and to individuals, in order to create a new debt, to be paid (if at all possible, to be paid in whole or in part) only by new usuries; and all this for the Nabob of Arcot, or, rather, for Mr. Benfield and the corps of the Nabob's creditors and their *soucars*. Thus these miserable Indian princes are continued in their seats, for no other purpose than to render them, in the first instance, objects of every species of extortion, and, in the second, to force them to become, for the sake of a momentary shadow of reduced authority, a sort of subordinate tyrants, the ruin and calamity, not the fathers and cherishers of their people.

Cruel arrangement respecting the means of irrigating Tanjore.

But take this tribute only as a mere charge (without title, cause, or equivalent) on this people; what one step has been taken to furnish grounds for a just calculation and estimate of the proportion of the burden and the ability? None; not an attempt at it. They do not adapt the burden to the strength, but they estimate the strength of the bearers by the burden they impose. Then what care is taken to leave a fund sufficient to the future reproduction of the revenues that are to bear all these loads? Every one but tolerably conversant in Indian affairs must know that the existence of this little kingdom depends on its control over the River Cavery.[39] The benefits of Heaven to any community ought never to be connected with political arrangements, or made to depend on the personal conduct of princes, in which the mistake, or error, or neglect, or distress, or passion of a moment on either side may bring famine on millions, and ruin an innocent nation perhaps for ages. The means of the subsistence of mankind should be as immutable as the laws of nature, let power and dominion take what course they may. Observe what has been done with regard to this important concern. The use of this river is indeed at length given to the Rajah, and a power provided for its enjoyment *at his own charge;* but the means of furnishing that charge (and a mighty one it is) are wholly cut off. This use of the water, which ought to have no more connection than clouds, and rains, and sunshine, with the politics of the Rajah, the Nabob, or the Company, is expressly contrived as a means of enforcing demands and arrears of tribute.[40] This horrid and unnatural instrument of extortion had been a distinguishing feature in the enormities of the Carnatic politics that loudly called for reformation. But the food of a whole people is by the reformers of India conditioned on payments from its prince at a moment that he is overpowered with a swarm of their demands, without regard to the ability of either prince or people. In fine, by opening an avenue to the irruption of the Nabob of Arcot's creditors and *soucars*, whom every man who did not fall in love with oppression and corruption, on an experience of the calamities they produced, would have raised wall before wall, and mound before mound, to keep from a possibility of entrance, a more destructive enemy than Hyder Ali is introduced into that kingdom. By this part of their arrangement, in which they establish a debt to the Nabob of Arcot, in effect and substance they deliver over Tanjore, bound hand and foot, to Paul Benfield, the old betrayer, insulter, oppressor, and scourge of a country which has for years been an object of an unremitted, but, unhappily, an unequal struggle, between the bounties of Providence to renovate and the wickedness of mankind to destroy.

Injustice of Mr. Dundas in deciding between the Rajah of Tanjore and the Nabob of Arcot.

The right honorable gentleman talks of his fairness in determining the territorial dispute between the Nabob of Arcot and the prince of that country, when he superseded the determination of the Directors, in whom the law had vested the decision of that controversy. He is in this just as feeble as he is in every other part. But it is not necessary to say a word in refutation of any part of his argument. The mode of the proceeding sufficiently speaks the spirit of it. It is enough to fix his character as a judge, that he *never heard the Directors in defense of their adjudication, nor either of the parties in support of their respective claims.* It is sufficient for me that he takes from the Rajah of Tanjore by this pretended adjudication, or, rather, from his unhappy subjects, £40,000 a year of his and their revenue, and leaves upon his and their shoulders all the charges that can be made on the part of the Nabob, on the part of his creditors, and on the part of the Company, without so much as hearing him as to right or to ability. But what principally induces me to leave the affair of the territorial dispute between the Nabob and the Rajah to another day is this, that both the parties being stripped of their all, it little signifies under which of their names the unhappy, undone people are delivered over to the merciless *soucars*, the allies of that right honorable gentleman and the Chancellor of the Exchequer. In them ends the account of this long dispute of the Nabob of Arcot and the Rajah of Tanjore.

The right honorable gentleman is of opinion

39 This river rises in a chain of mountains called the Ghauts, near the Malibar coast, and, after a course of four hundred and fifty miles, flows into the sea through Tanjore. The vast rice plains of that country are dependent for their products on the waters of this river, which are turned upon the fields by means of embankments and canals.

40 This refers to the instructions of the Board of Control, which expressly provide that the use of water from the Cavery for the irrigation of his territory shall be enjoyed by the Rajah "only while he shall be punctual in paying his annual tribute to the Nabob."

that his judgment in this case can be censured by none but those who seem to act as if they were paid agents to one of the parties.[41] What does he think of his court of Directors? If they are paid by either the parties, by which of them does he think they are paid? He knows that their decision has been directly contrary to his. Shall I believe that it does not enter into his heart to conceive that any person can steadily and actively interest himself in the protection of the injured and oppressed without being well *paid* for his service? I have taken notice of this sort of discourse some days ago, so far as it may be supposed to relate to me. I then contented myself, as I shall now do, with giving it a cold, though a very direct contradiction. Thus much I do from respect to truth. If I did more, it might be supposed, by my anxiety to clear myself, that I had imbibed the ideas which, for obvious reasons, the right honorable gentleman wishes to have received concerning all attempts to plead the cause of the natives of India, as if it were a disreputable employment. If he had not forgot, in his present occupation, every principle which ought to have guided him, and, I hope, did guide him, in his late profession [the law], he would have known that he who takes a fee for pleading the cause of distress against power, and manfully performs the duty he has assumed, receives an honorable recompense for a virtuous service. But if the right honorable gentleman will have no regard to fact in his insinuations or to reason in his opinions, I wish him at least to consider that if taking an earnest part with regard to the oppressions exercised in India, and with regard to this most oppressive case of Tanjore in particular, can ground a presumption of interested motives, he is *himself* the most mercenary man I know. His conduct, indeed, is such that he is on all occasions the standing testimony against himself. He it was that first called to that case the attention of the House. The reports of his own committee are ample and affecting upon that subject; and as many of us as have escaped his massacre must remember the very pathetic picture he made of the sufferings of the Tanjore country on the day when he moved the unwieldy code of his Indian resolutions.[42] Has he not stated over and over again, in his reports, the ill treatment of the Rajah of Tanjore (a branch of the royal house of the Mahrattas, every injury to whom the Mahrattas felt as offered to themselves) as a main cause of the alienation of that people from the British power? And does he now think that, to betray his principles, to contradict his declarations, and to become himself an active instrument in those oppressions which he had so tragically lamented, is the way to clear himself of having been actuated by a pecuniary interest at the time when he chose to appear full of tenderness to that ruined nation?

Attack on Mr. Dundas in reply to his insinuations against Mr. Burke.

VIII. The right honorable gentleman is fond of parading on the motives of others, and on his own. As to himself, he despises the imputations of those who suppose that any thing corrupt could influence him in this his unexampled liberality of the public treasure. I do not know that I am obliged to speak to the motives of the ministry in the arrangements they have made of the pretended debts of Arcot and Tanjore. If I prove fraud and collusion with regard to public money on those right honorable gentlemen, I am not obliged to assign their motives, because no good motives can be pleaded in favor of their conduct. Upon that case I stand; we are at issue, and I desire to go to trial. This, I am sure, is not loose railing or mean insinuation, according to their low and degenerate fashion when they make attacks on the measures of their adversaries. It is a regular and juridical course and, unless I choose it, nothing can compel me to go farther.

Motives which led to the payment of these debts.

But since these unhappy gentlemen have dared to hold a lofty tone about their motives, and affect to despise suspicion, instead of being careful not to give cause for it, I shall beg leave to lay before you some general observations on what I conceive was their duty in so delicate a business.

If I were worthy to suggest any line of prudence to that right honorable gentleman, I would tell him that the way to avoid suspicion in the settlement of pecuniary transactions, in which great frauds have been very strongly presumed, is to attend to these few plain principles: First, to hear all parties equally, and not the managers for the suspected claimants only; not to proceed in the dark, but to act with as much publicity as possible; not to precipitate decision; to be religious in following the rules prescribed in the commission under which we act; and lastly, and above all, not to be fond of straining constructions to force a jurisdiction, and to draw to ourselves the management of a trust in its nature invidious and obnoxious to suspicion, where the plainest letter of the law does not compel it. If these few plain rules are observed, no corruption ought to be suspected; if any of them are violated, suspicion will attach in proportion. If all of them are violated, a corrupt motive of some kind or other will not only be suspected, but must be violently presumed.

Way for ministers to avoid suspicion.

The persons in whose favor all these rules

---

[41] This refers to an insinuation thrown out by Mr. Dundas, some days previous, that Mr. Burke was a *paid* agent of the Rajah of Tanjore. Nothing could be more false, and the only pretense for it was that William Burke, brother of Edmund, was in the Rajah's service. At that time, Mr. Burke simply repelled the insinuation. He now turns back Mr. Dundas' attack upon himself.

[42] Mr. Dundas was chairman of the Committee of Secrecy on Indian Affairs. In 1782 he made a number of voluminous reports on the subject, and introduced nearly a hundred resolutions to carry out his views. The "massacre" to which Mr. Burke sportively alludes, seems to have been the defeat of the Coalition Ministry in respect to their East India Bill, in accomplishing which Mr. Dundas bore a very active part.

have been violated, and the conduct of ministers toward them, will naturally call for your consideration, and will serve to lead you through a series and combination of facts and characters, if I do not mistake, into the very inmost recesses of this mysterious business. You will then be in possession of all the materials on which the principles of sound jurisprudence will found, or will reject the presumption of corrupt motives; or, if such motives are indicated, will point out to you of what particular nature the corruption is.

The payment of these debts owing to the parliamentary influence of Paul Benfield, the principal creditor.

Our wonderful minister [Mr. Pitt], as you all know, formed a new plan, a plan *insigne, recens, alio indictum ore*,[43] a plan for supporting the *freedom* of our Constitution by court intrigues, and for removing its *corruptions* by Indian delinquency![44] To carry that bold paradoxical design into execution, sufficient funds and apt instruments became necessary. You are perfectly sensible that a parliamentary reform occupies his thoughts day and night, as an essential member of this extraordinary project. In his anxious researches upon this subject, natural instinct, as well as sound policy, would direct his eyes, and settle his choice on Paul Benfield. Paul Benfield is the grand parliamentary reformer, the reformer to whom the whole choir of reformers bow, and to whom even the right honorable gentleman himself must yield the palm; for what region in the empire, what city, what borough, what county, what tribunal, in this kingdom, is not full of his labors?[45] Others have been only speculators; he is the grand practical reformer; and while the Chancellor of the Exchequer pledges in vain the man and the minister to increase the provincial members, Mr. Benfield has auspiciously and practically begun it. Leaving far behind him even Lord Camelford's generous design of bestowing Old Sarum on the Bank of England, Mr. Benfield has thrown in the borough of Cricklade to re-enforce the county representation! Not content with this, in order to station a steady phalanx for all future reforms, this public-spirited usurer, amid his charitable toils for the relief of India, did not forget the poor, rotten Constitution of his native country. For her, he did not disdain to stoop to the trade of a wholesale upholsterer for this House, to furnish it, not with the faded tapestry figures of antiquated merit, such as decorate, and may reproach some other houses, but with real, solid, living patterns of true modern virtue. Paul Benfield made (reckoning himself) no fewer than eight members in the last Parliament. What copious streams of pure blood must he not have transfused into the veins of the present!

But what is even more striking than the real services of this new-imported patriot is his modesty. As soon as he had conferred this benefit on the Constitution, he withdrew himself from our applause. He conceived that the duties of a member of Parliament (which, with the elect faithful, the true believers, the *Islam* of parliamentary reform, are of little or no merit, perhaps not much better than specious sins) might be as well attended to in India as in England, and the means of reformation to Parliament itself be far better provided. Mr. Benfield was, therefore, no sooner elected, than he set off for Madras, and defrauded the longing eyes of Parliament. We have never enjoyed in this House the luxury of beholding that minion of the human race, and contemplating that visage, which has so long reflected the happiness of nations.

Benfield did not take his seat in Parliament, but went to Madras.

It was, therefore, not possible for the minister to consult personally with this great man. What, then, was he to do? Through a sagacity that never failed him in these pursuits, he found out in Mr. Benfield's representative his exact resemblance. A specific attraction, by which he gravitates toward all such characters, soon brought our minister into a close connection with Mr. Benfield's agent and attorney, that is, with the grand contractor (whom I name to honor[46]), Mr. Richard Atkinson; a name that will be well remembered as long as the records of this House, as long as the records of the British treasury, as long as the monumental debt of England shall endure.

This gentleman, sir, acts as attorney for Mr. Paul Benfield. Every one who hears me is well acquainted with the sacred friendship, and the steady, mutual attachment, that subsists between him and the present minister. As many members as chose to attend in the first session of this Parliament can best tell their own feelings at the scenes which were then acted. How much that honorable gentleman was consulted in the original frame and fabric of the bill, commonly called Mr. Pitt's India Bill, is matter only of conjec-

Mr. Atkinson, his agent, active in framing Mr. Pitt's India Bill.

43 Extraordinary and new, uttered by no other mouth.

44 There is great keenness in this attack on Mr. Pitt as a parliamentary reformer. His "supporting the *freedom* of our Constitution by court intrigues" refers to his defeating Mr. Fox's East India Bill in the House of Lords by appealing secretly to the King, through Lord Temple, and obtaining a declaration that "whoever voted for the India Bill were not only not his friends [the King's], but that he should consider them his enemies." This use of the powerful influence of the sovereign to overrule the decisions of Parliament was considered by Mr. Burke and his friends as a direct blow at the "freedom of the Constitution." It was also a mode of "removing its corruptions by Indian delinquency," because Mr. Pitt was united with Paul Benfield and other Indian delinquents in opposing Mr. Fox's bill, and these men operated chiefly through the purchase of rotten boroughs, which Mr. Pitt had always treated as the great source of corruption to the Constitution. It was known that Mr. Pitt, out of an avowed regard to his former principles, intended to bring forward some plan of parliamentary reform this session. This called forth the terrible irony and sarcasm of this passage. After his failure in that plan, Mr. Pitt never again attempted parliamentary reform.

45 Quæ regio in terris nostri non plena laboris?

46 Quem gratia honoris nomino.

ture, though by no means difficult to divine. But the public was an indignant witness of the ostentation with which that measure was made his own, and the authority with which he brought up clause after clause, to stuff and fatten the rankness of that corrupt act. As fast as the clauses were brought up to the table, they were accepted. No hesitation—no discussion. They were received by the new minister, not with approbation, but with implicit submission. The reformation may be estimated by seeing who was the reformer. Paul Benfield's associate and agent was held up to the world as legislator of Hindostan! But it was necessary to authenticate the coalition between the men of intrigue in India and the minister of intrigue in England, by a studied display of the power of this their connecting link. Every trust, every honor, every distinction was to be heaped upon him. He was at once made a director of the India Company; made an alderman of London; and to be made, if ministry could prevail (and I am sorry to say how near, how very near they were prevailing), representative of the capital of this kingdom. But, to secure his services against all risk, he was brought in for a *ministerial* borough. On his part, he was not wanting in zeal for the common cause. His advertisements show his motives, and the merits upon which he stood. For your minister, this worn-out veteran submitted to enter into the dusty field of the London contest; and you all remember, that in the same virtuous cause he submitted to keep a sort of public office or counting-house, where the whole business of the last general election was managed. It was openly managed by the direct agent and attorney of Benfield. It was managed upon Indian principles, and for an Indian interest. This was the golden cup of abominations; this the chalice of fornications of rapine, usury, and oppression, which was held out by the gorgeous Eastern harlot; which so many of the people, so many of the nobles of this land, had drained to the very dregs. Do you think that no reckoning was to follow this lewd debauch? that no payment was to be demanded for this riot of public drunkenness and national prostitution? Here! you have it here before you. The principal of the grand election manager must be indemnified; accordingly, *the claims of Benfield and his crew must be put above all inquiry!*

His activity in Mr. Pitt's favor during the election of 1784, and its reward.

For several years, Benfield appeared as the chief proprietor, as well as the chief agent, director, and controller of this system of debt. The worthy chairman of the Company has stated the claims of this single gentleman on the Nabob of Arcot as amounting to five hundred thousand pounds. Possibly, at the time of the chairman's statement, they might have been as high. Eight hundred thousand pounds had been mentioned some time before; and, according to the practice of shifting the names of creditors in these transactions, and reducing or raising the debt itself at pleasure, I think it not impossible that at one period the name of Benfield might have stood before those frightful figures. But my best information goes to fix his share no higher than four hundred thousand pounds. By the scheme of the present ministry for adding to the principal twelve per cent. from the year 1777 to the year 1781, four hundred thousand pounds, that smallest of the sums ever mentioned for Mr. Benfield, will form a capital of £592,000 at six per cent. Thus, besides the arrears of three years, amounting to £106,500 (which, as fast as received, may be legally lent out at twelve per cent.), Benfield has received, by the ministerial grant before you, an annuity of £35,520 a year, charged on the public revenues.

Amount of Benfield's interest in these claims.

Our mirror of ministers of finance did not think this enough for the services of such a friend as Benfield. He found that Lord Macartney, in order to frighten the court of Directors from the object of obliging the Nabob to give *soucar* security for his debt, assured them that, if they should take that step, Benfield would infallibly be the *soucar*, and would thereby become the entire master of the Carnatic. What Lord Macartney thought sufficient to deter the very agents and partakers with Benfield in his iniquities was the inducement to the two right honorable gentlemen to order this very *soucar* security to be given, and to recall Benfield to the city of Madras, from the sort of decent exile into which he had been relegated by Lord Macartney. You must, therefore, consider Benfield as *soucar* security for £480,000 a year, which, at twenty-four per cent. (supposing him contented with that profit), will, with the interest of his old debt, produce an annual income of £149,520 a year.

Here is a specimen of the *new* and *pure* aristocracy created by the right honorable gentleman [Mr. Pitt], as the support of the Crown and Constitution, against the old, corrupt, refractory, natural interests of this kingdom; and this is the grand counterpoise against all odious coalitions of these interests.[47] A single Benfield outweighs them all. A criminal, who long since ought to have fattened the region kites with his offal, is, by his Majesty's ministers, enthroned in the government of a great kingdom, and enfeoffed with an estate which, in the comparison, effaces the splendor of all the nobility of Europe. To bring a little more distinctly into view the true secret of this dark transaction, I beg you particularly to advert to the circumstances which I am going to place before you.

The general corps of creditors, as well as Mr. Benfield himself, not looking well into futurity, nor presaging the minister of this day, thought it not expedient for their common interest that such a name as his should stand at the head of their list. It was therefore agreed among them that Mr. Benfield should disappear by making over his debt to Messrs. Taylor, Majendie,

Temporary withdrawal of Benfield's name from the list of creditors.

[47] This sneer refers to the attacks made by Mr. Pitt on Mr. Fox's coalition with Lord North.

and Call, and should, in return, be secured by their bond.

The debt thus exonerated of so great a weight of its odium, and otherwise reduced from its alarming bulk, the agents thought they might venture to print a list of the creditors. This was done for the first time in the year 1783, during the Duke of Portland's administration. In this list the name of Benfield was not to be seen. To this strong negative testimony was added the farther testimony of the Nabob of Arcot. That prince (or, rather, Mr. Benfield for him) writes to the court of Directors a letter full of complaints and accusations against Lord Macartney, conveyed in such terms as were natural for one of Mr. Benfield's habits and education to employ. Among the rest, he is made to complain of his Lordship's endeavoring to prevent an intercourse of politeness and sentiment between him [the Nabob] and Mr. Benfield; and, to aggravate the affront, he expressly declares Mr. Benfield's visits to be only on account of respect and of gratitude, as *no pecuniary transactions* subsisted between them!

Suit of Benfield which brought the mystery to light.

Such, for a considerable space of time, was the outward form of the loan of 1777, in which Mr. Benfield had no sort of concern. At length intelligence arrived at Madras that this debt, which had always been renounced by the court of Directors, was rather like to become the subject of something more like a criminal inquiry than of any patronage or sanction from Parliament. Every ship brought accounts, one stronger than the other, of the prevalence of the determined enemies of the Indian system. The public revenues became an object desperate to the hopes of Mr. Benfield; he therefore resolved to fall upon his associates, and, in violation of that faith which subsists among those who have abandoned all other, *commences a suit* in the Mayor's Court against Taylor, Majendie, and Call for the bond given to him, when he agreed to disappear for his own benefit as well as that of the common concern. The assignees of his debt, who little expected the springing of this mine even from such an engineer as Mr. Benfield, after recovering their first alarm, thought it best to take ground on the real state of the transaction. They divulged the whole mystery, and were prepared to plead that they had never received from Mr. Benfield any other consideration for the bond than a transfer, in trust for himself, of his demand on the Nabob of Arcot. A universal indignation arose against the perfidy of Mr. Benfield's proceedings. The event of the suit was looked upon as so certain, that Benfield was compelled to retreat as precipitately as he had advanced boldly; he gave up his bond, and was reinstated in his original demand, to wait the fortune of other claimants. At that time, and at Madras, this hope was dull indeed; but at home another scene was preparing.

It was long before any public account of this discovery at Madras had arrived in England that the present minister and his Board of Control thought fit to determine on the debt of 1777. The recorded proceedings at this time knew nothing of any debt to Benfield. There was his own testimony; there was the testimony of the list; there was the testimony of the Nabob of Arcot against it; yet such was the ministers' feeling of the true secret of this transaction, that they thought proper, in the teeth of all these testimonies, to give him license *to return to Madras!* Here the ministers were under some embarrassment. Confounded between their resolution of rewarding the good services of Benfield's friends and associates in England, and the shame of sending that notorious incendiary to the court of the Nabob of Arcot, to renew his intrigues against the British government, at the time they authorize his return, they forbid him, under the severest penalties, from any conversation with the Nabob or his ministers; that is, they forbid his communication with the very person on account of his dealings with whom they permit his return to that city! To overtop this contradiction, there is not a word restraining him from the freest intercourse with the Nabob's second son, the real author of all that is done in the Nabob's name, who, in conjunction with this very Benfield, has acquired an absolute dominion over that unhappy man, is able to persuade him to put his signature to whatever paper they please, and often without any communication of the contents. This management was detailed to them at full length by Lord Macartney, and they can not pretend ignorance of it.

Benfield permitted to return to Madras.

This proves collusive intercourse between the ministry and Benfield.

I believe, after this exposure of facts, no man can entertain a doubt of the collusion of ministers with the corrupt interest of the delinquents in India. Whenever those in authority provide for the interest of any person, on the real but concealed state of his affairs, without regard to his avowed, public, and ostensible pretenses, it must be presumed that they are in confederacy with him, because they act for him on the same fraudulent principles on which he acts for himself. It is plain that the ministers were fully apprised of Benfield's real situation, which he had used means to conceal while concealment answered his purposes. They were, or the person on whom they relied was, of the cabinet council of Benfield, in the very depth of all his mysteries. An honest magistrate compels men to abide by one story. An equitable judge would not hear of the claim of a man who had himself thought proper to renounce it. With such a judge his shuffling and prevarication would have damned his claims; such a judge never would have known, but in order to animadvert upon, proceedings of that character.

I have thus laid before you, Mr. Speaker, I think with sufficient clearness, the connection of the ministers with Mr. Atkinson at the general election; I have laid open to you the connection of Atkinson with Benfield; I have shown Benfield's employment of his wealth, in creating a parliamentary interest, to procure a ministerial protection; I have set before your eyes his large concern in the debt, his practices to hide that concern from the public eye, and the liberal protection which he has received from the minister. If this chain of circumstances do not lead you necessarily to conclude that the minister has paid to the avarice of Benfield the services done by Benfield's connections to his ambition, I do not know any thing short of the confession of the party that can satisfy you of his guilt. Clandestine and collusive practice can only be traced by combination and comparison of circumstances. To reject such combination and comparison is to reject the only means of detecting fraud; it is, indeed, to give it a patent and free license to cheat with impunity.

Inference from the whole as to the motives for the payment of the Nabob of Arcot's debts.

I confine myself to the connection of ministers, mediately or immediately, with only two persons concerned in this debt. How many others, who support their power and greatness within and without doors, are concerned originally, or by transfers of these debts, must be left to general opinion. I refer to the reports of the select committee for the proceedings of some of the agents in these affairs, and their attempts, at least, to furnish ministers with the means of buying General Courts, and even whole Parliaments, in the gross.

Ministers not charged with acting from pecuniary motives, but the love of power.

I know that the ministers will think it little less than acquittal, that they are not charged with having taken to themselves some part of the money of which they have made so liberal a donation to their partisans, though the charge may be indisputably fixed upon the corruption of their politics. For my part, I follow their crimes to that point to which legal presumptions and natural indications lead me, without considering what species of evil motive tends most to aggravate or to extenuate the guilt of their conduct; but if I am to speak my private sentiments, I think that in a thousand cases for one it would be far less mischievous to the public, and full as little dishonorable to themselves, to be polluted with direct bribery, than thus to become a standing auxiliary to the oppression, usury, and peculation of multitudes, in order to obtain a corrupt support to their power. It is by bribing, not so often by being bribed, that wicked politicians bring ruin on mankind. Avarice is a rival to the pursuits of many. It finds a multitude of checks, and many opposers, in every walk of life. But the objects of ambition are for the few; and every person who aims at indirect profit, and therefore wants other protection than innocence and law, instead of its rival, becomes its instrument. There is a natural allegiance and fealty due to this domineering, paramount evil, from all the vassal vices, which acknowledge its superiority, and readily militate under its banners; and it is under that discipline alone that avarice is able to spread, to any considerable extent, or to render itself a general public mischief. It is, therefore, no apology for ministers that they have not been bought by the East India delinquents, but that they have only formed an alliance with them for screening each other from justice, according to the exigence of their several necessities. That they have done so is evident; and the junction of the power of office in England with the abuse of authority in the East has not only prevented even the appearance of redress to the grievances of India, but I wish it may not be found to have dulled, if not extinguished, the honor, the candor, the generosity, the good nature, which used formerly to characterize the people of England. I confess I wish that some more feeling than I have yet observed for the sufferings of our fellow-creatures and fellow-subjects in that oppressed part of the world had manifested itself in any one quarter of the kingdom, or in any one large description of men.

Hence the oppressions of the Hindoos overlooked and neglected.

That these oppressions exist is a fact no more denied, than it is resented as it ought to be. Much evil has been done in India under the British authority. What has been done to redress it? We are no longer surprised at any thing. We are above the unlearned and vulgar passion of admiration.[48] But it will astonish posterity when they read our opinions in our actions, that, after years of inquiry, we have found out that the sole grievance of India consisted in this, that the servants of the Company there had not *profited* enough of their opportunities, nor drained it sufficiently of its treasures; when they shall hear that the very first and only important act of a commission, specially named by act of Parliament, is to charge upon an undone country, in favor of a handful of men in the humblest ranks of the public service, the enormous sum of perhaps four millions of sterling money!

It is difficult for the most wise and upright government to correct the abuses of remote delegated power, productive of unmeasured wealth, and protected by the boldness and strength of the same ill-got riches. These abuses, full of their own wild native vigor, will grow and flourish under mere neglect. But where the supreme authority, not content with winking at the rapacity of its inferior instruments, is so shameless and corrupt, as openly to give bounties and premiums for disobedience to its laws; when it will not trust to the activity of avarice in the pursuit of its own gains; when it secures public robbery by all the careful jealousy and attention with which it ought to protect property from such violence; the commonwealth then is become totally perverted from its purposes; neither God nor man will long endure it; nor will it long endure itself. In that case, there is an unnatural infection, a pestilential taint fermenting in the constitution of society, which fever and convulsions of some kind or other must throw off; or in which the vital powers, worsted in an un-

---

[48] *Nil admirari* prope res est una, Numici,
Sola qua possit facere et servare beatum.
Horace, Epist. vi.

Not to admire is all the art I know,
To make men happy, and to keep them so.

equal struggle, are pushed back upon themselves, and, by a reversal of their whole functions, fester to gangrene—to death; and instead of what was but just now the delight and boast of the creation, there will be cast out in the face of the sun a bloated, putrid, noisome carcass, full of stench and poison, an offense, a horror, a lesson to the world.

In my opinion, we ought not to wait for the fruitless instruction of calamity to inquire into the abuses which bring upon us ruin in the worst of its forms, in the loss of our fame and virtue.

Mr. Dundas' pretense that the subject is too *delicate* to be taken up.

But the right honorable gentleman [Mr. Dundas] says, in answer to all the powerful arguments of my honorable friend [Mr. Fox], "that this inquiry is of a delicate nature, and that the state will suffer detriment by the exposure of this transaction." But it is exposed. It is perfectly known in every member, in every particle, and in every way, except that which may lead to a remedy. He knows that the papers of correspondence are printed, and that they are in every hand.

He and delicacy are a rare and singular coalition. He thinks that to divulge our Indian politics may be highly dangerous. He! the mover! the chairman! the reporter of the Committee of Secrecy! he that brought forth in the utmost detail, in several vast, printed folios, the most recondite parts of the politics, the military, the revenues of the British empire in India! With six great chopping bastards [Reports of the Committee of Secrecy], each as lusty as an infant Hercules, this delicate creature blushes at the sight of his new bridegroom, assumes a virgin delicacy; or, to use a more fit, as well as a more poetic comparison, the person so squeamish, so timid, so trembling, lest the winds of heaven should visit too roughly, is expanded to broad sunshine, exposed like the sow of imperial augury, lying in the mud with all the prodigies of her fertility about her, as evidence of her delicate amours:

Triginta capitum fœtus enixa jacebit,
Alba, solo recubans, albi circum ubera nati.[49]

While discovery of the misgovernment of others led to his own power, it was wise to inquire; it was safe to publish; there was then no delicacy; there was then no danger. But when his object is obtained, and in his *imitation* he has outdone the crimes that he had reprobated in volumes of reports, and in sheets of bills of pains and penalties, then concealment becomes prudence, and it concerns the safety of the state that we should not know, in a mode of parliamentary cognizance, what all the world knows but too well; that is, in what manner he chooses to dispose of the public revenues to the CREATURES of his politics.

Peroration: The concerns of India, however perplexed or repulsive, can never cease to involve the honor and safety of the empire.

The debate has been long, and as much so on my part, at least, as on the part of those who have spoken before me. But long as it is, the more material half of the subject has hardly been touched on; that is, the corrupt and destructive system to which this debt has been rendered subservient, and which seems to be pursued with at least as much vigor and regularity as ever. If I considered your ease or my own, rather than the weight and importance of this question, I ought to make some apology to you, perhaps some apology to myself, for having detained your attention so long. I know on what ground I tread. This subject, at one time taken up with so much fervor and zeal, is no longer a favorite in this House. The House itself has undergone a great and signal revolution. To some the subject is strange and uncouth; to several harsh and distasteful; to the relics of the last Parliament it is a matter of fear and apprehension. It is natural for those who have seen their friends sink in the tornado which raged during the late shift of the monsoon, and have hardly escaped on the planks of the general wreck, it is but too natural for them, as soon as they make the rocks and quicksands of their former disasters, to put about their new-built barks, and, as much as possible, to keep aloof from this perilous lee-shore.

But let us do what we please to put India from our thoughts, we can do nothing to separate it from our public interest and our national reputation. Our attempts to banish this importunate duty will only make it return upon us again and again, and every time in a shape more unpleasant than the former. A government has been fabricated for that great province; the right honorable gentleman says, that therefore you ought not to examine into its conduct. Heavens! what an argument is this! We are not to examine into the conduct of the direction, because it is an old government; we are not to examine into this Board of Control, because it is a new one; then we are only to examine into the conduct of those who have no conduct to account for. Unfortunately, the basis of this new government has been laid on old, condemned delinquents, and its superstructure is raised out of

[49] Mr. Burke here accommodates to his purpose a passage of Virgil's Æneid, book iii., p. 391, in which the prophet Helenus gives a sign to Æneas indicative of the spot where he should build a city, and cease from his labors.

Cum tibi solicito secreto ad fluminis undam,
Littoreis ingens inventa sub ilicibus sus
Trigcnta capitum fœtus enixa jacebit,
Alba, solo recubans, albi circum ubera nati;
Is locus urbis erit, requies ea certa laborum.

Dryden has rendered the lines somewhat loosely, in the following manner:

When in the shady shelter of a wood,
And near the margin of a gentle flood,
Thou shalt behold *a sow upon the ground,*
With thirty sucking young encompass'd round,
The dam and offspring white as fallen snow,
These on thy city shall their name bestow,
And there shall end thy labor and thy woe.

No one will dispute the ingenuity of Mr. Burke in turning these lines to his purpose; but it will be a wonder to most men, that he, who wrote the description of the Queen of France, could ever have soiled his pages with such a passage as the one above.

prosecutors turned into protectors. The event has been such as might be expected. But if it had been otherwise constituted; had it been constituted even as I wished, and as the mover of this question had planned, the better part of the proposed establishment was in the publicity of its proceedings; in its perpetual responsibility to Parliament. Without this check, what is our government at home; even awed, as every European government is, by an audience formed of the other states of Europe, by the applause or condemnation of the discerning and critical company before which it acts? But if the scene on the other side of the globe, which tempts, invites, almost compels to tyranny and rapine, be not inspected with the eye of a severe and unremitting vigilance, shame and destruction must ensue. For one, the worst event of this day, though it may deject, shall not break or subdue me. The call upon us is authoritative. Let who will shrink back, I shall be found at my post. Baffled, discountenanced, subdued, discredited, as the cause of justice and humanity is, it will be only the dearer to me. Whoever, therefore, shall at any time bring before you any thing toward the relief of our distressed fellow-citizens in India, and toward a subversion of the present most corrupt and oppressive system for its government, in me shall find a weak, I am afraid, but a steady, earnest, and faithful assistant.

The motion for inquiry was voted down. Mr. Pitt was now at the height of his popularity, and had an overwhelming majority at his command, ready to sustain him in all his measures. The consequences were very serious to the finances of the country. Many years were necessarily occupied in paying so large a debt. In 1814 Mr. Hume publicly stated that, according to the best information he could obtain, the amount paid (interest included) was nearly *five millions of pounds;* nor was this all. Mr. Hume adds, "the knowledge of the fact that Mr. Dundas had in that manner admitted, without any kind of inquiry, the whole claims of the Consolidated Debt of 1777, served as a strong inducement to others to get from the Nabob obligations or bonds of any description, in hopes that some future good-natured president of the Board of Control would do the same for them. We accordingly find that an enormous debt of near *thirty* millions sterling was very soon formed after that act of Mr. Dundas, and urgent applications were soon again made to have the claims paid in the same manner." It now became necessary to make a thorough inquiry. A Board of Commissioners was appointed to examine into these new claims. After an investigation of many years, only £1,346,796 were allowed as good, thus showing that less than one part in twenty of all these claims could be regarded as true and lawful debts. It is the opinion of well-informed men that the claims of Benfield and his associates, if fairly investigated, would have been reduced in very near the same proportion.

But has Mr. Burke made out his case as to the *motives* of Mr. Pitt? Has he proved that these claims were allowed without inquiry, as a "recompense" to Benfield and the other creditors for their parliamentary influence? This question will be differently answered by different persons, according to their estimate of Mr. Pitt's character. Mill, in his British India, speaking of Mr. Burke's charge, says, "In support of it, he adduces as great a body of proof as it is almost ever possible to bring to a fact of such a description." He goes on to examine Mr. Dundas' defense, that the Nabob and others were allowed "to object" to these claims, and adds, "That this was a *blind* is abundantly clear, though it is possible that it stood as much between his own eyes and the light, as he was desirous of putting it between the light and eyes of other people." There was also another "blind," mentioned by Wraxall, viz., that these claims had, to some extent, changed hands, and that the innocent would suffer with the guilty, if any of them were disallowed. It is easy to see how strongly Mr. Pitt was tempted, at this critical moment of his life, to attach undue importance to such considerations. It was impossible to go back and lay bare all the frauds and crimes of the English residents in India. To prevent them hereafter was the great object. Once firmly seated in power, he was resolved to do it; and when he was brought off in triumph at the polls through the agency (to a considerable extent) of men like Benfield, in connection with the immense East India interest throughout the country, it was natural for him to feel that he must not be too scrupulous in respect to the past, but must rather aim in future at the prevention of all such evils. It is thus that the errors of political men spring from mingled motives; and while we can not doubt that Mr. Pitt was more or less influenced in this case, as in that of Mr. Hastings' impeachment, by his "avarice of power," we should be slow to admit that his conduct implies that dereliction of principle imputed to him by Mr. Burke.

EXTRACTS.

Peroration of the Opening Speech at the Trial of Warren Hastings.

In the name of the Commons of England, I charge all this villainy upon Warren Hastings, in this last moment of my application to you.

My Lords, what is it that we want here to a great act of national justice? Do we want a cause, my Lords? You have the cause of oppressed princes, of undone women of the first rank, of desolated provinces, and of wasted kingdoms.

Do you want a criminal, my Lords? When was there so much iniquity ever laid to the charge of any one? No, my Lords, you must not look to punish any other such delinquent from India. Warren Hastings has not left substance enough in India to nourish such another delinquent.

My Lords, is it a prosecutor you want? You have before you the Commons of Great Britain as prosecutors; and I believe, my Lords, that the sun, in his beneficent progress round the world, does not behold a more glorious sight than that of men, separated from a remote people by the material bounds and barriers of nature, united by the bond of a social and moral community—all the Commons of England resenting, as their own, the indignities and cruelties that are offered to all the people of India.

Do we want a tribunal? My Lords, no example of antiquity, nothing in the modern world, nothing in the range of human imagination, can supply us with a tribunal like this. My Lords, here we see virtually, in the mind's eye, that sacred majesty of the Crown, under whose authority you sit, and whose power you exercise. We see in that invisible authority, what we all feel in reality and life, the beneficent powers and protecting justice of his Majesty. We have here the heir-apparent to the Crown, such as the fond wishes of the people of England wish an heir-apparent of the Crown to be. We have here all the branches of the royal family, in a situation between majesty and subjection, between the Sovereign and the subject—offering a pledge, in that situation, for the support of the rights of the Crown and the liberties of the people, both which extremities they touch. My Lords, we have a great hereditary peerage here; those who have their own honor, the honor of their ancestors, and of their posterity, to guard, and who will justify, as they have always justified, that provision in the Constitution by which justice is made an hereditary office. My Lords, we have here a new nobility, who have risen, and exalted themselves, by various merits, by great military services, which have extended the fame of this country from the rising to the setting sun. We have those, who, by various civil merits and various civil talents, have been exalted to a situation which they well deserve, and in which they will justify the favor of their Sovereign and the good opinion of their fellow-subjects, and make them rejoice to see those virtuous characters, that were the other day upon a level with them, now exalted above them in rank, but feeling with them in sympathy what they felt in common with them before. We have persons exalted from the practice of the law, from the place in which they administered high, though subordinate justice, to a seat here, to enlighten with their knowledge, and to strengthen with their votes, those principles which have distinguished the courts in which they have presided.

My Lords, you have here, also, the lights of our religion; you have the bishops of England. My Lords, you have that true image of the primitive Church in its ancient form, in its ancient ordinances, purified from the superstitions and the vices which a long succession of ages will bring upon the best institutions. You have the representatives of that religion which says that their God is love, that the very vital spirit of their institution is charity—a religion which so much hates oppression, that when the God whom we adore appeared in human form, he did not appear in a form of greatness and majesty, but in sympathy with the lowest of the people, and thereby made it a firm and ruling principle that their welfare was the object of all government, since the person, who was the Master of Nature, chose to appear himself in a subordinate situation. These are the considerations which influence them, which animate them, and will animate them, against all oppression; knowing that He who is called first among them, and first among us all, both of the flock that is fed and of those who feed it, made himself "the servant of all."

My Lords, these are the securities which we have in all the constituent parts of the body of this House. We know them, we reckon, we rest upon them, and commit safely the interests of India and of humanity into your hands. Therefore, it is with confidence, that, ordered by the Commons,

I impeach Warren Hastings, Esquire, of high crimes and misdemeanors.

I impeach him in the name of the Commons of Great Britain, in Parliament assembled, whose parliamentary trust he has betrayed.

I impeach him in the name of all the Commons of Great Britain, whose national character he has dishonored.

I impeach him in the name of the people of India, whose laws, rights, and liberties he has subverted, whose property he has destroyed, whose country he has laid waste and desolate.

I impeach him in the name, and by virtue, of those eternal laws of justice which he has violated.

I impeach him in the name of human nature itself, which he has cruelly outraged, injured, and oppressed, in both sexes, in every age, rank, situation, and condition of life.

French Revolution: Errors at its Commencement.[1]

You began ill, because you began by despising every thing that belonged to you. You set up your trade without a capital. If the last generations of your country appeared without much luster in your eyes, you might have passed them by, and derived your claims from a more early race of ancestors. Under a pious predilection for those ancestors, your imaginations would have realized in them a standard of virtue and wisdom, beyond the vulgar practice of the hour, and you would have risen with the example to

[1] The extracts which follow under this head are taken from Mr. Burke's Reflections on the Revolution in France, and his Letters on the Regicide Peace.

whose imitation you aspired. Respecting your forefathers, you would have been taught to respect yourselves. You would not have chosen to consider the French as a people of yesterday, as a nation of low-born, servile wretches, until the emancipating year of 1789. In order to furnish, at the expense of your honor, an excuse to your apologists here for several enormities of yours, you would not have been content to be represented as a gang of Maroon slaves, suddenly broke loose from the house of bondage, and therefore to be pardoned for your abuse of the liberty to which you were not accustomed, and were ill fitted. Would it not, my worthy friend, have been wiser to have you thought, what I, for one, always thought you, a generous and gallant nation, long misled, to your disadvantage, by your high and romantic sentiments of fidelity, honor, and loyalty; that events had been unfavorable to you, but that you were not enslaved through any illiberal or servile disposition; that, in your most devoted submission, you were actuated by a principle of public spirit, and that it was your country you worshiped, in the person of your king? Had you made it to be understood that, in the delusion of this amiable error, you had gone farther than your wise ancestors; that you were resolved to resume your ancient privileges, while you preserved the spirit of your ancient and your recent loyalty and honor; or, if diffident of yourselves, and not clearly discerning the almost obliterated Constitution of your ancestors, you had looked to your neighbors in this land, who had kept alive the ancient principles and models of the old common law of Europe, meliorated and adapted to its present state—by following wise examples you would have given new examples of wisdom to the world. You would have rendered the cause of liberty venerable in the eyes of every worthy mind in every nation. You would have shamed despotism from the earth, by showing that freedom was not only reconcilable, but as, when well disciplined, it is, auxiliary to law. You would have had an unoppressive, but a productive revenue. You would have had a flourishing commerce to feed it. You would have had a free Constitution, a potent monarchy, a disciplined army, a reformed and venerated clergy, a mitigated, but spirited nobility, to lead your virtue, not to overlay it; you would have had a liberal order of commons, to emulate and to recruit that nobility; you would have had a protected, satisfied, laborious, and obedient people, taught to seek and to recognize the happiness that is to be found by virtue in all conditions; in which consists the true moral equality of mankind, and not in that monstrous fiction, which, by inspiring false ideas and vain expectations into men destined to travel in the obscure walk of laborious life, serves only to aggravate and imbitter that real inequality which it never can remove, and which the order of civil life establishes as much for the benefit of those whom it must leave in a humble state, as those whom it is able to exalt to a condition more splendid, but not more happy. You had a smooth and easy career of felicity and glory laid open to you, beyond any thing recorded in the history of the world; but you have shown that difficulty is good for man.

Compute your gains; see what is got by those extravagant and presumptuous speculations which have taught your leaders to despise all their predecessors, and all their contemporaries, and even to despise themselves, until the moment in which they became truly despicable. By following those false lights, France has bought undisguised calamities at a higher price than any nation has purchased the most unequivocal blessings! France has bought poverty by crime! France has not sacrificed her virtue to her interest, but she has abandoned her interest, that she might prostitute her virtue. All other nations have begun the fabric of a new government, or the reformation of an old, by establishing originally, or by enforcing with greater exactness, some rites or other of religion. All other people have laid the foundations of civil freedom in severer manners, and a system of a more austere and masculine morality. France, when she let loose the reins of regal authority, doubled the license of a ferocious dissoluteness in manners, and of an insolent irreligion in opinions and practices, and has extended through all ranks of life, as if she were communicating some privilege, or laying open some secluded benefit, all the unhappy corruptions that usually were the disease of wealth and power. This is one of the new principles of equality in France.

France, by the perfidy of her leaders, has utterly disgraced the tone of lenient council in the cabinets of princes, and disarmed it of its most potent topics. She has sanctified the dark, suspicious maxims of tyrannous distrust, and taught kings to tremble at (what will hereafter be called) the delusive plausibilities of moral politicians. Sovereigns will consider those who advise them to place an unlimited confidence in their people, as subverters of their thrones; as traitors who aim at their destruction, by leading their easy good nature, under specious pretenses, to admit combinations of bold and faithless men into a participation of their power. This alone (if there were nothing else) is an irreparable calamity to you and to mankind. Remember that your Parliament of Paris told your king that, in calling the states together, he had nothing to fear but the prodigal excess of their zeal in providing for the support of the throne. It is right that these men should hide their heads. It is right that they should bear their part in the ruin which their counsel has brought on their Sovereign and their country. Such sanguine declarations tend to lull authority asleep; to encourage it rashly to engage in perilous adventures of untried policy; to neglect those provisions, preparations, and precautions which distinguish benevolence from imbecility, and without which no man can answer for the salutary effect of any abstract plan of government or of freedom. For want of these, they have seen the medicine of the state corrupted into its poison. They have seen the French rebel against a mild and lawful monarch, with more fury, outrage, and insult, than ever any people has been known to rise against the most illegal usurper or the most sanguinary tyrant. Their resistance was made to concession; their revolt was from protection; their blow was aimed at a hand holding out graces, favors, and immunities.

This was unnatural. The rest is in order. They have found their punishment in their success. Laws overturned; tribunals subverted; industry without vigor; commerce expiring; the revenue unpaid, yet the people impoverished; a church pillaged, and a state not relieved; civil and military anarchy made the constitution of the kingdom; every thing human and divine sacrificed to the idol of public credit, and national bankruptcy the consequence; and, to crown all, the paper securities of new, precarious, tottering power, the discredited paper securities of impoverished fraud, and beggared rapine, held out as a currency for the support of an empire, in lieu of the two great recognized species that represent the lasting conventional credit of mankind, which disappeared and hid themselves in the earth from whence they came, when the principle of property, whose creatures and representatives they are, was systematically subverted.

Were all these dreadful things necessary? Were they the inevitable results of the desperate struggle of determined patriots, compelled to wade through blood and tumult to the quiet shore of a tranquil and prosperous liberty? No! nothing like it. The fresh ruins of France, which shock our feelings wherever we can turn our eyes, are not the devastation of civil war; they are the sad but instructive monuments of rash and ignorant counsel in time of profound peace. They are the display of inconsiderate and presumptuous, because unresisted and irresistible authority. The persons who have thus squandered away the precious treasure of their crimes, the persons who have made this prodigal and wild waste of public evils (the last stake reserved for the ultimate ransom of the state), have met in their progress with little, or rather with no opposition at all. Their whole march was more like a triumphal procession than the progress of a war. Their pioneers have gone before them, and demolished and laid every thing level at their feet. Not one drop of *their* blood have they shed in the cause of the country they have ruined. They have made no sacrifice to their projects of greater consequence than their shoe-buckles, while they were imprisoning their king, murdering their fellow-citizens, and bathing in tears, and plunging in poverty and distress, thousands of worthy men and worthy families. Their cruelty has not even been the base result of fear. It has been the effect of their sense of perfect safety in authorizing treasons, robberies, rapes, assassinations, slaughters, and burnings, throughout their harassed land; but the cause of all was plain from the beginning.

Seizure of the King and Queen of France.

History will record, that on the morning of the 6th of October, 1789, the King and Queen of France, after a day of confusion, alarm, dismay, and slaughter, lay down, under the pledged security of public faith, to indulge nature in a few hours of respite and troubled melancholy repose. From this sleep the Queen was first startled by the voice of the sentinel at her door, who cried out to her to save herself by flight—that this was the last proof of fidelity he could give—that they were upon him, and he was dead. Instantly he was cut down. A band of cruel ruffians and assassins, reeking with his blood, rushed into the chamber of the Queen, and pierced, with a hundred strokes of bayonets and poniards, the bed from whence this persecuted woman had but just time to fly almost naked, and, through ways unknown to the murderers, had escaped to seek refuge at the feet of a King and husband not secure of his own life for a moment.

This King, to say no more of him, and this Queen, and their infant children (who once would have been the pride and hope of a great and generous people) were then forced to abandon the sanctuary of the most splendid palace in the world, which they left swimming in blood, polluted by massacre, and strewed with scattered limbs and mutilated carcases. Thence they were conducted into the capital of their kingdom. Two had been selected from the unprovoked, unresisted, promiscuous slaughter, which was made of the gentlemen of birth and family who composed the King's body-guard. These two gentlemen, with all the parade of an execution of justice, were cruelly and publicly dragged to the block, and beheaded in the great court of the palace. Their heads were stuck upon spears, and led the procession; while the royal captives who followed in the train were slowly moved along, amid the horrid yells, and thrilling screams, and frantic dances, and infamous contumelies, and all the unutterable abominations of the furies of hell, in the abused shape of the vilest of women. After they had been made to taste, drop by drop, more than the bitterness of death, in the slow torture of a journey of twelve miles, protracted to six hours, they were, under a guard composed of those very soldiers who had thus conducted them through this famous triumph, lodged in one of the old palaces of Paris, now converted into a Bastile for kings.

The Queen of France and the Spirit of Chivalry.

I hear, and I rejoice to hear, that the great lady, the other object of the triumph, has borne that day (one is interested that beings made for suffering should suffer well), and that she bears all the succeeding days—that she bears the imprisonment of her husband, and her own captivity, and the exile of her friends, and the insulting adulation of addresses, and the whole weight of her accumulated wrongs, with a serene patience, in a manner suited to her rank and race, and becoming the offspring of a sovereign distinguished for her piety and her courage; that, like her, she has lofty sentiments; that she feels with the dignity of a Roman matron; that in the last extremity she will save herself from the last disgrace; and that, if she must fall, she will fall by no ignoble hand.

It is now sixteen or seventeen years since I saw the Queen of France, then the dauphiness, at Versailles; and surely never lighted on this orb, which she hardly seemed to touch, a more delightful vision. I saw her just above the horizon, decorating and cheering the elevated sphere she just began to move in, glittering like the morning star, full of life, and splendor, and joy. Oh! what a revolution! and what a heart must I have, to contemplate, without motion, that elevation and that fall! Little did I dream, when she added titles of veneration to those of enthusiastic, distant, respectful love, that she should ever be obliged to carry the sharp antidote against disgrace concealed in that bosom;[2] little did I dream that I should have lived to see such disasters fallen upon her in a nation of gallant men, in a nation of men of honor and of cavaliers. I thought ten thousand swords must have leaped from their scabbards to avenge even a look that threatened her with insult.[3] But the age of chivalry is gone; that of sophisters, economists, and calculators has succeeded; and the glory of Europe is extinguished forever. Never, never more shall we behold that generous loyalty to rank and sex, that proud submission, that dignified obedience, that subordination of the heart, which kept alive, even in servitude itself, the spirit of an exalted freedom. The unbought grace of life, the cheap defense of nations, the nurse of manly sentiment and heroic enterprise is gone! It is gone, that sensibility of principle, that chastity of honor, which felt a stain like a wound, which inspired courage while it mitigated ferocity, which ennobled whatever it touched, and under which vice itself lost half its evil by losing all its grossness.[4]

This mixed system of opinion and sentiment had its origin in the ancient chivalry; and the principle, though varied in its appearance by the varying state of human affairs, subsisted and influenced through a long succession of generations, even to the time we live in. If it should ever be totally extinguished, the loss, I fear, will be great. It is this which has given its character to modern Europe. It is this which has distinguished it under all its forms of government, and distinguished it to its advantage from the states of Asia, and, possibly, from those states which flourished in the most brilliant periods of the antique world. It was this which, without confounding ranks, had produced a noble equality, and handed it down through all the gradations of social life. It was this opinion which mitigated kings into companions, and raised private men to be fellows with kings. Without force or opposition, it subdued the fierceness of pride and power; it obliged sovereigns to sub-

[2] The "sharp antidote against disgrace" here mentioned was a *dagger*, which, it was then reported, the Queen carried in her bosom, with a view to end her life if any indignities should be offered her. See London Chris. Obs., vol. vi., p. 67. The report, however, proved to be incorrect.

[3] This image may have been suggested by the following lines of Milton's Paradise Lost, book i., line 664, which are correspondent in thought, though not coincident in expression:

He spake; and, to confirm his words, *out flew*
Millions of flaming swords, drawn from the thighs
Of mighty cherubim.

[4] It is hardly necessary to remark on the wide extent of reading and reflection involved in these three sentences. The whole history of the Middle Ages must have flashed across the mind of Mr. Burke as he wrote—the division of Europe into feudal dependencies, creating a "cheap defense of nations," in bodies of armed men always ready at a moment's call, without expense to the sovereign—the various orders of knights devoted to the service of the Monarch, and the honor and protection of the Fair, producing "that generous loyalty to rank and sex, that proud submission, that dignified obedience," which formed so peculiarly the spirit of chivalry. Individual instances would, no doubt, be present to his imagination, of men like Bayard, and hundreds of others, whose whole life was made up of "high thoughts seated in a heart of courtesy." It is here that we find the true type of Mr. Burke's genius, rather than in the brilliant imagery with which the paragraph commences.

When Mr. Burke speaks of vice as having "lost half its evil by losing all its grossness," he obviously refers not to the personal guilt of the man, but to the injurious effects he produces on society. Even in this sense, he would hardly have laid down so sweeping a proposition, except from the influence of one-sided views in a moment of excited feeling and imagination. Vice, in the higher classes, when connected with grace and refinement of manners, is certainly less offensive to taste, but it is more insidious and seductive. It is, in addition to this, a mere system of *hypocrisy*, for vice is degrading in its nature; and the covering of polish and refinement thrown over it is intended simply to deceive. Genuine faith and moral principle must die out under such a system; and we see how it was that French society became reduced to that terrible condition described by Mr. Gouverneur Morris, in a passage already quoted for another purpose. "There is one fatal principle which pervades all ranks; *it is a perfect indifference to the violation of engagements.* Inconstancy is so mingled in the blood, marrow, and very essence of this people, that, when a man of high rank and importance laughs to-day at what he seriously asserted yesterday, it is considered the natural order of things." How could it be otherwise, among a people who had taken it as a maxim that "*manners* are *morals?*" Such a maxim Mr. Burke would have rejected with horror; but his own remark is capable of being so understood, or, at least, so applied, as to give a seeming countenance to this corrupt sentiment. History, on which he so much relied, affords the completest testimony, that the ruin of states which have attained to a high degree of civilization has almost uniformly resulted from the polished corruption of the higher classes, and not from the "grossness" of the lower.

mit to the soft collar of social esteem; compelled stern authority to submit to elegance; and gave a domination vanquisher of laws, to be subdued by manners.

Political Influence of Established Opinions.

When ancient opinions and rules of life are taken away, the loss can not possibly be estimated. From that moment we have no compass to govern us; nor can we know distinctly to what port we steer. Europe, undoubtedly, taken in a mass, was in a flourishing condition the day on which your revolution was completed. How much of that prosperous state was owing to the spirit of our old manners and opinions is not easy to say; but as such causes can not be indifferent in their operation, we must presume that, on the whole, their operation was beneficial.

We are but too apt to consider things in the state in which we find them, without sufficiently adverting to the causes by which they have been produced, and, possibly, may be upheld. Nothing is more certain, than that our manners, our civilization, and all the good things which are connected with manners and with civilization, have, in this European world of ours, depended for ages upon two principles, and were indeed the result of both combined; I mean the spirit of a gentleman, and the spirit of religion. The nobility and the clergy, the one by profession, the other by patronage, kept learning in existence even in the midst of arms and confusions, and while governments were rather in their causes than formed. Learning paid back what it received to nobility and to priesthood; and paid it with usury, by enlarging their ideas, and by furnishing their minds. Happy if they had all continued to know their indissoluble union, and their proper place! Happy if learning, not debauched by ambition, had been satisfied to continue the instructor, and not aspired to be the master! Along with its natural protectors and guardians, learning will be cast into the mire, and trodden down under the hoofs of a swinish multitude.[5]

If, as I suspect, modern letters owe more than they are always willing to own to ancient manners, so do other interests which we value fully as much as they are worth. Even commerce, and trade, and manufacture, the gods of our economical politicians, are themselves, perhaps, but creatures; are themselves but effects, which, as first causes, we choose to worship. They certainly grew under the same shade in which learning flourished. They too may decay with their natural protecting principles. With you, for the present at least, they all threaten to disappear together. Where trade and manufactures are wanting to a people, and the spirit of nobility and religion remains, sentiment supplies, and not always ill-supplies their place; but if commerce and the arts should be lost in an experiment to try how well a state may stand without these old fundamental principles, what sort of a thing must be a nation of gross, stupid, ferocious, and, at the same time, poor and sordid barbarians, destitute of religion, honor, or manly pride, possessing nothing at present, and hoping for nothing hereafter?

Views of the English Nation.

When I assert any thing as concerning the people of England I speak from observation, not from authority; but I speak from the experience I have had in a pretty extensive and mixed communication with the inhabitants of this kingdom, of all descriptions and ranks, and after a course of attentive observation, begun in early life, and continued for near forty years. I have often been astonished, considering that we are divided from you but by a slender dike of about twenty-four miles, and that the mutual intercourse between the two countries has lately been very great, to find how little you seem to know of us. I suspect that this is owing to your forming a judgment of this nation from certain publications, which do very erroneously, if they do at all, represent the opinions and dispositions generally prevalent in England. The vanity, restlessness, petulence, and spirit of intrigue of several petty cabals, who attempt to hide their total want of consequence in bustle, and noise, and puffing, and mutual quotation of each other, makes you imagine that our contemptuous neglect of their abilities is a general mark of acquiescence in their opinions. No such thing, I assure you. Because half a dozen grasshoppers under a fern make the field ring with their importunate chink, while thousands of great cattle, reposed beneath the shadow of the British oak, chew the cud and are silent, pray do not imagine that those who make the noise are the only inhabitants of the field; that, of course, they are many in number; or that, after all, they are other than the little, shriveled, meager, hopping, though loud and troublesome insects of the hour.

I almost venture to affirm, that not one in a hundred among us participates in the "triumph" of the revolution society. If the King and Queen of France and their children were to fall into our hands by the chance of war, in the most acrimonious of all hostilities (I deprecate such an event, I deprecate such hostility), they would be treated with another sort of triumphal entry into London. We formerly have had a king of France

[5] See the fate of Bailly and Condorcet, supposed to be here particularly alluded to. Compare the circumstances of the trial and execution of the former with this prediction.

Mr. Burke has been accused, without the slightest reason, of here applying the phrase "swinish multitude" to the lower class of society in *general*, as a distinctive appellation. The language was obviously suggested by the scriptural direction, "Cast not you pearls before swine." Bailly and Condorcet did this, and experienced the natural consequences; and Mr. Burke says that such will always be the case, that "learning will be trodden under the hoofs of *a* (not *the*) swinish multitude."

in that situation; you have read how he was treated by the victor in the field; and in what manner he was afterward received in England. Four hundred years have gone over us; but I believe we are not materially changed since that period. Thanks to our sullen resistance to innovation; thanks to the cold sluggishness of our national character, we still bear the stamp of our forefathers. We have not (as I conceive) lost the generosity and dignity of thinking of the fourteenth century; nor, as yet, have we subtilized ourselves into savages. We are not the converts of Rousseau; we are not the disciples of Voltaire; Helvetius has made no progress among us. Atheists are not our preachers; madmen are not our lawgivers. We know that *we* have made no discoveries; and we think that no discoveries are to be made in morality; nor many in the great principles of government, nor in the ideas of liberty, which were understood long before we were born, altogether as well as they will be after the grave has heaped its mold upon our presumption, and the silent tomb shall have imposed its law on our pert loquacity. In England we have not yet been completely emboweled of our natural entrails; we still feel within us, and we cherish and cultivate those inbred sentiments which are the faithful guardians, the active monitors of our duty, the true supporters of all liberal and manly morals. We have not been drawn and trussed in order that we may be filled, like stuffed birds in a museum, with chaff, and rags, and paltry blurred shreds of paper about the rights of man. We preserve the whole of our feelings, still native and entire, unsophisticated by pedantry and infidelity. We have real hearts of flesh and blood beating in our bosoms. We fear God; we look up with awe to kings; with affection to Parliaments; with duty to magistrates; with reverence to priests; and with respect to nobility. Why? Because, when such ideas are brought before our minds, it is *natural* to be so affected; because all other feelings are false and spurious, and tend to corrupt our minds, to vitiate our primary morals, to render us unfit for rational liberty; and by teaching us a servile, licentious, and abandoned insolence, to be our low sport for a few holidays, to make us perfectly fit for, and justly deserving of slavery through the whole course of our lives.

You see, sir, that in this enlightened age I am bold enough to confess that we are generally men of untaught feelings; that instead of casting away all our old prejudices, we cherish them to a very considerable degree, and, to take more shame to ourselves, we cherish them because they *are* prejudices; and the longer they have lasted, and the more generally they have prevailed, the more we cherish them. We are afraid to put men to live and trade each on his own private stock of reason; because we suspect that the stock in each man is small, and that the individuals would do better to avail themselves of the general bank and capital of nations and of ages. Many of our men of speculation, instead of exploding general prejudices, employ their sagacity to discover the latent wisdom which prevails in them. If they find what they seek, and they seldom fail, they think it more wise to continue the prejudice, with the reason involved, than to cast away the coat of prejudice, and to leave nothing but the naked reason; because prejudice, with its reason, has a motive to give action to that reason, and an affection which will give it permanence. Prejudice is of ready application in the emergency; it previously engages the mind in a steady course of wisdom and virtue, and does not leave the man, hesitating in the moment of decision, skeptical, puzzled, and unresolved. Prejudice renders a man's virtue his habit, and not a series of unconnected acts. *Through just prejudice, his duty becomes a part of his nature.*

Theory of the English Constitution.

You will observe that, from Magna Charta to the Declaration of Right, it has been the uniform policy of our Constitution to claim and assert our liberties, as an *entailed inheritance* derived to us from our forefathers, and to be transmitted to our posterity, as an estate specially belonging to the people of this kingdom, without any reference whatever to any other more general or prior right. By this means our Constitution preserves a unity in so great a diversity of its parts. We have an inheritable Crown, an inheritable peerage, and a House of Commons and a people inheriting privileges, franchises, and liberties, from a long line of ancestors.

The policy appears to me to be the result of profound reflection, or, rather, the happy effect of following nature, which is wisdom without reflection, and above it. A spirit of innovation is generally the result of a selfish temper and confined views. *People will not look forward to posterity, who never look backward to their ancestors.* Besides, the people of England well know that the idea of inheritance furnishes a sure principle of conservation, and a sure principle of transmission, without at all excluding a principle of improvement. It leaves acquisition free; but it secures what it acquires. Whatever advantages are obtained by a state proceeding on these maxims are locked fast as in a sort of family settlement; grasped as in a kind of mortmain, forever. By a constitutional policy, working after the pattern of nature, we receive, we hold, we transmit, our government and our privileges, in the same manner in which we enjoy and transmit our property and our lives. The institutions of policy, the goods of fortune, the gifts of Providence, are handed down, to us and from us, in the same course and order. Our political system is placed in a just correspondence and symmetry with the order of the world, and with the mode of existence decreed to a permanent body composed of transitory parts, wherein, by the disposition of a stupendous wisdom, molding together the great mysterious incorporation of the human race, the whole, at one time.

is never old, or middle-aged, or young, but, in a condition of unchangeable constancy, moves on through the varied tenor of perpetual decay, fall, renovation, and progression. Thus, by preserving the method of nature in the conduct of the state, in what we improve, we are never wholly new; in what we retain, we are never wholly obsolete. By adhering in this manner, and on those principles, to our forefathers, we are guided not by the superstition of antiquarians, but by the spirit of philosophic analogy. In this choice of inheritance we have given to our frame of polity the image of a relation in blood; binding up the Constitution of our country with our dearest domestic ties; adopting our fundamental laws into the bosom of our family affections; keeping inseparable, and cherishing with the warmth of all their combined and mutually reflected charities, our state, our hearths, our sepulchres, and our altars.

Through the same plan of a conformity to nature in our artificial institutions, and by calling in the aid of her unerring and powerful instincts, to fortify the fallible and feeble contrivances of our reason, we have derived several other, and those no small benefits, from considering our liberties in the light of an inheritance. Always acting as if in the presence of canonized forefathers, the spirit of freedom, leading in itself to misrule and excess, is tempered with an awful gravity. This idea of a liberal descent inspires us with a sense of habitual, native dignity, which prevents that upstart insolence almost inevitably adhering to and disgracing those who are the first acquirers of any distinction. By this means our liberty becomes a noble freedom. It carries an imposing and majestic aspect. It has a pedigree and illustrating ancestors. It has its bearings and its ensigns armorial. It has its gallery of portraits, its monumental inscriptions, its records, evidences, and titles. We procure reverence to our civil institutions, on the principle upon which nature teaches us to revere individual men; on account of their age, and on account of those from whom they are descended. All your sophisters can not produce any thing better adapted to preserve a rational and manly freedom than the course that we have pursued, who have chosen our nature rather than our speculations, our breasts rather than our inventions, for the great conservatories and magazines of our rights and privileges.

Degrading Influence of Low Views in Politics.

When men of rank sacrifice all ideas of dignity to an ambition without a distinct object, and work with low instruments and for low ends, the whole composition becomes low and base. Does not something like this now appear in France? Does it not produce something ignoble and inglorious? a kind of meanness in all the prevalent policy? a tendency in all that is done to lower, along with individuals, all the dignity and importance of the state? Other revolutions have been conducted by persons, who, while they attempted or effected changes in the commonwealth, sanctified their ambition by advancing the dignity of the people whose peace they troubled. They had long views. They aimed at the rule, not at the destruction of their country. They were men of great civil and great military talents, and if the terror, the ornament of their age. They were not like Jew brokers contending with each other who could best remedy with fraudulent circulation and depreciated paper the wretchedness and ruin brought on their country by their degenerate councils. The compliment made to one of the great bad men of the old stamp (Cromwell) by his kinsman, a favorite poet of that time, shows what it was he proposed, and what, indeed, to a great degree, he accomplished in the success of his ambition.

"Still as *you* rise, the *state* exalted too,
Finds no distemper while 'tis changed by *you*;
Changed like the world's great scene, when, without noise,
The rising sun night's *vulgar* lights destroys."

These disturbers were not so much like men usurping power, as asserting their natural place in society. Their rising was to illuminate and beautify the world. Their conquest over their competitors was by outshining them. The hand that, like a destroying angel, smote the country, communicated to it the force and energy under which it suffered. I do not say (God forbid) I do not say that the virtues of such men were to be taken as a balance to their crimes, but they were some corrective to their effects. Such was, as I said, our Cromwell. Such were your whole race of Guises, Condés, and Colignis. Such the Richelieus, who in more quiet times acted in the spirit of a civil war. Such, as better men, and in a less dubious cause, were your Henry the Fourth and your Sully, though nursed in civil confusions, and not wholly without some of their taint. It is a thing to be wondered at to see how very soon France, when she had a moment to respire, recovered and emerged from the longest and most dreadful civil war that ever was known in any nation. Why? because, among all their massacres, they had not slain the *mind* in their country. A conscious dignity, a noble pride, a generous sense of glory and emulation, was not extinguished. On the contrary, it was kindled and inflamed. The organs, also, of the state, however shattered, existed. All the prizes of honor and virtue, all the rewards, all the distinctions remained. But your present confusion, like a palsy, has attacked the fountain of life itself. Every person in your country, in a situation to be actuated by a principle of honor, is disgraced and degraded, and can entertain no sensation of life except in a mortified and humiliated indignation.

True Theory of the Rights of Man.

Far am I from denying in theory; full as far is my heart from withholding in practice (if I were of power to give or to withhold) the *rea.*

rights of men. In denying their false claims of right, I do not mean to injure those which are real, and are such as their pretended rights would totally destroy. If civil society be made for the advantage of man, all the advantages for which it is made become his right. It is an institution of beneficence; and law itself is only beneficence acting by a rule. Men have a right to live by that rule; they have a right to do justice, as between their fellows, whether their fellows are in politic function or in ordinary occupation. They have a right to the fruits of their industry, and to the means of making their industry fruitful. They have a right to the acquisitions of their parents; to the nourishment and improvement of their offspring; to instruction in life, and to consolation in death. Whatever each man can separately do, without trespassing upon others, he has a right to do for himself; and he has a right to a fair portion of all which society, with all its combinations of skill and force, can do in his favor. In this partnership all men have equal rights, but not to equal things. He that has but five shillings in the partnership has as good a right to it as he that has five hundred pounds has to his larger proportion; but he has not a right to an equal dividend in the product of the joint stock; and as to the share of power, authority, and direction which each individual ought to have in the management of the state, that I must deny to be among the direct, original rights of man in civil society; for I have in my contemplation the civil, social man, and no other. It is a thing to be settled by convention.

If civil society be the offspring of convention, that convention must be its law. That convention must limit and modify all the descriptions of constitution which are formed under it. Every sort of legislative, judicial, or executory power, are its creatures. They can have no being in any other state of things; and how can any man claim, under the conventions of civil society, rights which do not so much as suppose its existence? rights which are absolutely repugnant to it? One of the first motives to civil society, and which becomes one of its fundamental rules, is, *that no man should be judge in his own cause.* By this each person has at once divested himself of the first fundamental right of uncovenanted man; that is, to judge for himself, and to assert his own cause. He abdicates all right to be his own governor. He inclusively, in a great measure, abandons the right of self-defense, the first law of nature. Men can not enjoy the rights of an uncivil and of a civil state together. That he may obtain justice, he gives up his right of determining what it is in points the most essential to him. That he may secure some liberty, he makes a surrender in trust of the whole of it.

Government is not made in virtue of natural rights, which may and do exist in total independence of it, and exist in much greater clearness, and in a much greater degree of abstract perfection; but their abstract perfection is their practical defect. By having a right to every thing they want every thing. Government is a contrivance of human wisdom to provide for human *wants.* Men have a right that these wants should be provided for by this wisdom. Among these wants is to be reckoned the want, out of civil society, of a sufficient restraint upon their passions. Society requires not only that the passions of individuals should be subjected, but that even in the mass and body, as well as in the individuals, the inclinations of men should frequently be thwarted, their will controlled, and their passions brought into subjection. This can only be done *by a power out of themselves,* and not, in the exercise of its function, subject to that will and to those passions which it is its office to bridle and subdue. In this sense, the restraints on men, as well as their liberties, are to be reckoned among their rights; but as the liberties and the restrictions vary with times and circumstances, and admit of infinite modifications, they can not be settled upon any abstract rule, and nothing is so foolish as to discuss them upon that principle.

The moment you abate any thing from the full rights of men each to govern himself, and suffer any artificial, positive limitation upon those rights, from that moment the whole organization of government becomes a consideration of convenience. This it is which makes the Constitution of a state, and the due distribution of its powers, a matter of the most delicate and complicated skill. It requires a deep knowledge of human nature and human necessities, and of the things which facilitate or obstruct the various ends which are to be pursued by the mechanism of civil institutions. The state is to have recruits to its strength, and remedies to its distempers. What is the use of discussing a man's abstract right to food or medicine? The question is upon the method of procuring and administering them. In that deliberation I shall always advise to call in the aid of the farmer and the physician rather than the professor of metaphysics.

The science of constructing a commonwealth, or renovating it, or reforming it, is, like every other experimental science, not to be taught *a priori.* Nor is it a short experience that can instruct us in that practical science, because the real effects of moral causes are not always immediate, but that which in the first instance is prejudicial may be excellent in its remoter operation, and its excellence may arise even from the ill effects it produces in the beginning. The reverse also happens; and very plausible schemes, with very pleasing commencements, have often shameful and lamentable conclusions. In states there are often some obscure and almost latent causes, things which appear at first view of little moment, on which a very great part of its prosperity or adversity may most essentially depend. The science of government being, therefore, so practical in itself, and intended for such practical purposes—a matter which requires experience, and even more experience than any person can gain in his whole life, however sagacious and observing he may be—it is with infinite caution that any man ought to venture upon pulling down an edifice which has answered in any tolerable degree, for ages, the common purposes of society, or on building it up again, without having models and patterns of approved utility before his eyes.

True Statesmanship.

The true lawgiver ought to have a heart full of sensibility. He ought to love and respect his kind, and to fear himself. It may be allowed to his temperament to catch his ultimate object with an intuitive glance, but his movements toward it ought to be deliberate. Political arrangement, as it is a work for social ends, is to be only wrought by social means. There mind must conspire with mind. Time is required to produce that union of minds which alone can produce all the good we aim at. Our patience will achieve more than our force. If I might venture to appeal to what is so much out of fashion in Paris, I mean to experience, I should tell you that in my course I have known, and, according to my measure, have co-operated with great men; and I have never yet seen any plan which has not been mended by the observations of those who were much inferior in understanding to the person who took the lead in the business. By a slow but well-sustained progress the effect of each step is watched; the good or ill success of the first gives light to us in the second; and so, from light to light, we are conducted with safety through the whole series. We see that the parts of the system do not clash. The evils latent in the most promising contrivances are provided for as they arise. One advantage is as little as possible sacrificed to another. We compensate, we reconcile, we balance. We are enabled to unite into a consistent whole the various anomalies and contending principles that are found in the minds and affairs of men. From hence arises not an excellence in simplicity, but one far superior, an excellence in composition. Where the great interests of mankind are concerned through a long succession of generations, that succession ought to be admitted into some share in the councils which are so deeply to affect them. If justice requires this, the work itself requires the aid of more minds than one age can furnish. It is from this view of things that the best legislators have been often satisfied with the establishment of some sure, solid, and ruling principle in government; a power like that which some of the philosophers have called a plastic nature; and having fixed the principle, they have left it afterward to its own operation.

The State consecrated in the Hearts of the People.

To avoid, therefore, the evils of inconstancy and versatility, ten thousand times worse than those of obstinacy and the blindest prejudice, we have consecrated the state, that no man should approach to look into its defects or corruptions but with due caution; that he should never dream of beginning its reformation by its subversion; that he should approach to the faults of the state as to the wounds of a father, with pious awe and trembling solicitude. By this wise prejudice we are taught to look with horror on those children of their country who are prompt rashly to hack that aged parent in pieces, and put him into the kettle of magicians, in hopes that, by their poisonous weeds and wild incantations, they may regenerate the paternal constitution, and renovate their father's life.

Society is, indeed, a contract. Subordinate contracts for objects of mere occasional interest may be dissolved at pleasure; but the state ought not to be considered as nothing better than a partnership agreement in a trade of pepper and coffee, calico or tobacco, or some other such low concern, to be taken up for a little temporary interest, and to be dissolved by the fancy of the parties. It is to be looked on with other reverence, because it is not a partnership in things subservient only to the gross animal existence of a temporary and perishable nature. It is a partnership in all science; a partnership in all art; a partnership in every virtue, and in all perfection. As the ends of such a partnership can not be obtained in many generations, it becomes a partnership not only between those who are living, but between those who are living, those who are dead, and those who are to be born. Each contract of each particular state is but a clause in the great primeval contract of eternal society, linking the lower with the higher natures, connecting the visible and invisible world, according to a fixed compact sanctioned by the inviolable oath which holds all physical and all moral natures each in their appointed place. This law is not subject to the will of those who, by an obligation above them, and infinitely superior, are bound to submit their will to that law. The municipal corporations of that universal kingdom are not morally at liberty at their pleasure, and on their speculations of a contingent improvement, wholly to separate and tear asunder the bands of their subordinate community, and to dissolve it into an unsocial, uncivil, unconnected chaos of elementary principles. It is the first and supreme necessity only, a necessity that is not chosen, but chooses; a necessity paramount to deliberation, that admits no discussion and demands no evidence, which alone can justify a resort to anarchy. This necessity is no exception to the rule, because this necessity itself is a part, too, of that moral and physical disposition of things to which man must be obedient by consent of force; but if that which is only submission to necessity should be made the object of choice, the law is broken, nature is disobeyed, and the rebellious are outlawed, cast forth, and exiled from this world of reason, and order, and peace, and virtue, and fruitful penitence, into the antagonist world of madness, discord, vice, confusion, and unavailing sorrow.

These, my dear sir, are, were, and I think long will be, the sentiments of not the least learned and reflecting part of this kingdom. They who are included in this description form their opinions on such grounds as such persons ought to form them. The less inquiring receive them from an authority which those whom Providence dooms to live on trust need not be ashamed to rely on. These two sorts of men move in the same direction, though in a different place. They both move with the order of the universe. They all know or feel this great ancient truth: "Quod illi principi et præpotenti Deo qui omnem hunc mundum regit, nihil eorum quæ quidem fiant in terris acceptius quam concilia et cœtus hominum jure sociati quæ civitates appellantur."[6] They take this tenet of the head and heart not from the great name which it immediately bears, nor from the greater from whence it is derived, but from that which alone can give true weight and sanction to any learned opinion, the common nature and common relation of men. Persuaded that all things ought to be done with reference, and referring all to the point of reference to which all should be directed, they think themselves bound, not only as individuals, in the sanctuary of the heart, or as congregated in that personal capacity, to renew the memory of their high origin and cast, but also in their corporate character, to perform their national homage to the Institutor, and Author and Protector of civil society; without which civil society man could not by any possibility arrive at the perfection of which his nature is capable, nor even make a remote and faint approach to it. They conceive that He who gave our nature to be perfected by our virtue, willed also the necessary means of its perfection. He willed, therefore, the state. He willed its connection with the source and original archetype of all perfection. They who are convinced of this His will, which is the law of laws, and the sovereign of sovereigns, can not think it reprehensible that this our corporate fealty and homage, that this our recognition of a seigniory paramount, I had almost said this oblation of the state itself, as a worthy offering on the high altar of universal praise, should be performed as all public solemn acts are performed, in buildings, in music, in decorations, in speech, in the dignity of persons, according to the customs of mankind, taught by their nature! that is, with modest splendor, with unassuming state, with mild majesty, and sober pomp. For those purposes they think some part of the wealth of the country is as usefully employed as it can be in fomenting the luxury of individuals. It is the public ornament. It is the public consolation. It nourishes the public hope. The poorest man finds his own importance and dignity in it, while the wealth and pride of individuals at every moment makes the man of humble rank and fortune sensible of his inferiority, and degrades and vilifies his condition. It is for the man in humble life, and to raise his nature, and to put him in mind of a state in which the privileges of opulence will cease, when he will be equal by nature, and may be more than equal by virtue, that this portion of the general wealth of his country is employed and sanctified.

The English people are also satisfied that to the great the consolations of religion are as necessary as its instructions. They, too, are among the unhappy. They feel personal pain and domestic sorrow. In these they have no privilege, but are subject to pay their full contingent to the contributions levied on mortality. They want this sovereign balm under their gnawing cares and anxieties, which, being less conversant about the limited wants of animal life, range without limit, and are diversified by infinite combinations in the wild and unbounded regions of imagination. Some charitable dole is wanting to these, our often very unhappy brethren, to fill the gloomy void that reigns in minds which have nothing on earth to hope or fear; something to relieve in the killing languor and over-labored lassitude of those who have nothing to do; something to excite an appetite to existence in the palled satiety which attends on all pleasures which may be bought, where nature is not left to her own process, where even desire is anticipated, and even fruition defeated by meditated schemes and contrivances of delight, and no interval, no obstacle is interposed between the wish and the accomplishment.

The Revolutionary Government of France.

Out of the tomb of the murdered monarchy in France has arisen a vast, tremendous, unformed specter, in a far more terrific guise than any which ever yet have overpowered the imagination and subdued the fortitude of man. Going straightforward to its end, unappalled by peril, unchecked by remorse, despising all common maxims and all common means, that hideous phantom overpowered those who could not believe it was possible she could at all exist. * *

The republic of regicide, with an annihilated revenue, with defaced manufactures, with a ruined commerce, with an uncultivated and half-depopulated country, with a discontented, distressed, enslaved, and famished people, passing with a rapid, eccentric, incalculable course, from the wildest anarchy to the sternest despotism, has actually conquered the finest parts of Europe, has distressed, disunited, deranged, and broke to pieces all the rest.

What now stands as government in France is struck at a heat. The design is wicked, immoral, impious, oppressive, but it is spirited and daring; it is systematic; it is simple in its principle; it has unity and consistency in perfection. In that country, entirely to cut off a branch of commerce, to extinguish a manufacture, to destroy the circulation of money, to violate credit, to suspend the course of agriculture, even to burn a city or to lay waste a province of their

[6] That nothing is more acceptable to the All-powerful Being who rules the world than those councils of men under the authority of law, which bear the name of states.—*Somnium Scipionis,* sect. iii.

own, does not cost them a moment's anxiety. To them, the will, the wish, the want, the liberty, the toil, the blood of individuals is as nothing. Individuality is left out of their scheme of government. The *state* is all in all. Every thing is referred to the production of force; afterward, every thing is trusted to the use of it. It is military in its principle, in its maxims, in its spirit, and in all its movements. The state has *dominion* and *conquest* for its sole objects; dominion over minds by proselytism, over bodies by arms.

Thus constituted, with an immense body of natural means, which are lessened in their amount only to be increased in their effect, France has, since the accomplishment of the revolution, a complete unity in its direction. It has destroyed every resource of the state which depends upon opinion and the good will of individuals. The riches of convention disappear. The advantages of nature in some measure remain; even these, I admit, are astonishingly lessened; the command over what remains is complete and absolute. They have found the short cut to the productions of nature, while others in pursuit of them are obliged to wind through the labyrinth of a very intricate state of society. They seize upon the fruit of the labor; they seize upon the laborer himself. Were France but half of what it is in population, in compactness, in applicability of its force, situated as it is, and being what it is, it would be too strong for most of the states of Europe, constituted as they are, and proceeding as they proceed. Would it be wise to estimate what the world of Europe, as well as the world of Asia, had to dread from Genghis Khan, upon a contemplation of the resources of the cold and barren spot in the remotest Tartary from whence first issued that scourge of the human race? Ought we to judge from the excise and stamp duties of the rocks, or from the paper circulation of the sands of Arabia, the power by which Mohammed and his tribes laid hold at once on the two most powerful empires of the world, beat one of them totally to the ground, broke to pieces the other, and, in not much longer space of time than I have lived, overturned governments, laws, manners, religion, and extended an empire from the Indus to the Pyrenees?

Material resources never have supplied, nor ever can supply the want of unity in design and constancy in pursuit; but unity in design, and perseverance and boldness in pursuit, have never wanted resources, and never will. We have not considered as we ought the dreadful energy of a state in which the property has nothing to do with the government. Reflect, again and again, on a government in which the property is in complete subjection, and where nothing rules but the mind of desperate men. The condition of a commonwealth not governed by its property was a combination of things which the learned and ingenious speculator Harrington, who has tossed about society into all forms, never could imagine to be possible. We have seen it; and if the world will shut their eyes to this state of things they will feel it more. The rulers there have found their resources in crimes. The discovery is dreadful; the mine exhaustless. They have every thing to gain, and they have nothing to lose. They have a boundless inheritance in hope; and there is no medium for them between the highest elevation and death with infamy.

Their Treatment of Embassadors from Foreign Powers.

To those who do not love to contemplate the fall of human greatness, I do not know a more mortifying spectacle than to see the assembled majesty of the crowned heads of Europe waiting as patient suitors in the ante-chamber of regicide. They wait, it seems, until the sanguinary tyrant *Carnot* shall have snorted away the fumes of the indigested blood of his sovereign. Then, when sunk on the down of usurped pomp, he shall have sufficiently indulged his meditation with what monarch he shall next glut his ravening maw, he may condescend to signify that it is his pleasure to be awake; and that he is at leisure to receive the proposals of his high and mighty clients for the terms on which he may respite the execution of the sentence he has passed upon them. At the opening of those doors, what a sight it must be to behold the plenipotentiaries of royal impotence, in the precedency which they will intrigue to obtain, and which will be granted to them according to the seniority of their degradation, sneaking into the regicide presence, and with the relics of the smile, which they had dressed up for the levee of their masters, still flickering on their curled lips, presenting the faded remains of their courtly graces to meet the scornful, ferocious, sardonic grin of a bloody ruffian, who, while he is receiving their homage, is measuring them with his eye, and fitting to their size the slider of his guillotine!

Illustration from a Case supposed in England.

To illustrate my opinions on this subject, let us suppose a case, which, after what has happened, we can not think absolutely impossible, though the augury is to be abominated, and the event deprecated with our most ardent prayers. Let us suppose, then, that our gracious Sovereign was sacrilegiously murdered; his exemplary Queen, at the head of the matronage of this land, murdered in the same manner; that those princesses, whose beauty and modest elegance are the ornaments of the country, and who are the leaders and patterns of the ingenuous youth of their sex, were put to a cruel and ignominious death, with hundreds of others, mothers and daughters, ladies of the first distinction; that the Prince of Wales and the Duke of York, princes the hope and pride of the nation, with all their brethren, were forced to fly from the knives of assassins—that the whole body of our excellent clergy were either massacred or robbed of all, and transported—the Christian religion, in all its denominations, forbidden and persecuted—the law, totally, fundamentally, and in all its parts, destroyed—the judges put to death by revolutionary tribunals—the peers and commons robbed to the last acre of their estates; massacred if they stayed, or obliged to seek life in flight, in exile, and in beggary—that the whole landed property should share the very same fate—that every military and naval officer of honor and rank, almost to a man, should be placed in the same description of confiscation and exile—that the principal merchants and bankers should be drawn out, as from a hen-coop, for slaughter—that the citizens of our greatest and most flourishing cities, when the hand and the machinery of the hangman were not found sufficient, should have been collected in the public squares, and massacred by thousands with cannon; if three hundred thousand others should have been doomed to a situation worse than death in noisome and pestilential prisons—in such a case, is it in the faction of robbers I am to look for my country? Would this be the England that you and I, and even strangers admired, honored, loved, and cherished? Would not the exiles of England alone be my government and my fellow-citizens? Would not their places of refuge be my temporary country? Would not all my duties and all my affections be there, and there only? Should I consider myself as a traitor to my country, and deserving of death, if I knocked at the door and heart of every potentate in Christendom to succor my friends, and to avenge them on their enemies? Could I, in any way, show myself more a patriot? What should I think of those potentates who insulted their suffering brethren; who treated them as vagrants, or, at least, as mendicants; and could find no allies, no friends, but in regicide murderers and robbers? What ought I to think and feel if, being geographers instead of kings, they recognized the desolated cities, the wasted fields, and the rivers polluted with blood, of this geometrical measurement, as the honorable member of Europe called England? In that condition, what should we think of Sweden, Denmark, or Holland, or whatever power afforded us a churlish and treacherous hospitality, if they should invite us to join the standard of our King, our laws, and our religion; if they should give us a direct promise of protection; if, after all this, taking advantage of our deplorable situation, which left us no choice, they were to treat us as the lowest and vilest of all mercenaries? If they were to send us far from the aid of our King and our suffering country, to squander us away in the most pestilential climates for a venal enlargement of their own territories, for the purpose of trucking them, when obtained, with those very robbers and murderers they had called upon us to oppose with our blood? What would be our sentiments, if, in that miserable service, we were not to be considered either as English, or as Swedes, Dutch, Danes, but as outcasts of the human race? While we were fighting those battles of their interest, and as their soldiers, how should we feel if we were to be excluded from all their cartels? How must we feel if the pride and flower of the English nobility and gentry, who might escape the pestilential clime and the devouring sword, should, if taken prisoners, be delivered over as rebel subjects, to be condemned as rebels, as traitors, as the vilest of all criminals, by tribunals formed of Maroon negro slaves, covered over with the blood of their masters, who were made free, and organized into judges for their robberies and murders? What should we feel under this inhuman, insulting, and barbarous protection of Muscovites, Swedes, or Hollanders? Should we not obtest Heaven, and whatever justice there is yet on earth? Oppression makes wise men mad; but the distemper is still the madness of the wise, which is better than the sobriety of fools. Their cry is the voice of sacred misery, exalted, not into wild raving, but into the sanctified frenzy of prophecy and inspiration—in that bitterness of soul, in that indignation of suffering virtue, in that exaltation of despair, would not persecuted English loyalty cry out with an awful warning voice, and denounce the destruction that waits on monarchs, who consider fidelity to them as the most degrading of all vices; who suffer it to be punished as the most abominable of all crimes; and who have no respect but for rebels, traitors, regicides, and furious negro slaves, whose crimes have broke their chains? Would not this warm language of high indignation have more of sound reason in it, more of real affection, more of true attachment, than all the lullabies of flatterers, who would hush monarchs to sleep in the arms of death?

Conduct expected from Mr. Pitt when the French broke off Negotiations for Peace in 1797.

After such an elaborate display had been made of the injustice and insolence of an enemy, who seems to have been irritated by every one of the means which had been commonly used with effect to soothe the rage of intemperate power, the natural result would be, that the scabbard, in which we in vain attempted to plunge our sword, should have been thrown away with scorn. It would have been natural, that, rising in the fullness of their might, insulted majesty, despised dignity, violated justice, rejected supplication, patience goaded into fury, would have poured out all the length of the reins upon all the wrath which they had so long restrained.[7] It might

[7] This passage was probably suggested by Virgil's description of Neptune, as seated in his chariot, and controlling his impatient steeds (book v., line 818), till willing at last to give full course to their swiftness,

———manibusque omnes effundit habenas.

He pours forth all the reins from out his hands.

In like manner, the attributes here personified, "insulted majesty," "despised dignity," &c., "pour out all the length of the reins upon all the wrath

have been expected, that, emulous of the glory of the youthful hero [the Austrian Archduke Charles] in alliance with him, touched by the example of what one man, well formed and well placed, may do in the most desperate state of affairs, convinced there is a courage of the cabinet full as powerful, and far less vulgar than that of the field, our minister would have changed the whole line of that unprosperous prudence, which hitherto had produced all the effects of the blindest temerity. If he found his situation full of danger (and I do not deny that it is perilous in the extreme), he must feel that it is also full of glory; and that he is placed on a stage, than which no muse of fire that had ascended the highest heaven of invention could imagine any thing more awful and august.[8] It was hoped that, in the swelling scene in which he moved, with some of the first potentates of Europe for his fellow-actors, and with so many of the rest for the anxious spectators of a part, which, as he plays it, determines forever their destiny and his own, like Ulysses, in the unraveling point of the epic story, he would have thrown off his patience and his rags together; and, stripped of unworthy disguises, he would have stood forth in the form and in the attitude of a hero.[9] On that day, it was thought he would have assumed the port of Mars; that he would bid to be brought forth from their hideous kennel (where his scrupulous tenderness had too long immured them) those impatient dogs of war, whose fierce regards affright even the minister of vengeance that feeds them; that he would let them loose, in famine, fever, plagues, and death upon a guilty race, to whose frame, and to all whose habit, order, peace, religion, and virtue are alien and abhorrent.[10] It was expected that he would at last have thought of active and effectual war; that he would no longer amuse the British lion in the chase of mice and rats; that he would no longer employ the whole naval power of Great Britain, once the terror of the world, to prey upon the miserable remains of a peddling commerce, which the enemy did not regard, and from which none could profit. It was expected that he would have reasserted whatever remained to him of his allies, and endeavored to recover those whom their fears had led astray; that he would have rekindled the martial ardor of his citizens; that he would have held out to them the example of their ancestry, the assertor of Europe, and the scourge of French ambition; that he would have reminded them of a posterity which, if this nefarious robbery, under the fraudulent name and false color of a government, should in full power be seated in the heart of Europe, must forever be consigned to vice, impiety, barbarism, and the most ignominious slavery of body and mind. In so holy a cause it was presumed that he would (as in the beginning of the war he did) have opened all the temples; and with prayer, with fasting, and with supplication (better directed than to the grim Moloch of regicide in France), have called upon us to raise that united cry, which has so often stormed Heaven, and with a pious violence forced down blessings upon a repentant people. It was hoped that, when he had invoked upon his endeavors the favorable regard of the Protector of the human race, it would be seen that his menaces to the enemy and his prayers to the Almighty were not followed, but accompanied, with correspondent action. It was hoped that his shrilling trumpet should be heard, not to announce a show, but to sound a charge.

Duties of the Higher Classes in carrying on the War.

In the nature of things it is not with their persons that the higher classes principally pay their contingent to the demands of war. There is another and not less important part which rests with almost exclusive weight upon them. They furnish the means

> "How war may best upheld,
> Move by her two main nerves, iron and gold,
> In all her equipage."—*Milton's Par. Lost.*

Not that they are exempt from contributing,

---

which they had so long restrained." We have few images in our language of equal force and beauty.

[8] See the prologue to Shakspeare's Henry V.:

> Oh for a *Muse of Fire* that would ascend
> The highest heaven of invention!

[9] The scene referred to is that near the close of the twenty-first book of the Odyssey, where Ulysses, who had appeared disguised as a beggar among the suitors of Penelope, finding that none of them could bend his bow, takes it in hand himself, amid the jeers of all, strings it with the ease of a lyre, and sends the arrow whizzing through the rings which had been suspended as a mark.

> ——But when the wary hero wise
> Had made his hand familiar with the bow,
> Poising it, and examining—at once—
> As when, in harp and song adept, a bard
> Strings a new lyre, extending, first, the chords,
> He knits them to the frame, at either end,
> With promptest ease; with such Ulysses strung
> His own huge bow, and with his right hand trill'd
> The nerve, which, in its quick vibration, sang
> As with a swallow's voice. Then anguish turn'd
> The suitors pale; and in that moment Jove
> Gave him his rolling thunder for a sign.
> Such most propitious notice from the son
> Of wily Saturn, hearing with delight,
> He seized a shaft which at the table side
> Lay ready drawn; but in his quiver's womb
> The rest yet slept, though destined soon to steep
> Their points in Grecian blood. He lodged the reed
> Full on the bow-string, drew the parted head
> Home to his breast, and aiming as he sat,
> At once dismissed it. Through the num'rous rings
> Swift flew the gliding steel, and, issuing, sped
> Beyond them.—*Cowper.*

He then pours out the arrows at his feet, and turns his bow on the suitors till they are all destroyed.

[10] Then should the warlike Harry like himself,
Assume the *port of Mars*, and at his heels,
Leasht in like hounds should *famine*, sword, and [fire,
Crouch for employment.

also, by their personal service in the fleets and armies of their country. They do contribute, and in their full and fair proportion, according to the relative proportion of their numbers in the community. They contribute all the *mind* that actuates the whole machine. The fortitude required of them is very different from the unthinking alacrity of the common soldier, or common sailor, in the face of danger and death; it is not a passion, it is not an impulse, it is not a sentiment; it is a cool, steady, deliberate principle, always present, always equable; having no connection with anger; tempering honor with prudence; incited, invigorated, and sustained by a generous love of fame; informed, moderated, and directed by an enlarged knowledge of its own great public ends; flowing in one blended stream from the opposite sources of the heart and the head; carrying in itself its own commission, and proving its title to every other command, by the first and most difficult command, that of the bosom in which it resides; it is a fortitude which unites with the courage of the field the more exalted and refined courage of the council; which knows as well to retreat as to advance; which can conquer as well by delay as by the rapidity of a march or the impetuosity of an attack; which can be, with Fabius, the black cloud that lowers on the tops of the mountains, or with Scipio, the thunderbolt of war; which, undismayed by false shame, can patiently endure the severest trial that a gallant spirit can undergo, in the taunts and provocations of the enemy, the suspicions, the cold respect, and "mouth honor" of those from whom it should meet a cheerful obedience; which, undisturbed by false humanity, can calmly assume that most awful moral responsibility of deciding when victory may be too dearly purchased by the loss of a single life, and when the safety and glory of their country may demand the certain sacrifice of thousands.

Sentiments becoming the Crisis.

Nor are sentiments of elevation in themselves turgid and unnatural. Nature is never more truly herself than in her grandest form. The Apollo of Belvidere (if the universal robber has yet left him at Belvidere) is as much in nature as any figure from the pencil of Rembrandt, or any clown in the rustic revels of Teniers. Indeed, it is when a great nation is in great difficulties that minds must exalt themselves to the occasion, or all is lost. Strong passion, under the direction of a feeble reason, feeds a low fever, which serves only to destroy the body that entertains it. But vehement passion does not always indicate an infirm judgment. It ofte accompanies, and actuates, and is even auxiliary to a powerful understanding; and when they both conspire and act harmoniously, their force is great to destroy disorder within, and to repel injury from abroad. If ever there was a time that calls on us for no vulgar conception of things, and for exertions in no vulgar strain, it is the awful hour that Providence has now appointed to this nation. Every little measure is a great error; and every great error will bring on no small ruin. Nothing can be directed above the mark that we must aim at; every thing below it is absolutely thrown away.

* * * * *

Who knows whether indignation may not succeed to terror, and the revival of high sentiment, spurning away the delusion of a safety purchased at the expense of glory, may not yet drive us to that generous despair, which has often subdued distempers in the state, for which no remedy could be found in the wisest councils?

MISCELLANEOUS.

William III. forming the Grand Alliance against Louis XIV.

The steps which were taken to compose, to reconcile, to unite, and to discipline all Europe against the growth of France, certainly furnish to a statesman the finest and most interesting part in the history of that great period. It formed the master-piece of King William's policy, dexterity, and perseverance. Full of the idea of preserving, not only a local civil liberty united with order, to our country, but to embody it in the political liberty, the order, and the independence of nations united under a natural head, the King called upon his Parliament to put itself into a posture "*to preserve to England the weight and influence it at present had on the councils and affairs* ABROAD. It will be requisite *Europe* should see you will not be wanting to yourselves."

Baffled as that monarch was, and almost heartbroken at the disappointment he met with in the mode he first proposed for that great end, he held on his course. He was faithful to his object; and in councils, as in arms, over and over again repulsed, over and over again he returned to the charge. All the mortifications he had suffered from the last Parliament, and the greater he had to apprehend from that newly chosen, were not capable of relaxing the vigor of his mind. He was in Holland when he combined the vast plan of his foreign negotiations. When he came to open his design to his ministers in England, even the sober firmness of Somers, the undaunted resolution of Shrewsbury, and the adventurous spirit of Montague and Orford, were staggered. They were not yet mounted to the elevation of the King. The cabinet (then the regency) met on the subject at Tunbridge Wells the 28th of August, 1698; and there, Lord Somers holding the pen, after expressing doubts on the state of the continent, which they ultimately refer to the King, as best informed, they give him a most discouraging portrait of the spirit of this nation. "So far as relates to England," say these ministers, "it would be want of duty not to give your majesty this clear account, that *there is a deadness and want of spirit in the nation universally*, so as not to be at all disposed to *entering into a new war*. That they seem to be *tired out with taxes* to a degree beyond what was discerned, till it appeared upon occasion of the *late elections*. This is the truth of the fact upon which your majesty will determine what resolution ought to be taken."

His majesty did determine, and did take and pursue his resolution. In all the tottering imbecility of a new government, and with Parliament totally unmanageable, he persevered. He persevered to expel the fears of his people by his fortitude—to steady their fickleness by his constancy—to expand their narrow prudence by his enlarged wisdom—to sink their factious temper in his public spirit. In spite of his people, he resolved to make them great and glorious; to make England, inclined to shrink into her narrow self, the arbitress of Europe, the tutelary angel of the human race. In spite of the ministers, who staggered under the weight that his mind imposed upon theirs, unsupported as they felt themselves by the popular spirit, he infused into them his own soul; he renewed in them their ancient heart; he rallied them in the same cause.

It required some time to accomplish this work. The people were first gained, and through them their distracted representatives. Under the influence of King William, Holland had rejected the allurements of every seduction, and had resisted the terrors of every menace. With Hannibal at her gates, she had nobly and magnanimously refused all separate treaty, or any thing which might for a moment appear to divide her affection or her interest, or even to distinguish her in identity from England.

The English House of Commons was more reserved. The principle of the Grand Alliance was not directly recognized in the resolution of the Commons, nor the war announced, though they were well aware the alliance was formed for the war. However, compelled by the returning sense of the people, they went so far as to fix the three great immovable pillars of the safety and greatness of England, as they were then, as they are now, and as they must ever be to the end of time. They asserted in general terms the necessity of supporting Holland; of keeping united with our allies; and maintaining the liberty of Europe; though they restricted their vote to the succors stipulated by actual treaty. But now they were fairly embarked, they were obliged to go with the course of the vessel; and the whole nation, split before into an hundred adverse factions, with a king at its head evidently declining to his tomb, the whole nation —Lords, Commons, and people—proceeded as one body, informed by one soul. Under the British union, the union of Europe was consolidated; and it long held together with a degree of cohesion, firmness, and fidelity, not known before or since in any political combination of that extent.

Just as the last hand was given to this immense and complicated machine, the master-workman died; but the work was formed on true mechanical principles; and it was as truly wrought. It went by the impulse it had received from the first mover. The man was dead; but the Grand Alliance survived, in which King William lived and reigned. That heartless and dispirited people, whom Lord Somers had represented, about two years before, as dead in energy and operation, continued that war, to which it was supposed they were unequal in mind and in means, for near thirteen years.

The Duke of Bedford's hold on his Property.[1]

The Crown has considered me after long service, the Crown has paid the Duke of Bedford by advance. He has had a long credit for any services which he may perform hereafter. He is secure, and long may he be secure, in his advance, whether he performs any services or not. But let him take care how he endangers the safety of that Constitution which secures his own utility or his own insignificance; or how he discourages those who take up even puny arms to defend an order of things, which, like the sun of heaven, shines alike on the useful and the worthless. His grants are ingrafted on the public law of Europe, covered with the awful hoar of innumerable ages. They are guarded by the sacred rules of prescription, found in that full treasury of jurisprudence from which the jejuneness and penury of our municipal law has, by degrees, been enriched and strengthened. This prescription I had my share (a very full share) in bringing to its perfection.[2] The Duke of Bedford will stand as long as prescriptive law endures; as long as the great stable laws of property, common to us with all civilized nations, are kept in their integrity, and without the smallest intermixture of laws, maxims, principles, or precedents of the grand revolution. They are secure against all changes but one. The whole revolutionary system, institutes, digest, code, novels, text, gloss, comment, are not only not the same, but they are the very reverse, and the reverse, fundamentally, of all the laws on which civil life has hitherto been upheld in all the governments of the world. The learned professors of the rights of man regarded prescription, not as a title to bar all claim, set up against all possession—but they look on prescription as itself a bar against the possessor and proprietor. They hold an immemorial possession to be no more than a long-continued, and therefore an aggravated injustice.

Such are *their* ideas, such *their* religion; and such *their* law. But as to *our* country and *our* race, as long as the well-compacted structure of our church and state, the sanctuary, the holy of

---

[1] This passage is taken from a letter to a Noble Lord, which was called forth by an insulting attack from the Duke of Bedford when Mr. Burke received his pension.

[2] Sir George Savile's Act, called the *Nullum Tempus* Act.

holies of that ancient law, defended by reverence, defended by power, a fortress at once and a temple,[3] shall stand inviolate on the brow of the British Sion—as long as the British monarchy, not more limited than fenced by the orders of the state, shall, like the proud Keep of Windsor, rising in the majesty of proportion, and girt with the double belt of its kindred and coeval towers, as long as this awful structure shall oversee and guard the subjected land—so long the mounds and dikes of the low, fat, Bedford level will have nothing to fear from the pick-axes of all the levelers of France. As long as our sovereign lord the King, and his faithful subjects, the lords and commons of this realm—the triple cord, which no man can break; the solemn, sworn, constitutional frank-pledge of this nation; the firm guarantees of each other's being and each other's rights; the joint and several securities, each in its place and order, for every kind and every quality of property and of dignity. As long as these endure, so long the Duke of Bedford is safe; and we are all safe together—the high from the blights of envy and the spoliations of rapacity; the low from the iron hand of oppression and the insolent spurn of contempt. Amen! and so be it, and so it will be,

Dum domus Æneæ Capitoli immobile saxum
Accolet; imperiumque pater Romanus habebit.[4]

Mr. Burke on the Death of his Son.

Had it pleased God to continue to me the hopes of succession, I should have been, according to my mediocrity, and the mediocrity of the age I live in, a sort of founder of a family; I should have left a son, who, in all the points in which personal merit can be viewed, in science, in erudition, in genius, in taste, in honor, in generosity, in humanity, in every liberal sentiment, and every liberal accomplishment, would not have shown himself inferior to the Duke of Bedford, or to any of those whom he traces in his line. His grace very soon would have wanted all plausibility in his attack upon that provision which belonged more to mine than to me. He would soon have supplied every deficiency, and symmetrized every disproportion. It would not have been for that successor to resort to any stagnant wasting reservoir of merit in me, or in any ancestry. He had in himself a salient, living spring of generous and manly action. Every day he lived he would have repurchased the bounty of the Crown, and ten times more, if ten times more he had received. He was *made* a public creature, and had no enjoyment whatever but in the performance of some duty. At this exigent moment, the loss of a finished man is not easily supplied.

But a Disposer whose power we are little able to resist, and whose wisdom it behooves us not at all to dispute, has ordained it in another manner, and (whatever my querulous weakness might suggest) a far better. The storm has gone over me, and I lie like one of those old oaks which the late hurricane has scattered about me. I am stripped of all my honors; I am torn up by the roots, and lie prostrate on the earth! There, and prostrate there, I most unfeignedly recognize the divine justice, and in some degree submit to it.

Character of Sir Joshua Reynolds.

Last night (February 23, 1792), in the sixty-ninth year of his age, died, at his house in Leicester Fields, Sir Joshua Reynolds.

His illness was long, but borne with a mild and cheerful fortitude, without the least mixture of any thing irritable or querulous, agreeably to the placid and even tenor of his whole life. He had from the beginning of his malady a distinct view of his dissolution, which he contemplated with that entire composure, that nothing but the innocence, integrity, and usefulness of his life, and an unaffected submission to the will of Providence, could bestow. In this situation he had every consolation from family tenderness, which his own kindness to his family had indeed well deserved.

Sir Joshua Reynolds was, on very many accounts, one of the most memorable men of his time. He was the first Englishman who added the praise of the elegant arts to the other glories of his country. In taste, in grace, in facility, in happy invention, and in the richness and harmony of coloring, he was equal to the greatest masters of the most renowned ages. In portrait he went beyond them; for he communicated to that description of the art, in which English artists are the most engaged, a variety, a fancy, and a dignity derived from the higher branches, which even those who professed them in a superior manner did not always preserve when they delineated individual nature. His portraits remind the spectator of the invention of history and the amenity of landscape. In painting portraits, he appeared not to be raised upon that platform, but to descend upon it from a higher sphere. His paintings illustrate his lessons, and his lessons seem to be derived from his paintings.

He possessed the theory as perfectly as the practice of his art. To be such a painter, he was a profound and penetrating philosopher.

In full happiness of foreign and domestic fame, admired by the expert in art and by the learned in science, courted by the great, caressed by sovereign powers, and celebrated by distinguished poets, his native humility, modesty, and candor never forsook him, even on surprise or provocation; nor was the least degree of arrogance or assumption visible to the most scrutinizing eye, in any part of his conduct or discourse.

His talents of every kind—powerful from nature, and not meanly cultivated by letters—his social virtues in all the relations and all the hab-

[3] *Templum in modum arcis.* Tacitus of the temple of Jerusalem.

[4] While on the Capitol's unshaken rock,
The Ænean race shall dwell, and Father Jove
Rule o'er the Empire.
Virgil's Æneid, book ix., line 448.

itudes of life, rendered him the center of a very great and unparalleled variety of agreeable societies, which will be dissipated by his death. He had too much merit not to excite some jealousy, too much innocence to provoke any enmity. The loss of no man of his time can be felt with more sincere, general, and unmixed sorrow.

HAIL AND FAREWELL!

DETACHED SENTIMENTS AND MAXIMS.[1]

Never was there a jar or discord between genuine sentiment and sound policy. Never, no, never, did nature say one thing and wisdom say another.

The meditations of the closet have infected senates with a subtle frenzy, and inflamed armies with the brands of the furies.

We are alarmed into reflection; our minds are purified by terror and pity; our weak, unthinking pride is humbled under the dispensations of a mysterious wisdom.

The road to eminence and power, from obscure condition, ought not to be made too easy, nor a thing too much of course. The temple of honor ought to be seated on an eminence. If it be opened through virtue, let it be remembered that virtue is never tried but by some difficulty and some struggle.

Public virtue, being of a nature magnificent and splendid, instituted for great things, and conversant about great concerns, requires abundant scope and room, and can not spread and grow under confinement, and in circumstances straitened, narrow, and sordid.

All persons possessing any portion of power ought to be strongly and awfully impressed with an idea that they act in *trust*, and that they are to account for their conduct in that trust to the one great master, author, and founder of society.

They who administer in the government of men, in which they stand in the person of God himself, should have high and worthy notions of their function and destination. Their hope should be full of immortality.

It is with the greatest difficulty that I attempt to separate policy from justice. *Justice is itself the great standing policy of civil society*, and any eminent departure from it, under any circumstances, lies under the suspicion of being no policy at all.

In all mutations (if mutations must be), the circumstance which will serve most to blunt the edge of their mischief, and to promote what good may be in them, is, that they should find us with our minds *tenacious of justice, and tender of property*.

A man, full of warm, speculative benevolence, may wish society otherwise constituted than he finds it; but a good patriot, and a true politician, always considers how he shall make the most of the existing materials of his country. A disposition to *preserve*, and an ability to *improve*, taken together, would be my standard of a statesman. Every thing else is vulgar in the conception, perilous in the execution.

It is one of the excellencies of a method, in which time is among the assistants, that its operation is slow, and, in some cases, almost imperceptible.

It can not be too often repeated, line upon line, precept upon precept, until it comes into the currency of a proverb, *to innovate is not to reform*.

It is the degenerate fondness for taking *short cuts*, and little fallacious facilities, that has in so many parts of the world created governments with arbitrary powers.

Rage and frenzy will pull down more in half an hour, than prudence, deliberation, and foresight can build up in a hundred years.

I shall always consider that liberty as very equivocal in her appearance, which has not wisdom and justice for her companions, and does not lead prosperity and plenty in her train.

What is liberty without wisdom and without virtue? It is the greatest of all possible evils; for it is folly, vice, and madness, without tuition or restraint.

The strong struggle in every individual to *preserve possession* of what he has found to belong to him and to distinguish him, is one of the securities against injustice and despotism implanted in our nature. It operates as an instinct to secure property, and to preserve communities in a settled state. What is there to shock in this? Nobility is a graceful ornament to the civil order. It is the Corinthian capital of polished society.

It is a sour, malignant, envious disposition, without taste for the reality, or for any image or representation of virtue, that sees with joy the unmerited fall of what had long flourished in splendor and in honor.

The perennial existence of bodies corporate and their fortunes, are things particularly suited to a man who has long views; who meditates designs that require time in fashioning, and which propose duration when they are accomplished.

None can aspire to act greatly, but those who are of force greatly to suffer.

Strong instances of self-denial operate powerfully on our minds; and a man who has no wants has obtained great freedom and firmness, and even dignity.

[1] A few of these sentences have been very slightly modified or abridged, in order to give them the character of distinct propositions, but in no way affecting the sense.

Difficulty is a severe instructor, set over us by the supreme ordinance of a parental guardian and legislator, who knows us better than we know ourselves, as he loves us better too.

Pater ipse colendi
Haud facilem esse viam voluit.[2]

He that wrestles with us strengthens our nerves and sharpens our skill.

It has been the glory of the great masters in all the arts to confront and to overcome; and when they have overcome the first difficulty, to turn it into an instrument for new conquests over new difficulties.

Hypocrisy delights in the most sublime speculations; for, never intending to go beyond speculation, it costs nothing to have it magnificent.

Men who are too much confined to *professional and faculty habits*, and, as it were, inveterate in the recurrent employment of that narrow circle, are rather disabled than qualified for whatever depends on the knowledge of mankind, on experience in mixed affairs, on a comprehensive, connected view of the various complicated external and internal interests which go to the formation of that multifarious thing called a state.[3]

Turbulent, discontented men of quality, in proportion as they are puffed up with personal pride and arrogance, generally despise their own order.

The great must submit to the dominion of prudence and of virtue, or none will long submit to the dominion of the great.

Living law, full of reason, and of equity and justice (as it is, or it should not exist), ought to be severe and awful too; or the words of menace, whether written on the parchment roll of England, or cut into the brazen tablet of Rome, will excite nothing but contempt.

Men and states, to be secure, must be respected. Power, and eminence, and consideration, are things not to be begged. They must be commanded; and those who supplicate for mercy from others, can never hope for justice through themselves.

The blood of man should never be shed but to redeem the blood of man. It is well shed for our family, for our friends, for our God, for our country, for our kind. The rest is vanity; the rest is crime.

In a conflict between nations, that state which is resolved to hazard its existence rather than to abandon its objects, must have an infinite advantage over that which is resolved to yield rather than to carry its resistance beyond a certain point.

It is often impossible, in political inquiries, to find any proportion between the apparent force of any *moral causes* we may assign, and their known operation. Some states, at the very moment when they seemed plunged in unfathomable abysses of disgrace and disaster, have suddenly emerged; they have begun a new course and opened a new reckoning; and even in the depths of their calamity, and on the very ruins of the country, have laid the foundations of a towering and durable greatness.

There is a *courageous wisdom:* there is also a false, *reptile prudence*, the result, not of caution, but of fear. The eye of the mind is dazzled and vanquished. An abject distrust of ourselves, an extravagant admiration of the enemy, present us with no hope but in a compromise with his pride, by a submission to his will.

Parsimony is not economy. Expense, and great expense, may be an essential part in true economy, which is a distributive virtue, and consists not in saving, but in selection. Parsimony requires no providence, no sagacity, no powers of combination, no comparison, no judgment. Mere instinct, and that not an instinct of the noblest kind, may produce this false economy in perfection. The other economy has larger views. It demands a discriminating judgment, and a firm, sagacious mind.

If wealth is the obedient and laborious slave of virtue and of public honor, then wealth is in its place, and has its use. If we command our wealth, we shall be rich and free; if our wealth commands us, we are poor indeed.

No sound ought to be heard in the church but the healing voice of Christian charity. Those who quit their proper character to assume what does not belong to them, are, for the greater part, ignorant both of the character they leave and of the character they assume. They have nothing of politics *but the passions they excite.* Surely the church is a place where one day's truce ought to be allowed to the dissensions and animosities of mankind.

Steady, independent minds, when they have an object of so serious a concern to mankind as government under their contemplation, will disdain to assume the part of satirists and declaimers.

Those persons who creep into the hearts of most people, who are chosen as the companions of their softer hours, and their reliefs from care and anxiety, are never persons of shining qualities or strong virtues. It is rather *the soft green of the soul* on which we rest our eyes that are fatigued with beholding more glaring objects.

When pleasure is over, we relapse into indifference, or, rather, we fall into a soft tranquillity, which is *tinged with the agreeable color of the former sensation.*

Nothing tends so much to the corruption of science as to suffer it to stagnate: *these waters must be troubled before they can exert their virtues.*

---

[2] The Father of our race himself decrees
That culture shall be hard.
Virgil's Georgics, i., 121.

[3] See, also, on this subject, the sketch of Mr. George Grenville's character, page 251.

It is better to cherish virtue and humanity by leaving much to free will, even with some loss to the object, than to attempt to make men mere machines and instruments of a political benevolence. The world, on the whole, will gain by a liberty without which virtue can not exist.

The dignity of every occupation wholly depends upon the quantity and the kind of virtue that may be exerted in it

The degree of estimation in which any profession is held becomes the standard of the estimation in which the professors hold themselves.

It is generally in the season of prosperity that men discover their real temper, principles, and designs.

Nothing but the possession of some power can, with any certainty, discover what at the bottom is the true character of any man.

All men that are ruined, are ruined on the side of their natural propensities.

Good men do not suspect that their destruction is attempted through their virtues.

True humility is the low, but deep and firm foundation of all real virtue.

While shame keeps its watch, virtue is not wholly extinguished in the heart, nor will moderation be utterly exiled from the minds of tyrants.

The punishment of real tyrants is a noble and awful act of justice; and it has with truth been said to be consolatory to the human mind.

The arguments of tyranny are as contemptible as its force is dreadful.

Wisdom is not the most severe corrector of folly.

The love of lucre, though sometimes carried to a ridiculous, sometimes to a vicious excess, is the grand cause of prosperity to all states.

Good order is the foundation of all good things.

Whoever uses instruments, in finding helps, finds also impediments.

It is ordained, in the eternal constitution of things, that men of intemperate minds can not be free. Their passions forge their fetters.

Some persons, by hating vices too much, come to love men too little.

There are some follies which baffle argument, which go beyond ridicule, and which excite no feeling in us but disgust.

Men are as much blinded by the extremes of misery as by the extremes of prosperity. Desperate situations produce desperate councils and desperate measures.

They who always labor can have no true judgment. They never give themselves time to cool. They can never plan the future by the past.

Men who have an interest to pursue are extremely sagacious in discovering the true seat of power.

In all bodies, those who will lead must also, in a considerable degree, follow.

The virtues and vices of men in large towns are sociable; they are always in garrison; and they come embodied and half disciplined into the hands of those who mean to form them for civil or military action.

The elevation of mind, to be derived from fear, will never make a nation glorious.

The vice of the ancient democracies, and one cause of their ruin, was, that they ruled by *occasional* decrees (psephismata), which broke in upon the tenor and consistency of the laws.

Those who execute public *pecuniary* trusts, ought, of all men, to be the most strictly held to their duty.

Nothing turns out to be so oppressive and unjust as a feeble government.

HENRY GRATTAN.

HENRY GRATTAN was born at Dublin on the third day of July, 1746. His father was an eminent barrister, and acted for many years as recorder of that city, which he also represented for a time in the Parliament of Ireland.

In the year 1763, young Grattan entered Trinity College, Dublin, where he was distinguished for the brilliancy of his imagination and the impetuosity of his feelings. Having graduated in 1767, with an honorable reputation, he repaired to London, and became a member of the Middle Temple. His mind, however, was at first too exclusively occupied with literary pursuits to allow of his devoting much time to the study of the law. Politics next engaged his attention. The eloquence of Lord Chatham drew him as an eager listener to the debates in Parliament, and acted with such fascination upon his mind as seemed completely to form his destiny. Every thing was forgotten in the one great object of cultivating his powers as a public speaker. To emulate and express, though in the peculiar forms of his own genius, the lofty conceptions of the great English orator, was from this time the object of his continual study and most fervent aspirations.

In 1772 he returned to Ireland, where he was admitted to the bar; and in 1775 he became a member of the Irish Parliament, under the auspices of Lord Charlemont. He, of course, joined the ranks of Opposition, and united at once with Mr. Flood and the leading patriots of the day, in their endeavors to extort from the English minister the grant of free trade for Ireland. The peculiar circumstances of the country favored their design. The corps of Irish Volunteers had sprung into existence upon the alarm of invasion from France, and was marshaled throughout the country, to the number of nearly fifty thousand, for the defense of the island. With a semblance of some connection with the government, it was really an army unauthorized by the laws, and commanded by officers of their own choosing. Such a force could obviously be turned, at any moment, against the English; and, seizing on the advantage thus gained, Mr. Grattan, in 1779, made a motion, which was afterward changed into a direct resolution, that "nothing but a free trade could save the country from ruin." It was passed with enthusiasm by the great body of the House; and the nation, with arms in their hands, echoed the resolution as the watch-word of their liberties. Lord North and his government were at once terrified into submission. They had tampered with the subject, exciting hopes and expectations only to disappoint them, until a rebellion in Ireland was about to be added to a rebellion in America. In the emphatic words of Mr. Burke, "a sudden light broke in upon us all. It broke in, not through well-contrived and well-disposed windows, but through flaws and breaches—through the yawning chasms of our ruin." Every thing they asked was freely granted; and Ireland, as the English minister imagined, was propitiated.

But Mr. Grattan had already fixed his eye on a higher object—the complete independence of the Irish Parliament. By an act of the sixth year of George the First, it was declared that Ireland was a subordinate and dependent kingdom; that the Kings, Lords, and Commons of England had power to make laws to bind Ireland; that the Irish House of Lords had no jurisdiction, and that all proceedings before that court were void. This arbitrary act Mr. Grattan now determined to set aside. He availed himself of the enthusiasm which pervaded the nation, and, reminding them that the concessions just made might be recalled at any moment, if England continued to bind Ireland by her enactments, he urged them to a DECLARATION OF RIGHT, denying the claim of the British Parliament to make laws for Ireland. His friends endeavored to dissuade him from bringing the subject before the Irish Parliament; but the voice of the nation was with him, and on the 19th of April, 1780, he made his memorable motion for a Declaration of Irish Right. His speech on that occasion, which is the first in this selection, "was the most splendid piece of eloquence that had ever been heard in Ireland." As a specimen of condensed and fervent argumentation, it indicates a high order of talent; while in brilliancy of style, pungency of application, and impassioned vehemence of spirit, it has rarely, if ever, been surpassed. The conclusion, especially, is one of the most magnificent passages in our eloquence.

Mr. Grattan's motion did not then pass, but he was hailed throughout Ireland as the destined deliverer of his country. No Irishman had ever enjoyed such unbounded popularity. He animated his countrymen with the hope of ultimate success; he inspired them with his own imaginative and romantic spirit, and awakened among them a feeling of nationality such as had never before existed. He taught them to cherish Irish affections, Irish manners, Irish art, Irish literature; and endeavored, in short, to make them a distinct people from the English in every respect but one, that of being governed by the same sovereign. Nothing could be more gratifying to the enthusiastic spirit of that ardent and impulsive race; and though it was impossible that such a plan should succeed, he certainly stamped his own character, in no ordinary degree, on the mind of the nation. That peculiar kind of eloquence, especially, which prevails among his countrymen, though springing, undoubtedly, from the peculiarities of national temperament, was rendered doubly popular by the brilliant success of Mr. Grattan, who presents the most perfect exhibition of the highly-colored and impassioned style of speaking in which the Irish delight, with but few of its faults, or, rather, for the most part, with faults in the opposite direction.

With this ascendency over the minds of the people, Mr. Grattan spent nearly two years in preparing for the next decisive step. The Volunteers held their famous meeting at Dungannon in February, 1782, and passed unanimously a resolution drawn up by Mr. Grattan, that "a claim of any body of men, other than the King, Lords, and Commons of Ireland, to make laws to bind this kingdom, is unconstitutional, illegal, and a grievance." This resolution was virtually a declaration of war in case the act of Parliament complained of, was not repealed. It was adopted throughout the country, not merely by shouting thousands at mass meetings, but by armed regiments of citizens and owners of the soil, and by grand juries at judicial assizes. The administration of Lord North was now tottering to its fall. The avowed friends of Ireland, Lord Rockingham, Lord Shelburne, and Mr. Fox, took his place in March, 1782; and Mr. Grattan determined at once to try the sincerity of their feelings. He therefore gave notice that, on the 16th of the ensuing April, he should repeat his motion, in the Irish House of Commons, for a Declaration of Irish Right. It was a trying moment for the new Whig administration. To concede at such a time, when the Irish stood with arms in their hands, was to lay England at their feet. Mr. Fox, therefore, seconded by Burke, Sheridan, Sir Philip Francis, Colonel Barré, and other distinguished Irishmen, pleaded for delay. Lord Charlemont brought the message to the bedside of Mr. Grattan, who was confined by a severe illness, and received for reply, "NO TIME! NO TIME! The Irish leaders are pledged to the people; they can not postpone the question; it is *public property*." When the day arrived, Mr. Grattan, to the surprise of all who knew his debilitated state, made his appearance in the House, and delivered a speech, the second one in these extracts, which won universal admiration for its boldness, sublimity, and compass of thought. Lord Charlemont remarked afterward, in speaking of this effort, and of Mr. Grattan's weakness of health when he came forward, that "if ever spirit could be said to act independent of body, it was on that occasion." It was in vain for the friends of the minister to resist. The resolutions were carried almost by acclamation. Mr. Fox, when he heard the result, decided instantly to yield, declaring that he would rather see Ireland wholly separated from the crown of England than held in subjection by force. He, therefore, soon after brought in a bill for repealing the act of the sixth of George First.

As an expression of their gratitude for these services, the Parliament of Ireland voted the sum of £100,000 to purchase Mr. Grattan an estate. His feelings led him, at first, to decline the grant; but, as his patrimony was inadequate to his support in the new position he occupied, he was induced, by the interposition of his friends, to accept one *half* the amount.

Mr. Flood had been greatly chagrined at the ascendency gained by Mr. Grattan, and he now endeavored to depreciate his efforts by contending that the "simple repeal" of the act of the sixth of George First was of no real avail; that the English Parliament must pass a distinct act, *renouncing* all claim to make law for Ireland. Every one now sees that the pretense was a ridiculous one; but he succeeded in confusing and agitating the minds of the people on this point, until he robbed Mr. Grattan, to a considerable extent, of the honor of his victory. He came out, at last, into open hostility, stigmatizing him as "a *mendicant* patriot, subsisting on the public accounts—who, bought by his country for a sum of money, had sold his country for prompt payment." Mr. Grattan instantly replied in a withering piece of invective, to be found below, depicting the character and political life of his opponent, and ingeniously darkening every shade that rested on his reputation.

As most of the extracts in this selection are taken from the early speeches of Mr. Grattan, it will be unnecessary any farther to trace his history. Suffice it to say, that, although he lost his popularity at times, through the influence of circumstances or the arts of his enemies, he devoted himself throughout life to the defense of his country's interests. He was vehemently opposed to the union with England; but his countrymen were so much divided that it was impossible for any one to prevent it. At a later period (1805), he became a member of the Parliament of Great Britain, where he uniformly maintained those principles of toleration and popular government which he had supported in Ireland. He was an ardent champion of Catholic Emancipation, and may be said to have died in the cause. He had undertaken, in 1820, to present the Catholic Petition, and support it in Parliament, notwithstanding the remonstrances of his medical attendants, who declared it would be at the hazard of his life. "I should be happy," said he, "to die in the discharge of my duty." Exhausted by the journey, he did die almost immediately after his arrival in London, May 14th, 1820, at the age of seventy, and was buried, with the highest honors of the nation, in Westminster Abbey. His character was irreproachable; and Sir James Mackintosh remarked, in speaking of his death in the House of Commons, "He was as eminent in his observance of all the duties of private life, as he was heroic in the discharge of his public ones." "I never knew a man," said Wilberforce, "whose patriotism and love for his country seemed so completely to extinguish all private interests, and to induce him to look invariably and exclusively to the public good."

The personal appearance and delivery of Mr. Grattan are brought vividly before us in one of the lively sketches of Charles Phillips. "He was short in stature, and unprepossessing in appearance. His arms were disproportionately long. His walk was a stride. With a person swinging like a pendulum, and an abstracted air, he seemed always in thought, and each thought provoked an attendant gesticulation. How strange it is, that a mind so replete with grace, and symmetry, and power, and splendor, should have been allotted such a dwelling for its residence! Yet so it was; and so, also, was it one of his highest attributes that his genius, by its 'excessive light,' blinded his hearers to his physical imperfections. It was the victory of mind over matter." "The chief difficulty in this great speaker's way was the first five minutes. During his exordium laughter was imminent. He bent his body almost to the ground, swung his arms over his head, up, and down, and around him, and added to the grotesqueness of his manner a hesitating tone and drawling emphasis. Still, there was an earnestness about him that at first besought, and, as he warmed, enforced, nay, commanded attention."

The speeches of Mr. Grattan afford unequivocal proof, not only of a powerful intellect, but of high and original genius. There was nothing commonplace in his thoughts, his images, or his sentiments. Every thing came fresh from his mind, with the vividness of a new creation. His most striking characteristic was, condensation and rapidity of thought. "Semper instans sibi," pressing continually upon himself, he never dwelt upon an idea, however important; he rarely presented it under more than one aspect; he hardly ever stopped to fill out the intermediate steps of his argument. His forte was reasoning, but it was "logic on fire;" and he seemed ever to delight in flashing his ideas on the mind with a sudden, startling abruptness. Hence, a distinguished writer has spoken of his eloquence as a "combination of *cloud*, *whirlwind*, and *flame*"—a striking representation of the occasional obscurity and the rapid force and brilliancy of his style. But his incessant effort to be strong made him sometimes unnatural. He seems to be continually straining after effect. He wanted that calmness and self-possession which mark the highest order of minds, and show their consciousness of great strength. When he had mastered his subject, his subject mastered him. His great efforts have too much the air of harangues. They sound more like the battle speeches of Tacitus than the orations of Demosthenes.

His style was elaborated with great care. It abounds in metaphors, which are always striking, and often grand. It is full of antithesis and epigrammatic turns, which give it uncommon point and brilliancy, but have too often an appearance of labor and affectation. His language is select. His periods are easy and fluent—made up of short clauses, with but few or brief qualifications, all uniting in the expression of some one leading thought. His rhythmus is often uncommonly fine. In the peroration of his great speech of April 19th, 1780, we have one of the best specimens in our language of that admirable adaptation of the sound to the sense which distinguished the ancient orators.

Though Mr. Grattan is not a safe model in every respect, there are certain purposes for which his speeches may be studied with great advantage. Nothing can be better suited to break up a dull monotony of style—to give raciness and point—to teach a young speaker the value of that terse and expressive language which is, to the orator especially, the finest instrument of thought.

SPEECH

OF MR. GRATTAN IN THE IRISH HOUSE OF COMMONS IN MOVING A DECLARATION OF IRISH RIGHT, DELIVERED APRIL 19, 1780.

INTRODUCTION.

Ireland had been treated by the English, for three centuries, like a conquered nation. A Parliament had indeed been granted her, but a well known statute, called Poynings' Act, had so abridged the rights of that Parliament, as to render it almost entirely dependent on the English Crown. By the provisions of this act, which was passed in 1494, through the agency of Sir Edward Poynings, then Lord Deputy of Ireland, no session of the Irish Parliament could be held without a license previously obtained from the King of England in council, on the recommendation of the Deputy and his council in Ireland. Thus, the English government had power to prevent the Irish Parliament from ever assembling, except for purposes which the King saw reason to approve. At a later period, there was indeed a relaxation of the severity of this act, but the restraints still imposed were borne reluctantly by the Irish, and gave rise at times to violent struggles. Under such an administration, the commercial and manufacturing interests of Ireland were wholly sacrificed to those of the English; the exportation of woolen goods, and of most other articles of English manufacture, and also the direct import of foreign articles, being denied the Irish. These restrictions had been removed in part, as already stated, on the ground of "*expediency*," by an act of the British Parliament, passed December 13, 1779, under the terror of the Irish Volunteers; and Mr. Grattan, with the same instrument of compulsion in his hands, now moved the Irish Parliament to a Declaration of Right, which should deny the authority of England to make laws for Ireland—an authority asserted by an act of the British Parliament, passed in the sixth year of George I.

SPEECH, &c.

I have entreated an attendance on this day, that you might, in the most public manner, *deny the claim* of the British Parliament to make law for Ireland, and with one voice lift up your hands against it.

Duty of resisting at the earliest moment possible.

If I had lived when the ninth of William took away the woolen manufacture, or when the sixth of George the First took away your Constitution, I should have made a covenant with my own conscience, to seize the first reasonable moment of rescuing my country from the ignominy of such acts of power; or, if I had a son, I should have administered to him an oath that he would consider himself as a person separate and set apart for the discharge of so important a duty.

Upon the same principle am I now come to move a Declaration of Right, the first moment occurring in my time, in which such a declaration could be made with any chance of success, and without an aggravation of oppression.

The commercial concessions not satisfactory.

Sir, it must appear to every person that, notwithstanding the import of sugar, and export of woolens,[1] the people of this country are not satisfied; something remains—the greater work is behind—the public heart is not well at ease. To promulgate our satisfaction, to stop the throats of millions with the votes of Parliament, to preach homilies to the Volunteers, to utter invectives against the people under the pretense of affectionate advice, is an attempt, weak, suspicious and inflammatory.

[1] These were a part of the concession made by Lord North.

You can not dictate to those whose sense you are instructed to represent.

Your ancestors, who sat within these walls, lost to Ireland trade and liberty. You, by the assistance of the people, have recovered trade. You owe the kingdom a CONSTITUTION; she calls upon you to restore it.

The ground of public discontent seems to be, "We have gotten commerce, but not freedom." The same power which took away the export of woolen and the export of glass, may take them away again. The repeal is partial, and the ground of repeal is a principle of expediency.

Case of Ireland and of America compared.

Sir, *expedient* is a word of appropriated and tyrannical import—expedient is a word selected to express the reservation of authority, while the exercise is mitigated—expedient is the ill-omened expression in the repeal of the American Stamp Act. England thought it "expedient" to repeal that law. Happy had it been for mankind if, when she withdrew the exercise, she had not reserved the right. To that reservation she owes the loss of her American empire, at the expense of millions; and America the seeking of liberty through a scene of bloodshed. The repeal of the Woolen Act, similarly circumstanced, pointed against the principle of our liberty, may be a subject for illuminations to a populace, or a pretense for apostacy to a courtier, but can not be a subject of settled satisfaction to a free born, an intelligent and an injured community.

It is, therefore, they [the people of Ireland] consider the free trade as a trade *de facto*, not *de jure*—a *license* to trade under the Parliament of England, not a free trade under the charter of Ireland—a tribute to her strength, to maintain which she must continue in a state of armed preparation, dreading the approach of a general peace, and attributing all she holds dear to the calamitous condition of the British interest in every quarter of the globe. This dissatisfaction, founded upon a consideration of the liberty we have lost, is increased when they consider the opportunity they are losing; for, if this nation, after the death-wound given to her freedom, had fallen on her knees in anguish, and besought the Almighty to frame an occasion in which a weak and injured people might recover their rights, prayer could not have asked, nor God have formed, a moment more opportune for the restoration of liberty, than this in which I have the honor to address you.

Free trade not granted to Ireland as a *right*.

England now smarts under the lesson of the American war. The doctrine of imperial legislature she feels to be pernicious—the revenues and monopolies annexed to it she found to be untenable. Her enemies are a host pouring upon her from all quarters of the earth—her armies are dispersed—the sea is not her's—she has no minister, no ally, no admiral, none in whom she long confides, and no general whom she has not disgraced. The balance of her fate is in the hands of Ireland. You are not only her last connection—you are the only nation in Europe that is not her enemy. Besides, there does, of late, a certain damp and supineness overcast her arms and councils, miraculous as that vigor which has lately inspirited yours. With you every thing is the reverse. Never was there a Parliament in Ireland so possessed of the confidence of the people. You are now the greatest political assembly in the world. You are at the head of an immense army; nor do we only possess an unconquerable force, but a certain unquenchable fire, which has touched all ranks of men like a visitation. Turn to the growth and spring of your country, and behold and admire it!

The situation of England enables the Irish to demand their rights.

Where do you find a nation who, upon whatever concerns the rights of mankind, expresses herself with more truth or force, perspicuity or justice — not in the set phrases of the scholiast; not the tame unreality of the courtier; not the vulgar raving of the rabble; but the genuine speech of liberty, and the unsophisticated oratory of a free nation. See her military ardor, expressed not in forty thousand men conducted by instinct, as they were raised by inspiration, but manifested in the zeal and promptitude of every young member of the growing community. Let corruption tremble! Let the enemy, foreign or domestic, tremble! but let the friends of liberty rejoice at these means of safety and this hour of redemption—an enlightened sense of public right, a young appetite for freedom, a solid strength, and a rapid fire, which not only put a Declaration of Right within your power, but put it out of your power to decline one! Eighteen counties are at your bar. There they stand, with the compact of Henry, with the charter of John, and with all the passions of the people! "Our lives are at your service; but our liberties—we received them from God, we will not resign them to man!" Speaking to you thus, if you repulse these petitioners, you abdicate the office of Parliament, you forfeit the rights of the kingdom, you repudiate the instructions of your constituent, you belie the sense of your country, you palsy the enthusiasm of the people, and you reject that good which not a minister—not a Lord North—not a Lord Buckinghamshire—not a Lord Hillsborough, but a certain providential conjuncture, or, rather, the hand of God, seems to extend to you.

Spirit of the Irish nation.

I read Lord North's propositions, and I wish to be satisfied, but I am controlled by a *paper* (for I will not call it a law); it is the sixth of George First. [Here the clerk, at Mr. Grattan's request, read from the Act of the sixth of George I., "that the kingdom of Ireland hath been, is, and of right ought to be, subordinate to and dependent upon the Imperial Crown of Great Britain, as being inseparably united to and annexed thereunto; and that the King's Majesty, by and with the consent of the Lords spiritual and temporal, and the Commons of Great Britain in Parliament assembled, hath, and of right ought to have, full power and authority to make laws and statutes of sufficient force and validity to *bind* the kingdom and the people of Ireland.]

I will ask the gentlemen of the long robe, *is* this the law? I ask them whether it is not the *practice?* I appeal to the judges of the land, whether they are not in a course of declaring that the Parliament of England naming Ireland, binds her? I appeal to the magistrates of Ireland whether they do not, from time to time, execute certain acts of the British Parliament? I appeal to the officers of the army, whether they do not confine and execute their fellow-subjects by virtue of the Mutiny Act of England? And I appeal to this House whether a country so circumstanced is free? Where is the freedom of trade? Where is the security of property? Where the liberty of the people? I here, in this Declaratory Act, see my country proclaimed a slave! I see every man in this House enrolled a bondsman! I see the judges of the realm, the oracles of the law, borne down by an unauthorized power! I see the magistrates prostrate; and I see Parliament witness to these infringements, and silent! I therefore say, with the voice of three millions of people, that, notwithstanding the import of sugar, and export of woolen and kerseys, beetle-wood and prunellas, nothing is safe, satisfactory, or honorable; nothing, except a Declaration of Right! What! Are you, with three millions of men at your back, with charters in one hand and arms in the other, afraid to say, We are a free people? Are you—the greatest House of Commons that ever sat in Ireland, that want but this one act to equal that English House of Commons which passed the

This act is enforced.

The Declaration therefore demanded.

Petition of Right, or that other, which passed the Declaration—are you, are *you* afraid to tell the British Parliament that you are a free people? Are the cities and the instructing counties, who have breathed a spirit that would have done honor to old Rome, when Rome did honor to mankind—are they to be free by connivance? Are the military associations — those bodies whose origin, progress, and deportment have transcended, equaled, at least, any thing in modern or ancient story, in the vast line of Northern array—are they to be free by *connivance?* What man will settle among you? Who will leave a land of liberty and a settled government for a kingdom controlled by the Parliament of another country; whose liberty is a thing by stealth; whose trade a thing by permission; whose judges deny her charters; whose Parliament leaves every thing at random; where the hope of freedom depends on the chance that the jury shall despise the judge stating a British act, or a rabble stop the magistrate in the execution of it, rescue your abdicated privileges by anarchy and confusion, and save the Constitution by trampling on the government?

Nothing less can satisfy the people.

But I shall be told that these are groundless jealousies, and that the principal cities, and more than one half the counties of the kingdom, are misguided men, raising those groundless jealousies. Sir, they may say so, and they may hope to dazzle with illuminations, and they may sicken with addresses, but the public imagination will never rest, nor will her heart be well at ease; never, so long as the Parliament of England claims or exercises legislation over this country. So long as this shall be the case that very free trade (otherwise a perpetual attachment) will be the cause of new discontent. It will create a pride and wealth, to make you feel your indignities; it will furnish you with strength to bite your chain; the liberty withheld poisons the good communicated. The British minister mistakes the Irish character. Had he intended to make Ireland a slave, he should have kept her a beggar. There is no middle policy. Win her heart by a restoration of her right, or cut off the nation's right hand; greatly emancipate, or fundamentally destroy! We may talk plausibly to England; but so long as she exercises a power to bind this country, so long are the nations in a state of war. The claims of the one go against the liberty of the other, and the sentiments of the latter go to oppose those claims to the last drop of her blood.

The English Opposition, therefore, are right; mere trade will not satisfy Ireland. They judge of us by other great nations; by the English nation, whose whole political life has been a struggle for liberty. They judge of us with a true knowledge and just deference for our character, that a country enlightened as Ireland, armed as Ireland, and injured as Ireland, will be satisfied with nothing less than liberty. I admire that public-spirited merchant[3] who spread consternation at the Custom-house, and, despising the example which great men afforded, tendered for entry prohibited manufactures, and sought, at his private risk, the liberty of his country. With him, I am convinced, it is necessary to agitate the question of right. In vain will you endeavor to keep it back; the passion is too natural, the sentiment too irresistible; the question comes on of its own vitality. You must reinstate the laws.

No ground of fear for consequences.

There is no objection to this resolution except fears. I have examined your fears; I pronounce them to be frivolous. If England is a tyrant, it is you have made her so. It is the slave that makes the tyrant, and then murmurs at the master whom he himself has constituted. I do allow, on the subject of commerce, England was jealous in the extreme; and I do say, it was commercial jealousy; it was the spirit of monopoly. The woolen trade and the Act of Navigation had made her tenacious of a comprehensive legislative authority, and, having now ceded that monopoly, there is nothing in the way of our liberty except our own corruption and pusillanimity. Nothing can prevent your being free, except yourselves; it is not in the disposition of England, it is not in the interest of England, it is not in her force. What! can eight millions of Englishmen, opposed to twenty millions of French, seven millions of Spanish, to three millions of Americans, reject the alliance of three millions in Ireland? Can eight millions of British men, thus outnumbered by foes, take upon their shoulders the expense of an expedition to enslave Ireland? Will Great Britain, a wise and magnanimous country, thus tutored by experience and wasted by war, the French navy riding her channel, send an army to Ireland to levy no tax, to enforce no law, to answer no end whatever, except to spoliate the charters of Ireland, and enforce a barren oppression?

England offered substantially the same thing to America.

What! has England lost thirteen provinces? has she reconciled herself to this loss, and will she not be reconciled to the liberty of Ireland? Take notice, that the very Constitution which I move you to declare, Great Britain herself offered to America: it is a very instructive proceeding in the British history. In 1778 a commission went out with powers to cede to the thirteen provinces of America totally and radically the legislative authority claimed over her by the British Parliament;[4] and the commissioners, pursuant to their powers, did offer to all, or any of the American states, the total surrender of the legislative authority of the British Parliament. I will read you their letter to the Congress. [Here the letter was read, surrendering the power, as aforesaid]. What! has England of-

[3] Alderman Horan, who offered goods for entry at the Irish Custom-house, which had been prohibited by an English act of Parliament, for the purpose of trying the validity of the Act of the sixth of George the First.

[4] This is the commission referred to in such severe terms by Mr. Burke in a speech delivered at Bristol. See page 297.

fered this to the resistance of America, and will she refuse this to the loyalty of Ireland? But, though you do not hazard disturbance by agreeing to this resolution, you do most exceedingly hazard tranquillity by rejecting it. Do not imagine that the question will be over when this motion shall be negatived. No! it will recur in a vast variety of shapes and diversity of places. Your constituents have instructed you, in great numbers, with a powerful uniformity of sentiment, and in a style not the less awful because full of respect. They will find resources in their own virtue, if they have found none in yours. Public pride and conscious liberty, wounded by repulse, will find ways and means of vindication. You are in that situation in which every man, every hour of the day, may shake the pillars of the state. Every court may swarm with questions of right, every quay and wharf with prohibited goods. What shall the judges, what the commissioners, do upon such occasion? Shall they comply with the laws of Ireland against the claims of England, and stand firm where you have trembled? Shall they, on the other hand, not comply; and shall they persist to act against the law? Will you punish them, will you proceed against them, for not showing a spirit superior to your own? On the other hand, will you not punish them? Will you leave your liberties to be trampled on by those men? Will you bring them and yourselves, all constituted orders, executive power, judicial power, parliamentary authority, into a state of odium, impotence, and contempt; transferring the task of defending public right into the hands of the populace, and leaving it to the judges to break the laws, and to the people to assert them? Such would be the consequence of false moderation, of irritating timidity, of inflammatory palliations, of the weak and corrupt hope of compromising with the court before you have emancipated the country.

I have answered the only semblance of a solid reason against the motion. I will now try to remove some lesser pretenses, some minor impediments; for instance: first, that we have a resolution of the same kind already in our journals. But how often was the Great Charter confirmed? Not more frequently than your rights have been violated. Is one solitary resolution, declaratory of your rights, sufficient for a country, whose history, from the beginning unto the end, has been a course of violation?

Less important objection obviated.

The fact is, every new breach is a reason for a new repair; every new infringement should be a new declaration, lest charters should be overwhelmed by precedents, and a nation's rights lost in oblivion, and the people themselves lose the memory of their own freedom.

I shall hear of *ingratitude*, and name the argument to despise it. I know the men who use it are not grateful. They are insatiate; they are public extortioners, who would stop the tide of public prosperity, and turn it to the channel of their own wretched emolument. I know of no species of gratitude which should prevent my country from being free; no gratitude which should oblige Ireland to be the slave of England. In cases of robbery or usurpation, nothing is an object of gratitude, except the thing stolen, the charter spoliated. A nation's liberty can not, like her money, be rated and parceled out in gratitude. No man can be grateful or liberal of his conscience, nor woman of her honor, nor nation of her liberty. There are certain impartable, inherent, invaluable properties not to be alienated from the person, whether body politic or body natural. With the same contempt do I treat that charge which says that Ireland is insatiable; seeing that Ireland asks nothing but that which Great Britain has robbed her of—her rights and privileges. To say that Ireland is not to be satisfied with liberty, because she is not satisfied with slavery, is folly.

I laugh at that man who supposes that Ireland will not be content with a free trade and a free Constitution; and would any man advise her to be content with less?

I shall be told that we hazard the modification of the law of Poynings, and the Judges Bill, and the Habeas Corpus Bill, and the Nullum Tempus Bill; but I ask, have you been for years begging for these little things, and have you not yet been able to obtain them? And have you been contending against a little body of eighty men, in Privy Council assembled, convocating themselves into the image of a Parliament, and ministering your high office; and have you been contending against one man, an humble individual, to you a leviathan—the English Attorney General, exercising Irish legislation in his own person, and making your parliamentary deliberations a blank, by altering your bills or suppressing them; have you not been able to quell this little monster? Do you wish to know the reason? I will tell you; because you have not been a Parliament, nor your country a people. Do you wish to know the remedy? *Be* a Parliament, become a nation, and those things will follow in the train of your consequence.

I shall be told that tithes are shaken, being vested by force of English acts. But in answer to that, I observe, time may be a title, but an English Act of Parliament certainly can not. It is an authority which, if a judge would charge, no jury would find, and which all the electors of Ireland have already disclaimed—disclaimed unequivocally, cordially, and universally.

Sir, this is a good argument for an act of title, but no argument against a Declaration of Right. My friend, who sits above me, has a bill of confirmation.[5] We do not come unprepared to Parliament. I am not come to shake property, but to confirm property, and to restore freedom. The nation begins to form—we are moldering into a people; freedom asserted, property secured, and the army, a mercenary band, likely to be dependent on your Parliament, restrained by law.

[5] A bill to be immediately introduced on passing the Declaration, by which all laws of the English Parliament affecting property were to be confirmed by the Irish Parliament.

Never was such a revolution accomplished in so short a time, and with such public tranquillity. In what situation would those men, who call themselves friends of constitution and of government, have left you? They would have left you without a title (as they stole it) to your estates, without an assertion of your Constitution, or a law for your army; and this state of private and public insecurity, this anarchy, raging in the kingdom for eighteen months, these mock-moderators would have had the presumption to call peace.

Appeal to the principle of the Revolution of 1688.

The King has no other title to his Crown than that which you have to your liberty. Both are founded, the throne and your freedom, upon the right vested in the subject to resist by arms, notwithstanding their oaths of allegiance, any authority attempting to impose acts of power as laws; whether that authority be one man or a host, the second James or the British Parliament, every argument for the house of Hanover is equally an argument for the liberties of Ireland. The Act of Settlement[6] is an act of rebellion, or the sixth of George the First an act of usurpation. I do not refer to doubtful history, but to living record, to common charters, to the interpretation England has put on those charters (an interpretation made, not by words only, but crowned by arms), to the revolution she has formed upon them, to the King she has established, and, above all, to the oath of allegiance solemnly plighted to the house of Stuart, and afterward set aside in the instance of a grave and moral people, absolved by virtue of those very charters; and as any thing less than liberty is inadequate to Ireland, so is it dangerous to Great Britain. We are too near the British nation; we are too conversant with her history; we are too much fired by her example to be any thing less than equals; any thing less, we should be her bitterest enemies. An enemy to that power which smote us with her mace, and to that Constitution from whose blessings we were excluded, to be ground, as we have been, by the British nation, bound by her Parliament, plundered by her Crown, threatened by her enemies, and insulted with her protection, while we returned thanks for her condescension, is a system of meanness and misery which has expired in our determination and in her magnanimity.

Precedents not of binding force.

That there are precedents against us, I allow; acts of power I would call them, not precedents; and I answer the English pleading such precedents, as they answered their Kings when they urged precedents against the liberty of England. Such things are the tyranny of one side, the weakness of the other, and the *law* of neither. We will not be bound by them; or rather, in the words of the Declaration of Right, no doing, judgment, or proceeding to the contrary shall be brought into precedent or example. Do not, then, tolerate a power, the power of the British government, over this land, which has no foundation in necessity, or utility, or empire, or the laws of England, or the laws of Ireland, or the laws of nature, or the laws of God. Do not suffer that power, which banished your manufacturers, dishonored your peerage, and stopped the growth of your people. Do not, I say, be bribed by an export of woolen, or an import of sugar, and suffer that power, which has thus withered the land, to have existence in your pusillanimity. Do not send the people to their *own* resolves for liberty, passing by the tribunals of justice, and the high court of Parliament; neither imagine that, by any formation of apology, you can palliate such a commission to your hearts, still less to your children, who will sting you in your grave for interposing between them and their Maker, and robbing them of an immense occasion, and losing an opportunity which you did not create and can never restore.

Peroration.

Hereafter, when these things shall be history, your age of thraldom, your sudden resurrection, commercial redress, and miraculous armament,[7] shall the historian stop at *liberty*, and observe, that here the principal men among us were found wanting, were awed by a weak ministry, bribed by an empty treasury; and when liberty was within their grasp, and her temple opened its folding doors, fell down, and were prostituted at the threshold?

I might, as a constituent, come to your bar and demand my liberty. I do call upon you by the laws of the land, and their violation; by the instructions of eighteen counties; by the arms, inspiration, and providence of the present moment—tell us the rule by which we shall go; assert the law of Ireland; declare the liberty of the land! I will not be answered by a public lie, in the shape of an amendment; nor, speaking for the subjects' freedom, am I to hear of faction. I wish for nothing but to breathe in this our island, in common with my fellow-subjects, the air of liberty. I have no ambition, unless it be to break your chain and contemplate your glory. I never will be satisfied so long as the meanest cottager in Ireland has a link of the British chain clanking to his rags. He may be naked, he shall not be in irons. And I do see the time at hand; the spirit is gone forth; the Declaration of Right is planted; and though great men should fall off, yet the cause shall live; and though he who utters this should die, yet the immortal fire shall outlast the humble organ who conveys it, and the breath of liberty, like the word of the holy man, will not die with the prophet, but survive him.[8]

---

[6] This was an act of the British Parliament settling the line of succession to the British Crown on the descendants of the Princess Sophia of Hanover, to the exclusion of the Stuarts.

[7] Referring to the rapid formation of the volunteer corps.

[8] The reader will be interested to observe the *rhythmus* of the last three paragraphs; so slow and dignified in its movement; so weighty as it falls on the ear; so perfectly adapted to the sentiments expressed in this magnificent passage. The effect will be heightened by comparing it with the rapid and iambic movement of the passage containing Mr. Erskine's description of the Indian chief, page 696.

Mr. Grattan then moved the Declaration of Right; but the power of the English government was too great in the Irish House of Commons, and he was voted down. He renewed the motion two years after, in connection with the speech which follows.

SPEECH

OF MR. GRATTAN IN THE IRISH HOUSE OF COMMONS ON MAKING HIS SECOND MOTION FOR A DECLARATION OF IRISH RIGHT, DELIVERED APRIL 16, 1782.

INTRODUCTION.

DURING the two years which had elapsed since the preceding speech, great changes had taken place, both in England and in Ireland, which made the passing of the Declaration certain, if strongly insisted upon by the people. Mr. Grattan, therefore, in moving it a second time, uses not so much the language of argument or persuasion, as of assured triumph. He speaks of it in his first sentence as if already carried.

SPEECH,[1] &c.

The object already secured.

I am now to address a free people. Ages have passed away, and this is the first moment in which you could be distinguished by that appellation. I have spoken on the subject of your liberty so often, that I have nothing to add, and have only to admire by what Heaven-directed steps you have proceeded, until the whole faculty of the nation is braced up to the act of her own deliverance. I found Ireland on her knees. I watched over her with an eternal solicitude, and have traced her progress from injuries to arms, and from arms to liberty. Spirit of Swift—spirit of Molyneux[2]—your genius has prevailed—Ireland is now a nation—in that new character I hail her; and, bowing to her august presence, I say, *Esto perpetua!*[3]

Comparison of Ireland with other countries.

She is no longer a wretched colony, returning thanks to her Governor for his rapine, and to her King for his oppression; nor is she now a fretful, squabbling sectary, perplexing her little wits, and firing her furious statutes with bigotry, sophistry, disabilities, and death, to transmit to posterity insignificance and war. Look to the rest of Europe. Holland lives on the memory of past achievements. Sweden has lost her liberty. England has sullied her great name by an attempt to enslave her colonies! You are the only people—you, of the nations in Europe, are now the only people—who excite admiration; and in your present conduct, you not only exceed the present generation, but you equal the past. I am not afraid to turn back and look antiquity in the face. The Revolution, that great event—whether you call it ancient or modern, I know not—was tarnished with bigotry. The great deliverer—for such I must ever call the Prince of Nassau—was blemished by oppression. He assented to—he was forced to assent to acts which deprived the Catholics of religious, and all the Irish of civil and commercial rights, though the Irish were the only subjects in these islands who had fought in his defense. But you have sought liberty on her own principles. See the Presbyterians of Bangor petition for the Catholics of the South! You, with difficulties innumerable, with dangers not a few, have done what your ancestors wished, but could not accomplish; and what your posterity may preserve, but will never equal. You have molded the jarring elements of your country into a nation, and have rivaled those great and ancient states whom you were taught to admire, and among whom you are now to be recorded.

Her inferior advantages.

In this proceeding you had not the advantages which were common to other great countries—no monuments, no trophies, none of those outward and visible signs of greatness, such as inspire mankind, and connect the ambition of the age which is coming on with the example of that which is going off, and forms the descent and concatenation of glory. No! You have not had any great act recorded among all your misfortunes; nor have you one public tomb to assemble the crowd, and speak to the living the language of integrity and freedom. Your historians did not supply the want of monuments. On the contrary, those narrators of your misfortunes who should have felt for your wrongs, and have punished your oppressors with oppression's natural scourge, the moral indignation of history, compromised with public villainy, and trembled; they recited your violence, they suppressed your provocation, and *wrote in* the chain that entrammeled their country. I am come to break that chain; and I congratulate my country, who, without any of the advantages I speak of, going forth, as it were, with nothing but a stone and a sling, and what oppression could not take away, the favor of Heaven, accomplished her own redemption, and left you nothing to add, and every thing to admire. You want no trophy now—the records of Parliament are the evidence of your glory.

I beg to observe, that the deliverance of Ireland has proceeded from her own right hand

---

[1] This speech and the preceding are from a copy corrected by Mr. Grattan, and published in 1821.

[2] William Molyneux, the mathematician and astronomer, was originally bred to the law, and, being deeply interested for his countrymen, he wrote his celebrated work on the rights of the Irish Parliament, the first and ablest work ever produced on the subject. He was born in 1656, and died in 1698.

[3] Let her endure forever.

I rejoice at it; for, had the great acquisition of your freedom proceeded from the bounty of England, that great work would have been defective — would have been defective both in renown and security. It was necessary that the soul of the country should have been exalted by the act of her own redemption, and that England should withdraw her claim by operation of treaty, and not of mere grace and condescension. A gratuitous act of Parliament, however express, would have been revocable; but the repeal of her claim, under operation of treaty, is not. In that case, the Legislature is put in *covenant*, and bound by the law of nations, the only law that can legally bind Parliament. Never did this country stand so high. England and Ireland treat *ex æquo*. Ireland transmits to the King her claim of right, and requires of the Parliament of England the repeal of her claim of power, which repeal the English Parliament is to make under the force of a treaty, which depends on the law of nations—a law which can not be repealed by the Parliament of England. I rejoice that the people are a party to this treaty, because they are bound to preserve it. There is not a man of forty shillings freehold that is not associated in this our claim of right, and bound to die in its defense—cities, counties, associations, Protestants, and Catholics. It seems as if the people had joined in one great sacrament. A flame has descended from heaven on the intellect of Ireland, and plays round her head with a concentrated glory.

Her deliverance achieved by herself.

There are some who think, and a few who declare, that the associations to which I refer are illegal. Come, then, let us try the charge. And first, I ask, what were the grievances? An army imposed on us by another country—that army rendered perpetual—the Privy Council of both countries made a part of our Legislature—our Legislature deprived of its originating and propounding power—another country exercising over us supreme legislative authority—that country disposing of our property by its judgments, and prohibiting our trade by its statutes! These were not grievances, but spoliations; they left you nothing. When you contended against them, you contended for the whole of your condition. When the minister asks by what right, we refer him to our Maker. We sought our privileges by the right which we have to defend our property against a robber, our life against a murderer, our country against an invader, whether coming with civil or military force, a foreign army, or a foreign Legislature. This is a case that wants no precedent. The revolution wanted no precedent; for such things arrive to reform a course of bad precedents, and, instead of being founded on precedent, become such. The gazing world, whom they came to save, begins by doubt and concludes by worship. Let other nations be deceived by the sophistry of courts—Ireland has studied politics in the lair of oppression; and, taught by suffering, comprehends the right of subjects and the duty of kings. Let other nations imagine that subjects are made for the Monarch; but we conceive that kings, and Parliaments like kings, are made for the subject. The House of Commons, honorable and right honorable as it may be; the Lords, noble and illustrious as we pronounce them, are not original, but derivative. Session after session they move their periodical orbit about the source of their being—the NATION. Even the King—Majesty—must fulfill her due and tributary course round that great luminary; and, created by its beam and upheld by its attraction, must incline to that light or go out of the system.

Defense of the Volunteer Associations.

Ministers—we mean the ministers who have been dismissed;[4] I rely on the good intentions of the present—former ministers, I say, have put questions to us. We beg to put questions to them. They desired to know by what authority this nation had acted. This nation desires to know by what authority *they* acted. By what authority did government enforce the articles of war? By what authority does government establish the post-office? By what authority are our merchants bound by the East India Company's charter? By what authority has Ireland one hundred years been deprived of her export trade? By what authority are her peers deprived of their judicature? By what authority has that judicature been transferred to the peers of Great Britain, and our property, in its last resort, referred to the decision of a non-resident, unauthorized, illegal, and unconstitutional tribunal? Will ministers say it was the authority of the British Parliament? On what ground, then, do they place the question between the government on one side, and the people on the other? The government, according to their own statement, has been occupied to supersede the lawgiver of the country, and the people to restore him. His Majesty's late ministers thought they had quelled the country when they bought the newspapers, and they represented us as wild men, and our cause as visionary; and they pensioned a set of wretches to abuse both; but we took little account of them or their proceedings, and we waited, and we watched, and we moved, as it were, on our native hills, with the minor remains of our parliamentary army, until that minority became *Ireland!* Let those ministers now go home, and congratulate their king on the deliverance of his people. Did you imagine that those little parties, whom, three years ago, you beheld in awkward squads parading the streets, would arrive to such distinction and effect? What was the cause? For it was not the sword of the volunteer, nor his muster, nor his spirit, nor his promptitude to put down accidental disturbance, public discord, nor his own unblamed and distinguished deportment: this was much; but there was more than this. The

Argument retorted on the opposers of the Declaration.

[4] Lord North and his associates are here referred to. The "present" ministers were Lord Rockingham, Lord Shelburne, Mr. Fox, &c., composing the Whig administration, which followed that of Lord North.

upper orders, the property and the abilities of the country, formed with the Volunteer; and the volunteer had sense enough to obey them. This united the Protestant with the Catholic, and the landed proprietor with the people. There was still more than this—there was a continence which confined the corps to limited and legitimate objects. There was a principle which preserved the corps from adultery with French politics. There was a good taste which guarded the corps from the affectation of such folly. This, all this, made them bold; for it kept them innocent, it kept them rational. No vulgar rant against England, no mysterious admiration of France, no crime to conceal, no folly to blush for, they were what they professed to be; and that was nothing less than society asserting her liberty according to the frame of the British Constitution—her inheritance to be enjoyed in perpetual connection with the British empire. I do not mean to say that there were not divers violent and unseemly resolutions. The immensity of the means was inseparable from the excess. Such are the great works of nature—such is the sea; but, like the sea, the waste and excess were lost in the immensity of its blessings, benefits, and advantage; and now, having given a Parliament to the people, the Volunteers will, I doubt not, leave the people to Parliament, and thus close, pacifically and majestically, a great work, which will place them above censure and above panegyric. Those associations, like other institutions, will perish; they will perish with the occasion that gave them being; and the gratitude of their country will write their epitaph:

"This phenomenon, the departed Volunteer, justified by the occasion, with some alloy of public evil, did more public good to Ireland than all her institutions. He restored the liberties of his country; and thus, from his grave, he answers his enemies."

England and Ireland now confederate.

Connected by freedom, as well as by allegiance, the two nations, Great Britain and Ireland, form a constitutional confederacy as well as an empire. The Crown is one link, the Constitution another; and, in my mind, the latter link is the most powerful. You can get a king any where; but England is the only country with whom you can get and participate a free Constitution. This makes England your natural connection, and her king your natural as well as your legal sovereign. This is a connection, not as Lord Coke has idly said, not as Judge Blackstone has foolishly said, not as other judges have ignorantly said, by conquests; but, as Molyneux has said, and as I now say, by compact—*that compact is a free Constitution*.

Essential principles of the Confederacy.

Suffer me now to state some of the things essential to that free Constitution. They are as follows: The independency of the Irish Parliament—the exclusion of the British Parliament from any authority in this realm—the restoration of the Irish judicature, and the exclusion of that of Great Britain. As to the perpetual Mutiny Bill, it must be more than limited—it must be effaced. That bill must fall, or the Constitution can not stand. That bill was originally limited by this House to two years, and it returned from England without the clause of limitation. What! a bill making the army independent of Parliament, and perpetual? I protested against it then; I have struggled with it since; and I am now come to destroy this great enemy of my country. The perpetual Mutiny Bill must vanish out of the statute book. The excellent tract of Molyneux was burned—it was not answered, and its flame illumined posterity. This evil paper shall be burned; but burned like a felon, that its execution may be a peace-offering to the people, and that a Declaration of Right may be planted on its guilty ashes. A new Mutiny Bill must be formed, after the manner of England, and a Declaration of Right flaming in its preamble. As to the legislative powers of the Privy Council, I conceive them to be utterly inadmissible, against the Constitution, against the privileges of Parliament, and against the dignity of the realm. Do not imagine such power to be a theoretical evil; it is, in a very high degree, a practical evil. I have here an inventory of bills, altered and injured by the interference of the Privy Councils—Money Bills originated by them—Protests by the Crown, in support of those Money Bills—prorogation following those Protests. I have a Mutiny Bill of 1780, altered by the Council and made perpetual—a bill in 1778, where the Council struck out the clause repealing the Test Act—a Militia Bill, where the Council struck out the compulsory clause, requiring the Crown to proceed to form a militia, and left it optional to his majesty's ministers whether there should be a militia in Ireland. I have the Money Bill of 1775, when the Council struck out the clause enabling his majesty to take a part of our troops for general service, and left it to the minister to withdraw the forces against act of Parliament. I have to state the altered Money Bill of 1771; the altered Money Bill of 1775; the altered Money Bill of 1780. The day would expire before I could recount their ill doings. I will never consent to have men—God knows whom—ecclesiastics, &c., &c.; men unknown to the constitution of Parliament, and only known to the minister who has breathed into their nostrils an unconstitutional existence—steal to their dark divan, which they call the Council, to do mischief, and make nonsense of bills which their Lordships, the House of Lords, or we, the House of Commons, have thought good and meet for the people. No! These men have no legislative qualifications; they shall have no legislative power. 1st. The repeal of the perpetual Mutiny Bill, and the dependency of the Irish army on the Irish Parliament; 2d. The abolition of the legislative power of the Council; 3d. The abrogation of the claim of England to make law for Ireland; the exclusion of the English House of Peers, and of the English King's Bench from any judicial authority in this realm; the restoration of the Irish Peers to their final judicature; the independency of the Irish Parliament in its sole and exclusive Legislature—these are my terms.

Mr. Grattan now moved the Declaration of Right, which was carried almost without a dissenting voice; and a bill soon after passed the British Parliament, ratifying the decision by repealing the obnoxious act of George I.

The Parliament of Ireland was at last independent; but the beneficial results, so glowingly depicted by Mr. Grattan, were never realized; all were sacrificed and lost through a spirit of selfishness and faction. The Protestants of Ireland were divided into two parties, the Aristocracy and the Patriots. The former were exclusive, selfish, and arrogant; the latter were eager for reform, but too violent and reckless in the measures they employed to obtain it. The Parliament of Ireland was a *borough* Parliament, the members of the House of Commons being, in no proper sense, representatives of the people, but put in their places by a comparatively small number of individuals belonging to the higher classes. These classes, while they were among the foremost to demand that "England should not give law to Ireland," were equally determined that the Irish Parliament, in making laws, should do it for the peculiar benefit of the Aristocracy, and the support of their hereditary influence. The Patriots, on the other hand, demanded Parliamentary Reform, and clamored for universal suffrage. To enforce their claims, they assembled a Convention of the Volunteers at Dublin in 1783, with a view to influence, and perhaps overawe the Parliament. Their success would have been certain if they had gone one step farther, and proposed to impart the privileges they enjoyed to the Roman Catholics, by making them voters. But this the Protestants of neither party were willing to do. The Romanists comprised three quarters of the population; very few of them could read or write; and both parties—the Patriots as well as the Aristocracy—equally shrunk from the experiment of universal suffrage among this class of their fellow-citizens. Under these circumstances, the call for Parliamentary Reform was very faintly echoed by the great body of the people. The Convention of Volunteers had none of that power which they had previously exerted on the question of Parliamentary Independence. A bill was brought into the House of Commons by Mr. Flood for extending the right of suffrage, but it was voted down in the most decisive manner. The bitterest animosities now prevailed, and new subjects of contention arose from time to time. Associations were formed, at a later period, under the name of United Irishmen, designed to promote the cause of liberty. Rash men, in many instances, gained the ascendency; an insurrection was planned, and in part commenced; and measures of great severity were resorted to by the British government to restore order. The more sober part of the community became weary of these contentions, and some began to look to a union with England as the only safeguard of their persons and property. The British ministry had the strongest motives to urge on this measure in order to prevent future troubles; and in the year 1800, to a great extent by the use of bribes, the union was effected, and from this time the Parliament of Ireland became extinct.

INVECTIVE

OF MR. GRATTAN AGAINST MR. FLOOD, DELIVERED OCTOBER 28, 1783.

It has been said by Mr. Flood, that "the pen would fall from the hand, and the fetus of the mind would die unborn," if men had not a privilege to maintain a right in the Parliament of England to make law for Ireland. The affectation of zeal, and a burst of forced and metaphorical conceits, aided by the arts of the press, gave an alarm which, I hope, was momentary, and which only exposed the artifice of those who were wicked, and the haste of those who were deceived.

But it is not the slander of an evil tongue that can defame me. I maintain my reputation in public and in private life. No man who has not a bad character can ever say that I deceived; no country can call me cheat. But I will suppose such a public character. I will suppose such a man to have existence. I will begin with his character in its political cradle, and I will follow him to the last state of political dissolution.

I will suppose him, in the first stage of his life, to have been intemperate; in the second, to have been corrupt; and in the last, seditious; that after an envenomed attack on the persons and measures of a succession of viceroys, and after much declamation against their illegalities and their profusion, he took office, and became a supporter of government when the profusion of ministers had greatly increased, and their crimes multiplied beyond example; when your money bills were altered without reserve by the Council; when an embargo was laid on your export trade, and a war declared against the liberties of America. At such a critical moment, I will suppose this gentleman to be corrupted by a great sinecure office to muzzle his declamation, to swallow his invectives, to give his assent and vote to the ministers, and to become a supporter of government, its measures, its embargo, and its American war. I will suppose that he was suspected by the government that had bought him, and in consequence thereof, that he thought proper to resort to the acts of a trimmer, the last sad refuge of disappointed ambition; that, with respect to the Constitution of his country, that part, for instance, which regarded the Mutiny Bill, when a clause of reference was introduced, whereby the articles of war, which were, or hereafter might be, passed in England, should be current in Ireland without the interference of her Parliament—when such a clause was in view, I will suppose this gentleman to have *absconded.* Again, when the bill was made perpetual, I will suppose him again to have absconded; but a year and a half after the bill had passed, then I will suppose this gentleman to have come forward, and to say that your Constitution had been destroyed by the Perpetual Bill. With regard to that part of the Constitution that relates to the law of Poynings, I will suppose the gentleman to have made many a long, very long disquisition before he took office, but, after he received office, to have been as silent on that subject as before he had been loquacious. That, when money bills, under color of that law, were altered, year after year, as in 1775 and 1776, and when the bills so altered were resumed and passed, I will suppose that gentleman to have absconded or acquiesced, and to have supported the minister who made the alteration; but when he was dismissed from office, and a member introduced a bill to remedy this evil, I will suppose that this gentleman inveighed against the mischief, against the remedy, and against the person of the introducer, who did that duty which he himself for seven years had abandoned. With respect to that part of the Constitution which is connected with the repeal of the 6th of George the First, when the inadequacy of the repeal was debating in the House, I will suppose this gentleman to make no kind of objection; that he never named, at that time, the word renunciation; and that, on the division on that subject, he absconded; but when the office he had lost was given to another man, that he came forward, and exclaimed against the measure; nay, that he went into the public streets to canvass for sedition; that he became a rambling incendiary, and endeavored to excite a mutiny in the Volunteers against an adjustment between Great Britain and Ireland, of liberty and repose, which he had not the virtue to make, and against an administration who had the virtue to free the country without buying the members.

With respect to commerce, I will suppose this gentleman to have supported an embargo which lay on the country for three years, and almost destroyed it; and when an address in 1778, to open her trade, was propounded, to remain silent and inactive. And with respect to that other part of her trade, which regarded the duty on sugar, when the merchants were examined in 1778, on the inadequate protecting duty, when the inadequate duty was voted, when the act was recommitted, when another duty was proposed, when the bill returned with the inadequate duty substituted, when the altered bill was adopted, on every one of those questions I will suppose the gentleman to abscond; but a year and a half after the mischief was done, he out of office, I will suppose him to come forth, and to tell his country that her trade had been destroyed by an inadequate duty on English sugar, as her Constitution had been ruined by a Perpetual Mutiny Bill! In relation to three fourths of our fellow-subjects, the Catholics, when a bill was introduced to grant them rights of property and religion, I will suppose this gentleman to have come forth to give his negative to their pretensions. In the same manner, I will suppose him to have opposed the institution of the Volunteers, to which we owe so much, and that he went to a meeting in his own county to prevent their establishment; that he himself kept out of their associations; that he was almost the only man in this House that was not in uniform, and that he never was a Volunteer until he ceased to be a placeman, and until he became an incendiary.

With regard to the liberties of America, which were inseparable from ours, I will suppose this gentleman to have been an enemy, decided and unreserved; that he voted against her liberty, and voted, moreover, for an address to send four thousand Irish troops to cut the throats of the Americans; that he called these butchers "armed negotiators," and stood with a metaphor in his mouth, and a bribe in his pocket, a champion against the rights of America, the only hope of Ireland, and the only refuge of the liberties of mankind. Thus defective in every relationship, whether to Constitution, commerce, or toleration, I will suppose this man to have added much private improbity to public crimes; that his probity was like his patriotism, and his honor on a level with his oath. He loves to deliver panegyrics on himself. I will interrupt him, and say, "Sir, you are much mistaken if you think that your talents have been as great as your life has been reprehensible. You began your parliamentary career with an acrimony and personality which could have been justified only by a supposition of virtue. After a rank and clamorous opposition you became, on a sudden, *silent;* you were silent for seven years; you were silent on the greatest questions; and you were silent for money! In 1773, while a negotiation was pending to sell your talents and your turbulence, you absconded from your duty in Parliament; you forsook your law of Poynings; you forsook the questions of economy, and abandoned all the old themes of your former declamation. You were not at that period to be found in the House. You were seen, like a guilty spirit, haunting the lobby of the House of Commons, watching the moment in which the question should be put, that you might vanish. You were descried with a criminal anxiety, retiring from the scenes of your past glory; or you were perceived coasting the upper benches of this House like a bird of prey, with an evil aspect and a sepulchral note, meditating to pounce on its quarry. These ways—they were not the ways of honor—you practiced pending a negotiation which was to end either in your sale or your sedition. The former taking place, you supported the rankest measures that ever came before Parliament; the embargo of 1776, for instance. 'O, fatal embargo, that breach of law, and ruin of commerce!' You supported the unparalleled profusion and jobbing of Lord Harcourt's scandalous ministry—the address to support the American war—the other address to send four thousand men, which you had yourself declared to be necessary for the defense of Ireland, to fight against the liberties of America, to which you had declared yourself a friend. You, sir, who delight to utter execrations against the American commissioners of 1778, on account of their hostility to America—you, sir, who manufacture stage thunder against Mr. Eden for his anti-American principles—you, sir, whom it pleases to chant a hymn to the immortal Hampden—you, sir, approved of the tyranny exercised against America; and you, sir, voted four thousand Irish troops to cut the throats of the Americans fighting for their freedom, fighting for your freedom, fighting for the great principle, LIBERTY! But you found, at last (and this should be an eternal lesson to men of your craft and cunning), that the King had only dishonored you; the court had bought, but would not trust you; and, having voted for the worst measures, you remained, for seven years, the creature of *salary*, without the confidence of government. Mortified at the discovery, and stung by disappointment, you betake yourself to the sad expedients of duplicity. You try the sorry game of a trimmer in your progress to the acts of an incendiary. You give no honest support either to the government or the people. You, at the most critical period of their existence, take no part; you sign no non-consumption agreement; you are no Volunteer; you oppose no Perpetual Mutiny Bill; no altered Sugar Bill; you declare that you lament that the Declaration of Right should have been brought forward; and observing, with regard to both prince and people, the most impartial treachery and desertion, you justify the suspicion of your Sovereign, by betraying the government, as you had sold the people, until, at last, by this hollow conduct, and for some other steps, the result of mortified ambition, being dismissed, and another person put in your place, you fly to the ranks of the Volunteers and canvass for mutiny; you announce that the country was ruined by other men during that period in which she had been sold by you. Your logic is, that the repeal of a declaratory law is not the repeal of a law at all, and the effect of that logic is, an English act affecting to emancipate Ireland, by exercising over her the legislative authority of the British Parliament. Such has been your conduct; and at such conduct every order of your fellow-subjects have a right to exclaim! The merchant may say to you—the constitutionalist may say to you—the American may say to you—and I, *I* now say, and say to your beard, sir—*you are not an honest man!*"

INVECTIVE

OF MR. GRATTAN AGAINST MR. CORRY, DELIVERED DURING THE DEBATE ON THE UNION OF IRELAND TO ENGLAND, FEBRUARY 14, 1800.

Has the gentleman done? Has he completely done? He was unparliamentary from the beginning to the end of his speech. There was scarce a word that he uttered that was not a violation of the privileges of the House; but I did not call him to order. Why? Because the limited talents of some men render it impossible for them to be severe without being unparliamentary; but before I sit down I shall show him how to be severe and parliamentary at the same time. On any other occasion I should think myself justifiable in treating with silent contempt any thing which might fall from that honorable member; but there are times when the insignificance of the accuser is lost in the magnitude of the accusation. I know the difficulty the honorable gentleman labored under when he attacked me, conscious that, on a comparative view of our characters, public and private, there is nothing he could say which would injure me. The public would not believe the charge. I despise the falsehood. If such a charge were made by an honest man, I would answer it in the manner I shall do before I sit down. But I shall first reply to it when not made by an honest man.

The right honorable gentleman has called me "an unimpeached traitor." I ask, why not "traitor," unqualified by any epithet? I will tell him; it was because he dare not. It was the act of a coward, who raises his arm to strike, but has not courage to give the blow. I will not call him a villain, because it would be unparliamentary, and he is a privy counselor. I will not call him fool, because he happens to be Chancellor of the Exchequer; but I say he is one who has abused the privilege of Parliament and the freedom of debate, to the uttering language which, if spoken out of the House, I should answer only with a *blow*. I care not how high his situation, how low his character, how contemptible his speech; whether a privy counselor or a parasite, my answer would be a blow. He has charged me with being connected with the rebels. The charge is utterly, totally, and meanly false. Does the honorable gentleman rely on the report of the House of Lords for the foundation of his assertion? If he does, I can prove to the committee there was a physical impossibility of that report being true; but I scorn to answer any man for my conduct, whether he be a political coxcomb, or whether he brought himself into power by a false glare of courage or not. I scorn to answer any wizard of the Castle, throwing himself into fantastical airs;

but if an honorable and independent man were to make a charge against me, I would say, "You charge me with having an intercourse with rebels, and you found your charge upon what is said to have appeared before a committee of the Lords. Sir, the report of that committee is totally and egregiously irregular." I will read a letter from Mr. Nelson, who had been examined before that committee; it states that what the report represents him as having spoken is *not what he said.* [Mr. Grattan here read the letter from Mr. Nelson, denying that he had any connection with Mr. Grattan, as charged in the report; and concluded by saying, "*never was misrepresentation more vile than that put into my mouth by the report.*"]

From the situation that I held, and from the connections I had in the city of Dublin, it was necessary for me to hold intercourse with various descriptions of persons. The right honorable member might as well have been charged with a participation in the guilt of those traitors; for he had communicated with some of those very persons on the subject of parliamentary reform. The Irish government, too, were in communication with some of them.

The right honorable member has told me I deserted a profession where wealth and station were the reward of industry and talent. If I mistake not, that gentleman endeavored to obtain those rewards by the same means; but he soon deserted the occupation of a barrister for those of a parasite and pander. He fled from the labor of study to flatter at the table of the great. He found the Lords' parlor a better sphere for his exertions than the hall of the Four Courts; the house of a great man a more convenient way to power and to place; and that it was easier for a statesman of middling talents to sell his friends than a lawyer of no talents to sell his clients.

For myself, whatever corporate or other bodies have said or done to me, I, from the bottom of my heart, forgive them. I feel I have done too much for my country to be vexed at them. I would rather that they should not feel or acknowledge what I have done for them, and call me traitor, than have reason to say I sold them. I will always defend myself against the assassin; but with large bodies it is different. To the people I will bow; they may be my enemy—I never shall be theirs.

At the emancipation of Ireland, in 1782, I took a leading part in the foundation of that Constitution which is now endeavored to be destroyed. Of that Constitution I was the author; in that Constitution I glory; and for it the honorable gentleman should bestow praise, not invent calumny. Notwithstanding my weak state of body, I come to give my last testimony against this Union, so fatal to the liberties and interest of my country. I come to make common cause with these honorable and virtuous gentlemen around me; to try and save the Constitution; or if not save the Constitution, at least to save our characters, and remove from our graves the foul disgrace of standing apart while a deadly blow is aimed at the independence of our country.

The right honorable gentleman says I fled from the country, after exciting rebellion; and that I have returned to raise another. No such thing. The charge is false. The civil war had not commenced when I left the kingdom; and I could not have returned without taking a part. On the one side there was the camp of the rebel; on the other, the camp of the minister, a greater traitor than that rebel. The strong-hold of the Constitution was nowhere to be found. I agree that the rebel who rises against the government should have suffered; but I missed on the scaffold the right honorable gentleman. Two desperate parties were in arms against the Constitution. The right honorable gentleman belonged to one of those parties, and deserved death. I could not join the rebel—I could not join the government. I could not join torture—I could not join half-hanging—I could not join free quarter. I could take part with neither. I was, therefore, absent from a scene where I could not be active without self-reproach, nor indifferent with safety.

Many honorable gentlemen thought differently from me. I respect their opinions; but I keep my own; and I think now, as I thought then, *that the treason of the minister against the liberties of the people was infinitely worse than the rebellion of the people against the minister.*

I have returned, not, as the right honorable member has said, to raise another storm—I have returned to discharge an honorable debt of gratitude to my country, that conferred a great reward for past services, which, I am proud to say, was not greater than my desert. I have returned to protect that Constitution of which I was the parent and the founder, from the assassination of such men as the honorable gentleman and his unworthy associates. They are corrupt—they are seditious—and they, at this very moment, are in a conspiracy against their country. I have returned to refute a libel, as false as it is malicious, given to the public under the appellation of a report of the committee of the Lords. Here I stand, ready for impeachment or trial: I dare accusation. I defy the honorable gentleman; I defy the government; I defy the whole phalanx. Let them come forth. I tell the ministers I will neither give them quarter nor take it. I am here to lay the shattered remains of my constitution on the floor of this House, in defense of the liberties of my country.

* * * * * *

My guilt or innocence have little to do with the question here. I rose with the rising fortunes of my country—I am willing to die with her expiring liberties. To the voice of the people I will bow, but never shall I submit to the calumnies of an individual hired to betray them and slander me. The indisposition of my body has left me, perhaps, no means but that of lying down with fallen Ireland, and recording upon her tomb my dying testimony against the flagitious corruption that has murdered her independence.

The right honorable gentleman has said that this was not my place—that, instead of having a voice in the councils of my country, I should now stand a culprit at her bar—at the bar of a court of criminal judicature, to answer for my treasons. The Irish people have not so read my history; but let that pass; if I am what he said I am, the people are not therefore to forfeit their Constitution. In point of argument, therefore, the attack is bad—in point of taste or feeling, if he had either, it is worse—in point of fact, it is false, utterly and absolutely false—as rancorous a falsehood as the most malignant motives could suggest to the prompt sympathy of a shameless and a venal defense. The right honorable gentleman has suggested examples which I should have shunned, and examples which I should have followed. I shall never follow his, and I have ever avoided it. I shall never be ambitious to purchase public scorn by private infamy—the lighter characters of the model have as little chance of weaning me from the habits of a life spent, if not exhausted, in the cause of my native land. Am I to renounce those habits now forever, and at the beck of whom? I should rather say of what—half a minister—half a monkey—a 'prentice politician, and a master coxcomb. He has told you that what he said of me here, he would say any where. I believe he would say thus of me in any place where he thought himself safe in saying it. Nothing can limit his calumnies but his fears—in Parliament he has calumniated me to-night, in the King's courts he would calumniate me to-morrow; but had he said or dared to insinuate one half as much elsewhere, the indignant spirit of an honest man would have answered the vile and venal slanderer with—a blow.

CHARACTER OF LORD CHATHAM.

The Secretary stood alone. Modern degeneracy had not reached him. Original and unaccommodating, the features of his character had the hardihood of antiquity. His august mind overawed Majesty; and one of his Sovereigns [George III.] thought royalty so impaired in his presence, that he conspired to remove him, in order to be relieved from his superiority.[1] No state chicanery, no narrow system of vicious politics, no idle contest for ministerial victories, sunk him to the vulgar level of the great; but, overbearing, persuasive, and impracticable, his object was England—his ambition was fame. Without dividing, he destroyed party; without corrupting, he made a venal age unanimous. France sunk beneath him; with one hand he smote the house of Bourbon, and wielded in the other the democracy of England. The sight of his mind was infinite, and his schemes were to affect, not England, not the present age only, but Europe and posterity. Wonderful were the means by which these schemes were accomplished, always seasonable, always adequate, the suggestions of an understanding animated by ardor, and enlightened by prophecy.

The ordinary feelings which make life amiable and indolent—those sensations which soften and allure, and vulgarize, were unknown to him. No domestic difficulties, no domestic weakness, reached him; but, aloof from the sordid occurrences of life, and unsullied by its intercourse, he came occasionally into our system to counsel and decide.

A character so exalted, so strenuous, so various, so authoritative, astonished a corrupt age, and the Treasury trembled at the name of Pitt through all her classes of venality. Corruption imagined, indeed, that she found defects in this statesman, and talked much of the inconsistency of his glory, and much of the ruin of his victories—but the history of his country and the calamities of the enemy answered and refuted her.

Nor were his political abilities his only talents; his eloquence was an era in the Senate. Peculiar and spontaneous, familiarly expressing gigantic sentiments and instinctive wisdom—not like the torrent of Demosthenes, or the splendid conflagration of Tully, it resembled, sometimes the thunder, and sometimes the music of the spheres. Like Murray [Lord Mansfield], he did not conduct the understanding through the painful subtilty of argumentation; nor was he, like Townsend,[2] forever on the rack of exertion, but rather lightened upon the subject, and reached the point by the flashings of his mind, which, like those of his eye, were felt, but could not be followed.

Upon the whole, there was in this man something that could create, subvert, or reform; an understanding, a spirit, and an eloquence to summon mankind to society, or to break the bonds of slavery asunder, and rule the wildness of free minds with unbounded authority; something that could establish or overwhelm empire, and strike a blow in the world that should resound through its history.

---

[1] See page 63.

[2] Mr. Charles Townsend. See his character in Burke's speech on American Taxation.

MR. SHERIDAN.

Richard Brinsley Sheridan was born at Dublin in September, 1751. His father, Thomas Sheridan, author of the first attempt at a Pronouncing Dictionary of our language, was a distinguished teacher of elocution, and during most of his life was connected with the stage. This fact very naturally turned the attention of young Sheridan, even from his boyhood, to theatrical composition; and, being driven to strenuous exertion in consequence of an early marriage, he became a dramatic writer at the age of twenty-four. His first production was The Rivals, which, by the liveliness of its plot and the exquisite humor of its dialogue, placed him at once in the first rank of comic writers. His next work was the opera of The Duenna, which was performed seventy-five times during the season in which it was first produced, and yielded him a very large profit. In the year 1776, in conjunction with two friends, he purchased Garrick's half of the Drury Lane Theater; and becoming proprietor of the other half at the end of two years, he gave his father the appointment of manager. He now produced his School for Scandal, which has been regarded by many as the best comedy in our language. This was followed by The Critic, which was equally admirable as a farce; and here ended, in 1779, his "legitimate offerings on the shrine of the Dramatic Muse." He still, however, retained his proprietorship in Drury Lane, which would have furnished an ample support for any one but a person of his expensive and reckless habits.

Mr. Sheridan had cherished from early life a very lively interest in politics; and now that his thirst for dramatic fame was satiated, his ambition rose higher, and led him to seek for new distinction in the fields of oratory. He had already made the acquaintance of Lord John Townsend, Mr. Windham, and other distinguished members of the Whig party, and was desirous of forming a political connection with Mr. Fox. To promote this object, Townsend made a dinner-party early in 1780, at which he brought them together. Speaking of the subject afterward, he said, "I told Fox that all the notions he might have conceived of Sheridan's talents and genius from the 'Rivals,' &c., would fall infinitely short of the admiration of his astonishing powers which I was sure he would entertain at the first interview. Fox told me, after breaking up from dinner, that he had always thought Hare, after my uncle, Charles Townsend, the wittiest man he had ever met with, but that Sheridan surpassed them both, infinitely." Sheridan, on his side, formed the strongest attachment for Mr. Fox as a man and a political leader, and was soon after placed on terms of equal intimacy with Mr. Burke. He was admitted to Brooks's Club-house, the head-quarters of the Whigs,[1] and soon after became a member for Stafford, at an expense of £2000.

Mr. Sheridan's maiden speech was delivered on the 20th of November, 1780. The House listened to him with marked attention, but his appearance did not entirely satisfy the expectations of his friends. Woodfall, the reporter, used to relate that

[1] The following lines of Tickell give the character of Brooks:

> And know, I've bought the best Champagne from Brooks;
> From liberal Brooks, whose speculative skill
> Is hasty credit and a distant bill;
> Who, nursed in clubs, disdains a vulgar trade,
> Exults to trust, and blushes to be paid.

Nothing could be more convenient for a man of Sheridan's habits than so indulgent a creditor.

Sheridan came up to him in the gallery, when the speech was ended, and asked him, with much anxiety, what he thought of his first attempt. "I am sorry to say," replied Woodfall, "that I don't think this is your line—you had better have stuck to your former pursuits." Sheridan rested his head on his hand for some minutes, and then exclaimed, with vehemence, "It is *in* me, and it shall *come out of me!*" He now devoted himself with the utmost assiduity, quickened by a sense of shame, to the cultivation of his powers as a speaker; and having great ingenuity, ready wit, perfect self-possession, and a boldness amounting almost to effrontery, he made himself at last a most dexterous and effective debater.

During the short administration of the Marquess of Rockingham, in 1782, Mr. Sheridan came into office as Under Secretary of State; but on the decease of Rockingham, he resigned in common with Fox, Burke, and others, when Lord Shelburne was made prime minister in preference to Mr. Fox. Mr. William Pitt now came into the ministry, at the age of twenty-three, as Chancellor of the Exchequer, and undertook, soon after, to put down Mr. Sheridan by a contemptuous allusion to his theatrical pursuits. "No man," said he "admires more than I do the abilities of that right honorable gentleman—the elegant sallies of his thought, the gay effusions of his fancy, his dramatic turns, and his epigrammatic point. If they were reserved for the *proper* stage, they would no doubt receive the plaudits of the audience; and it would be the fortune of the right honorable gentleman, "sui plausu gaudere theatri."[2] Mr. Sheridan replied to this insolent language, with admirable adroitness, in the following words: "On the particular sort of personality which the right honorable gentleman has thought proper to make use of, I need not comment. The propriety, the taste, and the *gentlemanly* point of it must be obvious to this House. But let me assure the right honorable gentleman that I do now, and will, at any time he chooses to repeat this sort of allusion, meet it with the most perfect good humor. Nay, I will say more. Flattered and encouraged by the right honorable gentleman's panegyric on my talents, if I ever engage again in the composition he alludes to, I may be tempted to an act of presumption, and attempt an improvement on one of Ben Jonson's best characters, that of the *Angry Boy*, in the Alchymist." The effect was irresistible. The House was convulsed with laughter; and Mr. Pitt came very near having the title of the Angry Boy fastened on him for the remainder of his life.

When the administration of Lord Shelburne gave way to the Coalition Ministry of Mr. Fox and Lord North, in 1783, Sheridan was again brought into office as Secretary of the Treasury. The defeat of Mr. Fox's East India Bill threw him out of power at the close of the same year; and from that time, for more than twenty-two years, he was a strenuous and active opponent of Mr. Pitt.

In the year 1787, Mr. Burke, who had devoted ten years to the investigation of English atrocities in India, called forth the entire strength of the Whig party for the impeachment of Warren Hastings. To Mr. Sheridan he assigned the management of the charge relating to the Begums or princesses of Oude. It was a subject peculiarly suited to his genius; and, aided by an intimate knowledge of the facts, which was supplied him by the researches of Burke, he brought forward the charge in the House of Commons, on the 7th of February, 1787. His speech on this occasion was so imperfectly reported that it may be said to be wholly lost. It was, however, according to the representation of all who heard it, an astonishing exhibition of eloquence. The whole assembly, at the conclusion, broke forth into expressions of tumultuous applause. Men of all parties vied with each other in their encomiums; and Mr. Pitt concluded his remarks by saying that "an abler speech was perhaps *never delivered.*" A motion was made to adjourn, that the House might have time to recover their calmness and "collect their reason," after the excitement they had

[2] To exult in the applause of his *own* theater.

undergone; and Mr. Stanhope, in seconding the motion, declared that he had come to the House prepossessed in favor of Mr. Hastings, but that nothing less than a miracle could now prevent him from voting for his impeachment. Twenty years after, Mr. Fox and Mr. Windham, two of the severest judges in England, spoke of this speech with undiminished admiration. The former declared it to be the best speech ever made in the House of Commons. The latter said that "the speech deserved all its fame, and was, in spite of some faults of taste, such as were seldom wanting in the literary or in the parliamentary performances of Sheridan, the greatest that had been delivered within the memory of man."[3]

When the Commons voted to impeach Mr. Hastings, Sheridan was chosen one of the managers, and had assigned to him the charge relating to the Begums of Oude. He was thus called upon to reproduce, as far as possible, his splendid oration of the preceding year, in presence of an assembly still more dignified and august, and under circumstances calculated to inflame all his ambition as an orator and a man. The expectation of the public was wrought up to the highest pitch. During the four days on which he spoke, the hall was crowded to suffocation; and such was the eagerness to obtain seats, that fifty guineas were in some instances paid for a single ticket. These circumstances, undoubtedly, operated to the injury of Mr. Sheridan. They aggravated those "faults of taste" which were spoken of by Mr. Windham. They led him into many extravagances of language and sentiment; and though all who heard it agreed in pronouncing it a speech of astonishing power, it must have been far inferior in true eloquence to his great original effort in the House of Commons. His success in these two speeches was celebrated by Byron in the following lines, which are, however, much more applicable to Burke than to Sheridan:

> When the loud cry of trampled Hindostan
> Arose to Heaven, in her appeal to man,
> His was the thunder—his the avenging rod—
> The wrath—the delegated voice of God,
> Which shook the nations through his lips, and blazed,
> Till vanquished senates trembled as they praised.

Contrary to what might have been expected, Mr. Sheridan never attempted, in after life, that lofty strain of eloquence which gained him such rapturous applause on this occasion. "Good sense and wit were the great weapons of his oratory—shrewdness in detecting the weak points of an adversary, and infinite powers of raillery in exposing them." This is exactly the kind of speaking which has always been

[3] It was natural, in respect to such a speech, that some erroneous or exaggerated statements should have been given to the public. There is an anecdote related by Bissett, in his Reign of George III., which must be regarded in this light. Bissett says, "The late Mr. Logan, well known for his literary efforts, and author of a masterly defense of Mr. Hastings, went that day to the House, prepossessed for the accused and against the accuser. At the expiration of the first hour, he said to a friend, 'All this is declamatory assertion without proof;' when the second was finished, 'This is a wonderful oration;' at the close of the third, 'Mr. Hastings has acted unjustifiably;' the fourth, 'Mr. Hastings is a most atrocious criminal;' and at last, 'Of all monsters of iniquity, the most enormous is Warren Hastings!'"

Now the natural and almost necessary impression made by this story is, that Mr. Logan, *previous* to hearing this speech, had written his "masterly defense of Mr. Hastings;" and that, being thus "prepossessed" and committed in favor of the accused, he experienced the remarkable change of views and feelings here described. But the fact is, his defense of Hastings was written *after* the speech in question was delivered; and Mr. Logan therein charged the Commons with having acted, in their impeachment of Hastings, "from motives of personal animosity—not from regard to public justice." It is incredible that a man of Mr. Logan's character—a distinguished clergyman of the Church of Scotland—should have written such a pamphlet, or brought such a charge, only a few months after he had expressed the views of Mr. Hastings ascribed to him above. This anecdote must, therefore, have related to some other person who was confounded with Mr. Logan, and may be numbered with the many uncertainties which are current under the name of Literary History.

most popular in the House of Commons. It made Mr. Sheridan much more formidable to Mr. Pitt, during his long and difficult administration, than many in the Opposition ranks of far greater information and reasoning abilities. Notwithstanding his habitual indolence, and the round of conviviality in which he was constantly engaged, Sheridan contrived to pick up enough knowledge of the leading topics in debate to make him a severe critic on the measures of Mr. Pitt. If authorities or research were necessary, he would frankly say to his friends who desired his aid, "You know I am an ignoramus—here I am—instruct me, and I'll do my best." And such was the quickness and penetration of his intellect, that he was able, with surprising facility, to make himself master of the information thus collected for his use, and to pour it out with a freshness and vivacity which were so much the greater because his mind was left free and unencumbered by the effort to obtain it. A curious instance is mentioned of his boldness on such occasions, when his materials happened to fail him. In 1794, when he came to reply to the argument of Mr. Hastings' counsel on the Begum charge, his friend, Mr. Michael Angelo Taylor, undertook to read for him any papers which it might be necessary to bring forward in the course of his speech. One morning, when a certain paper was called for, Mr. Taylor asked him for the bag containing his documents. Sheridan replied, in a whisper, that he *had neither bag nor papers*—that they must contrive, by dexterity and boldness, to get on without them. The Lord Chancellor, in a few moments, called again for the minutes of evidence. Taylor pretended to send for the bag, and Sheridan proceeded with the utmost confidence, as if nothing had happened. Within a few minutes the "*papers*" were again demanded, when Mr. Fox ran up to Taylor, and inquired anxiously for the bag. "The man *has* no bag," says Taylor, in a whisper, to the utter discomfiture of Mr. Fox. Sheridan, in the mean time, went on—taking the facts for granted—in his boldest strain. When stopped by the court, and reproved for his negligence in not bringing forward the evidence, he assumed an indignant tone, and told the Chancellor that, "as a manager of the impeachment in behalf of the Commons, he should conduct the case as he thought fit, that it was his most ardent desire to be perfectly correct in what he stated; and that, should he fall into error, the *printed minutes* of the evidence would correct him!"

With all this apparent negligence, however, the papers of Mr. Sheridan, after his death, disclosed one remarkable fact, that his *wit* was most of it studied out beforehand. His commonplace book was found to be full of humorous thoughts and sportive turns, put down usually in a crude state just as they occurred to his mind, and afterward wrought into form for future use. To this collection we may trace a large part of those playful allusions, keen retorts, sly insinuations, and brilliant sallies—the jest, the frolic, and the fun—which flash out upon us in his speeches in a manner so easy, natural, and yet unexpected, that no one could suspect them of being any thing but the spontaneous suggestions of the moment. His biographer has truly said that, in this respect, "It was the fate of Mr. Sheridan throughout life—and in a great degree, perhaps his policy—to gain credit for excessive indolence and carelessness, while few persons, with so much natural brilliancy of talents, ever employed more art and circumspection in their display."

Mr. Sheridan usually took part in every important debate in Parliament, and gained much applause, in 1803, by a speech of uncommon eloquence, in which he endeavored to unite all parties for the defense of the country, when threatened with invasion by France. In the course of this speech, he turned the ridicule of the House upon Mr. Addington, the prime minister, in a way which was not soon forgotten. Mr. Addington was one of those "respectable" half-way men with whom it is difficult to find fault, and yet whom nobody confides in or loves. He was the son of an eminent physician, and there was something in his air and manner which savored of the profession, and had given him, to a limited extent, the appellation of "The Doctor." Mr. Sheridan, in the course of his speech, adverting to the personal dislike of many to Mr. Addington, quoted the lines of Martial:

> Non amo te, Sabine, nec possum dicere quare;
> Hoc tantum possum dicere, non amo te;

and added the English parody:

> I do not like you, *Doctor* Fell;
> The reason why I can not tell;
> But this, I'm sure, I know full well,
> I do not like you, *Doctor* Fell.

His waggish emphasis on the word doctor, and his subsequent repetition of it in the course of his speech, called forth peals of laughter; and thenceforth the minister was generally known by the name of the *Doctor*.[4] The Opposition papers took up the title, and twisted and tortured it into every form of attack, till Mr. Addington was borne down and driven from office by mere ridicule—a weapon which is often more fatal than argument to men of moderate abilities in high political stations.

Mr. Sheridan had always lived beyond his means, and was utterly ruined in 1809, by the burning of the Drury Lane Theater, which comprised all his property. He was also betrayed by his convivial habits into gross intemperance. Wine being no longer of sufficient strength to quicken his faculties for conversation or debate, stronger liquors were substituted. A person sitting one evening in a coffee-house, near St. Stephen's Chapel, saw, to his surprise, a gentleman with papers before him, after taking tea, pour the contents of a decanter of brandy into a tumbler, and drink it off without dilution. He then gathered up his papers and went out. Shortly after, the spectator, on entering the gallery of the House of Commons, heard the brandy-drinker, to his astonishment, deliver a long and brilliant speech. It was Mr. Sheridan! The natural consequences of such a life were not slow in overtaking him: he soon became bankrupt in character and health, as well as in fortune. The relief which he occasionally obtained from his friends served only to protract his misery. He was harassed with writs and executions, at the moment when he was sinking under disease; and a sheriff's officer, but for the intervention of his physician, would have carried him in his blanket to prison. A powerful writer in the Morning Post now called the attention of the public to his wretched condition. "Oh! delay not to draw aside the curtain within which that proud spirit hides its sufferings. Prefer ministering in the chambers of sickness to mustering at 'the splendid sorrows which adorn the hearse'—I say, *life* and *succor* against Westminster Abbey and a funeral!" Men of all ranks were roused. His chamber was crowded with sympathizing friends, but it was too late. He died on the 7th of July, 1816, at the age of sixty-four, a melancholy example of brilliant talents sacrificed to a love of display and convivial indulgence. He was buried with great pomp in the only spot of the Poet's Corner which remained unoccupied. His pall was borne by royal and noble dukes, by earls and marquesses, and his funeral procession was composed of the most distinguished nobility and gentry of the kingdom.[5]

[4] The Scottish members having deserted Mr. Addington in some debate about this time, Mr. Sheridan convulsed the House by suddenly exclaiming, in the words of the messenger to Macbeth, *Doctor*, "the THANES fly from thee!"

[5] Mr. Moore, in the following lines, gave vent to his feelings at the conduct of those who deserted Sheridan in his poverty, but crowded around his death-bed and flocked to his funeral with all the tokens of their early respect and affection:

> How proud they can press to the funeral array
> Of him whom they shunn'd in his sickness and sorrow—
> How bailiffs may seize his last blanket to-day,
> Whose pall shall be held up by nobles to-morrow!

Wraxall, in his Posthumous Memoirs, vol. i., 36–8, gives the following description of Mr. Sheridan's person and manner of speaking in his best days, before intemperance had begun its ravages on his body or mind. "His countenance and features had in them something peculiarly pleasing, indicative at once of intellect, humor, and gayety. All these characteristics played about his lips when speaking, and operated with inconceivable attraction; for they anticipated, as it were, to the eye the effect produced by his oratory on the ear; thus opening for him a sure way to the heart or the understanding. Even the tones of his voice, which were singularly mellifluous, aided the general effect of his eloquence; nor was it accompanied by Burke's unpleasant Irish accent. Pitt's enunciation was unquestionably more imposing, dignified, and sonorous; Fox displayed more argument, as well as vehemence; Burke possessed more fancy and enthusiasm; but Sheridan won his way by a sort of fascination."

"He possessed a ductility and versatility of talents which no public man in our time has equaled; and these intellectual endowments were sustained by a suavity of temper that seemed to set at defiance all attempts to ruffle or discompose it. Playing with his irritable or angry antagonist, Sheridan exposed him by sallies of wit, or attacked him with classic elegance of satire; performing this arduous task in the face of a crowded assembly, without losing for an instant either his presence of mind, his facility of expression, or his good humor. He wounded deepest, indeed, when he smiled, and convulsed his hearers with laughter while the object of his ridicule or animadversion was twisting under the lash. Pitt and Dundas, who presented the fairest marks for his attack, found, by experience, that though they might repel, they could not confound, and still less could they silence or vanquish him. In every attempt that they made, by introducing personalities, or illiberal reflections on his private life and literary or dramatic occupations, to disconcert him, he turned their weapons on themselves. Nor did he, while thus chastising his adversary, alter a muscle of his own countenance; which, as well as his gestures, seemed to participate, and display the unalterable serenity of his intellectual formation. Rarely did he elevate his voice, and never except in subservience to the dictates of his judgment, with the view to produce a corresponding effect on his audience. Yet he was always heard, generally listened to with eagerness, and could obtain a hearing at almost any hour. Burke, who wanted Sheridan's nice tact and his amenity of manner, was continually coughed down, and on those occasions he lost his temper. Even Fox often tired the House by the repetitions which he introduced into his speeches. Sheridan never abused their patience. Whenever he rose, they anticipated a rich repast of wit without acrimony, seasoned by allusions and citations the most delicate, yet obvious in their application."

Still, it should be remembered that such desertion is the inevitable fate of degrading vice, and especially of the beastly intemperance to which Sheridan had so long been abandoned. Large contributions had previously been made for his relief, but his improvidence knew no bounds; and he had for some time reduced himself to such a state that few of his old acquaintances could visit him without pain, or (it may be added) without the deepest mortification to himself, though they might wish, after his death, to do honor to his memory as a man of genius.

SPEECH

OF MR. SHERIDAN ON SUMMING UP THE EVIDENCE ON THE SECOND, OR BEGUM CHARGE AGAINST WARREN HASTINGS, DELIVERED BEFORE THE HOUSE OF LORDS, SITTING AS A HIGH COURT OF PARLIAMENT, JUNE, 1788.

INTRODUCTION.

THE Begums, or *princesses* referred to in this speech, were the mother and widow of the celebrated Sujah Dowlah, Nabob of Oude, a kingdom on the upper waters of the Ganges. At his death, he bequeathed for their support large yearly revenues from the government lands, called *jaghires*,[1] in addition to the treasures he had accumulated during his reign. He left his throne to Asoph Dowlah, a son by the younger Begum, who proved to be a man of weak intellect and debauched habits, and who soon became a mere vassal of the East India Company, under the government of Mr. Hastings. To secure his subjection, and guard against invasion from the neighboring states, Mr. Hastings compelled him to take large numbers of British troops into his pay; thus relieving the Company of enormous expense, and subjecting the natives to the severest exactions from men ostensibly placed among them for their protection. Single officers of the British army were known to have accumulated fortunes of several hundred thousand pounds during a few years service in Oude. Nearly the whole kingdom was thus reduced from a state of the highest prosperity, to beggary and ruin. The young Nabob was unable to make his regular payments of tribute, until, at the close of 1780, a debt of £1,400,000 stood against him on the Company's books.

Mr. Hastings was, at this time, in the most pressing want of money. He had powerful enemies at Calcutta; his continuance in office depended on his being able to relieve the Company at once from its financial difficulties; and to do this effectually was the object of his memorable journey into upper India, in July, 1780. He looked to two sources of supply, Benares and Oude; and from one or both of these, he was determined to extort the means of relief from all his embarrassments. In respect to Benares, Mr. Mill states, in his British India, that Cheyte Sing, the Rajah of that kingdom, had paid his tribute "with an exactness rarely exemplified in the history of the tributary princes of Hindostan." But the same system had been adopted with him, as with the Nabob of Oude; and when he at last declared his inability to pay, Mr. Hastings threw him into prison during the journey mentioned above, deprived him of his throne, and stripped him of all his treasures. They proved, however, to be only £200,000, a sum far short of what Mr. Hastings expected, for he had always supposed the Rajah to be possessed of immense hoards of wealth.

Disappointed in his first object, the Governor General now turned his attention to Oude. He knew the young Nabob would be ready, on almost any terms, to purchase deliverance from the troops which were quartered on his kingdom. He accordingly appointed a meeting with him at Chunar, a fortress of Benares, September 19th, 1781. Here the Nabob secretly offered him a bribe of £100,000. Mr. Hastings took it; whether with the intention to keep it as his own or pay it over to the Company, does not certainly appear. The transaction, however, soon became public, and the money was finally paid over, but not without a letter from Mr. Hastings to the Board of Directors, intimating in the most significant terms his anxiety to retain the money. On this point, Mr. Sheridan touches with great force in the progress of his speech. But Asoph Dowlah was not to escape so easily. A much larger sum than £100,000 was needed, and he was at length driven to an arrangement by which it was agreed, in the words of Mr. Mill, "that his Highness should be relieved from the expense, which he was unable to bear, of the English troops and gentlemen; and he, on his part, engaged to strip the Begums of both their treasures and their *jaghires*, delivering to the Governor General the proceeds."—*Brit. India*, iv., 375. In other words, he was to rob his mother and his grandmother, not only of all their property, but of the yearly income left by his father for their support.

But it was easier for the Nabob to promise than to perform. Such were the struggles of nature and religion in his breast, that for three months he hesitated and delayed, while Mr. Hastings, who was in the utmost need of money, was urging him to the performance. Finally, Mr. Middleton, the Resident at Oude, was ordered to cut the matter short—"to supersede the authority of the Nabob, and perform the necessary measures by the operation of English troops," if there was any further delay. Under this threat, Asoph resumed the *jaghires;* but declared, in so doing, that it was "an act of compulsion." The treasures were next to be seized. They were stored in the Zenana or Harem at Fyzabad, where the princesses resided; a sacred inclosure, guarded with superstitious veneration by the religion of the Hindoos, against access of all except its own inmates. A body of English troops, under the guidance of Mr. Middleton, marched to Fyzabad, on the 8th of January, 1782, and demanded the treasures. They were

---

[1] The lands thus farmed were also called *jaghires*, and those who farmed them *jaghiredars*.

refused, and the town and castle were immediately taken by storm. The Zenana was now in the power of the English; but Mr. Middleton shrunk from an act of profanation which would probably have created a general revolt throughout Oude, and endeavored to break the spirit of the Begums by other means. He threw into prison their two ministers of state, aged men of the highest distinction; abridged them of their food, till they were on the borders of starvation; tortured them with the lash; deprived the inmates of the Zenana of their ordinary supply of provisions, till they were on the point of perishing of want; and thus succeeded in extorting property to the amount of £600,000, leaving these wretched women nothing for their support or comfort, not even their common household utensils.

Such was the charge which Mr. Sheridan was now to lay before the House of Lords, on the fourteenth day of the trial, Mr. Fox having previously submitted that which related to the treatment of Cheyte Sing. The facts in this case were not denied by Mr. Hastings as to any of the important particulars. His defense was this: (1.) That the property did not belong to the Begums. (2.) That their plunder was demanded by state necessity. (3.) That they had rebelled against him by attempting to assist Cheyte Sing, when deposed; by inducing the *jaghiredars*, or farmers of the *jaghires*, to resist their resumption; and by promoting insurrections in Oude. To get affidavits on these points, Mr. Hastings had sent his friend, Sir Elijah Impey, Chief Justice of Bengal, some hundreds of miles into Oude. (4.) That he was not responsible for the cruelties practiced on the Begums and their ministers, because he had given no direct order on that subject. Such was Mr. Hastings' defense before the House of Commons; and hence Mr. Sheridan shaped his speech before the House of Lords to meet these points.

After disclaiming, in his exordium, those vindictive feelings so loudly charged upon the managers by Mr. Hastings' friends:

I. He proves by the testimony of Lord Cornwallis the wretched condition to which Oude was reduced; charges all its calamities on the misgovernment and violence of Mr. Hastings; and shows that it was nevertheless extremely difficult, at such a distance, to produce the full evidence which might be desired of what every one knew to be the fact.

II. He then dwells at large on the evidence. (1.) That afforded by Mr. Hastings himself, in the *contradictory* nature of his various defenses before the House of Commons. (2.) That which went to show the character and station of the Begums, and their perfect right to the property they held. The latter is proved by the explicit decision of the Council at Calcutta, sanctioned by Mr. Hastings himself, after deliberate inquiry; and also by the guarantees of the Company, founded on that decision.

III. He briefly touches on the plea of State Necessity, and rejects it with indignation, as wholly inapplicable to a case like this.

IV. He takes up the treaty at Chunar for plundering the Begums, and the pretexts by which it had been justified. Here he comments with great severity on the conduct of Impey in taking the affidavits, and his appearance before the Lords as a witness—goes at great length in an examination of the affidavits—shows by a comparison of dates and by other circumstances, that the whole of this defense was an *after-thought*, resorted to by Mr. Hastings, subsequent to the treaty, to excuse his conduct—and that there were causes enough for the commotions in Oude, arising out of the oppression of the English, without any intervention of the Begums.

V. He describes the scenes connected with the resumption of the *jaghires*, and the cruelties inflicted upon the Begums and their ministers to extort the treasures.

VI. He charges all these crimes and cruelties upon Mr. Hastings, as committed by his authorized agents, and rendered necessary by his express instructions.

This speech, considered as a *comment on evidence*, is one of great ability, notwithstanding the imperfect manner in which it is reported. It was a task for which Mr. Sheridan's mind was peculiarly fitted. His keen sagacity, ready wit, and thorough knowledge of the human heart, had here the widest scope for their exercise. He shows uncommon tact in sifting testimony, detecting motives, and exposing the subterfuges, contradictions, and falsehoods of Mr. Hastings and his friends. Intermingled with the examination of the evidence, there is a great deal of keen satire and bitter sarcasm, which must have told powerfully on the audience, especially when set off by that easy, pointed, and humorous style of delivery, in which Mr. Sheridan so greatly excelled. When he rises into a higher strain, as in examining Mr. Hastings' plea of "state necessity," or describing the desperation of the natives, throwing themselves on the swords of the soldiery, under the cruel exactions of Major Hanney, he is truly and powerfully eloquent. His attempts to be pathetic or sentimental, as in his famous description of Filial Piety, are an utter failure. It is this passage, in connection with his constant tendency to strain after effect, which has led some, at the present day, to underrate the talents of Mr. Sheridan, and treat him as a mere ranter. His biographer, Mr. Moore, suggests that many of the blemishes in his printed speeches may be ascribed to the bad taste of his reporter, who makes even Mr. Fox talk, at times, in very lofty and extravagant language. This may to a certain extent be true, but we can not doubt that the "faults of taste" spoken of by Mr. Windham lay in this direction. Sheridan looked upon the audience in Westminster Hall with the eye of an actor. He saw the admirable opportunity which it afforded him for scenic effect; and he obviously resorted to *clap-trap* in many passages, which he contrived to make most of his audience feel were his best ones, when they were really his worst. Still, these form only a small part of the speech, and there are many passages to which we can not deny the praise of high and genuine eloquence.

SPEECH, &c.

My Lords,—I shall not waste your Lordships' time nor my own, by any preliminary observations on the importance of the subject before you, or on the propriety of our bringing it in this solemn manner to a final decision. My honorable friend [Mr. Burke], the principal mover of the impeachment, has already executed the task in a way the most masterly and impressive. He, whose indignant and enterprising genius, roused by the calls of public justice, has, with unprecedented labor, perseverance, and eloquence, excited one branch of the Legislature to the vindication of our national character, and through whose means the House of Commons now makes this embodied stand in favor of man against man's iniquity, need hardly be followed on the *general* grounds of the prosecution.

The prosecution not dictated by vindictive feelings.

Confiding in the dignity, the liberality, and intelligence of the tribunal before which I now have the honor to appear in my delegated capacity of a manager, I do not, indeed, conceive it necessary to engage your Lordships' attention for a single moment with any introductory animadversions. But there is one point which here presents itself that it becomes me not to overlook. Insinuations have been thrown out that my honorable colleagues and myself are actuated by motives of malignity against the unfortunate prisoner at the bar. An imputation of so serious a nature can not be permitted to pass altogether without comment; though it comes in so loose a shape, in such whispers and oblique hints as to prove to a certainty that it was made in the consciousness, and, therefore, with the circumspection of falsehood.

I can, my Lords, most confidently aver, that a prosecution more disinterested in all its motives and ends; more free from personal malice or personal interest; more perfectly public, and more purely animated by the simple and unmixed spirit of justice, never was brought in any country, at any time, by any body of men, against any individual. What possible resentment can we entertain against the unfortunate prisoner? What possible interest can we have in his conviction? What possible object of a personal nature can we accomplish by his ruin? For myself, my Lords, I make this solemn asseveration, that I discharge my breast of all malice, hatred, and ill will against the prisoner, if at any time indignation at his crimes has planted in it these passions; and I believe, my Lords, that I may with equal truth answer for every one of my colleagues.

We are, my Lords, anxious, in stating the crimes with which he is charged, to keep out of recollection the person of the unfortunate prisoner. In prosecuting him to conviction, we are impelled only by a sincere abhorrence of his guilt, and a sanguine hope of remedying future delinquency. We can have no private incentive to the part we have taken. We are actuated singly by the zeal we feel for the public welfare, and by an honest solicitude for the honor of our country, and the happiness of those who are under its dominion and protection.

With such views, we really, my Lords, lose sight of Mr. Hastings, who, however great in some other respects, is too insignificant to be blended with these important circumstances. The unfortunate prisoner is, at best, to my mind, no mighty object. Amid the series of mischiefs and enormities to *my sense* seeming to surround him, what is he but a petty nucleus, involved in its *laminæ*, scarcely seen or heard of?

This prosecution, my Lords, was not, as is alleged, "begot in prejudice, and nursed in error." It originated in the clearest conviction of the wrongs which the natives of Hindostan have endured by the maladministration of those in whose hands this country had placed extensive powers; which ought to have been exercised for the benefit of the governed, but which was used by the prisoner for the shameful purpose of oppression. I repeat with emphasis, my Lords, that nothing personal or malicious has induced us to institute this prosecution. It is absurd to suppose it. We come to your Lordships' bar as the representatives of the Commons of England; and, as acting in this public capacity, it might as truly be said that the Commons, in whose name the impeachment is brought before your Lordships, were actuated by enmity to the prisoner, as that we, their deputed organs, have any private spleen to gratify in discharging the duty imposed upon us by our principals.

Does not endanger Mr. Hastings' life.

Your Lordships will also recollect and discriminate between impeachment for *capital* offenses and impeachment for high crimes and misdemeanors. In an impeachment of the former kind, when the life of an individual is to be forfeited on conviction, if malignity be indulged in giving a strong tincture and coloring to facts, the tenderness of man's nature will revolt at it; for, however strongly indignant we may be at the perpetration of offenses of a gross quality, there is a feeling that will protect an accused person from the influence of malignity in such a situation; but where no traces of this malice are discoverable, where no thirst for blood is seen, where, seeking for exemplary more than sanguinary justice, an impeachment is brought for high crimes and misdemeanors, malice will not be imputed to the prosecutors if, in illustration of the crimes alleged, they should adduce every possible circumstance in support of their allegations. Why will it not? Because their ends have nothing abhorrent to human tenderness. Because, in such a case as the present, for instance, all that is aimed at in convicting the prisoner is a temporary seclusion from the society of his countrymen, whose name he has tarnished by his crimes, and a deduction from the enormous spoils which he has accumulated by his greedy rapacity.

I. The only matter which I shall, in this stage

of my inquiry, lay before your Lordships, in order to give you an impression of the influence of the crimes on the prisoner over the country in which they were committed, is to refer to some passages in a letter of the Earl of Cornwallis.[1]

Wretched condition of Oude, and Mr. Hastings' responsibility therefor.

You see, my Lords, that the British government, which ought to have been a blessing to the powers in India connected with it, has proved a scourge to the natives, and the cause of desolation to their most flourishing provinces.

Behold, my Lords, this frightful picture of the consequences of a government of violence and oppression! Surely the condition of wretchedness to which this once happy and independent prince is reduced by our cruelty, and the ruin which in some way has been brought upon his country, call loudly upon your Lordships to interpose, and to rescue the national honor and reputation from the infamy to which both will be exposed, if no investigation be made into the causes of their calamities, and no punishment inflicted on the authors of them. By policy as well as justice, you are vehemently urged to vindicate the English character in the East; for, my Lords, it is manifest that the native powers have so little reliance on our faith, that the preservation of our possessions in that division of the world can only be effected by convincing the princes that a religious adherence to its engagements with them shall hereafter distinguish our India government.[2]

To these letters what answer shall we return? Let it not, my Lords, be by words, which will not find credit with the natives, who have been so often deceived by our professions, but by deeds which will assure them that we are at length truly in earnest. It is only by punishing those who have been guilty of the delinquencies which have ruined the country, and by showing that future criminals will not be encouraged or countenanced by the ruling powers at home, that we can possibly gain confidence with the people of India. This alone will revive their respect for us, and secure our authority over them. This alone will restore to us the alienated attachment of the much-injured Nabob, silence his clamors, heal his grievances, and remove his distrust. This alone will make him feel that he may cherish his people, cultivate his lands, and extend the mild hand of parental care over a fertile and industrious kingdom, without dreading that prosperity will entail upon him new rapine and extortion. This alone will inspire the Nabob with confidence in the English government, and the subjects of Oude with confidence in the Nabob. This alone will give to the soil of that delightful country the advantages which it derived from a beneficent Providence, and make it again what it was when invaded by an English spoiler, the garden of India.

Nothing but the punishment of the guilty can restore the confidence of the natives.

It is in the hope, my Lords, of accomplishing these salutary ends, of restoring character to England and happiness to India, that we have come to the bar of this exalted tribunal.

In looking round for an object fit to be held out to an oppressed people, and to the world as an example of national justice, we are forced to fix our eyes on Mr. Hastings. It is he, my Lords, who has degraded our fame, and blasted our fortunes in the East. It is he who has tyrannized with relentless severity over the devoted natives of those regions. It is he who must atone, as a victim, for the multiplied calamities he has produced!

Mr. Hastings the real criminal.

But though, my Lords, I designate the prisoner as a proper subject of exemplary punishment, let it not be presumed that I wish to turn the sword of justice against him merely because some example is required. Such a wish is as remote from my heart as it is from equity and law. Were I not persuaded that it is impossible I should fail to render the evidence of his crimes as conclusive as the effects of his conduct are confessedly afflicting, I should blush at having selected him as an

Not to be condemned without decisive evidence.

1 Here Mr. Sheridan read the letter of Lord Cornwallis, then Governor General of India, which stated that he had been received by the Nabob Vizier [Asoph Dowlah] with every mark of friendship and respect; but that the attentions of the court of Lucknow [the capital of Oude] did not prevent his seeing the desolation that overspread the face of the country, the sight of which had shocked his very soul; that he spoke to the Nabob on the subject, and earnestly recommended to him to adopt some system of government which might restore the prosperity of his kingdom and make his people happy; that the degraded prince replied to his Lordship, "that as long as the demands of the English government upon the revenue of Oude should remain unlimited, he, the Nabob, could have no interest in establishing economy, and that, while they continued to interfere in the internal regulations of the country, it would be in vain for him to attempt any salutary reform; for that his subjects knew he was only a cipher in his own dominions, and therefore laughed at and despised his authority aud that of his subjects.

The revenue of Oude, before its connection with the English, exceeded *three millions* of pounds sterling a year, and was levied without any deterioration of the country. Within a very few years the country was reduced, by the exactions of the Company and its agents, in connection with the misgovernment of the Nabob, to the condition described above by Lord Cornwallis.

2 To prove the necessity of bringing such a conviction to the mind of every native prince, Mr. Sheridan read a letter to Lord Cornwallis from Captain Kirkpatrick, who was resident at the court of the great Mahratta chief, Madajee Scindia. This letter stated that the new system of moderation introduced by his Lordship was certainly the only one to give stability to the British empire in India; but also observed that, as the princes of that country had so frequently had cause to lament the infidelity of engagements, it would require time, and repeated proofs of good faith, to convince them of the honesty of the professions thus held out to them; that ambition, or a desire of conquest, should no longer be encouraged by British councils, and that a most scrupulous adherence to all treaties and engagements should be the basis of our future political transactions.

object of retributive justice. If I invoke this heavy penalty on Mr. Hastings, it is because I honestly believe him to be a flagitious delinquent, and by far the most so of all those who have contributed to ruin the natives of India and disgrace the inhabitants of Britain. But while I call for justice upon the prisoner, I sincerely desire to render him justice. It would indeed distress me, could I imagine that the weight and consequence of the House of Commons, who are a party in this prosecution, could operate in the slightest degree to his prejudice; but I entertain no such solicitude or apprehension. It is the glory of the Constitution under which we live, that no man can be punished without guilt, and this guilt must be publicly demonstrated by a series of clear, legal, manifest evidence, so that nothing dark, nothing oblique, nothing authoritative, nothing insidious, shall work to the detriment of the subject. It is not the peering suspicion of apprehended guilt. It is not any popular abhorrence of its wide-spread consequences. It is not the secret consciousness in the bosom of the judge which can excite the vengeance of the law, and authorize its infliction! No! In this good land, as high as it is happy, because as just as it is free, all is definite, equitable, and exact. The laws must be satisfied before they are incurred; and ere a hair of the head can be plucked to the ground, *legal guilt* must be established by *legal proof*.

Peculiar difficulty of obtaining evidence in this case.

But this cautious, circumspect, and guarded principle of English jurisprudence, which we all so much value and revere, I feel at present in some degree inconvenient, as it may prove an impediment to public justice; for the managers of this impeachment labor under difficulties with regard to evidence that can scarcely occur in any other prosecution. What! my Lords, it may perhaps be asked, have none of the considerable persons who are sufferers by his crimes arrived to offer at your Lordships' bar their testimony, mixed with their execrations against the prisoner? No—there are none. These sufferers are persons whose manners and prejudices keep them separate from all the world, and whose religion will not permit them to appear before your Lordships. But are there no witnesses, unprejudiced spectators of these enormities, ready to come forward, from the simple love of justice, and to give a faithful narrative of the transactions that passed under their eyes? No—there are none. The witnesses whom we have been compelled to summon are, for the most part, the emissaries and agents employed, and involved in these transactions; the wily accomplices of the prisoner's guilt, and the supple instruments of his oppressions. But are there collected no written documents or authentic papers, containing a true and perfect account of his crimes? No—there are none.[3] The only papers we have procured are written by the party himself, or the participators in his proceedings, who studied, as it was their interest, though contrary to their duty, to conceal the criminality of their conduct, and, consequently, to disguise the truth.

But though, my Lords, I dwell on the difficulties which the managers have to encounter with respect to the evidence in this impeachment, I do not solicit indulgence, or even mean to hint, that what we have adduced is in any material degree defective. Weak no doubt it is in some parts, and deplorable, as undistinguished by any compunctious visitings of repenting accomplices. But there is enough, and enough in sure validity, notwithstanding every disadvantage and impediment, to abash the front of guilt no longer hid, and to flash those convictions on the minds of your Lordships, which should be produced.

Examination of evidence.

II. I now proceed, my Lords, to review the evidence.

Mr. Hastings' inconsistency

(1.) The first article which I shall notice must, I think, be considered pretty strong. It is the defense, or rather the *defenses*, of the prisoner before the House of Commons: for he has already made four: three of which he has since abandoned and endeavored to discredit. I believe it is a novelty in the history of criminal jurisprudence, that a person accused should first set up a defense, and afterward strive to invalidate it. But this, certainly, has been the course adopted by the prisoner; and I am the more surprised at it, as he has had the full benefit of the ablest counsel. Rescued from his own devious guidance, I could hardly have imagined that he would have acted so unwisely or indecently, as to evince his contempt of one House of Parliament by confessing the impositions which he had practiced on the other. But by this extraordinary proceeding, he has given, unwarily, to your Lordships a pledge of his *past truth*, in the *acknowledged falsehood* of his present conduct.

In every court of law in England, the confession of a criminal, when not obtained by any

[3] This is finely and truly put. The managers had the severest difficulties to encounter in respect to evidence. It would naturally be expected that some, at least, of the victims of Mr. Hastings' policy would appear in person to convict him of his crimes. Mr. Erskine, on the trial of Stockdale, refers to this fact in a passage of extraordinary dexterity and force. He contrasts the present case with that of Verres, in which hundreds flocked from Sicily to Rome, as witnesses against their oppressor; but the princes of Hindostan, though suffering a thousandfold greater oppressions, could not, for reasons hinted at by Mr. Sheridan, be brought from the other side of the globe to confront the author of their ruin. Nearly all the English residents in India sided with Hastings, either because they had shared in the robbery of India, or because they believed that his extortions and cruelties were the only means by which the British power could have been maintained in that country. These residents could not, therefore, be expected to come forward as witnesses against him. It was only, as Mr. Sheridan states, from his own papers, and the testimony of those who participated in his crimes, that evidence could be obtained; and it was proper that the court should be apprised at the outset of the extreme difficulty under which the Managers labored in regard to evidence.

promise of favor or lenity, or by violent threats, is always admitted as conclusive evidence against himself. And if such confession were made before a grave and respectable assembly of persons competent to take cognizance of crimes, there is no doubt but that it would have due weight, because it is fair to presume that it must be voluntary, and not procured by any undue or improper means. The prisoner has, in his defense, *admitted many facts;* and it is the intention of the managers, accordingly, to urge in support of the charges his admission of them. For, when he did it, he was speaking the language not of inconsiderate rashness and haste, but of deliberate consideration and reflection, as will appear to your Lordships by a passage which I shall cite from the introduction to the defense read by Mr. Hastings himself at the bar of the House of Commons. He employs the following words: "Of the discouragement to which I allude, I shall mention but two points, and these it is incumbent upon me to mention, because they relate to effects which the justice of this honorable House may, and I trust will, avert. The first is an obligation to my being at all committed in my defense; since, in so wide a field for discussion, it would be impossible not to admit some things of which an advantage might be taken to turn them into evidence against myself, whereas *another* might as well use as I could, or better, the same materials of my defense, without involving me in the same consequences. But I am sure the honorable House will yield me its protection against the cavils of unwarranted inference, and if truth can tend to convict me, I am content to be myself the channel to convey it. The other objection lies in my own breast. It was not till Monday last that I formed the resolution, and I knew not then whether I might not, in consequence, be laid under the obligation of preparing and completing in five days (and in effect so it proved) the refutation of charges which it has been the labor of my accuser, armed with all the powers of Parliament, to compile during as many years of almost undisturbed leisure."

Here, then, my Lords, the prisoner has, upon deliberation, committed his defense to paper; and after having five days to consider whether he should present it or not, he actually delivers it himself to the House of Commons as one founded in truth, and triumphantly remarks, that "if truth could tend to convict him, he was willing to be himself the channel to convey it."

But what is his language *now* that he has the advice of counsel?[4] Why, that there is not a word of truth in what he delivered to the House of Commons *as* truth! He did not, it seems, himself prepare the defense which he read as his own before that body. He employed others to draw it up. Major Scott comes to your bar, and represents Mr. Hastings, as it were, *contracting* for a character, to be made ready to his hands. Knowing, no doubt, that the accusation of the Commons had been drawn up by a committee, he thought it necessary, as a point of punctilio, to answer it by a committee also. For himself, he had no knowledge of the facts! no recollection of the circumstances! He commits his defense wholly to his friends! He puts his memory in trust, and duly nominates and appoints commissioners to take charge of it! One furnishes the raw material of fact, the second spins the argument, and the third twines up the conclusion; while Mr. Hastings, with a master's eye, is cheering them on, and overlooking the loom. To Major Scott he says, "you have my *good faith* in your hands—take care of my *consistency*—manage my *veracity* to the best advantage!" "Mr. Middleton, you have my *memory* in commission!" "Mr. Shore, make me out a good *financier!*" "Remember, Mr. Impey, you have my *humanity* in your hands!"[5] When this product of their skill was done, he brings it to the House of Commons, and says, "I was equal to the task. I knew the difficulties, but I scorned them: here is the *truth*, and if the truth tends to convict me, I am content myself to be the channel of it." His friends hold up their heads and say, "What noble magnanimity! This *must* be the effect of real innocence!"

But this journeyman's work, after all, is found to be defective. It is good enough for the House of Commons, but not for your Lordships. The prisoner now presents himself at your bar, and his only apprehension seems to arise from what had been thus done for him. He exclaims, "I am careless of what the managers say or do. Some of them have high passions, and others have bitter words, but these I heed not. Save me from the peril of my own panegyric; snatch me from my own friends. Do not believe a syllable of what I said before! I can not submit now to be tried, as I imprudently challenged, by the account which I have myself given of my own transactions!" Such is the language of the prisoner, by which it appears that truth is not natural to him, but that falsehood comes at his beck. Truth, indeed, it is said, lies deep, and requires time and labor to gain; but falsehood swims on the surface, and is always at hand.

It is in this way, my Lords, that the prisoner shows you how he sports with the dignity and feelings of the House by asserting that to be false, and not entitled to credit this day, which, on a former, he had averred to be truth itself. Indeed, from this avowal and disavowal of de-

[4] Mr. Hastings' counsel told him that he had committed himself imprudently in some parts of the defense which he delivered in at the bar of the House of Commons. He, therefore, introduced his friend, Major Scott, to prove that the paper had been drawn up by Mr. Middleton, Mr. Shore, and others—that Mr. Hastings had not even read it through, and ought not, therefore, to be held responsible for its contents.

[5] The keenness of this satire can be understood only by one who has entered fully into the character of the men here brought forward—the convenient elasticity of memory in Middleton, the abandonment of Impey to every excess of cruelty which would promote the designs of Hastings, &c.

fenses, and from the present defense differing from all the former which have been delivered to your Lordships, it does seem that Mr. Hastings thinks he may pursue this course just as far as best suits his convenience or advantage. It is not at all improbable, if he should deem it expedient, that he will hereafter abandon the one now submitted to you, and excuse himself by saying, "It was not made by me, but by my counsel, and I hope, therefore, your Lordships will give no credit to it." But if he will abide by this, his last revised and amended defense, I will join issue with him upon it, and prove it to be in numerous places void of truth, and almost every part of it unfounded in argument as well as fact.

Character of the Begums and their right to the property.

(2.) I am now to advert more particularly to the evidence in support of the allegations of the charge on which the prisoner is arraigned. We have already shown, most satisfactorily, that the Begums of Oude were of high birth and distinguished rank; the elder, or grandmother of the reigning prince being the daughter of a person of ancient and illustrious lineage, and the younger, or prince's mother, of descent scarcely less noble. We have also shown, with equal clearness, by the testimony of several witnesses, how sacred is the residence of women in India. To menace, therefore, the dwelling of these princesses with violation, as the prisoner did, was a species of torture, the cruelty of which can only be conceived by those who are conversant with the peculiar customs and notions of the inhabitants of Hindostan.

Reverence paid to the higher classes of females in India.

We have nothing in Europe, my Lords, which can give us an idea of the manners of the East. Your Lordships can not even learn the right nature of the people's feelings and prejudices from any history of other Mohammedan countries—not even from that of the Turks; for *they* are a mean and degraded race in comparison with many of these great families, who, inheriting from their Persian ancestors, preserve a purer style of prejudice and a loftier superstition. Women there are not as in Turkey—they neither go to the mosque nor to the bath. It is not the thin vail alone that hides them; but, in the inmost recesses of their Zenana, they are kept from public view by those reverenced and protected walls, which, as Mr. Hastings and Sir Elijah Impey admit, are held sacred even by the ruffian hand of warfare, or the more uncourteous hand of the law. But, in this situation, they are not confined from a mean and selfish policy of man, or from a coarse and sensual jealousy. Enshrined, rather than immured, their habitation and retreat is a sanctuary, not a prison—their jealousy is their own—a jealousy of their own honor, that leads them to regard liberty as a degradation, and the gaze of even admiring eyes as inexpiable pollution to the purity of their fame and the sanctity of their honor.

Such being the general opinion (or prejudices, let them be called) of this country, your Lordships will find that whatever treasures were given or lodged in a Zenana of this description must, upon the evidence of the thing itself, be placed beyond the reach of resumption. To dispute with the counsel about the original right to those treasures—to talk of a title to them by the Mohammedan law! Their title to them is the title of a saint to the relics upon an altar, placed there by Piety, guarded by holy Superstition, and to be snatched from thence only by Sacrilege.[6]

What, now, my Lords, do you think of the tyranny and savage apathy of a man who could act in open defiance of those prejudices which are so interwoven wtth the very existence of the females of the East, that they can be removed only by death? What do your Lordships think of the atrocity of a man who could threaten to profane and violate the sanctuary of the princesses of Oude, by declaring that he would storm it with his troops, and expel the inhabitants from it by force? There is, my Lords, displayed in the whole of this black transaction a wantonness of cruelty and ruffian-like ferocity that, happily, are not often incident even to the most depraved and obdurate of our species.[7]

Had there been in the composition of the prisoner's heart one generous propensity, or lenient disposition even slumbering and torpid, it must have been awakened and animated into kindness and mercy toward these singularly interesting females. Their character, and situation at the time, presented every circumstance to disarm hostility, and to kindle the glow of manly sympathy; but no tender impression could be made on his soul, which is as hard as adamant, and as black as sin. Stable as the everlasting hills in its schemes and purposes of villainy, it has never once been shaken by the cries of affliction, the claims of charity, or the complaints of injustice. With steady and undeviating step he marches on to the consummation of the abominable projects of wickedness which are engendered and contrived in its gloomy recesses. What his soul prepares his hands are ever ready to execute.

It is true, my Lords, that the prisoner is conspicuously gifted with the energy of vice, and

[6] Mr. Law, one of the counsel for Mr. Hastings, endeavored, in his reply, to throw ridicule on this metaphor, by asking how the Begum could be considered a "saint," or how the camels, which formed part of the treasure, could be placed on an "*altar*." This called forth one of Mr. Sheridan's keen retorts. "This is the first time in my life," said he, "in which I ever heard of 'special pleading' on a metaphor, or a 'bill of indictment' against a trope; but such is the turn of the learned counsel's mind, that when he attempts to be *humorous*, no jest can be found, and when *serious*, no fact is visible."

[7] Middleton, the instrument of Hastings in these cruelties, shows, in a letter of excuse to his master, how sacred the Zenana, or Harem, was considered among the Hindoos. "No man," he says, "*can* enter the walls of the Zenana—scarcely in the case of acting against an open enemy." It will be seen hereafter, how this threat was executed, and how Middleton himself shrunk from its literal performance.

the firmness of indurated sensibility. These are the qualities which he assiduously cultivates, and of which his friends vauntingly exult. They have, indeed, procured him his triumphs and his glories. Truly, my Lords, they have spread his fame, and erected the sombre pyramids of his renown.

That the treasures, my Lords, of the Zenana, the object of the prisoner's rapacity, and the incentive to his sacrilegious violation of this hallowed abode of the princesses of Oude, were their *private property*, justly acquired, and legally secured, and not the *money of the state*, as is alleged, has been clearly and incontestably demonstrated. It must be recollected how conclusive was the testimony, both positive and circumstantial, which we brought to support this point. Believing that it must have pressed itself upon your memories, I shall avoid here the tediousness of a detailed recapitulation. Permit me, however, to call your attention to a very brief summary of it.

Proof that the treasures were the private property of the Begums.

It is in complete evidence before you that Sujah ul Dowlah, the husband of the elder [younger] Begum, entertained[8] the warmest affection for his wife, and the liveliest solicitude for her happiness. Endeared to him by the double ties of conjugal attachment, and the grateful remembrance of her exemplary conduct toward him in the season of his severest misfortunes and accumulated distress, he seems, indeed, to have viewed her with an extravagance of fondness bordering on enthusiasm. You know, my Lords, that when the Nabob [Sujah Dowlah] was reduced, by the disastrous defeat which he sustained at Buxar, to the utmost extremity of adverse fortune, she, regardless of the danger and difficulties of the enterprise, fled to him, for the purpose of administering to his misery the solace of tenderness; and, prompted by the noblest sentiment, took along with her, for his relief, the jewels with which he had enriched her in his happier and more prosperous days. By the sale of these he raised a large sum of money, and retrieved his fortunes. After this generous and truly exemplary conduct on her part, the devotion of the husband to the wife knew no bounds. Can any farther proof be required of it than the appointment of his son, by her [Asoph Dowlah, the reigning Nabob], as the successor to his throne? With these dispositions, then, toward his wife, and from the manifest ascendency which she had acquired over him, is it, my Lords, I ask, an unwarrantable presumption that he did devise to her the treasures which she claimed? On the question of the legal right which the Nabob had to make such a bequest I shall not now dwell; it having been already shown, beyond disputation, by the learned manager [Mr. Adam] who opened the charge, that, according to the theory as well as the practice of the Mohammedan law, the reigning prince *may* alienate and dispose of either real or personal property. And it farther appears, my Lords, from the testimony which has been laid before you, that the younger Begum, or the Nabob's [Asoph Dowlah] mother, lent money to her son, amounting to twenty-six lacs of rupees, for which she received, as a pledge, his bonds. Here is the *evidentia rei* that the money so lent was acknowledged to be hers; for no one borrows his own money and binds himself to repay it!

Origin of the claim that they were public property.

But, my Lords, let us look into the origin of this pretended claim to the Begum's treasures. We hear nothing of it till the Nabob [Asoph] became embarrassed by the enormous expense of maintaining the military establishments to which he was compelled by the prisoner. Then, as a dernier resort, the title to the treasures was set up, as the property of the Crown, which could not be willed away. This, truly, was the dawn of the claim. Not long afterward, we detect the open interference of Mr. Hastings in this fraudulent transaction. It was, indeed, hardly to be expected that he would permit so favorable an occasion to escape of indulging his greedy rapacity. We find, accordingly, that Mr. Bristow, the resident at the court of Lucknow [the capital of Oude], duly received instructions to support, with all possible dexterity and intrigue, the pretensions of the Nabob. The result of the negotiation which in consequence took place, was, that the mother, as well to relieve the distresses of her son, as to secure a *portion* of her property, agreed finally to cancel his bond for the twenty-six lacs of rupees already lent, and to pay him thirty additional lacs, or £300,000, making in the whole £560,000 sterling. Part of this sum it was stipulated should be paid in goods contained in the Zenana, which, as they consisted of arms and other implements of war, the Nabob alleged to be the property of the state, and refused to receive in payment. The point, however, being referred to the Board at Calcutta, Mr. Hastings then, it is important to remark, *vindicated* the right of the Begums to all the goods of the Zenana, and brought over a majority of the council to his opinion. The matter in dispute being thus adjusted, a treaty between the mother and son was formally entered into, and to which the English became parties, guaranteeing its faithful execution. In consideration of the money paid to him by the mother, the son agreed to release all claim to the landed and remaining parts of the personal estate, left by his father Sujah ul Dowlah to the princess his widow. Whatever, therefore, might have been her title to this property before, her right, under this treaty and the guarantee, became as legal, as strong, and obligatory, as the laws of India, and the laws of nations, could possibly make it.

Decided by Mr. Hastings to belong to the Begums.

And confirmed to them by treaty.

But, my Lords, notwithstanding the opinion which Mr. Hastings so strenuously supported in

[8] Mr. Sheridan here inadvertently puts "elder" for "younger," as is obvious from his subsequent statement. The elder Begum was Sujah Dowlah's mother, and grandmother of the reigning Nabob, Asoph Dowlah, as stated by Mr. Sheridan on a preceding page.

the council at Calcutta of the absolute right of the princess to all the property in the Zenana, yet when it became convenient to his nefarious purposes to disown it, he, with an effrontery which has no example, declared that this recorded decision belonged not to him, but to the majority of the council! That, in short, being reduced to an inefficient minority in the council, he did not consider himself as responsible for any of their acts, either of those he opposed or those he approved. My Lords, you are well acquainted with the nature of majorities and minorities; but how shall I instance this new doctrine? It is as if Mr. Burke, the great leader of this prosecution, should, some ten years hence, revile the managers, and commend Mr. Hastings! What, sir, might one of us exclaim to him, do you, who instigated the inquiry, who brought the charge against him, who impeached him, who convinced me, by your arguments, of his guilt, speak of Mr. Hastings in this plausive style? Oh! but sir, replies Mr. Burke, this was done in the House of Commons, where, at the time, I was one of an inefficient minority, and, consequently, I am not responsible for any measure, either those I opposed or approved!

Mr. Hastings' subterfuge to avoid the argument.

If, my Lords, at any future period, my honorable friend should become so lost to truth, to honor, and consistency, as to speak in this manner, what must be the public estimation of his character? Just such was the conduct of the prisoner in avowing that he did not consider himself responsible for the measures which he approved while controlled in the council by General Clavering, Colonel Monson, and Mr. Francis, the only halcyon season that India saw during his administration.

But, my Lords, let it be observed that the claims of the Nabob to the treasures of the Begums were, at this time, the only plea alleged for the seizure. These were founded on a passage of the Koran, which is perpetually quoted, but never proved. Not a word was then mentioned of the strange rebellion which was afterward conjured up, and of which the existence and the notoriety were equally a secret! a disaffection which was at its height at the very moment when the Begums were dispensing their liberality to the Nabob, and exercising the greatest generosity to the English in distress! a disturbance without its parallel in history, which was raised by two *women*, carried on by *eunuchs*, and finally suppressed by an *affidavit!!*[9]

The sole pretense for the Nabob's claim was at first a passage of the Koran.

No one, my Lords, can contemplate the seizure of this treasure, with the attendant circumstances of aggravation, without being struck with horror at the complicated wickedness of the transaction We have already seen the noblest heroism and magnanimity displayed by the mother Begum. It was she, my Lords, you will recollect, who extricated, by the most generous interposition, her husband Sujah Dowlah from the rigors of his fortune after the fatal battle of Buxar. She even saved her son, the reigning Nabob, from death, at the imminent hazard of her own life. She, also, as you know, gave to her son his throne. A son so preserved, and so befriended, Mr. Hastings did arm against his benefactress, and his mother. He invaded the rights of that prince, that he might compel him to violate the laws of nature, and the obligations of gratitude, by plundering his parent. Yes, my Lords, it was the prisoner who cruelly instigated the son against the mother. That mother, who had twice given life to her son, who had added to it a throne, was (incredible as it may appear), by the compulsion of that man at your bar, to whose guardianship she was bequeathed by a dying husband—by that man, who is wholly insensible to every obligation which sets bounds to his rapacity and his oppression, was she pillaged and undone! But the son was not without his excuse. In the moment of anguish, when bewailing his hapless condition, he exclaimed that it was the English who had driven him to the perpetration of such enormities. "It is they who have reduced me. They have converted me to their use. They have made me a slave, to compel me to become a monster."

Cruelty of compelling the Nabob to seize the treasures.

Let us now, my Lords, turn to the negotiations of Mr. Middleton with the Begums in 1778, when the "discontents of the superior Begum would have induced her to leave the country, unless her authority was sanctioned and her property secured by the guarantee of the Company."[10] This guarantee the counsel of Mr. Hastings have thought it necessary to deny; knowing that if the agreements with the elder Begum were proved, it would affix to their client the guilt of all the sufferings of the women of the Khord Mahal [dwelling of the female rela-

The guarantee given to the elder Begum establishes her right.

[9] The force of this sarcasm upon Mr. Impey and his affidavits will be better understood when the reader comes to Mr. Sheridan's examination of Hastings' second pretense for seizing the treasures, namely, that the Begums and their ministers had fomented a rebellion against the Nabob.

[10] Early in 1778, the elder Begum became so much dissatisfied with her grandson's urgency for money, under the pressure of Mr. Hastings, that she meditated a withdrawal from his dominions, and a pilgrimage to Mecca. The English resident at Oude, Mr. Middleton, in common with the Nabob, was opposed to her departure. She demanded, as the condition of remaining, that the Board at Calcutta should *guarantee* her property against the exactions of her grandson. This property, consisting chiefly of certain *jaghires*, or grants of revenue, was given her by her son Sujah Dowlah, not merely for her own support, but that of his numerous female relations, "the women of the Khord Mahal," spoken of below. Mr. Middleton represented to the Board at Calcutta that her claims were just. Whether a formal guarantee was given (as Mr. Sheridan attempts to show), is doubtful; still, it is certain, as he proves, that the property of the Begum in her *jaghires* was exempted from taxation by the Board, which was the fullest admission of her rights.

tives of the Nabob], the revenues for whose support were secured by the same engagement. In treating this part of the subject, the principal difficulty arises from the uncertain evidence of Mr. Middleton, who, though concerned in the negotiation of four treaties, could not recollect affixing his signature to *three* out of that number! It can, however, be shown, even by his evidence, that a treaty was signed in October, 1778, wherein the rights of the elder Begum were fully recognized; a provision secured for the women and children of the late Vizier in the Khord Mahal; and that these engagements received the fullest sanction of Mr. Hastings. These facts are, moreover, confirmed by the evidence of Mr. Purling, a gentleman who delivered himself fairly, and as having no foul secrets to conceal. Mr. Purling swears he transmitted copies of these engagements, in 1780, to Mr. Hastings at Calcutta; the answer returned was, "that, in arranging the taxes of the other districts, he should pass over the *jaghires* of the Begums." No notice was then taken of any impropriety in the transactions in 1778, nor any notice given of an intended revocation of those engagements.

Meeting of Hastings with the Nabob at Chunar, when the present of £100,000 was made.

In June, 1781, however, when General Clavering and Colonel Monson were no more, and Mr. Francis had returned to Europe, all the *hoard* and *arrear* of collected evil burst out without restraint, and Mr. Hastings determined on his journey to the Upper Provinces. It was then, that, without adverting to intermediate transactions, he met with the Nabob Asoph Dowlah at Chunar, and received from him the mysterious present of £100,000. To form a proper idea of this transaction, it is only necessary to consider the respective situations of him who gave and of him who received this present. It was not given by the Nabob from the superflux of his wealth, nor in the abundance of his esteem for the man to whom it was presented. It was, on the contrary, a prodigal bounty, drawn from a country depopulated by the natural progress of British rapacity. It was after the country had felt still other calamities—it was after the angry dispensations of Providence had, with a progressive severity of chastisement, visited the land with a famine one year, and with a Colonel Hanney the next—it was after he, this Hanney, had returned to retrace the steps of his former ravages—it was after he and his voracious crew had come to plunder ruins which himself had made, and to glean from desolation the little that famine had spared, or rapine overlooked; *then* it was that this miserable bankrupt prince, marching through his country, besieged by the clamors of his starving subjects, who cried to him for protection through their cages—meeting the curses of some of his subjects, and the prayers of others—with famine at his heels, and reproach following him—then it was that this prince is represented as exercising this act of prodigal bounty to the very man whom he here reproaches—to the very man whose policy had extinguished his power, and whose creatures had desolated his country. To talk of a free-will gift! It is audacious and ridiculous to name the supposition. It was not a free-will gift. What was it, then? Was it a bribe? Or was it extortion? I shall prove it was both—it was an act of gross bribery and of rank extortion. The *secrecy* which marked this transaction is not the smallest proof of its criminality. When Benarum Pundit had, a short time before, made a present to the Company of a lac of rupees, Mr. Hastings, in his own language, deemed it "worthy the praise of being recorded." But in this instance, when ten times that sum was given, neither Mr. Middleton nor the council were acquainted with the transaction, until Mr. Hastings, four months afterward, felt himself compelled to write an account of it to England; and the intelligence returned thus circuitously to his friends in India! It is peculiarly observable in this transaction, how much the *distresses* of the different parties were at variance. The first thing Mr. Hastings does is to leave Calcutta in order to go to the relief of the distressed Nabob. The second thing is to take one hundred thousand pounds *from* that distressed Nabob, on account of the distressed Company. The third thing is, to ask of the distressed Company this very same hundred thousand pounds on account of the distresses of Mr. Hastings! There never were three distresses that seemed so little reconcilable with one another. This money, the prisoner alleges, was appropriated to the payment of the army. But here he is unguardedly contradicted by the testimony of his friend, Major Scott, who shows it was employed for no such purpose. My Lords, through all these windings of mysterious hypocrisy, and of artificial concealment, is it not easy to discern the sense of hidden guilt?[11]

Plea of State Necessity.

III. Driven from every other hold, the prisoner is obliged to resort, as a justification of his enormities, to the stale pretext of State Necessity! Of this last disguise, it is my duty to strip him. I will venture to say, my Lords, that no one instance of real necessity can be adduced. The necessity which the prisoner alleges listens to whispers for the purpose of crimination, and deals in rumor to prove its own existence. *His* a State Necessity! No, my Lords, that imperial tyrant, *State Neces-*

[11] The officers of the East India Company were forbidden by its laws to receive presents; but Mr. Hastings did accept the offered gift from Asoph Dowlah. "The Nabob," says Mr. Mill, "was totally unprovided with the money; the gift could be tendered only in bills, which were drawn on one of the great bankers of the country. As the intention of concealing the transaction should not be imputed to Mr. Hastings unless as far as evidence appears, so in this case the disclosure can not be imputed as a virtue, since no prudent man would have risked the chance of discovery which the publicity of a banker's transactions implied. Mr. Hastings informed the Directors of what he had received, in a letter dated January 20, 1782, *and in very plain terms requested their permission to make the money his own.*" —*British India*, iv., 409.

sity, is yet a generous despot—bold in his demeanor, rapid in his decisions, though terrible in his grasp. What he does, my Lords, he dares avow; and avowing, scorns any other justification, than the high motives that placed the iron scepter in his hand. Even where its rigors are suffered, its apology is also known; and men learn to consider it in its true light, as a power which turns occasionally aside from just government, when its exercise is calculated to prevent greater evils than it occasions. But a quibbling, prevaricating necessity, which tries to steal a pitiful justification from whispered accusations and fabricated rumors—no, my Lords, that is *no* State Necessity! Tear off the mask, and you see coarse, vulgar avarice lurking under the disguise. The State Necessity of Mr. Hastings is a juggle. It is a being that prowls in the dark. It is to be traced in the ravages which it commits, but never in benefits conferred or evils prevented. I can conceive justifiable occasions for the exercise even of outrage, where high public interests demand the sacrifice of private right. If any great man, in bearing the arms of his country—if any admiral, carrying the vengeance and the glory of Britain to distant coasts, should be driven to some rash acts of violence, in order, perhaps, to give food to those who are shedding their blood for their country—there is a State Necessity in such a case, grand, magnanimous, and all-commanding, which goes hand in hand with honor, if not with use! If any great general, defending some fortress, barren, perhaps, itself, but a pledge of the pride and power of Britain—if such a man, fixed like an imperial eagle on the summit of his rock, should strip its sides of the verdure and foliage with which it might be clothed, while covered on the top with that cloud from which he was pouring down his thunders on the foe—would he be brought by the House of Commons to your bar?[12] No, my Lords, never would his grateful and admiring countrymen think of questioning actions which, though accompanied by private wrong, yet were warranted by real necessity. But is the State Necessity which is pleaded by the prisoner, in defense of his conduct, of this description? I challenge him to produce a single instance in which any of his private acts were productive of public advantage, or averted impending evil.

Treaty of Chunar for the robbery of the Begums.

IV. We come now to the treaty of Chunar, which preceded the acceptance of the bribe to which we have already alluded. This transaction, my Lords, had its beginning in corruption, its continuance in fraud, and its end in violence. The first proposition of the Nabob was, that our army should be removed and all the English be recalled from his dominions. He declared, to use his own language, that "the English are the bane and ruin of my affairs. Leave my country to myself, and all will yet be recovered." He was aware, my Lords, that though their predecessors had exhausted his revenue; though they had shaken the tree till nothing remained upon its leafless branches, yet that a new flight was upon the wing to watch the first buddings of its prosperity, and to nip every promise of future luxuriance. To the demands of the Nabob, Mr. Hastings finally acceded. The bribe was the price of his acquiescence. But with the usual perfidy of the prisoner, this condition of the treaty never was performed. You will recollect, my Lords, that Mr. Middleton was asked whether the orders which were pretended to be given for the removal of the English were, in any instance, carried into effect? To this question he refused at first to answer, as tending to criminate himself. But when his objection was overruled, and it was decided that he should answer, so much was he agitated that he lost all memory. It turned out, however, by an amended recollection, that he never received any *direct order* from Mr. Hastings. But, my Lords, who can believe that a direct order is necessary when Mr. Hastings wants the services of Mr. Middleton? Rely upon it, a hint is sufficient to this servile dependent and obsequious parasite. Mr. Hastings has only to turn his *eye toward him*—that eye at whose scowl princes turn pale—and his wishes are obeyed.

Bad faith of Mr. Hastings.

But, my Lords, this is not the only instance in which the Nabob was duped by the bad faith of the prisoner. In the agreement relative to the resumption of the *jaghires*, the prince had demanded and obtained leave to resume those of certain individuals; but Mr. Hastings, knowing that there were some favorites of the Nabob whom he could not be brought to dispossess, defeated the permission, without the least regard to the existing stipulations to the contrary, by making the order general.

Such, my Lords, is the conduct of which Mr. Hastings is capable, not in the moment of cold or crafty policy, but in the hour of confidence, and during the effervescence of his gratitude for a favor received! Thus did he betray the man to whose liberality he stood indebted. Even the gratitude, my Lords, of the prisoner seems perilous; for we behold here the danger which actually awaited the return he made to an effusion of generosity!

He defends it by pretending that the Begums had rebelled.

The fact is, my Lords, as appears from the clearest evidence, that when Mr. Hastings left Calcutta he had two resources in view, Benares and Oude. The first having failed him, in consequence of the unexpected insurrection which terminated, unhappily for him, in the capture of Bedjigar, he turned his attention to Oude, previously, however. desolating the former province, which he was unable to pillage, destroying and cutting off the very sources of life. Thus frustrated in his original design, the genius of the prisoner, ever fertile in expedients, fixed itself on the treasures of the Begums, and now devised, as an apology for the signal act of cruelty and rapacity which he was meditating, the memorable rebellion; and, to

[12] This glowing picture was no doubt suggested by Sir Gilbert Elliot's noble defense of the Rock of Gibraltar a few years before.

substantiate the participation of these unfortunate princesses in it, he dispatched the Chief Justice of India to collect materials.[13]

The conduct of Sir Elijah Impey in this business, with all deference to the protest which he has entered against being spoken of in a place where he can not have the privilege of replying, I do not think ought to be passed over without animadversion. Not that I mean to say any thing harsh of this elevated character, who was selected to bear forth and to administer to India the blessings of English jurisprudence. I will not question either his feebleness of memory, or dispute in any respect the convenient doctrine which he has set up in his vindication, "that what he ought to have done it is likely he actually did perform." I have always thought, my Lords, that the appointment of the Chief Justice to so low and nefarious an office as that in which he was employed is one of the strongest aggravations of Mr. Hastings' guilt. That an officer, the purity and luster of whose character should be maintained even in the most domestic retirement; that he, who, if consulting the dignity of British justice, ought to have continued as stationary as his court at Calcutta; that such an exalted character, I repeat, as the Chief Justice of India, should have been forced on a circuit of five hundred miles for the purpose of transacting such a business, was a degradation without example, and a deviation from propriety which has no apology. But, my Lords, this is, in some degree, a question which is to be abstracted for the consideration of those who adorn and illumine the seats of justice in Britain, and the rectitude of whose deportment precludes the necessity of any farther observation on so opposite a conduct.

Mr. Impey his agent for collecting evidence.

The manner, my Lords, in which Sir Elijah Impey delivered his evidence deserves, also, your attention. He admitted, you will recollect, that, in giving it, he never answered without looking equally to the *probability* and the *fact* in question. Sometimes he allowed circumstances of which he said he had no recollection beyond the mere "probability" that they had taken place. By consulting in this manner what was "probable" and the contrary, he may certainly have corrected his memory at times. I am, at all events, content to accept of this mode of giving his testimony, provided that the converse of the proposition has also a place; and that where a circumstance is *improbable*, a similar degree of credit may be subtracted from the testimony of the witness. Five times in the House of Commons, and twice in this court, for instance, has Sir Elijah Impey borne testimony that a rebellion was raging at Fyzabad [the abode of the Begums], at the period of his journey to Lucknow [the residence of the Nabob]. Yet, on the eighth examination, he contradicted all the former, and declared that what he meant was, that the rebellion *had* been raging, and the country was then in some degree restored to quiet. The reasons he assigned for the former errors were, that he had forgotten a letter received from Mr. Hastings, informing him that the rebellion was quelled, and that he had also forgotten his own proposition of traveling *through* Fyzabad to Lucknow! With respect to the letter, nothing can be said, as it is not in evidence; but the other observation can scarcely be admitted when it is recollected that, in the House of Commons, Sir Elijah Impey declared that it was his proposal to travel through Fyzabad, which had originally brought forth the intelligence that the way was obstructed by the rebellion, and that in consequence of it he altered his route and went by the way of Illahabad. But what is yet more singular is, that on his return he again would have come by the way of Fyzabad, if he had not been once more informed of the danger; so that, had it not been for these friendly informations, the Chief Justice would have run plump into the very focus of the rebellion!

His appearance as witness before the Lords.

These, my Lords, are the pretexts by which the fiction of a rebellion was endeavored to be forced on the public credulity; but the trick is now discovered, and the contriver and the executer are alike exposed to the scorn and derision of the world.

There are two circumstances here which are worthy of remark. The first is, that Sir Elijah Impey, when charged with so dangerous a commission as that of procuring evidence to prove that the Begums had meditated the expulsion of the Nabob from the throne, and the English from Bengal, twice intended to pass through the city of their residence. But, my Lords, this *giddy* chief justice disregards business. He wants to see the country! Like some *innocent* school-boy, he takes the primrose path, and amuses himself as he goes! He thinks not that his errand is in danger and death, and that his party of pleasure ends in loading others with irons. When at Lucknow, he never mentions the affidavits to the Nabob. No! He is too polite. Nor, from the same courtesy, to Mr. Hastings. He is, indeed, a master of ceremonies in justice!

Improbabilities in his testimony.

When examined, the witness sarcastically re-

[13] In regard to this pretended rebellion in favor of Cheyte Sing of Benares, Mr. Mill has the following remarks as the result of subsequent impartial investigation. "The insurrection at Benares happened on the 16th of August, and the treaty was signed at Chunar on the 19th of September. The Begums, who had first to hear of the insurrection at Benares [some hundred miles off], and then spread disaffection throughout a great kingdom, had, therefore, little time for the contraction of guilt. And what was the proof upon the strength of which the Begums were selected for a singular and aggravated punishment? No direct proof whatever. Hardly an attempt is made to prove any thing except a *rumor*. Mr. Hastings' friends are produced in great numbers to say that they heard a *rumor!* But before a just judgment can be pronounced, the party accused should be heard in defense. Was this justice afforded to the Begums? Not a tittle. Mr. Hastings pronounced judgment, and sent his instrument, the Nabob, to inflict punishment, *in the first place.* Some time after this was done, he proceeded to collect evidence!"—*British India,* iv., 381-2.

marked "that there must have been a sworn interpreter, from the looks of the manager." How I looked, Heaven knows! but such a physiognomist there is no escaping. He sees a sworn interpreter in my looks! He sees the manner of taking an oath in my looks! He sees the Basin of the Ganges in my looks! As for himself, he looks only at the *tops* and *bottoms* of affidavits! In seven years he takes care never to look at these swearings; but when he does examine them, he *knows less* than before![14]

The other circumstance, my Lords, to which I have alluded, is, that it is fair to presume that Sir Elijah Impey was dissuaded by Mr. Hastings and Middleton from passing by the way of Fyzabad, as they well knew that if he approached the Begums he would be convinced by their reception of him as the friend of the Governor General, that nothing could be more foreign from the truth than their suspected disaffection. Neither should it escape your notice, my Lords, that while he was taking evidence at Lucknow in the face of day, in support of the charge of rebellion against the princesses, the Chief Justice heard not a word either from the Nabob or his minister, though he frequently conversed with both, of any treasonable machinations or plottings! Equally unaccountable does it appear, that Sir Elijah Impey, who advised the taking of these affidavits for the safety of the prisoner at your bar, did not *read* them at the time to see whether or not they were adequate to this purpose!

At length, it seems, he did read the affidavits, but not till after having declared on oath that he thought it unnecessary. To this he acknowledged he was induced "by having been misled by one of the managers on the part of the Commons, who, by looking at a book which he held in his hand, had entrapped him to own that a sworn interpreter was present when he received these affidavits, and that he was perfectly satisfied with his conduct on the occasion."

Now, my Lords, how I, by merely looking into a book, could *intimate* the presence of an interpreter, and could also *look* the satisfaction conceived by the Chief Justice on the occasion, when it clearly appears by the evidence that there was *no* interpreter present, are points which I believe he alone can explain!

I will concede to the witness, as he seems desirous it should be done, that he did not strictly attend to form when taking these affidavits. I will admit that he merely directed the Bible to be offered to the whites, and the Koran to the blacks, and packed up their depositions in his wallet without any examination. Or, I will admit that he glanced them over in India, having previously cut off all communication between his eye and his mind, so that nothing was transferred from the one to the other. Extraordinary as these circumstances certainly are, I will, nevertheless, admit them all; or if it be preferred by the prisoner, I will admit that the affidavits were legally and properly taken; for, in whatever light they may be received, I will prove that they are not sufficient to sustain a single allegation of criminality against those they were designed to inculpate.

But it is to these documents, my Lords, such as they are, that the defense of the prisoner is principally confided; and on the degree of respect which may be given to them by your Lordships does the event of this trial materially depend.

Antecedent presumptions against the charges in the affidavits.

Considered, therefore, in this view, I shall presently solicit your Lordships' attention, while I examine them at some length, and with some care. But before I enter into the analysis of the testimony, permit me to remind the court that the charge against the princesses of Oude, to substantiate which these affidavits were taken, consisted originally of two allegations. They were accused of a *uniform spirit of hostility to the British government*, as well as *the overt act of rebellion*. But, my Lords, the first part of the charge the counsel for the prisoner has been compelled to abandon, not being able to get one fact out of the whole farrago of these depositions to support it.

When the half of an accusation is thus deserted for the want of proof, is it not natural for us to suspect the whole? I do not say that it absolutely shows the falsity of it, nor do I mean to employ such an argument; but I maintain that it should influence the mind so far as to make it curious and severely inquisitive into the other branch of the charge, and to render it distrustful of its truth.

But in this particular case the court have an additional motive for jealousy and suspicion. It will not escape the recollection of your Lordships, in weighing the validity of the allegation which now remains to be considered, namely, "that the Begums influenced the jaghiredars,[15] and excited the discontents in Oude," what were the circumstances in which it arose, and by whom it was preferred. You will bear in mind,

[14] An examination of the Minutes of Evidence at the trial will show that Mr. Sheridan was fully justified in this severe treatment of Impey. The latter acknowledged that he went from Benares, where this business was concerted between him and Mr. Hastings, to Lucknow, the capital of Oude, for the express purpose of taking the affidavits, though his jurisdiction did not extend to the province of Oude. "What the affidavits contained," he says, "I did not know; nor do I know at present, for I have never read them." He adds, that "he did not know *whether the persons who swore to them had ever read them.*" At the time of taking the affidavits of the natives, not so much as a sworn interpreter was present, as he admitted, though he endeavored to turn off the matter with a jest on Mr. Sheridan's "looks." See Minutes of Evidence, page 622 to 651. Mr. Mill remarks on this point, "The examination of Sir Elijah Impey, upon the subject of affidavits, discloses a curious scene, in which it appears that one object alone was in view, namely, that of getting support to any allegations which Mr. Hastings had set up."—*British India*, iv., 383.

[15] Persons holding jaghires.

my Lords, that it appears in evidence that Mr. Hastings left Calcutta in the year 1781, for the avowed purpose of collecting a large sum of money, and that he had only two resources. Failing in Benares, as we have already seen, he next lays his rapacious hand on the treasures of the Begums. Here, then, we have in the person of the prisoner both the accuser and the judge. With much caution, therefore, should this judge be heard, who has, apparently at least, a profit in the conviction, and an interest in the condemnation of the party to be tried. I say nothing of the gross turpitude of such a double character, nor of the frontless disregard of all those feelings which revolt at mixing offices so distinct and incompatible.

The next point which I wish to press on your Lordships' consideration, previously to my taking up the affidavits, is the infinite improbability of the attempt which is alleged to have been made by the Begums to dethrone the Nabob and exterminate the English. Estimating the power of the princesses at the highest standard, it manifestly was not in their reach to accomplish any overthrow, decisive or even momentary, of their sovereign, much less of the English. I am not so weak, however, as to argue that, because the success of an enterprise seems impossible, and no adequate reason can be assigned for undertaking it, that it will therefore never be attempted; or that, because the Begums had no interest in exciting a rebellion, or sufficient prospect of succeeding in it, they are innocent of the charge. I can not look at the prisoner without knowing, and being compelled to confess that there *are* persons of such a turn of mind as to prosecute mischief without interest; and that there *are* passions of the human soul which lead, without a motive, to the perpetration of crimes.

I do not, therefore, my Lords, wish it to be understood that I am contending that the charge is rendered, by the matter I have stated, absolutely false. All I mean is, that an accusation, made under such circumstances, should be received with much doubt and circumspection; and that your Lordships, remembering how it is preferred, will accompany me through the discussion of the affidavits, free and uninfluenced by any bias derived from the positive manner in which the guilt of the Begums has been pronounced.

Examination of the affidavits.

We now come to the examination of this mass of evidence which Mr. Hastings conceives of so much consequence to his acquittal on the present charge. In the defense which has been submitted to your Lordships, the prisoner complains most bitterly that the chief mover of the prosecution treated these affidavits in his *peculiar manner*. What the *peculiar manner* of my honorable friend [Mr. Burke], here alluded to, was, I can not tell. But I will say, that if he treated them in any other way than as the most rash, irregular, and irrelevant testimony which was ever brought before a judicial tribunal, he did not do as they deserved. The prisoner has had, moreover, the hardihood to assert that they were taken for the purpose of procuring the best possible information of the state of the country, and of the circumstances of the insurrection; and being, therefore, merely accessary evidence in the present case, were entitled to more weight. This I declare, without hesitation, to be a falsehood. They were taken, I aver, for the sole and exclusive purpose of vindicating the plunder of the Begums. They were taken to justify what was afterward to be done. Disappointed at Benares, he turned to the remaining resource, the treasures of the princesses; and prepared, as a pretext for his meditated robbery, these documents.

I shall proceed to examine the affidavits severally, as far as they relate to the charge against the Begums.[16] They really contain, my Lords, nothing except vague rumor and improbable surmise. It is stated, for example, by one of these deponents, a black officer in a regiment of sepoys, that having a considerable number of persons as hostages in a fort where he commanded, who were sent thither by Colonel Hannay, the country people surrounded the fort and demanded their release; but instead of complying with their demand, he put twenty of these hostages to death; and on a subsequent day the heads of eighteen more were struck off, including the head of a great Rajah. In consequence of this last execution, the populace became exceedingly exasperated, and among the crowd several persons were heard to say, that the Begums had offered a reward of a thousand rupees for the head of every European; one hundred for the head of every sepoy officer, and ten for the head of a common sepoy. Now, my Lords, it appears pretty clearly that no such reward was ever offered; for, when this garrison evacuated the fort, the people told Captain Gordon, who then commanded it, that if he would deliver up his arms and baggage, they would permit him and his men to continue their march unmolested. So little did the people, indeed, think of enriching themselves by this process of decapitation, that, when the detachment of British forces was reduced to *ten men*, and when of course the slaughter of them would have been a work of no danger or difficulty, they were still permitted to proceed on their route without any interruption.

Mere hearsay.

Captain Gordon himself *supposes* that the Be-

---

16 "We pretend not," says the reporter, "to give more than a mere summary, and that a very brief one, of this part of Mr. Sheridan's speech. In the discussion of these affidavits he was very copious, reading, comparing, and commenting on the whole with an uncommon degree of force, acuteness, and eloquence; sometimes employing too the severest sarcasm, and wit the most pungent and brilliant.

Speaking of the testimony of one of the officers of the army, who had given three affidavits in the same day, he observed 'that he had sworn once—then again—and made nothing of it; then comes he with another and swears a third time, and in *company* does better. *Single-handed*, he can do nothing; but succeeds by *platoon swearing*, and *volleys of oaths!*'"

gums encouraged the country people to rise, because, when he arrived at the bank of the River Saunda Nutta, at the opposite side of which stands the town of Nutta, the Fowzdar, or Governor, who commanded there for the Bow [younger] Begum, in whose jaghire the town lay, did not *instantly* send boats to carry him and his men over the river; and because the Fowzdar [governor] pointed two or three guns across the river. Even admitting this statement to be true, I can not see how it is to affect the Begums. Where is the symptom of hostility? Surely it was the duty of the commanding officer of the fort not to let any troops pass until he ascertained who they were, and for what purpose they came. To have done otherwise would have been unmilitary, and a violation of the most sacred duties of his station. But, my Lords, after a while Captain Gordon crosses the river, and finds himself in a place of safety as soon as he enters a town which was under *the authority of the Begums*, where he was treated with kindness, and afterward sent with a *protecting guard* to Colonel Hannay. This last circumstance, which is mentioned in the first affidavit of Captain Gordon, is suppressed in the second, for what purpose it is obvious. But let us attend to the testimony of Hyder Beg Cawn, who, as the minister of the Nabob, was the person, certainly, of all others, the best acquainted with the transactions then passing in the country. Though with every source of intelligence open to him, and swearing both to rumor and to fact, he does not mention a syllable in proof of the pretended rebellion, which was to dethrone his sovereign, nor even hint at any thing of the kind.

Surmises.

Neither, my Lords, is the evidence of the English officers more conclusive. That of Mr. Middleton, which has been so much relied upon, contains but a single passage which is at all pertinent, and this is not legal evidence. He says, "there was *a general report* that the Begums had given much encouragement and some aid to the jaghiredars in resisting the resumption, and that he had *heard* there had been a good disposition in them toward the Rajah Cheyte Sing. His evidence is mere hearsay. He knows nothing of himself. He saw no insurrection. He met with no unfriendly dispositions. But on the mere rumors which he had stated did this conscientious servant of Mr. Hastings with promptitude execute the scheme of plunder which his master had devised.

Rumors.

The testimony of Colonel Hannay is of the same description. He simply states that "three Zimindars *told* him that they were credibly informed that the Begums had a hostile design against the Nabob. When asked who these Zemindars were, he replied that he was not at liberty to disclose their names. They had made the communication to him under an express injunction of secrecy, which he could not violate.

There is also the deposition of a Frenchman, which is drawn up quite in the style of magnificence and glitter which belongs to his nation. He talks of having penetrated immeasurable wilds; of having seen tigers and other prowling monsters of the forest; of having surveyed mountains, and navigated streams; of having been entertained in palaces and menaced with dungeons; of having heard a *number of rumors*, but that he never saw any rebellious or hostile appearances.

Such, my Lords, are the contents of these memorable depositions, on which the prisoner relies as a vindication of an act of the most transcendent rapacity and injustice of which there is any record or tradition.

I know, my Lords, that if I were in a court of law, sitting merely to try the question of the validity of this testimony, to rise in order to comment upon it, I should be prevented from proceeding. By the bench I should be asked, "What do you mean to do? There is nothing in these affidavits upon which we can permit you for a minute to occupy the time of the court. There is not, from the beginning to the end, one particle of legal, substantial, or even defensible proof. There is nothing except hearsay and rumor." But though, my Lords, I am persuaded that such would be the admonition which I should receive from the court, yet, being exceedingly anxious to meet every thing at your Lordships' bar on which the prisoner can build the smallest degree of dependence, I must pray your indulgence while I examine separately the points which are attempted to be set up by these affidavits.

They are three in number:

Mr. Hastings' charges against the Begums.

1. That the Begums gave assistance to Cheyte Sing, Rajah of Benares.

2. That they encouraged and assisted the *jaghiredars* to resist the resumption of the *jaghires*. And,

3. That they were the principal movers of all the commotions in Oude.

These, my Lords, are the three allegations that the affidavits are to sustain, and which are accompanied with the general charge that the Begums were in rebellion.

(1.) Charge of rebellion.

(1.) Of the rebellion here pretended, I can not, my Lords, find a trace. With the care and indefatigable industry of an antiquary, hunting for some precious vestige which is to decide the truth of his speculations, have I searched for the evidence of it. Though we have heard it spoken of with as much certainty as the one which happened in Scotland in the year 1745, not the slightest appearance of it can I discover. I am unable to ascertain either the time when, or the place where it raged. No army has been seen to collect; no battle to be fought; no blood to be spilt. It was a rebellion which had for its object the destruction of no human creature but those who *planned* it—it was a rebellion which, according to Mr. Middleton's expression, no man, either *horse* or *foot*, ever marched to quell! The Chief Justice was the only one who took the field against it. The force against which it was raised instantly *withdrew* to give it elbow-room; and even then, it was a rebellion which perversely showed itself in acts of *hospitality* to the Nabob whom it was to dethrone, and to the English whom it was to extirpate! Beginning in *nothing*, it continued *without raging*, and ended *as it originated!*

If, my Lords, rebellions of this mysterious nature can happen, it is time to look about us. Who can say that one does not now exist which menaces our safety? Perhaps at the very moment I am speaking one ravages our city! Perhaps it may be lying *perdue* in a neighboring village! Perhaps, like the ostentatious encampment which has given celebrity to Brentford and Ealing, it may have fixed its quarters at Hammersmith or Islington, ready to pour down its violence at the approach of night!

But, my Lords, let us endeavor to fix the time when this horrid rebellion occurred. To the first of August, 1781, it is clear there was none. At this date letters were received from Colonel Morgan, the commanding officer of Oude, who is silent on the subject. On the 27th of September, he gives an account of some insurrections *at Lucknow*, the seat of the court, but of *none at Fyzabad*, where the Begums resided. Nearly of the same date there is a letter from Major Hannay, then at the Rajah's court, in which the state of his affairs are described, but no suspicion expressed of his being assisted by the Begums.

At this time, therefore, there was certainly no rebellion or disaffection displayed. Nay, we find, on the contrary, the Nabob going to visit his mother, the very princess who is charged with revolting against his authority. But, my Lords, it is alleged that he was attended by two thousand horse, and the inference is drawn by the counsel of the prisoner that he took this military force to quell the insurrection; to confirm which they appealed to Mr. Middleton, who, being asked whether these troops were well appointed, caught in an instant a gleam of *martial memory*,[17] and answered in the affirmative. Unfortunately, however, for the martial memory of Mr. Middleton, it is stated by Captain Edwards, who was with the Nabob as his aid-de-camp, that there were not more than five or six hundred horse, and these so bad and miserably equipped that they were unable to keep up with him, so that very few were near his person or within the reach of his command. That of these few, the most were mutinous from being ill paid, and were rather disposed to promote than put down any insurrection. But, my Lords, I will concede to the prisoner the full amount of military force for which he anxiously contends. I will allow the whole two thousand cavalry to enter in a gallop into the very city of Fyzabad. For, has not Captain Edwards proved that they were only the usual guard of the Nabob? Has not, moreover, Mr. Middleton himself declared, rather indiscreetly, I confess, "that it is the constant custom of the princes of India to travel with a great equipage, and that it would be considered an unpardonable disrespect to the person visited were they to come unescorted." This, my Lords, is really the truth. The Indian princes never perform a journey without a splendid retinue. The habits of the East require ostentation and parade. They do not, as the princes of Europe —who, sometimes from one motive and sometimes from another, at times from political views and at times from curiosity, travel, some to France to learn manners, and others to England to learn liberty—choose to be relieved from the pomps of state and the drudgery of equipage. But, my Lords, perhaps, in this instance, the Nabob, wishing to adapt himself to the service on which he was going, did dispense with his usual style. Hearing of a rebellion without an army, he may have thought that it could only, with propriety, be attacked by a *prince* without a *guard!*

It has also been contended, my Lords, in proof of this rebellion, that one thousand Nudgies were raised at Fyzabad and sent to the assistance of Cheyte Sing.

It is deemed a matter of no consequence that the officer second in command to the Rajah [Cheyte Sing], has positively sworn that these troops came from Lucknow, and not from Fyzabad.[18] This the prisoner wishes to have considered as only the trifling mistake of the name of one capital for another. But he has found it more difficult to get over the fact which has been attested by the same witness, that the troops were of a different description from those in the service of the Begums, being *matchlock*, and not *swords* men. It is, therefore, manifest that the troops were not furnished by the princesses, and it seems highly probable that they did come from Lucknow; not that they were sent by the Nabob, but by some of the powerful *jaghiredars* who have uniformly avowed an aversion to the English.

It has been more than once mentioned, by some of the witnesses, my Lords, that Sabid Ally, the younger son of the Bow [younger] Begum, was deeply and criminally concerned in these transactions. Why was he, therefore, permitted to escape with impunity? To this question Sir Elijah Impey gave a very satisfactory answer, when he informed us that the young man was miserably poor, and a bankrupt. Here is a complete solution of the enigma. There never enters into the mind of Mr. Hastings a suspicion of treason where there is no *treasure!* Sabid Ally found, therefore, protection in his poverty, and safety in his insolvency. My Lords, the political sagacity of Mr. Hastings exhibits the converse of the doctrine which the experience of history has established. Hitherto it has generally been deemed that the possession of property attaches a person to the country which contains it, and makes him cautious how he hazards any enterprise which might be productive of in-

[17] This alludes to Mr. Middleton having declared, on a former occasion, that he had no memory for *military affairs*.

[18] That is, they came from the residence of the *Nabob*, not of the Begums.

novation, or draw upon him the suspicion or displeasure of government; and that, on the contrary, the needy, having no permanent stake, are always desperate, and easily seduced into commotions which promise any change; but, my Lords, the prisoner, inverting this doctrine, has, in the true spirit of rapacity and speculation which belongs to him, never failed to recognize loyalty in *want*, and to discern treason in *wealth!*

Proofs of the Begum's fidelity.

Allow me now, my Lords, to lay before you some of those proofs which we have collected of the steady friendship and good dispositions of the Begums, to the English interests. I have in my hands a letter from one of them, which I will read, complaining of the cruel and unjust suspicions that were entertained of her fidelity.[19] Your Lordships must perceive the extraordinary energy which the plain and simple language of truth gives to her representations. Her complaints are eloquence; her supplications, persuasion; her remonstrances, conviction.

Case of Captain Gordon.

I call, moreover, the attention of the court to the interference of the Bow [younger] Begum in behalf of Captain Gordon, by which his life was saved, at a moment when, if the princesses wished to strike a blow against the English, they might have done it with success. This man, whose life was thus preserved, and who, in the first burst of the natural feelings of his heart, poured forth his grateful acknowledgments of the obligation, afterward became the instrument of the destruction of his protectress. I will produce the letter wherein he thanks her for her interference, and confesses that he owes his life to her bounty.[20]

It has been asked, with an air of some triumph, why Captain Gordon was not called to the bar? Why call him to the bar? Would he not, as he has done in his affidavit, suppress the portion of testimony we require? I trust that he may never be brought to swear in this case till he becomes sensible of his guilt, and feels an ardent, contrite zeal to do justice to his benefactress, and to render her the most ample atonement for the injuries which she has sustained by his ingratitude and wickedness. The conduct of Captain Gordon, in this instance, is so astonishingly depraved, that I confess I am in some degree disposed to incredulity. I can scarcely believe it possible that, after having repeatedly acknowledged that he owed his life and liberty to her beneficent hand, he could so far forget these obligations as spontaneously, and of his own free will, to come forward, and expend a part of that breath which she had preserved, in an affidavit by which her ruin was to be effected! My knowledge of the human heart will hardly permit me to think that any rational being could deliberately commit an act of such wanton atrocity. I must imagine that there has been some scandalous deception; that, led on by Mr. Middleton, he made his deposition, ignorant to what purpose it would be applied. Every feeling of humanity recoils at the transaction viewed in any other light. It is incredible, that any intelligent person could be capable of standing up in the presence of God, and of exclaiming, "To you, my benevolent friend, the breath I now draw, next to Heaven, I owe to you. My existence is an emanation from your bounty. I am indebted to you beyond all possibility of return, and therefore my *gratitude* shall be your *destruction!*"

If, my Lords, if I am right in my conjecture, that Captain Gordon was thus seduced into the overthrow of his benefactress, I hope he will present himself at your bar, and, by stating the imposition which was practiced upon him, vindicate his own character, and that of human nature, from this foul imputation.

---

19 The following is the letter: "The disturbances of Colonel Hannay and Mr. Gordon were made a pretense for seizing my jaghire. The state of the matter is this: When Colonel Hannay was by Mr. Hastings ordered to march to Benares, during the troubles of Cheyte Sing, the Colonel, *who had plundered the whole country, was incapable of proceeding, from the union of thousands of Zemindars, who had seized this favorable opportunity.* They harassed Mr. Gordon near Junivard, and the Zemindars of that place and Acherpore opposed his march from thence, till he arrived near Saunda. As the Saunda Nutta, from its overflowing, was difficult to cross without a boat, Mr. Gordon sent to the Fouzdar (Governor) to supply him. He replied, that the boats were all in the river, but would assist him, according to orders, as soon as possible. Mr. Gordon's situation would not admit of his waiting; he forded the Nutta upon his elephant, and was hospitably received and entertained by the Fouzdar for six days. In the mean time, a letter was received by me from Colonel Hannay, desiring me to escort Mr. Gordon to Fyzabad. As my friendship for the English was always sincere, I readily complied, and sent some companies of Nejeebs to escort Mr. Gordon and all his effects to Fyzabad; where, having provided for his entertainment, I effected his junction with Colonel Hannay. The letters of thanks received from both these gentlemen, upon this occasion, are still in my possession, copies of which I gave in charge to Major Gilpin, to be delivered to Mr. Middleton, that he might forward them to the Governor General. To be brief, those who have loaded me with accusations *are now clearly convicted of falsehood*; but is it not extraordinary that, notwithstanding the justness of my cause, nobody relieves my misfortunes! My prayers have been constantly offered to Heaven for your arrival. Report has announced it, for which reason I have taken up the pen, and request you will not place implicit confidence in my accusers, but, weighing in the scale of justice *their falsehood and my representations*, you will exert your influence in putting a period to the misfortunes with which I am overwhelmed."

20 Mr. Sheridan read the following letter of Colonel Gordon: "Begum Saib, of exalted dignity and generosity, &c., whom God preserve."

After presenting the usual compliments of servitude, &c., in the customary manner, my address is presented. "Your gracious letter, in answer to the petition of your servant from Goondah, exalted me. From the contents I became unspeakably impressed with the honor it conferred. May the Almighty protect that royal purity, and bestow happiness, increase of wealth, and prosperity. *The welfare of your servant is entirely owing to your favor and benevolence, &c., &c.*"

The original letters which passed on this occasion between Captain Gordon and the Begum were transmitted by her to Mr. Middleton, for the purpose of being shown to the Governor General. These letters Mr. Middleton endeavored to conceal. His letter-book, into which they were transcribed, is despoiled of those leaves which contained them. When questioned about them, he said that he had deposited Persian copies of the letters in the office at Lucknow, and that he did not bring translations of them with him to Calcutta, because he left the former city the very next day after receiving the originals; but, my Lords, I will boldly assert that this pretext is a *black and barefaced perjury*. It can be proved that Middleton received the letters at least a month before he departed from Lucknow. He left that city on the 17th of October, and he received them on the 20th of the preceding month. Well aware that by these documents the purity of the Begum's intentions would be made manifest; that, while accused of disaffection, their attachment was fully displayed, he, as their punishment was predetermined, found it necessary to suppress the testimonials of their innocence; but, my Lords, these letters, covered as they were by every artifice which the vilest ingenuity could devise to hide them, have been discovered, and are now bared to view by the aid of that Power to whom all creation must bend—to whom nothing, in the whole system of thought or action, is impossible; who can invigorate the arm of infancy with a giant's nerve; who can bring light out of darkness, and good out of evil; can view the confines of hidden mischief, and drag forth each minister of guilt from amid his deeds of darkness and disaster, reluctant, alas! and unrepenting, to exemplify, at least, if not atone, and to qualify any casual sufferings of innocence by the final doom of its opposite; to prove there are the never failing corrections of God, to make straight the obliquity of man!

My Lords, the prisoner, in his defense, has ascribed the benevolent interposition of the Begum in favor of Captain Gordon to her knowledge of the successes of the English. This is an imputation as ungenerous as it is false. The only success which the British troops met with at this time was that of Colonel Blair, on the third of September; but he himself acknowledged, that another victory gained at such a loss would be equal to a defeat. The reports that were circulated throughout the country, so far from being calculated to strike the princesses with awe of the English, were entirely the reverse. These were, that Mr. Hastings had been slain at Benares, and that the English had sustained the most disastrous defeats.[21]

But, my Lords, to remove every doubt from your minds, I will recur to what never fails me—the evidence of the prisoner against himself. In a letter to the council, which is on record, he confesses that, from the 22d of August to the 22d of September, he was confined in a situation of the utmost hazard; that his safety during this period was exceedingly precarious, and that the affairs of the English were generally thought to be unfavorable in the extreme. In his defense, however, Mr. Hastings has forgotten entirely these admissions. It certainly appears that the princesses demonstrated the firmness of their attachment to the British; not in the season of prosperity or triumph; not from the impulse of fear, nor the prospect of future protection; but that they, with a magnanimity almost unexampled, came forward at a moment when the hoard of collected vengeance was about to burst over our heads; when the measure of European guilt in India was completely filled by the oppressions which had just been exercised on the unfortunate Cheyte Sing; and when offended Heaven seemed, at last, to interfere to change the meek dispositions of the natives, to awaken their resentment, and to inspirit their revenge.

(2.) Charge of inducing the *jaghiredars* to resist.

(2.) On the *second* allegation, my Lords, namely, "that the Begums encouraged and aided the *jaghiredars*," I do not think it necessary to say much. It is evident, from the letters of Mr. Middleton, that no such aid was required to awaken resentments, which must, indeed, unavoidably have arisen from the nature of an affair in which so many powerful interests were involved. The *jaghires* depending were of an immense amount, and as their owners, by the resumption of them, would be at once reduced to poverty and distress, they wanted surely no new instigation to resistance. It is ridiculous to attempt to impute to the Begums, without a shadow of proof, the inspiring of sentiments which must inevitably have been excited in the breast of every *jaghiredar* by the contemplation of the injury and injustice which were intended to be done him. Reluctant to waste the time of the court, I will dismiss the discussion of this charge by appealing to your Lordships individually to determine, whether, on a proposal being made to *confiscate* your several estates (and the cases are precisely analogous), the incitements of any two ladies of this kingdom would be at all required to kindle your resentments and to rouse you to opposition?

(3.) Charge of exciting commotions in Oude. These the result of English rapacity.

(3.) The commotions, my Lords, which prevailed in Oude have also been attributed to the Begums, and constitute the *third* and remaining allegation against them. But these disorders, I confidently aver, were, on the contrary, the work of the English, which I will show by the most incontestible evidence.

They were produced by their rapacity and violence, and not by the "perfidious artifices" of these old women. To drain the province of its money, every species of cruelty, of extortion, of rapine, of stealth was employed by the emissaries of Mr. Hastings. The Nabob perceived the growing discontents among the people, and, alarmed at the consequences, endeavored, by the

[21] This alludes to the reports which went abroad after the rising of the people of Benares in favor of their Rajah Cheyte Sing against Mr. Hastings. He was, as stated in the next paragraph, in a situation of extreme hazard for a month after that event.

strongest representations, to rid his devoted country of the oppressions of its invaders, and particularly from the vulture grasp of Colonel Hannay; swearing by Mohammed that if "this tyrant were not removed he would quit the province," as a residence in it was no longer to be endured.[22] Thus this mild people suffered for a while in barren anguish and ineffectual bewailings. At length, however, in their meek bosoms, where injury never before begot resentment, nor despair aroused to courage, increased oppression had its effect. They determined on resistance. They collected round their implacable foe [Colonel Hannay], and had nearly sacrificed him. So deeply were they impressed with the sense of their wrongs, that they would not even accept of life from their oppressors. They threw themselves upon the swords of the soldiery, and sought death as the only termination of their sorrows and persecutions. Of a people thus injured and thus feeling, it is an audacious fallacy to attribute their conduct to any external impulse. My Lords, the true cause of it is to be traced to the first-born principles of man. It grows with his growth; it strengthens with his strength. It teaches him to understand; it enables him to feel. For where there is human fate, can there be a penury of human feeling? Where there is injury, will there not be resentment? Is not despair to be followed by courage? The God of battles pervades and penetrates the inmost spirit of man, and, rousing him to shake off the burden that is grievous, and the yoke that is galling, reveals the law written on his heart, and the duties and privileges of his nature.

Desolation of Oude; its causes and effects.

If, my Lords, a stranger had at this time entered the province of Oude, ignorant of what had happened since the death of Sujah Dowlah—that prince who with a savage heart had still great lines of character, and who, with all his ferocity in war, had, with a cultivating hand, preserved to his country the wealth which it derived from benignant skies and a prolific soil—if, observing the wide and general devastation of fields unclothed and brown; of vegetation burned up and extinguished; of villages depopulated and in ruin; of temples unroofed and perishing; of reservoirs broken down and dry, this stranger should ask, "what has thus laid waste this beautiful and opulent land; what monstrous madness has ravaged with wide-spread war; what desolating foreign foe; what civil discords; what disputed succession; what religious zeal; what fabled monster has stalked abroad, and, with malice and mortal enmity to man, withered by the grasp of death every growth of nature and humanity, all means of delight, and each original, simple principle of bare existence?" the answer would have been, not one of these causes! No wars have ravaged these lands and depopulated these villages! No desolating foreign foe! No domestic broils! No disputed succession! No religious, superserviceable zeal! No poisonous monster! No affliction of Providence, which, while it scourged us, cut off the sources of resuscitation! No! This damp of death is the mere effusion of British amity! We sink under the pressure of their support! We writhe under their perfidious gripe! They have embraced us with their protecting arms, and lo! these are the fruits of their alliance!

What then, my Lords, shall we bear to be told that, under such circumstances, the exasperated feelings of a whole people, thus spurred on to clamor and resistance, were excited by the poor and feeble influence of the Begums? After hearing the description given by an eye-witness [Colonel Naylor, successor of Hannay][23] of the paroxysm of fever and delirium into which despair threw the natives when on the banks of the polluted Ganges, panting for breath, they tore more widely open the lips of their gaping wounds, to accelerate their dissolution; and while their blood was issuing, presented their ghastly eyes to heaven, breathing their last and fervent prayer that the dry earth might not be suffered to drink their blood, but that it might rise up to the throne of God, and rouse the eternal Providence to avenge the wrongs of their country—will it be said that all this was brought about by the incantations of these Begums in their secluded Zenana; or that they could inspire this enthusiasm and this despair into the breasts of a people who felt no grievance, and had suffered no torture? What motive, then, could have such influence in their bosom? What motive! That which nature, the common parent, plants in the bosom of man; and which, though it may be less active in the Indian than in the Englishman, is still congenial with, and makes a part of his being. That feeling which tells him that man was never made to be the property of man; but that, when in the pride and insolence of power, one human creature dares to tyrannize over another, it is a power usurped, and resistance is a duty. That principle which tells him that resistance to power usurped is not merely a duty which he owes to himself and to his neighbor, but a duty which he owes to his God, in asserting and maintaining the rank which he gave him in his creation. That principle which neither the rudeness of ignorance can stifle, nor the enervation of refinement extinguish! That principle which makes it base for a man to suffer when he ought to act; which, tending to preserve to the species the

[22] When Colonel Hannay entered the service of the Nabob, being sent there by Hastings with British troops, he was a man in debt. He was described by one of the witnesses as "involved in his circumstances." At the end of three years, he was understood to have realized a fortune of *three hundred thousand pounds sterling!* See Minutes of Evidence, p. 390, 391. It is not wonderful that such a man should have awakened the resistance so eloquently described in this and the next paragraph.

[23] This is the most graphic and powerful description to be found in the speeches of Mr. Sheridan. It is almost entirely free from those "faults of taste" which were so common in his most labored passages.

original designations of Providence, spurns at the arrogant distinctions of man, and indicates the independent quality of his race.

I trust, now, that your Lordships can feel no hesitation in acquitting the unfortunate princesses of this allegation. But though the innocence of the Begums may be confessed, it does not necessarily follow, I am ready to allow, that the prisoner must be guilty. There is a possibility that he might have been deluded by others, and incautiously led into a false conclusion. If this be proved, my Lords, I will cheerfully abandon the present charge. But if, on the other hand, it shall appear, as I am confident it will, that in his subsequent conduct there was a mysterious concealment denoting conscious guilt; if all his narrations of the business be found marked with inconsistency and contradiction, there can be, I think, a doubt no longer entertained of his criminality.

Mr. Hastings never believed the Begums to be guilty.

It will be easy, my Lords, to prove that such concealment was actually practiced. From the month of September, in which the seizure of the treasures took place, till the succeeding January, no intimation whatever was given of it by Mr. Hastings to the council at Calcutta. But, my Lords, look at the mode in which this concealment is attempted to be evaded. The first pretext is, *the want of leisure!* Contemptible falsehood! He could amuse his fancy at this juncture with the composition of Eastern tales, but to give an account of a rebellion which convulsed an empire, or of his acquiring so large an amount of treasure, he had *no time!*

Proved by his concealment and false pretexts.

The second pretext is, that all communication between Calcutta and Fyzabad was cut off. This is no less untrue. By comparing dates, it will be seen that letters, now in our possession, passed at this period between Mr. Middleton and the prisoner. Even Sir Elijah Impey has unguardedly declared that the road leading from the one city to the other was as clear from interruption as that between London and any of the neighboring villages. So satisfied am I, indeed, on this point, that I am willing to lay aside every other topic of criminality against the prisoner, and to rest this prosecution alone on the question of the validity of the reasons assigned for the concealment we have alleged. Let those, my Lords, who still retain any doubts on the subject, turn to the prisoner's narrative of his journey to Benares. They will there detect, amid a motley mixture of cant and mystery, of rhapsody and enigma, the most studious concealment.

It may, perhaps, be asked, why did Mr. Hastings use all these efforts to vail this business? Though it is not strictly incumbent on me to give an answer to the question, yet I will say that he had obviously a reason for it. Looking to the natural effect of deep injuries on the human mind, he thought that oppression must beget resistance. The attempt which the Begums might be driven to make in their own defense, though really the *effect*, he was determined to represent as the *cause* of his proceedings. He was here only repeating the experiment which he so successfully performed in the case of Cheyte Sing. Even when disappointed in those views by the natural meekness and submission of the princesses, he could not relinquish the scheme; and hence, in his letter to the court of Directors January 5th, 1782, he represents the *subsequent* disturbances in Oude as the cause of the violent measures he had adopted *two months* previous to the existence of these disturbances! He there congratulates his masters on the seizure of the treasures which he declares, by the law of Mohammed, were the property of Asoph ul Dowlah.

These accounted for.

My Lords, the prisoner more than once assured the House of Commons that the inhabitants of Asia believed him to be a preternatural being, gifted with good fortune or the peculiar favorite of Heaven; and that Providence never failed to take up and carry, by wise, but hidden means, every project of his to its destined end. Thus, in his blasphemous and vulgar puritanical jargon, did Mr. Hastings libel the course of Providence. Thus, according to him, when his corruptions and briberies were on the eve of exposure, Providence inspired the heart of Nuncomar to commit a low, base crime, in order to save him from ruin.[24] Thus, also, in his attempts on Cheyte Sing, and his plunder of the Begums, Providence stepped forth, and inspired the one with resistance and the other with rebellion, to forward his purposes! Thus, my Lords, did he arrogantly represent himself as a man not only the favorite of Providence, but as one for whose sake Providence departed from the eternal course of its own wise dispensations, to assist his administration by the elaboration of all that is deleterious and ill; *heaven-born forgeries—inspired treasons--Providential rebellions!* arraigning that Providence

Mr. Hastings' pretense of a special providence in his favor.

"Whose works are goodness, and whose ways are right."

[24] Nuncomar, as stated on a preceding page, was a Hindoo of high rank, who accused Hastings to the Council at Calcutta of having put up offices to sale, and of receiving bribes for allowing offenders to escape punishment. The accusation was malicious, and possibly false; but a majority of the Council, who were unfriendly to Hastings, declared it to be fully sustained. At this moment, Nuncomar was charged, through Hastings' instrumentality, with having *forged a bond*. For this offense, which, among the natives of India, would hardly be considered criminal, Hastings had him arraigned, not before a Hindoo court, but before the Supreme Court of Bengal, over which Impey presided as Chief Justice. Here, to the astonishment of all, Nuncomar was sentenced to die, under the laws of England, and not of his own country. Every one expected that Impey would have respited Nuncomar, and that Hastings would have been satisfied with his conviction, without demanding his blood. The Council interposed for the deliverance of Nuncomar in the most energetic manner, but Hastings was inflexible. Impey, the instrument of his vengeance, refused all delay, and Nuncomar was hung like a felon, to the horror of all India.

Want of consistency in his falsehood and crimes.

It does undoubtedly, my Lords, bear a strange appearance, that a man of reputed ability, like the prisoner, even when acting wrongly, should have recourse to so many bungling artifices, and spread so thin a vail over his deceptions. But those who are really surprised at this circumstance must have attended very little to the demeanor of Mr. Hastings. Through the whole of his defense upon this charge, sensible that truth would undo him, he rests his hopes on falsehood. Observing this rule, he has drawn together a set of falsehoods without consistency, and without connection; not knowing, or not remembering, that there is nothing which requires so much care in the fabrication, as a system of lies. The series must be regular and unbroken; but his falsehoods are eternally at variance, and demolish one another. Indeed, in all his conduct, he seems to be actuated but by one principle, to do things contrary to the established form. This architect militates against the first principles of the art. He begins with the frieze and the capital, and lays the base of the column at the top. Thus turning his edifice upside down, he plumes himself upon the novelty of his idea, till it comes tumbling about his ears. Rising from these ruins, he is soon found rearing a similar structure. He delights in difficulties, and disdains a plain and secure foundation. He loves, on the contrary, to build on a precipice, and to encamp on a mine. Inured to falls, he fears not danger. Frequent defeats have given him a hardihood, without impressing a sense of disgrace.

Some men may unite prudence and crime.

It was once, my Lords, a maxim, as much admitted in the practice of common life as in the schools of philosophy, that where Heaven is inclined to destroy, it begins with frenzying the intellect. "Quem Deus vult perdere prius dementat." This doctrine the right honorable manager (Mr. Burke), who opened generally to your Lordships the articles of impeachment, still farther extended. He declared that the co-existence of *vice* and *prudence* was incompatible; that the vicious man, being deprived of his best energies, and curtailed in his proportion of understanding, was left with such a short-sighted penetration as could lay no claim to *prudence*. This is the sentiment of my noble and exalted friend, whose name I can never mention but with respect and admiration due to his virtue and talents; whose proud disdain of vice can only be equaled by the ability with which he exposes and controls it; to whom I look up with homage; whose genius is commensurate with philanthropy; whose memory will stretch itself beyond the fleeting objects of any little partial shuffling—through the whole wide range of human knowledge and honorable aspiration after good—as large as the system which forms life—as lasting as those objects which adorn it; but in this sentiment, so honorable to my friend, I can not implicitly agree.[25] If the true definition of prudence be the successful management and conduct of a purpose to its end, I can at once bring instances into view where this species of prudence belonged to minds distinguished by the atrocity of their actions. When I survey the history of a Philip of Macedon, of a Cesar, of a Cromwell, I perceive great guilt successfully conducted, if not by legitimate discretion, at least by a consummate *craft*, or by an all-commanding sagacity, productive of precisely the same effects. These, however, I confess, were isolated characters, who left the vice they dared to follow either in the state of dependent vassalage, or involved it in destruction. Such is the perpetual law of nature, that virtue, whether placed in a circle more contracted or enlarged, moves with sweet concert. There is no dissonance to jar; no asperity to divide; and that harmony which makes its felicity at the same time constitutes its protection. Of vice, on the contrary, the parts are disunited, and each in barbarous language clamors for its pre-eminence. It is a scene where, though one domineering passion may have sway, the others still press forward with their dissonant claims; and, in the moral world, effects waiting on their causes, the discord which results, of course, insures defeat.

Not so with Mr. Hastings.

In this way, my Lords, I believe the failure of Mr. Hastings is to be explained, and such, I trust, will be the fate of all who shall emulate his character or his conduct. The doctrine of my friend, from what I have said, can, therefore, hold only in those minds which can not be satisfied with the indulgence of a single crime; where, instead of one base master passion having the complete sway, to which all the faculties are subject, and on which alone the mind is bent, there is a combustion and rivalry among a number of passions yet baser, when pride, vanity, avarice, lust of power, cruelty, all at once actuate the human soul and distract its functions; all of them at once filling their several spaces, some in their larger, some in their more contracted orbits; all of them struggling for pre-eminence, and each counteracting the other. In such a mind, undoubtedly, great crimes can never be accompanied by prudence. There is a fortunate disability, occasioned by the contention, that rescues the human species from the villainy of the intention. Such is the original denunciation of nature. Not so with the nobler passions. In the breast where they reside, the harmony is never interrupted by the number. A perfect and substantial agreement gives an accession of vigor to each, and, spreading their influence in every direction, like the divine intelligence and benignity from which they flow, they ascertain it to the individual by which they are possessed, and communicate it to the society of which he is a member.

The Nabob his mere vassal.

My Lords, I shall now revert again to the claims made on the princesses of Oude. The counsel for the prisoner have labored to impress on the court the idea that the Nabob was a prince sovereignly independent,

[25] The reader will at once see the object of Mr. Sheridan in thus apparently differing from Mr. Burke. It was to arrest attention, by an ingenious turn of thought, and thus to set forth his views in stronger relief.

and in no degree subject to the control of Mr. Hastings; but, after the numberless proofs we have adduced of his being, on the contrary, a mere cipher in the hands of the Governor General, your Lordships will require of them, to create such a conviction on your minds, much more conclusive evidence than any which they have hitherto presented. I believe, both as regards the resumption of the *jaghires*, and especially the seizure of the treasures, they will find it very difficult to show the independence of the prince.[26]

The seizure of the treasure not first proposed by the Nabob.

It has, my Lords, been strenuously contended on our parts, that the measure of seizing the treasures originated *with the prisoner*, and in maintenance of the position we have brought forward a chain of testimony clear, and, we think, satisfactory; but the counsel for the prisoner, on the other hand, assert with equal earnestness, that the proposition for seizing the treasures came originally from *the Nabob*. It is therefore incumbent on them to support their assertion by proof, as we have done. Certainly the best evidence of the fact would be the exhibition of the letter of the Nabob to Mr. Hastings, in which they allege the proposition was made. Why, then, is not this document, which must at once settle all disputation on the subject, produced? The truth is, there is no such letter. I peremptorily deny it, and challenge the prisoner and his counsel to produce a letter or paper containing any proposition of the kind coming immediately from the prince.

It was the result of a conspiracy set on foot by Mr. Hastings.

My Lords, the seizure of the treasures and the jaghires was the effect of a dark *conspiracy*, in which six persons were concerned. Three of the conspirators were of a higher order. These were Mr. Hastings, who may be considered as the principal and leader in this black affair; Mr. Middleton, the English resident at Lucknow; and Sir Elijah Impey. The three inferior or subordinate conspirators were, Hyder Beg Khan, the nominal minister of the Nabob, but in reality the creature of Mr. Hastings, Colonel Hannay, and Ali Ibrahim Khan.

Sir Elijah Impey was intrusted by Mr. Hastings to carry his orders to Mr. Middleton, and to concert with him the means of carrying them into execution. The Chief Justice, my Lords, being a principal actor in the whole of this iniquitous business, it will be necessary to take notice of some parts of the evidence which he has delivered upon oath at your Lordships' bar.

Exposure, in passing, of Impey's subterfuges.

When asked, what became of the Persian affidavit, sworn before him, after he had delivered them to Mr. Hastings, he replied that *he really did not know!* He was also asked, if he had them translated, or knew of their having been translated, or had any conversation with Mr. Hastings on the subject of the affidavits. He replied, "that he knew nothing at all of their having been translated, and that he had no conversation whatever with Mr. Hastings on the subject of the affidavits after he had delivered them to him." He was next asked whether he did not think it a little singular that he should not have held any conversation with the Governor General on a subject of so much moment as that of the affidavits which he had taken. His answer was, that he did not think it singular, because he left Chunar the very day after he delivered the affidavits to Mr. Hastings. By this answer the witness certainly meant it should be understood that when he quitted Chunar he left the Governor General behind him; but it appears, from letters written by the witness himself, and which we have already laid before the court, that he arrived at Chunar on the 1st of December, 1781; that he then began to take the affidavits, and, when completed, he and Mr. Hastings *left Chunar in company*, and set out on the road to Benares; and that, after being together from the first to the sixth of the month, the former took leave of the latter, and proceeded on his journey to Calcutta. Here, then, my Lords, we detect a subterfuge artfully contrived to draw you into a false conclusion! There is also another part of the witness's evidence which is entitled to as little credit. He has sworn that *he knew nothing of the Persian affidavits having been translated.* Now, my Lords, we formerly produced a letter from Major William Davy, the confidential secretary and Persian translator to the Governor General, in which he states that he made an affidavit before Sir Elijah Impey at Buxar, on the 12th of December, just six days after Sir Elijah parted from Mr. Hastings, swearing that the papers annexed to the affidavits were *faithful translations of the Persian affidavits!* What shall we say, my Lords, of such testimony? I will make only one remark upon it, which I shall borrow from an illustrious man; "that no one could tell where to look for truth, if it could not be found on the *judgment seat*, or know what to credit, if the affirmation of a *judge* was not to be trusted."

Impey sent as an agent to induce the Nabob to propose, as from *himself*, to seize the treasures.

I have, my Lords, before observed, that the Chief Justice was intrusted by the prisoner to concert with Mr. Middleton the means of carrying into execution the order of which he was the bearer from the Governor General to the resident. These orders do not appear any where in writing, but your Lordships are acquainted with their purport. The court must recollect that Mr. Middleton was instructed by them to persuade the Nabob to propose, as from *himself* to Mr. Hastings, the seizure of the Begum's treasures. That this was really so, appears undeniably as well from the tenor of Mr. Middleton's letter on the subject, as from the prisoner's account of the business in his defense. Evidently, Mr. Hastings was on this occasion hobbled by difficulties which put all his ingenuity into requisition. He was aware that it must seem extraordinary, that at the very moment he

[26] This claim is directly in the face of Mr. Hastings' own statement, in the Minutes of Consultation, where he says that Asoph ul Dowlah, by the treaty made upon the death of his father, "became eventually and *necessarily* the vassal of the Company." See quotation in Mill, vol. iv., 268.

was confiscating the property of the Begums, on the plea of their treasonable machinations, he should stipulate that an annual allowance equal almost to the produce of that property should be secured to them. Though he had accused the princesses of rebellion, by which, of course, their treasures were forfeited to the state, yet he was reluctant to appear as the principal in seizing them.

This shows Mr. Hastings knew the seizure to be unjust.

Do not, my Lords, these embarrassments prove that the prisoner was sensible of the injustice of his proceedings? *If the princesses were in rebellion, there could be no ground for his demurring to seize their property.* The consciousness of their innocence could alone, therefore, make him timid and irresolute. To get rid at once of his difficulties, he resorts to the expedient which I have before stated, namely, of giving directions to Sir Elijah Impey that Mr. Middleton should urge the Nabob to propose, as from himself, the seizure of the treasures. My Lords, the unhappy prince, without a will of his own, consented to make the proposal, as an alternative for the resumption of the *jaghires;* a measure to which he had the most unconquerable reluctance. Mr. Hastings, as it were to indulge the Nabob, agreed to the proposal; rejoicing, at the same time, that his scheme had proved so far successful; for he thought this proposal, coming from the Nabob, would free him from the odium of so unpopular a plundering. But the artifice was too shallow; and your Lordships are now able to trace the measure to its source. The court will see from the evidence that Mr. Hastings suggested it to Sir Elijah Impey, that Sir Elijah Impey might suggest it to Middleton, that Middleton might suggest it to the Nabob, *that his Highness might suggest it to Mr. Hastings;* and thus the suggestion returned to the place from which it had originally set out!

Confirmation from a letter of Middleton.

One single passage of a letter, written by Middleton to Mr. Hastings on the 2d of December, 1781, will make this point as clear as day. He informs the Governor General that "the Nabob, wishing to evade the measure of resuming the *jaghires*, had sent him a message to the following purport: that if the measure proposed was intended to procure the payment of the balance due to the Company, he could better and more expeditiously effect that object by taking from his mother the treasures of his father, which he asserted to be in her hands, and to which he claimed a right, founded on the laws of the Koran; and that it would be sufficient that he [Mr. Hastings] would hint his opinion upon it, *without giving a formal sanction* to the measure proposed." Mr. Middleton added, "the resumption of the *jaghires* it is necessary to suspend till I have your answer to this letter."

In the first place, it is clear from this letter that, though the Nabob consented to make the desired proposal for seizing the treasures, it was only as an alternative; for it never entered into his head both to seize the treasures and resume the *jaghires.* The former measure he wished to substitute in the room of the latter, and by no means to couple them together. But Mr. Hastings was too nice a reasoner for the prince. He insisted that one measure should be carried into execution, because the Nabob had proposed it; and the other, because he himself determined upon it.

It also appears that the Nabob was *taught* to plead his right to the treasures, as founded upon the laws of the Koran. Not a word was said about the guarantee and treaty which had *barred* that right, whatever it might have been! But, my Lords, if all Mr. Hastings would have the world believe is true, he [the Nabob] had still a much better title—one against which the treaty and guarantee could not be raised, and this was the *treason* of the Begums, by which they forfeited all their property to the state, and every claim upon English protection. On this right by forfeiture, the Nabob, however, was silent. Being a stranger to the rebellion, and to the treason of his parents, he was reduced to the necessity of reviving a right under the laws of the Koran, which the treaty and guarantee had forever extinguished.

This letter, moreover, contains this remarkable expression, namely, "that it would be sufficient to hint his [Mr. Hastings'] *opinion upon it, without giving a formal sanction to the measure proposed.*" Why this caution? If the Begums were guilty of treason, why should he be fearful of declaring to the world that it was not the practice of the English to protect rebellious subjects, and prevent their injured sovereigns from proceeding against them according to law?—that he considered the treaty and guarantee, by which the Begums held their property, as no longer binding upon the English government, who consequently could have no farther right to interfere between the Nabob and his rebellious parents, but must leave him at liberty to punish or forgive them as he should think fit? But, my Lords, instead of holding this language, which manliness and conscious integrity would have dictated, had he been convinced of the guilt of the Begums, Mr. Hastings wished to derive all possible advantage from *active* measures against them, and at the same time so far to save appearances, as that he might be thought to be *passive* in the affair.

Letters and papers suppressed which might afford other proof.

My Lords, in another part of the same letter, Mr. Middleton informs the Governor General "that he sent him, at the same time, a letter from the Nabob on the subject of seizing the treasures." This letter has been suppressed. I challenge the counsel for the prisoner to produce it, or to account satisfactorily to your Lordships for its not having been entered upon the Company's records. Nor is this, my Lords, the only suppression of which we have reason to complain. The affidavit of Goulass Roy, who lived at Fyzabad, the residence of the Begums, and who was known to be their enemy, is also suppressed. No person could be so well informed of their guilt, if they had been guilty, as Goulass Roy, who resided upon the spot where levies were said to have been made for Cheyte Sing by their order. If, therefore, his testimony had not destroyed the charge of a rebellion on the part of the Begums, there is no doubt but it would have been carefully preserved. The information of Mr. Scott has, moreover, been withheld from us. This gentleman lived unmolested at Taunda, where Sumshire Khan commanded for the Begums, and where he carried on an extensive manufacture without the least hinderance from this supposed disaffected governor. Mr. Scott was at Taunda too when it was said that the Governor pointed the guns of the fort upon Captain Gordan's party. If this circumstance, my Lords, did really happen, Mr. Scott must have heard of it, as he was himself at the time under the protection of those very guns. Why, then, is not the examination of this gentleman produced? I believe your Lordships are satisfied that, if it had supported the allegations against Sumshire Khan, it would have been canceled.

Middleton not perhaps fully confided in by Mr. Hastings.

It is not clear to me, my Lords, that, as servile a tool as Mr. Middleton was, the prisoner intrusted him with *every* part of his intentions throughout the business of the Begums. He certainly mistrusted, or pretended to mistrust him, in his proceedings relative to the resumption of the *jaghires*. When it began to be rumored abroad that terms so favorable to the Nabob as he obtained in the treaty of Chunar—by which Mr. Hastings consented to withdraw the temporary brigade, and to remove the English gentlemen from Oude—would never have been granted, if the Nabob had not bribed the parties concerned in the negotiation to betray the interests of the Company, Mr. Hastings *confirmed* the report by actually charging Mr. Middleton and his assistant resident, Mr. Johnson, with having accepted of bribes. They both joined in the most solemn assurances of their innocence, and called God to witness the truth of their declarations. Mr. Hastings, after this, appeared satisfied; possibly the consciousness that he had in his own pocket the only bribe which was given on the occasion, the £100,000, might have made him the less earnest in prosecuting any farther inquiry into the business.

The instructions given him not always committed to writing.

A passage in a letter from Mr. Hastings shows that he did not think proper to commit to writing all the orders which he wished Mr. Middleton to execute; for there Mr. Hastings expresses his doubts of the resident's "firmness and activity; and, above all, of his *recollection* of his instructions and their importance; and said, that if he, Mr. Middleton, could not rely on his own power, and the means he possessed for performing those services, he would *free him from the charge*, and proceed to Lucknow and undertake it himself." My Lords, you must presume that the instructions here alluded to were *verbal;* for had they been written, there could be no danger of their being forgot. I call upon the counsel to state the nature of those instructions, which were deemed of so much importance, that the Governor was so greatly afraid Mr. Middleton would not recollect them, and which, nevertheless, *he did not dare to commit to writing*.

This accounted for by the fact that Middleton dreaded to resume the *jaghires*.

To make your Lordships understand some other expressions in the above passage, I must recall to your memory, that it has appeared in evidence that Mr. Middleton had a strong objection to the resumption of the *jaghires;* which he thought a service of so much danger, that he removed Mrs. Middleton and his family when he was about to enter upon it; for he expected resistance not only from the Begums, but from the Nabob's own aumeels [agents]; who, knowing that the prince was a reluctant instrument in the hands of the English, thought they would please him by opposing a measure to which he had given his authority *against his will*. Middleton undoubtedly expected the whole country would unanimously rise against him; and therefore it was, my Lords, that he suspended the execution of the order of resumption, until he should find whether the seizure of the treasures, proposed *as an alternative*, would be accepted *as such*. The prisoner pressed him to execute the order for resuming the *jaghires*, and offered to go himself upon that service if he should decline it. Middleton at last, having received a thundering letter from Mr. Hastings, by which he left him to act under "a dreadful responsibility," set out for Fyzabad.

My Lords, for all the cruelties and barbarities that were executed there, the Governor General in his narrative says, he does not hold himself answerable, because he commanded Middleton to be personally present during the whole of the transaction, until he should complete the seizing of the treasures and resuming the jaghires. But for what purpose did he order Middleton to be present? I will show, by quoting the orders verbatim: "You yourself must be personally present; you must not allow any negotiation or forbearance, but must prosecute both services, until the Begums are at the entire mercy of the Nabob." These peremptory orders, given under "a dreadful responsibility," were not issued, my Lords, as you see, for purposes of *humanity;* not that the presence of the resident might restrain the violence of the soldier; but that he might be *a watch upon the Nabob*, to steel his heart against the feelings of returning nature in his breast, and prevent the possibility of his relenting, or granting any terms to his mother and grandmother. This, truly, was the abominable motive which induced the prisoner to command the personal attendance of Middleton, and yet, my Lords, he dares to say that he is not responsible for the horrid scene which ensued. [Here Mr. Sheridan was taken ill, and retired for a while to try if in the fresh air he could recover, so as that he might conclude all he had to say upon the evidence on the second charge. Some time after, Mr. Fox informed their Lordships that Mr.

Sheridan was much better, but that he felt he was not sufficiently so to be able to do justice to the subject he had in hand. The managers therefore hoped their Lordships would be pleased to appoint a future day, on which Mr. Sheridan would finish his observations on the evidence.

Upon this, their Lordships returned to their own House, and adjourned the court.]

Middleton's letters brought to light by a breach between him and Hastings.

My Lords, permit me to remind you, that when I had last the honor of addressing you, I concluded with submitting to the court the whole of the correspondence, as far as it could be obtained, between the principal and agents in the nefarious plot carried on against the Nabob Vizier and the Begums of Oude. These letters demand of the court the most grave and deliberate attention, as containing not only a narrative of that foul and unmanly conspiracy, but also a detail of the motives and ends for which it was formed, and an exposition of the trick and quibble, the prevarication and the untruth with which it was then acted, and is now attempted to be defended. It will here be naturally inquired, with some degree of surprise, how the private correspondence which thus establishes the guilt of its authors came to light? This was owing to a mutual resentment which broke out about the middle of December, 1782, between the parties. Mr. Middleton, on the one hand, became jealous of the abatement of Mr. Hastings' confidence; and the Governor General was incensed at the tardiness with which the resident proceeded.

Cause of this breach.

From this moment, shyness and suspicion between the principal and the agent took place. Middleton hesitated about the expediency of resuming the *jaghires*, and began to doubt whether the advantage would be equal to the risk. Mr. Hastings, whether he apprehended that Middleton was retarded by any return of humanity or sentiments of justice, by any secret combination with the Begum and her son, or a wish to take the *lion's share* of the plunder to himself, was exasperated at the delay. Middleton represented the unwillingness of the Nabob to execute the measure—the low state of his finances—that his troops were mutinous for want of pay—that his life had been in danger from an insurrection among them—and that in this moment of distress he had offered one hundred thousand pounds, in addition to a like sum paid before, as an equivalent for the resumption which was demanded of him. Of this offer, however, it now appears, *the Nabob knew nothing!* In conferring an obligation, my Lords, it is sometimes contrived, from motives of delicacy, that the name of the donor shall be concealed from the person obliged; but here it was reserved for Middleton to refine this sentiment of delicacy, so as to leave the person *giving utterly ignorant of the favor he bestowed!*

Middleton accused by Hastings.

But notwithstanding these little differences and suspicions, Mr. Hastings and Mr. Middleton, on the return of the latter to Calcutta in October, 1782, lived in the same style of friendly collusion and fraudulent familiarity as formerly. After, however, an intimacy of about six months, the Governor General very unexpectedly arraigns his friend before the board at Calcutta. It was on this occasion that the prisoner, rashly for himself, but happily for the purposes of justice, produced these letters. Whatever, my Lords, was the meaning of this proceeding—whether it was a juggle to elude inquiry, or whether it was intended to make an impression at Fyzabad—whether Mr. Hastings drew up the charge, and instructed Mr. Middleton how to prepare the defense; or whether the accused composed the charge, and the accuser the defense, there is discernible in the transaction the same habitual collusion in which the parties lived, and the prosecution ended, as we have seen, in a rhapsody, a repartee, and a poetical quotation by the prosecutor!

The private letters thus brought to light, more worthy of confidence than the public ones.

The *private letters*, my Lords, are the only part of the correspondence thus providentially disclosed, which is deserving of attention. They were written in the confidence of private communication, without any motives to palliate and color facts, or to mislead. The counsel for the prisoner have, however, chosen to rely on the *public* correspondence, prepared, as appears on the very face of it, for the concealment of fraud and the purpose of deception. They, for example, dwelt on a letter from Mr. Middleton, dated December, 1781, which intimates some supposed contumacy of the Begums; and this they thought countenanced the proceedings which afterward took place, and particularly the resumption of the jaghires; but, my Lords, you can not have forgotten, that both Sir Elijah Impey and Mr. Middleton declared, in their examination at your bar, that the letter was totally false. Another letter, which mentions "the determination of the Nabob to resume the *jaghires*," was also dwelt upon with great emphasis; but it is in evidence that the Nabob, on the contrary, could not, by any means, be induced to sanction the measure; that it was not, indeed, till Mr. Middleton had actually issued his own *Perwannas* [warrants] for the collection of the rents, that the Prince, to avoid a state of the lowest degradation, consented to give it the appearance of his act.

In the same letter, the resistance of the Begums to the seizure of their treasures is noticed as an instance of *female levity*, as if their defense of the property assigned for their subsistence was a matter of censure, or that they merited a reproof for feminine lightness, because they urged an objection to being *starved!*

The opposition, in short, my Lords, which *was expected* from the princesses, was looked to as a justification of the proceedings which afterward happened. There is not, in the *private* letters, the slightest intimation of the anterior rebellion, which by prudent *after-thought* was so greatly magnified. There is not a syllable of those dangerous machinations which were to dethrone the Nabob, nor of those sanguinary artifices by which the English were to be extirpated. It is indeed said, that if such measures were rigorously pursued, as had been set on foot, the people might be driven from murmurs to resistance, and rise up in arms against their oppressors.

Where, then, my Lords, is the proof of this mighty rebellion? It is contained alone, where it is natural to expect it, in the *fabricated* correspondence between Middleton and Hastings, and in the affidavits collected by Sir Elijah Impey!

The gravity of the business on which the Chief Justice was employed on this occasion, contrasted with the vivacity, the rapidity, and celerity of his movements, is exceedingly curious. At one moment he appeared in Oude, at another in Chunar, at a third in Benares, procuring testimony, and in every quarter exclaiming, like Hamlet's Ghost, "Swear!" To him might also have been applied the words of Hamlet to the Ghost, "What, Truepenny! are you there?"[27] But the similitude goes no farther. He was never heard to give the injunction,

> "Taint not thy mind, nor let thy soul contrive
> Against thy *mother* aught!"[28]

Resumption of the *jaghires*, and seizure of the Begums' treasures.

V. It is, my Lords, in some degree worthy of your observation, that not one of the private letters of Mr. Hastings has at any time been disclosed. Even Middleton, when all confidence was broken between them by the production of his private correspondence at Calcutta, either feeling for his own safety, or sunk under the fascinating influence of his master, did not dare attempt a retaliation! The letters of Middleton, however, are sufficient to prove the situation of the Nabob, when pressed to the resumption of the *jaghires*. He is there described as being sometimes lost in sullen melancholy—at others, agitated beyond expression, exhibiting every mark of agonized sensibility. Even Middleton was moved by his distresses to interfere for a temporary respite, in which he might become more reconciled to the measure. "I am fully of opinion," said he, "that the despair of the Nabob must impel him to violence. I know, also, that the violence must be fatal to himself; but yet I think, that with his present feelings, he will disregard all consequences."

Reluctance of the Nabob.

Mr. Johnson, the assistant resident, also wrote to the same purpose. The words of his letter are memorable. "He thought it would require a *campaign* to execute the orders for the resumption of the *jaghires!*" A campaign against whom? Against the Nabob, our friend and ally, who had *voluntarily* given the order!! This measure, then, which we have heard contended was for his good and the good of his country, could truly be only enforced by a campaign! Such is British justice! Such is British humanity! Mr. Hastings guarantees to the allies of the Company their prosperity and his protection. The former he secures by sending an army to plunder them of their wealth and to desolate their soil. The latter produces the misery and the ruin of the protected. His is the protection which the vulture gives to the lamb, which covers while it devours its prey; which, stretching its baleful pinions and hovering in mid air, disperses the kites and lesser birds of prey, and saves the innocent and helpless victim from all talons but its own.

Want of principle displayed in the correspondence between Hastings and his agents.

It is curious, my Lords, to remark, that in the correspondence of these creatures of Mr. Hastings, and in their earnest endeavors to dissuade him from the resumption of the *jaghires*, not a word is mentioned of the measure being contrary to honor—to faith; derogatory to national character; unmanly or unprincipled. Knowing the man to whom they were writing, their only arguments were, that it was contrary to *policy* and to *expediency*. Not one word do they mention of the just claims which the Nabob had to the gratitude and friendship of the English. Not one syllable of the treaty by which we were bound to protect him. Not one syllable of the relation which subsisted between him and the princesses they were about to plunder. Not one syllable is hinted of justice or mercy. All which they addressed to him was the apprehension that the money to be procured would not be worth the danger and labor with which it must be attended. There is nothing, my Lords, to be found in the history of human turpitude; nothing in the nervous delineations and penetrating brevity of Tacitus; nothing in the luminous and luxuriant pages of Gibbon, or of any other historian, dead or living, who, searching into measures and characters with the rigor of truth, presents to our abhorrence depravity in its blackest shapes, which can equal, in the grossness of the guilt, or in the hardness of heart with which it was conducted, or in low and groveling motives, the acts and character of the prisoner.[29] It was he who, in the base desire of stripping two helpless women, could stir the son to rise up in vengeance against them; who, when that son had certain touches of nature in his breast, certain feelings of an

[27] *Ghost* (from beneath the stage). Swear!
Hamlet. Ah ha, boy, say'st thou so? Art thou there, Truepenny?—*Shakspeare's Hamlet,* Act I., scene 5.

[28] This is the instruction of the Ghost to Hamlet:

> But howsoever thou pursuest this act,
> Taint not thy mind, nor let thy soul contrive
> Against thy mother aught. Leave that to Heaven!
> *Hamlet,* Act I., scene 5.

[29] Mr. Gibbon was present when this compliment was paid to his history, and considered it sufficiently important to be noticed in his Memoir of himself. "Before my departure from England," he says, "I was present at the august spectacle of Mr. Hastings' trial, in Westminster Hall. It is not my province to absolve or condemn the Governor of India, but Mr. Sheridan's eloquence demanded my applause; nor could I hear without emotion the personal compliment which he paid me in the presence of the British nation."

One of Sheridan's Whig friends, who was scandalized by this allusion to the Tory historian, asked the orator, when he sat down, how he came to compliment Gibbon with the epithet "luminous." Sheridan, whose love of fun never deserted him under any circumstances, instantly replied, in a half-whisper, "I said *voluminous*."

awakened conscience, could accuse him of entertaining peevish objections to the plunder and sacrifice of his mother; who, having finally divested him of all thought, all reflection, all memory, all conscience, all tenderness and duty as a son, all dignity as a monarch; having destroyed his character and depopulated his country, at length brought him to violate the dearest ties of nature, in countenancing the destruction of his parents. This crime, I say, has no parallel or prototype in the Old World or the New, from the day of original sin to the present hour. The victims of his oppression were confessedly destitute of all power to resist their oppressors. But their debility, which from other bosoms would have claimed some compassion, at least with respect to the mode of suffering, with him only excited the ingenuity of torture. Even when every feeling of the Nabob was subdued; when, as we have seen, my Lords, nature made a last, lingering, feeble stand within his breast; even then, that cold spirit of malignity, with which his doom was fixed, returned with double rigor and sharper acrimony to its purpose, and compelled the child to inflict on the parent that destruction of which he was himself reserved to be the final victim.

Great as is this climax, in which, my Lords, I thought the pinnacle of guilt was attained, there is yet something still more transcendently flagitious. I particularly allude to his [Hastings'] infamous letter, falsely dated the 15th of February, 1782, in which, at the very moment that he had given the order for the entire destruction of the Begums, and for the resumption of the *jaghires*, he expresses to the Nabob the warm and lively interest which he took in his welfare; the sincerity and ardor of his friendship; and that, though his presence was eminently wanted at Calcutta, he could not refrain from coming to his assistance, and that in the mean time he had sent four regiments to his aid; so deliberate and cool, so hypocritical and insinuating, is the villainy of this man! What heart is not exasperated by the malignity of a treachery so barefaced and dispassionate? At length, however, the Nabob was on his guard. He could not be deceived by this mask. The offer of the four regiments developed to him the object of Mr. Hastings. He perceived the dagger bunglingly concealed in the hand, which was treacherously extended as if to his assistance. From this moment the last faint ray of hope expired in his bosom. We accordingly find no further confidence of the Nabob in the prisoner. Mr. Middleton now swayed his iron scepter without control. The *jaghires* were seized. Every measure was carried. The Nabob, mortified, humbled, and degraded, sunk into insignificance and contempt. This letter was sent at the very time when the troops surrounded the walls of Fyzabad; and then began a scene of horrors, which, if I wished to inflame your Lordships' feelings, I should only have occasion minutely to describe —to state the violence committed on that palace which the piety of the kingdom had raised for the retreat and seclusion of the objects of its pride and veneration! It was in these shades, rendered sacred by superstition, that innocence reposed. Here venerable age and helpless infancy found an asylum! If we look, my Lords, into the whole of this most wicked transaction, from the time when this treachery was first conceived, to that when, by a series of artifices the most execrable, it was brought to a completion, the prisoner will be seen standing aloof, indeed, but not inactive. He will be discovered reviewing his agents, rebuking at one time the pale conscience of Middleton, at another relying on the stouter villainy of Hyder Beg Cawn.[30] With all the calmness of veteran delinquency, his eye will be seen ranging through the busy prospect, piercing the darkness of subordinate guilt, and disciplining with congenial adroitness the agents of his crimes and the instruments of his cruelty.

His hypocritical letter: The seizure of the jaghires.

The feelings, my Lords, of the several parties at the time will be most properly judged of by their respective correspondence. When the Bow [younger] Begum, despairing of redress from the Nabob, addressed herself to Mr. Middleton, and reminded him of the guarantee which he had signed, she was instantly promised that the amount of her *jaghire* should be made good, though he said he could not interfere with the sovereign decision of the Nabob respecting the lands. The deluded and unfortunate woman "thanked God that Mr. Middleton was at hand for her relief." At this very instant he was directing every effort to her destruction; for he had actually written the orders which were to take the collection out of the hands of her agents! But let it not be forgotten, my Lords, when the Begum was undeceived —when she found that British faith was no protection—when she found that she should leave the country, and prayed to the God of nations not to grant his peace to those who remained behind—there was still no charge of rebellion, no recrimination made to all her reproaches for the broken faith of the English; that, when stung to madness, she asked "how long would be her reign," there was no mention of her disaffection. The stress is therefore idle, which the counsel for the prisoner have strove to lay on these expressions of an injured and enraged woman. When at last, irritated beyond bearing, she denounced infamy on the heads of her oppressors, who is there that will not say that she spoke in a *prophetic* spirit; and that what she then predicted has not, even to its last letter, been accomplished?[31] But did Mr. Middleton, even to

Effect on the Begums.

[30] This was the Nabob's minister, but a creature of Mr. Hastings.

[31] In his speech before the House of Commons, Mr. Sheridan thus remarks on Mr. Hastings' accusation against the Begums, "that they complained of the injustice that was done them."

"God of heaven! had they not a right to complain? After the violation of a solemn treaty, plundered of their property, and on the eve of the last extremity of misery, were they to be deprived of the

this violence, retort any particle of accusation? No! he sent a *jocose* reply, stating that he had received such a letter under her seal, but that, from its contents, he could not suspect it to come from her; and begged, therefore, that she would endeavor to detect the *forgery!* Thus did he add to foul injuries the vile aggravation of a *brutal jest*. Like the tiger, he showed the savageness of his nature by grinning at his prey, and fawning over the last agonies of his unfortunate victim!

Declared by Middleton to be innocent.

The letters, my Lords, were then inclosed to the Nabob, who, no more than the rest, made any attempt to justify himself by imputing any criminality to the Begums. He only sighed a hope that his conduct to his parents had drawn no shame upon his head; and declared his intention to punish, not any disaffection in the Begums, but some officious servants who had dared to foment the misunderstanding between them and himself. A letter was finally sent to Mr. Hastings, about six days before the seizure of the treasures from the Begums, declaring their innocence; and referring the Governor General, in proof of it, to Captain Gordon, whose life they had protected, and whose safety should have been their justification. This inquiry was never made. It was looked on as unnecessary, because the conviction of their innocence was too deeply impressed already.

His parental feelings contrasted with his abuse of filial piety in the Nabob.

The counsel, my Lords, in recommending an attention to the public in reference to the private letters, remarked particularly that one of the latter should not be taken in evidence, because it was evidently and abstractedly private, relating the anxieties of Mr. Middleton on account of the illness of his son. This is a singular argument indeed. The circumstance, however, undoubtedly merits strict observation, though not in the view in which it was placed by the counsel. It goes to show, that some, at least, of the persons concerned in these transactions felt the force of those ties which their efforts were directed to tear asunder; that those who could ridicule the respective attachment of a mother and a son; who could prohibit the reverence of the son to the mother; who could deny to maternal debility the protection which filial tenderness should afford, were yet sensible of the straining of those chords by which they are connected. There is something in the present business, with all that is horrible to create aversion, so vilely loathsome, as to excite disgust. It is, my Lords, surely superfluous to dwell on the sacredness of the ties which those aliens to feeling, those apostates to humanity, thus divided. In such an assembly as the one before which I speak, there is not an eye but must look reproof to this conduct, not a heart but must anticipate its condemnation. *Filial piety!* It is the primal bond of society. It is that instinctive principle which, panting for its proper good, soothes, unbidden, each sense and sensibility of man. It now quivers on every lip. It now beams from every eye. It is that gratitude which, softening under the sense of recollected good, is eager to own the vast, countless debt it never, alas! can pay, for so many long years of unceasing solicitudes, honorable self-denials, life-preserving cares. It is that part of our practice where duty drops its awe, where reverence refines into love. It asks no aid of memory. It needs not the deductions of reason. Pre-existing, paramount over all, whether moral law or human rule, few arguments can increase, and none can diminish it. It is the sacrament of our nature; not only the duty, but the indulgence of man. It is his first great privilege. It is among his last most endearing delights. It causes the bosom to glow with reverberated love. It requites the visitations of nature, and returns the blessings that have been received. It fires emotion into vital principle. It changes what was instinct into a master passion; sways all the sweetest energies of man; hangs over each vicissitude of all that must pass away; and aids the melancholy virtues in their last sad tasks of life, to cheer the languors of decrepitude and age; and

"Explore the thought, explain the aching eye!"[32]

But, my Lords, I am ashamed to consume so much of your Lordships' time in attempting to give a cold picture of this sacred impulse, when I behold so many breathing testimonies of its influence around me; when every countenance in this assembly is beaming, and erecting itself into the recognition of this universal principle!

The expressions contained in the letter of Mr. Middleton, of tender solicitude for his son, have been also mentioned, as a proof of the amiableness of his affections. I confess that they do not tend to raise his character in my estimation. Is it not rather an aggravation of his guilt, that he, who thus felt the anxieties of a parent, and who, consequently, must be sensible of the reciprocal feelings of a child, could be brought to tear asunder, and violate in others, all those dear and sacred bonds? Does it not enhance the turpitude of the transaction, that it was not the result of idiotic ignorance or brutal indifference? I aver that his guilt is increased and magnified by these considerations. His criminality would have been less had he been insensible to tenderness—less,

ultimate resource of impotent wretchedness, lamentation, and regret? Was it a crime, that they should crowd together in fluttering trepidation, like a flock of unresisting birds, on seeing the felon kite, who, having darted at one devoted bird and missed his aim, singled out a new object, and was springing on his prey with redoubled vigor in his wing, and keener vengeance in his eye?"

32 This line occurs in the beautiful passage which closes Pope's Epistle to Dr. Arbuthnot. Mr. Sheridan, in quoting it, inadvertently changed the word *asking* into *aching*, and thus lessened the finely graphic effect of the original.

Me, let the tender office long engage
To rock the cradle of reposing age,
With lenient arts extend a mother's breath,
Make languor smile, and smooth the bed of death,
Explore the thought, explain the asking eye,
And keep a while one parent from the sky!

if he had not been so thoroughly acquainted with the true quality of parental love and filial duty.

Seizure of the treasures.

The *jaghires* being seized, my Lords, the Begums were left without the smallest share of that pecuniary compensation promised by Mr. Middleton, as an equivalent for the resumption. And as tyranny and injustice, when they take the field, are always attended by their camp followers, paltry pilfering and petty insult, so in this instance, the goods taken from the princesses were sold at a mock sale at an inferior value. Even gold and jewels, to use the language of the Begums, instantly lost their value when it was known that they came from them. Their ministers were imprisoned, to extort the deficiency which this fraud occasioned; and every mean art was employed to justify a continuance of cruelty toward them. Yet this was small to the frauds of Mr. Hastings. After extorting upward of £600,000, he forbade Mr. Middleton to come to a *conclusive settlement* with the princesses. He knew that the treasons of our allies in India had their origin solely in the wants of the Company. He could not, therefore, say that the Begums were entirely innocent, until he had consulted the General Record of Crimes, *the Cash Account of Calcutta!* His prudence was fully justified by the event; for there was actually found a balance of *twenty-six lacs* more against the Begums, which £260,000 worth of treason had never been dreamed of before. "Talk not to us," said the Governor General, "of their guilt or innocence, but as it suits the Company's *credit!* We will not try them by the Code of Justinian, nor the Institutes of Timur. We will not judge them either by British laws, or their local customs! No! we will try them by the *Multiplication Table;* we will find the guilty by the *Rule of Three;* and we will condemn them according to the unerring rules of—COCKER'S *Arithmetic!*"

Justified by Mr. Hastings on the ground of policy.

My Lords, the prisoner has said in his defense, that the cruelties exercised toward the Begums were not of his order. But in another part of it he avows, "that whatever were their distresses, and whoever was the agent in the measure, it was, in his opinion, reconcilable to justice, honor, and sound policy." By the testimony of Major Scott, it appears, that though the defense of the prisoner was not drawn up by himself, yet that this paragraph he wrote with his *own proper hand.* Middleton, it seems, had confessed his share in these transactions with some degree of compunction, and solicitude as to the consequences. The prisoner observing it, cries out to him, "give me the pen, I will defend the measure as just and necessary. I will take something upon myself. Whatever part of the load you can not bear, my *unburdened* character shall assume! Your conduct I will crown with my irresistible approbation. Do you find *memory* and I will find *character*, and thus twin warriors we will go into the field, each in his proper sphere of action, and assault, repulse, and contumely shall all be set at defiance."

If I could not prove, my Lords, that those acts of Mr. Middleton were in reality the acts of Mr. Hastings, I should not trouble your Lordships by combating them; but as this part of his criminality can be incontestably ascertained, I appeal to the assembled legislators of this realm to say whether these acts were justifiable on the score of *policy*. I appeal to all the august presidents in the courts of British justice, and to all the learned ornaments of the profession, to decide whether these acts were reconcilable to *justice*. I appeal to the reverend assemblage of prelates feeling for the general interests of humanity and for the honor of the religion to which they belong, to determine whether these acts of Mr. Hastings and Mr. Middleton were such as a Christian ought to perform, or a man to avow.

Cruelties inflicted on the Begum's ministers.

My Lords, with the ministers of the Nabob [Bahar Ally Cawn and Jewar Ally Cawn] was confined in the same prison that arch rebel Sumshire Cawn, against whom so much criminality has been charged by the counsel for the prisoner. We hear, however, of no inquiry having been made concerning his treason, though so many were held respecting the *treasures* of the others. With all his guilt, he was not so far noticed as to be deprived of his *food*, to be complimented with *fetters*, or even to have the satisfaction of being *scourged*, but was *cruelly* liberated from a dungeon, and *ignominiously* let loose on his parole!

[Here Mr. Sheridan read the following order from Mr. Middleton to Lieutenant Rutledge in relation to the Begum's ministers, dated January 28, 1782:

"SIR,—When this note is delivered to you by Hoolas Roy, I have to desire that you order the two prisoners to be put *in irons, keeping them from all food, &c., agreeably to my instructions of yesterday.* NATH. MIDDLETON."]

The Begums' ministers, on the contrary, to extort from them the disclosure of the place which concealed the treasures, were, according to the evidence of Mr. Holt, after being fettered and imprisoned, led out on a scaffold, and this array of terrors proving unavailing, the *meek*-tempered Middleton, as a dernier resort, menaced them with a confinement in the fortress of Churnargar. Thus, my Lords, was a British garrison made the *climax of cruelties!* To English arms, to English officers, around whose banners humanity has ever entwined her most glorious wreath, how will this sound? It was in this fort, where the British flag was flying, that these helpless prisoners were doomed to deeper dungeons, heavier chains, and severer punishments. Where that flag was displayed which was wont to cheer the depressed, and to dilate the subdued heart of misery, these venerable but unfortunate men were fated to encounter every aggravation of horror and distress. It, moreover, appears that they were both cruelly flogged, though one was above seventy years of age. Being charged with disaffection, they vindicated their innocence—"Tell us where are the remaining treasures," was the reply. "It is only treachery to your immediate sovereigns, and you will then be fit associates for the representatives of British faith and British justice in India!" Oh Faith! Oh Justice! I conjure you by your sacred names to depart for a moment from this place, though it be your peculiar residence; nor hear your names profaned by such a sacrilegious combination as that which I am now compelled to repeat—where all the fair forms of nature and art, truth and peace, policy and honor, shrink back aghast from the deleterious shade—where all existences, nefarious and vile, have sway—where, amid the black agents on one side and Middleton with Impey on the other, the great figure of the piece—characteristic in his place, aloof and independent from the puny profligacy in his train, but far from idle and inactive, turning a malignant eye on all mischief that awaits him; the multiplied apparatus of temporizing expedients and intimidating instruments, now cringing on his prey, and fawning on his vengeance—now quickening the limping pace of craft, and forcing every stand that retiring nature can make to the heart; the attachments and the decorums of life; each emotion of tenderness and honor; and all the distinctions of national pride; with a long catalogue of crimes and aggravations beyond the reach of thought for human malignity to perpetrate or human vengeance to punish; *lower* than *perdition—blacker* than *despair!*[33]

The Begums themselves treated with great severity.

It might, my Lords, have been hoped, for the honor of the human heart, that the Begums were themselves exempted from a share in these sufferings, and that they had been wounded only through the sides of their ministers. The reverse of this, however, is the fact. Their palace was surrounded by a guard, which was withdrawn by Major Gilpin to avoid the growing resentments of the people, and replaced by Mr. Middleton, through his fears of that "dreadful responsibility" which was imposed upon him by Mr. Hastings. The women, also, of the Khord Mahal, who were not involved in the Begums' supposed crimes; who had raised no *sub-rebellion* of their own; and who, it has been proved, lived in a distinct dwelling, were causelessly implicated, nevertheless, in the same punishment. Their residence surrounded with guards, they were driven to despair by famine, and when they poured forth in sad procession, were beaten with bludgeons, and forced back by the soldiery to the scene of madness which they had quitted. These are acts, my Lords, which, when told, need no comment. I will not offer a single syllable to awaken your Lordships' feelings; but leave it to the facts which have been stated to make their own impression.[34]

Mr. Hastings responsible for the conduct of his agents.

VI. The inquiry which now only remains, my Lords, is, whether Mr. Hastings is to be answerable for the crimes committed by his agents? It has been fully proved that Mr. Middleton signed the treaty with the superior Begum in October,

[33] This apostrophe to Faith and Justice is finely conceived, and, if carried out with the simplicity and conciseness which a man like Lord Chatham would have given it, might have formed one of the most magnificent passages in our language. But it was the besetting sin of Mr. Sheridan to *overdo*. He has here marred a noble idea by overlaying it with accessories—by an accumulation of circumstances and of glaring epithets, which divert the attention from the leading thought, and thus, to a great extent, destroy the effect.

It might be a useful exercise for the student in oratory, to write out this passage in more simple and concise terms, such as we may suppose would have been used by Lord Chatham or Lord Erskine.

[34] All these statements have been confirmed by subsequent investigations; and Mr. Mill has added others connected with them, which are necessary to fill out the picture. "The Begums gave up the treasures; but the eunuchs were not yet released. More money was absolutely required, and new severities were employed. The sufferings to which they were thus exposed drew from the eunuchs the offer of an engagement for the payment of the demanded sum, which they undertook to complete within the period of one month, from their *own* credit and effects. The engagement was taken, but the confinement of the eunuchs was not relaxed; the mother and grandmother of the Nabob remained under guard; and the resident was commanded to make with them *no settlement whatsoever*. The prisoners entreated their release, declaring their inability to procure any farther sums of money while they remained in confinement. So far from any relaxation of their sufferings, higher measures of severity were enjoined. After they had lain two months in irons, the commanding officer advised a temporary release from fetters on account of their health, which was rapidly sinking; but the instructions of the resident compelled him to refuse the smallest mitigation of their torture. They were threatened with being removed to Lucknow [to the fortress of Chunargar], where they would only be subjected to severer coercion, unless they performed, without delay, what they averred themselves unable to perform. They were accordingly soon after removed to Lucknow, and cruelties inflicted upon them, of which the nature is not disclosed; of which the following letter, addressed by the assistant resident to the commanding officer of the English guard, is a disgraceful proof. 'Sir,—The Nabob having determined to inflict *corporeal punishment* upon the prisoners under your guard, this is to desire that his officers, when they come, may have free access to the prisoners, and be permitted to do with them as they shall see proper.' The women in the Zenana, in the mean while, were, at various times, deprived of food, till they were on the point of perishing for want. The rigors went on increasing till the month of December [that is, for nearly a year], when the resident, convinced by his own experience, and the representation of the officer commanding the guard by which the princesses were coerced, that every thing which force could accomplish was already performed, removed, of his own authority, the guard from the palace of the Begums, and set at liberty their ministers."—See *British India*, iv., 392-98.

Mr. Hastings is referred to by the resident throughout, as *requiring* all these severities. If any thing could add to the horror which they awaken, it is the fact that he hypocritically pretended to believe that the Nabob wished them to be inflicted, and taught the victims of his cruelty to ascribe their final release to his own clemency. The resident was directed to inform them that the Governor General was "the spring from whence they were restored to their dignity and consequence."

1778. He also acknowledged signing some others of a different date, but could not *recollect* the authority by which he did it! These treaties were recognized by Mr. Hastings, as appears by the evidence of Mr. Purling, in the year 1780. In that of October, 1778, the *jaghire* was secured, which was allotted for the support of the women in the Khord Mahal. But still the prisoner pleads that he is not accountable for the cruelties which were exercised. His is the plea which tyranny, aided by its prime minister, treachery, is always sure to set up. Mr. Middleton has attempted to strengthen this ground by endeavoring to claim the whole infamy in those transactions, and to monopolize the guilt! He dared even to aver, that he had been condemned by Mr. Hastings for the ignominious part he had acted. He dared to avow this, because Mr. Hastings was on his trial, and he thought he never would be arraigned; but in the face of this court, and before he left the bar, he was compelled to confess that it was for the *lenience*, and not the *severity* of his proceedings, that he had been reproved by the prisoner.

No excuse that he did not order these cruelties by name.

It will not, I trust, be concluded, that, because Mr. Hastings has not marked every passing shade of guilt, and because he has only given the bold outline of cruelty, he is therefore to be acquitted. It is laid down by the law of England, that law which is the perfection of reason, that a person ordering an act to be done by his agent is answerable for that act with all its consequences, "quod facit per alium, facit per se."[35] Middleton was appointed, in 1777, the confidential agent, the *second self* of Mr. Hastings. The Governor General ordered the measure. Even if he never saw, nor heard afterward of its consequences, he was therefore answerable for every pang that was inflicted, and for all the blood that was shed. But he did hear, and that instantly, of the whole. He wrote to accuse Middleton of forbearance and of neglect! He commanded him to work upon the hopes and fears of the princesses, and to leave no means untried, until, to speak his own language, which was better suited to the banditti of a cavern, "he obtained possession of the secret hoards of the old ladies." He would not allow even of a delay of two days to smooth the compelled approaches of a son to his mother, on this occasion! His orders were peremptory. After this, my Lords, can it be said that the prisoner was ignorant of the acts, or not culpable for their consequences? It is true, he did not direct the guards, the famine, and the bludgeons; he did not weigh the fetters, nor number the lashes to be inflicted on his victims; but yet he is just as guilty as if he had borne an active and personal share in each transaction. It is as if he had commanded that the heart should be torn from the bosom, and enjoined that no blood should follow. He is in the same degree accountable to the *law*, to his *country*, to his *conscience*, and to his God!

His measures not chargeable on the council, who were deceived.

The prisoner has endeavored also to get rid of a part of his guilt, by observing that he was but one of the supreme council, and that all the rest had sanctioned those transactions with their approbation. Even if it were true that others did participate in the guilt, it can not tend to diminish his criminality. But the fact is, that the council erred in nothing so much as in a reprehensible credulity given to the declarations of the Governor General. They knew not a word of those transactions until they were finally concluded. It was not until the January following that they saw the mass of falsehood which had been published under the title of "Mr. Hastings' Narrative." They were, then, unaccountably duped to permit a letter to pass, dated the 29th of November, intended to seduce the Directors into a belief that they had received intelligence at that time, which was not the fact. These observations, my Lords, are not meant to cast any obloquy on the council; they undoubtedly were deceived; and the deceit practiced on them is a decided proof of his consciousness of guilt. When tired of corporeal infliction, Mr. Hastings was gratified by insulting the understanding. The coolness and reflection with which this act was managed and concerted raises its enormity and blackens its turpitude. It proves the prisoner to be that monster in nature, a *deliberate and reasoning tyrant!* Other tyrants of whom we read, such as a Nero, or a Caligula, were urged to their crimes by the impetuosity of passion. High rank disqualified them from advice, and perhaps equally prevented reflection. But in the prisoner we have a man born in a state of mediocrity; bred to mercantile life; used to system; and accustomed to regularity; who was accountable to his masters, and therefore was compelled to think and to deliberate on every part of his conduct. It is this cool deliberation, I say, which renders his crimes more horrible, and his character more atrocious.

The inquiry ordered deprecated by Mr. Hastings.

When, my Lords, the Board of Directors received the advices which Mr. Hastings thought proper to transmit, though unfurnished with any other materials to form their judgment, they expressed very strongly their doubts, and properly ordered an inquiry into the circumstances of the alleged disaffection of the Begums, declaring it, at the same time, to be a debt which was due to the honor and justice of the British nation. This inquiry, however, Mr. Hastings thought it absolutely necessary to elude. He stated to the council, in answer, "that it would revive those animosities that subsisted between the Begums and the Nabob [Asoph Dowlah], which had then subsided. If the former were inclined to appeal to a foreign jurisdiction, they were the best judges of their own feeling, and should be left to make their own complaint." All this, however, my Lords, is nothing to the magnificent paragraph which concludes this communication. "Besides," says

[35] This adage, though often quoted thus, is, properly, "*Qui* facit per alium, facit per se." He who acts through another does the thing himself.

His remarks about the Majesty of Justice.

he, "I hope it will not be a departure from official language to say, that the *Majesty of Justice* ought not to be approached without solicitation. She ought not to descend to inflame or provoke, but to withhold her judgment until she is called on to determine." What is still more astonishing, is, that Sir John Macpherson, who, though a man of sense and honor, is rather Oriental in his imagination, and not learned in the sublime and beautiful from the immortal leader of this prosecution, was caught by this bold, bombastic quibble, and joined in the same words, "that the *majesty of justice* ought not to be approached without solicitation." But, my Lords, do you, the judges of this land, and the expounders of its rightful laws, do you approve of this mockery, and call it the character of justice, which takes the *form of right* to excite wrong? No, my Lords, justice is not this halt and miserable object; it is not the ineffective bawble of an Indian pagod; it is not the portentous phantom of despair; it is not like any fabled monster, formed in the eclipse of reason, and found in some unhallowed grove of superstitious darkness and political dismay! No, my Lords. In the happy reverse of all this, I turn from the disgusting caricature to the real image! *Justice* I have now before me august and pure! The abstract idea of all that would be perfect in the spirits and the aspirings of men!—where the mind rises; where the heart expands; where the countenance is ever placid and benign; where her favorite attitude is to stoop to the unfortunate; to hear their cry and to help them; to rescue and relieve, to succor and save; majestic, from its mercy; venerable, from its utility; uplifted, without pride; firm, without obduracy; beneficent in each preference; lovely, though in her frown!

Peroration.

On that Justice I rely: deliberate and sure, abstracted from all party purpose and political speculation; not on words, but on facts. You, my Lords, who hear me, I conjure, by those rights which it is your best privilege to preserve; by that fame which it is your best pleasure to inherit; by all those feelings which refer to the first term in the series of existence, the original compact of our nature, our controlling rank in the creation. This is the call on all to administer to truth and equity, as they would satisfy the laws and satisfy themselves, with the most exalted bliss possible or conceivable for our nature; the self-approving consciousness of virtue, when the condemnation we look for will be one of the most ample mercies accomplished for mankind since the creation of the world! My Lords, I have done.

CHARLES JAMES FOX.

Charles James Fox was born on the 24th of January, 1749, and was the second son of Henry Fox (the first Lord Holland), and Lady Georgiana Lennox, daughter of the second Duke of Richmond. The father, as heretofore mentioned, was the great antagonist of Lord Chatham. He was a man of amiable feelings, but dissolute habits; poor (as the natural consequence) during most of his life, and governed in his politics by the master principle of the Walpole school—love of power for the sake of money. In 1757, he obtained the appointment of Paymaster of the Forces. This office, as then managed, afforded almost boundless opportunities for acquiring wealth; and so skillfully did he use his advantages, that within eight years he amassed a fortune of several hundred thousand pounds. A part of this money he spent in erecting a magnificent house on his estate at Kingsgate, in the Isle of Thanet. "Upon a bleak promontory," says one of his contemporaries, "projecting into the German Ocean, he constructed a splendid villa worthy of Lucullus, and adorned it with a colonnade in front of the building, such as Ictinus might have raised by order of Pericles." Here Charles spent a portion of his early years, and the estate fell to him, as a part of his patrimony, after his father's death.

Lord Holland's oldest son, Stephen, being affected with a nervous disease which impaired his faculties, Charles, who gave early proofs of extraordinary talent, became the chief object of pride and hope to the family. His father resolved to train him up for public life, and to make him what he himself had always endeavored to be, *a leader in fashionable dissipation*, and yet an *orator* and a *statesman*. He had lived in the days of Bolingbroke, and it would almost seem as if he intended to make that gifted but profligate adventurer the model of his favorite child. He began by treating him with extreme indulgence. His first maxim was, "Let nothing be done to break his spirit," and with this view he permitted no one either to contradict or to punish the boy. On the contrary, he encouraged him in the wildest whims and caprices. When about five years old, Charles was standing one day by his father as he wound up his watch, and said, "I have a great mind to break that watch." "No, Charles, that would be foolish." "But indeed I must do it—I *must*." "Nay," replied the father, "if you have so violent an inclination, I won't balk it," giving the watch to the boy, who instantly dashed it on the floor. Amid all this indulgence, however, his studies were not neglected; he showed surprising quickness in performing his tasks, and the same ready and retentive memory for which he was remarkable in after life. His father made him, from childhood, his companion and equal, encouraging him to converse freely at table, and to enter into all the questions discussed by public men who visited the family. Charles usually acquitted himself to the admiration of all, and was no doubt indebted to this early habit of thinking and speaking with freedom, for that frankness and intrepidity, amounting often to rashness, which distinguished him as an orator. Lord Holland, in the mean time, was steadily aiming at the object he had in view. He wrought upon his son's pride; he inflamed him with that love of superiority which is usually the most powerful excitement of genius; he continually pointed him to public life, as the great theater of his labors and triumphs.

Under such influences, his progress at a private school of distinction, where he was sent from childhood, was uncommonly rapid; the severe discipline pursued having the effect at once to repress his irregularities, and to turn his passion for superiority in the right direction. Here he laid the foundation of that intimate acquaintance with the classics, for which he was distinguished beyond most men of his age. He can hardly be said to have *studied* Latin or Greek after he was sixteen years old. So thoroughly was he grounded in these languages from boyhood, that he read them throughout life much as he read English, and could turn to the great authors of antiquity at any moment, not as a mental effort, but for the recreation and delight he found in their pages. This was especially true of the Greek writers, which were then less studied in England than at present. He took up Demosthenes as he did the speeches of Lord Chatham, and dwelt with the same zest on the Greek tragedians as on the plays of Shakspeare. As an instance of this, Mr. Trotter, who attended him at the close of life, mentions, that Mr. Fox once entered the room, just as he was beginning to read the Alcestis of Euripides. "You will soon find something you like," said he; "tell me when you come to it." Mr. Fox, who had not opened the book for many years, watched the reader's countenance till he came to the description of Alcestis, after praying for her children, as she mourned so pathetically over her lot, when he broke out with a kind of triumph at the effect produced by the exquisite tenderness of the passage. In the wildest excesses of his life, the classics were still his companions; in the midst of public business, he corresponded with Gilbert Wakefield on the nicest questions of Greek criticism; he usually led to the subject in conversation with literary men; and we see in the Memoirs of the poet Campbell what delight he expressed at their first interview, in finding how perfectly they agreed on some disputed points in Virgil. As an orator, he was much indebted to his study of the Greek writers for the simplicity of his taste, his severe abstinence from every thing like mere ornament, the terseness of his style, the point and stringency of his reasonings, and the all-pervading cast of *intellect* which distinguishes his speeches, even in his most vehement bursts of impassioned feeling.

Charles was next sent to Eaton, where he joined associates who were less advanced than himself in classical literature. This made him a leader in their studies and amusements. In every thing that called for eloquence, especially, whether in public meetings or private debate, or the contentions of the play-ground, he held an acknowledged pre-eminence. On such occasions, he always manifested those kind and generous feelings for which he was distinguished throughout life; espousing the cause of the weaker party, and exerting all his powers of oratory in behalf of those who were injured or neglected through prejudice or partiality for others. Never content with mediocrity, he endeavored to surpass his companions in every thing he undertook; and his habits of self-indulgence unfortunately taking a new direction, he now became a leader in all the dissipation of the school. To complete the mischief, his father took him, at the age of fourteen, on a trip to the Spa in Germany, at that time the great center of gambling for Europe; and, incredible as it may seem, he there initiated him in all the mysteries of the gaming-table! At the end of three months, Charles returned to Eaton with that fatal passion which so nearly proved his ruin for life, and immediately introduced gambling among his companions to an extent never before heard of in a public school. Under his influence, one of the boys, it is said, contracted debts of honor to the amount of *ten thousand pounds*, which he felt bound to pay when he arrived at manhood!

At the end of four years Charles was removed to Oxford, where he continued two years, still maintaining the highest rank as a scholar. Notwithstanding his love of pleasure, he must have devoted most of his time at the university to severe study; for his tutor, Dr. Newcombe, remarks, in a letter which Mr. Fox was fond of showing in after life, "Application like yours requires some intermission, and you are the only person with whom I have ever had connection, to whom I could say this." His studies were confined almost entirely to the classics and history; he paid but little attention to the mathematics, a neglect which he afterward lamented as injurious to his mental training; and perhaps for this reason he never felt the slightest interest, at this or any subsequent period, in those abstract inquiries which are designed to settle the foundations of moral and political science. Charles Butler having once mentioned to him that he had never read Smith's Wealth of Nations, "To tell you the truth," said Mr. Fox, "nor have I either. There is something in all these subjects which passes my comprehension; something so wide that I could never embrace them myself, nor find any one that did." This was one of the greatest defects in his character as a statesman. His tastes were too exclusively literary. With those habits of self-indulgence so unhappily created in childhood, he rarely did any thing but what he *liked*—he read poetry, eloquence, history, and elegant literature, because he loved them, and he read but little else. He had never learned to grapple with difficulties, except in connection with a subject which deeply interested his feelings. To secure some favorite object, he would now and then submit to severe drudgery, but he soon reverted to his old habits; and, with powers which, if rightly disciplined, would have enabled him to enter more easily than almost any man of his age into the abstrusest inquiries, he never mastered the principles of his own profession; he was not, in the strict sense of the term, a *scientific* statesman. He could discuss the Greek meters with Porson; and when a friend once insisted that a certain line in the Iliad could not be genuine because it contained measures not used by Homer, he was able, from his early recollections of the poet, instantly to adduce nearly twenty examples of the same construction. But he had no such acquaintance with the foundations of jurisprudence or the laws of trade; and at a period when the labors of Adam Smith were giving a new science to the world, and establishing the principles of political economy, the true source of the wealth of nations, he was obliged to say, "it is a subject which passes my comprehension." His deficiency in this respect was indeed less seen, because, being in opposition nearly all his life, he was rarely called to propose measures of finance; his chief business was to break down, and not to build up; yet he always felt the want of an early training in scientific investigation, correspondent to that he received in classical literature.

Mr. Fox left the University at the age of seventeen, and entered at once upon manhood. The light restraints imposed during his education being now removed, he became sole master of his own actions; and the prodigal liberality of his father supplied him with unbounded means of indulgence. For two years he traveled on the Continent, making great proficiency in Italian and French literature, and plunging, at the same time, into all the extravagance and vice of the most corrupt capitals of Europe. His father had succeeded, even beyond his intentions, in making him a 'leader in fashionable dissipation;' and he now began to fear that he had thus defeated his main design, that of training him up to be an 'orator and a statesman.' He recalled him from the Continent, and was compelled, in doing so (as afterward appeared from his banker's accounts), to pay *one hundred thousand pounds* of debt, contracted in two years! To wean him from habits which he had himself engendered, Lord Holland now resorted to the extraordinary expedient of having his son returned as a member of Parliament from Midhurst, a borough under his control, in May, 1768, being a year and eight months before he was eligible by law!

Under this return, Mr. Fox took his seat in the House, at the opening of Parliament in November, 1768. His deficiency in age was perhaps unknown; at all events, no one came forward to dispute his right. By education he was a Tory; he had distinguished himself when at Paris by some lively French verses reflecting severely on Lord Chatham; and in all his feelings, habits, and associations, he was opposed to the cause of popular liberty. He now came out a warm supporter of the Duke of Grafton, with whom his father was closely allied in politics, just after Junius's first attack on the administration of his Grace; and delivered his maiden speech, April 15th, 1769, in support of that flagrant outrage on the rights of the people, the seating of Colonel Luttrell, as a member of the House, in the place of John Wilkes. Horace Walpole speaks of him as distinguished for his "insolence" on this occasion, as well as "the infinite superiority of his parts." When Lord North came in as minister, in February, 1770, Mr. Fox, through the influence of his father, was appointed a junior Lord of the Admiralty, and three years after, one of the Lords of the Treasury. His time was now divided between politics and gambling, and he was equally devoted to both. In the House, he showed great, though irregular power as an orator, and at the gaming-table he often lost from five to ten thousand pounds at a single sitting. Though he differed from Lord North on the Royal Marriage Bill and Toleration Act, he sustained his Lordship in all his political measures, and even went at times beyond him—declaring that, for his part, he "paid no regard whatever to the voice of the people;" urging the imprisonment of Alderman Oliver and the Lord Mayor of London for the steps they took to guard the liberty of the press; and inveighing against Sergeant Glynn's motion respecting the rights of juries in cases of libel, the very rights which he himself afterward secured to them by an act of Parliament! To these views, derived from his father, and confirmed by all his present associates, he might very possibly have adhered through life, except for a breach which now took place between him and Lord North: so much do political principles depend on party connections and private interest. But his Lordship found Mr. Fox too warm and independent in his zeal; he sometimes broke the ranks and took his place as a leader; and in one instance, when Woodfall was brought to the bar of the House for making too free a use of his press, Mr. Fox proposed an amendment to a motion made by his Lordship, and actually carried it against him, under which Woodfall was committed to Newgate—a measure never contemplated by the ministry, and only calculated to injure them by its harshness. Such a violation of party discipline could not be overlooked, and it was decided at once to dismiss him. A day or two after (February 17th, 1774), as he was seated on the Treasury bench conversing with Lord North, the following note was handed him by the messenger of the House:

"Sir,—His Majesty has thought proper to order a new commission of the Treasury to be made out, *in which I do not perceive your name.* (Signed) North."

The cool contempt of this epistle shows the estimate in which he was held by the ministry, who plainly regarded him as a reckless gambler, whose friendship or hatred, notwithstanding all his talents, could never be of the least importance to any party. There was too much reason for this opinion. His father, after expending an enormous sum in paying his debts (one statement makes it £140,000 in the year 1773 alone), died about this time, leaving him an ample fortune, including his splendid estate in the Isle of Thanet; but the whole was almost immediately gone, sacrificed to the imperious passion which had taken such entire possession of his soul. Paris and London were equally witnesses to its power. The celebrated Madame Duffand, in a letter written at a somewhat later period, speaks of him and his companion, Colonel Fitzpatrick, as objects of curious speculation; but adds, in another letter—"Je ne saurais m'interesser à eux: ce sont des têtes absolument dérangées et sans espérance de retour."[1] The whole world, in fact, regarded him in very much the same way as Lord North.

It is probable that nothing but a blow like this, showing him the contempt into

[1] I could not interest myself in them: they are absolutely deranged in their minds, and there is no hope of their recovery.

which he had sunk, rousing all his pride, and driving him into the arms of new associates, whose talents commanded his respect, and whose instructions molded his political principles, could ever have saved Mr. Fox from the ruin in which he was involved. As it was, years passed away before he gained a complete mastery over this terrible infatuation; and it may here be stated, by way of anticipation, that his friends, at a much later period (1793), finding him involved, from time to time, in the most painful embarrassments from this cause, united in a subscription, with which they purchased him an annuity of £3000 a year, which could not be alienated, and after this testimony of their regard he wholly abstained from gambling.

The period at which Mr. Fox now stood was peculiarly favorable to the formation of new and more correct political principles. Hitherto he had none that could be called his own; he had never, probably, reflected an hour on the subject; he had simply carried out those high aristocratic feelings with which he was taught from childhood to look down upon the body of the people. But a change in the policy of Lord North now made *America* the great object of political interest. Within a few weeks, the Boston Port Bill and its attendant measures were brought forward, designed to starve a town of twenty thousand inhabitants, with the adjoining province, into submission; the charter of that province was violently set aside; a British governor was empowered to send persons three thousand miles across the Atlantic, to be tried in England for supposed offenses in America; and British troops were to be employed in carrying out these acts of violence and outrage. Mr. Fox was naturally one of the most humane of men; "He possessed," says Lord Erskine, "above all persons I ever knew, the most gentle and yet the most ardent spirit; he was tremblingly alive to every kind of private wrong or suffering; he had an indignant abhorrence of every species of cruelty, oppression, and injustice." With these feelings, quickened by the resentment which he naturally entertained against Lord North, it could not require much argument from Burke, Dunning, Barre, and the other leaders of the Opposition, into whose society he was now thrown, to make Mr. Fox enter with his whole soul into all their views of these violent, oppressive acts. He came out at once to resist them, and was the first man in the House who took the ground of denying the *right* of Parliament to tax the colonies without their consent. He affirmed that on this subject, "Just as the House of Commons stands to the House of Lords, so stands America with Great Britain;" neither party having authority to overrule or compel the other. He declared, "There is not an American but must reject and *resist* the principle and right." He accused Lord North of the most flagrant treachery to his adherents in New England. "You boast," said he, "of having friends there; but, rather than not make the ruin of that devoted country complete, even *your friends are to be involved in one common famine!*" His Lordship soon found that he had raised up a most formidable antagonist where he had least expected. Mr. Fox now entered into debate, not occasionally, as before, when the whim struck him, but earnestly and systematically, on almost every question that came up; and his proficiency may be learned from a letter of Mr. Gibbon (who was then a member of the House and a supporter of the ministry), in which, speaking of a debate on the subject of America (February, 1775), he says: "The principal men both days were Fox and Wedderburne, on opposite sides: the latter displayed his usual talents; the former, taking the vast compass of the question before us, discovered powers for regular debate *which neither his friends hoped nor his enemies dreaded.*"—Misc. Works, ii., 21.

Mr. Fox's sentiments respecting the treatment of America, though springing, perhaps, at first from humane feelings alone, or opposition to Lord North, involved, as their necessary result, an entire change of his political principles. He was now brought, for the first time, to look at public measures, not on the side of privilege or prerogative, but of the rights and interests of the people. From that moment, all the sympathies of his nature took a new direction, and he went on identifying himself more and more, to the end of life, with the popular part of the Constitution and the cause of free principles throughout the world. It was the test to which he brought every measure: it was his object, amid all the conflicts of party and personal interest, in his own expressive language, "to widen the basis of freedom—to infuse and circulate the spirit of liberty." As an orator, especially, he drew from this source the most inspiring strains of his eloquence. No English speaker, not even Lord Chatham himself, dwelt so often on this theme; no one had his generous sensibilities more completely roused; no one felt more strongly the need of a growing infusion of this spirit into the English government, as the great means of its strength and renovation. He urges this in a beautiful passage in his speech on Parliamentary Reform, "because it gives a power of which nothing else in governmeut is capable; because it incorporates every man with the state, and arouses every thing that belongs to the soul as well as the body of man; because it makes every individual feel that he is fighting for himself and not for another; that it is his own cause, his own safety, his own concern, his own dignity on the face of the earth, and his own interest in that identical soil, which he has to maintain. In this principle we find the key to all the wonders which were achieved at Thermopylæ: the principle of liberty alone could create those sublime and irresistible emotions; and it is in vain to deny, from the striking illustration that our times have given, that the principle is eternal, and that it belongs to the heart of man."

It was happy for Mr. Fox, in coming out so strongly against Lord North at the early age of twenty-five, that he enjoyed the friendship of some of the ablest men in the empire among the Whigs, on whom he could rely with confidence in forming his opinions and conducting his political inquiries. To Mr. Burke he could resort, in common with all the associates of that wonderful man, for every kind of knowledge on almost every subject; and he declared, at the time of their separation from each other in 1791, that "if he were to put all the political information which he had learned from books, all he had gained from science, and all which any knowledge of the world and its affairs had taught him, into one scale, and the improvement which he had derived from his right honorable friend's instruction and conversation were placed in the other, he should be at a loss to decide to which to give the preference." Mr. Dunning (afterward Lord Ashburton) was another leader among the Whigs, who, though less generally known as an orator from the imperfection of his voice and manner, was one of the keenest opponents in the House of those arbitrary acts into which George III. drove the Duke of Grafton and Lord North; and it can hardly be doubted that he had great influence with Mr. Fox at this time (though they were separated at a later period) in weaning him from his early predilections for the royal prerogative, and inspiring him with those sentiments which the Whigs expressed in their celebrated resolution (drawn up by Mr. Dunning himself), that "*the influence of the Crown has increased, is increasing, and* OUGHT TO BE DIMINISHED."[2]

[2] The reader will be interested in the following beautiful tribute to the memory of Lord Ashburton as an orator, from the pen of Sir William Jones: "His language was always pure, always elegant, and the best words dropped easily from his lips into the best places with a fluency at all times astonishing, and, when he had perfect health, really melodious. That faculty, however, in which no mortal ever surpassed him, and which all found irresistible, was his wit. This relieved the weary, calmed the resentful, and animated the drowsy; this drew smiles even from such as were the objects of it, and scattered flowers over a desert, and, like sunbeams sparkling on a lake, gave spirit and vivacity to the dullest and least interesting cause. Not that his accomplishments as an advocate consisted principally of volubility of speech or liveliness of raillery. He was endued with an intellect sedate yet penetrating, clear yet profound, subtle yet strong. His knowledge, too, was equal to his imagination, and his memory to his knowledge."—*Works*, vol. iv, p. 577.

The ambition of Mr. Fox was now directed to a single object, that of making himself *a powerful debater.* A debater, in the distinctive sense of the term, is described by a lively writer, as "one who goes out in all weathers"—one who, instead of carrying with him to the House a set speech drawn up beforehand, has that knowledge of general principles, that acquaintance with each subject as it comes up, that ready use of all his faculties, which enables him to meet every question where he finds it, to grapple with his antagonist at a moment's warning, and to avail himself of every advantage which springs from a perfect command of all his powers and resources. These qualities are peculiarly necessary in the British House of Commons, because the most important questions are generally decided at a single sitting; and there is no room for that pernicious custom so prevalent in the American Congress, of making interminable speeches to constituents under a semblance of addressing the House. In addition to great native quickness and force of mind, long-continued practice is requisite to make a successful debater. Mr. Fox once remarked to a friend, that he had literally gained his skill "at the expense of the House," for he had sometimes tasked himself, during an entire session, to speak on every question that came up, whether he was interested in it or not, as a means of exercising and training his faculties. He now found it necessary to be intimately acquainted with the history of the Constitution and the political relations of the country; and though he continued for some years to be a votary of pleasure, he had such wonderful activity of mind and force of memory, that he soon gained an amount of information on these topics such as few men in the House possessed, and was able to master every subject in debate with surprising facility and completeness. In all this he thought of but one thing—not language, not imagery, not even the best disposition and sequence of his ideas, but *argument:* how to put down his antagonist, how to make out his own case. His love of argument was, perhaps, the most striking trait in his character. Even in conversation (as noticed by a distinguished foreigner who was much in his society), he was not satisfied, like most men, to throw out a remark, and leave it to make its own way, he must *prove* it, and subject the remarks of others to the same test; so that *discussion* formed the staple of all his thoughts, and entered to a great extent into all his intercourse with others. With such habits and feelings, he rose, says Mr. Burke, "by slow degrees to be the most brilliant and accomplished debater the world ever saw." There was certainly nothing of envy or disparagement (though charged upon him with great bitterness by Dr. Parr) in Mr. Burke's selecting the term "debater" to express the distinctive character of Mr. Fox. The character is one which gives far more weight and authority to a speaker in Parliament, than the most fervid oratory when unattended by the qualities mentioned above. It was not denied by Mr. Burke, but rather intimated by his use of the word "brilliant," that Mr. Fox did superinduce upon those qualities an ardor and an eloquence by which (as every one knows) he gave them their highest effect. It is emphatically true, also, notwithstanding Dr. Parr's complaint of the expression, that Mr. Fox did rise "by slow degrees" to his eminence as an orator, an eminence of so peculiar a kind that no human genius could ever have attained it in any other way; and it is equally true, that whenever the name of Mr. Fox is mentioned, the first idea which strikes every mind is the one made thus prominent by Mr. Burke—we instantly think of him as "the most brilliant and accomplished *debater* the world ever saw." So much, indeed, was this the absorbing characteristic of his oratory, that nearly all his faults lay in this direction. He had made himself so completely an intellectual gladiator, that too often he thought of nothing but how to obtain the victory.

Notwithstanding the irregularities of his private life, to which Mr. Fox still unfortunately clung, he gradually rose as a speaker in Parliament, until, at the end of Lord North's administration, he was the acknowledged leader of the Whig party in the House. In many respects, he was peculiarly qualified for such a station. He had a fine, genial spirit, characteristic of the family, which drew his political friends around him with all the warmth of a personal attachment. "He was a man," said Mr. Burke, soon after their separation from each other, "who was *made* to be loved." His feelings were generous, open, and manly; the gaming-table had not made him, as it does most men, callous or morose; he was remarkably unassuming in his manners, yet frank and ardent in urging his views; he was above every thing like trick or duplicity, and was governed by the impulses of a humane and magnanimous disposition. These things, in connection with his tact and boldness, qualified him preeminently to be the leader of a Whig Opposition; while his rash turn of mind, resulting from the errors of his early training, would operate less to his injury in such a situation, and his very slight regard for political consistency would as yet have no opportunity to be developed.

It was with these characteristics, that, at the end of the long struggle which drove Lord North from power, Mr. Fox came into office as Secretary of State under Lord Rockingham, in March, 1782. This administration was terminated in thirteen weeks by the death of his Lordship, and Mr. Fox confidently expected to be made prime minister. But he had now to experience the natural consequences of his reckless spirit and disregard of character. The King would not, for a moment, entertain the idea of placing at the head of affairs a man who, besides his notorious dissipation, had beggared himself by gambling, and was still the slave of this ruinous passion. Nor was he alone in his feelings. Reflecting men of the Whig party, who were out of the circle of Mr. Fox's immediate influence, had long been scandalized by the profligacy of his life. In 1779, Dr. Price, who went beyond him in his devotion to liberal principles, remarked with great severity on his conduct, in a Fast Sermon which was widely circulated in print. "Can you imagine," said he, "that a spendthrift in his own concerns will make an economist in managing the concerns of others? that a wild gamester will take due care of the state of a kingdom? Treachery, vanity, and corruption must be the effects of dissipation, voluptuousness, and impiety. These sap the foundations of virtue; they render men necessitous and supple, ready at any time to fly to a court in order to repair a shattered fortune and procure supplies for prodigality." In addition to this, Mr. Fox had made himself personally obnoxious to George III., by another exhibition of his rashness. He had treated him with great indignity in his speeches on the American war, pointing directly to his supposed feelings and determinations in a manner forbidden by the theory of the Constitution, and plainly implying that he was governed by passions unbecoming his station as a King, and disgraceful to his character as a man. It is difficult to understand how Mr. Fox could allow himself in such language (whatever may have been his private convictions), if he hoped ever to be made minister; and it was certainly to be expected, for these reasons as well as those mentioned above, that the King would never place him at the head of the government while he could find any other man who was competent to fill the station. He accordingly made Lord Shelburne prime minister early in July, 1782, and Mr. Fox instantly resigned.

This step led to another which was the great misfortune of his life. Parties were so singularly balanced at the opening of the next Parliament, in December, 1782, that neither the minister nor any of his opponents had the command of the House. According to an estimate made by Gibbon, Lord Shelburne had one hundred and forty adherents, Lord North one hundred and twenty, and Mr. Fox ninety, leaving a considerable number who were unattached. Early in February, 1783, a report crept abroad, that a *coalition* was on the *tapis* between Mr. Fox and Lord North. The story was at first treated as an idle tale. A coalition of some kind was indeed expected, because the government could not be administered without an amalgamation of parties; but that Mr. Fox could ever unite with Lord North, after their bitter animosities and the glaring contrast of their principles on almost every question in politics, seemed utterly incredible. There was nothing of a personal nature to prevent an arrangement between Lord Shelburne and Lord North; but Mr. Fox had for years assailed his opponent in such language as seemed forever to cut them off from any intercourse as men, or any union of their interests as politicians. He had denounced him as "the most infamous of mankind," as "the greatest criminal of the state, whose *blood* must expiate the calamities he had brought upon his country;"[3] and, as if with the express design of making it impossible for him to enter into such an alliance, he had, only eleven months before, said of Lord North and his whole ministry in the House of Commons: "From the moment I should make any terms with one of them, I would rest satisfied to be called the most *infamous* of mankind. I could not for an instant think of a *coalition* with men who, in every public and private transaction as ministers, have shown themselves void of every principle of honor and honesty: in the hands of such men I would not trust my honor even for a minute."[4] Still, rumors of a coalition became more and more prevalent, until, on the 17th of February, 1783, says Mr. Wilberforce, in relating the progress of events, "When I reached the House, I inquired, 'Are the intentions of Lord North and Fox sufficiently known to be condemned?' 'Yes,' said Henry Banks, 'and the more strongly the better.'" The debate was on Lord Shelburne's treaty of peace with America; and every eye was turned to the slightest movements of the ex-minister and his old antagonist, until, at a late hour of the evening, Lord North came down from the gallery where he had been sitting, and *took his place by Mr. Fox.* His Lordship then arose, and attacked the treaty with great dexterity and force, as bringing disgrace upon the country by the concessions it made. Mr. Fox followed in the same strain, adding, in reference to himself and Lord North, that all causes of difference between them had ceased with the American war. The Coalition was now complete! The debate continued until nearly eight o'clock the next morning, when Lord Shelburne was defeated by a majority of sixteen votes, and was compelled soon after to resign.

Next came the Coalition Ministry. To this the King submitted with the utmost reluctance, after laboring in vain first to persuade Mr. Pitt to undertake the government, and then to obtain, as a personal favor from Lord North, the exclusion of Mr. Fox. So strong were the feelings of his Majesty, that he hesitated and delayed for *six weeks*, until, driven by repeated addresses from the House, he was compelled to yield; and this ill-fated combination came into power on the 2d of April, 1783, with the Duke of Portland as its head, and Mr. Fox and Lord North as principal secretaries of state. "The occurrence of this coalition," says Mr. Cooke, one of Mr. Fox's warmest admirers, "is greatly to be deplored, as an example to men who, without any of the power, may nevertheless feel inclined to imitate the errors of Fox. It is to be deplored as a blot on the character of a great man, as a precedent which strikes at the foundation of political morality, and as a weapon in the hands of those who would destroy all confidence in the honesty of public men."[5] The laxity of principle which it shows in Mr. Fox may be traced to the errors of his early education. It was the result of the pernicious habit in which he was trained of gratifying every desire without the least regard to consequences, and the still more pernicious maxims taught him by his father—"that brilliant talents would atone for every kind of delinquency, and that in politics, especially, any thing would be pardoned to a man of great designs and splendid abilities." Certain it is that Mr. Fox could never understand why he was condemned so severely for his union with Lord North. As an opponent, he had spoken of him, indeed, in rash and bitter terms, but never with a malignant spirit, for nothing

[3] Age of Pitt and Fox, vol. i., 145.

[4] Fox's Speeches, vol. ii., 39.

[5] History of Party, vol. iii., 316.

was farther from his disposition; and, knowing the character of the men, we can credit the statement of Mr. Gibbon, who was intimate with both, "that in their political contests these great antagonists had never felt any *personal* animosity; that their reconciliation was easy and sincere; and that their friendship had never been clouded by the shadow of suspicion and jealousy." Every one now feels that Mr. Fox uttered his real sentiments when he said, "It is not in my nature to bear malice or ill will; my friendships are perpetual; my enmities are not so: *amicitiæ sempiternæ, inimicitiæ placabiles.*" But he had thus far shown himself to the world only on the worst side of his character; and it is not surprising that most men considered him (what in fact he appeared to be on the face of the transaction) as a reckless politician, bent on the possession of power at whatever sacrifice of principle or consistency it might cost him. Even the warmest Whigs regarded him, to a great extent, in the same light. "From the moment this coalition was formed," says Bishop Watson, "I lost all confidence in public men." "The gazettes," says Sir Samuel Romilly in a letter to a friend, "have proclaimed to you the scandalous alliance between Fox and Lord North. It is not Fox alone, but his whole party; so much so that it is no exaggeration to say, that of all the public characters of this devoted country (Mr. Pitt only excepted), there is not a man who has, or deserves, the nation's confidence."[6]

The great measure of the Coalition ministry was Mr. Fox's East India Bill. Perilous as the subject was to a new administration lying under the jealousy of the people and the hostility of the King, it could not be avoided; and Mr. Fox met it with a fearless resolution, which at least demands our respect. The whole nation called for strong measures, and Mr. Fox gave them a measure stronger than any one of them had contemplated. He cut the knot which politicians had so long endeavored to untie. He annulled the charter of the East India Company, and, after providing for the payment of their debts, he took all their concerns into the hands of the government at home, placing the civil and military affairs of India under the control of a board of seven commissioners, and putting their commercial interests into the hands of a second board. to be managed for the benefit of the shareholders. Never, since the Revolution of 1688, has any measure of the government produced such a ferment in the nation. Lawyers exclaimed against the bill as a violation of chartered rights; all the corporate bodies of the kingdom saw in it a precedent which might be fatal to themselves; the East India Company considered it as involving the ruin of their commercial interests; and politicians regarded it as a desperate effort of Mr. Fox, after forcing his way into office against the wishes of the King, to set himself above the King's reach, and, by this vast accession of patronage, to establish his ministry for life. Mr. Fox had again to suffer the bitter consequences of his disregard of character. These objections were plausible, and some of the provisions of the bill were certainly *impolitic* for one situated like Mr. Fox. Yet Mr. Mill, in his British India, speaks of the alarm excited as one "for which the ground was extremely scanty, and for which, notwithstanding the industry and art with which the advantage was improved by the opposite party, it is difficult (considering the usual apathy of the public on much more important occasions) entirely to account."[7] As to the principal charge, Lord Campbell observes, in his Lives of the Chancellors, "No one at the present day believes that the framers of the famous East India Bill had the intention imputed to them of creating a power independent of the Crown."[8] And as to the other objections, it is obvious to remark, that *any* effectual scheme of Indian reform would, of necessity, encroach on the charter of the Company; that such encroachments must in any case be liable to abuse as precedents; and that if (as all agreed was necessary) the government at home assumed the civil and military administration of India, a large increase of patronage *must* fall into the hands of ministers,

[6] Memoirs, vol. i., p. 269. [7] Vol. iv., p. 475. [8] Vol. v., p. 551.

which others could abuse as easily as Mr. Fox. But the difficulty was, *no one knew how far to trust him!* His conduct had given boundless scope for jealousy and suspicion. He had put into the hands of his enemies the means of utterly ruining his character; and it is undoubtedly true, as stated by a late writer, that he was at this period regarded by the great body of the nation "as selfish, vicious, and destitute of virtue—by thousands he was looked upon as a man with the purposes of a Catiline and the manners of a Lovelace."[9]

Under all these difficulties, Mr. Fox placed his reliance on his majority in the House, and went forward with an unbroken spirit, trusting to time, and especially to the character of the men whom he should name as commissioners, for the removal of this wide-spread opposition. He introduced his bill on the 18th of November, 1783, in a speech explaining its import and design; and at the end of twelve days, after one of the hardest-fought battles which ever took place in the House, he closed the debate with a speech of great ability (to be found below), in reply to his numerous opponents, and especially to Mr. Dundas and Mr. Pitt. Believing (as almost every one now does) that Mr. Fox was far from being governed by the base motives ascribed to him—that, though ambitious in a high degree, and hoping, no doubt, to strengthen his ministry by this measure, his bill was dictated by generous and humane feelings, and was no more stringent than he felt the exigency of the case to demand—we can not but admire the dignity and manliness with which he stood his ground. He had every inducement, when he met this unexpected opposition, to shrink back, to modify his plan, to compromise with the East India Company, and to establish his power by uniting his interests with theirs. Even those who distrust his motives will therefore do honor to his spirit, and will be ready to say with Mr. Moore,[10] "We read his speech on the East India Bill with a sort of breathless anxiety, which no other political discourses, except those, perhaps, of Demosthenes, could produce. The importance of the stake which he risks—the boldness of his plan—the gallantry with which he flings himself into the struggle, and the frankness of personal feeling that breathes throughout, all throw around him an interest like that which encircles a hero of romance; nor could the most candid autobiography that ever was written exhibit the whole character of a man more transparently through it."

The bill passed the Commons by a vote of 217 to 103, but when it came up in the House of Lords it met with a new and more powerful resistance. Lord Temple, a near relative of Mr. Pitt, had obtained a private audience of the King, and represented the subject in such a light, that his Majesty commissioned him to say, that "whoever voted for the India Bill were not only not his friends, but that he should consider them his *enemies*." At its first reading, Lord Thurlow denounced it in the strongest terms; and turning to the Prince of Wales, who was present as a peer with the view to support the bill, he added, with a dark scowl as he looked him directly in the face, "I wish to see the Crown great and respectable, but if the present bill should pass, it will be no longer worthy of a man of honor to wear. The King may take the diadem from his own head and put it on the head of Mr. Fox." An instantaneous change took place among the peerage. The King's message through Lord Temple had been secretly but widely circulated among the Lords, especially those of the royal household, who had given their proxies to the ministry. These proxies were instantly withdrawn. Even Lord Stormont, a member of the cabinet, who at first supported the bill, changed sides after two days; the Prince of Wales felt unable to give Mr. Fox his vote; and the bill was rejected by a majority of ninety-five to seventy-six. The King hastened to town the moment he learned the decision of the Lords; and at twelve o'clock the same night, a messenger con-

[9] Age of Pitt and Fox, vol. i., p. 177.

[10] Life of Sheridan, vol. i., 215, Phila.

veyed to Mr. Fox and Lord North his Majesty's orders "that they should deliver up the seals of their offices, and send them by the under-secretaries, Mr. Frazer and Mr. Nepean, as a personal interview on the occasion would be disagreeable to him." The other ministers received their dismissal the next day in a note signed "Temple."

But the battle was not over. Mr. Fox had still an overwhelming majority in the House; and feeling that the interference of the King was an encroachment on the rights of the Commons, he resolved to carry his resistance to the utmost extremity. Accordingly, two days after, when Mr. Pitt came in as minister, he voted him down by so large a majority that a division was not even called for. Again and again he voted him down, demanding of him, in each instance, to resign in accordance with parliamentary usage, and bringing upon him at last a direct vote, "That after the expressed opinion of the House, the continuance of the present minister in office *is contrary to constitutional principles*, and injurious to the interests of his Majesty and the people." Earl Temple was terrified, and threw up his office within a few days, but Mr. Pitt stood firm. The contest continued for three months, during which Mr. Fox delayed the supplies from time to time, and distinctly intimated that he might *stop them entirely*, and prevent the passing of the Mutiny Bill, if Mr. Pitt did not resign.[11] But his impetuosity carried him too far. He was in this case, as in some others, his own worst enemy. The King's interference was certainly a breach of privilege, and, under other circumstances, the whole country would have rallied round Mr. Fox to resist it. But every one now saw that the real difficulty was his exclusion from office; and when he attempted to force his way back by threatening to suspend the operations of government, the nation turned against him more strongly than ever. They ascribed all that he did to mortified pride or disappointed ambition; they gave him no credit for those better feelings which mingled with these passions, and which he seems to have considered (so easily do men deceive themselves) as the only motives that impelled him to the violent measures he pursued.[12] Addresses now poured in upon the King from every quarter, entreating him not to yield. At a public meeting in Westminster Hall, Mr. Fox, who was present with a view to explain his conduct, was put down by cries of "No Great Mogul!" "No India tyrant!" "No usurper!" "No turn-coat!" "No dictator!" The city of London, once so strongly in his favor, now turned against him. Sir Horace Mann relates, that, going up to the King at this time with one of the addresses of the House against Mr. Pitt, he met the Lord Mayor of London and others who had just come down from presenting one in his favor; and on Sir Horace remarking, "I see I am among my friends," they replied, "We *were* your friends, but you have joined those who have set up a *Lord Protector!*" Such demonstrations of public feeling operated powerfully on the House.

[11] The bill for punishing mutiny in the army and navy is passed at each session for only one year. The power of withholding this bill and that which provides the annual supplies, gives the House of Commons, in the last extremity, an absolute control over ministers.

[12] One of the speeches in this selection, that of December 17th, 1784, has been given with a particular reference to this point. The reader will be interested to remark how completely the matter of this speech is made up of just sentiments and weighty reasonings—contempt of underhand dealing, scorn of court servility, detestation of that dark engine of *secret influence*, which had driven Lord Chatham and so many others from power. All this is expressed with a spirit and eloquence which Chatham alone could have equaled, but coming from Mr. Fox, it availed nothing. He stood in so false a position, that he could not even defend the popular part of the Constitution without turning the people more completely against him. The city of London, the most democratic part of the kingdom, thanked the King for that very interference which Toryism itself will not deny was a direct breach of the Constitution. But the people were taught to believe that Mr. Fox was aiming to make himself a "dictator" by the East India Bill, and they justified any measures which the King thought necessary for putting such a man down. Hardly any page of English history is more instructive than that which records the errors of Mr. Fox, and the pernicious consequences both to himself and others.

Mr. Fox's adherents gradually fell off, until, on a division at the end of eleven weeks, March 8th, 1784, his majority had sunk from fifty-four to a *single vote!* A shout of triumph now broke forth from the ministerial benches. The contest in the House was ended, and the question was carried at once to the whole country by a dissolution of Parliament.

The elections which followed, in April, 1784, went against the friends of Mr. Fox in every part of the kingdom; more than a hundred and sixty having lost their places, and become "Fox's Martyrs," in the sportive language of the day. In Westminster, which Mr. Fox and Sir Cecil Wray had represented in the preceding Parliament, the struggle was the most violent ever known—Wray in opposition to his old associate. At the end of eleven days, Mr. Fox was in a minority of three hundred and eighteen, and his defeat seemed inevitable, when relief came from a quarter never before heard of in a political canvass. Georgiana, Duchess of Devonshire, a woman of extraordinary beauty and the highest mental accomplishments, took the field in his behalf. She literally became the canvasser of Mr. Fox. She went from house to house soliciting votes; she sent her private carriage to bring mechanics and others of the lowest class to the polls; she appeared at the hustings herself in company with Mr. Fox; and on one occasion, when a young butcher turned the laugh upon her by offering his vote for a *kiss*, in the enthusiasm of the moment she took him at his word, and paid him on the spot! With such an ally, Mr. Fox's fortunes soon began to mend, and at the termination of forty days, when the polls were closed, he had a majority over Sir Cecil Wray of two hundred and thirty-five votes. This triumph was celebrated by a splendid procession of Mr. Fox's friends, most of them bearing *fox tails*, which gave rise to one of Mr. Pitt's best sarcasms. Some one having expressed his wonder how the people could procure such an immense number of foxes' tails; "That is by no means surprising," said Pitt; "this has been a good sporting year, and more *foxes* have been destroyed than in any former season. I think, upon an average, there has at least one Fox been run down in every borough of the kingdom!" The Prince of Wales showed the lively interest he had taken in the contest, by joining the procession on horseback in his uniform of a colonel of the Tenth Dragoons. A few days after, he celebrated the victory in a fête at Carlton House, attended by more than six hundred persons, the gentlemen being dressed in the costume of Mr. Fox, "buff and blue," and some even of the ladies wearing the same colors, with the "Fox laurel" on their heads, and the "Fox medal" suspended from their necks.

But Mr. Fox was not allowed to enjoy the fruits of his victory. Sir Cecil Wray demanded a *scrutiny* or revision of the poll, involving enormous expense, and a delay, perhaps, of years, in taking testimony as to disputed votes. All this time Mr. Fox was to be deprived of his seat—the object really aimed at in the whole transaction. The presiding officer lent himself to this design; he returned Lord Hood (the third candidate) as a member; and made a report to the House, that he had granted a scrutiny in relation to Sir Cecil Wray and Mr. Fox. There was no precedent for a scrutiny in a case like this, where the poll had been continued down to the very day before the meeting of Parliament, and the presiding officer was required by his writ to return *two* members for Westminster on the 18th of May, being the next day. If he could avoid this—if he was authorized (instead of doing the best he could) to reserve the question, and enter on a scrutiny after the session had commenced, it is obvious that the entire representation of the country would be in the hands of the returning officers. Any one of them, from party views or corrupt motives, might deprive a member of his seat as long as he saw fit, under the pretense (as in the present case) of satisfying his "conscience" by a protracted revision of the polls. The case came up early in the session, and Mr. Fox, being returned by a friend for the borough of Kirkwall, in the Orkney Isles, was enabled to join in the debate. Under any other circumstances Mr. Pitt would never have allowed his passions to become interested in such an affair; even if he thought the scrutiny legal, he would have seen the necessity of putting an end at once to a precedent so ob noxious to abuse. But the conflict of the last session seems to have poisoned his mind, and he showed none of that magnanimity which we should naturally expect in one who had achieved so splendid a victory at the recent elections. He assailed Mr. Fox in the language of taunt and ungenerous sarcasm, describing him as a man on whom a sentence of banishment had been passed by his country—as "driven by the impulse of patriotic indignation an exile from his native clime, to seek refuge on the stormy and desolate shores of the *Ultima Thule.*" Nothing could be more admirable than the firmness and elasticity of Mr. Fox's spirit under these depressing circumstances, stripped as he was of nearly all his former supporters in the House. He seemed, like the old Romans, to gather strength and courage from the difficulties that surrounded him. On the 8th of June, 1784, he discussed the subject of the Westminster scrutiny in one of the clearest and most fervid pieces of reasoning ever delivered in the House of Commons; adding, at the same time, some admonitions for Mr. Pitt and his other opponents, which effectually secured him against uncivil treatment in all their subsequent contests. Although the vote went against him at that time by a majority of 117, the House and the country soon became satisfied that the whole proceeding was dishonorable and oppressive; and, at the end of nine months, Mr. Pitt had the mortification to see his majority, so firm on every other subject, turning against him upon this, and, by a vote of 162 to 124, putting an end to the scrutiny and requiring an immediate return. Mr. Fox was accordingly returned the next day. The moment he took his seat as a member for Westminster, Mr. Fox moved, that all the proceedings in regard to the scrutiny be expunged from the journals of the House. This motion was supported by Mr. Scott, afterward Lord Eldon, who, on this occasion (the only one in his life), came out in opposition to Mr. Pitt; but the majority were unwilling to join him in so direct a vote of censure, and the motion was lost.[13] Mr. Fox recovered two thousand pounds damages from the presiding officer, the High Bailiff of Westminster, and a law was soon after passed providing against any farther abuses of this kind.

Mr. Fox was appointed one of the managers of the impeachment against Warren Hastings in 1786, and had assigned to him the second charge, relating to the oppressive treatment of Cheyte Sing, Rajah of Benares. This duty he performed in a manner which awakened general admiration, and fully sustained the high character he had already gained as a parliamentary orator.

In the autumn of 1788, while traveling in Italy, Mr. Fox was unexpectedly presented with the prospect of being called again to the head of affairs. The King became suddenly deranged; and if the malady continued, the Prince of Wales would, of course, be Regent, and Mr. Fox his prime minister. A messenger with this intelligence found him at Bologna, and urged his immediate return, as the session of Parliament was soon to commence. He started at once, and never quitted his chaise during the whole journey, traveling night and day until he reached London, on the 24th of November. At this time no definite anticipations could be formed in respect to the King's recovery. Parliament had voted a fortnight's recess, to allow time for deciding on the proper steps to be taken, and the political world was full of intrigue and agitation. It was the great object of the Prince and his future ministers to come in untrammeled—to

[13] Lord Eldon, speaking of this subject at a later period, said: "When the legality of the conduct of the High Bailiff of Westminster was before the House, all the lawyers on the ministerial side defended his right to grant a scrutiny. I thought their law bad, and I told them so. I asked Kenyon how he could answer *this*—that every writ or commission must be returned on the day on which it was made returnable. *He could not answer it.*"

have his authority as Regent, during his father's illness, established on the same footing as if he had succeeded to the throne by the King's death. The existing ministry, on the other hand, who believed the King might speedily recover, were desirous to impose such restrictions on the Regency as would prevent Mr. Fox and his friends from intrenching themselves permanently in power. It is curious to observe how completely the two parties changed sides under this new aspect of their political interests. Mr. Fox became the defender of the prerogative, and Mr. Pitt of the popular part of the Constitution. Before Mr. Fox returned from Italy, Lord Loughborough [Mr. Wedderburne] had devised a theory to meet the present case. He maintained that here (as in the case of natural death) "the administration of the government dovolved to him [the Prince of Wales] of *right*;" that it belonged to Parliament "not to confer, but to declare the right;" and it is now known that he actually advised the Prince, in secret, to assume the royal authority at a meeting of the Privy Council, and then to summon Parliament, in his *own* name, for the dispatch of business.[14] This theory, with one important modification, Mr. Fox took with him into the House. In a debate on the 10th of December, 1788, he maintained that during the incapacity of the King, the Prince "had as clear and express a right to assume the reins of government and exercise the power of sovereignty, as in the case of his Majesty's having undergone a natural and perfect demise;" but he added (limiting the theory of Lord Loughborough) that "as to this right, the Prince himself was not to judge *when* he was entitled to exercise it, but the two Houses of Parliament, as the organs of the nation, were alone qualified to pronounce *when* the Prince ought to take possession of and exercise this right."[15] Mr. Pitt, the moment he heard this doctrine, exclaimed to a friend who sat by him in the House, "Now I'll *unwhig* that gentleman for the rest of his life!" He instantly rose, and declared it to be "little less than treason against the Constitution: he pledged himself to prove that the Heir-apparent had no more right, in the case in question, to the exercise of the executive authority, than any other subject in the kingdom, and that it belonged entirely to the two remaining branches of the Legislature, in behalf of the nation at large, to make such a provision for supplying the temporary deficiency as they might think proper." Mr. Fox, either seeing that he had been misunderstood, or feeling that he had gone too far, explained himself, two days after, to have meant, that "from the moment the two Houses of Parliament *declared* the King unable to exercise the royal sovereignty, from *that* moment a right to exercise the royal authority attached to the Prince of Wales"—that "he must appeal to the court competent to decide whether it *belonged* to him or not, or must wait till that court itself made such a declaration."[16] This was apparently taking still lower ground; but even this Mr. Pitt maintained was equally false and unfounded. "He denied that the Prince had any *right* whatever;" he declared it "subversive of the principles of the Constitution to admit that the Prince of Wales might set *himself* on the throne during the lifetime of his father; he denied that Parliament were mere judges in this emergency, affirming that they acted for the entire body of the people in a case not provided for in the Constitution;" and affirmed it to be "a question of greater magnitude and importance even than the present exigency, a question that involved in it the principles of the Constitution, the protection and security of our liberties, and the safety of the state." A Regency Bill was now framed by the Ministers, making the Prince of Wales Regent, but committing the King's person to the care of the Queen, with the right of appointing the officers of the royal household. It provided that the Prince should have no power over the personal property of the King, and no authority either to create new peers, or to grant any pension, place, or reversion to be held after the King's recovery, except

[14] See a paper of Lord Loughborough on this subject in Campbell's Lives of the Chancellors, vol. vi., page 195.
[15] Speeches, vol. iii., page 401.
[16] Id. ib., page 407.

offices made permanent by law. Nearly four months were spent in debating this subject, every possible delay being interposed by Mr. Pitt, who was now confident of the King's early recovery. Accordingly, at the close of April, his Majesty was declared by the physicians to be restored to a sound state of mind; and Mr. Fox's prospect of office became more remote than ever, the King and the people being equally imbittered against him, as having again endeavored to establish himself in power by the use of violent and illegal means.[17] On the question so vehemently discussed at that time touching the rights of the Prince of Wales, there has been a diversity of opinion down to the present day. All agree in considering Lord Loughborough's theory as "a flimsy speculation;" but men have differed greatly as to Mr. Fox's doctrine. When the Regency question came up again, in 1810, an able writer in favor of the Prince remarked in the Edinburgh Review: "Strict legal right, which could be asserted and made good in a court of judicature, he [the Prince] certainly had none. It was observed, with more truth than decorum, by Mr. Pitt, that every individual of his father's subjects had as good a legal right to the Regency as his Royal Highness the Prince of Wales."[18] Lord Campbell, however, would seem to hold with Mr. Fox, when he says: "The next heir to the throne is *entitled*, during the continuance of this [the King's] disability, to carry on the executive government as Regent, with the same authority as if the disabled Sovereign were naturally dead;"[19] unless, indeed, he uses the word "entitled" in a looser sense to describe not what is strictly a *legal right*, but what is most accordant with the analogies of the Constitution and the nature of a hereditary monarchy. If so, he agrees with Lord Brougham, who nevertheless regarded the restrictions imposed on the Prince Regent as wise and necessary. After stating what he considered the argument from analogy, he says, in respect to this case: "There were reasons of a practical description which overbore these obvious considerations, and reconciled men's minds to such an anomalous proceeding. It seemed necessary to provide for the safe custody of the King's person, and for such a sure restoration of his powers as should instantly replace the scepter in his hand the very moment that his capacity to hold it should return. His Vicegerent must plainly have no control over this operation, neither over the royal patient's custody, nor over the resumption of his office and the termination of his own. But it would not have been very easy to cut off all interference on the Regent's part in this most delicate matter, had he been invested with the full powers of the Crown. So, in like manner, the object being to preserve things as nearly as possible in their present state, if those full powers had been exercised uncontrolled, changes of a nature quite irreversible might have been effected while the monarch's faculties were asleep; and not only he would have awakened to a new order of things, but the affairs of the country would have been administered under that novel dispensation by one irreconcilably hostile to it, while its author, appointed in the course of nature once more to rule as his successor, would have been living and enjoying all the influence acquired by his accidental, anticipated, and temporary reign. These considerations, and the great unpopularity of the Heir-apparent and his political associates, the Coalition party, enabled Mr. Pitt to carry his proposition of a Regency with restricted powers, established by a bill to which the two remaining branches alone of the crip-

[17] George III., throughout his whole life, believed that a conspiracy had been formed to prevent his remounting the throne. No explanations could ever relieve his mind from this error, and he always looked with abhorrence on those who resisted the limitations of the Regent's authority, and the transfer of his person to the custody of the Queen. The feelings of the nation were strongly excited in his behalf. Without sharing in his error, they considered him as treated with disrespect, and strongly condemned those who objected to the restrictions mentioned above. It was in this way, as well as by his East India Bill and Coalition, that Mr. Fox did more than any other man in the empire to remove the unpopularity of the King, and to draw his subjects around him in support and sympathy.

[18] Vol. xviii., page 91.

[19] Lives of the Chancellors, vol. vi., page 187.

pled Parliament had assented; instead of their addressing the Heir-apparent, declaring the temporary vacancy of the throne, and desiring him temporarily to fill it" When the same question came up again, in 1810, the Prince waived the claim of *right*, and yielded quietly to the restrictions enumerated above. These two precedents have settled the constitutional law and usage on this subject.

Mr. Fox's next conflict with his antagonist related to the Russian Armament, and here he carried the whole country with him in opposition to the warlike designs of the ministry. The courts of London and Berlin had demanded of the Empress of Russia, not only to desist from her war with Turkey, but to restore the numerous and important conquests she had made. Unwilling to provoke the resentment of these powerful and self-created arbiters; Catharine consented to yield every thing but a small station on the Black Sea called Ockzakow, with the dependent territory. Mr. Pitt, under a mistaken view of the importance of this fortress, peremptorily insisted on its surrender; the Empress, taking offense at this treatment, as peremptorily refused; and the British ministry made the most active preparations for war. When the subject came before Parliament, early in 1791, Mr. Fox put forth all his strength against this armament. Reflecting men throughout the country condemned Mr. Pitt for interfering in the contests of other nations; and, as the discussion went on in Parliament, ministers found their majority so much reduced, that they promptly and wisely gave up the point in dispute. Mr. Fox gained greatly in the public estimation by his conduct on this occasion. He appeared in his true character, that of a friend of peace; and was justly considered as having saved the country, probably from a long and bloody war, certainly from much unnecessary expense contemplated by the ministry. While this question was under discussion, he sent a friend, Mr. Adair, to St. Petersburgh, as it was generally supposed with confidential communications for the Empress. Mr. Burke, after his breach with Mr. Fox, spoke of this mission as involving, if not treason, at least a breach of the Constitution fraught with the most dangerous consequences. It is not easy to understand the ground of this severe charge. Mr. Fox was not in the secrets of the government, and could communicate nothing to the Empress which was not known to the world at large. He could only assure her that the English people were averse to war, and might, perhaps, exhort her not to lower her terms (though this was never proved); but as the two nations were still at peace, his communications with Catharine were certainly less objectionable than Burke's correspondence with Dr. Franklin during the American war, which he once proposed to read in Parliament, and which caused Lord New Haven to exclaim: "Do not my senses deceive me? Can a member of this Assembly not only avow his correspondence with a rebel, but dare to read it to us?"[20] There is one decisive fact which shows, that Mr. Adair's mission could not have been regarded by the King and ministry as it was by Mr. Burke. He was afterward sent as Envoy to the courts of Vienna and Constantinople. "The confidence of the Sovereign," as Dr. Parr remarks, "completely and visibly refutes the accusations of Mr. Burke." After Mr. Pitt was thus beaten off from the Russian Armament, Mr. Fox and his friends opened upon him one of the severest attacks he ever experienced, by proposing a vote of *censure*, on the ground that he had acted the part either of a bully or a coward—that he had disgraced the country by disarming, if there was just cause of war, and by arming if there was not. Mr. Fox's speech on that occasion will be found in this volume; it was one of his most powerful and characteristic efforts.

Mr. Fox likewise distinguished himself at this period by his efforts to defend the rights of juries. The law of libel, as laid down by Lord Mansfield in the case of Woodfall,[21] restricted the jury to the question of *fact*, "Was the accused guilty of publishing, and did he point his remarks at the government?" They were not allowed

[20] Wraxall's Memoirs, vol. ii., p. 277.

[21] See page 199.

to inquire into his motives, or the legality of what he said; and the real issue was, therefore, in the hands of the judges, who, being appointed by the Crown, were peculiarly liable to be swayed by court influences. This made the trial by jury in libel cases a mere nullity, and too often turned it into an instrument for crushing the liberty of the press. Mr. Burke took up the subject at the time of Woodfall's trial, and prepared a bill giving juries the right to judge of the law as well as the fact, but it was rejected by a large majority. This bill, in all its leading features, Mr. Fox brought forward again in the year 1791, after the famous trial of the Dean of St. Asaph, in which Mr. Erskine made his masterly argument on the rights of juries.[22] "When a man," said Mr. Fox, in urging his bill, "is accused of murder, a crime consisting of law and fact, the jury every day find a verdict of guilty, and this also is the case in felony and every criminal indictment. *Libels are the only exception, the single anomaly.*" "All will admit that a *writing* may be an overt act of treason; but suppose in this case the Court of King's Bench should charge the jury; 'Consider only whether the criminal *published* the papers—do not inquire into the nature of it—do not examine whether it corresponds to the definition of treason'—would Englishmen endure that death should be inflicted by the decision of a jury thus trammeled and overruled?" Mr. Pitt generously seconded Mr. Fox in this effort, and even raised Mr. Grenville to the House of Lords for the sake of giving the bill a more powerful support in that body, but Lord Thurlow succeeded in defeating it that session. It was passed, however, in 1792, notwithstanding the pertinacious opposition of the law Lords, Thurlow, Kenyon, and Bathurst; and Mr. Fox had the satisfaction of thus performing one of the most important services ever rendered to the liberty of the press.

The progress of our narrative has led us forward insensibly into the midst of the French Revolution. Some one, speaking of this convulsion, remarked to Mr. Burke, that it had shaken the whole world. "Yes," replied he, "and it has shaken the *heart of Mr. Fox* out of its place!" Certain it is that every thing Mr. Fox did or said on this subject, whether right or wrong, sprung directly from his heart, from the warm impulse of his humane and confiding nature. In fact, the leading statesmen of that day were all of them governed, in the part they took, far more by temperament and previous habits of thought, than by any deep-laid schemes of policy. Mr. Burke was naturally cautious. His great principle in government was prescription. With him abstract right was nothing, circumstances were every thing; so that his first inquiry in politics was, not what is true or proper in the nature of things, but what is practicable, what is expedient, what is wise and safe in the present posture of affairs. Hence, on the question of taxing America, he treated all discussions of the abstract right with utter contempt. "I do not enter into these metaphysical distinctions," said he, "I hate the sound of them." Mr. Fox, on the contrary, instantly put the question on the ground of *right;* all the sympathies of his nature were on the side of the colonies as injured and insulted. "There is not an American," said he, "but must reject and resist the principle and the right." With such feelings and habits of thought, it might have been foreseen from the beginning that Mr. Burke and Mr. Fox would be at utter variance respecting the French Revolution, carried on, as it was, upon the principle of the inherent "rights of man." The difficulty was greater, because each of them, to a certain extent, had the truth on his side. The right of self-government in a people, as Mr. Fox truly said, does not depend on precedent or the concessions of rulers, but is founded in the nature of things. "It is not because they *have* been free, but because they have a *right* to be free, that men demand their freedom." Mr. Burke, on the other hand, was equally correct in maintaining that the question of resistance is far from being a question of

[22] For this speech, see page 656.

mere abstract right. *Circumstances*, to a great extent, enter as an essential element into the decision of that question. No one is weak enough to suppose that any nation, however oppressed, can be justified in a rebellion which it is plainly impossible to carry through; or that self-government would be any thing but a curse to a people who are destitute of moral and political virtue. These are points, however, on which it is usually impossible to decide in the early stages of a revolution. A people sometimes *make* their destiny by the energy of their own will. The trials and privations through which they pass (as in the case of the seven United Provinces) prepare them for self-government. It was, therefore, natural for a man of Mr. Fox's sanguine temperament, especially with the example of America before him, to have confident hopes of the same auspicious results in France.

The first instance of popular violence that occurred was the attack on the Bastile (July 14th, 1789); and Mr. Fox, in referring to it in the House, quoted, very happily, from Cowper's Task (which had been recently published), the beautiful lines respecting that fortress:

> "Ye horrid towers, th' abode of broken hearts,
> Ye dungeons and ye cages of despair,
> That monarchs have supplied from age to age
> With music such as suits their sovereign ears:
> The sighs and groans of miserable men!
> There's not an English heart that would not leap
> To hear that ye were fall'n at last."

So far as this event was concerned, Mr. Burke's sympathies were entirely with Mr. Fox. He said it was impossible not to admire the spirit by which the attack was dictated; but the excesses which followed brought him out soon after as an opponent of the Revolution, while Mr. Fox, as might be expected from one of his ardent feelings, still clung to the cause he had espoused. He lamented those excesses as truly as Mr. Burke, but his hopeful spirit led him to believe they would speedily pass away. He ascribed them to the feelings naturally created by the preceding despotism, and thus insensibly became the apologist of the revolutionary leaders, as Mr. Burke was of the court and nobility.

The false position into which Mr. Fox was thus drawn was the great misfortune of his subsequent life. He had no feelings in common with the philosophizing assassins of France, and from the moment he learned their true character, and saw the utter failure of their experiments, it is much to be regretted that he should in any way have been led to appear as their advocate. And yet it seemed impossible for one of his cast of mind to avoid it. When Austria and Russia invaded France (July, 1792), for the avowed purpose of putting back the Bourbons on the throne, he felt (as the whole world now feel) that it was not only the worst possible policy, but a flagrant violation of national right. He sympathized with the French. He rejoiced, and proclaimed his joy in the House of Commons, when they drove out the invaders, and seized, in their turn, upon the Austrian Netherlands. So, too, on the questions in dispute between England and France, which soon after resulted in war, he condemned the course taken by his own government as harsh and insulting. He thus far sided with the French, declaring that the English ministry had provoked the war, and were justly chargeable with the calamities it produced. And when the French, elated by their success in the Netherlands, poured forth their armies on the surrounding nations, with the avowed design of carrying out the Revolution by fire and sword, Mr. Fox was even then led by his peculiar position to palliate what he had no wish to justify. He dwelt on the provocations they had received, and showed great ingenuity in proving that the spirit of conquest and treachery which characterized the Republic, was only the spirit of the Bourbons transfused into the new government—that *they* had taught the nation, and trained it up for ages, to be the plunderers of mankind. It is difficult to conceive, at the present day, how all this grated upon the ears of an immense majority of the English people. The world has learned many lessons from the French Revolution, and one of the most important is that which Mr. Fox was continually inculcating, that nations, however wrong may be their conduct, should be left to manage their internal concerns in their own way. But the doctrines of Mr. Burke had taken complete possession of the higher class of minds throughout the country. The French were a set of demons. They had murdered their king, and cast off religion; it was, therefore, the duty of surrounding nations to put them out of the pale of civilized society—to treat them as robbers and pirates; and whatever violence might result from such treatment was to be charged on the revolutionary spirit of the French. That spirit was certainly bad enough, and would very likely, under any circumstances, have produced war; but if Mr. Fox's advice had been followed, much of the enthusiasm with which the whole French nation rushed into the contest would have been prevented, and the fire of the Revolution might possibly have burned out within their own borders, instead of involving all Europe in the conflagration. But the great body of the English people were unprepared for such views, and Mr. Fox was the last man from whom they could hear any thing of this kind even with patience. His early mistakes as to the Revolution had made him the most unpopular man in the kingdom; and it must be admitted that, while he was right in the great object at which he aimed, the nature of the argument and the warmth of his feelings made him seem too often to be the advocate of the French, even in their worst excesses. It was hardly possible, indeed, to oppose the war without appearing to take part with the enemy. Even Mr. Wilberforce, when he made his motion against it in 1794, was very generally suspected of revolutionary principles. "When I first went to the levee," said he, "after moving my amendment, the King *cut* me." "Your friend Mr. Wilberforce," said Mr. Windham to Lady Spencer, "will be very happy any morning to hand your Ladyship to the guillotine!"

The name of Mr. Windham naturally suggests another event connected with Mr. Fox's views of the French Revolution. Nearly all his friends deserted him, and became his most strenuous opponents. Mr. Burke led the way, as already stated in the sketch of his life. The Duke of Portland, Lord Loughborough, Mr. Windham, and a large number of the leading Whigs, followed at a somewhat later period, leaving him with only a handful of supporters in the House to maintain the contest with Mr. Pitt. Any other man, in such circumstances, would have given up in despair, but Mr. Fox's spirit seemed always to rise in exact proportion to the pressure that was laid upon him. While he pleaded incessantly for peace with France, he maintained a desperate struggle for the rights of the English people during that memorable season of agitation and alarm from 1793 to 1797. His remedy for the disaffection which prevailed so extensively among the middling and lower classes, was that of Lord Chatham: "Remove their grievances, that will restore them to peace and tranquillity." "It may be asked," said he, "what would I propose to do in times of agitation like the present? I will answer openly. If there is a tendency in the Dissenters to discontent, because they conceive themselves to be unjustly suspected and cruelly calumniated, what would I do? I would instantly repeal the Test and Corporation Acts, and take from them, by such a step, all cause of complaint. If there are any persons tinctured with a republican spirit, because they think that the representative government would be more perfect in a republic, I would endeavor to amend the representation of the Commons, and to show that the House, though not chosen by all, can have no other interest than to prove itself the representative of all. If there are men dissatisfied in Scotland, or Ireland, or elsewhere, by reason of disabilities and exemptions, of unjust prejudices, and of cruel restrictions, I would repeal the penal statutes, which are a disgrace to our law books. If *I* were to issue a proclamation [the King had just issued one against seditious writings], this should be my proclamation: 'If any man has a grievance, let him bring it to the bar of the Commons' House of Parliament, with the firm persuasion of having it honestly investigated.' These are the subsidies that I would grant to government."

Such were, indeed, the *subsidia*, the support and strength in the hearts of his people, which the King of England needed. But George III. and his counselors at that time looked only to restriction and force. A repeal of the Corporation and Test Acts was not to be thought of (though strenuously urged by Mr. Fox), because Dr. Price and Dr. Priestley, who were leading Dissenters, had been warm friends of the French Revolution. The King would hear nothing of any relief for the Roman Catholics; his coronation oath required him to keep them in perpetual bondage. As to parliamentary reform, Mr. Fox himself, at an earlier period, saw no plan which he thought free from objections; and hence Mr. Moore, and others of his friends, have been led hastily to represent him as a cold, if not a hypocritical advocate of this measure. But from a private letter (see article *Fox*, in the Encyclopedia Britannica), it appears that his views at this time experienced a material change. "I think," said he, "we ought to go further toward agreeing with the democratic or popular party than at any former period." Accordingly, in May, 1797, he supported Mr. Grey's motion for reform in a speech (to be found below) of uncommon beauty and force. His great struggle, however, for the rights of the people was somewhat earlier, during the period which has been called (though with some exaggeration) the "Reign of Terror." Lord Loughborough, and the other Whigs who seceded to Mr. Pitt, had urged the ministry, with the proverbial zeal of new converts, into the most violent measures for putting down political discussion. The Habeas Corpus Act was suspended; the Traitorous Correspondence Bill made it high treason to hold intercourse with the French, or supply them with any commodities; the Treasonable Practice Bill was designed to construe into treason a conspiracy to levy war, even without an *overt act* amounting thereto; and the Seditious Meetings' Bill forbade any assembly of more than fifty persons to be held for political purposes, without the license of a magistrate. The two bills last mentioned were so hostile to the spirit of a free government, that even Lord Thurlow opposed them in the most vehement manner. It was during the discussion of the latter, that Mr. Fox made his famous declaration, that "if the bill should pass into a law, contrary to the sense and opinion of a great majority of the nation, and if the law, after it was passed, should be executed according to the rigorous provisions of the act, *resistance would not be a question of duty, but of prudence*."[23]

It was unfortunate for Mr. Fox that he was so often hurried into rash declarations of this kind. Threats are not usually the best mode of defending the cause of freedom. Nor is it true that men, under a representative government, have a right instantly to resist any law which the Legislature have regularly enacted, unless it be one diametrically opposed to the law of God. There is another remedy both in the judiciary and in the popular branch of the government. Mr. Fox's doctrine, that "a law, contrary to the *sense* and *opinion* of the great majority of the nation," may be rightfully resisted, is a species of "nullification" hitherto unknown in America. Another of his hasty expressions did him great injury about three years after. At a dinner of the Whig club in 1798, he gave as a toast, "The *Sovereignty* of the People of Great Britain." Exactly what he meant by this, it is difficult to say. He was a firm friend of the British Constitution, with its three estates of King, Lords, and Commons. He always declared himself to be against a republic; and he could not, therefore, have wished that the functions of sovereignty should be taken from the

[23] See Parliamentary History, vol. xxxiii., p. 456.

existing head of the government, and conferred on the body of the people or their representatives in Parliament. If he only meant that the King and Lords ought to yield in all cases to the deliberate and well-ascertained wishes of the people (a doubtful doctrine, certainly, in a mixed government), he took a very unfortunate mode of expressing his views. It is not wonderful, at all events, that the King considered it as a personal insult, and ordered his name to be struck from the list of Privy Counselors, a step never taken in any other case during his long reign, except in that of Lord George Germaine when convicted of a dereliction of duty, if not of cowardice, at the battle of Minden.

Mr. Pitt's ascendency in the House was now so complete, that Mr. Fox had no motive to continue his attendance in Parliament. He therefore withdrew from public business for some years, devoting himself to literary pursuits and the society of his friends. At no time does his character appear in so amiable a point of view. He had gradually worn out his vices. His marriage with Mrs. Armstead, which was announced at a later period, exerted the happiest influence on his character. This was truly, as a friend remarked, the golden season of his life. He devoted much of his time to the study of the classics, and especially of the Greek tragedians. At this time, also, he commenced his work on the Revolution of 1688, which was published after his death.

From this retirement he was temporarily called forth by an occurrence which led to one of the noblest efforts of his eloquence. In December, 1799, Bonaparte was elected First Consul of France for ten years; and the day after his induction into office, he addressed a letter to the King of England in his own hand, making proposals of peace. Mr. Pitt, however, refused even to *treat* with him on the subject. Upon the third of February, 1800, the question came before the House on a motion for approving the course taken by the ministry, and Mr. Fox again appeared in his place. Mr. Pitt, who felt the difficulty of his situation, had prepared himself beforehand with the utmost care. In a speech of five hours long, he went back to the origin of the war, brought up minutely all the atrocities of the Revolution, dwelt on the instability of the successive governments which had marked its progress, commented with terrible severity on the character and crimes of Bonaparte during the preceding four years, and justified on these grounds his backwardness to recognize the new government or to rely on its offers of peace. When he concluded, at four o'clock in the morning, Mr. Fox, who was always most powerful in reply, instantly rose and answered him in a speech of nearly the same length, meeting him on all the main topics with a force of argument, a dexterity in wresting Mr. Pitt's weapons out of his hands and turning them against himself, a keenness of retort, a graphic power of description, and an impetuous flow of eloquence, to which we find no parallel in any of his published speeches. Both these great efforts will be found in this collection, with all the documents which are necessary to a full understanding of the argument. Respecting one topic dwelt upon in these speeches, namely, the *justice* of the war with France, it may be proper to add a few words explanatory of Mr. Fox's views, to be followed by similar statements, on a future page, as to the ground taken by Mr. Pitt.

Mr. Fox held that the grievances complained of by the English, viz., the opening of the River Scheldt, the French Decree of Fraternity, and the countenance shown to disaffected Englishmen (points to be explained hereafter in notes to these speeches), ought to have been made the subject of full and candid negotiation. England was bound not only to state her wrongs, but to say explicitly what would satisfy her. But Mr. Pitt recalled the English embassador from Paris on the tenth of August, 1792 (when Louis XVI. became virtually a prisoner), *before* the occurrence of any of these events. He suspended the functions of M. Chauvelin, the French embassador at London, from the same date. He began to arm immediately after the alleged grievances took place; and when called upon by the French for an explanation of this armament, he declined to acknowledge their agents as having any diplomatic character, so that the points in dispute could not be regularly discussed; and after the execution of Louis XVI., he not only refused to accredit any minister from France, but sent M. Chauvelin out of the kingdom. Mr. Fox maintained that England, under these circumstances, was the aggressor, though the formal declaration of war came from France. He who shuts up the channel of negotiation while disputes are pending, is the author of the war which follows. No nation is bound to degrade herself by submitting to any clandestine modes of communication; she is entitled to that open, avowed, and honorable negotiation commonly employed by nations for the pacific adjustment of their disputes. Mr. Fox did not ask the ministry to treat with the new French government as having any existence *de jure*—he expressly waived this—but simply *de facto;* and as the English government had refused this, he held them responsible for the war. Such was his argument, and it was certainly one of great force. It may be true, as alleged by the friends of Mr. Pitt, that the French government were insincere in their offers and explanations; it is highly probable that the enthusiasm awakened by their triumph over their Austrian and Prussian invaders, had filled the nation with a love of conquest which would ultimately have led to a war with England. For this very reason, however, the course marked out by Mr. Fox ought to have been studiously followed. But Mr. Pitt shared in the common delusion of the day. He felt certain that France, split up as she was into a thousand factions, could not long endure the contest. "It will be a very short war," said he to a friend, "and certainly ended in one or two campaigns." Mr. Wilberforce, who at this time enjoyed his confidence, while he would not admit that the English were strictly the assailants, says in his Journal, "I had but too much reason to know that the ministry had not taken due pains to prevent its breaking out." As might be expected, Mr. Wilberforce united with Mr. Fox in condemning the refusal of Mr. Pitt to negotiate with Bonaparte.

But Mr. Fox's ardent desires for peace, though disappointed at this time, were soon after gratified by the treaty of Amiens, at the close of 1801. It proved, however, to be a mere truce. War was declared by England in January, 1803. To this declaration Mr. Fox was strenuously opposed, and made a speech against it, which Lord Brougham refers to as one of his greatest efforts. It does not so appear in any of the reports which have come down to us, and his Lordship perhaps confounded it with the speech of October, 1800, which he does not even mention.

Mr. Pitt, who had been again placed at the head of affairs, died in January, 1806; and Mr. Fox, at the end of twenty-two years, was called into the service of his country as Secretary of Foreign Affairs, on the 5th of February, 1806, through the instrumentality of Lord Grenville. His office was at that time the most important one under the government, and he may be considered as virtually minister. One of his first official acts was that of moving a resolution for an early abolition of the slave trade, which he had from the first united with Mr. Wilberforce in opposing. This resolution was carried by a vote of 114 against 15, and was followed up, the next session, by effectual measures for putting an end to this guilty traffic. He soon after entered on a negotiation for peace with France, which commenced in a somewhat singular manner. A Frenchman made his appearance at the Foreign Office, under the name of De la Grevilliere, and requested a private interview with Mr. Fox. He went on to say, that "it was necessary for the tranquillity of all crowned heads to put to death the ruler of France, and that a house had been hired at Passy for this purpose." On hearing these words, Mr. Fox drove him at once from his presence, and dispatched a communication to Talleyrand informing him of the facts. "I am not ashamed to confess to you who know me," said he, "that my confusion was extreme at finding myself led into conversation with an avowed assassin. I instantly ordered him to leave me. Our laws do not allow me to detain him, but I shall take care to have him landed at a sea-port as remote as possible from France." A reply was sent from Bonaparte, saying, among other things, "I recognize here the principles, honor, and virtue of Mr. Fox. Thank him on my part." In connection with this reply, Talleyrand stated, that the Emperor was ready to negotiate for a peace, "on the basis of the treaty of Amiens." Communications were accordingly opened on the subject, but at this important crisis Mr. Fox's health began to fail him. He had been taken ill some months before in consequence of exposure at the funeral of Lord Nelson, and his physicians now insisted that he should abstain for a time from all public duties. In July the disease was found to be dropsy of the chest, and, after lingering for three months, he died at the house of the Duke of Devonshire, at Chiswick, on the 13th of September, 1806. He was buried with the highest honors of the nation in Westminster Abbey, his grave being directly adjoining the grave of Lord Chatham, and close to that of his illustrious rival, William Pitt.

Mr. Fox was the most completely *English* of all the orators in our language. Lord Chatham was formed on the classic model—the express union of force, majesty, and grace. He stood raised above his audience, and launched the bolts of his eloquence like the Apollo Belvidere, with the proud consciousness of irresistible might. Mr. Fox stood on the floor of the House like a Norfolkshire farmer in the midst of his fellows: short, thick-set, with his broad shoulders and capacious chest, his bushy hair and eyebrows, and his dark countenance working with emotion, the very image of blunt honesty and strength.

His *understanding* was all English—plain, practical, of prodigious force—always directed to definite ends and objects, under the absolute control of sound common sense. He had that historical cast of mind by which the great English jurists and statesmen have been so generally distinguished. Facts were the staple of his thoughts; all the force of his intellect was exerted on the actual and the positive. He was the most practical speaker of the most practical nation on earth.

His *heart* was English. There is a depth and tenderness of feeling in the national character, which is all the greater in a strong mind, because custom requires it to be repressed. In private life no one was more guarded in this respect than Mr. Fox; he was the last man to be concerned in getting up a *scene*. But when he stood before an audience, he poured out his feelings with all the simplicity of a child. "I have seen his countenance," says Mr. Godwin, "lighten up with more than mortal ardor and goodness; I have been present when his voice was suffocated with tears." In all this, his powerful understanding went out the whole length of his emotions, so that there was nothing strained or unnatural in his most vehement bursts of passion. "His feeling," says Coleridge, "was all intellect, and his intellect was all feeling." Never was there a finer summing up; it shows us at a glance the whole secret of his power. To this he added the most perfect sincerity and artlessness of manner. His very faults conspired to heighten the conviction of his honesty. His broken sentences, the choking of his voice, his ungainly gestures, his sudden starts of passion, the absolute scream with which he delivered his vehement passages, all showed him to be deeply moved and in earnest, so that it may be doubted whether a more perfect delivery would not have weakened the impression he made.

Sir James Mackintosh has remarked, that "Fox was the most Demosthenean speaker since Demosthenes," while Lord Brougham says, in commenting on this passage, "There never was a greater mistake than the fancying a close resemblance between his eloquence and that of Demosthenes." When two such men differ on a point like this, we may safely say that both are in the right and in the wrong. As to certain qualities, Fox was the very reverse of the great Athenian; as to others, they had much in common. In whatever relates to the forms of oratory—symmetry, dignity, grace, the working up of thought and language to their most perfect expression —Mr. Fox was not only inferior to Demosthenes, but wholly unlike him, having no rhetoric and no ideality; while, at the same time, in the structure of his understanding, the modes of its operation, the soul and spirit which breathes throughout his eloquence, there was a striking resemblance. This will appear as we dwell for a moment on his leading peculiarities.

(1.) He had a luminous simplicity, which gave his speeches the most absolute unity of impression, however irregular might be their arrangement. No man ever kept the great points of his case more steadily and vividly before the minds of his audience.

(2.) He took every thing in the concrete. If he discussed principles, it was always in direct connection with the subject before him. Usually, however, he did not even discuss a subject—he grappled with an antagonist. Nothing gives such life and interest to a speech, or so delights an audience, as a direct contest of man with man.

(3.) He struck instantly at the heart of his subject. He was eager to meet his opponent at once on the real points at issue; and the moment of his greatest power was when he stated the argument against himself, with more force than his adversary or any other man could give it, and then seized it with the hand of a giant, tore it in pieces, and trampled it under foot.

(4.) His mode of enforcing a subject on the minds of his audience was to come back again and again to the strong points of his case. Mr. Pitt *amplified* when he wished to impress, Mr. Fox *repeated*. Demosthenes also repeated, but he had more adroitness in varying the mode of doing it. "Idem haud iisdem verbis."

(5.) He had rarely any preconceived method or arrangement of his thoughts. This was one of his greatest faults, in which he differed most from the Athenian artist. If it had not been for the unity of impression and feeling mentioned above, his strength would have been wasted in disconnected efforts.

(6.) Reasoning was his forte and his passion. But he was not a regular reasoner. In his eagerness to press forward, he threw away every thing he could part with, and compacted the rest into a single mass. Facts, principles, analogies, were all wrought together like the strands of a cable, and intermingled with wit, ridicule, or impassioned feeling. His arguments were usually personal in their nature, *ad hominem*, &c., and were brought home to his antagonist with stinging severity and force.

(7.) He abounded in *hits*—those abrupt and startling turns of thought which rouse an audience, and give them more delight than the loftiest strains of eloquence.

(8.) He was equally distinguished for his *side blows*, for keen and pungent remarks flashed out upon his antagonist in passing, as he pressed on with his argument.

(9.) He was often dramatic, personating the character of his opponents or others, and carrying on a dialogue between them, which added greatly to the liveliness and force of his oratory.

(10.) He had astonishing dexterity in evading difficulties, and turning to his own advantage every thing that occurred in debate.

In nearly all these qualities he had a close resemblance to Demosthenes.

In his language, Mr. Fox studied simplicity, strength, and boldness. "Give me an elegant Latin and a homely Saxon word," said he, "and I will always choose the latter." Another of his sayings was this: "Did the speech read well when reported? If so, it was a bad one." These two remarks give us the secret of his style as an orator.

The life of Mr. Fox has this lesson for young men, that early habits of recklessness and vice can hardly fail to destroy the influence of the most splendid abilities and the most humane and generous dispositions. Though thirty-eight years in public life, he was in office only eighteen months.

SPEECH

OF MR. FOX ON THE BILL FOR VESTING THE AFFAIRS OF THE EAST INDIA COMPANY IN THE HANDS OF CERTAIN COMMISSIONERS, FOR THE BENEFIT OF THE PROPRIETORS AND THE PUBLIC, DELIVERED IN THE HOUSE OF COMMONS, DECEMBER 1, 1783.

INTRODUCTION.

THE reader is already acquainted with the leading provisions of this bill, which were stated in the introduction to Mr. Burke's speech on the same subject. It was intended to place all the concerns of the East India Company in the hands of the British government. It abolished the courts of Directors and Proprietors, and divided the duties of the former between two distinct Boards. The first, having the entire government of India, civil and military, with the appointment and removal of officers, was to consist of seven Commissioners or Directors, to be chosen first by Parliament, and afterward by the Crown, and removable only in consequence of an address to the King from one of the Houses of Parliament. The other, having the management of the Company's commercial concerns, was to consist of nine Assistant Directors, appointed in the first instance by Parliament, and afterward by a major vote of the proprietors at an open poll. The bill was to remain in force four years, until after the next general election; and was accompanied by another, containing a variety of excellent regulations for the removal of abuses in India.

The debate was long and vehement. Burke had delivered his splendid speech of four hours in length, pouring forth a flood of information on the subject of India, such as no other man in England could have communicated. Dundas had attacked the bill with all his acuteness, and his perfect acquaintance with Indian affairs. Mr. Pitt had followed, denouncing it as a violation of chartered rights, designed to create an "imperium in imperio," which would place Mr. Fox above the King's control, and promising to bring forward another proposal "which would answer all the exigencies of the case without the violence and danger of this measure." It was at the end of such a debate, after two o'clock in the morning, that Mr. Fox rose to speak; and probably not a man in the kingdom but himself could have obtained a hearing under such circumstances, much less have commanded the fixed attention of the House for nearly three hours longer, as he did in this speech.

As he spoke in reply, his object was not so much to dwell on the positive side of the argument, which he had already done at the second reading of the bill, as to obviate objections, to turn back the reasoning of his antagonists upon themselves, and especially to relieve his character from the odium which rested upon it in consequence of his coalition with Lord North. As a specimen of uncommon dexterity in this respect, and of bold, indignant retort upon his antagonists, it has a high order of merit.

SPEECH, &c.

SIR,—The necessity of my saying something upon the present occasion is so obvious to the House, that no apology will, I hope, be expected from me in troubling them even at so late an hour.[1] I shall not enter much into a detail, or minute defense of the particulars of the bill before you, because few particular objections have been made. The opposition to it consists only in general reasonings, some of little application, and others totally aside from the point in question.

The bill has been combated through its past stages upon various principles; but, to the present moment, the House has not heard it canvassed upon its own intrinsic merits. The debate to-night has turned chiefly upon two points, namely, *violation of charter*, and *increase of influence;* and upon both these points I shall say a few words.

The honorable gentleman, who opened the debate [Mr. Powis], first demands my attention; not, indeed, for the wisdom of the observations which fell from him this night (acute and judicious though he is upon most occasions), but from the natural weight of all such characters in this country, the aggregate of whom should, I think, always decide upon public measures. His ingenuity, however, was never, in my opinion, exerted more ineffectually, upon more mistaken principles, and more inconsistent with the common tenor of his conduct, than in this debate.

Preliminary remarks on its connection with the cause of liberty.

The honorable gentleman charges me with abandoning that cause, which, he says in terms of flattery, I had once so successfully asserted. I tell him, in reply, that if he were to search the history of my life, he would find that the period of it in which I struggled most for the real, substantial cause of liberty is this very moment that I am addressing you. Freedom, according to my conception of it, consists in the safe and sacred possession of a man's property, governed by laws defined and certain; with many personal privileges, natural, civil, and religious, which

[1] Two o'clock in the morning.

he can not surrender without ruin to himself, and of which to be deprived by any other power is despotism. This bill, instead of subverting, is destined to stabilitate these principles; instead of narrowing the basis of freedom, it tends to enlarge it; instead of suppressing, its object is *to infuse and circulate the spirit of liberty.*

What is the most odious species of tyranny? Precisely that which this bill is meant to annihilate. That a handful of men, free themselves, should exercise the most base and abominable despotism over millions of their fellow-creatures; that innocence should be the victim of oppression; that industry should toil for rapine; that the harmless laborer should sweat, not for his own benefit, but for the luxury and rapacity of tyrannic depredation; in a word, that thirty millions of men, gifted by Providence with the ordinary endowments of humanity, should groan under a system of despotism, unmatched in all the histories of the world?[2] What is the end of all government? Certainly the happiness of the governed. Others may hold different opinions; but this is mine, and I proclaim it. What, then, are we to think of a government, whose good fortune is supposed to spring from the calamities of its subjects, whose aggrandizement grows out of the miseries of mankind? This is the kind of government exercised under the East India Company upon the natives of Hindostan; and the subversion of that infamous government is the main object of the bill in question.

Violation of charter justified.

I. But in the progress of accomplishing this end, it is objected that the charter of the Company should not be violated; and upon this point, sir, I shall deliver my opinion without disguise. A charter is a trust to one or more persons for some given benefit. If this trust be abused, if the benefit be not obtained, and that its failure arises from palpable guilt, or (what in this case is full as bad) from palpable ignorance or mismanagement, will any man gravely say that the trust should not be resumed and delivered to other hands?—more especially in the case of the East India Company, whose manner of executing this trust, whose laxity and languor produced, and tend to produce consequences diametrically opposite to the ends of confiding that trust, and of the institution for which it was granted? I beg of gentlemen to be aware of the lengths to which their arguments upon the intangibility of this charter may be carried. Every syllable virtually impeaches the establishment by which we sit in this House, in the enjoyment of this freedom, and of every other blessing of our government. Arguments of this kind are batteries against the main pillar of the British Constitution. Some men are consistent with their own private opinions, and discover the inheritance of family maxims when they question the principles of the Revolution; but I have no scruple in subscribing to the articles of that creed which produced it.[3] Sovereigns are sacred, and reverence is due to every king; yet, with all my attachments to the person of a first magistrate, had I lived in the reign of James the Second, I should most certainly have contributed my efforts, and borne part in those illustrious struggles which vindicated an empire from hereditary servitude, and recorded this valuable doctrine, *that trust abused is revocable.*

No man will tell me that a trust to a company of merchants stands upon the solemn and sanctified ground by which a trust is committed to a monarch; I am, therefore, at a loss to reconcile the conduct of men who approve that resumption of violated trust, which rescued and re-established our unparalleled and admirable Constitution with a thousand valuable improvements and advantages at the Revolution, and who, at this moment, rise up the champions of the East India Company's charter,[4] although the incapacity and incompetence of that Company to a due and adequate discharge of the trust deposited in them by that charter are themes of ridicule and contempt to all the world; and although, in consequence of their mismanagement, connivance, and imbecility, combined with the wickedness of their servants, the very name of an Englishman is detested, even to a proverb, throughout all Asia, and the national character is become degraded and dishonored. To rescue that name from odium, and redeem this character from disgrace, are some of the objects of the present bill; and gentlemen should, indeed, gravely weigh their opposition to a measure, which, with a thousand other points not less valuable, aims at the attainment of these objects.

Those who condemn the present bill as a violation of the chartered rights of the East India Company, condemn, on the same ground, I say again, the Revolution as a violation of the chartered rights of King James II.[5] He, with as much reason, might have claimed the property

[2] We have here one of Mr. Fox's peculiarities, on which much of his force depends, viz., terse and rapid enumeration—the crowding of many particulars into one striking mass of thought. His enumerations, however, are not made, like those of most men, for rhetorical effect; they are *condensed arguments,* as will be seen by analyzing this passage.

[3] Johnson decides the question in the same way with Mr. Fox, in his Taxation no Tyranny. "A charter is a grant of certain powers or privileges given to a part of the community for the advantage of the whole; and is therefore liable, by its nature, to change or to revocation. Every act of government aims at public good. A charter, which experience has shown to be detrimental to the nation, is to be repealed; because general prosperity must always be preferred to particular interest. If a charter be used to evil purposes, it is forfeited, as the weapon is taken away which is injuriously employed."

[4] Here is another characteristic of Mr. Fox, that of turning defense into attack. The reader of Demosthenes will remember how uniformly the same thing is done by the great Athenian orator.

[5] Mr. Fox gives us, thus early, one of those *repetitions* by which he was so much accustomed to enforce his reasonings. The statement, however, is finely varied by an expansion of the argument, and enlivened by that *dramatic* mode of presenting the thought, in which he so much delighted.

of dominion. But what was the language of the people? "No, you have no property in dominion. Dominion was vested in you, as it is in every chief magistrate, for the benefit of the community to be governed. It was a sacred trust, delegated by compact. You have abused the trust; you have exercised dominion for the purposes of vexation and tyranny—not of comfort, protection, and good order, and we therefore resume the power which was originally ours. We recur to the first principles of all government, the will of the many; and it is our will that you shall no longer abuse your dominion." The case is the same with the East India Company's government over a territory, as it has been said by Mr. Burke, of two hundred and eighty thousand square miles in extent, nearly equal to all Christian Europe, and containing thirty millions of the human race. It matters not whether dominion arises from conquest or from compact. Conquest gives no right to the conqueror to be a tyrant; and it is no violation of right to abolish the authority which is misused.

Objections answered.

II. Having said so much upon the general matter of the bill, I must beg leave to make a few observations upon the remarks of particular gentlemen; and first of the learned gentleman over against me [Mr. Dundas]. The learned gentleman has made a long, and, as he always does, an able speech; yet, translated into plain English, and disrobed of the dextrous ambiguity in which it has been enveloped, to what does it amount? To an establishment of the principles upon which this bill was founded, and an indirect confession of its necessity. He allows the frangibility of charters, when absolute occasion requires it; and admits that the charter of the Company should not prevent the adoption of a proper plan for the future government of India, if a proper plan can be achieved upon no other terms. The first of these admissions seems agreeable to the civil maxims of the learned gentleman's life, so far as a maxim can be traced in a political character so various and flexible;[6] and to deny the second of these concessions was impossible even for the learned gentleman, with a staring reason upon your table to confront him if he attempted it.[7] The learned gentleman's bill, and the bill before you, are grounded upon the same bottom, of abuse of trust, maladministration, debility, and incapacity in the Company and their servants. But the difference in the remedy is this: the learned gentleman's bill opens a door to an influence a hundred times more dangerous than any that can be imputed to this bill; and deposits in one man an arbitrary power over millions, not in England, where the evil of this corrupt ministry could not be felt, but in the East Indies, the scene of every mischief, fraud, and violence. The learned gentleman's bill afforded the most extensive latitude for malversation; the bill before you guards against it with all imaginable precaution. Every line in both the bills, which I have had the honor to introduce, presumes the possibility of bad administration, for every word breathes suspicion. This bill supposes that men are but men. It confides in no integrity; it trusts no character; it inculcates the wisdom of a jealousy of power, and annexes responsibility, not only to every *action*, but even to the *inaction* of those who are to dispense it. The necessity of these provisions must be evident, when it is known that the different misfortunes of the Company have resulted not more from what the servants *did*, than from what the *masters did not*.

To the probable effects of the learned gentleman's bill and this, I beg to call the attention of the House. Allowing, for argument's sake, to the Governor General of India, under the first-named bill [Mr. Dundas']. the most unlimited and superior abilities, with soundness of heart, and integrity the most unquestionable; what good consequences could be reasonably expected from his extraordinary, extravagant, and unconstitutional power, under the tenure by which he held it? Were his projects the most enlarged, his systems the most wise and excellent which human skill could devise; what fair hopes could be entertained of their eventual success, when, perhaps, before he could enter upon the execution of any measure, he may be recalled in consequence of one of those changes in the administrations of this country, which have been so frequent for a few years, and which some good men wish to see every year? Exactly the same reasons which banish all rational hope of benefit from an Indian administration under the bill of the learned gentleman, justify the duration of the proposed commission. If the dispensers of the plan of governing India (a place from which the answer of a letter can not be expected in less than twelve months) have not greater stability in their situations than a British ministry, adieu to all hopes of rendering our Eastern territories of any real advantage to this country; adieu to every expectation of purging or purifying the Indian system, of reform, of improvement, of reviving confidence, of regulating the trade upon its proper principles, of restoring tranquillity, of re-establishing the natives in comfort, and of securing the perpetuity of these blessings by the cordial reconcilement of the Indians with their former tyrants upon fixed terms of amity, friendship, and fellowship. I will leave the House and the kingdom to judge which is best calculated to accomplish those salutary ends; the bill of the learned gentleman, which leaves all to the discretion of one man, or the bill before you, which de-

[6] A side blow of this kind, in passing, is peculiarly characteristic of Mr. Fox.

[7] Mr. Dundas, as a member of the Shelburne ministry, had brought in a bill on the subject about seven months before. This gave the Governor General of Bengal a controlling power over the other two presidencies; and authorized him, when he saw fit, to act on his own responsibility, in opposition to the opinion of his own council. His bill also created a new Secretary of State for Indian affairs, with ample powers resembling, to a considerable extent, those of Mr. Fox's commissioners.

pends upon the duty of several men, who are in a state of daily account to this House, of hourly account to the ministers of the Crown, of occasional account to the proprietors of East India stock, and who are allowed sufficient time to practice their plans, unaffected by every political fluctuation.

But the learned gentleman wishes the appointment of an Indian Secretary of State in preference to these commissioners. In all the learned gentleman's ideas on the government of India, the notion of a new Secretary of State for the Indian department springs up, and seems to be cherished with the fondness of consanguinity.[8] But that scheme strikes me as liable to a thousand times more objections than the plan in agitation; nay, the learned gentleman had rather, it seems, the affairs of India were blended with the business of the office which I have the honor to hold. His good disposition toward me upon all occasions can not be doubted, and his *sincerity* in this opinion is unquestionable. I beg the House to attend to the reason which the learned gentleman gives for this preference, and to see the plights to which men even of his understanding are reduced who *must* oppose. He laughs at the responsibility of the Commissioners to this House, who, in his judgment, will find means of soothing and softening, and meliorating the members into an oblivion of their maladministration. What opinion has the learned gentleman of a Secretary of State? Does he think *him* so inert, so inactive, so incapable a creature, that, with all this vaunted patronage of the seven Commissioners in his own hands, the same means of soothing, and softening, and meliorating, are thrown away upon him? The learned gentleman has been for some years conversant with ministers; but his experience has taught him, it seems, to consider secretaries not only untainted and immaculate, but innocent, harmless, and incapable! In his time, secretaries were all *purity*, with every power of corruption in their hands; but so inflexibly attached to rigid rectitude, that no temptation could seduce them to employ that power for the purpose of corrupting, or, to use his own words, for soothing, or softening, or meliorating! The learned gentleman has formed his opinion of the simplicity and inaction of secretaries from that golden age of political probity when his own friends were in power, and when himself was every thing but a minister. This erroneous humanity of opinion arises from the learned gentleman's unsuspecting, unsullied nature, as well as from a commerce with only the best and purest ministers of this country, which has given him so favorable an impression of a Secretary of State that he thinks this patronage, so dangerous in the hands of seven Commissioners, perfectly safe in *his* hands.[9] I leave to the learned gentleman that pleasure which his mind must feel under the conviction with which he certainly gives this opinion; but I submit to every man who hears me, what would be the probable comments of the other side of the House, had I proposed either the erection of an Indian secretary, or the annexation of the Indian business to the office which I hold?

In the assemblage of the learned gentleman's objections, there is one still more curious than those I have mentioned. He dislikes this bill because it establishes an *imperium in imperio* [one government within another]. In the course of opposition to this measure, we have been familiarized to hear certain sentiments and particular words in this House, but directed, in reality, to *other* places [for the King]. I therefore take it for granted that the learned gentleman has not so despicable an idea of the good sense of the members, as to expect any more attention within these walls to such a dogma than has been shown to the favorite phrase of his honorable friend near him [Mr. Pitt], who calls a bill which backs this sinking Company with the credit of the state a *confiscation* of their property! I would only wish to ask the learned gentleman if he really holds the understanding even of the multitude in such contempt as to imagine this species of argument can have the very slightest effect? The multitude know the fallacy of it as well as the learned gentleman himself. They know that a dissolution of the East India Company has been wished for scores of years, by many good people in this country, for the very reason that it was an *imperium in imperio*. Yet the learned gentleman, with infinite gravity of face, tells you he dislikes this bill, because it establishes this novel and odious principle! Even a glance at this bill, compared with the present constitution of the Company, manifests the futility of this objection, and proves that the Company is, in its present form, a thousand times more an *imperium in imperio* than the proposed Commissioners. The worst species of government is that which can run counter to all the ends of its institution with impunity. Such exactly is the East India Company. No man can say that the Directors and proprietors have not, in numerous instances, merited severe infliction; yet who did ever think of a legal punishment for either body? Now the great feature of this bill is to render the Commissioners amenable, and to punish them upon delinquency.

The learned gentleman prides himself that his bill did not meddle with the *commerce* of the Company; and another gentleman, after acknowledging the folly of leaving the government in the hands of the Company, proposes to separate the commerce entirely from the domin-

[8] Had the Earl of Shelburne continued in power, it was understood that Mr. Dundas was to be the Indian secretary. Mr. Fox here stingingly alludes to this fact.

[9] These bitter sarcasms were aimed at Lord Shelburne, who was generally regarded as insincere and grasping. "His character," says a late writer, "was not simple; it was curiously artificial. Under the affectation of patriotism, he had a great craving for public honors. There was a vein of subtlety in his nature, and an appearance of insincerity in his manner, which deprived him of the confidence of his associates."—*Age of Fox and Pitt*, i., 109.

ion, and leave the former safe and untouched to the Company itself. I beg leave to appeal to every gentleman conversant in the Company's affairs, whether this measure is, in the nature of things, practicable at this moment. That the separation of the commerce from the government of the East may be ultimately brought about, I doubt not. But when gentlemen reflect upon the immediate state of the Company's affairs; when they reflect that their government was carried on for the sake of their commerce; that both have been blended together for such a series of years; when they review the peculiar, perplexed, and involved state of the eastern territories, their dissimilitude to every system in this part of the globe, and consider the deep and laborious deliberation with which every step for the establishment of a salutary plan of government, in the room of the present odious one, must be taken—the utter impossibility of instantly detaching the governing power from interference with the commercial body, will be clear and indubitable.

A gentleman has asked, Why not choose the Commissioners out of the [present] body of Directors; and why not leave the choice of the *Assistant* Directors in the Court of Proprietors? That is to say, why not do that which would infallibly undo all you are aiming at? I mean no general disparagement when I say that the body of the Directors have given memorable proofs that they are not the sort of people to whom any man can look for the success or salvation of India. Among them there are, without doubt, some individuals respectable both for their knowledge and integrity; but I put it to the candor of gentlemen, whether they are the species of men whose wisdom, energy, and diligence would give any promise of emancipating the East India concerns from their present disasters and disgraces. Indeed, both questions may be answered in two words. Why not choose the Directors, *who have ruined the Company?* Why not leave the power of election in the proprietors, *who have thwarted every good attempted by the Directors?*

The last point adverted to by the learned gentleman relates to *influence;* and upon his remarks, combined with what fell from some others upon the same subject, I beg leave to make a few observations. Much of my life has been employed to diminish the inordinate influence of the Crown. In common with others, I succeeded; and I glory in it.[10] To support that kind of influence which I formerly subverted, is a deed of which I shall never deserve to be accused. The affirmation with which I first introduced this plan, I now repeat. I reassert, that this bill as little augments the influence of the Crown as any measure which can be devised for the government of India, that presents the slightest promise of solid success; and that it tends to increase it in a far less degree than the bill proposed by the learned gentleman [Mr. Dundas]. The very genius of influence consists in hope or fear; fear of losing what we have, or hope of gaining more. Make these Commissioners removable at will, and you set all the little passions of human nature afloat. If benefit can be derived from the bill, you had better burn it than make the duration short of the time necessary to accomplish the plans it is destined for. *That* consideration pointed out the expediency of a fixed period, and in that respect it accords with the principle of the learned gentleman's bill, with this superior advantage, that, instead of leaving the Commissioners liable to all the influence which springs from the appointment of a Governor General, removable at pleasure, this bill invests them with the power, for the *time specified*, upon the same tenure that British judges hold their station; removable upon delinquency, punishable upon guilt; but fearless of power if they discharge their trust, liable to no seducement, and with full time and authority to execute their functions for the common good of the country, and for their own glory. I beg of the House to attend to this difference, and then judge upon the point of increasing the influence of the Crown, contrasted with the learned gentleman's bill.

The state of accusations against me upon this subject of *influence*, is truly curious. The learned gentleman [Mr. Dundas], in strains of emphasis, declares that this bill diminishes the influence of the Crown beyond all former attempts, and calls upon those who formerly voted with him in support of that influence, against our efforts to reduce it, and who now sit near me, to join him now in opposing my attempts to diminish that darling influence. He tells them I "out-Heroded Herod;" that I am outdoing all my former outdoings; and proclaims me as the merciless and insatiate enemy of the influence of the Crown.

Down sits the learned gentleman, and up starts an honorable gentleman [Mr. Martin], with a charge against me, upon the same subject, of a nature the *direct reverse*. I have fought under your banners, cries the honorable gentleman, against that fell giant, the influence of the Crown. I have bled in that battle which you commanded, and have a claim upon the rights of soldiership. You have conquered through us; and now that victory is in your arms, you turn traitor to our cause, and carry over your powers to the enemy. The fiercest of your former combatants in the cause of influence falls far short of you at this moment; your attempts in re-erecting this monster exceed all the exertions of your former foes. This night you will make the influence of the Crown a Colossus, that shall bestride the land and crush every impediment. I impeach you for treachery to your ancient principles! Come, come, and divide with us!!

This honorable gentleman, after a thrust or two at the Coalition, sits down; and while the House is perplexing itself to reconcile these wide

[10] Mr. Fox and his friends had long urged, and succeeded at last in passing, the celebrated resolution drawn up by Mr. Dunning, "That the influence of the Crown has increased, is increasing, and *ought to be diminished.*" He applies this principle very happily to the present case, by showing that the Commissioners must be raised above that influence, if they are to discharge their duty.

differences, the right honorable gentleman [Mr. Pitt] over the way confounds all past contradiction, by combining, in his own person, these extravagant extremes. He acknowledges that he has digested a paradox; and a paradox well he might call it, for never did a grosser one puzzle the intellects of a public assembly. By a miraculous kind of discernment, he has found out that the bill both *increases* and *diminishes* the influence of the Crown!

The bill diminishes the influence of the Crown, says one; you are wrong, says a second, it increases it: you are both right, says a third, for it both increases and diminishes the influence of the Crown! Now, as most members have one or other of these opinions upon the subject, the honorable gentleman can safely join with all parties upon this point; but few, I trust, will be found to join *him!*[11]

Thus, sir, is this bill combated, and thus am I accused. The nature and substance of these objections I construe as the strongest comment upon the excellence of the bill. If a more rational opposition *could* be made to it, no doubt it would. The truth is, it increases the influence of the Crown, and the influence of party, as little as possible; and if the reform of India, or any other matter, is to be postponed until a scheme be devised against which ingenuity, or ignorance, or caprice, shall not raise objections, the affairs of human life must stand still.

Conduct of Mr. Pitt.

I beg the House will attend a little to the manner in which the progress of this bill has been retarded, especially by the right honorable gentleman [Mr. Pitt]. First, the members were not all in town, and time was desired upon that account. Next, the finances of the East India Company were misstated by me, and time was desired to prove that. The time came, and the proofs were exhibited, counsel heard, and yet the issue was, that my former statement, instead of being controverted, became more established by the very proofs which were brought to overturn it. The honorable gentleman has misrepresented me to-night again. He has an evident pleasure in it, which, indeed, I can not prevent; but I can prevent this House and this country from believing him. He prefers the authority of his own conception (eager enough, in all conscience, to misunderstand me) of what I said, to my own repeated declarations of my own meaning. He supposes I mistake, because he wishes it. I never did say, the Company were absolute bankrupts to the amount of the debt; but I said there was immediate necessity of paying that given sum, without any immediate means of providing for it. The account of the Company's circumstances, presented last week, furnished matter of triumph to the honorable gentleman for the full space of three hours; that is to say, while counsel were at the bar. I made no objection to the account but this *trifling* one, that £12,000,000 were stated which ought not to appear at all there, and which were placed there only for delusion and fallacy. I never objected to the arithmetic of the account. The sums, I doubt not, were accurately cast up even to a figure. Yet the House will recollect that the honorable gentleman, about this very hour of that debate, endeavored to protract the business to the next day, upon assuring the House that the Company would then support their statement. I refused to accede, because I knew the matter to be mere shifting and maneuvering for a vote, and that the Company *could not* support their statement. Was I right? The House sees whether I was. The House sees the finance post is now totally abandoned, and for the best reason in the world, because it is no longer tenable. But the honorable gentleman is, indeed, a man of resources. He now gives me a *challenge;* and I beg the House to remark that I accept his challenge, and that I prophecy he will no more meet me upon this than upon the former points.[12]

But there is no limit to a youthful and vigorous fancy. The right honorable gentleman just now, in very serious terms, and with all his habitual gravity, engages, if the House will join in opposing us to-night, that he will digest and methodize a plan, the outline of which he has already conceived. He has nothing *now* to offer; but justly confiding in the fertility of his own imagination, and the future exercise of his faculties, he promises that he *will* bring a plan, provided the majority of this House will join him to-night. Now, if ever an idea was thrown out to pick up a stray vote or two in the heel of a debate, by a device, the idea thrown out a while ago by the honorable gentleman is precisely such. But if I can augur rightly from the complexion of the House, his present will have exactly the same success with all his past stratagems to oppose this bill.[13]

Answer to the pretense that the Company was taken unawares.

His learned friend [Mr. Dundas], with singular placidness, without smile or sneer, has said, "as this measure was probably decided upon some time since, the East India Company, *who could not expect such a blow*, ought to have been informed of the intended project. The Company was evidently unaware of this attack, and, in fairness, should have been apprised of it." Does the learned gentleman imagine that men are in their sober senses who listen to such caviling and quibbling opposition? The Company unaware of this attack! The learned gentleman's own labors, independent of any other intimation,

[11] Mr. Fox did not very often indulge in humor; he was usually too much in earnest to do it; but, in exposing the inconsistency of his opponents, he caught the very spirit of Lord North. Thus he gave the House the relief of a hearty laugh after a sitting of ten hours, and laid the foundation, at the same time, of the conclusion which he draws, that his scheme can not be far from right, when opposed on such contradictory grounds.

[12] Mr. Pitt had challenged Mr. Fox to discuss with him the particulars of a statement drawn out by the Company, to which Mr. Fox had objected.

[13] He was right; for the ministry had an accession of five votes this night above the former division.

had been an ample warning to the Company to be prepared. Every man in the kingdom, who reads a newspaper, expected something; and the only wonder with the nation was, how it could be so long delayed. The reports of the committees alarmed the public so much, for the honor of the country, and for the salvation of the Company, that all eyes were upon East India affairs. This sort of observation had, indeed, much better come from any other man in this House than from that identical gentleman.

If these were not sufficient to rouse the attention and diligence of the Company, his Majesty's speech at the commencement and conclusion of the late session of Parliament gave them note of preparation in the most plain and decisive terms. In his opening speech, his Majesty thus speaks to Parliament upon the subject of India:

"The regulation of a vast territory in Asia opens a large field for your wisdom, prudence, and foresight. I trust that you will be able to form some fundamental laws which may make their connection with Great Britain a blessing to India; and that you will take therein proper measures to give all foreign nations, in matters of foreign commerce, an entire and perfect confidence in the probity, punctuality, and good order of our government. You may be assured that whatever depends upon me shall be executed with a steadiness which can alone preserve that part of my dominions, or the commerce which arises from it."

The learned gentleman, who knows more of the dispositions of the Cabinet [Lord Shelburne's] at that time than I do, can better tell whether any measure of this nature was then intended. The words are very wide, and seem to portend, at least, something very important; but whether any thing similar to this measure was meant, as this passage seems to imply, or not, is indifferent to the point in question; this is clear from it, that it gives a very ceremonious warning to the East India Company; enough surely to expose the weakness and futility of the learned gentleman's remark. The changes and circumstances of the cabinet, in the course of the last session, can be the only excuse for the delay of some decisive measure with regard to India; and if, in addition to all these, any thing more is requisite to confirm the notoriety of Parliament's being to enter upon the business, the following paragraph of the King's closing speech, last July, completes the mass of evidence against the learned gentleman.

His Majesty, after intimating a belief that he shall be obliged to call his Parliament together earlier than usual, thus speaks:

"The consideration of the affairs of the East Indies will require to be resumed as early as possible, and to be pursued with a serious and unremitting attention." Superadd to all this the part of the King's opening speech this year upon India; and if the whole do not constitute sufficient testimony that the Company had full notice, nothing can.

Yet, notwithstanding all this, the learned gentleman accuses us of surprising the Company; and his right honorable friend [Mr. Pitt], in hopes his proposal of another bill may have weight in the division, repeats the hackneyed charge of precipitation, and forces the argument for delay in a taunt, "that we wish to get rid of our torments by sending this bill to the other House." The honorable gentleman's talents are splendid and various; but I assure him that all his efforts for the last eight days have not given me a single torment. Were I to choose a species of opposition to insure a ministerial tranquillity, it would be the kind of opposition which this bill has received; in which every thing brought to confute has tended to confirm, and in which the arguments adduced to expose the weakness have furnished materials to establish the wisdom of the measure. So impossible is it, without something of a tolerable cause, even for the right honorable gentleman's abilities to have effect, though his genius may make a flourishing and superior figure in the attempt!

Before I proceed to the other parts of the debate, I wish to say one word upon a remark of the learned gentleman [Mr. Dundas]; he says, that the clause relative to the zemindars was suggested by his observations.[14] God forbid I should detract from the merit, or diminish the desert of any man. Undoubtedly that excellent part of the regulation bill derives from the learned gentleman; and if he were in this House when I introduced the subject of India he would have known, that I did him full and complete justice upon that point.

Real grounds of the bill.

My noble friend [Lord John Cavendish] has said, this bill does not arise from the poverty of the Company, but that *liberal policy* and *national honor* demanded it. Upon the last day this bill was debated, I confined myself chiefly to the demonstration of the fallacy and imposture of that notable schedule presented by the East India Company; and, having proved its falsehood, I can now with the greater safety declare, that if every shilling of that fictitious property were real and forthcoming, a bill of this nature was not therefore the less necessary. I thought we were fully understood upon this point, from the opening speech in this business, which did not so degrade the measure as to say it originated in the poverty of the Company. This, as my noble friend rightly remarks, was the smallest reason for its adoption, and this opinion is not, as the right honorable gentleman [Mr. Pitt] insinuates, "shifting," but recognizing and recording the true grounds of the bill. If any misunderstanding, then, has hitherto taken place upon this head, it will, I trust, cease henceforth; and so odious a libel upon this country will not pass current, as that sordid motives only induced the government of England to that which we were bound to do, as politicians, as Christians, and as men, by every

[14] The zemindars, or native landlords, had a right of inheritance confirmed to them in Mr. Fox's second bill.

consideration which makes a nation respectable, great, and glorious!

Having vindicated the bill from this aspersion, and founded it upon that basis which every honest and sensible man in England must approve, I may be allowed to say, that some regard may be had even to the mean and mercenary upon this subject—a portion of whom we have here, in common with all other countries. Will such men endure with temper a constant drain upon this kingdom, for the sake of this monopolizing corporation? Will those, for instance, who clamor against a twopenny tax, afford, with good-humor, million after million to the East India Company? The Sinking Fund is at this moment a million the worse for the deficiency of the Company; and as the noble Lord [Lord J. Cavendish] says, an extent [execution] must in three weeks arrest their property, if Parliament does not interpose, or enable them to discharge a part of their debt to the Crown. Let those, therefore, who think the commerce ought to be instantly separated from the dominion (were that at this time possible), and who think it ought to be left wholly in the present hands, reflect that the formation of a vigorous system of government for India is not more incumbent upon us than the establishment of the eastern trade, upon such principles of solidity and fitness as shall give some just hopes that the public may be speedily relieved from the monstrous pressure of constantly supporting the indigence of the Company.

Notice of a personal attack made by Mr Pitt.

I have spoke of myself very often in the course of what I have said this night, and must speak still more frequently in the course of what I have to say. The House will see this awkward task is rendered indispensable, infinitely more having been said concerning *me*, during the debate, than concerning the question, which is the proper subject of agitation. The right honorable gentleman [Mr. Pitt] says, that nothing ever happened to give him an ill impression of my character, or to prevent a mutual confidence. He says rightly; there have been interchanges of civility, and amicable habits between us, in which I trust I have given him no cause to complain. But after pronouncing a brilliant eulogy upon me and my capacity to serve the country, the honorable gentleman considers me, at the same time, the most dangerous man in the kingdom. (Mr. Pitt said across the House, "*dangerous only from this measure.*" To which Mr. Fox instantly made this reply.) I call upon the House to attend to the honorable gentleman. He thinks me dangerous *only* from this measure, and confesses that hitherto he has seen nothing in my conduct to obliterate his good opinion. Compare this with his opposition during the last and the present session. Let every man reflect, that up to this moment the honorable gentleman deemed me worthy of confidence, and competent to my situation in the state. I thank him for the *support* he has afforded to the minister he thus esteemed, and shall not press the advantage he gives me, farther than leaving to himself to reconcile his practice and his doctrine in the best manner he can.[15]

The Coalition.

III. The honorable gentleman [Mr. Pitt] could not for one night pass by the *Coalition;* yet I think he might have chosen a fitter time to express his indignation against the noble Lord [Lord North] than the present moment. An attack upon the noble Lord in his presence, would bear a more liberal color; and the cause of his absence now would surely rather disarm than irritate a generous enemy![16] There are distinctions in hatred, and the direst foes upon such occasions moderate their aversion. The Coalition is, however, a fruitful topic; and the power of traducing it, which the weakest and meanest creatures in the country enjoy and exercise, is of course equally vested in men of rank and parts, though every man of parts and rank would not be apt to participate the privilege. Upon the Coalition, the honorable gentleman is welcome to employ his ingenuity, but upon another subject alluded to by him I shall beg leave to advise, nay, even to instruct him.

In what system of ethics will the honorable gentleman find the precept taught of ripping up old sores, and reviving animosities among individuals, of which the parties themselves retain no memory?[17] This kind of practice may incur a much worse charge than weakness of understanding, and subject a man to much greater imputations than are commonly applied to political mistakes of party violence. The soundness of the *heart* may be liable to suspicion, and the moral character be in danger of suffering by it in the opinion of mankind. To cover the heats and obliterate the sense of former quarrels between two persons, is a very distinguished virtue; to renew the subject of such differences, and attempt the revival of such disputes, deserves a name which I could give it, if that honorable gentleman had not forgotten himself, and fallen into some such deviation. He values himself, I doubt not, too much again to make a similar slip, and must even feel thankful to me for the counsel I thus take the liberty to give him.

An honorable gentleman under the gallery [Mr. Martin], to whom an abuse of the Coalition seems a sort of luxury, wishes that a starling were at the right hand of the chair to cry out "disgraceful Coalition!" Sir, upon this subject I shall say but a few words.

Defense of that measure.

The calamitous situation of this country required an administration whose stability could give it a tone of firmness with foreign nations, and promise some hope of restoring the faded glories of the country. Such

[15] There is a great dexterity in this retort, and something of that *over-reaching* in the assumption, that Mr. Pitt had "seen nothing in his conduct to obliterate his *good opinion,*" which we sometimes see in Demosthenes.

[16] Lord North left the House, in a state of indisposition, about midnight.

[17] Alluding to the passage quoted by Mr. Pitt from that famous speech of Mr. Fox's, which produced the duel between him and Mr. Adam.

an administration could not be formed without *some* junction of the parties; and if former differences were to be an insurmountable barrier to union, no chance of salvation remained for the country, as it is well known that four public men could not be found who had not at one time or other taken opposite sides in politics. The great cause of difference between us and the noble Lord in the blue ribbon [Lord North] no longer existed; his personal character stood high; and thinking it safer to trust him than those who had before deceived us, we preferred to unite with the noble Lord. A similar junction in 1757,[18] against which a similar clamor was raised, saved the empire from ruin, and raised it above the rivalship of all its enemies. The country, when we came into office, bore not a very auspicious complexion; yet, sir, I do not despair of seeing it once again resume its consequence in the scale of nations, and make as splendid a figure as ever. Those who have asserted the impossibility of our agreeing with the noble Lord and his friends were false prophets, for events have belied their augury. We have differed like men, and like men we have agreed.

A body of the best and honestest men in this House, who serve their country without any other reward than the glory of the disinterested discharge of their public duty, approved that junction, and sanctify the measure by their cordial support.

Such, sir, is this Coalition, which the state of the country rendered indispensable, and for which the history of every country records a thousand precedents; yet to this the term disgraceful is applied! Is it not extraordinary, then, that gentlemen should be under such spells of false delusion as not to see that if calling it disgraceful makes it so, these epithets operate with equal force against themselves? If the Coalition be disgraceful, what is the *anti-Coalition?* When I see the right honorable gentleman [Mr. Pitt] surrounded by the early objects of his political, nay, his hereditary[19] hatred, and hear him revile the Coalition, I am lost in the astonishment how men can be so blind to their own situation as to attempt to wound us in this particular point, possessed as we are of the power of returning the same blow, with the vulnerable part staring us directly in the face. If the honorable gentleman under the gallery [Mr. Martin] wishes that a starling were perched up on the right hand of the chair, I tell him that the wish is just as reasonable to have another starling upon the left hand of the chair, to chirp up *Coalition* against *Coalition*, and so harmonize their mutual disgrace, if disgrace there be.

With the same consistency, an honorable gentleman calls us *deserters!*[20] *Us!* A few cold and disaffected members fall off, then turn about, and, to palliate their own defection, call the body of the army *deserters!* *We* have not deserted; here we are, a firm phalanx. Deserted, indeed, we have been in the moment of disaster, but never dejected, and seldom complaining. Some of those who rose upon our wreck, and who eagerly grasped that power which we had the labor of erecting, now call us deserters. We retort the term with just indignation. Yet while they presume we have the attributes of men, they would expect us to have the obduracy of savages. They would have our resentments insatiate, our rancor eternal. In our opinion, an oblivion of useless animosity is much more noble; and in that the conduct of our accusers goes hand in hand with us. But I beg of the House, and I wish the world to observe, that although, like them, we have abandoned our enmities, we have not, like them, relinquished our friendships. There is a set of men, who, from the mere vanity of having consequence as *decisive* voters, object to all stable government. These men hate to see an administration so fixed as not to be movable by their vote. They assume their dignity on the mere negative merit of not accepting places; and in the pride of this self-denial, and the vanity of fancied independence, they object to every system that has a solid basis, because their consequence is unfelt. Of such men I can not be the panegyrist, and I am sorry that some such men are among the most estimable in the House.[21]

IV. An honorable gentleman advises me, for the future, not to mention the name of the Marquess of Rockingham, who, he says, would never countenance a bill of this kind. This is indeed imposing hard conditions upon those who have willingly suffered a sort of political martyrdom in the cause of that noble Lord's principles—those who surrendered pomp and power, rather than remain where his principles ceased to be fashionable, and were withering into contempt. I venerate the name of that noble Marquess, and shall ever mention it with love and reverence; but at no period of my life with more confidence than at this moment, when I say that his soul speaks in every line of the bill before you, for his soul speaks in every measure of virtue, wisdom, humane policy, general justice, and national honor. The name of the noble Lord, who enjoys his fortune, has been mentioned in this debate, and will be mentioned again by me. I will tell the honorable gentleman that this noble Lord [Earl Fitzwilliam], though not the issue of his loins, inherits, with his property, the principles of that noble Marquess in all their purity and soundness; and is as incapable as that noble Marquess himself, or as any man on earth,

Miscellaneous.

[18] That of Lord Chatham with the Duke of Newcastle.

[19] Mr. Jenkinson, Mr. Dundas, &c., sat near Mr. Pitt.

[20] This refers to the resignation of Mr. Fox, Mr. Burke, and the other Rockingham Whigs, when Lord Shelburne seized the reins of government.

[21] Alluding probably to Mr. Powys, who had been a friend of Mr. Fox, but would not vote with him after his junction with Lord North. Mr. Powys, at the opening of the debate, ascribed the obnoxious features of the present bill to Lord North, saying, "The *voice* is Jacob's voice, but the *hands* are the hands of Esau."

of countenancing any act which either immediately or ultimately tended to the prejudice of his country, or the injury of the Constitution.[22] I have had the honor of knowing the noble Earl from an early age. I have observed the motives of his actions; I am endeared to him by every tie of kindred sentiment and of mutual principle. A character more dignified and exalted exists not in the empire; a mind more firmly attached to the Constitution of his country. He is, what the nation would desire in the heir of Lord Rockingham, the only compensation that we could have for his loss.

An honorable gentleman on the other side [Mr. T. Pitt] has used violent terms against this bill and the movers of it. Sir, I tell that honorable gentleman [looking him directly in the face] that the movers of this bill are not to be browbeaten by studied gestures, nor frightened by tremulous tones, solemn phrases, or hard epithets. To arguments they are ready to reply; but all the notice they can take of assertions is to mark to the House that they are only assertions. The honorable gentleman again repeats his favorite language of our having *seized upon the government*. His Majesty changed his ministry last April, in consequence of a vote of this House; his Majesty did the same twelve months before [when Lord North was displaced], in consequence of a vote of this House. His Majesty, in so doing, followed the example of his predecessors; and his successors will, I doubt not, follow the example of his Majesty. The votes of Parliament have always decided upon the duration of the ministry, and always will, I trust. It is the nature of our Constitution; and those who dislike it had better attempt to alter it. The honorable gentleman called the change in 1782 a glorious one; this in 1783 a disgraceful one. Why? For a very obvious, though a very bad reason. The honorable gentleman assisted in effecting the first, and strenuously labored to prevent the second. The first battle he fought with us; the second against us, and we vanquished him. In 1782 his friends were *out*, and would be *in*. In 1783 his friends were *in*, nor *would* go out. Thus, having done without him what we once did with him, the House sees his motive. It is human nature, certainly; but certainly not the better part of human nature. He says he is no party man, and abhors a systematic opposition. I have always acknowledged myself to be a party man. I have always acted with a party in whose principles I have confidence; and if I had such an opinion of any ministry as the gentleman professes to have of us, I would pursue their overthrow by a systematic opposition. I have done so more than once, and I think that, in succeeding, I saved my country. Once the right honorable gentleman, as I have said, was with me, and our conduct was fair, manly, constitutional, and honorable. The next time he was against me, and our conduct was violent and unconstitutional, it was *treasonable!* And yet the means were in both instances the same—the means were the votes of this House!

A game of a two-fold quality is playing by the other side of the House upon this occasion, to which I hope the House, and I hope the kingdom, will attend. They are endeavoring to injure us through two channels at the same time; through a certain great quarter, and through the people. They are attempting to alarm the first by asserting that this bill increases the influence of ministry *against* the Crown; and rousing the people, under an idea that it increases the influence of the Crown *against them*. That they will fail in both, I doubt not. In the great quarter I trust they are well understood, and the princely mind of that high person is a security against their devices. They are running swiftly to take off whatever little imposition might have been put upon any part, even of the multitude; and I wish to rescue the character of the public understanding from the contemptuous implication, that it is capable of being gulled by such artifices. I feel for my country's honor when I say that Englishmen, free themselves, and fond of giving freedom to others, disdain these stratagems, and are equally above the silliness of crediting the revilers of this act, and the baseness of confederating or making common cause with those who would support a system which has dishonored this country, and which keeps thirty millions of the human race in wretchedness. I make allowances for the hair-brained, headstrong delusions of folly and ignorance, and the effects of design. To such evils every measure is liable, and every man must expect a portion of the consequence. But for the serious and grave determinations of the public judgment I have the highest value; I ever had, and ever shall have. If it be a weakness, I confess it, that to lose the good opinion of even the meanest man gives me some pain; and whatever triumph my enemies can derive from such a frame of mind they are welcome to. I do not, after the example of the honorable gentleman who began this debate [Mr. Powys], hold the opinion of constituents in disparagement. The clear and decided opinion of the more reasonable and respectable should, in my opinion, weigh with the member, upon the same principle that, I think, the voice of the nation should prevail in this House, and in every other place. But when the representative yields to the constituent, it should, indeed, be by the majority of the reasonable and respectable; and not, as we shall see in a day or two, some of the honestest men in England voting against the most popular tax ever introduced into this House, in direct opposition to their own conviction, and *not* upon the opinion of either the more respectable or reasonable class of their constituents.[23]

My noble friend [Sir John Cavendish], with

[22] Earl Fitzwilliam had been named by Mr. Fox as the first of the Commissioners under this bill. The names of the remainder were withheld until the bill should have passed.

[23] This refers to the Receipt Tax, for the repeal of which Alderman Newnham had made a motion a few days before.

his characteristic spirit, has said, that *we* never sought power by cabal, or intrigue, or underhand operations; and this he said in reply to an honorable gentleman [Mr. T. Pitt], whose conduct demonstrates that he thinks these the surest path for his friends. This bill, as a ground of contention, is farcical. This bill, if it admitted it, would be combated upon its intrinsic qualities, and not by abusing the Coalition or raising a clamor about influence. But why don't the gentlemen speak out fairly, as we do; and then let the world judge between us? Our love and loyalty to the sovereign are as ardent and firm as their own. Yet the broad basis of public character, upon which we received, is the principle by which we hope to retain this power, convinced that the surest road to the favor of the prince is by serving him with zeal and fidelity; that the safest path to popularity is by reducing the burden, and restoring the glory of the nation. Let those (looking at Mr. Jenkinson) who aim at office by *other* means, by inscrutable and mysterious methods, speak out; or, if they will not, let the world know it is because their arts will not bear examination, and that their safety consists in their obscurity.[24] *Our* principles are well known; and I should prefer to perish with them, rather than prosper with any other.

The honorable gentleman under the gallery [Mr. Martin] also says he dislikes systematic opposition. Whether perpetually rising up with peevish, capricious objections to every thing proposed by us deserve that name or not, I leave the gentleman himself to determine, and leave the House to reflect upon that kind of conduct which condemns the theory of its own constant practice. But I meet the gentleman directly upon the principle of the term. He dislikes systematic opposition; now I like it. A systematic opposition to a dangerous government is, in my opinion, a noble employment for the brightest faculties; and if the honorable gentleman thinks our administration a bad one, he is right to contribute to its downfall. Opposition is natural in such a political system as ours. It has subsisted in all such governments; and perhaps it is necessary. But to those who oppose, it is extremely essential that their manner of conducting it incur not a suspicion of their motives. If they appear to oppose from disappointment, from mortification, from pique, from whim, the people will be against them. If they oppose from public principle, from love of their country rather than hatred to administration from evident conviction of the badness of measures, and a full persuasion that in their resistance to men they are aiming at the public welfare, the people will be with them. We opposed upon *these* principles, and the people were with us; if we are opposed upon *other* principles, they will not be against us. Much labor has been employed to infuse a prejudice upon the present subject; but I have the satisfaction to believe that the labor has been fruitless, making a reasonable allowance for the mistakes of the uninformed, the first impressions of novelty, and the natural result of deliberate malice. We desire to be tried by the test of this bill, and risk our character upon the issue; confiding thoroughly in the good sense, the justice, and the spirit of Englishmen. Not lofty sounds, nor selected epithets, nor passionate declamation in this House, nor all the sordid efforts of interested men out of this House—of men whose acts in the East have branded the British name, and whose ill gotten opulence has been working through a thousand channels to delude and debauch the public understanding — can fasten odium upon this measure, or draw an obloquy upon the authors of it. We have been tried in the cause of the public, and until we desert that cause we are assured of public confidence and protection.

The honorable gentleman [Mr. Powys] has supposed for me a soliloquy, and has put into my mouth some things which I do not think are likely to be attributed to me. He insinuates that I was incited by avarice, or ambition, or party spirit. I have failings in common with every human being, besides my own peculiar faults; but of avarice I have indeed held myself guiltless. My abuse has been for many years even the profession of several people; it was their traffic, their livelihood; yet until this moment I knew not that avarice was in the catalogue of the sins imputed to me. Ambition I confess I have, but not ambition upon a narrow bottom, or built upon paltry principles. If, from the devotion of my life to political objects; if, from the direction of my industry to the attainment of some knowledge of the Constitution and the true interests of the British empire, the ambition of taking no mean part in those acts that elevate nations and make a people happy, be criminal, that ambition I acknowledge. And as to party spirit—that I feel it, that I have been ever under its impulse, and that I ever shall, is what I proclaim to the world. That I am one of a party —a party never known to sacrifice the interests, or barter the liberties of the nation for mercenary purposes, for personal emolument or honors —a party linked together upon principles which comprehend whatever is most dear and precious to free men, and essential to a free Constitution —is my pride and my boast.

The honorable gentleman has given me one assertion which it is my pride to make; he says that I am connected with a number of the first families in the country.[25] Yes, sir, I have a peculiar glory that a body of men, renowned for their ancestry, important for their possessions, distinguished for their personal worth, with all

[24] Mr. Jenkinson had entered life as the protégé of Lord Bute, and was looked upon for many years as the pivot of every court intrigue, the confidential agent of the King, and the prime mover in all kinds of secret influence; hence this pointed allusion. He was afterward known as Lord Hawkesbury, and at a subsequent period as Lord Liverpool.

[25] The Rockingham Whigs.

that is valuable to men at stake—hereditary fortunes and hereditary honors—deem me worthy of their confidence. With such men I am something—without them, nothing. My reliance is upon their good opinion; and in that respect, perhaps, I am fortunate. Although I have a just confidence in my own integrity, yet, as I am but man, perhaps it is well that I have no choice but between my own eternal disgrace and a faithful discharge of my public duty, while men of this kind are overseers of my conduct, while men whose uprightness of heart and spotless honor are even proverbial in the country [looking at Lord John Cavendish], are the vigils of my deeds, it is a pledge to the public for the purity and rectitude of my conduct. The prosperity and honor of the country are blended with the prosperity and honor of these illustrious persons. They have so much at stake, that if the country falls they fall with it; and to countenance any thing against its interest would be a suicide upon themselves. The good opinion and protection of these men is a security to the nation for my behavior, because if I lose them I lose my all.

Having said so much upon the extraneous subjects introduced by the honorable gentleman [Mr. Powys] into the debate, I shall proceed to make some observations upon the business in question. When the learned gentleman [Mr. Dundas] brought in his bill last year, the House saw its frightful features with just horror; but a very good method was adopted to soften the terrors of the extravagant power which that bill vested in the Governor General. The name of a noble Lord [Lord Cornwallis] was sent forth at the same time, whose great character lent a grace to a proposition which, destitute of such an advantage, could not be listened to for one moment. Now, sir, observe how differently we have acted upon the same occasion.

Earl Fitzwilliam has been spoken of here this day, in those terms of admiration with which his name is always mentioned. Take notice, however, that we did not avail ourselves of the fame of his virtue and abilities in passing this bill through the House.

If such a thing were to have taken place as the institution of an Indian secretaryship (according to the suggestions of some gentlemen), this noble Lord would certainly have been the very person whom, for my part, I should have advised his Majesty to invest with that office. Yet, although his erect mind and spotless honor would have held forth to the public the fullest confidence of a faithful execution of its duties, the objections in regard to influence upon a removable officer, are ten-fold in comparison with the present scheme. The House must now see, that with all the benefits we might derive from that noble Lord's character—that although his name would have imparted a sanctity, an ornament, and an honor to the bill, we ushered it in without that ceremony, to stand or fall by its own intrinsic merits, neither shielding it under the reputation nor gracing it under the mantle of any man's virtue. Our merit will be more in this, when the names of those are known whom we mean to propose to this House, to execute this commission. [Name them, said Mr. Arden, across the House.] I will not. I will not name them. The bill shall stand or fall by its own merits, without aid or injury from their character. An honorable gentleman has said these Commissioners will be made up of our "adherents and creatures." Sir, there is nothing more easy than to use disparaging terms; yet I should have thought the name of Earl Fitzwilliam would have given a fair presumption that the colleagues we shall recommend to this House for the co-execution of this business with that noble Lord, will not be of a description to merit these unhandsome epithets. I assure the honorable gentleman they are not. I assure him they are not men whose faculties of corrupting, or whose corruptibility, will give any alarm to this House, or to this country. They are men whose private and public characters stand high and untainted; who are not likely to countenance depredation, or participate the spoils of rapacity. They are not men to screen delinquency, or to pollute the service by disgraceful appointments. Would such men as Earl Fitzwilliam suffer unbecoming appointments to be made? Is Earl Fitzwilliam a man likely to do the dirty work of a minister? If they, for instance, were to nominate a Paul Benfield to go to India in the supreme council, would Earl Fitzwilliam subscribe to his appointment? This is the benefit of having a commission of high honor, chary of reputation, noble and pure in their sentiments, who are superior to the little jobs and traffic of political intrigue.[26]

But this bill, sir, presumes not upon the probity of the men; it looks to the future possibility of dissimilar successors, and to the morality of the present Commissioners, who are merely human, and therefore not incapable of alteration. Under all the caution of this bill, with the responsibility it imposes, I will take upon me to say that if the aggregate body of this Board determined to use all its power for the purpose of corruption, this House, and the people at large, would have less to dread from them, in the way of influence, than from a few Asiatics who would probably be displaced in consequence of this arrangement—some of whom will return to this country with a million, some with seven hundred thousand, some with five, besides the three or four hundred thousand of others, who are cut off in their career by the hand of Fate. An inundation of such wealth is far more dangerous than any influence that is likely to spring from a plan of government so constituted as this proposed—whether the operation of such a mass of wealth

26 The Commissioners, as named by Mr. Fox when the bill passed the House, were Earl Fitzwilliam, Chairman of the Board, the Honorable Frederick Montague, Lord Lewisham, the Honorable George Augustus North, eldest son of Lord North, Sir Gilbert Elliot, Baronet, Sir Henry Fletcher, Baronet, and Robert Gregory, Esq.

be considered in its probable effects upon the principles of the members of this House, or the manners of the people at large; more especially when a reflection that Orientalists are in general the most *exemplary* class of people in their morals, and in their deportment the most moderate, and corresponding with the distinction of their high birth and family, furnishes a very reasonable presumption that the expenditure of their money will be much about as honorable as its acquirement.[27]

I shall now, sir, conclude my speech with a few words upon the opinion of the right honorable gentleman [Mr. Pitt]. He says "he will stake his character upon the danger of this bill." I meet him in his own phrase, and oppose him, character to character. I risk my all upon the excellence of this bill. I risk upon it whatever is most dear to me, whatever men most value, the character of integrity, of talents, of honor, of present reputation and future fame. These, and whatever else is precious to me, I stake upon the constitutional safety, the enlarged policy, the equity, and the wisdom of this measure; and have no fear in saying (whatever may be the fate of its authors) that this bill will produce to this country every blessing of commerce and revenue; and that by extending a generous and humane government over those millions whom the inscrutable destinations of Providence have placed under us in the remotest regions of the earth, it will consecrate the name of England among the noblest of nations.

The vote was carried by a majority of 217 to 103. But when the bill reached the House of Lords, it was met and defeated by the influence of the King, as already mentioned in the sketch of Mr. Fox's life.

SPEECH

OF MR. FOX ON THE USE OF SECRET INFLUENCE TO DEFEAT HIS EAST INDIA BILL, DELIVERED IN THE HOUSE OF COMMONS, DECEMBER 17, 1783.

INTRODUCTION.

On the ninth of December, 1783, when Mr. Fox's East India Bill went up to the House of Lords, the ministry supposed themselves to possess the fullest evidence that it would pass that body by a decided majority. Within three days, however, rumors were in circulation of some extraordinary movements in the interior of the Court. It was affirmed that Lord Temple was closeted with the King on the eleventh, and that his Majesty had intrusted him with a message of some kind, expressing a strong disapprobation of the bill; which message his Lordship and others were circulating among the peers, and especially among the Lords of the Bedchamber and other members of the royal household who were more immediately connected with the King's person. On the fifteenth, the Duke of Portland, as head of the ministry, alluded to these rumors in the House of Lords. Lord Temple admitted that the interview referred to had taken place, but would neither acknowledge nor deny any thing farther touching the reports in question. It was evident, however, that a powerful impression had been made. Some peers who had given their proxies to the minister or his friends, withdrew them only a few hours before the time appointed for the second reading of the bill; and a letter was at length placed in the hands of the ministry, containing the message of the King which had produced these unexpected results. The substance of this letter is given in the speech below.

In view of these facts, before the bill had been decided upon by the Lords, Mr. Baker moved a resolution in the House of Commons, that "it is now necessary to declare, that to *report any opinion or pretended opinion of his Majesty* upon any bill or other proceeding depending in either House of Parliament, is a high crime and misdemeanor, derogatory to the honor of the Crown, a breach of the fundamental privileges of Parliament, and subversive of the Constitution of this country." In his remarks on the subject, Mr. Baker divided the criminality into two parts; first, the giving of secret advice to his Majesty; and, secondly, the use that had been made of the King's name for the purpose of influencing the votes of members of Parliament in a matter depending before them. He proved from the journals, that "any reference to the opinions of the King touching a bill before either House had always been judged a high breach of the privileges of Parliament." The motion was seconded by Lord Maitland, and was vehemently opposed by Mr. Pitt, who was a near relative of Lord Temple. Mr. Fox then delivered the following speech, in which he gave full vent to his indignation at the injustice done to ministers and the wound inflicted upon the Constitution by this interference.

SPEECH, &c.[1]

I did not intend, sir, to have said any thing in addition to that which has been already urged so ably in favor of the resolution now agitated. In my own opinion, its propriety and necessity are completely and substantially established. A few particulars, suggested in the course of the debate by gentlemen on the other side of the House,

[27] The adventurers to India, here called Orientalists, such as Paul Benfield, &c., were in most instances persons of no family, and of little worth or education. Hence the sneering terms here used.

[1] This speech has been slightly abridged by omitting a few passages in which the ideas were unnecessarily expanded.

may be thought, however, to merit some animadversion. And, once for all, *let no man complain of strong language.* Things are now arrived at such a crisis as renders it impossible to speak without warmth. Delicacy and reserve are criminal where the interests of Englishmen are at hazard. The various points in dispute strike to the heart; and it were unmanly and pusillanimous to wrap up in smooth and deceitful colors objects which, in their nature and consequences, are calculated to fill the House and the country with a mixture of indignation and horror.

Greatness of the interests involved.

This, at least, has made such an impression on my mind, that I never felt so much anxiety; I never addressed this House under such a pressure of impending mischief; I never trembled so much for public liberty as I now do. The question before the House involves the rights of Parliament in all their consequences and extent. These rights are the basis of our Constitution, and form the spirit of whatever discriminates the government of a free country. And have not these been threatened and assaulted? Can they exist a moment in opposition to such an interference as that which is supposed by the resolution, and has been stated by several honorable gentlemen to have taken place? No: human nature is not sufficiently perfect to resist the weight of such a temptation. When, therefore, shall the House assert its dignity, its independence, its prerogatives, by a resolute and unequivocal declaration of all its legal and constitutional powers, but in the instant of their danger? The disease, sir, is come to a crisis; and now is the juncture which destines the patient to live or die. We are called to sanctify or oppose an absolute extinction of all for which our ancestors struggled and expired. We are called to protect and defend, not only the stipulated franchises of Englishmen, but the sacred privileges of human nature. We are called to protract the ruin of the Constitution. The deliberations of this night must decide whether we are to be free men or slaves; whether the House of Commons be the palladium of liberty or the organ of despotism; whether we are henceforth to possess a voice of our own, or to be only the mechanical echo of secret influence. Is there an individual who feels for his own honor, callous to an apprehension of such a consequence as this? Does not every regard which he owes to a body that can not be degraded without his disgrace, that can not expire without involving his fate, rouse his indignation, and excite him to every exertion, both in his individual and delegated capacity, which can reprobate, suspend, or destroy a practice so inimical to public prosperity, as well as hostile to the very existence of this House?

Fact of interference.

But what is this resolution? It has been called, with great technical acuteness, a truism, which seems as incapable of discussion as it is of proof. The foundation of it, however, is a matter of such general and palpable notoriety, as to put every degree of skepticism to defiance. Rumors of a most extraordinary nature have been disseminated in no common way, and by no inferior agents. A noble Earl [Lord Temple] is said to have used the name of Majesty with the obvious and express intention of affecting the decisions of the Legislature concerning a bill, of infinite consequence to thirty millions of people, pending in Parliament. I tell gentlemen this is not a newspaper surmise, but something much stronger and more serious; there is a written record to be produced. This letter [pulling it out of his pocket] is not to be put in the balance with the lie of the day. It states, that "his Majesty allowed Earl Temple to say, that whoever voted for the India Bill were not only not his friends, but he should consider them as his enemies; and if these words were not strong enough, Earl Temple might use whatever words he might deem stronger, or more to the purpose." Is this parliamentary, or is it truth? Where is the man who dares to affirm the one or deny the other; or to say that he believes in his conscience such a rumor was not calculated to produce an immediate effect? It certainly tended, in the first instance, to vilify, in the grossest and most violent manner, the proceedings of Parliament. It says to the public, that we are not equal to our trust; that we either ignorantly or willfully betray the interest of our constituents; and that we are not to be guided in our decisions by their convictions or our own, but by that unseen and mysterious authority of which the Sovereign, his counselors, and the Legislature, are only the blind and passive instruments. Both Houses of Parliament are, consequently, parties in the contest, and reduced, by this unfortunate and wicked device, to the predicament of a man struggling for his life. We are robbed of our rights, with a menace of immediate destruction before our face. From this moment, farewell to every independent measure! Whenever the liberties of the people, the rights of private property, or the still more sacred and invaluable privileges of personal safety, invaded, violated, or in danger, are vindicated by this House, where alone they can be legally and effectually redressed, the hopes of the public, anxious, eager, and panting for the issue, are whispered away, and forever suppressed by the breath of secret influence. A Parliament thus fettered and controlled, without spirit and without freedom, instead of limiting, extends, substantiates, and establishes, beyond all precedent, latitude, or condition, the prerogatives of the Crown. But, though the British House of Commons were so shamefully lost to its own weight in the Constitution, were so unmindful of its former struggles and triumphs in the great cause of liberty and mankind, were so indifferent and treacherous to those primary objects and concerns for which it was originally instituted, I trust the characteristic spirit of this country is still equal to the trial; I trust Englishmen will be as jealous of secret influence as superior to open violence; I trust they are not more ready to defend their interests against foreign depredation and insult than to encounter and defeat this midnight conspiracy against the Constitution.

The proposition of this evening is, therefore,

founded on a fact the most extraordinary and alarming this country could possibly hear; a fact which strikes at the great bulwark of our liberties, and goes to an absolute annihilation, not only of our chartered rights, but of those radical and fundamental ones which are paramount to all charters, which were consigned to our care by the sovereign disposition of Nature, which we can not relinquish without violating the most sacred of all obligations; to which we are entitled, not as members of society, but as individuals and as men; the rights of adhering steadily and uniformly to the great and supreme laws of conscience and duty; of preferring, at all hazards, and without equivocation, those general and substantial interests which we have sworn to prefer; of acquitting ourselves honorably to our constituents, to our friends, to our own minds, and to that public whose trustees we are and for whom we act.

Greatness of the evil.

How often shall the friends of the noble Earl whom I have named be called upon to negative the proposition, by vouching for him his innocence of the charge? Will any of them lay their hand on their heart, and disavow the fact in that nobleman's name? Let them fairly, honorably, and decidedly put an end to that foul imputation which rests on his conduct, and the House must immediately dismiss the report as idle and ill founded. But, while no man comes honestly forward and takes truth by the hand, we must look to the consequence. This House must not lose sight of its rights and those of the community. The latter can subsist no longer than the former are safe. We now deliberate on the life and blood of the Constitution. Give up this point, and we seal our own quietus, and are accessory to our own insignificance or destruction.

Conduct of Lord Temple's friends when challenged to deny it.

But how is the question, thus unsuccessfully put to the friends and abettors of secret influence in this, answered, when put to the noble principal in the other House? Is he ready and eager to vindicate his own character, and rescue that of his Sovereign from so foul a reproach? No; but he replies in that mean, insidious, equivocal, and temporizing language, which tends to preserve the effect without boldly and manfully abiding by the consequences of the guilt. Such was the answer, as mysterious and ill-designed as the delinquency it was intended to conceal; and the man only, who could stoop to the baseness of the one, was the most likely in the world to screen himself behind the duplicity of the other. What, then, shall we infer from a system of acting and speaking thus guarded and fallacious, but that the device was formed to operate on certain minds, as it is rumored to have done; and that such a shallow and barefaced pretext could influence those only who, without honor or consistency, are endowed with congenial understandings!

Conduct of Lord Temple himself in the House of Lords.

Had this alarming and unconstitutional interference happened in matters of no consequence, or but of inferior consequence, the evil would not have appeared of such magnitude as it does. But let us consider the nature of the business which it is intended to impede or suppress. For nearly twenty years have the affairs of the East India Company, more or less, occasionally engrossed the attention of Parliament. Committees of this House, composed of the most able, industrious, and upright characters, have sat long, indefatigably, and assiduously, in calling forth, arranging, digesting, and applying every species of evidence which could be found. Reports of their honest and elaborate conduct are before the House.[2] The public feel the pressure of this monstrous and multifarious object. Gentlemen in opposition were, at least, not insensible to its necessity, its urgency, and its importance. A right honorable gentleman [Mr. W. Pitt], who has distinguished himself so much upon this occasion, protested very solemnly against all palliatives, expedients, or any abortive substitutes for radical and complete measures. To meet that right honorable gentleman's idea, as well as to suit the exigence of the case, the present bill was brought in. It has been called a rash, inconsiderate, and violent measure. The House is aware what discussion it has occasioned; and I dare any one to mention a single argument brought against it which has not been candidly and fairly tried, not by the weight of a majority, but by the force of plain and explicit reasoning. No bill was more violently and systematically opposed, investigated at greater length, or with more ability; passed the House under the sanction of a more respectable and independent majority; or had more the countenance and patronage of the country at large. How, then, did it succeed in the other House? What was the reception which, thus circumstanced, it received from their Lordships? Some degree of decency might have been expected from one branch of the Legislature to another. That respectable independence which ought to be the leading feature in their decisions is not incompatible with, but essential to such a mutual deference for the procedure of each, as must be the consequence of acting constitutionally. The bill, however, though matured and debated by all the abilities of this House, though urged by the most powerful of all arguments, necessity, and though recommended by almost two to one on every division it occasioned, will, in all probability, be lost.

Importance of the bill in question.

But, sir, I beseech the House to attend to the manner in which it is likely to meet such a fate. Is this to be effected by the voice of an independent majority? Can any man view the Lords of the Bedchamber in that respectable light? and the whole fortune of the measure now depends on their determination. The rumor, so often stated and

Means by which it is to be defeated.

[2] In the year 1781 two committees of the House of Commons, one a select and the other a secret committee, were appointed to inquire into the affairs of the East India Company, both at home and abroad. The reports of the select committee were twelve, and those of the secret committee six in number.

alluded to, was calculated and intended to answer an immediate and important end. I am far from saying that it ought. Those in high office and of elevated rank *should* prove themselves possessed of high and elevated sentiments; should join to an exquisite sense of personal honor the most perfect probity of heart; should discover as much dignity and strength of understanding as may be naturally expected from a superior education, the distinctions of fortune, and the example of the great and the wise. But how does this description agree with their mode of managing their proxies? These they cordially give in [to the ministry] before a rumor of the King's displeasure reaches their ears. The moment this intimation is made, on the same day, and within a few hours, matters appear to them in quite a different light, and the opinion which they embrace in the morning is renounced at noon. I am as ready as any man to allow, what is barely probable, that these Lords might receive new convictions, which, like a miracle, operated effectually and at once; and that, notwithstanding their proxies, from such a sudden and extraordinary circumstance, without hearing any debate or evidence on the subject, they might feel an immediate and unaccountable impulse to make their personal appearance, and vote according to their consciences. Who would choose to say that all this may not actually have been the case? There is certainly, however, a very uncommon coincidence in their Lordship's peculiar situation, and this unexpected revolution of sentiment; and, were I disposed to treat the matter seriously, the whole compass of language affords no terms sufficiently strong and pointed to mark the contempt which I feel for their conduct. It is an impudent avowal of political profligacy; as if that species of treachery were less infamous than any other. It is not merely a degradation of a station which ought to be occupied only by the highest and most exemplary honor, but forfeits their claim to the characters of gentlemen, and reduces them to a level with the meanest and the basest of the species; it insults the noble, the ancient, and the characteristic independence of the English peerage, and is calculated to traduce and vilify the British Legislature in the eyes of all Europe and to the latest posterity. By what magic nobility can thus charm vice into virtue I know not, nor wish to know; but in any other thing than politics, and among any other men than Lords of the Bedchamber, such an instance of the grossest perfidy would, as it well deserves, be branded with infamy and execration.

Motives for this interference.

Is there any thing, then, sir, more plain and obvious, than that this great, this important, this urgent measure, is become the handle of a desperate faction, whose principal object is power and place? It is the victim, not of open and fair reasoning, but of that *influence* which shuns the light and shrinks from discussion. Those who pledged their honor in its support, from an acknowledged conviction of its rectitude, its propriety, and utility, have broken that faith, and relinquished their own judgments, in consequence of a rumor that such a conduct would be personally resented by the Sovereign. What bill, in the history of Parliament, was ever so traduced, so foully misrepresented and betrayed in its passage through the different branches of the Legislature? The stroke which must decide the contest can not come from its real enemies, but its false friends; and its fate, without example in the annals of this House, will be handed down to the remotest posterity, not as a trophy of victory, but as a badge of treachery.

The real ambition of Mr. Fox.

Here, sir, the right honorable gentleman [Mr. Pitt], with his usual liberality, upbraids me with monopolizing, not only all the influence of the Crown, the patronage of India, and the principles of Whigism, but the whole of the royal confidence; but all such round, unqualified, and unfounded imputations must be contemptible, because they are not true; and the bitterest enemy, not lost to every sense of manliness, would scorn to become an accuser on grounds so palpably false. It is, indeed, as it has always been, my only ambition to act such a part in my public conduct as shall eventually give the lie to every species of suspicion which those who oppose me seem so anxious to create and circulate; and if to compass that by every possible exertion from which no man in the sound exercise of his understanding can honestly dissent, be a crime, I plead guilty to the charge. This I am not ashamed to avow the predominating passion of my life; and I will cherish it in spite of calumny, declamation, and intrigue, at the risk of all I value most in the world.

Lords in waiting on the King.

But, sir, in this monopoly of influence, the Lords of the Bedchamber ought, at least, for the sake of decency, to have been excepted. These, we all know, are constantly at the beck of whoever is minister of the day. How often have they not been stigmatized with the name of the household troops, who, like the Prætorian bands of ancient Rome,[3] are always prepared for the ready execution of every secret mandate! I remember a saying of an able statesman, whom, though I differed with him in many things, I have ever acknowledged to be possessed of many eminent and useful qualities. The sentence I allude to I have always admired for its boldness and propriety. It was uttered by the late George Grenville in experiencing a similar treachery; and would to God the same independent and manly sentiments had been inherited by all who bear the name! "I will never again," said he, "be at the head

[3] Gibbon, speaking of the Prætorian bands, says, "They derived their institution from Augustus. That crafty tyrant, sensible that laws might color, but that arms alone could maintain his usurped dominion, had gradually formed this powerful body of guards, in constant readiness to protect his person, to awe the Senate, and either to prevent or crush the first motions of rebellion."—*Hist. of the Decline and Fall*, ch. v.

of a string of janizaries, who are always ready to strangle or dispatch me on the least signal."

Where, sir, is that undue, that unconstitutional influence with which the right honorable gentleman upbraids me and those with whom I act? Are our measures supported by any other means than ministers have usually employed? In what, then, am I the "champion of influence?" Of the influence of sound and substantial policy, of open, minute, and laborious discussion, of the most respectable Whig interest in the kingdom, of an honorable majority in this House, of public confidence and public responsibility, I am proud to avail myself, and happy to think no man can bar my claim. But every sort of influence unknown to the Constitution, as base in itself as it is treacherous in its consequences, which is always successful because incapable of opposition, nor ever successful but when exerted in the dark, which, like every other monster of factious breed, never stalks abroad but in the absence of public principle, never assumes any other shape than a whisper, and never frequents any more public place of resort than the back stairs or closet at St. James's—all this secret, intriguing, and underhand influence I am willing and ready to forego. I will not even be the minister of a great and free people on any condition derogatory to my honor and independence as a private gentleman. Let those who have no other object than *place* have it, and hold it by the only tenure worthy of their acceptance, secret influence; but without the confidence of this House. as well as that of the sovereign, however necessary to my circumstances, and desirable to my friends, the dignity and emoluments of office shall never be mine.

Kind of influence sought by Mr. Fox.

The task, therefore, the gentleman has assigned me, of being the champion of influence, belongs more properly to himself, who has this night stood forward in defense of a practice which can not be indulged for a moment but at the imminent risk of every thing great and valuable which our Constitution secures. With what *consistency* he embarks in a cause so hostile and ominous to the rights and wishes of Englishmen, those who have known his connections and observed his professions will judge. Let him not, then, in the paroxysm of party zeal, put a construction on my conduct which it will not bear, or endeavor to stamp it with the impression of his own. For that influence which the Constitution has wisely assigned to the different branches of the Legislature, I ever have contended, and, I trust, ever shall. That of the Crown, kept within its legal boundaries, is essential to the practice of government; but woe to this country the moment its operations are not as public and notorious as they are sensible and effective! A great writer[4] has said that the English Constitution will perish when the legislative becomes more corrupt than the executive power. Had he been as sound a judge of the practice as of the theory of government, he might have added, with still greater truth, that we shall certainly lose our liberty when the deliberations of Parliament are decided, *not by the legal and usual, but by the illegal and extraordinary exertions of prerogative.*

Mr. Pitt the defender of secret influence.

The right honorable gentleman declares that if the King is thus prevented from consulting his peers, who are constitutionally styled the ancient and hereditary counselors of the Crown, or any other of his subjects, whenever he is pleased to call for it, he would be a captive on his throne, and the first slave in his own dominions. Does he, then, affect to think or allege that it is the desire of ministers to proscribe all social intercourse between his Majesty and his subjects? I will tell the right honorable gentleman thus far his argument goes, and that is something worse than puerility and declamation; it is disguising truth under such colors as are calculated to render it odious and detestable. The Lords are undoubtedly entitled to advise the throne collectively; but this does not surely entitle every noble individual to take his Majesty aside, and, by a shocking farrago of fiction and fear, poison the royal mind with all their own monstrous chimeras! Whoever knows the mode of digesting business in the cabinet must be sensible *that the least interference with any thing pending in Parliament must be dangerous to the Constitution.* The question is not, whether his Majesty shall avail himself of such advice as no one readily avows, but *who is answerable for such advice?* Is the right honorable gentleman aware that the responsibility of ministers is the only pledge and security the people of England possess against the infinite abuses so natural to the exercise of this power? Once remove this great bulwark of the Constitution, and we are in every respect the slaves and property of despotism. And is not this the necessary consequence of secret influence?

Secret influence not the prerogative of the Lords.

How, sir, are ministers situated on this ground? Do they not come into power with a halter about their necks, by which the most contemptible wretch in the kingdom may dispatch them at pleasure? Yes, they hold their several offices, not at the option of the sovereign, but of the very reptiles who burrow under the throne. They act the part of puppets, and are answerable for all the folly, the ignorance, and the temerity or timidity, of some unknown juggler behind the screen; they are not once allowed to consult their own, but to pay an implicit homage to the understandings of those whom to know were to despise. The only rule by which they are destined to extend authority over free men is a secret mandate which carries along with it no other alternative than obedience—or ruin! What man, who has the feelings, the honor, the spirit, or the heart of a man, would stoop to such a condition for any official dignity or emolument whatever? Boys, without judgment, experience of the sentiments suggested by the knowledge of the world, or the amiable decencies of a sound mind, may follow

Effect of secret influence on ministers.

[4] Montesquieu.—*Esprit des Lois,* liv. xi., ch. 6.

the headlong course of ambition thus precipitantly, and vault into the seat while the reins of government are placed in other hands; but the minister who can bear to act such a dishonorable part, and the country that suffers it, will be mutual plagues and curses to each other.[5]

Thus awkwardly circumstanced, the best minister on earth could accomplish nothing, nor on any occasion, however pressing and momentous, exert the faculties of government with spirit or effect. It is not in the human mind to put forth the least vigor under the impression of uncertainty. While all my best-meant and best-concerted plans are still under the control of a villainous whisper, and the most valuable consequences, which I flatter myself must have resulted from my honest and indefatigable industry, are thus defeated by secret influence, it is impossible to continue in office any longer either with honor to myself or success to the public. The moment I bring forward a measure adequate to the exigency of the state, and stake my reputation, or indeed whatever is most dear and interesting in life, on its merit and utility, instead of enjoying the triumphs of having acted fairly and unequivocally, all my labors, all my vigilance, all my expectations, so natural to every generous and manly exertion, are not only vilely frittered, but insidiously and at once whispered away by rumors, which, whether founded or not, are capable of doing irreparable mischief, and have their full effect before it is possible to contradict or disprove them.

The King's acting with his ministers the only ground of their being responsible.

So much has been said about the captivity of the throne, if his Majesty acts only in concert with his ministers, that one would imagine the spirit and soul of the British Constitution were yet unknown in this House. It is wisely established as a fundamental maxim, that "the King can do no wrong;" that whatever blunders or even crimes may be chargeable on the executive power, the Crown is still faultless. But how? Not by suffering tyranny and oppression in a free government to pass with impunity; certainly not; but the minister who advises or executes an unconstitutional measure does it at his peril; and he ought to know that Englishmen are not only jealous of their rights, but legally possessed of powers competent, on every such emergency, to redress their wrongs. What is the distinction between an absolute and a limited monarchy but this, that the sovereign in the one is a despot, and may do what he pleases; but in the other is himself subjected to the laws, and consequently not at liberty to advise with any one on public affairs *not responsible for that advice;* and the Constitution has clearly directed his negative to operate under the same wise restrictions. These prerogatives are by no means vested in the Crown to be exerted in a wanton and arbitrary manner. The good of the whole is the exclusive object to which all the branches of the Legislature and their different powers invariably point. Whoever interferes with this primary and supreme direction must, in the highest degree, be unconstitutional. Should, therefore, his Majesty be disposed to check the progress of the Legislature in accomplishing any measure of importance, either by giving countenance to an invidious whisper, or the exertion of his negative, without at the same time consulting the safety of his ministers, here would be an instance of maladministration, for which, on that supposition, the Constitution has provided no remedy. And God forbid that ever the Constitution of this country should be found defective in a point so material and indispensable to the public welfare!

Former operation of secret influence.

Sir, it is a public and crying grievance that we are not the first who have felt this secret influence. It seems to be a habit against which no change of men or measures can operate with success. It has overturned a more able and popular minister [Lord Chatham] than the present, and bribed him with a peerage, for which his best friends never cordially forgave him. The scenes, the times, the politics, and the system of the court may shift with the party that predominates, but this dark, mysterious engine is not only formed to control every ministry, but to enslave the Constitution. To this infernal spirit of intrigue we owe that incessant fluctuation in his Majesty's councils by which the spirit of government is so much relaxed, and all its minutest objects so fatally deranged. During the strange and ridiculous interregnum of last year,[6] I had not a doubt in my own mind with whom it originated; and I looked to an honorable gentleman [Mr. Jenkinson] opposite to me, the moment the grounds of objection to the East India Bill were stated. The same illiberal and plodding cabal which then invested the throne, and darkened the royal mind with ignorance and misconception, has once more been employed to act the same part. But how will the genius of Englishmen brook the insult? Is this enlightened and free country, which has so often and successfully struggled against every species of undue influence, to revert to those Gothic ages when princes were tyrants, ministers minions, and governments intriguing? Much and gloriously did this House fight and overcome the influence of the Crown by purging itself of ministerial dependents; but what was the contractors' bill, the Board of Trade, or a vote of the revenue officers, compared to a power equal to one third of the Legislature, unanswerable for and unlimited in its acting?[7] Against those we had always to contend; but we knew their strength, we saw their disposition; they fought under no covert, they were a powerful, not a sudden enemy. To compromise the matter therefore, sir, it would become this House to say,

[5] Mr. Pitt was at this time but twenty-four years old.

[6] Between the resignation of Lord Shelburne and the appointment of his successors.

[7] This refers to a bill excluding certain placemen from Parliament, and others from voting at elections, on the ground of their holding offices or contracts under the government.

"Rather than yield to a stretch of prerogative thus unprecedented and alarming, withdraw your secret influence, and whatever intrenchments have been made on the Crown we are ready to repair: take back those numerous and tried dependents who so often secured you a majority in Parliament; we submit to all the mischief which even this accession of strength is likely to produce; but, for God's sake, strangle us not in the very moment we look for success and triumph by an infamous string of Bed-chamber janizaries!"

Reply to Mr. Pitt as to resigning.

The right honorable gentleman has told us, with his usual consequence and triumph, that our duty, circumstanced as we are, can be attended with no difficulty whatever: the moment the Sovereign withdraws his confidence it becomes us to retire. I will answer him in my turn, that the whole system in this dishonorable business may easily be traced. Aware of that glorious and independent majority which added so much dignity and support to the measure which appears thus formidable to secret influence, they find all their efforts to oppose it here abortive; the private cabal is consequently convened, and an invasion of the throne, as most susceptible of their operations, proposed. It was natural to expect that I, for one, would not be backward to spurn at such an interference. This circumstance affords all the advantage they wished. I could not be easy in my situation under the discovery of such an insult; and this critical moment is eagerly embraced to goad me from office, to upbraid me with the meanness of not taking the hint, to remind me in public of the fate which I owe to secret advice. When that hour comes—and it may not be very distant—that shall dismiss me from the service of the public, the right honorable gentleman's example of lingering in office after the voice of the nation was that he should quit it, shall not be mine.[8] I did not come in by the fiat of Majesty, though by this fiat I am not unwilling to go out. I ever stood, and wish now and always to stand on public ground alone. I have too much pride ever to owe any thing to secret influence. I trust in God this country has too much spirit not to spurn and punish the minister that does!

Mr. Pitt's eagerness on the subject.

It is impossible to overlook or not to be surprised at the extreme eagerness of the right honorable gentleman about our places, when twenty-four hours, at most, would give him full satisfaction. Is it that some new information may be requisite to finish a system thus honorably begun? Or is the right honorable gentleman's youth the only account which can be given of that strange precipitancy and anxiety which he betrays on this occasion? It is, in my opinion, the best apology which can be urged in his behalf. Generosity and unsuspecting confidence are the usual disposition of this tender period. The friends of the right honorable gentleman, I doubt not, will soon teach him experience and caution; and when once he has known them as long, received as many of their promises, and seen their principles as much tried as I have done, he may not, perhaps, be quite so prodigal of his credulity as he now is. Is he apprised of the lengths these men would go to serve their own selfish and private views? that their public spirit is all profession and hypocrisy? and that the only tie which unites and keeps them together is that they are known only to each other, and that the moment of their discord puts a period to their strength and consequence?

Consequences of a change of ministry on such grounds.

If, however, a change must take place, and a new ministry is to be formed and supported, not by the confidence of this House, or of the public, but by the sole authority of the Crown, I, for one, shall not envy that right honorable gentleman his situation. From that moment I put in my claim for a monopoly of Whig principles. The glorious cause of freedom, of independence, and of the Constitution, is no longer his, but mine. In this I have lived; in this I will die. It has borne me up under every aspersion to which my character has been subjected. The resentments of the mean and the aversions of the great, the rancor of the vindictive and the subtlety of the base, the dereliction of friends and the efforts of enemies, have not all diverted me from that line of conduct which has always struck me as the best. In the ardor of debate, I may have been, like all other men, betrayed into expressions capable of misrepresentation; but the open and broad path of the Constitution has uniformly been mine. I never was the tool of any junto. I accepted of office at the obvious inclination of this House; I shall not hold it a moment after the least hint from them to resume a private station.

Mr. Pitt's situation if he comes in as minister on such grounds.

The right honorable gentleman is, however, grasping at place on very different grounds. He is not called to it by a majority of this House; but, in defiance of that majority, stands forth the advocate and candidate for secret influence. How will he reconcile a conduct thus preposterous to the Constitution with those principles for which he has pledged himself to the people of England? By what motives can he be thus blind to a system which so flatly and explicitly gives the lie to all his former professions? Will secret influence conciliate that confidence to which his talents, connections, and principles entitle him, but which the aspect under which he must now appear to an indignant and insulted public effectually bars his claim? Will secret influence unite this House in the adoption of measures which are not his own, and to which he only gives the sanction of his name to save them from contempt? Will secret influence draw along with it that affection and cordiality from all ranks without which the movements of government must be absolutely at a stand? Or, is he weak and violent enough to imagine that his Majesty's mere nomination will singly weigh against the constitutional influence of all these considerations?

[8] This refers to Mr. Pitt's continuing for a time in office the year before, when Lord Shelburne, to whose ministry he belonged, was defeated.

For my own part, it has been always my opinion that this country can labor under no greater misfortune than a ministry without strength and stability. The tone of government will never recover so as to establish either domestic harmony or foreign respect, without a permanent administration; and whoever knows any thing of the Constitution, and the present state of parties among us, must be sensible that this great blessing is only and substantially to be obtained and realized in connection with public confidence. It is undoubtedly the prerogative of the Sovereign to choose his own servants; but the Constitution provides that these servants shall not be obnoxious to his subjects by rendering all their exertions, thus circumstanced, abortive and impracticable. The right honorable gentleman had, therefore, better consider how much he risks by joining an arrangement thus hostile to the interests of the people; that they will never consent to be governed by secret influence; and that all the weight of his private character, all his eloquence and popularity, will never render the midnight and despotic mandates of an interior cabinet acceptable to Englishmen.

Respect due to the King.

When I say in what manner and to what ends the wisdom and experience of our ancestors have thus directed the exercise of all the royal prerogatives, let me not be understood as meaning in any degree to detract from those dutiful regards which all of us owe, as good citizens and loyal subjects, to the prince who at present fills the British throne. No man venerates him more than I do, for his personal and domestic virtues. I love him as I love the Constitution, for the glorious and successful efforts of his illustrious ancestors in giving it form and permanency. The patriotism of these great and good men must endear, to every lover of his country, their latest posterity. The King of England can never lose the esteem of his people, while they remember with gratitude the many obligations which they owe to his illustrious family. Nor can I wish him a greater blessing than that he may reign in the hearts of his subjects, and that their confidence in his government may be as hearty and sincere as their affection for his person.

The motion was carried by a majority of 73.

SPEECH

OF MR. FOX ON THE WESTMINSTER SCRUTINY, DELIVERED IN THE HOUSE OF COMMONS, JUNE 8, 1784.

INTRODUCTION.

THE leading facts respecting the Middlesex election of 1784 have already been given in the sketch of Mr. Fox's life. His contest with Sir Cecil Wray lasted forty days, and when the polls were closed there was a majority for Mr. Fox of two hundred and thirty-five votes.

Great care had been taken throughout the contest to prevent false voting. At the suggestion of Lord Mahon, acting for Sir Cecil Wray, it was agreed, before opening the polls, that eleven inspectors and five friends should be constantly present on each side; and that whenever a person was challenged, his case should be reserved, and no vote allowed him until his claims were thoroughly investigated. A large part of Mr. Fox's votes were subjected to this test, and toward the close of the polls hardly one was received "without an appeal to the presiding officer, and a decision that such vote was good."[1] Some of these decisions may have been hasty, but after such an arrangement Sir Cecil Wray ought to have acquiesced: to dispute the vote was unfair and uncandid in the extreme. But he did dispute it. Before the result was declared, he delivered to the presiding officer, Thomas Corbett, High Bailiff of Westminster, a list of bad votes which had been polled, as he affirmed, by Mr. Fox, and demanded a *scrutiny*, or re-examination of the entire poll. This was granted by Mr. Corbett on the 17th of May, 1784, when, by the writ under which he acted, he was bound to return two members for Westminster on the 18th, being *the next day!* Two questions, therefore, arose; first, whether a scrutiny into an election so conducted could be fairly and properly demanded; and, secondly, whether the presiding officer had a legal right to grant a scrutiny which ran beyond the time prescribed in his writ.

Parliament met May 18th, 1784, and Mr. Fox, who had been returned by a friend as member for Kirkwall, in the Orkneys, took his seat for that borough. Within a few days, the subject was brought before the House. Mr. Corbett appeared at the bar, and read a long paper in defense of his conduct. Witnesses were examined, counsel were heard on both sides, and the subject was discussed in the House, from time to time, under various aspects.

On the 8th of June, Mr. Wellbore Ellis offered the following resolution: "That it appearing to the House that Thomas Corbett, Esquire, bailiff of the Liberty of the City of Westminster, having received a precept from the Sheriff of Middlesex for electing two citizens to serve in Parliament for the said city; and having taken and finally closed the poll on the 17th day of May last, being the day next before the day for the return of the said writ, he be now directed forthwith to make return of his precept, and the names of members chosen in pursuance thereof." During the debate which followed Mr. Fox delivered the following speech, in which,

---

[1] Parliamentary History, xxiv., 844.

I. He examines the evidence by which Mr. Corbett had endeavored to justify his granting the scrutiny.

II. He discusses the question of law in respect to such a measure.

III. He enters into remarks of a more general nature respecting the authors of this scrutiny, the expense it involved, the alternative suggested of issuing a writ for a new election; and repels the intimation of Mr. Pitt, that he "ought not again to disturb the peace of the city of Westminster!"

A circumstance occurred at the commencement of the speech which turned greatly to the advantage of Mr. Fox. He began by complaining of a want of courtesy in the mode of carrying on the debate, and added, "But I have no reason to expect *indulgence*, nor do I know that I shall meet with bare *justice* in this House." Murmurs of disapprobation broke forth from a large part of the House, in which the minister had an overwhelming majority. Mr. Fox was at once roused to the utmost. His ordinary embarrassment and hesitation in commencing a speech instantly passed away. He repeated the words; he challenged his opponents to make a motion for taking them down with a view to his being censured; he referred to Mr. Grenville's bill in proof that the House was considered as peculiarly liable to act unjustly in such cases; he turned upon Lord Mulgrave, Lord Mahon, and Lord Kenyon, who had just spoken, commenting in the severest terms on the treatment they had shown him, and affirming that he might reasonably object to them as judges to decide in his cause; and repeated, for the fourth time, "*I have no reason to expect indulgence, nor do I know that I shall meet with bare justice in this House.*" Never was a great assembly more completely subdued. From that moment, he was heard with the utmost respect and attention. He had remarked, in going to the House, that this would be one of the best speeches he ever made. It proved so; and if the subject had been equal to his manner of treating it, embracing great national interests, instead of the details of a contested election, roused to the utmost as he was, he would probably have made it the greatest speech he ever delivered.

SPEECH, &c.

Mr. Speaker,—Before I enter upon the consideration of this question, I can not help expressing my surprise, that those who sit over against me [the ministry] should have been hitherto silent in this debate. Common candor might have taught them to urge whatever objections they have to urge against the motion of my honorable friend [Mr. Ellis] before this time; because, in that case, I should have had an opportunity of replying to their arguments; and sure it would have been fair to allow me the slight favor of being the last speaker upon such a subject. But, sir, I have no reason to expect indulgence, nor do I know that I shall meet with bare justice in this House.[2] Sir, I say that I have no reason to expect *indulgence*, nor do I know that I shall meet with *bare justice* in this House.[3]

Mr. Speaker, there is a regular mode of checking any member of this House for using improper words in a debate; and that is, to move to have the improper words taken down by the Clerk, for the purpose of censuring the person who has spoke them. If I have said any thing unfit for this House to hear, or me to utter—if any gentleman is offended by any thing that fell from me, and has sense enough to point out and spirit to correct that offense, he will adopt that parliamentary and *gentleman-like* mode of conduct; and that he may have an opportunity of doing so, I again repeat, *that I have no reason to expect* INDULGENCE, *nor do I know that I shall meet with* BARE JUSTICE *in this House.*

Sir, I am warranted in the use of these words, by events and authorities that leave little to be doubted and little to be questioned. The treatment this business has received within these walls, the extraordinary proceedings which have sprung from it, the dispositions which have been manifested in particular classes of men, all concur to justify the terms I have adopted, and to establish the truth of what I have asserted.

If the declaration I have made had happened not to have been supported by the occurrences I allude to, the very consideration of Mr. Grenville's bill is of itself sufficient to vindicate what I have said. That bill, sir, originated in a belief that this House, in the aggregate, was an unfit tribunal to decide upon contested elections. It viewed this House, as every popular assembly should be viewed, as a mass of men capable of political dislike and personal aversion; capable of too much attachment and too much animosity; capable of being biased by weak and by wicked motives; liable to be governed by ministerial influence, by caprice, and by corruption. Mr. Grenville's bill viewed this House as endued with these capacities; and judging it therefore incapable of determining upon controverted elections with impartiality, with justice, and with equity, it deprived it of the means of mischief, and formed a judicature as complete and ample perhaps as human skill can constitute.[4] That I am debarred the benefits of that celebrated bill is clear beyond all doubt, and thrown entirely upon the mercy, or, if you please, upon the wisdom of this House. Unless, then, we are to suppose that human nature is totally altered within a few months—unless we can be so grossly credulous as to imagine that the pres-

[2] Expressions of disapprobation from the ministerial side of the House.

[3] Expressions of disapprobation repeated.

[4] Mr. Grenville's bill enacted that the persons to try disputed elections shall be drawn out of a glass to the number of forty-nine; that the parties in the dispute shall strike from these names alternately without assigning any reason until they reduce the number to thirteen; that these thirteen shall be governed by positive law, and sworn upon oath to administer strict justice.

ent is purged of all the frailties of former Parliaments—unless I am to surrender my understanding, and blind myself to the extraordinary conduct of this House, in this extraordinary business, for the last fortnight—I may say, and say with truth, "*that I expect no indulgence, nor do I know that I shall meet with bare justice in the House.*"

There are in this House, sir, many persons to whom I might, upon every principle of equity, fairness, and reason, object as judges to decide upon my cause, not merely from their acknowledged enmity to me, to my friends, and to my politics, but from their particular conduct upon this particular occasion. To a noble Lord [Lord Mulgrave] who spoke early in this debate, I might rightly object as a judge to try me, who, from the fullness of his prejudice to me and predilection for my opponents, asserts things in direct defiance of the evidence which has been given at your bar. The noble Lord repeats again that "tricks" were used at my side in the election, although he very properly omits the epithet which preceded that term when he used it in a former debate. But does it appear in *evidence* that any tricks were practiced on my part? Not a word. Against him, therefore, who, in the teeth of the depositions on your table, is prompted by his enmity toward me to maintain what the evidence (the ground this House is supposed to go upon) absolutely denies, I might object with infinite propriety as a judge in this cause.

There is another judge, sir, to whom I might object with greater reason if possible than to the last. A person evidently interested in increasing the numbers of my adversaries upon the poll, but who has relinquished his right as an elector of Westminster, that his voting may not disqualify him from being a judge upon the committee to decide this contest. A person too, sir, who in the late election scrupled not to act as an agent, an avowed, and indeed an active agent, to my opponents.[5] Is there any interruption, sir? I hope not. I am but stating a known fact, that a person who is to pronounce a judgment this night in this cause, avoided to exercise one of the most valuable franchises of a British citizen, only that he might be a nominee for my adversaries; concluding that his industry upon the committee would be of more advantage to their cause than a solitary vote at the election. This, sir, I conceive would be a sufficient objection to him as a judge to try me.

A third person there is [Mr., afterward Lord Kenyon] whom I might in reason challenge upon this occasion. A person of a sober demeanor, who, with great diligence and exertion in a very respectable and learned profession, has raised himself to considerable eminence; a person who fills one of the first seats of justice in this kingdom, and who has long discharged the functions of a judge in an inferior but very honorable situation. This person, sir, has upon this day professed and paraded much upon the impartiality with which he should discharge his conscience in his judicial capacity as a member of Parliament in my cause. Yet this very person, insensible to the rank he maintains, or should maintain in this country, abandoning the gravity of his character as a member of the Senate, and losing sight of the sanctity of his station, both in this House and out of it,[6] even in the very act of delivering a judicial sentence, descends to minute and mean allusions to former politics—comes here stored with the intrigues of past times, and instead of the venerable language of a good judge and a great lawyer, attempts to entertain the House by quoting, or by *mis*quoting, words supposed to have been spoken by me in the heat of former debates, and in the violence of contending parties, when my noble friend [Lord North] and I opposed each other. This demure gentleman, sir, this great lawyer, this judge of law, and equity, and constitution, also enlightens this subject, instructs and delights his hearers, by reviving this necessary intelligence, that when I had the honor of first sitting in this House for Midhurst, I was not full twenty-one years of age! And all this he does for the honorable purpose of sanctifying the High Bailiff of Westminster in defrauding the electors of their representation in this House, and robbing me of the honor of asserting and confirming their right by sitting as their representative! Against him, therefore, sir, and against men like him, I might justly object as a judge or as judges to try my cause; and it is with perfect truth I once more repeat, "*that I have no reason to expect indulgence, nor do I know that I shall meet with bare justice in this House.*"

Sir, I understand that the learned gentleman I have just alluded to (I was not in the House during the first part of his speech) has insinuated that I have no right to be present during this discussion, and that hearing me is an indulgence. Against the principle of that assertion, sir, and against every syllable of it, I beg leave, in the most express terms, directly to protest. I maintain, that I not only have a right to speak, but a positive and clear right to vote upon this occasion; and I assure the House that nothing but the declaration I have made in the first stage of this business should prevent me from doing so. As to myself, if I were the only person to be aggrieved by this proceeding, if the mischief of it extended not beyond me, I should rest thoroughly and completely satisfied with the great and brilliant display of knowledge and abilities which have been exhibited by the learned gentlemen [Mr. Erskine and others], who appeared

[5] Here Lord Mahon started up in much agitation, and exposed himself to the House as the person alluded to. He appeared inclined to call Mr. Fox to order, but his friends prevented him. His Lordship, as already stated, was an avowed and active agent of Sir Cecil Wray during the election, and had been placed by his nomination on the joint committee selected by the two parties to conduct the scrutiny.

[6] We have, in this enumeration of qualities, one of those *side-blows* so common with Mr. Fox, as he is pressing forward to his main point.

for me and for my constituents at your bar. If I alone was interested in the decision of this matter, their exertions, combined with the acute and ingenious treatment this question has received from many gentlemen on this side of the House, whose arguments are, as learned as they are, evidently unanswerable, would have contented me. But a sense of duty superior to all personal advantage calls on me to exert myself at this time. Whatever can best encourage and animate to diligence and to energy; whatever is most powerful and influencing upon a mind not callous to every sentiment of gratitude and honor, demand at this moment the exercise of every function and faculty that I am master of. This, sir, is not my cause alone; it is the cause of the English Constitution; the cause of the electors of this kingdom; and it is in particular the especial cause of the most independent, the most spirited, the most kind, and generous body of men that ever concurred upon a subject of public policy. It is the cause of the Electors of Westminster; the cause of those who, upon many trials, have supported me against hosts of enemies; of those who upon a recent occasion, when every art of malice, of calumny, and corruption; every engine of an illiberal and shameless system of government; when the most gross and monstrous fallacy [as to the East India Bill] that ever duped and deceived a credulous country have been propagated and worked with all imaginable subtlety and diligence, for the purpose of rendering me unpopular throughout the empire, have, with a steadiness, with a sagacity, with a judgment becoming men of sense and spirit, defeated all the miserable malice of my enemies; vindicated themselves from the charge of caprice, and changeableness, and fluctuation; and, with a generosity that binds me to them by every tie of affection, supported me through the late contest, and accomplished a victory against all the arts and power of the basest system of oppression that ever destined the overthrow of any individual.[7]

If, by speaking in this House (where many perhaps may think I speak too much), I have acquired any reputation; if I have any talents, and that attention to public business has matured or improved those talents into any capability of solid service, the present subject and the present moment, beyond any other period of my life, challenge and call them into action.[8] When added to the importance of this question upon the English Constitution, combined with the immediate interest I feel personally in the fate of it, I am impelled by the nobler and more forcible incitement of being engaged in the cause of those to whom the devotion of all I have of diligence or ability would be but a slight recompense for their zeal, constancy, firm attachment, and unshaken friendship to me upon all occasions, and under all circumstances.

There are two leading points of view in which this question should be considered. The first is, whether the High Bailiff of Westminster has had sufficient evidence to warrant his granting a scrutiny, *supposing that he possessed a legal discretion to grant it*. The second, whether any returning officer can *by law* grant a scrutiny, even upon the completest evidence of its necessity, which scrutiny can not commence till after the day on which the writ is returnable.

It is of little consequence in which order the question is taken up. I shall

Examination of the evidence.

I. First proceed upon the *evidence*.

(1.) The great defense of the High Bailiff is built upon the circumstance of Sir Cecil Wray and his agents having furnished him with regular lists of bad votes on my part; and to prove that these lists were delivered they have brought a witness who knows not a syllable of the truth of the contents of the list! The witness who drew the affidavit which affirms those bad votes to have polled for me, upon cross-examination appears equally ignorant of the *truth* of the affidavits; and therefore the burden of the proof rested upon the evidence of Affleck, whose testimony, nevertheless, after four hours examination, is expunged from your books as inadmissible. Expunged, however, though it is, I wish the House to recollect the answers he gave concerning the descriptions of the bad voters which are imputed to me, and to the stated number of them. The number is said to be one hundred and forty-three; and the House will recollect that, although I repeatedly pressed the witness to name some of them, he could not even name one. I questioned Affleck particularly whether the one hundred and forty-three were persons who did not exist where they pretended to reside; his answer was that some did reside in the streets as mentioned in the poll-books, and that others could not be found at all. Those who could not be found at all (if any such there were) might fairly be deemed bad votes, but the other class of voters involved a question of law; and I submit to the House whether, if the evidence of this man, instead of being rejected as incompetent, had actually been admitted, the whole tenor of it, instead of exculpating, would not in the strongest sense tend to criminate the High Bailiff. Had he known his duty, or been disposed to discharge it, this he would have said to such a reporter. "You may be, and most likely are, interested in deceiving me. After much argument and discussion I, as the sole judge in this court, have admitted these to be legal votes, which you (of whom I know nothing) affirm to be only lodgers or non-residents. My situation is too solemn to be affected by such information, and therefore I dismiss it as unfit for me to proceed upon."

This should have been the High Bailiff's conduct, but his conduct is the exact reverse of it.

[7] This fine burst of eloquence is highly characteristic of the speaker; not lofty or imaginative, but simple, terse, bold, and springing from those generous sentiments which were the master-spirit of Mr. Fox's oratory.

[8] The reader of Cicero will at once trace the opening of this sentence to the exordium of the oration for the poet Archias.

He receives this species of information, and from this sort of men; and not only so, but accepts affidavits imputing bribery to some persons who canvassed for me, acknowledging at the same moment that he had no cognizance of bribery; and never once inquires into the truth of the charge, nor whether any credit is due to the deposer, nor even who the deposer is. All this the High Bailiff does in concert with my adversaries, secretly, collusively, without even once giving me or any one of my agents the very slightest idea that any such intercourse had subsisted between him [the judge of the court] and one of the parties litigating that upon which he was to exercise his judicial function.

To have received such information with the least attention was in itself criminal enough; but studiously, cautiously, and deliberately to have concealed it from me was base and wicked in the extreme. Had I been apprised of these machinations, I might have established the falsehood of every accusation; and surely, if justice had been the object of the High Bailiff, he would not rest one moment until he communicated to me the burden of these informations and affidavits, especially if he meant to overturn the whole tide of precedents, and to innovate upon the practice of all the returning officers that ever lived in this kingdom, in granting a scrutiny to commence after the return of the writ. If truth was his aim, the obvious mode of ascertaining it was to have given the other party an opportunity of knowing the charges brought against them; to let them have the chance of contradicting their accusers; and if we failed in falsifying these informations, the High Bailiff would have had this presumption in his favor, that it was only because we could not. But, sir, not this nor any thing like it did the High Bailiff of Westminster. So far from acting like an impartial judge, he appears to have been the agent, or rather the mere tool of my opponents; and every syllable of these informations upon which he acted might have been, for aught he knew, the vilest mass of falsehood and perjury that ever thwarted the course of justice. I say then, sir, if the High Bailiff absolutely possessed a legal discretion in granting a scrutiny, to have granted it upon this sort of evidence, and under these circumstances, was, to say no worse of it, an act that can not be justified upon any obvious principle of law, reason, common sense, or common equity.

(2.) But what will the candid part of the House think of this High Bailiff when they consider that the grounds of his vindication at your bar differ as much as light and darkness, from his vindication in the vestry of Covent Garden, upon granting the scrutiny? And here, sir, I have to lament that the paper which he read to this House as his defense, which the gentlemen opposite to me [the ministry], for reasons as honorable, perhaps, to themselves as to the High Bailiff, so strenuously opposed being laid on the table, is now impossible to be produced. That paper, sir, would have enabled me, from his own words, to have proved to you that the principle he avowed at your bar, as the rule that governed him in this business, is exactly and directly the very reverse of the principle he pretended to act upon at the time of granting the scrutiny. Fortunately, however, this fact is established in clear and unquestioned evidence before you. Mr. O'Bryen's testimony is complete and decisive to that point. His words were, "that the High Bailiff in the vestry, upon granting the scrutiny, *disclaimed* the informations delivered to him by Sir Cecil Wray and his agents—that he replied with peevishness and some displeasure to Sir Cecil for having mentioned them—that he declared he believed he had never read them; certainly never with any attention—that he threw them aside unnoticed—that they had not the least operation upon his judgment; and that they did not, in the very slightest sense, influence his determination in granting the scrutiny." These were his words. Atkinson, upon cross-examination, was obliged to acknowledge this; and Grojan's want of memory upon it goes of itself a great way to establish the truth, if it required farther corroboration.

Now, let the House and the world judge of this High Bailiff, who, upon granting the scrutiny, affects to be insulted at the supposition of his acting upon this *ex parte* information, and yet rests all his defense at the bar of this House upon that very *ex parte* information which, but a fortnight before, he disclaimed and despised!!

Without adverting to his shameful and scandalous conduct (which, if he had one spark of feeling, would make him blush to show his face, much less to avow the act) in holding this fraudulent intercourse with my enemies, cautiously concealing that any such intercourse subsisted between them, treacherously betraying the cause of justice, which his situation bound him to support inviolate, and basely lending himself to one party for the ruin of the other, can any thing better show his iniquity than varying the grounds of his defense according to the variation of scene, and the pressure of exigency. This continual shifting demonstrates that he has no honest defense to make; put the most favorable construction possible upon his conduct, and the best of the alternatives marks him a hypocrite, at the least. If he has spoken truth in the vestry, he is an arrant liar before this House; or if he vindicates himself before you upon pure principles, he has grossly and wickedly deceived me and all who heard the contempt he expressed in the vestry for that information upon which he has expatiated at the bar of this House with such extraordinary reverence.[9]

So much for the consistency of the High Bailiff, respecting his alleged motives in granting a scrutiny.

(3.) It is said upon the other side of the House that the poll was not a scrutiny, and said, in ex-

[9] This is one of those *repetitions*, so often spoken of as a peculiarity of Mr. Fox. He manages it admirably in this case; varying the mode of statement, and crushing into one mass the preceding charges of fraudulent collusion and gross inconsistency on the part of Mr. Corbett.

press contradiction to the evidence produced at your bar. Never was a poll a scrutiny, unless the poll in question was such. It is established by respectable testimony at your bar that the poll was an *absolute* scrutiny.[10] It is proved that the parish books were constantly at the hustings, and each voter's name, profession, and description collated with the books. It is proved that when the names of voters could not be found in the parish books (which was often the case, and yet the votes perfectly legal) a gentleman in the interest of each side frequently went to the very street in which the voter said he lived; that the vote was suspended until that inquiry was made; and that the decision was always governed by the report of the inquirers in such case. Was this or was it not a scrutiny? But it is said that the poll was "crammed" at one time, and hence an inference is drawn that the poll was not a scrutiny. This is strange reasoning, surely. To support this inference, it should be proved that votes were excepted to, and yet admitted in the hurry without examination or inquiry. Does this appear to be the case? Nothing like it. With all Mr. Grojan's disposition to shelter the High Bailiff, with all his power of memory at one time, and his want of it at another, does he assert any such thing? No, sir; he could not with truth, and even he could not venture upon *this* without truth. Did you ever hear, or did such a thing ever happen, as that a returning officer of his *own* accord should reject any votes not excepted to by the contending parties? Certainly not. These votes, therefore, in whose legality the candidates themselves agreed, must be justly presumed by the High Bailiff to be unexceptionable; and from hence to suppose that the poll was no scrutiny, is weak in the extreme. In the early part of the election, it was the natural wish of each candidate to get upon the head of the poll. Each brought up as many friends as possible, and this accounts for what they call cramming the poll. Respecting the High Bailiff's difficulty in forming an opinion as to which of the two had the greater number of legal votes, had *I* been the lowest upon the poll at the close of the election, there might have been some little color for his affectation of scruples. Why? because upon the days when the poll was most crammed, when the greatest numbers polled, and when there was least inquiry and least examination into their legality, *Sir Cecil Wray had a very great majority over me*. I began to gain upon my adversary, not when thousands polled of a day, but when only few hundreds and less than a hundred polled each day—at a time when there was sufficient leisure to scrutinize the votes, and when the most acute, the most jealous and sharp inquiry took place as to the qualification of each voter that was perhaps ever practiced in any court of hustings.

(4.) With a view to exculpate this High Bailiff, his deputy, Mr. Grojan, related an incident which I shall notice; and the exultation of the opposite side of the House, at the time of that relation, renders that notice the more necessary. It was this: He asked a man which way the street lay in which he lived, and the man said it was *that way*, pointing his hand toward Drury Lane. "I immediately suspected him, and afterward rejected him," says Mr. Grojan. Now, sir, this story happens to be strictly true; and true to the confusion of those who relate it for the vindication of the High Bailiff. Were my election to depend upon the merits of a single vote, I do not know that I should prefer any other inhabitant of this great city before *that very man* then rejected by Mr. Grojan; for in all Westminster there is not a better qualified, a more undoubted legal voter than that identical person. And what is the fact, sir? That this honest, ignorant man came to poll with liquor in his head; and embarrassed by the scene, by the shouting, and by the manner, perhaps, of the question, made that absurd reply. These events, sir, were not unfrequent at that hustings; and when one considers the facility of puzzling such men in all places, when one considers that Mr. Grojan is not of all men living the most embarrassed in the exercise of his duty, nor exactly the most anxious for the comments of by-standers upon his conduct, there is little wonder that honest, uninformed men, surrounded by thousands, with half a dozen inspectors plaguing them with different questions at the same moment, in the midst of noise and huzzaing, in that state of hilarity, perhaps, which is too frequent at general elections, should sometimes give a foolish, unconnected answer to such interrogatories as generally come from Mr. Grojan.

(5.) I understand that a learned gentleman has said that *he* would have closed the poll long before the High Bailiff proclaimed his intention of doing so. I do not mean to argue the legality of that position with the learned gentleman. That the fact was exactly otherwise is all that is necessary for me to maintain. It is in evidence before you that he did not close it until the 17th of May; and that he then closed it not from deficiency of voters, but for the express purpose of enabling himself to make his return by the 18th, the day on which the writ was returnable. The first and the only notice I had of his intention to close the poll was on the Thursday preceding (May 13th); and I do confess, and have always declared, that my object was to continue the poll during the three intermediate days, that the High Bailiff may be obliged to assign this as his reason, since the act of closing the poll was his own act. In this I hold myself perfectly justifiable. During these three days I confess it was my wish to protract the poll, but I solemnly deny that it was ever prolonged by me a single hour more; and also deny that up to the 13th of May, I had any proposal or any offer that I could notice for closing it.

(6.) Attempts have been made to prove, and that is the last head of evidence I shall touch

[10] Mr. Fox does not mean that there was a scrutiny, in the technical sense of the term; but that the election was so conducted, under the arrangement mentioned above, as to give it all the substantial attributes of a scrutiny.

upon, that insinuations came from us at a certain period of the poll of demanding a scrutiny. That some of my friends might have expressed that intention is very probable; but give me leave to say, sir, that if I had myself formally demanded it there is no rule of law that warrants a conclusion against me on account of my own conduct as a party. A thousand motives there may be to justify me in demanding of the High Bailiff that which it would be perfectly right in him to refuse. If, in any case of litigation, a judge should grant to one of the parties whatever he wished, how could he ever come to a just decision? Or who would ever be defeated, whatever may be the badness of his cause?

But, sir, has it been offered to you in proof, or is there a man that can say I ever did for one moment entertain the idea, much less express it, that a scrutiny could go on *after* the day on which the writ was returnable? Sir, I do assure you, so absurd, so preposterous, so pernicious a thought never once possessed me. I had occasion very maturely to consider this subject at the first Westminster election. Lord Lincoln then demanded a scrutiny, which the High Bailiff granted, and which the noble Lord afterward relinquished. I remember to have investigated the matter then. I consulted the greatest dead and living authorities, the best books, and the most learned men in my circle; and the result was that the granting a scrutiny before the return of the writ was legal; but no book, no lawyer, no man before this time ever to my knowledge maintained that a scrutiny could be continued, much less begun, *after* the day on which the writ was returnable.

Then say my enemies, why did *you* expect the High Bailiff to grant you a scrutiny, which you must know could not be finished before the 18th of May?—and at that I see the gentlemen on the opposite benches [the ministry] exult a little. But, sir, it is a weak and childish exultation. Do they think, or if they deceive themselves, can they believe the public will think that I could have been so gross an idiot as to suppose a scrutiny of this election could be over before the 18th, with the instance of Vandeput and Trentham staring me in the face; where an unfinished scrutiny lasted above five months? Can they imagine I could hope a scrutiny in this case, where upward of three thousand voters polled more than at the contested election of Vandeput and Trentham, could by any possible means be over before the 18th? Surely not. A tolerable knowledge of Mr. Thomas Corbett, the High Bailiff of Westminster, gave me no extravagant hopes of success in any scrutiny where he was to be the sole judge. All, therefore, I ever meant was, that an *inquiry* might take place previous to the 18th; which inquiry might enable us to form the train and order of the necessary evidence, that we might the better know how to discover the different species of bad votes, and class under their various heads those which were doubtful, those which were suspected, and those which were positively illegal; and so far to methodize, arrange, and simplify the business before the return, that we might go on in the committee under Granville's bill with the greater facility and expedition, and with less expense; and this would have been a material point of preparation for us. This, sir, was all I ever meant by a scrutiny before Mr. Corbett, and all that any man of common fairness and liberality can suppose I meant.

(7.) A noble Lord over against me [Lord Mulgrave], in his zeal to exculpate the High Bailiff, charges me with having intimidated him, and charges it upon the evidence of Mr. Grojan. That noble Lord, disdaining all regard to consistency whenever he thinks he can impute a fault to us, at the same moment that he asserts the High Bailiff was intimidated, pronounces a flashy panegyric upon the firmness and intrepidity of the very man he affirms to have been thus terrified. But, sir, the High Bailiff *was* threatened—and how? Was it by threats of assaulting him? No. Was it by holding up the fear of danger to him by mobs or riots? No. Was it by a menace of taking away his books, breaking the peace of the hustings, and interrupting him in the discharge of his duty? No, no; but it was by warning him of the consequences of unjust partialities, false or corrupt decisions; it was by threatening him with legal punishment if he did not make the law of the land the rule of his conduct. Grojan tells you that he believes these threats sometimes induced the High Bailiff to make decisions in my favor, contrary to his judgment. Yet this is the man whose firmness and intrepidity the noble Lord commends so much, and whom the government of this country is straining every nerve to bear harmless through this unprecedented business. An officer whose deputy, as a palliation of greater guilt, defends by saying that he committed a palpable breach of his duty, and only because he is threatened with legal punishment if he acts against law! Sir, for my own part I believe there is as much sincerity in the noble Lord's panegyric as there is veracity in the deputy Bailiff's inference from these threats. All I wish however, is, that you would properly notice this species of intimidation. It is an intimidation, sir, the influence of which I hope will reach every man, every magistrate in this country, however splendid his station, however lifted up above his fellow-creatures in office or dignity. *To keep before his eyes the danger of a vicious or a wanton breach of the law of the land.* Would to God this House were in a capacity to become an object of those consequences, which the verdict of a jury would determine to follow the violation of the laws! With what content, with what confidence should I submit my cause to such a tribunal![11]

---

[11] This paragraph is worthy of being dwelt upon, as showing some of Mr. Fox's most striking peculiarities. (1.) He instantly turns his defense into an attack, by exposing the "inconsistency" of Lord Mulgrave. (2.) He adopts his favorite mode of question and answer, by which he so often gives

Having now, Mr. Speaker, gone through the various depositions that have been made before you—having, from the evidence, shown that the alleged grounds of the High Bailiff's first granting this scrutiny were the direct reverse of those he declares to this House to have been his motives—having shown that he was in habits of clandestine intercourse with my opponents—having shown that he was in the constant course of receiving *ex parte* information in an illicit and shameful secrecy—having shown that he positively and solemnly denied this series of iniquitous proceeding in the vestry, which he boldly avows at your bar—having shown that the poll was as much a scrutiny as any poll can possibly be—having explained my views in the event of my demanding a scrutiny—having described the species of intimidation used to this man, and confirmed that, so far from exculpating, it tends deeply to criminate him—having shown this, sir, and shown it by the evidence which you have heard at your bar, I shall conclude this part of my subject with submitting to every man of honor and candor who hears me, whether he really thinks that the High Bailiff of Westminster exercised a sound and honest discretion in granting a scrutiny, supposing for argument sake that he actually possessed a legal power to grant it.

Recapitulation.

II. The remainder of what I have to say shall be directed to prove that he had no such power, and to lay before you the fatal effects of such a precedent as the loss of this question will afford.

Question of law.

I am not a professional man, and can not be supposed to speak with the information of professional gentlemen upon a legal subject. There are, however, general and fixed principles of common sense which serve to guide an unlearned man upon a subject of this kind.[12] Four different ways occur to me by which in a case of doubt the law may be discovered and ascertained. First of all, I should look into the statute-book upon the table; if, upon searching there, I find *an act of Parliament* upon the point in dispute, doubt and conjecture cease at once, and all is clear and certain. But if there should be found no act to regulate the case in question, I should then, in the second place, have recourse to practice and precedent, and inquire what has been done in similar cases on similar occasions. In other words, I should try what is the *common law*. If I find practice and precedent direct me, then every thing is plain and easy; but if no statute and no precedent should be found by which I could steer in this ambiguity, my next obvious resort would be to *legal analogies*, to cases which, though not precisely the same in all points, are yet perfectly similar in principle. If in this department of research I find any thing to direct me, there too all will be smooth, intelligible, and certain; but if I find no positive statute, nor precedent, nor practice at common law, and no legal analogy, whereby I might discover the fact, there is then much difficulty, indeed, but not an insurmountable one. Still I should make an effort, and my last and fourth resort should be to the experience and understanding of mankind—to those arguments which common sense suggests—to fair conclusions deducible from fair reasoning, founded upon the immutable principles of policy and expediency.

Now, sir, if some of these various modes of defining the law should happen to favor me upon the present subject, and that others should unfortunately militate against me, still I may be right in my position; but not with that fullness of conviction, that clearness of certainty which I might wish. The case, however, is so entirely otherwise, that I do venture to affirm, and engage to prove to the satisfaction of every man capable of being satisfied, that not only nothing in any of these different ways of attaining the fact does operate in the slightest degree against me, but that *all* and *each* concur in supporting me, and demonstrating the illegality and violence of my enemies in the present business. I do, therefore, assert, that the High Bailiff of Westminster, in granting this scrutiny, has violated the law of the land, by the combined force and testimony of these four tests:

By the statutes.

By the common law.

By the analogies of law.

By policy and expediency.

(1.) First, as to the *statutes*. The act of the tenth and eleventh of William III. was made for the avowed purpose of checking the bad conduct of returning officers. The preamble of the bill and every clause in it proves this to have been the object of enacting it. As the part of it which relates to returns is merely directory, it is gross and absurd to construe it in any other manner than that which makes it answer the evident purpose for which it is enacted. It requires that the writs for any future Parliament shall be returned on or before the day that Parliament is called to meet—that the return shall be made to the clerk of the crown, which clerk of the crown is authorized to receive four shillings for every knight and two shillings for every burgess. It imposes a penalty upon the sheriff if he does not make his return on or before this day.

Now observe the construction given by the opposite side of the House to this plain, intelligible

liveliness and force to a statement. (3.) He shows what the intimidation consisted in, viz., pointing out the consequences of a *breach of law*. Thus he flashes his defense upon the mind, in the very act of stating what he did. (4.) He adroitly rounds off by applying the whole to his present situation; expressing his fervent wish that every member of that House could feel himself liable to the punishment of the laws, if through party prejudice, or any other cause, he gave his vote unjustly. The manner in which all this is wrought into a single paragraph, and poured at once upon the mind, is truly admirable.

[12] The reader will be struck with the beauty of this preparation for the legal argument by a brief view of the sources from which it was to be deduced. The argument itself is one of the finest in our language for clearness, condensation, and binding force.

statute. It is true, say they, this act is binding upon a sheriff, but not at all upon a mayor or bailiff! Why? Because a mayor or bailiff are not mentioned! True, they are not mentioned; and probably the action I spoke of some time ago might not lie against the High Bailiff, not that he has not openly transgressed the spirit of the law, but because the penal part of every statute is to be construed according to the strict letter of the act. But I submit to the House whether they ever heard so low, so vile, so dirty a quibble; whether they ever heard so base a perversion of common sense, as to suppose the Legislature of this country to have been such a set of idiots, such a herd of miserable beings, as that in an act made for the avowed and declared purpose of correcting and punishing the misconduct of returning officers, they should have provided against the partialities, and corruption, and roguery of sheriffs, and have left the nation at the mere mercy of mayors and bailiffs, without restraint, redress, or punishment? This is the construction put upon this act by his Majesty's ministers, the patrons of this High Bailiff, although they see those express words in the body of the act—"that the clerk of the crown shall receive at the time of these returns (which returns must be made on or before the day of the meeting of such new Parliament) four shillings for every knight, and two shillings for every burgess." Why mention the burgess, if that act is not meant to compel the return of the writ under which he is chosen? Was there ever such an outrage upon common sense, as to maintain, although they see the fee stated for the burgess to pay, though they see the return required proceeding from the sheriff's precept to the mayor or bailiff, that the *mayor* or *bailiff* is not obliged to make return within the time prescribed by the same act; that is, *on or before the day that the new Parliament shall be called to meet?*

But there is another point which defines the meaning of the Legislature to a certainty, and that is the exception in favor of new writs upon *vacancies*. In that case, there is an obligation that the return be made within fourteen days after the election upon that vacancy. Is it consistent with reason, or, rather, is it not making downright nonsense of this act, to suppose that it should compel a return within a certain time in cases of *vacancy*, but that upon a *general election* all should lie at the mere will and pleasure of the returning officer? Will the gentlemen urge the same contemptible reasoning here, and assert that the compulsion in this case only respects the returns of the knights of the shire? What? That an act should be made to prevent the collusion and knavery of returning officers, yet that it extends only to the preclusion of frauds in returning about one hundred because they are knights of the shire! and leaves the remaining four hundred at the discretion of every mayor or bailiff! Sheriffs are, in general, of a much superior rank and character to the other returning officers; yet the wittol caution which the honorable interpreters of this act impute to the English Legislature is, that they guarded against abuses from that class of returning officers whose fortune and sphere of life presumed *most* for their integrity, and made no provision whatever for the possible misconduct of that very description of returning officers whose situation gave the *least* pledge or security for honest and uncorrupt conduct! If I am not mistaken, this species of reasoning carries with it its own refutation.

A noble Lord over against me (Lord Mulgrave) has advanced a singular kind of argument, indeed, touching the intention of this act of King William. He has read to you from the journals an instruction to the committee appointed to bring it in, which instruction suggests to them the introduction of a clause to secure the returns for cities and boroughs within the specified time; and, in a style of inference peculiar to himself, he concludes that as the express words [mayor and bailiff] do not appear in the statute, the Legislature never meant to include the returning officers of cities and boroughs.

Now I will take upon me to say, that every other man in this country (that noble Lord and those who concur with him in opposition to my honorable friend's motion excepted), capable of understanding the sense of an act of Parliament, will draw the direct converse of his conclusion from the non-insertion of that clause. The sole view of this statute was to correct the abuses of returning officers. The instruction from the House to the Committee proves that the disease *extended* to mayors and bailiffs. The omission of that clause, therefore, clearly demonstrates that the framers of the act thought the suggestion fully comprehended in the act as it stands, and that it would be mere tautology and needless repetition to be more explicit. What a miserable Legislature must that be which, in the act of applying a remedy to an acknowledged evil, creates ten times a greater than that which it endeavors to cure. Those who made this law were, in my opinion, good politicians; but they were evidently not good prophets; for they did not foresee that an hour would come when men should rise up, and put such a construction upon their labors as marked them for the most despicable set of drivelers that ever insulted society under the appellation of law-makers. In a word, sir, I contend that the statute of King William is decisively and completely with us.

The 23d of Henry the Sixth is likewise with us, and does afford me a legal remedy against the High Bailiff, of which I shall most certainly avail myself.[13] That act authorizes the sheriff to issue his precepts to the returning officers of cities and boroughs. It requires that they shall make a return to the sheriff, and gives the person chosen and not returned an action, which *must be brought within three months after the meeting of Parliament*. From this it is evident that the return of the writ, and of the precept proceeding from the writ, must be at one and the same time,

[13] He did so afterward, and obtained damages from Mr. Corbett to the amount of £2000.

viz., by the meeting of the Parliament; for otherwise observe what rank nonsense this statute would be. The misconduct of returning officers made it necessary to give a power of legal punishment to the party *chosen* and *not returned.* That power is here given; but if we can suppose that the act does not compel the return to be positively made by the meeting of Parliament, the penalty is all a farce; for who will make a return that will subject him to a civil action, if it be in his power to avoid it. Whether the return be true or false, therefore, it is as clear as daylight that *some* return must be made by the meeting of Parliament, for it is insulting common sense to say that the man who incurs a legal penalty shall have a legal power of evading it. That is to say, that a returning officer may, *of his own authority*, prolong his return until the three months pass away, *within which time alone* the action can commence for the punishment of this gross abuse!

I have, therefore, sir, no difficulty in saying, and I am confident every fair man agrees in the truth of it, that these two acts, in their letter as well as their spirit, demonstrate that the High Bailiff of Westminster, in granting this scrutiny, has positively broken the statute law of the land.

(2.) The second point to which I shall advert in the arrangement of this argument is the point of practice, or what the *common law* is upon this occasion. And the best way to show that the High Bailiff of Westminster's return is against both the one and the other, is to observe this fact, that in all the records of Parliament, in all the annals of elections, and in the history of this country, not a single precedent can be found to justify this extraordinary return. The main and evident drift of it was to deprive me of the benefit of Mr. Grenville's bill; and to accomplish this end, do but observe how many obvious modes of return he has passed by. Had the bailiff done his duty, and returned Lord Hood and me, Sir Cecil Wray would not have been injured, for he would instantly petition, and the merits of the election would be tried by a committee upon their oaths. Had the bailiff, doubting, as he pretends, the legality of my majority, returned, as he undoubtedly might have done, Lord Hood and Sir Cecil Wray, then *I* should have petitioned, and one of Mr. Grenville's committees would have redressed me. Had he returned Lord Hood alone, still it was cognizable by Grenville's bill. A petition against an undue return would have been presented, and this House infallibly prevented all interference in the matter, except in appointing the committee. Or, if he had returned the three candidates, the double return would have entitled it to a priority of hearing (upon that great and fundamental maxim that the first object was to have the House complete), and a committee under Grenville's bill would instantly have tried the merits of the return, and rescued the case from the prejudices and party influence of the House of Commons. At all events, my sitting here for Kirkwall rendered an immediate discussion and decision upon the business indispensable, as petitions complaining of pluralities of election are always heard in order, next to double returns. Thus you see with what dexterity this has been managed.

This curious return had two views. First, to exclude me from sitting for Westminster. Secondly, to deprive me of the advantage of Mr. Grenville's bill. And, sir, does any man think this return was the fabrication of Mr. Thomas Corbett? The party spirit and personal rancor, so visible in his defense before this House, confirm that he has all the disposition, if not all the ability in the world, to do me every mischief. Yet I can not be persuaded, when I consider who *they* are that take the lead in his vindication before this House, and when I observe how very familiar they appear to be with this *historical* return[14] (as my noble friend has well called it), that so peculiar, so ingenious, and so original a fragment as this could ever have been his sole production. In a word, sir, this accursed historical return, this return unmatched, and unprecedented in the history of Parliament, is the only species of return that could have robbed me and the independent electors of Westminster of a fair hearing before that admirable judicature instituted by Mr. Grenville's bill.

A learned gentleman who appears at your bar for the High Bailiff, admits that no instance of this kind ever happened before; and to induce the House to support his client, he says it will never happen again. How he comes to know that a line of conduct so convenient to a minister, so well suited to those who have the power to oppress, and a disposition to exert every power against those they dislike [will not be repeated], the learned gentleman himself best understands. But surely, after such an admission, to pray the sanction of this House for an act allowedly unprecedented, is somewhat singular. The learned gentleman's prophecy is surprising, it is true; but the argument drawn from that prophecy is still more surprising. Grant the scrutiny, says he, in this case; but you certainly *never will do the like again.* Perpetrate the most gross and glaring injustice deliberately, for you never will commit a similar outrage hereafter! A good understanding, however, seems to prevail between those within and those outside of the bar. And the intimation of a learned gentleman over against me, of an intention to bring in a bill to regulate this matter in future, does in a great measure account for the prediction of the High Bailiff's counsel, that this iniquitous precedent will be no example for future imitation. Now, sir, I take the first opportunity of saying that a bill declaring the law, after a decision directly contrary to law, shall be opposed by me with all the faculties and force I am master of. This is no new principle with me. I have ever set myself against the affectation of applying a remedy upon erroneous decisions, subversive of law in supreme courts of judicature. In the case of the determination concerning general bonds of

14 So called from its detailing the facts of the case.

resignation of Church livings in the House of Lords last year, a bill passed there and was sent afterward to this House, the purport of which was to declare the law in that case, after a determination which reversed the uniform current of decisions in Westminster Hall for a series of ages.[15] Such a bill would have been most fatal in its example, because it would have taken away the only check, restraint, and control, upon courts of dernier appeal. It would take away the general public inconvenience arising from the false determinations of superior courts. I opposed that bill, sir, and opposed it with success, for this House rejected it. I shall oppose the bill suggested by the learned gentleman upon the same principle, and every other bill of the same tendency; for sure there can not be a more barefaced violence of decency and justice, a grosser mockery of the common sense of mankind, than to authorize a scrutiny in direct opposition to the whole tide of precedents, and exactly subversive of positive law, because you intend to bring in a bill to prevent the repetition in future time of so scandalous and shocking a proceeding.

An incident occurs to me which will be proper to mention here. Much discussion formerly took place upon this subject of regulating scrutinies, and especially at the time of the Oxfordshire election; concerning which election I shall presently trouble the House with a few observations. Great pains and labor were employed then with a view to frame an act of Parliament upon the subject; and a great man, whose name I mention only with the purest respect and reverence for his character [Lord Mansfield], took an active part, and gave the whole attention of his extensive and shining talents to the business. Yet, after the most deliberate and mature consideration of the subject, even he abandoned it, in a despair of being able to accomplish any system of management, from which many evils and various disadvantages impossible to be remedied, might not flow. All attempts to regulate scrutinies by act of Parliament were then consequently given up. The learned gentleman [Mr. Harding] will excuse me if I can not easily believe that he will effect that which Lord Mansfield relinquished as impracticable; and even this consideration would be an additional motive with me, for not hastily assenting to a bill of the complexion suggested by him to the House upon the present subject.

I have said that this business had no precedent in the annals of Parliament. The gentlemen on the other side do not attempt, because they dare not, to show that this High Bailiff is justified by any. The only cases they venture to touch upon are the cases of Oxford and Westminster; and yet these two cases are fundamentally and altogether against them. Could they cite any instances more apposite, undoubtedly they would never have alluded to those, which, under a hope of giving some color to the matter in question, do absolutely, positively, and substantially make against them. If out of the mass of precedents I were to choose one, to prove the grossness of this proceeding, I think it would be the very case of Oxfordshire. The candidates who at that election were lowest on the poll demanded a scrutiny, and the sheriff granted it. Every one knows that the sheriff carried his partialities for the losing candidates, who demanded the scrutiny to the greatest lengths; yet, partial as he was, and although his friends were diminishing their opponent's majority daily by the scrutiny, he gave them notice that his duty bound him to stop the scrutiny for the purpose of making his *return on the day the writ was returnable.* He accordingly stopped it, and made his return. If this sheriff, interested as he was for those who were gaining by the scrutiny, conceived it possible for him to be sanctioned by any law or precedent in making a special return, and going on with the scrutiny, would he not have done so? Undoubtedly he would; and the kind of return he made proves that he would, if he thought he might. Unwilling that those who were obnoxious to him should sit in the House, he returns all the four candidates; and this he does as the last and greatest act of friendship he could confer on his friends, previous to the extinction of his authority, viz., the return of the writ. I do not say that in making this double return the sheriff did right. But right or wrong, it proves this, that all the service he could render his friends he did. Does any one doubt that the two candidates, thus aided by the sheriff, and in the act of growing daily upon their adversaries by the scrutiny, would not have preferred the partial, the kind, and favoring tribunal of their determined friend the sheriff, to the House of Commons, had they supposed that any thing could justify him in continuing the scrutiny after the meeting of Parliament? But so frightful an idea was never cherished; and they held themselves bound forever in gratitude to the sheriff for having included them in his return. An honorable gentleman, whom I see in his place, but who I believe neither sees nor hears me at this moment,[16] knows full well that all I am stating relative to the Oxfordshire election is strictly true. He can not easily have forgotten the part he took in that memorable transaction. He engaged eagerly in the contest, and embarked in that interest which I should certainly have embraced had I been of an age to form an opinion, and to act upon it. That honorable gentleman can attest the veracity of this recital; but it were vain flattery, I fear, to hope that he will rise up to-night, and vindicate, by his voice and his vote, the principles of the cause he then supported, and which gained his friends the election.

He must remember that a long discussion took place in this House, touching the right of a cer-

15 Case of Fytche and the Bishop of London.

16 Mr. Jenkinson, who was fast asleep upon the treasury bench, and whom Mr. Pitt awoke when Mr. Fox alluded to him.

tain class of copyhold tenants who voted for those who had the majority upon the poll; and that the disqualification of this description of voters seated those in the House who were lowest upon the poll and the scrutiny. And here I must observe, what a strong and unanswerable confirmation of the point I am endeavoring to establish springs from a careful review of the Oxfordshire case. The cause of the unsuccessful candidates was pleaded at the bar by one of the greatest characters of that time, and one of the greatest ornaments of this; I mean Lord Camden, *quem gratia honoris nomino!*[17] A question was agitated to ascertain a peculiar qualification, which bore the most inauspicious, and as it afterward proved, the most fatal aspect toward his clients. If any objection to determine the point upon that ground could possibly be supported, does any one doubt that his ingenuity and penetration would not have discovered it? Does any one doubt that he would have enforced that objection with all that perspicuity and fervor of eloquence which so much characterize that noble Lord? But the idea of a sheriff's withholding a return on account of a scrutiny never once occurred to him, nor to those who managed it within the bar; nor do I believe, until this time (to answer the laudable purpose of the present moment), did it ever enter into the head of any man as legal or practicable.

So much for the Oxfordshire case, which I maintain goes with us in all its points and principles.

With respect to the Westminster case in 1749. A learned gentleman [Mr. Harding], who has spoken with much liveliness, but without one word of legal argument, tells you that the scrutiny then and the scrutiny now are cases exactly in point. In contradiction to that, I affirm that not the least similitude subsists between them. In this case the writ is returnable upon the 18th day of May; in that *no* precise time is mentioned for the return; and here consists the whole difference. Every one knows that the election of Trentham and Vandeput was upon a *vacancy* in consequence of Lord Trentham's accepting a seat at the Board of Admiralty. Upon a general election the King calls a Parliament for the dispatch of great and urgent affairs, and he calls it to meet upon a particular day. Now, sir, observe, if there be no compulsion upon returning officers to make their returns by that express time, what is to become of the great and urgent affairs for the dispatch of which his Majesty calls a Parliament?

Can you reconcile, for one moment, that the nation should be bound by laws and burdened with taxes to which they did not consent; that the King should have no Parliament, and the people no representatives to dispatch the weighty and urgent affairs they are called to consider by a particular day, only because it is the whim or fancy, or wickedness of a returning officer, at his leisure, to keep them employed in the long, laborious business of a scrutiny? But *during the existence* of Parliament, when a writ issues upon a *vacancy*, no particular day is named for its return. A poll or a scrutiny (which means only the continuation of the poll in another form) may be carried on, because it does not in the least infringe upon the exigency of the writ; because no particular time is mentioned for the return; and because his Majesty does not call upon that individual representative to come upon a precise day, for the dispatch of great and urgent affairs that affect his people, as upon a general election. This, therefore, constitutes the distinction, and it is a wide and a material distinction. The grievance from the absence of one representative is slight, and the law in that case admits a scrutiny; but in the other case, to withhold the return beyond the time appointed, is infringing the exigency, and violating the terms on which it was issued, which are, that the Parliament must meet upon that *express day, for that express purpose.*

Why there should be this distinction—why the compulsion of a return by a specified period should not exist as well in cases of vacancy as of general election, is not now the point in dispute. If it be, as I think it is, a defect, it only serves to prove that in the best works of human wisdom there are flaws and imperfections. Our aim is to find out *what* is the law, not *why* it is the law; and, from the whole, it is clear that the High Bailiff of Westminster, in overstepping this distinction, and granting a scrutiny to commence after the day of the general return, has broken every statute that appears upon this subject in your books, and gone in the face of every precedent that can be found in your journals.

(3.) The third ground upon which I shall take up this subject is upon that of the *analogies of law.* Upon this I shall detain the House only with a few words; not only because my ignorance of that profession disqualifies me from treating the point fully, but because all that can be said has been urged with the greatest force and effect possible by the learned gentlemen who appeared at your bar in my behalf; the proof of which is, that not a position they have advanced upon the legal analogies has been controverted by the learned gentlemen who pleaded for the High Bailiff without the bar, or those venerable judges and crown lawyers who have attempted to defend him within the bar. Little, therefore, remains for me to say. But little as I affect to have of information upon this part of the subject, I have enough to know that wherever the gentlemen on the other side have attempted to assimilate this case with legal analogies, they have completely and entirely failed. They have endeavored to establish that an officer may *go on* to execute the object for which the writ was issued from the courts in Westminster Hall, even after the day on which the writ is returnable. Yes, sir, he may go on; but how? Upon the authority of the expired writ? No, by no means! He goes on by a *new* power given him by that court whence the writ originally issues, to complete that which the premature expiration of his first

17 Whom I name only to praise.

commission prevented his accomplishing. In a word, the court has the power of rendering effectual its own process, and therefore grants a writ of *venditioni exponas*, where the sheriff has not been able to sell the goods levied under the first writ, and grants many other writs of different titles, for the purpose of completing that process the court has begun. But has any man said, that without a fresh authority, any sheriff, or any officer of any court of law, can proceed a single step under the old writ, one single hour after the day named for its return? I say, no, sir. There is not one man, however ignorant in other things, who does not know that all the authorities of all writs are defunct and extinct on the day named for their return. It is admitted that the court can grant a new power to complete its own process. Now, sir, to show the gentlemen on the other side that they have not a shred of analogy to support them, I will suppose, for a moment, that the writ under which the High Bailiff carried on this election had been issued from *this* court, what writ, or what legal authority can *you* give him to finish that which he says is still depending? None, I say, sir. A court of law can effectuate its own process by giving its officer a new power on the demise of the old; but did you ever hear of *one* court granting an authority to accomplish the purpose of a writ issued from *another?* Never. Such a thing was never heard of. And how stands the fact here; that the Court of Chancery issues the writ, and the House of Commons (another court) is to send forth a fresh writ to finish that which has not been finished under the King's writ issuing from chancery, the duration of which ceased on the 18th of May! See the infinite absurdity into which these poor attempts to make out analogies involve the supporters of the High Bailiff. Will they say, though this House can not issue a supplemental power, the usual officer for making out parliamentary writs can? Try it, sir, and you will puzzle all the writ-framers belonging to the House. I will venture to say, that all the skill of the Crown-office, and all the skill of the Court of Chancery combined, will be at a loss in what shape or mode to frame an instrument so exotic and hideous. I will not push this point further, satisfied that no candid man can have a second opinion upon the subject; and shall conclude this part of my speech with affirming that the statutes, the precedents, and analogies of law assert and establish the truth of my honorable friend's motion; and that, by those three tests, I am clearly entitled to the judgment of this House against the conduct of the High Bailiff of Westminster.

(4.) The fourth and last ground of consideration is upon that of *expediency*, of sound sense, and of general policy. And here I shall have as little trouble as upon the three former grounds, to establish every position, and to show the House the iniquity of this proceeding. The conduct of this bailiff not only violates the spirit and letter of every law, but absolutely, in so far, subverts the main principles of the British Constitution. When the King calls a new Parliament, the fair presumption is, that the "great and urgent affairs" for which he calls them together demand their immediate deliberation. It is clear that our ancestors were extremely cautious that nothing should prevent or obstruct their meeting; and, lest returning officers should be instrumental to this obstruction, all the statutes, and all the precedents that bear upon this matter, confirm their jealousy, and prove their diligence to guard against abuses. The misconduct of returning officers, the facility of evil, and the dangerous consequences resulting from it, were the evident and avowed cause of making those laws which I have mentioned, and which were avowedly intended to restrain them. Let but the conduct of the High Bailiff of Westminster be sanctified this night by this House, and I challenge the ingenuity of mankind to show a more effectual mode of putting the nation into the hands of returning officers.

What security can any man have that a Parliament shall meet when the King calls it, if you establish this precedent? An honorable friend of mine who has this day spoken for the first time [Sir James Erskine], and who has exhibited a power of fancy and force of argument that give a high promise of his making a splendid figure in this House, has said, it was possible the House of Commons of England might, upon the assembling of a new Parliament, be confined to the members from Scotland, where all scrutinies precede elections, and where the positiveness of the law precludes the commission of these knaveries. Now, although the brilliant fancy of my honorable friend might, perhaps, have stretched the possibility a little too far, is there a man who will engage, that this case once sanctified, the example will not be followed to the most calamitous excess? The exact number of five hundred and thirteen English members might not, indeed, be absent upon the meeting of a new Parliament; but will any man say why twenty, why sixty, why one hundred, nay, why two hundred might not, by the ignorance, by the caprice, by the folly, by the stupidity, or (what is more analogous to the case in question) by the baseness or treachery of a returning officer, remain unreturned? Here I must notice the low, the little, the miserable allusions which are so frequently made by those over against me, to the place that did me the honor of sending me to Parliament.[18] But it is a poor and pitiful kind of triumph. Much as they may affect to exult, nothing can be clearer than their disappointment upon the occasion; and the petition lately presented against my seat for Kirkwall proves their mortification to a certainty. And indeed it appears, from the conduct of government, that Scotland is the only place that could return me; as the same shameless persecution would, no doubt, have followed me in any other place in England. Fortunately, there was one part of the kingdom where their oppression

[18] Mr. Pitt, as already stated, had spoken of Mr. Fox as an "exile driven to seek refuge on the stormy and desolate shores of the *Ultima Thule.*"

could not prosper, and from which their violence and injustice could not exclude me.

Sir, I do really believe that the supporters of this extraordinary business look but a short way, and do not at all calculate or count upon its probable effects. If there had not been an act of Parliament expressly to regulate scrutinies in the city of London, who can say that at this moment, when laws are to be made as serious and interesting as any that ever passed in this country—when great and weighty impositions must be laid upon the subjects—when new and important regulations are to be entered upon concerning the commerce, the credit, and revenues of the nation—who can say that at this time the capital of the country, so deeply and supremely interested in all these objects, might not be deprived of representation as well as the city of Westminster? But, sir, I beg pardon. I am doing injustice. The sheriffs of London are too well acquainted with their duty, and too zealous for the honorable discharge of it, to have been guilty of so gross an outrage upon the laws of the land, or lent themselves to be the vile and sordid instruments of so base a business.

But the character of an officer is a weak security against the abuse of an office. Under men less informed, and less tenacious of their official reputation, who can say (if an express act had not rendered it impossible) that the patrons of Sir Cecil Wray, who are also patrons of Mr. Atkinson,[19] might not practice the same stratagem in the city of London, and by that maneuver prevent the wishes and the sentiments of the capital from being declared in this House, through the constitutional organ of their representatives? They, sir, I affirm, are weak and foolish men, rash and giddy politicians, who, by supporting a measure of this kind, become parties in a precedent, capable of producing consequences which strike at the source and root of all legislation; for it is the fundamental maxim of our Constitution, that the consent of the people by their representatives is essential and indispensable to those laws that are to govern them.

Upon this, however, a curious sort of reasoning is adopted, and a noble Lord [Lord Mulgrave] sees no evil in a defect of representatives for Westminster, as it is *virtually* represented by those who sit here for other places. In the principle that every member is bound to the common interest of all, I certainly do agree; but I beg leave to set myself wholly against the general argument of virtual representation. We have too much of virtual, and too little of real representation in this House. And to the present hour I never heard that the most determined enemy to a parliamentary reform ever urged that the virtual representation of the country was so complete a substitute for real representation as to deem it wise and salutary upon slight occasions, or upon any occasion, to lessen that which is already much too little. The whole tide of reasoning has, on the contrary, run in the other channel; and the great argument for a parliamentary reform has been founded upon this very defect of real representation, which the noble Lord over against me is so zealous to diminish. As the honorable gentleman near him, however [Mr. Pitt], is the professed friend of that reform, in the representation of the people of this country, which I have in common with him, so long labored in vain to accomplish, I shall hope to see him stating this very case of Westminster, to induce the House to adopt the motion which will be made upon that subject by my honorable friend [Mr. Sawbridge] in a few days. Of the prosperity of that motion I now entertain real confidence. The boasted power in this House of the right honorable gentleman insures success to any measure he abets. No question, therefore, can be entertained of attaining it, if the honorable gentleman is serious upon the subject; for surely the people of England can never be persuaded that the majority, which supported the minister in vindicating a direct violation of the law of the land, in the person of Mr. Corbett, could have failed him in endeavoring to effect an object so long looked for, so loudly called for, and so essentially necessary to the security of the Constitution and the good of the nation, as a reform in the palpably defective representation of the people in this House.

The same noble Lord attempts to strengthen his cause with a species of argument still more extraordinary, if possible, than the former, although of nearly the same nature. He tells you, that representing Westminster has been a mere naval honor; and after stating the choice of Lord Rodney when on foreign service, leads you to this inference, that the electors of Westminster are wholly unsolicitous whether they are represented or not. This is rating the electors of Westminster at a low estimate indeed; but I, sir, who know them better than the noble Lord, deny that they are so insensible to the blessings of the British Constitution as his argument pretends. The electors of Westminster have rescued themselves from this imputation. Sir, they are seriously anxious to be represented, and they tell you so. But I remember when absence *was* deemed a disqualification for naval officers upon a Westminster election. I remember when Lord Hood was in the zenith of his fame, that persons now in my eye [looking at Lord Mahon] urged his absence to the electors as a ground of rejection; and advised them to prefer Sir Cecil Wray, who was present and able to represent them, to Lord Hood, who was absent and unable.[20] This, though not my argument (whose opinion is uniformly that all electors of all places should elect

[19] This would seem to be Mr. Richard Atkinson, the agent of Paul Benfield, spoken of by Mr. Burke in his speech on the Nabob of Arcot's debts, who had just been defeated in London at the general election.

[20] This kind of home thrust, by referring to some past incident, is one of Mr. Fox's most striking peculiarities. So, likewise, is the turn given in the next sentence, respecting the *coalition* of one who so hated Coalitions.

the men of their choice), was the exact argument of the present supporters of Lord Hood in favor of that of Sir Cecil Wray, who *then* opposed him, but who *now*—in his enmity to any junction after past opposition, in his utter abhorrence of all coalitions—is linked with that very Lord Hood in ties of friendship and good faith, which *he* certainly never will violate.

Efforts, sir, have been made to explain the act of George II. to the exculpation of this High Bailiff; and his supporters affect to justify him upon his declared difficulty in making up his "conscience." Why, sir, the very act they attempt to shield him under is his strongest condemnation. The oath imposed in that act only binds him to decide to "the best of his judgment" by a limited time. Lives there one man who shall say, "this man would have incurred the penalties of perjury if he had returned the majority upon the poll?" Lives there one man who thinks the disquietude of his conscience alone prompted him to make the return he has made, when they must see a thousand instances every day of decisions of conscience, in cases a thousand times more ambiguous and solemn? I will ask the House whether this High Bailiff has appeared to them, in the course of this business, so spotless, so immaculate, so consistent, as to induce them to give him credit for a delicacy of nerve, and a tenderness of scruple beyond any other man living? Every person in the exercise of a judicial function stands precisely in his predicament. What would become of us if a judge were forever to delay justice, until he could make up his conscience to the minutest point of precise accuracy upon every doubt? There are few cases upon which a man can not form *some* opinion. All that is required here is to form the best opinion he can; and if seven weeks did not afford the High Bailiff time enough to determine, it is surely hard with those who are obliged to decide almost immediately in the most important interests of humanity. My honorable friend who made this motion, with that weight and wisdom that accompany all his observations, has adverted to the case of jurors. Have you, then, patience at this man's pretense of conscience, when you reflect that twelve men must all concur before they go out of court, in a judgment which perhaps consigns a fellow-creature to an ignominious death? The case may be doubtful too, and yet they must all concur in a few hours, at most. It is unnecessary to push this point farther. I appeal to the House. There are feelings which even party prejudices can not dispossess us of. We owe to each other a certain candor; and I am sure I should be thoroughly satisfied to put this matter to the private answer of any man who hears me; if I were only to ask him, upon his honor as a gentleman, whether he really believes the return of this High Bailiff is an act of *conscience?* And, whether he thinks, if *I* stood in Sir Cecil Wray's place, and *he* had my majority, we should ever have heard of this man's difficulty in giving judgment; or ever been insulted with this mockery of his scruples?[21]

To show, in another striking point of view, that this scrutiny is against the law, let the House reflect for a moment upon its utter inefficacy to enable the High Bailiff to form a judgment, as that is the pretended cause of it. What *means* has he of exploring those things which he now affects to entertain doubts upon? He can command no witness; he can compel no appearance. He has no legal authority for penetrating the obscurity of any fact like other judges; he can administer no oath; he can impart no remedy to the party aggrieved by so tedious and vexatious a process; he can award no costs; he can try no offense that occurs in the execution of this important duty; he is governed by no precedents; he is bound by no decisions: what he affirms to-day he may deny to-morrow; he has, in a word, all the means of doing injustice, and no one power or competent faculty to do justice. Yet to this species of tribunal is this House going (in violation of law and practice) to send me and my cause, on purpose to evade one which is full, adequate, effective, and vigorous—I mean, a committee under Grenville's bill.

A noble Lord expresses his suspicions of the sincerity of my praises of Grenville's bill, and says he imagines there is "a snake in the grass." It is most true, that I had my doubts upon the effects of that bill, when it first passed into a law. But, sir, it is exerting the worst tyranny upon the understanding of men, if they are to be forever condemned for having entertained doubts upon a subject purely theoretical. Extinct is every idea of freedom, and lost is the boasted liberty of debate, and the spirit of free thinking in this country, if men are to be debarred from profiting by practice, and changing opinion upon the conviction of experiment. All I can say, sir, is, that the many salutary effects of that bill have long since completely converted me; and I do assure you, in great sincerity, that no man living reveres and loves it more than I do. There can be no stronger proof of its superior excellence, than that the evasion of it is the only possible means by which his Majesty's ministers could perpetrate this gross act of injustice. The most infallible of all tests, the test of repeated practice, asserts its virtues; and my attachment to it is not a little increased, for that it resembles that inestimable right—one of the few that Englishmen have yet to boast—the trial by jury. Oh that it were possible to mold this House into the size and character of a jury!—of twelve men acting indeed upon conscience, and sworn upon oath to give a true verdict according to evidence!

[21] There can hardly be found any where a passage which is a more complete "settler" than this paragraph about Mr. Corbett's conscience. There is a sort of power in it which no speaker but Demosthenes ever so fully possessed—strong common sense, brief but irresistible reasoning, keen sarcasm, manly appeal, all wrought together in the tersest language, and vivified by the warmest emotion.

How easy should I feel concerning the issue of this discussion!

In addition to all these arguments, will the House reflect that this scrutiny is not final in deciding the right of sitting here?[22] Will they reflect that, after all the waste of time, after all the expense, all the labor, all the fatigue, which are indispensable upon it, its termination (whenever it may happen) is but the commencement of another process before a judicature, capable and competent to administer justice, with a new series of expense, and labor, and fatigue? And who can tell us when this scrutiny shall conclude? The granting it is not more illegal and oppressive than the duration is uncertain and indefinite. Who can promise when such a conscience as Corbett's will be quieted? And who will venture to say that, after one, two, three, or ten years' investigation, the High Bailiff's *conscience* may not be as unsatisfied, even upon the scrutiny, as it appears at this moment, after a seven weeks' poll?

"But," say the supporters of the High Bailiff, "this House will take care that there is no vexatious delay in the business, and will from time to time call upon him for a return, or for the cause that may prevent his making one." I understand that argument perfectly well, sir; and it is of itself sufficient to show the grossness of this proceeding. *When* the bailiff will be called on to make a return, and *when* he will obey that call, can be very easily conceived, indeed. If it were possible for this man, in the course of this scrutiny, to strike off from my numbers so many as would place Sir Cecil Wray on the head of the poll, I have not the smallest doubt that all delays, subsequent to such an event, would appear just as frivolous, as vexatious and oppressive to the gentlemen on the opposite bench [the Ministry], and to the High Bailiff's *conscience*, as the whole proceeding now appears to me, and to the injured electors of Westminster. Upon all the considerations, therefore, that I have mentioned—the inordinate expense; the inefficacy of the tribunal; the obvious necessity of afterward resorting to a more adequate and competent judicature; the certainty that this precedent will be the source of future oppressions; the dangerous example of it to other returning officers, who, under the sanction of this case, can give full scope to their partialities, their caprices, and corruptions; the circumstance of depriving so great and respectable a body of men of their representation in this House; the recognizing that dreadful doctrine, that a King may be without a Parliament, and the people without representation, at the mere will and bare discretion of any low, mean, ignorant, base, and wretched being, who may happen to be a returning officer —from all these considerations, therefore, I am convinced, and I hope I have convinced this House, that if no statute could be found upon the subject; that if the common law were silent, and that legal analogies gave no light upon the subject, even upon the grounds of common sense and expediency, the law is clear and intelligible. But when all these concur to define and to decide the law; when positive statutes, when practice and precedents, when the analogies of law, and the arguments of expediency, founded upon the immutable principles of wisdom, reason, and sound policy, ALL combine and unite to establish and to assert it, can I have any fear to say that this motion ought to pass, and that the High Bailiff of Westminster, instead of being permitted to proceed with this scrutiny, should instantly make a return of members for Westminster?

Some gentlemen have argued that this motion does not agree with the prayer of the petition [previously presented by Mr. Fox]. Let it be recollected, sir, that the petition was presented by me with a view of its being referred to a committee.[23] Really, sir, if there is not enough of candor to admit this assertion without being explained, there seems but little chance of a fair hearing, or of a fair construction, upon points much more material. I again declare it was presented for the purpose I have described. A majority of this House decided that the petition was not cognizable by Mr. Grenville's bill; and it was upon a suggestion from the other side of the House that I presented it the same day, to save time, and prayed that counsel might be heard at the bar in favor of it. The sole object of that petition was, that this House might order such a return as would come under the jurisdiction of a committee; the motion before you goes precisely to the same point, and to no other.

To that argument, if it deserves the name of argument, that we are inconsistent in desiring the High Bailiff to make a return, when we contend that all his authority under that writ is completely defunct, it is almost unnecessary to reply, because it evidently defeats itself. In contending that the High Bailiff was *functus officio*[24] on the 18th of May, we are fortified by law; and, in desiring he would make *some* return, we are justified by precedent.

We contend, and contend with truth, that the writ under which the High Bailiff carried on the election, being returnable on the 18th of May, on that very day deprived the bailiff of all judicial authority, and devested him of all legal power under that writ. To proceed with a scrutiny is a great act of authority; to tell us who have, in his opinion, the majority of legal votes, is not. That this House should order a returning officer to commence a scrutiny several days after the positive day on which his writ was returnable, can not be paralleled by a single case in all the history of Parliament. That it should order a returning officer, who tells you he proceeded to an election, carried on a poll for a sufficient time, and that he then closed that poll of his own au-

[22] The question could be brought up again after the return was made, and tried before a committee of the House under Mr. Grenville's bill.

[23] Here the minister shook his head, as if to deny the fact.

[24] Discharged from further duty.

thority, to make a return, *has* happened again and again. We do not desire him to exercise any jurisdiction under that writ *now;* we only desire him to acquaint us with the fruits of the jurisdiction which he *has* exercised under it. I have done so and so, says the High Bailiff. "Tell us what you mean," is all we say. "I have, on such a day, proceeded to an election," says he; "I have carried on a poll for forty days; I have, on the day before the return of the writ, closed that poll, of my own authority." All this we understand. In all this you did your duty. Only tell us who are the candidates chosen upon this long poll? We do not mean to say you have at present any authority to do any thing under that writ; all we want to know is, what you did when you *had* authority under it? Let the House reflect upon this fair and reasonable distinction, and they will see the paltriness of those quibbles, the misery of those low subterfuges, which imply that we would bring "a dead man to life;" and which imply an inconsistency between the motion and the arguments advanced in support of it.

What, I beg leave to ask, has appeared to the House extraordinary or uncommon in the election for Westminster, that justifies this matchless violence? In all the variety of evidence they have heard at the bar, has there been a proof of one single bad vote of my side? Not one. But there was much *hearsay* that I had bad votes. Sir Cecil Wray and his agents told the High Bailiff they *heard* I had. Good God, sir, am I addressing men of common sense? Did any of you ever yet hear of an election wherein the losing candidate did not charge bad votes and bad practices upon the fortunate candidate? Peevishness upon miscarriage is perhaps an error, but it is the habit of human nature; and was the High Bailiff of Westminster so unhackneyed in the ways of men, as to be unapprized of this frailty; or are the discontents of Sir Cecil Wray, and the loose accusations of his agents, the extraordinary things which the House sees in the Westminster election, to justify this proceeding? Is the length of the election one of these uncommon incidents? By no means. The same thing happened at Bristol, where, without doubt, a scrutiny would have been granted, if the returning officer had thought the law would bear him out in it. The same thing happened at Lancaster, where a scrutiny was demanded and refused, and where, when the connections of one of the candidates[25] are considered, no doubt can be entertained that every stratagem to procrastinate, every scheme to perplex, every expedient to harass, all that a disposition not the mildest when victorious, nor the most patient when vanquished, all that wealth, all that the wantonness of wealth could do, would have been exerted; and where a plan so admirably calculated for litigation, for vexation, for expense, for oppression, as a scrutiny, would not have been admitted, were it found legal or practicable.

Let the House reflect for a moment upon the facility of a collusion in a case of this sort, to keep a candidate from his seat, whose right to it is clear, unquestioned, and unquestionable. Suppose that not one single bad vote had been given for Lord Hood in the late election, and that the noble Lord were not (he best knows why) resigned and easy under this proceeding, what could be more hard and cruel than his situation? Does not the House see that ministers will be enabled by this precedent to exclude an obnoxious candidate for an indefinite space of time, even though his majority be the most undoubted possible, and his election the fairest in the world? It is only for the losing candidate to demand, and for the returning officer to grant, a scrutiny. These are some of the evils that present themselves upon the recognition of this practice as right and legal. For my part, I see nothing in the late election for Westminster peculiar and distinct from many other elections, but this singly, *that I was one of the candidates.* In that light it is already seen by every cool, dispassionate, and sensible man; and that the whole nation will contemplate and construe the business of this night as an act of personal oppression, I am thoroughly convinced; nor can they think otherwise, when they learn that in all the law books of this country, in all your journals, in all the histories of Parliament, in all the annals of elections, in this great land of elections, where, from time to time, all that power, all that ingenuity, all that opulence could devise or execute, has been tried in elections—where, in the vast mass of cases that have happened, in all the multiplied variety of singular and curious contests we read and hear of, *nothing is found that assimilates with, or authorizes this scrutiny, under these circumstances*—not even by the worst of men, in the worst of times.

Remarks of a more general nature.

III. (1.) I will acquit the honorable gentleman over against me [Mr. Pitt] of being the author, or being a voluntary instrument in this vile affair; and in that concession, sir, I do not give him much. It is but crediting him for a little common sense, indeed, when I suppose that, from a regard to that government of which he is the nominal leader, from a regard to his own character with the world at this time, and his reputation with posterity, he acts his part in this business not without concern. That he may be accusable of too servile a compliance is probable enough; but of a free agency in it I believe he is guiltless. Not to him, sir, but to its true cause, do I attribute this shameful attack—to that black, that obstinate, that stupid spirit which, by some strange infatuation, pervades, and has pervaded the councils of this country throughout the whole course of this unfortunate and calamitous reign—to that weak, that fatal, that damnable system, which has been the cause of all our disgraces and all our miseries—to those *secret advisers*, who hate with rancor and revenge with cruelty—to those malignant men, whose character it is to harass the object of their enmity with a relentless and insatiate spirit of revenge; to those, sir, and not to

[25] Mr. Lowther, the nephew of Sir James Lowther.

the honorable gentleman, do I impute this unexampled persecution.[26]

(2.) Having said so much as to the real authors of this measure, there remains another consideration with which I am desirous to impress the House. It is a consideration, however, which in policy I ought to conceal, because it will be an additional incitement to my enemies to proceed in their career with vigor; but it will nevertheless show the extreme oppression and glaring impolicy of this scrutiny—I mean the consideration of expense.

I have had a variety of calculations made upon the subject of this scrutiny, and the lowest of all the estimates is £18,000. This, sir, is a serious and an alarming consideration. But I know it may be said (and with a pitiful triumph it perhaps will be said) that this is no injury to me, inasmuch as *I* shall bear but a small portion of the burden; but this, sir, to me, is the bitterest of all reflections!

Affluence is, on many accounts, an enviable state; but if ever my mind languished for and sought that situation, it is upon this occasion; it is to find that, when I can bear but a small part of this enormous load of wanton expenditure, the misfortune of my being obnoxious to bad men in nigh authority should extend beyond myself; it is when I find that those friends whom I respect for their generosity, whom I value for their virtues, whom I love for their attachment to me, and those spirited constituents to whom I am bound by every tie of obligation, by every feeling of gratitude, should, besides the great and important injury they receive in having no representation in the popular Legislature of this country, be forced into a wicked waste of idle and fruitless costs, only because they are too kind, too partial to me. This, sir, is their crime; and for their adherence to their political principles, and their personal predilection for me, they are to be punished with these complicated hardships.

These, sir, are sad and severe reflections; and although I am convinced they will infuse fresh courage into my enemies, and animate them the more to carry every enmity to the most vexatious and vindictive extremity, still it shows the wickedness of this scrutiny, and the fatality of its effects as an example for future ministers.

(3.) Little remains for me now to say upon this subject; and I am sure I am unwilling to trespass more upon the House than is barely necessary. I can not, however, omit to make an observation upon an argument of two learned gentlemen,[27] who concluded two very singular speeches with this very singular position, that the House had only to choose between issuing a new writ or ordering the scrutiny; that in its lenity it might adopt the latter method, but that their opinion was for issuing a new writ. Now, sir, if I, who think the old writ totally annihilated—who think that its powers and authorities have been completely extinct since the 18th of May—had delivered such an opinion, there would have been nothing in it inconsistent. And I should certainly be for issuing a new writ in preference to a scrutiny, if the law, the reason of the thing, and the practice of Parliament, did not convince me that the High Bailiff, having finished the election on the 17th, might make a return as of that day. But for the learned gentlemen who contend that the old writ is still in full vigor and force; who think that the High Bailiff has acted constitutionally and legally, and that a scrutiny may go on after the return of the writ—for those gentlemen to assert that the issuing a new one would be the fitter measure, is indeed extraordinary. But, sir, against that position, that the House might order the scrutiny to proceed, as a measure of *lenity*, I beg leave directly to oppose myself! I beg leave to deprecate such lenity, such oppressive, such cruel lenity!

To issue a new writ is a severe injustice, and a great hardship; but if I am forced to the alternative, if I am driven to the necessity of choosing between two evils, I do implore the House rather to issue a new writ than to order this scrutiny. Nothing can possibly be half so injurious, half so burdensome, half so vexatious to me and to my friends, as this scrutiny; and it is evidently ineffectual, as it can not be supposed that I should finally submit to the decision of a tribunal from which I have so little justice to expect. There is nothing, I assure the House, to which I should not rather resort than to the *conscience* of Mr. Thomas Corbett; upon whom I do not expect that the translation of the scene from Covent Garden to St. Ann's, or proceeding upon a scrutiny instead of a poll, will operate such conversions as to give me any hope of his displaying any other character, or appearing in any other light than that in which I have seen him upon many occasions in his official capacity. Therefore, sir, if it be only the alternative, I beg that the issuing a new writ may be the alternative you will adopt. In that case, I assure the honorable gentleman [Mr. Pitt] that I shall immediately apply to him for one of the Chiltern Hundreds to vacate my seat for Kirkwall, and instantly throw myself, as my only chance for the honor of sitting in this House, upon the good opinion of the electors of Westminster—who, in a season of frenzy and general delusion; who, when artifice, fallacy, and imposture prevailed but too successfully in other parts of the country, discovered a sagacity, a firmness, and a steadiness superior to the effects of a vulgar and silly clamor; and who, upon the very spot, the very scene of action, manifested that they understood and despised the hypocrisy, the fraud, and falsehood which gulled and duped their fellow-subjects in other places. In the event of a new election, I do anticipate future triumphs more brilliant, more splendid, if possible, than those I had lately the honor of en-

[26] This refers to that system of secret influence with the King, supposed to have commenced with Lord Bute, which was so much complained of at the beginning of this reign. Here Mr. Fox alludes particularly to Lord Temple's communications with the King, respecting the East India Bill, and the events dependent thereon.

[27] The Lord Advocate and Mr. Hardinge.

joying. Little fear do I feel of success with the electors of Westminster, who will not, I am sure, abandon me until I desert those principles which first recommended me to their favor!

(4.) A person of great rank in this House [Mr. Pitt] has thrown out a hint or threat, I know not which to call it, in a former debate, "that I should not again disturb the peace of the city of Westminster." Good God, sir! did any man ever hear such aggravating, such insulting insinuations? *I* disturb the peace of Westminster! Is that honorable gentleman not contented with breaking every law, with violating every statute, with overturning every analogy and every precedent, to accomplish this business; but must he, at the very moment he thus makes a deep breach in the English Constitution, complete the catalogue of injury, by adding pertness and personal contumely to every species of rash and inconsiderate violence! I, I disturb the peace of this city, who have three times had the honor of representing it in this House! I, who was favored with the free suffrages of its electors, long, long before any of those who lately opposed me were ever talked of, ever thought of for such a distinction! Every man qualified to sit in Parliament has a right to offer himself wherever he thinks proper; and it is indecent, daring, and audacious in any man, to insinuate that he ought not to disturb the peace of the place. I therefore hope, sir, that a language so peculiarly false and unbecoming toward me, and so directly repugnant to the genius and spirit of the Constitution, will meet with the disapprobation it deserves *in* this House, as it certainly will be received with merited odium and execration *out* of this House.

Upon the generous protection of the electors of this city I shall certainly throw myself, in case of a new writ; and, in doing so, sir, well I am aware what a series of *various* difficulties I have to encounter. Expenses at elections, in despite of every effort to reduce them, still continue most exorbitant; and how ill matched in funds and *certain* inexhaustible resources I stand with my opponents, is indeed very unnecessary to explain. But, sir, it is not in the article of expenses that I should most dread the operation of that power that sustains my adversaries—that *power* which discovers itself in characters that can not be mistaken, through every part of this transaction. I must be blind not to see that the hand of government appears throughout this matter. When I consider the extreme care employed in preparing it for the measures which have been taken in this House in consequence of it—when I consider the evident determination not to let it rest here—when I consider the extraordinary zeal and anxiety of particular persons in this House to shelter and to sanctify this High Bailiff—when I consider the situation of those who take the lead, and are most active in his vindication—when I consider the indifference of my adversaries to the expenses which result from this scrutiny, but which expenses must be a severe stroke upon the spirit and independence of those by whom I am supported—when I consider that all that artifice could dictate and power could execute have been exerted upon this occasion, I can have no doubt that the hand of a revengeful government pervades it all. The opposition of such a government upon an election is a discouraging circumstance; and the likelihood of renewing again those events which I have witnessed within the last two months, is indeed a formidable and terrific prospect.

When I look back, sir, to all the shameful and shocking scenes of the Westminster election—when I consider that my enemies practiced all that was possible of injustice, indecency, and irreverence in their efforts to overwhelm me—when I consider the gross, the frontless prostitution of names too sacred to be mentioned[28]—when I consider that all the influence of all the various branches of government was employed against me, in contempt of propriety and defiance of law—when I consider that a body of men was brought, in the appearance of constables, to the place of election, under the command of a magistrate, and against the express opinion of all the other magistrates of Westminster—that these constables broke that peace they were bound to preserve, and created a riot which proved fatal to one of their own body—when I consider that this was made the pretense of a wanton, and indecent, and unconstitutional introduction of the military, in violation of all that has been done by our ancestors to keep sacred the freedom of election—when I consider that the lives of innocent men were deemed light and trivial impediments to the gratification of that implacable spirit of revenge, which appears through the whole of this business—when I consider that several men of the lower order of life, whose only crime was appearing in my interest, were confined for many weeks in a prison, and obliged to stand trial,[29] and that others, of the higher rank, ingenious and amiable men, valuable for their qualities, respectable for their characters, distinguished for their abilities, and every way meriting the esteem of mankind, were also attacked without the show of a pretense, and obliged to undergo the ceremony of a public acquittal from the foul crime of murder—when I consider that palpable perjury, and subornation of perjury were employed to accomplish the sanguinary object of this base conspiracy—when I consider that the malignity of my enemies has stopped at nothing, however gross and wicked, to ruin me and all that appeared in my interest—when I consider all this, sir, I can not, indeed, but look with some anxiety to the circumstance of a new election.

I am not, it is well known, sir, of a melancholy complexion, or of a desponding turn of

[28] Reference is here made to the use of the King's name by Lord Temple and others, to defeat Mr. Fox.

[29] They were acquitted on that trial. Mr. O'Bryen, who is next referred to, was indicted for murder, but no evidence whatever was produced against him, and he was of course discharged.

mind; yet the idea of again combating this host of oppressions might, in other situations, deter me from the risk. But I owe too much to the electors of Westminster ever to abandon them from any dread of any consequences; and I do assure you that I should conceive a new writ, with the hazard of all these hardships, as a great indulgence and favor, compared to that mockery, that insult upon judicature, a scrutiny under Mr. Thomas Corbett.

Sir, I have nothing more to say upon this subject. Whatever may be the fate of the question, it will be a pleasing reflection to me that I have delivered my opinions at full upon a point so important to that great and respectable body of men, to whom I am so much indebted; and I sincerely thank the House for the honor of their patience and attention through so long a speech.

To the honorable gentleman over against me [Mr. Pitt] I will beg leave to offer a little advice. If he condemns this measure, let him not stoop to be the instrument of its success. Let him well weigh the consequences of what he is about, and look to the future effect of it upon the nation at large. Let him take care, that when they see all the powers of his administration employed to overwhelm an individual, men's eyes may not open sooner than they would if he conducted himself within some bounds of decent discretion, and not thus openly violate the sacred principles of the Constitution. A moderate use of his power might the longer keep people from reflecting upon the extraordinary means by which he acquired it. But if the honorable gentleman neglects his duty, I shall not forget mine. Though he may exert all the influence of his situation to harass and persecute, he shall find that we are incapable of unbecoming submissions: *There is a principle of resistance in mankind which will not brook such injuries; and a good cause and a good heart will animate men to struggle in proportion to the size of their wrongs, and the grossness of their oppressors.* If the House rejects this motion, and establishes the fatal precedent which follows that rejection, I confess I shall begin to think there is little to be expected from such a House of Commons. But let the question terminate as it may, I feel myself bound to maintain an unbroken spirit through such complicated difficulties. And I have this reflection to solace me, that this unexampled injustice could never have succeeded but by the most dangerous and desperate exertions of a government, which, rather than not wound the object of their enmity, scrupled not to break down all the barriers of law; to run counter to the known custom of our ancestors; to violate all that we have of practice and precedent upon this subject; and to strike a deep blow into the very vitals of the English Constitution, without any other inducement, or temptation, or necessity, except the malignant wish of gratifying an inordinate and implacable spirit of resentment.

These eloquent reasonings, and the significant appeal at the close, were lost upon Mr. Pitt. He had taken his ground, and Mr. Ellis' motion was negatived by a majority of 117. Still the mind of the country was affected precisely as Mr. Fox declared it would be. The scrutiny was more and more regarded as dishonorable and unjust; especially when, at the expiration of eight months, Mr. Fox was found to have lost only *eighteen* votes, as compared with his antagonist. All this time had been spent upon two out of seven parishes, and how long the investigation might be continued no one could predict. On Feb. 9th, 1785, another motion was made for an immediate return. This was rejected by a greatly diminished majority. The motion was renewed at the close of the same month, when the majority against it was reduced to *nine.* On the third of March, 1785, it was made again, and Mr. Pitt now endeavored to stave it off by moving an adjournment; but perfectly as he was master of his majority on every other subject, they deserted him here. His motion was negatived by a vote of 162 to 124. The original motion was carried, and the next day the High Bailiff made a return of Mr. Fox.

SPEECH

OF MR. FOX ON THE RUSSIAN ARMAMENT, DELIVERED IN THE HOUSE OF COMMONS, MARCH 1, 1792.

INTRODUCTION.

THIS was the most galling attack ever made by Mr. Fox on his great antagonist. The circumstances of the case were these. Turkey having commenced war against Russia in 1788, Joseph, Emperor of Austria, espoused the cause of the Russians, and attacked the Turks. At the end of two years, however, Joseph died, and his successor, Leopold, being unwilling to continue the contest, resolved on peace. He therefore called in the mediation of England and Prussia at the Congress of Reichenbach; and the three allied powers demanded of the Empress of Russia to unite in making peace on the principle of the *status quo,* that is, of giving up all the conquests she had gained during the war. To this Catharine strongly objected, and urged the formation of a new Christian kingdom out of the Turkish provinces of Bessarabia, Moldavia, and Wallachia, over which her grandson Constantine was expected to be ruler. This the allied powers refused, on the ground of its giving too great a preponderance to Russia; and the Empress, being unable to resist so strong an alliance, consented finally to relinquish all her conquests, with the exception of the fortress of Oczakow (pronounced *Otchakoff*), at the mouth of the Dnieper, on the Black Sea, and a desert tract of country dependent thereon, which was valuable only as a security for her former conquests. England and Prussia, however, insisted on her restoring Oczakow, to which they attached undue importance as the supposed key of Constantinople, distant about one hundred and ninety miles. The pride of Catharine was touched, and she indignantly refused. Mr. Pitt instantly prepared for war, and with his views and feelings at that time he would probably have thrown himself into the contest with all the energy and determination which marked his character.

But when he brought the subject before Parliament, he found that both sides of the House shrunk back. His majority carried him through, indeed, but with diminished numbers; and as the question came up again and again under different forms, it became obvious that the nation would never sustain him on so narrow an issue; for it seemed preposterous to every one to think of plunging England into war about a fortress in the wilds of Tartary, which hardly any man in the kingdom had ever heard of before. He therefore wisely determined to recede, though much to the mortification of some of his friends, and particularly of the Duke of Leeds, his foreign secretary, who instantly resigned under a sense of the disgrace brought upon government. Still Mr. Pitt continued his preparations for war (fearing, no doubt, that the Empress might rise in her demands), and thus brought upon himself new charges of wasting the public money, since it turned out that Catharine was still ready to abide by her original terms. On those terms the matter was finally adjusted, Mr. Pitt pledging himself that Turkey should accept them within four months, or be abandoned to her fate. Accordingly, peace was concluded on this basis between the Empress and the Porte, in August, 1791, and Oczakow has remained from that time in the hands of the Russians.

At the next session of Parliament, early in 1792, the Opposition seized upon this as a favorable opportunity to attack Mr. Pitt. He had placed himself, they affirmed, in a dilemma from which it was impossible for him to escape. If Oczakow was so important as to justify threats of war, and the expenditure of so large a sum for its recovery, he deserved a vote of censure for giving it up; if not so important, he equally deserved censure for endangering the peace of the nation, and adding, by his rashness, to the weight of the public burdens. Whether he had acted the part of a coward or a bully, he had equally disgraced the nation, and deserved its sternest reproof. Such were the views with which Mr. Whitbread moved his celebrated resolutions, on the 29th of March, 1792, condemning Mr. Pitt as having been "guilty of *gross misconduct* tending to incur unnecessary expense, and to diminish the influence of the British nation in Europe."

The debate occupied two nights, probably the most painful ones Mr. Pitt ever spent in the House of Commons. He was ingeniously defended on the ground of the balance of power, by Mr. Jenkinson, Mr. Grant, and Mr. Dundas (though some of his adherents gave him up, and joined in the general reprobation); and was lashed unmercifully by Mr. (afterward Earl) Grey, Sir Philip Francis, Mr. Sheridan, Mr. Windham, and others. Mr. Sheridan, speaking of the plea that ministers had obtained the navigation of the Dniester as a "*radoucissement*," said, "The Empress, with a vein of sarcasm, granted them their *sweetener*, but required them to go to the Porte and demand the same on their part. The entry of the Grand Vizier (Mr. Pitt) into the divan, accompanied by the Reis Effendi (Mr. Dundas), must have been a very curious spectacle! What sort of reception and dialogue must have taken place? 'What glorious terms have you procured with your grand fleet? Have you humbled Russia? Does she tremble at your power? Does she crouch? Have you burned her fleets for us? Have you demolished St. Petersburgh?' A melancholy No! must be the answer. 'What! does she not repent that she provoked you? But *have you made her give up Oczakow?* That your sovereign has pledged himself for.' The reply must be, 'Nothing of all this! We have engaged, if you do not comply with every tittle she demanded of you before we presumed to interfere, that *we will abandon you to all the consequences of the war!*'" Mr. Windham, speaking of the unimportance of Oczakow as a ground of arming, said, "Their political object was almost a nothing, and that nothing they have failed to obtain! They have not even the plea of a great and glorious failure. They aimed at trifling objects, and their success has been still more diminutive. It reminds one of the account of an invalid who could swallow nothing, and *even that would not stay on his stomach!* Or, to express it more classically,

Nil habuit Codrus, attamen infelix ille,
Perdidit totum nil!"[1]

Mr. Pitt bore the whole in silence, resolved, when the attack was through, to sum up briefly in his own defense, and throw himself on his majority. But Mr. Fox held back, obviously with a view to defeat the plan; until, at the end of the first evening, Mr. Dundas called upon him by name to come forward, claiming for Mr. Pitt a right to the closing turn. Mr. Fox denied the right, but promised (as there was not then enough time left) to open the debate the next evening, if the House would adjourn over. This was accordingly done, and, on the evening of the first of March, he delivered the following speech. Lord Brougham has spoken of it as perhaps the ablest, and certainly the most characteristic, of all Mr. Fox's productions. The occasion was one which gave the fullest scope for his favorite mode of attack, the *argumentum ad hominem*, the exposure of inconsistencies, the detection of what he considered the secret

[1] Codrus had nothing, yet, unhappy man,
He all that nothing lost!

motives of his opponents, and the bitterest invectives against Mr. Pitt's conduct, as bringing indelible disgrace on the country. The reader will mark the dexterity and force with which he wrests from the hands of Mr. Pitt's friends every weapon they had used in his defense—the ingenuity with which he shapes and interprets every act of the minister into a ground of condemnation—the closeness with which he holds him to the point, and the incessant goading to which he subjects him, on the horns of the dilemma mentioned above.

SPEECH, &c.

Reasons for not speaking before.

Sir,—After the challenge which was thrown out to me, in the speech of a right honorable gentleman [Mr. Dundas], last night, I consider it my duty to trouble you somewhat at length on this important question. But before I enter into the consideration of it, I will explain why I did not obey a call made, and repeated several times, in a manner not very consistent either with the freedom of debate, or with the order which the right honorable gentleman [Mr. Pitt] himself has prescribed for the discussion of this day. Why any members should think themselves entitled to call on an individual in that way, I know not; but why I did not yield to the call is obvious. It was said by an honorable gentleman, last night, to be the wish of the minister to hear all that could be said on the subject, before he should rise to enter into his defense. If so, it certainly would not become me to prevent him from hearing any other gentleman who might be inclined to speak on the occasion; and as he particularly alluded to me, I thought it respectful to give way to gentlemen, that I might not interrupt the course which he has chosen, as it seems he reserves himself till I have spoken.

Mr. Pitt no right to claim the last word.

This call on me is of a singular nature. A minister is accused of having rashly engaged the country in a measure by which we have suffered disaster and disgrace, and when a motion of censure is made, he chooses to reserve himself, and speak after every one, that no means may be given to reply to his defense—to expose its fallacy, if fallacious, or to detect its misrepresentations, if he shall choose to misrepresent what may be said. If the right honorable gentleman is truly desirous of meeting the charges against him, and has confidence in his ability to vindicate his conduct, why not pursue the course which would be manly and open? Why not go into a committee, as was offered him by the honorable gentleman who made the motion [Mr. Whitbread], in which the forms of this House would have permitted members on each side to answer whatever was advanced by the other, and the subject would have received the most ample discussion? Instead of this honorable course, he is determined to take all advantages. He screens himself by a stratagem which no defendant in any process in this country could enjoy; since no man put upon his defense in any court of justice could so contrive as not only to prevent all reply to his defense, but all refutation of what he may assert, and all explanation of what he may misrepresent.

Such are the advantages which the right honorable gentleman [Mr. Pitt] is determined to seize in this moment of his trial; and, to confess the truth, never did man stand so much in need of every advantage! Never was there an occasion in which a minister was exhibited to this House in circumstances so ungracious as those under which he at present appears. Last session of Parliament, we had no fewer than four debates upon the question of the armament, in which the right honorable gentleman involved this country, without condescending to explain the object which he had in view. The minority of this House stood forth against the monstrous measure of involving the country, without unfolding the reason. The minister proudly and obstinately refused, and called on the majority to support him. We gave our opinion at large on the subject, and with effect, as it turned out, on the public mind. On that of the right honorable gentleman, however, we were not successful; for what was his conduct? He replied to us, "I hear what you say. I could answer all your charges; but I know my duty to my King too well to submit, at this moment, to expose the secrets of the state, and to lay the reasons before you of the measure on which I demand your confidence. I choose rather to lie for a time under all the imputations which you may heap upon me, trusting to the explanations which will come at last." Such was explicitly his language. However I might differ from the right honorable gentleman in opinion, I felt for his situation. There was in this excuse some shadow of reason by which it might be possible to defend him, when the whole of his conduct came to be investigated. I thought it hard to goad him, when, perhaps, he considered it as unsafe to expose what he was doing. But when the conclusion of the negotiation had loosed him from his fetters, when he had cast off the trammels that bound him, I thought that, like the horse described by Homer (if I remembered, I would quote the lines), exulting in the fresh pastures after he had freed himself from the bridle, the right honorable gentleman would have been eager to meet us with every sort of explanation and satisfaction.[1] I thought that, restrained

His former refusals, and his present backwardness, to explain.

[1] The lines referred to are those near the end of the sixth book of the Iliad, in which Paris, after being withheld for a time from the combat, is represented as rushing to meet the foe with all the eagerness of a horse escaped from the stalls, when he seeks his accustomed pastures.

'Ως δ' ὅτε τις στατὸς ἵππος, ἀκοστησας ἐπὶ φάτνῃ,
δεσμὸν ἀπορρήξας θείῃ πεδίοιο κροαίνων,
εἰωθὼς λούεσθαι ἐϋρρεῖος ποταμοῖο,
κυδιόων· ὑψοῦ δὲ κάρη ἔχει, ἀμφὶ δὲ χαῖται
ὤμοις ἀΐσσονται· ὁ δ' ἀγλαΐηφι πεποιθὼς,
ῥίμφα ἑ γοῦνα φέρει μετά τ' ἤθεα καὶ νομὸν ἵππων.

by no delicacy, and panting only for the moment that was to restore him to the means of developing, and of expatiating upon every part of his conduct that was mysterious; of clearing up that which had been reprobated; of repelling on the heads of his adversaries those very accusations with which they had loaded him—the right honorable gentleman would have had but one wish, that of coming forward in a bold and manly manner, and endeavoring to make his cause good against us in the face of the world. Has he done so? Has he even given us the means of inquiring fully and fairly into his conduct? No such thing. He lays before us a set of papers, sufficient, indeed, as I shall contend, to found a strong criminal charge of misconduct against him, but evidently mutilated, garbled, and imperfect, with a view of precluding that full inquiry which his conduct demands, and which we had every reason to expect he would not have shrunk from on this day. We call for more. They are denied us. Why? "Because," say the gentlemen on the other side, "unless the papers now before you show there is ground for accusation, and unless you agree to accuse, it is not safe or proper to grant you more." But is this a defense for the right honorable gentleman? Do these papers exculpate him? Directly the reverse. *Prima facie* they condemn him. They afford us, in the first instance, the proof of disappointment. They show us that we have not obtained what we aimed to obtain; and they give us no justification of the right honorable gentleman for that disappointment. I have heard much ingenuity displayed to maintain that there was no guilt. But what is the fallacy of this argument? When we called for papers during the Spanish negotiation [as to Nootka Sound], we were answered, "the negotiation was pending, and it was unsafe to grant them."[2] Very well. But when it was over, and the same reasons for withholding them could not be said to exist, we were told, "Look to the result. The nation is satisfied with what we have got, and you must lay a ground of criminality before we can admit your principle of calling for papers." Thus we were precluded from all inquiry into that business. But now the right honorable gentleman, conscious that the country feels somewhat differently, admits the ground of criminality to have been laid, by producing those documents on your table, imperfect as they are. It is from his own confession, therefore, that I am to pronounce him guilty, until he proves himself not to be so; and it is enough for me to contend that the papers now before us afford him *prima facie* no justification, but, on the contrary, afford strong proof of his guilt, inasmuch as they evince a complete failure in the object he aimed to extort. Sir, the right honorable gentleman is sensible how much these circumstances render it necessary for him to take every possible advantage his situation can give him. Instead, therefore, of showing himself anxious to come forward, or thinking it his duty to explain, why it was inconvenient or impolitic for him to state last year the true grounds on which he had called upon us to arm, what was the object of that armament, and why he had abandoned it, he lays a few papers on the table, and contents himself with an appeal unheard of before: "If you have any thing to say against me, speak out, speak all. I will not say a word till you have done. Let me hear you one after another. I will have all the advantage of the game—none of you shall come behind me; for as soon as you have all thrown forth what you have to say, I will make a speech, which you shall not have an opportunity to contradict, and I will throw myself on my majority, that makes you dumb forever." Such is the situation in which we stand, and such is the course which the right honorable gentleman thinks it honorable to pursue! I cheerfully yield to him the ground he chooses to occupy, and I will proceed, in obedience to the call personally addressed to me, frankly to state the reasons for the vote of censure, in which I shall this night agree.

I. Much argument has been used on topics not unfit, indeed, to be mixed with this question, but not necessary; topics which undoubtedly may be incidentally taken up, but which are not essential to the discussion. In this class I rank what has been said upon the balance of Europe. Whether the insulated policy which disdained all continental connection whatever, as adopted at the beginning of the present reign—whether the system of extensive foreign connection, so eagerly insisted on by a young gentleman who spoke yesterday for the first time [Mr. Jenkinson, afterward Lord Liverpool]—or whether the medium between these two be our interest, are certainly very proper topics to be discussed, but as certainly not *essential* topics to this question. Of the three, I confidently pronounce the middle line the true political course of this country. I think that, in our situation, every continental connection is to be determined by its own merits. I am one of those who hold that a total inattention to foreign connections might be, as it has proved, very injurious to this country. But if I am driven to choose between the two extremes,

Mr. Pitt not excused by the doctrine of the balance of power.

The wanton courser thus with reins unbound
Breaks from his stall, and beats the trembling ground;
Pamper'd and proud, he seeks the wonted tides,
And laves, in height of blood, his shining sides;
His head now freed, he tosses to the skies;
His mane dishevel'd o'er his shoulders flies;
He snuffs the females in the distant plain,
And springs, exulting, to his fields again.—*Pope.*

[2] In 1789, a Spanish frigate broke up a small trading establishment of the English at Nootka Sound, alleging that Spain had an exclusive right to all the Pacific coast from Cape Horn to the sixteenth degree of north latitude. Mr. Pitt entered into negotiations on the subject, which could not then be made public; and in order to enforce his demands, he applied to Parliament in 1790 for a large increase of military and naval force. It was granted, and Spain yielded the point during the same year. She restored Nootka Sound, and conceded to England the right of carrying on a free navigation and her fisheries in the North Pacific Ocean.

between that of standing insulated and aloof from all foreign connections, and trusting for defense to our own resources, and that system as laid down in the speech of an honorable gentleman [Mr. Jenkinson], who distinguished himself so much last night, to the extent to which he pressed it, I do not hesitate to declare that my opinion is for the first of those situations. I should prefer even total disunion to that sort of connection, to preserve which we should be obliged to risk the blood and the resources of the country in every quarrel and every change that ambition or accident might bring about in any part of the Continent of Europe. But in the question before us, I deny that I am driven to either of these extremes. The honorable gentleman, who spoke with all the open ingenuousness, as well as the animation of youth, seemed himself to dread the extent to which his own doctrines would lead him. He failed, therefore, to sustain the policy of the system he described, in that part where it can alone apply, namely, to the degree in which it is necessary for us to support a balance of power. Holland, for instance, he states to be our natural ally. Granted. "To preserve Holland, and that she may not fall into the arms of France, we must make an alliance with Prussia." Good. But Prussia may be attacked by Austria. "Then we must make an alliance with the Ottoman Porte, that they may fall on Austria." Well, but the Porte may be attacked by Russia. "Then we must make an alliance with Sweden, that she may fall on Russia." By the way, I must here remind him that he totally forgot even to mention Poland, as if that country, now become in some degree able to act for itself, from the change in its Constitution, was of no moment, or incapable of influencing in any manner this system of treaties and attacks. His natural ingenuity pointed out to him that, in casting up the account of all this, it would not produce a favorable balance for England, and he evaded the consequence of his own principle, by saying that *perhaps* Russia would not attack the Porte! "for when we speculate on extreme cases (says the honorable gentleman) we have a right to make allowances. It is fair to expect that when we are in alliance with the Porte, Russia will feel too sensibly the importance of the commercial advantages she enjoys in her intercourse with this country to risk the loss of them by an attack on her." Are we, then, to suppose, in a scene of universal contest and warfare, that this ambitious power, who is reproached as perpetually and systematically aiming at the destruction of the Porte, and while the rest of Europe was at peace, has been in a state of restless and unceasing hostility with her, will then be the only power at peace, and let slip so favorable an opportunity of destroying her old enemy, simply because she is afraid of losing her trade with you in the Baltic? If the honorable gentleman means to state this as a rational conjecture, I would ask him to look to the fact. *Did* her sense of these advantages restrain her in the late war, or compel her to desist from the demands she made before we began to arm? Certainly not. We find, from the documents before us, that she adhered to one uniform, steady course, from which neither the apprehension of commercial loss, nor the terrors of our arms, influenced her one moment to recede. What, then, are we to conclude from this intricate system of balances and counterbalances, and those dangerous theories with which the honorable gentleman seemed to amuse himself? Why, that these are speculations too remote from our policy; that in some parts, even according to the honorable gentleman's argument, they may be defective, after all, and consequently, that if the system he builds upon it fails in one of its possibilities, it fails in the whole of them. Such must ever be the fate of systems so nicely constructed. But it is not true that the system necessary to enable this country to derive the true benefit from the Dutch alliance ought to be founded upon those involved and mysterious politics which make it incumbent upon us, nay, which prove its perfection, by compelling us to stand forward the principals in every quarrel, the Quixotes of every enterprise, the agitators in every plot, intrigue, and disturbance, which are every day arising in Europe to embroil one state of it with another. I confess that my opinions fall infinitely short of these perilous extremes; that possibly my genius is too scanty, and my understanding too limited and feeble, for the contemplation of their consequences; and that I can speculate no farther than on connections immediately necessary to preserve us, safe and prosperous, from the power of our open enemies, and the encroachment of our competitors. This I hold to be the only test by which the merits of an alliance can be tried. I did think, for instance, that when the intrigues of France threatened to deprive us of our ancient ally, Holland, it was wise to interfere, and afterward to form an alliance by which that evil might be prevented.[3] But to push the system farther is pernicious. Every link in the chain of confederacies, which has been so widely expatiated upon by the member already alluded to, carries us more and more from the just point. By this extension the broad and clear lines of your policy become narrower and less distinct, until at last the very trace of them is lost.

Other topics have been introduced into the discussion. The beginning of the war between Russia and the Porte has been referred to. What possible connection that has with our armament I know not, but of that I shall have occasion to speak by and by.[4]

II. I come, however, sir, to a question more immediately before us, and that is, the value and importance attached, in the minds of his

[3] In 1788, there were serious dissensions in Holland, and France manifested her intentions to interpose, with a view of gaining an ascendency among the Dutch. England and Prussia instantly united to prevent it; and Mr. Pitt went largely into preparations for war, which had the approbation and concurrence of the whole English nation.

[4] See page 508.

Majesty's ministers, to the fortress of Oczakow; and here I must beg leave to say, that they have not once attempted to answer the arguments so judiciously and ably enforced by my honorable friend who made this motion. It was explicitly stated by the gentlemen on the other side, as the only argument for our interference at all, that the balance of Europe was threatened with great danger if Oczakow was suffered to remain in the hands of Russia. Of no less importance did ministers last year state this fortress of Oczakow, than as if it were indeed the *talisman* on which depended the fate of the whole Ottoman empire. But if this, from their own admission, was true last year, what has happened to alter its value? If it then excited the alarms of his Majesty's ministers for the safety of Europe, what can enable them now to tell us that we are perfectly secure? If it was true that her bare possession of Oczakow would be so dangerous, what must be the terror of Europe, when they see our negotiators put Russia into the way of seizing even Constantinople itself? This was the strong argument of my honorable friend [Mr. Whitbread], and which he maintained with such solid reasoning that not the slightest answer has been given to it. To illustrate the value of Oczakow, however, one honorable gentleman [Mr. Grant] went back to the reign of Elizabeth, and even to the days of Philip and Demosthenes. He told us that when Demosthenes, urging the Athenians to make war on Philip, reproached them with inattention to a few towns he had taken, the names of which they scarcely knew, telling them that those towns were the keys by which he would in time invade and overcome Greece, he gave them a salutary warning of the danger that impended. But if the opponents of that great orator had prevailed, if they had succeeded in inducing their countrymen to acquiesce in the surrender not only of those towns, but of considerably more, as in the present instance, with what face would he afterward have declared to his countrymen, "True it was that these sorry and nameless towns were the keys to the Acropolis itself; but you have surrendered them, and what is the consequence? You are now in a state of the most perfect security. You have now nothing to fear. You have now the prospect of sixteen years of peace before you!" I ask, sir, what would have been the reception even of Demosthenes himself, if he had undertaken to support such an inconsistency?

Inconsistency of ministers in their estimate of Oczakow, and their conduct respecting it.

Let us try this, however, the other way. In order to show that his Majesty's ministers merit the censure which is proposed, I will admit that the preservation of the Turks *is* necessary for the security of a balance of power. I trust, at the same time, that this admission, which I make merely for the argument, will not be disingenuously quoted upon me, as hypothetical statements too commonly are, for admissions of fact. What will the right honorable gentleman gain by it? The Turks, by his arrangement, are left in a worse situation than he found them; for, previous to his interference, if Russia had gone to Constantinople, he would have been unfettered by the stipulations which bind him now, and he and his ally might have interfered to save the Porte from total destruction. But at present the possible and total extirpation of the Ottoman power is made to depend on a point so precarious as their accepting the proposal which the right honorable gentleman thought fit to agree to for them within the space of four months.[5] And what is this proposal? Why, that the Turks should give up, not only the war they had begun, but this very Oczakow, which of itself was sufficient, in the hands of Russia, to overturn the balance. If, therefore, it was so important to recover Oczakow, it is not recovered, and ministers ought to be censured. If unimportant, they ought never to have demanded it. If so unimportant, they ought to be censured for arming; but if so important as they have stated it, they ought to be censured for disarming without having gotten it. Either way, therefore, the argument comes to the same point, and I care not on which side the gentlemen choose to take it up; for whether Oczakow be, as they told us last year, the key to Constantinople, on the preservation of which to Turkey the balance of Europe depended, or, as they must tell us now, of no comparative importance, their conduct is equally to be condemned for disarming, and pusillanimously yielding up the object, in the first instance; for committing the dignity of their Sovereign, and hazarding the peace of their country, in the second.

Dilemma for ministers.

But they tell us it is unfair to involve them in this dilemma. There was a middle course to be adopted. Oczakow was certainly of much importance; but this importance was to be determined upon by circumstances. Sir, we are become nice, indeed, in our political arithmetic. In this calculating age we ascertain to a scruple what an object is really worth. Thus it seems that Oczakow was worth an armament, but not worth a war; it was worth a threat, but not worth carrying that threat into execution! Sir, I can conceive nothing so degrading and dishonorable as such an argument. To hold out a menace without ever seriously meaning to enforce it, constitutes, in common language, the true description of a bully. Applied to the transactions of a nation, the disgrace is deeper, and the consequences fatal to its honor. Yet such is the precise conduct the King's ministers have made the nation hold in the eyes of Europe, and which they defend by an argument that, if urged in private life, would stamp a man with the character of a coward and a bully, and sink him to the deepest abyss of infamy and degradation. Sure I am that this distinction never suggested itself to the reflection of a noble Duke [the Duke of Leeds], whose

No escape from this dilemma.

[5] Mr. Pitt, as already stated, when he gave up Oczakow, agreed that Turkey should accede to these terms within four months, or be abandoned to her fate.

conduct throughout the whole of this business has evinced the manly character of his mind, unaccustomed to such calculations! From him we learn the fact. He said in his place that his colleagues thought it fit to risk a threat to recover Oczakow, but would not risk a war for it. Such conduct was not for him. It might suit the characters of his colleagues in office; it could not his. But they say it might be worth a war *with* the public opinion, but worth nothing *without* it! I can not conceive any case in which a great and wise nation, having committed itself by a menace, can withdraw that menace without disgrace. The converse of the proposition I can easily conceive. That there may be a place, for instance, not fit to be asked at all, but which being asked for, and with a menace, it is fit to insist upon. This undoubtedly goes to make a nation, like an individual, cautious of committing itself, because there is no ground so tender as that of honor. How do ministers think on this subject? Oczakow was every thing by itself; but when they added to Oczakow the honor of England, it became nothing! Oczakow, by itself, threatened the balance of Europe. Oczakow and national honor united weighed nothing in the scale! Honor is, in their political arithmetic, a *minus* quantity, to be subtracted from the value of Oczakow! Sir, I am ashamed of this reasoning; nor can I reflect on the foul stain it has fixed on the English name, without feeling mortified and humbled indeed! Their late colleague, the noble Duke [of Leeds], urged his sentiments with the feelings that became him—feelings that form a striking contrast to those that actuate the right honorable gentleman. He told his country, that when he had made up his mind to the necessity of demanding Oczakow, it was his opinion that it might have been obtained without a war; but having once demanded it, he felt it his duty not to shrink from the war that might ensue from the rejection of that demand, and preferred the resignation of his office to the retracting that opinion. Far different was the conduct of the right honorable gentleman [Mr. Pitt], though his advice was the same; and small were the scruples he felt in tarnishing the honor of his Sovereign, whose name he pledged to this demand, and afterward obliged him to recede from it.

Public opinion: Ministers ought to have resigned if it was adverse to their settled convictions.

III. They tell us, however, and seem to value themselves much upon it, that, in abandoning the object for which they had armed, they acted in conformity to public opinion. Sir, I will fairly state my sentiments on this subject. It is right and prudent to consult the public opinion. It is frequently wise to attend even to public prejudices on subjects of such infinite importance, as whether they are to have war or peace. But if, in the capacity of a servant to the Crown, I were to see, or strongly to imagine that I saw any measures going forward that threatened the peace or prosperity of the country, and if the emergency were so pressing as to demand the sudden adoption of a decisive course to avert the mischief, I should not hesitate one moment to act upon my own responsibility. If, however, the public opinion did not happen to square with mine; if, after pointing out to them the danger, they did not see it in the same light with me; or if they conceived that another remedy was preferable to mine, I should consider it as due to my King, due to my country, due to my own honor, to *retire*, that they might pursue the plan which they thought better by a fit instrument—that is, by a man who thought with them. Such would be my conduct on any subject where conscientiously I could not surrender my judgment. If the case was doubtful, or the emergency not so pressing, I should be ready, perhaps, to sacrifice my opinion to that of the public; but one thing is most clear in such an event as this, namely, that I ought to give the public the means of forming an accurate estimate.

They ought, at least, on their own principles, to have ascertained it beforehand.

Do I state this difference fairly? If I do, and if the gentleman over against me will admit that in the instance before us the public sentiment ought to have influenced them, it follows that the public sentiment ought to have been consulted before we were committed in the eyes of Europe, and that the country ought to have had the means, and the information necessary to form their judgment upon the true merits of this question. Did the King's ministers act thus? Did they either take the public opinion, or did they give us the means of forming one? Nothing like it. On the 28th of March, 1791, the message was brought down to this House. On the 29th, we passed a vote of approbation, but no *opinion* was asked from us, no *explanation* was given us. So far from it, we were expressly told our advice was not wanted; that we had nothing to do with the prerogative of the Crown to make war; that all our business was to give confidence. So far with regard to this House. I can not help thinking this conduct somewhat hard upon the majority, who certainly might have counted for something in the general opinion, when the right honorable gentleman was collecting it, if he meant fairly so to do. I grant, indeed, that there are many ways by which the feeling and temper of the public may be tolerably well known out of this House as well as in it. I grant that the opinion of a respectable meeting at Manchester, of a meeting at Norwich, of a meeting at Wakefield, of public bodies of men in different parts of England, might give the right honorable gentleman a correct idea of the public impression.[6] Permit me to say, also, that in the speeches of the minority of this House, he might find the ground of public opinion, both as to what might give it rise, and what might give it countenance. But was the *majority* of this House the only body whose dispositions were not worth consulting? Will the minister say, "I traveled to Norwich, to York, to Manchester, to Wake-

[6] Public meetings were held in these and in other places, and resolutions passed hostile to the measures of the minister.

field, for opinions;" "I listened to the minority; I looked to Lord Stormont, to the Earl of Guilford; but as to you, my trusty majority, I neglected you! I had other business for you! It is not your office to give opinions; *your business is to confide!* You must pledge yourself, in the first instance, to all I can ask from you, and perhaps some time in the next year I may condescend to let you know the grounds on which you are acting." Such is the language he holds, if his conduct were to be explained by words, and a conduct more indecent or preposterous is not easily to be conceived; for it is neither more nor less than to tell us, "When I thought the Ottoman power in danger, I asked for an armament to succor it. You approved, and granted it to me. The public sense was against me, and, without minding you, I yielded to that sense. My opinion, however, remains still the same; though it must be confessed that I led you into giving a sanction to my schemes, by a species of reasoning which it appears the country has saved itself by resisting. But they were to blame. I yet think that the exact contrary of what was done ought to have been done, and that the peace and safety of Europe depended upon it. But never mind how you voted, or how directly opposite to the general opinion, with which I complied, was that opinion I persuaded you to support. *Vote now that I was right in both;* in the opinion I still maintain, and in my compliance with its opposite! The peace of Europe is safe. *I keep my place, and all is right again.*"[7]

Mr. Pitt's conduct on this subject insulting to his adherents.

But after all, the right honorable gentleman did not act from any deference to the public opinion; and to prove this, I have but to recall to your recollection dates. The message was brought down, as I said before, on the 28th of March; and in less than a week, I believe in four days, afterward, before it was possible to collect the opinion of any one public body of men, their whole system was reversed. The change, therefore, could not come from the country, even had they been desirous of consulting it. But I have proved that they were not desirous to have an opinion from any quarter. They came down with their purposes masked and vailed to this House, and tried all they could to preclude inquiry into what they were doing. These are not the steps of men desirous of acting by opinion. I hold it, however, to be now acknowledged, that it was not the public opinion, but that of the minority in this House, which compelled the ministers to relinquish their ill-advised projects; for a right honorable gentleman, who spoke last night [Mr. Dundas], confessed the truth in his own frank way. "We certainly," said he, "do not know that the opinion of the public was against us; we only know that a *great party* in this country was against us, and therefore we apprehended that, though one campaign might have been got through, at the beginning of the next session they would have interrupted us in procuring the supplies." I believe I quote the right honorable gentleman correctly. And here, sir, let me pause, and thank him for the praise which he gives the gentlemen on this side the House. Let me indulge the satisfaction of reflecting, that though we have not the emoluments of office, nor the patronage of power, yet we are not excluded from great influence on the measures of government. We take pride to ourselves, that at this moment we are not sitting in a committee of supply, voting enormous fleets and armies to carry into execution this calamitous measure. To us he honestly declares this credit to be due; and the country will, no doubt, feel the gratitude they owe us for having saved them from the miseries of war.[8]

Not true, however, that Mr. Pitt did yield to public opinion.

Was driven from his ground by the Opposition in Parliament.

An honorable gentleman, indeed [Mr. Jenkinson], has told us that our opposition to this measure in its commencement occasioned its having been abandoned by the ministers; but he will not allow us the merit of having saved the country from a war by our interposition, but charges us with having prevented their obtaining the terms demanded, which would have been got without a war. I am glad to hear this argument; but must declare, in the name of the minority, that we think ourselves most unfairly treated by it, and forced into a responsibility that belongs in no manner whatsoever to our situation. The minister, when repeatedly pressed on this subject during the last session, was uniform in affirming that he had reasons for his conduct, to his mind so cogent and unanswerable, that he was morally certain of the indispensable necessity of the measures he was pursuing. He has said the same since, and to this hour continues his first conviction. If, therefore, the right honorable gentleman [Mr. Pitt] thought so, and thought, at the same time, that our arguments were likely to mislead the country from its true interests, *why did he continue silent?* If public support was so necessary to him, that without it, as he tells us now, he could not proceed a single step, why did he suffer us to corrupt the passions, to blind and to pervert the understandings of the public, to a degree that compelled his sacrifice of this essential measure? Why did he quietly, and without concern, watch the prevalence of our false arguments? Why did he sanction their progress, by never answering them, when he knew the consequence must necessarily be to defeat his dearest object, and put the safety of his country to the hazard? Why did he not oppose some antidote to our poison? But,

But the failure of his negotiations not chargeable to the Opposition.

[7] There is nothing in the whole speech more characteristic of Mr. Fox, than the ingenuity with which he turns the conduct of Mr. Pitt into an insult to his "faithful majority," and the force he gives it by putting the whole into Mr. Pitt's own mouth.

[8] Nothing could be more adroit than the manner in which Mr. Dundas' remark is here converted into an acknowledgment that the minority had saved the country from war, and a little below, that they were not "a *faction*," as represented by others.

having neglected to do this (because of his duty to preserve state secrets, as he would have us believe), what semblance of right, what possible pretext has he to come forward now, and accuse *us* of thwarting his views, or to cast the responsibility of his failure and disgrace upon *us*, whose arguments he never answered, and to whom he obstinately and invariably refused all sort of information, by which we might have been enabled to form a better judgment, and possibly to agree with him on this subject? Another right honorable gentleman, however [Mr. Dundas], judges more fairly of us, and I thank him for the handsome acknowledgment he paid to the true character of the gentlemen on this side of the House; for by owning that, because we did not happen to approve of this armament, it was abandoned, he acknowledges another fact—that we are not what another honorable gentleman [Mr. Steele] chose to represent us, a *faction*, that indiscriminately approves of every thing, right and wrong. This is clearly manifest from his own admissions; for, giving up when they found we condemned, they must have begun in the idea that we should approve. We approved in the case of Holland, and in that of Spain. In the first case we did so, because the rectitude of the thing was so clear and manifest, that every well-wisher to England must have done it. We did so in the case of Spain, because the objects were explained to us. The insult given, and the reparation demanded, were both before us. But had the right honorable gentleman any right, because we agreed to the Dutch and Spanish armaments, to anticipate the consent of Opposition to the late one. It was insulting to impute the possibility to us! What, agree to take the money out of the pockets of the people, without an insult explained, or an object held up! It is said the object was stated, and that the means only were left to conjecture; that the *object* proposed to the House was an armament to make a peace, and Oczakow was supposed to be the *means* by which that peace was to be effected. Sir, it is almost constantly my misfortune to be differing from the right honorable gentleman [Mr. Pitt] about the import of the words *object* and *means*. In my way of using these words, I should have directly transposed them, and called the armament the *means* of effecting peace, and Oczakow the *object* of that armament. And the event proves that ministers thought as I should have done; for they gave up that object, because they knew they could get the end they proposed by their armament without it. This object, indeed, whatever was its importance; whether it was or was not, as we have alternately heard it asserted and denied, the key of Constantinople; nay, as some wild and fanciful people had almost persuaded themselves, the key to our possessions in the East Indies, the King's ministers have completely renounced; and seem, by their conduct, to have cared very little what became of that or Constantinople itself. The balance of Europe, however, is perfectly safe, they tell us; and on that point we have nothing more to apprehend. The enormous accession of power to Russia, from the possession of Oczakow, so far from affecting Great Britain, is not likely, according to what the ministers must assure us, to disturb the tranquillity of her nearest neighbors. That Oczakow, therefore, was at any time an object sufficient to justify their interference, I have stated many reasons for concluding will not be alleged this night.

Pretense that Russia was the aggressor, a false one.

IV. Some of the gentlemen on the other side, indeed, have advanced other grounds, and told us (I confess it is for the first time) that in this war the Empress of Russia was the aggressor; that on her part the war was offensive; and that it became us to interfere to stop her progress. They tell us of various encroachments in the Kuban [a part of Tartary], of hostilities systematically carried on in violation of treaties, and many other instances; not one of which they have attempted to prove by a single document, or have rested on any other foundation than their own assertions. But to these, sir, I shall oppose the authority of ministers themselves; for, in one of the dispatches of the Duke of Leeds to Mr. Whitworth [British minister to Russia], he desires him to communicate to the court of Petersburgh, that if they will consent to make peace with the Turks on the *status quo*,[9] the allies will consent to guarantee the Crimea to them, "*the object of the war*," as he states it to be. I desire no further proof than this, that we always considered the Turks as the aggressors; for it follows, that where any place in the possession of one power is made the object of a war by another, the power claiming that object is the aggressor. If, for example, we were at war with Spain, and Gibraltar the object, Spain, of course, would be the aggressor: the contrary, if the Havana were the object. The King of England, therefore, by the dispatch which I have quoted, has, in words and in fact, acknowledged the Turks to have been the aggressors in this war, by making pretensions to a province solemnly ceded to Russia in the year 1783. I can scarcely think that ministers mean to contend that cession by treaty does not give right to possession. Where are we to look, therefore, to ascertain the right of a country to any place or territory, but to the *last* treaty? To what would the opposite doctrine lead? France might claim Canada, ceded in 1763, or we Tobago, ceded in 1783. It might be urged that they took advantage of our dispute with our own colonies, and that the treaty gave no right. Canada, Jamaica, every thing, might be questioned. Where would be the peace of Europe, if these doctrines were to be acted on? Every country must continue in a state of endless perplexity, armament, and preparations. But, happily for mankind, a different principle prevails in the law of nations. There the last treaty gives the right; and upon that we must aver, that if, as the dispatch says, the Crimea was the object, the *Turk was the aggressor*.[10]

[9] State of things previous to the war.

[10] On this subject, Mr. Whitbread said in his opening speech, "It was stated by Count Osterman, in

V. What, therefore, was the right claimed by the right honorable gentleman to enter into this dispute? I will answer. The right of a proud man, anxious to play a lofty part. France had gone off the stage. The character of the miserable disturber of empires was vacant, and he resolved to boast and vapor, and play his antic tricks and gestures on the same theater. And what has been the first effect of this new experiment upon the British nation? That, in the pride and zenith of our power, we have miserably disgraced ourselves in the eyes of Europe; that the name of his Majesty has been sported with, and stained; that the people of England have been inflamed, their commerce disturbed, the most valuable citizens dragged from their houses [by press-warrants], and half a million of money added to the public burdens. And here, sir, in justice to my own feelings, I can not pass over wholly in silence the fate of that valuable body of our fellow-citizens who are more particularly the victims of these false alarms, and by whom the most bitter portion of the common calamity must be borne. I am compelled to admit that every state has a right, in the season of danger, to claim the services of all, or any of its members; that the "*salus populi suprema lex est.*[11] Tenderness and consideration in the use of such extensive powers is all I can recommend to those whose business it is to call them into action. But here I must lament, in common with every feeling mind, that unnecessary barbarity which dragged them from their homes, deprived them of their liberty, and tore them from the industrious exercise of those modes of life by which they earned support for their families, wantonly, cruelly, and without pretext, because *without the smallest intention of employing them.* The gentlemen well know what I state to be a fact; for they know that their system was changed, and their object abandoned, before even they had begun to issue press-warrants!

Real motives of Mr. Pitt's intervention.

VI. I return, sir, to the disgraceful condition in which the right honorable gentleman has involved us. Let us see whether what I have said on this point be not literally true. The Empress of Russia offered, early in the year 1790, to depart from the terms she had at first thrown out, namely, that Bessarabia, Wallachia, and Moldavia should be independent of the Ottoman power. This, it appears, she yielded upon the amicable representations of the allied powers, and substituted in the room of them those conditions which have since been conceded to her, namely, that the Dniester should be the boundary between the two empires, and all former treaties should be confirmed. "Then," say ministers, "if we gained this by simple negotiation, what may we not gain by an armament?" Thus judging of her pusillanimity by their own, they threatened her. What did she do? Peremptorily refused to depart one atom from her last conditions; and this determination, I assert, was in the possession of his Majesty's ministers long before the armament. They knew not only this, early in the month of March, 1791, but likewise the resolution of the Empress not to rise in her demands, notwithstanding any farther success that might attend her arms. The memorial of the court of Denmark, which they have, for reasons best known to themselves, refused us, but which was circulated in every court, and published in every newspaper in Europe, fully informed them of these matters. But the King's ministers, with an absurdity of which there is no example, called upon the country to arm. Why? Not because they meant to employ the armament against her, but in the fanciful hope that, because, in an amicable negotiation, the Empress had been prevailed upon not to press the demand of Wallachia, Moldavia, and Bessarabia as independent sovereignties, they should infallibly succeed by arming, and not employing that armament, in persuading her to abandon all the rest! And what was the end? Why, that after pledging the King's name in the most deliberate and solemn manner; after lofty vaporing, menacing, promising, denying, turning, and turning again; after keeping up the parade of an armament for four months, accompanied with those severe measures [pressing seamen, &c.], to be regretted even when necessary, to be reprobated when not, the right honorable gentleman crouches humbly at her feet; entreats, submissively supplicates of her moderation, that she will grant him some small trifle of what he asks, if it is but

Disgrace brought upon the country by Mr. Pitt's conduct.

his letter to Mr. Whitworth and Count Goltze, dated June 6th, 1791, that the courts of London and Berlin at the time avowed that Russia had been unjustly attacked." Mr. Pitt, therefore, could not but admit, in his reply to Mr. Fox, that "in point of strict fact, the Turks were aggressors" in commencing the war. Still, he contended, that "such had been the conduct of Russia toward the Porte, and such the indubitable proof of her hostile intentions toward that power, that although the Turks struck the first blow, the war might fairly be termed a defensive one." This statement was undoubtedly true, and is confirmed by Belsham, in his Memoirs of the reign of George III., vol. iv., 258. It is there shown that Catharine and the Emperor Joseph met at Cherson in 1787—that "the Turkish Empire at this period presenting an easy and inviting prospect of conquest, a negotiation was set on foot, with *this view*, between the two imperial courts"—that "scarcely did she [Catharine] deign to affect concealment of her hostile intentions; and over one of the gates of the city she caused to be inscribed, 'This is the gate which leads to BYZANTIUM;'" and that "the Ottoman Porte, fully apprised of the machinations of the imperial courts, took a hasty resolution, notwithstanding her own extreme unpreparedness for commencing offensive operations, to publish an immediate declaration of war against Russia, in the hope, probably, of being able to conciliate the Emperor [Joseph] before his plan of hostilities was matured." In this the Turks did not succeed. Joseph, according to his agreement, immediately united with Catharine in the war; and no one doubts that the dismemberment of the Turkish Empire had been concerted between them; so that Mr. Pitt was correct in saying the Turks were acting on the defensive.

[11] The highest law is the safety of the state.

by way of a boon; and finding at last that he can get nothing, either by threats or his prayers, gives up the whole precisely as she insisted upon having it!

The right honorable gentleman, however, is determined that this House shall take the whole of this disgrace upon itself. I heard him with much delight, on a former day, quote largely from that excellent and philosophical work, "The Wealth of Nations."[12] In almost the first page of that book he will find it laid down as a principle that, by a division of labor in the different occupations of life, the objects to which it is applied are perfected, time is saved, dexterity improved, and the general stock of science augmented; that by joint effort and reciprocal accommodation the severest tasks are accomplished, and difficulties surmounted, too stubborn for the labor of a single hand. Thus, in the building of a great palace, we observe the work to be parceled out into different departments, and distributed and subdivided into various degrees, some higher, some lower, to suit the capacities and condition of those who are employed in its construction. There is the architect that invents the plan, and erects the stately columns. There is the dustman and the nightman to clear away the rubbish. The right honorable gentleman applies these principles to his politics; and, in the division and cast of parts for the job we are now to execute for him, has reserved for himself the higher and more respectable share of the business, and leaves all the dirty work to us. Is he asked why the House of Commons made the armament last year? He answers, "The House of Commons did not make the armament! I made it. The House of Commons only approved of it." Is he asked why he gave up the object of the armament, after he had made it? "I did not give it up!" he exclaims. "I think the same of its necessity as ever. It is the House of Commons that gives it up! It is the House that supports the nation in their senseless clamor against my measures. It is to this House that you must look for the shame and guilt of your disgrace." To himself he takes the more conspicuous character of menacer. It is he that distributes provinces, and limits empires; while he leaves to this House the humbler office of licking the dust, and begging forgiveness;

"Not mine these groans—
These sighs that issue, or these tears that flow."

"I am forced into these submissions by a low, contracted, groveling, mean-spirited, and ignorant people!" But this is not all. It rarely happens that in begging pardon (when men determine upon that course) they have not some benefit in view, or that the profit to be got is not meant to counterbalance, in some measure, the honor to be sacrificed. Let us see how the right honorable gentleman managed this. On the first indication of hostile measures against Russia, one hundred and thirty-five members of this House divided against the adoption of them. This it was, according to a right honorable gentleman who spoke in the debate yesterday [Mr. Dundas], that induced ministers to abandon their first object; but not like the Duke of Leeds, who candidly avowed, that if he could have once brought himself to give up the claim of Oczakow, he would not have stood out for the razing its fortifications, or any such terms. The ministers determine that the nation, at least, shall reap no benefit from the reversal of their system. "You have resisted our projects," say they; "you have discovered and exposed our incapacity; you have made us the ridicule of Europe, and such we shall appear to posterity; you have defeated, indeed, our intentions of involving you in war; but *you* shall not be the gainers by it! you shall not save your money! We abandon Oczakow, as you compel us to do; but we will keep up the armament if it is only to spite you!"

Determined to act this dishonorable part, their next care was to do it in the most disgraceful manner; and as they had dragged Parliament and their King through the dirt and mire, they resolved to exhibit them in this offensive plight to the eyes of Europe. To do this, they did not care to trust to the minister we had at Petersburgh—a gentleman distinguished for amiable manners, and by the faithful, the vigilant, and the able discharge of his duty. Why was the management of the negotiation taken from him? Was he too proud for this service? No man is too proud to do his duty; and of all our foreign ministers, Mr. Whitworth[13] I should think the very last to whom it could be reproached that he is remiss in fulfilling the directions he receives, in their utmost strictness. But a new man was to be found; one whose reputation for talents and honor might operate, as they hoped, as a sort of set-off against the incapacity he was to cure, and the national honor he was deputed to surrender. Was it thus determined, because, in looking round their diplomatic body, there was no man to be selected from it, whose character assimilated with the dirty job he was to execute? As there was honor to be sacrificed, a stain to be fixed upon the national character, engagements to be retracted, and a friend to be abandoned; did it never occur to them that there was *one man* upon their diplomatic list who would have been pronounced by general acclamation thoroughly qualified in soul and qualities for this service? Such a person they might have found, and not so occupied as to make it inconvenient to employ him. They

He now seeks to transfer the disgrace to the Commons.

And saddles the country with unnecessary expense.

He next sacrifices the public honor by his mode of negotiating.

[12] Mr. Fox, in order to relieve the minds of his hearers from a continual stream of invective, now turns off for a few moments to Adam Smith's doctrine of a division of labor, and then makes it the starting-point of a new attack, to which he gives double life and force by his dramatic mode of putting the subject.

[13] Afterward Lord Whitworth, and embassador at the court of Bonaparte during the peace of Amiens.

would have found him absent from his station, under the pretense of attending his duty in this House, though he does not choose often to make his appearance here.[14] Instead of this, however, they increased the dishonor that they doomed us to suffer, by sending a gentleman endowed with every virtue and accomplishment, who had acquired, in the service of the Empress of Russia, at an early period of his life, a character for bravery and enterprise that rendered him personally esteemed by her, and in whom fine talents and elegant manners, ripened by habit and experience, had confirmed the flattering promise of his youth. Did they think that the shabbiness of their message was to be done away by the worth of the messenger? If I were to send a humiliating apology to any person, would it change its quality by being intrusted to Lord Rodney, Admiral Pigot, my honorable friend behind me [General Burgoyne], Lord Cornwallis, Sir Henry Clinton, Sir William Howe, or any other gallant and brave officer? Certainly not.

It was my fortune, in very early life, to have set out in habits of particular intimacy with Mr. Faulkener, and however circumstances may have intervened to suspend that intimacy, circumstances arising from wide differences in political opinion, they never have altered the sentiments of private esteem which I have uniformly felt for him; and with every amiable and conciliating quality that belongs to man, I know him to be one from whom improper submissions are the least to be expected. Well, sir, these gentlemen, Mr. Whitworth and Mr. Faulkener, commence the negotiation by the offer of three distinct propositions, each of them better than the other, and accompany it with an expression somewhat remarkable, namely, that this negotiation is to be as unlike all the others as possible, and to be "*founded in perfect candor.*" To prove this, they submit at once to the Russian ministers "all that their instructions enable them to propose." Who would not have imagined, according to the plain import of these words, that unless the Empress had assented to one of these propositions, all amicable interposition would have been at an end, and war the issue? The "perfect candor" promised in the beginning of their note, leads them to declare explicitly, that unless the fortifications of Oczakow be razed, or the Turks are allowed, as an equivalent, to keep both the banks of the Dniester, the allies can not propose any terms to them. What answer do they receive? An unequivocal rejection of every one of their propositions; accompanied, however, with a declaration, to which I shall soon return, that the navigation of that river shall be free to all the world, and a reference to those maxims of policy which have invariably actuated the Empress of Russia in her intercourse with neutral nations, whose commerce she has at all times protected and encouraged. With this declaration the British plenipotentiaries declare themselves perfectly contented; nay, more, they engage that if the Turks should refuse these conditions, and continue obstinate longer than four months, the allied courts "will abandon the termination of the war to the events it may produce." And here ends forever all care for the Ottoman empire, all solicitude about the balance of power. The right honorable gentleman will interpose no further to save either, but rests the whole of a measure, once so indispensable to *our* safety, upon this doubtful issue, whether the Turks will accept in December those very terms which in July the British ministers *could not venture to propose to them!*

Comparison of Mr. Pitt's conduct with that of Louis XIV. in the most trying circumstances.

Sir, we may look in vain to the events of former times for a disgrace parallel to what we have suffered. Louis the Fourteenth, a monarch often named in our debates, and whose reign exhibits more than any other the extremes of prosperous and of adverse fortune, never, in the midst of his most humiliating distresses, stooped to so despicable a sacrifice of all that can be dear to man. The war of the succession, unjustly begun by him, had reduced his power, had swallowed up his armies and his navies, had desolated his provinces, had drained his treasures, and deluged the earth with the blood of the best and most faithful of his subjects. Exhausted by his various calamities, he offered his enemies at one time to relinquish all the objects for which he had begun the war. That proud monarch sued for peace, and was content to receive it from our moderation. But when it was made a condition of that peace, that he should turn his arms against his grandson, and compel him by force to relinquish the throne of Spain, humbled, exhausted, conquered as he was, misfortune had not yet bowed his spirit to conditions so hard as these. We know the event. He persisted still in the war, until the folly and wickedness of Queen Anne's ministers enabled him to conclude the peace of Utrecht, on terms considerably less disadvantageous even than those he had himself proposed. And shall *we*, sir, the pride of our age, the terror of Europe, submit to this humiliating sacrifice of our honor? Have *we* suffered a defeat at Blenheim? Shall we, with our increasing prosperity, our widely diffused capital, our navy, the just subject of our common exultation, ever-flowing coffers, that enable us to give back to the people what, in the hour of calamity, we were compelled to take from them; flushed with a recent triumph over Spain [respecting Nootka

[14] Lord Auckland is understood to have been the object of this fierce attack, which was certainly unfair and ungentlemanly, as directed against one who, not being present, had no opportunity to speak in his own defense. Mr. Pitt, in his reply, asked Mr. Fox whether "it was decent or manly to go out of his way to allude, in an unhandsome manner, to an honorable gentleman in his absence, who was supposed to have been employed in a diplomatic capacity;" and declared that "no man who had been honored with the office of a minister at foreign courts had ever discharged his duty more ably, more honestly, or in a manner more creditable to himself, or advantageous to his country, than the honorable gentleman so illiberally alluded to."—*Parliamentary History*, xxix., 998.

Sound], and yet more than all, while our old rival and enemy was incapable of disturbing us, shall it be for us to yield to what France disdained in the hour of her sharpest distress, and exhibit ourselves to the world, the sole example in its annals of such an abject and pitiful degradation?[15]

Pretenses for continuing the armament: (1.) That the Emperor might have imposed harder conditions on the Turks.

VII. But gentlemen inform us now, in justification, as I suppose they mean it, of all these measures, that to effect a peace between Russia and the Porte was only the ostensible cause of our armament, or at least was not the sole cause; and that ministers were under some apprehension lest the Emperor of Germany, if the allies were to disarm, should insist on better terms from the Turks than he had agreed to accept by the convention of Reichenbach. This I can not believe. When his Majesty sends a message to inform his Parliament that he thinks it necessary to arm for a specific purpose, I can not suppose that a *falsehood* has been put into his Majesty's mouth, and that the armament which he proposes as necessary for one purpose is intended for another! If the right honorable gentleman shall tell me, that although the war between Russia and the Porte was the real cause of equipping the armament, yet that being once equipped, it was wise to keep it up when no longer wanted on that account, because the Emperor seemed inclined to depart from the convention of Reichenbach; then I answer, that it was his duty to have come with a second message to Parliament, expressly stating this new object, with the necessary information to enable the House to judge of its propriety. Another of

(2.) That the Empress of Russia might have risen in her demands.

the arguments for continuing the armament after the object was relinquished, is, that Russia might have insisted on harder terms, not conceiving herself bound by offers which we had refused to accept. I perfectly agree with gentlemen, that after the repeated offer of those terms on the part of Russia, and the rejection of them by us, the Empress was not bound to adhere to them in all possible events and contingencies. If the war had continued, she would have had a right to further indemnification for the expense of it. But was it not worth the minister's while to try the good faith of the Empress of Russia, after she had so solemnly pledged herself to all Europe that she would *not* rise in her demands? The experiment would have been made with little trouble, by the simple expedient of sending a messenger to ask the question. The object of his armament would have suffered little by the delay, as an answer from the Russian court might have been had in five or six weeks. Was it reasonable in ministers to suppose, that because, in the early part of the negotiation, the Empress had shown so much regard to us as actually to give up whatever pretensions she had formed to other provinces of the Turkish empire, solely with the view of obtaining our concurrence to the principle on which she offered to make peace, she would revert to those very pretensions the instant she had obtained that concurrence on our part, for the benefit of which she had sacrificed them? Surely, as I have said, it was worth while to make the experiment; but simple and obvious as this was, a very different course was adopted. Oczakow, indeed, was relinquished *before* the armament began, as we may find by comparing the date of the press-warrants with that of the Duke of Leed's resignation. As soon as the King's message was delivered to Parliament, a messenger was dispatched to Berlin with an intimation of the resolution to arm. This, perhaps, was rashly done as the ministry might have foreseen that the measure would probably meet with opposition, and much time could not have been lost by waiting the event of the first debate. No sooner was the division [upon the debate] known, than a second messenger was sent off to overtake and stop the dispatches of the first; and this brings me to another argument, which I confess appears to me very unlikely to help them out. They tell

(3.) That a continuance of the armament was necessary, until the views of Prussia could be known.

us, that the King of Prussia having armed in consequence of our assurances of support, we could not disarm before we knew the sentiments of the court of Berlin, without the imputation of leaving our ally in the lurch. Did we wait for the sentiments of that court to determine whether Oczakow was to be given up or not? Sir, when that measure was resolved upon, *the right honorable gentleman actually had abandoned his ally;* and that such was the sense of the court of Berlin, I believe can be testified by every Englishman who was there at the time. No sooner did the second messenger arrive, and the contents of his dispatches become known, than a general indignation rose against the conduct of the right honorable gentleman; and I am well enough informed on the subject to state to this House, that not an Englishman could show his face in that capital without exposing himself to mortification, perhaps to insult. But, between the 28th of March, 1791, when the message was brought down to this House, and the 2d or 3d of April, when the second messenger was dispatched with the news that ministers had abandoned the object of it, the armament could not have been materially advanced. Why, then, was it persisted in? The right honorable gentleman can not argue that he kept up the armament in compliance with his engagements with Prussia, when the armament, in fact, did not exist, and when it had been begun but four or five days previous to his renouncing the object of it. That could not have been his motive. What,

[15] We have here an instance of the admirable use which Mr. Fox sometimes made of history in his orations. The case selected was perfectly suited to his purpose; and the brief but masterly sketch which he gives of the circumstances and conduct of the French monarch, as contrasted with those of the British minister, was suited to awaken the keenest sense of disgrace in the minds of an English audience. In respect to style alone, it is one of the best specimens we have in our eloquence of terse and powerful language.

then, was the motive? Why, that he was too proud to own his error, and valued less the money and tranquillity of the people than the appearance of firmness, when he had renounced the reality. False shame is the parent of many crimes.[16] By false shame a man may be tempted to commit a murder, to conceal a robbery. Influenced by this false shame, the ministers robbed the people of their money, the seamen of their liberty, their families of support and protection, and all this to conceal that they had undertaken a system which was not fit to be pursued. If they say that they did this, apprehensive that, without the terror of an armament, Russia would not stand to the terms which they had refused to accept, they do no more than acknowledge that, by the insolence of their arming and the precipitancy of their submission, they had either so provoked her resentment, or excited her contempt, that she would not even condescend to agree to her own propositions when approved by them. But however they might have thought her disposed to act on this subject, it was at least their duty to try whether such would have been her conduct or not.

The free navigation of the Dniester no real gain.

VIII. To prove that the terms to which they agreed at last were the same with those they before rejected, all I feel it necessary for me to observe is, that the free navigation of the River Dniester, the only novelty introduced into them, was implied in proposing it as a boundary; for it is a well-known rule that the boundary between two powers must be as free to the one as to the other. True, says the minister, but we have got the free navigation for the subjects of other powers, particularly for those of Poland. If this be an advantage, it is one which he has gained by concession; for if he had not agreed that the river should be the boundary, the navigation would not have been free. The Turks offered no such stipulation, had they been put in possession of both the banks. Besides which, as a noble Duke, whom I have already quoted, well observed, it is an advantage, whatever may be its value, which can subsist only in time of peace. It is not, I suppose, imagined that the navigation will be free in time of war. They have, then, got nothing that deserves the name of a "modification," a term, I must here observe, the use of which is not justified even by the original memorial, where the sense is more accurately expressed by the French word "*radoucissement*." Was it, then, for some *radoucissement* [softening] that they continued their armament? Was it to say to the Empress, when they had conceded every thing, "We have given you all you asked, give us something that we may hold out to the public, something that we may use against the minority; that minority whom we have endeavored to represent as your allies. We have sacrificed our allies, the Turks, to you. You can do no less than sacrifice your allies, the minority, to us?" If I had been to advise the Empress on the subject, I would have counseled her to grant the British minister something of this sort. I would even have advised her to raze the fortifications of Oczakow, if he had insisted on it. I would have appealed from her policy to her generosity, and said, "Grant him this as an *apology*, for he stands much in need of it. His whole object was to appear to gain something, no matter what, by continuing the armament; and even in this last pitiful and miserable object he has failed." If, after all, I ask, whether these terms *are* contained in the peace that we have concluded for the Turks, or, rather, which the Turks concluded for themselves, the answer is, "We have no authentic copy of it." Is this what we have got by our arms, by distressing our commerce, dragging our seamen from their homes and occupations, and squandering our money? Is this the efficacy of our interference, and the triumph of our wisdom and our firmness? The Turks have at length concluded a peace, of which they do not even condescend to favor us with a copy, so that we know what it is only by report, and the balance of Europe, late in so much danger, and of so much importance, is left for them to settle without consulting us! Is it for this that we employed such men as Mr. Faulkener and Mr. Whitworth? They were sent to negotiate for the materials of a speech, and failed. But what are the complaints that private friendship has a right to make, compared with those of an insulted public? Half a million of money is spent, the people alarmed and interrupted in their proper pursuits by the apprehension of a war, and for what? For the restoration of Oczakow? No! Oczakow is not restored. To save the Turks from being too much humbled? No. They are now in a worse situation than they would have been had we never armed at all. If Russia had persevered in that system of encroachment of which she is accused, we could, as I observed before, then have assisted them unembarrassed. We are now tied down by treaties, and fettered by stipulations. We have even guaranteed to Russia what we before said it would be unsafe for the Turks to yield, and dangerous to the peace of Europe for Russia to possess. This is what the public have got by the armament. What, then, was the *private motive?*

> Scilicet, ut Turno contingat regia conjux,
> Nos, animæ viles, inhumata infletaque turba,
> Sternamur campis.[17]

---

16 The reader can not fail to remark how adroitly this mention of Mr. Pitt's pride and false shame is used by Mr. Fox to introduce anew some of the leading topics of reproach—lavish expenditure, pressing of seamen, &c. He thus keeps the great points of his case continually in view, at one time by incidental references in passing, at another by extended and formal repetitions.

17 That Turnus may obtain a royal spouse,
We abject souls, unburied and unwept,
Lie scattered on the plains.

The lines are taken from the Æneid of Virgil, book xi., line 371, and are part of Drances' speech in which he charges Turnus with sacrificing the

Tendency of such conduct to destroy confidence in the English Constitution.

IX. The minister gained, or thought he was to gain, an excuse for his rashness and misconduct; and to purchase this excuse was the public money and the public quiet wantonly sacrificed. There are some effects, which, to combine with their causes, is almost sufficient to drive men mad! That the pride, the folly, the presumption of a single person shall be able to involve a whole people in wretchedness and disgrace, is more than philosophy can teach mortal patience to endure. Here are the true weapons of the enemies of our Constitution! Here may we search for the source of those seditious writings, meant either to weaken our attachment to the Constitution, by depreciating its value, or which loudly tell us that we have no Constitution at all. We may blame, we may reprobate such doctrines; but while we furnish those who circulate them with arguments such as these; while the example of this day shows us to what degree the fact is true, we must not wonder if the purposes they are meant to answer be but too successful.[18] They argue, that a Constitution can not be right where such things are possible; much less so when they are practiced without punishment. This, sir, is a serious reflection to every man who loves the Constitution of England. Against the vain theories of men, who project fundamental alterations upon grounds of mere speculative objection, I can easily defend it; but when they recur to these facts, and show me how we may be doomed to all the horrors of war by the caprice of an individual who will not even condescend to explain his reasons, I can only fly to this House, and exhort you to rouse from your lethargy of confidence into the active mistrust and vigilant control which is your duty and your office. Without recurring to the dust to which the minister has been humbled, and the dirt he has been dragged through, if we ask, for what has the peace of the public been disturbed? For what is that man pressed and dragged like a felon to a service that *should* be honorable? we must be answered, for some three quarters of a mile of barren territory on the banks of the Dniester! In the name of all we value, give us, when such instances are quoted in derogation of our Constitution, some right to answer, that these are not its principles, but the monstrous abuses intruded into its practice. Let it not be said, that because the executive power, for an adequate and evident cause, may adopt measures that require expense without consulting Parliament, we are to convert the exception into a rule; to reverse the principle; and that it is now to be assumed, that the people's money may be spent for any cause, or for none, without either submitting the exigency to the judgment of their representatives, or inquiring into it afterward, unless we can make out ground for a criminal charge against the executive government. Let us disclaim these abuses, and return to the Constitution.

I am not one of those who lay down rules as universal and absolute; because I think there is hardly a political or moral maxim which is universally true; but I maintain the general rule to be, that before the public money be voted away, the occasion that calls for it should be fairly stated, for the consideration of those who are the proper guardians of the public money. Had the minister explained his system to Parliament before he called for money to support it, and Parliament had decided that it was not worth supporting, he would have been saved the mortification and disgrace in which his own honor is involved, and, by being furnished with a just excuse to Prussia for withdrawing from the prosecution of it, have saved that of his Sovereign and his country, which he has irrevocably tarnished. Is unanimity necessary to his plans? He can be sure of it in no manner, unless he explains them to this House, who are certainly much better judges than he is of the degree of unanimity with which they are likely to be received. Why, then, did he not consult us? Because he had other purposes to answer in the use he meant to make of his majority. Had he opened himself to the House at first, and had we declared against him, he might have been stopped in the first instance: had we declared for him, we might have held him too firmly to his principle to suffer his receding from it as he has done. Either of these alternatives he dreaded. It was his policy to decline our opinions, and to exact our confidence; that thus having the means of acting either way, according to the exigencies of his personal situation, he might come to Parliament and tell us what our opinions ought to be; which set of principles would be most expedient to shelter him from inquiry, and from punishment. It is for this he comes before us with a poor and pitiful excuse, that for want of the unanimity he expected, there was reason to fear, if the war should go to a second campaign, that it might be obstructed. Why not speak out, and own the real fact? He feared that a second campaign might occasion the loss of his place. Let him keep but his place, he cares not what else he loses. With other men, reputation and glory are the objects of ambition; power and place are coveted but as the means of these. For the minister, power and place are sufficient of themselves. With them he is content; for them he can calmly sacrifice every proud distinction that ambition covets, and every noble prospect to which it points the way!

Miscellaneous concluding remarks.

X. Sir, there is yet an argument which I have not sufficiently noticed. It has been said, as a ground for his defense, that he was prevented from gaining what he demanded by our opposition; and, but for this, Russia would have complied, and never would have hazarded a war. Sir, I believe the direct contrary, and my belief is as good as their asser-

people in a useless war, simply that he might receive Lavinia as his bride.

[18] Mr. Fox shows great dexterity in thus retorting upon Mr. Pitt those charges of weakening the British Constitution, which were brought against himself and friends so often at this time, in consequence of his admiration of the French Revolution.

tion, unless they will give us some proof of its correctness. Until then, I have a right to ask them, what if Russia had not complied? Worse and worse for him! He must have gone on, redoubling his menaces and expenses, the Empress of Russia continuing inflexible as ever, but for the salutary opposition which preserved him from his extremity of shame. I am not contending that armaments are never necessary to enforce negotiations; but it is one, and that not the least, of the evils attending the right honorable gentleman's misconduct, that by keeping up the parade of an armament, never meant to be employed, he has, in a great measure, deprived us of the use of this method of negotiating, whenever it may be necessary to apply it effectually; for if you propose to arm in concert with any foreign power, that power will answer, "What security can you give me that you will persevere in that system? You say you can not go to war, unless your people are unanimous." If you aim to negotiate against a foreign power, that power will say, "I have only to persist—the British minister may threaten, but he dare not act—he will not hazard the loss of his place by a war." A right honorable gentleman [Mr. Dundas], in excuse for withholding papers, asked what foreign power would negotiate with an English cabinet, if their secrets were likely to be developed, and exposed to the idle curiosity of a House of Commons? I do not dread such a consequence; but if I must be pushed to extremes, if nothing were left me but an option between opposite evils, I should have no hesitation in choosing. "Better have no dealings with them at all," I should answer, "if the right of inquiry into every part of a negotiation they think fit, and of knowing why they are to vote the money of their constituents, be denied the House of Commons." But there is something like a reason why no foreign power will negotiate with us, and that a much better reason than a dread of disclosing their secrets, in the right honorable gentleman's example. I declare, therefore, for the genius of our Constitution, against the practice of his Majesty's ministers; I declare that the duties of this House are, vigilance in preference to secrecy, deliberation in preference to dispatch. Sir, I have given my reasons for supporting the motion for a vote of censure on the minister. I will listen to his defense with attention, and I will retract wherever he shall prove me to be wrong.

Mr. Pitt closed the debate with great ability. He insisted on the necessity of restraining the ambition of Russia, and complained that Mr. Fox "had pushed his arguments, for the purpose of aggravation, to a degree of refinement beyond all reason." The vote was then taken, and stood 244 in his favor, and 116 against him. The country acquiesced in this decision, though most persons condemned his taking a stand on such narrow ground as the occupation of Oczakow. Subsequent events have proved that Mr. Pitt's jealousy of the growing power of Russia was well founded; and it has long been the settled policy of the other powers of Europe, at all hazards to prevent the Czar from becoming master of Constantinople.

SPEECH

OF MR. FOX IN FAVOR OF MR. GREY'S MOTION FOR PARLIAMENTARY REFORM, DELIVERED IN THE HOUSE OF COMMONS, MAY 26, 1797.

INTRODUCTION.

Mr. Fox had always professed to be in favor of Parliamentary Reform, though he did not agree in the details of any of the schemes which had been hitherto proposed, and he was not, perhaps, fully persuaded that those schemes could be so modified as to accomplish the desired object. But on this occasion he seems to have given his support to Mr. Grey's motion, with a sincere desire that it might prevail. The country was in a most disastrous state; the French had subdued all their enemies on the Continent, and England was left to maintain the contest single-handed; the pressure of commercial difficulties had rendered it necessary to suspend specie payments by law; great distress prevailed throughout the nation; there was much angry feeling and despondency both in England and Scotland, and a hostility to the government in Ireland, which soon after resulted in open rebellion. Under these circumstances, Mr. Fox felt that the prospects of Great Britain were gloomy in the extreme, and that measures were called for calculated to inspire the nation with increased confidence and interest in the government. As essential to this end, he urged a reform in Parliament which should give the people their just share in the Constitution; and he took occasion, at the same time, to inveigh against the measures of Mr. Pitt as hurrying on the country to the brink of ruin.

This speech bears internal evidence of having been corrected, to some extent, by Mr. Fox or his friends. While it has all the elasticity of spirit and rapidity of progress which mark his other speeches, it has greater polish and beauty than most of his parliamentary efforts, especially in an admirable passage toward the close, in which he speaks of the energy imparted to the ancient republics by the Spirit of Liberty.

SPEECH,[1] &c.

Sir,—Much and often as this question has been discussed, and late as the hour is, I feel it my duty to make some observations, and to deliver my opinion on a measure of high importance at all times, but which, at the present period, is become infinitely more interesting than ever.

Reform demanded by the condition of the country.

I fear, however, that my conviction on this subject is not common to the House. I fear that we are not likely to be agreed as to the importance of the measure, nor as to the necessity; since, by the manner in which it has been discussed this night, I foresee that, so far from being unanimous on the proposition, we shall not be agreed as to the situation and circumstances of the country itself, much less as to the nature of the measures which, in my mind, that situation and those circumstances imperiously demand. I can not suppress my astonishment at the tone and manner of gentlemen this day. The arguments that have been used would lead the mind to believe that we are in a state of peace and tranquillity, and that we have no provocation to any steps for improving the benefits we enjoy, or retrieving any misfortune that we have incurred. To persons who feel this to be our situation, every proposition tending to meliorate the condition of the country must be subject of jealousy and alarm; and if we really differ so widely in sentiment as to the state of the country, I see no probability of an agreement in any measure that is proposed. All that part of the argument against reform which relates to the danger of innovation is strangely misplaced by those who think with me, that, so far from procuring the mere *chance* of practical benefits by a reform, it is *only* by a reform that we can have a chance of rescuing ourselves from a state of extreme peril and distress. Such is my view of our situation. I think it is so perilous, so imminent, that though I do not feel conscious of despair—an emotion which the heart ought not to admit—yet it comes near to that state of hazard when the sentiment of despair, rather than of hope, may be supposed to take possession of the mind. I feel myself to be the member of a community, in which the boldest man, without any imputation of cowardice, may dread that we are not merely approaching to a state of extreme peril, but of absolute dissolution; and with this conviction impressed upon my mind, gentlemen will not believe that I disregard all the *general* arguments that have been used against the motion on the score of the danger of innovation from any disrespect to the honorable members who have urged them, or to the ingenuity with which they have been pressed, but because I am firmly persuaded that they are totally inapplicable to the circumstances under which we come to the discussion. With the ideas that I entertain, I can not listen for a moment to suggestions that are applicable only to other situations and to other times; for unless we are resolved pusillanimously to wait the approach of our doom, to lie down and die, we must take bold and decisive measures for our deliverance. We must not be deterred by meaner apprehensions. We must combine all our strength, fortify one another by the communion of our courage; and, by a seasonable exertion of national wisdom, patriotism, and vigor, take measures for the chance of salvation, and encounter with unappalled hearts all the enemies, foreign and internal—all the dangers and calamities of every kind which press so heavily upon us. Such is my view of our present emergency; and, under this impression, I can not, for a moment, listen to the argument of danger arising from innovation, since our ruin is inevitable if we pursue the course which has brought us to the brink of the precipice.

Reform not sought from those party feelings which spring from a desire of office.

But before I enter upon the subject of the proposition that has been made to us, I must take notice of an insinuation that has, again and again, been flung out by gentlemen on the other side of the House as to party feelings, in which they affect to deplore the existence of a spirit injurious to the welfare of the public. I suspect, by the frequent repetition of this insinuation, that they are desirous of making it believed, or that they understand themselves by the word party feelings an unprincipled combination of men for the pursuit of office and its emoluments, the eagerness after which leads them to act upon feelings of personal enmity, ill-will, and opposition to his Majesty's ministers. If such be their interpretation of party feelings, I must say that I am utterly unconscious of any such feeling; and I am sure that I can speak with confidence for my friends, that they are actuated by no motives of so debasing a nature. But if they understand by party feelings, that men of honor, who entertain similar principles, conceive that those principles may be more beneficially and successfully pursued by the force of mutual support, harmony, and confidential connection, then I adopt the interpretation, and have no scruple in saying that it is an advantage to the country; an advantage to the cause of truth and the Constitution; an advantage to freedom and humanity; an advantage to whatever honorable object they may be engaged in, that men pursue it with the united force of party feeling; that is to say, pursue it with the confidence, zeal, and spirit which the communion of just confidence is likely to inspire. And if the honorable gentlemen apply this description of party feeling to the pursuit in which we are engaged, I am equally ready to say, that the disastrous condition of the empire ought to animate and invigorate the union of all those who feel it to be their duty to check and arrest a career that threatens us with such inevitable ruin; for, surely, those who

[1] Two or three paragraphs of this speech are omitted, relating, not to the question of reform, but to old contests between Mr. Fox and Mr. Pitt.

think that party is a good thing for ordinary occasions must admit that it is peculiarly so on emergencies like the present. It is peculiarly incumbent upon men who feel the value of united exertion, to combine all their strength to extricate the vessel when in danger of being stranded.

The discussion, from its very nature, involves a certain degree of personality.

But gentlemen seem to insinuate that this union of action is directed more against persons than measures, and that allusions ought not to be made to the conduct of particular men. It is not easy to analyze this sort of imputation, for it is not easy to disjoin the measure from its author, nor to examine the origin and progress of any evil without also inquiring into and scrutinizing the motives and the conduct of the persons who gave rise to it. How, for instance, is it possible for us to enter into the discussion of the particular question now before the House, without a certain mixture of personal allusion? We complain that the representation of the people in Parliament is defective. How does this complaint originate? From the conduct of the majorities in Parliament. Does not this naturally lead us to inquire whether there is not either something fundamentally erroneous in our mode of election, or something incidentally vicious in the treatment of those majorities? We surely must be permitted to inquire whether the fault and calamity of which we complain is inherent in the institution (in which case nothing personal is to be ascribed to ministers, as it will operate, in a more or less degree, in all the circumstances in which we may find ourselves); or whether it is an occasional abuse of an original institution, applicable only to these times and to these men, in which case they are peculiarly guilty, while the system of representation itself ought to stand absolved.

I put the question in this way, in order to show that a certain degree of personality is inseparable from the discussion, and that gentlemen can not with justice ascribe to the bitterness of party feelings, what flows out of the principle of free inquiry. Indeed, this is a pregnant example of there being nothing peculiarly hostile to persons in this subject; it is not a thing now taken up for the first time, meditated and conceived in particular hostility to the right honorable the Chancellor of the Exchequer. Be it remembered, that he himself has again and again introduced and patronized the same measure, and that on all the occasions on which he has brought it forward it has invariably received my approbation and support. When he brought it forward first, in the year 1782, in a time of war and of severe public calamity, I gave to the proposition my feeble support. Again, when he brought it forward in 1783, at a time when I was in a high office in his Majesty's service, I gave it my support. Again, in 1785, when the right honorable gentleman himself was in place, and renewed his proposition, it had my countenance and support. I have invariably declared myself a friend to parliamentary reform, by whomsoever proposed; and though in all the discussions that have taken place, I have had occasion to express my doubt as to the efficacy of the particular mode, I have never hesitated to say that the principle itself was beneficial; and that though not called for with the urgency which some persons, and, among others, the right honorable gentleman, declared to exist, I constantly was of opinion that it ought not to be discouraged. Now, however, that all doubt upon the subject is removed by the pressure of our calamities, and the dreadful alternative seems to be, whether we shall sink into the most abject thraldom, or continue in the same course until we are driven into the horrors of anarchy, I can have no hesitation in saying, that the plan of recurring to the principle of melioration which the Constitution points out, is become a desideratum to the people of Great Britain. Between the alternatives of base and degraded slavery on the one side, or of tumultuous, though, probably, short-lived anarchy on the other, though no man would hesitate to make his choice, yet, if there be a course obvious and practicable, which, without either violence or innovation, may lead us back to the vigor we have lost, to the energy that has been stifled, to the independence that has been undermined, and yet preserve every thing in its place, a moment ought not to be lost in embracing the chance which this fortunate provision of the British system has made for British safety.

Reform early proposed by Mr. Pitt, in which he was supported by Mr. Fox.

No argument against reforming England to be drawn from the case of France.

This is my opinion, and it is not an opinion merely founded upon theory, but upon actual observation of what is passing in the world. I conceive that if we are not resolved to shut our eyes to the instructive lessons of the times, we must be convinced of the propriety of seasonable concession. I see nothing in what is called the lamentable example of France, to prove to me that timely acquiescence with the desires of the people is more dangerous than obstinate resistance to their demands; but the situations of Great Britain and France are so essentially different, there is so little in common between the character of England at this day, and the character of France at the commencement of the Revolution, that it is impossible to reason upon them from parity of circumstances or of character. It is not necessary for me, I am sure, to enter into any analysis of the essential difference between the character of a people that had been kept for ages in the barbarism of servitude, and a people who have enjoyed for so long a time the light of freedom. But we have no occasion to go to France for examples; another country, nearer to our hearts, with which we are better acquainted, opens to us a book so legible and clear, that he must be blind indeed who is not able to draw from it warning and instruction; it holds forth a lesson which is intelligible to dullness itself. Let us look to Ireland, and see how remarkably the arguments and reasoning of this day tally with the arguments and reasoning that unfortunately prevailed in the sister kingdom, and by which the King's ministers were fatally able to overpower the voice of reason and patriotism, and stifle all attention to the prayers and applications of the people.

It is impossible for any coincidence to be more perfect. We are told that there are in England, as it is said there were in Ireland, a small number of persons desirous of throwing the country into confusion, and of alienating the affections of the people from the established government. Permit me, Mr. Speaker, in passing to observe, that the right honorable the Chancellor of the Exchequer did not represent my learned friend [Mr. Erskine] quite correctly, when he stated that my learned friend admitted the existence of such men. On the contrary, the argument of my learned friend was hypothetical; he said, *if* it be true, as it is so industriously asserted, that such and such men do exist in the country, then surely in wisdom you ought to prevent their number from increasing, by timely conciliation of the body of moderate men who desire only reform. In this opinion I perfectly acquiesce with my learned friend. I believe that the number of persons who are discontented with the government of the country, and who desire to overthrow it, is very small indeed. But the right honorable gentleman [Mr. Pitt] says that the friends of moderate reform are few, and that no advantage is to be gained by conceding to this very small body what will not satisfy the violent, which, he contends, is the more numerous party; and he vehemently demands to know whom he is to divide, whom to separate, and what benefit he is to obtain from this surrender? To this I answer, that if there be two bodies [the rash and the moderate], it is wisdom, it is policy, to prevent the one from falling into the other, by granting to the moderate what is just and reasonable. If the argument of the right honorable gentleman be correct, the necessity for concession is more imperious; it is only by these means that you can check the spirit of proselytism, and prevent a conversion that by-and-by will be too formidable for you to resist. Mark this, and see how it applies to the precedent of Ireland. In the report that has been made by the Parliament of that kingdom on the present disorders, it is said that, so long ago as the year 1791, there existed some societies in that country which harbored the desire of separation from England, and which wished to set up a republican form of government. The report does not state what was the precise number of those societies in 1791; it declares, however, that the number was small and insignificant. From small beginnings, however, they have increased to the alarming number of one hundred thousand men in the province of Ulster only. By what means have they so increased, and who are the proselytes that swell their numbers to so gigantic a size? Obviously the men who had no such design originally; obviously the persons who had no other object in view in all the petitions which they presented, than Catholic emancipation and reform in Parliament. This is also admitted by the report. The spirit of reform spread over the country; they made humble, earnest, and repeated applications to the Castle[2] for redress; but there they found a fixed determination to resist every claim, and a rooted aversion to every thing that bore even the color of reform. They made their applications to all the considerable characters in the country, who had on former occasions distinguished themselves by exertions in the popular cause; and of these justly eminent men I desire to speak as I feel, with the utmost respect for their talents and virtues. But, unfortunately, they were so alarmed by the French Revolution, and by the cry which had been so artfully set up by ministers, of the danger of infection, that they could not listen to the complaint. What was the consequence? These bodies of men, who found it vain to expect it from the government at the Castle, or from the Parliament, and having no where else to recur for redress, joined the societies, which the report accuses of cherishing the desire of separation from England; and became converts to all those notions of extravagant and frantic ambition, which the report lays to their charge, and which threaten consequences so dreadful and alarming that no man can contemplate them without horror and dismay.

Argument from the case of Ireland as to increasing disaffection by denying reform.

What, then, is the lesson to be derived from this example, but that the comparatively small societies of 1791 became strong and formidable by the accession of the many who had nothing in common with them at the outset? I wish it were possible for us to draw the line more accurately between the small number that the report describes to have had mischievous objects originally in view, and the numerous bodies who were made converts by the neglect of their petition for constitutional rights. Is it improbable that the original few were not more than ten or twenty thousand in number? What, then, do I learn from this? That the impolitic and unjust refusal of government to attend to the applications of the moderate, made eighty or ninety thousand proselytes from moderation to violence.[3] This is the lesson which the book of Ireland exhibits! Can you refuse your assent to the moral? Will any man argue, that if reform had been conceded to the eighty or ninety thousand moderate petitioners, you would have this day to deplore the union of one hundred thousand men, bent on objects so extensive, so alarming, so calamitous? I wish to warn you by this example. Every argument that you have heard used this day was used at Dublin. In the short-sighted pride and obstinacy of the government, they turned a deaf ear to the supplicant; they have now, perhaps, in the open field to brave the assertor. Unwarned, untutored by example, are you still to go on with the same contemptuous and stubborn pride? I by no means think that Great Britain is at this moment in the same situation as Ireland. I by no means think that the

[2] The residence of the Lord Lieutenant of Ireland.

[3] The societies spoken of were those of the United Irishmen, which embraced a pretty large part of the entire population in some parts of the island.

discontents of this country have risen to such a height as to make us fear for the general peace of the country; but I deprecate the course which has been pursued in Ireland. What England is now, Ireland was in 1791. What was said of the few, they have now applied to the many; and as there are discontents in this country, which we can neither dissemble nor conceal, let us not, by an unwise and criminal disdain, irritate and fret them into violence and disorder. The discontents may happily subside; but a man must be sanguine indeed in his temper, or dull in his intellect, if he would leave to the operation of chance what he might more certainly obtain by the exercise of reason. Every thing that is dear and urgent to the minds of Englishmen presses upon us; in the critical moment at which I now address you, a day, an hour, ought not to elapse, without giving to ourselves the chance of this recovery.

The existing discontent in England demands reform.

When government is daily presenting itself in the shape of weakness that borders on dissolution—unequal to all the functions of useful strength, and formidable only in pernicious corruption—weak in power, and strong only in influence—am I to be told that such a state of things can go on with safety to any branch of the Constitution? If men think that, under the impression of such a system, we can go on without a recurrence to first principles, they argue in direct opposition to all theory and all practice. These discontents can not, in their nature, subside under detected weakness and exposed incapacity. In their progress and increase (and increase they must), who shall say that a direction can be given to the torrent, or that, having broken its bounds, it can be kept from overwhelming the country? Sir, it is not the part of statesmen, it is not the part of rational beings, to amuse ourselves with such fallacious dreams; we must not sit down and lament over our hapless situation; we must not deliver ourselves up to an imbecile despondency that would hasten the approach of danger; but, by a seasonable and vigorous measure of wisdom, meet it with a sufficient and a seasonable remedy. We may be disappointed. We may fail in the application, for no man can be certain of his footing on ground that is unexplored; but we shall at least have a chance for success—we shall at least do what belongs to legislators and to rational beings on the occasion, and I have confidence that our efforts would not be in vain. I say that we should give ourselves a chance, and, I may add, the best chance for deliverance; since it would exhibit to the country a proof that we had conquered the first great difficulty that stood in the way of bettering our condition—that we had conquered ourselves. We had given a generous triumph to reason over prejudice; we had given a deathblow to those miserable distinctions of Whig and Tory, under which the warfare has been maintained between pride and privilege, and, through the contention of our rival jealousies, the genuine rights of the many have been gradually undermined and frittered away. I say, that this would be giving us the best chance; because, seeing every thing go on from bad to worse—seeing the progress of the most scandalous waste countenanced by the most criminal confidence, and that the effrontery of corruption no longer requires the mask of concealment—seeing liberty daily infringed,[4] and the vital springs of the nation insufficient for the extravagance of a dissipated government, I must believe that, unless the people are mad or stupid, they will suspect that there is something fundamentally vicious in our system, and which no reform would be equal to correct. Then, to prevent all this, and to try if we can effect a reform without touching the main pillars of the Constitution, without changing its forms, or disturbing the harmony of its parts, without putting any thing out of its place, or affecting the securities which we justly hold to be so sacred, is, I say, the only chance which we have for retrieving our misfortunes by the road of quiet and tranquillity, and by which national strength may be recovered without disturbing the property of a single individual.

Recent petitions show that the House, as now constituted, does not possess the confidence of the country.

It has been said that the House possesses the confidence of the country as much as ever. This, in truth, is as much as to say that his Majesty's ministers possess the confidence of the country in the same degree as ever, since the majority of the House support and applaud the measures of the government, and give their countenance to all the evils which we are doomed to endure. I was very much surprised to hear any proposition so unaccountable advanced by any person connected with ministers, particularly as the noble Lord [Hawkesbury] had, but a sentence or two before, acknowledged that there had been, to be sure, a number of petitions presented to his Majesty for the dismission of his ministers. The one assertion is utterly incompatible with the other, unless he means to assert that the petitions which have been presented to the Throne are of no importance. The noble Lord can hardly, I think, speak in this contemptuous manner of the petitions from Middlesex, London, Westminster, Surrey, Hampshire, York, Edinburgh, Glasgow, and many other places, unless he means to insinuate that they are proofs only of our very great industry, and that they are not the genuine sense of the districts from which they come. If the noble Lord ascribes them to our industry, he gives us credit for much more merit of that kind than we are entitled to. It certainly is not the peculiar characteristic of the present Opposition, that they are very industrious in agitating the public mind. But, grant to the noble Lord his position—be it to our industry that all these petitions are to be ascribed. If industry could procure them, was it our moderation, our good will and forbearance, that have made us, for more than fourteen years, relax from this industry, and never bring forward

[4] This refers to the operation of the Treason and Sedition Bills, which restricted the holding of public meetings, extended the laws of high treason, and subjected persons found guilty of seditious libels to transportation beyond the seas.

these petitions until now? No, sir, it is not to our industry that they are to be ascribed now, nor to our forbearance that they did not come before. The noble Lord will not give us credit for this forbearance; and the consequence is, that he must own, upon his imputation of industry, that the present is the first time that we were sure of the people, and that these petitions are a proof that at length the confidence of the people in ministers is shaken. That it is so, it is in vain for the noble Lord to deny. They who in former times were eager to show their confidence by addresses have now been as eager to express their disapprobation in petitions for their removal. How, then, can we say that the confidence of the people is not shaken? Is confidence to be always against the people, and never for them? It is a notable argument, that because we do not find at the *general election* very material changes in the representation, the sentiments of the people continue the same, in favor of the war, and in favor of his Majesty's ministers. The very ground of the present discussion gives the answer to this argument. Why do we agitate the question of parliamentary reform? Why, but because a general election *does not afford to the people the means of expressing their views; because this House is not a sufficient representative of the people.* Gentlemen are fond of arguing in this circle. When we contend that ministers have not the confidence of the people, they tell us that the House of Commons is the faithful representative of the sense of the country. When we assert that the representation is defective, and show, from the petitions to the Throne, that the House does not speak the voice of the people, they turn to the general election, and say, that at this period the people had an opportunity of choosing faithful organs of their opinion; and because very little or no change has taken place in the representation, the sense of the people must be the same. Sir, it is in vain for gentlemen to shelter themselves by this mode of reasoning. We assert that, under the present form and practice of elections, we can not expect to see any remarkable change produced by a general election. We must argue from experience. Let us look back to the period of the American war. It will not be denied by the right honorable gentleman, that toward the end of the war, it became extremely unpopular, and that the King's ministers lost the confidence of the nation. In the year 1780 a dissolution took place, and then it was naturally imagined by superficial observers, who did not examine the real state of the representation, that the people would have returned a House of Commons that would have unequivocally spoken their sentiments on the occasion. What was the case? I am able to speak with considerable precision. At that time I was much more than I am at present in the way of knowing personally the individuals returned, and of making an accurate estimate of the accession gained to the popular side by that election. I can take upon me to say, that the change was very small indeed: not more than three or four persons were added to the number of those who had from the beginning opposed the disastrous career of the ministers in that war. I remember that, upon that occasion, Lord North made use of precisely the same argument as that which is now brought forward: "What!" said he; "can you contend the war is unpopular, after the declaration in its favor that the people have made by their choice of representatives? The general election is the proof that the war continues to be the war of the people of England." Such was the argument of Lord North, and yet it was notoriously otherwise; so notoriously otherwise, that the right honorable gentleman, the present Chancellor of the Exchequer, made a just and striking use of it, to demonstrate the necessity of parliamentary reform.[5] He referred to this event as to a demonstration of this doctrine. "You see," said he, "that so defective, so inadequate is the present practice, at least of the elective franchise, that no impression of national calamity, no conviction of ministerial error, no abhorrence of disastrous war, is sufficient to stand against that corrupt influence which has mixed itself with election, and which drowns and stifles the popular voice." Upon this statement, and upon this unanswerable argument, the right honorable gentleman acted in the year 1782. When he proposed a parliamentary reform, he did it expressly on the ground of the experience of 1780, and he made an explicit declaration, that we had no other security by which to guard ourselves against the return of the same evils. He repeated this warning in 1783 and in 1785. It was the leading principle of his conduct. "Without a reform," said he, "the nation can not be safe; this war may be put an end to, but what will protect you against another? As certainly as the spirit which engendered the present war actuates the secret councils of the Crown, will you, under the influence of a defective representation, be involved again in new wars, and in similar calamities." This was his argument in 1782; this was his prophecy; and the right honorable gentleman was a true prophet. Precisely as he pronounced it, the event happened; another war took place; and I am sure it will not be considered as an aggravation of its character that it is at least equal in disaster to the war of which the right honorable gentleman complained. "The defect of representation," he said, "is the national disease; and unless you apply a remedy directly to that disease, you must inevitably take the consequences with which it is pregnant." With such an authority, can any man deny that I reason right? Did not the right honorable gentleman demonstrate his case? Good God! what a fate is that of the right honorable gentleman, and in

False reasoning on the subject.

Illustration from the elections at the close of the American war.

Mr. Pitt's argument and warning.

[5] This was in Mr. Pitt's speech in favor of Parliamentary Reform, delivered in 1782; and we have here a striking instance of the dexterity and force with which Mr. Fox took the arguments of his opponents and turned them against themselves. The pungency and eloquence with which he turns upon Mr. Pitt at the close of the paragraph, are surprisingly great.

what a state of whimsical contradiction does he stand! During the whole course of his administration, and particularly during the course of the present war, every prediction that he has made, every hope that he has held out, every prophecy that he has hazarded, has failed; he has disappointed the expectations that he has raised; and every promise that he has given has proved to be fallacious; yet, for these very declarations, and notwithstanding these failures, we have called him a wise minister. We have given him our confidence on account of his predictions, and have continued it upon their failure. The *only* instance in which he really predicted what has come to pass, we treated with stubborn incredulity. In 1785, he pronounced the awful prophecy, "Without a parliamentary reform the nation will be plunged into new wars; without a parliamentary reform you can not be safe against bad ministers, nor can even good ministers be of use to you." Such was his prediction; and it has come upon us. It would seem as if the whole life of the right honorable gentleman, from that period, had been destined by Providence for the illustration of his warning. If we were disposed to consider him as a real enthusiast, and a bigot in divination, we might be apt to think that he had himself taken measures for the verification of his prophecy; for he might now exclaim to us, with the proud fervor of success, "You see the consequence of not listening to the oracle. I told you what would happen; it is true that your destruction is complete; I have plunged you into a new war; I have exhausted you as a people; I have brought you to the brink of ruin, but I told you beforehand what would happen; I told you that, without a reform in the representation of the people, no minister, however wise, could save you; *you denied me my means, and you take the consequence!*"

Answer to the argument from the supposed strength of the government.

The right honorable gentleman speaks, sir, of the strength of government. But what symptom of strength does it exhibit? Is it the *cordiality* of all the branches of the national force?[6] Is it the *harmony* that happily reigns in all the departments of the executive power? Is it the reciprocal *affection* that subsists between the government and the people? Is it in the *energy* with which the people are eager to carry into execution the measures of the administration, from the heartfelt conviction that they are founded in wisdom, favorable to their own freedom, and calculated for national happiness? Is it because our resources are flourishing and untouched, because our vigor is undiminished, because our spirit is animated by success, and our courage by our glory? Is it because government have, in a perilous situation, when they have been obliged to call upon the country for sacrifices, shown a conciliating tenderness and regard for the rights of the people, as well as a marked disinterestedness and forbearance on their own parts, by which they have, in an exemplary manner, made their own economy to keep pace with the increased demands for the public service? Are these the sources of the strength of government? I forbear, sir, to push the inquiry. I forbear to allude more particularly to symptoms which no man can contemplate at this moment without grief and dismay. It is not the declarations of right honorable gentlemen that constitute the strength of a government. That government is alone strong which possesses the hearts of the people; and will any man contend that we should not be more likely to add strength to the state, if we were to extend the basis of the popular representation? Would not a House of Commons freely elected be more likely to conciliate the support of the people? If this be true in the abstract, it is certainly our peculiar duty to look for this support in the hour of difficulty. What man who foresees a hurricane is not desirous of strengthening his house? Shall nations alone be blind to the dictates of reason? Let us not, sir, be deterred from this act of prudence by the false representations that are made to us. France is the phantom that is constantly held out to terrify us from our purpose. Look at France; it will not be denied but that she stands on the broad basis of free representation. Whatever other views the government of France may exhibit, and which may afford just alarm to other nations, it can not be denied that her representative system has proved itself capable of vigorous exertion.

Argument for reform from the energy of popular governments among the ancients and in France.

Now, sir, though I do not wish you to imitate France; and though I am persuaded you have no necessity for any terror of such imitation being forced upon you, yet I say that you ought to be as ready to adopt the virtues as you are steady in averting from the country the vices of France. If it is clearly demonstrated that genuine representation alone can give solid power, and that in order to make government strong, the people must make the government, you ought to act on this grand maxim of political wisdom thus demonstrated, and call in the people, according to the original principles of your system, to the strength of your government. In doing

[6] The keenness of the sarcasm involved in these questions will be seen by adverting to the state of the country at this time, which was partially referred to in the Introduction. About a month before, the fleet at Spithead had broken out into a general mutiny, and, notwithstanding the measures of Parliament designed to remove their discontent, they had renewed the mutiny only four days previous to the delivery of this speech. The King, as head of the "executive power," felt so much pressed by the unpopularity of Mr. Pitt, that he was supposed to be seriously contemplating a change of ministers. Mr. Fox also alludes to the wide-spread commercial embarrassments, the suspension of specie payments, the general distress which prevailed among the people, their loss of energy and spirit as the natural consequence, the diminished resources of the government, and the victories of France on the Continent, which had left England to continue the war alone. In addition to this, he refers to the lavish expenditures of the government, and the favoritism shown to their friends and adherents.

this, you will not innovate, you will not imitate. In making the people of England a constituent part of the government of England, you do no more than restore the genuine edifice designed and framed by our ancestors. An honorable baronet spoke of the instability of democracies, and says that history does not give us the example of one that has lasted eighty years. Sir, I am not speaking of pure democracies, and therefore his allusion does not apply to my argument. Eighty years, however, of peace and repose would be pretty well for any people to enjoy, and would be no bad recommendation of a pure democracy. I am ready, however, to agree with the honorable baronet, that, according to the experience of history, the ancient democracies of the world were vicious and objectionable on many accounts; their instability, their injustice, and many other vices, can not be overlooked. But surely, when we turn to the ancient democracies of Greece, when we see them in all the splendor of arts and of arms, when we see to what an elevation they carried the powers of man, it can not be denied that, however vicious on the score of ingratitude or injustice, they were, at least, the pregnant source of national strength, and that in particular they brought forth this strength in a peculiar manner in the moment of difficulty and distress. When we look at the democracies of the ancient world, we are compelled to acknowledge their oppression of their dependencies, their horrible acts of injustice and of ingratitude to their own citizens; but they compel us also to admiration by their vigor, their constancy, their spirit, and their exertions in every great emergency in which they were called upon to act. We are compelled to own that this gives a power of which no other form of government is capable. Why? Because it incorporates every man with the state, because it arouses every thing that belongs to the soul as well as to the body of man; because it makes every individual feel that he is fighting for himself, and not for another; that it is his own cause, his own safety, his own concern, his own dignity on the face of the earth, and his own interest in that identical soil which he has to maintain; and accordingly we find that whatever may be objected to them on account of the turbulency of the passions which they engendered, their short duration, and their disgusting vices, they have exacted from the common suffrage of mankind the palm of strength and vigor. Who that reads the Persian war—what boy, whose heart is warmed by the grand and sublime actions which the democratic spirit produced, does not find in this principle the key to all the wonders which were achieved at Thermopylæ and elsewhere, and of which the recent and marvelous acts of the French people are pregnant examples? He sees that the principle of liberty only could create the sublime and irresistible emotion; and it is in vain to deny, from the striking illustration that our own times have given, that the principle is eternal, and that it belongs to the heart of man. Shall we, then, refuse to take the benefit of this invigorating principle? Shall we refuse to take the benefit which the wisdom of our ancestors resolved that it should confer on the British Constitution? With the knowledge that it can be reinfused into our system without violence, without disturbing any one of its parts, are we become so inert, so terrified, or so stupid, as to hesitate for one hour to restore ourselves to the health which it would be sure to give? When we see the giant power that it confers upon others, we ought not to withhold it from Great Britain. How long is it since we were told in this House that France was a blank in the map of Europe, and that she lay an easy prey to any power that might be disposed to divide and plunder her? Yet we see that, by the mere force and spirit of this principle, France has brought all Europe to her feet. Without disguising the vices of France, without overlooking the horrors that have been committed, and that have tarnished the glory of the Revolution, it can not be denied that they have exemplified the doctrine that *if you wish for power you must look to liberty.* If ever there was a moment when this maxim ought to be dear to us, it is the present. We have tried all other means; we have had recourse to every stratagem that artifice, that influence, that cunning could suggest; we have addressed ourselves to all the base passions of the nation; we have addressed ourselves to pride, to avarice, to fear; we have awakened all the interested emotions; we have employed every thing that flattery, every thing that address, every thing that privilege could effect: we have tried to terrify them into exertion, and all has been unequal to our emergency. Let us try them by the only means which experience demonstrates to be invincible; let us address ourselves to their love; let us identify them with ourselves; let us make it their own cause as well as ours! To induce them to come forward in support of the state, let us make them a part of the state; and this they become the very instant you give them a House of Commons which is the faithful organ of their will. Then, sir, when you have made them believe and feel that there can be but one interest in the country, you will never call upon them in vain for exertion. Can this be the case as the House of Commons is now constituted? Can they think so if they review the administration of the right honorable gentleman, every part of which must convince them that the present representation is a mockery and a shadow?

A real and not a virtual representation of the people demanded by the conduct of recent Parliaments.

There has been, at different times, a great deal of dispute about virtual representation. Sir, I am no great advocate of these nice subtleties and special pleadings on the Constitution; much depends upon appearance as well as reality. I know well that a popular body of five hundred and fifty-eight gentlemen, if truly independent of the Crown, would be a strong barrier to the people. But the House of Commons should not only be, but appear to be, the representatives of the people; the system should satisfy the prejudices and the pride, as well as the reason of the people; and you never can expect to give that just impression which a House of Commons ought to make on the people, until you derive it unequivocally from them. It is asked, why gentlemen who were against a parliamentary reform on former occasions should vote for it now. Ten years ago men might reasonably object to any reform of the system, who ought now, in my opinion, to be governed by motives that are irresistible in its favor. They might look back with something like satisfaction and triumph to former Parliaments, and console themselves with the reflection that, though in moments of an ordinary kind, in the common course of human events, Parliament might abate from its vigilance, and give ministers a greater degree of confidence than was strictly conformable with representative duty—yet there was a point beyond which no artifice of power, no influence of corruption, could carry them; that there were barriers in the British Constitution over which the House of Commons never would leap, and that the moment of danger and alarm would be the signal for the return of Parliament to its post. Such might have been the reasoning of gentlemen on the experience of former Parliaments; and with this rooted trust in the latent efficacy of Parliament, they might have objected to any attempt that should cherish hopes of a change in the system itself. But what will the same gentlemen say after the experience of the last and the present Parliament? What reliance can they have for any one vestige of the Constitution that is yet left to us? Or rather, what privilege, what right, what security, has not been already violated? "Quid intactum nefasti liquimus?"[7] And seeing that in no one instance have they hesitated to go the full length of every outrage that was conceived by the minister; that they have been touched by no scruples, deterred by no sense of duty, corrected by no experience of calamity, checked by no admonition or remonstrance; that they have never made out a single case of inquiry; that they have never interposed a single restraint upon abuse; may not gentlemen consistently feel that the reform which they previously thought unnecessary is now indispensable?

No argument to be derived from the personal honor of borough representatives.

We have heard to-day, sir, all the old arguments about honor on the one side being as likely as honor on the other; that there are good men on both sides of the House; that a man upon the one side of the House as well as upon the other, may be a member for a close borough; and that he may be a good man, sit where he may. All this, sir, is very idle language; it is not the question at issue. No man disputes the existence of private and individual integrity; but, sir, this is not *representation*. If a man comes here as the proprietor of a burgage tenure, he does not come here as the representative of the people. The whole of this system, as it is now carried on, is as outrageous to morality as it is pernicious to just government; it brings a scandal on our character, which not merely degrades the House of Commons in the eyes of the people; it does more, it undermines the very principles of integrity in their hearts, and gives a fashion to dishonesty and imposture. They hear of a person receiving four or five thousand pounds as the purchase-money of a seat for a close borough; and they hear the very man who received and put the money into his pocket make a vehement speech in this House against bribery! They see him move for the commitment to prison of a poor, unfortunate wretch at your bar, who has been convicted of taking a single guinea for his vote in the very borough, perhaps, where he had publicly and unblushingly sold his influence, though, under the horrors of a war which he had contributed to bring upon the country, that miserable guinea was necessary to save a family from starving! Sir, these are the things that paralyze you to the heart; these are the things that vitiate the whole system; that spread degeneracy, hypocrisy, and sordid fraud over the country, and take from us the energies of virtue, and sap the foundations of patriotism and spirit. The system that encourages so much vice ought to be put an end to; and it is no argument, that because it lasted a long time without mischief, it ought now to be continued when it is found to be pernicious; it has arisen to a height that defeats the very end of government; *it must sink under its own weakness*. And this, sir, is not a case peculiar to itself, but inseparable from all human institutions. All the writers of eminence upon forms of government have said that, in order to preserve them, frequent recurrence must be had to their original principle. This is the opinion of Montesquieu, as well as of Machiavelli. Gentlemen will not be inclined to dispute the authority of the latter, on this point at least; and he says, that without this recurrence they grow out of shape, and deviate from their general form. It is only by recurring to former principles that any government can be kept pure and unabused. But, say gentlemen, if any abuses have crept into our system, have we not a corrective whose efficacy has been proved, and of which every body approves? Have we not Mr. Grenville's bill, as an amendment to the Constitution? An amendment it is; an amendment which acknowledges the deficiency. It is an avowal of a defective practice. It is a strong argument for reform, because it would not be necessary if the plan of representation were sufficient. But, sir, there is a lumping consideration, if I may be allowed the phrase, which now more than ever ought to make every man a convert to parliamentary reform; there is an annual revenue of twenty-three millions sterling collected by the executive government from the people. Here, sir, is the despot of election; here is the new power that has grown up to a magnitude, that bears down before it every defensive barrier established by our ancestors for the protection of the people. *They* had no such tyrant to control; they had no such enemy to oppose. Against every thing that was known, against

Danger from the patronage of the ministry.

[7] What, in our wickedness, have we left untouched?

every thing that was seen, they did provide; but it did not enter into the contemplation of those who established the checks and barriers of our system, that they would ever have to stand against a revenue of twenty-three millions a year! The whole landed rental of the kingdom is not estimated at more than twenty-five millions a year, and this rental is divided and dispersed over a large body, who can not be supposed to act in concert, or to give to their power the force of combination and unity. But it is said, that though the government is in the receipt of a revenue of twenty-three millions a year, it has not the expenditure of that sum, and that its influence ought not to be calculated from what it receives, but from what it has to pay away. I submit, however, to the good sense, and to the personal experience of gentlemen who hear me, if it be not a manifest truth that influence depends almost as much upon what they have to receive as upon what they have to pay? And if this be true of the influence which individuals derive from the rentals of their estates, and from the expenditure of that rental, how much more so is it true of government, who, both in the receipt and expenditure of this enormous revenue, are actuated by one invariable principle—that of extending or withholding favor in exact proportion to the submission or resistance to their measures, which the individuals make? Compare this revenue, then, with that against which our ancestors were so anxious to protect us, and compare this revenue with all the bulwarks of our Constitution in preceding times, and you must acknowledge that, though those bulwarks were sufficient to protect us in the days of King William and Queen Anne, they are not equal to the enemy we have now to resist.

Benefits to be expected from reform.

But it is said, what will this reform do for us? Will it be a talisman sufficient to retrieve all the misfortunes which we have incurred? I am free to say that it would not be sufficient, unless it led to reforms of substantial expense, and of all the abuses that have crept into our government. But at the same time, I think it would do this, I think it would give us the chance, as I said before, of recovery. It would give us, in the first place, a Parliament vigilant and scrupulous, and that would insure to us a government active and economical. It would prepare the way for every rational improvement, of which, without disturbing the parts, our Constitution is susceptible. It would do more; it would open the way for exertions infinitely more extensive than all that we have hitherto made. The right honorable gentleman says that we have made exertions. True. But what are they in comparison with our necessity? The right honorable gentleman says, that when we consider our situation compared with that of countries which have taken another line of conduct, we ought to rejoice. I confess, sir, that I am at a loss to conceive what country the right honorable gentleman has in view in this comparison. Does he mean to assert that the nations who preferred the line of neutrality to that of war have fallen into a severer calamity than ourselves? Does he mean to say that Sweden, or that Denmark, has suffered more by observing an *imprudent* neutrality, than England or Austria by *wisely* plunging themselves into a war? Or does he mean to insinuate that Prussia has been the victim of its impolicy, in getting out of the conflict on the first occasion? If this be the interpretation of the right honorable gentleman's argument, I do not believe that he will get many persons to subscribe to the justice of his comparison. But probably he alludes to the fate of Holland. If this be the object to which he wishes to turn our eyes, he does it unjustly. Holland acted under the despotic mandate of that right honorable gentleman; and Holland, whatever she has suffered, whatever may be her present situation, lays her calamities to the charge of England. I can not, then, admit of the argument, that our situation is comparatively better than that of the nations who altogether kept out of the war; or, being drawn into it in the first instance, corrected their error, and restored to themselves the blessings of peace.

Reform proposed by Mr. Gray.

I come now to consider the specific proposition of my honorable friend, and the arguments that have been brought against it. Let me premise, that however averse gentlemen may be to any specific proposition of reform, if they are friendly to the principle, they ought to vote for the present question, because it is merely a motion for leave to bring in a bill. An opposition to such a motion comes with a very ill grace from the right honorable gentleman, and contradicts the policy for which he strenuously argued. In 1785, he moved for leave to bring in a bill on a specific plan, and he fairly called for the support of all those who approved of the principle of reform, whatever might be the latitude of their ideas on the subject; whether they wished for more or less than his proposition, he thought that they should agree to the introduction of the bill, that it might be freely discussed in the committee, in hopes that the united wisdom of the House might shape out something that would be generally acceptable. Upon this candid argument I, for one, acted. I did not approve of his specific proposition, and yet I voted with him for leave to bring in the bill. And this, sir, has generally happened to me on all the former occasions, when propositions have been made. Though I have constantly been a friend to the principle, I have never before seen a specific plan that had my cordial approbation. That which came nearest, and of which I the least disapproved, was the plan of an honorable gentleman who is now no more [Mr. Flood]. He was the first person who suggested the idea of extending what might be proper to add to representation, to housekeepers, as to a description of persons the best calculated to give efficacy to the representative system. My honorable friend's plan, built upon this idea, is an improvement of it, since it is not an attempt even to vary the form and outline, much less to new-model the representation of the people; it keeps every thing in its place; it neither varies the number, nor changes the name, nor diverts the course of any part of our system; it corrects without change; it extends without destruction of any established right; it restores simply what has been injured by abuse, and reinstates what time has moldered away; no man can have a right to complain of genuine property assailed; no habit even, no mode of thinking, no prejudice, will be wounded; it traces back the path of the Constitution from which we have wandered, but it runs out into no new direction.

It leaves the county representation,

A noble Lord says that the county representation must be good, that it must be approved of; be it so: this proposes to leave the county representation where it is; I wish so to leave it. I think that representation ought to be of a *compound* nature. The counties may be considered as territorial representation, as contradistinguished from popular; but, in order to embrace all that I think necessary, I certainly would not approve of any farther extension of this branch of the representation. It has been asked whether the rights of corporations ought not to be maintained. That is a matter for farther discussion. I have no hesitation in saying that my opinion leans the other way; but if it should be thought so, it may be so modified in the bill. There is no reasonable objection to its introduction on account of our not now agreeing with all its parts. My honorable friend, with all his abilities, and all the industry with which he has digested his proposition, does not presume to offer it as a perfect plan. He does not call upon you to adopt all his notions, nor does he think that every part of his plan will be found to quadrate with the abstract principles of representation. He looks to what is practicable in the condition in which we are placed, not to what a new people might be tempted to hazard. My opinion, however unimportant it may be, goes with my honorable friend. I think there is enough of enterprise and vigor in the plan to restore us to health, and not enough to run us into disorder. I agree with him, because I am firmly of opinion, with all the philosophical writers on the subject, that *when a country is sunk into a situation of apathy and abuse, it can only be recovered by recurring to first principles*.

and extends the right of voting to all householders.

Now, sir, I think that, acting on this footing, to extend the right of election to housekeepers is the best and most advisable plan of reform. I think, also, that it is the most perfect recurrence to first principles—I do not mean to the first principles of society, nor the abstract principles of representation—but to the first known and recorded principles of our Constitution. According to the early history of England, and the highest authorities on our parliamentary Constitution, I find this to be the case. It is the opinion of the celebrated Glanville, that in all cases where no particular right intervenes, the common law right of paying scot and lot was the right of election in the land.[8] This, sir, was the opinion of Sergeant Glanville, and of one of the most celebrated committees of which our parliamentary history has to boast; and this, in my opinion, is the safest line of conduct you can adopt. But it is said that extending the right of voting to housekeepers may, in some respects, be compared to universal suffrage. I have always deprecated universal suffrage, not so much on account of the confusion to which it would lead, as because I think that we should in reality lose the very object which we desire to obtain; because I think it would, in its nature, embarrass and prevent the deliberative voice of the country from being heard. I do not think that you augment the deliberative body of the people by counting all the heads; but that, in truth, you confer on individuals, by this means, the power of drawing forth numbers, who, without deliberation, would implicitly act upon their will. My opinion is, that the best plan of representation is that which shall bring into activity the greatest number of independent voters; and that that is defective which would bring forth those whose situation and condition take from them the power of deliberation. I can have no conception of that being a good plan of election which should enable individuals to bring regiments to the poll. I hope gentlemen will not smile if I endeavor to illustrate my position by referring to the example of the other sex. In all the theories and projects of the most absurd speculation, it has never been suggested that it would be advisable to extend the elective suffrage to the female sex. And yet, justly respecting, as we must do, the mental powers, the acquirements, the discrimination, and the talents, of the women of England, in the present improved state of society—knowing the opportunities which they have for acquiring knowledge—that they have interests as dear and as important as our own, it must be the genuine feeling of every gentleman who hears me, that all the superior classes of the female sex of England must be more capable of exercising the elective suffrage with deliberation and propriety than the uninformed individuals of the lowest class of men to whom the advocates of universal suffrage would extend it. And yet, why has it never been imagined that the right of election should be extended to women? Why! but because by the law of nations, and perhaps also by the law of nature, that sex is dependent on ours; and because, therefore, their voices would be governed by the relation in which they stand in society. Therefore it is, sir, that, with the exception of *companies*, in which the right of voting merely affects property, it has never been in the contemplation of the most absurd theorists to extend the elective franchise to the other sex. The desideratum to be obtained is independent voters; and that, I say, would be a defective system that should bring regiments of soldiers, of servants,

This does not involve universal suffrage, which is to be deprecated.

[8] Those who paid parish taxes according to their ability, were said to "pay scot and lot."

and of persons whose low condition necessarily curbed the independence of their minds. That, then, I take to be the most perfect system which shall include the greatest number of independent electors, and exclude the greatest number of those who are necessarily, by their condition, dependent. I think that the plan of my honorable friend draws this line as discreetly as it can be drawn, and it by no means approaches to universal suffrage. It would neither admit, except in particular instances, soldiers nor servants. Universal suffrage would extend the right to three millions of men, but there are not more than seven hundred thousand houses that would come within the plan of my honorable friend; and when it is considered, that out of these some are the property of minors, and that some persons have two or more houses, it would fix the number of voters for Great Britain at about six hundred thousand; and I call upon gentlemen to say whether this would not be sufficiently extensive for deliberation on the one hand, and yet sufficiently limited for order on the other. This has no similarity to universal suffrage; and yet, taking the number of representatives as they now stand, it would give to every member about fifteen hundred constituents.

Objection to boroughs, that their representatives are compelled to obey the instructions of the proprietors who send them.

It has often been a question, both within and without these walls, how far representatives ought to be bound by the instructions of their constituents. It is a question upon which my mind is not altogether made up, though I own I lean to the opinion that, having to legislate for the empire, they ought not to be altogether guided by instructions that may be dictated by local interests. I can not, however, approve of the very ungracious manner in which I sometimes hear expressions of contempt for the opinion of constituents. They are made with a very bad grace in the first session of a septennial Parliament; particularly if they should come from individuals who, in the concluding session of a former Parliament, did not scruple to court the favor of the very same constituents by declaring that they voted against their conscience in compliance with their desire, as was the case of an honorable alderman of the city of London. But, sir, there is one class of constituents whose instructions it is considered as the implicit duty of members to obey. When gentlemen represent populous towns and cities, then it is a disputed point, whether they ought to obey their voice, or follow the dictates of their own conscience; but if they represent a noble Lord or a noble Duke, then it becomes no longer a question of doubt; and he is not considered as a man of honor who does not implicitly obey the orders of his single constituent! He is to have no conscience, no liberty, no discretion of his own; he is sent here by my Lord this or the Duke of that, and if he does not obey the instructions he receives, he is not to be considered as a man of honor and a gentleman. Such is the mode of reasoning that prevails in this House. Is this fair? Is there any reciprocity in this conduct? Is a gentleman to be permitted, without dishonor, to act in opposition to the sentiments of the city of London, of the city of Westminster, or of the city of Bristol; but if he dares to disagree with the Duke, or Lord, or Baronet, whose representative he is, must he be considered as unfit for the society of men of honor?

This, sir, is the chicane and tyranny of corruption; and this, at the same time, is called *representation!* In a very great degree the county members are held in the same sort of thraldom. A number of peers possess an overweening interest in the county, and a gentleman is no longer permitted to hold his situation than as he acts agreeably to the dictates of those powerful families. Let us see how the whole of this stream of corruption has been diverted from the side of the people to that of the Crown; with what constant, persevering art every man who is possessed of influence in counties, corporations, or boroughs, that will yield to the solicitations of the court, is drawn over to that phalanx which is opposed to the small remnant of popular election. I have looked, sir, to the machinations of the present minister in this way, and I find that, including the number of additional titles, the right honorable gentleman has made no fewer than one hundred and fifteen peers in the course of his administration; that is to say, he has bestowed no fewer than one hundred and fifteen titles, including new creations and elevations from one rank to another. How many of these are to be ascribed to national services, and how many to parliamentary interest, I leave the House to inquire. The country is not blind to these arts of influence, and it is impossible that we can expect them to continue to endure them.[9]

Reform necessary and unavoidable.

Now, sir, having shown this to be the state of our representation, I ask what remedy there can be other than reform. What can we expect, as the necessary result of a system so defective and vicious in all its parts, but increasing calamities, until we shall be driven to a convulsion that would overthrow every thing? If we do not apply this remedy in time, our fate is inevitable. Our most illustrious patriots—the men whose memories are the dearest to Englishmen, have long ago pointed out to us parliamentary reform as the only means of redressing national grievance. I need not inform you that Sir George Savile was its most strenuous advocate; I need not tell you that the venerable and illustrious Camden was through life a steady adviser of seasonable reform; nay, sir, to a certain degree we have the authority of Mr. Burke himself for the propriety of correcting the abuses of our system; for gentlemen will remember the memorable answer which he gave to the argument that was used for our right of taxing America, on the score of

[9] Mr. Burke's Bill of Economical Reform took away a very large number of sinecure offices, which ministers had been accustomed to use as means of patronage and reward. Mr. Pitt therefore resorted to the expedient of raising men to the peerage, as a means of influence, to an extent which was generally and justly complained of.

their being *virtually* represented, and that they were in the same situation as Manchester, Birmingham, and Sheffield. "What!" said Mr. Burke, "when the people of America look up to you with the eyes of filial love and affection, will you turn to them the *shameful* parts of the Constitution?" With the concurring testimony of so many authorities for correcting our abuses, why do we hesitate? Can we do any harm by experiment? Can we possibly put ourselves into a worse condition than that in which we are? What advantages we shall gain I know not. I think we shall gain many. I think we shall gain at least the chance of warding off the evil of confusion, growing out of accumulated discontent. I think we shall save ourselves from the evil that has fallen upon Ireland. I think we shall satisfy the moderate, and take even from the violent (if any such there be) the power of increasing their numbers and of making converts to their schemes. This, sir, is my solemn opinion, and upon this ground it is that I recommend with earnestness and solicitude the proposition of my honorable friend.

Intimation that Mr. Fox designed to withdraw, to some extent, from the House.

And now, sir, before I sit down, allow me to make a single observation with respect to the character and conduct of those who have, in conjunction with myself, felt it their duty to oppose the progress of this disastrous war. I hear it said, "You do nothing but mischief when you are here; and yet we should be sorry to see you away." I do not know how we shall be able to satisfy the gentlemen who feel toward us in this way. If we can neither do our duty without mischief, nor please them with doing nothing, I know but of one way by which we can give them content, and that is by putting an end to our existence. With respect to myself, and I believe I can also speak for others, I do not feel it consistent with my duty totally to secede from this House. I have no such intention; but, sir, I have no hesitation in saying, that, after seeing the conduct of this House; after seeing them give to ministers their confidence and support, upon convicted failure, imposition, and incapacity; after seeing them deaf and blind to the consequences of a career that penetrates the hearts of all other men with alarm, and that neither reason, experience, nor duty, are sufficiently powerful to influence them to oppose the conduct of government; I certainly do think I may devote more of my time to my private pursuits, and to the retirement which I love, than I have hitherto done; I certainly think I need not devote much of it to fruitless exertions, and to idle talk, in this House. Whenever it shall appear that my efforts may contribute in any degree to restore us to the situation from which the confidence of this House in a desperate system and an incapable administration, has so suddenly reduced us, I shall be found ready to discharge my duty.[10]

Peroration: The tendency of things, for years, has been to aggrandize the Crown at the expense of the people.

Sir, I have done. I have given my advice. I propose the remedy, and fatal will it be for England if pride and prejudice much longer continue to oppose it. The remedy which is proposed is simple, easy, and practicable; it does not touch the vitals of the Constitution; and I sincerely believe it will restore us to peace and harmony. Do you not think that you *must* come to parliamentary reform soon? and is it not better to come to it now, when you have the power of deliberation, than when, perhaps, it may be extorted from you by convulsion? There is as yet time to frame it with freedom and discussion; it will even yet go to the people with the grace and favor of a spontaneous act. What will it be when it is extorted from you with indignation and violence? God forbid that this should be the case! but now is the moment to prevent it; and now, I say, wisdom and policy recommend it to you, when you may enter into all the considerations to which it leads, rather than to postpone it to a time when you will have nothing to consider but the number and the force of those who demand it. It is asked, whether liberty has not gained much of late years, and whether the popular branch ought not, therefore, to be content? To this I answer, that if liberty has gained much, *power has gained more*. Power has been indefatigable and unwearied in its encroachments. Every thing has run in that direction through the whole course of the present reign. This was the opinion of Sir George Savile, of the Marquis of Rockingham, and of all the virtuous men who, in their public life, proved themselves to be advocates for the rights of the people. They saw and deplored the tendency of the Court; they saw that there was a determined spirit in the secret advisers of the Crown to advance its power, and to encourage no administration that should not bend itself to that pursuit. Accordingly, through the whole reign, no administration which cherished notions of a different kind has been permitted to last; and nothing, therefore, or next to nothing, has been gained to the side of the people, but every thing to that of the Crown, in the course of this reign. During the whole of this period, we have had no more than three administrations, one for twelve months, one for nine, and one for three months, that acted upon the popular principles of the early part of this century: nothing, therefore, I say, has been gained to the people, while the constant current has run toward the Crown; and God knows what is to be the consequence, both to the Crown and the country! I believe that we are come to the last moment of possible remedy. I believe that at this moment the enemies of both are few; but I firmly believe that what has been seen in Ireland will be experienced also here; and that if we are to go on in the same career with convention bills and acts of exasperation of all kinds, the few will soon become the many, and that we shall have to pay a severe retribution for our present pride. What a noble Lord said some time ago of France may be applicable to this very subject—"What!" said he, "negotiate with France? with

[10] Mr. Fox did for some time discontinue a regular attendance on the House.

men whose hands are reeking with the blood of their Sovereign? What, shall we degrade ourselves by going to Paris, and there asking in humble, diplomatic language, to be on a good understanding with them?" Gentlemen will remember these lofty words; and yet we have come to this humiliation; we have negotiated with France; and I should not be surprised to see the noble Lord himself (Hawkesbury) going to Paris, not at the head of his regiment, but on a diplomatic mission to those very regicides, to pray to be upon a good understanding with them. Shall we, then, be blind to the lessons which the events of the world exhibit to our view? Pride, obstinacy, and insult, must end in concessions, and those concessions must be humble in proportion to our unbecoming pride. Now is the moment to prevent all these degradations; the monarchy, the aristocracy, the people themselves, may now be saved; it is only necessary, at this moment, to conquer our own passions. Let those ministers whose evil genius has brought us to our present condition retire from the post to which they are unequal. I have no hesitation in saying, that the present administration neither can nor ought to remain in place. Let them retire from his Majesty's councils, and then let us, with an earnest desire of recovering the country, pursue this moderate scheme of reform, under the auspices of men who are likely to conciliate the opinion of the people. I do not speak this, sir, from personal ambition. A new administration ought to be formed: I have no desire, no wish to make a part of any such administration; and I am sure that such an arrangement is feasible, and that it is capable of being done without me. My first and chief desire is to see this great end accomplished. I have no wish to be the person, or to be one of the persons, to do it; but though my inclination is for retirement, I shall always be ready to give my free and firm support to any administration that shall restore to the country its outraged rights, and re-establish its strength upon the basis of free representation; and therefore, sir, I shall certainly give my vote for the proposition of my honorable friend.

On a division, the numbers were, Yeas, 93; Noes, 253. Mr. Grey's motion was therefore rejected.

SPEECH

OF MR. FOX ON THE REJECTION OF BONAPARTE'S OVERTURES FOR PEACE, DELIVERED IN THE HOUSE OF COMMONS, FEBRUARY 3, 1800.

INTRODUCTION.

Napoleon Bonaparte, having usurped the government of France, became First Consul in December, 1799; and, as an air of moderation seemed appropriate under these circumstances, he made overtures of peace to the King of England, in a letter written with his own hand. Mr. Pitt, who had no belief in the permanence of his power, rejected his offers in terms which were certainly rude, if not insulting. Some of them will be given hereafter in notes to this speech.

The correspondence in question was laid before Parliament, and, on the 3d of February, 1800, a motion was made by Mr. Dundas approving of the course taken, and pledging the country for a vigorous prosecution of the war. After Mr. Whitbread, Mr. Canning, and Mr. Erskine had spoken, Mr. Pitt rose, and held the House in fixed attention for nearly five hours by one of the most masterly orations he ever pronounced in Parliament. Mr. Fox then delivered the following speech in reply; and never were these two great orators brought into more direct competition, or the distinctive features of their eloquence exhibited in finer contrast.

Mr. Pitt, instead of entering at once on the reasons for refusing at that time to negotiate, treated the rise of Napoleon as only a new stage of the French Revolution, and thus dextrously prepared the way for going back to consider.

I. The origin of the war, maintaining that France was the sole aggressor throughout the whole conflict.

II. The atrocities of the French in overrunning and subjugating a large part of Europe during the preceding eight years.

III. The genius and spirit of the Revolution, as "an insatiable love of aggrandizement, an implacable spirit of destruction against all the civil and religious institutions of every country."

IV. The instability of the system, as marked from the first by sudden and great changes.

V. The past history and character of Napoleon, whom he depicted in the darkest colors, as devoid of all faith, the inveterate enemy of England, and the cruel oppressor of every country he had overrun. His power he represented as wholly unstable, and insisted that England ought never to enter into a treaty with him until, "from *experience* and the *evidence of facts*, we are convinced that such a treaty is admissible." On these grounds he defended his refusal to negotiate. This speech should be taken up previous to the one before us, if the reader intends to enter fully into the merits of the case.

Mr. Fox, in reply, without the exactness of Mr. Pitt's method, touches upon most of these points, and adverts to others with great pungency and force.

He condemns Mr. Pitt for reviving the early animosities of the contest as a reason for refusing to treat, since on this principle the war must be eternal.

He censures the severe and unconciliating terms in which a respectful offer of negotiation had been rejected.

He insists, in regard to the origin of the war, that Austria and Prussia (so long the allies of England) were undeniably the aggressors; that England provoked the contest by harsh treatment of the French minister; that, in relation to her grievances, she ought from the first to have stated definitely to the French what would satisfy her; that she ought, especially, to have accepted the mediation urged upon her by France, before a single blow had been struck, with a view to prevent the contest; that the English were, therefore, far from being guiltless as to the origin of the war, while the French, in all their aggressions, had been simply carrying out the principles taught them by the Bourbons, whom Mr. Pitt now proposed to restore.

While condemning the atrocities of the French, he sets off against them the outrages practiced on Poland and other countries by the powers in league with England; and exposes the inconsistency of refusing, on the ground of *character*, to treat with the French, while such rank oppressors were taken into the strictest alliance.

He dwells upon the fact, that Mr. Pitt, who now refused to treat on account of the outrages of the French and the instability of their government, had *himself* twice opened negotiations (in 1796 and 1797) in the midst of these very outrages, while the existing governments were confessedly of the most unstable kind, and comments with great severity upon Mr. Pitt's explanation of his conduct on those occasions.

Finally, in reference to the question, "When is this war to end?" he considers the grounds on which Mr. Pitt had intimated a willingness to treat with Bonaparte, if the Bourbons could not be restored, viz., "*experience* and the evidence of facts;" he adverts for a moment to some of the charges brought against the First Consul; and, recurring again to the grounds stated, inquires, "Where, then, is this war, which is pregnant with all these horrors, to be carried? Where is it to stop? *Not till we establish the house of Bourbon*"—or, at least, not until we have had due "*experience*" of Bonaparte's intentions. "So that we are called upon to go on merely as a *speculation*"—"to keep Bonaparte some time longer at war, as a state of *probation*"—"to try an EXPERIMENT, if he will not behave himself better than heretofore!" With this thought he concludes, in the boldest and most eloquent strain of mingled argument, irony, and invective which he ever produced.

The speech is admirably reported, and was considered by most who heard it as the ablest Mr. Fox ever made.

SPEECH, &c.

Mr. Speaker,—At so late an hour of the night, I am sure you will do me the justice to believe that I do not mean to go at length into the discussion of this great question. Exhausted as the attention of the House must be, and unaccustomed as I have been of late to attend in my place, nothing but a deep sense of my duty could have induced me to trouble you at all, and particularly to request your indulgence at such an hour.

A new era in the war, but the old arguments used for its continuance.

Sir, my honorable and learned friend [Mr. Erskine] has truly said, that the present is a new era in the war, and the right honorable gentleman opposite to me [Mr. Pitt] feels the justice of the remark; for, by traveling back to the commencement of the war, and referring again to all the topics and arguments which he has so often and so successfully urged upon the House, and by which he has drawn them on to the support of his measures, he is forced to acknowledge that, at the end of a seven years' conflict, we are come but to a new era in the war, at which he thinks it necessary only to press all his former arguments to induce us to persevere. All the topics which have so often misled us—all the reasoning which has so invariably failed—all the lofty predictions which have so constantly been falsified by events—all the hopes which have amused the sanguine, and all the assurances of the distress and weakness of the enemy which have satisfied the unthinking, are again enumerated and advanced as arguments for our continuing the war. What! at the end of seven years of the most burdensome and the most calamitous struggle in which this country ever was engaged, are we again to be amused with notions of finance, and calculations of the exhausted resources of the enemy, as a ground of confidence and of hope? Gracious God! were we not told five years ago that France was not only on the brink and in the jaws of ruin, but that she was actually sunk into the gulf of bankruptcy? Were we not told, as an unanswerable argument against treating, "that she could not hold out another campaign—that nothing but peace could save her—that she wanted only time to recruit her exhausted finances—that to grant her repose was to grant her the means of again molesting this country, and that we had nothing to do but persevere for a short time, in order to save ourselves forever from the consequences of her ambition and her jacobinism?" What! after having gone on from year to year upon assurances like these, and after having seen the repeated refutations of every prediction, are we again to be gravely and seriously assured, that we have the same prospect of success on the *same identical grounds?* And, without any other argument or security, are we invited, at this new era of the war, to conduct it upon principles which, if adopted and acted upon, may make it eternal? If the right honorable gentleman shall succeed in prevailing on Parliament and the country to adopt the principles which he has advanced this night, I see no possible termination to the contest. No man can see an end to it; and upon the assurances and predictions which have so uniformly failed, we are called upon not merely to refuse all negotiation, but to countenance principles and views as distant from wisdom and justice, as they are in their nature wild and impracticable.

Ministers censurable for using harsh language in declining to negotiate.

I must lament, sir, in common with every genuine friend of peace, the harsh and unconciliating language which ministers have held to the French, and which they have even made use of in their answer to a respectful offer of a negotiation.[1] Such language has ever been considered as extremely unwise, and has ever been reprobated by diplomatic men. I remember with pleasure the terms in which Lord Malmesbury, at Paris, in the year 1796, replied to expressions of this sort, used by M. de la Croix. He justly said, "that offensive and injurious insinuations were only calculated to throw new obstacles in the way of accommodation, and that it was not by revolting reproaches nor by reciprocal invective that a sincere wish to accomplish the great work of pacification could be evinced."[2] Nothing could be more proper nor more wise than this language; and such ought ever to be the tone and conduct of men intrusted with the very important task of treating with a hostile nation. Being a sincere friend to peace, I must say with Lord Malmesbury, that it is not by reproaches and by invective that we can hope for a reconciliation; and I am convinced, in my own mind, that I speak the sense of this House, and, if not of this House, certainly of a majority of the people of this country, when I lament that any unprovoked and unnecessary recriminations should be flung out, by which obstacles are put in the way of pacification. I believe it is the prevailing sentiment of the people, that we ought to abstain from harsh and insulting language; and in common with them, I must lament that both in the papers of Lord Grenville, and this night, such license has been given to invective and reproach.[3]

The original and early circumstances of the war not now the question.

For the same reason, I must lament that the right honorable gentleman [Mr. Pitt] has thought proper to go at such length, and with such severity of minute investigation, into all the early circumstances of the war, which (whatever they were) are nothing to the present purpose, and ought not to influence the present feelings of the House. I certainly shall not follow him through the whole of this tedious detail, though I do not agree with him in many of his assertions. I do not know what impression his narrative may make on other gentlemen; but I will tell him fairly and candidly, he has not convinced me. I continue to think, and until I see better grounds for changing my opinion than any that the right honorable gentleman has this night produced, I shall continue to think, and to say, plainly and explicitly, "that this country was the aggressor in the war."

The British allies, Austria and Prussia, undeniably the aggressors.

But with regard to Austria and Prussia—is there a man who, for one moment, can dispute that they were the aggressors? It will be vain for the right honorable gentleman to enter into long and plausible reasoning against the evidence of documents so clear, so decisive—so frequently, so thoroughly investigated. The unfortunate monarch, Louis XVI., himself, as well as those who were in his confidence, has borne decisive testimony to the fact, that between him and the Emperor [Leopold of Austria] there was an intimate correspondence and a perfect understanding. Do I mean by this that a positive treaty was entered into for the dismemberment of France? Certainly not. But no man can read

[1] The language referred to was of the following kind. As a reason for refusing to negotiate, Lord Grenville goes back to the *origin* of the war, declaring it to have been "an *unprovoked* attack" on the part of France. He says it sprung out of "a system, to the prevalence of which France justly ascribes all her present miseries, and which has involved all the rest of Europe in a long and destructive warfare, of a nature long since unknown to the practice of civilized nations"—he assumes that this system "*continues* to prevail; that the most solemn treaties have only prepared a way for fresh aggressions;" and ascribes to the French those "gigantic objects of ambition, and those restless schemes of destruction, which have endangered the very existence of civil society." In addition to this, he tells the French people, through their new ruler, that they ought at once *to take back the Bourbons;* that "the best and most natural pledge" they can give of a desire for peace, is "the restoration of that line of princes which for so many centuries maintained the French nation in prosperity at home, and consideration and respect abroad." He tells Bonaparte in direct terms, that England can not *trust* him; that there is "no sufficient evidence of the principles by which the new government will be directed; no reasonable ground by which to judge of its stability." Such language deserved the censures passed upon it by Mr. Fox. Nothing could more irritate the French people than to talk to them of restoring that hated dynasty against which they had so lately rebelled. Nothing was more calculated to provoke Bonaparte to the utmost, and to foster a desire to invade England (which he attempted some years after), than personal reflections of this kind on the stability of his government.

[2] This is one of Mr. Fox's characteristic arguments, *ad hominem.* It was Mr. Pitt (through his embassador) who thus reproved the French minister, M. de la Croix, for certain harsh expressions used during the negotiations for peace in 1796; and Mr. Fox now turns the reproof back upon Mr. Pitt, in language dictated by himself.

[3] Warmly as Mr. Wilberforce was attached to Mr. Pitt, he expressed himself still more strongly on this subject in a letter to a friend. "I must say I was shocked at Lord Grenville's letter; for though our government must feel adverse to any measure which might appear to give the stamp of our authority to Bonaparte's new dignity, yet I must say that unless they have some better reason than I fear they possess for believing that he is likely to be hurled from his throne, it seems a desperate game to play —to offend, and insult, and thereby irritate, this vain man beyond the hope of forgiveness."—*Life,* 215.

the declarations which were made at Mantua,[4] as well as at Pilnitz, as they are given by M. Bertrand de Molville, without acknowledging that this was not merely an intention; but a *declaration* of an intention, on the part of the great powers of Germany, to interfere in the internal affairs of France, for the purpose of regulating the government, against the opinion of the people. This, though not a plan for the partition of France, was, in the eye of reason and common sense, an aggression against France. The right honorable gentleman denies that there was such

Declaration of Pilnitz.

a thing as a treaty of Pilnitz. Granted. But was there not a Declaration which amounted to an act of hostile aggression?[5] The two powers, the Emperor of Germany and the King of Prussia, made a public declaration, that they were determined to employ their forces, in conjunction with those of the other Sovereigns of Europe, "to put the King of France in a situation to establish, in perfect liberty, the foundations of a monarchical government equally agreeable to the rights of Sovereigns and the welfare of the French." Whenever the other princes should agree to co-operate with them, "*then, and in that case*, their Majesties were determined to act promptly, and by mutual consent, with the forces necessary to obtain the end proposed by all of them. In the mean time, they declared that they would give orders for their troops to be ready for actual service." Now, I would ask gentlemen to lay their hands upon their hearts, and say with candor what the true and fair construction of this Declaration was—whether it was not a menace and an insult to France, since, in direct terms, it declared, that whenever the other powers should concur, they would attack France, then at peace with them, and then employed only in domestic and internal regulations? Let us suppose the case to be that of Great Britain. Will any gentleman say that if two of the great powers should make a public declaration, that they were determined to make an attack on this kingdom as soon as circumstances should favor their intention; that they only waited for this occasion, and that in the mean time they would keep their forces ready for the purpose, it would not be considered by the Parliament and people of this country as a hostile aggression? And is there any Englishman in existence who is such a friend to peace as to say that the nation could retain its honor and dignity if it should sit down under such a menace? I know too well what is due to the national character of England to believe that there would be two opinions on the case, if thus put home to our own feelings and understandings. We must, then, respect in others the indignation which such an act would excite in ourselves; and when we see it established, on the most indisputable testimony, that both at Pilnitz and at Mantua declarations were made to this effect, it is idle to say that, as far as the Emperor and the King of Prussia were concerned, they were not the aggressors in the war.

"Oh! but the decree of the 19th of November, 1792."[6] That, at least, the right honorable

---

[4] The Count d'Artois, brother of the King of France, met the Emperor Leopold of Austria, the King of Sardinia, and the King of Spain, at Mantua, in May, 1791, and, on his representation, these monarchs entered into an agreement to march one hundred thousand men to the borders of France, in expectation that the French people, terrified at the approach of the allied powers, would seek safety by submitting themselves to Louis XVI., and asking his mediation; but Louis, hoping at that time to restore the monarchy by his own efforts, discouraged the immediate execution of the plan. See *Mignet*, p. 119; *Alison's History of Europe*, vol. i., p. 571, third edition.

[5] The following is a copy of this celebrated Declaration, which led to a general war in Europe. It was framed in August, 1791, at Pilnitz, a fortress in Saxony, by the Emperor Leopold and the King of Prussia, and was given to the Count d'Artois, that he might use it to induce the other courts of Europe to enter into a league for restoring Louis XVI.

"His Majesty the Emperor, and his Majesty the King of Prussia, having heard the desires and representations of Monsieur and of his royal highness the Count d'Artois, declare jointly, that they regard the situation in which his Majesty the King of France actually is, as an object of common interest to all the Sovereigns of Europe. They hope that this concern can not fail to be acknowledged by the powers whose assistance is claimed; and that in consequence they will not refuse to employ jointly with their said Majesties the most efficacious means, in proportion to their forces, to place the King of France in a state to settle in the most perfect liberty the foundations of a monarchical government, equally suitable to the rights of Sovereigns and the welfare of the French. Then and in that case, their said Majesties are decided to act quickly and with one accord with the forces necessary to obtain the common end proposed. In the mean time they will give suitable orders to their troops, that they may be ready to put themselves in motion."—*Alison's History of Europe*, vol. i., p. 574, third edition.

The French justly regarded this as a hostile act, and, after calling in vain for an explanation from the Emperor, who had marched large bodies of troops to their borders, they declared war against Austria on the 20th of April, 1792. Prussia instantly united with Austria, and, three months after, July 25th, 1792, the Duke of Brunswick invaded France at the head of one hundred and thirty-eight thousand Austrian and Prussian troops.

[6] This famous "Decree of Fraternity" was passed under the following circumstances. The allied Austrian and Prussian armies, under the Duke of Brunswick, were beaten back by the French, who immediately pressed forward into the Austrian Netherlands; and made themselves masters of the country by the decisive battle of Jemmape, November 6th, 1792. When the news reached Paris, the decree in question was passed in the exultation felt at this and other victories of the republic. It was in the following words:

"The National Convention declare, in the name of the French nation, they will grant fraternity and assistance to all those people who wish to procure liberty. And they charge the executive power to send orders to the generals to give assistance to such people; and to defend citizens who have suffered, and are now suffering, in the cause of liberty."—*Alison*, vol. i., p. 592, third edition.

The reader will decide whether to consider it with

gentleman says, you must allow to be an act of aggression, not only against England, but against all the Sovereigns of Europe. I am not one of those, sir, who attach much interest to the general and indiscriminate provocations thrown out at random, like this resolution of the 19th of November, 1792. I do not think it necessary to the dignity of any people to notice and to apply to themselves menaces without particular allusion, which are always unwise in the power which uses them, and which it is still more unwise to treat with seriousness. But if any such idle and general provocation to nations is given, either in insolence or in folly, by any government, it is a clear first principle, that an *explanation* is the thing which a magnanimous nation, feeling itself aggrieved, ought to demand; and if an explanation be given which is not satisfactory, it ought clearly and distinctly to say so. There should be no ambiguity, no reserve, on the occasion. Now we all know, from documents on our table, that M. Chauvelin [the French minister] did give an explanation of this silly decree. He declared, "in the name of his government, that it was never meant that the French government should favor insurrections; that the decree was applicable only to those people who, after having acquired their liberty by conquest, should demand the assistance of the Republic; but that France would respect, not only the independence of England, but also that of her allies with whom she was not at war." This was the explanation of the offensive decree. "But this explanation was not satisfactory." Did you *say so* to M. Chauvelin? Did you tell him that you were not content with this explanation? and when you dismissed him, afterward, on the death of the King [of France], did you say that this explanation was unsatisfactory? No. You did no such thing; and I contend, that unless you demanded *further* explanations, and they were refused, you have no right to urge the decree of the 19th of November as an act of aggression. In all your conferences and correspondence with M. Chauvelin, did you hold out to him *what terms would satisfy you?* Did you give the French the power or the means of settling the misunderstanding which that decree, or any other of the points at issue, had created? I maintain, that when a nation refuses to state to another the thing which would satisfy her, she shows that she is not actuated by a desire to preserve peace between them; and I aver that this was the case here. The Scheldt, for instance. You now say that the navigation of the Scheldt was one of your causes of complaint.[7] Did you explain yourself on that subject? Did you make it one of the grounds for the dismissal of M. Chauvelin? Sir, I repeat it, that *a nation, to justify itself in appealing to the last solemn resort, ought to prove that it has taken every possible means, consistent with dignity, to demand the reparation and redress which would be satisfactory; and if she refuses to explain what would be satisfactory, she does not do her duty, nor exonerate herself from the charge of being the aggressor.*

Decree of the French National Convention.

Explanation of this decree by the French minister at London.

If not satisfactory, the ministry were bound to say so, and declare what would satisfy.

The right honorable gentleman has this night, for the first time, produced a most important paper; the instructions which were given to his Majesty's minister at the court of St. Petersburgh, about the end of the year 1792, to induce her Imperial Majesty to join her efforts with those of his Britannic Majesty, to prevent, by their joint mediation, the evils of a general war. Of this paper, and of the existence of any such document, I, for one, was wholly ignorant. But I have no hesitation in saying that I entirely approve of the instructions which appear to have been given; and I am sorry to see the right honorable gentleman disposed rather to take blame to himself than credit for having written them. He thinks that he shall be subject to the imputation of having been rather too slow to apprehend the dangers with which the French Revolution was fraught, than that he was forward and hasty—"Quod solum excusat, hoc solum miror in illo."[8] I do not agree with him. I by no means think that he was blamable for too much confidence in the good intentions of the French. I think the tenor and composition of this paper was excellent—the instructions conveyed in it wise, and that it wanted but one essential thing to have entitled it to general approbation, namely, *to have been acted upon!* The clear nature and intent of that paper I take to be, that our ministers were to solicit the court of Petersburgh to join with them in a declaration to the French government, stating explicitly what course of conduct, with respect to their foreign relations, they thought necessary to the general peace and security of Europe, and what, if complied with, would have induced them to mediate for that purpose. This was a proper, wise, and legitimate course of proceeding. Now, I ask you, sir, whether, if this paper had been communicated to Paris, at the end of the year 1792, instead of Petersburgh, it would not have been productive of most seasonable benefits to mankind; and, by informing the French in time of the means by which they might have secured the mediation of Great Britain, have not only avoided the rupture with this country, but have also restored general peace to

The plan of uniting with Russia to prevent the war would have been praiseworthy if only acted upon.

Mr. Fox, as an empty vaunt, or with Mr. Pitt, as a declaration of war against all the thrones of Europe.

[7] When the French conquered the Austrian Netherlands (as mentioned in the preceding note), they forcibly opened the navigation of its principal river, the Scheldt, down to the sea. This had been closed for nearly one hundred and fifty years, out of regard to the rights of Holland (through which it entered the ocean), under the provisions of the treaty of Westphalia, which settled the political relations of modern Europe. Holland and her protector, England, had just ground of complaint for the aggression, though it was too unimportant in itself to justify a war.

[8] The only thing he excuses is the only thing in him which I admire.

the continent? The paper, sir, was excellent in its intentions; but its merit was all in the composition. It was a fine theory, which ministers did not think proper to carry into practice. It was very much like what the right honorable gentleman at the head of the Board of Control [Mr. Dundas] said some years ago of the commercial system upon which we have maintained our government in the East Indies. "Nothing could be more moral, more beautiful, and benevolent, than the instructions which were sent out to our governors; but unfortunately those instructions had been confined to the registers of the corporation; they were to be found only in the minute-books of Leadenhall Street. Their beneficial effects had never been felt by the people, for whose protection and happiness the theories were framed."[9] In the same manner, this very commendable paper, so well digested, and so likely to preserve us from the calamities of war, was never communicated to the French; never acted upon; never known to the world until this day; nay, on the contrary, at the very time that ministers had drawn up this paper, they were insulting M. Chauvelin in every way, until about the 23d or 24th of January, 1793, when they finally dismissed him, without stating any one ground upon which they were willing to preserve terms with the French.[10]

England the aggressor in dismissing M. Chauvelin.

But "France," it seems, "then declared war against us; and she was the aggressor, because the declaration came from her." Let us look at the circumstances of this transaction on both sides. Undoubtedly the declaration was made by them; but is a declaration the only thing which constitutes the commencement of a war? Do gentlemen recollect that, in consequence of a dispute about the commencement of war, respecting the capture of a number of ships, an article was inserted in our treaty with France, by which it was positively stipulated that in future, to prevent all disputes, the act of the *dismissal* of a minister from either of the two courts should be held and considered as tantamount to a declaration of war?[11] I mention this, sir, because when we are idly employed in this retrospect of the origin of a war which has lasted so many years, instead of turning our eyes only to the contemplation of the means of putting an end to it, we seem disposed to overlook every thing on our own parts, and to search only for grounds of imputation on the enemy. I almost think it an insult on the House to detain them with this sort of examination. Why, sir, if France was the aggressor, as the right honorable gentleman says she was

[9] It is striking to see how dexterously Mr. Fox turns back Mr. Dundas' words upon himself in this case, as he did those of Lord Malmesbury upon Mr. Pitt on a preceding page.

[10] As the treatment of M. Chauvelin formed the hinge of the controversy between Mr. Fox and Mr. Pitt, it will be proper briefly to remind the reader of the principal dates and facts. M. Chauvelin was sent to London as French minister by Louis XVI. When that monarch was virtually deposed by the events of August 10th, 1792, M. Chauvelin was informed that his functions as minister were suspended, and though new credentials were sent him by the existing French government, they were not received. Informal communications did, however, pass between him and Lord Grenville, the Secretary of Foreign Affairs, but the tone of his Lordship was considered, not only by the French, but by Mr. Fox and his friends, as offensive, and even insulting. M. Chauvelin was addressed as *styling himself* plenipotentiary of France, and reminded that all *official* communication with that country had ceased. He was told that France "must *confine* herself within her own territory, without insulting other governments, without disturbing their tranquillity, without violating their rights." Such language, when France had been asking the mediation of England to prevent a general war in Europe, and while she was offering explanations of her decrees, was strongly condemned by Mr. Fox. Even if but little confidence could be reposed in the sincerity of the French, this treatment was felt to be wrong and irritating. On the 24th of January, 1793, three days after Louis XVI. was beheaded, the following note was addressed to M. Chauvelin by Lord Grenville: "I am charged to notify you, sir, that the character with which you have been invested at this court, and the functions which have so long been suspended, being now entirely terminated by the fatal death of his Most Christian Majesty, you have no longer any public character here; and his Majesty has thought proper to order that you should retire from the kingdom within the term of eight days."

Mr. Pitt justified his sending M. Chauvelin out of the kingdom on this ground, that by the death of Louis XVI. he was reduced to the character of a private individual; and was ordered to leave the country under the Alien Act, which authorized the government to send out of the kingdom any foreigners they thought proper.

[11] This was the treaty of Commerce and Navigation made with France by Mr. Pitt, September 26th, 1786. The second article contains the provision here referred to. Mr. Pitt could answer Mr. Fox's argument only by saying, "This article does not *now* apply. I made the treaty with the regal government of France, and it can not be pleaded in behalf of the new government, which I have not recognized." But unfortunately for Mr. Pitt, he *was continuing to act upon the Commercial Treaty as a treaty still in force.* And how could he do this, and yet not be subject to the article respecting the dismissal of a minister? By acting upon the treaty, he did in fact *recognize* the new government. This was Mr. Fox's argument in his letter to the electors of Westminster. "Every contract," says he, "must be at an end when the contracting parties have no longer any existence in their own persons, or by their representatives. After the tenth of August, 1792, the political existence of Louis XVI. (who was the contracting party in the Treaty of Commerce) was completely annihilated. The only question, therefore, is, whether the Executive Council of France did or did not *represent* the political power so annihilated? If we say they did not, the contracting party has no longer *any* political existence, either in his own person or by representation, and the treaty becomes null and void. If we say they did, then we have actually *acknowledged* them as representatives (for the time at least) of what was the executive government of France." Hence the dismissal of M. Chauvelin was, by the provisions of an existing treaty, a virtual declaration of war. So Mr. Fox contended.

throughout, did not Prussia call upon us for the stipulated number of troops, according to the article of the definitive treaty of alliance subsisting between us, by which, in case that either of the contracting parties was attacked, they had a right to demand the stipulated aid? and the same thing again may be asked when we were attacked. The right honorable gentleman might here accuse himself, indeed, of reserve; but it unfortunately happened, that *at the time* the point was too clear on which side the aggression lay. Prussia was too sensible that the war could not entitle her to make the demand, and that it was not a case within the scope of the defensive treaty. This is evidence worth a volume of subsequent reasoning; for if, at the time when all the facts were present to their minds, they could not take advantage of existing treaties, and that too when the courts were on the most friendly terms with one another, it will be manifest to every thinking man that *they were sensible they were not authorized to make the demand.*

France was attacked in her *internal*, and not merely in her *external* concerns.

I really, sir, can not think it necessary to follow the right honorable gentleman into all the minute details which he has thought proper to give us respecting the first aggression; but that Austria and Prussia were the aggressors, not a man in any country, who has ever given himself the trouble to think at all on the subject, can doubt. Nothing could be more hostile than their whole proceedings. Did they not declare to France, that it was her internal concerns, not her external proceedings, which provoked them to confederate against her? Look back to the proclamations with which they set out.[12] Read the declarations which they made themselves to justify their appeal to arms. They did not pretend to fear her ambition—her conquests—her troubling her neighbors; but they accused her of new-modeling her own government. They said nothing of her aggressions abroad. They spoke only of her clubs and societies at Paris.

The aggressions of the French utterly wrong, but conducted on Bourbon principles.

Sir, in all this, I am not justifying the French; I am not trying to absolve them from blame, either in their internal or external policy. I think, on the contrary, that their successive rulers have been as bad and as execrable, in various instances, as any of the most despotic and unprincipled governments that the world ever saw. I think it impossible, sir, that it should have been otherwise. It was not to be expected that the French, when once engaged in foreign wars, should not endeavor to spread destruction around them, and to form plans of aggrandizement and plunder on every side. Men bred in the school of the house of Bourbon could not be expected to act otherwise.[13] They could not have lived so long under their ancient masters without imbibing the restless ambition, the perfidy, and the insatiable spirit of the race. They have imitated the practice of their great prototype, and, through their whole career of mischiefs and of crimes, have done no more than servilely trace the steps of their own Louis XIV. If they have overrun countries and ravaged them, they have done it upon Bourbon principles; if they have ruined and dethroned Sovereigns, it is entirely after the Bourbon manner; if they have even fraternized with the people of foreign countries, and pretended to make their cause their own, they have only faithfully followed the Bourbon example. They have constantly had Louis, the Grand Monarque, in their eye. But it may be said, that this example was long ago, and that we ought not to refer to a period so distant. True, it is a remote period applied to the man, but not so of the principle. The principle was never extinct; nor has its operation been suspended in France, except, perhaps, for a short interval, during the administration of Cardinal Fleury; and my complaint against the Republic of France is, not that she has generated new crimes—not that she has promulgated new mischief—but that she has adopted and acted upon the principles which have been so fatal to Europe under the practice of the house of Bourbon. It is said, that where-ever the French have gone, they have introduced revolution—they have sought for the means of disturbing neighboring states, and have not been content with mere conquest. What is this but adopting the ingenious scheme of Louis XIV.? He was not content with merely overrunning a state. Whenever he came into a new territory, he established what he called his chamber of claims, a most convenient device, by which he inquired whether the conquered country or province had any dormant or disputed claims—any cause of complaint—any unsettled demand upon any other state or province—upon which he might wage war upon such state, thereby discover again ground for new devastation, and gratify his ambition by new acquisitions. What have the republicans done more atrocious, more Jacobinical than this? Louis went to war with Holland. His pretext was, that Holland had not treated him with sufficient *respect*. A very just and proper cause for war indeed!

Treaties were made with the Bourbons, and ought now to be made with the French, without going back to the *origin* of the war.

This, sir, leads me to an example which I think seasonable, and worthy the attention of his Majesty's ministers. When our Charles II., as a short exception to the policy of his reign, made the triple alliance for the protection of Europe, and particularly of Holland, against the ambition of Louis XIV., what was the conduct of that great, virtuous, and most

12 The manifesto of the Duke of Brunswick when he invaded France, declared that "all persons found in arms against the allied powers should be punished as *rebels* to their King; and in case the King and Queen were not immediately *set at liberty*, the city of Paris was threatened with the horrors of military execution, with avenging punishment and total destruction."

13 There is great adroitness in thus tracing the French spirit of aggression to the principles and practice of the Bourbons, especially as Mr. Pitt, in refusing to treat with Bonaparte, had pointed to the restoration of the Bourbons as the most certain mode of preparing the way for peace.

able statesman, M. de Witt, when the confederates came to deliberate upon the terms upon which they should treat with the French monarch? When it was said that he had made unprincipled conquests, and that he ought to be forced to surrender them all, what was the language of that great and wise man? "No," said he; "I think we ought not to look back to the origin of the war so much as the means of putting an end to it. If you had united in time to prevent these conquests, well; but now that he has made them, he stands upon the ground of conquest, and we must agree to treat with him, not with reference to the origin of the conquest, but with regard to his present posture. He has those places, and some of them we must be content to give up as the means of peace; for conquest will always successfully set up its claims to indemnification." Such was the language of this minister, who was the ornament of his time; and such, in my mind, ought to be the language of statesmen, with regard to the French, at this day; and the same ought to have been said at the formation of the confederacy. It was true that the French had overrun Savoy; but they had overrun it upon Bourbon principles; and, having gained this and other conquests before the confederacy was formed, they ought to have treated with her rather for future security, than for past correction. States in possession, whether monarchical or republican, will claim indemnity in proportion to their success; and it will never so much be inquired by what right they gained possession, as by what means they can be prevented from enlarging their depredations. Such is the safe practice of the world; and such ought to have been the conduct of the powers when the reduction of Savoy made them coalesce. The right honorable gentleman may know more of the secret particulars of their overrunning Savoy than I do; but certainly, as they have come to my knowledge, it was a most Bourbon-like act. A great and justly celebrated historian, I mean Mr. Hume, a writer certainly estimable in many particulars, but who is a childish lover of Princes, talks of Louis XIV. in very magnificent terms. But he says of him, that, though he managed his enterprises with great skill and bravery, he was unfortunate in this, *that he never got a good and fair pretense for war*. This he reckons among his misfortunes. Can we say more of the republican French? In seizing on Savoy, I think they made use of the words "*convénances morales et physiques*."[14] These were her reasons. A most Bourbon-like phrase. And I therefore contend, that as we never scrupled to treat with the princes of the house of Bourbon on account of their rapacity, their thirst of conquest, their violation of treaties, their perfidy, and their restless spirit, so, I contend, we ought not to refuse to treat with their republican imitators.

Ministers could not pretend ignorance of the unprincipled manner in which the French had seized on Savoy. The Sardinian minister complained of the aggression, and yet no stir was made about it. The courts of Europe stood by and saw the outrage; and our ministers saw it. The right honorable gentleman will in vain, therefore, exert his powers to persuade me of the interest he takes in the preservation of the rights of nations, since, at the moment when an interference might have been made with effect, no step was taken, no remonstrance made, no mediation negotiated, to stop the career of conquest. All the pretended and hypocritical sensibility "for the rights of nations, and for social order," with which we have since been stunned, can not impose upon those who will take the trouble to look back to the period when this sensibility ought to have roused us into seasonable exertion. At that time, however, the right honorable gentleman makes it his boast that he was prevented, by a sense of neutrality, from taking any measures of precaution on the subject. I do not give the right honorable gentleman much credit for his spirit of neutrality on the occasion. It flowed from the sense of the country at the time, the great majority of which was clearly and decidedly against all interruptions being given to the French in their desire of regulating their own internal government.

Savoy ought to have been protected *at the time*, and not now made the ground of continuing the war.

But this neutrality, which respected only the internal rights of the French, and from which the people of England would never have departed but for the impolitic and hypocritical cant which was set up to arouse their jealousy and alarm their fears, was very different from the great principle of political prudence which ought to have actuated the councils of the nation, on seeing the first steps of France toward a career of external conquest. My opinion is, that when the unfortunate King of France offered to us, in the letter delivered by M. Chauvelin and M. Talleyrand, and even entreated us to mediate between him and the allied powers of Austria and Prussia, they [ministers] ought to have accepted of the offer, and exerted their influence to save Europe from the consequence of a system which was then beginning to manifest itself.[15] It was,

England ought to have accepted the mediation urged upon her by France.

[14] Conveniences moral and physical.

[15] Early in 1792 the King of France sent a letter to the King of England, through Talleyrand and Chauvelin, requesting the latter to mediate between France and the allied powers, Austria and Prussia. "I consider," says Louis, "the success of the alliance in which I wish you to concur with as much zeal as I do, as of the highest importance; I consider it as necessary to the stability of the respective Constitutions of our two kingdoms; and I will add that our union ought to *command peace to Europe*." A few weeks after, the French monarch again applied to the King of England, through M. Chauvelin, "to interpose, and, by his wisdom and influence, avert, while there is still time, the progress of the confederacy formed against France, and which threatened the peace, the liberties, and the happiness of Europe." After an interval of twenty days, July 8, 1792, the British government declined. The Duke of Brunswick invaded France at the close of the same month.

at least, a question of prudence; and as we had never refused to treat and to mediate with the old princes on account of their ambition or their perfidy, we ought to have been equally ready now, when the same principles were acted upon by other men. I must doubt the sensibility which could be so cold and so indifferent at the proper moment for its activity. I fear that there were at that moment the germs of ambition rising in the mind of the right honorable gentleman, and that he was beginning, like others, to entertain hopes that something might be obtained out of the coming confusion. What but such a sentiment could have prevented him from overlooking the fair occasion that was offered for preventing the calamities with which Europe was threatened? What but some such interested principle could have made him forego the truly honorable task, by which his administration would have displayed its magnanimity and its power? But for some such feeling, would not this country, both in wisdom and in dignity, have interfered, and, in conjunction with the other powers, have said to France, "You ask for a mediation. We will mediate with candor and sincerity, but we will at the same time declare to you our apprehensions. We do not trust to your assertion of a determination to avoid all foreign conquest, and that you are desirous only of settling your own Constitution, because your language is contradicted by experience and the evidence of facts. You are Frenchmen, and you can not so soon have forgotten and thrown off the Bourbon principles in which you were educated. You have already imitated the bad practice of your princes. You have seized on Savoy without a color of right. But here we take our stand. Thus far you have gone, and we can not help it; but you must go no farther. We will tell you distinctly what we shall consider as an attack on the balance and the security of Europe; and, as the condition of our interference, we will tell you also the securities that we think essential to the general repose." This ought to have been the language of his Majesty's ministers when their mediation was solicited; and something of this kind they evidently thought of when they sent the instructions to Petersburgh which they have mentioned this night, but upon which they never acted. Having not done so, I say they have no right to talk now about the violated rights of Europe, about the aggression of the French, and about the origin of the war in which this country was so suddenly afterward plunged. Instead of this, what did they do? They hung back; they avoided explanation; they gave the French no means of satisfying them; and I repeat my proposition—when there is a question of peace and war between two nations, *that government feels itself in the wrong which refuses to state with clearness and precision what she should consider as a satisfaction and a pledge of peace.*

The irreligion of the French no ground for refusing to treat.

Sir, if I understand the true precepts of the Christian religion, as set forth in the New Testament, I must be permitted to say, that there is no such thing as a rule or doctrine by which we are directed, or can be justified, in waging a war for religion. The idea is subversive of the very foundations upon which it stands, which are those of peace and good will among men. Religion never was and never can be a justifiable cause of war; but it has been too often grossly used as the pretext and the apology for the most unprincipled wars.

Though the French have done wrong, recrimination, at this late period, would render the war eternal.

I have already said, and I repeat it, that the conduct of the French to foreign nations can not be justified. They have given great cause of offense, but certainly not to all countries alike. The right honorable gentlemen opposite to me have made an indiscriminate catalogue of all the countries which the French have offended, and, in their eagerness to throw odium on the nation, have taken no pains to investigate the sources of their several quarrels. I will not detain you, sir, by entering into the long detail which has been given of their aggressions and their violences; but let me mention Sardinia as one instance which has been strongly insisted upon. Did the French attack Sardinia when at peace with them? No such thing. The King of Sardinia had accepted of a subsidy from Great Britain; and Sardinia was, to all intents and purposes, a belligerent power. Several other instances might be mentioned; but though. perhaps, in the majority of instances, the French may be unjustifiable, is this the moment for us to dwell upon these enormities—to waste our time, and inflame our passions by criminating and recriminating upon each other? There is no end to such a war. I have somewhere read, I think in Sir Walter Raleigh's History of the World, of a most bloody and fatal battle which was fought by two opposite armies, in which almost all the combatants on both sides were killed, "because," says the historian, "though they had offensive weapons on both sides, they had none for defense." So, in this war of words, if we are to use only offensive weapons—if we are to indulge only in invective and abuse, the contest must be eternal.

The French may recriminate on the powers allied with England.

If this war of reproach and invective is to be countenanced, may not the French with equal reason complain of the outrages and horrors committed by the powers opposed to them? If we must not treat with the French on account of the iniquity of their former transactions, ought we not to be as scrupulous of connecting ourselves with other powers equally criminal? Surely, sir, if we must be thus rigid in scrutinizing the conduct of an enemy, we ought to be equally careful in not committing ourselves, our honor, and our safety, with an ally who has manifested the same want of respect for the rights of other nations. Surely, if it is material to know the character of a power with whom you are about only to treat for peace, it is more material to know the character of allies with whom you are about to enter into the closest connection of friendship, and for whose exertions you are about to pay. Now, sir, what was the conduct of your own allies to Poland? Is there a single atrocity of the French, in Italy, in Switzerland, in Egypt, if you please, more unprincipled and inhuman than that of Russia, Austria, and Prussia, in Poland? What has there been in the conduct of the French to foreign powers; what in the violation of solemn treaties; what in the plunder, devastation, and dismemberment of unoffending countries; what in the horrors and murders perpetrated upon the subdued victims of their rage in any district which they have overrun, worse than the conduct of those three great powers in the miserable, devoted, and trampled on kingdom of Poland, and who have been, or are, our allies in this war for religion and social order, and the rights of nations? "Oh! but you regretted the partition of Poland!" Yes, regretted! you regretted the violence, and that is all you did. You united yourselves with the actors; you, in fact, by your acquiescence, confirmed the atrocity. But they are your allies; and though they overran and divided Poland, there was nothing, perhaps, in the manner of doing it which stamped it with peculiar infamy and disgrace. The hero of Poland [Suwarrow], perhaps, was merciful and mild! He was "as much superior to Bonaparte in bravery, and in the discipline which he maintained, as he was superior in virtue and humanity!" He was animated by the purest principles of Christianity, and was restrained in his career by the benevolent precepts which it inculcates! Was he? Let unfortunate Warsaw, and the miserable inhabitants of the suburb of Praga in particular, tell! What do we understand to have been the conduct of this magnanimous hero, with whom, it seems, Bonaparte is not to be compared? He entered the suburb of Praga, the most populous suburb of Warsaw; and there he let his soldiery loose on the miserable, unarmed, and unresisting people. Men, women, and children, nay, infants at the breast, were doomed to one indiscriminate massacre! Thousands of them were inhumanly, wantonly butchered! And for what? Because they had dared to join in a wish to meliorate their own condition as a people, and to improve their Constitution, which had been confessed by their own Sovereign to be in want of amendment. And such is the hero upon whom the cause of religion and social order is to repose! And such is the man whom we praise for his discipline and his virtue, and whom we hold out as our boast and our dependence; while the conduct of Bonaparte unfits him to be even treated with as an enemy?[16]

Switzerland was scandalously abused, but England first invited her to depart from her neutrality.

But the behavior of the French toward Switzerland raises all the indignation of the right honorable gentleman, and inflames his eloquence. I admire the indignation which he expresses, and I think he felt it, in speaking of this country, so dear and so congenial to every man who loves the sacred name of liberty. "He who loves liberty," says the right honorable gentleman, "thought himself at home on the favored and happy mountains of Switzerland, where she seemed to have taken up her abode under a sort of implied compact, among all other states, that she should not be disturbed in this her chosen asylum." I admire the eloquence of the right honorable gentleman in speaking of this country of liberty and peace, to which every man would desire, once in his life at least, to make a pilgrimage! But who, let me ask him, first proposed to the Swiss people to *depart from the neutrality*, which was their chief protection, and to join the confederacy against the French? I aver that a noble relation of mine [Lord Robert Fitzgerald], then the minister of England to the Swiss Cantons, was instructed, in direct terms, to propose to the Swiss, by an official note, to break from the safe line they had laid down for themselves, and to tell them, "in such a contest neutrality was criminal." I know that noble Lord too well, though I have not been in habits of intercourse with him of late, from the employments in which he has been engaged, to suspect that he would have presented such a paper without the express instructions of his court, or that he would have gone beyond those instructions.

Tuscany and Genoa solicited in the same way.

But was it only to Switzerland that this sort of language was held? What was our language also to Tuscany and Genoa? An honorable gentleman [Mr. Canning] has denied the authenticity of a pretended letter which has been circulated, and ascribed to Lord Harvey. He says, it is all a fable and a forgery. Be it so; but is it also a fable that Lord Harvey did speak in terms to the Grand Duke, which he considered as offensive and insulting? I can not tell, for I was not present; but was it not, and is it not believed? Is it a fable that Lord Harvey went into the closet of the Grand Duke, laid his watch on the table, and demanded, in a peremptory manner, that he should, within a certain number of minutes

[16] Praga was taken in the manner here described, on the 4th of November, 1794. Thirteen thousand Poles covered the field of battle without the walls, two thousand perished in the Vistula, nearly fifteen thousand were made prisoners by the Russians, and about twelve thousand were butchered in the way described by Mr. Fox. This led to the third and last partition of Poland, in 1795. This battle was the one which Campbell describes with so much power in his Pleasures of Hope, though many, in consequence of his using the word *Prague* ["Prague's proud arch" or bridge] instead of *Praga*, have been led to suppose that another Polish city was referred to. The capture of the place is described in the following lines:

The sun went down, nor ceased the carnage there,
Tumultuous murder shook the midnight air;
On Prague's proud arch the fires of ruin glow,
His blood-dyed waters murmuring far below;
The storm prevails, the rampart yields away,
Bursts the wild cry of horror and dismay!
Hark! as the smoldering piles with thunder fall,
A thousand shrieks for hopeless mercy call!
Earth shook—red meteors flashed along the sky,
And conscious Nature shudder'd at the cry!

(I think I have heard within a quarter of an hour), determine, aye or no, to dismiss the French minister, and order him out of his dominions, with the menace, that if he did not, the English fleet should bombard Leghorn? Will the honorable gentleman deny this also? I certainly do not know it from my own knowledge; but I know that persons of the first credit, then at Florence, have stated these facts, and that they have never been contradicted. It is true that, upon the Grand Duke's complaint of this indignity, Lord Harvey was recalled; but was the *principle* recalled? was the mission recalled? Did not ministers persist in the demand which Lord Harvey had made, perhaps ungraciously? and was not the Grand Duke forced, in consequence, to dismiss the French minister? and did they not drive him to enter into an unwilling war with the republic? It is true that he afterward made his peace, and that, having done so, he was treated severely and unjustly by the French; but what do I conclude from all this, but that we have no right to be scrupulous, we who have violated the respect due to peaceable powers ourselves, in this war, which, more than any other that ever afflicted human nature, has been distinguished by the greatest number of disgusting and outrageous insults by the great to the smaller powers. And I infer from this, also, that the instances not being confined to the French, but having been perpetrated by every one of the allies, and by England as much as by others, we have no right, either in personal character, or from our own deportment, to refuse to treat with the French on this ground. Need I speak of your conduct to Genoa also? Perhaps the note delivered by Mr. Drake was also a forgery. Perhaps the blockade of the port never took place. It is impossible to deny the facts, which were so glaring at the time. It is a painful thing to me, sir, to be obliged to go back to these unfortunate periods of the history of this war, and of the conduct of this country; but I am forced to the task by the use which has been made of the atrocities of the French as an argument against negotiation. I think I have said enough to prove, that if the French have been guilty, we have not been innocent. Nothing but determined incredulity can make us deaf and blind to our own acts, when we are so ready to yield an assent to all the reproaches which are thrown out on the enemy, and upon which reproaches we are gravely told to continue the war.

Case of Venice.

"But the French," it seems, "have behaved ill every where. They seized on Venice, which had preserved the most exact neutrality, or rather," as it is hinted, "had manifested symptoms of friendship to them." I agree with the right honorable gentleman, it was an abominable act. I am not the apologist, much less the advocate, of their iniquities; neither will I countenance them in their pretenses for the injustice. I do not think that much regard is to be paid to the charges which a triumphant soldiery bring on the conduct of a people whom they have overrun. Pretenses for outrage will never be wanting to the strong, when they wish to trample on the weak; but when we accuse the French of having seized on Venice, after stipulating for its neutrality, and guaranteeing its independence, we should also remember the excuse that they made for the violence, namely, that their troops had been attacked and murdered. I say I am always incredulous about such excuses; but I think it fair to hear whatever can be alleged on the other side. We can not take one side of a story only. Candor demands that we should examine the whole before we make up our minds on the guilt. I can not think it quite fair to state the view of the subject of one party as indisputable fact, without even mentioning what the other party has to say for itself. But, sir, is this all? Though the perfidy of the French to the Venetians be clear and palpable, was it worse in morals, in principle, and in example, than the conduct of Austria? My honorable friend [Mr. Whitbread] properly asked, "Is not the receiver as bad as the thief?" If the French seized on the territory of Venice, did not the Austrians agree to receive it? "But this," it seems, "is not the same thing." It is quite in the nature, and within the rule of diplomatic morality, for Austria to receive the country which was thus seized upon unjustly. "The Emperor took it as a compensation. It was his by barter. He was not answerable for the guilt by which it was obtained." What is this, sir, but the false and abominable reasoning with which we have been so often disgusted on the subject of the slave trade? Just in the same manner have I heard a notorious wholesale dealer in this inhuman traffic justify his abominable trade. "I am not guilty of the horrible crime of tearing that mother from her infants; that husband from his wife; of depopulating that village; of depriving that family of their sons, the support of their aged parents! No, thank Heaven! I am not guilty of this horror. I only bought them in the fair way of trade. They were brought to the market; they had been guilty of crimes, or they had been made prisoners of war; they were accused of witchcraft, of obi, or of some other sort of sorcery; and they were brought to me for sale. I gave a valuable consideration for them. But God forbid that I should have stained my soul with the guilt of dragging them from their friends and families!" Such has been the precious defense of the slave trade, and such is the argument set up for Austria in this instance of Venice. "I did not commit the crime of trampling on the independence of Venice; I did not seize on the city; I gave a *quid pro quo*. It was a matter of barter and indemnity; I gave half a million of human beings to be put under the yoke of France in another district, and I had these people turned over to me in return!"[17] This, sir, is the defense of Austria;

[17] By the treaty of Campo Formio, concluded October 17th, 1797, France ceded to Austria the whole of the Venetian territory east of the Adige, includ ing that part of Istria, Dalmatia, &c., which had

and under such detestable sophistry is the infernal traffic in human flesh, whether in white or black, to be continued, and even justified! At no time has that diabolical traffic been carried to a greater length than during the present war, and that by England herself, as well as Austria and Russia.

Not true that *both* France and the Ministers have united all Europe against French aggression.

"But France," it seems, "has roused all the nations of Europe against her;" and the long catalogue has been read to you, to prove that she must have been atrocious to provoke them all. Is it true, sir, that she has roused them all? It does not say much for the address of his Majesty's ministers, if this be the case. What, sir! have all your negotiations, all your declamation, all your money, been squandered in vain? Have you not succeeded in stirring the indignation, and engaging the assistance of a single power? But you do yourselves injustice. Between the crimes of France and your money the rage *has* been excited, and full as much is due to your seductions as to her atrocities. My honorable and learned friend [Mr. Erskine] was correct, therefore, in his argument; for you can not take both sides of the case; you can not accuse France of having provoked all Europe, and at the same time claim the merit of having roused all Europe to join you.

Character of one of the allies of England, Paul I. of Russia.

You talk, sir, of your allies. I wish to know who your allies are? Russia is one of them, I suppose. Did France attack Russia? Has the *magnanimous* Paul taken the field for social order and religion, or on account of personal aggression?[18] The Emperor of Russia has declared himself Grand Master of Malta, though his religion is as opposite to that of the Knights as ours is; and he is as much considered a heretic by the Church of Rome as we are. The King of Great Britain might, with as much reason and propriety, declare himself the head of the order of the Chartreuse monks. Not content with taking to himself the commandery of this institution of Malta, Paul has even created a married man a Knight, contrary to all the most sacred rules and regulations of the order; and yet this ally of ours is fighting for religion! So much for his religion. Let us see his regard to social order! How does he show his abhorrence of the principles of the French, in their violation of the rights of other nations? What has been his conduct to Denmark? He says to her, "You have seditious clubs at Copenhagen; no Danish vessel shall therefore enter the ports of Russia!" He holds a still more despotic language to Hamburgh. He threatens to lay an embargo on her trade; and he forces her to surrender up men who are claimed by the French as their citizens, whether truly or not, I do not inquire. He threatens her with his own vengeance if she refuse, and subjects her to that of the French if she comply. And what has been his conduct to Spain? He first sends away the Spanish minister from Petersburgh, and then complains, as a great insult, that his minister was dismissed from Madrid! This is one of our allies; and he has declared that the object for which he has taken up arms, is to replace the ancient race of the house of Bourbon on the throne of France, and that he does this for the cause of religion and social order! Such is the respect for religion and social order which he himself displays, and such are the examples of it with which we coalesce!

The atrocities of the French no argument against negotiation, for Mr. Pitt has already treated with them for peace.

No man regrets, sir, more than I do, the enormities that France has committed; but how do they bear upon the question as it at present stands? Are we forever to deprive ourselves of the benefits of peace, because France has perpetrated acts of injustice? Sir, we can not acquit ourselves upon such ground. We *have* negotiated. With the knowledge of these acts of injustice and disorder, we have treated with them twice; yet the right honorable gentleman can not enter into negotiation with them again; and it is worth while to attend to the reasons that he gives for refusing their offer. The Revolution itself is no more an objection now than it was in the year 1796, when he did negotiate. For the government of France at that time was surely as unstable as it is at present. The crimes of the French, the instability of their government, did not then prevent him; and why are they to prevent him now? He negotiated with a government as unstable, and, baffled in that negotiation, he did not scruple to open another at Lisle in the year 1797. We have heard a very curious account of these negotiations this day, and, as the right honorable gentleman has emphatically told us, an *honest* account of them. He says he has no scruple in avowing that he apprehended danger from the success of his own efforts to procure a pacification, and that he was not displeased at its failure. He

Remarks on that negotiation.

formerly belonged to the Venetian republic. All Europe was scandalized at the eagerness with which the Emperor, who had commenced the war as the defender of the weak and the protector of social order against the common destroyer, grasped the spoils which were offered him at the close of the contest.

[18] Paul I. of Russia, father of the Emperors Alexander and Nicholas. His conduct had for some time been singular, and even foolish. When the Knights of Malta were driven out by Bonaparte, Paul received them at St. Petersburgh, and was greatly delighted to be chosen their Grand Master, directing that no communications should be received from foreign governments which did not address him in this character. He also interfered in the internal concerns of Denmark, Sweden, Hamburgh, and Spain, in the way alluded to by Mr. Fox. Mr. Pitt had said of him, a few months before, in the House of Commons, "There is no reason, no ground, to fear that this *magnanimous* prince will ever desert a cause in which he is so sincerely engaged." Hence Mr. Fox's sarcasm respecting the "magnanimous" Paul. But he did desert the allies, and make peace with the French, about this time. He was probably insane, and was assassinated March 11th, 1801, and succeeded by his son, the Emperor Alexander.

was sincere in his endeavors to treat, but he was not disappointed when they failed. I wish accurately to understand the right honorable gentleman. His declaration on the subject, then, I take to be, that though sincere in his endeavors to procure peace in 1797, yet he apprehended greater danger from accomplishing his object, than from the continuance of war; and that he felt this apprehension from the comparative views of the probable state of peace and war at that time. I hope I state the right honorable gentleman correctly. I have no hesitation in allowing the fact that a state of peace, immediately after a war of such violence, must, in some respects, be a state of insecurity; but does this not belong, in a certain degree, to all wars? and are we never to have peace, because that peace may be insecure? But there was something, it seems, so peculiar in this war, and in the character and principles of the enemy, that the right honorable gentleman thought a peace in 1797 would be comparatively more dangerous than war. Why, then, did he treat? I beg the attention of the House to this point. He treated "because the unequivocal sense of the people of England was declared to be in favor of a negotiation." The right honorable gentleman, therefore, confesses the truth, that in 1797 the people were for peace. I thought so at the time, but you all recollect that, when I stated it in my place, it was denied. "True," ministers said, "you have procured petitions, but we have petitions also. We all know in what strange ways petitions may be procured, and how little they deserve to be considered as the sense of the people." This was their language at the time; but now we find these petitions *did* speak the sense of the people, and that it was on this side of the House only the sense of the people was spoken. The majority spoke a contrary language! It hence follows that the unequivocal sense of the people of England may be spoken by the minority of this House, and that it is not always by the test of numbers that an honest decision is to be ascertained. This House decided against what the right honorable gentleman knew to be the sense of the country; but he himself acted upon that sense against the vote of Parliament.

Mr. Pitt compelled to negotiate by the voice of the people.

The negotiation in 1796 went off, as my honorable and learned friend [Mr. Erskine] has said, upon the question of Belgium; or, as the right honorable gentleman asserts, upon a question of principle. He negotiated to please the people, but it was defeated on account of a "monstrous principle advanced by France, incompatible with all negotiation." This is now said. Did the right honorable gentleman say so *at the time?* Did he fairly and candidly inform the people of England that they broke off the negotiation because the French had urged a basis that it was totally impossible for England at any time to grant? No such thing. On the contrary, when the negotiation broke off, they [the ministry] published a manifesto, "renewing, in the face of Europe, the solemn declaration, that whenever the enemy should be disposed to enter on the work of a general pacification in a spirit of conciliation and equity, nothing should be wanting on their part to contribute to the accomplishment of that great object."[19] And, accordingly, in the year 1797, notwithstanding this "incompatible principle," and with all the enormities of the French on their heads, they opened a new negotiation at Lisle. They did not wait for any retraction of this incompatible principle; they did not wait even till overtures were made to them; but they solicited and renewed a negotiation themselves.[20] I do not blame them for this, sir; I say only that it is an argument against the assertion of an "incompatible principle." It is a proof that they did not *then* think as the right honorable gentleman now says they thought, but that they yielded to the sentiments of the nation, who were generally inclined to peace, against their own judgment; and, from a motive which I shall come to presently, they had no hesitation, on account of the first rupture, to renew the negotiation. It was renewed at Lisle; and this the French broke off, after the Revolution at Paris on the 4th of September, 1797. What was the conduct of ministers upon this occasion? One would have thought, that with the fresh insult at Lisle in their minds, with the recollection of their failure the year before at Paris, if it had been true that they found an incompatible principle, they would have talked a warlike language, and would have announced to their country and to all Europe, that peace was not to be obtained; that they must throw away the scabbard, and think only of the means of continuing the contest. No such thing. They put forth a Declaration, in which they said that they should look with anxious expectation for the moment when the government of France should show a disposition and spirit corresponding with their own; and renewing before all Europe the solemn declaration, that at the very moment when the brilliant victory of Lord Duncan might have justified them to demand more extravagant terms, they were willing, if the calamities of war could be closed, to conclude peace on the same

Inconsistency of Mr. Pitt in accounting for the failure of that negotiation.

19 There is here no inconsistency. The "principle" referred to was this, that the French would not treat, except on the ground of *retaining all the territory of other countries* which they had incorporated into their republic. This they said with particular reference to a restoration of the Netherlands to Austria. The English "manifesto" did *at the time* say of this, "A pretension in itself so extravagant could in no instance have been admitted, or even listened to for a moment."—See *Parliamentary History,* vol. xxxii., p. 1437.

20 Here, again, there was no inconsistency. Early in 1797, Austria had given up the contest, and *ceded the Netherlands to France.* This removed the whole difficulty which existed the preceding year. England did not in 1797 ask France to part with any of her territory, and therefore there was no *reason* for any "restriction of this incompatible principle," as preliminary to treating.

moderate and equitable principles and terms which they had before proposed. Such was their declaration upon that occasion; and in the discussions which we had upon it in this House, ministers were explicit. They said that, by that negotiation, there had been given to the world what might be regarded as an unequivocal test of the sincerity and disposition of a government toward peace or against it. For those who refuse discussion show that they are disinclined to pacification; and it is therefore, they said, always to be considered as a test, that the party who refuses to negotiate is the party who is disinclined to peace. This they themselves set up as the criterion. Try them now, sir, by it. An offer is made them. They rashly, and I think rudely, refuse it. Have they, or have they not, broken their own test?

The restoration of the Bourbons a condition of treating.

But they say "they have not refused all discussion." They have put a case. They have expressed a wish for the restoration of the house of Bourbon, and have declared that to be an event which would immediately remove every obstacle to negotiation. Sir, as to the restoration of the house of Bourbon, if it shall be the wish of the people of France, I, for one, will be perfectly content to acquiesce. I think the people of France, as well as every other people, ought to have the government which they like best, and the form of that government, or the persons who hold it in their hands, should never be an obstacle with me to treat with the nation for peace, or to live with them in amity. But as an Englishman, sir, and actuated by English feelings, I surely can not wish for the restoration of the house of Bourbon to the Throne of France. I hope that I am not a man to bear heavily upon any unfortunate family. I feel for their situation; I respect their distresses; but as a friend of England, I can not wish for their restoration to the power which they abused. I can not forget that the whole history of the last century is little more than an account of the wars and the calamities arising from the restless ambition, the intrigues, and the perfidy of the house of Bourbon.

Reply to Mr. Canning's argument from the address to William III.

I can not discover, in any part of the labored defense which has been set up for not accepting the offer now made by France, any argument to satisfy my mind that ministers have not forfeited the test which they held out as infallible in 1797. An honorable gentleman [Mr. Canning] thinks that Parliament should be eager only to approach the Throne with declarations of their readiness and resolution to support his Majesty in the further prosecution of the war without inquiry; and he is delighted with an address, which he has found upon the journals, to King William, in which they pledged themselves to support him in his efforts to resist the ambition of Louis XIV. He thinks it quite astonishing how much it is in point, and how perfectly it applies to the present occasion. One would have thought, sir, that in order to prove the application, he would have shown that an offer had been respectfully made by the Grand Monarque to King William, to treat, which he had peremptorily, and in very irritating terms, refused; and that, upon this, the House of Commons had come forward, and with one voice declared their determination to stand by him, with their lives and fortunes, in prosecuting the just and necessary war. Not a word like this; and yet the honorable gentleman finds it exactly a parallel case, and a model for the House on this day to imitate. I really think, sir, he might as well have taken any other address upon the journals, upon any other topic, as this address to King William. It would have been equally in point, and would have equally served to show the honorable gentleman's talent for reasoning.

Remarks on Mr. Canning's attack on the Duke of Bedford.

Sir, I can not here overlook another instance of this honorable gentleman's candid style of debating, and of his respect for Parliament. He has found out, it seems, that in former periods of our history, and even in periods which have been denominated good times, intercepted letters have been published;[21] and he reads from the gazette instances of such publication. Really, sir, if the honorable gentleman had pursued the profession to which he turned his thoughts when younger, he would have learned that it was necessary to find cases a little more apposite. And yet, full of his triumph on this notable discovery, he has chosen to indulge himself in speaking of a most respectable and a most honorable person as any that his country knows, and who is possessed of as sound an understanding as any man that I have the good fortune to be acquainted with, in terms the most offensive and disgusting, on account of words which he may be supposed to have said in another place.[22] He has spoken of that noble person, and of his intellect, in terms which, were I disposed to retort, I might say, show himself to be possessed of an intellect which would justify me in passing over in silence any thing that comes from him. Sir, the noble person did not speak of the mere act of publishing the intercepted correspondence; and the honorable gentleman's reference to the gazettes of former periods is, therefore, not in point. The noble Duke complained of the manner in which these intercepted letters had been published, not of the fact itself of their publication; for, in the introduction and notes to those letters, the *ribaldry* is such, that they are not screened from the execration of every honorable mind even by their extreme stupidity. The honorable gentleman [Mr. Canning] says, that he must treat with indifference the intellect of a man who can ascribe the present scarcity of corn to the war. Sir, I think there is nothing either absurd or unjust in such an opinion. Does not the war necessarily, by its magazines, and still more by its expeditions, increase consumption? But when

[21] Mr. Canning had justified the publication of the intercepted correspondence of the French from Egypt by the British government.

[22] This refers to the Duke of Bedford's speech in the House of Lords.

we learn that corn is at this very moment sold in France for less than half the price which it bears here, is it not fair to suppose that, but for the war and its prohibitions, a part of that grain would be brought to this country, on account of the high price which it would command, and that, consequently, our scarcity would be relieved from their abundance? I speak, of course, only upon report; but I see that the prices quoted in the French markets are less, by one half, than the prices in England. There was nothing, therefore, very absurd in what fell from the noble person; and I would really advise the honorable gentleman, when he speaks of persons distinguished for every virtue, to be a little more guarded in his language. I see no reason why he and his friends should not leave to persons in another place, holding the same opinions as themselves, the task of answering what may be thrown out there. Is not the phalanx sufficient? It is no great compliment to their talents, considering their number, that they can not be left to the task of answering the few to whom they are opposed; but perhaps the honorable gentleman has too little to do in this House, and is to be sent there himself. In truth, I see no reason why even he might not be sent, as well as some others who have been raised to the peerage.[23] But while he continues with us, I really think that the honorable gentleman will find full employment for all his talents in answering the arguments which are urged in this House, without employing them in disparaging one of the finest understandings in this kingdom.

Motives of Mr. Pitt's negotiation in 1797.

And now, sir, to return to the subject of the negotiation in 1797. It is, in my mind, extremely material to attend to the account which the minister gives of his memorable negotiation of 1797, and of his motives for entering into it. In all questions of peace and war, he says, many circumstances must necessarily enter into the consideration; and that they are not to be decided upon by the extremes. The determination must be made upon a balance and a comparison of the evils or the advantages upon the one side and the other, and that one of the greatest considerations is that of finance. In 1797, the right honorable gentleman confesses he found himself peculiarly embarrassed as to the resources for the war, if they were to be found in the old and usual way of the funding system. Now, though he thought, upon his balance and comparison of considerations, that the evils of war would be fewer than those of peace, yet they would only be so, provided that he could establish "a new and solid system of finance" in the place of the old and exhausted funding system; and to accomplish this scheme, it was necessary to have the unanimous assent and approbation of the people. To procure unanimity, he pretended to be a friend to negotiation, though he did not wish for the success of that negotiation, but hoped only through that means he should bring the people to agree to his *new and solid system of finance.* I trust I state the right honorable gentleman fairly. I am sure that I mean to do so. With these views, then, what does he do? Knowing that, contrary to his declarations in this House, the opinion of the people of England was generally for peace, he enters into a negotiation, in which, as the world believed at the time, and even until this day, he completely failed. No such thing, sir. *He completely succeeded!* For his object was not to gain peace. It was to gain over the people of this country to a "new and solid system of finance"—that is, to the raising a great part of the supplies within the year, to the triple assessment, and to the tax upon income! And how did he gain them over? By pretending to be a friend of peace, which he was not; and by opening a negotiation which he secretly wished might not succeed! The right honorable gentleman says that in all this he was honest and sincere. He negotiated fairly, and would have obtained the peace, if the French had shown a disposition correspondent to his own; but he rejoiced that their conduct was such as to convince the people of England of the necessity of concurring with him in the views which he had, and in granting him the supply which he thought essential to their posture at the time. Sir, I will not say that in all this he was not honest to his own purpose, and that he has not been honest in his declarations and confessions this night; but I can not agree *that he was honest to this House, or honest to the people of this country.* To this House it was not honest to make them counteract the sense of the people, as he knew it to be expressed in the petitions upon the table, nor was it honest to the country to act in a disguise, and to pursue a secret purpose unknown to them, while affecting to take the road which they pointed out. I know not whether this may not be honesty in the political ethics of the right honorable gentleman; but I know that it would be called by a very different name in the common transactions of society, and in the rules of morality established in private life. I know of nothing in the history of this country that it resembles, except, perhaps, one of the most profligate periods—the reign of Charles II., when the sale of Dunkirk might probably have been justified by the same pretense. That monarch also declared war against France, and did it to cover a negotiation by which, in his difficulties, he was to gain a "*solid system of finance.*"

He ought now to treat out of regard to the wishes of the nation.

But, sir, I meet the right honorable gentleman on his own ground. I say that you ought to treat on the same principle on which you treated in 1797, in order to gain the cordial co-operation of the people. We want "experience and the evidence of facts." Can there be any evidence of facts equal to that of a frank, open, and candid negotiation. Let us see whether Bonaparte will

[23] This sneer was founded on the fact that Mr. Pitt, being in want of the means of patronage, had raised persons to the peerage, as a reward for political services, to an extent which was considered discreditable to the ministry and degrading to the House of Lords.

display the same temper as his predecessors. If he shall do so, then you will confirm the people of England in their opinion of the necessity of continuing the war, and you will revive all the vigor which you roused in 1797. Or will you not do this until you have a reverse of fortune? Will you never treat but when you are in a situation of distress, and when you have occasion to impose on the people?

The restoration of the Bourbons is really made a *sine qua non.*

But you say you have not refused to treat. You have stated a case in which you will be ready immediately to enter into a negotiation, viz., the restoration of the house of Bourbon. But you deny that this is a *sine qua non;* and in your nonsensical language, which I do not understand, you talk of "limited possibilities," which may induce you to treat without the restoration of the house of Bourbon. But do you state what they are? Now, sir, I say, that if you put one case upon which you declare that you are willing to treat immediately, and say that there are other possible cases which may induce you to treat hereafter, without mentioning what these possible cases are, you do state a *sine qua non* of immediate treaty. Suppose that I have an estate to sell, and I say my demand is £1000 for it. For that sum I will sell the estate immediately. To be sure, there may be other terms upon which I may be willing to part with it; but I mention nothing of them. The £1000 is the only condition that I state at the time. Will any gentleman assert that I do not make the £1000 the *sine qua non* of the immediate sale? Thus you say the restoration of the Bourbons is not the only possible ground; but you give no other. This is your project. Do you demand a counter project? Do you follow your own rule? Do you not do the thing of which you complained in the enemy? You seemed to be afraid of receiving another proposition; and, by confining yourselves to this one point, you make it in fact, though not in terms, your *sine qua non.*

Ridiculous to look for "experience" of Bonaparte's peaceable intentions by keeping him at war.

But the right honorable gentleman, in his speech, does what the official note avoids. He finds there the convenient words, "experience and the evidence of facts." Upon these he goes into detail; and in order to convince the House that new evidence is required, he reverts to all the earliest acts and crimes of the Revolution; to all the atrocities of all the governments that have passed away; and he contends that he must have experience that these foul crimes are repented of, and that a purer and a better system is adopted in France, by which he may be sure that they will be capable of maintaining the relations of peace and amity. Sir, these are not conciliatory words; nor is this a practicable ground to gain experience. Does he think it possible that evidence of a peaceable demeanor can be obtained in war? What does he mean to say to the French consul? "Until you shall, in *war*, behave yourself in a *peaceable* manner, I will not treat with you!" Is there not in this something extremely ridiculous? In duels, indeed, we have often heard of such language. Two gentlemen go out and fight, when, having discharged their pistols at one another, it is not unusual for one of them to say to the other, "Now I am satisfied. I see that you are a man of honor, and we are friends again." There is something, by-the-by, ridiculous, even here. But between nations it is more than ridiculous. It is criminal. It is a ground which no principle can justify, and which is as impracticable as it is impious. That two nations should be set on to *beat* one another into friendship, is too abominable even for the fiction of romance; but for a statesman seriously and gravely to lay it down as a system upon which he means to act, is monstrous. What can we say of such a test as he means to put the French government to, but that it is hopeless? It is in the nature of war to inflame animosity; to exasperate, not to soothe; to widen, not to approximate. So long as this is to be acted upon, I say, it is in vain to hope that we can have the evidence which we require.

Mr. Pitt's four possible cases in which he would treat with Bonaparte

The right honorable gentleman, however, thinks otherwise; and he points out four distinct possible cases, besides the re-establishment of the Bourbon family, in which he would agree to treat with the French.

(1.) "If Bonaparte shall conduct himself so as to convince him that he has abandoned the principles which were objectionable in his predecessors, and that he will be actuated by a more moderate system." I ask you, sir, if this is likely to be ascertained in war? It is the nature of war not to allay, but to inflame the passions; and it is not by the invective and abuse which have been thrown upon him and his government, nor by the continued irritations which war is sure to give, that the virtues of moderation and forbearance are to be nourished.

(2.) "If, contrary to the expectations of ministers, the people of France shall show a disposition to acquiesce in the government of Bonaparte." Does the right honorable gentleman mean to say, that because it is a usurpation on the part of the present chief, that therefore the people are not likely to acquiesce in it? I have not time, sir, to discuss the question of this usurpation, or whether it is likely to be permanent; but I certainly have not so good an opinion of the French, nor of any people, as to believe that it will be short-lived, *merely* because it was a usurpation, and because it is a system of military despotism. Cromwell was a usurper; and in many points there may be found a resemblance between him and the present Chief Consul of France. There is no doubt but that, on several occasions of his life, Cromwell's sincerity may be questioned, particularly in his self-denying ordinance, in his affected piety, and other things; but would it not have been insanity in France and Spain to refuse to treat with him because he was a usurper or wanted candor? No, sir, these are not the maxims by which governments are actuated. They do not inquire so much into the means by which power may have been acquired, as into the fact of where the power resides. The people did acquiesce in the government of Cromwell. But it may be said that the splendor of his talents, the vigor of his administration, the high tone with which he spoke to foreign nations, the success of his arms, and the character which he gave to the English name, induced the nation to acquiesce in his usurpation; and that we must not try Bonaparte by his example. Will it be said that Bonaparte is not a man of great abilities? Will it be said that he has not, by his victories, thrown a splendor over even the violence of the Revolution, and that he does not conciliate the French people by the high and lofty tone in which he speaks to foreign nations? Are not the French, then, as likely as the English in the case of Cromwell, to acquiesce in his government? If they should do so, the right honorable gentleman may find that this possible predicament may fail him. He may find that though one power may make war, it requires two to make peace. He may find that Bonaparte was as insincere as himself in the proposition which he made; and in his turn he may come forward and say, "I have no occasion now for concealment. It is true that, in the beginning of the year 1800, I offered to treat, not because I wished for peace, but because the people of France wished for it; and besides, my old resources being exhausted, and there being no means of carrying on the war without 'a new and solid system of finance,' I pretended to treat, because I wished to procure the unanimous assent of the French people to this 'new and solid system of finance.' Did you think I was in earnest? You were deceived. I now throw off the mask. I have gained my point, and I reject your offers with scorn."[24] Is it not a very possible case that he may use this language? Is it not within the right honorable gentleman's *knowledge of human nature?*[25] But even if this should not be the case, will not the very test which you require, the acquiescence of the people of France in his government, give him an advantage-ground in the negotiation which he doos not now possess? Is it quite sure, that when he finds himself safe in his seat, he will treat on the same terms as at present, and that you will get a better peace some time hence than you might reasonably hope to obtain at this moment? Will he not have one interest less to do it? and do you not overlook a favorable occasion for a chance which is exceedingly doubtful? These are the considerations which I would urge to his Majesty's ministers against the dangerous experiment of waiting for the acquiescence of the people of France.

(3.) "If the allies of this country shall be less successful than they have every reason to expect they will be, in stirring up the people of France against Bonaparte, and in the further prosecution of the war." And,

(4.) "If the pressure of the war should be heavier upon us than it would be convenient for us to continue to bear." These are the other two possible emergencies in which the right honorable gentleman would treat even with Bonaparte. Sir, I have often blamed the right honorable gentleman for being disingenuous and insincere. On the present occasion I certainly can not charge him with any such thing. He has made to-night a most honest confession. He is open and candid. He tells Bonaparte fairly what he has to expect. "I mean," says he, "to do every thing in my power to raise up the people of France against you; I have engaged a number of allies, and our combined efforts shall be used to excite insurrection and civil war in France. I will strive to murder you, or to get you sent away. If I succeed, well; but if I fail, then I will treat with you. My resources being exhausted; even my 'solid system of finance' having failed to supply me with the means of keeping together my allies, and of feeding the discontents I have excited in France; then you may expect to see me renounce my high tone, my attachment to the house of Bourbon, my abhorrence of your crimes, my alarm at your principles; for then I shall be ready to own that, on the balance and comparison of circumstances, there will be less danger in concluding a peace than in the continuance of war!" Is this political language for one state to hold to another? And what sort of peace does the right honorable gentleman expect to receive in that case? Does he think that Bonaparte would grant to baffled insolence, to humiliated pride, to disappointment and to imbecility, the same terms which he would be ready to give now? The right honorable gentleman can not have forgotten what he said on another occasion,

"Potuit quæ plurima virtus
Esse, fuit. Toto certatum est corpore regni."[26]

---

[24] It is a curious fact that Mr. Fox, in putting these words into the mouth of Bonaparte, hit precisely on the sentiments he entertained at this crisis. He says in his Memoirs, as dictated to Montholon, "I had then need of war; a treaty of peace which should have derogated from that of Campo Formio, and annulled the creations of Italy, would have withered every imagination. Mr. Pitt's answer accordingly was impatiently expected. When it arrived, *it filled me with a secret satisfaction. His answer could not have been more favorable!* From that moment I foresaw that, with such impassioned antagonists, I would have no difficulty in reaching the highest destinies."—Vol. i., 33, 34.

[25] This was a "palpable hit." A few months before, Mr. Pitt had made a descent upon Holland, which he declared, from "his knowledge of human nature," *must* be successful in rousing the Dutch against their French rulers. As it proved a miserable failure, he got many hints from Mr. Sheridan and Mr. Fox respecting "*his knowledge of human nature.*"

[26] See Virgil's Æneid, book xi., line 313. The words are those of the Latin King in relation to his war with Æneas.

Valor has done its utmost: we have fought
With the embodied force of all the realm!

On a former occasion, Mr. Pitt had said that the contest ought never to be given up, until England

He would then have to repeat his words, but with a different application. He would have to say, "All our efforts are vain. We have exhausted our strength. Our designs are impracticable, and we must sue to you for peace."

Sir, what is the question to-night? We are called upon to support ministers in refusing a frank, candid, and respectful offer of negotiation, and to countenance them in continuing the war. Now I would put the question in another way. Suppose that ministers had been inclined to adopt the line of conduct which they pursued in 1796 and 1797, and that to-night, instead of a question on a war address, it had been an address to his Majesty to thank him for accepting the overture, and for opening a negotiation to treat for peace: I ask the gentlemen opposite; I appeal to the whole five hundred and fifty-eight representatives of the people, to lay their hands upon their hearts, and to say whether they would not have cordially voted for such an address. Would they, or would they not? Yes, sir, if the address had breathed a spirit of peace, your benches would have resounded with rejoicings, and with praises of a measure that was likely to bring back the blessings of tranquillity. On the present occasion, then, I ask for the vote of no gentlemen but of those who, in the secret confession of their conscience, admit, at this instant, while they hear me, that they would have cheerfully and heartily voted with the minister for an address directly the reverse of the one proposed. If every such gentleman were to vote with me, I should be this night in the greatest majority that ever I had the honor to vote with in this House. I do not know that the right honorable gentleman would find, even on the benches around him, a single individual who would not vote with me. I am sure he would not find many. I do not know that in this House I could single out the individual who would think himself bound by consistency to vote against the right honorable gentleman on an address for negotiation. There may be some, but they are very few. I do know, indeed, one most honorable man in another place, whose purity and integrity I respect, though I lament the opinion he has formed on this subject, who would think himself bound, from the uniform consistency of his life, to vote against an address for negotiation. Earl Fitzwilliam would, I verily believe, do so. He would feel himself bound, from the previous votes he has given, to declare his objection to all treaty. But I own I do not know more in either House of Parliament. There may be others, but I do not know them. What, then, is the House of Commons come to, when, notwithstanding their support given to the right honorable gentleman in 1796 and 1797, on his entering into negotiation; notwithstanding their inward conviction that they would vote with him this moment for the same measure; who, after supporting the minister in his negotiation for a solid system of finance, can now bring themselves to countenance his abandonment of the ground he took, and to support him in refusing all negotiation! What will be said of gentlemen who shall vote in this way, and yet feel, in their consciences, that they would have, with infinitely more readiness, voted the other?

Appeal to the House, that they and the whole nation desire peace, and not a continuance of the war.

Sir, we have heard to-night a great many most acrimonious invectives against Bonaparte, against all the course of his conduct, and against the unprincipled manner in which he seized upon the reins of government. I will not make his defense. I think all this sort of invective, which is used only to inflame the passions of this House and of the country, exceedingly ill timed, and very impolitic. But I say I will not make his defense. I am not sufficiently in possession of materials upon which to form an opinion on the character and conduct of this extraordinary man. On his arrival in France, he found the government in a very unsettled state, and the whole affairs of the Republic deranged, crippled, and involved. He thought it necessary to reform the government; and he did reform it, just in the way in which a military man may be expected to carry on a reform. He seized on the whole authority for himself. It will not be expected from me that I should either approve or apologize for such an act. I am certainly not for reforming governments by such expedients; but how this House can be so violently indignant at the idea of military despotism, is, I own, a little singular, when I see the composure with which they can observe it nearer home; nay, when I see them regard it as a frame of government most peculiarly suited to the exercise of free opinion, on a subject the most important of any that can engage the attention of a people. Was it not the system which was so *happily* and so *advantageously* established of late, all over Ireland, and which even now the government may, at its pleasure proclaim over the whole of that kingdom? Are not the persons and property of the people left, in many districts, at this moment, to the entire will of military commanders? and is not this held out as peculiarly proper and advantageous, at a time when the people of Ireland are freely, and with unbiased judgments, to discuss the most interesting question of a legislative union? Notwithstanding the existence of martial law, so far do we think Ireland from being enslaved, that we presume it precisely the period and the circumstances under which she may best declare her free opinion! Now, really, sir, I can not think that gentlemen, who talk in this way about Ireland, can, with a good grace, rail at military despotism in France.

The military despotism of Bonaparte has its counterpart in martial law as applied to Ireland.

But, it seems, "Bonaparte has broken his oaths. He has violated his oath of fidelity to the Constitution of the third year." Sir, I am not one of those who hold that any such oaths ought ever to be exacted. They are seldom or

Charge against Bonaparte, that he had violated his oaths to the government.

was compelled to adopt these words as her own. Mr. Fox now ingeniously gives them a new turn.

ever of any effect; and I am not for sporting with a thing so sacred as an oath. I think it would be good to lay aside all such oaths. Who ever heard that, in revolutions, the oath of fidelity to the former government was ever regarded, or even that, when violated, it was imputed to the persons as a crime? In times of revolution, men who take up arms are called rebels. If they fail, they are adjudged to be traitors; but who before ever heard of their being perjured? On the restoration of King Charles II., those who had taken up arms for the commonwealth were stigmatized as rebels and traitors, but not as men forsworn. Was the Earl of Devonshire charged with being perjured, on account of the allegiance he had sworn to the house of Stuart, and the part he took in those struggles which preceded and brought about the Revolution? The violation of oaths of allegiance was never imputed to the people of England, and will never be imputed to any people. But who brings up the question of oaths? He who strives to make twenty-four millions of persons violate the oaths they have taken to their present Constitution, and who desires to re-establish the house of Bourbon by such violation of their vows. I put it so, sir, because, if the question of oaths be of the least consequence, it is equal on both sides! He who desires the whole people of France to perjure themselves, and who hopes for success in his project only upon their doing so, surely can not make it a charge against Bonaparte that he has done the same!

Retort on Mr. Pitt respecting oaths

"Ah! but Bonaparte has declared it as his opinion, that the two governments of Great Britain and of France can not exist together. After the treaty of Campo Formio, he sent two confidential persons, Berthier and Monge, to the Directory, to say so in his name." Well, and what is there in this absurd and puerile assertion, if it were ever made? Has not the right honorable gentleman, in this House, said the same thing? In this, at least, they resemble one another! They have both made use of this assertion; and I believe that these two illustrious persons are the only two on earth who think it! But let us turn the tables. We ought to put ourselves at times in the place of the enemy, if we are desirous of really examining with candor and fairness the dispute between us. How may they not interpret the speeches of ministers and their friends, in both houses of the British Parliament? If we are to be told of the idle speech of Berthier and Monge, may they not also bring up speeches, in which it has not been merely hinted, but broadly asserted, that "the two Constitutions of England and France could not exist together?" May not these offenses and charges be reciprocated without end? Are we ever to go on in this miserable squabble about words? Are we still, as we happen to be successful on the one side or the other, to bring up these impotent accusations, insults, and provocations against each other; and only when we are beaten and unfortunate, to think of treating? Oh! pity the condition of man, gracious God! and save us from such a system of malevolence, in which all our old and venerated prejudices are to be done away, and by which we are to be taught to consider war as the natural state of man, and peace but as a dangerous and difficult extremity!

Retort in respect to Bonaparte's saying that France and England could not exist together.

Sir, this temper must be corrected. It is a diabolical spirit, and would lead to an interminable war. Our history is full of instances that, where we have overlooked a proffered occasion to treat, we have uniformly suffered by delay. At what time did we ever profit by obstinately persevering in war? We accepted at Ryswick the terms we had refused five years before, and the same peace which was concluded at Utrecht might have been obtained at Gertruydenberg; and as to security from the future machinations or ambition of the French, I ask you, what security you ever had or could have. Did the different treaties made with Louis XIV. serve to tie up his hands, to restrain his ambition, or to stifle his restless spirit? At what time, in old or in recent periods, could you safely repose on the honor, forbearance and moderation of the French government? Was there *ever* an idea of refusing to treat, because the peace might be afterward insecure? The peace of 1763 was not accompanied with securities; and it was no sooner made, than the French court began, as usual, its intrigues. And what security did the right honorable gentleman exact at the peace of 1783, in which he was engaged? Were we rendered secure by that peace? The right honorable gentleman knows well that, soon after that peace, the French formed a plan, in conjunction with the Dutch, of attacking our India possessions, of raising up the native powers against us, and of driving us out of India; as they were more recently desirous of doing, only with this difference, that the cabinet of France formerly entered into this project in a moment of profound peace, and when they conceived us to be lulled into a perfect security. After making the peace of 1783, the right honorable gentleman and his friends went out, and I, among others, came into office. Suppose, sir, that we had taken up the jealousy upon which the right honorable gentleman now acts, and had refused to ratify the peace which he had made. Suppose that we had said—No! France is acting a perfidious part; we see no security for England in this treaty; they want only a respite, in order to attack us again in an important part of our dominions, and we ought not to confirm the treaty. I ask you, would the right honorable gentleman have supported us in this refusal? I say, that upon his present reasoning he ought. But I put it fairly to him, would he have supported us in refusing to ratify the treaty upon such a pretense? He certainly ought not, and I am sure he would not; but the course of reasoning which he now assumes would have justified his taking such a ground. On the contrary, I am persuaded that he would have said, "This

This disposition to protract war condemned by history.

security is a refinement upon jealousy. You have security, the only security that you can ever expect to get. It is the present interest of France to make peace. She will keep it, if it be her interest. She will break it, if it be her interest. Such is the state of nations; and you have nothing but your own vigilance for your security."

"It is not the interest of Bonaparte," it seems, "sincerely to enter into a negotiation, or, if he should even make peace, sincerely to keep it." But how are we to decide upon his sincerity? By refusing to treat with him? Surely, if we mean to discover his sincerity, we ought to hear the propositions which he desires to make. "But peace would be unfriendly to his system of military despotism." Sir, I hear a great deal about the short-lived nature of military despotism. I wish the history of the world would bear gentlemen out in this description of it. Was not the government erected by Augustus Cesar a military despotism? and yet it endured for six or seven hundred years. Military despotism, unfortunately, is too likely in its nature to be permanent, and it is not true that it depends on the life of the first usurper. Though half of the Roman Emperors were murdered, yet the military despotism went on; and so it would be, I fear, in France. If Bonaparte should disappear from the scene, to make room, perhaps, for a Berthier, or any other general, what difference would that make in the quality of French despotism, or in our relation to the country? We may as safely treat with a Bonaparte, or with any of his successors, be they whom they may, as we could with a Louis XVI., a Louis XVII., or a Louis XVIII. There is no difference but in the name. Where the power essentially resides, thither we ought to go for peace.

Reply as to Bonaparte's motives to continue the war.

But, sir, if we are to reason on the fact, I should think that it is the interest of Bonaparte to make peace. A lover of military glory, as that general must necessarily be, may he not think that his measure of glory is full; that it may be tarnished by a reverse of fortune, and can hardly be increased by any new laurels? He must feel that, in the situation to which he is now raised, he can no longer depend on his own fortune, his own genius, and his own talents, for a continuance of his success. He must be under the necessity of employing other generals, whose misconduct or incapacity might endanger his power, or whose triumphs even might affect the interest which he holds in the opinion of the French. Peace, then, would secure to him what he has achieved, and fix the inconstancy of fortune. But this will not be his only motive. He must see that France also requires a respite—a breathing interval, to recruit her wasted strength. To procure her this respite, would be, perhaps, the attainment of more solid glory, as well as the means of acquiring more solid power, than any thing which he can hope to gain from arms, and from the proudest triumphs. May he not, then, be zealous to secure this fame, the only species of fame, perhaps, that is worth acquiring? Nay, granting that his soul may still burn with the thirst of military exploits, is it not likely that he is disposed to yield to the feelings of the French people, and to consolidate his power by consulting their interests? I have a right to argue in this way when suppositions of his insincerity are reasoned upon on the other side. Sir, these aspersions are, in truth, always idle, and even mischievous. I have been too long accustomed to hear imputations and calumnies thrown out upon great and honorable characters, to be much influenced by them. My honorable and learned friend [Mr. Erskine] has paid this night a most just, deserved, and eloquent tribute of applause to the memory of that great and unparalleled character, who is so recently lost to the world.[27] I must, like him, beg leave to dwell a moment on the venerable GEORGE WASHINGTON, though I know that it is impossible for me to bestow any thing like adequate praise on a character which gave us, more than any other human being, the example of a perfect man; yet, good, great, and unexampled as General Washington was, I can remember the time when he was not better spoken of in this House than Bonaparte is at present. The right honorable gentleman who opened this debate [Mr. Dundas] may remember in what terms of disdain, of virulence, even of contempt, General Washington was spoken of by gentlemen on that side of the House.[28] Does he not recollect with what marks of indignation any member was stigmatized as an enemy to his country who mentioned with common respect the name of General Washington? If a negotiation had then been proposed to be opened with that great man, what would have been said? Would you treat with a rebel, a traitor! What an example would you not give by such an act! I do not know whether the right honorable gentleman may not yet possess some of his old prejudices on the subject. I hope not: I hope by this time we are all convinced that a republican government, like that of America, may exist without danger or injury to social order, or to established monarchies. They have happily shown that they can maintain the relations of peace and amity with other states. They have shown, too, that they are alive to the feelings of honor; but they do not lose sight of plain good sense and discretion. They have not refused to negotiate with the French, and they have accordingly the hopes of a speedy termination of every difference.[29] We cry up their con-

He may see reason to seek peace.

[27] The news of Washington's death, which took place December 14th, 1799, had just arrived in England.

[28] This hit was directed against Mr. Dundas, because he was one of Lord North's ministry, who had poured out this abuse upon Washington.

[29] It is curious to observe how adroitly Mr. Fox turns back upon his opponent almost every argument he uses. Thus, in the present case, Mr. Pitt had enumerated the Americans among those whom the French had injured and insulted. Mr. Fox replies that the Americans did not for this reason re-

duct, but we do not imitate it. At the beginning of the struggle, we were told that the French were setting up a set of wild and impracticable theories, and that we ought not to be misled by them; that they were phantoms with which we could not grapple. Now we are told that we must not treat, because, out of the lottery, Bonaparte has drawn such a prize as military despotism. Is military despotism a theory? One would think that that is one of the practical things which ministers might understand, and to which *they* would have no particular objection. But what is our present conduct founded on but a theory, and that a most wild and ridiculous theory? For what are we fighting? Not for a principle; not for security; not for conquest; but merely for an experiment and a speculation, to discover whether a gentleman at Paris may not turn out a better man than we now take him to be.

Difficulties in the way of the return of the Bourbons.

My honorable friend [Mr. Erskine] has been censured for an opinion which he gave, and I think justly, that the change of property in France since the Revolution must form an almost insurmountable barrier to the return of the ancient proprietors. "No such thing," says the right honorable gentleman, "nothing can be more easy. Property is depreciated to such a rate, that the purchasers would easily be brought to restore the estates." I think differently. It is the character of every such convulsion as that which has ravaged France, that an infinite and undescribable load of misery is inflicted upon private families. The heart sickens at the recital of the sorrows which it engenders. The Revolution did not imply, though it may have occasioned, a total change of property; the restoration of the Bourbons does imply it; and such is the difference. There is no doubt but that if the noble families had foreseen the duration and the extent of the evils which were to fall upon their heads, they would have taken a very different line of conduct; but they unfortunately flew from their country. The King and his advisers sought foreign aid, and a confederacy was formed to restore them by military force. As a means of resisting this combination, the estates of the fugitives were confiscated and sold. However compassion may deplore their case, it can not be said that the thing is unprecedented. The people have always resorted to such means of defense. Now the question is, how this property is to be got out of their hands. If it be true, as I have heard it said, that the purchasers of national and forfeited estates amount to one million and a half of persons, I see no hopes of their being forced to deliver up their property; nor do I even know that they ought. I doubt whether it would be the means of restoring tranquillity and order to a country, to attempt to divest a body of one million and a half of inhabitants, in order to reinstate a much smaller body. I question the policy, even if the thing were practicable; but I assert, that such a body of new proprietors forms an insurmountable barrier to the restoration of the ancient order of things. Never was a revolution consolidated by a pledge so strong.

Increased by a declaration of Louis XVIII.

But, as if this were not of itself sufficient, Louis XVIII., from his retirement at Mittau, puts forth a manifesto, in which he assures the friends of his house that he is about to come back with all the powers that formerly belonged to his family. He does not promise to the people a Constitution which might tend to conciliate their hearts; but, stating that he is to come with all the old *régime*, they would naturally attach to it its proper appendages of bastiles, *lettres de cachet*, *gabelle*, &c.; and the *noblesse*, for whom this proclamation was peculiarly conceived, would also naturally feel that, if the monarch was to be restored to all his privileges, they surely were to be reinstated in their estates without a compensation to the purchasers. Is this likely to make the people wish for the restoration of royalty? I have no doubt but there may be a number of Chouans in France, though I am persuaded that little dependence is to be placed on their efforts.[30] There may be a number of people dispersed over France, and particularly in certain provinces, who may retain a degree of attachment to royalty; how the government will contrive to compromise with that spirit I know not. I suspect, however, that Bonaparte will try. His efforts have been already turned to that object; and, if we may believe report, he has succeeded to a considerable degree. He will naturally call to his recollection the precedent which the history of France itself will furnish. The once formidable insurrection of the Huguenots was completely stifled, and the party conciliated, by the policy of Henry IV., who gave them such privileges, and raised them so high in the government, as to make some persons apprehend danger therefrom to the unity of the empire. Nor will the French be likely to forget the revocation of the edict; one of the memorable acts of the house of Bourbon, which was never surpassed in atrocity, injustice, and impolicy, by any thing that has disgraced Jacobinism. If Bonaparte shall attempt with the Chouans some similar arrangement to that of Henry IV., who will say that he is likely to fail? He will meet with no great obstacle to success from the influence which our ministers have established with the chiefs, or in the attachment and dependence which they have on our protection. For what has the right honorable gentleman told them, in stating the con-

---

fuse to negotiate; but by showing their readiness to do so, had the hopes of a speedy termination of their differences with France. In this he refers to the mission of Oliver Ellsworth, Chief Justice of the United States, Patrick Henry, and W. V. Murray, in 1799, to settle terms of peace between France and the United States. Their mission was successful, and an amicable adjustment took place a few months after.

[30] The Chouans were Royalists, particularly those on the Loire, who rose against the revolutionary government.

tingencies in which he will treat with Bonaparte? He will excite a rebellion in France. He will give support to the Chouans, if they can stand their ground; but he will not make common cause with them; for, unless they can depose Bonaparte, send him into banishment, or execute him, he will abandon the Chouans, and treat with this very man, whom, at the same time, he describes as holding the reins and wielding the powers of France for purposes of unexampled barbarity.

Retort upon Mr. Pitt as to cruelties practiced at Naples.

Sir, I wish the atrocities, of which we hear so much, and which I abhor as much as any man, were, indeed, unexampled. I fear that they do not belong exclusively to the French. When the right honorable gentleman speaks of the extraordinary successes of the last campaign, he does not mention the horrors by which some of these successes were accompanied. Naples, for instance, has been, among others, what is called *delivered;* and yet, if I am rightly informed, it has been stained and polluted by murders so ferocious, and by cruelties of every kind so abhorrent, that the heart shudders at the recital. It has been said, not only that the miserable victims of the rage and brutality of the fanatics were savagely murdered, but that, in many instances, their flesh was eaten and devoured by the cannibals, who are the advocates and the instruments of social order! Nay, England is not totally exempt from reproach, if the rumors which are circulated be true. I will mention a fact, to give ministers the opportunity, if it be false, to wipe away the stain that it must otherwise affix on the British name. It is said, that a party of the republican inhabitants of Naples took shelter in the fortress of the Castel de Uovo. They were besieged by a detachment from the royal army, to whom they refused to surrender; but demanded that a British officer should be brought forward, and to him they capitulated. They made terms with him under the sanction of the British name. It was agreed that their persons and property should be safe, and that they should be conveyed to Toulon. They were accordingly put on board a vessel; but, before they sailed, their property was confiscated, numbers of them taken out, thrown into dungeons, and some of them, I understand, notwithstanding the British guarantee, actually executed![31]

Peroration.

Where then, sir, is this war, which on every side is pregnant with such horrors, to be carried? Where is it to stop? Not till we establish the house of Bourbon! And this you cherish the hope of doing, because you have had a successful campaign. Why, sir, before this you have had a successful campaign. The situation of the allies, with all they have gained, is surely not to be compared now to what it was when you had taken Valenciennes, Quesnoy, Condé, &c., which induced some gentlemen in this House to prepare themselves for a march to Paris. With all that you have gained, you surely will not say that the prospect is brighter now than it was then. What have you gained but the recovery of a part of what you before lost? One campaign is successful to you; another to them; and in this way, animated by the vindictive passions of revenge, hatred, and rancor, which are infinitely more flagitious, even, than those of ambition and the thirst of power, you may go on forever; as, with such black incentives, I see no end to human misery.

And all this without an intelligible motive. All this because you may gain a better peace a year or two hence! So that we are called upon to go on merely as a speculation. We must keep Bonaparte for some time longer at war, as a state of probation. Gracious God, sir! is war a state of probation? Is peace a rash system? Is it dangerous for nations to live in amity with each other? Are your vigilance, your policy, your common powers of observation, to be extinguished by putting an end to the horrors of war? Can not this state of

[31] All this was literally true, and took place in the summer of 1799. Lord Nelson was the officer referred to: he was led by his infatuated attachment to Lady Hamilton, the favorite of the Queen of Naples, into conduct which has left an indelible stain on his memory. After the retreat of the French from Southern Italy, the leaders of the republican government, which had been organized at Naples, were besieged in the castles of Uovo and Nuovo by the Cardinal Ruffo at the head of the Royalists. The remainder of the story will be given in the words of Mr. Southey, the biographer of Nelson. "They [these castles] were strong places, and there was reason to apprehend that the French fleet might arrive to relieve them. Ruffo proposed to the garrison to capitulate, on condition that their persons and property should be guaranteed, and that they should, at their own option, either be sent to Toulon or remain at Naples, without being molested either in their persons or families. This capitulation was accepted; it was signed by the Cardinal, and the Russian and Turkish commanders, and, lastly, by Captain Foote, as commander of the British force. About six-and-thirty hours afterward, Nelson arrived in the bay, with a force, which had joined him during his cruise, consisting of seventeen sail of the line, with seventeen hundred troops on board, and the Prince Royal of Naples in the Admiral's ship. A flag of truce was flying on the castles and on board the Sea-horse. Nelson made a signal to *annul the treaty,* declaring that he would grant rebels no other terms than those of unconditional submission. The Cardinal objected to this; nor could all the arguments of Nelson, Sir W. Hamilton, and Lady Hamilton, who took an active part in the conference, convince him that a treaty of such a nature, solemnly concluded, could honorably be set aside. He retired at last, silenced by Nelson's authority, but not convinced. Captain Foote was sent out of the bay; and the garrisons, taken out of the castles under pretense of carrying the treaty into effect, *were delivered over as rebels to the vengeance of the Sicilian court.*—A deplorable transaction! A stain upon the memory of Nelson, and the honor of England! To palliate it would be in vain; to justify it would be wicked: there is no alternative, for one who will not make himself a participator in guilt, but to record the disgraceful story with sorrow and with shame."—*Life of Nelson in Harper's Family Library,* vol. vi., 177-8.

probation be as well undergone without adding to the catalogue of human sufferings? "But we must *pause!*" What! must the bowels of Great Britain be torn out—her best blood be spilled—her treasure wasted—that you may make an experiment? Put yourselves, oh! that you would put yourselves in the field of battle, and learn to judge of the sort of horrors that you excite! In former wars a man might, at least, have some feeling, some interest, that served to balance in his mind the impressions which a scene of carnage and of death must inflict. If a man had been present at the battle of Blenheim, for instance, and had inquired the motive of the battle, there was not a soldier engaged who could not have satisfied his curiosity, and even, perhaps, allayed his feelings. They were fighting, they knew, to repress the uncontrolled ambition of the Grand Monarch. But if a man were present now at a field of slaughter, and were to inquire for what they were fighting—"Fighting!" would be the answer; "they are not fighting; they are *pausing*." "Why is that man expiring? Why is that other writhing with agony? What means this implacable fury?" The answer must be, "You are quite wrong, sir, you deceive yourself—they are not fighting—do not disturb them—they are merely *pausing!* This man is not expiring with agony—that man is not dead—he is only *pausing!* Lord help you, sir! they are not angry with one another; they have now no cause of quarrel; but their country thinks that there should be a *pause*. All that you see, sir, is nothing like fighting—there is no harm, nor cruelty, nor bloodshed in it whatever: it is nothing more than a *political pause!* It is merely to try an experiment—to see whether Bonaparte will not behave himself better than heretofore; and in the mean time we have agreed to a *pause*, in pure friendship!" And is this the way, sir, that you are to show yourselves the advocates of order? You take up a system calculated to uncivilize the world—to destroy order—to trample on religion—to stifle in the heart, not merely the generosity of noble sentiment, but the affections of social nature; and in the prosecution of this system, you spread terror and devastation all around you.

Sir, I have done. I have told you my opinion. I think you ought to have given a civil, clear, and explicit answer to the overture which was fairly and handsomely made you. If you were desirous that the negotiation should have included all your allies, as the means of bringing about a general peace. you should have told Bonaparte so. But I believe you were afraid of his agreeing to the proposal. You took that method before. Ay, but you say the people were anxious for peace in 1797. I say they are friends to peace now; and I am confident that you will one day acknowledge it. Believe me, they are friends to peace; although by the laws which you have made, restraining the expression of the sense of the people, public opinion can not now be heard as loudly and unequivocally as heretofore. But I will not go into the internal state of this country. It is too afflicting to the heart to see the strides which have been made by means of, and under the miserable pretext of this war, against liberty of every kind, both of power of speech and of writing; and to observe in another kingdom the rapid approaches to that military despotism which we affect to make an argument against peace. I know, sir, that public opinion, if it could be collected, would be for peace, as much now as in 1797; and that it is only by public opinion, and not by a sense of their duty, or by the inclination of their minds, that ministers will be brought, if ever, to give us peace.

I conclude, sir, with repeating what I said before: I ask for no gentleman's vote who would have reprobated the compliance of ministers with the proposition of the French government. I ask for no gentleman's support to-night who would have voted against ministers, if they had come down and proposed to enter into a negotiation with the French. But I have a right to ask, and in honor, in consistency, in conscience, I have a right to expect, the vote of every honorable gentleman who would have voted with ministers in an address to his Majesty, diametrically opposite to the motion of this night.

These eloquent reasonings are said to have produced a powerful effect on the House, but Mr. Pitt's political adherents could not desert him on a question of this nature. Not to have passed the address approving of his conduct, would have been the severest censure, and it was accordingly carried by a vote of 265 to 64.

Bonaparte made this the occasion of appealing to a new class of feelings among the French. Hitherto *liberty* had been the rallying word in calling them to arms; the First Consul now addressed their sense of honor, and roused all by the appeal. Russia had already withdrawn from the contest, leaving Austria as the only ally of England on the Continent. Bonaparte instantly assembled his troops on the Rhine and Alps; made his celebrated passage of the St. Bernard in the month of June; crushed the Austrian power in Italy by the battle of Marengo (June 17th, 1800); and concluded the campaign in forty days! In Germany, the Austrians were again defeated by Moreau in the battle of Hohenlinden (Dec. 3d, 1800), and compelled to sue for peace, which was concluded between them and the French by Napoleon about a year after this debate, Feb. 9th, 1801. Mr. Pitt resigned nine days after, chiefly (as became afterward known) in consequence of a difference with the King on the subject of Catholic Emancipation.

Mr. Addington [afterward Lord Sidmouth] succeeded as minister, and in a short time opened negotiations for peace, the preliminaries of which were signed Oct. 1st, 1801. These were followed by the treaty of Amiens, which was concluded about six months after, March 27th, 1802.

WILLIAM PITT.

William Pitt, the younger, was born at Hayes, in Kent, on the 28th of May, 1759, and was the second son of Lord Chatham and of Lady Hester Grenville, Countess of Temple. His constitution was so weak from infancy that he was never placed at a public school, but pursued his studies as he was able, from time to time, under a private tutor, at his father's residence in the country. After eight years spent in this way, half of which time, however, was lost through ill health, he was sent, at the age of fourteen, to the University of Cambridge; and so great had been his proficiency, notwithstanding all his disadvantages, that, according to his tutor, Dr. Prettyman, afterward Bishop of Lincoln, "in Latin authors he seldom met with difficulty; and it was no uncommon thing for him to read into English six or eight pages of Thucydides which he had not previously seen, without more than two or three mistakes, and sometimes without even one." His ardor of mind and love of study may be inferred from a letter written by his father at this time, which gives a beautiful view of the familiarity and affection which always reigned in the intercourse of Lord Chatham with his children. "Though I indulge with inexpressible delight the thought of your returning health, I can not help being a little in pain lest you should make more haste than good speed to be well. You may, indeed, my sweet boy, better than any one, practice this sage dictum [festina lentè] without any risk of being *thrown out* (as little James would say) in the chase of learning. All you want at present is *quiet;* with this, if your ardor to excel can be kept in till you are stronger, you will make noise enough. How happy the task, my noble, amiable boy, to caution you only against pursuing too much all those liberal and praiseworthy things, to which less happy natures are perpetually to be spurred and driven! I will not teaze you with too long a lecture in favor of inaction and a competent stupidity—your two best tutors and companions at present. You have time to spare: consider there is but the *Encyclopedia;* and when you have mastered all that, what will remain? You will want, like Alexander, another world to conquer! Your mamma joins me in every word, and we know how much your affectionate mind can sacrifice to our earnest and tender wishes. Vive, vale, is the increasing prayer of your truly loving father. Chatham."

But all these cautions were unavailing. His constitution was so frail, and his strength so much reduced by the illness referred to, that during the first three years of his college life he was never able to keep his terms with regularity; It was not until the age of eighteen that he gained permanent health, and from that time onward few persons had greater powers of application to the most exhausting study or business. But though his early life at Cambridge seems to have been "one long disease," his quickness and accuracy of thought made up for every deficiency arising from bodily weakness. His whole soul from boyhood had been absorbed in one idea—that of becoming a distinguished orator; and when he heard, at the age of seven, that his father had been raised to the peerage, he instantly exclaimed, "Then I must take his place in the House of Commons." To this point all his efforts were now directed, with a zeal and constancy which knew of no limits but the weakness of his frame, and which seemed almost to triumph over the infirmities of nature. His studies at the University were continued nearly seven years, though with frequent intervals of residence under his father's roof; and the reader will be interested to know how the greatest of English orators trained his favorite son for the duties of public life.

Three things seem to have occupied his time and attention for many years, viz., the classics, the mathematics, and the logic of Aristotle applied to the purposes of debate. His mode of translating the classics to his tutor was a peculiar one. He did not construe an author in the ordinary way, but after reading a passage of some length in the original, he turned it at once into regular English sentences, aiming to give the ideas with great exactness, and to express himself, at the same time, with idiomatic accuracy and ease. Such a course was admirably adapted to the formation of an English style, distinguished at once for copiousness, force, and elegance. To this early training Mr. Pitt always ascribed his extraordinary command of language, which enabled him to give every idea its most felicitous expression, and to pour out an unbroken stream of thought, hour after hour, without once hesitating for a word, or recalling a phrase, or sinking for a moment into looseness or inaccuracy in the structure of his sentences. One of the great English metaphysicians was spoken of by Voltaire as "a reasoning machine," and the mind of Mr. Pitt might, in the same way, be described as a fountain ever flowing forth in clear, expressive, and commanding diction. In most persons, such a mode of translating would have a tendency to draw off the mind from the idiomatic forms of the original to those of our own language, but it was otherwise with him. "He was a nice observer," says Dr. Prettyman, "of the different styles of the authors read, and alive to all their various and characteristic excellences. The quickness of his comprehension did not prevent close and minute application. When alone, he dwelt for hours upon striking passages of an orator or historian, in noticing their turns of expression, marking their manner of arranging a narrative, or of explaining the avowed or secret motives of action. He was in the habit of copying any eloquent passage, or any beautiful or forcible expression, which occurred in his reading." The poets, in the mean time, had a large share of his attention; his memory was stored with their finest passages; and few men ever introduced a quotation in a more graceful manner, or with a closer adaptation to the circumstances of the case. "So anxious was he to be acquainted with every Greek poet, that he read with me," says his tutor, "at his own request, the obscure and generally uninteresting work of Lycophron, and with an ease, at first sight, which, if I had not witnessed it, I should have considered beyond the compass of the human intellect. The almost intuitive quickness with which he saw the meaning of the most difficult passages of the most difficult authors, made an impression on my mind which time can never efface. I am persuaded that, if a play of Menander or Æschylus, or an ode of Pindar, had been suddenly found, he would have understood it as soon as any professed scholar." Dr. Prettyman adds, that there was scarcely a Greek or Latin classical writer of any eminence, the *whole of whose works* Mr. Pitt had not read to him, in this thorough and discriminating manner, before the age of twenty.

The mathematics, in the mean time, had their daily share of attention, being regularly intermingled with his classical studies. Here he was equally successful, showing surprising promptitude and acuteness in mastering the greatest difficulties, and especially in solving problems in algebra, trigonometry, &c.—an employment which, though many consider it as dull and useless, is better fitted than almost any mental exercise to give penetration, sagacity, and fixedness of thought, and to establish the habit of never leaving a subject until all its intricacies are fully explored. When we remember the high standard of mathematical study at Cambridge, we learn with surprise that, in addition to all his attainments in the classics, "he was master of *every thing* usually known by young men who obtain the highest academical honors, and felt a great desire to fathom still farther the depths of the pure mathematics." "When the connection of tutor and pupil was about to cease between us," says Dr. Prettyman, "from his entering on the study of the law, he expressed a hope that he should find leisure and opportunity to read Newton's Principia *again* with me after some summer circuit; and, in the later periods of his life, he frequently declared that no portion of his time had been more usefully employed than that which had been devoted to these studies, not merely from the new ideas and actual knowledge thus acquired, but also on account of the improvement which his mind and understanding had received from the habit of close attention and patient investigation."

In regard to dialectics, Dr. Prettyman gives us less information as to the course pursued; but Mr. Pitt being asked by a friend how he had acquired his uncommon talent for *reply*, answered at once that he owed it to the study of Aristotle's Logic in early life, and the habit of applying its principles to all the discussions he met with in the works he read and the debates he witnessed. Dr. Prettyman thus describes a mode of studying the classics, which opened to Mr. Pitt the widest scope for such an exercise of his powers: "It was a favorite employment with him to compare opposite speeches on the same subject, and to examine how each speaker managed his own side of the argument, or answered the reasoning of his opponent. This may properly be called a study peculiarly useful to the future lawyer or statesman. The authors whom he preferred for this purpose were Livy, Thucydides, and Sallust. Upon these occasions his observations were often committed to paper, and furnished a topic for conversation at our next meeting." But he carried this practice still farther. He spent much of his time at London during the sessions of Parliament, and as he listened to the great speakers of the day, Burke, Fox, Sheridan, and others, he did so, not to throw his mind on the swelling tide of their eloquence, not even to analyze their qualities as orators, and catch the excellences of each with a view to his own improvement, but to see how he could *refute* the arguments on the one side, or *strengthen* them on the other, as he differed or agreed with the speakers. It was this practice which enabled him to rise, at the end of a debate of ten or twelve hours, extending over a vast variety of topics, and reply to the reasonings of every opponent with such admirable dexterity and force, while he confirmed the positions of his friends, and gave a systematic thoroughness to the whole discussion, such as few speakers in Parliament have ever been able to attain.

This severe training prepared Mr. Pitt to enter with ease and delight into the abstrusest questions in moral and political science. Locke on the Human Understanding was his favorite author upon the science of mind; he soon mastered Smith's Wealth of Nations, which was first published when he was a member of college; he gave great attention to an able course of lectures by Dr. Halifax on the Civil Law; and, in short, whatever subject he took up, he made it his chief endeavor to be deeply grounded in its *principles*, rather than extensively acquainted with mere details. "Multum haud multa" was his motto in pursuing these inquiries, and, indeed, in most of his studies for life. The same maxim gave a direction to his reading in English literature. He had the finest parts of Shakspeare by heart. He read the best historians with great care. Middleton's Life of Cicero, and the political and historical writings of Bolingbroke, were his favorite models in point of style; he studied Barrow's sermons, by the advice of his father, for copiousness of diction, and was intimately acquainted with the sacred Scriptures, not only as a guide of his faith and practice, but, in the language of Spenser, as the true "*well* of English undefiled."

How far Lord Chatham contributed by direct instruction to form the mind and habits of his son, it is difficult now to say. That he inspired him with his own lofty and generous sentiments; that he set integrity, truth, and public spirit before him as the best means of success even in politics; that he warned him against that fashionable dissipation which has proved the ruin of half the young English nobility; that he made him feel intensely the importance of *character* to a British statesman; that, in short, he pursued a course directly opposite to that of Lord Holland with his favorite son, is obvious from what remains to us of his correspondence, and from the results that appear in the early life of Mr. Pitt. But there is no evidence that he took any active part in his intellectual training. Dr. Prettyman says "the *only* wish ever expressed by his Lordship relative to Mr. Pitt's studies, was that I would read Polybius with him;" and we should naturally conclude, from the character of Lord Chatham, and the confidence he had in the talents and industry of his son, that having settled the general outline of his studies, he left his mind to its own free growth, subject only to those occasional influences which would, of course, be felt when they met in the intervals of collegiate study. Such, at least, is the only inference we can draw from the statements contained in the biographies of the father and the son; from all the letters between them which have come down to us; and especially from the course which Lord Chatham pursued with his favorite nephew, Lord Camelford, as shown in his correspondence afterward published. There must, therefore, have been an entire mistake in the statements of Coleridge on this subject. In a bitter, disparaging sketch of Mr. Pitt, written in early life, under the influence of hostile feelings, he says: "His father's rank, fame, political connections, and parental ambition were his *mold*—he was *cast* rather than *grew*. A palpable election, a conscious predestination controlled the free agency and transfigured the individuality of his mind, and that which he *might* have been was compelled into that which he *was* to be. From his early childhood, it was his father's custom to make him stand upon a chair and declaim before a large company, by which exercise, practiced so frequently, and continued for so many years, he acquired a premature and unnatural dexterity in the combination of words, which must, of necessity, have diverted his attention from present objects, obscured his impressions, and deadened his genuine feelings." This story of his declaiming from a chair is not alluded to either by Dr. Prettyman in his Life of Mr. Pitt, or by Mr. Thackeray in his Memoirs of Lord Chatham. That the boy sometimes *recited* the speeches of others in a circle of family friends is not improbable, for it was at that time a very common practice in England; but if Coleridge meant that Lord Chatham set a child, under fourteen years of age, to "declaim," or make speeches *of his own*, "before a large assembly," and that Mr. Pitt thus "acquired a premature and unnatural dexterity in the combination of words," productive of all the evils stated, it is what few men would believe, except from a desire to make out some favorite theory.[1] Mr. Coleridge's theory (for he could do nothing without one) was intended to *run down* Mr. Pitt as having "an education of words," which "destroys genius;" as "a being who had no feelings connected with man or nature, no spontaneous impulses, no unbiased and desultory studies, nothing that constitutes individuality of intellect, nothing that teaches brotherhood or affection." So much for theory; we may learn the *fact* from the testimony of his tutor and of his most intimate companions. Dr. Prettyman says: "Mr. Pitt now began [at the age of sixteen] to mix with other young men of his own age and station in life then resident in Cambridge, and no one was ever more admired and beloved by his acquaintances and friends. He was always the same person in company, abounding in playful and quick repartee." Mr. Wilberforce, who became his most intimate friend at the age of twenty, remarks: "He was the wittiest man I ever knew, and, what was quite peculiar to himself, had at all times his wit under entire control.

[1] In America the word *declaim* is often used for *recite* in the English sense of the term; *i. e.*, to pronounce the speech of another when committed to memory. But in England it is very rarely used in this sense; and the context seems to show that such could not have been the meaning of Coleridge.

Others appeared struck by the unwonted association of brilliant images; but every possible combination of ideas seemed always present to his mind, and he could at once produce whatever he desired. I was one of those who met to spend an evening in memory of Shakspeare, at the Boar's Head, East Cheap. Many professed wits were present, but Pitt was the most amusing of the party, and the readiest and most apt in the required allusions. He entered with the same energy into all our different amusements."

The truth is, Mr. Pitt had by nature a mind of such peculiar and unyielding materials, that Lord Chatham would have been wholly unable (whatever might be his wishes) to mold or fashion it after any preconceived model of his own. With some general resemblance in a few points, it has rarely happened in the case of two individuals so highly gifted, and placed in such similar circumstances, that a son has been so entirely unlike a father in all the leading traits of his intellectual character. It may interest the reader to dwell for a moment on some of the differences between them, before we follow Mr. Pitt into the scenes of public life. Lord Chatham, with all his splendid abilities, was still pre-eminently a man of feeling and impulse, governed by the suggestions of an ardent imagination, hasty in his resolves, wanting in self-command, irregular and often changeable in his plans and purposes. Mr. Pitt, with all his burning energy, was equally the man of *intellect*, deficient in imagination, gifted with extraordinary powers of abstract reasoning, having all his faculties brought into complete subjection to his will; so wary and circumspect in the midst of his boldest schemes, that Mr. Fox declared "he had never caught him tripping in a single instance" during a twenty years' contest; inflexible in his determinations, regular and symmetrical in the entire structure of his character. Both were lofty and assuming, but these qualities in Lord Chatham were connected with a love of display, with ceremonious manners notwithstanding the warmth of his affections, and a singular delight in the forms of office and state; while Mr. Pitt had the severe simplicity of one of the early Romans, with a coldness of address, as he advanced in life, which was repulsive to every one except his most intimate friends. Lord Chatham loved fame, and was influenced more than he would have been willing to acknowledge by a desire for popularity and a regard to the opinion of others. Mr. Pitt loved power: he cared but little for office except as it gave him command over others. Without a particle of vanity, he had excessive pride; he despised popularity, and looked with contempt on the vulgar, "among whom he included a large proportion of the peerage and commonalty of England." Mr. Pitt had less genius than his father, but greater strength of mind; and while the one swayed the feelings of his countrymen by the vehemence of his own, the other guided their wills and formed their purposes by the intense energy of his understanding.

Mr. Pitt lost his father in 1778, and being left in straitened circumstances, applied himself to the law as affording the most direct means of support, and was called to the bar on the 12th of June, 1780. He rode the western circuit during that and the next year, having causes put occasionally into his hands which he managed with great skill and success, especially one which he argued before Judge Buller, in a manner that awakened the admiration of the bar, and another before Lord Mansfield, on granting the writ of *habeas corpus* to a man charged with murder, in which he received the warmest applause from that distinguished jurist. He was a favorite with his brethren of the circuit, one of whom remarks: "Among the lively men of his own time of life, Pitt was always the most animated and convivial in the many hours of leisure which occur to young men on circuit. He joined all the little excursions to Southampton, Weymouth, and such parties of amusement as were habitually formed. He was extremely popular. His name and reputation for high acquirements at the University commanded the attention of his seniors. His wit and good humor endeared him to the younger part of the bar. After he became minister he continued to ask his old circuit intimates to dine with him, and his manners remained unchanged."

In January, 1781, he was returned as member of Parliament from Appleby, a borough belonging to Sir James Lowther. He immediately joined the Opposition under Burke and Fox, at a time when Lord North, besides the revolt of the American colonies, was engaged in a war with France, Spain, and Holland. His maiden speech was delivered on the twenty-sixth of the next month, and being wholly unpremeditated, gave a surprising exhibition of the readiness and fertility of his mind. One of Mr. Burke's bills on Economical Reform was under debate, and when Lord Nugent rose to oppose it, Mr. Byng, a member from Middlesex, asked Mr. Pitt to come forward in reply. He partly assented, but afterward changed his mind, and determined not to speak. Byng, who understood him otherwise, the moment Lord Nugent sat down, called out "Pitt, Pitt," and the cry at once became general throughout the House. At first he declined; but finding that the House were bent on hearing him, he rose with entire self-possession, took up the argument with all the dexterity and force of a practiced debater, and threw over the whole a glow, an elegance, a richness of thought and fervor of emotion, which called forth a round of applause from every quarter of the House. Burke took him by the hand, declaring that he was "not merely a chip of the old block, but the old block itself." Fox carried him to Brookes' when the House adjourned, and had him enrolled among the *élite* of the Whigs; and the nation felt that the mantle had fallen upon one who was already qualified to go forth in "the spirit and power" of his illustrious predecessor. He spoke but twice that session; and at the close of it, as some one was remarking, "Pitt promises to be one of the first speakers that was ever heard in Parliament," Mr. Fox, who was passing at the moment, turned instantly round and replied, "*He is so already.*" Thus, at the age of twenty-two, when most men are yet in the rudiments of political science, and just commencing their first essays in oratory, he placed himself at a single bound in the foremost rank of English statesmen and orators, at the proudest era of English eloquence. What is still more wonderful, he became, not by slow degrees, like Mr. Fox, but, as it were, by "inspiration" (in the language of Lord Brougham), one of the most accomplished *debaters* in the British Parliament.

At the next session, commencing in November, 1781, Mr. Pitt entered into debate on the broadest scale, and made the most strenuous exertions to put an end to the American war. The defeat of Cornwallis had rendered the contest absolutely hopeless; and he denounced it as one which "wasted the blood and treasure of the kingdom without even a rational object." But he avoided the error of Fox; he made no personal attack on the King. With that forecast which marked all his actions, in opposing the favorite measure of his sovereign, he did nothing to wound his pride or to rouse his resentment. He put the responsibility on his ministers, where the Constitution rests it, and inveighed against them as men, "who, by their fatal system, had led the country, step by step, to the most calamitous and disgraceful situation to which a once flourishing and glorious empire could possibly be reduced—a situation which threatened the final *dissolution* of the state, if not prevented by timely, wise, and vigorous efforts." A few days after, he again called forth a burst of admiration by one of those classical allusions, united to the keenest sarcasm, with which his early productions were so often adorned. In a speech on the army estimates, while commenting with great severity on a contradiction in the statements of Lord North and Lord George Germaine, he saw the two (who were seated near each other) conversing with great earnestness, while Welbore Ellis, Treasurer of the Navy, was interposing between them as if to impart some seasonable information. Stopping in the middle of a sentence, and turning the eyes of the whole House upon the group, he said, in a significant tone, "I will *pause* until the Nestor of the Treasury Bench shall settle the difference between Agamemnon and Achilles." The suddenness of the stroke, and the idea especially of making Lord George an *Achilles* after the part he acted at the battle of Minden, produced a roar of laughter throughout the House, which was instantly followed by a tumult of applause. It was by such means that Mr. Pitt always took care to repress any disposition to treat his remarks with levity or disrespect.

At the end of a few weeks, Lord North was driven from office, and the Rockingham administration came into power, March 19, 1782, with Mr. Fox and Lord Shelburne as principal secretaries of state. Various stations, and among them one of great emolument, the vice-treasurership of Ireland, were offered Mr. Pitt, but he declined them all, having resolved, with that lofty feeling which always marked his character, never to take office until he could come in at once as a member of the cabinet.

The Rockingham ministry was terminated by the death of its chief, at the end of thirteen weeks. Lord Shelburne succeeded, and with him brought in Mr. Pitt as Chancellor of the Exchequer and leader of the House of Commons. Such an event had never before happened in the history of English politics. The conduct of the entire finances of the empire had hitherto been reserved for men of tried experience. Godolphin, Oxford, Walpole, Pelham, Grenville, Townsend, and North, had risen by slow degrees to this weighty and responsible office. Mr. Pitt alone received it at once without passing through any subordinate station, at the age of *twenty-three*, and the country hailed him with joy as worthy to take his father's place in the management of the highest concerns of the empire. Lord Shelburne now made peace (October 30, 1782), on terms quite as favorable as could have been expected, after the disgraceful results of Lord North's contest with America and France. But it was already obvious that his Lordship, though head of the government, was not master of the House of Commons. Mr. Fox, who had seceded when the new ministry came in, held the balance of power between them and Lord North: some union of parties was, therefore, indispensable, or the government could not go on, and Mr. Pitt was commissioned to negotiate with Mr. Fox for a return to power. Their in terview was short. Fox instantly demanded whether, under the proposed arrangement, Lord Shelburne was still to remain prime minister. Pitt replied that nothing else had ever been contemplated. "I can not," said Fox, warmly, "ever consent to hold office under his Lordship." "And I certainly have not come here," replied Pitt, "to *betray* Lord Shelburne." They parted, and never again met under a private roof. From the entire contrariety of their habits and feelings, they could never have acted except as political opponents. Fox now united with Lord North, and voted down the ministry, as already mentioned, on the 17th of February, 1783. Four days after, Lord John Cavendish followed up the blow by moving a resolution involving a severe censure upon ministers, for the terms on which they had concluded peace. The debate was a long one, and Mr. Fox reserved himself for the close of the evening, obviously intending to overwhelm his young antagonist and put an end to the discussion by the force and severity of his remarks.[2] The moment he sat down, Mr. Pitt rose, to the surprise of all, and grappled at once in argument with "the most accomplished debater the world ever saw." Though imperfectly reported, his speech contains passages which he never surpassed in his long and brilliant career of eloquence. Some of them will here be given, and the reader can not fail to admire the dignity with which he faces his opponent, the compact energy of his defense touching the con-

[2] Mr. Pitt was seriously indisposed during this debate, and, as Mr. Wilberforce states, was "actually holding Solomon's porch door (a portico behind the House) open while vomiting during Fox's speech, to which he was to reply."

cessions made in the treaty, and the lofty spirit of self-assertion with which he turns back the assault of Mr. Fox, and vindicates his conduct and his motives.

"Sir, revering as I do the great abilities of the honorable gentleman who spoke last, I lament, in common with the House, when those abilities are misemployed, as on the present question, to inflame the imagination and mislead the judgment. I am told, sir, 'he does not envy me the triumph of my situation on this day,' a sort of language which becomes the *candor* of that honorable gentleman as ill as his *present* principles. The triumphs of party, sir, with which this self-appointed minister seems so highly elate, shall never seduce *me* into any inconsistency which the busiest suspicion shall presume to glance at. *I* will never engage in political enmities without a public cause! I will never forego such enmities without the public approbation; nor will *I* be *questioned* and *cast off* in the face of this House *by one virtuous and dissatisfied friend!* [3] These, sir, the sober and durable triumphs of reason over the weak and profligate inconsistencies of party violence; these, sir, the steady triumphs of virtue over success itself, shall be mine, not only in my present situation, but through every future condition of my life—triumphs which no length of time shall diminish, which no change of principle shall ever sully."

Having dwelt at large on the disgraces and dangers of the country at the close of the American war, Mr. Pitt now asks, "Could Lord Shelburne, thus surrounded with scenes of ruin, affect to *dictate* the terms of peace? Are these articles seriously compared with those of the peace of Paris in 1763?" This leads him to speak of the elevated position in which the country was at that time left by his father, and from this he passes to defend the concessions made by Lord Shelburne.

"I feel, sir, at this instant, how much I have been animated in my childhood by the recital of England's victories. I was taught, sir, by one whose memory I shall ever revere, that at the close of a war far different, indeed, from this, she had dictated the terms of peace to submissive nations. This, in which I have something more than a common interest, was the memorable era of England's glory. But that era has passed; she is under the awful and mortifying necessity of employing a language which corresponds to her true condition: the visions of her power and pre-eminence are passed away.

"*We have acknowledged American independence.* That, sir, was a needless form: the incapacity of the noble Lord who conducted our affairs [Lord North]; the events of war; and even a vote of this House, had already granted what it was impossible to withhold.

"*We have ceded Florida.* We have obtained Providence and the Bahama Islands.

"*We have ceded an extent of fishery on the coast of Newfoundland.* We have established an extensive right to the most valuable banks.

"*We have restored St. Lucia and given up Tobago.* We have regained Grenada, Dominica, St. Kitts, Nevis, and Montserrat, and have wrested Jamaica from her impending danger. In Africa we have ceded Goree, the grave of our countrymen; and we possess Senegambia, the best and most healthy settlement.

"*We have likewise permitted his most Christian Majesty to repair his harbor of Dunkirk.* The humiliating clause for its destruction was inserted, sir, after *other* wars than the past; and the immense expense attending its repair will still render the indulgence of no value to the French.

"*In the East Indies*, where alone we had power to dictate the terms of peace, we have restored what was useless to ourselves, and scarcely tenable in a continuance of the war.

"*But we have abandoned the American Loyalists to their implacable enemies.* Little, sir, are those unhappy men befriended by such language in this House; nor shall we give much assistance to their cause, or add stability to the reciprocal confidence of the two states, if we already impute to Congress a violence and injustice which decency forbids us to suspect. Would a continuance of the war have been justified on the single principle of assisting these unfortunate men? or would a continuance of the war, if so justified, have procured them a more certain indemnity? Their hopes must have been rendered desperate, indeed, by any additional distresses of Britain; those hopes which are now revived by the timely aid of peace and reconciliation.

"These are the ruinous conditions to which this country, engaged with four powerful states, and exhausted in all its resources, thought fit to subscribe for the dissolution of that alliance, and the immediate enjoyment of peace. Let us examine what is left with a manly and determined courage. Let us strengthen ourselves against inveterate enemies, and reconciliate our ancient friends. *The misfortunes of individuals and of kingdoms, when laid open and examined with true wisdom, are more than half redressed;* and to this great object should be directed all the virtue and abilities of this House. Let us feel our calamities—let us bear them, too, like men!

[3] This was one of Mr. Pitt's severest sarcasms. Sir Cecil Wray, Mr. Powys, and others, who had long been connected with Mr. Fox as political adherents and personal friends, had put to him during this debate the most painful interrogatories respecting his coalition with Lord North, and renounced all connection with him if that measure was consummated.

"But, sir, I fear I have too long engaged your attention to no real purpose; and that the public safety is this day risked, without a blush, by the malice and disappointment of faction. The honorable gentleman who spoke last [Mr. Fox] has declared, with that sort of consistency that marks his conduct, 'Because he is prevented from *prosecuting* the noble Lord in the blue ribbon [Lord North] to the satisfaction of public justice, he will heartily *embrace* him as his friend.' So readily does he reconcile extremes, and love the man whom he wishes to prosecute! With the same spirit, sir, I suppose he will cherish this peace, too—*because he abhors it!*"

We have here another instance of that keen and polished sarcasm which Mr. Pitt had more perfectly at command than any orator in our language, and which enabled him, as Charles Butler remarks, "to inflict a wound even in a single member of a sentence, that could never be healed." From this passing notice of Mr. Fox, he turns to Lord Shelburne, for whom he had a personal attachment as a friend and adherent of his father, and bestows upon him the following splendid eulogium:

"This noble Earl, like every other person eminent for ability, and acting in the first department of a great state, is undoubtedly an object of envy to some, as well as of admiration to others. The obloquy to which his capacity and situation have raised him, has been created and circulated with equal meanness and address; but his merits are as much above my panegyric, as the arts to which he owes his defamation are beneath my attention. When, stripped of his power and emoluments, he once more descends to private life without the invidious appendages of place, men will see him through a different medium, and perceive in him qualities which richly entitle him to their esteem. That official superiority which at present irritates their feelings, and that capacity of conferring good offices on those he prefers, which all men are fond of possessing, will not then be any obstacle to their making an impartial estimate of his character. But notwithstanding a sincere predilection for this nobleman, whom I am bound by every tie to treat with sentiments of deference and regard, I am far from wishing him retained in power against the public approbation; and if his removal can be innocently effected, if he can be compelled to resign without entailing all those mischiefs which seem to be involved in the resolution now moved, great as his zeal for his country is, powerful as his abilities are, and earnest and assiduous as his endeavors have been to rescue the British empire from the difficulties that oppress her, I am persuaded he will retire, firm in the dignity of his own mind, conscious of his having contributed to the public advantage, and, if not attended with the fulsome plaudits of a mob, possessed of that substantial and permanent satisfaction which arises from the habitual approbation of an upright mind. I know him well; and dismiss him from the confidence of his sovereign and the business of the state when you please, to this transcendent consolation he has a title, which no accident can invalidate or affect. It is the glorious reward of doing well, of acting an honest and honorable part. By the difficulties he encountered on his accepting the reins of government, by the reduced state in which he found the nation, and by the perpetual turbulence of those who thought his elevation effected at their own expense, he has certainly earned it dearly; and with such a solid understanding, and so much goodness of heart as stamp his character, he is in no danger of losing it."

Mr. Pitt next took up the Coalition, which had not yet assumed any definite shape, and delighted the House with one of those sudden *hits* as to its going on to be consummated, which have always so peculiar a power in a large and promiscuous assembly.

"I repeat it, sir, it is not this treaty, it is the Earl of Shelburne alone whom the movers of this question are desirous to wound. This is the object which has raised this storm of faction; this is the aim of the unnatural Coalition to which I have alluded. If, however, the baneful alliance is not already formed—if this ill-omened marriage is not already solemnized, I know *a just and lawful impediment*—and, in the name of the public safety, I HERE FORBID THE BANS!"

Pausing for a moment during the applause which followed this bold image, he then addressed himself to Mr. Fox with a proud consciousness of integrity, glancing at the same time at the supposed motives of those, lately the bitterest enemies, who were now transformed into bosom friends.

"My own share in the censure, pointed by the motion before the House against his Majesty's ministers, I will bear with fortitude, because my own heart tells me I have not acted wrong. To this monitor, which never did, and, I trust, never will deceive me, I shall confidently repair, as to an adequate asylum from all clamor which interested faction can raise. I was not very eager to come in, and shall have no great reluctance to go out, whenever the public are disposed to dismiss me from their service. It has been the great object of my short official existence to do the duties of my station with all the ability and address in my power, and with a fidelity and honor which should bear me up, and give me confidence, under every possible contingency or disappointment.

I can say, with sincerity, I never had a wish which did not terminate in the dearest interests of the nation. I will, at the same time, imitate the honorable gentleman's candor, and confess that I too have my ambition. High situation and great influence are desirable objects to most men, and objects which I am not ashamed to pursue—which I am even solicitous to possess, whenever they can be acquired with honor and retained with dignity. On these conditions, I am not less ambitious to be great and powerful than it is natural for a young man, with such brilliant examples before him, to be. But even these objects I am not beneath relinquishing, the moment my duty to my country, my character, and my friends, renders such a sacrifice indispensable. Then I hope to retire, not disappointed, but triumphant; triumphant in the conviction that my talents, humble as they are, have been earnestly, zealously, and strenuously employed, to the best of my apprehension, in promoting the truest welfare of my country; and that, however I may stand chargeable with weakness of understanding or error of judgment, nothing can be imputed to me in my official capacity which bears the most distant connection with an interested, a corrupt, or a dishonest intention.

"But it is not any part of my plan, when the time shall come that I quit my present station, to threaten the repose of my country, and erect, like the honorable gentleman, *a fortress and a refuge for disappointed ambition.* The self-created and self-appointed successors to the present administration have asserted, with much confidence, that this is likely to be the case. I can assure them, however, when they come from that side of the House to this, I will for one most cordially accept the exchange. The only desire I would indulge and cherish on the subject, is, that the service of the public may be ably, disinterestedly, and faithfully performed. To those who feel for their country as I wish to do, and will strive to do, it matters little who are out or in; but it matters much that her affairs be conducted with wisdom, with firmness, with dignity, and with credit. Those intrusted to my care I shall resign, let me hope, into hands much better qualified to do them justice than mine. But I will not mimic the parade of the honorable gentleman in avowing an indiscriminate opposition to whoever may be appointed to succeed. I will march out with no warlike, no hostile, no menacing protestations; but hoping the new administration will have no other object in view than the real and substantial welfare of the community at large; that they will bring with them into office those truly public and patriotic principles which they formerly held, but which they abandoned in opposition; that they will save the state, and promote the great purposes of public good, with as much steadiness, integrity, and solid advantage, as I am confident it must one day appear the Earl of Shelburne and his colleagues have done. I promise them, beforehand, my uniform and best support on every occasion, where I can honestly and conscientiously assist them."

He had now carried the House to the utmost point of interest and expectation. Something more directly relating to himself was obviously yet to come; and it is not wonderful that the ablest of the eloquent men before him, when they saw the perilous height to which he had raised his audience, felt he could never descend to his own personal concerns without producing in the minds of his hearers a painful shock and revulsion of feeling. But no, his crowning triumph was yet to come.

"Unused as I am to the factions and jarring clamors of this day's debate, I look up to the independent part of the House, and to the public at large, if not for that impartial approbation which my conduct deserves, at least for that acquittal from blame to which my innocence entitles me. My earliest impressions were in favor of the noblest and most disinterested modes of serving the public: these impressions are still dear, and will, I hope, remain forever dear to my heart: I will cherish them as a legacy infinitely more valuable than the greatest inheritance. On these principles alone I came into Parliament, and into place; and I now take the whole House to witness, that *I* have not been under the necessity of *contradicting one public declaration I have ever made.*[4]

"I am, notwithstanding, at the disposal of this House, and with their decision, whatever it shall be, I will cheerfully comply. It is impossible to deprive me of those feelings which must always result from the sincerity of my best endeavors to fulfill with integrity every official engagement. You may take from me, sir, the privileges and emoluments of place, but you can not, and you shall not, take from me those habitual and warm regards for the prosperity of Great Britain, which constitute the honor, the happiness, the pride of my life, and which, I trust, death alone can extinguish. And, with this consolation, the loss of power, sir, and the loss of fortune, though I affect not to despise them, I hope I soon shall be able to forget."

Here he went on to quote the beautiful lines of Horace in respect to Fortune (Odes, book iii. Ode 29, line 53–6):

[4] The reader can not have forgotten the declaration of Mr. Fox, made only a few months before, that nothing could ever induce him to think of a coalition with Lord North, and that he was willing to be considered as *infamous* if he ever formed one. See page 445.

Laudo manentem; si celeres quatit
Pennas, resigno quæ dedit—

when the thought struck him that the next words, "*et mea virtute me involvo*," would appear unbecoming if taken (as they might be) for a compliment to himself. Mr. Wraxall, who was present, describes him as instantly casting his eyes upon the floor, while a momentary silence elapsed, which turned upon him the attention of the whole House. He drew his handkerchief from his pocket, passed it over his lips, and then, recovering as it were from his temporary embarrassment, he struck his hand with great force upon the table, and finished the sentence in the most emphatic manner, omitting the words referred to:

Laudo manentem; si celeres quatit
Pennas, resigno quæ dedit, [*et mea*
Virtute me involvo] probamque
Pauperiem sine dote quæro.[5]

"The effect was electric; and the cheers with which his friends greeted him as he sat down, were followed with that peculiar kind of buzz, which is a higher testimony to oratorical merit than the noisier manifestations of applause."[6]

Lord North, in following Mr. Pitt that night, spoke of his eloquence as "amazing;" and added, "It is no small presumption of my innocence that I could hear his thunder without being dismayed, and even listen to it with a mixture of astonishment and delight."[7] But the Coalition was too strong to be dissolved. The vote of censure was passed by a majority of seventeen, and the Earl of Shelburne resigned.

The King now sent for Mr. Pitt, and urged him, in the most pressing terms, to accept the office of prime minister; but, with that strength of judgment which never deserted him in the most flattering or the most adverse circumstances, he steadfastly rejected the offer, satisfied that it would be impossible to resist the combined force of Lord North and Mr. Fox in the House. To gratify the King, however, while endeavoring to form a ministry to his mind, Mr. Pitt remained in office for six weeks, carrying on the government with a dignity of deportment, and an ease and dexterity in the dispatch of business, which excited the admiration of all, and produced the frequent remark, "there is no need of a ministry while Mr. Pitt is here." In the mean time, the King, though urged by repeated addresses from the House, continued to shrink back from the Coalition; and it is now known that he seriously meditated a retirement to Hanover, as the only means of relief from the painful situation to which he was reduced. It was Thurlow that deterred him from so hazardous a step. "Your Majesty may go to your Electoral dominions," said the Chancellor, bluntly; "nothing is easier; but you may not find it so easy to return when you grow tired of staying there. James II. did the same; *your Majesty must not follow his example*." He therefore advised the King to submit with patience, assuring him that the Coalition could not remain long in power without committing some error which

5 While propitious, I praise her, and bless her glad stay;
But if, waving her light wings, she flies far away,
[Why, wrapped in my virtue], her gifts I resign
And honest, though poor, I shall never repine.

6 More than twenty years after, Mr. Canning, while defending himself under circumstances somewhat similar, in respect to Catholic emancipation, began to quote the passage so finely turned by Pitt; but as he uttered the words "Laudo manentem," it suddenly occurred to him how they had been used before, and he instantly varied them, in his graceful manner, saying, "or, rather, to use the paraphrase of Dryden,"

"I can applaud her when she's kind;
But when she dances in the wind,
And shakes her wings, and will not stay,
I puff the prostitute away."

7 Age of Pitt and Fox, page 155.

would lay them open to successful attack. The King saw the wisdom of his advice. He permitted the Coalition ministry to be formed, April 2, 1783, but with an express reservation that he was to be understood as no way concerned in their measures.

Soon after the close of this session, Mr. Pitt visited France in company with Mr. Wilberforce, and spent some months in studying the institutions of the country. He was treated with great distinction; and, as Mr. Wilberforce states, "it was hinted to him, through the intervention of Horace Walpole, that he would be an acceptable suitor for the daughter of the celebrated Necker, afterward Madame De Staël. Necker is said to have offered to endow her with a fortune of £14,000 a year." But he declined the proposal, and remained unmarried to the end of life.[8] With all the diversity of his powers, there were two characters which Mr. Pitt would have been quite unable to sustain—to play the part of the lover or the husband would have been equally beyond his reach.

The measure foretold by Thurlow came earlier than was expected. During the first week of the next session (November 18th, 1783), Mr. Fox brought forward his *East India Bill.* In opposing this scheme, Mr. Pitt spoke the sentiments of most men in the kingdom. The firmest Whigs, like Lord Camden, the most strenuous enemies of oppression, like Wilberforce, united with the supporters of the Crown and the entire moneyed interest of the country to denounce it in the strongest terms. There were two features which exposed the bill to this general reprobation. First, it put the civil and military government of India in the hands of Commissioners, appointed, not, as usual in such cases, by the Crown, but by Parliament. Considering the manner in which Fox came into office, this was calculated to awaken the very worst suspicions. It looked like a direct defiance of the sovereign—like a determination on the part of the Coalitionists to make use betimes of their ascendency in Parliament, and establish themselves so firmly in power, through this immense increase of patronage, that the King would be unable to remove them. As already stated in the memoir of Mr. Fox, few men at the present day believe he had any such scheme of desperate ambition. He was actuated, there is reason to think, by humane sentiment. He did not mean to have his plan crippled in its execution by the personal animosity of the King, and he therefore gave to Parliament the *first* appointment of the Commissioners for four years; and while he expected, no doubt, to add greatly to the strength of his administration by these means, the idea of his aiming at an *imperium in imperio*, or "a perpetual dictatorship" over England, is now generally discarded. Still, the jealousy which prevailed was perfectly natural. Mr. Fox had made it for himself; and Mr. Pitt used it against him, only as the best men in the kingdom believed it to be founded in truth. Secondly, the bill stripped the Company of all their commercial rights, and placed their property in the hands of another board of Commissioners. This was a much more doubtful measure. "It was tantamount," as Lord Camden truly said, "to a commission of bankruptcy or a commission of lunacy against them; it pronounced them to be unable to proceed in their trade, either from want of property or from want of mental capacity." Nothing could justify it but the extremest necessity; and though Mr. Fox was convinced of that necessity, he ought, in prudence at least, to have delayed such a measure until the other part of his plan had been tried; until experience had shown that the

8 The reason which he was reported to have given, viz., that "he was married to his country," if not a mere jest, was probably, as Lord Brougham remarks, a fabrication of the day, like the words ("Oh, my country!") which were represented to have been the last that he uttered on his death-bed. "Such things," as his Lordship justly remarks, "were too theatrical for so great a man, and of too vulgar a cast for so consummate a performer, had he stooped to play a part in such circumstances."

abuses in India were incapable of redress by a change of its civil and military government—that the Company were fit only to be treated as bankrupts or lunatics. It is unnecessary to dwell on the means by which the East India Bill was defeated, and the Coalition ministry driven from power. They have been detailed in the memoir of Mr. Fox. What share Mr. Pitt had in Lord Temple's communications with the King has never been made known; but the course taken was regarded by all concerned as an extreme measure on the part of the Crown to repel an extreme measure of Mr. Fox, which endangered the rights of the King and the balance of the Constitution. The great body of the people gave it their sanction, and rejoiced in a step which they would have resisted, in almost any other case, as an invasion of their rights.

Mr. Pitt now came in as Prime Minister at the age of *twenty-four* (December 22d, 1783), under circumstances wholly without precedent in the history of English politics. Against him was arrayed an overwhelming majority in the House, led on by the most eloquent men of the age, inflamed by a sense of injury and disappointed ambition. So hopeless did his prospect appear, that a motion for a new writ to fill his place for the borough of Appleby was received with a general shout of laughter. In the contest which followed, and which turned the eyes of the whole empire on the House of Commons for nearly three months, the young minister's situation was not only trying beyond measure, in a political point of view, but, as Wraxall observes, "appeared at times to be not wholly exempt from personal danger. Fox might be said, without exaggeration, to hold suspended over his head the severest marks of the indignation of the offended House. His removal from the King's presence and councils as an enemy of his country—his impeachment or his commitment to the Tower—any or all of these propositions might, nay, might *certainly* have been carried in moments of effervescence, when the passions of a popular assembly, inflamed by such a conductor as Fox, seemed to be ripe for any acts of violence."[9] Under these circumstances, Mr. Pitt displayed a presence of mind, a skill and boldness in repelling attack, a dexterity in turning the weapons of his adversaries against themselves, and making the violence of their assault the very means of their final discomfiture, which we can not even now contemplate, as remote spectators of the scene, without wonder and admiration. Mr. Fox's first step was to demand, rather than request of the King, that Parliament should not be *dissolved*, intimating, in his speech on the subject, that it would not be safe to adopt such a measure "merely to suit the convenience of an ambitious young man." Mr. Pitt, who had wisely determined to fight the battle for a new Parliament *in* and *through* the present House, replied by a friend (for he had not yet been re-elected as a member), that he had no designs of this sort, and "that if any idea of proroguing or dissolving Parliament should be entertained *any where*, Mr. Pitt would instantly resign." To make himself still more sure, Mr. Fox next moved a resolution, declaring "the payment of any public money for services, voted in the present session, after Parliament should be prorogued or dissolved (if such events should take place before an act should have passed appropriating the supplies for such services), to be a high crime and misdemeanor." To this Mr. Pitt made no objection, and the motion was carried by general consent. These things combined brought Mr. Pitt apparently to the feet of Mr. Fox. The majority were not to be broken down by a new election, and if they stopped the supplies, he had no longer the resource of proroguing Parliament, and using the money on hand as absolutely *necessary* for continuing the government: he must resign, or bring the country at once into a state of anarchy. So certain did Mr. Fox consider the result, that he said on the floor of the House, "To talk of the permanency of such an administration would be only *laughing at and insulting them;*" and at the close

[9] Historical Memoirs, vol. iv., p. 724.

of the same speech, he spoke of "the *youth* of the Chancellor of the Exchequer, and the *weakness* incident to his early period of life, as the only possible excuse for his temerity!"

The Mutiny Bill had been already delayed by Mr. Fox for a month, and the same decisive step was soon after taken with the supplies. Mr. Pitt was thus distinctly warned of the inevitable consequences of his persisting in a refusal to resign, while he was insulted for many weeks by one resolution after another, passed by large majorities, reflecting in the severest terms on the means by which he had gained power, and declaring that his ministry did not possess the confidence of the House or the country. As to the first point, he repelled with indignation the charge of having come into office by indirect or unworthy means. "I declare," said he, "that I came up no *back stairs*. When my Sovereign was pleased to send for me, in order to know whether I would accept of employment, I was compelled to go to the royal closet; *but I know of no secret influence!* My own integrity forms my protection against such a concealed agent; and whenever I discover it, the House may rest assured I will not remain one hour in the cabinet! I will neither have the *meanness* to act upon advice given by others, nor the *hypocrisy* to pretend, when the measures of an administration in which I occupy a place are censured, that they were not of my advising. If any *former* ministers are hurt by these charges, *to them be the sting!*[10] Little did I conceive that I should ever be accused within these walls as the abettor or the tool of secret influence! The nature and the singularity of the imputation only render it the more contemptible. This is the sole reply that I shall ever deign to make. The probity and rectitude of my private, as well as of my public principles, will ever constitute my sources of action. I never will be responsible for measures not my own, nor condescend to become the instrument of any secret advisers whatever. With respect to the questions put to me on the subject of a dissolution of Parliament, it does not become me to comment on the expressions composing the gracious answer of the sovereign, delivered by him from the Throne. Neither will I compromise the royal prerogative, nor bargain it away in the House of Commons!"

The King, whose residence was then at Windsor, waited with deep emotion for a daily account of the conflict going on in the House; and such was his anxiety during part of the time, that *hourly* expresses were sent him with a report of the debates. It was, indeed, more his battle than that of the ministry. His correspondence shows that he had resolved to stake every thing on the firmness of Mr. Pitt. His honor as a sovereign forbade the thought of his receiving back Lord North and Mr. Fox, after the means they were using to force themselves again into power: if Mr. Pitt sunk in the conflict, it was the King's determination to sink with him. After a night of the greatest disaster, when the ministry had been five times beaten—twice on questions directly involving their continuance in office—his Majesty wrote to Mr. Pitt in the following terms: "As to myself, I am perfectly composed, as I have the self-satisfaction of feeling that I have done my duty. Though I think Mr. Pitt's day will be fully taken up in considering with the other ministers what measures are best to be adopted in the present crisis, yet, that no delay may arise from my absence, I shall dine in town, and consequently be ready to see him in the evening, if he should think that would be of utility. At all events, I am ready to take any step that may be proposed to oppose this faction, and to struggle to the last period of my life. But I can never submit to throw myself into its power. If they at the end succeed, *my line is a clear one, and to which I have fortitude enough to submit.*" These words, pointing directly to a withdrawal from England (with the case of James II. in

[10] Lord North felt this blow so keenly, that Wraxall says, he had never but once seen him so much agitated during his whole parliamentary career.

full view), if not to consequences even more fatal, must have wrought powerfully on the mind of Mr. Pitt. It was not merely his love of office or scorn of being beaten that nerved him with such energy for the conflict; it was sympathy and respect for his Sovereign, and the hope of averting those terrible civil commotions which seemed inevitable if Mr. Fox, at the head of the Commons, drove the King, supported by the nobility, into the desperate measure contemplated.[11]

As the contest went on, Mr. Pitt having been beaten on an East India Bill which he introduced, Mr. Fox moved the same night for leave to bring in another of his own, which he declared to be the same as his former one in all its essential principles. He then turned to Mr. Pitt, and demanded to know whether the King would dissolve Parliament to prevent the passing of such a bill. All eyes were turned to the treasury bench, and a scene ensued of the most exciting nature. "Mr. Pitt," says the Parliamentary History, "*sat still*—the members on all sides calling upon him in vain to rise."[12] Sir Grey Cooper then broke out into some very severe remarks, and closed with saying, that if the gentleman persisted in his silence, the House ought "to *come to a resolution*" on the subject. "On Mr. Pitt's sitting still, the cry was very loud of *Move, move!*" calling on Sir Grey to bring forward a resolution. Mr. Fox then made some very cutting observations on "the sulky silence of the gentleman," his treating the House with so little decency," &c., when "the House still called most vehemently on Mr. Pitt to rise." General Conway now came out with great warmth, and attacked the character and motives of ministers in the bitterest terms, declaring that "the present ministry, originating in darkness and secrecy, maintained themselves by artifice. All their conduct was dark and intricate. They existed by *corruption*, and they were now about to dissolve Parliament, after sending their agents about the country to bribe men." Mr. Pitt now rose, not to answer the interrogatories put him, but with a call *to order*. As Conway was advanced in years, Pitt treated him with respect, but demanded that he should "*specify* the instances of corruption" charged; and told him that "what he could not prove, *he ought never to assert*." "No man," said he, in his loftiest tone, "shall draw me aside from the purpose which, on mature deliberation, I have formed. Individual members have no right to call upon me for replies to questions involving in them great public considerations. Nor is it incumbent on me to answer interrogatories put in the harsh language that has been used." Turning again to Conway, whose age ought to have taught him more moderation, he reproved his intemperance of language in a way which called forth a burst of applause from the House, by quoting the noble reply of Scipio to Fabius, "Si nullâ aliâ re, modestiâ certe et temperando linguam *adolescens senem* vicero!"[13]

Some of Mr. Fox's friends now became anxious for a *compromise*. Among them was Mr. Powys, who had been so scandalized by the Coalition and the East India Bill, that he joined Mr. Pitt in opposing them, but went back to Fox the moment he was dismissed and Pitt was put in his place. He now urged a coalition between them as the only possible means of giving peace and harmony to the country.

[11] The King's determination was again expressed in a letter to Mr. Pitt, written on the morning of the day when Lord Effingham moved a resolution in the House of Lords, condemning the conduct of the majority in the Commons. "I trust," said he, "that the House of Lords will this day feel, that the hour is come for which the wisdom of our ancestors established that respectable corps in the state, to prevent either the Crown or the Commons from encroaching on the rights of each other. Indeed, should not the Lords boldly stand forth, this Constitution must soon be changed; for if the two only remaining privileges of the Crown are infringed—that of negativing bills which have passed both Houses of Parliament, and that of naming the ministers to be employed—I can not but feel, as far as regards my person, that I can be no *longer of utility to this country, nor can with honor continue in this island*."

[12] See the report of this debate, vol. xxiv., 421-4.

[13] Youth as I am, I will conquer the aged, if in nothing else, at least in modesty and command over my tongue.

He proposed to remove the difficulty as to Lord North (whom Fox could not desert) by raising him to the Upper House. "I did not," said he, "approve of the coalition between the late secretary [Mr. Fox] and the noble Lord. The ambition of the former was certainly laudible in itself, though he was not very delicate in the means of its gratification; still the noble Lord must not be disgraced. He shines, indeed, no longer except with a borrowed light. He is a man of whom I can not say laudandus; but *ornandus, tollendus.*" His Lordship, with his accustomed suavity and wit, in alluding to Powys' observation about his shining with "a borrowed light," observed, that "a classical expression had been applied to him, though with the difference of a monosyllable—*non* laudandus—sed ornandus, tollendus." "I hope," continued he, "*tollendus* is not to be taken in the worst sense: it is not meant to *kill* me! It is only intended I should be *ornandus*—or, in vulgar English, *kicked up stairs!* But, sir, I have no inclination to be kicked up stairs. I should be very unwilling to stand in the way of any political agreement which might be beneficial to the country, but I will not go up to the House of Peers. An acceptance of the peerage would place me in Agrippina's situation—

"'Je vois mes honneurs croître, et tomber mon crédit.'"[14]

No one knew better than Lord North how to soften the asperity of debate by good-humored pleasantry or elegant allusion.

A large number of country gentlemen had now become so anxious for a coalition (which Fox himself proposed), that a meeting, attended by nearly seventy members of the House, was held at St. Alban's Tavern, under the auspices of Powys and Mr. Grovesnor of Chester. On applying to the Duke of Portland, as head of the Opposition, they received for answer, that the only obstacle in the way was "*Mr. Pitt's being in office.*" He was required to resign as preliminary to negotiation! The King, though with great reluctance, consented to receive some of the Opposition "as a respectable part of one [a ministry] on a broad basis," but insisted on "their giving up the idea of having the administration in *their own hands.*" In accordance with these views, Mr. Pitt refused to resign, and when afterward reproached by Mr. Powys on the subject, said, "The honorable gentleman has talked of the fortress which I occupy, and has declared that *he* did not wish me to march out with a halter about my neck. Sir, the only fortress that I know of, or desire ever to defend, is the fortress of the Constitution. To preserve it, I will resist every attack and every seduction. With what regard, either to my own personal honor or to public principle, could I change my armor, and meanly beg to be received as a volunteer under the forces of the enemy? But, sir, I have declared, again and again, only prove to me that there is but a reasonable hope—show me even but the most distant prospect—that my resignation will at all contribute to restore peace to the country, and I will instantly resign. But, sir, I declare, at the same time, I *will not resign* as a preliminary to negotiation. I will not abandon this situation, in order to throw myself on the *mercy* of the right honorable gentleman. He calls me now a nominal minister—the mere puppet of secret influence. Sir, it is because I will not consent to become a merely nominal minister of his creation—it is because I disdain to become the puppet of that right honorable gentleman, that I will not resign. Neither shall his contemptuous expressions provoke me to resignation. My own honor and reputation I never will resign. That I am now standing on the rotten ground of secret influence I will not allow; nor yet will I quit my ground in order to put myself under the right honorable gentleman's *protection*—in order to accept of my nomination at his hands—to become a poor, self-condemned, helpless, and unprofitable minister in his train; a minister, perhaps, in some way serviceable to that right honorable

[14] The line is from Racine's Britannicus (Act i., Scene 1):

I see my honors rise, my credit sink.

gentleman, but totally unserviceable to my King and to my country. If I have, indeed, submitted to become the puppet and minion of the Crown, why should he condescend to receive me into his band?"

It was in this speech that Mr. Pitt, with reference to Fox's boasts of the great names that adorned the Opposition, broke forth into his splendid eulogium on Lord Camden. "Sir, I am not afraid to match the minority against the majority, either on the score of independence, of property, of long hereditary honors, of knowledge of the law and Constitution, of all that can give dignity to the peerage. Mr. Speaker, when I look round me, when I see near *whom* I am standing (Lord Camden was present at the debate), I am not afraid to place in the front of that battle—for at that battle the noble peer was not afraid to buckle on his armor and march forth, as if inspired with his youthful vigor, to the charge—I am not afraid to place foremost that noble and illustrious peer—venerable as he is for his years—venerable for his abilities—venerated throughout the country for his attachment to our glorious Constitution—high in honors—and possessing, as he does, in these tumultuous times, an equanimity and dignity of mind, that render him infinitely superior to *the wretched party spirit* with which the world may fancy us to be infected!"

In concluding his speech, Mr. Pitt thus defied Mr. Fox to stop the supplies. "The right honorable gentleman tells you, sir, that he means not to stop the supplies again to-night, but that he shall only *postpone* them occasionally. He *has* stopped them once, because the King did not listen to the voice of his Commons. He now ceases to stop them, though the same cause does not cease to exist. Now, sir, what is all this but a mere bravado?—a bravado calculated to alarm the country, but totally ineffectual to the object. I grant, indeed, that if the money destined to pay the public creditors is voted, one great part of the mischief is avoided. But, sir, let not this House think it a small thing to stop the money for all *public services*. Let us not think that, while such prodigious sums of money flow into the public coffers without being suffered to flow out again, the circulation of wealth in the country will not be stopped, nor the public credit affected. It has been said, 'How is it possible that Parliament should trust public money in the hands of those in whom they have expressly declared that they can not confide?' What, sir, is there any thing, then, in *my* character so flagitious? Am I, the Chief Minister of the Treasury, so suspected of alienating the public money to my own, or any other sinister purpose, that I am not to be trusted with the ordinary issues?" (A cry of No, no, from the Opposition.) "Why, then, sir," he exclaimed, seizing on the admission with instant effect, "*if they renounce the imputation, let them also renounce the argument!*"

It was not without reason that Mr. Fox had been desirous of a compromise; the whole country had begun to move "*for Pitt and the King*." Addresses in favor of the ministry now poured in from every part of the kingdom. London led the way, and sent a deputation to Mr. Pitt's residence, in Berkeley Square, preceded by the City Marshal and Sheriffs, to present him with the freedom of the city in a gold box of one hundred guineas in value, "as a mark of gratitude for, and approbation of, his zeal and assiduity in supporting the legal prerogatives of the Crown, and the constitutional rights of the people." Mr. Fox's majority now began to diminish, until, on the 27th of February, it was reduced to *nine*. On the 8th of March he made his last great effort in a "Representation to the King," drawn up in powerful language, containing reasons for the removal of ministers. So great was the anxiety to be present at this debate, that the gallery was filled to overflowing more than six hours before the House assembled. The debate was opened by Mr. Fox's moving that this Representation be entered on the records of the House; it continued till midnight, and when the vote was taken he had only *one majority!* Tremendous cheers now broke forth from the Treasury benches: the Coalition was defeated; the Mutiny Bill was passed; Parliament was soon after dissolved; and the nation was called upon to decide, at the hustings, between Fox and Pitt.[15]

The people ratified at the polls what they had declared in their addresses to the King and ministry. Never was there so complete a revolution in any House of Commons. More than a hundred and sixty of Mr. Fox's friends lost their seats; and at the opening of the new Parliament, May 18th, 1784, it might truly be said, in the words of Lord Campbell, "No administration in England ever was in such a triumphant position as that of Mr. Pitt, when, after the opposition it had encountered, the nation, applauding the choice of the Crown, declared in its favor, and the Coalition leaders, with their immense talents, family interest, and former popularity, found difficulty to obtain seats in the House of Commons."[16] From this period for seventeen years, and, after a short interval, during three years more, Mr. Pitt swayed the destinies of England under circumstances, for the most part, more perilous and appalling than have fallen to the lot of any British statesman in modern times. As to his leading measures, men differ now almost as much as during the heat of the contest, in the judgment they pronounce between him and his great opponent. But there is more candor in estimating the *motives* and *intentions* of both. Very few, at the present day, would call in question the honor, the integrity, or the sincere patriotism of William Pitt. All, too, have come to feel that, in deciding on the conduct of public men during the French Revolution, the question is not so much, 'Who was in the right,' as 'Who was least in the wrong.' Facts, also, are beginning to come out through the diaries of such men as Mr. Wilberforce, Lord Malmesbury, &c., who knew the secret history of the times, which put a new face upon many transactions, or on the motives in which they originated; but half a century must still elapse before the world will have the means of forming a full and impartial estimate of Mr. Pitt's administration. All that can here be attempted is a brief survey of his most important measures, commencing with those of the eight years previous to the war with France, and then touching lightly on the grounds and conduct of that fearful contest. Reference will occasionally be made to the opinions of Lord Campbell in his Lives of the Chancellors, not only because his judgments have been formed from the most recent information, but because his views, when favorable to Mr. Pitt, may be relied upon the more as coming from a strong political opponent.

The first measure of Mr. Pitt was a bill for the better government of India. It differed from that of Mr. Fox chiefly in the two particulars mentioned above: it left

[15] The reader may be interested to see the state of the vote at the several divisions which took place during this contest. It was as follows:

January 12th,	232 to 193;	majority 39.	February 18th,	208 to 196;	majority 12.
" "	196 to 142;	" 54.	" 20th,	197 to 177;	" 20.
" 16th,	205 to 184;	" 21.	" "	177 to 156;	" 21.
" 23d,	222 to 214;	" 8.	" 27th,	175 to 168;	" 7.
February 2d,	223 to 204;	" 19.	March 1st,	201 to 189;	" 12.
" 3d,	211 to 187;	" 24.	" 5th,	171 to 162;	" 9.
" 16th,	186 to 157;	" 29.	" 8th,	191 to 190;	" 1.

It was the *press*, to a great extent, which carried Mr. Pitt triumphantly through this struggle. The East India Company felt their existence to be staked on his success, and they spared no efforts or expense to rouse the nation in his behalf. From the day Mr. Fox introduced his bill into the House, a committee of the proprietors sat uninterruptedly at Leadenhall Street, for many weeks, sounding the alarm throughout the kingdom; and from that time, down to his final defeat in the general elections of 1784, they used every instrument in their power to defeat his designs. Among other things, caricatures were employed with great effect, some of them very ingenious and laughable. One of them, called the Triumphant Entry of Carlo Khan, represented Fox in the splendid costume of a Mogul emperor, seated on the body of an elephant, upon which was stuck the queer, fat, good-humored face of Lord North, while Burke strutted in front as a trumpeter with his instrument in full blast, sounding the praises of the Great Man. (See peroration of his speech on the East India Bill.)

[16] Lives of the Chancellors, vol. v., p. 566.

the commercial concerns of the Company in the hands of the Directors; and, instead of the seven Commissioners of Mr. Fox, it established a Board of Control, appointed by the Crown, whose members come in and go out with the ministry, and exercise the government of India in conjunction with the Directors. "The joint sway," says Lord Campbell, "of the Court of Directors and the Board of Control being substituted for the arbitrary rule of the "Seven Kings," our Eastern empire has been governed with wisdom, with success, and with glory."[17]

Early in 1785, Mr. Pitt brought forward a plan of Reform in Parliament. On this subject he had, from early life, entered with great warmth into the feelings of his father, and had twice before (in 1782 and 1783) moved similar resolutions, supported by able speeches, though without success. He now took it up as minister. His plan was to disfranchise thirty-six decayed boroughs (making due compensation to the owners), and transfer the representation, consisting of nearly a hundred members, to the counties and unrepresented large towns. He also proposed to extend the right of voting in populous places to the inhabitants in general. Mr. Fox strenuously resisted the proposed compensation, and the friends of reform being thus divided, Mr. Pitt was beaten by a majority of 248 to 174. As he never brought up the subject again, he has been accused by some of insincerity; but we learn his true feelings from a record in the diary of Mr. Wilberforce: "At Pitt's all the day. It (reform) goes on well: sat up late chatting with Pitt, who has good hopes of the country—noble and patriotic heart! To town (next day)—House—Parliamentary Reform—*terribly disappointed and beat.*"[18] It is not surprising that, after being defeated three times, he should be in no haste to revive the subject again, especially as the King was strongly opposed to the measure; nor does it show any want of sincerity in his early efforts, that he afterward changed his views as to the expediency of agitating the question. Even Lord Brougham, with all his disposition to censure Mr. Pitt, says "the alarms raised by the French Revolution, and its cognate excitement among ourselves, justified a reconsideration of the opinions originally entertained on our parliamentary system, and might induce an honest alteration of them."[19]

At this time, also, Mr. Pitt proposed two measures which the reader may recollect as denounced in bitter terms by Mr. Burke, in his speech on the Nabob of Arcot's Debts.[20] Neither of them deserved these censures. The first related to fees in the public offices, and, instead of being designed "to draw some resource out of the crumbs dropped from the trenchers of penury," was intended to abolish sinecures which, in some cases, yielded £16,000 a year. The bill was passed almost unanimously, and proved highly useful. The other was intended to give Ireland the benefits of free trade. Every one now sees that Mr. Pitt's plan was wise and salutary. Lord Campbell speaks of "the propositions for commercial union with Ireland, which do so much honor to the memory of Mr. Pitt, and not only show that he was disposed to govern that country with justice and liberality, but that, being the first disciple of Adam Smith who had been in power, he thoroughly understood, and was resolved to carry into effect, the principles of free trade."[21] He was defeated, however, partly through the clamor raised by the English traders and manufacturers, and partly by the unfounded jealousy of the Irish. Moore says, in his Life of Sheridan, "the acceptance of the terms then proffered by the minister might have averted much of the evil of which she [Ireland] was afterward the victim."[22]

In 1786, Mr. Pitt brought forward his celebrated plan for paying the national debt

[17] Lives of the Chancellors, vol. v., p. 561.

[18] Lord Campbell gives a letter from Lord Camden on this subject, which he says "affords strong evidence of the Premier's sincerity."—Lives of the Chancellors, vol. v., p. 332.

[19] Sketch of Pitt.—Statesmen of the Times of George III.

[20] See page 332–3.

[21] Lives of the Chancellors, vol. v., p. 569.

[22] Vol. i., p. 231.

of £239,000,000, by means of a Sinking Fund. The suggestion came from Dr. Price, who offered three schemes to the ministry; and it has often been said that Mr. Pitt "chose the worst." True it is that on the other two the debt would have been paid sooner, but they were more complicated, and required an annual outlay to begin with, which Mr. Pitt clearly saw the country could never endure. He, therefore, chose the plan which, though less expeditious, was the only one he deemed practicable. It was founded on the fact that he had a *surplus* revenue of £900,000 a year. To this £100,000 might be added from taxes without burdening the country; and "this sum of one million a year, improved at compound interest by being regularly invested in public stocks, would, in twenty-eight years, amount to four millions a year at the supposed interest of five per cent., a sum which would pay off one hundred millions of three per cents." The scheme was professedly founded on the continuance of peace. While this remained, the surplus could be relied on without adding any new debt; and, as the nations of Europe seemed tired of war after the exhausting contest from which they had just escaped, Mr. Pitt not unnaturally hoped that England might enjoy so long a season of repose as to place her Sinking Fund on high and safe ground before the occurrence of another war. But unfortunately, within seven years, there commenced the most terrible conflict in which the country was ever engaged. The surplus failed; and, though the form of a Sinking Fund was kept up, it became from this time a mere bubble—paying a debt with one hand while borrowing with the other. This was not the Sinking Fund devised by Dr. Price and Mr. Pitt. If the peace in Europe had been as lasting then as since the fall of Bonaparte, and the original plan had been faithfully carried out, the fund would probably by this time have extinguished a large part, if not the whole, of the public debt.

Mr. Pitt's Commercial Treaty with France, in 1787, was the first step on the part of England toward those enlarged principles of national intercourse which now so generally prevail. His armament against France, the same year, in behalf of Holland, was applauded by all; that against Spain, in 1790, was ultimately approved by Mr. Fox;[23] that against Russia, in 1791, was promptly and wisely given up (as already stated) when the voice of the nation declared against it.[24]

The ground taken by Mr. Pitt on the exciting question of the Regency has already been stated in the memoir of Mr. Fox;[25] the measures he then proposed now form an acknowledged part of the constitutional law on this subject. His change of policy in regard to the impeachment of Mr. Hastings was mentioned in the memoir of Mr. Burke.[26] Mr. Wilberforce always ascribed it to a growing conviction of Mr. Hastings' guilt; but the personal considerations referred to in the memoir are believed by most persons to have had a powerful influence with the ministry.

Mr. Pitt was a warm advocate of the immediate abolition of the slave trade, and in 1792 made the most eloquent speech on this subject ever delivered in the House of Commons.[27] Lord Brougham speaks of him in the harshest terms for not making this a ministerial question, and compelling his adherents to unite with him at once in a vote for suppressing the traffic. It may be doubted, however, whether a great moral question of this kind ought ever to be carried by mere force. Years of inquiry and argument are often necessary to make the removal, even of enormous abuses, either permanent or useful. The King and his whole family remained to the last, strenuous opponents of the abolition of the slave trade. Most of the nobility, for a long time, had the same feelings; and nearly all the mercantile interest of the kingdom resisted it for many years with their utmost strength. Some of the ablest of Mr. Pitt's colleagues were vehemently opposed to what they regarded as a rash and impracticable scheme, while they professed a sincere desire for a gradual abolition

[23] See page 508. [24] See page 501. [25] See page 451.
[26] See page 223. [27] See page 579.

of the traffic. It certainly does honor to Mr. Pitt, that, under these circumstances, he never wavered or shrunk back. He gave Mr. Wilberforce all the influence of his personal and official character; he spoke and voted for immediate abolition. If he had gone farther, and attempted what Lord Brougham condemns him so bitterly for not doing, he would probably have put an end at once to his ministry, without the slightest advantage, and perhaps with serious detriment, to the cause he had espoused.

In 1791, it became the duty of Mr. Pitt to frame a new Constitution for Canada. He did it upon wise and liberal principles. He forever took away the question which led to the American war, that of taxing the colonies for the sake of revenue. The British Parliament now expressly relinquished the right of laying any taxes except for the regulation of trade (to which the Americans were always ready to submit); and, in order to guard this point more fully, Mr. Pitt provided that the proceeds even of these taxes should go to the provincial assemblies, and not to the government at home. It was much for George III. to make such concessions.

The financial measures of Mr. Pitt, during the period under review, were highly successful. He took the government at the end of Lord North's wars, with an unfunded debt of thirty millions sterling, and a national income wholly unequal to the expense of even a moderate peace establishment. There were large claims to be provided for in favor of the American Loyalists; there was a system of enormous fraud in the collection of the public revenues to be searched out and collected; there were permanent arrangements to be made for commercial intercourse with America and some countries of Europe; and the vast concerns of India, all resting back on the treasury at home, were to be reduced to order and placed on a new foundation. In carrying out his plans, he had to fight his way at every step against the acutest and most eloquent men of England; and he did it under the disadvantage of having no common ground of argument on which to meet them, since they were ignorant of the principles of Adam Smith, while the popular maxims and prejudices of the day were all on their side. Within five years the debt was funded and reduced five millions of pounds, notwithstanding the expense of two armaments, and other outlays to the amount of six millions. An entire and most beneficial change was made in the manner of collecting the customs and auditing the public accounts, requiring more than three thousand distinct resolutions of Parliament to carry the plan into effect.[28] Under this system, the public revenue went on gradually increasing, until early in 1792 he "felt justified in proposing a repeal of the most burdensome imposts, and an addition of £400,000 to the annual million already appropriated as a Sinking Fund. In respect, then, to the first eight years of Mr. Pitt's administration, it was not, perhaps, too much for Mr. Gibbon to say, that "in all his researches in ancient and modern history, he had nowhere met with a parallel—with one who at so early a period of life had so important a trust reposed in him, which he had discharged with so much credit to himself and advantage to the kingdom."

We now come to the course adopted by Mr. Pitt respecting the Revolution in France and a war with that country. This, as Lord Brougham remarks, "is the *main* charge against him." It is obvious that, whatever may have been his errors on this subject, he had every possible motive to desire the continuance of peace. On this depended all his plans of finance, and especially the success of his Sinking Fund, to which he looked as the proudest memorial of his greatness as a statesman. That he did ardently desire it, no one doubts; and so sanguine were his expectations, that he remarked in the House of Commons, about the middle of 1792, "England had never a fairer prospect of a long continuance of peace. I think we may confidently reckon upon peace for *ten years*." Mr. Burke had previously expressed similar views.

[28] See Prettyman's Life of Pitt, vol. ii., p. 215; Belsham's Memoirs of the Reign of George III., vol. iv., p. 123; Wade's British History, p. 559.

England had no longer any thing to fear from her hereditary rival. "France," said he, "in a political light, is to be considered as *expunged* out of the system of Europe." At this moment (July 25th, 1792) Austria and Prussia invaded France for the avowed purpose of restoring Louis XVI. to all his rights as an absolute monarch. It is unnecessary to say that this step kindled the fire which soon after wrapped the whole of Europe in one general conflagration. But it is now known that England had no privity or concern in this invasion. On the contrary, Mr. Pitt declined all communication with Austria on the subject, and declared to Prussia his unalterable resolution to maintain neutrality and avoid all interference with the internal concerns of France.[29] It is also known that, some months after, he endeavored to put a stop to the contest, by "negotiating," in the words of Mr. Wilberforce, "with the principal European powers for the purpose of obtaining a joint representation to France, assuring her that if she would formally engage to keep within her own limits, and not molest her neighbors, she should be suffered to settle her own internal government and constitution without interference."[30] This negotiation was broken off in the midst by the execution of Louis XVI., and Mr. Pitt thus failed in his efforts to arrest the war on the Continent.

When the French drove out the Austrians and Prussians, they seized, in turn, on the Austrian Netherlands, early in November, 1792. Here arose the first point of collision between England and France. The Republican rulers forced the passage of the River Scheldt from the Netherlands down to the sea. This river had been closed, under the provisions of the treaty of Westphalia, for a century and a half, out of regard to the rights of Holland, through which it flows, and England was bound by treaty to defend those rights. A second point of collision was the French Decree of Fraternity, passed November 19, 1792, by the National Assembly, declaring that the French "would grant *fraternity* and *assistance* to all those people who wish to procure liberty, and charged the executive power to send orders to their generals to give assistance to such people as have suffered, or are now suffering, in the cause of liberty." This was considered as a declaration of war against all the monarchies of Europe, and a direct call upon their subjects to rise in rebellion. It was brought home to England by the fact, that delegates from societies in London and elsewhere, consisting of many thousands, were received at the bar of the French National Convention nine days after the publication of this decree, where they declared their intention to "adopt the French form of government, and establish a National Convention in Great Britain." The President of the Convention replied in very significant terms: "Royalty in Europe is either destroyed or on the point of perishing; and the Declaration of Rights placed by the side of thrones is a devouring fire which will consume them. The festival which you have celebrated in honor of the French Revolution is *the prelude to the festival of nations!*" There is no doubt that the French, at this time, expected a revolution in England.

These aggressions and insults would have justified the English government in demanding ample reparation. But there was a difficulty as to the mode of negotiating. When Louis XVI. was made a prisoner of the Convention by the events of August 10th, 1792, his government ceased, and Mr. Pitt recalled the English embassador from Paris, and suspended the functions of M. Chauvelin, the French embassador at London. How, then, were the two countries to communicate? This soon after became a practical question. England began to arm, which she might reasonably do under existing circumstances. The French government instructed M. Chauvelin, who remained at London, to demand whether this armament was directed against France, tendering at the same time an explanation of the Decree of Fraternity as

[29] See his statements on this subject, page 611.

[30] See Life, page 125, Philadelphia edition. See, also, page 612 of this volume.

not aimed at England, and proposing to negotiate in relation to the Scheldt. What was Mr. Pitt now to do? No one would expect him instantly to recognize the National Convention as *de jure* the government of France. Mr. Fox proposed to treat with them as the government *de facto;* but this is a distinction which has sprung up chiefly since the French Revolution, and it is easy to see how strong a repugnance George III. and most of the English must have felt to any recognition of the new government, while they held their King as a prisoner, and were calling on the subjects of every other monarch in Europe to join with them in rebellion. Mr. Pitt took a middle course. He did not refuse to communicate with the French rulers, but he declined to receive the paper of M. Chauvelin as "an *official* communication." He did, however, reply "under a form neither regular nor official," telling him, "If France is really desirous of maintaining friendship and peace with England, she must show herself disposed to renounce her views of aggression and aggrandizement, and confine herself within her own territory, without insulting other governments, without disturbing their tranquillity, without violating their rights." Within less than a month the King of France was beheaded. M. Chauvelin, whose functions had been suspended during the imprisonment of Louis, was now dismissed and sent out of the kingdom; and seven days after, France declared war against England. Such is an exact representation of the facts. It is certainly to be regretted that Mr. Pitt did not adopt the course recommended by Mr. Fox, and thus take from France all pretense of putting him in the wrong. But in passing a sentence on his conduct we are not to be influenced by our knowledge of the result. He acted under the prevailing delusion that, even if war took place, it could not be severe or calamitous. "It must certainly be ended," said he to a friend, "in one or two campaigns." He acted as most men act who feel strong, in dealing with those whom they consider as weak. He acted, also, under the belief (which subsequent events proved correct) that the French were insincere in their disavowals, that they only wished to gain time. The French Minister of War is now understood to have said at this juncture, "We have three hundred thousand men in arms, and we must make them march as far away as their legs will carry them, or they will return and cut our throats." From the moment of their triumph in the Austrian Netherlands, the policy of the French government was war. On the other hand, George III. and the great body of the English people were equally bent on fighting. "If a stop is not put to French principles," said he, "there will not be a king left in Europe in a few years."[31] The only stop then thought of was to shut out these principles by war, and to put down the authors of them as enemies of the human race. "Had Mr. Pitt refused to go to war," says a late writer, who was by no means friendly to his measures, "he would have been driven from power by the united voice of king and people; and his successor, whether Whig or Tory, would have been compelled to pursue the course of policy which was only reluctantly followed by that celebrated statesman."[32] The war, therefore, was not Mr. Pitt's war; it was equally the war of the English and of the French nation.

As to "French principles," which were an object of so much terror to the King, they had, no doubt, to some extent, gained a foothold among the middling and lower classes. Paine's Rights of Man, and other publications of a still more radical character, were widely circulated; and it has since been stated on high authority, that "the soldiers were every where tampered with." "You have a great estate," said one of these radical reformers to General Lambton; "we shall soon divide it among us." "You will presently spend it in liquor," replied the general, "and what will you do then?" "Why, then *we will divide again!*"

[31] Nicholl's Recollections of George III., p. 400.

[32] Wade's British History, p. 572.

Between 1793 and 1795 very stringent measures were adopted for putting down this spirit. Acts of Parliament were passed, as already stated in the memoir of Mr. Fox, suspending the Habeas Corpus Act, imposing severe restrictions on the holding of political meetings, and giving a wider extent to the crime of treason. They were designed, however, only as temporary measures, and were limited to three years. Still, they brought great reproach on Mr. Pitt, though it now appears that they originated not with him, but with the followers of Mr. Burke, who had been recently brought into the ministry. Lord Campbell, speaking of this period, says, "Now began that system of policy for the repression of French principles, which has caused the period in which it prevailed to be designated, in the language of exaggeration, 'the Reign of Terror.' I think the system was unwise, and that Lord Loughborough is chiefly answerable for it. I am afraid that, if he did not originate, he actively encouraged it, and that he, as the organ of the alarmist party, forced it upon the reluctant Prime Minister. Pitt had not only come forward in public life on the popular side, but I believe that his propensities continued liberal, and that, if he could have fulfilled his wishes, he would have emancipated the Catholics—he would have abolished slavery—he would have established free trade—and he would have reformed the House of Commons. His regard for the liberty of the press he had evinced by carrying Fox's Libel Bill by the influence of government, notwithstanding the furious opposition of Lord Chancellor Thurlow. He was likewise particularly adverse to any stringent measures against reformers, being aware that, having himself very recently belonged to that body, he would appear rather in an invidious light as the persecutor of his former associates. But he found that he could not adhere to constitutional laws and constitutional practices, without the disruption of his administration."[33] During this period, also, occurred those state trials, arising out of some wild attempts at parliamentary reform, in which Erskine was so much distinguished. Some reproach has fallen upon Mr. Pitt for allowing them to go on. It appears, however, from the statement of Lord Campbell, that "Lord Loughborough was the principal adviser of them. He had surrendered himself to the wildest apprehensions of Burke, he feared that any encouragement to parliamentary reform was tantamount to rebellion; and he believed that general bloodshed would be saved by the sacrifice of a few individuals. * * * When the plan was first proposed of arresting the members of the Corresponding Society, and proceeding capitally against them, it is said that Pitt, who had studied the law, expressed some disapprobation of the notion of 'constructive treason,' but he did not like to rely upon the objection that the Duke of Richmond and himself had supported similar doctrines, and no doubt in his heart he believed that, under the pretense of parliamentary reform, deeper designs were now carried on. The Attorney and Solicitor General, being consulted by the Chancellor, gave an opinion that the imputed conspiracy to change the form of government was a compassing of the King's death within the meaning of the statute of Edward III.—and the King himself, upon this opinion, was eager for the prosecutions. So in an evil hour an order was made that they should be instituted, and warrants were signed for the arrest of the supposed traitors." "Happily, English juries," adds Lord Campbell, "and the returning sober sense of the English people, at last saved public liberty from the great peril to which it was then exposed." * * * "To the credit of George III., when the whole subject was understood by him, he rejoiced in the acquittals, and, laying all the blame on the Chancellor, he said, 'You have got us into the wrong box, my Lord, you have got us into the wrong box. Constructive treason won't do, my Lord, constructive treason won't do.'"[34]

Mr. Pitt saw, within three years from the commencement of the war, how idle it was to think of refusing to recognize the French Republic as forming part of the po-

[33] Lives of the Chancellors, vol. vi., p. 254. [34] Id. ib., p. 266.

litical system of Europe. She had extorted that recognition from all around her at the point of the bayonet, and had nearly doubled her territory and dependencies at the expense of her neighbors. He therefore brought down a message from the King, acknowledging her government as established under the Directory in October, 1795, and in October, 1796, sent a plenipotentiary to Paris with proposals of peace. His terms were highly liberal. He offered to restore the conquests he had made from France, being all her rich colonies in the East and West Indies, receiving nothing in return, and only asking for Austria, as the ally of England, a similar restoration of the territory which had been wrested from her by the French. This the Directory refused, and, after a short negotiation, ordered the English embassador to quit Paris in twenty-four hours.

The next year, 1797, was one of the darkest seasons that England had known for centuries. In April, Austria was compelled to sue for peace, leaving the English to carry on the contest single-handed; and at the moment when this intelligence arrived, a mutiny had broken out in the fleets both at the Nore and Spithead, more extensive and threatening than has ever occurred in the English navy; while Ireland was on the brink of rebellion, and actually had deputies in France soliciting the aid of her troops. Never were the funds so low, even in the worst periods of the American war. These events were ushered in by the greatest calamity that can befall a commercial people, a drain of specie arising from the operation of the war, which endangered the whole banking system of the country. Whether Mr. Pitt was to blame or not for the causes which produced this drain, it is certain that his daring resolution saved the country in this alarming crisis. He issued an order of the Privy Council, February 26th, 1797, requiring the Bank of England *to suspend specie payments.* He might have avoided the personal hazard thus incurred by throwing the responsibility on Parliament, which was then in session—the order, indeed, was generally considered as unconstitutional; but the case would not admit of delay, a single night's debate on such a question might have destroyed all credit throughout the kingdom. Parliament and the country justified the course he took, while the bankers in every part of the empire united to sustain him. The mutiny was quelled by a judicious union of firmness and concession; Ireland was held down for another year; and Great Britain, instead of being plunged into the gulf of national and individual bankruptcy as predicted by Mr. Fox, was placed on a vantage ground, which enabled her to sustain the pressure of the war without injury to her financial system. It is not wonderful that the friends of Mr. Pitt were loud in their applause of "the pilot that weathered the storm."

About the middle of the same year, July, 1797, Mr. Pitt renewed his proposals of peace. He sent Lord Malmesbury to Lisle, offering, as in the former case, to restore all his conquests, and, as Austria was now out of the way, demanding nothing in return. There were at this juncture two parties in the Directory, one for peace and the other for war; and the negotiation changed its aspect, from time to time, during the two months of its continuance, as the one or the other obtained the mastery. It is a curious circumstance, showing the difficulties he had to encounter, that a similar division existed in his own cabinet; so that among the "astounding disclosures" made in Lord Malmesbury's diary, we find that it was necessary for his Lordship to send two sets of dispatches every time he communicated with his government, one of a more general nature to be read by Lord Loughborough and his associates, who were bent on defeating the negotiation, and the other for Mr. Pitt, Lord Grenville, and Mr. Dundas! The violent part of the Directory at last prevailed. War became the policy of the government, and Lord Malmesbury was dismissed. The French were to be deluded with new visions of conquest. Bonaparte was sent to subdue Egypt, and thus open a pathway to India; and the whole of Hindostan, with its hundred and fifty millions of inhabitants, was to become a tributary of the Republic. Mr. Pitt laid the subject before Parliament, November 10th, 1797, in a masterly speech, which is given in this collection. Parliament, without one dissenting voice, approved of his conduct, and united in the emphatic declaration, "We know that great exertions are wanted; we are ready to make them; and are, at all events, determined to stand or fall by the laws, liberties, and religion of our country." The people came forward with that noble spirit and unanimity which has always distinguished the English in times of great peril, and subscribed fifteen hundred thousand pounds, not as a loan, but as a voluntary gift for carrying on the war.

The Directory lasted a little more than four years, and then yielded to the power of Bonaparte, who usurped the government, and became First Consul in December, 1799. He immediately proposed a peace, and it was now Mr. Pitt's turn to reject the offer. Wounded by the insults which he had received in the two preceding negotiations, doubting whether the power of the First Consul would be at all more permanent than that of others who had gone before him, and convinced, at all events, that he could not be sincere in his offer, since the genius and interests of Bonaparte led only to war, Mr. Pitt declined to negotiate on the subject. It appeared afterward, as already stated, that Bonaparte did not wish for peace. When the question came before Parliament, February 3d, 1800, he delivered the third of his speeches contained in this volume. It is the most elaborate of all his efforts; and though worse reported than the other two, so far as language is concerned (Mr. Canning, indeed, says that Mr. Pitt suffered more in this respect than any orator of his day), it can hardly be too much admired for its broad and luminous statements, the closeness of its reasonings, and the fervor of its appeals.

In 1800, Mr. Pitt accomplished his favorite plan of a legislative union of Ireland with Great Britain. But he was unable to effect it without a distinct intimation to the Roman Catholics that they should receive, as a reward for their acquiescence, the boon of emancipation which they had been so long seeking. He did this without the privity of the King, and knowing his scruples on the subject, but still with a firm belief that his Majesty, in attaining so great an object, would yield those scruples to the wishes of the most enlightened men in the kingdom. But the moment he disclosed his plan to his colleagues, Lord Loughborough, says Lord Campbell, "set secretly to work, and composed a most elaborate and artful paper, showing forth the dangers likely to arise from Mr. Pitt's plan, in a manner admirably calculated to make an impression on the royal mind." The King was thus fortified against the proposal before Mr. Pitt had time to present his reasons; and, adopting the course he had taken with the East India Bill of Mr. Fox, declared at the levee, with a view to have his words circulated, "that he should consider any person who voted for the measure proposed by his minister as *personally indisposed toward himself!*" Mr. Pitt justly considered this as a direct exclusion from the public service, and so informed the cabinet, January 22d, 1800, having held the office of Prime Minister between sixteen and seventeen years. It was generally supposed at the time that he retired with a view to open a more easy way for negotiating a peace with France. He certainly desired peace, but the circumstances here stated were the true cause of his withdrawing from the government.

Mr. Addington (afterward Lord Sidmouth) succeeded him, and Mr. Pitt gave the new minister a cordial support. Mr. Wilberforce, in his diary, says, "Pitt has really behaved with a magnanimity unparalleled in a politician, and is wishing to form for Addington the best and strongest possible administration." He approved of the peace; and again, when the rupture took place, he gave the declaration of war, June 18th, 1803, his warmest support. His speech on this occasion (which, through an accident in the gallery, was never reported) is said by Lord Brougham to have "excelled all his other performances in vehement and spirit-stirring declamation; and this may be the more easily believed when we know that Mr. Fox, in his reply, said, 'The orators of antiquity would have admired, probably would have envied it.' The last half hour is described as having been one unbroken torrent of the most majestic declamation."

Mr. Addington had a timidity and inertness which wholly unfitted him for carrying on the war. The people were clamorous for a change of ministers, and Mr. Pitt was again called to the head of affairs, May 12th, 1804. Lord Brougham has reproached him for accepting office without insisting upon Catholic emancipation; but his former step had thrown the King into a fit of derangement for nearly three weeks, a new agitation of the subject might have produced the same result, and, as it was now obvious that emancipation could never be granted during the life of George III., Mr. Pitt, surely, was not to exclude himself from office on a mere point of etiquette, without the slightest advantage to the cause. He now formed his last great coalition against Bonaparte, but the battle of Austerlitz (December 2d, 1805) was a death blow to his hopes. Worn out with care and anxiety, his health had been declining for some months. On the 21st of January, 1806, the Bishop of Lincoln apprised him that his end was approaching. Mr. Pitt heard him with perfect composure, and after a few moments, rising as he spoke, and clasping his hands with the utmost fervor, he exclaimed, "I throw myself *entirely* (laying a strong emphasis on the last word) upon the mercy of God through the merits of Christ." He now arranged all his secular concerns with perfect calmness, and died at a quarter past four, Thursday morning, the 23d of January, 1806, in the forty-seventh year of his age. He was buried near his father in Westminster Abbey, and his debts, amounting to £40,000, were paid by the public. Mr. Wilberforce, who knew him more intimately than any other man, has given this testimony to his character: "Mr. Pitt had his foibles, and of course they were not diminished by so long a continuance in office; but for a clear and comprehensive view of the most complicated subject in all its relations; for that fairness of mind which disposes a man to follow out, and, when overtaken, to recognize the truth; for magnanimity, which made him ready to change his measures when he thought the good of the country required it, though he knew he should be charged with inconsistency on account of the change; for willingness to give a fair hearing to all that could be urged against his own opinions, and to listen to the suggestions of men whose understandings he knew to be inferior to his own; for personal purity, disinterestedness, integrity, and love of country, I have never known his equal. His strictness in regard to truth was astonishing, considering the situation he so long filled."

In person, Mr. Pitt was tall and slender; his features were somewhat harsh, but lighted up with intelligence by the flashes of his eye; his gesture was animated, but devoid of grace; his articulation was remarkably full and clear, filling the largest room with the volume of sound. His manner of entering the House was strikingly indicative of his absorption in the business before him. "From the instant he passed the doorway," says Wraxall, "he advanced up the floor with a quick and firm step, his head erect and thrown back, looking neither to the right nor the left, nor favoring with a nod or a glance any of the individuals seated on either side, among whom many who possessed £5000 a year would have been gratified even by so slight a mark of attention." Those who knew him best as a speaker expatiated with delight on "the perfection of his arrangement, the comprehensiveness of his reasonings, the power of his sarcasm, the magnificence of his declamation, the majestic tone of his voice, the legislative authority of his manner, and his felicitous observance of the temper of his audience." Mr. Canning has given the following sketch of his character, which will form an appropriate conclusion to this memoir.

"The character of this illustrious statesman early passed its ordeal. Scarcely had he attained the age at which reflection commences, when Europe with astonishment beheld him filling the first place in the councils of his country, and managing the vast mass of its concerns with all the vigor and steadiness of the most matured wisdom. Dignity—strength—discretion—these were among the masterly qualities of his mind at its first dawn. He had been nurtured a statesman, and his knowledge was of that kind which always lay ready for practical application. Not dealing in the subtleties of abstract politics, but moving in the slow, steady procession of reason, his conceptions were reflective, and his views correct. Habitually attentive to the concerns of government, he spared no pains to acquaint himself with whatever was connected, however minutely, with its prosperity. He was devoted to the state. Its interests engrossed all his study and engaged all his care. It was the element alone in which he seemed to live and move. He allowed himself but little recreation from his labors. His mind was always on its station, and its activity was unremitted.

"He did not hastily adopt a measure, nor hastily abandon it. The plan struck out by him for the preservation of Europe was the result of prophetic wisdom and profound policy. But, though defeated in many respects by the selfish ambition and short-sighted imbecility of foreign powers—whose rulers were too venal or too weak to follow the flight of that mind which would have taught them to outwing the storm—the policy involved in it has still a secret operation on the conduct of surrounding states. His plans were full of energy, and the principles which inspired them looked beyond the consequences of the hour.

"He knew nothing of that timid and wavering cast of mind which dares not abide by its own decision. He never suffered popular prejudice or party clamor to turn him aside from any measure which his deliberate judgment had adopted. He had a proud reliance on himself, and it was justified. Like the sturdy warrior leaning on his own battle-ax, conscious where his strength lay, he did not readily look beyond it.

"As a debater in the House of Commons, his speeches were logical and argumentative. If they did not often abound in the graces of metaphor, or sparkle with the brilliancy of wit, they were always animated, elegant, and classical. The strength of his oratory was intrinsic; it presented the rich and abundant resource of a clear discernment and a correct taste. His speeches are stamped with inimitable marks of originality. When replying to his opponents, his readiness was not more conspicuous than his energy. He was always prompt and always dignified. He could sometimes have recourse to the sportiveness of irony, but he did not often seek any other aid than was to be derived from an arranged and extensive knowledge of his subject. This qualified him fully to discuss the arguments of others, and forcibly to defend his own. Thus armed, it was rarely in the power of his adversaries, mighty as they were, to beat him from the field. His eloquence, occasionally rapid, electric, and vehement, was always chaste, winning, and persuasive—not awing into acquiescence, but arguing into conviction. His understanding was bold and comprehensive. Nothing seemed too remote for its reach or too large for its grasp.

"Unallured by dissipation and unswayed by pleasure, he never sacrificed the national treasure to the one, or the national interest to the other. To his unswerving integrity the most authentic of all testimony is to be found in that unbounded public confidence which followed him throughout the whole of his political career.

"Absorbed as he was in the pursuits of public life, he did not neglect to prepare himself in silence for that higher destination, which is at once the incentive and reward of human virtue. His talents, superior and splendid as they were, never made him forgetful of that Eternal Wisdom from which they emanated. The faith and fortitude of his last moments were affecting and exemplary."

SPEECH

OF MR. PITT ON THE ABOLITION OF THE SLAVE TRADE, DELIVERED IN THE HOUSE OF COMMONS, APRIL 2, 1792.

INTRODUCTION.

NUMEROUS petitions for the abolition of the African slave trade were presented to Parliament at the session of 1787–8. On the 9th of May, 1788, Mr. Pitt, acting for Mr. Wilberforce, who was confined by illness, moved that "the subject be taken up early the next session." This was accordingly done on the 19th of May, 1789, when Mr. Wilberforce laid open the enormities of this traffic in a speech of great compass and power. So conclusive were his statements, that Mr. Pitt was prepared to carry through the measure by an immediate vote; but yielded, at last, to a demand for the examination of witnesses in behalf of the slave merchants, remarking, however, that "he could by no means submit to the ultimate procrastination of so important a business." Every artifice was now used to protract the inquiry. The passions of the colonists were inflamed; the wealth and influence of the great commercial towns engaged in the trade, Liverpool, Bristol, &c., were arrayed against the measure; the revolution in St. Domingo, and the insurrection in Dominica, furnished plausible arguments to alarm the timid; the speedy depopulation of the West India Islands, with the loss of seventy millions sterling of property, was urged as the inevitable result; until the nation was staggered, and many well-wishers of the cause began to waver in their opinions. Some of Mr. Pitt's warmest supporters were of this number, and especially Mr. Dundas, with whom it was impossible for him to break, so that he felt himself no longer able to make it a ministerial question, or to insist on its being carried as a measure of the government. In the mean time, Mr. Wilberforce and his friends were not idle. Evidence of the most conclusive kind was collected from every quarter, and presented in so clear a light, as to relieve the public mind from the terrors which had been thrown around the subject, and to give a full exhibition of the unparalleled atrocities of the traffic, as then actually carried on.

Early in 1792, five hundred and seventeen petitions against the slave trade were laid before Parliament; and on the 2d of April, Mr. Wilberforce made a motion, supported by an able speech, for its *immediate suppression.* After a protracted debate, Mr. Dundas rose, and, declaring himself to be in favor of the ultimate extinction of the trade, pleaded for delay, insisting that the object aimed at by Mr. Wilberforce would be secured with far greater ease and certainty by a gradual than by an immediate abolition. Mr. Addington, the Speaker, followed him in the same strain. This called forth a reply from Mr. Pitt in the speech before us, being one of the ablest pieces of mingled argument and eloquence which he ever produced. He first took up the question of *expediency,* comparing the two schemes of gradual and immediate abolition; and while he put down Mr. Dundas and Mr. Addington completely on every point, he showed admirable tact in so doing it, as to leave no room for mortified feeling or personal resentment. He then proceeded to his main ground, that of *right.* "I now come to AFRICA! Why ought the slave trade to be abolished? Because it is *incurable injustice.* How much stronger, then, is the argument for immediate than for gradual abolition!" On this topic he put forth all his strength, exposing, in tones of lofty and indignant eloquence, the complicated enormities of a system which had made the shores of Africa for centuries a scene of cruelty and bloodshed, and brought infamy on the character of Christian nations engaged in this guilty traffic. Mr. Wilberforce says in his Journal, "Windham, who has no love for Pitt, tells me that Fox and Grey, with whom he walked home from this debate, agreed in thinking Pitt's speech one of the most extraordinary displays of eloquence they had ever heard. For the last twenty minutes he really seemed to be inspired."—P. 111.

SPEECH, &c.

MR. SPEAKER,—At this hour of the morning [four o'clock], I am afraid, sir, I am too much exhausted to enter so fully into the subject before the committee as I could wish; but if my bodily strength is in any degree equal to the task, I feel so strongly the magnitude of this question, that I am extremely earnest to deliver my sentiments, which I rise to do with more satisfaction, because I now look forward to the issue of this business with considerable hope of success.

The debate has this night taken a turn which, though it has produced a variety of new suggestions, has, upon the whole, contracted this question into a much narrower point than it was ever brought into before.

Ground narrowed by the debate.

I can not say that I quite agree with the right honorable gentleman over the way [Mr. Fox], for I am far from deploring all that has been said by my two honorable friends [Mr. Dundas and Mr. Addington]. I rather rejoice that they have now brought

All agree that the trade must be suppressed.

this subject to a fair issue; that something, at least, is already gained, and that the question has taken altogether a new course this night.[1] It is true, a difference of opinion has been stated, and has been urged with all the force of argument that could be given to it. But permit me to say that this difference has been urged upon principles very far removed from those which were maintained by the opponents of my honorable friend [Mr. Wilberforce], when he first brought forward his motion. There are very few of those who have spoken this night, who have not thought it their duty to declare their full and entire concurrence with my honorable friend in promoting the abolition of the slave trade as their ultimate object. However we may differ as to the time and manner of it, we are agreed in the abolition itself; and my honorable friends have expressed their agreement in this sentiment with that sensibility upon the subject, which humanity does most undoubtedly require. I do not, however, think they yet perceive what are the necessary consequences of their own concession, or follow up their own principles to their just conclusion.

The present question simply one of time.

The point now in dispute between us is a difference merely as to the period of time at which the abolition of the slave trade ought to take place. I therefore congratulate this House, the country, and the world, that this great point is gained. That we may now consider this trade as having received its condemnation; that its sentence is sealed; that this curse of mankind is seen by the House in its true light; and that the greatest stigma on our national character which ever yet existed is about to be removed; and, sir, which is still more important, that mankind, I trust, in general, are now likely to be delivered from *the greatest practical evil that has ever afflicted the human race;* from the severest and most extensive calamity recorded in the history of the world!

Ground of discussion.

In proceeding to give my reasons for concurring with my honorable friend [Mr. Wilberforce] in his motion, I shall necessarily advert to those topics which my honorable friends near me [Dundas and Addington] have touched upon, and which they stated to be their motives for preferring a gradual, and, in some degree, a distant abolition of the slave trade, to the more immediate and direct measure now proposed to you. Beginning as I do, with declaring that, in this respect, I differ completely from my right honorable friends near me, I do not, however, mean to say that I differ as to one observation which has been pressed rather strongly by them. If they can show that their proposition of a gradual abolition is more likely than ours to secure the object which we have in view; that by proceeding gradually we shall arrive more speedily at our end, and attain it with more certainty, than by a direct vote immediately to abolish; if they can show to the satisfaction both of myself and the committee, that our proposition has more the *appearance* of a speedy abolition than the *reality* of it, undoubtedly they will in this case make a convert of me, and my honorable friend who moved the question. They will make a convert of every man among us who looks to this (which I trust we all do) as a question not to be determined by theoretical principles or enthusiastic feelings, but considers the practicability of the measure, aiming simply to effect his object in the shortest time, and in the surest possible manner.[2] If, however, I shall be able to show that our measure proceeds more directly to its object, and secures it with more certainty, and within a less distant period; and that the slave trade will on our plan be abolished sooner than on theirs, may I not then hope that my right honorable friends will be as ready to adopt our proposition, as we should in the other case be willing to accede to theirs?

Preliminary inquiry: Can immediate abolition be enforced?

One of my right honorable friends has stated that an act passed here for the abolition of the slave trade would not secure its abolition. Now, sir, I should be glad to know why an act of the British Legislature, enforced by all those sanctions which we have undoubtedly the power and the right to apply, is not to be effectual; at least, as to every material purpose? Will not the executive power have the same appointment of the officers and the courts of judicature, by which all the causes relating to this subject must be tried, that it has in other cases? Will there not be the same system of law by which we now maintain a monopoly of commerce? If the same law, sir, be applied to the prohibition of the slave trade which is applied in the case of other contraband commerce, with all the same means of the country to back it, I am at a loss to know why the actual and total abolition is not as likely to be effected in this way, as by any plan or project of my honorable friends, for bringing about a gradual termination of it.[3] But my observation is extremely fortified by what fell from my honorable friend who spoke last. He has told you, sir, that if you

The laws are certainly strong enough.

[1] It is one characteristic of Mr. Pitt to open a discussion by some striking remark of this kind—some difference between him and a preceding speaker, some distinction, &c., &c.—which gives him an opportunity to state his ground with great clearness, and to place the question on its true footing. This throws a light forward upon the entire course he has to traverse, and conduces greatly to that luminous exposition of a subject for which he was so much celebrated.

[2] It is hardly necessary to remark how soon Mr. Pitt enters (as in these three sentences) on one of those *amplifications* by which he was accustomed to enforce his thoughts, presenting them in detail under different aspects upon which the mind might dwell.

[3] Mr. Pitt was much accustomed to argue, as in these four sentences, by *exhaustion*—by taking all the suppositions belonging to the case, and deducing the result. The turn which he next gives to the argument, by making Mr. Addington testify against himself, is an instance of the extraordinary sagacity for which he was distinguished in sifting the arguments of others.

will have patience with it for a few years, the slave trade must drop of itself, from the increasing dearness of the commodity imported, and the increasing progress, on the other hand, of internal population. Is it true, then, that the importations are so expensive and disadvantageous already, that the internal population is even now becoming a cheaper resource? I ask, then, if you leave to the importer no means of importation but by smuggling, and if, besides all the present disadvantages, you load him with all the charges and hazards of the smuggler, by taking care that the laws against smuggling are in this case watchfully and rigorously enforced, is there any danger of any considerable supply of fresh slaves being poured into the islands through this channel? And is there any real ground of fear, because a few slaves may have been smuggled in or out of the islands, that a bill will be useless and ineffectual on any such ground? The question under these circumstances will not bear a dispute.

Mr. Addington's argument turned against himself.

I. Perhaps, however, my honorable friends may take up another ground, and say, "It is true your measure would shut out further importations more immediately; but we do not mean to shut them out immediately. We think it right, on grounds of general expediency, that they should not be immediately shut out." Let us, therefore, now come to this question of the *expediency* of making the abolition distant and gradual, rather than immediate.

Expediency.

The argument of expediency, in my opinion, like every other argument in this disquisition, will not justify the continuance of the slave trade for one unnecessary hour. Supposing it to be in our power, which I have shown it is, to enforce the prohibition from this present time, the expediency of doing it is to me so clear, that if I went on this principle alone, I should not feel a moment's hesitation. What is the argument of expediency stated on the other side? It is doubted whether the deaths and births in the islands are, as yet, so nearly equal as to insure the keeping up a sufficient stock of laborers. In answer to this, I took the liberty of mentioning in a former year what appeared to me to be the state of population at that time. My observations were taken from documents which we have reason to judge authentic, and which carried on the face of them the conclusions I then stated; they were the clear, simple, and obvious result of a careful examination which I made into this subject, and any gentleman who will take the same pains may arrive at the same degree of satisfaction.

Population question.

These calculations, however, applied to a period of time that is now four or five years past. The births were then, in the general view of them, nearly equal to the deaths; and, as the state of population was shown, by a considerable retrospect, to be regularly increasing, an excess of births must, before this time, have taken place.

(1.) Births among the slaves nearly or quite equal to the deaths.

Another observation has been made as to the disproportion of the sexes. This, however, is a disparity which existed in any material degree only in former years; it is a disparity of which the slave trade has been itself the cause, which will gradually diminish as the slave trade diminishes, and must entirely cease if the trade shall be abolished; but which, nevertheless, is made the very plea for its continuance. I believe this disproportion of the sexes, taking the whole number of the islands, Creole as well as imported Africans, the latter of whom occasion all the disproportion, is not now by any means considerable.

(2.) The disparity of the sexes has ceased.

But, sir, I also showed that the great mortality, which turned the balance so as to make the deaths appear more numerous than the births, arose too from the imported Africans, who die in extraordinary numbers in the seasoning. If, therefore, the importation of negroes should cease, every one of the causes of mortality which I have now stated would cease also; nor can I conceive any reason why the present number of laborers should not maintain itself in the West Indies, except it be from some artificial cause, some fault in the islands; such as the impolicy of their governors, or the cruelty of the managers and officers whom they employ. I will not reiterate all that I said at that time, or go through island by island. It is true there is a difference in the ceded islands; and I state them possibly to be, in some respects, an excepted case. But we are not now to enter into the subject of the mortality in clearing new lands. It is, sir, undoubtedly another question; the mortality here is ten-fold; neither is it to be considered as the carrying on, but as the setting on foot a slave trade for the purpose of peopling the colony; a measure which I think will not now be maintained. I therefore desire gentlemen to tell me fairly, whether the period they look to is not now arrived; whether, at this hour, the West Indies may not be declared to *have actually attained a state in which they can maintain their population?* And upon the answer I must necessarily receive, I think I could safely rest the whole of the question.

(3.) Abolition would remove one great source of mortality, that among the imported negroes.

One honorable gentleman has rather ingeniously observed, that one or other of these two assertions of ours must necessarily be false: that either the population must be decreasing, which we deny, or, if the population is increasing, that the slaves must be perfectly well treated (this being the cause of such population), which we deny also. That the population is rather increasing than otherwise, and also that the general treatment is by no means so good as it ought to be, are both points which have been separately proved by different evidences; nor are these two points so entirely incompatible. The ill treatment must be very great, indeed, in order to diminish materially the population of any race of people. That it is not so extremely great as to do this, I will admit. I will even admit, if you please, that this charge may possibly have been some

His opponents' dilemma on this subject set aside.

times exaggerated; and I certainly think that it applies less and less as we come nearer to the present times.[4]

Dilemma turned back on its author.

But let us see how this contradiction of ours, as it is thought, really stands, and how the explanation of it will completely settle our minds on the point in question. Do the slaves diminish in numbers? It can be nothing but ill treatment that causes the diminution. This ill treatment the abolition must and will restrain. In this case, therefore, we ought to vote for the abolition. On the other hand, do you choose to say that the slaves clearly increase in numbers? Then you want no importations, and, in this case also, you may safely vote for the abolition. Or, if you choose to say, as the third and only other case which can be put, and which perhaps is the nearest to the truth, that the population is nearly stationary, and the treatment neither so bad nor so good as it might be; then surely, sir, it will not be denied that this, of all others, is, on each of the two grounds, the proper period for stopping farther supplies; for your population, which you own is already stationary, will thus be made undoubtedly to increase from the births, and the good treatment of your present slaves, which I am now supposing is but very moderate, will be necessarily improved also by the same measure of abolition. I say, therefore, that these propositions, contradictory as they may be represented, are in truth not at all inconsistent, but even come in aid of each other, and lead to a conclusion that is decisive. And let it be always remembered that, in this branch of my argument, I have only in view the well-being of the West Indies, and do not now ground any thing on the African part of the question.

(4.) Any remaining difficulties can and ought to be removed by the colonial governments.

But, sir, I may carry these observations respecting the islands much farther. It is within the power of the colonists, and it is then their indispensable duty to apply themselves to the correction of those various abuses by which population is restrained. The most important consequences may be expected to attend colonial regulations for this purpose. With the improvement of internal population, the condition of every negro will improve also; his liberty will advance, or, at least, he will be approaching to a state of liberty. Nor can you increase the happiness, or extend the freedom of the negro, without adding in an equal degree to the safety of the islands, and of all their inhabitants. Thus, sir, in the place of slaves, who naturally have an interest directly opposite to that of their masters, and are therefore viewed by them with an eye of constant suspicion, you will create a body of valuable citizens and subjects, forming a part of the same community, having a common interest with their superiors in the security and prosperity of the whole.

They have every motive of interest to better the condition of their slaves.

And here let me add, that in proportion as you increase the happiness of these unfortunate beings, you will undoubtedly increase in effect the quantity of their labor also. Gentlemen talk of the diminution of the labor of the islands! I will venture to assert that, even if in consequence of the abolition there were to be some decrease in the number of hands, the quantity of work done, supposing the condition of the slaves to improve, would by no means diminish in the same proportion; perhaps would be far from diminishing at all. For if you restore to this degraded race the true feelings of men; if you take them out from among the order of brutes, and place them on a level with the rest of the human species, they will then work with that energy which is natural to men, and their labor will be productive, in a thousand ways, above what it has yet been; as the labor of a man is always more productive than that of a mere brute.

This proved from facts furnished by the West Indians themselves.

It generally happens that in every bad cause information arises out of the evidence of its defenders themselves, which serves to expose in one part or other the weakness of their defense. It is the characteristic of such a cause, that if it be at all gone into, even by its own supporters, it is liable to be ruined by the contradictions in which those who maintain it are forever involved.

They testify, that a slave does twice the work when laboring for himself.

The committee of the Privy Council of Great Britain sent over certain queries to the West India islands, with a view of elucidating the present subject; and they particularly inquired whether the negroes had any days or hours allotted to them in which they might work for themselves. The assemblies in their answers, with an air of great satisfaction, state the labor of the slaves to be moderate, and the West India system to be well calculated to promote the domestic happiness of the slaves. They add, "that proprietors are not compelled by law to allow their slaves any part of the six working days of the week for themselves, but that it is the general practice to allow them one afternoon in every week out of crop-time; which, with such hours as they choose to work on Sundays, is time amply sufficient for their own purposes." Now, therefore, will the negroes, or I may rather say, do the negroes work for their own emolument? I beg the committee's attention to this point. The Assembly of Grenada proceeds to state—I have their own words for it, "that though the negroes are allowed the afternoons of only one day in every week, they will do as much work in that afternoon, when employed for their own benefit, as in the whole day when employed in their master's service."

This a decisive argument for improving their condition.

Now, sir, I will desire you to burn all my calculations; to disbelieve, if you please, every word I have said on the present state of population; nay, I will admit, for the sake of argument, that the numbers are decreasing, and the productive labor at present

[4] Mr. Pitt's peculiar dexterity in reply is here shown, in the ease with which he extricates himself from this dilemma and turns it upon his opponent in the next paragraph.

insufficient for the cultivation of those countries; and I will then ask, whether the increase in the *quantity of labor* which is reasonably to be expected from the improved condition of the slaves is not, by the admission of the islands themselves, by their admission not merely of an argument but a fact, far more than sufficient to counterbalance any decrease which can be rationally apprehended from a defective state of their population? Why, sir, a negro, if he works for himself, and not for a master, will do double work! This is their own account. If you will believe the planters, if you will believe the Legislature of the islands, the productive labor of the colonies would, in case the negroes worked as free laborers instead of slaves, be literally doubled. Half the present laborers, on this supposition, would suffice for the whole cultivation of our islands on the present scale! I therefore confidently ask the House, whether, in considering the whole of this question, we may not fairly look forward to an improvement in the condition of these unhappy and degraded beings; not only as an event desirable on the ground of humanity and political prudence; but also as a means of increasing, very considerably indeed, even without any increasing population, the productive industry of the islands?

When gentlemen are so nicely balancing the past and future means of cultivating the plantations, let me request them to put this argument into the scale; and the more they consider it, the more will they be satisfied that both the solidity of the principle which I have stated, and the fact which I have just quoted, in the very words of the Colonial Legislature, will bear me out in every inference I have drawn. I think they will perceive, also, that it is the undeniable duty of this House, on the grounds of true policy, immediately to sanction and carry into effect that system which insures these important advantages; in addition to all those other inestimable blessings which follow in their train.

Expediency demands this improvement.

If, therefore, the argument of expediency, as applying to the West India islands, is the test by which this question is to be tried, I trust I have now established this proposition, namely, that whatever tends most speedily and effectually to meliorate the condition of the slaves, is undoubtedly, on the ground of expediency, leaving justice out of the question, the main object to be pursued.

And therefore demands a suppression of the slave trade.

That the immediate abolition of the slave trade will most eminently have this effect, and that it is the only measure from which this effect can in any considerable degree be expected, are points to which I shall presently come; but before I enter upon them, let me notice one or two farther circumstances.

Other considerations leading to the same conclusion.

We are told, and by respectable and well-informed persons, that the purchase of new negroes has been injurious instead of profitable to the planters themselves; so large a proportion of these unhappy wretches being found to perish in the seasoning. Writers well versed in this subject have even advised that, in order to remove the temptation which the slave trade offers to expend large sums in this injudicious way, the door of importation should be shut. This very plan we now propose, the mischief of which is represented to be so great as to outweigh so many other momentous considerations, has actually been recommended by some of the best authorities, as one highly requisite to be adopted on the very principle of advantage to the islands; not merely on that principle of general and political advantage on which I have already touched, but for the advantage of the very individuals who would otherwise be most forward in purchasing slaves.

(a.) The purchase of new negroes from slavers tends to impoverish the planters.

On the part of the West Indies it is urged, "the planters are in debt: they are already distressed; if you stop the slave trade, they will be ruined." Mr. Long, the celebrated historian of Jamaica, recommends the stopping of importations, as a receipt for enabling the plantations which are embarrassed to get out of debt. I will quote his words. Speaking of the usurious terms on which money is often borrowed for the purchase of fresh slaves, he advises "the laying a duty equal to a prohibition on all negroes imported for the space of four or five years, except for re-exportation." "Such a law," he proceeds to say, "would be attended with the following good consequences. It would put an immediate stop to these extortions. It would enable the planter to retrieve his affairs by preventing him from running in debt, either by renting or purchasing of negroes. It would render such recruits less necessary, by the redoubled care he would be obliged to take of his present stock, the preservation of their lives and health. And, lastly, it would raise the value of negroes in the island. A North American province, by this prohibition alone for a few years, from being deeply plunged in debt, has become independent, rich, and flourishing." On this authority of Mr. Long I rest the question, whether the prohibition of further importations is that rash, impolitic, and completely ruinous measure, which it is so confidently declared to be with respect to our West India plantations.

Indemnification not refused, but the case must be clearly made out.

I do not, however, mean, in thus treating this branch of the subject, absolutely to exclude the question of indemnification on the supposition of possible disadvantages affecting the West Indies through the abolition of the slave trade. But when gentlemen set up a claim of compensation merely on those general allegations, which are all that I have yet heard from them, I can only answer, let them produce their case in a distinct and specific form; and if upon any practicable or reasonable grounds it shall claim consideration, it will then be time enough for Parliament to decide upon it.

I now come to another circumstance of great weight, connected with this part of the question. I mean the danger to which the islands are exposed from those negroes who are newly imported. This, sir, like the observation which I lately made, is no mere speculation of ours; for here, again, I refer you to Mr. Long, the historian of Jamaica. He treats particularly of the dangers to be dreaded from the introduction of Coromantine negroes; an appellation under which are comprised several descriptions of Africans obtained on the Gold Coast, whose native country is not exactly known, and who are purchased in a variety of markets, having been brought from some distance inland. With a view of preventing insurrections, he advises that, "by laying a duty equal to a prohibition, no more of these Coromantines should be bought;" and, after noticing one insurrection which happened through their means, he tells you of another in the following year, in which thirty-three Coromantines, most of whom had been newly imported, suddenly rose, and in the space of an hour murdered and wounded no less than nineteen white persons.

(*b*.) Insurrections to be dreaded chiefly from imported negroes, not those born in the islands.

To the authority of Mr. Long, both in this and other parts of his work, I may add the recorded opinion of the committee of the House of Assembly of Jamaica itself; who, in consequence of a rebellion among the slaves, were appointed to inquire into the best means of preventing future insurrections. The committee reported, "that the rebellion had originated (like most or all others) with the Coromantines;" and they proposed that a bill should be brought in "for laying a higher duty on the importation of these particular negroes," which was intended to operate as a prohibition.

But the danger is not confined to the importation of Coromantines. Mr. Long, carefully investigating as he does the causes of such frequent insurrections, particularly at Jamaica, accounts for them from the greatness of its general importations. "In two years and a half," says he, "twenty-seven thousand negroes have been imported." "No wonder we have rebellions! Twenty-seven thousand in two years and a half!" Why, sir, I believe that in some late years there have been as many imported into the same island within the same period! Surely, sir, when gentlemen talk so vehemently of the safety of the islands, and charge us with being so indifferent to it; when they speak of the calamities of St. Domingo, and of similar dangers impending over their own heads at the present hour, it ill becomes them to be the persons who are crying out for further importations. It ill becomes them to charge upon us the crime of stirring up insurrections—upon us who are only adopting the very principles which Mr. Long—which in part even the Legislature of Jamaica itself laid down in the time of danger, with an avowed view to the prevention of any such calamity.

The House, I am sure, will easily believe it is no small satisfaction to me, that among the many arguments for prohibiting the slave trade which crowd upon my mind, the security of our West India possessions against internal commotions, as well as foreign enemies, is among the most prominent and most forcible. And here let me apply to my two right honorable friends, and ask them, whether in this part of the argument they do not see reason for immediate abolition? Why should you any longer import into those countries that which is the very seed of insurrection and rebellion? Why should you persist in introducing those latent principles of conflagration, which if they should once burst forth, may annihilate in a single day the industry of a hundred years? Why will you subject yourselves, with open eyes, to the evident and imminent risk of a calamity which may throw you back a whole century in your profits, in your cultivation, in your progress to the emancipation of your slaves; and disappointing at once every one of these golden expectations, may retard, not only the accomplishment of that happy system which I have attempted to describe, but may cut off even your opportunity of taking any one introductory step? Let us begin from this time! Let us not commit these important interests to any further hazard! Let us prosecute this great object from this very hour! Let us vote that the abolition of the slave trade shall be immediate, and not left to I know not what future time or contingency! Will my right honorable friends answer for the safety of the islands during any imaginable intervening period? Or do they think that any little advantages of the kind which they state, can have any weight in that scale of expediency in which this great question ought undoubtedly to be tried.

The suppression of the trade, therefore, brings no hazard, but great security to the West Indies

Thus stated, and thus alone, sir, can it be truly stated, to what does the whole of my right honorable friend's argument, on the head of expediency, amount? It amounts but to this: The colonies, on the one hand, would have to struggle with some few difficulties and disadvantages at the first, for the sake of obtaining on the other hand immediate security to their leading interests; of insuring, sir, even their own political existence; and for the sake also of immediately commencing that system of progressive improvement in the condition of slaves, which is necessary to raise them from the state of brutes to that of rational beings, but which never can begin *until the introduction of these new, disaffected, and dangerous Africans into the same gangs shall have been stopped.* If any argument can in the slightest degree justify the severity that is now so generally practiced in the treatment of the slaves, it must be the introduction of these Africans. It is the introduction of these Africans that renders all idea of emancipation for the present so chimerical, and the very mention of it so dreadful. It is the introduction of these Africans that keeps down the condition of all plantation negroes. Whatever system of treatment is deemed necessary by the planters to be adopted toward these new Africans, extends itself to the other slaves also; instead, therefore, of deferring the hour when you will finally put an end to importations, vainly pur-

Argument summed up.

posing that the condition of your present slaves should previously be mended, you must, in the very first instance, stop your importations, if you hope to introduce any rational or practicable plan, either of gradual emancipation or present general improvement.

II. Being now done with this question of expediency as affecting the islands, I come next to a proposition advanced by my right honorable friend [Mr. Dundas], which appeared to intimate that, on account of some patrimonial rights of the West Indies, the prohibition of the slave trade might be considered as an invasion of their legal inheritance.

Claim of *Patrimonial right.*

Now, in answer to this proposition, I must make two or three remarks, which I think my right honorable friend will find some considerable difficulty in answering.

I observe, then, that his argument, if it be worth any thing, applies just as much to gradual as immediate abolition. I have no doubt, that at whatever period he might be disposed to say the abolition should actually take place, this defense will equally be set up; for it certainly is just as good an argument against an abolition seven or seventy years hence, as against an abolition at this moment. It supposes we have no right whatever to stop the importations; and even though the injury to our plantations, which some gentlemen suppose to attend the measure of immediate abolition, should be admitted gradually to lessen by the lapse of a few years, yet in point of principle the absence of all right of interference would remain the same. My right honorable friend, therefore, I am sure will not press an argument not less hostile to his proposition than to ours.

(1.) As strong against a gradual as against an immediate suppression of the traffic.

But let us investigate the foundation of this objection, and I will commence what I have to say by putting a question to my right honorable friend. It is chiefly on the presumed ground of our being bound by a parliamentary sanction heretofore given to the African slave trade, that this argument against the abolition is rested. Does, then, my right honorable friend, or does any man in this House think, that the slave trade has received any such parliamentary sanction as must place it more out of the jurisdiction of the Legislature forever after, than the other branches of our national commerce? I ask, is there any one regulation of any part of our commerce, which, if this argument be valid, may not equally be objected to, on the ground of its affecting some man's patrimony, some man's property, or some man's expectations? Let it never be forgotten that the argument I am canvassing would be just as strong if the possession affected were small, and the possessors humble; for on every principle of justice, the property of any single individual, or small number of individuals, is as sacred as that of the great body of West Indians. Justice ought to extend her protection with rigid impartiality to the rich and to the poor, to the powerful and to the humble. If this be the case, in what a situation does my right honorable friend's argument place the Legislature of Britain? What room is left for their interference in the regulation of any part of our commerce? It is scarcely possible to lay a duty on any one article which may not, when first imposed, be said in some way to affect the property of individuals, and even of some entire classes of the community. If the laws respecting the slave trade imply a contract for its perpetual continuance, I will venture to say, there does not pass a year without some act equally pledging the faith of Parliament to the perpetuating of some other branch of commerce. In short, I repeat my observation, that no new tax can be imposed, much less can any prohibitory duty be ever laid on any branch of trade that has before been regulated by Parliament, if this principle be once admitted.

(2.) The slave trade never had the sanction of Parliament.

This claim would imply a sanction and pledge for the perpetuity of *every* thing subjected to taxation.

Before I refer to the acts of Parliament by which the public faith is said to be pledged, let me remark, also, that a contract for the continuance of the slave trade must, on the principles which I shall presently insist on, have been void, even from the beginning; for if this trade is an outrage upon justice, and only another name for fraud, robbery, and murder, will any man urge that the Legislature could possibly by any pledge whatever incur the obligation of being an accessary, or, I may even say, a principal in the commission of such enormities, by sanctioning their continuance? As well might an individual think himself bound by a promise to commit an assassination. I am confident gentlemen must see that our proceeding on such grounds would infringe all the principles of law, and subvert the very foundation of morality.

(3.) A pledge for the perpetuity of the slave trade being unjust, would be invalid.

Let us now see how far these acts themselves show that there is that sort of parliamentary pledge to continue the African slave trade. The act of 23 George II., c. xxxi., is that by which we are supposed to be bound up by contract, to sanction all those horrors now so incontrovertibly proved. How surprised, then, sir, must the House be to find that, by a clause of their very act, some of these outrages are expressly forbidden! It says: "No commander or master of a ship trading to Africa, shall by fraud, force, or violence, or by any indirect practice whatsoever, take on board or carry away from the coast of Africa, any negro, or native of the said country, or commit any violence on the natives, to the prejudice of the said trade, and that every person so offending shall for every such offense forfeit," &c. When it comes to the penalty, sorry am I to say, that we see too close a resemblance to the West India law, which inflicts the payment of £30 as the punishment for murdering a negro. The price of blood in Africa is £100, but even this penalty is enough to prove that the act at least does not sanction, much less does it engage to perpetuate enormities; and the whole trade has now been demonstrated to be a mass, a system of enormities; of

Acts of Parliament examined.

enormities which incontrovertibly bid defiance not only to this clause, but to every regulation which our ingenuity can devise and our power carry into effect. Nothing can accomplish the object of this clause but an extinction of the trade itself.

Motive for these enactments.

But, sir, let us see what was the motive for carrying on the trade at all. The preamble of the act states it: "Whereas, the trade to and from Africa is very advantageous to Great Britain, and necessary for the supplying the plantations and colonies thereunto belonging with a sufficient number of negroes at reasonable rates, and for that purpose the said trade should be carried on," &c. Here, then, we see what the Parliament had in view when it passed this act; and I have clearly shown that not one of the occasions on which it grounded its proceedings now exists. I may then plead, I think, the very act itself as an argument for the abolition. If it is shown that, instead of being "very advantageous" to Great Britain, this trade is the most destructive that can well be imagined to her interests; that it is the ruin of our seamen; that it stops the extension of our manufactures; if it is proved, in the second place, that it is not now necessary for the "supplying our plantations with negroes;" if it is further established that this traffic was from the very beginning contrary to the first principles of justice, and consequently that a pledge for its continuance, had one been attempted to be given, must have been completely and absolutely void; where then, in this act of Parliament, is the contract to be found by which Britain is bound, as she is said to be, never to listen to her own true interests, and to the cries of the natives of Africa? Is it not clear that all argument, founded on the supposed pledged faith of Parliament, makes against those who employ it? I refer you to the principles which obtain in other cases. Every trade act shows undoubtedly that the Legislature is used to pay a tender regard to all classes of the community. But if for the sake of moral duty, of national honor, or even of great political advantage, it is thought right, by authority of Parliament, to alter any long-established system, Parliament is competent to do it. The Legislature will undoubtedly be careful to subject individuals to as little inconvenience as possible; and if any peculiar hardship should arise that can be distinctly stated and fairly pleaded, there will ever, I am sure, be a liberal feeling toward them in the Legislature of this country, which is the guardian of all who live under its protection. On the present occasion, the most powerful considerations call upon us to abolish the slave trade; and if we refuse to attend to them on the alleged ground of pledged faith and contract, we shall depart as widely from the practice of Parliament as from the path of moral duty. If, indeed, there is any case of hardship which comes within the proper cognizance of Parliament, and calls for the exercise of its liberality—well! But such a case must be reserved for calm consideration, as a matter distinct from the present question.

The same motive justifies the suppression of the slave trade.

I beg pardon for dwelling so long on the argument of expediency, and on the manner in which it affects the West Indies. I have been carried away by my own feelings on some of these points into a greater length than I intended, especially considering how fully the subject has been already argued. The result of all I have said is, that there exists no impediment, no obstacle, no shadow of reasonable objection on the ground of pledged faith, or even on that of national expediency, to the abolition of this trade. On the contrary, all the arguments drawn from those sources plead for it, and they plead much more loudly, and much more strongly in every part of the question, for an immediate than for a gradual abolition.

Injustice of the trade.

III. But now, sir, I come to Africa. That is the ground on which I rest, and here it is that I say my right honorable friends do not carry their principles to their full extent. Why ought the slave trade to be abolished? *Because it is incurable* INJUSTICE! How much stronger, then, is the argument for immediate than gradual abolition! By allowing it to continue even for one hour, do not my right honorable friends weaken—do not they desert, their own argument of its injustice? If on the ground of injustice it ought to be abolished at last, why ought it not now? Why is injustice to be suffered to remain for a single hour? From what I hear without doors, it is evident that there is a general conviction entertained of its being far from just, and from that very conviction of its injustice some men have been led, I fear, to the supposition that the slave trade never could have been permitted to begin, but from some strong and irresistible necessity; a necessity, however, which, if it was fancied to exist at first, I have shown can not be thought by any man whatever to exist at present. This plea of necessity, thus presumed, and presumed, as I suspect, from the circumstance of injustice itself, has caused a sort of acquiescence in the continuance of this evil. Men have been led to place it in the rank of those necessary evils which are supposed to be the lot of human creatures, and to be permitted to fall upon some countries or individuals, rather than upon others, by that Being whose ways are inscrutable to us, and whose dispensations, it is conceived, we ought not to look into. The origin of evil is, indeed, a subject beyond the reach of the human understanding; and the permission of it by the Supreme Being, is a subject into which it belongs not to us to inquire. But where the evil in question is a moral evil which a man can scrutinize, and where that moral evil has its origin with ourselves, let us not imagine that we can clear our consciences by this general, not to say irreligious and impious way of laying aside the question. If we reflect at all on this subject, we must see that every necessary evil supposes that some other and greater evil would be incurred were it removed. I therefore desire to ask, what can

Plea of necessity unfounded.

be that greater evil which can be stated to overbalance the one in question? I know of no evil that ever has existed, nor can imagine any evil to exist, worse than the tearing of EIGHTY THOUSAND PERSONS annually from their native land, by a combination of the most civilized nations in the most enlightened quarter of the globe; but more especially by that nation which calls herself the most free and the most happy of them all. Even if these miserable beings were proved guilty of every crime before you take them off, of which however not a single proof is adduced, ought *we* to take upon ourselves the office of executioners? And even if we condescend so far, still can we be justified in taking them, unless we have clear proof that they are criminals?

Guilt and dishonor of the trade, even if the slaves were criminals.

But if we go much farther; if we ourselves tempt them to sell their fellow creatures to us, we may rest assured that they will take care to provide by every method, by kidnapping, by village-breaking, by unjust wars, by iniquitous condemnations, by rendering Africa a scene of bloodshed and misery, a supply of victims increasing in proportion to our demand. Can we, then, hesitate in deciding whether the wars in Africa are their wars or ours? It was our arms in the River Cameroon, put into the hands of the trader, that furnished him with the means of pushing his trade; and I have no more doubt that they are British arms, put into the hands of Africans, which promote universal war and desolation, than I can doubt their having done so in that individual instance.

English capital and arms directly used in kidnapping.

I have shown how great is the enormity of this evil, even on the supposition that we take only convicts and prisoners of war. But take the subject in the other way; take it on the grounds stated by the right honorable gentleman over the way; and how does it stand? Think of EIGHTY THOUSAND persons carried away out of their country, by *we know not what means;* for crimes imputed; for light or inconsiderable faults; for debt, perhaps; for the crime of witchcraft; or a thousand other weak and scandalous pretexts! Besides all the fraud and kidnapping, the villainies and perfidy, by which the slave trade is supplied. Reflect on these eighty thousand persons thus annually taken off! There is something in the horror of it, that surpasses all the bounds of imagination. Admitting that there exists in Africa something like to courts of justice; yet what an office of humiliation and meanness is it in us, to take upon ourselves to carry into execution the partial, the cruel, iniquitous sentences of such courts, as if we also were strangers to all religion, and to the first principles of justice.

Horrors of the result.

But that country, it is said, has been in some degree civilized, and civilized by us. It is said they have gained some knowledge of the principles of justice. What, sir, have they gained the principles of justice from *us?* Is their civilization brought about by us! Yes, we give them enough of our intercourse to convey to them the means, and to initiate them in the study of mutual destruction. We give them just enough of the forms of justice to enable them to add the pretext of legal trials to their other modes of perpetrating the most atrocious iniquity. We give them just enough of European improvements, to enable them the more effectually to turn Africa into a ravaged wilderness. Some evidences say that the Africans are addicted to the practice of gambling; that they even sell their wives and children, and ultimately themselves. Are these, then, the legitimate sources of slavery? Shall we pretend that we can thus acquire an honest right to exact the labor of these people? Can we pretend that we have a right to carry away to distant regions men of whom we know nothing by authentic inquiry, and of whom there is every reasonable presumption to think that those who sell them to us have no right to do so? But the evil does not stop here. I feel that there is not time for me to make all the remarks which the subject deserves, and I refrain from attempting to enumerate half the dreadful consequences of this system. Do you think nothing of the ruin and the miseries in which so many other individuals, still remaining in Africa, are involved in consequence of carrying off so many myriads of people? Do you think nothing of their families which are left behind; of the connections which are broken; of the friendships, attachments, and relationships that are burst asunder? Do you think nothing of the miseries in consequence, that are felt from generation to generation; of the privation of that happiness which might be communicated to them by the introduction of civilization, and of mental and moral improvement? A happiness which you withhold from them so long as you permit the slave trade to continue. What do you yet know of the internal state of Africa? You have carried on a trade to that quarter of the globe from this civilized and enlightened country; but such a trade, that, instead of diffusing either knowledge or wealth, it has been the check to every laudable pursuit. Instead of any fair interchange of commodities; instead of conveying to them, from this highly favored land, any means of improvement, you carry with you that noxious plant by which every thing is withered and blasted; under whose shade nothing that is useful or profitable to Africa will ever flourish or take root. Long as that continent has been known to navigators, the extreme line and boundaries of its coasts is all with which Europe has yet become acquainted; while other countries in the same parallel of latitude, through a happier system of intercourse, have reaped the blessings of a mutually beneficial commerce. But as to the whole interior of that continent, you are, by your own principles of commerce, as yet entirely shut out. Africa is known to you only in its skirts. Yet even there you are able to infuse a poison that spreads its contagious effects from one end of it to the other; which penetrates to its very center, corrupting every part to which it reaches. You there subvert the

Effects of English civilization upon Africa.

whole order of nature; you aggravate every natural barbarity, and furnish to every man living on that continent, motives for committing, under the name and pretext of commerce, acts of perpetual violence and perfidy against his neighbor.

England should be eager to remove the guilt and shame of this perversion of her commerce.

Thus, sir, has the perversion of British commerce carried misery instead of happiness to one whole quarter of the globe. False to the very principles of trade, misguided in our policy, and unmindful of our duty, what astonishing—I had almost said, what *irreparable* mischief, have we brought upon that continent! How shall we hope to obtain, if it be possible, forgiveness from Heaven for those enormous evils we have committed, if we refuse to make use of those means which the mercy of Providence hath still reserved to us, for wiping away the guilt and shame with which we are now covered. If we refuse even this degree of compensation; if, knowing the miseries we have caused, we refuse even now to put a stop to them, how greatly aggravated will be the guilt of Great Britain! and what a blot will these transactions forever be in the history of this country! Shall we, then, delay to repair these injuries, and to begin rendering justice to Africa? Shall we not count the days and hours that are suffered to intervene, and to delay the accomplishment of such a work? Reflect what an immense object is before you; what an object for a nation to have in view, and to have a prospect, under the favor of Providence, of being now permitted to attain! I think the House will agree with me in cherishing the ardent wish to enter without delay upon the measures necessary for these great ends; and I am sure that the immediate abolition of the slave trade is the first, the principal, the most indispensable act of policy, of duty, and of justice, that the Legislature of this country has to take, if it is indeed their wish to secure those important objects to which I have alluded, and which we are bound to pursue by the most solemn obligations.

Refutation of objections. (1.) That other nations will not unite in abolishing the trade.

There is, however, one argument set up as a universal answer to every thing that can be urged on our side; whether we address ourselves to the understandings of our opponents, or to their hearts and consciences. It is necessary I should remove this formidable objection; for, though not often stated in distinct terms, I fear it is one which has a very wide influence. The slave trade system, it is supposed, has taken so deep root in Africa, that it is absurd to think of its being eradicated; and the abolition of that share of trade carried on by Great Britain, and especially if her example is not followed by other powers, is likely to be of very little service. Give me leave to say, in reply to so dangerous an argument, that we ought to be extremely sure, indeed, of the assumption on which it rests, before we venture to rely on its validity; before we decide that an evil which we ourselves contribute to inflict is incurable, and on that very plea, refuse to desist from bearing our part in the system which produces it. You are not sure, it is said, that other nations will give up the trade, if you should renounce it. I answer, if this trade is as criminal as it is asserted to be, or if it has in it a thousandth part of the criminality, which I and others, after thorough investigation of the subject, charge upon it, God forbid that we should hesitate in determining to relinquish so iniquitous a traffic, even though it should be retained by other countries. God forbid, however, that we should fail to do our utmost toward inducing other countries to abandon a bloody commerce, which they have probably been, in a good measure, led by our example to pursue. God forbid that we should be capable of wishing to arrogate to ourselves the glory of being singular in renouncing it!

I tremble at the thought of gentlemen's indulging themselves in this argument; an argument as pernicious as it is futile. "We are friends," say they, "to humanity. We are second to none of you in our zeal for the good of Africa; but the French will not abolish—the Dutch will not abolish. We wait, therefore, on prudential principles, till they join us, or set us an example."

England, as most guilty, ought to lead the way.

How, sir, is this enormous evil ever to be eradicated, if every nation is thus prudentially to wait till the concurrence of all the world shall have been obtained? Let me remark, too, that there is no nation in Europe that has, on the one hand, plunged so deeply into this guilt as Britain; or that is so likely, on the other, to be looked up to as an example, if she should have the manliness to be the first in decidedly renouncing it. But, sir, does not this argument apply a thousand times more strongly in a contrary way?[5] How much more justly may other nations point to us, and say, "Why should we abolish the slave trade, when Great Britain has not abolished? Britain, free as she is, just and honorable as she is, and deeply, also, involved as she is in this commerce above all nations, not only has not abolished, but has refused to abolish. She has investigated it well; she has gained the completest insight into its nature and effects; she has collected volumes of evidence on every branch of the subject. Her Senate has deliberated—has deliberated again and again; and what is the result? She has gravely and solemnly determined to sanction the slave trade. She sanctions it at least for a while—her Legislature, therefore, it is plain, sees no guilt in it, and has thus furnished us with the strongest evidence that she can furnish—of the justice unquestionably—and of the policy also, in a certain measure, and in certain cases at least, of permitting this traffic to continue."

Other nations may be expected to follow.

This, sir, is the argument with which we furnish the other nations of Europe, if we again refuse to put an end to the slave trade. Instead, therefore, of imagining, that by choosing to presume on their

[5] This taking an opponent's argument "in the *contrary* way," is one of Mr. Pitt's most characteristic modes of confuting an antagonist.

continuing it, we shall have exempted ourselves from guilt, and have transferred the whole criminality to them; let us rather reflect that, on the very principle urged against us, we shall henceforth have to answer for their crimes, as well as our own. We have strong reasons to believe that it depends upon us, whether other countries will persist in this bloody trade or not. Already we have suffered one year to pass away, and now the question is renewed, a proposition is made for gradual, with the view of preventing immediate abolition. I know the difficulty that exists in attempting to reform long-established abuses; and I know the danger arising from the argument in favor of delay, in the case of evils which, nevertheless, are thought too enormous to be borne, when considered as perpetual. But by proposing some other period than the present, by prescribing some condition, by waiting for some contingency, or by refusing to proceed till a thousand favorable circumstances unite together; perhaps until we obtain the general concurrence of Europe (a concurrence which I believe never yet took place at the commencement of any one improvement in policy or in morals), year after year escapes, and the most enormous evils go unredressed. We see this abundantly exemplified, not only in public, but in private life. Similar observations have been often applied to the case of personal reformation. If you go into the street, it is a chance but the first person who crosses you is one,

Qui recte vivendi prorogat horam.[6]

We may wait; we may delay to cross the stream before us, till it has run down; but we shall wait forever, for the river will still flow on, without being exhausted. We shall be no nearer the object which we profess to have in view, so long as the step, which alone can bring us to it, is not taken. Until the actual, the only remedy is applied, we ought neither to flatter ourselves that we have as yet thoroughly laid to heart the evil we affect to deplore; nor that there is as yet any reasonable assurance of its being brought to an actual termination.

(2.) That the African race can not be civilized, but are doomed to barbarism.

It has also been occasionally urged, that there is something in the disposition and nature of the Africans themselves which renders all prospect of civilization on that continent extremely unpromising. "It has been known," says Mr. Frazer, in his evidence, "that a boy has been put to death who was refused to be purchased as a slave." This single story was deemed by that gentleman a sufficient proof of the barbarity of the Africans, and of the inutility of abolishing the slave trade. My honorable friend, however, has told you that this boy had previously run away from his master three several times; that the master had to pay his value, according to the custom of the country, every time he was brought back; and that partly from anger at the boy for running away so frequently, and partly to prevent a still farther repetition of the same expense, he determined to put him to death. Such was the explanation of the story given in the cross-examination. This, sir, is the signal instance that has been dwelt upon of African barbarity. This African, we admit, was unenlightened, and altogether barbarous; but let us now ask, what would a *civilized* and *enlightened West Indian*, or a body of West Indians, have done in any case of a parallel nature? I will quote you, sir, a law, passed in the West Indies, in the year 1722, which, in turning over the book I happened just now to cast my eye upon; by which law, this very same crime of running away, is, by the Legislature of the island, by the grave and deliberate sentence of that enlightened Legislature, *punished with death;* and this, not in the case only of the *third* offense, but even in the very *first* instance. It is enacted, "that if any negro or other slave shall withdraw himself from his master for the term of six months; or any slave that was absent, shall not return within that time, it shall be adjudged felony, and every such person shall suffer death." There is another West India law, by which every negro's hand is armed against his fellow-negroes, by his being authorized to kill a runaway slave, and even having a reward held out to him for doing so. Let the House now contrast the two cases. Let them ask themselves which of the two exhibits the greater barbarity? Let them reflect, with a little candor and liberality, whether on the ground of any of those facts, and loose insinuations as to the sacrifices to be met with in the evidence, they can possibly reconcile to themselves the excluding of Africa from all means of civilization; whether they can possibly vote for the continuance of the slave trade upon the principle that the Africans have shown themselves to be a race of *incorrigible barbarians.*

The West India planters equally barbarous in some of their laws.

Resumption of the question whether other nations will unite in abolishing the trade.

I hope, therefore, we shall hear no more of the moral impossibility of civilizing the Africans, nor have our understandings and consciences again insulted, by being called upon to sanction the slave trade, until other nations shall have set the example of abolishing it. While we have been deliberating upon the subject, one nation, not ordinarily taking the lead in politics, nor by any means remarkable for the boldness of its councils, has determined on a gradual abolition;[7] a determination, indeed, which, since it permits for a time the existence of the slave trade, would be an unfortunate pattern for our imitation. France,

[6] This line, with the remainder of the passage as referred to in the next sentence, is found in the Epistles of Horace, Book i., Epist. 2, lines 41–3:

Qui recte vivendi prorogat horam,
Rusticus expectat dum defluat amnis, at ille
Labitur et labetur in omne volubilis ævum.

He who delays the hour of living well,
Stands like the rustic on a river's brink,
To see the stream run out; but on it flows,
And still shall flow with current never ceasing.

[7] The country referred to was Denmark, which, two years after the delivery of this speech (in 1794), made a law that the slave trade should cease at the end of *ten* years, i. e., in 1804.

it is said, will take up the trade if we relinquish it. What? Is it supposed that in the present situation of St. Domingo, of an island which used to take three fourths of all the slaves required by the colonies of France, she, of all countries, will think of taking it up? What countries remain? The Portuguese, the Dutch, and the Spaniards. Of those countries, let me declare it is my opinion that, if they see us renounce the trade after full deliberation, they will not be disposed, even on principles of policy, to rush further into it. But I say more. How are they to furnish the capital necessary for carrying it on? If there is any aggravation of our guilt, in this wretched business, greater than another, it is that we have stooped to be the carriers of these miserable beings from Africa to the West Indies for all the other powers of Europe. And now, sir, if we retire from the trade altogether, I ask, where is that fund which is to be raised at once by other nations, equal to the purchase of 30 or 40,000 slaves? A fund which, if we rate them at £40 or £50 each, can not make a capital of less than a million and a half, or two millions of money. From what branch of their commerce is it that these European nations will draw together a fund to feed this monster? to keep alive this detestable commerce? And even if they should make the attempt, will not that immense chasm, which must instantly be created in the other parts of their trade, from which this vast capital must be withdrawn in order to supply the slave trade, be filled up by yourselves? Will not these branches of commerce which they must leave, and from which they must withdraw their industry and their capitals, in order to apply them to the slave trade, be then taken up by British merchants? Will you not even in this case find your capital flow into these deserted channels? Will not your capital be turned from the slave trade to that natural and innocent commerce from which they must withdraw their capitals in proportion as they take up the traffic in the flesh and blood of their fellow creatures?

The committee sees, I trust, how little ground of objection to our proposition there is in this part of our adversaries' argument.

The civilization of Africa a leading object of the measure proposed.

Having now detained the House so long, all that I will further add shall be on that important subject, the civilization of Africa, which I have already shown that I consider as the leading feature in this question. Grieved am I to think that there should be a single person in this country, much more that there should be a single member in the British Parliament, who can look on the present dark, uncultivated, and uncivilized state of that continent as a ground for continuing the slave trade; as a ground not only for refusing to attempt the improvement of Africa, but even for hindering and intercepting every ray of light which might otherwise break in upon her, as a ground for refusing to her the common chance and the common means with which other nations have been blessed, of emerging from their native barbarism.

Here, as in every other branch of this extensive question, the argument of our adversaries pleads against them; for surely, sir, the present deplorable state of Africa, especially when we reflect that her chief calamities are to be ascribed to us, calls for our generous aid, rather than justifies any despair on our part of her recovery, and still less any further repetition of our injuries.

Argument from history as to the prospect of African civilization.

I will not much longer fatigue the attention of the House; but this point has impressed itself so deeply on my mind, that I must trouble the committee with a few additional observations. Are we justified, I ask, on any theory, or by any one instance to be found in the history of the world, from its very beginning to this day, in forming the supposition which I am now combating? Are we justified in supposing that the particular practice which we encourage in Africa, of men's selling each other for slaves, is any symptom of a barbarism that is incurable? Are we justified in supposing that even the practice of offering up human sacrifices proves a total incapacity for civilization? I believe it will be found, and perhaps much more generally than is supposed, that both the trade in slaves, and the still more savage custom of offering human sacrifices, obtained in former periods, throughout many of those nations which now, by the blessings of Providence, and by a long progression of improvements, are advanced the furthest in civilization. I believe, sir, that, if we will reflect an instant, we shall find that this observation comes directly home to our own selves; and that, on the same ground on which we now are disposed to proscribe Africa forever, from all possibility of improvement, we ourselves might, in like manner, have been proscribed, and forever shut out from all the blessings which we now enjoy.

England once polluted by human sacrifices, and a mart of slaves.

There was a time, sir, which it may be fit sometimes to revive in the remembrance of our countrymen, when even human sacrifices are said to have been offered in this island. But I would especially observe on this day, for it is a case precisely in point, that the very practice of the slave trade once prevailed among us. Slaves, as we may read in Henry's History of Great Britain, were formerly an established article of our exports. "Great numbers," he says, "were exported like cattle from the British coast, and were to be seen exposed for sale in the Roman market." It does not distinctly appear by what means they were procured; but there was unquestionably no small resemblance, in this particular point, between the case of our ancestors and that of the present wretched natives of Africa; for the historian tells you that "adultery, witchcraft, and debt, were probably some of the chief sources of supplying the Roman market with British slaves; that prisoners taken in war were added to the number; and that there might be among them some unfortunate gamesters who, after having lost all their goods, at length staked themselves, their wives, and their children." Every one of these sources of slavery has been stated, and almost precisely in the same terms, to be at this hour a source of slavery in Africa. And these circumstances, sir, with a solitary instance or two of human sacrifices, furnish the alleged proofs that Africa labors under a natural incapacity for civilization; that it is enthusiasm and fanaticism to think that she can ever enjoy the knowledge and the morals of Europe; that Providence never intended her to rise above a state of barbarism; that Providence has irrevocably doomed her to be only a nursery for slaves for us free and civilized Europeans. Allow of this principle, as applied to Africa, and I should be glad to know why it might not also have been applied to ancient and uncivilized Britain. Why might not some Roman senator, reasoning on the principles of some honorable gentlemen, and pointing to British barbarians, have predicted with equal boldness, "there is a people that will never rise to civilization—there is a people destined never to be free—a people without the understanding necessary for the attainment of useful arts; depressed by the hand of Nature below the level of the human species; and created to form a supply of slaves for the rest of the world." Might not this have been said, according to the principles which we now hear stated, in all respects as fairly and as truly of Britain herself, at that period of her history, as it can now be said by us of the inhabitants of Africa?

Contrast of her present condition, yet engaged in keeping others barbarians.

We, sir, have long since emerged from barbarism. We have almost forgotten that we were once barbarians. We are now raised to a situation which exhibits a striking contrast to every circumstance by which a Roman might have characterized us, and by which we now characterize Africa. There is, indeed, one thing wanting to complete the contrast, and to clear us altogether from the imputation of acting even to this hour as barbarians; for we continue to this hour a barbarous traffic in slaves; we continue it even yet, in spite of all our great and undeniable pretensions to civilization. We were once as obscure among the nations of the earth, as savage in our manners, as debased in our morals, as degraded in our understandings, as these unhappy Africans are at present. But in the lapse of a long series of years, by a progression slow, and for a time almost imperceptible, we have become rich in a variety of acquirements, favored above measure in the gifts of Providence, unrivaled in commerce, pre-eminent in arts, foremost in the pursuits of philosophy and science, and established in all the blessings of civil society. We are in the possession of peace, of happiness, and of liberty. We are under the guidance of a mild and beneficent religion; and we are protected by impartial laws, and the purest administration of justice. We are living under a system of government which our own happy experience leads us to pronounce the best and wisest which has ever yet been framed; a system which has become the admiration of the world. From all these blessings we must forever have been shut out, had there been any truth in those principles which some gentlemen have not hesitated to lay down as applicable to the case of Africa. Had those principles been true, we ourselves had languished to this hour in that miserable state of ignorance, brutality, and degradation, in which history proves our ancestry to have been immersed. Had other nations adopted these principles in their conduct toward us; had other nations applied to Great Britain the reasoning which some of the senators of this very island now apply to Africa; ages might have passed without our emerging from barbarism; and we who are enjoying the blessings of British civilization, of British laws, and British liberty, might, at this hour, have been little superior, either in morals, in knowledge, or refinement, to the rude inhabitants of the coast of Guinea.

Her duty to extend the boon to Africa.

If, then, we feel that this perpetual confinement in the fetters of brutal ignorance would have been the greatest calamity which could have befallen us; if we view with gratitude and exultation the contrast between the peculiar blessings we enjoy, and the wretchedness of the ancient inhabitants of Britain; if we shudder to think of the misery which would still have overwhelmed us had Great Britain continued to the present times to be a mart for slaves to the more civilized nations of the world, through some cruel policy of theirs, God forbid that *we* should any longer subject Africa to the same dreadful scourge, and preclude the light of knowledge, which has reached every other quarter of the globe, from having access to her coasts.

Peroration: animating prospects in the discharge of this duty.

I trust we shall no longer continue this commerce, to the destruction of every improvement on that wide continent; and shall not consider ourselves as conferring too great a boon, in restoring its inhabitants to the rank of human beings. I trust we shall not think ourselves too liberal, if, by abolishing the slave trade, we give them the same common chance of civilization with other parts of the world, and that we shall now allow to Africa the opportunity, the hope, the prospect of attaining to the same blessings which we ourselves, through the favorable dispensations of Divine Providence, have been permitted, at a much more early period, to enjoy. If we listen to the voice of reason and duty, and pursue this night the line of conduct which they prescribe, some of us may live to see a reverse of that picture from which we now turn our eyes with shame and regret. We may live to behold the natives of Africa engaged in the calm occupations of industry, in the pursuits of a just and legitimate commerce. We may behold the beams of science and philosophy breaking in upon their land, which at some happy period in still later times may blaze with full luster; and joining their influence to that of pure religion, may illuminate and invigorate the most distant extremities of that immense continent. Then may we hope that even Africa, though last of all the quarters of the globe, shall enjoy at length, in the evening of her days, those blessings which have descended so plentifully upon us in a much earlier period of the world. Then, also, will Europe, participating in her improvement and prosperity, receive an ample recompense for the tardy kindness (if kindness it can be called) of no longer hindering that continent from extricating herself out of the darkness which, in other more fortunate regions, has been so much more speedily dispelled.

———Nos que ubi primus equis oriens afflavit anhelis;
Illic sera rubens accendit lumina vesper.[8]

Then, sir, may be applied to Africa those words, originally used, indeed, with a different view:

His demum exactis———
Devenêre locos lætos, et amœna vireta
Fortunatorum nemorum, sedesque beatas;
Largior hic campos Æther et lumine vestit.
Purpuero:[9]

It is in this view, sir—it is an atonement for our long and cruel injustice toward Africa, that the measure proposed by my honorable friend most forcibly recommends itself to my mind. The great and happy change to be expected in the state of her inhabitants, is, of all the various and important benefits of the abolition, in my estimation, incomparably the most extensive and important.[10]

I shall vote, sir, against the adjournment; and I shall also oppose to the utmost every proposition which in any way may tend either to prevent, or even to postpone for an hour, the total abolition of the slave trade: a measure which, on all the various grounds which I have stated, we are bound, by the most pressing and indispensable duty, to adopt.

So great was the impression made by this speech, that nearly all the spectators present supposed the vote would be carried almost by acclamation. But the private, pecuniary interests which bore upon the House were too weighty to be overcome, and Mr. Dundas' plan of a gradual abolition had the preference by a majority of sixty-eight votes. Mr. Dundas now brought forward his scheme in detail, which was passed by a majority of nineteen, but the bill was lost in the House of Lords. The subject came up, through the indefatigable labors of Mr. Wilberforce, session after session, until in 1806, after Mr. Pitt's death, a resolution was passed declaring "that the slave trade was inconsistent with justice, humanity, and sound policy, and that measures ought to be taken for its immediate abolition." A bill to this effect was finally passed, February 6th, 1807; and January 1st, 1808, was fixed upon for the termination of the traffic on the part of the English.

America, in the mean time, had gone in advance on this subject, and stood foremost among the nations in her measure, for the suppression of the slave trade. In 1794, it was enacted that no person in the United States should *fit out any vessel there* for the purpose of carrying on any traffic in slaves to any foreign country, or for procuring from any foreign country the inhabitants thereof to be disposed of as slaves. In 1800, it was enacted that it should be unlawful for any citizen of the United States *to have any property in any vessel* employed in transporting slaves from one foreign country to another, or to *serve on board* any vessel so employed. In 1807, it was enacted that after the first of January 1808, no slaves should be imported into the United States. The slave trade was declared to be piracy by the American Congress in 1820, and by the British Parliament in 1824.

---

[8] This passage is taken from Virgil's description of the zodiac in his Georgics (book i., lines 230–50), and of the sun's progress through the constellations, so that Morning rises on one side of the globe, while Evening follows in slow succession on the other. This Mr. Pitt beautifully applies to the successive rising of the light of science on the two continents of Europe and of Africa.

On us, while early Dawn with panting steeds,
Breathes at his rising, ruddy Eve for *them*
Lights up her fires slow-coming.

[9] These words introduce Virgil's description of the Elysian fields in his region of departed spirits (Æneid, book vi., lines 637–41).

These rites performed, they reach those happy fields,
Gardens, and groves, and seats of living joy,
Where the pure ether spreads with wider sway,
And throws a purple light o'er all the plains.

[10] The last four paragraphs of this speech, together with three others at the opening of the third head, "But now, sir, I come to Africa," are specimens of that lofty declamation with which Mr. Pitt so often raised and delighted the feelings of the House. His theme in such cases was usually his *country*—what she had been, what she might be, what she ought to accomplish. His amplifications are often in the best manner of Cicero, adapted to modern times.

SPEECH

OF MR. PITT ON THE RUPTURE OF NEGOTIATIONS WITH FRANCE, DELIVERED IN THE HOUSE OF COMMONS, NOVEMBER 10, 1797.

INTRODUCTION.

FRANCE having declared war against Austria, April 20th, 1792, and against England, February 1st, 1793, all the leading powers of Europe united with the latter, and the contest soon became general. At the end of four years, the French had triumphed over their adversaries throughout the Continent; all the allies of England were driven from the field, and the Spaniards and Dutch were forced to turn their arms against her. The English, on the other hand, were every where victorious on the ocean, and had taken all her colonies from France, some valuable islands in the West Indies from Spain, and the Cape of Good Hope and the island of Ceylon from Holland, now the Batavian Republic.

But the internal condition of England made Mr. Pitt desirous of peace, and while his adversaries had nothing to restore, he had large possessions of theirs which he was willing to surrender as the price of a general pacification. Accordingly, on the fourth of July, 1797, he opened negotiations with the French at Lisle, through Lord Malmesbury, who had been sent the preceding year to Paris on the same mission, though without success. There were two parties at this time in the French government—the one moderate, the other violent and extreme. Hence, in conducting the negotiation, there was a continual fluctuation and studied delay on the part of the French, until the violent party prevailed in the revolutionary movement of September 4th, 1797, when they broke off the negotiation, twelve days after, in a rude and insulting manner. Mignet gives a solution of their conduct in his History of the French Revolution: "The Directory, at this time without money, without the support of a party at home, with no other aid than that of the army, and no other means of influence than a continuation of its victories, was not in a condition to consent to a general peace. *War was necessary to its existence.*. An immense body of troops could not be disbanded without danger." The nation was therefore to be dazzled, and the army employed, by an expedition for the conquest of Egypt, as the high road to the English possessions in India. Jomini admits, in his History of the Wars of the Revolution, that "Europe was convinced, on this occasion at least, that the cabinet of St. James had evinced more moderation than a Directory whose proceedings were worthy of the days of Robespierre."

On the 24th of October, 1797, the King of England issued a "Declaration respecting the Negotiation for Peace with France," part of which will here be given, as a specimen of the noble and commanding style of Mr. Pitt in his state papers.

"HIS MAJESTY directed his minister to repair to France furnished with the most ample powers, and instructed to communicate at once an explicit and detailed proposal and plan of peace, reduced into the shape of a regular treaty, just and moderate in its principles, embracing all the interests concerned, and extending to every subject connected with the restoration of public tranquillity.

"To this proceeding, open and liberal beyond example, the conduct of his Majesty's enemies opposes the most striking contrast. From them no counter-project has ever yet been obtained; no statement of the extent or nature of the conditions on which they would conclude any peace with these kingdoms. Their pretensions have always been brought forward either as *detached* or as *preliminary* points, distinct from the main object of negotiation, and accompanied in every instance with an express reserve of further and unexplained demands.

"The points which, in pursuance of this system, the plenipotentiaries of the enemy proposed for separate discussion in their first conferences with his Majesty's minister, were at once frivolous and offensive; none of them productive of any solid advantage to France, but all calculated to raise new obstacles in the way of peace. And to these demands was soon after added another, in its form unprecedented, in its substance extravagant, and such as could only originate in the most determined and inveterate hostility. The principle of mutual compensation (before expressly admitted by common consent as the just and equitable basis of negotiation) was now disclaimed; every idea of moderation or reason, every appearance of justice, was disregarded; and a concession was required from his Majesty's plenipotentiary, as a preliminary and indispensable condition of negotiation, which must at once have superseded all the objects, and precluded all the means of treating. France, after incorporating with her own dominions so large a portion of her conquests, and affecting to have deprived herself, by her own internal regulations, of the power of alienating these valuable additions of territory, did not scruple to demand from his Majesty the absolute and unconditional surrender of all that the energy of his people, and the valor of his fleets and armies, have conquered in the present war, either from France or from her allies. She required that the power of Great Britain should be confined within its former limits, at the very moment when her own dominion was extended to a degree almost unparalleled in history. She insisted that in proportion to the increase of danger the means of resistance should be diminished; and that his Majesty should give up, without compensation, and into the hands of his enemies, the necessary defenses of his possessions, and the future safeguards of his empire. Nor was even this demand brought forward as constituting the terms of peace, but *the price of negotiation;* as the condition on which alone his Majesty was to be allowed to learn what further unexplained demands were still reserved, and to what greater sacrifices these unprecedented concessions of honor and safety were to lead!

"To France, to Europe, and to the world, it must be manifest, that the French government (while they persist in their present sentiments) leave his Majesty without an alternative, unless he were prepared to surrender and sacrifice to the undisguised ambition of his enemies the honor of his crown and the safety of his dominions. It must be manifest, that, instead of showing, on their part, any inclination to meet his Majesty's pacific overtures on any moderate terms, they have never brought themselves to state *any* terms (however exorbitant) on which they were ready to conclude peace. * * * * * * The rupture of the negotiation is not, therefore, to be ascribed to any pretensions (however inadmissible) urged as the price of peace; not to any ultimate difference on terms, however exorbitant; but to the evident and fixed determination of the enemy to prolong the contest, and to pursue, at all hazards, their hostile designs against the prosperity and safety of these kingdoms.

"While this determination continues to prevail, his Majesty's earnest wishes and endeavors to restore peace to his subjects must be fruitless. But his sentiments remain unaltered. He looks with anxious expectation to the moment when the government of France may show a disposition and spirit in any degree corresponding to his own. And he renews, even now, and before all Europe, the solemn declaration, that, in spite of repeated provocations, and at the very moment when his claims have been strengthened and confirmed by that fresh success which, by the blessing of Providence, has recently attended his arms, he is yet ready (if the calamities of war can now be closed) to conclude peace on the same moderate and equitable principles and terms which he has before proposed. The rejection of such terms must now, more than ever, demonstrate the implacable animosity and insatiable ambition of those with whom he has to contend, and to them alone must the future consequences of the prolongation of the war be ascribed.

"His Majesty has an anxious, but a sacred, indispensable duty to fulfill: he will discharge it with resolution, constancy, and firmness. Deeply as he must regret the continuance of a war, so destructive in its progress, and so burdensome even in its success, he knows the character of the brave people whose interests and honor are intrusted to him. These it is the first object of his life to maintain; and he is convinced that neither the resources nor the spirit of his kingdoms will be found inadequate to this arduous contest, or unequal to the importance and value of the objects which are at stake. He trusts that the favor of Providence, by which they have always hitherto been supported against all their enemies, will be still extended to them; and that, under this protection, his faithful subjects, by a resolute and vigorous application of the means which they possess, will be enabled to vindicate the independence of their country, and to resist with just indignation the assumed superiority of an enemy, against whom they have fought with the courage, and success, and glory of their ancestors, and who aims at nothing less than to destroy at once whatever has contributed to the prosperity and greatness of the British empire; all the channels of its industry, and all the sources of its power; its security from abroad, its tranquillity at home; and, above all, that Constitution, on which alone depends the undisturbed enjoyment of its religion, laws, and liberties."

This Declaration was laid before the House of Lords, November 8th, 1797, and an Address to the Throne was passed without a single dissenting voice, approving of the course taken, and closing with these words: "We know that great exertions are necessary; we are prepared to make them; and placing our firm reliance on that Divine protection which has always hitherto been extended to us, we will support your Majesty to the utmost, and stand or fall with our religion, laws, and liberties." This address was sent down to the Commons on the tenth, and every one supposed it would be adopted there with equal unanimity. But Sir John Sinclair, a well-meaning but weak man, who was apprehensive that the tone of the Declaration might produce increased hostility among the French people, proposed a substitute, which dwelt in feeble language on "the various calamities to which nations in a state of hostility were necessarily exposed;" "deplored the continuance of a war which had already occasioned such an expense of treasure and of blood," and expressed a hope of "speedily renewing a negotiation so favorable to the interests of humanity." This substitute he proposed, while, with singular inconsistency, he condemned the ministry for the anxiety they had shown to prevent the conference from being broken off, declaring himself "perfectly astonished at the mean and degrading manner in which ministers had carried on the negotiation." He was followed by Earl Temple, a young relative of Mr. Pitt, who, in a maiden speech, took up the latter idea in a way perfectly consistent with his principles (which were those of Mr. Burke), and carried it much further, condemning ministers for negotiating at all, and going back to the origin and conduct of the war in a spirit which (if carried out) would have rendered it eternal.

Mr. Pitt, in his peculiar mode of giving a bold relief to his position at the opening of a speech, seized on the opportunity thus presented, and placed himself at once at the middle point between these two extremes; and after showing the extravagance of each, went on to state the measures by which he had endeavored to obtain peace, in one of the finest specimens of luminous *exposition*, intermingled with impassioned feeling, to be found in our language.

SPEECH, &c.

Sir,—Having come to this House with the firm conviction that there never existed an occasion when the unanimous concurrence of the House might be more justly expected than on a proposal to agree in the sentiments contained in the address which has been read, I must confess myself considerably disappointed, in some degree, even by the speech of my noble relation [Lord Temple], much as I rejoice in the testimony which he has given of his talents and abilities, and still more by the speech of the honorable baronet [Sir John Sinclair], and by the amendment which he has moved. I can not agree with the noble Lord in the extent to which he has stated his sentiments, that we ought to rejoice that peace was not made; much less, sir, can I feel desirous to accept on the part of myself, or my colleagues, either from my noble kinsman, or any other person, the approbation which he was pleased to express of the manner in which we have concluded the negotiation—We *have not concluded the negotiation*—the negotiation has been concluded by others. We have not been suffered to continue it. Our claim to merit, if we have any, our claim to the approbation of our country, is, that we persisted in every attempt to conduct that negotiation to a pacific termination, as long as our enemies left us not the prospect, but the *chance* or *possibility* of doing so, consistently with our honor, our dignity, and our safety. We lament and deplore the disappointment of the sincere wishes which we felt, and of the earnest endeavors which we employed; yet we are far from suffering those sentiments to induce us to adopt the unmanly line of conduct that has been recommended by the honorable baronet. This is not the moment to dwell only on our disappointment, suppress our indignation, or to let our courage, our constancy, and our determination be buried in expressions of unmanly fear or unavailing regret. Between these two extremes it is that I trust our conduct is directed; and in calling upon the House to join in sentiments between those extremes, I do trust, that if we can not have the unanimous opinion, we shall have the general and ready concurrence both of the House and of the country.

Mr. Pitt's position between the extremes of the two preceding speakers.

I. Sir, before I trouble the House (which I am not desirous of doing at length) with a few points which I wish to recapitulate, let me first call to your minds the general nature of the amendment which the honorable baronet has, under these circumstances, thought fit to propose, and the general nature of the observations by which he introduced it. He began with deploring the calamities of war, on the general topic that all war is calamitous. Do I object to this sentiment? No. But is it our business, at a moment when we feel that the continuance of that war is owing to the animosity, the implacable animosity of our enemy, to the inveterate and insatiable ambition of the present frantic government of France—not of the *people* of France, as the honorable baronet unjustly stated; is it our business at that moment to content ourselves with merely lamenting in commonplace terms the calamities of war? and forgetting that it is part of the duty which, as representatives of the people, we owe to our government and our country, to state that the continuance of those evils upon ourselves, and upon France, too, is the fruit only of the conduct of the enemy, that it is to be imputed to them, and not to us?

Preliminary discussion: (1.) Sir John Sinclair's amendment.

Sir, the papers which were ordered to be laid on the table have been in every gentleman's hand, and on the materials which they furnish we must be prepared to decide. Can there be a doubt that all the evils of war, whatever may be their consequences, are to be imputed solely to his Majesty's enemies? Is there any man here prepared to deny that the delay in every stage of the negotiation, and its final rupture, are proved to be owing to the evasive conduct, the unwarrantable pretensions, the inordinate ambition, and the implacable animosity of the enemy? I shall shortly state what are the points (though it is hardly necessary that I should state them, for they speak loudly for themselves) on which I would rest that proposition. But if there is a man who doubts it, is it the honorable baronet? Is it he who makes this amendment, leaving out every thing that is honorable to the character of his own country, and seeming to court some new complaisance on the part of the French Directory? The honorable baronet, who, as soon as he has stated the nature of his amendment, makes the first part of his speech a charge against his Majesty's ministers, for even having *commenced* the negotiation in the manner and under the circumstances in which they did commence it—who makes his next charge their having *persevered* in it, when violations of form and practice were insisted upon in the earliest stage of it? Does he discover that the French government, whom we have accused of insincerity, have been sincere from the beginning to the end of the negotiation? Or, after having accused his Majesty's ministers for commencing and persevering in it, is the honorable baronet so afraid of being misconstrued into an idea of animosity against the people of France, that he must disguise the *truth* —must do injustice to the character and cause of his own country, and leave unexplained the cause of the continuance of this great contest? Let us be prepared to probe that question to the bottom, to form our opinion upon it, and to render our conduct conformable to that opinion. This I conceive to be a manly conduct, and, especially at such a moment, to be the indispensable duty of the House.

The French government responsible for the continuance of the war.

But let not the honorable baronet imagine there is any ground for his apprehension, that by adopting the language of the Address, which ascribes the continuance of the war to the ambition of the enemy, he will declare a system of endless animosity between the nations of Great Britain and France. I say directly the contrary.[1] He who scruples to declare that in the present moment the government of France are acting as much in contradiction to the known wishes of the French nation as to the just pretensions and anxious wishes of the people of Great Britain—he who scruples to declare *them* [the government] the authors of this calamity—deprives us of the consolatory hope which we are inclined to cherish of some future change of circumstances more favorable to our wishes. It is a melancholy spectacle, indeed, to see in any country, and on the ruin of any pretense of liberty, however nominal, shallow, or delusive a system of tyranny erected, the most galling, the most horrible, the most undisguised in all its parts and attributes that has stained the page of history, or disgraced the annals of the world. But it would be much more unfortunate, if, when we see that the same cause carries desolation through France which extends disquiet and fermentation through Europe—it would be worse, indeed, if we attributed to the nation of France that which is to be attributed only to the unwarranted and usurped authority which involves them in misery, and would, if unresisted, involve Europe with them in one common ruin and destruction. Do we state this to be animosity on the part of the people of France? Do we state this in order to raise up an implacable spirit of animosity against that country? Where is one word to that effect in the declaration to which the honorable gentleman has alluded? He complains much of this declaration, because it tends to perpetuate animosity between two nations which one day or other must be at peace—God grant that day may be soon! But what does that Declaration express upon the subject? Does it express that because the present existing government of France has acted as it has acted, we forego the wish or renounce the hope that some new situation may lead to happier consequences? On the contrary, his Majesty's language is distinctly this: "While this determination continues to prevail on the part of his enemies, his Majesty's earnest wishes and endeavors to restore peace to his subjects must be fruitless, but his sentiments remain unaltered. He looks with anxious expectation to the moment when the government of France may show a temper and spirit in any degree corresponding with his own." I wish to know whether words can be found in the English language which more expressly state the contrary sentiment to that which the honorable baronet imputes. They not only disclaim animosity against the people of France in consequence of the conduct of its rulers, but do not go the length of declaring that, after all this provocation, even with the *present* rulers, all treaty is impracticable. Whether it is probable that, acting on the principles upon which they have acquired their power, and while that power continues, they will listen to any system of moderation or justice at home or abroad, it is not now necessary to discuss. But for one, I desire to express my cordial concurrence in the sentiment, so pointedly expressed in that passage of the Declaration in which his Majesty, notwithstanding all the provocation he has received, and even after the recent successes which by the blessing of Providence have attended his arms, declares his readiness to adhere to the same moderate terms and principles which he proposed at the time of our greatest difficulties, and to conclude peace on that ground, if it can now be obtained, even with this very government.

The Declaration which asserts this, not calculated to perpetuate hostility among the French people.

I am sensible that while I am endeavoring to vindicate his Majesty's servants against the charges of the honorable baronet (which are sufficiently, however, refuted by the early part of his own speech), I am incurring, in some degree, the censure of the noble Lord to whom I before alluded. According to his principles and opinions, and of some few others in this country, it is matter of charge against us, that we even harbor in our minds, at this moment, a wish to conclude peace upon the terms which we think admissible with the present rulers of France. I am not one of those who can or will join in that sentiment. I have no difficulty in repeating what I stated before, that in their present spirit, after what they have said, and still more, after what they have done, I can entertain *little hope* of so desirable an event. I have no hesitation in avowing (for it would be idleness and hypocrisy to conceal it) that, for the sake of mankind in general, and to gratify those sentiments which can never be eradicated from the human heart, I should see with pleasure and satisfaction the termination of a government whose conduct and whose origin is such as we have seen that of the government of France. But that is not the object—that ought not to be the principle of the war. Whatever wish I may entertain in my own heart, and whatever opinion I may think it fair or manly to avow, I have no difficulty in stating that, violent and odious as is the character of that government, I verily believe, in the present state of Europe, that if we are not wanting to ourselves, if, by the blessing of Providence, our perseverance and our resources should enable us to make peace with France upon terms in which we taint not our character, in which we do not abandon the sources of our wealth, the means of our strength, the defense of what we already possess—if we maintain our equal pretentions and assert that rank which we are entitled to hold among nations—the moment peace can be obtained on such terms, be the form of government in France what it may, peace is desirable, peace is then

(2.) Earl Temple's remarks.

However small the present hope, England ought always to be ready to treat when it can be done with safety.

[1] This mode of turning an argument round and presenting it with startling force under directly the contrary aspect, has already been mentioned as a striking characteristic of Mr. Pitt. The ease and dexterity with which he does it are truly admirable.

anxiously to be sought. But unless it is attained on such terms, there is no extremity of war—there is no extremity of honorable contest—that is not preferable to the name and pretense of peace, which must be, in reality, a disgraceful capitulation, a base, an abject surrender of every thing that constitutes the pride, the safety, and happiness of England.[2]

These, sir, are the sentiments of my mind on this leading point, and with these sentiments I shape my conduct between the contending opinions of the noble Lord and of the honorable baronet. But there is one observation of the honorable baronet on which I must now more particularly remark. He has discovered that we state the Directory of France to have been all along insincere, and yet take merit for having commenced a negotiation which we ought never to have commenced without being persuaded of their sincerity. This supposed contradiction requires but a few words to explain it. I believe that those who constitute the *present* government of France never were sincere for a moment in the negotiation. From all the information I have obtained, and from every conjecture I could form, I, for one, never was so duped as to believe them sincere. But I did believe, and I thought I knew, that there was a prevailing wish for peace, and a predominant sense of its necessity growing and confirming itself in France, and founded on the most obvious and most pressing motives. I did see a spirit of reviving moderation gradually gaining ground, and opening a way to the happiest alterations in the general system of that country. I did believe that the violence of that portion of the executive government which, by the late strange revolution of France, unhappily for France itself and for the world, has gained the ascendency, would have been restrained within some bounds—that ambition must give way to reason—that even frenzy itself must be controlled and governed by necessity. These were the hopes and expectations I entertained. I did, notwithstanding, feel that even from the outset, and in every step of that negotiation, those who happily had not yet the full power to cut it short in the beginning—who dared not trust the public eye with the whole of their designs—who could not avow all their principles—unfortunately, nevertheless, did retain from the beginning power enough to control those who had a better disposition, and to mix in every part of the negotiation (which they could not then abruptly break off) whatever could impede, embarrass, and perplex, in order to throw upon us, if possible, the odium of its failure.

Answer to Sir John Sinclair's charge of inconsistency.

Sir, the system of France is explained by the very objections that are made against our conduct. The violent party could not, as I have stated, at once break off the treaty on their part, but they wished to drive England to the rupture. They had not strength enough to reject all negotiation, yet they had strength enough to mix in every step those degradations and insults, those inconsistent and unwarranted pretensions in points even of subordinate importance, which reduced ministers to that option which I have described; but which they decided in a way that has exposed them to the censure of the honorable baronet. We chose rather to incur the blame of sacrificing punctilios (at some times essential) rather than afford the enemy an opportunity of evading this plain question. "Is there any ground, and, if any, what, upon which you are ready to conclude?" To that point it was our duty to drive them. We have driven them to that point. They would tell us *no* terms, however exorbitant and unwarrantable, upon which they would be ready to make peace. What would have been the honorable baronet's expedient to avoid this embarrassment? It would have been (as he has this day informed us) an address which he had thought of moving in the last session, and which, indeed, I should have been less surprised had he moved, than if the House had concurred in it. We would have moved that no project should be given in till the enemy were prepared to present a counter-project. If it was a great misfortune that that address was not moved, I am afraid some of the guilt belongs to me; because the honorable baronet did suggest such an idea, and I did with great sincerity and frankness tell him that, if he was really a friend to peace, there was no motion he could make so little calculated to promote that object; and I did prevail upon the honorable baronet to give up the intention. If I am right in the supposition I have stated—if I am right in thinking that our great object was to press France to this point, and to put the question, "If you have any terms to offer, what are they?"—was there any one way by which we could make it so difficult for them to retain any pretense of a desire of peace as to speak out ourselves, and call upon them either for agreement, or for modification, or for some other plan in their turn? By not adopting the honorable baronet's plan, we have put the question beyond dispute, whether peace was attainable at last, and whether our advances would or would not be met on the part of France. And I shall, to the latest hour of my life, rejoice that we were fortunate enough to place this question in the light which defies the powers of misrepresentation; in which no man can attempt to perplex it; and in which it presents itself this day for the decision of the House and of the nation, and calls upon every individual who has at stake the public happiness and his own, to determine for himself whether this is or is not a crisis which requires his best exertions in the defense of his country.

Conduct of the violent party in the French government.

How met by the British government.

Sir John Sinclair's plan.

II. To show which, I shall now proceed, notwithstanding the reproach which has been thrown on our line of conduct, to show the system even of obstinate forbearance, with which we endeav-

[2] We have here one of those fine amplifications in which Mr. Pitt was accustomed to enlarge and dwell upon the more important parts of a subject, in order to deepen the impression.

ored to overcome preliminary difficulties—the determined resolution on our part to overlook all minor obstacles, and to come to the real essence of discussion upon the terms of peace. To show this, it is not necessary to do more than to call to the recollection of the House the leading parts of the Declaration of his Majesty; I mean to leave that part of the subject, also, without the possibility of doubt or difference of opinion. It is certainly true that, even previous to any of the circumstances that related to the preliminary forms of the negotiation, the prior conduct of France had offered to any government that was not sincerely and most anxiously bent upon peace, sufficient ground for the continuance of hostilities. It is true that, in the former negotiation at Paris, Lord Malmesbury was finally sent away, not upon a question of terms of peace—not upon a question of the cession of European or Colonial possessions, but upon the haughty demand of a previous preliminary, which should give up every thing on the part of the allies; and which should leave them afterward every thing to ask, or rather to require. It is true, it closed in nearly the same insulting manner as the second mission. It is true, too, that subsequent to that period, in the preliminaries concluded between the Emperor and France, it was agreed to invite the allies of each party to a congress; which, however, was never carried into execution.[3] It was under these circumstances that his Majesty, in the earnest desire of availing himself of that spirit of moderation which had begun to show itself in France, determined to renew those proposals which had been before slighted and rejected. But when this step was taken, what was the conduct of those who have gained the ascendency in France? On the first application to know on what ground they were disposed to negotiate, wantonly, as will be shown by the sequel, and for no purpose but to prevent even the opening of the conferences, they insisted upon a mode of negotiation very contrary to general usage and convenience—contrary to the mode in which they had terminated war with any of the belligerent powers, and directly contrary to any mode which they themselves afterward persisted in following in this very negotiation with us! They began by saying they would receive no proposals for *preliminaries*, but that conferences should be held for the purpose of concluding at once a *definitive* treaty.[4]

Exposition of the conduct of the French government as compared with that of the English.

(1.) Conduct of the French in the previous negotiation of 1796.

(2.) The dictatorial tone from the commencement, as to the nature of the negotiation.

His Majesty's answer was, that it was his desire to adopt that mode only which was most likely to accelerate the object in view; and the powers of his plenipotentiary would apply to either object, either preliminary or definitive. They appeared content with his answer, but what was the next step? In the simple form of granting a passport for the minister, at the moment they were saying they preferred a definitive peace, because it was the most expeditious—in that very passport, which in all former times has only described the character of the minister, without entering into any thing relating to the *terms* or *mode* of negotiating—they insert a condition relative to his powers, and that inconsistent with what his Majesty had explained to be the nature of the powers he had intended to give, and with which they had apparently been satisfied. They made it a passport not for a minister coming to conclude peace generally, but applicable only to a definitive and *separate* peace.[5]

(3.) Gross impropriety in the passport they sent to the English minister.

This proceeding was in itself liable to the most obvious objection. But it is more important, as an instance to show how, in the simplest part of the transaction, the untractable spirit of France discovered itself. It throws light on the subsequent part of the transaction; and shows the inconsistencies and contradictions of their successive pretensions. As to the condition then made in the passport for the first time, that the negotiation should be for a separate peace, his Majesty declared that he had no choice between a definitive and a preliminary treaty; but as to a separate peace, his honor and good faith, with regard to his ally the Queen of Portugal, would not permit it. He, therefore, stated his unalterable determination to agree to no treaty in which Portugal should not be included; expressing, at the same time, his readiness that France should treat on the part of Holland and Spain.

On this occasion, the good faith of this country prevailed. The system of violence and despotism was not then ripe, and therefore his Majesty's demand to treat for Portugal

Passport changed.

[3] This was at Leoben, in April, 1797, when the preliminaries of peace were settled between France and Austria, which led to the treaty of Campo Formio.

[4] This refusal to discuss "the preliminaries of peace," as proposed by Lord Grenville (in accordance with established usage), was contained in the first note from the French minister. He put the negotiation on the ground of England's coming forward immediately with *her* "overtures and proposals," and insisted that "negotiations should be set on foot at once for a *definitive* treaty." See his Note in Parliamentary History, vol. xxxiii., page 909.

[5] The passport addressed to the officers of the French police was in the following words:

"Allow to pass freely —— ——, furnished with the full powers of his Britannic Majesty for the purpose of negotiating, concluding, and signing a definitive and *separate* treaty of peace with the French Republic."

Here the word *separate* was inserted in direct contravention of the arrangement between the two governments, and was obviously intended to make difficulty. England had agreed to negotiate for a definitive, but not for a separate treaty; she could not give up Portugal, which had long been under her protection. The French Directory plainly designed to draw Mr. Pitt into a dilemma: if he accepted the passport, and afterward undertook to treat for Portugal, the negotiation could be broken off on the ground that he went beyond the terms established by the passport; if he refused the passport, it was easy to say he had broken off the negotiation when acceded to by France.

was acquiesced in by the Directory. They, at the same time, undertook to treat on their part for their allies, Holland and Spain, as well as for themselves; though in the subsequent course of the negotiation, they pretended to be without sufficient power to treat for either.

(4.) Use of insulting language by the French as to the British government and embassador.

I must here entreat the attention of the House to the next circumstance which occurred. When the firmness of his Majesty, his anxious and sincere desire to terminate the horrors of war, and his uniform moderation overcame the violence, and defeated the designs of the members of the executive government of France, they had recourse to another expedient, the most absurd, as well as the most unjustifiable. They adverted to the rupture of the former negotiation, as if that rupture was to be imputed to his Majesty; and this insinuation was accompanied with a personal reflection upon the minister who was sent by his Majesty to treat on the part of this country.[6] His Majesty, looking anxiously as he did to the conclusion of peace, disdained to reply otherwise than by observing that this was not a fit topic to be agitated at the moment of renewing a negotiation, and that the circumstances of the transaction were well enough known to Europe and to the world. And the result of this negotiation has confirmed, what the former had sufficiently proved, that his Majesty could not have selected, in the ample field of talents which his dominions furnish, any person better qualified to do justice to his sincere and benevolent desire to promote the restoration of Peace, and his firm and unalterable determination to maintain the dignity and honor of his kingdom.

(5.) Exchange of powers, those of the French commissioners less ample than those of the English embassador.

In spite of these obstacles and others more minute, the British plenipotentiary at length arrived at Lisle. The full powers were transmitted to the respective governments, and were found unexceptionable; though the supposed defect of these full powers is, three months after, alleged as a cause for the rupture of the negotiation! And what is more remarkable, it did so happen that the French full powers were, on the face of them, much more limited than ours; for they only enabled the commissioners of the Directory to act according to the instructions they were to receive from time to time. On this point it is not necessary now to dwell; but I desire the House to treasure it in their memory, when we come to the question of pretense for the rupture of the negotiation.

(6.) The English at once offered their project in a treaty fully drawn out.

Then, sir, I come to the point in which we have incurred the censure of the honorable baronet, for delivering in on our part a project. To his opinion I do not subscribe, for the reasons that I stated before. But can there be a stronger proof of his Majesty's sincerity than his waving so many points important in themselves, rather than suffer the negotiation to be broken off? What was our situation?

Reasons for so doing: (a) France demanded a *definitive* treaty.

We were to treat with a government that had in the outset expressed that they would treat only definitively, and from every part of their conduct which preceded the meeting of our plenipotentiary and their commissioners, we might have expected that they would have been prepared to answer our project almost in twenty-four hours after it was delivered.

(b) England had nothing to receive from her enemy, but had simply to say what she was willing to give up.

We stood with respect to France in this predicament—we had nothing to ask of them. The question only was, how much we were to give of that which the valor of his Majesty's arms had acquired from them and from their allies. In this situation, surely, we might have expected that, before we offered the price of peace, they would at least have condescended to say what were the sacrifices which they expected us to make. But, sir, in this situation, what species of project was it that was presented by his Majesty's minister? A project the most distinct, the most particular, the most conciliatory and moderate, that ever constituted the first words spoken by any negotiator. And yet of this project what have we heard in the language of the French government? What have we seen dispersed through all Europe, by that press in France which knows no sentiments but what the French police dictates? What have we seen dispersed by that *English* press which knows no other use of English liberty but servilely to retail and transcribe French opinions? We have been told that it was a project that refused to

---

[6] The following are the words which charge the rupture of the preceding negotiation on the English: "The Directory requires that it shall be established as a principle, that each English packet-boat which shall have brought over either the plenipotentiary or a courier shall not be allowed to make any stay." "The Directory desires, at the same time, that the couriers should not be sent too frequently; *the frequent sending them having been one of the principal causes of the rupture of the preceding negotiation.*"

Nothing more frivolous could be conceived of as a reason for such a rupture. Nothing of this kind was mentioned *at the time.* The French minister did in one instance inquire, whether it was necessary for Lord Malmesbury to send a courier to England every time he received a communication from the Directory—a question which seems plainly to have been designed as a taunt; and his Lordship coolly replied, that he should do it "as often as the official communications made to him required *special* instructions."

The "personal reflection" on Lord Malmesbury was in the following words: "The Directory *consents* that the negotiation shall be opened by Lord Malmesbury. *Another choice* would, however, have appeared to the Directory to augur more favorably for a speedy conclusion of peace." This was a gratuitous insult. Lord Malmesbury was distinguished for his courteous deportment, and no complaint had been made of him by the French government. Even Belsham, who was so rabid against Mr. Pitt and his friends, that Fox once said concerning his Memoirs of the Reign of George III., "how can a man write history in this way?" admits that his Lordship "was uniformly mild and temperate, his manners polite and pleasing."—Vol. vi., page 322. It is plain the Directory meant to force Mr. Pitt, by their treatment, to break off the negotiation.

embrace the terms of negotiation! Gentlemen have read the papers; how does that fact stand? In the original project, we agreed to give up the conquests we had made from France and her allies, with certain exceptions. For those exceptions a blank was left, in order to ascertain whether France was desirous that the exceptions should be divided between her and her allies, or whether she continued to insist upon a complete compensation, and left England to look for compensation only to her allies. France, zealous as she pretends to be for her allies, had no difficulty in authorizing her ministers to declare that she must retain every thing for *herself*. This blank was then filled up; and it was then distinctly stated how little, out of what we had, we demanded to keep. In one sense, it remains a blank still: we did not attempt to preclude France from any other mode of filling it up; but while we stated the utmost extent of our own views, we left open to full explanation whatever points the government of France could desire. We called upon them, and repeatedly solicited them to state something as to the nature of the terms which they proposed, if they objected to ours. It was thus left open to modification, alteration, or concession. But this is not the place, this is not the time, in which I am to discuss whether those terms, in all given circumstances, or in the circumstances of that moment, were or were not the ultimate terms upon which peace ought to be accepted or rejected, if it was once brought to the point when an ultimatum could be judged of. I will not argue whether some greater concession might not have been made with the *certainty* of peace, or whether the terms proposed constituted an offer of peace upon more favorable grounds for the enemy than his Majesty's ministers could justify. I argue not the one question or the other. It would be inconsistent with the public interest and our duty, that we should here state or discuss it. All that I have to discuss is, whether the terms, upon the face of them, appear honorable, open, frank, distinct, sincere, and a pledge of moderation; and I leave it to the good sense of the House whether there can exist a difference of opinion upon this point.

The blanks for English concessions, when filled up, were still subject to further negotiation.

Sir, what was it we offered to renounce to France? In one word, all that we had taken from them. What did this consist of? The valuable, and almost under all circumstances, the impregnable island of Martinique; various other West India possessions; Saint Lucia, Tobago, the French part of Saint Domingo, the settlements of Pondicherry and Chandernagore; all the French factories and means of trade in the East Indies; and the islands of Saint Pierre and Miquelon. And for what were these renunciations to be made? For peace, and for peace only. And to whom? To a nation which had obtained from his Majesty's dominions in Europe nothing in the course of the war—which had never met our fleets but to add to the catalogue of our victories, and to swell the melancholy lists of their own captures and defeats. To a power which had never separately met the arms of this country by land, but to carry the glory and prowess of the British name to a higher pitch; and to a country whose commerce is unheard of; whose navy is annihilated; whose distress, confessed by themselves (however it may be attempted to be dissembled by their panegyrists in this or any other country), is acknowledged by the sighs and groans of the people of France, and proved by the expostulations and remonstrations occasioned by the violent measures of its executive government—such was the situation in which we stood—such the situation of the enemy when we offered to make those important concessions as the price of peace. What was the situation of the allies of France? From Spain—who, from the moment she had deserted our cause and enlisted on the part of the enemy, only added to the number of our conquests, and to her own indelible disgrace—we made claim of one island, the island of Trinidad—a claim not resting on the mere naked title of possession to counterbalance the general European aggrandizement of France, but as the price of something that we had to give, by making good the title to the Spanish part of Saint Domingo, which Spain had ceded without right, and which cession could not be made without our guarantee. To Holland—having in our hands the whole means of their commerce, the whole source of their wealth—we offered to return almost all that was valuable and lucrative to them, in the mere consideration of commerce. We desired, in return, to keep what to them, in a pecuniary point of view, would be only a burden [the Cape of Good Hope and the island of Ceylon]; in a political view worse than useless, because they had not the means to keep it—what (had we granted it) would have been a sacrifice, not to them, but to France—what would in future have enabled her to carry on her plan of subjugation against the eastern possessions of Holland itself, as well as against those of Great Britain.[7] All that we asked was not indemnification for what we had suffered, but the means of preserving our own possessions and the strength of our naval empire. We did this at a time when our enemy was feeling the pressure of war; and who looks at the question of peace without some regard to the relative situation of the country with which you are contending? Look, then, at their trade; look at their means; look at the posture of their affairs; look at what we hold, and at the means we have of defending ourselves, and our enemy of resisting us, and tell me whether this offer was or was not a proof of sincerity, and a pledge of moderation. Sir, I should be ashamed of arguing it. I confess I am apprehensive we may have gone too far in the first proposals we made, rather than shown any backwardness in the negotiation, but it is unnecessary to argue this point.

(7.) Concessions offered by England.

[7] The concessions offered by England were so ample that all Europe, and even Mr. Belsham, pronounced them highly liberal.

(8.) The French now insist on the discussion of *preliminaries*.

Our proposal was received and allowed by the French plenipotentiaries, and transmitted for the consideration of the Directory. Months had elapsed in sending couriers weekly and daily from Paris to Lisle, and from Lisle to Paris. They taught us to expect, from time to time, a consideration of this subject, and an explicit answer to our project. But the first attempt of the Directory to negotiate, after having received our project, is worthy of remark. They required that we, whom they had summoned to a *definitive* treaty, should stop and discuss *preliminary* points, which were to be settled without knowing whether, when we had agreed to them all, we had advanced one inch. We were to discuss, (1) whether his Majesty would renounce the title of King of France, a harmless feather at most in the crown of England. We were to discuss, (2) whether we would restore those ships taken at Toulon, the acquisition of valor, and which we were entitled upon every ground to hold. We were to discuss, (3) whether we would renounce the mortgage which we might possess on the Netherlands, and which engaged much of the honorable baronet's attention; but it does so happen that what the honorable baronet considered as so important was of no importance at all; for a mortgage on the Netherlands we have none, and consequently we have none to renounce. Therefore, upon that condition, which they had no right to ask, and we had no means of granting, we told them the true state of the case, and that it was not worth talking about.[8]

(9.) They next demand the surrender of *all* the conquests made by England, as a preliminary.

The next point which occurred is of a nature which is difficult to dwell upon without indignation. We were waiting the fulfillment of a promise which had been made repeatedly, of delivering to our embassador a counter-project, when they who had desired us to come for the purpose of concluding a definitive treaty, propose that we should subscribe, as a *sine qua non preliminary*, that we were ready, in the first instance, to consent to give up all that we had taken, and then to hear what they had further to ask![9] Is it possible to suppose that such a thing could be listened to by any country that was not prepared to prostrate itself at the feet of France; and in that abject posture to adore its conqueror, to solicit new insults, to submit to demands still more degrading and ignominious, and to cancel at once the honor of the British name? His Majesty had no hesitation in refusing to comply with such insolent and unwarrantable demands. Here, again, the House will see that the spirit of the violent part of the French government which, had the insolence to advance this proposition, had not acquired power and strength in that state of the negotiation to adhere to it. His Majesty's explanations and remonstrances for a time prevailed; and an interval ensued in which we had a hope that we were advancing to a pacification. His Majesty's refusal of this demand was received by the French plenipotentiaries with assurances of a pacific disposition, was transmitted to their government, and was seconded by a continued and repeated repetition of promises that a counter-project should be presented—pretending that they were under the necessity of sending to their allies an account of what passed, and that they were endeavoring to prevail on them to accede to proposals for putting an end to the calamities of war—to terminate the calamities of that war into which those allies were *forced;* in which they were retained by France alone; and in which they purchased nothing but sacrifices to France and misery to themselves. We were told, indeed, in a conference that followed, that they had obtained an answer; but that not being sufficiently satisfactory, it was sent back to be considered! This continued during the whole period, until that dreadful catastrophe of the 4th of September, 1797. Even after that event, the same pretense was held out: they peremptorily promised the counter-project in four days; the same pacific professions were renewed, and our minister was assured that the change of circumstances in France should not be a bar to the pacification. Such was the uniform language of the plenipotentiaries in the name of the government—how it is proved by their actions, I have already stated to the House. After this series

[8] It may be remarked as to the first of these preliminary points, that all the French kings for three centuries had allowed this part of the title of the English monarch ("King of France") to stand at the head of treaties, and it was, therefore, certainly frivolous to raise any question about it. As to the second, touching the ships taken at Toulon, there was more plausibility in the claim, because they were given up on the condition of being "restored in the event of peace." But they were given up by French *Royalists* to create a diversion against the Republic, and the peace referred to was, therefore, plainly a peace with the regal government, and not with a revolutionary body like the Directory. The third preliminary related to a lien which England had on the hereditary possessions of Austria, as security for certain loans made to the Emperor; and the Directory demanded to know whether the Austrian Netherlands (then incorporated into France) were considered as subject to this lien. Mr. Pitt answered them as stated in the text.

[9] This extraordinary demand was made on the ground (never mentioned or alluded to before) that "there exists in the public and secret treaties by which the French Republic is bound to its allies, Spain and the Batavian Republic, articles by which those powers respectively guarantee the territories possessed by each of them before the war. The French government, unable to detach itself from these engagements, establishes as an *indispensable preliminary* of the negotiation for the peace with England, the consent of his Britannic Majesty to the *restitution* of all the possessions which he occupies, not only from the French Republic, but further and formally, of those of Spain and of the Batavian Republic." It is obvious that this was an afterthought to impede the negotiation, and that France, which overruled Spain and Holland at her will, had no difficulty on this subject except as she chose to make one.

of professions, what was the first step taken [by the French], to go on with the negotiation in this spirit of conciliation? Sir, the first step was to renew (as his Majesty's Declaration has well stated), in a shape still more offensive, the former inadmissible and rejected demand—the rejection of which had been acquiesced in by themselves two months before; and during all which time we had been impatiently waiting for the performance of their promises. That demand was the same that I have already stated in substance, that Lord Malmesbury should explain to them not only his powers, but also his instructions; and they asked not for the formal extent of his power, which would give solidity to what he might conclude in the King's name, but they asked an irrevocable pledge that he would consent to give up all that we had taken from them and from their allies without knowing how much more they had afterward to ask![10] It is true, they endeavored to convince Lord Malmesbury that, although an avowal of his instructions was demanded, it would never be required that he should act upon it—since there was a great difference between knowing the extent of the powers of a minister and insisting upon their exercise. And here I would ask the honorable baronet whether he thinks if, in the first instance, we had given up all to the French plenipotentiaries, they would have given it all back again to us? Suppose I was embassador from the French Directory, and the honorable baronet was embassador from Great Britain, and I were to say to him, "Will you give up all you have gained; it would only be a handsome thing in you as an Englishman, and no ungenerous use shall be made of it?" would the honorable baronet expect me, as a French embassador, to say I am instructed, from the good nature of the Directory, to say you have acted handsomely, and I now return what you have so generously given? Should we not be called children and drivelers, if we could act in this manner? And, indeed, the French government could be nothing but children and drivelers if they could suppose that we should have acceded to such a proposal. But they are bound, it seems, by sacred treaties! They are bound by immutable laws! They are sworn, when they make peace to return every thing to their allies! And who shall require of France, for the safety of Europe, to depart from its own pretensions to honor and independence?

(10.) They finally demand of Lord Malmesbury that, if he has not power to do this, he shall *obtain* it from his government.

If any person can really suppose that this country could have agreed to such a proposition, or that such a negotiation was likely to lead to a good end; all I can say is, that with such a man I will not argue. I leave others to imagine what was likely to have been the end of a negotiation in which it was to have been settled as a preliminary that you were to give up *all that you have gained;* and when, on the side of your enemy, not a word was said of what he had to propose afterward. They demand of your embassador to show to them, not only his powers, but also his instructions, before they explain a word of theirs; and they tell you, too, that you are never to expect to hear what their powers are, until you shall be ready to accede to every thing which the Directory may think fit to require. This is certainly the substance of what they propose; and they tell you, also, that they are to carry on the negotiation from the instructions which their plenipotentiaries are to receive from time to time from them. You are to have no power to instruct your embassador! You are to show to the enemy at once all you have in view! And they will only tell you from time to time, as to them shall seem meet, what demands they shall make.

Impossible for England to grant this.

It was thus it was attempted, on the part of the French, to commence the negotiation. In July, this demand was made to Lord Malmesbury. He stated that his powers were ample. In answer to this, they went no farther than to say that if he had no such power as what they required, he should send to England to obtain it. To which he replied, that he had not, nor should he have it if he sent. In this they acquiesce, and attempt to amuse us for two months. At the end of that time, the plenipotentiaries say to Lord Malmesbury, not what they said before, send to England for power to accede to proposals which you have already rejected; but *go* to England yourself for such powers, in order to obtain peace.

Recapitulation.

Such was the winding up of the negotiation. Such was the way in which the prospect of peace has been disappointed by the conduct of France; and I must look upon the dismissal of Lord Malmesbury as the last stage of the negotiation, because the undisguised insult by which it was pretended to be kept up for ten days after Lord Malmesbury was sent away, was really below comment. You send him to ask for those powers which you were told he had not, and in the refusal of which you acquiesced. You have asked as a preliminary that which is monstrous and exorbitant. That preliminary you were told would not be complied with, and yet the performance of that preliminary you made the *sine qua non* conditions of his return! Such was the last step by which the French government has shown that it had feeling enough left to think it necessary to search for some pretext to color its proceedings. But they are such proceedings that no pretext or artifice can cover them, as will appear more particularly from the papers officially communicated to the House.

But here the subject does not rest. If we look to the whole complexion of this transaction, the

[10] The words used were these: "There is a decree of the Directory, that in case Lord Malmesbury shall declare himself not to have the necessary powers for agreeing to all the restitutions which the laws and treaties which bind the French Republic make indispensable, he *shall return in twenty-four hours to his court to ask for sufficient powers*." As the Directory knew the English could not grant this, certainly as a *preliminary*, such a communication was a direct dismissal of Lord Malmesbury.

duplicity, the arrogance, and violence which has appeared in the course of the negotiation, if we take from thence our opinion of its general result, we shall be justified in our conclusion—not that the people of France—not that the whole government of France—but that part of the government which had too much influence, and has now the whole ascendency, never was sincere—was determined to accept of no terms but such as would make it neither durable nor safe; such as could only be accepted by this country by a surrender of all its interests, and by a sacrifice of every pretension to the character of a great, a powerful, or an independent nation.

A revolutionary government, and not the French people, responsible for their acts.

This, sir, is inference no longer. You have their own open avowal. You have stated in the subsequent declaration of France itself that it is not against your commerce, that it is not against your wealth, it is not against your possessions in the East, or your colonies in the West, it is not against even the source of your maritime greatness, it is not against any of the appendages of your empire, but against the very essence of liberty, against the foundation of your independence, against the citadel of your happiness, against your Constitution itself, that their hostilities are directed. They have themselves announced and proclaimed the proposition, that what they mean to bring with their invading army is the genius of *their* liberty. I desire no other word to express the subversion of the British Constitution, and the substitution of the most malignant and fatal contrast—the annihilation of British liberty, and the obliteration of every thing that has rendered you a great, a flourishing, and a happy people.

They are directed against the very existence of the British empire.

This is what is at issue. For this are we to declare ourselves in a manner that deprecates the rage which our enemy will not dissemble, and which will be little moved by our entreaty! Under such circumstances, are we ashamed or afraid to declare, in a firm and manly tone, our resolution to defend ourselves, or to speak the language of truth with the energy that belongs to Englishmen united in such a cause? Sir, I do not scruple, for one, to say, *If I knew nothing by which I could state to myself a probability of the contest terminating in our favor, I would maintain that the contest, with its worst chances, is preferable to an acquiescence in such demands.*

Issue now before the country.

If I could look at this as a dry question of prudence; if I could calculate it upon the mere grounds of interest, I would say, if we love that degree of national power which is necessary for the independence of the country and its safety; if we regard domestic tranquillity, if we look at individual enjoyment from the highest to the meanest among us, there is not a man whose stake is so great in the country that he ought to hesitate a moment in sacrificing any portion of it to oppose the violence of the enemy—nor is there, I trust, a man in this happy and free nation whose stake is so small that would not be ready to sacrifice his life in the same cause. If we look at it with a view to *safety*, this would be our conduct. But if we look at it upon the principle of true honor, of the character which we have to support, of the example which we have to set to the other nations of Europe; if we view rightly the lot in which Providence has placed us, and the contrast between ourselves and all the other countries in Europe, gratitude to that Providence should inspire us to make every effort in such a cause. There may be danger; but on the one side there is danger accompanied with honor; on the other side, there is danger with indelible shame and disgrace: upon such an alternative, Englishmen will not hesitate. I wish to disguise no part of my sentiments upon the grounds on which I put the issue of the contest. I ask, whether up to the principles I have stated, we are prepared to act? Having done so, my opinion is not altered: my hopes, however, are animated by the reflection that the means of our safety are in our own hands; for there never was a period when we had more to encourage us. In spite of heavy burdens, the radical strength of the nation never showed itself more conspicuous; its revenue never exhibited greater proofs of the wealth of the country; the same objects which constitute the blessings we have to fight for, furnish us with the means of continuing them. But it is not upon that point I rest. There is one great resource, which I trust will never abandon us, and which has shone forth in the English character, by which we have preserved our existence and fame as a nation, which I trust we shall be determined never to abandon under any extremity; but shall join hand and heart in the solemn pledge that is proposed to us, and declare to his Majesty *that we know great exertions are wanted; that we are prepared to make them; and are, at all events, determined to stand or fall by the* Laws, Liberties, *and* Religion *of our country.*

Peroration: Appeal to the honor and the interests of all.

The House was completely electrified by this speech. Sir John Sinclair, at the suggestion of Mr. Wilberforce, withdrew his motion for an amendment, and the Address was passed (as in the House of Lords) without one dissenting voice. The great body of the nation, with their characteristic energy in times of danger, rallied around King and Parliament. A subscription was raised of fifteen hundred thousand pounds sterling, as a voluntary donation to meet the increased expenses of the war; and Mr. Pitt was permitted so to modify his system of taxation as to produce a vast accession to the regular income of the government. This relieved him from his main difficulty, and enabled him to renew the contest with increased vigor.

The Directory sent Bonaparte to invade Egypt early in 1798, and Turkey immediately declared war against France. Russia now entered eagerly into the contest; and Austria, which had been negotiating with the French at Radstadt, since the treaty of Campo Formio, respecting the concerns of the German Empire, encouraged by the advance of the Russians, again resorted to arms. Thus was formed the third great confederacy against France, which was sustained by immense subsidies furnished by Mr. Pitt out of the increased means now placed at his disposal. The scene of warfare at the close of 1798, and throughout the year 1799, was extended over the whole surfaee of Italy, along the banks of the Rhine, amid the marshes and canals of Holland, and among the lakes and mountains of Switzerland. France, after gigantic efforts, lost all Italy, with the exception of Genoa, but retained her borders upon the Rhine and the barriers of the Alps. Russia withdrew from the contest in the autumn of 1799.

The Directory had now become extremely unpopular throughout France, but no party was strong enough to relieve the country from its arrogance and rapacity, until Bonaparte suddenly returned from Egypt, and, throwing himself on the army for support, usurped the government on the 9th of November, 1799. A new Constitution was immediately formed, under which Bonaparte was nominated First Consul for ten years, and this was adopted by a vote throughout France of 3,012,659 to 1562. The new government was inaugurated with great pomp on the 24th of December, 1799. Bonaparte made every effort to unite and pacify the people; and with a view to present himself before Europe as governed by a spirit of moderation, he instantly dispatched a courier to England with proposals for negotiating a peace. This brings us to the subject of the next speech.

SPEECH

OF MR. PITT ON AN ADDRESS TO THE THRONE APPROVING OF HIS REFUSAL TO NEGOTIATE WITH BONAPARTE FOR A PEACE WITH FRANCE, DELIVERED IN THE HOUSE OF COMMONS, FEBRUARY 3, 1800.

INTRODUCTION.

On the 25th of December, 1799, the day after he was inaugurated as First Consul of France, Bonaparte addressed a letter to the King of England, written with his own hand, and couched in the following terms:

"Called by the wishes of the French nation to occupy the first magistracy of the Republic, I think it proper, on entering into office, to make a direct communication to your Majesty. The war which for eight years has ravaged the four quarters of the world, must it be eternal? Are there no means of coming to an understanding? How can the two most enlightened nations of Europe, powerful and strong beyond what their safety and independence require, sacrifice to ideas of vain greatness the benefits of commerce, internal prosperity, and the happiness of families? How is it that they do not feel that peace is of the first necessity as well as of the first glory? These sentiments can not be foreign to the heart of your Majesty, who reigns over a free nation, and with the sole view of rendering it happy. Your Majesty will only see in this overture my sincere desire to contribute efficaciously, for the second time, to a general pacification, by a step speedy, entirely of confidence, and disengaged from those forms which, necessary perhaps to disguise the dependence of weak states, prove only in those which are strong the mutual desire of deceiving each other. France and England, by the abuse of their strength, may still for a long time, to the misfortune of all nations, retard the period of their being exhausted. But I will venture to say it, the fate of all civilized nations is attached to the termination of a war which involves the whole world. Of your Majesty, &c. BONAPARTE."

From the feelings expressed by Mr. Pitt in the preceding speech, we should naturally have expected him to embrace this overture with promptitude, if not with eagerness. But the resentment which he justly felt at the evasive and insulting conduct of the Directory during the last negotiation, seems wholly to have changed his views, and he rejected the proposal in terms which were too much suited to awaken a similar resentment in the new French rulers. The reply of Lord Grenville went back to the *commencement* of the war, declaring it to have been "an unprovoked attack" on the part of the French. It assumed, that "this system *continues* to prevail," and that on the part of England "no defense but that of open and steady hostility can be availing." In reference to peace, it pointed to the *restoration of the Bourbons*, as "the best and most natural pledge of its reality and permanence;" and while the English minister did not "claim to prescribe to France what shall be her form of government," he did say, as to any ground of confidence in the one recently organized, "Unhappily no such security hitherto exists; no sufficient evidence of the principles by which the new government will be directed; *no reasonable ground by which to judge of its stability*." The French minister, Talleyrand, replied to these remarks in a pointed note, and Lord Grenville closed the correspondence in a letter reaffirming his former positions.

These communications were laid before the House of Commons, February 3d, 1800, when an Address was proposed by Mr. Dundas, approving of the course taken by ministers. He was followed by Mr. Whitbread. Mr. Canning, and Mr. [afterward Lord] Erskine, who complained in strong terms of the uncourteous language used by Lord Grenville. Mr. Pitt then rose, and without making any defense on this point, or touching directly upon the question, "Why should we not *now* treat?" took up the subject on the broadest scale, going back to the origin of the war, the atrocities of the French in overrunning a large part of Europe during the last ten years, the genius and spirit of the Revolution, the instability of its successive governments, his motives for treating with such men on a former occasion, and the character and deeds of Bonaparte from the commencement of his career as a military chieftain. This was the most elaborate oration ever delivered by Mr. Pitt. Of the vast variety of facts brought forward or referred to, very few have ever been disputed; they are arranged in luminous order, and grow out of each other in regular succession; they present a vivid and horrible picture of the miseries inflicted upon Europe by revolutionary France, while the provocations of her enemies are thrown entirely into the background.

It will interest the reader to compare this speech with the reply of Mr. Fox, in respect to the *stand-point* of the speaker. That of Mr. Fox was this, that peace is the *natural* state of human society, and ought, therefore, to be made, unless there is clear evidence that the securities for its continuance are inadequate. Mr. Pitt's *stand-point* was this, that as the war existed, and sprung out of a system of perfidy and violence unparalleled in the history of the world, it ought not to be ended except on *strong and direct evidence* that there were adequate securities for the continuance of peace if made. The question was whether the new government under Bonaparte offered those securities. But Mr. Pitt showed great dexterity in treating this government as merely a new phase of the Revolution, and thus bringing all the atrocities of the past to bear on the question before the House. His speech was admirably adapted to a people like the English, jealous of France as their hereditary rival, conscious of their resources, and prepared to consider a continuation of the contest, as the safest means of defending "their liberties, their laws, and their most holy religion."

Some of the facts referred to in this speech have been already explained in connection with Mr. Fox's reply on this subject, as given on a preceding page. For the convenience of the reader, however, these explanations will, in a few instances, be given again.

SPEECH, &c.

Sir,—I am induced, at this period of the debate, to offer my sentiments to the House, both from an apprehension that at a later hour the attention of the House must necessarily be exhausted, and because the sentiment with which the honorable and learned gentleman [Mr. Erskine] began his speech, and with which he has thought proper to conclude it, places the question precisely on that ground on which I am most desirous of discussing it. The learned gentleman seems to assume as the foundation of his reasoning, and as the great argument for immediate treaty, that every effort to overturn the system of the French Revolution must be unavailing; and that it would be not only imprudent, but almost impious to struggle longer against that order of things which, on I know not what principle of predestination, he appears to consider as immortal. Little as I am inclined to accede to this opinion, I am not sorry that the honorable gentleman has contemplated the subject in this serious view. I do, indeed, consider the French Revolution as the severest trial which the visitation of Providence has ever yet inflicted upon the nations of the earth; but I can not help reflecting, with satisfaction, that this country, even under such a trial, has not only been exempted from those calamities which have covered almost every other part of Europe, but appears to have been reserved as a refuge and asylum to those who fled from its persecution, as a barrier to oppose its progress, and perhaps ultimately as an instrument to deliver the world from the crimes and miseries which have attended it.

Reasons for dwelling on the origin of the war, and the atrocities of the French Revolution.

Under this impression, I trust the House will forgive me, if I endeavor, as far as I am able, to take a large and comprehensive view of this important question. In doing so, I agree with my honorable friend [Mr. Canning] that it would, in any case, be impossible to separate the present discussion from the former crimes and atrocities of the French Revolution; because both the papers now on the table, and the whole of the learned gentleman's argument, force upon our consideration the origin of the war, and all the material facts which have occurred during its continuance. The learned gentleman [Mr. Erskine] has revived and retailed all those arguments from his own pamphlet, which had before passed through thirty-seven or thirty-eight editions in print, and now gives them to the House embellished by the graces of his personal delivery. The First Consul has also thought fit to revive and retail the chief arguments used by all the opposition speakers and all the opposition publishers in this country during the last seven years. And (what is still more material) the question itself, which is now immediately at issue —the question whether, under the present circumstances, there is such a prospect of security from any treaty with France as ought to induce us to negotiate, can not be properly decided upon without retracing, both from our own experience and from that of other nations, the nature, the causes, and the magnitude of the danger against which we have to guard, in order to judge of the security which we ought to accept.

Three opinions, one of which must be held by those who are in favor of negotiation.

I say, then, that before any man can concur in opinion with that learned gentleman; before any man can think that the substance of his Majesty's answer is any other than the safety of the country required; before any man can be of opinion that, to the overtures made by the enemy, at such a time and under such circumstances, it would have been safe to return an answer concurring in the negotiation—he must come within one of the three following descriptions: He must either believe that the French Revolution neither does now exhibit, nor has at any time exhibited such circumstances of danger, arising out of the very nature of the system, and the internal state and condition of France, as to leave to foreign powers no adequate ground of security in negotiation; or, secondly, he must be of opinion that the change which has recently taken place has given that security which, in the former stages of the Revolution, was wanting; or, thirdly, he must be one who, believing that the danger exists, not undervaluing its extent nor mistaking its nature, nevertheless thinks, from his view of the present pressure on the country, from his view of its situation and its prospects, compared with the situation and prospects of its enemies, that we are, with our eyes open, bound to accept of inadequate security for every thing that is valuable and sacred, rather than endure the pressure, or incur the risk which would result from a farther prolongation of the contest.[1]

In discussing the last of these questions, we shall be led to consider what inference is to be drawn from the circumstances and the result of our own negotiations in former periods of the war; whether, in the comparative state of this country and France, we now see the same reason for repeating our then unsuccessful experiments; or whether we have not thence derived the lessons of experience, added to the deductions of reason, marking the inefficacy and danger of the very measures which are quoted to us as precedents for our adoption.

Origin of the war.

I. Unwilling, sir, as I am to go into much detail on ground which has been so often trodden before; yet, when I find the learned gentleman, after all the information which he must have received, if he has read any of the answers to his work (however ignorant he might be when he wrote it) still giving the sanction of his authority to the supposition that the order to M. Chauvelin [French minister] to depart from this kingdom was the cause of the war between this country and France, I do feel it necessary to say a few words on that part of the subject.

Error in the note of the French government.

Inaccuracy in dates seems to be a sort of fatality common to all who have written on that side of the question; for even the writer of the note to his Majesty is not more correct, in this respect, than if he had taken his information only from the pamphlet of the learned gentleman. The House will recollect the first professions of the French Republic, which are enumerated, and enumerated truly, in that note. They are tests of every thing which would best recommend a government to the esteem and confidence of foreign powers, and the reverse of every thing which has been the system and practice of France now for near ten years. It is there stated that their first principles were love of peace, aversion to conquest, and respect for the independence of other countries. In the same note it seems, indeed, admitted that they since have violated all those principles; but it is alleged that they have done so only in consequence of the provocation of other powers. One of the first of those provocations is stated to have consisted in the various outrages offered to their ministers, of which the example is said to have been set by the King of Great Britain in his conduct to M. Chauvelin. In answer to this supposition, it is only necessary to remark, that before the example was given, before Austria and Prussia are supposed to have been thus encouraged to combine in a plan for the partition of France, that plan, if it ever existed at all, had existed and been acted upon for above eight months. France and Prussia had been at war eight months before the dismissal of M. Chauvelin. So much for the accuracy of the statement.[2]

Contradiction of Mr. Erskine as to the origin of the war.

I have been hitherto commenting on the arguments contained in the Notes. I come now to those of the learned gentleman. I understand him to say that the dismissal of M. Chauvelin was the real cause, I do not say of the general war, but of the rupture between France and England; and the learned gentleman states particularly that this dismissal rendered all discussion of the points in dispute impossible. Now I desire to meet distinctly every part of this assertion. I maintain, on the contrary, that an opportunity was given for discussing every matter in dispute between France and Great Britain as fully as if a regular and accredited French minister had been resident here; that the causes of war, which existed at the beginning, or arose during the course of this discussion, were such as would have justified,

[1] In distributing his opponents into these three classes, Mr. Pitt follows his usual course of opening his speech with a striking statement which reaches forward into the subsequent discussion.

[2] Mr. Erskine here observed that this was not the statement of his argument. Mr. Pitt replied that he had not yet come to Mr. Erskine, but was speaking of the statement made by the French government in their Note. It can not be, however, that Mr. Pitt had that Note before him when he made these remarks. The passage referred to is in the following words: "As soon as the French Revolution had broken out, almost all Europe entered into a league for its destruction. The aggression was real long time before it was public. Internal resistance was excited; its opponents were favorably received; their extravagant declamations were supported; the French nation was insulted in the person of its agents; and England set particularly this example by the dismissal of the minister accredited to her. Finally, France was, in fact, attacked in her independence, in her honor, and in her safety, long time before war was declared."—Parl. Hist., vol. xxxiv., p. 1201. It is obvious that the writer is here giving a mere general summation of supposed wrongs, without professing to arrange them in the exact order of time. He does not say, as Mr. Pitt represents, that "one of the *first* of those provocations" was the ill treatment of French ministers, of which "the *example* was set by the King of Great Britain." He does not even mention Austria or Prussia, much less does he speak of their being "encouraged to combine in a plan for the partition of France," by "the example" referred to. And yet it is only by assuming this that Mr. Pitt makes out his argument, and then sneers at "the accuracy of the statement."

twenty times over, a declaration of war on the part of this country; that all the explanations on the part of France were evidently unsatisfactory and inadmissible, and that M. Chauvelin had given in a peremptory ultimatum, declaring that if these explanations were not received as sufficient, and if we did not immediately disarm, our refusal would be considered as a declaration of war. After this followed that scene which no man can even now speak of without horror, or think of without indignation; that murder and regicide from which I was sorry to hear the learned gentleman date the beginning of the legal government of France.[3]

Ground of M. Chauvelin's dismissal.

Having thus given in their ultimatum, they added, as a further demand (while we were smarting under accumulated injuries, for which all satisfaction was denied) that we should instantly receive M. Chauvelin as their embassador, with new credentials, representing them in the character which they had just derived from the murder of their sovereign. We replied, "he came here as the representative of a sovereign whom you have put to a cruel and illegal death; we have no satisfaction for the injuries we have received, no security from the danger with which we are threatened. Under these circumstances we will not receive your new credentials. The former credentials you have yourselves recalled by the sacrifice of your King."

Sent out of the country as a private individual.

What, from that moment, was the situation of M. Chauvelin? He was reduced to the situation of a private individual, and was required to quit the kingdom under the provisions of the Alien Act, which, for the purpose of securing domestic tranquillity, had recently invested his Majesty with the power of removing out of this kingdom all foreigners suspected of revolutionary principles. Is it contended that he was then less liable to the provisions of that act than any other individual foreigner, whose conduct afforded to government just ground of objection or suspicion? Did his conduct and connections here afford no such ground? or will it be pretended that the bare act of refusing to receive fresh credentials from an infant republic, not then acknowledged by any one power of Europe, and in the very act of heaping upon us injuries and insults, was of itself a cause of war? So far from it, that even the very nations of Europe, whose wisdom and moderation have been repeatedly extolled for maintaining neutrality, and preserving friendship with the French Republic, remained for years subsequent to this period without receiving from it any accredited minister, or doing any one act to acknowledge its political existence.

A refusal to recognize the new government no ground of hostilities on the part of the French.

In answer to a representation from the belligerent powers, in December, 1793, Count Bernstorff, the minister of Denmark, officially declared that "it was well known that the National Convention had appointed M. Grouville minister plenipotentiary at Denmark, but that it was also well known that he had neither been received nor acknowledged in that quality." And as late as February, 1796, when the same minister was at length, for the first time, received in his official capacity, Count Bernstorff, in a public note, assigned this reason for that change of conduct: "So long as no other than a revolutionary government existed in France, his Majesty *could* not acknowledge the minister of that government; but now that the French Constitution is completely organized, and a regular government established in France, his Majesty's obligation ceases in that respect, and M. Grouville will therefore be acknowledged in the usual form." How far the court of Denmark was justified in the opinion that a revolutionary government then no longer existed in France, it is not now necessary to inquire; but whatever may have been the fact in that respect, the *principle* on which they acted is clear and intelligible, and is a decisive instance in favor of the proposition which I have maintained.

Aggressions of France.

Is it, then, necessary to examine what were the terms of that ultimatum with which we refused to comply? Acts of hostility had been openly threatened against our allies; a hostility founded upon the assumption of a right which would at once supersede the whole law of nations. The pretended right to open the Scheldt we discussed at the time, not so much on account of its immediate importance (though it was important both in a maritime and commercial view) as on account of the general principle on which it was founded.[4] On the

[3] Here, again, Mr. Pitt founds his attack upon a mistake. Mr. Erskine, as reported in the Parliamentary History, did not say "the beginning of *legal* government," but "when France cut off her most unfortunate monarch, and established her *first republic*, she had an embassador at our court."—Vol. xxxiv., p. 1289. His language may have been confused or obscure, but it is hardly conceivable that Mr. Erskine, through any haste or inadvertence, could have been betrayed into the absurdity of saying that there never was a *legal* government in France until the 21st of January, 1793.

Nor does Mr. Pitt appear to have understood Mr. Erskine more correctly when he represents him, a few sentences before, as affirming that the dismissal of M. Chauvelin "rendered all discussion of the points in dispute *impossible*." No statement of this kind appears in the printed speech. He and his friends only maintained that the treatment of this gentleman, after the imprisonment and death of Louis XVI., was so harsh and irritating as to defeat all the objects of negotiation. It was a matter of public notoriety that *informal* communications did pass between the two governments; but the agents of France were denied all public and accredited character, an indignity (as Mr. Erskine and his friends maintained) which was tantamount to breaking off all friendly intercourse, and which threw upon England, in their view, the responsibility of the war which followed.

[4] When the Austrians and Prussians, who invaded France under the Duke of Brunswick, were driven back, the French in return attacked the Austrian Netherlands, and became masters of the country by the battle of Jemappe, November 6th, 1792. They

same arbitrary notion they soon afterward discovered that sacred law of nature which made the Rhine and the Alps the legitimate boundaries of France, and assumed the power, which they have affected to exercise through the whole of the Revolution, of superseding, by a new code of their own, all the recognized principles of the law of nations. They were, in fact, actually advancing toward the republic of Holland, by rapid strides, after the victory of Jemappe, and they had ordered their generals to pursue the Austrian troops into any neutral country, thereby explicitly avowing an intention of invading Holland. They had already shown their moderation and self-denial, by incorporating Belgium with the French Republic. These lovers of peace, who set out with a sworn aversion to conquest, and professions of respect for the independence of other nations; who pretend that they departed from this system only in consequence of your aggression, themselves, in time of peace, while you were still confessedly neutral, without the pretense or shadow of provocation, wrested Savoy from the King of Sardinia, and had proceeded to incorporate it likewise with France.[5] These were their aggressions at this period, and more than these. They had issued a universal declaration of war against all the thrones of Europe, and they had, by their conduct, applied it particularly and specifically to you. They had passed the decree of the 19th of November, 1792, proclaiming the promise of French succor to all nations who should manifest a wish to become free;[6] they had, by all their language as well as their example, shown what they understood to be freedom; they had sealed their principles by the deposition of their sovereign; they had applied them to England by inviting and encouraging the addresses of those seditious and traitorous societies, who, from the beginning, favored their views, and who, encouraged by your forbearance, were even then publicly avowing French doctrines, and anticipating their success in this country—who were hailing the progress of those proceedings in France which led to the murder of its King; they were even then looking to the day when they should behold a National Convention in England formed upon similar principles.[7]

And what were the explanations they offered on these different grounds of offense? As to Holland: they told you the Scheldt was too insignificant for you to trouble yourselves about, and therefore it was to be decided as they chose, in breach of positive treaty, which they had themselves guaranteed, and which we, by our alliance, were bound to support.[8] If, however, after the war was over, Belgium should have consolidated its liberty (a term of which we

Explanations of the French.

immediately forced the passage of the Scheldt (the principal river of the country) down to the sea. This had been closed for nearly one hundred and fifty years, out of regard to the rights of Holland (through which it entered the ocean), under the provisions of the treaty of Westphalia (1648), which established the international relations of modern Europe. England, as the protector of Holland, justly complained of this, chiefly, however, as Mr. Pitt remarks, on account of the general principle avowed by the French of setting aside the provisions of the treaty of Westphalia.

[5] Savoy had been invaded by the French in September, 1792, on the ground that the King of Sardinia had united at Mantua with Austria and Spain in agreeing to march one hundred thousand troops to the borders of France. See page 531. The people united to a considerable extent with the French, and sent deputations from their clubs to Paris. On the 27th of November, 1792, the National Convention erected Savoy into an eighty-fourth department of France, in direct defiance of the existing Constitution, which interdicted any permanent extension of the territory.

[6] This celebrated decree was passed by the National Convention in the tumult of joy which followed the victory at Jemappe. They resolved to adopt in other countries the course taken in Savoy, and hence framed this document in the following words:

"The National Convention declare, in the name of the French nation, they will grant fraternity and assistance to all those people who wish to procure liberty. And they charge the executive power to send orders to the generals to give assistance to such people, and to defend citizens who have suffered, and are now suffering, in the cause of liberty."—*Alison*, vol. i., p. 592, third edition.

The reader will see (in note 9) M. Chauvelin's disclaimer in respect to this decree, of any intention on the part of the French to "favor insurrections or excite disturbance in any neutral or friendly country whatever"—"particularly Holland, so long as that power adheres to the principles of her neutrality." Mr. Pitt, of course, had no confidence in the sincerity of these declarations.

[7] Within ten days after the decree of November 19th was passed, an English "Society for Constitutional Information" sent delegates to Paris, who presented at the bar of the National Convention an address congratulating that body on "the glorious triumph of liberty on the 10th of August," when the King was deposed. These delegates take upon them to predict "that, after the example given by France, revolutions will become easy. Reason is about to make a rapid progress; and it would not be extraordinary if, in a much less time than can be imagined, the French should send addresses of congratulation to a National Convention in England." M. Gregoire, the President of the Convention, replied in a high-flown style, praising the English as having afforded illustrious examples to the universe. "The shades of Hampden and Sydney," said he, "hover over your heads; and the moment without doubt approaches when the French will bring congratulations to the National Convention of Great Britain. Generous Republicans! your appearance among us prepares a subject for history!" The French were egregiously deceived, no doubt, by these demonstrations of a comparatively small number of individuals in England, and really expected great results. The English government had certainly grounds of serious complaint against the Convention for receiving the deputation in this manner.

[8] Austria had endeavored, in 1784, to force the navigation of the Scheldt, but France had interfered and guaranteed to Holland her exclusive right to the lower part of that river. This guarantee England was bound to maintain by a subsequent alliance which she formed with Holland.

now know the meaning, from the fate of every nation into which the arms of France have penetrated), then Belgium and Holland might, if they pleased, settle the question of the Scheldt, by separate negotiation between themselves. With respect to aggrandizement, they assured us that they would retain possession of Belgium by arms no longer than they should find it necessary to the purpose already stated, of consolidating its liberty. And with respect to the decree of the 19th of November, 1792, applied as it was pointedly to you, by all the intercourse I have stated with all the seditious and traitorous part of this country, and particularly by the speeches of every leading man among them, they contented themselves with asserting that the declaration conveyed no such meaning as was imputed to it, and that, so far from encouraging sedition, it could apply only to countries where a great majority of the people should have already declared itself in favor of a revolution: a supposition which, as they asserted, necessarily implied a total absence of all sedition.

Effect of admitting their explanation of the decree of November 19.

What would have been the effect of admitting this explanation? to suffer a nation, and an armed nation, to preach to the inhabitants of all the countries in the world, that they themselves were slaves, and their rulers tyrants; to encourage and invite them to revolution, by a previous promise of French support, to whatever might call itself a majority, or to whatever France might declare to be so. This was their explanation; and this, they told you, was their ultimatum.[9]

But was this all? Even at that very moment, when they were endeavoring to induce you to admit these explanations, to be contented with the avowal, that France offered herself as a general guarantee for every successful revolution, and would interfere only to sanction and confirm whatever the free and uninfluenced choice of the people might have decided, what were their orders to their generals on the same subject? In the midst of these amicable explanations with you, came forth a decree which I really believe must be effaced from the minds of gentlemen opposite to me, if they can prevail upon themselves for a moment to hint even a doubt upon the origin of this quarrel, not only as to this country, but as to all the nations of Europe with whom France has been subsequently engaged in hostility. I speak of the decree of the 15th of December, 1792. This decree, more even than all the previous transactions, amounted to a universal declaration of war against all thrones, and against all civilized governments. It said, wherever the armies of France shall come (whether within countries then at war or at peace is not distinguished), in all those countries it shall be the first care of their generals to introduce the principles and the practice of the French Revolution; to demolish all privileged orders, and every thing which obstructs the establishment of their new system.[10]

Still more violent decree of December 15, 1792.

Extensive application of this decree.

If any doubt is entertained whither the armies of France were intended to come; if it is contended that they referred only to those nations with whom they were then at war, or with whom, in the course of this contest, they might be driven into war; let it be remembered that at this very moment they had actually given orders to their generals to pursue the Austrian army from the Netherlands into Holland, with whom they were at that time in peace. Or, even if the construction contended for is admitted, let us see what would have been its application, let us look at the list of their aggressions, which was read by my right honorable friend [Mr. Dundas] near me. With whom have they been at war since the period of this declaration? With all the nations of Europe save two (Sweden and Denmark), and if not with these two, it is only because, with every provocation

[9] The communication here spoken of as an ultimatum was made through M. Chauvelin, December 27, 1792, and contained the following words: "The Executive Council of the French Republic, thinking it a duty which they owe to the French nation not to leave it in a state of suspense into which it has been thrown by the late measures of the British government, have authorized him [M. Chauvelin] to demand with openness, whether France ought to consider England as a neutral or hostile power; at the same time being solicitous that not the smallest doubt should exist respecting the disposition of France toward England, and of its desire to remain in peace." In allusion to the decree of the 19th of November [for this decree see note 6], M. Chauvelin says, "that the French nation absolutely reject the idea of that false interpretation by which it might be supposed that the French Republic should favor insurrections, or excite disturbance in any neutral or friendly country whatever. In particular, they declare in the most solemn manner, that France will not attack Holland so long as that power adheres to the principles of her neutrality." As to the navigation of the Scheldt, M. Chauvelin affirms it "to be a question of too little importance to be made the sole cause of a war, and that it could only be used as a pretext for a premeditated aggression. On this fatal supposition (he says) the French nation will accept war; but such a war would be the war not of the British nation, but of the British ministry against the French Republic; and of this he conjures them well to consider the terrible responsibility."

[10] This decree was even more violent than Mr. Pitt has here described. It required the French generals, (1.) To proclaim wherever they marched their armies the abolition of all existing feudal and manorial rights, together with all imposts, contributions, and tithes; (2.) To declare the sovereignty of the people, and the suppression of all existing authorities; (3.) To convoke the people for the establishment of a provisional government; (4.) To place all the property of the Prince and his adherents, and the property of all public bodies, both civil and religious, under the safeguard of the French Republic; (5.) To provide, as soon as possible, for the organization of a free and popular form of government.—*Ann. Reg.*, vol. xxxiv., p. 155.

There can be no doubt that the Convention at this time had extravagant notions of extending their principles of liberty by force. "A blind and groundless confidence," says Marshal St. Cyr, "had taken possession of their minds; they thought only of dethroning kings by their decrees."

that could justify defensive war, those countries have hitherto acquiesced in repeated violations of their rights, rather than recur to war for their vindication. Wherever their arms have been carried it will be a matter of short subsequent inquiry to trace whether they have faithfully applied these principles. If in *terms*, this decree is a denunciation of war against all governments; if in *practice* it has been applied against every one with which France has come into contact; what is it but the deliberate code of the French Revolution, from the birth of the Republic, which has never once been departed from, which has been enforced with unremitted rigor against all the nations that have come into their power?

Designed to be applied to all nations.

If there could otherwise be any doubt whether the application of this decree was intended to be universal, whether it applied to all nations, and to England particularly; there is one circumstance which alone would be decisive—that nearly at the same period it was proposed [by M. Baraillon], in the National Convention, to declare expressly that the decree of November 19th was confined to the nations with whom they were *then* at war; and that proposal was *rejected* by a great majority, by that very Convention from whom we were desired to receive these explanations as satisfactory.

Instructions to their generals.

Such, sir, was the nature of the system. Let us examine a little farther, whether it was from the beginning intended to be acted upon in the extent which I have stated. At the very moment when their threats appeared to many little else than the ravings of madmen, they were digesting and methodizing the means of execution, as accurately as if they had actually foreseen the extent to which they have since been able to realize their criminal projects. They sat down coolly to devise the most regular and effectual mode of making the application of this system the current business of the day, and incorporating it with the general orders of their army; for (will the House believe it!) this confirmation of the decree of November 19th was accompanied by an exposition and commentary addressed to the general of every army of France, containing a schedule as coolly conceived, and as methodically reduced, as any by which the most quiet business of a justice of peace, or the most regular routine of any department of state in this country could be conducted. Each commander was furnished with one general blank formula of a letter for all the nations of the world! The people of France to the people of ———, Greeting, "We are come to expel your tyrants." Even this was not all; one of the articles of the decree of the fifteenth of December was expressly, "that those who should show themselves so brutish and so enamored of their chains as to refuse the restoration of their rights, to renounce liberty and equality, or to preserve, recall, or treat with their prince or privileged orders, were not entitled to the distinction which France, in other cases, had justly established between government and people; and that such a people ought to be treated according to the rigor of war, and of conquest." Here is their love of peace; here is their aversion to conquest; here is their respect for the independence of other nations!

Such the circumstances under which M. Chauvelin was sent out of the country.

It was then, after receiving such explanations as these, after receiving the ultimatum of France, and after M. Chauvelin's credentials had ceased, that he was required to depart. Even at that period, I am almost ashamed to record it, we did not on our part shut the door against other attempts to negotiate, but this transaction was immediately followed by the declaration of war, proceeding not from England in vindication of her rights, but from France, as the completion of the injuries and insults they had offered. And on a war thus originating, can it be doubted by an English House of Commons whether the aggression was on the part of this country or of France? or whether the manifest aggression on the part of France was the result of any thing but the principles which characterize the French Revolution?

What, then, are the resources and subterfuges by which those who agree with the learned gentleman are prevented from sinking under the force of this simple statement of facts? None but what are found in the insinuation contained in the note from France, that this country had, *previous* to the transactions to which I have referred, encouraged and supported the combination of other powers directed against them.[11]

---

[11] It is only an act of justice to remind the reader that Mr. Erskine, at the commencement of Mr. Pitt's speech, expressly disclaimed the ground here imputed to him and his friends. See Note 2. Throughout his speech, he based his position (whether it was a true or false one) on other grounds. He did not claim that Mr. Pitt had acted in concert with Austria and Prussia in the declaration of Pilnitz, or in any of their other measures *previous* to the suspension of M. Chauvelin's functions as French minister. And Mr. Fox, in his reply to the speech before us, admitted that England had maintained her neutrality down to that time. See page 532. But they insisted that, after the imprisonment of Louis XVI. (August 10th, 1792), France was not treated "as a civilized nation"—the English minister was ordered to leave Paris—M. Chauvelin's powers were suspended; and when Mr. Fox moved, December 15th, 1792, "that a minister be sent to Paris to treat with those persons who *provisionally exercise* the executive government of France" (thus avoiding a recognition of them as a government), Mr. Pitt refused. See Parl. Hist., vol. xxx., p. 80. They affirmed that the tone of Lord Grenville, in his subsequent informal communications with M. Chauvelin, was harsh and irritating—that England ought to have come frankly forward and negotiated as to her grievances in respect to the opening of the Scheldt, the decree of November the 19th, the speech of M. Gregoire, &c., stating explicitly what would satisfy her—that she ought especially to have accepted the mediation urged upon her by Louis XVI. and the French National Assembly early in 1792. See note to Mr. Fox's speech, page 535. They affirmed that there was at least a *possibility* that in this way the war might have been prevented—that, at all events, England was bound to have made the trial before she commenced arming against France—that if she

Facts showing the hostile intentions of France.

Upon this part of the subject, the proofs which contradict such an insinuation are innumerable. In the first place, the evidence of dates; in the second place, the admission of all the different parties in France; of the friends of Brissot, charging on Robespierre the war with this country, and of the friends of Robespierre charging it on Brissot, but both acquitting England; the testimonies of the French government during the whole interval, since the declaration of Pilnitz and the pretended treaty of Pavia; the first of which had not the slightest relation to any project of partition or dismemberment; the second of which I firmly believe to be an absolute fabrication and forgery, and in neither of which, even as they are represented, any reason has been assigned for believing that this country had any share. Even M. Talleyrand himself was sent by the constitutional king of the French, after the period when that concert which is now charged must have existed, if it existed at all, with a letter from the King of France, expressly thanking his Majesty for the neutrality which he had uniformly observed.[12] The same fact is confirmed by the concurring evidence of every person who knew any thing of the plans of the King of Sweden in 1791; the only sovereign who, I believe, at that time meditated any hostile measures against France, and whose utmost hopes were expressly stated to be, that England would not oppose his intended expedition; by all those, also, who knew any thing of the conduct of the Emperor or the King of Prussia; by the clear and decisive testimony of M. Chauvelin himself in his dispatches from hence to the French government, since published by their authority; by every thing which has occurred since the war; by the publications of Dumourier; by the publications of Brissot; by the facts that have since come to light in America, with respect to the mission of M. Genet, which show that hostility against this country was decided on by France long before the period when M. Chauvelin was sent from hence;[13] besides this, the reduction of our peace establishment in the year 1791, and continued to the subsequent year, is a fact from which the inference is indisputable; a fact which, I am afraid, shows not only that we were not waiting for the occasion of war, but that, in our partiality for a pacific system, we had indulged ourselves in a fond and credulous security, which wisdom and discretion would not have dictated. In addition to every other proof, it is singular enough that, in a decree, on the eve of a declaration of war on the part of France, it is expressly stated, as for the first time, that England was then departing from that system of neutrality *which she had hitherto observed.*

Direct proof that England had no connection with Austria and Prussia on their first attack on France.

But, sir, I will not rest merely on these testimonies or arguments, however strong and decisive. I assert distinctly and positively, and I have the documents in my hand to prove it, that from the middle of the year 1791, upon the first rumor of any measure taken by the Emperor of Germany, and till late in the year 1792, we not only were no parties to any of the projects imputed to the Emperor, but, from the political circumstances in which we stood with relation to that court, we wholly declined all communications with him on the subject of France. To Prussia, with whom we were in connection, and still more decisively to Holland, with whom we were in close and intimate correspondence, we uniformly stated our unalterable resolution to maintain neutrality, and avoid interference in the internal affairs of France, as long as France should refrain from hostile measures against us and our allies. No minister of England had any authority to treat with foreign states, even provisionally, for any warlike concert, till after the battle of Jemappe; till a period subsequent to the repeated provocations which had been offered to us, and subsequent particularly to the decree of fraternity of the 19th of November; even then, to what object was it that the concert which we wished to establish, was to be directed? If we had then rightly cast the true character of the French Revolution, I can not now deny that we should have been better justified in a very different conduct. But it is material to the present argument to declare what that conduct actually was, because it is of itself sufficient to confute all the pretexts by which the advocates of France have so long labored to perplex the question of aggression.

had done so, and failed through the violent councils of the French Assembly, she would have stood blameless before the world in the contest that followed—that, having neglected to do so, she was justly to be considered as in part, at least, the author of the war; and that Mr. Pitt, at all events, had no right to go back to these questions, and the subsequent atrocities of the French, *as a reason for refusing now to negotiate.*

12 This was at the time when the mediation was requested, which has just been spoken of in the preceding note.

13 In Genet's secret instructions (which he published at a later period), it is stated that France had a particular interest in acting efficiently against England; and America was, if possible, to be drawn into the contest. As a preliminary step, the American government were to be induced to unite with France in a league, "to befriend the empire of liberty wherever it can be extended—to guarantee the sovereignty of the people—and to punish those powers who keep up *an exclusive colonial and commercial system,* by declaring that their vessels shall not be received in the ports of the contracting parties." The last clause was pointed particularly against England. Whether Mr. Pitt referred to any thing beyond the disclosures in these instructions is uncertain. The instructions themselves prove but little, for they were drawn up January 4th, 1793, only three weeks before Chauvelin was sent out of England, and five months after his functions as minister were suspended. Mr. Pitt had, perhaps, forgotten the dates when he said "*long* before the period when M. Chauvelin was sent hence;" or perhaps he fairly inferred that a systematic attack of this kind upon England, through her commerce, must have taken a considerable time in its preparation.

At that period Russia had at length conceived, as well as ourselves, a natural and just alarm for the balance of Europe, and applied to us to learn our sentiments on the subject. In our answer to this application we imparted to Russia the principles upon which we then acted, and we communicated this answer to Prussia, with whom we were connected in defensive alliance. I will state shortly the leading part of those principles. A dispatch was sent from Lord Grenville to his Majesty's minister in Russia, dated the 29th of December, 1792, stating a desire to have an explanation set on foot on the subject of the war with France. I will read the material parts of it.

Ground taken in a communication to Russia.

"The two leading points on which such explanation will naturally turn are the line of conduct to be followed previous to the commencement of hostilities, and with a view, if possible, to avert them; and the nature and amount of the forces which the powers engaged in this concert might be enabled to use, supposing such extremities to be unavoidable.

"With respect to the first, it appears, on the whole, subject, however, to future consideration and discussion with the other powers, that the most advisable step to be taken would be, that sufficient explanation should be had with the powers at war with France, in order to enable those not hitherto engaged in the war to propose to that country terms of peace. That these terms should be the withdrawing their arms within the limits of the French territory; the abandoning their conquests, the rescinding any acts injurious to the sovereignty or rights of any other nations, and the giving, in some public and unequivocal manner, a pledge of their intention no longer to foment troubles or to excite disturbances against other governments. In return for these stipulations, the different powers of Europe who should be parties to this measure might engage to abandon all measures, or views of hostility against France, or interference in their internal affairs, and to maintain a correspondence and intercourse of amity with the existing powers in that country, with whom such a treaty may be concluded. If, as the result of this proposal so made by the powers acting in concert, these terms should not be accepted by France, or being accepted, should not be satisfactorily performed, the different powers might then engage themselves to each other to enter into active measures for the purpose of obtaining the ends in view; and it may be considered whether, in such case, they might not reasonably look to some indemnity for the expenses and hazards to which they would necessarily be exposed."

The dispatch then proceeded to the second point, that of the forces to be employed, on which it is unnecessary now to speak.

Now, sir, I would really ask any person who has been from the beginning the most desirous of avoiding hostilities, whether it is possible to conceive any measure to be adopted in the situation in which we then stood which could more evidently demonstrate our desire, after repeated provocations, to preserve peace, on any terms consistent with our safety; or whether any sentiment could now be suggested which would have more plainly marked our moderation, forbearance, and sincerity? In saying this I am not challenging the applause and approbation of my country, because I must now confess that we were too slow in anticipating that danger of which we had, perhaps, even then sufficient experience, though far short, indeed, of that which we now possess, and that we might even then have seen, what facts have since but too incontestably proved, that nothing but vigorous and open hostility can afford complete and adequate security against revolutionary principles, while they retain a proportion of power sufficient to furnish the means of war.

II. I will enlarge no farther on the origin of the war. I have read and detailed to you a system which was in itself a declaration of war against all nations, which was so intended, and which has been so applied, which has been exemplified in the extreme peril and hazard of almost all who for a moment have trusted to treaty, and which has not at this hour overwhelmed Europe in one indiscriminate mass of ruin, only because we have not indulged, to a fatal extremity, that disposition which we have, however, indulged too far; because we have not consented to trust to profession and compromise, rather than to our own valor and exertion, for security against a system, from which we never shall be delivered till either the principle is extinguished, or till its strength is exhausted.

Atrocities of the French in carrying out their revolutionary system.

I might, sir, if I found it necessary, enter into much detail upon this part of the subject; but at present I only beg leave to express my readiness at any time to enter upon it, when either my own strength or the patience of the House will admit of it; but I say, without distinction, against every nation in Europe, and against some out of Europe, the principle has been faithfully applied. You can not look at the map of Europe, and lay your hand upon that country against which France has not either declared an open and aggressive war, or violated some positive treaty, or broken some recognized principle of the law of nations.

Extent of the subject.

This subject may be divided into various periods. There were some acts of hostility committed previous to the war with this country, and very little, indeed, subsequent to that declaration, which abjured the love of conquest. The attack upon the papal state, by the seizure of Avignon, in 1791, was accompanied with specimens of all the vile arts and perfidy that ever disgraced a revolution. Avignon was separated from its lawful sovereign, with whom not even the pretense of quarrel existed, and forcibly incorporated in the tyranny of one and indivisible France.[14] The

Aggressions of France upon various countries before her war with England.

[14] This city with the adjoining province, lying on the Rhone, in the south of France, had been for more than four centuries the property of the papal government. For seventy years (from 1305 to 1377) it was the residence of the popes, and was afterward

same system led, in the same year, to an aggression against the whole German empire, by the seizure of Porentrui, part of the dominions of the Bishop of Basle. Afterward, in 1792, unpreceded by any declaration of war, or any cause of hostility, and in direct violation of the solemn pledge to abstain from conquest, they made war against the King of Sardinia, by the seizure of Savoy, for the purpose of incorporating it, in like manner, with France. In the same year, they had proceeded to the declaration of war against Austria, against Prussia, and against the German empire, in which they have been justified only on the ground of a rooted hostility, combination, and league of sovereigns, for the dismemberment of France. I say that some of the documents, brought to support this pretense are spurious and false. I say that even in those that are not so, there is not one word to prove the charge principally relied upon, that of an intention to effect the dismemberment of France, or to impose upon it, by force, any particular Constitution. I say that, as far as we have been able to trace what passed at Pilnitz, the Declaration there signed referred to the imprisonment of Louis XVI., its immediate view was to effect his deliverance, if a concert sufficiently extensive could be formed with other sovereigns for that purpose. It left the internal state of France to be decided by the King restored to his liberty, with the free consent of the states of his kingdom, and it did not contain one word relative to the *dismemberment* of France.[15]

Import of the Declaration of Pilnitz.

In the subsequent discussions, which took place in 1792, and which embraced at the same time all the other points of jealousy which had arisen between the two countries, the Declaration of Pilnitz was referred to, and explained on the part of Austria in a manner precisely conformable to what I have now stated. The amicable explanations which took place, both on this subject and on all the matters in dispute, will be found in the official correspondence between the two courts, which has been made public; and it will be found, also, that as long as the negotiation continued to be conducted through M. Delessart, then minister for foreign affairs, there was a great prospect that those discussions would be amicably terminated; but it is notorious, and has since been clearly proved on the authority of Brissot himself, that the violent party in France considered such an issue of the negotiation as likely to be fatal to their projects, and thought, to use his own words, that "war was necessary to consolidate the Revolution." For the express purpose of producing the war, they excited a popular tumult in Paris; they insisted upon and obtained the dismissal of M. Delessart. A new minister was appointed in his room, the tone of the negotiation was immediately changed, and an ultimatum was sent to the Emperor, similar to that which was afterward sent to this country, affording him no satisfaction on his just grounds of complaint, and requiring him, under those circumstances, to disarm. The first events of the contest proved how much more France was prepared for war than Austria,[16] and afford a strong confirmation of the proposition which I maintain,

Shown by subsequent evidence.

governed by a vice-legate. The National Assembly seized it in 1790, and at the close of the next year annexed it to the French Republic.

[15] Mr. Erskine and his friends did not maintain that the Declaration of Pilnitz was aimed at "the *dismemberment* of France," and yet they considered it as a just ground of her declaring war against Austria. "It was," said Mr. Fox in his reply to this speech, "a declaration of an intention on the part of the great powers of Germany, to interfere in the internal affairs of France for the purpose of *regulating the government* against the opinion of the people. This, though not a plan for the *partition* of France, was in the eye of reason and common sense an *aggression* against France." The Declaration was in the following words, and was given to the Count d'Artois, brother of Louis XVI., in August, 1791, for the purpose of being used to combine the other powers of Europe against the existing French government:

"His Majesty the Emperor, and his Majesty the King of Prussia, having heard the desires and representations of Monsieur and of his royal highness the Count d'Artois, declare jointly that they regard the situation in which his Majesty the King of France actually is as an object of common interest to all the sovereigns of Europe. They hope that this concern can not fail to be acknowledged by the powers whose assistance is claimed; and that in consequence they will not refuse to employ jointly with their said Majesties the most efficacious means, in proportion to their forces, *to place the King of France in a state to settle in the most perfect liberty the foundations of a monarchical government, equally suitable to the rights of sovereigns and the welfare of the French.* Then and in that case, their said Majesties are decided to act quickly and with one accord with the forces necessary to obtain the common end proposed. In the mean time they will give suitable orders to their troops, that they may be ready to put themselves in motion."—*Alison's Hist. of Europe*, vol. i., p. 574, third edition.

The reader will observe that Mr. Pitt has inserted in his statement one very important clause not to be found in this document, viz.: "it left the internal state of France to be decided by the King restored to his liberty, *with the free consent of the states of his kingdom.*" He also omitted one important clause, viz., that this should be done "in a manner equally suitable to the rights of *sovereigns* and the welfare of the French." "Of *sovereigns*"—not of the King of France alone—clearly indicating that *monarchical power* in Europe was to be effectually provided for, and thus opening the way for other monarchs to interfere in deciding on the proper adjustment of the internal affairs of France.

[16] This shows the rashness and ignorance with which the allies rushed into the war. All the royal troops of France were infected with the spirit of the Revolution. Bonaparte, in his exile, speaking of this subject, said, "It was neither the volunteers nor the recruits who saved the Republic; it was the one hundred and eighty thousand old troops of the monarchy and the discharged veterans whom the Revolution impelled to the frontiers. Part of the recruits deserted, part died, a small portion only remained. who, in process of time, formed good soldiers."

that no offensive intention was entertained on the part of the latter power.

War was then declared against Austria, a war which I state to be a war of aggression on the part of France. The King of Prussia had declared that he should consider war against the Emperor or empire as war against himself. He had declared that, as a coestate of the empire, he was determined to defend their rights; that, as an ally of the Emperor, he would support him to the utmost against any attack; and that, for the sake of his own dominions, he felt himself called upon to resist the progress of French principles, and to maintain the balance of power in Europe. With this notice before them, France declared war upon the Emperor, and the war with Prussia was the necessary consequence of this aggression, both against the Emperor and the empire.

Reasons for Prussia's uniting with Austria.

The war against the King of Sardinia follows next. The declaration of that war was the seizure of Savoy by an invading army —and on what ground? On that which has been stated already. They had found out, by some light of nature, that the Rhine and the Alps were the natural limits of France. Upon that ground Savoy was seized; and Savoy was also incorporated with France.

Case of Sardinia.

Here finishes the history of the wars in which France was engaged antecedent to the war with Great Britain, with Holland, and with Spain. With respect to Spain, we have seen nothing which leads us to suspect that either attachment to religion, or the ties of consanguinity, or regard to the ancient system of Europe, was likely to induce that court to connect itself in offensive war against France. The war was evidently and incontestably begun by France against Spain.

Spain.

The case of Holland is so fresh in every man's recollection, and so connected with the immediate causes of the war with this country, that it can not require one word of observation. What shall I say, then, on the case of Portugal? I can not, indeed, say that France ever declared war against that country. I can hardly say even that she ever made war, but she required them to make a treaty of peace, as if they had been at war; she obliged them to purchase that treaty; she broke it as soon as it was purchased; and she had originally no other ground of complaint than this, that Portugal had performed, though inadequately, the engagements of its ancient defensive alliance with this country in the character of an auxiliary—a conduct which can not of itself make any power a principal in a war.

Holland and Portugal.

I have now enumerated all the nations at war at that period, with the exception only of Naples. It can hardly be necessary to call to the recollection of the House the characteristic feature of revolutionary principles which was shown, even at this early period, in the personal insult offered to the King of Naples, by the commander of a French squadron riding uncontrolled in the Mediterranean, and (while our fleets were yet unarmed) threatening destruction to all the coast of Italy.

Naples,

It was not till a considerably later period that almost all the other nations of Europe found themselves equally involved in actual hostility; but it is not a little material to the whole of my argument, compared with the statement of the learned gentleman, and with that contained in the French note, to examine at what period this hostility extended itself. It extended itself, in the course of 1796, to the states of Italy which had hitherto been exempted from it. In 1797 it had ended in the destruction of most of them; it had ended in the virtual deposition of the King of Sardinia; it had ended in the conversion of Genoa and Tuscany into democratic republics; it had ended in the revolution of Venice, in the violation of treaties with the new Venetian Republic; and, finally, in transferring that very republic, the creature and vassal of France, to the dominion of Austria.

and the other Italian states.

I observe from the gestures of some honorable gentlemen that they think we are precluded from the use of any argument founded on this last transaction. I already hear them saying that it was as criminal in Austria to receive as it was in France to give. I am far from defending or palliating the conduct of Austria upon this occasion. But because Austria, unable at last to contend with the arms of France, was forced to accept an unjust and insufficient indemnification for the conquests France had made from it, are we to be debarred from stating what, on the part of France, was not merely an unjust acquisition, but an act of the grossest and most aggravated perfidy and cruelty, and one of the most striking specimens of that system which has been uniformly and indiscriminately applied to all the countries which France has had within its grasp? This only can be said in vindication of France (and it is still more a vindication of Austria) that, practically speaking, if there is any part of this transaction for which Venice itself has reason to be grateful, it can only be for the permission to exchange the embraces of French fraternity for what is called the despotism of Vienna.[17]

Reply as to Austria's receiving Venice from the French.

Let these facts and these dates be compared with what we have heard. The honorable gentleman has told us, and the author of the note from France has told us also, that all the French con-

Attack on Mr. Erskine as if approving of the French aggressions.

[17] Austria, being worsted in the contest, made peace with the French in 1797, and, as a recompense for her sacrifices, and for leaving the German states on the Rhine at the mercy of the conqueror, received Venice and the adjacent territory, which had just been seized, under circumstances of great perfidy and violence, by the French. Alison, with all his partiality for the allies, says of this transaction, "It is darker in atrocity than the partition of Poland, and has only excited less indignation in subsequent years because it was attended with no heroism or dignity in the vanquished."—Vol. iii., p. 276, third edition.

quests were produced by the operations of the allies. It was, when they were pressed on all sides, when their own territory was in danger, when their own independence was in question, when the confederacy appeared too strong, it was then they used the means with which their power and their courage furnished them, and, "attacked upon all sides, they carried every where their defensive arms." I do not wish to misrepresent the learned gentleman, but I understood him to speak of this sentiment with approbation. The sentiment itself is this, that if a nation is unjustly attacked in any one quarter by others, she can not stop to consider by whom, but must find means of strength in other quarters, no matter where; and is justified in attacking, in her turn, those with whom she is at peace, and from whom she has received no species of provocation. Sir, I hope I have already proved, in a great measure, that no such attack was made upon France; but, if it was made, I maintain that the whole ground on which that argument is founded can not be tolerated. In the name of the laws of nature and nations, in the name of every thing that is sacred and honorable, I demur to that plea; and I tell that honorable and learned gentleman that he would do well to look again into the law of nations before he ventures to come to this House to give the sanction of his authority to so dreadful and execrable a system.[18]

The note of the French government, at least, justified those atrocities.

I certainly understood this to be distinctly the tenor of the learned gentleman's argument, but as he tells me he did not use it, I take it for granted he did not intend to use it. I rejoice that he did not; but at least, then, I have a right to expect that the learned gentleman should now transfer to the French note some of the indignation which he has hitherto lavished upon the declarations of this country. This principle, which the learned gentleman disclaims, the French note avows; and I contend, without the fear of contradiction, it is the principle upon which France has uniformly acted. But while the learned gentleman disclaims this proposition, he certainly will admit that he has himself asserted, and maintained in the whole course of his argument, that the pressure of the war upon France imposed upon her the necessity of those exertions which produced most of the enormities of the Revolution, and most of the enormities practiced against the other countries of Europe. The House will recollect that, in the year 1796, when all these horrors in Italy were beginning, which are the strongest illustrations of the general character of the French Revolution, we had begun that negotiation to which the learned gentleman has referred. England then possessed numerous conquests. England, though not having at that time had the advantage of three of her most splendid victories, England even then appeared undisputed mistress of the sea. England, having then engrossed the whole wealth of the colonial world; England, having lost nothing of its original possessions; England then comes forward, proposing a general peace, and offering—what? offering the surrender of all that it had acquired, in order to obtain—what? Not the dismemberment, not the partition of ancient France, but the return of a part of those conquests, no one of which could be retained, but in direct contradiction to that original and solemn pledge which is now referred to as the proof of the just and moderate disposition of the French Republic. Yet even this offer was not sufficient to procure peace, or to arrest the progress of France in her *defensive operations* against other unoffending countries!

The offer of England to restore her numerous conquests as the price of peace, rejected by France.

Answer to Mr. Erskine as to the causes which terminated the negotiation of 1796.

From the pages, however, of the learned gentleman's pamphlet (which, after all its editions, is now fresher in his memory than in that of any other person in this House or in the country), he is furnished with an argument, on the result of the negotiation, on which he appears confidently to rely. He maintains that the single point on which the negotiation was broken off was the question of the possession of the Austrian Netherlands, and that it is, therefore, on that ground only that the war has, since that time, been continued. When this subject was before under discussion, I stated, and I shall state again (notwithstanding the learned gentleman's accusation of my having endeavored to shift the question from its true point), that the question then at issue was not whether the Netherlands should *in fact* be restored; though even on that question I am not (like the learned gentleman) unprepared to give any opinion. I am ready to say, that to leave that territory in the possession of France would be obviously dangerous to the interests of this country, and is inconsistent with the policy which it has uniformly pursued at every period in which it has concerned itself in the general system of the continent. But it was not on the decision of this question of expediency and policy, that the issue of the negotiation then turned. What was required of us by France was, not merely that we should acquiesce in her retaining the Netherlands, but that, as a *preliminary* to all treaty, and before entering upon the discussion of terms, we should recognize the principle that whatever France, in time of war, had *annexed* to the Republic must remain inseparable forever, and could not become the subject of negotiation. I say that, in refusing such a preliminary, we

[18] Mr. Erskine here said across the House that he had never maintained any such proposition. His line of argument was certainly a very different one, as will be seen from the passage of his speech alluded to. "Was it imagined that a powerful nation, so surrounded, would act merely on the defensive, or that, in the midst of a revolution which the confederacy of nations had rendered terrible, the *rights* of nations would be respected? No; we gave the different French governments, by our conduct, a *pretext* for jealousy of every other European state, and, *in a manner,* goaded them on to the accomplishment of all the conquests which had since been the subject of *just* lamentation and complaint."—*Parl. Hist.*, vol. xxxiv., p. 1291.

were only resisting the claim of France to arrogate to itself the power of controlling, by its own separate and municipal acts, the rights and interests of other countries, and molding, at its discretion, a new and general code of the law of nations.

Subsequent conduct of France.

In reviewing the issue of this negotiation, it is important to observe that France, who began by abjuring a love of conquest, was desired to give up nothing of her own, not even to give up all that she had conquered; that it was offered to her to receive back all that had been conquered from her; and when she rejected the negotiation for peace upon these grounds, are we then to be told of the unrelenting hostility of the combined powers, for which France was to revenge itself upon other countries, and which is to justify the subversion of every established government, and the destruction of property, religion, and domestic comfort, from one end of Italy to the other? Such was the effect of the war against Modena, against Genoa, against Tuscany, against Venice, against Rome, and against Naples, all of which she engaged in, or prosecuted, subsequent to this very period.

England renewed the offer in 1797.

After this, in the year 1797, Austria had made peace; England and its ally, Portugal (from whom we could expect little active assistance, but whom we felt it our duty to defend), alone remained in the war. In that situation, under the pressure of necessity, which I shall not disguise, we made another attempt to negotiate. In 1797, Prussia, Spain, Austria, Naples, having successively made peace, the princes of Italy having been destroyed, France having surrounded itself, in almost every part in which it is not surrounded by the sea, with revolutionary republics, England made another offer of a different nature. It was not now a demand that France should restore any thing. Austria having made a peace upon her own terms, England had nothing to require with regard to her allies, she asked no restitution of the dominions added to France in Europe. So far from retaining any thing French out of Europe, we freely offered them all, demanding only, as a poor compensation, to retain a part of what we had acquired by arms from Holland, then identified with France. This proposal also, sir, was proudly refused, in a way which the learned gentleman himself has not attempted to justify, indeed of which he has spoken with detestation. I wish, since he has not finally abjured his duty in this House, that that detestation had been stated earlier; that he had mixed his own voice with the general voice of his country on the result of that negotiation.[20]

Conduct of France after this second refusal of peace.

Let us look at the conduct of France immediately subsequent to this period. She had spurned at the offers of Great Britain; she had reduced her continental enemies to the necessity of accepting a precarious peace; she had (in spite of those pledges repeatedly made and uniformly violated) surrounded herself by new conquests on every part of her frontier but one. That one was Switzerland. The first effect of being relieved from the war with Austria, of being secured against all fears of continental invasion on the ancient territory of France, was their unprovoked attack against this unoffending and devoted country. This was one of the scenes which satisfied even those who were the most incredulous that France had thrown off the mask, "*if indeed she had ever worn it.*" It collected, in one view, many of the characteristic features of that revolutionary system which I have endeavored to trace—the perfidy which alone rendered their arms successful—the pretexts of which they availed themselves to produce division and prepare the entrance of Jacobinism in that country—the proposal of armistice, one of the known and regular engines of the Revolution, which was, as usual, the immediate prelude to military execution, attended with cruelty and barbarity, of which there are few examples. All these are known to the world. The country they attacked was one which had long been the faithful ally of France, which, instead of giving cause of jealousy to any other power, had been for ages proverbial for the simplicity and innocence of its manners, and which had acquired and preserved the esteem of all the nations of Europe; which had almost, by the common consent of mankind, been exempted from the sound of war, and marked out as a land of Goshen, safe and untouched in the midst of surrounding calamities.

To Switzerland.

Look, then, at the fate of Switzerland, at the circumstances which led to its destruction. Add this instance to the catalogue of aggression against all Europe, and then tell me whether the system I have described has not been prosecuted with an unrelenting spirit, which can not be subdued in adversity, which can not be appeased in prosperity, which neither solemn professions, nor the general law of nations, nor the obligation of treaties (whether previous to the Revolution or subsequent to it), could restrain from the subversion of every state into which, either by force or fraud, their arms could penetrate. Then tell me, whether the disasters of Europe are to be charged upon the provocation of this country and its allies, or on the inherent principle of the French Revolution, of which the natural result produced so much misery and carnage in France, and carried desolation and terror over so large a portion of the world.

To America.

Sir, much as I have now stated, I have not finished the catalogue. America, almost as much as Switzerland, perhaps, contributed to that change which has taken place in the minds of those who were originally partial to the principles of the French government. The hostility against America followed a long course

[20] The following was the occasion of this severe blow. When France broke off the negotiations of 1797, and Mr. Pitt brought the subject before the House in the speech already given in this collection, Mr. Erskine and his friends did not attend. They condemned the conduct of France, and had no wish to oppose the Address, but had not the magnanimity to appear in their places and vote for it.

of neutrality adhered to under the strongest provocations, or rather of repeated compliances to France, with which we might well have been dissatisfied. It was on the face of it unjust and wanton; and it was accompanied by those instances of sordid corruption which shocked and disgusted even the enthusiastic admirers of revolutionary purity, and threw a new light on the genius of revolutionary government.[21]

To Malta and Egypt.

After this, it remains only shortly to remind gentlemen of the aggression against Egypt, not omitting, however, to notice the capture of Malta in the way to Egypt. Inconsiderable as that island may be thought, compared with the scenes we have witnessed, let it be remembered that it is an island of which the government had long been recognized by every state of Europe, against which France pretended no cause of war, and whose independence was as dear to itself and as sacred as that of any country in Europe. It was in fact not unimportant, from its local situation to the other powers of Europe; but in proportion as any man may diminish its importance, the instance will only serve the more to illustrate and confirm the proposition which I have maintained. The all-searching eye of the French Revolution looks to every part of Europe, and every quarter of the world, in which can be found an object either of acquisition or plunder. Nothing is too great for the temerity of its ambition, nothing too small or insignificant for the grasp of its rapacity. From hence Bonaparte and his army proceeded to Egypt. The attack was made, pretenses were held out to the natives of that country in the name of the French King, whom they had murdered. They pretended to have the approbation of the Grand Seignior, whose territories they were violating; their project was carried on under the profession of a zeal for Mohammedanism; it was carried on by proclaiming that France had been reconciled to the Mussulman faith, had abjured that of Christianity, or, as he in his impious language termed it, of *the sect of the Messiah*.[22]

India finally aimed at.

The only plea which they have since held out to color this atrocious invasion of a neutral and friendly territory, is that it was the road to attack the English power in India. It is most unquestionably true that this was one and a principal cause of this unparalleled outrage; but another, and an equally substantial cause (as appears by their own statements) was the division and partition of the territories of what they thought a falling power. It is impossible to dismiss this subject without observing that this attack against Egypt was accompanied by an attack upon the British possessions in India, made on true revolutionary principles. In Europe, the propagation of the principles of France had uniformly prepared the way for the progress of its arms. To India, the lovers of peace had sent the messengers of Jacobinism, for the purpose of inculcating war in those distant regions on Jacobin principles, and of forming Jacobin clubs, which they actually succeeded in establishing; and which in most respects resembled the European model, but which were distinguished by this peculiarity, that they were required to swear in one breath hatred to tyranny, the love of liberty, and the destruction of all kings and sovereigns, except the good and faithful ally of the French Republic, *Citizen* Tippoo![23]

Genius and spirit of the French revolutionary system.

III. What, then, was the nature of this system? Was it any thing but what I have stated it to be? an insatiable love of aggrandizement, an implacable spirit of destruction against all the civil and religious institutions of every country. This is the first moving and acting spirit of the French Revolution; this is the spirit which animated it at its birth, and this is the spirit which will not desert it till the moment of its dissolution, "which grew with its growth, which strengthened with its strength," but which has not abated under its misfortunes, nor declined in its decay. It has been invariably the same in every period, operating more or less, according as accident or circumstances might assist it; but it has been inherent in the Revolution in all its stages; it has equally belonged to Brissot, to Robespierre, to Tallien, to Reubel, to Barras, and to every one of the leaders of the Directory, but to none more than to Bonaparte, in whom now all their powers are united. What are its characters? Can it be accident that produced them? No, it is only from the alliance of the most horrid principles, with the most horrid means, that such miseries could have been brought upon Europe. It is this paradox which we must always keep in mind when we are discussing any question relative to the effects of the French Revolution. Groaning under every degree of misery, the victim of its own crimes, and as I once before expressed in this House, asking pardon of God and of man for the miseries which it has brought

[21] All this was emphatically true. France preyed on the commerce of America in the most wanton manner, and when redress was asked in 1797, large *bribes* for the officers of the government (£50,000 sterling) were directly demanded of the American embassadors, besides some millions of money for the public service. But America continued to negotiate; and a few months after Bonaparte became First Consul, an amicable adjustment was effected.

[22] In his proclamation to the inhabitants of Cairo, December 28th, 1798, Bonaparte says (addressing the teachers in the mosques): "Instruct the people, that since the world has existed it was written, that, after having destroyed the enemies of Islamism (Mohammedanism), *and destroyed the cross*, I should come from the farthest part of the west to fulfill the task which was imposed upon me."—*Annual Register*, vol. xl., p. 265.

[23] Tippoo Saib "the despot of Mysore," was the son and successor of the celebrated Hyder Ali, and was in the closest alliance with the French. Barruel affirms, in his History of Jacobinism, that French emissaries from Pondicherry formed secret societies among the nations of India for the propagation of their principles; and Mr. Pitt humorously adds an exception made in favor of *Citizen* Tippoo, in administering their oaths.

upon itself and others, France still retains (while it has neither left means of comfort, nor almost of subsistence to its own inhabitants) new and unexampled means of annoyance and destruction against all the other powers of Europe.

Its leading principles.

Its first fundamental principle was to bribe the poor against the rich, by proposing to transfer into new hands, on the delusive notion of equality, and in breach of every principle of justice, the whole property of the country. The practical application of this principle was to devote the whole of that property to indiscriminate plunder, and to make it the foundation of a revolutionary system of finance, productive in proportion to the misery and desolation which it created. It has been accompanied by an unwearied spirit of proselytism, diffusing itself over all the nations of the earth: a spirit which can apply itself to all circumstances and all situations, which can furnish a list of grievances, and hold out a promise of redress equally to all nations; which inspired the teachers of French liberty with the hope of alike recommending themselves to those who live under the feudal code of the German empire; to the various states of Italy, under all their different institutions; to the old republicans of Holland, and to the new republicans of America; to the Catholic of Ireland, whom it was to deliver from Protestant usurpation; to the Protestant of Switzerland, whom it was to deliver from popish superstition; and to the Mussulman of Egypt, whom it was to deliver from Christian persecution; to the remote Indian, blindly bigoted to his ancient institutions; and to the natives of Great Britain, enjoying the perfection of practical freedom, and justly attached to their Constitution, from the joint result of habit, of reason, and of experience. The last and distinguishing feature is a perfidy which nothing can bind, which no tie of treaty, no sense of the principles generally received among nations, no obligation, human or divine, can restrain. Thus qualified, thus armed for destruction, the genius of the French Revolution marched forth, the terror and dismay of the world. Every nation has in its turn been the witness, many have been the victims of its principles; and it is left for us to decide whether we will compromise with such a danger, while we have yet resources to supply the sinews of war, while the heart and spirit of the country is yet unbroken, and while we have the means of calling forth and supporting a powerful co-operation in Europe.

Much more might be said on this part of the subject; but if what I have said already is a faithful, though only an imperfect sketch of those excesses and outrages which even history itself will hereafter be unable fully to represent and record, and a just representation of the principle and source from which they originated, will any man say that we ought to accept a precarious security against so tremendous a danger? Much more—will he pretend, after the experience of all that has passed in the different stages of the French Revolution, that we ought to be deterred from probing this great question to the bottom, and from examining, without ceremony or disguise, whether the change which has recently taken place in France is sufficient now to give security, not against a common danger, but against such a danger as that which I have described?

Instability of its successive governments.

IV. In examining this part of the subject, let it be remembered that there is one other characteristic of the French Revolution as striking as its dreadful and destructive principles: I mean the instability of its government, which has been of itself sufficient to destroy all reliance, if any such reliance could at any time have been placed on the good faith of any of its rulers. Such has been the incredible rapidity with which the revolutions in France have succeeded each other, that I believe the names of those who have successively exercised absolute power, under the pretense of liberty, are to be numbered by the years of the Revolution, and by each of the new Constitutions, which, under the same pretense, has in its turn been imposed by force on France: all of which alike were founded upon principles which professed to be universal, and was intended to be established and perpetuated among all the nations of the earth. Each of these will be found, upon an average, to have had about two years as the period of its duration.

Under this revolutionary system, accompanied with this perpetual fluctuation and change, both in the form of the government and in the persons of the rulers, what is the security which has hitherto existed, and what new security is now offered? Before an answer is given to this question, let me sum up the history of all the revolutionary governments of France, and of their characters in relation to other powers, in words more emphatical than any which I could use—the memorable words pronounced, on the eve of this last Constitution, by the orator[24] who was selected to report to an assembly, surrounded by a file of grenadiers, the new form of liberty which it was destined to enjoy under the auspices of General Bonaparte. From this reporter, the mouth and organ of the new government, we learn this important lesson: "It is easy to conceive why peace was not concluded before the establishment of the constitutional government. The only government which then existed described itself as revolutionary; it was, in fact, only the tyranny of a few men who were soon overthrown by others, and it consequently presented no stability of principles or of views, no security either with respect to men or with respect to things.

"It should seem that that stability and that security ought to have existed from the establishment, and as the effect of the constitutional system; and yet they did not exist more, perhaps even less, than they had done before. In truth, we did make some partial treaties; we

[24] Vide the speech of Boulay de la Meuthe in the Council of Five Hundred, at St. Cloud, 19th Brumaire (9th November), 1799.

signed a continental peace, and a general congress was held to confirm it; but these treaties, these diplomatic conferences, appear to have been the source of a new war, more inveterate and more bloody than before.

"Before the 18th Fructidor (4th September) of the fifth year, the French government exhibited to foreign nations so uncertain an existence that they refused to treat with it. After this great event, the whole power was absorbed in the Directory; the legislative body can hardly be said to have existed; treaties of peace were broken, and war carried every where, without that body having any share in those measures. The same Directory, after having intimidated all Europe, and destroyed, at its pleasure, several governments, neither knowing how to make peace or war, or how even to establish itself, was overturned by a breath, on the 13th Prairial (18th June), to make room for other men, influenced perhaps by different views, or who might be governed by different principles.

"Judging, then, only from notorious facts, the French government must be considered as exhibiting nothing fixed, neither in respect to men or to things." Here, then, is the picture, down to the period of the last revolution, of the state of France under all its successive governments!

V. Having taken a view of what it was, let us now examine what it is. In the first place, we see, as has been truly stated, a change in the description and form of the sovereign authority. A supreme power is placed at the head of this nominal republic, with a more open avowal of military despotism than at any former period; with a more open and undisguised abandonment of the names and pretenses under which that despotism long attempted to conceal itself. The different institutions, republican in their form and appearance, which were before the instruments of that despotism, are now annihilated; they have given way to the absolute power of one man, concentrating in himself all the authority of the state, and differing from other monarchs only in this, that (as my honorable friend [Mr. Canning] truly stated it) he wields a sword instead of a scepter. What, then, is the confidence we are to derive either from the frame of the government, or from the character and past conduct of the person who is now the absolute ruler of France?

Character of the system under the consulate of Bonaparte.

Had we seen a man of whom we had no previous knowledge suddenly invested with the sovereign authority of the country; invested with the power of taxation, with the power of the sword, the power of war and peace, the unlimited power of commanding the resources, of disposing of the lives and fortunes of every man in France; if we had seen at the same moment all the inferior machinery of the Revolution, which, under the variety of successive shocks, had kept the system in motion, still remaining entire, all that, by requisition and plunder, had given activity to the revolutionary system of finance, and had furnished the means of creating an army, by converting every man who was of age to bear arms into a soldier, not for the defense of his own country, but for the sake of carrying the war into the country of the enemy; if we had seen all the subordinate instruments of Jacobin power subsisting in their full force, and retaining (to use the French phrase) all their original organization; and had then observed this single change in the conduct of their affairs, that there was now *one man*, with no rival to thwart his measures, no colleague to divide his powers, no council to control his operations, no liberty of speaking or writing, no expression of public opinion to check or influence his conduct; under such circumstances, should we be wrong to pause, or wait for the evidence of facts and experience, before we consented to trust our safety to the forbearance of a single man, in such a situation, and to relinquish those means of defense which have hitherto carried us safe through all the storms of the Revolution? if we were to ask what are the principles and character of this stranger, to whom fortune has suddenly committed the concerns of a great and powerful nation?

But is this the actual state of the present question? Are we talking of a stranger of whom we have heard nothing? No, sir: we have heard of him; we, and Europe, and the world, have heard both of him and of the satellites by whom he is surrounded, and it is impossible to discuss fairly the propriety of any answer which could be returned to his overtures of negotiation without taking into consideration the inferences to be drawn from his personal character and conduct. I know it is the fashion with some gentlemen to represent any reference to topics of this nature as invidious and irritating; but the truth is, that they rise unavoidably out of the very nature of the question. Would it have been possible for ministers to discharge their duty, in offering their advice to their sovereign, either for accepting or declining negotiation, without taking into their account the reliance to be placed on the disposition and the principles of the person on whose disposition and principles the security to be obtained by treaty must, in the present circumstances, principally depend? Or would they act honestly or candidly toward Parliament and toward the country if, having been guided by these considerations, they forbore to state, publicly and distinctly, the real grounds which have influenced their decision; and if, from a false delicacy and groundless timidity, they purposely declined an examination of a point, the most essential toward enabling Parliament to form a just determination on so important a subject?

Character of Bonaparte.

What opinion, then, are we led to form of the pretensions of the Consul to those particular qualities for which, in the official note, his personal character is represented to us as the surest pledge of peace? We are told this is his second attempt at general pacification. Let us see, for a moment, how his attempt has been conducted. There is, indeed, as the learned gentleman has said, a word in the first declaration which refers to general peace, and which

His proposals.

states this to be the second time in which the Consul has endeavored to accomplish that object. We thought fit, for the reasons which have been assigned, to decline altogether the proposal of treating, under the present circumstances, but we, at the same time, expressly stated that, whenever the moment for treaty should arrive, we would in no case treat but in conjunction with our allies. Our general refusal to negotiate at the present moment does not prevent the Consul from renewing his overtures; but are they renewed for the purpose of general pacification? Though he had hinted at general peace in the terms of his first note; though we had shown by our answer that we deemed negotiation, even for general peace, at this moment inadmissible; though we added that, even at any future period, we would treat only in conjunction with our allies, what was the proposal contained in his last note? To treat for a separate peace between Great Britain and France.

His former conduct toward England.

Such was the second attempt to effect *general pacification*—a proposal for a *separate* treaty with Great Britain. What had been the first? The conclusion of a separate treaty with Austria; and there are two anecdotes connected with the conclusion of this treaty, which are sufficient to illustrate the disposition of this pacificator of Europe. This very treaty of Campo Formio was ostentatiously professed to be concluded with the Emperor for the purpose of enabling Bonaparte to take the command of the army of England, and to dictate a separate peace with this country on the banks of the Thames.[25] But there is this additional circumstance, singular beyond all conception, considering that we are now referred to the treaty of Campo Formio as a proof of the personal disposition of the Consul to general peace. He sent his two confidential and chosen friends, Berthier and Monge, charged to communicate to the Directory this treaty of Campo Formio; to announce to them that one enemy was humbled, that the war with Austria was terminated, and, therefore, that now was the moment to prosecute their operations against this country; they used on this occasion the memorable words, "*The kingdom of Great Britain and the French Republic can not exist together.*" This, I say, was the solemn declaration of the deputies and embassadors of Bonaparte himself, offering to the Directory the first-fruits of this first attempt at general pacification.

His violation of oaths to preceding governments.

So much for his disposition toward general pacification. Let us look next at the part he has taken in the different stages of the French Revolution, and let us then judge whether we are to look to him as the security against revolutionary principles. Let us determine what reliance we can place on his engagements with other countries, when we see how he has observed his engagements to his own. When the Constitution of the third year was established under Barras, that Constitution was imposed by the arms of Bonaparte, then commanding the army of the triumvirate in Paris. To that Constitution he then swore fidelity. How often he has repeated the same oath I know not, but twice, at least, we know that he has not only repeated it himself, but tendered it to others, under circumstances too striking not to be stated.

His support of the violent party in the Directory.

Sir, the House can not have forgotten the Revolution of the 4th of September, which produced the dismissal of Lord Malmesbury from Lisle. How was that revolution procured? It was procured chiefly by the promise of Bonaparte, in the name of his army, decidedly to support the Directory in those measures which led to the infringement and violation of every thing that the authors of the Constitution of 1795, or its adherents, could consider as fundamental, and which established a system of despotism inferior only to that now realized in his own person. Immediately before this event, in the midst of the desolation and bloodshed of Italy, he had received the sacred present of new banners from the Directory; he delivered them to his army with this exhortation: "Let us swear, fellow-soldiers, by the manes of the patriots who have died by our side, eternal hatred to the enemies of the Constitution of the third year." That very Constitution which he soon after enabled the Directory to violate, and which, at the head of his grenadiers, he has now finally destroyed. Sir, that oath was again renewed, in the midst of that very scene to which I have last referred; the oath of fidelity to the Constitution of the third year was administered to all the members of the Assembly then sitting, under the terror of the bayonet, as the solemn preparation for the business of the day; and the morning was ushered in with swearing attachment to the Constitution, that the evening might close with its destruction.

His perfidy and violence toward the states of Italy.

If we carry our views out of France, and look at the dreadful catalogue of all the breaches of treaty, all the acts of perfidy at which I have only glanced, and which are precisely commensurate with the number of treaties which the Republic have made (for I have sought in vain for any one which it has made and which it has not broken), if we trace the history of them all from the beginning of the Revolution to the present time, or if we select those which have been accompanied by the most atrocious cruelty, and marked the most strongly with the characteristic features of the Revolution, the name of Bonaparte will be found allied to more of them than that of any other that can be handed down in the history of the crimes and miseries of the last ten years. His name will be recorded with the horrors committed in Italy, in the memorable campaign of 1796 and 1797, in the Milanese, in Genoa, in Modena, in Tuscany, in Rome, and in Venice.

His entrance into Lombardy was announced by a solemn proclamation, issued on the 27th of

[25] At that time (1797) the French threatened to invade Great Britain, and had collected for this purpose large bodies of troops on the sea-coast, under the name of the Army of England.

April, 1796, which terminated with these words: Lombardy. "Nations of Italy! the French army is come to break your chains, the French are the friends of the people in every country; your religion, your property, your customs, shall be respected." This was followed by a second proclamation, dated from Milan 20th of May, and signed "*Bonaparte*," in these terms: "Respect for property and personal security. Respect for the religion of countries, these are the sentiments of the government of the French Republic and of the army of Italy. The French victorious, consider the nations of Lombardy as their brothers." In testimony of this fraternity, and to fulfill the solemn pledge of respecting property, this very proclamation imposed on the Milanese a provisional contribution to the amount of twenty millions of livres, or near one million sterling, and successive exactions were afterward levied on that single state to the amount, in the whole, of near six millions sterling. The regard to religion and to the customs of the country was manifested with the same scrupulous fidelity. The churches were given up to indiscriminate plunder. Every religious and charitable fund, every public treasure, was confiscated. The country was made the scene of every species of disorder and rapine. The priests, the established form of worship, all the objects of religious reverence, were openly insulted by the French troops; at Pavia, particularly, the tomb of St. Augustin, which the inhabitants were accustomed to view with peculiar veneration, was mutilated and defaced; this last provocation having roused the resentment of the people, they flew to arms, surrounded the French garrison and took them prisoners, but carefully abstained from offering any violence to a single soldier. In revenge for this conduct, Bonaparte, then on his march to the Mincio, suddenly returned, collected his troops, and carried the extremity of military execution over the country. He burned the town of Benasco, and massacred eight hundred of its inhabitants; he marched to Pavia, took it by storm, and delivered it over to general plunder, and published, at the same moment, a proclamation, of the 26th of May, ordering his troops to shoot all those who had not laid down their arms and taken an oath of obedience, and to burn every village where the tocsin should be sounded, and to put its inhabitants to death.

The transactions with Modena were on a smaller scale, but in the same character. Modena. Bonaparte began by signing a treaty, by which the Duke of Modena was to pay twelve millions of livres, and neutrality was promised him in return; this was soon followed by the personal arrest of the Duke, and by a fresh extortion of two hundred thousand sequins. After this he was permitted, on the payment of a farther sum, to sign another treaty, called a *convention de sureté*, which of course was only the prelude to the repetition of similar exactions.

Nearly at the same period, in violation of the rights of neutrality and of the treaty which Tuscany. had been concluded between the French Republic and the Grand Duke of Tuscany in the preceding year, and in breach of a positive promise given only a few days before, the French army forcibly took possession of Leghorn, for the purpose of seizing the British property which was deposited there and confiscating it as prize; and shortly after, when Bonaparte agreed to evacuate Leghorn, in return for the evacuation of the island of Elba, which was in possession of the British troops, he insisted upon a separate article, by which, in addition to the plunder before obtained, by the infraction of the law of nations, it was stipulated that the Grand Duke should pay the expense which the French had incurred by this invasion of his territory.

In the proceedings toward Genoa we shall find not only a continuance of the same system Genoa. of extortion and plunder, in violation of the solemn pledge contained in the proclamations already referred to, but a striking instance of the revolutionary means employed for the destruction of independent governments. A French minister was at that time resident at Genoa, which was acknowledged by France to be in a state of neutrality and friendship; in breach of this neutrality Bonaparte began, in the year 1796, with the demand of a loan. He afterward, from the month of September, required and enforced the payment of a monthly subsidy, to the amount which he thought proper to stipulate. These exactions were accompanied by repeated assurances and protestations of friendship; they were followed, in May, 1797, by a conspiracy against the government, fomented by the emissaries of the French embassy, and conducted by the partisans of France, encouraged, and afterward protected by the French minister. The conspirators failed in their first attempt. Overpowered by the courage and voluntary exertions of the inhabitants, their force was dispersed, and many of their number were arrested. Bonaparte instantly considered the defeat of the conspirators as an act of aggression against the French Republic; he dispatched an aid-de-camp with an order to the Senate of this independent state; first, to release all the French who were detained; secondly, to punish those who had arrested them; thirdly, to declare that *they had no share in the insurrection;* and fourthly, to disarm the people. Several French prisoners were immediately released, and a proclamation was preparing to disarm the inhabitants, when, by a second note, Bonaparte required the arrest of the three inquisitors of state, and immediate alterations in the Constitution. He accompanied this with an order to the French minister to quit Genoa, if his commands were not immediately carried into execution; at the same moment his troops entered the territory of the Republic, and shortly after, the councils, intimidated and overpowered, abdicated their functions. Three deputies were then sent to Bonaparte to receive from him a new Constitution. On the 6th of June, after the conferences at Montebello, he signed a convention, or rather issued a decree, by which he fixed the new form of their government; he himself named provisionally all the members who were to compose it, and he required the payment of seven millions of livres as the price of the subversion of their Constitution and their independence. These transactions require but one short comment. It is to be found in the official account given of them at Paris; which is in these memorable words: "General Bonaparte has pursued the only line of conduct which could be allowed in the representative of a nation which has supported the war only to procure the solemn acknowledgment of the right of nations, to change the form of their government. He contributed nothing toward the revolution of Genoa, but he seized the first moment to acknowledge the new government, as soon as he saw that it was the result of the wishes of the people."[26]

Rome. It is unnecessary to dwell on the wanton attacks against Rome, under the direction of Bonaparte himself in the year 1796, and in the beginning of 1797, which terminated first by the treaty of Tolentino concluded by Bonaparte, in which, by enormous sacrifices, the Pope was allowed to purchase the acknowledgment of his authority as a sovereign prince; and secondly, by the violation of that very treaty, and the subversion of the papal authority by Joseph Bonaparte, the brother and the agent of the general, and the minister of the French Republic to the Holy See. A transaction accompanied by outrages and insults toward the pious and venerable Pontiff, in spite of the sanctity of his age and the unsullied purity of his character, which even to a Protestant seem hardly short of the guilt of sacrilege.

Venice. But of all the disgusting and tragical scenes which took place in Italy in the course of the period I am describing, those which passed at Venice are perhaps the most striking and the most characteristic. In May, 1796, the French army, under Bonaparte, in the full tide of its success against the Austrians, first approached the territories of this republic, which from the commencement of the war had observed a rigid neutrality. Their entrance on these territories was, as usual, accompanied by a solemn proclamation in the name of their general, "Bonaparte to the republic of Venice." "It is to deliver the finest country in Europe *from the iron yoke of the proud house of Austria*, that the French army has braved obstacles the most difficult to surmount. Victory in union with justice has crowned its efforts. The wreck of the enemy's army has retired behind the Mincio. The French army, in order to follow them, passes over the territory of the republic of Venice; but it will never forget that ancient friendship unites the two republics. Religion, government, customs, and property shall be respected. That the people may be without apprehension, the most severe discipline shall be maintained. All that may be provided for the army shall be faithfully paid for in money. The general-in-chief engages the officers of the republic of Venice, the magistrates, and the priests, to make known these sentiments to the people, in order that confidence may cement that friendship which has so long united the two nations. Faithful in the path of honor as in that of victory, the French soldier is terrible only to the enemies of his liberty and his government."—BONAPARTE.

This proclamation was followed by exactions similar to those which were practiced against Genoa, by the renewal of similar professions of friendship and the use of similar means to excite insurrection. At length, in the spring of 1797, occasion was taken from disturbances thus excited, to forge in the name of the Venetian government, a proclamation hostile to France, and this proceeding was made the ground for military execution against the country, and for effecting by force the subversion of its ancient government and the establishment of the democratic forms of the French Revolution. This revolution was sealed by a treaty, signed in May, 1797, between Bonaparte and commissioners appointed on the part of the new and revolutionary government of Venice. By the second and third secret articles of this treaty, Venice agreed to give as a ransom, to secure itself against all further exactions or demands, the sum of three millions of livres in money, the value of three millions more in articles of naval supply, and three ships of the line; and it received in return the assurances of the friendship and support of the French Republic. Immediately after the signature of this treaty, the arsenal, the library, and the palace of St. Marc were ransacked and plundered, and heavy additional contributions were imposed upon its inhabitants. And, in not more than four months afterward, this very republic of Venice, united by alliance to France, the creature of Bonaparte himself, from whom it had received the present of French liberty, was by the same Bonaparte transferred, under the treaty of Campo Formio, to "*that iron yoke of the proud house of Austria*," to deliver it from which he had represented in his first proclamation to be the great object of all his operations.

His conduct in Egypt. Sir, all this is followed by the memorable expedition into Egypt; which I mention, not merely because it forms a principal article in the catalogue of those acts of violence and perfidy in which Bonaparte has been engaged; not merely because it was an enterprise peculiarly his own, of which he was himself the planner, the executor, and the betrayer; but chiefly because when from thence he retires to a different scene to take possession of a new throne, from which he is to speak upon an equality with the kings and governors of Europe, he leaves behind him, at the moment of his departure, a specimen, which can not be mistaken, of his principles of negotiation. The intercepted correspondence which has been alluded to in this debate, seems to afford the strongest ground to believe that his offers to the Turkish government to evacuate Egypt were made solely with a view to gain time; that the ratification of any treaty on this subject was to be delayed with the view of finally eluding its performance, if any change of circumstances favorable to the French should oc-

[26] Rédacteur Officiel, June 30, 1797.

cur in the interval. But whatever gentlemen may think of the intention with which these offers were made, there will at least be no question with respect to the credit due to those professions by which he endeavored to prove in Egypt his pacific dispositions. He expressly enjoins his successor strongly and steadily to insist, in all his intercourse with the Turks, that he came to Egypt with no hostile design, and that he never meant to keep possession of the country; while, on the opposite page of the same instructions, he states in the most unequivocal manner his regret at the discomfiture of his favorite project of colonizing Egypt, and of maintaining it as a territorial acquisition. Now, sir, if in any note addressed to the Grand Vizier or the Sultan, Bonaparte had claimed credit for the sincerity of his professions, that he came to Egypt with no view hostile to Turkey, and solely for the purpose of molesting the British interests, is there any one argument now used to induce us to believe his present professions to us, which might not have been equally urged on that occasion? Would not those professions have been equally supported by solemn asseveration, by the same reference which is now made to personal character, with this single difference, that they would have then had one instance less of hypocrisy and falsehood, which we have since had occasion to trace in this very transaction?

He may have motives to negotiate,

It is unnecessary to say more with respect to the credit due to his professions, or the reliance to be placed on his general character. But it will, perhaps, be argued that whatever may be his character, or whatever has been his past conduct, he has now an interest in making and observing peace. That he has an interest in making peace is at best but a doubtful proposition, and that he has an interest in preserving it is still more uncertain. That it is his interest to negotiate, I do not indeed deny. It is his interest, above all, to engage this country in separate negotiation, in order to loosen and dissolve the whole system of the confederacy on the continent, to palsy at once the arms of Russia, or of Austria, or of any other country that might look to you for support; and then either to break off his separate treaty, or if he should have concluded it, to apply the lesson which is taught in his school of policy in Egypt; and to revive at his pleasure those claims of indemnification which *may have been reserved to some happier period.*[27]

but none to make peace.

This is precisely the interest which he has in negotiation. But on what grounds are we to be convinced that he has an interest in concluding and observing a solid and permanent pacification? Under all the circumstances of his personal character, and his newly acquired power, what other security has he for retaining that power but the sword? His hold upon France is the sword, and he has no other. Is he connected with the soil, or with the habits, the affections, or the prejudices of the country? He is a stranger, a foreigner, and a usurper. He unites in his own person every thing that a pure republican must detest; every thing that an enraged Jacobin has abjured; every thing that a sincere and faithful royalist must feel as an insult. If he is opposed at any time in his career, what is his appeal? *He appeals to his fortune;* in other words, to his army and his sword. Placing, then, his whole reliance upon military support, can he afford to let his military renown pass away, to let his laurels wither, to let the memory of his trophies sink in obscurity? Is it certain that, with his army confined within France, and restrained from inroads upon her neighbors, that he can maintain, at his devotion, a force sufficiently numerous to support his power? Having no object but the possession of absolute dominion, no passion but military glory, is it to be reckoned as certain that he can feel such an interest in permanent peace as would justify us in laying down our arms, reducing our expense, and relinquishing our means of security, on the faith of his engagements? Do we believe that, after the conclusion of peace, he would not still sigh over the lost trophies of Egypt, wrested from him by the celebrated victory of Aboukir, and the brilliant exertions of that heroic band of British seamen; whose influence and example rendered the Turkish troops invincible at Acre? Can he forget that the effect of these exploits enabled Austria and Russia, in one campaign, to recover from France all which she had acquired by his victories, to dissolve the charm, which for a time fascinated Europe, and to show that their generals, contending in a just cause, could efface even by their success and their military glory, the most dazzling triumphs of his victorious and desolating ambition?

Would have the strongest motives to break a peace if made.

Can we believe, with these impressions on his mind, that if, after a year, eighteen months, or two years of peace had elapsed, he should be tempted by the appearance of fresh insurrection in Ireland, encouraged by renewed and unrestrained communication with France, and fomented by the fresh infusion of Jacobin principles; if we were at such a moment without a fleet to watch the ports of France, or to guard the coasts of Ireland, without a disposable army, or an embodied militia, capable of supplying a speedy and adequate re-enforcement, and that he had suddenly the means of transporting thither a body of twenty or thirty thousand French troops; can we believe that, at such a moment, his ambition and vindictive spirit would be restrained by the recollection of engagements or the obligation of treaty? Or if, in some new crisis of difficulty and danger to the Ottoman empire, with no British navy in the Mediterranean, no confederacy formed, no force collected to support it, an opportunity should present itself for resuming the abandoned expedition to Egypt, for renewing the avowed and favorite project of conquering and colonizing that rich and fertile country, and of opening the way to wound some of the vital interests of England, and to plunder the treasures of the East,

---

27 Vide intercepted correspondence from Egypt.

in order to fill the bankrupt coffers of France? Would it be the interest of Bonaparte, under such circumstances, or his principles, his moderation, his love of peace, his aversion to conquest, and his regard for the independence of other nations—would it be all or any of these that would secure us against an attempt which would leave us only the option of submitting without a struggle to certain loss and disgrace, or of renewing the contest which we had prematurely terminated, without allies, without preparation, with diminished means, and with increased difficulty and hazard?

No evidence of the stability of his power.

Hitherto I have spoken only of the reliance which we can place on the professions, the character, and the conduct of the present First Consul; but it remains to consider the stability of his power. The Revolution has been marked throughout by a rapid succession of new depositaries of public authority, each supplanting its predecessor. What grounds have we to believe that this new usurpation, more odious and more undisguised than all that preceded it, will be more durable? Is it that we rely on the particular provisions contained in the code of the pretended Constitution, which was proclaimed as accepted by the French people as soon as the garrison of Paris declared their determination to exterminate all its enemies, and before any of its articles could even be known to half the country, whose consent was required for its establishment?

His new Constitution creates a military despotism.

I will not pretend to inquire deeply into the nature and effects of a Constitution which can hardly be regarded but as a farce and a mockery. If, however, it could be supposed that its provisions were to have any effect, it seems equally adapted to two purposes, that of giving to its founder, for a time, an absolute and uncontrolled authority, and that of laying the certain foundation of disunion and discord, which, if they once prevail, must render the exercise of all the authority under the Constitution impossible, and leave no appeal but to the sword.

Most unstable of all kinds of power.

Is, then, military despotism that which we are accustomed to consider as a stable form of government? In all ages of the world it has been attended with the least stability to the persons who exercised it, and with the most rapid succession of changes and revolutions. In the outset of the French Revolution, its advocates boasted that it furnished a security forever, not to France only, but to all countries in the world, against military despotism; that the force of standing armies was vain and delusive; that no artificial power could resist public opinion; and that it was upon the foundation of public opinion alone that any government could stand. I believe that in this instance, as in every other, the progress of the French Revolution has belied its professions; but, so far from its being a proof of the prevalence of public opinion against military force, it is, instead of the proof, the strongest exception from that doctrine which appears in the history of the world. Through all the stages of the Revolution, military force has governed, and public opinion has scarcely been heard. But still I consider this as only an exception from a general truth. I still believe that in every civilized country, not enslaved by a Jacobin faction, public opinion is the only sure support of any government. I believe this with the more satisfaction, from a conviction that, if this contest is happily terminated, the established governments of Europe will stand upon that rock firmer than ever; and, whatever may be the defects of any particular Constitution, those who live under it will prefer its continuance to the experiment of changes which may plunge them in the unfathomable abyss of revolution, or extricate them from it only to expose them to the terrors of military despotism. And to apply this to France, I see no reason to believe that the present usurpation will be more permanent than any other military despotism which has been established by the same means, and with the same defiance of public opinion.

All these facts call for delay and stronger evidence.

What, then, is the inference I draw from all that I have now stated? Is it that we will in *no case* treat with Bonaparte? I say no such thing. But I say, as has been said in the answer returned to the French note, that we ought to wait for "*experience and the evidence of facts*" before we are convinced that such a treaty is admissible. The circumstances I have stated would well justify us if we should be slow in being convinced; but on a question of peace and war, every thing depends upon degree and upon comparison. If, on the one hand, there should be an appearance that the policy of France is at length guided by different maxims from those which have hitherto prevailed; if we should hereafter see signs of stability in the government which are not now to be traced; if the progress of the allied army should not call forth such a spirit in France as to make it probable that the act of the country itself will destroy the system now prevailing; if the danger, the difficulty, the risk of continuing the contest should increase, while the hope of complete ultimate success should be diminished; all these, in their due place, are considerations which, with myself and, I can answer for it, with every one of my colleagues, will have their just weight. But at present these considerations all operate one way; at present there is nothing from which we can presage a favorable disposition to change in the French councils. There is the greatest reason to rely on powerful co-operation from our allies; there are the strongest marks of a disposition in the interior of France to active resistance against this new tyranny; and there is every ground to believe, on reviewing our situation and that of the enemy, that, if we are ultimately disappointed of that complete success which we are at present entitled to hope, the continuance of the contest, instead of making our situation comparatively worse, will have made it comparatively better.

If, then, I am asked how long are we to persevere in the war, I can only say that no period can be accurately assigned. Considering the importance of obtaining complete security for the objects for which we contend, we ought not to be discouraged too soon; but on the contrary, considering the importance of not impairing and exhausting the radical strength of the country, there are limits beyond which we ought not to persist, and which we can determine only by estimating and comparing fairly, from time to time, the degree of security to be obtained by treaty, and the risk and disadvantage of continuing the contest.

No definite period can be assigned.

But, sir, there are some gentlemen in the House who seem to consider it already certain that the ultimate success to which I am looking is unattainable. They suppose us contending only for the restoration of the French monarchy, which they believe to be impracticable, and deny to be desirable for this country. We have been asked in the course of this debate: Do you think you can impose monarchy upon France, against the will of the nation? I never thought it, I never hoped it, I never wished it. I have thought, I have hoped, I have wished, that the time might come when the effect of the arms of the allies might so far overpower the military force, which keeps France in bondage, as to give vent and scope to the thoughts and actions of its inhabitants. We have, indeed, already seen abundant proof of what is the disposition of a large part of the country; we have seen almost through the whole of the Revolution the western provinces of France deluged with the blood of its inhabitants, obstinately contending for their ancient laws and religion. We have recently seen, in the revival of that war, fresh proof of the zeal which still animates those countries in the same cause. These efforts (I state it distinctly, and there are those near me who can bear witness to the truth of the assertion) were not produced by any instigation from hence; they were the effects of a rooted sentiment prevailing through all those provinces forced into action by the "law of the hostages" and the other tyrannical measures of the Directory, at the moment when we were endeavoring to discourage so hazardous an enterprise. If, under such circumstances, we find them giving proofs of their unalterable perseverance in their principles; if there is every reason to believe that the same disposition prevails in many other extensive provinces of France; if every party appears at length equally wearied and disappointed with all the successive changes which the Revolution has produced; if the question is no longer between monarchy, and even the pretense and name of liberty, but between the ancient line of hereditary princes on the one hand, and a military tyrant, a foreign usurper, on the other; if the armies of that usurper are likely to find sufficient occupation on the frontiers, and to be forced at length to leave the interior of the country at liberty to manifest its real feeling and disposition; what reason have we to anticipate, that the restoration of monarchy under such circumstances is impracticable?

The object is not to force monarchy upon France.

The learned gentleman has, indeed, told us that almost every man now possessed of property in France must necessarily be interested in resisting such a change, and that therefore it never can be effected.[28] If that single consideration were conclusive against the possibility of a change, for the same reason the Revolution itself, by which the whole property of the country was taken from its ancient possessors, could never have taken place. But though I deny it to be an insuperable obstacle, I admit it to be a point of considerable delicacy and difficulty. It is not, indeed, for us to discuss minutely what arrangement might be formed on this point to conciliate and unite opposite interests. But whoever considers the precarious tenure and depreciated value of lands held under the revolutionary title, and the low price for which they have generally been obtained, will think it, perhaps, not impossible that an ample compensation might be made to the bulk of the present possessors, both for the purchase-money they have paid and for the actual value of what they now enjoy; and that the ancient proprietors might be reinstated in the possession of their former rights, with only such a temporary sacrifice as reasonable men would willingly make to obtain so essential an object.

Inquiry whether the changes of property in France would prevent the restoration of the Bourbons.

The honorable and learned gentleman, however, has supported his reasoning on this part of the subject, by an argument which he undoubtedly considers as unanswerable—a reference to what would be his own conduct in similar circumstances; and he tells us that every landed proprietor in France must support the present order of things in that country from the same motive that he and every proprietor of three per cent. stock would join in the defense of the Constitution of Great Britain. I must do the learned gentleman the justice to believe that the habits of his profession must supply him with better and nobler motives for defending a Constitution, which he has had so much occasion to study and examine, than any he can derive from the value of his proportion, however large, of three per cents, even supposing them to continue to increase in price as rapidly as they have done during the last three years, in which the security and prosperity of the country has been established by following a system directly opposite to the counsels of the learned gentleman and his friends.

Hit at Mr. Erskine as to the rise of three per cent. stock in the English funds.

The learned gentleman's illustration, however, though it fails with respect to himself, is hap-

[28] An immense amount of confiscated property had passed into new hands during the Revolution. Mr. Erskine had correctly argued that if this was to be restored to the former proprietors, nearly all France had the strongest motives to resist the return of the Bourbons. The obstacle plainly would have been insurmountable; and when they did return in 1814, nothing of this kind was attempted.

pily and aptly applied to the state of France; and let us see what inference it furnishes with respect to the probable attachment of moneyed men to the continuance of the revolutionary system, as well as with respect to the general state of public credit in that country. I do not, indeed, know that there exists precisely any fund of three per cents in France, to furnish a test for the patriotism and public spirit of the lovers of French liberty. But there is another fund which may equally answer our purpose. The capital of three per cent. stock which formerly existed in France has undergone a whimsical operation, similar to many other expedients of finance which we have seen in the course of the Revolution. This was performed by a decree which, as they termed it, *republicanized* their debt; that is, in other words, struck off at once two thirds of the capital, and left the proprietors to take their chance for the payment of interest on the remainder. This remnant was afterward converted into the present five per cent. stock. I had the curiosity very lately to inquire what price it bore in the market, and I was told that the price had somewhat risen from confidence in the new government, and was actually as high as *seventeen.* I really at first supposed that my informer meant seventeen years purchase for every pound of interest, and I began to be almost jealous of revolutionary credit; but I soon found that he literally meant seventeen pounds for every hundred pounds capital stock of five per cent., that is a little more than three and a half years' purchase. So much for the value of revolutionary property, and for the attachment with which it must inspire its possessors toward the system of government to which that value is to be ascribed!

And the low state of the French funds.

On the question, sir, how far the restoration of the French monarchy, if practicable, is desirable, I shall not think it necessary to say much. Can it be supposed to be indifferent to us or to the world, whether the throne of France is to be filled by a Prince of the house of Bourbon, or by him whose principles and conduct I have endeavored to develop? Is it nothing, with a view to influence and example, whether the fortune of this last adventurer in the lottery of revolutions shall appear to be permanent? Is it nothing whether a system shall be sanctioned which confirms, by one of its fundamental articles, that general transfer of property from its ancient and lawful possessors, which holds out one of the most terrible examples of national injustice, and which has furnished the great source of revolutionary finance and revolutionary strength against all the powers of Europe?

Desirableness of the return of the Bourbons.

In the exhausted and impoverished state of France, it seems for a time impossible that any system but that of robbery and confiscation, any thing but the continued torture, which can be applied only by the engines of the Revolution, can extort from its ruined inhabitants more than the means of supporting in peace the yearly expenditure of its government. Suppose, then, the heir of the house of Bourbon reinstated on the throne, he will have sufficient occupation in endeavoring, if possible, to heal the wounds, and gradually to repair the losses of ten years of civil convulsion; to reanimate the drooping commerce, to rekindle the industry, to replace the capital, and to revive the manufactures of the country. Under such circumstances, there must probably be a considerable interval before such a monarch, whatever may be his views, can possess the power which can make him formidable to Europe; but while the system of the Revolution continues, the case is quite different. It is true, indeed, that even the gigantic and unnatural means by which that Revolution has been supported are so far impaired; the influence of its principles and the terror of its arms so far weakened; and its power of action so much contracted and circumscribed, that against the embodied force of Europe, prosecuting a vigorous war, we may justly hope that the remnant and wreck of this system can not long oppose an effectual resistance.

They could not, if restored, be formidable to the rest of Europe.

But, supposing the confederacy of Europe prematurely dissolved; supposing our armies disbanded, our fleets laid up in our harbors, our exertions relaxed, and our means of precaution and defense relinquished; do we believe that the revolutionary power, with this rest and breathing time given it to recover from the pressure under which it is now sinking, possessing still the means of calling suddenly and violently into action whatever is the remaining physical force of France, under the guidance of military despotism; do we believe that this revolutionary power, the terror of which is now beginning to vanish, will not again prove formidable to Europe? Can we forget that in the ten years in which that power has subsisted, it has brought more misery on surrounding nations, and produced more acts of aggression, cruelty, perfidy, and enormous ambition than can be traced in the history of France for the centuries which have elapsed since the foundation of its monarchy, including all the wars which, in the course of that period, have been waged by any of those sovereigns, whose projects of aggrandizement and violations of treaty afford a constant theme of general reproach against the ancient government of France? And if not, can we hesitate whether we have the best prospect of permanent peace, the best security for the independence and safety of Europe from the restoration of the lawful government, or from the continuance of revolutionary power in the hands of Bonaparte?

But the power of Bonaparte, in the event of a premature peace, might be terribly employed.

In compromise and treaty with such a power, placed in such hands as now exercise it, and retaining the same means of annoyance which it now possesses, I see little hope of permanent security. I see no possibility at this moment of such a peace as would justify that liberal intercourse which is the essence of real amity; no chance of termin-

No security that peace with him will be permanent.

ating the expenses or the anxieties of war, or of restoring to us any of the advantages of established tranquillity; and, as a sincere lover of peace, I can not be content with its nominal attainment. I must be desirous of pursuing that system which promises to attain, in the end, the permanent enjoyment of its solid and substantial blessings for this country and for Europe. As a sincere lover of peace, I will not sacrifice it by grasping at the shadow when the reality is not substantially within my reach.

Cur igitur pacem nolo? Quia infida est, quia periculosa, quia esse non potest.[29]

If, sir, in all that I have now offered to the House, I have succeeded in establishing the proposition that the system of the French Revolution has been such as to afford to foreign powers no adequate ground for security in negotiation, and that the change which has recently taken place has not yet afforded that security; if I have laid before you a just statement of the nature and extent of the danger with which we have been threatened, it would remain only shortly to consider whether there is any thing in the circumstances of the present moment to induce us to accept a security confessedly inadequate against a danger of such a description.

Mr. Pitt's reasons for negotiating in 1796–7.

It will be necessary here to say a few words on the subject on which gentlemen have been so fond of dwelling, I mean our former negotiations, and particularly that at Lisle, in 1797. I am desirous of stating frankly and openly the true motives which induced me to concur in then recommending negotiation; and I will leave it to the House and to the country to judge whether our conduct at that time was inconsistent with the principles by which we are guided at present. That revolutionary policy which I have endeavored to describe, that gigantic system of prodigality and bloodshed by which the efforts of France were supported, and which counts for nothing the lives and the property of a nation, had at that period driven us to exertions which had, in a great measure, exhausted the ordinary means of defraying our immense expenditure, and had led many of those who were the most convinced of the original justice and necessity of the war, and of the danger of Jacobin principles, to doubt the possibility of persisting in it, till complete and adequate security could be obtained. There seemed, too, much reason to believe that, without some new measure to check the rapid accumulation of debt, we could no longer trust to the stability of that funding system by which the nation had been enabled to support the expense of all the different wars in which we have engaged in the course of the present century. In order to continue our exertions with vigor, it became necessary that a new and solid system of finance should be established, such as could not be rendered effectual but by the general and decided concurrence of public opinion. Such a concurrence in the strong and vigorous measures necessary for the purpose could not then be expected, but from satisfying the country, by the strongest and most decided proofs, that peace, on terms in any degree admissible, was unattainable.

The negotiation, though unsuccessful, produced the happiest results in England.

Under this impression, we thought it our duty to attempt negotiation, not from the sanguine hope, even at that time, that its result could afford us complete security, but from the persuasion that the danger arising from peace, under such circumstances, was less than that of continuing the war with precarious and inadequate means. The result of those negotiations proved that the enemy would be satisfied with nothing less than the sacrifice of the honor and independence of the country. From this conviction, a spirit and enthusiasm was excited in the nation which produced the efforts to which we are indebted for the subsequent change in our situation. Having witnessed that happy change, having observed the increasing prosperity and security of the country from that period, seeing how much more satisfactory our prospects now are than any which we could then have derived from the successful result of negotiation, I have not scrupled to declare that I consider the rupture of the negotiation, on the part of the enemy, as a fortunate circumstance for the country. But because these are my sentiments at this time, after reviewing what has since passed, does it follow that we were at that time insincere in endeavoring to obtain peace? The learned gentleman, indeed, assumes that we were, and he even makes a concession, of which I desire not to claim the benefit. He is willing to admit that, on our principles and our view of the subject, insincerity would have been justifiable. I know, sir, no plea that would justify those who are intrusted with the conduct of public affairs in holding out to Parliament and to the nation one object, while they were, in fact, pursuing another. I did, in fact, believe, at the moment, the conclusion of peace, if it could have been obtained, to be preferable to the continuance of the war under its increasing risks and difficulties. I therefore wished for peace; I sincerely labored for peace. Our endeavors were frustrated by the act of the enemy. If, then, the circumstances are since changed; if what passed at that period has afforded a proof that the object we aimed at was unattainable; and if all that has passed since has proved that, provided peace had been then made, it could not have been durable, are we bound to repeat the same experiment, when every reason against it is strengthened by subsequent experience, and when the inducements which led to it at that time have ceased to exist?

Peroration. Increase of resources.

When we consider the resources and the spirit of the country, can any man doubt that if adequate security is not now to be obtained by treaty, we have the means of prosecuting the contest without material difficulty or danger, and with a reasonable prospect

[29] Why, then, am I against peace? Because it is faithless, because it is dangerous, because it can not be maintained.

of completely attaining our object? I will not dwell on the improved state of public credit, on the continually increasing amount, in spite of extraordinary temporary burdens, of our permanent revenue, on the yearly accession of wealth to an extent unprecedented even in the most flourishing times of peace, which we are deriving, in the midst of war, from our extended and flourishing commerce; on the progressive improvement and growth of our manufactures; on the proofs which we see on all sides of the uninterrupted accumulation of productive capital; and on the active exertion of every branch of national industry which can tend to support and augment the population, the riches, and the power of the country?

Recent victories.

As little need I recall the attention of the House to the additional means of action which we have derived from the great augmentation of our disposable military force, the continued triumphs of our powerful and victorious navy, and the events which, in the course of the last two years, have raised the military ardor and military glory of the country to a height unexampled in any period of our history.

Skill and valor of our allies.

In addition to these grounds of reliance on our own strength and exertions, we have seen the consummate skill and valor of the arms of our allies proved by that series of unexampled success in the course of the last campaign, and we have every reason to expect a coöperation on the continent, even to a greater extent, in the course of the present year. If we compare this view of our own situation with every thing we can observe of the state and condition of our enemy—if we can trace him laboring under equal difficulty in finding men to recruit his army, or money to pay it—if we know that in the course of the last year the most rigorous efforts of military conscription were scarcely sufficient to replace to the French armies, at the end of the campaign, the numbers which they had lost in the course of it—if we have seen that that force, then in possession of advantages which it has since lost, was unable to contend with the efforts of the combined armies—if we know that, even while supported by the plunder of all the countries which they had overrun, those armies were reduced, by the confession of their commanders, to the extremity of distress, and destitute not only of the principal articles of military supply, but almost of the necessaries of life—if we see them now driven back within their own frontiers, and confined within a country whose own resources have long since been proclaimed by their successive governments to be unequal either to paying or maintaining them —if we observe that since the last revolution no one substantial or effectual measure has been adopted to remedy the intolerable disorder of their finances, and to supply the deficiency of their credit and resources—if we see through large and populous districts of France, either open war levied against the present usurpation, or evident marks of disunion and distraction, which the first occasion may call forth into a flame—if, I say, sir, this comparison be just, I feel myself authorized to conclude from it, not that we are entitled to consider ourselves certain of ultimate success, not that we are to suppose ourselves exempted from the unforeseen vicissitudes of war; but that, considering the value of the object for which we are contending, the means for supporting the contest, and the probable course of human events, we should be inexcusable, if at this moment we were to relinquish the struggle on any grounds short of entire and complete security; that from perseverance in our efforts under such circumstances, we have the fairest reason to expect the full attainment of our object; but that at all events, even if we are disappointed in our more sanguine hopes, we are more likely to gain than to lose by the continuation of the contest; that every month to which it is continued, even if it should not in its effects lead to the final destruction of the Jacobin system, must tend so far to weaken and exhaust it, as to give us at least a greater comparative security in any termination of the war; that, on all these grounds, this is not the moment at which it is consistent with our interest or our duty to listen to any proposals of negotiation with the present ruler of France; but that we are not, therefore, pledged to any *unalterable* determination as to our future conduct; that in this we must be regulated by the course of events; and that it will be the duty of his Majesty's ministers from time to time to adapt their measures to any variation of circumstances, to consider how far the effects of the military operations of the allies or of the internal disposition of France correspond with our present expectations; and, on a view of the whole, to compare the difficulties or risks which may arise in the prosecution of the contest with the prospect of ultimate success, or of the degree of advantage to be derived from its further continuance, and to be governed by the result of all these considerations in the opinion and advice which they may offer to their sovereign.

Exhausted state of the French.

Notwithstanding the deep impression made by Mr. Fox in reply, the address was carried by a vote of 265 to 64. The result, however, painfully disappointed the expectations of Mr. Pitt. It seemed to be his fate, throughout the war, to be deceived on the two points dwelt upon in his peroration, viz., the skill and valor of his allies and the exhausted state of the French. The former were uniformly out-generaled and defeated, while the latter grew continually in spirit and resources. The reader will see at the conclusion of Mr. Fox's speech in reply to this, a slight sketch of the events which followed during the two subsequent years—the entire discomfiture of the allies, their withdrawal from the contest, the resignation of Mr. Pitt, and the conclusion of the peace of Amiens in 1802, to the great joy of the English.

LORD ERSKINE.

THOMAS ERSKINE, youngest son of the Earl of Buchan, was born at Edinburgh, on the 10th day of January, 1750. The family had once been eminent for rank and wealth; but their ample patrimony being gradually wasted, the income of their estates was at last reduced to two hundred pounds a year. To conceal their poverty, they removed to the capital from an old castle, which was all that was left of their wide domains; and "in a small and ill-furnished room in an upper *flat*, or story, of a lofty house in the old town of Edinburgh, first saw the light the Honorable Thomas Erskine, the future defender of Stockdale, and Lord Chancellor of Great Britain."

Young Erskine displayed in very early life that quickness of intellect and joyous hilarity of spirits for which he was so remarkable throughout his professional career. He was kept for some years at the High School of Edinburgh, and then removed to the University of St. Andrew's, where he spent less than two years. His early education was, therefore, extremely limited. He had but little knowledge of Latin, and none of Greek.[1] In the rudiments of English literature, however, he was uncommonly well instructed for one of his age. He profited greatly by conversation with his mother, who was a woman of uncommon strength of mind, and owed much of the daring energy of his character to her example and instructions. Being accustomed, notwithstanding the poverty of the family, to associate from childhood with persons of high rank and breeding, he early acquired that freedom and nobleness of manner for which he was so much distinguished in after life. He was the favorite of all who knew him—of his masters, his school-mates, and the families in which he visited. Full of fun and frolic, with a lively fancy, ready wit, and unbounded self-reliance, he found his chief delight in society; and probably laid the foundation, at this early period, of those extraordinary powers of conversation to which he was greatly indebted for his subsequent success. He was one of the few who seem to have gained by being left chiefly to themselves in their early years. If he had less learning, he had more freedom and boldness; and when the time arrived for his entering into the conflicts of the bar, it is not surprising that, with high native talent, extraordinary capacity for application, and a self-confidence amounting to absolute egotism, he was able to put forth his powers, under the impulse of strong motive, with prodigious effect, and to make himself, without any preparatory training, one of the most ready and eloquent speakers of the age.

He showed a great desire from boyhood to be fitted for one of the learned professions, and had even then his dreams of distinction in eloquence; but the poverty of his father forbade the attempt. At the age of fourteen, he was placed as a midshipman in the navy, and was commended to the particular care of his captain by Lord Mansfield, who took a lively interest in the Buchan family. He now spent four years in visiting various parts of the globe, particularly the West Indies and the coast of North America. He was often on shore; and it was probably on one of

[1] Lord Brougham speaks of him as having "*hardly any* access to the beauties of Attic eloquence, whether in prose or verse;" but Lord Campbell goes farther, and says, "he learned little of Greek *beyond the alphabet.*"

these occasions that he witnessed that meeting of an Indian chief with the governor of a British colony, which he described so graphically in his defense of Stockdale, and made the starting-point of one of the noblest bursts of eloquence in our language.

At the end of four years he returned to England ; the ship was paid off, and he was cast without employment on the world. At this moment of deep perplexity his father died, leaving him but a scanty pittance for his support. After consulting with his friends, he saw no course but to try his fortune in the army; and accordingly he spent the whole of his little patrimony in purchasing an ensign's commission in the Royals, or First Regiment of Foot. The regiment remained for some years at home, and was quartered, from time to time, in different provincial towns. Erskine, with his habitual buoyancy of spirits, mingled in the best society of the places where he was stationed, and attracted great attention by the elegance of his manners and the brilliancy of his conversation. He at last became entangled with an affair of the heart ; and was married in April, 1770, at the age of twenty, to a lady of respectable family, though without fortune—the daughter of Daniel Moore. Esq., member of Parliament for Marlow.

This rash step would to most persons have been the certain precursor of poverty and ruin ; but in his case it was a fortunate one. It served to balance his mind, to check his natural volatility, to impress him with a sense of new obligations and higher duties. The regiment was ordered to Minorca, where he spent two years in almost uninterrupted leisure. In the society of his wife, he now entered on the systematic study of English literature, and probably no two years were ever better spent for the purposes of mental culture. As a preparation for his future efforts in oratory, they were invaluable. In addition to his reading in prose, he devoted himself with great ardor to the study of Milton and Shakspeare. A large part of the former he committed to memory, and became so familiar with the latter, that "he could almost, like Porson, have held conversations on all subjects for days together in the phrases of the great English dramatist." Here he acquired that fine choice of words, that rich and varied imagery, that sense of harmony in the structure of his sentences, that boldness of thought and magnificence of expression, for which he was afterward so much distinguished. It may also be remarked, that there are passages in both these writers which are the exact counterpart of the finest eloquence of the ancients. The speeches, in the second book of the Paradise Lost, have all the condensed energy and burning force of expression which belong to the great Athenian orator. The speech of Brutus, in Shakspeare's Julius Cæsar, has all the stern majesty of Roman eloquence. That of Anthony over the dead body of Cæsar is a matchless exhibition of the art and dexterity of insinuation which characterized the genius of the Greeks. It is not in regard to poetry alone that we may say of these great masters,

> Hither, as to a fountain,
> Other suns repair, and in their urns
> Draw golden light.

In respect to eloquence, also, to use the words of Johnson, slightly varied, he who would excel in this noblest of arts must give his days and nights to the study of Milton and Shakspeare.

In the year 1772 the regiment returned to England, and the young ensign obtained a furlough of six months. Most of this time he spent in the best society of London ; and Boswell speaks of Johnson and himself as dining, April 6, 1772, with "a young officer in the regimentals of the Scots Royals, who talked with a vivacity, fluency, and precision which attracted particular attention." It was Erskine, who, with his characteristic boldness, entered at once into a literary discussion with Johnson, disputing his views on the comparative merits of Fielding and Richardson in a manner which rather gained him the favor of the great English moralist.

At the end of six years from his entering the army, when he had reached the rank of Lieutenant, the attention of Erskine was by mere accident directed to the bar. Being stationed, during the summer of 1774, in a country town where the Assizes were held, he rambled one day into court; and Lord Mansfield, who presided, having noticed his uniform, was led to inquire his name. Finding that it was the boy whom he had aided ten years before in going to sea, he invited him to a seat on the bench, briefly stating the principal points of the case, and showing him other civilities which were peculiarly gratifying under such circumstances. Erskine listened with the liveliest interest. The counsel were considered skillful and eloquent; but it often occurred to him, in the course of the argument on both sides, how much more clearly and forcibly he could have presented certain points and urged them on the minds of the jury. "And why not be a lawyer?" was the thought which instantly forced itself on his mind. "Why not carry out the early aspirations of boyhood?" Any one of a less sanguine temperament would have felt the attempt to be hopeless, burdened as he was with a young and growing family, and wholly destitute of any means of subsistence except his commission, which must, of course, be relinquished if he entered on the study of the law. But Erskine's whole life was one of daring enterprise. The very difficulty of an undertaking seemed only to impel him forward with greater eagerness. Being invited to dinner by Lord Mansfield, who was delighted with his conversational powers, he brought out at the close of the evening the question which was already beating at his heart, "Is it impossible for me to become a lawyer?" Mansfield, who admired his talents and spirit, did not utterly discourage him, and this was enough for one of his sanguine temperament. He consulted his mother, who had the same habit of looking on the bright side of things, and who perfectly understood the force of his character, and found to his delight that she was almost as eager as he was to see him enter on the undertaking. He accordingly became a member of Lincoln's Inn, about the middle of 1775. His term of legal study might be materially abridged by his taking a degree at one of the universities, and to this he was entitled, as son of a nobleman, without passing an examination, if he kept his regular terms. He therefore became a member of Trinity College, Cambridge, early in 1776, paying no attention whatever to the studies of the place, and contriving, at the same time, to keep his terms at Lincoln's Inn. He still retained his office in the army as a means of support, having obtained leave of absence for six months, and at the end of this time sold out his commission and husbanded his resources to the utmost. He lived in a small village just out of London; and Reynolds, the comic writer, says, in his "Life and Times," "The young student resided in small lodgings near my father's villa at Hampstead, and openly avowed that he lived on cow-beef, because he could not afford any of a superior quality; he dressed shabbily, and expressed the greatest gratitude to Mr. Harris for occasional free admissions to Covent Garden, and used boastingly to exclaim to my father, "Thank fortune, out of my own family, I don't know a Lord." In July, 1778, he was called to the bar, and according to all ordinary experience of the profession in London, he had reason to expect a delay of some years before his business would support his family.

But the early life of Erskine was full of singular adventure. Not long after his call to the bar, he was dining with a friend, and happened to speak of a Captain Baillie, whose case at that time awakened great interest in the public mind. As Lieutenant Governor of Greenwich Hospital, Baillie had discovered enormous abuses in the management of the institution (which was used for political purposes), and had publicly charged them on Lord Sandwich, First Lord of the Admiralty. For this he was prosecuted on a charge of a libel, at the instance of Sandwich, who kept, however, behind the scenes to avoid any opportunity of bringing him before the court on the merits of the case. As the trial was soon to come on, Erskine remarked on this conduct at table with great severity, not knowing that Baillie *was present as one of the guests.* The captain was delighted with what he heard; and learning that his volunteer advocate was a young lawyer, as yet without business, who had himself been a sailor, declared to a friend that he should at least have one brief. Accordingly, Erskine's first retainer of a guinea was put into his hands the next day, and it never occurred to him but that he was the only counsel in the case. As the trial approached, however, he found there were four distinguished advocates before him, and he also found they had so little hope of success, that they advised Baillie, at a consultation, to pay the costs, and in this way escape trial, as the prosecutors had kindly proposed. Erskine alone dissented. "My advice, gentlemen," said he, "may savor more of my former profession than my present, but I am against consenting." "You are the man for me," said Baillie, hugging the young advocate in his arms; "I will never give up."

The case came on before Lord Mansfield in the afternoon of November 23d, 1778. The senior counsel of Baillie consumed the time till late in the evening, in showing cause why the rule should be dismissed; and no one expecting Erskine to come forward, the case was adjourned until the next day. The court was crowded in the morning, as the Solicitor General was expected to speak in support of the rule, and, just as Lord Mansfield was about to call upon him to proceed, Erskine rose, unknown to nearly every individual in the room except his Lordship, and said, in a mild but firm tone, "My Lord, *I am likewise counsel for the author of this supposed libel,* * * * and when a British subject is brought before a court of justice only for having ventured to attack abuses which owe their continuance to the danger of attacking them, * * * I can not relinquish the privilege of doing justice to such merit, I will not give up even my share of the honor of repelling and exposing so odious a prosecution." The whole audience was hushed into a pin-fall silence, and he then went on to ask in regard to his client, "*Who is he? What was his duty? What has he written? To whom has he written? and what motive induced him to write?*" Taking these inquiries as the heads of his speech, he went on, in brief but eloquent terms, to show that Baillie, as Lieutenant Governor of the Hospital, was bound in duty to expose the abuses of the institution—that he had written nothing on the subject but what was undeniably true—that he had written it for the information of the Governors of the Hospital, who ought to be informed on such a subject—and that his only motive in writing had been the protection of those who had lost their limbs and periled their lives in fighting the battles of their country. In closing, he turned from Captain Baillie to the First Lord of the Admiralty, "Indeed, Lord Sandwich," said he, "has in my mind—" [Mansfield here reminded him that Lord Sandwich was not before the court, when Erskine, borne away by his feelings, instantly broke forth], "I know he is not formally before the court, but for that very reason *I will bring him before the court!* He has placed these men [the prosecutors] in the front of the battle, in hopes to escape under their shelter; but I will not join in the battle with them; *their* vices, though screwed up to the highest pitch of human depravity, are not of dignity enough to vindicate the combat with *me.* I will drag *him* to light, who is the dark mover behind this scene of iniquity. I assert, that the Earl of Sandwich has but one road to escape out of this business without pollution and disgrace, and *that is,* by publicly disavowing the acts of the prosecutors, and restoring Captain Baillie to his command. If he does this, then his offense will be no more than the too common one of having suffered his own personal interest to prevail over his public duty, in placing his voters in the hospital. But if, on the contrary, he continues to protect the prosecutors, in spite of the evidence of their guilt, which has excited the abhorrence of the numerous audience that crowd this court; *if he keeps this injured man suspended, or dares to turn that suspension into a removal, I shall then not scruple to declare him an accomplice in their guilt, a shameless oppressor, a disgrace to his rank, and a traitor to his trust.*" * * "FINE AND IMPRISONMENT! The man deserves a *palace* instead of a *prison* who prevents the palace, built by the public bounty of his country, from being converted into a dungeon, and who sacrifices his own security to the interests of humanity and virtue." Considering all the circumstances of the case, it is not surprising that Lord Campbell should pronounce this "the most wonderful forensic effort which we have in our annals." It is hardly necessary to say that the decision was for the defendant; the rule was dismissed with costs.

Never did a single case so completely make the fortune of any individual. Erskine entered Westminster Hall that morning not only in extreme poverty, but with no reasonable prospect of an adequate subsistence for years. He left it a rich man. He received thirty retainers from attorneys who were present, it is said, while retiring from the hall. Not only was his ambition gratified, but the comfort and independence of those whose happiness he had staked on his success as a lawyer were secured for life. Some one asked him, at a later period, how he dared to face Lord Mansfield so boldly on a point where he was clearly out of order, when he beautifully replied, "I thought of my children as plucking me by the robe, and saying, 'Now, father, is the time to get us bread.'" His business went on rapidly increasing, until he had an annual income of £12,000.

The next year he added to his reputation by a masterly defense of Admiral Keppel before a court-martial at Portsmouth. His experience in naval affairs recommended him for this service, and he performed it with unabated zeal for thirteen days, which were spent in examining witnesses and arguing points of order, after which he wrote out the speech which the Admiral read to the court. This was followed by a unanimous verdict of acquittal; and so strongly did Keppel feel the value of the young advocate's services, that he addressed him a note in token of his gratitude containing a present of a thousand pounds, adding, "I shall ever rejoice in this commencement of a *friendship* which I hope daily to improve." Erskine, with the boyish hilarity which always marked his character, hastened to the villa of the Reynoldses, and, displaying his bank-notes, exclaimed, "Voila the non-suit of cow-beef, my good friends."

He came into the House five years after, in November, 1783, as a supporter of the Coalition ministry of Mr. Fox and Lord North. Nearly all the lawyers being on the other side, great reliance was placed on his services by the friends of the new government. But they were sorely disappointed. His habits were not suited to parliamentary debate. His understanding was eminently a legal one; he wanted the stimulus and encouragement of a listening court and jury; and was embarrassed by the presence of sneering opponents ready to treat him with personal indignity. His vanity now turned to his disadvantage, and put him in the power of his antagonists. When he commenced his maiden speech, says Mr. Croly, in his Life of George IV., "Mr. Pitt, evidently intending to reply, sat with pen and paper in his hand, prepared to catch the arguments of his formidable adversary. He wrote a word or two. Erskine proceeded; but, with every additional sentence, Pitt's attention to the paper relaxed, his look became more careless, and he obviously began to think the orator less and less worthy of his attention. At length, while every eye in the House was fixed upon him, with a contemptuous smile he dashed the pen through the paper, and flung them on the floor. Erskine never recovered from this expression of disdain; his voice faltered, he struggled through the remainder of his speech, and sank into his seat dispirited and shorn of his fame." Sheridan remarked to him at a later period, "I'll tell you how it happens, Erskine; you are *afraid* of Pitt, and that is the flabby part of your character." There was too much truth in the remark. Erskine could bear any thing but contempt. He recovered himself, however, at a later period of life, and made quite a number of very able and eloquent speeches; in fact, he would have stood high as a parliamentary orator, if he had not so completely outshone himself by the brilliancy of his efforts in Westminster Hall.

"As an advocate in the forum," says Lord Campbell, "I hold him to be without an equal in ancient or modern times." What is rare in one of so brilliant a genius, he had no less power with the court than with the jury. It was remarked of him, as of Scarlett, that "he had invented a machine by the secret use of which, in court, he could make the head of a judge nod assent to his propositions; whereas his rivals, who tried to pirate it, always made the same head move from side to side." He was certainly not a profound lawyer, as the result of original investigation; his short period of study rendered this impossible. But he had the power of availing himself more completely than almost any man that ever lived, of the knowledge collected for his use by others. His speech on the Rights of Juries, in the case of the Dean of St. Asaph, is universally admitted to show "a depth of learning which would have done honor to Selden or Hale;" and so completely had he thrown his mind into the case, and made himself master of what black-letter lawyers spent months in searching out as the materials of his brief, that he poured forth all this learning, in his argument before the court, with the freshness and precision of one who had spent his life in such researches. He always, indeed, grasped a cause so firmly, that he never forgot a principle or a decision, an analogy or a fact which made for his client, while he showed infinite dexterity in avoiding the difficulties of his case, and turning to his own advantage the unexpected disclosures which sometimes come out in the progress of a trial. Nothing could be more incorrect than the idea of some, that Erskine owed his success chiefly to the warmth and brilliancy of his genius. The dryest special pleader never managed a cause with greater caution. Even in his Indian Chief, in the case of Stockdale (p. 696), a passage which verges more toward poetry than any thing in our eloquence, he was still, as a writer in the Edinburgh Review remarks, "*feeling his way* every step he took." His boldness was equal to his caution. In his defense of the liberty of the press, and of the rights of the subject when assailed by the doctrine of constructive treason, he had some of the severest conflicts with the court which any advocate was ever called to maintain. When the jury, in the case of the Dean of St. Asaph, brought in their verdict, "Guilty of publishing *only*," which would have the effect of clearing the defendant, Justice Buller, who presided, acting on the principle then held by the court, considered it beyond their province to make this addition, and determined they should withdraw it. Erskine, on the other hand, seized upon the word the moment it was uttered, and demanded to have it recorded. After some sparring between him and the court, he put the question to the foreman, "Is the word *only* to stand as a part of the verdict?" "Certainly," was the reply. "Then I insist it shall be recorded," says Erskine. "The verdict," says Buller, "must be misunderstood: let me understand the jury." "The jury," replied Erskine, "do understand their verdict." *Buller*. "Sir, I will not be interrupted." *Erskine*. "I stand here as an advocate for a brother citizen, and I desire the word *only* may be recorded." *Buller*. "SIT DOWN, SIR. REMEMBER YOUR DUTY, OR I SHALL BE OBLIGED TO PROCEED IN ANOTHER MANNER." *Erskine*. "YOUR LORDSHIP MAY PROCEED IN WHAT MANNER YOU THINK FIT; I KNOW MY DUTY AS WELL AS YOUR LORDSHIP KNOWS YOURS. I SHALL NOT ALTER MY CONDUCT." The spirit of the judge sunk before the firmness of the advocate; no attempt was made to carry the threat into execution.

It was this mixture of boldness and caution, it was the keen sagacity and severe logic of Erskine, which laid the foundation of his unrivaled power over a jury. It was owing to these qualities that, when he threw into his argument all the strength of his ardent feelings, and all that beauty and richness of illustration which his glowing fancy supplied, no one ever suspected him of wishing to play upon their passions; the appeal was still so entirely to their intellect, that the jury gave him their sympathies without hesitation or reserve. And if he seemed to digress for a moment from the line of his reasoning, as he sometimes did for the sake of relieving the minds of his auditors, he still showed the same sagacity in turning even this to the furtherance of his argument, for he always brought back with him from these excursions some weighty truth which he had gathered by the way, and which served to give a new and startling force to the urgency of his appeal. To these qualities he added a good-humored cheerfulness in the most difficult cases, which put him on the best terms with the court and jury. They wished him to succeed, even when they had made up their minds that he must fail. It is easy to see the advantage he thus gained. Sometimes, under his management, the worst cause seemed wholly to change its aspect; as in the case of Hadfield (given below), in which Kenyon, who presided, showed himself at first to be strongly prejudiced against the prisoner, but had his views so entirely changed that, at the close of Erskine's argument, he took the extraordinary step of recommending to the Attorney General not to proceed in the case, but to allow an immediate acquittal. Only one trait more will be added to his character as an advocate. He was uniformly kind to the younger members of the profession. He was the last man on earth to injure or depress a rival. When Sir James Mackintosh made his celebrated defense in the case of Peltier—a case which he might naturally expect, from his superior age and devotion to a free press, would have been committed to his care—he showed no mean jealousy; he attended the trial, and, before retiring to bed that night, addressed a note to the young advocate expressing his warmest admiration of the defense, as "one of the most splendid monuments of genius, learning, and eloquence."

Nine of Mr. Erskine's ablest arguments are given in this collection. It is unnecessary here to dwell upon their merits or the circumstances out of which they sprung: these are detailed at large in the Introductions which precede the speeches. The writer would only urge upon the general student in oratory not to pass over, as belonging exclusively to the lawyer, the four great arguments of Erskine in the cases of Lord George Gordon, of the Dean of St. Asaph, of Hardy, and of Hadfield. The technical terms are briefly explained in notes, so that no embarrassment need arise from this cause. As specimens of acute and powerful reasoning, enlivened occasionally by glowing eloquence, they are among the finest efforts of genius in our language. Nothing can be more useful to our young orators of any profession, than to make themselves perfectly acquainted with these admirable specimens of reasoning, whatever toil it may cost them. Such productions, as Johnson said of a similar class of writings, "are bark and steel to the mind."

Mr. Erskine, as already mentioned, came into Parliament in 1783, as the friend and supporter of Mr. Fox. He adhered to him in all his reverses, and at last shared in his success. When Lord Grenville and Mr. Fox came into power in 1806, Erskine was appointed Lord Chancellor, thus verifying a prediction which he made twenty-seven years before, just after he was called to the bar, and which (for he was inclined to be superstitious) he probably ascribed to some supernatural agency. "Willie," said he to his friend William Adam, after a long silence, as they were riding together over a blasted heath between Lewes and Guilford, in 1779, "Willie, the time will come when I shall be Lord Chancellor, and the Star of the Thistle shall blaze on my bosom!" His dream was now accomplished. But the office of Lord Chancellor was one to which he was very little suited. All his practice had lain in another direction; he was wholly unacquainted with the laws of property, so essential to the decision of cases in chancery; and "the doctrines which prevail in the courts of equity," as Sir Samuel Romilly remarked, "were to him almost like the laws of a foreign country." He had always thrown contempt upon proceedings in these courts; and was sometimes taunted with his pathetic appeal to Lord Kenyon, when recommending that his client should apply to chancery for redress: "Would your Lordship send a *dog* you loved there?" Still, he endeavored to gain what information he could on the subject at his period of life, and said humorously to Romilly, who excelled in this knowledge of these proceedings, "You must make me a chancellor now, that *I may afterward make you one.*" Though he added no honor to the office, he did not disgrace it. None of his decisions except one were ever called in question, and that was affirmed by the House of Lords. He presided with dignity, and when he retired from office, as he did at the end of thirteen months, Sir Arthur Pigot addressed him in the name of the bar, expressing "their grateful sense of the kindness shown them while he presided."

The remainder of Erskine's life was saddened by poverty, and unworthy of his early fame. The usages of the profession forbade his returning to the bar; the pension on which he retired was small; the property he had gained was wasted in speculations; and his early sense of character was unhappily lost, to some extent, in the general wreck of his fortunes. He died on a visit to Scotland, at Almondell, the residence of his sister-in-law, on the 17th of November, 1823, in the seventy-third year of his age.

The oratory of Erskine owed much of its impressiveness to his admirable delivery. He was of the medium height, with a slender but finely-turned figure, animated and graceful in gesture, with a voice somewhat shrill but beautifully modulated, a countenance beaming with emotion, and an eye of piercing keenness and power. "Juries," in the words of Lord Brougham, "have declared that they felt it impossible to remove their looks from him, when he had riveted, and, as it were, fascinated them by his first glance; and it used to be a common remark of men who observed his motions, that they resembled those of a *blood-horse;* as light, as limber, as much betokening strength and speed, as free from all gross superfluity or encumbrance."

His style was chaste, forcible, and harmonious, a model of graceful variety, without the slightest mannerism or straining after effect. His rhythmus was beautiful; that of the passage containing his Indian Chief is surpassed by nothing of the kind in our language. His sentences were sometimes too long—a fault which arose from the closeness and continuity of his thought.

The exordium with which Erskine introduced a speech was always natural, ingenious, and highly appropriate; none of our orators have equaled him in this respect. The arrangement of the matter which followed was highly felicitous; and he had this peculiarity, which gave great unity and force to his arguments, that "he proposed," in the words of another, "a *great leading principle*, to which all his efforts were referable and subsidiary—which ran through the whole of his address, governing and elucidating every part. As the principle was a true one, whatever might be its application to that particular case, it gave to his whole speech an air of honesty and sincerity which it was difficult to resist."

[2] The Rev. Dr. Emmons, one of the acutest reasoners among the divines of New England, was accustomed (as the writer is directly informed) to read the Massachusetts Reports as they came out, for the pleasure and benefit they afforded him as specimens of powerful reasoning. Would not our young divines find similar benefit from the study of great legal arguments like these of Erskine?

SPEECH

OF MR. ERSKINE IN BEHALF OF LORD GEORGE GORDON WHEN INDICTED FOR HIGH TREASON, DELIVERED BEFORE THE COURT OF THE KING'S BENCH, FEBRUARY 5, 1781.

INTRODUCTION.

Lord George Gordon, a member of the House of Commons, was a young Scottish nobleman of weak intellect and enthusiastic feelings. He had been chosen president of the Protestant Association, whose object was to procure the repeal of Sir George Saville's bill in favor of the Catholics.[1] In this capacity, he directed the association to meet him in St. George's Fields, and proceed thence to the Parliament House with a petition for the repeal of the bill. Accordingly, about forty thousand persons of the middling classes assembled on Friday, the 2d of June, 1780, and, after forming a procession, moved forward till they blocked up all the avenues to the House of Commons. They had no arms of any kind, and were most of them orderly in their conduct, though individuals among them insulted some members of both Houses who were passing into the building, requiring them to put blue cockades on their hats, and to cry "No Popery!"

Lord George presented the petition, but the House refused to consider it at that time, by a vote of 192 to 6. The multitude now became disorderly, and after the House adjourned, bodies of men proceeded to demolish the Catholic chapels at the residences of the foreign ministers. From this moment the whole affair changed its character. Desperate men, many of them thieves and robbers, took the lead. Not only were Catholic chapels set on fire, but the London prisons were broken open and destroyed; thirty-six fires were blazing at one time during the night; the town was for some days completely in the power of the multitude; Lord Mansfield's house was destroyed; the breweries and distilleries were broken open, and the mob became infuriated with liquor; and for a period there was reason to apprehend that the whole of the metropolis might be made one general scene of conflagration. The military were at last called in from the country, and, after a severe conflict, the mob was put down; but not until nearly five hundred persons had been killed or wounded, exclusive of those who perished from the effects of intoxication.

The government had been taken by surprise: no adequate provision was made to guard against violence; and, as the riots went on, all authority for a time seemed to be paralyzed or extinct. When order was at last restored, the magistrates, as is common with those who have neglected their duty, endeavored to throw the blame on others—they resolved to make Lord George Gordon their scapegoat. He was accordingly arraigned for high treason; and such was the excitement of the public mind, such the eagerness to have some one punished, that he was in imminent danger of being made the victim of public resentment. It was happy for him that, in addition to Mr. (afterward Lord) Kenyon, his senior counsel, a man of sound mind, but wholly destitute of eloquence, he had chosen Mr. Erskine, as a Scotchman, to aid in his defense. It was the means probably of saving his life.

The Attorney General opened the case in behalf of the Crown, contending (1.) That the prisoner, in assembling the multitude round the two Houses of Parliament, was guilty of high treason, if he did so with a view to overawe and intimidate the Legislature, and enforce his purposes by numbers and violence (a doctrine fully confirmed by the court); and (2.), That the overt acts proved might be fairly *construed* into such a design, and were the only evidence by which a traitorous intention, in such a case, could be shown. When the evidence for the Crown was received, Mr. Kenyon addressed the jury in behalf of Lord George Gordon, but in a manner so inefficient that, when he sat down, "the friends of Lord George were in an agony of apprehension." According to the usual practice, Mr. Erskine should now have followed, before the examination of his client's witnesses. But he adroitly changed the order, claiming as a privilege of the prisoner (for which he adduced a precedent) to have the evidence in his favor received at once. His object was, by meeting the evidence of the Crown with that of Lord George's witnesses as early as possible, to open a way for being heard with more favor by the jury, and of commenting upon the evidence on *both* sides as compared together. The Rev. Mr. Middleton, a member of the Protestant Association, swore that he had watched the prisoner's conduct, and that he appeared to be always actuated by the greatest loyalty to the King and attachment to the Constitution—that his speeches at the meetings of the association, at Coachmakers' Hall, never contained an expression tending directly or indirectly to a repeal of the bill by *force*—that he desired the people not even to carry sticks in the procession, and begged that riotous persons might be delivered to the constables. Mr. Evans, an eminent surgeon, declared that he saw Lord George Gordon in the center of one of the divisions in St. George's Fields, and that it appeared from his conduct and expressions that he wished and endeavored to prevent all disorder.

---

1 The reader has already seen Mr. Burke's admirable exposition of the reasons for Sir George Saville's bill, in his speech at Bristol, pages 299–310.

This was confirmed by others; and it was proved by decisive evidence that the bulk of the people round the Parliament House and in the lobby were not members of the Association, but idlers, vagabonds, and pickpockets, who had thrust themselves in; so that the persons who insulted the members were of a totally different class from those who formed the original procession. The Earl of Lonsdale swore that he took the prisoner home from the House in his carriage; that great multitudes surrounded Lord George, inquiring the fate of the petition; that he answered it was uncertain, and *earnestly entreated them to retire to their homes and be quiet.*

The evidence was not closed until after midnight, when Mr. Erskine addressed the jury in the following speech. Lord Campbell says of it, "Regularly trained to the profession of the law—having practiced thirty years at the bar—having been Attorney General above seven years—having been present at many trials for high treason, and having conducted several myself—I again peruse, with increased astonishment and delight, the speech delivered on this occasion by him, who had recently thrown aside the scarlet uniform of a subaltern in the army, which he had substituted for the blue jacket of a midshipman, thrust upon him while he was a school-boy. Here I find not only great acuteness, powerful reasoning, enthusiastic zeal, and burning eloquence, but the most masterly view ever given of the English law of high treason, the foundation of all our liberties."—*Lives of the Chancellors,* vol. vi., page 408.

SPEECH, &c.

Exordium: Amount of evidence in favor of the prisoner.

Gentlemen of the Jury,—Mr. Kenyon having informed the court that we propose to call no other witnesses, it is now my duty to address myself to you as counsel for the noble prisoner at the bar, the whole evidence being closed. I use the word *closed*, because it certainly is not finished, since I have been obliged to leave the seat in which I sat, to disentangle myself from the volumes of men's names, which lay there under my feet, whose testimony, had it been necessary for the defense, would have confirmed all the facts that are already in evidence before you.[1]

Indulgence due to the speaker.

Gentlemen, I feel myself entitled to expect, both from you and from the court, the greatest indulgence and attention. I am, indeed, a greater object of your compassion than even my noble friend whom I am defending. He rests secure in conscious innocence, and in the well-placed assurance that it can suffer no stain in your hands. Not so with ME. I stand before you a troubled, I am afraid a *guilty* man, in having presumed to accept of the awful task which I am now called upon to perform—a task which my learned friend who spoke before me, though he has justly risen, by extraordinary capacity and experience, to the highest rank in his profession, has spoken of with that distrust and diffidence which becomes every Christian in a cause of blood. If Mr. Kenyon has such feelings, think what mine must be. Alas! gentlemen, who am I? A young man of little experience, unused to the bar of criminal courts, and sinking under the dreadful consciousness of my defects. I have, however, this consolation, that no ignorance nor inattention on my part can possibly prevent you from seeing, under the direction of the Judges, that the Crown has established no case of treason.

Transition: Reasons for discussing the law of treason.

Gentlemen, I did expect that the Attorney General, in opening a great and solemn state prosecution, would have at least indulged the advocates for the prisoner with his notions on the law, as applied to the case before you, in less general terms.[2] It is very common, indeed, in little civil actions, to make such obscure introductions by way of *trap*. But in criminal cases it is unusual and unbecoming; because the right of the Crown to reply, even where no witnesses are called by the prisoner, gives it thereby the advantage of replying, without having given scope for observations on the principles of the opening, with which the reply must be consistent.

Greatness of the crime.

One observation he has, however, made on the subject, in the truth of which I heartily concur, viz., that the crime of which the noble person at your bar stands accused, is the very highest and most atrocious that a member of civil life can possibly commit; because it is not, like all other crimes, merely an injury to society from the breach of some of its reciprocal relations, but is an attempt utterly to dissolve and destroy society altogether.

Hence it is most exactly defined.

In nothing, therefore, is the wisdom and justice of our laws so strongly and eminently manifested as in the rigid, accurate,

[1] Mr. Erskine shows great dexterity in turning a slight circumstance at the opening of his speech, into a means of impressing the jury *from the first* with a sense of his client's innocence. He had sat thus far in the front row, with large files of papers at his feet, but he now stepped back to obtain greater freedom of movement; and this he represents as done to escape from "the volumes of men's names" who stood ready to confirm the evidence in favor of Lord Gordon! So the next paragraph, though in form a plea for indulgence to himself as a young speaker, is in fact the strongest possible assumption of the prisoner's innocence, since the *guilt* referred to consisted in his venturing to endanger, by his inexperience, the cause of one who stood secure himself "in conscious innocence." There is hardly any thing for which Mr. Erskine deserves more to be studied, than his thus making every circumstance conspire to produce the desired impression. All is so easy and natural, that men never think of it as the result of design or premeditation, and here lies his consummate skill as an advocate.

[2] The reader can not fail to remark how admirably one thought grows out of another in the transition, all of them important and all preparing the mind to be deeply interested in the discussion of the subject to which it leads, the nature of high treason. The same characteristic runs throughout the whole speech.

cautious, explicit, unequivocal definition of what shall constitute this high offense. For, high treason consisting in the breach and dissolution of that allegiance which binds society together, if it were left ambiguous, uncertain, or undefined, all the other laws established for the personal security of the subject would be utterly useless; since this offense, which, from its nature, is so capable of being created and judged of by the rules of political expediency on the spur of the occasion, would be a rod at will to bruise the most virtuous members of the community, whenever virtue might become troublesome or obnoxious to a bad government.

A potent engine of tyranny if overstrained.

Injuries to the persons and properties of our neighbors, considered as individuals, which are the subjects of all other criminal prosecutions, are not only capable of greater precision, but the powers of the state can be but rarely interested in straining them beyond their legal interpretation. But if treason, where the government is directly offended, were left to the judgment of its ministers, without any boundaries—nay, without the most broad, distinct, and inviolable boundaries marked out by the law—there could be no public freedom. The condition of an Englishman would be no better than a slave's at the foot of a Sultan; since there is little difference whether a man dies by the stroke of a saber, without the forms of a trial, or by the most pompous ceremonies of justice, if the crime could be made at pleasure by the state to fit the fact that was to be tried. Would to God, gentlemen of the jury, that this were an observation of theory alone, and that the page of our history was not blotted with so many melancholy, disgraceful proofs of its truth! But these proofs, melancholy and disgraceful as they are, have become glorious monuments of the wisdom of our fathers, and ought to be a theme of rejoicing and emulation to us. For, from the mischiefs constantly arising to the state from every extension of the ancient law of treason, the ancient law of treason has been always restored, and the Constitution at different periods washed clean; though, unhappily, with the blood of oppressed and innocent men.

High treason defined.

I. When I speak of the ancient law of treason, I mean the venerable statute of King Edward the Third, on which the indictment you are now trying is framed—a statute made, as its preamble sets forth, for the more precise definition of this crime, which has not, by the common law, been sufficiently explained; and consisting of different and distinct members, the plain unextended letter of which was thought to be a sufficient protection to the person and honor of the Sovereign, and an adequate security to the laws committed to his execution. I shall mention only two of the number, the others not being in the remotest degree applicable to the present accusation.[3]

(1.) *To compass or imagine the death of the King:* such imagination or purpose of the mind (visible only to its great Author) being manifested by some open act; an institution obviously directed, not only to the security of his natural person, but to the stability of the government; since the life of the Prince is so interwoven with the Constitution of the state, that an attempt to destroy the one is justly held to be rebellious conspiracy against the other.

(2.) (which is the crime charged in the indictment) *To levy war against him in his realm:* a term that one would think could require no explanation, nor admit of any ambiguous construction, among men who are willing to read laws according to the plain signification of the language in which they are written; but which has, nevertheless, been an abundant source of that *constructive* cavil which this sacred and valuable act was made expressly to prevent. The real meaning of this branch of it, as it is bottomed in policy, reason, and justice; as it is ordained in plain unambiguous words; as it is confirmed by the precedents of justice, and illustrated by the writings of the great lights of the law in different ages of our history, I shall, before I sit down, impress upon your minds as a safe, unerring standard by which to measure the evidence you have heard. At present I shall only say, that far and wide as judicial decisions have strained the construction of levying war beyond the warrant of the statute, to the discontent of some of the greatest ornaments of the profession, they hurt not me. As a citizen I may disapprove of them, but as advocate for the noble person at your bar, I need not impeach their authority. For none of them have said more than this, "that war may be levied against the King in his realm, not only by an insurrection to change or to destroy the fundamental Constitution of the government itself by rebellious war; but, by the same war, to endeavor to suppress the execution of the laws it has enacted, or to violate and overbear the protection they afford, not to individuals (which is a private wrong), but to any general class or description of the community, *by premeditated open acts of violence, hostility, and force.*"

Criterion of high treason.

Gentlemen, I repeat these words, and call solemnly on the judges to attend to what I say, and to contradict me if I mistake the law, "*By premeditated open acts of violence, hostility, and force,*" nothing equivocal, nothing ambiguous, no intimidations or overawings, which signify nothing precise or certain (because what frightens one man or set of men may have no effect upon another), but that which *compels* and *coerces—open violence and force.*

Gentlemen, this is not only the whole text; but I submit it to the learned judges, under whose correction I am happy to speak, an accurate ex-

[3] In this statement of the law of treason, perfectly fair and accurate as it is, there is one thing which marks the consummate skill of Mr. Erskine. He shapes it throughout with a *distinct reference to the facts of the case,* as they were afterward to come out in evidence. The points made most prominent are the points he had occasion afterward to use. Thus the jury were prepared, without knowing it, to look at the evidence under aspects favorable to the prisoner.

planation of the statute of treason, as far as it relates to the present subject, taken in its utmost extent of judicial construction; and which you can not but see, not only in its letter, but in its most strained signification, is confined to acts which *immediately*, *openly*, and *unambiguously* strike at the very root and being of government, and not to any other offenses, however injurious to its peace.

All attempts to widen the crime have been wisely repressed.

Such were the boundaries of high treason marked out in the reign of Edward the Third; and as often as the vices of bad princes, assisted by weak submissive Parliaments, extended state offenses beyond the strict letter of that act, so often the virtue of better princes and wiser Parliaments brought them back again. A long list of new treasons, accumulated in the wretched reign of Richard the Second, from which (to use the language of the act that repealed them) "no man knew what to do or say for doubt of the pains of death," were swept away in the first year of Henry the Fourth, his successor; and many more, which had again sprung up in the following distracted arbitrary reigns, putting tumults and riots on a footing with armed rebellion, were again leveled in the first year of Queen Mary, and the statute of Edward made once more the standard of treasons. The acts, indeed, for securing his present Majesty's illustrious House from the machinations of those very Papists, who are now so highly in favor, have, since that time, been added to the list. But these not being applicable to the present case, the ancient statute is still our only guide; which is so plain and simple in its object, so explicit and correct in its terms, as to leave no room for intrinsic error; and the wisdom of its authors has shut the door against all extension of its plain letter; declaring, in the very body of the act itself, that nothing out of that plain letter should be brought within the pale of treason by *inference* or *construction*, but that, if any such cases happened, they should be referred to the Parliament.

These restrictions approved by the highest authority.

This wise restriction has been the subject of much just eulogium by all the most celebrated writers on the criminal law of England. Lord Coke says the Parliament that made it was on that account called *Benedictum*, or Blessed; and the learned and virtuous Judge Hale, a bitter enemy and opposer of constructive treason, speaks of this sacred institution with that enthusiasm which it can not but inspire in the breast of every lover of the just privileges of mankind.

Definition applied to the present case.

Gentlemen, in these mild days, when juries are so free and judges so independent, perhaps all these observations might have been spared as unnecessary. But they can do no harm; and this history of treason, so honorable to England, can not (even imperfectly as I have given it) be unpleasant to Englishmen. At all events, it can not be thought an inapplicable introduction to saying that Lord George Gordon, who stands before you indicted for that crime, is not, *can not* be guilty of it, unless he has levied war against the King in his realm, contrary to the plain letter, spirit, and intention of the act of the twenty-fifth of Edward the Third—to be extended by no new or occasional construction, to be strained by no fancied analogies, to be measured by no rules of political expediency, to be judged of by no theory, to be determined by the wisdom of no individual, however wise, but to be expounded by the simple, genuine letter of the law.

The prisoner responsible only for the *original* object of the assemblage.

Gentlemen, the only overt act charged in the indictment, is the assembling the multitude, which we all of us remember went up with the petition of the Associated Protestants, on the second day of last June. In addressing myself to a humane and sensible jury of Englishmen, sitting in judgment on the life of a fellow-citizen, more especially under the direction of a court so filled as this is, I trust I need not remind you that the purposes of that multitude, as *originally* assembled on that day, and the purposes and acts of him who assembled them, are the sole objects of investigation. All the dismal consequences which followed, and which naturally link themselves with this subject in the firmest minds, must be altogether cut off, and abstracted from your attention, further than the evidence warrants their admission. If the evidence had been *co-extensive* with these consequences; if it had been proved that the same multitude, under the direction of Lord George Gordon, had afterward attacked the Bank, broke open the prisons, and set London in a conflagration, I should not now be addressing you. Do me the justice to believe that I am neither so foolish as to imagine I could have defended him, nor so profligate to wish it if I could. But when it has appeared, not only by the evidence in the cause, but by the evidence of the thing itself—by the issues of life, which may be called the evidence of Heaven—that these dreadful events were either entirely unconnected with the assembling of that multitude to attend the petition of the Protestants, or, at the very worst, the unforeseen, undesigned, unabetted, and deeply regretted consequences of it, I confess the seriousness and solemnity of this trial sink and dwindle away. Only abstract from your minds all that misfortune, accident, and the wickedness of others have brought upon the scene, and the cause requires no advocate. When I say that it requires no advocate, I mean that it requires no argument to screen it from the guilt of *treason*. For though I am perfectly convinced of the purity of my noble friend's intentions, yet I am not bound to defend his prudence, nor to set it up as a pattern for imitation; since you are not trying him for imprudence, for indiscreet zeal, or for want of foresight and precaution, but for a deliberate and malicious predetermination to overpower the laws and government of his country, by hostile, rebellious force.

The indictment charges that they were *armed*.

The indictment, therefore, first charges that the multitude assembled on the 2d of June "were armed and arrayed in a warlike manner;" which, indeed, if it had omitted to charge, we should not have troubled you with any defense at all, because no judgment could have been given on so defective an indictment. For the statute never meant to put an unarmed assembly of citizens on a footing with armed rebellion; and the crime, whatever it is, must always appear on the record to warrant the judgment of the court.

What constitutes arming and levying war.

It is certainly true that it has been held to be matter of evidence, and dependent on circumstances, what numbers, or species of equipment and order, though not the regular equipment and order of soldiers, shall constitute an army, so as to maintain the averment in the indictment of a warlike array; and, likewise, what kind of violence, though not pointed at the King's person, or the existence of the government, shall be construed to be war against the King. But as it has never yet been maintained in argument, in any court of the kingdom, or even speculated upon in theory, that a multitude, without either weapons offensive or defensive of any sort or kind, and yet not supplying the want of them by such acts of violence as multitudes sufficiently great can achieve without them, was a hostile army within the statute; as it has never been asserted by the wildest adventurer in constructive treason, that a multitude, armed with nothing, threatening nothing, and doing nothing, was an army levying war; I am entitled to say that the evidence does not support the first charge in the indictment; but that, on the contrary, it is manifestly false — false in the knowledge of the Crown, which prosecutes it—false in the knowledge of every man in London, who was not bed-ridden on Friday the 2d of June, and who saw the peaceable demeanor of the Associated Protestants.

Case of Damaree inapplicable.

But you will hear, no doubt, from the Solicitor General (for they have saved all their intelligence for the reply) that fury supplies arms; *furor arma ministrat;* and the case of Damaree[4] will, I suppose, be referred to; where the people assembled had no banners or arms, but only clubs and bludgeons: yet the ringleader, who led them on to mischief, was adjudged to be guilty of high treason for levying war. This judgment it is not my purpose to impeach, for I have no time for digression to points that do not press upon me. In the case of Damaree, the mob, though not regularly armed, were provided with such weapons as best suited their mischievous designs. Their designs were, besides, open and avowed, and all the mischief was done that could have been accomplished, if they had been in the completest armor. They burned Dissenting meeting-houses protected by law, and Damaree was taken at their head, *in flagrante delicto* [in the crime itself], with a torch in his hand, not only in the very act of destroying one of them, but leading on his followers, *in person*, to the *avowed* destruction of all the rest. There could, therefore, be no doubt of his purpose and intention, nor any great doubt that the perpetration of such purpose was, from its generality, high treason, if perpetrated by such a force as distinguishes a felonious riot from a treasonable levying of war.[5] The principal doubt, therefore, in that case was, whether such an unarmed, riotous force was *war*, within the meaning of the statute; and on that point very learned men have differed; nor shall I attempt to decide between them, because in this one point they all agree. Gentlemen, I beseech you to attend to me here. I say on this point they all agree, that it is the *intention* of assembling them which forms the guilt of treason. I will give you the words of high authority, the learned Foster, whose private opinions will, no doubt, be pressed upon you as a doctrine and law, and which, if taken together, as all opinions ought to be, and not extracted in smuggled sentences to serve a shallow trick, I am contented to consider as authority.

The *intention* constitutes the essence of the crime.

That great judge, immediately after supporting the case of Damaree, as a levying war within the statute, against the opinion of Hale in a similar case, namely, the destruction of bawdy-houses,[6] which happened in his time, says, "The true criterion, therefore, seems to be—*Quo animo* did the parties assemble?—with what intention did they meet?" On that issue, then, in which I am supported by the whole body of the criminal law of England, concerning which there are no practical precedents of the courts that clash, nor even abstract opinions of the closet that differ, I come forth with boldness to meet the Crown. For, even supposing that peaceable multitude—though not hostilely arrayed—though without one species of weapon among them—though assembled without plot or disguise by a public advertisement, exhorting, nay, commanding peace, and inviting the magistrates to be present to restore it, if broken—though composed of thousands who are now standing around you, unimpeached and unreproved, yet who are all principals in treason, if such assembly was treason; supposing, I say, this multitude to be, nevertheless, an army within the statute, still the great question would remain behind, on which the guilt or innocence of the accused must singly depend, and which it is your exclusive province to determine, namely, whether they were assembled by my noble client for the traitorous purpose charged in the indictment? For war must not only be levied, but it must be levied against the King in his realm; *i. e.*, either directly against his person to alter the Constitution of the government, of which he is the head, or to suppress the laws committed to his execution *by rebellious force*. You must find that Lord George Gordon assembled these men

[4] In this case, a mob assembled for the purpose of destroying all the Protestant Dissenting meeting-houses, and actually pulled down two.—8 State Trials, 218. Foster, 208.

[5] To constitute a treasonable levying of war there must be an insurrection; there must be force accompanying that insurrection; and it must be for an object of a general nature. Regina *v.* Frost, 9 Carrington and Payne, 129.

[6] 1 Hale, 132.

with that traitorous intention. You must find not merely a riotous, illegal petitioning—not a tumultuous, indecent importunity to influence Parliament, not the compulsion of motive, from seeing so great a body of people united in sentiment and clamorous supplication—but the absolute, unequivocal compulsion of force, from the hostile acts of numbers united in rebellious conspiracy and arms.

This is the issue you are to try, for crimes of all denominations consist wholly in the purpose of the human will producing the act. "Actus non facit reum nisi mens sit rea." The act does not constitute guilt, unless *the mind* be guilty. This is the great text from which the whole moral of penal justice is deduced. It stands at the top of the criminal page, throughout all the volumes of our humane and sensible laws, and Lord Chief Justice Coke, whose chapter on this crime is the most authoritative and masterly of all his valuable works, ends almost every sentence with an emphatical repetition of it.

The intention must be proved traitorous by some open act.

The indictment *must* charge an open *act*, because the purpose of the mind, which is the object of trial, can only be known by actions. Or, again to use the words of Foster, who has ably and accurately expressed it, "the traitorous purpose is the treason; the overt act, the means made use of to effectuate the intentions of the heart." But why should I borrow the language of Foster, or of any other man, when the language of the indictment itself is lying before our eyes? What does it say? Does it directly charge the overt act as in itself constituting the crime? No; it charges that the prisoner "maliciously and traitorously did *compass, imagine, and intend to raise and levy war and rebellion against the King;*" this is the malice prepense of treason; and that to fulfill and bring to effect *such traitorous compassings and intentions*, he did, on the day mentioned in the indictment, actually assemble them, and levy war and rebellion against the King. Thus the law, which is made to correct and punish the wickedness of the heart, and not the unconscious deeds of the body, goes up to the fountain of human agency, and arraigns the lurking mischief of the soul, dragging it to light by the evidence of open acts. The hostile *mind* is the crime; and, therefore, unless the matters that are in evidence before you do, beyond all doubt or possibility of error, convince you that the prisoner is a determined traitor *in his heart*, he is not guilty.

The same is true of homicide and other crimes.

It is the same principle which creates all the various degrees of homicide, from that which is excusable to the malignant guilt of murder. The fact is the same in all. The death of the man is the imputed crime; but the *intention* makes all the difference; and he who killed him is pronounced a murderer—a simple felon—or only an unfortunate man, as the circumstances, by which his mind has been deciphered to the jury, show it to have been cankered by deliberate wickedness, or stirred up by sudden passions.

These principles applied to the case of the prisoner.

Here an immense multitude was, beyond all doubt, assembled on the second of June. But whether HE that assembled them be guilty of high treason, of a high misdemeanor, or only of a breach of the act of King Charles the Second[7] against tumultuous petitioning (if such an act still exists), depends wholly upon the evidence of his purpose in assembling them, to be gathered by you, and by you alone, from the whole tenor of his conduct; and to be gathered, not by inference, or probability, or reasonable presumption, but, in the words of the act, *provably;* that is, in the full, unerring force of demonstration. You are called, upon your oaths, to say, *not* whether Lord George Gordon assembled the multitudes in the place charged in the indictment, for that is not denied; but whether it appears, by the facts produced in evidence for the Crown when confronted with the proofs which we have laid before you, that he assembled them in hostile array and with a hostile mind, to take the laws into his own hands by main force, and to dissolve the Constitution of the government, unless his petition should be listened to by Parliament.

That is *your* exclusive province to determine. The court can only tell you what acts the law, in its general theory, holds to be high treason, on the general assumption that such acts proceed from traitorous purposes. But they must leave it to *your* decision, and to *yours* alone, whether the acts proved appear, in the present instance, under all the circumstances, to have arisen from the causes which form the essence of this high crime.

Summation.

Gentlemen, you have now heard the law of treason; first, in the abstract, and secondly, as it applies to the general features of the case; and you have heard it with as much sincerity as if I had addressed you upon my oath from the bench where the judges sit. I declare to you solemnly, in the presence of that great Being at whose bar we must all hereafter appear, that I have used no one art of an advocate, but have acted the plain unaffected part of a Christian man, instructing the consciences of his fellow-citizens to do justice. If I have deceived you on this subject, I am myself deceived; and if I am misled through ignorance, my ignorance is incurable, for I have spared no

[7] By 13 Car. II., st. 1, c. 5, passed in consequence of the tumults on the opening of the memorable Parliament of 1640, it is provided that no petition to the King or either House of Parliament, for any alteration in Church or State, shall be signed by above twenty persons, unless the matter thereof be approved by three justices of the peace, or the major part of the grand jury in the county; and in London by the Lord Mayor, Aldermen, and Common Council: nor shall any petition be presented by more than ten persons at a time. But *under* these regulations, it is declared by the Bill of Rights, 1 W. and M., st. 2, c. 2, that the subject hath a right to petition. Lord Mansfield told the jury that the court were clearly of opinion that this statute, 13 Car. II., was not in any degree affected by the Bill of Rights, but was still in force. Dougl., 571.

pains to understand it. I am not stiff in opinions; but before I change any of those that I have given you to-day, I must see some direct monument of justice that contradicts them. For the law of England pays no respect to theories, however ingenious, or to authors, however wise; and therefore, unless you hear me refuted by a series of direct precedents, and not by vague doctrine, *if you wish to sleep in peace, follow me.*

The evidence brought to the test of these principles.

II. And now the most important part of our task begins, namely, the application of the evidence to the doctrines I have laid down. For trial is nothing more than the reference of facts to a certain rule of action, and a long recapitulation of them only serves to distract and perplex the memory, without enlightening the judgment, unless the great standard principle by which they are to be measured is fixed, and rooted in the mind. When that is done (which I am confident has been done by you), every thing worthy of observation falls naturally into its place, and the result is safe and certain.

Reasons of the restrictions on the Catholics.

Gentlemen, it is already in proof before you (indeed it is now a matter of history), that an act of Parliament passed in the session of 1778, for the repeal of certain restrictions, which the policy of our ancestors had imposed upon the Roman Catholic religion, to prevent its extension, and to render its limited toleration harmless; restrictions, imposed *not* because our ancestors took upon them to pronounce that faith to be offensive to God, but because it was incompatible with good faith to man—being utterly inconsistent with allegiance to a Protestant government, from their oaths and obligations, to which it gave them not only a release, but a crown of glory, as the reward of treachery and treason.

It was, indeed, with astonishment that I heard the Attorney General stigmatize those wise regulations of our patriot ancestors with the title of factious and cruel impositions on the consciences and liberties of their fellow-citizens. Gentlemen, they were, *at the time*, wise and salutary regulations; regulations to which this country owes its freedom, and his Majesty his crown—a crown which he wears under the strict entail of professing and protecting that religion which they were made to repress; and which I know my noble friend at the bar joins with me, and with all good men, in wishing that he and his posterity may wear forever.[8]

It is not my purpose to recall to your minds the fatal effects which bigotry has, in former days, produced in this island. I will not follow the example the Crown has set me, by making an attack upon your passions, on subjects foreign to the object before you. I will not call your attention from those flames, kindled by a villainous banditti (which they have thought fit, in defiance of evidence, to introduce), by bringing before your eyes the more cruel flames, in which the bodies of our expiring, meek, patient, Christian fathers were, little more than a century ago, consuming in Smithfield. I will not call up from the graves of martyrs all the precious holy blood that has been spilled in this land, to save its established government and its reformed religion from the secret villainy and the open force of Papists. The cause does not stand in need even of such honest arts; and I feel my heart too big voluntarily to recite such scenes, when I reflect that some of my own, and my best and dearest progenitors, from whom I glory to be descended, ended their innocent lives in prisons and in exile, *only because they were Protestants.*

These laws very suddenly repealed by Sir George Saville's bill.

Gentlemen, whether the great lights of science and of commerce, which, since those disgraceful times, have illuminated Europe, may, by dispelling these shocking prejudices, have rendered the Papists of this day as safe and trusty subjects as those who conform to the national religion established by law, I shall not take upon me to determine. It is wholly unconnected with the present inquiry. We are not trying a question either of divinity or civil policy; and I shall, therefore, not enter at all into the motives or merits of the act that produced the Protestant petition to Parliament. It was certainly introduced by persons who can not be named by any good citizen without affection and respect.[9] But this I will say, without fear of contradiction, that it was sudden and unexpected; that it passed with uncommon precipitation, considering the magnitude of the object; that it underwent no discussion; and that the heads of the Church, the constitutional guardians of the national religion, were never consulted upon it. Under such circumstances, it is no wonder that many sincere Protestants were alarmed; and they had a right to spread their apprehensions. It is the privilege and the duty of all the subjects of England to watch over their religious and civil liberties,

8 After the strong statements of Burke respecting this law (see p. 299), the reader will be surprised at these assertions of Mr. Erskine. He was probably influenced by his feelings as a Scotchman whose ancestors had been cruelly persecuted by the Catholics. Twenty-six years after, when Lord Chancellor, he was opposed to allowing Catholic officers in England to hold commissions in the army, as they had been permitted to do in Ireland since 1793; declaring that on this subject he thought "religiously and morally exactly as the King did." He here gives great prominence to his views of the original necessity of the law, confirming them by pointed references in the next paragraph to the persecuting spirit of Popery, in order to enforce his next leading thought; namely, that the Protestant Association originated in justifiable feelings, a point which was important to the defense of his client. This mode of shaping one part of his speech to prepare the way for and support of another, is one of the most admirable qualities of Mr. Erskine, and is worthy of being studied with great attention by the young orator.

9 The bill was brought in by Sir George Saville, and supported, among others, by Mr. Dunning, Mr. Thurlow, and Lord Beauchamp, and passed into an act without any opposition in the House of Commons, and with very slight opposition in the Lords, and the King was known to have been favorable to it.

and to approach either their representatives or the Throne with their fears and their complaints—a privilege which has been bought with the dearest blood of our ancestors, and which is confirmed to us by law, as our ancient birth-right and inheritance.

Origin and design of the Protestant Association.

Soon after the repeal of the act, the Protestant Association began, and, from small beginnings, extended over England and Scotland. A deed of association was signed, *by all legal means* to oppose the growth of Popery; and which of the advocates for the Crown will stand up and say that such an union was illegal? Their union was perfectly constitutional; there was no obligation of secrecy; their transactions were all public; a committee was appointed for regularity and correspondence; and circular letters were sent to all the dignitaries of the Church, inviting them to join with them in the protection of the national religion.

Lord George Gordon as its president perfectly blameless.

All this happened before Lord George Gordon was a member of, or the most distantly connected with it; for it was not till November, 1779, that the London Association made him an offer of their chair, by a unanimous resolution, communicated to him, unsought and unexpected, in a public letter, signed by the secretary in the name of the whole body; and from that day, to the day he was committed to the Tower, I will lead him by the hand in your view, that you may see there is no blame in him. Though all his behavior was unreserved and public, and though watched by wicked men for purposes of vengeance, the Crown has totally failed in giving it such a context as can justify, in the mind of any reasonable man, the conclusion it seeks to establish.

Examination of evidence for the Crown.

This will fully appear hereafter; but let us first attend to the evidence on the part of the Crown.

The first witness to support this prosecution is,

William Hay—a bankrupt in fortune he acknowledges himself to be, and I am afraid he is a bankrupt in conscience. Such a scene of impudent, ridiculous inconsistency would have utterly destroyed his credibility in the most trifling civil suit; and I am, therefore, almost ashamed to remind you of his evidence, when I reflect that you will never suffer it to glance across your minds on this solemn occasion.

This man, whom I may now, without offense or slander, point out to you as a dark Popish spy, who attended the meetings of the London Association to pervert their harmless purposes, conscious that the discovery of his character would invalidate all his testimony, endeavored at first to conceal the activity of his zeal, by denying that he had seen any of the destructive scenes imputed to the Protestants. Yet, almost in the same breath, it came out, by his own confession, that there was hardly a place, public or private, where riot had erected her standard, in which he had not been; nor a house, prison, or chapel, that was destroyed, to the demolition of which he had not been a witness. He was at Newgate, the Fleet, at Langdale's, and at Coleman Street; at the Sardinian Embassador's, and in Great Queen Street, Lincoln's Inn Fields. What took him to Coachmakers' Hall? He went there, as he told us, to watch their proceedings, because he expected no good from them; and to justify his prophecy of evil, he said, on his examination by the Crown, that, as early as December, he had heard some alarming republican language. What language did he remember? "Why, that the Lord Advocate of Scotland was called only Harry Dundas!" Finding this too ridiculous for so grave an occasion, he endeavored to put some words about the breach of the King's coronation oath[10] into the prisoner's mouth, as proceeding from himself; which it is notorious he read out of an old Scotch book, published near a century ago, on the abdication of King James the Second.

Attend to his cross-examination. He was *sure* he had seen Lord George Gordon at Greenwood's room in January; but when Mr. Kenyon, who knew Lord George had never been there, advised him to recollect himself, he desired to consult his notes. First, he is positively sure, from his memory, that he had seen him there: then he says, he can not trust his memory without referring to his papers. On looking at them, they contradict him; and he then confesses that he never saw Lord George Gordon at Greenwood's room in January, when his note was taken, *nor at any other time*. But why did he take notes? He said it was because he foresaw what would happen. How fortunate the Crown is, gentlemen, to have such friends to collect evidence by anticipation! When did he begin to take notes? He said, on the 21st of February, which was the *first* time he had been alarmed at what he had seen and heard, although, not a minute before, he had been reading a note taken at Greenwood's room in January, and had sworn that he had attended their meetings, from apprehensions of consequences, as early as December.

Mr. Kenyon, who now saw him bewildered in a maze of falsehood, and suspecting his notes to have been a villainous fabrication to give the show of correctness to his evidence, attacked him with a shrewdness for which he was wholly unprepared. You remember the witness had said that he always took notes when he attended any meetings where he expected their deliberations might be attended with dangerous consequences. "Give me one instance," says Mr. Kenyon, "in the whole course of your life, where you ever took notes before." Poor Mr. Hay was thunderstruck; the sweat ran down his face, and his countenance bespoke despair—not recollection: "Sir, I must have an instance; tell me when and where?" Gentlemen, it was now too late; *some* instance he was obliged to give, and, as it was evident to every body that he had one still to choose, I think he might have chosen a better. "*He had taken notes at the General Assembly of*

[10] Hay swore that Lord Gordon had declared that the King had broken his coronation oath.

the Church of Scotland, six-and-twenty years before!!" What! did he apprehend dangerous consequences from the deliberations of the grave elders of the Kirk? Were they levying war against the King? At last, when he is called upon to say to whom he communicated the intelligence he had collected, the spy stood confessed indeed. At first he refused to tell, saying he was his friend, and that he was not obliged to give him up; and when forced at last to speak, it came out to be Mr. Butler, a gentleman universally known, and who, from what I know of him, I may be sure never employed him, or any other spy, because he is a man every way respectable, but who certainly is not only a Papist, but the person who was employed in all their proceedings, to obtain the late indulgences from Parliament.[11] He said Mr. Butler was his particular friend, yet professed himself ignorant of his religion. I am sure he could not be desired to conceal it. Mr. Butler makes no secret of his religion. It is no reproach to any man who lives the life he does. But Mr. Hay thought it of moment to his own credit in the cause, that he himself might be thought a Protestant, unconnected with Papists, and not a Popish spy.

So ambitious, indeed, was the miscreant of being useful in this odious character, through every stage of the cause, that, after staying a little in St. George's Fields, he ran home to his own house in St. Dunstan's church-yard, and got upon the leads, where he swore he saw *the very same man* carrying *the very same flag* he had seen in the fields. Gentlemen, whether the petitioners employed the same standard-man through the whole course of their peaceable procession is certainly totally immaterial to the cause, but the circumstance is material to show the wickedness of the man. "How," says Mr. Kenyon, "do you know that it was the same person you saw in the fields? Were you acquainted with him?" "No." "How then?" "Why, he looked like a brewer's servant." *Like a brewer's servant!* "What, were they not all in their Sunday's clothes?" "Oh! yes, they were all in their Sunday's clothes." "Was the man with the flag then alone in the dress of his trade?" "No." "Then how do you know he was a brewer's servant?" Poor Mr. Hay!—nothing but sweat and confusion again! At last, after a hesitation, which every body thought would have ended in his running out of court, he said, "he knew him to be a brewer's servant, *because there was something particular in the cut of his coat, the cut of his breeches, and the cut of his stockings!"*

You see, gentlemen, by what strange means villainy is detected. Perhaps he might have escaped from me, but he sunk under that shrewdness and sagacity, which ability, without long habits, does not provide. Gentlemen, you will not, I am sure, forget, whenever you see a man about whose apparel there is any thing particular, to set him down for a *brewer's servant.*

Mr. Hay afterward went to the lobby of the House of Commons. What took him there? He thought himself in danger; and therefore, says Mr. Kenyon, you thrust yourself voluntarily into the very center of danger. That would not do. Then he had a particular friend, whom he knew to be in the lobby, and whom he apprehended to be in danger. "Sir, who was that particular friend? Out with it. Give us his name instantly." All in confusion again. Not a word to say for himself; and the name of this person who had the honor of Mr. Hay's friendship, will probably remain a secret forever.[12]

It may be asked, are these circumstances material? and the answer is obvious: they are material; because, when you see a witness running into every hole and corner of falsehood, and, as fast as he is made to bolt out of one, taking cover in another, you will never give credit to what that man relates, as to any possible matter which is to affect the life or reputation of a fellow-citizen accused before you. God forbid that you should. I might, therefore, get rid of this wretch altogether without making a single remark on that part of his testimony which bears upon the issue you are trying; but the Crown shall have the full benefit of it all. I will defraud it of nothing he has said. Notwithstanding all his folly and wickedness, let us for the present take it to be true, and see what it amounts to. What is it he states to have passed at Coachmakers' Hall? That Lord George Gordon desired the multitude to behave with unanimity and firmness, as the Scotch had done. Gentlemen, there is no manner of doubt that the Scotch behaved with unanimity and firmness in resisting the relaxation of the penal laws against Papists, and that by that unanimity and firmness they succeeded;[13] but it was by the *constitutional* unanimity and firmness of the great body of the people of Scotland whose example Lord George Gordon recommended, and not by the riots and burning which they attempted to prove had been committed in Edinburgh in 1778.

I will tell you myself, gentlemen, as one of the people of Scotland, that there then existed, and still exist, eighty-five societies of Protestants, who have been, and still are, uniformly firm in opposing every change in that system of laws established to secure the Revolution; and Parliament gave way in Scotland to their united voice, and not to the fire brands of the rabble. It is the duty of Parliament to listen to the voice of the people, for they are the servants of the people. And when the Constitution of church or state is believed, whether truly or falsely, to be in danger, I hope there never will be wanting men (notwithstanding the proceedings of to-day) to desire the people to persevere and be firm. Gentlemen, has the Crown proved that the Protestant brethren of the London Association fired the mass-

11 Mr. Charles Butler, author of the Reminiscences.

12 Nothing could be finer than the way in which Mr. Erskine sifts this evidence and detects its falsehood.

13 The violent popular opposition manifested toward the proposed act extending the Roman Catholic Relief Bill to Scotland, caused it to be abandoned.

houses in Scotland or acted in rebellious opposition to law, so as to entitle it to wrest the prisoner's expressions into an excitation of rebellion against the state, or of violence against the properties of English Papists, by setting up their firmness as an example? Certainly not. They have not even proved the naked fact of such violences, though such proof would have called for no resistance; since to make it bear as rebellious advice to the Protestant Association of London, it must have been first shown that such acts had been perpetrated or encouraged by the Protestant societies in the North.

Who has dared to say this? No man. The rabble in Scotland certainly did that which has since been done by the rabble in England, to the disgrace and reproach of both countries. But in neither country was there found one man of character or condition, of any description, who abetted such enormities, nor any man, high or low, of any of the Associated Protestants, here or there, who were either convicted, tried, or taken on suspicion.

As to what this man heard on the 29th of May, it was nothing more than the proposition of going up in a body to St. George's Fields to consider how the petition should be presented, with the same exhortations to firmness as before. The resolution made on the motion has been read, and when I come to state the evidence on the part of my noble friend, I will show you the impossibility of supporting any criminal inference from what Mr. Hay afterward puts in his mouth in the lobby, even taking it to be true. I wish here to be accurate [looking on a card on which he had taken down his words]. He says: "Lord George desired them to continue steadfastly to adhere to so good a cause as theirs was; promised to persevere in it himself, and hoped, though there was little expectation at present from the House of Commons that they would meet with redress from their *mild and gracious Sovereign*, who, no doubt, would recommend it to his ministers to repeal it." This was all he heard, and I will show you how this wicked man himself (if any belief is to be given to him) entirely overturns and brings to the ground the evidence of Mr. Bowen,[14] on which the Crown rests singly for the proof of words which are more difficult to explain. Gentlemen, was this the language of rebellion? If a multitude were at the gates of the House of Commons to command and insist on a repeal of this law, why encourage their hopes by reminding them that they had a mild and gracious Sovereign? If war was levying against him, there was no occasion for his mildness and graciousness. If he had said, "Be firm and persevere, we shall meet with redress from the *prudence* of the Sovereign," it might have borne a different construction; because, whether he was gracious or severe, his prudence might lead him to submit to the necessity of the times. The words sworn to were, therefore, perfectly clear and unambiguous—"Persevere in your zeal and supplications, and you will meet with redress from a mild and gracious King, who will recommend it to his ministers to repeal it." Good God! if they were to wait till the King, whether from benevolence or fear, should direct his minister to influence the proceedings of Parliament, how does it square with the charge of instant coercion or intimidation of the House of Commons? If the multitude were assembled with the premeditated design of producing immediate repeal by terror or arms, is it possible to suppose that their leader would desire them to be quiet, and refer them to those qualities of the Prince, which, however eminently they might belong to him, never could be exerted on subjects in rebellion to his authority? In what a labyrinth of nonsense and contradiction do men involve themselves, when, forsaking the rules of evidence, they would draw conclusions from words in contradiction to language and in defiance of common sense?

The next witness that is called to you by the Crown is Mr. Metcalf. He was not in the lobby, but speaks only to the meeting in Coachmakers' Hall, on the 29th of May, and in St. George's Fields. He says that at the former, Lord George reminded them that the Scotch had succeeded by their unanimity—and hoped that no one who had signed the petition would be ashamed or afraid to show himself in the cause; that he was ready to go to the gallows for it; that he would not present the petition of a lukewarm people; that he desired them to come to St. George's Fields, distinguished with blue cockades, and that they should be marshaled in four divisions. Then he speaks to having seen them in the fields in the order which has been described; and Lord George Gordon in a coach surrounded by a vast concourse of people, with blue ribbons, forming like soldiers, but was not near enough to hear whether the prisoner spoke to them or not. Such is Mr. Metcalf's evidence; and after the attention you have honored me with, and which I shall have occasion so often to ask again on the same subject, I shall trouble you with but one observation, namely, that it can not, without absurdity, be supposed that if the assembly at Coachmakers' Hall had been such conspirators as they are represented, their doors would have been open to strangers, like this witness, to come in to report their proceedings.

The next witness is Mr. Anstruther,[15] who speaks to the language and deportment of the noble prisoner, both at Coachmakers' Hall, on the 29th of May, and afterward on the 2d of June, in the lobby of the House of Commons. It will be granted to me, I am sure, even by the advocates of the Crown, that this gentleman, not only from the clearness and consistency of his testimony, but from his rank and character in the world, is infinitely more worthy of credit than Mr. Hay, who went before him. And from the circumstances of irritation and confusion under which the Rev. Mr. Bowen confessed himself to have heard and seen, what he told you he heard

[14] The Chaplain of the House of Commons.

[15] This gentleman was a member of Parliament.

and saw, I may likewise assert, without any offense to the reverend gentleman, and without drawing any parallel between their credits, that where their accounts of this transaction differ, the preference is due to the former. Mr. Anstruther very properly prefaced his evidence with this declaration: "I do not mean to speak accurately to words; it is impossible to recollect them at this distance of time." I believe I have used his very expression, and such expression it well became him to use in a *case of blood.* But words, even if they could be accurately remembered, are to be admitted with great reserve and caution, when the purpose of the speaker is to be measured by them. They are transient and fleeting; frequently the effect of a sudden transport, easily misunderstood, and often unconsciously misrepresented. It may be the fate of the most innocent language to appear ambiguous, or even malignant, when related in mutilated, detached passages, by people to whom it is not addressed, and who know nothing of the previous design either of the speaker or of those to whom he spoke. Mr. Anstruther says that he heard Lord George Gordon desire the petitioners to meet him on the Friday following, in St. George's Fields, and that if there were fewer than twenty thousand people, he would not present the petition, as it would not be of consequence enough; and that he recommended to them the example of the Scotch, who, by their firmness, had carried their point.

Gentlemen, I have already admitted that they did by firmness carry it. But has Mr. Anstruther attempted to state any one expression that fell from the prisoner to justify the positive, unerring conclusion, or even the presumption, that the firmness of the Scotch Protestants, by which the point was carried in Scotland, was the resistance and riots of the rabble? No, gentlemen; he singly states the words, as he heard them in the hall on the 29th, and all that he afterward speaks to in the lobby, repels so harsh and dangerous a construction. The words sworn to at Coachmakers' Hall are, "that he recommended temperance and firmness." Gentlemen, if his motives are to be judged by words, for Heaven's sake let these words carry their popular meaning in language. Is it to be presumed, without proof, that a man means *one* thing because he says *another?* Does the exhortation to temperance and firmness apply most naturally to the constitutional resistance of the Protestants of Scotland, or to the outrages of ruffians who pulled down the houses of their neighbors? Is it possible, with decency, to say, in a court of justice, that the recommendation of temperance is the excitation to villainy and frenzy? But the words, it seems, are to be construed, not from their own signification, but from that which follows them, viz., "by that the Scotch carried their point." Gentlemen, is it in evidence before you that by rebellion the Scotch carried their point? or that the indulgences to Papists were not extended to Scotland because the rabble had opposed their extension? Has the Crown authorized either the court or its law servants to tell you so? Or can it be decently maintained that Parliament was so weak or infamous as to yield to a wretched mob of vagabonds at Edinburgh what it has since refused to the earnest prayers of a hundred thousand Protestants of London? No, gentlemen of the jury, Parliament was not, I hope, so abandoned. But the ministers knew that the Protestants of Scotland were to a man abhorrent of that law. And though they never held out resistance, if government should be disposed to cram it down their throats by force, yet such violence to the united sentiments of a whole people appeared to be a measure so obnoxious, so dangerous, and withal so unreasonable, that it was wisely and judiciously dropped, to satisfy the general wishes of the nation, and not to avert the vengeance of those low incendiaries whose misdeeds have rather been talked of than proved.

Thus, gentlemen, the exculpation of Lord George's conduct on the 29th of May is sufficiently established by the very evidence on which the Crown asks you to convict him. For, in recommending *temperance and firmness after the example of Scotland*, you can not be justified in pronouncing that he meant more than the firmness of the grave and respectable people in that country, to whose constitutional firmness the Legislature had before acceded, instead of branding it with the title of rebellion; and who, in my mind, deserve thanks from the King for temperately and firmly resisting every innovation which they conceived to be dangerous to the national religion, independently of which his Majesty (without a new limitation by Parliament) has no more title to the crown than I have.

Such, gentlemen, is the whole amount of all my noble friend's previous communication with the petitioners, whom he afterward assembled to consider how their petition should be presented. This is all, not only that men of credit can tell you on the part of the prosecution, but all that even the worst vagabond who ever appeared in a court—the very scum of the earth—thought himself safe in saying, upon oath, on the present occasion. Indeed, gentlemen, when I consider my noble friend's situation, his open, unreserved temper, and his warm and animated zeal for a cause which rendered him obnoxious to so many wicked men—speaking daily and publicly to mixed multitudes of friends and foes, on a subject which affected his passions—I confess I am astonished that no other expressions than those in evidence before you have found their way into this court. That they have not found their way is surely a most satisfactory proof that there was nothing in his heart which even youthful zeal could magnify into guilt, or that want of caution could betray.

Gentlemen, Mr. Anstruther's evidence, when he speaks of the lobby of the House of Commons, is very much to be attended to. He says, "I saw Lord George leaning over the gallery," which position, joined with what he mentioned of his talking with the chaplain, marks the time, and casts a strong doubt on Bowen's testimony, which you will find stands, in this only material part of it, single and unsupported. "I then heard him," continues Mr. Anstruther, "tell them they had been called a mob in the House, and that peace-officers had been sent to disperse them (peaceable petitioners); but that by steadiness and firmness they might carry their point; as he had no doubt his Majesty, who was a gracious prince, would send to his ministers to repeal the act, when he heard his subjects were coming up for miles round, and wishing its repeal." How coming up? In rebellion and arms to compel it? No! all is still put on the *graciousness* of the Sovereign, in listening to the unanimous wishes of his people. If the multitude then assembled had been brought together to intimidate the House by their firmness, or to coerce it by their numbers, it was ridiculous to look forward to the King's influence over it, when the collection of future multitudes should induce him to employ it. The expressions were therefore quite unambiguous; nor could malice itself have suggested another construction of them, were it not for the fact that the House was at that time surrounded, not by the petitioners, whom the noble prisoner had assembled, but by a mob who had mixed with them, and who, therefore, when addressed by him, were instantly set down as his followers. He thought he was addressing the sober members of the association, who, by steadiness and perseverance, could understand nothing more than perseverance in that conduct he had antecedently prescribed, as steadiness signifies a uniformity, not a change of conduct; and I defy the Crown to find out a single expression, from the day he took the chair at the association to the day I am speaking of, that justifies any other construction of steadiness and firmness than that which I put upon it before.

What would be the feelings of our venerable ancestors, who framed the statute of treasons to prevent their children being drawn into the snares of death, unless *provably* convicted by overt acts, if they could hear us disputing whether it was treason to desire harmless, unarmed men to be firm and of good heart, and to trust to the graciousness of their King?

Here Mr. Anstruther closes his evidence, which leads me to Mr. Bowen, who is the only man—I beseech you, gentlemen of the jury, to attend to this circumstance—Mr. Bowen is the only man who has attempted, directly or indirectly, to say that Lord George Gordon uttered a syllable to the multitude in the lobby concerning the destruction of the mass-houses in Scotland. Not one of the Crown's witnesses; not even the wretched, abandoned Hay, who was kept, as he said, in the lobby the whole afternoon, from anxiety for his pretended friend, has ever glanced at any expression resembling it. They all finish with the expectation which he held out, from a mild and gracious Sovereign. Mr. Bowen alone goes on further, and speaks of the successful riots of the Scotch. But he speaks of them in such a manner, as, so far from conveying the hostile idea, which he seemed sufficiently desirous to convey, tends directly to wipe off the dark hints and insinuations which have been made to supply the place of proof upon that subject—a subject which should not have been touched on without the fullest support of evidence, and where nothing but the most unequivocal evidence ought to have been received. He says, "his Lordship began by bidding them be quiet, peaceable, and steady"—not "*steady*" alone; though, if that had been the expression, singly by itself, I should not be afraid to meet it; but, "*Be quiet,* PEACEABLE, *and steady.*" Gentlemen, I am indifferent what other expressions of dubious interpretation are mixed with these. For you are trying whether my noble friend came to the House of Commons with a decidedly hostile mind; and as I shall, on the recapitulation of our own evidence, trace him in your view, without spot or stain, down to the very moment when the imputed words were spoken, you will hardly forsake the whole innocent context of his behavior, and torture your inventions to collect the blackest system of guilt, starting up in a moment, without being previously concerted, or afterward carried into execution.

First, what are the words by which you are to be convinced that the Legislature was to be frightened into compliance, and to be coerced if terror should fail? "Be quiet, *peaceable*, and steady; you are a good people; yours is a good cause: his Majesty is a *gracious* monarch, and when he hears that all his people, ten miles round, are collecting, he will send to his ministers to repeal the act." By what rules of construction can such an address to unarmed, defenseless men be tortured into treasonable guilt? It is impossible to do it without pronouncing, even in the total absence of all proof of fraud or deceit in the speaker, that *quiet* signifies *tumult and uproar*, and that *peace* signifies *war and rebellion.*

I have before observed that it was most important for you to remember that, with this exhortation to quiet and confidence in the King, the evidence of all the other witnesses closed. Even Mr. Anstruther, who was a long time afterward in the lobby, heard nothing further; so that if Mr. Bowen had been out of the case altogether, what would the amount have been? Why, simply, that Lord George Gordon, having assembled an unarmed, inoffensive multitude in St. George's Fields, to present a petition to Parliament, and finding them becoming tumultuous, to the discontent of Parliament and the discredit of the cause, desired them not to give it up, but to continue to show their zeal for the legal object in which they were engaged; to manifest that zeal *quietly and peaceably*, and not to despair of success; since, though the House was not disposed to listen to it, they had a gracious Sovereign, who would second the wishes of his people. This is the sum and substance of the whole. They were not, even by any one ambiguous expression, encouraged to trust to their numbers, as sufficient to overawe the House, or to their strength to compel it, or to the prudence of the state in yielding to necessity, but to the indulgence of the King, in compliance with the wishes of his people. Mr. Bowen, however, thinks proper to proceed; and I beg that you will attend to the sequel of his evidence. He stands single in all the rest that he says, which might entitle me to ask you absolutely to reject it. But I have no objection to your believing every word of it, *if you can:* because, if inconsistencies prove any thing, they prove that there was nothing of that deliberation in the prisoner's expressions which can justify the inference of guilt. I mean to be correct as to his words [*looking at his words which he had noted down*]. He says "that Lord George told the people that an attempt had been made to introduce the bill into Scotland, and that they had no redress till the mass-houses were pulled down. That Lord Weymouth[16] then sent official assurances that it should not be extended to them." Gentlemen, why is Mr. Bowen called by the Crown to tell you this? The reason is plain: because the Crown, conscious that it could make no case of treason from the rest of the evidence, in sober judgment of law; aware that it had proved no purpose or act of force against the House of Commons, to give countenance to the accusation, much less to warrant a conviction, found it necessary to hold up the noble prisoner as the wicked and cruel author of all those calamities in which every man's passions might be supposed to come in to assist his judgment to decide. They therefore made him speak in enigmas to the multitude: not telling them *to do* mischief in order to succeed, but that *by* mischief in Scotland success had been obtained.

But were the mischiefs themselves that did happen here of a sort to support such a conclusion? Can any man living, for instance, believe that Lord George Gordon could possibly have excited the mob to destroy the house of that great and venerable magistrate, who has presided so long in this high tribunal that the oldest of us do not remember him with any other impression than the awful form and figure of justice: a magistrate who had always been the friend of the Protestant Dissenters against the ill-timed jealousies of the Establishment—his countryman, too—and, without adverting to the partiality not unjustly imputed to men of that country, a man of whom any country might be proud? No, gentlemen, it is not credible that a man of noble birth and liberal education (unless agitated by the most implacable personal resentment which is not imputed to the prisoner) could possibly consent to the burning of the house of Lord Mansfield.[17]

If Mr. Bowen, therefore, had ended here, I can hardly conceive such a construction could be decently hazarded consistent with the testimony of the witnesses we have called. How much less, when, after the dark insinuations which such expressions might otherwise have been argued to convey, the very same person, on whose veracity or memory they are only to be believed, and who must be credited or discredited *in toto*, takes out the sting himself by giving them such an immediate context and conclusion as renders the proposition ridiculous, which his evidence is brought forward to establish; for he says that Lord George Gordon instantly afterward addressed himself thus: "Beware of evil-minded persons who may mix among you and do mischief, the blame of which will be imputed to you."

Gentlemen, if you reflect on the slander which I told you fell upon the Protestants in Scotland by the acts of the rabble there, I am sure you will see the words are capable of an easy explanation. But as Mr. Bowen concluded with telling you that he heard them in the midst of noise and confusion, and as I can only take them from *him*, I shall not make an attempt to collect them into one consistent discourse, so as to give them a decided meaning in favor of my client, because I have repeatedly told you that words imperfectly heard and partially related can not be so reconciled. But this I will say—that he must be a ruffian, and not a lawyer, who would dare to tell an English jury that such ambiguous words, hemmed closely in between others not only innocent but meritorious, are to be adopted to constitute guilt, by rejecting both introduction and sequel, with which they are absolutely irreconcilable and inconsistent: For if ambiguous words, when coupled with actions, decipher the mind of the actor, so as to establish the presumption of guilt, will not such as are plainly innocent and unambiguous go as far to repel such presumption? Is innocence more difficult of proof than the most malignant wickedness? Gentlemen, I see your minds revolt at such shocking propositions. I beseech you to forgive me. I am afraid that my zeal has led me to offer observations which I ought in justice to have believed every honest mind would suggest to itself with pain and abhorrence without being illustrated and enforced.

I now come more minutely to the evidence on the part of the prisoner.

Examination of the evidence for the prisoner.

I before told you that it was not till November, 1779, when the Protestant Association was already fully established, that Lord George Gordon was elected President by the unanimous voice of the whole body, unlooked for and unsolicited. It is surely not an immaterial circumstance that at the very first meeting where his Lordship presided, a dutiful and respectful petition, the same which was afterward presented to Parliament, was read and approved of; a petition which, so far from containing any thing threatening or offensive, con-

[16] Then Secretary for the Southern Department.

[17] This reference to Lord Mansfield, then seated on the bench as presiding judge at the age of eighty-six, is not only appropriate and beautiful in itself, but, as managed by Mr. Erskine, forms a most convincing proof in favor of Lord George Gordon. This was one of Mr. Erskine's excellences, that he never went out of his case for an illustration or a picture which refreshed the mind, but he brought back with him an ***argument***.

veyed not a very oblique reflection upon the behavior of the people in Scotland. It states, that as England and that country were now one, and as official assurances had been given that the law should not pass there, they hoped the *peaceable* and *constitutional deportment of the English* Protestants would entitle them to the approbation of Parliament.

It appears by the evidence of Mr. Erasmus Middleton,[18] a very respectable clergyman, and one of the committee of the Association, that a meeting had been held on the 4th of May, at which Lord George was not present; that at that meeting a motion had been made for going up with the petition in a body, but which not being regularly put from the chair, no resolution was come to upon it; and that it was likewise agreed on, but in the same irregular manner, that there should be no other public meeting previous to the presenting the petition. That this last resolution occasioned great discontent, and that Lord George was applied to by a large and respectable number of the Association to call another meeting, to consider of the most prudent and respectful method of presenting their petition: but it appears that, before he complied with their request, he consulted with the committee on the propriety of compliance, who all agreeing to it except the Secretary, his Lordship advertised the meeting which was afterward held on the 29th of May. The meeting was, therefore, the act of the *whole* Association. As to the original difference between my noble friend and the committee on the expediency of the measure, it is totally immaterial; since Mr. Middleton, who was one of the number who differed from him on that subject (and whose evidence is, therefore, infinitely more to be relied on), told you that his whole deportment was so clear and unequivocal, as to entitle him to assure you on his most solemn oath, that he in his conscience believed his views were perfectly constitutional and pure. This most respectable clergyman further swears that he attended all the previous meetings of the society, from the day the prisoner became President to the day in question; and that, knowing they were objects of much jealousy and malice, he watched his behavior with anxiety, lest his zeal should furnish matter for misrepresentation; but that he never heard an expression escape him which marked a disposition to violate the duty and subordination of a subject, or which could lead any man to believe that his objects were different from the avowed and legal objects of the Association. We could have examined thousands to the same fact, for, as I told you when I began to speak, I was obliged to leave my place to disencumber myself from their names.

This evidence of Mr. Middleton's as to the 29th of May, must, I should think, convince every man how dangerous and unjust it is in witnesses, however perfect their memories, or however great their veracity, to come into a criminal court where a man is standing for his life or death, retailing scraps of sentences which they had heard by thrusting themselves, from curiosity, into places where their business did not lead them; ignorant of the views and tempers of both speakers and hearers, attending only to a part, and, perhaps innocently, misrepresenting that part, from not having heard the whole.

The witnesses for the Crown all tell you that Lord George said he would not go up with the petition unless he was attended by twenty thousand people who had signed it. There they think proper to stop, as if he had said nothing further; leaving you to say to yourselves, what possible purpose could he have in assembling such a multitude on the very day the House was to receive the petition? Why should he urge it, when the committee had before thought it inexpedient? And why should he refuse to present it unless so attended? Hear what Mr. Middleton says. He tells you that my noble friend informed the petitioners that if it was decided they were *not* to attend to consider how their petition should be presented, he would with the greatest pleasure go up with it *alone*. But that, if it was resolved they should attend it in person, he expected twenty thousand at the least should meet him in St. George's Fields, for that otherwise the petition would be considered as a forgery; it having been thrown out in the House and elsewhere that the repeal of the bill was not the serious wish of the people at large, and that the petition was a mere list of names on parchment, and not of men in sentiment. Mr. Middleton added, that Lord George adverted to the same objections having been made to many other petitions, and he, therefore, expressed an anxiety to show Parliament how many were actually interested in its success, which he reasonably thought would be a strong inducement to the House to listen to it. The language imputed to him falls in most naturally with this purpose: "I wish Parliament to see who and what you are; dress yourselves in your best clothes"—which Mr. Hay (who, I suppose, had been reading the indictment) thought it would be better to call "ARRAY YOURSELVES." He desired that not a stick should be seen among them, and that, if any man insulted another, or was guilty of any breach of the peace, he was to be given up to the magistrates. Mr. Attorney General, to persuade you that this was all color and deceit, says, "How was a magistrate to face forty thousand men? How were offenders in such a multitude to be amenable to the civil power?" What a shameful perversion of a plain, peaceable purpose! To be sure, if the multitude had been assembled to resist the magistrate, offenders could not be secured. But they themselves were ordered to apprehend all offenders among them, and to deliver them up to justice. They themselves were to surrender their fellows to civil authority if they offended.

The prisoner can not be censured without condemning the government.

But it seems that Lord George ought to have foreseen that so great a multitude could not be collected without mischief. Gentlemen, we are not trying whether he might or ought to

[18] The first witness called for the prisoner.

have foreseen mischief, but whether he wickedly and traitorously *preconcerted and designed it.* But if *he* be an object of censure for not foreseeing it, what shall we say to GOVERNMENT, that took no step to prevent it, that issued no proclamation, warning the people of the danger and illegality of such an assembly? If a peaceable multitude, with a petition in their hands, be an army, and if the noise and confusion inseparable from numbers, though without violence or the purpose of violence, constitute war, what shall be said of that GOVERNMENT which remained from Tuesday to Friday, knowing that an army was collecting to levy war by public advertisement, yet had not a single soldier, no, nor even a constable, to protect the state?

Gentlemen, I come forth to do that for government which its own servant, the Attorney General, has not done. I come forth to rescue it from the eternal infamy which would fall upon its head, if the language of its own advocate were to be believed. But government has an unanswerable defense. It neither did nor could possibly enter into the head of any man in authority to prophesy—human wisdom could not divine that wicked and desperate men, taking advantage of the occasion which, perhaps, an imprudent zeal for religion had produced, would dishonor the cause of all religions, by the disgraceful acts which followed.

Why, then, is it to be said that Lord George Gordon is a traitor, who, without proof of any hostile purpose to the government of his country, only did not foresee *what no body else foresaw*—what those people whose business it is to foresee every danger that threatens the state, and to avert it by the interference of magistracy, though they could not but read the advertisement, neither did nor could possibly apprehend?[19]

Answer to the pretense of deception on the part of the prisoner.

How are these observations attempted to be answered? Only by asserting, without evidence or even reasonable argument, that all this was color and deceit. Gentlemen, I again say that it is scandalous and reproachful, and not to be justified by any duty which can possibly belong to an advocate at the bar of an English court of justice, to declare, without any proof or attempt at proof, that all a man's expressions, however peaceable, however quiet, however constitutional, however loyal, are all fraud and villainy. Look, gentlemen, to the issues of life, which I before called the evidence of Heaven: I call them so still. Truly may I call them so, when, out of a book compiled by the Crown from the petition in the House of Commons, and containing the names of all who signed it, and which was printed in order to prevent any of that number being summoned upon the jury to try this indictment, *not one criminal, or even a suspected name is to be found, among this defamed host of petitioners!*

After this, gentlemen, I think the Crown ought, in decency, to be silent. I see the effect this circumstance has upon you, and I know I am warranted in my assertion of the fact. If I am not, why did not the Attorney General produce the record of some convictions, and compare it with the list? I thank them, therefore, for the precious compilation, which, though they did not produce, they can not stand up and deny.

Solomon [Job] says, "Oh that mine adversary had written a book!" My adversary *has* written a book, and out of it I am entitled to pronounce, that it can not again be decently asserted that Lord George Gordon, in exhorting an innocent and unimpeached multitude to be peaceable and quiet, was exciting them to violenee against the state.

What is the evidence, then, on which this connection with the mob is to be proved? *Only that they had blue cockades.*[20] Are you or am I answerable for every man who wears a blue cockade? If a man commits murder in my livery or in yours, without command, counsel, or consent, is the murder ours? In all *cumulative*, constructive treasons, you are to judge from the tenor of a man's behavior, not from crooked and disjointed parts of it. "Nemo repente fuit turpissimus."[21] No man can possibly be guilty of *this* crime by a sudden impulse of the mind, as he may of some others; and, certainly, Lord George Gordon stands upon the evidence at Coachmakers' Hall as pure and white as snow. He stands so upon the evidence of a man who had differed with him as to the expediency of his conduct, yet who swears that from the time he took the chair till the period which is the subject of inquiry, there was no blame in him.

You, therefore, are bound as Christian men to believe that, when he came to St. George's Fields that morning, he did not come there with the hostile purpose of repealing a law by rebellion.

But still it seems all his behavior at Coachmakers' Hall was color and deceit. Let us see, therefore, whether this body of men, when assembled, answered the description of that which I have stated to be the purpose of him who assembled them. Were they a multitude arrayed for terror or force? On the contrary, you have heard, upon the evidence of men whose veracity is not to be impeached, that they were sober, decent, quiet, peaceable tradesmen; that they were all of the better sort; all well-dressed and well-behaved; and that there was not a man among them who had any one weapon, offensive or defensive. Sir Philip Jennings Clerke[22] tells

[19] This was the great turning-point of the case, and it would have been impossible to state it in more simple or more powerful terms.

[20] The members of the Association, at the meeting of St. George's Fields, were distinguished by wearing cockades, on which were inscribed the words "No Popery!"

[21] No one has ever at once reached the extreme point of wickedness.

[22] This gentleman, in giving evidence on behalf of the prisoner, deposed to the peaceable behavior of the members of the Association, who formed the original procession to carry up the petition, and whom he distinguished from the mob which after

you, he went into the Fields; that he drove through them, talked to many individuals among them, who all told him that it was not their wish to persecute the Papists, but that they were alarmed at the progress of their religion from their schools. Sir Philip further told you, that he never saw a more peaceable multitude in his life; and it appears upon the oaths of all who were present,[23] that Lord George Gordon went round among them, desiring peace and quietness.

Mark his conduct, when he heard from Mr. Evans[24] that a low, riotous set of people were assembled in Palace Yard. Mr. Evans, being a member of the Protestant Association, and being desirous that nothing bad might happen from the assembly, went in his carriage with Mr. Spinage to St. George's Fields, to inform Lord George that there were such people assembled (probably Papists), who were determined to do mischief. The moment he told him of what he heard, whatever his original plan might have been, he instantly changed it on seeing the impropriety of it. "Do you intend," said Mr. Evans, "to carry up all these men with the petition to the House of Commons?" "Oh no! no! not by any means; I do not mean to carry them all up." "Will you give me leave," said Mr. Evans, "to go round to the different divisions, and tell the people it is not your Lordship's purpose?" He answered, "By all means." And Mr. Evans accordingly went, but it was impossible to guide such a number of people, peaceable as they were. They were all desirous to go forward; and Lord George was at last obliged to leave the Fields, exhausted with heat and fatigue, beseeching them to be peaceable and quiet. Mrs. Whitingham set him down at the House of Commons; and at the very time that he thus left them in perfect harmony and good order, it appears, by the evidence of Sir Philip Jennings Clerke, that Palace Yard was in an uproar, filled with mischievous boys and the lowest dregs of the people.

Gentlemen, I have all along told you that the Crown was aware that it had no case of treason, without connecting the noble prisoner with consequences, which it was in some luck to find advocates to state, without proof to support it. I can only speak for myself, that, small as my chance is (as times go) of ever arriving at high office, I would not accept of it on the terms of being obliged to produce against a fellow-citizen that which I have been witness to this day. For Mr. Attorney General perfectly well knew the innocent and laudable motive with which the *protection* was given, that he exhibited as an evidence of guilt;[25] yet it was produced to insinuate that Lord George Gordon, knowing himself to be the ruler of those villains, set himself up as a savior from their fury. We called Lord Stormont to explain this matter to you, who told you that Lord George Gordon came to Buckingham House, and begged to see the King, saying, he might be of great use in quelling the riots; and can there be on earth a greater proof of conscious innocence? For if he had been the wicked mover of them, would he have gone to the King to have confessed it, by offering to recall his followers from the mischiefs he had provoked? No! But since, notwithstanding a public protest issued by himself and the Association, reviling the authors of mischief, the Protestant cause was still made the pretext, he thought his public exertions might be useful, as they might tend to remove the prejudices which wicked men had diffused. The King thought so likewise, and therefore (as appears by Lord Stormont) refused to see Lord George till he had given the test of his loyalty by such exertions. But sure I am, our gracious sovereign meant no trap for innocence, nor ever recommended it as such to his servants.

Paper given by the prisoner to protect a house from being burned.

Lord George's language was simply this: "The multitude pretend to be perpetrating these acts, under the authority of the Protestant petition; I assure your Majesty they are not the Protestant Association, and I shall be glad to be of any service in suppressing them." I say, BY GOD, that man is a ruffian who shall, after this, presume to build upon such honest, artless conduct, as an evidence of guilt.[26] Gentlemen, if

ward assembled tumultuously about the House of Commons.

[23] Sir James Lowther, another of the prisoner's witnesses, proved that Lord George Gordon and Sir Philip Jennings Clerke accompanied him in his carriage from the House, and the former entreated the multitudes collected to disperse quietly to their homes.

[24] A surgeon, who also was examined for the defense, and deposed that he saw Lord George Gordon in the midst of one of the companies in St. George's Fields, and that it appeared his wish at that time, from his conduct and expressions, that, to prevent all disorder, he should not be attended by the multitude across Westminster Bridge. This gentleman's evidence was confirmed by that of other witnesses.

[25] A witness, of the name of Richard Pond, called in support of the prosecution, had sworn that, hearing his house was about to be pulled down, he applied to the prisoner for protection, and in consequence received the following document signed by him: "All true friends to Protestants, I hope, will be particular, and do no injury to the property of any true Protestant, as I am well assured the proprietor of this house is a staunch and worthy friend to the cause.—G. GORDON."

[26] The effect produced on the jury and spectators by this sudden burst of feeling, is represented by eye-witnesses to have been such as to baffle all powers of description. It was wholly unpremeditated, the instantaneous result of that sympathy which exists between a successful speaker and his audience. In uttering this appeal to his Maker, Mr. Erskine's tone was one of awe and deep reverence, without the slightest approach toward the profane use of the words, but giving them all the solemnity of a judicial oath. The magic of his eye, gesture, and countenance beaming with emotion, completed the impression, and made it irresistible. It was a thing which no man could do but once in his life. Mr. Erskine attempted it again in the House of Commons, and utterly failed.

Lord George Gordon had been guilty of high treason (as is assumed to-day) in the face of the whole Parliament, how are all its members to defend themselves from the misprision[27] of suffering such a person to go at large and to approach his sovereign? The man who conceals the perpetration of treason is himself a traitor; but they are all perfectly safe, for nobody thought of treason till fears arising from another quarter bewildered their senses. The King, therefore, and his servants, very wisely accepted his promise of assistance, and he flew with honest zeal to fulfill it. Sir Philip Jennings Clerke tells you that he made use of every expression which it was possible for a man in such circumstances to employ. He begged them, for God's sake, to disperse and go home; declared his hope that the petition would be granted, but that rioting was not the way to effect it. Sir Philip said he felt himself bound, without being particularly asked, to say every thing he could in protection of an injured and innocent man, and repeated again, that there was not an art which the prisoner could possibly make use of, that he did not zealously employ; but that it was all in vain. "I began," says he, "to tremble for myself, when Lord George read the resolution of the House, which was hostile to them, and said their petition would not be taken into consideration till they were quiet." But did he say, "therefore go on to burn and destroy?" On the contrary, he helped to pen that motion, and read it to the multitude, as one which he himself had approved. After this he went into the coach with Sheriff Pugh, in the city; and there it was, in the presence of the very magistrate whom he was assisting to keep the peace, that he *publicly* signed the protection which has been read in evidence against him; although Mr. Fisher, who now stands in my presence, confessed in the Privy Council that he himself had granted similar protections to various people—*yet he was dismissed, as having done nothing but his duty.*

This is the plain and simple truth; and for this just obedience to his Majesty's request, do the King's servants come to-day into his court, where he is supposed in person to sit, to turn that obedience into the crime of high treason, and to ask you to put him to death for it.

Recapitulation.

Gentlemen, you have now heard, upon the solemn oaths of honest, disinterested men, a faithful history of the conduct of Lord George Gordon, from the day that he became a member of the Protestant Association to the day that he was committed a prisoner to the Tower. And I have no doubt, from the attention with which I have been honored from the beginning, that you have still kept in your minds the principles to which I entreated you would apply it, and that you have measured it by that standard.

You have, therefore, only to look back to the whole of it together; to reflect on all you have heard concerning him; to trace him in your recollection through every part of the transaction; and, considering it with one manly, liberal view, to ask your own honest hearts, whether you can say that this noble and unfortunate youth is a wicked and deliberate traitor, who deserves by your verdict to suffer a shameful and ignominious death, which will stain the ancient honors of his house forever.

The crime which the Crown would have fixed upon him is, that he assembled the Protestant Association round the House of Commons, not merely to influence and persuade Parliament by the earnestness of their supplications, but actually to coerce it by hostile, rebellious force; that, finding himself disappointed in the success of that coercion, he afterward incited his followers to abolish the legal indulgences to Papists, which the object of the petition was to repeal, by the burning of their houses of worship, and the destruction of their property, which ended, at last, in a general attack on the property of all orders of men, religious and civil, on the public treasures of the nation, and on the very being of the government.[28]

To support a charge of so atrocious and unnatural a complexion, the laws of the most arbitrary nations would require the most incontrovertible proof. Either the villain must have been taken in the overt act of wickedness, or, if he worked in secret upon others, his guilt must have been brought out by the discovery of a conspiracy, or by the consistent tenor of criminality. The very worst inquisitor that ever dealt in blood would vindicate the torture, by plausibility at least, and by the semblance of truth.

What evidence, then, will a jury of Englishmen expect from the servants of the Crown of England, before they deliver up a brother accused before them to ignominy and death? What proof will their consciences require? What will their plain and manly understandings accept of? What does the immemorial custom of their fathers, and the written law of this land, warrant them in demanding? Nothing less, in any case of blood, than the clearest and most unequivocal conviction of guilt. But in this case the Act has not even trusted to the humanity and justice of our general law, but has said, in plain, rough, expressive terms—*provably;* that is, says Lord Coke, *not upon conjectural presumptions, or inferences, or strains of wit*, but upon direct and plain proof. "For the King, Lords, and Commons," continues that great lawyer, "did not use the word *probably*, for then a common argument might have served, but *provably*, which signifies the highest force of demonstration." And what evidence, gentlemen of the jury, does the Crown offer to you in compliance with these sound and sacred doctrines of justice? A few

27 Misprision of treason consists in the bare knowledge and concealment of treason, without any degree of assent thereto, for any assent makes the party a principal traitor,—*Blackstone's Comm.*, iv., 120.

28 At the time of the interference of the military, the mob had attacked the Pay Office, and were attempting to break into the Bank; and, to aid the work of the incendiaries, a large party had been sent to cut the pipes of the New River.

broken, interrupted, disjointed words, without context or connection—uttered by the speaker in agitation and heat—heard, by those who relate them to you, in the midst of tumult and confusion—and even those words, mutilated as they are, in direct opposition to, and inconsistent with repeated and earnest declarations delivered at the very same time and on the very same occasion, related to you by a much greater number of persons, and absolutely incompatible with the whole tenor of his conduct. Which of us all, gentlemen, would be safe, standing at the bar of God or man, if we were not to be judged by the regular current of our lives and conversations, but by detached and unguarded expressions, picked out by malice, and recorded, without context or circumstances, against us? Yet such is the only evidence on which the Crown asks you to dip your hands, and to stain your consciences, in the innocent blood of the noble and unfortunate youth who stands before you—on the single evidence of the words you have heard from their witnesses (for of what but words have you heard?), which, even if they had stood uncontroverted by the proofs that have swallowed them up, or unexplained by circumstances which destroy their malignity, could not, at the very worst, amount in law to more than a breach of the Act against tumultuous petitioning (if such an act still exists); since the worst malice of his enemies has not been able to bring up one single witness to say that he ever *directed*, *countenanced*, or *approved* rebellious force against the Legislature of this country. It is, therefore, a matter of astonishment to me that *men can keep the natural color in their cheeks* when they ask for human life, even on the Crown's original case, though the prisoner had made no defense.

But will they still continue to ask for it after what they have heard? I will just remind the Solicitor General, before he begins his reply, what matter he has to encounter. He has to encounter this: That the going up in a body was not even originated by Lord George, but by others in his absence—that when proposed by him officially as chairman, it was adopted by the *whole* Association, and consequently was *their* act as much as his—that it was adopted, not in a conclave, but with open doors, and the resolution published to all the world—that it was known, of course, to the ministers and magistrates of the country, who did not even signify to him, or to any body else, its illegality or danger—that decency and peace were enjoined and commanded—that the regularity of the procession, and those badges of distinction, which are now cruelly turned into the charge of an hostile array against him, were expressly and publicly directed for the preservation of peace and the prevention of tumult—that while the House was deliberating, he repeatedly entreated them to behave with decency and peace, and to retire to their houses, though he knew not that he was speaking to the enemies of his cause—that when they at last dispersed, no man thought or imagined that treason had been committed—that he retired to bed, where he lay unconscious that ruffians were ruining him by their disorders in the night—that on Monday he published an advertisement, reviling the authors of the riots; and, as the Protestant cause had been wickedly made the pretext for them, solemnly enjoined all who wished well to it to be obedient to the laws (nor has the Crown even attempted to prove that he had either given, or that he afterward gave secret instructions in opposition to that public admonition)—that he afterward begged an audience to receive the King's commands—that he waited on the ministers—that he attended his duty in Parliament—and when the multitude (among whom there was not a man of the associated Protestants) again assembled on the Tuesday, under pretense of the Protestant cause, he offered his services, and read a resolution of the House to them, accompanied with every expostulation which a zeal for peace could possibly inspire—that he afterward, in pursuance of the King's direction, attended the magistrates in their duty; honestly and honorably exerting all his powers to quell the fury of the multitude; a conduct which, to the dishonor of the Crown, has been scandalously turned against him, by criminating him with protections granted publicly in the coach of the Sheriff of London, whom he was assisting in his office of magistracy; although protections of a similar nature were, to the knowledge of the whole Privy Council, granted by Mr. Fisher himself, who now stands in my presence unaccused and unreproved, but who, if the Crown that summoned him durst have called him, would have dispersed to their confusion the slightest imputation of guilt.

Cause of the prosecution.

What, then, has produced this trial for high treason, or given it, when produced, the seriousness and solemnity it wears? What but the inversion of all justice, by judging from *consequences*, instead of from *causes* and *designs?* What but the artful manner in which the Crown has endeavored to blend the petitioning in a body, and the zeal with which an animated disposition conducted it, with the melancholy crimes that followed? crimes which the shameful indolence of our magistrates—which the total extinction of all police and government suffered to be committed in broad day, and in the delirium of drunkenness, by an unarmed banditti, without a head—without plan or object—and without a refuge from the instant gripe of justice: a banditti with whom the associated Protestants and their president had no manner of connection, and whose cause they overturned, dishonored, and ruined.

How unchristian, then, is it to attempt, without evidence, to infect the imaginations of men who are sworn, dispassionately and disinterestedly, to try the trivial offense of assembling a multitude with a petition to repeal a law (which has happened so often in all our memories), by blending it with the fatal catastrophe, on which every man's mind may be supposed to retain some degree of irritation! O fie! O fie! Is the intellectual seat of justice to be thus impiously shaken? Are your benevolent propensities to be thus disappointed and abused? Do they wish you, while you are listening to the evidence, to connect it with unforeseen consequences, in spite of reason and truth? Is it their object to hang the millstone of prejudice around his innocent neck to sink him? If there be such men, may Heaven forgive them for the attempt, and inspire you with fortitude and wisdom to discharge your duty with calm, steady, and reflecting minds!

Peroration.

Gentlemen, I have no manner of doubt that you will.[29] I am sure you can not but see, notwithstanding my great inability, increased by a perturbation of mind (arising, thank God! from no dishonest cause), that there has been not only no evidence on the part of the Crown to fix the guilt of the late commotions upon the prisoner, but that, on the contrary, we have been able to resist the probability, I might almost say the possibility of the charge, not only by living witnesses, whom we only ceased to call because the trial would never have ended, but by the evidence of all the blood that has paid the forfeit of that guilt already; an evidence that I will take upon me to say is the strongest and most unanswerable which the combination of natural events ever brought together since the beginning of the world for the deliverance of the oppressed: since, in the late numerous trials for acts of violence and depredation, though conducted by the ablest servants of the Crown, with a laudable eye to the investigation of the subject which now engages us, no one fact appeared which showed any plan, any object, any leader; since, out of forty-four thousand persons who signed the petition of the Protestants, not one was to be found among those who were convicted, tried, or even apprehended on suspicion; and since, out of all the felons who were let loose from prisons, and who assisted in the destruction of our property, not a single wretch was to be found who could even attempt to save his own life by the plausible promise of giving evidence to-day.

What can overturn such a proof as this? Surely a good man might, without superstition, believe that such a union of events was something more than natural, and that a Divine Providence was watchful for the protection of innocence and truth.

I may now, therefore, relieve you from the pain of hearing me any longer, and be myself relieved from speaking on a subject which agitates and distresses me. Since Lord George Gordon stands clear of every hostile act or purpose against the Legislature of his country, or the properties of his fellow-subjects—since the whole tenor of his conduct repels the belief of the *traitorous intention* charged by the indictment—my task is finished. I shall make no address to your passions. I will not remind you of the long and rigorous imprisonment he has suffered; I will not speak to you of his great youth, of his illustrious birth, and of his uniformly animated and generous zeal in Parliament for the Constitution of his country. Such topics might be useful in the balance of a doubtful case; yet, even then, I should have trusted to the honest hearts of Englishmen to have felt them without excitation. At present, the plain and rigid rules of justice and truth are sufficient to entitle me to your verdict.

The jury, after being charged by Lord Mansfield, withdrew at three o'clock in the morning, and speedily returned with the verdict — Not Guilty. The decision was satisfactory, in a high degree, to all reflecting men. Even those who considered his conduct as deeply criminal, felt with Dr. Johnson: "I am glad Lord George Gordon has escaped, rather than a precedent should be established of hanging a man for constructive treason."

SPEECH

OF MR. ERSKINE ON THE RIGHTS OF JURIES, DELIVERED BEFORE THE COURT OF KING'S BENCH, IN THE CASE OF THE DEAN OF ASAPH, NOVEMBER 15, 1784.

INTRODUCTION.

Sir William Jones, just before he went to India in 1783, wrote a small tract in favor of Parliamentary Reform, entitled a "Dialogue between a Gentleman and a Farmer," which was published by his brother-in-law Dr. Shipley, dean of St. Asaph, with an advertisement stating his reasons for so doing. Though harmless in its tendency, it gave umbrage to some high Tories of the neighborhood, and the Dean was indicted, at their instance, for printing a seditious libel. The trial came on at Shrewsbury, August 6th, 1784, and Mr. Bearcroft, counsel for the prosecution, satisfied that no English jury would ever find it a libel (as the court, in fact, afterward declared there was nothing in it illegal) took the

---

[29] This peroration is remarkable for the quiet and subdued tone which reigns throughout it. A less skillful advocate would have closed with a powerful appeal to the feelings of the jury. But Mr. Erskine, with that quick instinct which enabled him to read the emotions of men in their countenances, saw that his cause was gained. He chose, therefore, to throw over his concluding remarks the appearance of a perfect understanding between him and the jury, that the verdict of acquittal was already made up in their minds, so that any appeal to their feelings would be wholly out of place. His allusion to the providence of God as watching over the innocent, beautifully coincides with this sentiment; and in his closing sentence he does not ask a decision in his favor, but takes it as a matter of course.

ground that this was *no question* for them to decide—that they were bound to find the defendant guilty if they believed he had caused it to be *published*, and that it was "*of* and *concerning* the King and his government"—leaving him to move the court in arrest of judgment, or to bring a writ of error if its sentiments and language were claimed to be innocent. Mr. Erskine, for the defendant, argued the question to the jury on the supposition of their having a right to judge whether it was a libel or not. But Mr. Justice Buller charged the jury in accordance with the claim of Mr. Bearcroft, telling them, as Lord Mansfield had done in the case of Woodfall, that they must bring in the defendant guilty if they were satisfied he had published the tract, leaving the question whether it was libelous or not for the court to decide. The jury, however, gave their verdict "guilty of publishing *only*," which would have been tantamount to an acquittal. But the Judge having objected strongly to this finding, the jury withdrew, and returned with a verdict, "Guilty of publishing, but whether a libel or not we do not find."

In Michaelmas term following, November 8th, 1784, Mr. Erskine moved for a new trial on the ground of misdirection on the part of the judge. A rule *nisi* having been granted, the case came on for argument on the 15th, when he made the following speech. Lord Campbell says, "Erskine's addresses to the court in moving, and afterward in supporting his rule, display beyond all comparison the most perfect union of argument and eloquence ever exhibited in Westminster Hall. He laid down five propositions most logically framed and connected—which, if true, completely established his case—and he supported them with a depth of learning which would have done honor to Selden or Hale, while he was animated by an enthusiasm which was peculiarly his own. Though appealing to judges who heard him with aversion or indifference, he was as spirited as if the decision had depended on a favorable jury, whose feelings were entirely under his control. So thoroughly had he mastered the subject, and so clear did he make it, that he captivated alike old black-letter lawyers and statesmen of taste and refinement." —*Lives of the Lord Chancellors*, vol. vi., 433–4.

The following are the five propositions mentioned by Lord Campbell, which had been previously delivered to the judges in nearly the same terms:

I. "That when a bill of indictment is found, or an information filed, charging any crime or misdemeanor known to the law of England, and the party accused puts himself upon the country by pleading the general issue—Not Guilty; the jury are GENERALLY charged with his deliverance from that CRIME, and not SPECIALLY from the *fact* or *facts*, in the commission of which the indictment or information charges the crime to consist; much less from any single fact, to the exclusion of others charged upon the same record."

II. "That no act, which the law in its general theory holds to be criminal constitutes in itself a crime, abstracted from the mischievous *intention* of the actor; and that the intention (even where it becomes a simple inference of legal reason from a fact established) may and ought to be collected by the JURY, with the Judge's assistance; because the act charged, though established as a fact in a trial on the general issue, does not necessarily and unavoidably establish the criminal intention by any abstract conclusion of law—the establishment of the fact being still no more than full *evidence* of the crime, but not the crime itself; unless the jury render it so themselves, by referring it voluntarily to the court by special verdict."

III. "That the case of a libel forms no legal exception to the general principles which govern the trial of all other crimes; that the argument for the difference, namely, because the whole charge [in the prosecution for a libel] always appears on the record—is false in fact, and that, even if true, it would form no substantial difference in law."

IV. "That where a writing indicted as a libel neither contains, nor is averred by the indictment to contain, any slander of an individual (so as to fall within those rules of law which protect personal reputation), but whose criminality is charged to consist (as in the present instance) in its tendency to stir up general discontent—the trial of such an indictment neither involves, nor can in its obvious nature involve, any abstract question of law for the judgment of a court, but must wholly depend upon the judgment of the jury on the tendency of the writing itself to produce such consequences, when connected with all the circumstances which attended its publication."

V. "That in all cases where the mischievous intention (which is agreed to be the essence of the crime) can not be collected by simple inference from the fact charged, because the defendant goes into evidence to rebut such inference, the intention then becomes a pure, unmixed question of fact, for the consideration of the jury."

This speech has a peculiar interest for the lawyer, but the general reader will be amply repaid for giving it the closest attention. The young orator of any profession will find the study of it one of the best means of mental discipline, and will rise from the perusal of it with increased admiration of Lord Erskine as a logician and an orator.

SPEECH, &c.

I AM now to have the honor to address myself to your Lordship in support of the rule granted to me by the court upon Monday last; which, as Mr. Bearcroft has truly said, and seemed to mark the observation with peculiar emphasis, is a rule for a new trial. Much of my argument, according to his notion, points another way; whether its direction be true, or its force adequate to the object, it is now my business to show.

In rising to speak at this time, I feel all the

advantage conferred by the reply over those whose arguments are to be answered; but I feel a disadvantage likewise, which must suggest itself to every intelligent mind. In following the objections of so many learned persons, offered under different arrangements upon a subject so complicated and comprehensive, there is much danger of being drawn from that method and order which can alone fasten conviction upon unwilling minds, or drive them from the shelter which ingenuity never fails to find in the labyrinth of a desultory discourse. The sense of that danger, and my own inability to struggle against it, led me originally to deliver up to the court certain written and maturely considered PROPOSITIONS, from the establishment of which I resolved not to depart, nor to be removed, either in substance or in order, in any stage of the proceedings, and by which I must therefore this day unquestionably stand or fall.

Necessity of a very exact order of argument.

Pursuing this system, I am vulnerable two ways, and in two ways only. Either it must be shown that my propositions are not valid in law, or, admitting their validity, that the learned judge's charge to the jury at Shrewsbury was not repugnant to them: there can be no other possible objections to my application for a new trial. My duty today is, therefore, obvious and simple: it is, first, to re-maintain those propositions, and then to show that the charge delivered to the jury at Shrewsbury was founded upon the absolute denial and reprobation of them.

Only two possible modes of evading its force.

I. I begin, therefore, by saying again, in my own original words, That when a bill of indictment is found, or an information filed, charging any crime or misdemeanor known to the law of England, and the party accused puts himself upon the country by pleading the general issue—not guilty; the jury are GENERALLY charged with his deliverance from that *crime*, and not SPECIALLY from the *fact* or *facts*, in the commission of which the indictment or information charges the crime to consist; much less from any single fact, to the exclusion of others charged upon the same record.

First Proposition.

II. That no act, which the law in its general theory holds to be criminal, constitutes in itself a crime, abstracted from the mischievous *intention* of the actor; and that the intention (even where it becomes a simple inference of legal reasons from a fact or facts established), may and ought to be collected by the JURY, with the judge's assistance; because the act charged, though established as a fact in a trial on the general issue, does not necessarily and unavoidably establish the criminal intention by any abstract conclusion of the law: the establishment of the fact being still no more than full *evidence* of the crime, but not the crime itself; unless the jury render it so themselves, by referring it voluntarily to the court by special verdict.

Second Proposition.

These two propositions, though worded with cautious precision, and in technical language, to prevent the subtlety of legal disputation in opposition to the plain understanding of the world, neither do nor were intended to convey any other sentiment than this, namely, that in all cases where the law either directs or permits a person accused of a crime to throw himself upon a jury for deliverance, by pleading *generally* that he is not guilty; the JURY, thus legally appealed to, may deliver him from the accusation by a general verdict of acquittal founded (as in common sense it evidently must be) upon an INVESTIGATION as *general* and comprehensive as the charge itself from which it is a general deliverance.

Restatement of these propositions.

Having said this, I freely confess to the court that I am much at a loss for any further illustration of my subject, because I can not find any matter by which it might be further illustrated, so clear or so indisputable, either in fact or in law, as the very proposition itself upon which this trial has been brought into question. Looking back upon the ancient Constitution, and examining with painful research the original jurisdictions of the country, I am utterly at a loss to imagine from what sources these novel limitations of the rights of juries are derived. Even the bar is not yet trained to the discipline of maintaining them. My learned friend Mr. Bearcroft[1] solemnly abjures them. He repeats to-day what he avowed at the trial, and is even jealous of the imputation of having meant less than he expressed. For, when speaking this morning of the *right* of the jury to judge of the whole charge, your Lordship corrected his expression, by telling him he meant the *power*, and not the *right*; he caught instantly at your words, disavowed your explanation, and, with a consistency which does him honor, declared his adherence to his original admission in its full and obvious extent. "I did not mean," said he, "merely to acknowledge that the jury have the *power*, for their power nobody ever doubted. If a judge was to tell them they had it not, they would only have to laugh at him, and convince him of his error, by finding a GENERAL verdict, which must be recorded: I meant, therefore, to consider it as a *right*, as an important privilege, and of great value to the Constitution." Thus Mr. Bearcroft and I are perfectly agreed; I never contended for more than he has voluntarily conceded. I have now his express authority for repeating, in my own former words, that the jury have not merely the *power* to acquit, upon a view of the whole charge, without control or punishment, and without the possibility of their acquittal being annulled by any other authority; but that they have *a constitutional, legal right to do it; a right fit to be exercised;* and intended, by the wise founders of the government, to be a protection to the lives and liberties of Englishmen, against the encroachments and perversions of authority in the hands of fixed magistrates.

The recent limitations on the rights of juries a departure from original usage.

Concession of opposing counsel.

But this candid admission on the part of Mr.

[1] One of the counsel for the prosecution.

Bearcroft, though very honorable to himself, is of no importance to me; since, from what has already fallen from your Lordship, I am not to expect a ratification of it from the court; it is therefore my duty to establish it. I feel all the importance of my subject, and nothing shall lead me to-day to go out of it. I claim all the attention of the court, and the right to state every authority which applies, in my judgment, to the argument, without being supposed to introduce them for other purposes than my duty to my client and the Constitution of my country warrants and approves.

The court having expressed another opinion, their attention claimed.

It is not very usual, in an English court of justice, to be driven back to the earliest history and original elements of the Constitution, in order to establish the first principles which mark and distinguish English law: they are always assumed, and, like axioms in science, are made the foundations of reasoning without being proved. Of this sort our ancestors, for many centuries, must have conceived the right of an English jury to decide upon every question which the forms of the law submitted to their final decision; since, though they have immemorially exercised that supreme jurisdiction, we find no trace in any of the ancient books of its ever being brought into question. It is but as yesterday, when compared with the age of the law itself, that judges, unwarranted by any former judgments of their predecessors, without any new commission from the Crown, or enlargement of judicial authority from the Legislature, have sought to fasten a limitation upon the rights and privileges of jurors, totally unknown in ancient times, and palpably destructive of the very end and object of their institution.

The right of a jury to decide on the *law* as well as facts in the case, an original principle of English jurisprudence.

No fact, my Lord, is of more easy demonstration; for the history and laws of a free country lie open, even to vulgar inspection.

During the whole Saxon era, and even long after the establishment of the Norman government, the whole administration of justice, criminal and civil, was in the hands of the *people*, without the control or intervention of any judicial authority, delegated to fixed magistrates by the Crown. The tenants of every manor administered civil justice to one another in the Court Baron of their Lord; and their crimes were judged of in the Leet,[2] every suitor of the manor giving his voice as a juror, and the steward being only the registrar, and not the judge.

(1.) The lowest courts, both Baron and Leet.

On appeals from these domestic jurisdictions to the county court, and to the tourn (circuit) of the sheriff, or in suits and prosecutions originally commenced in either of them, the sheriff's authority extended no further than to summon the jurors, to compel their attendance, ministerially to regulate their proceedings, and to enforce their decisions. And even where he was specially empowered by the King's writ of *justicies*[3] to proceed in causes of superior value, no judicial authority was thereby conferred upon himself, but only a more enlarged jurisdiction ON THE JURORS, who were to try the cause mentioned in the writ. It is true that the sheriff can not now intermeddle in pleas of the Crown; but with this exception, which brings no restrictions on juries, these jurisdictions remain untouched at this day: intricacies of property have introduced other forms of proceeding, but the Constitution is the same.

(2.) The County and Sheriff's Court.

This popular judicature was not confined to particular districts, or to inferior suits and misdemeanors, but pervaded the whole legal Constitution. For, when the Conqueror, to increase the influence of his crown, erected that great superintending court of justice in his own palace to receive appeals criminal and civil from every court in the kingdom, and placed at the head of it the *capitalis justiciarius totius Angliæ* [Chief Justiciary of all England], of whose original authority the Chief Justice of this court is but a partial and feeble emanation: even that great magistrate was in the *Aula Regis* [King's Court] merely ministerial; every one of the King's tenants, who owed him service in right of a *barony*, had a seat and a voice in that high tribunal; and the office of justiciar was but to record and to enforce their judgments.[4]

(3.) The King's Court of William the Conqueror.

In the reign of King Edward the First, when this great office was abolished, and the present courts at Westminster established by a distribution of its powers,[5] the barons preserved that supreme superintending jurisdiction which never belonged to the Justiciar, but to *themselves* only as the jurors in the King's Court—a jurisdiction which, when nobility, from being territorial and feudal, became personal and honorary, was assumed and exer-

(4.) The House of Lords as a court.

---

[2] The Court Baron belonged more particularly to a manor, and the Court Leet to a hundred, which was the smallest civil division in Saxon times.—See Jacobs's Law Dictionary.

[3] The Writ of Justicies was a writ directed to the sheriff in some special cases, by virtue of which he might hold plea of debt in his county court for a large sum, whereas, by his ordinary power, he was limited to sums under forty shillings.

[4] The King's Court was composed of the Chief Justiciary, the Chancellor, the Constable, Marshal, Chamberlain, Steward, and Treasurer, with any others whom the King might appoint. The Court of Exchequer, in which all revenue matters were transacted, formed a branch of this court. The Chief Justiciary was the greatest subject in England: besides presiding in the King's Court, and in the Exchequer, he was originally, by virtue of his office, the Regent of the kingdom during the absence of the Sovereign.

[5] Though Edward settled the jurisdiction of the several courts, the separation of the Exchequer first, and afterward the Common Pleas, from the King's Court, took place long before. The detachment of the latter had its beginning, in Madox's opinion, as early as in the reign of Richard the First; but it was completely established by the Magna Charta of 17 John, and then first made stationary at Westminster

cised by the peers of England, who, without any delegation of judicial authority from the Crown, form to this day the supreme and final court of English law, judging in the last resort for the whole kingdom, and sitting upon the lives of the peerage, in their ancient and genuine character, as the *pares* of one another.[6]

With the advance of commerce, the jury ceased to be judges of the *law* in certain cases of property,

When the courts at Westminster were established in their present forms, and when the civilization and commerce of the nation had introduced more intricate questions of justice, the judicial authority in civil cases could not but enlarge its bounds. The rules of property in a cultivated state of society became by degrees beyond the compass of the unlettered multitude, and with certain well-known restrictions undoubtedly fell to the judges; yet more, perhaps, from necessity than by consent, as all judicial proceedings were artfully held in the Norman language, to which the people were strangers.[7] Of these *changes* in judicature, immemorial custom, and the acquiescence of the Legislature, are the evidence which establish the jurisdiction of the courts on the true principle of English law, and measure the extent of it by their ancient practice.

but not in cases of crimes.

But no such evidence is to be found of the least relinquishment or abridgment of popular judicature, *in cases of crimes;* on the contrary, every page of our history is filled with the struggles of our ancestors for its preservation.

Reasons for the distinction.

The law of property changes with new objects, and becomes intricate as it extends its dominion; but crimes must ever be of the same easy investigation. They consist wholly in intention, and the more they are multiplied by the policy of those who govern, the more absolutely the public freedom depends upon the people's preserving the entire administration of criminal justice to themselves. In a question of property between two private individuals, the Crown can have no possible interest in preferring the one to the other; but it may have an interest in crushing both of them together, in defiance of every principle of humanity and justice, if they should put themselves forward in a contention for public liberty, against a government seeking to emancipate itself from the dominion of the laws. No man in the least acquainted with the history of nations or of his own country, can refuse to acknowledge, that if the administration of criminal justice were left in the hands of the Crown or its deputies, no greater freedom could possibly exist than government might choose to tolerate from the convenience or policy of the day.

[6] During a trial before the House of Peers, every peer present on the trial has always been judge both of the law and the fact. Hence no special verdict can be given on the trial of a peer.

[7] All pleadings were, by order of William the Conqueror, conducted in Norman-French. By act 36 Edward III., cap. 15 (A.D. 1363), the use of the French language in legal proceedings was abolished.

This distinction confirmed by Blackstone,

My Lord, this important truth is no discovery or assertion of mine, but is to be found in every book of the law: Whether we go up to the most ancient authorities, or appeal to the writings of men of our own times, we meet with it alike in the most emphatical language. Mr. Justice Blackstone, by no means biased toward democratical government, having in the third volume of his Commentaries explained the excellence of the trial by jury in civil cases, expresses himself thus (vol. iv., p. 349): "But it holds much stronger in criminal cases, since, in times of difficulty and danger, more is to be apprehended from the violence and partiality of judges appointed by the Crown, in suits between the King and the subject, than in disputes between one individual and another, to settle the boundaries of private property. Our law has, therefore, wisely placed this strong and two-fold barrier of a presentment and trial by jury between the liberties of the people and the prerogative of the Crown. Without this barrier, justices of *oyer* and *terminer* named by the Crown might, as in France or in Turkey, imprison, dispatch, or exile any man that was obnoxious to government, by an instant declaration that such was their will and pleasure. So that the liberties of England can not but subsist so long as this palladium remains sacred and inviolate, not only from all open attacks, which none will be so hardy as to make, but also from all secret machinations which may sap and undermine it."

and by Bracton.

But this remark, though it derives new force in being adopted by so great an authority, was no more an original in Mr. Justice Blackstone than in me: the institution and authority of juries is to be found in Bracton, who wrote about five hundred years before him. "The *curia* [court] and the *pares* [jury]," says he, "were necessarily the judges in all cases of life, limb, crime, and disherison of the heir *in capite*. The King could not decide, for then he would have been both prosecutor and judge; neither could his justices, for they represent him."

Further evidence of an entire distinction between civil and criminal cases.

Notwithstanding all this, the learned judge [Mr. Buller] was pleased to say at the trial, that there was no difference between civil and criminal cases.[8] I say, on the contrary, independent of these authorities, that there is not, even to vulgar observation, the remotest similitude between them.

[8] In his charge to the jury, in the case of the Dean of St. Asaph, Mr. Justice Buller had said, "The law acts equally and justly, as the pamphlet itself states: it is equal between the prosecutor and defendant; and whatever appears upon the record is not for our decision here, but may be the subject of future consideration in the court out of which the record comes: and afterward, if either party thinks fit, they have a right to carry it to the *dernier resort*, and have the opinion of the House of Lords upon it; and, therefore, that has been the uniform and established answer, *not only in criminal but civil cases. The law is the same in both, and there is not a gentleman round this table who does not know that is the constant and uniform answer which is given in such cases.*"

There are four capital distinctions between prosecutions for crimes and civil actions, every one of which deserves consideration:

First, in the jurisdiction necessary to found the charge.

Secondly, in the manner of the defendant's pleading it.

Thirdly, in the authority of the verdict which discharges him.

Fourthly, in the independence and security of the jury from all the consequences in giving it.

Jurisdiction.

(1.) As to the first, it is unnecessary to remind your Lordships that, in a civil case, the party who conceives himself aggrieved states his complaint to the court—avails himself at his own pleasure of its process—compels an answer from the defendant by its authority—or, taking the charge *pro confesso* against him on his default, is entitled to final judgment and execution for his debt, without any interposition of a jury. But in criminal cases it is otherwise; the court has no cognizance of them, without leave from the people forming a grand inquest. If a man were to commit a capital offense in the face of all the judges of England, their united authority could not put him upon his trial. They could file no complaint against him, even upon the records of the supreme criminal court, but could only commit him for safe custody, which is equally competent to every common justice of the peace. The grand jury alone could arraign him, and in their discretion might likewise finally discharge him, by throwing out the bill, the names of all your Lordships as witnesses on the back of it. If it shall be said that this exclusive power of the grand jury does not extend to lesser misdemeanors, which may be prosecuted by information; I answer, that for that very reason it becomes doubly necessary to preserve the power of the other jury which is left. In the rules of pleading, there is no distinction between *capital* and *lesser* offenses; and the defendant's plea of not guilty (which universally prevails as the legal answer to every information or indictment, as opposed to special pleas to the court in civil actions), and the necessity imposed upon the Crown to join the general issue, are absolutely decisive of the present question [*i. e.*, as to jurisdiction].

Manner of the defendant's pleading. This shuts out the law from the jury in civil cases,

(2.) Every lawyer must admit that the rules of pleading were originally established to mark and to preserve the distinct jurisdictions of the court and the jury, by a *separation* of the law from the fact, wherever they were intended to be separated. A person charged with owing a debt, or having committed a trespass, &c., &c., if he could not deny the facts on which the actions were founded, was obliged to submit his justification for matter of law by a special plea to the court upon the record; to which plea the plaintiff might *demur*,[9] and submit the legal merits to the judges. By this arrangement, no power was ever given to the jury, by an issue joined before them, but when a right of decision, as comprehensive as the issue, went along with it. If a defendant in such civil actions pleaded the general issue instead of a special plea, aiming at a *general* deliverance from the charge, by showing his justification to the jury at the trial, the court protected its own jurisdiction, by refusing all evidence of the facts on which such justification was founded. The extension of the general issue beyond its ancient limits, and in deviation from its true principle, has, indeed, introduced some confusion into this simple and harmonious system; but the law is substantially the same. No man, at this day, in any of those actions where the ancient forms of our jurisprudence are still wisely preserved, can possibly get at the opinion of a jury upon any question not intended by the Constitution for their decision. In actions of debt, detinue, breach of covenant, trespass, or replevin, the defendant can only submit the mere fact to the jury, the law must be pleaded to the court. If, dreading the opinion of the judges, he *conceals* his justification under the cover of a general plea, in hopes of a more favorable construction of his defense at the trial, its very existence can never even come within the knowledge of the jurors. Every legal defense must arise out of the facts; and the authority of the judge is interposed to prevent their appearing before a tribunal which, in such cases, has no competent jurisdiction over them.

By imposing this necessity of pleading every legal justification to the court, and by this exclusion of all evidence on the trial beyond the negation of the fact, the courts indisputably intended to establish, and did in fact effectually secure, the judicial authority over legal questions from all encroachment or violation. And it is impossible to find a reason in law or in common sense, why the same boundaries between the fact and the law should not have been at the same time extended to criminal cases by the same rules of pleading, if the jurisdiction of the jury had been designed to be limited to the *fact*, as in civil actions.

but never in criminal cases.

But no such boundary was ever made or attempted—on the contrary, every person charged with any crime by an indictment or information has been in all times, from the Norman Conquest to this hour, not only permitted, but even bound, to throw himself upon his country for deliverance, by the general plea of "Not guilty," and may submit his *whole* defense to the jury, whether it be a negation of the fact or a justification of it in law. The judge has no authority, as in a civil case, to refuse such evidence at the trial as out of the issue, and as *coram non judice* [not before the judge]—an authority which in common sense he certainly would have, if the jury had no higher jurisdiction in the one case than in the other. The general plea thus sanctioned by immemorial custom, so *blends* the law and the fact together, as to be inseparable but by the voluntary

[9] *I. e.*, might allege that, admitting the facts, the justification set up is not sufficient in law, which would be a question for the decision of the court, and not of the jury.

act of the jury in finding a *special* verdict.[10] The general investigation of the whole charge is, therefore, before them; and although the defendant admits the fact laid in the information or indictment, he nevertheless, under his general plea, gives evidence of *others* which are collateral, referring them to the judgment of the jury as a legal excuse or justification, and receives from their verdict a complete, general, and conclusive deliverance. Mr. Justice Blackstone, in the fourth volume of his Commentaries, page 339, says: "The traitorous or felonious intent are the points and very gist of the indictment, and must be answered directly by the general negative, 'Not guilty;' and the jury will take notice of any *defensive* matter, and give their verdict accordingly, as effectually as if it were specially pleaded." This, therefore, says Sir Matthew Hale, in his Pleas of the Crown, page 258, is, upon all accounts, the most advantageous plea for the defendant: "It would be a most unhappy case for the judge himself, if the prisoner's fate depended upon his directions—unhappy also for the prisoner; for if the judge's opinion must rule the verdict, the trial by jury would be useless."

The authority of the verdict, and the protection of the jury in giving it.

(3 and 4.) My Lord, the conclusive operation of the verdict when given [in a criminal case], and the security of the jury from all consequences in giving it, render the contrast between criminal and civil cases striking and complete. No new trial can be granted, as in a civil action. Your Lordships, however you may disapprove of the acquittal, have no authority to award one; for there is no precedent of any such upon record; and the discretion of the court is circumscribed by the law. Neither can the jurors be attainted by the Crown.[11] In Bushel's case, Vaughan's Reports, page 146, that learned and excellent judge expressed himself thus: "There is no case in all the law of an attaint for the King, nor any opinion but that of Thyrning's, 10th of Henry IV., title Attaint, 60 and 64, for which there is no warrant in law, though there be other specious authority against it, touched by none that have argued this case."

Lord Mansfield. To be sure it is so.

Mr. Erskine. Since that is clear, my Lord, I shall not trouble the court further upon it. Indeed, I have not been able to find any one authority for such an attaint, but a *dictum* in Fitzherbert's Natura Brevium, page 107; and on the other hand, the doctrine of Bushel's case is expressly agreed to in very modern times: vide Lord Raymond's Reports, vol. i., page 469.

Recapitulation of the points of difference between civil and criminal cases.

If, then, your Lordships reflect but for a moment upon this comparative view of criminal and civil cases which I have laid before you, how can it be seriously contended, not merely that there is no difference, but that there is any the remotest similarity between them? In the one case, the power of accusation begins from the court; in the other, from the people only, forming a grand jury. In the one, the defendant must plead a special justification, the merits of which can only be decided by the judges; in the other, he may throw himself for general deliverance upon his country. In the first, the court may award a new trial, if the verdict for the defendant be contrary to the evidence or the law; in the last, it is conclusive and unalterable. And, to crown the whole, the King never had that process of attaint which belonged to the meanest of his subjects.

General inference as to the rights of juries in criminal cases.

When these things are attentively considered, I might ask those who are still disposed to deny the right of the jury to investigate the whole charge, whether such a solecism can be conceived to exist in any human government, much less in the most refined and exalted in the world, as that a power of supreme judicature should be conferred [on the jury] at random by the blind forms of the law, where no right was intended to pass with it, and which was upon no occasion and under no circumstance to be exercised—which, though exerted notwithstanding in every age and in a thousand instances to the confusion and discomfiture of fixed magistracy, should never be checked by authority, but should continue on, from century to century, the revered guardian of liberty and of life, arresting the arm of the most headstrong government in the worst of times; without any power in the Crown or its judges to touch, without its consent, the meanest wretch in the kingdom, or even to ask the reason and principle of the verdict which acquits him. That such a system should prevail in a country like England, without either the original institution or the acquiescing sanction of the Legislature, is impossible. Believe me, my Lord, *no talents can reconcile, no authority can sanction such an absurdity: the common sense of the world revolts at it.*

Views of Justice Foster.

Having established this important right in the jury, beyond all possibility of cavil or controversy, I will now show your Lordships that its existence is not merely consistent with the theory of the law, but is illustrated and confirmed by the universal practice of all judges; not even excepting Mr. Justice Foster himself, whose writings have been cited in support of the contrary opinion. How a man expresses his *abstract* ideas is of but little importance when an appeal can be made to his plain directions to others, and to his own particular conduct; but even none of his expressions, when properly considered and understood, militate against my position.

In his justly celebrated book on the Criminal Law, page 256, he expresses himself thus: "The construction which the law putteth upon fact

[10] A special verdict is one in which the jury find only the *facts*, and leave the law to be decided by the court.

[11] An attaint is a writ to inquire whether a jury of twelve men gave a false verdict (Finch, 484), that so the judgment following thereupon may be reversed, and the jury punished. Very few instances of attaints appear later than the sixteenth century.

STATED AND AGREED OR FOUND by a jury, *is in all cases undoubtedly the proper province of the court.*" Now, if the adversary is disposed to stop here, though the author never intended he should, as is evident from the rest of the sentence, yet I am willing to stop with him, and to take it as a substantive proposition; for the slightest attention must discover that it is not repugnant to any thing which I have said. Facts *stated and agreed*, or facts *found* by a jury (which amount to the same thing), constitute a *special verdict;* and who ever supposed that the law upon a special verdict was not the province of the court? Where, in a trial upon a general issue, the parties choose to agree upon facts and to state them, or the jury choose voluntarily to find them without drawing the legal conclusion themselves, who ever denied that in such instances the court is to draw it? That Foster meant nothing more than that the court was to judge of the law, when the jury thus voluntarily *prays* its assistance by special verdict, is evident from his words which follow, for he immediately goes on to say: "*In cases of doubt and real difficulty, it is therefore commonly recommended to the jury to state facts and circumstances in a special verdict.*" But neither here, nor in any other part of his works, is it said or insinuated that they are *bound* to do so, but at their own free discretion. Indeed, the very term *recommended* admits the contrary, and requires no commentary. I am sure I shall never dispute the wisdom or expediency of such a recommendation in those cases of doubt, because the more I am contending for the existence of such an important right, the less it would become me to be the advocate of rashness and precipitation in the exercise of it. It is no denial of jurisdiction to tell the greatest magistrate upon earth to take good counsel in cases of real doubt and difficulty. Judges upon trials, whose authority to state the law is indisputable, often refer it to be more solemnly argued before the court. And this court itself often holds a meeting of the twelve judges before it decides on a point upon its own records, of which the others have confessed no cognizance till it comes before them by the writ of error of one of the parties. These instances are monuments of wisdom, integrity, and discretion; but they do not bear, in the remotest degree, upon *jurisdiction.* The sphere of jurisdiction is measured by what may or may not be decided by any given tribunal with legal effect, not by the rectitude or error of the decision. If the jury, according to these authorities, may determine the whole matter by their verdict, and if the verdict, when given, is not only final and unalterable, but must be enforced by the authority of the judges, and executed, if resisted, by the whole power of the state—upon what principle of government or reason can it be argued not to be law? That the jury are in this exact predicament is confessed by Foster, for he concludes with saying that *when the law is clear, the jury, under the direction of the court, in point of law may, and if they are well advised will, always find a general verdict conformably to such directions.*

His doctrine, relied on by the other side, relates properly to *special* verdicts.

This is likewise consistent with my position. If the law be clear, we may presume that the judge states it clearly to the jury; and if he does, undoubtedly the jury, if they are well advised, will find according to such directions. For they have not a capricious discretion to *make* law at their pleasure, but are bound in conscience, as well as judges are, to find it truly; and, generally speaking, the learning of the judge who presides at the trial affords them a safe support and direction.

The same practice of judges in stating the law to the jury, as applied to the particular case before them, appears likewise in the case of the King against Oneby, 2d Lord Raymond, page 1494. "On the trial the judge directs the jury thus: 'If you believe such and such witnesses who have sworn to such and such facts, *the killing of the deceased appears to be with malice prepense;* but if you do not believe them, then you ought to find him guilty of manslaughter; and the jury may, if they think proper, give a general verdict of murder or manslaughter: *but if they decline* giving a general verdict, and *will* find the facts specially, the court is then to form their judgment from the facts found, whether the defendant be guilty or not guilty, that is, whether the act was done with malice and deliberation or not.'" Surely language can express nothing more plainly or unequivocally, than that, where "the general issue" is pleaded to an indictment, the *law* and the *fact* are both before the jury; and that the former can never be separated from the latter, for the judgment of the court, unless by their *own spontaneous act* For the words are, "if they *decline* giving a general verdict, and *will* find the facts specially, the court is *then* to form their judgment from the facts found." So that, after a general issue joined, the authority of the court only commences when the jury chooses to decline the decision of the law by a general verdict—the right of declining which legal determination, is a privilege conferred on them by the statute of Westminster 2d, and by no means a restriction of their powers.

Case in Lord Raymond shows that the jury have the right of deciding as to the *law.*

But another very important view of the subject remains behind. Supposing I had failed in establishing that contrast between criminal and civil cases, which is now too clear not only to require, but even to justify another observation, the argument would lose nothing by the failure. The similarity between criminal and civil cases derives all its application to the argument from the learned judge's supposition, that the jurisdiction of the jury over the *law* was never contended for in the latter, and consequently, on a principle of equality, could not be supported in the former—whereas I *do* contend for it, and can incontestably establish it in both. This application of the argument is plain from the words of the charge: "If the jury could find the law, it would undoubtedly

Reply to an argument of Justice Buller.

hold in civil cases as well as criminal; but was it ever supposed that a jury was competent to say the operation of a fine, or a recovery, or a warranty; which are mere questions of law?"[12]

To this question I answer, that the competency of the jury in such cases *is* contended for to the full extent of my principle, both by Lyttleton and by Coke. They can not, indeed, decide upon them *de plano* [in the abstract, or aside from the facts], which, as Vaughan truly says, is unintelligible, because an *unmixed* question of law can by no possibility come before them for decision. But whenever (which very often happens) the operation of a fine, a recovery, a warranty, or any other record or conveyance known to the law of England comes forward, mixed with the fact on the general issue, the jury have then most unquestionably a right to determine it. And what is more, no other authority possibly can; because, when the general issue is permitted by law, these questions can not appear on the record for the judgment of the court, and although it can grant a new trial, yet the same question must ultimately be determined by another jury. This is not only self-evident to every lawyer, but, as I said, is expressly laid down by Lyttleton in the 368th section: "Also in such case where the inquest may give their verdict at large, if they will take upon them the knowledge of the law upon the matter, they may give their verdict generally as it is put in their charge; as in the case aforesaid they may well say that the lessor did not disseize the lessee, if they will." Coke, in his commentary on this action, confirms Lyttleton, saying that in doubtful cases they should find *specially* for fear of an attaint. And it is plain that the statute of Westminster the 2d was made either to give or to confirm the right of the jury to find the matter specially, leaving their jurisdiction over the law as it stood by the common law. The words of the statute of Westminster 2d, chapter 30th, are, "*Ordinatum est quod justitiarii ad assisas capiendas assignati*, NON COMPELLANT *juratores dicere precisè si sit disseisina vel non; dummodo voluerint dicere veritatem facti et petere auxilium justitiariorum.*"[13] From these words it should appear that the jurisdiction of the jury over the law, when it came before them on the general issue, was so vested in them by the Constitution, that the exercise of it in all cases had been considered to be compulsory upon them, and that this was a legislative relief from that compulsion in the case of an assize of disseizin. It is equally plain, from the remaining words of the act, that their jurisdiction remained as before: "*Sed si spontè velint dicere quod disseisina est vel non, admittatur eorum veredictum sub suo periculo.*"[14]

But the most material observation upon this statute, as applicable to the present subject, is, that the terror of the attaint from which it was passed to relieve them, having (as has been shown) no existence in cases of *crime*, the act only extended to relieve the jury, at their discretion, from finding the law in civil actions. Consequently, it is only from custom, and not from positive law, that they are not *even compellable* to give a general verdict involving a judgment of law on every criminal trial.

General conclusion as to the duty of the judge and the right of the jury.

These principles and authorities certainly establish, that it is the duty of the judge, on every trial where the general issue is pleaded, to give to the jury his opinion on the law as applied to the case before them; and that they must find a general verdict, comprehending a judgment of law, unless they *choose* to refer it specially to the court.

Yet the judge, in this case, violates that duty and these rights, and still demands a general verdict.

But we are here in a case where it is contended that the duty of the judge is the direct contrary of this; that he is to give no opinion at all to the jury upon the law as applied to the case before them; that they likewise are to refrain from all consideration of it, and yet that the very same general verdict, comprehending both fact and law, is to be given by them as if the whole legal matter had been summed up by the one, and found by the other.

I confess I have no organs to comprehend the principle on which such a practice proceeds. I contended for nothing more at the trial than the very practice recommended by Foster and Lord Raymond. I addressed myself to the jury upon the law with all possible respect and deference, and, indeed, with very marked personal attention to the learned judge. So far from urging the jury dogmatically to think for themselves without his constitutional assistance, I called for his opinion on the question of libel. I said that if he should tell them distinctly the paper indicted was libelous, though I should not admit that they were bound at all events to give effect to it if they felt it to be innocent, yet I was ready to agree that they ought not to go against the charge without great consideration; but that if he should shut himself

[12] A *fine* was an amicable composition (originally of an actual, and afterward of a fictitious suit) adopted principally as a mode of putting an *end* (*finis*) to all controversies respecting certain tenures or estates. A *common recovery* was a judgment recovered in a fictitious suit, and its principal use was to enable a tenant in tail to bar not only the estate tail, but also all remainders over, and to acquire an absolute estate in fee simple. Fines and recoveries are now abolished by 3 and 4 Wm. IV., c. 74, and more simple modes of assurance employed to effect their objects. A *warranty* was a covenant real annexed to lands, whereby the grantor of the estate, for himself and his heirs, did warrant and secure to the grantee the estate so granted, and covenanted to yield other lands and tenements equal to the value of the estate granted, in case of the grantee being evicted.

[13] Be it enacted, that the justices for holding the assizes shall not *compel* the jury to say decisively whether there is a *disseizin* or not, provided they are willing to find the truth of the *fact*, and ask the aid of the court.—A *disseizin* is the act of wrongfully depriving a person of land or certain other kinds of property, of which he was actually *seized* or in possession.

[14] But if they choose to say of their own accord, that there is or is not a *disseizin*, let their verdict be received at their own risk.

up in silence, giving no opinion at all upon the criminality of the paper, from which alone any guilt could be fastened on the publisher, and should narrow their consideration to the *publication*, I entered my protest against their finding a verdict affixing the epithet of *guilty* to the mere fact of publishing a paper; the *guilt* of which had not been investigated. If, after this address to the jury, the learned judge had told them that in his opinion the paper was a libel, but still leaving it to their judgments, and likewise the defendant's evidence to their consideration, had further told them that he thought it did not exculpate the publication; and if in consequence of such directions the jury had found a verdict for the Crown, I should never have made my present motion for a new trial; because I should have considered such a verdict of "guilty" as founded upon the opinion of the jury on the whole matter as left to their consideration, and must have sought my remedy by arrest of judgment on the record.

But the learned judge took a directly contrary course. He gave no opinion at all on the guilt or innocence of the paper; he took no notice of the defendant's evidence of *intention;* he told the jury, in the most explicit terms, that neither the one nor the other was within their jurisdiction. Upon the mere fact of *publication*, he directed a general verdict comprehending the epithet of *guilty*, after having expressly withdrawn from the jury every consideration of the merits of the paper published or the intention of the publisher, from which it is admitted on all hands the *guilt* of publication could alone have any existence.

Ground of motion for a new trial.

My motion is, therefore, founded upon this obvious and simple principle—that the defendant has had, in fact, NO TRIAL, having been found *guilty* without any investigation of his *guilt*, and without any power left to the jury to take cognizance of his innocence. I undertake to show that the jury could not possibly conceive or believe, from the judge's charge, that they had any *jurisdiction* to acquit him, however they might have been impressed even with the merit of the publication, or convinced of his meritorious intention in publishing it. Nay, what is worse, while the learned judge totally deprived them of their whole jurisdiction over the question of libel, and the defendant's seditious intention, he, at the same time, directed a general verdict of guilty, which comprehended a *judgment upon both!*

Founded on the plain import of the judge's charge.

When I put this construction on the learned judge's direction, I found myself wholly on the language in which it was communicated; and it will be no answer to such construction that no such restraint was *meant* to be conveyed by it. If the learned judge's intentions were even the direct contrary of his expressions, yet if, in consequence of that which was expressed, though not intended, the jury were abridged of a jurisdiction which belonged to them by law, and in the exercise of which the defendant had an interest, he is equally a sufferer, and the verdict given under such misconception of authority is equally void: my application ought, therefore, to stand or fall by the charge itself, upon which I disclaim all disingenuous caviling. I am certainly bound to show that, from the general result of it, fairly and liberally interpreted, the jury could not conceive that they had any right to extend their consideration beyond the bare fact of publication, so as to acquit the defendant by a judgment on the legality of the Dialogue, or the honesty of the intention in publishing it.

Proof that the jury must have understood the judge. that they could not acquit if they found the fact of publication.

In order to understand the learned judge's direction, it must be recollected that it was addressed to them in answer to me, who had contended for nothing more than that these two considerations ought to rule the verdict; and it will be seen that the charge, on the contrary, not only excluded both of them by general inference, but by expressions, arguments, and illustrations the most studiously selected to convey that exclusion, and to render it binding on the consciences of the jury. After telling them, in the very beginning of his charge, that the single question for their decision was, whether the defendant had published the pamphlet, he declared to them that it was not even *allowed to him, as the judge trying the cause*, to say whether it was or was not a libel; for that if he should say it was no libel, and they, following his direction, should acquit the defendant, they would thereby deprive the prosecutor of his writ of error upon the record, which was one of his dearest birthrights.

He told them that equality between the parties forbade it.

The law, he said, was equal between the prosecutor and the defendant; that a verdict of acquittal would close the matter forever, depriving him of his appeal; and that whatever, therefore, was upon the record *was not for their decision*, but might be carried, at the pleasure of either party, to the House of Lords. Surely, language could not convey a limitation upon the right of the jury over the question of libel, or the intention of the publisher, more positive or more universal. It was positive, inasmuch as it held out to them that such a jurisdiction could not be entertained without injustice. It was universal, because the principle had no special application to the particular circumstances of that trial; but subjected every defendant, upon every prosecution for a libel, to an inevitable conviction on the mere proof of publishing *any thing*, though both judge and jury might be convinced that the thing published was innocent, and even meritorious.

Effect of this.

My Lord, I make this commentary without the hazard of contradiction from any man whose reason is not disordered. For if the prosecutor, in every case, has a birthright by law to have the question of libel left open upon the record, which it can only be by a verdict of conviction on the single fact of publishing; no legal right can at the same time exist in the jury to shut out that question by a verdict of acquittal founded upon the merits of the publication, or the innocent mind of the publisher. Rights that are repugnant and contradictory can not be coexistent. The jury can never have a constitutional right to do an act beneficial to the defendant which, when done, deprives the prosecutor of a right which the same Constitution has vested in him. No right can belong to one person, the exercise of which, in *every instance*, must necessarily work a wrong to another. If the prosecutor of a libel has, in *every* instance, the privilege to try the merits of his prosecution before the judges, the jury can have no right, in *any* instance, to preclude his appeal to them, by a general verdict for the defendant.

The jury, therefore, from this part of the charge, must necessarily have felt themselves absolutely limited (I might say even in their powers) to the fact of publication; because the highest restraint upon good men is to convince them that they can not break loose from it without injustice; and the power of a good subject is never more effectually destroyed than when he is made to believe that the exercise of it will be a breach of his duty to the public, and a violation of the laws of his country.

This pretense of equality examined.

But since equal justice between the prosecutor and the defendant is the pretense for this abridgment of jurisdiction, let us examine a little how it is affected by it. Do the prosecutor and the defendant really stand upon an equal footing by this mode of proceeding? With what decency this can be alleged, I leave those to answer who know that it is only by the indulgence of Mr. Bearcroft, of counsel for the prosecution, that my reverend client is not at this moment in *prison*, while we are discussing this notable equality![15] Besides, my Lord, the judgment of this court, though not final in the Constitution, and therefore not binding on the prosecutor, is absolutely conclusive on the defendant. If your Lordships pronounce the record to contain no libel, and arrest the judgment on the verdict, the prosecutor may carry it to the House of Lords, and, pending his writ of error, it remains untouched by your Lordship's decision. But if judgment be against the defendant, it is only at the *discretion of the Crown* (as it is said), and not of right, that he can prosecute any writ of error at all. And even if he finds no obstruction in that quarter, it is but at the best an appeal for the benefit of public liberty, from which he himself can have no personal benefit; for the writ of error being no supersedeas, the punishment is inflicted on him in the mean time. In the case of Mr. Horne,[16] this court imprisoned him for publishing a libel upon its own judgment, pending his appeal from its justice; and he had suffered the utmost rigor which the law imposed upon him as a criminal, at the time that the House of Lords, with the assistance of the twelve judges of England, were gravely assembled to determine whether he had been guilty of any crime. I do not mention this case as hard or rigorous on Mr. Horne as an individual—it is the general course of practice; but surely that practice ought to put an end to this argument of *equality* between prosecutor and prisoner! It is adding insult to injury, to tell an innocent man who is in a dungeon, pending his writ of error, and of whose innocence both judge and jury were convinced at the trial, that he is in equal scales with his prosecutor, who is at large, because he has an opportunity of deciding, *after* the expiration of his punishment, that the prosecution had been unfounded and his sufferings unjust. By parity of reasoning, a prisoner in a capital case might be hanged in the mean time, for the benefit of equal justice, leaving his executors to fight the battle out with his prosecutor upon the record, through every court in the kingdom; by which at last his attainder might be reversed, and the blood of his posterity remain uncorrupted. What justice can be more *impartial* or *equal?*

So much for this right of the prosecutor of a libel to *compel* a jury, in every case, generally to convict a defendant on the fact of publication, or to find a special verdict—a right unheard of before since the birth of the Constitution—not even founded upon any equality in fact, even if such a shocking parity could exist in law, and not even contended to exist in any other case, where private men become the prosecutors of crimes for the ends of public justice. It can have, generally speaking, no existence in any prosecution for felony; because the general description of the crime in such indictments, for the most part, shuts out the legal question in the particular instance from appearing on the record. For the same reason, it can have no place even in appeals of death, &c., the only cases where prosecutors appear as the revengers of their own private wrongs, and not as the representatives of the Crown.

The judge also told the jury that established precedents confined them to the mere question of publication.

The learned judge proceeded next to establish the same universal limitation upon the power of the jury, from the history of different trials, and the practice of former judges who presided at them; and while I am complaining of what I conceive to be injustice, I must take care not to be unjust myself. I certainly do not, nor ever did, consider the learned judge's misdirection in his charge to be peculiar to himself. It was only the resistance of the defendant's evidence, and what passed after the jury returned into court with the verdict, that I ever considered to be a departure from all precedents. The rest had undoubtedly the sanction of several modern cases; and I wish, therefore, to be distinctly understood that I partly found my motion for a new trial in opposition to these decisions. It is my duty to speak with deference of all the judgments of this court; and I feel an additional respect for some of those I am about to combat, because they are your Lordship's; but, comparing them with

---

15 Lord Mansfield ordered the Dean to be committed to prison on the motion for the new trial, and said he had no discretion to suffer him to be at large, without consent, after his appearance in court, on conviction. Upon which, Mr. Bearcroft gave his consent that the Dean should remain at large upon bail.

16 Afterward Mr. Horne Tooke. For the circumstances of that case, see note 28 of this speech.

the judgments of your predecessors for ages, which is the highest evidence of English law, I must be forgiven if I presume to question their authority.

My Lord, it is necessary that I should take notice of some of them as they occur in the learned judge's charge. For, although he is not responsible for the rectitude of those precedents which he only cited in support of it, yet the defendant is unquestionably entitled to a new trial, if their principles are not ratified by the court; for whenever the learned judge cited precedents to warrant the limitation on the province of the jury imposed by his own authority, it was such an adoption of the doctrines they contained as made them a rule to the jury in their decision.

Discussion of precedents.

First, then, the learned judge, to overturn my argument with the jury for their jurisdiction over the whole charge, opposed your Lordship's established practice for eight-and-twenty years; and the weight of this great authority was increased by the general manner in which it was stated; for I find no expressions of your Lordship's, in any of the reported cases, which go the length contended for. I find the practice, indeed, fully warranted by them; but I do not meet with the *principle*, which can alone vindicate that practice, fairly and distinctly avowed.

(1.) Lord Mansfield's decisions.

The learned judge then referred to the charge of Chief Justice Raymond, in the case of the King and Franklin, in which the universal limitation contended for is, indeed, laid down, not only in the most unequivocal expressions, but the ancient jurisdiction of juries, resting upon all the authorities I have cited, treated as a ridiculous notion which had been just taken up, a little before the year 1731, and which no man living had ever dreamed of before. The learned judge observed, that Lord Raymond stated to the jury on Franklin's trial that there were three questions: the first was, the fact of publishing the "Craftsman," secondly, whether the averments in the information were true; but that the third, viz., whether it was a libel, was merely a question of *law*, with which the jury *had nothing to do*, as had been then of late thought by some people who ought to have known better. This direction of Lord Raymond's was fully ratified and adopted in all its extent, and given to the jury on the present trial, with several others of the same import, as an unerring guide for their conduct. And surely human ingenuity could not frame a more abstract and universal limitation upon their right to acquit the defendant by a general verdict; for Lord Raymond's expressions amount to an absolute denial of the right of the jury to find the defendant not guilty, if the publication and innuendos are proved. "Libel or no libel, is a question of law, with which you, the jury, *have nothing to do.*" How, then, can they have any right to give a general verdict consistently with this declaration? Can any man in his senses collect that he has a right to decide on that with which he has nothing to do? But it is needless to comment on these expressions, for the jury were likewise told by the learned judge [Buller] himself that, if they believed the fact of publication, they were *bound* to find the defendant guilty; and it will hardly be contended that a man has a right to refrain from doing that which he is bound to do.

(2.) Lord Raymond's.

Mr. Cowper, as counsel for the prosecution [against the Dean of St. Asaph] took upon him to explain what was meant by this expression; and I seek for no other construction: "The learned judge," said he, "did not mean to deny the right of the jury, but only to convey that there was a religious and moral obligation upon them to refrain from the exercise of it." Now—if the principle which imposed that obligation had been alleged to be *special*, applying only to the particular case of the Dean of St. Asaph, and consequently consistent with the right of the jury to a more enlarged jurisdiction in *other* instances—telling the jury that they were bound to convict, on proof of publication, might be plausibly construed into a recommendation to refrain from the exercise of their right in *that case*, and not to a *general* denial of its existence. But the moment it is recollected that the principle which bound them was not *particular* to the instance, but abstract and universal, binding alike in *every* prosecution for a libel, it requires no logic to pronounce the expression to be an absolute, unequivocal, and universal denial of the right. Common sense tells every man that to speak of a person's right to do a thing, which yet, in every possible instance where it might be exerted he is religiously and morally bound not to exert, is not even sophistry, but downright vulgar nonsense. But the jury were not only limited by these modern precedents, which certainly have an existence, but were, in my mind, limited with still greater effect by the learned judge's declaration, that some of those ancient authorities on which I had principally relied for the establishment of their jurisdiction, had not merely been overruled, but were altogether inapplicable. I particularly observed how much ground I lost with the jury, when they were told from the bench that even in Bushel's case, on which I had so greatly depended, the very reverse of my doctrine had been expressly established—the court having said unanimously in that case, according to the learned judge's statement, that if the jury be asked what the law is, they can not say, and having likewise ratified in express terms the maxim, *Ad quæstionem legis non respondent juratores.*[17]

Explanation of the doctrine by the counsel for the prosecution.

My Lord, this declaration from the bench, which I confess not a little staggered and surprised me, rendered it my duty to look again into Vaughan, where Bushel's case is reported. I have performed that duty, and now take upon me positively to say that the words of Lord Chief Justice Vaughan, which the learned judge considered as a judge

Bushel's case misstated by Justice Buller.

[17] The jury do not decide the qnestion of law.

ment of the court, denying the jurisdiction of the jury over the law, where a general issue is joined before them, were, on the contrary, made use of by that learned and excellent person to expose the *fallacy* of such a misapplication of the maxim alluded to by the counsel against Bushel; declaring that it had no reference to any case where the law and the fact were incorporated by the plea of not guilty, and confirming the right of the jury to find the law upon every such issue, in terms the most emphatical and expressive. This is manifest from the whole report.

Statement of the case.

Bushel, one of the jurors on the trial of Penn and Mead, had been committed by the court for finding the defendant not guilty, against the direction of the court in matter of law; and being brought before the court of Common Pleas by *habeas corpus*, this cause of commitment appeared upon the face of the return to the writ. It was contended by the counsel against Bushel, upon the authority of this maxim, that the commitment was legal, since it appeared by the return that Bushel had taken upon him to find the law against the direction of the judge, and had been, therefore, legally imprisoned for that contempt. It was upon that occasion that Chief Justice Vaughan, with the concurrence of the whole court, repeated the maxim, *Ad quæstionem legis non respondent juratores*, as cited by the counsel for the Crown, but denied the application of it to impose any restraint upon jurors trying any crime upon the general issue. His language is too remarkable to be forgotten, and too plain to be misunderstood. Taking the words of the return to the *habeas corpus*, viz., "That the jury did acquit against the direction of the court in matter of law"—"These words," said this great lawyer, "taken literally and *de plano*, are insignificant and unintelligible; for no issue can be joined of matter of law; no jury can be charged with the trial of matter of law barely. No evidence ever was or can be given to a jury of what is law or not; nor any oath given to a jury to try matter of law *alone;* nor can any attaint lie for such a false oath. Therefore we must take off this vail and color of words, which make a show of being something, but are in fact nothing; for if the meaning of these words, '*Finding against the direction of the court in matter of law*,' be, that if the judge, having heard the evidence given in court (for he knows no other), shall tell the jury, upon this evidence, that the law is for the plaintiff or the defendant, and they, under the pain of fine and imprisonment, are to find accordingly, every one sees that the jury is but a troublesome delay, great charge, and of no use in determining right and wrong; which were a strange and new-found conclusion, after a trial so celebrated for many hundreds of years in this country."

Vaughan's argument.

Lord Chief Justice Vaughan's argument is, therefore, plainly this: Adverting to the arguments of the counsel, he says, "You talk of the maxim *ad quæstionem legis non respondent juratores*, but it has no sort of application to your subject. The words of your return, viz., that Bushel did acquit against the direction of the court in matter of law, are unintelligible, and, as applied to the case, impossible. The jury could not be asked, in the abstract, what was the law; they could not have an issue of the law joined before them; they could not be sworn to try it. *Ad quæstionem legis non respondent juratores;* therefore, to say literally and *de plano* that the jury found the law against the judge's direction, is absurd. They could not be in a situation to find it—an unmixed question of law could not be before them—the judge could not give any positive directions of law upon the trial, for the law can only arise out of facts, and the judge can not know what the facts are till the jury have given their verdict. Therefore," continued the Chief Justice, "let us take off this vail and color of words, which make a show of being something, but are in fact nothing; let us get rid of the fallacy of applying a maxim, which truly describes the jurisdiction of the courts over issues of law, to destroy the jurisdiction of jurors, in cases where law and fact are blended together upon a trial; since, if the jury at the trial are bound to receive the law from the judge, every one sees that it is a mere mockery, and of no use in determining right and wrong."

This is the plain common sense of the argument; and it is impossible to suggest a distinction between its application to Bushel's case and to the present, except that the right of imprisoning the jurors was there contended for, in order to enforce obedience to the directions of the judge. But this distinction, if it deserves the name, though held up by Mr. Bearcroft as very important, is a distinction without a difference. For if, according to Vaughan, the free agency of the jury over the whole charge, uncontrolled by the judge's direction, constitutes the whole of that ancient mode of trial, it signifies nothing by what means that free agency is destroyed; whether by the imprisonment of conscience or of body; by the operation of their virtues or of their fears. Whether they decline exerting their jurisdiction, from being told that the exertion of it is a contempt of religious and moral order, or a contempt of the court punishable by imprisonment, their jurisdiction is equally taken away.

Restatement: the defendant has had no trial.

My Lord, I should be very sorry improperly to waste the time of the court; but I can not help repeating once again, that if, in consequence of the learned judge's directions, the jury, from a just deference to learning and authority, from a nice and modest sense of duty, felt themselves not at liberty to deliver the defendant from the whole indictment, HE HAS NOT BEEN TRIED. Because, though he was entitled by law to plead generally that he was not guilty, though he did, in fact, plead it accordingly, and went down to trial upon it, the jury have not been permitted to try that issue, but have been directed to find, at all events, a general verdict of guilty, with a positive injunction not to investigate the guilt, or even to listen to any evidence of innocence.

My Lord, I can not help contrasting this trial with that of Colonel Gordon's but a few sessions past in London: I had in my hand but this moment an accurate note of Mr. Baron Eyre's charge to the jury on that occasion; but I will not detain the court by looking for it among my papers, because I believe I can correctly repeat the substance of it.

Argument against Justice Buller: Baron Eyre's decision in the case of Gordon.

Lord Mansfield. The case of the King against Cosmo Gordon?

Mr. Erskine. Yes, my Lord: Colonel Gordon was indicted for the murder of General Thomas, whom he had killed in a duel, and the question was whether, if the jury were satisfied of that fact, the prisoner was to be convicted of murder? That was, according to Foster, as much a question of *law* as libel or no libel, but Mr. Baron Eyre did not, therefore, feel himself at liberty to withdraw it from the jury. After stating (greatly to his honor) the hard condition of the prisoner, who was brought to trial for life in a case where the positive law and the prevailing manners of the times were so strongly in opposition to one another, that he was afraid the punishment of individuals would never be able to beat down an offense so sanctioned, he addressed the jury nearly in these words: "Nevertheless, gentlemen, I am bound to declare to you what the law is as applied to this case, in all the different views in which it can be considered by you upon the evidence. *Of this law and of the facts as you shall find them, your verdict must be compounded;* and I persuade myself that it will be such an one as to give satisfaction to your own consciences."

Statement of the case.

Now, if Mr. Baron Eyre, instead of telling the jury that a duel, however fair and honorably fought, was murder by the law of England, and, leaving them to find a general verdict under that direction, had said to them, that whether such a duel was murder or manslaughter, was a question with which neither he nor they had any thing to do, and on which he should, therefore, deliver no opinion, and had directed them to find that the prisoner was guilty of killing the deceased in a deliberate duel, telling them that the court would settle the rest, that would have been directly consonant to the case of the Dean of St. Asaph's. By this direction the prisoner would have been in the hands of the court, and the judges, not the jury, would have decided upon the life of Colonel Gordon.

But the two learned judges differ most essentially indeed. Mr. Baron Eyre conceives himself bound in duty to state the law as applied to the particular facts, and to leave it to the jury. Mr. Justice Buller says he is not bound, nor even allowed so to state or apply it, and withdraws it entirely from their consideration. Mr. Baron Eyre tells the jury that their verdict is to be compounded of the fact and the law. Mr. Justice Buller, on the contrary, that it is to be confined to the fact only, the law being the exclusive province of the court. My Lord, it is not for me to settle differences of opinion between the judges of England, nor to pronounce which of them is wrong; but since they are contradictory and inconsistent, I may hazard the assertion that they can not both be right. The authorities which I have cited, and the general sense of mankind which settles every thing else, must determine the rest.

Difference between Eyre and Buller.

My Lord, I come now to a very important part of the case, untouched, I believe, before in any of the arguments on this occasion.

I mean to contend that the learned judge's charge to the jury can not be supported even upon its own principles. For, supposing the court to be of opinion that all I have said in opposition to these principles is inconclusive, and that the question of libel, and the intention of the publisher, were properly withdrawn from the consideration of the jury, still I think I can make it appear that such a judgment would only render the misdirection more palpable and striking.

Justice Buller wrong in his charge, even on his own principles.

I may safely assume that the learned judge must have meant to direct the jury either to find a general or a special verdict; or, to speak more generally, that one of these two verdicts must be the object of every charge; because I venture to affirm that neither the records of the courts, the reports of their proceedings, nor the writings of lawyers, furnish any account of a third. There can be no middle verdict between both; the jury must either try the whole issue generally, or find the facts specially, referring the legal conclusion to the court.

Every verdict must be either *general* or *special.*

I may affirm, with certainty, that the general verdict *ex vi termini* is universally as comprehensive as the issue, and that, consequently, such a verdict on an indictment, upon the general issue "not guilty," universally and unavoidably involves a judgment of law as well as fact, because the charge comprehends both, and the verdict, as has been said, is coextensive with it. Both Coke and Lyttleton give this precise definition of a general verdict; for they both say, that if the jury will find the law, they may do it by a general verdict, which is ever as large as the issue. If this be so, it follows by necessary consequence that if the judge means to direct the jury to find generally against a defendant, he must leave to their consideration every thing which goes to the constitution of such a general verdict, and is therefore bound to permit them to come to, and to direct them how to form, that general conclusion from the law and the fact, which is involved in the term "guilty." For it is ridiculous to say that guilty is a *fact;* it is a conclusion of law from a fact, and therefore can have no place in a special verdict, where the legal conclusion is by the court.

Every *general* verdict must be coextensive with the issue.

In this case the defendant is charged, not with having published this pamphlet, but with having published a certain false, scandalous, and wicked libel, with a seditious and libelous intention. He pleads that he is not guilty in manner

The issue in this case was not the mere fact of publishing, but of doing so with a libelous intent.

and form as he is accused; which plea is admitted on all hands to be a denial of the whole charge, and consequently does not merely put in issue the fact of publishing the pamphlet, but the truth of the whole indictment, that is, the publication of the libel set forth in it, with the intention charged by it. When this issue comes down for trial, the jury must either find the whole charge or a part of it; and admitting, for argument' sake, that the judge has a right to dictate either of these two courses, he is undoubtedly bound in law to make his direction to the jury conformable to the one or the other. If he means to confine the jury to the fact of publishing, considering the guilt of the defendant to be a legal conclusion for the court to draw from that fact, specially found on the record, he ought to direct the jury to find that fact without affixing the *epithet* of "guilty" to the finding. But if he will have a general verdict of "guilty," which involves a judgment of law as well as fact, he *must* leave the law to the consideration of the jury. For when the word "guilty" is pronounced by them, it is so well understood to comprehend every thing charged by the indictment, that the associate or his clerk instantly records that the defendant is guilty "in manner and form as he is accused"—that is, not simply that he has *published* the pamphlet contained in the indictment, but that he is *guilty of publishing the libel with the wicked intentions charged on him by the record.*

Effect of a general verdict of *guilty* in such a case.

Now, if this effect of a general verdict of "guilty" is reflected on for a moment, the illegality of directing one upon the bare fact of publishing, will appear in the most glaring colors. The learned judge says to the jury, "Whether this be a libel is not for your consideration. I can give no opinion on that subject without injustice to the prosecutor; and as to what Mr. Jones swore[18] concerning the defendant's motives for the publication, that is likewise not before you; for if you are satisfied in point of fact that the defendant *published* this pamphlet, you are bound to find him *guilty*." Why GUILTY, my Lord, when the consideration of guilt is withdrawn? He confines the jury to the finding of a *fact*, and enjoins them to leave the legal conclusion from it to the court. Yet, instead of directing them to make that fact the subject of a *special* verdict, he desires them in the same breath to find a general one—to draw the conclusion without any attention to the premises; to pronounce a verdict which, upon the face of the record, includes a judgment upon their oaths that the paper is a libel, and that the publisher's intentions in publishing it were wicked and seditious, although neither the one nor the other made any part of their consideration! My Lord, such a verdict is a monster in law, without precedent in former times, or root in the Constitution. If it be true, on the principle of the charge itself, that the fact of publication was all that the jury were to find, and all that was necessary to establish the defendant's guilt—if the thing published be a libel, why was not that fact found, like all other facts, upon special verdicts? Why was an epithet, which is a legal conclusion from the fact, extorted from a jury who were restrained from forming it themselves? The verdict must be taken to be general or special: if general, it has found the whole issue without a coextensive examination: if special, the word "guilty," which is a conclusion from facts, can have no place in it. Either this word "guilty" is operative, or unessential; an epithet of substance, or of form. It is impossible to controvert that proposition, and I give the gentlemen their choice of the alternative. If they admit it to be operative and of real substance—or, to speak more plainly, that the fact of publication found *specially*, without the epithet of "guilty," would have been an imperfect verdict, inconclusive of the defendant's guilt, and on which no judgment could have followed—then it is impossible to deny that the defendant has suffered injustice. For such an admission confesses that a criminal conclusion from a fact has been obtained from the jury, without permitting them to exercise that judgment which might have led them to a conclusion of innocence; and that the word "guilty" has been obtained from them at the trial *as a mere matter of form*, although the verdict without it, stating only the fact of publication which they were directed to find, to which they thought the finding alone enlarged, and beyond which they had never enlarged their inquiry, would have been an absolute verdict of acquittal. If, on the other hand, to avoid this insuperable objection to the charge, the word "guilty" is to be reduced to a mere word of form, and it is to be contended that the fact of publication, found specially, would have been tantamount; be it so. Let the verdict be so recorded; let the word "guilty" be expunged from it, and I instantly sit down. I trouble your Lordships no further. I withdraw my motion for a new trial, and I will maintain, in arrest of judgment, that the Dean is not convicted. But if this is not conceded to me, and the word "guilty," though argued to be but form, and though, as such, obtained from the jury, is still preserved upon the record, and made use of against the defendant as substance, it will then become us (independently of all con-

[18] Mr. Edward Jones was called for the defense, and deposed that he was a member of the Flintshire Committee; that it was intended by them to print the Dialogue in Welsh; that the Dean said he had received the pamphlet so late from Sir William Jones that he had not had time to read it; that he told the Dean that he had collected the opinions of gentlemen, which were, that it might do harm; and that, thereupon, the Dean told him that he was obliged to him for his information; that he should be sorry to publish any thing that tended to sedition; and it was for that reason that it was not published in Welsh. He further stated that it was not till after the Dialogue had been spoken of in very opprobrious terms, and the Dean's character reflected on, that the Dean stated he felt bound to show that it was not seditious, and therefore determined to publish it.

siderations as lawyers) to consider a little how that argument is to be made consistent with the honor of gentlemen, or that fairness of dealing which can not but have place wherever justice is administered.

The word *guilty* shown not to be one of mere form by supposing the facts found in a *special* verdict.

But in order to establish that the word "guilty" is a word of essential substance; that the verdict would have been imperfect without it; and that, therefore, the defendant suffers by its insertion; I undertake to show your Lordship, upon every principle and authority of law, that if the fact of publication (which is all that was left to the jury) had been found by *special* verdict, no judgment could have been given on it. My Lord, I will try this by taking the fullest finding which the facts in evidence could possibly have warranted. Supposing, then, for instance, that the jury had found that the defendant published the paper according to the tenor of the indictment; that it was written of and concerning the King and his government; and that the innuendoes were likewise as averred, K. meaning the present King, and P. the present Parliament of Great Britain; on such a finding, no judgment could have been given by the court, even if the record had contained a complete charge of a libel. No principle is more unquestionable, than that to warrant any judgment upon a special verdict, the court which can presume nothing that is not visible on the record, must see sufficient matter upon the face of it, which, if taken to be true, is conclusive of the defendant's guilt. They must be able to say, "If this record be true, the defendant can not be innocent of the crime which it charges on him." But from the facts of such a verdict the court could arrive at no such legitimate conclusion; for it is admitted on all hands, and, indeed, expressly laid down by your Lordship, in the case of the King against Woodfall, that the publication even of a libel is not *conclusive* evidence of guilt; for that the defendant may give evidence of an innocent publication.[19]

The word *guilty*, therefore, essential to conviction.

Looking, therefore, upon a record containing a good indictment of a libel, and a verdict finding that the defendant published it, but without the epithet of "guilty," the court could not pronounce that he published it with the malicious intention which is the essence of the crime.[20] They could not say what might have passed at the trial; for any thing that appeared to them, he might have given such evidence of innocent motive, necessity, or mistake, as might have amounted to excuse or justification. They would say that the facts stated upon the verdict would have been fully sufficient, in the absence of a legal defense, to have warranted the judge to have directed, and the jury to have given a general verdict of guilty, comprehending the intention which constitutes the crime; but that to warrant the bench, which is ignorant of every thing at the trial, to *presume* that intention, and thereupon to pronounce judgment on the record, the jury must not merely find full evidence of the crime, but such facts as compose its legal definition. This wise principle is supported by authorities which are perfectly familiar.

Parallel cases of special verdict.

If, in action of trover,[21] the plaintiff proves property in himself, possession in the defendant, and a demand and refusal of the thing charged to be converted; this evidence unanswered is full proof of a conversion; and if the defendant could not show to the jury why he had refused to deliver the plaintiff's property on a legal demand of it, the judge would direct them to find him guilty of the conversion. But on the same facts found by *special* verdict, no judgment could be given by the court. The judges would say, "If the special verdict contains the whole of the evidence given at the trial, the jury should have found the defendant guilty; for the conversion was fully proved; but we can not declare these facts to amount to a conversion, for the defendant's *intention* was a fact which the jury should have found from the evidence, over which we have no jurisdiction." So, in the case put by Lord Coke—I believe in his first Institute 115—if a *modus* is found to have existed beyond memory till within thirty years before the trial, the court can not, upon such facts found by special verdict, pronounce against the MODUS;[22] but any one of your Lordships would tell the jury, that upon such evidence they were warranted in finding against it. In all cases of prescription, the universal practice of judges is to direct juries, by analogy to the statute of limitations, to decide against incorporeal rights, which for many years have been relinquished; but such modern relinquishments, if stated upon the record by *special* verdict, would in no instance warrant a judgment against any prescription. The principle of the difference is obvious and universal. The court looking at a rec-

Principle on which the distinction rests.

[19] Lord Mansfield's words were, "There may be cases where the fact of the publication even of a libel, may be justified, or excused as lawful or innocent; for no fact which is not criminal, even though the paper be a libel, can amount to a publication of which a defendant ought to be found guilty.

[20] A libel is defined to be a malicious defamation expressed in printing, or writing, or by signs and pictures, &c., tending to injure the reputation of another, and thereby exposing such person to public hatred, contempt, or ridicule.

[21] Trover is an action which may be maintained by any person who has either an absolute or special property in goods, for recovering the value of such goods from another, who having, or being supposed to have, obtained possession of such goods by lawful means, has wrongfully converted them to his own use.

[22] A *modus decimandi* [mode of taking tithes]. commonly called a *modus* only, is where there is, by custom, a particular manner of tithing allowed, different from the general law of taking tithes in *kind*, which are the actual tenth part of the annual increase. By 2 and 3 Wm. IV., c. 100, the time required to establish a *modus* is now much shortened; but previously to this act, a *modus*, to be good, must have been proved to have existed from the time of legal memory, that is, from the first year of Richard the First, A.D. 1189.

ord can presume nothing; it has nothing to do with reasonable probabilities, but is to establish legal certainties by its judgments. Every crime is, like every other complex idea, capable of a legal definition. If *all* the component parts which go to its formation are put as facts upon the record, the court can pronounce the perpetrator of them a criminal; but if any of them are wanting, it is a chasm in fact, and can not be supplied. Wherever *intention* goes to the essence of the charge, *it must be found by the jury*—it must be either *comprehended* under the word guilty in the general verdict, or specifically found as a fact by the special verdict. This was solemnly decided by the court in Huggins's case, in 2d Lord Raymond, 1581, which was a special verdict of murder from the Old Bailey. It was an indictment against John Huggins and James Barnes, for the murder of Edward Arne. The indictment charged that Barnes made an assault upon Edward Arne, being in the custody of the other prisoner Huggins, and detained him for six weeks in a room newly built over the common sewer of the prison, where he languished and died; the indictment further charged, that Barnes and Huggins well knew that the room was unwholesome and dangerous; the indictment then charged that the prisoner Huggins, of his malice aforethought, was present, aiding and abetting Barnes to commit the murder aforesaid. This was the substance of the indictment.

Decided in Huggins's case that whenever *intention* enters into the charge it is involved in the verdict of guilty.

The special verdict found that Huggins was warden of the Fleet by letters patent; that the other prisoner Barnes was servant to Huggins, deputy in the care of all the prisoners, and of the deceased, a prisoner there. That the prisoner Barnes, on the 7th of September, put the deceased Arne in a room over the common sewer, which had been newly built, knowing it to be newly built and damp, and situated as laid in the indictment; *and that, fifteen days before the prisoner's death,* HUGGINS *likewise well knew that the room was new built, damp, and situated as laid. They found that, fifteen days before the death* of the prisoner, Huggins was present in the room, and saw him there under duress of imprisonment, *but then and there turned away, and Barnes locked the door, and that from that time till his death the deceased remained locked up.*

It was argued before the twelve judges, in Sergeants' Inn, whether Huggins was guilty of murder. It was agreed that he was not answerable *criminally*, for the act of his deputy, and could not be guilty, unless the criminal intention was brought personally home to himself. And it is remarkable how strongly the judges required the fact of knowledge and malice to be stated on the face of the verdict, as opposed to *evidence* of intention, and inference from a fact.

The court said, "It is chiefly relied on that Huggins was present in the room, and saw Arne *sub duritie imprisonamenti, et se avertit* [under duress of imprisonment, and turned away]; but he might be present, and not know all the circumstances; the words are VIDIT *sub duritie* [he *saw* under duress]; but he might *see* him under duress, and not *know* he was under duress; it was answered that, seeing him under duress, evidently means, he knew he was under duress. But, says the court, "We can not take things by inference in this manner; his seeing is but evidence of his knowledge of these things; and, therefore, the jury, if the fact would have borne it, should have found that Huggins knew he was there without his consent; which not being done, we can not intend these things nor infer them; we must judge of facts, and not from the evidence of facts;" and cited Kelynge, 78; that whether a man be aiding and abetting a murder is matter of fact, and ought to be expressly found by a jury.

The application of these last principles and authorities to the case before the court is obvious and simple. The criminal intention is a *fact*, and must be found by the jury; and that finding can only be expressed upon the record by the general verdict of guilty which comprehends it, or by the special enumeration of such facts as do not merely amount to evidence of, but which completely and conclusively constitute the crime. But it has been shown, and is indeed admitted, that the publication of a libel is only *prima facie* evidence of the complex charge in the indictment, and not such a fact as amounts in itself, when specially stated, to conclusive guilt. For, as the judges can not tell how the criminal inference from the fact of publishing a libel, might have been rebutted at the trial; no judgment can follow from a *special* finding that the defendant published the paper indicted, according to the tenor laid in the indictment. It follows from this, that if the jury had only found the *fact* of publication (which was all that was left to them) *without affixing the epithet of guilty* (which could only be legally affixed by an investigation not permitted to them); a *venire facias de novo* [a writ for a new trial] must have been awarded because of the uncertainty of the verdict as to the criminal intention: Whereas, it will now be argued, that if the court shall hold the Dialogue to be a libel, the defendant is fully convicted; because the verdict does not merely find that he PUBLISHED, which is a finding consistent with innocence, but finds him GUILTY of publishing, which is a finding of the criminal publication charged by the indictment.

Principle applied to this case.

My Lord, how I shall be able to defend my innocent client against such an argument, I am not prepared to say. I feel all the weight of it; but that feeling surely entitles me to greater attention, when I complain of that which subjects him to it, without the warrant of the law. It is the weight of such an argument that entitles me to a new trial; for the Dean of St. Asaph is not only found guilty, without any investigation of his guilt by the jury, but without that question being even open to your Lordships on the record! Upon the record the court can only say the Dialogue is, or is not, a libel; but if it should pronounce it to be one, the criminal intention of the defendant in publishing

The extreme injustice of such a case.

it is taken for granted by the word guilty; although it has not only not been tried, but evidently appears, from the verdict itself, not to have been found by the jury. Their verdict is, "Guilty of publishing; but whether a libel or not, they do not find." And it is, therefore, impossible to say that they can have found a criminal motive in publishing a paper, on the criminality of which they have formed no judgment. Printing and publishing that which is legal, contains in it no crime. The guilt must arise from the publication of a *libel;* and there is, therefore, a palpable repugnancy on the face of the verdict itself, which first finds the Dean guilty of publishing, and then renders the finding a nullity by pronouncing *ignorance in the jury whether the thing published comprehends any guilt!*

To conclude this part of the subject, the epithet of guilty—as I set out with at first—must either be taken to be substance or form. If it be substance, and, as such, conclusive of the *criminal* intention of the publisher, should the thing published be hereafter adjudged to be a libel, I ask a new trial, because the defendant's guilt in that respect has been found without having been tried; if, on the other hand, the word GUILTY is admitted to be but a word of form, then let it be expunged, and I am not hurt by the verdict.

Third Proposition. Remarks on the distinction set up to rebut this doctrine.

III. Having now established, according to my first two Propositions, that the jury upon every general issue, joined in a criminal case, have a constitutional jurisdiction over the whole charge; I am next, in support of my Third, to contend, That the case of a libel forms no legal exception to the general principles which govern the trial of all other crimes; that the argument for the difference, namely, because the whole charge [in a prosecution for a libel] always appears on the record—is false in fact, and that, even if true, it would form no substantial difference in law.

(1.) The distinction false in fact—a part only of a publication may be indicted.

As to the first, I still maintain that the whole case does by no means necessarily appear on the record. The Crown may indict *part* of the publication, which may bear a criminal construction when separated from the context, and the context omitted having no place in the indictment, the defendant can neither demur to it, nor arrest the judgment after a verdict of guilty; because the court is absolutely circumscribed by what appears on the record, and the record contains a legal charge of a libel.

If the defendant could read the other facts, this would do him no good, on Justice Buller's principles.

I maintain, likewise, that, according to the principles adopted upon this trial, he is equally shut out from such defense before the jury. For though he may read the explanatory context in evidence, yet he can derive no advantage from reading it, if they are tied down to find him guilty of publishing the matter which is contained in the indictment, however its innocence may be established by a view of the whole work. The only operation which, looking at the context, it can have upon a jury, is to convince them that the matter upon the record, however libelous when taken by itself, was not intended to convey the meaning which the words indicted import in language, when separated from the general scope of the writing. But upon the principle contended for, they could not acquit the defendant upon any such opinion, for that would be to take upon them the prohibited question of libel, which is said to be matter of law for the Court.

Reply to Mr. Bearcroft.

My learned friend, Mr. Bearcroft, appealed to his audience with an air of triumph, whether any sober man could believe that an English jury, in the case I put from Algernon Sidney, would convict a defendant of publishing the Bible, should the Crown indict a member of a verse which was blasphemous in itself if separated from the context.[23] My Lord, if my friend had attended to me, he would have found that, in considering such supposition as an absurdity, he was only *repeating my own words!* I never supposed that a jury would act so wickedly, or so absurdly, in a case where the principle contended for by my friend Mr. Bearcroft carried so palpable a face of injustice, as in the instance which I selected to expose it; and which I, therefore, selected to show that there were cases in which the supporters of the doctrine were ashamed of it, and obliged to deny its operation.

If the jury can acquit from a view of the *rest* of the work, this subverts the principle of the opposing counsel.

For it is impossible to deny that, if the jury can look at the context, in the case put by Sidney, and acquit the defendant on the merits of the thing published, they may do it in cases which will directly operate against the principle he seems to support. This will appear from other instances, where the injustice is equal, but not equally striking. Suppose the Crown were to select some passages from Locke upon government; as, for instance, "that there is no difference *between the King and the Constable, when either of them exceeds his authority.*" That assertion, under certain circumstances, if taken by itself, without the context, might be highly seditious, and the question, therefore, would be, *quo animo* it was written. Perhaps the real meaning of the sentence might not be discoverable by the immediate context without a view of the whole chapter—perhaps of the whole book. Therefore—to do justice to the defendant, upon the very principle by which Mr. Bearcroft, in answering Sidney's case, can alone acquit the publisher of his Bible—the jury must look into

[23] The case supposed a bookseller having published the Bible, and being indicted thus, "That, intending to promote atheism and irreligion, he had blasphemously printed and published the following false and profane libel—'There is no God;'" and, in moving for the rule *Nisi,* Mr. Erskine argued, that consistently with the principles which governed the judge, in the Dean of St. Asaph's case, the court would in such a case forbid the jury looking at the context, by which it would appear that the words formed part only of a verse in the Psalms, "The fool hath said in his heart, there is no God," and would direct them only to consider the *fact,* whether the defendant published the words last in the indictment.

the whole Essay on Government, and form a judgment of the design of the author, and the meaning of his work.

Lord Mansfield. To be sure, they may judge from the whole work.

Mr. Erskine. And what is this, my Lord, but determining the question of libel which is denied to-day? For if a jury may acquit the publisher of any part of Mr. Locke on Government, from a judgment arising out of a view of the whole book, though there be no innuendoes[24] to be filled up as facts in the indictment, what is it that bound the jury to convict the Dean of St. Asaph, as the publisher of Sir William Jones's Dialogue, on the *bare fact of publication*, without the right of saying that his observations, as well as Mr. Locke's, were speculative, abstract, and legal?

For if so, they may acquit in any and all cases.

Lord Mansfield. They certainly may, in all cases, go into the whole context.

Mr. Erskine. And why may they go into the context? Clearly, my Lord, to enable them to form a correct judgment of the meaning of the part indicted, even though no particular meaning be submitted to them by averments in the indictment. And, therefore, the very permission to look at the context for such a purpose (where there are no innuendoes to be filled up by them as facts) is a plausible admission of all I am contending for, namely, the right of the jury to judge of the merits of the paper, and the intention of its author.

But it is said, that though a jury have a right to decide that a paper, criminal as far as it appears on the record, is, nevertheless, legal when explained by the whole work of which it is a part; yet that they shall have no right to say that the *whole* work itself, if it happens to be all indicted, is innocent and legal. This proposition, my Lord, upon the bare stating of it, seems too preposterous to be seriously entertained; yet there is no alternative between maintaining it in its full extent, and abandoning the whole argument. If the defendant is indicted for publishing part of the verse in the Psalms, "There is no God," it is asserted that the jury *may* look at the context, and, seeing that the whole verse did not maintain that blasphemous proposition, but only that the *fool* had said so in his heart, may acquit the defendant upon a judgment that it is no libel to impute such imagination to a fool; but if the whole verse had been indicted, namely, "The fool has said in his heart, There is no God," the jury, on the principle contended for, *would be restrained* from the same judgment of its legality, and must convict of blasphemy on the fact of publishing, leaving the question of libel untouched on the record.

Absurdity of saying that they can not acquit because the *whole* work is indicted.

If, in the same manner, only part of this very dialogue had been indicted instead of the whole, it is said, even by your Lordship, that the jury might have read the context, and then, notwithstanding the fact of publishing, might have collected from the whole its abstract and speculative nature, and have acquitted the defendant upon that judgment of it. And yet it is contended that they have no right to form the *same* judgment of it upon the present occasion, although the whole be before them upon the face of the indictment, but are bound to convict the defendant upon the fact of publishing, notwithstanding they should have come to the same judgment of its legality, which it is admitted they might have come to on trying an indictment for the publication of a part!! Really, my Lord, the absurdities and gross departures from reason, which must be hazarded to support this doctrine, are endless.

Application to the present case.

The criminality of the paper is said to be a question of law, yet the *meaning* of it, from which alone the legal interpretation can arise, is admitted to be a question of fact! If the text be so perplexed and dubious as to require innuendoes to explain, to point out and to apply obscure expression or construction, the jury alone, as judges of fact, are to interpret and to say what sentiments the author must have meant to convey by his writing. Yet, if the writing be so plain and intelligible as to require no averments of its meaning, it then becomes so obscure and mysterious as to be a question of law, and beyond the reach of the very same men, who, but a moment before, were interpreters for the judges; and though its object be most obviously peaceable, and its author innocent, they are bound to say, upon their oaths, that it is wicked and seditious, and the publisher of it guilty! As a question of fact, the jury are to try the real sense and construction of the words indicted, by comparing them with the context; and yet, if that context itself, which affords the comparison, makes part of the indictment, the whole becomes a question of law, and they are then bound down to convict the defendant on the fact of publishing it, without any jurisdiction over the meaning! To complete the juggle, the intention of the publisher may likewise be shown as a fact by the evidence of any extrinsic circumstances, such as the context, to explain the writing, or the circumstances of mistake or ignorance under which it was pub lished; and yet, in the same breath, the intention is pronounced to be an inference of law from the act of publication, which the jury can not exclude, but which must depend upon the future judgment of the court!

Absurdity still further exposed.

But the danger of this system is no less obvious than its absurdity. I do not believe that its authors ever thought of inflicting death upon En-

[24] By an innuendo in indictments and other pleadings is meant an explanation of something supposed to be implied in what is published or given to the world. In the legal sense, it is a statement of the covert meaning contained in some word, phrase, &c. Thus, in an action against a man for the words "He is a thief," if, in any previous part of the record, the words had been charged to have been spoken of and concerning the plaintiff, in any subsequent part the defendant's meaning in the use of the word "*He*." in "*He is a thief*," may be explained by innuendo, "*thereby meaning the said plaintiff*."

glishmen, without the interposition of a jury; yet its establishment would unquestionably extend to annihilate the substance of that trial in every prosecution for high treason, where the publication of any writing was laid as the overt act. I illustrated this by a case, when I moved for a rule, and called upon my friends for an answer to it; but no notice has been taken of it by any of them. This was just what I expected: when a convincing answer can not be found to an objection, those who understand controversy never give strength to it by a weak one. I said, and I again repeat, that if an indictment charges that a defendant did traitorously intend, compass, and imagine the death of the King, and, in order to carry such treason into execution, published a paper, which it sets out *literatim* on the face of the record, the principle which is laid down to-day would subject that person to the pains of death by the single authority of the judges, without leaving any thing to the jury, but the bare fact of publishing the paper. For if that fact were proved, and the defendant called no witnesses, the judge who tried him would be warranted, nay bound in duty by the principle in question, to say to the jury, "Gentlemen, the overt act of treason charged upon the defendant is the publication of this paper, intending to compass the death of the King; the fact is proved, and you are, therefore, bound to convict him: the treasonable *intention* is an inference of law from the act of publishing; and if the thing published does not, upon a future examination, intrinsically support that inference, the court will arrest the judgment, and your verdict will not affect the prisoner."

The danger equal to the absurdity, as shown in a supposed prosecution for treason.

My Lord, I will rest my whole argument upon the analogy between these two cases, and give up every objection to the doctrine when applied to the one, if, upon the strictest examination, it shall not be found to apply equally to the other. If the *seditious* intention be an inference of law, from the fact of publishing the paper which this indictment charges to be a libel, is not the *treasonable* intention equally an inference from the fact of publishing that paper, which the other indictment charges to be an overt act of treason? In the one case, as in the other, the writing or publication of a paper is the whole charge; and the substance of the paper so written or published makes all the difference between the two offenses. If that substance be matter of law where it is a seditious libel, it must be matter of law where it is an act of treason; and if, because it is law, the jury are excluded from judging it in the one instance, their judgment must suffer an equal abridgment in the other.

The two cases compared.

The consequence is obvious. If the jury, by an appeal to their consciences, are to be thus limited in the free exercise of that right which was given them by the Constitution, to be a protection against judicial authority, where the weight and majesty of the crown is put into the scale against an obscure individual, the freedom of the press is at an end. For how can it be said that the press is free because every thing may be published without a previous license, if the publisher of the most meritorious work which the united powers of genius and patriotism ever gave to the world may be prosecuted by information of the King's Attorney General, without the consent of the grand jury—may be convicted by the petty jury, on the mere fact of publishing (who, indeed, without perjuring themselves, must on this system inevitably convict him), and must then depend upon judges, who may be the supporters of the very administration whose measures are questioned by the defendant, and who must, therefore, either give judgment against him or against themselves.

The doctrine contended for by the Crown puts the liberty of the press in the hands of the judges.

To all this Mr. Bearcroft shortly answers, Are you not in the hands of the same judges, with respect to your property, and even to your life, when special verdicts are found in murder, felony, and treason? In these cases do prisoners run any hazard from the application of the law by the judges, to the facts found by the juries? Where can you possibly be safer?

The case is different with indictments for other crimes.

My Lord, this is an argument which I can answer without indelicacy or offense, because your Lordship's mind is much too liberal to suppose that I insult the court by general observations on the principles of our legal government. However safe we might be, or might think ourselves, the Constitution never intended to invest judges with a *discretion* which can not be tried and measured by the plain and palpable standard of law; and in all the cases put by Mr. Bearcroft, no such loose discretion is exercised as must be entertained by a judgment on a seditious libel, and therefore the cases are not parallel.

On a special verdict for murder, the life of the prisoner does not depend upon the religious, moral, or philosophical ideas of the judges, concerning the nature of homicide. No; precedents are searched for, and if he is condemned at all, he is judged exactly by the same rules as others have been judged by before him. His conduct is brought to a precise, clear, intelligible standard, and cautiously measured by it; it is the law, therefore, and not the judge, which condemns him. It is the same in all indictments or civil actions for slander upon individuals.

Reputation is a personal right of the subject—indeed, the most valuable of any—and it is, therefore, secured by law, and all injuries to it clearly ascertained. Whatever slander hurts a man in his trade—subjects him to danger of life, liberty, or loss of property—or tends to render him infamous—is the subject of an action, and, in some instances, of an indictment.[25] But in all these cases where the *malus animus* is found by the jury, the judges are in like manner a safe repository of the legal consequence; because

[25] The general rule is, that wherever an action will lie for slander, without laying special damages, an indictment will lie for the same words, if reduced to writing and published.

such libels may be brought to a well-known standard of strict and positive law: they leave no discretion in the judges. The determination of what words, when written or spoken of another, are actionable, or the subject of an indictment, leaves no more latitude to a court sitting in judgment on the record, than a question of title does in a special verdict in ejectment.

But I beseech your Lordship to consider by what rule the legality or illegality of this Dialogue is to be decided by the court as a question of law upon the record. Mr. Bearcroft has admitted in the most unequivocal terms—what, indeed, it was impossible for him to deny—that every part of it, when viewed in the abstract, was legal; but he says, there is a great distinction to be taken between speculation and exhortation, and that it is this latter which makes it a libel. I readily accede to the truth of the observation; but how your Lordship is to determine that difference as a question of law, is past my comprehension. For if the Dialogue, in its phrase and composition, be general, and its libelous tendency arises from the purpose of the writer to raise discontent by a seditious application of legal doctrines, that purpose is surely a question of fact, if ever there was one, and must, therefore, be distinctly averred in the indictment, to give the cognizance of it as a fact to the jury, without which no libel can possibly appear upon the record. This is well known to be the only office of the innuendo; because the judges can presume nothing which the strictest rules of grammar do not warrant them to collect intrinsically from the writing itself.

Circumscribed by the record, your Lordship can form no judgment of the tendency of this Dialogue to excite sedition by any thing but the mere words. You must look at it as if it was an old manuscript dug out of the ruins of Herculaneum. You collect nothing from the time when, or the circumstances under which, it was published—the person by whom, and those among whom, it was circulated. Yet these may render a paper, at one time and under some circumstances, dangerously wicked and seditious, which, at another time and under different circumstances, might be innocent and highly meritorious. If puzzled by a task so inconsistent with the real sense and spirit of judicature, your Lordship should spurn the fetters of the record, and, judging with the reason rather than the infirmities of men, should take into your consideration the state of men's minds on the subject of equal representation at this moment, and the great disposition of the present times to revolution in government—if, reading the record with these impressions, your Lordships should be led to a judgment not warranted by an abstract consideration of the record—then, besides that such a judgment would be founded on facts not in evidence before the court, and not within its jurisdiction if they were, let me further remind your Lordships that, even if those objections to the premises were removed, the conclusion would be no conclusion of *law*. Your decision on the subject might be very sagacious as politicians, as moralists, as philosophers, or as licensers of the press; but they would have no resemblance to the judgments of an English court of justice, because it could have no warrant from the act of your predecessors, nor afford any precedent to your successors.

Transition to the fourth proposition: Advantages of adopting it.

But all these objections are perfectly removed, when the seditious tendency of a paper is considered as a question of fact. We are then relieved from the absurdity of legal discussion, separated from all the facts from which alone the law can arise. The jury can do what (as I observed before) your Lordships can not do in judging by the record—they can examine by evidence all those circumstances that tend to establish the seditious tendency of the paper, from which the court is shut out—they may know themselves, or it may be proved before them, that it has excited sedition already—they may collect from witnesses that it has been widely circulated and seditiously understood—or, if the prosecution (as is wisest) precedes these consequences, and the reasoning must be *à priori*, surely gentlemen living in the country are much better judges than your Lordship, what has or has not a tendency to disturb the neighborhood in which they live, and that very neighborhood is the forum of criminal trial.

If they know that the subject of the paper is the topic that agitates the country around them—if they see danger in that agitation, and have reason to think that the publisher must have intended it—they say he is guilty. If, on the other hand, they consider the paper to be legal, and enlightened in principle, likely to promote a spirit of activity and liberty in times when the activity of such a spirit is essential to the public safety, and have reason to believe it to be written and published in that spirit, they say, as they ought to do, that the writer or the publisher is not guilty. Whereas your Lordships' judgment upon the language of the record must ever be in the pure abstract; operating blindly and indiscriminately upon all times, circumstances, and intentions; making no distinction between the glorious attempts of a Sidney or a Russell, struggling against the terrors of despotism under the Stuarts, and those desperate adventurers of the year forty-five, who libeled the person, and excited rebellion against the mild and gracious government of our late excellent sovereign King George the Second.

The jury as likely as the court to decide with justice.

My Lord, if the independent gentlemen of England are thus better qualified to decide from cause of knowledge, it is no offense to the court to say that they are full as likely to decide with impartial justice as judges appointed by the Crown. Your Lordships have but a life interest in the public property, but they have an inheritance in it for their children. Their landed property depends upon the security of the government, and no man who wantonly attacks it can hope or expect to escape from the selfish lenity of a jury. On the first principles of human action they must lean heavily against him. It is only when the pride of Englishmen is insulted by such doctrines as I am opposing to-day, that they may be betrayed into a verdict delivering the guilty, rather than surrender the rights by which alone innocence in the day of danger can be protected.

Fourth Proposition.

IV. I venture, therefore, to say, in support of one of my original Propositions, That where a writing indicted as a libel neither contains, nor is averred by the indictment to contain, any slander of an individual, so as to fall within those rules of law which protect personal reputation, but whose criminality is charged to consist, as in the present instance, in its tendency to stir up general discontent—the trial of such an indictment neither involves, nor can in its obvious nature involve, any abstract question of law for the judgment of a court, but must wholly depend upon the judgment of the jury on the tendency of the writing itself to produce such consequences, when connected with all the circumstances which attended its publication.

This proposition no one has attempted directly to refute.

It is unnecessary to push this part of the argument further, because I have heard nothing from the bar against the position which it maintains. None of the gentlemen have, to my recollection, given the court any one single reason, good or bad, why the *tendency* of a paper to stir up discontent against government, separated from all the circumstances which are ever shut out from the record, ought to be considered as an abstract question of law. They have not told us where we are to find any matter in the books to enable us to argue such questions before the court, or where your Lordships yourselves are to find a rule for your judgments on such subjects. I confess that to me it looks more like legislation or arbitrary power than English judicature. If the court can say this is a criminal writing—*not* because we know that mischief was intended by its author, or is even contained in itself, but because fools, believing the one and the other, may do mischief in their folly—the suppression of such writings, under particular circumstances, may be wise policy in a state; but upon what principle it can be criminal law in England, to be settled in the abstract by judges, I confess with humility that I have no organs to understand.

Answer to an *indirect* attempt at refutation.

Mr. Leycester [counsel for the Crown] felt the difficulty of maintaining such a proposition by any argument of law, and therefore had recourse to an argument of fact. "If," says my learned friend, "what is or is not a seditious libel, be not a question of law for the court, but of fact for the jury, upon what principle do defendants, found guilty of such libels by a general verdict, defeat the judgment for error on the record; and what is still more in point, upon what principle does Mr. Erskine himself, if he fails in his present motion, mean to ask your Lordships to arrest this very judgment by saying that the Dialogue is not a libel?"

My Lord, the observation is very ingenious, and God knows the argument requires that it should be; but it is nothing more. The arrest of judgment which follows after a verdict of guilty for publishing a writing, which, on inspection of the record, exhibits to the court no specific offense against the law, is no impeachment of my doctrine. I never denied such a jurisdiction to the court. *My* position is, that no man shall be punished for the criminal breach of any law, until a jury of his equals have pronounced him guilty in *mind* as well as in *act*. *Actus non facit reum nisi mens sit rea.*[26]

But I never asserted that a jury had the power to *make* criminal law, as well as to administer it; and, therefore, it is clear that they can not deliver over a man to punishment, if it appears by the record of his accusation—which it is the office of judicature to examine—that he has not offended against any positive law; because, however criminal he may have been in his disposition, which is a fact established by the verdict, yet statute and precedents can alone decide what is by law an *indictable* offense.

If, for instance, a man were charged by an indictment with having held a discourse in words highly seditious, and were found guilty by the jury, it is evident that it is the province of the court to arrest that judgment. Why? Because, though the jury have found that he spoke the words as laid in the indictment, with the seditious intention charged upon him, which they, and they only, could find; yet, as the words are not *punishable by indictment*, as when committed to writing, the court could not pronounce judgment. The declaration of the jury, that the defendant was guilty in manner and form as accused, could evidently never warrant a judgment, if the accusation itself contained no charge of an offense against the law.

In the same manner, if a butcher were indicted for privately putting a sheep to causeless and unnecessary torture in the exercise of his trade, but not in public view, so as to be productive of evil example, and the jury should find him guilty, I am afraid no judgment could follow; because, though done *malo animo*, yet neither statute nor precedent have, perhaps, determined it to be an indictable offense; it would be difficult to draw the line. An indictment would not lie for every inhuman neglect of the sufferings of the smallest innocent animals which Providence has subjected to us:

"Yet the poor beetle which we tread upon,
In corporeal suffering feels a pang as great
As when a giant dies."

A thousand other instances might be brought of acts base and immoral, and prejudicial in their consequences, which are yet not indictable by law.

In the case of the King against Brewer, in Cowper's Reports, it was held that *knowingly* exposing to sale and selling gold under sterling for standard gold is not indictable; because the act refers to goldsmiths only, and private cheat-

[26] It is not the act which makes a man guilty, but the intention.

ing is not a common-law offense.[27] Here, too, the declaration of the jury that the defendant is guilty in manner and form as accused, does not change the nature of the accusation. The verdict does not go beyond the charge; and if the charge be invalid in law, the verdict must be invalid also. All these cases, therefore, and many similar ones which might be put, are clearly consistent with my principle. I do not seek to erect jurors into legislators or judges. There must be a rule of action in every society, which it is the duty of the Legislature to create, and of judicature to expound when created. I only support their right to determine guilt or innocence where the crime charged is blended by the general issue with the intention of the criminal; more especially when the quality of the act itself, even independent of that intention, is not measurable by any precise principle or precedent of law, but is inseparably connected with the time when, the place where, and the circumstances under which the defendant acted.

Pro cuting officers do commonly act on the principle of this proposition in their arguments to the jury.

My Lord, in considering libels of this nature, as opposed to slander on individuals, to be mere questions of fact, or, at all events, to contain matter fit for the determination of the jury, I am supported not only by the general practice of courts, but even of those very practicers themselves, who, in prosecuting for the Crown, have maintained the contrary doctrine. Your Lordships will, I am persuaded, admit that the general practice of the profession—more especially of the very heads of it, prosecuting too, for the public—is strong evidence of the law. Attorneys-general have seldom entertained such a jealousy of the King's judges in state prosecutions as to lead them to make presents of jurisdiction to juries, which did not belong to them of right by the Constitution of the country. Neither can it be supposed that men in high office and of great experience should in every instance, though differing from each other in temper, character, and talents, uniformly fall into the same absurdity of declaiming to juries upon topics totally irrelevant, when no such inconsistency is found to disfigure the professional conduct of the same men in other cases. Yet I may appeal to your Lordship's recollection, without having recourse to the state trials, whether, upon every prosecution for a seditious libel within living memory, the Attorney General has not uniformly stated such writings at length to the jury, pointed out their seditious tendency which rendered them criminal, and exerted all his powers to convince them of their illegality, as the very point on which their verdict for the Crown was to be founded.

Cases in point.

On the trial of Mr. Horne, for publishing an advertisement in favor of the widows of those American subjects who had been *murdered* by the King's troops at Lexington,[28] did the present Chancellor [Lord Thurlow], then Attorney General, content himself with saying that he had proved the publication, and that the criminal quality of the paper which raised the legal inference of guilt against the defendant, was matter for the court? No, my Lord; he went at great length into its dangerous and pernicious tendency, and applied himself with skill and ability to the understandings and the consciences of the jurors. This instance is in itself decisive of his opinion. That great magistrate could not have acted thus upon the principle contended for to-day. He never was an idle declaimer: close and masculine argument is the characteristic of his understanding.

The character and talents of the late Lord Chief Justice De Grey no less entitle me to infer his opinion from his uniform conduct. In all such prosecutions, while he was in office, he held the same language to juries; and particularly in the case of the King against Woodfall[29]—to use the expression of a celebrated writer on the occasion [Junius]—"he tortured his faculties for more than an hour, to convince them that Junius's letter was a libel."[30]

The opinions of another Crown lawyer, who has since passed through the first offices of the law, and filled them with the highest reputation, I am not driven to collect alone from his language as an Attorney General, because he carried them with him to the seat of justice. Yet one case is too remarkable to be omitted. Lord Camden, prosecuting Dr. Shebbeare, told the jury that he did not desire their verdict upon any other principle than their solemn conviction of the truth of the information, which charged the defendant with a wicked design to alienate the hearts of the subjects of this country from their king upon the throne.

To complete the account: my learned friend Mr. Bearcroft, though last, not least in favor, upon this very occasion, spoke above an hour to the jury at Shrewsbury, to convince them of the *libelous* tendency of the Dialogue, which soon afterward the learned judge desired them wholly to dismiss from their consideration, as matter with which they had no concern! The real fact

[27] But cheating has since been made a statutable offense, particularly by 7 and 8 Geo. IV.

[28] Mr. Horne (afterward Horne Tooke), in 1775, being a member of the "Society for Constitutional Information," and eager for celebrity, moved, at a meeting of that society, "That a subscription be raised for the widows, orphans, and aged parents of their American fellow-subjects, who, preferring death to slavery, were, for this reason only, *murdered* by the King's troops at Lexington and Concord, on the 19th of April, 1775." The sum of £100 was voted, and Mr. Horne took on himself the responsibility of signing the order for transmitting it to Dr. Franklin; in consequence of which he was prosecuted, and sentenced to pay £200, to be imprisoned one year, and to find securities for three.

[29] Woodfall, the printer, was prosecuted in 1770 for the publication of the celebrated Letter of Junius to the King. On the trial before Lord Mansfield, in consequence of his Lordship's direction to the jury, excluding from them the question of the letter being a libel or not, a verdict was returned of "Guilty of *printing and publishing only*."

[30] See the Preface to "Junius's Letters"

is that the doctrine is too absurd to be acted upon—too distorted in principle to admit of consistency in practice. It is contraband in law, and can only be smuggled by those who introduce it. It requires great talents and great address to hide its deformity; in vulgar hands it becomes contemptible.

Practice of the courts.

Having supported the rights of juries, by the uniform practice of Crown lawyers, let us now examine the question of authority, and see how this court itself, and its judges, have acted upon trials for libels in former times; for, according to Lord Raymond, in Franklin's case,[31] as cited by Mr. Justice Buller, at Shrewsbury, the principle I am supporting had, it seems, been only broached about the year 1731, by some men of party spirit, and then, too, for the very first time. My Lord, such an observation in the mouth of Lord Raymond proves how dangerous it is to take up as doctrine every thing flung out at *Nisi Prius;* above all, upon subjects which engage the passions and interests of government. The most solemn and important trials with which history makes us acquainted, discussed, too, at the bar of this court, when filled with judges the most devoted to the Crown, afford the most decisive contradiction to such an unfounded and unguarded assertion.

Case of the seven bishops.

In the famous case of the seven bishops,[32] the question of libel or no libel was held unanimously by the Court of King's Bench trying the cause at the bar, to be matter for the consideration and determination of the jury; and the bishops' petition to the King, which was the subject of the information, was accordingly delivered to them, when they withdrew to consider of their verdict.

Thinking this case decisive, I cited it at the trial, and the answer it received from Mr. Bearcroft was, that it had no relation to the point in dispute between us, for that the bishops were acquitted, not upon the question of libel, but because the delivery of the petition to the King was held to be no publication.

I was not a little surprised at this statement, but my turn of speaking was then past. Fortunately, to-day it is my privilege to speak last, and I have now lying before me the fifth volume of the State Trials, where the case of the bishops is printed, and where it appears that the publication was expressly proved—that nothing turned upon it in the judgment of the court, and that the charge turned wholly upon the question of libel, which was expressly left to the jury by every one of the judges. Lord Chief Justice Wright, in summing up the evidence, told them that a question had at first arisen about the publication, it being insisted on that the delivery of the petition to the King had not been proved; that the court was of the same opinion; and that he was just going to direct them to find the bishops not guilty, when in came my Lord President (such sort of witnesses were, no doubt, always at hand when wanted), who proved the delivery to his Majesty. "Therefore," continued the Chief Justice, "if you believe it was the same petition, it is a publication sufficient, and we must, therefore, come to inquire whether it be a libel." He then gave his reasons for thinking it within the case *de libellis famosis* [defamatory libels], and concluded by saying to the jury, "In short, I must give you my opinion: I do take it to be a libel; if my brothers have any thing to say to it, I suppose they will deliver their opinion." What opinion? not that the jury had no jurisdiction to judge of the matter, but an opinion for the express purpose of enabling them to give that judgment which the law required at their hands.

Mr. Justice Holloway then followed the Chief Justice; and so pointedly was the question of libel or no libel, and not the publication, the only matter which remained in doubt, and which the jury, with the assistance of the court, were to decide upon, that when the learned judge went into the facts which had been in evidence, the Chief Justice said to him, "Look you; by-the-way, brother, I did not ask you to sum up the evidence, but only to deliver your opinion to the jury, whether it be a libel or no." The Chief Justice's remark, though it proves my position, was, however, very unnecessary; for, but a moment before, Mr. Justice Holloway had declared he did not think it was a libel, but, addressing himself to the jury, had said, "*It is left to you, gentlemen.*"

Mr. Justice Powell, who likewise gave his opinion that it was no libel, said to the jury, "*But the matter of it is before you, and I leave the issue of it to God and your own consciences.*" And so little was it in the idea of any one of the court that the jury ought to found their verdict solely upon the evidence of the publication, without attending to the criminality or innocence of the petition, that the Chief Justice himself consented, on their withdrawing from the bar, that they should carry with them all the materials for coming to a judgment as comprehensive as the charge; and, indeed, expressly directed that the information, the libel, the declarations under the great seal, and even the statute book, should be delivered to them.

The happy issue of this memorable trial, in the acquittal of the bishops by the jury, exercising jurisdiction over the whole charge, freely granted to them as legal, even by King James's judges, is admitted by two of the gentlemen [for the Crown] to have prepared and forwarded the glorious era of the Revolution. Mr. Bower, in particular, spoke with singular enthusiasm concerning this verdict, choosing—for reasons sufficiently obvious—to ascribe it to a *special miracle* wrought for the safety of the nation, rather than to the right lodged in the jury to save it by its laws and Constitution!

My learned friend, finding his argument like nothing upon the earth, was obliged to ascend

[31] See *antè*, p. 666.

[32] Committed to the Tower by James II., A.D. 1688, and prosecuted for petitioning the King against their being required to promulgate his second declaration of indulgence in favor of the Roman Catholics.

to heaven to support it. Having admitted that the jury not only acted like just men toward the bishops, but as patriot citizens toward their country, and not being able, without the surrender of his whole argument, to allow either their public spirit or their private justice to have been consonant to the laws, he is driven to make them the instruments of divine Providence to bring good out of evil; and holds them up as men inspired by God to perjure themselves in the administration of justice, in order, by-the-by, to defeat the effects of that wretched system of judicature, which he is defending to-day as the Constitution of England! For if the King's judges could have decided the petition to be a libel, the Stuarts might yet have been on the throne.

Mr. Bower on the case of the bishops.

My Lord, this is an argument of a priest, not of a lawyer; and even if faith, and not law, were to govern the question, I should be as far from subscribing to it as a religious opinion. No man believes more firmly than I do, that God governs the whole universe by the gracious dispensations of his providence, and that all the nations of the earth rise and fall at his command; but, then, this wonderful system is carried on by the natural, though, to us, the often hidden, relation between effects and causes, which wisdom adjusted from the beginning, and which foreknowledge at the same time rendered sufficient, without disturbing either the laws of nature or of civil society. The prosperity and greatness of empires ever depended, and ever must depend, upon the use their inhabitants make of their reason in devising wise laws, and the spirit and virtue with which they watch over their just execution; and it is impious to suppose that men who have made no provision for their own happiness or security in their attention to their government, are to be saved by the interposition of Heaven in turning the hearts of their tyrants to protect them.

But if every case in which judges have left the question of libel to juries in opposition to law, is to be considered as a miracle, England may vie with Palestine; and Lord Chief Justice Holt steps next into view as an apostle; for that great judge, in Tutchin's case, left the question of libel to the jury, in the most unambiguous terms. After summing up the evidence of writing and publishing, he said to them as follows: "You have now heard the evidence, and you are to consider whether Mr. Tutchin be guilty. They say they are innocent papers, and no libels; and they say nothing is a libel but what reflects upon some particular person. But this is a very strange doctrine—to say it is not a libel reflecting on the government, endeavoring to possess the people, that the government is maladministered by corrupt persons, that are employed in such or such stations, either in the navy or army. To say that corrupt officers are appointed to administer affairs, is certainly a reflection on the government. If people should not be called to account for possessing the people with an ill opinion of the government, no government can subsist. For it is very necessary for all governments that the people should have a good opinion of it; and nothing can be worse to any government than to endeavor to procure animosities as to the management of it; this has always been looked upon as a crime, and no government can be safe without it be punished."

Chief Justice Holt in the case of Tutchin.

Having made these observations, did the Chief Justice tell the jury that whether the publication in question fell within that principle, so as to be a libel on government was a matter of law for the court, with which they had no concern? Quite the contrary: he considered the seditious tendency of the paper as a question for their sole determination, saying to them,

"Now you are to consider whether these words I have read to you do not tend to beget an ill opinion of the administration of government; to tell us that those that are employed know nothing of the matter, and those that do know are not employed. Men are not adapted to offices, but offices to men, out of a particular regard to their interest, and not to their fitness for the places. This is the purport of these papers."

In citing the words of judges in judicature, I have a right to suppose their discourse to be pertinent and relevant, and that, when they state the defendant's answer to the charge, and make remarks on it, they mean that the jury should exercise a judgment under their direction. This is the practice we must certainly impute to Lord Holt, if we do him the justice to suppose that he meant to convey the sentiments which he expressed. So that, when we come to sum up this case, I do not find myself so far behind the learned gentleman, even in point of express authority; putting all reason, and the analogies of law which unite to support me, wholly out of the question. There is Court of King's Bench against Court of King's Bench; Chief Justice Wright against Chief Justice Lee; and Lord Holt against Lord Raymond. As to living authorities, it would be invidious to class them; but it is a point on which I am satisfied myself, and on which the world will be satisfied likewise, if ever it comes to be a question.[33]

Comparison of authorities.

But even if I should be mistaken in that particular, I can not consent implicitly to receive any doctrine as the law of England, though pronounced to be such by magistrates the most respectable, if I find it to be in direct violation of the very first principles of English judicature. The great jurisdictions of the country are unalterable except by Parliament, and, until they are changed by that authority, they ought to remain sacred: the judges have no power over them. What parliamentary abridgment has been made upon the rights of juries since the trial of the bishops, or since Tutchin's case, when they were fully recognized by this court? None. Lord Raymond and Lord Chief Justice Lee ought, therefore, to have looked there—to their predecessors—for the law, instead of setting up a new one for their successors.

[33] Lord Camden is the one here opposed to Mansfield.

But supposing the court should deny the legality of all these propositions, or, admitting their legality, should resist the conclusions I have drawn from them: then I have recourse to my last proposition, in which I am supported even by all those authorities, on which the learned judge relies for the doctrines contained in his charge; to wit:

Fifth Proposition.

V. "That, in all cases where the mischievous intention, which is agreed to be the essence of the crime, can not be collected by simple inference from the fact charged, because the defendant goes into evidence to rebut such inference, the intention then becomes a pure unmixed question of fact, for the consideration of the jury."

Authorities in favor of the proposition.

I said the authorities of the King against Woodfall and Almon were with me. In the first, which is reported in fifth Burrow, your Lordship expressed yourself thus: "Where an act, in itself indifferent, becomes criminal when done with a particular intent, there the intent must be proved and found. But where the act itself is unlawful, as in the case of a libel, the PROOF of justification or excuse lies on the defendant; *and in failure thereof, the law implies a criminal intent.*" Most luminously expressed to convey this sentiment, namely, that when a man publishes a libel, and has nothing to say for himself—no explanation or exculpation—a criminal intention need not be proved. I freely admit that it need not; it is an inference of common sense, not of law. But the publication of a libel does not exclusively show criminal intent, but is only an implication of law, in failure of the defendant's proof. Your Lordship immediately afterward, in the same case, explained this further. "There may be cases where the publication may be justified or excused as lawful or innocent; FOR NO FACT WHICH IS NOT CRIMINAL, *though the paper* BE A LIBEL, can amount to SUCH a publication of which a defendant ought to be found guilty." But no question of that kind arose at the trial, that is, at the trial of Woodfall. Why? Your Lordship immediately explained why—"*Because the defendant called no witnesses;*" expressly saying, that the publication of a libel is not in itself a crime, unless the intent be criminal; and that it is not merely in mitigation of punishment, but that *such* a publication does not warrant a verdict of guilty.

In the case of the King against Almon, a magazine, containing one of Junius's letters, was sold at Almon's shop: there was proof of that sale at the trial. Mr. Almon called no witnesses, and was found guilty. To found a motion for a new trial, an affidavit was offered from Mr. Almon that he was not privy to the sale, nor knew his name was inserted as a publisher; and that this practice of booksellers being inserted as publishers by their correspondents, without notice, was common in the trade.

Your Lordship said, "Sale of a book in a bookseller's shop, is *prima facie* evidence of publication by the master, and the publication of a libel is *primâ facie* evidence of criminal intent: it stands good, till answered by the defendant: it must stand till contradicted or explained; *and if not contradicted, explained, or exculpated, becomes tantamount to conclusive, when the defendant calls no witnesses.*"

Mr. Justice Aston said, "*Primâ facie* evidence *not answered*, is sufficient to ground a verdict upon: if the defendant had a sufficient excuse, he might have proved it at the trial: his having neglected it where there was no surprise, is no ground for a new one." Mr. Justice Willes and Mr. Justice Ashurst agreed upon those express principles.

These cases declare the law, beyond all controversy, to be, that publication, even of a libel, is no conclusive proof of guilt, but only *primâ facie* evidence of it till answered; and that, if the defendant can show that his intention was not criminal, he completely rebuts the inference arising from the publication; because, though it remains true that he published, yet, according to your Lordship's express words, it is not such a publication of which a defendant ought to be found guilty. Apply Mr. Justice Buller's summing up to this law, and it does not require even a legal apprehension to distinguish the repugnancy.

The advertisement was proved to convince the jury of the Dean's motive for publishing; Mr. Jones's testimony went strongly to aid it;[34] and the evidence to character, though not sufficient in itself, was admissible to be thrown into the scale. But not only no part of this was left to the jury, but the whole of it was expressly removed from their consideration, although, in the cases of Woodfall and Almon, it was as expressly laid down to be within their cognizance, and a complete answer to the charge, if satisfactory, to the minds of the jurors.

Only two arguments in favor of Justice Buller's charge.

In support of the learned judge's charge, there can be, therefore, but the two arguments, which I stated on moving for the rule. Either that the defendant's evidence, namely, the advertisement—Mr. Jones's evidence in confirmation of its being *bonâ fide*—and the evidence to character, to strengthen that construction—were not sufficient proof that the Dean believed the publication meritorious, and published it in vindication of his honest intentions; or else that, even admitting it to establish that fact, it did not amount to such an exculpation as to be evidence on Not Guilty, so as to warrant a verdict. I still give the learned judge the choice of the alternative.

Remarks on the first.

As to the first, namely, whether it showed honest intention in point of fact, that was a question for the jury. If the learned judge had thought it was not sufficient evidence to warrant the jury's believing that the Dean's motives were such as he had declared them, I conceive he should have given his opinion of it as a point of evidence, and left it there. I can not condescend to go further; it would be ridiculous to argue a self-evident proposition.

As to the second, namely, that even if the

[34] For Mr. Jones's testimony, see note 18.

jury had believed, from the evidence, that the Dean's intention was wholly innocent, it would not have warranted them in acquitting, and, therefore, should not have been left to them upon Not Guilty. That argument can never be supported. For if the jury had declared, "We find that the Dean published this pamphlet; whether a libel or not, we do not find: and we find further, that, believing it in his conscience to be meritorious and innocent, he, *bonâ fide*, published it with the prefixed advertisement, as a vindication of his character from the reproach of seditious intentions, and not to excite sedition:" it is impossible to say, without ridicule, that on such a special verdict the court could have pronounced a criminal judgment.

Remarks on the second.

Then why was the consideration of that evidence, by which those facts might have been found, withdrawn from the jury, after they brought in a verdict guilty of publishing ONLY, which, in the King against Woodfall, was simply said not to negative the criminal intention, because the defendant called no witnesses? Why did the learned judge confine his inquiries to the innuendoes, and finding them agreed in, direct the epithet of guilty, without asking the jury if they believed the defendant's evidence to rebut the criminal inference? Some of them positively meant to negative the criminal inference by adding the word *only*, and all would have done it, if they had thought themselves at liberty to enter upon that evidence. But they were told expressly that they had nothing to do with the consideration of that evidence, which, if believed, would have warranted that verdict. The conclusion is evident; if they had a right to consider it, and their consideration might have produced such a verdict, and if such a verdict would have been an acquittal, it must be a misdirection.

"But," says Mr. Bower, "if this advertisement prefixed to the publication, by which the Dean professed his innocent intention in publishing it, should have been left to the jury as evidence of that intention, to found an acquittal on, even taking the Dialogue to be a libel, no man could ever be convicted of publishing any thing, however dangerous; for he would only have to tack an advertisement to it by way of preface, professing the excellence of its principles and the sincerity of its motives, and his defense would be complete." My Lord, I never contended for any such position. If a man of education, like the Dean, were to publish a writing so palpably libelous that no ignorance or misapprehension imputable to such a person could prevent his discovering the mischievous design of the author, no jury would believe such an advertisement to be *bonâ fide*, and would, therefore, be bound in conscience to reject it, as if it had no existence. The effect of such evidence must be to convince the jury of the defendant's purity of mind, and must, therefore, depend upon the nature of the writing itself, and all the circumstances attending its publication. If, upon reading the paper, and considering the whole of the evidence, they have reason to think that the defendant did not believe it to be illegal, and did not publish it with the seditious purpose charged by the indictment, he is not guilty upon any principle or authority of law, and would have been acquitted even in the Star Chamber; for it was held by that court, in Lambe's case, in the eighth year of King James the First, as reported by Lord Coke, who then presided in it, that every one who should be convicted of a libel must be the writer or contriver, or a *malicious* publisher, *knowing* it to be a libel.

Answer to Mr. Bower as to the advertisement.

This case of Lambe being of too high authority to be opposed, and too much in point to be passed over, Mr. Bower endeavors to avoid its force by giving it a new construction of his own: He says, that not knowing a writing to be a libel, in the sense of that case, means, not knowing the contents of the thing published; as by conveying papers sealed up, or having a sermon and a libel, and delivering one by mistake for the other. In such cases, he says, *ignorantia facti excusat*, because the mind does not go with the act; *sed ignorantia legis non excusat*;[35] and, therefore, if the party knows the contents of the paper which he publishes, his mind goes with the act of publication, though he does not find out any thing criminal, and he is bound to abide by the legal consequences.

Mr. Bower's attempt to evade the force of Lambe's case.

This is to make criminality depend upon the consciousness of an act, and not upon the knowledge of its quality, which would involve lunatics and children in all the penalties of criminal law; for whatever they do is attended with consciousness, though their understanding does not reach to the consciousness of offense. The publication of a libel, not believing it to be one after having read it, is a much more favorable case than publishing it unread by mistake; the one, nine times in ten, is a culpable negligence, which is no excuse at all. For a man can not throw papers about the world without reading them, and afterward say he did not know their contents were criminal. But if a man reads a paper, and not believing it to contain any thing seditious, having collected nothing of that tendency himself, publishes it among his neighbors as an innocent and useful work, he can not be convicted as a criminal publisher. *How* he is to convince the jury that his purpose was innocent, though the thing published be a libel, must depend upon *circumstances*—and these circumstances he may, on the authority of all the cases, ancient and modern, lay before the jury in evidence; because, if he can establish the innocence of his mind, he negatives the very gist of the indictment.

Reply: Intention constitutes the essence of the crime.

"In all crimes," says Lord Hale, in his Pleas of the Crown, "the intention is the principal consideration; it is the mind that makes the taking of another's goods to be felony, or a bare trespass only: it is impossible to prescribe all the

[35] This old adage, "Ignorance of a *fact* may excuse, but not of *law*," proceeds on the principle that men are bound to know the *law* of their country, but not every *fact* that may be connected with their conduct and actions.

circumstances evidencing a felonious intent, or the contrary; but the same must be left to the attentive consideration of judge *and jury:* wherein the best rule is, *in dubiis*, rather to incline to acquittal than conviction."

In the same work, he says, "By the statute of Philip and Mary, touching importation of coin counterfeit of foreign money, it must, to make it treason, be with the intent to utter and make payment of the same; and the intent in this case may be tried and found by circumstances of FACT, by words, letters, and a thousand evidences besides the bare doing of the fact."

This principle is illustrated by frequent practice, where the intention is found by the jury as a fact in a special verdict. It occurred, not above a year ago, at East Grinstead, on an indictment for burglary, before Mr. Justice Ashurst, where I was myself counsel for the prisoner. It was clear upon the evidence that he had broken into the house by force, in the night, but I contended that it appeared from proof that he had broken and entered with an intent to rescue his goods, which had been seized that day by the officers of excise; which rescue, though a capital felony by modern statute, was but a trespass, *temp. Henry VIII.*, and consequently not a burglary.

Mr. Justice Ashurst saved this point of law, which the twelve judges afterward determined for the prisoner. But in order to create the point of law, it was necessary that the prisoner's intention should be ascertained as a fact; and, for this purpose, the learned judge directed the jury to tell him with what intention they found that the prisoner broke and entered the house, which they did by answering, "To rescue his goods," which verdict was recorded.

In the same manner, in the case of the King against Pierce, at the Old Bailey, the intention was found by the jury as a fact in the special verdict. The prisoner, having hired a horse and afterward sold him, was indicted for felony; but the judges, doubting whether it was more than a fraud, unless he originally hired him intending to sell him, recommended it to the jury to find a special verdict, comprehending their judgment of his intention, from the evidence. Here the quality of the act depended on the intention, which intention it was held to be the exclusive province of the jury to determine, before the judges could give the act any legal denomination.

The error arises from confounding civil and criminal cases.

My Lord, I am ashamed to have cited so many authorities to establish the first elements of the law; but it has been my fate to find them disputed. The whole mistake arises from confounding criminal with civil cases. If a printer's servant, without his master's consent or privity, inserts a slanderous article against me in his newspaper, I ought not in justice to indict him; and if I do, the jury *on such proof* should acquit him; but it is no defense against an action, for he is responsible to me *civiliter* for the damage which I have sustained from the newspaper, which is his property. Is there any thing new in this principle? So far from it, that every student knows it is as applicable to all other cases. But people are resolved, from some fatality or other, to distort every principle of law into nonsense, when they come to apply it to printing; as if none of the rules and maxims which regulate all the transactions of society had any reference to it.

If a man, rising in his sleep, walks into a china shop, and breaks every thing about him, his being asleep is a complete answer to an *indictment* for a trespass; but he must answer in an *action* for every thing he has broken.

If the proprietor of the York coach, though asleep in his bed at that city, has a drunken servant on the box at London, who drives over my leg and breaks it, he is responsible to me in damages for the accident; but I can not indict him as the criminal author of my misfortune. What distinction can be more obvious and simple?

Let us only, then, extend these principles, which were never disputed in other criminal cases, to the crime of publishing a libel; and let us, at the same time, allow to the jury, as our forefathers did before us, the same jurisdiction in that instance which we agree in rejoicing to allow them in all others, and the system of English law will be wise, harmonious, and complete.

Peroration.

My Lord, I have now finished my argument, having answered the several objections to my five original propositions, and established them by all the principles and authorities which appear to me to apply, or to be necessary for their support. In this process I have been unavoidably led into a length not more inconvenient to the court than to myself, and have been obliged to question several judgments which had been before questioned and confirmed.

They, however, who may be disposed to censure me for the zeal which has animated me in this cause, will at least, I hope, have the candor to give me credit for the sincerity of my intentions. It is surely not my interest to stir up opposition to the decided authorities of the court in which I practice. With a seat here within the bar, at my time of life, and looking no further than myself, I should have been contented with the law as I found it, and have considered *how little* might be said with decency, rather than *how much;* but feeling as I have ever done upon the subject, it was impossible I should act otherwise. It was the first command and counsel to my youth, always to do what my conscience told me to be my duty, and to leave the consequences to God. I shall carry with me the memory, and, I hope, the practice, of this parental lesson to the grave. I have hitherto followed it, and have no reason to complain that the adherence to it has been even a temporal sacrifice: I have found it, on the contrary, the road to prosperity and wealth, and shall point it out as such to my children. It is impossible, in this country, to hurt an honest man; but even if it were possible, I should little deserve that title, if I could, upon any principle, have consented to tamper or temporize with a question which involves, in its determination and its consequences, the liberty of the press, and, in that liberty, the very existence of every part of the public freedom.

Notwithstanding this powerful argument, the court, through Lord Mansfield, gave a unanimous decision in favor of Justice Buller's doctrine, and discharged the rule for a new trial.[36] But they afterward allowed an arrest of judgment, finding, on examination, that there was nothing illegal in the Dialogue. Mr. Erskine, referring to the subject in his speech on the trial of Paine, said: "I ventured to maintain this very right of a jury over questions of libel before a noble and revered magistrate of the most exalted understanding, and the most uncorrupted integrity. He treated me, not with contempt, indeed, for of that his nature was incapable; but he put me aside with indulgence, as you do a child when it is lisping its prattle out of season." At the present day, however, most lawyers agree in the opinion expressed by Lord Campbell, that the doctrine of Mansfield, though it had obtained in the courts for a century, was a departure from the original principles of the English common law on this subject.

The decision now made, confirming that in the case of Woodfall, was considered as finally establishing the fatal principle, that the question of *libel or no libel* was one for the judges alone to decide—thus putting the liberty of the press beyond the reach of a jury, in the hands of the court. The public mind became greatly agitated on the subject. Mr. Erskine's argument was written out and widely circulated; and a way was thus prepared for a declaratory law, affirming the right of the jury "to give their verdict on the *whole matter* in issue," and ordering that "they shall not be required or directed by the court to find the defendant or defendants guilty merely on the proof of the publication by such defendant or defendants, of the papers charged to be a libel." Mr. Fox introduced a bill to this effect into the House of Commons, in 1791. When passed there, it was once defeated and again resisted by Thurlow, Kenyon, Bathurst, and all the judges in the House of Lords, but was finally passed, June 1st, 1792, chiefly through the exertions of Lord Camden. "I have said," says the distinguished jurist already mentioned, "and I still think, that this great constitutional triumph is mainly to be ascribed to Lord CAMDEN, who had been fighting in the cause for half a century, and uttered his last words in the House of Lords in its support: but without the invaluable assistance of ERSKINE, as counsel of the Dean of St. Asaph, the Star Chamber might have been re-established in this country."

SPEECH

OF MR. ERSKINE IN BEHALF OF JOHN STOCKDALE WHEN TRIED FOR A LIBEL ON THE HOUSE OF COMMONS, DELIVERED BEFORE THE COURT OF KING'S BENCH, DECEMBER 9, 1789.

INTRODUCTION.

MR. STOCKDALE was a London bookseller, who published a pamphlet, written by a Scottish clergyman named Logan, while the trial of Warren Hastings was going on, reflecting severely on the House of Commons for their proceedings therein. Mr. Fox, one of the managers of the impeachment, brought this publication before the House, as impugning the motives of those who had proposed the trial, and moved that the Attorney General be directed to prosecute the author and publisher of the pamphlet for a libel on the Commons. The fact of publication was admitted, and the case, therefore, turned on the true nature of the crime alleged.

In this speech Mr. Erskine has stated, with admirable precision and force, the great principles involved in the law of libel: namely, that every composition of this kind is to be taken as a *whole*, and not judged of by detached passages; that if its general spirit and intention are good, it is not to be punished for hasty or rash expressions thrown off in the heat of discussion, and which might even amount to libels when considered by themselves; that the interests of society demand great freedom in canvassing the measures of government; and that if a publication is decent in its language and peaceable in its import, much indulgence ought to be shown toward its author, when his real design is to discuss the subject, and not to bring contempt on the government—though in doing so he may be led, by the strength of his feelings, to transcend the bounds of candor and propriety.

---

[36] It is curious that so accurate a man as Lord Mansfield should have made so entire a mistake upon one point embraced in his decision. In maintaining that, from the time of the Revolution of 1688, the doctrine of Justice Buller had been universally received and acknowledged he quoted the following lines from a ballad by Mr. Pulteney concerning Sir Philip Yorke, the Attorney General, to prove that even "the popular party, in those days, had no idea of assuming that the jury had a right to determine upon a question of *law*."

> For Sir Philip well knows
> That his innuendoes
> Will serve him no longer
> In verse or in prose;
> For twelve honest men have decided the cause,
> Who are judges of *fact*, though not judges of *laws*.

Now it happens that the last line was written and published thus by Pulteney in the Craftsman:

> Who are judges *alike* of the *facts* and the LAWS!

—See *Erskine's Speeches*, vol. i., p. 216, New York.

This is universally considered the finest of Mr. Erskine's speeches, "whether we regard the wonderful skill with which the argument is conducted—the soundness of the principles laid down, and their happy application to the case—the exquisite fancy with which they are embellished and illustrated—or the powerful and touching language in which they are conveyed. It is justly regarded by all English lawyers as a consummate specimen of the art of addressing a jury—as a standard, a sort of precedent for treating cases of libel, by keeping which in his eye a man may hope to succeed in special pleading his client's case within its principle, who is destitute of the talent required even to comprehend the other and higher merits of his original. By these merits it is recommended to lovers of pure diction—of copious and animated description—of lively, picturesque, and fanciful illustration—of all that constitutes, if we may so speak, the poetry of eloquence."—*Edinburgh Review*, vol. xvi., p. 109.

SPEECH, &c.

Extraordinary confidence reposed in the speaker by the defendant.

GENTLEMEN OF THE JURY,—Mr. Stockdale, who is brought as a criminal before you for the publication of this book, has, by employing me as his advocate, reposed what must appear to many an extraordinary degree of confidence; since, although he well knows that I am personally connected in friendship with most of those whose conduct and opinions are principally arraigned by its author,[1] he nevertheless commits to my hands his defense and justification.

This created by the impartiality of the English bar.

From a trust apparently so delicate and singular, vanity is but too apt to whisper an application to some fancied merit of one's own; but it is proper, for the honor of the English bar, that the world should know that such things happen to all of us daily, and of course; and that the defendant, without any knowledge of me, or any confidence that was personal, was only not afraid to follow up an accidental retainer, from the knowledge he has of the general character of the profession. Happy, indeed, is it for this country that, whatever interested divisions may characterize *other places*, of which I may have occasion to speak to-day, however the counsels of the highest departments of the state may be occasionally distracted by personal considerations, they never enter these walls to disturb the administration of justice. Whatever may be our public principles, or the private habits of *our* lives, they never cast even a shade across the path of our professional duties. If this be the characteristic even of the bar of an English court of justice, what sacred impartiality may not every man expect from its jurors and its bench?

What impartiality, then, may we not expect of the court and jury?

Admitted principles applicable to the case.

As, from the indulgence which the court was yesterday pleased to give to my indisposition, this information was not proceeded on when you were attending to try it, it is probable you were not altogether inattentive to what passed at the trial of the other indictment, prosecuted also by the House of Commons. Without, therefore, a restatement of the same principles, and a similar quotation of authorities to support them, I need only remind you of the law applicable to this subject, as it was then admitted by the Attorney General, in concession to my propositions, and confirmed by the higher authority of the court, namely, that every information or indictment must contain such a description of the crime that,

First, the defendant may know what crime it is which he is called upon to answer.

Secondly, the jury may appear to be warranted in their conclusion of guilty or not guilty.

And, thirdly, the court may see such a precise and definite transgression upon the record, as to be able to apply the punishment which judicial discretion may dictate, or which positive law may inflict.

It was admitted also to follow as a mere corollary from these propositions, that where an information charges a writing to be composed or published of and concerning the Commons of Great Britain, with an intent to bring that body into scandal and disgrace with the public, the author can not be brought within the scope of such a charge, unless the jury, on examination and comparison of the *whole matter* written or published, shall be satisfied that the particular passages charged as criminal, when explained by the context, and considered as part of one entire work, were meant and intended by the author to vilify the House of Commons as a BODY, and were written of and concerning them IN PARLIAMENT ASSEMBLED.

These principles being settled, we are now to see what the present information is.

The crime charged.

It charges that the defendant—"unlawfully, wickedly, and maliciously devising, contriving, and intending to asperse, scandalize, and vilify the Commons of Great Britain in Parliament assembled; and most wickedly and audaciously to represent their proceedings as corrupt and unjust, and to make it believed and thought as if the Commons of Great Britain in Parliament assembled were a most wicked, tyrannical, base, and corrupt set of persons, and to bring them into disgrace with the public—the defendant published — *What?* Not those latter ends of sentences which the Attorney General has read from his brief, as if they had followed one another in order in this book. Not those scraps and tails of passages which are patched together upon this record, and pronounced in one breath, as if they existed without intermediate matter in the same page, and without context any where. No! This is not the accusation, even mutilated as it is; for the information charges *that, with intention to vilify*

[1] Mr. Erskine was not only a great admirer of Mr. Burke, but he was in the constant habit of referring to his productions in terms of the highest admiration.

the House of Commons, the defendant published the whole book, describing it on the record by its title: "A Review of the Principal Charges against Warren Hastings, Esq., late Governor General of Bengal:" in which, among other things, the matter particularly selected is to be found.[2]

Question for the jury to decide.

Your inquiry, therefore, is not confined to this, whether the defendant published those selected parts of it; and whether, looking at them as they are distorted by the information, they carry, in fair construction, the sense and meaning which the innuendoes put upon them; but whether the author of the entire work—I say the *author*, since, if he could defend himself, the publisher unquestionably can—whether the author wrote the volume which I hold in my hand, as a free, manly, *bonâ fide* disquisition of criminal charges against his fellow-citizen. Or whether the long, eloquent discussion of them, which fills so many pages, was a mere cloak and cover for the introduction of the supposed scandal imputed to the selected passages; the mind of the writer all along being intent on traducing the House of Commons, and not on fairly answering their charges against Mr. Hastings? This, gentlemen, is the principal matter for your consideration. And therefore, if, after you shall have taken the book itself into the chamber which will be provided for you, and shall have read the whole of it with impartial attention—if, after the performance of this duty, you can return here, and with clear consciences pronounce upon your oaths that the impression made upon you by these pages is, that the author wrote them with the wicked, seditious, and corrupt intentions charged by the information—you have then my full permission to find the defendant guilty. But if, on the other hand, the general tenor of the composition shall impress you with respect for the author, and point him out to you as a man mistaken, perhaps, himself, but not seeking to deceive others—if every line of the work shall present to you an intelligent, animated mind, glowing with a Christian compassion toward a fellow-man, whom he believed to be innocent, and with a patriot zeal for the liberty of his country, which he considered as wounded through the sides of an oppressed fellow-citizen—if *this* shall be the impression on your consciences and understandings, when you are called upon to deliver your verdict—then hear from me that you not only work private injustice, but break up the press of England, and surrender her rights and liberties forever, if you convict the defendant.

Charge made out by selecting passages, and omitting the intervening matter.

Gentlemen, to enable you to form a true judgment of the meaning of this book and of the intention of its author, and to expose the miserable juggle that is played off in the information, by the combination of sentences which, in the work itself, having no bearing upon one another, I will first give you the publication as it is charged upon the record, and presented by the Attorney General in opening the case for the Crown; and I will then, by reading the interjacent matter, which is studiously kept out of view, convince you of its true interpretation.

The information, beginning with the first page of the book, charges as a libel upon the House of Commons the following sentence: "The House of Commons has now given its final decision with regard to the merits and demerits of Mr. Hastings. The Grand Inquest of England have delivered their charges, and preferred their impeachment; their allegations are referred to proof; and from the appeal to the collective wisdom and justice of the nation in the supreme tribunal of the kingdom, the question comes to be determined whether Mr. Hastings be guilty or not guilty?"

It is but fair, however, to admit that this first sentence, which the most ingenious malice can not torture into a criminal construction, is charged by the information rather as introductory to what is made to follow it than as libelous in itself. For the Attorney General, from this introductory passage in the first page, goes on at a leap to page thirteenth, and reads—almost without a stop, as if it immediately followed the other—this sentence: "What credit can we give to multiplied and accumulated charges, when we find that they originate from misrepresentation and falsehood?"

From these two passages thus standing together, without the intervenient matter which occupies thirteen pages, one would imagine that—instead of investigating the probability or improbability of the guilt imputed to Mr. Hastings—instead of carefully examining the charges of the Commons, and the defense of them which had been delivered before them, or which was preparing for the Lords—the author had immediately, and in a moment after stating the mere fact of the impeachment, decided that the act of the Commons originated from misrepresentation and falsehood.

Gentlemen, in the same manner a vail is cast over all that is written in the next seven pages; for, knowing that the context would help to the true construction, not only of the passages charged before, but of those in the sequel of this information, the Attorney General, aware that it would convince every man who read it that there was no intention in the author to calumniate the House of Commons, passes over, by another leap, to page twenty; and in the same manner, without drawing his breath, and as if it directly followed the two former sentences in the first and thirteenth pages, reads from page twentieth: "An impeachment of error in judgment with regard to the quantum of a fine, and for an intention that never was executed and never known to the offending party, characterizes a tribunal of inquisition rather than a Court of Parliament."

From this passage, by another vault, he leaps over one-and-thirty pages more, to page fifty-

[2] The principal parts selected by the Attorney General are specified and commented on by Mr. Erskine in a subsequent part of this speech.

one, where he reads the following sentence, which he mainly relies on, and upon which I shall by-and-by trouble you with some observations: "Thirteen of them passed in the House of Commons, not only without investigation, but without being read; and the votes were given without inquiry, argument, or conviction. A majority had determined to impeach; opposite parties met each other, and 'jostled in the dark, to perplex the political drama, and bring the hero to a tragic catastrophe.'"

From thence, deriving new vigor from every exertion, he makes his last grand stride over forty-four pages more, almost to the end of the book, charging a sentence in the ninety-fifth page.

So that out of a volume of one hundred and ten pages, the defendant is only charged with a few scattered fragments of sentences, picked out of three or four. Out of a work consisting of about two thousand five hundred and thirty lines, of manly, spirited eloquence, only forty or fifty lines are culled from different parts of it, and artfully put together, so as to rear up a libel, out of a false context, by a supposed connection of sentences with one another, which are not only entirely independent, but which, when compared with their antecedents, bear a totally different construction. In this manner, the greatest works upon government, the most excellent books of science, the sacred Scriptures themselves, might be distorted into libels, by forsaking the general context, and hanging a meaning upon selected parts. Thus, as in the text put by Algernon Sidney, "The fool hath said in his heart, there is no God," the Attorney General, on the principle of the present proceeding against this pamphlet, might indict the publisher of the Bible for blasphemously denying the existence of heaven, in printing, "There is no God," for these words alone, without the context, would be selected by the information, and the Bible, like this book, would be underscored to meet it. Nor could the defendant, in such a case, have any possible defense, unless the jury were permitted to see, *by the book itself*, that the verse, instead of denying the existence of the Divinity, only imputed that imagination to a *fool*.

Any book might in this way be convicted of error.

Gentlemen, having now gone through the Attorney General's reading, the book shall presently come forward and speak for itself. But before I can venture to lay it before you, it is proper to call your attention to how matters stood at the time of its publication: without which the author's meaning and intention can not possibly be understood.[3]

Preliminary considerations before taking up the book.

The Commons of Great Britain, in Parliament assembled, had accused Mr. Hastings, as Governor General of Bengal, of high crimes and misdemeanors; and their jurisdiction, for that high porpose of national justice, was unquestionably competent. But it is proper you should know the nature of this inquisitorial capacity. The Commons, in voting an impeachment, may be compared to a grand jury finding a bill of indictment for the Crown. Neither the one nor the other can be supposed to proceed but upon the matter which is brought before them; neither of them can find guilt without accusation, nor the truth of accusation without evidence. When, therefore, we speak of the "accuser," or "accusers," of a person indicted for any crime, although the grand jury are the accusers *in form*, by giving effect to the accusation, yet, in common parlance, we do not consider *them* as the responsible authors of the prosecution. If I were to write of a most wicked indictment, found against an innocent man, which was preparing for trial, nobody who read it would conceive I meant to stigmatize the grand jury that found the bill; but it would be inquired immediately, who was the prosecutor, and who were the witnesses on the back of it? In the same manner, I mean to contend, that if this book is read with only common attention, the whole scope of it will be discovered to be this: That, in the opinion of the author, Mr. Hastings had been accused of maladministration in India, from the heat and spleen of political divisions in Parliament, and not from any zeal for national honor or justice; that the impeachment did not originate from government, but from a faction banded against it, which, by misrepresentation and violence, had fastened it on an unwilling House of Commons; that, prepossessed with this sentiment (which, however unfounded, makes no part of the present business, since the publisher is not called before you for defaming individual members of the Commons, but for a contempt of the Commons as a body), the author pursues the charges, article by article; enters into a warm and animated vindication of Mr. Hastings, by regular answers to each of them; and that, as far as the mind and soul of a man can be visible, I might almost say embodied in his writings, his intention throughout the whole volume appears to have been to charge with injustice the *private accusers* of Mr. Hastings, and not the House of Commons as a body; which undoubtedly rather reluctantly gave way to, than heartily adopted the impeachment.[4] This will be found to be the palpable scope of the book; and no man who can read English, and who, at the same time, will have the candor and common sense to take up his impressions from what is written in it, instead of bringing his

(1.) Character and conduct of the House in impeaching Mr. Hastings.

[3] One of the most admirable things in this defense was the introduction of this preliminary matter. Before comparing the book with the charges, Mr. Erskine here brings forward the character sustained by the Commons, and the error they committed in allowing the charges against Hastings to be published to the world. He thus shows the *necessity* of some defense on the part of the accused. He next awakens sympathy in his favor by a powerful description of the trial, and of the talent arrayed against his client in Westminster Hall.

[4] This distinction between the individual opponents of Mr. Hastings and the House to which they belonged, was one of the turning-points of the case, and was used by Mr. Erskine with great effect when he came to comment on the pamphlet.

own along with him to the reading of it, can possibly understand it otherwise.

But it may be said, that admitting this to be the scope and design of the author, what right had he to canvass the merits of an accusation upon the records of the Commons, more especially while it was in the course of legal procedure? This, I confess, might have been a serious question, but the Commons, *as prosecutors of this information*, seem to have waived or forfeited their right to ask it. Before they sent the Attorney General into this place, to punish the publication of answers to their charges, they should have recollected that their own want of circumspection in the maintenance of their privileges, and in the protection of persons accused before them, had given to the public the charges themselves, which *should* have been confined to their own journals. The course and practice of Parliament might warrant the printing of them for the use of their own members; but there the publication should have stopped, and all further progress been resisted by authority. If they were resolved to consider answers to their charges as a contempt of their privileges, and to punish the publication of them by such severe prosecutions, it would have well become them to have begun first with those printers who, by publishing the charges themselves throughout the whole kingdom, or rather throughout the whole civilized world, were anticipating the passions and judgments of the public against a subject of England upon his trial, so as to make the publication of *answers* to them not merely a privilege, but a debt and duty to humanity and justice. The Commons of Great Britain claimed and exercised the privileges of questioning the innocence of Mr. Hastings by their impeachment: but as, however questioned, it was still to be presumed and protected, until guilt was established by a judgment, he whom they had accused had an equal claim upon their justice, to guard him from prejudice and misrepresentation until the hour of trial.

(2.) The House provoked this attack by allowing the charges against Hastings to be published.

Had the Commons, therefore, by the exercise of their high, necessary, and legal privileges, kept the public aloof from all canvass of their proceedings, by an early punishment of printers, who, without reserve or secrecy, had sent out *the charges* into the world from a thousand presses in every form of publication, they would have then stood upon ground to-day from whence no argument of policy or justice could have removed them; because nothing can be more incompatible with either than appeals to the many upon subjects of judicature, which, by common consent, a few are appointed to determine, and which must be determined by facts and principles, which the multitude have neither leisure nor knowledge to investigate. But then, let it be remembered that it is for those who have the authority to accuse and punish, to set the example of, and to enforce this reserve, which is so necessary for the ends of justice. Courts of law, therefore, in England, never endure the publication of their records. A prosecutor of an indictment would be attached for such a publication; and, upon the same principle, a defendant would be punished for anticipating the justice of his country, by the publication of his defense, the public being no party to it, until the tribunal appointed for its determination be open for its decision.

Such a procedure contrary to all judicial usage.

Gentlemen, you have a right to take judicial notice of these matters, without the proof of them by witnesses. For jurors may not only, without evidence, found their verdicts on facts that are notorious, but upon what they know privately themselves, after revealing it upon oath to one another. Therefore, you are always to remember that this book was written when the *charges* against Mr. Hastings, to which it is an answer, were, *to the knowledge of the Commons* (for we can not presume our watchmen to have been asleep), publicly hawked about in every pamphlet, magazine, and newspaper in the kingdom. You well know with what a curious appetite these charges were devoured by the whole public, interesting as they were, not only from their importance, but from the merit of their composition; certainly not so intended by the honorable and excellent composer to oppress the accused, but because the commonest subjects swell into eloquence under the touch of his sublime genius. Thus, by the remissness of the Commons, who are now the prosecutors of this information, a subject of England, who was not even charged with contumacious resistance to authority, much less a proclaimed outlaw, and therefore fully entitled to every protection which the customs and statutes of the kingdom hold out for the protection of British liberty, saw himself pierced with the arrows of thousands and ten thousands of libels.

These things, though not in evidence, are properly before the jury.

Gentlemen, before I venture to lay the book before you, it must be yet further remembered (for the fact is equally notorious) that under these inauspicious circumstances the trial of Mr. Hastings at the bar of the Lords had actually commenced long before its publication.

There the most august and striking spectacle was daily exhibited which the world ever witnessed. A vast stage of justice was erected, awful from its high authority, splendid from its illustrious dignity, venerable from the learning and wisdom of its judges, captivating and affecting from the mighty concourse of all ranks and conditions which daily flocked into it, as into a theater of pleasure. There, when the whole public mind was at once awed and softened to the impression of every human affection, there appeared, day after day, one after another, men of the most powerful and exalted talents, eclipsing by their accusing eloquence the most boasted harangues of antiquity; rousing the pride of national resentment by the boldest invectives against broken faith and violated treaties, and shaking the bosom with alternate pity and horror by the most glowing pictures of insulted nature and humanity; ever animated and ener-

(3.) Description of the trial.

getic, from the love of fame, which is the inherent passion of genius; firm and indefatigable, from a strong prepossession of the justice of their cause.

Gentlemen, when the author sat down to write the book now before you, all this terrible, unceasing, exhaustless artillery of warm zeal, matchless vigor of understanding, consuming and devouring eloquence, united with the highest dignity, was daily, and without prospect of conclusion, pouring forth upon one private unprotected man, who was bound to hear it, in the face of the whole people of England, with reverential submission and silence. I do not complain of this, as I did of the publication of the charges, because it is what the law allowed and sanctioned in the course of a public trial. But when it is remembered that we are not angels, but weak, fallible men, and that even the noble judges of that high tribunal are clothed beneath their ermines with the common infirmities of man's nature, it will bring us all to a proper temper for considering the book itself, which will in a few moments be laid before you. But first, let me once more remind you, that it was under all these circumstances, and amid the blaze of passion and prejudice, which the scene I have been endeavoring faintly to describe to you might be supposed likely to produce, that the author, whose name I will now give to you, sat down to compose the book which is prosecuted to-day as a libel.

The history of it is very short and natural.

Origin of the pamphlet.

The Rev. Mr. Logan, minister of the Gospel at Leith, in Scotland, a clergyman of the purest morals, and, as you will see by-and-by, of very superior talents, well acquainted with the human character, and knowing the difficulty of bringing back public opinion after it is settled on any subject, took a warm, unbought, unsolicited interest in the situation of Mr. Hastings, and determined, if possible, to arrest and suspend the public judgment concerning him. He felt for the situation of a fellow-citizen exposed to a trial which, whether right or wrong, is undoubtedly a severe one—a trial certainly not confined to a few criminal acts like those we are accustomed to, but comprehending the transactions of a whole life, and the complicated policies of numerous and distant nations—a trial which had neither visible limits to its duration,[5] bounds to its expense, nor circumscribed compass for the grasp of memory or understanding—a trial which had, therefore, broke loose from the common form of decision, and had become the universal topic of discussion in the world, superseding not only every other grave pursuit, but every fashionable dissipation.

Gentlemen, the question you have, therefore, to try upon all this matter is extremely simple. It is neither more nor less than this: At a time when the charges against Mr. Hastings were, by the implied consent of the Commons, in every hand, and on every table—when, by their managers, the lightning of eloquence was incessantly consuming him, and flashing in the eyes of the public—when every man was with perfect impunity saying, and writing, and publishing, just what he pleased of the supposed plunderer and devastator of nations—would it have been criminal *in Mr. Hastings himself* to have reminded the public that he was a native of this free land, entitled to the common protection of her justice, and that he had a defense, in his turn, to offer to them, the outlines of which he implored them, in the mean time, to receive as an antidote to the unlimited and unpunished poison in circulation against him? THIS IS, without color or exaggeration, the true question you are to decide. For I assert, without the hazard of contradiction, that if Mr. Hastings himself could have stood justified or excused in your eyes for publishing this volume in his own defense, the author, if he wrote it *bonâ fide* to defend him, must stand equally excused and justified; and if the author be justified, the publisher can not be criminal, unless you have evidence that it was published by him, with a different spirit and intention from those in which it was written. The question, therefore, is correctly what I just now stated it to be: Could *Mr. Hastings* have been condemned to infamy for writing this book?

Question for the jury to decide, in view of these facts.

Ground of the defense.

Gentlemen, I tremble with indignation, to be driven to put such a question in England. Shall it be endured, that a subject of this country (instead of being arraigned and tried for some single act in her ordinary courts, where the accusation, as soon, at least, as it is made public, is followed within a few hours by the decision) may be impeached by the Commons for the transactions of twenty years—that the accusation shall spread as wide as the region of letters—that the accused shall stand, day after day, and year after year, as a spectacle before the public, which shall be kept in a perpetual state of inflammation against him; yet that he shall not, without the severest penalties, be permitted to submit any thing to the judgment of mankind in his defense? If this be law (which it is for you to-day to decide), such a man has NO TRIAL! That great hall, built by our fathers for English justice, is no longer a court, but an altar; and an Englishman, instead of being judged in it by GOD AND HIS COUNTRY, IS A VICTIM AND A SACRIFICE![6]

You will carefully remember that I am not

[5] The trial began 13th February, 1788, and was protracted until 17th April, 1795 (occupying one hundred and forty-eight days), when Mr. Hastings was acquitted by a large majority on every separate article charged against them. The costs of the defense amounted to £76,080.

[6] In the next paragraph Mr. Erskine shows that peculiar caution which he always maintained in his boldest flights. He instantly comes back to the rights of the House, and the propriety with which the managers had conducted. He thus took care to impress his hearers, in his most impassioned passages, with the feeling that all he said was in the exercise of the severest judgment—that he was never borne away by mere emotion in his most fervent appeals. This gave great weight to his more glowing passages.

presuming to question either the right or duty of the Commons of Great Britain to impeach; neither am I arraigning the propriety of their selecting, as they have done, the most extraordinary persons for ability which the age has produced, to manage their impeachment. Much less am I censuring the managers themselves, charged with the conduct of it before the Lords, who are undoubtedly bound, by their duty to the House and to the public, to expatiate upon the crimes of the persons whom they had accused. None of these points are questioned by me, nor are in this place questionable. I only desire to have it decided whether, if the Commons, when national expediency happens to call in their judgment for an impeachment, shall, instead of keeping it on their own records, and carrying it with due solemnity to the Peers for trial, permit it, without censure and punishment, to be sold like a common newspaper in the shop of my client, so crowded with their own members that no plain man, without privilege of Parliament, can hope even for a sight of the fire in the winter's day, every man buying it, reading it, and commenting upon it—the gentleman himself who is the object of it, or his friend in his absence, may not, without stepping beyond the bounds of English freedom, put a copy of what is thus published into his pocket, and send back to the very same shop for publication a *bonâ fide*, rational, able answer to it; in order that the bane and antidote may circulate together, and the public be kept straight till the day of decision. If you think, gentlemen, that this common duty of self-preservation to the accused himself, which nature writes as a law upon the hearts of even savages and brutes, is nevertheless too high a privilege to be enjoyed by an impeached and suffering Englishman; or if you think it beyond the offices of humanity and justice, when brought home to the hand of a brother or a friend, you will say so by your verdict of guilty; the decision will then be *yours*; and the consolation *mine*, that I have labored to avert it. A very small part of the misery which will follow from it is likely to light upon *me*; the rest will be divided among *yourselves and your children*.

Recapitulation.

Gentlemen, I observe plainly and with infinite satisfaction, that you are shocked and offended at my even supposing it possible you should pronounce such a detestable judgment; and that you only require of me to make out to your satisfaction, as I promised, that the real scope and object of this book is a *bonâ fide* defense of Mr. Hastings, and not a cloak and cover for scandal on the House of Commons. I engage to do this, and I engage for nothing more. I shall make an open, manly defense. I mean to torture no expressions from their natural constructions, to dispute no innuendoes on the record, should any of them have a fair application; nor to conceal from your notice any unguarded, intemperate expressions, which may, perhaps, be found to chequer the vigorous and animated career of the work. Such a conduct might, by accident, shelter the defendant; but it would be the surrender of the very principle on which alone the liberty of the English press can stand; and I shall never defend any man from a temporary imprisonment by the permanent loss of my own liberty, and the ruin of my country. I mean, therefore, to submit to you that though you should find a few lines in page thirteen or twenty-one; a few more in page fifty-one, and some others in other places; containing expressions bearing on the House of Commons, even as a body, which, if written as independent paragraphs by themselves, would be indefensible libels, yet, that you have a right to pass them over in judgment, provided the substance clearly appears to be a *bonâ fide* conclusion, arising from the honest investigation of a subject which it was lawful to investigate, and the questionable expressions, the visible effusion of a zealous temper, engaged in an honorable and legal pursuit. After this preparation, I am not afraid to lay the book in its genuine state before you.

Transition to an examination of the pamphlet.

The pamphlet begins thus: "The House of Commons has now given its final decision with regard to the merits and demerits of Mr. Hastings. The Grand Inquest of England have delivered their charges, and preferred their impeachment; their allegations are referred to proof; and, from the appeal to the collective wisdom and justice of the nation in the supreme tribunal of the kingdom, the question comes to be determined, whether Mr. Hastings be guilty or not guilty?"

Comments thereon.

Now if, immediately after what I have just read to you—which is the first part charged by the information—the author had said, "Will accusations, built on such a baseless fabric, prepossess the public in favor of the impeachment? What credit can we give to multiplied and accumulated charges, when we find that they originate from misrepresentation and falsehood?" every man would have been justified in pronouncing that he was attacking the House of Commons; because the groundless accusations mentioned in the second sentence could have no reference but to the House itself mentioned by name in the first and only sentence which preceded it.

But, gentlemen, to your astonishment I will now read *what intervenes* between these two passages. From this you will see, beyond a possibility of doubt, that the author never meant to calumniate the House of Commons, but to say that the accusations of Mr. Hastings before the whole House grew out of a Committee of Secrecy established some years before, and was afterward brought forward by the spleen of private enemies and a faction in the government. This will appear not only from the grammatical construction of the words, but from what is better than words, from the meaning which a person writing as a friend of Mr. Hastings must be supposed to have intended to convey. Why should such a friend attack the House of Commons? Will any man gravely tell me that the House of Commons, *as a body*, ever wished to impeach Mr. Hastings? Do we not all know that they constantly hung back from it, and hardly knew where they were, or what to do when they found themselves entangled with it? My learned friend, the Attorney General, is a member of this Assembly: perhaps he may tell you by-and-by what HE thought of it, and whether he ever marked any disposition in the majority of the Commons hostile to Mr. Hastings. But why should I distress my friend by the question? the fact is sufficiently notorious; and what I am going to read from the book itself—which is left out in the information—is too plain for controversy.

"Whatever may be the event of the impeachment, the proper exercise of such power is a valuable privilege of the British Constitution, a formidable guardian of the public liberty and the dignity of the nation. *The only danger is, that, from the influence of faction, and the awe which is annexed to great names, they may be prompted to determine before they inquire, and to pronounce judgment without examination.*"

Here is the clue to the whole pamphlet. The author trusts to, and respects, the House of Commons, but is afraid their mature and just examination may be disturbed by *faction*. Now, does he mean government by *faction?* Does he mean the majority of the Commons by *faction?* Will the House, which is the prosecutor here, sanction that application of the phrase; or will the Attorney General admit the majority to be the true innuendo of *faction?* I wish he would; I should then have gained something at least by this extraordinary debate. But I have no expectation of the sort; such a concession would be too great a sacrifice to any prosecution, at a time when every thing is considered as faction that disturbs the repose of the minister in Parliament. But, indeed, gentlemen, some things are too plain for argument. The author certainly means *my* friends, who, whatever qualifications may belong to them, must be contented with the appellation of *faction*, while they oppose the minister in the House of Commons; but the House having given this meaning to the phrase of faction for its own purposes, can not in decency change the interpretation, in order to convict my client. I take that to be beyond the privilege of Parliament.

The same bearing upon individual members of the Commons, *and not on the Commons as a body*, is obvious throughout. Thus, after saying, in page ninth, that the East India Company had thanked Mr. Hastings for his meritorious services—which is unquestionably true—he adds, "that mankind would abide by their deliberate decision, rather than by the intemperate assertion of a *committee*."

This he writes after the impeachment was found by the Commons at large. But he takes no account of their proceedings; imputing the whole to the original committee—that is, the *Committee of Secrecy*[7]—so called, I suppose, from their being the authors of twenty volumes in folio, which will remain a secret to all posterity, as nobody will ever read them. The same construction is equally plain from what immediately follows: "The report of the *Committee of Secrecy* also states that the happiness of the native inhabitants of India has been deeply affected, their confidence in English faith and lenity shaken and impaired, and the character of this nation wantonly and wickedly degraded."

Here, again, you are grossly misled by the omission of nearly twenty-one pages. For the author, though he is here speaking of this committee *by name*, which brought forward the charges to the notice of the House, and which he continues to do onward to the next selected paragraph, yet, by arbitrarily sinking the whole context, he is taken to be speaking to the House as a *body*, when, in the passage next charged by the information, he reproaches the *accusers* of Mr. Hastings; although, so far is he from considering them as the House of Commons, that in the very same page he speaks of the articles as the charges not even of the committee, but of Mr. Burke alone, the most active and intelligent member of that body, having been circulated in India by a relation of that gentleman: "The charges of Mr. Burke have been carried to Calcutta, and carefully circulated in India."

Now if we were considering these passages of the work as calumniating a body of gentlemen, many of whom I must be supposed highly to respect, or as reflecting upon my worthy friend whose name I have mentioned, it would give rise to a totally different inquiry, which it is neither my duty nor yours to agitate. But surely, the more that consideration obtrudes itself upon us, the more clearly it demonstrates that the author's whole direction was against the individual accusers of Mr. Hastings, and not against the House of Commons, which merely trusted to the matter they had collected.

Although, from a caution which my situation dictates, as representing another, I have thought it my duty thus to point out to you the real intention of the author, as it appears by the fair construction of the work, yet I protest, that in my own apprehension it is very immaterial whether he speaks of the committee or of the House, provided you shall think the whole volume a *bonâ fide* defense of Mr. Hastings. This is the great point I am, by all my observations, endeavoring to establish, and which, I think, no man who reads the following short passages can doubt. Very intelligent persons have, indeed, considered them, if founded in facts, to render every other amplification unnecessary. The first of them is as follows: "It was known at that time that Mr. Hastings had not only descended from a public to a private station, but that he was persecuted

[7] The Secret Committee and the Select Committee for inquiring into the general management of the state of affairs in India were first appointed in 1781. In 1782, the committees having made their reports, which were exceedingly voluminous, Mr. Dundas, the chairman of the Secret Committee, moved no less than one hundred and eleven resolutions, and concluded with a censure on the conduct of Warren Hastings.

with accusations and impeachments. But none of these *suffering millions* have sent their complaints to this country; not a sigh nor a groan has been wafted from India to Britain. On the contrary, testimonies the most honorable to the character and merit of Mr. Hastings have been transmitted by those very princes whom he has been supposed to have loaded with the deepest injuries."

Here, gentlemen, we must be permitted to pause together a little; for, in examining whether these pages were written as an honest answer to the charges of the Commons, or as a prostituted defense of a notorious criminal, whom the writer believed to be guilty, truth becomes material at every step. For if, in any instance, he be detected of a willful misrepresentation, he is no longer an object of your attention.

Comparison of the case of Hastings with that of Verres.

Will the Attorney General proceed, then, to detect the hypocrisy of our author, by giving us some details of the *proofs* by which these personal enormities have been established, and which the writer must be supposed to have been acquainted with? I ask this as the defender of Mr. Stockdale, not of Mr. Hastings, with whom I have no concern. I am sorry, indeed, to be so often obliged to repeat this protest; but I really feel myself embarrassed with those repeated coincidences of defense which thicken on me as I advance, and which were, no doubt, overlooked by the Commons when they directed this interlocutory inquiry into his conduct. I ask, then, as counsel for Mr. Stockdale, whether, when a great state criminal is brought for justice at an immense expense to the public, accused of the most oppressive cruelties, and charged with the robbery of princes and the destruction of nations, it is not open to any one to ask, Who are his accusers? What are the sources and the authorities of these shocking complaints? Where are the embassadors or memorials of those princes whose revenues he has plundered? Where are the witnesses for those unhappy men in whose persons the rights of humanity have been violated? How deeply buried is the blood of the innocent, that it does not rise up in retributive judgment to confound the guilty! These, surely, are questions which, when a fellow-citizen is upon a long, painful, and expensive trial, humanity has a right to propose; which the plain sense of the most unlettered man may be expected to dictate, and which all history must provoke from the more enlightened. When CICERO impeached VERRES[8] before the great tribunal of Rome, of similar cruelties and depredations in *her* provinces, the Roman people were not left to such inquiries. All Sicily surrounded the Forum, demanding justice upon her plunderer and spoiler, with tears and imprecations. It was not by the eloquence of the orator, but by the cries and tears of the miserable, that Cicero prevailed in that illustrious cause. Verres fled from the oaths of his accusers and their witnesses, and not from the voice of Tully. To preserve the fame of his eloquence, he composed his five celebrated speeches, but they were never delivered against the criminal, because he had fled from the city, appalled with the sight of the persecuted and the oppressed. It may be said that the cases of Sicily and India are widely different; perhaps they may be; whether they are or not, is foreign to my purpose. I am not bound to deny the possibility of answers to such questions; I am only vindicating *the right to ask them.*[9]

Gentlemen, the author, in the other passage which I marked out to your attention, goes on thus: "Lord Cornwallis and Sir John Macpherson, his successors in office, have given the same voluntary tribute of approbation to his measures as Governor General of India. A letter from the former, dated the 10th of August, 1786, gives the following account of our dominions in Asia: 'The native inhabitants of this kingdom are the happiest and best protected subjects in India; our native allies and tributaries confide in our protection; the country powers are aspiring to the friendship of the English; and from the King of Tidore, toward New Guinea, to Timur Shah, on the banks of the Indus, there is not a state that has not *lately* given us proofs of confidence and respect.'"

Still pursuing the same test of sincerity, let us examine this defensive allegation.

Will the Attorney General say that he does not believe such a letter from Lord Cornwallis ever existed? No: for he knows that it is as authentic as any document from India upon the table of the House of Commons. What, then, is the letter? "The native inhabitants of this kingdom, says Lord Cornwallis (writing from the very spot), are the happiest and best protected subjects in India," &c., &c., &c. The inhabitants of *this kingdom! Of what kingdom?* Of the very kingdom which Mr. Hastings has just returned from governing for thirteen years, and for the misgovernment and desolation of which he stands every day as a criminal, or rather as a spectacle, before us. This is matter for serious reflection, and fully entitles the author to put the question which immediately follows: "Does this authentic account of the administration of Mr. Hastings, and of the state of India, correspond with the gloomy picture of despotism and despair drawn by the *Committee of Secrecy?*"

Had that picture been even drawn by the House of Commons itself, he would have been

[8] Verres, as prætor and governor of Sicily, was guilty of such extortion and oppression, that the Sicilian people brought an accusation against him in the Senate, and Cicero conducted the impeachment. Verres was defended by Hortensius, the celebrated Roman orator; but, aware of the justice of the accusation, he left Rome without waiting the result.

[9] This passage was probably suggested by one in Mr. Sheridan's speech on the Begum Charge (page 409), where he is showing the difficulties under which the Managers labored in procuring their evidence. Nothing could be happier than Mr. Erskine's application of the case of Verres to illustrate the point—nothing more vivid than his picture of the scene.

fully justified in asking this question; but you observe it has no bearing on it; the last words not only entirely destroy that interpretation, but also the meaning of the very next passage, which is selected by the information as criminal, namely, "What credit can we give to multiplied and accumulated charges, when we find that they originate from misrepresentation and falsehood?"

This passage, which is charged as a libel on the Commons, when thus compared with its immediate antecedent, can bear but one construction. It is impossible to contend that it charges misrepresentation on the House that found the impeachment, but upon the *Committee of Secrecy* just before adverted to, who were supposed to have selected the matter, and brought it before the whole House for judgment.

I do not mean, as I have often told you, to vindicate any calumny on that honorable committee, or upon any individual of it, any more than upon the Commons at large; BUT THE DEFENDANT IS NOT CHARGED BY THIS INFORMATION WITH ANY SUCH OFFENSES.

Let me here pause once more to ask you, whether the book in its genuine state, as far as we have advanced in it, makes the same impression on your minds now as when it was first read to you in detached passages; and whether, if I were to tear off the first part of it which I hold in my hand, and give it to you as an entire work, the first and last passages, which have been selected as libels on the Commons, would now appear to be so, when blended with the interjacent parts? I do not ask your answer; I shall have it in your verdict. The question is only put to direct your attention in pursuing the remainder of the volume to this main point—IS IT AN HONEST, SERIOUS DEFENSE? For this purpose, and as an example for all others, I will read the author's entire answer to the first article of charge concerning Cheyte Sing, the Zemindar of Benares, and leave it to your impartial judgments to determine whether it be a mere cloak and cover for the slander imputed by the information to the concluding sentence of it, which is the only part attacked; or whether, on the contrary, that conclusion itself, when embodied with what goes before it, does not stand explained and justified?

"The first article of impeachment," continues our author, "is concerning Cheyte Sing, the Zemindar of Benares. Bulwart Sing, the father of this Rajah, was merely an *aumil*, or farmer and collector of the revenues for Sujah ul Dowlah, Nabob of Oude, and Vizier of the Mogul empire. When, on the decease of his father, Cheyte Sing was confirmed in the office of collector for the Vizier, he paid £200,000 as a gift, or nuzzeranah, and an additional rent of £30,000 per annum."

Case of Cheyte Sing.

"As the father was no more than an *aumil* [agent], the son succeeded only to his rights and pretensions. But by a sunnud [decree] granted to him by the Nabob Sujah Dowlah in September, 1773, through the influence of Mr. Hastings, he acquired a legal title to property in the land, and was raised from the office of *aumil* to the rank of Zemindar. About four years after the death of Bulwart Sing, the Governor General and council of Bengal obtained the sovereignty paramount of the province of Benares. On the transfer of this sovereignty the governor and council proposed a new grant to Cheyte Sing, confirming his former privileges, and conferring upon him the addition of the sovereign rights of the Mint, and the powers of criminal justice with regard to life and death. He was then recognized by the Company as one of their Zemindars: a tributary subject, or feudatory vassal, of the British empire in Hindostan. The feudal system, which was formerly supposed to be peculiar to our Gothic ancestors, has always prevailed in the East. In every description of that form of government, notwithstanding accidental variations, there are two associations expressed or understood; one for internal security, the other for external defense. The King or Nabob confers protection on the feudatory baron as tributary prince, on condition of an annual revenue in the time of peace, and of military service, partly commutable for money, in the time of war. The feudal incidents in the Middle Ages in Europe, the fine paid to the superior on *marriage*, *wardship*, *relief*, &c., correspond to the annual tribute in Asia. Military service in war, and extraordinary aids in the event of extraordinary emergencies, were common to both."

"When the Governor General of Bengal, in 1778, made an extraordinary demand on the Zemindar of Benares for five lacks of rupees, the British empire, in that part of the world, was surrounded with enemies which threatened its destruction. In 1779, a general confederacy was formed among the great powers of Hindostan for the expulsion of the English from their Asiatic dominions. At this crisis the expectation of a French armament augmented the general calamities of the country. Mr. Hastings is charged by the committee with making his first demand under the false pretense that hostilities had commenced with France. Such an insidious attempt to pervert a meritorious action into a crime is new, even in the history of impeachments. On the 7th of July, 1778, Mr. Hastings received private intelligence from an English merchant at Cairo, that war had been declared by Great Britain on the 23d of March, and by France on the 30th of April. Upon this intelligence, considered as authentic, it was determined to attack all the French settlements in India. The information was afterward found to be premature; but in the latter end of August a secret dispatch was received from England, authorizing and appointing Mr. Hastings to take the measures which he had already adopted in the preceding month. The Directors and the Board of Control have expressed their approbation of this transaction by liberally rewarding Mr. Baldwyn, the merchant, for sending the earliest intelligence he could procure to Bengal. It was two days after Mr. Hastings's information of the French war, that he formed the resolution of exacting the five lacks of rupees from Cheyte Sing, and would have made similar exactions from all the dependencies of the company in India, had they been in the same circumstances. The fact is, that the great Zemindars of Bengal pay as much to government as their lands can afford. Cheyte Sing's collections were above fifty lacks, and his rent not twenty-four."

"The right of calling for extraordinary aids and military service in times of danger being universally established in India, as it was formerly in Europe during the feudal times, the subsequent conduct of Mr. Hastings is explained and vindicated. The Governor General and Council of Bengal having made a demand upon a tributary Zemindar for three successive years, and that demand having been resisted by their vassal, they are justified in his punishment. The necessities of the company, in consequence of the critical situation of their affairs in 1781, calling for a high fine—the ability of the Zemindar, who possessed near two crores of rupees in money and jewels, to pay the sum required—his backwardness to comply with the demands of his superiors—his disaffection to the English interest, and desire of revolt, which even then began to appear, and were afterward conspicuous, fully justify Mr. Hastings in every subsequent step of his conduct. In the whole of his proceedings, it is manifest that he had not early formed a design hostile to the Zemindar, but was regulated by events which he could neither foresee nor control. When the necessary measures which he had taken for supporting the authority of the company, by punishing a refractory vassal, were thwarted and defeated by the barbarous massacre of the British troops, and the rebellion of Cheyte Sing, the appeal was made to arms, an unavoidable revolution took place in Benares, and the Zemindar became the author of his own destruction."

Here follows the concluding passage, which is arraigned by the information:

"The decision of the House of Commons on this charge against Mr. Hastings is one of the most singular to be met with in the annals of Parliament. The minister, who was followed by the majority, vindicated him in every thing that he had done, and found him blamable only for what he intended to do; justified every step of his conduct, and only criminated his proposed intention of converting the crimes of the Zemindar to the benefit of the state, by a fine of fifty lacks of rupees. An impeachment of error in judgment with regard to the *quantum* of a fine, and for an intention that never was executed, and never known to the offending party, characterizes a tribunal of *inquisition* rather than a court of Parliament."

Gentlemen, I am ready to admit that this sentiment might have been expressed in language more reserved and guarded; but you will look to the sentiment itself, rather than to its dress—to the mind of the writer, and not to the bluntness with which he may happen to express it. It is obviously the language of a warm man, engaged in the honest defense of his friend, and who is brought to what he thinks a just conclusion in argument, which, perhaps, becomes offensive in proportion to its truth. Truth is undoubtedly no warrant for writing what is reproachful of any private man. If a member of society lives within the law, then, if he offends, it is against God alone, and man has nothing to do with him; and if he transgress the laws, the libeler should arraign him before them, instead of presuming to try him himself. But as to writings on *general subjects*, which are not charged as an infringement on the rights of individuals, but as of a seditious tendency, it is far otherwise. When, in the progress either of legislation or of high national justice in Parliament, they who are amenable to no law are supposed to have adopted, through mistake or error, a principle which, if drawn into precedent, might be dangerous to the public, I shall not admit it to be a libel in the course of a legal and *bonâ fide* publication, to state that such a principle had *in fact* been adopted. The people of England are not to be kept in the dark touching the proceedings of their own representatives. Let us, therefore, coolly examine this supposed offense, and see what it amounts to.

First, was not the conduct of the right honorable gentleman, whose name is here mentioned, exactly what it is represented? Will the Attorney General, who was present in the House of Commons, say that it was not? Did not the minister vindicate Mr. Hastings in what he *had done*,[10] and was not his consent to that article of the impeachment founded on the *intention only* of levying a fine on the Zemindar for the service of the state, beyond the quantum which he, the minister, thought reasonable? What else is this but an impeachment of error in judgment in the quantum of a fine?

So much for the first part of the sentence, which, regarding Mr. Pitt only, is foreign to our purpose. And as to the last part of it, which imputes the sentiments of the minister to the majority that followed him with their votes on the question, that appears to me to be giving handsome credit to the majority for having voted from conviction, and not from courtesy to the minister. To have supposed otherwise, I dare not say, would have been a more *natural* libel, but it would certainly have been a greater one. The sum and substance, therefore, of the paragraph is only this—that an impeachment for an error in judgment is not consistent with the theory or the practice of the English government. So say I. I say, without reserve, speaking merely in the abstract, and not meaning to decide upon the merits of Mr. Hastings's cause, that an impeachment for an error in judgment is contrary to the whole spirit of English criminal justice, which, though not binding on the House of Commons, ought to be a guide to its proceedings. I say that the extraordinary jurisdiction of impeach-

[10] Mr. Pitt expressed his opinion that, admitting the right of Mr. Hastings to tax the Zemindar, his general conduct in the business had been unnecessarily severe.

ment ought never to be assumed to expose error or to scourge misfortune, but to hold up a terrible example to corruption and *willful* abuse of authority by extra legal pains. If public men are always punished with due severity when the source of their misconduct appears to have been selfishly corrupt and criminal, the public can never suffer when their errors are treated with gentleness. From such protection to the magistrate, no man can think lightly of the charge of magistracy itself, when he sees, by the language of the saving judgment, that the only title to it is an honest and zealous intention. If, at this moment, gentlemen, or indeed in any other in the whole course of our history, the people of England were to call upon every man in this impeaching House of Commons who had given his voice on public questions, or acted in authority, civil or military, to answer for the issues of our councils and our wars, and if honest single intentions for the public service were refused as answers to impeachments, we should have many relations to mourn for, and many friends to deplore. For my own part, gentlemen, I feel, I hope, for my country as much as any man that inhabits it; but I would rather see it fall, and be buried in its ruins, than lend my voice to wound any minister, or other responsible person, however unfortunate, who had fairly followed the lights of his understanding and the dictates of his conscience for their preservation.

Gentlemen, this is no theory of mine; it is the language of English law, and the protection which it affords to every man in office, from the highest to the lowest trust of government. In no one instance that can be named, foreign or domestic, did the Court of King's Bench ever interpose its extraordinary jurisdiction, by information, against any magistrate for the widest departure from the rule of his duty, without *the plainest and clearest proof of corruption.* To every such application, not so supported, the constant answer has been, Go to a grand jury with your complaint. God forbid that a magistrate should suffer from an error in judgment, if his purpose was honestly to discharge his trust. We can not stop the ordinary course of justice; but wherever the court has a discretion, such a magistrate is entitled to its protection. I appeal to the noble judge, and to every man who hears me, for the truth and universality of this position. And it would be a strange solecism, indeed, to assert that, in a case where the supreme court of criminal justice in the nation would refuse to interpose an extraordinary though a legal jurisdiction, on the principle that the ordinary execution of the laws should never be exceeded, but for the punishment of malignant guilt, the Commons, in their higher capacity, growing out of the same Constitution, should reject that principle, and stretch them still further by a jurisdiction still more eccentric. Many impeachments have taken place, because the law *could not* adequately punish the objects of them; but who ever heard of one being set on foot because the law, upon principle, *would not* punish them? Many impeachments have been adopted for a *higher* example than a prosecution in the ordinary courts, but surely never for a *different* example. The matter, therefore, in the offensive paragraph is not only an indisputable truth, but a truth in the propagation of which we are all deeply concerned.

Whether Mr. Hastings, in the particular instance, acted from corruption or from zeal for his employers, is what I have nothing to do with; it is to be decided in judgment; my duty stops with wishing him, as I do, an honorable deliverance. Whether the minister or the Commons meant to found this article of the impeachment on mere error, without corruption, is likewise foreign to the purpose. The author could only judge from what was said and done on the occasion. He only sought to guard the principle, which is a common interest, and the rights of Mr. Hastings under it. He was, therefore, justified in publishing that an impeachment, founded in error in judgment, was, to all intents and purposes, illegal, unconstitutional, and unjust.

Gentlemen, it is now time for us to return again to the work under examination. The author having discussed the whole of the first article through so many pages, without even the imputation of an incorrect or intemperate expression, except in the concluding passage (the meaning of which I trust I have explained), goes on with the same earnest disposition to the discussion of the second charge respecting the princesses of Oude, which occupies *eighteen* pages, not one syllable of which the Attorney General has read, and on which there is not even a glance at the House of Commons. The whole of this answer is, indeed, so far from being a mere cloak for the introduction of slander, that I aver it to be one of the most masterly pieces of writing I ever read in my life. From thence he goes on to the charge of contracts and salaries, which occupies *five* pages more, in which there is not a glance at the House of Commons, nor a word read by the Attorney General. He afterward defends Mr. Hastings against the charges respecting the opium contracts. Not a glance at the House of Commons; not a word by the Attorney General. And, in short, in this manner he goes on with the others, to the end of the book.

Now, is it possible for any human being to believe that a man, having no other intention than to vilify the House of Commons (as this information charges), should yet keep his mind thus fixed and settled as the needle to the pole, upon the serious merits of Mr. Hastings's defense, without ever straying into matter even questionable, except in the two or three selected parts out of two or three hundred pages? This is a forbearance which could not have existed, if calumny and detraction had been the malignant objects which led him to the inquiry and publication. The whole fallacy, therefore, arises from holding up to view a few detached passages, and carefully concealing the general tenor of the book.

Having now finished most, if not all of these *critical* observations, which it has been my duty to make upon this unfair mode of prosecution, it is but a tribute of common justice to the Attorney General (and which my personal regard for him makes it more pleasant to pay), that none of my commentaries reflect in the most distant manner upon him; nor upon the Solicitor for the Crown, who sits near me, who is a person of the most correct honor; far from it. The Attorney General having orders to prosecute in consequence of the address of the House to his Majesty, had no choice in the mode—no means at all of keeping the prosecutors before you in countenance, but by the course which has been pursued. But so far has he been from enlisting into the cause those prejudices, which it is not difficult to slide into a business originating from such exalted authority, he has honorably guarded you against them; pressing, indeed, severely upon my client with the weight of his ability, but not with the glare and trappings of his high office.

Gentlemen, I wish that my strength would enable me to convince you of the author's singleness of intention, and of the merit and ability of his work, by reading the whole that remains of it. But my voice is already nearly exhausted; I am sorry my client should be a sufferer by my infirmity. One passage, however, is too striking and important to be passed over; the rest I must trust to your private examination. The author having discussed all the charges, article by article, sums them all up with this striking appeal to his readers:

"The authentic statement of facts which has been given, and the arguments which have been employed, are, I think, sufficient to vindicate the character and conduct of Mr. Hastings, even on the maxims of European policy. When he was appointed Governor General of Bengal, he was invested with a discretionary power to promote the interests of the India Company, and of the British empire in that quarter of the globe. The general instructions sent to him from his constituents were, '*That in all your deliberations and resolutions, you make the safety and prosperity of Bengal your principal object, and fix your attention on the security of the possessions and revenues of the company.*' His superior genius sometimes acted in the spirit, rather than complied with the letter of the law; but he discharged the trust, and preserved the empire committed to his care, in the same way, and with greater splendor and success than any of his predecessors in office; his departure from India was marked with the lamentations of the natives and the gratitude of his countrymen; and, on his return to England, he received the cordial congratulations of that numerous and respectable society, whose interests he had promoted, and whose dominions he had protected and extended."

Collateral defense of Mr. Hastings.

Gentlemen of the jury—if this be a willfully false account of the instructions given to Mr. Hastings for his government, and of his conduct under them, the author and publisher of this defense deserves the severest punishment, for a mercenary imposition on the public. But if it be true that he was directed to make the *safety and prosperity of Bengal the first object of his attention*, and that, under his administration, it has been safe and prosperous; if it be true that the security and preservation of our possessions and revenues in Asia were marked out to him as the great leading principle of his government, and that those possessions and revenues, amid unexampled dangers, *have* been secured and preserved; then a question may be unaccountably mixed with your consideration, much beyond the consequence of the present prosecution, involving, perhaps, the merit of the impeachment itself which gave it birth—a question which the Commons, as prosecutors of Mr. Hastings, should, in common prudence, have avoided; unless, regretting the unwieldy length of their proceedings against him, they wish to afford him the opportunity of this strange anomalous defense. For, although I am neither his counsel, nor desire to have any thing to do with his guilt or innocence; yet, in the collateral defense of my client, I am driven to state matter which may be considered by many as hostile to the impeachment. For if our dependencies have been secured, and their interests promoted, I am driven, in the defense of my client, to remark, that it is mad and preposterous to bring to the standard of justice and humanity the exercise of a dominion founded upon violence and terror. It *may* and *must* be true that Mr. Hastings has repeatedly offended against the rights and privileges of Asiatic government, if he was the faithful deputy of a power which could not maintain itself for an hour without trampling upon both. He may and must have offended against the laws of God and nature, if he was the faithful viceroy of an empire wrested in blood from the people to whom God and nature had given it. He may and must have preserved that unjust dominion over timorous and abject nations by a terrifying, overbearing, insulting superiority, if he was the faithful administrator of your government, which, having no root in consent or affection—no foundation in similarity of interests—no support from any one principle which cements men together in society, could only be upheld by alternate stratagem and force. The unhappy people of India, feeble and effeminate as they are from the softness of their climate, and subdued and broken as they have been by the knavery and strength of civilization, still occasionally start up in all the vigor and intelligence of insulted nature. To be governed at all, they must be governed with a rod of iron; and our empire in the East would, long since, have been lost to Great Britain, if civil skill and military prowess had not united their efforts to support an authority—which Heaven never gave—by means which it never can sanction.[11]

[11] Mr. Hastings was unquestionably guilty of nearly all the acts charged upon him by Mr. Burke. Still it was felt by the court, and at last by the public at large, that great allowance ought to be made for him when it was remembered that he completely restored the finances of the country, which he found in the utmost disorder; that he established the British empire in India on a firm basis, at a time when, under a less energetic government than his own, it would

Gentlemen, I think I can observe that you are touched with this way of considering the subject, and I can account for it. I have not been considering it through the cold medium of books, but have been speaking of man and his nature, and of human dominion, from what I have seen of them myself among reluctant nations submitting to our authority. I know what they feel, and how such feelings can alone be repressed. I have heard them in my youth from a naked savage, in the indignant character of a prince surrounded by his subjects, addressing the governor of a British colony, holding a bundle of sticks in his hand, as the notes of his unlettered eloquence. "Who is it," said the jealous ruler over the desert, encroached upon by the restless foot of English adventure—"who is it that causes this river to rise in the high mountains, and to empty itself into the ocean? Who is it that causes to blow the loud winds of winter, and that calms them again in summer? Who is it that rears up the shade of those lofty forests, and blasts them with the quick lightning at his pleasure? The same Being who gave to you a country on the other side of the waters, and gave ours to us, and by this title we will defend it," said the warrior, throwing down his tomahawk upon the ground, and raising the war-sound of his nation. These are the feelings of subjugated man all round the globe; and depend upon it, nothing but fear will control where it is vain to look for affection.[12]

The Indian Chief.

These reflections are the only antidotes to those anathemas of superhuman eloquence which have lately shaken these walls that surround us, but which it unaccountably falls to my province, whether I will or no, a little to stem the torrent of, by reminding you that you have a mighty sway in Asia, which can not be maintained by the finer sympathies of life, or the practice of its charities and affections. What will *they* do for you when surrounded by two hundred thousand men with artillery, cavalry, and elephants, calling upon you for their dominions which you have robbed them of? Justice may, no doubt, in such a case forbid the levying of a fine to pay a revolting soldiery; a treaty may stand in the way of increasing a tribute to keep up the very existence of the government; and delicacy for women may forbid all entrance into a Zenana for money, whatever may be the necessity for taking it.[13] All these things must ever be occurring. But under the pressure of such constant difficulties, so dangerous to national honor, it might be better, perhaps, to think of effectually securing it altogether, by recalling our troops and our merchants, and abandoning our Oriental empire. Until this be done, neither religion nor philosophy can be pressed very far into the aid of reformation and punishment. If England, from a lust of ambition and dominion, will insist on maintaining despotic rule over distant and hostile nations, beyond all comparison more numerous and extended than herself, and gives commission to her viceroys to govern them with no other instructions than to preserve them, and to secure permanently their revenues, with what color of consistency or reason can she place herself in the moral chair, and affect to be shocked at the execution of her own orders; adverting to the exact measure of wickedness and injustice necessary to their execution, and complaining only of *the excess* as the immorality, considering her authority as a dispensation for breaking the commands of God, and the breach of them as only punishable when contrary to the ordinances of man?

Such a proceeding, gentlemen, begets serious reflection. It would be better, perhaps, for the masters and the servants of all such governments to join in supplication, that the great Author of violated humanity may not confound them together in one common judgment.

Gentlemen, I find, as I said before, I have not sufficient strength to go on with the remaining parts of the book. I hope, however, that notwithstanding my omissions, you are now completely satisfied that, whatever errors or misconceptions may have misled the writer of these pages, the justification of a person whom he believed to be innocent, and whose accusers had themselves appealed to the public, was the single object of his contemplation. If I have succeeded in that object, every purpose which I had in addressing you has been answered.

It only now remains to remind you that another consideration has been strongly pressed upon you, and, no doubt, will be insisted on in reply. You will be told that the matters which I have been justifying as legal. and even meritorious, have therefore not been made the subject of complaint; and that whatever intrinsic merit parts of the book may be supposed or even admitted to possess, such merit can afford no justification to the selected passages, some of which, even with the context, carry the meaning charged by the information, and which are indecent animadversions on authority. To this I would answer (still protesting as I do against the application of any one of the innuendoes), that if you are firmly persuaded of the singleness and purity of the author's intentions, you

If the writer was honest in his intentions, he ought not to be punished for an occasional excess.

inevitably have fallen altogether; and, in addition to this, he was constantly pressed by the Directors of the East India Company for remittances of money, which could only be extorted by oppression. Although his government was arbitrary, yet it was popular among the natives, being milder and more just than that of their own princes; while he himself was respected for the unusual regard which he paid to native prejudices and customs, and his patronage of literature and the fine arts.

[12] The reader will be struck with the rapid flow of the rhythmus in this speech of the Indian chief, so admirably corresponding in its iambic structure with the character of the speaker. It should be read aloud in connection with a correspondent passage of Mr. Grattan, already remarked upon for its slow and majestic movement. See page 390.

[13] See introduction to Mr. Sheridan's speech, p. 405–6.

are not bound to subject him to infamy, because, in the zealous career of a just and animated composition, he happens to have tripped with his pen into an intemperate expression in one or two instances of a long work. If this severe duty were binding on your consciences, the liberty of the press would be an empty sound, and no man could venture to write on any subject, however pure his purpose, without an attorney at one elbow and a counsel at the other.

Evils of too severe a restriction on the press.

From minds thus subdued by the terrors of punishment, there could issue no works of genius to expand the empire of human reason, nor any masterly compositions on the general nature of government, by the help of which the great commonwealths of mankind have founded their establishments; much less any of those useful applications of them to critical conjunctures, by which, from time to time, our own Constitution, by the exertion of patriot citizens, has been brought back to its standard. Under such terrors, all the great lights of science and civilization must be extinguished; for men can not communicate their free thoughts to one another with a lash held over their heads. It is the nature of every thing that is great and useful, both in the animate and inanimate world, to be wild and irregular, and we must be contented to take them with the alloys which belong to them, or live without them. Genius breaks from the fetters of criticism, but its wanderings are sanctioned by its majesty and wisdom when it advances in its path: subject it to the critic, and you tame it into dullness. Mighty rivers break down their banks in the winter, sweeping away to death the flocks which are fattened on the soil that they fertilize in the summer: the few may be saved by embankments from drowning, but the flock must perish for hunger. Tempests occasionally shake our dwellings and dissipate our commerce; but they scourge before them the lazy elements, which without them would stagnate into pestilence.[14] In like manner, Liberty herself, the last and best gift of God to his creatures, must be taken just as she is: you might pare her down into bashful regularity, and shape her into a perfect model of severe, scrupulous law, but she would then be Liberty no longer; and you must be content to die under the lash of this inexorable justice which you had exchanged for the banners of Freedom.

General principle as to the liberty of the press.

If it be asked where the line to this indulgence and impunity is to be drawn, the answer is easy. The liberty of the press, *on general subjects*, comprehends and implies as much strict observance of positive law as is consistent with perfect purity of intention, and equal and useful society. What that latitude is, can not be promulgated in the abstract, but must be judged of in the particular instance, and consequently, upon this occasion, must be judged of by you, without forming any possible precedent for any other case; and where can the judgment be possibly so safe as with the members of that society which alone can suffer, if the writing is calculated to do mischief to the public? You must, therefore, try the book by that criterion, and say whether the publication was premature and offensive, or, in other words, whether the publisher is bound to have suppressed it until the public ear was anticipated and abused, and every avenue to the human heart or understanding secured and blocked up? I see around me those by whom, by-and-by, Mr. Hastings will be most ably and eloquently defended;[15] but I am sorry to remind my friends that, but for the right of suspending the public judgment concerning him till their season of exertion comes round, the tongues of angels would be insufficient for the task.

Gentlemen, I hope I have now performed my duty to my client: I sincerely hope that I have; for, certainly, if ever there was a man pulled the other way by his interests and affections—if ever there was a man who should have trembled at the situation in which I have been placed on this occasion, it is myself, who not only love, honor, and respect, but whose future hopes and preferments are linked, from free choice, with those who, from the mistakes of the author, are treated with great severity and injustice. These are strong retardments; but I have been urged on to activity by considerations which can never be inconsistent with honorable attachments, either in the political or social world—the love of justice and of liberty, and a zeal for the Constitution of my country, which is the inheritance of our posterity, of the public, and of the world. These are the motives which have animated me in defense of this person, who is an entire stranger to me—whose shop I never go to—and the author of whose publication, as well as Mr. Hastings, who is the object of it, I never spoke to in my life.

A regard to human frailty to be observed in administering justice.

One word more, gentlemen, and I have done. Every human tribunal ought to take care to administer justice, as we look hereafter to have justice administered to ourselves. Upon the principle on which the Attorney General prays sentence upon my client—God have mercy upon us! Instead of standing before him in judgment with the

[14] This is one of the finest amplifications in English oratory, beautiful in itself, justified by the importance of the subject which it enforces, and admirably suited to produce the designed impression. The seminal idea was probably suggested by a remark of Burke, whose writings Mr. Erskine incessantly studied. "*It is the nature of all greatness not to be exact.*"—See page 252. We see in this case, how a man of genius may borrow from another, without detracting in the least from the freshness and originality with which his ideas are expressed and applied. At the present day, there can be very little of that originality which presents an idea *for the first time*. All that can be expected is, that we *make it our own*, and apply it to new purposes.

[15] Mr. Law (afterward Lord Ellenborough), Mr. Plumer, and Mr. Dallas.

hopes and consolations of Christians, we must call upon the mountains to cover us; for which of us can present, for omniscient examination, a pure, unspotted, and faultless course? But I humbly expect that the benevolent Author of our being will judge us as I have been pointing out for your example. Holding up the great volume of our lives in his hands, and regarding the general scope of them; if he discovers benevolence, charity, and good-will to man beating in the heart, where he alone can look; if he finds that our conduct, though often forced out of the path by our infirmities, has been in general well directed; his all-searching eye will assuredly never pursue us into those little corners of our lives, much less will his justice select them for punishment, without the general context of our existence, by which faults may be sometimes found to have grown out of virtues, and very many of our heaviest offenses to have been grafted by human imperfection upon the best and kindest of our affections. No, gentlemen, believe me, this is not the course of divine justice, or there is no truth in the Gospels of Heaven. If the general tenor of a man's conduct be such as I have represented it, he may walk through the shadow of death, with all his faults about him, with as much cheerfulness as in the common paths of life; because he knows that, instead of a stern accuser to expose before the Author of his nature those frail passages which, like the scored matter in the book before you, checkers the volume of the brightest and best-spent life, his mercy will obscure them from the eye of his purity, and our repentance blot them out forever.

All this would, I admit, be perfectly foreign and irrelevant, if you were sitting here in a case of property between man and man, where a strict rule of law must operate, or there would be an end of civil life and society. It would be equally foreign, and still more irrelevant, if applied to those shameful attacks upon private reputation which are the bane and disgrace of the press; by which whole families have been rendered unhappy during life, by aspersions, cruel, scandalous, and unjust. Let such libelers remember that no one of my principles of defense can, at any time or upon any occasion, ever apply to shield THEM from punishment; because such conduct is not only an infringement of the rights of men, as they are defined by strict law, but is absolutely incompatible with honor, honesty, or mistaken good intention. On such men let the Attorney General bring forth all the artillery of his office, and the thanks and blessings of the whole public will follow him. But this is a totally different case. Whatever private calumny may mark this work, it has not been made the subject of complaint, and we have therefore nothing to do with that, nor any right to consider it. We are trying whether the public could have been considered as offended and endangered if Mr. Hastings himself, in whose place the author and publisher have a right to put themselves, had, under all the circumstances which have been considered, composed and published the volume under examination. That question can not, in common sense, be any thing resembling a question of LAW, but is a pure question of FACT, to be decided on the principles which I have humbly recommended. I, therefore, ask of the court that the book itself may now be delivered to you. Read it with attention, and as you shall find it, pronounce your verdict.

This trial took place before the passing of Mr Fox's Libel Bill; and Lord Kenyon charged the jury that they were not to consider whether the pamphlet was libelous, but simply whether it had been published by the defendant. Under these circumstances, they spent two hours in deliberation, but finally broke through the instructions of the court, and found the defendant NOT GUILTY, thus anticipating the rights soon after secured to juries by an act of Parliament.

SPEECH

OF MR. ERSKINE IN BEHALF OF JOHN FROST, WHEN INDICTED FOR UTTERING SEDITIOUS WORDS, DELIVERED BEFORE THE COURT OF KING'S BENCH, MARCH, 1793.

INTRODUCTION

THIS was the first trial under what has been called the "Reign of Terror." Mr. Frost was a London attorney of eminence, who had just returned from a visit to France, at that time under the government of the Convention, and hastening toward the revolutionary crisis. He dined with an agricultural society at a coffee-house, on the 6th of November, 1792. On his coming down from the private room, where he had been dining, into the public coffee-room, between nine and ten in the evening, he was addressed by a person of the name of Yatman, who, knowing Mr. Frost, and that he had just returned from the continent, said to him, "Well, how do they go on in France?" Upon which Mr. Frost, who was much heated with wine, exclaimed, "I am for equality, and no King." Mr. Yatman replied, "What! no King in this country?" and Mr. Frost then repeated, "Yes, no King; there ought to be no King." And it was for the use of this language, and for nothing beyond this, that the indictment was preferred.

SPEECH, &c.

GENTLEMEN OF THE JURY,—I rise to address you under circumstances so peculiar, that I consider myself entitled, not only for the defendant arraigned before you, but personally for myself, to the utmost indulgence of the court. I came down this morning with no other notice of the duty cast upon me in this cause, nor any other direction for the premeditation necessary to its performance, than that which I have ever considered to be the safest and the best—namely, the records of the court, as they are entered here for trial, where, for the ends of justice, the charge must always appear with the most accurate precision, that the accused may know what crime he is called upon to answer, and his counsel how he may defend him. Finding, therefore, upon the record which arraigns the defendant, a simple, unqualified charge of seditious words, unconnected, and uncomplicated with any extrinsic events, I little imagined that the conduct of my client was to receive its color and construction from the present state of France, or rather of all Europe, as affecting the condition of England. I little dreamed that the 6th of November (which, reading the indictment, I had a right to consider like any other day in the calendar) was to turn out an *epoch* in this country (for so it is styled in the argument); and that, instead of having to deal with idle, thoughtless words, uttered over wine, through the passage of a coffee-house, with whatever at any time might belong to them, I was to meet a charge of which I had no notice or conception, and to find the loose dialogue, which, even upon the face of the record itself, exhibits nothing more than a casual sudden conversation, exalted to an accusation of the most premeditated, serious, and alarming nature—verging upon high treason itself, by its connection with the most hostile purposes to the state, and assuming a shape still more interesting from its dangerous connection with certain mysterious conspiracies, which, in confederacy with French republicans, threaten, *it seems*, the Constitution of our once happy country.

Embarrassment arising from the Crown having traveled out of the record.

Gentlemen, I confess myself much unprepared for a discussion of this nature, and a little disconcerted at being so. For although, as I have said, I had no notice from the record that the politics of Europe were to be the subject of discourse, yet experience ought to have taught me to expect it; for what act of government has, for a long time past, been carried on by any other means? *When* or *where* has been the debate, or *what* has been the object of authority, in which the affairs of France have not taken the lead? The affairs of France have, indeed, become the common stalking-horse for all state purposes. I know the honor of my learned friend,[1] too well to impute to him the introduction of them for any improper or dishonorable purpose. I am sure he connects them in his own mind with the subject, and thinks them legally before you: I am bound to think so, because the general tenor of his address to you has been manly and candid. But I assert that neither the actual condition of France, nor the supposed condition of this country, are, or can be, in any shape, before you; and that upon the trial of this indictment, supported only by the evidence you have heard, the words must be judged of as if spoken by any man or woman in the kingdom, at any time from the Norman Conquest to the moment I am addressing you.

Unjust to involve the case of the defendant with French politics.

I admit, indeed, that the particular time in which words are spoken, or acts committed, may most essentially alter their quality and construction, and give to expressions or conduct, which in another season might have been innocent, or at least indifferent, the highest and most enormous guilt. But, for that very reason, the supposed particularity of the present times, as applicable to the matter before you, is absolutely shut out from your consideration—shut out upon the plainest and most obvious principle of justice and law; because, wherever *time* or *occasion* mix with an act, affect its quality, and constitute or enhance its criminality, they then become an essential part of the misdemeanor itself, and must consequently be charged as such upon the record. I plainly discover I have his Lordship's assent to this proposition. If, therefore, the Crown had considered this cause originally in the serious light in which it considers it to-day, it has wholly mistaken its course. If it had considered the government of France as actively engaged in the encouragement of disaffection to the monarchy of England, and that her newly-erected republic was set up by her as the great type for imitation and example here; if it had considered that numbers, and even classes of our countrymen, were ripe for disaffection, if not for rebellion; and that the defendant, as an emissary of France, had spoken the words with the premeditated design of undermining our government—this situation of things might and ought to have been put *as facts upon the record*, and as facts established by evidence, instead of resting, as they do to-day, upon assertion. By such a course the crime, indeed, would have become of the magnitude represented; but, on the other hand, as the conviction could only have followed from the proof, the defendant, upon the evidence of to-day, must have an hour ago been acquitted. Not a syllable has been proved of any emissaries from France to debauch our monarchical principles; not even an insinuation in evidence that, if there were any such, the defendant was one of them; not a syllable of proof, either directly or indirectly, that the condition of the country, when the words were uttered, differed from its ordinary condition in times of prosperity and peace. It is, therefore, a new and most compendious mode of justice, that the facts which wholly constitute, or, at all events, lift up the dignity and danger of the offense, should not be charged upon record, *because they could not be proved*, but are to be taken for granted in the argument, so as to produce the same effect upon the trial and in the punishment, as if they had been actually charged and completely established. If the affairs of France, as they are supposed to affect this country, had been introduced without a warrant from the

If these were connected with the crime, they should have been included in the indictment.

[1] The Attorney General, Sir A. Macdonald.

charge or the evidence, I should have been wholly silent concerning them; but as they have been already mixed with the subject, in a manner so eloquent and affecting as, too probably, to have made a strong impression, it becomes my duty to endeavor at least to remove it.

Views expressed by the counsel for the Crown.

The late revolutions in France have been represented to you as not only ruinous to their authors, and to the inhabitants of that country, but as likely to shake and disturb the principles of this and all other governments. You have been told, that though the English people are generally well affected to their government—ninety-nine out of one hundred, upon Mr. Attorney General's own statement—yet that wicked and designing men have long been laboring to overturn it; that nothing short of the wise and spirited exertions of the present government (of which this prosecution is, it seems, one of the instances) have hitherto averted, or can continue to avert, the dangerous contagion which misrule and anarchy are spreading over the world; that bodies of Englishmen, forgetting their duty to their own country and its Constitution, have congratulated the Convention of France upon the formation of their monstrous government; and that the conduct of the defendant must be considered as a part of a deep-laid system of disaffection, which threatens the establishments of this kingdom.

These things not before the jury in evidence.

Gentlemen, this state of things having no support whatever from any evidence before you, and resting only upon opinion, I have an equal right to mine; having the same means of observation with other people of what passes in the world; and as I have a very clear one upon this subject, I will give it you in a few words.

Mr. Erskine's views directly the reverse.

I am of opinion, then, that there is not the smallest foundation for the alarm which has been so industriously propagated; in this I am so far from being singular, that I verily believe the authors of it are themselves privately of the same way of thinking. But it was convenient for certain persons,[2] who had changed their principles, to find some plausible pretext for changing them. It was convenient for those who, when out of power, had endeavored to lead the public mind to the necessity of reforming the corruptions of our own government, to find any reasons for their continuance and confirmation, when they operate as engines to support themselves in the exercise of powers which were only odious when in other hands. For this *honorable* purpose, the sober, reflecting, and temperate character of the English nation was to be represented as fermenting into sedition, and into an insane contempt for the revered institutions of their ancestors. For this honorable purpose, the wisest men—the most eminent for virtue—the most splendid in talents—the most independent for rank and property in the country, were, for no other crime than their perseverance in those sentiments which certain persons had originated and abandoned,[3] to be given up to the licentious pens and tongues of hired defamation; to be stabbed in the dark by anonymous accusations; and to be held out to England and to the whole world, as conspiring, under the auspices of cut-throats, to overturn every thing sacred in religion, and venerable in the ancient government of our country. Certain it is, that the whole system of government, of which the business we are now engaged in is no mean specimen, came upon the public with the suddenness of a clap of thunder, without one act to give it foundation, from the very moment that notice was given of a motion in Parliament to reform the representation of the people.[4] Long, long, before that time the "Rights of Man," and other books, though not complained of, had been written; equally long before it, the addresses to the French government, which have created such a panic, had existed; but as there is a "give and take" in this world, they passed unregarded. Leave but the practical corruptions, and they are contented to wink at the speculations of theorists, and the compliments of public-spirited civility. But the moment the national attention was awakened to look at things in practice, and to seek to reform corruptions at home, from that moment, as at the ringing of a bell, the whole hive began to swarm, and every man in his turn has been stung.

The defendant formerly associated with Mr. Pitt as a friend of parliamentary reform.

This, gentlemen, is the real state of the case; and I am so far from pushing the observation beyond its bearing for the defense of a client, that I am ready to admit Mr. Frost, in his conduct, has not been wholly invulnerable, and that, in some measure, he has brought this prosecution upon himself. Gentlemen, Mr. Frost must forgive me, if I take the liberty to say that, with the best intentions in the world, he formerly pushed his observations and conduct respecting government further than many would be disposed to follow him. I can not disguise or conceal from you, that I find his name in this green-book, as associated with Mr. Pitt and the Duke of Richmond, at the Thatched House Tavern, in St. James's Street.[5] I find him, also, the correspondent of the former; and that I discover in their publications on the structure and conduct of the House of Commons, expressions which, however merited, and in my

[2] Among the principal were Mr. Burke, the Prince of Wales, the Duke of Portland, and Lords Spencer, Mansfield, Fitzwilliam, and Loughborough.

[3] In allusion to Mr. Pitt's altered opinions as to parliamentary reform.

[4] Mr. Charles Grey, at the request of the Society of "The Friends of the People," on the 30th April, 1792, gave notice of his intention to bring forward, in the ensuing session, a motion to this effect.

[5] Mr. Erskine read the minute (in Mr. Pitt's own handwriting) of a meeting of members of Parliament, and of members of several committees of counties and cities, held at the Thatched House Tavern, at which Mr. Frost was present, on the 18th of May, 1782, and at which resolutions were passed in approbation of Mr. Pitt's motion, on the 7th of May previous, on the subject of the representation of the people in Parliament.

opinion commendable, would now be considered, not merely as intemperate and unguarded, but as highly criminal.[6]

Reasons for his now being prosecuted.

Gentlemen, the fashion of this world speedily passeth away. We find these glorious restorers of equal representation determined, as *ministers*, that, so far from every man being an elector, the metropolis of the kingdom should have no election at all; but should submit to the power, or to the softer allurements, of the Crown. Certain it is, that, for a short season, Mr. Frost being engaged professionally as agent for the government candidate, did not (indeed, he could not) oppose this inconsistency between the doctrine and practice of his friends; and in this interregnum of public spirit, he was, in the opinion of government, a perfect patriot, a faithful friend to the British Constitution. As a member of the law, he was, therefore, trusted with government business in matters of revenue, and was, in short, what all the friends of government, of course, are, the best and most approved—to save words, he was like the rest of them, *just what he should be*. But the election being over, and, with it, professional agency, and Mr. Frost, as he lawfully might, continuing to hold his former opinions (which were still avowed and gloried in, though not acted on, by his ancient friends), he, unfortunately, did not change them the other day, when they were thrown off by others. On the contrary, he rather seems to have taken fire with the prospect of reducing them to practice; and being, as I have shown you, bred in a school which took the lead in boldness of remonstrance of all other reformers before or since, he fell, in the heat and levity of wine, into expressions which have no correspondence with his sober judgment; which would have been passed over or laughed at in you or me, but which, coming from him, were never to be forgiven by government. This is the genuine history of his offense. For this he is to be the subject of prosecution—not the prosecution of my learned friend—not the prosecution of the Attorney General—not the prosecution of his Majesty; but the prosecution of Mr. Yatman, who wishes to show you his great loyalty to the state and Constitution, which were in danger of falling, had it not been for the drugs of this worthy apothecary.

Remarks on the French Revolution,

With regard to the new government of France, since the subject has been introduced, all I can say of it is this, that the good or evil of it belongs to themselves. They had a right, like every other people upon earth, to change their government; the system destroyed was a system disgraceful to free and rational beings; and if they have neither substituted, nor shall hereafter substitute, a better in its stead, they must eat the bitter fruits of their own errors and crimes. As to the horrors which now disfigure and desolate that fine country, all good men must undoubtedly agree in condemning and deploring them, but they may differ, nevertheless, in deciphering their causes. Men to the full as wise as those who pretend to be wiser than Providence, and stronger than the order of things, may, perhaps, reflect that a great fabric of unwarrantable power and corruption could not fall to the ground without a mighty convulsion—that the agitation must ever be in proportion to the surface agitated—that the passions and errors inseparable from humanity must heighten and swell the confusion; and that, perhaps, the crimes and ambition of other nations, under the mask of self-defense and humanity, may have contributed not a little to aggravate them—may have tended to imbitter the spirits and to multiply the evils which they condemn—to increase the misrule and anarchy which they seek to disembroil, and in the end to endanger their own governments, which by carnage and bloodshed, instead of by peace, improvement, and wise administration, they profess to protect from the contagion of revolution.

and the feelings it had awakened in England.

As to the part which bodies of men in England have taken, though it might, in some instances, be imprudent and irregular, yet I see nothing to condemn, or to support, the declamation which we daily hear upon the subject. The congratulations[7] of Englishmen were directed to the fall of corrupt and despotic power in France, and were animated by a wish of a milder and freer government—happier for that country, and safer for this. They were, besides, addressed to France when she was at peace with England, and when no law was, therefore, broken by the expression of opinion or satisfaction. They were not congratulations on the murders which have since been committed, nor on the desolations which have since overspread so large a portion of the earth, neither were they traitorous to the government of this

[6] The following are copies of Mr. Pitt's letters:

"Lincoln's Inn, Friday, May 10th.

"Dear Sir,—I am extremely sorry that I was not at home when you and the other gentlemen from the Westminster Committee did me the honor to call.

"May I beg the favor of you to express that I am truly happy to find that the motion of Tuesday last has the approbation of such zealous friends to the public, and to assure the committee that my exertions shall never be wanting in support of a measure, *which I agree with them in thinking essentially necessary to the independence of Parliament and the liberty of the people.*

"I have the honor to be, with great respect and esteem, sir, your most obedient and most humble servant, W. Pitt.

"John Frost, Esq., Percy Street."

"Lincoln's Inn, May 12th, 1782.

"Sir,—I have received the favor of your note, and shall be proud to receive the honor intended me by the gentlemen of the Middlesex Committee, at the time you mention.

"I am, with great regard, sir, your most humble servant, W. Pitt.

"John Frost, Esq., Percy-Street."

[7] Mr. Erskine alluded to the addresses sent from several political societies in England to the French National Assembly, which, in the expressions of their warm approbation of the new government established in France, bordered closely on sedition against the English government.

country. This we may safely take in trust, since not one of them, even in the rage of prosecution, has been brought before a criminal court. For myself, I never joined in any of these addresses, but what I have delivered concerning them is all I have been able to discover; and government itself, as far as evidence extends, has not been more successful. I would, therefore, recommend it to his Majesty's servants, to attend to the reflections of an eloquent writer [Mr. Burke] at present high in their confidence and esteem, who has admirably exposed the danger and injustice of general accusations. "This way of proscribing the citizens by denominations and general descriptions, dignified by the name of reason of state, and security for Constitutions and commonwealths, is nothing better at bottom than the miserable invention of an ungenerous ambition, which would fain hold the sacred trust of power, without any of the virtues or energies that give a title to it; a receipt of policy, made up of a detestable compound of malice, cowardice, and sloth. They would govern men against their will; but in that government would be discharged from the exercise of vigilance, providence, and fortitude; and, therefore, that they may sleep on their watch, consent to take some one division of the society into partnership of the tyranny over the rest. But let government, in whatever form it may be, comprehend the whole of its justice, and restrain the suspicious by its vigilance; let it keep watch and ward; let it discover by its sagacity, and punish by its firmness, all delinquency against its power, whenever it exists in the overt acts, and then it will be as safe as God and nature intended it should be. Crimes are the acts of individuals, and not of denominations; and, therefore, arbitrarily to class men under general descriptions, in order to proscribe and punish them in the lump for a presumed delinquency, of which, perhaps, but a part—perhaps none at all—are guilty, is, indeed, a compendious method, and saves a world of trouble about proof; but such a method, instead of being law, is an act of unnatural rebellion against the legal dominion of reason and justice; and a vice, in any Constitution that entertains it, which at one time or other will certainly bring on its ruin."[8]

Crime charged upon the defendant.

Gentlemen, let us now address ourselves to the cause, disembarrassed by foreign considerations; let us examine what the charge upon the record is, and see how it is supported by the proofs. For, unless the whole indictment, or some one count of it, be in form and substance supported by the evidence, the defendant must be acquitted, however in other respects you may be dissatisfied with his imprudence and indiscretion. The indictment charges, "That the defendant being a person of an impious, depraved, seditious disposition, and maliciously intending to disturb the peace of the kingdom; to bring our most serene Sovereign into hatred and contempt with all the subjects of the realm, and to excite them to discontent against the government; he the said defendant, his aforesaid wicked contrivances and intentions to complete, perfect, and render effectual, on the 6th day of November," spoke the words imputed to him by the Crown. This is the indictment, and it is drawn with a precision which marks the true principle of English criminal law. It does not merely charge the speaking of the words, leaving the wicked intention to be supplied and collected by necessary and unavoidable inference, because such inference may or may not follow from the words themselves, according to circumstances, which the evidence alone can disclose. It charges therefore the wicked intention as a fact, and as constituting the very essence of the crime, stating, as it must state, to apprise the defendant of the crime alleged against him, the overt act, by which such malicious purpose was displayed, and by which he sought to render it effectual. No man can be criminal without a criminal intention—*actus non facit reum nisi mens sit rea.*[9] God alone can look into the heart, and man, could he look into it, has no jurisdiction over it, until society is disturbed by its actions; but the criminal mind being the source of all criminality, the law seeks only to punish actions which it can trace to evil disposition—it pities our errors and mistakes—makes allowances for our passions, and scourges only our crimes.

Intention is essential to the crime.

Concessions of the counsel for the Crown.

Gentlemen, my learned friend the Attorney General, in the conclusion of his address to you, did more than ratify these propositions. With a liberality and candor very honorable to himself, and highly advantageous to the public which he represents, he said to you, that if the expressions charged upon the defendant should turn out, in your opinion, to be unadvised and unguarded, arising on the sudden, and unconnected with previous bad intention, he should not even insist upon the strictness of the law, whatever it might be, nor ask a verdict, but such as between man and man, acting upon moral and candid feelings, ought to be asked and expected. These were the suggestions of his own just and manly disposition, and he confirmed them by the authority of Mr. Justice Foster, whose works are so deservedly celebrated. But judging of my unfortunate client, not from his own charity, but from the false information of others, he puts a construction upon an expression of this great author which destroys much of the intended effect of his doctrine—a doctrine which I will myself read again to you, and by the right interpretation of which I desire the defendant may stand or fall. In the passage read to you, Foster says, "As to mere words, they differ widely from writings in point of real malignity and proper evidence; they are often the effect of mere heat of blood, which in some natures, otherwise well disposed, carrieth the man beyond the bounds of prudence; they are always liable to great misconstruction, from the

[8] Mr. Burke's speech at Bristol. See page 308.

[9] This act does not make a man guilty without the intention.

ignorance or inattention of the hearers, and too often from a motive truly criminal." Foster afterward goes on to contrast such loose words, "*not relative to any act or design*," for so he expresses himself, with "words of advice and persuasion *in contemplation of some traitorous purpose actually on foot or intended, and in prosecution of it*." Comparing this rule of judgment with the evidence given, one would have expected a consent to the most favorable judgment—one would have almost considered the quotation as a tacit consent to an acquittal. But Mr. Attorney General, still looking through the false medium of other men's prejudices, lays hold of the words "otherwise well disposed," and ingrafts upon them this most extraordinary requisition. Show me, he says, that Mr. Frost is *otherwise well disposed*. Let him bring himself within the meaning of Foster, and *then* I consent that he shall have the fullest benefit of his indulgent principle of judgment. Good God, gentlemen, are we in an English court of justice? Are we sitting in judgment before the Chief Justice of England, with the assistance of a jury of Englishmen? And am I in such a presence to be called upon to prove the good disposition of my client, before I can be entitled to the protection of those rules of evidence which apply equally to the just and to the unjust, and by which an evil disposition must be proved before it shall even be suspected? I came here to resist and to deny the existence of legitimate and credible proof of disloyalty and disaffection; and am I to be called upon to prove that my client has not been, nor is, disloyal or disaffected? Are we to be deafened with panegyrics upon the English Constitution, and yet to be deprived of its first and distinguishing feature, that innocence is to be presumed until guilt be established? Of what avail is that sacred maxim, if, upon the bare assertion and imputation of guilt, a man may be deprived of a rule of evidence, the suggestion of wisdom and humanity, as if the rule applied only to those who need no protection, and who were never accused? If Mr. Frost, by any previous overt acts, by which alone any disposition, good or evil, can be proved, had shown a disposition leading to the offense in question, it was evidence for the Crown. Mr. Wood,[10] whose learning is unquestionable, undoubtedly thought so, when, with the view of crimination, he asked where Mr. Frost had been before the time in question, for he is much too correct to have put an irregular and illegal question in a criminal case: I must, therefore, suppose his right to ask it appeared to him quite clear and established, and I have no doubt that it was so. Why, then, did he not go on and follow it up, by asking what he had done in France—what declarations he had made *there*—or what part he proposed to act *here*, upon his return? The charge upon the record is, that the words were uttered with malice and premeditation; and Mr. Attorney General properly disclaims a conviction upon any other footing. Surely, then, it was open to the Crown, upon every principle of common sense, to have proved the previous malice by all previous discourses and previous conduct *connected with the accusation*. And yet, after having wholly and absolutely failed in this most important part of the proof, we are gravely told that the Crown having failed in the *affirmative*, we must set about establishing the *negative!* for that otherwise we are not within the pale or protection of the very first and paramount principles of the law and government of the country!

Mode of evading the consequences of this concession.

Having disposed of this stumbling-block in the way of sound and indulgent judgment, we may now venture to examine this mighty offense as it is proved by the witnesses for the Crown, supposing the facts neither to have been misstated from misapprehension, nor willfully exaggerated.

Mr. Frost, the defendant, a gentleman who, upon the evidence, stands wholly unimpeached of any design against the public peace, or any indisposition to the Constitution of the kingdom, appears to have dined at the tavern over the Percy coffee-house. This he did not with a company met upon any *political* occasion, good or evil, but, as has been admitted in the opening, with a society for the encouragement of agriculture, consisting of most reputable and inoffensive persons, neither talking nor thinking about government, or its concerns: so much for the preface to this dangerous conspiracy. The company did not retire till the bottle had made many merry circles; and it appears, upon the evidence for the Crown, that Mr. Frost, to say the least, had drunk very freely. But was it with the evil intention imputed to him that he went into this coffee-house to circulate his opinions, and to give effect to designs he had premeditated? He could not possibly go home *without* passing through it; for it is proved that there was no other passage into the street from the room where he had dined. But having got there by accident, did he even then stop by design, and collect an audience to scatter sedition? So far from it, that Mr. Yatman, the very witness against him, admits that he *interrupted* him as he passed in silence toward the street, and fastened the subject of France upon him. Every word which passed (for the whole is charged upon the very record as a dialogue with this witness) was in answer to his entrapping questions, introduced with the familiarity of a very old acquaintance, and in a sort of banter, too, which gave a turn to the conversation that renders it ridiculous, as well as wicked, to convert it into a serious plan of mischief: "Well," says Mr. Yatman, "well, Mr. Equality, so you have been in France—when did you arrive? I suppose you are for equality, and no Kings?" "O yes," says Mr. Frost, "certainly I am for equality; I am for no Kings." Now, beyond all question, when this answer was made, whether in jest or in earnest, whether when drunk or sober, it neither had, nor could have, the remotest relation to England or its government. France

Evidence against the defendant examined.

The defendant's language referred to France, not to England.

[10] One of the counsel for the prosecution.

had just abolished its new Constitution of monarchy, and set up a republic. She was at that moment divided and in civil confusion on the subject; the question, therefore, and the answer, as they applied to France, were sensible and relevant; but to England or to English affairs they had not (except in the ensnaring sequel) the remotest application. Had Yatman, therefore, ended here, the conversation would have ended, and Mr. Frost would have been the next moment in the street. But still the question is forced upon him, and he is asked, "What! no Kings in England?" although his first answer had no connection with England; the question, therefore, was self-evidently a snare, to which he answered, "No Kings in England;" which seemed to be all that was wanted, for in a moment every thing was confusion and uproar. Mr. Frost, who had neither delivered nor meant to deliver any serious opinion concerning government, and finding himself injuriously set upon, wished, as was most natural, to explain himself, by stating to those around him what I have been just stating to you. But all in vain; they were in pursuit of the immortal fame of the very business we are engaged in at this moment, and were resolved to hold their advantage. His voice was immediately drowned by the clamors of insult and brutality; he was baited on all sides like a bull, and left the coffee-house without the possibility of being heard either in explanation or defense. An indictment was immediately preferred against him, and from that moment the public ear has been grossly and wickedly abused upon the subject, his character shamefully calumniated, and his cause prejudged before the day of trial.

To accuse under such circumstances destructive of all human confidence.

Gentlemen it is impossible for me to form any other judgment of the impression which such a proceeding altogether is likely to make upon your minds, but from that which it makes upon my own. In the first place, is society to be protected by the breach of those confidences, and in the destruction of that security and tranquillity which constitute its very essence every where, but which, till of late, most emphatically characterized the life of an Englishman? Is government to derive dignity and safety by means which render it impossible for any man who has the least spark of honor to step forward to serve it? Is the time come when obedience to the law and correctness of conduct are not a sufficient protection to the subject, but that he must measure his steps, select his expressions, and adjust his very looks in the most common and private intercourses of life? Must an English gentleman in future fill his wine by a measure, lest, in the openness of his soul, and while believing his neighbors are joining with him in that happy relaxation and freedom of thought which is the prime blessing of life, he should find his character blasted, and his person in a prison? Does any man put such constraint upon himself in the most private moment of his life, that he would be contented to have his loosest and lightest words recorded, and set in array against him in a court of justice? Thank God, the world lives very differently, or it would not be worth living in. There are moments when jarring opinions may be given without inconsistency — when Truth herself may be sported with without the breach of veracity—and where well-imagined nonsense is not only superior to, but is the very index to wit and wisdom. I might safely assert—taking, too, for the standard of my assertion the most honorably correct and enlightened societies in the kingdom—that if malignant spies were properly posted, scarcely a dinner would end without a duel and an indictment.

Illustration from case supposed.

When I came down this morning, and found, contrary to my expectation, that we were to be stuffed into this miserable hole in the wall,[11] to consume our constitutions: suppose I had muttered along through the gloomy passages—"What, is this cursed trial of Hastings going on again? Are we to have no respite? Are we to die of the asthma in this damned corner? I wish to God that the roof would come down and abate the impeachment, Lords, Commons, and all together." Such a *wish*, proceeding from the mind, would be desperate wickedness, and the serious expression of it a high and criminal contempt of Parliament. Perhaps the bare utterance of such words, even without meaning, would be irreverent and foolish. But still, if such expressions had been gravely imputed to me as the result of a malignant mind, seeking the destruction of the Lords and Commons of England, how would they have been treated in the House of Commons on a motion for my expulsion? How! The witness would have been laughed out of the House before he had half finished his evidence, and would have been voted to be too great a blockhead to deserve a worse character. Many things are, indeed, wrong and reprehensible, that neither do nor can become the objects of criminal justice, because the happiness and security of social life, which are the very end and object of all law and justice, forbid the communication of them; because the spirit of a gentleman, which is the most refined morality, either shuts men's ears against what should not be heard, or closes their lips with the sacred seal of honor.

Society in no danger from liberality on this subject.

This tacit but well-understood and delightful compact of social life is perfectly consistent with its safety. The security of free governments, and the unsuspecting confidence of every man who lives under them, are not only compatible, but inseparable. It is easy to distinguish where the public duty calls for the violation of the private one. Criminal intention, but not indecent levities—not even grave opinions unconnected with conduct, are to be exposed to the magistrate; and when men (which happens but seldom), without the honor or the sense to make the due distinctions, force complaints upon governments which they can neither approve of nor refuse to act upon, it becomes the

[11] The King's Bench sat in the small Court of Common Pleas.

office of juries—as it is yours to-day—to draw the true line in their judgments, measuring men's conduct by the safe standards of human life and experience.

Gentlemen, the misery and disgrace of society, under the lash of informers, running before the law and hunting men through the privacies of domestic life, is described by a celebrated speaker [Mr. Burke] with such force and beauty of eloquence, that I will close my observations on this part of the subject by repeating what can not, I am persuaded, be uttered among Englishmen without sinking deep into their hearts: "A mercenary informer knows no distinction. Under such a system, the obnoxious people are slaves, not only to the government, but they live at the mercy of every individual; they are at once the slaves of the whole community and of every part of it; and the worst and most unmerciful men are those on whose goodness they must depend. In this situation men not only shrink from the frowns of a stern magistrate, but are obliged to fly from their very species. The seeds of destruction are sown in civil intercourse, and in social habitudes. The blood of wholesome kindred is infected. Their tables and beds are surrounded with snares. All the means given by Providence to make life safe and comfortable are perverted into instruments of terror and torment. This species of universal subserviency, that makes the very servant who waits behind your chair the arbiter of your life and fortune, has such a tendency to degrade and abase mankind, and to deprive them of that assured and liberal state of mind which alone can make us what we ought to be, that I vow to God, I would sooner bring myself to put a man to immediate death for opinions I disliked, and so to get rid of the man and his opinions at once, than to fret him with a feverish being, tainted with the jail distemper of a contagious servitude, to keep him above ground, an animated mass of putrefaction, corrupted himself, and corrupting all about him."[12]

All private espionage peculiarly adverse to English institutions.

If these sentiments apply so justly to the reprobation of persecution for opinions—even for opinions which the laws, however absurdly, inhibit—for opinions though certainly and maturely entertained—though publicly professed, and though followed up by corresponding conduct; how irresistibly do they devote to contempt and execration all eaves-dropping attacks upon loose conversations, casual or convivial, more especially when proceeding from persons conforming to all the religious and civil institutions of the state, unsupported by general and avowed profession, and not merely unconnected with conduct, but scarcely attended with recollection or consciousness! Such a vexatious system of inquisition, the disturber of household peace, began and ended with the Star Chamber. The venerable law of England never knew it. Her noble, dignified, and humane policy soars above the little irregularities of our lives, and disdains to enter our closets without a warrant founded upon complaint. Constructed by man to regulate human infirmities, and not by God to guard the purity of angels, it leaves to us our thoughts, our opinions, and our conversations, and punishes only overt acts of contempt and disobedience to her authority.

Evidence of this from the provisions of law.

Gentlemen, this is not the specious phrase of an advocate for his client; it is not even my exposition of the spirit of our Constitution; but it is the phrase and letter of the law itself. In the most critical conjunctures of our history, when government was legislating for its own existence and continuance, it never overstepped this wise moderation. To give stability to establishments, it occasionally bridled opinions concerning them, but its punishments, though sanguinary, laid no snares for thoughtless life, and took no man by surprise.

Of this the act of Queen Anne,[13] which made it high treason to deny the right of Parliament to alter the succession, is a striking example. The hereditary descent of the Crown had been recently broken at the Revolution by a minority of the nation, with the aid of a foreign force, and a new inheritance had been created by the authority of the new establishment, which had but just established itself. Queen Anne's title, and the peaceable settlement of the kingdom under it, depended wholly upon the constitutional power of Parliament to make this change. The superstitions of the world and reverence for antiquity, which deserves a better name, were against this power and the use which had been made of it; the dethroned King of England was living in hostile state at our very doors, supported by a powerful monarch at the head of a rival nation—and our own kingdom itself full of factious plots and conspiracies, which soon after showed themselves in open rebellion.

If ever, therefore, there was a season when a narrow jealousy could have been excusable in a government—if ever there was a time when the sacrifice of some private liberty to common security would have been prudent in a people, it was at such a conjuncture. Yet mark the reserve of the crown, and the prudence of our ancestors in the wording of the statute. Although the denial of the right of Parliament to alter the succession was tantamount to the denial of all legitimate authority in the kingdom, and might be considered as a sort of abjuration to the laws, yet the statute looked at the nature of man, and to the private security of individuals in society, while it sought to support the public society itself. It did not, therefore, dog men into taverns and coffee-houses, nor lurk for them at corners, nor watch for them in their domestic enjoyments. The act provides, "That every person who should maliciously, advisedly, and directly, by *writing* or *printing*, affirm that the Queen was not the rightful Queen of these realms, or that the Pretender had any right or title to the Crown, or that any other person had any right or title, otherwise than according to

[12] See Mr. Burke's speech at Bristol, page 301.

[13] Sixth Anne, c. 7.

the acts passed since the Revolution for settling the succession, or that the Legislature hath not sufficient authority to make laws for limiting the succession, should be guilty of high treason, and suffer as a traitor;" and then enacts, "That if any person shall *maliciously*, and *directly*, by *preaching*, *teaching*, or *advised speaking*, declare and maintain the same, he shall incur the penalties of a *præmunire*."

Remarks of Foster.

"I will make a short observation or two," says Foster, "on the act. First. The positions condemned by them had as direct a tendency to involve these nations in the miseries of an intestine war, to incite her Majesty's subjects to withdraw their allegiance from her, and to deprive her of her crown and royal dignity, as any general doctrine, any declaration not relative to actions or designs, could possibly have; and yet in the case of bare words, positions of this dangerous tendency, though maintained maliciously, advisedly, and directly, and even in the solemnities of preaching and teaching, are not considered as overt acts of treason.

"Secondly. In no case can a man be *argued* into the penalties of the act by inferences and conclusions drawn from what he hath affirmed; the criminal position must be *directly* maintained to bring him within the compass of the act.

"Thirdly. Nor will every rash, hasty, or unguarded expression, owing, perhaps, to natural warmth, or thrown out in the heat of disputation, render any person criminal within the act; the criminal doctrine must be maintained *maliciously and advisedly*."

He afterward adds, "Seditious writings are permanent things, and if published, they scatter the poison far and wide. They are acts of deliberation, capable of satisfactory proof, and not ordinarily liable to misconstruction; at least, they are submitted to the judgment of the court, naked and undisguised, as they came out of the author's hands. Words are transient and fleeting as the wind; the poison they scatter is, at the worst, confined to the narrow circle of a few hearers; they are frequently the effect of a sudden transport, easily misunderstood, and often misreported."

His principles founded in the nature of things.

Gentlemen, these distinctions, like all the dictates of sound policy, are as obvious to reason as they are salutary in practice. What a man *writes* that is criminal and pernicious, and what he disseminates when written, is conclusive of his purpose. He manifestly must have deliberated on what he wrote, and the distribution is also an act of deliberation. *Intention* in such cases is not, therefore, matter of legal proof, but of reasonable inference, unless the accused, by proof on his side, can rebut what reason must otherwise infer: since he who writes to others undoubtedly seeks to bring over other minds to assimilate with his own. So he who advisedly speaks to others upon momentous subjects, may be presumed to have the same intention. Yet so frail is memory—so imperfect are our natures—so dangerous would it be to place *words*, which, to use the language of Foster, are transient and fleeting, upon a footing with deliberate *conduct*, that the criminating letter of the law itself interposes the check, and excludes the danger of a rash judgment, by curiously selecting from the whole circle of language an expression which can not be mistaken; for nothing said upon the sudden, without the evidence of a context, and sequel in thought or conduct, can in common sense deserve the title of *advised speaking*. Try the matter before you upon the principle of the statute of Queen Anne, and examine it with the caution of Foster.

Application of these principles to the present case.

Supposing, then, that instead of the words imputed by this record, the defendant, coming half drunk through this coffee-house, had, in his conversation with Yatman, denied the right of Parliament to alter the succession, could he have been adjudged to suffer death for high treason under the statute of Queen Anne? Reason and humanity equally revolt at the position, and yet the decision asked from you is precisely that decision. For if you could not have found [his language] "*advised speaking*" to bring it within that statute of treason, so neither can you find it as the necessary evidence of the intention charged by the present indictment, which intention constitutes the misdemeanor.

If any thing were wanting to confirm these principles of the law and the commentaries of its ablest judges, as applicable to words—it is in another way emphatically furnished by the instance before us. In the zeal of these coffee-house politicians to preserve the defendant's expressions, they were instantly to be put down in writing, and signed by the persons present. Yet the paper read by Colonel Bullock,[14] and written, as he tells you, at the very moment with that intention, contains hardly a single word, from the beginning to the end of it, either in meaning or expression, the same as has been related by the witnesses. It sinks, in the first place, the questions put to the defendant, and the whole dialogue, which is the best clue to the business, and records, "that Mr. Frost came into the coffee-house and *declared*," an expression which he never used, and which wears the color of deliberation, "that he wished to see equality prevail in this country," another expression, which it is now agreed on all hands he never uttered, and which conveys a very different idea from saying, in answer to an impertinent or taunting question, "Oh yes, I am for equality." I impute nothing at all to Colonel Bullock, who did not appear to me to give his evidence unfairly—he read his paper as he wrote. But this is the very strength of my observation:

[14] The paper was as follows: "Percy coffee-house, 6th of November, 1792. We, the undermentioned, do hereby certify that at about 10 o'clock this evening, Mr. John Frost came into this coffee-room, and did then and in our presence openly declare that he wished to see equality prevail in this country, and no King, in a loud and factious way; and upon being asked whether he meant that there should be no King in this country, he answered 'Yes.'" The paper was not signed.

for suppose the case had not come for months to trial, the other witnesses (and honestly too) might have let their memories lean on the written evidence, and thus you would have been trying, and perhaps condemning the defendant for speaking words, stripped too of their explanatory concomitants, which it stands confessed at this moment were never spoken at all.

Pernicious influence of associations for the purpose of prosecuting in such cases.

Gentlemen, the disposition which has of late prevailed to depart from the wise moderation of our laws and Constitution, under the pretext, or from the zeal of preserving them, and which has been the parent of so many prosecutions, is an awful monument of human weakness. These associators to prosecute, who keep watch of late upon our words and upon our looks, are associated, it seems, to preserve our excellent Constitution from the contagion of France, where an arbitrary and tyrannous democracy, under the color of popular freedom, destroys all the securities and blessings of life. But how does it destroy them? How, but by the very means that these new partners of executive power would themselves employ, if we would let them—by inflicting, from a mistaken and barbarous state necessity, the severest punishments for offenses never defined by the law—by inflicting them upon suspicion instead of evidence, and in the blind, furious, and indiscriminate zeal of persecution, instead of by the administration of a sober and impartial jurisprudence. Subtracting the horrors of invading armies which France can not help, what other mischief has she inflicted upon herself? From what has she suffered but from this undisciplined and cruel spirit of accusation and rash judgment? A spirit that will look at nothing dispassionately, and which, though proceeding from a zeal and enthusiasm for the most part honest and sincere, is, nevertheless, as pernicious as the wicked fury of demons when it is loosened from the sober dominion of slow and deliberate justice. What is it that has lately united all hearts and voices in lamentation? What but these judicial executions, which we have a right to style murder, when we see the ax falling, and the prison closing upon the genuine expressions of the inoffensive heart—sometimes for private letters to friends, unconnected with conduct or intention—sometimes for momentary exclamations in favor of royalty, or some other denomination of government different from that which is established.

These are the miseries of France, the unhappy attendants upon revolution; and united as we all are in deploring them, upon what principle of common sense shall we vex and terrify the subjects of our own country in the very bosom of peace, and disgust them with the government, which we wish them to cherish, by unusual, irritating, and degrading prosecutions?

Indeed, I am very sorry to say that we *hear* of late too much of the excellence of the British government, and *feel* but too little of its benefits. They, too, who pronounce its panegyrics, are those who alone prevent the entire public from acceding to them. The eulogium comes from a suspected quarter, when it is pronounced by persons enjoying every honor from the Crown, and treating the people upon all occasions with suspicion and contempt. The three estates of the kingdom are co-ordinate, all alike representing the dignity, and jointly executing the authority of the nation; yet all our loyalty seems to be wasted upon one of them. How happens it else that we are so exquisitely sensible, so tremblingly alive to every attack upon the Crown or the nobles that surround it, *yet so completely careless of what regards the once respected and awful Commons of Great Britain?*

Prevailing tendencies on this subject, and their danger.

If Mr. Frost had gone into every coffee-house, from Charing Cross to the Exchange, lamenting the dangers of popular government, reprobating the peevishness of opposition in Parliament, and wishing, in the most advised terms, that we could look up to the throne and its excellent ministers alone for quiet and comfortable government, do you think that we should have had an indictment? I ask pardon for the supposition; I can discover that you are laughing at me for its absurdity. Indeed, I might ask you whether it is not the notorious language of the highest men, in and out of Parliament, to justify the alienation of the popular part of the government from the spirit and principle of its trust and office, and to prognosticate the very ruin and downfall of England, from a free and uncorrupted representation of the great body of the people? I solemnly declare to you, that I think the whole of this system leads inevitably to the dangers we seek to avert. It divides the higher and the lower classes of the nation into adverse parties, instead of uniting and compounding them into one harmonious whole. It embitters the people against authority, which, when they are made to feel and know is but their own security, they must, from the very nature of man, unite to support and cherish. I do not believe that there is any set of men to be named in England—I might say, that I do not know an individual who seriously wishes to touch the Crown, or any branch of our excellent Constitution; and when we hear peevish and disrespectful expressions concerning any of its functions, depend upon it, it proceeds from some practical variance between its theory and its practice. These variances are the fatal springs of disorder and disgust. They lost America, and in that unfortunate separation laid the foundation of all that we have to fear; yet, instead of treading back our steps, we seek recovery in the system which brought us into peril. Let government in England always take care to make its administration correspond with the true spirit of our genuine Constitution, and nothing will ever endanger it. Let it seek to maintain its corruptions by severity and coercion, and neither laws nor arms will support it. These are my sentiments; and I advise you, however unpopular they may be at this moment, to consider them before you repel them.

If the defendant, among others, has judged too lightly of the advantages of our government reform his errors by a beneficial experience o. them. Above all, let him feel its excellence to-day in its beneficence; let him compare in his trial the condition of an English subject with that of a citizen of France, which he is supposed in theory to prefer. These are the true criterions by which, in the long run, individuals and nations become affectionate to governments, or revolt against them. Men are neither to be talked nor written into the belief of happiness and security when they do not practically feel them, nor talked or written out of them when they are in the full enjoyment of their blessings: but if you condemn the defendant upon this sort of evidence, depend upon it, he must have his adherents, and, as far as that goes, I must be one of them.

Peroration: Let him that is without sin among you cast the first stone.

Gentlemen, I will detain you no longer, being satisfied to leave you, as conscientious men, to judge the defendant as you yourselves would be judged; and if there be any among you who can say to the rest that he has no weak or inconsiderate moments—that all his words and actions, even in the most thoughtless passages of his life, are fit for the inspection of God and man, he will be the fittest person to take the lead in a judgment of "Guilty," and the properest foreman to deliver it with good faith and firmness to the court.

I know the privilege that belongs to the Attorney General to reply to all that has been said; but perhaps, as I have called no witnesses, he may think it a privilege to be waived. It is, however, pleasant to recollect, that if it should be exercised, even with his superior talents, his honor and candor will guard it from abuse.

The Attorney General having exercised his privilege of reply, Lord Kenyon summed up; and the jury, after a consultation of an hour and a half, returned a verdict of "Guilty." Mr. Frost was sentenced to be imprisoned in Newgate six months, to stand one hour in the pillory, and to be struck off the roll of attorneys, whereby he was ruined for life.

SPEECH

OF MR. ERSKINE FOR MR. BINGHAM ON A TRIAL FOR ADULTERY, DELIVERED IN THE COURT OF KING'S BENCH, FEBRUARY 24, 1794.

INTRODUCTION.

THIS was almost the only case in which Mr. Erskine ever appeared as counsel for the defendant in a trial of this kind. All his sympathies and feelings were with the bereaved party; and so fervid were his appeals on such occasions, that in many instances he gained an amount of damages which swept the entire property of the defendant.

But the circumstances of this case were so peculiar, that Mr. Erskine felt himself authorized to appear for the defense. Mr. Bingham, afterward the Earl of Lucan, had formed an early attachment for Lady Elizabeth Fauconberg, which was warmly reciprocated by the latter. They were engaged to be married, and had the expectation of an early union, when the match was broken off by her parents in favor of Mr. Howard, afterward the Duke of Norfolk, and she was compelled to marry one whom she regarded with disgust and even abhorrence. She bore him a son within sixteen months after their marriage; but her affections continued to be passionately fixed on Mr. Bingham (who had at first avoided her society); a renewed intercourse gradually sprung up between them; her husband naturally became alienated by the growing hostility of her feelings; and after mutual upbraidings, she left him at the end of four years, and eloped with Mr. Bingham. It was certainly proper that they should now be divorced, especially as she was expected to give birth speedily to a child by the latter; but through a singular anomaly in the English laws, a divorce could be obtained only by Mr. Howard's bringing an action in *damages* against Mr. Bingham for depriving him of "the comfort and society of his wife!"

Mr. Erskine's management of the case was truly admirable. The entire simplicity with which he commences—his disclaimer of all idea of being eloquent, or of making any address to the feelings of the jury—the dry detail of *dates* with which he enters on the facts of the case, so perfectly suited to do away all suspicion on that subject—his pointed exposure of the opposing counsel's statements without evidence to support them—the vivid picture which he brings before the mind of the ill-fated daughter "given up to the plaintiff by the infatuation of parents, and stretched upon her bridal bed as upon a rack"—the bold burst of passion with which he exclaims, "Mr. Howard was never *married*"—"he was himself the *seducer*"—"imagine my client to be *plaintiff*, and what damages are you not prepared to give him, and yet he is here as *defendant!*"—the solemn lessons for the nobility which he deduces from the case, so instructive in themselves, and so peculiarly adapted to strengthen his cause—every thing, in short, conspires to make this speech, though brief, one of the most perfect exhibitions of power over the minds of a jury, to be found in the eloquence of our language.

SPEECH, &c.

GENTLEMEN OF THE JURY,—My learned friend, as counsel for the plaintiff, has bespoke an address from me, as counsel for the defendant, which you must not, I assure you, expect to hear.

He has thought it right (partly in courtesy to me, as I am willing to believe, and in part for the purposes of his cause) that you should suppose you are to be addressed with eloquence which I never possessed, and which, if I did, I should be incapable at this moment of exerting; because the most eloquent man, in order to exert his eloquence, must have his mind free from embarrassment on the occasion on which he is to speak—I am not in that condition. My learned friend has expressed himself as the friend of the plaintiff's family. He does not regard that family more than I do; and I stand in the same predicament toward my own honorable client and his relations. I know him and them, and because I know them, I regard them also: my embarrassment, however, only arises at being obliged to discuss this question in a public court of justice, because; could it have been the subject of private reference, I should have felt none at all in being called upon to settle it.

None of the eloquence to be expected which the opposing counsel had predicted.

Forbidden by the embarrassing situation of the speaker.

Gentlemen, my embarrassment is abundantly increased, when I see present a noble person, high, very high in rank in this kingdom, but not higher in rank than he is in my estimation: I speak of the noble Duke of Norfolk, who most undoubtedly must feel not a little at being obliged to come here as a witness for the defendant in the cause of a plaintiff so nearly allied to himself. I am persuaded no man can have so little sensibility, as not to feel that a person in my situation must be greatly embarrassed in discussing a question of this nature before such an audience, and between such parties as I have described.

Gentlemen, my learned friend desired you would take care not to suffer argument, or observation, or eloquence to be called into the field, to detach your attention from the evidence in the cause, upon which alone you ought to decide; I wish my learned friend, at the moment he gave you that caution, had not *himself* given testimony of a fact to which he stood the solitary witness. I wish he had not introduced *his own evidence*, without the ordinary ceremony of being sworn. I will not follow his example. I will not tell you what I know from the conversation of my client, nor give evidence of what I know myself. My learned friend tells you that nothing can exceed the agony of mind his client has suffered, and that no words can describe his adoration of the lady he has lost: these most material points of the cause rest, however, altogether on the *single, unsupported, unsworn evidence of the* COUNSEL for the plaintiff. No RELATION has been called upon to confirm them, though we are told that the whole house of Fauconberg, Bellasyse, and Norfolk are in the avenues of the court, ready, it seems, to be called at my discretion: and yet my learned friend is himself the only witness; though the facts (and most material facts, indeed, they would have been) might have been proved by so many illustrious persons.

Error of the opposing counsel in giving testimony without being under oath.

Now, to show you how little disposed I am to work upon you by any thing but by proof; to convince you how little desirous I am to practice the arts of speech as my only artillery in this cause, I will begin with a few plain *dates*, and, as you have pens in your hands, I will thank you to write them down. I shall begin with stating to you what my cause is, and shall then prove it—not by myself, but by witnesses.

Statement of the case.

The parties were married on the 24th of April, 1789. The child that has been spoken of, and in terms which gave me great satisfaction, as the admitted son of the plaintiff, blessed with the affection of his parent, and whom the noble person to whom he may become heir can look upon without any unpleasant reflection—that child was born on the 12th of August, 1791. Take that date, and my learned friend's *admission*, that this child must have been the child of Mr. Howard; an admission which could not have been rationally or consistently made, but upon the implied admission that no illicit connection had existed *previously* by which its existence might have been referred to the defendant. On this subject, therefore, the plaintiff must be silent. He can not say the parental mind has been wrung; he can not say hereafter, "NO SON OF MINE SUCCEEDING"[1]—he can say none of these things. This child was born on the 12th of August, 1791, and as Mr. Howard is *admitted* to be the author of its existence (which he must have been, if at all, in 1790), I have a right to say that, during all that interval, this gentleman could not have had the least reasonable cause of complaint against Mr. Bingham. His jealousy must, of course, have begun *after* that period; for, had there been grounds for it before, there could be no sense in the admission of his counsel, nor any foundation for that parental consolation which was brought forward in the very front of the cause.

Marriage of the parties, and birth of their child.

The next dry date is, therefore, the 24th of July, 1793; and I put it to his Lordship, that there is no manner of evidence which can be pressed into this cause *previous* to that time. Let me next disembarrass the cause from another assertion of my learned friend, namely, that a divorce can not take place before the birth of this child; and that, if the child happens to be a son, which is *one* contingency—and if the child so born does not die, which is *another* contingency—and if the noble Duke dies without issue, which is a *third* contingency—*then* this child might inherit the honors of the house of Norfolk. That I deny. My recent experience tells me the contrary. In a case where Mr. Stewart, a gentleman of Ireland, stood in a similar predicament, the Lords and Commons of England not only passed an Act of Divorce between him and his lady, but, on finding there was no access on the part of the husband, and that the child was not his, they bastardized the issue.

Time of Mrs. Howard's elopement.

Error of the opposing counsel as to divorce.

What, then, remains in this cause? Gentle-

[1] Macbeth. Act iii., Scene 2

men, there remains only this: In what manner, when you have heard my evidence (for this is a cause which, like all others, must stand upon evidence), the plaintiff shall be able to prove, what I have the noble judge's authority for saying he *must* prove, namely, *the loss of the comfort and society of his wife, by the seduction of the defendant*. THAT is the very gist of the action. The loss of her affection, and of domestic happiness, are the only legal foundations of his complaint.

True point at issue.

Now, before any tning can be *lost*, it must have *existed;* before any thing can be taken away from a man, he must have had it; before the seduction of a woman's affections from her husband can take place, he must have possessed her affections.

Gentlemen, my friend, Mr. Mingay, acknowledges this to be the law, and he shapes his case accordingly. He represents his client, a branch of a most illustrious house, as casting the eyes of affection upon a *disengaged* woman, and of rank equal to, or, at least, suitable to his own. He states a marriage of mutual affection, and endeavors to show that this young couple, with all the ardor of love, flew into each other's embraces. He shows a child, the fruit of that affection, and finishes with introducing the seductive adulterer coming to disturb all this happiness, and to destroy the blessings which he describes. He exhibits the defendant coming with all the rashness and impetuosity of youth, careless of the consequences, and thinking of nothing but how he could indulge his own lustful appetite at the expense of another man's honor; while the unhappy husband is represented as watching with anxiety over his beloved wife, anxious to secure her affections, and on his guard to preserve her virtue. Gentlemen, if such a case, or any thing resembling it, is established, I shall leave the defendant to whatever measure of damages you choose, in your resentment, to inflict.

Representations of opposing counsel.

In order, therefore, to examine this matter (and I shall support every syllable that I utter with the most precise and uncontrovertible proofs), I will begin with drawing up the curtains of this blessed marriage-bed, whose joys are supposed to have been nipped in the bud by the defendant's adulterous seduction.

True state of facts.

Nothing, certainly, is more delightful to the human fancy than the possession of a beautiful woman in the prime of health and youthful passion; it is beyond all doubt the highest enjoyment which God, in his benevolence, and for the wisest purposes, has bestowed upon his own image. I reverence, as I ought, that mysterious union of mind and body which, while it continues our species, is the source of all our affections; which builds up and dignifies the condition of human life; which binds the husband to the wife by ties more indissoluble than laws can possibly create, and which, by the reciprocal endearments arising from a mutual passion, a mutual interest, and a mutual honor, lays the foundation of that parental affection which dies in the brutes with the necessities of nature, but which reflects back again upon the human parents the unspeakable sympathies of their offspring, and all the sweet, delightful relations of social existence. While the curtains, therefore, are yet closed upon this bridal scene, your imaginations will naturally represent to you this charming woman endeavoring to conceal sensations which modesty forbids the sex, however enamored, too openly to reveal, wishing, beyond adequate expression, what she must not even attempt to express, and seemingly resisting what she burns to enjoy.

Alas, gentlemen! you must now prepare to see in the room of this a scene of horror and of sorrow. You must prepare to see a noble lady, whose birth surely required no further illustration; who had been courted to marriage before she ever heard even her husband's name; and whose affections were irretrievably bestowed upon, and pledged to, my honorable and unfortunate client; you must behold her given up to the plaintiff by the infatuation of parents, and stretched upon this bridal-bed as upon a rack; torn from the arms of a beloved and impassioned youth, himself of noble birth, only to secure the honors of a higher title; a legal victim on the altar of Heraldry.

The lady's previous engagement and loathing repugnance to the marriage.

Gentlemen, this is no high coloring for the purposes of a cause; no words of an advocate can go beyond the plain, unadorned effect of the evidence. I will prove to you that when she prepared to retire to her chamber she threw her desponding arms around the neck of her confidential attendant, and wept upon her as a criminal preparing for execution. I will prove to you that she met her bridegroom with sighs and tears—the sighs and tears of afflicted love for Mr. Bingham, and of rooted aversion to her husband. I think I almost hear her addressing him in the language of the poet—

> "I tell thee, Howard,
> Such hearts as ours were never pair'd above:
> Ill-suited to each other; join'd, not match'd;
> Some sullen influence, a foe to both,
> Has wrought this fatal marriage to undo us.
> Mark but the frame and temper of our minds,
> How very much we differ. Ev'n this day,
> That fills thee with such ecstasy and transport,
> To me brings nothing that should make me bless it,
> To think it better than the day before,
> Or any other in the course of time,
> That duly took its turn, and was forgotten."

Gentlemen, this was not the sudden burst of youthful disappointment, but the fixed and settled habit of a mind deserving of a happier fate I shall prove that she frequently spent her nights upon a couch, in her own apartments, dissolved in tears; that she frequently declared to her woman that she would rather go to Newgate than to Mr. Howard's bed; and it will appear, by his own confession, that for months subsequent to the marriage she obstinately refused him the privileges of a husband.

To all this, it will be said by the plaintiff's counsel (as it has, indeed, been hinted already), that disgust and alienation from her husband could not but be expected; but that it arose from her affection for Mr. Bingham. Be it so, gentlemen. I read-

Mr. Bingham in no sense the seducer.

ily admit, that if Mr. Bingham's acquaintance with the lady had commenced *subsequent to the marriage*, the argument would be irresistible, and the criminal conclusion against him unanswerable. But has Mr. Howard a right to instruct his counsel to charge my honorable client with seduction, when *he himself* was the SEDUCER? My learned friend deprecates the power of what he terms my pathetic eloquence. Alas, gentlemen! if I possessed it, the occasion forbids its exertion, because Mr. Bingham has only to defend *himself*, and can not demand damages from Mr. Howard for depriving him of what was *his* by a title superior to any law which man has a moral right to make. Mr. Howard was NEVER MARRIED! God and nature forbid the bans of such a marriage. If, therefore, Mr. Bingham this day could have, by me, addressed to you his wrongs in the character of a plaintiff demanding reparation, what damages might I not have asked for him; and, without the aid of this imputed eloquence, what damages might I not have expected?

I would have brought before you a noble youth, who had fixed his affections upon one of the most beautiful of her sex, and who enjoyed hers in return. I would have shown you their suitable condition; I would have painted the expectation of an honorable union; and would have concluded by showing her to you in the arms of another, by the legal prostitution of parental choice in the teeth of affection; with child by a rival, and only reclaimed at last, after so cruel and so afflicting a divorce, with her freshest charms despoiled, and her very morals in a manner impeached, by asserting the purity and virtue of her original and spotless choice. Good God! imagine my client to be PLAINTIFF, and what damages are you not prepared to give him? and yet he is here as DEFENDANT, and damages are demanded against HIM. Oh, monstrous conclusion!

Gentlemen, considering my client as perfectly safe under these circumstances, I may spare a moment to render this cause beneficial to the public.

It involves in it an awful lesson; and more instructive lessons are taught in courts of justice than the Church is able to inculcate. Morals come in the cold abstract from pulpits; but men smart under them practically when we lawyers are the preachers.

Admonitions to the aristocracy of England arising out of such facts.

Let the aristocracy of England, which trembles so much for itself, take heed to its own security. Let the nobles of England, if they mean to preserve that pre-eminence which, in some shape or other, must exist in every social community, take care to support it by aiming at that which is creative, and alone creative, of real superiority. Instead of matching themselves to supply wealth, to be again idly squandered in debauching excesses, or to round the quarters of a family shield; instead of continuing their names and honors in cold and alienated embraces, amid the enervating rounds of shallow dissipation, let them live as their fathers of old lived before them. Let them marry as affection and prudence lead the way, and in the ardors of mutual love, and in the simplicities of rural life, let them lay the foundation of a vigorous race of men, firm in their bodies, and moral from early habits; and instead of wasting their fortunes and their strength in the tasteless circles of debauchery, let them light up their magnificent and hospitable halls to the gentry and peasantry of the country, extending the consolations of wealth and influence to the poor. Let them but do this; and, instead of those dangerous and distracting divisions between the different ranks of life, and those jealousies of the multitude so often blindly painted as big with destruction, we should see our country as one large and harmonious family, which can never be accomplished amid vice and corruption, by wars or treaties, by informations *ex officio* for libels, or by any of the tricks and artifices of the state.[2] Would to God this system had been followed in the instance before us! Surely the noble house of Fauconberg needed no further illustration; nor the still nobler house of Howard, with blood enough to have inoculated half the kingdom. I desire to be understood to make these observations as general moral reflections, and not personally to the families in question; least of all to the noble house of Norfolk, the head of which is now present; since no man, in my opinion, has more at heart the liberty of the subject and the honor of our country.

Their application to this case.

Nothing done by Mr. Bingham to produce further alienation.

Having shown the feeble expectation of happiness from this marriage, the next point to be considered is this: Did Mr. Bingham take advantage of that circumstance to increase the disunion? I answer, No. I will prove to you that he conducted himself with a moderation and restraint, and with a command over his passions, which I confess I did not expect to find, and which in young men is not to be expected. I shall prove to you, by Mr. Greville, that, on this marriage taking place with the betrothed object of his affections, he went away a desponding man. His health declined; he retired into the country to restore it; and it will appear that for months afterward he never saw this lady until by mere accident he met her. And then, so far was he from endeavoring to renew his connection with her, that she came home in tears, and said he frowned at her as he passed. This I shall prove to you by the evidence in the cause.

Gentlemen, that is not all. It will appear that, when he returned to town, he took no manner of notice of her; and that her unhappiness was beyond all power of expression. How, indeed, could it be otherwise, after the account I have given you of the marriage? I shall prove, besides, by a gentleman who married one of the daughters of a person to whom this country is deeply indebted for his eminent and meritorious service [Marquis Cornwallis], that, from her utter reluctance to her husband, although in every respect honorable and correct in his manners and

[2] This was during the progress of those oppressive state trials in which Mr. Erskine was so largely engaged.

behavior, he was not allowed even the privileges of a husband, for months after the marriage. This I mentioned to you before, and only now repeat it in the statement of the proofs. Nothing better, indeed, could be expected. Who can control the will of a mismatched, disappointed woman? Who can restrain or direct her passions? I beg leave to assure Mr. Howard (and I hope he will believe me when I say it), that I think his conduct toward this lady was just such as might have been expected from a husband who saw himself to be the object of disgust to the woman he had chosen for his wife, and it is with this view only that I shall call a gentleman to say how Mr. Howard spoke of this supposed, but, in my mind, impossible object of his adoration. How, indeed, is it possible to adore a woman when you know her affections are riveted to another? It is unnatural! A man may have that appetite which is common to the brutes, and too indelicate to be described; but he can never retain an affection which is returned with detestation. Lady Elizabeth, I understand, was, at one time, going out in a phaeton: "There she goes," said Mr. Howard; "God damn her—I wish she may break her neck; I should take care how I got another." This may seem unfeeling behavior; but in Mr. Howard's situation, gentlemen, it was the most natural thing in the world, for they cordially hated one another. At last, however, the period arrived when this scene of discord became insupportable, and nothing could exceed the generosity and manly feeling of the noble person (the Duke of Norfolk), whose name I have been obliged to use in the course of this cause, in his interference to effect that separation which is falsely imputed to Mr. Bingham. He felt so much commiseration for this unhappy lady, that he wrote to her in the most affecting style. I believe I have got a letter from his Grace to Lady Elizabeth, dated Sunderland, July the 27th, that is, three days after their separation; but before he knew it had actually taken place: it was written in consequence of one received from Mr. Howard upon the subject. Among other things he says, "*I sincerely feel for you.*" Now if the Duke had not known at that time that Mr. Bingham had her earliest and legitimate affections, she could not have been an object of that pity which she received. She *was*, indeed, an object of the sincerest pity; and the sum and substance of this mighty seduction will turn out to be no more than this, that she was affectionately received by Mr. Bingham after the final period of voluntary separation. At four o'clock this miserable couple had parted *by consent*, and the chaise was not ordered till she might be considered as a single woman by the abandonment of her husband. Had this separation been *legal* and *formal*, I should have applied to his Lordship, upon the most unquestionable authorities, to nonsuit the plaintiff; for this action being founded upon the loss of the wife's society, it must necessarily fall to the ground if it appears that the society, though not the marriage union, was interrupted by a previous act of his own. In that hour of separation, I am persuaded he never considered Mr. Bingham as an object of resentment or reproach. He was the author of his own misfortunes, and I can conceive him to have exclaimed, in the language of the poet, as they parted,

Exasperation of Mr. Howard at his wife's conduct.

Their separation.

"Elizabeth never loved me.
Let no man, after me, a woman wed
Whose heart he knows he has not; though she [brings
A mine of gold, a kingdom, for her dowry.
For let her seem, like the night's shadowy queen,
Cold and contemplative—he can not trust her:
She may, she will, bring shame and sorrow on him;
The worst of sorrows, and the worst of shames."

You have, therefore, before you, gentlemen, two young men of fashion, both of noble families, and in the flower of youth: the proceedings, though not collusive, can not possibly be vindictive; they are indispensably preliminary to the dissolution of an inauspicious marriage, which never should have existed. Mr. Howard may, then, profit by a useful though an unpleasant experience, and be happier with a woman whose mind he may find disengaged; while the parents of the rising generation, taking warning from the lesson which the business of the day so forcibly teaches, may avert from their families, and the public, that bitterness of disunion, which, while human nature continues to be itself, will ever be produced to the end of time, from similar conjunctures.

The suit necessary to procure a divorce, but not one that authorizes damages.

Gentlemen, I have endeavored so to conduct this cause as to offend no man. I have guarded against every expression which could inflict unnecessary pain; and, in doing so, I know that I have not only served my client's interests, but truly represented his honorable and manly disposition. As the case before you can not be considered by any reasonable man as an occasion for damages, I might here properly conclude. Yet, that I may omit nothing which might apply to any possible view of the subject, I will close by reminding you that my client is a member of a numerous family; that, though Lord Lucan's fortune is considerable, his rank calls for a corresponding equipage and expense; he has other children—one already married to an illustrious nobleman, another yet to be married to some man who must be happy indeed if he shall know her value. Mr. Bingham, therefore, is a man of no fortune; but the heir only of, I trust, a very distant expectation. Under all these circumstances, it is but fair to believe that Mr. Howard comes here for the reasons I have assigned, and not to take money out of the pocket of Mr. Bingham to put into his own. You will, therefore, consider, gentlemen, whether it would be creditable for you to offer what it would be disgraceful for Mr. Howard to receive.

At least the damages should be merely nominal.

So completely had Mr. Erskine borne away the minds of the jury by this speech, that as some of them afterward stated, they had resolved to bring in a verdict for the defendant, with *heavy damages to be paid him by the plaintiff!* And even when the judge reminded them, in his charge, that no blame could be imputed to Mr. Howard, who was left in total ignorance of the previous engagement—that his wife's vows at the altar ought to have been respected by Mr. Bingham, not only at first, but to the end—that the defendant ought never to have allowed an intimacy to be renewed which led to such deplorable consequences—that he was liable to render a compensation to the plaintiff under these circumstances—and that they could not be justified in affixing a brand upon the latter by giving trifling damages—still they gave him but five hundred pounds, when the sum usually awarded, at that time, between persons of a wealthy condition, was from ten to fifteen thousand pounds.

SPEECH

OF MR. ERSKINE IN BEHALF OF THOMAS HARDY WHEN INDICTED FOR HIGH TREASON, DELIVERED BEFORE THE COURT OF KING'S BENCH, NOVEMBER 1, 1794.

INTRODUCTION.

THOMAS HARDY was a shoemaker in London, and secretary of the "London Corresponding Society," whose professed object was to promote parliamentary reform—having branch societies in most parts of the kingdom. Rash and inflammatory speeches were undoubtedly made at the meetings of these associations, and many things contained in their letters among themselves, and their addresses to the public, were highly objectionable. "The grand object of these associations," says Mr. Belsham, who probably was well acquainted with their designs, "was unquestionably to effect a reform in Parliament upon the visionary, if not pernicious principles of the Duke of Richmond—universal suffrage and annual election. They contained a considerable proportion of concealed republicans, converts to the novel and extravagant doctrine of Paine; and there can be no doubt but that *these* people hoped, and perhaps in the height of their enthusiasm believed, that a radical reform in Parliament upon democratic principles would eventually lead to the establishment of a democratic government." Still, it is generally understood that the bulk of the members were attached to the Constitution.

The government became alarmed at their proceedings, and instead of prosecuting for a *misdemeanor* those who could be proved to have used seditious language, they unhappily determined, at the instance of Lord Loughborough, to indict Hardy, Horne Tooke, and eleven others for high treason.

The act laid hold of was that of proposing a National Convention, avowedly for the purpose of promoting parliamentary reform; but the government maintained that the real design was to use the convention, if assembled, as an instrument of changing the government. The indictment, therefore, alleged,

1. That Hardy and the others, in calling this convention, did conspire to excite insurrection, subvert and alter the Legislature, depose the King, and "bring and put our said Lord the King to death."

2. The overt acts charged were attempting to induce persons, through the press, and by letters and speeches, to send delegates to a convention called for the above-mentioned purposes; and also the preparation of a few pikes in some populous places, which, as the parties concerned maintained, were provided as a defense against illegal attacks.

The case was opened on Tuesday, the 28th of October, 1794, by a speech from the Attorney General, Sir John Scott [afterward Lord Eldon], of nine hours in length. Never before had a trial for treason occupied more than one day; but in this instance the court sat during an entire week until after midnight, commencing every morning at eight o'clock. The Crown occupied the whole time, till after midnight Friday evening, with evidence against the prisoner; and Mr. Erskine then begged an adjournment to a somewhat later hour than usual the next day, that he might have time to look over his papers and make ready for the defense. To this the court objected as an improper delay of the jury, and proposed that the prisoner's witnesses should be examined while Mr. Erskine was preparing his reply. The following dialogue then ensued: *Erskine.* "I should be sorry to put the jury to any inconvenience; I do not shrink from my duty, but I assure your Lordship that during the week I have been nearly without natural rest, and that my physical strength is quite exhausted." *Eyre, C.J.* "What is it you ask for?" *Erskine.* "As I stated before, the Attorney General found it necessary to consume nine hours; I shall not consume half that time if I have an opportunity of doing that which I humbly request of the court." *Eyre, C.J.* "We have offered you an expedient, neither of you say whether you accept it?" Mr. Gibbs, the other counsel for the prisoner, spurned the proposal, and Mr. Erskine requested an adjournment until twelve the next day, as essential to the fair defense of one who was on trial for his life. The Chief Justice, with apparent reluctance, agreed to eleven. *Erskine.* "I should be glad if your Lordships would allow another hour." *Eyre, C.J.* "I feel so much for the situation of the jury, that, on their account, I can not think of it." *Erskine.* "My Lord, I never was placed in such a situation in the whole course of my practice before; however, I will try to do my duty." *Jury.* "My Lord, we are extremely willing to allow Mr. Erskine another hour, if your Lordship thinks proper." *Eyre, C.J.* "As the jury ask it for you, I will not refuse you."

"Cheered by this good omen," says Lord Campbell, "Erskine went home, and, after a short repose, arranged the materials of a speech which will last forever.' He began at two o'clock on Saturday afternoon, and spoke seven hours—a period that seemed very short to his hearers, and in reality was so, considering the subjects he had to deal with, and the constitutional learning, powerful reasoning, the wit, and the eloquence which he condensed into it. This wonderful performance must be studied as a *whole* by all who are capable of understanding its merits; for the enunciation of principles is so connected with the inferences to be drawn from the evidence, and there is such an artful, though seemingly natural succession of topics, to call for the pity and the indignation of the jury—to captivate their affections and to convince their understandings—that the full beauty of detached passages can not be properly appreciated."

SPEECH, &c.

Thanks to the jury for their indulgence.

GENTLEMEN OF THE JURY,—Before I proceed to the performance of the momentous duty which is at length cast upon me, I desire, in the first place, to return my thanks to the judges for the indulgence I have received in the opportunity of addressing you at this later period of the day than the ordinary sitting of the court, when I have had the refreshment which nature but too much required, and a few hours' retirement, to arrange a little in my mind that immense matter, the result of which I must now endeavor to lay before you. I have to thank *you*, also, gentlemen, for the very condescending and obliging manner in which *you* so readily consented to this accommodation. The court could only speak for itself, referring me to *you*, whose rest and comfort had been so long interrupted. I shall always remember your kindness.

The praises bestowed on the Constitution are merited only as it secures equal and impartial justice.

Before I advance to the regular consideration of this great cause, either as it regards the evidence or the law, I wish first to put aside all that I find in the speech of my learned friend, the Attorney General, which is either collateral to the merits, or in which I can agree with him. First, then, IN THE NAME OF THE PRISONER, and speaking *his* sentiments, which are well known to be my own also, I concur in the eulogium which you have heard upon the Constitution of our wise forefathers: But before this eulogium can have any just or useful application, we ought to reflect upon what it is which entitles this Constitution to the praise so justly bestowed upon it. To say nothing at present of its most essential excellence, or rather the very soul of it, viz., the share the people ought to have in their government, by a pure representation, for the assertion of which the prisoner stands arraigned as a traitor before you—what is it that distinguishes the government of England from the most despotic monarchies? What but the security which the subject enjoys in a trial and judgment by his equals; rendered doubly secure as being part of a system of law which no expediency can warp, and which no power can abuse with impunity

The evils of the French Revolution a warning not to stretch the laws to the injury of private right.

The Attorney General's second preliminary observation I equally agree to. I anxiously wish with him that you may bear in memory the anarchy which is desolating France. Before I sit down, I may, perhaps, in my turn, have occasion to reflect a little upon its probable causes; but, waiting a season for such reflections, let us first consider what the evil is which has been so feelingly lamented as having fallen on that unhappy country. It is, that under the dominion of a barbarous state necessity, every protection of law is abrogated and destroyed. It is, that no man can say, under such a system of alarm and terror, that his life, his liberty, his reputation, or any one human blessing, is secure to him for a moment. It is, that if accused of federalism, or moderatism, or incivism, or of whatever else the changing fashions and factions of the day shall have lifted up into high treason against the state, he must see his friends, his family, and the light of heaven no more: the accusation and the sentence being the same, following one another as the thunder pursues the flash. Such has been the state of England—such is the state of France; and how, then, since they are introduced to you for application, ought they, in reason and sobriety, to be applied? If this prosecution has been commenced (as is asserted) to avert from Great Britain the calamities incident to civil confusion, leading in its issues to the deplorable condition of France, I call upon you, gentlemen, to avert such calamity from falling upon my client, and, through his side, upon yourselves and upon our country. Let not him suffer under vague expositions of tyrannical laws, more tyrannically executed. Let not him be hurried away to predoomed execution, from an honest enthusiasm for the public safety. I ask for him a trial by this applauded Constitution of our country. I call upon you to administer the law to him, according to our own wholesome institutions, by its strict and rigid letter. However you may eventually disapprove of any part of his conduct, or, viewing it through a false medium, may think it even wicked, I claim for him, as a subject of England, that the *law* shall decide upon its criminal denomination. I protest, in his name, against all appeals to speculations concerning *consequences*, when the law commands us to look only to *intentions*. If the state be threatened with evils, let Parliament administer a prospective remedy, but let the prisoner hold his life under the law.[1]

[1] Nothing could be more admirable than the turn given in this exordium to the remarks of the Attorney General. The prisoner and his eleven companions were in great danger of being sacrificed to the dread of French principles. The jury, though

Gentlemen, I ask this solemnly of the court, whose justice I am persuaded will afford it to me. I ask it more emphatically of you, the jury, who are called upon your oaths to make a true deliverance of your countryman from this charge. But lastly, and chiefly, I implore it of Him in whose hands are all the issues of life—whose humane and merciful eye expands itself over all the transactions of mankind; at whose command nations rise and fall, and are regenerated; without whom not a sparrow falleth to the ground—I implore it of God himself, that He will fill your minds with the spirit of justice and of truth, so that you may be able to find your way through the labyrinth of matter laid before you—a labyrinth in which no man's life was ever before involved in the annals of British trial, nor, indeed, in the whole history of human justice or injustice.

The indictment.

Gentlemen, the first thing in order is to look at the indictment itself; of the whole of which, or of some integral part, the prisoner must be found guilty, or be wholly discharged from guilt.

Crime alleged. A conspiracy to bring about the *natural* death of the King.

The indictment charges that the prisoners did maliciously and traitorously conspire, compass, and imagine, "*to bring and put our Lord the King to death.*" And that to fulfill, perfect, and bring to effect their most evil and wicked purpose (that is to say, of bringing and putting the King to death), "they met, conspired, consulted, and agreed among themselves, and other false traitors unknown, to cause and procure a convention to be assembled within the kingdom, *with intent*" (I am reading the very words of the indictment, which I entreat you to follow in the notes you have been taking with such honest perseverance)—"*with intent, and in order* that the persons so assembled at such convention, should and might traitorously, and in defiance of the authority, and against the will of Parliament, subvert and alter, and cause to be subverted and altered, the Legislature, rule, and government of the country, and to depose the King from the royal state, title, power, and government thereof." This is the first and great leading overt act in the indictment. And you observe that it is not charged as being treason substantively and in *itself*, but only as it is committed in *pursuance* of the treason against the King's person, antecedently imputed. For the charge is not, that the prisoners conspired to assemble a convention to *depose* the King, but that they conspired and compassed his *death*, and that, in order to accomplish that wicked and detestable purpose (*i. e.*, in order to fulfill the traitorous intention of the mind against his *life*), they conspired to assemble a convention with a view to depose him.[2] The same observation applies alike to all the other counts or overt acts upon the record, which manifestly, indeed, lean upon the establishment of the first for their support. They charge the publication of different writings, and the provision of arms, not as distinct offenses, but as acts done to excite to the assembling of the same convention, and to maintain it when assembled; but, above all, and which must never be forgotten, because they also uniformly charge these different acts as committed in fulfillment of the same traitorous purpose, TO BRING THE KING TO DEATH. You will, therefore, have three distinct matters for consideration upon this trial; *First.* What share (if any) the prisoner had, in concert with others, in assembling *any* convention, or meeting of subjects within this kingdom; *Second.* What were the acts to be done by this convention when assembled; and, *Third.* What was the view, purpose, and intention of those who projected its existence This third consideration, indeed, comprehends, or rather precedes and swallows up the other two. Because, before it can be material to decide upon the views of the convention, as pointed to the subversion of the rule and order of the King's political authority (even if such views could be ascribed to it, and brought home even personally to the prisoner), we shall have to examine whether that criminal conspiracy against the established order of the community was hatched and engendered by a wicked contemplation to destroy the *natural life and person* of the King, and whether the acts charged and established by the evidence were done in pursuance and in fulfillment of the same traitorous purpose.

Further proof that this is the crime alleged.

Gentlemen, this view of the subject is not only correct, but self-evident. The subversion of the King's political government, and all conspiracies to subvert it, are crimes of great magnitude and enormity, which the law is open to punish; but neither of

gentlemen of high intelligence and respectability, were zealous adherents of the ministry, and committed to the support of their measures as members of the Loyal Associations of the metropolis. Most of the evidence for the Crown had been previously *published,* and undoubtedly read by the jury under circumstances calculated to produce the worst impressions on their minds. The subject had been brought before Parliament by Mr. Pitt. The case had been prejudged; a conspiracy had been charged on the prisoner and his companions by an act of Parliament; and the Habeas Corpus Act had actually been suspended through fear of this conspiracy! Under these circumstances, it seemed hardly possible for any jury to give the prisoner a fair hearing. This accounts for the extreme anxiety manifested by Mr. Erskine throughout the whole of this speech. The lives of eleven others besides the prisoner were suspended on the issue of this one argument. These considerations will induce the reader to follow Mr. Erskine, with unwonted interest, through all the windings of this intricate case.

[2] Here Mr. Erskine takes his first stand, and gives us the foundation of the entire legal argument which follows. There were two kinds of treason—one the "compassing the King's death," and the other "levying war to depose him." Now the indictment had charged the *former* on the prisoner; and although it had also mentioned the latter, this became *subordinate* to the former; so that the thing to be proved against the prisoners was, that in the alleged conspiracy they directly intended to destroy the *natural* life of the King.

them are the crimes before you. The prisoner is not charged with a conspiracy against the King's political government, but against his *natural life*. He is not accused of having merely taken steps to depose him from his authority, but with having done so *with the intention to bring him to death.* It is the act with the *specific intention*, and not the act alone, which constitutes the charge. The act of conspiring to depose the King may, indeed, be *evidence*, according to circumstances, of an intention to destroy his natural existence; but never, as a proposition of law, can it constitute the intention itself. Where an act is done in pursuance of an intention, surely the intention must first exist; a man can not do a thing in fulfillment of an intention, unless his mind first *conceives* that intention. The doing of an act, or the pursuit of a system of conduct, which leads in probable consequences to the death of the King, may legally (if any such be before you) affect the consideration of the traitorous purpose charged by the record; and I am not afraid of trusting you with the evidence. How far any given act, or course of acting, *independent* of intention, may lead probably or inevitably to any natural or political consequence, is what we have no concern with. These may be curious questions of casuistry or politics; but it is wickedness and folly to declare that consequences unconnected even with intention or consciousness, shall be synonymous in law with the traitorous mind, although the traitorous mind alone is arraigned, as constituting the crime.

Part First: The law of treason involved in this case.

I. Gentlemen, the first question consequently for consideration, and to which I must, therefore, earnestly implore the attention of the court, is this—WHAT IS THE LAW UPON THIS MOMENTOUS SUBJECT? And recollecting that I am invested with no authority, I shall not presume to offer you any thing of my own. Nothing shall proceed from myself upon this part of the inquiry, but that which is merely introductory, and necessary to the understanding of the authorities on which I mean to rely for the establishment of doctrines, not less essential to the general liberties of England, than to the particular consideration which constitutes our present duty.

(1.) The treason in question directed against the *natural* life of the King, &c.

First, then, I maintain, that that branch of the statute 25th of Edward the Third, which declares it to be high treason, "*when a man doth compass or imagine the death of the King, of his lady the Queen, or of his eldest son and heir,*" was intended to guard, by a higher sanction than felony, the NATURAL LIVES of the King, Queen, and Prince; and that no act, therefore (either inchoate or consummate), of resistance to, or rebellion against, the King's regal capacity, amounts to high treason of compassing his death, unless where they can be charged upon the indictment, and proved to the satisfaction of the jury at the trial, as overt acts committed by the prisoner, in *fulfillment* of a traitorous intention to destroy the King's natural life.

It *consists* in the intention to destroy that natural life.

Secondly, that the compassing the King's death, or, in other words, the traitorous intention to destroy his *natural existence*, is the treason, and not the overt acts, which are only laid as manifestations of the traitorous intention; or, in other words, as *evidence* competent to be left to a jury to prove it—that no conspiracy to levy war against the King, nor any conspiracy against his regal character or capacity, is a good overt act of compassing his death, unless some force be exerted, or in contemplation, against the King's person; and that such force, so exerted or in contemplation, is not substantively the treason of compassing, but only competent in point of law to establish it, if the jury, by the verdict of guilty, draw that conclusion of fact from the evidence of the overt act.

The existence of this intention is a *fact* to be inferred by the jury, from the overt acts, and not a deduction of law.

Thirdly, that the charge in the indictment, of compassing the King's death, is not laid as legal inducement or introduction, to follow as a legal inference from the establishment of the overt act, but is laid as an averment of A FACT; and, as such, the very gist of the indictment, to be affirmed or negatived by the verdict of Guilty or Not guilty.[3]

The doctrines of Hale and other great authorities not controverted in those positions.

It will not (I am persuaded) be suspected by the Attorney General, or by the court, that I am about to support these doctrines by opposing my own judgment to the authoritative writings of the venerable and excellent Lord Hale, whose memory will live in this country, and throughout the enlightened world, as long as the administration of pure justice shall exist. Neither do I wish to oppose any thing which is to be found in the other learned authorities principally relied upon by the Crown, because all my positions are perfectly consistent with a right interpretation of them; and because, even were it otherwise, I could not expect successfully to oppose them by any reasonings of my own, which can have no weight, but as they shall be found at once consistent with acknowledged authorities, and with the established principles of the English law. I can do this with the greater security, because my respectable and learned friend, the Attorney General, has not cited cases which have been the disgrace of this country in former times, nor asked you to sanction by your judgment those bloody murders, which are recorded by them as acts of English justice; but, as might be expected of an honorable man, his expositions of the law (though

[3] The statement contained in these three propositions, if admitted, overthrew at once the entire argument of the Attorney General as to the question of law. He had blended, as it were, the two kinds of treason mentioned in the preceding note. He insisted that it was enough for him to prove that the prisoner's acts amounted to a "levying of war" against the King's government, and that this, by the *intendment of law,* was a compassing of his death. Mr. Erskine shows that the jury must take the *whole* as a question of *fact*—"Did he aim to destroy the King's *natural* life." This question he lays on the consciences of the jury.

I think them frequently erroneous) are drawn from the same sources, which I look up to for doctrines so very different. I find, indeed, throughout the whole range of authorities (I mean those which the Attorney General has properly considered as deserving that name and character) very little contradiction. As far as I can discover, much more entanglement has arisen from now and then a tripping in the *expression*, than from any difference of sentiment among eminent and virtuous judges, who have either examined or sat in judgment upon this momentous subject.[4]

A very wide field of argument opened by the peculiar circumstances of the case.

Gentlemen, before I pursue the course I have prescribed to myself, I desire most distinctly to be understood, that in my own judgment the most successful argument that a conspiracy to *depose* the King does not necessarily establish the treason charged upon this record, is totally beside any possible judgment that you can have to form upon the evidence before you. The truth is, throughout the whole volumes [of evidence] that have been read, I can trace nothing that even points to the imagination of such a conspiracy; and, consequently, the doctrines of Coke, Hale, and Foster, on the subject of high treason, might equally be detailed in any other trial that has ever been proceeded upon in this place. But, gentlemen, I stand in a fearful and delicate situation. As a supposed attack upon the King's civil authority has been transmuted, by *construction*, into a murderous conspiracy against his natural person. in the same manner, and by the same arguments, a conspiracy to overturn that civil authority by direct force has again been assimilated, by *further* construction, to a design to undermine monarchy by changes wrought through public opinion, enlarging gradually into universal will; so that I can admit no false proposition, however aside I may think it from rational application. For as there is a constructive *compassing*, so also there is constructive *deposing;* and I can not, therefore, possibly know what either of them is separately, nor how the one may be argued to involve the other. There are, besides, many prisoners whose cases are behind, and whose lives may be involved in your present deliberation; their names have been already stigmatized, and their conduct arraigned in the evidence you have heard, as a part of the conspiracy. It is these considerations which drive me into so large a field of argument, because, by sufficiently ascertaining the law in the outset, they who are yet looking up to it for protection may not be brought into peril.

Gentlemen, I now proceed to establish, that a compassing of the death of the King, within the twenty-fifth of Edward the Third, which is the charge against the prisoner, consists in a traitorous intention against his NATURAL LIFE; and that nothing short of your firm belief of that detestable intention, from overt acts which you find him to have committed, can justify his conviction. That I may keep my word with you in building my argument upon nothing of my own, I hope my friend Mr. Gibbs [his associate in the defense] will have the goodness to call me back if he finds me wandering from my engagement, that I may proceed step by step upon the most venerable and acknowledged authorities of the law.

Evidence from authorities: Lord Hale.

In this process I shall begin with Lord Hale, who opens this important subject by stating the reason of passing the statute of the twenty-fifth of Edward the Third, on which the indictment is founded. Lord Hale says, in his Pleas of the Crown (vol. i., page 82), that "at common law there was a great latitude used in raising offenses to the crime and punishment of treason, by way of interpretation and arbitrary *construction*, which brought in great uncertainty and confusion. Thus, accroaching (i. e., encroaching on) *royal power*, was a usual charge of treason anciently, though a very uncertain charge; so that no man could tell what it was, or what defense to make to it." Lord Hale then goes on to state various instances of vexation and cruelty, and concludes with this striking observation: "By these and the like instances that might be given, it appears how *arbitrary and uncertain* the law of treason was before the statute of twenty-fifth of Edward the Third, whereby it came to pass that almost every offense that was, or seemed to be, a breach of the faith and allegiance due to the King, was by *construction*, *consequence*, and *interpretation*, raised into the offense of high treason." This is the lamentation of the great Hale upon the state of this country previous to the passing of the statute, which, he says, was passed as a remedial law, to put an end to them. And Lord Coke, considering it in the same light, says, in his third Institute, page 2, "The Parliament which passed this statute was called (as it well deserved) *Parliamentum Benedictum;* and the like honor was given to it by the different statutes which from time to time brought back treasons to its standard, all agreeing in magnifying and extolling this blessed act." Now this statute, which has obtained the panegyric of these great men, whom the Chief Justice in his charge looked up to for light and for example, and whom the Attorney General takes also for his guide, would very little have deserved the high eulogium bestowed upon it, if, though avowedly passed to destroy uncertainty in criminal justice, and to beat down the arbitrary constructions of judges, lamented by Hale as disfiguring and dishonoring the law, it had, nevertheless, been so worded as to give birth to *new* constructions and uncertainties, instead of destroying the old ones. It would but ill have entitled itself to the denomination of a blessed statute, if it had not, in its enacting letter, which professed to remove doubts, and to ascertain the law, made use of

[4] Here Mr. Erskine throws out, in passing, a reference to the explanation which he intends to give of the apparent contradiction of the books to his positions as here laid above. Nothing is more remarkable than the dexterity with which he thus prepares the way for what is coming, and makes his speeches a compacted system of thought.

expressions the best known and understood; and it will be found, accordingly, that it cautiously did so.

Meaning of the words "compassing the King's death."

In selecting the expression of COMPASSING THE DEATH, it employed a term of the most fixed and appropriate signification in the language of English law, which not only no judge or counsel, but which no attorney or attorney's clerk, could misunderstand; because, in former ages, before the statute compassing the death of *any man* had been a felony, and what had amounted to such compassing, had been settled in a thousand instances. To establish this, and to show also, by no reasoning of mine, that the term "compassing the death" was intended by the statute, when applied to the King, as high treason, to have the same signification as it had obtained in the law when applied to the subject as a felony, I shall refer to Mr. Justice Foster, and even to a passage cited by the Attorney General himself, which speaks so unequivocally and unanswerably for itself as to mock all commentary. "The ancient writers," says Foster, "in treating of felonious homicide, considered the felonious *intention* manifested by plain facts, in the same light, in point of guilt, as homicide itself. The rule was, *voluntas reputatur pro facto;*[5] and while this rule prevailed, the nature of the offense was expressed by the term *compassing the death.* This rule has been long laid aside as too rigorous in the case of common persons. But in the case of the King, Queen, and Prince, the statute of treasons has, with great propriety, *retained* it in its full extent and vigor; and, in describing the offense, has likewise *retained* the ancient mode of expression, when a man doth 'compass or imagine the death of our Lord the King,' &c., and thereof be upon sufficient proof, provablement, attainted of open deed, by people of his condition: the words of the statute descriptive of the offense, must, therefore, be strictly pursued in every indictment for this species of treason. It must charge that the defendant did traitorously compass and imagine the King's death; and then go on and charge the several acts made use of by the prisoner to effectuate his traitorous purpose. For 'the compassing the King's death' is the treason, and the overt acts are charged as the *means* made use of to effectuate the intentions and imaginations of the heart. And, therefore, in the case of the regicides, the indictment charged that they did traitorously compass and imagine the death of the King, and the cutting off the head was laid as the overt act, and the person who was supposed to have given the mortal stroke was convicted on the same indictment."

This concluding instance, though at first view it may appear ridiculous, is well selected as an illustration. Because, though in that case there could be no possible doubt of the intention, since the act of a deliberate execution involves, in common sense, the intention to destroy life, yet still the anomaly of the offense, which exists *wholly* in the INTENTION, and not in the overt act, required the preservation of the form of the indictment. It is surely impossible to read this commentary of Foster without seeing the true purpose of the statute. The common law had anciently considered, even in the case of a fellow-subject, the malignant intention to destroy, as equivalent to the act itself. But that noble spirit of humanity which pervades the whole system of our jurisprudence, had, before the time of King Edward the Third, eat out and destroyed this rule, too rigorous in its general application; but, as Foster truly observes in the passage I have read, "This rule, too rigorous in the case of the subject, the statute of treasons retained in the case of the King, and retained also the very expression used by the law when compassing the death of a subject was felony."

The common law use of the phrase shows its meaning in the statute.

The statute, therefore, being expressly made to remove doubts, and accurately to define treason, adopted the ancient expression of the common law, as applicable to felonious homicide, meaning that the life of the Sovereign should remain an exception, and that *voluntas pro facto*, the wicked intention for the deed itself (as it regarded *his* sacred life), should continue for the rule; and, therefore, says Foster, the statute, meaning to retain the law which was before general, retained also the expression. It appears to me, therefore, incontrovertible, not only by the words of the statute itself, but upon the authority of Foster, which I shall follow up by that of Lord Coke and Hale (contradicted by no syllable in their works, as I shall demonstrate), that the statute, as it regarded the security of the King's life, did not mean to enact a new security never known to the common law in other cases; but meant to suffer a common law rule, which formerly existed universally, which was precisely known, but which was too severe in common cases, to remain as an exception in favor of the King's security. I do, therefore, positively maintain, not as advocate merely, but in my own person, that, within the letter and meaning of the statute, nothing can be a compassing the death of the King that would not, in ancient times, have been a felony in the case of a subject. For otherwise Foster and Coke, as will be seen, are very incorrect when they say the statute *retained* the old law, and the appropriate word to express it; for if it went *beyond* it, it would, on the contrary, have been a new rule unknown to the common law, enacted for the first time, for the preservation of the King's life. Unquestionably, the Legislature might have made such a rule; but we are not inquiring what it might have enacted, but what it has enacted. But I ought to ask pardon for having relapsed into any argument of my own upon this subject, when the authorities are more express to the purpose than any language I can use. For Mr. Justice Foster himself expressly says—*Discourse 1st, of High Treason*, p. 207, "All the words descriptive of the offense, name-

Nothing a compassing the King's death which would not have been felony toward a fellow-subject.

[5] The will is taken for the deed.

ly, 'If a man doth compass or imagine, and thereof be attainted of open deed,' are plainly borrowed from the common law, and therefore must bear the *same* construction they did at common law." Is this distinct? I will read it to you again: "All the words descriptive of the offense, namely, 'If a man doth compass or imagine, and thereof be attainted of open deed,' are plainly borrowed from the common law, and therefore must bear the same construction they did at common law."

Gentlemen, Mr. Justice Foster is by no means singular in his doctrine. Lord Coke, the oracle of the law, and the best oracle that one can consult, when standing for a prisoner charged with treason, as he was the highest prerogative lawyer that ever existed, maintains the same doctrine. Even he, even Coke, the infamous prosecutor of Raleigh,[6] whose character with posterity, as an Attorney General, my worthy and honorable friend would disdain to hold, to be author of all his valuable works; yet even this very Lord Coke himself holds precisely the same language with Foster. For, in his commentary on this statute, in his *3d Institute*, p. 5, when he comes to the words, "Doth compass," he says, "Let us see, first, what the compassing the death of a *subject* was before the making of this statute, when *voluntas reputabatur pro facto*." Now what is the plain English of this? The commentator says, "I am going to instruct you, the student, who are to learn from me the law of England, what is a compassing of the death of the King. But that I can not do but by first carrying you to look into what was the compassing the death of a subject at the ancient common law; because the statute having made a compassing, as applied to the King, the crime of high treason, which, at common law, was felony in the case of a subject, it is impossible to define the one without looking back to the records which illustrate the other." This is so directly the train of Lord Coke's reasoning, that, in his own singularly precise style of commentating, he immediately lays before his reader a variety of instances from the ancient records and year books, of compassing the subject's death. And what are they? Not acts wholly collateral to attacks upon life, dogmatically laid down by the law from speculations upon probable or possible consequences; but assaults *with intent to murder*; conspiracies to waylay the person with the same intention; and other *murderous* machinations. These were [the] only compassings before the statute against the subject's life; and the extension of the expression was never heard of in the law, till introduced by the craft of political judges when it became applicable to crimes against the state.

Same views maintained by Lord Coke.

Here, again, I desire to appeal to the highest authorities for this source of constructive treason. Although the statute of Edward the Third had expressly directed that nothing should be declared to be treason but cases within its enacting letter, yet Lord Hale says, in his Pleas of the Crown, page 83, that "things were so carried by parties and factions, in the succeeding reign of Richard the Second, that this statute was but little observed but as this or that party got the better. So the crime of high treason was in a manner arbitrarily imposed and adjudged to the disadvantage of the party that was to be judged; which, by various vicissitudes and revolutions, mischiefed all parties, first and last, and left a great unsettledness and unquietness in the minds of the people, and was one of the occasions of the unhappiness of that King."

Lord Hale on the extension of the crime of treason.

"All this mischief was produced by the statute of the 21st of Richard the Second, which enacted, That every man that compasseth or pursueth the death of the King, or *to depose him*, or to render up his homage liege, or he that raiseth people, and rideth against the King, to make war within his realm, and of that be duly attainted and adjudged, shall be adjudged a traitor, of high treason against the Crown."

Act of Richard Second.

"This," says Lord Hale, "was a great snare to the subject, insomuch that the statute, 1st of Henry Fourth, which repealed it, recited that no man knew how he ought to behave himself, to do, speak, or say, for doubt of such pains of treason; and, therefore, wholly to remove the prejudice which might come to the King's subjects, the statute 1st of Henry the Fourth, chap. 10, was made, which brought back treason to the standard of the 25th of Edward the Third."

Now if we look to this statute of Richard the Second, which produced such mischiefs, what are they? As far as it re-enacted the treason of compassing the King's death, and levying war, it only re-enacted the statute of Edward the Third. But it went beyond it by the loose construction of compassing to depose the King, and raising the people, and riding to make war, or a compassing to depose him—terms new to the common law. The actual *levying* of force to imprison or depose the King, was already and properly high treason, within the second branch of the statute. So that this statute of Richard the Second enlarged only the crime of *compassing*, making it extend to a compassing to imprison or depose, which are the great objects of an actual levying of war, and putting a compassing to levy war on a footing with the actual levying it. It seems, therefore, most astonishing that any judge could be supposed to have decided, as an abstract rule of law, that a compassing to imprison or depose the King was high treason, substantively, without a previous compassing of his death. For it was made so by this statute, 21st of Richard the Second, and reprobated, stigmatized, and repealed by the statute 1st of Henry the Fourth, chap. 10, "And so little effect," says Mr. Justice Blackstone, "have over-violent laws to prevent any crime, that, within two years after this new law of treason respecting imprisonment and deposing, this very prince was both deposed and murdered."

Its extent.

Gentlemen, this distinction, made by the hu-

[6] See page 277 for his abusive treatment of Raleigh.

mane statute of Edward the Third, between treason against the King's natural life, and rebellion against his civil authority, and which the act of Richard the Second, for a season, broke down, is founded in wise and sound policy. A successful attack may be made upon the King's person by the malignity of an individual, without the combination of extended conspiracy, or the exertions of rebellious force; the law, therefore, justly stands upon the watch to crush the first overt manifestation of so evil and detestable a purpose. Considering the life of the chief magistrate as infinitely important to the public security, it does not wait for the possible consummation of a crime, which requires neither time, combination, nor force to accomplish, but considers the traitorous *purpose* as a consummated treason. But the wise and humane policy of our forefathers extended the severity of the rule, *voluntas pro facto*, no further than they were thus impelled and justified by the necessity. And, therefore, an intention to levy war and rebellion, not consummated, however manifested by the most overt acts of conspiracy, was not declared to be treason, and upon the plainest principle in the world, namely, that the King's REGAL capacity, guarded by all the force and authority of the state, could not, like his NATURAL existence, be overthrown or endangered in a moment, by the first machinations of the traitorous mind of an individual, or even by the unarmed conspiracy of numbers; and, therefore, this humane and exalted institution, measuring the sanctions of criminal justice by the standard of civil necessity, thought it sufficient to scourge and dissipate unarmed conspirators by a less vindictive proceeding.

Reasons for the distinction in the statute of Edward III.

These new treasons were, however, at length all happily swept away on the accession of King Henry the Fourth, which brought the law back to the standard of Edward the Third. And, indeed, in reviewing the history of this highly favored island, it is most beautiful, and, at the same time, highly encouraging to observe by what an extraordinary concurrence of circumstances, under the superintendence of a benevolent Providence, the liberties of our country have been established. Amid the convulsions arising from the maddest ambition and injustice, and while the state was alternately departing from its poise on one side, and on the other the great rights of mankind were still insensibly taking root and flourishing. Though sometimes monarchy threatened to lay them prostrate, though aristocracy occasionally undermined them, and democracy, in her turn, rashly trampled on them, yet they have ever come safely round at last. This awful and sublime contemplation should teach us to bear with one another when our opinions do not quite coincide; extracting final harmony from the inevitable differences which ever did, and ever must, exist among men.[7]

This extension of the crime done away with by Henry IV.

Gentlemen, the act of Henry the Fourth was scarcely made when it shared the same fate with the venerable law which it restored. Nobody regarded it. It was borne down by factions, and, in those days, there were no judges, as there are now, to hold firm the balance of justice amid the storms of state. Men could not then, as the prisoner can to-day, look up for protection to magistrates independent of the Crown,[8] and awfully accountable in character to an enlightened world. As fast as arbitrary constructions were abolished by one statute, unprincipled judges began to build them up again, till they were beat down by another. To recount their strange treasons would be tiresome and disgusting; but their system of construction, in the teeth of positive law, may be well illustrated by two lines from Pope—

But the statute disregarded.

> "Destroy his fib and sophistry in vain,
> The creature 's at his dirty work again."

This system, both judicial and parliamentary, became, indeed, so intolerable in the interval between the reign of Henry the Fourth, and that of Philip and Mary,[9] that it produced, in the first year of the latter reign, the most remarkable statute that ever passed in England,[10] repealing not only all former statutes upon the subject, except that of Edward the Third, but also stigmatizing, upon the records of Parliament, the arbitrary constructions of judges, and limiting them, in all times, to every letter of the statute. I will read to you Lord Coke's commentary upon the subject. In his third Institute, page 23, he says, "Before the act of the 25th of Edward the Third, so many treasons had been made and declared, and in such sort penned, as not only the ignorant and unlearned people, but also learned and expert

Statute in the time of Mary.

[7] This is one of the many instances in which Mr. Erskine digresses for a moment to relieve the minds of his auditors, but he does it only to gather a striking general truth, which, in returning, he applies with new force to the case in hand.

[8] At the recommendation of George III., soon after his accession, the judges were made independent of the Crown, by holding their offices for life at a certain fixed salary.

[9] Among the new treasons created during this interval, particularly in the reign of Henry VIII., may be reckoned the following: namely, clipping money, breaking prison or rescue when the prisoner is committed for treason, burning houses to extort money, stealing of cattle by Welshmen, counterfeiting foreign coin, willful poisoning, execrations against the King, calling him opprobrious names by public writing, counterfeiting the sign manual or signet, refusing to abjure the Pope, deflowering, or marrying without the royal license any of the King's children, sisters, aunts, nephews, or nieces, bare solicitation of the chastity of the queen or princess, or advances made by themselves, marrying with the King by a woman not a virgin, without previously discovering to him her previous unchaste life, judging or believing (manifested by an overt act) the King to have been lawfully married to Anne of Cleve, derogating from the King's royal style and title, impugning his supremacy, assembling riotously to the number of twelve, and not dispersing on proclamation.

[10] 1 Mary, stat. 1, c. i.

men, were trapped and snared, * * so as the mischief before Edward the Third, of the uncertainty of what was treason and what not, became so frequent and dangerous, as that the safest and surest remedy was, by this excellent act of Mary, to abrogate and repeal all but [except] only such as are specified and expressed in this statute of Edward the Third. By which law the safety of both the King and of the subject, and the preservation of the common weal, were wisely and sufficiently provided for, and in such certainty that *nihil relictum est arbitrio judicis*.[11]

Intent and meaning of that statute of Mary.

The whole evil, indeed, to be remedied and avoided, by the act of Queen Mary, was the *arbitrium judicis*, or judicial construction beyond the letter of the statute. The statute [of Edward III.] itself was perfect, and was restored in its full vigor; and to suppose, therefore, that when an act was expressly made, because judges had built treasons by constructions beyond the law, they were to be left, consistently with their duty, to go on building again, is to impute a folly to the Legislature which never yet was imputed to the framers of this admirable statute. But this absurd idea is expressly excluded, not merely by the statute, according to its plain interpretation, but according to the direct authority of Lord Coke himself, in his commentary upon it. For he goes on to say, "Two things are to be observed: first, that the word *expressed*, in the statute of Mary, excludes all implications or inferences whatsoever; secondly, that no former attainder, judgment, precedent, resolution, or opinion of judges, or justices, of high treason, other than such as are specified and expressed in the statute of Edward the Third, are to be followed or drawn into example. For the words be plain and direct; that from henceforth no act, deed, or offense shall be taken, had, deemed, or adjudged to be high treason, but only such as are declared and expressed in the said act of the 25th of Edward the Third, any act of Parliament or statute after 25th of Edward the Third, or any other declaration or matter, to the contrary notwithstanding."

Shown by its preamble.

Gentlemen, if the *letter* of the statute of Mary, when coupled with Lord Coke's commentary, required further illustration, it would amply receive it from the PREAMBLE, which ought to be engraved on the heart of every man who loves the King, or who is called to any share in his councils; for, as Lord Coke observes in the same commentary: It truly recites that "the state of a King standeth and consisteth more assured by the love and favor of the subjects toward their Sovereign, than in the dread and fear of laws, made with rigorous and extreme punishment; and that laws, justly made for the preservation of the common weal, without extreme punishment or penalty, are more often and for the most part better kept and obeyed, than laws and statutes made with extreme punishment."

[11] Nothing was left to the arbitrary decision of the judge.

But, gentlemen, the most important part of Lord Coke's commentary on this statute is yet behind, which I shall presently read to you, and to which I implore your most earnest attention. I will show you by it, that the unfortunate man, whose innocence I am defending, is arraigned before you of high treason, upon evidence not only wholly repugnant to this particular statute, but such as never yet was heard of in England upon any capital trial; evidence which, even with all the attention you have given to it, I defy any one of you, at this moment, to say of what it consists; evidence, which (since it must be called by that name) I tremble for my boldness in presuming to stand up for the life of a man, when I am conscious that I am incapable of understanding from it, even what acts are imputed to him; evidence, which has consumed four days in the reading; not in reading the acts of the prisoner, but the unconnected writings of men unknown to one another, upon a hundred different subjects; evidence, the very listening to which has deprived me of the sleep which nature requires; which has filled my mind with unremitting distress and agitation, and which, from its discordant, unconnected nature, has suffered me to reap no advantage from the indulgence, which I began with thanking you for; but which, on the contrary, has almost set my brain on fire, with the vain endeavor of collecting my thoughts upon a subject never designed for any rational course of thinking.[12]

Remarks of Lord Coke.

Let us, therefore, see how the unexampled condition I am placed in falls in with Lord Coke upon this subject, whose authority is appealed to by the Crown itself; and let us go home and burn our books if they are to blazon forth the law by eulogium, and accurately to define its protector, which yet the subject is to be totally cut off from, when, even under the sanction of these very authors, he stands upon his trial for his existence. Lord Coke says, in the same Commentary, page 12, that the statute had not only accurately defined the charge, but the nature of the proof on which alone a man shall be attainted of any of the branches of high treason. "It is to be observed," says he, "that the word in the act of Edward the Third is *provablement;* that is, upon direct and manifest proof, not upon conjectural presumptions, or inferences, or strains of wit, but upon good and sufficient proof. And herein the adverb *provably* hath a great force, and signifieth a direct plain proof, which word the Lords and Commons in Parliament did use, for that the offense of treason was

[12] We have here one of those sallies of feeling which sometimes occur in the midst of Erskine's arguments. An immense mass of evidence in the shape of correspondence had been brought forward by the Crown, for the purpose of showing, among other things, the treasonable designs of another society, called the "Constitutional Society," and that the "London Corresponding Society," of which Hardy was the secretary, was closely connected with it, and advocated the same principles. No wonder that Erskine spoke with impatience of such a mode of aiming at the lives of men.

so heinous, and was so heavily and severely punished, as none other the like, and therefore the offender must be *provably* attainted, which words are as forcible as upon direct and manifest proof. Note, the word is not *probably*, for then *commune argumentum* might have served, but the word is '*provably* be attainted.'"

Nothing can be so curiously and tautologously labored as this commentary, of even that great prerogative lawyer Lord Coke, upon this single word in the statute. And it manifestly shows that, so far from its being the spirit and principle of the law of England, to *loosen* the construction of this statute, and to adopt rules of construction and proof, unusual in trials for other crimes, on the contrary, the Legislature did not even leave it to the judges to apply the ordinary rules of legal proof to trials under it, but admonished them to do justice in that respect in the very body of the statute.

Lord Hale treads in the same path with Lord Coke, and concludes this part of the subject by the following most remarkable passage (vol. i., chap. xi., 86):

Remarks of Lord Hale.

"Now, although the crime of high treason is the greatest crime against faith, duty, and human society, and brings with it the greatest and most fatal dangers to the government, peace, and happiness of a kingdom or state; and, therefore, is deservedly branded with the highest ignominy, and subjected to the greatest penalties that the laws can inflict; it appears, first, how necessary it was that there should be some *known*, *fixed*, *settled* boundary for this great crime of treason, and of what great importance the statute of 25th of Edward the Third was, in order to that end. Second, how dangerous it is to depart from the *letter* of that statute, and to multiply and enhance crimes into treason by ambiguous and general words, such as accroaching royal power, subverting fundamental laws, and the like. And third, how dangerous it is by *construction* and *analogy*, to make treasons where the *letter* of the law has not done it. For such a method admits of no limits or bounds, but runs as far and as wide as the wit and invention of accusers, and the detestation of persons accused, will carry men."

Application of them to the present case.

Surely, the admonition of this supereminent judge ought to sink deep into the heart of every judge, and of every juryman, who is called to administer justice under this statute; above all, in the times and under the peculiar circumstances which assemble us in this place. Honorable men, feeling, as they ought, for the safety of government, and the tranquillity of the country, and naturally indignant against those who are supposed to have brought them into peril, ought, for that very cause, to proceed with more abundant caution, lest they should be surprised by their resentments or their fears. They ought to advance, in the judgments they form, by slow and trembling steps; they ought even to fall back and look at every thing again, lest a false light should deceive them, admitting no fact but upon the foundation of clear and precise evidence, and deciding upon no intention that does not result with equal clearness from the fact. This is the universal demand of justice in every case, criminal or civil. How much more, then, in this, when the judgment is every moment in danger of being swept away into the fathomless abyss of a thousand volumes; where there is no anchorage for the understanding; where no reach of thought can look round in order to compare their points, nor any memory be capacious enough to retain even the imperfect relation that can be collected from them!

Illustration from the impeachment of Warren Hastings.

Gentlemen, my mind is the more deeply affected with this consideration by a very recent example in that monstrous phenomenon which, under the name of a trial, has driven us out of Westminster Hall for a large portion of my professional life. No man is less disposed than I am to speak lightly of great state prosecutions, which bind to their duty those who have no other superiors, nor any other control; last of all am I capable of even glancing a censure against those who have led to or conducted the impeachment, because I respect and love many of them, and know them to be among the best and wisest men in the nation. I know them, indeed, so well, as to be persuaded that, could they have foreseen the vast field it was to open, and the length of time it was to occupy, they never would have engaged in it.[13] For I defy any man, not illuminated by the Divine Spirit, to say, with the precision and certainty of an English judge deciding upon evidence before him, that Mr. Hastings is guilty or not guilty!—for who knows what is before him, or what is not? Many have carried what they knew to their graves, and the living have lived long enough to forget it. Indeed, I pray God that such another proceeding may never exist in England; because I consider it as a dishonor to the Constitution, and that it brings, by its example, insecurity into the administration of justice. Every man in civilized society has a right to hold his life, liberty, property, and reputation, under plain laws that can be well understood and is entitled to have some limited specific part of his conduct compared and examined by their standard. But he ought not for seven years, no, nor for seven days, to stand as a criminal before the highest human tribunal, until judgment is bewildered and confounded, to come at last, perhaps, to defend himself, broken down with fatigue and dispirited with anxiety, which, indeed, is my own condition at this moment, who am only stating the case of another. What, then, must be the condition of the unfortunate person whom you are trying?

The next great question is, how the admonitions of these great writers are to be reconciled

[13] It was the good fortune of Mr. Erskine to remedy, in his own person, the evil thus complained of, when he presided as Chancellor on the trial of Lord Melville. He insisted that the House of Lords should sit daily, like every other criminal tribunal, till the verdict was delivered; and thus completed the case in fourteen days.

with what is undoubtedly to be found in other parts of their works.[14] I think, then, I do not go too far, when I say that it ought to be the inclination of every person's mind who is considering the meaning of any writer (particularly if he be a person of superior learning and intelligence), to reconcile as much as possible all he says upon any subject, and not to adopt such a construction as necessarily raises up one part in direct opposition to another. The law itself, indeed, adopts this sound rule of judgment in the examination of every matter which is laid before it for a sound construction; and the judges, therefore, are bound by duty, as well as reason, to adopt it.

The foregoing statements reconciled with what the same writers have elsewhere said.

It appears to me, then, that the only ambiguity which arises, or can possibly arise, in the examination of the great authorities, and in the comparison of them with themselves, or with one another, is from not rightly understanding the meaning of the term OVERT ACT as applied to this species of treason. The moment you get right upon the true meaning and signification of this expression, the curtain is drawn up, and all is light and certainty.

The key to this is the sense they give to the phrase *overt act*.

Gentlemen, an overt act of the high treason charged upon this record, I take, with great submission to the court, to be plainly and simply this: The high treason charged is the compassing or imagining (in other words, the intending or designing) the death of the King—I mean his *natural* death—which being a hidden operation of the mind, an "overt act" is any thing which legally *proves* the existence of such traitorous design and intention. I say, then, that the *design* against the King's natural life is the high treason under the first branch of the statute; and whatever is *evidence* that may be legally laid before a jury to judge of the traitorous intention, is a legal overt act; because an overt act is nothing but legal evidence embodied upon the record.

Meaning of the phrase.

The charge of compassing being a charge of intention, which, without a manifestation by conduct, no human tribunal could try, the statute requires, by its very letter (but without which letter reason must have presumed), that the intention to cut off the sovereign should be manifested by an open act. And as a prisoner charged with an intention could have no notice how to defend himself without the charge of *actions* from whence the intention was to be imputed to him, it was always the practice, according to the sound principles of English law, to state upon the face of the indictment the overt act, which the Crown charges, as the means made use of by the prisoner to effect his traitorous purpose; and as this rule was too frequently departed from, the statute of the seventh of King William[15] enacted, for the benefit of the prisoner, that no evidence should ever be given of any overt act not charged in the indictment.[16] The charge, therefore, of the overt acts in the indictment, is the *notice* (enacted by statute to be given to the prisoner for his protection) of the means by which the Crown is to submit to the jury the existence of the traitorous purpose, which is the crime alleged against him, and in pursuance of which traitorous purpose the overt acts must also be charged to have been committed. Whatever, therefore, is relevant or competent *evidence* to be received in support of the traitorous intention, is a legal overt act; and what acts are competent to that purpose is (as in all other cases) matter of law for the judges. But whether, after the overt acts are received upon the record as competent, and are established by proof upon the trial, they be sufficient or insufficient, in the particular instance, to convince the jury of the traitorous compassing or intention, is a mere matter of *fact*, which, from its very nature, can be reduced to no other standard than that which each man's own conscience and understanding erects in his mind as the arbiter of his judgment. This doctrine is by no means new, nor peculiar to high treason. It pervades the whole law, and may be well illustrated in a memorable case lately decided upon writ of error in the House of Lords, and which must be in the memory of all the judges now present who took a part in its decision. There the question was, whether, upon the establishment of a number of facts by legal evidence, the defendant had knowledge of a fact, the knowing of which would leave him without defense. To draw that question from the jury to the judges, I demurred to the evidence, saying, that though each part of it was legally admitted, it was for the law, by the mouth of the judges, to pronounce whether this fact of knowledge could legally be inferred from it. But the Lords, with the assent of all the judges, decided, to my perfect satisfaction, that such a demurrer to the evidence was irregular and invalid; that the province of the jury over the *effect* of evidence ought not to be so transferred to the judges, and converted into matter of law; that what was relevant evidence to come before a jury was the province of the court, but that the *conclusion* to be drawn from admissible evidence was the unalienable province of the country.

Reasons for specifying the overt act.

These reasons show that the overt act constitutes the *evidence* of the crime.

Thus it belongs to the jury to decide on that evidence.

To apply that reasoning to the case before us. The matter to be inquired of here is the *fact* of the prisoner's intention, as, in the case I have just

[14] Mr. Erskine here comes to the second great division of his legal argument. It is really an answer to the argument of the Attorney General, though in another form. His object is to show how the authorities adduced by the Crown could be reconciled with his preceding statement of the law. This he does with an ingenuity and force which can not fail to interest the reader.

[15] 7 and 8 William III., c. iii., s. 8.

[16] That is, any overt act amounting to a distinct, independent charge. But if an overt act, not charged in the indictment, amount to a direct proof of any other overt act which is charged, it may be given in evidence to prove such overt act.

cited, it was the fact of the defendant's knowledge.

So the jury are here to decide whether the acts charged were aimed at the *natural* life of the King.

The charge of a conspiracy to depose the King is, therefore, laid before you to establish that intention. Its competency to be laid before you for that purpose is not disputed. I am only contending (with all reason and authority on my side) that it is to be submitted to your consciences and understandings, whether, even if you believed the overt act, you believe also that it proceeded from a traitorous machination against the *life* of the King. I am only contending that these *two* beliefs must coincide to establish a verdict of guilty.[17] I am not contending that, under [certain] circumstances, a conspiracy to depose the King, and to annihilate his regal capacity, may not be strong and satisfactory evidence of the intention to destroy his life—I only contend that in this, as in every other instance, it is for YOU to collect or not to collect this treason against the King's life, according to the result of your conscientious belief and judgment, from the acts of the prisoner laid before you, and that the establishment of the overt act, even if it were established, does not *establish the treason against the King's life by a consequence of law*. On the contrary, I affirm that the overt act, though punishable in another shape as an independent crime, is a dead letter upon this record, unless you believe, exercising your exclusive jurisdiction over the facts laid before you, that it was committed in accomplishment of the treason against THE NATURAL LIFE OF THE KING.

Peculiar nature of this crime.

Gentlemen, this particular crime of compassing the King's death is so complete an anomaly, being wholly seated in *unconsummated* intention, that the law can not depart from describing it according to its real essence, even when it is followed by his death. A man can not be indicted for *killing* the King, as was settled in the case of the Regicides of Charles I., after long consultation among all the judges. It was held that the very words of the statute must be pursued; and that, although the King was actually murdered, the prisoners who destroyed him could not be charged with the *act* itself, as high treason, but with the "compassing" of his death—the very act of the executioner in beheading him being only laid as the "overt act" upon the record. There, though the overt act was so connected with, as to be even inseparable from the traitorous intention, yet they were not confounded because of the effect of the precedent in dissimilar cases. And although the Regicides came to be tried immediately on the restoration of the King, in the dayspring of his authority, and before high prerogative judges, and under circumstances when, in any country but England, their trial would have been a mockery, or their execution have been awarded without even the forms of trial; yet in England, that sacred liberty which has forever adorned the Constitution, refused to sacrifice to zeal or enthusiasm either the substance or the forms of justice. Hear what the Chief Baron pronounced upon that occasion: "These persons are to be proceeded with according to the laws of the land, and I shall speak nothing to you but what are the words of the law. By the statute of Edward the Third, it is made high treason to compass and imagine the death of the King: in no case else imagination or compassing, without an actual effect, is punishable by law." He then speaks of the sacred life of the King, and, speaking of the treason, says, "The treason consists in the wicked imagination which is not apparent; but when this poison swells out of the heart, and breaks forth into action, in that case it is high treason. Then, what is an overt act of an imagination, or compassing of the King's death? Truly it is any thing which *shows* what the imagination of the heart is."

Views of Lord Hale.

Further evidence in support of this principle.

Indeed, gentlemen, the proposition is so clear that one gets confounded in the argument from the very simplicity of it. But still I stand in a situation which I am determined, at all events, to fulfill to the utmost; and I shall, therefore, not leave the matter upon these authorities, but will bring it down to our own times, repeating my challenge to have one single authority produced in contradiction. Lord Coke, in his *3d Institute*, pages 11 and 12, says, "The indictment must charge that the prisoner traitorously compassed and imagined the death and destruction of the King." He says, too, "There must be a compassing or imagination; for an act without compassing, intent, or imagination, is not within the Act, as appeareth by the express letter thereof: *Et actus non facit reum nisi mens sit rea.*" Nothing in language can more clearly illustrate my proposition. The indictment, like every other indictment, must charge distinctly and specifically the crime. That charge must, therefore, be in the very words of the statute which creates the crime—the crime created by the statute, not being the perpetration of any *act*, but being, in the rigorous severity of the law, the very *contemplation*, *intention*, and *contrivance* of a purpose directed to an act. That contemplation, purpose, and contrivance must be found to exist, without which, says Lord Coke, there can be no compassing; and as the intention of the mind can not be investigated without the investigation of conduct, the overt act is required by the statute, and must be laid in the indictment and proved. It follows from this deduction, that upon the clear principles of the English law, every act may be laid as an overt act of compassing the King's death, which may be reasonably considered to be relevant and competent to *manifest* that intention. For were it otherwise, it would be shutting out

[17] This was the great point on which Erskine rested his hopes of success. If he could fasten this responsibility on the jury, and make them act under it, he felt that his cause was safe. But the danger was, that, adopting the Attorney General's principles, they might consider "the writing of letters," &c., mentioned by Lord Hale, as *tending* ultimately to subvert the monarchy, and thus be led to a verdict of guilty. Hence the intense earnestness with which he goes on to argue this point.

from the view of the jury certain conduct of the prisoner, which might, according to circumstances, serve to manifest the criminal intention of his mind. Hence, as more than one overt act may be laid, and even overt acts of different kinds, though not in themselves substantively treason, the judges [in the case of the Regicides] appear to have been justified in law, when they ruled them to be overt acts of compassing the death of the King. For, they are such acts as before the statute of King William (which required that the indictment should charge all overt acts) *would* have been held to be relevant proof—of which relevancy of proof the judges are to judge as matter of law—and, therefore, being relevant proof, must also be relevant matter of charge, because nothing can be relevantly charged which may not also be relevantly admitted to proof. These observations explain, to the meanest capacity, in what sense Lord Coke must be understood, when he says, on the very same page, that "A preparation to depose the King, and to take the King by force and strong hand, until he has yielded to certain demands, is a sufficient overt act to *prove* the compassing of the King's death." He does not say, *as a proposition of law*, that he who prepares to seize the King, compasseth his death; but that a preparation to seize him is a sufficient overt act *to prove* the compassing; and he directly gives the reason, "Because of the strong *tendency* it has to that end." This latter sentence destroys all ambiguity.[18] I perfectly agree with Lord Coke, and I think every judge would so decide, upon the general principles of law and evidence, without any resort to his authority for it; and for this plain and obvious reason: The judges who are by law to decide upon the relevancy or competency of the proof, in every matter, criminal and civil, have immemorially sanctioned the indispensable necessity of charging the traitorous intention as the crime, before it was required by the statute of King William. As the crime is in its nature invisible and inscrutable, until manifested by such conduct as in the eye of reason is indicative of the intention, which constitutes the crime; no overt act is, therefore, held to be sufficient to give jurisdiction, even to a jury to draw the inference in fact of the traitorous purpose, but such acts from whence it may be reasonably inferred. And, therefore, as the restraint and imprisonment of a prince has a greater tendency to his destruction than in the case of a private man, such conspiracies are admitted to be laid as overt acts, upon this principle—that if a man does an act from whence either an inevitable or a mainly probable consequence may be expected to follow, much more if he persists deliberately in a course of conduct, leading certainly or probably to any given consequence, it is reasonable to believe that he foresaw such consequence, and by pursuing his purpose with that foreknowledge, the intention to produce the consequence may be fairly imputed. But then all this is matter of fact for the jury from the evidence, not matter of law for the court, further than it is the privilege and duty of the judge to direct the attention of the jury to the evidence, and to state the law as it may result from the different views the jury may entertain of the facts. And if such acts could not be laid as overt acts, they could not be offered in evidence; and if they could not be offered in evidence, the *mind* of the prisoner, which it was the object of the trial to lay open as a clue to his intention, would be shut up and concealed from the jury, whenever the death of the Sovereign was sought by circuitous but obvious means, instead of by a direct and murderous machination. But when they are thus submitted, as matter of charge and evidence, to prove the traitorous purpose which is the crime, the security of the King and of the subject is equally provided for. All the matter which has a relevancy to the crime is chargeable and provable, not substantively to raise from their establishment a *legal* inference, but to raise a presumption in *fact*, capable of being weighed by the jury, with all the circumstances of the transaction, as offered to the Crown and the prisoner. And it is the province of the jury finally to say—not what was the possible or the probable consequence of the overt act laid in the indictment, but whether it has brought them to a safe and conscientious judgment of the guilt of the prisoner, *i. e.*, of his guilt in compassing the death of the King, which is the treason charged in the indictment. Lord Hale is if possible, more direct and explicit upon the subject. He says, page 107, "The words 'compass' or 'imagine' are of a great latitude; they refer to the purpose or design of the mind or will, though the purpose or design takes not effect. But compassing or imagining singly of itself, is an *internal* act, and, without something to *manifest* it, could not possibly fall under any judicial cognizance but of God alone; and therefore this statute requires such an *overt* act as may render the compassing or imagining capable of a trial and sentence by human judicatures." Now, can any man possibly derive from such a writing (proceeding, too, from an author of the character of Lord Hale), that an overt act of compassing might, in his judgment, be an act committed *inadvertently* without the intention? Can any man gather from it, that a man, by falling into bad company, can be drawn in to be guilty of this species of treason by rash conduct, while the love of his Sovereign was glowing in his bosom? Can there be any particular acts which can entitle a judge or counsel to pronounce, *as a matter of law*, what another man intends? or that what a man intends is *not* a matter of *fact?* Is there any man that will meet the matter fairly, and advance and support that naked proposition! At all events, it is certainly not a proposition to be dealt with publicly, because the man whose mind is capable even of conceiving it should be treas-

Lord Hale.

[18] Mr. Erskine had quoted from Lord Coke on a preceding page in support of his views respecting high treason (p. 718), and he here gives his promised reconciliation of Coke's statements, which had appeared contradictory.

ured up in a museum, and exhibited there as a curiosity, for money.

Summing up on this point with an incidental appeal to the feelings of the jury.

Gentlemen, all I am asking, however, from my argument, and I defy any power of reason upon earth to move me from it, is this—that the prisoner being charged with *intending the King's death*, YOU are to find whether this charge be founded or unfounded. I say, therefore, put upon the record what else you will—prove what you will—read these books over and over again—and let us stand here a year and a day in discoursing concerning them—still the question must return at last to what YOU, and YOU ONLY, can resolve—*Is he guilty of that base, detestable intention to destroy the King?* NOT whether you incline to *believe* that he is guilty; NOT whether you *suspect*, nor whether it be *probable;* NOT whether he *may* be GUILTY; no, but that PROVABLY HE IS GUILTY. If you can say this upon the evidence, it is your duty to say so, and you may, with a tranquil conscience, return to your families; though, by your judgment, the unhappy object of it must return no more to his. Alas! gentlemen, what do I say? HE has no family to return to. The affectionate partner of his life has already fallen a victim to the surprise and horror which attended the scene now transacting. But let that melancholy reflection pass. It should not, perhaps, have been introduced—it certainly ought to have no effect upon you who are to judge upon your oaths. I do not stand here to desire you to commit perjury from compassion; but at the same time, my earnestness may be forgiven, since it proceeds from a weakness common to us all. I claim no merit with the prisoner for my zeal; it proceeds from a selfish principle inherent in the human heart—I am counsel, gentlemen, for myself. In every word I utter, I feel that I am pleading for the safety of my own life, for the lives of my children after me, for the happiness of my country, and for the universal condition of civil society throughout the world.[19]

Return to Lord Hale's views of an overt act in a case of compassing the King's death.

But let us return to the subject, and pursue the doctrine of Lord Hale upon the true interpretation of the term *overt act*, as applicable to this branch of treason. Lord Hale says, and I do beseech most earnestly the attention of the court and jury to this passage—"If men conspire the death of the King, and thereupon provide weapons, or send letters, this is an overt act within the statute." Take this to pieces, and what does it amount to? "If men conspire the death of the King," *that* is the first thing, *viz.*, the *intention*, "and thereupon," that is, in pursuance of that *wicked intention*, "provide weapons, or send letters for the execution thereof," *i. e.*, for the execution of that destruction of the King which they have meditated, "this is an overt act within the statute." Surely the meaning of all this is self-evident. If the intention be against the King's life, though the conspiracy does not immediately and directly point to his death, yet still the overt act will be sufficient, if it be something which has so direct a tendency to that end, as to be competent rational evidence of the intention to obtain it. But the instances given by Lord Hale himself furnish the best illustration: "If men conspire to imprison the King by *force and a strong hand* until he has yielded to certain demands, and *for that purpose gather company or write letters*, that is an overt act to *prove* the compassing the King's death, as it was held in Lord Cobham's case by all the judges."[20] In this sentence Lord Hale does not depart from that precision which so eminently distinguishes all his writings. He does not say that if men conspire to imprison the King until he yields to certain demands, and for that purpose to do so and so, *this* is high treason. No, nor even an overt act of high treason, though he might in legal language correctly have said so. But, to prevent the possibility of confounding the treason with matter which may be legally charged as relevant to the *proof* of it, he follows Lord Coke's expression, in the third Institute, and says, "This is an overt act to *prove* the compassing of the King's death." And as if by this mode of expression he had not done enough to keep the ideas asunder, and from abundant regard for the rights and liberties of the subject, he immediately adds, "But, then, there must be an overt act to *prove* that conspiracy; and then that overt act to prove such design, is an overt act to *prove* the compassing of the death of the King." The language of this sentence labors in the ear from the excessive caution of the writer. Afraid that his reader should jump too fast to his conclusion upon a subject of such awful moment, he pulls him back after he has read that a conspiracy to imprison the King is an overt act to prove the compassing of his death; and says to him, But recollect that there must be an overt act to *prove*, in the first place, that conspiracy to imprison the King, and even then that intention to imprison him so manifested by the overt act is but in its turn an overt act to *prove* the compassing or intention to destroy the King. Nor does the great and benevolent Hale rest even here, but after this almost tedious perspicuity, he begins the next sentence with this fresh

[19] There was consummate skill when Mr. Erskine thus glanced at the death of Mrs. Hardy, in seeming almost to condemn himself for doing so, since this placed him before the jury as one who did not seek to work on their passions. The turn he next gives the thought is peculiarly fine—he was speaking for himself—for his children—for the world—and he was therefore *bound* to express these feelings.

[20] Lord Cobham took part in the rash conspiracy of Raleigh against James I., A.D. 1604. He was tried and convicted, and condemned to death, but subsequently pardoned.

It will occur at once to the reader that this passage in Lord Hale was the strong-hold of the Attorney General. The "writing of letters" to call the convention was the great thing charged in the present case. Mr. Erskine, therefore, delayed the consideration of this passage from Hale till he had got out his doctrine strongly from Coke, and showed its reasons. Then he takes up Lord Hale and gives a decisive answer.

caution and limitation, "*But then this must be intended of a conspiracy forcibly to detain and imprison the King.*" What, then, is a conspiracy forcibly to imprison the King? Surely it can require no explanation: it can only be a direct machination to seize and detain his PERSON by rebellious force. Will this expression be satisfied by a conspiracy to seize *speculatively* upon his authority by the publication of pamphlets, which, by the inculcation of republican principles, may in the eventual circulation of a course of years, perhaps in a course of centuries, in this King's time, or in the time of a remote successor, debauch men's minds from the English Constitution; and, by the destruction of monarchy, involve the life of the Monarch? Will any man say that this is what the law means by a conspiracy against the King's government, supposing even that a conspiracy against his government were synonymous with a design upon his life? Can any case be produced where a person has been found guilty of high treason, under this branch of the statute, where no war has been actually levied, unless where the conspiracy has been a forcible invasion of the King's personal liberty or security? I do not mean to say that a conspiracy to levy war may not, in many instances, be laid as an overt act of compassing the King's death, because the war may be mediately or immediately pointed distinctly to his destruction or captivity; and, as Lord Hale truly says, "small is the distance between the prisons and graves of princes." But multiply the instances as you will, still the principle presents itself. The truth of this very maxim, built upon experience, renders an overt act of this description rational and competent *evidence* to be left to a *jury* of a design against the King's life. But it does not, therefore, change the nature of the crime, nor warrant any court to declare the overt act to be *legally and conclusively indicative* of the traitorous intention. For if this be once admitted to be law, and the jury are bound to find the treason upon their belief of the existence of the overt act, the trial by the country is at an end, and the judges are armed with an arbitrary, uncontrollable dominion over the lives and liberties of the nation.

These doctrines belong to the whole system of law.

Gentlemen, I will now proceed to show you that the doctrines which I am insisting on have been held by all the great judges of this country, in even the worst of times; and that they are, besides, not at all peculiar to the case of high treason, but pervade the whole system of the criminal law. Mr. Justice Foster, so justly celebrated for his writings, lays down the rule thus: It may be laid down as a general rule, that "indictments founded upon penal statutes, *especially the most penal*, must pursue the statute so as to bring the party within it." And this general rule is so expressly allowed to have place in high treason, that it is admitted, on all hands, that an indictment would be radically and incurably bad, unless it charged the compassing of the King's death as the leading and fundamental averment, and unless it formally charged the overt act to be committed in order to effectuate the traitorous purpose. Nobody ever denied this proposition; and the present indictment is framed accordingly. Now, it is needless to say, that if the benignity of the general law requires this precision in the indictment, the *proof* must be correspondingly precise, otherwise the subject would derive no benefit from the strictness of the indictment. That strictness can have no other meaning in law or common sense, than the *protection* of the prisoner; for if, though the indictment must directly charge a breach of the very LETTER of the statute, the prisoner could, nevertheless, be convicted by evidence not amounting to a breach of the LETTER, then the strictness of the indictment would not only be no protection to the prisoner, but a direct violation of the first principles of justice, criminal and civil, which call universally for the proof of all material averments in every legal proceeding. But Mr. Justice Foster expressly adverts to the necessary severity of proof, as well as of charge. He says, "although a case is brought within the *reason* of a penal statute, and within the *mischief* to be prevented, yet, if it does not come within the unequivocal *letter*, the benignity of the law interposeth." If the law, then, be thus severe in the interpretation of every penal proceeding, even down to an action for the killing of a hare or a partridge, are its constructions only to be enlarged and extended as to the statute of high treason, although the single object of passing it was to guard against constructions?

The Attorney General admits it; though he contradicts himself afterward.

Gentlemen, the reason of the thing is so palpably and invincibly in favor of this analogy, that it never met with a direct opposition. The Attorney General himself distinctly admits it, in one part of his address to you, though he seems to deny it in another. I hope that when I state one part of his speech to be in diametrical opposition to another, he will not suppose that I attribute the inconsistency to any defect either in his understanding or his heart. Far from it—they arise, I am convinced, from some of the authorities not being sufficiently understood.

In the beginning of his speech, he admits that the evidence must be satisfactory and convincing as to the intention; but in the latter part he seems, as it were, to take off the effect of that admission. I wish to give you the very words. I took them down at the time; and if I do not state them correctly, I desire to be corrected. "I most distinctly disavow," said my honorable friend, "every case of construction. I most distinctly disavow any like case of treason not within the letter of the statute. I most distinctly disavow cumulative treason. I most distinctly disavow enhancing guilt by parity of reason. The question undoubtedly is, whether the proof be full and satisfactory to your reasons and consciences, that the prisoner is guilty of the treason of compassing the King's death." Gentlemen, I hope that this will always with equal honor be admitted. Now, let us see how the rest of the learned gentleman's speech falls in with this. For he goes on to say, that it is by no means necessary that the distinct, specific intention should pre-exist the overt act. "If the overt act," says he, "be deliberately committed, it is a compassing." But how so, if the *intention* be admitted to be the treason? What benefit is obtained by the rigorous demand of the statute, that the compassing of the King's death shall be charged by the *indictment* as the crime, if a crime different, or short of it, can be substituted for it in the *proof?* And how can the statute of Richard the Second be said to be repealed, which made it high treason to compass to depose the King, independently of intention upon his life, if the law shall declare, notwithstanding the repeal, that they are synonymous terms, and that the one conclusively involves the other?

Mr. Erskine's doctrines confirmed by the State Trials.

Gentlemen, if we examine the most prominent cases which have come in judgment before judges of the most unquestionable authority, and, after the Constitution had become fixed, you will find every thing that I have been saying to you justified and confirmed.

Case of Sir John Friend.

The first great state trial, after the Revolution, was the case of Sir John Friend, a conspirator in the assassination plot.[21] Sir John Friend was indicted for compassing and imagining the death of King William. The overt acts charged and principally relied on, were, first, the sending Mr. Charnock into France to King James, to desire him to persuade the French King to send forces over to Great Britain, to levy war against, and to depose the King, and that Mr. Charnock was actually sent; and, secondly, the preparing men to be levied to form a corps to assist in the restoration of the Pretender,[22] and the expulsion of King William, of which Sir John Friend was to be the colonel. In this case, if the proofs were not to be wholly discredited, and the overt acts were consequently established, they went rationally to convince the mind of every man of the pre-existing intention to destroy the King. The conspiracy was not to do an act which, though it might lead eventually and speculatively to the King's death, might not be foreseen or designed by those who conspired together. The conspiracy was not directed to an event probably leading to another and a different one, and from the happening of which second, a third, still different, might be engendered, which third might again lead, in its consequences, to a fourth state of things, which might, in the revolution of events, bring on the death of the King, though never compassed or imagined. Friend's conspiracy, on the contrary, had for its *direct* and *immediate* object the restoration of the Pretender to the throne, by the junction of foreign and rebellious force. In my opinion (and I am not more disposed than others to push things beyond their mark in the administration of criminal justice), Sir John Friend, if the evidence against him found credit with the jury, could have no possible defense; since the evidence went directly to prove the dispatch of Charnock to France, under his direction, to invite the French King to bring over the Pretender into England, and to place him on the throne. The intention, therefore, of Sir John Friend to cut off King William was a clear inference from the overt act in question. It was not an inference of *law* for the court, but of *fact* for the jury, under the guidance of plain common sense; because the consequence of the Pretender's regaining the throne must have been the attainder of King William by act of Parliament. Some gentlemen seem to look as if they thought not; but I should be glad to hear the position contradicted. I repeat, that if the Pretender had been restored as King of England, the legal consequence would have been, that King William would have been a traitor and a usurper, and subject as such to be tried at the Old Bailey, or wherever else the King, who took his place, thought fit to bring him to judgment. From these premises, therefore, there could be no difficulty of inferring the intention. If, then, a case ever existed where, from the clearness of the inference, the province of the jury might have been overlooked, and the overt act confounded with the treason, it was in the instance of Friend; but so far was this from being the case, that you will find, on the contrary, every thing I have been saying to you, since I began to address you, summed up and confirmed by that most eminent magistrate, Lord Chief Justice Holt, who presided at that trial.

Difference between this case and the one under trial.

He begins thus: "Gentlemen of the Jury, look ye, the treason that is mentioned in the indictment is conspiring, compassing, and imagining the death of the King. To prove the conspiracy and design of the King's death, two principal overt acts are insisted on." He does not consider the overt act of conspiracy and consultation to be the treason, but evidence (as it undoubtedly was in that case) to prove the compassing the death. The Chief Justice then states the two overt acts above mentioned, and sums up the evidence for and against the prisoner, and leaves the intention to the jury *as matter of fact*. For it is not till afterward that he comes to an-

[21] In 1695, the year after the death of Queen Mary, which event it was considered would considerably weaken the authority of the King (William III.), several of the Jacobites conspired to seize his person, and convey him to France, and, in case of resistance, to assassinate him; and messengers were sent to St. Germain, where James II. was then staying, under the protection of the French government, to demand a commission for the purpose (which was, however, refused), and to make arrangements for a descent upon England. The principal parties connected with this conspiracy were, the Earl of Aylesbury, Lord Montgomery, Sir John Fenwick, Sir John Friend, Captain Charnock, Captain Porter, and Mr. Goodman.

[22] Mr. Erskine departs from general usage in giving James II. the name of the Pretender. After his death, in 1701, his son, the Chevalier de St. George, assumed the title of James III.; and as this was a mere pretense, without legal right, in the view of the English nation, he was stigmatized with the title of Pretender.

swer the prisoner's objection in point of law, as the Chief Justice in terms puts it—"There is another thing," said Lord Chief Justice Holt, "he did insist upon, *and that is matter of law.*" The statute 25th Edward the Third was read, which is the great statute about treason, and that does contain divers species of treason, and declares what shall be treason: one treason is the compassing and imagining the death of the King; another is the levying war. "Now," says he, (*i. e.*, Friend), "here is no war actually levied; and a bare conspiracy to levy war does not come within the law against treason." To pause here a little: Friend's argument was this, Whatever my intentions might be—whatever my object of levying war might have been—whatever might have been my design to levy it—however the destruction of the King might have been effected by my conspiracy, if it had gone on—and however it might have been my intention that it should, it is not treason within the 25th of Edward the Third. To which Holt replied, a little incorrectly in language, but right in substance: "Now for that I must tell you, if there be only a conspiracy to levy war, it is not treason;" that is, it is not a substantive treason: it is not a treason in the abstract. "But if the design and conspiracy be either to kill the King, or to depose him, or imprison him, or put any force or restraint upon him" (*i. e.*, personal restraint by force), "and the way of effecting these purposes is by levying a war, there the conspiracy and consultation, to levy war for that purpose, is high treason, though no war be levied; for such consultation and conspiracy is an overt act proving the compassing the death of the King." But what sort of war is it, the bare conspiracy to levy which is an overt act to prove a design against the King's life, though no war be actually levied? Gentlemen, Lord Holt himself illustrates this matter so clearly, that if I had any thing at stake short of the honor and life of the prisoner, I might sit down as soon as I had read it; for if one did not know it to be an extract from an ancient trial, one would say it was admirably and accurately written for the present purpose. It is a sort of prophetic bird's-eye view of what we are engaged in at this moment: "There may be war levied" (continues Lord Holt in Friend's case) "without any design upon the King's person, which, if *actually levied*, is high treason; though purposing and designing such a levying of war is not so. As, for example: if persons do assemble themselves, and act with force, in opposition to some law, and hope thereby to get it repealed; this is a levying war, and treason, though the *purposing and designing* of it is not so. So when they endeavored, in great numbers, with force, to make reformation of their own heads, without pursuing the methods of the law, that is a levying war, but the *purpose and designing* is not so. But if there be, as I told you, a purpose and design to destroy the King, *and*" (not *or* to depose him, but *and* to depose him) "to depose him from his throne, which is proposed and designed to be effected by war that is to be levied; such a conspiracy and consultation to levy war for the bringing this to pass" (that is, for bringing the King's death to pass) "is an overt act of high treason. So that, gentlemen, as to that objection which he [Friend] makes, in point of law, it is of no force, if there be evidence sufficient to convince you that he did conspire to levy war for such an end." And he concludes by again leaving the intention expressly to the jury.

The doctrine established by the case of Sir John Friend.

It is the *end*, therefore, for which the war is to be levied, and not the conspiracy to do any act, which the law considers as a levying of war, that constitutes an overt act of treason against the King's life. The most rebellious movements toward a reform in *government*, not directed against the *King's person*, will not, according to Lord Holt, support the charge before you. I might surround the House of Commons with fifty thousand men, for the express purpose of forcing them, by duress, to repeal any law that is offensive to me, or to pass a bill for altering elections, without being a possible object of this prosecution. Under the other branch of the statute, I might, indeed, be convicted of levying war, but not of compassing the King's death; and if I only conspired and meditated this rising to repeal laws by rebellion, I could be convicted of nothing but a high misdemeanor. I would give my friends the case upon a special verdict, and let them hang me if they could. How much more might I give it them if the conspiracy imputed was not to effect a reform by violence, but, as in the case before us, by pamphlets and speeches, which might produce universal suffrage, which universal suffrage might eat out and destroy aristocracy, which destruction might lead to the fall of monarchy, and, in the end, to the death of the King. Gentlemen, if the cause were not too serious, I should liken it to the play with which we amuse our children: this is the cow with the crumpled horn, which gored the dog, that worried the cat, that ate the rat, &c., ending in "the house which Jack built." I do, therefore, maintain, upon the express authority of Lord Holt, that, to convict a prisoner charged with this treason, it is absolutely necessary that you should be satisfied of his *intention against the King's life*, as charged in the indictment; and that no design against the King's *government* will even be a legal overt act to be left to a jury as the evidence of such an intention (much less the substantive and consummate treason), unless the conspiracy be directly pointed against the person of the King.

Case of Lord George Gordon.

The case of Lord George Gordon is opposed to this as a high and modern decision; and the Attorney General descended, indeed, to a very humble and lowly authority, when he sought to maintain his argument by my own speech as counsel for that unfortunate person.[23] The passage of it alluded to lies at this

[23] Sir John Scott, in opening the case, had read a passage from this speech, in a triumphant tone, as if confirming his views in respect to treason from the lips of Mr. Erskine himself.

moment before me; and I shall repeat it and remaintain it to-day. But let it first be recollected that Lord George Gordon was not indicted for compassing or imagining the King's death, under the first branch of the statute, but for levying war under the second. It never, indeed, entered into the conception of any man living, that such an indictment could have been maintained or attempted against him. I appeal to one of your Lordships now present, for whose learning and capacity I have the greatest and highest respect, and who sat upon that trial, that it was not insinuated from the bar, much less adjudged by the court, that the evidence had any bearing upon the first branch of treason. I know that I may safely appeal to Mr. Justice Buller for the truth of this assertion; and nothing, surely, in the passage from my address to the jury has the remotest allusion to assimilate a conspiracy against the King's *government* (collateral to his person) with a treason against his *life*. My words were: "*To compass or imagine the death of the King;* such imagination, or purpose of the mind, visible only to its great Author, being manifested by some open act;' an institution obviously directed, not only to the security of his natural person, but to the stability of the government; the life of the Prince being so interwoven with the Constitution of the state, that an attempt to destroy the one is justly held to be a rebellious conspiracy against the other."

Explanation of Mr. Erskine's speech in that case.

What is this but to say that the King's sacred life is guarded by higher sanctions than the ordinary laws, because of its more inseparable connection with the public security, and that an attempt to destroy it is, therefore, made treason against the state. But the Attorney General is, I am sure, too correct in his logic to say that the converse of the proposition is, therefore, maintained, and that an attack upon the King's authority, without design upon his person, is affirmed by the same expression to be treason against his life. His correct and enlarged mind is incapable of such confusion of ideas.

But it is time to quit what fell from me upon this occasion, in order to examine the judgment of the court, and to clothe myself with the authority of that great and venerable magistrate, whose memory will always be dear to me, not only from the great services he rendered to his country in the administration of her justice, but on account of the personal regard and reverence I had for him when living.

Lord Mansfield's charge.

Lord Mansfield, in delivering the law to the jury upon Lord George Gordon's trial (I appeal to the trial itself, and to Mr. Justice Buller, now present, who agreed in the judgment), expressly distinguished between the safety provided for the King's natural person, by the first branch of the statute, and the security of his executive power under the second. That great judge never had an idea that the natural person of the King and the majesty of the King were the same thing, nor that the treasons against them were synonymous; he knew, on the contrary, for he knew all that was to be known, that as substantive crimes they never had been blended. I will read his own words. "There are two kinds of levying war—one against the *person* of the King, to imprison, to dethrone, or to kill him, or to make him change measures, or remove counselors; the other, which is said to be levied against the majesty of the King, or, in other words, against him in his regal capacity, as when a multitude rise and assemble to attain by force and violence any object of a general public nature; that is levying war against the majesty of the King; and most reasonably so held, because it tends to dissolve all the bonds of society, to destroy property, and to overturn government; and by force of arms to restrain the King from reigning according to law." But then observe, gentlemen, *the war must be actually levied;* and here, again, I appeal to Mr. Justice Buller, for the words of Lord Mansfield, expressly referring for what he said to the authority of Lord Holt, in Sir John Friend's case already cited: "Lord Chief Justice Holt, in Sir John Friend's case, says, 'If persons do assemble themselves and act with force, in opposition to some law which they think inconvenient, and hope thereby to get it repealed, this is a levying war, and treason.' In the present case [Gordon's] it don't rest upon an implication that they hoped by opposition to a law to get it repealed; but the prosecution proceeds upon the direct ground, that the object was, by *force and violence*, to compel the Legislature to repeal a law; and, therefore, without any doubt, I tell you the joint opinion of us all, that if this multitude assembled *with intent, by acts of force and violence*, to compel the Legislature to repeal a law, it is high treason."

It sustains Mr. Erskine in the ground he now takes.

Let these words of Lord Mansfield be taken down, and then show me the man, let his rank and capacity be what they may, who can remove me from the foundation on which I stand, when I maintain that a conspiracy to levy war for the objects of reformation is not only *not* the high treason charged by this indictment when not directly pointed against the King's person, but that even the actual *levying* it would not amount to the constitution of the crime. But this is the least material part of Lord Mansfield's judgment, as applicable to the present question; for he expressly considers *the intention* of the prisoner, whatever be the act of treason alleged against him, to be all in all. So far from holding the probable, or even inevitable, consequence of the thing done as constituting the quality of the act, he pronounces them to be nothing as separated from the criminal *design* to produce them. Lord George Gordon assembled an immense multitude around the House of Commons; a system so opposite to that of the persons accused before this commission, that it appears from the evidence they would not even allow a man to come among them, because he had been Lord George's attorney. The Lords and Commons were absolutely blockaded in the chambers of Parliament: and if control was the intention of the prisoner

[Gordon], it must be wholly immaterial what were the deliberations that were to be controlled; whether it was the continuance of Roman Catholics under penal laws, the repeal of the Septennial Act, or a total change of the structure of the House of Commons, that was the object of violence, the attack upon the Legislature of the country would have been the same. That the multitude were actually assembled round the Houses, and brought there by the prisoner, it was impossible for me, as his counsel, even to think of denying; nor that their tumultuous proceedings were not in effect productive of great intimidation, and even danger, to the Lords and Commons, in the exercise of their authority; neither did I venture to question the law, that the assembling the multitude *for that purpose* was levying war within the statute. Upon these facts, therefore, applied to the doctrines we have heard upon this trial, there would have been nothing in Lord George Gordon's case to try; he must have been instantly, without controversy, convicted. But Lord Mansfield did not say to the jury (according to the doctrines that have been broached here), that if they found the multitude, assembled by the prisoner, were in fact palpably intimidating and controlling the Parliament in the exercise of their functions, he was guilty of high treason, whatever his *intentions* might have been. He did not tell them that the inevitable consequence of assembling a hundred thousand people round the Legislature, being a control on their proceedings, was therefore a levying war; though collected from folly and rashness, without the *intention* of violence or control. If this had been the doctrine of Lord Mansfield, there would, as I said before, have been nothing to try; for I admitted, in terms, that his conduct was the extremity of rashness, and totally inconsistent with his rank in the country, and his station as a member of the House of Commons. But the venerable magistrate never for a moment lost sight of the grand ruling principle of criminal justice, that crimes have no seat but in the mind; and upon the prisoner's *intention*, and upon his *intention alone*, he expressly left the whole matter to the jury, with the following directions, which I shall read *verbatim* from the trial:

"Having premised these several propositions and principles, the subject-matter for your consideration naturally resolves itself into two points.

"First. Whether this multitude did assemble and commit acts of violence, with intent to terrify and compel the Legislature to repeal the act called Sir George Saville's. If upon this point your opinion should be in the negative, that makes an end of the whole, and the prisoner ought to be acquitted. But if your opinion should be that the intent of this multitude, and the violence they committed, was to force a repeal, there arises a second point—

"Whether the prisoner at the bar incited, encouraged, promoted, or assisted in raising this insurrection, and the terror they carried with them, with the INTENT of forcing a repeal of this law.

"Upon these two points, which you will call your attention to, depends the fate of this trial; for if either the multitude had no such intent, or supposing they had, if the prisoner was no cause, did not excite, and took no part in conducting, counseling, or fomenting the insurrection, the prisoner ought to be acquitted; and there is no *pretense* that he personally concurred in any act of violence."

I therefore consider the case of Lord George Gordon as a direct authority in my favor.

Comments on a case *supposed* by the Attorney General.

To show that a conspiracy to depose the King, independently of ulterior intention against his life, is high treason within the statute, the Attorney General next supposes that traitors had conspired to depose King William, but still to preserve him as Stadtholder in Holland, and asks whether that conspiracy would not be a compassing his death. To that question I answer, that it would not have been a compassing the death of King William, provided the conspirators could have convinced the jury that their firm and *bonâ fide* intention was to proceed no further, and that, under that belief and impression, the jury (as they lawfully might) had negatived, by their finding, the fact of the intention against the King's natural existence. I have no doubt at all that, upon such a finding, no judgment of treason could be pronounced; but the difficulty would be to meet with a jury who, upon the bare evidence of such a conspiracy, would find such a verdict. There might be possible circumstances to justify such a negative of the intention, but they must come from the prisoner. In such a case the Crown would rest upon the conspiracy to depose, which would be *primâ facie* and cogent evidence of the compassing, and leave the hard task of rebutting it on the defendant—I say the hard task, because the case put is of a direct rebellious force, acting against the King; not only abrogating his authority, but imprisoning, and expelling his person from the kingdom. I am not seeking to abuse the reasons and consciences of juries in the examination of facts, but am only resisting the confounding them with arbitrary propositions of law.

Summing up of this head.

Gentlemen, I hope I have now a right to consider that the existence of high treason charged against the unfortunate man before you, *is a matter of fact for your consideration upon the evidence.* To establish this point has been the scope of all that you have been listening to with so much indulgence and patience. It was my intention to have further supported myself by a great many authorities, which I have been laboriously extracting from the different books of the law; but I find I must pause here, lest I consume my strength in this preliminary part of the case, and leave the rest defective.

Part Second: Sole cause of this prosecution, efforts to procure a reform in Parliament.

Gentlemen, the persons named in the indictment are charged with a conspiracy to subvert the rule, order, and government of this country; and it is material that you should observe most particularly the means by which it alleges this purpose was to be accomplished. The charge is not of a conspiracy to hold the convention in Scotland, which was actually held there; nor of the part they took in its actual proceedings; but the overt act, to which all the others are subsidiary and subordinate, is a supposed conspiracy to hold a convention in England, which never in fact was held. Consequently, all the vast load of matter which it has been decided you should hear, that does not immediately connect itself with the charge in question, is only laid before you—as the court has repeatedly expressed it—to prove that, in point of fact, such proceedings were had, the *quality* of which is for your judgment.[24] So far, and so far only, as they can be connected with the prisoner, and the act which he stands charged with, are they left to you, as evidence of the *intention* with which the holding of the second convention [that in England] was projected.

Call of a convention for this purpose.

THIS INTENTION is, therefore, the whole cause. The charge is not the agreement to hold a convention—which it is notorious, self-evident, and even admitted that they intended to hold—but the agreement to hold it for the purpose alleged, of assuming all the authority of the state, and in fulfillment of the main intention against the life of the King. Unless, therefore, you can collect this *double* intention from the evidence before you, the indictment is not maintained.

The acts charged as a conspiracy were not covert or concealed, but open to the whole world.

Gentlemen, the charge being of a conspiracy, which, if made out in point of fact, involved beyond all controversy, and within the certain knowledge of the conspirators, the lives of every soul that was engaged in it; the first observation which I shall make to you (because in reason it ought to precede all others) is, that every act done by the prisoners, and every sentence written by them, in the remotest degree connected with the charge, or offered in evidence to support it, were done and written in the public face of the world. The transactions which constitute the whole body of the proof, were not those of a day, but in regular series for two years together. They were not the peculiar transaction of the prisoners, but of immense bodies of the King's subjects, in various parts of the kingdom, assembled without the smallest reserve, and giving to the public, through the channel of the daily newspapers, a minute and regular journal of their whole proceedings. Not a syllable have we heard read, in the week's imprisonment we have suffered, that we had not all of us read for months and months before the prosecution was heard of; and which, if we are not sufficiently satiated, we may read again upon the file of every coffee-house in the kingdom. It is admitted distinctly by the Crown, that a reform in the House of Commons is the ostensible purpose of all the proceedings laid before you, and that the attainment of that object only is the grammatical sense of the great body of the written evidence. It rests, therefore, with the Crown, to show by legal proof that this ostensible purpose, and the whole mass of correspondence upon the table, was only a cloak to conceal a hidden machination, to subvert by force the entire authorities of the kingdom, and to assume them to themselves. Whether a reform of Parliament be a wise or an unwise expedient; whether, if it were accomplished, it would ultimately be attended with benefits, or dangers, to the country, I will not undertake to investigate, and for this plain reason, because it is wholly foreign to the subject before us. But when we are trying the integrity of men's intentions, and are examining whether their complaints of defects in the representation of the House of Commons be *bonâ fide*, or only a mere stalking-horse for treason and rebellion, it becomes a most essential inquiry, whether they be the first who have uttered these complaints—whether they have taken up notions for the first time, which never occurred to others; and whether, in seeking to interfere practically in an alteration of the Constitution, they have manifested, by the novelty of their conduct, a spirit inconsistent with affection for the government, and subversive of its authority. Gentlemen, I confess for one (for I think the safest way of defending a person for his life before an enlightened tribunal, is to defend him ingenuously), I confess for one, that if the defects in the Constitution of Parliament, which are the subject of the writings, and the foundation of all the proceedings before you, had never occurred to other persons at other times, or, if not new, they had only existed in the history of former conspiracies, I should be afraid you would suspect, at least, that the authors of them were plotters of mischief. In such a case I should naturally expect that you would ask yourselves this question—Why should it occur to the prisoner at the bar, and to a few others, in the year 1794, immediately after an important revolution in another country, to find fault, on a sudden, with a Constitution which had endured for ages, without the imputation of defect, and which no good subject had ever thought of touching with the busy hand of reformation? I candidly admit that such a question would occur to the mind of every reasonable man, and could admit no favorable answer. But surely this admission entitles me, on the other hand, to the concession, that if, in comparing their writings, and examining their conduct with the writings and conduct of the best and most unsuspected persons in the best and most unsuspected times, we find them treading in the paths which have distinguished their highest superiors; if we find them only exposing the same defects, and pursuing the same or similar courses for their removal—it would be the height of wickedness and injustice to torture expressions, and pervert conduct into treason and rebellion, which had recently lifted up others to the love of the nation, to the confidence of the Sovereign, and to all the honors of the state. The

The plan of parliamentary reform no novelty, but sanctioned by the highest names of the country.

[24] In other words, the court had admitted the evidence as to the Scottish convention (which occupied so much time, as the reader will see hereafter), merely as showing that the prisoners were previously in a *state of mind* which might lead to treason in the proposed English convention.

natural justness of this reasoning is so obvious, that we have only to examine into the fact. Considering, then, under what auspices the prisoners are brought before you, it may be fit that I should set out with reminding you that the great Earl of Chatham began and established the fame and glory of his life upon the very cause[25] which my unfortunate clients were engaged in, and that he left it as an inheritance to the present minister of the Crown, as the foundation of his fame and glory after him.[26] His fame and glory were, accordingly, raised upon it, and if the Crown's evidence had been carried as far back as it might have been (for the institution of only one of the two London Societies is before us), you would have found that the Constitutional Society owed its earliest credit with the country, if not its very birth, to the labor of the present minister,[27] and its professed principles to his Grace the Duke of Richmond, high also in his Majesty's present councils,[28] whose plan of reform has been clearly established by the whole body of the written evidence, and by every witness examined for the Crown, to have been the type and model of all the societies in the supposed conspiracy, and uniformly acted upon in form and in substance by the prisoner before you, up to the very period of his confinement.

Duke of Richmond's plan of reform.

Gentlemen, the Duke of Richmond's plan was universal suffrage and annual Parliaments; and urged, too, with a boldness which, when the comparison comes to be made, will leave in the back-ground the strongest figures in the writings on the table. I do not say this sarcastically. I mean to speak with the greatest respect of his Grace, both with regard to the wisdom and integrity of his conduct; for although I have always thought in politics with the illustrious person [Mr. Fox] whose letter was read to you, although I think with Mr. Fox that annual Parliaments and universal suffrage would be nothing like an improvement in the Constitution; yet I confess that I find it easier to say so than to answer the Duke of Richmond's arguments on the subject. I must say, also, speaking of his Grace from a long personal knowledge, which began when I was counsel for his relation, Lord Keppel,[29] that, independently of his illustrious rank, which secures him against the imputation of trifling with its existence, he is a person of an enlarged understanding, of extensive reading, and of much reflection. His book can not, therefore, be considered as the effusion of rashness and folly, but as the well-weighed, though perhaps erroneous, conclusions drawn from the actual condition of our affairs, namely, that without a speedy and essential reform in Parliament (and there my opinion goes along with him) the very being of the country, as a great nation, would be lost. This plan of the Duke of Richmond was the grand main-spring of every proceeding we have to deal with. You have had a great number of loose conversations reported from societies, on which no reliance can be had. Sometimes they have been garbled by spies, sometimes misrepresented by ignorance; and even, if correct, have frequently been the extravagances of unknown individuals, not even uttered in the presence of the prisoner, and totally unconnected with any design. For whenever their proceedings are appealed to, and their real object examined by living members of them, brought before you by the Crown, to testify them under the most solemn obligations of truth, they appear to have been following, in form and in substance, the plans adopted within our memories, not only by the Duke of Richmond, but by hundreds of the most eminent men in the kingdom.

Influence of the Duke of Richmond's views upon Ireland.

The Duke of Richmond formally published his plan of reform in the year 1780, in a letter to Lieutenant Colonel Sharman,[30] who was at that time practically employed upon the same object in Ireland. This is a most material part of the case, because you are desired to believe that the terms CONVENTION and DELEGATES, and the holding the one, and sending the other, were all collected from what had recently happened in France, and were meant as the formal introduction of her republican Constitution. But they who desire you to believe all this, do not believe it themselves; because they know certainly—and it has, indeed, already been proved by their own witnesses—that conventions of reformers were held in Ireland, and delegates regularly sent to them, while France was under the dominion of her ancient government. They knew full well that Colonel Sharman, to whom the Duke's letter was addressed, was, at that very moment, supporting a convention in Ireland, at the head of ten thousand men in arms, for the defense of their country, without any commission from the King any more than poor Franklow had, who is now in Newgate for regimenting sixty. These volunteers asserted and saved the liberties of Ireland; and the King would, at this day, have had no more subjects in Ireland than he now has in America, if they had been treated as traitors to the government. It was never imputed to Colonel Sharman and the volunteers that they were in rebellion. Yet they had arms in their hands, which

[25] See remarks of Lord Chatham, page 105, on the necessity of parliamentary reform.

[26] Mr. Pitt, who, on his first entry on political life, strenuously advocated parliamentary reform.

[27] See note in trial of Frost, page 700.

[28] Master General of the Ordnance.

[29] In the early part of the year 1779, Mr. Erskine appeared as counsel for Admiral Keppel, who was tried by a court-martial on charges preferred against him by Sir Hugh Palliser, respecting his conduct in the partial and unsatisfactory action with the French fleet off Ushant, and honorably acquitted.

[30] In this letter, and also in an address to the county of Sussex, the Duke asserted that it was vain for the people to look to the House of Commons for redress; that they could find it only in themselves; that they ought to assert their right, and not to desist till they should have established a House of Commons truly representing every man in the kingdom.

the prisoners never dreamed of having; while a grand general convention was actually sitting under their auspices at the Royal Exchange of Dublin, attended by regular delegates from all the counties in Ireland.[31] And who were these delegates? I will presently tear off their names from this paper, and hand it to you. They were the greatest, the best, and proudest names in Ireland; men who had the wisdom to reflect (before it was too late for reflection) that greatness is not to be supported by tilting at inferiors, till, by the separation of the higher from the lower orders of mankind, every distinction is swept away in the tempest of revolution; but in the happy harmonization of the whole community—by conferring upon the people their rights—sure of receiving the auspicious return of affection, and of insuring the stability of the government, which is erected upon that just and natural basis. Gentlemen, they who put this tortured construction on conventions and delegates, know also that repeated meetings of reforming societies, both in England and Scotland, had assumed about the same time the style of conventions, and had been attended by regular delegates, long before the phrase had, or could have, any existence in France; and that upon the very model of these former associations a formal convention was actually sitting at Edinburgh, with the Lord Chief Baron of Scotland in the chair, for promoting a reform in Parliament, at the very moment the Scotch convention, following its example, assumed that title.

To return to this letter of the Duke of Richmond: It was written to Colonel Sharman, in answer to a letter to his Grace, desiring to know his plan of reform, which he accordingly communicated by the letter which is in evidence. This plan was neither more nor less than that adopted by the prisoners, of surrounding Parliament (unwilling to reform its own corruptions), not by armed men, or by importunate multitudes, but by the still and universal voice of a whole people claiming their known and unalienable rights. This is so precisely the plan of the Duke of Richmond, that I have almost borrowed his expressions. His Grace says, "The lesser reform has been attempted with every possible advantage in its favor; not only from the zealous support of the advocates for a more effectual one, but from the assistance of men of great weight, both in and out of power. But with all these temperaments and helps, it has failed. Not one proselyte has been gained from corruption, nor has the least ray of hope been held out from any quarter that the House of Commons was inclined to adopt any other mode of reform. The weight of corruption has crushed this more gentle, as it would have defeated any more efficacious plan in the same circumstances. From that quarter, therefore, I have nothing to hope. IT IS FROM THE PEOPLE AT LARGE THAT I EXPECT ANY GOOD; and I am convinced that the only way to make them feel that they are really concerned in the business is to contend for their full, clear, and indisputable rights of universal representation." Now, how does this doctrine apply to the defense of the prisoner? I maintain that it has the most decisive application; because this book has been put into the hands of the Crown witnesses, who have one and all of them recognized it, and declared it to have been, *bonâ fide*, the plan which they pursued.

All the witnesses of the Crown prove that the accused acted on the principles of the Duke of Richmond.

But are the Crown's witnesses worthy of credit? If they are not, let us return home, since there is no evidence at all, and the cause is over. All the guilt, if any there be, proceeds from their testimony. If they are not to be believed, they have proved nothing; since the Crown can not force upon you that part of the evidence which suits its purpose, and ask you to reject the other which does not. The witnesses are either entirely credible, or undeserving of all credit, and I have no interest in the alternative. This is precisely the state of the cause. For, with regard to all the evidence that is written, let it never be forgotten, that it is not upon me to defend my clients against it, but for the Crown to extract from it the materials of accusation. They do not contend that the treason is upon the surface of it, but in the latent intention; which intention must, therefore, be supported by extrinsic proof; but which is, nevertheless, directly negatived and beat down by every witness they have called, leaving them nothing but commentaries and criticisms against both fact and language, to which, for the present, I shall content myself with replying in the authoritative language of the court, in the earliest stage of their proceedings. [Charge of Chief Justice Eyre to the grand jury.]

This is not to be treated as a mere pretext, without decisive proof.

"If there be ground to consider the professed purpose of any of these associations (a reform in Parliament) as mere color, and as a pretext held out in order to cover deeper designs—designs against the whole Constitution and government of the country—the case of those embarked in such designs is that which I have already considered. Whether this be so or not, is mere matter of fact; as to which I shall only remind you, that an inquiry into a charge of this nature, which undertakes to make out that the ostensible purpose is a mere vail, under which is concealed a traitorous conspiracy, requires cool and deliberate examination, and the most attentive consideration; and that the result should be perfectly clear and satisfactory. In the affairs of common life, no man is justified in imputing to another a meaning contrary to what he himself expresses, but upon the fullest evidence." To this (though it requires nothing to support it, either in reason or authority) I desire to add the direction of Lord Chief Justice Holt to the jury, on the trial of Sir William Perkyns:[32]

[31] The origin and history of the volunteer forces in Ireland has already been stated. See page 296. At a later period, a national convention was held at Dublin under their auspices.

[32] Sir William Perkyns was a violent Jacobite,

"Gentlemen, it is not fit that there should be any strained or forced construction put upon a man's actions when he is tried for his life. You ought to have a full and satisfactory evidence that he is guilty, before you pronounce him so."

In this assimilation of the writings of the societies to the writings of the Duke of Richmond and others, I do not forget that it has been truly said by the Lord Chief Justice, in the course of this very cause, that ten or twenty men's committing crimes furnishes no defense for other men in committing them. Certainly it does not, and I fly to no such sanctuary. But in trying the prisoner's *intentions*, and the intentions of those with whom he associated and acted, if I can show them to be only insisting upon the same principles that have distinguished the most eminent men for wisdom and virtue in the country, it will not be very easy to declaim or argue them into the pains of death, while our bosoms are glowing with admiration at the works of those very persons [Burke, &c.] who would condemn them.

Mr. Burke's views respecting the House of Commons.

Gentlemen, it has been too much the fashion of late to overlook the genuine source of all human authority, but more especially totally to forget the character of the British House of Commons as a representative of the people. Whether this has arisen from that Assembly's having itself forgotten it, would be indecent for me to inquire into or to insinuate. But I shall preface the authorities which I mean to collect in support of the prisoner, with the opinion on that subject of a truly celebrated writer,[33] whom I wish to speak of with great respect; I should, indeed, be ashamed, particularly at this moment, to name him invidiously, while he is bending beneath the pressure of a domestic misfortune, which no man out of his own family laments more sincerely than I do. No difference of opinion can ever make me forget to acknowledge the sublimity of his genius, the vast reach of his understanding, and his universal acquaintance with the histories and constitutions of nations. I also disavow the introduction of these writings, with the view of involving the author in any apparent inconsistencies, which would tend, indeed, to defeat rather than to advance my purpose. I stand here today to claim at your hands a fair and charitable interpretation of human conduct, and I shall not set out with giving an example of uncharitableness. A man may have reason to change his opinions, or perhaps the defect may be in myself, who collect that they are changed. I leave it to God to judge of the heart—my wish is that Christian charity may prevail—that the public harmony, which has been lost, may be restored—that all England may reunite in the bonds of love and affection—and that, when the court is broken up by the acquittal of the prisoners, all heart-burnings and animosities may cease; that, while yet we work in the light, we may try how we can save our country by a common effort; and that, instead of shamelessly setting one half of society against the other by the force of armed associations and the terrors of courts of justice, our spirits and our strength may be combined in the glorious cause of our country. By this, I do not mean in the cause of the present war,[34] which I protest against as unjust, calamitous, and destructive; but this is not the place for such a subject—I only advert to it to prevent mistake or misrepresentation.

The history and character of the English House of Commons was formerly thus described by Mr. Burke: "The House of Commons was supposed originally to be no part of the standing government of this country, but was considered as a control issuing immediately from the people, and speedily to be resolved into the mass from whence it arose: in this respect it was in the higher part of government what juries are in the lower. The capacity of a magistrate being transitory, and that of a citizen permanent, the latter capacity, it was hoped, would, of course, preponderate in all discussions, not only between the people and the standing authority of the Crown, but between the people and the fleeting authority of the House of Commons itself. It was hoped that, being of a middle nature, between subject and government, they would feel, with a more tender and a nearer interest, every thing that concerned the people, than the other remoter and more permanent parts of Legislature.

"Whatever alterations time and the necessary accommodation of business may have introduced, this character can never be sustained, unless the House of Commons shall be made to bear some stamp of the actual disposition of the people at large; it would (among public misfortunes) be an evil more natural and tolerable, that the House of Commons should be infected with every epidemical frenzy of the people, as this would indicate some consanguinity, some sympathy of nature with their constituents, than that they should, in all cases, be wholly untouched by the opinions and feelings of the people out of doors. By this want of sympathy they would cease to be a House of Commons.

"The virtue, spirit, and essence of a House of Commons consists in its being the express image of the feelings of the nation. It was not instituted to be a control *upon* the people, as of late it has been taught, by a doctrine of the most pernicious tendency, but as a control *for* the people."

Actual constitution of the House of Commons.

He then goes on to say, that to give a technical shape, a color, dress, and duration to popular opinion, is the true office of a House of Commons. Mr. Burke is unquestionably correct. The control *upon* the

and a party not only in the conspiracy for the restoration of James, mentioned *ante*, p. 728, note, but also in a plot for the assassination of King William, on the road between Richmond and Turnham Green. The plot was discovered through some of the underlings, who were to aid in the attempt on the King's life, and Sir William Perkyns was tried for treason, and executed at Tyburn.

[33] Mr. Burke, whose son was at the point of death.

[34] The war with France consequent on the execution of Louis XVI.

people is the King's majesty, and the hereditary privileges of the Peers; the balance of the State is the control *for* the people upon both, in the existence of the House of Commons. But how can that control exist *for* the people, unless they have the actual election of the House of Commons, which, it is most notorious, they have not? I hold in my hand a state of the representation which, if the thing were not otherwise notorious, I would prove to have been lately offered in proof to the House of Commons, by an honorable friend of mine now present,[35] whose motion I had the honor to second, where it appeared that twelve thousand people return near a majority of the House of Commons, and those, again, under the control of about two hundred. But though these facts were admitted, all redress, and even discussion, was refused. What ought to be said of a House of Commons that so conducts itself, it is not for me to pronounce. I will appeal, therefore, to Mr. Burke, who says, "that a House of Commons, which in all disputes between the people and administration presumes against the people, which punishes their disorders, but refuses even to inquire into their provocations, is an *unnatural, monstrous* state of things in the Constitution."

Still stronger language of Mr. Burke.

But this is nothing. Mr. Burke goes on afterward to give a more full description of Parliament, and in stronger language (let the Solicitor General[36] take it down for his reply) than any that has been employed by those who are to be tried at present as conspirators against its existence. I read the passage, to warn you against considering hard words against the House of Commons as decisive evidence of treason against the King. The passage is in a well-known work, called "Thoughts on the Causes of the present Discontents;" and such discontents will always be present while their causes continue. The word *present* will apply just as well now, and much better than to the time [1770] when the honorable gentleman wrote his book; for we are now in the heart and bowels of another war, and groaning under its additional burdens. I shall, therefore, leave it to the learned gentleman who is to reply, to show us what has happened since our author wrote, which renders the Parliament less liable to the same observations now.

"It must be always the wish of an unconstitutional statesman, that a House of Commons, who are entirely dependent upon him, should have every right of the people entirely dependent upon their pleasure. For it was soon discovered that the forms of a free, and the ends of an arbitrary government, were things not altogether incompatible.

"The power of the Crown, almost dead and rotten as prerogative, has grown up anew, with much more strength and far less odium, under the name of *influence*. This influence, which operated without noise and violence; which converted the very antagonist into the instrument of power; which contained in itself a perpetual principle of growth and renovation; and which the distresses and the prosperity of the country equally tended to augment, was an admirable substitute for a prerogative which, being only the offspring of antiquated prejudices, had molded in its original stamina irresistible principles of decay and dissolution."

What is this but saying that the House of Commons is a settled and scandalous abuse fastened *upon* the people, instead of being an antagonist power *for* their protection; an odious instrument of power in the hands of the Crown, instead of a popular balance *against* it? Did Mr. Burke mean that the prerogative of the Crown, properly understood and exercised, was an antiquated prejudice? Certainly not, because his attachment to a properly balanced monarchy is notorious. Why, then, is it to be fastened upon the prisoners, that they stigmatize monarchy, when they also exclaim *only against its corruptions?* In the same manner, when he speaks of the abuses of *Parliament*, would it be fair to Mr. Burke to argue, from the strict legal meaning of the expression, that he included, in the censure on Parliament, the King's person, or majesty, which is part of the Parliament? In examining the work of an author you must collect the sense of his expressions from the subject he is discussing; and if he is writing of the House of Commons as it affects the structure and efficacy of the government, you ought to understand the word Parliament so as to meet the sense and obvious meaning of the writer. Why, then, is this common justice refused to others? Why is the word Parliament to be taken in its strictest and least obvious sense against a poor shoemaker [Hardy], or any plain tradesman at a Sheffield club, while it is interpreted in its popular, though less correct acceptation, in the works of the most distinguished scholar of the age? Add to this, that the cases are not at all similar. Mr. Burke uses the word Parliament throughout, when he is speaking of the House of Commons, without any concomitant words which convey an explanation, but the sense of his subject; whereas Parliament is fastened upon the prisoner as meaning something beyond the House of Commons, when it can have no possible meaning beyond it; since from the beginning to the end it is joined with the words "representation of the people"—"the representation of the people in Parliament." Does not this most palpably mean the House of Commons, when we know that the people have no representation in either of the other branches of the government.

Evidence that Mr. Fox, Lord Grey, and others did not consider the prisoner as aiming to subvert the government.

A letter has been read in evidence from Mr. Hardy to Mr. Fox, where he says their object was universal representation. Did Mr. Fox suppose, when he received this letter, that it was from a nest of republicans, clamoring

[35] Mr. (afterward Lord) Grey, who brought forward a motion for reform, in the session of 1792, in consequence of the resolution of the Society of Friends of the People, of which he and Mr. Erskine were members.

[36] Sir John Mitford, afterward Lord Redesdale.

publicly for a universal representative Constitution like that of France? If he had, would he have sent the answer he did, and agreed to present their petition? They wrote also to the Society of the Friends of the People, and invited them to send delegates to the convention.[37] The Attorney General, who has made honorable and candid mention of that body, will not suppose that it would have contented itself with refusing the invitation in terms of cordiality and regard, if, with all the knowledge they had of their transactions, they had conceived themselves to have been invited to the formation of a body which was to overrule and extinguish all the authorities of the state. Yet, upon the perversion of these two terms, Parliament and Convention, against their natural interpretation, against a similar use of them by others, and against the solemn explanation of them by the Crown's own witness, this whole fabric of terror and accusation stands for its support. Letters, it seems, written to other people, are to be better understood by the gentlemen round this table, who never saw them till months after they were written, than by those to whom they were addressed and sent; and no right interpretation, forsooth, is to be expected from writings when pursued in their regular series, but they are to be made distinct by binding them up in a large volume, alongside of others totally unconnected with them, and the very existence of whose authors was unknown to one another.

Other language of Mr. Burke.

I will now, gentlemen, resume the reading of another part of Mr. Burke, and a pretty account it is of this same Parliament: "They who will not conform their conduct to the public good, and can not support it by the prerogative of the Crown, have adopted a new plan. They have totally abandoned the shattered and old-fashioned fortress of prerogative, and made a lodgment in the strong-hold of Parliament itself. If they have any evil design to which there is no ordinary legal power commensurate, they bring it into Parliament. There the whole is executed from the beginning to the end; and the power of obtaining their object absolute, and the safety in the proceeding perfect; no rules to confine, nor after-reckonings to terrify. For Parliament can not, with any great propriety, punish others for things in which they themselves have been accomplices. Thus its control upon the executory power is lost."

This is a proposition universal. It is not that the popular control was lost under this or that administration, but generally that the people have no control in the House of Commons. Let any man stand up and say that he disbelieves this to be the case; I believe he would find nobody to believe him. Mr. Burke pursues the subject thus: "The distempers of monarchy were the great subjects of apprehension and redress in the *last* century—in *this*, the distempers of Parliament." Here the word Parliament and the abuses belonging to it are put in express opposition to the monarchy, and can not, therefore, comprehend it; the distempers of Parliament, then, are objects of serious apprehension and redress. What distempers? Not of this or that year, but the habitual distempers of Parliament. And then follows the nature of the remedy, which shows that the prisoners are not singular in thinking that it is by THE VOICE OF THE PEOPLE ONLY that Parliament can be corrected. "It is not in Parliament alone," says Mr. Burke, "that the remedy for parliamentary disorders can be completed; and hardly, indeed, can it begin there. Until a confidence in government is re-established, the people ought to be excited to a more strict and detailed attention to the conduct of their representatives. Standards for judging more systematically upon their conduct ought to be settled in the meetings of counties and corporations, and frequent and correct lists of the voters in all important questions ought to be procured. By such means something may be done."

It was the same sense of the impossibility of a reform in Parliament, without a general expression of the wishes of the people, that dictated the Duke of Richmond's letter: all the petitions in 1780[38] had been rejected by Parliament. This made the Duke of Richmond exclaim, that from that quarter no redress was to be expected, and that from the people alone he expected any good; and he, therefore, expressly invited them to claim and to assert an equal representation as their indubitable and unalienable birth-right—how to assert their rights, when Parliament had already refused them without even the hope, as the Duke expressed it, of listening to them any more. Could the people's rights, under such circumstances, be asserted without rebellion? Certainly they might; for rebellion is, when bands of men within a state oppose themselves by violence to the general will, as expressed or implied by the public authority; but the sense of a *whole people*, peaceably collected, and operating by its natural and certain effect upon the public councils, is not rebellion, but is paramount to, and the parent of, authority itself.

The true remedy for discontent is to acknowledge the rights of the people.

Gentlemen, I am neither vindicating nor speaking the language of inflammation or discontent. I shall speak nothing that can disturb the order of the state—I am full of devotion to its dignity and tranquillity, and would not for worlds let fall an expression in this or in any other place that could lead to disturbance or disorder. But for that very reason I speak with firmness of THE RIGHTS OF THE PEOPLE, and am anxious for the redress of their complaints, because I believe a system of attention to them to be a far better security and establishment of every part of the government, than those that are employed to preserve them.

[37] This society was composed of some of the first nobility and gentry of the kingdom—such as Lord Grey, Lord John Russell, &c.

[38] In that year Parliament was overwhelmed with innumerable petitions on the subject of the increasing influence of the Crown, the abuse of prerogative and the rights of the people.

The state and government of a country rest for their support on the great body of the people; and I hope never to hear it repeated in any court of justice, that peaceably to convene the people upon the subject of their own privileges can lead to the destruction of the King — they are the King's worst enemies who hold this language. It is a most dangerous principle that the Crown is in jeopardy if the people are acquainted with their rights, and that the collecting them together, to consider of them, leads inevitably to the destruction of the Sovereign. Do these gentlemen mean to say that the King sits upon his throne without the consent, and in defiance of the wishes, of the great body of his people, and that he is kept upon it by a few individuals who call themselves his friends, in exclusion of the rest of his subjects? Has the King's inheritance no deeper or wider roots than this? Yes, gentlemen, it has—it stands upon the love of the people, who consider their own inheritance to be supported by the King's constitutional authority. This is the true prop of the Throne; and the love of every people upon earth will forever uphold a government founded, as ours is, upon reason and consent, as long as government shall be itself attentive to the general interests which are the foundations and the ends of all human authority. Let us banish, then, these unworthy and impolitic fears of an unrestrained and an enlightened people; let us not tremble at the rights of man, but, by giving to men their rights, secure their affections; and, through their affections, their obedience. Let us not broach the dangerous doctrine that the rights of Kings and of men are incompatible. Our government at the Revolution began upon their harmonious incorporation; and Mr. Locke defended King William's title upon no other principle than the rights of man. It is from the revered work of Mr. Locke, and not from the Revolution in France, that one of the papers in the evidence, the most stigmatized, most obviously flowed. For it is proved that Mr. Yorke held in his hand Mr. Locke upon Government, when he delivered his speech on the Castle Hill at Sheffield,[39] and that he expatiated largely upon it. Well, indeed, might the witnesses say he expatiated largely, for there are many well-selected passages taken verbatim from the book; and here, in justice to Mr. White,[40] let me notice the fair and honorable manner in which, in the absence of the clerk, he read this extraordinary performance. He delivered it not merely with distinctness, but in a manner so impressive, that I believe every man in court was affected by it.

The language charged not always proper; but neither language nor acts indicate evil intentions.

Gentlemen, I am not driven to defend every expression. Some of them are improper undoubtedly, rash; and inflammatory; but I see nothing in the whole taken together, even if it were connected with the prisoner, that goes at all to an evil purpose in the writer. But Mr. Attorney General has remarked upon this proceeding at Sheffield (and whatever falls from a person of his rank and just estimation, deserves great attention)—he has remarked that it is quite apparent they had resolved not to *petition.* They had certainly resolved not *at that season* to petition, and that seems the utmost which can be maintained from the evidence. But supposing they had negatived the measure altogether, is there no way by which the people may actively associate for the purposes of a reform in Parliament, but to consider of a petition to the House of Commons? Might they not legally assemble to consider the state of their liberties, and the conduct of their representatives? Might they not legally form conventions or meetings (for the name is just nothing) to adjust a plan of rational union for a wise choice of representatives when Parliament should be dissolved? May not the people meet to consider their interests preparatory to, and independently of, a petition for any specific object? My friend seems to consider the House of Commons as a substantive and permanent part of the Constitution. He seems to forget that the Parliament dies a natural death; that the people then re-enter into their rights, and that the exercise of them is the most important duty that can belong to social man. How are such duties to be exercised with effect, on momentous occasions, but by concert and communion? May not the people, assembled in their elective districts, resolve to trust no longer those by whom they have been betrayed? May they not resolve to vote for no man who contributed by his voice to this calamitous war, which has thrown such grievous and unnecessary burdens upon them? May they not say, "We will not vote for those who deny we are their constituents, nor for those who question our clear and natural right to be equally represented?" Since it is illegal to carry up petitions, and unwise to transact any public business attended by multitudes, because it tends to tumult and disorder, may they not, for that very reason, depute, as they have done, the most trusty of their societies to meet with one another to consider, without the specific object of petitions, how they may claim, by means which are constitutional, their imprescriptible rights?

Reply to the Attorney General as to urging universal suffrage.

And here I must advert to an argument employed by the Attorney General, that the views of the societies toward universal suffrage carried in themselves (however sought to be effected) an implied force upon Parliament. For that, supposing by invading it with the vast pressure, not of the public arm, but of the public sentiment of the nation, the influence of which upon that assembly is admitted ought to be weighty, it could have prevailed upon the Commons to carry up a bill to the King for universal representation and annual Parliaments, his Majesty was bound to reject it; and could not, without a breach of his coronation oath, consent to pass it into an act. I can not conceive where my friend met with this law, or what he can possibly mean by asserting

[39] Mr. Yorke was a member of the London Corresponding Society, and was appointed a delegate from that society to similar societies at Sheffield and other places.

[40] The Solicitor to the Treasury.

that the King can not, consistently with his coronation oath, consent to any law that can be stated or imagined, presented to him as the act of the two Houses of Parliament. He could not, indeed, consent to a bill sent up to him framed by a convention of delegates assuming legislative functions. If my friend could have proved that the societies, sitting as a Parliament, had sent up such a bill to his Majesty, I should have thought the prisoner, as a member of such a Parliament, was at least in a different situation from that in which he stands at present. But as this is not one of the chimeras whose existence is contended for, I return back to ask upon what authority it is maintained, that universal representation and annual Parliaments could not be consented to by the King, in conformity to the wishes of the other branches of the Legislature. On the contrary, one of the greatest men that this country ever saw, considered universal representation to be such an inherent part of the Constitution, as that the King himself might grant it by his prerogative, even without the Lords and Commons—and I had never heard the position denied upon any other footing than the Union with Scotland. But be that as it may, it is enough for my purpose that the maxim, that the King might grant universal representation, as a right before inherent in the whole people to be represented, stands upon the authority of Mr. Locke, the man, next to Sir Isaac Newton, of the greatest strength of understanding that England, perhaps, ever had; high, too, in the favor of King William, and enjoying one of the most exalted offices in the state.[41] Mr. Locke says, book ii., c. xiii., sect. 157 and 158: "Things of this world are in so constant a flux, that nothing remains long in the same state. Thus people, riches, trade, power, change their stations, flourishing mighty cities come to ruin, and prove, in time, neglected desolate corners, while other unfrequented places grow into populous countries, filled with wealth and inhabitants. But things not always changing equally, and private interest often keeping up customs and privileges, when the reasons of them are ceased, it often comes to pass, that in governments, where part of the legislative consists of representatives chosen by the people, that, in tract of time, this representation becomes very unequal and disproportionate to the reasons it was at first established upon. To what gross absurdities the following of custom, when reason has left it, may lead, we may be satisfied when we see the bare name of a town of which there remains not so much as the ruins, where scarce so much housing as a sheep-cote, or more inhabitants than a shepherd, is to be found, sends as many representatives to the grand assembly of law-makers, as a whole county, numerous in people and powerful in riches.[42] This strangers stand amazed at, and every one must confess needs a remedy."

Views of Mr. Locke.

"*Salus populi suprema lex*, is certainly so just and fundamental a rule, that he who sincerely follows it can not dangerously err. If, therefore, the executive, who has the power of convoking the legislative, observing rather the true proportion, than fashion of representation, regulates, not by old custom, but by true reason, the number of members in all places that have a right to be distinctly represented, which no part of the people, however incorporated, can pretend to, but in proportion to the assistance which it affords to the public, it can not be judged to have set up a new legislative, but to have restored the old and true one, and to have rectified the disorders which succession of time had insensibly, as well as inevitably, introduced; for it being the interest as well as intention of the people to have fair and equal representation, whoever brings it nearest to that, is an undoubted friend to, and establisher of, the government, and can not miss the consent and approbation of the community; prerogative being nothing but a power, in the hands of the Prince, to provide for the public good, in such cases, which, depending upon unforeseen and uncertain occurrences, certain and unalterable laws could not safely direct; whatsoever shall be done manifestly for the good of the people, and the establishing the government upon its true foundations, is, and always will be, just prerogative. Whatsoever can not but be acknowledged to be of advantage to the society, and people in general, upon just and lasting measures, will always, when done, justify itself; and whenever the people shall choose their representatives upon just and undeniably equal measures, suitable to the original frame of the government, it can not be doubted to be the will and act of the society, whoever permitted or caused them so to do." But as the very idea of universal suffrage seems now to be considered not only to be dangerous to, but absolutely destructive of, monarchy, you certainly ought to be reminded that the book which I have been reading, and which my friend kindly gives me a note to remind you of, was written by its immortal author in defense of King William's title to the Crown; and when Dr. Sacheverel ventured to broach those doctrines of power and non-resistance, which, under the same establishments, have now become so unaccountably popular, he was impeached[43] by the people's representatives for denying their rights, which had been asserted and established at the glorious era of the Revolution.

[41] He was one of the Commissioners of Trade and Plantations.

[42] Mr. Locke alluded to Old Sarum, in Wiltshire, in which a few fragments of foundation-walls are the only traces of a town ever having existed. It was totally deserted in the reign of Henry VIII.; but yet, up to the passing of the Reform Bill, in 1832, when the borough was disfranchised, Old Sarum was represented in Parliament.

[43] A. D. 1709. Being found guilty, he was prohibited from preaching for three years, and his two sermons, which had given so much offense, were ordered to be burned by the common hangman. The famous decree passed in the Convocation of the University of Oxford, asserting the absolute authority and indefeasible right of princes, was also ordered to be, in like manner, committed to the flames.

Part Third: Examination of the evidence for the Crown.

Gentlemen, if I were to go through all the matter which I have collected upon this subject, or which obtrudes itself upon my mind, from common reading in a thousand directions, my strength would fail long before my duty was fulfilled. I had very little when I came into court, and I have abundantly less already; I must, therefore, manage what remains to the best advantage. I proceed, therefore, to take a view of such parts of the evidence as appear to me to be the most material for the proper understanding of the case. I have had no opportunity of considering it, but in the interval which the indulgence of the court and your own has afforded me, and that has been for a very few hours this morning. But it occurred to me, that the best use I could make of the time given to me was, if possible, to disembroil this chaos; to throw out of view every thing irrelevant, which only tended to bring chaos back again; to take what remained in order of time; to select certain stages and resting-places; to review the effect of the transactions, as brought before us, and then to see how the written evidence is explained by the testimony of the witnesses who have been examined.

(1.) London Corresponding Society.

The origin of the Constitutional Society not having been laid in evidence before you, the first thing, both in point of date, and as applying to show the objects of the different bodies, is the original address and resolution of the London Corresponding Society on its first institution, and when it first began to correspond with the other, which had formerly ranked among its members so many illustrious persons.[44] Before we look to the matter of this [latter] institution, let us recollect that the objects of it were given without reserve to the public, as containing the principles of the [former] association. And I may begin with demanding, whether the annals of this country, or, indeed, the universal history of mankind, afford an assistance of a *plot* and *conspiracy* voluntarily given up in its very infancy to government, and the whole public; and of which—to avoid the very thing that has happened, the arraignment of conduct at a future period, and the imputation of secrecy where no secret was intended—a regular notice by letter was left with the Secretary of State, and a receipt taken at the public office, as a proof of the publicity of their proceeding, a[illegible] the sense they entertained of their innocen[illegible][45] For the views and objects of the society, we must look to the institution itself, which you are, indeed, desired to look at by the Crown; for their intentions are not considered as deceptions in this instance, but as plainly revealed by the very writing itself.

Motto of the society.

Gentlemen, there was a sort of silence in the court—I do not say an affected one, for I mean no possible offense to any one—but there seemed to be an effect expected from beginning, not with the address itself, but with the very bold motto to it, though in verse:

"Unbless'd by virtue, government a league
Becomes, a circling junto of the great
To rob by law; Religion mild, a yoke
To tame the stooping soul, a trick of state
To mask their rapine, and to share the prey.
Without it, what are Senates, but a face
Of consultation deep and reason free,
While the determined voice and heart are sold?
What, boasted freedom, but a sounding name?
And what election, but a market vile,
Of slaves self-barter'd?"

I almost fancy I heard them say to me, "What think you of that to set out with? Show me the parallel of that." Gentlemen, I am sorry, for the credit of the age we live in, to answer, that it *is* difficult to find the parallel, because the age affords no such poet as he who wrote it. These are the words of Thomson; and it is under the banners of his proverbial benevolence that these men are supposed to be engaging in plans of anarchy and murder—under the banners of that great and good man, whose figure you may still see in the venerable shades of Hagley, placed there by the virtuous, accomplished, and public-spirited Lyttelton: the very poem, too, written under the auspices of his Majesty's royal father, when heir-apparent to the Crown of Great Britain, nay, within the very walls of Carlton House, which afforded an asylum to matchless worth and genius in the person of this great poet. It was under the roof of a Prince of Wales that the poem of Liberty was written; and what better return could be given to a Prince for his protection, than to blazon, in immortal numbers, the only sure title to the Crown he was to wear—the freedom of the people of Great Britain? And it is to be assumed, forsooth, in the year 1794, that the unfortunate prisoner before you was plotting treason and rebellion, because, with a taste and feeling beyond his humble station, his first proceeding was ushered into view under the hallowed sanction of this admirable person, the friend and the defender of the British Constitution; whose countrymen are preparing at this moment (may my name descend among them to the latest posterity!) to do honor to his immortal memory. Pardon me, gentlemen, for this desultory digression—I must express myself as the current of my mind will carry me.[46]

---

[44] Previous to the formation of the London Corresponding Society, there existed another called the Society for Constitutional Information. This was founded by some of the most distinguished Whigs of the kingdom. Soon after the commencement of the French Revolution, it was joined by Horne Tooke and others of more radical views, and many of its original members left it. This society took the lead in sending a deputation to the National Convention of France, an act which was highly censured as derogatory to the English government. They also passed a vote of thanks to Thomas Paine for his work entitled the Rights of Man. Much of the evidence in the present case was intended to identify the Corresponding Society with the Constitutional Society, and thus to load Hardy with the odium of their proceedings.

[45] This was done by the Corresponding Society, partly, no doubt, in the spirit of bravado.

[46] Th[illegible]mson was born at Ednam in Scotland, and

If we look at the whole of the institution itself, it exactly corresponds with the plan of the Duke of Richmond, as expressed in the letters to Colonel Sharman, and to the High Sheriff of Sussex. This plan they propose to follow, in a public address to the nation, and all their resolutions are framed for its accomplishment; and I desire to know in what they have departed from either, and what they have done which has not been done before, without blame or censure, in the pursuance of the same object. I am not speaking of the libels they may have written, which the law is open to punish, but what part of their conduct has, as applicable to the subject in question, been unprecedented? I have at this moment in my eye an honorable friend of mine, and a distinguished member of the House of Commons [Mr. Fox], who, within my own remembrance, I believe in 1780, sat publicly at Guildhall, with many others, some of them magistrates of the city, as a convention of delegates for the same objects. And what is still more in point, just before the convention began to meet at Edinburgh, whose proceedings have been so much relied on, there was a convention regularly assembled, attended by delegates from all the counties of Scotland, for the express and avowed purpose of altering the constitution of Parliament—not by rebellion, but by the same means employed by the prisoner. The Lord Chief Baron of Scotland sat in the chair, and was assisted by some of the first men in that country, and, among others, by an honorable person to whom I am nearly allied, who is at the very head of the bar in Scotland, and most avowedly attached to the law and the Constitution.[47]

The object of the society was to carry out the plan of the Duke of Richmond.

In proposing a convention, they had high authorities.

These gentlemen, whose good intentions never fell into suspicion, had presented a petition for the alteration of election laws, which the House of Commons had rejected, and on the spur of that very rejection they met in a convention at Edinburgh, in 1793. The style of their first meeting was "A Convention of Delegates, chosen from the counties of Scotland, *for altering and amending the laws concerning Elections*"—not for considering how they might be best amended—not for petitioning Parliament to amend them, but for altering and amending the election laws. The proceedings of these meetings were regularly published, and I will prove that their first resolution, as I have read it to you, was brought up to London, and delivered to the editor of the Morning Chronicle, by Sir Thomas Dundas, lately created a peer of Great Britain, and paid for by him as a public advertisement. Now, suppose any man had imputed treason or sedition to these honorable persons, what would have been the consequence? He would have been considered as an infamous libeler and traducer, and deservedly hooted out of civilized life. Why, then, are different constructions to be put upon similar transactions? Why is every thing to be held up as *bonâ fide* when the example is set, and *malâ fide* when it is followed? Why have I not as good a claim to take credit for honest purpose in the poor man I am defending, against whom not a contumelious expression has been proved, as when we find the same expressions in the mouths of the Duke of Richmond or Mr. Burke? I ask nothing more from this observation, than that a sober judgment may be pronounced from the quality of the acts which can be fairly established; each individual standing responsible only for his own conduct, instead of having our imaginations tainted with cant phrases, and a farrago of writings and speeches, for which the prisoner is not responsible, and for which the authors, if they be criminal, are liable to be brought to justice.

First Scottish convention.

But it will be said, gentlemen, that all the constitutional privileges of the people are conceded—that their existence was never denied or invaded—and that their right to petition and to meet for the expression of their complaints, founded or unfounded, was never called in question. These, it will be said, are the rights of subjects—but that "the rights of man" are what alarms them. Every man is considered as a traitor who talks about the rights of man; but this bugbear stands upon the same perversion with its fellows.

Prejudice against these latter conventions because they speak of the rights of man.

The rights of man are the foundation of all government, and to secure them is the only reason of men's submitting to be governed. It shall not be fastened upon the unfortunate prisoner at the bar, nor upon any other man, that because these natural rights were asserted in France, by the destruction of a government which oppressed and subverted them—a process happily effected here by slow and imperceptible improvements—that, therefore, they can only be so asserted in England, where the government, through a gradation of improvement, is well calculated to protect them. We are, fortunately, not driven in this country to the terrible alternatives which were the unhappy lot of France, because we have had a happier destiny in the forms of a free Constitution. This, indeed, is the express language of many of the papers before you that have been complained of—especially of one alluded to by the Attorney General, as having been written by a gentleman with whom I am particularly acquainted. And though in that spirited composition there are, perhaps, some expressions proceeding from warmth which he may not desire me critically to justify, yet I will venture to affirm, from my own personal knowledge, that there is not a man in court more honestly public-spirited and zealously devoted to the Constitution of King, Lords, and Commons, than the honorable gentleman I allude to [Felix Vaughan, Esq., barrister-at-law]: it is the *phrase*, therefore, and not the sentiment expressed by it, that can

Defense of the phrase.

an association was formed at this time, of which Erskine was a member, to erect a monument to his memory in his native village. This was finally accomplished at an expense of £300.

[47] The Honorable Henry Erskine, Mr. Erskine's brother, then Dean of the Faculty of Advocates, at Edinburgh.

alone give justifiable offense. It is, it seems, a *new* phrase commencing in revolutions, and never used before in discussing the rights of British subjects, and, therefore, can only be applied in the sense of those who framed it. But this is so far from being the truth, that the very phrase sticks in my memory, from the memorable application of it to the rights of subjects, under this and every other establishment, by a gentleman whom you will not suspect of using it in any other sense. The rights of man were considered by Mr. Burke, at the time that the great uproar was made upon a supposed invasion of the East India Company's charter, to be the foundation of, and paramount to, all the laws and ordinances of a state. The ministry, you may remember, were turned out for Mr. Fox's India Bill,[48] which their opponents termed an attack upon the chartered rights of man, or, in other words, upon the abuses supported by a monopoly in trade. Hear the sentiments of Mr. Burke, when the natural and chartered rights of men are brought into contest. Mr. Burke, in his speech in the House of Commons, expressed himself thus: "The first objection is, that the bill is an attack on the chartered rights of men. As to this objection, I must observe that the phrase, "the chartered rights *of men*," is full of affectation, and very unusual in the discussion of privileges conferred by charters of the present description. But it is not difficult to discover what end that ambiguous mode of expression, so often reiterated, is meant to answer.

Mr. Burke on this subject.

"The rights of men, that is to say, the natural rights of mankind, are, indeed, sacred things; and if any public measure is proved mischievously to affect them, the objection ought to be fatal to that measure, even if no charter at all could be set up against it. And if these natural rights are further affirmed and declared by express covenants, clearly defined and secured against chicane, power, and authority, by written instruments and positive engagements, they are in a still better condition: they then partake not only of the sanctity of the object so secured, but of that solemn public faith itself, which secures an object of such importance. Indeed, this formal recognition, by the sovereign power, of an original right in the subject, can never be subverted but by rooting up the holding radical principles of government, and even of society itself."

Duke of Richmond on the same subject.

The Duke of Richmond, also, in his public letter to the High Sheriff of Sussex, rests the rights of the people of England upon the same horrible and damnable principle of the rights of man. Let gentlemen, therefore, take care they do not pull down the very authority which they come here to support. Let them remember that his Majesty's family was called to the throne upon the very principle that the ancient kings of this country had violated these sacred trusts. Let them recollect, too, in what the violation was charged to consist: it was charged by the Bill of Rights to consist in cruel and infamous trials, in the packing of juries, and in disarming the people, whose arms are their unalienable refuge against oppression. But did the people of England assemble to make this declaration? No! because it was unnecessary. The sense of the people, against a corrupt and scandalous government, dissolved it, by almost the ordinary forms by which the old government itself was administered. King William sent his writs to those who had sat in the former Parliament; but will any man, therefore, tell me that that Parliament re-organized the government without the will of the people? and that it was not their consent which entailed on King William a particular inheritance, to be enjoyed under the dominion of the law?

Paine's book called forth by the denial of constitutional principles.

Gentlemen, it was the denial of these principles, asserted at the Revolution in England, that brought forward the author of the "Rights of Man," and stirred up this controversy which has given such alarm to government. But for this, the literary labors of Mr. Paine had closed. He asserts it himself in his book, and every body knows it. It was not the French Revolution, but Mr. Burke's Reflections upon it, followed up by another work on the same subject, as it regarded things in England, which brought forward Mr. Paine, and which rendered his works so much the object of attention in this country. Mr. Burke denied positively the very foundation upon which the Revolution of 1688 must stand for its support, namely, the right of the people to change their government; and he asserted, in the teeth of his Majesty's title to the Crown, that no such right in the people existed. This is the true history of the Second Part of the "Rights of Man." The First Part had little more aspect to this country than to Japan; it asserted the right of the people of France to act as they had acted, but there was little which pointed to it as an example for England. There had been a despotic authority in France, which the people had thrown down, and Mr. Burke seemed to question their right to do so. Mr. Paine maintained the contrary in his answer; and, having imbibed the principles of republican government during the American Revolution, he mixed with the controversy many coarse and harsh remarks upon monarchy, as established even in England, or in any possible form. But this was collateral to the great object of his work, which was to maintain the right of the people to choose their government. This was the right which was questioned, and the assertion of it was most interesting to many who were most strenuously attached to the English government. For men may assert the right of every people to choose their government, without seeking to destroy their own. This accounts for many expressions imputed to the unfortunate prisoners, which I have often uttered myself, and shall continue to utter every day of my life, and call upon the spies of government to record them. I will say any where, without fear —nay, I will say here, where I stand, that an at-

[48] See *ante*, page 313.

tempt to interfere, by despotic combination and violence, with any government which a people choose to give to themselves, whether it be good or evil, is an oppression and subversion of the natural and inalienable rights of man; and though the government of this country should countenance such a system, it would not only be still legal for me to express my detestation of it, as I here deliberately express it, but it would become my interest and my duty. For if combinations of despotism can accomplish such a purpose, who shall tell me what other nation shall not be the prey of their ambition? Upon the very principle of denying to a people the right of governing themselves, how are we to resist the French, should they attempt by violence to fasten their government upon us? Or what inducement would there be for resistance to preserve laws which are not, it seems, our own, but which are unalterably imposed upon us? The very argument strikes, as with a palsy, the arm and vigor of the nation. I hold dear the privileges I am contending for, not as privileges hostile to the Constitution, but as necessary for its preservation; and if the French were to intrude by force upon the government of our own free choice, I should leave these papers, and return to a profession that, perhaps, I better understand.[49]

(2.) Letter of Norwich reformers, and reply.

The next evidence relied on, after the institution of the Corresponding Society, is a letter written to them from Norwich, dated the 11th of November, 1792, with the answer, dated the 26th of the same month. It is asserted that this correspondence shows they aimed at nothing less than the total destruction of the monarchy, and that they, therefore, vail their intention under covert and ambiguous language. I think, on the other hand, and I shall continue to think so, as long as I am capable of thought, that it was impossible for words to convey more clearly the explicit avowal of their original plan for a constitutional reform in the House of Commons. This letter from Norwich, after congratulating the Corresponding Society on its institution, asks several questions arising out of the proceedings of other societies in different parts of the kingdom, which they profess not thoroughly to understand.

The Sheffield people (they observe) seemed at first determined to support the Duke of Richmond's plan only, but that they had afterward observed a disposition in them to a more moderate plan of reform proposed by the Friends of the People in London; while the Manchester people, by addressing Mr. Paine (whom the Norwich people had not addressed), seemed to be intent on republican principles only. They [the Norwich people], therefore, put a question, not at all of distrust or suspicion, but *bonâ fide*, if ever there was good faith between men, whether the Corresponding Society meant to be satisfied with the plan of the Duke of Richmond? or whether it was their private design to rip up monarchy by the roots, and place democracy in its stead? Now hear the answer, from whence it is inferred that this last is their intention. They begin their answer with recapitulating the demand of their correspondent, as regularly as a tradesman, who has had an order for goods, recapitulates the order, that there may be no ambiguity in the reference or application of the reply, and then they say, as to the objects they have in view, they refer them to their addresses. "You will thereby see that we mean to disseminate political knowledge, and thereby engage the judicious part of the nation to demand the recovery of their lost rights in annual Parliaments; the members of these Parliaments owing their election to unbought suffrages." They then desire them to be careful to avoid all dispute, and say to them, "Put monarchy, democracy, and even religion quite aside;" and "let your endeavors go to increase the numbers of those who desire a full and equal representation of the people, and leave to a Parliament, so chosen, to reform all existing abuses, and if they don't answer, at the year's end, you may choose others in their stead." The Attorney General says this is lamely expressed. I, on the other hand, say that it is not only not lamely expressed, but anxiously worded to put an end to dangerous speculations. Leave all theories undiscussed; do not perplex yourselves with abstract questions of government; endeavor practically to get honest representatives; and if they deceive you—then, what?—bring on a revolution? No! *Choose others in their stead!* They refer, also, to their Address, which lay before their correspondent, which Address expresses itself thus: "Laying aside all claim to originality, we claim no other merit than that of reconsidering and verifying what has already been urged in our common cause by the Duke of Richmond and Mr. Pitt, and their then honest party."

Pretense that language of the reformers was a mere cover.

When the language of the letter, which is branded as ambiguous [by the counsel for the Crown], thus stares them in the face as an undeniable answer to the charge, they then have recourse to the old refuge of *mala fides;* all this, they say, is but a cover for hidden treason. But I ask you, gentlemen, in the name of God, and as fair and honest men, what reason upon earth there is to suppose that the writers of this letter did not mean what they expressed? Are you to presume, in a court of justice, and upon a trial for life, that men write with duplicity in their most confidential correspondence, even to those with whom they are confederated? Let it be recollected, also, that if this correspondence was calculated for deception, the deception must have been understood and agreed upon by all parties concerned—for otherwise you have a conspiracy among persons who are at cross purposes with one another—consequently, the conspiracy, if this be a branch of it, is a conspiracy of thousands and ten thousands, from one end of the kingdom to the other, who are all guilty, if any of the prisoners are guilty. Upward of forty thousand persons, upon the low-

[49] The reader is already aware that Mr. Erskine had served successively in the navy and army, before studying for the law.

est calculation, must alike be liable to the pains and penalties of the law, and hold their lives as tenants at will of the ministers of the Crown. In whatever aspect, therefore, this prosecution is regarded, new difficulties and new uncertainties and terrors surround it.

The next thing in order which we have to look at, is the convention at Edinburgh. It appears that a letter had been written by Mr. Skirving,[50] who was connected with reformers in Scotland, proceeded avowedly upon the Duke of Richmond's plan, proposing that there should be a convention from the societies assembled at Edinburgh. Now you will recollect, in the opening, that the Attorney General considered all the great original sin of this conspiracy and treason to have originated with the societies in London; that the country societies were only tools in their hands, and that the Edinburgh Convention was the commencement of their projects. And yet it plainly appears that this convention originated from neither of the London societies, but had its beginning at Edinburgh, where, just before, a convention had been sitting for the reform in Parliament, attended by the principal persons in Scotland. And, surely, without adverting to the nationality so peculiar to the people of that country, it is not at all suspicious that, since they were to hold a meeting for similar objects, they should make use of the same style for their association; and that their deputies should be called delegates, when delegates had attended the other convention from all the counties, and whom they were every day looking at in their streets, in the course of the very same year that Skirving wrote his letter on the subject. The views of the Corresponding Society, as they regarded this convention, and consequently the views of the prisoner, must be collected from the written instructions to the delegates, unless they can be falsified by matter which is collateral. If I constitute an agent, I am bound by what he does, but always with this limitation—for what he does within the scope of his agency. If I constitute an agent to buy horses for me, and he commits high treason, it will not, I hope, be argued, that I am to be hanged. If I constitute an agent for any business that can be stated, and he goes beyond his instructions, he must answer for himself beyond their limits; for beyond them he is not my representative. The acts done, therefore, at the Scotch Convention, whatever may be their quality, are evidence to show that, in point of fact, a certain number of people got together, and did any thing you choose to call illegal. But, as far as it concerns me, if I am not present, you are limited by my instructions, and have not advanced a single step upon your journey to convict me. The instructions to Skirving have been read, and speak for themselves; they are strictly legal, and pursue the avowed object of the society; and it will be for the Solicitor General to point out, in his reply, any counter or secret instructions, or any collateral conduct, contradictory of the good faith with which they were written. The instructions are in these words: "The delegates are instructed, on the part of this society, to assist in bringing forward and supporting any *constitutional* measure for procuring a real representation of the Commons of Great Britain." What do you say, gentlemen, to this language? How are men to express themselves who desire a constitutional reform? The object and the mode of effecting it were equally legal. This is most obvious from the conduct of the Parliament of Ireland, acting under directions from England; they passed the Convention Bill, and made it only a misdemeanor, knowing that, by the law as it stood, it was no misdemeanor at all. Whether this statement may meet with the approbation of others, I care not; I know the fact to be so, and I maintain that you can not prove upon the convention which met at Edinburgh, and which is charged to-day with high treason, one thousandth part of what, at last, worked up government in Ireland to the pitch of voting it a misdemeanor.

(3.) The second Edinburgh Convention.

Did not originate in London influence.

The prisoners not responsible for its doings, except as they instructed their delegates.

Gentlemen, I am not vindicating any thing that can promote disorder in the country, but I am maintaining that the worst possible disorder that can fall upon a country is, when subjects are deprived of the sanction of clear and unambiguous laws. If wrong is committed, let punishment follow according to the measure of that wrong. If men are turbulent, let them be visited by the laws according to the measure of their turbulency. If they write libels upon government, let them be punished according to the quality of those libels. But you must not, and will not, because the stability of the monarchy is an important concern to the nation, confound the nature and distinctions of crimes, and pronounce that the life of the Sovereign has been invaded, because the privileges of the people have been, perhaps, irregularly and hotly asserted. You will not, to give security to government, repeal the most sacred laws instituted for our protection, and which are, indeed, the only consideration for our submitting at all to government. If the plain letter of the statute of Edward III. applies to the conduct of the prisoners, let it, in God's name, be applied; but let neither their conduct, nor the law that is to judge it, be tortured by construction; nor suffer the transaction, from whence you are to form a dispassionate conclusion of intention, to be magnified by scandalous epithets, nor overwhelmed in an undistinguishable mass of matter, in which you may be lost and bewildered, having missed the only parts which could have furnished a clue to a just or rational judgment.

Laws rendered ambiguous by construction the worst of evils.

[50] The Secretary to the Edinburgh Convention. He, together with Maurice Margaret and Joseph Gerald (two of the London delegates), was arrested at Edinburgh, in 1794, for sedition: all of them were found guilty, and sentenced to fourteen years' transportation. All his papers were seized by the magistrate at the same time.

Gentlemen, this religious regard for the liberty of the subject against constructive treason is well illustrated by Dr. Johnson, the great author of our English Dictionary, a man remarkable for his love of order, and for high principles of government, but who had the wisdom to know that the great end of government, in all its forms, is the security of liberty and life under the law. This man, of masculine mind, though disgusted at the disorder which Lord George Gordon created, felt a triumph in his acquittal, and exclaimed, as we learn from Mr. Boswell, "I hate Lord George Gordon, but I am glad he was not convicted of this constructive treason; for though I hate him, I love my country and myself." This extraordinary man no doubt remembered, with Lord Hale, that, when the law is broken down, injustice knows no bounds, but runs as far as the wit and invention of accusers, or the detestation of persons accused, will carry it. You will pardon this almost perpetual recurrence to these considerations; but the present is a season when I have a right to call upon you by every thing sacred in humanity and justice—by every principle which ought to influence the heart of man, to consider the situation in which I stand before you. I stand here for a poor, unknown, unprotected individual, charged with a design to subvert the government of the country and the dearest rights of its inhabitants—a charge which has collected against him a force sufficient to crush to pieces any private man. The whole weight of the Crown presses upon him; Parliament has been sitting upon *ex parte* evidence for months together; and rank and property is associated, from one end of the kingdom to the other, to avert the supposed consequences of the treason.[51] I am making no complaint of this. But surely it is an awful summons to impartial attention; surely it excuses me for so often calling upon your integrity and firmness to do equal justice between the Crown, so supported, and an unhappy prisoner, so unprotected.

Views of Dr. Johnson.

Hardship of the prisoner's situation.

Gentlemen, I declare that I am utterly astonished, on looking at the clock, to find how long I have been speaking; and that, agitated and distressed as I am, I have yet strength enough remaining for the remainder of my duty. At every peril to my health it shall be exerted; for even if this cause should miscarry, I know I shall have justice done me for the honesty of my intentions. But what is that to the public and posterity? What is it to them, when it is plain, if this evidence can convict of high treason, that no man can be said to have a life which is his own? For how can he possibly know by what engines it may be snared, or from what unknown sources it may be attacked and overpowered? Such a monstrous precedent would be as ruinous to the King as to his subjects. We are in a crisis of our affairs, which, putting justice out of the question, calls in sound policy for the greatest prudence and moderation. At a time when other nations are disposed to subvert their establishments, let it be our wisdom to make the subject feel the practical benefits of our own: let us seek to bring good out of evil. The distracted inhabitants of the world will fly to us for sanctuary, driven out of their countries from the dreadful consequences of not attending to seasonable reforms in government—victims to the folly of suffering corruptions to continue till the whole fabric of society is dissolved and tumbles into ruin. Landing upon our shores, they will feel the blessing of security, and they will discover in what it consists. They will read this trial, and their hearts will palpitate at your decision. They will say to one another—and their voices will reach to the ends of the earth—"May the Constitution of England endure forever! the sacred and yet remaining sanctuary for the oppressed! Here, and here only, the lot of man is cast in security! What though authority, established for the ends of justice, may lift itself up against it! What though the House of Commons itself should make an *ex parte* declaration of guilt! What though every species of art should be employed to entangle the opinions of the people, which in other countries would be inevitable destruction; yet, in England, in enlightened England, all this will not pluck a hair from the head of innocence. The jury will still look steadfastly to the law, as the great polar star, to direct them in their course. As prudent men, they will set no example of disorder, nor pronounce a verdict of censure on authority, or of approbation or disapprobation beyond their judicial province; but, on the other hand, they will make no political sacrifice, but deliver a plain, honest man from the toils of injustice." When your verdict is pronounced, this will be the judgment of the world; and if any among ourselves are alienated in their affections to government, nothing will be so likely to reclaim them. They will say, Whatever we have lost of our control in Parliament, we have yet a sheet-anchor remaining to hold the vessel of the state amid contending storms. We have still, thank God, a sound administration of justice secured to us, in the independence of the judges, in the rights of enlightened juries, and in the integrity of the bar—ready at all times, and upon every possible occasion, whatever may be the consequences to themselves, to stand forward in defense of the meanest man in England, when brought for judgment before the laws of the country.

Motives for impartial justice at the present crisis.

To return to this Scotch convention. Their papers were all seized by government. What their proceedings were, they best know; we can

[51] The following are the facts here referred to. On the 12th of April, 1794, the King sent a message to Parliament announcing the existence of seditious societies. The prisoners were arrested, and the Habeas Corpus Act was suspended on the 24th of the same month. The papers found on the premises of Hardy and others were published by way of vindication, and the subject was long under discussion in Parliament. Loyal associations to support the government were formed, in the mean time, in various places.

only see what parts they choose to show us. But from what we have seen, does any man seriously believe that this meeting at Edinburgh meant to assume and to maintain by force all the functions and authorities of the state? Is the thing within the compass of human belief? If a man were offered a dukedom and twenty thousand pounds a year for trying to believe it, he might *say* he believed it—as what will not man say for gold and honors?—but he never, in fact, could believe that this Edinburgh meeting was a Parliament for Great Britain. How, indeed, could he, from the proceedings of a few peaceable, unarmed men, discussing, in a constitutional manner, the means of obtaining a reform in Parliament; and who, to maintain the club, or whatever you choose to call it, collected a little money from people who were well disposed to the cause; a few shillings one day, and perhaps as many pence another? I think, as far as I could reckon it up, when the report from this great committee of supply was read to you, I counted that there had been raised, in the first session of this Parliament, fifteen pounds, from which, indeed, you must deduct two bad shillings, which are literally noticed in the account. Is it to be endured, gentlemen, that men should gravely say, that this body assumed to itself the offices of Parliament? that a few harmless people, who sat, as they profess, to obtain a full representation of the people, were themselves, even in their own imaginations, the complete representation which they sought for? Why should they sit from day to day to consider how they might obtain what they had already got? If their object was a universal representation of the whole people, how is it credible they could suppose that universal representation to exist in themselves—in the representatives of a few societies, instituted to obtain it for the country at large? If they were themselves the nation, why should the language of every resolution be, that reason ought to be their grand engine for the accomplishment of their object, and should be directed to convince the nation to speak to Parliament in a voice that must be heard? The proposition, therefore, is too gross to cram down the throats of the English people, and this is the prisoner's security. Here, again, he feels the advantage of our free administration of justice. This proposition, on which so much depends, is not to be reasoned out on parchment, to be delivered privately to magistrates for private judgment. No. He has the privilege of appealing loud (as he now appeals by me) to an enlightened assembly, full of eyes, and ears, and intelligence, where speaking to a jury is, in a manner, speaking to a nation at large, and flying for sanctuary to its universal justice.

Nothing treasonable in the Edinburgh Convention.

Gentlemen, the very work of Mr. Paine, under the banners of which this supposed rebellion was set on foot, refutes the charge it is brought forward to support. Mr. Paine, in his preface, and throughout his whole book, reprobates the use of force against the most evil governments, and the contrary was never imputed to him. If his book had been written in pursuance of the design of force and rebellion, with which it is now sought to be connected, he would, like the prisoners, have been charged with an overt act of high treason; but such a proceeding was never thought of. Mr. Paine was indicted [in 1792] for a misdemeanor, and the misdemeanor was argued to consist not in the falsehood that a nation has no right to choose or alter its government, but in seditiously exciting the nation, without cause, to exercise that right. A learned Lord [Lord Chief Baron Macdonald] now on this bench, addressed the jury as Attorney General upon this principle. His language was this: "The question is not what the people have a right to do, for the people are, undoubtedly, the foundation and origin of all government. But the charge is, for seditiously calling upon the people, without cause or reason, to exercise a right which would be sedition, supposing the right to be in them; for though the people might have a right to do the thing suggested, and though they are not excited to the doing it by force and rebellion, yet, as the suggestion goes to unsettle the state, the propagation of such doctrines is seditious." There is no other way, undoubtedly, of describing that charge. I am not here entering into the application of it to Mr. Paine, whose counsel I was, and who has been tried already. To say that the people have a right to change their government, is, indeed, a truism. Every body knows it, and they exercised the right [in 1688], otherwise the King could not have had his establishment among us. If, therefore, I stir up individuals to oppose by force the general will, seated in the government, it may be treason; but to induce changes in a government, by exposing to a whole nation its errors and imperfections, can have no bearing upon such an offense. The utmost which can be made of it is a misdemeanor, and that, too, depending wholly upon the judgment which the jury may form of the intention of the writer. The courts for a long time, indeed, assumed to themselves the province of deciding upon this intention, as a matter of law, conclusively inferring it from the act of publication. I say the courts *assumed* it, though it was not the doctrine of Lord Mansfield, but handed down to him from the precedents of judges before his time. But even in that case, though the publication was the crime, not, as in this case, the intention, and though the quality of the thing charged, when not rebutted by evidence for the defendant, had so long been considered to be a legal inference, yet the Legislature, to support the province of the jury, and in tenderness for liberty, has lately altered the law upon this important subject.[52] If, therefore, we were not assembled, as we are, to consider of the existence of high treason against the King's life, but only of a misdemeanor for seditiously disturbing his

Paine, whose principles they avowed, was opposed to violence.

It is not treason to propose changes in the government.

[52] See the concluding remarks on Mr. Erskine's speech upon the rights of juries, page 683.

title and establishment, by the proceedings for a reform in Parliament, I should think the Crown, upon the very principle which, under the libel law, must now govern such a trial, quite as distant from its mark. Because, in my opinion, there is no way by which his Majesty's title can more firmly be secured, or by which (above all, in our times) its permanency can be better established, than by promoting a more full and equal representation of the people, by peaceable means; and by what other means has it been sought, in this instance, to be promoted?

The conduct of the convention when broken up, shows that violence was not intended.

Gentlemen, when the members of this convention were seized, did they attempt resistance? Did they insist upon their privileges as subjects under the laws, or as a Parliament enacting laws for others? If they had said or done any thing to give color to such an idea, there needed no spies to convict them. The Crown could have given ample indemnity for evidence from among themselves. The societies consisted of thousands and thousands of persons, some of whom, upon any calculation of human nature, might have been produced. The delegates who attended the meetings could not be supposed to have met with a different intention from those who sent them; and if the answer to that be, that the constituents are involved in the guilt of their representatives, we get back to the monstrous position which I observed you before to shrink back from, with visible horror, when I stated it; namely, the involving in the fate and consequence of this single trial *every man* who corresponded with these societies, or who, as a member of societies in any part of the kingdom, consented to the meeting which was assembled, or which was in prospect. But I thank God I have nothing to fear from such hydras, when I see before me such just and honorable men to hold the balance of justice.

Gentlemen, the dissolution of this Parliament speaks as strong a language as its conduct when sitting. How was it dissolved? When the magistrates entered, Mr. Skirving was in the chair, which he refused to leave. He considered and asserted his conduct to be legal, and therefore informed the magistrate he must exercise his authority, that the dispersion might appear to be involuntary, and that the subject, disturbed in his rights, might be entitled to his remedy. The magistrate on this took Mr. Skirving by the shoulder, who immediately obeyed; the chair was quitted in a moment, and this great Parliament broken up! What was the effect of all this proceeding at the time, when whatever belonged to it must have been best understood? Were any of the parties indicted for high treason? Were they indicted even for a breach of the peace in holding the convention? None of these things. The law of Scotland, arbitrary as it is, was to be disturbed to find a *name* for their offense,[53] and the rules of trial to be violated, to convict them. They were denied their challenges to their jurors, and other irregularities were introduced, so as to be the subject of complaint in the House of Commons.

Apology for the warmth of the prisoners when the Edinburgh reformers were tried and sentenced.

Gentlemen, in what I am saying I am not standing up to vindicate all that was published during these proceedings, more especially those things which were written in consequence of the trials I have just alluded to.[54] But allowance must be made for a state of heat and irritation. They saw men whom they believed to be persecuted for what they believed to be innocent. They saw them the victims of sentences which many would consider as equivalent to, if not worse than, judgment of treason[55]—sentences which, at all events, had never existed before, and such as I believe never will again with impunity. But since I am on the subject of *intention*, I shall conduct myself with the same moderation which I have been prescribing. I will cast no aspersions, but shall content myself with lamenting that these judgments were productive of consequences which rarely follow from authority discreetly exercised. How easy is it, then, to dispose of as much of the evidence as consumed half a day in the anathemas against the Scotch judges! It appears that they came to various resolutions concerning them; some good, some bad, and all of them irregular. Among others, they compare them to Jefferies, and wish that they who imitate his example may meet his fate. What then? Irreverent expressions against judges are not acts of high treason! If they had assembled round the Court of Justiciary, and hanged them in the execution of their offices, it would not have been treason within the statute. I am no advocate for disrespect to judges, and think that it is dangerous to the public order; but, putting aside the insult upon the judges now in authority, the reprobation of Jefferies is no libel, but an awful and useful memento to wicked men. Lord Chief Justice Jefferies denied the privilege of English law to an innocent man. He refused it to Sir Thomas Armstrong,[56] who in vain pleaded in bar of his outlawry that he was out of the realm when he was exacted (an ob-

Defense of their language in respect to Jefferies.

[53] They were indicted for *leasing making*, by which was meant stirring up sedition.

[54] The London Societies took a deep interest in Skirving and the other Scottish reformers, who had been condemned to transportation for fourteen years to Botany Bay. They spoke of this in strong terms of indignation, as it deserved, and this was now made their crime.

[55] The *legality* of the sentence in the case of these men, as well as of Muir and Palmer, has been called in question; it being maintained by many that outlawry without transportation was all that the law allowed.

[56] Sir Thomas Armstrong was seized in Holland for having been engaged in Monmouth's conspiracy against James II. in 1683; and as it was apprehended that sufficient evidence could not be procured to obtain a verdict against him even from the subservient juries of that time, he was condemned and executed without a trial, under the pretense that he was not entitled to claim one, as he had not surrendered himself after outlawry.

jection so clear that it was lately taken for granted in the case of Mr. Purefoy). The daughter of this unfortunate person, a lady of honor and quality, came publicly into court to supplicate for her father, and what were the effects of her supplications, and of the law in the mouth of the prisoner? "Sir Thomas Armstrong," said Jefferies, "you may amuse yourself as much as you please with the idea of your innocence, but you are to be hanged next Friday;" and upon the natural exclamation of a daughter at this horrible outrage against her parent, he said, "Take that woman out of court;" which she answered by a prayer that God Almighty's judgments might light upon him. Gentlemen, they did light upon him; and when, after his death, which speedily followed this transaction, the matter was brought before the House of Commons, under that glorious Revolution which is asserted throughout the proceedings before you, the judgment against Sir Thomas Armstrong was declared to be a murder under color of justice! Sir Robert Sawyer, the Attorney General, was expelled the House of Commons for his misdemeanor in refusing the writ of error; and the executors of Jefferies were commanded to make compensation to the widow and the daughter of the deceased. These are great monuments of justice; and although I by no means approve of harsh expressions against authority which tend to weaken the holdings of society, yet let us not go beyond the mark in our restraints, nor suppose that men are dangerously disaffected to the government, because they feel a sort of pride and exultation in events which constitute the dignity and glory of their country.

The treatment of the Scottish reformers very generally condemned.

Gentlemen, this resentment against the proceedings of the courts in Scotland was not confined to those who were the objects of them, It was not confined even to the friends of a reform in Parliament. A benevolent public, in both parts of the island, joined them in the complaint; and a gentleman of great moderation, and a most inveterate enemy to parliamentary reform, as thinking it not an improvement of the government, but nevertheless a lover of his country and its insulted justice, made the convictions of the delegates the subject of a public inquiry. I speak of my friend Mr. William Adam, who brought these judgments of the Scotch judges before the House of Commons, arraigned them as contrary to law, and proposed to reverse them by the authority of Parliament. Let it not, then, be matter of wonder that these poor men, who were the immediate victims of this injustice, and who saw their brethren expelled from their country by an unprecedented and questionable judgment, should feel like men on the subject, and express themselves as they felt.

Proof from the conduct of the accused that reform by force was not intended.

Gentlemen, amid the various distresses and embarrassments which attend my present situation, it is a great consolation that I have marked, from the beginning, your vigilant attention and your capacity to understand; it is, therefore, with the utmost confidence that I ask you a few plain questions, arising out of the whole of these Scotch proceedings. In the first place, then, do you believe it to be possible that, if these men had really projected the convention as a traitorous usurpation of the authorities of Parliament, they would have invited the Friends of the People, in Frith Street, to assist them, when they knew that this society was determined not to seek the reform of the Constitution but by means that were constitutional, and from whom they could neither hope for support nor concealment of evil purposes? I ask you, next, if their objects had been traitorous, would they have given them, without disguise or color, to the public and to the government in every common newspaper? And yet it is so far from being a charge against them that they concealed their objects by hypocrisy or guarded conduct, that I have been driven to admit the justice of the complaint against them, for unnecessary inflammation and exaggeration. I ask you, further, whether, if the proceedings thus published and exaggerated had appeared to government, who knew every thing belonging to them, in the light they represent them to you to-day, they could possibly have slept over them with such complete indifference and silence? For it is notorious that after this convention had been held at Edinburgh; after, in short, every thing had been said, written, and transacted, on which I am now commenting, and after Mr. Paine's book had been for above a year in universal circulation—ay, up to the very day when Mr. Grey gave notice, in the House of Commons, of the intention of the Friends of the People for a reform in Parliament, there was not even a single indictment on the file for a misdemeanor; but, from that moment, when it was seen that the cause was not beat down or abandoned, the Proclamation made its appearance, and all the proceedings that followed had their birth. I ask you, lastly, gentlemen, whether it be in human nature, that a few unprotected men, conscious, in their own minds, that they had been engaged and detected in a detestable rebellion to cut off the King, to destroy the administration of justice, and to subvert the whole fabric of the government, should turn round upon their country, whose ruin they had projected, and whose most obvious justice attached on them, complaining, forsooth, that their delegates, taken by magistrates in the very act of high treason, had been harshly and illegally interrupted in a meritorious proceeding? The history of mankind never furnished an instance, nor ever will, of such extravagant, preposterous, and unnatural conduct! No, no, gentlemen. All their hot blood was owing to their firm persuasion, dictated by conscious innocence, that the conduct of their delegates had been legal, and might be vindicated against the magistrates who obstructed them. In that they might be mistaken; I am not arguing that point at present. If they are hereafter indicted for a misdemeanor, and I am counsel in that cause, I will then tell you what I think of it. Sufficient unto the day is the good or evil thereof. It is sufficient for the present one, that the legality or illegality of the business has no relation to the crime that it is imputed to the prisoner.

(4.) The sending of delegates to France by the two London societies.

The next matter that is alleged against the authors of the Scotch Convention, and the societies which supported it, is their having sent addresses of friendship to the Convention of France. These addresses are considered to be a decisive proof of republican combination, verging closely in themselves upon an overt act of treason. Gentlemen, if the dates of these addresses are attended to, which come no lower down than November, 1792, we have only to lament that they were but the acts of private subjects, and that they were not sanctioned by the state itself. The French nation, about that period, under their new Constitution, or under their new anarchy—call it which you will—were, nevertheless, most anxiously desirous of maintaining peace with this country. But the King was advised to withdraw his embassador from France, upon the approaching catastrophe of its most unfortunate Prince—an event which, however to be deplored, was no justifiable cause of offense to Great Britain. France desired nothing but the regeneration of her own government; and if she mistook the road to her prosperity, what was that to us? But it was alleged against her in Parliament, that she had introduced spies among us, and held correspondence with disaffected persons, for the destruction of our Constitution. This was the charge of our minister, and it was, therefore, considered just and necessary, for the safety of the country, to hold France at arm's length, and to avoid the very contagion of contact with her at the risk of war. But, gentlemen, this charge against France was thought by many to be supported by no better proofs than those against the prisoner. In the public correspondence of the embassador from the French King, and upon his death, as minister from the Convention, with his Majesty's Secretary of State, documents which lie upon the table of the House of Commons, and which may be made evidence in the cause, the executive council repelled with indignation all the imputations, which to this very hour are held out as the vindications of quarrel. "If there be such persons in England," says Monsieur Chauvelin, "has not England laws to punish them? France disavows them—such men are not Frenchmen." The same correspondence conveys the most solemn assurances of friendship down to the very year 1792, a period subsequent to all the correspondence and addresses complained of. Whether these assurances were faithful, or otherwise—whether it would have been prudent to have depended on them, or otherwise—whether the war was advisable or unadvisable, are questions over which we have no jurisdiction. I only desire to bring to your recollection, that a man may be a friend to the rights of humanity and to the imprescriptible rights of social man, which is now a term of derision and contempt—that he may feel to the very soul for a nation beset by the sword of despots, and yet be a lover of his own country and its Constitution.

France was then at peace with England.

Mr. Burke publicly expressed his sympathy with the Americans though in arms against England.

Gentlemen, the same celebrated person, of whom I have had occasion to speak so frequently, is the best and brightest illustration of this truth. Mr. Burke, indeed, went a great deal further than requires to be pressed into the present argument. He maintained the cause of justice and of truth against all the perverted authority and rash violence of his country, and expressed the feelings of a Christian and a patriot in the very heat of the American war—boldly holding forth our victories as defeats, and our successes as calamities and disgraces. "It is not instantly," said Mr. Burke, "that I can be brought to rejoice when I hear of the slaughter and captivity of long lists of those names which have been familiar to my ears from my infancy, and to rejoice that they have fallen under the sword of strangers, whose barbarous appellations I scarcely know how to pronounce. The glory acquired at the White Plains by Colonel Rhalle has no charms for me; and I fairly acknowledge that I have not yet learned to delight in finding Fort Knyphausen in the heart of the British dominions."[57] If this had been said or written by Mr. Yorke at Sheffield, or by any other member of these societies, heated with wine at the Globe Tavern, it would have been trumpeted forth as decisive evidence of a rebellious spirit, rejoicing in the downfall of his country. Yet the great author, from whose writings I have borrowed, approved himself to be the friend of this nation at that calamitous crisis, and had it pleased God to open the understandings of our rulers, his wisdom might have averted the storms that are now thickening around us. We must not, therefore, be too severe in our strictures upon the opinions and feelings of men as they regard such mighty public questions. The interests of a nation may often be one thing, and the interests of its government another; but the interests of those who hold government for the hour is at all times different from either. At the time many of the papers before you were circulated on the subject of the war with France, many of the best and wisest men in this kingdom began to be driven by our situation to these melancholy reflections. Thousands of persons, the most firmly attached to the principles of our Constitution, and who never were members of any of these societies, considered, and still consider, Great Britain as the aggressor against France. They considered, and still consider, that she had a right to

Others may have similar views respecting the French without any treasonable designs.

[57] See Mr. Burke's letter to the Sheriff of Bristol. Colonel Rhalle was a Hessian officer, who distinguished himself at the battle of White Plains, in November, 1776. A few days after, General Knyphausen, a German officer in the British service, led the way in attacking Fort Washington, on the Hudson, a little above New York; and from this circumstance, probably, his name was given to the fort by the British while it remained in their possession.

choose a government for herself, and that it was contrary to the first principles of justice, and, if possible, still more repugnant to the genius of our own free Constitution, to combine with despots for her destruction. And who knows but that the external pressure upon France may have been the cause of that unheard-of state of society which we complain of? Who knows whether, driven as she has been to exertions beyond the ordinary vigor of a nation, she has not thus gained that unnatural and giant strength which threatens the authors of it with perdition? These are melancholy considerations, but they may reasonably and, at all events, lawfully be entertained. We owe obedience to government in our actions, but surely our opinions are free.

(5.) Proposal for a convention in England.

Gentlemen, pursuing the order of time, we are arrived at length at the proposition to hold another convention, which, with the supposed support of it by force, are the only overt acts of high treason charged upon this record. For, strange as it may appear, there is no charge whatever before you of any one of those acts or writings, the evidence of which consumed so many days in reading, and which has already nearly consumed my strength in only passing them in review before you. If every line and letter of all the writings I have been commenting upon were admitted to be traitorous machinations, and if the convention in Scotland was an open rebellion, it is conceded to be foreign to the present purpose, unless as such criminality in them might show the *views* and *objects* of the persons engaged in them. On that principle only the court has over and over again decided the evidence of them to be admissible; and on the same principle I have illustrated them in their order as they happened, that I might lead the prisoner in your view up to the very point and moment when the treason is supposed to have burst forth into the overt act for which he is arraigned before you.

All the treason to be found here, if any where.

The transaction respecting this second convention, which constitutes the principal, or, more properly, the only overt act in the indictment, lies in the narrowest compass, and is clouded with no ambiguity. I admit freely every act which is imputed to the prisoner, and listen not so much with fear as with curiosity and wonder to the treason sought to be connected with it.

Hardy's letter to the Constitutional Society.

You will recollect, that the first motion toward the holding of a second convention originated in a letter to the prisoner from a country correspondent, in which the legality of the former was vindicated, and its dispersion lamented. This letter was answered on the 27th of March, 1794, and was read to you in the Crown's evidence in these words:

"March 27, 1794.

"CITIZEN,—I am directed by the London Corresponding Society to transmit the following resolutions to the Society for Constitutional Information, and to request the sentiments of that society respecting the important measures which the present juncture of affairs seems to require.

"The London Corresponding Society conceives that the moment is arrived when a full and explicit declaration is necessary from all the friends of freedom—whether the late illegal and unheard-of prosecutions and sentences[58] shall determine us to abandon our cause, or shall excite us to pursue a radical reform, with an ardor proportioned to the magnitude of the object, and with a zeal as distinguished on our own parts as the treachery of others in the same glorious cause is notorious. The Society for Constitutional Information is, therefore, required to determine whether or no they will be ready, when called upon, to act in conjunction with this and other societies to obtain a fair representation of the people—whether they concur with us in seeing the necessity of a speedy convention, for the purpose of obtaining, in a constitutional and legal method, a redress of those grievances under which we at present labor, and which can only be effectually removed by a full and fair representation of the people of Great Britain. The London Corresponding Society can not but remind their friends that the present crisis demands all the prudence, unanimity, and vigor, that may or can be exerted by MEN and BRITONS; nor do they doubt but that manly firmness and consistency will finally, and they believe shortly, terminate in the full accomplishment of all their wishes.

"I am, fellow-citizen,
"(In my humble measure),
"A friend to the rights of man,
"(Signed) T. HARDY, *Secretary*."

They then resolve that there is no security for the continuance of any right but in equality of *laws*—not in equality of *property*—the ridiculous bugbear by which you are to be frightened into injustice; on the contrary, throughout every part of the proceedings, and most emphatically in Mr. Yorke's speech (so much relied on), the beneficial subordinations of society, the security of property, and the prosperity of the landed and commercial interests, are held forth as the very objects to be attained by the reform in the representation which they sought for.

The object of this was the same as of the former convention, which was confessedly not treasonable.

In examining this first moving toward a second convention, the first thing to be considered is, what reason there is, from the letter I have just read to you, or from any thing that appears to have led to it, to suppose that a different sort of convention was projected from that [at Edinburgh] which had been before assembled and dispersed. The letter says, *another* British Convention, and it describes the same objects as the first. Compare all the papers for the calling this second convention with those for assembling the first, and you will find no difference, except that they mixed with them extraneous and libelous matter arising obviously from the irritation produced by the sailing of the transports with their brethren condemned to exile.

[58] Those of Muir and others, mentioned above.

These papers have already been considered, and separated, as they ought to be, from the charge.

Conference between the two societies.

I will now lay before you all the remaining operations of this formidable conspiracy, up to the prisoner's imprisonment in the Tower. Mr. Hardy having received the letter just adverted to regarding a second convention, the Corresponding Society wrote the letter of the 27th of March, and which was found in his handwriting, and is published in the first Report, page 11. This letter, inclosing the resolutions they had come to upon the subject, was considered by the Constitutional Society on the next day, the 28th of March, the ordinary day for their meeting, when they sent an answer to the Corresponding Society, informing them that they had received their communication—that they heartily concurred with them in the objects they had in view, and invited them to send a delegation of their members to confer with them on the subject.

The objects of their conference.

Now what were the objects they concurred in, and what was to be the subject of conference between the societies by their delegates? Look at the letter, which distinctly expresses its objects and the means by which they sought to effect them. Had these poor men (too numerous to meet all together, and therefore renewing the cause of parliamentary reform by delegation from the societies) any reason to suppose that they were involving themselves in the pains of treason, and that they were compassing the King's death, when they were redeeming (as they thought) his authority from probable downfall and ruin? Had treason been imputed to the delegates before? Had the imagining the death of the King ever been suspected by any body? Or, when they were prosecuted for misdemeanors, was the prosecution considered as an indulgence conferred upon men whose lives had been forfeited? And is it to be endured, then, in this free land—made free, too, by the virtue of our forefathers, who placed the King upon his throne to maintain this freedom—that forty or fifty thousand people, in the different parts of the kingdom, assembling in their little societies to spread useful knowledge, and to diffuse the principles of liberty—which the more widely they are spread, the surer is the condition of our free government—are in a moment, without warning, without any law or principle to warrant it, and without precedent or example, to be branded as traitors, and to be decimated as victims for punishment! The Constitutional Society having answered the letter of the 27th of March, in the manner I stated to you, committees from each of the two societies were appointed to confer together. The Constitutional Society appointed Mr. Joyce, Mr. Kidd, Mr. Wardle, and Mr. Holcroft, all indicted; and Mr. Sharpe, the celebrated engraver, not indicted, but examined as a witness by the Crown. Five were appointed by the Corresponding Society to meet these gentlemen; namely, Mr. Baxter, Mr. Moore, Mr. Thelwall, and Mr. Hodgson, all indicted, and Mr. Lovatt, against whom the bill was thrown out. These gentlemen met at the house of Mr. Thelwall, on the 11th of April, 1794, and there published the resolutions already commented on, in conformity with the general objects of the two societies, expressed in the letter of the 27th of March, and agreed to continue to meet on Mondays and Thursdays for further conference on the subject. The first Monday was the 14th of April, of which we have heard so much, and no meeting was held on that day. The first Thursday was the 17th of April, but there was no meeting; the 21st of April was the second Monday, but there was still no meeting; the 24th of April was the second Thursday, when the five of the Corresponding Society attended, but, nobody coming to meet them from the other, nothing, of course, was transacted. On Monday, the 28th of April, three weeks after their first appointment, this bloody and impatient band of conspirators, seeing that a Convention Bill was in projection, and that Hessians were landing on our coasts, at last assembled themselves; and now we come to the point of action.[59] Gentlemen, they met; they shook hands with each other; they talked over the news and the pleasures of the day; they wished one another a good evening, and retired to their homes: it is in vain to hide it, they certainly did all these things. The same *alarming* scene was repeated on the three following days of meeting, and on Monday, May the 12th, would, but for the vigilance of government, have probably again taken place; but on that day Mr. Hardy was arrested, his papers seized, and the conspiracy which pervaded this devoted country was dragged into the face of day. To be serious, gentlemen, you have literally the whole of it before you in the meetings I have just stated; in which you find ten gentlemen, appointed by two peaceable societies, conversing upon the subject of a constitutional reform in Parliament, publishing the result of their deliberations, without any other arms than one supper-knife; which, when I come to the subject of arms, I will in form lay before you. Yet for this, and for this alone, you are asked to devote the prisoner before you, and his unfortunate associates, to the pains and penalties of death; and not to death alone, but to the eternal stigma and infamy of having conceived the detestable and horrible design of dissolving the government of

Difficulty of bringing it about.

Actual result.

59 A body of Hessian troops were landed on the Isle of Wight, from Germany, in 1794, in readiness for a projected expedition against France. The Opposition insisted that such an introduction of foreign troops, without the consent of Parliament, was illegal; but the motions declaratory of the illegality of the proceedings were negatived, and Mr. Pitt refused to countenance a Bill of Indemnity. This, though well intended by Mr. Pitt, was an unfortunate measure. Many considered it as designed to put down free discussion by force. The great evil was, that it gave an opening for rash men to mislead the people, and represent these troops as called in to enslave them. There is reason to believe that this was one main reason why some were induced to prepare pikes and other weapons.

their country, and of striking at the life of their Sovereign, who had never given offense to them, nor to any of his subjects.

No mention of arms when the arrests first took place.

Gentlemen, as a conspiracy of this formidable extension, which had no less for its object than the sudden annihilation of all the existing authorities of the country, and of every thing that supported them, could not be even gravely stated to have an existence, without contemplation of force to give it effect, it was absolutely necessary to impress upon the public mind, and to establish by formal evidence upon the present occasion, that such a force was actually in preparation. This most important and indispensable part of the cause was attended with insurmountable difficulties, not only from its being unfounded in fact, but because it had been expressly negatived by the whole conduct of government. For, although the motions of all these societies had been watched for two years together—though spies had regularly attended, and collected regular journals of their proceedings, yet when the first report was finished, and the Habeas Corpus Act suspended upon the foundation of the facts contained in it, there was not to be found, from one end of it to the other, even the insinuation of arms. I believe that this circumstance made a great impression upon all the thinking, dispassionate part of the public, and that the materials of the first report were thought to furnish but a slender argument to support such a total eclipse of liberty. No wonder, then, that the discovery of a pike, in the interval between the two reports, should have been highly estimated. I mean no reflections upon government, and only state the matter as a man of great wit very publicly reported it. He said that the discoverer, when he first beheld the long-looked-for pike, was transported beyond himself with enthusiasm and delight, and that he hung over the rusty instrument with all the raptures of a fond mother, who embraces her first-born infant, "and thanks her God for all her travail past."

(6.) Preparation of pikes. Views of the Sheffield reformers.

In consequence of this discovery, whoever might have the merit of it, and whatever the discoverer might have felt upon it, persons were sent by government (and properly sent) into all corners of the kingdom, to investigate the extent of the mischief. The fruit of this inquiry has been laid before you, and I pledge myself to sum up the evidence which you have had upon the subject, not by parts, or by general observations, but in the same manner as the court itself must sum it up to you, when it lays the whole body of the proof with fidelity before you. Notwithstanding all the declamations upon French anarchy, I think I may safely assert that it has been distinctly proved by the evidence that the Sheffield people were for universal representation in a British House of Commons. This appears to have been the general sentiment, with the exception of one witness, whose testimony makes the truth and *bona-fides* of the sentiments far more striking: the witness I allude to (George Widdison), whose evidence I shall state in its place, seems to be a plain, blunt, honest man, and, by-the-by, which must never be forgotten of any of them, the Crown's witness. I am not interested in the veracity of any of them; for (what I have frequently remarked) the Crown must take them for better for worse: it must support each witness, and the whole body of its evidence throughout. If you do not believe the whole of what is proved by a witness, what confidence can you have in part of it, or what part can you select to confide in? If you are deceived in part, who shall measure the boundaries of the deception? This man says he was at first for universal suffrage—Mr. Yorke had persuaded him, from all the books, that it was the best—but that he afterward saw reason to think otherwise, and was not for going the length of the Duke of Richmond; but that all the other Sheffield people were for the Duke's plan—a fact confirmed by the cross-examination of every one of the witnesses. You have, therefore, positively and distinctly, upon the universal authority of the evidence of the Crown, the people of Sheffield, who are charged as at the head of a republican conspiracy, proved to be associated on the very principles which, at different times, have distinguished the most eminent persons in this kingdom; and the charge made upon them, with regard to arms, is cleared up by the same universal testimony.

Reason for the preparation of these pikes.

You recollect that, at a meeting held upon the Castle-hill, there were two parties in the country; and it is material to attend to what these two parties were. In consequence of the King's proclamation,[60] a great number of honorable, zealous persons, who had been led by a thousand artifices to believe that there was a just cause of alarm in the country, took very extraordinary steps for support of the magistracy. The publicans were directed not to entertain persons who were friendly to a reform of Parliament; and alarms of change and of revolution pervaded the country, which became greater and greater as our ears were hourly assailed with the successive calamities of France. Others saw things in an opposite light, and considered that these calamities were made the pretext for extinguishing British liberty. Heart-burnings arose between the two parties; and some—I am afraid a great many—wickedly or ignorantly interposed in a quarrel which zeal had begun. The societies were disturbed in their meetings, and even the private dwellings of many of their members were illegally violated. It appears by the very evidence to the Crown, by which the cause must stand or fall, that many of the friends of reform were daily insulted, their houses threatened to be pulled

60 This proclamation was issued on the 21st of May, 1792, and was directed against seditious meetings, and publications. In support of this proclamation, associations were formed in many places to sustain the government, and the magistrates took very stringent measures, which were in some instances hasty and irritating.

down, and their peaceable meetings beset by pretended magistrates, without the process of the law. These proceedings naturally suggested the propriety of having arms for self-defense, the first and most unquestionable privilege of man, in or out of society, and expressly provided for by the very letter of English law. It was ingeniously put by the learned counsel, in the examination of a witness, that it was complained of among them that very little was sufficient to obtain a warrant from some magistrates, and that, therefore, it was as well to be provided for those who might have warrants as for those who had none. Gentlemen, I am too much exhausted to pursue or argue such a difference, even if it existed upon the evidence. If the societies in question (however mistakenly) considered their meetings to be legal, and the warrants to disturb them to be beyond the authority of the magistrate to grant, they had a right, at the peril of the legal consequences, to stand upon their defense; and it is no transgression of the law, much less high treason against the King, to resist his officers when they pass the bounds of their authority. So much for the general evidence of arms; and the first and last time that even the name of the prisoner is connected with the subject, is by a letter he received from a person of the name of Davison. I am anxious that this part of the case should be distinctly understood, and I will, therefore, bring back this letter to your attention. The letter is as follows:

Letter from Sheffield proposing to Hardy the preparation of pikes in London.

"FELLOW-CITIZEN,—The barefaced aristocracy of the present administration has made it necessary that we should be prepared to act on the defensive, against any attack they may command their newly-armed minions to make upon us. A plan has been hit upon, and, if encouraged sufficiently, will, no doubt, have the effect of furnishing a quantity of pikes to the patriots, great enough to make them formidable. The blades are made of steel, tempered and polished after an approved form. They may be fixed into any shafts (but *fir* ones are recommended) of the girt of the accompanying hoops at the top end, and about an inch more at the bottom.

"The blades and hoops (more than which can not properly be sent to any great distance) will be charged one shilling. Money to be sent with the orders.

"As the institution is in its infancy, immediate encouragement is necessary.

"Orders may be sent to the Secretary of the Sheffield Constitutional Society. [*Struck out.*]

"RICHARD DAVISON.

"Sheffield, April 24, 1794."

Gentlemen, you must recollect (for if it should escape you, it might make a great difference) that Davison directs the answer to this letter to be sent to Robert Moody at Sheffield, to prevent post-office suspicion; and that he also incloses in it a similar one which Mr. Hardy was to forward to Norwich, in order that the society at that place might provide pikes for themselves, in the same manner that Davison was recommending, through Hardy, to the people of London. Now what followed upon the prisoner's receiving this letter? It is in evidence by this very Moody, to whom the answer was to be sent, and who was examined as a witness by the Crown, that he *never received any answer to the letter;* and, although there was a universal seizure of papers, no such letter, nor any other, appeared to have been written. And, what is more, the letter to Norwich, from Davison, inclosed in his letter to Hardy, *was never forwarded*, but was found in his custody when he was arrested, three weeks afterward, folded up in the other, and unopened, as he received it. Good God! what is become of the humane sanctuary of English justice? Where is the sense and meaning of the term *provably* in the statute of King Edward, if such evidence can be received against an English subject on a trial for his life? If a man writes a letter to me about pikes, or about any thing else, can I help it? And is it evidence (except to acquit me of suspicion) when it appears that nothing is done upon it? Mr. Hardy never before corresponded with Davison—he never desired him to write to him—how, indeed, could he desire him, when his very existence was unknown to him? He never returned an answer—he never forwarded the inclosed to Norwich; he never even communicated the letter itself to his own society, although he was its secretary, which showed he considered it as the unauthorized officious correspondence of a private man; he never acted upon it at all, nor appears to have regarded it as dangerous or important, since he neither destroyed nor concealed it! Gentlemen, I declare I hardly know in what language to express my astonishment, that the Crown can ask you to shed the blood of the man at the bar upon such foundations. Yet this is the whole of the written evidence concerning arms; for the remainder of the plot rests for its foundation upon the parole evidence, the whole of which I shall pursue with precision, and not suffer a link of the chain to pass unexamined.

Hardy did not reply to the letter.

William Camage was the first witness. He swore that the Sheffield societies were frequently insulted, and threatened to be dispersed; so that the people in general thought it necessary to defend themselves against illegal attacks. The justices having officiously intruded themselves into their peaceable and legal meetings, they thought they had a right to be armed; but they did not claim this right under the law of nature, or by theories of government, but as ENGLISH SUBJECTS, under the government of ENGLAND; for they say in their paper, which has been read by the Crown that would condemn them, that they were entitled by the "BILL of RIGHTS" to be armed. Gentlemen, they state their title truly. The preamble of that statute enumerates the offenses of King James the Second; among the chief of which was his causing his subjects to be disarmed, and then our ancestors claim this violated right as their indefeasible inheritance. Let

Witnesses in respect to the preparation of pikes: Camage.

us, therefore, be cautious how we rush to the conclusion that men are plotting treason against the King, because they are asserting a right, the violation of which has been adjudged against a King to be treason against the people. And let us not suppose that English subjects are a banditti, for preparing to defend their legal liberties with pikes, because pikes may have been accidentally employed in another country to destroy both liberty and law. Camage says he was spoken to by this Davison about three dozen of pikes. What then? He is the Crown's witness, whom they offer to you as the witness of truth; and he started with horror at the idea of violence, and spoke with visible reverence for the King: saying, God forbid that he should touch him; but he, nevertheless, had a pike for himself. Indeed, the manliness with which he avowed it gave an additional strength to his evidence. "No doubt," says he, "I had a pike, but I would not have remained an hour a member of the society, if I had heard a syllable that it was in the contemplation of any body to employ pikes or any other arms against the King or the government. We meant to petition Parliament, through the means of the Convention of Edinburgh, thinking that the House of Commons would listen to this expression of the general sentiments of the people; for it had been thrown out, he said, in Parliament, that the people did not desire it themselves."

Broomhead. Mr. Broomhead, whose evidence I have already commented upon, a sedate, plain, sensible man, spoke also of his affection to the government, and of the insults and threats which had been offered to the people of Sheffield. He says, "I heard of arms on the Castle-hill, but it is fit this should be distinctly explained. A wicked hand-bill, to provoke and terrify the multitude, had been thrown about the town in the night, which caused agitation in the minds of the people; and it was then spoken of as being the right of every individual to have arms for defense; but there was no idea ever started of resisting, much less of attacking the government. I never heard of such a thing. I fear God," said the witness, "and honor the King; and would not have consented to send a delegate to Edinburgh but for peaceable and legal purposes."

Widdison. The next evidence upon the subject of arms is what is proved by Widdison, to which I beg your particular attention, because, if there be any reliance upon his testimony, it puts an end to every criminal imputation upon Davison, through whom, in the strange manner already observed upon, Hardy could alone be criminated. This man, Widdison, who was both a turner and a hair-dresser, and who dressed Davison's hair, and was his most intimate acquaintance, gives you an account of their most confidential conversations upon the subject of the pikes, when it is impossible that they could be imposing upon one another! He declares upon his solemn oath that Davison, without even the knowledge or authority of the Sheffield society, thinking that the same insults might be offered to the London societies, wrote the letter to Hardy, "*of his own head*," as the witness expressed it, and that he, Widdison, made the pike-shafts, to the number of a dozen and a half. Davison, he said, was his customer. He told him that people began to think themselves in danger, and he therefore made the handles of the pikes for sale, to the number of a dozen and a half, and one likewise for himself, without conceiving that he offended against any law. "I love the King," said Widdison, "as much as any man, and all that I associated with did the same. I would not have stayed with them if they had not. Mr. Yorke often told me privately, that he was for universal representation—and so were we all—THE DUKE OF RICHMOND'S PLAN WAS OUR ONLY OBJECT." This was the witness who was shown the Duke's letter, and spoke to it as being circulated and as the very creed of the societies. This evidence shows, beyond all doubt, the genuine sentiments of these people, because it consists of their most confidential communications with one another; and the only answer, therefore, that can possibly be given to it is, that the witnesses who deliver it are imposing upon the court. But this—as I have wearied you with reiterating—*the Crown can not say*. For, in that case, their whole proof falls to the ground together, since it is only from the same witnesses that the very existence of these pikes and their handles comes before us; and, if you suspect their evidence *in part*, for the reasons already given, it must be *in toto* rejected. My friend is so good as to furnish me with this further observation: that Widdison said he had often heard those who call themselves aristocrats say, that if an invasion of the country should take place, they would begin with destroying their enemies at home, that they might be unanimous in the defense of their country.

John Hill was next called. He is a cutler, and was employed by Davison to make the blades for the pikes. He saw the letter which was sent to Hardy, and knew that it was sent, lest there should be the same call for defense in London against illegal attacks upon the societies—for that at Sheffield they were daily insulted, and that the opposite party came to his own house, fired muskets under the door, and threatened to pull it down. He swears that they were, to a man, faithful to the King, and that the reform proposed was in the Commons House of Parliament. Hill.

John Edwards was called, further to connect the prisoner with the combination of force. Edwards. But so far from establishing it, he swore, upon his cross-examination, that his only reason for going to Hardy's was, that he wanted a pike for his own defense, without connection with Davison or with Sheffield, and without concert or correspondence with any body. He had heard, he said, of the violences at Sheffield, and of the pikes that had been made there for defense; that Hardy, on his application, showed him the letter, which, as has appeared, he never showed to any other person. This is the whole sum and substance of the evidence which applies to the charge of pikes, after the closest investigation, under the sanction, and by the aid of Parliament itself. It is evidence which, so far from establishing the fact, would have been a satisfactory answer to almost any testimony by which such a fact could have been supported; for in this unparalleled proceeding, the prisoner's counsel is driven by his duty to dwell upon the detail of the Crown's proofs, because the whole body of it is the completest answer to the indictment which even a free choice itself could have selected. It is further worthy of your attention, that as far as the evidence proceeds from these plain, natural sources, which the Crown was driven to for the necessary foundation of the proceedings before you, it has been simple, uniform, natural, and consistent. Whenever a different complexion was to be given to it, it was only through the medium of spies and informers, and of men, independently of their infamous trade, of the most abandoned and profligate characters.

Testimony of government spies and informers.

Before I advert to what has been sworn by this description of persons, I will give you a wholesome caution concerning them, and, having no eloquence of my own to enforce it, I will give it to you in the language of the same gentleman whose works are always seasonable, when moral or political lessons are to be rendered delightful. Look, then, at the picture of society, as Mr. Burke has drawn it, under the dominion of spies and informers. I say, under their *dominion*, for a resort to spies may, on occasions, be justifiable, and their evidence, when confirmed, may deserve implicit credit. But I say under the *dominion* of spies and informers, because the case of the Crown must stand *alone* upon their evidence, and upon their evidence, not only unconfirmed, but in direct contradiction to every witness not an informer or a spy, and in a case, too, where the truth, whatever it is, lies within the knowledge of forty or fifty thousand people. Mr. Burke says—I believe I can remember it without reference to the book—

Mr. Burke in respect to such men.

"A mercenary informer knows no distinction. Under such a system, the obnoxious people are slaves, not only to the government, but they live at the mercy of every individual; they are at once the slaves of the whole community, and of every part of it; and the worst and most unmerciful men are those on whose goodness they most depend.

"In this situation men not only shrink from the frowns of a stern magistrate, but are obliged to fly from their very species. The seeds of destruction are sown in civil intercourse and in social habitudes. The blood of wholesome kindred is infected. The tables and beds are surrounded with snares. All the means given by Providence to make life safe and comfortable, are perverted into instruments of terror and torment. This species of universal subserviency that makes the very servant who waits behind your chair the arbiter of your life and fortune, has such a tendency to degrade and abuse mankind, and to deprive them of that assured and liberal state of mind which alone can make us what we ought to be, that I avow to God, I would sooner bring myself to put a man to immediate death for opinions I disliked, and so to get rid of the man and his opinions at once, than to fret him with a feverish being, tainted with the jail distemper of a contagious servitude, to keep him above ground, an animated mass of putrefaction, corrupted himself, and corrupting all about him."[61]

Alexander.

Gentlemen, let me bring to your recollection the deportment of the first of this tribe, Mr. Alexander—who could not in half an hour even tell where he had lived, or why he had left his master. Does any man believe that he had forgotten these most recent transactions of his life? Certainly not—but his history would have undone his credit, and must, therefore, be concealed. He had lived with a linen-draper, whose address we could scarcely get from him, and they had parted because they had words. What were the words? We were not to be told that. He then went to a Mr. Killerby's, who agreed with him at twenty-five guineas a year. Why did he not stay there? He was obliged, it seems, to give up this lucrative agreement, because he was obliged to attend here as a witness. Gentlemen, Mr. Killerby lives only in Holborn; and was he obliged to give up a permanent engagement with a tradesman in Holborn, because he was obliged to be absent at the Old Bailey for five minutes in one single day? I asked him if he had told Mr. White, the Solicitor for the Treasury, who would not have been so cruel as to deprive a man of his bread, by keeping him upon attendance which might have been avoided by a particular notice. The thing spoke for itself—he had never told Mr. White. But had he ever told Mr. Killerby? For how else could he know that his place was inconsistent with his engagement upon this trial? No, he had never told him! How, then, did he collect that his place was inconsistent with his duty here? This question never received any answer. You saw how he dealt with it, and how he stood stammering, not daring to lift up his countenance in any direction—confused—disconcerted—and confounded.

(7.) Story about knives. Mr. Groves.

Driven from the accusation upon the subject of pikes, and even from the very color of accusation, and knowing that nothing was to be done without the proof of arms, we have got this miserable, solitary knife, held up to us as the engine which was to destroy the Constitution of this country; and Mr. Groves, an Old Bailey solicitor, employed as a spy upon the occasion, has been selected to give probability to this monstrous absurdity, by his *respectable* evidence. I understand that this same gentleman has carried his system of spying to such a pitch as to practice it since this unfortunate man has been standing a prisoner before you, proffering himself, as a friend, to the committee preparing his defense, that he might discover to the Crown the materials by which he

[61] See speech at Bristol, page 301.

meant to defend his life. I state this only from report, and I hope in God I am mistaken; for human nature starts back appalled from such atrocity, and shrinks and trembles at the very statement of it. But as to the perjury of this miscreant, it will appear palpable beyond all question, and he shall answer for it in due season. He tells you he attended at Chalk Farm;[62] and that there, forsooth, among about seven or eight thousand people, he saw two or three persons with knives. He might, I should think, have seen many more, as hardly any man goes without a knife of some sort in his pocket. He asked, however, it seems, where they got these knives, and was directed to Green, a hair-dresser, who deals besides in cutlery; and accordingly this notable Mr. Groves went (as he told us) to Green's, and asked to purchase a knife; when Green, in answer to him, said, "Speak low, for my wife is a damned aristocrat." This answer was sworn to by the wretch, to give you the idea that Green, who had the knives to sell, was conscious that he kept them for an illegal and wicked purpose, and that they were not to be sold in public. The door, he says, being ajar, the man desired him to speak low, from whence he would have you understand that it was because this aristocratic wife was within hearing. This, gentlemen, is the testimony of Groves; and Green himself is called as the next witness, and called by whom? Not by me—I know nothing of him, he is the Crown's own witness. He is called to confirm Groves's evidence. But *not being a spy*, he declared solemnly upon his oath (and I can confirm his evidence by several respectable people) that the knives in question lie constantly, and lay then, in his open shop-window, in what is called the show-glass, where cutlers, like other tradesmen, expose their ware to public view; and that the knives differ in nothing from others publicly sold in the Strand, and every other street in London; that he bespoke them from a rider, who came round for orders in the usual way—that he sold only fourteen in all. and that they were made up in little packets, one of which Mr. Hardy had, who was to choose one for himself, but four more were found in his possession, because he was arrested before Green had an opportunity of sending for them.

Contradicted by Green, who sold the knives.

Gentlemen, I think the pikes and knives are now completely disposed of. But something was said also about guns; let us, therefore, see what that amounts to. It appears that Mr. Hardy was applied to by Samuel Williams, a gun-engraver, who was not even a member of any society, and who asked him if he knew any body who wanted a gun. Hardy said he did not; and undoubtedly, upon the Crown's own showing, it must be taken for granted that if at that time he had been acquainted with any plan of arming, he would have given a different answer, and would have jumped at the offer. About a fortnight afterward, however (Hardy in the interval having become acquainted with Franklow), Williams called to buy a pair of shoes, and then Hardy, recollecting his former application, referred him to Franklow, who had in the most public manner raised the forty men, who were called the Loyal Lambeth Association. So that, in order to give this transaction any bearing upon the charge, it became necessary to consider Franklow's association as an armed conspiracy against the government—though the forty people who composed it were collected by public advertisement—though they were enrolled under public articles—and though Franklow himself, as appears from the evidence, attended publicly at the Globe Tavern in his uniform, while the cartouch-boxes and the other accoutrements of these secret conspirators lay openly upon his shop-board, exposed to the open view of all his customers and neighbors! This story, therefore, is not less contemptible than that which you must have all heard concerning Mr. Walker, whom I went to defend at Lancaster, where that respectable gentleman was brought to trial upon such a trumped-up charge, supported by the solitary evidence of one Dunn, a most infamous witness.[63] But what was the end of that prosecution? I recollect it to the honor of my friend, Mr. Law, who conducted it for the Crown, who, knowing that there were persons whose passions were agitated upon these subjects at that moment, and that many persons had enrolled themselves in societies to resist conspiracies against the government, behaved in a most manful and honorable manner—in a manner, indeed, which the public ought to know, and which I hope it never will forget. He would not even put me upon my challenges to such persons, but withdrew them from the panel; and when he saw the complexion of the affair, from the contradiction of the infamous witness whose testimony supported it, he honorably gave up the cause.

(8.) Story about guns.

Gentlemen, the evidence of Lynam does not require the same contradiction which fell upon Mr. Groves, because it destroys itself by its own intrinsic inconsistency. I could not, indeed, if it were to save my life, undertake to state it to you. It lasted, I think, about six or seven hours, but I have marked, under different parts of it, passages so grossly contradictory, matter so impossible, so inconsistent with any course of conduct, that it will be sufficient to bring these parts to your view, to destroy all the rest. But let us first examine in what manner this matter, such as it is, was recorded. He professed to speak from notes, yet I observed him frequently looking up to the ceiling while he was speaking. When I said to him, Are you now speaking from a note? Have you got any note of what you are now saying? He answered, "Oh no; this is from recollection." Good God

Lynam.

62 A place in the country, a little out of London, where a meeting of the reformers was held.

63 Mr. Walker, of Manchester, with some others, was indicted. in 1794, at the Lancaster Assizes, for a conspiracy to overthrow the government. The prosecution depended on the evidence of an informer of the name of Dunn, who was afterward convicted of perjury at the very same Assizes.

Almighty! Recollection mixing itself with notes in a case of high treason! He did not even take down the words; nay, to do the man justice, he did not even affect to have taken the words, but only the substance, as he himself expressed it. Oh, excellent evidence! The substance of words taken down by a spy, and supplied, when defective, by his memory! But I must not call him a spy; for it seems he took them *bonâ fide* as a delegate, and yet *bonâ fide* as an informer. What a happy combination of fidelity! faithful to serve, and faithful to betray! correct to record for the business of the society, and correct to dissolve and to punish it! What, after all, do the notes amount to? I will advert to the parts I alluded to. They were, it seems, to go to Frith Street, to sign the declaration of the Friends of the Liberty of the Press, which lay there already signed by between twenty and thirty members of the House of Commons, and many other respectable and opulent men; and then they were to begin civil confusion, and the King's head and Mr. Pitt's were to be placed on Temple Bar! Immediately after which, we find them resolving unanimously to thank Mr. Wharton for his speech to support the glorious Revolution of 1688, which supports the very throne that was to be destroyed! which same speech they were to circulate in thousands, for the use of the societies throughout the kingdom. Such incoherent, impossible matter, proceeding from such a source, is unworthy of all further concern.

(9.) Atrocious charge against Hardy, touching the crimes of Watt.

Thus driven out of every thing which relates to arms, and from every other matter which can possibly attach upon life, they have recourse to an expedient which I declare fills my mind with horror and terror. It is this: The Corresponding Society had, you recollect, two years before, sent delegates to Scotland, with specific instructions peacefully to pursue a parliamentary reform. When the convention which they were sent to was dispersed, they sent *no others*; for they were arrested when only considering of the propriety of another convention. It happened that Mr. Hardy was the secretary during the period of these Scotch proceedings, and the letters, consequently, written by him, during that period, were all official letters from a large body, circulated by him in point of form. When the proposition took place for calling a second convention, Mr. Hardy continued to be secretary, and in that character signed the circular letter read in the course of the evidence, which appears to have found its way, in the course of circulation, into Scotland. This single circumstance has been admitted as the foundation of receiving in evidence against the prisoner a long transaction, imputed to one Watt, at Edinburgh, whose very existence was unknown to Hardy. This Watt had been employed by government as a spy, but at last caught a Tartar in his spyship; for, in endeavoring to urge innocent men to a project which never entered into their imaginations, he was obliged to show himself ready to do what he recommended to others; and the tables being turned upon him, he was hanged by his employers. This man Watt read from a paper designs to be accomplished, but which he never intended to attempt, and the success of which he knew to be visionary. To suppose that Great Britain could have been destroyed by such a rebel as Watt, would be, as Dr. Johnson says, "to expect that a great city might be drowned by the overflowing of its kennels." But whatever might be the peril of Watt's conspiracy, what had Hardy to do with it? The people with Watt were five or six persons, wholly unknown to Hardy, and not members of any society of which Mr. Hardy was a member. I vow to God, therefore, that I can not express what I feel, when I am obliged to state the evidence by which he is sought to be affected. A letter, namely, the circular letter signed by Hardy, for calling another convention, is shown to George Ross, who says he received it from one Stock, who belonged to a society which met in Nicholson Street, in Edinburgh, and that he sent it to Perth, Strathaven, and Paisley, and other places in Scotland. The single, unconnected evidence of this public letter, finding its way into Scotland, is made the foundation of letting in the whole evidence which hanged Watt, against Hardy, *who never knew him!* Government hanged its own spy in Scotland upon that evidence, and it may be sufficient evidence for that purpose. I will not argue the case of a dead man, and, above all, of such a man; but I will say, that too much money was spent upon this performance, as I think it cost government about fifty thousand pounds. M'Ewen says that Watt read from a paper to a committee of six or seven people, of which he, the witness, was a member, that gentlemen residing in the country were not to leave their habitations under pain of death; that an attack was to be made in the manner you remember, and that the Lord Justice Clerk and the Judges were to be cut off by these men in buckram—and then an address was to be sent to the King, desiring him to dismiss his ministers and put an end to the war, or he might expect bad consequences. WHAT IS ALL THIS TO MR. HARDY? How is it possible to affect him with any part of this? Hear the sequel, and then judge for yourselves. Mr. Watt said (that is, the man who is hanged, said), after reading the paper, that he, Watt, *wished* to correspond with Mr. Hardy in a safe manner! So that, because a ruffian and scoundrel, whom I never saw or heard of, chooses, at the distance of four hundred miles, to say, that he wishes to correspond with me, I am to be involved in the guilt of his actions! It is not proved or insinuated, that Mr. Hardy ever saw, or heard of, or knew that such men were in being as Watt or Downie; nor is it proved, or asserted, that any letter was, in fact, written by either of them to Hardy, or to any other person. No such letter has been found in his possession, nor a trace of any connection between them and any member of any English society. The truth, I believe, is, that nothing was intended by Watt but to entrap others to obtain a reward for himself, and he has been amply and justly rewarded. Gentlemen, I desire to be understood to be making no attacks upon government. I have wished throughout the whole cause that good intentions may be imputed to it, but I really confess that it requires some ingenuity for government to account for the original existence of all this history, and its subsequent application to the present trial. They went down to Scotland after the arrest of the prisoners, in order, I suppose, that we might be taught the law of high treason by the Lord Justice Clerk of Edinburgh, and that there should be a sort of *rehearsal* to teach the people of England to administer English laws. For, after all this expense and preparation, no man was put upon his trial, or even arraigned under the special commission in Scotland, but these two men—one for reading this paper, and the other for not dissenting from it when it was read—and, with regard to this last unfortunate person, the Crown thought it indecent (as it would, indeed, have been indecent and scandalous) to execute the law upon him. A gentleman upon his jury said, he would die rather than convict Downie without a recommendation of mercy, and he was only brought over to join in the verdict under the idea that he would not be executed, and, accordingly, he has not suffered execution. If Downie, then, was an object of mercy, or rather of justice, though he was in the very room with Watt, and heard distinctly the proposition, upon what possible ground can they demand the life of the prisoner at the bar, on account of a connection with the very same individual, though he never corresponded with him, nor saw him, nor heard of him—to whose very being he was an utter stranger?

Appeal to the justice and humanity of the jury.

Gentlemen, it is impossible for me to know what impression this observation makes upon you, or upon the court; but I declare I am deeply impressed with the application of it. How is a man to defend himself against such implications of guilt? Which of us all would be safe, standing at the bar of God or man, if he were even to answer for all his own expressions, without taking upon him the crimes or rashnesses of others? This poor man has, indeed, none of his own to answer for. Yet how can he stand safely in judgment before you, if, in a season of alarm and agitation, with the whole pressure of government upon him, your minds are to be distracted with criminating materials brought from so many quarters, and of an extent which mocks all power of discrimination? I am conscious that I have not adverted to the thousandth part of them. Yet I am sinking under fatigue and weakness; I am at this moment scarcely able to stand up while I am speaking to you, deprived, as I have been, for nights together, of every thing that deserves the name of rest, repose, or comfort. I, therefore, hasten, while yet I may be able, to remind you once again of the great principle into which all I have been saying resolves itself.

Recapitulation of principles.

Gentlemen, my whole argument, then, amounts to no more than this, that before the crime of compassing THE KING'S DEATH can be found by you, the jury, whose province it is to judge of its existence, it must be believed by you to have existed in point of fact. Before you can adjudge a FACT, you must *believe* it—not *suspect* it, or *imagine* it, or *fancy* it—but BELIEVE it. And it is impossible to impress the human mind with such a reasonable and certain belief as is necessary to be impressed, before a Christian man can adjudge his neighbor to the smallest penalty, much less to the pains of death, without having such evidence as a reasonable mind will accept of, as the infallible test of truth. And what is that evidence? Neither more nor less than that which the Constitution has established in the courts for the general administration of justice—namely, that the evidence convinces the jury, beyond all reasonable doubt, that the criminal *intention*, constituting the crime, existed in the mind of the man upon trial, and was the main-spring of his conduct. The rules of evidence, as they are settled by law, and adopted in its general administration, are not to be overruled or tampered with. They are founded in the charities of religion, in the philosophy of nature, in the truths of history, and in the experience of common life; and whoever ventures rashly to depart from them, let him remember that it will be meted to him in the same measure, and that both God and man will judge him accordingly.

No precedents can set aside these principles.

These are arguments addressed to your reasons and consciences, not to be shaken in upright minds by any precedent, for no precedents can sanctify injustice. If they could, every human right would long ago have been extinct upon the earth. If the state trials in bad times are to be searched for precedents, what murders may you not commit? What law of humanity may you not trample upon? What rule of justice may you not violate? What maxim of wise policy may you not abrogate and confound? If precedents in bad times are to be implicitly followed, why should we have heard any evidence at all? You might have convicted without any evidence, for many have been so convicted, and in this manner murdered, even by acts of Parliament. If precedents in bad times are to be followed, why should the Lords and Commons have investigated these charges, and the Crown have put them into this course of judicial trial, since, without such a trial, and even after an acquittal upon one, they might have attainted all the prisoners by act of Parliament? They did so in the case of Lord Strafford. There are precedents, therefore, for all such things. But such precedents as could not for a moment survive the times of madness and distraction which gave them birth—precedents which, as soon as the spurs of the occasions were blunted, were repealed, and execrated even by Parliaments which (little as I may think of the present) ought not to be compared with it; Parliaments sitting in the darkness of former times—in the night of freedom—before the principles of government were developed, and before the Constitution became fixed. The last of these precedents, and all the proceedings upon it, were ordered to be taken off the file and burned, to the intent that the same might no longer be visible in after ages—an order dictated, no doubt, by a pious tenderness for national honor, and meant as a charitable covering for the crimes of our fathers. But it was a sin against posterity—it was a treason against society; for, instead of commanding them to be burned, they should rather have directed them to be blazoned in large letters upon the walls of our courts of justice, that, like the characters deciphered by the prophet of God to the Eastern tyrant, they might enlarge and blacken in your sights, to terrify you from acts of injustice.

Motives for adhering to the strict letter of the law.

In times when the whole habitable earth is in a state of change and fluctuation—when deserts are starting up into civilized empires around you; and when men, no longer slaves to the prejudices of particular countries, much less to the abuses of particular governments, enlist themselves, like the citizens of an enlightened world, into whatever communities their civil liberties may be best protected—it never can be for the advantage of this country to prove that the strict, unextended letter of her laws is no security to its inhabitants. On the contrary, when so dangerous a lure is every where held out to emigration, it will be found to be the wisest policy of Great Britain to set up her happy Constitution—the strict letter of her guardian laws, and the proud condition of equal freedom, which her highest and her lowest subjects ought equally to enjoy—it will be her wisest policy to set up these first of human blessings against those charms of change and novelty which the varying condition of the world is hourly displaying, and which may deeply affect the population and prosperity of our country. In times when the subordination to authority is said to be every where but little felt, it will be found to be the wisest policy of Great Britain to instill into the governed an almost superstitious reverence for the strict security of the laws; which, from their equality of principle, beget no jealousies or discontent; which, from their equal administration, can seldom work injustice; and which, from the reverence growing out of their mildness and antiquity, acquire a stability in the habits and affections of men far beyond the force of civil obligation—whereas, severe penalties and arbitrary constructions of laws intended for security, lay the foundations of alienation from every human government, and have been the cause of all the calamities that have come, and are coming upon the earth.

Argument against using violence with the people derived from the Netherlands.

Gentlemen, what we read of in books makes but a faint impression upon us compared to what we see passing under our eyes in the living world. I remember the people of another country, in like manner, contending for a renovation of their Constitution, sometimes illegally and turbulently, but still devoted to an honest end. I myself saw the people of Brabant so contending for the ancient Constitution of the good Duke of Burgundy. How was this people dealt by? All who were only contending for their own rights and privileges, were supposed to be, of course, disaffected to the Emperor. They were handed over to courts constituted for the emergency, as this is, and the Emperor marched his army through the country till all was peace—but such peace as there is in Vesuvius or Ætna, the very moment before they vomit forth their lava, and roll their conflagrations over the devoted habitations of mankind. When the French approached, the fatal effects were suddenly seen of a government of constraint and terror: the well-affected were dispirited, and the disaffected inflamed into fury.[64] At that moment, the Archduchess fled from Brussels, and the Duke of Saxe-Teschen was sent express to offer the *joyeuse entrée* so long petitioned for in vain. But the season of concession was past, the storm blew from every quarter, and the throne of Brabant departed forever from the house of Burgundy. Gentlemen, I venture to affirm that, with other counsels, this fatal prelude to the last revolution in that country might have been averted. If the Emperor had been advised to make the concessions of justice and affection to his people, they would have risen in a mass to maintain their Prince's authority, interwoven with their own liberties; and the French, the giants of modern times, would, like the giants of antiquity, have been trampled in the mire of their own ambition.

Authority of Mr. Burke in favor of conciliating the people.

In the same manner, a far more splendid and important crown passed away from his Majesty's illustrious brow—THE IMPERIAL CROWN OF AMERICA. The people of that country, too, for a long season, contended as subjects, and often with irregularity and turbulence, for what they felt to be their rights; and oh, gentlemen! that the inspiring and immortal eloquence of that man, whose name I have so often mentioned, had then been heard with effect! What was his language to this country when she sought to lay burdens on America, not to support the dignity of the Crown, or for the increase of national revenue, but to raise a fund for the purpose of corruption; a fund for maintaining those tribes of hireling skip-jacks, which Mr. Tooke so well contrasted with the hereditary nobility of England? Though America would not bear this imposition, she would have borne any useful or constitutional burden to support the parent state.

"For that service—for all service," said Mr. Burke, "whether of revenue, trade, or empire, my trust is in her interest in the British Constitution. My hold of the colonies is in the close affection which grows from common names, from kindred blood, from similar privileges and equal protection. These are ties which, though light as air, are as strong as links of iron. Let the colonies always keep the idea of their civil rights associated with your governments, they will cling and grapple to you, and no force under

[64] This refers to the invasion of the Netherlands by the armies of the French Republic after the battle of Jemappe, in 1792.

heaven will be of power to tear them from their allegiance. But let it be once understood that your government may be one thing, and their privileges another; that these two things may exist without any mutual relation; the cement is gone; the cohesion is loosened; and every thing hastens to decay and dissolution. As long as you have the wisdom to keep the sovereign authority of this country as the sanctuary of liberty, the sacred temple consecrated to our common faith, wherever the chosen race and sons of England worship freedom, they will turn their faces toward you. The more they multiply, the more friends you will have; the more ardently they love liberty, the more perfect will be their obedience. Slavery they can have any where. It is a weed that grows in every soil. They may have it from Spain, they may have it from Prussia. But until you become lost to all feeling of your true interest and your natural dignity, freedom they can have from none but you. This is the commodity of price, of which you have the monopoly. This is the true act of navigation, which binds to you the commerce of the colonies, and, through them, secures to you the wealth of the world. Is it not the same virtue which does every thing for us here in England? Do you imagine, then, that it is the Land-tax Act which raises your revenue? that it is the annual vote in the Committee of Supply which gives you your army? or that it is the Mutiny Bill which inspires it with bravery and discipline? No! surely no! It is the love of the people, it is their attachment to their government, from the sense of the deep stake they have in such a glorious institution, which gives you your army and your navy, and infuses into both that liberal obedience, without which your army would be a base rabble, and your navy nothing but rotten timber."

Gentlemen, to conclude—my fervent wish is, that we may not conjure up a spirit to destroy ourselves, nor set the example here of what in another country we deplore. Let us cherish the old and venerable laws of our forefathers. Let our judicial administration be strict and pure; and let the jury of the land preserve the life of a fellow-subject, who only asks it from them upon the same terms under which they hold their own lives, and all that is dear to them and their posterity forever. Let me repeat the wish with which I began my address to you, and which proceeds from the very bottom of my heart. May it please God, who is the Author of all mercies to mankind, whose providence, I am persuaded, guides and superintends the transactions of the world, and whose guardian spirit has forever hovered over this prosperous island, to direct and fortify your judgments. I am aware I have not acquitted myself to the unfortunate man who has put his trust in me, in the manner I could have wished; yet I am unable to proceed any further; exhausted in spirit and in strength, but confident in the expectation of justice. There is one thing more, however, that (if I can) I must state to you, namely, that I will show, by as many witnesses as it may be found necessary or convenient for you to hear upon the subject, that the views of the societies were what I have alleged them to be—that whatever irregularities or indiscretions they might have committed, their purposes were honest; and that Mr. Hardy's, above all other men, can be established to have been so. I have, indeed, an honorable gentleman [Mr. Francis] in my eye at this moment, to be called hereafter as a witness, who being desirous, in his place as a member of Parliament, to promote an inquiry into the seditious practices complained of, Mr. Hardy offered himself voluntarily to come forward, proffered a sight of all the papers, which were afterward seized in his custody, and tendered every possible assistance to give satisfaction to the laws of his country, if found to be offended. I will show, likewise, his character to be religious, temperate, humane, and moderate, and his uniform conduct all that can belong to a good subject and an honest man. When you have heard this evidence, it will, beyond all doubt, confirm you in coming to the conclusion which, at such great length (for which I entreat your pardon), I have been endeavoring to support.

Peroration.

As Mr Erskine drew near to the close of this speech, his voice failed him, so that for the last ten minutes he could only speak in a whisper, leaning on the table for support. The impression made upon his audience, as they hung with breathless anxiety on his lips, while he stood before them in this exhausted state, is said to have been more thrilling and profound than at any period of his long professional career.

The moment he ended, the hall was filled with acclamations, which were taken up and repeated by the vast multitudes that surrounded the building and blocked up the streets. Erskine made a noble use of his popularity. Recovering his voice, he went out and addressed the crowd, exhorting them to maintain order and confide in the justice of their country. He then requested them to disperse and retire to their own homes; and, within a few minutes, they were all gone, leaving the streets to a stillness like that of midnight.

On Monday morning, the evidence for the prisoner was received, after which Mr. Gibbs summed up in his defense, and the Solicitor General, Sir John Mitford, closed in behalf of the Crown. The jury were out three hours, and returned with a verdict of NOT GUILTY.

As the other cases stood on the same ground, it was supposed the government would stop here. But they determined to make one more effort, by arraigning Horne Tooke, the celebrated philologist. Tooke was then nearly sixty years old, with a frame broken down by disease, but having all the self-confidence of his early days, when he entered the lists with Junius. Mr. Erskine was his counsel; but he wrote a note from prison, saying that, in addition to this, he was determined to speak in his own defense. He had done so three years before, in his suit with Mr. Fox; and he thus began his address to the jury: "Gentlemen, there are here three parties to be considered —*you*, *Mr. Fox*, and *myself*. As for the *judge* and the *crier*, they are sent here to preserve order, and they are both well paid for their trouble." Mr. Erskine, remembering the past, answered Tooke's note proposing to speak, by simply saying, "You'll be *hanged* if you do;" to which Tooke instantly replied, "I'll be hanged if *I don't*," and went on to keep his word! When arraigned for trial, and asked, "By whom will you be tried?" he looked round some seconds on the court in a significant manner, and exclaimed, "I *would* be tried by God and my country! But—" He then asked liberty to sit with his counsel; and the court, on consultation, granted it as "an indulgence to his age." "My Lord," said he, "if I were judge, the word *indulgence* should never issue from my lips. My Lord, you have no indulgence to show; you are bound to be just; to do that which is ordered!" It is wonderful that Mr. Erskine was able to keep Tooke from being hanged, when he went on, throughout the whole cause, examining witnesses, and making remarks in the same spirit. But the case of Hardy had decided the principle, and Tooke was acquitted. The other prisoners were then discharged.

Mr. Erskine's prediction proved correct when he told the jury that indulgence to the prisoners in this case would be found the best way to check a factious spirit among the people. "The verdict of acquittal," says the editor of his speeches, "instead of giving encouragement to whatever spirit of sedition may have existed at that period, produced a universal spirit of content and confidence in the people. Nothing, indeed, could more properly excite such sentiments than so memorable a proof of safety under the laws."

SPEECH

OF MR. ERSKINE AGAINST THOMAS WILLIAMS FOR THE PUBLICATION OF PAINE'S AGE OF REASON, BEFORE LORD KENYON AND A SPECIAL JURY, ON THE 24th OF JULY, 1797.

INTRODUCTION.

Williams was a bookseller of infamous character in London, and was prosecuted by the Society for the Suppression of Vice and Immorality, for publishing Paine's abusive attack on Christianity entitled the Age of Reason. Mr. Erskine was counsel for the prosecution, and opened the case. The plea set up by the defendant was, that such an attack was no crime against the government; and Mr. Erskine's remarks were, therefore, directed chiefly to one point, viz., that "the Christian religion is the very foundation of the laws of the land." He draws the line with great clearness and precision between a legitimate inquiry into the evidences of our religion, and a scurrilous and insulting attack on its institutions, calculated to destroy the influence of all religious belief upon the minds of men, and to set them free from the restraints of conscience, the obligations of an oath, and all the other bonds which unite society together. This speech contains a fuller exhibition than any other, of Mr. Erskine's powers of *declamation* in the best sense of the term—of lofty and glowing amplification on subjects calculated to awaken sublime sentiments, and thus to enforce the argument out of which it springs.

SPEECH, &c.

Gentlemen of the Jury,—The charge of blasphemy, which is put upon the record against the printer of this publication, is not an accusation of the servants of the Crown, but comes before you sanctioned by the oaths of a grand jury of the country. It stood for trial upon a former day; but it happening, as it frequently does, without any imputation on the gentlemen named in the panel, that a sufficient number did not appear to constitute a full special jury, I thought it my duty to withdraw the cause from trial till I could have the opportunity, which is now open to me, of addressing myself to you, who were originally appointed to try it. I pursued this course, however, from no jealousy of the common juries appointed by the laws for the ordinary service of the court, since my whole life has been one continued experience of their virtues, but because I thought it of great importance that those who were to decide upon a cause so very momentous to the public should have the highest possible qualifications for the decision. That they should not only be men capable, from their education, of forming an enlightened judgment, but that their situations should be such as to bring them within the full view of their enlightened country, to which, in character and in estimation, they were in their own turns to be responsible.

Reasons for delaying the trial till the jury originally summoned could take up the case.

Not having the honor, gentlemen, to be sworn for the King, as one of his counsel, it has fallen much oftener to my lot to defend indictments for libels, than to assist in the prosecution of them. But I feel no embarrassment from that recollection, since I shall not be found to-day to express a sentiment or to utter an expression, inconsistent with those invaluable principles for which I have uniformly contended in the defense of others. Nothing that I have ever said, either professionally or personally, for the liberty of the press, do I mean to deny, to contradict, or counteract. On the contrary, I desire to preface the discourse I have to make to you, with reminding you that it is your most solemn duty to take care it suffers no injury in your hands. A free and unlicensed press, *in*

No invasion intended on the liberty of the press.

the just and legal sense of the expression, has led to all the blessings, both of religion and government, which Great Britain, or any part of the world, at this moment enjoys, and is calculated still further to advance mankind to higher degrees of civilization and happiness. But this freedom, like every other, must be limited to be enjoyed, and, like every human advantage, may be defeated by its abuse.

Nature of the proposed defense.

Gentlemen, the defendant stands indicted for having published this book, which I have only read from the obligations of professional duty, and which I rose from the reading of with astonishment and disgust. Standing here with all the privileges belonging to the highest counsel for the Crown, I shall be entitled to reply to any defense that shall be made for the publication. I shall wait with patience till I hear it. Indeed, if I were to anticipate the defense which I hear and read of, it would be defaming, by anticipation, the learned counsel who is to make it. For if I am to collect it, even from a formal notice given to the prosecutors in the course of the proceedings, I have to expect that, instead of a defense conducted according to the rules and principles of English law and justice, the foundation of all our laws, and the sanctions of all our justice, are to be struck at and insulted. What is the force of that jurisdiction which enables the court to sit in judgment? What but the oath which his Lordship as well as yourselves have sworn upon the Gospel to fulfill. Yet in the King's Court, where his Majesty is himself also sworn to administer the justice of England in the King's Court, who receives his high authority under a solemn oath to maintain the *Christian religion*, as it is promulgated by God in the Holy Scriptures, I am nevertheless called upon, as counsel for the prosecution, to produce a certain book described in the indictment to be the Holy Bible. No man deserves to be upon the rolls of the court who dares, as an attorney, to put his name to such a notice. It is an insult to the authority and dignity of the court of which he is an officer; since it seems to call in question the very foundations of its jurisdiction. If this is to be the spirit and temper of the defense; if, as I collect from that array of books which are spread upon the benches behind me, this publication is to be vindicated by an attack on all the truths which the Christian religion promulgates to mankind, let it be remembered that such an argument was neither suggested nor justified by any thing said by me on the part of the prosecution. *In this stage of the proceedings*, I shall call for reverence to the sacred Scriptures, not from their merits, unbounded as they are, but from their authority in a Christian country; not from the obligations of conscience, but from the rules of law. For my own part, gentlemen, I have been ever deeply devoted to the truths of Christianity, and my firm belief in the Holy Gospel is by no means owing to the prejudices of education, though I was religiously educated by the best of parents, but arises from the fullest and most continued reflections of my riper years and understanding. It forms at this moment the great consolation of a life which, as a shadow, must pass away; and without it, indeed, I should consider my long course of health and prosperity, perhaps too long and uninterrupted to be good for any man, only as the dust which the wind scatters, and rather as a snare than as a blessing. Much, however, as I wish to support the authority of the Scriptures, from a reasoned consideration of them, I shall repress that subject for the present. But if the defense shall be as I have suspected, to bring them at all into argument or question, I shall then fulfill a duty which I owe not only to the court, as counsel for the prosecution, but to the public, to state what I feel and know concerning the evidences of that religion which is reviled without being examined, and denied without being understood.

A denial of that on which the whole judicial system of the kingdom rests.

Use and importance of a free press.

I am well aware that by the communications of a free press, all the errors of mankind, from age to age, have been dissipated and dispelled; and I recollect that the world, under the banners of *reformed* Christianity, has struggled through persecution to the noble eminence on which it stands at this moment, shedding the blessings of humanity and science upon the nations of the earth. It may be asked by what means the Reformation would have been effected if the books of the reformers had been suppressed, and the errors of condemned and exploded superstitions had been supported as unquestionable by the state, founded upon those very superstitions formerly, as it is at present, upon the doctrines of the Established Church? or how, upon such principles, any reformation, civil or religious, can in future be effected? The solution is easy. Let us examine what are the genuine principles of the liberty of the press, as they regard writings upon general subjects, unconnected with the personal reputations of private men, which are wholly foreign to the present inquiry. They are full of simplicity, and are brought as near perfection by the law of England as, perhaps, is consistent with any of the frail institutions of mankind.

Principles which regulate the freedom of the press in matters civil and religious.

Although every community must establish supreme authorities, founded upon fixed principles, and must give high powers to magistrates to administer laws for the preservation of the government itself, and for the security of those who are to be protected by it; yet, as infallibility and perfection belong neither to human establishments nor to human individuals, it ought to be the policy of all free establishments, as it is most peculiarly the principle of our own Constitution, to permit the most unbounded freedom of discussion, even by detecting errors in the Constitution or administration of the very government itself, so as that decorum is observed which every state must exact from its subjects, and which imposes no restraint upon any intellectual composition, fairly, honestly, and decently addressed to the consciences and understandings of men. Upon this principle I have an unquestionable right — a right which the best subjects have exercised—to examine the principles and structure of the Constitution, and by fair, manly reasoning, to question the practice of its administrators. I have a right to consider and to point out errors in the one or in the other; and not merely to reason upon their existence, but to consider the means of their reformation. By such free, well-intentioned, modest, and dignified communication of sentiments and opinions all nations have been gradually improved, and milder laws and purer religions have been established. The same principles which vindicate civil contentions, honestly directed, extend their protection to the sharpest controversies on religious faiths. This rational and legal course of improvement was recognized and ratified by Lord Kenyon as the law of England, in a late trial at Guildhall, when he looked back with gratitude to the labors of the reformers, as the fountains of our religious emancipation, and of the civil blessings that followed in their train. The English Constitution, indeed, does not stop short in the toleration of religious *opinions*, but liberally extends it to *practice*. It permits every man, even publicly, to worship God according to his own conscience, though in marked dissent from the national establishment, so as he professes *the general faith*, which is the sanction of all our moral duties, and the only pledge of our submission to the system which constitutes a state. Is not this system of freedom of controversy and freedom of worship, sufficient for all the purposes of human happiness and improvement? and will it be necessary for either that the law should hold out indemnity to those who wholly abjure and revile the government of their country, or the religion on which it rests for its foundation?

Distinction between legitimate inquiry and scurrilous invective.

I expect to hear, in answer to what I am now saying, much that will offend me. My learned friend, from the difficulties of his situation, which I know, from experience, how to feel for very sincerely, may be driven to advance propositions which it may be my duty, with much freedom to reply to; and the law will sanction that freedom. But will not the ends of justice be completely answered by the right to point out the errors of his discourse in terms that are decent and calculated to expose its defects? or will any argument suffer, or will public justice be impeded, because neither private honor and justice, nor public decorum, would endure my telling my very learned friend that he was a fool, a liar, and a scoundrel, in the face of the court, because I differed from him in argument or opinion? This is just the distinction between a book of free legal controversy and the book which I am arraigning before you. Every man has a legal right to investigate, *with modesty and decency*, controversial points of the Christian religion; but no man, consistently with a law which only exists under its sanctions, has a right not only broadly to deny its very existence, but to pour forth a shocking and insulting invective, which the lowest establishments in the gradations of civil authority ought not to be permitted to suffer, and which soon would be borne down by insolence and disobedience, if they did.

Illustration from parallel cases.

The same principle pervades the whole system of the law, not merely in its abstract theory, but in its daily and most applauded practice. The intercourse between the sexes, and which, properly regulated, not only continues, but humanizes and adorns our natures, is the foundation of all the thousand romances, plays, and novels which are in the hands of every body. Some of them lead to the confirmation of every virtuous principle; others, though with the same profession, address the imagination in a manner to lead the passions into dangerous excesses. But though the law does not nicely discriminate the various shades which distinguish these works from one another, so as that it suffers many to pass, through its liberal spirit, that upon principle might be suppressed, would it or does it tolerate, or does any decent man contend that it ought to pass by unpunished, libels of the most shameless obscenity, manifestly pointed to debauch innocence, and to blast and poison the morals of the rising generation? This is only another illustration to demonstrate the obvious distinction between the works of an author who fairly exercises the powers of his mind in investigating doctrinal points in the religion of any country, and him who attacks the rational existence of every religion, and brands with absurdity and folly the state which sanctions, and the obedient tools who cherish, the delusion. But this publication appears to me to be as mischievous and cruel in its probable effects, as it is manifestly illegal in its principles; because it strikes at the best, sometimes, alas! the only refuge and consolation amid the distresses and afflictions of the world. The poor and humble, whom it affects to pity, may be stabbed to the heart by it. They have more occasion for firm hopes beyond the grave than those who have greater comforts to render life delightful. I can conceive a distressed, but virtuous man, surrounded by children, looking up to him for bread when he has none to give them, sinking under the last day's labor, and unequal to the next, yet still looking up with confidence to the hour when all tears shall be wiped from the eyes of affliction, bearing the burden laid upon him by a mysterious Providence which he adores, and looking forward with exultation to the *revealed* promises of his Creator, when he shall be greater than the greatest, and happier than the happiest of mankind. What a change in such a mind might be wrought by such a merciless publication? Gentlemen, whether these remarks are the overcharged declamations of an accusing counsel, or the just reflections of a man anxious for the public freedom, which is best secured by the morals of a nation, will be best settled by an appeal to the passages in the work, that are selected in the indictment for your consideration and judgment. You are at liberty to connect them with every context and sequel, and to bestow upon them the mildest interpretation. [Here Mr. Erskine read and

Importance of religious consolations to persons in poverty and affliction.

commented upon several of the selected passages.]

Gentlemen, it would be useless and disgusting to enumerate the other passages within the scope of the indictment. How any man can rationally vindicate the publication of such a book, in a country where the Christian religion is the very foundation of the law of the land, I am totally at a loss to conceive, and have no wish to discuss. How is a tribunal, whose whole jurisdiction is founded upon the solemn belief and practice of what is denied as falsehood, and reprobated as impiety, to deal with such an anomalous defense? Upon what principle is it even offered to the court, whose authority is contemned and mocked at? If the religion proposed to be called in question is not previously adopted in belief, and solemnly acted upon, what authority has the court to pass any judgment at all of acquittal or condemnation? Why am I now, or upon any other occasion, to submit to your Lordship's authority? Why am I now, or at any time, to address twelve of my equals, as I am now addressing you, with reverence and submission? Under what sanction are the witnesses to give their evidence, without which there can be no trial? Under what obligations can I call upon you, the jury, representing your country, to administer justice? Surely upon no other than that you are sworn to administer it under the oaths you have taken. The whole judicial fabric, from the King's sovereign authority to the lowest office of magistracy, has no other foundation. The whole is built, both in form and substance, upon the same oath of every one of its ministers, to do justice, "*as God shall help them hereafter*." What God? and what hereafter? That God, undoubtedly, who has commanded Kings to rule, and judges to decree with justice; who has said to witnesses, not by the voice of nature, but in revealed commandments, "*thou shalt not bear false witness against thy neighbor;*" and who has enforced obedience to them by the revelation of the unutterable blessings which shall attend their observances, and the awful punishments which shall await upon their transgressions.

The book subversive of the foundation of government.

But it seems this course of reason, and the time and the person are at last arrived, that are to dissipate the errors which have overspread the past generations of ignorance! The believers in Christianity are many, but it belongs to the few that are wise to correct their credulity! Belief is an act of reason; and superior reason may, therefore, dictate to the weak. In running the mind along the numerous list of sincere and devout Christians, I can not help lamenting that Newton had not lived to this day, to have had his shallowness filled up with this new flood of light. But the subject is too awful for irony. I will speak plainly and directly. Newton was a Christian! Newton, whose mind burst forth from the fetters cast by nature upon our finite conceptions; Newton, whose science was truth, and the foundation of whose knowledge of it was philosophy. Not those visionary and arrogant assumptions which too often usurp its name, but philosophy resting upon the basis of mathematics, which, like figures, can not lie. Newton, who carried the line and rule to the utmost barriers of creation, and explored the principles by which, no doubt, all created matter is held together and exists. But this extraordinary man, in the mighty reach of his mind, overlooked, perhaps, the errors which a minuter investigation of the created things on this earth might have taught him of the essence of his Creator. What shall then be said of the great Mr. Boyle, who looked into the organic structure of all matter, even to the brute inanimate substances which the foot treads on. Such a man may be supposed to have been equally qualified with Mr. Paine, to "look through nature, up to nature's God." Yet the result of all his contemplation was the most confirmed and devout belief in all which the other holds in contempt as despicable and driveling superstition. But this error might, perhaps, arise from a want of due attention to the foundations of human judgment, and the structure of that understanding which God has given us for the investigation of truth. Let that question be answered by Mr. Locke, who was to the highest pitch of devotion and adoration a Christian. Mr. Locke, whose office was to detect the errors of thinking, by going up to the fountains of thought, and to direct into the proper track of reasoning the devious mind of man, by showing him its whole process, from the first perceptions of sense to the last conclusions of ratiocination; putting a rein, besides, upon false opinion, by practical rules for the conduct of human judgment.

Mr. Paine compared with the believers in Christianity.

Newton.

Boyle.

Locke.

But these men were only deep thinkers, and lived in their closets, unaccustomed to the traffic of the world, and to the laws which practically regulate mankind. Gentlemen, in the place where you now sit to administer the justice of this great country, above a century ago the never-to-be-forgotten Sir Matthew Hale presided, whose faith in Christianity is an exalted commentary upon its truth and reason, and whose life was a glorious example of its fruits in man; administering human justice with a wisdom and purity drawn from the pure fountain of the Christian dispensation, which has been, and will be, in all ages, a subject of the highest reverence and admiration.

Hale.

But it is said by Mr. Paine that the Christian fable is but the tale of the more ancient superstitions of the world, and may be easily detected by a proper understanding of the mythologies of the heathens. Did Milton understand those mythologies? Was *he* less versed than Mr. Paine in the superstitions of the world? No: they were the subject of his immortal song; and though shut out from all recurrence to them, he poured them forth from the stores of a memory rich with all that man ever knew, and laid them in their order as the illustration of that real and exalted faith, the unquestionable source of that fervid genius, which

Pretense that Christianity is only a myth of earlier times.

cast a sort of shade upon all the other works of man:

He pass'd the bounds of flaming space,
Where angels tremble while they gaze;
He saw, till, blasted with excess of light,
He clos'd his eyes in endless night![1]

But it was the light of the *body* only that was extinguished; "the celestial light shone inward," and enabled him to "justify the ways of God to man." The result of his thinking was, nevertheless, not the same as Mr. Paine's. The mysterious incarnation of our blessed Savior, which the "Age of Reason" blasphemes in words so wholly unfit for the mouth of a Christian, or for the ear of a court of justice, that I dare not and will not give them utterance, Milton made the grand conclusion of PARADISE LOST, the rest of his finished labors, and the ultimate hope, expectation, and glory of the world:

A Virgin is his mother, but his sire
The power of the Most High: he shall ascend
The throne hereditary, and bound his reign
With earth's wide bounds, his glory with the heavens.

The immortal poet having thus put into the mouth of the angel the prophecy of man's redemption, follows it with that solemn and beautiful admonition, addressed in the poem to our great First Parent, but intended as an address to his posterity through all generations:

This having learned, thou hast attained the sum
Of wisdom: hope no higher, though all the stars
Thou knew'st by name, and all th' ethereal powers,
All secrets of the deep, all Nature's works,
Or works of God in heaven, air, earth, or sea,
And all the riches of this world enjoy'st,
And all the rule one empire; only add
Deeds to thy knowledge answerable, add faith,
Add virtue, patience, temperance; add love,
By name to come call'd Charity, the soul
Of all the rest: then wilt thou not be loth
To leave this Paradise, but shalt possess
A paradise within thee, happier far.

Thus you find all that is great, or wise, or splendid, or illustrious among created beings—all the minds gifted beyond ordinary nature, if not inspired by their universal Author for the advancement and dignity of the world, though divided by distant ages, and by the clashing opinions distinguishing them from one another, yet joining, as it were, in one sublime chorus to celebrate the truths of Christianity, and laying upon its holy altars the never-fading offerings of their immortal wisdom.

Against all this concurring testimony, we find suddenly, from Mr. Paine, that the Bible teaches nothing but "lies, obscenity, cruelty, and injustice." Did the author or publisher ever read the sermon of *Christ upon the Mount*, in which, the great principles of our faith and duty are summed up? Let us all but read and practice it, and lies, obscenity, cruelty, and injustice, and all human wickedness, would be banished from the world.

Morality of the New Testament.

Gentlemen, there is but one consideration more, which I can not possibly omit, because, I confess, it affects me very deeply. Mr. Paine has written largely on public liberty and government; and this last performance has, on that account, been more widely circulated, and principally among those who attached themselves from principle to his former works. This circumstance renders a public attack upon *all revealed religion*, from such a writer, infinitely more dangerous. The religious and moral sense of the people of Great Britain is the great anchor which alone can hold the vessel of the state amid the storms which agitate the world. If I could believe, for a moment, that the mass of the people were to be debauched from the principles of religion, which form the true basis of that humanity, charity, and benevolence that has been so long the national characteristic, instead of mixing myself, as I sometimes have done, in political reformations, I would rather retire to the uttermost corners of the earth to avoid their agitation; and would bear, not only the imperfections and abuses complained of in our own wise establishment, but even the worst government that ever existed in the world, rather than go to the work of reformation with a multitude set free from all the charities of Christianity, who had no sense of God's existence but from Mr. Paine's observation of nature, which the mass of mankind have no leisure to contemplate; nor any belief of future rewards and punishments to animate the good in the glorious pursuit of human happiness, nor to deter the wicked from destroying it even in its birth. But I know the people of England better. They are a religious people; and, with the blessing of God, as far as it is in my power, I will lend my aid to keep them so. I have no objections to the freest and most extended discussions upon doctrinal points of the Christian religion; and, *though the law of England does not permit it*, I do not dread the reasoned arguments of Deists against the existence of Christianity itself, because, as was said by its divine author, if it is of God, it will stand. An intellectual book, however erroneous, addressed to the intellectual world upon so profound and complicated a subject, can never work the mischief which this indictment is calculated to repress. Such works will only employ the minds of men enlightened by study in a deeper investigation of a subject well worthy of their profound and continued contemplation. The powers of the mind are given for human improvement in the progress of human existence. The changes produced by such reciprocations of lights and intelligences are certain in their progressions, and make their way imperceptibly, as conviction comes upon the world, by the final and irresistible power of truth. If Christianity be founded in falsehood, let us become Deists in this manner, and I am contented. But this book hath no such object and no such capacity; it presents no arguments to the wise and enlightened. On the contrary, it treats the faith and opinions of the wisest with the most shocking

Tendency of the book to destroy all social order, so that despotism itself would be a refuge from its results.

1 Grey's Ode on the Progress of Poetry.

contempt, and stirs up men without the advantages of learning or sober thinking to a total disbelief of every thing hitherto held sacred, and, consequently, to a rejection of all the laws and ordinances of the state, which stand only upon the assumption of their truth.

Peroration: The friends of civil liberty should be the last persons to attack Christianity.

Gentlemen, I can not conclude without expressing the deepest regret at all attacks upon the Christian religion by authors who profess to promote the civil liberties of the world. For under what other auspices than Christianity have the lost and subverted liberties of mankind in former ages been reasserted? By what zeal, but the warm zeal of devout Christians, have English liberties been redeemed and consecrated? Under what other sanctions, even in our own days, have liberty and happiness been extending and spreading to the uttermost corners of the earth? What work of civilization, what commonwealth of greatness has the bald religion of nature ever established? We see, on the contrary, the nations that have no other light than that of nature to direct them, sunk in barbarism or slaves to arbitrary governments; while, since the Christian era, the great career of the world has been slowly, but clearly, advancing lighter at every step, from the awful prophecies of the Gospel, and leading, I trust, in the end, to universal and eternal happiness. Each generation of mankind can see but a few revolving links of this mighty and mysterious chain; but, by doing our several duties in our allotted stations, we are sure that we are fulfilling the purposes of our existence. You, I trust, will fulfill yours this day!

The jury found a verdict of Guilty, without retiring from their seats.

SPEECH

OF MR. ERSKINE IN BEHALF OF JAMES HADFIELD, WHEN INDICTED FOR HIGH TREASON, DELIVERED BEFORE THE COURT OF KING'S BENCH, JUNE 26, 1800.

INTRODUCTION.

James Hadfield was an invalid soldier of the British army, and was indicted for firing a pistol at the King in the Drury Lane Theater. He was defended on the ground that he acted under a strong *delusion*, producing a settled insanity on one subject, while he appeared entirely rational upon every other. Lord Campbell says this "was Erskine's last, and perhaps his greatest display of genius in defending a party prosecuted by the Crown. It is now, and ever will be, studied by medical men for its philosophic views of mental disease—by lawyers for its admirable distinctions as to the degree of alienation of mind which will exempt from final responsibility—by logicians for its severe and connected reasoning; and by all lovers of genuine eloquence for its touching appeals to human feeling."—*Lives of the Chancellors*, vol. vi., page 520.

SPEECH, &c.

Gentlemen of the Jury,—The scene which we are engaged in, and the duty which I am not merely *privileged*, but *appointed* by the authority of the court to perform, exhibits to the whole civilized world a perpetual monument of our national justice.[1]

The peculiarity of the proceeding in a case like this an honor to English justice.

The transaction, indeed, in every part of it, as it stands recorded in the evidence already before us, places our country, and its government, and its inhabitants, upon the highest pinnacle of human elevation. It appears that, upon the 15th day of May last, his Majesty, after a reign of forty years, not merely in sovereign power, but spontaneously in the very hearts of his people, was openly shot at (or to all appearance shot at) in a public theater [Drury Lane], in the center of his capital, and amid the loyal plaudits of his subjects, YET NOT A HAIR OF THE HEAD OF THE SUPPOSED ASSASSIN WAS TOUCHED. In this unparalleled scene of calm forbearance, the King himself, though he stood first in personal interest and feeling, as well as in command, was a singular and fortunate example. The least appearance of emotion on the part of that august personage must unavoidably have produced a scene quite different, and far less honorable than the court is now witnessing. But his Majesty remained unmoved, and the person *apparently* offending was only secured, without injury or reproach, for the business of this day.

Greater protection given to an assailant of the King than of any private individual.

Gentlemen, I agree with the Attorney General[2] (indeed, there can be no possible doubt) that if the same pistol had been maliciously fired by the prisoner, in the same theater, at the meanest man within its walls, he would have been brought to immediate trial, and, if guilty, to immediate execution. He would have heard the charge against him for the first time when the indictment was read upon his arraignment. He would have been

---

[1] This is, perhaps, the most felicitous of Mr. Erskine's exordiums. It turns upon a fact highly gratifying to the minds of an English jury, and leading directly to the great thought which needed to be urged at the outset, viz., that no regard for the King's safety should lead to any hasty or prejudiced judgments. The same thought is admirably introduced in a different connection at the close.

[2] Sir John Mitford, afterward Lord Redesdale, and Lord Chancellor of Ireland.

a stranger to the names, and even to the existence, of those who were to sit in judgment upon him, and of those who were to be the witnesses against him. But upon the charge of even this murderous attack upon the King himself, he is covered all over with the armor of the law. He has been provided with counsel by the King's own judges, and not of *their* choice, but of *his own*.[3] He has had a copy of the indictment ten days before his trial.[4] He has had the names, descriptions, and abodes of all the jurors returned to the court; and the highest privilege of peremptory challenges derived from, and safely directed by that indulgence.[5] He has had the same description of every witness who could be received to accuse him; and there must at this hour be *twice* the testimony against him which would be legally competent to establish his guilt on a similar prosecution by [in behalf of] the meanest and most helpless of mankind.

Gentlemen, when this melancholy catastrophe happened, and the prisoner was arraigned for trial, I remember to have said to some now present, that it was, at first view, difficult to bring those indulgent exceptions to the general rules of trial within the principle which dictated them to our humane ancestors in cases of treasons against the political government, or of *rebellious* conspiracy against the person of the King. In these cases, the passions and interests of great bodies of powerful men being engaged and agitated, a counterpoise became necessary to give composure and impartiality to criminal tribunals; but a *mere murderous* attack upon the King's person, not at all connected with his political character, seemed a case to be ranged and dealt with like a similar attack upon any private man.

Difficult, at first view, to see the reason of this difference.

But the wisdom of the law is greater than any man's wisdom; how much more, therefore, than mine! An attack upon the King is considered to be parricide against the state, and the jury and the witnesses, and even the judges, are the children. It is fit, on that account, that there should be a solemn pause before we rush to judgment; and what can be a more sublime spectacle of justice than to see a statutable disqualification of a whole nation for a limited period, a fifteen days' *quarantine* before trial, lest the mind should be subject to the contagion of partial affections!

That reason assigned.

From a prisoner so protected by the benevolence of our institutions, the utmost good faith would, on his part, be due to the public if he had consciousness and reason to reflect upon the obligation. The duty, therefore, devolves on *me;* and, *upon my honor*, it shall be fulfilled. I will employ no artifices of speech. I claim only the strictest protection of the law for the unhappy man before you. I should, indeed, be ashamed if I were to say any thing of the rule *in the abstract* by which he is to be judged, which I did not honestly feel; I am sorry, therefore, that the subject is so difficult to handle with brevity and precision. Indeed, if it could be brought to a clear and simple criterion, which could admit of a dry admission or contradiction, there might be very little difference, *perhaps none at all*, between the Attorney General and myself, upon the principles which ought to govern your verdict. But this is not possible, and I am, therefore, under the necessity of submitting to you, and to the judges, for their direction (and at greater length than I wish), how I understand this difficult and momentous subject.

The obligations imposed by this distinction on the counsel for the prisoner.

The law, as it regards this most unfortunate infirmity of the human mind, like the law in all its branches, aims at the utmost degree of precision; but there are some subjects, as I have just observed to you, and the present is one of them, upon which it is extremely difficult to be precise. The general principle is clear, but the application is most difficult.

The law on this subject necessarily indefinite in its application.

It is agreed by all jurists, and is established by the law of this and every other country, that it is the REASON OF MAN which makes him accountable for his actions; and that the deprivation of reason acquits him of crime. This principle is indisputable; yet so fearfully and wonderfully are we made, so infinitely subtle is the spiritual part of our being, so difficult is it to trace with accuracy the effect of diseased intellect upon human action, that I may appeal to all who hear me, whether there are any causes more difficult, or which, indeed, so often confound the learning of the judges themselves, as when insanity, or the effects and consequences of insanity, become the subjects of legal consideration and judgment. I shall pursue the subject as the Attorney General has properly discussed it. I shall consider insanity, as it annuls a man's dominion over property, as it dissolves his contracts, and other acts, which otherwise would be binding, and as it takes away his responsibility for crimes. If I could draw the line in a moment between these two views of the subject, I am sure the judges will do me the jus-

The exercise of *reason* essential to the existence of crime.

[3] By 7 Will. III., cap. 3, sec. 1, a person charged with high treason is allowed to make his defense by counsel, not exceeding two in number, to be selected by himself and assigned to him by the court; and by sec. 2 of the same statute, no person shall be convicted of high treason but upon the oaths of two lawful witnesses, unless he shall willingly, and without violence, confess the same.

[4] The statute 7 Anne, cap. 21, directs that all persons indicted for high treason shall have a copy of the indictment, together with a list of the witnesses to be produced against them on the trial, and of the jurors impanneled, with their professions and places of abode respectively, delivered to them ten days before trial, and in the presence of two or more witnesses. But now, by 39 and 40 Geo. III., cap. 93, and 5 and 6 Vict., cap. 51, the proceedings in trials for high treason in compassing the death or bodily harm of the Queen are assimilated to those in trials for murder.

[5] On a trial for high treason, the prisoner is allowed a peremptory challenge of thirty-five jurors; that is, one under the number of three full juries. This is the effect of 1 and 2 Philip and Mary, cap. 10, sec. 7.

tice to believe that I would fairly and candidly do so; but great difficulties press upon my mind, which oblige me to take a different course.

It is not mere weakness of mind, but deprivation of reason, which operates as an excuse.

I agree with the Attorney General, that the law, in neither civil nor criminal cases, will measure the degrees of men's understandings. A *weak* man, however much below the ordinary standard of human intellect, is not only responsible for crimes, but is bound by his contracts, and may exercise dominion over his property. Sir Joseph Jekyll, in the Duchess of Cleveland's case, took the clear, legal distinction, when he said, "The law will not measure the sizes of men's capacities, so as they be *compos mentis*."

Lord Coke.

Lord Coke, in speaking of the expression *non compos mentis*, says, "Many times (as here) the Latin word expresses the true sense, and calleth him not *amens*, *demens*, *furiosus*, *lunaticus*, *fatuus*, *stultus*, or the like, for *non compos mentis* is the most sure and legal." He then says, "*Non compos mentis* is of four sorts: first, *ideota* [an idiot], which from his nativity, by a perpetual infirmity, is *non compos mentis*; secondly, he that by sickness, grief, or other accident, wholly loses his memory and understanding; thirdly, a lunatic that hath sometimes his understanding, and sometimes not; *aliquando gaudet lucidis intervallis* [has sometimes lucid intervals]; and, therefore, he is called *non compos mentis* so long as he hath not understanding."

But notwithstanding the precision with which this great author points out the different kinds of this unhappy malady, the nature of his work, in this part of it, did not open to any illustration which it can now be useful to consider. In his fourth Institute he is more particular; but the admirable work of Lord Chief Justice Hale, in which he refers to Lord Coke's pleas of the Crown, renders all other authorities unnecessary.

Lord Hale.

Lord Hale says, "There is a partial insanity of mind, and a total insanity. The former is either in respect to things, *quoad hoc vel illud insanire* [to be insane as to this or that]. Some persons that have a competent use of reason in respect of some subjects, are yet under a particular *dementia* [deprivation of reason] in respect of some particular discourses, subjects, or applications; or else it is partial in respect of *degrees*; and this is the condition of very many, especially melancholy persons, who for the most part discover their defect in excessive fears and griefs, and yet are not wholly destitute of the use of reason; and this partial insanity seems not to excuse them in the committing of any offense for its matter capital. For, doubtless, most persons that are felons of themselves and others, are under a degree of partial insanity when they commit these offenses. It is very difficult to define the invisible line that divides perfect and partial insanity; but it must rest upon circumstances duly to be weighed and considered both by judge and jury, lest on the one side there be a kind of inhumanity toward the defects of human nature; or, on the other side, too great an indulgence given to great crimes."

Marked distinction between civil and criminal cases.

Nothing, gentlemen, can be more accurately nor more humanely expressed; but the application of the rule is often most difficult. I am bound, besides, to admit that there is a wide distinction between civil and criminal cases. If, in the former, a man appears, upon the evidence, to be *non compos mentis*, the law avoids his act, though it can not be traced or connected with the morbid imagination which constitutes his disease, and which may be extremely partial in its influence upon conduct; but to deliver a man from responsibility for *crimes*, above all, for crimes of great atrocity and wickedness, I am by no means prepared to apply this rule, however well established when property only is concerned.

This shown in the case of Greenwood.

In the very recent instance of Mr. Greenwood (which must be fresh in his Lordship's recollection), the rule in civil cases was considered to be settled. That gentleman, while insane, took up an idea that a most affectionate brother had administered poison to him. Indeed, it was the prominent feature of his insanity. In a few months he recovered his senses. He returned to his profession as an advocate; was sound and eminent in his practice, and in all respects a most intelligent and useful member of society; but he could never dislodge from his mind the morbid delusion which disturbed it; and under the pressure, no doubt, of that diseased prepossession, he disinherited his brother. The cause to avoid this will was tried here. We are not now upon the evidence, but upon the principle adopted as the law. The noble and learned judge, who presides upon this trial, and who presided upon that, told the jury, that if they believed Mr. Greenwood, when he made the will, to have been *insane*, the will could not be supported, whether it had disinherited his brother or not; that the act, no doubt, strongly confirmed the existence of the false idea which, if believed by the jury to amount to *madness*, would equally have affected his testament, if the brother, instead of being disinherited, had been in his grave; and that, on the other hand, if the unfounded notion did not amount to madness, its influence could not vacate the devise.[6] This principle of law appears to be sound and reasonable, as it applies to civil cases, from the extreme difficulty of tracing with precision the secret motions of a mind, deprived by disease of its soundness and strength.

Whenever, therefore, a person may be considered *non compos mentis*, all his *civil* acts are void, whether they can be referred or not, to the morbid impulse of his malady, or even though, to all *visible appearances*, totally separated from it. But I agree with Mr. Justice Tracey, that it is not every man of an idle, frantic appearance and behavior, who is to be considered as a lunatic, either as it regards obligations or crimes; but that he must appear to the jury to be *non compos mentis*, in the legal acceptation of the term; and that, not at any anterior period, which can have

[6] The jury in that case found for the will; but after a contrary verdict in the Common Pleas, a compromise took place.

no bearing upon any case whatsoever, but at *the moment* when the contract was entered into, or the crime committed.

Nature of the insanity which in most cases operates as an excuse.

The Attorney General, standing undoubtedly upon the most revered authorities of the law, has laid it down that to protect a man from *criminal* responsibility, there must be a TOTAL *deprivation of memory and understanding.* I admit that this is the very expression used, both by Lord Coke and by Lord Hale; but the true interpretation of it deserves the utmost attention and consideration of the court. If a total deprivation of memory was intended by these great lawyers to be taken in the *literal* sense of the words; if it was meant, that, to protect a man from punishment, he must be in such a state of prostrated intellect as not to know his name, nor his condition, nor his relation toward others—that if a husband, he should not know he was married; or, if a father, could not remember that he had children, nor know the road to his house, nor his property in it—then no such madness ever existed in the world. It is IDIOCY alone which places a man in this helpless condition; where, from an *original* mal-organization, there is the human frame alone without the human capacity; and which, indeed, meets the very definition of Lord Hale himself, when, referring to Fitzherbert, he says, "Idiocy, or fatuity *à nativitate, vel dementia naturalis,* is such a one as described by Fitzherbert, who knows not to tell twenty shillings, nor knows his own age, or who was his father." But in all the cases which have filled Westminster Hall with the most complicated considerations—the lunatics, and other insane persons who have been the subjects of them, have not only had memory, in my sense of the expression—they have not only had the most perfect knowledge and recollections of all the relations they stood in toward others, and of the acts and circumstances of their lives, but have, in general, been remarkable for subtlety and acuteness. Defects in their reasonings have seldom been traceable—the disease consisting in the delusive sources of thought; all their deductions within the scope of the malady being founded upon the *immovable* assumption of matters as *realities,* either without any foundation whatsoever, or so distorted and disfigured by fancy as to be almost nearly the same thing as their creation. It is true, indeed, that in some, perhaps in many cases, the human mind is stormed in its citadel, and laid prostrate under the stroke of frenzy; these unhappy sufferers, however, are not so much considered, by physicians, as maniacs, but to be in a state of delirium as if from fever. There, indeed, all the ideas are overwhelmed—for reason is not merely disturbed, *but driven wholly from her seat.* Such unhappy patients are unconscious, therefore, except at short intervals, even of external objects; or, at least, are wholly incapable of considering their relations. Such persons, *and such persons alone* (except idiots), *are wholly deprived of their* UNDERSTANDINGS, in the Attorney General's seeming sense of that expression. But these cases are not only extremely rare, but never can become the subjects of judicial difficulty. There can be but one judgment concerning them. In other cases, reason is not driven from her seat, but distraction sits down upon it along with her, holds her, trembling, upon it, and frightens her from her propriety.[7] Such patients are victims to delusions of the most alarming description, which so overpower the faculties, and usurp so firmly the place of realities, as not to be dislodged and shaken by the organs of perception and sense: in such cases the images frequently vary, but in the same subject are generally of the same terrific character. Here, too, no judicial difficulties can present themselves; for who could balance upon the judgment to be pronounced in cases of such extreme disease? Another class, branching out into almost infinite subdivisions, under which, indeed, the former, and every case of insanity, may be classed, is, where the delusions are not of that frightful character, but infinitely various and often extremely *circumscribed;* yet where imagination (*within the bounds of the malady*) still holds the most uncontrollable dominion over reality and fact. These are the cases which frequently mock the wisdom of the wisest in judicial trials; because such persons often reason with a subtlety which puts in the shade the ordinary conceptions of mankind. Their conclusions are just, and frequently profound; but the premises from which they reason, *when within the range of the malady,* are uniformly false—not false from any defect of knowledge or judgment, but because a delusive image, the inseparable companion of real insanity, is thrust upon the subjugated understanding, incapable of resistance, because unconscious of attack.

Not mere idiocy.

But a permanent *delusion* of some sort making things appear real which are not so.

This delusion must, in criminal cases, be directly *connected* with the unlawful act.

Delusion, therefore, where there is no frenzy or raving madness, is the true character of insanity. Where it can not be predicated of a man standing for life or death for a crime, he ought not, in my opinion, to be acquitted; and if courts of law were to be governed by any other principle, every departure from sober, rational conduct would be an emancipation from criminal justice. I shall place my claim to your verdict upon no such dangerous foundation. I must convince you, not only that the unhappy prisoner was a lunatic, within my own definition of lunacy, but that the act in question was the *immediate, unqualified offspring of the disease.* In *civil* cases, as I have already said, the law avoids every act of the lunatic during the period of the lunacy, although the delusion may be extremely circumscribed; although the mind may be quite sound in all that is not within the shades of the very partial eclipse; and although the act to be avoid-

[7] And *frights* the isle from her *propriety.—Othello,* act ii., sc. 3. The reader can not fail to remark the strength and beauty of the images used here, and in other passages above and below to describe the different kinds of madness.

ed can in no way be connected with the influence of the insanity—but to deliver a lunatic from responsibility to *criminal* justice, above all in a case of such atrocity as the present, the relation between the disease and the act should be apparent. Where the connection is doubtful, the judgment should certainly be most indulgent, from the great difficulty of diving into the secret sources of a disordered mind; but still, I think that, as a doctrine of law, *the delusion and the act should be connected.*

The doctrine should be held very strictly on this subject.

You perceive, therefore, gentlemen, that the prisoner, in naming me for his counsel, has not obtained the assistance of a person who is disposed to carry the doctrine of insanity in his defense so far as even books would warrant me in carrying it. Some of the cases—that of Lord Ferrers, for instance—which I shall consider hereafter, as distinguished from the present—would not, in my mind, bear the shadow of an argument, as a defense against an indictment for murder. I can not allow the protection of insanity to a man who only exhibits violent passions and malignant resentments, acting upon *real circumstances;* who is impelled to evil by no morbid delusions; but who proceeds upon the ordinary perceptions of the mind. I can not consider such a man as falling within the protection which the law gives, and is bound to give, to those whom it has pleased God, for mysterious causes, to visit with this most afflicting calamity.

Principle restated.

He alone can be so emancipated, whose disease (call it what you will) consists, not merely in seeing with a prejudiced eye, or with odd and absurd particularities, differing, in many respects, from the contemplations of sober sense, upon the actual existence of things; but *he only*, whose reasoning and corresponding conduct, though governed by the ordinary dictates of reason, proceed upon something which has no foundation or existence.

Such was the insanity of the prisoner.

Gentlemen, it has pleased God so to visit the unhappy man before you; to shake his reason in its citadel; to cause him to build up as realities the most impossible phantoms of the mind, and to be impelled by them as motives *irresistible:* the whole fabric being nothing but the unhappy vision of his disease—existing nowhere else—having no foundation whatsoever in the very nature of things.

He had the full possession of his mind on other subjects.

Gentlemen, it has been stated by the Attorney General, and established by evidence which I am in no condition to contradict, nor have, indeed, any interest in contradicting, that, when the prisoner bought the pistol which he discharged at or *toward* his Majesty, he was well acquainted with the nature and use of it; that, as a soldier, he could not but know, that in his hands it was a sure instrument of death; that, when he bought the gunpowder, he knew it would prepare the pistol for its use; that, when he went to the playhouse, he knew he was going there, and knew every thing connected with the scene, as perfectly as any other person. I freely admit all this; I admit, also, that every person who listened to his conversation, and observed his deportment upon his apprehension, must have given precisely the evidence delivered by his Royal Highness the Duke of York, and that nothing like insanity appeared to those who examined him. But what then? I conceive, gentlemen, that *I* am more in the habit of examination than either that illustrious person or the witnesses from whom you have heard this account. Yet I well remember (indeed, I never can forget it), that since the noble and learned Judge has presided in this court, I examined, for the greater part of a day, in this very place, an unfortunate gentleman, who had indicted a most affectionate brother, together with the keeper of a mad-house at Hoxton [Dr. Sims], for having imprisoned him as a lunatic, while, according to his evidence, he was in his perfect senses. I was, unfortunately, not instructed in what his lunacy consisted, although my instructions left me no doubt of the fact; but, not having the clue, he completely foiled me in every attempt to expose his infirmity. You may believe that I left no means unemployed which long experience dictated, but without the smallest effect. The day was wasted, and the prosecutor, by the most affecting history of unmerited suffering, appeared to the judge and jury, and to a humane English audience, as the victim of the most wanton and barbarous oppression. At last Dr. Sims came into court, who had been prevented, by business, from an earlier attendance, and whose name, by-the-by, I observe to-day in the list of the witnesses for the Crown. From Dr. Sims I soon learned that the very man whom I had been above an hour examining, and with every possible effort which counsel are so much in the habit of exerting, believed himself to be *the Lord and Savior of mankind;* not merely at the time of his confinement, which was alone necessary for my defense, but during the whole time that he had been triumphing over every attempt to surprise him in the concealment of his disease! I then affected to lament the indecency of my ignorant examination, when he expressed his forgiveness, and said, with the utmost gravity and emphasis in the face of the whole court, "I AM THE CHRIST;" and so the cause ended. Gentlemen, this is not the only instance of the power of concealing this malady. I could consume the day if I were to enumerate them; but there is one so extremely remarkable, that I can not help stating it.

Similar case.

Another similar case.

Being engaged to attend the assizes at Chester upon a question of lunacy, and having been told that there had been a memorable case tried before Lord Mansfield in this place, I was anxious to procure a report of it. From that great man himself (who, within these walls, will ever be reverenced, being then retired, in his extreme old age, to his seat near London, in my own neighborhood) I obtained the following account of it: "A man of the name of Wood," said Lord Mansfield, "had indicted Dr. Monro for keeping him as a prisoner (I believe in the same mad-house at Hoxton) when he was sane. He underwent the most severe examination by the defendant's counsel without exposing his complaint; but Dr. Battye, having come upon the bench by me, and having desired me to ask him what was become of the PRINCESS whom he had corresponded with in cherry-juice, he showed in a moment what he was. He answered, that there was nothing at all in that, because, having been (as every body knew) imprisoned in a high tower, and being debarred the use of ink, he had no other means of correspondence but by writing his letters in cherry-juice, and throwing them into the river which surrounded the tower, where the Princess received them in a boat. There existed, of course, no tower, no imprisonment, no writing in cherry-juice, no river, no boat; but the whole the inveterate phantom of a morbid imagination. I immediately," continued Lord Mansfield, "directed Dr. Monro to be acquitted. But this man, Wood, being a merchant in Philpot Lane, and having been carried through the City in his way to the mad-house, he indicted Dr. Monro over again, for the trespass and imprisonment *in London*, knowing that he had lost his cause by speaking of the Princess at Westminster. And such," said Lord Mansfield, "is the extraordinary subtlety and cunning of madmen, that when he was cross-examined on the trial in London, as he had successfully been before, in order to expose his madness, all the ingenuity of the bar, and all the authority of the court, could not make him say a syllable upon that topic, which had put an end to the indictment before, although he still had the same indelible impression upon his mind, as he signified to those who were near him; but, conscious that the delusion had occasioned his defeat at Westminster, he obstinately persisted in holding it back."[8]

Application of these cases to the present question.

Now, gentlemen, let us look to the application of these cases. I am not examining, for the present, whether either of these persons ought to have been acquitted, if they had stood in the place of the prisoner now before you. That is quite a distinct consideration, which we shall come to hereafter. The direct application of them is only this, that if I bring before you such evidence of the prisoner's insanity as, *if believed to have really existed*, shall, in the opinion of the court, as the rule for your verdict in point of law, be sufficient for his deliverance, then that you ought not to be shaken in giving full credit to such evidence, notwithstanding the report of those who were present at his apprehension, who describe him as discovering no symptom whatever of mental incapacity or disorder. For I have shown you that insane persons frequently appear in the utmost state of ability and composure, even in the highest paroxysms of insanity, except when frenzy is the characteristic of the disease. In this respect, the cases I have cited to you have the most decided application, because they apply to the overthrow of the whole of the evidence (admitting, at the same time, the truth of it), by which the prisoner's case can alone be encountered.

This delusion may exist in cases where the subject of it can distinguish between right and wrong.

But it is said that whatever delusions may overshadow the mind, every person ought to be responsible for crimes *who has the knowledge of good and evil*. I think I can presently convince you, that there is something too general in this mode of considering the subject; and you do not, therefore, find any such proposition in the language of the celebrated writer alluded to by the Attorney General in his speech. Let me suppose that the character of an insane delusion consisted in the belief that some given person was any brute animal, or an inanimate being (and such cases have existed), and that upon the trial of such a lunatic for murder, you firmly, upon your oaths, were convinced, upon the uncontradicted evidence of a hundred persons, that he believed the man he had destroyed to have been a potter's vessel. Suppose it was quite impossible to doubt that fact, *although to all other intents and purposes he was sane*; conversing, reasoning, and acting, as men not in any manner tainted with insanity, converse, and reason, and conduct themselves. Let me suppose further, that he believed the man whom he destroyed, but whom he destroyed as a potter's vessel, to be the property of another; and that he had malice against such supposed person, and that he meant to injure him, knowing the act he was doing to be malicious and injurious, and that, in short, he had full knowledge of all the principles of good and evil. Yet it would be possible to convict such a person of murder, if, from the influence of his disease, he was ignorant of the relation he stood in to the man he had destroyed, and was utterly *unconscious* that he had struck at the life of a human being. I only put this case, and many others might be brought as examples to illustrate that the knowledge of good and evil is too general a description.

These principles substantially admitted by the Attorney General.

I really think, however, that the Attorney General and myself do not, in substance, very materially differ. From the whole of his most able speech, taken together, his meaning may, I think, be thus collected; that where the act which is criminal, is done under the dominion of malicious mischief and wicked intention, although such insanity might exist in a corner of the mind, as might avoid the acts of the delinquent as a lunatic in a *civil* case, yet that he ought not to be protected, if malicious mischief, and not insanity, had impelled him to the act for which he was *criminally* to answer; because, in such a case, the act might be justly ascribed to malignant motives, and not to the dominion of disease. I am not disposed to dispute such a proposition, in a case which would apply to it, and I can well conceive such cases may exist. The question, therefore, which you will have to try, is this:

The real question before the jury

Whether, when this unhappy man discharged the pistol in a direction which

[8] The evidence at Westminster was then proved against him by the short-hand writer.

convinced, and ought to convince, every person that it was pointed at the person of the King, he meditated mischief and violence to his Majesty, or whether he came to the theater (*which it is my purpose to establish*) under the dominion of the most melancholy insanity that ever degraded and overpowered the faculties of man. I admit that when he bought the pistol, and the gunpowder to load it, and when he loaded it, and came with it to the theater, and lastly, when he discharged it; every one of these acts would be overt acts of compassing the King's death, if at all or *any* of these periods he was actuated by that *mind and intention*, which would have constituted murder in the case of an individual, supposing the individual had been actually killed. I admit, also, that the mischievous, and, in this case, traitorous intention must be inferred from all these acts, unless *I can rebut the inferences by proof.* If I were to fire a pistol toward you, gentlemen, where you are now sitting, the act would undoubtedly infer the malice. *The whole proof, therefore, is undoubtedly cast upon* ME.

Was the motive of the prisoner a permanent delusion of the kind described.

In every case of treason, or murder, which are precisely the same, except that the unconsummated intention in the case of the King is the same as the actual murder of a private man, the jury must impute to the person whom they condemn by their verdict, *the motive* which constitutes the crime. And your province to-day will, therefore, be to decide whether the prisoner, when he did the act, was under the uncontrollable dominion of insanity, and was impelled to it by a *morbid delusion;* or whether it was the act of a man who, though occasionally mad, or even at the time not perfectly collected, was yet not actuated by the disease, but by the suggestion of a wicked and malignant disposition.

I admit, therefore, freely, that if, after you have heard the evidence which I hasten to lay before you, of the state of the prisoner's mind, and close up to the very time of this catastrophe, you shall still not feel yourselves clearly justified in negativing the wicked motives imputed by this indictment, I shall leave you in the hands of the learned judges to declare to you the law of the land, and shall not seek to place society in a state of uncertainty by any appeal addressed only to your compassion. I am appointed by the court to claim for the prisoner the full protection of the law, but not to misrepresent it in his protection.

Gentlemen, the facts of this melancholy case lie within a narrow compass.

Early life of the prisoner.

The unfortunate person before you was a soldier. He became so, I believe, in the year 1793—and is now about twenty-nine years of age. He served in Flanders, under the Duke of York, as appears by his Royal Highness's evidence; and being a most approved soldier, he was one of those singled out as an orderly man to attend upon the person of the Commander-in-Chief. You have been witnesses, gentlemen, to the calmness with which the prisoner has sitten in his place during the trial. There was but one exception to it. You saw the emotion which overpowered him when the illustrious person now in court took his seat upon the bench. Can you then believe, from the evidence, for I do not ask you to judge as physiognomists, or to give the rein to compassionate fancy; but can there be any doubt that it was the generous emotion of the mind, on seeing the Prince, under whom he had served with so much bravery and honor? Every man, certainly, must judge for himself. I am counsel, not a witness, in the cause. But it is a most striking circumstance, as you find from the Crown's evidence, that when he was dragged through the orchestra under the stage, and charged with an act for which he considered his life as forfeited, he addressed the Duke of York with the same enthusiasm which has marked the demeanor I am adverting to. Mr. Richardson, who showed no disposition in his evidence to help the prisoner, but who spoke with the calmness and circumspection of truth, and who had no idea that the person he was examining was a lunatic, has given you the account of the burst of affection on his first seeing the Duke of York, against whose father and sovereign he was supposed to have had the consciousness of treason. The King himself, whom he was supposed to have so malignantly attacked, never had a more gallant, loyal, or suffering soldier. His gallantry and loyalty will be proved; his sufferings speak for themselves.

His attachment as a soldier to his commanding officer.

His wounds.

About five miles from Lisle, upon the attack made on the British army, this unfortunate soldier was in the fifteenth light dragoons, in the thickest of the ranks, exposing his life for his Prince, whom he is supposed to-day to have sought to murder. The first wound he received is most materially connected with the subject we are considering; you may see the effect of it now.[9] The point of a sword was impelled against him with all the force of a man urging his horse in battle. When the court put the prisoner under my protection, I thought it my duty to bring Mr. Cline to inspect him in Newgate. It will appear by the evidence of that excellent and conscientious person, who is known to be one of the first anatomists in the world, that from this wound one of two things must have happened: either, that by the immediate operation of surgery the displaced part of the skull must have been taken away, or been forced inward on the brain. The second stroke, also, speaks for itself: you may now see its effects. [Here Mr. Erskine touched the head of the prisoner.] He was cut across all the nerves which give sensibility and animation to the body, and his head hung down almost dissevered, until by the act of surgery it was placed in the position you now see it. But thus, almost destroyed, he still recollected his duty, and continued to maintain the glory of his country, when a sword divided the membrane of his neck where it terminates in the head; yet he still kept his place,

9 Mr. Erskine put his hand to the prisoner's head, who stood by him at the bar of the court.

though his helmet had been thrown off by the blow which I secondly described, when by another sword he was cut into the very brain—you may now see its membrane uncovered. Mr. Cline will tell you that he examined these wounds, and he can better describe them. I have myself seen them, but am no surgeon; from his evidence you will have to consider their consequences. It may be said that many soldiers receive grievous wounds without their producing insanity. So they may, undoubtedly; but we are upon *the fact*. There was a discussion the other day, whether a man who had been seemingly hurt by a fall beyond remedy could get up and walk. The people around said it was impossible; but he did get up and walk, and so there was an end to the impossibility. The effects of the prisoner's wounds were known by the *immediate* event of insanity, and Mr Cline will tell you that it would have been strange, indeed, if any other event had followed. We are not here upon a case of insanity arising from the spiritual part of man, as it may be affected by hereditary taint, by intemperance, or by violent passions, the operations of which are various and uncertain; but we have to deal with a species of insanity more resembling what has been described as idiocy, proceeding from original malorganization. *There* the disease is, from its very nature, *incurable*; and so where a man (like the prisoner) has become insane from *violence to the brain, which permanently affects its structure*, however such a man may appear occasionally to others, his disease is *immovable*. If the prisoner, therefore, were to live a thousand years, he *never* could recover from the consequence of that day.

But this is not all. Another blow was still aimed at him, which he held up his arm to avoid, when his hand was cut into the bone. It is an afflicting subject, gentlemen, and better to be spoken of by those who understand it; and, to and all further description, he was then thrust almost through and through the body with a bayonet, and left in a ditch among the slain.

He was afterward carried to a hospital, where he was known by his tongue to one of his countrymen, who will be examined as a witness, who found him, not merely as a wounded soldier deprived of the powers of his body, but bereft of his senses forever.

The madness that followed.

He was affected from the very beginning with that species of madness which, from violent agitation, fills the mind with the most inconceivable imaginations, wholly unfitting it for all dealing with human affairs, according to the sober estimate and standard of reason. He imagined that he had constant intercourse with the Almighty Author of all things; that the world was coming to a conclusion; and that, like our blessed Savior, he was to *sacrifice himself for its salvation*. So obstinately did this morbid image continue, that you will be convinced he went to the theater to perform, as he imagined, that blessed sacrifice; and, because he would not be guilty of suicide, though called upon by the imperious voice of Heaven, he wished that by the appearance of crime his life might be taken away from him by others. This bewildered, extravagant species of madness appeared immediately after his wounds, on his first entering the hospital; and on the very same account he was discharged from the army on his return to England, which the Attorney General very honorably and candidly seemed to intimate.

The peculiar nature of the delusion under which he labored.

Manifested in an attempt to destroy his own child.

To proceed with the proofs of his insanity *down to the very period of his supposed guilt*. This unfortunate man before you is the father of an infant of eight months; and I have no doubt, that if the boy had been brought into court (but this is a grave place for the consideration of justice, and not a theater for stage effect)—I say, I have no doubt whatever, that if this poor infant had been brought into court, you would have seen the unhappy father wrung with all the emotions of parental affection. Yet, upon the Tuesday preceding the Thursday when he went to the playhouse, you will find his disease still urging him forward, with the impression *that the time was come* when he must be destroyed for the benefit of mankind; and in the confusion, or, rather, delirium of this wild conception, he came to the bed of the mother, who had this infant in her arms, and endeavored to dash out its brains against the wall. The family was alarmed; and the neighbors being called in, the child was, with difficulty, rescued from the unhappy parent, who, in his madness, would have destroyed it.

Comparison of his feelings at that time and when he fired at the King.

Now let me, for a moment, suppose that he had succeeded in the accomplishment of his insane purpose; and the question had been, whether he was guilty of murder. Surely, the affection for this infant, up to the very moment of his distracted violence, would have been conclusive in his favor. But not more so than his loyalty to the King, and his attachment to the Duke of York, as applicable to the case before us; yet at that very period, even of extreme distraction, he conversed as rationally on all other subjects as he did with the Duke of York at the theater. The prisoner knew perfectly that he was the husband of the woman and the father of the child. The tears of affection ran down his face at the very moment that he was about to accomplish its destruction. During the whole of this scene of horror, he was not at all deprived of memory; in the Attorney General's sense of the expression; he could have communicated, at that moment, every circumstance of his past life, and every thing connected with his present condition, *except only the quality of the act he was meditating*. In *that*, he was under the overruling dominion of a morbid imagination, and conceived that he was acting against the dictates of nature in obedience to the superior commands of Heaven, which had told him, that the moment he was dead, and the infant with him, all nature was to be changed, and all mankind were to be redeemed by his dissolution. There was not an idea in his mind, from the beginning to the end, of the destruction of the King. On the contrary, he always maintained his loyalty—lamented that he could not go again to fight his battles in the field; and it will be proved, that only a few days before the period in question, being present when a song was sung, indecent, as it regarded the person and condition of his Majesty, he left the room with loud expressions of indignation, and immediately sang "God save the King," with all the enthusiasm of an old soldier, who had bled in the service of his country.

His prevailing sentiment of *loyalty* one of the strongest points in the case.

I confess to you, gentlemen, that this last circumstance, which may, to some, appear insignificant, is, in my mind, most momentous testimony. For if this man had been in the habit of associating with persons inimical to the government of our country, so that mischief might have been fairly argued to have mixed itself with madness (which, by-the-by, it frequently does); if it could in any way have been collected that, from his disorder, more easily inflamed and worked upon, he had been led away by disaffected persons to become the instrument of wickedness; if it could have been established that such had been his companions and his habits, I should have been ashamed to lift up my voice in his defense. I should have felt that, however his mind might have been weak and disordered, yet if his understanding sufficiently existed to be methodically acted upon as an instrument of malice, I could not have asked for an acquittal. But you find, on the contrary, in the case before you, that, notwithstanding the opportunity which the Crown has had, and which, upon all such occasions, it justly employs to detect treason, either against the person of the King or against his government, *not one witness* has been able to fix upon the prisoner before you any one companion, of even a doubtful description, or any one expression from which disloyalty could be inferred, while the whole history of his life repels the imputation. His courage in defense of the King and his dominions, and his affection for his son, in such unanswerable evidence, all speak aloud against the presumption that he went to the theater with a mischievous intention.

Peculiarity of his feelings on attempting the King's life.

To recur again to the evidence of Mr. Richardson, who delivered most honorable and impartial testimony. I certainly am obliged to admit, that what a prisoner says for himself, when coupled at the very time with an overt act of wickedness, is no evidence whatever to alter the obvious quality of the act he has committed. If, for instance, I, who am now addressing you, had fired the same pistol toward the box of the King, and, having been dragged under the orchestra and secured for criminal justice, I had said that I had no intention to kill the King, but was weary of my life, and meant to be condemned as guilty; would any man, who was not himself insane, consider that as a defense? Certainly not: because it would be without the whole foundation of the prisoner's previous condition, part of which it is even difficult to apply closely and directly by strict evidence, without taking his undoubted insanity into consideration, because it is his unquestionable insanity which alone stamps the effusions of his mind with sincerity and truth.

He felt it necessary to do something which would lead to his being put to death *judicially*.

The idea which had impressed itself, but in most confused images, upon this unfortunate man, was, *that he must be destroyed, but ought not to destroy himself*. He once had the idea of firing over the King's carriage in the street; but then he imagined he should be immediately killed, which was not the mode of propitiation for the world. And as our Savior, before his passion, had gone into the garden to pray, this fallen and afflicted being, after he had taken the infant out of bed to destroy it, returned also to the garden, saying, as he afterward said to the Duke of York, "that all was not over —that a great work was to be finished;" and there he remained in prayer, the victim of the same melancholy visitation.

Comparison of this case with that of Lord Ferrers.

Gentlemen, these are the facts, freed from even the possibility of artifice or disguise; because the testimony to support them will be beyond all doubt. In contemplating the law of the country, and the precedents of its justice to which they must be applied, I find nothing to challenge or question. I approve of them throughout. I subscribe to all that is written by Lord Hale. I agree with all the authorities cited by the Attorney General, from Lord Coke; but above all, I do most cordially agree in the instance of convictions by which he illustrated them in his able address.[10] I have now lying before me the case of Earl Ferrers: unquestionably there could not be a shadow of doubt, and none appears to have been entertained, of his guilt. I wish, indeed, nothing more than to contrast the two cases; and so far am I from disputing either the principle of that condemnation, or the evidence that was the foundation of it, that I invite you to examine whether any two instances in the whole body of the criminal law are more diametrically opposite to each other than the case of Earl Ferrers and that now before you. Lord Ferrers was divorced from his wife by act of Parliament; and a person of the name of Johnson, who had been his steward, had taken part with the lady in that proceeding, and had conducted the business in carrying the act through the two Houses. Lord Ferrers consequently wished to turn him out of a farm which he occupied under him; but his estate being in trust, Johnson was supported by the trustees in his possession. There were, also, some differences respecting coal-mines; and in consequence of both transactions, Lord Ferrers took up the most violent resentment against him. Let me

[10] The reader will remark, that in the cases which Mr. Erskine goes on to consider, the statement of the facts is not only clear and beautiful in itself, but is shaped throughout with a particular reference to the case of Hadfield, so as to bring out the points of contrast in strong relief, and thus open the way for the distinctions which follow. This kind of *preparation* is one of Mr. Erskine's greatest excellence.

here observe, gentlemen, that this was not a resentment founded upon any *illusion;* not a resentment forced upon a distempered mind by fallacious images, but depending upon *actual circumstances and real facts;* and, acting like any other man under the influence of malignant passions, he repeatedly declared that he would be revenged on Mr. Johnson, particularly for the part he had taken in depriving him of a contract respecting the mines.

Now, suppose Lord Ferrers could have showed that no difference with Mr. Johnson had ever existed regarding his wife at all—that Mr. Johnson had never been his steward—and that he had only, from delusion, believed so when his situation in life was quite different. Suppose, further, that an *illusive imagination* had *alone* suggested to him that he had been thwarted by Johnson in his contract for these coal-mines, there never having been any contract at all for coal-mines—in short, that the whole basis of his enmity was without any foundation in nature, and had been shown to have been a *morbid image* imperiously fastened upon his mind. Such a case as that would have exhibited a character of insanity in Lord Ferrers extremely different from that in which it was presented by the evidence to his peers. Before them, he only appeared as a man of turbulent passions, whose mind was disturbed by no fallacious images of things without existence; whose quarrel with Johnson was founded *upon no illusions*, but upon existing facts; whose resentment proceeded to the fatal consummation with all the ordinary indications of mischief and malice; and who conducted his own defense with the greatest dexterity and skill. WHO, THEN, COULD DOUBT THAT LORD FERRERS WAS A MURDERER? When the act was done, he said, "I am glad I have done it. He was a villain, and I am revenged." But when he afterward saw that the wound was probably mortal, and that it involved consequences fatal to himself, he desired the surgeon to take all possible care of his patient; and, conscious of his crime, kept at bay the men who came with arms to arrest him: showing, from the beginning to the end, nothing that does not generally accompany the crime for which he was condemned. He was proved, to be sure, to be a man subject to unreasonable prejudices, addicted to absurd practices, and agitated by violent passions. But the act was not done under the dominion of uncontrollable disease; and whether the mischief and malice were substantive, or marked in the mind of a man whose passions bordered upon, or even amounted to insanity, it did not convince the Lords that, under all the circumstances of the case, he was not a fit object of criminal justice.

In the same manner, Arnold, who shot at Lord Onslow, and who was tried at Kingston soon after the Black Act passed on the accession of George I. Lord Onslow having been very vigilant as a magistrate in suppressing clubs, which were supposed to be set on foot to disturb the new government, Arnold had frequently been heard to declare that Lord Onslow would ruin his country; and although he appeared from the evidence to be a man of most wild and turbulent manners, yet the people round Guildford, who knew him, did not, in general, consider him to be insane. His counsel could not show that any morbid *delusion* had ever overshadowed his understanding. They could not show, as I shall, that just before he shot at Lord Onslow, he had endeavored to destroy his own beloved child. It was a case of *human-resentment.*

With that of Arnold.

I might instance, also, the case of Oliver, who was indicted for the murder of Mr. Wood, a potter, in Staffordshire. Mr. Wood had refused his daughter to this man in marriage. My friend, Mr. Milles, was counsel for him at the assizes. He had been employed as a surgeon and apothecary by the father, who forbid him his house, and desired him to bring in his bill for payment; when, in the agony of disappointment, and brooding over the injury he had suffered, on his being admitted to Mr. Wood to receive payment, he shot him upon the spot. The trial occupied great part of the day; yet, for my own part, I can not conceive that there was any thing in the case for a jury to deliberate on. He was a man acting upon *existing facts*, and upon *human resentments* connected with them. He was at the very time carrying on his business, which required learning and reflection, and, indeed, a reach of mind beyond the ordinary standard, being trusted by all who knew him as a practitioner in medicine. Neither did he go to Mr. Wood's under the influence of *illusion;* but he went to destroy the life of a man who was placed exactly in the circumstances which the mind of the criminal represented him. He went to execute vengeance on him for refusing his daughter. In such a case there might, no doubt, be passion approaching to frenzy; but there wanted that characteristic of madness to emancipate him from criminal justice.

With that of Oliver.

There was another instance of this description in the case of a most unhappy woman, who was tried, in Essex, for the murder of Mr. Errington, who had seduced and abandoned her and the children she had borne to him. It must be a consolation to those who prosecuted her, that she was acquitted, as she is at this time in a most undoubted and deplorable state of insanity. But I confess, if I had been upon the jury who tried her, I should have entertained great doubts and difficulties; for, although the unhappy woman had before exhibited strong marks of insanity, arising from grief and disappointment, yet she acted upon *facts* and *circumstances* which had an *existence*, and which were calculated, upon the ordinary principles of human action, to produce the most violent resentment. Mr. Errington having just cast her off, and married another woman, or taken his under his protection, her jealousy was excited to such a pitch as occasionally to overpower her understanding; but when she went to Mr. Errington's house, where she shot him, she went with the express and deliberate purpose of shooting him. That fact was unquestionable. She went there

With that of the murderer of Mr. Errington.

with a resentment long rankling in her bosom, bottomed on an existing foundation. She did not act under *a delusion*, that he had deserted her when he had not, but took revenge upon him for an actual desertion. But still the jury, in the humane consideration of her sufferings, pronounced the insanity to be predominant over resentment, and they acquitted her.

But let me suppose (which would liken it to the case before us) that she had never cohabited with Mr. Errington; that she never had had children by him; and, consequently, that he neither had, nor could possibly have deserted or injured her. Let me suppose, in short, that she had never seen him in her life, but that her resentment had been founded on the morbid delusion that Mr. Errington, who had never seen her, had been the author of all her wrongs and sorrows; and that, under that *diseased* impression, she had shot him. If that had been the case, gentlemen, she would have been acquitted upon the opening, and no judge would have sat to try such a cause. The *act itself* would have been decisively characteristic of madness, because, being founded upon nothing existing, it could not have proceeded from malice, which the law requires to be charged and proved, in every case of murder, as the foundation of a conviction.

Application to the case in hand.

Let us now recur to the cause we are engaged in, and examine it upon those principles by which I am ready to stand or fall, in the judgment of the court. You have a man before you who will appear, upon the evidence, to have received those almost deadly wounds which I described to you, producing the immediate and immovable effects which the eminent surgeon, whose name I have mentioned, will prove that they could not but have produced. It will appear that, from that period, he was visited by the severest paroxysms of madness, and was repeatedly confined with all the coercion which it is necessary to practice upon lunatics; yet, what is quite decisive against the imputation of treason against the person of the King, his loyalty never forsook him. Sane or insane, it was his very characteristic to love his Sovereign and his country, although the delusions which distracted him were sometimes, *in other respects*, as contradictory as they were violent.

Striking instances of the prisoner's delusions.

Of this inconsistency, there was a most striking instance on only the Tuesday before the Thursday in question, when it will be proved that he went to see one Truelet, who had been committed by the Duke of Portland as a lunatic. This man had taken up an idea that our Savior's second advent, and the dissolution of all human beings, were at hand; and conversed in this strain of madness. This mixing itself with the insane delusion of the prisoner, he immediately broke out upon the subject of his own propitiation and sacrifice for mankind, although only the day before he had exclaimed that the Virgin Mary was a whore; that Christ was a bastard; that God was a thief; and that he and this Truelet were to live with him at White Conduit House, and there to be enthroned together. His mind, in short, was overpowered and overwhelmed with distraction.

Case reviewed and its leading points presented.

The charge against the prisoner is the overt act of compassing the death of the King, in firing a pistol at his Majesty—an act which only differs from murder, inasmuch as the bare compassing is equal to the accomplishment of the malignant purpose; and it will be *your* office, under the advice of the judge, to decide by your verdict to which of the two impulses of the mind you refer the act in question. You will have to decide, whether you attribute it wholly to mischief and malice, or wholly to insanity, or to the one mixing itself with the other. If you find it attributable to mischief and malice *only*, LET THE MAN DIE. The law demands his death for the public safety. If you consider it as conscious malice and mischief mixing itself with insanity, I leave him in the hands of the court, to say how he is to be dealt with; it is a question too difficult for me. I do not stand here to disturb the order of society, or to bring confusion upon my country But if you find that the act was committed wholly under the dominion of insanity; if you are satisfied that he went to the theater contemplating his own destruction only; and that, when he fired the pistol, he did not *maliciously* aim at the person of the King—you will then be bound, even upon the principle which the Attorney General himself humanely and honorably stated to you, to acquit this most unhappy prisoner.

If, in bringing these considerations hereafter to the standard of the evidence, any doubts should occur to you on the subject, the question for your decision will then be, which of the two alternatives is the most probable—a duty which you will perform in the exercise of that reason of which, for wise purposes, it has pleased God to deprive the unfortunate man whom you are trying. Your sound understandings will easily enable you to distinguish *infirmities*, which are misfortunes, from *motives*, which are crimes. Before the day ends, the evidence will be decisive upon this subject.

No evidence of any pretense or fraud when seized.

There is, however, another consideration, which I ought distinctly to present to you; because I think that more turns upon it than any other view of the subject; namely, whether the prisoner's defense can be impeached for artifice or fraud. I admit, that if, at the moment when he was apprehended, there can be fairly imputed to him any pretense or counterfeit of insanity, it would taint the whole case, and leave him without protection. But for such a suspicion there is not even a shadow of foundation. It is repelled by the whole history and character of his disease, as well as of his life, independent of it. If you were trying a man, under the Black Act, for shooting at another, and there was a doubt upon the question of malice, would it not be important, or rather decisive evidence, that the prisoner had no resentment against the prosecutor; but that, on the contrary, he was a man whom he had always loved and served? Now the prisoner was maimed, cut down, and destroyed, in the service of the King.

Peroration: The King's life has never been aimed at amid all the imputed excesses of reform.

Gentlemen, another reflection presses very strongly on my mind, which I find it difficult to suppress. In every state there are political differences and parties, and individuals disaffected to the system of government under which they live as subjects. There are not many such, I trust, in this country. But whether there are many or any of such persons, there is one circumstance which has peculiarly distinguished his Majesty's life and reign, and which is in itself as a host in the prisoner's defense, since, amid all the treasons and all the seditions which have been charged on reformers of government as conspiracies to disturb it, no hand or voice has been lifted up against the person of the King. There have, indeed, been unhappy lunatics who, from ideas too often mixing themselves with insanity, have intruded themselves into the palace, but no malicious attack has ever been made upon the King to be settled by a trial. His Majesty's character and conduct have been a safer shield than guards, or than laws. Gentlemen, I wish to continue to that sacred life that best of all securities. I seek to continue it under that protection where it has been so long protected. We are not to do evil that good may come of it; we are not to stretch the laws to hedge round the life of the King with a greater security than that which the Divine Providence has so happily realized.

It is safest when guarded by impartial justice, without excited feelings or any excess of zeal.

Perhaps there is no principle of religion more strongly inculcated by the sacred scriptures than that beautiful and encouraging lesson of our Savior himself upon confidence in the Divine protection: "Take no heed for your life, what ye shall eat, or what ye shall drink, or wherewithal ye shall be clothed; but seek ye first the kingdom of God, and all these things shall be added unto you." By which it is undoubtedly not intended that we are to disregard the conservation of life, or to neglect the means necessary for its sustentation; nor that we are to be careless of whatever may contribute to our comfort and happiness; but that we should be contented to receive them as they are given to us, and not seek them in the violation of the rule and order appointed for the government of the world. On this principle, nothing can more tend to the security of his Majesty and his government, than the scene which this day exhibits in the calm, humane, and impartial administration of justice; and if, in my part of this solemn duty, I have in any manner trespassed upon the just security provided for the public happiness, I wish to be corrected. I declare to you, solemnly, that my only aim has been to secure for the prisoner at the bar, whose life and death are in the balance, that he should be judged rigidly by the evidence and the law. I have made no appeal to your passions—you have no right to exercise them. This is not even a case in which, if the prisoner be found guilty, the royal mercy should be counseled to interfere. He is either an accountable being, or not accountable. If he was *unconscious* of the mischief he was engaged in, the law is a corollary, and he is not guilty. But if, when the evidence closes, you think he was conscious, and maliciously meditated the treason he is charged with, it is impossible to conceive a crime more vile and detestable; and I should consider the King's life to be ill attended to, indeed, if not protected by the full vigor of the laws, which are watchful over the security of the meanest of his subjects. It is a most important consideration, both as it regards the prisoner, and the community of which he is a member. Gentlemen, I leave it with you.

Lord Kenyon, who presided at the trial, appeared, it is said, much prejudiced against the prisoner while the evidence for the Crown was taken. But when Mr. Erskine had stated the principle upon which he grounded his defense, and when his Lordship found that the facts came up to the case opened for the prisoner, he delivered to the Attorney General the opinion of the court, that the case should not be proceeded in. A verdict of acquittal was, therefore, given, without any reply for the Crown, and the prisoner was placed in confinement at Bedlam. He remained there to an extreme old age, perfectly rational on most subjects, but liable to strong delusions, which rendered it unsafe to discharge him.

In consequence of the attack of Hadfield upon George III., the peculiar provisions of the laws, referred to by Mr. Erskine in his exordium, were changed. Though he assigned very ingenious reasons for giving to a person who attempted the life of the King greater advantages as to trial, and as to the degree of evidence by which the change was to be established, than were granted in the case of a similar attempt on a subject, it was generally felt that this was neither wise nor safe. Hence the statute 39 and 40, George III., c. 93, was passed, by which it is enacted, that in all cases of high treason, in compassing or imagining the death of the King, and of misprision of such treason, where the overt act of such treason shall be alleged in the indictment to be the assassination of the King, or a direct attempt against his life or person, the person accused shall be indicted and tried in the same manner in every respect, and upon the like evidence, as if he was charged with murder, but the judgment and execution shall be the same as in other cases of high treason.

SPEECH

OF MR. ERSKINE FOR THE REV. GEORGE MARKHAM AGAINST JOHN FAWCETT, ESQ., FOR CRIMINAL CONVERSATION WITH HIS WIFE, DELIVERED BEFORE THE DEPUTY SHERIFF OF MIDDLESEX AND A SPECIAL JURY, MAY 4, 1802, ON AN INQUISITION OF DAMAGES.

INTRODUCTION.

WITH all the varied abilities of Mr. Erskine, there was nothing in which he was thought so much to excel as the management of cases of adultery. He was almost uniformly retained for the complainant; and some of the most thrilling strains of his eloquence were on this subject. He obtained greater damages than any other advocate in England; and some even complained that, with Kenyon on the bench and Erskine at the bar, the judgments of juries in such cases became absolutely vindictive.

In the present instance, there was no room for denial or exculpation, and the case went by default. It was, therefore, simply a hearing as to the amount of damages; and was referred by the court to a special jury, convened by the Under Sheriff in a private room at the King's Arms Tavern, Westminster. Eloquence, under such circumstances, would seem to be almost out of the question; and Mr. Erskine, therefore, entered on the subject in the quiet manner of a private individual conversing with a few old acquaintances in a parlor of their own dwellings. But he instantly passed to a topic always interesting to an Englishman, the peculiar character of an English jury; and touched their pride by the suggestion—one which runs throughout the whole speech—that the defendant, dreading the exposure of a public trial, had thrust the jury aside into a private room to cover his crimes for money. He then lays open the facts of the case in a narration of uncommon simplicity and beauty; dwells on the peculiarly aggravating circumstances which attended it; and takes the ground, that a *full recompense* (so far as money could give it) ought to be made to the plaintiff for the loss and suffering he had sustained. The damages were laid at £20,000, a sum more than double the defendant's entire property. Still Mr. Erskine contends that these damages ought to be awarded in *full*, as an act of simple justice to Mr. Markham, and as a warning to others for the protection of families in the intimacy of private friendship. On this last topic, he presents considerations founded on the structure of society, which are worthy of so fervent an admirer and student of Mr. Burke.

It is a striking fact, that on so hackneyed a theme, necessarily involving a limited range of considerations, Mr. Erskine has nothing commonplace—no strained expressions, no extravagant sensibility, no *clap-trap* of any kind. In such a case, a man often shows his ability quite as much by what he does *not* say, as by what he does say; and we find Mr. Erskine here, as every where else, a perfect model of a *business speaker*, keeping his exuberant powers of fancy, sentiment, and pathos in the strictest subordination to the realities of his case.

SPEECH, &c.

MR. SHERIFF, AND GENTLEMEN OF THE JURY,—In representing the unfortunate gentleman who has sustained the injury which has been stated to you by my learned friend, Mr. Holroyd, who opened the pleadings, I feel one great satisfaction—a satisfaction founded, as I conceive, on a sentiment perfectly constitutional. I am about to address myself to men whom I PERSONALLY KNOW; to men, honorable in their lives, moral, judicious; and capable of correctly estimating the injuries they are called upon to condemn in their character of jurors. THIS, gentlemen, is the only country in the world where there is such a tribunal as the one before which I am now to speak; for, however in other countries such institutions as our own may have been set up of late, it is only by that maturity which it requires ages to give to governments—by that progressive wisdom which has slowly ripened the Constitution of our country—that it is possible there can exist such a body of men as YOU are. It is the great privilege of the subjects of England that they judge one another. It is to be recollected that, although we are in this private room, all the sanctions of justice are present. It makes no manner of difference, whether I address you in the presence of the under sheriff, your respectable chairman, or with the assistance of the highest magistrate of the state.

Character and circumstances of the jury.

The defendant has, on this occasion, suffered judgment by default: *other* adulterers have done so before him. Some have done so under the idea that, by suffering judgment against them, they had retired from the public eye—from the awful presence of the judge; and that they came into a corner where there was not such an assembly of persons to witness their misconduct, and where it was to be canvassed before persons who might be less qualified to judge the case to be addressed to them.

Object of the defendant in suffering the case to go by default.

It is not long, however, since such persons have had an opportunity of judging how much they were mistaken in this respect. The largest damages, in cases of adultery, have been given in this place. By this place, I do not mean the particular room in which we are now assembled, but under inquisitions directed to the sheriff; and the instances to which I allude are of modern, and, indeed, recent date.

His probable mistake.

Gentlemen, after all the experience I have had, I feel myself, I confess, considerably embarrassed in what manner to address you. There are some subjects that harass and overwhelm the mind of man. There are some kinds of distresses one knows not how to deal with. It is impossible to contemplate the situation of the plaintiff without being disqualified, in some degree, to represent it to others with effect. It is no less impossible for you, gentlemen, to receive on a sudden the impressions which have been long in *my* mind, without feeling overpowered with sensations which, after all, had better be absent, when men are called upon, in the exercise of duty, to pronounce a legal judgment.

Transition: Painful nature of the subject to be presented.

The plaintiff is the third son of his Grace the Archbishop of York, a clergyman of the Church of England; presented, in the year 1791, to the living of Stokeley, in Yorkshire; and now, by his Majesty's favor, Dean of the Cathedral of York. He married, in the year 1789, Miss Sutton, the daughter of Sir Richard Sutton, Bart., of Norwood, in Yorkshire, a lady of great beauty and accomplishments, most virtuously educated, and who, but for the crime of the defendant, which assembles you here, would, as she has expressed it herself, have been the happiest of womankind. This gentleman having been presented, in 1791, by his father, to this living, where, I understand, there had been no resident rector for forty years, set an example to the Church and to the public, which was peculiarly virtuous in a man circumstanced as he was; for, if there can be any person more likely than another to protect himself securely with privileges and indulgences, it might be supposed to be the son of the metropolitan of the province. This gentleman, however, did not avail himself of the advantage of his birth and station. Although he was a very young man, he devoted himself entirely to the sacred duties of his profession; at a large expense he repaired the rectory-house for the reception of his family, as if it had been his own patrimony, while, in his extensive improvements, he adopted only those arrangements which were calculated to lay the foundation of an innocent and peaceful life. He had married this lady, and entertained no other thoughts than that of cheerfully devoting himself to all the duties, public and private, which his situation called upon him to perform.

Narration: Mr. Markham's marriage and institution in the ministry.

About this time, or soon afterward, the defendant became the purchaser of an estate in the neighborhood of Stokeley, and, by such purchase, an inhabitant of that part of the country, and the neighbor of this unfortunate gentleman. It is a most affecting circumstance, that the plaintiff and the defendant had been bred together at Westminster School; and in my mind it is still more affecting, when I reflect what it is which has given to that school so much rank, respect, and illustration. It has derived its highest advantages from the reverend father of the unfortunate gentleman whom I represent.[1] It was the School of Westminster which gave birth to that learning which afterward presided over it, and advanced its character. However some men may be disposed to speak or write concerning public schools, I take upon me to say they are among the wisest of our institutions. Whoever looks at the national character of the English people, and compares it with that of all the other nations upon the earth, will be driven to impute it to that reciprocation of ideas and sentiments which fill and fructify the mind in the early period of youth, and to the affectionate sympathies and friendships which rise up in the human heart before it is deadened or perverted by the interests and corruptions of the world. These youthful attachments are proverbial, and, indeed, few instances have occurred of any breaches of them; because a man, before he can depart from the obligations they impose, must have forsaken every principle of virtue, and every sentiment of manly honor. When, therefore, the plaintiff found his old school-fellow and companion settled in his neighborhood, he immediately considered him as his brother. Indeed, he might well consider him as a brother, since, after having been at Westminster, they were *again* thrown together in the same college at Oxford; so that the friendship they had formed in their youth became cemented and consolidated upon their first entrance into the world. It is no wonder, therefore, that when the defendant came down to settle in the neighborhood of the plaintiff, he should be attracted toward him by the impulse of his former attachment. He recommended him to the Lord Lieutenant of the county, and, being himself a magistrate, he procured him a share in the magistracy. He introduced him to the respectable circle of his acquaintances. He invited him to his house, and cherished him there as a friend. It is *this* which renders the business of to-day most affecting, as it regards the plaintiff, and wicked in the extreme, as it relates to the defendant, because the confidences of friendship conferred the opportunities of seduction. The plaintiff had no pleasures or affections beyond the sphere of his domestic life; and except in his occasional residences at York, which were but for short periods, and at a very inconsiderable distance from his home, he constantly reposed in the bosom of his family. I believe it will be impossible for my learned friend to invade his character. on the contrary, he will

Mr. Fawcett's removal into the same neighborhood.

Their intimacy in early life.

Mr. Markham's confidence and cordial reception of his friend.

[1] Dr. Markham, afterward Archbishop of York, was for some years at the head of the Westminster School, and was so much distinguished for his learning and his tact in drawing out the abilities of his pupils, that he was chosen to be private tutor of the Prince of Wales and his brother the Duke of York.

be found to have been a pattern of conjugal and parental affection.

Mr. Fawcett being thus settled in the neighborhood, and thus received by Mr. Markham as his friend and companion, it is needless to say he could harbor no suspicion that the defendant was meditating the seduction of his wife; there was nothing, indeed, in his conduct, or in the conduct of the unfortunate lady, that could administer any cause of jealousy to the most guarded or suspicious temper. Yet, dreadful to relate, and it is, indeed, the bitterest evil of which the plaintiff has to complain, a criminal intercourse, for nearly *five years* before the discovery of the connection, had most probably taken place.

Mr. Fawcett's abuse of that confidence to the purposes of seduction.

I will leave you to consider what must have been the feelings of such a husband, upon the fatal discovery that his wife, and such a wife, had conducted herself in a manner that not merely deprived him of her comfort and society, but placed him in a situation too horrible to be described. If a man without children is suddenly cut off by an adulterer from all the comforts and happiness of marriage, the discovery of *his* condition is happiness itself when compared with that to which the plaintiff is reduced. When children, by a woman, lost forever to the husband, by the arts of the adulterer, are begotten in the unsuspected days of virtue and happiness, there remains a consolation; mixed, indeed, with the most painful reflections, yet a consolation still. But what is the plaintiff's situation? He does not know at *what time* this heavy calamity fell upon him—he is tortured with the most afflicting of all human sensations. When he looks at the children, whom he is by law bound to protect and provide for, and from whose existence he ought to receive the delightful return which the union of instinct and reason has provided for the continuation of the world, he knows not whether he is lavishing his fondness and affection upon his own children, or upon the seed of a villain sown in the bed of his honor and his delight. He starts back with horror, when, instead of seeing his own image reflected from their infant features, he thinks he sees the destroyer of his happiness—a midnight robber introduced into his house, under professions of friendship and brotherhood—a plunderer, not in the repositories of his treasure, which may be supplied, or lived without, "*but there where he had garnered up his hopes, where either he must live or bear no life.*"[2]

Peculiar aggravation of the misery into which the plaintiff is plunged.

In this situation, the plaintiff brings his case before you, and the defendant attempts no manner of defense. He admits his guilt—he renders it unnecessary for me to go into any proof of it; and the only question, therefore, that remains, is for you to say what shall be the consequences of his crime, and what verdict you will pronounce against him. You are placed, therefore, in a situation most momentous to the public. You have a duty to discharge, the result of which not only deeply affects the present generation, but which remotest posterity will contemplate to your honor or dishonor. On your verdict it depends whether persons of the description of the defendant, who have cast off all respect for religion, who laugh at morality, when it is opposed to the gratification of their passions, and who are careless of the injuries they inflict upon others, shall continue their impious and destructive course with impunity. On your verdict it depends whether such men, looking to the proceedings of courts of justice, shall be able to say to themselves, that there are *certain limits* beyond which the damages of juries are not to pass. On your verdict it depends whether men of large fortunes shall be able to adopt this kind of reasoning to spur them on in the career of their lusts: "*There are many chances that I may not be discovered at all; there are chances that, if I am discovered, I may not be the object of legal inquiry—and supposing I should, there are certain damages, beyond which a jury can not go. They may be large, but still within a certain compass. If I can not pay them myself, there may be persons belonging to my family who will pity my situation: somehow or other the money may be raised, and I may be delivered from the consequences of my crime.*" I TRUST THE VERDICT OF THIS DAY WILL SHOW MEN WHO REASON THUS THAT THEY ARE MISTAKEN.

Duty of the jury to the plaintiff and to the public in assessing damages.

The action for adultery, like every other action, is to be considered according to the extent of the injury which the person complaining to a court of justice has received. If he has received an injury, or sustained a loss that can be estimated directly in money, there is then no other medium of redress, but in moneys numbered according to the extent of the proof. I apprehend it will not be even stated by the counsel for the defendant, that if a person has sustained a loss, and can show it is to any given extent, he is not entitled to the *full measure* of it in damages. If a man destroys my house or furniture, or deprives me of a chattel, I have a right, beyond all manner of doubt, to recover their corresponding values in money, and it is no answer to me to say that he who has deprived me of the advantage I before possessed is in no situation to render me satisfaction. A verdict pronounced upon such a principle, in any of the cases I have alluded to, would be set aside by the court, and a new trial awarded. It would be a direct breach of the oaths of jurors, if, impressed with a firm conviction that a plaintiff had received damages to a given amount, they retired from their duty, because they felt commiseration for a defendant, even in a case where he might be worthy of compassion from the injury being unpremeditated and inadvertent.

The suffering party entitled in every case to a full compensation for the injury sustained.

But there are other wrongs which can not be estimated in money:

[2] But there, where I had garnered up my heart,
Where either I must live, or bear no life,
The fountain from the which my current runs,
Or else dries up; to be discarded *thence!*
Othello, Act iv., Sc. 9.

You can not minister to a *mind* diseased.[3]

You can not redress a man who is wronged beyond the possibility of redress: the law has no means of restoring to him what he has lost. God himself, as he has constituted human nature, has no means of alleviating such an injury as the one I have brought before you. While the sensibilities, affections, and feelings he has given to man remain, it is impossible to heal a wound which strikes so deep into the soul. When you have given to a plaintiff, in damages, all that figures can number, it is as nothing; he goes away hanging down his head in sorrow, accompanied by his wretched family, dispirited and dejected. Nevertheless, the law has given a civil action for adultery, and, strange to say, it has given *nothing else.* The law commands that the injury shall be compensated (as far as it is practicable) IN MONEY, because courts of *Civil* Justice have no other means of compensation THAN *money;* and the only question, therefore, and which *you* upon your oaths are to decide, is this: has the plaintiff sustained an injury up to the extent which he has complained of? Will twenty thousand pounds place him in the same condition of comfort and happiness that he enjoyed before the adultery, and which the adulterer has deprived him of? You know that it will not. Ask your own hearts the question, and you will receive the same answer. I should be glad to know, then, upon what principle, as it regards the *private* justice, which the plaintiff has a right to, or upon what principle, as the example of that justice affects the public and the remotest generations of mankind, you can reduce this demand even in a single farthing.

If money can not ...lly repair the ...ong, the award ...t, for this ...ry reason, to be ...ost ample.

This is a doctrine which has been frequently countenanced by the noble and learned Lord [Lord Kenyon] who lately presided in the Court of King's Bench; but his Lordship's reasoning on the subject has been much misunderstood, and frequently misrepresented. The noble Lord is supposed to have said, that although a plaintiff may not have sustained an injury by adultery to a given amount, yet that large damages, for the sake of public example, should be given. He never said any such thing. He said that which law and morals dictated to him, and which will support his reputation as long as law and morals have a footing in the world. He said that every plaintiff had a right to recover damages *up to the extent of the injury he had received*, and that public example stood in the way of showing *favor* to an adulterer, by reducing the damages below the sum which the jury would otherwise consider as the lowest compensation for the wrong. If the plaintiff shows you that he was a most affectionate husband; that his parental and conjugal affections were the solace of his life; that for nothing the world could bestow in the shape of riches or honors would he have bartered one moment's comfort in the bosom of his family, he shows you a wrong *that no money can compensate.* Nevertheless, if the injury is only mensurable in money, and if you are sworn to make upon your oaths a pecuniary compensation, though I can conceive that the damages when given to the extent of the declaration, and you can give no more, may fall short of what your consciences would have dictated, yet I am utterly at a loss to comprehend upon what principle they can be *lessened.* But then comes the defendant's counsel, and says, "It is true that the injury can not be compensated by the sum which the plaintiff has demanded; but you will consider the miseries my client must suffer, if you make him the object of a severe verdict. You must, therefore, regard him with compassion; though I am ready to admit the plaintiff is to be compensated for the injury he has received.

Views of Lord Kenyon as to amount of damages.

Here, then, Lord Kenyon's doctrine deserves consideration. "He who will mitigate damages below the fair estimate of the wrong which he has committed, must do it upon some principle which the policy of the law will support."

Damages not to be mitigated without positive cause shown by the defendant.

Let me, then, examine, whether the defendant is in a situation which entitles him to have the damages against him *mitigated*, when private justice to the injured party calls upon you to give them TO THE UTMOST FARTHING. The question will be, on what principle of mitigation he can stand before you. I had occasion, not a great while ago, to remark to a jury, that the wholesome institutions of the civilized world came seasonably in aid of the dispensations of Providence for our well-being in the world. If I were to ask, what it is that prevents the prevalence of the crime of incest, by taking away those otherwise natural impulses, from the promiscuous gratification of which we should become like the beasts of the field, and lose all the intellectual endearments which are at once the pride and the happiness of man? What is it that renders our houses pure and our families innocent? It is that, by the wise institutions of all civilized nations, there is placed a kind of guard against the human passions, in that sense of impropriety and dishonor, which the law has raised up, and impressed with almost the force of a second nature. This wise and politic restraint beats down, by the habits of the mind, even a propensity to incestuous commerce, and opposes those inclinations which nature, for wise purposes, has implanted in our breasts at the approach of the other sex. It holds the mind in chains against the seductions of beauty. It is a moral feeling in perpetual opposition to human infirmity. It is like an angel from heaven placed to guard us from propensities which are evil. It is *that* warning voice, gentlemen, which enables you to embrace

No such cause in this case.

On the contrary, the severest guards necessary to protect society in cases of the closest intimacy.

[3] Canst thou not minister to a mind diseased,
Pluck from the memory a rooted sorrow,
Raze out the written troubles of the brain,
And with some sweet oblivious antidote
Cleanse the stuffed bosom of that perilous stuff
Which weighs upon the heart?
Macbeth, Act v., Sc. 3.

your daughter, however lovely, without feeling that you are of a different sex. It is *that* which enables you, in the same manner, to live familiarly with your nearest female relations, without those desires which are natural to man.

Application of the principle to the case of friendship.

Next to the tie of blood (if not, indeed, before it) is the sacred and spontaneous relation of friendship. The man who comes under the roof of a married friend, ought to be under the dominion of the same moral restraint; and, thank God, generally is so, from the operation of the causes which I have described. Though not insensible to the charms of female beauty, he receives its impressions under an habitual reserve, which honor imposes. Hope is the parent of desire, and honor tells him he must not hope. Loose thoughts may arise, but they are rebuked and dissipated:

"Evil into the mind of God or man
May come and go, so unapproved, and leave
No spot or blame behind."—*Milton.*

Gentlemen, I trouble you with these reflections, that you may be able properly to appreciate the guilt of the defendant, and to show you, that you are not in a case where large allowances are to be made for the ordinary infirmities of our imperfect natures. When a man does wrong in the heat of *sudden* passion—as, for instance, when, upon receiving an affront, he rushes into immediate violence, even to the deprivation of life, the humanity of the law classes his offense among the lower degrees of homicide; it supposes the crime to have been committed before the mind had time to parley with itself. But is the criminal act of such a person, however disastrous may be the consequence, to be compared with that of the defendant? Invited into the house of a friend—received with the open arms of affection, as if the same parents had given them birth and bred them—in THIS situation, this most monstrous and wicked defendant deliberately perpetrated his crime; and, shocking to relate, not only continued the appearances of friendship after he had violated its most sacred obligations, but continued them as a cloak to the barbarous repetitions of his offense—writing letters of regard, while, perhaps, he was the father of the last child, whom his injured friend and companion was embracing and cherishing as his own! What protection can such conduct possibly receive from the humane consideration of the law for sudden and violent passions? A passion for a woman is progressive; it does not, like anger, gain an uncontrolled ascendency in a moment, nor is a modest matron to be seduced in a day. Such a crime can not, therefore, be committed under the resistless dominion of *sudden* infirmity; it must be *deliberately*, *willfully*, and *wickedly* committed. The defendant could not possibly have incurred the guilt of this adultery without often passing through his mind (for he had the education and principles of a gentleman) the very topics I have been insisting upon before you for his condemnation. Instead of being suddenly impelled toward mischief, without leisure for such reflections, he had innumerable difficulties and obstacles to contend with. He could not but hear, in the first refusals of this unhappy lady, every thing to awaken conscience, and even to excite horror. In the arguments he must have employed to seduce *her* from *her* duty, he could not but recollect and willfully trample upon *his own*. He was a year engaged in the pursuit; he resorted repeatedly to his shameful purpose, and advanced to it at such intervals of time and distance, as entitle me to say, that he determined in cold blood to enjoy a future and momentary gratification, at the expense of every principle of honor which is held sacred among gentlemen, even where no laws interpose their obligations or restraints.

Abuse of friendship by the defendant.

A jury the chief vindicators of society in such cases.

I call upon you, therefore, gentlemen of the jury, to consider well this case—for it is *your* office to keep human life in tone; *your* verdict must decide whether such a case can be indulgently considered, without tearing asunder the bonds which unite society together.

Aggravations in the present instance.

Gentlemen, I am not preaching a religion which men can scarcely practice. I am not affecting a severity of morals beyond the standard of those whom I am accustomed to respect, and with whom I associate in common life. I am not making a stalking-horse of adultery, to excite exaggerated sentiment. This is not the case of a gentleman meeting a handsome woman in a public street or in a place of public amusement; where, finding the coast clear for his addresses, without interruption from those who should interrupt, he finds himself engaged (probably the successor of another) in a vain and transitory intrigue. It is not the case of him who, night after night, falls in with the wife of another, to whom he is a stranger, in the boxes of a theater, or other resorts of pleasure, inviting admirers by indecent dress and deportment, unattended by any thing which bespeaks the affectionate wife and mother of many children. Such connections may be of evil example; but I am not here to reform public manners, but to demand private justice. It is impossible to assimilate the sort of cases I have alluded to, which ever will be occasionally occurring, with this atrocious invasion of household peace—this portentous disregard of every thing held sacred among men, good or evil. Nothing, indeed, can be more affecting than even to be called upon to state the evidence I must bring before you. I can scarcely pronounce to you that the victim of the defendant's lust was the mother of nine children, seven of them females and infants, unconscious of their unhappy condition, deprived of their natural guardian, separated from her forever, and entering the world with a dark cloud hanging over them. But it is not in the descending line alone that the happiness of this worthy family is invaded. It hurts me to call before you the venerable progenitor of both the father and the children, who has risen by extraordinary learning and piety to his eminent rank in the Church; and who, instead of receiving, unmixed and undisturbed, the best consolation of age, in counting up the number of his descendants, carrying down the name and honor of his house to future times, may be forced to turn aside his face from *some of them* that bring to his remembrance the wrongs which now oppress him, and which it is his duty to forget, because it is his, otherwise impossible, duty to forgive them.

Gentlemen, if I make out this case by evidence (and if I do not, forget every thing you have heard, and reproach me for having abused your honest feelings), I have established a claim for damages that has no parallel in the annals of fashionable adultery. It is rather like the entrance of Sin and Death into this lower world. The undone pair were living like our first parents in Paradise, till this demon saw and envied their happy condition. Like them, they were in a moment cast down from the pinnacle of human happiness into the very lowest abyss of sorrow and despair. In one point, indeed, the resemblance does not hold, which, while it aggravates the crime, redoubles the sense of suffering. It was not from an enemy, but from a friend, that this evil proceeded. I have just had put into my hand a quotation from the Psalms upon this subject, full of that unaffected simplicity which so strikingly characterizes the sublime and sacred poet:

It is one almost without parallel in the history of such offenses.

"It is not an open enemy that hath done me this dishonor, for then I could have borne it.

"Neither was it mine adversary that did magnify himself against me; for then, peradventure, I would have hid myself from him.

"But it was even *thou*, my companion, my guide, mine own familiar friend."

This is not the language of counsel, but the inspired language of truth. I ask you solemnly, upon your honors and your oaths, if you would exchange the plaintiff's former situation for his present, for a hundred times the compensation he requires at your hands. I am addressing myself to affectionate husbands and to the fathers of beloved children. Suppose I were to say to you, There is twenty thousand pounds for you: embrace your wife for the last time, and the child that leans upon her bosom and smiles upon you—retire from your house, and make way for the adulterer—wander about an object for the hand of scorn to point its slow and moving finger at—think no more of the happiness and tranquillity of your former state—I have destroyed them forever. But never mind—don't make yourself uneasy—here is a draft upon my banker, it will be paid at sight—there is no better man in the city. I can see you think I am mocking you, gentlemen, and well you may; but it is the very pith and marrow of this cause. It is impossible to put the argument in mitigation of damages in plain English, without talking such a language, as appears little better than an insult to your understandings, dress it up as you will.

But it may be asked—if no money can be an adequate, or, indeed, any compensation, why is Mr. Markham a plaintiff in a CIVIL ACTION? Why does he come here for money? Thank God, gentlemen, IT IS NOT MY FAULT. I take honor to myself, that I was one of those who endeavored to put an end to this species of action, by the adoption of a more salutary course of proceeding. I take honor to myself, that I was one of those who supported in Parliament the adoption of a law to pursue such outrages with the terrors of criminal justice. I thought then, and I shall always think, that every act *malum in se* directly injurious to an individual, and most pernicious in its consequences to society, should be considered to be a misdemeanor. Indeed, I know of no other definition of the term. The Legislature, however, thought otherwise, and I bow to its decision; but the business of this day may produce some changes of opinion on the subject. I never meant that *every* adultery was to be similarly considered. Undoubtedly, there are cases where it is comparatively venial, and judges would not overlook the distinctions. I am not a pretender to any extraordinary purity. My severity is confined to cases in which there can be but one sentiment among men of honor, as to the offense, though they may differ in the mode and measure of its correction.

Mr. Erskine's exertions to have this made a criminal offense.

It is this difference of sentiment, gentlemen, that I am alone afraid of. I fear you may think there is a sort of limitation in verdicts, and that you may look to precedents for the amount of damages, though you can find no precedent for the magnitude of the crime; but you might as well abolish the action altogether, as lay down a principle which limits the consequences of adultery to what it may be convenient for the adulterer to pay. By the adoption of such a principle, or by any mitigation of severity, arising even from an insufficient reprobation of it, you unbar the sanctuary of domestic happiness, and establish a sort of license for debauchery, to be sued out like other licenses, at its price. A man has only to put money into his pocket, according to his degree and fortune, and he may then debauch the wife or daughter of his best friend, at the expense he chooses to go to. He has only to say to himself, what Iago says to Roderigo in the play,

Dangerous consequences of mitigating damages in cases of this kind.

Put money in thy purse—go to—put money in thy purse.[4]

Persons of immense fortunes might, in this way, deprive the best men in the country of their domestic satisfactions, with what to them might be considered as impunity. The most abandoned profligate might say to himself, or to other profligates, "I have suffered judgment by default—let them send down their deputy-sheriff to the King's Arms Tavern; I shall be concealed from the eye of the public—I have drawn upon my banker for the *utmost damages*, and I have as much more to spare to-morrow, if I can find another woman whom I would choose to enjoy at such a price." In this manner I have seen a rich delinquent, too

[4] Othello, Act i., Scene 3.

lightly fined by courts of criminal justice, throw down his bank-notes to the officers, and retire with a deportment, not of contrition, but contempt.

For these reasons, gentlemen, I expect from you to-day the full measure of damages demanded by the plaintiff. Having given such a verdict, you will retire with a monitor within eonfirming that you have done right; you will retire in sight of an approving public, and an approving Heaven. Depend upon it, the world can not be held together without morals; nor can morals maintain their station in the human heart without religion, which is the corner-stone of the fabric of human virtue.

Peroration: Religious institutions (including marriage) restored in France.

We have lately had a most striking proof of this sublime and consoling truth in *one* result, *at least*, of the Revolution which has astonished and shaken the earth. Though a false philosophy was permitted, *for a season*, to raise up her vain fantastic front, and to trample down the Christian establishments and institutions, yet, on a sudden, God said, "Let there be light, and there was light." The altars of religion were restored—not purged, indeed, of human errors and superstitions, not reformed in the just sense of reformation; yet the Christian religion is still re-established—leading on to further reformation; fulfilling the hope, that the doctrines and practice of Christianity shall overspread the face of the earth.

Gentlemen, as to us, WE have nothing to wait for. We have long been in the center of light. We have a true religion and a free government, AND YOU ARE THE PILLARS AND SUPPORTERS OF BOTH.

Duty of a jury in England, where these institutions have always been cherished and revered.

I have nothing further to add, except that, since the defendant committed the injury complained of, he has sold his estate, and is preparing to remove into some other country. Be it so. Let him *remove;* but YOU will have to pronounce the penalty of his *return*. It is for YOU to declare whether such a person is worthy to be a member of our community. But if the feebleness of your jurisdiction, or a commiseration which destroys the exercise of it, shall shelter such a criminal from the consequences of his crimes, individual security is gone, and the rights of the public are unprotected. Whether this be our condition or not, I shall know by your verdict.

The jury gave £7000 damages—being the full amount of the defendant's property. The money could not be collected, as Mr. Fawcett had fled the country; but the verdict operated as a sentence of perpetual banishment against him.

MR. CURRAN.

John Philpot Curran was born at Newmarket, an obscure village in the northwest corner of the county of Cork, Ireland, on the 24th of July, 1750. The family was in low circumstances, his father being seneschal, or collector of rents, to a gentleman of small property in the neighborhood. He was a man, however, of vigorous intellect, and acquirements above his station; while his wife was distinguished for that bold, irregular strength of mind, that exuberance of imagination and warmth of feeling, which were so strikingly manifested in the character of her favorite son.

The peculiar position of his father brought the boy, from early life, into contact with persons of every class, both high and low; and he thus gained that perfect knowledge of the mind and heart of his countrymen, and that kindling sympathy with their feelings, which gave him more power over an Irish jury than any other man ever possessed. Though sent early to school, his chief delight was in society—in fun, frolic, mimicry, and wild adventure. The country fairs, which were frequent in his native village, were his especial delight; and, as he moved in the crowded streets, among the cattle and the pigs, the horse-dealers and frieze-dealers, the matchmakers and the peddlers, he had his full share of the life, and sport, and contention of the scene. He was a regular attendant on dances and wakes; and dwelt with the deepest interest on the old traditions about the unfinished palace of Kanturk, in the neighborhood, or listened to the stories concerning the rapparees of King William's wars, or to "the strains of the piper as he blew the wild notes to which Alister M'Donnel marched to battle at Knocknanois, and the wilder ones in which the woman mourned over his corse." Every thing conspired from his earliest years to give him freedom and versatility of mind; to call forth the keenest sagacity as to character and motives; to produce a quick sense of the ridiculous; to cherish that passionate strength of feeling which expressed itself equally in tears and laughter; to make him, at once, of *reality* and *imagination* "all compact."

When he was about fourteen years old, as he was rolling marbles one morning, and playing his tricks in the ball-alley, he attracted the notice of an elderly gentleman who was passing by. It was the Rev. Mr. Boyse, a clergyman of the Church of England, who held the rectorship of the parish. The family of Curran were attendants on his ministry, and he had heard much of the brightness and promise of the boy. He invited him to his house, and was so much pleased with his frank and hearty conversation, that he offered at once to instruct him in the classics, with a view to his entering Trinity College, Dublin. Young Curran was ready for any thing that could gratify his curiosity. He removed to the Rectory; he devoted himself to study, though with occasional outbreaks of his love of fun and frolic; he made such proficiency that, within three years, he fairly outran his patron's ability to teach him; he was then removed by Mr. Boyse to a school at Middleton, and supported partly at his expense; and was prepared for the University in 1769, at the age of nineteen.

Here he studied the classics especially, with great ardor, perfecting himself so fully both in the Latin and Greek languages, that he could read them with ease and pleasure throughout life. His exertions were rewarded by honors and emoluments which very nearly provided for his support while in college; and he carried with him into life an enthusiasm for these studies which never subsided, amid all the multiplied cares of business and politics. For a long time he read Homer once every year;

Mr. Phillips speaks of seeing him, late in life, on board a Holyhead packet in a storm, absorbed in the Æneid, while every one around was deadly sick; and in the last journey he ever took, Horace and Virgil were still, as in early life, his traveling companions. He was also distinguished at college for his love of metaphysical inquiries and subtle disquisition. He showed great ingenuity in the discussion of subjects; and his companions were so much struck with his dexterity and force on a certain occasion, that they declared, with one consent, that "the bar, and the bar alone, was the proper profession for the talents of which he had that day given such striking proof." "He accepted the omen," says his son, "and never after repented of his decision."[1]

Having completed his college course, and qualified himself for the degree of Master of Arts, in 1773, he removed to London, and commenced the study of the law in the Middle Temple. Here he was supported in part by a wealthy friend, but his life in London was "a hard one." He spent his mornings, as he states, "in reading even to exhaustion," and the rest of the day in the more congenial pursuits of literature, and especially in unremitted efforts to perfect himself as a speaker. His voice was bad, and his articulation so hasty and confused, that he went among his schoolfellows by the name of "stuttering Jack Curran." His manner was awkward, his gesture constrained and meaningless, and his whole appearance calculated only to produce laughter, notwithstanding the evidence he gave of superior abilities. All these faults he overcame by severe and patient labor. Constantly on the watch against bad habits, he practiced daily before a glass, reciting passages from Shakspeare, Junius, and the best English orators. He frequented the debating societies, which then abounded in London; and though mortified at first by repeated failures, and ridiculed by one of his opponents as "Orator Mum," he surmounted every difficulty. "He turned his shrill and stumbling brogue," says one of his friends, "into a flexible, sustained, and finely-modulated voice; his action became free and forcible; he acquired perfect readiness in thinking on his legs;" he put down every opponent by the mingled force of his argument and wit, and was at last crowned with the universal applause of the society, and invited by the president to an entertainment in their behalf. Well might one of his biographers say, "His oratorical training was as severe as any Greek ever underwent."

Mr. Curran married during his residence in London, with but little accession to his fortune, and, returning soon after to Ireland, commenced the practice of the law in Dublin, at the close of 1775. He soon rose into business, because he *could not do without it;* verifying the remark of Lord Eldon, that some barristers succeed by great talents, some by high connections, some by miracle, but the great majority by *commencing without a shilling*." Within four years, he gained an established reputation and a lucrative practice; and at this time, 1779, he united with Mr. Yelverton, afterward Lord Avonmore, in forming a Society, called "The Monks of the Order of St. Patrick," embracing a large part of the wit, literature, eloquence, and public virtue of the metropolis of Ireland. From the title familiarly given its members of the "Monks of the Screw," it has been supposed by many to have been chiefly a drinking-club. So far was this from being the case, that, by an express regulation, every thing stronger than beer was excluded from the meeting. "It was a union,"

[1] Mr. Curran's feelings toward Mr. Boyse, who sent him to College, were expressed in a story he once told at his own table. "Thirty-five years after," said he, "returning one day from court, I found an old gentleman seated in my drawing-room, with his feet on each side of the marble chimney-piece, and an air of being perfectly at home. He turned—it was my friend of *the ball-alley!* I could not help bursting into tears. 'You are right, sir, you are right! The chimney-piece is yours, the pictures are yours, the house is yours: *you gave me all*—my friend, my father!' He went with me to Parliament, and I saw the tears glistening in his eyes when he saw his poor little Jackey rise to answer a *Right Honorable.* He is gone, sir. This is his wine—let us drink his health!"

says one acquainted with its proceedings, "of strong minds, brought together like electric clouds by affinity, and flashing as they joined. They met, and shone, and warmed—they had great passions and generous accomplishments, and, like all that was then good in Ireland, they were heaving for want of freedom." Nearly thirty years after, when the angry politics of the day had thrown Lord Avonmore and his friend into hostile parties, so that they were no longer on speaking terms, Mr. Curran adverted to the meetings of this society in arguing a case before Lord Avonmore, as Chief Baron of the Exchequer, in a manner which was deeply interesting to those who witnessed it. After delicately alluding to his Lordship, as differing from the Chief Justice of England on a point of law, and as having "derived his ideas from the purest fountains of Athens and Rome," Mr. Curran expressed his hope that such would be the decision of the court, embracing as it did members of the society referred to. "And this soothing hope," said he, "I draw from the dearest and tenderest recollections of my life—from the remembrance of those Attic nights, and those refections of the gods, which we have spent with those admired, and respected, and beloved companions who have gone before us; over whose ashes the most precious tears of Ireland have been shed. [Here Lord Avonmore became so much affected that he could not refrain from tears.] Yes, my good Lord, I see you do not forget them. I see their sacred forms passing in sad review before your memory. I see your pained and softened fancy recalling those happy meetings, where the innocent enjoyment of social mirth became expanded into the nobler warmth of social virtue, and the horizon of the board became enlarged into the horizon of man—where the swelling heart conceived and communicated the pure and generous purpose—where my slenderer and younger taper imbibed its borrowed light from the more matured and redundant fountain of yours. Yes, my Lord, we can remember those nights without any other regret than that they can never more return; for,

> "We spent them not in toys, or lust, or wine,
> But search of deep philosophy,
> Wit, eloquence, and poesy,
> Arts which I loved—for they, my friend, were thine."—Cowley.[2]

The space allowed to this sketch will not permit any minute detail of Mr. Curran's labors at the bar or in public life. Nor was there any thing in either which calls for an extended notice. He was a member of the Irish House of Commons from 1783 to 1797, and entered warmly into the cause of emancipation and reform; but he was never distinguished as a parliamentary orator. His education was forensic; his feelings and habits fitted him pre-eminently to act on the minds of a jury, and for more than twenty years he had an unrivaled mastery over the Irish bar. His speeches at state trials arising out of the United Irish conspiracy, were the most splendid efforts of his genius. He condemned insurrection; but he felt that the people had been goaded to madness by the oppression of the government, and for nearly six years he tasked every effort of his being to save the victims of misguided and unsuccessful resistance. He did it at the hazard of his life. As he drove to town at this period from his residence in a neighboring village, he was in daily expectation of being shot at. The court-room was crowded with troops during some of the trials, with a view, it was believed, of intimidating the jury or the advocates of the prisoners. "*What's that?*" exclaimed Mr. Curran, as a clash of arms was heard from the soldiery at the close of one of his bold denunciations of the course

[2] Lord Avonmore, in whose breast political resentment was easily subdued by the same noble tenderness of feeling which distinguished Charles J. Fox. upon a more celebrated occasion, could not withstand this appeal to his heart. The moment the court rose, his Lordship sent for his friend, and threw himself into his arms, declaring that unworthy artifices had been used to separate them, and that they should never succeed in future.

pursued by the government. Some who stood near him seemed, from their looks and gestures, about to offer him personal violence, when he fixed his eye sternly upon them, and added, "*You may assassinate, but you shall not intimidate me!*" "They were not mere clients for whom he pleaded," says his biographer, "they were friends for whose safety he would have coined his blood; they were patriots who had striven by means which he thought desperate or unsuited to himself for the freedom of their country. He came in the spirit of love and mercy, inspired by genius and commissioned by Heaven to walk on the waters with these patriots, and lend them his hand when they were sinking. He pleaded for some who, nevertheless, were slaughtered; but was his pleading therefore in vain? Did he not convert many a shaken conscience, sustain many a frightened soul? Did he not keep the life of genius, if not of hope, in the country? Did he not help to terrify the government into the compromise which they so ill kept? He did all this, and more. His speeches will ever remain less as models of eloquence than as examples of patriotism and undying exhortations to justice and liberty."

In 1803 there was another attempt at insurrection, which Mr. Curran regarded with very different emotions. It was that of Robert Emmett. Whatever we may think of the motives or the genius of this extraordinary young man, there can be but one opinion of the enterprise in which he was engaged. It was, from the first, rash and hopeless. He was just from college, with no character throughout the country to give him authority as a leader, and no experience in the conduct of affairs; hasty in his judgments, obstinate to an extreme in his resolves, and fatally deceived by weak or false advisers. The moment he began to move, the ground sunk under him. "His attempt," as remarked by a friend of his principles, "had not the dignity of even partial success, and did a vast injury to the country." To Mr. Curran it was peculiarly afflictive, because it commenced with the murder of his old friend, Lord Chief Justice Kilwarden, in the streets of Dublin. In addition to this, Emmett had won the affections of Sarah Curran without the knowledge of her father; a correspondence between them was found among his papers; and Mr. Curran was thus brought under the suspicions of the government, was compelled to undergo the interrogatories of the Privy Council, and had the pain of being laid under obligations to the generosity of the Attorney General, while his character was exposed to obloquy, and the cause he had espoused subjected to the basest imputations from his political opponents. It is not, therefore, surprising that he refused to defend Emmett—defense was, indeed, impossible—or even to see him. Nor, perhaps, is it surprising that his feelings continued to be so much wounded at Sarah's clandestine engagement and its results, as to make her home an unhappy one; so that she left his house, married without love, and carried her broken heart to an early grave in a foreign land.[3] To complete his wretchedness, Mr. Curran, through the villainy of a friend, was called to suffer the severest calamity which a husband can ever endure.

The remaining events of his life can be briefly told. On the accession of the Whigs to power, under Lord Grenville, in 1806, he was appointed Master of the Rolls. But the bench was not his place. He was but poorly fitted for its duties; and, though he discharged them with a moderate degree of ability, it was always with reluctance. To assuage the melancholy which now preyed upon him, he carried his former habits of conviviality to a still greater extent. He surrounded himself with gay companions, especially at his dinner-table; "and when roused," says one of his biographers, "he used to run over jokes of every kind, good, bad, and indifferent. No epigram too delicate, no mimicry too broad, no pun too little, and no metaphor too bold for him. He wanted to be happy, and to make others so, and rattled away for mere enjoyment. These afternoon dinner sittings were seldom pro-

[3] See Washington Irving's story of the Broken Heart, in his Sketch Book.

longed very late; but they made up in vehemence what they wanted in duration." But his health failed him, and in 1814 he resigned the Mastership of the Rolls. He now traveled, spending most of his time in England, but occasionally visiting Paris and other places on the Continent. In the spring of 1817, while dining with his friend, Thomas Moore, he had a slight attack of paralysis. His physician ordered him at once to the south of Europe; and, to arrange his affairs, he went over to Ireland for the last time. He returned to London, and was attacked with apoplexy, of which he died, after lingering a few days, on the 14th of October, 1817.

Mr. Curran was short of stature, with a swarthy complexion, and "an eye that glowed like a live coal." His countenance was singularly expressive; and, as he stood before a jury, he not only read their hearts with a searching glance, but he gave them back his own, in all the fluctuations of his feelings, from laughter to tears. His gesture was bold and empassioned; his articulation was uncommonly distinct and deliberate; the modulations of his voice were varied in a high degree, and perfectly suited to the widest range of his eloquence.

His power lay in the variety and strength of his emotions. He delighted a jury by his wit; he turned the court-room into a scene of the broadest farce by his humor, mimicry, or fun; he made it "a place of tears," by a tenderness and pathos which subdued every heart; he poured out his invective like a stream of lava, and inflamed the minds of his countrymen almost to madness by the recital of their wrongs. His rich and powerful imagination furnished the materials for these appeals, and his instinctive knowledge of the heart taught him how to use them with unfailing success. He relied greatly for effect on his power of painting to the eye; and the actual condition of the country for months during the insurrection, and after it, furnished terrific pictures for his pencil. Speaking of the ignorance which prevailed in England as to the treatment of the Irish, he said, "If you wished to convey to the mind of an English matron the horrors of that period, when, in defiance of the remonstrances of the ever-to-be-lamented Abercromby, our poor people were surrendered to the brutality of the soldiery by the authority of the state, you would vainly attempt to give her a *general* picture of lust, and rapine, and murder, and conflagration. By endeavoring to comprehend every thing, you would convey nothing. When the father of poetry wishes to portray the movements of contending armies and an embattled field, he *exemplifies*, he does not describe. So should your story to her keep clear of generalities. You should take a cottage, and place the affrighted mother with her orphan daughters at the door, the paleness of death in her face, and more than its agonies in her heart—her aching heart, her anxious ear struggling through the mist of closing day to catch the approaches of desolation and dishonor. The ruffian gang arrives—the feast of plunder begins—the cup of madness kindles in its circulation—the wandering glances of the ravisher become concentrated upon the shrinking and devoted victim. You need not dilate—you need not expatiate; the unpolluted matron to whom you tell the story of horror beseeches you not to proceed; she presses her child to her heart—she drowns it in her tears—her fancy catches more than an angel's tongue could describe; at a single view she takes in the whole miserable succession of force, of profanation, of despair, of death. So it is in the question before us."

The faults of Mr. Curran arose from the same source as his excellences. They lay chiefly on the side of *excess;* intense expressions, strained imagery, overwrought passion, and descriptions carried out into too great minuteness of circumstance. But he spoke for the people; the power he sought was *over the Irish mind;* and, in such a case, the cautious logic and the Attic taste of Erskine, just so far as they existed, would only have weakened the effect. There are but few parts of our country where Curran would be a safe model for the bar; but our mass meetings will be swayed most powerfully by an eloquence conceived in the spirit of the great Irish Orator.

SPEECH

OF MR. CURRAN IN BEHALF OF ARCHIBALD HAMILTON ROWAN WHEN INDICTED FOR THE PUBLICATION OF A SEDITIOUS LIBEL, DELIVERED JANUARY 29, 1794.

INTRODUCTION.

MR. ROWAN was a gentleman of wealth and respectability in Dublin, who acted as secretary of the Society of United Irishmen for that city. Associations under this name were now taking the place of the Irish Volunteers,[1] who ten years before had so powerful an influence on the politics of Ireland. Their original object was to promote Catholic emancipation and a reform in Parliament. The society to which Mr. Rowan belonged was one of the earliest, and the views of its members, as stated by the son and biographer of Curran, "did not extend beyond a *constitutional* reform." It should not be confounded with the subsequent associations which, under the same title, aimed at a revolution.

In 1792, the government issued a proclamation against seditious associations, which was no doubt directed against the United Irishmen. The chairman of the Dublin Society, Dr. Drennan, drew up a reply addressed to the Volunteers of Ireland, and Mr. Rowan signed it as secretary. Its language was vehement and unguarded. "Citizen soldiers, to arms! Take up the shield of freedom and the pledge of peace—peace, the motive and end of your virtuous institution. War, an occasional duty, should never be your occupation; every man should become a soldier in defense of his rights." The best construction that could be put on such language, was that Ireland was again to be converted into a camp, as in 1780, for the sake of showing England that her rights and interests must not be trifled with. The construction put upon it by the government was that of a summons to prepare for insurrection, and it is not improbable that the feelings of Drennan would have led him to such a result. But Mr. Rowan, as stated by Charles Phillips, had no such intentions. "He was a man of the kindest nature, with a touch of the romantic. Never was there a man less capable of crime, or more likely to commit an indiscretion. He never thought of himself, but if he saw toward another even the semblance of oppression, at all cost and at all hazard he stood forth to redress or to resist it. He was no mere political adventurer; he was a man of large possessions; the interests of Ireland and his own were identified." He signed this address, but he never gave it circulation; the man who did distribute it, and who greatly resembled Mr. Rowan, was named Willis, and was never indicted.

Drennan and Rowan were brought before the Court of King's Bench for a seditious libel, not by a presentment of the grand jury, but by an information of the Attorney General. The former was acquitted on a mere point of form; the trial of the latter gave rise to this speech. In justice to Mr. Curran, one thing should be remembered in perusing it. Mr. Rowan had given directions that his counsel should aim not so much to obtain his acquittal as *to defend his principles*. This accounts for the want of that close argument on the exact point at issue, which has been the chief objection to this speech. Its true title would be, A Vindication of Mr. Rowan's motives, of the Irish Volunteers, of a Free Press, and of Catholic Emancipation.

SPEECH, &c.

GENTLEMEN OF THE JURY,—When I consider the period at which this prosecution is brought forward; when I behold the *extraordinary safeguard*[2] of armed soldiers, resorted to, no doubt, for the preservation of peace and order; when I catch, as I can not but do, the throb of public anxiety, which beats from one end to the other of this hall; when I reflect on what may be the fate of a man of the most beloved personal character, of one of the most respected families of our country—himself the only individual of that family—I may almost say of that country, who can look to that possible fate with unconcern? Feeling, as I do, all these impressions, it is in the honest simplicity of my heart I speak, when I say that I never rose in a court of justice with so much embarrassment as upon this occasion.

Causes of embarrassment in entering on the defense.

If, gentlemen, I could entertain a hope of finding refuge for the disconcertion of my mind in the perfect composure of yours; if I could suppose that those awful vicissitudes of human events, which have been stated or alluded to, could leave your judgments undisturbed and your hearts at ease, I know I should form a most erroneous opinion of your character. I entertain no such chimerical hopes; I form no such unworthy opinions; I expect not

Only resource in the candor and justice of the jury.

[1] For an account of this corps, see note 5 to Mr. Burke's speech previous to the Bristol election, page 296, and the Memoir of Mr. Grattan, page 383.

[2] Alluding to a guard of soldiers which was brought into court just at the opening of the trial. Mr. Curran, in alluding to this fact, very naturally shaped his exordium into a beautiful resemblance to that of Cicero, in his oration for Milo.

that your hearts can be more at ease than my own; I have no right to expect it; but I have a right to call upon you in the name of your country, in the name of the living God, of whose eternal justice you are now administering that portion which dwells with us on this side of the grave, to discharge your breasts, as far as you are able, of every bias of prejudice or passion; that if my client is guilty of the offense charged upon him, you may give tranquillity to the public by a firm verdict of conviction; or if he is innocent, by as firm a verdict of acquittal; and that you will do this in defiance of the paltry artifices and senseless clamors that have been resorted to in order to bring him to his trial with anticipated conviction. And, gentlemen, I feel an additional necessity of thus conjuring you to be upon your guard, from the able and imposing statement which you have just heard on the part of the prosecution. I know well the virtues and the talents of the excellent person who conducts that prosecution; I know how much he would disdain to impose upon you by the trappings of office; but I also know how easily we mistake the lodgment which character and eloquence can make upon our feelings, for those impressions that reason, and fact, and proof, only ought to work upon our understandings.

Perhaps, gentlemen, I shall act not unwisely in waving any further observation of this sort, and giving your minds an opportunity of growing cool and resuming themselves, by coming to a calm and uncolored statement of mere facts, premising only to you that I have it in the strictest injunction from my client to defend him upon facts and evidence only, and to avail myself of no technical artifice or subtilty that could withdraw his cause from the test of that inquiry which it is your province to exercise, and to which only he wishes to be indebted for an acquittal.

Preliminary remarks. Hardships of Mr. Rowan in the early stages of the prosecution.

In the month of December, 1792, Mr. Rowan was arrested on an information charging him with the offense for which he is now on his trial. He was taken before an honorable personage now on that bench, and admitted to bail. He remained a considerable time in this city, soliciting the threatened prosecution, and offering himself to a fair trial by a jury of his country; but it was not then thought fit to yield to that solicitation; nor has it now been thought proper to prosecute him in the ordinary way, by sending up a bill of indictment to a grand jury. I do not mean by this to say that informations *ex officio* are always oppressive or unjust; but I can not but observe to you, that when a petty jury is called upon to try a charge not previously found by the grand inquest, and supported by the naked assertion only of the King's prosecutor, the accusation labors under a weakness of probability which it is difficult to assist. If the charge had no cause of dreading the light; if it was likely to find the sanction of a grand jury, it is not easy to account why it deserted the more usual, the more popular, and the more constitutional mode, and preferred to come forward in the ungracious form of *ex officio* information.

If such bill had been sent up and found, Mr. Rowan would have been tried at the next commission; but a speedy trial was not the wish of his prosecutors. An information was filed, and when he expected to be tried upon it, an error, it seems, was discovered in the record. Mr. Rowan offered to wave it, or consent to any amendment desired. No. That proposal could not be accepted. A trial must have followed. That information, therefore, was withdrawn, and a new one filed; that is, in fact, a third prosecution was instituted upon the same charge. This last was filed on the eighth day of last July. Gentlemen, these facts can not fail of a due impression upon you. You will find a material part of your inquiry must be, whether Mr. Rowan is pursued as a criminal or hunted down as a victim. It is not, therefore, by insinuation or circuity, but it is boldly and directly that I assert, that oppression has been intended and practiced upon him; and by those facts which I have stated I am warranted in the assertion.

Backwardness of the Crown to bring him to trial.

His demand, his entreaty to be tried was refused; and why? A hue and cry was to be raised against him; the sword was to be suspended over his head; some time was necessary for the public mind to become heated by the circulation of artful clamors of anarchy and rebellion; those same clamors which, with more probability, and not more success, had been circulated before through England and Scotland. In this country the causes and the swiftness of their progress were as obvious, as their folly has since become to every man of the smallest observation. I have been stopped myself with, "Good God, sir, have you heard the news?" No, sir, what? "Why one French emissary was seen traveling through Connaught in a post-chaise, and scattering from the windows as he passed, little doses of political poison, made up in square bits of paper; another was actually surprised in the fact of seducing our good people from their allegiance, by discourses upon the indivisibility of French robbery and massacre, which he preached in the French language to a congregation of Irish peasants!"

The design was to overwhelm him with prejudice.

Such are the bugbears and spectres to be raised to warrant the sacrifice of whatever little public spirit may remain among us; but time has also detected the imposture of these Cock-lane apparitions, and you can not now, with your eyes open, give a verdict without asking your consciences this question: Is this a fair and honest precaution? Is it brought forward with the single view of vindicating public justice, and promoting public good?

And here let me remind you that you are not convened to try the guilt of a libel affecting the personal character of any private man. I know no case in which a jury ought to be more severe than when personal calumny is conveyed through

Difference between a personal libel and the freest remarks on the government.

a vehicle, which ought to be consecrated to public information; neither, on the other hand, can I conceive any case in which the firmness and the caution of a jury should be more exerted than when a subject is prosecuted for a libel on the state. The peculiarity of the British Constitution (to which, in its fullest extent, we have an undoubted right, however distant we may be from the actual enjoyment), and in which it surpasses every known government in Europe, is this, that its only professed object is the general good, and its only foundation the general will. Hence the people have a right, acknowledged from time immemorial, fortified by a pile of statutes, and authenticated by a revolution that speaks louder than them all, to see whether abuses have been committed, and whether their properties and their liberties have been attended to as they ought to be. This is a kind of subject which I feel myself overawed when I approach. There are certain fundamental principles which nothing but necessity should expose to a public examination. They are pillars, the depth of whose foundation you can not explore without endangering their strength; but let it be recollected that the discussion of such topics should not be condemned in me, nor visited upon my client. The blame, if any there be, should rest only with those who have forced them into discussion. I say, therefore, it is the right of the people to keep an eternal watch upon the conduct of their rulers; and in order to that, the freedom of the press has been cherished by the law of England. In private defamation, let it never be tolerated; in wicked and wanton aspersion upon a good and honest administration, let it never be supported; not that a good government can be exposed to danger by groundless accusation, but because a bad government is sure to find in the detected falsehood of a licentious press a security and a credit which it could never otherwise obtain.

Great freedom of remark on their rulers the right of the people.

I have said that a good government can not be endangered—I say so again; for whether it be good or bad, can never depend upon assertion; the question is decided by simple inspection—to try the tree, look at its fruit; to judge of the government, look at the people. What is the fruit of good government? "The virtue and happiness of the people." Do four millions of people in this country gather those fruits from that government, to whose injured purity, to whose spotless virtue and violated honor, this seditious and atrocious libeler is to be immolated upon the altar of the Constitution? To you, gentlemen of that jury, who are bound by the most sacred obligation to your country and your God, to speak nothing but the truth, I put the question—Do they gather these fruits? are they orderly, industrious, religious, and contented? do you find them free from bigotry and ignorance, those inseparable concomitants of systematic oppression? or, to try them by a test as unerring as any of the former, are they *united?* The period has now elapsed in which considerations of this extent would have been deemed improper to a jury; happily for these countries, the Legislature of each has lately changed, or, perhaps, to speak more properly, revived and restored the law respecting trials of this kind.[3] For the space of thirty or forty years, a usage had prevailed in Westminster Hall, by which the judges assumed to themselves the decision of the question, whether libel or not. But the learned counsel for the prosecution are now obliged to admit that this is a question for the jury only to decide. You will naturally listen with respect to the opinion of the court, but you will receive it as matter of advice, not as matter of law; and you will give it credit, not from any adventitious circumstances of authority, but merely so far as it meets the concurrence of your own understandings.

What, then, is existing government of Ireland?

Give me leave, now, to state to you the charge as it stands upon the record: It is, that Mr. Rowan, "being a person of a wicked and turbulent disposition, and maliciously designing and intending to excite and diffuse among the subjects of this realm of Ireland, discontents, jealousies, and suspicions of our Lord the King and his government, and disaffection and disloyalty to the person and government of our said Lord the King, and to raise very dangerous seditions and tumults within this kingdom of Ireland and to draw the government of this kingdom into great scandal, infamy, and disgrace; and to incite the subjects of our said Lord the King to attempt, by force and violence, and with arms, to make alterations in the government, state, and Constitution of this kingdom; and to incite his Majesty's said subjects to tumult and anarchy, and to overturn the established Constitution of this kingdom, and to overawe and intimidate the Legislature of this kingdom by armed force," did "maliciously and seditiously" publish the paper in question.

Charge against Mr. Rowan.

Gentlemen, without any observation of mine, you must see that this information contains a direct charge upon Mr. Rowan; namely, that he did, with the intents set forth in the information, publish this paper, so that here you have, in fact, two or three questions for your decision: first, the matter of fact of the publication; namely, Did Mr. Rowan publish that paper? If Mr. Rowan did not, in fact, publish that paper, you have no longer any question on which to employ your minds. If you think that he was, in fact, the publisher, then, and not till then, arises the great and important subject to which your judgments must be directed. And that comes shortly and simply to this, is the paper a libel; and did he publish it with the intent charged in the information? But whatever you may think of the abstract question, whether the paper be libelous or not, and of which paper it has not even been insinuated that he is the author, there can be no ground for a verdict against him, unless you also are persuaded that what he did was done with a

Three things must combine to authorize his conviction.

[3] Alluding to Mr. Fox's Libel Bill.

criminal design. I wish, gentlemen, to simplify, and not to perplex; I, therefore, say again, if these three circumstances conspire—that he published it, that it was a libel, and that it was published with the purposes alleged in the information, you ought unquestionably to find him guilty; if, on the other hand, you do not find that all these circumstances concurred; if you can not, upon your oaths, say that he published it, if it be not in your opinion a libel, and if he did not publish it with the intention alleged; I say, upon the failure of any one of these points, my client is entitled, in justice, and upon your oaths, to a verdict of acquittal.

Topics to be discussed in meeting the charge. (1.) The Volunteers of Ireland.

Gentlemen, Mr. Attorney General has thought proper to direct your attention to the state and circumstances of public affairs at the time of this transaction; let me also make a few retrospective observations on a period at which he has but slightly glanced; I speak of the events which took place before the close of the American war. You know, gentlemen, that France had espoused the cause of America, and we became thereby engaged in war with that nation. *Heu nescia mens hominum futuri!*[4] Little did that ill-fated Monarch know that he was forming the first causes of those disastrous events that were to end in the subversion of his throne, in the slaughter of his family, and the deluging of his country with the blood of his people. You can not but remember, that at a time when we had scarcely a regular soldier for our defense; when the old and the young were alarmed and terrified with the apprehension of invasion, Providence seemed to have worked a sort of miracle in our favor. You saw a band of armed men come forth at the great call of nature, of honor, and their country. You saw men of the greatest wealth and rank; you saw every class of the community give up its members, and send them armed into the field, to protect the public and private tranquillity of Ireland. It is impossible for any man to turn back to that period without reviving those sentiments of tenderness and gratitude which then beat in the public bosom; to recollect amid what applause, what tears, what prayers, what benedictions, they walked forth among spectators, agitated by the mingled sensations of terror and reliance, of danger and protection, imploring the blessings of Heaven upon their heads, and its conquest upon their swords. That illustrious, and adored, and *abused* body of men, stood forward and assumed the title which, I trust, the ingratitude of their country will never blot from its history, "THE VOLUNTEERS OF IRELAND."

Give me leave, now, with great respect, to put one question to you: Do you think the assembling of that glorious band of patriots was an insurrection? Do you think the invitation to that assembling would have been sedition? They came under no commission but the call of their country; unauthorized and unsanctioned, except by public emergency and public danger. I ask, was that meeting an insurrection or not? I put another question: If any man had then published a call on that body, and stated that war was declared against the state—that the regular troops were withdrawn—that our coasts were hovered round by the ships of the enemy—that the moment was approaching when the unprotected feebleness of age and sex, when the sanctity of habitation, would be disregarded and profaned by the brutal ferocity of a rude invader: if any man had then said to them, "Leave your industry for a while, that you may return to it again, and come forth in arms for the public defense." I put this question boldly to you, gentlemen. It is not the case of the Volunteers of that day; it is the case of my client at this hour, which I put to you. Would that call have been then pronounced in a court of justice, or by a jury on their oaths, a criminal and seditious invitation to insurrection? If it would not have been so then, upon what principle can it be so now? What is the force and perfection of the law? It is the permanency of the law; it is, that whenever the fact is the same, the law is also the same; it is, that the law remains a written, monumented, and recorded letter, to pronounce the same decision upon the same facts, whenever they shall arise. I will not affect to conceal it; you know there has been an artful, ungrateful, and blasphemous clamor raised against these illustrious characters, the saviors of the kingdom of Ireland. Having mentioned this, let me read a few words of the paper alleged to be criminal: "You first took up arms to protect your country from foreign enemies, and from domestic disturbance. For the same purposes, it now becomes necessary that you should resume them."

Their formation not a seditious act.

If not, then the call on them to come forth again, not sedition.

I should be the last in the world to impute any want of candor to the right honorable gentleman who has stated the case on behalf of the prosecution; but he has certainly fallen into a mistake, which, if not explained, might be highly injurious to my client. He supposed that this publication was not addressed to the old Volunteers, but to new combinations of them, formed upon new principles, and actuated by different motives. You have the words to which this construction is imputed upon the record; the meaning of his mind can be collected only from those words which he has made use of to convey it. The guilt imputable to him can only be inferred from the meaning ascribable to those words. Let his meaning then be fairly collected by resorting to them. Is there a foundation to suppose that this address was directed to any such body of men as has been called a banditti, with what justice, it is unnecessary to inquire, and not to the old Volunteers? As

This call made on the old corps, not any new organization.

[4] The passage is from the Æneid of Virgil, book x., line 501, and relates to Turnus, and his bringing down upon himself the calamities which at last overtook him.

Nescia mens hominum fati sortisque futuræ.
Such are the minds of men!
Unconscious of their fate and coming fortune.

to the sneer at the word *citizen soldiers*, I should feel that I was treating a very respected friend with an insidious and unmerited unkindness, if I affected to expose it by any gravity of refutation. I may, however, be permitted to observe, that those who are supposed to have disgraced this expression by adopting it, have taken it from the idea of the British Constitution, "that no man, in becoming a soldier, ceases to be a citizen." Would to God, all enemies as they are, that that unfortunate people had borrowed more from that sacred source of liberty and virtue; and would to God, for the sake of humanity, that they had preserved even the little they did borrow. If even there could be an objection to that appellation, it must have been strongest when it was first assumed.[5] To that period the writer manifestly alludes; he addresses those who first took up arms: "You first took up arms to protect your country from foreign enemies and from domestic disturbance. For the same purposes, it is now necessary that you should resume them." Is this applicable to those who had never taken up arms before? "A proclamation," says this paper, "has been issued in England, for embodying the militia, and a proclamation has been issued by the Lord Lieutenant and Council in Ireland for repressing all seditious associations. In consequence of both these proclamations, it is reasonable to apprehend danger from abroad and danger at home." God help us; from the situation of Europe at that time, we were threatened with too probable danger from abroad, and I am afraid it was not without foundation that we were told our having something to dread at home.

It was justified by the proclamation of the government.

I find much abuse has been lavished on the disrespect with which the proclamation is treated in that part of the paper alleged to be a libel. To that my answer for my client is short; I do conceive it competent to a British subject—if he thinks that a proclamation has issued for the purpose of raising false terrors, I hold it to be not only the privilege, but the duty of a citizen to set his countrymen right with respect to such misrepresented danger; and until a proclamation in this country shall have the force of law, the reason and grounds of it are surely, at least, questionable by the people. Nay, I will go further; if an actual law had received the sanction of the three estates, if it be exceptionable in any matter, it is warrantable to any man in the community to state, in a becoming manner, his ideas upon it. And I should be at a loss to know, if the positive laws of Great Britain are thus questionable, upon what ground the proclamation of an Irish government should not be open to the animadversion of an Irish subject.

It was made with honest intentions.

Whatever be the motive, or from whatever quarter it arises, says this paper, "alarm has arisen." Gentlemen, do you not know that to be the fact? It has been stated by the Attorney General, and most truly, that the most gloomy apprehensions were entertained by the whole country. "You Volunteers of Ireland, are therefore summoned to arms at the instance of government, as well as by the responsibility attached to your character, and the permanent obligations of your institution." I am free to confess, if any man assuming the liberty of a British subject, to question public topics, should, under the mask of that privilege, publish a proclamation inviting the profligate and seditious, those in want and those in despair, to rise up in arms to overawe the Legislature, to rob us of whatever portion of the blessings of a free government we possess, I know of no offense involving greater enormity. But that, gentlemen, is the question you are to try. If my client acted with an honest mind and fair intention, and having, as he believed, the authority of government to support him in the idea that danger was to be apprehended, did apply to that body of so known and so revered a character, calling upon them by their former honor, the principle of their glorious institution, and the great stake they possessed in their country; if he interposed, not upon a fictitious pretext, but a real belief of actual and imminent danger, and that their arming at that critical moment was necessary to their country, his intention was not only innocent, but highly meritorious. It is a question, gentlemen, upon which you only can decide; it is for you to say whether it was criminal in the defendant to be so misled, and whether he is to fall a sacrifice to the prosecution of that government by which he was so deceived. I say, again, gentlemen, you can look only to his own words as the interpreter of his meaning, and to the state and circumstances of his country, as he was made to believe them, as the clue to his intention. The case, then, gentlemen, is shortly and simply this: a man of the first family, and fortune, and character, and property among you, reads a proclamation, stating the country to be in danger from abroad and at home, and thus alarmed — thus, upon authority of the prosecutor, alarmed, applies to that august body, before whose awful presence sedition must vanish and insurrection disappear. You must surrender, I hesitate not to say it, your oaths to unfounded assertion, if you can submit to say that such an act of such a man, so warranted, is a wicked and seditious libel. If he was a dupe, let me ask you who was the impostor? I blush and I shrink with shame and detestation from that meanness of dupery, and servile complaisance, which could make that dupe a victim to the accusation of that impostor.

You perceive, gentlemen, that I am going into the merits of this publication, before I apply myself to the question which is first in order of time, namely, whether the publication, in point of fact, is to be ascribed to Mr. Rowan or not. I have been unintentionally led into this violation of order. I should effect no purpose of either brevity or clearness, by returning to the more methodical course of observation. I have been naturally

[5] The old volunteers often used the phrase "*citizen soldiers.*"

drawn from it by the superior importance of the topic I am upon, namely, the merit of the publication in question.

This publication, if ascribable at all to Mr. Rowan, contains four distinct subjects. The first the invitation to the Volunteers to arm. Upon that I have already observed; but those that remain are surely of much importance, and no doubt are prosecuted as equally criminal. The paper next states the necessity of a reform in Parliament; it states, thirdly, the necessity of an emancipation of the Catholic inhabitants of Ireland; and, as necessary to the achievement of all these objects, does, fourthly, state the necessity of a general delegated convention of the people.

(2.)Parliamentary reform: The freest discussion of this subject allowed in England.

It has been alleged that Mr. Rowan intended by this publication to excite the subjects of this country to effect an alteration in the form of your Constitution. And here, gentlemen, perhaps you may not be unwilling to follow a little further than Mr. Attorney General has done, the idea of a late prosecution in Great Britain upon the subject of a public libel. It is with peculiar fondness I look to that country for solid principles of constitutional liberty and judicial example. You have been pressed in no small degree with the manner in which this publication marks the different orders of our Constitution, and comments upon them. Let me show you what boldness of animadversion on such topics is thought justifiable in the British nation, and by a British jury. I have in my hand the report of the trial of the printers of the Morning Chronicle for a supposed libel against the state, and of their acquittal: let me read to you some passages from that publication, which a jury of Englishmen were in vain called upon to brand with the name of libel.

Extracts from the Morning Chronicle.

"Claiming it as our indefeasible right to associate together, in a peaceable and friendly manner, for the communication of thoughts, the formation of opinions, and to promote the general happiness, we think it unnecessary to offer any apology for inviting you to join us in this manly and benevolent pursuit. The necessity of the inhabitants of every community endeavoring to procure a true knowledge of their rights, their duties, and their interests, will not be denied, except by those who are the slaves of prejudice, or interested in the continuation of abuses. As men who wish to aspire to the title of freemen, we totally deny the wisdom and the humanity of the advice, to approach the defects of government with 'pious awe and trembling solicitude.' What better doctrine could the Pope or the tyrants of Europe desire? We think, therefore, that the cause of truth and justice can never be hurt by temperate and honest discussions; and that cause which will not bear such a scrutiny must be systematically or practically bad. We are sensible that those who are not friends to the general good, have attempted to inflame the public mind with the cry of 'Danger,' whenever men have associated for discussing the principles of government; and we have little doubt but such conduct will be pursued in this place. We would, therefore, caution every honest man, who has really the welfare of the nation at heart, to avoid being led away by the prostituted clamors of those who live on the sources of corruption. We pity the fears of the timorous; and we are totally unconcerned respecting the false alarms of the venal.

"We view with concern the frequency of wars. We are persuaded that the interests of the poor can never be promoted by accession of territory, when bought at the expense of their labor and blood; and we must say, in the language of a celebrated author, 'We, who are only the people, but who pay for wars with our substance and our blood, will not cease to tell Kings,' or governments, 'that to them alone wars are profitable; that the true and just conquests are those which each makes at home by comforting the peasantry, by promoting agriculture and manufactures, by multiplying men, and the other productions of nature; that then it is that kings may call themselves the image of God, whose will is perpetually directed to the creation of new beings. If they continue to make us fight and kill one another, in uniform, we will continue to write and speak until nations shall be cured of this folly.' We are certain our present heavy burdens are owing, in a great measure, to cruel and impolitic wars; and therefore we will do all on our part, as peaceable citizens who have the good of the community at heart, to enlighten each other, and protest against them.

"The present state of the representation of the people calls for the particular attention of every man who has humanity sufficient to feel for the honor and happiness of his country; to the defects and corruptions of which we are inclined to attribute unnecessary wars, oppressive taxes, &c. We think it a deplorable case when the poor must support a *corruption* which is calculated to oppress them; when the laborer must give his money to afford the means of preventing him having a voice in its disposal; when the lower classes may say, "We give you our money, for which we have toiled and sweated, and which would save our families from cold and hunger; but we think it more hard that there is nobody whom we have delegated to see that it is not improperly and wickedly spent. We have none to watch over *our* interests. The rich only are represented.

"An equal and uncorrupt representation would, we are persuaded, save us from heavy expenses, and deliver us from many oppressions. We will, therefore, do our duty to procure this reform, which appears to us of the utmost importance.

"In short, we see with the most lively concern an army of placemen, pensioners, &c., fighting in the cause of corruption and prejudice, and spreading the contagion far and wide.

"We see with equal sensibility the present outcry against reforms, and a proclamation (tending to cramp the liberty of the press, and discredit the true friends of the people) receiving the support of numbers of our countrymen.

"We see burdens multiplied, the lower classes

sinking into poverty, disgrace, and excesses, and the means of those shocking abuses increased for the purpose of revenue.

"We ask ourselves, 'Are we in England?' Have our forefathers fought, bled, and conquered for liberty? And did they not think that the fruits of their patriotism would be more abundant in peace, plenty, and happiness?

"Is the condition of the poor never to be improved?

"Great Britain must have arrived at the highest degree of national happiness and prosperity, and our situation must be too good to be mended, or the present outcry against reforms and improvements is inhuman and criminal. But we hope our condition will be speedily improved, and to obtain so desirable a good is the object of our present association: a union founded on principles of benevolence and humanity; disclaiming all connection with riots and disorder, but firm in our purpose, and warm in our affections for liberty.

"Lastly, we invite the friends of freedom throughout Great Britain to form similar societies, and to act with unanimity and firmness, till the people be too wise to be imposed upon, and their influence in the government be commensurate with their dignity and importance. *Then shall we be free and happy.*" Such, gentlemen, is the language which a subject of Great Britain thinks himself warranted to hold, and upon such language has the corroborating sanction of a British jury been stamped by a verdict of acquittal. Such was the honest and manly freedom of publication; in a country, too, where the complaint of abuses has not half the foundation it has here. I said I loved to look to England for principles of judicial example; I can not but say to you, that it depends on your spirit whether I shall look to it hereafter with sympathy or with shame.

The motives of the accused were upright and patriotic.

Be pleased now, gentlemen, to consider whether the statement of the imperfection in your representation has been made with a desire of inflaming an attack upon the public tranquillity, or with an honest purpose of procuring a remedy for an actually existing grievance. It is impossible not to revert to the situation of the times; and let me remind you, that whatever observations of this kind I am compelled thus to make in a court of justice, the uttering of them in this place is not imputable to my client, but to the necessity of defense imposed upon him by this extraordinary prosecution.

Importance of an actual and fair representation of the people in Parliament.

Gentlemen, the representation of your people is the vital principle of their political existence. Without it they are dead, or they live only to servitude; without it there are two estates acting upon and against the third, instead of acting in co-operation with it; without it, if the people are oppressed by their judges, where is the tribunal to which their judges can be amenable? Without it, if they are trampled upon and plundered by a minister, where is the tribunal to which the offender shall be amenable? Without it, where is the ear to hear, or the heart to feel, or the hand to redress their sufferings? Shall they be found, let me ask you, in the accursed bands of imps and minions that bask in their disgrace, and fatten upon their spoils, and flourish upon their ruin? But let me not put this to you as a merely speculative question. It is a plain question of fact: rely upon it, physical man is every where the same; it is only the various operations of moral causes that gives variety to the social or individual character and condition. How otherwise happens it that modern slavery looks quietly at the despot, on the very spot where Leonidas expired? The answer is easy; Sparta has not changed her climate, but she has lost that government which her liberty could not survive.

Has Ireland such a representation?

I call you, therefore, to the plain question of fact. This paper recommends a reform in Parliament: I put that question to your consciences; do you think it needs that reform? I put it boldly and fairly to you; do you think the people of Ireland are represented as they ought to be? Do you hesitate for an answer? If you do, let me remind you that, until the last year, three millions of your countrymen have, by the express letter of the law, been excluded from the reality of actual, and even from the phantom of virtual representation. Shall we, then, be told that this is only the affirmation of a wicked and seditious incendiary? If you do not feel the mockery of such a charge, look at your country; in what state do you find it? Is it in a state of tranquillity and general satisfaction? These are traces by which good are ever to be distinguished from bad governments, without any very minute inquiry or speculative refinement. Do you feel that a veneration for the law, a pious and humble attachment to the Constitution, form the political morality of the people? Do you find that comfort and competency among your people which are always to be found where a government is mild and moderate, where taxes are imposed by a body who have an interest in treating the poorer orders with compassion, and preventing the weight of taxation from pressing sore upon them?

The question a proper one for consideration.

Gentlemen, I mean not to impeach the state of your representation; I am not saying that it is defective, or that it ought to be altered or amended; nor is this a place for me to say whether I think that three millions of the inhabitants of a country whose whole number is but four, ought to be admitted to any efficient situation in the state. It may be said, and truly, that these are not questions for either of us directly to decide; but you can not refuse them some passing consideration at least, when you remember that on this subject the real question for your decision is, whether the allegation of a defect in your Constitution is so utterly unfounded and false, that you can ascribe it only to the malice and perverseness of a wicked mind, and not to the innocent mistake of an ordinary understanding; whether it may not be mistake; whether it can be only sedition.

And here, gentlemen, I own I can not but regret that one of our countrymen should be criminally pursued for asserting the necessity of a reform, at the very moment when that necessity seems admitted by the Parliament itself; that this unhappy reform shall, at the same moment, be a subject of legislative discussion and criminal prosecution. Far am I from imputing any sinister design to the virtue or wisdom of our government; but who can avoid feeling the deplorable impression that must be made on the public mind, when the demand for that reform is answered by a criminal information! I am the more forcibly impressed by this consideration, when I consider that when this information was first put on the file, the subject was transiently mentioned in the House of Commons. Some circumstances retarded the progress of the inquiry there, and the progress of the information was equally retarded here. On the first day of this session, you all know, that subject was again brought forward in the House of Commons, and, as if they had slept together, this prosecution was also revived in the Court of King's Bench, and that before a jury taken from a panel partly composed of those very members of Parliament who, in the House of Commons, must debate upon this subject as a measure of public advantage, which they are here called upon to consider as a public crime.[6]

rliament them-res con-lering it.

This paper, gentlemen, insists upon the necessity of emancipating the Catholics of Ireland, and that is charged as a part of the libel. If they had kept this prosecution impending for another year, how much would remain for a jury to decide upon, I should be at a loss to discover. It seems as if the progress of public reformation was eating away the ground of the prosecution. Since the commencement of the prosecution, this part of the libel has unluckily received the sanction of the Legislature. In that interval, our Catholic brethren have obtained that admission which, it seems, it was a libel to propose.[7] In what way to account for this, I am really at a loss. Have any alarms been occasioned by the emancipation of our Catholic brethren? Has the bigoted malignity of any individuals been crushed? Or, has the stability of the government, or has that of the country been weakened? Or, are one million of subjects stronger than three millions? Do you think that the benefit they received should be poisoned by the stings of vengeance? If you think so, you must say to them, "You have demanded your emancipation, and you have got it; but we abhor your persons, we are outraged at your success; and we will stigmatize, by a criminal prosecution, the relief which you have obtained from the voice of your country." I ask you, gentlemen, do you think, as honest men, anxious for the public tranquillity, conscious that there are wounds not yet completely cicatrized, that you ought to speak this language at this time, to men who are too much disposed to think that in this very emancipation they have been saved from their own Parliament by the humanity of their Sovereign? Or, do you wish to prepare them for the revocation of these improvident concessions? Do you think it wise or humane, at this moment, to insult them, by sticking up in a pillory the man who dared to stand forth their advocate? I put it to your oaths, do you think that a blessing of that kind, that a victory obtained by justice over bigotry and oppression, should have a stigma cast upon it by an ignominious sentence upon men bold and honest enough to propose that measure; to propose the redeeming of religion from the abuses of the Church—the reclaiming of three millions of men from bondage, and giving liberty to all who had a right to demand it—giving, I say, in the so much censured words of this paper, "UNIVERSAL EMANCIPATION!" I speak in the spirit of the British law, which makes liberty commensurate with, and inseparable from, the British soil—which proclaims, even to the stranger and the sojourner, the moment he sets his foot upon British earth, that the ground on which he treads is holy, and consecrated by the genius of UNIVERSAL EMANCIPATION. No matter in what language his doom may have been pronounced; no matter what complexion incompatible with freedom an Indian or an African sun may have burned upon him; no matter in what disastrous battle his liberty may have been cloven down; no matter with what solemnities he may have been devoted upon the altar of slavery; the first moment he touches the sacred soil of Britain, the altar and the god sink together in the dust; his soul walks abroad in her own majesty; his body swells beyond the measure of his chains that burst from around him, and he stands redeemed, regenerated, and disenthralled, by the irresistible genius of UNIVERSAL EMANCIPATION.[8]

(3.) Catholic emancipation.

[Here Mr. Curran was interrupted by a sudden burst of applause from the court and hall. After some time, silence was restored by the authority of Lord Clonmel, who acknowledged the pleasure which he himself felt at the brilliant display of professional talent, but disapproved of any intemperate expressions of applause in a court of justice. Mr. Curran then proceeded:]

Gentlemen, I am not such a fool as to ascribe any effusion of this sort to any merit of mine. It is the mighty theme, and not the inconsiderable advocate, that can excite interest in the hearer. What you hear is but the testimony which

It is not the individual, but the cause, that demands strong statements.

[6] The jury was taken from a panel containing the names of a number of members of Parliament.

[7] In 1793, after the prosecution was commenced, a bill passed the Irish Parliament giving the right of suffrage to Catholics, and conferring a large part of the rights and privileges desired.

[8] The origin of this fine passage may be traced to the following lines of Cowper:

Slaves can not breathe in England; if their lungs
Receive our air, that moment they are free;
They touch our country, and their shackles fall.
Task, book ii.

nature bears to her own character; it is the effusion of her gratitude to that Power which stamped that character. And, gentlemen, permit me to say, that if my client had occasion to defend his cause by any mad or drunken appeals to extravagance or licentiousness, I trust in God, I stand in that situation, that, humble as I am, he would not have resorted to me to be his advocate. I was not recommended to his choice by any connection of principle or party, or even private friendship; and, saying this, I can not but add, that I consider not to be acquainted with such a man as Mr. Rowan a want of personal good fortune. Gentlemen, upon this great subject of reform and emancipation, there is a latitude and boldness of remark, justifiable in the people, and necessary to the defense of Mr. Rowan, for which the habits of professional studies, and technical adherence to established forms, have rendered me unfit. It is, however, my duty, standing here as his advocate, to make some few observations to you, which I conceive to be material.

The interests of England and Ireland inseparable.

Gentlemen, you are sitting in a country that has a right to the British Constitution, and which is bound by an indissoluble union with the British nation. If you were now even at liberty to debate upon that subject—if you even were not by the most solemn compacts, founded upon the authority of your ancestors and of yourselves, bound to that alliance, and had an election now to make, in the present unhappy state of Europe—if you had heretofore been a stranger to Great Britain, you would now say, we will enter into society and union with you:

Commune periculum,
Una salus ambobus erit.[9]

But to accomplish that union, let me tell you, you must learn to become like the English people: it is vain to say you will protect their freedom, if you abandon your own. The pillar whose base has no foundation can give no support to the dome under which its head is placed; and if you profess to give England that assistance which you refuse to yourselves, she will laugh at your folly, and despise your meanness and insincerity.

Disposition of England to depress the other parts of the empire.

Let us follow this a little further; I know you will interpret what I say with the candor in which it is spoken. England is marked by a natural avarice of freedom, which she is studious to engross and accumulate, but most unwilling to impart, whether from any necessity of her policy, or from her weakness, or from her pride, I will not presume to say; but that so is the fact, you need not look to the East or to the West—you need only look to yourselves. In order to confirm that observation, I would appeal to what fell from the learned counsel for the Crown, that notwithstanding the alliance subsisting for two centuries past, between the two countries, the date of liberty in one goes no further back than the year 1784. If it required additional confirmation, I should state the case of the invaded American, and the subjugated Indian, to prove that the policy of England has ever been to govern her connections more as colonies than allies; and it must be owing to the great spirit, indeed, of Ireland, if she shall continue free. Rely upon it, she will ever have to hold her course against an adverse current; rely upon it, if the popular spring does not continue firm and elastic, a short interval of debilitated nerve and broken force will send you down the stream again, and reconsign you to the condition of a province.

Ireland kept down and governed by a faction.

If such should become the fate of your Constitution, ask yourselves what must be the motive of your government? It is easier to govern a province by a faction, than to govern a co-ordinate country by co ordinate means. I do not say it is now, but it will be always thought easiest by *the managers of the day*, to govern the Irish nation by the agency of such a faction, as long as this country shall be found willing to let her connection with Great Britain be preserved only by her own degradation. In such a precarious and wretched state of things, if it shall ever be found to exist, the true friend of Irish liberty and British connection will see that the only means of saving both must be, as Lord Chatham expressed it, "the infusion of new health and blood into the Constitution." He will see how deep a stake each country has in the liberty of the other; he will see what a bulwark he adds to the common cause, by giving England a co-ordinate and co-interested ally, instead of an oppressed, enfeebled, and suspected dependent; he will see how grossly the credulity of Britain is abused by those who make her believe that her solid interest is promoted by our depression; he will see the desperate precipice to which she approaches, by such a conduct, and, with an animated and generous piety, he will labor to avert her danger. But, gentlemen of the jury, what is likely to be his fate? The interest of the Sovereign must be forever the interest of his people, because his interest lives beyond his life; it must live in his fame—it must live in the tenderness of his solicitude for an unborn posterity—it must live in the heart-attaching bond, by which millions of men have united the destinies of themselves and their children with his, and call him by the endearing appellation of King and father of his people.

But what can be the interest of such a government as I have described? Not the interest of the King, not the interest of the people; but the sordid interest of the hour; the interest in deceiving the one, and in oppressing and deforming the other; the interest of unpunished rapine and unmerited favor; that odious and abject interest that prompts them to extinguish public spirit in punishment or in bribe; and to pursue every man even to death who has sense to see, and integrity and firmness enough to abhor and to oppose them. What, therefore, I say, gentlemen, will be the fate of the man who embarks

---

[9] To both alike one danger and one safety.

The words are those of Æneas, addressed to his father as he was bearing him from Troy.—*Æneid*, book ii., 709–10.

in an enterprise of so much difficulty and danger? I will not answer it. Upon that hazard has my client put every thing that can be dear to man: his fame, his fortune, his person, his liberty, and his children; but with what event your verdict only can answer, and to that I refer your country.

Gentlemen, there is a fourth point remaining. Says this paper, "for both these purposes, it appears necessary that provincial conventions should assemble preparatory to the convention of the Protestant people. The delegates of the Catholic body are not justified in communicating with individuals, or even bodies of an inferior authority, and therefore an assembly of a similar nature and organization is necessary to establish an intercourse of sentiment, a uniformity of conduct, a united cause, and a united nation. If a convention on the one part does not soon follow, and is not connected with that on the other, the common cause will split into partial interests; the people will relax into inattention and inertness; the union of affection and exertion will dissolve, and too probably some local insurrection, instigated by the malignity of our common enemy, may commit the character and risk the tranquillity of the island, which can be obviated only by the influence of an assembly arising from, and assimilated with the people, and whose spirit may be, as it were, knit with the soul of the nation—unless the sense of the Protestant people be, on their part, as fairly collected and as judiciously directed, unless individual exertion consolidates into collective strength, unless the particles unite into one mass, we may perhaps serve some person or some party for a little, but the public not at all. The nation is neither insolent, nor rebellious, nor seditious. While it knows its rights, it is unwilling to manifest its powers. It would rather supplicate administration to anticipate revolution by well-timed reform, and to save their country in mercy to themselves."

(4.) Call of a convention.

Gentlemen, it is with something more than common reverence, it is with a species of terror, that I am obliged to tread this ground. But what is the idea put in the strongest point of view. "We are willing not to manifest our powers, but to supplicate administration to anticipate revolution, that the Legislature may save the country in mercy to itself."

True import of the words.

Let me suggest to you, gentlemen, that there are some circumstances which have happened in the history of this country, that may better serve as a comment upon this part of the case than any I can make. I am not bound to defend Mr. Rowan as to the truth or wisdom of the opinions he may have formed. But if he did really conceive the situation of the country to be such that the not redressing her grievances might lead to a convulsion, and of such an opinion not even Mr. Rowan is answerable here for the wisdom, much less shall I insinuate any idea of my own upon so awful a subject; but if he did so conceive the fact to be, and acted from the fair and honest suggestion of a mind anxious for the public good, I must confess, gentlemen, I do not know in what part of the British Constitution to find the principle of his criminality.

No guilt in them if the motive was right.

But, gentlemen, be pleased further to consider that he can not be understood to put the fact on which he argues on the authority of his assertion. The condition of Ireland was as open to the observation of every other man as to that of Mr. Rowan. What, then, does this part of the publication amount to? In my mind, simply to this: "the nature of oppression in all countries is such that, although it may be borne to a certain degree, it can not be borne beyond that degree. You find it exemplified in Great Britain. You find the people of England patient to a certain point; but patient no longer. That infatuated monarch James II experienced this. The time did come when the measure of popular suffering and popular patience was full; when a single drop was sufficient to make the waters of bitterness to overflow. I think this measure in Ireland is brimful at present. I think the state of representation of the people in Parliament is a grievance. I think the utter exclusion of three millions of people is a grievance of that kind that the people are not likely long to endure; and the continuation of which may plunge the country into that state of despair which wrongs exasperated by perseverance never fail to produce." But to whom is even this language addressed? Not to the body of the people, on whose temper and moderation, if once excited, perhaps not much confidence could be placed; but to that authoritative body whose influence and power would have restrained the excesses of the irritable and tumultuous; and for that purpose expressly does this publication address the Volunteers. "We are told that we are in danger. I call upon you, the great constitutional saviors of Ireland, to defend the country to which you have given political existence; and use whatever sanction your great name, your sacred character, and the weight you have in the community, must give you to repress wicked designs, if any there are."

Their reference to the case of England.

"We feel ourselves strong. The people are always strong. The public chains can only be riveted by the public hands. Look to those devoted regions of southern despotism. Behold the expiring victim on his knees, presenting the javelin reeking with his blood to the ferocious monster who returns it into his heart. Call not that monster the tyrant. He is no more than the executioner of that inhuman tyranny which the people practice upon themselves, and of which he is only reserved to be a later victim than the wretch he has sent before. Look to a nearer country, where the sanguinary characters are more legible; whence you almost hear the groans of death and torture. Do you ascribe the rapine and murder of France to the few names that we are execrating here? or do you not see that it is the frenzy of an infuriated multitude abusing its own strength, and practicing those hideous abominations upon itself. Against the violence of this strength let your virtue and influence be our safeguard."

What criminality, gentlemen of the jury, can you find in this? What at any time? But I ask you, particularly at this momentous period, what guilt can you find in it? My client saw the scene of horror and blood which covers almost the face of Europe. He feared that causes, which he thought similar, might produce similar effects; and he seeks to avert those dangers by calling the united virtue and tried moderation of the country into a state of strength and vigilance. Yet this is the conduct which the prosecution of this day seeks to stigmatize; and this is the language for which this paper is reprobated to-day, as tending to turn the hearts of the people against their Sovereign, and inviting them to overturn the Constitution.

Not designed to create, but prevent disturbance in Ireland.

Let us now, gentlemen, consider the concluding part of this publication. It recommends a meeting of the people to deliberate on constitutional methods of redressing grievances. Upon this subject I am inclined to suspect that I have in my youth taken up crude ideas, not founded, perhaps, in law; but I did imagine that when the Bill of Rights restored the right of petitioning for the redress of grievances, it was understood that the people might boldly state among themselves that grievances did exist; that they might lawfully assemble themselves in such a manner as they might deem most orderly and decorous. I thought I had collected it from the greatest luminaries of the law. The power of petitioning seemed to me to imply the right of assembling for the purpose of deliberation. The law requiring a petition to be presented by a limited number, seemed to me to admit that the petition might be prepared by any number whatever, provided, in doing so, they did not commit any breach or violation of the public peace. I know that there has been a law passed in the Irish Parliament of last year which may bring my former opinion into a merited want of authority. That law declares, "that no body of men may delegate a power to any similar number, to act, think, or petition for them!" If that law had not passed, I should have thought that the assembling by a delegated convention was recommended, in order to avoid the tumult and disorder of a promiscuous assembly of the whole mass of the people. I should have conceived, before that act, that any law to abridge the orderly appointment of the few to consult for the interest of the many, and thus force the many to consult by themselves, or not at all, would in fact be a law not to restrain, but to promote insurrection. But that law has spoken, and my error must stand corrected. Of this, however, let me remind you. You are to try this part of the publication by what the law was then: not by what it is now. How was it understood until last session of Parliament? You had both in England and Ireland, for the last ten years, these delegated meetings. The Volunteers of Ireland, in 1782, met by delegation; they framed a plan of parliamentary reform; they presented it to the representative wisdom of the nation. It was not received; but no man ever dreamed that it was not the undoubted right of the subject to assemble in that manner. They assembled, by delegation, at Dungannon; and to show the idea then entertained of the legality of their public conduct, that same body of Volunteers was thanked by both Houses of Parliament, and their delegates most graciously received at the Throne. The other day you had delegated representatives for the Catholics of Ireland, publicly elected by the members of that persuasion, and sitting in convention in the heart of your capital, carrying on an actual treaty with the existing government, and under the eye of your own Parliament, which was then assembled; you have seen the delegates from that convention carry the complaints of their grievances to the foot of the throne, from whence they brought back to that convention the auspicious tidings of that redress which they had been refused at home.

The right of holding conventions implied in the right of petition.

A recent law has forbidden it.

But Mr. Rowan not to be tried by that law.

Such, gentlemen, have been the means of popular communication and discussion, which, until the last session, have been deemed legal in this country, as, happily for the sister kingdom, they are yet considered there.

I do not complain of this act as any infraction of popular liberty; I should not think it becoming in me to express any complaint against a law, when once become such. I observe only, that one mode of popular deliberation is thereby taken utterly away, and you are reduced to a situation in which you never stood before. You are living in a country where the Constitution is rightly stated to be only ten years old—where the people have not the ordinary rudiments of education. It is a melancholy story that the lower orders of the people here have less means of being enlightened than the same class of people in any other country. If there be no means left by which public measures can be canvassed, what will be the consequence? Where the press is free, and discussion unrestrained, the mind, by the collision of intercourse, gets rid of its own asperities; a sort of insensible perspiration takes place in the body politic, by which those acrimonies, which would otherwise fester and inflame, are quietly dissolved and dissipated. But now, if any aggregate assembly shall meet, they are censured; if a printer publishes their resolutions, he is punished: rightly, to be sure, in both cases, for it has been lately done. If the people say, let us not create tumult, but meet in delegation, they can not do it; if they are anxious to promote parliamentary reform in that way, they can not do it; the law of the last session has, for the first time, declared such meetings to be a crime. What then remains? The liberty of the press *only*—that sacred palladium which no influence, no power, no minister, no government, which nothing but the depravity, or folly, or corruption of a jury, can ever destroy.

Under this law the freedom of the press doubly important.

And what calamities are the people saved

from, by having public communication left open to them? I will tell you, gentlemen, what they are saved from, and what the government is saved from; I will tell you, also, to what both are exposed by shutting up that communication. In one case, sedition speaks aloud and walks abroad; the demagogue goes forth; the public eye is upon him; he frets his busy hour upon the stage; but soon either weariness, or bribe, or punishment, or disappointment, bears him down, or drives him off, and he appears no more. In the other case, how does the work of sedition go forward? Night after night the muffled rebel steals forth in the dark, and casts another and another brand upon the pile, to which, when the hour of fatal maturity shall arrive, he will apply the torch. If you doubt of the horrid consequence of suppressing the effusion even of individual discontent, look to those enslaved countries where the protection of despotism is supposed to be secured by such restraints. Even the person of the despot there is never in safety. Neither the fears of the despot nor the machinations of the slave have any slumber—the one anticipating the moment of peril, the other watching the opportunity of aggression. The fatal crisis is equally a surprise upon both: the decisive instant is precipitated without warning—by folly on the one side, or by frenzy on the other; and there is no notice of the treason till the traitor acts. In those unfortunate countries—one can not read it without horror—there are officers whose province it is to have the water which is to be drunk by their rulers sealed up in bottles, lest some wretched miscreant should throw poison into the draught.

Benefits to the government from a free press.

But, gentlemen, if you wish for a nearer and more interesting example, you have it in the history of your own revolution. You have it at that memorable period, when the Monarch [James II.] found a servile acquiescence in the ministers of his folly—when the liberty of the press was trodden under foot—when venal sheriffs returned packed juries, to carry into effect those fatal conspiracies of the few against the many—when the devoted benches of public justice were filled by some of those foundlings of fortune who, overwhelmed in the torrent of corruption at an early period, lay at the bottom like drowned bodies while soundness or sanity remained in them; but at length, becoming buoyant by putrefaction, they rose as they rotted, and floated to the surface of the polluted stream, where they were drifted along, the objects of terror, and contagion, and abomination.[10]

Illustration from English history.

In that awful moment of a nation's travail, of the last gasp of tyranny and the first breath of freedom, how pregnant is the example! The press extinguished, the people enslaved, and the prince undone. As the advocate of society, therefore—of peace—of domestic liberty—and the lasting union of the two countries—I conjure you to guard the liberty of the press, that great sentinel of the state, that grand detector of public imposture; guard it, because, when it sinks, there sinks with it, in one common grave, the liberty of the subject and the security of the Crown.

Gentlemen, I am glad that this question has not been brought forward earlier; I rejoice for the sake of the court, of the jury, and of the public repose, that this question has not been brought forward till now. In Great Britain, analogous circumstances have taken place. At the commencement of that unfortunate war which has deluged Europe with blood, the spirit of the English people was tremblingly alive to the terror of French principles; at that moment of general paroxysm, to accuse was to convict. The danger looked larger to the public eye, from the misty region through which it was surveyed. We measure inaccessible heights by the shadows which they project, where the lowness and the distance of the light form the length of the shade.

Recent panic in the sister island, and its disgraceful consequences.

There is a sort of aspiring and adventurous credulity which disdains assenting to obvious truths, and delights in catching at the improbability of circumstances, as its best ground of faith. To what other cause, gentlemen, can you ascribe that, in the wise, the reflecting, and the philosophic nation of Great Britain, a printer has been found guilty of a libel, for publishing those resolutions, to which the present minister of that kingdom had actually subscribed his name? To what other cause can you ascribe, what in my mind is still more astonishing, in such a country as Scotland, a nation cast in the happy medium between the spiritless acquiescence of submissive poverty, and the sturdy credulity of pampered wealth; cool and ardent, adventurous and persevering; winging her eagle flight against the blaze of every science, with an eye that never winks, and a wing that never tires; crowned as she is with the spoils of every art, and decked with the wreath of every muse; from the deep and scrutinizing researches of her Hume, to the sweet and simple, but not less sublime and pathetic morality of her Burns—how, from the bosom of a country like that, genius and character, and talents, should be banished to a distant, barbarous soil; condemned to pine under the horrid communion of vulgar vice and base-born profligacy, for twice the period that ordinary calculation gives to the continuance of human life?[11] But I will not further press any idea

[10] It may not be ungratifying to hear the manner in which this passage was suggested to the speaker's mind. A day or two before Mr. Rowan's trial, one of Mr. Curran's friends showed him a letter that he had received from Bengal, in which the writer, after mentioning the Hindoo custom of throwing the dead into the Ganges, added, that he was then upon the banks of that river, and that, as he wrote, he could see several bodies floating down its stream. The orator, shortly after, while describing a corrupted bench, recollected this fact, and applied it as above.—*Life of Curran, by his Son*, vol. i., p. 316.

[11] Alluding to the banishment of the Scotch Reformers, Muir, Palmer, &c.

that is painful to me, and I am sure must be painful to you. I will only say, you have now an example of which neither England nor Scotland had the advantage. You have the example of the panic, the infatuation, and the contrition of both. It is now for you to decide whether you will profit by their experience of idle panic and idle regret, or whether you merely prefer to palliate a servile imitation of their frailty, by a paltry affectation of their repentance. It is now for you to show that you are not carried away by the same hectic delusions, to acts of which no tears can wash away the consequences or the indelible reproach.

An Irish jury ought to profit by these errors.

Gentlemen, I have been warning you by instances of public intellect suspended or obscured; let me rather excite you by the example of that intellect recovered and restored. In that case which Mr. Attorney General has cited himself, I mean that of the trial of Lambert in England, is there a topic of invective against constituted authorities, is there a topic of abuse against every department of British government that you do not find in the most glowing and unqualified terms in that publication, for which the printer of it was prosecuted, and acquitted by an English jury? See, too, what a difference there is between the case of a man publishing his own opinion of facts, thinking that he is bound by duty to hazard the promulgation of them, and without the remotest hope of any personal advantage, and that of a man who makes publication his trade. And saying this, let me not be misunderstood; it is not my province to enter into any abstract defense of the opinions of any man upon public subjects. I do not affirmatively state to you that these grievances, which this paper supposes, do in fact exist; yet I can not but say that the movers of this prosecution have forced that question upon you. Their motives and their merits, like those of all accusers, are put in issue before you; and I need not tell you how strongly the motive and merits of any *informer* ought to influence the fate of his accusation.

They ought also to be influenced by a more recent change of feeling in England.

I agree most implicitly with Mr. Attorney General that nothing can be more criminal than an attempt to work a change in the government by armed force, and I entreat that the court will not suffer any expression of mine to be considered as giving encouragement or defense to any design to excite disaffection, to overawe or to overturn the government. But I put my client's case upon another ground. If he was led into an opinion of grievances where there were none; if he thought there ought to be a reform where none was necessary, he is answerable only for his intention. He can be answerable to you in the same way only that he is answerable to that God before whom the accuser, the accused, and the judge must appear together; that is, not for the clearness of his understanding, but for the purity of his heart.

Mr. Rowan answerable only for his *intentions*, not for his errors of judgment.

Gentlemen, Mr. Attorney General has said that Mr. Rowan did by this publication (supposing it to be his) recommend, under the name of equality, a general, indiscriminate assumption of public rule by every the meanest person in the state. Low as we are in point of public information, there is not, I believe, any man, who thinks for a moment, that does not know that all which the great body of the people of any country can have from any government, is a fair encouragement to their industry, and protection for the fruits of their labor. And there is scarcely any man, I believe, who does not know that if a people could become so silly as to abandon their stations in society, under pretense of governing themselves, they would become the dupes and the victims of their own folly. But does this publication recommend any such infatuated abandonment, or any such desperate assumption? I will read the words which relate to that subject. "By liberty we never understood unlimited freedom, nor by equality the leveling of property or destruction of subordination." I ask you with what justice, upon what principle of common sense, you can charge a man with the publication of sentiments the very reverse of what his words avow; and that, when there is no collateral evidence, where there is no foundation whatever, save those very words, by which his meaning can be ascertained? or, if you do adopt an arbitrary principle of imputing to him *your* meaning instead of his own, what publication can be guiltless or safe? It is a sort of accusation that I am ashamed and sorry to see introduced in a court acting on the principles of the British Constitution.

No leveling principles contained in the Address.

In the bitterness of reproach it was said, "out of thine own mouth will I condeman thee." From the severity of justice I demand no more. See if, in the words that have been spoken, you can find matter to acquit or to condemn. "By liberty we never understood unlimited freedom, nor by equality the leveling of property, nor the destruction of subordination. This is a calumny invented by that faction, or that gang, which misrepresents the King to the people, and the people to the King; traduces one half of the nation to cajole the other; and, by keeping up distrust and division, wishes to continue the proud arbitrators of the fortune and fate of Ireland." Here you find that meaning disclaimed as a calumny, which is artfully imputed as a crime.

I say, therefore, gentlemen of the jury, as to the four parts into which the publication must be divided, I answer thus:

Recapitulation.

It calls upon the *Volunteers*. Consider the time, the danger, the authority of the prosecutors themselves for believing that danger to exist; the high character, the known moderation, the approved loyalty of that venerable institution; the similarity of the circumstances between the period at which they are summoned to take arms, and that in which they have been called upon to reassume them. Upon this simple ground, gentlemen, you will decide whether this part of the publication was libelous and criminal, or not.

As to *reform*, I could wish to have said nothing upon it. I believe I have said enough. If he thought the state required it, he acted like an honest man. For the rectitude of the opinion he was not answerable. He discharged his duty in telling the country that he thought so.

As to the *emancipation* of the Catholics, I can not but say that Mr. Attorney General did very wisely in keeping clear of that. Yet, gentlemen, I need not tell you how important a figure it was intended to make upon the scene, though, from unlucky accidents, it has become necessary to expunge it during the rehearsal.

Of the concluding part of this publication, the *Convention* which it recommends, I have spoken already. I wish not to trouble you with saying more upon it. I feel that I have already trespassed much upon your patience. In truth, upon a subject embracing such a variety of topics, a rigid observance either of conciseness or arrangement could, perhaps, scarcely be expected. It is, however, with pleasure I feel I am drawing to a close, and that only one question remains, to which I beg your attention.

Want of evidence to bring home the publication of the Address to Mr. Rowan.

Whatever, gentlemen, may be your opinion of the meaning of this publication, there yet remains a great point for you to decide upon; namely, whether, in point of fact, this publication be imputable to Mr. Rowan or not; whether he did publish it or not. And two witnesses are called to that fact, one of the name of *Lyster*, and the other of the name of *Morton*. You must have observed that Morton gave no evidence upon which that paper could even have been read; he produced no paper; he identified no paper; so that in point of law, there was no evidence to be given to a jury; and, therefore, it turns entirely upon the evidence of the other witness. He has stated that he went to a public meeting, in a place where there was a gallery crowded with spectators; and that he there got a printed paper, the same which has been read to you.

Only one witness, and he impeached.

I know you are well acquainted with the fact that the credit of every witness must be considered by, and rest with the jury. They are the sovereign judges of that circumstance; and I will not insult your feelings by insisting on the caution with which you should watch the testimony of a witness that seeks to affect the liberty, or property, or character of your fellow-citizens. Under what circumstances does this evidence come before you? The witness says he has got a commission in the army by the interest of a lady, from a person then high in administration. He told you that he made a memorandum upon the back of that paper, it being his general custom, when he got such papers to make an endorsement upon them; that he did this from mere fancy; that he had no intention of giving any evidence on the subject; he took it with no such view.

Comments on his testimony.

There is something whimsical enough in this curious story. Put his credit upon the positive evidence adduced to his character. Who he is I know not. I know not the man; but his credit is impeached. Mr. Blake was called; he said he knew him. I asked him, "Do you think, sir, that Mr. Lyster is or is not a man deserving credit upon his oath?" If you find a verdict of conviction, it can be only upon the credit of Mr. Lyster. What said Mr. Blake? Did he tell you that he believed he was a man to be believed upon his oath? He did not attempt to say that he was. The best he could say was, that he would hesitate. Do you believe Blake? Have you the same opinion of Lyster's testimony that Mr. Blake has? Do you know Lyster? If you do know him, and know that he is credible, your knowledge should not be shaken by the doubts of any man. But if you do not know him, you must take his credit from an unimpeached witness, swearing that he would hesitate to believe him.

A strong circumstance against him.

In my mind there is a circumstance of the strongest nature that came out from Lyster on the table.[12] I am aware that a very respectable man, if impeached by surprise, may not be ready prepared to repel a wanton calumny by contrary testimony. But was Lyster unapprised of this attack upon him? What said he? "I knew that you had Blake to examine against me. You have brought him here for that purpose." He knew the very witness that was to be produced against him; he knew that his credit was impeached, and yet he produced no person to support that credit. What said Mr. Smyth? "From my knowledge of him, I would not believe him upon his oath."

Mr. Attorney General. I beg pardon, but I must set Mr. Curran right. Mr. Lyster said he heard Blake would be here, but not in time to prepare himself.

Mr. Curran. But what said Mrs. Hatchell? Was the production of that witness a surprise upon Mr. Lyster? her cross-examination shows the fact to be the contrary. The learned counsel, you see, was perfectly apprised of a chain of private circumstances, to which he pointed his questions. Did he know these circumstances by inspiration? No; they could come only from Lyster himself. I insist, therefore, the gentleman knew his character was to be impeached; his counsel knew it; and not a single witness has been produced to support it. Then consider, gentlemen, upon what ground you can find a verdict of conviction against my client, when the only witness produced to the fact of publication is impeached, without even an attempt to defend his character. Many hundreds, he said, were at that meeting; why not produce one of them to swear to the fact of such a meeting? One he has ventured to name; but he was certainly very safe in naming a person who, he has told you, is not in the kingdom, and could not, therefore, be called to confront him.

Gentlemen, let me suggest another observation or two. If still you have any doubt as to

[12] In the Irish courts the witness gives his testimony seated in a chair, on a raised platform called the *table*.

the guilt or innocence of the defendant, give me leave to suggest to you what circumstances you ought to consider in order to found your verdict. You should consider the character of the person accused, and in this your task is easy. I will venture to say there is not a man in this nation more known than the gentleman who is the subject of this prosecution, not only by the part he has taken in public concerns, and which he has taken in common with many, but still more so by that extraordinary sympathy for human affliction which, I am sorry to think, he shares with so small a number. There is not a day that you hear the cries of your starving manufacturers in your streets, that you do not also see the advocate of their sufferings. That you do not see his honest and manly figure, with uncovered head soliciting for their relief, searching the frozen heart of charity for every string that can be touched by compassion, and urging the force of every argument and every motive, save that which his modesty suppresses; the authority of his own generous example. Or, if you see him not there, you may trace his steps to the private abode of disease, and famine, and despair; the messenger of Heaven, bearing with him food, and medicine, and consolation. Are these the materials of which anarchy and public rapine are to be formed? Is this the man on whom to fasten the abominable charge of goading on a frantic populace to mutiny and bloodshed? Is this the man likely to apostatize from every principle that can bind him to the state, his birth, his property, his education, his character, and his children? Let me tell you, gentlemen of the jury, if you agree with his prosecutors in thinking that there ought to be a sacrifice of such a man, on such an occasion, and upon the credit of such evidence, you are to convict him—never did you, never can you give a sentence, consigning any man to public punishment with less danger to his person or to his fame; for where could the hireling be found to fling contumely or ingratitude at his head, whose private distress he had not labored to alleviate, or whose public condition he had not labored to improve.

Argument derived from the character of the accused.

I can not, however, avoid adverting to a circumstance that distinguishes the case of Mr. Rowan from that of a late sacrifice in a neighboring kingdom.[13] The severer law of that country, it seems, and happy for them that it should, enables them to remove from their sight the victim of their infatuation. The more merciful spirit of our law deprives you of that consolation. His sufferings must remain forever before your eyes a continual call upon your shame and your remorse. But those sufferings will do more; they will not rest satisfied with your unavailing contrition, they will challenge the great and paramount inquest of society. The man will be weighed against the charge, the witness, and the sentence; and impartial justice will demand, why has an *Irish* jury done this deed? The moment he ceases to be regarded as a criminal, he becomes of necessity an accuser. And, let me ask you, what can your most zealous defenders be prepared to answer to such a charge? When your sentence shall have sent him forth to that stage [the pillory] which guilt alone can render infamous, let me tell you he will not be like a little statue upon a mighty pedestal, diminishing by elevation. But he will stand a striking and imposing object upon a monument, which, if it does not, and it can not, record the atrocity of his crime, must record the atrocity of his conviction. And upon this subject credit me when I say that I am still more anxious for you than I can possibly be for him. I can not but feel the peculiarity of your situation. Not the jury of his own choice, which the law of England allows, but which ours refuses,[14] collected in that box by a person certainly no friend to Mr. Rowan, certainly not very deeply interested in giving him a very impartial jury. Feeling this, as I am persuaded you do, you can not be surprised, however you may be distressed at the mournful presage with which an anxious public is led to fear the worst from your possible determination. But I will not, for the justice and honor of our common country, suffer my mind to be borne away by such melancholy anticipations. I will not relinquish the confidence that this day will be the period of his sufferings; and however merciless he has been hitherto pursued, that your verdict will send him home to the arms of his family and the wishes of his country. But if, which Heaven forbid, it hath still been unfortunately determined that, because he has not bent to power and authority, because he would not bow down before the golden calf and worship it, he is to be bound and cast into the furnace; I do trust in God that there is a redeeming spirit in the Constitution which will be seen to walk with the sufferer through the flames, and to preserve him unhurt by the conflagration.

Peroration: Mr. Rowan, if condemned, must suffer in Ireland.

At the conclusion of this speech, there was another universal burst of applause, throughout the court and hall, for some minutes, which was again silenced by the interference of Lord Clonmel. "Mr. Curran," says Charles Phillips, "used to relate a ludicrous incident which attended his departure from court after the trial. His path was instantly beset by the populace, who were bent on chairing him. He implored—he entreated—all in vain. At length, assuming an air of authority, he addressed those nearest to him: "I desire, gentlemen, that you will desist." "I laid great emphasis," says Curran, "on the word 'desist,' and put on my best suit of dignity. However, my next neighbor, a gigantic, brawny chairman, eyeing me with a somewhat contemptuous affection, from top to toe, bellowed out to his companion, 'Arrah, blood and turf! Pat, don't

[13] Alluding to the banishment of Muir, Palmer, &c.

[14] In making up the jury, Mr. Rowan was not allowed the same right of challenging which is enjoyed in England.

mind the little *crachur;* here, pitch him up this minute upon my *showlder.*' Pat did as he was desired; the 'little crachur' was carried, *nolens volens*, to his carriage, and drawn home by an applauding populace."

The jury brought in a verdict of Guilty, and Mr. Rowan was sentenced to pay £500, and to be imprisoned two years. Within a short time, however, he escaped from prison and fled to America, where he remained for many years, but finally returned to Ireland and had all further punishment remitted.

SPEECH

OF MR. CURRAN IN BEHALF OF PETER FINNERTY WHEN INDICTED FOR A LIBEL, DELIVERED BEFORE JUSTICE DOWNS IN THE COMMISSION COURT, DECEMBER 22, 1797.

INTRODUCTION.

MR. FINNERTY was the printer of a newspaper published at Dublin called the Press, and was indicted for publishing a severe letter, signed MARCUS, addressed to the Lord Lieutenant of Ireland, in reference to the execution of William Orr.

Orr was a farmer of the Presbyterian sect—a man of pious, gentle, and gallant character, greatly respected and beloved in the county of Antrim, where he lived. He was prosecuted for administering an oath to a United Irishman, and for so doing was *condemned to death!* Some of the jury made an affidavit, immediately after the trial, that they acted under intimidation in convicting him, and that spirits were introduced into the jury room. It was likewise ascertained that the principal witness against Orr was a man of infamous character, whose word could not be relied on. These things were certified to the Lord Lieutenant with a view to Orr's being pardoned. He was accordingly respited to allow time for consideration; a second, and then a third respite was granted, and the feeling became general that his pardon was secured; when, to the astonishment and horror of the public, he was hanged at the expiration of seven days, surrounded by large bodies of troops collected to overawe the people. He died with great calmness, leaving a written declaration of his entire innocence.

The public indignation was now universal. Medals were struck and circulated bearing the inscription, "Remember Orr;" his name became a watch-word even in England; Mr. Fox spoke of him as a martyr; and the toast, "The ministers in Orr's place," was often heard in both countries. The letters of MARCUS expressed the general sentiment of the people respecting his execution; and this was thought by the government a favorable opportunity for crushing Finnerty's paper, in which it was published—the only remaining paper in Ireland which had not been bought out or broken down by the government.

"Mr. Curran's address to the jury in this case," says his son, "must be considered, if not the finest, at least the most surprising specimen of his oratorical powers. He had no time for preparation; it was not till a few minutes before the case commenced that his brief was handed him. During the progress of the trial, he had occasion to speak at unusual length to questions of law that arose upon the evidence, so that his speech to the jury could necessarily be no other than a sudden, extemporaneous effusion; and it was, perhaps, a secret, and not unjustifiable, feeling of pride at having so acquitted himself upon such an emergency that inclined his own mind to prefer it to any of his other efforts."

SPEECH, &c.

[Mr. Curran, after a few observations on the right of the jury under the Libel Bill of Mr. Fox, proceeded thus:]

Remarks on the extraneous matter introduced by the counsel for the Crown.

And now, gentlemen, let us come to the immediate subject of the trial, as it is brought before you by the charge in the indictment, to which it ought to have been confined; and also, as it is presented to you by the statement of the learned counsel who has taken a much wider range than the mere limits of the accusation, and has endeavored to force upon your consideration extraneous and irrelevant facts, for reasons which it is my duty to explain. The indictment states simply that Mr. Finnerty has published a false and scandalous libel upon the Lord Lieutenant of Ireland, tending to bring his government into disrepute, and to alienate the affections of the people; and one would have expected that, without stating any other matter, the counsel for the Crown would have gone directly to the proof of this allegation. But he has not done so; he has gone to a most extraordinary length, indeed, of preliminary observation, and an allusion to facts, and sometimes an assertion of facts, at which, I own, I was astonished, until I saw the drift of these allusions and assertions. Whether you have been fairly dealt with by him, or are now honestly dealt with by me, you must be judges.

His insinuations against the general character of the newspaper containing the piece complained of.

He has been pleased to say that this prosecution is brought against this letter signed MARCUS, merely as a part of what he calls a system of attack upon government by the paper called the Press. As to this I will only ask you whether you are fairly dealt with? Whether it is fair treatment to men upon their oaths, to insinuate to them, that the general character of a newspaper (and that general character founded merely upon the assertion of the prosecutor) is to have any influence upon their minds when they are to judge of a particular publication? I will only ask you what men you must be supposed to be when it is thought that even in a court of justice, and with the eyes of the nation upon you, you can be the dupes of that trite and exploded expedient, so scandalous of late in this country, of raising a vulgar and mercenary cry against whatever man or whatever principle it is thought necessary to put down; and I shall therefore merely leave it to your own pride to suggest upon what foundation it could be hoped that a senseless clamor of that kind could be echoed back by the yell of a jury upon their oaths. I trust you see that this has nothing to do with the question.

His pretense of seeking to promote the liberty of the press by this prosecution.

Gentlemen of the jury, other matters have been mentioned, which I must repeat for the same purpose—that of showing you that they have nothing to do with the question. The learned counsel has been pleased to say, that he comes forward in this prosecution as the real advocate for the liberty of the press, and to protect a mild and merciful government from its licentiousness; and he has been pleased to add, that the Constitution can never be lost while its freedom remains, and that its licentiousness alone can destroy that freedom. As to that, gentlemen, he might as well have said that there is only one mortal disease of which a man can die. I can die the death inflicted by tyranny; and when he comes forward to extinguish this paper in the ruin of the printer by a state prosecution, in order to prevent its dying of licentiousness, you must judge how candidly he is treating you, both in the fact and in the reasoning. Is it in Ireland, gentlemen, that we are told licentiousness is the only disease that can be mortal to the press? Has he heard of nothing else that has been fatal to the freedom of publication? I know not whether the printer of the Northern Star may have heard of such things in his captivity, but I know that his wife and children are well apprised that a press may be destroyed in the open day, not by its own licentiousness, but by the licentiousness of a military force.[1]

Proof from facts that governments prosecute for very different reasons.

As to the sincerity of the declaration that the state has prosecuted in order to assert the freedom of the press, it starts a train of thought, of melancholy retrospect and direful prospect, to which I did not think the learned counsel would have wished to commit your minds. It leads you naturally to reflect at what times, from what motives, and with what consequences the government has displayed its patriotism by prosecutions of this sort. As to the motives, does history give you a single instance in which the state has been provoked to these conflicts, except by the fear of truth, and by the love of vengeance? Have you ever seen the rulers of any country bring forward a prosecution from motives of filial piety, for libels upon their departed ancestors? Do you read that Elizabeth directed any of those state prosecutions against the libels which the divines of her time had written against her Catholic sister; or against the other libels which the same gentlemen had written against her Protestant father? No, gentlemen, we read of no such thing; but we know she did bring forward a prosecution from motives of personal resentment, and we know that a jury was found time-serving and mean enough to give a verdict which she was ashamed to carry into effect!

I said the learned counsel drew you back to the times that have been marked by these miserable conflicts. I see you turn your thoughts to the reign of the second James. I see you turn your eyes to those pages of governmental abandonment, of popular degradation, of expiring liberty, of merciless and sanguinary persecution; to that miserable period, in which the fallen and abject state of man might have been almost an argument in the mouth of the atheist and blasphemer against the existence of an all-just and an all-wise First Cause; if the glorious era of the Revolution that followed it had not refuted the impious inference, by showing that if man descends, it is not in his own proper motion;[2] that it is with labor and with pain, and that he can continue to sink only until, by the force and pressure of the descent, the spring of his immortal faculties acquires that recuperative energy and effort that hurries him as many miles aloft. He sinks but to rise again. It is at that period that the state seeks for shelter in the destruction of the press; it is in a period like that that the tyrant prepares for the attack upon the people, by destroying the liberty of the press; by taking away that shield of wisdom and of virtue, behind which the people are invulnerable, in whose pure and polished convex, ere the lifted blow has fallen, he beholds his own image, and is turned into stone.[3] It is at those periods that the honest man dares not speak, because truth is too dreadful to be told; it is then humanity has no ears, because humanity has no tongue. It is then the proud man scorns to speak, but like a physician baffled by the wayward excesses of a dying patient, retires indignantly from the bed of an unhappy wretch, whose ear is too fastidious to bear the sound of wholesome advice, whose palate is too debauched to bear the salutary bitter of the medicine that might redeem him; and therefore leaves him to the felonious piety of the slaves that talk to him of life, and strip him before he is cold.

I do not care, gentlemen, to exhaust too much of your attention by following this subject through the last century with much minuteness; but the facts are too recent in your minds not to show

[1] The Northern Star was a paper published in Belfast, which was broken down and destroyed by the government in the way here referred to.

[2] See the speech of Moloch in Milton's Paradise Lost, book ii.:

In our proper motion we ascend
Up to our native seat; descent and fall
To us are adverse.

[3] The allusion here is to the shield of Minerva, having the head of Medusa in its center, which turned the beholder into stone.

you that the liberty of the press and the liberty of the people sink and rise together, and that the liberty of speaking and the liberty of acting have shared exactly the same fate. You must have observed in England that their fate has been the same in the successive vicissitudes of their late depression; and sorry I am to add that this country has exhibited a melancholy proof of their inseparable destiny, through the various and further stages of deterioration down to the period of their final extinction; when the Constitution has given place to the sword, and the only printer in Ireland who dares to speak for the people is now in the dock.

The preceding remarks rendered necessary by the course of the prosecuting attorney.

Gentlemen, the learned counsel has made the real subject of this prosecution so small a part of his statement, and has led you into so wide a range, certainly as necessary to the object, as inapplicable to the subject of this prosecution, that I trust you will think me excusable in somewhat following his example. Glad am I to find that I have the authority of the same example for coming at last to the subject of this trial. I agree with the learned counsel that the charge made against the Lord Lieutenant of Ireland is that of having grossly and inhumanly abused the royal prerogative of mercy, of which the King is only the trustee for the benefit of the people. The facts are not controverted. It has been asserted that their truth or falsehood is indifferent, and they are shortly these, as they appear in this publication.

Narration of the facts which gave rise to the letter of Marcus.

William Orr was indicted for having administered the oath of a United Irishman. Every man now knows what that oath is; that it is simply an engagement, first, to promote a brotherhood of affection among men of all religious distinctions; secondly, to labor for the attainment of a parliamentary reform; and, thirdly, an obligation of secrecy, which was added to it when the convention law made it criminal and punishable to meet by any public delegation for that purpose. After remaining upward of a year in jail, Mr. Orr was brought to his trial; was prosecuted by the state; was sworn against by a common informer by the name of Wheatley, who himself had taken the obligation, and was convicted under the Insurrection Act, which makes the administering such an obligation felony of death. The jury recommended Mr. Orr to mercy. The judge, with a humanity becoming his character, transmitted the recommendation to the noble prosecutor in this case [the Lord Lieutenant]. Three of the jurors made solemn affidavit in court that liquor had been conveyed into their box; that they were brutally threatened by some of their fellow-jurors with capital prosecution if they did not find the prisoner guilty; and that, under the impression of those threats, and worn down by watching and intoxication, they had given a verdict of guilty against him, though they believed him, in their conscience, to be innocent. That further inquiries were made, which ended in a discovery of the infamous life and character of the informer; that a respite was therefore sent once, and twice, and thrice, to give time, as Mr. Attorney General has stated, for his Excellency to consider whether mercy *could* be extended to him or not; and that, with a knowledge of all these circumstances, his Excellency did finally determine that mercy *should not* be extended to him, and that he was accordingly executed upon that verdict.

That letter does not, as pretended by the Attorney General, reflect in the least on the judges in that case.

Of this publication, which the indictment charges to be false and seditious, Mr. Attorney General is pleased to say that the design of it is to bring the courts of justice into contempt. As to this point of fact, gentlemen, I beg to set you right. To the administration of justice, so far as it relates to the judges, this publication has not even an allusion in any part mentioned in this indictment. It relates to a department of justice that can not begin until the duty of the judge is closed. Sorry should I be that, with respect to this unfortunate man, any censure should be flung on those judges who presided at his trial, with the mildness and temper that became them, upon so awful an occasion as the trial of life and death. Sure am I, that if they had been charged with inhumanity or injustice, and if they had condescended at all to prosecute the reviler, they would not have come forward in the face of the public to say, as has been said this day, that it was immaterial whether the charge was true or not. Sure I am, their first object would have been to show that it was false; and ready, should I have been an eye-witness of the fact, to have discharged the debt of ancient friendship, of private respect, and of public duty, and upon my oath, to have repelled the falsehood of such an imputation. Upon this subject, gentlemen, the presence of those venerable judges restrains what I might otherwise have said, nor should I have named them at all if I had not been forced to do so, and merely to undeceive you, if you have been made to believe their characters to have any community of cause whatever with the Lord Lieutenant of Ireland. To *him* alone it is confined, and against *him* the charge is made, as strongly, I suppose, as the writer could find words to express it, "that the Viceroy of Ireland has cruelly abused the prerogative of royal mercy, in suffering a man under such circumstances to perish like a common malefactor." For this Mr. Attorney General calls for your conviction as a false and scandalous libel, and after stating himself every fact that I have repeated to you, either from his statement or from the evidence, he tells you that you ought to find it false, though he almost in words admits that it is not false, and has resisted the admission of the evidence by which we offered to prove every word of it to be true.

It was directed wholly against the Lord Lieutenant.

Parties in this case.

And here, gentlemen, give me leave to remind you of the parties before you. The traverser[4] is a printer, who follows that pro-

[4] The name of *traverser* is usually given to the defendant in the Irish courts.

fession for bread, and who at a time of great public misery and terror, when the people are restrained by law from debating under any delegated form; when the few constituents that we have are prevented by force from meeting in their own persons to deliberate or to petition; when every other newspaper in Ireland is put down by force, or purchased by the administration (though here, gentlemen, perhaps I ought to beg your pardon for stating without authority, I recollect, when we attempted to examine as to the number of newspapers in the pay of the Castle, that the evidence was objected to), at a season like this, Mr. Finnerty has had the courage, perhaps the folly, to print the publication in question, from no motive under heaven of malice or vengeance, but in the mere duty which he owes to his family and to the public. His prosecutor is the King's minister in Ireland. In that character does the learned gentleman mean to say that his conduct is not a fair subject of public observation? Where does he find his authority for that in the law or practice of the sister country? Have the virtues, or the exalted station, or the general love of his people preserved the sacred person even of the royal master of the prosecutor from the asperity and the intemperance of public censure, unfounded as it ever must be, with any personal respect to his Majesty, justice, or truth? Have the gigantic abilities of Mr. Pitt, have the more gigantic talents of his great antagonist, Mr. Fox, protected either of them from the insolent familiarity, and, for aught I know, the injustice with which writers have treated them? What latitude of invective has the King's minister escaped upon the subject of the present war? Is there an epithet of contumely or of reproach, that hatred or that fancy could suggest, that are not publicly lavished upon him? Do you not find the words, "advocate of despotism—robber of the public treasure—murderer of the King's subjects—debaucher of the public morality—degrader of the Constitution—tarnisher of the British empire," by frequency of use lose all meaning whatsoever, and dwindling into terms, not of any peculiar reproach, but of ordinary appellation? And why, gentlemen, is this permitted in that country? I will tell you why. Because in that country they are yet wise enough to see that the measures of the state are the proper subjects for the freedom of the press; that the principles relating to *personal* slander do not apply to rulers or to ministers; that to publish an attack upon a *public* minister, without any regard to truth, but merely because of its tendency to a breach of the peace, would be ridiculous in the extreme. What breach of the peace, gentlemen, I pray you, is it in such a case? Is it the tendency of such publications to provoke Mr. Pitt, or Mr. Dundas, to break the head of the writer, if they should happen to meet him? No, gentlemen. In that country this freedom is exercised, because the people feel it to be their right, and it is wisely suffered to pass by the state, from a consciousness that it would be vain to oppose it; a consciousness confirmed by the event of every incautious experiment. It is suffered to pass from a conviction that, in a court of justice at least, the bulwarks of the Constitution will not be surrendered to the state, and that the intended victim, whether clothed in the humble guise of honest industry, or decked in the honors of genius, and virtue, and philosophy; whether a Hardy or a Tooke will find certain protection in the honesty and spirit of an English jury.

The conduct of the Lord Lieutenant a fair ground of animadversion.

Boldness of English writers in this respect.

Reasons for its being permitted.

But, gentlemen, I suppose Mr. Attorney will scarcely wish to carry his doctrine altogether so far. Indeed, I remember, he declared himself a most zealous advocate for the liberty of the press. I may, therefore, even according to him, presume to make some observations on the conduct of the existing government. I should wish to know how far he supposes it to extend. Is it to the composition of lampoons and madrigals, to be sung down the grates by ragged ballad-mongers, to kitchen maids and footmen? I will not suppose that he means to confine it to those ebullitions of Billingsgate, to those cataracts of ribaldry and scurrility that are daily spouting upon the miseries of our wretched fellow-sufferers, and the unavailing efforts of those who have vainly labored in their cause.[5] I will not suppose that he confines it to the poetic license of a birth-day ode. The laureate would not use such language! in which case I do entirely agree with him, that the truth or the falsehood is as perfectly immaterial to the law as it is to the laureate, as perfectly unrestrained by the law of the land as it is by any law of decency, or shame, or modesty, or decorum. But as to the privilege of censure or blame, I am sorry that the learned gentleman has not favored you with *his* notion of the liberty of the press. Suppose an Irish viceroy acts "a very little absurdly." May the press venture to be "respectfully comical upon that absurdity?" The learned counsel does not, at least in terms, give a negative to that. But let me treat you honestly, and go further, to a more material point. Suppose an Irish viceroy does an act that brings scandal upon his master; that fills the mind of a reasonable man with the fear of approaching despotism; that leaves no hope to the people of preserving themselves and their children from chains, but in common confederacy for common safety. What is an honest man in that case to do? I am sorry the right honorable advocate for the liberty of the press has not told you his opinion, at least in any express words. I will, therefore, venture to give you my humbler thoughts upon the subject.

What are the Attorney General's views as to the rights of the press?

I think an honest man ought to tell the people frankly and boldly of their peril, and, I must say, I can imagine no villainy greater than that of his holding a traitorous silence at such a crisis, except the villainy and

Statement of those rights.

[5] Mr. Curran here refers to the abuse poured out by the government papers in Ireland against the friends of reform.

baseness of prosecuting him, or of finding him guilty for such an honest discharge of his public duty. And I found myself on the known principle of the Revolution of England, namely, that the Crown itself may be abdicated by certain abuses of the trust reposed, and that there are possible excesses of arbitrary power, which it is not only the right, but the bounden duty of every honest man to resist at the risk of his fortune and his life. Now, gentlemen, if this reasoning be admitted, and it can not be denied, if there be any possible event in which the people are obliged to look only to themselves, and are justified in doing so, can you be so absurd as to say that it is lawful to the people to act upon it when it unfortunately does arrive; but that it is criminal in any man to tell them that the miserable event has actually arrived, or is imminently approaching? Far am I, gentlemen, from insinuating that (extreme as it is) our misery has been matured into any deplorable crisis of this kind, from which I pray that the Almighty God may forever preserve us. But I am putting my principle upon the strongest ground, and most favorable to my opponents; namely, that it never can be criminal to say any thing of the government but what is false; and I put this in the extreme, in order to demonstrate to you *a fortiori*, that the privilege of speaking truth to the people, which holds in the last extremity, must also obtain in every stage of inferior importance; and that however a court may have decided before the late act [the Libel Act of Mr. Fox] that the truth was immaterial in case of libel, that since that act no honest jury can be governed by such a principle.

The Attorney General charges as libelous a statement which he acknowledges to be true.

Be pleased now, gentlemen, to consider the grounds upon which this publication is called a libel, and criminal. Mr. Attorney tells you it tends to excite sedition and insurrection. Let me again remind you that the truth of this charge is not denied by the noble prosecutor. What is it, then, that tends to excite sedition and insurrection? "The act that is charged upon the prosecutor, and is not attempted to be denied." And, gracious God! gentlemen of the jury, is the public statement of the King's representative this? "I have done a deed that must fill the mind of every feeling or thinking man with horror and indignation, that must alienate every man that knows it, from the King's government, and endanger the separation of this distracted empire; the traverser has had the guilt of publishing this fact, which I myself acknowledge, and I pray you to find him guilty." Is this the case which the Lord Lieutenant of Ireland brings forward? Is this the principle for which he ventures, at a dreadful crisis like the present, to contend in a court of justice? Is this the picture which he wishes to hold out of himself, to the justice and humanity of his own countrymen? Is this the history which he wishes to be read by the poor Irishman of the south and of the north, by the sister nation, and the common enemy.

But *ought* not the press to tell the truth?

With the profoundest respect, permit me humbly to defend his Excellency, even against his own opinion. The guilt of this publication, he is pleased to think, consists in this, that it tends to insurrection. Upon what can such a fear be supported? After the multitudes which have perished in this unhappy nation within the last three years, and which has been borne with a patience unparalleled in the story of nations, can any man suppose that the fate of a single individual could lead to resistance or insurrection? But suppose that it might, what ought to be the conduct of an honest man? Should it not be to apprise the government and the country of the approaching danger? Should it not be to say to the viceroy, "You will drive the people to madness if you persevere in such bloody counsels; you will alienate the Irish nation; you will distract the common force; and you will invite the common enemy." Should not an honest man say to the people, "the measure of your affliction is great, but you need not resort for remedy to any desperate expedients. If the King's minister is defective in humanity or wisdom, his royal master and your beloved sovereign is abounding in both." At such a moment, can you be so senseless as not to feel that any one of you ought to hold such language, or is it possible you could be so infatuated as to punish the man who was honest enough to hold it? Or is it possible that you could bring yourselves to say to your country, that at such a season the press ought to sleep upon its post, or to act like the perfidious watchman on his round that sees the villain wrenching the door, or the flames bursting from the windows, while the inhabitant is wrapped in sleep, and cries out, "Past five o'clock; the morning is fair, and all well!"

Would it have been a libel to tell the truth respecting the cases of Russell and Sydney?

On this part of the case I shall only put one question to you. I do not affect to say that it is similar in all its points; I do not affect to compare the humble fortunes of Orr with the sainted names of Russell or of Sydney; still less am I willing to find any likeness between the present period and the year 1683. But I will put a question to you completely parallel in principle. When that unhappy and misguided Monarch had shed the sacred blood which their noble hearts had matured into a fit cement of revolution, if any honest Englishman had been brought to trial for daring to proclaim to the world his abhorrence of such a deed, what would you have thought of the English jury that could have said, "We know in our hearts that what he said was true and honest; but we will say, upon our oaths, that it was false and criminal; and we will, by that base subserviency, add another item to the catalogue of public wrongs, and another argument for the necessity of an appeal to Heaven for redress.

Gentlemen, I am perfectly aware that what I say may be easily misconstrued; but if you listen to me with the same fairness that I address you, I can not be misunderstood. When I show you the full extent of your political rights and remedies; when I answer those slanderers of British liberty who degrade the Monarch into a despot, who degrade the steadfastness of law into the waywardness of will; when I show you the inestimable stores of political wealth so dearly acquired by our ancestors, and so solemnly bequeathed; and when I show you how much of that precious inheritance has yet survived all the prodigality of their posterity, I am far from saying that I stand in need of it all upon the present occasion. No, gentlemen, far, indeed, am I from such a sentiment. No man more deeply than myself deplores the present melancholy state of our unhappy country. Neither does any man more fervently wish for the return of peace and tranquillity through the natural channels of mercy and of justice. I have seen too much of force and of violence, to hope much good from the continuance of them on one side, or retaliation from another. I have seen too much of late of political rebuilding, not to have observed that to demolish is not the shortest way to repair. It is with pain and anguish that I should search for the miserable right of breaking ancient ties, or going in quest of new relations or untried adventures. No, gentlemen, the case of my client rests not upon these sad privileges of despair. I trust that as to the fact, namely, the intention of exciting insurrection, you must see it can not be found in this publication; that it is the mere idle, unsupported imputation of malice, or panic, or falsehood. And that as to the law, so far has he been from transgressing the limits of the Constitution, that whole regions lie between him and those limits which he has not trod; and which I pray to Heaven it may never be necessary for any of us to tread.

The present case is far from calling for the application of the above principles in their full extent.

Gentlemen, Mr. Attorney General has been pleased to open another battery upon this publication, which I do trust I shall silence; unless I flatter myself too much in supposing that hitherto my resistance has not been utterly unsuccessful. He abuses it for the foul and insolent familiarity of its address. I do clearly understand his idea; he considers the freedom of the press to be the license of offering that paltry adulation which no man ought to stoop to utter or to hear; he supposes the freedom of the press ought to be like the freedom of a King's jester, who, instead of reproving the faults of which majesty ought to be ashamed, is base and cunning enough, under the mask of servile and adulatory censure, to stroke down and pamper those vices of which it is foolish enough to be vain. He would not have the press presume to tell the Viceroy that the prerogative of mercy is a trust for the benefit of the subject, and not a gaudy feather stuck in the diadem to shake in the wind, and by the waving of the gaudy plumage to amuse the vanity of the wearer. He would not have it say to him that the discretion of the Crown, as to *mercy*, is like the discretion of a court of justice as to *law*, and that in the one case as well as the other, wherever the propriety of the exercise of it appears, it is equally a matter of right. He would have the press all fierceness to the people, and all sycophancy to power; he would have it consider the mad and phrenetic depopulations of authority like the awful and inscrutable dispensations of Providence, and say to the unfeeling and despotic spoiler, in the blasphemed and insulted language of religious resignation, "the Lord hath given, and the Lord hath taken away, blessed be the name of the Lord!"

Examination of the charge that Marcus was insolent and vulgar.

But let me condense the generality of the learned gentleman's invective into questions that you can conceive. Does he mean that the air of this publication is rustic and uncourtly? Does he mean that when Marcus presumed to ascend the steps of the castle, and to address the Viceroy, he did not turn out his toes as he ought to have done? But, gentlemen, you are not a jury of dancing-masters. Or does the learned gentleman mean that the language is coarse and vulgar? If this be his complaint, my client has but a poor advocate. I do not pretend to be a mighty grammarian, or a formidable critic; but I would beg leave to suggest to you in serious humility, that a FREE PRESS can be supported only by the ardor of men who feel the prompting sting of real or supposed capacity; who write from the enthusiasm of virtue or the ambition of praise, and over whom, if you exercise the rigor of grammatical censorship, you will inspire them with as mean an opinion of your integrity as your wisdom, and inevitably drive them from their post; and if you do, rely upon it, you will reduce the spirit of publication, and with it the press of this country, to what it for a long interval has been, the register of births, and fairs, and funerals, and the general abuse of the people and their friends.

The meaning of this charge.

But, gentlemen, in order to bring this charge of insolence and vulgarity to the test, let me ask you whether you know of *any* language which could have adequately described the idea of mercy denied where it ought to have been granted, or of any phrase vigorous enough to convey the indignation which an honest man would have felt upon such a subject? Let me beg of you for a moment to suppose that any one of *you* had been the writer of this very severe expostulation with the Viceroy, and that you had been the witness of the whole progress of this never-to-be-forgotten catastrophe. Let me suppose that you had known the charge upon which Mr. Orr was apprehended, the charge of abjuring that bigotry which had torn and disgraced his country; of pledging himself to restore the people of his country to their place in the Constitution; and of binding himself never to be the betrayer of his fellow-laborers in that enterprise—that you had seen him upon that charge removed from his industry, and confined in a jail—that through the slow and lingering progress of twelve tedious months you had seen him confined in a dungeon, shut out from the common use of air and of his own limbs—that day after day you had marked the unhappy captive, cheer-

The charge brought to the test of facts.

ed by no sound but the cries of his family, or the clanking of his chains; that you had seen him at last brought to his trial—that you had seen the vile and perjured informer deposing against his life—that you had seen the drunken, and worn-out, and terrified jury give in a verdict of death —that you had seen the same jury, when their returning sobriety had brought back their consciences, prostrate themselves before the humanity of the bench, and pray that the mercy of the Crown might save their characters from the reproach of an involuntary crime, their consciences from the torture of eternal self-condemnation, and their souls from the indelible stain of innocent blood.

Let me suppose that you had seen the respite given, and that contrite and honest recommendation transmitted to that seat where mercy was presumed to dwell — that new and before unheard of crimes are discovered against the informer — that the royal mercy seems to relent, and that a new respite is sent to the prisoner—that time is taken, as the learned counsel for the Crown has expressed it, to see whether mercy *could* be extended or not!—that after that period of lingering deliberation passed, a *third* respite is transmitted—that the unhappy captive himself feels the cheering hope of being restored to a family that he had adored, to a character that he had never stained, and to a country that he had ever loved—that you had seen his wife and children upon their knees, giving those tears to gratitude which their locked and frozen hearts could not give to anguish and despair, and imploring the blessings of eternal Providence upon his head, who had graciously spared the father, and restored him to his children—that you had seen the olive branch sent into his little ark, but no sign that the waters had subsided.

"Alas!
Nor wife, nor children more shall he behold,
Nor friends, nor sacred home!"[6]

No seraph mercy unbars his dungeon, and leads him forth to light and life, but the minister of death hurries him to the scene of suffering and of shame, where, unmoved by the hostile array of artillery and armed men, collected together to secure, or to insult, or to disturb him, he dies with a solemn declaration of his innocence, and utters his last breath in a prayer for the liberty of his country! Let me now ask you, if any of you had addressed the public ear upon so foul and monstrous a subject, in what language would you have conveyed the feelings of horror and indignation? Would you have stooped to the meanness of qualified complaint? would you have been mean enough? but I entreat your forgiveness, I do not think meanly of you. Had I thought so meanly of you, I could not suffer my mind to commune with you as it has done. Had I thought you that base and vile instrument, attuned by hope and by fear, into discord and falsehood, from whose vulgar string no groan of suffering could vibrate, no voice of integrity or honor could speak — let me honestly tell you, I should have scorned to fling my hand across it; I should have left it to a fitter minstrel. If I do not, therefore, grossly err in my opinion of you, I could use no language upon such a subject as this that must not lag behind the rapidity of your feelings, and that would not disgrace those feelings if it attempted to describe them.

Gentlemen, I am not unconscious that the learned counsel for the Crown seemed to address you with a confidence of a very different kind; he seemed to expect a kind and respectful sympathy from you with the feelings of the castle, and the griefs of chided authority. Perhaps, gentlemen, he may know you better than I do. If he does, he has spoken to you as he ought. He has been right in telling you that if the reprobation of this writer is weak, it is because his genius could not make it stronger; he has been right in telling you that his language has not been braided and festooned as elegantly as it might; that he has not pinched the miserable plaits of his phraseology, nor placed his patches and feathers with that correctness of millinery which became so exalted a person. If you agree with him, gentlemen of the jury, if you think that the man who ventures at the hazard of his own life, to rescue from the deep, "the drowned honor of his country,"[7] must not presume upon the guilty familiarity of plucking it up by the locks, I have no more to say. Do a courteous thing. Upright and honest jurors, find a civil and obliging verdict against the printer! And when you have done so, march through the ranks of your fellow-citizens to your own homes, and *bear their looks as ye pass along*. Retire to the bosom of your families and your children, and when you are presiding over the morality of the parental board, tell those infants, who are to be the future men of Ireland, the history of this day. Form their young minds by your precepts, and confirm those precepts by your own example; teach them how discreetly allegiance may be perjured on the table, or loyalty be forsworn in the jury box. And when you have done so, tell them the story of Orr. Tell them of his captivity, of his children, of his hopes, of his disappointments, of his courage, and of his death; and when you find your little hearers hanging upon your lips, when you see their eyes overflow with sympathy and sorrow, and their young hearts bursting with the pangs of anticipated orphanage, tell them that YOU *had the boldness and the injustice to stigmatize the man who had dared to publish the transaction!*

The way in which the Attorney General expected this subject to be treated.

Gentlemen, I believe I told you before that the conduct of the viceroy was a small part, indeed, of the subject of this trial. If the vindication of his mere personal character had been, as it ought to have been, the sole object

The object of this prosecution reaches far beyond the vindication of the Lord Lieutenant.

[6] See Thomson's description, in his Winter, of a man perishing in a snow-storm.

[7] "And pluck up drowned honor by the locks." *Shakspeare's 1st Part of Henry IV.*, Act I., Sc. 4.

of this prosecution, I should have felt the most respectful regret at seeing a person of his high consideration come forward in a court of public justice in one and the same breath to admit the truth, and to demand the punishment of a publication like the present; to prevent the chance he might have had of such an accusation being disbelieved, and by a prosecution like this, to give to the passing stricture of a newspaper, that life, and body, and action, and reality, that proves it to all mankind, and makes the record of it indelible. Even as it is, I do own I feel the utmost concern that his name should have been soiled by being mixed in a question of which it is the mere pretext and scape-goat. Mr. Attorney was too wise to state to you the real question, or the object which he wished to be answered by your verdict. Do you remember that he was pleased to say that this publication was a base and foul misrepresentation of the virtue and wisdom of the government, and a false and audacious statement to the world, that the King's government in Ireland was base enough to pay informers for taking away the lives of the people? When I heard this statement to-day, I doubted whether you were aware of its tendency or not. It is now necessary that I should explain it to you more at large.

The contest of the government and the people

You can not be ignorant of the great conflict between prerogative and privilege which hath convulsed the country for the last fifteen years. When I say privilege, you can not suppose that I mean the privileges of the House of Commons; I mean the privileges of the people. You are no strangers to the various modes by which the people labored to approach their object. Delegations, conventions, remonstrances, resolutions, petitions to the Parliament, petitions to the Throne. It might not be decorous in this place to state to you with any sharpness the various modes of resistance that were employed on the other side. But you all of you seem old enough to remember the variety of acts of Parliament that have been made, by which the people were deprived, session after session, of what they had supposed to be the known and established fundamentals of the Constitution; the right of public debate, the right of public petition, the right of bail, the right of trial, the right of arms for self-defense; until at last even the relics of popular privilege became superseded by military force; the press extinguished; and the state found its last intrenchment in the grave of the Constitution. As little can you be strangers to the tremendous confederations of hundreds of thousands of our countrymen, of the nature and the objects of which such a variety of opinions have been propagated and entertained.[8]

The writer of this letter has presumed to censure the recall of Lord Fitzwilliam as well as the measures of the present Viceroy. Into this subject I do not enter; but you can not yourselves forget that the conciliatory measures of the former noble Lord had produced an almost miraculous unanimity in this country; and much do I regret, and sure I am that it is not without pain you can reflect how unfortunately the conduct of his successor has terminated. His intentions might have been the best. I neither know them nor condemn them; but their terrible effects you can not be blind to. Every new act of coercion has been followed by some new symptom of discontent, and every new attack provoked some new paroxysm of resentment or some new combination of resistance. In this deplorable state of affairs, convulsed and distracted within, and menaced by a most formidable enemy from without, it was thought that public safety might be found in union and conciliation, and repeated applications were made to the Parliament of this kingdom for a calm inquiry into the complaints of the people. These applications were made in vain. Impressed by the same motives, Mr. Fox brought the same subject before the Commons of England, and ventured to ascribe the perilous state of Ireland to the severity of its government. Even his stupendous abilities, excited by the liveliest sympathy with our sufferings, and animated by the most ardent zeal to restore the strength with the union of the empire, were repeatedly exerted without success. The fact of discontent was denied; the fact of coercion was denied; and the consequence was, the coercion became more implacable, and the discontent more threatening and irreconcilable. A similar application was made, in the beginning of this session, in the Peers of Great Britain, by our illustrious countryman, Lord Moira, of whom I do not wonder that my learned friend should have observed how much virtue can fling pedigree into the shade, or how much the transient honor of a body inherited from man is obscured by the luster of an intellect derived from God. He, after being an eye-witness of this country, presented the miserable picture of what he had seen; and, to the astonishment of every man in Ireland, the existence of those facts was ventured to be denied. The conduct of the present Viceroy was justified and applauded; and the necessity of continuing that conduct was insisted upon as the only means of preserving the Constitution, the peace, and the prosperity of Ireland. The moment the learned counsel had talked of this publication as a false statement of the conduct of the government and the condition of the people, no man could be at a loss to see that that awful question which had been dismissed from the Commons of Ireland, and from the Lords and Commons of Great Britain, is now brought forward to be tried by a side wind, and in a collateral way, by a criminal prosecution.

The severe measures of the Lord Lieutenant.

The discontent thus created has been publicly denied.

I tell you, therefore, gentlemen of the jury, it is not with respect to Mr. Orr that your verdict is now sought. You are called upon, on your oaths, to say that the government is wise and mer-

[8] Mr. Curran here refers to the societies of United Irishmen, which were formed every where throughout the land just in proportion as the restrictions took place which are enumerated above.

ciful; that the people are prosperous and happy; that military law ought to be continued; that the British Constitution could not, with safety, be restored to this country; and that the statements of a contrary import by your advocates in either country were libelous and false. I tell you these are the questions; and I ask you, can you have the front to give the expected answer in the face of a community who know the country as well as you do? Let me ask you how you could reconcile with such a verdict the jails, the tenders, the gibbets, the conflagrations, the murders, the proclamations that we hear of every day in the streets, and see every day in the country. What are the processions of the learned counsel himself, circuit after circuit? Merciful God, what is the state of Ireland, and where shall you find the wretched inhabitant of this land! You may find him, perhaps, in a jail, the only place of security, I had almost said of ordinary habitation; you may see him flying, by the conflagration of his own dwelling; or you may find his bones bleaching on the green fields of his country; or he may be found tossing upon the surface of the ocean, and mingling his groans with those tempests, less savage than his persecutors, that drift him to a returnless distance from his family and his home. And yet, with these facts ringing in the ears, and staring in the face of the prosecutor, you are called upon to say, on your oaths, that these facts do not exist. You are called upon, in defiance of shame, of truth, of honor, *to deny the sufferings under which you groan, and to flatter the persecution that tramples you under foot.*

The chief object of the prosecution is to obtain a declaration in favor of the government.

But the learned gentleman is further pleased to say that the traverser has charged the government with the encouragement of informers. This, gentlemen, is another small fact that you are to deny at the hazard of your souls, and upon the solemnity of your oaths. You are upon your oaths to say to the sister country, that the government of Ireland uses no such abominable instruments of destruction as informers. Let me ask you honestly, what do you feel, when in my hearing, when in the face of this audience, you are called upon to give a verdict that every man of us, and every man of you, knows by the testimony of his own eyes to be utterly and absolutely false? I speak not now of the public proclamation of informers, with a promise of secrecy and of extravagant reward. I speak not of the fate of those horrid wretches who have been so often transferred from the table to the dock, and from the dock to the pillory;[9] I speak of what your own eyes have seen day after day, during the course of this commission, from the box where you are now sitting—the number of horrid miscreants who avowed upon their oaths that they had come from the very seat of government, from the Castle, where they had been worked upon by the fear of death and the hopes of compensation to give evidence against their fellows—[I speak of the well-known fact] that the *mild* and *wholesome* counsels of this government are holden over these catacombs of living death, where the wretch that is buried a man lies till his heart has time to fester and dissolve, and is then dug up a witness.

Also a declaration that informers are not employed by the executive.

Is this fancy, or is it fact? Have you not seen him after his resurrection from that tomb, after having been dug out of the region of death and corruption, make his appearance upon the table, the living image of life and of death, and the supreme arbiter of both? Have you not marked, when he entered, how the stormy wave of the multitude retired at his approach? Have you not marked how the human heart bowed to the supremacy of his power in the undissembled homage of deferential horror? How his glance, like the lightning of heaven, seemed to rive the body of the accused and mark it for the grave, while his voice warned the devoted wretch of woe and death—a death which no innocence can escape, no art elude, no force resist, no antidote prevent. There was an antidote—*a juror's oath*—but even that adamantine chain, which bound the integrity of man to the throne of eternal justice, is solved and melted in the breath that issues from the *informer's mouth.* Conscience swings from her mooring, and the appalled and affrighted juror consults his own safety in the surrender of the victim:

The appearance of the informer in court.

> ————Et quæ sibi quisque timebat,
> Unius in miseri exitium conversa tulere.[10]

Gentlemen, I feel I must have tired your patience, but I have been forced into this length by the prosecutor, who has thought fit to introduce those extraordinary topics, and to bring a question of mere politics to trial, under the form of a criminal prosecution. I can not say I am surprised that this has been done, or that you should be solicited by the same inducements and from the same motives, as if your verdict was a vote of approbation. I do not wonder that the government of Ireland should stand appalled at the state to which we are reduced. I wonder not that they should start at the public voice, and labor to stifle or to contradict it. I wonder not that at this arduous crisis, when the very existence of the empire is at stake, when its strongest and most precious limb is not girt with the sword for battle, but pressed by the tourniquet for amputation; when they find the coldness of death already begun in those extremities where it never ends, that they are terrified at what they have done, and wish to say to the surviving parties of that empire, "they can not

Peroration: Not wonderful that the government seek to cover their dishonor by the verdict of a jury; but no jury can thus cover it.

[9] There were many government witnesses at this time, who so obviously perjured themselves in their testimony, that they were taken immediately to the criminal's box (the dock), and thence, on conviction, to the *pillory*, where they were sentenced to stand for their perjuries.

[10] And thus what each was dreading for himself,
On the devoted head of one poor wretch
They turned.—*Virgil's Æneid*, book ii., line 130.

say that we did it." I wonder not that they should consider their conduct as no immaterial question for a court of criminal jurisdiction, and wish anxiously, as on an inquest of blood, for the kind acquittal of a friendly jury. I wonder not that they should wish to close the chasm they have opened by flinging you into the abyss. But trust me, my countrymen, you might perish in it, but you could not close it. Trust me, if it is yet possible to close it, it can be done only by truth and honor. Trust me, that such an effect could no more be wrought by the sacrifice of a jury than by the sacrifice of Orr. As a state measure, the one would be as unwise and unavailing as the other. But while you are yet upon the brink, while you are yet visible, let me, before we part, remind you once more of your awful situation. The law upon this subject gives you supreme dominion. Hope not for much assistance from his Lordship. On such occasions, perhaps, the duty of the court is to be cold and neutral. I can not but admire the dignity he has supported during this trial; I am grateful for his patience. But let me tell you it is not his province to fan the sacred flame of patriotism in the jury box. As he has borne with the little extravagances of the law, do you bear with the little failings of the press. Let me, therefore, remind you, that though the day may soon come when our ashes shall be scattered before the winds of heaven, the memory of what you do can not die. It will carry down to your posterity your honor or your shame. In the presence, and in the name of that ever-living God, I do therefore conjure you to reflect that you have your characters, your consciences, that you have also the character, perhaps the ultimate destiny, of your country in your hands. In that awful name, I do conjure you to have mercy upon your country and upon yourselves, and so to judge now as you will hereafter be judged; and I do now submit the fate of my client, and of that country which we yet have in common to your disposal.

Mr. Finnerty was found guilty by the jury, and was brought up for sentence the following day. He stated that he had been taken to Alderman Alexander's office, and there threatened with public whipping if he did not give up the name of the author of MARCUS. He refused to do it, and was sentenced to stand in the pillory one hour, and be imprisoned two years, which punishment he suffered.

SPEECH

OF MR. CURRAN AGAINST THE MARQUESS OF HEADFORT FOR ADULTERY WITH THE WIFE OF THE REV. CHARLES MASSY, BEFORE BARON SMITH AND A SPECIAL JURY, DELIVERED JULY 27, 1804.

INTRODUCTION.

THE REV. CHARLES MASSY, son of Sir Hugh Massy, Bart., was a clergyman of the Church of England, and was married to Miss Rosslewyn, a lady of extraordinary beauty, in 1796. By her he had one son. In 1803, the Marquess of Headfort, an officer in the army, was quartered in the neighborhood with his regiment, and was received to the hospitalities of Mr. Massy's house. As the Marquess was more than fifty years of age, Mr. Massy had no suspicions of any evil design on the part of his guest, and admitted him to the most familiar intercourse with his family. The occasion was laid hold of for seducing Mrs. Massy, who eloped with the Marquess on the Sunday after Christmas, while her husband was performing service in his own church.

The damages were laid at £40,000. All the facts of the case were admitted; and the only thing urged for the defendant in mitigation of damages was that Mr. Massy had brought this calamity on himself by allowing his wife to associate too freely with the Marquess. It gave a melancholy interest to Mr. Curran's speech that he had himself suffered the same injury under the same circumstances, and that the defense of the man who had injured him was precisely the same. Mr. Curran was, therefore, arguing his own cause in defending his client against these imputations, and exposing the guilt of the seducer.

SPEECH, &c.

Power of just sentiments over the minds of men.

NEVER, so clearly as in the present instance, have I observed that safeguard of justice which Providence has placed in the nature of man. Such is the imperious dominion with which truth and reason wave their scepter over the human intellect, that no solicitation, however artful, no talent, however commanding, can reduce it from its allegiance. In proportion to the humility of our submission to its rule, do we rise into some faint emulation of that ineffable and presiding divinity, whose characteristic attribute it is to be coerced and bound by the inexorable laws of its own nature, so as to be *all-wise* and *all-just* from necessity, rather than election. You have seen it, in the learned advocate who has preceded me, most peculiarly and strikingly illustrated. You have seen even his great talents, perhaps the first in any country, languishing under a cause too weak to carry him, and too heavy to be carried by him. He was forced to dismiss his natural candor and sincerity, and, having no merits in his case, to substitute the dignity of his own manner, the resources of his own ingenuity, over the overwhelming difficulties with which he was surrounded. Wretched client! unhappy advocate! What a combination do you form! But such is the condition of guilt—its commission mean and tremulous—its defense artificial and insincere—its prosecution candid and simple—its condemnation dignified and austere. Such has been the defendant's guilt—such his defense—such shall be my address, and such, I trust, your verdict.

The reparation demanded.

The learned counsel has told you that this unfortunate woman is not to be estimated at forty thousand pounds. Fatal and unquestionable is the truth of this assertion. Alas! gentlemen, she is no longer worth any thing—faded, fallen, degraded, and disgraced, she is worth less than nothing. But it is for the honor, the hope, the expectation, the tenderness, and the comforts that have been blasted by the defendant, and have fled forever, that you are to remunerate the plaintiff, by the punishment of the defendant. It is not her present value which you are to weigh—but it is her value at that time, when she sat basking in a husband's love, with the blessing of Heaven on her head, and its purity in her heart. When she sat among her family, and administered the morality of the parental board—estimate that past value—compare it with its present deplorable diminution—and it may lead you to form some judgment of the severity of the injury and the extent of the compensation.

The jury ought to be governed by their sensibilities in the damages they give.

The learned counsel has told you, you ought to be cautious, because your verdict can not be set aside for excess. The assertion is just, but has he treated you fairly by its application? His cause would not allow him to be fair—for why is the rule adopted in this single action? Because, this being peculiarly an injury to the most susceptible of all human feelings—it leaves the injury of the husband to be ascertained by the sensibility of the jury; and does not presume to measure the justice of their determination by the cold and chilly exercise of its own discretion. In any other action, it is easy to calculate. If a tradesman's arm is cut off, you can measure the loss which he has sustained; but the wound of feeling, and the agony of the heart can not be judged by any standard with which I am acquainted. You are, therefore, unfairly dealt with, when you are called on to appreciate the present suffering of the husband by the present guilt, delinquency, and degradation of his wife. As well might you, if called on to give compensation to a man for the murder of his dearest friend—to find the measure of his injury by weighing the ashes of the dead. But it is not, gentlemen of the jury, by weighing the ashes of the dead, that you would estimate the loss of the survivor.

Amount of damages given in other cases.

The learned counsel has referred you to other cases and other countries for instances of moderate verdicts. I can refer you to some authentic instances of just ones. In the next county, £15,000 against a subaltern officer. In Travers and M'Carthy, £5000 against a servant. In Tighe against Jones, £10,000 against a man not worth a shilling. What, then, ought to be the rule, where rank, and power, and wealth, and station have combined to render the example of his crime more dangerous—to make his guilt more odious—to make the injury to the plaintiff more grievous, because more conspicuous? I affect no leveling familiarity, when I speak of persons in the higher ranks of society. Distinctions of orders are necessary, and I always feel disposed to treat them with respect. But when it is my duty to speak of the crimes by which they are degraded, I am not so fastidious as to shrink from their contact, when to touch them is essential to their dissection. In this action, the condition, the conduct, and circumstances of the party are justly and peculiarly the objects of your consideration.

Condition of the parties in the present case.

Who are the parties? The plaintiff, young, amiable, of family and education. Of the generous disinterestedness of his heart, you can form an opinion, even from the evidence of the defendant, that he declined an alliance which would have added to his fortune and consideration, and which he rejected for an unportioned union with his present wife. She, too, at that time young, beautiful, and accomplished; and feeling her affection for her husband increase, in proportion as she remembered the ardor of his love, and the sincerity of his sacrifice. Look now to the defendant! I blush to name him! I blush to name a rank which he has tarnished, and a patent that he has worse than canceled. High in the army—high in the state—the hereditary counselor of the King—of wealth incalculable—and to this last I advert with an indignant and contemptuous satisfaction, because, as the only instrument of his guilt and shame, it will be the means of his punishment, and the source of compensation for his guilt.

The defendant's guilt acknowledged.

But let me call your attention distinctly to the questions you have to consider. The first is the fact of guilt. Is this noble Lord guilty? His counsel knew too well how they would have mortified his vanity, had they given the smallest reason to doubt the splendor of his achievement. Against any such humiliating suspicion, he had taken the most studious precaution by the publicity of the exploit. And here in this court, and before you, and in the face of the country, has he the unparalleled effrontery of disdaining to resort even to a *confession of innocence*. His guilt established, your next question is the damages you should give. You have been told that the amount of the damages should depend on circumstances. You will consider these circumstances, whether of aggravation or mitigation. His learned counsel contend that the plaintiff has been the author of his own suffering, and ought to receive no compensation for the ill consequences of his own conduct. In what part of the evidence do you find any foundation for that assertion? He indulged her, it seems, in dress. Generous and attached, he probably indulged her in that point beyond his means; and the defendant now impudently calls on you to find an excuse for the adulterer, in the fondness and liberality of the husband.

But you have been told that the husband *connived*. Odious and impudent aggravation of injury—to add calumny to insult, and outrage to

The pretense that Mr. Massy had connived, or at least been indiscreet.

dishonor. From whom, but a man hackneyed in the paths of shame and vice — from whom, but from a man having no compunctions in his own breast to restrain him, could you expect such brutal disregard for the feelings of others? From whom, but the cold-blooded, veteran seducer—from what, but from the exhausted mind, the habitual community with shame—from what, but the habitual contempt of virtue and of man, could you have expected the arrogance, the barbarity, and folly of so foul, because so false an imputation? He should have reflected, and have blushed, before he suffered so vile a topic of defense to have passed his lips. But, ere you condemn, let him have the benefit of the excuse, if the excuse be true. You must have observed how his counsel fluttered and vibrated between what they called connivance and injudicious confidence; and how, in affecting to distinguish, they have confounded them both together. If the plaintiff has connived, I freely say to you, do not reward the wretch who has prostituted his wife and surrendered his own honor—do not compensate the pander of his own shame, and the willing instrument of his own infamy. But as there is no sum so low to which such a defense, if true, ought not to reduce your verdict, so neither is any so high to which such a charge ought not to inflame it, if such a charge be false. Where is the single fact in this case on which the remotest suspicion of connivance can be hung? Odiously has the defendant endeavored to make the softest and most amiable feelings of the heart the pretext of his slanderous imputations. An ancient and respectable prelate, the husband of his wife's sister, was chained down to the bed of sickness, perhaps to the bed of death. In that distressing situation, my client suffered that wife to be the bearer of consolation to the bosom of her sister—he had not the heart to refuse her—and the softness of his nature is now charged on him as a crime! He is now insolently told that he connived at his dishonor, and that he ought to have foreseen that the mansion of sickness and of sorrow would have been made the scene of assignation and of guilt. On this charge of connivance I will not further weary you, or exhaust myself—I will add nothing more, than that it is as false as it is impudent; that, in the evidence, it has not a color of support; and that by your verdict you should mark it with reprobation. The other subject, namely, that he was indiscreet in his confidence, does, I think, call for some discussion—for I trust you see that I affect not any address to your passions by which you may be led away from the subject. I presume merely to separate the parts of this affecting case, and to lay them item by item before you, with the coldness of detail, and not with any coloring or display of fiction or of fancy. Honorable to himself was his unsuspecting confidence; fatal must we admit it to have been, when we look to the abuse committed upon it; but where was the *guilt* of this indiscretion? He did admit this noble Lord to pass his threshold as his guest. Now the charge which this noble Lord builds on this indiscretion is, "Thou fool! thou hast confidence in my honor, and that was a guilty indiscretion—thou simpleton, thou thoughtest that an admitted and cherished guest would have respected the laws of honor and hospitality, and thy indiscretion was guilt. Thou thoughtest that he would have shrunk from the meanness and barbarity of requiting kindness with treachery, and thy indiscretion was guilt."

Not one fact to justify this pretense.

The necessary consequences of admitting this defense.

Gentlemen, what horrid alternative in the treatment of wives would such reasoning recommend? Are they to be immured by worse than Eastern barbarity? Are their principles to be depraved, their passions sublimated, every finer motive of action extinguished by the inevitable consequences of thus treating them like slaves? Or is a liberal and generous confidence in them to be the passport of the adulterer, and the justification of his crime?

Mr. Massy did repose confidence.

Honorably but fatally for his own repose, he was neither jealous, suspicious, nor cruel. He treated the defendant with the confidence of a friend, and his wife with the tenderness of a husband. He did leave to the noble Marquess the physical possibility of committing against him the greatest crime which can be perpetrated against a being of an amiable heart and refined education. In the middle of the day, at the moment of divine worship, when the miserable husband was on his knees, directing the prayers and thanksgiving of his congregation to their God, that moment did the remorseless adulterer choose to carry off the deluded victim from her husband—from her child—from her character—from her happiness—as if not content to leave his crime confined to its miserable aggravations, unless he also gave it a cast and color of factitious sacrilege and impiety. Oh! how happy had it been when he arrived at the bank of the river with the ill-fated fugitive, ere yet he had committed her to that boat, of which, like the fabled bark of Styx, the exile was eternal—how happy at that moment, so teeming with misery and with shame, if you, my Lord, had met him, and could have accosted him in the character of that good genius which had abandoned him. How impressively might you have pleaded the cause of the father, of the child, of the mother, and even of the worthless defendant himself. You would have said, "Is this the requital that you are about to make for the respect, and kindness, and confidence in your honor? Can you deliberately expose this young man in the bloom of life, with all his hopes yet before him? Can you expose him, a wretched outcast from society, to the scorn of a merciless world? Can you set him adrift upon the tempestuous ocean of his own passions, at this early season when they are most headstrong; and can you cut him out from the moorings of those domestic obligations, by whose cable he might ride at safety from their turbulence? Think, if you can

Supposed remonstrance with the Marquess.

conceive it, what a powerful influence arises from the sense of home, from the sacred religion of the hearth in quelling the passions, in reclaiming the wanderings, in correcting the disorders of the human heart. Do not cruelly take from him the protection of these attachments. But if you have no pity for the father, have mercy, at least, upon his innocent and helpless child. Do not condemn him to an education scandalous or neglected. Do not strike him into that most dreadful of all human conditions, the orphanage that springs not from the grave, that falls not from the hand of Providence or the stroke of death; but comes before its time, anticipated and inflicted by the remorseless cruelty of parental guilt." For the poor victim herself, not yet immolated, while yet balancing upon the pivot of her destiny, your heart could not be cold, nor your tongue be wordless. You would have said to him, "Pause, my Lord, while there is yet a moment for reflection. What are your motives, what your views, what your prospects, from what you are about to do? You are a married man, the husband of the most amiable and respectable of women; you can not look to the chance of marrying this wretched fugitive. Between you and such an event there are two sepulchers to pass. What are your inducements? Is it love, think you? No. Do not give that name to any attraction you can find in the faded refuse of a violated bed. Love is a noble and generous passion; it can be founded only on a pure and ardent friendship, on an exalted respect, on an implicit confidence in its object. Search your heart; examine your judgment. Do you find the semblance of any one of these sentiments to bind you to her? What could degrade a mind to which nature or education had given port or stature, or character, into a friendship for her? Could you repose upon her faith? Look in her face, my Lord: she is at this moment giving you the violation of the most sacred of human obligations as the pledge of her fidelity. She is giving you the most irrefragable proof that as she is deserting her husband for you, so she would without scruple abandon you for another. Do you anticipate any pleasure you might feel in the possible event of your becoming the parents of a common child? She is at this moment proving to you that she is as dead to the sense of parental as of conjugal obligation, and that she would abandon your offspring to-morrow with the same facility with which she now deserts her own. Look then at her conduct as it is, as the world must behold it, blackened by every aggravation that can make it either odious or contemptible, and unrelieved by a single circumstance of mitigation that could palliate its guilt or retrieve it from abhorrence.

"Mean, however, and degraded as this woman must be, she will still (if you take her with you) have strong and heavy claims upon you. The force of such claims does certainly depend upon circumstances. Before, therefore, you expose her fate to the dreadful risk of your caprice or ingratitude, in mercy to her, weigh well the confidence she can place in your future justice and honor. At that future time, much nearer than you think, by what topics can her cause be pleaded to a sated appetite, to a heart that repels her, to a just judgment, in which she never could have been valued or respected? Here is not the case of an unmarried woman, with whom a pure and generous friendship may insensibly have ripened into a more serious attachment, until at last her heart became too deeply pledged to be reassumed. If so circumstanced, without any husband to betray, or child to desert, or motive to restrain, except what related solely to herself, her anxiety for your happiness made her overlook every other consideration, and commit her destiny to your honor; in such a case (the strongest and the highest that man's imagination can suppose), in which you, at least, could see nothing but the most noble and disinterested sacrifice; in which you could find nothing but what claimed from you the most kind and exalted sentiment of tenderness, and devotion, and respect, and in which the most fastidious rigor would find so much more subject for sympathy than blame—let me ask you, could you, even in that case, answer for your own justice and gratitude? I do not allude to the long and pitiful catalogue of paltry adventures, in which, it seems, your time has been employed—the coarse and vulgar succession of casual connections, joyless, loveless, and unendeared. But do you not find upon your memory some trace of an engagement of the character I have sketched? Has not your sense of what you would owe in such a case, and to such a woman, been at least once put to the test of experiment? Has it not once, at least, happened that such a woman, with all the resolution of strong faith, flung her youth, her hope, her beauty, her talent, upon your bosom, weighed you against the world, which she found but a feather in the scale, and took you as an equivalent?[1] How did you then acquit yourself? Did you prove yourself worthy of the sacred trust reposed in you? Did your spirit so associate with hers as to leave her no room to regret the splendid and disinterested sacrifice she had made? Did her soul find a pillow in the tenderness of yours, and a support in its firmness? Did you preserve her high in her own consciousness, proud in your admiration and friendship, and happy in your affection? You might have so acted (and the man that was worthy of her would have perished rather than not so act) as to make her delighted with having confided so sacred a trust to his honor. Did you so act? Did she feel that, however precious to your heart, she was still more exalted and honored in your reverence and respect? Or did she find you coarse and paltry, fluttering and unpurposed, unfeeling and ungrateful? You found her a fair and blushing flower, its beauty and its fragrance bathed in the dews

[1] This reference to a previous elopement of another with the Marquess, and his desertion of her, must have operated with great force on the minds of the jury.

of heaven. Did you so tenderly transplant it as to preserve that beauty and fragrance unimpaired? Or did you so rudely cut it as to interrupt its nutriment, to waste its sweetness, to blast its beauty, to bow down its faded and sickly head? And did you at last fling it, like 'a loathsome weed, away?' If, then, to such a woman, so clothed with every title that could ennoble, and exalt, and endear her to the heart of man, you could be cruelly and capriciously deficient, how can a wretched fugitive like this, in every point her contrast, hope to find you just? Send her, then, away. Send her back to her home, to her child, to her husband, to herself."

The conduct of the Marquess in the elopement.

Alas, there was none to hold such language to this noble defendant; he did not hold it to himself. But he paraded his despicable prize in his own carriage, with his own retinue, his own servants. This veteran Paris hawked his enamored Helen, from this western quarter of the island, to a sea-port in the eastern, crowned with the acclamations of a senseless and grinning rabble, glorying and delighted, no doubt, in the leering and scoffing admiration of grooms, and hostlers, and waiters, as he passed. In this odious contempt of every personal feeling, of public opinion, of common humanity, did he parade this woman to the seaport, whence he transported his precious cargo to a country where her example may be less mischievous than in her own; where I agree with my learned colleague in heartily wishing he may remain with her forever. We are too poor, too simple, too unadvanced a country for the example of such achievements. When the relaxation of morals is the natural growth and consequence of the great progress of arts and wealth, it is accompanied by a refinement that makes it less gross and shocking. But for such palliations we are at least a century too young.

Public morals require exemplary damages.

I advise you, therefore, most earnestly to rebuke this budding mischief, by letting the wholesome vigor and chastisement of a liberal verdict speak what you think of its enormity. In every point of view in which I can look at the subject, I see you are called upon to give a verdict of bold, and just, and indignant, and exemplary compensation. The injury of the plaintiff demands it from your justice. The delinquency of the defendant provokes it by its enormity. The rank on which he has relied for impunity calls upon you to tell him that crime does not ascend to the rank of the perpetrator, but the perpetrator sinks from his rank and descends to the level of his delinquency. The style and mode of his defense is a gross aggravation of his conduct, and a gross insult upon you. Look upon the different subjects of his defense as you ought, and let him profit by them as he deserves. Vainly presumptuous upon his rank, he wishes to overawe you by the despicable consideration. He next resorts to a cruel aspersion upon the character of the unhappy plaintiff, whom he had already wounded beyond the possibility of reparation. He has ventured to charge him with connivance. As to that, I will only say, gentlemen of the jury, do not give this vain boaster a pretext for saying that if the husband connived in the offense, the jury also connived in the reparation.

The pretense that Mr. Massy was not perfectly judicious when he suspected some evil.

But he has pressed another curious topic upon you. After the plaintiff had cause to suspect his designs, and the likelihood of their being fatally successful, he did not then act precisely as he ought. Gracious God, what an argument for him to dare to advance! It is saying thus to him, "I abused your confidence, your hospitality; I laid a base plan for the seduction of the wife of your bosom; I succeeded at last, so as to throw in upon you that most dreadful of all suspicions to a man fondly attached, proud of his wife's honor, and tremblingly alive to his own; that you were possibly a dupe to the confidence in the wife as much as in the guest. In this so pitiable distress, which I myself had studiously and deliberately contrived for you—between hope and fear, and doubt and love, and jealousy and shame; one moment shrinking from the cruelty of your suspicion, the next fired with indignation at the facility and credulity of your acquittal—in this labyrinth of doubt, in this frenzy of suffering, you were not collected and composed. You did not act as you might have done if I had not worked you to madness; and upon that very madness which I have inflicted upon you, upon the very completion of my guilt and of your misery, I will build my defense. You will not act critically right, and therefore are unworthy of compensation." Gentlemen, can you be dead to the remorseless atrocity of such a defense! And shall not your honest verdict mark it as it deserves?

The difficulty of his situation.

But let me go a little further; let me ask you, for I confess I have no distinct idea of what should be the conduct of a husband so placed, and who is to act critically right. Shall he lock her up or turn her out? Or enlarge or abridge her liberty of acting as she pleases? Oh, dreadful Areopagus of the tea-table! How formidable thy inquests, how tremendous thy condemnations! In the first case, he is brutal and barbarous—an odious Eastern despot. In the next, What! turn an innocent woman out of his house, without evidence or proof, but merely because he is vile and mean enough to suspect the wife of his bosom, and the mother of his child! Between these extremes, what intermediate degree is he to adopt? I put this question to you, do you at this moment, uninfluenced by any passion, as you now are, but cool and collected, and uninterested as you must be, do you see clearly this proper and exact line which the plaintiff should have pursued? I much question if you do. But if you did or could, must you not say that he was the last man from whom you should expect the coolness to discover or the steadiness to pursue it? And yet this is the outrageous and insolent defense that is put forward to you. My miserable client, when his brain was on fire, and every fiend of hell was let loose upon his heart, he should then, it seems, have placed himself before his mirror, he should have taught the stream of agony to flow decorously down his forehead. He should have composed his features to harmony, he should have writhed with grace and groaned in melody.

The pretense that Mrs. Massy encouraged attentions.

But look farther to this noble defendant and his honorable defense: the wretched woman is to be successively the victim of seduction and of slander. She, it seems, received marked attentions. Here, I confess, I felt myself not a little at a loss. The witnesses could not describe what these marked attentions were or are. They consisted not, if you believe the witness that swore to them, in any personal approach or contact whatsoever, nor in any unwarrantable topics of discourse. Of what materials, then, were they composed? Why, it seems, a gentleman had the insolence at table to propose to her a glass of wine, and she, O most abandoned lady! instead of flying, like an angry parrot, at his head, and besmirching and bescratching him for his insolence, tamely and basely replies, "Port, sir, if you please." But, gentlemen, why do I advert to this folly, this nonsense? Not, surely, to vindicate from censure the most innocent and the most delightful intercourse of social kindness, of harmless and cheerful courtesy; "where virtue is, these are most virtuous." But I am soliciting your attention and your feeling to the mean and odious aggravation—to the unblushing and remorseless barbarity of falsely aspersing the wretched woman he had undone. One good he has done, he has disclosed to you the point in which he *can feel;* for how imperious must that avarice be which could resort to so vile an expedient of frugality? Yes, I will say that, with the common feelings of a man, he would have rather suffered his £30,000 a year to go as compensation to the plaintiff than saved a shilling of it by so vile an expedient of economy. He would rather have starved with her in a jail, he would rather have sunk with her into the ocean, than have so vilified her—than have so degraded himself.

The first time the Marquess has been sued for such conduct.

But it seems, gentlemen, and, indeed, you have been told, that long as the course of his gallantries has been (and he has grown gray in the service), it is the first time he has been called upon for damages. To how many might it have been fortunate if he had not that impunity to boast? Your verdict will, I trust, put an end to that encouragement to guilt that is built upon impunity. The devil, it seems, has saved the noble Marquess harmless in the past; but your verdict will tell him the term of that indemnity is expired, that his old friend and banker has no more effects in his hands, and that if he draws any more upon him, he must pay his own bills himself. You will do much good by doing so. You may not enlighten his conscience nor touch his heart, but his frugality will understand the hint. It will adopt the prudence of age, and deter him from pursuits in which, though he may be insensible of shame, he will not be regardless of expense. You will do more, you will not only punish him in his tender point, but you will weaken him in his strong one—his money. We have heard much of this noble Lord's wealth, and much of his exploits, but not much of his accomplishments or his wit. I know not that his verses have soared even to the poet's corner. I have heard it said that an ass laden with gold could find his way through the gate of the strongest city. But, gentlemen, lighten the load upon his back, and you will completely curtail the mischievous faculty of a grave animal, whose momentum lies not in his agility, but his weight; not in the quantity of motion, but the quantity of his matter.

Large damages ought to be given to punish the defendant's ostentation of his crime.

There is another ground on which you are called upon to give most liberal damages, and that has been laid by the unfeeling vanity of the defendant. This business has been marked by the most elaborate publicity. It is very clear that he has been allured by the glory of the chase, and not the value of the game. The poor object of his pursuit could be of no value to him, or he could not have so wantonly, and cruelly, and unnecessarily abused her. He might easily have kept this unhappy intercourse an unsuspected secret. Even if, he wished for her elopement, he might easily have so contrived it that the place of her retreat would be profoundly undiscoverable. Yet, though even the expense (a point so tender to his delicate sensibility) of concealing could not be a one fortieth of the cost of publishing her, his vanity decided him in favor of glory and publicity. By that election he has in fact put forward the Irish nation, and its character, so often and so variously calumniated, upon its trial before the tribunal of the empire; and your verdict will this day decide, whether an Irish jury can feel with justice and spirit upon a subject that involves conjugal affection and comfort, domestic honor and repose—the certainty of issue—the weight of public opinion—the gilded and presumptuous criminality of overweening rank and station. I doubt not but he is at this moment reclined on a silken sofa, anticipating that submissive and modest verdict by which you will lean gently on his errors; and expecting, from your patriotism, no doubt, that you will think again and again before you condemn any great portion of the immense revenue of a great absentee to be detained in the nation that produced it, instead of being transmitted, as it ought, to be expended in the splendor of another country. He is now probably waiting for the arrival of the report of this day, which I understand a famous note-taker has been sent hither to collect. (Let not the gentleman be disturbed.) Gentlemen, let me assure you it is more, much more the trial of you, than of the noble Marquess, of which this imported recorder is at this moment collecting the materials.

The kind of report of the trial which the Marquess may be supposed to expect.

His noble employer is now expecting a report to the following effect: "Such a day came on to be tried at Ennis, by a special jury, the cause of Charles Massy against the most noble the Marquess of Headfort. It appeared that the plaintiff's wife was young, beautiful, and captivating. The plaintiff himself a person fond of this beautiful creature to distraction, and both doting on their child; but the noble Marquess approached her; the plume of glory nodded on his head. Not the Goddess Minerva, but the Goddess Venus had lighted upon his casque, 'the fire that never tires—such as many a lady gay had been dazzled with before.' At the first advance she trembled, at the second she struck to the redoubted son of Mars and pupil of Venus. The jury saw it was not his fault (it was an Irish jury); they felt compassion for the tenderness of the mother's heart, and for the warmth of the lover's passion. The jury saw on the one side a young, entertaining gallant, on the other a beauteous creature, of charms irresistible. They recollected that Jupiter had been always successful in his amours, although Vulcan had not always escaped some awkward accidents. The jury was composed of fathers, brothers, husbands—but they had not the vulgar jealousy that views little things of that sort with rigor; and wishing to assimilate their country in every respect to England, now that they are united to it, they, like English gentlemen, returned to their box with a verdict of sixpence damages and sixpence costs." Let this be sent to England. I promise you your odious secret will not be kept better than that of the wretched Mrs. Massy. There is not a bawdy chronicle in London in which the epitaph which you would have written on yourselves will not be published, and our enemies will delight in the spectacle of our precocious depravity, in seeing that we can be rotten before we are ripe. I do not suppose it, I do not, can not, will not, believe it. I will not harrow up myself with the anticipated apprehension.

Large damages due for the breach of hospitality.

There is another consideration, gentlemen, which I think most imperiously demands even a vindictive award of exemplary damages, and that is the breach of hospitality. To us peculiarly does it belong to avenge the violation of its altar. The hospitality of other countries is a matter of necessity or convention; in savage nations of the first, in polished of the latter; but the hospitality of an *Irishman* is not the running account of posted and legered courtesies, as in other countries; it springs, like all his qualities, his faults, his virtues—directly from his heart. The heart of an Irishman is by nature bold, and he confides; it is tender, and he loves; it is generous, and he gives; it is social, and he is hospitable. This sacrilegious intruder has profaned the religion of that sacred altar so elevated in our worship, so precious to our devotion; and it is our privilege to avenge the crime. You must either pull down the altar and abolish the worship, or you must preserve its sanctity undebased. There is no alternative between the universal exclusion of all mankind from your threshold, and the most rigorous punishment of him who is admitted and betrays. This defendant has been so trusted, has so betrayed, and you ought to make him a most signal example.

Peroration: The injury done to the plaintiff and the protection due to society are both to be considered in awarding damages.

Gentlemen, I am the more disposed to feel the strongest indignation and abhorrence at this odious conduct of the defendant, when I consider the deplorable condition to which he has reduced the plaintiff, and perhaps the still more deplorable one that he has in prospect before him. What a progress has he to travel through before he can attain the peace and tranquillity which he has lost? How like the wounds of the body are those of the mind! How burning the fever! How painful the suppuration! How slow, how hesitating, how relapsing the process to convalescence! Through what a variety of suffering, what new scenes and changes, must my unhappy client pass, ere he can reattain, should he ever reattain, that health of soul of which he has been despoiled by the cold and deliberate machinations of this praticed and gilded seducer? If, instead of drawing upon his incalculable wealth for a scanty retribution, you were to stop the progress of his despicable achievements by reducing him to actual poverty, you could not even so punish him beyond the scope of his offense, nor reprise the plaintiff beyond the measure of his suffering. Let me remind you that in this action the law not only empowers you, but that its policy commands you to consider the public example, as well as the individual injury, when you adjust the amount of your verdict. I confess I am most anxious that you should acquit yourselves worthily upon this important occasion. I am addressing you as fathers, husbands, brothers. I am anxious that a feeling of those high relations should enter into, and give dignity to your verdict. But I confess it, I feel a ten-fold solicitude when I remember that I am addressing you as my countrymen, as Irishmen, whose characters as jurors, as gentlemen, must find either honor or degradation in the result of your decision. Small as must be the distributive share of that national estimation that can belong to so unimportant an individual as myself, yet do I own I am tremblingly solicitous for its fate. Perhaps it appears of more value to me, because it is embarked on the same bottom with yours; perhaps the community of peril, of common safety, or common wreck gives a consequence to my share of the risk, which I could not be vain enough to give it, if it were not raised to it by that mutuality. But why stoop to think at all of myself, when I know that you, gentlemen of the jury, when I know that our country itself are my clients on this day, and must abide the alternative of honor or of infamy, as you shall decide. But I will not despond; I will not dare to despond. I have every trust, and hope, and confidence in you. And to that hope I will add my most fervent prayer to the God of all truth and justice, so to raise, and enlighten, and fortify your minds, that you may so decide as to preserve to yourselves while you live, the most delightful of all recollections, that of acting justly, and to transmit to your children the most precious of all inheritances, the memory of your virtue.

The damages were fixed by the jury at ten thousand pounds.

SIR JAMES MACKINTOSH.

James Mackintosh was the son of a captain in the British army, and was born at Aldourie, near Inverness, in Scotland, on the 24th of October, 1765. He was very early remarkable for his love of reading, making it his constant employment, whether at home or abroad, and being accustomed, when a mere child, to take his book and dinner with him into the wild hills around his father's residence, where he gave up the whole day in some secluded nook to his favorite employment.

At the age of ten, he was sent to a boarding-school at a small town called Fortrose, where he soon made such proficiency in his studies that "the name of *Jamie Mackintosh* was synonymous, all over the country side, with a prodigy of learning." He early assisted his instructor in teaching the younger boys, and before he reached his thirteenth year, he showed a singular love of politics and extemporaneous speaking. "It was at this period," says his instructor, the Reverend Mr. Wood, "that Fox and North made such brilliant harangues on the American war. Jamie espoused the cause of liberty, and called himself a *Whig;* and such was his influence among his school-fellows, that he prevailed on some of the older ones, instead of playing at ball, and such out-of-door recreations, to join him in the school-room during the hours of play, and assist at debates in what they called the *House of Commons*, on the political events of the day. When Jamie ascended the rostrum, he harangued until his *soprano* voice failed him. One day he was Fox, another Burke, or some leading member of the Opposition; and when no one ventured to reply to his arguments, he would change sides for the present, personate North, and endeavor to combat what he conceived to be the strongest parts of his own speech. When I found out this singular amusement of the boys," adds Mr. Wood, "I had the curiosity to listen when Jamie was on his legs. I was greatly surprised and delighted with his eloquence in the character of Fox, against some supposed or real measure of the minister. His voice, though feeble, was musical, and his arguments so forcible that they would have done credit to many an adult."

At the age of fifteen he was placed at King's College, Aberdeen, and at once showed his predilection for those abstract inquiries in which he spent so large a part of his life. Though a mere boy, his favorite books were Priestley's Institutes of Natural and Revealed Religion, Beattie on Truth, and Warburton's Divine Legation, which last delighted him, as he stated in after life, more than any book he ever read. He soon after made the acquaintance of Robert Hall, then a student at Aberdeen, who was deeply interested in the same pursuits, and though both were diligent in their classical studies, they gave their most strenuous and unwearied labors to a joint improvement in philosophy. They read together; they sat side by side at lecture; they were constant companions in their daily walks. In the classics, they united in reading much of Xenophon and Herodotus, and more of Plato; and so far did they carry it, says the biographer of Hall, that, "exciting the admiration of some and the envy of others, it was not unusual for their class-fellows to point at them and say, 'There go Plato and Herodotus!' But the arena, in which they most frequently met was that of morals and metaphysics. After having sharpened their weapons by reading, they often repaired to the spacious sands on the sea-shore, and, still more frequently, to the picturesque scenery on the banks of the Don, above the old town, to discuss with eagerness the various subjects to which their attention had been directed. There was scarcely an important position in Berkeley's Minute Philosopher, in Butler's Analogy, or in Edwards on the Will, over which they had not thus debated with the utmost intensity. Night after night, nay, month after month, they met only to study or dispute, yet no unkindly feeling ensued. The process seemed rather, like blows in the welding of iron, to knit them more closely together." From this union of their studies, and the discussions which ensued, Sir James afterward declared himself to have "learned more than from all the books he ever read;" while Mr. Hall expressed his opinion throughout life, that Sir James "had an intellect more like that of Bacon than any person of modern times."

Having taken his degree of Bachelor of Arts at the age of nineteen, Mr. Mackintosh repaired to Edinburgh in 1784, and commenced the study of medicine. Here he was soon received as a member of the Speculative Society, an association for debate which then exerted a powerful influence over the University, and was the means of training some of the most distinguished speakers which Scotland has ever produced. In this exciting atmosphere, his early passion for extemporaneous speaking, in connection with his subsequent habits of debate, gained the complete ascendency; so that, although his medical studies were not wholly neglected, a large part of his time was given to those miscellaneous subjects which would furnish topics for the Society, and that desultory reading and speculation in which he always delighted.

After four years spent at Edinburgh, Mr. Mackintosh went to London in 1788, with a view to medical practice, but found no immediate prospect of business, and but little encouragement for the future. His father died about this time, leaving him a very scanty patrimony; and, as he married soon after, without adding to his property, he was driven, like Burke in early life, to the public press for the means of support. He wrote from the first with uncommon force and elegance, and was thus introduced to the acquaintance of some distinguished literary men, chiefly of the extreme Whig party. He was much in the society of Horne Tooke, and found great delight in the rich, lively, and sarcastic conversation of that extraordinary man; while Tooke, though jealous, and sparing of praise, was so struck with his talents for argument, that he declared him "a very *formidable* adversary across a table." He now took to the study of the law in connection with his labors for the press, and never, probably, were his exertions greater or better directed than at this time, or more conducive to his intellectual improvement. Desultory reading and speculation without any definite object, were the bane of his life; but he was now held to his daily task, and, under the pressure of want, the encouragement of his friends, and the kindling delight which he felt in high literary excellence, he was daily forming those habits of rich and powerful composition for which he was afterward so much distinguished.

In 1792 he published his first great work, the "Vindiciæ Gallicæ," or "Defense of the French Revolution against the accusations of the Right Honorable Edmund Burke." It was a daring attempt for a young man of twenty-six to enter the lists with such an opponent, celebrated beyond any man of the age for his powers as a writer, and regarded as an oracle by nearly all among the middling and higher classes, who looked with horror and dismay at the Revolution which this unknown adventurer came forward to defend. Not to have failed utterly in such an attempt was no mean praise. But he did more. He brought to the work an honest and dauntless enthusiasm; a large stock of legal and constitutional learning; a style which, though inferior in richness to that of his great antagonist, was not only elegant and expressive, but often keen and trenchant; and his success was far beyond his most sanguine expectations. Three editions were called for in rapid succession; Mr. Fox quoted the work with applause in the House of Commons; and even Mr

Burke, who had been treated by Mr. Mackintosh with the respect due to his great talents, spoke of its spirit and execution in the kindest terms. Mr. Canning, who was accustomed, at that period, to treat every thing that favored the Revolution with ridicule or contempt, told a friend that he read the book, on its first coming out, "with as much admiration as he had ever felt."

The Revolution turned out very differently, in most respects, from what Mr. Mackintosh had hoped, and he saw reason to change some of the opinions expressed in this work. He afterward made the acquaintance of Mr. Burke, and remarked, in a letter to him, about four years after, "For a time I was seduced by what I thought *liberty*, and ventured to oppose, without ever ceasing to venerate, that writer who had nourished my understanding with the most wholesome principles of political wisdom. Since that time a melancholy experience has undeceived me on many subjects in which I was then the dupe of my own enthusiasm. I can not say (and you would despise me if I dissembled) that I can even now assent to all your opinions on the present politics of Europe.[1] But I can with truth affirm that I subscribe to your general principles, and am prepared to shed my blood in defense of the laws and Constitution of my country."[2]

In the latter part of 1795, Mr. Mackintosh was called to the bar, and in 1799 he formed the plan of giving lectures on the Law of Nature and of Nations. The subject was peculiarly suited to his philosophical cast of mind, and had long occupied his attention. Being in want of a hall for the purpose, he asked the Benchers of Lincoln's Inn to grant him the use of theirs; and when some demur was made on account of the sentiments expressed in his Vindiciæ Gallicæ, he printed the Introductory Lecture as a prospectus of the course. It was truly and beautifully said by Thomas Campbell, "If Mackintosh had published nothing else than this Discourse, he would have left a perfect monument of his intellectual strength and symmetry; and even supposing that essay had been recovered only imperfect and mutilated—if but a score of its consecutive sentences could be shown, they would bear a testimony to his genius as decided as the bust of Theseus bears to Grecian art among the Elgin marbles." The Lord Chancellor [Loughborough], ashamed of the delay among the Benchers, interposed decisively, and procured the use of the hall; and the Prime Minister, Mr. Pitt, "always liberally inclined," as one of his opponents in politics has described him, wrote a private letter to Mr. Mackintosh, saying, "The plan you have marked out appears to me to promise more useful instruction and just reasoning on the principles of government than I have ever met with in any treatise on the subject." The lectures now went forward, and Lincoln's Inn Hall was daily filled with an auditory such as never before met on a similar occasion. Lawyers, members of Parliament, men of letters, and gentlemen from the country, crowded the seats; and the Lord Chancellor, who, from a pressure of public business, was unable to attend, received a full report of each lecture in writing, and was loud in their praise.

In such a course of lectures the name of Grotius could not fail to have a prominent place, and the reader will be delighted with the following sketch of his character, which has rarely, if ever, been equaled by any thing of the kind in our language.

"So great is the uncertainty of posthumous reputation, and so liable is the fame, even of the greatest men, to be obscured by those new fashions of thinking and writing which succeed each

1 Mr. Mackintosh here refers to Mr. Burke's views respecting the war with France, which he openly condemned in opposition to Mr. Burke; nor did he ever agree with him on a number of points mentioned in the sketch of Mr. Burke in this volume, p. 231. His change consisted mainly in withdrawing his defense of the Revolution as actually conducted, and agreeing with Mr. Burke that the nation was not prepared for liberty.

2 When Mr. Mackintosh visited Paris during the peace of Amiens, some of the French literati to whom he was introduced complimented him on his defense of their Revolution. "Gentlemen," said he, in reply, "since that time you have entirely *refuted me!*"

other so rapidly among polished nations, that Grotius, who filled so large a space in the eyes of his cotemporaries, is now, perhaps, known to some of my readers only by name. Yet, if we fairly estimate both his endowments and his virtues, we may justly consider him as one of the most memorable men who have done honor to modern times. He combined the discharge of the most important duties of active and public life with the attainment of that exact and various learning which is generally the portion only of the recluse student. He was distinguished as an advocate and a magistrate, and he composed the most valuable works on the law of his own country. He was almost equally celebrated as a historian, a scholar, a poet, and a divine; a disinterested statesman, a philosophical lawyer, a patriot who united moderation with firmness, and a theologian who was taught candor by his learning. Unmerited exile did not damp his patriotism; the bitterness of controversy did not extinguish his charity. The sagacity of his numerous and fierce adversaries could not discover a blot on his character; and in the midst of all the hard trials and galling provocations of a turbulent political life, he never once deserted his friends when they were unfortunate, nor insulted his enemies when they were weak. In times of the most furious civil and religious faction he preserved his name unspotted, and he knew how to reconcile fidelity to his own party with moderation toward his opponents."

The Introductory Lecture closed in the following beautiful manner:

"I know not whether a philosopher ought to confess that, in his inquiries after truth, he is *biased* by any consideration, even by the love of virtue; but I, who conceive that a real philosopher ought to regard truth itself chiefly on account of its subserviency to the happiness of mankind, am not ashamed to confess that I shall feel a great consolation at the conclusion of these lectures if, by a wide survey and an exact examination of the conditions and relations of human nature, I shall have confirmed but one individual in the conviction that justice is the permanent interest of all men, and of all commonwealths. To discover one new link of that eternal chain, by which the Author of the universe has bound together the happiness and the duty of his creatures, and indissolubly fastened their interests to each other, would fill my heart with more pleasure than all the fame with which the most ingenious paradox ever crowned the most ingenious sophist."

Mr. Mackintosh now devoted himself to his profession with the most flattering prospects of success; but his thoughts were soon after directed to a judicial station, either in Trinidad or India, which he had the prospect of obtaining, and which he considered as more suited to his habits and cast of mind. While this matter was pending, he made his celebrated speech in favor of M. Peltier, which is given in this collection. The case was a singular one. Peltier was a French royalist, who resided in London, and published a newspaper in the French language, in which he spoke with great severity of Bonaparte, then First Consul of France. It would seem hardly possible that a man like Bonaparte could feel the slightest annoyance at such attacks; but it is said to have been the weak point in his character, and that he was foolishly sensitive on this subject. At all events, as the two countries were then at peace, he made a formal demand of the English ministry to punish Peltier for "a libel on a friendly government." A prosecution was accordingly commenced, and Mr. Mackintosh, in defending Peltier, was brought into the same dilemma with that of Demosthenes in his Oration for the Crown. Equity was on his side, but the law was against him; and his only hope (as in the case of Demosthenes) was that of pre-occupying the minds of the jury with a sense of national honor and public justice, and bearing them so completely away by the fervor of his eloquence, as to obtain a verdict of acquittal from their feelings, without regard to the strict demands of law. His theme was the *freedom of the English press*—its right and duty to comment on the crimes of the proudest tyrants; and he maintained (with great appearance of truth) that the real object of Bonaparte, after destroying every vestige of free discussion throughout the Continent, was to silence the press of England as to his conduct and designs. He told the jury, after dwelling on the extinction of the liberty of the press abroad, "One asylum of free discussion is still inviolate. There is still one spot in Europe where man can freely exercise his reason on the most important concerns of society—where he can boldly publish his judgment on the acts of the proudest and most powerful tyrants. The press of England is still free. It is guarded by the free Constitution of our forefathers; it is guarded by the hearts and arms of Englishmen; and I trust I may venture to say, that if it be to fall, it will fall only under the ruins of the British empire. It is an awful consideration, gentlemen: every other monument of European liberty has perished: that ancient fabric, which has been gradually reared by the wisdom and virtue of our fathers, still stands. It stands (thanks be to God!) solid and entire; but it stands alone, and it stands amid ruins." Still, as the law was, the jury felt bound to convict Peltier.

We have hardly any thing in our eloquence conceived in a finer spirit, or carried out in a loftier tone of sentiment and feeling, than the appeals made in this oration. It would have been just as sure to succeed before an Athenian tribunal, as that of Demosthenes to fail in an English court of law. Lord Erskine was present during its delivery, and before going to bed addressed the following note to Mr. Mackintosh:

"DEAR SIR,—I can not shake off from my nerves the effect of your powerful and most wonderful speech, which so completely disqualifies you for Trinidad or India. I could not help saying to myself, as you were speaking, '*O terram illam beatam quæ hunc virum acciperit, hanc ingratam si ejicerit, miseram si amiserit.*'[3] I perfectly approve the verdict, but the manner in which you opposed it I shall always consider as one of the most splendid monuments of genius, literature, and eloquence.

"Yours ever, T. ERSKINE."

When the speech was published, Mr. Mackintosh sent a copy to his friend Robert Hall, and soon after received a letter, containing, among other things, the following passage: "Accept my best thanks for the trial of Peltier, which I read, so far as your part in it is concerned, with the highest delight and instruction. I speak my sincere sentiments when I say, it is the most extraordinary assemblage of whatever is most refined in address, profound in political and moral speculation, and masterly in eloquence, which it has ever been my lot to read in the English language."

A few months after, Mr. Mackintosh was appointed Recorder of Bombay, and at the same time received the honors of knighthood. He arrived in India about the middle of 1804, and spent eight years in that country, devoting all the time he could gain from the duties of the bench to the more congenial pursuits of literature. He wrote several interesting pieces during this period, and particularly a sketch of Mr. Fox's character, which will be found below, and which has always been regarded as one of the best delineations ever given of that distinguished statesman. His appointment to India was, on the whole, injurious to his intellectual growth. He needed beyond most men to be kept steadily at work, under the impulse of great objects and strong motives urging him to the utmost exertion of his powers. Had he remained at the bar, he might have surpassed Erskine in learning, and rivaled him in skill as an advocate, while his depth and amplitude of thought would have furnished the richest materials for every occasion that admitted of eloquence. But he now relapsed into his old habits of desultory reading and ingenious speculation. He projected a number of great works, and labored irregularly in collecting materials; but his health sunk under the enervating effects of the climate, and he returned to England at the end of eight years, disappointed in his expectations and depressed in spirit, bringing with him a vast amount of matter for books which were never to be completed.

So highly were his talents appreciated, that immediately after his return in 1812, he was offered a seat in the House of Commons by the government, and also by his old Whig friends. He chose the latter, and continued true to liberal principles to the end of his days.

[3] The words are taken from the peroration of Cicero's oration for Milo, in which he deplores the exile which must befall his client if he loses his cause.

Happy the land that shall receive him! Ungrateful the country that shall cast him out! miserable if she finally lose him!

In 1818 he was appointed Professor of Law and of General Politics at Haileybury College, an institution designed to prepare young men for the service of the East India Company. His lectures embraced a course of four years, extending through four months of each year. He endeared himself greatly to his pupils by his kind and conciliating manners, while his extraordinary learning, and the high reputation he had with the public, made him the object of their respect and veneration. This situation he held nine years, and resigned it in 1827. During all this time he took an active part in politics, entering warmly into every important debate in Parliament, and writing numerous articles for the Edinburgh Review. He also wrote, in 1829, a Dissertation on the Progress of Ethical Philosophy, which was first published as a supplement to the Encyclopedia Britannica, and soon after printed in an 8vo volume by itself. To these he added, in the three subsequent years, several volumes of an abridged history of England, and a work on the Revolution of 1688, which was published after his death. Under the administration of Earl Grey, he was appointed a member of the Board of Control, and took an active part in the great struggle for parliamentary reform.

As a speaker in Parliament he was instructive rather than bold and exciting. His residence in India had so debilitated his constitution, and his habits of speculation had so completely gained the ascendency, that he never spoke with that lofty enthusiasm and fervor of emotion which distinguished his defense of Peltier. He had, says an able cotemporary, "perhaps more than any man of his time, that *mitis sapientia* which formed the distinguishing characteristic of the illustrious friend of Cicero, and which wins its way into the heart, while it at once enlightens and satisfies the understanding." He died on the 30th of May, 1832, in the sixty-seventh year of his age, perhaps more regretted and less envied than any public man of his age.

SPEECH

OF MR. MACKINTOSH IN BEHALF OF JEAN PELTIER WHEN TRIED FOR A LIBEL ON NAPOLEON BONAPARTE, DELIVERED IN THE COURT OF KING'S BENCH, FEBRUARY 21, 1803.

INTRODUCTION

THE leading circumstances of this trial have been already stated in the preceding memoir.

In 1802, Mr. Peltier commenced a French newspaper in London, designed to expose the *ambiguous* conduct of Bonaparte, who, though only First Consul in name, was assuming the power and dignity of the regal office. Hence he called his paper L'AMBIGU, and put on the frontispiece the figure of a sphynx (emblematic of mystery), with a head which strikingly resembled that of Bonaparte, *wearing a crown.* Its pages were filled with instances of the despotism of the First Consul, some violent and some ridiculous, and hence he also called it "Variétés atroces et amusantes." It was characterized, on the whole, by great bitterness, one of the numbers containing an ode, written in the name of Chenier—so distinguished at once for his talents and his Jacobin principles—which directly hinted at the assassination of Bonaparte. In another, there was an intimation of the same kind in a short poem from a Dutch patriot. A third contained a parody on a speech in Sallust, that of Lepidus against Sylla, which was plainly pointed at the First Consul as having assumed the Dictatorship.

These things gave so much annoyance to Bonaparte, that he actually demanded of the English government to send Peltier out of the kingdom;[1] and when this was refused, he insisted, as France was then at peace with England, that Mr. Peltier should be *prosecuted* by the English Attorney General for "a libel on a friendly government!" Upon this subject, the laws of England were strict even to severity. Convictions had been frequent in past times; and only four years before, John Vint had been sentenced to an imprisonment of six months and a fine of one hundred pounds; for using the following words respecting the conduct of the Czar of Russia: "The Emperor Paul is rendering himself obnoxious to his subjects by various acts of tyranny, and ridiculous in the eyes of Europe by his inconsistency. He has lately passed an edict to prohibit the exportation of deals and other naval stores. In consequence of this ill-judged law, a hundred sail of vessels are likely to return to this country without freight." When these harmless words had been visited with such a penalty, it was impossible for the government to avoid taking up the case of Peltier, and he was accordingly brought before the Court of King's Bench, Lord Ellenborough presiding, by an information from the Attorney General, Mr. Percival, afterward Prime Minister.

It was a singular spectacle for the English government to appear as prosecutor of a poor French Royalist for bitter words about Bonaparte, when the Prime Minister of England had so lately poured out against him one of the most terrible invectives ever uttered by human lips. But the First Consul held them firmly to the execution of their laws; and when the trial came on, two French officers of high rank made their appearance in the court room, *and took their seats by the jury-box, directly in front of the counsel for the Crown and prisoner!*

Mr. Percival opened the case in a mild and gentlemanly address, insisting on the three points mentioned above, and reminded the jury that as Bonaparte was head of a government now at peace with England, he was entitled to the protection of her laws. Mr. Mackintosh followed in the speech before us. Without directly alluding to the presence of the French officers, he took the ground that the real object of this prosecution was *to break down the only remaining free press in Europe;* and appealed to the jury for its protection, with a compass and richness of thought, a grandeur of sentiment, and an impassioned warmth of feeling, such as no court, either in ancient or modern times, had ever witnessed.

SPEECH, &c.

GENTLEMEN OF THE JURY,—The time is now come for me to address you in behalf of the unfortunate gentleman who is the defendant on this record.

I must begin with observing, that though I know myself too well to ascribe to any thing but to the kindness and good nature of my learned friend, the Attorney General, the unmerited praises which he has been pleased to bestow on me, yet, I will venture to say, he has done me no more than justice in supposing that in this place, and on this occasion, where I exercise the functions of an inferior minister of justice, an inferior minister, indeed, but a minister of justice still, I am incapable of lending myself to the passions of any client, and that I will not make the proceedings of this court subservient to any political purpose. Whatever is respected by the laws and government of my country shall, in this place, be respected by me. In considering matters that deeply interest the quiet, the

No indecorum contemplated toward the head of a government at peace with England.

[1] See Howell's State Trials, vol. xxviii., p. 566.

safety, and the liberty of all mankind, it is impossible for me not to feel warmly and strongly; but I shall make an effort to control my feelings however painful that effort may be, and where I can not speak out but at the risk of offending either sincerity or prudence, I shall labor to contain myself and be silent.

Still the defense of the accused demands a frank and fearless statement of the truth.

I can not but feel, gentlemen, how much I stand in need of your favorable attention and indulgence. The charge which I have to defend is surrounded with the most invidious topics of discussion; but they are not of my seeking. The case and the topics which are inseparable from it are brought here by the prosecutor. Here I find them, and here it is my duty to deal with them, as the interests of Mr. Peltier seem to me to require. He, by his choice and confidence, has cast on me a very arduous duty, which I could not decline, and which I can still less betray. He has a right to expect from me a faithful, a zealous, and a fearless defense; and this his just expectation, according to the measure of my humble abilities, shall be fulfilled. I have said a fearless defense. Perhaps that word was unnecessary in the place where I now stand. Intrepidity in the discharge of professional duty is so common a quality at the English bar, that it has, thank God, long ceased to be a matter of boast or praise. If it had been otherwise, gentlemen, if the bar could have been silenced or overawed by power, I may presume to say that an English jury would not this day have been met to administer justice. Perhaps I need scarce say that my defense *shall* be fearless, in a place where fear never entered any heart but that of a criminal. But you will pardon me for having said so much when you consider who the real parties before you are.

Part First: Preliminary considerations: Parties in the present case.

I. Gentlemen, the real prosecutor is the master of the greatest empire the civilized world ever saw. The defendant is a defenseless, proscribed exile. He is a French Royalist, who fled from his country in the autumn of 1792, at the period of that memorable and awful emigration when all the proprietors and magistrates of the greatest civilized country of Europe were driven from their homes by the daggers of assassins; when our shores were covered, as with the wreck of a great tempest, with old men, and women, and children, and ministers of religion, who fled from the ferocity of their countrymen as before an army of invading barbarians.

The greatest part of these unfortunate exiles, of those, I mean, who have been spared by the sword, who have survived the effect of pestilential climates or broken hearts, have been since permitted to revisit their country. Though despoiled of their all, they have eagerly embraced even the sad privilege of being suffered to die in their native land.

The defendant a voluntary victim of loyalty and honor.

Even this miserable indulgence was to be purchased by compliances, by declarations of allegiance to the new government, which some of these suffering Royalists deemed incompatible with their consciences, with their dearest attachments, and their most sacred duties. Among these last is Mr. Peltier. I do not presume to blame those who submitted, and I trust you will not judge harshly of those who refused. You will not think unfavorably of a man who stands before you as the voluntary victim of his loyalty and honor. If a revolution (which God avert) were to drive us into exile, and to cast us on a foreign shore, we should expect, at least, to be pardoned by generous men, for stubborn loyalty, and unseasonable fidelity to the laws and government of our fathers.

The publisher of a French newspaper for his support.

This unfortunate gentleman had devoted a great part of his life to literature. It was the amusement and ornament of his better days. Since his own ruin and the desolation of his country, he has been compelled to employ it as a means of support. For the last ten years he has been engaged in a variety of publications of considerable importance; but since the peace, he has desisted from serious political discussion, and confined himself to the obscure journal which is now before you; the least calculated, surely, of any publication that ever issued from the press, to rouse the alarms of the most jealous government; which will not be read in England, because it is not written in our language; which can not be read in France, because its entry into that country is prohibited by a power whose mandates are not very supinely enforced, nor often evaded with impunity; which can have no other object than that of amusing the companions of the author's principles and misfortunes, by pleasantries and sarcasms on their victorious enemies. There is, indeed, gentlemen, one remarkable circumstance in this unfortunate publication; it is the only, or almost the only journal which still dares to espouse the cause of that royal and illustrious family, which but fourteen years ago was flattered by every press and guarded by every tribunal in Europe. Even the court in which we are met affords an example of the vicissitudes of their fortune. My learned friend has reminded you that the last prosecution tried in this place, at the instance of a French government, was for a libel on that magnanimous princess, who has since been butchered in sight of her palace.

His work incapable of doing the slightest injury to the French government.

Liable, nevertheless, to be prosecuted for libel.

I do not make these observations with any purpose of questioning the general principles which have been laid down by my learned friend. I must admit his right to bring before you those who libel any government recognized by his Majesty, and at peace with the British empire. I admit that, whether such a government be of yesterday, or a thousand years old; whether it be a crude and bloody usurpation, or the most ancient, just, and paternal authority upon earth, we are *here* equally bound, by his Majesty's recognition, to protect it against libelous attacks.[2] I admit that, dur-

[2] The reader will at once see Mr. Mackintosh's motive in making the extreme concessions which follow as to Clarendon and others. Principles

ing our usurpation, Lord Clarendon had published his history at Paris, or the Marquess of Montrose his verses on the murder of his sovereign, Mr. Cowley his Discourse on Cromwell's government, and if the English embassador had complained, the President De Molí, or any other of the great magistrates who then adorned the Parliament of Paris, however reluctantly, painfully, and indignantly, might have been compelled to have condemned these illustrious men to the punishment of libelers. I say this only for the sake of bespeaking a favorable attention from your generosity, and compassion to what will be feebly urged in behalf of my unfortunate client, who has sacrificed his fortune, his hopes, his connections, his country, to his conscience; who seems marked out for destruction in this his last asylum.

The defendant hitherto protected by the government.

That he still enjoys the security of this asylum, that he has not been sacrificed to the resentment of his powerful enemies, is perhaps owing to the firmness of the King's government. If that be the fact, gentlemen; if his Majesty's ministers have resisted applications to expel this unfortunate gentleman from England, I should publicly thank them for their firmness, if it were not unseemly and improper to suppose that they could have acted otherwise—to thank an English government for not violating the most sacred duties of hospitality; for not bringing indelible disgrace on their country.[3]

He now looks for protection to an English jury.

But be that as it may, gentlemen, he now comes before you, perfectly satisfied that an English jury is the most refreshing prospect that the eye of accused innocence ever met in a human tribunal; and he feels with me the most fervent gratitude to the Protector of empires that, surrounded as we are with the ruins of principalities and powers, we still continue to meet together, after the manner of our fathers, to administer justice in this her ancient sanctuary.

Part Second: The real question at issue. The preservation of a free press in Europe.

II. There is another point of view in which this case seems to me to merit your most serious attention. I consider it as the first of a long series of conflicts between the greatest power in the world and the only free press remaining in Europe.[4] No man living is more thoroughly convinced than I am that my learned friend, Mr. Attorney General, will never degrade his excellent character; that he will never disgrace his high magistracy by mean compliances, by an immoderate and unconscientious exercise of power; yet I am convinced, by circumstances, which I shall now abstain from discussing, that I am to consider this as the first of a long series of conflicts between the greatest power in the world and the only free press now remaining in Europe. Gentlemen, this distinction of the English press is new; it is a proud and melancholy distinction. Before the great earthquake of the French Revolution had swallowed up all the asylums of free discussion on the Continent, we enjoyed that privilege, indeed, more fully than others; but we did not enjoy it exclusively. In great monarchies, the press has always been considered as too formidable an engine to be intrusted to unlicensed individuals. But in other Continental countries, either by the laws of the state, or by long habits of liberality and toleration in magistrates, a liberty of discussion has been enjoyed, perhaps sufficient for most useful purposes. It existed, in fact, where it was not protected by law; and the wise and generous connivance of governments was daily more and more secured by the growing civilization of their subjects. In Holland, in Switzerland, in the imperial towns of Germany, the press was either legally or practically free. Holland and Switzerland are no more; and since the commencement of this prosecution, fifty imperial towns have been erased from the list of independent states by one dash of the pen. Three or four still preserve a precarious and trembling existence. I will not say by what compliances they must purchase its continuance. I will not insult the feebleness of states, whose unmerited fall I do most bitterly deplore.[5]

Freedom of discussion in the smaller states on the Continent.

Position of those states, and the influence of their press on the larger powers.

These governments were in many respects one of the most interesting parts of the ancient system of Europe. Unfortunately for the repose of mankind, great states are compelled, by regard to their own safety, to consider the military spirit and martial habits of their people as one of the main objects of their policy. Frequent hostilities seem almost the necessary condition of their greatness; and, without being great, they can not long remain safe. Smaller states exempted from this cruel necessity—a hard condition of greatness, a bitter satire on human nature—devoted themselves to the arts of peace, to the cultivation of literature, and the improvement of reason. They became places of refuge for free and fearless discussion; they were the impartial

which reach so far, and involve such consequences, must be often set aside, and he hoped to induce the jury to do so in the present instance.

[3] What is here stated hypothetically, Mr. Peltier afterward declared to be the fact. Bonaparte had directly demanded of the government to *banish* Peltier, and he was saved only by the firmness of ministers. An intimation of this fact was designed to touch the pride of the jury when called upon to carry out the demands of the First Consul.

[4] It was not for mere effect that Mr. Mackintosh put his cause on this high ground. He had recently returned from Paris, and was perfectly satisfied that Bonaparte intended to break down all discussion which might weaken his power. If the peace of Amiens had continued for ten years, and he could prosecute effectually in English courts, what might not have been the result?

[5] The digression which follows, touching the smaller states of Europe, is not only beautiful in itself, and conceived in a fine spirit of philosophy, but prepares the way for coming back, with increased force and interest, to the *press of England* as the only remaining instrument of free discussion in Europe.

spectators and judges of the various contests of ambition which from time to time disturbed the quiet of the world. They thus became peculiarly qualified to be the organs of that public opinion which converted Europe into a great republic, with laws which mitigated, though they could not extinguish ambition; and with moral tribunals to which even the most despotic sovereigns were amenable. If wars of aggrandizement were undertaken, their authors were arraigned in the face of Europe. If acts of internal tyranny were perpetrated, they resounded from a thousand presses throughout all civilized countries. Princes on whose will there were no legal checks, thus found a moral restraint which the most powerful of them could not brave with absolute impunity. They acted before a vast audience, to whose applause or condemnation they could not be utterly indifferent. The very constitution of human nature, the unalterable laws of the mind of man, against which all rebellion is fruitless, subjected the proudest tyrants to this control. No elevation of power, no depravity, however consummate, no innocence, however spotless, can render man wholly independent of the praise or blame of his fellow-men.

The security of these states one of the most striking facts in the history of Europe.

These governments were, in other respects, one of the most beautiful and interesting parts of our ancient system. The perfect security of such inconsiderable and feeble states, their undisturbed tranquillity amid the wars and conquests that surrounded them, attested, beyond any other part of the European system, the moderation, the justice, the civilization to which Christian Europe had reached in modern times. Their weakness was protected only by the habitual reverence for justice, which, during a long series of ages, had grown up in Christendom. This was the only fortification which defended them against those mighty monarchs to whom they offered so easy a prey. And till the French Revolution, this was sufficient. Consider, for instance, the situation of the Republic of Geneva. Think of her defenseless position, in the very jaws of France; but think also of her undisturbed security, of her profound quiet, of the brilliant success with which she applied to industry and literature, while Louis XIV. was pouring his myriads into Italy before her gates. Call to mind, if ages crowded into years have not effaced them from your memory, that happy period, when we scarcely dreamed more of the subjugation of the feeblest republic of Europe than of the conquest of her mightiest empire; and tell me, if you can imagine a spectacle more beautiful to the moral eye, or a more striking proof of progress in the noblest principles of true civilization.

All of them now subjugated, and their press enslaved.

These feeble states—these monuments of the justice of Europe — the asylum of peace, of industry, and of literature—the organs of public reason—the refuge of oppressed innocence and persecuted truth, have perished with those ancient principles which were their sole guardians and protectors. They have been swallowed up by that fearful convulsion which has shaken the uttermost corners of the earth. They are destroyed and gone forever.

The liberty of the press now confined to England as its last asylum in Europe.

One asylum of free discussion is still inviolate. There is still one spot in Europe where man can freely exercise his reason on the most important concerns of society, where he can boldly publish his judgment on the acts of the proudest and most powerful tyrants. The press of England is still free. It is guarded by the free Constitution of our forefathers. It is guarded by the hearts and arms of Englishmen, and I trust I may venture to say that if it be to fall, it will fall only under the ruins of the British empire.

It is an awful consideration, gentlemen. Every other monument of European liberty has perished. That ancient fabric which has been gradually reared by the wisdom and virtue of our fathers still stands. It stands, thanks be to God! solid and entire; but it stands alone, and it stands amid ruins.

Restatement of the question at issue.

In these extraordinary circumstances, I repeat that I must consider this as the first of a long series of conflicts between the greatest power in the world and the only free press remaining in Europe. And I trust that you will consider yourselves as the advanced guard of liberty, as having this day to fight the first battle of free discussion against the most formidable enemy that it ever encountered. You will therefore excuse me, if, on so important an occasion, I remind you, at more length than is usual, of those general principles of law and policy on this subject which have been handed down to us by our ancestors.

Part Third: The law in respect to political libels.

III. Those who slowly built up the fabric of our laws never attempted any thing so absurd as to define, by any precise rule, the obscure and shifting boundaries which divide libel from history or discussion. It is a subject which, from its nature, admits neither rules nor definitions. The same words may be perfectly innocent in one case, and most mischievous and libelous in another. A change of circumstances, often apparently slight, is sufficient to make the whole difference. These changes, which may be as numerous as the variety of human intentions and conditions, can never be foreseen nor comprehended under any legal definitions, and the framers of our law have never attempted to subject them to such definitions. They left such ridiculous attempts to those who call themselves philosophers, but who have, in fact, proved themselves most grossly and stupidly ignorant of that philosophy which is conversant with human affairs.

Necessarily variable in its application, according to the circumstances of the case and of the times.

Liable to become severe and oppressive if executed to the letter.

The principles of the law of England on the subject of political libel are few and simple, and they are necessarily so broad, that, without a habitually mild administration of justice, they might encroach materially on the liberty of political discussion. Every publication which is intended to vilify either our own government or the government of any foreign state in amity with this kingdom, is, by the law of England, a libel.

Means of protection against this severity.

To protect political discussion from the danger to which it would be exposed by these wide principles, if they were severely and literally enforced, our ancestors trusted to various securities—some growing out of the law and Constitution, and others arising from the character of those public officers whom the Constitution had formed, and to whom its administration is committed. They trusted,

(a) In the character of the prosecuting officers.

in the first place, to the moderation of the legal officers of the Crown, educated in the maxims and imbued with the spirit of a free government; controlled by the superintending power of Parliament, and peculiarly watched in all political prosecutions by the reasonable and wholesome jealousy of their fellow-subjects. And I am bound to admit that, since the glorious era of the Revolution [1688], making due allowance for the frailties, the faults, and the occasional vices of men, they have, upon the whole, not been disappointed. I know that in the hands of my learned friend that trust will never be abused. But, above all, they confided in the moderation and good sense of juries, popular in their origin,

(b) And still more in the sound judgment and feelings of the jury.

popular in their feelings, popular in their very prejudices, taken from the mass of the people, and immediately returning to that mass again. By these checks and temperaments they hoped that they should sufficiently repress malignant libels, without endangering that freedom of inquiry which is the first security of a free state. They knew that the offense of a political libel is of a very peculiar nature, and differing in the most important particulars from all other crimes. In all other cases, the most severe execution of law can only spread terror among the guilty; but in political libels it inspires even the innocent with fear.

Peculiar evils of severity in the case of political libels.

This striking peculiarity arises from the same circumstances which make it impossible to define the limits of libel and innocent discussion; which make it impossible for a man of the purest and most honorable mind to be always perfectly certain whether he be within the territory of fair argument and honest narrative, or whether he may not have unwittingly overstepped the faint and varying line which bounds them. But, gentlemen, I will go further. This is the only offense where severe and frequent punishments not only intimidate the innocent, but deter men from the most meritorious acts, and from rendering the most important services to their country. They indispose and disqualify men for the discharge of the most sacred duties which they owe to mankind. To inform the public on the conduct of those who administer public affairs requires courage and conscious security. It is always an invidious and obnoxious office; but it is often the most necessary of all public duties. If it is not done boldly, it can not be done effectually, and it is not from writers trembling under the uplifted scourge that we are to hope for it.

Peculiar inducements for England to admit an exposure of wrongs committed in other countries.

There are other matters, gentlemen, to which I am desirous of particularly calling your attention. These are the circumstances in the condition of this country which have induced our ancestors, at all times, to handle with more than ordinary tenderness that branch of the liberty of discussion which is applied to the conduct of foreign states. The relation of this kingdom to the commonwealth of Europe is so peculiar, that no history, I think, furnishes a parallel to it. From the moment in which we abandoned all projects of continental aggrandizement, we could have no interest respecting the state of the Continent but the interests of national safety and of commercial prosperity. The paramount interest of every state—that which comprehends every other—is *security*. And the

(a) Her security depends on the maintenance of justice throughout Europe.

security of Great Britain requires nothing on the Continent but the uniform observance of justice. It requires nothing but the inviolability of ancient boundaries and the sacredness of ancient possessions, which, on these subjects, is but another form of words for justice. A nation which is herself shut out from the possibility of continental aggrandizement can have no interest but that of preventing such aggrandizement in others. We can have no interest of safety but the preventing of those encroachments which, by their immediate effects, or by their example, may be dangerous to ourselves. We can have no interest of ambition respecting the Continent. So that neither our real, nor even our apparent interests, can ever be at variance with justice.

(b) Her commercial prosperity.

As to commercial prosperity, it is, indeed, a secondary, but it is still a very important branch of our national interests, and it requires nothing on the continent of Europe but the *maintenance of peace*, as far as the paramount interest of security will allow.[6]

Whatever ignorant or prejudiced men may affirm, no war was ever gainful to a commercial

[6] It hardly need be mentioned that a feeling prevailed on 'Change that "the acquittal of Peltier would be considered in France as tantamount to a declaration of war." This feeling the jury were very likely to entertain, and while Mr. Mackintosh could not allude to it in direct terms, it was his object to attack it indirectly, and set it aside. Hence he goes on to expatiate in beautiful language, and with great ingenuity and truth, on the importance of peace to the commercial prosperity of England. This coincidence with the feelings of the jury as mercantile men would naturally give him their confidence; and he then leads them on to see that peace is best promoted, on the whole, by maintaining the cause of political justice throughout Europe; that entire freedom of remark on the part of the English press is favorable to this object; and that the policy of England has never been to purchase peace by withholding her writers from the freest expression of their opinions respecting the crimes of other governments. Considered in this light, the reader will see in the passage which follows an admirable instance of rhetorical skill.

nation. Losses may be less in some, and incidental profits may arise in others. But no such profits ever formed an adequate compensation for the waste of capital and industry which all wars must produce. Next to peace, our commercial greatness depends chiefly on the affluence and prosperity of our neighbors. A commercial nation has, indeed, the same interest in the wealth of her neighbors that a tradesman has in the wealth of his customers. The prosperity of England has been chiefly owing to the general progress of civilized nations in the arts and improvements of social life. Not an acre of land has been brought into cultivation in the wilds of Siberia or on the shores of the Mississippi which has not widened the market for English industry. It is nourished by the progressive prosperity of the world, and it amply repays all that it has received. It can only be employed in spreading civilization and enjoyment over the earth; and by the unchangeable laws of nature, in spite of the impotent tricks of government, it is now partly applied to revive the industry of those very nations who are the loudest in their senseless clamors against its pretended mischiefs. If the blind and barbarous project of destroying English prosperity could be accomplished, it could have no other effect than that of completely beggaring the very countries who now stupidly ascribe their own poverty to our wealth.

This dependent on the peace and prosperity of other nations.

Under these circumstances, gentlemen, it became the obvious policy of the kingdom, a policy in unison with the maxims of a free government, to consider with great indulgence even the boldest animadversions of our political writers on the ambitious projects of foreign states.

And these are promoted by exposing the designs of ambitious rulers abroad.

Bold, and sometimes indiscreet as these animadversions might be, they had, at least, the effect of warning the people of their danger, and of rousing the national indignation against those encroachments which England has almost always been compelled in the end to resist by arms. Seldom, indeed, has she been allowed to wait till a provident regard to her own safety should compel her to take up arms in defense of others. For as it was said by a great orator of antiquity that no man ever was the enemy of the republic who had not first declared war against him, so I may say, with truth, that no man ever meditated the subjugation of Europe who did not consider the destruction or the corruption of England as the first condition of his success.[7] If you examine history, you will find that no such project was ever formed in which it was not deemed a necessary preliminary, either to detach England from the common cause or to destroy her. It seems as if all the conspirators against the independence of nations might have sufficiently taught other states that England is their natural guardian and protector; that she alone has no interest but their preservation; that her safety is interwoven with their own. When vast projects of aggrandizement are manifested, when schemes of criminal ambition are carried into effect, the day of battle is fast approaching for England. Her free government can not engage in dangerous wars without the hearty and affectionate support of her people. A state thus situated can not without the utmost peril silence those public discussions which are to point the popular indignation against those who must soon be enemies. In domestic dissensions, it may sometimes be the supposed interest of government to overawe the press. But it never can be even their apparent interest when the danger is purely foreign. A King of England who, in such circumstances, should conspire against the free press of this country, would undermine the foundations of his own throne; he would silence the trumpet which is to call his people round his standard.

Such an exposure rouses to resistance.

It aids England in her work among the nations of guarding public justice.

Our ancestors never thought it their policy to avert the resentment of foreign tyrants by enjoining English writers to contain and repress their just abhorrence of the criminal enterprises of ambition. This great and gallant nation, which has fought in the front of every battle against the oppressors of Europe, has sometimes inspired fear, but, thank God, she has never felt it. We know that they are our real, and must soon become our declared foes. We know that there can be no cordial amity between the natural enemies and the independence of nations. We have never adopted the cowardly and short-sighted policy of silencing our press, of breaking the spirit and palsying the hearts of our people for the sake of a hollow and precarious truce. We have never been base enough to purchase a short respite from hostilities by sacrificing the first means of defense; the means of rousing the public spirit of the people, and directing it against the enemies of their country and of Europe.[8]

Never her policy to check animadversion on foreign despotism.

She has never sacrificed her national spirit for an uncertain peace.

Gentlemen, the public spirit of a people, by which I mean the whole body of those affections which unites men's hearts to the commonwealth, is in

National spirit the great source of strength to a state.

[7] The words are those of Cicero in his second oration against Anthony, "Quonam meo fato, Patres Conscripti, fieri dicam, ut nemo, his annis viginti, reipublicæ fuerit hostis, qui non bellum eodem tempore mihi quoque indixerit?" How has it happened, Conscript Fathers, that no one has come out as an enemy of the republic, for these last twenty years, who did not at the same time declare war against me?

[8] Here Mr. Mackintosh reaches the point aimed at in the last three paragraphs, viz., that *the jury must not sacrifice Mr. Peltier to propitiate Bonaparte*, and adds force to his admonition by reminding them of what was becoming daily more manifest, that the peace of Amiens was only "a hollow and precarious truce." Sooner, probably, than he expected—only seventeen days after—the King sent a message to Parliament which showed that war was inevitable. It accordingly commenced May 18, 1803. The noble passage which follows as to the means of cherishing *national spirit* was, therefore, peculiarly appropriate.

various countries composed of various elements, and depends on a great variety of causes. In this country, I may venture to say that it mainly depends on the vigor of the popular parts and principles of our government, and that the spirit of liberty is one of its most important elements. Perhaps it may depend less on those advantages of a free government, which are most highly estimated by calm reason, than upon those parts of it which delight the imagination, and flatter the just and natural pride of mankind. Among these we are certainly not to forget the political rights which are not uniformly withheld from the lowest classes, and the continual appeal made to them in public discussion, upon the greatest interests of the state. These are undoubtedly among the circumstances which endear to Englishmen their government and their country, and animate their zeal for that glorious institution which confers on the meanest of them a sort of distinction and nobility unknown to the most illustrious slaves, who tremble at the frown of a tyrant. Whoever were unwarily and rashly to abolish or narrow these privileges, which it must be owned are liable to great abuse, and to very specious objections, might perhaps discover too late that he had been dismantling his country. Of whatever elements public spirit is composed, it is always and every where the chief defensive principle of a state. It is perfectly distinct from courage. Perhaps no nation, certainly no European nation, ever perished from an inferiority of courage. And undoubtedly no considerable nation was ever subdued in which the public affections were sound and vigorous. It is public spirit which binds together the dispersed courage of individuals and fastens it to the commonwealth. It is, therefore, as I have said, the chief defensive principle of every country. Of all the stimulants which arouse it into action, the most powerful among us is certainly the press; and it can not be restrained or weakened without imminent danger that the national spirit may languish, and that the people may act with less zeal and affection for their country in the hour of its danger.

That spirit dependent on preserving the freedom of the press.

These principles, gentlemen, are not new—they are genuine old English principles. And though in our days they have been disgraced and abused by ruffians and fanatics, they are in themselves as just and sound as they are liberal; and they are the only principles on which a free state can be safely governed. These principles I have adopted since I first learned the use of reason, and I think I shall abandon them only with life.

Part Fourth: Explanation and defense of Mr. Peltier's publications.

IV. On these principles I am now to call your attention to the libel with which this unfortunate gentleman is charged. I heartily rejoice that I concur with the greatest part of what has been said by my learned friend, Mr. Attorney General, who has done honor even to his character by the generous and liberal principles which he has laid down. He has told you that he does not mean to attack *historical narrative*. He has told you that he does not mean to attack *political discussion*. He has told you, also, that he does not consider every intemperate word into which a writer, fairly engaged in narration or reasoning, might be betrayed, as a fit subject for prosecution. The essence of the crime of libel consists in the malignant mind which the publication proves, and from which it flows. A jury must be convinced, before they find a man guilty of libel, that his intention was to libel, not to state facts which he believed to be true, or reasonings which he thought just. My learned friend has told you that the liberty of history includes the right of publishing those observations which occur to intelligent men when they consider the affairs of the world; and I think he will not deny that it includes also the right of expressing those sentiments which all good men feel on the contemplation of extraordinary examples of depravity or excellence.

First Ground: If he published *historically* what others said, he is not liable.

One more privilege of the historian, which the Attorney General has not named, but to which his principles extend, it is now my duty to claim on behalf of my client; I mean the right of *republishing, historically*, those documents, whatever their original malignity may be, which display the character and unfold the intentions of governments, or factions, or individuals. I think my learned friend will not deny that a historical compiler may innocently republish in England the most insolent and outrageous declaration of war ever published against his Majesty by a foreign government. The intention of the original author was to vilify and degrade his Majesty's government; but the intention of the compiler is only to gratify curiosity, or, perhaps, to rouse just indignation against the calumniator whose production he republishes. His intention is not libelous — his republication is therefore not a libel. Suppose this to be the case with Mr. Peltier. Suppose him to have republished libels with a merely historical intention. In that case it can not be pretended that he is more a libeler than my learned friend, Mr. Abbott [junior counsel for the Crown, afterward Lord Tenterden], who read these supposed libels to you when he opened the pleadings. Mr. Abbott republished them to you, that you might know and judge of them—Mr. Peltier, on the supposition I have made, also republished them, that the public might know and judge of them.

His paper was designed to expose the factions in France, and to hold forth their language and feelings.

You already know that the general plan of Mr. Peltier's publication was to give a picture of the cabals and intrigues, of the hopes and projects of French factions. It is undoubtedly a natural and necessary part of this plan to republish all the serious and ludicrous pieces which these factions circulate against each other. The ode ascribed to Chenier or Ginguené I do really believe to have been written at Paris, to have been circulated there, to have been there attributed to some one of these writers, to have been sent to England as their work, and as such to have been republished by Mr. Peltier. But I am not sure that I have evidence to convince you of the truth of this. Suppose that I have not; will my learned friend say that my client must necessarily be convicted? I, on the contrary, contend that it is for my learned friend to show that it is not a historical republication. Such it professes to be, and that profession it is for him to disprove. The profession may indeed be "a mask;" but it is for my friend to pluck off the mask, and expose the libeler, before he calls upon you for a verdict of guilty.

Such an exposure has always been permitted in England.

If the general lawfulness of such republications be denied, then I must ask Mr. Attorney General to account for the long impunity which English newspapers have enjoyed. I must request him to tell you why they have been suffered to republish all the atrocious, official and unofficial libels which have been published against his Majesty for the last ten years, by the Brissots, the Marats, the Dantons, the Robespierres, the Barreres, the Talliens, the Reubells, the Merlins, the Barrases, and all that long line of bloody tyrants who oppressed their own country and insulted every other which they had not the power to rob. What must be the answer? That the English publishers were either innocent, if their motive was to gratify curiosity, or praiseworthy, if their intention was to rouse indignation against the calumniators of their country. If any other answer be made, I must remind my friend of a most sacred part of his duty—the duty of protecting the honest fame of those who are absent in the service of their country. Within these few days we have seen, in every newspaper in England, a publication, called the Report of Colonel Sebastiani, in which a gallant British officer [General Stuart] is charged with writing letters to procure assassination. The publishers of that infamous report are not, and will not be prosecuted, because their intention is not to libel General Stuart. On any other principle, why have all our newspapers been suffered to circulate that most atrocious of all libels against the King and people of England, which purports to be translated from the Moniteur of the ninth of August, 1802—a libel against a Prince who has passed through a factious and stormy reign of forty-three years, without a single imputation on his personal character; against a people who have passed through the severest trials of national virtue with unimpaired glory—who alone in the world can boast of mutinies without murder, of triumphant mobs without massacre, of bloodless revolutions, and of civil wars unstained by a single assassination. That most impudent and malignant libel which charges such a King of such a people, not only with having hired assassins, but with being so shameless, so lost to all sense of character, as to have bestowed on these assassins, if their murderous projects had succeeded, the highest badges of public honor, the rewards reserved for statesmen and heroes—the order of the Garter—the order which was founded by the heroes of Cressy and Poitiers—the garter which was worn by Henry the Great and by Gustavus Adolphus, which might now be worn by the hero who, on the shores of Syria [Sir Sydney Smith]—the ancient theater of English chivalry—has revived the renown of English valor and of English humanity—that unsullied garter which a detestable libeler dares to say is to be paid as the price of murder.

If I had now to defend an English publisher for the republication of that abominable libel, what must I have said in his defense? I must have told you that it was originally published by the French government in their official gazette; that it was republished by the English editor to gratify the natural curiosity, perhaps to rouse the just resentment of his English readers. I should have contended, and, I trust, with success, that his republication of a libel was not libelous; that it was lawful, that it was laudable. All that would be important, at least all that would be essential in such a defense, I now state to you on behalf of Mr. Peltier; and if an English newspaper may safely republish the libels of the French government against his Majesty, I shall leave you to judge whether Mr. Peltier, in similar circumstances, may not with equal safety republish the libels of Chenier against the First Consul. On the one hand, you have the assurances of Mr. Peltier in the context that this ode is merely a republication—you have also the general plan of his work, with which such a republication is perfectly consistent. On the other hand, you have only the suspicions of Mr. Attorney General that this ode is an original production of the defendant.

Second Ground: If he wrote *satirically* to expose the principles of French Jacobins, he is not liable.

But supposing that you should think it his production, and that you should also think it a libel, even in that event, which I can not anticipate, I am not left without a defense. The question will still be open, "Is it a libel on Bonaparte, or is it a libel on Chenier or Ginguené?" This is not an information for a libel on Chenier; and if you should think that this ode was produced by Mr. Peltier, and ascribed by him to Chenier, for the sake of covering that writer with the odium of Jacobinism, the defendant is entitled to your verdict of not guilty. Or if you should believe that it is ascribed to Jacobinical writers for the sake of *satirizing* a French Jacobinical faction, you must also, in that case, acquit him. Butler puts seditious and immoral language into the mouth of rebels and fanatics; but Hudibras is not for that reason a libel on morality or government. Swift, in the most exquisite piece of irony in the world (his argument against the abolition of Christianity), uses the language of those shallow, atheistical coxcombs whom his satire was intended to scourge. The scheme of his irony required some levity and even some profaneness of language. But nobody was ever so dull as to doubt whether Swift meant to satirize Atheism or religion. In the same manner, Mr. Peltier, when he wrote a satire on French Jacobinism, was compelled to ascribe to Jacobins a Jacobinical hatred of government. He was obliged, by dramatic propriety, to put into their mouths those anarchical maxims which are complained of in his ode. But it will be said, these incitements to insurrection are here directed against the authority of Bonaparte. This proves nothing, because they must have been so directed, if the ode were a satire on Jacobinism. French Jacobins must inveigh against Bonaparte, because he exercises the powers of government. The satirist who attacks them must transcribe their sentiments and adopt their language.

When writing an ode in the name of Chenier, he *must* express the sentiments of a Jacobin.

I do not mean to say, gentlemen, that Mr. Peltier feels any affection, or professes any allegiance to Bonaparte. If I were to say so, he would disown me. He would disdain to purchase an acquittal by the profession of sentiments which he disclaims and abhors. Not to love Bonaparte is no crime. The question is not whether Mr. Peltier loves or hates the First Consul, but whether he has put revolutionary language into the mouth of Jacobins with a view to paint their incorrigible turbulence, and to exhibit the fruits of Jacobinical revolutions to the detestation of mankind.

Now, gentlemen, we can not give a probable answer to this question without previously examining two or three questions, on which the answer to the first must very much depend. Is there a faction in France which breathes the spirit, and is likely to employ the language of this ode? Does it perfectly accord with their character and views? Is it utterly irreconcilable with the feelings, opinions, and wishes of Mr. Peltier? If these questions can be answered in the affirmative, then I think you must agree with me that Mr. Peltier does not in this ode speak his own sentiments, that he does not here vent his own resentment against Bonaparte; but that he personates a Jacobin, and adopts his language for the sake of satirizing his principles.

Proof that he spoke not his own feelings, but those of a Jacobin.

Line of argument.

These questions, gentlemen, lead me to those political discussions which, generally speaking, are in a court of justice odious and disgusting. Here, however, they are necessary, and I shall consider them only as far as the necessities of this cause require.

Gentlemen, the French Revolution—I must pause after I have uttered words which present such an overwhelming idea. But I have not now to engage in an enterprise so far beyond my force as that of examining and judging that tremendous Revolution. I have only to consider the character of the factions which it must have left behind it.[9]

(a) French Revolution, and origin of Jacobinism.

The French Revolution began with great and fatal errors. These errors produced atrocious crimes. A mild and feeble monarchy was succeeded by bloody anarchy, which very shortly gave birth to military despotism. France, in a few years, described the whole circle of human society.

All this was in the order of nature. When every principle of authority and civil discipline, when every principle which enables some men to command, and disposes others to obey, was extirpated from the mind by atrocious theories, and still more atrocious examples; when every old institution was trampled down with contumely, and every new institution covered in its cradle with blood; when the principle of property itself, the sheet-anchor of society, was annihilated; when in the persons of the new possessors, whom the poverty of language obliges us to call proprietors, it was contaminated in its source by robbery and murder, and it became separated from that education and those manners, from that general presumption of superior knowledge and more scrupulous probity which form its only liberal titles to respect; when the people were taught to despise every thing old, and compelled to detest every thing new, there remained only one principle strong enough to hold society together, a principle utterly incompatible, indeed, with liberty and unfriendly to civilization itself, a tyrannical and barbarous principle; but in that miserable condition of human affairs, a refuge from still more intolerable evils. I mean the principle of military power which gains strength from that confusion and bloodshed in which all the other elements of society are dissolved, and which, in these terrible extremities, is the cement that preserves it from total destruction.

The crimes of the Revolution prepared the way for a military despotism.

Under such circumstances, Bonaparte usurped the supreme power in France. I say *usurped*, because an illegal assumption of power is a usurpation. But usurpation in its strongest moral sense, is scarcely applicable to a period of lawless and savage anarchy. The guilt of military usurpation, in truth, belongs to the author of those confusions which sooner or later give birth to such a usurpation.

Bonaparte's usurpation of that despotism.

Thus, to use the words of the historian: "By recent as well as all ancient example, it became evident that illegal violence, with whatever pretenses it may be covered, and whatever object it may pursue, must inevitably end at last in the arbitrary and despotic government of a single person."[10] But though the government of Bonaparte has silenced the revolutionary factions, it has not and it can not have extinguished them. No human power could reimpress upon the minds of men all those sentiments and opinions which the sophistry and anarchy of fourteen years had obliterated. A faction must exist which breathes the spirit of the ode now before you.

But the Jacobin spirit still remains.

It is, I know, not the spirit of the quiet and

[9] As Mr. Mackintosh had written in favor of the French Revolution at its early stages, and changed his views as he saw its progress and inevitable tendency, he is throughout this speech the more explicit in expressing his abhorrence of its principles and its results.

[10] Hume's History of England, vol. vii., p. 220.

submissive majority of the French people. They have always rather suffered than acted in the Revolution. Completely exhausted by the calamities through which they have passed, they yield to any power which gives them repose. There is, indeed, a degree of oppression which rouses men to resistance; but there is another and a greater, which wholly subdues and unmans them. It is remarkable that Robespierre himself was safe till he attacked his own accomplices. The spirit of men of virtue was broken and there was no vigor of character left to destroy him, but in those daring ruffians who were the sharers of his tyranny.

Not among the common people who have quietly submitted.

As for the wretched populace who were made the blind and senseless instrument of so many crimes, whose frenzy can now be reviewed by a good mind with scarce any moral sentiment but that of compassion; that miserable multitude of beings, scarcely human, have already fallen into a brutish forgetfulness of the very atrocities which they themselves perpetrated. They have already forgotten all the acts of their drunken fury. If you ask one of them, Who destroyed that magnificent monument of religion and art? or who perpetrated that massacre? they stupidly answer, the Jacobins! though he who gives the answer was probably one of these Jacobins himself; so that a traveler, ignorant of French history, might suppose the Jacobins to be the name of some Tartar horde who, after laying waste France for ten years, were at last expelled by the native inhabitants. They have passed from senseless rage to stupid quiet. Their delirium is followed by lethargy.

They are stupidly ignorant on the subject,

In a word, gentlemen, the great body of the people of France have been severely trained in those convulsions and proscriptions which are the school of slavery. They are capable of no mutinous, and even of no bold and manly political sentiments. And if this ode professed to paint their opinions, it would be a most unfaithful picture. But it is otherwise with those who have been the actors and leaders in the scene of blood. It is otherwise with the numerous agents of the most indefatigable, searching, multiform, and omnipresent tyranny that ever existed, which pervaded every class of society which had ministers and victims in every village in France.

and trained to subjection.

Some of them, indeed, the basest of the race, the sophists, the rhetors, the poet-laureates of murder, who were cruel only from cowardice and calculating selfishness, are perfectly willing to transfer their venal pens to any government that does not disdain their infamous support. These men, Republicans from servility, who published rhetorical panegyrics on massacre, and who reduced plunder to a system of ethics, are as ready to preach slavery as anarchy. But the more daring, I had almost said, the more respectable ruffians, can not so easily bend their heads under the yoke. These fierce spirits have not lost

Some, especially literary men, have sold their services to the government.

But others still retain the fiercest spirit of Jacobinism.

"The unconquerable will,
And study of revenge, immortal hate."[11]

They leave the luxuries of servitude to the mean and dastardly hypocrites, to the Belials and Mammons of the infernal faction. They pursue their old end of tyranny under their old pretext of liberty. The recollection of their unbounded power renders every inferior condition irksome and vapid; and their former atrocities form, if I may so speak, a sort of moral destiny which irresistibly impels them to the perpetration of new crimes. They have no place left for penitence on earth. They labor under the most awful proscription of opinion that ever was pronounced against human beings. They have cut down every bridge by which they could retreat into the society of men. Awakened from their dreams of Democracy, the noise subsided that deafened their ears to the voice of humanity; the film fallen from their eyes which hid from them the blackness of their own deeds; haunted by the memory of their inexpiable guilt; condemned daily to look on the faces of those whom their hands made widows and orphans, they are goaded and scourged by these *real* furies, and hurried into the tumult of new crimes, which will drown the cries of remorse, or, if they be too depraved for remorse, will silence the curses of mankind.[12] Tyrannical power is their only refuge from the just vengeance of their fellow-creatures. Murder is their only means of usurping power. They have no taste, no occupation, no pursuit but power and blood. If their hands are tied, they must at least have the luxury of murderous projects. They have drunk too deeply of human blood ever to relinquish their cannibal appetite.

Such a faction exists in France. It is numerous; it is powerful; and it has a principle of fidelity stronger than any that ever held together a society. *They are banded together by despair of forgiveness, by the unanimous detestation of mankind.* They are now contained by a severe and stern government. But they still meditate the renewal of insurrection and massacre; and they are prepared to renew the worst and most atrocious of their crimes, that crime against posterity and against human nature itself, that crime of which the latest generations of mankind may feel the fatal consequences—the crime of degrading and prostituting the sacred name of liberty.[13]

Their number great in France.

---

[11] Milton's Paradise Lost, book ii.

[12] The furies in ancient mythology were considered as "hunters of men," who pursued the guilty as they fled before them, whether into retirement or the crowded scenes of life, and inflicted upon them the just punishment of their crimes.

[13] There is a depth of thought, a power of combination, and a glow of eloquence in this description of the French Jacobins, which Burke alone could have equaled. There is also a startling air of paradox in saying that these faithless villains were united by "a principle of fidelity stronger than any that ever held a society together." The thought flashes across the mind, What can that principle be? and the next sentence gives a complete answer: "They

They are more respectable than their fellows who have joined the government.

I must own, that however paradoxical it may appear, I should almost think not worse, but more meanly of them if it were otherwise. I must then think them destitute of that which I will not call courage, because that is the name of a virtue; but of that ferocious energy which alone rescues ruffians from contempt. If they were destitute of that which is the heroism of murderers, they would be the lowest as well as the most abominable of beings.

It is impossible to conceive any thing more despicable than wretches who, after hectoring and bullying over their meek and blameless sovereign and his defenseless family, whom they kept so long in a dungeon trembling for their existence—whom they put to death by a slow torture of three years, after playing the Republican and the tyrannicide to women and children, become the supple and fawning slaves of the first government that knows how to wield the scourge with a firm hand.

In no sense are they true Republicans.

I have used the word Republican because it is the name by which this atrocious faction describes itself. The assumption of that name is one of their crimes. They are no more Republicans than Royalists. They are the common enemies of all human society. God forbid that by the use of that word I should be supposed to reflect on the members of those respectable Republican communities which did exist in Europe before the French Revolution. That Revolution has spared many monarchies, but it has spared no republic within the sphere of its destructive energy. One republic only now exists in the world—a republic of English blood, which was originally composed of Republican societies, under the protection of a monarchy, which had, therefore, no great and perilous change in their internal constitution to effect; and of which, I speak it with pleasure and pride, the inhabitants, even in the convulsions of a most deplorable separation, displayed the humanity as well as valor which, I trust I may say, they inherited from their forefathers.

Nor does a Republican government seem adapted to the old monarchies of Europe.

Nor do I mean by the use of the word "Republican" to confound this execrable faction with all those who, in the liberty of private speculation, may prefer a Republican form of government. I own that, after much reflection, I am not able to conceive an error more gross than that of those who believe in the possibility of erecting a republic in any of the old monarchical countries of Europe, who believe that in such countries an elective supreme magistracy can produce any thing but a succession of stern tyrannies and bloody civil wars. It is a supposition which is belied by all experience, and which betrays the greatest ignorance of the first principles of the constitution of society. It is an error which has a false appearance of superiority over vulgar prejudice; it is, therefore, too apt to be attended with the most criminal rashness and presumption, and too easy to be inflamed into the most immoral and anti-social fanaticism. But as long as it remains a mere quiescent error, it is not the proper subject of moral disapprobation.

But such Jacobins exist in France, having exactly the feelings of the ode written in the name of Chenier.

If then, gentlemen, such a faction, falsely calling itself Republican, exists in France, let us consider whether this ode speaks their sentiments, describes their character, agrees with their views. Trying it by the principle I have stated, I think you will have no difficulty in concluding that it is agreeable to the general plan of this publication to give a historical and satirical view of the Brutuses and brutes of the republic—of those who assumed and disgraced the name of Brutus,[14] and who, under that name, sat as judges in their mock tribunals, with pistols in their girdles, to anticipate the office of the executioner on those unfortunate men whom they treated as rebels, for resistance to Robespierre and Couthon.

(b) These feelings have nothing in common with those of Mr. Peltier.

I now come to show you that this ode can not represent the opinions of Mr. Peltier. He is a French Royalist. He has devoted his talents to the cause of his King. For that cause he has sacrificed his fortune and hazarded his life. For that cause he is proscribed and exiled from his country. I could easily conceive powerful topics of Royalist invective against Bonaparte; and if Mr. Peltier had called upon Frenchmen by the memory of St. Louis and Henry the Great, by the memory of that illustrious family which reigned over them for seven centuries, and with whom all their martial renown and literary glory are so closely connected; if he had adjured them by the spotless name of that Louis XVI., the martyr of his love for his people, which scarce a man in France can now pronounce but in the tone of pity and veneration; if he had *thus* called upon them to change their useless regret

---

are banded together by despair of forgiveness, by the unanimous detestation of mankind." Demosthenes sometimes uses paradox to rouse the attention of his hearers, but he has no instance of it equal to this.

Madame De Stäel, in her "Ten Years of Exile," thus speaks of this passage. "It was during this stormy period of my existence that I received the speech of Mr. Mackintosh; and there read his description of a *Jacobin*, who had made himself an object of terror during the Revolution to children, women, and old men, and who was now bending himself double under the rod of the Corsican, who tears from him, even to the last atom, that liberty for which he pretended to have taken arms. This *morceau* of the finest eloquence touched me to my very soul; it is the privilege of superior writers sometimes unwittingly to solace the unfortunate in all countries and at all times. France was in a state of such complete silence around me, that this voice, which suddenly responded to my soul, seemed to me to come down from heaven—*it came from a land of liberty!*"

She afterward translated the whole speech into French, and thus made it widely known on the Continent.

[14] Citizen *Brutus*, president of the Military Commission, at Marseilles, in January, 1794.

and their barren pity into generous and active indignation; if he had reproached the conquerors of Europe with the disgrace of being the slaves of an upstart stranger; if he had brought before their minds the contrast between their country under her ancient monarch—the source and model of refinement in manners and taste—and since their expulsion the scourge and the opprobrium of humanity; if he had exhorted them to drive out their ignoble tyrants and to restore their native sovereign; I should then have recognized the voice of a Royalist. I should have recognized language that must have flowed from the heart of Mr. Peltier, and I should have been compelled to acknowledge that it was pointed against Bonaparte.

These, or such as these, must have been the topics of a Royalist, if he had published an invective against the First Consul. But instead of these or similar topics, what have we in this ode? On the supposition that it is the invective of a Royalist, how is it to be reconciled to common sense? What purpose is it to serve? To whom is it addressed? To what interests does it appeal? What passions is it to rouse? If it be addressed to Royalists, then I request, gentlemen, that you will carefully read it, and tell me whether, on that supposition, it can be any thing but the ravings of insanity, and whether a commission of lunacy be not a proceeding more fitted to the author's case than a conviction for a libel. On that supposition, I ask you whether it does not amount in substance to such an address as the following? "Frenchmen, Royalists, I do not call upon you to avenge the murder of your innocent Sovereign, the butchery of your relations and friends, the disgrace and oppression of your country! I call upon you by the hereditary right of Barras, transmitted through a long series of ages, by the beneficent government of Merlin and Reubell, those worthy successors of Charlemagne, whose authority was as mild as it was lawful—I call upon you to revenge on Bonaparte the despotism of that Directory who condemned the far greater part of yourselves to beggary and exile, who covered France with Bastiles and scaffolds; who doomed the most respectable remaining members of their community—the Pichegrues, the Barbe Marbois, the Barthélemis—to a lingering death in the pestilential wilds of Guiana. I call upon you to avenge on Bonaparte the cause of those councils of five hundred or of two hundred, of elders or of youngsters, those disgusting and nauseous mockeries of representative assemblies—those miserable councils which sycophant sophists had converted into machines for fabricating decrees of proscription and confiscation, which not only proscribed unborn thousands, but, by a refinement and innovation in rapine, visited the sins of the children upon the fathers, and beggared parents, not for the offenses, but for the misfortunes of their sons. I call upon you to restore this Directory and these councils, and all this horrible profanation of the name of a republic, and to punish those who delivered you from them. I exhort you to reverence the den of these banditti as 'the sanctuary of the laws,' and to lament the day in which this intolerable nuisance was abated as 'an unfortunate day.' Last of all, I exhort you once more to follow that deplorable chimera—the first lure that led you to destruction—the sovereignty of the people—though I know, and you have bitterly felt, that you never were so much slaves in fact as since you have been sovereigns in theory!"

The sentiments of that ode would be nonsense in the mouth of Mr. Peltier as a Royalist.

Let me ask, Mr. Attorney General, whether, upon his supposition, I have not given you a faithful translation of this ode; and I think I may safely repeat that if this be the language of a Royalist addressed to Royalists, it must be the production of a lunatic. But on my supposition, every thing is natural and consistent. You have the sentiments and language of a Jacobin. It is therefore *probable*, if you take it as a historical republication of a Jacobin piece. It is *just*, if you take it as a satirical representation of Jacobin opinions and projects.

Equally nonsensical if they are supposed to take a Jacobin dress to promote the designs of a Royalist.

Perhaps it will be said that this is the production of a Royalist writer, who assumes a Republican *disguise* to serve Royalist purposes; but if my learned friend chooses that supposition, I think an equal absurdity returns upon him in another shape. We must, then, suppose it to be intended to excite Republican discontent and insurrection against Bonaparte. It must, then, be taken as addressed to Republicans. Would Mr. Peltier in that case have disclosed his name as the publisher? Would he not much rather have circulated the ode in the name of Chenier, without prefixing his own, which was more than sufficient to warn his Jacobinical readers against all his counsels and exhortations. If he had circulated it under the name of Chenier only, he would, indeed, have hung out Republican colors; but by prefixing his own, he appears without disguise. You must suppose him then to say: "Republicans! I, your mortal enemy for fourteen years, whom you have robbed of his all, whom you have forbidden to revisit his country under pain of death, who, from the beginning of the Revolution, unceasingly poured ridicule upon your follies, and exposed your crimes to detestation, who in the cause of my unhappy Sovereign braved your daggers for three years, and who escaped almost by miracle from your assassins in September, who has since been constantly employed in warning other nations by your example, and in collecting the evidence upon which history will pronounce your condemnation; I, who at this moment deliberately choose exile and honorable poverty, rather than give the slightest mark of external compliance with your abominable institutions; I, your most irreconcilable and indefatigable enemy, offer you counsel which you know can only be a snare into which I expect you to fall, though by the mere publication of my name I have sufficiently forewarned you that I can have no aim but that of your destruction."

I ask you again, gentlemen, is this common sense? Is it not as clear, from the name of the author, that it is not addressed to Jacobins, as, from the contents of the publication, that it is not addressed to Royalists? It may be the genuine work of Chenier, for the topics are such as he would employ. It may be a satire on Jacobinism, for the language is well adapted to such a composition. But it can not be a Royalist's invective against Bonaparte, intended by him to stir up either Royalists or Republicans to the destruction of the First Consul.

The ode was, therefore, either written by Chenier or designed to expose his sentiment.

I can not conceive it to be necessary that I should minutely examine this poem to confirm my construction. There are one or two passages on which I shall make a few observations. The first is the contrast between the state of England and that of France, of which an ingenious friend has favored me with a translation, which I shall take the liberty of reading to you.[15]

Comments on particular passages.

Her glorious fabric England rears
  On law's fixed base alone;
Law's guardian pow'r while each reveres,
England! thy people's freedom fears
  No danger from the Throne.

For there, before the almighty Law,
High birth, high place, with pious awe,
  In reverend homage bend:
There man's free spirit, unconstrain'd
Exults, in man's best rights maintain'd.
Rights, which by ancient valor gain'd,
  From age to age descend.

Britons, by no base fear dismay'd,
  May power's worst acts arraign:
Does tyrant force their rights invade?
They call on Law's impartial aid,
  Nor call that aid in vain.

Hence, of her sacred charter proud,
With every earthly good endow'd,
  O'er subject seas unfurl'd,
Britannia waves her standard wide,
Hence, sees her freighted navies ride
Up wealthy Thames' majestic tide,
  The wonder of the world.

Here, at first sight, you may perhaps think that the consistency of the Jacobin character is not supported, that the Republican disguise is thrown off, that the Royalist stands unmasked before you; but, on more consideration, you will find that such an inference would be too hasty. The leaders of the Revolution are now reduced to envy that British Constitution which, in the infatuation of their presumptuous ignorance, they once rejected with scorn. They are now slaves, as they themselves confess, because twelve years ago they did not believe Englishmen to be free. They can not but see that England is the only popular government in Europe, and they are compelled to pay a reluctant homage to the justice of English principles. The praise of England is too striking a satire on their own government to escape them; and I may accordingly venture to appeal to all those who know any thing of the political circles of Paris, whether such contrasts between France and England as that which I have read to you be not the most favorite topics of the opponents of Bonaparte. But in the very next stanza,

Cependant, encore affligée
Par l'odieuse hérédité,
Londres de titres surchargée,
Londres n'a pas *l'Egalité*.[16]

You see, that though they are forced to surrender an unwilling tribute to our liberty, they can not yet renounce all their fantastic and deplorable chimeras. They endeavor to make a compromise between the experience on which they can not shut their eyes, and the wretched systems to which they still cling. Fanaticism is the most incurable of all mental diseases; because in all its forms, religious, philosophical, or political, it is distinguished by a sort of mad contempt for experience, which alone can correct the errors of practical judgment. And these democratical fanatics still speak of the odious principle of "hereditary government." They still complain that we have not "equality." They know not that this odious principle of inheritance is our bulwark against tyranny; that if we had their pretended equality, we should soon cease to be the objects of their envy. These are the sentiments which you would naturally expect from half-cured lunatics. But once more I ask you, whether they can be the sentiments of Mr. Peltier? Would he complain that we have too much monarchy, or too much of what they call aristocracy? If he has any prejudices against the English government, must they not be of an entirely opposite kind?

I have only one observation more to make on this poem. It relates to the passage which is supposed to be an incitement to assassination.[17] In my way of considering the subject, Mr. Peltier is not answerable for that passage, whatever its demerits may be. It is put into the mouth of a Jacobin; and it will not, I think, be affirmed that if it were an incitement to assassinate, it would be very unsuitable to his character. Experience, and very recent experience, has abundantly proved how widely the French Revolution has blackened men's imaginations, what a daring and desperate cast it has given to their characters, how much it has made them regard the most extravagant projects of guilt

Comments on the part supposed to recommend the assassination of Bonaparte.

[15] We learn from Mr. Mackintosh's son that Mr. Canning was the author of this beautiful translation.

[16] A literal translation affords the best means of judging in this case, and such a translation will, therefore be given—"London, still suffering under the evils of hereditary rank, wealth, &c.; London, burdened with titles [of nobility, &c.], *has no equality!*"

[17] The words were these, alluding to the death of Cesar by the hand of Brutus:

"Rome, dans ce revers funeste,
Pour te venger au moins il reste
Un poignard aux derniers Romains."

Rome, in this sad reverse, there remains, at least, a dagger to avenge thee among the last Romans.

as easy and ordinary expedients; and to what a horrible extent it has familiarized their minds to crimes which before were only known among civilized nations by the history of barbarous times, or as the subject of poetical fiction. But, thank God, gentlemen, we in England have not learned to charge any man with inciting assassination, not even a member of that atrocious sect who have revived political assassination in Christendom, except when we are compelled to do so by irresistible evidence. Where is that evidence here? In general, it is immoral, because indecent to speak with levity, still more to anticipate with pleasure, the destruction of any human being. But between this immorality and the horrible crime of inciting to assassination, there is a wide interval indeed. The real or supposed author of this ode gives you to understand that he would hear with no great sorrow of the destruction of the First Consul. But surely the publication of that sentiment is very different from an exhortation to assassinate.

But, says my learned friend, why is the example of Brutus celebrated? Why are the French reproached with their baseness in not copying that example? Gentlemen, I have no judgment to give on the act of Marcus Brutus. I rejoice that I have not. I should not dare to condemn the acts of brave and virtuous men in extraordinary and terrible circumstances, and which have been, as it were, consecrated by the veneration of so many ages. Still less should I dare to weaken the authority of the most sacred rules of duty by praises which would be immoral, even if the acts themselves were in some measure justified by the awful circumstances under which they were done. I am not, in the words of Mr. Burke, the panegyrist of "those instances of doubtful public spirit at which morality is perplexed, reason is staggered, and from which affrighted nature recoils."

But whatever we may think of the act of Brutus, surely my learned friend will not contend that every allusion to it, every panegyric on it which has appeared for eighteen centuries, in prose and verse, is an incitement to assassination. From the *Conspicuæ Divina Phillipica Famæ*, down to the last school-boy declamation, he will find scarce a work of literature without such allusions, and not very many without such panegyrics. I must say that he has construed this ode more like an Attorney General than a critic in poetry. According to his construction, almost every fine writer in our language is a preacher of murder.[18]

Comment on the lines ascribed to a Dutch patriot.

Having said so much on the first of these supposed libels, I shall be very short on the two that remain—the verses ascribed to a Dutch patriot, and the parody of the speech of Lepidus. In the first of these, the piercing eye of Mr. Attorney General has again discovered an incitement to assassinate—the most learned incitement to assassinate that ever was addressed to such ignorant ruffians as are most likely to be employed for such nefarious purposes![19] An obscure allusion to an obscure and perhaps fabulous part of Roman history, to the supposed murder of Romulus, about which none of us know any thing, and of which the Jacobins of Paris and Amsterdam probably never heard. But the *apotheosis!* Here my learned friend has a little forgotten himself. He seems to argue as if apotheosis always presupposed death. But he must know that Augustus, and even Tiberius and Nero, were deified during their lives, and he can not have forgotten the terms in which one of the court poets of Augustus speaks of his master's divinity:

——Præsens divus habebitur
Augustus adjectis Britannis
Imperio.[20]

If any modern rival of Augustus should choose that path to Olympus,[21] I think he will find it more steep and rugged than that by which Pollux and Hercules climbed to the ethereal towers, and that he must be content with purpling his lips with Burgundy on earth, as he has very little chance of purpling them with nectar among the gods.

They express only a wish for Bonaparte's death, not for his assassination.

The utmost that can seriously be made of this passage is, that it is a wish for a man's death. I repeat that I do not contend for the decency of publicly declaring such wishes, or even for the propriety of entertaining them; but the distance between

[18] The quotation above is from the tenth satire of Juvenal, line 125.

Divine Phillipic of illustrious fame.

The poet refers to the second Oration of Cicero against Anthony, containing the well-known passage, "Cæsare interfecto statim cruentum alte extollens Marcus Brutus pugionem, Ciceronem nominatim exclamavit, atque ei recuperatam libertatem est gratulatus."

Akenside has given a free translation of the words in his celebrated lines on moral sublimity.

'Look then abroad through nature, to the range
Of planets, suns, and adamantine spheres
Wheeling unshaken through the void immense;
And speak, O man! does this capacious scene
With half that kindling majesty dilate
Thy strong conception, as when *Brutus rose*
Refulgent from the stroke of Cæsar's fate,
Amid the crowd of patriots; and his arm
Aloft extending, like eternal Jove
When guilt brings down the thunder, call'd aloud
On TULLY'S *name, and shook his crimson steel,*
And bade the Father of his Country hail!
For lo! the tyrant prostrate on the dust,
And Rome again is free!

Pleasures of the Imagination, Book i.

[19] The passage referred to is at the close of a short poem, entitled "*Vœu d'un bon Patriot,*" Wish of a good patriot:

"Enfin (et Romulus nous rappelle la chose)
Je fais vœu—dès demain qu'il ait *l'apothéose!*"
Finally (and Romulus recalls the thing to mind),
I wish that on the morrow he may have his *apotheosis.*

[20] A present GOD, Augustus shall be worshiped,
With Britons added to his wide domains.
Horace, Odes, Book iii., Ode 5.

[21] Alluding to any attempt that Bonaparte might make to invade England.

such a wish and a persuasive to murder is immense. Such a wish for a man's death is very often little more than a strong, though, I admit, not a very decent way of expressing detestation for his character.

But without pursuing this argument any further, I think myself entitled to apply to these verses the same reasoning which I have already applied to the first supposed libel on Bonaparte. If they be the real composition of a pretended Dutch patriot, Mr. Peltier may republish them innocently. If they be a satire on such pretended Dutch patriots, they are not a libel on Bonaparte. Granting, for the sake of argument, that they did entertain a serious exhortation to assassinate, is there any thing in such an exhortation inconsistent with the character of these pretended patriots?

Character of the Dutch Jacobins.

They who were disaffected to the mild and tolerant government of their flourishing country, because it did not exactly square with all their theoretical whimsies; they who revolted from that administration as tyrannical, which made Holland one of the wonders of the world for protected industry, for liberty of action and opinion, and for a prosperity which I may venture to call the greatest victory of man over hostile elements; they who called in the aid of the fiercest tyrants that Europe ever saw, who served in the armies of Robespierre, under the impudent pretext of giving liberty to their country, and who have finally buried in the same grave its liberty, its independence, and perhaps its national existence, they are not men entitled to much tenderness from a political satirist, and he will scarcely violate dramatic propriety if he impute to them any language, however criminal and detestable. They who could not brook the authority of their old, lazy, good-natured government, are not likely to endure with patience the yoke of that stern domination which they have brought upon themselves, and which, as far as relates to them, is only the just punishment of their crimes. They who call in tyrants to establish liberty, who sacrifice the independence of their country under pretense of reforming its internal constitution, are capable of every thing.

More odious than any, except those of Ireland.

I know nothing more odious than their character, unless it be that of those who invoked the aid of the oppressors of Switzerland to be the deliverers of Ireland! Their guilt has, indeed, peculiar aggravations. In the name of liberty, they were willing to surrender their country into the hands of tyrants, the most lawless, faithless, and merciless that ever scourged Europe; who, at the very moment of their negotiation, were covered with the blood of the unhappy Swiss, the martyrs of real independence and of real liberty. Their success would have been the destruction of the only free community remaining in Europe—of England, the only bulwark of the remains of European independence. Their means were the passions of an ignorant and barbarous peasantry, and a civil war, which could not fail to produce all the horrible crimes and horrible retaliations of the last calamity that can befall society—a servile revolt. They sought the worst of ends by the most abominable of means. They labored for the subjugation of the world at the expense of crimes and miseries which men of humanity and conscience would have thought too great a price for the deliverance of mankind.

Parody on the speech of Lepidus.

The last of these supposed libels is the parody on the speech of Lepidus, in the fragments of Sallust. It is certainly a very ingenious and happy parody of an original, attended with some historical obscurity and difficulty, which it is no part of our present business to examine.[22] This parody is said to have been clandestinely placed among the papers of one of the most amiable and respectable men in France, M. Camille Jordan, in order to furnish a pretext for involving that excellent person in a charge of conspiracy. This is said to have been done by a spy of Fouché. Now, gentlemen, I take this to be a satire on Fouché, on his manufacture of plots—on his contrivances for the destruction of innocent and virtuous men—and I should admit it to be a libel on Fouché, if it were possible to libel him. I own that I should like to see Fouché appear as a plaintiff, seeking reparation for his injured character, before any tribunal safe from his fangs, where he had not the power of sending the judges to Guiana or Madagascar. It happens that we know something of the history of M. Fouché from a very credible witness against him—from himself. You will perhaps excuse me for reading to you some passages of his letters in the year 1793, from which you will judge whether any satire can be so severe as the portrait he draws of himself.

Applied to Fouché

Quotations from his letters.

"Convinced that there are no innocent men in this infamous city,[23] but those who are opposed and loaded with irons by the assassins of the people,[24] we are on our guard against the *tears of repentance!* nothing can disarm our severity. They have not yet dared to solicit the repeal of our first decree for the *annihilation of the city of Lyons!* but scarcely any thing has yet been done to carry it into execution." (Pathetic!) "The demolitions are too slow. More rapid means are necessary to republican impatience. The explosion of the mine and the devouring activity of the flames can alone adequately represent the omnipotence of the people." (Unhappy populace, always the pretext, the instrument, and the victim of political crimes!) "Their will can not be checked like that of tyrants. It ought to have the effects of thunder!" The next specimen of this worthy gentleman which I shall give, is in a speech to the Jacobin Club of Paris, on the 21st of De-

[22] This parody seems not to have originated with Peltier, but to have been made in Paris during the Revolution.

[23] The unhappy city of Lyons.

[24] He means the murderers who were condemned to death for their crimes.

cember, 1793, by his worthy colleague in the mission to Lyons, Collot d'Herbois:

"We are accused" (you, gentlemen, will soon see how unjustly) "of being cannibals, men of blood; but it is in counter-revolutionary petitions, hawked about for signature by aristocrats, that this charge is made against us. They examine with the most scrupulous attention how the counter-revolutionists are put to death, and they affect to say that they are not killed at one stroke." (He speaks for himself and his colleague Fouché, and one would suppose that he was going to deny the fact,—but nothing like it.) "Ah! Jacobins, did Chalier[25] die at the first stroke, &c.? A drop of blood poured from generous veins goes to my heart" (humane creature!), "but I have no pity for conspirators." (He, however, proceeds to state a most undeniable proof of his compassion.) "We caused two hundred to be shot at once, and it is charged upon us as a crime!" (Astonishing! that such an act of humanity should be called a crime!) "They do not know that it is a proof of our sensibility! When twenty criminals are guillotined, the last of them dies twenty deaths; but these two hundred conspirators perished at once. They speak of sensibility, *we also are full of sensibility!* The *Jacobins have all the virtues!* They are *compassionate, humane, generous!*" (This is somewhat hard to be understood, but it is perfectly explained by what follows.) "But they reserve these sentiments for the patriots who are their brethren, which the aristocrats never will be."

The only remaining document with which I shall trouble you is a letter from Fouché to his amiable colleague Collot d'Herbois, which, as might be expected in a confidential communication, breathes all the native tenderness of his soul. "Let us be *terrible*, that we may run no risk of being feeble or *cruel*. Let us annihilate in our wrath, at a single blow, all rebels, all conspirators, all traitors" (comprehensive words in his vocabulary), "to spare ourselves the pain, the long agony of punishing like kings!" (Nothing but philanthropy in this worthy man's heart.) "Let us exercise justice after the example of nature. Let us avenge ourselves like a people. Let us strike like the thunder-bolt; and let even the ashes of our enemies disappear from the soil of liberty! Let the perfidious and ferocious English be attacked from every side. Let the whole republic form a volcano to pour devouring lava upon them. May the infamous island which produced these monsters, who no longer belong to humanity, be forever buried under the waves of the ocean! Farewell, my friend! Tears of joy stream from my eyes" (we shall soon see for what), "they deluge my soul."

[Then follows a little postscript, which explains the cause of this excessive joy, so hyperbolical in its language, and which fully justifies the indignation of the humane writer against the "ferocious English," who are so stupid and so cruel as never to have thought of a benevolent massacre, by way of sparing themselves the pain of punishing individual criminals.]

"*We have only one way of celebrating victories. We send this evening two hundred and thirteen rebels to be shot!*"

Such, gentlemen, is M. Fouché, who is said to have procured this parody to be mixed with the papers of my excellent friend, Camille Jordan, to serve as a pretext for his destruction. Fabricated plots are among the most usual means of such tyrants for such purposes; and if Mr. Peltier intended to libel (shall I say?) Fouché by this composition, I can easily understand both the parody and the history of its origin. But if it be directed against Bonaparte to serve Royalist purposes, I must confess myself wholly unable to conceive why Mr. Peltier should have stigmatized his work and deprived it of all authority and power of persuasion, by prefixing to it the infamous name of Fouché.

Comments on the title of Mr. Peltier's paper.

On the same principle, I think one of the observations of my learned friend, on the title of this publication, may be retorted on him. He has called your attention to the title, "L'Ambigu, ou Variétés atroces et amusantes." Now, gentlemen, I must ask whether, had these been Mr. Peltier's own invectives against Bonaparte, he would himself have branded them as "atrocious." But if they be specimens of the opinions and invectives of a French faction, the title is very natural, and the epithets are perfectly intelligible. Indeed, I scarce know a more appropriate title for the whole tragic comedy of the Revolution than that of "atrocious and amusing varieties."

In other parts of his paper he may have been flippant or severe, but he has not been libelous.

My learned friend has made some observations on other parts of this publication, to show the spirit which animates the author, but they do not seem to be very material to the question between us. It is no part of my case that Mr. Peltier has spoken with some unpoliteness, with some flippancy, with more severity than my learned friend may approve, of factions and of administrations in France. Mr. Peltier can not love the Revolution, or any government that has grown out of it and maintains it. The Revolutionists have destroyed his family, they have seized his inheritance, they have beggared, exiled, and proscribed himself. If he did not detest them he would be unworthy of living, and he would be a base hypocrite if he were to conceal his sentiments. But I must again remind you that this is not an information for not sufficiently honoring the French Revolution, for not showing sufficient reverence for the consular government. These are no crimes among us. England is not yet reduced to such an ignominious dependence. Our hearts and consciences are not yet in the bonds of so wretched a slavery. This is an information for a libel on Bonaparte, and if you believe the principal intention of Mr. Peltier to have been to republish the writings or to satirize the character of other individuals, you must acquit him of a libel on the First Consul.

[25] This Chalier was the Marat of Lyons.

Here, gentlemen, I think I might stop, if I had only to consider the defense of Mr. Peltier. I trust that you are already convinced of his innocence. I fear I have exhausted your patience, as I am sure I have very nearly exhausted my own strength. But so much seems to me to depend on your verdict, that I can not forbear from laying before you some considerations of a more general nature.

Part Fourth: Appeal to the examples of former times as showing the sentiments becoming the present crisis.

Believing, as I do, that we are on the eve of a great struggle; that this is only the first battle between reason and power; that you have now in your hands, committed to your trust, the only remains of free discussion in Europe, now confined to this kingdom—addressing you, therefore, as the guardians of the most important interests of mankind; convinced that the unfettered exercise of reason depends more on your present verdict than on any other that was ever delivered by a jury, I can not conclude without bringing before you the sentiments and examples of our ancestors in some of those awful and perilous situations by which Divine Providence has in former ages tried the virtue of the English nation. We are fallen upon times in which it behooves us to strengthen our spirits by the contemplation of great examples of constancy. Let us seek for them in the annals of our forefathers.

(1.) The age of Elizabeth.

The reign of Queen Elizabeth may be considered as the opening of the modern history of England, especially in its connection with the modern system of Europe, which began about that time to assume the form that it preserved till the French Revolution. It was a very memorable period, of which the maxims ought to be engraven on the head and heart of every Englishman. Philip II., at the head of the greatest empire then in the world, was openly aiming at universal domination, and his project was so far from being thought chimerical by the wisest of his cotemporaries that, in the opinion of the great Duke of Sully, he must have been successful, "if, by a most singular combination of circumstances, he had not at the same time been resisted by two such strong heads as those of Henry IV. and Queen Elizabeth." To the most extensive and opulent dominions, the most numerous and disciplined armies, the most renowned captains, the greatest revenue, he added also the most formidable power over opinion. He was the chief of a religious faction, animated by the most atrocious fanaticism, prepared to second his ambition by rebellion, anarchy, and regicide in every Protestant state. Elizabeth was among the first objects of his hostility. That wise and magnanimous Princess placed herself in the front of the battle for the liberties of Europe. Though she had to contend at home with his fanatical faction, which almost occupied Ireland, which divided Scotland, and was not of contemptible strength in England, she aided the oppressed inhabitants of the Netherlands in their just and glorious resistance to his tyranny; she aided Henry the Great in suppressing the abominable rebellion which anarchical principles had excited and Spanish arms had supported in France, and after a long reign of various fortune, in which she preserved her unconquered spirit through great calamities and still greater dangers, she at length broke the strength of the enemy, and reduced his power within such limits as to be compatible with the safety of England and of all Europe. Her only effectual ally was the spirit of her people, and her policy flowed from that magnanimous nature which in the hour of peril teaches better lessons than those of cold reason. Her great heart inspired her with a higher and a nobler wisdom—which disdained to appeal to the low and sordid passions of her people even for the protection of their low and sordid interests, because she knew, or, rather, she felt, that these are effeminate, creeping, cowardly, short-sighted passions, which shrink from conflict even in defense of their own mean objects. In a righteous cause, she roused those generous affections of her people which alone teach boldness, constancy, and foresight, and which are therefore the only safe guardians of the lowest as well as the highest interests of a nation. In her memorable address to her army, when the invasion of the kingdom was threatened by Spain, this woman of heroic spirit disdained to speak to them of their ease and their commerce, and their wealth and their safety. No! She touched another chord—she spoke of their national honor, of their dignity as Englishmen, of "the foul scorn that Parma or Spain *should dare* to invade the borders of her realms." She breathed into them those grand and powerful sentiments which exalt vulgar men into heroes, which led them into the battle of their country, armed with holy and irresistible enthusiasm; which even cover with their shield all the ignoble interests that base calculation and cowardly selfishness tremble to hazard, but shrink from defending.[26] A sort of prophetic instinct, if I may so speak, seems to have revealed to her the importance of that great instrument for rousing and guiding the minds of men, of the effects of which she had no experience, which, since her time, has changed the condition of the world, but which few modern statesmen have thoroughly understood or wisely employed; which is, no doubt, connected with many ridiculous and degrading details, which has produced, and which may again produce terrible mischiefs, but of which the influence must, after all, be considered as the most certain effect and the most efficacious cause of civilization, and which, whether it be a blessing or a curse, is the most powerful engine that a politician can move—I mean the press.

She was the first to avail herself of the press to awaken the spirit of the country.

It is a curious fact that in the year of the Armada, Queen Elizabeth caused to be printed the first gazettes that ever appeared in England; and I own, when I consider that this mode of rousing a national spirit was then absolutely unexampled, that she could have no assurance of

[26] We have but few strains of eloquence in our language more noble or more inspiring for a people like the English than this passage.

its efficacy from the precedents of former times, I am disposed to regard her having recourse to it as one of the most sagacious experiments, one of the greatest discoveries of political genius, one of the most striking anticipations of future experience that we find in history. I mention it to you to justify the opinion that I have ventured to state of the close connection of our national spirit with our press, even our periodical press. I can not quit the reign of Elizabeth without laying before you the maxims of her policy, in the language of the greatest and wisest of men. Lord Bacon, in one part of his discourse on her reign, speaks thus of her support of Holland: "But let me rest upon the honorable and continual aid and relief she hath given to the distressed and desolate people of the Low Countries—a people recommended unto her by ancient confederacy and daily intercourse, by their cause so innocent and their fortune so lamentable!" In another passage of the same discourse, he thus speaks of the general system of her foreign policy as the protector of Europe, in words too remarkable to require any commentary. "Then it is her government, and her government alone, that hath been the sconce and fort of all Europe, which hath let this proud nation from overrunning all. If any state be yet free from his factions erected in the bowels thereof; if there be any state wherein this faction is erected that is not yet fired with civil troubles; if there be any state under his protection that enjoyeth moderate liberty, upon whom he tyrannizeth not, it is the mercy of this renowned Queen that standeth between them and their misfortunes!"

(2.) Succor of the Huguenots in the days of Louis XIV.

The next great conspirator against the rights of men and of nations, against the security and independence of all European states, against every kind and degree of civil and religious liberty, was Louis XIV. In his time the character of the English nation was the more remarkably displayed, because it was counteracted by an apostate and perfidious government. During great part of his reign, you know that the throne of England was filled by princes who deserted the cause of their country and of Europe, who were the accomplices and the tools of the oppressor of the world,[27] who were even so unmanly, so unprincely, so base, as to have sold themselves to his ambition; who were content that he should enslave the Continent, if he enabled them to enslave Great Britain. These princes, traitors to their own royal dignity and to the feelings of the generous people whom they ruled, preferred the condition of the first slave of Louis XIV. to the dignity of the first freemen of England; yet even under these princes, the feelings of the people of this kingdom were displayed, on a most memorable occasion, toward foreign sufferers and foreign oppressors. The Revocation of the Edict of Nantes threw fifty thousand French Protestants on our shores. They were received as I trust the victims of tyranny ever will be in this land, which seems chosen by Providence to be the home of the exile, the refuge of the oppressed. They were welcomed by a people high-spirited as well as humane, who did not insult them by clandestine charity; who did not give alms in secret lest their charity should be detected by the neighboring tyrants! No! They were publicly and nationally welcomed and relieved. They were bid to raise their voice against their oppressor, and to proclaim their wrongs to all mankind. They did so. They were joined in the cry of just indignation by every Englishman worthy of the name. It was a fruitful indignation, which soon produced the successful resistance of Europe to the common enemy. Even then, when Jeffreys disgraced the bench which his Lordship [Lord Ellenborough] now adorns, no refugee was deterred by prosecution for libel from giving vent to his feelings, from arraigning the oppressor in the face of all Europe.

(3.) Aid given to Holland when invaded by the same monarch.

During this ignominious period of our history, a war arose on the Continent, which can not but present itself to the mind on such an occasion as this; the only war that was ever made on the avowed ground of attacking a free press. I speak of the invasion of Holland by Louis XIV. The liberties which the Dutch gazettes had taken in discussing his conduct were the sole cause of this very extraordinary and memorable war, which was of short duration, unprecedented in its avowed principle, and most glorious in its event for the liberties of mankind. That republic, at all times so interesting to Englishmen—in the worst times of both countries our brave enemies; in their best times our most faithful and valuable friends—was then charged with the defense of a free press against the oppressor of Europe, as a sacred trust for the benefit of all generations. They felt the sacredness of the deposit, they felt the dignity of the station in which they were placed, and though deserted by the un-English government of England, they asserted their own ancient character, and drove out the great armies and great captains of the oppressor with defeat and disgrace. Such was the result of the only war hitherto avowedly undertaken to oppress a free country because she allowed the free and public exercise of reason. And may the God of justice and liberty grant that such may ever be the result of wars made by tyrants against the rights of mankind, especially against that right which is the guardian of every other.

(4.) Support of King William in fighting the battle of Europe against Louis XIV.

This war, gentlemen, had the effect of raising up from obscurity the great Prince of Orange, afterward King William III., the deliverer of Holland, the deliverer of England, the deliverer of Europe; the only hero who was distinguished by such a happy union of fortune and virtue that the objects of his ambition were always the same with the interests of humanity; perhaps the only man who devoted the whole of his life exclusively to the service of mankind. This most illustrious

[27] Charles II. and James II. They both received regular pensions from the French Monarch.

benefactor of Europe, this "hero without vanity or passion," as he has been justly and beautifully called by a venerable prelate [Dr. Shipley, Bishop of St. Asaph], who never made a step toward greatness without securing or advancing liberty, who had been made Stadtholder of Holland for the salvation of his own country, was soon after made King of England for the deliverance of ours. When the people of Great Britain had once more a government worthy of them, they returned to the feelings and principles of their ancestors, and resumed their former station and their former duties as protectors of the independence of nations. The people of England, delivered from a government which disgraced, oppressed, and betrayed them, fought under William as their forefathers had fought under Elizabeth, and after an almost uninterrupted struggle of more than twenty years, in which they were often abandoned by fortune, but never by their own constancy and magnanimity, they at length once more defeated those projects of guilty ambition, boundless aggrandizement, and universal domination, which had a second time threatened to overwhelm the whole civilized world. They rescued Europe from being swallowed up in the gulf of extensive empire, which the experience of all times points out as the grave of civilization; where men are driven by violent conquest and military oppression into lethargy and slavishness of heart; where, after their arts have perished with the mental vigor from which they spring, they are plunged by the combined power of effeminacy and ferocity into irreclaimable and hopeless barbarism. Our ancestors established the safety of their own country by providing for that of others, and rebuilt the European system upon such firm foundations that nothing less than the tempest of the French Revolution could have shaken it.

(5.) Bold animadversions of the English press on Louis XIV. in time of peace with France.

This arduous struggle was suspended for a short time by the peace of Ryswick. The interval between that treaty and the war of the succession enables us to judge how our ancestors acted in a very peculiar situation, which requires maxims of policy very different from those which usually govern states. The treaty which they had concluded was in truth and substance only a truce. The ambition and the power of the enemy were such as to render real peace impossible. And it was perfectly obvious that the disputed succession of the Spanish Monarch would soon render it no longer practicable to preserve even the appearance of amity. It was desirable, however, not to provoke the enemy by unseasonable hostility; but it was still more desirable, it was absolutely necessary, to keep up the national jealousy and indignation against him who was soon to be their open enemy. It might naturally have been apprehended that the press might have driven into premature war a Prince who, not long before, had been violently exasperated by the press of another free country. I have looked over the political publications of that time with some care, and I can venture to say that at no period were the system and projects of Louis XIV. animadverted on with more freedom and boldness than during that interval. Our ancestors and the heroic Prince who governed them, did not deem it wise policy to disarm the national mind for the sake of prolonging a truce. They were both too proud and too wise to pay so great a price for so small a benefit.

Increased influence of newspapers on political subjects.

In the course of the eighteenth century, a great change took place in the state of political discussion in this country. I speak of the multiplication of newspapers. I know that newspapers are not very popular in this place, which is, indeed, not very surprising, because they are known here only by their faults. Their publishers come here only to receive the chastisement due to their offenses. With all their faults, I own I can not help feeling some respect for whatever is a proof of the increased curiosity and increased knowledge of mankind; and I can not help thinking that if somewhat more indulgence and consideration were shown for the difficulties of their situation, it might prove one of the best correctives of their faults, by teaching them that self-respect which is the best security for liberal conduct toward others: But however that may be, it is very certain that the multiplication of these channels of popular information has produced a great change in the state of our domestic and foreign politics. At home, it has, in truth, produced a gradual revolution in our government. By increasing the number of those who exercise some sort of judgment on public affairs, it has created a substantial democracy, infinitely more important than those democratical forms which have been the subject of so much contest. So that I may venture to say, England has not only in its forms the most democratical government that ever existed in a great country, but in substance has the most democratical government that ever existed in any country; if the most *substantial* democracy be that state in which the greatest number of men feel an interest and express an opinion upon political questions, and in which the greatest number of judgments and wills concur in influencing public measures.

Increased boldness of their tone as to foreign governments.

The same circumstances gave great additional importance to our discussion of continental politics. That discussion was no longer, as in the preceding century, confined to a few pamphlets, written and read only by men of education and rank, which reached the multitude very slowly and rarely. In newspapers an almost daily appeal was made, directly or indirectly, to the judgment and passions of almost every individual in the kingdom, upon the measures and principles not only of his own country, but of every state in Europe. Under such circumstances, the tone of these publications, in speaking of foreign governments, became a matter of importance. You will excuse me, therefore, if, before I conclude, I remind you of the general nature of their language on one or two very remarkable occasions, and of the boldness with which they arraigned the crimes of powerful sovereigns, without any check from the laws and magistrates of their own country. This toleration, or rather this protection, was too long and uniform to be accidental. I am, indeed, very much mistaken if it be not founded upon a policy which this country can not abandon without sacrificing her liberty and endangering her national existence.

(6.) Denunciation by the English press of those who were engaged in the first partition of Poland.

The first remarkable instance which I shall choose to state of the unpunished and protected boldness of the English press, of the freedom with which they animadverted on the policy of powerful sovereigns, is the partition of Poland in 1772; an act not, perhaps, so horrible in its means, nor so deplorable in its immediate effects, as some other atrocious invasions of national independence which have followed it; but the most abominable in its general tendency and ultimate consequences of any political crime recorded in history, because it was the first practical breach in the system of Europe, the first example of atrocious robbery perpetrated on unoffending countries which have been since so liberally followed, and which has broken down all the barriers of habit and principle which guarded defenseless states. The perpetrators of this atrocious crime were the most powerful sovereigns of the Continent, whose hostility it certainly was not the interest of Great Britain wantonly to incur. They were the most illustrious princes of their age, and some of them were, doubtless, entitled to the highest praise for their domestic administration, as well as for the brilliant qualities which distinguished their characters. But none of these circumstances, no dread of their resentment, no admiration of their talents, no consideration for their rank, silenced the animadversion of the English press. Some of you remember, all of you know, that a loud and unanimous cry of reprobation and execration broke out against them from every part of this kingdom. It was perfectly uninfluenced by any considerations of our own mere national interest, which might perhaps be supposed to be rather favorably affected by that partition. It was not, as in some other countries, the indignation of rival robbers, who were excluded from their share of the prey. It was the moral anger of disinterested spectators against atrocious crimes, the gravest and the most dignified moral principle which the God of justice has implanted in the human heart; that of which the dread is the only restraint on the actions of powerful criminals, and of which the promulgation is the only punishment that can be inflicted on them. It is a restraint which ought not to be weakened. It is a punishment which no good man can desire to mitigate.

That great crime was spoken of as it deserved in England. Robbery was not described by any courtly circumlocutions. Rapine was not called policy; nor was the oppression of an innocent people termed a *mediation* in their domestic differences. No prosecutions, no criminal informations followed the liberty and the boldness of the language then employed. No complaints even appear to have been made from abroad, much less any insolent menaces against the free Constitution which protected the English press. The people of England were too long known throughout Europe for the proudest potentate to expect to silence our press by such means.

Contributions to the Poles after the second partition.

I pass over the second partition of Poland in 1792. You all remember what passed on that occasion, the universal abhorrence expressed by every man and every writer of every party, the succors that were publicly preparing by large bodies of individuals of all parties for the oppressed Poles.

Severe tone of the English press toward the authors of the final dismemberment, though allies of England.

I hasten to the final dismemberment of that unhappy kingdom, which seems to me the most striking example in our history of the habitual, principled, and deeply rooted forbearance of those who administer the law toward political writers. We were engaged in the most extensive, bloody, and dangerous war that this country ever knew; and the parties to the dismemberment of Poland were our allies, and our only powerful and effective allies. We had every motive of policy to court their friendship. Every reason of state seemed to require that we should not permit them to be abused and vilified by English writers. What was the fact? Did any Englishman consider himself at liberty, on account of temporary interests, however urgent, to silence those feelings of humanity and justice which guard the certain and permanent interests of all countries? You all remember that every voice, and every pen, and every press in England were unceasingly employed to brand that abominable robbery. You remember that this was not confined to private writers, but that the same abhorrence was expressed by every member of both Houses of Parliament who was not under the restraints of ministerial reserve. No minister dared even to blame the language of honest indignation which might be very inconvenient to his most important political projects; and I hope I may venture to say that no English assembly would have endured such a sacrifice of eternal justice to any miserable interest of an hour. Did the law-officers of the Crown venture to come into a court of justice to complain of the boldest of the publications of that time? They did not. I do not say that they felt any disposition to do so. I believe that they could not. But I do say that if they had; if they had spoken of the necessity of confining our political writers to cold narrative and unfeeling argument; if they had informed the jury that they did not prosecute history, but invective; that if private writers be at all to blame great princes, it must be with moderation and decorum, the sound heads and honest hearts of an English jury would have confounded such sophistry, and declared by their verdict that moderation of language is a relative term, which varies with the subject to which it is applied; that atrocious crimes are not to be related as calmly and coolly as indifferent or tri-

The same language held in Parliament.

fling events; that if there be a decorum due to exalted rank and authority, there is also a much more sacred decorum due to virtue and to human nature, which would be outraged and trampled under foot by speaking of guilt in a lukewarm language, falsely called moderate.

(7.) Indignant language of the press when the liberties of Switzerland were destroyed by France.

Soon after, gentlemen, there followed an act, in comparison with which all the deeds of rapine and blood perpetrated in the world are innocence itself—the invasion and destruction of Switzerland, that unparalleled scene of guilt and enormity; that unprovoked aggression against an innocent country, which had been the sanctuary of peace and liberty for three centuries; respected as a sort of sacred territory by the fiercest ambition; raised, like its own mountains, beyond the region of the storms which raged around on every side; the only warlike people that never sent forth armies to disturb their neighbors; the only government that ever accumulated treasures without imposing taxes, an innocent treasure, unstained by the tears of the poor, the inviolate patrimony of the commonwealth, which attested the virtue of a long series of magistrates, but which at length caught the eye of the spoiler, and became the fatal occasion of their ruin! Gentlemen, the destruction of such a country, "its cause so innocent, and its fortune so lamentable!" made a deep impression on the people of England. I will ask my learned friend, if we had then been at peace with the French Republic, whether we must have been silent spectators of the foulest crimes that ever blotted the name of humanity! whether we must, like cowards and slaves, have repressed the compassion and indignation with which that horrible scene of tyranny had filled our hearts?[28] Let me suppose, gentlemen, that Aloys Reding, who has displayed in our times the simplicity, magnanimity, and piety of ancient heroes, had, after his glorious struggle, honored this kingdom by choosing it as his refuge; that after performing prodigies of valor at the head of his handful of heroic peasants on the field of Morgarten, where his ancestor, the *Landmann Reding*, had, five hundred years before, defeated the first oppressors of Switzerland, he had selected this country to be his residence, as the chosen abode of liberty, as the ancient and inviolable asylum of the oppressed; would my learned friend have had the boldness to have said to this hero, "that he must hide his tears" (the tears shed by a hero over the ruins of his country!) "lest they might provoke the resentment of *Reubell* or *Rapinat!* that he must smother the sorrow and the anger with which his heart was loaded; that he must breathe his murmurs low, lest they might be overheard by the oppressor!" Would this have been the language of my learned friend? I know that it would not. I know that by such a supposition I have done wrong to his honorable feelings, to his honest English heart. I am sure that he knows as well as I do, that a nation which should *thus* receive the oppressed of other countries would be preparing its own neck for the yoke. He knows the slavery which such a nation would deserve, and must speedily incur. He knows that sympathy with the unmerited sufferings of others, and disinterested anger against their oppressors, are, if I may so speak, the masters which are appointed by Providence to teach us fortitude in the defense of our own rights; that selfishness is a dastardly principle, which betrays its charge and flies from its post; and that those only can defend themselves with valor who are animated by the moral approbation with which they can survey their sentiments toward others, who are ennobled in their own eyes by a consciousness that they are fighting for justice as well as interest; a consciousness which none can feel but those who have felt for the wrongs of their brethren. These are the sentiments which my learned friend would have felt. He would have told the hero. "Your confidence is not deceived; this is still that England, of which the history may, perhaps, have contributed to fill your heart with the heroism of liberty. Every other country of Europe is crouching under the bloody tyrants who destroyed your country. *We* are unchanged; we are still the same people which received with open arms the victims of the tyranny of Philip II. and Louis XIV. We shall not exercise a cowardly and clandestine humanity! Here we are not so dastardly as to rob you of your greatest consolation. Here, protected by a free, brave, and high-minded people, you may give vent to your indignation; you may proclaim the crimes of your tyrants, you may devote them to the execration of mankind; there is still one spot upon earth in which they are abhorred, without being dreaded!"

If during the French Revolution England had been at peace with France, what ought to have been the course of the English press?

I am aware, gentlemen, that I have already abused your indulgence, but I must entreat you to bear with me for a short time longer, to allow me to suppose a case which might have occurred, in which you will see the horrible consequences of enforcing rigorously principles of law, which I can not counteract, against political writers. We might have been at peace with France during the whole of that terrible period which elapsed between August, 1792 and 1794, which has been usually called the reign of Robespierre! The only series of crimes, perhaps, in history, which, in spite of the common disposition to exaggerate extraordinary facts, has been beyond measure underrated in public opinion. I say this, gentlemen, after an investigation, which, I think,

[28] In the spring of 1798, Aloys Reding, here spoken of, met the French army on the field of Morgarten, as chief magistrate of the Canton of Schweitz, and with a handful of men broke their ranks and put them to flight. But he was at last overpowered by numbers, his country subjugated, and himself thrown at first into prison and afterward driven into exile. He was born in 1755 and died in 1818, retaining to the last his hatred of French revolutionary principles, and especially of Bonaparte. Zschokke, in his history of the fall of the democratic Cantons of Switzerland, has thrown a romantic interest around the name of Reding.

entitles me to affirm it with confidence. Men's minds were oppressed by atrocity and the multitude of crimes; their humanity and their indolence took refuge in skepticism from such an overwhelming mass of guilt; and the consequence was, that all these unparalleled enormities, though proved not only with the fullest historical, but with the strictest judicial evidence, were at the time only half believed, and are now scarcely half remembered. When these atrocities were daily perpetrating, of which the greatest part are as little known to the public in general as the campaigns of Genghis Khan, but are still protected from the scrutiny of men by the immensity of those voluminous records of guilt in which they are related, and under the mass of which they will be buried till some historian be found with patience and courage enough to drag them forth into light, for the shame, indeed, but for the instruction of mankind—when these crimes were perpetrating, which had the peculiar malignity, from the pretexts with which they were covered, of making the noblest objects of human pursuit seem odious and detestable; which has almost made the names of liberty, reformation, and humanity synonymous with anarchy, robbery, and murder; which thus threatened not to extinguish every principle of improvement, to arrest the progress of civilized society, and to disinherit future generations of that rich succession, which they were entitled to expect from the knowledge and wisdom of the present, but to destroy the civilization of Europe, which never gave such a proof of its vigor and robustness as in being able to resist their destructive power—when all these horrors were acting in the greatest empire of the Continent, I will ask my learned friend, if we had then been at peace with France, how English writers were to relate them so as to escape the charge of libeling a friendly government?[29]

When Robespierre, in the debates in the National Convention on the mode of murdering their blameless Sovereign, objected to the formal and tedious mode of murder called a trial, and proposed to put him immediately to death, "on the principles of insurrection," because, to doubt the guilt of the King would be to doubt of the innocence of the Convention; and if the King were not a traitor, the Convention must be rebels; would my learned friend have had an English writer state all this with "*decorum and moderation?*" Would he have had an English writer state that though this reasoning was not perfectly agreeable to our national laws, or perhaps to our national prejudices, yet it was not for him to make any observations on the judicial proceedings of foreign states?

When Marat, in the same Convention, called for two hundred and seventy thousand heads, must our English writers have said that the remedy did, indeed, seem to their weak judgment rather severe; but that it was not for them to judge the conduct of so illustrious an assembly as the National Convention, or the suggestions of so enlightened a statesman as M. Marat?

When that Convention resounded with applause at the news of several hundred aged priests being thrown into the Loire, and particularly at the exclamation of Carrier, who communicated the intelligence, "What a revolutionary torrent is the Loire"—when these suggestions and narrations of murder, which have hitherto been only hinted and whispered in the most secret cabals, in the darkest caverns of banditti, were triumphantly uttered, patiently endured, and even loudly applauded by an assembly of seven hundred men, acting in the sight of all Europe, would my learned friend have wished that there had been found in England a single writer so base as to deliberate upon the most safe, decorous, and polite manner of relating all these things to his countrymen?

When Carrier ordered five hundred children under fourteen years of age to be shot, the greater part of whom escaped the fire from their size, when the poor victims ran for protection to the soldiers, and were bayoneted clinging round their knees! *would my friend*—but I can not pursue the strain of interrogation. It is too much. It would be a violence which I can not practice on my own feelings. It would be an outrage to my friend. It would be an insult to humanity. No! Better, ten thousand times better, would it be that every press in the world were burned; that the very use of letters were abolished; that we were returned to the honest ignorance of the rudest times, than that the results of civilization should be made subservient to the purposes of barbarism, than that literature should be employed to teach a toleration for cruelty, to weaken moral hatred for guilt, to deprave and brutalize the human mind. I know that I speak my friend's feelings as well as my own when I say God forbid that the dread of any punishment should ever make any Englishman an accomplice in so corrupting his countrymen, a public teacher of depravity and barbarity!

Mortifying and horrible as the idea is, I must remind you, gentlemen, that even at that time, even under the reign of Robespierre, my learned friend, if he had then been Attorney General, might have been compelled by some most deplorable necessity to have come into this court to ask your verdict against the libelers of Barrère and Collot d'Herbois. Mr. Peltier then employed his talents against the enemies of the human race, as he has uniformly and bravely done. I do not believe that any peace, any political considerations, any fear of punishment would have silenced him. He has shown too much honor, and constancy, and intrepidity, to be shaken by such circumstances as these.

My learned friend might then have been compelled to have filed a criminal information against Mr. Peltier, for "wickedly and maliciously intending to vilify and degrade Maximilian Robespierre, President of the Committee of Public Safety of the French Republic!" He might

[29] We see in this passage a tendency which Mackintosh had, in common with Burke, to overload a sentence with too many particulars. He condemned it himself in after life, when remarking on this speech.

have been reduced to the sad necessity of appearing before you to belie his own better feelings, to prosecute Mr. Peltier for publishing those sentiments which my friend himself had a thousand times felt, and a thousand times expressed. He might have been obliged even to call for punishment upon Mr. Peltier for language which he and all mankind would forever despise Mr. Peltier if he were not to employ. Then, indeed, gentlemen, we should have seen the last humiliation fall on England; the tribunals, the spotless and venerable tribunals of this free country reduced to be the ministers of the vengeance of Robespierre! What could have rescued us from this last disgrace? *The honesty and courage of a jury.* They would have delivered the judges of this country from the dire necessity of inflicting punishment on a brave and virtuous man, because he spoke truth of a monster. They would have despised the threats of a foreign tyrant, as their ancestors braved the power of oppression at home.

Peroration: Conduct of an English jury in the times of Cromwell.

In the court where we are now met, Cromwell twice sent a satirist on his tyranny to be convicted and punished as a libeler, and in this court, almost in sight of the scaffold streaming with the blood of his Sovereign, within hearing of the clash of his bayonets which drove out Parliament with contumely, two successive juries rescued the intrepid satirist [Lilburne] from his fangs, and sent out with defeat and disgrace the usurper's Attorney General from what he had the insolence to call *his* court! Even then, gentlemen, when all law and liberty were trampled under the feet of a military banditti; when those great crimes were perpetrated on a high place and with a high hand against those who were the objects of public veneration, which, more than any thing else, break their spirits and confound their moral sentiments, obliterate the distinctions between right and wrong in their understanding, and teach the multitude to feel no longer any reverence for that justice which they thus see triumphantly dragged at the chariot-wheels of a tyrant; even then, when this unhappy country, triumphant, indeed, abroad, but enslaved at home, had no prospect but that of a long succession of tyrants wading through slaughter to a throne—*even then, I say, when all seemed lost, the unconquerable spirit of English liberty survived in the hearts of English jurors.* That spirit is, I trust in God, not extinct; and if any modern tyrant were, in the drunkenness of his insolence, to hope to overawe an English jury, I trust and I believe that they would tell him, "Our ancestors braved the bayonets of Cromwell; we bid defiance to yours. *Contempsi Catiline gladios—non pertimescam tuos!*"[30]

Their duty at the present crisis.

What could be such a tyrant's means of overawing a jury? As long as their country exists, they are girt round with impenetrable armor. Till the destruction of their country, no danger can fall upon them for the performance of their duty, and I do trust that there is no Englishman so unworthy of life as to desire to outlive England. But if any of us are condemned to the cruel punishment of surviving our country—if, in the inscrutable counsels of Providence, this favored seat of justice and liberty, this noblest work of human wisdom and virtue, be destined to destruction, which I shall not be charged with national prejudice for saying would be the most dangerous wound ever inflicted on civilization; at least let us carry with us into our sad exile the consolation that we ourselves have not violated the rights of hospitality to exiles—that we have not torn from the altar the suppliant who claimed protection as the voluntary victim of loyalty and conscience!

Gentlemen, I now leave this unfortunate gentleman in your hands. His character and his situation might interest your humanity; but, on his behalf, I only ask justice from you. I only ask a favorable construction of what can not be said to be more than ambiguous language, and this you will soon be told, from the highest authority, is a part of justice.

Lord Ellenborough charged the jury that any publication which tends to degrade, revile, and defame persons in considerable situations of power and dignity in foreign countries, may be taken to be and treated as a libel, and particularly where it has a tendency to interrupt the pacific relations between the two countries. If the publication contains a plain and manifest incitement and persuasion addressed to others to assassinate and destroy the persons of such magistrates, as the tendency of such a publication is to interrupt the harmony subsisting between two countries, the libel assumes a still more criminal complexion.

His Lordship also showed it to be his decided opinion that the words could not be taken *ironically*, as suggested by Mr. Mackintosh. The jury, therefore, found the defendant GUILTY, without leaving their seats; but as war broke out almost immediately, Mr. Peltier was not brought up for sentence, but was at once discharged.

---

[30] This was the exclamation of Cicero to Anthony at the close of his second oration against him. "Defendi rempublicam adolescens; non deseram senex: contempsi Catilinæ gladios; non pertimescam tuos." I defended the republic in my youth, I will not desert her in my age; I have despised the daggers of Catiline, and I shall not fear yours.

The whole of this peroration of Cicero is worthy of the reader's attentive perusal.

The pointed reference to Bonaparte in this and a preceding sentence was called forth, no doubt, by the conduct of the French officers already mentioned. Being functionaries of the Consular government, their appearing at this time in court, their seating themselves alongside of the jury, and in a place directly suited to an inspection of the counsel, as if they meant to hold the Attorney General to his duty, and to face down the advocate of the prisoner—these things had all the appearance of a design to overrule the decision; and it is rather surprising that such conduct did not stir the spirit of an English jury.

CHARACTER OF CHARLES J. FOX.

Mr. Fox united in a most remarkable degree the seemingly repugnant characters of the mildest of men and the most vehement of orators. In private life he was gentle, modest, placable, kind; of simple manners, and so averse from parade and dogmatism, as to be not only unostentatious, but even somewhat inactive in conversation. His superiority was never felt, but in the instruction which he imparted, or in the attention which his generous preference usually directed to the more obscure members of the company. The simplicity of his manners was far from excluding that perfect urbanity and amenity which flowed still more from the mildness of his nature than from familiar intercourse with the most polished society of Europe. His conversation, when it was not repressed by modesty or indolence, was delightful. The pleasantry, perhaps, of no man of wit had so unlabored an appearance. It seemed rather to escape from his mind than to be produced by it. He had lived on the most intimate terms with all his cotemporaries, distinguished by wit, politeness, philosophy, learning, or the talents of public life. In the course of thirty years, he had known almost every man in Europe whose intercourse could strengthen, or enrich, or polish the mind. His own literature was various and elegant. In classical erudition, which, by the custom of England, is more peculiarly called learning, he was inferior to few professed scholars. Like all men of genius, he delighted to take refuge in poetry from the vulgarity and irritation of business. The character of his mind was displayed in his extraordinary partiality for the poetry of the two most poetical nations or, at least, languages of the west—those of the Greeks and of the Italians. He disliked political conversation, and never willingly took any part in it.

To speak of him justly as an orator would require a long essay. Every where natural, he carried into public something of that simple and negligent exterior which belonged to him in private. When he began to speak, a common observer might have thought him awkward; and even a consummate judge could only have been struck with the exquisite justness of his ideas, and the transparent simplicity of his manners. But no sooner had he spoken for some time, than he was changed into another being. He forgot himself and every thing around him. He thought only of his subject. His genius warmed, and kindled as he went on. He darted fire into his audience. Torrents of impetuous and irresistible eloquence swept along their feelings and conviction. He certainly possessed above all moderns that union of reason, simplicity, and vehemence which formed the prince of orators. He was the most Demosthenean speaker since Demosthenes. "I knew him," says Mr. Burke, in a pamphlet written after their unhappy difference, "when he was nineteen; since which time he has risen, by slow degrees, to be the most brilliant and accomplished debater that the world ever saw." The quiet dignity of a mind roused only by great objects, the absence of petty bustle, the contempt of show, the abhorrence of intrigue, the plainness and downrightness, and the thorough good nature which distinguished Mr. Fox, seem to render him no very unfit representative of that old English national character, which if it ever changed, we should be sanguine, indeed, to expect to see succeeded by a better. The simplicity of his character inspired confidence, the ardor of his eloquence roused enthusiasm, and the gentleness of his manners invited friendship. "I admired," says Mr. Gibbon, "the powers of a superior man, as they are blended in his attractive character, with all the softness and simplicity of a child; no human being was ever more free from any taint of malignity, vanity, or falsehood." From these qualities of his public and private character, it probably arose that no English statesman ever preserved during so long a period of adverse fortunes, so many affectionate friends and so many zealous adherents. The union of ardor in public sentiment, with mildness in social manner, was in Mr. Fox an hereditary quality. The same fascinating power over the attachment of all who came within his sphere is said to have belonged to his father; and those who know the survivors of another generation will feel that this delightful quality is not yet extinct in the race.

Perhaps nothing can more strongly prove the deep impression made by this part of Mr. Fox's character than the words of Mr. Burke, who in January, 1797, six years after all intercourse between them had ceased, speaking to a person honored with some degree of Mr. Fox's friendship, said, "To be sure, he is a man made to be loved!" and these emphatical words were uttered with a fervor of manner which left no doubt of their heartfelt sincerity.

These few hasty and honest sentences are sketched in a temper too sober and serious for intentional exaggeration, and with too pious an affection for the memory of Mr. Fox, to profane it by intermixture with the factious brawls and wrangles of the day. His political conduct belongs to history. The measures which he supported or opposed may divide the opinion of posterity, as they have divided those of the present age. But he will most certainly command the unanimous reverence of future generations, by his pure sentiments toward the commonwealth, by his zeal for the civil and religious rights of all men, by his liberal principles favorable to mild government, to the unfettered exercise of the human faculties, and the progressive civilization of mankind, by his ardent love for a country, of which the well-being and greatness were, indeed, inseparable from his own glory, and by his profound reverence for that free Constitution, which he was universally admitted to understand better than any other man of his age, both in an exactly legal and a comprehensively philosophical sense.

MR. CANNING.

George Canning was born in London on the 11th of April, 1770. His father, who belonged to an Irish family of distinction, had been disinherited for marrying beneath his rank, and was trying his fortune as a barrister in the English metropolis with very scanty means of subsistence. He died one year after the birth of his son, leaving a widow, with three young children, wholly destitute of property, and dependent for support on her own exertions.

Under these circumstances, Mrs. Canning, who was a woman of extraordinary force of character, first set up a small school, and soon after attempted the stage. She was successful in her provincial engagements, especially at Bath and Exeter; and in the latter place she married a linen-draper of the name of Hunn, who was passionately attached to theatrical performances, and united with her in the employment of an actor. A few years after, she was again left a widow by the death of Mr. Hunn; but her profession gave her a competent independence, until she saw her son raised to the highest honors of the state, and was permitted to share in the fruits of his success.[1]

George was educated under the care of his uncle, Mr. Stratford Canning, a London merchant, out of the proceeds of a small estate in Ireland, which was left him by his grandmother. He was first sent to school at Hyde Abbey, near Winchester, where he made uncommon proficiency in the rudiments of Latin and Greek, and was particularly distinguished for his love of elegant English literature. On one occasion, when a mere child, being accidentally called upon to repeat some verses, he commenced with one of the poems of Mr. Gray, and never stopped or faltered until he had gone through the entire volume. His mother's employment naturally led him to take a lively interest in speaking, and especially in acting dialogues; and in one instance, when the boys performed parts out of the Orestes of Euripides, previous to a vacation, he portrayed the madness of the conscience-stricken matricide with a force and tenderness which called forth the liveliest applause of the audience.

Before he was fifteen, George went to Eton, and carried with him a high reputation for writing Latin and Greek verses, which always confers distinction in the great schools of England. He was at once recognized as a boy of surprising genius and attainments; and he used the influence thus gained in promoting his favorite pursuit, that of elegant English literature. When a little more than sixteen, he induced the boys to establish a weekly paper called the Microcosm, to which he contributed largely, and acted as principal editor. Its pages bore such striking marks of brilliancy and wit, as to attract the attention of the leading reviews; and the work became the means of training up some of the most distinguished men of the age to those habits of *early composition*, which Sir James Mackintosh speaks of as indispensable to the character of a truly great writer.

[1] It is a high testimony to Mr. Canning's manliness and warmth of heart, that he never attempted to throw any covering over his mother's early history, but treated her openly throughout life with the utmost reverence and affection. He visited her at her residence in Bath as often as his public employments would permit, and never allowed any business, however urgent, to prevent him from writing to her every Sunday of his life. He obtained pensions for his mother and sisters; and when attacked on the subject, defended himself to the satisfaction of all by saying that, in retiring from his office of Under Secretary in 1801, he was entitled to a pension of £500 a year, and had only procured the settlement of a fair equivalent on his dependent relatives.

His attention, while at Eton, was also strongly turned to extemporaneous speaking. He joined a society for debate, in which the Marquess of Wellesley, Earl Grey and other distinguished statesmen had gone before him in their preparation as orators, and had introduced all the forms of the House of Commons. The Speaker was in the chair; the minister, with his partisans, filled the Treasury benches, and were faced by the most strenuous Opposition that Eton could muster. The enthusiasm with which Canning and his companions entered into these mimic contests was but little inferior to what they felt in the real ones that followed, and for which they were thus preparing the way. Canning, especially, showed throughout life the influence of his early habits of *writing* in conjunction with extemporaneous debate. His speeches bear proofs on every page of the effects of the pen in forming his spoken style. On every important debate, he wrote much beforehand, and composed more in his mind, which flowed forth spontaneously, and mingled with the current of his thoughts, in all the fervor of the most prolonged and excited discussion. Hence, while he had great ease and variety, he never fell into that negligence and looseness of style which we always find in a purely extemporaneous speaker.

After standing foremost among his companions at Eton in all the lower forms, George became "captain" of the school, and was removed to Christ Church, Oxford, in October, 1787. The accuracy and ripeness of his scholarship turned upon him the eyes of the whole University, and justified his entering, even when a *freshman*, into competition for the Chancellor's first prize, which he gained by a Latin poem entitled "Iter ad Meccam Religionis Causâ Susceptum." The distinction which he thus early acquired, he maintained, throughout his whole college course, by a union of exemplary diligence with a maturity of judgment, refinement of taste, and brilliancy of genius far beyond his years. In Mr. Canning we have one of the happiest exhibitions of the results produced by the classical course pursued at Eton and Oxford, which, "whatever may be its defects, must be owned," says Sir James Mackintosh, "when taken with its constant appendages, to be eminently favorable to the cultivation of sense and taste, as well as to the development of wit and spirit." The natural effect, however, of this incessant competition, in connection with the early tendencies of his mind and his remarkable success, was to cherish that extreme sensitiveness to the opinion of others, that delight in superiority, that quick sense of his own dignity, that sensibility to supposed neglect or disregard, which, with all his attractive qualities, made him in early life not always a pleasant companion, and sometimes involved him in the most serious difficulties. But, though he never lost his passion for distinction, it was certainly true of him, as said by another, "As he advanced in years, his fine countenance, once so full of archness or petulance, was ennobled by the expression of thought and feeling; he now pursued that lasting praise which is not to be earned without praiseworthiness; and if he continued to be a lover of fame, he also passionately loved the glory of his country."

Mr. Canning left the University in the twenty-second year of his age, and after giving a few months to the study of the law, was invited by Mr. Pitt, who had heard of his extraordinary talents, to take a seat in Parliament as a regular supporter of the government. His first predilections were in favor of Whig principles. He had been intimate with Mr. Sheridan from early life, but differed from him wholly in respect to the French Revolution, and was thus prepared to look favorably on the proposals of Mr. Pitt. After mutual explanations, he accepted the offer, and was returned to Parliament from one of the ministerial boroughs at the close of 1793, in the twenty-fourth year of his age.

Mr. Canning's maiden speech was in favor of a subsidy to the King of Sardinia, and was delivered on the 31st of January, 1794. It was brilliant, but wanting in solidity and judgment; and in general it may be remarked, that he rose *slowly* into those higher qualities as a speaker, for which he was so justly distinguished during the later years of his life. He was from the first easy and fluent; he knew how to play with an argument when he could not answer it; he had a great deal of real wit, and too much of that ungenerous raillery and sarcasm, by which an antagonist may be made ridiculous, and the audience turned against him, without once meeting the question on its true merits. There was added to this an air of disregard for the feelings of others, and even of willingness to offend, which doubled the sense of injury every blow he struck; so that during the first ten years of his parliamentary career, he never made a speech, it was said, on which he particularly plumed himself, without making likewise an enemy for life. He was continually acting, as one said who put the case strongly, like "the head of the sixth form at Eton: squibbing the 'doctor,' as Mr. Addington was called—fighting my Lord Castlereagh—cutting heartless jokes on poor Mr. Ogden—flatly contradicting Mr. Brougham—swaggering over the Holy Alliance—quarreling with the Duke of Wellington—perpetually involved in some personal scrape." These habits, however, gradually wore off as he advanced in life, and his early political opponents were warmest in their commendations of his conduct at the close of his political career.

In 1797, Mr. Canning projected the Anti-Jacobin Review, in conjunction with Mr. Jenkinson and Mr. Ellis (afterward Lords Liverpool and Seaford), Mr. Frere, and other writers of the same stamp. Mr. Gifford was editor, and its object was to *bear down* the Radical party in politics and literature, and to turn upon them the contempt of the whole nation by the united force of argument and ridicule. It took the widest range, from lofty and vehement reasoning to the keenest satire and the most bitter personal abuse. It applied the lash with merciless severity to all the extravagances of the day in taste and sentiment—the mawkish sensibility of the Della Cruscan school, the incongruous mixtures of virtue and vice in the new German drama, and the various *improvements* in literature introduced by Holcroft, Thelwall, and others among the Radical reformers. Such an employment was perfectly suited to the taste of Mr. Canning. It was an exercise of ingenuity in which he always delighted; and a large part of the keenest wit, the most dextrous travesty, and the happiest exhibitions of the laughable and burlesque, were the productions of his pen. The most striking poetical effusions were his. Among these, the "Knife-grinder," and the "Loves of Mary Pottinger," are admirable in their way, and will hold their place among the amusing extravaganzas of our literature, when the ablest political diatribes of the Anti-Jacobin are forgotten.[2]

[2] The reader may be pleased, as a specimen, to see Mr. Canning's sapphics on the Knife-grinder, intended as a burlesque on a fashionable poet's extreme sensibility to the sufferings of the poor, and his reference of all their distresses to political causes. It was also designed to ridicule his hobbling verse and abrupt transitions.

THE FRIEND OF HUMANITY AND THE KNIFE-GRINDER.

Friend of Humanity.

Needy knife-grinder! whither are you going?
Rough is the road; your wheel is out of order;
Bleak blows the blast; your hat has got a hole in't,
So have your breeches!

Weary knife-grinder! little think the proud ones,
Who in their coaches roll along the turnpike-
Road, what hard work 'tis crying all day, "Knives and
Scissors to grind O!"

Tell me, knife-grinder, how came you to grind knives?
Did some rich man tyrannically use you?
Was it the squire? or parson of the parish?
Or the attorney?

In July, 1800, Mr. Canning married Miss Joan Scott, daughter of General Scott, and sister to Lady Tichfield, afterward Duchess of Portland. She had a fortune of £100,000, which placed him at once in circumstances of entire independence, while he gained an increase of influence by his family alliances.

In a sketch like this, only the leading incidents can be given in the political career of Mr. Canning. He was actively engaged in public life for nearly thirty-four years, eleven of which were spent in connection with Mr. Pitt. His first office was that of Under Secretary of State. He went out with his patron during Mr. Addington's brief ministry, and came in with him again, as Treasurer of the Navy, in 1804. On Mr. Pitt's death, early in 1806, he was not included (as he had reason to expect) in Lord Grenville's arrangements, and went into opposition. During his whole life, he was the ardent champion of the "Great Minister's" principles, and the defender of his fame. In the London Quarterly for August, 1810, he gave an estimate of Mr. Pitt's character and a defense of his political life, which for ingenuity of thought, richness of fancy, and splendor of diction, has never been surpassed in the periodical literature of our language. It came warm from his heart. He truly said to his constituents at Liverpool, "In the grave of Mr. Pitt my political allegiance lies buried."

On the accession of the Duke of Portland to power (March, 1807), Mr. Canning became Secretary of Foreign Affairs, and for the first time a member of the cabinet. But, at the end of two years, he had a personal altercation with Lord Castlereagh (then Secretary of War), resulting in a duel, which not only threw both of them out of office, but dissolved the Portland ministry.

Mr. Canning now remained out of power nearly five years, though regular in his attendance on Parliament. He took independent ground during Mr. Percival's ministry of a year and a half, and delivered at this time his celebrated speech on the Bullion Question, exposing the current fallacy, "It is not paper that has fallen, but gold which has risen," and calling, in the strongest terms, for the resumption of cash

---

Was it the squire, for killing of his game? or
Covetous parson, for his tithes distraining?
Or roguish lawyer, made you lose your little
All in a lawsuit?

(Have you not read the Rights of Man, by Tom Paine?)
Drops of compassion tremble on my eyelids,
Ready to fall, as soon as you have told your
Pitiful story.

Knife-grinder.

Story! why bless you! I *have none to tell*, sir;
Only last night a drinking at the Checkers,
This poor old hat and breeches, as you see, were
Torn in a scuffle.

Constables came up for to take me into
Custody; they took me before the justice;
Justice Oldmixon put me in the parish-
stocks for a vagrant.

I should be glad to drink your honor's health in
A pot of beer, if you will give me sixpence;
But, for my part, I never love to meddle
With politics, sir.

Friend of Humanity.

I give thee sixpence! I will see thee hang'd first!
Wretch! whom no sense of wrongs can rouse to vengeance.
Sordid, unfeeling, reprobate, degraded,
Spiritless outcast!

[*Kicks the knife-grinder, overturns his wheel, and exit in a transport of republican enthusiasm and universal philanthropy.*]

payments. This speech, though interesting no longer to the general reader, has been truly characterized as "one of the most powerful and masterly specimens on record of chaste and reasoning eloquence." The question lay out of Mr. Canning's ordinary range of thought, and the ability with which he took it up proved (what his friends had always said) that no man could more promptly, or with greater effect, turn the whole force of his mind on any new subject, however foreign to his ordinary pursuits. Under his friend Lord Liverpool [Mr. Jenkinson], who followed Mr. Percival in June, 1812, he gave his cordial support to the ministry, though excluded from office by his views in favor of Catholic emancipation. To him especially, at this period, was Lord Wellington indebted for an enthusiastic support during his long and terrible conflict in Spain. It was under the policy and guidance of Canning, as Secretary of Foreign Affairs in 1808, that this conflict commenced; and he never ceased to animate the country to fresh sacrifices and efforts in battling with Bonaparte for the rescue of the Peninsula. It was the first favorable opportunity ever presented for carrying out the continental policy of Mr. Pitt, and it was always the theme of Mr. Canning's proudest exultations. "If there is any part of my political conduct," said he, "in which I *glory*, it is that in the face of every difficulty, discouragement, and prophecy of failure, *mine* was the hand which committed England to an alliance with Spain."

In 1812, Mr. Canning was invited to stand as a candidate for Liverpool, and, though powerfully opposed by Mr. Brougham, he carried his election, and was again returned, on three subsequent occasions, with continually increasing majorities. Two speeches to his constituents at Liverpool will be found below; they are some of the best specimens of his eloquence.

In 1814, he was sent as embassador extraordinary to the court of Lisbon, and being attacked on this subject, after his return to the House, in 1816, he made his defense in a speech of remarkable ability and manliness, which has, however, but little interest for the reader at the present day, because filled up chiefly with matters of personal detail. The same year [1816] he was made President of the Board of Indian Control, and thus brought again into the ministry. From this time England was agitated for six or eight years by the rash movements of the Radical reformers, which led ministers to adopt measures of great, perhaps undue stringency, to preserve the public peace. Mr. Canning took strong ground on this subject, and was severely attacked in a pamphlet understood to be from the pen of Sir Philip Francis. His extreme sensitiveness to such attacks showed itself in an extraordinary way. He addressed a private letter to the author of the pamphlet, through Ridgeway, the publisher, telling him, "*You are a liar and a slanderer, and want courage only to be an assassin.*" Even on dueling principles, no man was bound to come forward under such a call; and the challenge which Mr. Canning endeavored to provoke was not given.

In 1822, he was appointed Governor General of India, but, at the moment when he was ready to embark for Calcutta, the office of Secretary of Foreign Affairs became vacant by the sudden death of the Marquess of Londonderry [Lord Castlereagh], and Mr. Canning was called to this important station on the 16th of February, 1823. It was a crisis of extreme difficulty. France was at that moment collecting troops to overthrow the constitutional government of Spain, and was urging the other allied powers, then assembled in congress at Verona, to unite in the intervention. Mr. Canning instantly dispatched the Duke of Wellington to Verona with the strongest remonstrances of the British government against the proposed invasion of Spain; and, at the opening of the next Parliament, explained and defended the views of the ministry in a manner which called forth the warmest applause of Mr. Brougham and most of his other political opponents.[3] Early in 1825, Mr. Canning took the import-

[3] On this subject, see Mr. Brougham's speech, page 904.

ant step of recognizing the independence of the Spanish provinces in South America, a measure which made him deservedly popular in every part of the kingdom. In December, 1826, actuated by the same liberal sentiments, he made his celebrated speech on giving aid to Portugal, when threatened with invasion from Spain. It will be found below, and has been generally regarded as the master-piece of his eloquence, not only for the felicity of its arrangement and the admirable grace and spirit with which his points are pressed, but for the large and statesmanlike views he takes of European politics, and his prophetic foresight of the great contest of *principles* which was even then coming on.[4]

As to all questions of foreign policy—the most important by far of any at that period—Mr. Canning was virtually minister from February, 1823, when he was appointed Secretary of Foreign Affairs. He had so entirely the confidence of Lord Liverpool, that *his* intellect was the presiding one in the cabinet; and as Lord Liverpool's health began to decline, the burden of the government rested upon him more and more. In 1827, his Lordship died of a paralytic shock; and on April 12th of that year, Mr. Canning was made Prime Minister in form. The Duke of Wellington, Mr. Peel, and nearly all his Tory colleagues, threw up their places at once, out of hostility to Catholic emancipation, which they saw must prevail if he remained in power—the very men who, two years after, under the strong compulsion of public sentiment, carried that same emancipation through both houses of Parliament! But they sacrificed Mr. Canning before they could be made to do it. A keen and unrelenting opposition now sprung up; and some who, only a few months before, had made him "the god of their idolatry," were foremost in denouncing him as "the most profligate minister that was ever in power." Unfortunately, at this crisis, his health failed him. He had been brought to the brink of the grave, at the commencement of the year, by an illness contracted at the funeral of the Duke of York; and with his peculiar sensitiveness, heightened by disease, he could not endure the bitter personal altercations to which he was continually exposed. He was singularly situated. Standing between the two great parties of the country, he agreed with the Whigs on the subjects of Catholic emancipation, foreign policy, and commercial regulation, while he differed from them as to parliamentary reform, and the repeal of the Test Act: Still, they gave him a generous support; and he could rely on the wit of Tierney and the scathing eloquence of Brougham to defend him against the attacks of those who were so lately his servile dependents or his admiring friends. He had reached the summit of his ambition—but it was only to die! His ardent mind bore him up for a brief season, but was continually exhausting the springs of life within. His last act was one of his worthiest—that of signing the treaty of London for the deliverance of Greece. He transacted public business until a few days before his death, and died on the 8th of August, 1827, in the fifty-eighth year of his age.[5]

As a fitting close of this memoir, the reader will be interested in the following beautiful sketch of Mr. Canning's character by Sir James Mackintosh, slightly abridged and modified in the arrangement of its parts.

"Mr. Canning seems to have been the best model among our orators of the adorned style. The splendid and sublime descriptions of Mr. Burke—his comprehensive and profound views of general principles—though they must ever delight and instruct the reader, must be owned to have been digressions which diverted the mind of the hearer from the object on which the speaker ought to have kept it steadily fixed.

[4] See the remarkable passage on this subject, page 882.

[5] "Canning," says a late writer, "would have attained to old age, but for his sleepless nights. Down to the year 1826, he had no organic disease whatever. His constitution was untouched; but his brain, at night, was active for hours after he retired to bed. He has himself, in a letter to Sir W. Knighton, given a graphic picture of a night of torture."

Sheridan, a man of admirable sense and matchless wit, labored to follow Burke into the foreign regions of feeling and grandeur. The specimens preserved of his most celebrated speeches show too much of the exaggeration and excess to which those are peculiarly liable who seek by art and effort what nature has denied. By the constant part which Mr. Canning took in debate, he was called upon to show a knowledge which Sheridan did not possess, and a readiness which that accomplished man had no such means of strengthening and displaying. In some qualities of style Mr. Canning surpassed Mr. Pitt. His diction was more various—sometimes more simple—more idiomatical, even in its more elevated parts. It sparkled with imagery, and was brightened by illustration; in both of which Mr. Pitt, for so great an orator, was defective.

"Had he been a dry and meager speaker, Mr. Canning would have been universally allowed to have been one of the greatest masters of argument; but his hearers were so dazzled by the splendor of his diction that they did not perceive the acuteness and the occasional excessive refinement of his reasoning; a consequence which, as it shows the injurious influence of a seductive fault, can with the less justness be overlooked in the estimate of his understanding. Ornament, it must be owned, when it only pleases or amuses, without disposing the audience to adopt the sentiments of the speaker, is an offense against the first law of public speaking; it obstructs instead of promoting its only reasonable purpose. But eloquence is a widely-extended art, comprehending many sorts of excellence, in some of which ornamented diction is more liberally employed than in others, and in none of which the highest rank can be attained without an extraordinary combination of mental powers.

"No English speaker used the keen and brilliant weapon of wit so long, so often, or so effectively, as Mr. Canning. He gained more triumphs, and incurred more enmity by it than by any other. Those whose importance depends much on birth and fortune are impatient of seeing their own artificial dignity, or that of their order, broken down by derision; and perhaps few men heartily forgive a successful jest against themselves, but those who are conscious of being unhurt by it. Mr. Canning often used this talent imprudently. In sudden flashes of wit, and in the playful description of men or things, he was often distinguished by that natural felicity which is the charm of pleasantry, to which the air of art and labor is more fatal than to any other talent. The exuberance of fancy and wit lessened the gravity of his general manner, and perhaps also indisposed the audience to feel his earnestness where it clearly showed itself. In that important quality he was inferior to Mr. Pitt,

"'Deep on whose front engraven,
Deliberation sat, and public care;'[6]

and no less inferior to Mr. Fox, whose fervid eloquence flowed from the love of his country, the scorn of baseness, and the hatred of cruelty, which were the ruling passions of his nature.

"On the whole, it may be observed that the range of Mr. Canning's powers as an orator was wider than that in which he usually exerted them. When mere statement only was allowable, no man of his age was more simple. When infirm health compelled him to be brief, no speaker could compress his matter with so little sacrifice of clearness, ease, and elegance. As his oratorical faults were those of youthful genius, the progress of age seemed to purify his eloquence, and every year appeared to remove some speck which hid, or at least dimmed, a beauty. He daily rose to larger views, and made, perhaps, as near approaches to philosophical principles as the great difference between the objects of the philosopher and those of the orator will commonly allow.

"Mr. Canning possessed, in a high degree, the outward advantages of an orator.

6 Paradise Lost, book ii.

His expressive countenance varied with the changes of his eloquence; his voice, flexible and articulate, had as much compass as his mode of speaking required. In the calm part of his speeches, his attitude and gesture might have been selected by a painter to represent grace rising toward dignity.

"In social intercourse Mr. Canning was delightful. Happily for the true charm of his conversation, he was too busy not to treat society as more fitted for relaxation than for display. It is but little to say that he was neither disputatious, declamatory, nor sententious—neither a dictator nor a jester. His manner was simple and unobtrusive; his language always quite familiar. If a higher thought stole from his mind, it came in its conversational undress. From this plain ground his pleasantry sprang with the happiest effect; and it was nearly exempt from that alloy of taunt and banter which he sometimes mixed with more precious materials in public contest. He may be added to the list of those eminent persons who pleased most in their friendly circle. He had the agreeable quality of being more easily pleased in society than might have been expected from the keenness of his discernment and the sensibility of his temper: still, he was liable to be discomposed, or even silenced, by the presence of any one whom he did not like. His manner in company betrayed the political vexations or anxieties which preyed on his mind: nor could he conceal that sensitiveness to public attacks which their frequent recurrence wears out in most English politicians. These last foibles may be thought interesting as the remains of natural character, not destroyed by refined society and political affairs.

"In some of the amusements or tasks of his boyhood there are passages which, without much help from fancy, might appear to contain allusions to his greatest measures of policy, as well as to the tenor of his life, and to the melancholy splendor which surrounded his death. In the concluding line of the first English verses written by him at Eton, he expressed a wish, which has been singularly realized, that he might

"'Live in a blaze, and in a blaze expire.'

It is a striking coincidence, that the statesman, whose dying measure was to mature an alliance for the deliverance of Greece, should, when a boy, have written English verses on the slavery of that country; and that in his prize poem at Oxford, on the Pilgrimage to Mecca—a composition as much applauded as a modern Latin poem can aspire to be—he should have so bitterly deplored the lot of other renowned countries now groaning under the same barbarous yoke,

"'Nunc satrapæ imperio et sævo subdita Turcæ.'[7]

"To conclude: He was a man of fine and brilliant genius, of warm affections of a high and generous spirit—a statesman who, at home, converted most of his opponents into warm supporters; who, abroad, was the sole hope and trust of all who sought an orderly and legal liberty, and who was cut off in the midst of vigorous and splendid measures, which, if executed by himself or with his own spirit, promised to place his name in the first class of rulers, among the founders of lasting peace and the guardians of human improvement."

[7] Now to the satrap and proud Turk subjected.

SPEECH

OF MR. CANNING ON THE FALL OF BONAPARTE, DELIVERED AT LIVERPOOL, JANUARY 10, 1814.

INTRODUCTION.

MR. CANNING was elected member for Liverpool, in opposition to Mr. Brougham, in the autumn of 1812, and at the end of fourteen months he visited his constituents to congratulate them on the success of the Allies on the Continent, which had filled all England with exultation and triumph.

After the retreat of Bonaparte from Moscow, in the winter of 1812–13, nearly all Europe combined for his overthrow; and though he still maintained the contest, his fall was rendered certain by the advance of an overpowering force from every quarter to invade the French territory.

The speech of Mr. Canning on this occasion, for selectness of thought, for beauty of language, for ardor and enthusiasm, was perhaps superior to any of his productions.

SPEECH, &c.

GENTLEMEN, as your guest, I thank you from my heart for the honorable and affectionate reception which you have given me. As the representative of Liverpool, I am most happy in meeting my constituents again, after a year's experience of each other, and a year's separation; a year, the most eventful in the annals of the world, and comprising within itself such a series of stupendous changes as might have filled the history of an age.

Acknowledgment of kindness.

Gentlemen, you have been so good as to couple with my name the expression of your acknowledgments for the attention which I have paid to the interests of your town. You, gentlemen, I have no doubt, recollect the terms upon which I entered into your service; and you are aware, therefore, that I claim no particular acknowledgment at your hands for attention to the interests of Liverpool, implicated as they are with the general interests of the country. I trust, at the same time, that I have not been wanting to all or to any of you in matters of local or individual concern. But I should not do fairly by you, if I were not to take this opportunity of saying that a service (which certainly I will not pretend to describe as without some burden in itself) has been made light to me, beyond all example, by that institution which your munificence and provident care have established: I mean the office in London, through which your correspondence with your members is now carried on. I had no pretension, gentlemen, to this singular mark of your consideration; but neither will it, I hope, be thought presumptuous in me to confess, that I might not have been able to discharge the service which I owe you, in a way which would have satisfied my own feelings as well as yours —that I might, in spite of all my endeavors, have been guilty of occasional omissions, if I had not been provided with some such medium of communication with my constituents. Of an absent and meritorious individual, it is as pleasing as it is just to speak well; and I do no more than justice to the gentleman [Mr. John Backhouse] whom you have appointed to conduct the office in question (with whom I had no previous acquaintance), in bearing public testimony to his merit, and in assuring you that it would be difficult to find any one who would surpass him in zeal, intelligence, and industry.

Regard for the interests of the speaker's constituents.

Having dispatched what it was necessary for me to say on these points, I know, gentlemen, that it is your wish, and I feel it to be my duty, that I should now proceed to communicate to you my sentiments on the state of public affairs, with the same frankness which has hitherto distinguished all our intercourse with each other. That duty is one which it does not now require any effort of courage to perform. To exhort to sacrifices, to stimulate to exertion, to shame despondency, to divert from untimely concession, is a duty of a sterner sort, which you found me not backward to discharge, at a period when, from the shortness of our acquaintance, I was uncertain whether my freedom might not offend you. My task of to-day is one at which no man can take offense. It is to mingle my congratulations with your rejoicings on the events which have passed and are passing in the world.

View of public affairs.

If, in contemplating events so widely (I had almost said so tremendously) important, it be pardonable to turn one's view for a moment to local and partial considerations, I may be permitted to observe, that, while to Great Britain, while to all Europe, while to the world and to posterity, the events which have recently taken place are matter of unbounded and universal joy, there is no collection of individuals who are better entitled than the company now assembled in this room (in great part, I presume, identically the same, and altogether representing the same interests and feelings as that of which I took leave, in this room, about fourteen months ago) to exult in the present state of things, and to derive from it, in addition to their share of the general joy, a distinct and special satisfaction.

Sources of joy and exultation for Englishmen.

Alarming predictions which have failed.

We can not forget, gentlemen, the sinister omens and awful predictions under which we met and parted in October, 1812. The penalty denounced upon you for your election of me was embarrassment to the rich and famine to the poor. I was warned that, when I should return to renew my acquaintance with my constituents, I should find the grass growing in your streets. In spite of that denunciation, you did me the honor to elect me; in spite of that warning, I venture to meet you here again. It must be fairly confessed that this is not the season of the year to estimate correctly the amount of superfluous and unprofitable vegetation with which your streets may be teeming; but, without presuming to limit the power of productive nature, it is at least satisfactory to know that the fields have not been starved to clothe your quays with verdure; that it is not by economizing in the scantiness of the harvest that nature has reserved her vigor for the pastures of your Exchange.

This failure owing not to the choice of men,

But, gentlemen, I am sure you feel, with me, that these are topics which I treat with levity only because they are not, nor were, at the time when they were seriously urged, susceptible of a serious argument; they did not furnish grounds on which any man would rest his appeal to your favor, or on which your choice of any man could be justified. If I have condescended to revert to them at all, it is because I would leave none of those recollections untouched which the comparison of our last meeting with the present, I know, suggests to your minds as well as to my own; and because I would, so far as in me lies, endeavor to banish from all future use, by exposing their absurdity, topics which are calculated only to mislead and to inflame. That the seasons would have run their appointed course, that the sun would have shone with as genial a warmth, and the showers would have fallen with as fertilizing a moisture, if you had not chosen me for your representative, is an admission which I make without much apprehension of the consequence. Nor do I wish you to believe that your choice of any other than me would have delayed the return of your prosperity, or prevented the revival of your commerce.

but adherence to great principles.

I make these admissions without fear, so far as concerns the choice between individuals. But I do not admit that it was equally indifferent upon what principles that choice should be determined. I do not admit, that if the principles which it was then recommended to you to countenance had unfortunately prevailed in Parliament, and, through the authority of Parliament, had been introduced into the counsels of the country, they would not have interfered with fatal operation, not indeed to arrest the bounty of Providence, to turn back the course of the seasons, and to blast the fertility of the earth, but to stop that current of political events which, "taken at the flood," has placed England at the head of the world.

Perseverance in these principles the source of the present triumphs.

Gentlemen, if I had met you here again on this day in a state of public affairs as doubtful as that in which we took leave of each other; if confederated nations had been still arrayed against this country, and the balance of Europe still trembling in the scale, I should not have hesitated now, as I did not hesitate then, to declare my decided and unalterable opinion, that perseverance, under whatever difficulties, under whatever privations, afforded the only chance of prosperity to you, because the only chance of safety to your country; and the only chance of safety to the country, because the only chance of deliverance to Europe. Gentlemen, I should be ashamed to address you now in the tone of triumph, if I had not addressed you then in that of exhortation. I should be ashamed to appear before you shouting in the train of success, if I had not looked you in the face and encouraged you to patience under difficulties. It is because my acquaintance with you commenced in times of peril and embarrassment, and because I then neither flattered nor deceived you, that I now not only offer to you my congratulations, but put in my claim to yours, on the extinction of that peril, on the termination of that embarrassment, and on the glorious issue to which exertion and endurance have brought that great struggle in which our honor and our happiness were involved.

Gentlemen, during the course of a political life, nearly coeval with the commencement of the war, I have never given one vote, I have never uttered one sentiment, which had not for its object the consummation now happily within our view.

Elevated position of England.

I am not ashamed, and it is not unpleasing or unprofitable, to look back upon the dangers which we have passed, and to compare them with the scene which now lies before us. We behold a country inferior in population to most of her continental neighbors, but multiplying her faculties and resources by her own activity and enterprise, by the vigor of her Constitution, and by the good sense of her people; we behold her, after standing up against a formidable foe throughout a contest, in the course of which every one of her allies, and at times all of them together, have fainted and failed—nay, have been driven to combine with the enemy against her—we behold her, at this moment, rallying the nations of Europe to one point, and leading them to decisive victory.

If such a picture were merely the bright vision of speculative philosophy, if it were presented to us in the page of the history of ancient times, it would stir and warm the heart. But, gentlemen, this country is our own; and what must be the feelings which arise, on such a review, in the bosom of every son of that country? What must be the feelings of a community such as I am now addressing, which constitutes no insignificant part of the strength of the nation so described; which has suffered largely in her privations, and may hope to participate proportionably in her reward? What (I may be permitted to add) must be the feelings of one who is chosen to represent that community, and who finds himself in that honorable station at the moment of triumph, only because he discountenanced despair in the moment of despondency?

The consequence of adhering to her long-established principles.

From the contemplation of a spectacle so mighty and magnificent as this, I should disdain to turn aside to the controversies of party. Of principles, however, it is impossible not to say something; because our triumph would be incomplete, and its blessings might be transient, if we could be led astray by any sophistry; if we could consent, in a sort of compromise of common joy, to forget or to misstate the causes from which that triumph has sprung. All of one mind, I trust and believe we are, in exulting at the success of our country; all of one mind, I trust, we now are throughout this land, in determining to persevere, if need be, in strenuous exertion to prosecute, and I hope, to perfect the great work so happily in progress. But we know that there are some of those who share most heartily in the public exultation, who yet ascribe effects, which happily can not be disputed, to causes which may justly be denied. No tenderness for disappointed prophecies, gentlemen, ought to induce us thus to disconnect effect and cause. It would lead to errors which might be dangerous, if unwarily adopted and generally received.

These not changed, as pretended, during the contest.

We have heard, for instance, that the war has now been successful, because the principles on which the war was undertaken have been renounced; that we are at length blessed with victory, because we have thrown away the banner under which we entered into the contest; that the contest was commenced with one set of principles, but that the issue has been happily brought about by the adoption of another. Gentlemen, I know of no such change. If we have succeeded, it has not been by the renunciation, but by the prosecution of our principles; if we have succeeded, it has not been by adopting new maxims of policy, but by upholding, under all varieties of difficulty and discouragement, old, established, inviolable principles of conduct.

But the people brought to act with their rulers.

We are told that this war has of late become *a war of the people*, and that by the operation of that change alone the power of imperial France has been baffled and overcome. Nations, it is said, have at length made common cause with their sovereigns, in a contest which heretofore had been a contest of sovereigns only. Gentlemen, the fact of the change might be admitted, without, therefore, admitting the argument. It does not follow that the people were not at all times equally interested in the war (as those who think as I do have always contended that they were), because it may be, and must be admitted that the people, in many countries, were for a time deluded. They who argue against us say that jarring interests have been reconciled. We say that gross delusions have been removed. Both admit the fact that sovereigns and their people *are* identified. But it is for them, who contend that this has been effected by change of principles, to specify the change. What change of principles or of government has taken place among the nations of Europe? We are the best judges of ourselves—what change has taken place *here?* Is the Constitution other than it was when we were told (as we often were told in the bad times) that it was a doubt whether it were worth defending? Is the Constitution other than it was when we were warned that peace on any terms must be made, as the only hope of saving it from popular indignation and popular reform?

The powers which have achieved the victory.

There is yet another question to be asked. By what power, in what part of the world, has that final blow been struck which has smitten the tyrant to the ground? I suppose, by some enlightened republic; by some recently-regenerated government of pure philanthropy and uncorrupted virtue; I suppose, by some nation which, in the excess of popular freedom, considers even a representative system as defective, unless each individual interferes directly in the national concerns; some nation of enlightened patriots, every man of whom is a politician in the coffee-house, as well as in the Senate: I suppose it is from some such government as this that the conqueror of autocrats, the sworn destroyer of monarchical England, has met his doom. I look through the European world, gentlemen, in vain: I find there no such august community. But in another hemisphere I do find such a one, which, no doubt, must be the political David by whom the Goliath of Europe has been brought down. What is the name of that glorious republic, to which the gratitude of Europe is eternally due—which, from its innate hatred to tyranny, has so perseveringly exerted itself to liberate the world, and at last has successfully closed the contest? Alas, gentlemen, such a republic I do indeed find; and I find it enlisted, and (God be thanked!) enlisted alone, under the banner of the despot.[1] But where was the blow struck? Where? Alas for theory! In the wilds of despotic Russia. It was followed up on the plains of Leipsic—by Russian, Prussian, and Austrian arms.

Patriotism chiefly an instinctive feeling.

But let me not be mistaken. Do I, therefore, mean to contend—do I therefore, give to our antagonists in the argument the advantage of ascribing to us the base tenet that an absolute monarchy is better than a free government? God forbid! What I mean is this, that, in appreciating the comparative excellence of political institutions, in estimating the force of national spirit, and the impulses of national feeling, it is idle—it is mere pedantry, to overlook the affections of nature. The order of nature could not subsist among mankind, if there were not an *instinctive* patriotism; I do not say unconnected with, but prior and para-

[1] This slant at America was, of course, to be expected in time of war, and had quite as little bitterness in it as we should naturally look for in a man of Mr. Canning's temperament, at a moment of so much exultation.

mount to, the desire of political amelioration. It may be very wrong that it should be so. I can not help it. Our business is with fact. And surely it is not to be regretted that tyrants and conquerors should have learned, from the lessons of experience, that the first consideration suggested to the inhabitant of any country by a foreign invasion, is, not whether the political constitution of the state be faultlessly perfect or not, but whether the altar at which he has worshiped—whether the home in which he has dwelt from his infancy—whether his wife and his children—whether the tombs of his forefathers—whether the place of the Sovereign under whom he was born, and to whom he, therefore, owes (or, if it must be so stated, fancies that he, therefore, owes) allegiance, shall be abandoned to violence and profanation.

Delusion on this subject produced by the French Revolution.

That, in the infancy of the French Revolution, many nations in Europe were, unfortunately, led to believe and to act upon a different persuasion, is undoubtedly true; that whole countries were overrun by reforming conquerors, and flattered themselves with being proselytes till they found themselves victims. Even in this country, as I have already said, there have been times when we have been called upon to consider whether there was not something at home which must be mended before we could hope to repel a foreign invader with success.

It is fortunate for the world that this question should have been tried, if I may so say, to a disadvantage; that it should have been tried in countries where no man in his senses will say that the frame of political society is such as, according to the most moderate principles of regulated freedom, it ought to be; where, I will venture to say, without hazarding the imputation of being myself a visionary reformer, political society is not such as, after the successes of this war, and from the happy contagion of the example of Great Britain, it is sure gradually to become. It is fortunate for the world that this question should have been tried on its own merits; that, after twenty years of controversy, we should be authorized, by undoubted results, to revert to nature and to truth, and to disentangle the genuine feelings of the heart from the obstructions which a cold, presumptuous, generalizing philosophy had wound around them.

A love of one's native soil the foundation of patriotism.

One of the most delightful poets of this country, in describing the various proportions of natural blessings and advantages dispensed by Providence to the various nations of Europe, turns from the luxuriant plains and cloudless skies of Italy to the rugged mountains of Switzerland, and inquires whether there, also, in those barren and stormy regions, the "patriot passion" is found equally imprinted on the heart? He decides the question truly in the affirmative; and he says, of the inhabitant of those bleak wilds,

> Dear is that shed to which his soul conforms,
> And dear that hill which lifts him to the storms;
> And, as a child, when scaring sounds molest,
> Clings close and closer to the mother's breast,
> So the loud torrent and the whirlwind's roar
> But bind him to his native mountains more.[2]

What Goldsmith thus beautifully applied to the physical varieties of soil and climate has been found no less true with respect to political institutions. A sober desire of improvement, a rational endeavor to redress error, and to correct imperfection in the political frame of human society, are not only natural, but laudable in man. But it is well that it should have been shown, by irrefragable proof, that these sentiments, even where most strongly and most justly felt, supersede not that devotion to native soil which is the foundation of national independence. And it is right that it should be understood and remembered, that the spirit of national independence alone, aroused where it had slumbered, enlightened where it had been deluded, and kindled into enthusiasm by the insults and outrages of an all-grasping invader, has been found sufficient, without internal changes and compromises of sovereigns or governments with their people —without relaxations of allegiance and abjurations of authority, to animate, as with one pervading soul, the different nations of the continent; to combine, as into one congenial mass, their various feelings, passions, prejudices; to direct these concentrated energies with one impulse against the common tyrant; and to shake (and, may we not hope? to overthrow) the *Babel* of his iniquitous power.

But no country can stand insulated.

Gentlemen, there is another argument, more peculiarly relating to our own country, which has at times been interposed to discourage the prosecution of the war. That this country is sufficient to its own defense, sufficient to its own happiness, sufficient to its own independence; and that the complicated combinations of continental policy are always hazardous to our interests, as well as burdensome to our means, has been, at several periods of the war, a favorite doctrine, not only with those who, for other reasons, wished to embarrass the measures of the government, but with men of the most enlightened minds, of the most benevolent views, and the most ardent zeal for the interests as well as the honor of their country. May we not flatter ourselves, that upon this point, also, experience has decided in favor of the course of policy which has been actually pursued?

The interests of England indissolubly connected with those of other nations.

Can any man now look back upon the trial which we have gone through, and maintain that, at any period during the last twenty years, the plan of insulated policy could have been adopted, without having in the event, at this day, prostrated England at the foot of a conqueror? Great, indeed, has been the call upon our exertions; great, indeed, has been the drain upon our resources; long and wearisome has the struggle been; and late is the moment at which peace is brought within our reach. But even though the

[2] Goldsmith's Traveler.

difficulties of the contest may have been enhanced, and its duration protracted by it, yet is there any man who seriously doubts whether the having associated our destinies with the destinies of other nations be or be not that which, under the blessing of Providence, has eventually secured the safety of all?

Peace could not have been safely made at any earlier period.

It is at the moment when such a trial has come to its issue, that it is fair to ask of those who have suffered under the pressure of protracted exertion (and of whom rather than of those who are assembled around me—for by whom have such privations been felt more sensibly?)—it is now, I say, the time to ask whether, at any former period of the contest, such a peace could have been made as would at once have guarded the national interests and corresponded with the national character? I address myself now to such persons only as think the character of a nation an essential part of its strength, and consequently of its safety. But if, among persons of that description, there be one who with all his zeal for the glory of his country, has yet at times been willing to abandon the contest in mere weariness and despair, of such a man I would ask, whether he can indicate the period at which he now wishes that such an abandonment had been consented to by the government and the Parliament of Great Britain?

Not when Bonaparte first usurped power.

Is it when the continent was at peace—when, looking upon the map of Europe, you saw one mighty and connected system, one great luminary, with his attendant satellites circulating around him; at that period could this country have made peace, and have remained at peace for a twelvemonth? What is the answer? Why, that the experiment was tried. The result was the renewal of the war.

Not during the prevalence of the continental system.

Was it at a later period, when the continental system had been established? When two thirds of the ports of Europe were shut against you? When but a single link was wanting to bind the continent in a circling chain of iron, which should exclude you from intercourse with other nations? At that moment peace was most earnestly recommended to you. At that moment, gentlemen, I first came among you. At that moment I ventured to recommend to you perseverance, patient perseverance; and to express a hope that, by the mere strain of an unnatural effort, the massive bonds imposed upon the nations of the continent might, at no distant period, burst asunder. I was heard by you with indulgence—I know not whether with conviction. But is it now to be regretted that we did not at that moment yield to the pressure of our wants or of our fears? What has been the issue? The continental system was completed, with the sole exception of Russia, in the year 1812. In that year the pressure upon this country was undoubtedly painful. Had we yielded, the system would have been immortal. We persevered, and, before the conclusion of another year, the system was at an end: at an end, as all schemes of violence naturally terminate, not by a mild and gradual decay, such as waits upon a regular and well-spent life, but by sudden dissolution; at an end, like the breaking up of a winter's frost. But yesterday the whole continent, like a mighty plain covered with one mass of ice, presented to the view a drear expanse of barren uniformity; to-day, the breath of heaven unbinds the earth, the streams begin to flow again, and the intercourse of human kind revives.

Can we regret that we did not, like the fainting traveler, lie down to rest—but, indeed, to perish—under the severity of that inclement season? Did we not more wisely to bear up, and to wait the change?

Right for England to exult in the results of her long privations.

Gentlemen, I have said that I should be ashamed, and in truth I should be so, to address you in the language of exultation, if it were merely for the indulgence, however legitimate, of an exuberant and ungovernable joy. But they who have suffered great privations have a claim not merely to consolation, but to something more. They are justly to be compensated for what they have undergone, or lost, or hazarded, by the contemplation of what they have gained.

Her pre-eminence among the nations of Europe.

We have gained, then, a rank and authority in Europe, such as, for the life of the longest liver of those who now hear me, must place this country upon an eminence which no probable reverses can shake. We have gained, or rather we have recovered, a splendor of military glory, which places us by the side of the greatest military nations in the world. At the beginning of this war, while there was not a British bosom that did not beat with rapture at the exploits of our navy, there were few who would not have been contented to compromise for that reputation alone; to claim the sea as exclusively our province, and to leave to France and the other continental powers the struggle for superiority by land. That fabled deity, whom I see portrayed upon the wall,[3] was considered as the exclusive patron of British prowess in battle; but in seeming accordance with the beautiful fiction of ancient mythology, our Neptune, in the heat of contest, smote the earth with his trident, and up sprang the fiery war-horse, the emblem of military power.

The benefits to Europe by which she has gained it.

Let Portugal, now led to the pursuit of her flying conquerors—let liberated Spain—let France, invaded in her turn by those whom she had overrun or menaced with invasion, attest the triumphs of the army of Great Britain, and the equality of her military with her naval fame. And let those who, even after the triumphs of the Peninsula had begun, while they admitted that we had, indeed, wounded the giant in the heel, still deemed the rest of his huge frame invulnerable—let them now behold him reeling under the blows of united nations, and acknowledge at once the might of British arms and the force of British example.

[3] A figure of Neptune.

I do not say that these are considerations with a view to which the war, if otherwise terminable, ought to have been purposely protracted; but I say that, upon the retrospect, we have good reason to rejoice that the war was not closed ingloriously and insecurely, when the latter events of it have been such as have established our security by our glory.

I say we have reason to rejoice, that, during the period when the continent was prostrate before France—that, especially during the period when the continental system was in force, we did not shrink from the struggle; that we did not make peace for present and momentary ease, unmindful of the permanent safety and greatness of this country; that we did not leave unsolved the momentous questions, whether this country could maintain itself against France, unaided and alone; or with the continent divided; or with the continent combined against it; whether, when the wrath of the tyrant of the European world was kindled against us with seven-fold fury, we could or could not walk unharmed and unfettered through the flames?

I say we have reason to rejoice that, throughout this more than *Punic* war, in which it has so often been the pride of our enemy to represent herself as the Rome, and England as the Carthage, of modern times (with at least this color for the comparison, that the utter destruction of the modern Carthage has uniformly been proclaimed to be indispensable to the greatness of her rival)—we have, I say, reason to rejoice that, unlike our assigned prototype, we have not been diverted by internal dissensions from the vigorous support of a vital struggle; that we have not suffered distress nor clamor to distract our counsels, or to check the exertions of our arms.

The war has been uniformly advocated as the means of an honorable peace.

Gentlemen, for twenty years that I have sat in Parliament, I have been an advocate of the war. You knew this when you did me the honor to choose me as your representative. I then told you that I was the advocate of the war, because I was a lover of peace; but of a peace that should be the fruit of honorable exertion, a peace that should have a character of dignity, a peace that should be worth preserving, and should be likely to endure. I confess I was not sanguine enough, at that time, to hope that I should so soon have an opportunity of justifying my professions. But I know not why, six weeks hence, such a peace should not be made as England may not only be glad, but proud to ratify. Not such a peace, gentlemen, as that of Amiens—a short and feverish interval of unrefreshing repose. During that peace, which of you went or sent a son to Paris, who did not feel or learn that an Englishman appeared in France shorn of the dignity of his country; with the mien of a suppliant, and the conscious prostration of a man who had consented to purchase his gain or his ease by submission? But let a peace be made to-morrow, such as the allies have now the power to dictate, and the meanest of the subjects of this kingdom shall not walk the streets of Paris without being pointed out as the compatriot of Wellington; as one of that nation whose firmness and perseverance have humbled France and rescued Europe.

Is there any man that has a heart in his bosom who does not find, in the contemplation of this contrast alone, a recompense for the struggles and the sufferings of years?

The result not only glorious, but most beneficial.

But, gentlemen, the doing right is not only the most honorable course of action—it is also the most profitable in its result. At any former period of the war, the independence of almost all the other countries, our allies would have been to be purchased with sacrifices profusely poured out from the lap of British victory. Not a throne to be re-established, not a province to be evacuated, not a garrison to be withdrawn, but this country would have had to make compensation, out of her conquests, for the concessions obtained from the enemy. Now, happily, this work is already done, either by our efforts or to our hands. The peninsula free—the lawful commonwealth of European states already, in a great measure, restored, Great Britain may now appear in the congress of the world, rich in conquests, nobly and rightfully won, with little claim upon her faith or her justice, whatever may be the spontaneous impulse of her generosity or her moderation.

Such, gentlemen, is the situation and prospect of affairs at the moment at which I have the honor to address you. That you, gentlemen, may have your full share in the prosperity of your country, is my sincere and earnest wish. The courage with which you bore up in adverse circumstances eminently entitles you to this reward.

For myself, gentlemen, while I rejoice in your returning prosperity, I rejoice also that our connection began under auspices so much less favorable; that we had an opportunity of knowing each other's minds in times when the minds of men are brought to the proof—times of trial and difficulty. I had the satisfaction of avowing to you, and you the candor and magnanimity to approve, the principles and opinions by which my public conduct has uniformly been guided, at a period when the soundness of those opinions and the application of those principles was matter of doubt and controversy. I thought, and I said, at the time of our first meeting, that the cause of England and of civilized Europe must be ultimately triumphant, if we but preserved our spirit untainted and our constancy unshaken. Such an assertion was, at that time, the object of ridicule with many persons: a single year has elapsed, and it is now the voice of the whole world.

Gentlemen, we may, therefore, confidently indulge the hope that our opinions will continue in unison; that our concurrence will be as cordial as it has hitherto been, if unhappily any new occasion of difficulty or embarrassment should hereafter arise.

At the present moment, I am sure, we are equally desirous to bury the recollection of all our differences with others in that general feeling of exultation in which all opinions happily combine.

SPEECH

OF MR. CANNING ON RADICAL REFORM, DELIVERED TO HIS CONSTITUENTS AT LIVERPOOL, MARCH 18, 1820.

INTRODUCTION.

ENGLAND was in a very agitated state during the year 1819. Pecuniary distress was nearly universal, and the agricultural, manufacturing, and commercial interests were reduced to the lowest point of depression.

Sir Francis Burdett, Mr. Hunt, Lord Cochrane, and others, ascribed nearly all the sufferings of the country to one cause, viz., the want of parliamentary reform, and made the most strenuous efforts in favor of *annual* Parliaments and *universal suffrage*. Nothing could be more injurious than these efforts to the cause of genuine reform, as advocated by Earl Grey, especially considering the means adopted by the radical reformers to accomplish their object. Itinerant lecturers traversed the country, gathering immense crowds of the lower classes, and inflaming their minds by a sense of injury and oppression. Bodies of men, amounting sometimes to fifty thousand, marched to the place of meeting in regular array, with banners bearing the inscription "Liberty or Death!" and others of a similar import. The magistrates became alarmed, and the measures used to prevent mischief were sometimes unduly severe, and in one instance (that of the meeting at Manchester, August 16th) were attended with the most deplorable consequences.

It was the general sentiment of the country, that some measures should be adopted to prevent these evils, and at the meeting of Parliament in November, 1819, the ministry introduced bills for the following purposes, which, from their number, were called the "Six Acts." 1. To take away the right of traversing in cases of misdemeanor; 2. To punish any person found guilty on a second conviction of libel, by fine, imprisonment, and banishment for life; 3. To prevent seditious meetings, requiring the names of seven householders to the requisition, which in future convened any meeting for the discussion of subjects connected with Church or State; 4. To prohibit military training, except under the authority of a magistrate or Lord Lieutenant; 5. To subject cheap periodical pamphlets, on political subjects, to a duty similar to that of newspapers; 6. A bill giving magistrates the power of entering houses by night or by day, for the purpose of seizing arms believed to be collected for unlawful purposes. These bills were all carried by large majorities; the entering houses *by night*, and the severity of the restrictions on the press, were chiefly objected to; but there appeared a general concurrence in the necessity of strong measures.

Soon after these acts were passed, a new election took place; and Mr. Canning came forward to vindicate the above measures, and also to resist every attempt at parliamentary reform by identifying the whole plan with these radical views. The speech is certainly a very able one, and will interest the reader as giving the Tory side of the argument, though it by no means meets the question as presented by such reformers as Earl Grey and Mr. Brougham.

SPEECH, &c.

Recent political evils.

GENTLEMEN,—Short as the interval is since I last met you in this place on a similar occasion, the events which have filled up that interval have not been unimportant. The great moral disease which we then talked of as gaining ground on the community has, since that period, arrived at its most extravagant height; and since that period, also, remedies have been applied to it, if not of permanent cure, at least of temporary mitigation.

The remedies applied.

Gentlemen, with respect to those remedies—I mean with respect to the transactions of the last short session of Parliament, previous to the dissolution—I feel that it is my duty, as your representative, to render to you some account of the part which I took in that assembly to which you sent me; I feel it my duty also, as a member of the government by which those measures were advised. Upon occasions of such trying exigency as those which we have lately experienced, I hold it to be of the very essence of our free and popular Constitution, that an unreserved interchange of sentiment should take place between the representative and his constituents; and if it accidentally happens that he who addresses you as your representative, stands also in the situation of a responsible adviser of the Crown, I recognize in that more rare occurrence a not less striking or less valuable peculiarity of that Constitution under which we have the happiness to live—by which a minister of the Crown is brought into contact with the great body of the community, and the service of the King is shown to be a part of the service of the people.

Gentlemen, it has been one advantage of the transactions of the last session of Parliament, that while they were addressed to meet the evils which had grown out of charges heaped upon the House of Commons, they had also, in a great measure, falsified the charges themselves.

I would appeal to the recollection of every man who now hears me—of any the most careless estimator of public sentiment, or the most indifferent spectator of public events, whether any country, in any two epochs, however distant, of its history, ever presented such a contrast with itself as this country in November, 1819, and this country in February, 1820? Do I exaggerate when I say, that there was not a man of property who did not tremble for his possessions?—that there was not a man of retired and peaceable habits who did not tremble for the tranquillity and security of his home?—that there was not a man of orderly and religious principles who did not fear that those principles were about to be cut from under the feet of succeeding generations? Was there any man who did not apprehend the Crown to be in danger? Was there any man attached to the other branches of the Constitution who did not contemplate with anxiety and dismay the rapid and apparently irresistible diffusion of doctrines hostile to the very existence of Parliament as at present constituted, and calculated to excite not hatred and contempt merely, but open and audacious force, especially against the House of Commons? What is, in these respects, the situation of the country now? Is there a man of property who does not feel the tenure by which he holds his possessions to have been strengthened? Is there a man of peace who does not feel his domestic tranquillity to have been secured? Is there a man of moral and religious principles who does not look forward with better hope to see his children educated in those principles?—who does not hail, with renewed confidence, the revival and re-establishment of that moral and religious sense which had been attempted to be obliterated from the hearts of mankind?

Signal change in the condition of the country.

Well, gentlemen, and what has intervened between the two periods? A calling of that degraded Parliament; a meeting of that scoffed at and derided House of Commons; a concurrence of those three branches of an imperfect Constitution, not one of which, if we are to believe the radical reformers, lived in the hearts, or swayed the feelings, or commanded the respect of the nation; but which, despised as they were while in a state of separation and inaction, did, by a co-operation of four short weeks, restore order, confidence, a reverence for the laws, and a just sense of their own legitimate authority.

This change produced by the action of the so much complained of Parliament.

Another event, indeed, has intervened, in itself of a most painful nature, but powerful in aiding and confirming the impressions which the assembling and the proceedings of Parliament were calculated to produce. I mean the loss which the nation has sustained by the death of a Sovereign, with whose person all that is venerable in monarchy has been identified in the eyes of successive generations of his subjects; a Sovereign whose goodness, whose years, whose sorrows and sufferings must have softened the hearts of the most ferocious enemies of kingly power; whose active virtues, and the memory of whose virtues, when it pleased Divine Providence that they should be active no more, have been the guide and guardian of his people through many a weary and many a stormy pilgrimage; scarce less a guide, and quite as much a guardian, in the cloud of his evening darkness, as in the brightness of his meridian day.[1]

That such a loss, and the recollections and reflections naturally arising from it, must have had a tendency to revive and refresh the attachment to monarchy, and to root that attachment deeper in the hearts of the people, might easily be shown by reasoning; but a feeling, truer than all reasoning, anticipates the result, and renders the process of argument unnecessary. So far, therefore, has this great calamity brought with it its own compensation, and conspired to the restoration of peace throughout the country with the measures adopted by Parliament.

And, gentlemen, what was the character of those measures? The best eulogy of them I take to be this: it may be said of them, as has been said of some of the most consummate productions of literary art, that, though no man beforehand had exactly anticipated the scope and the details of them, there was no man, when they were laid before him, who did not feel that they were precisely such as he would himself have suggested. So faithfully adapted to the case which they were framed to meet, so correctly adjusted to the degree and nature of the mischief they were intended to control, that, while we all feel that they have done their work, I think none will say there has been any thing in them of excess or supererogation.

Regulation of large public meetings.

We were loudly assured by the reformers, that the test throughout the country by which those who were ambitious of seats in the new Parliament would be tried, was to be — whether they had supported those measures. I have inquired, with as much diligence as was compatible with my duties here, after the proceedings of other elections, and I protest I know no place yet, besides the hustings of Westminster and Southwark, at which that menaced test has been put to any candidates. To me, indeed, it was not put as a test, but objected as a charge. You know how that charge was answered; and the result is to me a majority of 1300 out of 2000 voters upon the poll.

But, gentlemen, though this question has not, as was threatened, been the watch-word of popular elections, every other effort has, nevertheless, been industriously employed to persuade the people that their liberties have been essentially abridged by the regulation of popular meetings. Against that one of the measures passed by Parliament, it is that the attacks of the radical reformers have been particularly directed. Gentlemen, the first answer to this averment is, that the act leaves untouched all the constitutional modes of assembly which have been known to the nation since it became free. We are fond of dating our freedom from the Revolution. I should be glad to know in what period since the

The interdict of immense masses meeting, no restraint on the liberty of the people.

[1] This refers to the King's derangement from 1811.

Revolution (up to a very late period indeed, which I will specify)—in what period of those reigns growing out of the Revolution—I mean, of the first reigns of the house of Brunswick—did it enter into the head of man, that such meetings could be holden, or that the Legislature would tolerate the holding of such meetings, as disgraced this kingdom for some months previous to the last session of Parliament? When, therefore, it is asserted that such meetings were never before suppressed, the simple answer is, they were never before systematically attempted to be holden.

Such meetings unknown to the Constitution.

I verily believe the first meeting of the kind that was ever attempted and tolerated (I know of none anterior to it) was that called by Lord George Gordon, in St. George's Fields, in the year 1780, which led to the demolition of chapels and dwelling-houses, the breaking of prisons, and the conflagration of London. Was England never free till 1780? Did British liberty spring to light from the ashes of the metropolis? What! was there no freedom in the reign of George the Second? None in that of George the First? None in the reign of Queen Anne or of King William? Beyond the Revolution I will not go. But I have always heard that British liberty was established long before the commencement of the late reign; nay, that in the late reign (according to popular politicians) it rather sunk and retrograded; and yet never till that reign was such an abuse of popular meetings, dreamed of, much less erected into a right not to be questioned by magistrates, and not to be controlled by Parliament.

All social rights liable to restriction for the general good.

Do I deny, then, the general right of the people to meet, to petition, or to deliberate upon their grievances? God forbid! But social right is not a simple, abstract, positive, unqualified term. Rights are, in the same individual, to be compared with his duties; and rights in one person are to be balanced with the rights of others. Let us take this right of meeting in its most extended construction and most absolute sense. The persons who called the meeting at Manchester tell you that they had a right to collect together countless multitudes to discuss the question of parliamentary reform; to collect them when they would and where they would, without consent of magistrates, or concurrence of inhabitants, or reference to the comfort or convenience of the neighborhood. May not the peaceable, the industrious inhabitant of Manchester say, on the other hand, "I have a right to quiet in my house; I have a right to carry on my manufactory, on which not my existence only and that of my children, but that of my workmen and their numerous families depends. I have a right to be protected in the exercise of this my lawful calling; I have a right to be protected, not against violence and plunder only, against fire and sword, but against the terror of these calamities, and against the risk of these inflictions; against the intimidation or seduction of my workmen; or against the distraction of that attention and the interruption of that industry, without which neither they nor I can gain our livelihood. I call upon the laws to afford me that protection; and if the laws in this country can not afford it, depend upon it, I and my manufacturers must emigrate to some country where they can." Here is a conflict of rights, between which what is the decision? Which of the two claims is to give way? Can any reasonable being doubt? Can any honest man hesitate? Let private justice or public expediency decide, and can the decision by possibility be other than that the peaceable and industrious shall be protected—the turbulent and mischievous put down?

These immense mass meetings not essential to the right of petition.

But what similarity is there between tumults such as these and an orderly meeting, recognized by the law for all legitimate purposes of discussion or petition? God forbid that there should not be modes of assembly by which every class of this great nation may be brought together to deliberate on any matters connected with their interest and their freedom. It is, however, an inversion of the natural order of things, it is a disturbance of the settled course of society, to represent discussion as every thing, and the ordinary occupations of life as nothing. To protect the peaceable in their ordinary occupations is as much the province of the laws, as to provide opportunities of discussion for every purpose to which it is necessary and properly applicable. The laws do both; but it is no part of the contrivance of the laws that immense multitudes should wantonly be brought together, month after month, and day after day, in places where the very bringing together of a multitude is of itself the source of terror and of danger.

They are directly opposed to the spirit of the English laws.

It is no part of the provision of the laws, nor is it in the spirit of them, that such multitudes should be brought together at the will of unauthorized and irresponsible individuals, changing the scene of meeting as may suit their caprice or convenience, and fixing it where they have neither property, nor domicil, nor connection. The spirit of the law goes directly the other way. It is, if I may so express myself, eminently a spirit of corporation. Counties, parishes, townships, guilds, professions, trades, and callings, form so many local and political subdivisions, into which the people of England are distributed by the law; and the pervading principle of the whole is that of vicinage or neighborhood; by which each man is held to act under the view of his neighbors; to lend his aid to them, to borrow theirs; to share their councils, their duties, and their burdens; and to bear with them his share of responsibility for the acts of any of the members of the community of which he forms a part.

Observe, I am not speaking here of the reviled and discredited statute law only, but of that venerable common law to which our reformers are so fond of appealing on all occasions, against the statute law by which it is modified, explained, or enforced. Guided by the spirit of the one, no less than by the letter of the other, what man is there in this country who can not point to the portion of society to which he belongs? If injury is sustained, upon whom is the injured person expressly entitled to come for redress? Upon the hundred, or the division in which he has sustained the injury. On what principle? On the principle, that as the individual is amenable to the division of the community to which he specially belongs, so neighbors are answerable for each other. Just laws, to be sure, and admirable equity, if a stranger is to collect a mob which is to set half Manchester on fire; and the burned half is to come upon the other half for indemnity, while the stranger goes off unquestioned, to excite the like tumult and produce the like danger elsewhere!

Their results might easily be foreseen.

That such was the nature, such the tendency, nay, that such, in all human probability, might have been the result, of meetings like that of the 16th of August, who can deny? Who that weighs all the particulars of that day, comparing them with the rumors and the threats that preceded it, will dispute that such might have been the result of that very meeting, if that meeting, so very legally assembled, had not, by the happy decision of the magistrates, been so very illegally dispersed?

They were called in a way to avoid the operation of the law.

It is, therefore, not in consonance, but in contradiction to the spirit of the law, that such meetings have been holden. The law prescribes a corporate character. The callers of these meetings have always studiously avoided it. No summons of freeholders—none of freemen—none of the inhabitants of particular places or parishes—no acknowledgment of local or political classification. Just so at the beginning of the French Revolution; the first work of the reformers was to loosen every established political relation, every legal holding of man to man; to destroy every corporation, to dissolve every subsisting class of society, and to reduce the nation into individuals, in order afterward to congregate them into mobs.

Such was the obvious design.

Let no person, therefore, run away with the notion that these things were done without design. To bring together the inhabitants of a particular division, or men sharing a common franchise, is to bring together an assembly of which the component parts act with some respect and awe of each other. Ancient habits, which the reformers would call prejudices; preconceived attachments, which they would call corruption; that mutual respect which makes the eye of a neighbor a security for each man's good conduct, but which the reformers would stigmatize as a confederacy among the few for dominion over their fellows; all these things make men difficult to be moved, on the sudden, to any extravagant and violent enterprise. But bring together a multitude of individuals, having no permanent relation to each other—no common tie but what arises from their concurrence as members of that meeting, a tie dissolved as soon as the meeting is at an end; in such an aggregation of individuals there is no such mutual respect, no such check upon the proceedings of each man from the awe of his neighbor's disapprobation; and if ever a multitudinous assembly can be wrought up to purposes of mischief, it will be an assembly so composed.

Ought never to be confounded with the legalized meetings of the people.

How monstrous is it to confound such meetings with the genuine and recognized modes of collecting the sense of the English people! Was it by meetings such as these that the Revolution was brought about, that grand event to which our antagonists are so fond of referring? Was it by meetings in St. George's Fields? in Spa Fields? in Smithfield? Was it by untold multitudes collected in a village in the north? No! It was by the meeting of corporations, in their corporate capacity; by the assembly of recognized bodies of the state; by the interchange of opinions among portions of the community known to each other, and capable of estimating each other's views and characters. Do we want a more striking mode of remedying grievances than this? Do we require a more animating example? And did it remain for the reformers of the present day to strike out the course by which alone Great Britain could make and keep herself free?

Some one ought to be responsible for the holding of public meetings.

Gentlemen, all power is, or ought to be, accompanied by responsibility. Tyranny is irresponsible power. This definition is equally true, whether the power be lodged in one or many; whether in a despot, exempted by the form of government from the control of the law; or in a mob, whose numbers put them beyond the reach of law. Idle, therefore, and absurd, to talk of freedom where a mob domineers! Idle, therefore, and absurd, to talk of liberty, when you hold your property, perhaps your life, not indeed at the nod of a despot, but at the will of an inflamed, an infuriated populace! If, therefore, during the reign of terror at Manchester, or at Spa Fields, there were persons in this country who had a right to complain of tyranny, it was they who loved the Constitution, who loved the monarchy, but who dared not utter their opinions or their wishes until their houses were barricaded, and their children sent to a place of safety. That was tyranny! and so far as the mobs were under the control of a leader, that was despotism! It was against that tyranny, it was against that despotism, that Parliament at length raised its arm.

Personal responsibility checks their abuse.

All power, I say, is vicious that is not accompanied by proportionate responsibility. Personal responsibility prevents the abuse of individual power; responsibility of character is the security against the abuse of collective power, when exercised by bodies of men whose existence is permanent and defined. But strip such bodies of these qualities, you degrade them into multitudes, and then what security have you against any thing that they may do or resolve, knowing that, from the moment at which the meeting is at an end, there is no human being responsible for their proceedings? The meeting at Manchester, the meeting at Birmingham, the meeting at Spa Fields or Smithfield, what pledge could they give to the nation of the soundness or sincerity of their designs? The local character of Manchester, the local character of Birmingham, was not pledged to any of the proceedings to which their names were appended. A certain number of ambulatory tribunes of the people, self-elected to that high function, assumed the name and authority of whatever place they thought proper to select for a place of meeting; the rostrum was pitched, sometimes here, sometimes there, according to the fancy of the mob or the patience of the magistrates; but the proposition and the proposer were in all places nearly alike; and when, by a sort of political ventriloquism, the same voice had been made to issue from half a dozen different corners of the country, it was impudently assumed to be a concord of sweet sounds, composing the united voice of the people of England!

The cause of liberty has not suffered by the remedies adopted.

Now, gentlemen, let us estimate the mighty mischief that has been done to liberty by putting down meetings such as I have described. Let us ask what lawful authority has been curtailed; let us ask what respectable community has been defrauded of its franchise; let us ask what municipal institutions have been violated by a law which fixes the migratory complaint to the spot whence it professes to originate, and desires to hear of the grievance from those by whom that grievance is felt—which leaves to Manchester, as Manchester, to Birmingham, as Birmingham, to London, as London, all the free scope of utterance which they have at any time enjoyed for making known their wants, their feelings, their wishes, their remonstrances; which leaves to each of these divisions its separate authority—to the union of all, or of many of them, the aggregate authority of such a consent and co-operation; but which denies to any itinerant hawker of grievances the power of stamping their names upon his wares; of pretending, because he may raise an outcry *at* Manchester or *at* Birmingham, that he therefore speaks the sense of the town which he disquiets and endangers; or, still more preposterously, that because he has disquieted and endangered half a dozen neighborhoods in their turn, he is, therefore, the organ of them all, and through them, of the whole British people.

Such are the stupid fallacies which the law of the last session has extinguished! and such are the object and effect of the measures which British liberty is not to survive!

Parliamentary Reform.

To remedy the dreadful wound thus inflicted upon British liberty—to restore to the people what the people have not lost—to give a new impulse to that spirit of freedom which nothing has been done to embarrass or restrain, we are invited to alter the constitution of that assembly through which the people share in the Legislature; in short, to make a *radical reform in the House of Commons*.

What is meant by it?

It has always struck me as extraordinary that there should be persons prepared to entertain the question of a change in so important a member of the Constitution, without considering in what way that change must affect the situation of the other members, and the action of the Constitution itself.

I have, on former occasions, stated here, and I have stated elsewhere, questions on this subject, to which, as yet, I have never received an answer. "You who propose to reform the House of Commons, do you mean to restore that branch of the Legislature to the same state in which it stood at some former period? or do you mean to reconstruct it on new principles?"

Perhaps a moderate Reformer or Whig will answer, that he means only to restore the House of Commons to what it was at some former period. I then beg to ask him—and to that question, also, I have never yet received an answer—"At what period of our history was the House of Commons in the state to which you wish to restore it?"

The Commons never more truly popular than at present.

The House of Commons must, for the purpose of clear argument, be considered in two views. First, with respect to its agency as a third part in the Constitution; secondly, with respect to its composition, in relation to its constituents. As to its agency as a part of the Constitution, I venture to say, without hazard, as I believe, of contradiction, that there is no period in the history of this country in which the House of Commons will be found to have occupied so large a share of the functions of government as at present. Whatever else may be said of the House of Commons, this one point, at least, is indisputable, that from the earliest infancy of the Constitution, the power of the House of Commons has been growing, till it has almost, like the rod of Aaron, absorbed its fellows. I am not saying whether this is or is not as it ought to be. I am merely saying why I think that it can not be intended to complain of the want of power, and of a due share in the government, as the defect of the modern House of Commons.

I admit, however, very willingly, that the greater share of power the House of Commons exercises, the more jealous we ought to be of its composition; and I presume, therefore, that it is in this respect, and in relation to its constituents, that the state of that House is contended to want revision. Well, then, at what period of our history was the composition of the history of the House of Commons materially different from what it is at present? Is there any period of our history in which the rights of election were not as various, in which the influence of property was not as direct, in which recommendations of candidates were not as efficient, and some boroughs as close as they are now? I ask for information; but that information, plain and simple as it is, and necessary, one should think, to a clear understanding, much more to a grave decision of the point at issue, I never, though soliciting it with all humility, have ever yet been able to obtain from any reformer, Radical or Whig.

The objects of the Radical reformer inconsistent with monarchy.

The Radical reformer, indeed, to do him justice, is not bound to furnish me with an answer to this question, because with *his* view of the matter, precedents (except one, which I shall mention presently) have nothing to do. The Radical reformer would, probably, give to my first question an answer very different from that which I have supposed his moderate brother to give. He will tell me fairly, that he means not simply to bring the House of Commons back, either to the share of power which it formerly enjoyed, or to the modes of election by which it was formerly chosen; but to make it what, according to him, it ought to be — a direct, effectual representative of the people; representing them not as a delegate commissioned to take care of their interests, but as a deputy appointed to speak their will. Now to this view of the matter I have no other objection than this: that the British Constitution is a limited monarchy; that a limited monarchy is, in the nature of things, a mixed government; but that such a House of Commons as the Radical reformer requires would, in effect, constitute a pure democracy—a power, as it appears to me, inconsistent with any monarchy, and unsusceptible of any limitation.

The question of a republic not the one before us.

I may have great respect for the person who theoretically prefers a republic to a monarchy. But even supposing me to agree with him in his preference, I should have a preliminary question to discuss, by which he, perhaps, may not feel himself embarrassed; which is this, whether I, born as I am (and as *I* think it is my good fortune to be) under a monarchy, am quite at liberty to consider myself as having a clear stage for political experiments; whether I should be authorized, if I were convinced of the expediency of such a change, to withdraw monarchy altogether from the British Constitution, and to substitute an unqualified democracy in its stead; or whether, whatever changes I may be desirous of introducing, I am not bound to consider the Constitution which I find as at least circumscribing the range, and in some measure prescribing the nature of the improvement.

But the direct tendency of the present scheme is to destroy the monarchy.

For my own part, I am undoubtedly prepared to uphold the ancient monarchy of the country, by arguments drawn from what I think the blessings which we have enjoyed under it; and by arguments of another sort, if arguments of another sort shall ever be brought against it. But all that I am now contending for is, that whatever reformation is proposed, should be considered with some reference to the established Constitution of the country. That point being conceded to me, I have no difficulty in saying, that I can not conceive a Constitution of which one third part shall be an assembly delegated by the people—not to consult for the good of the nation, but to speak, day by day, the people's will—which must not, in a few days' sitting, sweep away every other branch of the Constitution that might attempt to oppose or control it. I can not conceive how, in fair reasoning, any other branch of the Constitution should pretend to stand against it. If government be a matter of will, all that we have to do is to collect the will of the nation, and, having collected it by an adequate organ, that will is paramount and supreme. By what pretension could the House of Lords be maintained in equal authority and jurisdiction with the House of Commons, when once that House of Commons should become a direct deputation, speaking the people's will, and that will the rule of the government? In one way or other the House of Lords must act, if it be to remain a concurrent branch of the Legislature. Either it must uniformly affirm the measures which come from the House of Commons, or it must occasionally take the liberty to reject them. If it uniformly affirm, it is without the shadow of authority. But to presume to reject an act of the deputies of the whole nation!—by what assumption of right could three or four hundred great proprietors set themselves against the national will? Grant the reformers, then, what they ask, on the principles on which they ask it, and it is utterly impossible that, after such a reform, the Constitution should long consist of more than one body, and that one body a popular assembly.

Proof from past history.

Why, gentlemen, is this theory? or is it a theory of mine? If there be, among those who hear me, any man who has been (as in the generous enthusiasm of youth any man may blamelessly have been) bitten by the doctrines of reform, I implore him, before he goes forward in his progress to embrace those doctrines in their radical extent, to turn to the history of the transactions in this country in the year 1648, and to examine the bearings of those transactions on this very question of radical reform.[2] He will find, gentlemen, that the House of Commons of that day passed the following resolution:

"*Resolved*, That the people are, under God, the original of all just power."

Well! can any sentiment be more just and reasonable? Is it not the foundation of all the liberties of mankind? Be it so. Let us proceed. The House of Commons followed up this resolution by a second, which runs in something like these terms:

"*Resolved*, That the Commons of England, assembled in Parliament, being chosen by and representing the people, *have the supreme authority* of this nation."

In this resolution the leap is taken. Do the Radical reformers deny the premises or the inference? or do they adopt the whole of the tempting precedent before them?

But the inference did not stop there. The House of Commons proceeded to deduce from these propositions an inference, the apparently logical dependence of which upon these propositions I wish I could see logically disproved.

"*Resolved* (without one dissenting voice), That whatsoever is enacted and declared law by the Commons of England, assembled in Parliament, hath the force of law, and all the people of this nation are included thereby, *although the consent and concurrence of the King and House of Peers be not had thereunto.*"

[2] It is hardly necessary to remind the reader, that Mr. Canning here goes back to the days of Cromwell and the deposition of Charles I.

Such was the theory: the practical inferences were not tardy in their arrival after the theory. In a few weeks the House of Peers was voted useless. We all know what became of the Crown.

Such the result of radical reform.

Such, I say, were the radical doctrines of 1648, and such the consequences to which they naturally led. If we are induced to admit the same premises now, who is it, I should be glad to know, that is to guarantee us against similar conclusions?

And this the only consistent scheme.

These, then, are the reasons why I look with jealousy at schemes of parliamentary reform. I look at them with still more jealousy, because, in one of the two classes of men who co-operate in support of that question, I never yet found any two individuals who held the same doctrines: I never yet heard any intelligible theory of reform, except that of the Radical reformers. Theirs, indeed, it is easy enough to understand. But as for theirs, I certainly am not yet fully prepared. I, for my part, will not consent to take one step, without knowing on what principle I am invited to take it, and (which is, perhaps, of more consequence) without declaring on what principle, I will *not* consent that any step, however harmless, shall be taken.

No change to be attempted without settling the *principle* on which it is made.

What more harmless than to disfranchise a corrupt borough in Cornwall, which has exercised its franchise amiss, and brought shame on itself, and on the system of which it is a part? Nothing. I have no sort of objection to doing, as Parliament has often done in such cases (supposing always the case to be proved), to disfranchising the borough, and rendering it incapable of abusing its franchise in future. But though I have no objection to doing this, I will *not* do it on the principle of speculative improvement. I do it on the principle of specific punishment for an offense. And I will take good care that no inference shall be drawn from my consent in this specific case, as to any sweeping concurrence in a scheme of general alteration.

Boroughs properly disfranchised for their crimes.

Nay, I should think it highly disingenuous to suffer the Radical reformers to imagine that they had gained a single step toward the admission of their theory, by any such instance of particular animadversion on proved misconduct. I consent to such disfranchisement; but I do so, not with a view of furthering the Radical system—rather of thwarting it. I am willing to wipe out any blot on the present system, because I mean the present system to stand. I will take away a franchise, because it has been practically abused; not because I am at all disposed to inquire into the origin or to discuss the utility of all such franchises, any more than I mean to inquire, gentlemen, into your titles to your estates. Disfranchising Grampound (if that is to be so), I mean to save Old Sarum.

Now, sir, I think I deal fairly with the Radical reformers; more fairly than those who would suffer it to be supposed by them that the disfranchisement of Grampound is to be the beginning of a system of reform: while they know, and I hope mean as well as I do, *not* to reform (in the sense of change) but to preserve the Constitution. I would not delude the reformers, if I could; and it is quite useless to attempt a delusion upon persons quite as sagacious in their generation as any moderate reformers or anti-reformers of us all. They know full well that the Whigs have no more notion than I have of parting with the close boroughs. Not they, indeed! A large, and perhaps the larger, part of them are in their hands. Why, in the assembly to which you send me, gentlemen, some of those who sit on the same side with me represent, to be sure, less popular places than Liverpool—but on the bench immediately over against me, I descry, among the most eminent of our rivals for power, scarce any other sort of representatives than members for close, or, if you will, for rotten boroughs. To suppose, therefore, that our political opponents have any thoughts of getting rid of the close boroughs, would be a gross delusion; and, I have no doubt, they will be quite as fair and open with the reformers on this point as I am.

But not on the principle of reforming the representation

It endangers the monarchy of England.

And why, gentlemen, is it that I am satisfied with a system which, it is said, no man can support who is not in love with corruption? Is it that I, more than any other man, am afraid to face a popular election? To the last question you can give the answer. To the former I will answer for myself. I do verily believe, as I have already said, that a complete and perfect democratical representation, such as the reformers aim at, can not exist as part of a mixed government. It may exist, and, for aught I know or care, may exist beneficially as a whole. But I am not sent to Parliament to inquire into the question whether a democracy or a monarchy be the best. My lot is cast under the British monarchy. Under that I have lived—under that I have seen my country flourish—under that I have seen it enjoy as great a share of prosperity, of happiness, and of glory, as I believe any modification of human society to be capable of bestowing; and I am not prepared to sacrifice or to hazard the fruit of centuries of experience, of centuries of struggles, and of more than one century of liberty, as perfect as ever blessed any country upon the earth, for visionary schemes of ideal perfectibility, or for doubtful experiments even of possible improvement.

The government to be taken as it is.

I am, therefore, for the House of Commons as a part, and not as the whole, of the government. And as a part of the government, I hold it to be frantic to suppose, that from the election of members of Parliament you can altogether exclude, by any contrivance, even if it were desirable to do so, the influence of property, rank, talents, family connection, and whatever else, in the radical language of the day, is considered as intimidation or corruption. I believe that if a reform, to the extent of that demanded by the Radical reformers, were granted, you would, before an annual election came round, find that there were new connections grown up which you must again destroy, new influence acquired which you must dispossess of its authority; and that in these fruitless attempts at unattainable purity, you were working against the natural current of human nature.

I believe, therefore, that, contrive how you will, some such human motives of action will find room to operate in the election of members of Parliament. I think that this must and ought to be so, unless you mean to exclude from the concerns of the nation all inert wealth, all inactive talent, the retired, the aged, and the infirm; all who can not face popular assemblies or engage in busy life; in short, unless you have found some expedient for disarming property of influence, without (what I hope we are not yet ripe for) the abolition of property itself.

Varied modes of election best for the House.

I would have by choice—if the choice were yet to be made—I would have in the House of Commons great variety of interests, and I would have them find their way there by a great variety of rights of election; satisfied that uniformity of election would produce any thing but a just representation of various interests. As to the close boroughs, I know that through them have found their way into the House of Commons men whose talents have been an honor to their kind, and whose names are interwoven with the brightest periods in the history of their country. I can not think that system altogether vicious which has produced such fruits. Nor can I think that there should be but one road into that assembly, or that no man should be presumed fit for the deliberations of a Senate, who has not had the nerves previously to face the storms of the hustings.

I need not say, gentlemen, that I am one of the last men to disparage the utility and dignity of popular elections. I have good cause to speak of them in far different language. But, among numberless other considerations which endear to me the favors which I have received at your hands, I confess it is one that, as your representative, I am enabled to speak my genuine sentiments on this (as I think it) vital question of parliamentary reform, without the imputation of shrinking from popular canvass, or of seeking shelter for myself in that species of representation which, as an element in the composition of Parliament, I never shall cease to defend.

The most violent reformers are willing to sit for boroughs.

In truth, gentlemen, though the question of reform is made the pretext of those persons who have vexed the country for some months, I verily believe that there are very few even of them who either give credit to their own exaggerations, or care much about the improvements which they recommend. Why, do we not see that the most violent of the reformers of the day are aiming at seats in that assembly, which, according to their own theories, they should have left to wallow in its own pollution, discountenanced and unredeemed? It is true, that if they found their way there, they might endeavor to bring us to a sense of our misdeeds, and to urge us to redeem our character by some self-condemning ordinance; but would not the authority of their names, as our associates, have more than counterbalanced the force of their eloquence as our reformers?

But, gentlemen, I am for the whole Constitution. The liberty of the subject as much depends on the maintenance of the constitutional prerogatives of the Crown—on the acknowledgment of the legitimate power of the other House of Parliament, as it does in upholding that supreme power (for such is the power of the purse in one sense of the word, though not in the sense of the resolution of 1648) which resides in the democratical branch of the Constitution. Whatever beyond its just proportion was gained by one part, would be gained at the expense of the whole; and the balance is now, perhaps, as nearly poised as human wisdom can adjust it. I fear to touch that balance, the disturbance of which must bring confusion on the nation.

Such a subject ought not to be tampered with.

Gentlemen, I trust there are few, very few, reasonable and enlightened men ready to lend themselves to projects of confusion. But I confess I very much wish that all who are not ready to do so would consider the ill effect of any countenance given publicly or by apparent implication, to those whom in their hearts and judgments they despise. I remember that most excellent and able man, Mr. Wilberforce, once saying in the House of Commons that he "never believed an opposition really to wish mischief to the country; that they only wished just so much mischief as might drive their opponents out, and place themselves in their room." Now, gentlemen, I can not help thinking that there are some persons tampering with the question of reform something in the same spirit. They do not go so far as the reformers; they even state irreconcilable differences of opinion; but to a certain extent they agree, and even co-operate with them. They co-operate with them in inflaming the public feeling not only against the government, but against the support given by Parliament to that government, in the hope, no doubt, of attracting to themselves the popularity which is lost to their opponents, and thus being enabled to correct and retrieve the errors of a displaced administration. Vain and hopeless task to raise such a spirit and then to govern it! They may stimulate the steeds into fury, till the chariot is hurried to the brink of a precipice; but do they flatter themselves that they can then leap in, and, hurling the incompetent driver from his seat, check the reins just in time to turn from the precipice and avoid the fall? I fear they would attempt it in vain. The impulse once given may be too impetuous to be controlled; and intending only to change the guidance of the machine, they may hurry it and themselves to irretrievable destruction.

May every man who has a stake in the country, whether from situation, from character, from wealth, from his family, and from the hopes of his children—may every man who has a sense of the blessings for which he is indebted to the form of government under which he lives, see that the time is come at which his decision must be taken, and, when once taken, steadfastly acted upon—for or against the institutions of the British monarchy! The time is come at which there is but that line of demarkation. On which side of that line we, gentlemen, shall range ourselves, our choice has long ago been made. In acting upon that our common choice, with my best efforts and exertions, I shall at once faithfully represent your sentiments, and satisfy my own judgment and conscience.

SPEECH

OF MR. CANNING, DELIVERED AT PLYMOUTH, IN THE YEAR 1823.

INTRODUCTION.

Mr. Canning having visited Plymouth and inspected the Dock-yards in 1823, the freedom of the town was presented him through the Mayor and other public officers. He returned thanks in the following speech, which was much admired at the time not only for the political views which it expressed, but especially for his beautiful allusion to the ships in ordinary as an emblem of England while reposing in the quietude of peace.

SPEECH, &c.

Mr. Mayor and Gentlemen,—I accept with thankfulness, and with greater satisfaction than I can express, this flattering testimony of your good opinion and good will. I must add that the value of the gift itself has been greatly enhanced by the manner in which your worthy and honorable Recorder has developed the motives which suggested it, and the sentiments which it is intended to convey.

The life of every public man subject to scrutiny.

Gentlemen, your recorder has said very truly, that whoever in this free and enlightened state, aims at political eminence, and discharges political duties, must expect to have his conduct scrutinized, and every action of his public life sifted with no ordinary jealousy, and with no sparing criticism; and such may have been my lot as much as that of other public men. But, gentlemen, unmerited obloquy seldom fails of an adequate, though perhaps tardy, compensation. I must think myself, as my honorable friend has said, eminently fortunate, if such compensation as he describes has fallen to me at an earlier period than to many others; if I dare flatter myself (as his partiality has flattered me), that the sentiments that you are kind enough to entertain for me, are in unison with those of the country; if, in addition to the justice done me by my friends, I may, as he has assured me, rely upon a candid construction, even from political opponents.

Success depends on very simple principles.

But, gentlemen, the secret of such a result does not lie deep. It consists only in an honest and undeviating pursuit of what one conscientiously believes to be one's public duty—a pursuit which, steadily continued, will, however detached and separate parts of a man's conduct may be viewed under the influence of partialities or prejudices, obtain for it, when considered as a whole, the approbation of all honest and honorable minds. Any man may occasionally be mistaken as to the means most conducive to the end which he has in view; but if the end be just and praiseworthy, it is by that he will be ultimately judged, either by his contemporaries or by posterity.

The views of a British politician should be confined to the interests of Great Britain.

Gentlemen, the end which I confess I have always had in view, and which appears to me the legitimate object of pursuit to a British statesman, I can describe in one word. The language of modern philosophy is wisely and diffusely benevolent; it professes the perfection of our species, and the amelioration of the lot of all mankind. Gentlemen, I hope that my heart beats as high for the general interest of humanity—I hope that I have as friendly a disposition toward other nations of the earth, as any one who vaunts his philanthropy most highly; but I am contented to confess that, in the conduct of political affairs, the grand object of my contemplation is the interest of England.

This involves no principle of selfishness.

Not, gentlemen, that the interest of England is an interest which stands isolated and alone. The situation which she holds forbids an exclusive selfishness; her prosperity must contribute to the prosperity of other nations, and her stability to the safety of the world. But intimately connected as we are with the system of Europe, it does not follow that we are, therefore, called upon to mix ourselves on every occasion, with a restless and meddling activity, in the concerns of the nations which surround us. It is upon a just balance of conflicting duties, and of rival, but sometimes incompatible advantages, that a government must judge when to put forth its strength, and when to husband it for occasions yet to come.

The peace of the world the great ultimate object.

Our ultimate object must be the peace of the world. That object may sometimes be best attained by prompt exertions—sometimes by abstinence from interposition in contests which we can not prevent. It is upon these principles that, as has been most truly observed by my worthy friend, it did not appear to the government of this country to be necessary that Great Britain should mingle in the recent contest between France and Spain.

Your worthy recorder has accurately classed the persons who would have driven us into that contest. There were undoubtedly among them those who desired to plunge this country into the difficulties of war, partly from the hope that those difficulties would overwhelm the administration; but it would be most unjust not to admit that there were others who were actuated by nobler principles and more generous feelings, who would have rushed forward at once from the sense of indignation at aggression, and who deemed that no act of injustice could be perpetrated from one end of the universe to the other, but that the sword of Great Britain should leap from its scabbard to avenge it. But as it is the province of law to control the excess even of laudable passions and propensities in individuals, so it is the duty of government to restrain within due bounds the ebullition of national sentiment, and to regulate the course and direction of impulses which it can not blame. Is there any one among the latter class of persons described by my honorable friend (for to the former I have nothing to say) who continues to doubt whether the government did wisely in declining to obey the precipitate enthusiasm which prevailed at the commencement of the contest in Spain?[1] Is there any body who does not now think that it was the office of government to examine more closely all the various bearings of so complicated a question, to consider whether they were called upon to assist a united nation, or to plunge themselves into the internal feuds by which that nation was divided—to aid in repelling a foreign invader, or to take part in a civil war? Is there any man that does not now see what would have been the extent of burdens that would have been cast upon this country? Is there any one who does not acknowledge that, under such circumstances the enterprise would have been one to be characterized only by a term borrowed from that part of the Spanish literature with which we are most familiar—Quixotic; an enterprise romantic in its origin, and thankless in the end?

But peace should be sought by being ready for war.

But while we thus control even our feelings by our duty, let it not be said that we cultivate peace either because we fear, or because we are unprepared for war; on the contrary, if eight months ago the government did not hesitate to proclaim that the country was prepared for war, if war should be unfortunately necessary, every month of peace that has since passed has but made us so much the more capable of exertion. The resources created by peace are means of war. In cherishing those resources, we but accumulate those means. *Our present repose is no more a proof of inability to act, than the state of inertness and inactivity in which I have seen those mighty masses that float in the waters above your town, is a proof that they are devoid of strength, and incapable of being fitted out for action. You well know, gentlemen, how soon one of those stupendous masses, now reposing on their shadows in perfect stillness—how soon, upon any call of patriotism, or of necessity, it would assume the likeness of an animated thing, instinct with life and motion—how soon it would ruffle, as it were, its swelling plumage—how quickly it would put forth all its beauty and its bravery, collect its scattered elements of strength, and awaken its dormant thunder. Such as is one of these magnificent machines when springing from inaction into a display of its might—such is England herself, while, apparently passive and motionless, she silently concentrates the power to be put forth on an adequate occasion.*[2] But God forbid that that occasion should arise. After a war sustained for near a quarter of a century—sometimes single-handed, and with all Europe arranged at times against her, or at her side, England needs a period of tranquillity, and may enjoy it without fear of misconstruction. Long may we be enabled, gentlemen, to improve the blessings of our present situation, to cultivate the arts of peace, to give to commerce, now reviving, greater extension, and new spheres of employment, and to confirm the prosperity now generally diffused throughout this island. Of the blessing of peace, gentlemen, I trust that this borough, with which I have now the honor and happiness of being associated, will receive an ample share. I trust the time is not far distant, when that noble structure of which, as I learn from your Recorder, the box with which you have honored me, through his hands, formed a part, that gigantic barrier against the fury of the waves that roll into your harbor, will protect a commercial marine not less considerable in its kind than the warlike marine of which your port has been long so distinguished an asylum, when the town of Plymouth will participate in the commercial prosperity as largely as it has hitherto done in the naval glories of England.

[1] See this subject explained in the introduction to Mr. Brougham's speech respecting it, page 904.

[2] It will interest the reader to compare this passage with one conceived in the same spirit by the poet Campbell, on the launching of a ship of the line.

"Those who have ever witnessed the spectacle of the launching of a ship of the line will perhaps forgive me for adding this to the examples of the sublime objects of artificial life. Of that spectacle I can never forget the impression, and of having witnessed it reflected from the faces of ten thousand spectators. They seem yet before me—I sympathize with their deep and silent expectation, and with their final burst of enthusiasm. It was not a vulgar joy, but an affecting national solemnity. When the vast bulwark sprang from her cradle, the calm water on which she swung majestically round, gave the imagination a contrast of the stormy element on which she was soon to ride. All the days of battle, and the nights of danger which she had to encounter—all the ends of the earth which she had to visit—and all that she had to do and to suffer for her country, rose in awful presentiment before the mind; and when the heart gave her a benediction, it was like one pronounced on a living being."—*Essay on English Poetry.*

SPEECH

OF MR. CANNING ON AFFORDING AID TO PORTUGAL WHEN INVADED FROM SPAIN, DELIVERED IN THE HOUSE OF COMMONS, DECEMBER 12, 1826.

INTRODUCTION.

ENGLAND had been for nearly two centuries the ally and protector of Portugal, and was bound to defend her when attacked.

In 1826, a body of absolutists, headed by the Queen Dowager and the Marquess of Chaves, attempted to destroy the existing Portuguese government, which had been founded on the basis of constitutional liberty. This government had been acknowledged by England, Franee, Austria, and Russia. It was, however, obnoxious to Ferdinand, king of Spain; and Portugal was invaded from the Spanish territory by large bodies of Portuguese absolutists, who had been there organized with the connivance, if not the direct aid, of the Spanish government.

The Portuguese government now demanded the assistance of England. Five thousand troops were, therefore, instantly ordered to Lisbon, and Mr. Canning came forward in this speech to explain the reasons of his prompt intervention. "This," says his biographer, "is the master-piece of his eloquence. In propriety and force of diction—in excellence of appropriate and well-methodized arrangement—in elevation of style and sentiment; and in all the vigorous qualities of genuine manly eloquence—boldness—judgment—firmness, it fully sustains its title to the high eulogy given it by Mr. Brougham at the close of the debate."

SPEECH, &c.

Design of the speaker.

MR. SPEAKER,—In proposing to the House of Commons to acknowledge, by an humble and dutiful address, his Majesty's most gracious message, and to reply to it in terms which will be, in effect, an echo of the sentiments and a fulfillment of the anticipations of that message, I feel that, however confident I may be in the justice, and however clear as to the policy of the measures therein announced, it becomes me, as a British minister, recommending to Parliament any step which may approximate this country even to the hazard of a war, while I explain the grounds of that proposal, to accompany my explanation with expressions of regret.

High sense entertained of the importance of peace.

I can assure the House, that there is not within its walls any set of men more deeply convinced than his Majesty's ministers—nor any individual more intimately persuaded than he who has now the honor of addressing you—of the vital importance of the continuance of peace to this country and to the world. So strongly am I impressed with this opinion—and for reasons of which I will put the House more fully in possession before I sit down—that I declare there is no question of doubtful or controverted policy—no opportunity of present national advantage—no precaution against remote difficulty—which I would not gladly compromise, pass over, or adjourn, rather than call on Parliament to sanction, at this moment, any measure which had a tendency to involve the country in war. But, at the same time, sir, I feel that which has been felt, in the best times of English history, by the best statesmen of this country, and by the Parliaments by whom those statesmen were supported—I feel that there are two causes, and but two causes, which can not be either compromised, passed over, or adjourned. These causes are, adherence to the national faith, and regard for the national honor.

But national faith and honor demand the proposed measures.

Sir, if I did not consider both these causes as involved in the proposition which I have this day to make to you, I should not address the House, as I now do, in the full and entire confidence that the gracious communication of his Majesty will be met by the House with the concurrence of which his Majesty has declared his expectation.

Part First. Treaty obligations to Portugal.

In order to bring the matter which I have to submit to you, under the cognizance of the House, in the shortest and clearest manner, I beg leave to state it, in the first instance, divested of any collateral considerations. It is a case of law and of fact: of national law on the one hand, and of notorious fact on the other; such as it must be, in my opinion, as impossible for Parliament, as it was for the government, to regard in any but one light; or to come to any but one conclusion upon it.

Early origin of those obligations.

Among the alliances by which, at different periods of our history, this country has been connected with the other nations of Europe, none is so ancient in origin, and so precise in obligation—none has continued so long, and been observed so faithfully—of none is the memory so intimately interwoven with the most brilliant records of our triumphs, as that by which Great Britain is connected with Portugal. It dates back to distant centuries; it has survived an endless variety of fortunes. Anterior in existence to the accession of the house of Braganza to the throne of Portugal—it derived, however, fresh vigor from that event; and never, from that epoch to the present hour, has the independent monarchy of Portugal ceased to be nurtured by the friendship of Great Britain. This alliance has never been seriously interrupted; but it has been renewed by repeated sanctions. It has been maintained under difficulties by which the fidelity of other alliances were shaken, and has been vindicated in fields of blood and of glory.

No one has ever felt that they ought to be broken off.

That the alliance with Portugal has been always unqualifiedly advantageous to this country—that it has not been sometimes inconvenient and sometimes burdensome—I am not bound nor prepared to maintain. But no British statesman, so far as I know, has ever suggested the expediency of shaking it off; and it is assuredly not at a moment of need that honor and, what I may be allowed to call national sympathy, would permit us to weigh, with an over-scrupulous exactness, the amount of difficulties and dangers attendant upon its faithful and steadfast observance. What feelings of national honor would forbid, is forbidden alike by the plain dictates of national faith.

Solemnly renewed in 1815.

It is not at distant periods of history, and in by-gone ages only, that the traces of the union between Great Britain and Portugal are to be found. In the last compact of modern Europe, the compact which forms the basis of its present international law—I mean the treaty of Vienna of 1815—this country, with its eyes open to the possible inconveniences of the connection, but with a memory awake to its past benefits, solemnly renewed the previously existing obligations of alliance and amity with Portugal. I will take leave to read to the House the third article of the treaty concluded at Vienna, in 1815, between Great Britain on the one hand, and Portugal on the other. It is couched in the following terms: "The treaty of Alliance, concluded at Rio de Janeiro, on the 19th of February, 1810, being founded on circumstances of a temporary nature, which have happily ceased to exist, the said treaty is hereby declared to be void in all its parts, and of no effect; *without prejudice, however, to the ancient treaties of alliance, friendship, and guarantee, which have so long and so happily subsisted between the two Crowns, and which are hereby renewed by the high contracting parties, and acknowledged to be of full force and effect.*"

Circumstances connected with that renewal.

In order to appreciate the force of this stipulation—recent in point of time, recent, also, in the sanction of Parliament—the House will, perhaps, allow me to explain shortly the circumstances in reference to which it was contracted. In the year 1807, when, upon the declaration of Bonaparte, that the house of Braganza had ceased to reign, the King of Portugal, by the advice of Great Britain, was induced to set sail for the Brazils; almost at the very moment of his most faithful Majesty's embarkation, a secret convention was signed between his Majesty and the King of Portugal, stipulating that, in the event of his most faithful Majesty's establishing the seat of his government in Brazil, Great Britain would never acknowledge any other dynasty than that of the house of Braganza on the throne of Portugal. That convention, I say, was contemporaneous with the migration to the Brazils; a step of great importance at the time, as removing from the grasp of Bonaparte the sovereign family of Braganza. Afterward, in the year 1810, when the seat of the King of Portugal's government was established at Rio de Janeiro, and when it seemed probable, in the then apparently hopeless condition of the affairs of Europe, that it was likely long to continue there, the secret convention of 1807, of which the main object was accomplished by the fact of the emigration to Brazil, was abrogated, and a new and public treaty was concluded, into which was transferred the stipulation of 1807, binding Great Britain, so long as his faithful Majesty should be compelled to reside in Brazil, not to acknowledge any other sovereign of Portugal than a member of the house of Braganza. That stipulation which had hitherto been *secret*, thus became *patent*, and part of the known law of nations.

In the year 1814, in consequence of the happy conclusion of the war, the option was afforded to the King of Portugal of returning to his European dominions. It was then felt that, as the necessity of his most faithful Majesty's absence from Portugal had ceased, the ground for the obligation originally contracted in the secret convention of 1807, and afterward transferred to the patent treaty of 1810, was removed. The treaty of 1810 was, therefore, annulled at the Congress of Vienna; and in lieu of the stipulation not to acknowledge any other sovereign of Portugal than a member of the house of Braganza, was substituted that which I have just read to the House.

Annulling the treaty of 1810, the treaty of Vienna renews and confirms (as the House will have seen) all *former* treaties between Great Britain and Portugal, describing them as "ancient treaties of alliance, friendship, and guarantee;" as having "long and happily subsisted between the two Crowns;" and as being allowed, by the two high contracting parties, to remain "in full force and effect."

England bound, not by this, but by previous treaties to protect Portugal.

What, then, is the force—what is the effect of those ancient treaties? I am prepared to show to the House what it is. But before I do so, I must say, that if all the treaties to which this article of the treaty of Vienna refers, had perished by some convulsion of nature, or had by some extraordinary accident been consigned to total oblivion, still it would be impossible not to admit, as an incontestible inference from this article of the treaty of Vienna alone, that in a moral point of view, there is incumbent on Great Britain, a decided obligation to act as the effectual defender of Portugal. If I could not show the letter of a single antecedent stipulation, I should still contend that a solemn admission, only ten years old, of the existence at that time of "treaties of alliance, friendship, and guarantee," held Great Britain to the discharge of the obligations which that very description implies. But fortunately there is no such difficulty in specifying the nature of those obligations. All of the preceding treaties exist—all of them are of easy reference—all of them are known to this country, to Spain, to every nation of the civilized world. They are so numerous, and their general result is so uniform, that it may be sufficient to select only two of them to show the nature of all.

By treaty of 1661.

The first to which I shall advert is the treaty of 1661, which was concluded at the time of the marriage of Charles the Second, with the Infanta of Portugal. After reciting the marriage, and making over to Great Britain, in consequence of that marriage, first, a considerable sum of money, and, secondly, several important places, some of which, as Tangier, we no longer possess; but others of which, as Bombay, still belong to this country, the treaty runs thus: "In consideration of all which grants, so much to the benefit of the King of Great Britain and his subjects in general, and of the delivery of those important places to his said Majesty and his heirs forever, &c., the King of Great Britain does profess and declare, with the consent and advice of his council, that he will take the interest of Portugal and all its dominions to heart, defending the same with his utmost power by sea and land, *even as England itself;*" and it then proceeds to specify the succors to be sent, and the manner of sending them.

By treaty of 1703.

I come next to the treaty of 1703, a treaty of alliance cotemporaneous with the Methuen treaty, which has regulated, for upward of a century, the commercial relations of the two countries. The treaty of 1703 was a tripartite engagement between the States General of Holland, England, and Portugal. The second article of that treaty sets forth, that "If ever it shall happen that the Kings of Spain and France, either the present or the future, that both of them together, or either of them separately, shall make war, or give occasion to suspect that they intend to make war upon the kingdom of Portugal, either on the continent of Europe, or on its dominions beyond the seas; her Majesty the Queen of Great Britain, and the Lords the States General, shall use their friendly offices with the said Kings, or either of them, in order to persuade them to observe the terms of peace toward Portugal, and not to make war upon it." The third article declares, "That in the event of these good offices not proving successful, but altogether ineffectual, so that war should be made by the aforesaid Kings, or by either of them upon Portugal, the above-mentioned powers of Great Britain and Holland shall make war with all their force upon the aforesaid Kings or King who shall carry hostile arms into Portugal; and toward that war which shall be carried on in Europe, they shall supply twelve thousand men, whom they shall arm and pay, as well when in quarters as in action; and the said high allies shall be obliged to keep that number of men complete, by recruiting it from time to time at their own expense."

Further discussion of these two treaties.

I am aware, indeed, that with respect to either of the treaties which I have quoted, it is possible to raise a question—whether variation of circumstances or change of times may not have somewhat relaxed its obligations. The treaty of 1661, it might be said, was so loose and prodigal in the wording—it is so unreasonable, so wholly out of nature, that any one country should be expected to defend another, "*even as itself;*" such stipulations are of so exaggerated a character, as to resemble effusions of feeling, rather than enunciations of deliberate compact. Again, with respect to the treaty of 1703, if the case rested on that treaty alone, a question might be raised, whether or not, when one of the contracting parties—Holland—had since so changed her relations with Portugal, as to consider her obligations under the treaty of 1703 as obsolete—whether or not, I say, under such circumstances, the obligation on the remaining party be not likewise void. I should not hesitate to answer both these objections in the negative. But without entering into such a controversy, it is sufficient for me to say that the time and place for taking such objections was at the Congress at Vienna. Then and there it was that if you, indeed, considered these treaties as obsolete, you ought frankly and fearlessly to have declared them to be so. But then and there, with your eyes open, and in the face of all modern Europe, you proclaimed anew the ancient treaties of alliance, friendship, and guarantee, "so long subsisting between the Crowns of Great Britain and Portugal," as still "acknowledged by Great Britain," and still "of full force and effect." It is not, however, on specific articles alone—it is not so much, perhaps, on either of these ancient treaties, taken separately, as it is on the spirit and understanding of the whole body of treaties, of which the essence is concentrated and preserved in the treaty of Vienna, that we acknowledge in Portugal a right to look to Great Britain as her ally and defender.

General inference as to treaty obligations.

Part Second. This protection now demanded.

This, sir, being the state, morally and politically, of our obligations toward Portugal; it is obvious that when Portugal, in apprehension of the coming storm, called on Great Britain for assistance, the only hesitation on our part could be—not whether that assistance was due, supposing the occasion for demanding it to arise, but simply whether that occasion—in other words, whether the *casus fœderis* had arisen.

Answer to the objections of some that the government had moved too slowly.

I understand, indeed, that in some quarters it has been imputed to his Majesty's ministers that an extraordinary delay intervened between the taking of the determination to give assistance to Portugal and the carrying of that determination into effect. But how stands the fact? On Sunday, the third of this month, we received from the Portuguese embassador a direct and formal demand of assistance against a hostile aggression from Spain. Our answer was, that although rumors had reached us through France, his Majesty's government had not that accurate information—that official and precise intelligence of facts—on which they could properly found an application to Parliament. It was only on last Friday night that this precise information arrived. On Saturday his Majesty's confidential servants came to a decision. On Sunday that decision received the sanction of his Majesty. On Monday it was communicated to both Houses of Parliament; and this day, sir, at the hour in which I have the honor of addressing you, the troops are on their march for embarkation.

They were bound to have evidence to act on.

I trust, then, sir, that no unseemly delay is imputable to government. But undoubtedly, on the other hand, when the claim of Portugal for assistance—a claim clear, indeed, in justice, but at the same time fearfully spreading in its possible consequences, came before us, it was the duty of his Majesty's government to do nothing on hearsay. The eventual force of the claim was admitted; but a thorough knowledge of facts was necessary before the compliance with that claim could be granted. The government here labored under some disadvantage. The rumors which reached us through Madrid were obviously distorted, to answer partial political purposes; and the intelligence through the press of France, though substantially correct, was, in particulars, vague and contradictory. A measure of grave and serious moment could never be founded on such authority; nor could the ministers come down to Parliament until they had a confident assurance that the case which they had to lay before the Legislature was true in all its parts.

That evidence delayed by the nature of the Portuguese government.

But there was another reason which induced a necessary caution. In former instances, when Portugal applied to this country for assistance, the whole power of the state in Portugal was vested in the person of the monarch. The expression of his wish, the manifestation of his desire, the putting forth of his claim, was sufficient ground for immediate and decisive action on the part of Great Britain, supposing the *casus fœderis* to be made out. But, on this occasion, inquiry was in the first place to be made whether, according to the new Constitution of Portugal, the call upon Great Britain was made with the consent of all the powers and authorities competent to make it, so as to carry with it an assurance of that reception in Portugal for our army, which the army of a friend and ally had a right to expect. Before a British soldier should put his foot on Portuguese ground, nay, before he should leave the shores of England, it was our duty to ascertain that the step taken by the Regency of Portugal was taken with the cordial concurrence of the Legislature of that country. It was but this morning that we received intelligence of the proceedings of the Chambers at Lisbon, which establishes the fact of such concurrence. This intelligence is contained in a dispatch from Sir W. A'Court, dated 29th of November, of which I will read an extract to the House. "The day after the news arrived of the entry of the rebels into Portugal, the ministers demanded from the Chambers an extension of power for the executive government, and the permission to apply for foreign succors, in virtue of ancient treaties, in the event of their being deemed necessary. The deputies gave the requisite authority by acclamation; and an equally good spirit was manifested by the peers, who granted every power that the ministers could possibly require. They even went further, and, rising in a body from their seats, declared their devotion to their country, and their readiness to give their personal services, if necessary, to repel any hostile invasion. The Duke de Cadaval, president of the Chamber, was the first to make this declaration; and the minister who described this proceeding to me, said it was a movement worthy of the good days of Portugal!"

Proof that the interposition of England is needed.

I have thus incidentally disposed of the supposed imputation of delay in complying with the requisition of the Portuguese government. The main question, however, is this: Was it obligatory upon us to comply with that requisition? In other words, had the *casus fœderis* arisen? In our opinion it had. Bands of Portuguese rebels, armed, equipped, and trained in Spain, had crossed the Spanish frontier, carrying terror and devastation into their own country, and proclaiming sometimes the brother of the reigning Sovereign of Portugal, sometimes a Spanish Princess, and sometimes even Ferdinand of Spain, as the rightful occupant of the Portuguese throne. These rebels crossed the frontier, not at one point only, but at several points; for it is remarkable that the aggression, on which the original application to Great Britain for succor was founded, is not the aggression with reference to which that application has been complied with.

Portugal invaded from Spain in different quarters.

The attack announced by the French newspapers was on the north of Portugal, in the province of Tras-os-Montes; an official account of which has been received by his Majesty's government only this day. But on Friday an account was received of an invasion in the south of Portugal, and of the capture of Villa Viciosa, a town lying on the road from the southern frontier to Lisbon. This new fact established even more satisfactorily than a mere confirmation of the attack first complained of would have done, the systematic nature of the aggression of Spain against Portugal. One hostile irruption might have been made by some single corps escaping from their quarters—by some body of stragglers, who might have evaded the vigilance of Spanish authorities; and one such accidental and unconnected act of violence might not have been conclusive evidence of cognizance and design on the part of those authorities; but when a series of attacks are made along the whole line of a frontier, it is difficult to deny that such multiplied instances of hostility are evidence of concerted aggression.

The invasion a Spanish one in fact.

If a single company of *Spanish* soldiers had crossed the frontier in hostile array, there could not, it is presumed, be a doubt as to the character of that invasion. Shall bodies of men, armed, clothed, and regimented by Spain, carry fire and sword into the bosom of her unoffending neighbor, and shall it be pretended that no attack, no invasion has taken place, because, forsooth, these outrages are committed against Portugal by men to whom Portugal had given birth and nurture? What petty quibbling would it be to say, that an invasion of Portugal from Spain was not a *Spanish* invasion, because Spain did not employ her own troops, but hired mercenaries to effect her purpose? And what difference s it, except as an aggravation, that the mercenaries in this instance were natives of Portugal.

England will not interfere between the Portuguese at home.

I have already stated, and I now repeat, that it never has been the wish or the pretension of the British government to interfere in the internal concerns of the Portuguese nation. Questions of that kind the Portuguese nation must settle among themselves. But if we were to admit that hordes of traitorous refugees from Portugal, with Spanish arms, or arms furnished or restored to them by Spanish authorities, in their hands, might put off their country for one purpose, and put it on again for another—put it off for the purpose of attack, and put it on again for the purpose of impunity—if, I say, we were to admit this juggle, and either pretend to be deceived by it ourselves, or attempt to deceive Portugal, into a belief that there was nothing of external attack, nothing of foreign hostility, in such a system of aggression—such pretense and attempt would, perhaps, be only ridiculous and contemptible; if they did not require a much more serious character from being employed as an excuse for infidelity to ancient friendship, and as a pretext for getting rid of the positive stipulations of treaties.

But this is a case of aggression from abroad.

This, then, is the case which I lay before the House of Commons. Here is, on the one hand, an undoubted pledge of national faith—not taken in a corner—not kept secret between the parties, but publicly recorded among the annals of history, in the face of the world. Here are, on the other hand, undeniable acts of foreign aggression, perpetrated, indeed, principally through the instrumentality of domestic traitors, but supported with foreign means, instigated by foreign councils, and directed to foreign ends. Putting these facts and this pledge together, it is impossible that his Majesty should refuse the call that has been made upon him; nor can Parliament, I am convinced, refuse to enable his Majesty to fulfill his undoubted obligations. I am willing to rest the whole question of to-night, and to call for the vote of the House of Commons upon this simple case, divested altogether of collateral circumstances; from which I especially wish to separate it, in the minds of those who hear me, and also in the minds of others, to whom what I now say will find its way. If I were to sit down this moment, without adding another word, I have no doubt but that I should have the concurrence of the House in the address which I mean to propose.

In protecting Portugal, England does not war on Spain.

When I state this, it will be obvious to the House, that the vote for which I am about to call upon them, is a vote for the defense of Portugal, not a vote for war against Spain. I beg the House to keep these two points entirely distinct in their consideration. For the former I think I have said enough. If, in what I have now further to say, I should bear hard upon the Spanish government, I beg that it may be observed that, unjustifiable as I shall show their conduct to have been—contrary to the law of nations, contrary to the law of good neighborhood, contrary, I might say, to the laws of God and man—with respect to Portugal—still I do not mean to preclude a *locus pœnitentiæ*, a possibility of redress and reparation. It is our duty to fly to the defense of Portugal, be the assailant who he may. And, be it remembered, that, in thus fulfilling the stipulation of ancient treaties, of the existence and obligation of which all the world are aware, we, according to the universally admitted construction of the law of nations, neither make war upon that assailant, nor give to that assailant, much less to any other power, just cause of war against ourselves.

Part Third. View of the political state of Portugal with reference to the duties of England.

Sir, he present situation of Portugal is so anomalous, and the recent years of her history are crowded with events so unusual, that the House will, perhaps, not think that I am unprofitably wasting its time, if I take the liberty of calling its attention, shortly and succinctly, to those events, and to their influence on the political relations of Europe. It is known that the consequence of the residence of the King of Portugal in Brazil was to raise the latter country from a colonial to a metropolitan condition; and that, from the time when the King began to contemplate his return to Portugal, there grew up in Brazil a desire of independence that threatened dissension, if not something like civil contest, between the European and American dominions of the house of Braganza. It is known, also, that Great Britain undertook a mediation between Portugal and Brazil, and induced the King to consent to a separation of the two Crowns—confirming that of Brazil on the head of his eldest son. The ink with which this agreement was written was scarcely dry, when the unexpected death of the King of Portugal produced a new state of things, which reunited on the same head the two Crowns which it had been the policy of England, as well as of Portugal and of Brazil, to separate. On that occasion, Great Britain, and another European court closely connected with Brazil, tendered advice to the Emperor of Brazil, now become King of Portugal, which advice it can not be accurately said that his Imperial Majesty followed, because he had decided for himself before it reached Rio de Janeiro; but in conformity with which advice, though not in consequence of it, his Imperial Majesty determined to abdicate the Crown of Portugal in favor of his eldest daughter. But the Emperor of Brazil had done more.

Separation of Brazil from Portugal.

What had not been foreseen—what would have been beyond the province of any foreign power to advise—his Imperial Majesty had accompanied his abdication of the Crown of Portugal with the grant of a free constitutional charter for that kingdom.

A constitutional government established in the latter.

It has been surmised that this measure, as well as the abdication which it accompanied, was the offspring of our advice. No such thing—Great Britain did not suggest this measure. It is not her duty nor her practice to offer suggestions for the internal regulation of foreign states. She neither approved nor disapproved of the grant of a constitutional charter to Portugal: her opinion upon that grant was never required. True it is, that the instrument of the constitutional charter was brought to Europe by a gentleman of high trust in the service of the British government. Sir C. Stuart had gone to Brazil to negotiate the separation between that country and Portugal. In addition to his character of Plenipotentiary of Great Britain, as the mediating power, he had also been invested by the King of Portugal with the character of his most faithful Majesty's Plenipotentiary for the negotiation with Brazil. That negotiation had been brought to a happy conclusion; and therewith the British part of Sir C. Stuart's commission had terminated. But Sir C. Stuart was still resident at Rio de Janeiro, as the Plenipotentiary of the King of Portugal, for negotiating commercial arrangements between Portugal and Brazil. In this latter character it was that Sir C. Stuart, on his return to Europe, was requested by the Emperor of Brazil to be the bearer to Portugal of the new constitutional charter. His Majesty's government found no fault with Sir C. Stuart for executing this commission; but it was immediately felt that if Sir C. Stuart were allowed to remain at Lisbon, it might appear, in the eyes of Europe, that England was the contriver and imposer of the Portuguese Constitution. Sir C. Stuart was, therefore, directed to return home forthwith, in order that the Constitution, if carried into effect there, might plainly appear to be adopted by the Portuguese nation itself, not forced upon them by English interference.

This not done through English interference.

As to the merits, sir, of the new Constitution of Portugal, I have neither the intention nor the right to offer any opinion. Personally, I may have formed one; but as an English minister, all I have to say is, "May God prosper this attempt at the establishment of constitutional liberty in Portugal! and may that nation be found as fit to enjoy and to cherish its new-born privileges, as it has often proved itself capable of discharging its duties among the nations of the world!"

The merits of this government not now the question.

I, sir, am neither the champion nor the critic of the Portuguese Constitution. But it is admitted on all hands to have proceeded from a legitimate source—a consideration which has mainly reconciled continental Europe to its establishment; and to us, as Englishmen, it is recommended by the ready acceptance which it has met with from all orders of the Portuguese people. To that Constitution, therefore, thus unquestioned in its origin, even by those who are most jealous of new institutions—to that Constitution, thus sanctioned in its outset by the glad and grateful acclamations of those who are destined to live under it—to that Constitution, founded on principles, in a great degree, similar to those of our own, though differently modified—it is impossible that Englishmen should not wish well. But it would not be for us to force that Constitution on the people of Portugal, if they were unwilling to receive it, or if any schism should exist among the Portuguese themselves, as to its fitness and congeniality to the wants and wishes of the nation. It is no business of ours to fight its battles. We go to Portugal in the discharge of a sacred obligation, contracted under ancient and modern treaties. When there, nothing shall be done by us to enforce the establishment of the Constitution; but we must take care that nothing shall be done by others to prevent it from being fairly carried into effect. Internally, let the Portuguese settle their own affairs; but with respect to external force, while Great Britain has an arm to raise, it must be raised against the efforts of any power that should attempt forcibly to control the choice, and fetter the independence of Portugal.

It is acknowledged to be a legitimate one, and approved by the people.

Has such been the intention of Spain? Whether the proceedings which have lately been practiced or permitted in Spain, were acts of a government exercising the usual power of prudence and foresight (without which a government is, for the good of the people which live under it, no government at all), or whether they were the acts of some secret illegitimate power—of some furious fanatical faction, over-riding the counsels of the ostensible government, defying it in the capital, and disobeying it on the frontiers—I will not stop to inquire. It is indifferent to Portugal, smarting under her wrongs—it is indifferent to England, who is called upon to avenge them—whether the present state of things be the result of the intrigues of a faction, over which, if the Spanish government has no control, it ought to assume one as soon as possible—or of local authorities, over whom it has control, and for whose acts it must, therefore, be held responsible. It matters not, I say, from which of these sources the evil has arisen. In either case, Portugal must be protected; and from England that protection is due.

This government is assailed from Spain.

It would be unjust, however, to the Spanish government, to say that it is only among the members of that government that an unconquerable hatred of liberal institutions exists in Spain. However incredible the phenomenon may appear in this country, I am persuaded that a vast majority of the Spanish nation entertain a decided attachment to arbitrary power, and a predilection for absolute government. The more liberal institutions of countries in the neighborhood have not yet extended their influence into Spain, nor awakened any sympathy in the mass of the Spanish

Free institutions are obnoxious to most of the Spanish people.

people. Whether the public authorities of Spain did or did not partake of the national sentiment, there would almost necessarily grow up between Portugal and Spain, under present circumstances, an opposition of feelings which it would not require the authority or the suggestions of the government to excite and stimulate into action. Without blame, therefore, to the government of Spain—out of the natural antipathy between the two neighboring nations—the one prizing its recent freedom, the other hugging its traditionary servitude—there might arise mutual provocations and reciprocal injuries which, perhaps, even the most active and vigilant ministry could not altogether restrain. I am inclined to believe that such has been, in part at least, the origin of the differences between Spain and Portugal. That in their progress they have been adopted, matured, methodized, combined, and brought into more perfect action, by some authority more united and more efficient than the mere feeling disseminated through the mass of the community, is certain; but I do believe their origin to have been as much in the real sentiment of the Spanish population, as in the opinion or contrivance of the government itself.

If the government of Spain has not acted in this case, England does not war on her.

Whether this be or be not the case, is precisely the question between us and Spain. If, though partaking in the general feelings of the Spanish nation, the Spanish government has, nevertheless, done nothing to embody those feelings, and to direct them hostilely against Portugal; if all that has occurred on the frontiers has occurred only because the vigilance of the Spanish government has been surprised, its confidence betrayed, and its orders neglected—if its engagements have been repeatedly and shamefully violated, not by its own good-will, but against its recommendation and desire—let us see some symptoms of disapprobation, some signs of repentance, some measures indicative of sorrow for the past, and of sincerity for the future. In that case, his Majesty's message, to which I propose this night to return an answer of concurrence, will retain the character which I have ascribed to it—that of a measure of defense for Portugal, not a measure of resentment against Spain.

Facts as to existing differences between Portugal and Spain.

With these explanations and qualifications, let us now proceed to the review of facts. Great desertions took place from the Portuguese army into Spain, and some desertions took place from the Spanish army into Portugal. In the first instance, the Portuguese authorities were taken by surprise; but in every subsequent instance, where they had an opportunity of exercising a discretion, it is but just to say that they uniformly discouraged the desertions of the Spanish soldiery. There exist between Spain and Portugal specific treaties, stipulating the mutual surrender of deserters. Portugal had, therefore, a right to claim of Spain that every Portuguese deserter should be forthwith sent back. I hardly know whether from its own impulse, or in consequence of our advice, the Portuguese government waved its right under those treaties; very wisely reflecting that it would be highly inconvenient to be placed by the return of their deserters in the difficult alternative of either granting a dangerous amnesty, or ordering numerous executions. The Portuguese government, therefore, signified to Spain that it would be entirely satisfied if, instead of surrendering the deserters, Spain would restore their arms, horses, and equipments; and, separating the men from their officers, would remove both from the frontiers into the interior of Spain. Solemn engagements were entered into by the Spanish government to this effect—first with Portugal, next with France, and afterward with England. Those engagements, concluded one day, were violated the next. The deserters, instead of being disarmed and dispersed, were allowed to remain congregated together near the frontiers of Portugal, where they were enrolled, trained, and disciplined for the expedition which they have since undertaken. It is plain that in these proceedings there was perfidy somewhere. It rests with the Spanish government to show that it was not with them. It rests with the Spanish government to prove that, if its engagements have not been fulfilled—if its intentions have been eluded and unexecuted—the fault has not been with the government, and that it is ready to make every reparation in its power.

Apparent perfidy on the part of Spain.

France and England equally insulted by her conduct.

I have said that these promises were made to France and to Great Britain as well as to Portugal. I should do a great injustice to France if I were not to add, that the representations of that government upon this point to the cabinet of Madrid, have been as urgent, and, alas! as fruitless, as those of Great Britain. Upon the first irruption into the Portuguese territory, the French government testified its displeasure by instantly recalling its embassador; and it further directed its charge d'affaires to signify to his Catholic Majesty, that Spain was not to look for any support from France against the consequences of this aggression upon Portugal. I am bound, I repeat, in justice to the French government, to state, that it has exerted itself to the utmost in urging Spain to retrace the steps which she has so unfortunately taken. It is not for me to say whether any more efficient course might have been adopted to give effect to their exhortations; but as to the sincerity and good faith of the exertions made by the government of France, to press Spain to the execution of her engagements, I have not the shadow of a doubt, and I confidently reckon upon their continuance.

It will be for Spain, upon knowledge of the step now taken by his Majesty, to consider in what way she will meet it. The earnest hope and wish of his Majesty's government is, that she may meet it in such a manner as to avert any ill consequences to herself from the measure into which we have been driven by the unjust attack upon Portugal.

Sir, I set out with saying that there were reasons which entirely satisfied my judgment that nothing short of a point of national faith or national honor would justify, at the present moment, any voluntary approximation to the possibility of war. Let me be understood, however, distinctly as not meaning to say that I dread war in a good cause (and in no other may it be the lot of this country ever to engage!) from a distrust of the strength of the country to commence it, or of her resources to maintain it. I dread it, indeed—but upon far other grounds: I dread it from an apprehension of the tremendous consequences which might arise from any hostilities in which we might now be engaged. Some years ago, in the discussion of the negotiations respecting the French war against Spain, I took the liberty of adverting to this topic. I then stated that the position of this country in the present state of the world was one of neutrality, not only between contending nations, but between conflicting principles; and that it was by neutrality alone that we could maintain that balance, the preservation of which I believed to be essential to the welfare of mankind. I then said, that I feared that the next war which should be kindled in Europe would be a war not so much of armies as of opinions. Not four years have elapsed, and behold my apprehension realized! It is, to be sure, within narrow limits that this war of opinion is at present confined; but it *is* a war of opinion that Spain (whether as government or as nation) is now waging against Portugal; it is a war which has commenced in hatred of the new institutions of Portugal. How long is it reasonable to expect that Portugal will abstain from retaliation? If into that war this country shall be compelled to enter, we shall enter into it with a sincere and anxious desire to mitigate rather than exasperate—and to mingle only in the conflict of arms, not in the more fatal conflict of opinions. But I much fear that this country (however earnestly she may endeavor to avoid it) could not, in such case, avoid seeing ranked under her banners all the restless and dissatisfied of any nation with which she might come in conflict. It is the contemplation of this new *power* in any future war which excites my most anxious apprehension. It is one thing to have a giant's strength, but it would be another to use it like a giant. The consciousness of such strength is, undoubtedly, a source of confidence and security; but in the situation in which this country stands, our business is not to seek opportunities of displaying it, but to content ourselves with letting the professors of violent and exaggerated doctrines on both sides feel, that it is not their interest to convert an umpire into an adversary. The situation of England, amid the struggle of political opinions which agitates more or less sensibly different countries of the world, may be compared to that of the Ruler of the Winds, as described by the poet:

Peroration: The next great war in Europe will be one of *opinions*.

"Celsâ sedet Æolus arce,
Sceptra tenens; mollitque animos et temperat iras;
Ni faciat, maria ac terras cœlumque profundum
Quippe ferant rapidi secum, verrantque per auras."[1]

The consequence of letting loose the passions at present chained and confined, would be to produce a scene of desolation which no man can contemplate without horror; and I should not sleep easy on my couch, if I were conscious that I had contributed to precipitate it by a single moment.

This, then, is the reason—a reason very different from fear—the reverse of a consciousness of disability—why I dread the recurrence of hostilities in any part of Europe; why I would bear much, and would forbear long; why I would (as I have said) put up with almost any thing that did not touch national faith and national honor, rather than let slip the furies of war, the leash of which we hold in our hands—not knowing whom they may reach, or how far their ravages may be carried. Such is the love of peace which the British government acknowledges; and such the necessity for peace which the circumstances of the world inculcate. I will push these topics no further.

I return, in conclusion, to the object of the Address. Let us fly to the aid of Portugal, by whomsoever attacked, because it is our duty to do so; and let us cease our interference where that duty ends. We go to Portugal not to rule, not to dictate, not to prescribe constitutions, but to defend and to preserve the independence of an ally. We go to plant the standard of England on the well-known heights of Lisbon. Where that standard is planted, foreign dominion shall not come.

The House gave an almost unanimous support to an Address approving of the measures adopted; and the insurrection was at once suppressed in every part of Portugal.

Mr. Canning gained very great and merited applause by this intervention in behalf of a constitutional government. His prediction that the next great war in Europe would be one of *opinions*, is yet to be accomplished; and events since the usurpation of Louis Napoleon Bonaparte, at the close of 1851, seem clearly to indicate that such a contest may not be far remote.

---

[1] Æolus sits upon his lofty tower
And holds the scepter, calming all their rage:
Else would they bear sea, earth, and heaven profound
In rapid flight, and sweep them through the air.
Virgil's Æneid, book i., lines 56–9.

EXTRACTS.

FOREIGN ENLISTMENT BILL. APRIL 16, 1823.

WHAT, sir! is it to become a maxim with this country that she is ever to be a belligerent? Is she never, under any possible state of circumstances, to remain neutral? If this proposition be good for any thing, it must run to this extent—that our position, insulated as it is from all the rest of the world, moves us so far from the scene of continental warfare, that we ought always to be belligerent—that we are bound to counteract the designs of Providence, to reject the advantages of nature, and to render futile and erroneous the description of the poet, who has said, to our honor, that we were less prone to war and tumult, on account of our happy situation, than the neighboring nations that lie conterminous with one another. But wherefore this dread of a neutrality? If gentlemen look to the page of history, they will find that for centuries past, whenever there has been a war in Europe, we have almost always been belligerent. The fact is undoubtedly so; but I am not prepared to lay it down as a principle, that if, at the beginning of a war, we should happen to maintain a species of neutrality, it was an unnatural thing that we should do so. Gentlemen say that we must be drawn into a war, sooner or later. Why, then, I answer, let it be later. I say, if we are to be drawn into a war, let us be drawn into it on grounds clearly British. I do not say—God forbid I should—that it is no part of the duty of Great Britain to protect what is termed the balance of power, and to aid the weak against the insults of the strong. I say, on the contrary, that to do so is her bounden duty; but I affirm, also, that we must take care to do our duty to ourselves. The first condition of engaging in any war—the *sine quâ non* of every such undertaking—is, that the war must be just; the second, that being just in itself, we can also with justice engage in it; and the third, that being just in its nature, and it being possible for us justly to embark in it, we can so interfere without detriment or prejudice to ourselves. I contend that he is a visionary politician who leaves this last condition out of the question; and I say further, that though the glorious abandonment of it may sound well in the generous speech of an irresponsible orator—with the safety of a nation upon his lips, and none of the responsibility upon his shoulders—it is matter deeply to be considered; and that the minister who should lay it out of his view, in calling on the country to undertake a war, would well deserve that universal censure and reprobation with which the noble Lord opposite has this night menaced me. If it be wise for a government, though it can not prevent an actual explosion, to endeavor to circumscribe the limits, and to lessen the duration of a war, then I say that the position we have taken in the present instance is of more probable efficacy than that in which we should have stood had we suffered ourselves to be drawn into a participation in the contest. Participation, did I say? Sir! is there any man who hears me—is there any man acquainted with the history of the country for the last twenty years, who does not know the way in which Great Britain has been accustomed to participate in a war? Do not gentlemen know that if we now enter into a war, we must take the whole burden of it upon ourselves, and conduct the whole force and exertions of the peninsula? But supposing such to be our course, how different must be our situation, as compared with former periods. When we last became the defenders of Spain, we fought for and with a united people. What would be the case at present? Any interference on our parts in favor of Spain must commence with an attempt to unite contending factions, and to stimulate men of opposite interests and opposite feelings to one grand and simultaneous effort. Now I do not hesitate to say that the man who would undertake to do this under present circumstances, must either be possessed of supernatural means of information, or of a hardihood which I may envy, but shall not attempt to imitate. I say that those men will not consult the true dignity of the country, who, finding fault with the part we have adopted, wish to indemnify themselves by endeavoring to make us perform that part amiss. Our course is neutrality—strict neutrality; and in the name of God, let us adhere to it. If you dislike that course—if you think it injurious to the honor or interests of the country—drive from their places those neutral ministers who have adopted it; but until you are prepared to declare war, you are bound to adhere to and to act upon the system which ministers have laid down.

I stated, a few evenings ago, that we could have no difficulty in the course which we had to pursue in observance of a strict neutrality. We have spent much time in teaching other powers the nature of a strict neutrality; and, generally speaking, we found them most reluctant scholars. All I now call upon the House to do, is to adopt the same course which it has recommended to neutral powers upon former occasions. If I wished for a guide in a system of neutrality, I should take that laid down by America in the days of the Presidency of Washington and the Secretaryship of Jefferson

---

ON THE KING'S SPEECH. FEBRUARY 15, 1825.

I NOW turn to that other part of the honorable and learned gentleman's [Mr. Brougham] speech, in which he acknowledges his acquiescence in the passages of the address echoing the satisfaction felt at the success of the liberal commercial principles adopted by this country, and at the steps taken for recognizing the new states of America. It does happen, however, that the honorable and learned gentleman being not unfrequently a speaker in this House, nor very concise in his speeches, and touching occasionally, as he proceeds, on almost every subject within the range of his imagination, as well as making some observations on the matter in hand—and having at different periods proposed and supported every innovation of which the law or Constitution of the country is susceptible—it is impossible to innovate, without appearing to borrow from him. Either, therefore, we must remain forever absolutely locked up as in a northern winter, or we must break our way out by some mode already suggested by the honorable and learned gentleman, and then he cries out, "Ah, I was there before you! That is what I told you to do; but as you would not do it then, you have no right to do it now." In Queen Anne's reign there lived a very sage and able critic, named Dennis, who, in his old age, was the prey of a strange fancy, that he had himself written all the good things in all the good plays that were acted. Every good passage he met with in any author he insisted was his own. "It is none of his," Dennis would always say; "no, it's mine!" He went one day to see a new tragedy. Nothing particularly good to his taste occurred, till a scene in which a great storm was represented. As soon as he heard the thunder rolling over head, he exclaimed, "That's my thunder!" So it is with the honorable and learned gentleman; it's all his thunder. It will henceforth be impossible to confer any boon, or make any innovation, but he will claim it as his thunder, But it is due to him to acknowledge that he does not claim every thing; he will be content with the exclusive merit of the liberal measures relating to trade and commerce. Not desirous of violating his own principles, by claiming a monopoly of foresight and wisdom, he kindly throws overboard to my honorable and learned friend [Sir J. Mackintosh] near him, the praise of South America. I should like to know whether, in some degree, this also is not his thunder. He thinks it right itself; but lest we should be too proud if he approved our conduct *in toto*, he thinks it wrong in point of time. I differ from him essentially; for if I pique myself on any thing in this affair, it is the time. That, at some time or other, states which had separated themselves from the mother country should or should not be admitted to the rank of independent nations, is a proposition to which no possible dissent could be given. The whole question was one of time and mode. There were two modes: one a reckless and headlong course, by which we might have reached our object at once, but at the expense of drawing upon us consequences not highly to be estimated; the other was more strictly guarded in point of principle; so that, while we pursued our own interests, we took care to give no just cause of offense to other powers.

On unlawful Societies in Ireland. February 15, 1825.

In the next place, are we prepared to say that these and other acts of the Catholic Association have no tendency to excite and inflame animosities? I affirm, without hesitation, that they have directly that tendency; and in support of this affirmation I must beg leave to recur, however solemnly warned against the recurrence, to an expression which I was the first to bring to the notice of the House, but which has been since the subject of repeated animadversion; I mean the adjuration "by the *hate* you bear to Orangemen," which was used by the association in their address to the Catholics of Ireland.

Various and not unamusing have been the attempts of gentlemen who take the part of the association, to get rid of this most unlucky phrase, or at least to dilute and attenuate its obvious and undeniable meaning. It is said to be unfair to select one insulated expression as indicating the general spirit of the proceedings of any public body. Granted; if the expression had escaped in the heat of debate, if it had been struck out by the collision of argument, if it had been thrown forth in haste, and had been, upon reflection, recalled. But if the words are found in a document which was prepared with care and considered with deliberation—if it is notorious that they were pointed out as objectionable when they were first proposed by the framers of the address, but were, nevertheless, upon argument retained—surely we are not only justified in receiving them as an indication, at least, of the *animus* of those who used them; but we should be rejecting the best evidence of that *animus*, if we passed over so well-weighed a manifestation of it.

Were not this felt by honorable gentlemen on the other side to be true, we should not have seen them so anxious to put forced and fanciful constructions on a phrase which is as plain in its meaning as any which the hand of man ever wrote or the eye of man ever saw. The first defense of this phrase was by an honorable member from Ireland, who told us that the words do not convey the same meaning in the Irish language which we in England naturally attach to them. I do not pretend to be conversant with the Irish language; and must, therefore, leave that apology to stand for what it may be worth, on the learned gentleman's erudition and authority. I will not follow every other gentleman who has strained his faculties to explain away this unfortunate expression; but will come at once to my honorable and learned friend [Sir James Mackintosh], the member for Knaresborough, to whom the palm in this contest of ingenuity must be conceded by all his competitors. My honorable friend has expended abundant research and subtilty upon this inquiry, and having resolved the phrase into its elements in the crucible of his philosophical mind, has produced it to us purified and refined to a degree that must command the admiration of all who take delight in metaphysical alchemy. My honorable and learned friend began by telling us that, after all, *hatred* is no bad thing in itself. "I hate a Tory," says my honorable friend—"and another man hates a cat; but it does not follow that he would hunt down the cat, or I the Tory," Nay, so far from it—hatred, if it be properly managed, is, according to my honorable friend's theory, no bad preface to a rational esteem and affection. It prepares its votaries for a reconciliation of differences—for lying down with their most inveterate enemies, like the leopard and the kid, in the vision of the prophet.

This dogma is a little startling, but it is not altogether without precedent. It is borrowed from a character in a play which is, I dare say, as great a favorite with my learned friend as it is with me—I mean the comedy of *The Rivals;* in which *Mrs. Malaprop*, giving a lecture on the subject of marriage to her niece (who is unreasonable enough to talk of liking as a necessary preliminary to such a union), says, "What have you to do with your likings and your preferences, child? depend upon it, it is safest to begin with a little aversion. I am sure I hated your poor dear uncle like a blackamoor before we were married; and yet you know, my dear, what a good wife I made him." Such is my learned friend's argument to a hair.

But finding that this doctrine did not appear to go down with the House so glibly as he had expected, my honorable and learned friend presently changed his tack, and put forward a theory, which, whether for novelty or for beauty, I pronounce to be incomparable; and, in short, as wanting nothing to recommend it but a slight foundation in truth. "True philosophy," says my honorable friend, "will always contrive to lead men to virtue by the instrumentality of their conflicting vices. The virtues, where more than one exist, may live harmoniously together; but the vices bear mortal antipathy to one another, and therefore furnish to the moral engineer the power by which he can make each keep the other under control." Admirable!—but, upon this doctrine, the poor man who has but one single vice must be in a very bad way. No *fulcrum*, no moral power for effecting *his* cure. Whereas his more fortunate neighbor, who has two or more vices in his composition, is in a fair way of becoming a very virtuous member of society. I wonder how my learned friend would like to have this doctrine introduced into his domestic establishment. For instance, suppose that I discharge a servant because he is addicted to liquor, I could not venture to recommend him to my honorable and learned friend; it might be the poor man's *only* fault, and therefore clearly incorrigible. But if I had the good fortune to find out that he was also addicted to stealing, might I not, with a safe conscience, send him to my learned friend with a very strong recommendation, saying, I send you a man whom I know to be a drunkard; but I am happy to assure you he is also a thief: you can not do better than employ him; you will make his drunkenness counteract his thievery, and no doubt you will bring him out of the conflict a very moral personage. My honorable and learned friend, however, not content with laying down these new rules for reformation, thought it right to exemplify them in his own person, and, like Pope's *Longinus*, to be "himself the great sublime he drew." My learned friend tells us that Dr. Johnson was what he [Dr. Johnson himself] called *a good hater;* and that among the qualities which he hated most were two which my honorable friend unites in his own person—that of Whig and that of Scotchman. "So that," says my honorable friend, "if Dr. Johnson were alive, and were to meet me at the club, of which he was a founder, and of which I am now an unworthy member, he would probably break up the meeting rather than sit it out in such society." No, sir, not so. My honorable and learned friend forgets his own theory. If he had been *only* a Whig, or *only* a Scotchman, Dr. Johnson might have treated him as he apprehends; but being both, the great moralist would have said to my honorable friend, "Sir, you are too much of a Whig to be a good Scotchman; and, sir, you are too much of a Scotchman to be a good Whig." It is no doubt from the collision of these two vices in my learned friend's person, that he has become what I, and all who have the happiness of meeting him at the club, find him—an entirely faultless character.

For my own part, however, I must say, that I can not see any hope of obtaining the great moral victory which my learned friend has anticipated—of winning men to the practice of virtue by adjurations addressed to their peculiar vices. I believe, after all these ratiocinations and refinements, we must come back to the plain truth, which is felt even while it is denied—that the phrase "by the hate you bear to Orangemen," is an indefensible phrase; that it is at least—what alone I am contending that it is—incontestable evidence of the allegation that the Catholic Association does excite animosities in Ireland. It is an expression calculated to offend, provoke, and exasperate the Orangemen, however palatable to those whose hatred of Orangemen it predicates, and, to say the least, does not disapprove.

LORD BROUGHAM.

HENRY BROUGHAM is the last among the orators embraced in this collection; and as he is still living, only a brief notice will be given of his life and character.

The family was one of the most ancient in Westmoreland, England. Brougham Castle is older than the days of King John; and the manor connected with it, after passing out of the family for a time, was regained by purchase and entailed on the oldest descendant in the male line. Toward the close of the last century, it fell to a young man who was studying in the University of Edinburgh, and who married, while there, a niece of the celebrated historian, Dr. Robertson. The first-fruit of this union was a son named HENRY, who was born at Edinburgh in 1779.

The family appear to have resided chiefly or wholly in the Scottish capital; the boy received the rudiments of his education at the High School of Edinburgh, under the celebrated Dr. Adam, and was even then distinguished for his almost intuitive perception of whatever he undertook to learn. "He was wild, fond of pleasure, taking to study by starts, and always reading with more effect than others (when he did read), because it was for some specific object, the knowledge of which was to be acquired in the shortest possible time." We have here a perfect picture of Lord Brougham's mode of reading for life. Eager, restless, grasping after information of every kind, he has brought into his speeches a wider range of collateral thought than any of our orators, except Burke; and he has done it in just the way that might be expected from such a man, with inimitable freshness and power, but with those hasty judgments, that want of a profound knowledge of principles, and that frequent inaccuracy in details, which we always see in one who reads "for some specific object," instead of taking in the whole range of a science, and who is so much in a hurry, that he is constantly aiming to accomplish his task in "the shortest possible time."

He entered the University of Edinburgh in the sixteenth year of his age, and soon gained the highest distinction by his extraordinary mathematical attainments. He gave in solutions of some very difficult theorems, which awakened the admiration of his instructors; and before he was seventeen, produced an essay on the "Flection and Reflection of Light," which was estimated so highly as to be inserted in the Edinburgh Philosophical Transactions. His supposed discoveries, so far as they were correct, proved, indeed, to have been anticipated by earlier writers; but they were undoubtedly the result of his own investigation; and they showed so remarkable a talent for mathematical research, that he was rewarded, at a somewhat later period (1803), with an election as member of the Royal Society of Edinburgh. It is a curious fact that Lord Brougham has again taken up his favorite pursuits in optics at the age of seventy, and made recent communications to the French Institute, from his chateau at Cannes, in the south of France, on the same branch of science which called forth his early efforts in the University of Edinburgh.

Having completed his college course, Mr. Brougham entered with indefatigable zeal upon the study of the law, in conjunction with Jeffery, Horner, and several other young men, who, only a few years after, stood foremost among the leading advocates of the country. He had commenced the practice of extemporaneous speaking some years before in the Speculative Society, that great theater of debate for the University of Edinburgh. He now carried it to a still greater height in the immediate prospect of his professional duties, and "exercised the same superiority over his youthful competitors (though some of them were then and afterward remarkable for their ability) which he held at a later period as Chancellor over the House of Lords." He was called in due course to the Scottish bar, and commenced business in Edinburgh with the most encouraging prospects of success. In 1803, he published his first work, in two octavo volumes, entitled "The Colonial Policy of the European Powers," containing an immense amount of information, and distinguished by the daring spirit of philosophical inquiry which he carried into this vast and complicated subject. He now removed to London, and, in addition to his practice at the bar, entered warmly into politics; producing a volume on the "State of the Nation," which awakened the liveliest interest by its eloquent assertion of Whig principles, and ultimately procured him a seat in Parliament by means of the Russell family.

Before his removal to London, he united with the companions mentioned above in establishing the Edinburgh Review. He was for nearly twenty years one of its most regular contributors; and to him more than any other man was the work indebted for its searching analysis, its contemptuous and defiant spirit, its broad views of political subjects, and its eloquent exposition of Whig principles. Its motto,[1] whether selected by him or not, was designed to justify that condemnatory spirit which is so striking a trait in his character. A great part of his life has been spent in *beating down*; in detecting false pretensions whether in literature or politics; in searching out the abuses of long established institutions; in laying open the perversions of public charities; in exposing the cruelties of the criminal code; or in rousing public attention to a world of evils resulting from the irregularities in the administration of municipal law. The reader will be amused to trace this tendency of his mind, in turning over the four octavo volumes of his speeches as edited by himself, and observing their titles. We have "Military Flogging," with an exposure of its atrocities—"Queen Caroline," defended at the expense of her husband—"The Durham Clergy," lashed unmercifully for their insulting treatment of the Queen—"The Orders in Council," with the folly of abusing the Americans because they had suffered from the abuse of France—"Agricultural Distress" and "Manufacturing Distress," as resulting from the rashness and incompetency of ministers—"Army Estimates," under which millions were lavished for mere military show in time of peace—"The Holy Alliance," with its atrocious attack on the constitutional government of Spain through the instrumentality of France—"The Slave Trade"—"The Missionary Smith," murdered in Demerara under a false charge of having excited insurrection—"Negro Apprenticeship," its inadequacy and folly—"The Eastern Slave Trade," or the cruelty and guilt of transporting coolies from Hindostan to be made laborers in the West India Islands—"Law Reform"—"Parliamentary Reform"—"Education," and the abuse of Educational Charities—"Scotch Parliamentary and Burgh Reform"—"Scotch Marriage and Divorce Bill," showing that the existing laws are "the worst possible"—"The Poor Laws," with "the deplorably corrupting effects of this abominable system"—"Neutral Rights," exposing their invasion by Great Britain—"Administration of Law in Ireland," showing that "she had received penal statutes from England almost as plentifully as she had received blessings from the hands of Providence"—"Change of Ministry in 1834," with the gross, glaring, and almost incredible inconsistencies of Lord Wellington—"Business of Parliament," or "the abuses which prevail in the mode of conducting its business"—"Maltreatment of the North American Colonies"—"The Civil List," or men's voting an allowance to the Queen "under the influence of excited feelings, and without giving themselves time to reflect." No orator certainly, since the days of Pym and Charles I., could furnish such another list.

[1] "Judex damnatur dum nocens absolvitur," the judge is condemned when the guilty is suffered to escape.

The character of his eloquence corresponds to the subjects he has chosen. "For fierce, vengeful, and irresistible assault," says John Foster, "Brougham stands the foremost man in all this world." His attack is usually carried on under the forms of logic. For the materials of his argument he sometimes goes off to topics the most remote and apparently alien from his subject, but he never fails to come down upon it at last with overwhelming force. He has wit in abundance, but it is usually dashed with scorn or contempt. His irony and sarcasm are terrible. None of our orators have ever equaled him in bitterness.

His style has a hearty freshness about it, which springs from the robust constitution of his mind and the energy of his feelings. He sometimes disgusts by his use of Latinized English, and seems never to have studied our language in the true sources of its strength—Shakspeare, Milton, and the English Bible. His greatest fault lies in the structure of his sentences. He rarely puts forward a simple, distinct proposition. New ideas cluster around the original frame-work of his thoughts; and instead of throwing them into separate sentences, he blends them all in one; enlarging, modifying, interlacing them together, accumulating image upon image, and argument upon argument, till the whole becomes perplexed and cumbersome, in the attempt to crowd an entire system of thought into a single statement. Notwithstanding these faults, however, we dwell upon his speeches with breathless interest. They are a continual strain of impassioned argument, intermingled with fearful sarcasm, withering invective, lofty declamation, and the earnest majesty of a mind which has lost every other thought in the magnitude of its theme.

Lord Brougham has been in opposition during the greater part of his political life. He came in as Lord Chancellor with Earl Grey at the close of 1830, and retained his office about four years. Of late he has withdrawn, to a great extent, from public affairs, and spent a considerable part of his time on an estate which he owns in the south of France.

The following comparison between the subject of this sketch and his great parliamentary rival will interest the reader, as presenting the characteristic qualities of each in bolder relief from their juxtaposition. It is from the pen of one who had watched them both with the keenest scrutiny during their conflicts in the House of Commons. The scene described in the conclusion arose out of a memorable attack of Mr. Canning on Lord Folkestone for intimating, that he had "truckled to France." "The Lacedæmonians," said Mr. C., "were in the habit of deterring their children from the vice of intoxication by occasionally exhibiting their slaves in a state of disgusting inebriety. But, sir, there is a moral as well as a physical intoxication. Never before did I behold so perfect a personification of the character which I have somewhere seen described, as 'exhibiting the contortions of the Sibyl without her inspiration.' Such was the nature of the noble Lord's speech." Mr. Brougham took occasion, a few evenings after, to retort on Mr. Canning and repeat the charge, in the manner here described: but first we have a sketch of their characteristics as orators.

"Canning was airy, open, and prepossessing; Brougham seemed stern, hard, lowering, and almost repulsive. Canning's features were handsome, and his eye, though deeply ensconced under his eyebrows, was full of sparkle and gayety; the features of Brougham were harsh in the extreme: while his forehead shot up to a great elevation, his chin was long and square; his mouth, nose, and eyes seemed huddled together in the center of his face, the eyes absolutely lost amid folds and corrugations; and while he sat listening, they seemed to retire inward or to be vailed by a filmy curtain, which not only concealed the appalling glare which shot from them when he was aroused, but rendered his mind and his purpose a sealed book to the keenest scrutiny of man. Canning's passions appeared upon the open champaign of his face, drawn up in ready array, and moved to and fro at every turn of his own oration and every retort in that of his antagonist. Those of Brougham remained within, as in a citadel which no artillery could batter and no mine blow up; and even when he was putting forth all the power of his eloquence, when every ear was tingling at what he said, and while the immediate object of his invective was writhing in helpless and indescribable agony, his visage retained its cold and brassy hue; and he triumphed over the passions of other men by seeming to be without passion himself. When Canning rose to speak, he elevated his countenance, and seemed to look round for applause as a thing dear to his feelings; while Brougham stood coiled and concentrated, reckless of all but the power that was within himself.

"From Canning there was expected the glitter of wit and the glow of spirit—something showy and elegant; Brougham stood up as a being whose powers and intentions were all a mystery—whose aim and effect no living man could divine. You bent forward to catch the first sentence of the one, and felt human nature elevated in the specimen before you; you crouched and shrunk back from the other, and dreams of ruin and annihilation darted across your mind. The one seemed to dwell among men, to join in their joys, and to live upon their praise; the other appeared a son of the desert, who had deigned to visit the human race merely to make it tremble at his strength.

"The style of their eloquence and the structure of their orations were just as different. Canning arranged his words like one who could play skillfully upon that sweetest of all instruments, the human voice; Brougham proceeded like a master of every power of reasoning and the understanding. The modes and allusions of the one were always quadrable by the classical formulæ; those of the other could be squared only by the higher analysis of the mind; and they soared, and ran, and pealed, and swelled on and on, till a single sentence was often a complete oration within itself; but still, so clear was the logic, and so close the connection, that every member carried the weight of all that went before, and opened the way for all that was to follow after. The style of Canning was like the convex mirror, which scatters every ray of light that falls upon it, and shines and sparkles in whatever position it is viewed; that of Brougham was like the concave speculum, scattering no indiscriminate radiance, but having its light concentrated into one intense and tremendous focus. Canning marched forward in a straight and clear track; every paragraph was perfect in itself, and every coruscation of wit and of genius was brilliant and delightful; it was all felt, and it was felt all at once: Brougham twined round and round in a spiral, sweeping the contents of a vast circumference before him, and uniting and pouring them onward to the main point of attack.

"Such were the rival orators, who sat glancing hostility and defiance at each other during the session of eighteen hundred and twenty-three—Brougham, as if wishing to overthrow the Secretary by a sweeping accusation of having abandoned all principle for the sake of office; and the Secretary ready to parry the charge and attack in his turn. An opportunity at length offered. Upon that occasion the oration of Brougham was disjointed and ragged, and apparently without aim or application. He careered over the whole annals of the world, and collected every instance in which genius had prostituted itself at the footstool of power, or principle had been sacrificed for the vanity or the lucre of place; but still there was no allusion to Canning, and no connection, that ordinary men could discover, with the business before the House. When, however, he had collected every material which suited his purpose—when the mass had become big and black, he bound it about and about with the cords of illustration and argument; when its union was secure, he swung it round and round with the strength of a giant and the rapidity of a whirlwind, in order that its impetus and its effects might be the more tremendous; and while doing this, he ever and anon glared his eye, and pointed his finger, to make the aim and the direction sure. Canning himself was the first that seemed to be aware where and how terrible was to be the collision; and he kept writhing his body in agony and rolling his eye in fear, as if anxious to find some shelter from the impending bolt. The House soon caught the impression, and every man in it was glancing fearfully, first toward the orator, and then toward the Secretary. There was, save the voice of Brougham, which growled in that under tone of muttered thunder which is so fearfully audible, and of which no speaker of the day was fully master but himself, a silence as if the angel of retribution had been flaring in the faces of all parties the scroll of their personal and political sins. The stiffness of Brougham's figure had vanished; his features seemed concentrated almost to a point; he glanced toward every part of the House in succession; and, sounding the death-knell of the Secretary's forbearance and prudence with both his clinched hands upon the table, he hurled at him an accusation more dreadful in its gall, and more torturing in its effects, than had ever been hurled at mortal man within the same walls. The result was instantaneous—was electric. It was as when the thunder-cloud descends upon the Giant Peak; one flash—one peal—the sublimity vanished, and all that remained was a small and cold pattering of rain. Canning started to his feet, and was able only to utter the unguarded words, 'It is *false!*' to which followed a dull chapter of apologies. From that moment the House became more a scene of real business than of airy display and angry vituperation."

SPEECH

OF MR. BROUGHAM ON THE ARMY ESTIMATES, DELIVERED IN THE HOUSE OF COMMONS, MARCH 11, 1816.

INTRODUCTION.

LORD CASTLEREAGH and his ministry, elated by their triumph over Bonaparte at the battle of Waterloo, had the ambition of still continuing an immense military establishment after the return of peace had rendered it wholly unnecessary.

For the year 1816, they proposed a standing force of *one hundred and seventy-six thousand men,* when the country was suffering under extreme embarrassments in every branch of its industry. A part of these forces consisted of the Household Troops, as they were called, to the number of ten thousand men, supported for mere parade in London or its vicinity, and confessedly of no use except in the case of mobs, which were then wholly out of the question.

When the debate took place on the army estimates, March 11, 1816, Mr. Calcraft moved to reduce the appropriation for the Household Troops to one half the sum proposed, intending, if this motion prevailed, to carry out the principle of retrenchment into the other branches of the army. In support of this motion, Mr. Brougham delivered the following speech, which is marked by that mixture of bold assertion, rapid argument, and fervid declamation which so generally characterized his speaking.

SPEECH, &c.

The speaker called forth by challenges from the ministry.

SIR,—Although I on a former occasion delivered my opinion generally upon these estimates, yet I am anxious now to state my sentiments in more detail upon a subject of such great importance, and the rather because of the defiances flung out from the other side to all of us to go into the examination of it. I stand forward to take up the gauntlet which has thus been thrown down; and I affirm that the more minutely you scrutinize the several items of this bill, brought in against the country, the more objectionable you will find them.

Objection to new title of "Household Troops."

I object, in the first place, altogether to the large force of guards which it is intended to keep up; and I even protest, though that is a trifle in comparison, but I do protest against the new-fangled French name of Household Troops, under which they are designated—a name borrowed from countries where this portion of the national force is exclusively allotted to protect the Prince against a people in whom he can not trust—is the appointed means given him to maintain his arbitrary power—is the very weapon put into his hands to arm him against the liberties of his country. However appropriate the appellation may be there, it can not be endured in this nation, where the Sovereign ought never to have any reason for distrusting his subjects, and never can be intrusted with any force except that which the defense of his people requires. But the name is of far less importance than the thing. Has the noble Lord [Lord Castlereagh] made out any thing like a case for raising the amount of this force to more than double of what it was in 1791?

Objection to their number.

If any such proof had been given, I should not have been found among the opposers of the proposition. But the truth is, that, with all the professed anxiety of the noble Lord and his friends to go through the estimates, item by item; with all their pretended readiness and even desire to court full investigation; with all the bluster of their defiance to us, and the bravado more than once used, that we durst not grapple with the question in detail, they have themselves wholly shrunk from the inquiry, fled from all particulars, and abandoned all attempts at showing, in any one instance, from any one conclusion, with a view to any single circumstance in the present situation of the country, that there is the shadow of a ground for this increase of force. We had the subject debated generally, indeed, but at great length, a few days ago, on bringing up the report; and it had been repeatedly before the House on former occasions. We have now renewed the discussion on the motion for going into this committee. We have been in the committee for some hours. At this very advanced stage of the debate have we arrived, and though all the members of the government have addressed themselves to the question, many of them once and again, yet I defy any one to point out a single fact that has been stated, a single argument urged, a single topic used, to prove the necessity which alone can justify the scale these estimates are framed upon. It has, indeed, been said that 2400 of the guards are destined for France, where I suppose the army of occupation is required in order to demonstrate how tranquil our famous negotiators have left the whole Continent—how perfectly successful—how absolutely final—the grand settlement of all Europe is, upon which we so greatly plume ourselves, and upon which, above all, the political reputation of the noble Lord is built.[1] But sup-

[1] After the deposition of Bonaparte, the allied Sov-

pose I pass over this, and do not stop to ask what reason there can be for these 2400 men being guards, and not simply troops of the line—those troops required to maintain our final and conclusive settlement, and enforce the profound tranquillity in which Europe is every where enwrapt; suppose I admit, for argument' sake, and in my haste to get at the main question, that these 2400 guards may be necessary—what is to be said of all the rest? There remain no less than 7600 to account for. What reason has been assigned, what attempt ever made by the noble Lord to assign a reason why 3600 more guards should be wanted more than in Mr. Pitt's celebrated establishment of 1792? I desire, however, to have this explained—I demand the ground for this enormous augmentation of what you call your "household force"—I have a right to know why this increase is called for—I call for the reason of it, *and the reason I will have.* Deduct all you require, or say you require, for France; what has happened since Mr. Pitt's time to justify you in nearly doubling the number of the guards? That is the question, and it must be answered to Parliament and to the country—answered, not by vague generalities—by affected anxiety for discussion—by shallow pretenses of desire to have the fullest investigation—by blustering defiances to *us*—and swaggering taunts that we dare not investigate. We *do* investigate—we do advance to the conflict—we do go into the details—we do enter upon the items one by one; and the first that meets us on the very threshold, and as soon as we have planted a foot upon it, is this doubling of the guards. Then how do you defend *that?* Where is the ground for it? What is there to excuse it or to explain? Mr.

No disorders throughout the country to require these troops, as in 1792.

Pitt found 4000 enough in 1792—then what is there to make 7600 wanting now? Look at home. Is the country less peaceable now than it was then? Quite the contrary. It was then disturbed; it is now profoundly quiet. Then, although there was no insurrection, nor any thing that could be called by such a name, unless by those who sought a pretext for violating the Constitution, and, by suspending its powers, securing their own, yet still no man could call the state of the country tranquil. Universal discontent prevailed, here and there amounting to disaffection, and even breaking out into local disorders; rumors of plots floated every where about; while meetings were held—unmeasured language was used—wild schemes were broached—dangerous associations were formed. Though no man had a right to say that the government was entitled to pursue unconstitutional courses for meeting those evils, every man felt obliged to admit that there was reason for much anxiety—that the aspect of things was lowering; the alarm was a natural feeling—that the duty of the executive was to be vigilant and to be prepared. The fears of men, whose loyalty was unquestioned, though their wisdom might be doubted, led them a good deal further than this. Meetings were encouraged to address the Crown, and testify the resolution to support its prerogatives. Bonds were entered into for defending the Constitution, believed to be threatened. Pledges of life and fortune were given to stand by the established order of things, and resist to the death all violence that might be directed against it. Parliament was not alone in countenancing these measures, proceeding from alarm. Both Houses addressed the Throne; both joined in asserting the existence of great peril to the Constitution; both declared that the public peace was in danger from the designs of the evil-disposed. To read the language of those times, both in public meetings and their addresses, and in parliamentary debates, and resolutions of the two Houses, any one would have thought that a wide-spreading disaffection had shot through the land; that the materials of a vast rebellion were every where collected; and that the moment was tremblingly expected when some spark lighting on the mass should kindle the whole into a flame, and wrap the country in destruction. Yet in that state of things, and with these testimonies to its menacing aspect, Mr. Pitt, at the very time when he was patronizing the doctrines of the alarmists, encouraging their movements, and doing all he could to increase rather than allay their fears; when he was grounding on the panic that prevailed, those measures out of which his junction with a part of the Whigs arose, whereby he succeeded in splitting that formidable party—yet never dreamed of such a force as we are now told is necessary for preserving the public peace. He proposed no more than 4000 guards; and held that amount to be sufficient.

The increase not required for the security of the metropolis.

We are challenged to go into particulars; we are defied to grapple with the question in detail. Then I come to particulars and details with the noble Lord. The main duty of the guards is the London service—that is the district to which their force is peculiarly applicable. To keep the peace of this great metropolis is their especial province; and I grant the high importance of such functions. Then I ask when London was ever more quiet than at this moment? When were its numerous inhabitants ever more contented, more obedient to the laws, more disinclined to any thing like resistance? At what period of our history was the vast mass of the people, by whom we are surrounded, ever more peaceably disposed, more unlikely to engage in any thing approaching to tumult than now? Why, they have even given over going to public meetings; the very trade of the libeler languishes, if it be not at end, in the general tranquillity and stagnation of these quiet times. All is silence, and indifference, and dullness, and inertness, and assuredly inaction. To the unnatural and costly excitement of war has succeeded a state of collapse, perhaps from exhaustion, but possibly from contrast alone. The mighty events of the latter days, when the materials for the history of a

ereigns kept for a time a large body of troops in France, to secure the execution of the treaty made by the Bourbon government.

country were crowded into the space of a few months, have left the public mind listless and vacant. The stimulus is withdrawn, and change has had its accustomed sedative influence. They who had been gazing till their eyes ached, and they doubted if they were awake, upon the most prodigious sights ever presented in the political and the moral world—upon empires broken up and formed anew—dynasties extinguished or springing up—the chains cast off by not merely a people, but a hemisphere; and half the globe suddenly covered with free and independent states—wars waged, battles fought, compared to which the heroes of old had only been engaged in skirmishes and sallies—treaties made which disposed of whole continents, and span the fate of millions of men—could hardly fail to find the contemplation of peace flat, stale, and unprofitable. The eye that had been in vain attempting to follow the swift march of such gigantic events, could not dwell with much interest upon the natural course of affairs, so slow in its motion as to appear at rest. And hence, if ever there was a time of utter inaction, of absolute rest to the public mind, it is the hour now chosen for supposing that there exists some danger which requires defensive preparation, and the increase of the garrison with which the listless and motionless mass of the London population may be overawed. Why, my honorable and learned friend [the Attorney General] has had nobody to prosecute for some years past. It is above two years since he has filed an ex-officio information, unless in the exchequer against smugglers. Jacobinism, the bugbear of 1792, has for the past six years and more never been even named. I doubt if allusion to it has been made in this House, even in a debate upon a King's speech, since Mr. Pitt's death. And to produce a Jacobin, or a specimen of any other kindred tribe, would, I verily believe, at this time of day, baffle the skill and the perseverance of the most industrious and most zealous collector of political curiosities to be found in the whole kingdom. What, then, is the danger—what the speculation upon some possible and expected, but non-existing risk—which makes it necessary at this time to augment the force applied to preserve the peace of the metropolis? But I fear there are far other designs in this measure, than merely to preserve a peace which no man living can have the boldness to contend is in any danger of being broken, and no man living can have the weakness really to be apprehensive about. Empty show, vain parade, will account for the array being acceptable in some high quarters; in others, the force may be recommended by its tending to increase the powers of the executive government, and extend the influence of the prerogative. In either light, it is most disgustful, most hateful to the eye of every friend of his country, and every one who loves the Constitution—all who have any regard for public liberty, and all who reflect on the burdens imposed upon the people.

But if the internal state of the country offers not the shadow of justification for this increase of force, what shall we say of the state of foreign affairs? Above all, what shall we say of the comparison between the face of those affairs now and its aspect in 1792? That was really a period of external danger. Never was there greater room for anxiety; never had the statesmen, not of England only, but of all Europe, more cause for apprehension and alarm—more occasion for wakefulness to passing events—more ground for being prepared at every point. A prodigious revolution had unchained twenty-six millions of men in the heart of Europe, gallant, inventive, enterprising, passionately fond of military glory, blindly following the phantom of national renown. Unchained from the fetters that had for ages bound them to their monarchs, they were speedily found to be alike disentangled from the obligations of peaceful conduct toward their neighbors. But they stopped not here. Confounding the abuses in their political institutions with the benefits, they had swept away every vestige of their former polity; and, disgusted with the rank growth of corruption to which religion had afforded a shelter, they tore up the sacred tree itself, under whose shade France had so long adored and slept. To the fierceness of their warfare against all authority, civil and religious at home, was added the fiery zeal of proselytism abroad, and they had rushed into a crusade against all existing governments, and on behalf of all nations throughout Europe, proclaiming themselves the redressers of every grievance, and the allies of each people that chose to rebel against their rulers. The uniform triumph of these principles at home, in each successive struggle for supremacy, had been followed by success almost as signal against the first attempts to overpower them from without, and all the thrones of the Continent shook before the blast which had breathed life and spirit into all the discontented subjects of each of their trembling possessors.[2] This was the state of things in 1792, when Mr. Pitt administered the affairs of a nation, certainly far less exposed either to the force or to the blandishments of the revolutionary people, but still very far from being removed above the danger of either their arts or their arms; and the existence of peril in both kinds, the fear of France menacing the independence of her neighbors, the risk to our domestic tranquillity from a party at home strongly sympathizing with her sentiments, were the topics upon which both he and his adherents were most prone to dwell in all their discourses of state affairs. Yet in these circumstances, the country thus beset with danger, and the peace thus menaced, both from within and from without, Mr. Pitt was content with half the establishment we are now required to vote! But see only how vast the difference between the

Much less does the state of *foreign affairs* demand these forces.

[2] This is a favorable specimen of Mr. Brougham's free, bold, animated painting and declamation, always made directly subservient to his argument, and filling his speeches with life and interest.

present aspect of affairs and that which I have been feebly attempting to sketch from the records of recent history, no page of which any of us can have forgotten! The ground and cause of all peril is exhausted—the object of all the alarms that beset us in 1792 is no more—France no longer menaces the independence of the world, or troubles its repose. By a memorable reverse, not of fortune, but of Divine judgments meting out punishment to aggression, France, overrun, reduced, humbled, has become a subject of care and protection, instead of alarm and dismay. Jacobinism itself, arrested by the Directory, punished by the Consuls, reclaimed by the Emperor, has become attached to the cause of good order, and made to serve it with the zeal, the resources, and the address of a malefactor engaged by the police after the term of his sentence had expired. All is now, universally over the face of the world, wrapped in profound repose. Exhausted with such gigantic exertions as man never made before, either on the same scale or with the like energy, nations and their rulers have all sunk to rest. The general slumber of the times is every where unbroken; and if ever a striking contrast was offered to the eye of the observer by the aspect of the world at two different ages, it is that which the present posture of Europe presents to its attitude in Mr. Pitt's time, when, in the midst of wars and rumors of wars, foreign enemies and domestic treason vieing together for the mastery, and all pointed against the public peace, he considered a military establishment of half the amount now demanded to be sufficient for keeping the country quiet, and repelling foreign aggression, as well as subduing domestic revolt.

Respect for the valor of these troops no reason for still keeping them on foot.

Driven from the argument of necessity, as the noble Lord seemed to feel assured he should be the moment any one examined the case, he skillfully prepared for his retreat to another position, somewhat less exposed, perhaps, but far enough from being impregnable. You can not, he said, disband troops who have so distinguished themselves in the late glorious campaigns. This topic he urged for keeping up the guards. But I ask, which of our troops did not equally distinguish themselves? What regiment engaged in the wars failed to cover itself with their glories? This argument, if it has any force at all, may be used against disbanding a single regiment, or discharging a single soldier. Nay, even those who by the chances of war had no opportunity of displaying their courage, their discipline, and their zeal, would be extremely ill treated if they were now to be dismissed the service merely because it was their misfortune not to have enjoyed the same opportunity with others in happier circumstances of sharing in the renown of our victories. It is enough to have been deprived of the laurels which no one doubts they would equally have won had they been called into the field. Surely, surely, they might justly complain if to the disappointment were added the being turned out of the service, which no act of theirs had dishonored. I am now speaking the language of the noble Lord's argument, and not of my own. He holds it to be unfair toward the guards that they should be reduced, after eminently meritorious service—he connects merit with the military state—disgrace, or at least slight, with the loss of this station. He holds the soldier to be preferred, rewarded, and distinguished, who is retained in the army—him to be neglected or ill used, if not stigmatized, who is discharged. His view of the Constitution is, that the capacity of the soldier is more honorable and more excellent than that of the citizen. According to his view, therefore, the *whole army* has the same right to complain with the guards. But his view is not my view; it is not the view of the Constitution; it is not the view which I can ever consent to assume as just, and to inculcate into the army by acting as if it were just. I never will suffer it to be held out as the principle of our free and popular government that a man is exalted by being made a soldier, and degraded by being restored to the rank of a citizen. I never will allow it to be said that in a country blessed by having a civil, and not a military government; by enjoying the exalted station of a constitutional monarchy, and not being degraded to that of a military despotism, there is any pre-eminence whatever in the class of citizens which bears arms, over the class which cultivates the arts of peace. When it suits the purpose of some argument in behalf of a soldiery who have exceeded the bounds of the law in attacking some assembled force of the people, how often are we told from that bench of office, from the Crown side of the bar, nay, from the bench of justice itself, that by becoming soldiers, men cease not to be citizens, and that this is a glorious peculiarity of our free Constitution? Then what right can the noble Lord have to consider that the retaining men under arms, and in the pay of the state, is an exaltation and a distinction which they cease to enjoy if restored to the status of ordinary citizens? I read the Constitution in the very opposite sense to the noble Lord's gloss. I have not sojourned in congresses with the military representatives of military powers[3]—I have not frequented the courts, any more than I have followed the camps of these potentates—I have not lived in the company of crowned soldiers, all whose ideas are fashioned upon the rules of the drill and the articles of the fifteen maneuvers—all whose estimates of a country's value are framed on the number of troops it will raise, and who can no more sever the idea of a subject from that of a soldier, than if men were born into this world in complete armor, as Minerva started from Jupiter's head. My ideas are more humble and more civic, and the only

[3] The unusual course taken by Lord Castlereagh, as minister, of going himself to the various congresses on the Continent in 1815, instead of sending an embassador, had before this drawn forth the severest strictures from the Opposition, who considered him as inflated by vanity, and in danger of being seduced into measures unbecoming the representative of a free people.

language I know, or can speak, or can understand in this House, is the mother tongue of the old English Constitution. I will speak none other—I will suffer none other to be spoken in my presence. Addressing the soldier in that language—which alone above all other men in the country he ought to know—to which alone it peculiarly behooves us that he, the armed man, should be accustomed—I tell him, "You *have* distinguished yourself—all that the noble Lord says of you is true—nay, under the truth—you have crowned yourself with the glories of war. But chiefly you, the guards, you have outshone all others, and won for yourselves a deathless fame. Now, then, advance and receive your reward. Partake of the benefits you have secured for your grateful country. None are better than you entitled to share in the blessings, the inestimable blessings of peace—than you whose valor has conquered it for us. Go back, then, to the rank of citizens, which, for a season, you quitted at the call of your country. Exalt her glory in peace, whom you served in war; and enjoy the rich recompense of all your toils in the tranquil retreat from dangers, which her gratitude bestows upon you." I know this to be the language of the Constitution, and time was when none other could be spoken, or would have been understood in this House. I still hope that no one will dare use any other in the country; and, least of all, can any other be endured as addressed to the soldiery in arms, treating them as if they were the hired partisans of the Prince, a caste set apart for his service, and distinguished from all the rest of their countrymen, not a class of the people devoting themselves for a season to carry arms in defense of the nation, and when their services are wanted no more, retiring naturally to mix with and be lost in the mass of their fellow-citizens.

Nor does justice require it.

But it has been said that there is injustice and ingratitude in the country turning adrift her defenders as soon as the war is ended, and we are tauntingly asked, "Is this the return you make to the men who have fought your battles? When the peace comes which they have conquered, do you wish to starve them or send them off to sweep the streets?" I wish no such thing; I do not desire that they should go unrequited for their services. But I can not allow that the only, or the best, or even a lawful mode of recompensing them, is to keep on foot during peace the army which they compose, still less that it is any hardship whatever for a soldier to return into the rank of citizens when the necessity is at an end, which alone justified his leaving those ranks. Nor can I believe that it is a rational way of showing our gratitude toward the army, whose only valuable service has been to gain us an honorable peace, to maintain an establishment for their behoof, which must deprive the peace of all its value, and neutralize the benefits which they have conferred upon us.

See, too, the gross inconsistency of this argument with your whole conduct. How do you treat the common sailors who compose our invincible navy? All are at once dismissed. The Victory, which carried Nelson's flag to his invariable and undying triumphs, is actually laid up in ordinary, and her crew disbanded to seek a precarious subsistence where some hard fortune may drive them. Who will have the front to contend that the followers of Nelson are less the glory and the saviors of their country than the soldiers of the guards? Yet who is there candid enough to say one word in their behalf when we hear so much of the injustice of disbanding our army after its victories? Who has ever complained of that being done to the seamen which is said to be impossible in the soldier's case? But where is the difference? Simply this: That the maintenance of the navy in time of peace never can be dangerous to the liberties of the country, like the keeping up a standing army; and that a naval force gives no gratification to the miserable, paltry love of show which rages in some quarters, and is to be consulted in all the arrangements of our affairs, to the exclusion of every higher and worthier consideration.

These troops far more expensive than those of the line.

After the great constitutional question to which I have been directing your attention, you will hardly bear with me while I examine these estimates in any detail. This, however, I must say, that nothing can be more scandalous than the extravagance of maintaining the establishment of the guards at the expense of troops of the line, which cost the country so much less. Compare the charge of two thousand guards with an equal number of the line, and you will find the difference of the two amounts to be above £10,000 a year. It is true that this sum is not very large, and compared with our whole expenditure it amounts to nothing. But in a state burdened as ours is, there can be no such thing as a small saving; the people had far rather see millions spent upon necessary objects, than thousands squandered unnecessarily, and upon matters of mere superfluity; nor can any thing be more insulting to their feelings, and less bearable by them, than to see us here underrating the importance even of the most inconsiderable sum that can be added to or taken from the intolerable burdens under which they labor.

As for the pretext set up to-night that the question is concluded by the vote of last Friday, nothing can be more ridiculous. This House never can be so bound. If it could, then may it any hour be made the victim of surprise, and the utmost encouragement is held out to tricks and maneuvers. If you voted too many men before, you can now make that vote harmless and inoperative by withholding the supplies necessary for keeping those men on foot. As well may it be contended that the House is precluded from throwing out a bill on the third reading, because it affirmed the principle by its vote on the second, and sanctioned the details by receiving the committee's report.

The estimate before you is £385,000, for the support of eight thousand one hundred guards.

Adopt my honorable friend's amendment [Mr. Calcraft], and you reduce them to about four thousand, which is still somewhat above their number in the last peace.

Peroration: The speaker free from all responsibility if the injurious system is pursued.

Sir, I have done. I have discharged my duty to the country; I have accepted the challenge of the ministers to discuss the question; I have met them fairly, and grappled with the body of the argument. I may very possibly have failed to convince the House that this establishment is enormous and unjustifiable, whether we regard the burdened condition of the country, or the tranquil state of its affairs at home, or the universal repose in which the world is lulled, or the experience of former times, or the mischievous tendency of large standing armies in a constitutional point of view, or the dangerous nature of the arguments urged in their support upon the present occasion. All this I feel very deeply; and I am also very sensible how likely it is that, on taking another view, you should come to an opposite determination. Be it so; I have done my duty; I have entered my protest. It can not be laid to my charge that a force is to be maintained in profound and general peace twice as great as was formerly deemed sufficient when all Europe was involved in domestic troubles, and war raged in some parts, and was about to spread over the whole. It is not my fault that peace will have returned without its accustomed blessings; that our burdens are to remain undiminished; that our liberties are to be menaced by a standing army, without the pretense of necessity in any quarter to justify its continuance. The blame is not mine that a brilliant and costly army of household troops, of unprecedented numbers, is allowed to the Crown without the shadow of use, unless it be to pamper a vicious appetite for military show, to gratify a passion for parade, childish and contemptible; unless, indeed, that nothing can be an object of contempt which is at once dangerous to the Constitution of the country, and burdensome to the resources of the people. I shall further record my resistance to this system by my vote; and never did I give my voice to any proposition with more hearty satisfaction than I now do to the amendment of my honorable friend.

The amendment was voted down by a majority of eighty.

SPEECH

OF MR. BROUGHAM IN BEHALF OF WILLIAMS WHEN PROSECUTED FOR A LIBEL ON THE CLERGY OF DURHAM, DELIVERED AT DURHAM BEFORE THE COURT OF KING'S BENCH, AUGUST 9, 1822.

INTRODUCTION.

MR. WILLIAMS was editor of the Chronicle, a paper published at Durham, in the north of England, and distinguished for its assertion of free principles in Church and State.

When Queen Caroline died, August 7, 1821, the established clergy of Durham would not allow the bells of their churches to be tolled in the ordinary manner as a token of respect to her memory. This fact called out the following remarks from Mr. Williams, in his paper of August 10, 1821:

"So far as we have been able to judge from the accounts in the public papers, a mark of respect to her late Majesty has been almost universally paid throughout the kingdom, when the painful tidings of her decease were received, by tolling the bells of the cathedrals and churches. But there is one exception to this very creditable fact which demands especial notice. In this episcopal city, containing six churches independently of the cathedral, not a single bell announced the departure of the magnanimous spirit of the most injured of queens—the most persecuted of women. Thus the brutal enmity of those who embittered her mortal existence pursues her in her shroud.

"We know not whether any actual orders were issued to prevent this customary sign of mourning; but the omission plainly indicates the kind of spirit which predominates among our clergy. Yet these men profess to be followers of Jesus Christ, to walk in his footsteps, to teach his precepts, to inculcate his spirit, to promote harmony, charity, and Christian love! Out upon such hypocrisy! It is such conduct which renders the very name of our established clergy odious, till it stinks in the nostrils; that makes our churches look like deserted sepulchers, rather than temples of the living God; that raises up conventicles in every corner, and increases the brood of wild fanatics and enthusiasts; that causes our beneficed dignitaries to be regarded as usurpers of their possessions; that deprives them of all pastoral influence and respect; that, in short, has left them no support or prop in the attachment or veneration of the people. Sensible of the decline of their spiritual and moral influence, they cling to temporal power, and lose in their officiousness in political matters, even the semblance of the character of ministers of religion. It is impossible that such a system can last. It is at war with the spirit of the age, as well as with justice and reason, and the beetles who crawl about amid its holes and crevices act as if they were striving to provoke and accelerate the blow, which, sooner or later, will inevitably crush the whole fabric and level it with the dust."

Mr. Williams was prosecuted for these remarks as a libel on the clergy of Durham, and was defended by Mr. Brougham in the following speech, which for bitter irony and withering invective has hardly its equal in our language.

SPEECH, &c.

Gentlemen of the Jury,—My learned friend [Mr. Scarlett], the Attorney General for the Bishop of Durham, having at considerable length offered to you various conjectures as to the line of defense which he supposed I should pursue upon this occasion; having nearly exhausted every topic which I was *not* very likely to urge, and elaborately traced, with much fancy, all the ground on which I could hardly be expected to tread—perhaps it may be as well that *I* should now, in my turn, take the liberty of stating to you what really *is* the defendant's case, and that you should know from myself what I *do* intend to lay before you. As my learned friend has indulged in so many remarks upon what I shall not say, I may take leave to offer a single observation on what he has said; and I think I may appeal to any one of you who ever served upon a jury or witnessed a trial, and ask if you ever before this day saw a public prosecutor who stated his case with so much art and ingenuity—wrought up his argument with such pains—wandered into so large a field of declamation—or altogether performed his task in so elaborate and eloquent a fashion as the Attorney General has done upon the present occasion. I do not blame this course. I venture not even to criticise the discretion he has exercised in the management of his cause; and I am far, indeed, from complaining of it. But I call upon you to declare that inference which I think you must already have drawn in your own minds, and come to that conclusion at which I certainly have arrived—that he felt what a laboring case he had—that he was aware how very different his situation to-day is from any he ever before knew in a prosecution for libel—and that the extraordinary pressure of the difficulties he had to struggle with drove him to so unusual a course. He has called the defendant "*that unhappy man.*" Unhappy he will be, indeed; but not the only unhappy man in this country, if the doctrines laid down by my learned friend are sanctioned by your verdict; for those doctrines, I fearlessly tell you, must, if established, inevitably destroy the whole liberties of us all. Not that he has ventured to deny the right of discussion generally upon all subjects, even upon the present, or to screen from free inquiry the foundations of the Established Church, and the conduct of its ministers as a body (which I shall satisfy you are not even commented on in the publication before you). Far from my learned friend is it to impugn those rights in the abstract; nor, indeed, have I ever yet heard a prosecutor for libel—an Attorney General (and I have seen a good many in my time), whether of our Lord the King or our Lord of Durham, who, while in the act of crushing every thing like unfettered discussion, did not preface his address to the jury with "God forbid that the fullest inquiry should not be allowed." But then the admission had invariably a condition following close behind, which entirely retracted the concession—"provided always the discussion be carried on harmlessly, temperately, calmly"—that is to say, in such a manner as to leave the subject untouched, and the reader unmoved; to satisfy the public prosecutor, and to please the persons attacked.

Remarks on the speech of the Attorney General as showing how much he felt the difficulties of his case.

My learned friend has asked if the defendant knows that the Church is established by law? He knows it, and so do I. The Church is established by law, as the civil government—as all the institutions of the country are established by law—as all the offices under the Crown are established by law, and all who fill them are by the law protected. It is not more established, nor more protected, than those institutions, officers, and office-bearers, each of which is recognized and favored by the law as much as the Church; but I never yet have heard, and I trust I never shall; least of all do I expect, in the lesson which your verdict this day will read, to hear that those officers and office-bearers, and all those institutions, sacred and secular, and the conduct of all, whether laymen or priests, who administer them, are not the fair subjects of open, untrammeled, manly, zealous, and even vehement discussion, as long as this country pretends to liberty, and prides herself on the possession of a free press.

The Church, like the other institutions of the country, is established by law.

In the publication before you the defendant has not attempted to dispute the high character of the Church; on that Establishment, or its members generally, he has not endeavored to fix any stigma. Those topics, then, are foreign to the present inquiry, and I have no interest in discussing them; yet, after what has fallen from my learned friend, it is fitting that I should claim for this defendant, and for all others, the right to question—freely to question—not only the conduct of the ministers of the Established Church, but even the foundations of the Church itself. It is, indeed, unnecessary for my present purpose, because I shall demonstrate that the paper before you does not touch upon those points; but unnecessary though it be, as my learned friend has defied me, I will follow him to the field and say that if there is any one of the institutions of the country which, more emphatically than all the rest, justifies us in arguing strongly, feeling powerfully, and expressing our sentiments as well as urging our reasons with vehemence, it is that branch of the state which, because it is sacred, because it bears connection with higher principles than any involved in the mere management of worldly concerns—for that very reason, entwines itself with deeper feelings, and must needs be discussed, if discussed at all, with more warmth and zeal than any other part of our system is fitted to rouse. But if any hierarchy in all the world is bound on every principle of consistency—if any Church should be forward, not only to suffer, but pro-

It is liable, like them, to the severest scrutiny.

The Church of England ought especially to court that scrutiny.

voke discussion; to stand upon that title and challenge the most unreserved inquiry—it is the Protestant Church of England; first, because she has nothing to dread from it; secondly, because she is the very creature of free inquiry, the offspring of repeated revolutions, and the most reformed of the reformed churches of Europe. But surely if there is any one corner of Protestant Europe where men ought not to be rigorously judged in ecclesiastical controversy—where a large allowance should be made for the conflict of irreconcilable opinions—where the harshness of jarring tenets should be patiently borne, and strong, or even violent language be not too narrowly watched—it is this very realm, in which we live under three different ecclesiastical orders, and owe allegiance to a Sovereign who in one of his kingdoms is the head of the Church, acknowledged as such by all men; while, in another neither he nor any earthly being is allowed to assume that name—a realm composed of three great divisions, in one of which Prelacy is favored by law and approved in practice by an Episcopalian people; while in another it is protected, indeed, by law, but abjured in practice by a nation of sectaries, Catholic and Presbyterian; and in a third, it is abhorred alike by law and in practice, repudiated by the whole institutions of the country, scorned and detested by the whole of its inhabitants. His Majesty, almost at the time in which I am speaking, is about to make a progress through the northern provinces of this island, accompanied by certain of his chosen counselors—a portion of men who enjoy, unenvied, and in an equal degree, the admiration of other countries and the wonder of their own—and there the Prince will see much loyalty, great learning, some splendor, the remains of an ancient monarchy, and of the institutions which made it flourish.[1] But one thing he will not see. Strange as it may seem, and to many who hear me incredible, from one end of the country to the other he will see no such thing as a Bishop; not such a thing is to be found from the Tweed to John O'Groats; not a mitre; no, nor so much as a minor canon, or even a rural dean; and in all the land not one single curate, so entirely rude and barbarous are they in Scotland; in such outer darkness do they sit, that they support no cathedrals, maintain no pluralists, suffer non-residence; nay, *the poor benighted creatures are ignorant even of tithes!* Not a sheaf, or a lamb, or a pig, or the value of a plow-penny do the hapless mortals render from year's end to year's end! Piteous as their lot is, what makes it infinitely more touching is to witness the return of good for evil in the demeanor of this wretched race. Under all this cruel neglect of their spiritual concerns, they are actually the most loyal, contented, moral, and religious people any where, perhaps, to be found in the world. Let us hope (many indeed there are, not afar off, who will, with unfeigned devotion, pray) that his Majesty may return safe from the dangers of his excursion into such a country—an excursion most perilous to a certain portion of the Church, should his royal mind be infected with a taste for cheap establishments, a working clergy, and a pious congregation!

For the country is divided into different and opposing church organizations.

But compassion for our brethren in the North has drawn me aside from my purpose, which was merely to remind you how preposterous it is in a country of which the ecclesiastical polity, is framed upon plans so discordant, and the religious tenets themselves are so various, to require any very measured expressions of men's opinions upon questions of church government. And if there is any part of England in which an ample license ought more especially to be admitted in handling such matters, I say, without hesitation, it is this very Bishopric, where, in the nineteenth century, you live under a Palatine Prince, the Lord of Durham; where the endowment of the hierarchy—I may not call it enormous, but I trust I shall be permitted, without offense, to term splendid; where the Establishment—I dare not whisper—proves grinding to the people, but I will rather say is an *incalculable*, an *inscrutable* blessing—only it is prodigiously large—showered down in a profusion somewhat overpowering; and laying the inhabitants under a load of obligation *overwhelming* by its weight. It is in Durham, where the Church is endowed with a splendor and a power unknown in monkish times and Popish countries, and the clergy swarm in every corner an' it were the patrimony of St. Peter; it is here, where all manner of conflicts are at each moment inevitable between the people and the priests, that I feel myself warranted, on *their* behalf and for *their* protection—for the sake of the Establishment, and as the discreet advocate of that Church and that clergy; for the defense of their very existence—to demand the most unrestrained discussion for their title, and their actings under it. For them in this age to screen their conduct from investigation, is to stand self-convicted; to shrink from the discussion of their title is to confess a flaw; he must be the most shallow, the most blind of mortals who does not at once perceive that if that title is protected only by the strong arm of the law, it becomes not worth the parchment on which it is engrossed, or the wax that dangles to it for a seal. I have hitherto all along assumed that there is nothing impure in the practice under the system; I am admitting that every person engaged in its administration does every one act which he ought, and which the law expects him to do; I am supposing that up to this hour not one unworthy member has entered within its pale; I am even presuming that up to this moment not one of those individuals has stepped beyond the strict line of his sacred functions, or given the slightest offense or annoyance to any human being. I am taking it for granted that they all act the part of good shepherds, making

Durham, especially, ought to be open to the freest remarks.

[1] The King visited Scotland on this occasion for the first time, leaving London on the tenth of August, 1822, and spending nearly three weeks on his tour.

the welfare of their flock their first care, and only occasionally bethinking them of shearing, in order to prevent the too luxuriant growth of the fleece proving an encumbrance, or to eradicate disease. If, however, those operations be so constant that the flock actually live under the knife; if the shepherds are so numerous, and employ so large a troop of the watchful and eager animals that attend them (some of them, too, with a cross of the fox, or even the wolf, in their breed) can it be wondered at, if the poor creatures thus fleeced, and hunted, and barked at, and snapped at, and from time to time worried, should now and then bleat, dream of preferring the rot to the shears, and draw invidious, possibly disadvantageous comparisons between the wolf without and the shepherd within the fold—it can not be helped; it is in the nature of things that suffering should beget complaint; but for those who have caused the pain to complain of the outcry and seek to punish it—for those who have goaded to scourge and to gag, is the meanest of all injustice. It is, moreover, the most pitiful folly for the clergy to think of retaining their power, privileges, and enormous wealth, without allowing free vent for complaints against abuses in the Establishment and delinquency in its members; and in this prosecution they have displayed that folly in its supreme degree. I will even put it that there has been an attack on the hierarchy itself; I do so for argument's sake only; denying all the while that any thing like such an attack is to be found within the four corners of this publication.

Example of Milton in this respect.

But suppose it had been otherwise; I will show you the sort of language in which the wisest and the best of our countrymen have spoken of that Establishment. I am about to read a passage in the immortal writings of one of the greatest men, I may say, the greatest genius which this country or Europe has in modern times produced. You shall hear what the learned and pious Milton has said of prelacy. He is arguing against an Episcopalian antagonist, whom, from his worldly and unscriptural doctrines, he calls a "*Carnal Textman;*" and it signifies not that we may differ widely in opinion with this illustrious man; I only give his words as a sample of the license with which he was permitted to press his argument, and which in those times went unpunished: "That which he imputes as sacrilege to his country, is the only way left them to purge that abominable sacrilege out of the land, which none but the prelates are guilty of; who for the discharge of one single duty receive and keep that which might be enough to satisfy the labors of many painful ministers better deserving than themselves —who possess huge benefices for lazy performances, great promotions only for the exercise of a cruel disgospelling jurisdiction—who engross many pluralities under a non-resident and slumbering dispatch of souls—who let hundreds of parishes famish in one diocese, while they the prelates are mute, and yet enjoy that wealth that would furnish all those dark places with able supply; and yet they eat and yet they live at the rate of earls, and yet hoard up; they who chase away all the faithful shepherds of the flock, and bring in a dearth of spiritual food, robbing thereby the Church of her dearest treasure, and sending herds of souls starving to hell, while they feast and riot upon the labors of hireling curates, consuming and purloining even that which by their foundation is allowed and left to the poor, and the reparation of the Church. These are they who have bound the land with the sin of sacrilege, from which mortal engagement we shall never be free till we have totally removed with one labor, as one individual thing, prelaty and sacrilege." "Thus have ye heard, readers" (he continues, after some advice to the Sovereign to check the usurpations of the hierarchy), "how many shifts and wiles the prelates have invented to save their ill got booty. And if it be true, as in Scripture it is foretold, that pride and covetousness are the sure marks of those false prophets which are to come, then boldly conclude these to be as great seducers as any of the latter times. For between this and the judgment-day do not look for any arch-deceivers, who, in spite of reformation, will use more craft or less shame to defend their love of the world and their ambition, than these prelates have done."[2]

Example of Bishop Burnet.

If Mr. Williams had dared to publish the tithe part of what I have just read; if any thing in sentiment or in language approaching to it were to be found in his paper, I should not stand before you with the confidence which I now feel; but what he has published forms a direct contrast to the doctrines contained in this passage. Nor is such language confined to the times in which Milton lived, or to a period of convulsion when prelacy was in danger. I will show you that in tranquil, episcopal times, when the Church existed peacefully and securely as by law established, some of its most distinguished members, who have added to its stability as well as its fame, by the authority of their learning and the purity of their lives, the fathers and brightest ornaments of that Church, have used expressions nearly as free as those which I have cited from Milton, and ten-fold stronger than any thing attributed to the defendant. I will read you a passage from Bishop Burnet, one of those Whig founders of the Constitution, whom the Attorney General has so lavishly praised. He says, "I have lamented during my whole life that I saw so little true zeal among our clergy; I saw much of it in the clergy of the Church of Rome, though it is both ill directed and ill conducted; I saw much zeal, likewise, throughout the foreign churches."

Now comparisons are hateful to a proverb; and it is for making a comparison that the defendant is to-day prosecuted; for his words can have no application to the Church generally, except in the way of comparison. And with whom does the venerable Bishop here compare the clergy? Why, with anti-Christ—with the Church

[2] Apology for Smectymnus—published in 1642.

of Rome—casting the balance in her favor—giving the advantage to our ghostly adversary. Next comes he to give the Dissenters the preference over our own clergy; a still more invidious topic; for it is one of the laws which govern theological controversy almost as regularly as gravitation governs the universe, that the mutual rancor of conflicting sects is inversely as their distance from each other; and with such hatred do they regard those who are separated by the slightest shade of opinion, that your true intolerant priest abhors a pious sectary far more devoutly than a blasphemer or an atheist; yet to the sectary also does the good Bishop give a decided preference: "The Dissenters have a great deal (that is of zeal) among them, but I must own that the main body of our clergy has always appeared dead and lifeless to me; and instead of animating one another, they seem rather to lay one another asleep." "I say it with great regret" (adds the Bishop), "I have observed the clergy in all the places through which I have traveled, Papists, Lutherans, Calvinists, and Dissenters; but of them all, our clergy is much the most remiss in their labors in private, and the least severe in their lives. And let me say this freely to you, now I am out of the reach of envy and censure" (he bequeathed his work to be given to the world after his death), "unless a better spirit possess the clergy, arguments and, which is more, laws and authority will not prove strong enough to preserve the Church."[3]

Of Dr. Hartley.

I will now show you the opinion of a very learned and virtuous writer, who was much followed in his day, and whose book, at that time, formed one of the manuals by which our youth were taught the philosophy of morals to prepare them for their theological studies, I mean Dr. Hartley: "I choose to speak of what falls under the observation of all serious, attentive persons in the kingdom. The superior clergy are in general ambitious, and eager in the pursuit of riches—flatterers of the great, and subservient to party interest—negligent of their own particular charges, and also of the inferior clergy. The inferior clergy imitate their superiors, and in general take little more care of their parishes than barely what is necessary to avoid the censure of the law; and the clergy of all ranks are in general either ignorant, or, if they do apply, it is rather to profane learning, to philosophical or political matters, than in the study of the Scriptures, of the Oriental languages, and the Fathers. I say this is, in general, the case; that is, far the greater part of the clergy of all ranks in the kingdom are of this kind."

I here must state that the passage I have just read is very far from meeting my approval, any more than it speaks the defendant's sentiments, and especially in its strictures upon the inferior clergy; for certainly it is impossible to praise too highly those pious and useful men, the resident, working parish priests of this country. I speak not of the dignitaries, the pluralists and sinecurists, but of men neither possessing the higher preferments of the Church, nor placed in that situation of expectancy so dangerous to virtue; the hard-working, and I fear too often hard-living, resident clergy of this kingdom, who are an ornament to their station, and who richly deserve that which in too many instances is almost all the reward they receive, the gratitude and veneration of the people committed to their care. But I read this passage from Dr. Hartley, not as a precedent followed by the defendant; for he has said nothing approaching to it—not as propounding doctrine authorized by the fact; or which in reasoning he approves—but only for the purpose of showing to what lengths such discussion of ecclesiastical abuses (which, it seems, we are now, for the first time, to hold our peace about) was carried near a century ago, when the freedom of speech, now to be stifled as licentiousness, went not only unpunished, but unquestioned and unblamed.

Of a clergyman in Chester.

To take a much later period, I hold in my hand an attack upon the hierarchy by one of their own body—a respectable and beneficed clergyman in the sister county Palatine of Chester, who undertook to defend the Christian religion, itself the basis, I presume I may venture to call it, of the Church, against Thomas Paine. In the course of so pious a work, which he conducted most elaborately, as you may perceive by the size of this volume, he inveighs in almost every page against the abuses of the Establishment, but in language which I am very far from adopting. In one passage is the following energetic, and I may add, somewhat violent invective, which I will read, that you may see how a man, unwearied in the care of souls, and so zealous a Christian that he is in the act of confuting infidels and putting scoffers to silence, may yet, in the very course of defending the Church and its faith, use language, any one word of which, if uttered by the defendant, would make my learned friend shudder at the license of the modern press upon sacred subjects. "We readily grant, therefore, you see, my countrymen, that the corruptions of Christianity shall be purged and done away; and we are persuaded the wickedness of Christians so called, the lukewarmness of professors, and the reiterated attacks of infidels upon the Gospel, shall all, under the guidance of infinite Wisdom, contribute to accomplish this end."

I have read this sentence to show you the spirit of piety in which the work is composed; now see what follows:

"The lofty looks of lordly prelates shall be brought low; the supercilious airs of downy doctors and perjured pluralists shall be humbled; the horrible sacrilege of non-residents, who shear the fleece, and leave the flock thus despoiled to the charge of uninterested hirelings that care not for them, shall be avenged on their impious heads. Intemperate priests, avaricious clerks, and buckish parsons, those curses of Christendom, shall be confounded. All secular hierarchies in the Church shall be tumbled into ruin; luke-

[3] History of His own Times, ii., 641.

warm formalists of every denomination shall call to the rocks and mountains to hide them from the wrath of the Lamb."

This is the language—these are the lively descriptions—these the warm, and I will not hesitate to say, exaggerated pictures which those reverend authors present of themselves; these are the testimonies which they bear to the merits of one another; these are opinions coming, not from the enemy without, but from the true, zealous, and even intemperate friend within. And can it be matter of wonder that laymen should sometimes raise their voices tuned to the discords of the sacred choir? And are they to be punished for what secures to clergymen followers, veneration, and—preferment? But I deny that Mr. Williams is of the number of followers; I deny that he has taken a leaf or a line out of such books; I deny that there is any sentiment of this cast, or any expression approaching to those of Dr. Simpson, in the publication before you. But I do contend that if the real friends of the Church, if its own members can safely indulge in such language, it is ten thousand times more lawful for a layman, like the defendant, to make the harmless observations which he has published, and in which I defy any man to show me one expression hostile to our ecclesiastical Establishment.

If the clergy of the English Church are thus severe, the laity may certainly be free in their remarks.

[Mr. Brougham then read the following passage from the libel:]

"We know not whether any actual orders were issued to prevent this customary sign of mourning; but the omission plainly indicates the kind of spirit which predominates among our clergy. Yet these men profess to be followers of Jesus Christ, to walk in his footsteps, to teach his precepts, to inculcate his spirit, to promote harmony, charity, and Christian love! Out upon such hypocrisy!"

That you may understand the meaning of this passage, it is necessary for me to set before you the picture my learned friend was pleased to draw of the clergy of the Diocese of Durham, and I shall recall it to your minds almost in his own words. According to him, they stand in a peculiarly unfortunate situation; they are, in truth, the most injured of men. They all, it seems, entertained the same generous sentiment with the rest of their countrymen, though they did not express them in the old, free, English manner, by openly condemning the proceedings against the late Queen; and after the course of unexampled injustice against which she victoriously struggled had been followed by the needless infliction of inhuman torture, to undermine a frame whose spirit no open hostility could daunt, and extinguish a life so long embittered by the same foul arts—after that great Princess had ceased to harass her enemies (if I may be allowed thus to speak, applying, as they did, by the perversion of all language, those names to the victim which belong to the tormentor), after her glorious but unhappy life had closed, and that princely head was at last laid low by death, which, living, all oppression had only the more illustriously exalted—the venerable the Clergy of Durham, I am now told for the first time, though less forward in giving vent to their feelings than the rest of their fellow-citizens—though not so vehement in their indignation at the matchless and unmanly persecution of the Queen—though not so unbridled in their joy at her immortal triumph, nor so loud in their lamentations over her mournful and untimely end—*did, nevertheless, in reality, all the while deeply sympathize with her sufferings in the bottom of their reverend hearts!* When all the resources of the most ingenious cruelty hurried her to a fate without parallel—if not so clamorous as others, they did not feel the least of all the members of the community—their grief was in truth too deep for utterance—sorrow clung round their bosoms, weighed upon their tongues, stifled every sound—and, when all the rest of mankind, of all sects and of all nations, freely gave vent to feelings of our common nature, THEIR silence, the contrast which THEY displayed to the rest of their species, *proceeded from the greater depth of their affliction; they said the less, because they felt the more!* Oh! talk of hypocrisy after this! Most consummate of all the hypocrites! After instructing your chosen, official advocate to stand forward with such a defense—such an exposition of your motives—to dare utter the word "hypocrisy," and complain of those who charged you with it! This is indeed to insult common sense and outrage the feelings of the whole human race! If you were hypocrites before, you were downright, frank, honest hypocrites to what you have now made yourselves—and surely, for all you have ever done, or ever been charged with, your worst enemies must be satiated with the humiliation of this day, its just atonement, and ample retribution!

Comments on the representations made by the Attorney General touching the Durham clergy.

If Mr. Williams had known the hundredth part of this at the time of her Majesty's demise—if he had descried the least twinkling of the light which has now broke upon us as to the real motives of their actions—I am sure this cause would never have been tried; because to have made any one of his strictures upon their conduct, would have been not only an act of the blackest injustice—it would have been perfectly senseless. But can he be blamed for his ignorance, when such pains were taken to keep him in the dark? Can it be wondered at that he was led astray when he had only so false a guide to their motives as their conduct, unexplained, afforded? When they were so anxious to mislead by facts and deeds, is his mistake to be so severely criticised? Had he known the real truth, he must have fraternized with them; embraced them cordially; looked up with admiration to their superior sensibility; admitted that he who feels most, by an eternal law of our nature, is least disposed to express his feelings; and lamented that his own zeal was less glowing than theirs; but, ignorant and misguided as he was, it is no

Mr. Williams left in ignorance of the feelings now attributed to the Durham clergy.

great marvel that he did not rightly know the real history of their conduct, until about three quarters of an hour ago, when the truth burst in upon us that all the while they were generously attached to the cause of weakness and misfortune!

Yet they ought, from their function, to have felt thus.

Gentlemen, if the country, as well as Mr. Williams, has been all along so deceived, it must be admitted that it is not from the probabilities of the case. Judging beforehand, no doubt, any one must have expected the Durham clergy, of all men, to feel exactly as they are now, for the first time, ascertained to have felt. They are Christians; outwardly, at least, they profess the gospel of charity and peace; they beheld oppression in its foulest shape; malignity and all uncharitableness putting on their most hideous forms; measures pursued to gratify prejudices in a particular quarter, in defiance of the wishes of the people and the declared opinions of the soundest judges of each party; and all with the certain tendency to plunge the nation in civil discord. If for a moment they had been led away by a dislike of cruelty and of civil war, to express displeasure at such perilous doings, no man could have charged them with political meddling; and when they beheld truth and innocence triumph over power, they might, as Christian ministers, calling to mind the original of their own Church, have indulged without offense in some little appearance of gladness; a calm, placid satisfaction on so happy an event would not have been unbecoming their sacred station. When they found that her sufferings were to have no end; that new pains were inflicted in revenge for her escape from destruction, and new tortures devised to exhaust the vital powers of her whom open, lawless violence had failed to subdue—we might have expected some slight manifestation of disapproval from holy men who, professing to inculcate loving-kindness, tender-mercy, and good-will to all, offer up their daily prayers for those who are desolate and oppressed. When at last the scene closed, and there was an end of that persecution which death alone could stay; but when not even her unhappy fate could glut the revenge of her enemies; and they who had harassed her to death now exhausted their malice in reviling the memory of their victim; if among them had been found, during her life, some miscreant under the garb of a priest, who, to pay his court to power, had joined in trampling upon the defenseless; even such an one, bear he the form of a man, with a man's heart throbbing in his bosom, might have felt even *his* fawning, sordid, calculating malignity assuaged by the hand of death; even *he* might have left the tomb to close upon the sufferings of the victim. All probability certainly favored the supposition that the clergy of Durham would not take part against the injured because the oppressor was powerful; and that the prospect of emolument would not make them witness with dry eyes and hardened hearts the close of a life which they had contributed to embitter and destroy. But I am compelled to say that their whole conduct has falsified those expectations. They sided openly, strenuously, forwardly, officiously, with power, in the oppression of a woman whose wrongs this day they, for the first time, pretend to bewail in their attempt to cozen you out of a verdict, behind which they may skulk from the inquiring eyes of the people. Silent and subdued in their tone as they were on the demise of the unhappy Queen, they could make every bell in all their chimes peal when gain was to be expected by flattering present greatness. Then they could send up addresses, flock to public meetings, and load the press with their libels, and make the pulpit ring with their sycophancy, filling up to the brim the measure of their adulation to the reigning Monarch, Head of the Church, and Dispenser of its Patronage.

But their conduct was directly the reverse.

Hence the severe strictures of Mr. Williams.

In this contrast originated the defendant's feelings, and hence the strictures which form the subject of these proceedings. I say the publication refers exclusively to the clergy of this city and its suburbs, and especially to such parts of that clergy as were concerned in the act of disrespect toward her late Majesty, which forms the subject of the alleged libel; but I deny that it has any reference whatever to the rest of the clergy, or evinces any designs hostile either to the stability of the Church or the general character and conduct of its ministers. My learned friend has said that Mr. Williams had probably been bred a sectary, and retained sectarian prejudices. No argument is necessary to refute this supposition. The passage which has been read to you carries with it the conviction that he is no sectary, and entertains no schismatical views against the Church; for there is a more severe attack upon the sectaries themselves than upon the clergy of Durham. No man can have the least hesitation in saying that the sentiments breathed in it are any thing but those of a sectary. For myself, I am far from approving the contemptuous terms in which he has expressed himself of those who dissent from the Establishment; and I think he has not spoken of them in the tone of decent respect that should be observed to so many worthy persons, who, though they differ from the Church, differ from it on the most conscientious grounds. This is the only part of the publication of which I can not entirely approve, but it is not for this that he is prosecuted. Then, what is the meaning of the obnoxious remarks? Are they directed against the Establishment? Are they meant to shake or degrade it? I say that no man who reads them can entertain a moment's doubt in his mind that they were excited by the conduct of certain individuals, and the use which he makes of that particular conduct, the inference which he draws from it, is not invective against the Establishment, but a regret that it should by such conduct be lowered. He says no more than this: "These are the men who do the mischief; ignorant and wild fanatics are crowding the tabernacles, while the Church

These strictures were designed, not to injure, but to benefit the Established Church.

is deserted," and he traces, not with exultation, but with sorrow, the cause of the desertion of the Church, and the increase of conventicles. "Here," says he, "I have a fact which accounts for the clergy sinking in the estimation of the community, and I hold up this mirror, not to excite hostility toward the Established Church, nor to bring its ministers into contempt among their flocks, but to teach and to reclaim those particular persons who are the disgrace and danger of the Establishment, instead of being, as they ought, its support and its ornament." He holds up to them that mirror in which they may see their own individual misconduct, and calculate its inevitable effects upon the security and honor of the Establishment which they disgrace. This is no lawyer-like gloss upon the passage—no special pleading construction, or far-fetched refinement of explanation—I give the plain and obvious sense which every man of ordinary understanding must affix to it. If you say that such an one disgraces his profession, or that he is a scandal to the cloth he wears (a common form of speech, and one never more in men's mouths than within the last fortnight, when things have happened to extort an universal expression of pain, sorrow, and shame), do you mean by such lamentations to undermine the Establishment? In saying that the purity of the cloth is defiled by individual misconduct, it is clear that you cast no imputation on the cloth generally; for an impure person could not contaminate a defiled cloth. Just so has the defendant expressed himself, and in this light I will put his case to you. If he had thought that the whole Establishment was bad; that all its ministers were time-servers, who, like the spaniel, would crouch and lick the hand that fed it, but snarl and bite at one which had nothing to bestow—fawning upon rich and liberal patrons, and slandering all that were too proud or too poor to bribe them; if he painted the Church as founded upon imposture, reared in time-serving, cemented by sordid interest, and crowned with spite, and insolence, and pride—to have said that the Durham clergy disgraced such a hierarchy, would have been not only gross inconsistency, but stark nonsense. He must rather have said that they were worthy members of a base and groveling Establishment—that the Church was as bad as its ministers—and that it was hard to say whether they more fouled it or were defiled by it. But he has said nothing that can bring into jeopardy or discredit an institution which every one wishes to keep pure, and which has nothing to dread so much as the follies and crimes of its supporters.

Peroration: The English Church is its own worst enemy in seeking to crush freedom of remark.

Gentlemen, you have to-day a great task committed to your hands. This is not the age—the spirit of the times is not such—as to make it safe, either for the country or for the government, or for the Church itself, to vail its mysteries in secrecy; to plant in the porch of the temple a prosecutor brandishing his flaming sword, the process of the law, to prevent the prying eyes of mankind from wandering over the structure. These are times when men *will* inquire, and the day most fatal to the Established Church, the blackest that ever dawned upon its ministers, will be that which consigns this defendant, for these remarks, to the horrors of a jail, which its false friends, the chosen objects of such lavish favor, have far more richly deserved. I agree with my learned friend, that the Church of England has nothing to dread from external violence. Built upon a rock, and lifting its head toward another world, it aspires to an imperishable existence, and defies any force that may rage from without. But let it beware of the corruption engendered within and beneath its massive walls; and let all its well-wishers—all who, whether for religious or political interests, desire its lasting stability—beware how they give encouragement, by giving shelter to the vermin bred in that corruption, who "*stink and sting*" against the hand that would brush the rottenness away. My learned friend has sympathized with the priesthood, and innocently enough lamented that they possess not the power of defending themselves through the public press. Let him be consoled; they are not so very defenseless—they are not so entirely destitute of the aid of the press as through him they have represented themselves to be. They have largely used that press (I wish I could say "as not abusing it"), and against some persons very near me—I mean especially against the defendant, whom they have scurrilously and foully libeled through that great vehicle of public instruction, over which, for the first time, among the other novelties of the day, I now hear they have control. Not that they wound deeply or injure much; but that is no fault of theirs—without hurting, they give trouble and discomfort. The insect brought into life by corruption, and nestled in filth, though its flight be lowly and its sting puny, can swarm and buzz, and irritate the skin and offend the nostril, and altogether give nearly as much annoyance as the wasp, whose nobler nature it aspires to emulate: These reverend slanderers—these pious backbiters—devoid of force to wield the sword, snatch the dagger, and destitute of wit to point or to barb it, and make it rankle in the wound, steep it in venom to make it fester in the scratch. The much-venerated personages whose harmless and unprotected state is now deplored, have been the wholesale dealers in calumny, as well as largest consumers of the base article—the especial promoters of that vile traffic, of late the disgrace of the country—both furnishing a constant demand for the slanders by which the press is polluted, and prostituting themselves to pander for the appetites of others; and now they come to demand protection from retaliation, and shelter from just exposure; and, to screen themselves, would have you prohibit all scrutiny of the abuses by which they exist, and the malpractices by which they disgrace their calling. After abusing and well-nigh dismantling, for their own despicable purposes, the great engine of instruction, they would have you annihilate all that they have left of it, to secure their escape. They have the incredible assurance to expect that an English jury will conspire with them in this wicked design. They expect in vain! If all existing institutions and all public functionaries must henceforth be sacred from question among the people; if at length the free press of this country, and with it the freedom itself, is to be destroyed—at least let not the heavy blow fall from your hands. Leave it to some profligate tyrant; leave it to a mercenary and effeminate Parliament—a hireling army, degraded by the lash, and the readier instrument for enslaving its country; leave it to a pampered House of Lords—a venal House of Commons—some vulgar minion, servant-of-all-work to an insolent court—some unprincipled soldier, unknown, thank God! in our times, combining the talents of a usurper with the fame of a captain; leave to such desperate hands, and such fit tools, so horrid a work! But you an English jury, parent of the press, yet supported by it, and doomed to perish the instant its health and strength are gone—lift not you against it an unnatural hand. Prove to us that our rights are safe in your keeping; but maintain, above all things, the stability of our institutions, by well guarding their corner stone. Defend the Church from her worst enemies, who, to hide their own misdeeds, would vail her solid foundations in darkness; and proclaim to them, by your verdict of acquittal, that henceforward, as heretofore, all the recesses of the sanctuary must be visited by the continual light of day, and by that light its abuses be explored!

After the judge had summed up to the jury, they retired, and remained inclosed for above five hours. They then returned the following special verdict, viz.: "Guilty of so much of the matter in the first count as charges a libel upon the clergy residing in and near the city of Durham, and the suburbs thereof; and as to the rest of the first count, and the other counts of the information, Not Guilty."

Mr. Brougham now moved for a new trial, and obtained one; but the prosecutors did not again appear, and no judgment was therefore pronounced in the case. Thus Mr. Williams was let go free, as if he had been acquitted altogether by the jury.

SPEECH

OF MR. BROUGHAM ON THE INVASION OF SPAIN BY FRANCE, DELIVERED IN THE HOUSE OF COMMONS, FEBRUARY 4, 1823.

INTRODUCTION.

A CONSTITUTIONAL GOVERNMENT was established in Spain by the Cortes, or states of the kingdom, in the year 1812, and was recognized as legitimate by England, Russia, Prussia, and other leading powers. After being set aside by Ferdinand VII. in 1814, it was proclaimed anew in January, 1820, by the Spanish military, headed by Riego and other gallant officers, who rebelled against the tyranny of Ferdinand, and were sustained by a large part of the kingdom. The flame spread into Naples and Piedmont, where constitutional governments were also speedily established. This alarmed the Allied Powers, embracing Russia, Austria, Prussia, and France, who at once decreed the overthrow of the whole system. Naples and Piedmont were successively overrun by Austria, and the new governments destroyed. The fate of Spain was deferred two years longer, and was committed to France.

Ferdinand, in the mean time, had yielded to the wishes of his people, and in March, 1820, had sworn to maintain the Constitution, and to administer the laws according to its provisions. But his friends, with his connivance, attempted, in 1822, to restore him to absolute power by an insurrection; and failing in this, they established a regency in Catalonia, near the French borders, in the name of the "*imprisoned* King." France had before this begun to collect troops on the same borders, first under the name of a *sanitary cordon* to prevent the introduction of disease, and afterward of an army of observation. In December, 1822, Louis XVIII. demanded of the Spanish government to restore Ferdinand to absolute power, under penalty of an immediate invasion of the country by the French troops. Austria, Prussia, and Russia united in this demand, and urged it in the strongest terms. The government of Spain replied, on the 9th of January, 1823, in a note addressed to the different powers of Europe, repelling with indignation this interference of the Allied Sovereigns in the internal affairs of Spain.

Parliament met about three weeks after, February 4, 1823, and Mr. Canning, the Secretary of Foreign Affairs, had the same abhorrence which was felt by the nation at large for this crusade against the constitutional government of Spain. Within forty-eight hours after he came in as minister (September 18, 1822), he had sent the Duke of Wellington to the Congress at Verona with a remonstrance against the proposed intervention; and he now brought forward the subject in the King's speech, "His Majesty has declined being party to any proceedings at Verona which could be deemed an interference with the internal concerns of Spain; and his Majesty has since used, and continues to use, his most anxious endeavors to allay the irritation subsisting between the French and Spanish governments, and to avert, if possible, the calamity of war between France and Spain." The ground taken by the government was highly gratifying to the Whigs, and Mr. Brougham expressed their sentiments in the following speech. It is one of the most striking specimens we have of his leading characteristics—strong argument intermingled with bold declamation, scathing invective, irony, sarcasm, and contempt.

SPEECH, &c.

I rise in consequence of the appeal made to every member of the House by the gallant officer [Sir J. Yorke] who has just sat down, to declare my sentiments. I answer that appeal, which does credit to the honor, to the English feeling of that gallant officer; and I join with him, and with every man who deserves the name of Briton, in unqualified abhorrence and detestation of the audacious interference to which he has alluded; or, if that execration is at all qualified, it can only be by contempt and disgust at the canting hypocrisy of the language in which the loathsome principles of the tyrants are promulgated to the world. I have risen to make this declaration, called upon as I am, in common with every member, but I should ill discharge my duty if I did not mark my sense of the candor of the two honorable gentlemen [Mr. Childs and Mr. Wildman] who have moved and seconded the address, and express my satisfaction at what, in the House, however divided upon other points, will be almost, and certainly in the country will be quite unanimously felt to be the sound and liberal view which they have taken of this great affair. Indeed, I know not, circumstanced as they were, that they could go further; or even that his Majesty's ministers, in the present state of this very delicate question, ought to have gone beyond the communication of to-day. That communication, coupled with the commentary of the honorable mover, will be the tidings of joy, and the signal for exultation to England—it will spread gladness and exultation over Spain—will be a source of comfort to all other free states—and will bring confusion and dismay to the Allies, who, with a pretended respect, but a real mockery of religion and morality, make war upon liberty in the abstract; endeavor to crush national independence wherever it is to be found; and are now preparing, with their armed hordes, to carry into execution their frightful projects. That Spain will take comfort from the principles avowed in the House this evening, I am certain; and I am not less clear that the handful of men at present surrounding the throne of our nearest and most interesting neighbor [Louis XVIII.] (who, by-the-way, has, somehow or other, been induced to swerve from the prudent counsels which had, till of late, guided his course) will feel astonished and dismayed with the proceedings of this day, in proportion as others are encouraged.[1] Cheering, however, as is the prevalence of such sentiments; highly as they raise the character of the nation, and much as may be augured from their effects, still I think no man can deny that the country is at present approaching to a crisis such as has not occurred, perhaps, for above a century, certainly not since the French Revolution. Whether we view the internal condition of the kingdom, and the severe distress which press upon that most important and most useful branch of the community, the farmers; or cast our eyes upon our foreign relations, our circumstances must appear, to the mind of every thinking man, critical and alarming. They may, it is true, soon wear a better aspect, and we may escape the calamities of war; but he must be a bold, and possibly a rash man, certainly not a very thoughtful one, who can take upon him to foretell that so happy a fortune shall be ours.

Answer to the appeal of the last speaker.

Wise and honorable course taken by the ministry.

It is the deep consideration of these things which induces me to come forward and make a declaration of my principles; and to state that, with a strict adherence to the most rigid economy in every department, the reduction of establishments, which I am at all times, if not the first, at least among the foremost to support, and which is so necessary in the ordinary circumstances of the country, must now be recommended, with a certain modification, in order to adapt our policy to the present emergency. I am guilty of no inconsistency whatever in thus qualifying the doctrine of unsparing retrenchment; indeed, the greater the chance of some extraordinary demand upon our resources from the aspect of affairs abroad, the more imperious is the necessity of sparing every particle of expense not absolutely requisite. Economy to its utmost extent I still recommend as politic, and urge as due to the people of right; and every expense is now to be regarded as more inexcusable than ever, both because the country is suffering more severely, and because it may become necessary soon to increase some parts of our establishment. I say I am certainly not prepared to propose, or to suffer, as far as my voice goes, any the least reduction of our naval force, to the extent even of a single ship or seaman; on the contrary, I fear the time may not be distant when its increase will be required. Any such augmentation of the army I can not conceive to be justifiable in almost any circumstances; for, happen what may, a war on our part, carried on with the wasteful and scandalous profusion of the last, and upon the same vast scale, or any thing like it, is wholly out of the question.

Necessity of England's being ready for war.

[Mr. Brougham entered at some length into the internal state of the country—the indications of distress at the various meetings—the inconsistency of the violent attacks made upon the Norfolk Petition by those who had passed the Gold Coin Bill of 1811, which enacted the parts of the Norfolk plan most liable to objection—the inadequacy of any relief to be obtained from repeal of taxes that only affected small districts —the absolute necessity of repealing a large

[1] Louis XVIII., as here intimated, was, in the early part of his reign, a friend of constitutional principles, and pursued a policy which gained him the support of men of liberal sentiments throughout his kingdom. But at the assassination of the Duke of Berri in 1820, his feelings became alienated, and the ultra-Royalists gradually gained the ascendant in his councils.

amount of the taxes pressing generally on all classes—and for this purpose, he urged the necessity of a saving wherever it could be effected with safety; and, at any rate, of giving up the sinking fund. He then proceeded:]

I think, then, that if war were once commenced, we should soon be compelled to take some part in it, one way or other, and that, for such an emergency, every shilling which can be saved by the most rigid economy should be reserved. I think our intervention in some shape will become unavoidable. We are bound, for instance, to assist one party, our old ally Portugal, if she should be attacked; and it is not likely that she can remain neuter, if the present hateful conspiracy against Spain shall end in open hostility.[2] It is in this view of the question that I differ from the gallant officer [Sir J. Yorke] who last spoke, and I am glad that I could not collect from the honorable mover or seconder the ominous words "*strict neutrality*," as applied to this country in the threatened contest. A state of *declared* neutrality on our part would be nothing less than a practical admission of those principles which we all loudly condemn, and a license to the commission of all the atrocities which we are unanimous in deprecating. I will say, therefore, that it is the duty of his Majesty's ministers (with whom I should rejoice in co-operating on the occasion; and so, I am certain, would every one who now hears me, waving for a season all differences of opinion on lesser matters) to adopt and to announce the resolution, that when certain things shall take place on the Continent, they will be ready to assist the Spaniards—a measure necessary to avert evils, which even those the least prone to war (of which I avow myself one) must admit to be inevitable, should a wavering or pusillanimous course be pursued. Our assistance will be necessary to resist the wicked enforcement of principles contrary to the law of nations, and repugnant to the idea of national independence.

Her intervention may be demanded, especially in behalf of Portugal.

To judge of the principles now shamelessly promulgated, let any man read patiently, if he can, the declarations in the notes of Russia, Prussia, and Austria; and, with all due respect to those high authorities, I will venture to say that to produce any thing more preposterous, more absurd, more extravagant, better calculated to excite a mingled feeling of disgust and derision, would baffle any chancery or state-paper office in Europe. I shall not drag the House through the whole nauseous details; I will only select a few passages, by way of sample, from those notable productions of legitimate genius.

Conduct and designs of the Allied Powers.

In the communication from the minister of his Prussian Majesty, the [Spanish] Constitution of 1812, restored in 1820, and now established, is described as a system which, "confounding all elements, and all power, and assuming only the single principle of a permanent and legal opposition against the government, necessarily destroys that central and tutelary authority which constitutes the essence of the monarchical system." Thus far the King of Prussia, in terms which, to say the least, afforded some proof of the writer's knowledge of the monarchical system, and of the contrast which, in his opinion, it exhibited to the present government of Spain. The Emperor of Russia, in terms not less strong, calls the constitutional government of the Cortes, "that which the public reason of Europe, *enlightened by the experience of all ages*, stamps with its disapprobation;" and complains of its wanting the "conservative principle of social order." Where, in the conservative character of keeper of the peace of Europe, does his Imperial Majesty discover that the Constitution of Spain had been stamped with the disapprobation of the public reason of Europe? Let the House observe that the "public reason of Europe, enlightened by the experience of all ages," happens to be that of his Imperial Majesty *himself* for the last ten years exactly, and no more; for, notwithstanding that he had the "experience of all ages" before his eyes, he did, in the year 1812, enter into a treaty with Spain, with the same Cortes, under the same Constitution, not one iota of which had been changed up to that very hour. In that treaty, his Imperial Majesty, the Emperor of all the Russias, speaking of the then government, did use the very word by which he and his allies would themselves be designated—the word, by the abuse of which they are known—he did call the Spanish government of the Cortes "a *legitimate* government," that very government—that very Constitution—of which the Spaniards have not changed one word; and God forbid they should change even a letter of it, while they have the bayonet of the foreign soldier at their breast! I hope, if it has faults—and some faults it may have—that when the hour of undisturbed tranquillity arrives, the Spaniards themselves will correct them. If they will listen to the ardent wish of their best friends—of those who have marked their progress, and gloried in the strides they have made toward freedom and happiness—of those who would go to the world's end to serve them in their illustrious struggle—of those, above all, who would not have them yield an hair's breadth to force—my counsel would be to disarm the reasonable objections of their friends, but not to give up any thing to the menaces of their enemies. I shall not go more into detail at the present moment; for ample opportunities will occur of discussing this subject; but I will ask, in the name of common sense, can any thing be more absurd, more inconsistent, than that Spain should now be repudiated as illegitimate by those, some of whom have, in treaties with her, described her government in its present shape by the very term "legitimate government?" In the treaty of friendship and alliance, concluded in 1812,

(1.) The government now condemned by the Allied Powers was formerly recognized as legitimate.

[2] The reader is already aware, from the speech of Mr. Canning on a preceding page, that in 1826, this intervention became necessary in behalf of Portugal.

between the Emperor of all the Russias and the Spanish Cortes, Ferdinand being then a close prisoner in France, his Imperial Majesty [of Russia], by the third article, acknowledges in express terms the Cortes, "and the CONSTITUTION sanctioned and decreed by it." This article I cite from the collection of Treaties by Martens, a well known Germanic, and therefore a laborious and accurate compiler.

(2.) Intervention forbidden by the treaty of Aix-la-Chapelle.

But not only is the conduct of the Allies toward Spain inconsistent with the treaties of some among them with Spain—I will show that their principle of interference, in any manner of way, is wholly at variance with treaties recently made among themselves. I will prove that one of the fundamental principles of a late treaty is decidedly opposed to any discussion whatever among them respecting the internal situation of that country. By the 4th article of the treaty of Aix-la-Chapelle, November, 1818, it is laid down that a special congress may be held, from time to time, on the affairs of Europe. Using the words, and borrowing the hypocritical cant of their predecessors, the same three powers who basely partitioned Poland—who, while they despoiled a helpless nation of its independence, kept preaching about the quiet of Europe, the integrity of its states, and the morality and happiness of their people—talking daily about the desire of calm repose (the atmosphere, I well know, in which despotism loves to breathe, but which an ancient writer eloquently painted, when he said that tyrants mistake for peace the stillness of desolation[3])—following the vile cant of their ancestors—the Allies declared, at Aix-la-Chapelle, that their object was to secure the tranquillity, the peace (which I, giving them credit for sincerity, read the *desolation* of Europe), and that their fundamental principle should be, never to depart from a strict adherence to the law of nations. "Faithful to these principles" (continued this half-sermon, half-romance, and half-state-paper), "they will only study the happiness of their people, the progress of the peaceful arts, and attend carefully to the interests of morality and religion, of late years unhappily too much neglected"—here, again, following the example of the Autocratrix Catharine—the spoiler of Poland—who, having wasted and pillaged it, province after province, poured in hordes of her barbarians, which hewed their way to the capital through myriads of Poles, and there, for one whole day, from the rising of the sun to the going down thereof, butchered its unoffending inhabitants, unarmed men, and women, and infants; and not content with this work of undistinguishing slaughter, after the pause of the night had given time for cooling, rose on the morrow and renewed the carnage, and continued it throughout that endless day; and after this, a *Te Deum* was sung, to return thanks for her success over the *enemies*, that is, the natives of Poland. That mild and gentle Sovereign, in the midst of these most horrible outrages upon every feeling of human nature, issued a proclamation, in which she assured the Poles (I mean to give her very words) that she felt toward them "the solicitude of a tender mother, whose heart is only filled with sentiments of kindness for all her children." Who can, or who dares doubt that she was all she described herself; and who can, after the experience of the last year, dispute the legitimate descent of the allied powers, and the purity of their intentions toward Spain? But along with this declaration of the object of future congresses, came the article which I should like to see some German statist—some man versed in the manufacture of state papers—compare with, and reconcile (if it only may be done within a moderate compass) to the notes fashioned at Verona, not unlikely by the very hands which produced the treaty of Aix-la-Chapelle. The article is this: "Special congresses concerning the affairs of states not parties to this alliance, shall not take place, except" (and here I should like to know how Spain, which was no party to the alliance, has brought herself within the exception)—"*except in consequence of a formal invitation from such states*;" "and their embassadors shall assist at such congresses." How will any German commentator reconcile these contradictions? Here the interference in the internal affairs of Spain is not only not "by special invitation" from, but is in downright opposition to, the will of Spain. Thus stands the conduct of those Holy Allies diametrically opposed to their own professions and engagements, and by such means is the attempt now made to crush the independence of a brave people.

(3.) The reasons which have been given for this intervention.

But it is not in the case of Spain alone that the consideration of these papers is important—they furnish grounds of rational fear to all independent governments; for I should be glad to learn what case it is (upon the doctrines now advanced) to which this principle of interference may not be extended? or what Constitution or what act of state it is on which the authority to comment, criticise, and dictate may not be assumed? The House is not aware of the latitude to which the interference of those armed legislators may be, nay, actually is extended. The revolt of the colonies is distinctly stated as one ground of interposition! The allies kindly offer their "intervention" to restore this great branch of "the strength of Spain." There is no end of the occasions for interfering which they take. One is rather alarming—the accident of a sovereign having weak or bad ministers. Russia, forsooth, was anxious to see Ferdinand surrounded with "the most enlightened—most faithful of his subjects"—men "of tried integrity and superior talents"—men, in a word, who should be every way worthy of himself. So that, according to these wise men of Verona (and this is a consideration which should be looked to in some other countries as well as

(a) The extent of their application.

[3] Solitudinem faciunt pacem appellant.

Speech of Galgacus respecting the Romans, in *Tacitus' Life of Agricola*, cap. 30.

Spain), the existence of an inefficient or unprincipled administration, would be of itself a just ground of interference. The principle does not stop here. "Ruinous loans" form another ground, and "contributions unceasingly renewed;" "taxes which, for year after year, exhausted the public treasures and the fortunes of individuals"—these are instances in which the principle of interference may apply to other powers besides Spain; and I have no doubt that when the same doctrines are extended to certain countries, the preparatory manifesto will make mention of *agricultural* distress, *financial* embarrassment, and the *sinking fund*. But, to complete all the charges against Spain, the Russian Emperor finishes his invective with the awful assertion that, on the 7th of July, "blood was seen to flow in the palace of the King, and a civil war raged throughout the Peninsula." It is true that a revolt had been excited in some of the provinces. But by whom? An *ally*. It was produced by those cordons of troops which were posted [by France] on the Spanish frontier, armed with gold and with steel, and affording shelter and assistance by force, to those in whose minds disaffection had been excited by bribery. It is also true that blood has been shed. But would it not be supposed, by any person unacquainted with the fact, and who only read the statement in the manifesto, that this was blood shed in an attempt to dethrone Ferdinand, and introduce some new and unheard of form of government? At any rate, does not this statement plainly intend it to be supposed that the Constitutional party had made the onset, and shed royalist, if not royal blood? But what is the fact? A few persons were killed who had first attacked the Constitutionalists, in other words, mutinied against the established government—the government which the Emperor Alexander himself recognized as legitimate in 1812; and this he has now the audacity to call the shedding of blood by Spaniards in the palace of the King! As well might he accuse the People, the Parliament, and the Crown of England of causing "blood to flow in the palace of the King," for ordering their sentinels to fire on some person whom they found attempting to assassinate the Sovereign, as accuse the Spaniards of such a crime, for the events which happened in July, 1822.

(b) Some of them iniquitous and insulting.

I shall pass over many other heavy charges leveled at the Spaniards, in phrases of terrible import—as harboring a "disorganized philosophy," "indulging in dreams of fallacious liberty," and the want of "venerable and sacred rights," with which the Prussian note is loaded to repletion; and shall proceed to the Russian, which objects to the Spaniards their want of the "true conservative principle of social order"—or, in other words, of despotic power, in the hands of one man, for his own benefit, at the expense of all mankind besides; and to their not falling within the scope of those "grand truths," which, though they were ever in their mouths, were nowhere explained by any one of the three sovereigns. The Austrian note discourses largely of "the solid and venerable claims" which the Spanish nation has upon the rest of Europe; prays it to adopt a better form of government than it has at present; and calls upon it to reject a system which is at once "powerful and paralyzed." It would be disgusting to enter at any length into papers at once so despicable in their execution, and in their plan so abominably iniquitous. There is but one sentiment held regarding them out of the House; and my excuse for taking notice of them now, is my desire to call forth a similar expression of feeling from the House itself. Monstrous, and insolent, and utterly unbearable, as all of them are, I consider that of Russia to be more monstrous, more insolent, and more prodigiously beyond all endurance than the rest. It is difficult to determine which most to admire, the marvelous incongruity of her language and conduct now, with her former most solemn treaties, or the incredible presumption of *her* standing forward to lead the aggression upon the independence of all free and polished states. Gracious God! Russia! Russia! a power that is only half civilized—which, with all her colossal mass of physical strength, is still quite as much Asiatic as European—whose principles of policy, foreign and domestic, are completely despotic, and whose practices are almost altogether Oriental and barbarous! In all these precious documents there is, with a mighty number of general remarks, mixed up a wondrous affectation of honest principles—a great many words covering ideas that are not altogether clear and intelligible; or, if they happen to be so, only placing their own deformity in a more hideous and detestable light; but, for argument, or any thing like it, there is none to be found from the beginning to the end of them. They reason not, but speak one plain language to Spain and to Europe, and this is its sum and substance: "We have hundreds of thousands of hired mercenaries, and we will not stoop to reason with those whom we would insult and enslave."

(c) The reply of Spain an admirable one.

I admire the equal frankness with which this haughty language had been met by the Spanish government: the papers which it had sent forth are plain and laconic; and borrowing for liberty, the ancient privilege of tyrants—to let their will stand in the place of argument—they bluntly speak this language: "We are millions of freemen, and will not stoop to reason with those who threaten to enslave us." They hurl back the menace upon the head from which it issued, little caring whether it came from Goth, or Hun, or Calmuc; with a frankness that outwitted the craft of the Bohemian, and a spirit that defied the ferocity of the Tartar, and a firmness that mocks the obstinacy of the Vandal. If they find leagued against them the tyrants by whom the world is infested, they may console themselves with this reflection, that wherever there is an Englishman, either of the Old World or of the New—wherever there is a Frenchman, with the miserable exception of that little band which now, for a moment, sways the destinies of France in opposition to the wishes and interests of its gallant and liberal people—a people which, after enduring the miseries of the Revolution, and wading through its long and bloody wars, are entitled, Heaven knows, if ever any people were, to a long enjoyment of peace and liberty, so dearly and so honorably purchased—wherever there breathes an Englishman or a true-born Frenchman—wherever there beats a free heart or exists a virtuous mind, there Spain has a natural ally, and an inalienable friend.

(d) Retort which Spain might have given the Allies as to their own conduct.

For my own part, I can not but admire the mixture of firmness and forbearance which the government of Spain has exhibited. When the Allied Monarchs were pleased to adopt a system of interference with the internal policy of Spain—when they thought fit to deal in minute and paltry criticisms upon the whole course of its domestic administration—when each sentence in their manifestoes was a direct personal insult to the government, nay to every individual Spaniard—and when the most glaring attempts were made in all their state papers to excite rebellion in the country, and to stir up one class of the community against the other—it would not have surprised me if, in the replies of the Spanish government, some allusion had been made to the domestic policy of the Allied Sovereigns; or if some of the allegations which had been so lavishly cast upon it, had been scornfully retorted upon those who had so falsely and so insolently called them forth. What could have been more pardonable, nay, what more natural, than for the Spanish government to have besought his Prussian Majesty, who was so extremely anxious for the welfare and good government of Spain—who had shown himself so minute a critic on its laws and institutions, and who seemed so well versed in its recent history—to remember the promises which he had made some years ago to his own people, by whose gallant exertions, on the faith of those promises, he had regained his lost crown? What would have been more natural than to have suggested that it would be better, ay, and safer too in the end, to keep those promises, than to maintain, at his people's cost, and almost to their ruin, a prodigious army, only safely employed when in the act of ravaging the territories or putting down the liberties of his neighbors? The government of Spain would have had a right to make such representations, for his Prussian Majesty owed much, very much, to its exertions; indeed, the gallant resistance which it made to the invasion of Bonaparte had alone enabled Prussia to shake off the yoke; while, on the other hand, the Spaniards owed a debt of gratitude to the brave and honest people of Prussia for beginning the resistance to Bonaparte in the north.

Prussia.

Could any thing, I will also ask, have been more natural for the Spanish government, than to have asked the Emperor of Austria whether he who now pretended to be so scrupulously fond of strict justice in Ferdinand's case, when it cost him nothing, or must prove a gain, had always acted with equal justice toward others when he was himself concerned? Could any thing have been more natural than suggesting to him that, before he was generous to King Ferdinand, he might as well be just to King George; that he had better not rob the one to pay the other—nay, that he ought to return him the whole, or, at any rate, some part of the millions, principal and interest, which he owed him? a debt which, remaining unpaid, wastes the resources of a faithful ally of Spain, and tends mightily to cripple his exertions in her behalf. I wish likewise to know what could have been more natural—nay, if the doctrine of interference in the internal concerns of neighboring nations be at all admitted—what could have been more rightful, in a free people, than to have asked him how it happened that his dungeons were filled with all that was noble, and accomplished, and virtuous, and patriotic in the Milanese? to have called on him to account for the innocent blood which he had shed in the north of Italy? to have required at his hands satisfaction for the tortures inflicted in the vaults and caverns where the flower of his Italian subjects were now languishing? to have demanded of him some explanation of that iron policy which has consigned fathers of families the most virtuous and exalted in Europe, not to the relief of exile or death, but to a merciless imprisonment for ten, fifteen, and twenty years, nay, even for life, without a knowledge of the charge against them, or the crime for which they are punished?

Austria.

Even the Emperor Alexander himself, tender and sensitive as he is at the sight of blood flowing within the precincts of a royal palace—a sight so monstrous that, if his language could be credited, it had never before been seen in the history of the world—might have been reminded of passages in that history calculated to lessen his astonishment at least, if not to soothe his feelings; for the Emperor Alexander, if the annals of Russian story may be trusted, however pure in himself, and however happy in always having agents equally innocent, is nevertheless descended from an illustrious line of ancestors, who have, with exemplary uniformity, dethroned, imprisoned, and slaughtered husbands, brothers, and children. Not that I can dream of imputing those enormities to the parents, or sisters, or consorts; but it does happen that those exalted and near relations had never failed to reap the whole benefit of the atrocities, and had ever failed to bring the perpetrators to justice.[4] In these circumstances, if I had had the honor of being in the confidence of his Majesty of all the Russias, I should have been the last person in the world to counsel my

Russia.

[4] Paul I., father of the Emperor Alexander, was murdered by conspirators in his own palace, on the 11th of March, 1801. No one supposes that Alexander was personally concerned in the plot, though he succeeded to the government. But in no part of Europe have assassinations been so common in the royal line as in Russia, and there is singular force in the manner in which Mr. Brougham dwells on this topic.

Imperial Master to touch upon so tender a topic —I should humbly have besought him to think twice or thrice, nay, even a third and a fourth time, before he ventured to allude to so delicate a subject—I should, with all imaginable deference, have requested him to meddle with any other topic—I should have directed him by preference to every other point of the compass—I should have implored him rather to try what he could say about Turkey, or Greece, or even Minorca, on which he has of late been casting many an amorous glance—in short, any thing and every thing, before he approached the subject of "blood flowing within the precincts of a royal palace," and placed his allusion to it, like an artful rhetorician, upon the uppermost step of his climax.

(e) Retorts which might have been given as to their language about Bonaparte.

I find, likewise, in these self-same documents, a topic for which the Spanish government, had it been so inclined, might have administered to the Holy Alliance another severe lecture. I allude to the glib manner in which the three Potentates now talk of an individual who, let his failings or even his crimes be what they may, must always be regarded as a great and a resplendent character—who, because he was now no longer either upon a throne or at liberty, or even in life, is described by them, not merely as an ambitious ruler, not merely as an arbitrary tyrant, but as an upstart and an usurper. This is not the language which those Potentates formerly employed, nor is it the language which they were now entitled to use regarding this astonishing individual. Whatever epithets England, for instance, or Spain, may have a right to apply to his conduct, the mouths of the Allies, at least, are stopped: *they* can have no right to call him usurper—they who, in his usurpations, had been either most greedy accomplices or most willing tools. What entitles the King of Prussia to hold such language now? he who followed his fortunes with the most shameless subserviency, after the thorough beating he received from him, when trampled upon and trodden down in the year 1806? Before he had risen again and recovered the upright attitude of a man, he fell upon his knees, and still crouching before him who had made him crawl in the dust, kissed the blood-stained hand of Napoleon for leave to keep his Britannic Majesty's foreign dominions, the Electorate of Hanover, which the Prussian had snatched hold of while at peace with England. So the Emperor Alexander, after he had also undergone the like previous ceremony, did not disdain to lick up the crumbs which fell from the table of his more successful rival in usurpation. Little, it is true, was left by the edge of Gallic appetite; but rather than have nothing—rather than desert the true Russian principle of getting something on every occasion, either in Europe or in Asia (and of late years they have even laid claim to an almost indefinite naval dominion in America)—rather than forego the Calmuc policy for the last century and a half, of always adding something, be it ever so little, to what was already acquired, be it ever so great—he condescended to receive from the hand of Bonaparte a few square leagues of territory, with an additional population of some two or three thousand serfs. The object was trifling indeed, but it served to keep alive the principle. The tender heart of the father, overflowing, as his imperial grandmother had phrased it, with the milk of human kindness for all his children, could not be satisfied without receiving a further addition to their numbers; and therefore it is not surprising that, on the next occasion, he should be ready to seize, in more effectual exemplification of the principle, a share of the booty large in proportion as his former one had been small. The Emperor of Austria, too, who had entered before the others into the race for plunder, and never weary in ill doing, had continued in it till the very end—he who, if not an accomplice with the Jacobins of France in the spoliation of Venice, was at least a receiver of the stolen property—a felony, of which it was well said at the time in the House, that the receiver was as bad as the thief—that magnanimous Prince, who, after twenty years alternation of truckling and vaporing—now the feeble enemy of Bonaparte, now his willing accomplice—constantly punished for his resistance by the discipline invariably applied to those mighty Princes in the tenderest places, their capitals, from which they were successively driven—as constantly, after punishment, joining the persecutor, like the rest of them, in attacking and plundering his allies—ended by craving the honor of giving Bonaparte his favorite daughter in marriage. Nay, after the genius of Bonaparte had fallen under the still more powerful restlessness of his ambition—when the star of his destiny had waned, and the fortune of the Allies was triumphant, through the roused energies of their gallant people, the severity of the elements, his own turbulent passions and that without which the storms of popular ferment, and Russian winter, and his own ambition would have raged in vain, the aid of English arms, and skill, and gallantry—strange to tell, these very men were the first to imitate that policy against which they had inveighed and struggled, and to carry it further than the enemy himself in all its most detestable points. I maintain that it is so; for not even by his bitterest slanderers was Bonaparte ever accused of actions so atrocious as was the spoliation of Norway, the partition of Saxony, the transfer of Genoa, and the cession of Ragusa, perpetrated by those in whose mouths no sound had been heard for years but that of lamentation over the French attacks upon national independence.[5] It is too much, after such deeds as these—it is too much after the Allies had submitted to a long course of crouching before Bonaparte, accompanied by

[5] The annexation of Norway to Sweden, of Genoa to Sardinia, and other arrangements of territory made by the Allied Powers after the dethronement of Bonaparte, excited general indignation throughout the free countries of Europe.

every aggravation of disgrace—it is too much for them now to come forth and calumniate his memory for transactions in the benefits of which they participated at the time, as his accomplices, and the infamy of which they have since surpassed with the usual exaggeration of imitators. I rejoice that the Spaniards have only such men as these to contend with. I know that there are fearful odds when battalions are arrayed against principles. I may feel solicitous about the issue of such a contest. But it is some consolation to reflect that those embodied hosts are not aided by the merits of their chiefs, and that all the weight of character is happily on one side.

(f) Reasons for surprise and regret that Louis XVIII. should espouse this cause.

It gives me, however, some pain to find that a monarch so enlightened as the King of France has shown himself on various occasions, should have yielded obedience, even for an instant, to the arbitrary mandates of this tyrannic junto. I trust that it will only prove a temporary aberration from the sounder principles on which he has hitherto acted; I hope that the men who appear to have gained his confidence only to abuse it, will soon be dismissed from his councils; or if not, that the voice of the country, whose interests they are sacrificing to their wretched personal views, and whose rising liberties they seem anxious to destroy, in gratification of their hatred and bigotry, will compel them to pursue a more manly and more liberal policy. Indeed, the King of France has been persuaded, by the parasites who at present surround him, to go even beyond the principles of the Holy Alliance. He has been induced to tell the world that it is from the hands of a tyrant alone that a free people can hold a Constitution. That accomplished Prince—and all Europe acknowledges him to be, among other things, a finished scholar—can not but be aware that the wise and good men of former times held far other opinions upon this subject; and if I venture to remind him of a passage in a recently recovered work of the greatest philosopher of the ancient world, it is in the sincere hope that his Majesty will consider it with all the attention that is due to such high authority. That great man said, "Non in ulla civitate, nisi in qua summa potestas populi est, ullum domicilium libertas habet."[6] I recommend to his most Christian Majesty the reflection that this lesson came not only from the wisdom of so great a philosopher, but also from the experience of so great a statesman. I would have him remember that, like himself, he lived in times of great difficulty and of great danger—that he had to contend with the most formidable conspiracy to which the life, property, and liberty of the citizen had ever been exposed—that, to defeat it, he had recourse only to the powers of the Constitution—threw himself on the good-will of his patriotic countrymen—and only put forth the powers of his own genius, and only used the wholesome vigor of the law. He never thought of calling to his assistance the Allobroges, or the Teutones, or the Scythians of his day; and I now say that if Louis XVIII. shall call upon the modern Teutones or Scythians to assist him in this unholy war, the day their hordes move toward the Rhine, judgment will go forth against him, and his family, and his counselors; and the dynasty of Gaul has ceased to reign.

(4.) The real object is the destruction of free institutions throughout Europe,

What, I ask, are the grounds on which the necessity of this war is defended? It is said to be undertaken because an insurrection has broken out with success at Madrid. I deny this to be the fact. What is called an insurrection, was an attempt to restore the lawful Constitution of the country—a Constitution which was its established government, till Ferdinand overthrew it by means of a mutiny in the army; and, therefore, when a military movement enabled the friends of liberty to recover what they had lost, it is a gross perversion of language to call this recovery, this restoration, by the name of insurrection—an insidious confusion of terms, which can only be intended to blind the reason, or play upon the prejudices of the honest part of mankind. Let the pretext, however, for the war be what it may, the real cause of it is not hard to conjecture. It is not from hatred to Spain or to Portugal that the Allied Sovereigns are for marching their swarms of barbarians into the Peninsula—it is not against freedom on the Ebro, or freedom on the Mincio, they make war. No, it is against *freedom!*—against freedom wherever it is to be found—freedom by whomsoever enjoyed—freedom by whatever means achieved, by whatever institutions secured. Freedom is the object of their implacable hate. For its destruction they are ready to exhaust every resource of force and fraud. All the blessings which it bestows—all the establishments in which it is embodied, the monuments that are raised to it, and the miracles that are wrought by it—they hate with the malignity of demons, who tremble while they are compelled to adore; for they quiver by instinct at the sound of its name. And let *us* not deceive ourselves; these despots can have but little liking toward this nation and its institutions, more especially our Parliament and our press. As long as England remains unenslaved; as long as the Parliament continues a free and open tribunal, to which the oppressed of all nations under heaven can appeal against their oppressors, however mighty and exalted—and with all its abuses (and no man can lament them more than I do, because no man is more sensible of its intrinsic value, which those abuses diminish), with all its imperfections (and no man can be more anxious to remove them, because none wishes more heartily, by restoring its original purity, to make it entirely worthy of the country's love)—it is still far too pure and too free to please the taste of the con-

[6] Never has liberty had a home, except in a country where the power was in the hands of the people. The words are from the treatise of Cicero, De Republica, a considerable part of which was for the first time brought to light by Maio, and given to the world in the year 1822.

tinental despots—so long would England be the object of their hatred, and of machinations, sometimes carried on covertly, sometimes openly, but always pursued with the same unremitting activity, and pointed to the same end.

and the aggrandizement of Russia at the expense of Turkey.

But it is not free states alone that have to dread this system of interference; this plan of marching armies to improve the political condition of foreign nations. It is idle to suppose that those armed critics will confine their objections to the internal policy of popular governments. Can any one imagine that, if there be a portion of territory in the neighborhood of the Emperor Alexander peculiarly suited to his views, he will not soon be able to discover some fault, to spy out some flaw in its political institutions requiring his intervention, however little these may savor of democracy, supposing it even to be a part of the Ottoman government itself? If his Imperial Majesty be present in council with his consistory of jurists and diplomatists, I believe that it will be in vain for the Ulemah to send a deputation of learned Muftis, for the purpose of vindicating the Turkish institutions. These sages of the law may contend that the Ottoman government is of the most "venerable description"—that it has "antiquity in its favor"—that it is in full possession of "the conservative principle of social order" in its purest form—that it is replete with "grand truths;" a system "powerful and paralyzed"—that it has never lent an ear to the doctrines of a "disorganized philosophy"—never indulged in "vain theories," nor been visited by such things as "dreams of fallacious liberty." All this the learned and reverend deputies of the Ulemah may urge, and may maintain to be true as holy Koran; still "The Three Gentlemen of Verona," I fear, will turn a deaf ear to the argument, and set about prying for some imperfection in the "pure and venerable system"—some avenue by which to enter the territory; and, if they can not find a way, will probably not be very scrupulous about making one. The windings of the path may be hard to trace, but the result of the operation will be plain enough. In about three months from the time of deliberation, the Emperor Alexander will be found one morning at Constantinople—or, if it suit him, at Minorca—for he has long shown a desire to have some footing in what he pleasantly termed the "western provinces" of Europe, which, in the Muscovite tongue, signifies the petty territories of France and Spain, while Austria and Prussia will be invited to look for an indemnity elsewhere; the latter, as formerly, taking whatever the King of England may have on the Continent. The principles on which this band of confederated despots have shown their readiness to act are dangerous in the extreme, not only to free states (and to those to which no liberty can be imputed), but also to the states over which the very members of this unholy league preside.

Resistance to them is a matter of duty to all nations, and the duty of this country is especially plain. It behooves us, however, to take care that we rush not blindly into a war. An appeal to arms is the last alternative we should try, but still it ought never to be so foreign to our thoughts as to be deemed very distant, much less impossible; or so foreign from our councils as to leave us unprepared. Already, if there is any force in language, or any validity in public engagements, we are committed by the defensive treaties into which we have entered. We are bound by various ties to prevent Portugal from being overrun by an enemy. If (which Heaven avert!) Spain were overrun by foreign invaders, what would be the situation of Portugal? Her frontier on the side of Spain can scarcely be said to have an existence; there is no defending it any where; and it is in many places a mere imaginary line, that can only be traced on the page of the geographer; her real frontier is in the Pyrenees; her real defense is in their fastnesses and in the defense of Spain; whenever those passes are crossed, the danger which has reached Spain will hang over Portugal. If we acknowledge the force of treaties, and really mean that to be performed for which we engaged, though we may not be bound to send an army of observation to watch the motions of the French by land, because that would be far from the surest way of providing for the integrity of our ally, at least we are bound to send a naval armament; to aid with arms and stores; to have at all times the earliest information; and to be ready at any moment to give effectual assistance to our ancient ally. Above all things, we ought to do that which of itself will be a powerful British armament by sea and by land—repeal without delay the Foreign Enlistment Bill—a measure which, in my opinion, we ought never to have enacted, for it does little credit to us either in policy or justice. I will not, however, look backward to measures on the nature of which all may not agree; I will much rather look forward, to avoid every matter of vituperation, reserving all blame for the foreign tyrants whose profligate conduct makes this nation hate them with one heart and soul, and my co-operation for any faithful servant of the Crown, who shall, in performing his duty to his country, to freedom, and to the world, speak a language that is truly British—pursue a policy that is truly free—and look to free states as our best and most natural allies against all enemies whatsoever; allies upon principle, but whose friendship was also closely connected with our highest interests; quarreling with none, whatever may be the form of their government, for that would be copying the faults we condemn; keeping pace wherever we could, but not leaving ourselves a moment unprepared for war; not courting hostilities from any quarter, but not fearing the issue, and calmly resolved to brave it at all hazards, should it involve us in the affray with them all; determined to maintain, amid every sacrifice, the honor and dignity of the Crown, the independence of the country, the ancient law of nations, the supremacy of all

Peroration: Duty of England to be prepared for war.

separate states; all those principles which are cherished as most precious and most sacred by the whole civilized world.

The views of England were wholly disregarded by the Allied Sovereigns, and on the 9th of April, 1823, the French army of nearly one hundred thousand men, under the Duke of Angoulême, entered the Spanish territory. They were received with open arms by the priests and the lower classes of the people, and after some severe conflicts forced their way to Cadiz within six months, October 4th, 1823. The English having no treaty with Spain which laid the foundation of their interposing to assist her, remained neutral, prepared instantly to strike if Portugal should be attacked. Ferdinand was invested with absolute power; and in direct violation of the terms of capitulation, a persecuting and vindictive policy was adopted toward the partisans of the constitutional government. Riego was executed at Madrid, November 6th, and great cruelty exercised toward his leading associates. Portuguese absolutists now put forth every effort in their power, conjointly with Ferdinand, to break down the constitutional government of Portugal, and in 1826 that country was invaded from Spain. The result has been already stated in connection with Mr. Canning's speech on this subject. The insurrection was put down within two months, and Ferdinand, fearing an invasion from England, was driven from his favorite design.

The student in oratory will be interested, in connection with this speech, to read that of Mr. Webster on the Greek revolution, delivered in the House of Representatives of the United States, on the 19th of January, 1824. In the former part of this speech, the reader will find the subject of "Intervention" discussed not merely in the spirit of just invective against those concerned, but of searching analysis into its grounds and its consequences. He will find himself in communion with a mind of a much higher order than that of Lord Brougham—richer in its combinations, wider in its reach, more elevated in sentiment, more self-possessed in its loftiest flights of eloquence. Mr. Webster concludes this part of his subject in a passage which, though often quoted, may be given with peculiar propriety in this place, not only for the views which it presents of the remedy for these interventions, but for its prophetic intimations of the fate of the Duke of Augouleme and of the Bourbon race.

"It may, in the next place, be asked, perhaps, supposing all this to be true, what can *we* do? Are we to go to war? Are we to interfere in the Greek cause, or any other European cause? Are we to endanger our pacific relations? No, certainly not. What, then, the question recurs, remains for *us?* If we will not endanger our own peace; if we will neither furnish armies nor navies to the cause which we think the just one, what is there within *our* power?

"Sir, this reasoning mistakes the age. The time has been, indeed, when fleets, and armies,

and subsidies were the principal reliances even in the best cause. But, happily for mankind, there has arrived a great change in this respect. Moral causes come into consideration, in proportion as the progress of knowledge is advanced; and the *public opinion* of the civilized world is rapidly gaining an ascendency over mere brutal force. It is already able to oppose the most formidable obstruction to the progress of injustice and oppression; and, as it grows more intelligent and more intense, it will be more and more formidable. It may be silenced by military power, but it can not be conquered. It is elastic, irrepressible, and invulnerable to the weapons of ordinary warfare. It is that impassable, unextinguishable enemy of mere violence and arbitrary rule which, like Milton's angels,

"Vital in every part,
Can not, but by annihilating, die."

"Until this be propitiated or satisfied, it is vain for power to talk either of triumphs or of repose. No matter what fields are desolated, what fortresses surrendered, what armies subdued, or what provinces overrun. In the history of the year that has passed by us, and in the instance of unhappy Spain, we have seen the vanity of all triumphs, in a cause which violates the general sense of justice of the civilized world. It is nothing that the troops of France have passed from the Pyrenees to Cadiz; it is nothing that an unhappy and prostrate nation has fallen before them; it is nothing that arrests, and confiscation, and execution sweep away the little remnant of national resistance. There is an enemy that still exists to check the glory of these triumphs. It follows the conqueror back to the very scene of his ovations; it calls upon him to take notice that Europe, though silent, is yet indignant; it shows him that the scepter of his victory is a barren scepter; that it shall confer neither joy nor honor, but shall molder to dry ashes in his grasp. In the midst of his exultation it pierces his ear with the cry of injured justice; it denounces against him the indignation of an enlightened and civilized age; it turns to bitterness the cup of his rejoicing, and wounds him with the sting which belongs to the consciousness of having outraged the opinion of mankind."

It was, indeed, to the Duke of Angoulême and his family,

A *barren* scepter in their gripe,
Thence to be wrenched by an unlineal hand,
No son of theirs succeeding.

His uncle, Louis XVIII., died the next year; his father, Charles X., succeeded, and in less than six years was driven, with his branch of the family, from the throne (July, 1830); Louis Philippe, of the Orleans branch, succeeded, and met with the same fate in less than eighteen years (June, 1848); and the prediction of Lord Brougham as to Louis XVIII. and his dynasty was verified, even without his calling in "the modern Teutones and Scythians to assist him;" "judgment" *did* "go forth against him, and his family, and his counselors; and *the dynasty of the Gaul has ceased to reign!*"

SPEECH

OF LORD BROUGHAM ON PARLIAMENTARY REFORM, DELIVERED IN THE HOUSE OF LORDS, OCTOBER 7, 1831.

INTRODUCTION.

EARL GREY came into power November 22d, 1830, being the first Whig minister since the days of Lord Grenville in 1806–7. His life had been devoted to parliamentary reform, and he made this the leading object of his administration.

Ages had passed away since the apportionment of members for the House of Commons. The population of England had five-folded. Many of the largest towns in the kingdom, such as Liverpool, Manchester, &c., had sprung into existence, and were without representatives; while a large number of places, sending two members each to Parliament, had sunk into mere villages or hamlets, and some, like Old Sarum, Gatton, &c., were actually left without an inhabitant. These places passed into the hands, or under the control, of the nobility and men of wealth, so that seats in the House of Commons, by scores upon scores, were bought and sold in the market. When Lord Grey first took up the subject in 1793, he offered to prove that seventy-one peers, by direct nomination or influence, returned *one hundred and sixty-three members*, and ninety-one commoners *one hundred and thirty-nine members.* Thus, in England and Wales (exclusive of the forty-five for Scotland), *three hundred and two members*, being a decided majority of the Commons, were returned by one hundred and sixty-two individuals! These statements made a deep impression on the public mind; but such was the dread inspired by the French Revolution and its misguided friends in England, and such the reluctance of the higher classes to part with power, that every attempt at reform was instantly voted down, until 1830, when Earl Grey came into power.

On the first of March, 1831, the new ministry brought forward their Reform Bill in the House of Commons. It was designed to meet three evils: first, the appointment of members by individuals; secondly, the small number of voters in most boroughs and in the counties; and, thirdly, the expenses of elections. To meet the first evil, it proposed that sixty boroughs, enumerated in a schedule marked A, having each a population under two thousand, should be totally disfranchised; and that forty-seven others, in a schedule marked B, with a like population under four thousand, should each be allowed only one member. Weymouth, which sent four members, was to have but two. In this way, *one hundred and sixty-eight* vacancies would be created, which might be supplied by giving representatives to the large towns, and by increasing the number of county members. In respect to the second evil, it proposed to give the right of voting in boroughs to all householders paying a £10 rent, and in the counties to copyholders of £10 a year, and to leaseholders of £50 a year. In regard to the third evil, that of election expenses, it disfranchised all non-resident electors, thus saving vast sums paid for their transportation to the polls; and shortened the duration of elections by increasing the facilities for receiving votes.

This bill was debated in the Commons with great ability on both sides for seven weeks, and was finally rejected by a majority of *eight.* The ministry immediately tendered their resignations, but the King (William IV.), who was in favor of reform, refused to accept them; he preferred to dissolve Parliament, and refer the question to the decision of the people in a new House of Commons. The elections, in all places where the popular voice could prevail, went strongly for the bill, eighty of the county members being chosen under pledges to vote for reform.

The bill, with some slight modifications, was brought again into the House on the 24th of June, 1831. Here it was debated under various forms for nearly three months, and was finally passed on the 19th of September, by a majority of *one hundred and six.* It was now carried to the House of Lords, a large majority of whom were known to be bitterly opposed to the measure. The great body of the nation were equally resolved it should pass; petitions came in by thousands from every part of the kingdom; and the feeling seemed to be almost universal, "*through* Parliament or *over* Parliament, this measure must be carried."

In this state of the public mind, the House of Lords took up the subject on the 3d of October, 1831, and discussed it in a debate of five nights, which, "for skill, force, and variety of argument; for historical, constitutional, and classical information," says an able writer, "was never surpassed." Lord Brougham reserved himself until the fifth night; and after Lord Eldon had spoken with all the weight of his age and authority against the bill, the Lord Chancellor came down from the wool-sack to reply. His speech was intended as an answer to all the important arguments which had been urged against reform during this protracted discussion. He began in a mild and conciliatory manner, unwilling to injure his cause by the harshness in which he too commonly indulged, and answered a part of the arguments in a strain of good-humored wit and pleasantry which has rarely been surpassed. But after repeated interruptions

some of them obviously designed to put him down, he changed his tone, and spoke for nearly three hours more with a keenness of rebuke, a force of argument, and a boldness of declamation which secured him a respectful hearing, and extorted the confession from his adversary Lord Lyndhurst, that a more powerful speech of the kind had never been delivered in the House of Lords.

SPEECH, &c.

My Lords,—I feel that I owe some apology to your Lordships for standing in the way of any noble Lords[1] who wish to address you; but after much deliberation, and after consulting with several of my noble friends on both sides of the House, it did appear to us, as I am sure it will to your Lordships, desirable, on many grounds, that the debate should be brought to a close this night; and I thought I could not better contribute to that end than by taking the present opportunity of addressing you. Indeed, I had scarcely any choice. I am urged on by the anxiety I feel on this mighty subject, which is so great that I should hardly have been able to delay the expression of my opinion much longer; if I had, I feel assured that I must have lost the power to address you. This solicitude is not, I can assure your Lordships, diminished by my recollection of the great talents and brilliant exertions of those by whom I have been preceded in the discussion, and the consciousness of the difficulties with which I have to contend in following such men. It is a deep sense of these difficulties that induces me to call for your patient indulgence. For, although not unused to meet public bodies, nay, constantly in the habit, during many years, of presenting myself before great assemblies of various kinds, yet I do solemnly assure you that I never, until this moment, felt what deep responsibility may rest on a member of the Legislature in addressing either of its Houses. And if I, now standing with your Lordships on the brink of the most momentous decision that ever human assembly came to at any period of the world, and seeking to arrest you while it is yet time, in that position could, by any divination of the future, have foreseen in my earliest years that I should live to appear here, and to act as your adviser, on a question of such awful importance, not only to yourselves, but to your remotest posterity, I should have devoted every day and every hour of that life to preparing myself for the task which I now almost sink under—gathering from the monuments of ancient experience the lessons of wisdom which might guide our course at the present hour—looking abroad on our own times, and these not uneventful, to check by practice the application of those lessons—chastening myself, and sinking within me every infirmity of temper, every waywardness of disposition which might by possibility impede the discharge of this most solemn duty; but above all, eradicating from my mind every thing that, by any accident, could interrupt the most perfect candor and impartiality of judgment. I advance thus anxious and thus humbled to the task before me; but cheered, on the other hand, with the intimate and absolute persuasion that I have no personal interest to serve—no sinister views to resist—that there is nothing in my nature or in my situation which can cast even the shadow of a shade across the broad path, I will not say of legislative, but of judicial duty, in which I am now to accompany your Lordships.

Anxiety of the speaker in approaching the subject.

The preparation he would wish to have made.

I have listened, my Lords, with the most profound attention, to the debate on this question, which has lasted during the five past days; and having heard a vast variety of objections brought against this measure, and having also attended to the arguments which have been urged to repel those objections, I, careless whether I give offense in any quarter or no, must, in common fairness, say, on the one hand, that I am so far moved by some of the things which I have heard urged, as to be inclined toward the reconsideration of several matters on which I had conceived my mind to be fully made up; and, on the other, that in the great majority of the objections which have been ingeniously raised against this bill, I can by no means concur; but viewing them as calmly and dispassionately as ever man listened to the arguments advanced for and against any measure, I am bound by a sense of duty to say, that those objections have left my mind entirely unchanged as to the bulk of the principles upon which the bill is framed. If I presumed to go through those objections, or even through the majority of them, in detail, I should be entering upon a tedious and also a superfluous work; so many of them have been removed by the admirable speeches which you have already heard, that I should only be wasting your time were I once more to refute them; I should only be doing worse what my precursors have already done far better. I will begin, however, with what fell from a noble Earl [Earl Dudley] with whose display I was far less struck than others, because I was more accustomed to it—who, viewing this bill from a remote eminence, and not coming close, or even approaching near, made a *reconnoissance* of it too far off to see even its outworks—who, indulging in a vein of playful and elegant pleasantry, to which no man listens in private with more delight than myself, knowing how well it becomes the leisure hours and familiar moments of my noble friend, delivered with the utmost purity of diction, and the most felicitous aptness of allusion—I was going to say a discourse—but it was an exercise or essay—of the highest merit, which had only this fault, that it was an essay or exercitation on some other thesis, and not on this bill. It was as if some one had set to my noble friend, whose accom-

Answer to those who have spoken against the bill.

(1.) Lord Dudley.

[1] The Marquess of Cleveland and several others had risen and given way.

plishments I know—whose varied talents I admire, but in whom I certainly desiderate soundness of judgment and closeness of argument—a theme *de rebuspublicis*, or *de motû civium*, or *de novarum rerum cupiditate*[2]—on change, on democracies, on republicanism, on anarchy; and on these interesting but somewhat trite and even threadbare subjects, my noble friend made one of the most lucid, most terse, most classical, and, as far as such efforts will admit of eloquence, most eloquent exercitations that ever proceeded from mortal pen. My noble friend proceeded altogether on a false assumption; it was on a fiction of his own brain, on a device of his own imagination, that he spoke throughout. He first assumed that the bill meant change and revolution, and on change and revolution he predicted voluminously and successfully. So much for the critical merits of his performance; but, practically viewed, regarded as an argument on the question before us, it is to be wholly left out of view; it was quite beside the matter. If this bill be change and be revolution, there is no resisting the conclusions of my noble friend. But on that point I am at issue with him; and he begins by taking the thing in dispute for granted. I deny that this bill is change, in the bad sense of the word; nor does it lead to, nor has it any connection with revolution, except so far as it has a direct tendency to prevent revolution.

His argument assumes the very point at issue.

My noble friend, in the course of his essay, talked to you of this administration as one prone to change; he told you that its whole system was a system of changes; and he selected as the first change on which he would ring a loud peal, that which he said we had made in our system of finance. If he is so averse to our making alterations in our scheme of finance the very first year we have been in office, what does he think, I ask, of Mr. Pitt's budgets, of which never one passed without undergoing changes in almost every one tax, besides those altogether abandoned? If our budget had been carried as it was originally brought in, with a remission of the timber duty, and the candle duty, and the coal duty, it would have been distinguished beyond all others only as having given substantial relief to the people on those very trivial and unnecessary articles, I suppose, of human life—fire, and light, and lodging. Then, our law reform is another change which my noble friend charged the government with being madly bent on effecting. Scarcely had the Lord President of the Council risen to answer the objection raised against us on this score, than up started my noble friend to assert that he had not pressed any such objection into his service. My Lords, I am not in the habit of taking a note of what falls from any noble Lord in debate—it is not my practice—but by some fatality it did so happen that, while my noble friend was speaking, I took a note of his observations, of which I will take the liberty of reading you the very first line. "Change and revolution; all is change; among the first—law." I took that note, because I was somewhat surprised at the observation, knowing, as I did, that this law reform had met with the approbation of my noble friend himself; and, what was yet more satisfactory to my mind, it had received the sanction of your Lordships, and had been passed through all its stages without even a division. My noble friend then told us, still reconnoitering our position at a distance, or, at most, partaking in an occasional skirmish, but holding himself aloof from the main battle—he told us that this bill came recommended neither by the weight of ancient authority nor by the spirit of modern refinement; that this attack on our present system was not supported by the experience of the past, nor sanctioned by any appearance of the great mind of the master genius of our precursors in later times. As to the weight of ancient authority, skilled as my noble friend is in every branch of literary history, I am obliged to tell him he is inaccurate; and, because it may afford him some consolation in this his day of discomfiture and anguish, I will supply the defect which exists in his historical recollections; for an author, the first of satirists in any age—Dean Swift, with whom my noble friend must have some sympathy, since he closely imitates him in this respect, that as the Dean satirized, under the name of man, a being who had no existence save in his own imagination, so my noble friend attacks, under the name of the bill, a fancy of his own, a creature of his fertile brain, and which has no earthly connection with the real ink and parchment bill before you—Dean Swift, who was never yet represented as a man prone to change, who was not a Radical, who was not a Jacobin (for, indeed, those terms were in his day unknown)—Dean Swift, who was not even a Whig, but, in the language of the times, a regular, stanch, thick-and-thin Tory, while enumerating the absurdities in our system, which required an adequate and efficient remedy, says: "It is absurd that the boroughs, which are decayed, and destitute both of trade and population, are not extinguished" (or, as we should say, in the language of the bill, which was as unknown to Dean Swift as it is now to my noble friend, put into schedule A.), "because," adds the Dean, "they return members who represent nobody at all;" so here he adopts the first branch of the measure; and next he approves of the other great limb, for the second grand absurdity which he remarks is, "that several large towns are not represented, though they are filled with those who increase mightily the trade of the realm." Then as to shortening the duration of Parliaments, on which we have not introduced a single provision into the bill—if we had, what a cry should we have heard about the statesmen in Queen Anne's day, the great men who lived in the days of Blenheim, and during the period sung of by my noble friend, from Blenheim to Waterloo; how we should have been taunted with the Somerses

His charges against the ministry as being eager for innovation.

as regardless of ancient authority,

[2] Concerning public affairs, or civil commotions, or the love of political change

and Godolphins, and their cotemporaries, the Swifts and the Addisons! What would *they* have said of such a change? Yet what did the same Dean Swift, the cotemporary of Somers and Godolphin, the friend of Addison, who sang the glories of Blenheim, the origin of my noble friend's period—what did the Dean, inspired by all the wisdom of ancient times, say to shortening the duration of Parliaments? "I have a strong love for the good old fashion of Gothic Parliaments, which were only of one year's duration." Such is the ground, such the vouchers, upon the authority of which my noble friend, in good set phrase, sets the weight of ancient wisdom against the errors of the Reformers, and triumphs in the round denial that we have any thing in our favor like the sanction of authority; and it turns out, after all, that the wise men of the olden time promulgated their opinions on the subject in such clear, and decisive, and vigorous terms, that if they were living in our days, and giving utterance to the same sentiments, they would be set down rather for determined Radicals than for enemies of reform.

Then my noble friend, advancing from former times to our own, asked who and what they are that form the cabinet of the day? To such questions it would be unbecoming in me to hazard a reply. I do not find fault with my noble friend for asking them; I admit that it is fair to ask who are they that propound any measure, especially when it comes in the shape of a great change. The noble Earl then complained of our poverty of genius—absence of commanding talents—want of master minds—and even our destitution of eloquence, a topic probably suggested by my noble friend's [Lord Grey] display, who opened the debate, and whose efforts in that kind are certainly very different from those which the noble Earl seems to admire. But if it be a wise rule to ask by whom a measure is propounded before you give it implicit confidence, it certainly can not be an unwise rule to ask, on the other hand, who and what be they by whom that measure is resisted, before you finally reject it on their bare authority. Nor can I agree with a noble friend of mine [Lord Caernarvon], who spoke last night, and who laid down one doctrine on this subject at which I marveled greatly. It was one of his many allegories—for they were not metaphors, nor yet similes—some of them, indeed, were endless, especially when my noble friend took to the water, and embarked us on board of his ship—for want of steam, I thought we should never have got to the end of our voyage. When we reply to their arguments against our measure, by asking what reform they have got of their own to offer, he compares us to some host, who, having placed before his friends an uneatable dinner, which they naturally found fault with, should say, "Gentlemen, you are very hard to please; I have set a number of dishes before you which you can not eat; now, what dishes can you dress yourselves?" My noble friend says that such an answer would be very unreasonable; for, he asks, ingeniously enough, how *can* the guests dress a dinner, especially when they have not possession of the kitchen? But did it never strike him that the present is not the case of guests called upon to eat a dinner; it is one of rival cooks who want to get into our kitchen. We are here all on every side cooks—a synod of cooks (to use Dr. Johnson's phrase), and nothing but cooks; for it is the very condition of our being—the bond of our employment under a common master—that none of us shall ever taste the dishes we are dressing. The Commons House may taste it; but can the Lords? We have nothing to do but prepare the viands. It is, therefore, of primary importance, when the authority of the two classes of rival artists is the main question, to inquire what are our feats severally in our common calling. I ought, perhaps, to ask your Lordships' pardon for pursuing my noble friend's allegory; but I saw that it produced an impression by the cheers it excited, and I was desirous to show that it was in a most extraordinary degree inapplicable to the question, to illustrate which it was fetched from afar off. I, therefore, must think myself entitled to ask who and what be they that oppose us, and what dish they are likely to cook for us, when once again they get possession of the kitchen? I appeal to any candid man who now hears me, and I ask him whether, it being fair to consider who are the authors of the bill, it is not equally fair to consider from whom the objections come? I, therefore, trust that any impartial man, unconnected with either class of statesmen, when called upon to consider our claims to confidence before he adopts our measures, should, before he repudiates us in favor of our adversaries, inquire, Are they likely to cure the evils and remedy the defects, of which they admit the existence in our system? and are their motives such as ought to win the confidence of judicious and calmly reflecting men?

[Margin notes: And as destitute of talent. / Remarks in passing on an illustration of Lord Caernarvon.]

One noble Lord [Lord Winchelsea] there is whose judgment we are called upon implicitly to trust, and who expressed himself with much indignation, and yet with entire honesty of purpose, against this measure. No man is, in my opinion, more single-hearted; no man more incorruptible. But in his present enmity to this bill, which he describes as pregnant with much mischief to the Constitution, he gives me reason to doubt the soundness of the resolution which would take him as a guide, from the fact of his having been not more than five or six months ago most friendly to its provisions, and expressed the most unbounded confidence in the government which proposed it. Ought not this to make us pause before we place our consciences in his keeping—before we surrender up our judgment to his prudence—before we believe in his cry that the bill is revolution, and the destruction of the empire—when we find the same man delivered diametrically opposite opinions only six months ago?

[Margin notes: (2.) Lord Winchelsea. / His self-contradiction.]

Lord Winchelsea here shouted out "No."

The Lord Chancellor. Then I have been practiced upon, if it is not so; and the noble Earl's assertion should be of itself sufficient to convince me that I have been practiced on. But I can assure the noble Earl that this has been handed to me as an extract from a speech which he made to a meeting of the county of Kent, held at Maidstone, on the 24th of last March: "They have not got reform yet; but when the measure does come, as I am persuaded it will come, into the law of the land—" (a loud cry of "No," from the opposition Lords). Then, if noble Lords will not let me proceed quietly, I must begin again, and this time I will go further back. The speech represents the noble Earl to have said, "His Majesty's government is entitled to the thanks of the country. Earl Grey, with his distinguished talents, unites a political honesty not to be surpassed, and leaves behind him, at an immeasurable distance, those who have abandoned their principles and deceived their friends. The noble Lord is entitled to the eternal gratitude of his country for the manner in which he has brought forward this question. I maintain that he deserves the support of the country at large." And, my Lords, the way in which I was practiced on to believe that all this praise was not referable to the timber duties, but to reform, I shall now explain. It is in the next passage of the same speech: "They have not got reform yet; but when the measure does come, as I am persuaded it will come, into the law of the land, it will consolidate, establish, and strengthen our glorious Constitution; and not only operate for the general welfare and happiness of the country, but will also render an act of justice to the great and influential body of the people. The measure has not yet been introduced to that House of which I am a member." (Lord Winchelsea and his friends here cheered loudly.) Ay, but it had been debated in the House of Commons for near a month—it had been published in all books, pamphlets, and newspapers—it had been discussed in all companies and societies—and I will undertake to assert that there was not one single man in the county of Kent who did not know that Lord John Russell's bill was a bill for parliamentary reform. The speech thus concludes: "When the bill is brought forward in that House of which I am a member, I shall be at my post, ready to give it my most hearty and cordial"—opposition? no—"support." But why do I allude to this speech at all? Merely to show that if those who oppose the bill say to us, "Who are you that propound it?" and make our previous conduct a ground for rejecting it, through distrust of its authors, we have a right to reply to them with another question, and to ask, "Who are you that resist it, and what were your previous opinions regarding it?"

Proof.

Another noble Lord [Lord Mansfield] has argued this question with great ability and show of learning; and if we are to take him as our guide, we must also look at the panacea which he provides for us in case of rejection. That noble Lord, looking around him on all sides—surveying what had occurred in the last forty or fifty years—glancing above him and below him, around him and behind him—watching every circumstance of the past—anticipating every circumstance of the future—scanning every sign of the times—taking into his account all the considerations upon which a lawgiver ought to reckon—regarding also the wishes, the vehement desires, not to say absolute demands, of the whole country for some immediate reform—concentrates all his wisdom in this proposition—the result, the *practical result* of all his deliberations, and all his lookings about, and all his scannings of circumstances—the whole produce of his thoughts, by the value of which you are to try the safety of his counsels—namely, that you should suspend all your operations on this bill for two years, and, I suppose, two days, to give the people—what? breathing time. The noble Lord takes a leaf out of the book of the noble Duke near him—a leaf, which I believe the noble Duke himself would now wish canceled. The noble Duke, shortly before he proposed the great measure of Catholic emancipation, had said, "Before I can support that measure, I should wish that the whole question might sink into oblivion." But the proposition of the noble Earl, though based on the same idea, goes still further. "Bury," says he, "this measure of reform in oblivion for two years and two days, and then see, good people, what I will do for you." And then what will the noble Lord do for the good people? Why, nothing—neither more nor less than nothing. We, innocents that we were, fancied that the noble Lord must, after all his promises, really mean to do something; and thought that he had said somewhat of bribery—of doing a little about bribery—which was his expression; but when we mentioned our supposition that he really meant to go as far as to support a bill for the more effectual prevention of bribery at elections, the noble Lord told us he would do no such thing.

(3.) Lord Mansfield asks a delay of the question for two years.

The Earl of Mansfield. I gave no opinion on the point.

The Lord Chancellor. Exactly so. The noble Lord reserves his opinion as to whether he would put down bribery, for two years and two days; and when they are expired, he, peradventure, may inform us whether he will give us leave to bring in a bill to prevent bribery; not all kinds of bribery—that would be radical work—but as far as the giving away of ribbons goes, leaving beer untouched, and agreeably to the venerable practice of the olden time.

Another noble Lord, a friend of mine, whose honesty and frankness stamp all he says with still greater value than it derives from mere talent [Lord Wharncliffe], would have you believe that all the petitions under which your table now groans are indeed for reform, but not for this bill, which he actually says the people dislike. Now is not this a droll way for the people to act, if we are to take my noble friend's statement as true? First of all, it is an odd

(4.) Lord Wharncliffe. Denies that the petitions presented are in favor of the bill.

time they have taken to petition for reform, if they do not like this bill. I should say that if they petition for reform while this particular measure is passing through the House, it is a proof that the bill contains the reform they want. Surely, when I see the good men of this country —the intelligent and industrious classes of the community—now coming forward, not by thousands, but by hundreds of thousands, I can infer nothing from their conduct but that this is the bill, and the only bill, for which they petition? But if they really want some other than the bill proposes, is it not still more unaccountable that they should one and all petition, not for that other reform, but for this very measure? The proposition of my noble friend is, that they love reform in general, but hate this particular plan; and the proof of it is this, that their petitions all pray earnestly for this particular plan, and say not a word of general reform. Highly as I prize the integrity of my noble friend—much as I admire his good sense on other occasions—I must say that, on this occasion, I descry not his better judgment, and if I estimate how far he is a safe guide, either as a witness to facts or as a judge of measures, by his success in the present instance; in either capacity, I can not hesitate in recommending your Lordships not to follow him. As a witness to facts, never was failure more complete. The bill, said he, has no friends any where; and he mentioned Bond Street as one of his walks, where he could not enter a shop without finding its enemies abound. No sooner had Bond Street escaped his lips, than up comes a petition to your Lordships from nearly all its shop-keepers, affirming that their sentiments have been misrepresented, for they are all champions of the bill. My noble friend then says, "Oh, I did not mean the shop-keepers of Bond Street in particular; I might have said any other street, as St. James's equally." No sooner does that unfortunate declaration get abroad, than the shopkeepers of St. James's Street are up in arms, and forth comes a petition similar to that from Bond Street. My noble friend is descried moving through Regent Street, and away scamper all the inhabitants, fancying that he is in quest of anti-reformers—sign a requisition to the church-wardens—and the householders, one and all, declare themselves friendly to the bill. Whither shall he go —what street shall he enter, in what alley shall he take refuge—since the inhabitants of every street, and lane, and alley, feel it necessary, in self-defense, to become signers and petitioners, as soon as he makes his appearance among them? If harassed by reformers on land, my noble friend goes down to the water, the thousand reformers greet him, whose petition [Lambeth's] I this day presented to your Lordships. If he were to get into a hackney-coach, the very coachmen and their attendants would feel it their duty to assemble and petition. Wherever there is a street, an alley, a passage, nay, a river, a wherry, or a hackney-coach, these, because inhabited, become forbidden and *tabooed* to my noble friend. I may meet him not on "the accustomed hill," for Hay-hill, though short, has some houses on its slope, but on the south side of Berkeley Square, wandering "remote, unfriended, melancholy, slow"—for there he finds a street without a single inhabitant, and therefore without a single friend of the bill. If, in despair, he shall flee from the town to seek the solitude of the country, still will he be pursued by cries of "Petition, petition! The bill, the bill!" His flight will be through villages placarded with "The Bill"—his repose at inns holden by landlords who will present him with the *bill*—he will be served by reformers in the guise of waiters—pay tribute at gates where petitions lie for signing—and plunge into his own domains to be overwhelmed with the Sheffield petition, signed by 10,400 friends of the bill.

The way in which he is met by the people.

"Me miserable! which way shall I fly
Infinite wrath and infinite despair?
Which way I fly, Reform—myself Reform!"

for this is the most serious part of the whole—my noble friend is himself, after all, a reformer. I mention this to show that he is not more a safe guide on matters of opinion than on matters of fact. He is a reformer—he is not even a bit-by-bit reformer—not even a gradual reformer—but that which, at any other time than the present, would be called a wholesale and even a radical reformer. He deems that no shadowy unsubstantial reform—that nothing but an effectual remedy of acknowledged abuses will satisfy the people of England and Scotland; and this is a fact to which I entreat the earnest and unremitting attention of every man who wishes to know what guides are safe to follow on this subject. Many now follow men who say that reform is necessary, and yet object to this bill as being too large; that is, too efficient. This may be very incorrect; but it is worse; it is mixed up with a gross delusion which can never deceive the country; for I will now say, once for all, that every one argument which has been urged by those leaders is as good against moderate reform as it is against this bill. Not a single reason they give, not a topic they handle, not an illustration they resort to, not a figure of speech they use, not even a flower they fling about, that does not prove or illustrate the position of "*no reform.*" All their speeches, from beginning to end, are railing against the smallest as against the greatest change, and yet all the while they call themselves reformers! Are they, then, safe guides for any man who is prepared to allow any reform, however moderate, of any abuse, however glaring?

(5.) Lord Harrowby.

Of another noble Earl [Lord Harrowby], whose arguments, well selected and ably put, were yet received with such exaggerated admiration by his friends as plainly showed how pressing were their demands for a tolerable defender, we have heard it said, again and again, that no answer whatever has been given to his speech. I am sure I mean no disrespect to that noble Earl when I venture to remark the infinite superiority in all things, but especially in argument, of such speeches as those of the noble Marquess [Marquess Lansdowne] and the noble Viscount [Viscount Melbourne]. The former, in his most masterly answer, left but little of the speech for any other antagonist to destroy. The latter, while he charmed us with the fine eloquence that pervaded his discourse, and fixed our thoughts by the wisdom and depth of reflection that informed it, won all hearers by his candor and sincerity. Little, indeed, have they left for me to demolish; yet if any thing remain, it may be as well we should take it to pieces. But I am first considering the noble Earl in the light of one professing to be a safe guide for your Lordships. What, then, are his claims to the praise of calmness and impartiality? For the constant cry against the government is, "You are hasty, rash, intemperate men. You know not what you do; your adversaries are the true state physicians; look at their considerate deportment; imitate their solemn caution." This is the sort of thing we hear in private as well as public. "See such an one—*he* is a man of prudence, and a discreet (the olden times called such a *sad*) man; he is not averse to all innovation, but dislikes precipitancy; he is calm; just to all sides alike; never gives a hasty opinion; a safe one to follow; look how *he* votes." I have done this on the present occasion; and, understanding the noble Earl might be the sort of personage intended, I have watched him. Common consistency was, of course, to be, at all events, expected in this safe model—some connection between the premises and conclusion, the speech and the vote. I listened to the speech, and also, with many others, expected that an avowal of all, or nearly all the principles of the bill would have ended in a vote for the second reading, which might suffer the committee to discuss its details, the only subject of controversy with the noble Earl. But no such thing; he is a reformer, approves the principle, objecting to the details, and therefore he votes against it in the lump, details, principle, and all. But soon after his own speech closed, he interrupted another, that of my noble and learned friend [Lord Plunkett] to give us a marvelous sample of calm and impartial judgment.

Charges the ministry with rashness and precipitancy.

What do you think of the cool head, the unruffled temper, the unbiased mind of that man—most candid and most acute as he is, when not under the domination of alarm—who could listen, without even a gesture of disapprobation, to the speech of one noble Lord [Lord Mansfield], professedly not extemporaneous; for he, with becoming, though unnecessary modesty, disclaims the faculty of speaking offhand, but elaborately prepared, in answer to a member of the other House, and in further answer to a quarto volume, published by him—silent and unmoved, could hear another speech, made up of extracts from the House of Commons' debates—could listen and make no sign when a noble Marquess [Marquess Londonderry] referred to the House of Commons' speeches of my noble friend by his House of Commons' name, again and again calling him Charles Grey, without even the prefix of Mr.; nay, could *himself* repeatedly comment upon those very speeches of the other House—what will your Lordships say of the fatal effects of present fear in warping and distorting a naturally just mind, when you find this same noble Earl interrupt the Chancellor of Ireland [Lord Plunkett], because he most regularly, most orderly, referred to the public conduct of a right honorable Baronet [Sir Robert Peel], exhibited in a former Parliament, and now become a matter of history? Surely, surely, nothing more is wanted to show that all the rashness, all the heedlessness, all the unreflecting precipitancy is not to be found upon the right hand of the woolsack [ministerial side of the House]; and that they who have hurried across the sea, in breathless impatience, to throw out the bill, might probably, had they been at home, and allowed themselves time for sober reflection, have been found among the friends of a measure which they now so acrimoniously oppose! So much for the qualifications of the noble Lords to act safely as our guides, according to the general view of the question as one of mere authority, taken by my noble friend [Lord Dudley]. But I am quite willing to rest the subject upon a higher ground, and to take it upon reason, and not upon authority. I will therefore follow the noble Earl [Lord Harrowby] somewhat more closely through his argument, the boast of our antagonists.

And then shows the same things himself.

He began with historical matter, and gave a very fair and manly explanation of his family's connection with the borough of Tiverton. This, he said, would set him *rectus in curiâ*, as he phrased it. If by this he meant that he should thence appear to have no interest in opposing the bill, I can not agree with him; but certainly his narrative, coupled with a few additions by way of reference, which may be made to it, throws considerable light upon the system of rotten boroughs. The influence by which his family have so long returned the two members is, it seems, personal, and in no way connected with property. This may be very true; for certainly the noble Lord has no property within a hundred miles of the place; yet, if it is true, what becomes of the cry, raised by his Lordship, about property? But let that pass—the influence, then, is personal—ay, but it may be personal, and yet be *official* also. The family of the noble Earl has for a long series of years been in high office, ever since the time when its founder also laid the foundations of the borough connection, as Solicitor General. By some accident or other, they have always been connected with the government, as well as the borough. I venture to suspect that the matter of patronage may have had some share in cementing the attachment of the men of Tiverton to the house of Ryder. I take leave to suggest the bare possibility of many such men having always held local and other places—of the voters and their families having

Lord Harrowby may control Tiverton by official influence as well as by property.

always got on in the world through that patronage. If it should turn out that I am right, there may be no very peculiar blame imputable to the noble Earl and his Tiverton supporters; but it adds one to the numberless proofs that the borough system affords endless temptations to barter political patronage for parliamentary power—to use official influence for the purpose of obtaining seats in the Commons, and, by means of those seats, to retain that influence.

Proof that the bill does not necessarily exclude the sons of Peers from the House of Commons.

The noble Earl complained that the Reform Bill shut the doors of Parliament against the eldest sons of Peers, and thus deprived our successors of the best kind of political education. My Lords, I freely admit the justice of his panegyric upon this constitutional training, by far the most useful which a statesman can receive; but I deny that the measure proposed will affect it—will obstruct the passage to the House of Commons; it will rather clear and widen it to all who, like your Lordships' sons, ought there to come. My noble friend [Lord Goderich], who so admirably answered the noble Earl in a speech distinguished by the most attractive eloquence, and which went home to every heart from the honest warmth of feeling, so characteristic of his nature, that breathed through it—has already destroyed this topic by referring to the most notorious facts, by simply enumerating the open counties represented by peers' eldest sons. But I had rather take one instance for illustration, because an individual case always strikes into the imagination, and rivets itself deep in the memory. I have the happiness of knowing a young nobleman—whom to know is highly to esteem—a more virtuous, a more accomplished I do not know—nor have any of your Lordships, rich as you are in such blessings, any arrow in all your quivers of which you have more reason to be proud. He sat for a nomination borough; formed his own opinion; decided for the bill; differed with his family—they excluded him from Parliament, closing against him at least that avenue to a statesman's best education, and an heir-apparent's most valued preparation for discharging the duties of the peerage. How did this worthy scion of a noble stock seek to reopen the door thus closed, and resume his political schooling, thus interrupted by the borough patrons? Did he resort to another close borough, to find an avenue like that which he had lost under the present system, and long before the wicked bill had prevented young lords from duly finishing their parliamentary studies? No such thing. He threw himself upon a large community—canvassed a populous city—and started as a candidate for the suffrages of thousands, on the only ground which was open to such solicitation—he avowed himself a friend of the bill. *Mutato nomine de te.*[3] The borough that rejected him was Tiverton—the young nobleman was the heir of the house of Ryder—the patron was the noble Earl, and the place to which the ejected member resorted for the means of completing his political education in one house, that he might one day be the ornament of the other, was no small, rotten, nomination borough, but the great town of Liverpool.[4]

Lord Harrowby begged to set the noble and learned Lord right. He was himself abroad at the time, fifteen hundred miles off; and his family had nothing to do with the transaction. His son was not returned, because he did not offer himself. [*Cries of Hear!*]

Retort upon the Opposition for their contemptuous cheers.

The Lord Chancellor continued. I hope the noble Lords will themselves follow the course their cries seem to recommend, and endeavor to *hear*. Excess of noise may possibly deter some speakers from performing their duty; but my political education (of which we are now speaking) has been in the House of Commons; my habits were formed there; and no noise will stop me. I say so in tenderness to the noble persons who are so clamorous; and that, thus warned, they may spare their own lungs those exertions which can have no effect except on my ears, and perhaps to make me more tedious. As to the noble Earl's statement, by way of setting me right, it is wholly unnecessary, for I knew he was abroad—I had represented him as being abroad, and I had never charged him with turning out his son. The family, however, must have done it. (Lord Harrowby said *No.*) Then so much the better for my argument against the system, for then the borough itself had flung him out, and prevented him from having access to the political school. I believe the statement that the family had nothing to do with it, because the noble Earl makes it; but it would take a great deal of statement to make me believe that neither the patron nor the electors had any thing to do with the exclusion, and that the member had *voluntarily* given up his seat, and indeed his office with his seat, besides abandoning his political studies, when he could have continued them as representative of his father's borough.

His Lordship's main objection to the bill answered.

But the next argument of the noble Earl I am, above all, anxious to grapple with, because it brings me at once to a direct issue with him upon the great principle of the measure. The grand charge iterated by him, and re-echoed by his friends, is, that population, not property, is assumed by the

[3] Mutato nomine de te
Fabula narratur.

Change but the name, the tale is of yourself.

Horace, Satires, Book i., Sat. i., line 69, 70.

[4] Nothing could be more felicitous than this narration of Mr. Brougham, commencing so far off as to preclude all thought of any personal application, and gradually advancing until the fact comes out that a son of Lord Harrowby himself was thus brought into Parliament. Such a passage may serve as a *study* for the young orator. Let him remark how different the effect from that of a bald announcement of the *fact*, in contradiction of Lord Harrowby. Let him notice the delicate compliment contained in the passage, both to his Lordship and his son, and the force they give to the argument. In these and other respects the passage shows great dexterity and rhetorical skill.

bill as the basis of representation. Now this is a mere fallacy, and a gross fallacy. I will not call it a willful misstatement; but I will demonstrate that two perfectly different things are, in different parts of this short proposition, carefully confounded, and described under the same equivocal name. If, by basis of representation is meant the ground upon which it was deemed right, by the framers of the bill, that some places should send members to Parliament, and others not, then I admit that there is some foundation for the assertion; but then it only applies to the new towns, and also it has no bearing whatever upon the question. For the objection—and I think the sound objection—to taking mere population as a criterion in giving the elective franchise, is, that such a criterion gives you electors without a qualification, and is, in fact, universal suffrage. And herein, my Lords, consists the grievous unfairness of the statement I am sifting; it purposely mixes together different matters, and clothes them with an ambiguous covering, in order, by means of the confusion and the disguise, to insinuate that universal suffrage is at the root of the bill. Let us strip off this false garb. Is there in the bill any thing resembling universal suffrage? Is it not framed upon the very opposite principles? In the counties, the existing qualification by freehold is retained in its fullest extent; but the franchise is extended to the other kinds of property, copyhold and leasehold. It is true that tenants at will are also to enjoy it, and their estate is so feeble, in contemplation of law, that one can scarce call it property. But whose fault is that? Not the authors of the bill, for they deemed that terms of years alone should give a vote; but they were opposed and defeated in this by the son of my noble friend [the Duke of Buckingham] near me, and his fellow-laborers against the measure. Let us now look to the borough qualification. (*Some noise from conversation here took place.*) Noble Lords must be aware that the chancellor, in addressing your Lordships, stands in a peculiar situation. He alone speaks among his adversaries. Other peers are at least secure against being interrupted by the conversation of those in their immediate neighborhood. And for myself, I had far rather confront any distant cheers, however hostile, than be harassed by the talk of those close by. No practice in the House of Commons can ever accustom a person to this mode of annoyance, and I expect it, in fairness, to cease.[5]

The bill founds representation on *property* as well as population.

To resume the subject where I was forced to break off. I utterly deny that population is the test, and property disregarded, in arranging the borough representation. The franchise is conferred upon householders only. Is not this a restriction? Even if the right of voting had been given to all householders, still the suffrage would not have been universal; it would have depended on property, not on numbers; and it would have been a gross misrepresentation to call population the basis of the bill. But its framers restricted that generality, and determined that property, to a certain considerable amount, should alone entitle to elect. It is true, they did not take freehold tenure of land, as that qualification is inconsistent with town rights—nor did they take a certain amount of capital as the test—for that, besides its manifest inconvenience, would be a far more startling novelty than any the measure can be charged with. But the renting a £10 house is plainly a criterion both of property and respectability. It is said, indeed, that we have pitched this qualification too low—but are we not now debating on the principle of the bill? And is not the committee the place for discussing whether that principle should be carried into effect by a qualification of £10, or a higher? I have no objection, however, to consider this mere matter of detail here; and if I can satisfy the noble Earl that all over England, except in London and a few other great towns, £10 is not too low, I may expect his vote after all. Now, in small towns—I speak in the hearing of noble Lords who are well acquainted with the inhabitants of them—persons living in £10 houses are in easy circumstances. This is undeniably the general case. In fact, the adoption of that sum was not a matter of choice. We had originally preferred £20, but, when we came to inquire, it appeared that very large places had a most inconsiderable number of such houses. One town, for instance, with 17,000 or 18,000 inhabitants, had not twenty who rented houses rated at £20 a year. Were we to destroy one set of close boroughs, the Old Sarums and Gattons, which had at least possession to plead for their title, in order to create another new set of boroughs just as close, though better peopled? In the large town I have alluded to, there were not three hundred persons rated at £10. Occupiers of such houses, in some country towns, fill the station of inferior shop-keepers—in some, of the better kind of tradesmen—here they are foremen of work-shops—there, artisans earning good wages—sometimes, but seldom, laborers in full work; generally speaking, they are a class above want, having comfortable houses over their heads, and families and homes to which they are attached. An opinion has been broached, that the qualification might be varied in different places, raised in the larger towns, and lowered in the smaller. To this I myself, at one time, leaned very strongly; I deemed it a great improvement of the measure. If I have since yielded to the objections which were urged, and the authorities brought to bear against me, this I can very confidently affirm, that if any one shall propound it in the committee, he will find in me, I will not say a supporter, but certainly an ample security, that the doctrine, which I deem important, shall undergo a full, and candid, and scrutinizing discussion. I speak for myself only—I will not even fo my-

Proof of this fact.

[5] The repeated insults to which Lord Brougham was thus subjected soon induced him to change his tone, and we find him, on the next page and onward, assuming that bold defiant manner which was so natural to him in debate.

self say, that were the committee so to modify the bill, I would accept it thus changed. Candor prevents me from holding out any such prospect; but I do not feel called upon to give any decisive opinion now upon this branch of the details, not deeply affecting the principle; only, I repeat emphatically, that I shall favor its abundant consideration in the proper place—the committee.

My Lords, I have admitted that there is some truth in the assertion of population being made the criterion of title in towns to send representatives, though it has no application to the present controversy. Some criterion we were forced to take; for nobody holds that each place should choose members severally. A line must be drawn somewhere, and how could we find a better guide than the population? That is the general test of wealth, extent, importance; and therefore substantially, though not in name, it is really the test of property. Thus, after all, by taking population as the criterion of what towns shall send members, we get at property by almost the only possible road, and property becomes substantially the basis of the title to send representatives; as it confessedly is, in name as well as in substance, the only title to concur in the election of them. The whole foundation of the measure, therefore, and on which all its parts rest, is property alone, and not at all population.

Population is itself an indication of property.

But then, says the noble Earl, the population of a town containing four thousand souls may, for any provision to the contrary in the bill, be all paupers! Good God! Did ever man tax his ingenuity so hard to find an absurdly extreme case? What! a town of four thousand paupers! Four thousand inhabitants, and all quartered on the rates! Then, who is to pay the rates? But if extreme cases are to be put on the one side, why may not I put one on the other? What say you to close boroughs coming, by barter or sale, into the hands of Jew jobbers, gambling loan-contractors, and scheming attorneys, for the materials of extreme cases? What security do these afford against the machinations of aliens—ay, and of alien enemies? What against a nabob of Arcot's parliamentary and financial speculations? What against that truly British potentate naming eighteen or twenty of his tools members of the British House of Commons? But is this an extreme case, one that stands on the outermost verge of possibility, and beyond all reach of probable calculation? Why, it once happened; the Nabob Wallajah Cawn Bahauder had actually his eighteen or twenty members bought with a price, and sent to look after his pecuniary interests, as honest and independent members of Parliament. Talk now of the principle of property—the natural influence of great families—the sacred rights of the aristocracy—the endearing ties of neighborhood—the paramount claims of the landed interest! Talk of British duties to discharge—British trusts to hold—British rights to exercise! Behold the Sovereign of the Carnatic, who regards nor land, nor rank, nor connection, nor open country, nor populous city; but his eye fastens on the time-honored relics of departed greatness and extinct population—the walls of Sarum and Gatton; he arms his right hand with their venerable parchments, and, pointing with his left to a heap of star pagodas too massive to be carried along, lays siege to the citadel of the Constitution, the Commons House of Parliament, and its gates fly open to receive his well-disciplined band. Am I right in the assertion that a foreign Prince obtaining votes in Parliament, under the present system, is no extreme case? Am I wrong in treating with scorn the noble Earl's violent supposition of a town with four thousand souls, and all receiving parish relief?

When an extreme case is put to answer this argument, it may be met with another extreme case.

But who are they that object to the bill its disregard of property? Is a care for property that which peculiarly distinguishes the system *they* uphold? Surely the conduct of those who contend that property alone ought to be considered in fixing the rights of election, and yet will not give up one freeman of a corporation to be disfranchised, presents to our view a miracle of inconsistency. The right of voting, in freemen, is wholly unconnected with any property of any kind whatever; the being freemen is no test of being worth one shilling. Freemen may be, and very often are, common day-laborers, spending every week their whole weekly gains—menial servants, having the right by birth—men living in alms-houses—parish paupers. All who have been at contested elections for corporate towns know that the question constantly raised is upon the right to vote of freemen receiving parish relief. The voters in boroughs, under the present system, are such freemen, non-resident as well as resident (a great abuse, because the source of a most grievous expense to candidates), inhabitants paying scot and lot, which is only an imperfect form of the qualification intended by the bill to be made universal, under wholesome restrictions, and burgage tenants. I have disposed of the two first classes; there remains the last. Burgages, then, are said to be property and no doubt they resemble it a good deal more than the rights of freemen do. In one sense, property they certainly are. But whose? The Lord's who happens to have them on his estate. Are they the property of the voter, who, to qualify him for the purposes of election, receives his title by a mock conveyance at two o'clock in the afternoon, that he may vote at three for the nominee of the real owner, and at four returns it to the solicitor of that owner, to be ready for the like use at the next election? This is your present right of voting by burgage, and this you call a qualification by virtue of property. It is a gross abuse of terms. But it is worse; it is a gross abuse of the Constitution—a scandal and an outrage no longer to be endured. That a peer, or a speculating attorney, or a jobbing Jew, or a gambler from the Stock Exchange, by vesting in his own person the old

But the borough system has no regard to property, except that of the aristocracy.

walls of Sarum, a few pig-sties at Bletchingly, or a summer-house at Gatton, and making fictitious, and collusive, and momentary transfers of them to an agent or two, for the purpose of enabling them to vote as if they had the property, of which they all the while know they have not the very shadow, is in itself a monstrous abuse, in the form of a gross and barefaced cheat; and becomes the most disgusting hypocrisy, when it is seriously treated as a franchise by virtue of property.

The existing abuses in this respect will not be endured much longer.

I will tell those peers, attorneys, jobbers, loan-contractors, and the Nabob's agents, if such there still be among us, that the time is come when these things can no longer be borne, and an end *must* at length be put to the abuse which suffers the most precious rights of government to be made the subject of common barter—the high office of making laws to be conveyed by traffic, pass by assignment under a commission of bankrupt, or the powers of an insolvent act, or be made over for a gaming debt. If any one can be found to say that the abuses which enable a man to put his livery servants in the House of Commons as lawgivers, are essential parts of the British Constitution, he must have read its history with better eyes than mine; and if such person be right, I certainly am wrong—but if I am, then also are all those other persons far more in the wrong who have so lavishly, in all times and countries, sung the praises of the Constitution. I well remember, when I argued at that bar the great case of my noble friend [Lord Segrave] claiming a barony by tenure, it was again and again pressed upon me by the noble and learned Earl [Earl of Eldon], as a consequence of the argument absurd enough to refute it entirely, that a seat in this House might become vested, as he said, in a tailor, as the assignee of an insolvent's estate and effects. I could only meet this by humbly suggesting that the anomaly, the grossness of which I was forced to admit, already existed in every day's practice; and I reminded your Lordships of the manner in which seats in the other House of the Legislature are bought and sold. A tailor may by purchase, or by assignment under a bankruptcy, obtain the right of sending members to Parliament, and he may nominate himself —and the case has actually happened. A waiter at a gambling-house did sit for years in that House, holding his borough property, for aught I can tell, in security of a gambling debt. By means of that property, and right of voting, he advanced himself to the honors of the baronetcy. Fine writing has been defined to be right words in right places; so may fine acting be said to consist of right votes in right places, that is, on pinching questions; and in the discharge of my professional duty on the occasion of which I am speaking, I humbly ventured to approach a more awful subject, and to suggest the possibility of the worthy baronet rising still higher in the state; and, by persisting in his course of fine acting and judicious voting, obtaining at length a seat among your Lordships—which he would then have owed to a gambling debt. Certain it is, that the honors of the peerage have been bestowed before now upon right voters in right places.

Instances of enormous abuses of this kind.

Incidental defense of a recent creation of Peers.

While I am on this subject, I can not but advert to the remarks of my noble and learned friend [Lord Wynford] who was elevated from the bench to this House, and who greatly censured the ministers for creating some peers who happened to agree with them in politics. The coronation was, as all men know, forced upon us; nothing could be more against our will; but the Opposition absolutely insisted on having one, to show their loyalty; a creation of peers was the necessary consequence, and the self-same number were made as at the last coronation ten years ago. But we did not make our adversaries peers—we did not bring in a dozen men to oppose us—that is my noble friend's complaint; and we did not choose our peers for such merits as alone, according to his view, have always caused men to be ennobled. Merit, no doubt, has opened to many the doors of this House. To have bled for their country—to have administered the highest offices of the state—to have dispensed justice on the bench—to have improved mankind by arts invented, or enlightened them by science extended—to have adorned the world by letters, or won the more imperishable renown of virtue—these, no doubt, are the highest and the purest claims to public honors; and from some of these sources are derived the titles of some among us—to others, the purest of all, none can trace their nobility—and upon not any of them can one single peer in a score rest the foundation of his seat in this place. Service without a scar in the political campaign—constant presence in the field of battle at St. Stephen's chapel—absence from all other fights, from "Blenheim down to Waterloo" — but above all, steady discipline — right votes in right places—these are the precious, but, happily, not rare qualities, which have generally raised men to the peerage. For these qualities the gratitude of Mr. Pitt showered down his baronies by the score, and I do not suppose he ever once so much as dreamed of ennobling a man who had ever been known to give one vote against him.

Return to the subject of traffic in boroughs.

My Lords, I have been speaking of the manner in which owners of boroughs traffic, and exercise the right of sending members to Parliament. I have dwelt on no extreme cases; I have adverted to what passes every day before my eyes. See now the fruits of the system, also, by every day's experience. The Crown is stripped of its just weight in the government of the country by the masters of rotten boroughs; they may combine; they do combine, and their union enables them to dictate their own terms. The people are stripped of their most precious rights by the masters of rotten boroughs, for they have usurped the elective franchise, and thus gained an influence in Parliament which enables them to prevent its restoration. The best interests of the country are sacrificed by the masters of rotten boroughs, for their nominees must vote according to the interest not of the nation at large, whom they affect to represent, but of a few individuals, whom alone they represent in reality. But so perverted have men's minds become, by the gross abuse to which they have been long habituated, that the grand topic of the noble Earl [Lord Harrowby], and other debaters—the master-key which instantly unlocked all the sluices of indignation in this quarter of the House against the measure—which never failed, how often soever used, to let loose the wildest cheers, has been, that our reform will open the right of voting to vast numbers, and interfere with the monopoly of the few; while we invade, as it is pleasantly called, the property of the peers and other borough-holders. Why, say they, it absolutely amounts to representation! And wherefore should it not, I say? and what else ought it to be? Are we not upon the question of representation, and none other? Are we not dealing with the subject of a representative body for the people? The question is how we may best make the people's House of Parliament represent the people; and, in answer to the plan proposed, we hear nothing but the exclamations, "Why, this scheme of yours is a rank representation! It is downright election! It is nothing more nor less than giving the people a voice in the choice of their own representatives! It is absolutely most strange—unheard of—unimagined—and most abominable—intolerable—incredibly inconsistent and utterly pernicious novelty, that the members chosen should have electors, and *that the constituents should have something to do with returning the members!*"

Historical view: The present borough system not fixed and unchangeable.

But we are asked at what time of our history any such system as we propose to establish was ever known in England, and this appeal, always confidently made, was never more pointedly addressed than by my noble and learned friend [Lord Wynford] to me. Now I need not remind your Lordships that the present distribution of the right to send members is any thing rather than very ancient; still less has it been unchanged. Henry VIII. created twenty boroughs; Edward VI. made twelve; good Queen Elizabeth created one hundred and twenty, revived forty-eight; and in all, there were created and revived two hundred down to the Restoration. I need only read the words of Mr. Prynne upon the remote antiquity of our borough system. He enumerates sixty-four boroughs—fourteen in Cornwall alone—as all new; and he adds, "for the most part, the Universities excepted, very mean, poor, inconsiderable boroughs, set up by the late returns, practices of sheriffs, or ambitious gentlemen desiring to serve them, courting, bribing, feasting them for their voices, not by prescription or charter (some few excepted), since the reign of Edward IV., before whose reign they never elected or returned members to any English Parliament as now they do." Such, then, is the old and venerable distribution of representation time out of mind, had and enjoyed in Cornwall and in England at large. Falmouth and Bossiney, Lostwithiel and Grampound, may, it seems, be enfranchised, and welcome, by the mere power of the Crown. But let it be proposed to give Birmingham and Manchester, Leeds and Sheffield, members by an act of the Legislature, and the air resounds with cries of revolution!

Not the original Constitution of the kingdom.

But I am challenged to prove that the present system, as regards the elective franchise, is not the ancient parliamentary Constitution of the country—upon pain, says my noble and learned friend, of judgment going against me if I remain silent. My Lords, I will not keep silence, neither will I answer in my own person, but I will refer you to a higher authority, the highest known in the law, and in its best days, when the greatest lawyers were the greatest patriots. Here is the memorable report of the committee of the Commons in 1623–4, of which committee Mr. Sergeant Glanville was the chairman, of which report he was the author. Among its members were the most celebrated names in the law—Coke, and Selden, and Finch, and Noy, afterward Attorney General, and of known monarchical principles. The first resolution is this:

"There being no certain custom, nor prescription, who should be electors and who not, we must have recourse to common right, which, to this purpose, was held to be, that more than the freeholders only ought to have voices in the election; namely, *all men inhabitants, householders, resiants* [residents] *within the borough.*"

The bill not an innovation, but a return to old principles.

What, then, becomes of the doctrine that our bill is a mere innovation; that, by the old law of England, inhabitants householders had no right to vote; that owners of burgage tenements, and freemen of corporations, have in all times exclusively had the franchise? Burgage tenants, it is true, of old had the right, but in the way I have already described—not as now, the nominal and fictitious holders for an hour, merely for election purposes, but the owners of each, the real and actual proprietors of the tenement. Freemen never had it at all, till they usurped upon the inhabitants and thrust them out. But every householder voted in the towns without regard to value, as before the eighth of Henry VI. every freeholder voted without regard to value in the counties—not merely £10 householders, as we propose to restrict the right, but the holder of a house worth a shilling, as much as he whose house was worth a thousand pounds. But I have been appealed to; and I will take upon me to affirm, that if the Crown were to issue a writ to the sheriff, commanding him to send his precept to Birmingham or Manchester, requiring those towns to send burgesses to Parliament, the votes of *all* inhabitant householders must needs be taken, according to the exigency of the writ and precept, the right of voting at common law, and independent of any usurpation upon it, belonging to every resident householder. Are, then, the King's ministers innovators, revolutionists, wild projectors, idle dreamers of dreams and feigners of fancies, when they restore the ancient common law right, but not in its ancient common law extent, for they limit, fix, and contract it? They add a qualification of £10 to restrain it, as our forefathers, in the fifteenth century, restrained the county franchise by the freehold qualification.

Answer to objections against £10 voters.

But then we hear much against the qualification adopted; that is, the particular sum fixed upon, and the noble Earl [Lord Harrowby] thinks it will only give us a set of constituents busied in gaining their daily bread, and having no time to study and instruct themselves on state affairs. My noble friend, too [Lord Dudley], who lives near Birmingham, and may therefore be supposed to know his own neighbors better than we can, sneers at the statesmen of Birmingham and at the philosophers of Manchester. He will live—I tell him he will live to learn a lesson of practical wisdom from the statesmen of Birmingham, and a lesson of forbearance from the philosophers of Manchester. My noble friend was ill advised when he thought of displaying his talent for sarcasm upon one hundred and twenty thousand people in the one place, and one hundred and eighty thousand in the other. He did little, by such exhibitions, toward gaining a stock of credit for the order he belongs to—little toward conciliating for the aristocracy which he adorns, by pointing his little epigrams against such mighty masses of the people. Instead of meeting their exemplary moderation, their respectful demeanor, their affectionate attachment, their humble confidence, evinced in every one of the petitions, wherewithal they have in myriads approached the House, with a return of kindness, of courtesy, even of common civility, he has thought it becoming and discreet to draw himself up in the pride of hexameter and pentameter verse—skill in classic authors—the knack of turning fine sentences, and to look down with derision upon the knowledge of his unrepresented fellow-countrymen in the weightier matters of practical legislation. For myself, I, too, know where they are defective; I have no desire ever to hear them read a Latin line, or hit off in the mother tongue any epigram, whether in prose or in numerous verse. In these qualities they and I freely yield the palm to others. I, as their representative, yield it. I once stood as such elsewhere, because they had none of their own; and though a noble Earl [Lord Harrowby] thinks they suffer nothing by the want, I can tell him they did severely suffer in the greatest mercantile question of the day, the Orders in Council, when they were fain to have a professional advocate for their representative, and were only thus allowed to make known their complaints to Parliament. Again representing them here, for them I bow to my noble friend's immeasurable superiority in all things classical or critical. In book lore—in purity of diction—in correct prosody—even in elegance of personal demeanor, I and they, in his presence, hide, as well we may, our diminished heads. But to say that I will take my noble friend's judgment on any grave practical subject, on any thing touching the great interests of our commercial country, or any of those manly questions which engage the statesman, the philosopher in practice; to say that I could ever dream of putting the noble Earl's opinions, ay, or his knowledge, in any comparison with the bold, rational, judicious, reflecting, natural, and because natural, the trustworthy opinions of those honest men, who always give their strong natural sense fair play, having no affections to warp their judgment—to dream of any such comparison as this, would be, on my part, a flattery far too gross for any courtesy, or a blindness which no habits of friendship could excuse!

Retort on Lord Dudley for his contempt of Manchester and Birmingham politicians.

Evidence of their good sense and ability.

When I hear so much said of the manufacturers and artisans being an inferior race in the political world, I, who well know the reverse to be the fact, had rather not reason with their contemners, nor give my own partial testimony in their favor; but I will read a letter which I happen to have received within the three last days, and since the Derby meeting. "Some very good speeches were delivered," says the writer, "and you will perhaps be surprised when I tell you that much the best was delivered by a common mechanic. He exposed, with great force of reasoning, the benefits which the lower classes would derive from the Reform Bill, and the interest they had in being well governed. Not a single observation escaped him, during a long speech, in the slightest degree disrespectful to the House of Lords, and he showed as much good taste and good feeling as he could have done had he been a member of St. Stephen's. He is, of course, a man of talent; but there are many others also to be found not far behind him. The feeling in general is, that their capacity to judge of political measures is only despised by those who do not know them." These men were far from imputing to any of your Lordships, at that time, a contempt for their capacities. They had not heard the speech of the noble Earl, and they did not suspect any man in this House of an inclination to despise them. They did, however, ascribe some such contemptuous feelings—*horresco referens*—to a far more amiable portion of the aristocracy. "They think," pursues the writer, "they are only treated with contempt by a few women (I suppress the epithets employed), who, because they set the tone of fashion in London, think they can do so here too."

Some talent may be lost to the House by means of the bill, but this is incidental to a greater good.

The noble Earl behind [Lord Harrowby] addressed one observation to your Lordships, which I must in fairness confess I do not think is so easily answered as those I have been dealing with. To the Crown, he says, belongs the undoubted right, by the Constitution, of appointing its ministers and the other public servants; and it ought to have a free choice, among the whole community, of the men fittest to perform the varied offices of the executive government. But, he adds, it may so happen that, the choice having fallen on the most worthy, his constituents, when he vacates his seat, may not re-elect him, or he may not be in Parliament at the time of his promotion; in either case he is excluded till a general election; and even at a general election, a discharge of unpopular, but necessary duties, may exclude him from a seat through an unjust and passing, and, possibly, a local disfavor with the electors. I have frankly acknowledged that I feel the difficulty of meeting this inconvenience with an apt and safe remedy, without a great innovation upon the elective principle. In the committee, others may be able to discover some safe means of supplying the defect. The matter deserves fuller consideration, and I shall be most ready to receive any suggestion upon it. But one thing I have no difficulty in stating, even should the evil be found remediless, and that I have only the choice between taking the reform with this inconvenience, or perpetuating that most corrupt portion of our system, condemned from the time of Swift down to this day, and which even the most moderate and bit-by-bit reformers have now abandoned to its fate—my mind is made up, and I cheerfully prefer the reform.

Defense of the ministry for seeking support from the body of the people.

The noble Earl [Lord Harrowby] has told my noble friend at the head of the government [Lord Grey] that he might have occupied a most enviable position, had he only abstained from meddling with parliamentary reform. He might have secured the support and met the wishes of all parties. "He stood," says the noble Earl, "between the living and the dead."[6] All the benefit of this influence, and this following, it seems, my noble friend has forfeited by the measure of reform. My Lords, I implicitly believe the noble Lord's assertion, as far as regards himself. I know him to be sincere in these expressions, not only because he tells me so, which is enough, but because facts are within my knowledge thoroughly confirming the statement. His support, and that of one or two respectable persons around him, we should certainly have had. Believe me, my Lords, we fully appreciated the value of the sacrifice we made; it was not without a bitter pang that we made up our minds to forego this advantage. But I can not so far flatter those noble persons as to say that their support would have made the government sufficiently strong in the last Parliament. Honest, and useful, and creditable as it would have been, it never could have enabled us to go on for a night without the support of the people. I do not mean the populace—the mob; I never have bowed to them, though I never have testified any unbecoming contempt of them. Where is the man who has yielded less to their demands than he who now addresses you? Have I not opposed their wishes again and again? Have I not disengaged myself from them on their most favorite subject, and pronounced a demonstration, as I deemed it, of the absurdity and delusion of the ballot? Even in the most troublous times of party, who has gone less out of his course to pay them court, or less submitted his judgment to theirs? But if there is the mob, there is the people also. I speak now of the middle classes —of those hundreds of thousands of respectable persons—the most numerous, and by far the most wealthy order in the community; for if all your Lordship's castles, manors, rights of warren and rights of chase, with all your broad acres, were brought to the hammer, and sold at fifty years' purchase, the price would fly up and kick the beam when counterpoised by the vast and solid riches of those middle classes, who are also the genuine depositaries of sober, rational, intelligent, and honest English feeling. Unable though they be to round a period or point an epigram, they are solid, right-judging men, and, above all, not given to change. If they have a fault, it is that error on the right side, a suspicion of state quacks—a dogged love of existing institutions—a perfect contempt of all political nostrums.

Character and power of the Middle Classes.

They will neither be led astray by false reasoning nor deluded by impudent flattery; but so neither will they be scared by classical quotations or browbeaten by fine sentences; and as for an epigram, *they care as little for it as they do for a cannon-ball.* Grave—intelligent—rational—fond of thinking for themselves—they consider a subject long before they make up their minds on it; and the opinions they are thus slow to form they are not swift to abandon. It is an egregious folly to fancy that the popular clamor for reform, or whatever name you please to give it, could have been silenced by a mere change of ministers. The body of the people, such as I have distinguished and described them, had weighed the matter well, and they looked to the government and to the Parliament for an effectual reform. Doubtless they are not the only classes who so felt; at their backs were the humbler and numerous orders of the state; and may God of his infinite mercy avert any occasion for rousing the might which in peaceful times slumbers in their arms! To the people, then, it was necessary, and it was most fit that the government should look steadily for support—not to save this or that administration; but because, in my conscience, I do believe that no man out of the precincts of Bethlem Hospital—nay, no thinking man, not certainly the noble Duke, a most sagacious and reflecting man—can, in these times, dream of carrying on any government in despite of those middle orders of the state. Their support must be sought, if the government would endure—the support of the people, as distinguished from the populace, but connected with that populace, who look up to them as their kind and natural protectors. The middle class, in-

[6] This is a misapplication, apparently, of the noble allusion of one of our greatest orators (Mr. Wilberforce), who said of Mr. Pitt and Revolution—"*He stood between the living and the dead, and the plague was stayed.*"

deed, forms the link which connects the upper and the lower orders, and binds even your Lordships with the populace, whom some of you are wont to despise. This necessary support of the country it was our duty to seek (and I trust we have not sought it in vain), by salutary reforms, not merely in the representation, but in all the branches of our financial, our commercial, and our legal polity. But when the noble Earl talks of the government being able to sustain itself by the support of himself and his friends, does he recollect the strong excitement which prevailed last winter? Could we have steered the vessel of the state safely through that excitement, either within doors or without, backed by no other support? I believe he was then on the Bay of Naples, and he possibly thought all England was slumbering like that peaceful lake — when its state was more like the slumbers of the mountain upon its margin. "Stand between the living and the dead," indeed! Possibly we might; for we found our supporters among the latter class, and our bitter assailants among the former. True it is, the noble Earl would have given us his honest support; *his* acts would have tallied with his professions. But can this be said of others? Did they, who used nearly the same language, and avowed the same feelings, give any thing to the government but the most factious opposition? Has the noble Earl never heard of their conduct upon the timber duties, when, to thwart the administration, they actually voted against measures devised by themselves—ay, and threw them out by their division? Exceptions there were, no doubt, and never to be mentioned without honor to their names, some of the most noble that this House, or indeed any country of Europe can boast [Mr. T. P. Courtenay]. They would not, for spiteful purposes, suffer themselves to be dragged through the mire of such vile proceedings, and conscientiously refused to join in defeating the measures themselves had planned. These were solitary exceptions; the rest, little scrupulous, gave up all to wreak their vengeance on the men who had committed the grave offense, by politicians not to be forgiven, of succeeding them in their offices. I do not then think that, in making our election to prefer the favors of the country to those of the noble Earl, we acted unwisely, independent of all considerations of duty and of consistency; and I fear I can claim for our conduct no praise of disinterestedness.

Answer to the objection that the bill will make members *delegates* of their constituents,

My Lords, I have followed the noble Earl as closely as I could through his arguments, and I will not answer those who supported him with equal minuteness, because, in answering him, I have really answered all the arguments against the bill. One noble Lord [Lord Falmouth] seems to think he has destroyed it, when he pronounces, again and again, that the members chosen under it will be delegates. What if they were delegates? What should a representative be but the delegate of his constituents? But a man may be the delegate of a single person, as well as of a city or a town; he may be just as much a delegate when he has one constituent as when he has 5000—with this material difference, that, under a single constituent, who can turn him off in a moment, he is sure to follow the orders he receives implicitly, and that the service he performs will be for the benefit of one man, and not of many. The giving a name to the thing, and crying out Delegate! Delegate! proves nothing, for it only raises the question, who should be the delegator of this public trust—the people or the borough-holders? Another noble Lord [Lord Caernarvon], professing to wish well to the great unrepresented towns, complained of the bill on their behalf, because, he said, the first thing it does is to close up the access which they at present possess to Parliament, by the purchase of seats for mercantile men, who may represent the different trading interests in general. Did ever mortal man contrive a subtlety so absurd, so nonsensical as this? What! Is it better for Birmingham to subscribe, and raise £5000, for a seat at Old Sarum, than to have the right of openly and honestly choosing its own representative, and sending him direct to Parliament? Such horror have some men of the straight, open highway of the Constitution, that they would, rather than travel upon it, sneak into their seats by the dirty, winding by-ways of rotten boroughs.

and prevent mercantile men from buying seats in Parliament.

Folly of waiting till boroughs are disfranchised for crimes.

But the noble Earl behind [Lord Harrowby] professed much kindness for the great towns—he had no objection to give Birmingham, Manchester, and Sheffield representatives as vacancies might occur, by the occasional disfranchisement of boroughs for crimes. Was there ever any thing so fantastical as this plan of reform? In the first place, these great towns either ought to have members or they ought not. If they ought, why hang up the possession of their just rights upon the event of some other place committing an offense? Am I not to have my right till another does a wrong? Suppose a man wrongfully keeps possession of my close; I apply to him, and say, "Mr. Johnson, give me up my property, and save me and yourself an action of ejectment." Should not I have some cause to be surprised, if he answered, "Oh no, I can't let you have it till Mr. Thomson embezzles £10,000, and then I may get a share of it, and that will enable me to buy more land, and then I'll give you up your field." "But I want the field, and have a right to get it; not because Thomson has committed a crime, but because it is my field, and not yours—and I should be as great a fool as you are a knave, were I to wait till Thomson became as bad as yourself." I am really ashamed to detain your Lordships with exposing such wretched trifling.

A speech, my Lords, was delivered by my noble friend under the opposite gallery [Lord Radnor], which has disposed of much that remains of my task. I had purposed to show the mighty change which has been wrought in later times upon the opinions, the habits, and the intelligence of the people, by the universal diffusion of knowledge. But this has been done by my noble friend with an accuracy of statement, and a power of language which I should in vain attempt to follow; and there glowed through his admirable oration a natural warmth of feeling to which every heart instinctively responded. I have, however, lived to hear that great speech talked of in the language of contempt. A noble Lord [Lord Falmouth], in the fullness of his ignorance of its vast subject, in the maturity of his incapacity to comprehend its merits, described it as an amusing—a droll speech; and in this profound criticism a noble Earl [Earl Caernarvon] seemed to concur, whom I should have thought capable of making a more correct appreciation. Comparisons are proverbially invidious; yet I can not help contrasting that speech with another which I heard not very long ago, and of which my noble friend [Earl Caernarvon] knows something; one not certainly much resembling the luminous speech in question, but a kind of chaos of dark, disjointed figures, in which soft professions of regard for friends fought with hard censures on their conduct, frigid conceptions with fiery execution, and the lightness of the materials with the heaviness of the workmanship—

"Frigida pugnabant calidis, humentia siccis,
Mollia cum duris, sine pondere habentia pondus."[7]

A droll and amusing speech, indeed! It was worthy of the same speaker of whom both Mr. Windham and Mr. Canning upon one occasion said, that he had made the finest they ever heard. It was a lesson deeply impregnated with the best wisdom of the nineteenth century, but full also of the profoundest maxims of the seventeenth. There was not a word of that speech—not one proposition in its luminous context—one sentence of solemn admonition or of touching regret—fell from my noble friend [Lord Radnor]—not a severe reproof of the selfishness, nor an indignant exclamation upon the folly of setting yourselves against the necessary course of events, and refusing the rights of civilization to those whom you have suffered to become civilized—not a sentiment, not a topic, which the immortal eloquence and imperishable wisdom of Lord Bacon did not justify, sanction, and prefix.

The sole object of the government is to conform things to the progress of the times.

They who are constantly taunting us with subverting the system of the representation, and substituting a parliamentary Constitution unknown in earlier times, must be told that we are making no change—that we are not pulling down, but building up—or, at the utmost, adapting the representation to the altered state of the community. The system which was hardly fitted for the fourteenth century can not surely be adapted to the nineteenth. The innovations of time, of which our detractors take no account, are reckoned upon by all sound statesmen; and in referring to them, my noble friend [Lord Radnor] has only followed in the footsteps of the most illustrious of philosophers. "Stick to your ancient parliamentary system," it is said; "make no alteration; keep it exactly such as it was in the time of Harry the Third, when the two Houses first sat in separate chambers, and such as it has to this day continued!" This is the ignorant cry; this the very shibboleth of the party. But I have joined an issue with our antagonists upon the fact; and I have given the evidence of Selden, of Glanville, of Coke, of Noy, and of Prynne, proving to demonstration that the original right of voting has been subjected to great and hurtful changes—that the exclusive franchise of freemen is a usurpation upon householders—and that our measure is a restoration of the rights thus usurped upon. I have shown that the ministers are only occupied in the duty of repairing what is decayed, not in the work of destruction, or of violent change. Your Lordships were recently assembled at the great solemnity of the coronation. Do you call to mind the language of the primate, and in which the monarch swore, when the sword of kingly estate was delivered into his hands? "Restore the things that are gone into decay; maintain that which is restored; purify and reform what is amiss; confirm that which is in good order!" His sacred Majesty well remembers his solemn vow, to restore the Constitution, and to reform the abuses time has introduced; and I, too, feel the duty imposed on me, of keeping fresh in the recollection of the prince, whom it is my pride and my boast to serve, the parts of our system which fall within the scope of his vow. But if he has sworn to restore the decayed, so has he also sworn to maintain that which is restored, and to confirm that which wants no repairing; and what sacrifice soever may be required to maintain and confirm, that sacrifice I am ready to make, opposing myself, with my sovereign, to the surge that may dash over me, and saying to it, "Hitherto shalt thou come; here shall thy waves be stayed." For while that sovereign tells the enemies of all change, "I have sworn to restore!" so will he tell them who look for change only, "I have also sworn to maintain!"

Manifest absurdity of the present system.

"Stand by the whole of the old Constitution!" is the cry of our enemies. I have disposed of the issue of fact, and shown that what we attack is any thing but the old Constitution. But suppose, for argument's sake, the question had been decided against us—that Selden, Coke, Noy, Glanville, Prynne, were all wrong—that their doctrine and mine was a mere illusion, and rotten boroughs the ancient order of things—that it was a fundamental principle of the old Constitution to have members without constituents, boroughs without members, and a representative Parliament without electors. Suppose this to be the nature of the old, and much admired, and more bepraised, government of England. All this I will assume for the sake of the argument; and I solicit the attention of the noble Lords who main-

[7] The cold and hot contended—dry and wet—
Things hard and soft—those with weight and without it.—*Ovid's Metamp.* (*Chaos*), Book i., l. 19.

tain that argument, while I show them its utter absurdity. Since the early times of which they speak, has there been no change in the very nature of a seat in Parliament? Is there no difference between our days and those when the electors eschewed the right of voting, and a seat in Parliament, as well as the elective franchise, was esteemed a burden? Will the same principles apply to that age and to ours, when all the people of the three kingdoms are more eager for the power of voting than for any other earthly possession; and the chance of sitting in the House of Commons is become the object of all men's wishes? Even as late as the union of the Crowns, we have instances of informations filed in the courts of law to compel Parliament men to attend their duty, or punish them for the neglect—so ill was privilege then understood. But somewhat earlier we find boroughs petitioning to be relieved from the expense of sending members, and members supported by their constituents as long as they continued their attendance. Is it not clear that the parliamentary law applicable to that state of things can not be applied to the present circumstances, without in some respects making a violent revolution? But so it is in the progress of all those changes which time is perpetually working in the condition of human affairs. They are really the authors of change, who resist the alterations which are required to adjust the system, and adapt it to new circumstances; who forcibly arrest the progress of one portion amid the general advancement. Take, as an illustration, the state of our jurisprudence. The old law ordained that a debtor's property should be taken in execution. But in early times there were no public funds, no paper securities, no accounts at bankers; land and goods formed the property of all; and those were allowed to be taken in satisfaction of debts. The law, therefore, which only said, let land and goods be taken, excluded the recourse against stock and credits, although it plainly meant that all the property should be liable, and would clearly have attached stock and credits, had they then been known. But when nine tenths of the property of our richest men consist of stock and credits, to exempt these under pretense of standing by the old law, is manifestly altering the substance for the sake of adhering to the letter; and substituting for the old law, that all the debtor's property should be liable, a new and totally different law, that a small part only of his property should be liable. Yet in no part of our system has there been a greater change than in the estimated value attached to the franchise, and to a seat in Parliament, from the times when one class of the community anxiously shunned the cost of electing, and another as cautiously avoided being returned, to those when both classes are alike anxious to obtain these privileges. Then, can any reasonable man argue that the same law should be applied to two states of things so diametrically opposite? Thus much I thought fit to say, in order to guard your Lordships against a favorite topic, one sedulously urged by the adversaries of reform, who lead men astray by constantly harping upon the string of change, innovation, and revolution.

Answer to the argument, that it *works well.*

But it is said, and this is a still more favorite argument, the system works well. How does it work well? Has it any pretensions to the character of working well? What say you to a town of five or six thousand inhabitants, not one of whom has any more to do with the choice of its representatives than any of your Lordships sitting round that table—indeed, a great deal less—for I see my noble friend [the Duke of Devonshire] is there? It works well, does it? How works well? It would work well for the noble Duke, if he chose to carry his votes to market! Higher rank, indeed, he could not purchase than he has; but he has many connections, and he might gain a title for every one that bears his name. But he has always acted in a manner far more worthy of his own high character, and of the illustrious race of patriots from whom he descends, the founders of our liberties and of the throne which our Sovereign's exalted house fills; and his family have deemed that name a more precious inheritance than any title for which it could be exchanged. But let us see how the system works for the borough itself, and its thousands of honest, industrious inhabitants. My Lords, I once had the fortune to represent it for a few weeks; at the time when I received the highest honor of my life, the pride and exultation of which can never be eradicated from my mind but by death, nor in the least degree allayed by any lapse of time—the most splendid distinction which any subjects can confer upon a fellow-citizen—to be freely elected for Yorkshire, upon public grounds, and being unconnected with the county. From having been at the borough the day of the election, I can give your Lordships some idea how well the system works there. You may be returned for the place, but it is at your peril that you show yourself among the inhabitants. There is a sort of polling; that is, five or six of my noble friend's tenants ride over from another part of the country—receive their burgage qualifications—vote, as the enemies of the bill call it, "in right of property," that is, of the Duke's property—render up their title-deeds—dine, and return home before night. Being detained in court at York longer than I had expected on the day of this elective proceeding, I arrived too late for the chairing, and therefore did not assist at that awful solemnity. Seeing a gentleman with a black patch, somewhere about the size of a sergeant's coif, I expressed my regret at his apparent ailment; he said, "It is for a blow I had the honor to receive in representing you at the ceremony." Certainly no constituent ever owed more to his representative than I to mine; but the blow was severe, and might well have proved fatal. I understand this is the common lot of the members, as my noble friend [Lord Tankerville], who once sat for the place, I believe, knows; though there is some variety, as he is aware, in the mode of proceed-

Not for the inhabitants of the boroughs.

ing, the convenient neighborhood of a river with a rocky channel sometimes suggesting operations of another kind. I am very far, of course, from approving such marks of public indignation; but I am equally far from wondering that it should seek a vent; for I confess, that if the thousands of persons whom the well working of the present system insults with the farce of the Knaresborough election (and whom the bill restores to their rights) were to bear so cruel a mockery with patience, I should deem them degraded indeed.

It works well, does it? For whom? For the Constitution? No such thing. For borough proprietors it works well, who can sell seats or traffic in influence, and pocket the gains. Upon the Constitution it is the foulest stain, and eats into its very core.

It works well? For the people of England? For the people, of whom the many excluded electors are parcel, and for whom alone the few actual electors ought to exercise their franchise as a trust! No such thing. As long as a member of Parliament really represents any body of his countrymen, be they freeholders, or copyholders, or leaseholders—as long as he represents the householders in any considerable town, and is in either way deputed to watch over the interests of a portion of the community, and is always answerable to those who delegate him—so long has he a participation in the interests of the whole state, whereof his constituents form a portion—so long may he justly act as representing the whole community, having, with his particular electors, only a general coincidence of views upon national questions, and a rigorous coincidence where their special interests are concerned. But if he is delegated by a single man, and not by a county or a town, he does not represent the people of England; he is a jobber, sent to Parliament to do his own or his patron's work. But then we are told, and with singular exultation, how many great men have found their way into the House of Commons by this channel. My Lords, are we, because the only road to a place is unclean, not to travel it? If I can not get into Parliament, where I may render the state good service, by any other means, I will go that way, defiling myself as little as I can, either by the filth of the passage or the indifferent company I may travel with. I won't bribe; I won't job, to get in; but if it be the only path open, I will use it for the public good. But those who indulge in this argument about great men securing seats, do not, I remark, take any account of the far greater numbers of very little men who thus find their way into Parliament to do all manner of public mischief. A few are, no doubt, independent; but many are as docile, as disciplined in the evolutions of debate, as any troops the noble Duke had at Waterloo. One borough proprietor is well remembered, who would display his forces, command them in person, carry them over from one flank to the other, or draw them off altogether, and send them to take the field against the larks at Dunstable, that he might testify his displeasure. When conflicting bodies are pretty nearly matched, the evolutions of such a corps decide the fate of the day. The noble Duke [Wellington] remembers how doubtful even the event of Waterloo might have been had Grouchy come up in time. Accordingly, the fortunate leader of that parliamentary force raised himself to an Earldom and two Lord Lieutenancies, and obtained titles and blue ribbons for others of his family, who now fill most respectable stations in this House.

Not for the people of England.

The system, we are told, works well, because, notwithstanding the manner of its election, the House of Commons sometimes concurs immediately in opinion with the people; and, in the long run, is seldom found to counteract it. Yet sometimes, and on several of the most momentous questions, the run has, indeed, been a very long one. The slave trade continued to be the signal disgrace of the country, the unutterable opprobrium of the English name, for many years after it had been denounced in Parliament, and condemned by the people all in one voice. Think you this foul stain could have so long survived, in a reformed Parliament, the prodigious eloquence of my venerable friend, Mr. Wilberforce, and the unanimous reprobation of the country? The American war might have been commenced, and even for a year or two persevered in, for, though most unnatural, it was, at first, not unpopular. But could it have lasted beyond 1778, had the voice of the people been heard in their own House? The French war, which in those days I used to think a far more natural contest, having in my youth leaned to the alarmist party, might possibly have continued some years. But if the representation of the country had been reformed, there can be no reason to doubt that the sound views of the noble Earl [Lord Grey], and the immortal eloquence of my right honorable friend [Mr. Fox], whose great spirit, now freed from the coil of this world, may be permitted to look down complacent upon the near accomplishment of his patriotic desires, would have been very differently listened to in a Parliament unbiassed by selfish interests; and of one thing I am as certain as that I stand here, that ruinous warfare never could have lasted a day beyond the arrival of Bonaparte's letter in 1800.

It is always behind public sentiment.

But still it is said public opinion finds its way more speedily into Parliament upon great and interesting emergencies. How does it so? By a mode contrary to the whole principles of representative government—by sudden, direct, and dangerous impulses. The fundamental principle of our Constitution, the great political discovery of modern times—that, indeed, which enables a state to combine extent with liberty—the system of representation, consists altogether in the perfect delegation by the people, of their rights and the care of their interests, to those who are to deliberate and to act for them. It is not a delegation which shall make the representative a mere organ of the passing will, or mo-

When that sentiment reaches Parliament, it is by undesirable means.

mentary opinion, of his constituents. I am aware, my Lords, that in pursuing this important topic, I may lay myself open to uncandid inference touching the present state of the country; but I feel sure no such unfair advantage will be taken, for my whole argument upon the national enthusiasm for reform rests upon the known fact that it is the growth of half a century, and not of a few months; and, according to the soundest views of representative legislation, there ought to be a *general* coincidence between the conduct of the delegate and the sentiments of the electors. Now, when the public voice, for want of a regular and legitimate organ, makes itself, from time to time, heard within the walls of Parliament, it is by a direct interposition of the people, not in the way of a delegated trust, to make the laws; and every such occasion presents, in truth, an instance where the defects of our elective system introduce a recurrence to the old and barbarous schemes of government, known in the tribes and centuries of Rome, or the assemblies of Attica. It is a poor compensation for the faults of a system which suffers a cruel grievance to exist, or a ruinous war to last twenty or thirty years after the public opinion has condemned it, that some occasions arise when the excess of the abuse brings about a violent remedy, or some revolutionary shock, threatening the destruction of the whole.

The petitions against the present system show it does not work well.

But it works well! Then why does the table groan with the petitions against it, of all that people, for whose interests there is any use in it working at all? Why did the country at the last election, without exception, wherever they had the franchise, return members commissioned to complain of it, and amend it? Why were its own produce, the men chosen under it, found voting against it by unexampled majorities? Of eighty-two English county members, seventy-six have pronounced sentence upon it, and they are joined by all the representatives of cities and of great towns.

The combinations not to pay taxes show how odious the system is.

It works well! Whence, then, the phenomena of Political Unions—of the people every where forming themselves into associations to put down a system which you say well serves their interests? Whence the congregating of one hundred and fifty thousand men in one place, the whole adult male population of two or three counties, to speak the language of discontent, and refuse the payment of taxes? I am one who never have either used the language of intimidation, or will ever suffer it to be used toward me; but I also am one who regard those indications with unspeakable anxiety. With all respect for those assemblages, and for the honesty of the opinions they entertain, I feel myself bound to declare, as an honest man, as a minister of the Crown, as a magistrate, nay, as standing, by virtue of my office, at the head of the magistracy, that a resolution not to pay the King's taxes is unlawful. When I contemplate the fact, I am assured that not above a few thousands of those nearest the chairman could know for what it was they held up their hands. At the same time, there is too much reason to think that the rest would have acted as they did had they heard all that passed. My hope and trust is, that these men and their leaders will maturely reconsider the subject. There are no bounds to the application of such a power; the difficulty of counteracting it is extreme; and as it may be exerted on whatever question has the leading interest, and every question in succession is felt as of exclusive importance, the use of the power I am alluding to really threatens to resolve all government, and even society itself, into its elements. I know the risk I run of giving offense by what I am saying. To me, accused of worshiping the democracy, here is, indeed, a tempting occasion, if in that charge there were the shadow of truth. Before the great idol, the Juggernaut, with his hundred and fifty thousand priests, I might prostrate myself advantageously. But I am bound to do my duty, and speak the truth; of such an assembly I can not approve; even its numbers obstruct discussion, and tend to put the peace in danger—coupled with such a combination against payment of taxes, it is illegal; it is intolerable under any form of government; and as a sincere well-wisher to the people themselves, and devoted to the cause which brought them together, I feel solicitous, on every account, to bring such proceedings to an end.

Danger of these combinations.

This danger arises from denying the people their rights.

But, my Lords, it is for us to ponder these things well; they are material facts in our present inquiry. Under a system of real representation, in a country where the people possessed the only safe and legitimate channel for making known their wishes and their complaints, a Parliament of their own choosing, such combinations would be useless. Indeed, they must always be mere *brutum fulmen*, unless where they are very general; and where they are general, they both indicate the universality of the grievance and the determination to have redress. Where no safety-valve is provided for popular discontent, to prevent an explosion that may shiver the machine in pieces—where the people, and by the people, I repeat, I mean the middle classes, the wealth and intelligence of the country, the glory of the British name—where this most important order of the community are without a regular and systematic communication with the Legislature—where they are denied the Constitution which is their birth-right, and refused a voice in naming those who are to make the laws they must obey, impose the taxes they must pay, and control, without appeal, their persons as well as properties—where they feel the load of such grievances, and feel, too, the power they possess, moral, intellectual, and, let me add, without the imputation of a threat, physical—then, and only then, are their combinations formidable; when they are armed by their wrongs, far more formidable than any physical force—then, and only then, they become invincible.

Do you ask what, in these circumstances, we ought to do? I answer, simply our duty. If there were no such combinations in existence—no symptom of popular excitement—if not a man had lifted up his voice against the existing system, we should be bound to seek and to seize any means of furthering the best interests of the people, with kindness, with consideration, with the firmness, certainly, but with the prudence, also, of statesmen. How much more are we bound to conciliate a great nation anxiously panting for their rights—to hear respectfully their prayers—to entertain the measure of their choice with an honest inclination to do it justice; and if, while we approve its principle, we yet dislike some of its details, and deem them susceptible of modification, surely we ought, at any rate, not to reject their prayers for it with insult. God forbid we should so treat the people's desire; but I do fear that a determination is taken not to entertain it with calmness and impartiality. (Cries of *No! No!* from the Opposition.) I am glad to have been in error; I am rejoiced to hear this disclaimer, for I infer from it that the people's prayers are to be granted. You will listen, I trust, to the advice of my noble and learned friend [Lord Plunkett], who, with his wonted sagacity, recommended you to do as you would be done by. This wise and Christian maxim will not, I do hope, be forgotten. Apply it, my Lords, to the case before you. Suppose, for a moment, that your Lordships, in your wisdom, should think it expedient to entertain some bill regulating matters in which this House alone has any concern, as the hereditary privileges of the peerage, or the right of voting by proxy, or matters relative to the election of peers representing the aristocracy of Ireland and Scotland, or providing against the recurrence of such an extraordinary and, indeed, unaccountable event as that which decided on the Huntingdon peerage without a committee; suppose, after great exertions of those most interested, as the Scotch and Irish peers, or this House at large, your Lordships had passed it through all its stages by immense majorities, by fifty or a hundred to one, as the Commons did the Reform. (Cries of *No.*) I say an overwhelming majority of all who represented any body, all the members for counties and towns; but, to avoid caviling, suppose it passed by a large majority of those concerned, and sent down to the Commons, whom it only remotely affected. Well—it has reached that House; and suppose the members were to refuse giving your measure any examination at all in detail, and to reject it at once. What should you say? How should you feel, think you, when the Commons arrogantly turned round from your request, and said, "Let us fling out this silly bill without more ado; true, it regulates matters belonging exclusively to the Lords, and in which we can not at all interfere without violating the law of the land; but still, out with it for an aristocratic, oligarchical, revolutionary bill—a bill to be abominated by all who have a spark of the true democratic spirit in their composition." What should you think if the measure were on such grounds got rid of, without the usual courtesy of a pretended postponement, by a vote that this Lord's bill be rejected? And should you feel much soothed by hearing that some opposition Chesterfield had taken alarm at the want of politeness among his brethren, and, at two o'clock in the morning, altered the words, retaining their offensive sense—I ask, would such proceedings in the Commons be deemed by your Lordships a fair, just, candid opposition to a measure affecting your own seats and dignities only? Would you tolerate their saying, "We don't mind the provisions of this Lord's bill; we don't stop to discuss them; we won't parley with such a thing; we plainly see it hurts our interest, and checks our own patronage; for it is an aristocratic bill, and an oligarchical bill, and withal a revolutionary bill?" Such treatment would, I doubt not, ruffle the placid tempers of your Lordships; you would say somewhat of your order, its rights, and its privileges, and buckle on the armor of a well-founded and natural indignation. But your wonder would doubtless increase if you learned that your bill had been thus contemptuously rejected in its first stage by a House in which only two members could be found who disapproved of its fundamental principles. Yes, all avow themselves friendly to the principle; it is a matter of much complaint if you charge one with not being a reformer; but they can not join in a vote which only asserts that principle, and recognizes the expediency of some reform. Yes, the Commons all allow your peerage law to be an abomination; your privileges a nuisance: all cry out for some change as necessary, as imperative; but they, nevertheless, will not even listen to the proposition for effecting a change, which you, the most interested party, have devised and sent down to them. Where, I demand, is the difference between this uncourteous and absurd treatment of your supposed bill by the Commons, and that which you talk of giving to theirs? You approve of the principle of the measure sent up by the other House, for the sole purpose of amending its own Constitution; but you won't sanction that principle by your vote, nor afford its friends an opportunity of shaping its features, so as, if possible, to meet your wishes. Is this fair? Is it candid? Is it consistent? Is it wise? Is it, I ask you, is it at this time very prudent? Did the Commons act so by you in Sir Robert Walpole's time, when the bill for restraining the creation of peers went down from hence to that House? No such thing; though it afterward turned out that there was a majority of one hundred and twelve against it, they did not even divide upon the second reading. Will you not extend an equal courtesy to the bill of the Commons and of the people?

The people must be conciliated, not treated with contempt.

I am asked what great practical benefits are to be expected from this measure? And is it no benefit to have the government strike its roots into the hearts of the people? Is it no benefit to have a calm

Practical benefits to be expected from reform.

and deliberative, but a real organ of the public opinion, by which its course may be known, and its influence exerted upon state affairs regularly and temperately, instead of acting convulsively, and, as it were, by starts and shocks? I will only appeal to one advantage, which is as certain to result from this salutary improvement of our system as it is certain that I am addressing your Lordships. A noble Earl [Lord Winchelsea] inveighed strongly against the licentiousness of the press; complained of its insolence; and asserted that there was no tyranny more intolerable than that which its conductors now exercised. It is most true that the press has great influence, but equally true that it derives this influence from expressing, more or less correctly, the opinion of the country. Let it run counter to the prevailing course, and its power is at an end. But I will also admit that, going in the same general direction with public opinion, the press is oftentimes armed with too much power in particular instances; and such power is always liable to be abused. But I will tell the noble Earl upon what foundation this overgrown power is built. The press is now the only organ of public opinion. This title it assumes; but it is not by usurpation; it is rendered legitimate by the defects of your parliamentary Constitution; it is erected upon the ruins of real representation. The periodical press is the rival of the House of Commons; and it is, and it will be, the successful rival, as long as that House does not represent the people—but not one day longer. If ever I felt confident in any prediction, it is in this, that the restoration of Parliament to its legitimate office of representing truly the public opinion will overthrow the tyranny of which noble Lords are so ready to complain, who, by keeping out the lawful sovereign, in truth support the usurper. It is you who have placed this unlawful authority on a rock: pass the bill, it is built on a quicksand. Let but the country have a full and free representation, and to that will men look for the expression of public opinion, and the press will no more be able to dictate, as now, when none else can speak the sense of the people. Will its influence wholly cease? God forbid! Its just influence will continue, but confined within safe and proper bounds. It will continue, long may it continue, to watch the conduct of public men—to watch the proceedings even of a reformed Legislature—to watch the people themselves—a safe, an innoxious, a useful instrument, to enlighten and improve mankind! But its overgrown power—its assumption to speak in the name of the nation—its pretension to dictate and to command, will cease with the abuse upon which alone it is founded, and will be swept away, together with the other creatures of the same abuse, which now "fright our isle from its propriety."

Those portentous appearances, the growth of later times, those figures that stalk abroad, of unknown stature and strange form—unions of leagues, and musterings of men in myriads, and conspiracies against the exchequer; whence do they spring, and how come they to haunt our shores? What power engendered those uncouth shapes, what multiplied the monstrous births till they people the land? Trust me, the same power which called into frightful existence, and armed with resistless force the Irish Volunteers of 1782—the same power which rent in twain your empire, and raised up thirteen republics—the same power which created the Catholic Association, and gave it Ireland for a portion. What power is that? Justice denied—rights withheld—wrongs perpetrated—the force which common injuries lend to millions—the wickedness of using the sacred trust of government as a means of indulging private caprice—the idiotcy of treating Englishmen like the children of the South Sea Islands—the frenzy of believing, or making believe, that the adults of the nineteenth century can be led like children, or driven like barbarians! This it is that has conjured up the strange sights at which we now stand aghast! And shall we persist in the fatal error of combating the giant progeny, instead of extirpating the execrable parent? Good God! Will men never learn wisdom, even from their own experience? Will they never believe, till it be too late, that the surest way to prevent immoderate desires being formed, ay, and unjust demands enforced, is to grant in due season the moderate requests of justice? You stand, my Lords, on the brink of a great event; you are in the crisis of a whole nation's hopes and fears. An awful importance hangs over your decision. Pause, ere you plunge! There may not be any retreat! It behooves you to shape your conduct by the mighty occasion. They tell you not to be afraid of personal consequences in discharging your duty. I too would ask you to banish all fears; but, above all, that most mischievous, most despicable fear—the fear of being thought afraid. If you won't take counsel from me, take example from the statesman-like conduct of the noble Duke [Wellington], while you also look back, as you may, with satisfaction upon your own. He was told, and you were told, that the impatience of Ireland for equality of civil rights was partial, the clamor transient, likely to pass away with its temporary occasion, and that yielding to it would be conceding to intimidation. I recollect hearing this topic urged within this hall in July, 1828; less regularly I heard it than I have now done, for I belonged not to your number—but I heard it urged in the self-same terms. The burden of the cry was—it is no time for concession; the people are turbulent, and the Association dangerous. That summer passed, and the ferment subsided not; autumn came, but brought not the precious fruit of peace—on the contrary, all Ireland was convulsed with the unprecedented conflict which returned the great chief of the Catholics to sit in a Protestant Parliament; winter bound the earth in chains, but it controlled not the popular fury, whose surge, more deafening than the tempest, lashed the frail bulwarks of law founded upon

All the evils experienced in Ireland may be expected in England, if these rights are withheld.

injustice. Spring came; but no ethereal mildness was its harbinger, or followed in its train; the Catholics became stronger by every month's delay, displayed a deadlier resolution, and proclaimed their wrongs in a tone of louder defiance than before. And what course did you, at this moment of greatest excitement, and peril, and menace, deem it most fitting to pursue? Eight months before, you had been told how unworthy it would be to yield when men clamored and threatened. No change had happened in the interval, save that the clamors were become far more deafening, and the threats, beyond comparison, more overbearing. What, nevertheless, did your Lordships do? Your duty; for you despised the cuckoo-note of the season, "be not intimidated." You granted all that the Irish demanded, and you saved your country. Was there in April a single argument advanced which had not held good in July? None, absolutely none, except the new height to which the dangers of longer delay had risen, and the increased vehemence with which justice was demanded; and yet the appeal to your pride, which had prevailed in July, was in vain made in April, and you wisely and patriotically granted what was asked, and ran the risk of being supposed to yield through fear.

Delay will only aggravate the evil.

But the history of the Catholic claims conveys another important lesson. Though in right, and policy, and justice, the measure of relief could not be too ample, half as much as was received with little gratitude when so late wrung from you, would have been hailed twenty years before with delight; and, even the July preceding, the measure would have been received as a boon freely given, which, I fear, was taken with but sullen satisfaction in April, as a right long withheld. Yet, blessed be God, the debt of justice, though tardily, was at length paid, and the noble Duke won by it civic honors which rival his warlike achievements in lasting brightness—than which there can be no higher praise. What, if he had still listened to the topics of intimidation and inconsistency which had scared his predecessors? He might have proved his obstinacy, and Ireland would have been the sacrifice.

The aristocracy can not afford to alienate the minds of the people.

Apply now this lesson of recent history—I may say of our own experience to the measure before us. We stand in a truly critical position. If we reject the bill, through fear of being thought to be intimidated, we may lead the life of retirement and quiet, but the hearts of the millions of our fellow-citizens are gone forever; their affections are estranged; we and our order and its privileges are the objects of the people's hatred, as the only obstacles which stand between them and the gratification of their most passionate desire. The whole body of the aristocracy must expect to share this fate, and be exposed to feelings such as these. For I hear it constantly said that the bill is rejected by all the aristocracy. Favor, and a good number of supporters, our adversaries allow it has among the people; the ministers, too, are for it; but the aristocracy, say they, is strenuously opposed to it. I broadly deny this silly, thoughtless assertion. What, my Lords! the aristocracy set themselves in a mass against the people—they who sprang from the people—are inseparably connected with the people—are supported by the people—are the natural chiefs of the people! *They* set themselves against the people, for whom peers are ennobled—bishops consecrated—Kings anointed—the people to serve whom Parliament itself has an existence, and the monarchy and all its institutions are constituted, and without whom none of them could exist for an hour! The assertion of unreflecting men is too monstrous to be endured—as a member of this House, I deny it with indignation. I repel it with scorn, as a calumny upon us all. And yet there are those who even within these walls speak of the bill augmenting so much the strength of the democracy as to endanger the other orders of the state; and so they charge its authors with promoting anarchy and rapine. Why, my Lords, have its authors nothing to fear from democratic spoliation? The fact is, that there are members of the present cabinet, who possess, one or two of them alone, far more property than any two administrations within my recollection; and all of them have ample wealth. I need hardly say, I include not myself, who have little or none. But even of myself I will say, that whatever I have depends on the stability of existing institutions; and it is as dear to me as the princely possessions of any among you. Permit me to say, that, in becoming a member of your House, I staked my all on the aristocratic institutions of the state. I abandoned certain wealth, a large income, and much real power in the state, for an office of great trouble, heavy responsibility, and very uncertain duration. I say, I gave up substantial power for the shadow of it, and for distinction depending upon accident. I quitted the elevated station of representative for Yorkshire, and a leading member of the Commons. I descended from a position quite lofty enough to gratify any man's ambition, and my lot became bound up in the stability of this House. Then, have I not a right to throw myself on your justice, and to desire that you will not put in jeopardy all I have now left?

It is not the rabble alone who are in favor of the bill.

But the populace only, the rabble, the ignoble vulgar, are for the bill! Then what is the Duke of Norfolk, Earl Marshal of England? What the Duke of Devonshire? What the Duke of Bedford? (Cries of *order* from the Opposition.) I am aware it is irregular in any noble Lord that is a friend to the measure; its adversaries are patiently suffered to call peers even by their Christian and surnames. Then I shall be as regular as they were, and ask, Does my friend John Russell, my friend William Cavendish, my friend Harry Vane, belong to the mob, or to the aristocracy? Have they no possessions? Are they modern names? Are they wanting in Norman blood, or whatever else you pride yourselves on? The idea is too ludicrous to be seriously refuted; that the bill is only a favorite with the democracy, is a delusion so wild as to point a man's destiny toward St. Luke's. Yet many, both here and elsewhere, by dint of constantly repeating the same cry, or hearing it repeated, have almost made themselves believe that none of the nobility are for the measure. A noble friend of mine has had the curiosity to examine the list of peers, opposing and supporting it, with respect to the dates of their creation, and the result is somewhat remarkable. A large majority of the peers, created before Mr. Pitt's time, are for the bill; the bulk of those against it are of recent creation; and if you divide the whole into two classes, those ennobled before the reign of George III. and those since, of the former, fifty-six are friends, and only twenty-one enemies of the reform. So much for the vain and saucy boast that the real nobility of the country are against reform. I have dwelt upon this matter more than its intrinsic importance deserves, only through my desire to set right the fact, and to vindicate the ancient aristocracy from a most groundless imputation.

Peroration: Danger of delay.

My Lords, I do not disguise the intense solicitude which I feel for the event of this debate, because I know full well that the peace of the country is involved in the issue. I can not look without dismay at the rejection of the measure. But grievous as may be the consequences of a temporary defeat—temporary it can only be; for its ultimate, and even speedy success, is certain. Nothing can now stop it. Do not suffer yourselves to be persuaded that even if the present ministers were driven from the helm, any one could steer you through the troubles which surround you without reform. But our successors would take up the task in circumstances far less auspicious. Under them, you would be fain to grant a bill, compared with which the one we now proffer you is moderate indeed. Hear the parable of the Sibyl; for it conveys a wise and wholesome moral. She now appears at your gate, and offers you mildly the volumes—the precious volumes—of wisdom and peace. The price she asks is reasonable; to restore the franchise, which, without any bargain, you ought voluntarily to give; you refuse her terms—her moderate terms—she darkens the porch no longer. But soon, for you can not do without her wares, you call her back; again she comes, but with diminished treasures; the leaves of the book are in part torn away by lawless hands—in part defaced with characters of blood. But the prophetic maid had risen in her demands—it is Parliaments by the year—it is vote by the ballot—it is suffrage by the million! From this you turn away indignant, and for the second time she departs. Beware of her third coming; for the treasure you must have; and what price she may next demand, who shall tell? It may even be the mace which rests upon that wool-sack. What may follow your course of obstinacy, if persisted in, I can not take upon me to predict, nor do I wish to conjecture. But this I know full well, that, as sure as man is mortal, and to err is human, justice deferred enhances the price at which you must purchase safety and peace; nor can you expect to gather in another crop than they did who went before you, if you persevere in their utterly abominable husbandry, of sowing injustice and reaping rebellion.

But among the awful considerations that now bow down my mind, there is one which stands pre-eminent above the rest. You are the highest judicature in the realm; you sit here as judges, and decide all causes, civil and criminal, without appeal. It is a judge's first duty never to pronounce sentence in the most trifling case without hearing. Will you make this the exception? Are you really prepared to determine, but not to *hear*, the mighty cause upon which a nation's hopes and fears hang? You are. Then beware of your decision! Rouse not, I beseech you, a peace-loving, but a resolute people; alienate not from your body the affections of a whole empire. As your friend, as the friend of my order, as the friend of my country, as the faithful servant of my Sovereign, I counsel you to assist with your uttermost efforts in preserving the peace, and upholding and perpetuating the Constitution. Therefore, I pray and exhort you not to reject this measure. By all you hold most dear—by all the ties that bind every one of us to our common order and our common country, I solemnly adjure you—I warn you—I implore you—yea, on *my bended knees*, I supplicate you—reject not this bill!

So completely had Lord Brougham wrought up his own feelings and those of his hearers at the close of this speech, that it was nothing strained or unnatural—it was, in fact, almost a matter of course—for him to sink down upon one of his knees at the table where he stood, when he uttered the last words, "I *supplicate* you—reject not this bill!" But the sacrifice was too great a one for that proud nobility to make at once, and the bill was rejected by a majority of *forty-one*, of whom *twenty-one* belonged to the board of bishops of the Established Church.

The question, "*What will the Lords do?*" which had agitated and divided the public mind for some months, was now answered, and a burst of wounded and indignant feeling followed throughout the whole country. The London papers were many of them arrayed in mourning; some of the Lords who had opposed the bill were assaulted by the populace in the streets; others were burned in effigy in the neighborhoods where they lived; riots took place in many of the large towns, at which the property of the anti-Reformers was destroyed; and in the vicinity of Nottingham the ancient palace of the Duke of Newcastle was consumed by fire. The great body of the nation, while they disapproved of these excesses, were wrought up to the highest pitch of determination that, *come what might, the bill should be carried*. Public meetings, embracing a large part of the entire population, were held in all parts of the kingdom, and men of the highest standing and ability came forward to form them into one compact body, with the King in their midst, to press with the united force of millions on the House of Lords. Before such an array the aristocracy of England, for the first time, with all its wealth, and talent, and hereditary claims on the respect of the people, were seen to be utterly powerless. They were even treated with contempt. "The efforts of the Lords to stop the progress of reform," said the Rev. Sydney Smith at the Taunton meeting, "reminds me very forcibly of the great storm at Sidmouth, and of the conduct of the excellent *Mrs. Partington* on that occasion. In the winter of 1824, there set in a great flood upon that town; the tide rose to an incredible height, the waves rushed in upon the houses, and every thing was threatened with destruction. In the midst of this sublime and terrible storm, Dame Partington, who lived upon the beach, was seen at the door of her house with mop and pattens, trundling her mop, squeezing out the sea-water, and vigorously pushing away the Atlantic Ocean. The Atlantic was roused, Mrs. Partington's spirit was up, but I need not tell you that the contest was unequal. The Atlantic Ocean beat Mrs. Partington. She was excellent at a slop or a puddle, but she should not have meddled with a tempest. Gentlemen, be at your ease—be quiet and steady. You will beat Mrs. Partington."[8]

On the 12th of December, 1831, the bill was introduced into the House of Commons for the *third* time, and was passed by a majority of one hundred and sixty-two; but was rejected in the House of Lords on the 7th of May, 1832, by a majority of *thirty-nine*. The ministry instantly resigned, and the King, after an ineffectual effort to form another, invited them back, on the condition that he would *create enough new Lords to carry through the bill*. This ended the contest. To escape such an indignity, a large number of the anti-Reformers signified their intention of being absent when the bill came up anew, and it finally passed the Upper House on the 4th of June, 1832, by a vote of 106 to 22.

INAUGURAL DISCOURSE

OF MR. BROUGHAM WHEN ELECTED LORD RECTOR OF THE UNIVERSITY OF GLASGOW DELIVERED APRIL 6, 1825.

INTRODUCTION.

At Glasgow a Lord Rector is annually chosen by a major vote of the members of the University. The station is simply one of honor, like that of Chancellor in the English Universities, involving no share in the government or instruction, and is usually awarded to some public man who has a distinguished name in literature or politics.

When inducted into office, the Lord Rector returns thanks in an address which is usually short, as a mere matter of form and compliment, expressing his sense of the honor conferred, and his best wishes for the prosperity of the institution. Lord Brougham, however, when called to this office, took a different course. He prepared an elaborate address on "*the study of the Rhetorical Art, and the purposes to which a proficiency in this art should be made subservient.*" He urges the study of rhetoric, however, not in mere treatises on the subject, but (as in the case of the sculptor and painter) in the direct study of the great productions of the art itself, and especially of the Greek orators; of whom he affirms, "the works of the English chisel fall not more short of the wonders of the Acropolis, than the best productions of modern pens fall short of the chaste, finished, nervous, and overwhelming compositions of them "that fulmined over Greece." The discourse is full of striking remarks, many of them of great value as the result of the author's own experience, and it therefore forms a very appropriate close to this volume. One fact respecting it is certainly remarkable, that, containing so many and such extended quotations, it was written not at home among his books, but "during the business of the Northern Circuit."

DISCOURSE, &c.

It now becomes me to return my very sincere and respectful thanks for the kindness which has placed me in a chair filled at former times by so many great men, whose names might well make any comparison formidable to a far more worthy successor.

Reasons for a more extended address than usual.

While I desire you to accept this unexaggerated expression of gratitude, I am anxious to address you rather in the form which I now adopt, than in the more usual one of an unpremeditated discourse. I shall thus at least prove that the remarks which I deem it my duty to make are the fruit of mature reflection, and that I am unwilling to discharge an important office in a perfunctory manner.

Transition: Motives for diligence in a college life.

I feel very sensibly that if I shall now urge you by general exhortations to be instant in the pursuit of the learning which, in all its branches, flourishes under the kindly shelter of these roofs, I may weary you with the unprofitable repetition of a thrice-told tale; and if I presume to offer my advice touching the conduct of your studies, I may seem to trespass upon the province of those venerable persons under whose care you have the singular happiness to be placed. But I would nevertheless expose myself to either charge, for the sake of joining my voice with

8 It scarcely need be said that this mention of the good lady gave rise to the frequent occurrence of her name in the newspapers of the present day.

theirs in anxiously entreating you to believe how incomparably the present season is verily and indeed the most precious of your whole lives. It is not the less true, because it has been oftentimes said, that the period of youth is by far the best fitted for the improvement of the mind, and the retirement of a college almost exclusively adapted to much study. At your enviable age every thing has the lively interest of novelty and freshness; attention is perpetually sharpened by curiosity; and the memory is tenacious of the deep impressions it thus receives, to a degree unknown in after life; while the distracting cares of the world, or its beguiling pleasures, cross not the threshold of these calm retreats; its distant noise and bustle are faintly heard, making the shelter you enjoy more grateful; and the struggles of anxious mortals embarked upon that troublous sea are viewed from an eminence, the security of which is rendered more sweet by the prospect of the scene below. Yet a little while, and you too will be plunged into those waters of bitterness; and will cast an eye of regret, as now I do, upon the peaceful regions you have quitted forever. Such is your lot as members of society; but it will be your own fault if you look back on this place with repentance or with shame; and be well assured that, whatever time—ay, every hour—you squander here on unprofitable idling, will then rise up against you, and be paid for by years of bitter but unavailing regrets. Study, then, I beseech you, so to store your minds with the exquisite learning of former ages, that you may always possess within yourselves sources of rational and refined enjoyment, which will enable you to set at naught the grosser pleasures of sense, whereof other men are slaves; and so imbue yourselves with the sound philosophy of later days, forming yourselves to the virtuous habits which are its legitimate offspring, that you may walk unhurt through the trials which await you, and may look down upon the ignorance and error that surround you, not with lofty and supercilious contempt, as the sages of old times, but with the vehement desire of enlightening those who wander in darkness, and who are by so much the more endeared to us by how much they want our assistance.

Subject: The study of Rhetoric and its proper applications.

Assuming the improvement of his own mind and of the lot of his fellow-creatures to be the great end of every man's existence, who is removed above the care of providing for his sustenance, and to be the indispensable duty of every man, as far as his own immediate wants leave him any portion of time unemployed, our attention is naturally directed to the means by which so great and urgent a work may best be performed; and as in the limited time allotted to this discourse, I can not hope to occupy more than a small portion of so wide a field, I shall confine myself to two subjects, or rather to a few observations upon two subjects, both of them appropriate to this place, but either of them affording ample materials for an entire course of lectures—the study of the rhetorical art, by which useful truths are promulgated with effect, and the purposes to which a proficiency in this art should be made subservient.

Part First. The study of Rhetoric. This should be pursued chiefly among the Greek orators.

It is an extremely common error among young persons, impatient of academical discipline, to turn from the painful study of ancient, and particularly of Attic composition, and solace themselves with works rendered easy by the familiarity of their own tongue. They plausibly contend, that as powerful or captivating diction in a pure English style is, after all, the attainment they are in search of, the study of the best English models affords the shortest road to this point; and even admitting the ancient examples to have been the great fountains from which all eloquence is drawn, they would rather profit, as it were, by the classical labors of their English predecessors, than toil over the same path themselves. In a word, they would treat the perishable results of those labors as the standard, and give themselves no care about the immortal originals. This argument, the thin covering which indolence weaves for herself, would speedily sink all the fine arts into barrenness and insignificance. Why, according to such reasoners, should a sculptor or painter encounter the toil of a journey to Athens or to Rome? Far better work at home, and profit by the labor of those who have resorted to the Vatican and the Parthenon, and founded an English school adapted to the taste of our own country. Be you assured that the works of the English chisel fall not more short of the wonders of the Acropolis, than the best productions of modern pens fall short of the chaste, finished, nervous, and overwhelming compositions of them that "resistless fulmined over Greece." Be equally sure that, with hardly any exception, the great things of poetry and of eloquence have been done by men who cultivated the mighty exemplars of Athenian genius with daily and with nightly devotion. Among poets there is hardly an exception to this rule, unless may be so deemed Shakspeare, an exception to all rules, and Dante, familiar as a cotemporary with the works of Roman art, composed in his mother tongue, having taken, not so much for his guide as for his "master,' Virgil, himself almost a translator from the Greeks. But among orators I know of none among the Romans, and scarce any in our own times. Cicero honored the Greek masters with such singular observance, that he not only repaired to Athens for the sake of finishing his rhetorical education, but afterward continued to practice the art of declaiming in Greek; and although he afterward fell into a less pure manner through the corrupt blandishments of the Asian taste, yet do we find him ever prone to extol the noble perfections of his first masters, as something placed beyond the reach of all imitation. Nay, at a mature period of his life, he occupied himself in translating the greater orations of the

Inferiority of all English models.

Testimony of Cicero to the pre-eminence of Greek oratory.

Greeks, which composed almost exclusively his treatise "*De optimo genere Oratoris;*" as if to write a discourse on oratorial perfection were merely to present the reader with the two immortal speeches upon the Crown. Sometimes we find him imitating, even to a literal version, the beauties of those divine originals—as the beautiful passage of Æschines, in the Timarchus, upon the torments of the guilty, which the Roman orator has twice made use of, almost word for word; once in the oration for Sextus Roscius, the earliest he delivered, and again in a more mature effort of his genius, the oration against L. Piso.[1]

Inferiority of Roman eloquence as a model.

I have dwelt the rather upon the authority of M. Tullius, because it enables us at once to answer the question, Whether a study of the Roman orators be not sufficient for refining the taste? If the Greeks were the models of an excellence which the first of Roman orators never attained, although ever aspiring after it—nay, if so far from being satisfied with his own success, he even in those his masters found something which his ears desiderated (ita sunt avidæ et capaces; et semper aliquid immensum infinitumque desiderant [so eager are they and capacious, so continually desirous of something boundless and infinite])[2]—he either fell short while copying them, or he failed by diverting his worship to the false gods of the Asian school. In the one case, were we to rest satisfied with studying the Roman, we should only be imitating the imperfect copy, instead of the pure original—like him who should endeavor to catch a glimpse of some beauty by her reflection in a glass, that weakened her tints, if it did not distort her features. In the other case, we should not be imitating the same, but some less perfect original, and looking at the wrong beauty; not her whose chaste and simple attractions commanded the adoration of all Greece, but some garish damsel from Rhodes or Chios, just brilliant and languishing enough to captivate the less pure taste of half-civilized Rome.

The style and manner of Cicero not suited to the present day.

But there are other reasons too weighty to be passed over, which justify the same decided preference. Not to mention the incomparable beauty and power of the Greek language, the study of which alone affords the means of enriching our own, the compositions of Cicero, exquisite as they are for beauty of diction, often remarkable for ingenious argument and brilliant wit, not seldom excelling in deep pathos, are nevertheless so extremely rhetorical, fashioned by an art so little concealed, and sacrificing the subject to a display of the speaker's powers, admirable as those are, that nothing can be less adapted to the genius of modern elocution, which requires a constant and almost exclusive attention to the business in hand. In all his orations which were spoken (for, singular as it may seem, the remark applies less to those which were only written, as all the Verrine, except the first, all the Philippics, except the first and ninth, and the Pro Milone) hardly two pages can be found which a modern assembly would bear. Some admirable arguments on evidence, and the credit of witnesses, might be urged to a jury;[3] several passages, given by him on the merits of the case, and in defense against the charge, might be spoken in mitigation of punishment after a conviction or confession of guilt; but, whether we regard the political or forensic orations, the style, both in respect of the reasoning and the ornaments, is wholly unfit for the more severe and less trifling nature of modern affairs in the Senate or at he bar. Now it is altogether otherwise with the Greek masters. Changing a few phrases, which the difference of religion and of manners might render objectionable—moderating, in some degree, the virulence of invective, especially against private character, to suit the chivalrous courtesy of modern hostility—there is hardly one of the political or forensic orations of the Greeks that

That of the Greeks perfectly adapted to modern times.

[1] *Μὴ γὰρ οἴεσθε, τὰς τῶν ἀδικημάτων ἀρχὰς ἀπό θεῶν, ἀλλ' οὐχ ὑπ' ἀνθρώπων ἀσελγείας γίνεσθαι· μηδὲ τοὺς ἠσεβηκότας, καθάπερ ἐν ταῖς τραγῳδίαις, Ποινὰς ἐλαύνειν καὶ κολάζειν δασὶν ἡμμέναις· ἀλλ' αἱ προπετεῖς τοῦ σώματος ἡδοναί, καὶ τὸ μηδὲν ἱκανὸν ἡγεῖσθαι, ταῦτα πληροῖ τὰ λῃστήρια—ταῦτ' εἰς τὸν ἐπακτροκέλητα ἐμβιβάζει—ταῦτά ἐστιν ἑκάστῳ Ποινή, κ. τ. λ.*—'ΑΙΣΧΙΝ. *κατὰ Τιμάρχου.* Let no one think that crimes arise from the instigation of the gods, and not from the rash intemperance of men; or that the profane are driven and chastized, as we see them on the stage, by furies with blazing torches. The eager lusts of the flesh, and the insatiable desire for more—these swell the ranks of the robber, and crowd the deck of the pirate—these are to every one his own fury!

Nolite enim putare, quemadmodum in fabulis sæpenumero videtis, eos, qui aliquid impie scelerateque commiserint, agitari et perterreri Furiarum tædis ardentibus. Sua quemque fraus, et suus terror maxime vexat; suum quemque scelus agitat, amentiaque afficit; suæ malæ cogitationes conscientiæque animi terrent. Hæ sunt impiis assiduæ domesticæque Furiæ; quæ dies noctesque parentum pœnas a consceleratissimis filiis repetant.—*Pro Sexto Roscio Amerino.*

Nolite enim putare, ut in scena videtis, homines consceleratos impulsu deorum terreri Furiarum tædis ardentibus. Sua quemque fraus, suum facinus—suum scelus—sua audacia, de sanitate ac mente deturbat. Hæ sunt impiorum Furiæ—hæ flammæ—hæ faces.—*In Luc. Calp. Pisonem.*

The great improvement in Cicero's taste between the first and the second of these compositions is manifest, and his closer adherence to the original. He introduces the same idea, and in very similar language, in the Treatise *De Legg.*, Lib. 1.—*Brougham.*

[2] Orator., c. 29.

[3] There is a singular example of this in the remarks on the evidence and cross-examination in the oration for L. Flaccus, pointed out to me by my friend Mr. Scarlett (now Lord Abinger), the mention of whose name affords an illustration of my argument, for, as a more consummate master of the forensic art in all its branches never lived, so no man is more conversant with the works of his predecessors in ancient times. Lord Erskine, too, perhaps the first of judicial orators, ancient or modern, had well studied the noble remains of the classic age.—*Brougham*

might not be delivered in similar circumstances before our Senate or tribunals; while their funeral and other panegyrical discourses are much less inflated and unsubstantial than those of the most approved masters of the epideictic style, the French preachers and academicians. Whence this difference between the master-pieces of Greek and Roman eloquence? Whence but from the rigid steadiness with which the Greek orator keeps the object of all eloquence perpetually in view, never speaking for mere speaking's sake; while the Latin rhetorician, "*ingenii sui nimium amator*" [too fond of his own ingenuity], and, as though he deemed his occupation a trial of skill or display of accomplishments, seems ever and anon to lose sight of the subject-matter in the attempt to illustrate and adorn it; and pours forth passages sweet indeed, but unprofitable—fitted to tickle the ear, without reaching the heart. Where, in all the orations of Cicero, or of him who almost equals him, Livy, "*miræ facundiæ homo*" [admirable for his command of language],[4] shall we find any thing like those thick successions of short questions in which Demosthenes oftentimes forges, as it were, with a few rapidly following strokes, the whole massive chain of his argument; as in the Chersonese, *Εἰ δ' ἅπαξ διαφθαρήσεται καὶ διαλυθήσεται, τί ποιήσομεν, ἂν ἐπὶ Χεῤῥόνησον ἴῃ; κρινοῦμεν Διοπείθην; νὴ Δία. Καὶ τί τὰ πράγματα ἔσται βελτίω; ἀλλ' ἐνθένδε βοηθήσομεν αὐτοῖς· ἂν δ' ὑπὸ τῶν πνευμάτων μὴ δυνώμεθα; ἀλλὰ μὰ Δί' οὐχ ἥξει· καὶ τίς ἐγγυητής ἐστι τούτου;* [Let this force be once destroyed or scattered, and what are we to do if Philip marches on the Chersonese? Put Diopeithes on his trial? But how will that better our condition? And how shall we send them succor if prevented by the winds? But, by Jupiter, he will *not march!* And who is our surety for that?] or, comprising all of a long narrative that suits his argument in a single sentence, presenting a lengthened series of events at a single glance; as in the *Παραπρεσβεία*: *Πέντε γὰρ γεγόνασιν ἡμέραι μόναι, ἐν αἷς—οὗτος ἀπήγγειλε τὰ ψευδῆ—ὑμεῖς ἐπιστεύσατε—οἱ Φωκεῖς ἐπύθοντο—ἐνέδωκαν ἑαυτοὺς—ἀπώλοντο.* [There were only five days in which this man (Eschines, who had been sent as an embassador) brought back those lies—you believed—the Phocians listened—gave themselves up—*perished!*]

Qualities in which it surpasses the best specimens of modern debate.

But though the more business-like manner of modern debate approaches much nearer the style of the Greek than the Latin compositions, it must be admitted that it falls short of the great originals in the closeness, and, as it were, density of the argument; in the habitual sacrifice of all ornament to use, or rather in the constant union of the two; so that, while a modern orator too frequently has his speech parceled out into compartments, one devoted to argument, another to declamation, a third to mere ornament, as if he should say, "Now your reason shall be convinced; now I am going to rouse your passions; and now you shall see how I can amuse your fancy," the more vigorous ancient argued in declaiming, and made his very boldest figures subservient to, or rather an integral part of his reasoning. The most figurative and highly wrought passage in all antiquity is the famous oath in Demosthenes; yet, in the most pathetic part of it, and when he seems to have left the furthest behind him the immediate subject of his speech, led away by the prodigious interest of the recollections he has excited; when he is naming the very tombs where the heroes of Marathon lie buried, he instantly, not abruptly, but by a most felicitous and easy transition, returns into the midst of the main argument of his whole defense—that the merits of public servants, not the success of their councils, should be the measure of the public gratitude toward them—a position that runs through the whole speech, and to which he makes the funeral honors bestowed alike on all the heroes, serve as a striking and appropriate support. With the same ease does Virgil manage his celebrated transition in the Georgics; where, in the midst of the Thracian war, and while at an immeasurable distance from agricultural topics, the magician strikes the ground on the field of battle, where helmets are buried, and suddenly raises before us the lonely husbandman, in a remote age, peacefully tilling its soil, and driving his plow among the rusty armor and moldering remains of the warrior.[5]

The admirable variety of its topics.

But if a further reason is required for giving the preference to the Greek orators, we may find it in the greater diversity and importance of the subjects upon which their speeches were delivered. Besides the number of admirable orations and of written arguments upon causes merely forensic, we have every subject of public policy, all the great affairs of state, successively forming the topics of discussion. Compare them with Cicero in this particular, and the contrast is striking. His finest oration for matter and diction together is in defense of an individual charged with murder, and there is nothing in the case to give it a public interest, except that the parties were of opposite factions in the state, and the deceased a personal as well as political adversary of the speaker. His most exquisite performance in point of diction, perhaps the most perfect prose composition in the language, was addressed to one man, in palliation of another's having borne arms against him in a war with a personal rival. Even the Catilinarians, his most splendid decla-

[4] Quintilian.

[5] Georgicon, i., 493:

Scilicet et tempus veniet, cum finibus illis
Agricola, incurvo terram molitus aratro,
Exesa inveniet scabrâ rubigine pila:
Aut gravibus rastris galeas pulsabit inanes.
Grandiáque effossis mirabitur ossa sepulcris.

The time shall come when in these borders round,
The swain who turns the soil with crooked plow,
Shall javelins find, and spears eaten with rust;
Or with his harrows strike on empty helmets,
And see with wonder the gigantic bones
Of opened graves.

mations, are principally denunciations of a single conspirator; the Philippics, his most brilliant invectives, abuse of a profligate leader; and the Verrine orations, charges against an individual governor. Many, indeed almost all the subjects of his speeches, rise to the rank of what the French term *Causes célèbres;* but they seldom rise higher.[6] Of Demosthenes, on the other hand, we have not only many arguments upon cases strictly private, and relating to pecuniary matters (those generally called the Ἰδιωτικοὶ), and many upon interesting subjects, more nearly approaching public questions; as the speech against Midias, which relates to an assault on the speaker, but excels in spirit and vehemence, perhaps, all his other efforts; and some which, though personal, involve high considerations of public policy, as that most beautiful and energetic speech against Aristocrates; but we have all his immortal orations upon the state affairs of Greece—the Περὶ Στεφάνου, embracing the history of a twenty years' administration during the most critical period of Grecian story; and the Philippics, discussing every question of foreign policy, and of the stand to be made by the civilized world against the encroachments of the barbarians. Those speeches were delivered upon subjects the most important and affecting that could be conceived to the whole community; the topics handled in them were of universal application and of perpetual interest. To introduce a general observation, the Latin orator must quit the immediate course of his argument; he must for a moment lose sight of the object in view. But the Athenian can hardly hold too lofty a tone, or carry his view too extensively over the map of human affairs, for the vast range of his subject—the fates of the whole commonwealth of Greece, and the stand to be made by free and polished nations against barbaric tyrants.

After forming and chastening the taste by a diligent study of those perfect models, it is necessary to acquire correct habits of composition in our own language, first by studying the best writers, and next by translating copiously into it from the Greek. This is by far the best exercise that I am acquainted with for at once attaining a pure English diction, and avoiding the tameness and regularity of modern composition. But the English writers who really unlock the rich sources of the language are those who flourished from the end of Elizabeth's to the end of Queen Anne's reign; who used a good Saxon dialect with ease, but correctness and perspicuity—learned in the ancient classics, but only enriching their mother tongue where the Attic could supply its defects—not overlaying it with a profuse pedantic coinage of foreign words — well practiced in the old rules of composition, or rather collocation (σύνθεσις), which unite natural ease and variety

Practice in composition.

(1.) With a diligent study of the old English writers.

[6] The cause of this difference between the Greek and Roman orators has been so strikingly described by a learned friend of mine, in the following note upon the above passage, that the celebrity of his name, were I at liberty to mention it, is not required to attract the reader's notice. "In Athens," says he, "an incessant struggle for independence, for power, or for liberty, could not fail to rouse the genius of every citizen—to force the highest talent to the highest station—to animate her councils with a holy zeal—and to afford to her orators all that, according to the profoundest writers of antiquity, is necessary to the sublimest strains of eloquence. 'Magna eloquentia sicut flamma materia alitur, a motibus excitatur, urendo clarescit.' Hers were not the holiday contests of men who sought to dazzle by the splendor of their diction, the grace of their delivery, the propriety and richness of their imagery. Her debates were on the most serious business which can agitate men—the preservation of national liberty, honor, independence, and glory. The gifts of genius and the perfection of art shed, indeed, a luster upon the most vigorous exertions of her orators—but the object of their thunders was to stir the energies of the men of Athens, and to make tyrants tremble, or rivals despair. Rome, on the other hand, mistress of the world, at the time when she was most distinguished by genius and eloquence, owned no superior, hated no rival, dreaded no equal. Nations sought her protection, Kings bowed before her majesty; the bosom of her sole dominion was disturbed by no struggle for national power, no alarm of foreign danger. While she maintained the authority of her laws over the civilized earth, and embraced under the flattering name of allies those who could no longer resist her arms, the revolt of a barbarian King, or the contests of bordering nations with each other, prolonged only till she had decided between them, served to amuse her citizens or her Senate, without affecting their tranquillity. Her government, though essentially free, was not so popular as the Athenian. The severity of her discipline, and the gravity of her manners, disposed her citizens less to those sudden and powerful emotions which both excited and followed the efforts of the Greek orators. It seems, therefore, reasonable to conclude that the character of Roman eloquence would be distinguished more by art than by passion, by science than by nature. The divisions and animosities of party, no doubt, would operate, and did operate with their accustomed force. But these are not like the generous flame which animates a whole nation to defend its liberty or its honor. The discussion of a law upon which the national safety could not depend, the question whether this or that general should take the command of an army, whether this or that province should be allotted to a particular minister, whether the petition of a city to be admitted to the privileges of Roman citizens should be granted, or whether some concession should be made to a suppliant King; these, with the exception of the debates on the Catiline conspiracy, and one or two of the Philippics, form the subjects of a public nature, on which the mighty genius and consummate art of Cicero were bestowed. We are not, therefore, surprised to find that those of his orations in which he bears the best comparison with his rival Demosthenes were delivered in the forum in private causes. In some of these may be found examples of perhaps the very highest perfection to which the art can be carried, of clear, acute, convincing argument, of strong natural feeling, and of sudden bursts of passion; always, however, restrained by the predominating influence of a highly cultivated art—an art little concealed."—*Brougham.*

with absolute harmony, and give the author's ideas to develop themselves with the more truth and simplicity when clothed in the ample folds of inversion, or run from the exuberant to the elliptical without ever being either redundant or obscure. Those great wits had no foreknowledge of such times as succeeded their brilliant age, when styles should arise, and for a season prevail over both purity, and nature, and antique recollections — now meretriciously ornamented, more than half French in the phrase, and to mere figures fantastically sacrificing the sense—now heavily and regularly fashioned as if by the plumb and rule, and by the eye rather than the ear, with a needless profusion of ancient words and flexions, to displace those of our own Saxon, instead of temperately supplying its defects. Least of all could those lights of English eloquence have imagined that men should appear among us professing to teach composition, and ignorant of the whole of its rules, and incapable of relishing the beauties, or indeed apprehending the very genius of the language, should treat its peculiar terms of expression and flexion as so many inaccuracies, and practice their pupils in correcting the faulty English of Addison, and training down to the mechanical rhythm of Johnson the lively and inimitable measures of Bolingbroke.

(2.) With a steady observance of the compact energy of Greek composition.

But in exhorting you deeply to meditate on the beauties of our old English authors, the poets, the moralists, and perhaps more than all these, the preachers of the Augustan age of English letters, do not imagine that I would pass over their great defects when compared with the renowned standards of severe taste in ancient times. Addison may have been pure and elegant; Dryden airy and nervous; Taylor witty and fanciful; Hooker weighty and various; but none of them united force with beauty—the perfection of matter with the most refined and chastened style; and to one charge all, even the most faultless, are exposed—the offense unknown in ancient times, but the besetting sin of later days —they always overdid—never knowing or feeling when they had done enough. In nothing, not even in beauty of collocation and harmony of rhythm, is the vast superiority of the chaste, vigorous, manly style of the Greek orators and writers more conspicuous than in the abstinent use of their prodigious faculties of expression. A single phrase—sometimes a word—and the work is done—the desired impression is made, as it were, with one stroke, there being nothing superfluous interposed to weaken the blow or break its fall. The commanding idea is singled out; it is made to stand forward; all auxiliaries are rejected; as the Emperor Napoleon selected one point in the heart of his adversary's strength, and brought all his power to bear upon that, careless of the other points, which he was sure to carry if he won the center, as sure to have carried in vain if he left the center unsubdued. Far otherwise do modern writers make their onset; they resemble rather those campaigners, who fit out twenty little expeditions at a time to be a laughing-stock if they fail, and useless if they succeed; or if they do attack in the right place, so divide their forces, from the dread of leaving any one point unassailed, that they can make no sensible impression where alone it avails them to be felt.

Great error of modern speakers.

It seems the principle of such authors never to leave any thing unsaid that can be said on any one topic; to run down every idea they start; to let nothing pass; and leave nothing to the reader, but harass him with anticipating every thing that could possibly strike his mind. Compare with this effeminate laxity of speech the manly severity of ancient eloquence; or of him who approached it, by the happy union of natural genius with learned meditation; or of him who so marvelously approached still nearer with only the familiar knowledge of its least perfect ensamples. Mark, I do beseech you, the severe simplicity, the subdued tone of the diction, in the most touching parts of the "old man Eloquent's"[7] loftiest passages.

Manner of Demosthenes presented as a contrast.

In the oath, when he comes to the burial-place where they repose by whom he is swearing, if ever a grand epithet were allowable, it is here —yet the only one he applies is *ἀγαθοὺς—μὰ τοὺς ἐν Μαραθῶνι προκινδυνεύσαντας τῶν προγόνων—καὶ τοὺς ἐν Πλαταιαῖς παραταξαμένους—καὶ τοὺς ἐν Σαλαμῖνι ναυμαχήσαντας—καὶ τοὺς ἐπ' Ἀρτεμισίῳ, καὶ πολλούς ἑτέρους τοὺς ἐν τοῖς δημοσίοις μνήμασι κειμένους* ἈΓΑΘΟΥ͂Σ *ἄνδρας*.[8] When he would compare the effects of the Theban treaty in dispelling the dangers that compassed the state round about, to the swift passing away of a *stormy cloud*, he satisfies himself with two words, *ὥσπερ νέφος*—the theme of just admiration to succeeding ages; and when he

[7] Milton applied this phrase to Plato, as well he might; but of the orator it is yet more descriptive.

[8] We have no word in our language which is at once *simple* and *strong* enough to give the true force of *ἀγαθοὺς* in this passage. *Brave* is perhaps the nearest. *Gallant*, which Lord Brougham elsewhere uses, is wanting in that very attribute of simplicity which he here speaks of. The whole passage is, in fact, untranslatable. It is impossible to give the mere English reader any true conception of its majesty and force. We have no words corresponding to those fine participles which bring before the eye at the same moment an *act* and a *picture*, *προκινδυνεύσαντας, παραταξαμένους, ναυμάχήσαντας*. Add to this the magnificent roll of the sound, and the kindling associations in the mind of every Greek at the bare mention of Marathon, Platæa, Salamis, and Artemisium. It has all that there is in poetry to rouse the imagination, and all there is in truth to move the feelings and the heart.

The following is Lord Brougham's version of the passage, in his translation of the entire oration, made some years after:

"No! By your forefathers, who for that cause rushed upon destruction at Marathon, and by those who stood in battle array at Platæa, and those who fought the sea-fight at Salamis, and by the warriors of Artemisium, and by all the others who now repose in the sepulchers of the nation — GALLANT men!"

would paint the sudden approach of overwhelming peril to beset the state, he does it by a stroke the picturesque effect of which has not, perhaps, been enough noted—likening it to a *whirlwind* or a *winter torrent*, ὥσπερ σκηπτὸς ἢ χειμάῤῥους. It is worthy of remark, that in by far the first of all Mr. Burke's orations, the passage which is, I believe, universally allowed to be the most striking, owes its effect to a figure twice introduced in close resemblance to these two great expressions, although certainly not in imitation of either; for the original is to be found in Livy's description of Fabius's appearance to Hannibal. Hyder's vengeance is likened to "a black cloud, that hung for a while on the declivities of the mountains," and the people who suffered under its devastations are described as "enveloped in a whirlwind of cavalry." Whoever reads the whole passage will, I think, admit that the effect is almost entirely produced by those two strokes; that the amplifications which accompany them, as the "blackening of the horizon"—the "menacing meteor"—the "storm of unusual fire,"[9] rather disarm than augment the terrors of the original *black cloud;* and that the "goading spears of the drivers," and "the trampling of pursuing horses," somewhat abate the fury of the *whirlwind of cavalry.* Δουλεύουσί γε μαστιγούμενοι καὶ στρεβλούμενοι [They are slaves—*lashed and racked*], says the Grecian master, to describe the wretched lot of those who had yielded to the wiles of the conqueror, in the vain hope of securing their liberties in safety. Compare this with the choicest of Mr. Burke's invectives of derision and pity upon the same subject—the sufferings of those who made peace with regicide France—and acknowledge the mighty effect of relying upon a single stroke to produce a great effect—if you have the master-hand to give it. "The King of Prussia has hypothecated in trust to the Regicides his rich and fertile territories on the Rhine, as a pledge of his zeal and affection to the cause of liberty and equality. He has been robbed with unbounded liberty, and with the most leveling equality. The woods are wasted; the country is ravaged; property is confiscated; and the people are put to bear a double yoke, in the exactions of a tyrannical government, and in the contributions of a hostile conscription." "The Grand Duke of Tuscany, for his early sincerity, for his love of peace, and for his entire confidence in the amity of the assassins of his family, has been complimented with the name of the '*wisest Sovereign in Europe.*' This pacific Solomon, or his philosophic cudgeled ministry, cudgeled by English and by French, whose wisdom and philosophy between them have placed Leghorn in the hands of the enemy of the Austrian family, and driven the only profitable commerce of Tuscany from its only port."[10] Turn now for refreshment to the Athenian artist—Καλήν γ' οἱ πολλοὶ νῦν ἀπειλήφασιν 'Ωρειτῶν χάριν, ὅτι τοῖς Φιλίππου φίλοις ἐπέτρεψαν αὑτοὺς, τὸν δ' Εὐφραῖον ἐώθουν· καλὴν γ' ὁ δῆμος ὁ τῶν 'Ερετρίεων, ὅτι τούς ὑμετέρους μὲν πρέσβεις ἀπήλασε, Κλειτάρχῳ δ' ἐνέδωκεν αὑτόν· δουλεύουσί γε μαστιγούμενοι καὶ στρεβλούμενοι [Much, forsooth, did the Oreitœ gain when they yielded to the friends of Philip, and thrust out Euphræus; and much the people of Eretria, when they drove off your embassadors, and gave themselves up to Kleitarchus! They are now slaves—*lashed and racked*].—Phil. 3. Upon some very rare occasions, indeed, the orator, not content with a single blow, pours himself forth in a full torrent of invective, and then we recognize the man who was said of old to eat *shields* and *steel*—ἀσπίδας καὶ καταπέλτας ἐσθίων. But still the effect is produced without repetition or diffuseness. I am not aware of any such expanded passage as the invective in the Περὶ Στεφάνου against those who had betrayed the various states of Greece to Philip. It is, indeed, a noble passage; one of the most brilliant, perhaps the most highly colored of any in Demosthenes; but it is as condensed and rapid as it is rich and varied: ῎Ανθρωποι μιαροὶ καὶ κόλακες καὶ ἀλάστορες, ἠκρωτηριασμένοι τὰς ἑαυτῶν ἕκαστοι πατρίδας, τὴν ἐλευθερίαν προπεπωκότες πρότερον μὲν Φιλίππῳ, νῦν δὲ 'Αλεξάνδρῳ—τῇ γαστρί μετροῦντες καὶ τοῖς αἰσχίστοις τὴν εὐδαιμονίαν—τὴν δ' ἐλευθερίαν καὶ τὸ μηδένα ἔχειν δεσπότην αὑτῶν (ἃ τοῖς προτέροις ῞Ελλησιν ὅροι τῶν ἀγαθῶν ἦσαν καὶ κανόνες), ἀνατετροφότες (Περὶ Στεφ.). [Base and fawning creatures, wretches who have mutilated the glory each of his own native land—toasting away their liberties to the health first of Philip, then of Alexander; measuring their happiness by their gluttony and debauchery, but utterly overthrowing those rights of freemen, and that independence of any master, which the Greeks of former days regarded as the test and the summit of all felicity.][11] This requires no contrast to make its merit shine forth; but compare it with any of Cicero's invectives—that, for instance, in the third Catilinarian, against the conspirators, where he attacks them regularly under six different heads, and in above twenty times as many words; and ends with the known and very

His want of condensation.

[9] Quoting from memory, Lord Brougham here puts into the mouth of Mr. Burke one of the tamest of all possible expressions, "a storm of *unusual* fire," instead of the one actually used, "a storm of *universal* fire blasted every field, consumed every house, destroyed every temple." As *fire* was the chief instrument of destruction used by Hyder Ali, the mention of it (whether it served or not to disarm the terrors of the original black cloud) was essential to the truth of his description.

[10] Lord Brougham does injustice to Mr. Burke in this quotation. The passage, instead of being one of the "choicest," is one of the most careless, in point of style, to be found in the Regicide Peace.

[11] The object of chief abhorrence to the old Greeks is remarkably expressed in this passage: δεσπότης is the correlative of δοῦλος; and the meaning of δεσπότην ἔχειν αὑτῶν is, "having an owner or proprietor of themselves," that is, "being the property, the chattels of any one;" and this they justly deemed the last of human miseries. The addition of the cart-whip, and a tropical climate, would not probably have been esteemed by them an alleviation of the lot of slavery.—*Brougham.*

moderate jest of their commander keeping "Scortorum cohortem Prætoriam."

The great poet of modern Italy, Dante, approached nearest to the ancients in the quality of which I have been speaking. In his finest passages you rarely find an epithet; hardly ever more than one; and never two efforts to embody one idea. "*A guisa di Leon quando si posa*" [Like the lion when he lays himself down], is the single trait by which he compares the dignified air of a stern personage to the expression of the lion slowly laying him down. It is remarkable that Tasso copies the verse entire, but he destroys its whole effect by filling up the majestic idea, adding this line, "*Girando gli occhi e non movendo il passo*" [Casting around his eyes, but not hastening his pace]. A better illustration could not easily be found of the difference between the ancient and the modern style.[12] Another is furnished by a later imitator of the same great master. I know no passage of the *Divina Commedia* more excursive than the description of evening in the Purgatorio; yet the poet is content with somewhat enlarging on a single thought—the tender recollections which that hour of meditation gives the traveler, at the fall of the first night he is to pass away from home, when he hears the distant knell of the expiring day. Gray adopts the idea of the knell in nearly the words of the original, and adds eight other circumstances to it, presenting a kind of ground-plan, or at least a catalogue, an accurate enumeration (like a natural historian's) of every one particular belonging to nightfall, so as wholly to exhaust the subject, and leave nothing to the imagination of the reader. Dante's six verses, too, have but one epithet, *dolci*, applied to *amici*. Gray has thirteen or fourteen; some of them mere repetitions of the same idea which the verb or the substantive conveys—as *drowsy* tinkling *lulls*—the *moping* owl *complains*—the plowman *plods* his *weary* way. Surely, when we contrast the simple and commanding majesty of the ancient writers with the superabundance and diffusion of the exhaustive method, we may be tempted to feel that there lurks some alloy of bitterness in the excess of sweets.[13] This was

Dante as an instance of condensation among modern poets.

Gray an example of expansion.

[12] Lord Brougham here cites a number of passages from Dante, as specimens of the brief energy of his descriptions. In some of these cases, however, an explanation of the circumstances, or a longer quotation, is necessary to exhibit the true force and beauty of the original. These will therefore be given.

(1.) "The flight of doves." This passage, from the fifth Canto of the Inferno, relates to the ghosts of two lovers, Paulo and Francesca, whom the poet calls to him from a distance, that they may tell their mournful story. They come,

Quali colombe, dal disio chiamate,
Con l' ali aperte e ferme al dolce nido
Volan per l' äer dal voler portate.

As doves, by instinct led,
With outstretched wings and steady, through the air,
Seek their sweet nest, borne on by strong desire.

(2.) "The gnawing of a skull by a mortal enemy." The passage here referred to is from the most terrific description contained in the Inferno (Canto xxxiii.), where Count Ugolino has seized on the head of his enemy, the Archbishop of Pisa, from behind, as he endeavored to escape, and was gnawing into his skull like a dog. Ugolino turns at the call of the poet, *wipes his bloody jaws on the hair of his victim*, and tells the well-known story of his being shut up in a tower through the arts of his enemy, and left with his two sons and two grandsons to die the lingering death of starvation. Then follows the passage,

Quand' ebbe detto ciò, con gli occhi torti
Riprese 'l teschio misero *co' denti*,
Che furo all' osso, come d' un can, forti.

He spoke, and turning with his eyes askance,
Again he seized upon that wretched skull
With teeth strong grinding to the bone, like dog's!

(3.) "The venality and simoniacal practices of the Romish Church." In the Paradiso (Canto xvii.) the poet meets one of his ancestors, who predicts his banishment from Florence as procured for money of Boniface VIII., then Pope at Rome, and adds,

Lá dove Cristo tutto dì si merca.

There CHRIST himself is daily bought and sold!

(4.) "The perfidy of a Bourbon," viz., Charles of Valois, who, coming from France in the guise of peace, gained the mastery of Florence by a treachery which the poet could compare to nothing but that of Judas Iscariot. The image is that of a knight entering the lists of a tournament.

Senza arme n'esce, e solo con la lancia
Con la qual giostrò Giuda.

Unarmed he came, save only with the lance
That *Judas fought with!*

(5.) The pains of dependence (Paradiso xvii.).

Tu proverai sì come sa di sale
Il pane altrui, è com' è duro calle
Lo scendere e l' salir per l' altrui scale.

Thou shalt learn
How bitter is the taste of others' bread;
How hard the path to climb and to descend
Another's stairs!

[13] In this criticism, Lord Brougham falls into the not uncommon error of making one kind of excellence the standard in every case. He forgets that we may admire the rapid sketches of Dante without condemning the minuter pictures of Gray.

There is also a distinction to be made as to the proper place for dwelling on particulars and using epithets. When the mind is on the ascendant scale of feeling, and pressing forward to some great result. conciseness is demanded—detail and epithet are out of place. But when the pursuit is over, and we look back with tender or melancholy feelings on the past, it is natural to dwell in fond detail on the objects we have left behind, and to accumulate those epithets which mark their distinctive qualities. Thus when Othello, who was at first so rapid, so concise, so eager to go forward, feels himself at last to be a ruined man, and cries out, "Othello's occupation's gone," it is striking to observe how he dwells in minute detail, and with accumulated epithets, on those warlike scenes in which he once delighted.

Farewell the tranquil mind, farewell content,
Farewell the plumed troops, and the big war
That makes ambition virtue! oh, farewell!
Farewell the neighing steed, and the shrill trump,
The spirit-stirring drum, the ear-piercing fife,
The royal banner, and all quality,
Pride, pomp, and circumstance of glorious war!

so fully recognized by the wise ancients, that it became a proverb among them, as we learn from an epigram still preserved.

Εἰς τὴν μετριότητα.

Πᾶν τὸ περιττὸν ἄκαιρον, ἐπεὶ λόγος ἐστὶ παλαιὸς,
'Ως καὶ τοῦ μέλιτος τὸ πλέον ἐστὶ χολή.

[TO MODERATION.
All excess is inappropriate; hence the proverb,
Too much even of honey turns to gall.]

In addition to the general study of rhetoric each effort to be a labored one.

In forming the taste by much contemplation of those antique models, and acquiring the habits of easy and chaste composition, it must not be imagined that all the labor of the orator is ended, or that he may then dauntless and fluent enter upon his office in the public assembly. Much preparation is still required before each exertion, if rhetorical excellence is aimed at. I should lay it down as a rule, admitting of no exception, that a man will speak well in proportion as he has written much; and that with equal talents, he will be the finest extempore speaker, when no time for preparing is allowed, who has prepared himself the most sedulously when he had an opportunity of delivering a premeditated speech. All the exceptions which I have ever heard cited to this principle are apparent ones only; proving nothing more than that some few men of rare genius have become great speakers without preparation; in nowise showing that with preparation they would not have reached a much higher pitch of excellence. The admitted superiority of the ancients in all oratorial accomplishments is the best proof of my position; for their careful preparation is undeniable; nay, in Demosthenes (of whom Quintilian says that his style indicates more premeditation—*plus curæ*—than Cicero's) we can trace, by the recurrence of the same passage, with progressive improvements in different speeches, how nicely he polished the more exquisite parts of his compositions. I could point out favorite passages, occurring as often as three several times with variations, and manifest amendment.

Writing to be mingled with extemporaneous address.

This labor to be carried throughout the orator's whole course for life.

I am now requiring not merely great preparation while the speaker is learning his art, but after he has accomplished his education. The most splendid effort of the most mature orator will be always finer for being previously elaborated with much care. There is, no doubt, a charm in extemporaneous elocution, derived from the appearance of artless, unpremeditated effusion, called forth by the occasion, and so adapting itself to its exigencies, which may compensate the manifold defects incident to this kind of composition: that which is inspired by the unforeseen circumstances of the moment, will be of necessity suited to those circumstances in the choice of the topics, and pitched in the tone of the execution, to the feelings upon which it is to operate. These are great virtues: it is another to avoid the besetting vice of modern oratory—the overdoing every thing—the exhaustive method—which an off-hand speaker has no time to fall into, and he accordingly will take only the grand and effective view; nevertheless, in oratorical merit, such effusions must needs be very inferior; much of the pleasure they produce depends upon the hearer's surprise, that in such circumstances any thing can be delivered at all, rather than upon his deliberate judgment, that he has heard any thing very excellent in itself. We may rest assured that the highest reaches of the art, and without any necessary sacrifice of natural effect, can only be attained by him who well considers, and maturely prepares, and oftentimes sedulously corrects and refines his oration. Such preparation is quite consistent with the introduction of passages prompted by the occasion, nor will the transition from the one to the other be perceptible in the execution of a practiced master. I have known attentive and skillful hearers completely deceived in this matter, and taking for extemporaneous passages which previously existed in manuscript, and were pronounced without the variation of a particle or a pause. Thus, too, we are told by Cicero, in one of his epistles, that having to make, in Pompey's presence, a speech, after Crassus had very unexpectedly taken a particular line of argument, he exerted himself, and it appears successfully, in a marvelous manner, mightily assisted in what he said extempore by his habit of rhetorical preparation, and introducing skillfully, as the inspiration of the moment, all his favorite commonplaces, with some of which, as we gather from a good-humored joke at his own expense, Crassus had interfered: "Ego autem ipse, Dî Boni! quomodo *ἐνεπερπερευσάμην* novo auditori Pompeio! Si unquam mihi *περίοδοι*, si *καμπαὶ*, si *ἐνθυμήματα*, si *κατασκευαὶ*, suppeditaverunt, illo tempore. Quid multa? clamores. Etenim hæc erat *ὑπόθεσις*, de gravitate ordinis, de equestri concordia, de consensione Italiæ, de immortuis reliquiis conjurationis, de vilitate, de otio—nôsti jam in hâc materiâ sonitus nostros; tanti fuerunt, ut ego eo brevior sim, quod eos usque isthinc exauditos putem."—Ep. ad Att., i., 14.[14]

II. If, from contemplating the means of ac-

On the same principle, Gray's minuteness of detail, when meditating in a country church-yard, is perfectly appropriate. Every one's heart tells him that it is the nice and delicate shading of the picture that forms its chief excellence.

[14] This passage is a curious specimen of Cicero's habit of sportive boasting in familiar intercourse with his friends.

But for myself, good Gods, how I launched out before my new auditor Pompey! Then, if ever, I had an abundant supply of rounded sentences, graceful transitions, striking rhetorical proofs, and amplifications to illustrate and confirm my sentiments. Why should I say more? Shouts of applause followed. My subject was, the dignity of the Senate, the concord of the Knights, the union of all Italy, the expiring remains of the conspiracy—corruption destroyed, peace established. You know how I can raise my voice on these topics; and I now say the less, because it swelled so loud that I should think you might have heard it even at the distance you are off!

quiring eloquence, we turn to the noble purposes to which it may be made subservient, we at once perceive its prodigious importance to the best interests of mankind.

Part Second. The uses of eloquence.

The greatest masters of the art have concurred, and upon the greatest occasion of its display, in pronouncing that its estimation depends on the virtuous and rational use made of it. Let their sentiments be engraved on your memory in their own pure and appropriate diction. Καλὸν (says Æschines) *τὴν μὲν διάνοιαν προαιρεῖσθαι τὰ βέλτιστα, τὴν δὲ παιδείαν τὴν τοῦ ῥήτορος καὶ τὸν λόγον πείθειν τοὺς ἀκούοντας—εἰ δὲ μὴ, τὴν εὐγνωμοσύνην ἀεὶ προτακτέον τοῦ λόγου* [It is well that the intellect should choose the best objects, and that the education and eloquence of the orator should obtain the assent of his hearers; but if not, that sound judgment should be preferred to mere speech.] Ἔστι (says his illustrious antagonist) *δ' οὐχ ὁ λόγος τοῦ ῥήτορος τίμιος, οὐδ' ὁ τόνος τῆς φωνῆς, ἀλλὰ τὸ ταὐτὰ προαιρεῖσθαι τοῖς πολλοῖς* [It is not the language of the orator or the modulation of his voice that deserves your praise, but his seeking the same interests and objects with the body of the people].

Multiplied as the interests of society.

It is but reciting the ordinary praises of the art of persuasion, to remind you how sacred truths may be most ardently promulgated at the altar—the cause of oppressed innocence be most powerfully defended — the march of wicked rulers be most triumphantly resisted—defiance the most terrible be hurled at the oppressor's head. In great convulsions of public affairs, or in bringing about salutary changes, every one confesses how important an ally eloquence must be. But in peaceful times, when the progress of events is slow and even as the silent and unheeded pace of time, and the jars of a mighty tumult in foreign and domestic concerns can no longer be heard, then too she flourishes — protectress of liberty—patroness of improvement—guardian of all the blessings that can be showered upon the mass of human kind; nor is her form ever seen but on ground consecrated to free institutions. "Pacis comes, otiique socia, et jam bene constitutæ reipublicæ alumna eloquentia" [Eloquence is the companion of peace and the associate of leisure; it is trained up under the auspices of a well-established republic]. To me, calmly revolving these things, such pursuits seem far more noble objects of ambition than any upon which the vulgar herd of busy men lavish prodigal their restless exertions. To diffuse useful information—to further intellectual refinement, sure forerunner of moral improvement—to hasten the coming of the bright day when the dawn of general knowledge shall chase away the lazy, lingering mists, even from the base of the great social pyramid—this indeed is a high calling, in which the most splendid talents and consummate virtue may well press onward eager to bear a part. I know that I speak in a place consecrated by the pious wisdom of ancient times to the instruction of but a select portion of the community. Yet from this classic ground have gone forth those whose genius, not their ancestry, ennobled them; whose incredible merits have opened to all ranks the temple of science; whose illustrious example has made the humblest emulous to climb steeps no longer inaccessible, and enter the unfolded gates, burning in the sun. I speak in that city where Black having once taught, and Watt learned, the grand experiment was afterward made in our day, and with entire success; to demonstrate that the highest intellectual cultivation is perfectly compatible with the daily cares and toils of working-men; to show by thousands of living examples that a keen relish for the most sublime truths of science belongs alike to every class of mankind.

Men of the highest station and attainments summoned to the field of its labors.

To promote this, of all objects the most important, men of talents and of influence I rejoice to behold pressing forward in every part of the empire; but I wait with impatient anxiety to see the same course pursued by men of high station in society, and by men of rank in the world of letters. It should seem as if these felt some little lurking jealousy, and those were somewhat scared by feelings of alarm—the one and the other surely alike groundless. No man of science needs fear to see the day when scientific excellence shall be too vulgar a commodity to bear a high price. The more widely knowledge is spread, the more will they be prized whose happy lot it is to extend its bounds by discovering new truths, or multiply its uses by inventing new modes of applying it in practice. Their numbers will indeed be increased, and among them more Watts and more Franklins will be enrolled among the lights of the world, in proportion as more thousands of the working classes, to which Franklin and Watt belonged, have their thoughts turned toward philosophy; but the order of discoverers and inventors will still be a select few, and the only material variation in their proportion to the bulk of mankind will be, that the mass of the ignorant multitude being progressively diminished, the body of those will be incalculably increased who are worthy to admire genius, and able to bestow upon its possessors an immortal fame.

True knowledge and eloquence conducive to enlightened and stable government.

To those, too, who feel alarmed as statesmen, and friends of existing establishments, I would address a few words of comfort. Real knowledge never promoted either turbulence or unbelief; but its progress is the forerunner of liberality and enlightened toleration. Whoso dreads these, let him tremble; for he may be well assured that their day is at length come, and must put to sudden flight the evil spirits of tyranny and persecution which haunted the long night now gone down the sky. As men will no longer suffer themselves to be led blindfolded in ignorance, so will they no more yield to the vile principle of judging and treating their fellow-creatures, not according to the intrinsic merit of their actions, but according to the accidental and involuntary coincidence of their opinions. The great truth has finally gone forth to all the ends of the earth, THAT MAN SHALL NO MORE RENDER ACCOUNT TO MAN FOR HIS BELIEF, OVER WHICH HE HAS HIMSELF NO CONTROL. Henceforward, nothing shall prevail upon us to praise or to blame any one for that which he can no more change than he can the hue of his skin or the height of his stature.[15] Henceforward, treating with entire respect those who conscientiously differ from ourselves, the only practical effect of the difference will be, to make us enlighten the ignorance on one side or the other from which it springs, by instructing them, if it be theirs; ourselves, if it be our own, to the end that the only kind of unanimity may be produced which is desirable among rational beings—the agreement proceeding from full conviction after the freest discussion. Far then, very far, from the universal spread of knowledge being the object of just apprehension to those who watch over the peace of the country, or have a deep interest in the permanence of her institutions, its sure effect will be the removal of the only dangers that threaten the public tranquillity, and the addition of all that is wanting to confirm her internal strength.

Let me, therefore, indulge in the hope that, among the illustrious youths whom this ancient kingdom, famed alike for its nobility and its learning, has produced, to continue her fame through after ages, possibly among those I now address, there may be found some one—I ask no more—willing to give a bright example to other nations in a path yet untrodden, by taking the lead of his fellow-citizens, not in frivolous amusements, nor in the degrading pursuits of the ambitious vulgar, but in the truly noble task of enlightening the mass of his countrymen, and of leaving his own name no longer encircled, as heretofore, with barbaric splendor, or attached to courtly gewgaws, but illustrated by the honors most worthy of our rational nature—coupled with the diffusion of knowledge—and gratefully pronounced through all ages by millions whom his wise beneficence has rescued from ignorance and vice. To him I will say, "Homines ad Deos nullâ re propius accedunt quam salutem hominibus dando: nihil habet nec fortuna tua majus quam ut possis, nec natura tua melius quam ut velis servare quamplurimos" [In nothing do men approach more nearly to the Divinity than in ministering to the safety of their fellow-men; so that fortune can not give you any thing greater than the ability, or nature any thing better than the desire to extend relief to the greatest possible number]. This is the true mark for the aim of all who either prize the enjoyment of pure happiness, or set a right value upon a high and unsullied renown. And if the benefactors of mankind, when they rest from their pious labors, shall be permitted to enjoy hereafter, as an appropriate reward of their virtue, the privilege of looking down upon the blessings with which their toils and sufferings have clothed the scene of their former existence, do not vainly imagine that, in a state of exalted purity and wisdom, the founders of mighty dynasties, the conquerors of new empires, or the more vulgar crowd of evil-doers, who have sacrificed to their own aggrandizement the good of their fellow-creatures, will be gratified by contemplating the monuments of their inglorious fame—theirs will be the delight—theirs the triumph—who can trace the remote effects of their enlightened benevolence in the improved condition of their species, and exult in the reflection that the prodigious change they now survey, with eyes that age and sorrow can make dim no more—of knowledge become power—virtue sharing in the dominion—superstition trampled under foot—tyranny driven from the world—are the fruits, precious, though costly, and though late reaped, yet long-enduring, of all the hardships and all the hazards they encountered here below!

Peroration: The high object and reward of cultivated intellect.

15 This is one of those hasty statements so characteristic of Lord Brougham. In his eagerness to do away religious intolerance, he puts *belief*, or the assent we give to probable evidence, on the same footing with our assent to a mathematical demonstration; declaring it to be involuntary, and the result of a necessity of our nature. Such a sentiment does not need to be discussed. It is refuted by the universal experience of mankind. Every one knows—it has, indeed, passed into a proverb—that a man can make himself believe almost any thing he pleases. Under the influence of feeling and prejudice, men look only at the proof on one side; they turn away from evidence which makes against their wishes. Or, if they do contemplate it, every one knows it requires far more evidence to gain a man's assent against his wishes than in favor of them, so that Butler says in his Hudibras,

He who's convinced against his will,
Is of the same opinion still.

But, according to Lord Brougham, there is no room for the man's "will" in the case; it is wholly involuntary, a thing "over which he himself has no control!" All this he contradicts, under other aspects, on every page of his speeches. He condemns men for being *uncandid*, when such a thing as candor or the want of it could not exist on his scheme: nobody talks about *candor* in studying the mathematics. If there was ever a man who held others responsible for their opinions, it is Lord Brougham; he is perpetually finding fault with men for their political views. It is unnecessary to add, that the whole tenor of the Scriptures is against this principle. They make belief the condition of salvation, and represent it as springing from a right state of heart; "With the heart man believeth unto righteousness." They treat unbelief as sinful; "Ye believe not because of the hardness of your hearts." On Lord Brougham's principle, Paul was free from blame before his conversion, for he "Verily thought that he ought to do many things contrary to the name of Jesus of Nazareth;" but the Apostle decided differently, and declared his guilt to have been great, though he acted "ignorantly and in unbelief."

THE END.